# Encyclopedia of the Middle Ages

The Byzantine Empire
in the 9th C.
c. 1100
in 1349
Russia
Riga
Polotsk
Moscow
Lithuania
Gdansk
Novogrodek
Marienberg
Pomerania
Poznan
Gniezno
Poland
Chernihiv
Wroclaw
Silesia
Kiev
Kiev
Prague
Cracow
Ukraine
Bohemia
Lviv
Podolia
Moravia
Vienna
Pannonia
Galicia
Veszprem
Kalocsa
Crimea
Caucasus
Hungary
Moldavia
Caffa
Venice
Walachia
Serbia
Nicopolis
Georgia
Bosnia
Dubrovnik
Bulgaria
Trebizond
Byzantine Empire
Armenia
Constantinople
Ohrid
Thessalonica
Nicaea
Olympus
Cappadocia
Athos
Philadelphia
Lesbos
Cilicia
Edessa
Athens
Patmos
Aleppo
Antioch
Rhodes
Cyprus
Krak
Crete
Tripoli
Beirut
Damascus
Tyre
Acre
Tiberias
Caesarea
Jerusalem
Damietta
Bethlehem
Alexandria
Mansura
Scetis
Cairo
Egypt
Sinai
0
100
200
300
400 miles
0
200
400
600 kms

# Encyclopedia of the Middle Ages

# I

# A-J

Edited by

ANDRE VAUCHEZ

in conjunction with

BARRIE DOBSON

and

MICHAEL LAPIDGE

English translation by Adrian Walford

FD

EDITIONS
DU CERF
Paris

FITZROY DEARBORN
PUBLISHERS
Chicago and London

CITTÀ
NUOVA
Rome

First Published in the United Kingdom in 2000 by:
**James Clarke & Co**
**P.O. Box 60**
**Cambridge**
**CB1 2NT**
**England**

First Published in the United States of America in 2000 by:
**Fitzroy Dearborn Publishers**
**919 North Michigan Avenue**
**Chicago**
**Illinois 60611**
**USA**

This edition published by arrangement with James Clarke & Co

ISBN, Two Volume set: 1-57958-282-6

British Library and Library of Congress Cataloging in Publication Data are available



Printed in China by Midas

# Contents

## Volume I



## Volume II

# List of Maps

Places listed in the *Encyclopedia of the Middle Ages* are shown on the coloured maps in black (towns) and blue (monasteries). Unless specifically indicated for a particular date, borders between territories are not shown. In many cases borders were disputed. In addition the same name could be given to different regions at different times.

Volume I



Volume II



# Publisher's Note


The Publisher would like to thank those without whose help publication of the *Encyclopedia of the Middle Ages* would have been very much harder. In addition to the help and support of Professors Vauchez, Lapidge and Dobson, many others have provided valuable assistance.

In particular Adrian Walford's determination to ensure the publication of the *Encyclopedia* has gone far beyond the service of a translator – important though that has been. Laura Napran has devoted great time and energy to bibliographical help and to working on the maps. Professor Muri Rubin has read the whole book in proof and made many valuable suggestions for improvement. Dr Florentina Badalanova has helped to avoid serious errors in the sections on Eastern Europe.

That others are not individually thanked is not a reflection on the value of their assistance, but the size of the project and the number of people involved make it impossible to thank all.

# Preface

The *Encyclopedia of the Middle Ages* is the fruit of the labours of over 600 scholars from a wide range of disciplines, brought together by a small editorial team, itself supported by thirty subject experts, and by the project management (and financial investment) of the three publishers.

A human and intellectual investment of such importance and length – a space of ten years separates the beginning of work on the *Encyclopedia* from its publication in English – cannot be the result of mere luck or a happy combination of circumstances. Two main factors have contributed to making the present editorial project possible and even necessary. The first is the extraordinary development that has taken place in medieval studies everywhere, not just in the English-speaking world. A glance at such projects as the *International Medieval Bibliography* and *Medioevo Latino* shows a bibliographical explosion. This rapid growth is accompanied by a renewal of methods and approaches that has affected every medieval discipline, from history and art history to archaeology, philosophy and musicology. The time has clearly come to harvest and publish the fruits of this rich growth, to which most of the contributors to the *Encyclopedia of the Middle Ages* have themselves contributed.

But this synthesis of the research of the last half-century would have been impossible had not the Middle Ages meanwhile departed from the twilight in which it had vegetated and had not the perception of it visibly changed. In the early 1960s, the prevalent idea of it was that of an obscure, even obscurantist, period, marked by ignorance, and intolerance and sadly symbolised by the Inquisition. In one generation, thanks to historians to whom we are all in debt, of whom Georges Duby, Richard Southern, Jacques Le Goff and Patrick Geary are only a few distinguished examples), the Middle Ages have been rediscovered in all their richness an d put into a perspective closer to the reality. We do not intend to idealise a period that lasted nearly a thousand years (essentially from A.D. 500 to 1500) and was marked by harsh living conditions and behaviour whose brutality shocks our modern sensibilities, built as they are on ideas of tolerance and ideological pluralism. But what some see as the "darkness" of the Middle Ages should not make us overlook the greatness or undervalue the importance of this varied civilisation. So we have tried to present the whole range of medieval Europe, giving as much space to the East as to the West, and to show that the Middle Ages played an essential role in many fields such as land settlement, agricultural techniques, political institutions and even science. Umberto Eco has rightly reminded us in *The Name of the Rose* that spectacles were invented in the early 14th century.

The relatively restricted size of this *Encyclopedia*, when compared to the more exhaustive ones that have recently appeared in Germany and United States, forbids us any claim to exhaustiveness, and the choices we have made must be justified. The first of these is that of geographical scope. Writing for a European public primarily concerned with its own history (the work is being published in French and Italian as well as English), our centre of interest has been medieval Christendom – or rather Christendoms –, *i.e.* a set of regions extending from Iceland – or even, because of Vinland, from Canada – to Ethiopia and Central Asia. Articles devoted to other continents or civilisations appear only to the extent that Western Christians were aware of them and took an interest in them. However, the fact that the *Encyclopedia* is centred on the Christian world has led us to give plenty of space to those peoples and religions that were in contact with it over those thousand years; the Jews, since so many of them lived within Christendom itself, and the Muslims, with whom Eastern and Western Christians, though often in conflict, also had fruitful economic and cultural exchanges. We have also taken care to deal with the "pagan" peoples (Lithuanians, Lapps, Cumans, Mongols, etc.) whom the Christians of the Middle Ages sought, with mixed success, to draw into their orbit.

A final requirement has guided the choice of articles and the general orientation: to help Europeans of the third millennium identify with an inheritance that still marks their way of life and some of whose aspects still charm them, but whose meaning escapes them. With this intention, we have deliberately given a privileged place to philosophy, theology, spirituality, liturgy and iconography. In doing so, we have put ourselves into the mind of the time, which – whether Christian, Jewish or Muslim –, while not ignoring or scorning economic and social realities, always tried to put them into a religious, intellectual or moral perspective. We have put special emphasis on those aspects of medieval civilisation that are hardest for most contemporary people – strangers alike to the old humanist and scholastic education and to religious systems or ecclesiastical institutions – to understand. Our hope is that this work, which tries to bring its readers the most exact possible scholarly information, will help them understand better what Verlaine called the "enormous, delicate" Middle Ages, which have ceaselessly fascinated the European imagination since the beginning of the nineteenth century.

ANDRÉ VAUCHEZ

# Preface to the English Edition

In the world of scholarship and learning, one of the most startling and far-reaching phenomena of the past half-century has been the explosion of published work on medieval studies. The causes of the explosion are not easily identifiable, but they certainly include an ever more pervasive interest on both sides of the Atlantic in almost all aspects of the European Middle Ages. It is clear that one of the factors which has propelled the growth is the need felt by academic institutions (and, regrettably, governments) to measure individual scholarly performance, and the concomitant expectation that a young scholar will publish one book (or more) to achieve tenure, a second book to secure further promotion, and a substantial number of books and articles to attain to the highest academic posts. The impact of this explosion on the field of medieval studies – as probably on all scholarly disciplines – has been overwhelming. With countless books and articles on all aspects of medieval studies appearing each year, the possibility of exercising control over the scholarship published annually in even a small patch of the larger field of medieval studies becomes increasingly difficult, if not impossible; and, one might add, the more interdisciplinary the field, the greater the difficulty. Given these circumstances, it is not surprising that the past few decades have seen the creation of various sorts of bibliographies and encyclopedias designed to provide streamlined guidance to the essential scholarship on a given medieval topic. There is the massive and excellent (though unillustrated) *Lexikon des Mittetalters* (ed. G. Avella-Widhalm *et al.*, 9 vols. in 17, Munich and Zurich, 1977-99), and those limited to English may perhaps consult the twelve-volume *Dictionary of the Middle Ages* (ed. J.R. Strayer, New York, 1982-9). But because of their size and cost, these encyclopedias may be accessible in major libraries, but are scarcely affordable by individual scholars (a nine-volume edition of the *Lexikon des Mittelalters,* without index volumes, has recently been advertised at c. £1,800, almost $3,000). There is also a number of one-volume dictionaries and encyclopedias, which vary in quality, but in their nature are limited in scope and coverage.

There is thus a need for an encyclopedia of the Middle Ages on a scale smaller than the *Dictionary of the Middle Ages* and the *Lexikon des Mittetalters,* which, unlike them, would be affordable by individual scholars, and would provide the illustration which they regrettably lack. These considerations led a consortium of British, French and Italian publishers to approach André Vauchez, a scholar particularly well known in his native France and in Italy, but increasingly also in the English-speaking world, to edit the present work. Vauchez assembled a team of some 30 (largely French-speaking) scholars, with the aim of producing a comparatively inexpensive, illustrated, two-volume dictionary of the Middle Ages. The aim was from the first to create an encyclopedia using the best scholarship available in Europe and North America.

The resulting work is now published – in slightly different versions – in English, French and Italian. It containing some 3,200 articles of variable length by some 600 scholars, some 600 black and white illustrations and 30 colour plates.

The French edition is published by Editions du Cerf in Paris in two volumes as the *Dictionnaire encyclopédique du moyen âge.* Despite the excellence of most of the entries, many of them – in spite of the editor's aim of supplying each entry with relevant bibliography – lack bibliography altogether. From a non-French point of view, however, the most serious defect of the French version is its Franco-centric orientation. For example, medieval English subjects are given cursory, often inadequate, treatment, if they are treated at all (the French edition contained no article on Robin Hood or *Beowulf).*

The Italian edition, the *Dizionario enciclopedico del medioevo,* was overseen by Claudio Leonardi of the University of Florence, is published in three large volumes by Città Nuova. Leonardi and his collaborators were able to broaden the coverage by adding a number of useful articles.

The present English edition, translated by Adrian Walford from the French and Italian editions, while preserving the overall scope and lavish illustration of the French and Italian editions, contains an additional fifty or so entries, partly to enhance the English presence in the volume (articles on *Beowulf,* the Battle of Hastings and the so-called Peasants' Revolt of 1381 have been added, for example). In addition, however, the present English edition goes beyond the French and Italian editions, namely in the matter of bibliography. A concerted effort has been made to provide every article with relevant and up-to-date bibliography, and we hope that this feature will be found useful by users of this English *Encyclopedia of the Middle Ages.*

In any event, the scope of the present *Encyclopedia is* vast, covering the fields of archaeology, art, architecture, economics, education, geography, history, institutions, languages, literature, philosophy, religion, theology, law, science and politics, and spanning a period from the seventh century to the fifteenth. We are unaware of a comparable work of reference on the Middle Ages which offers so much detailed information at a price which individual medievalists will be able to afford.

It is hoped that it will be of value to scholars by providing them with information on fields outside their own expertise and in showing them the main sources for further research. Librarians, whether in academic institutions or in public libraries, will find it a useful one-stop guide. Students will be able to obtain a speedy overview of topics that they need. Publication of the *Encyclopedia of the Middle Ages* provides a happy means of inaugurating the new millennium for medievalists of all persuasions.

BARRIE. DOBSON
MICHAEL LAPIDGE

May 2000

# Bibliographical Abbreviations

ABMA *Auctores Britannici medii aevi*, London, etc., 1969f.
ABourg *Annales de Bourgogne. Revue historique*, Dijon, 1929f.
Abr-n. *Abr-nahrain. Department of Semitic Studies, University of Melbourne*, Leiden, 1959f.
ABret *Annales de Bretagne et des pays de l'Ouest*, Rennes, 1886f.
ABSHF *Annuaire-bulletin de la Société de l'histoire de France*, Paris, 1863f.
ACi *Analecta cisterciensia*, Rome, 1952f.
ActaSS *Acta sanctorum*, Antwerp, etc., 1643-1944 (70 vol.); 2nd ed. Venice, 1734-1770 (43 vol.); 3rd ed. Paris, 1863-1870 (60 vol.); re-ed. Paris, 1966-1971 (60 vol.).
ADGMA *Acta et diplomata Graeca medii aevi sacra et profana collecta*, F. Miklosich (ed.) *et al.*, Vienna, 1860-1890 (6 vol.); repr. Aalen, 1968.
ADipl *Archiv für Diplomatik, Schriftgeschichte, Siegel- und Wappenkunde*, Münster, etc., 1955f.
ADSPMa *Atti e memorie della (reale) deputazione di storia patria per le (provincie delle) Marche*, Ancona, 1895f.
AEM *Anuario de estudios medievales*, Barcelona, 1964f.
AEst *Annales de l'Est*, Nancy, 1887f.
AEt *Annales d'Éthiopie. Revue d'archéologie, de philosophie et d'histoire*, Addis Ababa, 1955f.
Aevum *Aevum. Rassegna di scienze storiche, linguistiche e filologiche*, Milan, 1927f.
AFH *Archivum franciscanum historicum*, Florence, etc., 1908f.
AFP *Archivum fratrum praedicatorum*, Rome, 1930 (1931)f.
AGKKN *Archief voor de geschiedenis van de Katholieke Kerk in Nederland*, Utrecht, etc., 1959f.
AHAH *Acta historiae artium Academiae scientiarum Hungaricae*, Budapest, 1953f.
AHAW.PH *Abhandlungen der Heidelberger Akademie der Wissenschaften. Philosophisch-historische Klasse*, Heidelberg, 1913f.
AHC *Annuarium historiae conciliorum*, Paderborn, etc., 1969f.
AHDL *Archives d'histoire doctrinale et littéraire du Moyen Âge*, Paris, 1926f.
AHES *Annales d'histoire économique et sociale*, Paris, 1929-1938 (then "Annales d'histoire sociale", 1939-1941; "Mélanges d'histoire sociale", 1942-1944; and "Annales").
AHMA *Analecta hymnica medii aevi*, G. Dreves (ed.), C. Blumes (ed.), Leipzig, 1886-1922 (55 vol.; re-ed. Frankfurt am Main, 1961); index 1978 (2 vol.).
AHP *Archivum historiae pontificiae*, Rome, 1963f.
AHR *The American Historical Review*, New York, etc., 1895f.
AIA *Archivo iberoamericano. Revista trimestal de estudios históricos sobre la orden Franciscana en España y sus misione*, Madrid, 1914f.
AIPh *Annuaire de l'Institut de philologie et d'histoire orientales et slaves*, Brussels, 1932f.
AIs *Annali dell'islàm*, Milan, etc., 1905-1926.
AJu *Archives juives*, Paris, 1965f.
ALKGMA *Archiv für Literatur- und Kirchengeschichte des Mittelalters*, H. Denifle (ed.),F. Ehrle (ed.), Berlin, etc., 1885-1900 (7 vol.).
ALMA *Archivum latinitatis medii aevi*, Brussels, 1924f.
AltprForsch *Altpreußische Forschungen*, Königsberg, 1924-1943.
AMidi *Annales du Midi. Revue archéologique, historique et philologique de la France méridionale*, Toulouse, 1889f.
AMin *Annales minorum*, L. Wadding (ed.) *et al.*, Lyon, 1625-1654; 2nd ed. 1731-1886; 3rd ed. 1931f.
AMNam *Analecta mediaevalia Namurcensia*, Louvain, etc., 1950f.
AMont *Analecta Montserratensia*, Barcelona, etc., 1917-1964.
AnBoll *Analecta bollandiana*, Brussels, 1882f.
And. *Al-Andalus. Revista de las Escuelas de estudios árabes de Madrid y Granada*, Madrid, 1933-1978 (then "Qan.").
Anglia *Anglia. Zeitschrift für englische Philologie*, Tübingen, etc., 1878f.
Annales *Annales. Économies, sociétés, civilisations*, Paris, 1946f. (sequel to "AHES").
ANor *Annales de Normandie*, Caen, 1951f.
Anton. *Antonianum. Periodicum philosophico-theologicum trimestre*, Rome, 1926f.
AOC *Archives de l'Orient chrétien*, Bucharest, Paris, 1932f.
AOL *Archives de l'Orient latin*, Paris, 1881-1884.
APEL *Arabic papyri in the Egyptian Library*, Cairo, 1934f.
APH *Acta Poloniae historica*, Rome, 1958f.
APraem *Analecta Praemonstratensia*, Tongerloo, 1925f.
AQDGMA *Ausgewählte Quellen zur deutschen Geschichte des Mittelalters*, Darmstadt, 1960f.
Arabica *Arabica. Revue d'études arabes*, Leiden, 1954f.
ArAt *Archives de l'Athos*, Paris, 1937f. (19 vol. issued).
ArBob *Archivum Bobiense*, Bobbio, 1979f.
ArMed *Archéologie médiévale*, Caen, 1971f.
ArtB *The Art Bulletin*, New York, etc., 1913f.
ASAN *Annales de la Société archéologique de Namur*, Namur, 1849f.
ASAW.PH *Abhandlungen der sächsischen Akademie der Wissenschaften. Philosophisch-historische Klasse*, Leipzig, 1915f.
ASLSP *Atti della Società Ligure di storia patria*, Genoa, 1858f.

ASNSP *Annali della reale Scuola normale superiore di Pisa*, Pisa, etc., 1873f.
ASRSP *Archivio della Società romana di storia patria*, Rome, 1878f.
ASSR *Archives de sciences sociales des religions*, Paris, 1973f.
Aug(L) *Augustiniana. Tijdschrift voor de studie van Sint Augustinus en de Augustijnenorde*, Louvain, 1951 f.
AUU *Acta universitatis Upsaliensis*, Uppsala, etc., 1959f.
BAC *Biblioteca de autores cristianos*, Madrid, 1944f.
BalS *Balkan Studies*, Thessalonica, 1960f.
BAr *Bulletin archéologique du Comité des travaux historiques et scientifiques*, Paris, 1883-1975.
BAug *Bibliothèque augustinienne*, Paris, 1936f.
BCRH *Bulletin de la Commission royale d'histoire de Belgique*, Brussels, 1834f.
BDLG *Blätter für deutsche Landesgeschichte*, Wiesbaden, 1937f.
BEC *Bibliothèque d'études coptes*, Cairo, 1919f. ("Publications de l'Institut français d'archéologie orientale du Caire").
BECh *Bibliothèque de l'École des chartes*, Paris, etc., 1839f.
BEFAR *Bibliothèque des Écoles françaises d'Athènes et de Rome*, Paris, 1877f.
BEHE *Bibliothèque de l'École des hautes études*, Paris, 1869f.
BenM *Benediktinische Monatsschrift zur Pflege religiösen und geistigen Leben*, Beuron, 1919-1958.
BEO *Bulletin d'études orientales de l'Institut français de Damas*, Beirut, etc., 1931f.
BEThL *Bibliotheca ephemeridum theologicarum Lovaniensium*, Louvain, etc., 1948f.
BFRPC *Bullarium franciscanum romanorum pontificum constitutiones, epistolas ac diplomata continens*, J. H. Sbaralea (ed.), C. Eubel (ed.), Rome, 1759-1904; suppl. 1780; Epitome 1908.
BGDS(H) *Beiträge zur Geschichte der deutschen Sprache und Literatur*, Halle, 1955-1979.
BGPhMA *Beiträge zur Geschichte der Philosophie und Theologie des Mittelalters*, M. Grabmann (ed.), Münster, 1891f.
BGQMA *Beiträge zur Geschichte und Quellenkunde des Mittelalters*, Berlin, etc., 1975f.
BHG *Bibliotheca hagiographica graeca*, Brussels, 1909 (3rd ed. 1957; 3 vol.; repr. 1986; "SHG", 8a); *Novum auctarium BHG*, 1984 ("SHG", 65).
BHL *Bibliotheca hagiographica latina antiquae et mediae aetatis*, Brussels, 1898-1901 (4 fasc. or 2 vol.; repr. 1992; "SHG", 6); *ibid., novum supplementum*, H. Fros (ed.), 1986 (2 vol.; "SHG", 70).
BHSt *Berliner historische Studien*, Berlin, 1980f.
Bib. *Biblica. Commentarii periodici ad rem biblicam scientifice investigandam*, Rome, 1920f.
BIHBR *Bulletin de l'Institut historique belge de Rome*, Rome, etc., 1919f.
BIIRHT *Bulletin d'information de l'Institut de Recherche et d'Histoire des Textes*, Paris, 1953-1963 (sequel to "PIRHT").
BISI *Bollettino dell'Istituto storico italiano per il Medio Evo (e archivio muratoriano)*, Rome, 1886f.
BLE *Bulletin de littérature ecclésiastique*, Toulouse, 1899f.
BM *Bulletin monumental*, Paris, etc., 1834f.
BMCL *Bulletin of Medieval Canon Law*, new series, Berkeley (CA), 1971f. (sequel to "Bulln. Institute of Medieval Canon Law", 1955-1970).
BMGS *Byzantine and Modern Greek Studies*, London, 1975f.
BNBelg *Biographie nationale, publiée par l'Académie de Belgique*, Brussels, 1866f.
BPH *Bulletin philologique et historique du Comité des travaux historiques et scientifiques*, Paris, 1913f.
BRUO A. B. Emden, *A Biographical Register of the University of Oxford to A.D. 1500*, Oxford, 1957-1959 (3 vol.).
BSAO *Bulletin de la societé des antiquaires de l'Ouest et des musées de Poitiers*, Poitiers, 1834f.
BSBS *Bollettino storico-bibliografico subalpino*, Turin, 1896f.
BSHAR *Bulletin de la Section historique de l'académie roumaine*, Bucharest, 1912-1942.
BSNAF *Bulletin de la Société nationale des antiquaires de France*, Paris, 1871f.
BSS *Bibliotheca Sanctorum. Istituto Giovanni XXIII nella pontificia università Lateranense*, Rome, 1962-1969 (12 vol.); indexes 1980; *Prima appendice*, 1987.
BSSV *Bollettino della Società di Studi Valdesi*, Torre Pellice, 1934f.
BThAM *Bulletin de théologie ancienne et médiévale*, Louvain, 1929f.
BTP *Bibliotheca theologiae practicae*, Lund, 1957f.
ByF *Byzantinische Forschungen*, Amsterdam, 1966f.
BySl *Byzantinoslavica. International Journal of Byzantine Studies*, Prague, 1929f.
ByZ *Byzantinische Zeitschrift*, Leipzig, etc., 1892f.
Byz. *Byzantion. Revue internationale des études byzantines*, Brussels, 1924f.
CAF *Congrès archéologique de France*, 1834f.
CaP *The Church at prayer. An introduction to the liturgy*, A. G. Martimort (ed.) *et al.*, London, 1986-1988 (4 vol.; translation of *L'Église en prière*, 2nd ed., Paris, 1983-1984).
CAr *Cahiers archéologiques*, Paris, 1945f.
Car. *Caritas. Zeitschrift für Caritaswissenschaft und Caritasarbeit*, Freiburg im Breisgau, 1896f.
Cath. *Catholicisme. Hier, aujourd'hui, demain*, G. Jacquemet (ed.), Paris, 1948f.
CAV *Collectanea Archivi Vaticani*, Vatican, 1968f.
CChr *Corpus Christianorum*, Turnhout, 1953f.
CChr.CM *CChr. Continuatio mediaevalis*, 1966f.
CChr.SG *CChr. Serie graeca*, 1974f.
CChr.SL *CChr. Serie latina*, 1953f.
CCist *Collectanea cisterciensia*, Scourmont, 1965f.
CCM *Cahiers de civilisation médiévale X^e-XII^e siècle*, Poitiers, 1958f.

| | |
|---|---|
| CCMon | *Corpus consuetudinum monasticarum*, K. Hallinger (ed.), Siegburg, 1963f. |
| CCSSM | *Convegni del Centro di Studi sulla spiritualità medievale*, Todi, 1957f. |
| CDHF | *Collection de documents inédits sur l'histoire de France*, Paris, 1835f. |
| CDios | *La Ciudad de Dios*, L'Escurial, etc., 1887f. |
| CE | *The Catholic Encyclopedia*, C. G. Herbermann (ed.), New York, 1907-1912 (15 vol.); index 1914; suppl. 1922; re-ed. 1950-1959 (18 vol.; then "NCE"). |
| CEFR | *Collection de l'École française de Rome*, Rome, 1972f. |
| CFa n | *Cahiers de Fanjeaux*, Fanjeaux, etc., 1966f. |
| CFHB | *Corpus fontium historiae byzantinae*, Berlin, etc., 1967f. |
| CFr | *Collectanea franciscana*, Rome, etc., 1931f. |
| CH | *Cahiers d'histoire*, Lyon, 1956f. |
| CHB | *Cambridge History of the Bible*, Cambridge 1963f. |
| CHFMA | *Classiques de l'histoire de France au Moyen Âge*, Paris, 1923f. |
| ChH | *Church History. American Society of Church History*, Chicago (IL), etc., 1932f. |
| CHIr | *Cambridge History of Iran*, Cambridge, 1968f. |
| CHR | *The Catholic Historical Review*, Washington (DC), 1915f. |
| CiSt | *Cistercian Studies. Bulletin of Monastic Spirituality*, Chimay, 1966f. |
| Cîteaux | *Cîteaux. Commentarii cistercienses*, Westmalle, etc., 1959f. (sequel to "CitN"). |
| CitN | *Cîteaux in de Nederlanden. Mededelingen over het Cisterciënser leven van de 12$^{e}$ tot de 18$^{e}$ eeuw*, Westmalle, 1950-1958 (then "Cîteaux"). |
| Clair-lieu | *Clair-lieu. Tijdschrift gewijd aan de geschiedenis der Kruisheeren*, Diest, 1943f. |
| CLD | *Cahiers Léopold Delisle*, Paris, 1947f. |
| CMCS | *Cambridge Medieval Celtic Studies*, Cambridge 1981f. |
| CMH | *Cambridge Medieval History*, Cambridge, 1911-1936; 2nd ed. 1966-1967 (8 vol.); 3rd ed. 1975f. |
| CMR | *Church Missionary Review*, London, 1907-1927. |
| CNL | *Cultura neolatina*, Modena, etc., 1941f. |
| COD | *Conciliorum oecumenicorum decreta*, H. Jedin (ed.), Fribourg, etc., 1962; 2nd ed. 1962; 3rd ed. G. Alberigo (ed.), Bologna, 1973. |
| Conc(F) | *Concilium. Revue internationale de théologie*, Paris, 1965f. |
| CPF | *Collection Les pères dans la foi*, Paris, 1977f.; new series 1979f. |
| CPG | *Clavis patrum Graecorum*, M. Geerard (ed.), 1974-1987 (5 vol.; "CChr.SG"). |
| CRAI | *Comptes rendus des séances de l'Académie des inscriptions et des belles-lettres*, Paris, 1857f. |
| CrSt | *Cristianesimo nella storia*, Bologna, 1980f. |
| CSCO | *Corpus scriptorum christianorum orientalium*, Paris, etc., 1903f. |
| CSCO.Sub | *CSCO. Subsidia*, 1950f. |
| CSEL | *Corpus scriptorum ecclesiasticorum latinorum*, Vienna, 1866f. |
| CSIC | *Consejo superior de investigaciones cientificas*, Madrid, 1953f. |
| CSMLT | *Cambridge Studies in Medieval Life and Thought*, Cambridge 1920-1930; 2nd series 1951-1969; 3rd series 1969f.; 4th series 1986f. |
| CStS | *Collected Studies Series*, London, Aldershot, 1970f. ("Variorum Reprint"). |
| CTom | *Ciencia tomista*, Madrid, etc., 1910f. |
| CTT | *Chrétiens de tous les temps. Textes du I$^{e}$ au XX$^{e}$ siècle*, Paris, 1963f. |
| CVSpir | *Cahiers de la vie spirituelle*, Paris, 1943-1954. |
| DA | *Deutsches Archiv für Erforschung des Mittelalters*, Cologne, etc., 1937f. ("MGH [Zeitschriften]"). |
| DACL | *Dictionnaire d'archéologie chrétienne et de liturgie*,F. Cabrol (ed.), H. Leclercq (ed.), Paris, 1903-1953 (15 vol.). |
| DAFC | *Dictionnaire apologétique de la foi catholique*, A. d'Alès, Paris, 1889; 4th ed. 1909-1928 (4 vol.); suppl. 1931. |
| DB | *Deutsche Bibliographie*, Frankfurt am Main, 1945f. |
| DBF | *Dictionnaire de biographie française*, Paris, 1923f. |
| DBI | *Dizionario biografico degli italiani*, Rome, 1960f. |
| DBS | *Dictionnaire de la Bible. Supplément*, L. Pirot (ed.) *et al.*, Paris, 1928f. |
| DDC | *Dictionnaire de droit canonique*, R. Naz (ed.), Paris, 1924f. |
| DEMA | *Dictionnaire encyclopédique du Moyen Âge*, A. Vauchez (ed.), Paris, 1997 (2 vol.). |
| DEF | *Dictionnaire des églises de France, Belgique, Luxembourg, Suisse*, Paris, 1966-1971 (5 vol.). |
| DEP | B. Mondin, *Dizionario Enciclopedico dei papi*, Rome, 1995. |
| DH | *Enchiridion symbolorum, definitionum et declarationum de rebus fidei et morum*, H. Denzinger (ed.), P. Hünermann (ed.), Freiburg im Breisgau, 1991 (37th ed.; 1st ed. 1854). |
| DHEE | *Diccionario de historia eclesiástica de España*, Q. Aldea Vaquero (ed.), T. Marin Martinez (ed.), J. Vives Gatell (ed.), Madrid, 1972f. |
| DHGE | *Dictionnaire d'histoire et de géographie ecclésiastiques*, A. Baudrillart (ed.), Paris, 1912f. |
| DHP | *Dictionnaire historique de la papauté*, P. Levillain (ed.), Paris, 1994. |
| DicRel | *Dictionnaire des religions*, P. Poupard (ed.), Paris, 1984. |
| DIP | *Dizionario degli Istituti di perfezione*, G. Pelliccia (ed.), G. Rocca (ed.), Rome, 1974f. |
| Div. | *Divinitas. Pontificae academiae theologicae Romanae commentarii*, Rome, 1957f. |
| DLFMA | *Dictionnaire des lettres françaises. Le Moyen Âge*, R. Bossuat (ed.), L. Pichard (ed.), G. Raynaud de Lage (ed.), G. Hasenohr (ed.), M. Zink (ed.), Paris, 1992 ("La Pochothèque"; 1st ed. 1964). |
| DMA | *Dictionary of the Middle Ages*, J. R. Strayer (ed.), New York, 1982-1989 (13 vol.). |
| DNB | *Dictionary of National Biography from the Earliest Times to 1900*, London, 1885-1900 (63 vol.); suppl. 1901 (3 vol.); 2nd ed. 1908-1909 (22 vol.); suppl. 1912 (3 vol.). |
| DoA | *Dictionary of Art*, J. Turner (ed.), London, New York, 1996 (34 vol.). |

| | |
|---|---|
| DomSt | *Dominican Studies*, Oxford, 1948f. |
| DOP | *Dumbarton Oaks Papers*, Cambridge (MA), etc., 1941f. |
| DPLR | *Dictionnaire pratique de liturgie romaine*, Paris, 1952. |
| DSp | *Dictionnaire de spiritualité, ascétique et mystique. Doctrine et histoire*, M. Viller (ed.), Paris, 1932-1994 (16 vol.); tables 1996. |
| DThC | *Dictionnaire de théologie catholique*, A. Vacant (ed.), E. Mangenot (ed.) *et al.*, Paris, 1903-1950 (15 vol.); index 1951-1972 (3 vol.). |
| DuCange | C. Du Cange, *Glossarium mediae et infimae latinitatis*, Paris, 1687 (3 vol.); 2nd ed. Niort, 1883-1887 (10 vol.); repr. Graz, 1954; suppl. 1970. |
| EAug | *Études augustiniennes*, Paris, 1954. |
| EC | *Enciclopedia cattolica*, P. Paschini (ed.), Vatican, etc., 1948-1954 (12 vol.); suppl. 1969. |
| ECR | *Eastern Churches Review*, Oxford, 1966-1978. |
| EdM | *Enzyklopädie des Märchens. Handwörterbuch zur historischen und vergleichenden Erzählforschung*, K. Ranke (ed.), Berlin, 1975f. |
| EE | *Estudios eclesiásticos*, Madrid, 1922f. |
| EEC | *Encyclopedia of the Early Church*, A. Di Berardino (ed.), Cambridge, 1992 (2 vol.; Eng. tr. of *Dizionario patristico*). |
| EEM | *East European Monographs*, New York, 1971f. |
| EETS | *Early English Text Society*, London, 1864f. |
| EHR | *English Historical Review*, London, 1886f. |
| EI(E) | *Encyclopaedia of Islam*, Leiden-London, 1913-1936 (4 vol.); suppl. 1938; new ed. Leiden, 1960- (10 vol. so far issued); suppl. 1980-1982 (6 fasc.); glossary 1997; index 1998 (2 vol.). |
| Elr | *Encyclopaedia Iranica*, E. Yarshater (ed.), London, 1982f. |
| EL | *Ephemerides Liturgicae*, Rome, 1887f. |
| EncIt | *Enciclopedia italiana di scienze, lettere ed arti*, Rome, 1929-1939; *Appendice* 1938-1981 (44 vol.). |
| EncKat | *Encyklopedia Katolicka*,F. Gryglewicza (ed.) *et al.*, Lublin, 1973f. |
| EncRel(E) | *The Encyclopedia of Religion*, M. Eliade (ed.), New York, London, 1987 (16 vol.). |
| EO | *Ecclesia orans. Periodica de scientiis liturgicis*, Rome, 1984f. |
| E0r | *Écho d'Orient*, Paris, Bucharest, etc., 1897-1943. |
| EPh | *Études philosophiques*, Paris, 1927-1945; new series 1946f. |
| ES | *Economia e storia*, Rome, 1954f. |
| EstB | *Estudios biblicos*, Madrid, 1929f. |
| EtCarm | *Études carmélitaines*, Paris, 1911-1964. |
| EtFr | *Études franciscaines*, Paris, 1899f. |
| EtFr.SA | *EtFr. Supplément annuel*, 1952-1972. |
| EThL | *Ephemerides theologicae Lovanienses*, Bruges, Louvain, etc., 1924f. |
| FBRG | *Forschungen zur byzantinischen Rechtsgeschichte*, Frankfurt am Main, 1976f. |
| FDA | *Freiburger Diözesan-Archiv*, Freiburg im Breisgau, 1865f. |
| FMSt | *Frühmittelalterliche Studien*, Berlin, 1967f. |
| FOEG | *Forschungen zur osteuropäischen Geschichte*, Berlin, Wiesbaden, etc., 1954f. |
| FoiCath | *Foi catholique*, Paris, 1908f. |
| Fr. | *Franciscana. Archief der Paters Minderbroeders*, Sint-Truiden, 1946f. |
| Francia | *Francia. Forschungen zur westeuropäischen Geschichte*, Munich, 1973f. |
| FrFr | *France franciscaine. Recherches de théologie, philosophie, histoire*, Paris, 1912-1939. |
| FrS | *Franciscan Studies*, Saint Bonaventure (NY), 1924f. |
| FS | *Franziskanische Studien*, Münster, etc., 1914f. |
| FSI | *Fonti per la storia d'Italia*, Rome, 1887f. |
| FVK | *Forschungen zur Volkskunde*, Düsseldorf, etc., 1930f. |
| GBA | *Gazette des Beaux-Arts*, Paris, 1859f. |
| GCFI | *Giornale critico della filosofia italiana*, Florence, etc., 1920f. |
| GermSac | *Germania sacra*, Berlin, 1929f.; new series 1962. |
| GGB | *Geschichtliche Grundbegriffe. Historisches Lexikon zur politisch-sozialen Sprache in Deutschland*, 0. Brunner (ed.) *et al.*, Stuttgart, 1972f. |
| Gn. | *Gnomon. Kritische Zeitschrift für die gesamte klassische Altertumswissenschaft*, Munich, etc., 1925f. |
| GRLMA | *Grundriss der romanischen Literaturen des Mittelalters*, H. R. Jauss (ed.) *et al.*, Heidelberg, 1968f. |
| HAW | *Handbuch der Altertumswissenschaft*, I. von Miller (ed.) *et al.*, Munich, 1922f. |
| HBS | *Publications. Henry Bradshaw Society*, London, 1891f. |
| HChr | *Histoire du christianisme des origines à nos jours*, J.-M. Mayeur (ed.), C. Pietri (ed.), A. Vauchez (ed.), M. Venard (ed.), Paris, 1990f. (vol. 4, *Évêques, moines et empereurs: 610-1054*, 1993; vol. 5, *Apogée de la papauté et expansion de la chrétienté: 1054-1274*, 1993; vol. 6, *Un temps d'épreuves: 1274-1449*, 1990; vol. 7, *De la réforme à la Réformation: 1450-1530*, 1994). |
| HCO | *Histoire des conciles œcuméniques*, Paris, 1962-1981 (12 vol.). |
| HDF | *Histoire des diocèses de France*, Paris, 1970f. |
| HDG | *Handbuch der Dogmengeschichte*, M. Schmaus (ed.) *et al.*, Freiburg im Breisgau, 1951f. |
| HDIEO | *Histoire du droit et des institutions de l'Église en Occident*, G. Le Bras (ed.), Paris, 1955f. |
| HE | *Histoire de l'Église depuis les origines jusqu'à nos jours*, A. Fliche (ed.), V. Martin (ed.), Paris, 1934f. |
| HelSac | *Helvetia sacra*, A. Bruckner (ed.), Sankt Gallen, Berne, 1972f. |
| Herm. | *Hermaea. Germanistische Forschungen*, Halle, 1905-1940; new series 1952f. |
| Hes. | *Hesperis. Archives berbères et bulletin de l'Institut des hautes études marocaines*, Paris, 1921-1959. |
| HGP | *Handbuch der Geschichte der Philosophie*, W. Totok (ed.), Frankfurt am Main, 1963f. |

| | |
|---|---|
| Hist(L) | *History. The Journal of the Historical Association*, London, 1912f. |
| Hist(P) | *Historica. Les sciences historiques en Tchécoslovaquie*, Prague, 1959f. |
| HistDog | *Histoire des dogmes*, Paris, 1953f. |
| HJ | *Historisches Jahrbuch der Görres-Gesellschaft*, Cologne, Munich, etc., 1880f. |
| HKG(J) | *Handbuch der Kirchengeschichte*, H. Jedin (ed.), Freiburg im Breisgau, etc., 1962-1979; suppl. 1970 (7 vol). |
| HLF | *Histoire littéraire de la France*, Paris, 1733-1763 (12 vol.); 1814-1927 (23 vol.); new ed. 1835f.; 3rd ed. 1974-1980 (17 vol.). |
| HMGOG | *Handelingen der Maatschappij voor Geschiedenis en Oudheidkunde te Gent*, Ghent, 1894-1923; new series 1944f. |
| HO | *Handbuch der Orientalistik*, Leiden, etc., 1984f. |
| HS | *Historische Studien*, E. Ebering (ed.) *et al.*, Berlin, etc., 1896f. |
| HSE | *Histoire et sociologie de l'Église*, Paris, 1962f. |
| HSSC | *Histoire des saints et de la sainteté chrétienne*, J. Delumeau (ed.), P. Riché (ed.), A. Vauchez (ed.), Paris, 1986f. |
| HThR | *The Harvard Theological Review*, Cambridge (MA), 1906f. |
| HUMC | *Histoire universelle des missions catholiques*, J. Delacroix (ed.), Paris, 1954-1959 (4 vol.). |
| HWP | *Historisches Wörterbuch der Philosophie*, J. Ritter (ed.) *et al.*, Basel, 1971f. |
| HZ | *Historische Zeitschrift*, Munich, 1859f. |
| IATG | S. M. Schwertner, *Internationales Abkürzungsverzeichnis für Theologie und Grenzgebiete: Zeitschriften, Serien, Lexika, Quellenwerke mit bibliographischen Angaben*, Berlin, 1974; 2nd ed. revised and enlarged, 1992 (ed. in "TRE" in 1976 and 1994). |
| IER | *The Irish Ecclesiastical Record*, Dublin, 1864-1968. |
| IMU | *Italia medioevale e umanistica*, Padua, 1959f. |
| InR | *Innes Review. Scottish Catholic Historical Studies*, Glasgow, 1950f. |
| Irén. | *Irénikon*, Amay-Chevetogne, etc., 1926f. |
| IS | *ltalia sacra*, Padua, 1959f. |
| ltBen | *Italia benedettina*, Cesena, 1979f. |
| JA | *Journal asiatique*, Paris, 1822f. |
| JAfH | *Journal of African History*, London, 1960f. |
| JBAA | *Journal of the British Archaeological Association*, London, 1845-1894; 2nd series 1895-1936; 3rd series 1937f. |
| JEconHist | *Journal of Economic History*, New York, 1941f. |
| JEH | *The Journal of Ecclesiastical History*, London, etc., 1950f. |
| JFLF | *Jahrbuch für fränkische Landesforschung*, Neustadt, etc., 1935f. |
| JGO | *Jahrbücher für Geschichte Osteuropas*, Munich, etc., 1936f. |
| JHI | *Journal of the History of Ideas*, New York, etc., 1940f. |
| JMH | *Journal of Medieval History*, Amsterdam, 1975f. |
| JMRS | *The Journal of Medieval and Renaissance Studies*, Durhan (NC), 1971f. |
| JÖB | *Jahrbuch der österreichischen Byzantinistik*, Vienna, etc., 1969f. |
| JRAS | *Journal of the Royal Asiatic Society of Great Britain and Ireland*, London, 1834f. |
| JRS | *Journal of Roman Studies*, London, 1911f. |
| JS | *Journal des savants*, Paris, 1665f. |
| JThS | *Journal of Theological Studies*, Oxford, etc., 1899f. |
| Jurist | *Jurist. Catholic University of America, School of Canon Law*, Washington (DC), 1941f. |
| JVABG | *Jahrbuch des Vereins für Augsburger Bistumsgeschichte*, Augsburg, 1967f. |
| Klio | *Klio. Beiträge zur alten Geschichte*, Leipzig, etc., 1906-1943. |
| KLNM(S) | *Kulturhistorisk Lexicon för nordisk medeltid från vikingetid till reformationstid*, Malmö, 1956-1978 (22 vol.). |
| KonGe | *Konziliengeschichte*, Paderborn, 1979f. |
| KonGe.D | *KonGe. Darstellungen*, Paderborn, 1980f. |
| Kyrios | *Kyrios. Vierteljahrsschrift für Kirchen- und Geistesgeschichte Osteuropas*, Berlin, 1936f. |
| Latomus | *Latomus. Revue d'études latines*, Brussels, 1937f. |
| LCI | *Lexikon der christlichen Ikonographie*, Freiburg im Breisgau, 1968-1976 (8 vol.); re-ed. 1990. |
| LdM | *Lexikon des Mittelalters*, Munich, Zurich, 1980f. |
| Leod. | *Leodium. Société d'art et d'histoire du diocèse de Liège*, Liège, 1908f. |
| LJ | *Liturgisches Jahrbuch*, Münster, 1951f. |
| LMD | *La Maison-Dieu. Revue de pastorale liturgique*, Paris, 1945f. |
| LP | *Liber pontificalis*, L. Duchesne (ed.), Paris, 1886 and 1892; 2nd ed. C. Vogel (ed.), 1955-1957 (3 vol.; "BEFAR"). |
| LQF | *Liturgiegeschichtliche Quellen und Forschungen*, Münster, 1928-1939. |
| LThK | *Lexikon für Theologie und Kirche*, M. Buchberger (ed.), Freiburg im Br, etc., 1930-1938 (10 vol.); 2nd ed. 1957-1968; 3rd ed. 1993f. |
| LV(L) | *Lumière et vie. Revue de formation et de réflexion théologique*, Lyon, 1951f. |
| MA | *Le Moyen Âge. Revue d'histoire et de philologie*, Brussels, etc., 1888f. |
| MAe | *Medium aevum*, Oxford, 1932f. |
| MAIBL | *Mémoires présentés par divers savants a l'Académie des inscriptions et belles-lettres de l'Institut de France*, Paris, 1843f. |
| Mansi | *Sacrorum conciliorum nova et amplissima collectio*, J. D. Mansi (ed.), Florence, 1759-1789 (31 vol.); new ed. Paris, etc., 1901-1927 (55 vol.); repr. Graz, 1960-1961 (59 vol.). |
| Maria | *Maria. Études sur la sainte Vierge*, M. du Manoir (ed.), Paris, 1949-1971 (8 vol.). |
| MCass | *Miscellanea Cassinese*, Montecassino, 1897f. |
| MDom | *Memorie domenicane. Rivista di religione, storia, arte*, Florence, etc., 1921f. |
| MEFRM | *Mélanges de l'École française de Rome. Moyen Âge, Temps modernes*, Rome, 1971f. |
| MeH | *Medievalia et humanistica*, Boulder (CO), 1943-1966; new series 1970. |

MeH(M) *Medievalia et humanistica*, Madrid, 1986f.
MF *Miscellanea francescana*, Rome, etc., 1936f.
MGH *Monumenta Germaniae historica inde ab a.C. 500 usque ad a. 1500*, K. vom Stein (ed.) *et al.*, Hanover, Munich, etc., 1819f. (mainly 5 groups of subseries: "Scriptores": 10 series; "Leges": 11 series; "Diplomata": 6 series; "Epistolae": 5 series; "Antiquitates": 4 series; numerous re-editions and supplements).
MGH.AA *MGH [Scriptores]. Auctores antiquissimi*, 1877-1919; re-ed. 1978-1985 (15 vol.).
MGH.B *MGH [Epistolae]. Die Briefe der deutschen Kaiserzeit*, 1949-1994; re-ed. 1977f. (7 vol.).
MGH.Cap *MGH [Leges]. Capitularia regum Francorum*, 1883-1897; re-ed. 1980-1984 (2 vol.).
MGH.Conc *MGH [Leges]. Concilia*, 1893f.; re-ed. 1979f. (7 vol.).
MGH.Const *MGH [Leges]. Constitutiones et acta publica imperatorum et regum*, 1893f.; re-ed. 1963f. (11 vol.).
MGH.D *MGH [Diplomata]. Diplomata (in folio)*, K. A.F. Pertz (ed.), 1872; re-ed. 1980 (1 vol.).
MGH.DR *MGH [Diplomata]. Diplomata regum et imperatorum Germaniae (Die Urkunden der deutschen Könige und Kaiser)*, 1879f.; re-ed. 1959f. (19 vol.).
MGH.Ep *MGH [Epistolae]. Epistolae (in quarto)*, 1887-1939; re-ed. 1978f. (8 vol.).
MGH.ES *MGH. Epistolae selectae*, 1916f.
MGH.F *MGH [Leges]. Fontes iuris Germanici antiqui*, 1869f.; re-ed. 1980f. (14 vol.); new series 1933f.; re-ed. 1973f. (6 vol.).
MGH.H *MGH. Hilfsmittel*, 1975f.; re-ed. 1987f. (15 vol.).
MGH.LF *MGH [Diplomata]. Laienfürsten- und Dynastenurkunden der Kaiserzeit*, 1, 1941-1949 (re-ed. 1995); *ibid.*, 2, 1997.
MGH.LL *MGH [Scriptores]. Libelli de lite imperatorum et pontificum saeculis XI. et XII. conscripti*, E. Dümmler (ed.) *et al.*, 1891-1897 (3 vol.).
MGH.PL *MGH [Antiquitates]. Poetae latini Medii Aevi*, 1881f.; re-ed. 1978f. (6 vol.; including "Poetae Latini aevi Carolini", vol. 1-4).
MGH.QG *MGH. Quellen zur Geistesgeschichte des Mittelalters*, 1955f.; re-ed. 1983f. (15 vol.).
MGH.SRG *MGH [Scriptores]. Scriptores rerum Germanicarum*, 1826f.; re-ed. 1965f. (67 vol.); new series 1922f.; re-ed. 1980f. (17 vol.).
MGH.SRL *MGH [Scriptores]. Scriptores rerum Langobardicarum et Italicarum saec. VI-IX*, G. Waitz (ed.), 1878; re-ed. 1988 (1 vol.).
MGH.SRM *MGH [Scriptores]. Scriptores rerum Merovingicarum*, B. Krusch (ed.) *et al.*, 1884-1920; re-ed. 1937f. (7 vol).
MGH.SS *MGH [Scriptores]. Scriptores (in folio)*, 1826f.; re-ed. 1963f. (37 vol.; also "in quarto").
MGSL *Mitteilungen der Gesellschaft für Salzburger Landeskunde*, Salzburg, 1860f.
MHF *Monuments historiques de la France*, Paris, 1936f.
MHP *Miscellanea historiae pontificae*, Rome, 1939f.
MIC.C *Monumenta iuris canonici. Corpus collectionum*, Rome, 1973f.
MIC.S *Monumenta iuris canonici. Subsidia*, Rome, 1965f.
MIDEO *Mélanges de l'Institut dominicain d'études orientales du Caire*, Cairo, etc., 1954f.
MIÖG *Mitteilungen des Instituts für Österreichische Geschichtsforschung*, Innsbruck, 1880f.
MIÖG.E *MIÖG. Ergänzungsband*, 1885f.
MJBK *Münchner Jahrbuch der bildenden Kunst*, Munich, 1906f.
MKHIF *Mitteilungen des Kunsthistorischen Instituts in Florenz*, Florence, etc., 1908f.
MLN *Modern Language Notes*, Baltimore (MD) ,1886f.
MM *Miscellanea mediaevalia*, Berlin, etc., 1962f.
MMAS *Münstersche Mittelalterschriften*, Munich, 1970f.
MOCC *Magnum oecumenicum Constantiense concilium de universali ecclesiae reformatione*, H. Von der Hardt (ed.), Frankfurt am Main, 1696-1742.
MOFPH *Monumenta ordinis fratrum praedicatorum historica*, Rome, 1896f.
MonBelg *Monasticon belge*, Liège, 1890f.
MonIt *Monasticon Italiae*, Cesena ,1981f.
MPhLJ *Mélanges de philosophie et de littérature juives*, Paris, 1956f.
MRSt *Medieval and Renaissance Studies. Proceedings*, Chapel Hill (NC), 1965f. ("Medieval and Renaissance Series").
MS *Mediaeval Studies. Pontifical Institute of Mediaeval Studies*, Toronto, etc., 1939f.
MSAO *Mémoires de la Société des antiquaires de l'Ouest,*Poitiers, 1935f.
MSHAB *Mémoires de la Société d'histoire et d'archéologie de Bretagne*, Rennes, 1920f.
MSHAL *Mémoires de la Société historique et archéologique de Langres*, Langres, 1847f.
MSHD *Mémoires de la Société pour l'histoire du droit et des institutions des anciens pays Bourguignons, Comtois et Romands*, Dijon, 1932f.
MSHP *Mémoires de la Société de l'histoire de Paris et de l'Île-de-France*, Paris, 1875-1930.
MSR *Mélanges de science religieuse*, Lille, 1944f.
Muséon *Le Muséon. Revue d'études orientales*, Louvain, etc., 1882f.
MUSJ *Mélanges de l'université Saint-Joseph*, Beirut, 1913f.
MySal *Mysterium salutis. Grundriß heilsgeschichtlicher Dogmatik*, Einsiedeln, 1965f.
NBA *Nuova Biblioteca Agostiniana*, Rome, 1965f.
NC(C) *Nouvelle Clio: l'histoire et ses problèmes. Collection*, Paris, 1969f.
NCE *New Catholic Encyclopedia*, W. J. McDonald (ed.) *et al.*, New York, etc., 1967f. (new ed. of "CE").
NDM *Nuovo dizionario di mariologia*, Rome, 1985.
NDB *Neue deutsche Biographie*, Berlin, 1953f.
NPM *Neuphilologische Mitteilungen*, Helsinki, 1899f.
NQRW *Notes and Queries for Readers and Writers, Collectors and Librarians*, London, 1849f.
NRTh *Nouvelle revue théologique. Museum Lessianum, section théologique*, Louvain, etc., 1869f.
NSchol *New Scholasticism*, Washington (DC), etc., 1927f.
OCA *Orientalia christiana analecta*, Rome, 1935f.

OGE *Ons geestelijk erf*, Antwerp, etc., 1927f.
OMT *Oxford Medieval Texts*, Oxford 1967f.
OrChr *Oriens christianus*, Rome, etc., 1901f.
OrChrA *Orientalia christiana analecta*, Rome, 1935f. (sequel to "OrChr").
OrChrP *Orientalia christiana periodica*, Rome, 1935f.
PaP *Past and Present, A Journal of Scientific History*, London, 1952f.
ParLi *Paroisse et liturgie*, Saint-André-lès-Bruges, 1946-1974.
PBA *Proceedings of the British Academy for the Promoting of Historical, Philosophical and Philological Studies*, London, 1903f.
PCS *Publications. Camden Society*, London, 1838-1872; new series 1871-1901 (called "Old Series"); 4th series 1975f.
PG *Patrologiae cursus completus. Series Graeca*, J.-P. Migne (ed.), Paris, 1857-1866 (167 vol.); index 1928-1936.
PHChr *Problèmes d'histoire du christianisme*, Brussels, 1970f.
PIASH *Proceedings of the Israel Academy of Sciences and Humanities*, Jerusalem, 1963f.
PIRHT *Publications de l'Institut de Recherche et d'Histoire des Textes*, Paris, 1952 (then "BIIRHT").
PL *Patrologiae cursus completus. Series Latina*, J.-P. Migne (ed.), Paris, 1841-1864 (217 vol. and 4 vol. of tables); suppl. 1958-1974 (5 vol.).
PLP *Prosopographisches Lexikon der Palaiologenzeit*, E. Trapp (ed.), Vienna, 1976-1994 (15 fasc.; "Österreichische Akademie der Wissenschaften. Veröffentlichungen der Kommission für Byzantinistik", 1).
PO *Patrologia orientalis*, Paris, etc., 1903f.
POC *Proche-Orient chrétien*, Jerusalem, 1951f.
PRE *Paulys Real-Encyclopädie der klassischen Altertumswissenschaft*, G. Wissowa (ed.), Stuttgart, 1894-1980.
PRE.S *PRE. Supplement*, 1903-1980.
ProvHist *Provence historique*, Marseille, 1950f.
PSc *Publications de "Scriptorium"*, Brussels, etc., 1947f.
PTS *Patristische Texte und Studien*, Berlin, 1963f.
Qan. *Al-Qantara. Revista de estudios árabes*, Madrid, 1980f. (sequel to "And.").
QFIAB *Quellen und Forschungen aus italienischen Archiven und Bibliotheken*, Tübingen, etc., 1898f.
QM *Quaderni medievali*, Bari, 1976f.
QSJ *Que sais-je?*, Paris, 1949f.
QSt *Quaderni storici*, Ancona, 1970f.
RAC *Reallexikon für Antike und Christentum*, F. J. Dölger (ed.), Stuttgart, 1950f.
Rals *Revue d'Alsace*, Strasbourg, etc., 1850f.
RAPC *Les Regestes des actes du patriarcat de Constantinople*, V. Grumel (ed.), Constantinople, 1932f. ("Le Patriarcat byzantin", 1).
RArte *Rivista d'arte*, Florence, 1904f.
RAuv *Revue d'Auvergne*, Clermont-Ferrand, 1884f.
RB *Revue biblique*, Paris, 1892f.
RBAHA *Revue belge d'archéologie et d'histoire de l'art*, Antwerp, etc., 1931f.
RBen *Revue bénédictine de critique, d'histoire et de littérature religieuses*, Maredsous, 1890f.
RBK *Reallexikon zur byzantinischen Kunst*, K. Wessel (ed.), Stuttgart, 1966f.
RBMA *Repertorium biblicum medii aevi*, F. Stegmüller (ed.), Madrid, 1950-1961.
RBMAS *Rerum Britannicarum medii aevi scriptores or Chronicles and Memorials of Great Britain and Ireland during the Middle Ages*, London, 1858-1896 (called "Rolls Series").
RBPH *Revue belge de philologie et d'histoire*, Brussels, 1922f.
RDC *Revue de droit canonique*, Strasbourg, 1951f.
RDK *Reallexikon zur deutschen Kunstgeschichte*, Stuttgart, 1933f.
REArm *Revue des études arméniennes*, Paris, 1920-1933; new series 1964f.
REAug *Revue des études augustiniennes*, Paris, 1955f.
REByz *Revue des études byzantines*, Paris, 1946f.
RechAug *Recherches augustiniennes*, Paris, 1958f.
RegBenSt *Regulae Benedicti studia. Annuarium internationale*, Hildesheim, 1972f.
REI *Revue des études islamiques*, Paris, 1927f.
REJ *Revue des études juives*, Paris, 1880f.
Ren. *Renovatio. Zeitschrift für das interdisziplinäre Gespräche*, Ratisbon, 1976f.
RESl *Revue des études slaves*, Paris, 1921f.
RevSR *Revue des sciences religieuses. Faculté catholique de théologie*, Strasbourg, etc., 1921f.
RGG *Die Religion in Geschichte und Gegenwart*, Tübingen, 1909-1913.
RH *Revue historique*, Paris, 1876f.
RHD *Revue d'histoire diplomatique*, Paris, 1887f.
RHDF *Revue d'histoire de droit français et étranger*, Paris, 1855f.
RHE *Revue d'histoire ecclésiastique*, Louvain, 1900f.
RHEF *Revue d'histoire de l'Église de France*, Paris, 1910f.
RHPhR *Revue d'histoire et de philosophie religieuse*, Strasbourg, 1921f.
RHR *Revue de l'histoire des religions*, Paris, 1880f. ("Annales du musée Guimet").
RHSp *Revue d'histoire de la spiritualité*, Paris, 1972f.
RHT *Revue d'histoire des textes*, Paris, 1971f.
RhV *Rheinische Vierteljahrsblätter*, Bonn, 1931f.

| | |
|---|---|
| RIS | *Rerum Italicarum scriptores*, L. A. Muratori (ed.), Città di Castello, etc., 1723-1751 (2nd ed. 1900f.). |
| RivAC | *Rivista di archeologia cristiana*, Rome, 1924f. |
| RLS | *Repertorium der lateinischen Sermones des Mittelalters für die Zeit 1150-1350*, J. B. Schneyer (ed.), Münster, 1969f. ("BGPhMA", 43). |
| RMab | *Revue Mabillon. Archives de la France monastique*, Paris, etc., 1905f. |
| RMAL | *Revue du Moyen Âge latin*, Paris, etc., 1945f. |
| RMM | *Revue de métaphysique et de morale*, Paris, 1893f. |
| RMoMu | *Revue du monde musulman*, Paris, 1906-1926 (then "REI"). |
| RNord | *Revue du Nord*, Lille, 1910f. |
| RNSP | *Revue néo-scolastique de philosophie*, Louvain, 1910-1945. |
| ROC | *Revue de l'Orient chrétien*, Paris, 1896-1936 (1946). |
| RöHM | *Römische historische Mitteilungen*, Graz, etc., 1956f. |
| Rom. | *Romania. Revue trimestrielle consacrée a l'étude des langues et des littératures romanes*, Paris, 1872f. |
| RQ | *Römische Quartalschrift für christliche Altertumskunde und für Kirchengeschichte*, Freiburg im Breisgau, 1887f. |
| RRH | *Revue roumaine d'histoire*, Bucharest, 1962f. |
| RSBN | *Rivista di studi bizantini e neoellenici*, Rome, 1964f. |
| RSCI | *Rivista di storia della Chiesa in Italia*, Rome, 1947f. |
| RSJB | *Recueils de la société Jean Bodin pour l'histoire comparative des institutions*, Brussels, 1936f. |
| RSPhTh | *Revue des sciences philosophiques et théologiques*, Paris, etc., 1907f. |
| RSR | *Recherches de science religieuse*, Paris, 1910f. |
| RTh(P) | *Revue théologique*, Paris, 1870-1890. |
| RThAM | *Recherches de théologie ancienne et médiévale*, Louvain, 1929f. |
| RThom | *Revue thomiste*, Bruges, etc., 1893f. |
| RThPh | *Revue de théologie et de philosophie et comptes rendus des principales publications scientifiques (à l'étranger)*, Lausanne, 1873f. |
| RTL | *Revue théologique de Louvain*, Louvain, 1970f. |
| SAC | *Studi di antichità cristiana*, Rome, etc., 1929f. |
| Saec. | *Saeculum. Jahrbuch für Universalgeschichte*, Munich, etc., 1950f. |
| SAGM | *Sudhoffs Archiv für Geschichte des Medizin und der Naturwissenschaften*, Wiesbaden, 1929f. |
| Sal. | *Salesianum. Pontificio ateneo salesiano*, Turin, 1939f. |
| SbWGF | *Sitzungsberichte der wissenschaftlichen Gesellschaft an der Johann Wolfgang Goethe-Universität*, Frankfurt am Main, Wiesbaden, 1962f. |
| SC | *Sources chrétiennes*, Paris, 1941f. |
| SCH | *Studies in Church History. American Society of Church History*, Chicago (IL), etc., 1933f. |
| SCH(L) | *Studies in Church History. Ecclesiastical History Society*, London, 1964f. |
| SCH(L).S | *SCH(L). Subsidia*, 1978f. |
| Schol. | *Scholastik. Vierteljahresschrift für Theologie und Philosophie*, Freiburg im Breisgau, 1926f. |
| Scr. | *Scriptorium. Revue internationale des études relatives aux manuscripts*, Antwerp, etc., 1946f. |
| SDHI | *Studia et documenta historiae et iuris*, Rome, 1935f. |
| SE | *Sacris erudiri. Jaarboek voor godsdienstwetenschappen*, Steenbrugge, etc., 1948f. |
| SeArm | *Seanchas Armhacha. Journal of the Armagh Diocesan Historical Society*, Armagh, 1954f. |
| Sef. | *Sefarad. Revista de la escuela de hebraicos*, Madrid, 1941f. |
| SFS | *Spicilegii Friburgensis subsidia*, Fribourg, 1963f. |
| SGSG | *Studi gregoriani per la storia di Gregorio VII e della riforma gregoriana*, Rome, 1947-1960. |
| SGSLE | *Studi gregoriani per la storia della libertas ecclesiae*, Rome, 1970f. (sequel to "SGSG"). |
| SHG | *Subsidia hagiographica*, Brussels, 1886f. |
| SHM | *Sources d'histoire mediévale*, Paris, 1965f. |
| SLH | *Scriptores latini Hiberniae*, Dublin, 1955f. |
| SMBO | *Studien und Mitteilungen aus dem Benediktiner-Orden*, Munich, 1882-1910 (then "SMGB"). |
| SMGB | *Studien un Mitteilungen zur Geschichte des Benediktinerordens und seiner Zweige*, Munich, 1911f. (sequel to "SMBO"). |
| SMGH | *Schriften der Monumenta Germaniae historica*, Stuttgart, Hanover, 1938f. (38 vol.; "MGH"). |
| SMH | *Studies in Medieval History*, Washington (DC), 1927-1933; new series 1938f. |
| SMRT | *Studies in Medieval and Reformation Thought*, Leiden, 1966f. |
| SOP | J. Quétif, J. Échard, *Scriptores ordinis praedicatorum recensiti*, Paris, 1719-1721 (2 vol.); re-ed. 1885-1914 (9 vol.); suppl. 1934. |
| SOPMA | T. Kaeppeli, *Scriptores ordinis praedicatorum medii aevi*, Rome, 1970-1993 (4 vol.). |
| Spec. | *Speculum. A Journal of Mediaeval Studies*, Cambridge (MA), 1926f. |
| SpicFri | *Spicilegium Friburgense. Texte zur Geschichte des kirchlichen Lebens*, Fribourg (Switzerland), 1957f. |
| SpOr | *Spiritualité orientale*, Bégrolles-en-Mauges, 1985f. |
| SQWFG | *Studien und Quellen zur westfälischen Geschichte*, Paderborn, 1957f. |
| SR | *Studies in Religion. Sciences religieuses. Canadian Corporation for Studies in Religion*, Toronto, 1971f. |
| SRo | *Storia di Roma*, Bologna, 1938. |
| SS | *Studi semitici*, Rome, 1958f. |
| SSAM | *Settimane di studio del Centro italiano di studi sull'alto medievo*, Spoleto, 1953f. |
| SSL | *Spicilegium sacrum Lovaniense*, Louvain, 1922f. |
| SSOSM | *Studi storici dell'Ordine dei Servi di Maria*, Rome, 1933f. |
| StAns | *Studia anselmiana. Philosophica et theologica*, Rome, 1933f. |

| | |
|---|---|
| StCan | *Studia canonica*, Ottawa, 1967f. |
| StGra | *Studia Gratiana. Post octava decreti saecularia auctore consilio commemorationi Gratianae instruendae edita*, Bologna, 1953-1978. |
| StIr.C | *Studia Iranica. Cahier*, Paris, 1982f. |
| StIsl | *Studia Islamica*, Paris, 1953f. |
| StMed | *Studi medievali*, Turin, etc., 1904f. |
| StMon | *Studia monastica*, Barcelona, 1959f. |
| StPat | *Studia Patavina. Rivista di filosofia e teologia*, Padua, 1954f. |
| STPIMS | *Studies and Texts. Pontifical Institute of Mediaeval Studies, St. Michael's College, University of Toronto*, Toronto, 1955f. |
| StSt | *Studi storici. Istituto storico italiano per il Medio Evo*, Rome, 1953f. |
| StT | *Studi e testi. Biblioteca apostolica Vaticana*, Vatican, 1900f. |
| StVen | *Studi veneziani*, Florence, 1966f. |
| SvKy | *Sveriges kyrkor*, Stockholm, 1921f. |
| Syr. | *Syria. Revue d'art oriental et d'archéologie*, Paris, 1920f. |
| TCCG | *Topographie chrétienne des cités de la Gaule des origines au milieu du VIII$^{e}$ siècle*, Paris, 1986f. |
| Theol(P) | *Théologie. Études publiées sous la dir. de la faculté de théologie s.j. de Lyon-Fourvière*, Paris, 1944f. |
| ThH | *Théologie historique*, Paris, 1963f. |
| Thom. | *Thomist. A Speculative Quarterly Review of Theology and Philosophy*, Washington (DC), etc., 1939f. |
| ThQ | *Theologische Quartalschrift*, Tübingen, etc., 1819f. |
| THS | *Transactions of the Royal Historical Society*, London, 1867f. |
| ThViat | *Theologia viatorum. Jahrbuch der kirchlichen Hochschule Berlin*, Berlin, 1948f. |
| TJHSE | *Transactions. Jewish Historical Society of England*, London, 1893f. |
| TMCB | *Travaux et mémoires du Centre de recherche d'histoire et civilisation de Byzance*, Paris, 1965f. (also the collection "TMCB. Monographies", 1982f.). |
| TP | *T'oung Pao. Archives concernant l'histoire, les langues, la géographie, l'ethnographie et les arts de l'Asie orientale*, Leiden, 1890f. |
| TPKR | *Theologická příloha Křesťanské revue* [Theological Supplement of Christian Review], Prague, 1968f. |
| Tr. | *Traditio. Studies in Ancient and Medieval History, Thought and Religion*, New York, etc., 1943f. |
| TRE | *Theologische Realenzyklopädie*, G. Krause (ed.), G. Müller (ed.), Berlin, 1974f. (contains "IATG"). |
| TRHS | *Transactions of the Royal Historical Society*, London, 1873f. |
| TSMÂO | *Typologie des sources du Moyen Âge occidental*, Turnhout, 1972f. |
| UnSa | *Unam sanctam*, Paris, 1937f. |
| VBW | *Vorträge der Bibliothek Warburg*, Leipzig, 1921-1931. |
| VerLex | *Deutsche Literatur des Mittelalters, Verfasserlexikon*, W. Stammler (ed.), Berlin, 1933-1955 (5 vol.); 2nd ed. K. Langosch (ed.), 1978f. |
| Verlex | *Die deutsche Literatur des Mittelalters. Verfasserlexikon*, Berlin, New York, 1978. |
| VetChr | *Vetera Christianorum*, Bari, 1964f. |
| VIEG | *Veröffentlichungen des Instituts für Europäische Geschichte Mainz*, Wiesbaden, etc., 1952f. |
| VieMon | *Vie monastique*, Bégrolles-en-Mauges, 1966f. |
| VKAMAG | *Vorträge und Forschungen. Konstanzer Arbeitskreis für Mittelalterliche Geschichte*, Konstanz, 1955f. |
| VL | *Vetus latina. Die Reste der altlateinischen Bibel*, Freiburg im Breisgau, 1949f. |
| VS.S | *Vie spirituelle. Supplément*, Paris, 1947-1969. |
| VSAM | *Vie spirituelle ascétique et mystique*, Paris, 1919-1945. |
| VSB | *Vies des saints et des bienheureux. Publié par les Bénédictins de Paris*, J. L. Baudot (ed.), L. Chaussin (ed.), Paris, 1935-1959. |
| WDGB | *Würzburger Diözesangeschichtsblätter*, Würzburg, 1933f. |
| WiWei | *Wissenschaft und Weisheit. Zeitschrift für augustinisch-franziskanische Theologie und Philosophie in der Gegenwart*, Freiburg im Breisgau, etc., 1934f. |
| WSlJb | *Wiener slavistisches Jahrbuch*, Vienna, 1950f. |
| ZBLG | *Zeitschrift für bayerische Landesgeschichte*, Munich, 1928. |
| ZDA | *Zeitschrift für deutsches Altertum und deutsche Literatur*, Berlin, etc., 1841f. |
| ZfKG | *Zeitschrift für Kunstgeschichte*, Munich, etc., 1932f. |
| ZGO | *Zeitschrift für die Geschichte des Oberrheins*, Karlsruhe, 1850f. |
| ZKTh | *Zeitschrift für katholische Theologie*, Vienna, etc., 1876f. |
| ZSRG.G | *Zeitschrift der Savigny-Stiftung für Rechtsgeschichte. Germanistische Abteilung*, Weimar, 1880f. |
| ZSRG.K | *Zeitschrift der Savigny-Stiftung für Rechtsgeschichte. Kanonische Abteilung*, Weimar, 1911f. |

**Other abbreviations**

| | | | | | |
|---|---|---|---|---|---|
| bibl. | bibliography | f. | and following | ms. | manuscript |
| BL | British Library | fasc. | fascicle | no. | number |
| BNF | Bibliothèque nationale de France | fig. | figure | re-ed. | re-edition |
| *c.* | *circa* | Fr. | French | repr. | ("reprint") |
| ch. | chapter | Ger. | German | ser. | series |
| comm. | commentary | *ibid.* | *ibidem* | suppl. | supplement |
| ed. | editor, edition | *id.* | *idem* | tr. | translator, translation |
| Eng. | English | intro. | introduction | vol. | volume |
| *et al.* | *et alii* (and others) | It. | Italian | V&A | Victoria and Albert Museum |

**Note on alphabetical order.**

Proper names such as John, Nicholas, Peter or Thomas are placed in the following order: popes, patriarchs, emperors, kings, others. However, John the Baptist and John the Evangelist stand at the head of their list, as do St Peter and St Paul. Likewise, names of religious orders (*e.g.* Saint James, Order of) precede place-names (*e.g.* Saint Andrews).

# A

***A LATERE.*** *Alexander III (reigned 1159 to 1181) was the first pope to apply to *legates having plenipotentiary powers the term *a latere papae*, which meant "on behalf of the pope". In the 13th c., the term *a latere* was increasingly reserved for missions of Roman *cardinals or high prelates of the Roman *Curia.

From the 12th c., the papacy had granted the archbishops of *Canterbury the title of permanent legates (*legati nati*), which did not rule out the sending of legates *a latere*. In fact, in England, access for legates *a latere* was often difficult.

R. C. Figueira, "'Legatus Apostolice sedis': the Pope's 'alter ego' according to Thirteenth-Century Canon Law", *StMed*, 3rd series, 27, 1986, 528-574.

Agostino Paravicini Bagliani

**AACHEN.** Aachen (Aix-la-Chapelle) is situated to the north of the Eifel massif. Its hot springs were known to the Romans, who left several abandoned thermal establishments there in *c.*375. The place is mentioned again in 765 when *Pippin the Short stayed there. But it was *Charlemagne's decision in the 800s to make this place his preferred residence that raised Aachen above the other royal residences of the Carolingian Empire.

Charlemagne built a group of buildings that aimed to fulfil all needs. Wooden constructions, doubtless the most numerous – *i.e.* domestic buildings – have now disappeared. Among stone buildings, traces have been found of the *aula palatina*, a great reception room, and a monumental gate that was the starting-point for the principal road, doubtless surmounted by a room where the emperor dispensed justice. All that survives to our day is the palatine chapel, dedicated to Our Lady, which housed Charlemagne's tomb and ensured the continuity of the place when, at the end of the 9th c., the royal *palace declined.

*Charlemagne's throne.* Aachen, Palatine Chapel, gallery of the westwork.

This chapel, built between 796 and 805 under the direction of Eudes of Metz, has a plan centred on an octagon surrounded by side-aisles surmounted by tribunes, the whole inscribed in a 16-sided polygon. On the west, a square room flanked by two staircase-towers gave access to the tribunes. It was in the tribunes that the emperor took his place, on a seat modelled on King *Solomon's throne and filled with *relics. From there, he could see the two *altars in the sanctuary to the east of the main body of the chapel, viz. the altar of the Virgin, below, and that of the Saviour, upstairs. He was also facing the main motif of the *mosaic that covered the cupola: *Christ acclaimed by the 24 elders of the *Apocalypse. By the *coronation of 936, *Otto I established the tradition that the German rulers had to be crowned in the chapel of Aachen, which became an obligation from 1356. Finally *Frederick Barbarossa, who had Charlemagne canonized in 1165, on that occasion granted a privilege making the town of Aachen a free town raised to the rank of capital of the *Empire.

This privilege shows that alongside the chapel and royal palace had developed an important centre of population, no doubt heir to the **vicus* that supplied Charlemagne's court. The town was given a wall in 1175, and in 1267 the municipal council built a town hall on the site of Charlemagne's reception room. The town lived mainly on cloth production and metalwork, such as copper and brass.

R.E. Sullivan, *Aix-la-Chapelle in the Age of Charlemagne*, Norman, 1963. – *Karolingische Kunst, Karl der Grosse*, W. Braunfels (ed.), 3, Düsseldorf, 1967. – C. Heitz, *L'Architecture religieuse carolingienne*, Paris, 1980. – L. Falckenstein, *Karl der Grosse und die Entstehung des Aachener Marienstiftes*, Munich, 1981.

Geneviève Bührer-Thierry

**ABBASIDS.** The Muslim Arab dynasty of the Abbasids ruled a large part of the Islamic lands in the East from 749 to 1258, with *Baghdad as their capital.

Descendants of an uncle of the Prophet, the Abbasids declared themselves members of his family and, as such, claimed power, which they seized in 749 to the detriment of the 'Alids. While maintaining dynastic custom and the principle of the oath of allegiance representing the free choice of the community, they considered themselves as belonging to the "elect" family, which appeared in the regnal names they adopted (*e.g.* al-Mansūr, "he to whom God gives victory").

The Empire that the Abbasid *caliphs had seized from the *Umayyad caliphs was from the outset deprived of its western part, *Spain. Then, the western and central *Maghreb having seceded, the Empire's orientation was more Asiatic than Mediterranean, all the more since the caliphs established themselves not in *Syria, but in *Iraq, at first near Kūfa, then in the new capital Baghdad, founded in 762. Baghdad remained the residence of the caliphs until 1258, except for the short period (836-892) when the rulers settled in the new town of Samarra.

The supports of the regime inaugurated by the Abbasids were different from those on which the Umayyads had leaned in their essentially Arab realm. The Abbasids had taken power with the help of an army made up of Khurasanians, at once Arabs and "clients", and they kept this army of professionals that had not existed before. They also surrounded themselves with *mawāli*, mainly Iranians, who took the place of some Syrian clients who served the Umayyads.

The army of the Abbasids underwent a new transformation when, early in the 9th c., Caliph al-Mu'tasim decided to recruit mercenary slaves of Turkish origin whom he installed in the town of Samarra. This was the first of such armies of slave or freed mercenaries, in every case strangers to the world of *Islam, whose existence characterised numerous Muslim dynasties.

The period lasting from 749 to 936, during which the caliphs governed, was marked by two important reigns. The first was that of Hārūn al-Rashīd (786-809) who, surrounded by his ministers, the Barmakids, left a reputation as an autocratic and unquiet ruler, living in a luxurious palace. It was this caliph who exchanged with *Charlemagne ambassadors apparently intended to regulate certain problems concerning the Latin clergy of *Jerusalem. The second was that of al-Ma'mūn (813-833), who was the first to encourage translations of Greek philosophical works and to support the *Mu'tazilite school of rationalizing theology. He tried also – without success – to reconcile the 'Alid and Abbasid branches of the Prophet's family.

Indeed, in the course of this period, the Abbasid caliphs did not succeed, despite various efforts, in putting an end to the opposition of the *Shi'ites, partisans of the 'Alid *imāms, the twelfth and last of whom disappeared at Samarra around 875, becoming the mahdi whose return is hoped for and expected.

This period was above all that of the setting up of the classical governmental institutions, the creation of the great legal schools (Malikism, Hanafism, Shafi'ism and Hanbalism), the first outlines of Muslim *theology, the flowering of a new prose and a new poetry, and finally an astonishing economic development of the Empire.

But with the start of the 10th c. began the decline of the caliphate at the same time as the dismemberment of the Empire. At Baghdad, the caliph, prey to a severe financial crisis, had to delegate military and financial powers to a grand *emir who, from 945, belonged to the Shi'ite Iranian family of the Buyids. From 1055 it was a sultan, belonging to the Turkish family of the *Seljuks, who played this role until the end of the 12th c., when a caliph succeeded in recovering his authority over a territory restricted to Iraq.

The Abbasid caliphate, which from 969 to 1171 had had a rival in the Fatimid caliphate of Egypt, disappeared in 1258 at the time of the capture of Baghdad by the *Mongols. However, some Abbasid princes were welcomed at *Cairo, where an Abbasid caliphate was to maintain itself, without power, until 1517.

D. Sourdel, *Le Vizirat abbasside*, Damascus, 1959-1960 (2 vol.). – H. Busse, *Chalif und Grosskönig*, Beirut, 1969. – *The Cambridge History of Islam*, Cambridge, 1970 (2 vol.). – M. A. Shaban, *Islamic History, 2, A. D. 750-1055*, Cambridge, 1976. – M. M. Ahsan, *Social Life under the Abbasids, 170-789 AH, 786-902 AD*, London, 1979. – M. O. Zaman, *Religion and Politics under the Early Abbasids*, Leiden, 1997. – D. Sourdel, *L'Etat impérial des califes abbassides*, Paris, 1999.

Dominique Sourdel

The tower of Samarra (Iraq). Minaret of the Friday mosque. Abbasid period, *c.*850.

**ABBESS.** A word derived from Late Latin *abbatissa*, in turn formed by analogy from *abbas* (*abbot, father): title of the superior in charge of the government of an independent monastery of *nuns. The female monasteries of the old monastic orders had abbesses; so did *canonesses, both those with *vows and those without vows; the *Poor Clares, who in the first Rule given them by Cardinal Ugolino (1218-1219) formally professed the Rule of St *Benedict, but in reality lived according to Ugolino's Rule; and the Conceptionists, founded by the blessed Beatrice da Silva (15th c.), at first *Cistercians, but from the early 16th c. rather *Franciscans.

The abbesses of some old monasteries, especially in *Germany, also became princesses of the Empire, with the honours and duties of that rank; they could be present or be represented at the diets of the Empire and at synods.

All abbesses elected for life received a liturgical blessing from the *bishop, like the former deaconesses; some also the abbatial *staff. The abbesses of the Poor Clares, for a long time elected for life but then only for three years, never received the liturgical blessing, nor did they have the staff. The abbesses of *Carthusian nunneries used the *maniple and the stole.

The council of Aachen in 789 ordered bishops to forbid abbesses to bless men or to impose the veil on *virgins (can. 75).

*Innocent III (*Register* XIII, n. 187: *PL*, 116, 356) condemned as an intolerable abuse the fact that certain abbesses of the dioceses of *Burgos and Palencia in Spain dared to bless their own nuns, hear *confessions, read the Gospel and preach.

In some *double monasteries, the abbess governed the monks as well as the nuns, as in the monastery of *Fontevraud in France (founded in 1099), and in the Order of *St Saviour founded by *St Bridget of Sweden at *Vadstena. When in 1222 the canonesses and clergy of *Quedlinburg (Saxony) refused to obey the orders of the abbess since she could not constrain them by *excommunication, she turned to *Honorius III, who backed her up with the reply inserted into the *Decretals* of *Gregory IX (ch. 12, X, I, 33), laying down that canonesses and clergy *abbatissae praefatae oboedientiam et reverentiam debitam impendentes, eius salubria monita et mandata observent.*

Famous in Italy is the abbey of San Benedetto di Conversano in Apulia, given in 1266 to Cistercian nuns, refugees from the Near East, whose abbess exercised, through a vicar, an almost episcopal jurisdiction in the abbatial fief of Castellana, almost into modern times.

In 1258 *Alexander IV granted the Vallombrosan abbey *nullius* of Fucecchio to the Poor Clares of Gattaiola at Lucca, who, giving the land to the Friars Minor in 1299, reserved the right to appoint to the ecclesiastical *benefices of the former abbey.

Another monastery whose abbess exercised temporal as well as spiritual jurisdiction was the Cistercian one of Santa Maria de *Las Huelgas near Burgos in Spain, founded in 1187 and from the start provided with great privileges. Here too the Crown and the upper nobility, to whom the abbesses often belonged, contributed to maintaining this extraordinary position into the 19th century. It ceased when Pius IX, with the constitution *Quam diversa* (12 July 1873), suppressed all quasi-episcopal ecclesiastical jurisdictions, *i.e.* not under the authority of the diocesan bishops, in Spain; a measure that came into effect on 20 May 1874.

K. H. Schäfer, *Die Kanonissenstifter im deutschen Mittelalter*, Stuttgart, 1907. – G. Mongelli, *Le abbadesse mitrate di S. Benedetto di Conversano*, Montevergine, 1960. – A. Pantoni, "Abbadessa", *DIP*, 1, 14-22. – M. de Fontette, *Les religieuses à l'âge classique du droit canonique*, Paris, 1970.

Maria Cristina Buschi

**ABBEY.** An abbey was a group of buildings occupied by a regular religious community, and was always directed, unlike other *convents or monasteries, by an *abbot. Thus Charterhouses, governed by a *prior, remain monasteries and not abbeys.

There were two categories of abbeys. The most common was the regular abbey that depended on the *bishop of the *diocese to which it belonged or, in case of *exemption, directly on the Holy See. Much more rare was the abbey called *nullius* which was not incorporated into any diocese and thus enjoyed a particular legal status. It possessed in fact its own territory with a distinct clergy and congregation. This was the case, *e.g.*, of the abbey of *Subiaco.

Originally, no rule imposed a particular ground-plan or architecture on the abbey. The monks thus reused existing buildings such as ancient Roman **villae* or built shelters of wattle and daub, similar to the rural dwellings of the time. Then, in the early Middle Ages, the rise of the *coenobitic life entailed the construction of more durable and better organised structures. Thus buildings with specific functions gradually came to predominate. The first monastic *Rules, without giving precise directives as to their construction, already mention the elements indispensable to every new abbey. We thus find places intended for the common life of the monks (*oratory, cells or dorter), others for utilitarian use (workshops, cellar, kitchen), and others reserved for the *laity, consecrated or not (lay-brothers' house, guest-house, infirmary). Among all the buildings making up an abbey, one was the focus of it: the church. This, called the abbey church or minster, was the heart of all monastic life. Sometimes placed at the centre, it was most often built at the highest point of the site in order to emphasize this vocation symbolically. At first intended solely for the monks, the abbey church was a restricted sanctuary; later it sometimes underwent an important development, imposed by the orientations and growth of the order. This was the case *e.g.* at *Cluny. But whether it was of exceptional size, as among the Cluniacs, or reserved for the intimacy of monks and lay-brothers, as among the *Cistercians, the abbey church was always the point of anchorage around which all the other buildings of the abbey were organised. The *cloister was usually to the south of the church, and around it radiated the buildings indispensable to common life. The plans of *Fontenay for the Order of Cîteaux and *Sankt Gallen for the Benedictines are considered models of organisation of monastic buildings.

J. M. Besse, "Abbaye", *DACL*, 1, 1, Paris, 1907, 25-39. – H. Beaunier, *Abbayes et prieurés de l'ancienne France*, Paris, 1913. – G. Jacquemet, "Abbaye", *Cath.*, 1, Paris, 1954, 7-14. – C. N. L. Brooke, W. Swaan, *The Monastic World 1000-1300*, London, 1974. – P. Fergusson, *Architecture of Solitude: Cistercian abbeys in twefth-century England*, Princeton (NJ), 1984. – C. Platt, *The Abbeys and Priories of Medieval England*, London, 1984.

Noëlle Deflou

**ABBO OF FLEURY (*c.*940-1004).** Born in the Orléanais, Abbo was offered very young by his parents to the monastery of *Fleury (Saint-Benoît-sur-Loire) where he was educated. After studying at *Paris and *Reims, Abbo returned to Fleury where, *c.*965, he was given the post of **scholasticus*. In 985-987 he lived at the monastery of *Ramsey. He entered into relations with *Dunstan, archbishop of Canterbury, at whose request he wrote the *Passion of Saint Edmund*, a small monument of Anglo-Saxon national history. In 988, Abbo became *abbot of Fleury. He was murdered in 1004 at La Réole, a dependency of Fleury, during a journey to Gascony. A *Life of Abbo*, composed by his disciple Aimoin, launched the cult of this abbot and *martyr (feast 13 Nov).

Abbo was at once a great scholar, a *canonist and a theoretician in ecclesial matters: a collection of grammatical questions, two treatises on the syllogisms and a series of scientific treatises (*astronomy, *computus) are all attributed to the saint. His "political" work was a practical response to the problems encountered at two tumultuous *councils held at Saint-Basle-de-Verzy (991) and *Saint-Denis (994), at which monks and *bishops of West Francia clashed on the question of *Rome's competence in conciliar matters and the status of monks within the Church. Champion of monastic freedom and the primacy of Rome, Abbo obtained from the *pope in 997 a privilege of *exemption that seems, in fact, to have come from his own pen; he wrote *letters, composed a *canonical collection and made a synthesis of his ideas on political theology in his *Apologia to Kings Hugh and Robert*. His contribution to ecclesial thought is of the very first importance; together with the Cluniacs, he was the theoretician of the society of orders, within which monks, cut off from the world and of a virginal purity, played the role of guides. In his *Apologeticus* and his *Letter 14*, he opened the debate on *simony, which was to have a great future in the course of the *Gregorian reform; Abbo defended the idea of one Church, the theory that material goods and spiritual goods were as inseparable as body and spirit , and the view that all possession of ecclesiastical property by the *laity was a heresy and an attack on the unity of Christ in two natures.

Abbo of Fleury, *PL*, 139, 1853. – Aimoin, *Life of Abbo*, *PL*, 139, 1853, 375-414. – Abbo of Fleury, *Commentarius in circulos beati Cyrilii et Dyonisii romani ac Bedae praefatio*, A. Cordoliani (ed.), in *RHE*, 44, 1949, 474-476. – Abbo of Fleury, *Syllogismorum categoricorum et hypotheticorum enodatio*, A. Van de Vyver (ed.), *Abbonis Floriacensis opera inedita*, 1, Bruges, 1966, 29-95. – Abbo of Fleury, *Passio sancti Edmundi*, M. Winterbottom (ed.), in *Three Lives of English Saints*, Toronto, 1972, 67-87. – Abbo of Fleury, *Quaestiones grammaticales*, A. Guerreau-Jalabert (ed.), Paris, 1982.

"Abbon de Fleury", *LdM*, 1, 1980, 16. – M. Mostert, *The Political Theology of Abbo of Fleury*, Hilversum, 1987. – "Abbon de Fleury", *DLFMA*, Paris, 1992, 1-2. – S. Gwara, "Three Acrostic Poems by Abbo of Fleury", *The Journal of Medieval Latin*, 2, 1992, 203-35. – E.M. Engelen, *Zeit, Zahl und Bild. Studien zur Verbindung von Philosophie und Wissenschaft bei Abbo von Fleury*, Berlin, 1993. – A. Gransden, "Abbo of Fleury's *Passio S. Eadmundi*", *Revue Bénédictine*, 105, 1995, 20-78. – M. Lapidge, P.S. Baker, "More Acrostic Verse by Abbo of Fleury", *The Journal of Medieval Latin*, 7, 1997, 1-32.

Dominique Iogna-Prat

**ABBO OF SAINT-GERMAIN (9th c.).** A strange war correspondent, Abbo, a monk of the monastery of *Saint-Germain-des-Prés, described the siege of *Paris by the *Vikings in 885-886. Having come from the west (*Neustria) to be educated by the scholar Aimoin, the young Abbo was present at the fighting and bargaining that ended in the retreat of the invaders. Impressed by these crucial events for the history of the *regnum Francorum* and *Christendom, and proud of his brilliant scholarship, some years later Abbo composed a small *epic in three songs (*Bellorum parisiacae urbis libri III*). Despite the faults inherent in the writer's exuberance and the pretentiousness of his style, the text offers valuable historical evidence of this period. It also provides access to the peculiar Latinity of these lesser Carolingian masters who oscillated between the Virgilian model (hexameters and gods!), the new forms of epic narrative (*cantilenae*) then being born, and the savour of proto-French that can sometimes be heard (*barcas* for *naues minores*).

*MGH.PL*, 4, 1, Berlin, 1899, 77-122 (re-ed. 1978). – *CHFMA*, 1942 (2nd ed., 1964).

J. Soubiran, "Prosodie et métrique des *Bella Parisiacae Urbis* d'Abbon", *JS*, 1965, 204-331. – P. Lendinara, "The Third Book of the *Bella Parisiacae Urbis* by Abbo of Saint-Germain-des-Prés and its Old English Gloss", *Anglo-Saxon England*, 15, 1986, 73-89.

Michel Banniard

**ABBOT.** The term *abba*, used to designate the superior of a religious community, means "father" and already contains in itself the fundamental meaning of the words "abbot" and "*abbess". Each of the monastic *Rules written in the first centuries confirms the role reserved for the abbot, whose model is given in chapter II of St *Benedict's Rule: "The abbot, judged worthy to be the head of a monastery, must always remember the title given him, and by his actions justify the name of 'superior', because we believe that in the monastery he holds the place of Christ, whose title he bears". He must account for his behaviour and that of his disciples.

The titles of abbot and abbess gave the houses they ruled the name of *abbeys, as opposed to *priories, *commanderies, *convents and other establishments not governed by abbots or abbesses. As well as superiors of monks, in the early Middle Ages abbots could be heads of *clerics or *canons, and abbesses superiors of *canonesses. Regular canons were also given abbots as superiors. Abbots and abbesses were normally elected by the community to rule, and were chosen from among its members, before receiving the blessing of the *bishop of the place (save in case of *exemption). This regime of *election knew many exceptions: superiors appointed or imposed by an outside authority (action of kings, princes, *advocates until the 12th c.), monks moved from one abbey to govern another (frequently in periods of *reform), non-regular abbots, called lay abbots, and commendatory abbots – when they were not monks or members of the order concerned (lay abbacy of the 9th and 10th cc., *commendation of the late Middle Ages). The presence of abbots "external" to the community led to the distinction of an abbatial **mensa*, to safeguard the rights of the monks.

Abbots had a spiritual and a temporal duty of equal importance, according to the definition given by whichever rule was observed. Their role was decisive; indeed the quality and dynamism of the superior guaranteed those of the community. The abbots of the great Benedictine monasteries, the oldest and richest, were prelates, considered equal to bishops, frequenting princely courts, holding great state, powerful landed lords; so their place was much coveted. Some abbots even had princely rank and, as direct vassals of the ruler, were at the head of little territorial principalities (*Fulda, *Monte Cassino). In England many abbots sat in the House of Lords. What has been said for abbots applied in many cases to abbesses, among whom stand out the noble ladies of some great Western monasteries.

P. Salmon, *L'Abbé dans la tradition monastique*, Paris, 1962. – F. Jakobi, *Wibald von Stablo und Korvey*, Münster, 1979. – A. de Vogüé, *Community and Abbot in the Rule of St. Benedict*, Kalamazoo, 1979-88. – "Abt", *LdM*, 1, 1980. – F. Felten, *Äbte und Laienäbte im Frankenreich*, Stuttgart, 1980. – F. Felten, "Herrschaft des Abtes", *Herrschaft und Kirche*, F. Prinz (dir.), Stuttgart, 1988, 147-296. – M. Bur, *Suger, abbé de Saint-Denis, régent de France*, Paris, 1991.

Michel Parisse

**ABBREVIATOR.** Attested from the 13th c., the abbreviators (*abreviator* or *breviator*) were *clerics in charge of drawing up minutes, and were dependent on the papal *notaries. Towards the end of the century, on the other hand, the "abbreviators of apostolic letters" were responsible for drawing up *letters; they were attached to the vice-chancellor. According to a constitution of *John XXII (*Cum ad sacrosanctae*, 1316), they received the same emoluments as the *scriptores*. In the 15th c., their prestige diminished, owing to the appearance of the papal dataries and secretaries.

E. Fournier, *DDC*, 1, 1935, 98-106. – P. Rabikauskas, *Diplomatica pontificia*, Rome, 1964. – T. Frenz, *I documenti pontifici nel medioevo e nell'età moderna*, Rome, 1989.

Agostino Paravicini Bagliani

**'ABDISHO OF NISIBIS (died 1318).** Metropolitan bishop of Nisibis (now Nusaybin, South-East Turkey) and *Armenia, he was the last of the great Syro-oriental authors. His work of philosophy and theology, entitled *The Pearl* – which he himself translated into Arabic – is chronologically the last exposition of Oriental doctrine. He is above all the author of a celebrated verse *Catalogue* which lists the works of his predecessors and constitutes our first history of Syro-oriental literature, handing down the titles of numerous works since lost. Finally he wrote a *Nomocanon*, bringing together the texts of civil and especially ecclesiastical law.

J. S. Assemani, *Bibliotheca orientalis clementino-vaticana*, 3, 1, Rome, 1725, 3-362 (Syriac text and Lat. tr.); repr. Hildesheim-New York, 1975 (for the *Catalogue*). – G. P. Badger, *The Nestorians and their Rituals*, 2, London, 1852 (Eng. tr.); repr. Farnborough, 1969, 361-379 (for the *Catalogue*).

Micheline Albert

**ABDUCTION.** All the Germanic laws condemned the abduction of young girls, *widows and *nuns. Certain laws imposed separation, or else the return of the woman to whoever held her *mundium* (power over the woman). The Salic law condemned the ravisher to payment of a fine of composition and banishment, without imposing the restitution of the girl. Finally it authorized the *family to take revenge. The Church equally firmly condemned abduction, which violated paternal authority and sapped *social order. Hence the punishment of the ravisher was *excommunication (Roman council of 743). These penalties do not seem to have been dissuasive, since abduction was very frequent in the early Middle Ages: *women were safe neither in their home, nor in the workshops where they worked, nor even on the road that took them to the home of their future husband. Such frequency is doubtless partly explained by the surrounding *violence, but still more by the matrimonial system itself. Balance between *kinship groups rested on a system of homogamic alliances. Legal *marriage, called *Muntehe*, thus implied the consent of the relatives and the transfer of *mundium* from the father (or his substitute) to the husband. Abduction appears on the contrary as a form of hypergamic marriage, which allowed young men to loosen the too heavy constraints of legal marriage, obtaining by force a wife capable of contributing an increase of nobility, wealth and power.

From the 7th c., a difference began to be made between abduction and *seductio*, *i.e.* the removal of a young girl with her consent. Abduction remained liable to separation or banishment; later, it became a nullifying impediment to marriage. But more tolerance was shown towards *seductio*, which was punished only by a fine. The resulting marriage was valid and could even take the form of a legal marriage, if the ravisher obtained the consent of the parents and publicly endowed his wife. The Church was doubtless responsible for this distinction, since removal with consent could appear as a form of consensual marriage. Hence Carolingian *bishops often encouraged parents to recognise the validity of unions concluded in this way. Later, the frequency of abductions seems to have progressively diminished, while consensual marriage prevailed. In the 12th c., the consent of the parents was no longer required and abduction became a marginal practice.

S. Kalifa, "Singularités matrimoniales chez les anciens germains: le rapt et le droit de la femme à disposer d'elle-même", *RHDF*, 1970, 199-225. – R. Köstler, "Raub-, Kauf- und Friedelehe bei den Germanen", *ZSGR.G*, 63, 1943, 92-136. – P. Mikat, "Ehe", *Handwörterbuch der Rechtsgeschichte*, 1, 815-816.

Régine Le Jan

***ABECEDARIUM.*** Elementary teaching in Antiquity and the Middle Ages consisted in learning firstly to read the letters of the alphabet. Exceptionally when a *child learned to read alone from a text, he passed directly from letters in disorder to words. But at *school the antique method was followed. The Venerable *Bede (*HE*, V, 2) tells how the bishop of Hexham taught a dumb man to speak: "'say *a*', the dumb man said *a*, 'say *b*', he said *b*, and so he answered the bishop by giving the name of each letter, then the bishop continued by asking him to read syllables and words". The schoolchild copied the letters on a tablet or on a piece of *parchment. In a 13th-c. sermon, we are told that the child went to school with the alphabet hanging from his belt. In the late Middle Ages, the child ate cakes in the form of letters or drank from bowls decorated with the alphabet. Some alphabets which have survived were preceded by a cross, whence the name "Christ-cross-row" or "criss-cross-row". At the start of the modern period embroidered alphabets began to be used; in some texts each letter is glossed, so as to be better remembered: *a* for "*amitié*", *b* for "*bonté*", *c* for "*crainte*", etc.

P. Riché, "Apprendre à lire et à écrire dans le haut Moyen Âge", *BSNAF*, 1978-1979, 193-203. – D. Alexandre-Bidon, "La lettre volée. Apprendre à lire à l'enfant au Moyen Âge", *Annales*, 1989, 953-992.

Pierre Riché

**ABELARD, PETER (1079-1142).** Peter Abelard was born at Le Pallet, near Nantes. According to his autobiography (*History of my misfortunes*), he was the son of a knight. Though the eldest, he renounced arms and decided to dedicate himself to studies, which were then reviving. First he studied logic with Roscelin at Loches and *William of Champeaux at *Paris, then theology with Anselm of Laon. He later taught both these disciplines at Paris, at the school of Notre-Dame (*c.*1112-1117). This was the period of his meeting with *Heloise, niece of canon Fulbert, their love, their clandestine marriage, and the birth of a son. When Fulbert took revenge by castrating Abelard, he and Heloise took the religious habit, he at *Saint-Denis, she at Argenteuil (1118). This celebrated episode reveals the ambiguity of the status of a *cleric merely in minor *orders, at a time when, owing to the *Gregorian reform, the gap between clerics and *laity was growing wider and when *marriage, regulated by an ever more rigorous law, was becoming precisely one of the decisive criteria of this distinction. Nevertheless it is not anachronistic to see, in the love of Heloise and Abelard, a moving example of that unhappy passion which gave rise to their immense literary fame.

Becoming a monk in 1118 (and later a priest), Abelard had an agitated monastic career. Soon embroiled with his brethren at Saint-Denis, he lived in various hermitages in *Champagne, notably that of the Paraclete where, *c.*1130, he installed Heloise, herself now *abbess of a women's community. Abelard had meanwhile been elected *abbot of Saint-Gildas at Rhuys in *Brittany. In fact, and though we cannot doubt the sincerity of his religious convictions, he found it difficult to submit to monastic discipline. Exposed to the hostility of the monks of Saint-Gildas, he left that monastery in *c.*1132. He then made frequent stays at the Paraclete and from this time date his autobiography and his correspondence with Heloise in which regret for lost love is mingled with spiritual advice.

But Abelard was primarily a professor; in this sphere he retained exceptional prestige and continually sought to resume his teaching, on his own account from now on. In 1121, it earned him a first doctrinal condemnation at the council of Soissons. Nevertheless we find Abelard in 1136 keeping a school at Paris, on Mont Sainte-Geneviève. It is not known whether his monastic situation had been regularized. However, his lessons once more aroused suspicion and, denounced by *William of Saint-Thierry to *Bernard of Clairvaux, he was summoned in 1140 (or 1141) before the council of Sens and was once again condemned at the insistence of St Bernard. This condemnation having been confirmed by the pope, Abelard retired to *Cluny, under the protection of Abbot *Peter the Venerable, and died on 21 April 1142 at the Cluniac priory of Saint-Marcel-lez-Chalon.

Abelard had at first been one of the protagonists of the scholarly revival of the 12th century. He had been one of the first to open, alongside the cathedral school, a "private" school where he taught freely, remunerated by his pupils; he was one of the first too to settle at Paris on the left bank. His influence as a professor had been great, despite the official condemnations; he trained several of the important Parisian *masters of the next generation (*Robert of Melun, *John of Salisbury, *Peter Lombard) and some of his pupils turn up at the Roman *Curia as *cardinals or even *popes (Celestine II and *Celestine III). Fascinated like many clerics of his time by the rise of *towns, sensitive to the atmosphere of freedom that characterised town life, long protected by the Garlandes, one of the most ambitious of the aristocratic clans surrounding *Louis VI, Abelard was also a sincere Christian. The violent hostility of *Cistercian circles towards him should not hide his adherence to the ideals of Church reform and his attraction towards certain forms of monastic life (notably *eremitism).

But Abelard's main originality obviously lay in his work and his thought. As well as *sermons (intended for the monks of Saint-Gildas or the nuns of the Paraclete) and religious *hymns, this work comprises firstly the *History of my misfortunes* (*Historia calamitatum*) and the correspondence exchanged with Heloise. Despite the reservations of some specialists (who see them as 13th-c. fakes), these documents are generally considered authentic and appear as exceptional evidence of both the personality of their authors and the mentality (ambition, *love, *marriage, religious *conversion) of the time.

Abelard's other writings flow out of his teaching. Some of them are in fact students' notes. They include firstly treatises on *logic (glosses on the various books of *Aristotle's "old logic" – doubtless all Abelard knew – and a *Dialectic*); though he had access to only a part of Aristotle's works (the rest was revealed at Paris after 1140), Abelard shows himself in these glosses a virtuoso dialectician; he also appears, though with nuances, as a "*nominalist" who refused to put *universals among things and classified them among the concepts (genera, *species) that allow us to describe the "manner of being" of things.

Then come his *Theologies*; three of these have survived, each of which had several successive versions. In these treatises, which were hit by the condemnations of 1121 and 1140, Abelard did not try, as he would be accused of, to "pierce the mysteries of faith" or to "understand God by human reason"; he defended himself from this charge, with evident sincerity, in several short *Apologies*. His ambition was solely to show that, thanks to the resources of *dialectic, it was possible to set out truths of dogma (*e.g.* the dogma of the *Trinity), statements not leading to contradictory propositions, unacceptable to *reason. Apart from their methodological interest (Abelard here inaugurated what would become the great scholastic method of the **quaestio*), these *Theologies* bear witness to the new spirit displayed by the public of the urban schools (a spirit obviously rejected by traditional theologians like St Bernard): the refinement of logical thought, the intellectual curiosity and increased confidence in reason favoured by the revival of towns and trade, would no longer accommodate the heavily dogmatic formulations of the old-style scriptural *gloss ("extraordinary in words, but without understanding or reason", said Abelard, not without some injustice, of Anselm of Laon), nor the allegories and subtle symbolism of monastic mysticism.

In direct line with and as an illustration of his *theology come Abelard's few exegetical works, especially the commentary on the epistle to the Romans and the **Sic et non* where he expounds how dialectic allows a resolution of the apparent contradictions of Scripture and the *Fathers. We may also cite a treatise on *ethics (*Ethics* or *Know thyself*) in which, without falling into subjectivism, Abelard puts conscious intention at the centre of his definition of *sin, and finally the *Dialogue* which is perhaps his last work, unfinished, and which seems to be a sort of philosophical and spiritual testament: in it Abelard arbitrates in a dialogue between "a philosopher, a Jew and a Christian" who appear to him in a "night vision". In a remarkable effort of synthesis, Abelard seems to have tried in this work not to oppose the doctrines compared, but to reconcile them in order to end in a triumph of a "complete Christianity, under its three instances: biblical, evangelical, philosophical" (J. Jolivet).

A complex personality, who lived painfully through the contradictions of his time, at once a pioneer of scholarly renewal and an intellectual who led to the flowering of *scholasticism, Abelard is one of the most engaging figures of the "12th-century renaissance".

Peter Abelard, *Ethics*, D. E. Luscombe (ed.), Oxford, 1971 (*OMT*). – *The Letters of Abelard and Heloise*, B. Radice (tr.), Harmondsworth, 1974. – Peter Abailard, *Sic et Non. A Critical Edition*, B. B. Boyer (ed.), R. McKeon (ed.), Chicago (IL), London, 1976-1977 (3 vol.).

É. Gilson, *Abelard and Heloise*, London, 1953. – J. Jolivet, *Arts du langage et théologie chez Abélard*, Paris, 1969. – J. Jolivet, *Abélard ou la Philosophie dans le langage*, Paris, 1969. – D. E. Luscombe, *The School of Peter Abelard. The Influence of Abelard's Thought in the Early Scholastic Period*, Cambridge, 1969. – *Pierre Abélard. Pierre le Vénérable. Les courants philosophiques, littéraires et artistiques en Occident au milieu du XIIe siècle*, Paris, 1975. – *Petrus Abaelardus (1079-1142). Person, Werk und Wirkung*, Trier, 1980. – *Abélard en son temps*, Paris, 1981. – J. Verger, J. Jolivet, *Bernard – Abélard ou le cloître et l'école*, Paris, 1982. – M. Fumagalli Beonio Brocchieri, *Eloisa e Abelardo*, Milan, 1984. – C.J. Mews, *Peter Abelard,* Aldershot, 1995. – J. Verger, *L'Amour castré. L'histoire d'Héloïse et Abélard*, Paris, 1996. – M.T. Clanchy, *Abelard: a Medieval Life*, Oxford, 1997. – J. Marenbon, *The Philosophy of Peter Abelard*, Cambridge, 1997. – C.J. Mews, *The Last Love Letters of Abelard and Heloise*, London, 2000.

Jacques Verger

**ABERDEEN.** According to late medieval tradition, a *bishopric was transferred from Mortlach (in Strathspey, Grampian Region) to Aberdeen in the 12th century. The dedication of the *cathedral was to St Machar; his dates are unknown, and nothing factual is known of his life. The bishopric covered most of north-east *Scotland between the rivers Dee and Spey. The cathedral stands near the mouth of the river Don; its nave is still in use, but the choir and transepts are ruined. Bishop William Elphinstone founded a *university at Aberdeen in 1495, and caused the legends of Scottish saints to be assembled in the nation's first printed book, the *Breviarium Aberdonense*, printed in *Edinburgh in 1509-1510. The town or burgh of Aberdeen grew up around a natural harbour at the mouth of the river Dee, about 5 kilometres south of the cathedral.

H. Boece [Boethius], *Murthlacensium et Aberdonensium Episcoporum Vitae*, J. Moir (ed,), Aberdeen, 1894.

*New Light on Medieval Aberdeen*, J.S. Smith (ed.), Aberdeen, 1985. – L. J. MacFarlane, *William Elphinstone and the Kingdom of Scotland, 1431-1514*, Aberdeen, 1985.

Alan Macquarrie

**ABJURATION.** In its most widespread sense, abjuration is the solemn renunciation of a heterodox doctrine. In the Middle Ages, it took place mainly in the context of the struggle against *heresy and became, from the 13th c., a key moment of inquisitorial procedure. The Dominican *Bernard Gui had the abjuration of heretics written down following their confessions. During the general *sermon, in the course of which the inquisitor made public the faults and penalties, the guilty solemnly renewed their abjuration: it was in fact the indispensable preliminary of penitence and pardon.

*Manuel de l'inquisiteur*, G. Mollat (ed.), Paris, 1927, 26-55, 127 (1st ed.). – "Abjuration", *DDC*, 1, 1935, 76-87.

Patrick Henriet

**ABLUTION.** The rite by which, after *communion, the priest washed the *chalice and paten used for the *mass and "purified" the fingers that had touched the eucharistic body of Christ before returning to secular activities. The aim of ablutions was to ensure the complete consumption of the eucharistic *species and avoid all involuntary profanation. The priest gathered up all the fragments on the *corporal and put them in the chalice; the chalice itself was then washed with wine, then with wine and water. With a great variety of practices according to *dioceses or religious *orders, ablutions in general took on more importance from the Carolingian period, taking place at the *altar or at the *piscina. They became a general custom in the 12th c., under the influence of the monastic liturgy; there were firstly one, then two, quite often three, and they were accompanied by devotional *prayers.

J.-A. Jungmann, *The Mass of the Roman Rite*, Westminster (MD), 1986.

Guy-Marie Oury

**ABRAHAM.** The Old Testament patriarch Abraham is a character of the first importance in *Genesis (14 chapters out of 50 are devoted to him: Gen 12-25) and the common ancestor of Jews, Christians and Muslims. Recognised as model of *faith (Gen 15, 6; Heb 11, 8), prototype of total obedience to God and spiritual father of all believers (Rom 4, 11-12), Abraham plays an important role in Christian iconography. The place accorded to him is especially linked to several themes.

Abraham is above all the ancestor of Christ (Mt 1, 1-17; Lk 3, 23-38), named insistently by Matthew's gospel (Mt 1, 1. 2. 17). As such, we find him in representations of Christ's genealogy where he is often put in direct relationship with King *David (Mt 1, 1). By assimilation to the theme of the *Tree of Jesse, we sometimes also find "Trees of Abraham", *e.g.* in the famous illustrated encyclopedia **Hortus deliciarum* (*c.*1200; manuscript destroyed).

The sacrifice of *Isaac (Gen 22) is one of the extremely popular scenes of Christian art, a polyvalent image, in which Abraham's deed is the symbol of unlimited confidence in God, as much as a typological *sign of death on the cross. During the Middle Ages, when the sacrificial value of the *Redemption was a prominent issue, preference was given to this symbolic relationship between the, so to speak, unfinished sacrifice of Isaac and the completed sacrifice of Christ, by frequently representing the sacrifice of Isaac in proximity to the Crucifixion. In the late Middle Ages, this scene appears especially in exemplars of the *Biblia pauperum* and the *Speculum humanae salvationis*.

Abraham's hospitality (Gen 18) played a primary role in the creation of the iconography of the *Trinity, in particular the type known as the "triandric Trinity" (three similar Persons). But it could also serve as a typological prefiguration of the *Annunciation (Klosterneuberg altar).

*The Sacrifice of Isaac.* Miniature from the *Paraphrase of Ælfric.* London, BL (Ms Claudius B IV).

"Father of all who believe", Abraham was also, by virtue of the parable of Dives and Lazarus (Lk 16, 19-31), the place of eternal rest of the just. The representations of "*Abraham's Bosom" that derived from this concept had considerable importance during the Middle Ages. First appearing in the West in the early 11th c. in the narrative context of Ottonian illustrated gospels (Aachen, cathedral treasury; Nuremburg, Germanisches Museum), the theme was perpetuated in this context (*Hortus deliciarum*, fol. 123 v°). But soon thereafter, separated from the gospel narrative, Abraham's Bosom was placed in the eschatological context as the depiction of the happy afterlife, *e.g.* in *Romanesque sculpture, in particular on the pilgrimage routes of Santiago de *Compostela (*Moissac, *Conques), and in cycles summing up sacred history from *Creation to the *Last Judgment (*Hortus deliciarum*, fol. 263 v°; or the so-called Psalter of Blanche of Castile, Paris, Bibliothèque de l'Arsenal, ms. 1186). In the Byzantine world, Abraham holding Lazarus on his knees was an integral part of images illustrating the Last Judgment. In French Romanesque *Bibles, Abraham's Bosom and the genealogical theme of *Adam and his descendants sometimes interpenetrate at the beginning of the first book of Chronicles (Souvigny Bible: Moulins, municipal library, ms. 1). Abraham's Bosom is also correlated with the iconography of Fatherhood (image of God holding the infant Son on his knees).

Apart from these particular scenes, the story of Abraham played an important role in narrative cycles illustrating manuscripts, more rarely on the walls of churches. One good example is a 12th-c. Mosan manuscript (Berlin, Kupferstichkabinett, ms. 78 A.6) representing seven scenes of the patriarch's life, some of them very rare.

E. Lucchesi Palli, "Abraham", *LCI*, 1, 1968, 20-35. – J. Gutmann, "The Sacrifice of Isaac: Variations on a Theme in Early Jewish and Christian Art", *Thiasos tôn Mousôn. Studien zu Antike und Christentum. Festschrift für Josef Fink zum 70. Geburtstag*, D. Ahrens (ed.), Vienna, 1984, 115-122. – J. H. Lowden, "Abraham", *Oxford Dictionary of Byzantium*, 1, New York-Oxford, 1991, 6. – A. Simon, "Abramo", *Enciclopedia dell'arte medievale*, 1, Rome, 1991, 57-60. – Y. Zaluska, "Antenati di Cristo", *Enciclopedia dell'arte medievale*, 2, Rome, 1991, 72-74. – J. Baschet, "Medieval Abraham. Between Fleshly Patriarch and Divine Father", *MLN*, 108, 1993, 738-758.

Yolanta Zaluska

**ABRAHAM BAR HIYYA (*c.*1065-1145).** Mathematician, astronomer-astrologer and philosopher of *Neoplatonist inspiration, Bar Hiyya, who perfectly mastered the Arabic language and culture, wrote several original texts in *Hebrew. Latin sources know him under the surname of *Savasorda*.

In *Barcelona, he collaborated with Plato of Tivoli in his work of *translation from Arabic to Latin. With the author's help, Plato adapted into Latin the Jewish scholar's main work on geometry, *The Treatise on Surface and Measures* (in Hebrew, *Ḥibbur ha-Meshiḥa we ha-Tishboreth*). Published under the title *Liber embadorum a Savasordo in hebraico compositus*, this work of practical geometry had a notable influence in medieval Europe. The learned 16th-c. Latin world knew part of Bar Hiyya's astronomical work through a Latin summary of his treatise: *The Form of the Earth and the Configuration of the Heaven* (in Hebrew, *Ṣurat ha-Areṣ*). His work on *eschatology and *astronomy *The Scroll of Him Who Unveils* (in Hebrew, *Megillat ha-Megalleh*) was partly translated into Latin in the 14th c., under the title *Liber de redemptione Israhel*, from a French version.

J. M. Millás Vallicrosa, "La Obra enciclopédica de R. Abraham bar Hiyya", *Estudios sobre historia de la ciencia española*, Barcelona, 1949, 219-262. – C. Sirat, *A History of Jewish Philosophy in the Middle Ages*, Cambridge, 1985.

Tony Lévy

**ABRAHAM IBN DA'UD (early 12th c. - *c.*1180).** Jewish philosopher, born at *Cordova, Abraham Ibn Da'ud lived mainly at *Toledo, where he may have suffered martyrdom. His main work, *Emuna rama* (*Sublime faith*), *Aristotelian in inspiration, turns on the problem of free *will. He was also the author of a historical work, *Sefer ha-qabbalah* (*Book of Tradition*). Some would see in him Dominic Gundisalvi's famous collaborator designated by the name *Avendaut* (Iohannes Avendaut Israelita, translator of *Avicenna's *De anima*), or even another famous translator, Iohannes Hispanus.

C. Sirat, *La philosophie juive médiévale en terre d'Islam*, Paris, 1988, 164-179. – T.A.M. Fontaine, *In Defence of Judaism: Abraham ibn Daud*, Assen, 1990. – M.-T. d'Alverny, *Avicenne en Occident*, Paris, 1993, 19-43.

Gilbert Dahan

**ABRAHAM IBN EZRA (1089-1164/1165).** Poet, grammarian, biblical exegete, philosopher, mathematician-astronomer and physician, Abraham ibn Ezra was born at Tudela in *Spain. His life had two periods: half a century in Spain and a quarter-century, from 1140, shared between Italy, France and England. During the first of these periods, he lived in contact with the great Spanish Jewish figures of the world of the general and religious sciences. During the second, he delivered his Arab-Jewish science to the scholars of the Jewish communities who took him in, leaving his numerous pupils nearly a hundred works. The Western world owes him its knowledge of *Hebrew grammar and the literal biblical *exegesis of the Spanish schools, of *Neoplatonist philosophy close to that of *Avicenna, and of Euclid's mathematical and astronomical calculations. His influence profoundly marked the Jewish and Christian intellectuals of the Middle Ages, particularly in the field of philology and *mathematics.

*Rabbi Abraham Ibn Ezra*, I. Twersky (ed.), J.M. Harris (ed.), Cambridge, 1993.

Michel Serfaty

**ABRAHAM'S BOSOM.** The conception of the dwelling of the just after death as a reunion with *Abraham, the Old Testament patriarch, appears in Jewish *apocrypha such as the *Fourth Book of Maccabees*, but especially in three gospel passages, the most important being the parable of Dives and Lazarus (Lk 16, 19-31; see also Mt 8, 11 and Lk 13, 28). After his death, Lazarus is borne "to the bosom of Abraham" (*in sinum Abrahae*) where he receives his consolation, while Dives, tormented in the infernal fire, vainly implores Abraham.

The bosom of Abraham (or the bosom of the three patriarchs, Abraham, *Isaac and *Jacob) became in the Middle Ages a favourite means of evoking the paradisal destiny of the just. Its importance was particularly great in the liturgy of the *dead, whose formulae often consisted in praying that the dead person's *soul be received into Abraham's bosom (*e.g.* the Roman prayer *Deus apud quem*: "Command the holy angels to take this soul in their arms and lead it to the bosom of the patriarch Abraham . . .").

In this context, as in the gospel parable, Abraham's bosom receives souls in the time between individual death and the *Last Judgment. But, despite the ideas of some authors like Tertullian, it would be wrong to make Abraham's bosom a neutral place, without reward or punishment, comparable to the Jewish Sheol. Even if certain expressions connected with Abraham's bosom (*refrigerium*, *requies*) suggest a *beatitude inferior to that enjoyed by the elect after the Last Judgment, many theologians emphasize the properly paradisal value of Abraham's bosom (*e.g.* *Julian of Toledo in the 7th c.). On the other hand, if Abraham's bosom usually designates a place for souls, it can also signify the *paradise in which the risen elect will live after the Last Judgment. Thus, for St *Thomas Aquinas, Abraham's bosom has two possible senses: before the coming of Christ, it corresponded to the *limbo of the patriarchs; but after the *Redemption, there is an equivalence between "Abraham's bosom" and "kingdom of *heaven" (*Summa theologiae*, Supp., 69, 4).

In iconography, Abraham's bosom is a way of representing paradise (the elect may be held on the patriarch's knees, covered by his cloak, or placed in a cloth). This image appeared in the East in the 9th c., in the West towards the year 1000; it was widely developed in the 11th-13th cc., both in illustrating the parable of Lazarus and in representations of the Last Judgment (Torcello *mosaic, portals of Gothic cathedrals). While in the East – where they resorted more readily to the three patriarchs – this figuration lasted beyond the Middle Ages, in the West it tended in the 14th and 15th cc. to be supplanted by other evocations of paradise (heavenly *Jerusalem, celestial court).

A. Mangenot, "Abraham (sein d')", *DThC*, 1, 1930, 111-116. – J. Ntedika, *L'Évocation de l'au-delà dans la prière pour les morts. Étude de patristique et de liturgie latines (IVe-VIIIe siècle)*, Paris-Louvain, 1971. – J. Baschet, "Medieval Abraham: between Fleshly Patriarch and Divine Father", *MLN*, 108, 1993, 738-758.

Jérôme Baschet

**ABRAVANEL, ISAAC (1437-1508).** Born at Lisbon, favourite of the Portuguese court until 1481, then from 1484 a familiar of the *Catholic Kings, Ferdinand of Aragon and Isabella of Castile, Isaac Abravanel tried and failed to annul the decree expelling the *Jews from *Spain in 1492. He chose exile and served successively the king of *Naples and, after travelling via Corfu, the republic of *Venice. He died in Venice. Esteemed by the powerful of this world for his talents as financier and diplomat, Abravanel was also a prolific exegete. In particular, he commented on nearly the whole biblical corpus and Moses *Maimonides's *Guide for the Perplexed*. He was also the author of a messianic trilogy, the *Keep of salvation*, aiming among other things to answer the arguments of Christian polemic against *Judaism, in which he announced the redemption for the first decades coming in the 16th century.

M.M. Kellner, *Dogma in Medieval Jewish Thought: from Maimonides to Abravanel*, Oxford, 1986. – J.-C. Attias, *Isaac Abravanel, La mémoire et l'espérance*, Paris, 1992.

Jean-Christophe Attias

**ABRUZZI.** The Abruzzi covered the whole south-east part of the duchy of *Spoleto. The region was characterised by the weakness of its urban network, destroyed at the time of the *Lombard invasions and partly recreated in the 13th c. with the foundation of L'Aquila and the development of Sulmona, and by the importance of its early medieval monastic settlements. Integrated into the Frankish political world from the 8th c., the Abruzzi had evident economic and cultural affinities with southern *Italy: viz. the influence of *Monte Cassino on the region in the 11th c., a political system derived from Lombard models, and the precocious development of transhumance. *Roger II annexed the region to the Norman kingdom of *Sicily in 1140.

"Abruzzo: storia", *EncIt*, 1, 1949, 142-143. – L. Feller, *Les Abruzzes médiévales. Territoire, économie et société en Italie centrale du IXe au XIIe siècle*, Rome, 1998 ("BEFAR", 300).

Laurent Feller

***ABSOLUTIO.*** *Absolutio*, derived from the Latin *absolvo*, to loosen or release, was a particular prayer for the *dead, accompanied by a rite. God is asked to acquit his servant who has just finished his life. The liturgy of the dead was often imagined as a sort of final combat to snatch from the *demon a soul that in some way belonged to him by his voluntary consent to *sin, and to attain God thanks to His all-powerful intervention acting through his *angels.

The rite took place after the funeral *mass, at the church, around the coffin; it was accompanied by the chanting of a response, marked by an aspersion and a censing, and ended with a prayer.

In the old forms, the celebration of mass was not essential to the *funeral itself (called the mass of the dead, but not necessarily in the presence of the body); *absolutio*, on the other hand, was an essential element, which could take place in the *cemetery; it ended each of the three or four watches of the vigil around the body.

H.-R. Philippeau, "Origine et évolution des rites funéraires", *Le Mystère de la mort et sa célébration*, Paris, 1956, 186-206.

Guy-Marie Oury

**ABSOLUTION.** In the early Church, the power to absolve sinners was reserved to the *bishop; it was exercised by priests as well after the introduction of private *penance. Only with the development of scholastic sacramental theory in the 12th and 13th cc. did the question of the power of absolution implied in the "power of the keys" became central to penitential discussion. Some argued that absolution by a priest freed a sinner from punishment alone, while others, beginning with *Peter Lombard, held that the priest held the power to absolve sinners from the *sin in itself as well as from punishment due for sin. For *Thomas Aquinas, absolution by the priest was the *form of the sacrament of penance, while *confession, *contrition and satisfaction were the matter. Through perfect contrition one could obtain pardon of sins without sacramental confession, but through the sacrament absolution could be obtained even without perfect contrition. Later theologians, mainly *Duns Scotus, considered that the sacrament consisted principally in the priest's absolution rather than in the actions of the penitent.

C. Vogel, *Le Pécheur et la pénitence au Moyen Âge*, Paris, 1969. – L. Hödl, "Die scholastische Busstheologie", *LdM*, 2, 1983, 1137-1141.

Patrick J. Geary

**ABSTRACTION.** In a general sense, abstraction is the act by which the *intellect considers an aspect of reality without taking into account the other aspects to which it is linked. There is total abstraction when the intellect "isolates" a *universal determination (*e.g.* animality) from its particular realizations (humanity or caninity), and formal abstraction when it "isolates" a form from its concrete subject. In the *Aristotelian noetic, abstraction is the operation by which the agent intellect takes hold of the intelligible element, universal and necessary, with which the material reality is pregnant. This theory, which aims to ensure the transition from empirical *knowledge to intellectual knowledge, is at the heart of the problem of relations between thought and the real.

M.-V. Leroy, "*Abstractio et separatio* d'après un texte controversé de saint Thomas", *RThom*, 48, 1948, 328-339.

Serge Bonino

## ACCLAMATIONS

**The West.** Brief formulae pronounced by the crowd, acclamations generally served to approve a man or a situation. In the earliest times of Christendom, the *bishop was chosen by acclamation of the assembly; the *Laudes regiae* were formulae of acclamation for great men.

Acclamation played a role in the liturgy throughout the Middle Ages, as witness certain formulae of the *mass or the *office: *Alleluia*, **Kyrie eleison*, *Deo gratias*. It provides one of the earliest proofs of the assembly's participation in the liturgy, and in this sense it is close to the *antiphon which was originally a response of the people to the chanting of the *psalm by the soloist.

E. Cantorowicz, *Laudes Regiae. A Study in Liturgical Acclamations and Medieval Ruler Worship*, Berkeley (CA), 1946. – G. Chew, "Acclamation", *The New Grove Dictionary*, 1, 1980, London, 35-36. – S. McCormick, *Eternal Victory. Triumphal Rulership in Late Antiquity, Byzantium and the Early Medieval West*, Cambridge, 1990.

Claire Maître

**Byzantium.** To acclaim especially a god was an old Near-Eastern tradition which spread into the Roman Empire for the benefit of the emperors and was maintained after its Christianisation. Thus the canons of the council of Sardica were adopted by the synod's response: "*placet*".

The Byzantine imperial ceremonies – *coronation, *marriage, birth of a *porphyrogenete, horse-races, celebration of a triumph – were pretexts for acclamations, codified according to circumstances, a good many of which were preserved by Constantine Porphyrogenitus in his *De Cerimoniis*. The appearance of an emperor took place amid complete silence, ensured by a special official, the *silentiarius*; then the people, represented by the demes, the senators and the dignitaries, reacted with rhythmic acclamations. The most crucial of these formulated the acquiescence of the *army, the senate and the people to a new emperor's accession to the throne. Any usurper, over and above the wearing of purple buttons, was careful to benefit from such acclamations, an indispensable step for whoever wished to be considered the legitimate *basileus*.

There was no room for improvisations, or else the *euphemiai* might be transformed into outrages (*disphemiai*), expression of a necessarily sacrilegious discontent, the Hippodrome being the appropriate place where the people of the capital expressed their wishes, or perhaps their hostility to imperial policy and those responsible for it. It was thus that the "Nika" insurrection of 532, which nearly dethroned Justinian, began. In the 9th and 10th cc., such accidents were unthinkable: everything was regulated by the orders of the *praepositus*, chants and responses were established in advance and followed age-old formulae, the rhythm being maintained by organs.

The promotion of senior dignitaries – caesar, *magister*, patrician – and higher officials such as *strategoi* also involved ceremonies in which the demes, who had obviously had no voice in the choice of these people, ritually acclaimed the beneficiaries.

C. Roueché, "Acclamations in the Late Roman Empire: New Evidence from Aphrodisias", *JRS*, 74, 1984, 181-199. – S. McCormick, *Eternal Victory. Triumphal Rulership in Late Antiquity, Byzantium and the Early Medieval West*, Cambridge, 1990. – N. Maliaras, *Die Orgel im byzantinischen Hofzeremoniell des 9. und des 10. Jahrhunderts. Eine Quellenuntersuchung*, Munich, 1991.

Jean-Claude Cheynet

***ACEDIA.*** *Acedia* or accidie is a chronic state of ennui and discouragement, a general atony of *soul and *body that prevents one from carrying out any manual, intellectual or spiritual activity. Its symptoms are instability, disgust for the way of life being led, the feeling of being abandoned by everyone, nostalgia for past life.

When Evagrius made his analysis and theory of *acedia* in the late 4th c., it was mainly as a monastic vice that attacked solitaries. In becoming secularized, the notion lost much of its substance. It was sometimes likened to *tristitia*, sometimes a synonym of laziness and spiritual torpor. It was in these impoverished forms that it survived in the West, after *Gregory the Great had removed it from the list of *capital sins, in *Hugh of Saint-Victor, Guillaume Peyraut and St *Thomas Aquinas.

S. Wenzel, "The Sin of Sloth, Acedia 700-1200", *Tr.*, 22, 1966, 73-102. – A. Guillaumont, *SC*, 170, 1971, 84-90. – A. Solignac, "Péchés capitaux", *DSp*, 12, 1, 1983, 853-862.

Paul Géhin

***ACHEIROPOIETOS.*** The term *acheiropoietos* (not made by human hands) was used in the New Testament with reference to the resurrected body (Mk 14, 58; 2 Cor 5, 1; Col 2, 11). In Byzantine use, it referred rather to miraculously produced *images, usually but not exclusively of Christ. The most famous was the Mandylion of Edessa, which, according to *legend, Christ himself made for his contemporary King Abgar. Acheiropoietic *icons date mostly from the period of the Byzantine wars against the Persians. The Mandylion of Edessa was translated in the 10th c. to *Constantinople, from which it ultimately disappeared. There are several Western candidates to be the original Mandylion.

A. Grabar, *L'Iconoclasme byzantin*, Paris, 1957, 31-33 ("Dossier archéologique").

Christopher Walter

**ACOLYTE.** The acolytate was the highest of the minor *orders. It is attested in Pope Cornelius's letter to Fabius of Antioch, which refers to a *deacon, a *subdeacon and six acolytes for each of the seven apostolic regions of Rome. The acolyte was the assistant of the subdeacon for the *Eucharist, particularly for *communion. His functions were conferred on him at his *ordination, when, in the earliest mention made of this service, the acolyte received a linen bag intended for the consecrated bread. Later he would receive a candlestick and a cruet to present the wine and the water; the prayer hopes that "he may be a faithful servitor of the altar".

A. Snijders, "'Acolythus cum ordinatur': eine historische Studie", *SE*, 9, 1957, 163-198. – A. Faivre, *Naissance d'une hiérarchie. Les premières étapes du cursus clérical, ThH*, 40, Paris, 1977.

Paul De Clerck

**ACRE.** A town on the Palestinian coast, Acre (*'Akkā*) appears in the Old Testament and at the time of the Ptolemies of Egypt. It was conquered by the Arabs at the start of the Caliphate of 'Umar (634-644), rebuilt in the reign of Caliph Mu'āwiya (661-680) and its *port refitted at the end of the 9th century. Its fame comes mainly from the role it played during the *crusades. *Baldwin I, king of *Jerusalem, took it from the *Fatimids in 1104 with the help of Genoese ships. Its favourable position as a harbour made it the point of convergence of the caravans from inner *Syria and the destination of all the Western fleets. Communes like *Genoa, *Marseille, *Venice and *Pisa were granted their own quarters and important privileges there. Western merchants sold mainly wood, *metals and cloth, and bought from Muslim merchants medicinal products, *spices, cotton, *silk, dyestuffs and various luxury goods (precious stones, porcelain, perfumes, precious woods). Customs duties, imposed especially on goods coming from the East, were levied at the royal market (*Funda regis*) in the north-east part of the town, and in the inner port quarter, at the court of the Chain, which also served as a court of justice for maritime affairs.

The town was reconquered by *Saladin on 9 July 1187, but on 12 July 1191, after a two-year siege, the Eastern Franks and those of the third crusade regained possession of it. After the treaty of Jaffa (1192) concluded between *Richard Coeur de Lion and Saladin, Acre became the capital of the second Latin kingdom. Its population increased, and the suburb or new town of Montmusard, which developed north of the city wall, was given its own wall during *Louis IX's visit to *Palestine after 1250.

But Acre in the 13th century was a deeply divided town. The Italian communes installed in their fortified quarters were at odds with each other: Pisans against Genoese in 1228, Venetians against Genoese from 1256 to 1258 during the war of St Sabas. The *military orders of *Templars and *Hospitallers, which each possessed a quarter in the town, also intervened more and more in the ceaseless conflicts that shook the kingdom after the Emperor *Frederick II's accession to the throne of Jerusalem in 1229. In

1231 a commune was formed around the anti-imperialist nobles led by the Ibelins, and managed the government of the town for ten years.

These divisions were all the more dangerous for Acre since the *Mamluks, installed in Egypt from 1250, began to lead an offensive *jihād* against the Franks after 1265. The fall of Acre on 18 May 1291 was the culmination of this Muslim reconquest and put an end to two centuries of Latin presence in Syria-Palestine. In the Mamluk period, Acre was no more than a ruined town: not until the mid 18th c. was it rebuilt.

M. Benvenisti, *The Crusaders in the Holy Land*, Jerusalem, 1970, 78-113. – J. Prawer, *Histoire du royaume latin de Jérusalem*, Paris, 1975, 543-557. – M. Balard, *Les croisades*, Paris, 1988, 60-62. – H.E. Mayer, *The Crusades*, 2nd ed., Oxford, 1988.

Anne-Marie Eddé

**ACROSTIC.** An acrostic is a poem whose subject, or the name of the author or dedicatee, can be read in a word or group of words, consisting of the first letter or first syllable – more rarely the last letter or last syllable – of each verse. This genre, quite popular during the early Middle Ages, notably in the court poetry of the Carolingian period, under the joint influence of the mannerist *rhetoric of Late Antiquity and the writing techniques proper to Celtic and Germanic poetry, suffered a relative eclipse in the course of the central Middle Ages before triumphing again in the 15th century. More than a mere exercise of pure literary virtuosity, it testifies to the extreme importance accorded by medieval writers to the *significans*, or even to the sacred character that they acknowledged to the letter: they were often invocations or texts of *prayers that were thus read vertically.

K. Krumbacher, "Die Akrostichis in der griechischen Kirchenpoesie", *Sitzungsberichte Bayer. Akademie der Wissenschaften*, 4, 1903, 551-691. – *DACL*, 1, 1907, 356-372. – P. Zumthor, *Langue, texte, énigme*, Paris, 1975, 25-54. – U. Ernst, *Carmen figuratum. Geschichte des Figuren-Gedichte von den antiken Ursprüngen bis zum Ausgang des Mittelalters*, Cologne-Weimar-Vienna, 1991. – S. Gwara, "Three Acrostic Poems by Abbo of Fleury", *Journal of Medieval Latin*, 1, 1992, 203-35. – M. Lapidge, P.S. Baker, "More Acrostic Verse by Abbo of Fleury", *Journal of Medieval Latin*, 7, 1997, 1-32.

Jean-Yves Tilliette

**ACT AND POTENCY.** The pair "act – potency" appears, in *Aristotle, in the context of the physical explanation of movement and, more widely, the metaphysical explanation of becoming. A notion too primordial to be defined, act can only be described inductively: it is then revealed as *being (*esse*) in its finished, perfect state. So act implies perfection, determination. Potency is deduced from the analysis of becoming: this postulates in effect an indeterminate substrate, relative non-being, but apt to become this or that. Potency, thus understood, is a real principle that composes with act, and it must be distinguished from logical potency or simple possibility, which exists only in the mind.

For *Thomas Aquinas, the pair act – potency has full transcendental value, *i.e.* it is a primary division of created being and occurs in its different categories, so it needs metaphysical consideration. Act and potency are not two "entities", of which it would be hard to see how their composition could constitute a true unity, but are two co-principles, really distinct, of all being. Act is prior to potency. Firstly in the logical order of *knowledge, since act enters into the definition of potency: sight is potency to see (act). Then in chronological order: if, in the subject, potency precedes act, the subject only actualizes its potency under the action of a *cause which is itself in act. Finally, in the order of perfection, since act is, in each being, a principle of determination and perfection, while potency is a principle of imperfection. The proper effect of potency is to receive the act and, subsequently, to limit and multiply it, while act, *per se*, betokening only perfection, is infinite and unique. So the pair act – potency lies at the heart of the problem of the one and the many.

Among the main realizations of the pair act – potency is the pair "accidents (act) – *substance (potency)", of which the pair "operation (act) – operative potency or *faculty (potency)" is a realization, or again the pair "substantial form (act) – matter (potency)". For St Thomas, the pair act – potency also applies to the most radical composition of created being, that of *esse* and essence: *esse* is the act of essence. Certainly, essence is act in its own *order, but it remains in potency in relation to *esse*, act of acts, which confers on it all its existential reality.

For *Duns Scotus, potency and act are no longer intrinsic principles of the existent, so much as properties of the existent *qua* existent: existential modes among which all being is divided. Potency is thus acknowledged a certain existence, independently of act.

L. Elders, *The Metaphysics of Being of St. Thomas Aquinas in a Historical Perspective*, New York, 1993, ch. 11 ("Being in act – being in potency").

Serge Bonino

**ACTIVE LIFE, CONTEMPLATIVE LIFE.** Formulated by Plato and *Aristotle, the doctrine of the two lives came to terms with biblical tradition in the Jew Philo. To the "practical" or active life, led within society, was opposed the "theoretical" or contemplative life, in which one isolated oneself in order to deal with God. The former must precede the latter, preparing man by the exercise of the human *virtues for the divine vision. Of this normal sequence of the two lives, Philo sees the figure in *Jacob, symbol of the ascetic, who becomes "Israel", *i.e.* "seeing God". With these two ways of life, the Alexandrian philosopher already connects the two forms of contemporary Jewish monasticism: the Essenes, whose existence was entirely communal, led the active life, while the Therapeutae, who spent six days out of seven in isolation, gave themselves to the contemplative life. This dichotomy would become current in Christian *monasticism, where *coenobites, living in community, were devoted in principle to "action" (ascetic purification), while hermits gave themselves up to *contemplation.

Expounded notably by *Cassian, this pattern could be applied to another pair: the pastor and the monk, one active, the other contemplative. Augustine, a monk turned *bishop, often developed this contrast, illustrated by the figures of Martha and Mary, *Peter and John, Leah and Rachel, or again by the two men, one working "in the fields", the other lying "in bed", taken by surprise on the day of the parousia (Mt 24, 40-41; Lk 17, 34). With Gregory Nazianzen, Augustine also advocated a mixed way of life, uniting action and contemplation, after the manner of his own existence as a pastor who remained faithful to the monastic ideal. It would be the same for *Gregory the Great, whose variations on this theme are particularly numerous and rich in biblical images, sometimes new (Penninah and Hannah, Merab and Michal, etc.).

But Augustine and Gregory often contrasted earthly life, where we give ourselves mainly to meritorious and purificatory action, with eternal contemplation, recompense of the future life. As for the contemplative life on earth, medieval literature would oscillate

*Woman carding wool.* Left bay of the north portal of Chartres cathedral, 13th c.

between a stricter concept, which reserved it for hermits, and a wider notion, which identified it with all monastic life, even communal. This second meaning was that which still prevails in our own day. But it is important not to forget that in the Middle Ages, the opposed term, "active life", did not just designate, as it does today, external activity for the profit of others, but also moral action on oneself to purify oneself by virtues and *ascesis, with a view to contemplating God down here and seeing him face to face hereafter.

F. Cayré, *La contemplation augustinienne*, Paris, 1954. – *Théologie de la vie monastique*, Paris, 1961. – A. Grilli, A. de Vogüé, "Vita attiva – Vita contemplativa – Vita mista", *DIP*, 10, Rome, 2000.

Adalbert de Vogüé

**ACTS OF BISHOPS.** Bishops' acts refer to the texts (*charters, *letters) issued by *bishops, whether or not through the intermediary of an episcopal *chancery. The earliest acts are *testaments, by which are designated long-term arrangements made by prelates on the eve of their death or on important occasions like the *foundations of abbeys. Until the 10th c., these documents are not numerous and come only from a few cities.

Bishops' charters begin to be issued in a regular way only in the 10th c., and even later in some regions. Their density is greatest at this time between the Rhine and the Loire, while their number begins to increase in the *Empire only from the mid 12th century. The French Midi, *Italy and *Spain are regions where bishops' acts were amply rivalled by the private acts delivered by *notaries in great numbers. Between the Loire and the Rhine, after a very clear domination of royal and imperial diplomas, bishops' acts caught up, then took the lead from the mid 11th century. Up to the early 13th c. and before the multiplication of private acts, lay and ecclesiastical, bishops' acts constituted a group of documents doubly coherent, in content and in form. Between 1000 and 1200 they provide a documentary mass that can be diplomatically analysed as fruitfully as royal diplomas and papal *bulls. Around 1200, the development of *officialities freed the bishop's chancery from having to deliver a great number of acts of no interest for the *diocese and its spiritual or patrimonial management.

For the formal and diplomatic presentation of episcopal acts, a distinction must be made between the Midi and the North. South of the Loire, though this limit has no absolute validity, episcopal charters copy the unequal form and indifferent presentation of private acts. The earliest ones have autograph subscriptions: those of other prelates for conciliar acts, those of officials and *canons of *chapters in other cases. The kinds of affairs dealt with are very diverse, but their number is relatively small compared to that of written acts in general. The present state of research on the acts of bishops in the French Midi is thus far behind that of the North by reason of their lesser importance. In *Catalonia, the dossier is much thicker than in the regions north of the Pyrenees, despite the role played by the archbishops of *Narbonne and Bordeaux in *Languedoc and *Aquitaine.

The cities of northern France and the Empire usually had an episcopal chancery, which borrowed its inspiration from the imperial and papal chanceries, as much for the formulary as for formal presentation. This chancery rested on a chancellor-canon, assisted by notaries, or scribes, more or less numerous, the group ensuring the quality and continuity of work dispatched. The number of episcopal acts issued by the chancery was directly related to the activity and authority of the group surrounding the bishop. Charters at this time show great solemnity: large *parchments, ornate writing, *seal, respect and repetition of formulae (invocation, title, preambles, final clauses, witnesses, chancery formulae). In this respect the model is given by the output of the bishops of the province of *Reims. The bishop was mainly invited to act in the following spheres: *foundation and restoration of religious communities, *donations and confirmations of properties, rulings on litigation. Prelates divided their acts into their personal actions and their role in authenticating the actions of third parties (mainly princes and nobles). The number of acts delivered increased particularly with the creation and expansion of monastic and canonical *orders in the 12th century. This also occasioned an increase in the number of charters prepared by the recipients and brought to the episcopal chancery for sealing. The 12th century was thus a period of apogee of episcopal acts by reason of their relative importance and the variety of subjects dealt with.

Alongside charters, which form the common lot of episcopal acts and whose preservation was ensured by community archives, a great number of letters were sent by the chancery itself, out of all proportion to the small number that have survived. Indeed they very quickly lost their topicality. What survive are those that were included in urgent dossiers, and those that found their way by chance into archives or intentionally into collections. Some celebrated correspondences could also be published: *e.g.* those of Archbishop *Hincmar of Reims, Bishops Frotaire of Toul and Lambert of Arras. They, more than the charters, faithfully reflect the work of the prelates, since in his correspondence the bishop could more fully express his personal capacity as jurist or theologian, his daily activities. For these reasons, it is regrettable that the letters have not been preserved in greater number.

A. Giry, *Manuel de diplomatique*, Paris, 1898 (bishops' acts). – *English Episcopal Acta*, 16 vols., Oxford, 1980-98. – *A propos des actes des évêques*, Nancy, 1991 (ed. of acts and *regesta*).

C. R. Cheney, *English Bishops' Chanceries, 1100-1250*, Manchester, 1950. – B.-M. Tock, *La Chancellerie des évêques d'Arras*, Paris, 1991. – B.-M. Tock, *Une chancellerie épiscopale au XIIe siècle: le cas d'Arras*, Louvain, 1991.

Michel Parisse

***AD EXTRA, AD INTRA.*** In Antiquity, these two expressions referred to human actions, *ad intra* designating operations of the subject that do not end in an exteriorization, *ad extra* being applied to action that is exteriorized. Taking up this anthropological distinction, *Thomas Aquinas (*De potentia*, q. 10, a. 1; *De veritate*, q. 7, a. 6) attempted a prudent application of this dual expression to the divinity. *God's actions *ad intra* concern the intra-trinitarian life, which is not communicable. Each *person of the *Trinity can produce actions that are proper to himself (*creation, *redemption, insufflation). God's action *ad extra* is his self-communication in the various *mirabilia* of salvation-history culminating in the Incarnation and the eucharistic presence.

H. Quilliet, "Ad intra, ad extra", *DThC*, 1, 1990, 398-400.

Michel Deneken

***AD LIMINA.*** *Gregory the Great ordered that the *bishops dependent on him should come on 29 June to the tombs of the apostles Peter and Paul (*limina apostolorum*). The annual obligation, which goes back to Pope *Zacharias (743), was extended by *Gregory VII († 1077) to the bishops of Christendom. According to a *Decretal of *Gregory IX († 1241), the *citramontani* bishops should go *ad limina* annually, the *ultramontani* every two years, and the *ultramarini* every three to five years. From the late 12th c., the bishops no longer had just to visit the tombs of the apostles, but also the *pope, to whom they had to give a report on the state of their *diocese. This evolution was justified in the 13th c. by the concept that "where the pope is, there is Rome".

J. Sägmüller, "Die Visitatio liminum bis Bonifaz VIII", *ThQ*, 81, 1900, 69-117. – M. Maccarrone, "Ubi est papa, ibi est Roma", *Romana Ecclesia Cathedri Petri*, 2, Rome, 1991, 1137-1156.

Agostino Paravicini Bagliani

**ADALARD OF CORBIE (751-826).** A cousin of *Charlemagne, Adalard was raised at court with his brother Wala. He retired to *Corbie where, after a stay at *Monte Cassino, he returned as *abbot (780). There he favoured the development of studies, in liaison with the great architects of the *Carolingian Renaissance: Angilbert, *Alcuin and *Paul the Deacon. He took part in the theological controversy over the procession of the *Holy Spirit. He was the first to conceive the idea of sending a monastic colony to *Saxony (this was *Corvey). To reform his *abbey, he composed Statutes (832) which served as a model for many other *foundations. His Life was written by *Paschasius Radbertus.

Paschasius Radbertus, "Vita Adalhardi", *PL*, 120, 1852, 1507-1556. – Paschasius Radbertus, *Charlemagne's Cousins*, A. Cabaniss (ed.), Syracuse (NY), 1967.

"Les Statuts. . .", L. Levillain (ed.), *MA*, 13, 1900, 238-386. – G. Hocquard, *Cath.*, 1, 1948, 118. – D. Ganz, *Corbie in the Carolingian Renaissance*, Sigmaringen, 1990.

Michel Sot

**ADALBERO OF LAON (*c.*950/957-1031).** Adalbero or Ascelin was born into an Ardennes family which included the dukes of Upper *Lorraine and three other Adalberos, bishops of *Metz (984-1005), *Verdun (984-988) and *Reims (969-989). After early studies, probably in the monastery of *Gorze (near Metz), he went to Reims doubtless in the train of his uncle, appointed *archbishop in 969. He was the pupil of *Gerbert, the future Pope Silvester II. In 974 he appears as *notary to the king of France, Lothar, who got him elected bishop of *Laon, 16 Jan 977. He remained there until his death, probably in 1031. He played an important political role in 989 when he treacherously delivered up to the new king, Hugh Capet, his competitor Charles of Lorraine (brother of King Lothair) who had taken refuge in the city of Laon. His relations with Hugh, then with his son Robert the Pious, would not always be good. Though he had rallied to the new dynasty, he retained a nostalgia for the old Carolingian grandeur. His literary work bears witness to these sentiments, especially his *Poem to King Robert*, written probably between 1027 and 1030. This is an unfinished composition, in four parts, of 433 verses in dactylic hexameters, in which satire and didacticism alternate. Its object is the order of the realm, whose regulator is the king himself. This is why Adalbero opens his poem with a symbolic eulogy of the king, who concentrates in himself – following a tripartite structure of Dumézilian type – *wisdom, strength and *beauty. In the second discourse, it is the realm which is divided into the three estates: those who pray, those who fight and those who *labour. By the rigour of his *justice, the king must see to it that the three orders do not transgress their proper bounds. The satirical part of the poem shows, in contrast, the forces of disorder: the *milites*, turbulent young warriors, and the Cluniac monks, under the leadership of their "king" *Odilo. The world is upside-down and the *bishops as well as the powerful see their traditional prerogatives under attack. This poem is the old bishop's last warning to King Robert, both approaching the end of their life. Earlier, Adalbero had written a theological poem, *De summa fidei*, of 327 verses; a *Rythmus satiricus*, a short satirical poem against Count Landri of Nevers; and a *letter to Bishop Fulk of Amiens, setting out the first principles of *dialectic in a pleasant way.

Adalbéron de Laon, *Poème au roi Robert*, C. Carozzi (ed.), Paris, 1979.

G. Hückel, *Les poèmes satiriques d'Adalbéron*, *Bibliothèque de la faculté des lettres de Paris*, 13, Paris, 1901. – R. T. Coolidge, *Adalbéro Bishop of Laon*, *Studies in Medieval and Renaissance History*, 2, Lincoln (NE), 1965. – G. Duby, *The Three Orders: Feudal Society Imagined*, Chicago, 1980.

Claude Carozzi

**ADALBERT OF PRAGUE (*c.*956-997).** Bishop, monk and *martyr, Adalbert of Prague is the great figure of the Christianization of the peoples of central Europe. Born into a Bohemian family, the Slavnik, rivals of the *Přemyslid dukes, he was educated from 972 to 981 at the cathedral *school of *Magdeburg. At his *confirmation he abandoned his Slav name Woytech and took that of his sponsor, Archbishop Adalbert. Becoming a cleric of the church of *Prague, he was elected its *bishop in 983.

His pastoral activity was opposed, and his struggle against customs and the *slave traffic, a source of revenue for Duke *Boleslas of Bohemia, was a failure. Discouraged, he left Prague in 988 for Italy, finally entering the monastery of Sts Boniface and Alexius in *Rome. In 992 he was recalled to *Bohemia under pressure from his *metropolitan *Willigis of Mainz. Though positive, owing to the links forged with the neighbouring princes Géza of Hungary and *Boleslas the Brave of Poland, this second sojourn met with the same difficulties. Convinced of the uselessness of his efforts, he returned to Rome (*c.*994/5), where he soon frequented the court of the young Emperor *Otto III, over whom he exercised a strong influence, developing in him an ardent spirituality. Invited back to Prague, he obtained, in case of failure, the right to wage missionary campaigns in Slav territory. In fact, access to his see was forbidden him by Boleslas of Bohemia, who had just massacred his family. Freed from his diocesan obligations, he undertook a journey to the great sanctuaries of France, then went to *Hungary and *Poland, where he prepared with his half-brother Gaudentius a *mission to the Prussians, east of the mouths of the Vistula. Taken prisoner, he was put to death on 23 April 997. Boleslas the Brave ransomed his body and deposited it at *Gniezno, his capital.

A reputation for *sanctity was formed with Otto III's support and culminated in his *canonization before December 999. In February 1000 the emperor went on pilgrimage to Gniezno and raised his *relics on a golden altar, also recognising the political and religious independence of Poland. Returning with portions of the body, he distributed them to churches founded under the saint's patronage. His cult spread in Poland, Hungary and above all *Bohemia, where his relics were transferred in 1038 and where the saint became an emblem of national identity. Adalbert's life is told by two biographers, one being probably the Roman John Canaparius, the other the Saxon Bruno of Querfurt. They insist on the exemplary monk, the ascetic full of *humility, the mystic. Historians place more emphasis on his noble origin and high rank, and on his links with the German church and Ottonian policy. But this image of an imperial missionary is not incompatible, given the spiritual perspectives of the year 1000, with that of the monk burning with *faith to the point of martyrdom.

A. Poppe, "Adalbert de Prague", *Histoire des saints et de la sainteté chrétienne*, 5, Paris, 1986, 62-69.

Patrick Corbet

*Otto II invests Adalbert as bishop of Prague.* Bronze door of Gniezno cathedral, Poland (detail).

**ADAM AND EVE.** Representation of our first parents was early, continuous and frequent in the Middle Ages. These images were based on the text of *Genesis, which gives two accounts of the creation of woman (Gen 1, 27-30 and 3, 21-22). The second, which subordinated woman to man, was much preferred in iconography. The common pattern of succession of scenes was fixed from the time of Leo I (440-461). It is found in four Carolingian *Bibles (Bible of Alcuin, Moutier-Grandval Bible, First Bible of Charles the Bald and Bible of St Paul's Without the Walls) which devote a whole page to the illustration of this theme, apparently derived from an early Christian manuscript. The account is divided among eight images: creation of Adam, extraction of a rib, presentation of Eve to Adam, prohibition of eating the fruit of the *tree of knowledge, temptation of Eve and original sin, God's discovery of the fault and shame of our parents, expulsion from the garden of Eden, labour of Adam and Eve. More detailed accounts also exist: frescos of the Roman basilicas of *St Peter's and *St Paul's Without the Walls (mid 5th c.), Cotton Bible and Vienna Bible (6th c.), mosaic in the cupola of the atrium of St Mark's, Venice (1220). The cycle is often supplemented by the sacrifice and murder of Abel, a formula very frequent in the central Middle Ages. From the late 13th c., in Italy (*Orvieto cathedral, campanile of *Florence cathedral, fountain of *Perugia), the cycle was also supplemented by the invention of the various arts.

In all cases, the account of the origin of mankind is given value by a development outside the strict framework of the seven days of *Creation. The importance accorded it comes from its general import: the original fault explains man's estrangement from God and, happy fault, permits man's *redemption by Christ, with whose characteristics the Creator is nearly always depicted. From the early Christian period developed the contrast of Adam and Christ, then that of Eve and *Mary: to the Romanesque cycles, cited above, correspond those of the life of Christ. This relationship is not *typological but shows the dynamic of salvation-history; it can be expressed by the juxtaposition of the two cycles (*e.g.* on the doors of *Hildesheim cathedral, late 10th - early 11th c.) or, very frequently from the 12th c., by synthetic images. Adam's skull is placed under the *cross that bears Christ; sometimes it is Adam himself who appears and collects the Saviour's blood. With Eve, he appears in Christ's *Descent into Limbo or in scenes of the *Last Judgment. The history of the wood of the cross itself is connected with the tree of knowledge and with Adam (fresco of the Invention of the Holy Cross by Agnolo Gaddi in the choir of Santa Croce, Florence, *c.*1385-1390). As for Eve, she is sometimes represented prostrate at the feet of the Virgin in *Majesty (fresco of Ambrogio *Lorenzetti at San Galgano, Montesiepi, *c.*1345).

Isolated images of Adam and Eve could bear different meanings. On the portals of cathedrals (Saint-Lazare at *Autun, portal of Adam at *Bamberg, Notre-Dame at *Reims), they evoke the *penitents pardoned by the Church. Finally, the Presentation of Eve to Adam enjoyed great popularity as the founding episode of the sacrament of *marriage.

S. Esche, *Adam und Eva. Sündenfall und Erlösung*, Düsseldorf, 1957. – E. Guldan, *Eva und Maria. Eine Antithese als Bildmotiv*, Graz-Cologne, 1966. – A. Masure, *Adam et Eve. Le thème d'Adam et Eve dans l'art*, Paris, 1967. – S. Esche-Braufels, "Adamo ed Eva", *Enciclopedia dell'arte medievale*, 1, Rome, 1991, 138-145.

Pierre Kerbrat

**ADAM DE LA HALLE (13th c.).** A **trouvère* born at *Arras *c.*1250, died in southern Italy before 1289, Adam de la Halle (or Adam le Bossu) left love songs and *jeu-partis* in accordance with the tradition of his time. He was more innovative as a musician in his

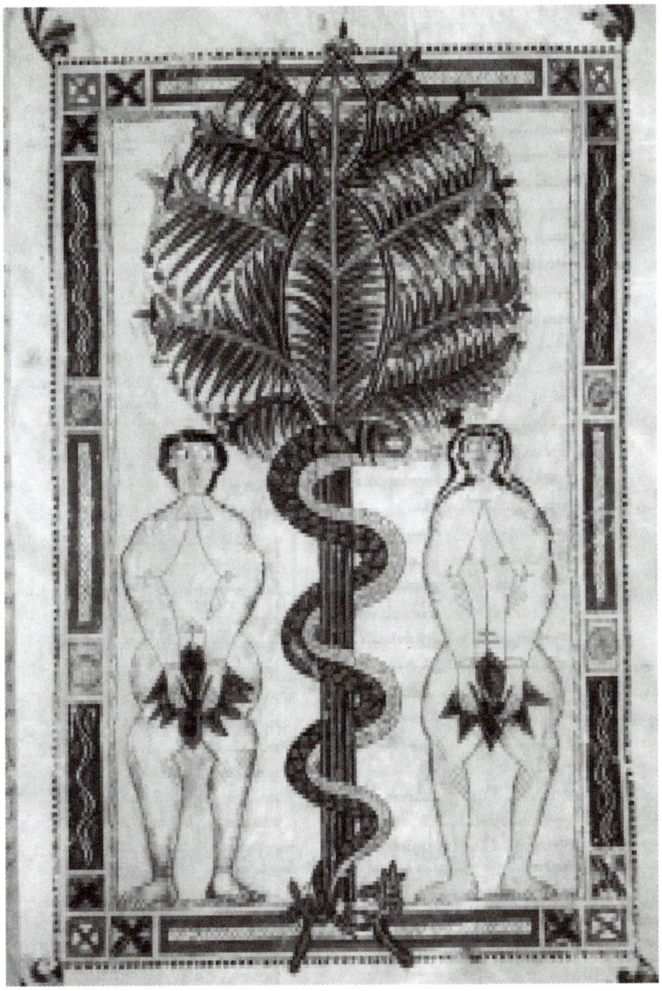

*Adam and Eve: the original sin.* Beatus of Liebana's *Commentary on the Apocalypse*, fol. 18 r°. Guadalupe, *c.*776-786. Madrid, Escorial Library.

*motets and rondeaux, introducing *polyphony into non-religious *music. He was the first dramatist to compose pieces in a purely secular spirit: the *Jeu de la feuillée* (1276) where with a group of friends he celebrates, with verve and impertinence, *friendship and the right it confers to say anything; and the *Jeu de Robin et Marion*, where he cleverly transposes the action of the *pastourelles*.

*The Lyrics and Melodies of Adam de la Halle*, D. H. Nelson (ed.), H. van der Werf (ed.), New York, 1985. – Adam de la Halle, *Oeuvres complètes*, P.-Y. Badel (ed.), Paris, 1995.

Pierre-Yves Badel

**ADAM MARSH (DE MARISCO) (died 1259).** A Franciscan scholar, died 18 Nov 1259. A pupil and friend of *Robert Grosseteste, he was a master of arts when he took the *Franciscan habit in 1232. He incepted in theology at *Oxford, the first of his order to do so, and taught it from 1247 to 1250. A noted biblical scholar, he collaborated with Grosseteste in Greek studies. He was counsellor to King *Henry III, Simon de Montfort and the archbishop of *Canterbury, Boniface of Savoy, and advised his order on *readers for the English Franciscan province. His letters are an important source for English political and Franciscan history.

J. S. Brewer, *Monumenta franciscana*, London, 1858, 77-489. – C. H. Lawrence, "The Letters of Adam Marsh and the Franciscan school at Oxford", *JEH*, 42, 1991, 218-238 (bibliography).

Clifford Hugh Lawrence

**ADAM OF BREMEN (died *c.*1081/1085).** Of Franconian origin, Adam of Bremen was probably a *canon of *Bamberg whence he was called by the archbishop of *Bremen, Adalbert. There he became director of the cathedral *school from 1069 at the latest. He died on 12 October, between 1081 and 1085. His most important work was the redaction of the *Gesta Hammaburgensis ecclesiae pontificum*, the earliest *chronicle of the diocese of *Hamburg-Bremen, undertaken in 1073-1075. It relates the history of the diocese from its beginnings under *Charlemagne (prefaced by the early history of the *Saxons) to the death of Archbishop Adalbert in 1072. The *Gesta* is divided into four books, the first of which ends at the death of Archbishop Unni (936), the second at that of Vezelin II (1043); the third book is entirely given over to the outstanding episcopate of Adalbert, and the fourth gives an ethnographical description of the *Scandinavian lands based, among other sources, on the oral testimony of the king of *Denmark, Sven Estridsen. To this whole, which he dedicated to the new archbishop, Liemar, Adam added appendixes (*scholia*) with his own hand. After his death, the manuscript, which had become hard to read by reason of the numerous additions, was rewritten and again supplemented. Adam's chronicle survives in 22 manuscripts.

The author's personality and his perception of the world appear exclusively in this work. The *Gesta* shows tokens of objectivity of which the psychologizing critique of Adalbert is not the least, but, written "for the glory of the Church of Bremen", it actually answered certain interests. Of these, one of the most important was a defence and illustration, historically underpinned and legitimized, of the deeply threatened rights of the Church of Bremen, notably its charge of the *mission to the Nordic peoples to which the diocese attached its glory. These threats, appearing in Adam's time, came from the Church of Denmark's hankering for autonomy, from the neighbouring dukes and also from *bishops who neglected the diocese in favour of an exaggerated service to the king. In this perspective, the chronicle can thus be read as a warning to Bishop Liemar, invested by the king, to defend the interests of the diocese as he should. Written before the outbreak of the *Investiture Contest and the appearance of the communal movement, the work takes up no position on the quarrel of the powers. However, as a major monument of the 11th c., it already clearly reflects, in its narratives and its internal contradictions, the tensions of a time of crisis and disruption, in the course of which the bishops became territorial princes.

Adam von Bremen, *Hamburgische Kirchengeschichte*, B. Schmeidler (ed.), *MGH.SRG*, 2, 1917 (re-ed. 1993). – *AQDGMA*, 11, W. Trillmich (ed.), Darmstadt (Ger. tr.).

A. Taylor, "Adam de Brême", *DHGE*, 1, 1912, 470-471. – R. Buchner, "Die politische Vorstellungswelt Adams von Bremen", *Archiv für kulturgeschichte*, 45, 1963, 15-50. – G. Theuerkauf, "Die Hamburgische Kirchengeschichte Adams von Bremen. Über Gesellschaftsformen und Weltbilder im 11. Jahrhundert", *Historiographia mediaevalis. Festschrift für F. J. Schmale*, Darmstadt, 1988, 118-137. – H.-W. Goetz, "Geschichtsschreibung und Recht. Zur rechtlichen Legitimierung des Bremer Erzbistums in der Chronik Adams von Bremen", *Recht und Alltag im Hanseraum. Festschrift G. Theuerkauf*, Hamburg, 1993.

Hans-Werner Goetz

**ADAM OF PETIT PONT (12th c.).** This *master of English origin taught the *liberal arts at *Paris between 1132 and 1148. He left an *Ars disserendi*, a treatise on *logic in which he was one of the first to use *Aristotle's "new logic", and a lexicographical collection, *De utensilibus*. Though a brilliant logician, he was controversial, as much for his character as for his style. His surname (his school was on the Petit Pont, between the Cité and the left bank) appeared late. Little is known of the end of his life; some say he died *c.*1159, others in 1181 as bishop of St Asaph in Wales.

L. Minio Paluello, "The *Ars disserendi* of Adam of Balsham Parvipontanus", *MRSt*, 3, 1954, 116-169. – P. Lendinara, "The *Oratio de utensilibus* . . . by Adam of Balsham", *Anglo-Norman Studies*, 15, 1992, 161-176.

Jacques Verger

**ADAM OF WODEHAM (*c.*1298-1358).** This *Franciscan taught the **Sentences* at *Oxford (1332), *Norwich (*c.*1330) and *London. Apart from his Oxford and Norwich commentaries (*Lectura secunda*), we have two treatises (*Tractatus de indivisibilibus*; *Tractatus alphabeticus*). He further explored the doctrines of *Ockham, whom he knew personally. His response to the question concerning the object of scientific *knowledge (*Sent.*, I, d. 1, q. 1) is among the most important innovations since he sketched out, for the first time, the thesis of the *complexe significabile*. The influence of this thinker preoccupied by logical and semantic problems on the theologians of his time, notably *Gregory of Rimini, is not negligible.

Adam de Wodeham, *Lectura secunda in librum primum Sententiarum*, R. Wood (ed.), St Bonaventure (NY), 1990 (3 vol.).

W. Courtenay, *Adam Wodeham*, Leiden, 1978.

Ruedi Imbach

**ADELARD OF BATH (*c.*1080-1160?).** According to the meagre biographical details we possess, Adelard of Bath was the son of a certain Fastrad. He was in the retinue of John of Villula, bishop of Bath and *Wells (1088-1122), who moved the see of the *bishopric to Bath in order to promote the town as a spa and a place of learning. It may have been John who sent Adelard to *Tours for his higher education. He later had students at *Laon, including a "nephew" – perhaps one of the young noblemen that Adelard had charge of as tutor – with whom he made a pact that he (Adelard) would investigate the learning of the Arabs to the best of his ability, whilst his nephew would master the unstable doctrines of the French. His treatise *On the same and the different* is dedicated to William, bishop of Syracuse, and indicates that Adelard spent some time in search of Greek learning in southern *Italy and *Sicily. The *Natural Questions*, on the other hand, purports to be the result of Adelard's investigation of "the studies of the Arabs" (*studia Arabum*) and refers to experiences at Mamistra and at Tarsus in *Cilicia. Adelard probably spent several years on the shores of the Mediterranean early in the 12th century. Eventually, however, he settled down in his native Bath where, probably with the assistance of the converted Jew from *Aragon, *Petrus Alfonsi, he made Latin versions from the Arabic of Euclid's *Elements*, a set of astronomical tables, two elementary works on *astrology and a book on talismans. Perhaps as late as 1149-1150 he composed a text on the *astrolabe, including in it a brief account of Ptolemaic *astronomy. He dedicated this to Prince Henry (who became King *Henry II in 1154). But it is as a geometer that he achieved his highest reputation. His translation of Euclid's *Elements*, perhaps also as a result of his own teaching in *mathematics, became the basis of geometrical speculation and adaptations of Euclid's work. One of the earliest centres where this appears to have taken place is *Chartres where an adaptation of Adelard's translation was included in Thierry of Chartres's *encyclopedia of the arts, the *Heptateuchon*. An English tradition can also be traced, which had close relations with scholarship in *Toledo.

Adelard of Bath, *Conversations with his Nephew*, C. Burnett (ed.), Cambridge, 1998.

C. H. Haskins, *Studies in the History of Mediaeval Science*, Cambridge (MA), 1927, 20-42 (2nd ed.). – C. Burnett, *Adelard of Bath: An English Scientist and Arabist of the early Twelfth Century, Warburg Institute Surveys and Texts*, 14, London, 1987. – A. G. Rigg, "Peter Alfonsi, Adelard of Bath", *A History of Anglo-Latin Literature 1066-1422*, Cambridge, 1992, 31-2. – L. Cochrane, *Adelard of Bath*, London, 1994.

Charles Burnett

**ADELHAUSEN.** Adelhausen was one of the four *Dominican convents of *Freiburg im Breisgau. Founded in 1245, it followed on from a community of women attested from 1234. Adelhausen, which numbered 70 sisters from the 13th c., had important possessions in Baden and *Alsace. Prioress Anna of Munzingen (first quarter of 14th c.) wrote the *Lives* of 36 sisters, in which she relates their *visions and mystical experiences. The Dominican *reform, coming from *Colmar, met strong opposition here. But in 1458 the Dominican chronicler J. Meyer, coming from Schoenensteinbach, reformed the convent.

*750 Jahre Dominikanerinnenkloster Adelhausen*, Freiburg im Breisgau, 1985.

Jean-Luc Eichenlaub

**ADELPHATON.** Byzantine monasteries, up against grave economic difficulties, got into the habit of giving monks, *clerics or even laymen, in exchange for gifts of money, an *adelphaton*, *i.e.* the right during their lifetime to board in the monastery without being subject to its rule. With time, *adelphata* could be sold or bequeathed. The *patriarchs fought in vain against the generalization of this practice, sometimes imposed by the civil authorities and hardly apt to contribute to respect for monastic discipline.

P. Lemerle, *Actes de Kutlumus*, 1988, 51 ("ArAt", 1; 2nd ed.). – *HChr*, 6, 1990, 173.

Marie-Hélène Congourdeau

**ADEODATUS II, POPE (died 676).** Roman by birth, probably the son of a monk, Adeodatus II is often considered the second of that name, Pope Deusdedit (615-618) having also been identified under the name Adeodatus. He was educated in the monastery of Sant'Erasmo al Celio, apparently a Greek foundation by culture, and was made *pope on 11 April 672. Like his predecessor Vitalian (657-672), he resolutely opposed the dogmatic line prevalent at *Constantinople, that of *monothelism. This orientation softened only with his successor Donus (676-678) and returned with Pope *Agatho (678-681), in a perspective of genuine dialogue. In the West, Adeodatus was in contact with the chief Churches of Britain (*Canterbury) and Gaul (*Tours). He died on 16 June 676, and is buried in *St Peter's.

*LP*, 1, 346-347. – F. Camobreco, "Il monastero di S. Erasmo sul Monte Celio", *ASRSP*, 28, 1905, 265-300. – J. Richards, *The Popes and Papacy in the Early Middle Ages*, London, 1979. – B. Mondin, *Dizionario enciclopedico dei papi*, Rome, 1995, 81.

Federico Marazzi

**ADHEMAR OF CHABANNES (989-1034).** Son of Limousin aristocracy, a monk of Saint-Cybard in Angoulême, educated at *Saint-Martial at Limoges, Adhemar was a talented and versatile scribe. His autograph manuscripts (over 1000 folios) contain editions, drawings, poetry, liturgy with musical notations, *sermons, *history, *computus, etc. Around 1025 he began a history of his time which survives in three recensions and, in its global scope and its attention to popular religious activity, resembles that of *Rodulfus Glaber.

In 1028, Adhemar became the impresario of the enormously popular cult of St Martial, attempting to promote the saint to the status of apostle. But a prior from Lombardy roundly defeated him in public debate, driving him from the city in disgrace. Adhemar returned to Angoulême and, after writing a long rambling *apologia*, concocted a whole dossier of *forgeries and fictional accounts in which he and Martial won the battle. In 1032-1033 he left this work at Saint-Martial before going on *pilgrimage to *Jerusalem, where he died. The monks at Saint-Martial used his forgeries to launch the apostolic cult successfully; and only late in the 20th century did medievalists realize the full extent of Adhemar's deception.

D. Gaborit-Chopin, "Les dessins d'Adémar de Chabannes", *BAr*, new series, 3, 1967, 163-225. – D. Callahan, "Adémar de Chabannes et la Paix de Dieu", *AMidi*, 89, 1977, 21-43. – R. Landes, *The Deceits of History: The Life and Times of Ademar de Chabannes*, Cambridge (MA)-London, 1995.

Richard Landes

**ADHEMAR OF LE PUY (*c.*1050-1098).** Adhemar of Monteil, bishop of *Le Puy from 1079 to his death in 1098, is known mainly as the spiritual leader of the first *crusade, which he accompanied as *legate to Pope *Urban II. He sprung from the illustrious Adhemar family, counts of Valentinois, lords of Monteil, Pierrelate, Donzère and other places, masters of the Rhône valley from Valence to Donzère, and had undoubtedly borne arms before entering the religious life. Elected *bishop, Adhemar devoted himself to his *diocese: according to tradition, it was he who composed the *Salve regina*, a hymn in honour of the sanctuary's patron, as well as the anthem of Le Puy. The bishop of Le Puy had already made a *pilgrimage to the *Holy Land in 1086, when the vassals of the Velay, led by Viscounts Pons and Heraclius of Polignac, had taken advantage of his absence to attack his Church's possessions and had taken control of them. On his return, Adhemar declared war on the usurpers, while leaving a way open for negotiation: the viscounts agreed to abandon their claims in exchange for a sum of 25,000 sous of Le Puy. Adhemar was a disciple of *Cluny and was closely associated with the battle that the Burgundian *abbey had fought for more than a century to rescue the Church from the tyranny of the temporal powers and regenerate ecclesiastical discipline; as such, he maintained close relations with the abbey of Saint-Chaffre du Monastier – in his diocese –, relations based on a common Cluniac idea of crusade. For this reason he was chosen by Urban II, a former Cluniac monk who became *pope in 1088. At *Clermont, where he came to preach the crusade before an immense crowd, the supreme pontiff gave the direction of the enterprise to Adhemar. A good organiser, the legate sought military leaders: from his own diocese, the viscount of Polignac, reconciled, joined his bishop and became his standard-bearer, followed by Pierre de Faÿ and Gérenton du Béage, who sold part of their property to equip themselves. Adhemar also recruited William VI, count of Auvergne. Above all he persuaded the powerful count of *Toulouse, Raymond of Saint-Gilles, who took command of one of the three armies of crusaders and committed himself never to return to Gaul, offering his life in combat against the infidels. A whole part of *Languedoc thus flocked to the bishop of Le Puy, who was able to find supplementary reinforcements outside the province, in his own land of Valence. The crusading army of the Midi, commanded by Adhemar and Raymond, after suffering some difficulties in *Dalmatia (attack by *Pechenegs in the service of Byzantium), reached the East: on the steppe plateau of Anatolia, it finally joined battle with the *Turks, at Dorylaeum (1 July 1097); it was the first great battle, which showed the military superiority of the Franks, and Adhemar, a former warrior, did not fear to don armour, fighting valiantly. A year later, the legate was struck down by plague and died at *Antioch, 1 Aug 1098, without having seen the capture of *Jerusalem, leaving the crusaders divided and less concerned with mysticism than with political prestige and material profits.

Raymond d'Agiles, "Historia Francorum qui ceperunt Hierusalemi", *Gesta Dei per Francos*, 1, J. Bongars (ed.), Hanover, 1611, 139. – Raymond d'Agiles, *ibid.*, M. Guizot (ed.), *Collection des mémoires relatifs à l'histoire de France...*, 21, Paris, 1824, 227-397. – Raymundus de Aguilers, *Historia Francorum qui ceperunt Iherusalem*, J. H. Hill, L. L. Hill (tr., intro, notes), Philadelphia (PA), 1968.

L. Bréhier, "Un évêque du Puy à la première Croisade, Adémar de Monteil", *Bulletin de la Société Académique du Puy et de la Haute-Loire*, 8, Le Puy-en-Velay, 1923, 221-248. – C. Erdmann, *The origins of the idea of Crusade*, Princeton (NJ), 1977.

Christian Lauranson-Rosaz

**ADMONT.** A Benedictine *abbey in Styria (Austria), founded in 1074 by Archbishop Gebhard of *Salzburg as a point of support for the *Gregorian reform. Endowed with numerous possessions in Austria, *Bavaria and Friuli, Admont had its apogee from the mid 12th c. with, notably, a very active *scriptorium*. Its most outstanding *abbots were Henry II (1275-1297), who at the same time played an important political role, and Engelbert (1297-1327), author of numerous writings, theological works, but also works bearing on natural *science and the theory of the *State. The womens' abbey founded in parallel in 1121 kept going until the early 16th century. Admont was rebuilt in the 18th c. in the baroque style and its *library survived the fire of 1865.

P. J. Wichner, *Geschichte des Stiftes Admont*, Graz, 1874-1880 (4 vol.). – R. List, *Stift Admont, Festschrift zur Neunhundertjahrfeier*, Ried, 1974. – M. Mannewitz, *Stift Admont*, Munich, 1989. – "Engelbert d'Admont", *VerLex* II, 535-549 (2nd ed.).

Werner Maleczek

**ADO OF VIENNE (died 875).** Born perhaps in Gâtinais, Ado was first a monk at Ferrières at the same time as *Lupus. He then stayed at *Prüm abbey under Abbot Markward between 841 and 853 and may later have gone to Italy. In any case he was at *Lyon, then a very important intellectual centre, around 858, in the entourage of Archbishop Remigius. There he wrote a *martyrology, for which he was content to follow that of *Florus, adding or modifying certain notices in a not very scrupulous way, while sheltering behind the authority of a pseudo-ancient Roman martyrology. His work nevertheless served as source to *Usuard. Promoted archbishop of *Vienne in 859-860, he was a very active pastor, keeping up good relations with Pope *Nicholas I, and maintained a very reserved attitude towards *Lothar II, ruler in Viennois after the death of Charles of Provence (863). At Vienne he wrote a *chronicle (from the beginnings to 870) and a *Vita* of St Theuderius (St Chef) and revised that of St Desiderius of Vienne. He died on 16 Dec 875 and was inscribed as a saint in the Roman martyrology.

*PL*, 123, 1852, 23-450.

H. Quentin, *Les Martyrologes historiques au Moyen Âge*, Paris, 1908. – M. Besson, "Adon", *DHGE*, 1, 1912, 685-686. – J. Dubois, G. Renaud, *Le Martyrologe d'Adon. Ses deux familles; ses trois recensions*, Paris, 1984.

Michel Rubellin

**ADOMNÁN (*c.*624-704).** Ninth *abbot of *Iona, St Adomnán was one of the great Irish Latin authors of the early Middle Ages. Little is known of his life. He first appears as an ambassador to King Aldfrith in Northumbria (686). He took part in the *council of the Irish Church that in 697 promulgated the "law of the innocents" that bears his name (*Cáin Adomnáin*). His renown rests on two Latin works: *De locis sanctis*, an account of the *Holy Land and the churches of *Constantinople as told to Adomnán by a Frankish bishop named Arculf; and the *Vita S. Columbae*, an acount of St *Columba, the founder of Iona. A corpus of commentaries on Virgil has come down under his name.

D. Meehan, *Adamnan's De locis sanctis*, Dublin, 1958 – *CChr.SL*, 175, 175-234. – *Adomnan's Life of Columba*, A. O. Anderson (ed.), M. O. Anderson (ed.), Oxford, 1991.

J.M. Picard, "The Purpose of Adomnán's *Vita Columbae*", *Peritia*, 1, 1982, 160-77. – A.D.S. MacDonald, "Aspects of the Monastery and Monastic Life in Adomnán's Life of Columba", *Peritia*, 3, 1984, 271-302. – R. Sharpe, *Adomnán of Iona: Life of St Columba*, Harmondsworth, 1995 (Eng. tr.).

Michael Lapidge

**ADOPTIANISM.** The name "adoptianism" is given to a heresy that appeared in the Iberian peninsula in the early 780s. It was in opposing the views of the cleric Migetius on the *Trinity that the archbishop of Toledo, *Elipandus, laid the basis of adoptianism. According to him, God had chosen Jesus to bear his message; but only the *Word emanated from the deity, thus *Christ was only the adoptive son of the Creator, his son "by appellation". This claim met with a certain success. It was taken up and spread in the Asturias and in *Galicia, then as far as *Septimania thanks to the activities of the bishop of Urgel, Felix. But it also came up against very strong resistance, led by *Beatus of Liébana and his disciple Etherius of Osma.

The debate took on such dimensions that before long it mobilized the main religious and political authorities of the Christian West. In 785, Pope *Adrian I wrote the prelates of the peninsula a doctrinal letter denouncing Elipandus's views. At the same period *Charlemagne took up the case of Felix of Urgel, a *suffragan of the *metropolitan of *Narbonne and so under his jurisdiction. Obliged to appear before a *synod that met at *Regensburg in 792, Felix retracted. He officially abjured at *Rome but, as soon as he was freed, he took shelter at Toledo and reaffirmed his adherence to the positions condemned at Regensburg. The affair was considered so serious that Charlemagne called a *council at *Frankfurt, in 794, in the presence of papal *legates. There, adoptianism was declared heretical and, at the sovereign's request, Adrian I wrote another letter in which he threatened with *anathema all those who rejected the assembly's conclusions. The council of Frankfurt had seen the first participation of *Alcuin, who then became the champion of orthodoxy against the deviant views coming from Toledo. Supported by the patriarch of Aquileia, *Paulinus, he engaged in a vigorous polemic with Felix.

In 799 *Leo III pronounced an anathema against Felix of Urgel. Charlemagne sent to him Leidrad, bishop of Lyon, Nefrid, bishop of Narbonne, and *Benedict, abbot of Aniane. Felix claimed to be convinced by their arguments and once more retracted in 800, at *Aachen. Charlemagne, having been fooled once, did not allow him to return to his *diocese and settled him at Lyon, where he died in 818. Elipandus, now alone at the head of his followers and apparently abandoned by most of his disciples, continued to hold firm. Despite Alcuin's efforts, he obstinately refused to retract and remained firm in his position until his death, *c.*807-808. Though adoptianism was finally reduced, the quarrel it aroused nevertheless remains of capital importance in the history of the *Mozarabic Church. Indeed it may be that the debate which set the primate of Toledo against Rome and Aachen contributed to the singularization and isolation of the Christian community of *Spain subject to Muslim rule.

M. Menendez Pelayo, *Historia de los heterodoxos espanoles*, 2, Santander, 1947, 7-58. – *HChr*, 4, 1993.

Daniel Baloup

**ADORATION.** The Middle Ages took from Antiquity the difference between the supreme worship due to *God (*latria*) and that due to the *angels and saints (*dulia*). In the early Middle Ages, especially in the East, the question of adoration was at the heart of the *iconoclastic quarrel. Popular religion made veneration of *icons a fundamental prop. The **Libri Carolini* condemn the adoration of *images (II, 15): adoration is an external act of worship, but involves the whole man. Indeed there can be no real difference between an external gesture and an internal attitude. For St *Thomas Aquinas, adoration is an exterior act of worship (*Summa theologiae*, $II^a$ $II^{ae}$, q. 82, a. 3); its forms and even its places are only a consequence of necessity (that of gathering communally, *e.g.* $II^a$ $II^{ae}$, q. 84, a. 1). Man cannot reach God through the senses, but visible *signs can provoke the *soul to turn to him ($II^a$ $II^{ae}$, q. 84, a. 2). God remains free in relation to forms; but Thomas insists on the communal value of the worship of adoration *par excellence* that is the *Eucharist ($II^a$ $II^{ae}$, q. 84, a. 3).

E. Beurlier, "Adoration", *DThC*, 1, 1990, 437-442.

Michel Deneken

**ADRIAN I, POPE (died 795).** A Roman, Adrian I was consecrated on 9 Feb 772 and died on Christmas day 795. From a politico-religious point of view, his was one of the most important pontificates of the whole Middle Ages. He came from a family prominent in post-Byzantine *Rome. In his first years he tried to bring back under control the quarrels between pro- and anti-Lombard factions in Rome, which had greatly weakened his predecessor Stephen III (768-772), by strengthening the pontiff's power of arbitration. *Charlemagne's descent into *Italy in 774, requested by Adrian himself, led to the fall of the *Lombard kingdom. Italy was thus opened up to the Europe of the *Franks, and at the same time the papal attempt to create a papal lordship over Rome and *Latium under Carolingian protection was accelerated. Adrian was also very active in dialogue with the Eastern Churches to resolve the crisis opened up by *iconoclasm.

*LP*, 1, 486-523. – E. Caspar, *Das Papsttum under frankischer Herrschaft*, Darmstadt, 1956, 35-113. – *DBI*, 1, 312-323.– *HE*, 6, 49-70, 107-153. – *Dizionario enciclopedico dei papi*, Rome, 1995, 95-96.

Federico Marazzi

**ADRIAN IV, POPE (*c.*1110/1120-1159).** Nicholas Breakspear owed his career to *Eugenius III who appointed him *cardinal-bishop of Albano, before 1150, and charged him with a mission to *Sweden (1152). Elected *pope on 4 Dec 1154, he took the name of Adrian IV. He was faced with a complex political situation. In 1155, he crowned the Emperor *Frederick Barbarossa, who helped him to get rid of *Arnold of Brescia. Without German help, he took the head of an anti-Norman coalition. Despite military failure, the treaty of *Benevento (18 June 1156), concluded with *William I, recognised papal sovereignty over the Norman kingdom, and this move aggravated the tensions with the *Empire. After the diet of *Besançon (1157) and the Constitutions of Roncaglia (1158), the pope found himself obliged to take the head of a new coalition bringing together the Lombard towns, the Byzantine emperor and the Normans, to protect the rights of *Rome. In the middle of the crisis, he died on 1 Sept 1159.

K. Schnith, "Adrien IV", *DHP*, 53-55. – *LP*, 2, 388-397. – P. Brezzi, "Lo scisma 'inter regnum et sacerdotium' al tempo di Federico Barbarossa", *Arch. Deput. Rom. St. patr.*, 64, 1940, 1-98. – W. Ullmann, "The Pontificate of Adrian IV", *Cambridge Historical Journal*, 11, 1953-1955, 233-252.

Pierre Kerbrat

**ADSO OF MONTIER-EN-DER (930-992).** **Scholasticus*, then *abbot of Montier-en-Der (south-west of Saint-Dizier), Adso was subsequently abbot of Saint-Bénigne at *Dijon and died on a journey to the Holy Places. He is known for a treatise *De ortu et tempore Antichristi*, written before 954 at the request of Queen Gerberge. In the orthodox tradition inaugurated by St Augustine, he opposed a popular belief that fixed the end of the world in the year 1000. But Adso also left important hagiographical work including a Life of St Mansuy, first bishop of Toul, and *Deeds and miracles* of St Basil, founder of the monastery of Verzy in the hills of *Reims in the late 6th century.

*Adso Dervensis. De ortu et tempore Antichristi*, D. Verhelst (ed.), Turnhout, 1976.

G. Hocquard, *Cath.*, 1, 1948, 163.

Michel Sot

**ADULTERY.** For the Church, adultery was primarily a *sin: it was the lapse of conjugal faith by one or other of the spouses ("The Christian religion condemns adultery in the same way in both sexes", says Gratian's **Decretum*). For the *laity, it was an exclusively female crime: like *Roman law, customary law blamed only the infidelity of the wife; only she risked introducing "clandestine" foreign elements into the *family. As a result, the judgment of adulterers was an object of rivalry between Church courts and secular *courts. In the 12th c., in the north and west of France, it was the former that prevailed (*e.g.* the "Établissements de Rouen", art. 32, admit that adultery "can only be judged by the hand of Holy Church"); but from the end of the century, in the Midi, in *Italy and in *Catalonia, the temporal authorities claimed to take cognizance of the judgment of adulterers, arguing from the nuisance to public order. In the 13th c. the competence of lay courts in the matter was general. While Church judges normally imposed simple penances, and sometimes fines, lay judges inflicted on adulterous women and their accomplices harsher sanctions, initially purely arbitrary: the guilty pair were "at the lord's mercy".

In the 13th c., however, common law was liberalized and came to set limits to repression: sometimes the court's action followed a complaint (*clameur*) by the deceived husband, sometimes it was conditioned by the "capture" of the lovers *in flagrante delicto*. The legal repression of adultery then became less frequent, since it was mainly a private affair. In point of fact, common-law texts regularly raise the supposition that the guilty pair were caught in the act by the husband: if he, carried away by righteous anger, "slays the man and the woman, or one of them" (Beaumanoir), he benefited, at least until the 13th c., from a complete absolutory excuse; from the 14th c. it was enough for him to ask the king for a letter of remission, easily granted. In the customary law of the Midi, from the late 12th c., the penalty for adultery was the *course*: the guilty pair had to run a ritual course, naked, to the sound of the trumpet, whipped here and there by the executioner. From the mid 13th c., however, the *course* could be redeemed: "*currant aut solvant* [let them run or pay!]". To this was added, for the woman, civil sanctions (loss of dowry, of her place in the community, etc.).

Despite the preachers and moralists who thundered at the end of the Middle Ages against the misconduct of wives and the laxity of repression, social reprobation towards adultery seems very muted: as popular literature shows very well, in this kind of affair it is the deceived husband who is ridiculous. It is clear that it was hardly worth his while in these conditions to publish his misfortune.

J.-M. Carbasse, "Currant nudi", *Droit, histoire et sexualité*, Paris, 1987, 83-102. – J.A. Brundage, *Law, Sex and Christian Society in Medieval Europe*, Chicago, 1987. – J.-M. Carbasse, *Introduction historique au droit pénal*, Paris, 1990 (bibliography).

Jean-Marie Carbasse

**ADVENT.** Advent (Latin *adventus*, coming), designates the weeks (numbering four in the post-Carolingian *Roman liturgy) preceding Christmas while being also the end of the year and, so to speak, the opening of *time onto the last days, what modern theology calls *eschatology. This duality between the expectation of Christmas and the eschatological expectation rests on the patristic idea of the double coming of Christ, at Christmas and at his second coming (parousia). To this double coming of Christ, St *Bernard proposed in piety to join a third, viz. the coming of the Saviour in people's souls. Wednesday and Friday of the third week of Advent celebrated respectively the Annunciation and *Visitation of the Virgin *Mary.

*CaP*, 4, *The Liturgy and Time*, London, 1986.

Pierre-Marie Gy

**ADVOCATE.** From the Latin *ad vocatus (auxilium)*, the advocate is one who is called (in aid), who speaks up in justice to defend his client's *cause.

Heir to the Roman courts, the advocate reappeared in the 12th-13th cc. and certainly before ecclesiastical jurisdictions. Local *councils specified the first professional rules: to have a legal training, to take an *oath before the *bishop and his *official, to respect secrecy, not to take on an unjust cause, not to plead for both parties, to tell the truth and to be content with a reasonable remuneration. The first incompatibilities also appeared. *Women, *serfs, *excommunicates or infamous persons could not be advocates; priests could not plead, except to defend the Church or the poor; religious, moreover, had to obtain the consent of their superior. It was also unacceptable to be both proxy and advocate. The council of *Lyon of 1274 devoted a whole chapter to advocates, the constitution *Properandum*, to suppress certain abuses. It again instructed them not to take on a bad cause and especially to moderate their fees. The organisation of the profession in secular *courts was modeled on that of advocates in ecclesiastical jurisdictions. The decisions of the council of Lyon were repeated in France notably by two *ordinances of 1274 and 1314. The definitive organisation of advocates was provided for by an ordinance of 13 Feb 1327, supplemented by a regulatory decree of the *Parlement of Paris in 1344.

R. Delachenal, *Les Avocats au Parlement de Paris*, Paris, 1887. – P. Fournier, *Les Officialités au Moyen Âge*, Paris, 1889, 32-36. – C. Lefevre, "La Constitution Properandum et les avocats de la Curie à la fin du XIII^e^ siècle", *1274, année charnière, mutations et continuités*, Paris, 1977, 525-531. – H. Vidal, "L'Avocat dans les décisions conciliares et synodales en France (XII^e^-XIII^e^ siècles)", *Revue de la Société Internationale d'Histoire de la Profession d'Avocat*, 3, Paris, 1990, 1-21.

Jean-Louis Gazzaniga

**ADVOCATE, ADVOCACY.** From the *Merovingian period, rulers granted churches an *immunity that protected them from the management and intervention of royal agents. Following a formula soon stereotyped, the latter were forbidden all entry into the immune territory, all legal action, all levying of taxes. To represent the interests of the church outside the immunity, the king put in place a representative, called *advocatus*, a person of modest origin, guarantor by his own property of the honesty of his management, and charged with defending before a *court the interests of the church entrusted to him. Great men were forbidden to take on advocacy of churches, so as to avoid all abusive behaviour. This prohibition was not always followed when the royal power lost its authority in the 9th century.

In the 10th c., advocacy underwent a slow evolution. Deprived by the 10th-c. monastic *reform movement of lay abbacy and of all identical lordship, which had given them free disposal of *abbeys, great men found a compensation in taking over the advocacy which allowed them to keep their control over the monastic temporality, often indispensable to the existence of their principality or lordship. To represent them, they put in place at their service local sub-advocates, who were their vassals, while they themselves became great advocates or principal advocates. As they tried to monopolize for their sole benefit the exercise of the right of *ban on church lands, there was often an establishment of regulations of advocacy, intended strictly to limit the advocate's rights of intervention to three annual visits, the exercise of *haute justice* only on the *appeal of the *abbot, and limited and precise levying of taxes.

While advocacy disappeared slowly in the kingdom of France in its old form and was replaced by a protection or a lordship of the *laity, in the *Empire it remained a very vigorous institution. The king normally reserved the concession of the advocacy of royal abbeys to his great vassals, *bishops doing likewise for their own abbeys. In certain cases monasteries obtained the right freely to choose their advocate, who, for many formerly private abbeys, was automatically taken from the founder's family. Using their prerogatives, many advocates built up a seignorial principality on monastic temporalities (counts of Boulogne and abbey of *Saint-Riquier, counts of *Luxemburg and advocacies of *Echternach and Saint-Maximin of *Trier, county of Salm in the Vosges and abbey of Senones).

F.-L. Ganshof, "L'immunité dans la monarchie franque", *RSJB*, 1, 1958 (2nd ed.). – E. Boshof, "Untersuchungen zur Kirchenvogtei in Lothringen im 10. und 11. Jahrhundert", *ZSRG.K*, 66, 1979, 55-119.

Michel Parisse

**ÆLFRIC (*c.*950-*c.*1010).** Ælfric, sometime abbot of Eynsham (appointed 1005), was one of the principal authors of Old English prose and was a characteristic product of the English Benedictine reform movement of the second half of the 10th century. He was a student of bishop *Æthelwold at *Winchester and subsequently (from 987) served as a *chaplain at Cerne Abbas (Dorset) for the ealdorman of the southwestern shires, Æthelweard. Much of his substantial corpus of Old English writings was produced at the instigation of this Æthelweard. The corpus includes: two sets of *Sermones catholici* or "Catholic Homilies", each set containing forty *homilies intended primarily for feasts of the *temporal; a set of *Lives of Saints*, which is not preserved intact, but which probably contained forty homilies for saints' days of the *sanctoral; a grammar of Latin (the earliest surviving Latin grammar in any European vernacular) with an accompanying glossary; a translation of parts of the Hexateuch; a Latin *vita* of his former master, Æthelwold; a Latin *customary for his community of monks at Eynsham; and a number of *letters, in Latin and English, on matters of ecclesiastical discipline (the "pastoral letters"). In his Latin writings, Ælfric reveals a concern with clarity and concise expression; in Old English, his prose is elegantly conceived but drawn from simple, unostentatious vocabulary. His later Old English prose writings use alliteration, modelled apparently on Old English verse; but this is the only stylistic affectation which Ælfric permitted himself. The range of his learning in patristic sources was extensive, and his homilies in particular enjoyed wide circulation in the 11th c. and into the 12th.

*Ælfric's Lives of Saints*, W. W. Skeat (ed.), Oxford, 1881-1900. – *Ælfrics Grammatik und Glossar*, J. Zupitza (ed.), H. Gneuss (rev.), Berlin, 1966. – *Homilies of Ælfric: a Supplementary Collection*, J. C. Pope (ed.), Oxford, 1967-1968. – *Ælfric's Catholic Homilies: the Second Series*, M. Godden (ed.), Oxford, 1979. – *Ælfric's Prefaces*, J. Wilcox (ed.), Durham, 1994. – *Ælfric's Catholic Homilies: the First Series*, P. Clemoes (ed.), Oxford, 1997. – *Ælfric's Letter to the Monks of Eynsham*, C. A. Jones (ed.), Cambridge, 1998.

M. McC. Gatch, *Preaching and Theology in Anglo-Saxon England: Ælfric and Wulfstan*, Toronto, 1977. – L. M. Reinsma, *Ælfric: an Annotated Bibliography*, New York, 1987. – L. Grundy, *Books and Grace: Ælfric's Theology*, London, 1991.

Michael Lapidge

**ÆLRED OF RIEVAULX (*c.*1109-1166).** Born at Hexham in England, Ælred received a good education. A friend of the son of the king of Scotland, he lived at his court and became its *seneschal. In 1135 he entered the abbey of Rievaulx, a daughter-house of *Clairvaux, where the teaching was much marked by the thought of St *Bernard. But it was the thought of St Augustine that most influenced him. Appointed novice-master in 1141, he was elected *abbot of Revesby, then of Rievaulx in 1146. He became ill in *c.*1156, died in 1166 and was venerated as a saint in the Middle Ages.

His works are historical (history of England and the saints of Northumbria) and spiritual (liturgical *sermons, biblical commentaries, monastic writings that earned him a renown comparable to that of St Bernard). Like Cicero, he wrote from his own experience about spiritual *friendship and reveals the maturity of a man of delicacy and acuteness. The work was prepared by the *Mirror of charity*, fruit of his teaching as novice-master and abbot. In it he shows the excellence of charity and the way that, through discernment and practice, leads to perfection and fruition (enjoyment), the supreme end of *love. His treatise on the institution of *recluses (*De institutione inclusarum*), written for his sister, had real popularity in the Middle Ages by reason of the development of this way of life. After recalling the origins of this life, he describes its rule and virtues, then expounds the *mysteries of *Christ, object of monastic *meditation, and propounds a reflection on the last things.

The permanent aim of his teaching is growth in spiritual life. To this end, the mysteries of Christ must be the object of permanent consideration, and Ælred returns to this ceaselessly. Faithful to Bernadine tradition, he does not separate *Mary from her Son and invites us to put her on, as we must put on Christ, for she is truly the mother of the faithful. Not only has she given us life, but, as helper and mediator, she makes it grow by cooperating with all our deeds to raise us up to Jesus, whom she unveils to the contemplative. This *contemplation through trials purifies us, because it necessitates silence of the faculties of *intellect and heart so as to be totally disoccupied with ourselves and others. But in the end, it is also the heavenly enjoyment that crowns the perfect charity which God realises in man. In practical life, the monk must alternate between the exercise of the *corporalia* (vigils, manual *labour, *fasting) and the *spiritualia* (*lectio*, *oratio*, *meditatio*) which characterise the *ascesis of body and spirit. This alternation is necessary to avoid falling into *acedia, the worst of evils for a monk.

Walter Daniel, *The Life of Ailred of Rievaulx*, M. Powicke (ed.), Oxford, 1978 (*OMT*). – Aelred, *Aelred of Rievaulx's De institutione inclusarum*, J. Ayto (ed.), A. Barratt (ed.), London, 1984. – Aelredi Rievallensis, *Opera omnia*, *CChr.CM*, 1971-1989. – Aelred, *Quand Jésus eut douze ans*, *SC*, 60, 1987 (2nd ed.).

*DSp*, 1, 1932, 225-234. – A. Hallier, *The Monastic Theology of Aelred of Rievaulx*, Spence (MA), 1969. – A. Hoste, *Bibliotheca Aelrediana*, Steenbrugge, 1962. – *Cistercian Studies Conference*, Kalamazoo (MI), 1981. – *DSp*, 13, 1988, 746-747. – A.G. Rigg, "Aelred of Rievaulx", *A History of Anglo-Latin Literature 1066-1422*, Cambridge, 1992, 61.

Jean-Baptiste Auberger

**ÆTHELBERT OF KENT (died 616).** King of Kent (560-616), Æthelbert (*Æthelberht*) is remembered as the king under whose patronage, in 597, Kent was converted to Christianity by *Augustine and the Roman monks sent by Pope *Gregory the Great. Æthelbert was aware of Christian practice before their arrival, because he had married the Frankish princess Bertha (daughter of Charibert) who was a practising Christian, and it was probably through Bertha's influence that he himself adopted Christianity. Most of our knowledge of him derives from *Bede (*Historia Ecclesiastica*, I, 25-26; II, 3-5), who also preserves the text of a letter sent to him by Pope Gregory (*HE*, I, 32). A code of laws in Æthelbert's name, though preserved only in a 12th-c. manuscript, is thought to contain genuine elements.

F. Liebermann, *Die Gesetze der Angelsachsen*, Halle, 1903-1916, 1, 3-8 (3 vol.). – N. Brooks, *The Early History of the Church of Canterbury*, Leicester, 1984, 3-11.

Michael Lapidge

**ÆTHELWOLD (904/909-984).** Æthelwold, the dynamic and powerful bishop of *Winchester (963-984), was one of the progenitors of the movement of reformed Benedictine *monasticism that transformed the English Church during the second half of the 10th century. The principal source for our knowledge of his life is the *Vita S. Æthelwoldi* by his pupil Wulfstan *Cantor*, written soon after the translation of the bishop's *relics in

996. From this *vita* we learn that Æthelwold was born in Wessex (904/909); that during his adolescence he was a member of the household of King Æthelstan (924-939); that he was ordained a priest and monk by Ælfheah, bishop of Winchester (934-951); and that, following the death of Æthelstan, he spent a decade or more at *Glastonbury studying with his colleague *Dunstan, then abbot of Glastonbury. Following this period, Æthelwold was given the delapidated monastery of Abingdon; during his abbacy there, he established the guidelines for reformed Benedictine monasticism so that, when he was appointed to Winchester, one of his first acts there was, with the support of King Edgar (whose tutor Æthelwold had been), to expel the secular *canons from the cathedral and to replace them with Benedictine monks from Abingdon. During the period of his episcopacy, he established or reformed a number of Benedictine monasteries, including Peterborough, Ely and Thorney. Following his discovery and translation of the relics of St Swithun (an obscure, but reportedly saintly, 9th-c. bishop of Winchester), Æthelwold undertook a massive reconstruction of the cathedral (called the Old Minster) at Winchester. He was the author of an English translation of the *Regula S. Benedicti* and of the Latin *customary known as the *Regularis concordia*; his authorship of corpora of *glosses to Aldhelm and to the Psalter has recently been demonstrated. He numbered among his pupils two of the most important Anglo-Latin authors of the late 10th c.: Wulfstan *Cantor* and *Ælfric, sometime abbot of Eynsham.

*Regularis Concordia*, T. Symons (ed.), London, 1953. – *Die angelsächsischen Prosabearbeitungen der Benediktinerregel*, A. Schröer (ed.), H. Gneuss (rev.), Darmstadt, 1964. – *Wulfstan of Winchester: the Life of St Æthelwold*, M. Lapidge (ed.), M. Winterbottom (ed.), Oxford, 1991 (*OMT*).

*Bishop Æthelwold*, B. Yorke (ed.), Woodbridge, 1988. – M. Gretsch, *The Intellectual Foundations of the English Benedictine Reform Movement*, Cambridge, 1998.

Michael Lapidge

**AFONSO I HENRIQUES (*c.*1109-1185).** Son of Count Henry of Burgundy and the infanta Teresa, Afonso I Henriques was count of *Portugal from 1128 and took the title of king in 1140. Three years later, to escape the tutelage of his Castilian neighbour, he chose to become a papal vassal. After conquering Lisbon in 1147, he firmly maintained the southern frontier of his kingdom on the Tagus, with the help of the *military orders. However the papacy, in the person of *Alexander III, did not recognise his title of king until 1179, six years before his death in 1185. He founded the Portuguese Church, in 1131 obtaining from the Holy See the attachment of all the Portuguese dioceses to the metropolis of *Braga.

J. V. Serrão, *História de Portugal, 1 (1080-1415)*, Lisbon, 1985.

Robert Durand

**AFRICA.** Until the dawn of the 15th c., Africa remained the continent least known to medieval geography, as witness the hesitations in vocabulary. *Africa* designated the province formed of the former territory of Carthage (149 BC), but the term was rapidly applied to all North Africa, land of the Whites, as opposed to *Aethiopia*, land of the Blacks, with faces burned by the sun according to the sense of the Greek word *aithiops*. The use of these terms by Pliny ensured their success during the medieval period. Africa was also the whole of the third continent, devolved, in the partition of the Biblical world, to Ham, son of Noah, as Asia was to Shem and Europe to Japhet. And it was this meaning that finally prevailed in texts as well as in cartography.

Ill defined, the African continent was also ill circumscribed. A dual vision was quite clearly perceived, North-South, White Africa and Black Africa, and West-East, Africa facing the Western Ocean and Africa facing the Ocean of the Indies. But it was not known how far the southern part and the eastern part extended. Towards the south, the obstacle was the torrid zone, long judged uninhabitable, or else the supposed presence of a great river, an arm of the Ocean Sea, surrounding the globe at the equator and preventing access to another continent where the Antipodes might lie. This is what appears from texts like *Isidore of Seville's *Etymologies* (XIV, 5, 17) or *mappae mundi* like those of some manuscripts of *Beatus or that of Lambert of Saint-Omer's *Liber Floridus*. Towards the east, the term "India" was applied indifferently to one or other shore of the Indian Ocean. Around 1320, the **mappa mundi* of Petrus Vesconte placed an *India parva que est Ethiopia* at the mouths of the Indus and another Ethiopia in Africa near the *Habesse terra Nigrorum*. In the early 15th c., Ptolemean *mappae mundi* still extended the horn of Africa immeasurably eastwards, making the Indian Ocean a closed sea.

This lack of knowledge of Africa is largely explained by the obstacle of the desert, which prevented access to the land of the Blacks and pushed Egypt towards Asia, medieval geography making Africa begin at the desert of Libya. It is also explained by the Islamic conquest which blocked the southern shores of the Mediterranean and prevented access to the Red Sea, as Renaud de Châtillon learned to his cost in his vain attempt to force the passage in 1183.

Up to the mid 13th c., medieval authors of descriptions of Africa merely repeat what had been handed down by Pliny and the authors of late Antiquity. In Isidore of Seville's *Etymologies* in the 7th c., as in *Honorius Augustodunensis's *Imago mundi* in *c.*1130, we find the list of Roman provinces of North Africa, Libya, Cyrenaica, Tripolitania, Byzacena, Getulia, Numidia, Mauritania, with their chief towns, Berenice, Carthage, Hippo etc . Then comes Ethiopia, "to the south", a desert zone where live the Garamantes and more or less fabulous peoples like the Troglodytes, amidst monstrous beasts and "all sorts of serpents unknown to man". This image of Africa passed into vernacular literature. Gossuin of Metz's *Image of the world* in *c.*1245 defined "Ethyope" as a land where people were "blacker than pitch", where the heat was such "that the land there seems to burn"; beyond it, there were only deserts full "of vermin and wild beasts".

Everything changed in the14th century. After the failure of the Vivaldi brothers in 1291 and Jaime Ferrer in 1346, progress in the arts of *navigation and ship-building made possible the colonization of the archipelagos, notably of the Canaries by the Castilians, before the expedition of Jean de Béthencourt and Cavelier de La Salle (1402-1406). But the decisive impulse was given by the Portuguese Prince Henry the Navigator and his brother Don Pedro in their impassioned search for *gold, *spices and the kingdom of *Prester John, which a better knowledge of Asia had led to being situated in Africa. Starting with the capture of Ceuta, in 1415, began the systematic reconnaissance of the Atlantic coast. Cape Bojador was passed in 1434 by Gil Eanes; in 1444, Cape Verde was reached by Dinis Dias and the mouth of the Senegal discovered by Nuño Tristao; in 1461, Diogo Afonso explored the Cape Verde archipelago; Joao de Santarém and Pero Escobar reached the equator in 1471. If Diogo Cao touched the southern point of the continent in 1486, it fell to Bartolomeu Dias 1487 to pass the famous Cape of Storms, before Vasco da Gama, by his success in reaching *India, made it the Cape of Good Hope, but this was in 1497-1498 and the *Middle Ages were over.

On the eastern side, relations were gradually formed with *Ethiopia, on which the monks of the Ethiopian monastery of Jerusalem had provided some information. The most famous embassy was that of the Portuguese Pero da Covilham, which set out from Lisbon in 1487 and was discovered in 1520 in the entourage of the Ethiopian ruler by another embassy, that of Francisco Alvares. Finally we possess the letter of the Genoese merchant Antonio Malfante (1447) indicating that he had reached Sigilmassa and the Touat by joining a caravan.

From then on Africa's image changed and was clarified. Already the *Libro del conoscimento* (*c.*1350), the work of an anonymous Franciscan, spoke of the Canaries, Madeira, the Azores, the kingdom of Dongola between the "Nile" (Niger) and the Rio d'Oro, as well as the kingdom of Guynoa on the banks of that same river, and gave the design of the flags of the various States. In the mid 15th c. appeared the accounts of travellers – the Venetian Alvise Cadamosto, the Genoese Antonietto Usodimare –, or syntheses of various accounts, like Eanes de Zurara's *Chronicle of Guinea*. Cartography made use of all this information, notably the *mappa mundi* of Angelino Dulcert (*c.*1330), the Catalan Atlas (1375) or the *mappa mundi* of Fra Mauro in 1457, to cite only the most famous.

But, though better known, Africa still remained misunderstood, marked by all that evoked negative feelings in the white man, the Black with the burnt face of the *Aethiops*.

*The Cambridge History of Africa*, 3, *c.1050-c.1600*, R. Oliver (ed.), Cambridge, 1977. – P. Chaunu, *European Expansion in the Later Middle Ages*, Amsterdam, 1979. – Y. Fall, *L'Afrique à la naissance de la cartographie moderne: les cartes majorquines (XIV$^e$-XV$^e$ siècle)*, Paris, 1982. – M. Mollat, *Les Explorateurs du XIII$^e$ au XVI$^e$ siècle. Premiers regards sur des mondes nouveaux*, Paris, 1984. – F. de Medeiros, *L'Occident et l'Afrique (XIII$^e$-XV$^e$ siècle)*, Paris, 1985. – J. Ki-Zerbo, *Histoire de l'Afrique Noire*, Paris, 1987. – M. Mund-Dopchie, *La Fortune du périple d'Hannon à la Renaissance et au XVII$^e$ siècle*, Namur, 1995 ("Collection d'études classiques", 8).

Christiane Deluz

**AGAPETUS II, POPE (died 955).** Roman, Agapetus was *pope from 10 May 946 to Dec 955, and is now buried in *St Peter's. He was one of the five popes who occupied the see during the two decades (933-954) in which the *princeps* *Alberic ruled *Rome. Compared to his immediate predecessors, he was perhaps the one who enjoyed the greatest autonomy. For the first time in this period, indeed, we have coins that bear the pope's full name (not just the monogram), together with that of the *princeps*. Agapetus certainly acted under pressure from Alberic in refusing to welcome *Otto of Saxony, who became king the same year, to Rome. But he did confer on Otto the power to decide the institution of new episcopal sees, in the context of the German advance eastward. He mediated in the conflict between the king of France, Louis IV, and Hugo, count of Paris.

*LP*, 2, 245. – P. Brezzi, *Roma e l'impero medioevale*, Bologna, 1947. – F. X. Seppelt, *Storia dei papi*, 1, 409-411. – B. Mondin, *Dizionario enciclopedico dei papi*, Rome, 1995, 129-130.

Federico Marazzi

**AGATHO, POPE (died 681).** Consecrated *pope 27 June 678, Agatho held the papacy until his death on 10 Jan 681. Sicilian by birth, he was the first of the eleven Greek or Greek-speaking pontiffs who occupied the papal see up to the mid 8th century. He played an important part in organising the preparations for the ecumenical *council of Constantinople, ordered by the Emperor Constantine IV, which was to discuss the doctrine of *monothelism (Roman synod of 680). The pontiff worked hard to find common ground with the Eastern churches. He was particularly committed to reinforcing relations between the Roman See and the Western Churches, especially those of Gaul and Britain, but always with a view to strengthening the papal role within the *oecumenos* of the Empire.

*LP*, 1, 350-358. – I. Daniele, "Agatone", *BSS*, 1, 341-342. – J. Richards, *The Popes and Papacy in the Early Middle Ages*, London, 1979. – B. Bischoff, M. Lapidge, *Biblical Commentaries from the Canterbury School of Theodore and Hadrian*, Cambridge, 1994, 140-143. – B. Mondin, *Dizionario enciclopedico dei papi*, Rome, 1995, 82-83.

Federico Marazzi

**AGES OF LIFE.** The medieval notion of the ages of life (*aetates vitae*) was based upon an amalgamation of classical, Christian and Arab sources, such as *Aristotle's *Parva naturalia*, *Avicenna's *Liber canonis*, Scripture and *Isidore of Seville's *Etymologiae*, aided by empirical observation. The entire universe had been endowed by the Creator with certain natural unifying laws that governed the transition from one stage of life to another. As the microcosmic reflection of all Creation, human spiritual, physical, intellectual and emotional development paralleled the seasonal, historical and planetary changes in the natural world, and was subject to the same cosmic laws. Each period possesses its own inherent strengths and weaknesses, which are the seeds for passage to the next period. A balanced life demands the equilibrium peculiar to each period. A variety of schemes were suggested, dividing life into three, four, six or seven ages, each of which is characterised by its own peculiar moral virtues and *vices and physical traits, largely the product of the changing proportions of the humours and the absence or lack of heat and moisture within the body. Although the precise length of each period may vary, the following periods were widely recognised: infancy (from birth to seven), was a time of innocence, purity and ignorance; childhood (seven to 14) was a time of malleability, openness, physical development and awakening religious consciousness; adolescence (14 to 21), of turmoil and sexual awakening, when crucial life choices, between the temptations of the flesh and the spirit, are taken; *youth (21 to 28/35) was a time of career, child-bearing and public responsibility; adulthood (28 to 48/50), one of physical and emotional maturity; old age (50 to 70), one of physical decay, decline and disillusionment; decrepitude (70 till death), a time of growing senility, bitterness and fear of death. Partly as a result of the improved quality of life, the later Middle Ages witnessed efforts to extend life and thus, by the Renaissance, the seven-stage scheme prevailed. The schematic view of the life cycle became a repositary for the discussion of such secondary themes as the path to *salvation, the learning process, the acquisition of virtue, and the foibles of humanity. A growing body of speculation regarding the topos of the ages, their parallels in the natural world and place in the plan of salvation, received wide popular currency in manuscript *illumination, *stained-glass windows, sculpture, vernacular literature and the minor arts.

S. Shahar, *Growing Old in the Middle Ages*, London, 1977. – J. A. Burrow, *The Ages of Man: A Study in Medieval Writing and Thought*, Oxford, 1986. – E. Sears, *The Ages of Man: Medieval Interpretations of the Life Cycle*, Princeton (NJ), 1986. – M. Goodich, *From Birth to Old Age. The Human Life Cycle in Medieval Thought. 1250-1350*, Lanham (MD), 1989.

Michael Goodich

**AGHLABIDS.** A 9th-c. Arab dynasty, the Aghlabids governed Ifrīkiya in the name of the *Abbasids, with *Kairouan as their capital. Rapidly becoming autonomous, the Aghlabids made Ifrīkiya the most powerful and prosperous state in the *Maghreb; from 827, they undertook the conquest of *Sicily. Irrigation works, planting of fruit trees, exploitation of mines and development of trade marked the economic revival. The Aghlabids were also great builders: they protected the coasts by *ribāts*, built the great *mosques of Sousse and Tunis and enlarged that of Kairouan. By developing Malikism, they made Kairouan one of the greatest religious centres in the Muslim world. In 909, the last Aghlabid fled before the threat of the *Fatimids.

M. Talbi, *L'Émirat aghlabide*, Paris, 1966.

Philippe Gourdin

**AGNES OF BOHEMIA (1205-1282).** Born in *Prague, Agnes was the daughter of Přemysl Otakar I, king of Bohemia (1197-1230), and Constance, sister of King *Andrew II of Hungary. For political reasons, her father betrothed her at the age of three to Boleslas, duke of *Silesia. On Boleslas's death she was approached to marry the son of Frederick II; then in *c.*1230 she was solicited by the emperor himself, now widowed, and by King *Henry III of England. Pope *Gregory IX intervened in 1233 to support Agnes's desire to become a nun; she then founded in Prague a hospital, a convent of Friars Minor and a monastery of *Poor Clares of which she became *abbess.

St *Clare of Assisi wrote her four letters between 1233 and 1253 and supported her in obtaining from the papacy the right to live without revenue or property. These missives as well as the *Legenda* allow an insight into Agnes's intense mystical life centred on the person of Christ the Spouse. Beatified in 1874, she was canonized in 1989 (feast 2 March).

*Acta SS*, Martii Boll., 1668, I, 502-532. – *BFRPC*, 1, 1759. – A. de Serent, "Agnès de Bohême", *DHGE*, 1, 1912, 977-979. – J. K. Vyskocil, *Legenda blashoslavene Anazky actyri lisky sv. Klary*, Prague, 1932. – G. Rocca, "Agnese di Boemia", *DIP*, 1, 1974, 154.

Élisabeth Lopez

**AGNUS DEI.** The singing of the *Agnus Dei* is one of the five sung parts of the ordinary of the *mass. In the eucharistic celebration, it is performed at the moment of the breaking of the bread by the celebrant priest. It was finally integrated into the *cursus* of the *Roman liturgy around 700. Its theological interpretation insists on the praise addressed to Christ at the very moment of offering the sacrifice of the Church, the *Eucharist. The content of numerous *tropes that came to enrich its melody and its content from the 10th c. developed this christological *exegesis.

G. Iversen, *Corpus troporum IV. Tropes de l'Agnus Dei*, Stockholm, 1980. – A. Ekenberg, *Cur cantatur? Die Funktion des liturgischen Gesanges nach den Autoren der Karolingerzeit*, Stockholm, 1987, 94-100.

Éric Palazzo

**AGOBARD OF LYON (*c.*769-840).** Archbishop of *Lyon (816-840). Probably born in *Septimania, he was at first doubtless part of the entourage of *Benedict of Aniane. In the late 8th c. he moved to Lyon where, as **chorepiscopus*, he was one of the closest collaborators of Bishop Leidrad in his work of material and spiritual restoration of the Church of Lyon. Aged and sick, Leidrad designated Agobard in his lifetime to succeed him (in 813?). This procedure having met with opposition, he could not take possession of his see until the council of Aachen in August 816 . Once *archbishop (he was the first to bear this title at Lyon), he was intensely active both in his diocese and in the Empire, as the important and varied work he left (25 letters and treatises and a poem) attests.

His career is divided into three stages, marked by the evolution of his relations with the imperial court. From 816 to 822, Agobard was part of the group of reforming *bishops and *abbots who worked to guide the actions of the new Emperor *Louis the Pious, notably imposing on him the celebrated *Ordinatio imperii* of 817 and the penance of Attigny (822). Various texts of this period betray the passion for unity that henceforth never ceased to animate him: dogmatic unity (he denounced the *superstition of those in his diocese who believed in the powers of *tempestarii* who were able to make hail and thunder; he refuted *adoptianism, after having had proof that Felix of Urgel, who died in exile at Lyon in 818, had in fact retracted nothing of his past errors); political and social unity (he protested against the legal division of the Empire that subjected the inhabitants of the Lyon region to the *lex Gombata*); and finally ecclesiological unity (aimed at in his description of the duties of *clerics and the reminder of the reverence that is their due).

From 823, the growing influence of the Empress Judith led Agobard to join the party of opponents of imperial policy. In five letters written between 823 and 828 to various correspondents including the emperor, he denounced in very vivid terms the dangers that the Church of Lyon would incur through the activities of the town's Jewish community, made possible in his eyes by the imperial protection from which it benefited. These texts, which show a very good knowledge of Jewish religious practices, in fact protest much more against the particular status – a real threat to unity, according to Agobard – thus accorded to the *Jews of Lyon than against *Judaism as such. On the question of *images, once more under discussion in the West in 825, Agobard wrote a quasi-iconoclastic treatise, very close to the ideas of *Claudius of Turin, to whom it has sometimes (wrongly) been attributed. He also reaffirmed the legitimacy of the possession of *property by the Church and protested against the spoliations it had suffered. But above all, Agobard sided more and more clearly against the emperor whom he accused of wanting to divide the Empire. Although he did not take a direct part in the first revolt of Louis's sons against their father in 830, he played a decisive role in that of 833, legitimizing *Lothar's uprising and justifying Pope Gregory IV's intervention on his side.

The final victory of Louis the Pious led to the condemnation of Agobard, deprived of his episcopal see at the assembly of Thionville in 835, which opened the final stage of his career. In exile in Italy, but kept in touch by his supporters who remained at Lyon (notably the deacon *Florus) with the activities of the famous *Amalarius of Trier, who was charged with administering the diocese of Lyon, Agobard set himself in two treatises to denounce his liturgical innovations as contrary to tradition and dangerous to the unity of the Church. Pardoned by Louis the Pious, he regained his see in 839, and died the following year at Saintonge.

The key that connects all his works is the very *Augustinian theme of the necessary unity of Christian society, pledge of salvation: unity in faith and prayer, unity of the Empire, unity of the Church around the bishops. Rediscovered by chance at Lyon early in the 17th c. and then edited, in those times of absolute monarchy and the struggle against Jansenism his works were not considered very orthodox. Not until the 19th c. would people start to take an interest in his work, though not without falling into *hagiography or anachronism. His "rationalism" was invoked, apropos of his writings against superstitions; he was also made a precursor of the Reformation! Finally, by isolating his texts against the Jews from the rest of his work, he was sometimes seen as an ancestor of contemporary antisemitism. Only by taking his work and his actions into overall account and replacing them in their context can these deformations be avoided from now on.

L. Van Acker, *Agobardi Lugdunensis opera omnia, CChr.CM*, 52, 1981.

A. Bressolles, *Saint Agobard, évêque de Lyon*, Paris, 1949. – E. Boshof, *Erzbischof Agobard von Lyon. Leben und Werk*, Cologne, 1969.

Michel Rubellin

**AGRICULTURAL TECHNIQUES.** Between the 10th and the 12th c., the diet of European man became essentially a cereal one, and agricultural techniques were primarily intended for "corn". The tools were multi-purpose and also served for kitchen gardening or industrial crops. Their basic material was wood, since iron remained rare and dear, though it was more common after the 10th century.

The spade (a wooden core partly covered in iron) and the hoe were the first utensils before the swing-plough which broke the soil and the plough which turned over the ground. In the early Middle Ages the latter was a heavy instrument with numerous oxen and wheels. It was simplified in the 13th c., lost its wheels and became more manageable. The use of one or other tool is not a criterion of development: both were adapted to different types of soil and different agrarian structures. On big well-run plots (those of the masters), the plough was more usual since it went faster than the spade and, all in all, demanded less iron, thus economizing on *metal and man-power, while the spade and hoe were the tools of the intensive agriculture of the *peasant holdings. Harvesting was done with a sickle, the grain being cut high or low according to how much straw was needed. The scythe, conceived in late Antiquity for cutting hay, could, from the 14th c., occasionally be used for oats and rye.

The reasons for the improvement in production must rather be sought in the multiplication of tasks: more frequent ploughing, drainage, development of sloping land, etc. It was men's *labour and perhaps their motivation that changed, rather than their material tools. Crop rotation properly so-called, obligatory collective organisation, only appeared quite late, in the 14th c., but a biennial or triennial rotation had long been practised. Triennial rotation distributed the work and the risks in a more balanced way, but it did not increase the value of the total output, nor was it a criterion of development. There was little fattening pasture and animal droppings were spread without making manure.

The great draught *animal of the West was the ox, with which the horse slowly began to be associated in the final medieval centuries. Medieval harness (yoke, collar, breast-strap) was not the result of a sudden innovation, but of long and regular adaptation since Antiquity. Archaeologists have recently found that the size of oxen varied. It increased from the iron age to the Roman period, then diminished during the Middle Ages and did not go up again until the 16th century. This variation (ten to fifteen centimetres) was perhaps in keeping with the occupation of the soil and the relative importance of lands sown with wheat.

D. Hall, *Medieval Fields*, Aylesbury, 1981. – P.J. Fowler, "Farming in the Anglo-Saxon Landscape: an Archaeologist's Review", *Anglo-Saxon England*, 9, 1982, 263-80. – J. Langdon, *Horses, Oxen and Technological Innovation*, Cambridge, 1986. – G. Comet, *Le paysan et son outil, essai d'histoire technique des céréales (France VIII*[e]*-XIII*[e] *siècles)*, Rome, 1992. – M.-C. Amouretti, G. Comet, *Hommes et techniques de l'Antiquité à la Renaissance*, Paris, 1993. – *Medieval Farming and Technology. The Impact of Agricultural Change in Northwest Europe*, G. Astill (ed.), J. Langdon (ed.), Leiden-New York-Cologne, 1997.

Georges Comet

**AGRICULTURE.** The main activity of medieval populations, agriculture had to provide for a diet normally composed of *bread or gruel, *wine or beer, and accompanying products (meat, fish, vegetables and fruits). In response to demographic growth and to put into cultivation the northern regions of the West, the techniques inherited from Antiquity were improved: use of the plough on heavy soils, perfecting of ox-teams, agricultural use of the horse, development of spring cultivation (barley, oats) in a system of three-year rotation assuring the natural recovery of the soil (fallow). But, unequally diffused, this technical progress was less important for the evolution of agriculture than the extension of the cultivated area and the work provided by *peasant families.

Turning their back on the ancient economy and the use of servile *labour, the lords of the Middle Ages favoured labour carried out under peasant tenure. Entrusted to a conjugal family – men and women worked in the fields – tenure became the usual form of agricultural exploitation, supplemented by seignorial equipment that gave rise to specific fees (banal *mill, oven and press). This transformation, begun in the Carolingian period and completed in the period of castellan lordship, intensified work on the land. The multiplication of these family cells made the countryside the theatre of an unprecedented development of the cultivated area, patiently conquered from *forest, marsh and litoral fen (polders). This agrarian conquest lastingly moulded the rural countryside (open-field, mixed wood and pasture-land, Mediterranean soils).

To limit the risks of a bad harvest, to ensure the feeding of the peasants and to respond to seignorial needs, polyculture was the rule. Wheat, destined for the white bread of the proprietors, gained ground without leading to the disappearance of less noble cereals (millet, spelt, rye, sorghum). Exploitation combined a variety of soils (arable land, vineyards, well cared-for *gardens), supplemented by rights of use in forests and on uncultivated lands (gathering, picking up wood, *animal husbandry). In time, speculative cultures developed under the influence of citizen proprietors (dye-plants, hops, sugar-cane, rice, silk-mulberries), while at the end of the Middle Ages regional specializations were being marked out (*vine-growing regions, animal husbandry in the *Alps).

Medieval agriculture was perhaps limited less by yields than by the compartmentalization of the economy. Although capable of producing surpluses in good years, it did not put populations beyond the reach of the dearths and *famines that natural conditions (*climate, *epidemics) or social conditions (wars) periodically provoked. As for technical knowledge, traditionally held and passed on by the peasants, it interested proprietors attentive to their revenues, wanting to know and improve the methods of good agriculture: some, such as Pietro de'Crescenzi in the early 14th c., took material from this knowledge to write treatises on agriculture.

R. Grand, R. Delatouche, *L'Agriculture au Moyen Âge, de la fin de l'empire romain au XVI*[e] *siècle*, Paris, 1950. – G. Duby, *Rural Economy and Country Life in the Medieval West*, London, 1968. – *The Agrarian History of England and Wales I: 2: A.D. 43-1042*, H.P.R. Finberg (ed.), Cambridge, 1972. – C.H. Berman, *Medieval Agriculture, the Southern French Countryside, and the Early Cistercians*, Philadelphia, 1986. – *The Agrarian History of England and Wales II: 1042-1350*, H.E. Hallam (ed.), Cambridge,

1988. – *L'Ambiente vegetale nell'alto Medioevo*, 1990 ("SSAM", 37). – *La Croissance agricole du haut Moyen Âge. Chronologie, modalités, géographie, Dixièmes Journées internationales d'histoire (Centre culturel de l'abbaye de Flaran), 9-11 septembre 1988*, Auch, 1990. – G. Comet, *Le Paysan et son outil. Essai d'histoire technique des céréales (France, VIIIe-XVe siècle)*, Paris-Rome, 1992 ("CEFR", 165).

Jean-Louis Gaulin

**AISTULF (died 756).** Aistulf was proclaimed king of the *Lombards and reigned from 749 to 756 at *Milan, while *Pavia was still held by his brother and predecessor Ratchis (744-749), who retired to *Monte Cassino. A warrior king, he reorganised armed service according to levels of wealth, and integrated the merchants into it. He opened a new phase of conquest against the Roman territories, Byzantine and papal. He occupied *Ravenna and benefited from the alliance of the Spoletans and Beneventans against *Rome, which he subjected to tribute (752), then besieged (756). Meanwhile Pope *Stephen II had obtained help from the *Franks. *Pippin the Short defeated Aistulf in 755 and 756 and obliged him to give St Peter the conquered territories, among them Ravenna, to the discontent of Byzantium. An alliance between Lombards and Byzantines was being prepared when Aistulf died accidentally.

O. Bertolini, "Astolfo", *DBI*, 4, 1962, 467-483. – P. Delogu, *Il regno Longobardo*, *Storia d'Italia*, G. Galasso (dir.), 1, Turin, 1980, 169-178.

Huguette Taviani-Carozzi

***AKATHISTOS*.** A Byzantine Marian hymn in 24 strophes (*kontakia*) whose *acrostics follow the order of the letters of the alphabet. An initial dedicatory strophe implores the protection of the Mother of God "great *strategos* of the celestial forces". The first twelve strophes sing the mystery of the Incarnation, following Matthew's infancy narrative, the next twelve, more lyrical in character, celebrate *Mary's praises. Each strophe is followed alternately by a short hymn in the form of a greeting or a litany.

This hymn, which undoubtedly dates from the 6th c., is said to have been solemnly sung during the siege of *Constantinople by the *Avars and Persians in 626, and preceded on that occasion by a new prologue suggested by Patriarch *Sergius. Composed for the feast of the Annunciation, it constitutes the framework of the office of the fifth Saturday in *Lent, but its use is much more frequent. In the course of time it has served as a model for many hymns called "akathistoi" because sung standing up.

From at least the 15th c. it has provided matter for numerous frescos or *icons, notably in the Balkans (*Serbia), Russia and *Moldavia.

E. Wellesz, *The Akathistos Hymn*, Copenhagen, 1957. – G. G. Preersseman, *Der Hymnos Akathistos von Abendland*, Fribourg, 1958-1960 (2 vol.). – F. Keller, "Die slavischen Fassungen des Akathistos", *Schweizerische Beiträge zum VIII. Internationalen Slavistenkongress in Zagreb und Ljubljana*, Bern, Frankfurt am Main, Las Vegas, 1979, 87-103.

Irénée-Henri Dalmais

**ALAIN DE LA ROCHE (*c.*1428-1475).** Of Breton origin, Alain de La Roche entered the *Dominicans of Dinan in *c.*1450 and, after some time at Paris, spent his whole career in the convents of the *Observance belonging to the congregation of Holland, Lille, Douai, *Ghent and Rostock. Very early, he showed a strong Marian piety: daily recital of the psalter of the Virgin or *rosary is said to have helped him overcome a moral crisis. Arising from this piety, he dedicated his life and work to the spread of this devotion, notably

*Ploughing*, from the *Codex Oppiano*, a treatise on hunting and fishing. 11th-c. manuscript. Venice, Bibliotheca Marciana.

through the *reform at Douai of a Dominican Marian confraternity which he intended to become a "universal union of the devotees of the rosary", and which was associated from 1470 with the spiritual benefits of the congregation of Holland.

A. Duval, "Rosaire", *DSp*, 12, 1988, 937-969.

Catherine Vincent

**ALAMANNI, ALAMANNIA.** The *Alamanni* appear in Roman sources in 213, when they formed a *gens populosa* that pressed on the *limes* in the region of the Main. Their name, which meant "mixture of men", in fact designated an aggregation of various tribes. A certain ethnic unity appears more clearly in the second half of the 4th c., but it is not certain whether, at the beginning of the 6th c., the people had been united under the authority of a single king. From the 4th c., the Alamanni never ceased to extend their territory, to the extent that at the beginning of the 6th c. it reached Langres and *Troyes in the west, Lech in the east and the Danube in the south. However, the area of Alaman colonization did not go beyond the Rhine, the Alamanni being content to exercise military control over the Roman cities of the West and South.

In 506, at Tolbiac, the *Franks inflicted a defeat on the Alamanni that led to Alamannia passing under *Merovingian control. The defeat also had profound repercussions on population: many families of the Alaman aristocracy emigrated with their followers towards Rhaetia, *Italy or *Burgundy, while others settled in the old Romanized regions of the upper Danube and upper Rhine (in *Alsace in particular). New centres of population, Franks but also Thuringians, later appeared in inner Alamannia. A new aristocracy was thus defined in the second half of the 6th c.: its culture participated in that of the whole of the eastern Merovingian kingdom.

In the 6th-7th cc., the country was administered on behalf of the East Frankish kings by dukes, though whether these were of Frankish or Alaman origin is unknown. In fact, their competence hardly went beyond the old Romanized regions. Frankish influence in inner Alamannia, east of the Rhine and north of Lake Constance, intensified under Chlotar II and *Dagobert (613-639): at this time the kings fixed Alamannic law and began to organise the country politically and religiously. Colonization and Christianization eventually led to the creation of the *dioceses of Basel, *Constance, *Strasbourg and *Augsburg, as well as the foundation of the monasteries of *Sankt Gallen and *Reichenau, so much so that the duchy of Alamannia, which appeared at the beginning of the 8th c. with Duke Gotfried, extended at this time to all Alamannia. Its rise, its power and its autonomy around 700 were part of the process of regionalization that characterised the 8th century. The hostility of the dukes towards the Pippinids and the policy followed by the *Carolingians of taking the peripheral regions in hand explain the brutal suppression of the duchy by Carloman in 746, following the bloody defeat of Cannstatt.

Carolingian Alamannia was at first subjected to a sort of military occupation, until *Charlemagne's marriage to the Alaman Hildegard facilitated the rallying of the aristocracy and the integration of the country into the Carolingian administrative system, but the process was only completed in the reign of *Louis the Pious.

R. Christlein, *Die Alamannen. Archäologie und lebendiges Volkes*, Stuttgart, 1978. – H. Keller, "Archäologie und Geschichte der Alamannen in merowingischer Zeit", *ZGO*, 129, 1981. – D. Geuenich, H. Keller, "Alamannen, Alamanien, Alamannisch im frühen Mittelalter", H. Wolfram, F. Daim, *Die Bayern und ihre Nachbarn*, 1, Vienna, 1985.

Régine Le Jan

**ALAN OF LILLE (*c.*1128-1203).** Born at Lille, Alan studied and then taught at *Paris. From *c.*1180 he was in southern France, at *Montpellier in particular. At the end of his life, he retired to *Cîteaux where he died in 1203; his tomb has been found (April 1960).

Before *Albert the Great († 1280), Alan of Lille merited the title *doctor universalis*. His works were numerous and varied. They were published in 1654 by C. de Visch, prior of the abbey of Dunes, then at Bruges, followed by *PL*, 210 (1855). Since then several of Alan's works have benefited from a new edition or studies; others have been discovered and published (thus the commentary on the *Pater*), but many *sermons remain unedited.

*De planctu naturae* is among Alan's first writings, apparently before 1171; a prose text, intercut with poems in different metres, *De planctu* criticizes man's vices, in particular sodomy, and denounces the failure of human nature, incapable on its own of preventing man from succumbing to the disorders of the senses. Some ten years later, the *Anticlaudianus* sings of the "perfect man" called for by *Nature, draws up a list of the *sciences and eulogizes the moral virtues inseparable from the intellectual *faculties. A much-read poem, handed down by numerous manuscripts, sometimes adapted and commented; it has benefited from a critical edition by R. Bossuat (Paris, 1955).

Also at Paris, between 1170 and 1180, he composed several works of *theology, often marked by the influence of *Gilbert of Poitiers. The *summa *Quoniam homines*, incomplete, known by a single manuscript, comprises treatises on *God, the *Trinity and the *angels (ed. P. Glorieux, *AHDL*, 20, 1953, 113-264). *De uirtutibus et uitiis* divides the virtues into "political", or natural and "catholic", or theological (ed. O. Lottin, *Mediaeval Studies*, 12, 1950, 20-56). The *Regulae caelestis iuris* study God, *man, the Incarnation and the *sacraments; here Alan applies to the field of theology the method of demonstration of the arts, in particular of geometry (ed. N. Häring, *AHDL*, 48, 1981, 97-226).

Probably associated with the anti-Cathar struggle during his stay in *Languedoc, Alan did not abate his literary activity, but he gave it a more pastoral character. *De fide catholica contra haereticos* (*PL*, 210, 305-430) studies successively the *Cathars (76 ch.), the *Waldenses (25 ch.), the *Jews (21 ch.) and the Muslims (14 ch.). As well as the *Distinctiones* explaining biblical terms in alphabetical order (*PL*, 210, 685-1012), he wrote *Expositiones* on the *Song of Songs, the *Lord's Prayer and the *Apostles' Creed.

It may be that the majority of the "diverse" sermons come from this period, to which the *Ars praedicandi* surely belongs; an anthology of biblical, patristic and secular citations grouped around virtues to be preached and *vices to be fought (*PL*, 210, 109-195). The *Ars* is sometimes accompanied in manuscripts by a *Liber sermonum*, a sort of model series of some 20 *homilies divided among the liturgical cycle.

Dedicated to Henri de Sully, archbishop of Bourges (1183-1193), and of very different lengths in the three manuscript traditions, the *Liber poenitentialis* aims to facilitate the administration of the sacrament of *penance; more generally, it aims to stimulate the zeal of pastors and contribute to a better spiritual and moral training (ed. J. Longère, 2 vol., Louvain-Lille, 1965, and *AHDL*, 32, 1965, 169-242).

M.-T. d'Alverny, *Alain de Lille. Textes inédits avec une introduction sur sa vie et ses oeuvres*, Paris, 1965.

G.R. Evans, *Alan of Lille*, Cambridge, 1983. – J. Ziolkowski, *Alan of Lille's Grammar of Sex*, Cambridge, 1985. – J. Longère, "Alain de Lille", *DLFMA*, 1992, 32-35.

Jean Longère

**ALBANIA, CAUCASIAN.** Caucasian Albania, between the Greco-Roman world and the Iranian world, has nothing to do with Albania in the Balkans: it sits under the south-east slopes of the Great *Caucasus. Its frontiers, like those of all the neighbouring States, varied at different times; it went at least as far as the Kura. Its capital Kabala was transferred to Barda'a-Partav, an active commercial centre, in the 6th c.; "Albanian" was still spoken there in the 10th century.

Albania was Christianized in the late 4th c. and received from *Armenia its own alphabet which allowed the circulation of the Albanian translation of the Scriptures. In this region close to *Iran, ritual stuffing with straw persisted longer than the cult of the moon, of Caucasian origin. Albania, at first linked to the Syro-Oriental Church, hesitated between Chalcedonianism (as in *Georgia) and the Armenian type of monophysitism which finally triumphed. But the *Khazar, Arab, Russian, *Turkish and *Mongol invasions overcame this little kingdom, where fine architectural monuments still exist. The Albanian-held monasteries in Jerusalem have disappeared.

Z. Aleksidze, *Georgian-Albanian Palimpsest on Mount Sinai and its Relevance to Caucasian Studies*, Tbilisi, 1998. – *Actes du premier colloque international sur l'Albanie du Caucase* (to appear).

Bernard Outtier

**ALBANIANS.** A nation of Thraco-Illyrian origin, in the Middle Ages the Albanians were ruled by the Byzantines (6th-14th cc.) and *Bulgars (9th-10th cc.) before succumbing to the *Turks (1479). The fourth *crusade (1203-1204) allowed the creation, among other things, of the independent principalities of Scuttari (Shkodër), governed by the Balsha family, and Durazzo (Durrës), dominated by the Thopia clan. Durrës (ancient Dyrrachion) was the starting-point of an important trans-Balkan route, the old Via Egnatia, connecting the Adriatic with *Constantinople. Installed at Valone (Vlorë), *Charles of Anjou proclaimed himself *rex Albaniae* in 1272, and the Angevin State continued to exist until 1380 under the name of duchy of Durazzo. The Albanians also came under Serbian (1345-1350) and Venetian (1392-1479) authority.

The rechristianization of the Albanians after the Slav *invasions of the 6th-7th cc. was the work of missionaries sent from Rome and Constantinople. At the time of the *iconoclast quarrel, Leo III the *Isaurian detached eastern Illyricum from the Western *patriarchate and attached it to the Church of Constantinople. During the Bulgar rule, a great part of Albanian territory, formerly under the jurisdiction of the archdiocese of Dyrrachion, was subjected to the authority of the archbishop of *Ohrid in Macedonia, while the dioceses of the North (Drivaste, Scuttari) remained under the jurisdiction of the metropolitan Church of Ragusa (*Dubrovnik), then under that of the archbishopric of Bar (Antivari), where an important council met in 1199 to promote the reform of the Church in Albania. This Church was divided between the two rites, Latin and Greek: the North remained under Roman obedience while the South recognised the jurisdiction of Constantinople. The religious orders, especially the Benedictines and mendicants, kept very close links with *Dalmatia. At the time of the *Ottoman occupation, delayed by the heroic resistance of *Scanderbeg (1444-1468), the *Catholic North and the *Orthodox South resisted Islamization, while the Centre became entirely Muslim.

William Adam, a learned Dominican and archbishop of Bar, said in *c.*1332 that "the Albanians have a language entirely different from Latin", but that "they make use of Latin script and use it in all their books". Of all the medieval literature in Albanian, only the liturgical texts from 1462 and a lexicon of Albanian, copied in 1497 by a German pilgrim, have survived.

Art of Byzantine inspiration reappeared towards the end of the 9th century. The finest churches, covered with *mosaics, *frescos and *icons, like that of St Mary at Berat in southern Albania, date from the period of prosperity (11th-12th cc.). The influence of Dalmatian and Venetian artists and craftsmen came with the settlement of the *Dominicans and *Franciscans in the towns bordering the Adriatic (Durrës) and the fortified citadels (Shkodër, Krujë).

L. Thalloczy, K. Jireček, M. Sufflay, *Acta et diplomata res Albaniae mediae aetatis illustrantia*, Vienna, 1913-1916 (2 vol.). – N. Jorga, *Brève histoire d'Albanie et du peuple albanais*, Bucharest, 1919. – S. Skendi, *Albania*, New York, 1956. – K. Frasheri, *Histoire de l'Albanie*, Tirana, 1964. – S. Pollo, A. Puto, *Histoire de l'Albanie des origines à nos jours*, Lyon, 1974, 31-106. – Z. Mirdita, *Krishtenizmi nder Shqiptarë* [Christianity in Albanian], Prizren-Zagreb, 1998.

Franjo Šanjek

**ALBERIC or AUBREY (died 1109).** Instigator of the Cistercian reform, Alberic was previously (*c.*1070) one of a small group of hermits in the forest of Collan (Côte-d'Or). Initiated into the *coenobitic life by Robert, prior of Saint-Ayoul de Provins, they founded *Molesmes. Robert became abbot and he prior. Growing tensions in the community on the subject of monastic observances were a severe trial to him and Abbot Robert allowed him to approach the legate *Hugh of Die at Lyon, who authorized the creation of *Cîteaux in 1098. Prior, then abbot in 1099, in 1100 he obtained confirmation and protection of the monastery from Pope *Paschal II. Austerity and simplicity characterised his life and the beginnings of Cîteaux, where he died in 1109.

*Cath.*, 1, 1948, 1014-1015.

Jean-Baptiste Auberger

**ALBERIC II OF SPOLETO (died 954).** Alberic II of Spoleto, or rather Alberic of Rome, was the son of Alberic, marquis of *Spoleto, and *Marozia, daughter of *Theophylact "senator of the Romans". After the death of Alberic I, Marozia married *Hugh of Provence, king of Italy, who installed himself at *Rome in 932; Alberic II expelled him, took the title of prince and maintained good relations with Byzantium and southern Italy. In 936 he concluded a truce with Hugh, whose daughter he married. He made the *Patrimony of St Peter a principality like those of the rest of the West, and supported monastic *reform with the help of *Odo of Cluny. Alberic II created "the scene on which was played out the decisive act of the great mutation of 10th-century *Latium" (P. Toubert). He left the *popes their autonomy, but on his death (954) he made the Romans promise to elect his son Octavian as pope (John XII).

G. Arnaldi, "Alberico di Roma", *DBI*, 1, 1960. – P. Toubert, *Les structures du Latium médiéval*, Rome, 1973.

Jean-Marie Martin

**ALBERIC III OF TUSCULUM (11th c.).** Alberic III of *Tusculum was descended from the powerful family founded in the 10th c. in *Latium by *Theophylact I, from which issued the two branches of *Crescentii and Tuscolani. In 1012, on the death of Pope Sergius IV and the patrician John II, the latter branch attained power by the successive election of two *popes, the two elder sons of Gregory of Tusculum: Theophilus, under the name of Benedict VIII, and then Romanus, under the name of John XIX. Both were brothers of Alberic III of Tusculum. Their rise to power was facilitated by their undeniable personal merit, but also by the detachment manifested by the Emperors *Henry II and Conrad II towards Roman affairs. In restoring papal authority at *Rome and in the *Patrimony of St Peter, as keystone of their family foundations, the young Tuscolani and their brother Alberic III, given responsiblity for the running of the ecclesiastical *patrimony, can be considered the first Roman architects of papal reform. Alberic III worked to limit the powers of the emperor, to recover the temporalities of the Holy See, alienated by the Crescentii popes, and to exploit them in the sole interests of the papacy and not of his family, whose territorial base in Latium was narrow and remained so.

P. Toubert, *Les structures du Latium médiéval*, Rome, 1973.

Françoise Gasparri

**ALBERT OF BEHAIM (before 1200 - *c.*1260).** Albert of Behaim or Bohemus, a Bavarian curialist, is known mainly as the *legate of *Gregory IX at the time of the *excommunication of *Frederick II, in 1239. His historical writings, which were important for the genesis of a Bavarian history – though primarily intended to defend the interests of the church of *Passau over which Albert watched, after 1246, as dean of the cathedral *chapter –, share the same hostility to the *Empire as the apocalyptic texts included in the surviving volume of his correspondence.

*Das Brief- und Memorialbuch des Albert Behaim*, T. Frenz (ed.), P. Herde (ed.) ("MGH. Briefe des späteren Mittelalters", 1; to appear).

P. Herde, "Albert Behaim", *LdM*, 1, 1980, 288. – J.-M. Moeglin, *Les Ancêtres du Prince*, Geneva, 1985, 37-44. – T. Frenz, "Apokalypse als Geschichtserklärung", *Ostbairische Grenzmarken*, 32, Passau, 1990, 48-55.

Martial Staub

**ALBERT OF BUXHÖVDEN (died 1229).** Canon, then bishop of *Bremen in 1199, Albert was one of the architects and executors of *Ostsiedlung* (German colonization of the territories east of the Elbe).

When Pope *Innocent III called for the defence of the Livonian church, Albert decided to resume the missionary work of Meinhard of Holstein. Setting out from *Lübeck in spring 1200 with 23 ships, the bishop headed an imposing troop of crusaders, composed of nobles from lower Germany and merchants. In 1201 he founded *Riga and, becoming bishop of Livonia in 1202, created the Order of *Knights of the Sword, with whom he soon came into conflict over the division of the conquered territories. Having been made a prince of the Empire in 1207 by *Philip of Swabia, he was obliged to give up a third of the order's lands, part of which he later recovered, and he died in 1229.

C. Higounet, *Les Allemands en Europe centrale et orientale au Moyen Âge*, Paris, 1989.

Simonne Abraham-Thisse

**ALBERT OF JERUSALEM (*c.*1150-1214).** Patriarch of *Jerusalem (1205-1214) and legislator of the *Carmelites, also called Albert of Vercelli, St Albert came from a noble family. Prior of the monastery of Santa Croce at Mortara in Lombardy, in 1184 he became bishop of *Bobbio, then bishop of Vercelli. Esteemed for his diplomatic ability, he served as mediator between Pope Clement III and *Frederick Barbarossa. In 1205 he was chosen as patriarch of Jerusalem and papal *legate to the *Holy Land. He settled at *Acre in 1206, since Jerusalem was then in the hands of the Muslims, and strove to arbitrate the quarrels among Christian princes. Towards 1207 he created a rule for the hermits of Mount Carmel, who had settled there since the mid 12th century. *Innocent III invited him to take part in the fourth *Lateran council, but he was murdered on 4 Sept 1214 by the Master of the Hospital of the Holy Spirit, whom he had just deposed.

P. Marie-Joseph, "Albert de Verceil", *DHGE*, 1, Paris, 1912, 1564-1567. – B. Edwards, "Introduction to the Rule of St Albert", *The Rule of Saint Albert*, Aylesford-Kensington, 1973, 12-13.

Anne-Marie Eddé

**ALBERT THE BEAR (*c.*1100-1170).** Member of the Ascanian dynasty, Albert was the first margrave of *Brandenburg (*marchio in Brandenborch*, from the late 1150s). The nickname "the Bear" was assigned him by Helmold of Bosau, who thus established a parallel with the Welf *Henry "the Lion", Albert's opponent and counterpart. Opponent over the possession of the duchy of *Saxony, which Albert never managed to seize from him despite imperial support. Counterpart in the east, where Albert's successes equalled those of the Welf in the matter of territorial extension (March of Brandenburg), colonization and Christianization.

*NDB*, 1, 1953, 160-161. – E. Schmidt, *Die Mark Brandenburg unter die Askanier*, Vienna, 1973. – *LdM*, 1, 1980, 316-317.

Joseph Morsel

**ALBERT THE GREAT (*c.*1200-1280).** St Albert was born at Lauingen in *Swabia, to a family of lesser nobility. In 1223 he was a student of Arts at *Padua where he met *Jordan of Saxony and, influenced by his preaching, decided to enter the *Dominican Order. Returning to Germany to study theology, he began a rapid career within the order's group of intellectuals, the conventual *readers. From 1235 onwards he taught in the convents of *Hildesheim, Freiberg, *Regensburg and *Strasbourg. During this period he wrote the *De natura boni*, a work in which, as well as the influence of Augustine, we already see a serious interest in *Aristotle, particularly in the first and still partial translation of the *Nicomachean Ethics* (*Ethica vetus*). In the early 1240s Albert was sent to *Paris to further his theological studies. After studying *Peter Lombard's **Sentences*, in 1245 he gained the degree of master of theology and taught for three years in the chair reserved for non-French Dominicans. The fruits of the work of this period are found in the *Commentary on the Sentences* and the so-called *Summa de creaturis*, a group of six theological works dealing with the *Creation, man, the cardinal virtues, the *sacraments, the Incarnation and the *Resurrection.

*Albert the Great*, by Tommaso da Modena (*c.*1325-*c.*1379), wall-painting, *c.*1352. Treviso, Seminary.

In 1248 Albert was transferred to *Cologne, charged with founding in the Rhineland metropolis the general *studium* of the Dominicans for the province of Germany. He was accompanied by the young student *Thomas Aquinas, who followed his *lectures on the *Corpus Dionysiacum* there (1249). The next year, 1250, marked a change in Albert's intellectual activity. If so far he had written and thought as a theologian while showing an interest in the doctrines of the philosophers of Antiquity, from now on his centre of gravity shifted decidedly towards *philosophy. At the general *studium*, he gave a series of courses on the complete text of Aristotle's *Nicomachean Ethics* (in *Robert Grosseteste's new translation), and at the same time began his systematic exposition of the *Corpus Aristotelicum*, whose most important stages were the *Physica* (1251), *De caelo*, *De generatione et meteora*, *Logic*, *De anima* (1254-1257), *Parva naturalia*, *De vegetabilibus*, *De animalibus* (1258-1263) and *Metaphysica* (after 1263). Albert's expositions, in the form of paraphrases, are characterised by explanatory digressions containing ample doxographies (collections of "opinions" of philosophers) and diffuse accounts of the positions expressed by the Greek and Islamic philosophical tradition, not just Aristotelian but also Platonic, according to the principle which says that "the philosopher's training is not complete unless it includes knowledge of two philosophies, that of Aristotle and that of Plato" (*Metaph.* I, 5, 15).

Meanwhile, Albert passed through several important steps in his career: from 1254 to 1257 he was provincial prior of the German Dominicans, in 1256-1257 he resided at the papal court, in 1260 he was elected bishop of *Regensburg. Two years later, having resigned this post and completed a long series of preaching journeys in Germany, he settled in 1264 in *Würzburg. The period immediately following saw the production of most of his commentaries on the *Bible, which comprise the important **Postillae* on the gospels of Matthew, Luke and John. Around 1268, probably at Strasbourg, Albert concluded the cycle of his philosophical expositions with his commentary on the *Liber de causis* (*De causis et processu universitatis*), which he still considered, following the Parisian tradition, to be a text of Aristotelian nature and content. From 1270 to his death in 1280 he resided at Cologne, where he laboured on his last work, the *Summa de mirabili scientia Dei*.

Albert owes his reputation, in the Middle Ages as in the modern period, mainly to his ample philosophical and scientific output, which almost entirely takes the form of exposition of the Aristotelian and pseudo-Aristotelian writings. This vast systematic project, which occupied Albert for some fifteen years, and whose object for him was to make the classical philosophical texts "comprehensible to the Latins" (*Phys.* I, 1, 1), freed the European arts *faculties for the first time from subjection to *Avicenna's paraphrases and *Averroes's commentaries, and was the necessary condition for the adoption of the Aristotelian texts in the programme of studies of the Dominican Order (ratified in 1259 by the general chapter of Valenciennes). Albert's commentaries, which aim to understand and explain the reasons for the various positions expressed in the philosophical tradition, rather than to censure them *a priori* on the basis of the dogmas of Christian *theology, are characterised by a fundamental cultural openness, which has led to a rather fruitless discussion among critics as to whether he shared as a theologian the ideas he professed as a philosopher. In reality, Albert's position on this point is very clear: the rationalist method of philosophy, exemplified at its highest point, but not exclusively (*II Sent.* 13, 2), by the whole of the *Corpus Aristotelicum*, is in his view the sole valid method for the scientific investigation of man and nature. In proceeding according to its scientific deductions, philosophy can and must totally abstract itself from *Revelation, *i.e.* the certainties of the **Credo* which serve as the basis of theological discourse. Thus the philosopher legitimately states, for example, that according to the principles of scientific *reason, there is no reason to conclude that the world will have an end (*De gen. et corr.* I, 1, 22). While it is true that the theologian knows with equal certainty that the world will end, it is nevertheless in consequence to a precise departure from the *order of nature, which depends on the free decision of *God and which as such does not deny, but on the contrary confirms, the legitimacy of scientific reasoning.

Albert was substantially convinced that the conflicts between philosophical reason and theological reason had their origin in precise departures from natural necessity (object of philosophico-scientific reason) due to the free intervention of God on the course of nature, documented by Revelation (object of theology). Apart from its epistemological value, Albert's position had a shattering political and cultural importance since, though it recognised the Revelation of the theologian as the ultimate forum of truth, it *de facto* delegitimized its claim to philosophical competence, legalizing pagan *science *en bloc*.

Albert's position was based on a solid, articulated philosophy of *nature, very far from the traditional symbolic interpretation then current among his colleagues of the theology faculty. According to Albert, the universe is governed by iron natural laws dependent on the influences exercised by the stars on the terrestrial world by their perfect and always regular movement (*Phys.* II, 2, 19). These influences are formal in nature, and are responsible for the regularity of the generative and corruptive processes of bodily nature, presiding over the ordered development of forms that, in matter, are in an incipient state (*Summa theologiae*, $II^a$, q. 1, 4, 1, 1).

In this cosmos governed by an astrologico-hermetizing type of necessity, a particular position belongs to *man by virtue of his *intellect, which frees him and makes him "a link between God and the world" (*Metaph.* I, 1, 1). Albert argues for man's *freedom and dignity both by theological analysis (the intellect is an image of God: *Summa theologiae*, $I^a$, q. 1, 4, 2, 1) and through a philosophical analysis of the universality of the cognitive function, made under the influence of Averroes (*De an.* III, 3, 1, 1). In the exercise of reason, the consequent recognition of the autonomy of the intellect as such, and the mental felicity that ensues, Albert sees the possibility of the fulfilment of the human essence. The Albertine doctrine of intellect and human felicity, into which flow Aristotelian and Averroist, as well as Platonic and hermetic motifs, would later be taken up and developed by the German Dominicans *Theodoric of Freiberg, Meister *Eckhart, Berthold of Moosburg and Johann *Tauler.

Albert the Great, *Opera omnia*, P. Jammy (ed.), Lyon, 1651 (21 vol.); A. and E. Borgnet (ed.), Paris, 1890-1899 (38 vol.); Münster, 1951 (20 vol. appeared, crit. ed., called "Cologne ed."). – W. Fauser, *Die Werke des Albertus Magnus in ihrer handschriftlichen Überlieferung*, Münster, 1982.

*HGP*, 2, 1970, 362-367 (bibl. up to 1966). – *Albertus Magnus, Doctor universalis: 1280-1980*, Mainz, 1980, 495-508 (bibl. 1967-1980). – I. Craemer-Ruegenberg, *Albertus Magnus*, Munich, 1980. – J. A. Weisheipl, *Albertus Magnus and the Sciences*, Toronto, 1980. – G. Wieland, *Ethica – Scientia practica. Die Anfänge der philosophischen Ethik im 13. Jahrhundert*, Münster, 1981. – B. Thomassen, *Metaphysik als Lebensform.*

*Untersuchungen zur Grundlegung der Metaphysik im Metaphysikkommentar Alberts des Grossen*, Münster, 1985. – L. Sturlese, *Die deutsche Philosophie im Mittelalter*, 1, Munich, 1993, 324-389.

Loris Sturlese

**ALBI.** A modest *vicus*, Albi owed its promotion to the administrative reforms of the 4th c., which made it the capital of a *civitas* and a *diocese. Its importance long remained minor, despite signs, from the 7th c., that it was a very lively cultural centre.

Around 900, the town was caught up in a growth that was accelerated by the establishment of the feudal system (construction of a *bridge over the Tarn, *c.*1040). New quarters burgeoned alongside the ancient city and the *bourg* of the *collegiate church of Saint-Salvi, and the whole was enclosed by a wall in *c.*1190.

The "great southern war" of the 12th c. allowed the Viscounts Trencavel to exclude the counts of *Toulouse from the town, but they themselves had to reckon with the *bishop, who managed to enlarge his *temporal power from before 1200. The crusade of summer 1209 confirmed the prelate as allodial lord of the town, with the support of the burghers to whom he conceded some franchises in 1220.

The solidarity between the bishop and the urban elites was kept up for a time against the king's officials, who established themselves there after 1229, but the oligarchy wanted more freedom. It adhered largely to *heresy, which suited well its spiritual trouble and developed a religious sociability in accordance with its requirements. From the time of St *Bernard's preaching in the Midi in 1145, the heretics were called Albigenses: the term arose from a regional context, but there is no doubt that the town was a *Cathar stronghold. Heresy appears there as an affair of notables, merchants, jurists and some nobles; a minority affair, far from being a popular movement, it undoubtedly affected less than five per cent of the population of Albi.

Political and spiritual conflict between the bishop and his flock reached its culminating point under Bernard de Castanet (1276-1308), who set up an "episcopal monarchy" in his diocese. With him, the *chapters of Saint-Salvi and of the cathedral of Sainte-Cécile, which had long played an essential role, lost much of their influence to the *mendicant orders, particularly the *Dominicans (these settled at Albi in 1276, the *Franciscans in 1242, the *Carmelites in 1311). The opulence of the bishopric allowed Bernard de Castanet to make a double monumental statement: a palace-fortress, the Berbie, and a cathedral that was heir to the Toulousan experiments of the 13th c., which he synthesized and systematized. The powerful mass of these buildings, conceived perhaps by the Catalan Pons Descoyl, makes them the magisterial illustration of an architecture of combat and proclamation.

The context of urban politics evolved with the setting up of the modern *State. A town of 10,000 inhabitants in 1343, at that time nearly 60 % of Albi's population were indigent, which made it a marvellous breeding-ground for the plague: this carried off two thirds of the population in 1348 and continued to strike every seven years or so, until the end of the 15th century. These recurrences favoured a government unshared by the oligarchy. The elites accepted the subjection of the town to the control of the king's officials, because they found a promotion and a guarantee in the monarchical system, of which the bishop himself became a cog.

At the end of the 15th c., with its municipal institutions and its *seigneurie*, the new State took over from the town. The decoration commissioned for Sainte-Cécile by the *Amboise family, princes of the Church and servants of the *monarchy, clearly expresses not only this change in government, but also the spiritual tendencies of the time and the *pastoral care that went with them.

"Albi", *Atlas historique des villes de France*, 1983. – J.-L. Biget, *Histoire d'Albi*, Toulouse, 1983. – J.-L. Biget, *La Cathédrale d'Albi*, 1984. – J.-L. Biget, J.-C. Hervé, Y. Thébert, "Expressions iconographiques et monumentales du pouvoir d'État en France et en Espagne à la fin du Moyen Âge: l'exemple d'Albi et de Grenade", *Culture et idéologie dans la genèse de l'État moderne*, Rome, 1985, 245-279. – J.-L. Biget, M. Escourbiac, *Sainte-Cécile d'Albi. Peintures*, Graulhet, 1994. – J.-L. Biget, M. Escourbiac, *Saint-Cécile d'Albi. Sculptures*, Graulhet, 1997.

Jean-Louis Biget

**ALBORNOZ, GIL (1310?-1367).** A protégé of Alfonso XI, Albornoz became archbishop of *Toledo (1338) and chancellor of the kingdom of *Castile; *legate of the Holy See during the crusade against the *Saracens of Andalusia, he distinguished himself at the battle of Tarifa (1340). Disgraced by King Peter the Cruel, he retired to *Avignon where *Clement VI appointed him titular *cardinal of San Clemente (1350).

*Innocent VI, in an attempt to restore order to the Papal States, made Albornoz his legate in *Italy (1353); in practice he would sometimes support, sometimes disavow his actions. In the territory of the *Patrimony of St Peter, Albornoz fought against Giovanni di Vico who was extending his power there; after some setbacks, *Orvieto and then *Viterbo were taken and, by the treaty of Montfiascone, Vico recognised the supremacy of the Church and received the vicariate at Corneto (1354).

Albornoz later campaigned in the *Marches and captured Galeotto *Malatesta, who signed a peace at Gubbio (1355), before entering Ancona where he built a fortress. But in *Romagna he came up against the influence of the *Visconti and, following their intrigues at Avignon, Albornoz was replaced by Cardinal Androin de la Roche, a mediocre character who compromised his predecessor's work (1357).

Albornoz returned to Avignon and Innocent VI restored his title of legate in 1358; this time he bore down on Francesco Ordelaffi, lord of Cesena and Forlì who capitulated in 1359. He recovered *Bologna where he installed his kinsman Blasco Fernandez as rector (1360). The town, threatened by the troops of Bernabò Visconti, was saved by a ruse of Albornoz (1361).

*Urban V prolonged the powers of his legate, cited Bernabò Visconti to appear at Avignon, condemned him as a heretic and preached a crusade against him. But Bernabò demanded the presence of a new legate as the price of his submission, and Albornoz was once more removed in favour of Androin de la Roche (1363) and appointed legate in the kingdom of *Naples. But before his departure he helped Androin, fought against the *Companies of Fortune and reconciled *Florence and *Pisa. At Avignon, calumnies were propagated against him by cardinals, but the pope wrote to him personally of his esteem for him. Albornoz was still able to complete the pacification of the Papal States, which was an indispensable precondition for the return of the papacy to Italy, but he died on 22 Aug 1367, when Urban V had reached Viterbo.

One of the greatest legates of the Avignonese papacy, he combined the qualities of a war leader with the gifts of a diplomat; victory once gained, he knew how to deal tactfully with his opponents by entrusting them with responsibilities which made them

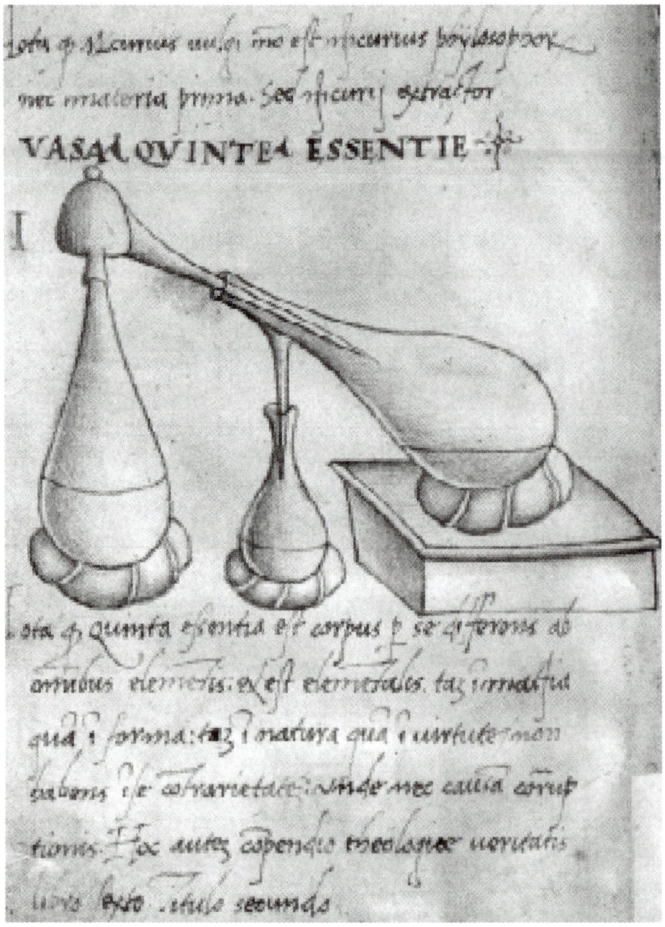


Treatise on alchemy. Vessel for the fifth essence. 15th-c. manuscript. Padua, University Library.

allies or subordinates of the Church; he did not hesitate several times successfully to oppose the fluctuating policy of the papacy; he also proved the qualities of a legislator and administrator by drawing up the *Constitutiones aegidianae*, which were applied in the Marches.

G. Mollat, *DHGE*, 1, 1912, 1717-1725. – E. Dupré-Theseider, *DBI*, 1960, 45-53. – J. Glenisson, G. Mollat, *L'Administration des États de l'Église au XIVe siècle. Correspondance des légats et vicaires généraux: Gil Albornoz et Androin de la Roche*, Paris, 1964. – *El cardenal Albornoz y el Colegio de España*, Bologna, 1972-1973 (3 vol.). – P. Colliva, *Il card. Albornoz, lo stato della Chiesa, le Constitutiones Aegidianae*, Bologna, 1977. – E. Saez, J. Trenchs Odena, *Diplomatario del cardenal Gil de Albornoz*, Barcelona, 1981. – J. Beneyto, *El cardenal Albornoz*, Madrid, 1986. – *Diplomatario del card. Gil de Albornoz, Cancilleria pontificia 1357-1389*, M. T. Ferrer (ed.), R. Sanz del Maza (ed.), Barcelona, 1995.

Anne-Marie Hayez

**ALCÁNTARA, ORDER OF.** A Hispanic *military order, it grew out of the confraternity of knights of San Julián del Pereiro, which was approved by *Alexander III in Oct 1176. The order, founded during the struggle against the Muslims, was subjected to the Order of *Calatrava in 1187 and adopted the *Cistercian rule. The conflict between the Sanjulianists and the Order of Calatrava ended in 1218 in a compromise by whose terms the former submitted and received the fortress of Alcántara on the Tagus, whose name they took. The Order of Alcántara developed mainly in Estremadura where it served the Crown against *Granada and *Portugal. In the 15th c., the order's masters involved it in the struggles of the *nobles while internal disorder grew; in 1501, the *Catholic Kings managed to get themselves appointed "perpetual administrators" of the order by the pope.

J. O'Callahan, "The Foundation of the Order of Alcántara", *CHR*, 47, 1962, 471-486. – "Ordenes Militares", *DHEE*, 1973. – D. W. Lomax, *Las Ordenes Militares en la Península Ibérica durante la Edad Media*, Salamanca, 1976.

Adeline Rucquoi

**ALCHEMY.** Despite some earlier traces, alchemy is considered to have been introduced to the West in the movement of scientific *translations from Arabic to *Latin, around the mid 12th c. (with that of the *Morienus* by Robert of Chester in 1144). The dominant theory of this alchemy, thus introduced, made sulphur and mercury the constituents of metals (it also had to take into account the theory of the four *elements). Of the *corpus* that circulated (largely apocryphally) under the name of Jābir ibn Hayyān, the *Liber de septuaginta* , *e.g.*, was transmitted to the West. Works attributed to Razi, like the *Liber secretorum*, were also translated. Among many other titles and authors, one text was of the first importance: *Avicenna's *De congelatione et conglutinatione lapidum* (translated *c.*1200) extracted from his *Kitāb al-Shifā*. Often put at the end of *Aristotle's *Meteorologica*, it frequently passed for the expression of the Greek philosopher's opinion on the transmutation of metals.

One of the first problems encountered by Western intellectuals was to find a place for this new discipline (which had the notable pecularity of being both an *ars* and a *scientia*) in the organisation of knowledge. Thus *Vincent of Beauvais, in his *Speculum naturale*, made it belong "to that natural part of philosophy which concerns minerals, as agriculture [belongs to] that which concerns plants".

Leaving aside those treatises apocryphally or doubtfully attributed to *Albert the Great, it is in the *De mineralibus* that Albert expounds his position on alchemy. He follows Avicenna in his statement that alchemists are incapable of transmuting metals and that at most they manage to modify accidental properties, leading only to simple imitations. Yet he recalls that Avicenna admitted the theoretical possibility of a transmutation of metals after their reduction to "prime matter". Albert, for whom art does not surpass *nature, shows that alchemy, like *medicine, can act instrumentally, by arranging matter in such a way that it can be transmuted by nature. The point of view expressed by *Roger Bacon in his authentic works is quite different. He makes alchemy a part of his *scientia experimentalis* that would be able to fight against the fraudulent *magic of *Antichrist. Thus he does not limit alchemy to the search for the transmutation of metals into *gold. For him the secret of alchemy is the search for an elixir, admittedly a *medicina* of metals, since it changes them into gold, but also a *medicina* of the body since it can "prolong life". He has a predilection for organic substances as starting-point for the operation. For him, art is capable of surpassing nature. *Medicina* could thus make matter, corruptible by definition, incorruptible.

From the late 13th c., Western alchemy, having assimilated and explored the contribution of translations from Arabic, took on greater autonomy in relation to its models and was constructed in a truly original way. Written some time between the 1260s and the first decades of the 14th c., the *Summa perfectionis* of Pseudo-Geber (in fact by the *Franciscan Paul of Taranto, according to W. Newman) no longer gives us a reflection conducted from outside by a thinker about alchemy, but an examination made by an alchemist. Pseudo-Geber seems to be the first to formulate the so-called theory of mercury alone, which attributes to sulphur a merely secondary role in the constitution of metals (thus replacing the sulphur-mercury theory). The import of this treatise was very great.

The *Pretiosa margarita novella* of Petrus Bonus of Ferrara, dated 1330, also contributes an original reflection. This work affirms the dual nature of alchemy: at once *scientia* and *donum Dei* (gift of God), since alchemical work is "partly natural and partly divine, *i.e.* above nature". If "sublimation" (transmutation of a metal into natural gold) remains within the realm of nature, the "fixation" or manufacture of the *lapis divinus*, which is capable of inducing these transmutations or these purifications, belongs to the religious supernatural. Also, the true alchemist has need of a supplement of divine illumination in order to bring his work to a conclusion. In this context, alchemy has a sacred meaning expressing the redemption of nature: Petrus is one of the first to bring out the parallel between *lapis* and Christ. He thus justifies the old theme of the secret and, with it, that of the dissimulation intended to reserve it only for the initiates who have received this indispensable supplement of illumination.

Also of great importance was the contribution of the Franciscan *John of Roquetaillade (Joannes de Rupescissa). His *Liber de consideratione quintae essentiae* dates from the years 1351-1352. Here it was not a question of making gold, but of giving the friars (vowed to *poverty) a substance capable of protecting their body against corruption, short of making it immortal, which God did not wish. This substance, itself not corruptible, was the "quintessence", likened to "water of life" – admittedly not ordinary alcohol, but a much purer alcohol. In the manner of the fifth celestial element which preserves the universe, this fifth terrestrial element preserves "the four qualities of the human body". In the *Liber lucis* (which also seems authentic), John justifies the revelation of the secret of the "healing of metals" in anticipation of the time when the Church will be dispossessed by Antichrist.

The multiplication in the 14th and 15th cc. of false attributions to famous names (such as Albert the Great, Roger Bacon or *Thomas Aquinas) attests that alchemy was now well anchored in the West. Among the most well-furnished *corpus*, that which circulated under the name of *Arnold of Villanova may include some authentic works (the *Rosarius*?). By contrast, the *corpus* attributed to Raymond *Lull is entirely apocryphal, though produced by authors inspired by *Lullism (Lull himself having rejected alchemy). The first of the series appears to be the *Testamentum* (dated 1332) followed by the *Codicillus*. A large place is given here to an "alchemical philosophy" which could not however be purely and simply "subalternated" to the natural philosophy of the scholastics.

It was precisely at the time of its fullest growth that alchemy suffered a number of attacks. In the years 1270-1280, the

The cloister of silence at the monastery of Santa Anna at Alcobaça (Portugal), built under King Dinis from 1303 to 1311.

*Portrait of Alcuin.* Manuscript. Bamberg, Staatsbibliothek (Ms Bibl. 1, fol. 5 v°).

authorities of the *mendicant orders forbade their members to practise it. The most celebrated condemnation was the *Decretal *Spondent quas non exhibent* of Pope *John XXII (1317) which, however, attacked this activity only as a possible source of falsification, and in any case had a fairly limited importance. Within the Church, many voices were not hostile or were even favourable to alchemy.

As we have seen, it was perhaps as a result of the failures of transmutation that alchemical discourse changed from the late 13th c.: either because of a broadening of the philosophical context in which speculations were formulated, or because it was thought that discursiveness had to be prolonged by a revelation, an intuition of divine origin – and authors were accused on this occasion of having misinterpreted the alchemical texts.

In this logic, the 15th c. saw few texts of any originality, but a development of allegorical alchemical expression, in both literary and iconographical form. Thus the *Book of the Holy Trinity* metaphorically superimposed *prophecy, *mysticism and alchemy.

L. Thorndike, *A History of Magic and Experimental Science*, New York, 1923-1958 (8 vol.). – E. J. Holmyard, *Alchemy*, Harmondsworth, 1957 (re-ed. 1968). – C. Crisciani, "La *Quaestio de alchimia* fra Duecento e Trecento", *Medioevo*, 2, Padua, 1976, 119-169. – *Preziosa margherita novella*, C. Crisciani (ed.), Florence, 1976. – R. Halleux, *Les Textes alchimiques*, Turnhout, 1979 ("TSMÂO", 32). – R. Halleux, "Les ouvrages alchimiques de Jean de Rupescissa", *HLF*, 41, 1981, 241-284. – R. Halleux, "Alchemy", *DMA*, 1, 1982, 134-140. – B. Obrist, *Les Débuts de l'imagerie alchimique, XIVe-XVe siècles*, Paris, 1982. – W. R. Newman, *The* Summa Perfectionis *of Pseudo-Geber: A Critical Edition, Translation and Study*, Leiden, New York, 1991. – M. Pereira, *L'oro dei filosofi: Saggio sulle idee di un alchimista del Trecento*, Spoleto, 1992. – *Alchimie et Philosophie à la Renaissance*, J.-C. Margolin, S. Matton (dir.), Paris, 1993. – *L'arte del sole e della luna. Alchimia e filosofia nel medioevo*, C. Crisciani (ed.), M. Pereira (ed.), Spoleto, 1996.

Nicolas Weill-Parot

**ALCOBAÇA.** A *Cistercian monastery, founded in 1152 by monks from *Clairvaux, at the confluence of the Alcoa and the Baça, 100 kilometres north of Lisbon. This foundation must be set in the general picture of the politics of the first Portuguese king, *Afonso Henriques, who was anxious both to conciliate the clergy and to ensure the development of lands recently taken from the Muslims. Indeed, it was mainly from the 13th c. that Cistercian colonization reached its full extent. From then on the abbey's political and cultural role grew ceaselessly.

Nothing is known of the original establishment, which was destroyed by the *Almohads in 1190. The present edifice (Alcobaça II) is an exact replica of Clairvaux, with the same *orientation of the church and the same arrangement of monastic buildings.

M. Cocheril, *Routier des abbayes cisterciennes du Portugal*, Paris, 1978.

Robert Durand

**ALCUIN (730-804).** Born in Northumbria in *c.*730 (when *Bede was still teaching there), his desire to study led Alcuin to enter the monastery *school of *York where he became the pupil and friend of Ælbert, archbishop of York (767-778). Accompanying his master, he discovered *Rome and the continent, where he came into contact with the intellectual elite of the Frankish kingdom. Entrusted in 781 by the archbishop of York with a mission to Rome, he met *Charlemagne at *Parma, a crucial interview. While remaining a *deacon of his monastery, he entered the king's service and ended by adopting France as his new country, where Charles made him his director of studies at court. Rewarded in 796 by being made *abbot of *Saint-Martin at Tours, the most powerful abbey in the kingdom, Alcuin retired there until his death.

An intelligent disciple of Bede, Alcuin saw for himself the indiscipline of spoken and written *Latin in the 8th c. (collective speech seemed to him still Latin, but corrupted). He applied himself to providing for the continent's intellectuals a mastery of a renovated Roman language: short treatises reopened access to the norms of *grammatica*, thanks to pedagogical procedures that made the works animated and readable: a *Grammar*, nourished especially on the *Etymologies* of *Isidore of Seville; a manual *On Orthography* (dedicated to Charles), compiled from *Cassiodorus and Bede; lessons drawn from Cicero (*De inuentione, De oratore*) and handed down in the form of a dialogue with the king, *On Rhetoric*; a treatise *On Dialectic* whose framework was provided by Isidore and *Boethius. These writings are clear and well constructed, in a limpid style.

Like *Paul the Deacon, Alcuin was ordered to restore the Latinity (*emendatio*) of religious texts: a revision of the *Bible; systematic rewriting of local hagiographical accounts (Lives of St Riquier, St Vaast, St *Willibrord, St *Martin – abridged from Sulpicius Severus). Mediator between arduous patristic works and an aristocracy longing for progress, he dictated a treatise *On the Trinity* and a *Commentary on St John's Gospel*, which borrowed from and simplified Augustine; then an exposition *On the Structure of the Soul*. To Count Guy he dedicated an abridged *On the Virtues* *and Vices*. To distract a court whose sovereign gave an example of intellectual curiosity, Alcuin wrote a brief *Discussions between Pippin and Professor Albinus* (this was, with Flaccus, one of his two nicknames) which raised 101 questions calling forth unexpected answers. The *Propositions to Stimulate the Wits of the Young* associate mathematical problems with simple mental exercises. Alcuin's correspondence is sprinkled with erudite notes intended for the sovereign (for example *On the Subject of Eclipses of the Moon*), based on a spirit of observation and *logic.

Familiar with the classical poets, Alcuin was himself a poet of quality, composing according to the principles of traditional metric, which he used with ease despite sporadic errors: *epitaphs, eulogies, bucolic entertainments; celebration of the *Saints of the Church of York*. Finally, more than 200 of his *letters survive (dating mainly from after 790).

Capable of encompassing all the degrees of teaching, from the most modest to the most erudite, Alcuin also played an essential part in the *Carolingian Renaissance by amplifying the work of legislation already begun under *Pippin. The reforming laws (*admonitiones*, inspired if not dictated by him) attest the firmness, breadth of views, and the great optimism of the restorer.

*PL*, 100-101, 1863. – *MGH.SRM*, 1, 1881 (re-ed. 1978). – *MGH.Ep*, 4, 1892. – *MGH.SRM*, 3, 4, 7, 1896-1920. – S. Allott, *Alcuin of York, his Life and Letters*, York, 1974 (repr. 1987). – Alcuin, *The Bishops, Kings and Saints of York*, P. Godman (ed.), Oxford, 1982 (*OMT*).

C. Leonardi, "Alcuino e la rinascita culturale carolingia", *Schede medievali*, 2, 1982, 32-53. – D. Bullough, "Alcuin and the Kingdom of Heaven: Liturgy, Theology and the Carolingian Age", *Carolingian Essays*, V.R. Blumenthal (ed.), Washington (DC), 1983. – R. McKitterick, *The Carolingians and the Written Word*, Cambridge, 1989. – F. Brunhölzl, *Histoire de la littérature latine du Moyen Âge*, 1 and 2, Turnhout, 1991, 29-46 and 267-272. – M. Banniard, *Viva Voce, Communication écrite et communication orale du IVe au IXe siècle en Occident latin*, Paris, 1992, 305-393. – J. Fleckenstein, "Alcuin im Kreis der Hofgelehrten Karls des Grossen", *Science in Western and Eastern Civilization in Carolingian Times*, P.L. Butzer (ed.), D. Lohrmann (ed.), Basel, 1993, 3-22.

Michel Banniard

**ALDHELM (*c.*640-709).** Aldhelm was the first English man of letters; the vast corpus of his Latin writings exercised profound influence on his contemporaries and formed an important part of the curriculum of Anglo-Saxon *schools. Born to a noble Wessex family in the first generation of English Christianity, Aldhelm studied at the famous *Canterbury school of *Theodore and *Hadrian, before becoming abbot of *Malmesbury in *c.*675 and bishop of Sherborne in 705. He is known to have established various churches in his *diocese (including one at Bradford-on-Avon). Various *letters by Aldhelm survive, as do several letters to Aldhelm from his students, which reveal clearly the influence exercised by his writings in matters of style. Unfortunately the 12th-c. *Vitae* of Aldhelm by Faricius and *William of Malmesbury are essays in hagiography, and contribute very little to our knowledge of Aldhelm's life. His writings are characterised by an extraordinary range of learning in both classical and patristic sources, and a penchant for very long sentences crammed with recherché vocabulary: they include a collection of *tituli* for churches within his diocese (*Carmina ecclesiastica*), a poem in rhythmical octosyllables on a journey to Cornwall and Devon, a prose treatise on *virginity (*De virginitate*) which is a *florilegium of accounts of various saints and *martyrs of the early church; a hexametrical version of the prose treatise (*Carmen de virginitate*), which concludes with the account of a battle between the *vices and the virtues; a collection of one hundred metrical *enigmata* or riddles, in which Aldhelm explores the mysteries of creation; and two treatises on metre.

*Aldhelmi Opera*, R. Ehwald (ed.), *MGH.AA*, 15, 1919.

M. Lapidge, M. Herren, *Aldhelm: the Prose Works*, Cambridge, 1979. – M. Lapidge, J. Rosier, *Aldhelm: the Poetic Works*, Cambridge, 1985. – A. Orchard, *The Poetic Art of Aldhelm*, Cambridge, 1994.

Michael Lapidge

**ALEPPO.** Aleppo (*Halab*) in northern *Syria has been known since the 20th century BC. Occupied by Greeks (*Beroia*), Romans and Byzantines, it fell to the Arabs in 637. In the *Umayyad Empire it played no important role, since *Damascus was the capital. During the first two *Abbasid centuries, it was sometimes under Iraqi influence, sometimes that of the Tulunid and then Ikhshidid governors of Egypt. In 944, for the first time since the arrival of the Arabs, it became the capital of a State founded by the Hamdanid *emir Sayf al-Dawla (944-967). The starting-point for expeditions against the Byzantines, Aleppo was also an important centre of literary activity. But this renaissance was short-lived: in 962 the town was taken and sacked by the Byzantines. In the 11th c. it was constantly disputed between Byzantines, *Fatimids and the small Arab dynasty of the Mirdassids. In 1086 it became part of the *Seljuk Empire under the control of Tutush, brother of Sultan Malikshāh, and then of his son Ridwān (1095-1113). When the Franks founded the States of Edessa and *Antioch in 1098, the territory of Aleppo was directly threatened. In 1128 the Turkish emir of Mosul, Zengi, established himself at Aleppo and consolidated Upper Mesopotamia and northern Syria under his authority, the first step towards Arab reunification. His son Nūr al-Dīn (1146-1174) continued his work from Aleppo, taking possession of Damascus (1154) and then Egypt (1169). Under *Saladin (1174-1193), Aleppo remained the region's third city after *Cairo and Damascus. In the 13th c., under the *Ayyubids, the town, protected by its restored citadel, extended beyond the ramparts, but family quarrels and dissensions within the army prevented it resisting the *Mongol invasion. The city was conquered and completely sacked in 1260. Retaken by the *Mamluks, it took more than a century to recover and not until the start of the 15th c. did it regain its prosperity.

The region of Aleppo, relatively fertile, produced cereals, olives, cotton and fruits. From *Iraq and Upper Mesopotamia it received the products of the East. From the Byzantine period and then under the Seljuks, it also traded with Anatolia. To the south, its merchants frequented Damascus and its products reached the ports of the Egyptian coast. Finally, in the 13th c., the peaceful co-existence established with the Franks allowed the Venetians to possess an establishment at Aleppo.

The population of Aleppo remained largely *Shi'ite from the 10th to the mid 12th century. After that, the *Sunni restoration brought about by Nūr al-Dīn, particularly through the construction of a great number of *madrasas*, colleges for the teaching of Sunni law and religious science, bore fruit, and in the 13th c. the two most influential communities were the Shafi'ites and the Hanifites. Aleppo became a very important cultural centre, and meeting-place of numerous professors and their students, while an important Jewish and Christian minority managed to maintain itself there.

J. Sauvaget, *Alep*, Paris, 1941. – J. Sauvaget, "Ḥalab", *EI(E)*, 3, 1971, 85-90. – Y. Tabbaa, *Constructions of power and piety in medieval Aleppo*, University Park (PA), 1997. – A.M. Eddé, *La principauté ayyoubide d'Alep (579/1183-658/1260)*, Stuttgart, 1999 (*Freiburger Islamstudien*, 21).

Anne-Marie Eddé

**ALEXANDER II, POPE (*c.*1010/1015-1073).** Anselmo da Baggio,son of a leading Milanese family, was educated from his youth at the cathedral school of *Milan. In 1056, thanks to the support of the Emperor *Henry III and Duke Godfrey of *Lorraine-Tuscany, he was appointed to the episcopal see of *Lucca. He kept this post throughout his life, even after his accession to the papacy. In his *diocese he worked in favour of reform by promoting the common life of *clerics, encouraging the veneration of saints, building St Martin's cathedral and reorganising the exploitation of episcopal lands. Being close to the circle of Roman reformers, he was sent to Milan as papal *legate with St *Peter Damian to appease the conflict between the archbishop and the *Patarine movement, of which he was long wrongly considered the initiator.

In 1063 he succeeded *Nicholas II. He had been chosen for his good relations with the imperial court, at the instigation of archdeacon Hildebrand, the real strongman of the papacy now emerging. Alexander II had to face the revolt of a pro-imperial aristocratic faction and the *schism of Honorius II, elected at Basel on 28 Oct 1061. The conflict was regulated in 1064 at the council of Mantua, convened by Archbishop Anno II of Cologne, *chancellor of the Empire.

Once installed, the *pope pursued his predecessor's efforts in the matter of disciplinary reform. The length of his pontificate permitted a reorganisation of Roman power; thus, the keeping of registers of letters was resumed in his reign. The decisions of Roman *synods, meeting at regular dates, were imposed more and more firmly in southern *Italy, previously oriented towards Byzantium. Great attention was given to *Spain where the *Mozarabic liturgy gave way to the *Roman liturgy. The first *indulgence for the warriors of the *Reconquest (1063), the giving of the standard of St Peter (*vexillum sancti Petri*) to various war leaders engaged in Spain and southern Italy, as well as to *William the Conqueror (1066), soon prepared the way for crusading zeal.

Though Alexander II's policy had none of the extremism of his successors, there was no lack of tensions between the Holy See and the *Empire. The conflict worsened from 1071 over the see of Milan, for which each of the powers supported a candidate. Atto, the candidate elected, who was close to Rome, had to flee from Milan. During Lent 1073, the pope ended by *excommunicating five of the emperor's advisers. Shortly after, at the heart of the crisis, Alexander II died, leaving *Gregory VII the task of regulating this conflict, harbinger of the *Investiture Contest.

A. R. Calderoni Masetti, "Anselmo da Baggio e la cattedrale di Lucca", *ASNSP*, 3rd series, 7, 1977, 91-116. – T. Schmidt, *Alexander II (1061-1073) und die römische Reformsgruppe seiner Zeit*, Stuttgart, 1977 ("Papst und Papstum", 11). – F. J. Schmale, "Synoden Papst Alexanders II (1061-1073): Anzahl, Termine, Entscheidungen", *AHC*, 11, 1979, 307-338. – T. Schmidt, "Alexandre II", *DHP*, 1994.

Pierre Kerbrat

**ALEXANDER III, POPE (died 1181).** Contemporary sources state that Rolando was the son of a Sienese (Ranutius). His attachment to the Bandinelli family appears only in 14th-c. Sienese chronicles. The future *pope has long been identified, apparently wrongly, with one of the great professors of law at *Bologna, *magister* Rolandus, author of a very important **summa*. But there is no clue allowing us to confirm that Rolando taught canon law at Bologna; *Huguccio speaks only of his teaching theology (*divina pagina*).

A *canon of *Pisa, he was appointed *cardinal (1150) and *chancellor of the Roman church (1153) by *Eugenius III. While *legate at the imperial diet of Besançon (1157), he was the protagonist and witness of a grave incident: having to translate a letter of Pope *Adrian IV, the imperial *chancellor Rainald of Dassel rendered the word *beneficium* by "*fief"; one of the two legates (perhaps Rolando himself), exasperated, exclaimed: "From whom then does the emperor hold the *Empire if not from the lord pope?". On the imperial side too, the reaction was very strong: the Count Palatine of *Wittelsbach even wanted to take the cardinal's life.

After the death of Adrian IV (at *Anagni, 1 Sept 1159), Rolando was elected pope by the majority of the cardinals (Rome, 7 Sept). His refusal incited a small number of cardinals favourable to *Frederick Barbarossa to elect instead the Roman cardinal Ottaviano Monticelli. But, his electors having maintained their decision, Rolando ended by accepting the office. Elected by at least four cardinal-bishops out of six, Alexander III could consider himself the legitimate pope. The emperor's decision to have the *election of Victor IV confirmed by a *council meeting at Pavia (15 Feb 1160) provoked a *schism that would last 18 years.

Alexander III sought refuge in France: at *Tours he called a council (1163) that had important legislative consequences. Peace between Barbarossa and the pope was sealed in Venice, 24 July 1177; the emperor kissed the pope's feet and performed his duty as *écuyer*. After ten years of exile, the pope could solemnly enter *Rome in 1178, and a year later, he held one of the most important *councils of the Middle Ages, at the *Lateran.

Alexander III produced a legislative work of extraordinary breadth (notably on *marriage) and defined with particular depth the doctrinal foundations of papal *authority. Clarity of expression and rigour of argument assured it lasting success; 470 *Decretals form the *Corpus iuris canonici.*

In summer 1179 the citizens of Rome elected a new *antipope, Innocent (III), and obliged Alexander to leave Rome. Old and sick, he died at Civita Castellana on 30 Aug 1181.

M. Pacaut, *Alexandre III*, Paris, 1956. – M. Baldwin, *Alexander III and the Twelfth Century*, Glen Rock, 1968. – R. Somerville, *Pope Alexander III and the Council of Tours, 1163*, Berkeley (CA), 1977, 27-29. *Rolando Bandinelli papa Alessandro III*, Siena, 1986. – I.S. Robinson, *The Papacy, 1073-1198*, Cambridge, 1990. – A. Paravicini Bagliani, *HChr*, 5, 1993.

Agostino Paravicini Bagliani

**ALEXANDER IV, POPE (*c.*1185-1261).** Reginald was a son of Philip, lord of Jenne, with possessions at *Subiaco and in the diocese of *Anagni. According to *Matthew Paris, he was the nephew of Pope *Gregory IX. A *canon of Anagni cathedral perhaps from 1208, he was already in contact with the papal court under *Honorius III. He very soon bore the title of *magister*, which seems to indicate that he had studied at university, though we have no information on this. *Chaplain to the pope (1221), Reginald was one of the main collaborators of Cardinal Ugolino, the future Gregory IX, whom he accompanied on his important legation in northern Italy. By appointing him firstly cardinal-deacon of Sant'Eustachio, then cardinal-bishop of Ostia, the pope gave him the cardinalician *titles that had been his own. Reginald was also placed in charge of the Apostolic *Camera. For the young *cardinal,

Gregory IX's pontificate was a period of intense diplomatic activity which made him one of the key figures of the *Curia. Between 1231 and 1232 he formed excellent relations with the Emperor *Frederick II. At the time of the transfer of the Curia to *Lyon (1245), *Innocent IV asked him to stay at Rome as apostolic vicar. Elected *pope on 12 Dec 1254, Alexander IV spent the whole of his pontificate outside Rome, then under the rule of Senator Brancaleone.

On many levels, his pontificate continued that of Innocent IV, notably towards the Latin East and the Empire of *Nicaea-Constantinople. With a view to *union with the Greeks, he opened negotiations, unfruitful, with the Emperor *Theodore II Lascaris; he conferred on the leader of the *Maronites the title of patriarch of Antioch. Alexander IV was the first pope to establish that the inquisitors could combat magical practices "manifestly" linked to *heresy. These particular cases concerned mainly divination and *sorcery, still vaguely defined, but, in general, the pope reaffirmed that "it is against heresy that the inquisitors must engage all their forces". In his actions, Alexander IV remained equally faithful to the commitments made in the course of his career as a cardinal. Thus he favoured the *Franciscans (he addressed some 40 *bulls to them), canonizing St *Clare and restoring the privileges suppressed by his predecessor. In particular, Alexander IV firmly took on the defence of the *mendicant orders in the conflict with the *secular clergy. On his death at *Viterbo, 25 May 1261, the papacy passed for a short decade into the hands of two prelates subject to the king of France.

*Les Registres d'Alexandre IV (1254-1261)*, C. Bourel de La Roncière (ed.) *et al.*, Paris, 1895-1959. – *Acta Alexandri P.P. IV, 1254-1261*, T.T. Haluscynskyj (ed.), M.M. Wojnar (ed.), Rome 1966.

A. Paravicini Bagliani, *Cardinali di Curia e familie cardinalizie*, 1, Padua, 1972, 51 f. – I.S. Robinson, *The Papacy, 1073-1198*, Cambridge, 1990. – A. Paravicini Bagliani, *HChr*, 5, 1993.

Agostino Paravicini Bagliani

**ALEXANDER NEVSKY (1220-1263).** Prince of *Novgorod (1228-1252), grand prince of *Vladimir (1252-1263). Son of Grand Prince Iaroslav Vsevolodovich, holder of a hereditary principality, Pereyaslavl'-Zalesskii, Alexander began his career at Novgorod, not without some interruptions due to the struggles of rival factions. One of the roles of the prince at Novgorod was to command the army, and it was as a military leader that Alexander distinguished himself: he managed several times to avoid the danger presented by Lithuanian raids (though he could not prevent the principality of his father-in-law Polock from passing under Lithuanian rule) and he repulsed Swedish and German incursions. Two of these combats, little attested by other sources, are fully described in the Life of Alexander. The first opposed the Novgorodians to the Swedes in 1240 at the mouth of the Neva (whence the surname *Nevsky*), the second to the *Teutonic Knights on the frozen waters of lake Peipus (1242), near *Pskov which had momentarily fallen into enemy hands. But neither of these seems to have had the importance accorded them by historiography, on the credit of a single source.

On the death of his father (1246), Alexander turned his ambition towards the grand principality of Vladimir. To obtain this, for six years he opposed his uncle and especially his brothers Andrei and Iaroslav who, like Prince *Daniel of Halych, favoured resistance to the *Mongols. Alexander, by contrast, was supported by the khan of the *Golden Horde, and after his brothers were defeated by a Mongol troop he was enthroned as grand prince of Vladimir (1252) and exercised power, directly or indirectly, over the whole of Northern *Russia, from now on cut off from Southern *Rus'. The circumstances of his accession to the status of grand prince had predetermined his policy: unfailing loyalty to the Mongols, which necessitated frequent and exhausting journeys to the Horde; pursuit of the defence of the western frontier. In both cases Alexander benefited, in the person of Metropolitan Cyril II, from the support of the Church, which had gained numerous fiscal privileges from the Mongols and had reason, after the fourth *crusade, to nourish anti-Latin feelings. The episode related in the Life, in which Alexander got rid of an envoy from Rome, is revealing of this attitude. His local canonization at Vladimir – but not at Novgorod – attests the limits of his reputation.

Even in our own day, in historiography, three images of this prince confront us: the valiant warrior whose sword stopped a massive offensive of the Latins conceived by Rome, the skilful diplomat who was able to lighten the consequences of the Mongol yoke, and the faithful servant of the foreign occupier.

W. Philipp, W. Leitsch, *FOEG*, 18, 1973, 55-72; *ibid.*, 25, 1978, 202-216. – J. Fennell, *The Crisis of Medieval Russia, 1200-1304*, London, 1983.

Vladimir Vodoff

**ALEXANDER OF HALES (before 1186-1245).** A *Franciscan, born at Hales Owen in Shropshire before 1186, master of arts before 1210, Alexander of Hales was, according to *Roger Bacon (*Opus minus*, London, 1859, 325-329), a good man, rich, a great *archdeacon of Coventry, loaded with honours, one of the great masters of *theology of his time. He kept a school at *Paris in *c.*1220-1221 and was the first to take *Peter Lombard's **Sentences* as his basic teachng text. In 1229, during the students' strike, he was bursar of the *masters and students who took refuge at Angers. On his return to Paris at the start of the school year 1236-1237 he took the Franciscan habit. This caused a Parisian sensation because of Alexander's importance and because the Order of Friars Minor was new and somewhat mistrusted. On his entry, the enthusiastic friars immediately gave him authority over the whole *studium*.

He arrived with a knowledge, a technique and a project that made him the creator of the Franciscan school. His learning was vast. During his years as master, he had assimilated the work of his predecessors and colleagues, *William of Auxerre with his *Summa aurea*, *Philip the Chancellor with his *Summa de bono*. He had to his credit an innovative work, since he had carried over a tried method from the reading of Scripture to that of the *Liber sententiarum* with the *Glossa in quatuor libris sententiarum*. His *Quaestiones disputatae "antequam esset frater"* initiated a search for new solutions to the trinitarian problem, notably by clarifying the notion of order among the divine persons.

Alexander also contributed a new technique. He had assimilated *Aristotle's *Organon* as the sole technique valid for intellectual research that would be profitable in *theology, and he had engineered a project, that of bringing together the knowledge of his time in a vast theological *encyclopedia. He conceived of the idea of the **summa* to which the Franciscan *studium* gave his name: *Summa fratris Alexandri*. His assistants, among them *John of La Rochelle, and his bachelors, among them *Eudes Rigaud, set to work and in 1245, at Alexander's death, the *Summa* represented a monument whose wealth of documentation and approach to the most difficult problems represented a considerable step forward. Alexander had provided the material, John of La Rochelle was the producer. Students and masters drew on it, including *Bonaventure and *Thomas Aquinas.

Hardly had he entered the Franciscan Order than Alexander was led to draw up, in 1241-1242, with John of La Rochelle, Eudes Rigaud, Robert of La Bassée and the *guardian of the Paris *convent, Geoffroy of Brie, the *Expositio quatuor magistrorum super regulam fratrum minorum.*

His still unedited works include the *Quaestiones disputatae "postquam fuit frater"* and the **Postillae in quatuor Evangelia.*

Alexandri Halensis, *Summa Theologica*, 3 vol., Quaracchi, 1924-1948 [*Summa fratris Alexandri*]. – *Expositio quatuor magistrorum super regulam fratrum minorum*, L. Oliger (ed.), Rome, 1950. – Magistri Alexandri Halensis, *Glossa in quatuor Libros Sententiarum Petri Lombardi*, 4 vol., Quaracchi, 1951-1957. – Magistri Alexandri de Hales, *Quaestiones disputatae "antequam esset frater"*, 3 vol., Quaracchi, 1960.

V. Doucet, "Maîtres franciscains de Paris", P. Glorieux, *Répertoire des Maîtres en théologie de Paris au XIIIe siècle*, *AFH*, Suppl., 27, 1934, 534-538. – E. Gossman, *Metaphysik und Heilsgeschichte*, Munich, 1964. – F. J. Catania, *Knowledge of God in Alexander of Hales and John Dun Scotus*, Kalamazoo, 1966. – W. H. Principe, *The Theology of the Hypostatic Union in the Early Thirteenth Century,* Vol. 2, Toronto, 1967. – V. Marcolino, *Das Altes Testament in der Heilsgeschichte*, Münster, 1970. – K.B. Osborne, "Alexander of Hales: Precursor and Promoter of Franciscan Theology", *The History of Franciscan Theology*, St Bonaventure (NY), 1994, 1-38.

Jacques-Guy Bougerol

**ALEXANDER OF ROES (late 13th c. - early 14th c.).** Son of a patrician family of *Cologne, in *c.*1280 Alexander of Roes entered the entourage of the Roman *cardinal Giacomo Colonna, to whom he dedicated the *Memoriale de prerogativa romani imperii.* His *noticia seculi* was finished early in 1288. The *Pavo*, a parable poem completed three years earlier, also expressed his political concerns: the ascent of the national States, which marked the decline of the imperial idea; and the papacy's understanding with the king of *France, which imperilled the tripartite equilibrium of the world: to the Romans, *sacerdotium*; to the French, *studium*; to the Germans, *regnum.*

H. Grundmann, H. Heimpel, *Die Schriften des Alexander von Roes*, Stuttgart, 1958. – M. Hamm, "Alexander von Roes", *VerLex*, 1, 1978, 222-226.

Agostino Paravicini Bagliani

**ALEXANDRIA**

**The town.** Alexandria was founded in 331 BC at the west end of the Egyptian delta. Under the *Byzantine Empire it was the "town" *par excellence*, as compared to the countryside (*chôra*) that constituted *Egypt, so much so that the famous men who came from that town were distinguished from their homonyms by the surname *politikos*. With the arrival of the Arab invaders, the situation changed: the Arabs set up their seat of government at Fusṭāṭ (from the Latin *fossatum* [ditch surrounding a military camp]) near what is now Old *Cairo. For some time Alexandria kept its former privileges, such as that of having a particular government (often Christian) called, as in the time of the Byzantine regime, *augustalios*, alongside a purely military governor, delegated by the central authority at al-Fusṭāṭ; but – and this shows clearly that Alexandria was no longer the capital – control of the whole country belonged to al-Fusṭāṭ alone.

At the start of the Arab period, Alexandria was called a "frontier town": as such, it had its own status, which continued to increase as Alexandria became the sole gateway for relations, commercial and otherwise, with the outside world. In particular, especially to begin with, the Arabs were dependent on the *Copts for all their naval requirements: the 7th-c. expeditions to *Cyprus, *Rhodes and *Sicily were all launched from Alexandria.

Likewise, Hellenistic influence continued to diminish, at least on the level of literary output, as the town became gradually more militarized and Arabized. Greek-speaking authors were few; some medical works were transmitted to the Arabs by Alexandrian scholars, but their role was much less important in this sphere than that of the East Syrians at *Baghdad; the same went for Arabic translation of Greek philosophical texts. But if literary output was gradually diminishing, the Greek language was always in use: we have bilingual (Greek-Arabic) *papyri up to 996, and this would be the language used by the (Coptic) patriarchal chancery: we possess an 8th-c. festal letter (*i.e.* announcing the date of Easter) written in Greek, as also were the synodal letters by which the patriarch of Alexandria announced his election to his colleague of *Antioch (just as the Roman pontiff has his documents addressed to the Catholic world drawn up in Latin, though the Vatican has long used Italian). It is true that only an Arabic version of these synodal letters exists, still unedited: the substratum seems to have been Greek, though the surviving Arabic version was established on a Coptic translation. That very probably lasted until about 1047/1048, the date of the first canons of a Coptic patriarch (Christodulos) drawn up in Arabic.

**The patriarchates.** The *council of Chalcedon (451) had been the cause of a schism, leading to the consecration of two *patriarchs of Alexandria. One of them was Greek (or "Chalcedonian") and was appointed by the Emperor *Heraclius as both patriarch and prefect of Egypt: as such, he had to sign the surrender of the Egyptian province and flee to *Constantinople before the invading troops. There were no Greek patriarchs from 651 to 742, but only resident or non-resident *topoteretes* (substitutes), and the patriarchs appointed between 742 and 1846 usually resided at Constantinople. They lived in Egypt again from 1846, the Hellene community having been increased by the great number of emigrants coming especially from Turkey and the islands, attracted by the hope of business. At that time, the Greek patriarch resumed the title not just of patriarch of Alexandria, but of all Africa.

The Coptic patriarch resided at Alexandria until *c.*965, after which he lived in various delta villages until *c.*1061, when he settled at Old Cairo, no doubt in order to be in touch with the civil authorities. At one time he was entitled archbishop of Fusṭāṭ and Miṣr (this word designated all Egypt or just Cairo, traditionally founded in 969), which led to friction with the titular bishop of the see of "Babylon" (Old Cairo). He later resumed the title of patriarch of Alexandria.

J. Faivre, "Alexandrie", *DHGE*, 2, 1912, 289-369. – A. Papadakis, "Alexandria, patriarchate of", *ODB*, 1, 61. – P. M. Fraser, "Alexandria, Christian and Medieval", *Coptic Encyclopedia*, 1, New York, 1991, 88-92 (bibliography).

René-Georges Coquin †

**ALEXIS, LEGEND OF SAINT.** The starting-point for the legend of St Alexis was probably the existence at Edessa, around the 5th c., of an ascetic famous for his extreme poverty and humility. Starting from this historical source, a *Life* was written in Syriac: it told the story of a "man of God" (anonymous in this first version) of a noble Roman family who, fleeing wealth and the marriage arranged by his parents, settled at Edessa as a stranger and mendicant, passing his nights in prayer; falling ill, he died at the hospital where he had been taken and was buried in the cemetery for indigent strangers; his sanctity being revealed, Bishop Rabbula had his tomb opened but the body had disappeared. Bishop Rabbula spent the rest of his life serving the poor and strangers, and the cult of the "man of God of Edessa" spread through the East.

Reaching *Constantinople in the 9th c., the legend was transformed. While the Oriental version made the man of God an image of Christ living as a poor stranger on earth, the Byzantine version insisted on the romantic side of the unknown saint: the "man of God", who received the name Alexis, saw his sanctity "proclaimed" at Edessa by an icon of the Mother of God, and was obliged to flee Edessa to preserve his humility. He returned to Rome where he spent the rest of his life as an anonymous mendicant in his parents' house. At his death, a voice from heaven revealed both his identity and his sanctity. This legend, which recentred the saint in Rome (his stay at Edessa being just a parenthesis), was popularized by a liturgical canon of Joseph the Hymnographer (*c.*810-*c.*883). It then migrated to Rome in the 10th c., through the establishment in that town of the Greco-Latin monastery of St Boniface. In the Latin versions of the legend, this church of St Boniface became the place of Alexis's marriage at the start of the *Life* and his burial at the end.

The legend was very popular in the West and in the Slav countries and there is even an Ethiopian version (in which Alexis has become the son of the Emperor Theodosius II). St Alexis is celebrated on 17 March in the Byzantine churches, and was on 17 July in the Latin rite until his suppression from the Roman *calendar in 1969.

F. M. Esteves Pereira, "La Légende grecque de l'homme de Dieu saint Alexis", *AnBoll* 19, 1900, 241 f. – J. P. Kirsch, "Alexis", *DHGE*, 2, 1914, 379-381. – C. E. Stebbins, "Les Origines de la légende de saint Alexis", *RBPH* 51, 1973, 497-507. – H. J. W. Drijvers, "Hellenistic and Oriental Origins", *The Byzantine Saint*, S. Hackel (ed.), Birmingham, 1981, 25-33.

Marie-Hélène Congourdeau

**ALEXIS OF MOSCOW (died 1378).** Metropolitan of *Kiev and all *Rus' (1354-1378), of Russian origin, and residing like his two predecessors at *Moscow, St Alexis worked to strengthen the Church. He favoured monasticism, but also Muscovite power, defending the rights of Dmitrii Donskoi during his minority (1358-1366), supporting him by any means against his opponents, guaranteeing the pro-*Mongol policy of the princes of Moscow and opposing the creation, in favour of *Cyprian, of a rival metropolis in *Lithuania. The first churchman to identify the cause of the Church with that of the princes of Moscow, he contributed to the process of dividing the former metropolis of Kiev.

J. Meyendorff, *Byzantium and the Rise of Russia*, Cambridge, 1981.

Vladimir Vodoff

**ALFONSINE TABLES.** A set of astronomical tables reputed to have been worked out at the prompting of *Alfonso X of Castile, the *Alfonsine Tables* are in fact the work of a Parisian team of scholars (Jean de Murs, Jean de Lignières, John of Saxony) – doubtless linked to each other by master-pupil relations – who between 1320 and 1327 established tables that bear no resemblance to what is known of Alfonso X's astronomical work. A second problem posed by the *Alfonsine Tables* is that of their content: the *editio princeps* (Venice, 1483) published under this title a vast collection of tables and canons (way of using tables) of which the actual *Alfonsine Tables* form only a part.

The object of the *Tables* was very limited: to bring together the numerical elements that would allow the longitudes of the planets to be calculated no matter what the date, despite the apparent irregularity of the planetary movements. Their organisation was part of a tradition that renounced Ptolemy's *Easy Tables* and which was developed by Arab astronomers whose works were translated or adapted into Latin before the 14th c. (tables of al-Khwarizmi, al-Battani, Azarquiel); the main work involved was to tabulate firstly the mean co-ordinates of the planets, co-ordinates that varied regularly over time, and secondly the corrections, called equations, which, according to a complex process, were applied to the mean co-ordinates to transform them into true co-ordinates.

If the organisation of the *Alfonsine Tables* thus remained largely traditional, their originality lay in very technical fields: systematic sexagesimalization of the expression of dates and mean co-ordinates, which gave the tables a real universality of application (in all calendars and in all places); adoption of a list of partly original equations; choice of tropic positions rather than sidereal positions for mean co-ordinates, contrary to what was done, following the Toledo tables, by the tables most commonly used before 1320; and especially the application to the discrepancy between the sidereal sphere and the tropic sphere of an altogether original movement that combined, with entirely new revolutions and periodicities, the slow movement of precession defined by Ptolemy and the so-called movement of access and recess devised by Thebit ben Qurra.

The *Alfonsine Tables*' qualities of universality, presentation and convenience of use, and their apparent precision, earned the Parisian astronomers' work a prodigious success, which made the *astronomy of the 14th to16th centuries an exclusively Alfonsine astronomy, ensuring the reputation of a king to whom they owed nothing. One of the most effective architects of this success was John of Saxony, whose canons supplemented the *Alfonsine Tables* in an almost institutional way; each of the three men responsible for the tables produced his own canons, but while two of them enjoyed only a marginal manuscript circulation, that of John of Saxony's canons was truly exceptional; naturally they are found accompanying the *Tables* in the latter's *editio princeps*.

*Les Tables alphonsines avec les canons de Jean de Saxe, édition, traduction et commentaire*, E. Poulle (ed.), 1984 ("SHM"). – E. Poulle, "The Alfonsine Tables and Alfonso X of Castile", *Journal for the History of Astronomy*, 19, 1988, 97-120.

Emmanuel Poulle

**ALFONSO V OF ARAGON (*c.*1396-1458).** The eldest son of Ferdinand (1412-1416), first king of *Aragon and count of *Barcelona of the Castilian house of Trastámara, Alfonso V succeeded his father in 1416. In 1419 he convoked the **Cortes* or *representative assemblies to finance his onerous Mediterranean programme; but his subjects demanded a greater part in the government, monopolized by his Castilian officials. In 1420 he waged war on *Genoa, pacifying a revolted *Sardinia, but failing to conquer *Corsica. In 1423 he tried unsuccessfully to take *Naples from Louis III of Anjou, heir of Queen Joanna II; in reprisal he sacked *Marseille, taking away the *relics of St Louis of Anjou. In 1435 the *Angevins of Naples, allies of *Milan and the papacy, inflicted on him the naval defeat of Ponza. During his captivity, however, he turned his gaoler Filippo Maria *Visconti, duke of Milan, into an ally: he conquered Naples in 1442. In Albania, he lent his support to *Scanderbeg against the *Turks, and tried to organise a crusade against them, but was taken up with a new conflict against Genoa (1454-1458). He never returned to his Hispanic principalities, which were ruled by his wife Maria of Castile. In *Catalonia, the situation deteriorated because of the revolt of the *remença*, enslaved peasantry, and the struggles between the Biga and the Busca at Barcelona; war against *Castile (1445-1454) aggravated the situation. On his death in 1458, Alfonso's brother John II inherited his Iberian states, while Ferrante, his illegitimate son by Lucrezia of Alagno, retained the kingdom of Naples.

The essential part of Alfonso's political activities took place in *Italy. He subjected Neapolitan institutions to increased centralism, granting the seven great offices of the Crown of Naples to his Iberian relations. His fiscal policy, like his monopoly of transhumance routes, met with strong opposition: from 1444 to 1446, the lords revolted. The king became a generous patron of the arts at Naples, where he surrounded himself with prestigious *humanists like Lorenzo *Valla, Leonardi Bruni of Arezzo, Leonardo Giovanni Pontano or Antonio Beccadelli of Palermo, author of a *De dictis et factis Alphonsi regis Aragonum*. He enriched his *library, encouraging the rise of the sciences: his major-domo Manuel Diez composed the *Treatise on horses*. In 1446 he ordered the construction of the Castel Nuovo, his fortified palace. The Majorcan architect Guillem Sagrera set the stamp of Catalan *Flamboyant Gothic on it. Pietro da Milano, helped by numerous sculptors, designed the antiquizing portal, with the aim of exalting the royal person, power and victories; his work is in the spirit of the *Renaissance. In 1449 the monarch invited the painter *Pisanello, trained at *Verona; he enriched his library with several Flemish pictures. Alfonso V thus forged the image of a humanist king, a friend to arts and letters.

A. Ryder, *Alfonso the Magnanimous King of Aragon, Naples and Sicily, 1396-1458*, Oxford, 1990.

Martin Aurell

**ALFONSO I OF ASTURIAS (died 757).** King of Asturias (739-757), son of Peter, Visigothic duke of Cantabria, and son-in-law of the semi-legendary Pelayo who by the victory of Covadonga (722) put an end to Muslim expansion and made the Asturian mountains a bastion of Christian resistance, Alfonso I was able to profit from political circumstances (a general rising of the Berbers [741], then a great drought [748-753] leading to the relaxation of military pressure from *Cordova) to extend his rule in all directions, in particular west towards *Galicia and south towards the Duero valley. Unable to hold the conquered area, he razed fortresses and towns, precipitated the exodus of the Muslim population and transferred north of the cordillera the Christians of Galicia and Meseta. Historiography long attributed to him the project of turning the territory north of the Duero into a desert. Though archaeology today attests the permanence of certain sites, the depopulation was still severe enough to require a new colonization in the 9th century.

The immigration of southern populations favoured the adoption of Visigothic traditions by the Asturian kingdom: Alfonso appears the true founder of the kingdom of Asturias.

Y. Bonnaz, "Divers aspects de la continuité wisigothique dans la monarchie asturienne", *Mélanges de la Casa de Velázquez*, Madrid, 1976, 81-99. – Y. Bonnaz, *Chroniques asturiennes (fin IXe siècle)*, Paris, 1987.

Michel Zimmermann

**ALFONSO VI OF CASTILE (1040-1109).** King from 1065 to 1109, firstly of *León, then in 1072 of León, *Castile and *Galicia, which, separated by his father, he reunified, from 1077 Alfonso entitled himself "*Imperator totius Hispaniae*". He annexed the Rioja and conquered *Toledo in 1085, becoming the most powerful ruler in the peninsula. He received tributes (*parias*) from the kingdoms of the *ta'ifas*.

He resisted the advance of the *Almoravids who defeated him at Zallaca in 1086 and Consuegra in 1097; in 1102 they took back *Valencia, which the *Cid had conquered for him in 1094.

Alfonso sought spouses of high lineage from beyond the *Pyrenees. The first king of León to strike *coinage, he conceded numerous *fueros* and strengthened ties with the abbey of *Cluny.

C. Estepa Díez, *El Reinado de Alfonso VI*, Madrid, 1985. – B. F. Reilly, *The Kingdom of Leon-Castilla under King Alfonso VI (1065-1109)*, Princeton (NJ), 1988.

Denis Menjot

**ALFONSO VIII OF CASTILE (1155-1214).** King of *Castile from 1158 to 1214, Alfonso VIII married Eleanor, daughter of *Henry II Plantagenet. He recaptured Cuenca from the Muslims in 1177. Defeated at Alarcos in 1195 by the *Almohads who took back from him all the places south of the Tagus, he took his revenge at Las *Navas de Tolosa in 1212.

He fought the kings of *León and *Portugal for control of frontier places, and took from *Navarre the left bank of the Ebro, Guipuzcoa and Alava with its capital Vitoria in 1200.

In 1172, Alfonso struck the first gold *maravedis*. He granted and confirmed *fueros* to Basque towns, and founded the monastery of *Las Huelgas at *Burgos in 1187.

J. González, *El Reino de Castilla en la época de Alfonso VIII*, 1946 (3 vol.; "CSIC"). – *Alfonso VIII y su época*, Madrid, 1992.

Denis Menjot

**ALFONSO X THE WISE (1221-1284).** King of *Castile and *León from 1252 to 1284. Son of Beatrice of Swabia, Alfonso X was elected Emperor of the Holy Roman Empire in 1257, but struggled vainly until 1275 to be crowned. He established a protectorate over the kingdom of Murcia in 1243 and conquered the kingdom of Niebla in 1262. He put down the revolt of the Muslims of Andalusia and Murcia in 1266 and organised the repopulation of these conquered territories; he also founded Villareal in 1255.

Alfonso granted *fairs at Alcalá de Henares, Badajoz, Murcia, *Seville, Guadalajara and Alcaraz. In 1272 he institutionalized the association of transhumant stockraisers, the *Mesta*. He established new direct and indirect taxes, and devalued the *coinage in 1265 and 1272.

At his prompting was organised the most formidable corpus of legal texts ever formed in Castile, from which emerged the *Espéculo*, the *Fuero Real* and the *Siete Partidas*, a monument of universal legal literature. Upon his initiative was created a literary work of encyclopedic character in which compilations and *translations from Arabic mingled with original productions: treatises of *astronomy, histories, written in Castilian (*Estoria de España* and the *Grande e General Estoria*), poems (the celebrated *Cantigas written in Galician*), treatises on *hunting, Book of the game of chess. He took Solomon as royal model.

King Alfonso X the Wise surrounded by his counsellors. Manuscript of *Las Cantigas de Santa Maria* (fol. 5 r°), late 13th c. Madrid, Escorial, Royal Library

A. Ballesteros Beretta, *Alfonso X el Sabio*, Barcelona-Murcia, 1963. – W. F. Von Schoen, *Alfonso de Castilla*, Madrid, 1966. – *Alfonso X, Catalogue expo. Tolède*, Madrid, 1984. – J. Valdeón, *Alfonso X el Sabio*, Valladolid, 1986. – *Alfonso X of Castile, the Learned King (1221-1284)*, F. Marquis-Villaneuva (ed.), C. Alberto Vega (ed.), Cambridge (MA), 1990. – M. González Jiménez, *Alfonso X el Sabio (1252-1284)*, Palencia, 1993 ("Corona de España. Reyes de Castilla y León", 2). – J. F. O'Callaghan, *The Learned King: the Reign of Alfonso of Castile*, Philadelphia, 1993. – J. F. O'Callaghan, *Alfonso X, the Cortes, and Government in Medieval Spain*, Aldershot, 1998.

Denis Menjot

**ALFONSO OF VALLADOLID (*c.*1270-1340).** A Jewish doctor of *Burgos, qualified in 1295, Alfonso of Valladolid (also called Abner of Burgos or Alfonso of Burgos), made desperate by the living conditions of the *Jews in exile, made a profession of Christian *faith in 1321. The first apostate to formulate an ideological justification of *conversion, he rejected the rationalist interpretations of the Torah and engaged in oral polemic with Jewish scholars. His *Moreh Zedek* survives in Castilian under the title *Mostrador de Justicia* (Master of Justice), as does his treatise *Minhat Kena'oth* (The Offering of Zeal) directed against Isaac Pulgar. His writings, along with *Raymond Martini's *Pugio Fidei* (Dagger of Faith), served as a source for polemics in Spanish Christian literature.

R. Chazan, "Maestre Alfonso of Valladolid and the New Missionizing", *REJ*, 143, 1-2, 1984, 83-94.

Sonia Fellous

**ALFONSO BUENHOMBRE (late 13th c. - 1353).** Alfonso Buenhombre (Alfonsus Bonihominis), a *Dominican missionary and polemist, born perhaps at *Toledo, led an adventurous life that took him notably to Egypt (1336), *Morocco (1337-1338) and Famagusta (1341). He was elected bishop of Morocco in 1344. His travels (and perhaps studies in one of the Dominican *studia linguarum*?) gave him a good knowledge of Arabic, allowing him to translate several texts: an apocryphal *History of the patriarch Joseph* (1336), a *Life* of St Anthony the Hermit (1341). He also presented as translations from Arabic a *Disputatio Abutalib Sarraceni et Samuelis Iudei* on the best religion (1339-40) and his best-known work, extremely widespread in the 14th c., the *Epistola rabbi Samuelis* (1339); in the latter case this is probably a fiction. This *Epistola* is an apology for the Christian faith, written in the character of a Jew addressing a co-religionist. We also owe him a *Tractatus contra malos medicos* (1342).

G. Meersseman, "La chronologie des voyages et des oeuvres du frère Alphonse Bonhomme", *AFH*, 10, 1940, 77-109. – T. Kaeppeli, *SOPMA*, 1, Rome, 1970, 48-55.

Gilbert Dahan

**ALFRED THE GREAT (849-899).** King of Wessex (871-899) and one of the greatest of *Anglo-Saxon kings. During his reign *England was under continual assault from *Viking armies; but through a combination of courage, brilliant military strategy and resourcefulness (he is credited with having designed an effective type of warship), Alfred was able eventually to defeat the Vikings and to establish a treaty (at Wedmore, 878) which secured peace from Viking attack for nearly a century. After the treaty Alfred set about re-establishing English *schools by inviting several foreign scholars (including the Welshman Asser, John the Old Saxon, and Grimbald of Saint-Bertin) to his court. With their help, Alfred himself translated into English a number of Latin works which in his view were essential to human knowledge: *Gregory the Great's *Regula pastoralis*, *Boethius's *De consolatione Philosophiae*,

Augustine's *Soliloquiae*, Orosius's *Historiae adversum paganos*, and the first fifty *psalms. He also established monasteries at Athelney and Shaftesbury.

S. Keynes, M. Lapidge, *Alfred the Great*, Harmondsworth, 1983. – A. J. Frantzen, *King Alfred*, Boston, 1986. – J.R. Maddicott, "Trade, Industry and the Wealth of King Alfred", *PaP*, 123, 1989, 3-51. – R. Abels, *Alfred the Great*, London, 1998.

Michael Lapidge

**ALGER OF LIÈGE (*c.*1070 - before 1136).** Monk and theologian. Formerly *deacon and **scholasticus* at *Liège, he was called to the service of the cathedral in 1101 by Bishop Otbert who made him his secretary, an office he kept under his successor Frederick. After Frederick's death in 1121, he joined *Cluny as a monk, became a priest and died before 1136. He is the author of two great treatises: *De sacramentis corporis et sanguinis dominici libri tres*, a remarkable defence of the dogma of the *Eucharist against *Berengar of Tours, and *De misericordia et iustitia*, in which he justifies the decisions of *Gregory VII on the relations of the Church and the *Empire and on simoniacs.

Algerus Leodiensis, *Opera*, *PL*, 180, 1855, 727-972.

L. Brigué, *Alger de Liège, un théologien de l'Eucharistie au début du XIIe siècle*, Paris, 1936.

André Cantin

**'ALĪ (*c.*598-661).** 'Alī son of Abū Talib, cousin and son-in-law of the prophet *Muḥammad, fourth *caliph, was born *c.*598 (*c.*23 before the *hejira) at *Mecca. Venerated by *Sunnis as well as *Shi'ites, but for markedly different reasons, and above all by mystics of all tendencies, he remains one of the most outstanding figures in *Islam. As a young adolescent, he was one of the first believers in Muḥammad's mission and soon joined him in his exile at *Medina. Soon after, he married the Prophet's daughter Fātima, during whose lifetime he took no other wife; from their marriage were born al-Hasan and al-Husayn. He took part in nearly all the military expeditions of Muḥammad's time; he showed, in particular during the battles of Badr, Khaybar and Hunayn, a bravery that later became legendary. During the reigns of the first two caliphs, Abū Bakr and 'Umar, Alī had no political responsibilities and took no part in any military expedition after the Prophet's death, even though the caliphate of 'Umar marked the beginning of the great Muslim conquests. If it is probable that he was solicited by the caliphs to give advice of a legal nature, by reason of his exemplary knowledge of the *Koran and the Prophetic Tradition, it is nevertheless doubtful whether this advice was followed in the political and economic spheres, especially by 'Umar who judged it probably too utopian for a State in full expansion. His opposition became more manifest under 'Uthmān, the third caliph. An intransigent believer in the scrupulous application of the Divine Law, 'Alī rebuked him many times for neglecting the scriptural *dicta*, going so far as to accuse him publicly of having introduced "blameworthy innovations" into the religion. His ambiguous attitude, sometimes favourable to the heterogeneous coalition that finally assassinated the caliph, ended by convincing the latter's partisans, particularly the powerful family of the *Umayyads, that he was an accomplice of the murderers. The opposition party, masters of the capital Medina, brought 'Alī to power, probably against his own wishes (656 [35 of the hejira]). The five years or so of 'Alī's caliphate were a succession of battles within a community torn apart by perpetual intrigues. He had to confront the rebellion led by his permanent enemy Āisha, the Prophet's widow, soon joined by the two Companions, Talha and al-Zubayr. It is hard to explain the reasons for this revolt, the more so since the individuals who led it were in part responsible for 'Uthmān's fate and were now demanding vengeance for his murder. The rebellion was put down in blood at the battle of the Camel. Equally obscure are the conditions which gave rise to the long conflict that set 'Alī against Mu'āwiya, head of the Umayyad family, cousin of 'Uthmān and governor of *Syria. After a week of a particularly bloody battle in the plain of Siffīn, the two parties agreed to resort to arbitration to determine whether or not 'Uthmān had been assassinated unjustly. If he had, 'Alī would lose his legitimacy. The procedure lasted long months. Meanwhile, 'Alī had to suppress at Nahrawān the seditious movement of the *Khārijites, believers in war to the death, who had arisen out of his own ranks. The arbitration ended in favour of the Umayyads, but 'Alī refused to submit to it, judging the sentence contrary to the Koran and the Tradition of the Prophet. During this time, Mu'āwiya had reconquered Egypt and Arabia, leaving 'Alī only the province of *Iraq. In 661 (40), 'Alī was stabbed in the *mosque of Kūfa by the Khārijite Ibn Muljam; he died of his wounds two days later and was buried not far from that town, in a place that later became the Shi'ite holy city of Najaf. Mu'āwiya became caliph, thus inaugurating the Umayyad period. The very contrasting portraits of 'Alī can be explained by the fact that his religious rigorism made him a mediocre politician. Faithful to the ascetic spirit of early Islam, he could not adapt to the requirements of the nascent Empire and lacked the political opportunism that made his predecessors or Mu'āwiya excellent diplomats. Venerated by the Sunnis because of his kinship with the Prophet and one of his most loyal Companions, 'Alī is considered by the Shi'ites as the personally designated successor of the Prophet, whose rights were usurped by the first caliphs. The first and father of the whole line of Shi'ite *imāms, 'Alī is perceived by the Shi'ites, and to a great extent by the mystics, not just as the prototype of the Muslim ideal but above all as an initiated sage, an inspired thaumaturge and the repositary of the esoteric content of the prophetic message. Some would even see in him a manifestation of the divine Attributes and Names. Numerous pronouncements of a mystical nature, public sermons, political addresses, poetry or wise sayings are attributed to him and have been collected, from very early on, in the compilations of Shi'ite traditions or in the *Nahj al-balāgha* (The way of maturity), a collection made in the 11th (5th) century.

L. Caetani, *AIs*, 9-10, 1926. – L. Veccia Vaglieri, "'Alī b. Abī Ṭālib", *EI(E)*, 1, 1960, 381-386. – H. Laoust, "Le rôle de Alī dans la sīra shiite", *REI*, 30, 1962. – J. Eliash, *Alī ibn Abī Tālib in ithnā asharī shii belief*, London, 1966. – E. Kohlberg, I. Poonawala, "Alī b. Abī Talib", *EIr*, 1983. – W. Madelung, *the Succession to Muḥammad*, Cambridge, 1997.

Mohammad Ali Amir-Moezzi

**ALL SAINTS.** The feast of All Saints was established in honour of the Virgin and the *martyr saints by Pope Boniface IV, and transferred to 1 Nov in the 9th century. In 609, the Pantheon was given to the Church by the Emperor Phocas and consecrated by Pope Boniface IV on 13 May to the Virgin and all the martyrs, under the name of *Sancta Maria ad martyres* (see *LP*, ed. Duchesne, I, 31). The feast of dedication was considered in Antiquity as that of the titular saint. Pope Gregory III (731-741) dedicated an altar at the far end of the main nave of *St Peter's basilica in honour of the Saviour, his mother, the holy apostles and all the martyr and confessor saints (*LP*, I, 417). In the 8th c., the Irish celebrated all the martyrs of the world on 17 April, and on 20 April all the saints and virgins of *Ireland, Britain and Europe, a feast placed, according to Eastern usage, close to *Easter. At the council of Riesbach in 798, Archbishop Arno of Salzburg (785-821) drew up the list of public holidays, including that of All Saints on 1 Nov, put on that day apparently in agreement with *Alcuin, a feast also appearing on that day in the *sacramentaries of *Saint-Martin at Tours, of which Alcuin was abbot from 796 to 804. It appears on the same day in the Metrical Calendar of York (late 8th c.). This feast prevailed in the Church in the 9th c., beginning with the Empire. In his martyrology, *Ado states that the celebration of this feast was prescribed in Gaul by the Emperor *Louis the Pious (814-840) at the request of Pope Gregory IV (827-844), who also on 1 Nov rededicated Sancta Maria Ad Martyres, though the **Liber pontificalis* does not mention this. The feast (solemn, with *vigil) is in any case attested in *Rome in the 10th c., when the town was open to Gallican influences. According to *Sicard of Cremona († 1215), Pope *Gregory VII suppressed the dedication of 13 May, keeping only that of 1 Nov. In the 13th c., the Dominican *Jacobus de Voragine in his **Golden Legend* assigned the feast four objectives: "First, to commemorate the consecration of a certain temple; second, to make up for omissions; third, to expiate our sins; fourth, to help us fulfil our vows" (ed. Graesse, *Legenda aurea*, CLXII [157]). The octave of the feast was instituted by *Sixtus IV (1471-1484).

A. Wilmart, "Un témoin anglo-saxon du calendrier métrique d'York", *RBen*, 46, 1934, 41-690. – J. Dubois, "La Toussaint", *VSB*, 11, 1954, 16-22. – P. Jounel, *Le Culte des saints dans les basiliques du Latran et du Vatican au XIIe siècle*, Rome, 1977, 103-106. – P. Jounel, *Le Renouveau du culte des saints dans la liturgie romaine*, Rome, 1986, 203-205. – L. Pietri, "Les Origines de la Toussaint", *Les Quatre Fleuves*, 25-26, Paris, 1988, 57-61.

Jean-Loup Lemaître

*Gospels. Wisdom between Prudence, Justice, Fortitude and Temperance.* 9th-c. miniature. Northern Franco-Insular School. Cambrai, Municipal Library (Ms 327, fol. 16 v°).

**ALLEGORY.** Starting from definitions inherited from ancient rhetoric, the Church *Fathers elucidated a properly theological conception of allegory. At the same time, following the example of late antique poetry, the writers of the Middle Ages composed works that we call allegorical.

Rhetoric bequeathed two definitions. One, very general, could apply to any trope: "Allegory is saying-something-else [*Allegoria est alieniloquium*]; we hear one thing and understand another" (*Isidore of Seville, *Etym.*, 1, 37, 22). The second makes allegory a continuous metaphor: "The shepherds shear their sheep: we transfer two words, shepherds and sheep, that of shepherds to prelates and that of sheep to their subjects" (Geoffrey of Vinsauf, *Poetria nova*, 938-940). Allegory is one of the tropes, to be compared with other tropes or figures of *analogy: metaphor, comparison.

Theology defined the place of allegory in the *exegesis of Scripture. According to a celebrated 13th-c. distich, "the letter teaches what happened, allegory what to believe, morality what to do, anagogy what to hope" (*littera gesta docet, quid credas allegoria, moralis quid agas, quid speres anagogia*). The Old Testament has four senses. The commentator can distinguish between the literal (or historical) sense of a text and its spiritual sense, which is subdivided into three: the allegorical (or typical) sense states the Good News prefigured in the sacred history, the moral (or tropological) sense draws a lesson from it for this life, the anagogical sense explains what the letter says about man's last end. Take the verse: "When Israel went forth from Egypt, the house of Jacob from a people of strange language, Judah became his sanctuary, Israel his dominion" (Ps 113 [114], 1); the letter of the text is the fact of the exodus from Egypt, the allegory the redemptive work of Christ, the moral sense the *conversion of the soul, the anagogy its entry into *eternal life (Dante, *Epistle to Can Grande*).

The allegory of the theologians is very different from that of the rhetoricians. The relation between the event and its allegorical sense is based on the structure of *Revelation. The sacred history related in the Old Testament foretells the work of Jesus related in the gospels. Two histories are put in relation to each other, two realities: in accordance with God's plan, the first finds its fulfilment in the second which gives it its full meaning. By contrast, the allegory of the rhetoricians replaces words with other words; it is a manner of speaking, a fiction (*fabula*), a product of human imagination.

As Scripture also resorted to figures and tropes (the arms of God), to fable (Jgs 9, 8-15), parables and the allegory of the rhetors, the theologians of the 13th c. were led to think out the connection between the two sorts of allegory. Effects connected with the use of *rhetoric were called the parabolical (or metaphorical) sense, and the theologians demonstrated that this sense is a subdivision of the literal sense: "The parabolic sense is contained in the literal sense; because words have a proper sense and a figurative sense, and the literal sense is not the figure, but that which it represents" (*Thomas Aquinas, *Summa theologiae*, 1a, q. 1, a. 10). When the word "fox" is taken metaphorically to mean "cunning man", the literal sense of fox is not its proper sense, but its metaphorical sense of cunning man. The literal sense is what the writer has in mind.

As for the secular writings, the works of pagan Antiquity, it follows from the theological definition of allegory that it is vain to seek four senses in them as in Scripture. Their literal sense is not sacred history; how could it find its fulfilment in the Incarnation? "Poetic fictions do not depart from the literal sense" (St Thomas, *Quodlibet*, 7, q. 6, a. 3). *John of Salisbury censures those who extend the exegetical method proper to the *Bible to texts studied by teachers of *grammar and rhetoric: "In the *liberal arts, where it is not realities but merely words that signify, whoever is not content with the primary sense of the letter is in error or seeks for interested ends to turn his hearers away from the understanding of the truth" (*Policraticus*, 7, 12). Yet it is possible to comment on pagan works; Christians have learned from the pagan exegetes of Homer, Virgil or Ovid to draw from mythology, whose garment is poetry, lessons both moral (relations between divinities are conflicts between passions of the soul) and physical (they are relations between the elements or the stars). Here the pagans spoke of allegory (Plutarch); the medievals dismissed this word and, in the 12th c., preferred the word *integumentum* (covering): "Allegory is a discourse that wraps up in a historical narrative a true sense different from the superficial sense: the combat of Jacob. Integument is a discourse that encloses a true sense in a fictional narrative: Orpheus. There history, here fiction, have a hidden value. Allegory concerns *theology, integument *philosophy" (Bernard Silvestris, *In Martianum Capellam*). To read Plato's *Timaeus*, the *Aeneid* and the *Metamorphoses* as *integumenta* is to draw from them the lessons of cosmogony and morality in which is the true meaning aimed at by the ancient authors.

In French, the word "allegory", which is rare, is mainly part of the vocabulary of the Bestiaries: the phoenix reborn from its ashes is an allegory of the dead and resurrected Christ. According to an old tradition, the created universe spoke of its Creator, or even of the devil, the Church and man. But "allegory" never designates an entire literary work, even a work of the Middle Ages. The *Roman de la Rose* is never called an allegory; no more is it called an integument, though one of its authors, Jean de Meung, was tempted by the latter term.

Medieval allegorical literature has antique models, brief forms like the *fable and the parable or great poems like the *Psychomachia* of the Christian Prudentius or the *Marriage of Mercury and Philology* of the pagan Martianus Capella. In this literature, the meaning of the narratives or descriptions is what the writer who has imagined them has in mind. Often the author invites his reader to seek beyond appearances a sense that he himself can make clear. Usually the narrative, presented as the effect of a *dream or *vision, partakes of a revelation whose mystery we must pierce. The narrative is supported by a long continuous metaphor: combat, marriage, journey. The characters are either souls without reason (animals, plants) or inanimate things (concepts, whether philosophical – *Nature, *Reason, Fortune –, moral – *Love, Avarice – or scientific – *Grammar, *Logic) to which are attributed reason, movement and speech. In the former case we have the Aesopic fable, but also narratives that bring beasts on stage only to arouse laughter or indignation at the conduct of men: the *Ecbasis cuiusdam captivi per tropologiam* (Flight of a captive to be understood as a trope, 11th c.) in which a calf (a young monk), who has left his farm (abbey) at the instigation of a wolf (a layman), is brought back by a fox (a monk); the *Ysengrimus* (*c.*1150), in which the wolf's misfortunes are the occasion for a satire on the Church and the world; the *Roman de Renart* and its French and foreign imitations; the *Roman de Fauvel*, the dun (or false) horse (*fauve, faux cheval*). Inanimate things are personified in poems that teach the verities of sacred or profane love; whether they have the dimensions of a philosophical epic or a, sometimes very brief, French **dit*, they cause us to reflect on man's place before God and in the natural and social universe. The narrative is subtended by a great metaphor, combat (Henri d'Andeli's *Bataille des sept Arts*), debate (the whole of the texts on the meeting of the four daughters of God, after Psalm 84, 11 [85, 10]), marriage (*Mariage des neuf filles du diable*) and especially journey or quest: journey towards the origins of the universe (Bernard Silvestris's *Cosmographia*), towards the powers that administer it or towards God (*Alan of Lille's *De planctu naturae* and *Anticlaudianus*), a walk in the garden of pleasure (*Roman de la Rose* of Guillaume de Lorris and Jean de Meung). The most fertile metaphor was that of the journey to the underworld: told in numerous French *Voies d'enfer et de paradis*, in the 14th c. it inspired the *Pèlerinages* of Guillaume de Digulleville, all works that have been eclipsed by *Dante's *Divine Comedy*.

C. S. Lewis, *The Allegory of Love: a Study in Medieval Tradition*, Oxford, 1936. – E. de Bruyne, *Études d'esthétique médiévale*, Bruges, 1946, 3, 302-333. – H. de Lubac, *Exégèse médiévale: les quatre sens de l'Écriture*, 1, 1-2, 2, Paris, 1959-1964. – J. Pépin, *Dante et la tradition de l'allégorie*, Montreal-Paris, 1970. – *Formen und Funktionen der Allegorie*, W. Haug (ed.), Stuttgart, 1979. – J. Whitman, *Allegory: the Dynamics of an Ancient and Medieval Technique*, Oxford, 1987. – *Allegoresis: the Craft of Allegory in Medieval Literature*, J. S. Russell (ed.), New York, 1988. – A. Strubel, *La Rose, Renart et le Graal: la littérature allégorique en France au XIII^e siècle*, Paris, 1989.

Pierre-Yves Badel

**ALMOHADS.** In *c.*1128, returning from a journey to the East to study, a Berber of the Masmūda tribe, Ibn Tūmart, began to preach in the *Maghreb a doctrine based on the affirmation of divine unicity (whence the name *al-muwahhidūn*, "unitarians"). Considering himself the envoy of God (*mahdī*), Ibn Tūmart settled at Tinmal, an isolated village in the Atlas, and undertook to reform the morals of the Berbers corrupted by the *Almoravids. His doctrine advocated a return to the sources of *Islam, in particular the *Koran and the *Sunna. From its origins, the movement was of an extreme rigorism and practised a policy of repression against the Malikite theologians. Its founder set up an organisation modeled on the tradition of the earliest times of Islam, while respecting the tribal particularism of the Berber groups. Below him was an inner council, then two assemblies, the Council of Ten and the Council of Fifty, consisting of representatives of the Masmūda tribes. With the exception of this last, the other elements of the Almohad hierarchy were fairly rapidly abandoned.

On the death of Ibn Tūmart (1130), his disciple Abd al-Mumīn took the title of Caliph (1130-1163) and engaged in a policy of military expansion, sometimes difficult, so that it took the Almohads nearly 20 years to conquer *Morocco. In 1147 they took Marrakesh, thus ending Almoravid rule, and made it their capital. Abd al-Mumīn then turned towards Salé where he assembled a great army destined to undertake the conquest of the central Maghreb. Algiers, Bougie and Constantine were occupied from 1152, and in 1159 the Almohads took Tunis. The same year, Mahdiya, Sfax and Tripoli were taken from the Normans. These conquests were complicated by several interventions in *Spain. Cadiz and Jérez recognised the authority of the Almohad *caliph in 1146 and *Seville was taken in 1147. Resistance was more difficult than foreseen, particularly in the region of *Valencia, and especially in the *Balearic islands: Minorca was not taken until 1202 and Palma de Majorca in 1203.

The Caliph Abū Yūsuf Yakūb's victory over the Christians at Alarcos in 1195 engendered a new awareness of danger; an appeal for a crusade launched by the archbishop of *Toledo led to the formation of an armed coalition which routed the Almohads at the battle of Las *Navas de Tolosa in 1212. This defeat, aggravated by economic difficulties and intolerance against Jews and men of letters, was the signal for an interior crisis which accelerated the decline of Almohad power in the peninsula. *Cordova fell into Christian hands in 1236, then Valencia (1238) and Seville (1248). In the Maghreb, a crisis marked by revolts in the towns and the repudiation of Almohad doctrine by Caliph al-Mamūn led to a period of political instability. The regions furthest from the capital then began to detach themselves from the Empire and, from 1229, the governor of Ifrīqiya declared himself independent, soon followed by those of Tlemcen and the central Maghreb. In Morocco, Zanāta nomad tribes of the plains managed to take Marrakesh (1269) and Tinmal (1276). The Almohad Empire then disappeared, giving way to new dynasties. While the Nasrids of *Granada managed to maintain a Muslim power in al-Andalus, the Maghreb broke up into three zones of influence: the *Merinids in Morocco, the Abdawadids at Tlemcen, and the Hafsids in Ifrīqiya.

A. Huici Miranda, *Historia politica del imperio almohade*, Tétuan, 1956-1959. – R. Le Tourneau, *The Almohad Movement in North Africa in the Twelfth and Thirteenth Centuries*, Princeton (NJ), 1969. – A. Laroui, *The History of the Maghrib*, Princeton (NJ), 1977.

Philippe Sénac

**ALMORAVIDS.** In the second quarter of the 11th c., on his return from a pilgrimage to *Mecca, the Sanhāja Berber chief Yahyā ben Ibrāhīm, supported by a Malikite *Sufi named Abd Allāh ben Yasīn, created a reforming movement which preachedg a strict Malikism, based on the teaching of the prescriptions of the *Koran and the *Sunna. The name of Almoravids was given to the followers of this movement, and came from the word *ribāt* (*al-Murābitūn*, people of the **ribāt*), designating a fortified convent whose location remains disputed (an island in the Atlantic or in the river Niger, to which Abd Allāh ben Yasīn retired). If the obligations and interdictions that flowed from the doctrine clashed with the customs and traditions of the Sanhāja tribes, the demographic expansion they enjoyed and their aversion for the Zanāta Berbers, who prevented them taking their troops in the direction of the plains of the Sous, quickly overcame the initial resistance. Under the leadership of two great military chiefs, Abū Bakr ben Umar and then Yūsuf ben Tāshfīn, the Almoravids threw themselves into a policy of conquest marked by the capture of Sijilmasa in *c.*1054, Awdagust in 1055 and Agmat in 1058. *Fez was subjected in 1063 and in *c.*1069 they founded the town of Marrakesh, destined to become the capital of the Empire. After having subjected Salé in 1073, then Tlemcen in 1075, Yūsuf ben Tāshfīn took Algiers (1083), the eastern limit of Almoravid expansion.

These successes soon attracted the attention of the Malikite jurists of al-Andalus, who wished to defend *Islam threatened by the Christian *Reconquest and put an end to the political anarchy that reigned in the realms of the Ta'ifas. The capture of *Toledo in 1085 by King *Alfonso VI of Castile led several Andalusian princes to request support from Emir Yūsuf ben Tāshfīn. He intervened three times: first in 1086, to inflict a bitter defeat on the Castilians at Sagrajas (Zallāka); in 1088, to beat the Christians a second time at Aledo; and finally in 1090, this time with the intention of undertaking the conquest of the peninsula on his own account. Progress, facilitated by the benevolent attitude of the population seduced by the motto of the Almoravids ("Propagate the truth, put down injustice, abolish illegal taxes"), was rapid: *Cordova and *Seville fell in 1091, then Badajoz and Lisbon in 1094, *Valencia in 1102. The arrogance of the Sanhāja Berbers, masters of the army

The minaret of the Kutubiyya at Marrakesh (Morocco). 12th c.

and administration where they were distinguished by the wearing of a veil (*lithām*), and the intransigence of the Malikite *fuqahā* gave rise to a protest movement that prevailed in proportion to the growth of the Christian threat, momentarily slowed down at the battle of Uclés in 1108. After having taken *Saragossa in 1118, the king of *Aragon Alfonso I the Battler reached Andalusia and threatened Murcia, Cordova and *Granada (1125). The expedition revealed the weakness of the Almoravid resistance and led to the deportation of numerous *Mozarabic communities to the *Maghreb. A burst of military activity allowed the Almoravids to beat the Aragonese at Fraga in 1134, but some years later, with the loss of Tortosa (1148) and Lérida (1149), the whole of the Ebro valley passed into Christian hands. At the same time, in the Maghreb, the *Almohads took Marrakesh in 1147, following a battle in which the last Almoravid *emir, Ishāk ben Alī, died. Almoravid rule then came to an end, apart from in the *Balearic islands and in Ifrīqiya where, under the Banū Ghāniya, it lasted into the early 13th century.

V. Lagardère, *Le Vendredi de Zallaqa, 23 octobre 1086*, Paris, 1989. – J. Bosch Vilá, *Los Almorávides*, Granada, 1990 (2nd ed.). – V. Lagardère, *Les Almoravids*, Paris, 1991.

Philippe Sénac

**ALMS.** *Thomas Aquinas defines alms as being "the work by which we give something to him who is in need, out of compassion and for the sake of God". Thus the word refers to the corporeal "*works of mercy", essentially aid in money, food or clothing, given to a neighbour in a situation of material distress.

*Alpha and Omega*, frontispiece of a manuscript of St Augustine's *Quaestiones in Heptateuchon*. Northern France, mid 8th c. Paris, BNF (Ms lat. 12168).

While the Jewish law limited almsgiving to brothers in the religion of believers, the teaching of Christ prescribed coming to the aid of all, pagans and enemies included, recommending moreover that it be done in humility and secret. The doctrine being thus defined, it remained to the Church *Fathers and the thinkers of the *scholastic period to work out its theological formulation. From Clement of Alexandria to Ambrose, from Cyprian to *Gregory the Great, the idea developed of the rich man as mere depositary of earthly goods, whose true proprietor was God: so he must distribute them generously to the poor, since he will have to render an account of their use in the afterlife. In the 13th c., St Thomas determined the conditions of interference between the superfluity of the rich and the necessity of the poor: in case of "extreme" necessity, the poor should receive help from all those who possess "relative" superfluity (*i.e.* goods whose absence does not put life in danger); it is then licit for the poor to take of this superfluity himself in order to save his life, in the name of the common destination of earthly goods, made for the whole of mankind and not for the satisfaction of some. In situations of "ordinary" necessity, the poor should be content with the "absolute" superfluity of him who possesses (*i.e.* that which merely permits him to have a more agreeable life).

In practice, more influenced by evangelical *pastoral care than by theological thought, almsgiving was, throughout the Middle Ages and especially from the 12th c., constantly encouraged by *clerics and presented as one of the favoured ways to gain *salvation. While the ordinary faithful always found close to them some mendicant to whom to "give alms", monasteries, monasteries and *chapters practised assistance to the destitute on a larger scale by collective distributions of food, willingly imitated by great personages: from the 13th c., *kings, princes, lords, *popes and *cardinals all had their "almonry". In the 14th c., that of the popes of *Avignon (the *Pignotta) daily offered a ration of bread to several hundred – at times even several thousand – hungry people and served complete meals to several dozen more. Finally the charitable *confraternities, many of which took the name "alms" or "charity", devoted themselves, especially during the last centuries of the Middle Ages, to the relief of indigents through "doles" of bread and clothing.

If the view held of the poor at the end of the period evolved in a rather negative way, it was nonetheless true that almsgiving, as a concrete illustration of the evangelical virtue of *charity, remained a requirement for every Christian, and was expressed at that time in many ways.

R. Brouillard, "Aumône", *Cath.*, 1, 1948, 1050-1056. – M. Mollat, *The Poor in the Middle Ages*, New Haven, 1986. – A. Vauchez, "Assistance et charité en Occident, XIII$^{e}$-XIV$^{e}$ siècles", *Domande e consumi, livelli e strutture, sec. XIII-XVIII (Prato, 1974)*, Prato, 1978, 151-162. – M. Rubin, *Charity and Community in Medieval Cambridge*, Cambridge, 1987.

Daniel Le Blévec

**ALPHA – OMEGA.** The first and last letters of the Greek alphabet, alpha and omega are employed by the Son of Man in the *Apocalypse three times (Rev 1, 18; 21, 6; 22, 13), where they signify that *Christ is "the beginning and the end of everything" (Rev 21, 6). Since the early Christian period these two characters have been associated with the labarum *XP* and sometimes suspended from the branches of the *X*. They have also been used in inscriptions, painting, sculpture and *objets d'art*, in apocalyptic cycles or to frame the figure of Christ. Examples include the *mosaic cross of Sant'Apollinare in Classe (6th c.), the lintel of Saint-Genis-des-Fontaines (1019-1020), and Christ blessing on an enamelled binding in the Musée de Cluny (1165-1170).

F. Cabrol, *DACL*, 1, 1907, 1-25.

Dominique Alibert

**ALPS.** Of Celtic origin, the word "Alps" means "high summit", "rock", and designates the largest and highest of the European mountain ranges, extending in the form of an arc 1000 kilometres long by some 250 kilometres wide, from the Mediteranean to the Danube. Furrowed by deep valleys and accessed easily by many passes, the Alps, which enjoy a privileged position at the heart of Europe, have never been a barrier but a thoroughfare and even, in the late Middle Ages, a veritable cultural crossroads, as attest, among other things, the wealth of painted decoration in its churches.

The climatic warming of the Alps during the early Middle Ages (5th-7th cc.), earlier than was once thought, favoured migrations and heavy colonization of the highlands in the 11th and 12th centuries. Many regions were abandoned during the demographic crisis of the 14th and 15th cc. and owing to a deterioration in *climate: the little ice age. But between the 10th and 15th cc., the considerable and permanent migrations that troubled the life of the *towns and *villages played a central role in the Alpine economy.

If, for the *Lombards, the Alps had remained primarily a natural frontier against barbarian *invasions, under the *Carolingians they became a place of strategic importance. A policy of control and colonization led to the multiplication of monasteries in both the western and eastern zones. In 726, a high Frankish official, Abbo, rector of the Maurienne and the Val di Susa, founded the abbey of *Novalesa situated at a key point on the Mont-Cenis route which allowed surveillance of communications between the two Alpine valleys. There are many examples of these Carolingian *foundations that, from Disentis to Müstair or Malles, bear witness to a veritable grip on the crossing points. The study of routes remains incontestably one of the best known aspects of Alpine historiography. Their role in the formation of political entities is such that we can talk of "lordships of routes". However, despite the example of the duchy of *Savoy, which was installed on the passes and "gate-keeper of the Alps", these "lands in the middle of the world" had some difficulty in establishing a clear symbolic space, and presenting themselves as a historically coherent territory. By contrast, the situation of "dual periphery" typical of frontier regions contributed to the birth of hinge areas, lands of refuge for *heretics, places where different cultures met and original experiences could be formulated. Great bourgeois and commercial centres, like the merchant town of Bolzano, were focal points of artistic innovation in the 14th century.

But it was the 15th c. that was truly the century of the Alps, as illustrated by the Savoy of Duke Amadeus VIII who became pope under the name of *Felix V. And with the councils of *Constance and *Basel, the Alpine region became the stage on which was played out the fate of *authority in the Church, accompanied by the beginnings of the *witch-hunt. While religious painting, supported by the impact of the *mendicant orders, especially the *Franciscans, saw an unprecedented success, the artistic effloresence reached its full capacity in secular cycles, sign of an authentic chivalric culture that is visible from the castle of La Manta near Saluzzo to that of Buon Consiglio at Trento.

*Die Alpen in der europäischen Geschichte des Mittelalters*, Konstanz-Stuttgart, 1965. – E. Castelnuovo, "Les Alpes, carrefour et lieu de rencontre des tendances artistiques au XVe siècle", *Études de lettres*, 2nd series, 10, Lausanne, 1967, 13-26. – P. Guichonnet, *Histoire et civilisation des Alpes*, Toulouse-Lausanne, 1980.

Dominique Rigaux

**ALSACE.** The geographical area bounded by the Vosges and the Rhine, the region of *Speyer and *Burgundy, Alsace, integrated into the Frankish kingdom, was originally part of *Alamannia. In the 7th c., having become Christian, it was divided between the dioceses of *Strasbourg in the north and Basel in the south, and possessed several great monasteries (Wissembourg, *Marmoutier, *Münster, *Murbach). Becoming a Frankish *duchy within *Austrasia, it was put under the authority of the Etichonid dynasty (named from Duke Eticho, father of St *Odile), and then divided by the *Carolingians into two counties: Nordgau and Sundgau. In 843, Alsace was included in the kingdom of *Lothar I, but detached from *Lotharingia in 910; from then on, it was part of the duchy of *Swabia and hence of the *Empire.

Alsace experienced a certain growth in activity in the 10th and 11th cc., owing to the works of the bishops of Strasbourg like Erkenbald and Werner, the foundation of Selz by the empress Adelaide (rise of Erstein and Andlau) and the destiny of a descendant of the Etichonid counts of Eguisheim, Pope *Leo IX. Around 1100, the first *Staufen imposed their presence and their policy in Alsace, notably by building *castles. *Lorraine influence

Altar of Gilduin, consecrated in 1096. Toulouse, basilica of Saint-Sernin.

was perceptible all along the Alsatian slope of the Vosges through the possessions of the bishops of *Metz (Marmoutier, Neuwiller), Lorraine *advocacy over the property of *Saint-Denis (Liepvre, Saint-Hippolyte), and Lorraine *abbeys (*vines and villages). *Cistercians, regular *canons and Benedictines peopled Alsace from the 12th century. *Frederick Barbarossa consolidated the imperial presence at Wissembourg, Haguenau and Brumath. Many towns developed along the Ill and at the foot of the Vosges, castles multiplied, notably on the rocky peaks of the North, economic, commercial and agricultural activity developed (Burgfelsen). Society was marked by structures of a Germanic character: *ministeriality, *Landgrafen*, ecclesiastical princes and castellans.

The later Middle Ages were marked by difficult times (*epidemics and war), urban expansion (nearly 70 towns), the creation of the decapolis which grouped together the imperial towns, the development of different laws in the north (Haguenau) and the south (*Colmar). The bishops of Strasbourg established an important *patrimony in the 14th c., and their town increased in size, hardly rivalled by Colmar to the south. Society was characterised by the influence of the urban patriciate on the one hand and the lesser ministerial nobility and robber knights on the other. Alsace benefited again from the development of trade in the Rhine valley, and from its important production of *wine. Traces of its intellectual life survived through the *library of Murbach, the writings of Otfrid of Wissemburg, Herrad of Hohenburg, *Gottfried von Strassburg and *Manegold of Lautenbach, the rise of *historiography and the early manifestations of *humanism (*Sélestat).

L. Sittler, *La Décapole alsacienne des origines à la fin du Moyen Âge*, Strasbourg, 1956. – M. Barth, *Handbuch der elsässischen Kirchen im Mittelalter*, Strasbourg, 1960. – F. J. Himly, *Atlas des villes médiévales d'Alsace*, Strasbourg, 1970. – F. Rapp, *Réformes et réformation à Strasbourg (1450-1525)*, Strasbourg, 1974. – *Histoire de Strasbourg*, F. Rapp (dir.), Toulouse, 1981. – *Histoire d'Alsace*, P. Dollinger (dir.), Toulouse, 1984 (4th ed.). – H. Büttner, *Geschichte des Alsass*, Sigmaringen, 1991 (2nd ed.).

Michel Parisse

**ALTAR.** The Christian altar is a central element of the Christian liturgy: around it and in terms of it are developed the liturgical area and its furniture.

A simple table (*mensa*) in the first centuries, its sole function was its use for the commemoration of the eucharistic meal. But,

*Renuccini Altarpiece.* Central panel: *Virgin and Child surrounded by Sts Francis, John the Baptist and Mary Magdalene* by Giovanni del Biondo, 1379. Florence, church of Santa Croce.

from an early time, the Christians conferred on the altar a symbolism nourished by many Old Testament passages on the subject of sacrifice. The altars installed in some *baptisteries in Antiquity sometimes contained *relics (*cippus*-altars or reliquary-altars): the symbolism of this arrangement touched on the very meaning of *baptism, the death and resurrection of the neophyte leading him to a new life. During the early Middle Ages, the multiplication of altars in monastic churches corresponded with the growth in the number of monk-priests, who celebrated several votive masses on the altars installed in the side-aisles and transept arms of the church. Influenced by the *Roman liturgy and its ecclesial space, the monks developed a particular symbolism around these secondary altars; each represented a Roman parish and the main altar symbolized *St Peter's basilica, true centre of the Roman liturgy.

At first, these altar arrangements did not directly influence forms of *architecture. From the second half of the 9th c. however, we see the creation of architectural forms that often owe their origin to altars and their organisation within the church, as *e.g.* at Saint-Bénigne at *Dijon and *Saint-Michel-de-Cuxa in the 11th century. In the *Romanesque period, sculptors developed on altars a decoration of geometrical motifs and plant and zoomorphic friezes or even human figures. As example, we may cite the magnificent altar table of the sculptor Bernard Gilduin (11th c.) at Saint-Sernin, *Toulouse. In the sphere of *goldsmiths' work, portable altars and altar frontals (**antependia*) show a christological and hagiographical iconography of great importance for medieval art. The golden altar given by *Henry II and his wife *Cunegund to Basel cathedral (made *c.*1019) also had room for the figures of the two imperial patrons, represented at Christ's feet.

Representations of altars in *illuminations are very numerous and help to supplement our knowledge of the object, its use and symbolic meaning, as shown by the pictures on copies of *Beatus's *Commentary on the Apocalypse*, one of which shows the souls of the *martyrs under the altar (Rev 6, 9-11).

J. Braun, *Der christliche Altar in seiner geschichtlichen Entwicklung*, Munich, 1924 (2 vol.). – J. Hubert, "Introïbo ad altare", *Revue de l'art*, 24, Paris, 1974, 9-21. – *Les Cahiers de Saint-Michel de Cuxa*, 13, Prades-Codalet, 1982. – *Italian Altarpieces, 1250-1550: Function and Design*, E. Borsook (ed.), F.S. Gioffredi (ed.), Oxford, 1994. – L.F. Jacobs, *Early Netherlandish Carved Altarpieces, 1380-1550*, Cambridge 1998.

Éric Palazzo

**ALTARPIECE, RETABLE.** The term "retable" comes from the Latin *retabulum*, which means "rear panel". Originally, the altarpiece was a fixed or movable construction, on the *altar, beside the table or raised up, sometimes also immediately behind it. From the outset, it was distinguished from the altar frontal (**antependium* or *paliotto*) intended to clothe the front face of the table or marble or stone block, though analogies of form and iconography existed between them. The altarpiece was raised above the *tabernacle and dominated the *reliquary inserted in the altar. In *cathedral churches, it masked the seat of honour reserved for the *bishop and obliged this to be moved. It appeared like a wall of *images, though it did not, like the Byzantine iconostasis, form a compartment, nor did it become, as in the baroque period, the centre of a decorative whole. It was, in some way, the expansion of the table of sacrifice, in accordance with the need for accompanying figuration that grew ceaselessly in the 11th c.: before this, we know no images placed on the altar, though there may have been *icons hung above it, *pale* in precious *goldsmiths' work or golden altars (Sant'Ambrogio, Milan, 9th c.; San Marco, Venice, the *pala d'oro*, commissioned by doge Falieri in 1105).

When, from the 13th c., it became established as an artistic genre in its own right, the altarpiece very often supplanted all other earlier decorative forms: according to inventories drawn up in the Middle Ages, its use was massive (48 altarpieces in the church of Our Lady at *Gdańsk, 45 in the *cathedral of Schleswig, 31 in that of *Regensburg, 20 in the church of Saint-Servais at Beaumont, in Hainaut). We need not exaggerate the connection of the altarpiece with the liturgy: quite apart from the fact that it was not indispensable to the eucharistic celebration (it appeared well after the formalization of the liturgy of the *mass), only a few late examples testify to a direct influence of the liturgy on its structures (altarpieces provided with eucharistic *tabernacles, as at St Martin's, Landshut; altarpieces representing the Last Supper in the centre, like that of Tilman Riemenschneider at Rothenburg). On the other hand, the altarpiece was a product of religious devotion, understood in the broad sense: it flourished, in fact, at the very moment when worship, as it was practised, could not remain the sole centre of attraction for the faithful in church and when paraliturgical forms served as pivots for the new *spirituality. Hence the close connection we remark between their iconography and a series of particular texts (*apocrypha, commentaries on Church *Fathers, biblical *exegesis). There ensued, during the 14th c. and also in the 15th, a clear tendency to tell a story (in the predella) or the coordinated presentation of the figures in the centre (the altar-*pala* and the iconography of the Sacra Conversazione).

J. Burckhardt, *The Altarpiece in Renaissance Italy*, P. Humfrey (ed.), Oxford, 1988.

P. Skubiszewski, "Le retable gothique sculpté: entre le dogme et l'univers humain", *Le Retable d'Issenheim et la Sculpture au nord des Alpes à la fin du Moyen Âge*, Colmar, 1989, 13-47. – J.B. Sobre, *Behind the Altar Table: the Development of the Painted Retable in Spain, 1350-1550*, Columbia, 1989. – P. Humphrey, M. Kemp, *The Altarpiece in the Renaissance*, Cambridge, 1990. – A. Chastel, *La Pala d'autel en Italie, des origines à 1500*, Paris, 1993. – *Italian Altarpieces, 1250-1550: Function and Design*, E. Borsook (ed.), F. S. Gioffredi (ed.), Oxford, 1994.

Daniel Russo

**ALVARO OF CORDOVA (9th c.).** Alvaro was the most illustrious figure, along with his fellow disciple Abbot *Eulogio, of the 9th-c. *Mozarabic "martyr movement", which struggled against the progress of *Islam – or even *Judaism – in the Christian ranks. He was not, however, among those sacrificial witnesses, whom he supported with all his literary talent. As well as Latin verses, a *Confessio*, a compilation of sentences of the *Fathers, we have a vigorous *apologetic *oeuvre*: *letters, and especially the *Vita* of Eulogio (martyred 859) and the *Indiculus luminosus*, written in 854 as a guide to those who doubted the aggression of Islam. A cultural combat as much as a religious one, which Alvaro, the best Latin writer of his country and century led with his pen, as others shed their blood for it.

E. P. Colbert, *The Martyrs of Cordoba*, Washington (DC), 1962. – K. Wolf, *Christian Martyrs in Muslim Spain*, Cambridge, 1988.

Gabriel Martinez

**ALVARO PELAYO (*c.*1275-1349).** Alvaro Pelayo or Pais (Alvarus Pelagius) studied *canon law and civil law at *Bologna, before becoming a *Franciscan in 1306. From 1330 to 1332, he was confessor to Pope *John XXII at *Avignon; in 1333 he became bishop of Sylves in *Portugal. His fundamental work, *De statu et planctu ecclesiae*, was written during his Avignon period and revised between 1335 and 1340. His *Speculum regum,* a summary of *De statu et planctu*, was written for Alfonso XI of Castile.

Alvaro Pelayo was a disciple of *James of Viterbo; like him, he was a theoretician of papal *plenitudo potestatis*. Impregnated with the doctrines of *Dionysius the Areopagite in particular, he applied the doctrine of hierarchies to the ecclesial institution: the *pope, successor of Peter and vicar of Christ, holds the same power as Christ himself. All members of the *civilitas christiana* are ordered for the same reason to the same *end, viz. *grace, *charity and unity, which are the bonds of perfection *in via*, in this world. It is the force of charity (*vis caritatis*) that associates people with each other on earth; and as, to attain a single end, it is not good for there to be several distinct *causes acting towards that one end, so in *Christendom there should be a single prince directing all men of that republic to its proper end. It is the pope who has received this position and power from Christ. Alvaro still recognises the autonomy of human nature and human society, but considers *temporal power as being in the Church and participating in spiritual power.

J. Morais Barbosa, *Lo* De Statu et planctu Ecclesiae. *Estudio critico*, Lisbon, 1982. – M. Damiata, *Alvaro Pelayo, teocratico scontento*, Florence, 1984.

Jeannine Quillet

**ALVERNA (LA VERNA).** "On this rough rock between the Tiber and the Arno / he took the supreme seal of Christ / which he bore for two years in his members"; these are the verses that *Dante (*Paradiso*, XI, 106-108) devotes to Alverna and the miraculous event that brought fame to this mountainous spur of the Apennines, in what is now the province of Arezzo, in the centre of Italy. The historical memory of the Friars Minor affirmed very early that there, in the summer of 1224, Brother *Francis received the *stigmata. The place became an eminent reference-point for the *Franciscan movement with the construction, from the 13th c., of various sacred buildings. A late tradition, without foundation, has it that from the second decade of the 13th c. the mountain was given to brother Francis and his first "friars" by Count Orlando of Chiusi.

C. Frugoni, *Francesco e l'invenzione delle stimmate. Una storia per parole e immagini fino a Bonaventura e Giotto*, Turin, 1993.

Grado G. Merlo

**AMALARIUS OF METZ (died after 850).** The Carolingian *liturgist and theologian Amalarius of Metz was a pupil of *Alcuin at *Tours before being appointed archbishop of *Trier in 811. During *Agobard's exile (*c.*834), he was also responsible for administering the diocese of *Lyon.

His work is marked by his presentation of the allegorical interpretation of the liturgy (notably set out in the *Liber officialis*). This method often displeased his contemporaries, who were attached to a less symbolic conception of commentaries on the liturgy. Amalarius also compiled an *antiphonary for the Church of *Metz, on the basis of the Gregorian antiphonary.

*Amalarii episcopi opera liturgica omnia*, J. M. Hanssens (ed.), *StT*, 138-140, 1948-1950.

R.-J. Hesbert, "L'antiphonaire d'Amalaire", *EL*, 94, 1980, 176-194.

Éric Palazzo

**AMALFI.** A small Italian city in Campania, clinging to the rocky slopes of its peninsula dominating the bay of Salerno, Amalfi is mentioned as a *bishopric in a letter of Pope *Gregory I in 596. It was under Byzantine rule until the 9th century, when it elected an indigenous *count and enjoyed a "peripheral autonomy" from Byzantium, while maintaining good relations with the *Fatimids of Ifriqiya. Obliged to take their resources from the sea, its inhabitants built ships and, thanks to the privileges they enjoyed in the *Byzantine Empire and the good reception they received in Barbary and then Egypt, from the 10th c. they enjoyed a precursory role in trade between East and West. The town was ruled by an aristocracy of counts, then prefects: foremost among these, in the 11th c., stand out the family of Mauro and Pantaleone, whose business connections extended throughout the East and rested on a triangular trade between southern *Italy, the Muslim world (Barbary, Egypt) and Byzantium. They founded a hospice at *Jerusalem, Santa Maria Latina near the *Holy Sepulchre, and Santa Maria Maggiore, which they entrusted to the Benedictine monks of *Cava dei Tirreni. After the capture of Jerusalem by the crusaders in 1099, these establishments were put under the authority of the monk Gerard who, early in the 12th c., transformed them into a *military order, the *Hospital of St John of Jerusalem.

Around 987, Pope John XV raised the episcopal see into an *archbishopric with four *suffragan bishops under its authority: Lettere, Scala, Minori and Capri. Several titulars stand out: John (1030-1050) was the teacher of the future Pope *Gregory VII; Peter, who had received a Greek education, was part of the embassy sent by Pope *Leo IX to *Constantinople in 1054; with *Humbert of Moyenmoutier and Frederick of Lorraine, he was responsible for the rupture between the Eastern and Western Churches. In 1112, Archbishop Mauro was sent by Pope *Paschal II to the *basileus* Alexius I *Comnenus. The Amalfitans also founded a monastery on Mount *Athos, which is attested until the 13th century, and seem to have played a moderating

*Sts Amandus and Baudemund*, manuscript of the *Life and miracles of St Amandus*, mid 12th c. Valenciennes, Municipal Library (Ms 501, fol. 58 v°).

role in the religious quarrels between East and West.

Culturally, Amalfi made a large contribution to the penetration of Byzantine works into the West. Hagiographical accounts, like the life of St *Irene or the miracles of St *Michael, were translated from Greek to *Latin by Amalfitans in *Constantinople. Above all, they made known in the West the refinement of Byzantine works of art, *chalices, crucifixes, candelabra, *tapestries and *silks, widely diffused at *Rome, *Monte Cassino and in numerous Italian churches. In addition to this, the seven bronze doors from Constantinople still adorn the *cathedrals and *basilicas of Amalfi, *St Paul's Without the Walls (Rome), Monte Cassino, Atrani, *Monte Sant'Angelo, Salerno and St Mark's (Venice). Amalfi also made a significant legal contribution, with the redaction of the maritime statute – the oldest in existence – known as the *Tabula de Amalphi*; made at various times, it would form the basis of all European commercial and maritime jurisprudence.

The conquest of the town by the *Normans (1073), then its pillage by the Pisans in 1135 and 1137, put an end to the major role played by Amalfi in East-West relations between the 9th and 11th centuries.

M. Del Treppo, A. Leone, *Amalfi medioevale*, Naples, 1977. – U. Schwarz, *Amalfi im frühen Mittelalter (9-11 Jahrh.). Untersuchungen zur Amalfitaner Uberlieferung*, Tübingen, 1978. – R.P. Bergman, *The Salerno Ivories: Ars Sacra from Medieval Amalfi*, Cambridge (MA), 1980. – *Istituzioni civili e organiszazione ecclesiastica nello stato medievale amalfitano*, Amalfi, 1986. – B. Figliuolo, "Amalfi e il Levante nel Medioevo", G. Airaldi (ed.), B. Z. Kedar (ed.), *I comuni italiani nel regno crociato di Gerusalemme*, 573-664. – S. Salomi (ed.), *Le porte di bronzo dall'antichità al secolo XIII*, Rome, 1990.

Michel Balard

**AMALRIC OF BENA (died *c.*1207), AMALRICIANS.** Amalric (Amaury) of Bena taught *logic and *theology at *Paris. His theological views, controversial in his lifetime, were condemned in 1210 as part of those of a group of theologians called the "Amalricians". These were mainly theses developed by a play of *dialectic from scriptural texts, or taken from Pseudo-*Dionysius and *John Scotus Eriugena, but whose conclusions contradicted dogma. One of the main disputed theses – "God is everything" – concerned the idea of *God as the *being of everything, not in the causal but the formal sense, which was seen as equivalent to *pantheism. It is difficult however to reconstruct Amalric's true thought since he is known only through his disciples.

C. Baeumker, *Contra Amaurianos. Ein anonymer wahrscheinlich dem Garnerius von Rochefort zugehöriger Traktat gegen die Amalrikaner aus dem Anfang des XIII. Jahrhunderts*, Münster, 1926. – C. Capelle, *Autour du décret de 1210: III, Amaury de Bène, étude sur son panthéisme formel*, Paris, 1932. – M.-T. d'Alverny, "Un fragment du procès des amauriciens", *AHDL*, 25-26, 1950-1951, 325-336.

Coloman Viola

**AMANDUS OF MAASTRICHT (*c.*600-676?/679?/684?).** Amandus, an Aquitanian noble, was a missionary *bishop without a see and at one time bishop of *Maastricht (648-650). From the cloister of Elnone (now Saint-Amand-les-Eaux) which he founded before 639, he carried on his missionary activity in the regions neighbouring the Schelde. His navigations led him to *Ghent, *Antwerp and probably *Frisia. An ardent preacher, he was received by the great whom he persuaded to found monasteries (Itte at Nivelles) or to retire to them (Rictrude at Marchiennes). After *missions in Vasconia and Carinthia, he returned to Elnone, where he died at a great age on 6 Feb (676, 679 or 684). Valenciennes, Municipal Library (Ms 501, fol. 58 v°).

*Vita Amandi*, 1, B. Krusch (ed.), *MGH.SRM*, 5, 1910, 431-483.

"Amand", *DHGE*, 2, 1942, 942-945. – E. de Moreau, *St. Amand, le principal évangélisateur de la Belgique*, Brussels, 1942. – "Amand", *LdM*, 1, 1980, 510-511.

Régine Le Jan

**AMATUS OF MONTE CASSINO (died before 1105).** Amatus, a Lombard born at Salerno, was a bishop before becoming a monk at *Monte Cassino. He was part of the group of scholars surrounding Abbot *Desiderius (1058-1087), and Peter the Deacon praises him as writer and poet. He wrote a poem on the apostles Peter and Paul, dedicated to *Gregory VII; we know the titles of two more works. Finally he was the author of a history of the Norman conquest of southern *Italy, written *c.*1083 and dedicated to Abbot Desiderius; we possess only a French translation made around 1300. In it he exalts the fidelity of the conquerors and presents Prince Richard and Duke *Robert Guiscard as models of magnanimity and humility.

*Storia de' Normanni di Amato di Montecassino*, V. De Bartholomaeis (ed.), Rome, 1935 ("FSI", 76). – A. Lentini, "Amato di Montecassino", *DBI*, 2, 1960.

Jean-Marie Martin

**AMBO.** The word (*ambôn*) is Greek and designates a raised-up place from which one speaks or proclaims something, but also a place where the speaker is seen by the assembly. The earliest ambos were like a tribune reached by several steps; the top was surrounded by a full balustrade on three sides; the part facing the congregation was provided with a fixed *lectern. There were sometimes two ambos, one for the first readings of the *mass; the other, higher, for the Gospel. The ambo was in wood, stone or even marble and was richly decorated. Italy has preserved a great many from the 12th and 13th cc., all of them masterpieces. Elsewhere, when the rood loft developed, it often carried tribunes for the readings.

G. Rohault de Fleury, *La Messe*, 3, Paris, 1883, 1-72. – *DACL*, 1, 1907, 1330-1347. – J. Jarry, "L'ambon dans la liturgie primitive de l'Église", *Syr.*, 40, 1963, 147-162.

Guy-Marie Oury

**AMBOISE, CARDINAL D' (1460-1510).** Georges d'Amboise combined a brilliant and sometimes chequered ecclesiastical career as a reforming prelate with a political and diplomatic career that made him one of the key figures of the late 15th and early 16th centuries. Abbot of Saint-Paul at Narbonne and of Grandselve, bishop of Montauban in 1489, almoner to the king, archbishop of *Narbonne in 1492, of *Rouen in 1493, he was *cardinal of St Sixtus in 1498 and *legate in France from 1501 to 1503.

Having sided with the duke of Orléans in 1487, at first he suffered some reverses, was imprisoned at Corbeil, and then played an essential political role from 1491, notably in the French monarchy's Italian policy. In 1498 he became a valued adviser of the new king, Louis XII, to whom he presented the Grande Ordonnance of Blois (regulating judiciary organisation and civil procedure), and whom he accompanied to *Italy in 1499. Amboise failed in his attempt to become pope in 1503, but rallied to Julius II, who felt obliged to him and entrusted him with the legation to *Avignon. He negotiated the treaty of Blois (1504) that gave the investiture of the Milanese to Louis XII, and took part in the Italian campaigns. Falling ill at Milan in July 1509, he returned to France and died at Lyon on 25 May 1510, very popular, the prosperity of the realm being considered all his own work. His château of Gaillon, begun in 1501, where he received the king in 1508, was the first example of the introduction of Italian architecture to France.

J. Sirmond, *La Vie du cardinal d'Amboise*, Paris, 1634. – A. Vogt, *DHGE*, 2, 1914, 1060-1072. – M. Prévost, *DBF*, 2, 1934, 491-503.

Nicole Lemaître

**AMBROSIAN CHANT.** Throughout the Middle Ages, the singing of the *Ambrosian liturgy retained characteristics of its own that distinguished it from Gregorian *plainchant, and even today it can be heard in *Milan cathedral. According to tradition, St Ambrose, bishop of Milan from 374 to 397, contributed to its development, notably by composing *hymns. The Milanese liturgy involved many *processions between the town's two *basilicas and the *baptistery, for which many chants have been preserved. Ambrosian chants are of a great variety of styles and forms, hard to classify into musical or stylistic categories. The modality of these chants does not belong to the system of octaechos by which we analyse *Gregorian chant.

T. Bailey, P. Merkley, *The Melodic Tradition of the Ambrosian Office-antiphons*, Ottawa, 1990. – T. Bailey, *Antiphon and Psalm in the Ambrosian Office*, Ottawa, 1994.

Claire Maître

Carved pulpit in the church of Santa Maria del Lago, Moscufo (Italy). The work of Nicodemo, mid 12th c.

**AMBROSIAN LITURGY.** The liturgy of the Church of *Milan claims to date back to St Ambrose who succeeded the Arian Archbishop Auxentius in the late 4th century. This liturgy's area of expansion was *Lombardy. It is a liturgy close to that of Rome, but marked by great originality. Milan having been one of the imperial capitals, some borrowings were made from the *Byzantine and *Gallican liturgies.

The development of this liturgy between the 4th and the 8th c. belongs partly to the sphere of conjecture, since the surviving liturgical documents nearly all belong to the Carolingian or post-Carolingian period. In them we find a good many elements common to the *Roman liturgy or the Romano-Frankish *sacramentaries, but the Ambrosian liturgy contrasts with the concision of the Roman tradition. It is impregnated with *theology.

Its most specific aspect is the chant. Its musical repertoire is related to what we call the Old Roman, which seems to be the early chant of the Roman Church (maintained up to the 12th c.), and to the *Gregorian chant that was widespread throughout Western *Christendom (except *Spain) from the late 8th century.

This liturgy survived through the medieval centuries, and kept its very particular appearance despite efforts in the 9th, 11th and 15th cc. to make Milan adopt the Roman liturgy.

P. Borella, *Il Rito ambrosiano*, Brescia, 1964 (bibliography). – A. M. Triacca, "Ambrosienne (Liturgie)", *Dictionnaire encyclopédique de la liturgie*, 1, D. Sartore (ed.), A. M. Triacca (ed.), Turnhout, 1992, 11-38 (Fr. tr.).

Guy-Marie Oury

*The Last Judgment.* Tympanum of the west portal of Amiens cathedral, 13th c.

**AMBROSIUS AUTPERTUS (died 784).** Born in *Provence, a monk at *San Vincenzo al Volturno in the Beneventano, Ambrosius Autpertus became its *abbot in 777. In 774 *Charlemagne had defeated the *Lombards, but had not subjugated the duchy of *Benevento: Autpertus's election aggravated the disputes between French and Lombard monks, and in late 778 he was forced to leave the monastery to the Lombard Poto and flee to *Spoleto. Summoned to *Rome by Charlemagne to resolve the conflict, he died on the way, perhaps murdered, in 784. A good writer, he composed a life of the monastery's founders (*Vita Paldonis, Tasonis et Tatonis*, *BHL* 6415), some *sermons, a *Conflictus vitiorum et virtutum* and a commentary on the *Apocalypse, his major work. In it he sets out an original mystical reading of the text (exploiting Augustine's heritage on the theme of the *Holy Spirit), totally unhistorical, tempered by the theme of the necessity of preaching (in line with *Gregory the Great). Among his sermons, a *De cupiditate* on the perfection of lay life, two more consecrated to the Virgin and one on the Transfiguration are all marked by an obvious mystical imprint.

*CChr.CM*, 27 and 27A, R. Weber (ed.), 1975 (2 vol.).

C. Leonardi, "Spiritualità di Ambrogio Autperto", *StMed*, 9, 1968, 1-131. – H. Riedinger, *LdM*, 1, 1980, 525.

Claudio Leonardi

**AMDA SION (died 1344).** Under Amda Sion's reign (1314-1344), which was one of the most brilliant in the history of the kingdom of *Ethiopia, Church and State experienced a remarkable expansion. He reorganised the army and made it a force capable of reducing the rebellions of the provincial governors and breaking Muslim attacks. He thus managed to restore the unity of the Empire, weakened under the Zagué, and push back the frontiers, at the same time ensuring a commercial opening to the Red Sea, on the coast of Eritrea. A skilful administrator, he set up an elaborate and effective feudal system. He also came into conflict with the Church, whose power had become offensive to the royal authority. Such was his renown that he was eulogized by his Muslim contemporary Al-Omari and from then on the West often confused his kingdom with that of *Prester John.

J. Perruchon, "Histoire des guerres d'Amda Syon, roi d'Éthiopie", *JA*, 14, 1889, 271-363, 381-493. – G. W. B. Huntingford, *The Glorious Victories of Amda Seyon, King of Ethiopia*, Oxford, 1965. – T. Tamrat, *Church and State in Ethiopia, 1270-1527*, Oxford, 1972.

Yvan G. Lepage

**AMICE.** *Amictorium* is the equivalent of the Greek *anabolos*, "that which is thrown around the neck". The great veil covering the neck and shoulders and provided with cords to attach it is a liturgical *vestment. It was originally worn above the alb, as was long done by the priests of *Lyon and *Milan, in accordance with the rules of their liturgy, but from the 13th c., elsewhere, it was worn under the alb. In fact it was placed on the head like a hood, then turned down when the other liturgical vestments had been put on; hence the sumptuous decoration of its upper border. The symbolic meaning given to the amice was that of moderation in speech; he who was allowed to wear it had to be "pure in word".

*Dictionnaire encyclopédique de la liturgie*, D. Sartore (ed.), A. M. Triacca (ed.), Turnhout, 1992 (Fr. tr.).

Guy-Marie Oury

**AMIENS CATHEDRAL.** Clues given by the *labyrinth, laid by the architect Renaud de Cormont in 1288, give precious information about the beginning of the construction of Amiens *cathedral: the impetus for the work came, under Bishop Évrard de Fouilloy in 1220, from the architect Robert de Luzarches. His plan, close to that of *Reims, differs from it mainly by the absence of transept towers. He sought the impression of size, obtained by the length of the building (145 m.), its height (42.5 m.) which was increased, doubtless following the example of *Beauvais, from that of the initial project, and finally by the width of the transept. This is carried on by the double aisles of the vertical bays of the choir, continued by a simple ambulatory onto which open five radiating chapels. The architect owed much to the model of *Chartres, from which he took the three-storey elevation and the use of piers of four engaged columns, whose function is to sculpt the stone with a play of light and accentuate the impression of verticality. Loftiness and luminosity are pushed to perfection in the apse (1236-1269), a masterpiece of **rayonnante* architecture, with its amply-lit triforium and its high lancets. Of the cathedral's *stained glass, unfortunately only irregular vestiges remain, which merely allow us to suppose its considerable importance in this mid 13th century.

The façade, made heavier by the strongly jutting buttresses, has three portals, whose sculpted programme, of extreme wealth, has the homogeneity of a rapid conception. The central portal is dedicated, like that of Notre-Dame in *Paris, to the *Last Judgment, with an impressive development of the tympanum, divided into four registers. The left portal exalts the theme of *Mary, the right portal is unusual in glorifying local hagiography, in the theme of the Life of St Firmin. Among the originalities of Amiénois iconography is the row of sixteen *prophets whose procession ensures the unity of the façade. Very much subordinated to the architecture, the sculpture of the façade has on the whole a rather massive severity.

H. Jantzen, *High Gothic: the Classic Cathedrals of Chartres, Reims and Amiens*, New York, 1962. – W. Sauerländer, *La Sculpture gothique en France, 1140-1270*, Paris, 1972 (1st ed. Munich, 1970). – A. Erlande-Brandenburg, "La façade de la cathédrale d'Amiens", *BM*, 135, 1977, 253-293. – A. Erlande-Brandenburg, *L'Art gothique*, Paris, 1983. – J. Thiébaut, *Les Cathédrales gothiques en Picardie*, Amiens, 1987.

Editorial staff

**AMPULLA, HOLY.** The Holy Ampulla was one of the main objects in the *coronation liturgy of the kings of France at *Reims; it commemorated the founding miracle of *Clovis's baptism in 498, and from the 9th c. the chrism that it contained was used for anointing the *kings at their *consecration. The first traces of the legend appear with the real founder of the royal Frankish ceremonies at Reims, Archbishop *Hincmar of Reims, in his account of the consecration of *Charles the Bald (869) as king of *Lotharingia, then in his *Life of Remigius* (*c.*880). A century later, *Flodoard gave a more complete version of Clovis's baptism. Clovis, a pagan unlike many barbarian rulers of Gaul and Germany who were *Arians, opted for Catholicism after his marriage with the *Burgundian princess Clotild (493). His baptism took place at Christmas 498 (or 499); Flodoard relates that in the press of the ceremony, the cleric carrying the holy oils could not reach the church. Then a *miracle happened: a dove descended from heaven with an ampulla (a liturgical phial) containing the chrism, which was mixed with the baptismal *water. It is hard to find the origin of this episode in the 9th c.: no mention of any discovery of the ampulla is recorded. But from Hincmar's first allusion, a confusion was set up between baptism and consecration. Clovis received no anointing: apart from biblical (Saul and *David) and *Visigothic precedents, Western kings were not anointed before *Pippin the Short. For Hincmar, what must have been no more than a simple catechumenal *oil became a chrism of unction. The confusion reappears in 9th-c. iconography, which sometimes depicts the *Baptism of Christ with a dove carrying an ampulla, but it is not possible to determine what meaning the analogy had. This confusion prepared the way for the royal *thaumaturgical miracle of the central Middle Ages, which derived not from the royal person, but from the power of this quasi-*sacrament, according to the Church's interpretation in the 13th century.

The ampulla was preserved in the abbey of St Remigius at Reims, being solemnly transported to the *cathedral for each coronation. Its importance appeared in 1429, when the rumour spread that the English wanted to steal it, and *Joan of Arc managed to convince *Charles VII to have himself consecrated at Reims. Early in the 14th c., an English Dominican, Nicholas of Stratton, made known the existence of a second ampulla miraculously delivered to *Thomas Becket by the Holy Virgin, destined for the anointing of the fifth English king after *Henry II. *Edward III did not use it because of the *pope's reservations, but in 1399 *Henry IV of Lancaster made it a part of the English ritual. A third ampulla, claimed to have been given to St *Martin to cure him, and preserved at *Marmoutier, allowed Henri IV, cut off from Reims, to have himself consecrated at *Chartres (1594). The ampulla of Reims was broken in 1793 by an envoy of the Convention. Despite the attempts of the Restoration, the existence of the ampulla coincided with that of the duration of the ambiguous relations between the Church and the French *Crown.

F. Oppenheimer, *The Legend of the Sainte Ampoule*, London, 1953. – A. Frolow, *Les Reliquaires de la vraie croix*, Paris, 1965.

Alain Boureau

**ANACLETUS II, ANTIPOPE (died 25 Jan 1138).** Piero Pierleoni, member of a powerful Roman family, studied at *Paris and became a monk at *Cluny. Called to *Rome by *Paschal II in 1116, he acquired an influential position in the *Sacred College under Paschal's pontificate and that of his successor *Calixtus II, who made him cardinal-priest. He then carried out numerous legations (England, Scotland, Ireland, Orkneys and France). On his return to Rome in 1145, he was kept at a relative distance by Honorius II and Chancellor Haimeric, close to the Frangipani family.

On the death of Honorius II (13 Feb 1130), Piero returned to centre stage. Haimeric had appointed a commission of eight *cardinals who proceeded to elect Gregorio Papereschi, who took the name *Innocent II. The majority of the cardinals, contesting the canonical *validity of this *election, elected Piero Pierleoni as *pope; he took the name Anacletus II. The regularity of both elections being disputable, it was the evolution of the ratio of strength between the two candidates that allowed a decision between them. Anacletus II, supported by his family, forced his rival to leave Rome. Outside the City, he was supported by the towns of central *Italy and the Po valley (*Milan), the bishops of *Aquitaine and the Norman *Roger II, on whom in Sept 1130 he conferred the hereditary royal title for *Sicily and the South of the peninsula. Meanwhile *Innocent II could soon count on the obedience of Germany, France, Castile, León and England, and the zeal of St *Bernard and Cardinal Haimeric in his favour was doubtless decisive. Strong in German support, Innocent II was able to enter Rome, take possession of the Lateran (30 April 1132) and crown King *Lothar emperor (8 June); but he could not maintain himself in the town after the departure of the imperial troops. Anacletus II managed to remain at Rome until his death, 25 Jan 1138, though his rival too was finally able to install himself there from 1 Nov 1137. Obedience to Anacletus II had never ceased to diminish, with the defection of the Italian towns: outside Rome, his sole lasting support was that of Roger II, following the traditional alliance with the reforming papacy. The *schism ended at Anacletus's death: though his partisans elected a successor to him (Victor IV), the latter abdicated after four months (29 May).

The schism of 1130 has given rise to numerous interpretations. The oldest explanation refers it to the conflicts between the Roman families of *Pierleoni and Frangipani. In the last half-century, the schism has been seen as the expression of a conflict of generations within the college of cardinals: Anacletus's partisans were holders of the reforming position inspired by the Cluniac monastic ideal, while those of Innocent II would have been more open to the new problems of society and the Church, after the *concordat of *Worms (H.-W. Klewitz, F.-J. Schmale). A recent tendency tends, by prosopographical work, to correct a too rigid vision of two sociologically opposed groups, while M. Stroll reevaluates the weight of the ratio of strength in the City and in the *Curia in relation to ideological positions.

H.-W. Klewitz, "Das Ende des Reformpapstums", *DA*, 1939, 371-412. – P.-F. Palumbo, *Lo Scisma del MCXXX*, Rome, 1942. – R. Manselli, "Anacleto II", *DBI*, 3, 1961, 17-19. – F.-J. Schmale, *Studien zum Schisma des Jahres 1130*, Cologne-Graz, 1961. – M. Stroll, *The Jewish Pope*, Leiden-New York, 1987. – M. Pacaut, "[Anaclet II]", *DHP*, 1994, 83-84.

Pierre Kerbrat

**ANAGNI.** An ancient city of pre-Roman origin (capital of the Ernici), situated south-east of *Rome. An episcopal see from the 5th c. (probably founded by Leo the Great), its ecclesiastical and political vicissitudes were largely influenced by the Holy See. The list of its *bishops can be reconstructed with some gaps throughout the early Middle Ages and shows the presence even in the Carolingian and post-Carolingian periods of prelates of *Lombard origin; this demonstrates that even after the Frankish conquest the Lombard ruling class did not immediately disappear from central *Italy. Anagni frequently offered hospitality to pontiffs, when for whatever reason they had to leave the Holy See. In 847, *e.g.*, the Saracen threat led Leo *IV to seek refuge there; in 963, expelled from Rome by the emperor *Otto I, so did John XII, who held a *council there with the prelates of the Roman Campagna. During a further papal sojourn at Anagni in 1062, *Alexander II, who had fled there to escape the men of the emperor and the antipope Cadalus, had Peter, of the Lombard family of the princes of Salerno, elected bishop. During his long episcopate, the most important in Anagni's medieval history, construction of the new *cathedral began, and at the time of *Urban II's stay there in 1088 the neighbouring *diocese of Trevi was annexed to the diocese. After having taken part in the first *crusade, Bishop Peter was canonized by *Paschal II five years after his death in 1105. In the 12th and 13th cc., papal sojourns at Anagni followed each other almost uninterruptedly, so that the city was often the scene of important political events. There in 1122 *Calixtus II issued the *bull that was the basis for the Concordat of Worms; there in 1160 *Alexander III excommunicated *Frederick Barbarossa in the cathedral; while in 1176, after the battle of Legnano, the same pope received the imperial legates, with whom he worked out the *pactum anagninum*, premise for the general peace that would be concluded at Venice in 1177. In the 13th c., Anagni gave birth to four pontiffs: *Innocent III, *Gregory IX, *Alexander IV and *Boniface VIII, which contributed to increasing the city's importance. There in 1227 Gregory IX proclaimed the *excommunication of *Frederick II of Swabia, guilty of having abandoned the crusade, and there three years later he received the imperial legates to negotiate the remission of the ban. Still at Anagni, during the period of polemic against the *mendicant orders in the pontificate of Alexander IV, were issued the disciplinary measures against the Franciscan *Gerard of Borgo San Donnino and the canon *William of Saint-Amour. In 1255 the same Alexander IV issued at Anagni the bull of *canonization of *Clare of Assisi. But the most famous episode of Anagni's medieval history was the capture of Boniface VIII by emissaries of *Philip the Fair of France and his subsequent liberation by the citizens of Anagni who rose up against the French. With the transfer of the papal see to *Avignon (1308-1376), a period of political and economic decline began for Anagni, to end only in the 15th century.

R. Ambrosi De Magistris, *Storia di Anagni*, 1889. – P. Zappasodi, *Anagni attraverso i secoli*, Anagni, 1908. – *Le iscrizioni urbani ad Anagni*, H. Solin (ed.), P. Tuomisto (ed.), Rome, 1996.

Andrea Tabarroni

**ANALOGY.** Analogues are what we call predicates whose formal contents (*rationes*) are neither identical (univocity) nor totally different (equivocity), but present a certain unity of meaning based on a direct relation or a similitude of relations. In the Middle Ages, this originally semantic instrument played a decisive role in the question of the constitution of the object of *metaphysics (so-called theory of analogy of *being). In *theology, analogy comes into the question of the divine names: how far can concepts expressing a created perfection be attributed to *God? The theory of the analogy of the divine names enables us to provide a basis for the validity of discourse on God, while respecting the transcendence of the object.

B. Montagnes, *La Doctrine de l'analogie de l'être d'après saint Thomas d'Aquin*, Louvain-Paris, 1963.

Serge Bonino

**ANAPHORA.** Literally "to carry upwards". In the Eastern liturgies it designates the Prayer of Oblation or Eucharistic Prayer (in Syriac, *Qurbana*). The oldest surviving formularies date from the 3rd and 4th cc. (*Apostolic Tradition*, *Euchologion* of Serapion, *Apostolic Constitutions*, VIII). The texts presently in use were fixed between the 5th and 8th centuries; some, in the Syriac tradition particularly rich in this field, are of more recent origin.

We can distinguish two great types of structure: Antiochene-Cappadocian (characteristic anaphorae: St Basil, St John Chrysostom or of the Apostles), and Egyptian (St Mark or St Cyril), depending on whether the epiclesis and the intercessions take place after or before the anamnesis. The number of anaphorae in use varies according to liturgy: they are particularly numerous in the Syriac tradition, while the *Byzantine liturgy keeps solely to the anaphorae named after St Basil and St John Chrysostom.

W. H. Frere, *The Anaphora or Great Eucharistic Prayer*, London, 1938. – A. Hänggi, I. Pahl, *Prex eucharistica*, Fribourg, 1968.

Irénée-Henri Dalmais

## ANATHEMA

**The West.** Anathema was the severest of the ecclesiastical penalties: not only did it exclude the guilty party from the Christian community, but also, according to Pope Adrian II (9th c.), who was merely repeating a common idea, it "sent [him] to *hell with the devil".

From the 12th c., anathema was confused with major *excommunication. It could be employed for any type of crime: thus in 1262 the archbishop of Bordeaux forbade cockfighting under pain of anathema. Theoretically permanent, it actually lasted only during the time of culpability.

"Anathème", *DACL*, 1, 2, 1907, 1926-1940. – "Anathème", *DDC*, 1, 1935, 512-516. – E. Vodola, *Excommunication in the Middle Ages*, Berkely, 1986, 14-16.

Patrick Henriet

**Byzantium.** From the Greek *anathema*, anathema was an ecclesiastical *sanction that banished the guilty person from the Church. The term dates back to the Septuagint (Dt 13, 15). Once anathematized, one was rejected from communion and suffered all the consequences of this exclusion up to the loss of eternal *salvation. There were also social and economic or even political implications for one against whom anathema was pronounced. It was the most severe ecclesiastical sanction; it had to be pronounced at an episcopal level, sparingly and after deep examination. Even in death, in popular imagination, the excommunicate was isolated, since his body did not decompose in the normal way unless the anathema was lifted. The lifting of the anathema was carried out at a special ceremony presided over by a *bishop.

K. M. Rhalles, *Poinikon dikaion tès Orthodoxou Anatolikès Ekklèsias*, Athens, 1907, 135-192.

Stavros Perentidis

## ANCHORITE, ANCHORESS

**The West.** Lay or religious, the anchorite was a person seeking the most perfect imitation of *Christ. His progress, animated by a profound faith, developed in a spirit of total humility, complete liberty and absolute love. To realise this lofty ideal, permanent or provisional retreat in a *desert place – edge of a *forest, marshy valley, ruins or caves – was one of the favourite ways of breaking with the world, in order to cast off the social mask and rediscover the identity of *man created in the image of *God. Despoiled of himself, he could then in some cases return to the world to convert it and transform it. Prophets and counsellors in daily life, medieval anchorites attracted companions and disciples who formed monastic communities, led great popular movements (the first *crusade) and were instigators of religious *orders like the *Camaldolese and *Carthusians. Their way of life sometimes aroused the mistrust of civil and ecclesiastical authorities, the *Benedictine Rule reserving this state for the more seasoned monks.

*L'Érémitisme en Occident jusque l'an Mil*, Milan, 1962. – J. Leclercq, *Aux sources de la spiritualité occidentale, étapes et constantes*, Paris, 1964. – A.K. Warren, "The Nun as Anchoress: England, 1100-1500", *Medieval Religious Women*, vol. 1, Kalamazoo (MI), 1984, 197-212. – A.K. Warren, *Anchorites and their Patrons in Medieval England*, Berkeley, 1985. – J. Heuclin, *Aux origines monastiques de la Gaule du Nord*, Lille, 1988. – M. E. Brunert, *Das Ideal der Wüstenaskese*, Münster, 1994.

Jean Heuclin

**Byzantium.** Etymologically, the anchorite is one who retires from the world (*anachôreô*) to find God by a rigorous *ascesis. There were numerous forms of anchoritic life: *eremitism, reclusion, *stylitism, anchoritic colonies. Complete solitude was rare. Most often the anchorites lived apart but accepted guests and disciples who could form a community. The *laura*, existing mainly in *Palestine, comprised anchorites who lived in solitude during the week and came together for the Sunday liturgy. Up to the end of the *Byzantine Empire, anchorites lived under the jurisdiction of *coenobitic monasteries. But anachoresis was reserved only for experienced monks, since the attacks of the *demon were more formidable there.

A.-J. Festugière, *Les moines d'orient*, 1, *Culture et sainteté*, Paris, 1961. – D. Papachryssanthou, "La vie monastique dans les campagnes byzantines du VIIIe au XIe siècle", *Byz.*, 43, 1973, 158 f.

Bernard Flusin

**ANDORRA.** Andorra is the largest of the small independent States of Europe, measuring 452 square kilometres. Situated on the south slopes of the *Pyrenees, it is a co-principality under the joint rule of the bishop of Urgel, in *Catalonia, and the President of the French Republic.

This mountainous territory was originally a fief of the Spanish *March, which *Louis the Pious ceded in 819 to the bishop of Urgel, a donation recognised by the *popes until 1099. After a gap of 50 years under other rulers, it returned to the bishops of Urgel. But they did not hold it peacefully: the fief was contested, especially in the first half of the 13th c. when it came under the ambitious eye of the counts of Foix, who finally prevailed at least in part. Their rights over the valley of Andorra were derived from the Caboets, to whom they had been ceded early in the 12th c. by the bishop of Urgel in exchange for protection. The bishop had reserved the right of sovereignty for himself, a fact contested when the Foix succeeded the Caboets.

On 8 Sept 1278 a pact of peaceful "co-lordship" (*pariatge*) was reached between the Foix and the bishop, though the bishop kept the title of "prince of Andorra", which he still holds. The agreement was ratified with the *placitum* of *Martin IV in 1282. The archives of Urgel cathedral – dedicated to St *Odo – keep these and other precious documents: a codex of the *Apocalypse (*codex de Beatus*), a codex of *Gregory the Great's *Dialogues* (10th c.), and others (of Silvester II, 1001; Benedict VIII, 1012; *Eugenius III, 1151; *Alexander III, 1163-1175). The rights of the counts of Foix passed, through marriage, via the kings of Navarre, to Henri IV who incorporated them in the crown of France.

Andorra's present institutional form dates from 1231: six parishes, each with a council presided over by a consul. Above these is a General Council of 24 members, holding legislative and executive power, in which the six parishes have equal representation.

J. Martines Mier, *Memoria sobre la fundación y origen de la ciudad de la Seo di Urgel*, Tortosa, 1884. – J. Wincke, *Documenta selecta*, Barcelona, 1936. – S. Lobet, *El medio y la vida en Andorra*, Barcelona, 1947. – J. Ortiz de Urbina, "Andorra", *EC*, 1, 1948, 1180-1181. – J. Sermet, *La nouvelle Andorre*, Clermont-Ferrand, 1963.

Attilio Stendardi

**ANDREW II OF HUNGARY (1177-1235).** King of *Hungary from 1205 to 1235, second son of Béla III (1172-1196). Having opposed his brother Imre I (1196-1204) several times, Andrew II inherited his throne in 1205. In 1200, he had married Gertrude of Meran, and their eldest daughter was St *Elizabeth of Hungary (1207-1231). Andrew made large *donations of the royal domains to his barons. After violent conflicts set the queen in opposition to the *nobility, Gertrude was assassinated in 1213. Fulfilling a vow of his father, in 1217 Andrew II took part in the fifth *crusade. Responding to the demands of the lesser nobility in process of formation (*servientes regis*), in 1222 he promulgated a Golden Bull to guarantee its constitutional rights – the first continental parallel to *Magna Carta (1215). From 1214, he had to share the kingdom with his eldest son, Béla IV (1235-1270), who became prince of *Transylvania in 1224 and followed an autonomous policy.

J. R. Sweeney, "Hungary in the Crusades 1169-1218", *The International History Review*, 3, Toronto, 1981, 467-481. – G. Kristó, *Die Arpaden-Dynastie*, Budapest, 1993, 240-265.

Gábor Klaniczay

**ANDREW OF LONGJUMEAU (13th c.).** A *Dominican missionary who, perhaps already instructed to bring the *relics of the *Passion to France (1239), brought letters from *Innocent IV to various Muslim princes and oriental prelates as well as to the *Mongols, meeting the *Nestorian Simeon Rabban-ata at Tabriz (1245-1247). At *Cyprus, *Louis IX charged him with an embassy that took him to Mongolia, whence he brought back an invitation to submit to the Mongols, but also information on the captive Christians in the Altai which decided William of Rubruck to go to the Mongol lands (1249-1251). It appears that he stayed and preached at Tunis before 1270.

P. Pelliot, "Les Mongols et la papauté", *ROC*, 24, 1924, 225-268; *ibid.*, 28, 1931-1932, 3-84.

Jean Richard

**ANDREW OF SAINT-VICTOR (died 1175).** Originally from England, Andrew was a pupil of *Hugh at the abbey of *Saint-Victor in Paris. While distancing himself from his master, he continued Hugh's literal *exegesis, confining himself to Old Testament commentaries. Called for the first time (1148/1149-1153) to the post of *abbot, he died at Wigmore (Wales) in October 1175. In his scriptural exegesis Andrew sets out an interpretation according to the scheme *littera-sensus-sententia*, a product of classical *rhetoric. The wide range of his sources (classical authors, Church *Fathers, Jewish exegetes) reflects a great humanist culture thus put at the service of *theology as exegesis.

*Angels of the heavenly host* by Ridolfo Guariento, 14th c. Padua, Museo Civico.

R. Berndt, *André de Saint-Victor (mort en 1175). Exégète et théologien*, *Bibliotheca Victorina*, 2, Turnhout, 1991. – M.A. Signer, "Peshat, Sensus Litteralis and Sequential Narrative: Jewish Exegesis and the School of St. Victor in the 12th Century", *The Frank Talmage Memorial Volume*, B. Walfish (ed.), 1, Haifa, 1993, 203-16.

Rainer Berndt

**ANGEL.** The term "angel" (Hebrew *mal'ak'*, Greek *angelos*, Latin *angelus* or *nuntius*) means a messenger, sent by God for a mission. The Scriptures provided the primary basis for the medieval treatment of angels, especially in the 9th-12th cc., when reflection on the biblical text, unlike subsequent practice, was more direct and immediate. But the more strictly doctrinal themes were provided mainly by Augustine (theory of creation and knowledge of angels, position of the good and the depraved), Pseudo-*Dionysius the Areopagite (subdivision of angels into hierarchies which receive purification, illumination and perfection from *God and transmit them in an orderly way to the ecclesiastical hierarchy) and *Gregory the Great (the angels, by divine mandate, are at man's service).

In the 9th c., the most important treatment of angels is that by the *Neoplatonist *John Scotus Eriugena, who translated Dionysius's writings and commented on his *Celestial Hierarchy.* He illustrates the orderly *participation of the celestial *intelligences in the supreme light of the divine *Word and gives an original development to two angelological themes. The first of these concerns teratological or monstrous symbolism, which consists in attributing to the angel a mixture of physical elements, anthropomorphic or zoomorphic (six wings, eyes, faces, feet). Eriugena emphasizes the great anagogical value of such symbolism, or its value in spurring men upwards: precisely because it is repugnant and radically dissimilar to the reality that it represents, the teratological symbol invites mortals not to dwell on it, but to transcend it in search of the intelligible, spiritual value whose vehicle it is, and which refers to God. The second theme concerns the *beatific vision of angels and men. Eriugena aligns himself not with the *Augustinian position, which affirms the possibility of a vision of God face to face in *heaven, but with the Greco-Dionysiac position in which God, because absolutely transcendent and invisible, remains unknowable in his essence both to the angels and to the blessed. He makes himself visible only in his theophanies: these are the result of his condescension to the creature, which is thus elevated to him and "divinized" and becomes his manifestation without ceasing to be a creature.

In the 11th c. the most prominent position is that of *Anselm of Canterbury. Indebted mainly to Augustine and Gregory the Great, and hence the expression of an angelological tendency particularly attentive to relations between men and angels (since both, similarly created and directly dependent on God, are together called to constitute the future heavenly city), he analyses at length the status of the angels before and after the fall, what they lost as a consequence, and asks whether the number of the elect in the heavenly city corresponds to that of the fallen angels, so as to make up the perfect number of rational creatures who contemplate God.

The 12th c. was the great period of medieval angelology. It is found mainly in the following genres of theological text: biblical commentaries (*e.g.* those of *Rupert of Deutz), commentaries on the *Celestial Hierarchy* (*e.g.* that of *Hugh of Saint-Victor), *sermons (*e.g.* those of *Bernard of Clairvaux) and collections of *Sentences (the best known being those of Peter Lombard). The main themes dealt with in exegetical commentaries and collections of Sentences are the moment of creation, the sin, the number, the body and the function of angels. It is asked whether their creation took place before or at the same time as that of the visible world. Especially central is the reflection on the fall of the angel (Lucifer) and the "lesser angels": their state at the moment of creation is investigated, *e.g.* whether they were immediately blessed; whether they sinned as soon as they were created or after a brief instant; whether their sin was one of envy or of pride; whether their fault was remediable, whether the elect in heaven will be able to occupy the vacant place of the fallen angels. Again it is considered whether the number of the angels is determinable, whether they are more or less than men; whether they have a body, and if so of what *nature, tangible and heavy like the human, or subtle, airy, luminous. But above all what is the role of an angel, and what is the function of the guardian angel: is there one for each person or does each protect more than one? In commentaries on the *Celestial Hierarchy*, on the other hand, the themes most often discussed are the hierarchical structure of the angelic world, its purifying, illumining and perfecting activity, and the Dionysian and Eriugenian theory of illumination and theophanies. Hugh of Saint-Victor protested vigorously against the latter, stating that, if the beatific vision consisted in seeing just an image of God, it would not be true *beatitude. Representing in this the most authentic Augustinian claims, he was the leader of a tradition that finally triumphed, leading in 1241 to the condemnation by the university of *Paris of the proposition "*Divina essentia in se nec ab homine nec ab angelo videtur* (The divine essence in itself is seen neither by men nor by angels)".

In the 13th c., the available material on angels was enlarged by the circulation of three groups of works: *John of Damascus's *De fide orthodoxa*, translated in the 12th c., which set out in clear and schematic form the angelological doctrines of the late antique Greek tradition (Gregory Nazianzen, Dionysius); the "Latin" *Corpus Dionysiacum* (which appeared around the middle of the century and was assiduously studied by Parisian theologians), complex and stratified, made up of several versions and extracts of Areopagitic writings, commentaries on the *Celestial Hierarchy*, apparatus of scholia and glosses; and *Peter Lombard's four books of *Sentences*, the second of which contained a treatise on angels with headings indicating subject-matter. This work became a real handbook, and the object of commentaries for those studying *theology at *university: in this new setting, therefore, meditation on the angel became an institutional exercise, either in the form of *lectures aiming at doctrinal exploration of the Lombard's text, or of *disputation with its own rules: arguments of authority and *reason for or against a particular angelological problem, solution, replies to *objections: angelology took on a "scientific" garb.

Two quite different events gave new direction to the debates of the 13th c.: the fourth *Lateran council (1215), and the acquisition of a new culture, this time more philosophical than theological, *i.e.* the Arab-peripatetic. Lateran IV confirmed against the *Cathar heresy that the principle of the universe is one, creator *ex nihilo* of all things visible and invisible, spiritual – *i.e.* angelic – and corporeal, and that the devil and his acolytes, originally created *good by God, became depraved by their own *will. In short, the angel is, like *man, a creature *ex nihilo*, endowed with *freedom: all this would be invoked as peculiar to Christian angelology against the ever-emergent temptations of necessarist emanationism, characteristic more of Arab-peripatetic angelology.

With the circulation of *Aristotle's psychological, physical and metaphysical works by his Arabic commentators, especially *Avicenna and *Averroes – but not forgetting the *De causis* and the works of Proclus –, theological reflection on angels came to be measured against new conceptions, no longer of revealed origin, not patristic, but pagan and philosophical: *e.g.* that of separate *intelligences, necessary and eternal emanations from an impersonal first principle, motors of celestial spheres of a universe without history and without end. In these conceptions, the angel's sympathy for man becomes *apatheia*. Against this metaphysicizing and naturalistic conception of angelology, however, the theologians made war. Those who had most occasion to confront it, *e.g.* *Albert the Great or *Thomas Aquinas (and later the Parisian censors of the condemnations of 1277), were in search of a sometimes difficult equilibrium; they asked, like Albert, whether the angels of the theologians were the same as the intelligences of the philosophers, while making use in their angelological claims of the enemy's conceptual apparatus, *i.e.* that offered by peripatetic and Neoplatonist physics, psychology and *metaphysics. Albert and Thomas had as their main interlocutors the Greeks and the Arabs, and for the first time the *Jews, such as *Avicebron and *Maimonides; *Bonaventure's dialogue, on the other hand, was mainly with the authors of the 12th c.: especially in his spiritual works, he constructed a peculiarly Franciscan theology of the angel, whose model of reference was St *Francis who received the *stigmata at the appearance of a winged Seraph carrying a cross. Of the angelology of the past, nothing would be lost in the 13th c.: all theories would be reinterpreted, clarified, systematized. New themes became favoured objects of investigation: the *nature, knowledge, communication, place, motion, dimensions of angels. It was asked whether angels were pure form or constituted of *form and matter (*hylomorphism); from the solution given arose another way of interpreting their principle of individuation: if they are pure forms, either they are distinguished from one another by *species or each of them is a species *per se*; if on the other hand they have a hylomorphic structure, they are distinguished individually. Questions were asked about the object of their knowledge – whether God himself, themselves, creatures, the material world, the future –, the means (the species) and modes of their knowledge, which cannot in any case be through the senses, and hence its difference from human *knowledge. The two types *par excellence* of communication of knowledge were examined: illumination and *language. Again it was asked whether the angel, without extension and dimensions, can be in a place, whether he can be in several places at the same time, whether several angels can together occupy the same space; and how the angel moves from one place to another, whether his movement is continuous or discontinuous, whether it depends on that of the heavens; and what is the angel's measure of duration, since God has his measure, which is eternity, and man too has his measure, which is *time.

In the 14th c., the angel became increasingly the object of subtle *scholastic exercises that developed, but also criticized, the forms of thought of earlier angelology. It is found especially in the works of *Dante: mainly in the *Convivio* and the theological poetry of the *Divine Comedy*. In the *Inferno,* Dante alludes to the singular position of the "neutral" angels: unlike the faithful or the rebellious angels, through indolence they made no choice, either in favour of *good or of *evil: but they were no less sinners. In the *Purgatorio,* he perceives the wealth of the angel in his dynamic function as God's messenger in the service of man. He accompanies him, exhorts him, purifies him, defends him in his arduous journey of *ascesis; finally, in the *Paradiso*, Dante understands the angel in his function of contemplating God solely, ceaselessly and joyously: and this according to the position that is proper to him, *i.e.* according to the rank he occupies in the hierarchical scale of the celestial creatures.

A. Vacant, "III. Angélologie dans l'Église latine depuis le temps des Pères jusqu'à saint Thomas d'Aquin" and "IV. Angélologie de saint Thomas d'Aquin et des scolastiques postérieures", *DThC*, 1, 1930, 1222-1248. – J. Daniélou, *Les Anges et leur mission d'après les Pères de l'Église*, Chevetogne, 1951. – P. Glorieux, *Autour de la spiritualité des anges*, Tournai, 1959. – G. Tavard, "Die Engel", *HDG*, 2, 2b, 1968, 1-78. – V. Klee, *Les Plus beaux textes sur les saints anges*, Paris, 1984. – M. Cacciari, *The Necessary Angel*, Albany (NY), 1994. – P. Faure, *Les Anges*, Paris, 1988. – R. Lavatori, *Gli angeli*, Genoa, 1991. – A. Amato, "L'Angelologia nella tradizione della Chiesa", *Angeli e demoni*, Bologna, 1992, 105-150. – M. L. Colish, "Early Scholastic Angelology", *RThAM*, 62, 1995, 80-109. - B. Faes de Mottoni, *San Bonaventura e la scala di Giacobbe, Letture di angelologia*, Naples, 1995.

Barbara Faes de Mottoni

**ANGELA OF FOLIGNO (*c.*1248-1309).** The greatest Italian mystic of the 14th c., born probably at Foligno. There is little sure information on Angela's life. It has been conjectured from the *Memorial*, a sort of spiritual biography written by her confessor Arnaldo da Foligno, that she was married and had several children. Converted to a life of chastity and penitence in *c.*1285, she was free to dedicate herself entirely to God after the "providential" death of all her family. Her conversion originated in a personal crisis, born of a profound and oppressive sense of *sin and a feeling of inability to make a complete confession. She tells how St Francis appeared to her in a vision and came to her aid, obtaining for her the grace of a general *confession thanks to which she was able to begin her spiritual journey. In 1291 she made a pilgrimage to Assisi and entered the Franciscan *Third Order, marking a new step in her spiritual journey.

Angela's works, while echoing various influences, in particular St *Bonaventure and the Victorines, have a specific originality of their own and exemplify a quite individual *spirituality.As well as the *Memorial*, 36 *Instructions* are attributed to her, comparable in their content to contemporary "negative theology". She spiritually influenced many people, including the Franciscan Spiritual *Ubertino da Casale. Her writings, or at least the texts concerning her, were submitted, for reasons still unclear, to the approval of Cardinal Giacomo *Colonna in 1309. She has the title of *beata* and is called *magistra theologorum* for her influence on the theologians of her time and for the esteem aroused, even later, by her writings.

*Il libro della beata A. da Foligno*, L. Thier (ed.), A. Calufetti (ed.), Grottaferrata, 1985 (crit. ed. of Latin text). – *Angela of Foligno: Complete Works*, P. Lachance (ed.), New York, 1993.

*Vita e spiritualità della beata Angela da Foligno, Atti del Convegno per il VII Centenario della conversione della beata Angela da Foligno (1285-1985)*, C. Schmitt (ed.), Perugia, 1987. – C. W. Bynum, *Holy feast and holy fast*, Berkeley (CA), 1987. – *Angela da Foligno, terziaria francescana*, Spoleto, 1992. – A. Pompei, "Concetto e pratica della penitenza in Margherita da Cortona e Angela da Foligno", *Francesco d'Assisi: intenzionalità teologico-pastorale delle Fonti Francescane*, Rome, 1994. – J. Dalarun, "Angèle de Foligno a-t-elle existé?", *Alla signorina. Mélanges offerts à Noëlle de la Blanchardière*, 1995, 59-97 ("CEFR", 204). – S. Andreoli, *Angela da Foligno, maestra spirituale*, Rome, 1996 (2nd ed.). – M. J. Higgins, "Angela of Foligno (1248-1309)", *Analecta Tor*, 158, 1996, 101-134.

Giulia Barone

**ANGELIC POPE.** The *papa angelicus*, or *pastor angelicus*, appears in medieval *apocalyptic literature as one who will inaugurate a new Church and a new world, of perfect sanctity. The first speculations on an ideal and saintly *pope who would transform the world appeared in the writings of *Joachim of Fiore († 1202). In his *Liber de Concordia Novi ac Veteri Testamenti* (Book of the Harmony of the Old and New Testaments) he declares that, before the end of the Age of the Son and the coming of *Antichrist, the preaching of the "universal pontiff of the new Jerusalem" will announce the coming of a new Christianity. In *c.*1270 some poems appeared announcing a last pope "of angelic life"; at the same time, the Franciscan *Roger Bacon († 1294) wrote of a pope to come whose holiness would be such that he would unite all the peoples, Greeks, Tartars and Muslims.

The election of Pope *Celestine V in 1294, followed by his abdication and the election of *Boniface VIII, triggered vast polemics on the subject of the angelic pope. Unlike Boniface, Celestine was generally held to be a holy and austere pope; so the figure of an angelic pope, sometimes contrasted with that of a pope who would be the Antichrist, was increasingly evoked and made the object of ever more numerous discussions. The Franciscan *Spirituals (who had Joachist tendencies and had benefited from Celestine's protection) were the main propagators of this papal myth; but it was a Dominican, Robert of Uzès († 1296), who first drew attention to the contrast between Celestine and Boniface and announced that a holy Franciscan would soon succeed them. Some of the first Spiritual writers, such as *Peter John Olivi, *Angelo of Clareno and *Ubertino da Casale, had little to say on this subject. The most valuable and influential studies were probably the work of their contemporary confrères, like the *Vaticinia de summis pontificibus* and the *Liber de Flore*. Most manuscripts of the *Vaticinia* comprise a number of brief, enigmatic texts concerning a series of popes, with captioned illustrations; the last five illustrations generally represent poor, saintly popes in the company of angels. The *Liber de Flore*, the first work to mention the expression *pastor angelicus*, describes the spectacular achievements of the last four popes, in co-operation with a Last World Emperor, who would be French.

The *Vaticinia* and the *Liber* influenced contemporary writers and even those of a later period, such as *Arnold of Villanova († 1313), *John of Roquetaillade († after 1365; his apocalyptic account ends with the description of a *pastor angelicus* who rules the Church after having conquered the Antichrist) and the widely read Telesphorus of Cosenza (active *c.*1386). The myth persisted into the time of reformers such as *Savonarola, who proclaimed the coming of a *papa santo*, and Martin Luther, who was himself identified as the angelic pope.

F. Baethgen, *Der Engelpapst*, Leipzig, 1943. – M. Reeves, *The Influence of Prophecy in the Later Middle Ages*, Oxford, 1969. – M. Reeves, *Joachim of Fiore and the Prophetic Future*, London, 1976, 59-82. – B. McGinn, "'Pastor angelicus': Apocalyptic Myth and Political Hope in the Fourteenth Century", *Santi e santità nel secolo XIV*, Perugia, 1989, 219-251. – "Fin du monde et signes des temps. . .", *CFan*, 27, 1992.

George Ferzoco

**ANGELICO, FRA (*c.*1400-1455).** An Italian friar preacher, born at Vicchio in the Mugello (province of Florence). We know almost nothing of the younger years of Guido son of Piero, except that he was a painter before entering the *Dominicans. On 31 Oct 1417, at his own request, he was inscribed in the Company of St Nicholas, one of the many *guilds of painters then existing at *Florence, several of whose members entered *orders. Between 1420 and 1422 Guido, named in religion Fra Giovanni, took the habit with the friars of Fiesole who belonged to the movement of the *Observance. There he became friends with Fra Antonino Pierozzi, the future St *Antoninus, and was influenced by *John Dominici, founder and first prior of the convent, and champion of renewal of the order.

At first, Fra Giovanni – not until more than 18 years after his death was he called "Angelico" – put his art at the service of his brethren. Between 1428 and 1435, date of the solemn *consecration of the conventual church, he painted at least five *altarpieces for the convent of Fiesole, among them the famous *Annunciation* in the Prado museum, which aroused Michelangelo's admiration, and the *Coronation of the Virgin* now in the Louvre. But it was in the *frescos of St Mark's convent, painted between 1438 and 1445, that he showed the full extent of a talent that allied Gothic traditions to the attainments of the Renaissance. Each cell contains a fresco whose very sober composition centres interest on the essential: the invitation to meditation, out of concern for the return to evangelical sources preached by the Observance.

In 1445, Pope *Eugenius IV called Fra Giovanni to *Rome to decorate the chapel of the Holy Sacrament (St Nicholas's chapel) at the Vatican, whose frescos are now lost. The painter then settled at the Dominican convent of Santa Maria della Minerva, residence of the order's master general. He ran an important studio, but remained that "modest, pious man" depicted by his biographers, and refused the archbishopric of Florence. He had close links with the pope, as with his successor *Nicholas V, first humanist pope of the *Renaissance, whose private chapel (capella Niccolina) he decorated between 1447 and 1450. In these paintings, which set out in parallel the lives of the martyr saints Stephen and Lawrence, a new role was accorded to architecture and landscape, translating the propositions of the *humanists into theological terms. Returning to Tuscany, he was from 1450 to 1452, without ceasing to paint, prior of the convent of San Domenico at Fiesole, to which he was always greatly attached. We know almost nothing of the last three years of one who was called in his lifetime "one of the most famous painters in Italy". He may have returned to Rome to collaborate in the restoration of the convent of Santa Maria della Minerva, in which he had already had a part during his first Roman sojourn. He died in that convent on 18 Feb 1455.

From 1517, his brethren gave him the title "blessed", but the Order of Preachers did not take the necessary steps for beatification until 400 years later. The process was impeded by the absence of an uninterrupted veneration. No miracle of his was known, no-one came to his tomb to celebrate a cult. It was by his painting that he finally obtained the glory of the altar in 1984, at the end of the longest and most original process of beatification.

G. C. Argan, *Fra Angelico et son siècle: étude biographique et critique*, Paris, 1955. – A. Berne-Joffroy, U. Baldini, *Tout l'oeuvre peint de Fra Angelico*, Paris, 1973. – *Beato Angelico, Miscellanea de studi*, Rome, 1984. – A. Hertz, H. Nils Loose, *Fra Angelico*, Paris, 1984 (Fr. tr.). – G. Didi-Huberman, *Fra Angelico*, Paris, 1990. – W. Hood, *Fra Angelico at San Marco*, New Haven, 1993. – W. Hood, "Angelico, Fra", *DoA*, 2, 30-40.

Dominique Rigaux

*The mystic wheel* by Fra Angelico (*c.*1400-1455). Florence, convent of San Marco

**ANGELO CLARENO (*c.*1255-1337).** A *Franciscan, leader of the **fraticelli* of central-southern Italy. In his youth, because of his position in favour of radical *poverty, rejected by the majority of the order, he spent several years in prison; he was freed in 1290. After a first stay in *Cilicia, he returned to Italy (1294) and was one of those who received verbal authorization from Pope *Celestine V to set up the autonomous congregation of *Pauperes eremite domini Celestini* (the *Celestines). To escape the order's hostility and that of *Boniface VIII, they took refuge in Greece for ten years. There Clareno collected and translated into Latin a large corpus of ascetic writings still largely unknown in the West, among them Basil's *Asceticon*, the Pseudo-Basilian *Constitutiones monasticae*, Pseudo-Macarius's *Opuscula ascetica* and *John Climacus's *Scala Paradisi*. Back in Italy (1307), he followed Cardinal Giacomo *Colonna to the Avignon *Curia, where he worked in vain to obtain full ecclesiastical recognition for the Poor Hermits, whose leader he had meanwhile become. The new pope, *John XXII, ordered the dissident Franciscans (called *fraticelli* from this time) to submit to the order's discipline. Clareno took refuge at *Subiaco (1318-1334), from where he maintained contacts with the communities of *fraticelli* of central-southern Italy; sought by the *Inquisition, he fled to Basilicata.

From 1312 to the eve of his death, his ecclesiastical and religious career is documented by the collection of 80 Latin *Epistulae*. They are addressed to his companions and a wider circle of friars and *laity concerned with following evangelical perfection. His correspondents are called to a rigorous ideal of *ascesis and poverty and exhorted to remain faithful to their promises. The question of the Franciscan identity of the Poor Hermits was finally resolved, thanks to the distinction between the Franciscan Order and the Franciscan life, to which alone it was important to remain faithful. His criticism of John XXII's positions on poverty went so far as to accuse the pope of *heresy. The *Expositio regulae* (1321-1323) interpreted the Franciscan Rule from the viewpoint of an evangelical radicalism nourished by Eastern patristic sources, especially on the theme of poverty. His most famous work is the *Chronicon seu Historia septem tribulationum ordinis minorum*, written between 1323 and 1326. After having characterised *Francis's vocation in terms of *sequela* as far as the cross, Clareno offers a coherent rereading of the first Franciscan century as a progressive flight from its original intention. The "seven tribulations" punctuate the conflict, prophecied by Francis, between the order's leadership and a minority of *Spirituals determined to remain faithful to their promises. The *Chronicon* is the main document of the attempted rereading of Franciscan history made by the spiritual and *fraticelli* minority, in explicit polemic against the order's official orientation as represented by St *Bonaventure.

L. von Auw, *Angelo Clareno et les Spirituels italiens*, Rome, 1979. – G. L. Potestà, *Angelo Clareno dai poveri eremiti ai fraticelli*, Rome, 1990.

Gian Luca Potestà

**ANGELUS.** Millet's painting is a fine illustration of the popular prayer of the *Angelus*. Three times a day – morning, mid-day and evening – the *Angelus* was rung on all the *bells of Christendom. Work stopped and three *Ave Marias* were recited with verses recalling the mystery of the Incarnation. The first document relating to the *Angelus* is an act of Pope *John XXII in 1318 approving the custom of reciting the *Ave Maria* three times, kneeling, each evening at the sound of the bell, and attaching spiritual favours to it. The morning ringing is mentioned early in the 14th c. in the *Parma Chronicle* (1317-1318). The mid-day *Angelus* is a much later development, which *Louis XI greatly encouraged in France. The evening ringing invited the faithful to commemorate the mystery of the Incarnation; that of mid-day was at first linked to the memory of the *Passion; the morning one, most commonly to the *Resurrection. Only in the 16th c. did remembrance of the mystery of the Incarnation become predominant for all three ringings, whence the name: "The Angel of the Lord announced to Mary. . ."

J. Fournée, *Histoire de l'Angelus*, Paris, 1991.

Guy-Marie Oury

**ANGELUS, DYNASTY OF.** A Byzantine dynasty that reigned from 1185 to 1204. The marriage of Constantine Angelus to Theodora, daughter of Alexius I Comnenus, founded the fortune of this previously obscure family, which became one of the branches of the *Comneni, from which the emperors chose numerous generals. Isaac Angelus, whose life was threatened by the suspicious Andronicus I Comnenus, took refuge in Hagia Sophia at *Constantinople and dared to appeal to the people, with unhoped-for success since Andronicus was overthrown and Isaac proclaimed emperor (1185-1195). After a brilliant victory, 7 Nov 1185, over the Normans who had just taken *Thessalonica, he could nevertheless not prevent the restoration in 1186 of a Bulgar-Vlach State ruled by the brothers Ivan and Peter Asen. In 1189 his negotiations with *Saladin drew on him the hostility of the German crusaders of *Frederick Barbarossa, to the extent that they dreamed for a time of seizing Constantinople. With Byzantine power declining on all sides, Isaac was challenged and overthrown by the army of the Western provinces, who were tired of defeats by the *Bulgars, in favour of his brother Alexius III (1195-1203).

The new emperor showed himself equally incapable of pushing back the *Turks or, despite some successes around 1200-1202, of reducing the Bulgars, now led by the terible Kaloyan. He deceived even his own supporters, which led to severe internal troubles. In 1195 Alexius resigned himself to paying tribute to the German emperor *Henry VI, from which he was freed by Henry's unexpected death. He multiplied concessions to the Italian towns, notably *Venice by a treaty of 1198, though safeguarding the Byzantine monopoly in the Black Sea. The *hyperpyron* was heavily devalued and the resources of an Empire run by often incompetent and venal governors visibly diminished. Worse still, the emperor let his nephew Alexius, Isaac's son, escape and seek refuge with his brother-in-law *Philip of Swabia, emperor of *Germany.

On Philip's advice, Alexius joined the crusaders of the fourth *crusade at Corfu and convinced them to modify their route so as to take him to Constantinople and establish him as emperor in return for the promise of important material help. Alexius appeared before Constantinople in July 1203, his uncle fled, and the people of the capital, not wishing to see the Latins enter by main force, took the aged Emperor Isaac II from his prison, put him back on the throne and opened the gates to his son. Alexius IV (July 1203 - Feb 1204) alienated both his Latin allies, by failing to keep his financial promises, and his subjects, by his fiscal demands and his supposed friendship for the Latins. Victim of a nationalist reaction, he was overthrown and assassinated by a relative, Alexius V *Ducas Murtzuphlus (Feb-April 1204), who could not prevent Constantinople falling to the Crusaders on 13 April 1204.

C. M. Brand, *Byzantium confronts the West (1180-1204)*, Cambridge (MA), 1968. – D. E. Queller, T. F. Madden, *The Fourth Crusade. The Conquest of Constantinople*, Philadelphia (PA), 1997.

Jean-Claude Cheynet

**ANGEVINS OF HUNGARY.** The Angevins of *Hungary were descended from the *Angevins of Naples. In 1269 *Charles I of Anjou concluded a double marriage treaty with the *Árpáds (*Charles II marrying Mary of Hungary and Ladislas IV the Cuman marrying Isabella of Anjou). This was the basis of the claims of Charles II's son Charles Martel († 1295), claims bequeathed to his son Charles I of Hungary (1309-1342) who became the heir of the Árpáds, extinct in 1301. Charles tried to obtain the inheritance of his cousin *Robert of Naples by marrying his son Andrew to Robert's grand-daughter Joanna (1345-1380). But Andrew was murdered in 1345. His death was the reason for the Hungarian campaigns at *Naples (1347-1352), led by Charles I's heir, Louis the Great (1342-1382). Louis also became king of *Poland in 1370. His Polish crown fell in 1384 to his daughter *Hedwig, who in 1386 married *Ladislas Jagiello, grand duke of *Lithuania. In Hungary, his daughter Mary succeeded him in 1382 and had another Angevin claimant, Charles III (1385-1386), murdered. In 1387, she married *Sigismund of Luxemburg and resigned power in Hungary to him.

E. G. Léonard, *Les Angevins de Naples*, Paris, 1954. – S. B. Vardy, G. Grosschmid, L. S. Domokos, *Louis the Great. King of Hungary and Poland*, New York, 1986. – G. Klaniczay, "Le Culte des saints dynastiques en Europe Centrale (Angevins et Luxembourg au XIV$^{e}$ siècle)", *L'Église et le peuple chrétien*, Rome, 1990, 221-247.

Gábor Klaniczay

**ANGEVINS OF NAPLES.** The Angevins of Naples, princes of French royal blood, were two successive families from *Anjou, who ruled the kingdom of *Naples in the late Middle Ages. It officially kept the name of Kingdom of *Sicily, which it had borne since its foundation in 1130; but Sicily fell into the power of the Crown of *Aragon in 1282. The first house of Anjou was founded by *Louis IX's youngest brother, Charles, who had received the county of Anjou in appanage from his father *Louis VIII. In 1246, a skilfully negotiated marriage added the county of *Provence to that of Anjou. Charles was then called on by the pope to conquer the kingdom of Sicily from the last Hohenstaufen, supporters of the Ghibelline party opposed to the papacy. Charles succeeded in this conquest, 1266-1268, but he subsequently lost Sicily, which remained separated from southern *Italy until the 16th century. Charles I's son Charles II gave Anjou as his daughter's dowry on the occasion of her marriage to Charles of Valois, brother of *Philip the Fair; and this Charles's son, King *Philip VI, reunited Anjou with the French Crown in 1328.

The second house of Anjou came from Louis, younger son of John the Good, who received the duchy of Anjou in appanage. Louis was chosen as heir by Joanna, queen of Naples of the first house of Anjou, who had no children (1380). But he and his successors had to dispute the kingdom with rivals, the most redoubtable of whom, Alfonso V, king of Aragon, finally expelled the Angevins from southern Italy in 1443.

The first house of Anjou-Naples numbered some great rulers. *Charles I, intelligent, energetic, authoritarian, ambitious, gave his possessions a solid administration.His wealth allowed Charles to conduct an active and wide-ranging diplomacy: in northern and central Italy, North Africa, the Balkans. But the fruits of this ambition were mediocre: the Crown of Aragon conquered Sicily and, by the time Charles died in 1285, the kingdom of Naples had fallen under the economic influence of the Florentine *bankers.

His son *Charles II, king from 1285 to 1309, was more prudent; his diplomacy enabled him to obtain the crown of *Hungary for his grandson. Successor to Charles II, and the most brilliant of the Angevin kings of Naples, was *Robert the Wise (1309-1343), a skilful politician, patron of the arts and good administrator. But he left as heir only a grand-daughter, Joanna I (1343-1382), who was intelligent but frivolous: she married four times, which caused complex wars, all the more since these unions were sterile. Her closest heir, Charles of Anjou-Durazzo, crowned king of Naples by the pope in 1381, had Joanna strangled the next year; but in 1380 she had adopted Louis of Anjou, brother of *Charles V of France. A war of succession ensued: Charles III of Durazzo defeated Louis I of Anjou, who died in Italy (1384); but Charles, engaged in the affairs of Hungary, was murdered there in 1386. His son Ladislas, who died in 1414, spent his reign fighting against the son of Louis I of Anjou, Louis II, whom the pope of *Avignon crowned king of Naples in 1389, while the popes of *Rome tended to support the house of Anjou-Durazzo. When the *Great Schism, which had been going since 1378, was reabsorbed in 1418 by the installation of a single *pope at Rome, this pope supported Ladislas's sister Joanna II, who alone had a right to his inheritance.

The new queen, capricious and dissolute, let several favourites govern. Louis II of Anjou had died in 1415, bequeathing his rights to his son Louis III. Joanna II first adopted *Alfonso V, king of Aragon, in 1421; but he wanted to remove the queen from power, and Joanna then adopted Louis III in 1423. The war between the two claimants ruined the kingdom of Naples. Louis died in 1434, transmitting his rights to his brother *René, who resumed the struggle against Alfonso V. Joanna II died in 1435. Alfonso was finally the victor in 1442; René, forced out of the kingdom of Naples, was never able to re-enter it, nor were his descendants.

The Angevins of Naples had begun by establishing a solidly structured monarchical power in an economically rich kingdom. They were thus able to conduct an active foreign policy, notably by installing a cadet branch in Hungary. But this expansion cost dear, and the loss of Sicily was irremediable. The economy came under the control of the great Florentine financiers and, after the death of Robert the Wise, dynastic struggles impoverished the Kingdom, which was devastated by mercenary troops of *condottieri* who sold their services dear to the party that offered most. These prolonged conflicts led to the ruin of the middle class and the towns, and strengthened out of all measure the baneful power of the feudal barons. The Angevin Kings thus left behind them a dissolving State: their sole positive attainment was the maintenance and development of cultural life, particularly at Naples which, though its *port declined, retained the excitement of a court city.

B. Croce, *Storia del regno di Napoli*, Bari, 1925; 4th ed., 1953. – E. G. Léonard, *Les Angevins de Naples*, Paris, 1954. – *Storia di Napoli*, 3-4, Naples, 1969-1975. – *Gli angioini di Napoli e di Ungheria*, Rome, 1974 ("Problemi di scienza e di cultura", 210). – *L'État angevin*, Rome, 1998 (*CEFR*, 245).

Georges Peyronnet

**ANGLES.** First mentioned by Tacitus, the Angles lived in what is now Schleswig-Holstein, where the toponym "Angeln" persists. Very close to the *Frisians by geographical origin and language, they settled with the Saxons and Jutes in Britain in the 5th and 6th centuries. They were known to Procopius (*Angiloi*), but especially to *Gregory the Great who sent them the *mission of *Augustine of Canterbury (597): to Gregory is attributed the pun "*non Angli sed angeli*". *Bede in his *Historia ecclesiastica gentis Anglorum* (731) distinguishes the three Germanic peoples established in Britain, but from this time the term *Angli* tends to designate them all, as with Gregory.

F. M. Stenton, *Anglo-Saxon England*, Oxford, 1971 (3rd ed.). – M. Richter, "Bede's Angli: Angles or English?", *Peritia*, 3, 1984, 99-114.

Bruno Judic

**ANGLO-NORMAN LANGUAGE AND LITERATURE.** The term "Anglo-Norman" designates the French dialect written and spoken in the British Isles between *William I's conquest in 1066 and the early 15th century. Despite being the official language of the English court until the reign of *Henry IV (1367-1413), Anglo-Norman does not seem to have supplanted the use of English either among the *nobility or among the populace. Though it is hard to measure the respective importance of the English and Anglo-Norman languages in everyday life, it remains certain that Anglo-Norman was employed in commercial transactions, in drawing up legal acts and in the official documents of the royal administration from the 13th century. Meanwhile, teaching in the *universities was done in French and *Latin until the mid 14th century. Anglo-Norman rapidly became the appanage of an instructed and cultivated English elite on whom the use of that language conferred a mark of social distinction.

The term "Anglo-Norman" is mainly used today as an adjective to evoke the literary output of that time. Rich in moral, religious and didactic works, the Anglo-Norman literature of the 12th-15th cc. is characterised by the diversity of its modes of expression. Saints' Lives composed in Anglo-Norman and vernacular adaptations of Latin *vitae* find an important place in the literary corpus (*e.g.* Lives of St *Edward the Confessor and St *Thomas Becket). Following the decrees of the *Lateran council (1215) and the council of Oxford (1222) recommending religious instruction for the *laity and annual *confession for all Christians, moralizing works multiplied first in England and later on the continent. Whether in the form of manuals (*Manuel des péchés*, *c.*1260) or didactic *treatises (Peter of Peckham's *Lumiere as Lais*, 1267), allegorical poems (*Robert Grosseteste's *Château d'Amour* written *c.*1215) or **exempla* (Nicole Bozon's *Contes moralisés*, *c.*1320), these works enjoyed a remarkable circulation in the 13th and 14th centuries. *Chronicles intended to forge the origins of the English nation enjoyed a parallel expansion from the 12th c. (Geffrei Gaimar's *Estoire des Englés*, *c.*1140), as did *romances (Thomas's *Tristan*, *c.*1172-1175), *lais* and **fabliaux*. This literature attained its full flowering in cultural exchanges between the British Isles and the continent: the **Chanson de Roland* in the Oxford version written in *c.*1100 and the *Jeu d'Adam*, the earliest religious piece we possess in French, composed *c.*1150.

M. D. Legge, *Anglo-Norman Literature and Its Background*, Oxford, 1963. – L. Stone, W. Rothwell, *Anglo-Norman Dictionary*, London, 1977-1985. – B. Merrilees, "Anglo-Norman Literature", *DMA*, 1982, 259-272.

Laurie Postlewate

**ANGLO-SAXONS**

**Anglo-Saxon Kingdoms.** The first Anglo-Saxon kingdoms evolved in the post-Roman period of Germanic settlement, when groups of invaders settled in *England under leaders to whom later king-lists and genealogies attributed royal status. These first Germanic polities are essentially prehistoric, however; rulers and peoples alike are shadowy or invisible, the nature and extent of their dominion correspondingly obscure. The territorial outlines of some of the earliest groupings, which may have occupied fractured units of late Roman Britain, can possibly be identified in the archaeological record. Early kingdoms were nevertheless

Anglo-Saxon carved cross (front) from Worcestershire. 8th c.

not simply territorial entities but consisted of units of government over peoples, on whom were imposed fiscal and military obligations. Relations shifted constantly as kingdoms contended for resources: as peoples which had once been independent came under the control of more powerful neighbours, weaker polities were absorbed and disappeared, occasional signs of their former existence being preserved in place-names and literary sources such as the "Tribal Hidage". The first kingdoms to be more than dimly lit by the historical record, those of the 7th c., had their origins in the more successful of these early kingdoms and are most likely to have begun to form in the second half of the 6th century. After 597 the Church played a role, in part by defining the character of kingship and supporting particular dynasties, but also by stabilizing the boundaries of kingdoms with the establishment of *dioceses. The process of assimilation continued throughout the 7th and 8th centuries. Despite the application of the term "the Heptarchy" to pre-Viking-Age England, it was probably never divided into seven kingdoms each ruled by a single king. Rather, there existed a multiplicity of kingdoms, many of which had more than one ruler. These kingdoms were characterised by diverse arrangements of power-sharing and territorial partition. A further development distinguished the rule of very powerful kings, who placed themselves at the head of larger confederacies. At times these regional hegemonies appear to have been extended to include all the southern kingdoms. Several 6th- and 7th-c. kings (three of them Northumbrian) are said by *Bede to have exercised such power. Mercia achieved a similar status, which rested on an essentially personal hegemony, under a series of powerful kings from the early 8th c. to the second quarter of the 9th, after which Wessex rose to dominance. By 865 the multiplicity of kingdoms had been reduced to four: Wessex, Mercia, East Anglia, and Northumbria. The threat posed by *Viking aggression and the subsequent establishment of Anglo-Scandinavian kingdoms in the North and East led to a long campaign of conquest by the kings of Wessex, unification being temporarily achieved by King Æthelstan (924-939) and finally accomplished under King Edgar (959-975). Regional separatism nonetheless persisted even until the *Norman Conquest.

F. M. Stenton, *Anglo-Saxon England*, Oxford, 1971 (3rd ed.). – *The Anglo-Saxons*, J. Campbell (ed.), London, 1982. – *The Origins of Anglo-Saxon Kingdoms*, S. Bassett (ed.), Leicester, 1989. – D. P. Kirby, *The Earliest English Kings*, London, 1991. – *The Anglo-Saxons from the Migration Period to the Eighth Century*, J. Hines (ed.), Woodbridge, 1997.

Lesley J. Abrams

**Art and culture.** During the Anglo-Saxon period, England was one of the wealthier countries of Europe. This wealth unfortunately attracted Viking pirates, but it was also used creatively for the commissioning of works of art and literature. Wealthy patronage is reflected in the lavish production of works of art throughout the period. Only in the 9th c., when Viking attacks brought artistic and intellectual life to a standstill, did the production of artefacts and manuscripts cease. The wealth of Anglo-Saxon artistic skill may still be appreciated in many media of expression: metalwork, *ivory carving, stone sculpture, manuscript decoration and *architecture, as well as literature, both in Old English and Latin. Representatives of perishable media which no doubt exhibited similar artistic excellence, such as wall-painting, *embroidery and wood carving, are represented only fragmentarily. The vast amount of surviving metalwork is impressive for the intricacy of its design and ornamentation (and more is recovered by archaeologists every year), famously so in objects such as the Sutton Hoo jewelry (7th c.), the Pentney brooches, the Fuller Brooch and the Alfred Jewel, to name but a few. Ivory carving is brilliantly represented by the Franks Casket, but also by many lesser known pieces. There survive thousands of examples of Anglo-Saxon stone carving from all over the country (though concentrated especially in Northumbria), often of superb intricacy, frequently in the form of standing crosses, such as the famous Ruthwell Cross. Some 180 illuminated manuscripts survive from Anglo-Saxon England; the finest examples of English manuscript decoration – *e.g.* the Book of Durrow, the Lindisfarne Gospels, the *Codex Amiatinus*, the Vespasian Psalter, the Benedictional of St Æthelwold, and many more – are unsurpassed anywhere in Europe. A substantial number of Anglo-Saxon churches still survive intact, most notably perhaps those at Jarrow, Brixworth, Bradford-on-Avon, Deerhurst and Escomb, but many more larger and more lavish churches have been recovered by excavation, notably the Old Minster at *Winchester and *Edward the Confessor's church at *Westminster.

Anglo-Saxon England boasts the richest vernacular literature of early medieval Europe. Some 30,000 lines of poetry survive, all in a distinctive Germanic literary form, and including such works as **Beowulf*, one of the masterpieces of medieval literature in any language, and elegiac poems such as *The Wanderer* and *The Seafarer*, as well as biblical, hagiographical and gnomic verse of many kinds. An even larger corpus of Old English prose survives, consisting largely of translations from Latin works, Saints' Lives and *homilies. Finally, a large (but insufficiently explored) corpus of Latin literature was produced in Anglo-Saxon England, including the writings of authors such as *Aldhelm, *Bede and *Alcuin, who were in the vanguard of European learning in their day, but also numerous lesser figures whose writing in many genres, including poetry, *history and *hagiography, will in most Anglo-Saxon centuries bear comparison with contemporary Latin literature produced on the Continent.

H. M. and J. Taylor, *Anglo-Saxon Architecture*, Cambridge, 1965-1978 (3 vol.). – J. Beckwith, *Ivory Carvings in Early Medieval England*, London, 1972. – E. Temple, *Anglo-Saxon Manuscripts 900-1066*, London, 1976. – J. J. G. Alexander, *Insular Manuscripts 6th to the 9th Century*, London,

1978. – C. R. Dodwell, *Anglo-Saxon Art: a New Perspective*, Manchester, 1982. – E. Fernie, *The Architecture of the Anglo-Saxons*, London, 1983. – *Corpus of Anglo-Saxon Stone Sculpture*, R. Cramp (ed.) *et al.*, London, 1984. – J. Backhouse, D. H. Turner, L. Webster, *The Golden Age of Anglo-Saxon Art, 966-1066*, London, 1984. – R. Deshman, *Anglo-Saxon and Anglo-Scandinavian Art: an Annotated Bibliography*, Boston, 1984. – D. M. Wilson, *Anglo-Saxon Art*, London, 1984. – S. B. Greenfield, D. G. Calder, *A New Critical History of Old English Literature*, New York, 1986. – *The Cambridge Companion to Old English Literature*, M. Godden (ed.), M. Lapidge (ed.), Cambridge, 1991. – *The Making of England. Anglo-Saxon Art and Culture AD 600-900*, L. Webster (ed.), J. Backhouse (ed.), London, 1991. – M. Lapidge, *Anglo-Latin Literature, 900-1066*, London, 1993. – M. Lapidge, *Anglo-Latin Literature, 600-899*, London, 1996.

Michael Lapidge

**ANI.** Capital of Bagratid *Armenia (991-1045) and seat of the *catholicos* after 991, Ani was situated on the right bank of the Aχurean, a northern tributary of the Araxes.

Enriched by the presence of the court and international commerce, the "town of a thousand and one churches" grew so rapidly that its walls – enclosing the citadel, upper and lower towns with paved streets, bordered with palaces, baths and shops – were enlarged after a generation to contain a tripled surface area and a population greater than that of contemporary European towns. The renown of its cathedral's architect gained him an invitation to repair the dome of Hagia Sophia at *Constantinople.

Given up to Byzantium in 1045 after the forced abdication of its last king, Ani was captured in 1064 by the *Seljuks who sold it in 1072 to the Shāddādid Kurds. Ani was recaptured in 1199 by the Zak'arids and its prosperity, attested by new monuments, persisted until the *Mongol conquest.

H. Manandian, *The Trade and Cities of Armenia in Relation to Ancient World Trade*, N. G. Garsoïan (tr.), Lisbon, 1965, 144-145, 148-152, 154, 173, 176-177, 179-187, 197-199. – *Ani*, Milan, 1984 ("Documenti di architettura armena", 12). – J.-M. Thierry, P. Donabédian, *Les arts arméniens*, Paris, 1987, 481-489.

Nina G. Garsoïan

**ANIMAL HUSBANDRY.** The recent contributions of archaeozoology allow us to supplement and clarify the impressionistic views of medieval animal husbandry given by texts and iconography. In fact, we can now know not only what animals were reared, but also in what proportion and for what purposes.

Excavations carried out on a hundred medieval European sites give concordant results as to the morphology of domestic animals. In general, we see a diminution in the size of most animals in relation to their Roman counterparts. Less obvious among ovines and equidae, it is particularly pronounced among bovines, whose mean height at the withers is hardly more than 110 cm (against 130 to 150 in the Roman period). This fall continues at least until the end of the 13th c., the movement not being reversed until the 15th century. Even horses, whose role in medieval society is known, do not totally escape this movement. These variations must be related, on the one hand, to the contraction of pastoral space in the central Middle Ages in parallel with demographic growth and correlative extension of cultures, and on the other, to the demographic catastrophes of the 14th c., which freed lands for the pasturing of beasts.

A study of the distribution of the main domestic areas shows a general predominance of bovines at all times in the Middle Ages. They are followed by ovines-caprines, except in the early Middle Ages when these were overtaken by pigs. However, a closer geographical exploration allows us, unsurprisingly, to oppose a Europe of bovines (north and centre) to a Europe of ovines (Mediterranean regions).

The aims of animal husbandry were many. Apart from scavenging dogs and hunting cats (present on many sites from the early Middle Ages), domestic *animals had several important functions. The use of bovines for their tractive force, omnipresent in texts and iconography, is confirmed by archeozoology which reveals the age attained by a great many of them at the time of slaughter. It was to ensure their maintenance that the land of every *village had to include, alongside the cultivated space (*ager*, "in-field"), a waste area (*saltus*, "outfield"). When the latter was too much reduced by *clearance, it was necessary to reorganise the land by grouping parcels together as fallow ground and submitting to the constraints of crop rotation. The use of the horse to draw the plough or the harrow was more limited, but signs of it are found in the plains of northern France from before the year 1000.

If the proportion of meat in the diet of medieval man remains an enigma, a quite precise idea can nonetheless be given of the different kinds consumed. Beef, mutton and pork provided almost the whole of his meat. Wild beasts (including cervids) and domestic fowls constituted only a very slender portion, but their progress is nevertheless perceptible from the 14th century.

The use of fleeces, *furs and hides for *clothing and footwear must not be forgotten. The raising of sheep specially for wool, in England and Spain, gave rise in the later Middle Ages to new fortunes, new activities, new institutions (like the Iberian *Mesta*) and new landscapes.

R. Trow-Smith, *A History of British Livestock Husbandry to 1700*, London, 1957. – R.-H. Bautier, "Les Mutations agricoles du XIV^e^ et XV^e^ siècles et les progrès de l'élevage", *BPH*, 1, 1969, 1-27. – J. Clutton-Brock, "The Animal Resources", *The Archaeology of Anglo-Saxon England*, D.M. Wilson (ed.), London, 1976. – *Le Monde animal et ses représentations au Moyen Âge, XI^e^-XV^e^ siècle, 15^e^ Congrès des Historiens médiévistes, Toulouse, 1984*, Toulouse, 1985. – J. Langdon, *Horses, Oxen, and Technological Innovation*, Cambridge, 1986. – K. Biddick, *The Other Economy: Pastoral Husbandry on a Medieval Estate*, Berkeley, 1989. – F. Audoin-Rouzeau, "Les Modifications du bétail et de sa consommation en Europe médiévale et moderne: le témoignage des ossements animaux archéologiques", *L'homme, l'animal domestique et l'environnement, du Moyen Âge au XVIII^e^ siècle, Nantes, 1992*, Nantes, 1993.

Robert Durand

**ANIMALS.** More than objects of science, animals were bearers of symbols and objects of exploitation throughout the medieval period.

Knowledge of animals progressed relatively little in the course of the Middle Ages. Most of the authors who interested themselves in animal life were indebted to *Isidore of Seville († 636), who gathered into his *Etymologiae* part of the observations, but also of the myths transmtted by Pliny in his *Natural History*. Isidore was used unquestioningly by the Venerable *Bede and *Rabanus Maurus in the 7th and 8th centuries. Not until the 12th c. did personal observation replace the authority of the Ancients, with the Benedictine abbess *Hildegard of Bingen (1098-1179), "the first true zoologist of the Christian Middle Ages" (R. Delort), though in her *Physics* she is still very much indebted to Genesis for her classification of animals, which was followed by her 13th-c. emulators *Vincent of Beauvais and Brunetto Latini. But the great master of medieval zoology is incontestably *Albert the Great (1193-1280) who, in *The Animals* and *The Nature of Places*, grappled with *Aristotle's *science, not without adding his

*Depiction of animals. Miniature from the San Pedro (Roda) Bible* from the monastery of Roda (Catalonia). 10th-11th c. Paris, BNF (Ms lat. 6, fol. 65 v°).

personal reflections, the fruit of methodical observation. However, these treatises were to find few echoes over the following centuries.

More than anatomy or physiology, medieval image-makers and preachers were interested, for the edification of the faithful, in the symbols of which many animals were the bearers. The rich medieval bestiary was inspired particularly by an anonymous oriental work, dating probably from the 2nd c., the **Physiologus*. Nearly fifty animals, among them the *dragon, the *unicorn and the gryphon, appear in it, each with a strong symbolic charge. Created by God for man's benefit, *i.e.* for his service or chastisement, animals could not be entirely bad. That is why the majority of them were credited with characters either positive or negative, according to time and place, but sometimes both at once. Moreover, their attributes could be transferred to man when he called himself by a name or a nickname borrowed from the animal world, a practice widespread in Germanic personal names in the early Middle Ages.

This same anthropocentric and utilitarian approach justified man's exploitation of animals. Besides a workforce, what he expected from the animal world was *food, *clothing and remedies. *Hunting occupies an important place in medieval literature as well as in statutory texts; however, archaeozoologists observe that game entered only sparingly into the medieval meat diet, at all levels of society. So we may suppose that even in the Middle Ages the risk of confrontation, through the hunt, between man and wild animals was as much the affirmation of a social situation as the satisfaction of a material need.

*La chasse au Moyen Âge. Colloque Nice, 1979*, Paris, 1980. – R. Delort, *Les Animaux ont une histoire*, Paris, 1984. – *Beasts and Birds of the Middle Ages*, W.B. Clarke (ed.), M.T.McMunn (ed.), Philadelphia, 1989. – L. Moulinier, "L'ordre du monde animal selon Hildegarde de Bingen (XIIe siècle)", *L'Homme, l'animal domestique et l'environment, Nantes, 1992*, Nantes, 1993. – C. Hicks, *Animals in Early Medieval Art*, Edinburgh, 1993. – *Animals in the Middle Ages*, N.C. Flores (ed.), New York, 1996.

Robert Durand

**ANJOU, ANGERS.** The region of Anjou (the old *pagus Andecavensis*), with no geological or structural unity, cut in two by the Loire basin which traverses it from side to side, is hard to discern before the year 1000. Only in the 11th c. did the conquests of the *counts of Anjou join the region of the Mauges, south of the Layon, to the county and the *diocese; at this date, the diocese of Angers (more extensive than the present diocese based on the *département* of Maine-et-Loire) had ceased to coincide with the county of Anjou, which included Sablé in the north, part of Touraine, and Loudun in the south. Nevertheless, Anjou was a relatively coherent territory, a creation of history.

Insecurity profoundly marked the last years of Antiquity and the early Middle Ages in Anjou. Subject to barbarian *invasions, taken by the Saxons, then by the *Franks, the town of Angers was reduced to little importance at this time; restricted from the late 3rd c. to an enclosure covering hardly nine hectares (as against 60 in the early Empire), the town was described by its bishop Thalasius († 462) as a *civitatula*. From the death of *Clovis to the approach of the *millennium, the history of Anjou was an uninterrupted succession of struggles and dramas; throughout the 6th c., Merovingian partitions integrated Anjou into ephemeral kingdoms, victims of their rulers' fratricidal rivalries; absorbed by *Neustria from 613, Anjou shared its agitated destinies. The sole events known from the *Merovingian period are the efforts at *evangelization undertaken by the *bishops.

The Christianization of Anjou is generally put in the 4th c., with the presence of the first bishop, Defensor, the election of St *Martin (372) and the appearance of Christian signs on tombs in the necropolis south-east of Angers. The evangelization of the countryside was undertaken by obscure local apostles, soon raised to the altars (Doucelin, Maxenceul, Vétérin); among them St Maurille, destroyer of idols in the region of Chalonnes, acquired such renown that the Angevins chose him as bishop († 453). Amidst the Merovingian anarchy, Christianization continued its progress thanks to the activities of bishops, several of whom were recognised as saints (Aubin, Lézin, Maimbeuf). Benedictine *monasticism was implanted at Angers (Saint-Étienne in *c.*530, soon called Saint-Aubin, and Saint-Serge) and in the territory (*Saint-Maur-de-Glanfeuil before 560, and Mont-Glonne). But the collapse of the *Carolingian State after the death of *Louis the Pious inaugurated a long period characterised by a conjunction of perils; for three quarters of a century from 852, the Bretons occupied the land west of the Maine and the Mayenne; from the second third of the 9th c., the Northmen, installed on an island in the Loire, periodically ravaged Anjou and occupied Angers (854, 872-873, 886). The defence of the realm then attached Anjou to the ancestors of the *Capetians, since the province was part of the military command of the regions between the Seine and the Loire entrusted to Robert the Strong, who was killed fighting the Normans at Brissarthe (866), and then to his son Eudes, who became king in 888. Faced with the collapse of monarchical *authority, the local dynasty of the Ingelgerians (named after its legendary founder Ingelger or Enjeuger) succeeded in making Anjou an autonomous and hereditary *territorial principality from the late 9th c., though these counts were no usurpers and never ceased to recognise the theoretical supremacy of the *kings at Paris.

From the reign of Count Fulk III Nerra (987-1040) to that of *Henry II Plantagenet (1151-1189), Anjou enjoyed a remarkable expansion that is generally considered its golden age. Angevin influence extended up the Loire and the three rivers (Mayenne, Sarthe and Loir). Thus was formed a Greater Anjou, advancing as far as Vendômois and Touraine (1044), incorporating Maine (1109) and *Normandy (1144); meanwhile Count Fulk V, distinguishing himself in the East on *crusade, became the first ruler of the Angevin dynasty of *Jerusalem (1131-1185). In 1152, Count Henry's marriage to Aliénor or *Eleanor (newly divorced from King *Louis VII of France) brought him *Aquitaine, and two years later he became king of *England. A veritable empire was born, extending from *Scotland to the *Pyrenees, at the centre of which was Anjou, where the count's power was from now on represented by a *seneschal. An unprecedented economic expansion characterised this period. Demographic pressure necessitated the rapid conquest of new lands; thanks to land *clearances, accompanied by the foundation of numerous new *bourgs*, *famines became less frequent and *agriculture was able to go beyond the stage of subsistence, as witness the spectacular extension of viticulture; the multiplication of *fairs, *markets and tolls responded to the renewal of trade. This movement accelerated the growth of Angers: the occupation of the right bank of the Maine was the essential step in the extension of the town from the 11th c., with the foundation of the monasteries of Saint-Nicolas (*c.*1010) and Notre-Dame-de-la-Charité (1028), kernels of the quarter of the Doutre.

The 11th and 12th cc. were also marked by transformations of society (still to be studied) and by a religious renewal illustrated particularly by the revival of Benedictine monasticism with the foundation of a multitude of *priories and the return to evangelical *poverty; hermits, soon transformed into itinerant preachers, aroused the enthusiasm of the crowds before forming their disciples into new communities (Nyoiseau, or La Roë and *Fontevraud, both founded by *Robert of Arbrissel). As for the *secular clergy, bishops like Renaud of Martigné and especially Ulger (1125-1148) were able to free them from the grip of the *laity and attach themselves to that of the count. At this date, for the first time ever, Anjou's personality was expressed in an architectural style of its own, Angevin Gothic (or Plantagenet style), inaugurated *c.*1150 in the nave of Angers *cathedral, which then spread across the whole of the West in the second half of the 12th century. Also in the 11th and 12th cc., the first Angevins eminent in letters and thought (*Marbod, Baldric of Bourgeuil, Ulger) appeared at the episcopal *school and in the *abbeys.

Part of an empire of European dimensions, Anjou found itself caught up in the conflict between Capetians and *Plantagenets. From 1205, the capture of Chinon made *Philip Augustus master of Anjou but, though the Capetian conquest was rapid, the transition from Angevin Anjou to a French Anjou fully integrated into the monarchichal unit took place gradually. The young *Louis IX built the powerful *castle that still exists at Angers and a new town wall to incorporate the whole built-up area, on both banks of the Maine. The peace and security thus restored were reinforced by the treaty of Paris (1258-1259) by whose terms *Henry III of England renounced all claim on the province. But from 1246, Anjou and Maine had been given in appanage to the king's youngest brother, *Charles; he founded the *Angevin house of Naples and a Mediterranean empire extending as far as Eastern Europe and the Near East, once more associating Anjou with a new and prodigious adventure. Reunited with the royal domain when Count Philip of Valois ascended the throne as *Philip VI (1328), Anjou was raised to a duchy in 1360 and given to Louis, second son of King John II the Good; the ducal house was maintained until 1480. In conformity with the status of appanages, the counts and then dukes had their own administration and their own personnel, but this persistence of Angevin autonomy should not deceive us; the Angevin princes contributed to favouring monarchical unification by copying their institutions from the royal model; being often absent, they let Parisian influence develop in all their domains.

Nave and choir of the cathedral of St Maurice, Angers. 13th c.

The prosperity of the 13th c. was succeeded, in Anjou as elsewhere, by the period of demographic and moral crisis of the 14th and 15th centuries. Although Angers never fell into enemy hands, Anjou, both "barrier and bulwark", issued from the *Hundred Years' War exhausted, devastated and ruined by financial exactions from all sides. The time of "Good King" *René, last

*Meeting of Sts Joachim and Anne at the Golden Gate.* Fresco by Giotto in the Scrovegni chapel, Padua. 1303-1309.

effective duke of Anjou (1434-1480), marked by the luxury of his *court, one of the most ostentatious of the time, was that of a final illusion that even allowed the Angevins to regard Bishop John-Michael (1439-1447) as a saint. But Anjou's loyalty to the *monarchy and the necessities of war had increased royal influence; in 1475, King *Louis XI gave Angers its municipal charter and, on the death of his uncle René, he united to the royal domain the duchy over which he already had power. He was merely legitimizing a *fait accompli*.

F. Uzureau, "Angers" and "Angers (diocèse)", *DHGE*, 3, 1924, 85-114. – *Histoire des Pays de Loire*, F. Lebrun (dir.), Toulouse, 1972. – *Atlas historique français*, 2: *Anjou*, R. Favreau (dir.), Paris, 1973 (2 vol.). – *Histoire d'Angers*, F. Lebrun (dir.), Toulouse, 1975. – *Le Diocèse d'Angers*, F. Lebrun (dir.), 1981 (*HDF*, 13).

Jean-Michel Matz

**ANNALS.** Accounts of events classified by year, annals arose out of Paschal tables, lists of annual dates on which the feast of *Easter was indicated. A monk, consulting these tables to know the date of Easter in the current year, would note in the margin some events that had seemed significant. These marginal notations were developed, then written down on their own account, without the Paschal table but keeping the number of the year. Thus in the 8th c. appeared what are called minor annals since the facts reported are linked to a precise place.

With the accession of the *Carolingians, court clerks tried to justify the *coup d'État* of 751 in the form of more developed annals, a sort of official palace history: these are the *Royal Frankish Annals*. In general however their yearly structure lent itself to the most elementary account, disengaged from any ideological purpose. These annals, called major annals by contrast to the former, are specifically Carolingian. They appeared with this dynasty and disappeared more or less along with it, those written by *Flodoard from 919 to 966 being the last. Meanwhile, the annals reflected the destiny of the *Empire. The *Royal Annals* were unique. They were continued in West Francia by the *Annals of Saint-Bertin* which cover the period 830-882 and in East Francia by the *Annals of Fulda*, at first up to 887, then continued up to 901. Also classified among major annals are the *Annals of Xanten*, going up to 873, and the *Annals of Saint-Vaast*, covering the period 873-899.

For scholars of the Middle Ages, annals are not *history. History implies wide perspectives, a desire to explain and demonstrate. Annals are merely materials for history, materials precious to us for their chronological precision, but often hardly worked into a form and always considered by the lettered as a minor literary genre.

B. W. Scholz, *Carolingian Chronicles*, Ann Arbor (MI), 1972. – *The Annals of St-Bertin*, J. L. Nelson (ed.), Manchester, 1991. – *The Annals of Fulda*, T. Reuter (ed.), Manchester, 1992.

R.L. Poole, *Chronicles and Annals*, Oxford, 1926. – M. McCormick, *Les Annales du haut Moyen Âge*, *TSMÂO*, 14, 1975. – H. White, *The content and the form*, Baltimore (MD), 1987.

Michel Sot

**ANNATES.** Taxes levying the revenue of the first year of a minor *benefice, annates were reserved for the Apostolic *Camera following a new collation. Invoking his financial needs, *Clement V reserved for himself for three years from 1 Feb 1306 the *annalia* of vacant benefices in England, Scotland and Ireland. *John XXII extended the principle to the whole of Christendom and definitively fixed the method of levying annates (*Si gratanter advertitis* and *Suscepti regiminis*, 1317). Annates were suppressed by the council of *Basel (21st session, 9 June 1448).

J.-P. Kirsch, *Die päpstlichen Annaten in Deutschland während des XIV. Jahrhunderts*, Paderborn, 1903. – G. Mollat, *DDC*, 1, 1935, 533-538.

Agostino Paravicini Bagliani

**ANNE AND JOACHIM.** No canonical text mentions the name of Anne: a tradition dating back to the first centuries makes her the wife of Joachim and mother of the Virgin *Mary (*Protogospel of James*, *Gospel of Pseudo-Matthew*).

The cult of St Anne was late and ephemeral in the West. It developed in the late Middle Ages in connection with the formulation of the Immaculate *Conception of the Virgin. A statue on the trumeau of the central door of the north transept of *Chartres cathedral shows us St Anne carrying the Virgin and Child. The main representations of herself and Joachim refer to the episode of their miraculous meeting at the Golden Gate of Jerusalem: *e.g.*, in the 13th c., with Joachim arriving on horseback at the Golden Gate, on the lintel of St Anne's door at Notre-Dame in *Paris. St Anne is also present in scenes of the life of Mary, such as the Education of the Virgin.

*Interpreting Cultural Symbols: Saint Anne in late Medieval Society*, K. Ashley (ed.), P. Sheingorn (ed.), Athens (GA), 1990.

Frédérique Trouslard

**ANNIVERSARIES.** Early in the 3rd c. the Christians seem to have got into the habit of commemorating the *dead on the anniversary of their decease, at first designated by the expression "*natales dies defunctorum*". Tertullian († 220) mentions eucharistic celebrations for the dead, each year, "*pro nataliciis*". Shortly afterwards, Cyprian († 258) mentions the establishment of calendars intended for the liturgical commemoration of the *martyrs. In the 4th and 5th cc., it was customary to pronounce panegyrics in memory of certain dignitaries, on the anniversary of their death: "*in anniversario*", according to a sermon of Augustine († 430).

In the *Carolingian period, the "anniversary" of the dead was a well-established form of commemoration, consisting of a liturgical service (*office or *mass) fixed on the anniversary of the decease and celebrated in perpetuity. We distinguish from anniversaries proper the first of these (later called mass "of the year's end"), which marked the end of the cycle of celebrations begun after the decease: in the 11th and 12th cc., many *acta* of *confraternities provided for celebrations for deceased monks and *clerics on the third, seventh and thirtieth days after their death and on the occasion of its first anniversary; after that, the dead were commemorated only by the reading of their name, each year, on the anniversary of their death.

Many *bishops and *abbots, but also laypeople, at first emperors and *kings, later mere lords, asked that after their death their "anniversary" be celebrated in perpetuity. More frequent services were sometimes demanded: each month, each week. In certain cases, it was specified that the anniversary was to comprise a "mass" and "vigils" (sung on the evening of the previous day). A sum was often provided for the *lighting and for a meal offered to the ecclesiastical community that performed the liturgical services. Demand growing, those responsible for the celebrations wrote down the date of anniversary services and the revenues assigned to them in *obituaries and "anniversary books". In the late Middle Ages, the cost of celebrating "anniversaries" was relatively moderate, which allowed the middle classes, well-off merchants and artisans, to have recourse to them.

J. Chiffoleau, *La Comptabilité de l'au-delà. Les hommes, la mort et la religion dans la région d'Avignon à la fin du Moyen Âge*, Rome, 1981, 334-339. – P. A. Février, "La Mort chrétienne", *Segni e riti nella Chiesa altomedievale occidentale*, 2, Spoleto, 1987, 928-934. – J. L. Lemaître, *Mourir à Saint-Martial. La commémoration des morts et les obituaires à Saint-Martial de Limoges du XI^e au XIII^e siècle*, Paris, 1989, 393-401. – V. Bainbridge, *Gilds in the medieval countryside: social and religious change in Cambridgeshire, c.1350-1558*, Woodbridge, 1996.

Michel Lauwers

**ANNUNCIATION (iconography).** The archangel *Gabriel's annunciation to *Mary coincided with the Incarnation of *Christ and formed the first act of the work of *Redemption. The textual sources of its representation are Lk 1, 26-28, and the *apocrypha (*Protogospel of James*, *Gospel of the Nativity of the Virgin*) vulgarized in the West by *Vincent of Beauvais (*Speculum historiale*, 3rd part of the *Speculum majus*, *c.*1257-1258) and *Jacobus de Voragine (*Legenda sanctorum, alias Lombardica hystoria*, *c.*1261-1266).

The scene shown is that of the archangel transmitting the divine message to the Elect (in 15th-c. Flemish painting, the reverse, painted in "grisaille", of *altarpieces like that of Jan *van Eyck's *Mystic Lamb* in the church of Saint-Bavon at *Ghent, *c.*1432). Ordinarily, the composition comprised a small number of persons, two or three, with or without the *Holy Spirit. The two main actors belong to two different universes, heavenly for one, earthly for the other: hence, in space, there is a conflict of horizontal and vertical lines. Stemming from this dual plain are the different roles, active for the archangel, passive for Mary, at least until the 13th c.; whence, also, the two scales of representation, the archangel

*The Annunciation.* Altarpiece by Simone Martini (*c.*1284-1344), 1333. Florence, Uffizi.

prominent (wings spread), Mary tucked away in a corner (chamber, oratory). The scene takes place in a mixed place, both open and enclosed, outdoors and indoors. When the characters are indoors, especially in the 14th c., the scene is always divided into two parts by a column (Simone *Martini, *Annunciation*, Florence, Uffizi, 1333) or by another artifice (attribute, like a vase containing a lily). In the 15th c., Mary is usually positioned inside a room or an oratory, while the archangel is outside, on a landscape background.

From the late 12th c., still more from the 13th, iconography changed under the effect of the progress of the Marian cult: the archangel kneels before Mary who is no longer altogether God's humble servant, but the ruler accepting homage. From being polarized, the composition becomes convergent: Mary tends to occupy the centre and appears as the main character towards whom the rays emanating from the Father are all directed (in the 15th c. especially). The moment chosen is that when, surprised by the archangel, Mary is reading *Isaiah's prophecy; so she is increasingly shown holding a book, reading it or turning away from it, in a room that takes on the aspect of a veritable study. Thus, in *Books of Hours, she is shown arms extended, palms open, turning away from a book before her (Moulins, BM, ms. 89, fol. 16); or a silent transmission of divine *grace may be suggested, Mary being depicted reading, or in any other position indicating her inner piety (Paris, bibliothèque de l'Arsenal, ms. 434, fol. 53). In the late 14th and in the 15th c., these types of representation are the reflection of a society in which oral recitation of *prayers was gradually giving way to silent prayer.

D. M. Robb, "The Iconography of the Annunciation in the Fourteenth and Fifteenth Centuries", *ArtB*, 18, 1936, 480-526. – J. Spencer, "Spatial Imagery of the Annunciation in Fifteenth-Century Florence", *ArtB*, 37, 1955, 273-280.

Daniel Russo

**ANSELM OF CANTERBURY (1033-1109).** Theologian, philosopher and archbishop of Canterbury, born at Aosta (Italy) in 1033. As a young man, he set off towards the north to seek out famous teachers. At *Bec, an innovative school had been set up by another educated and able Italian, *Lanfranc, who lectured on works of classical logic and rhetoric and taught the study of the *Bible. Anselm stayed at Bec and, when Lanfranc left for Caen, took charge of the teaching. In 1078 he was elected abbot of Bec.

Anselm described his first book, the *Monologion*, as a meditation on the divine being. His method of teaching had been to invite his monks to begin from what they knew of the good and to climb in their thought to higher and higher goods until they began to glimpse, not God himself, who is ultimately beyond human comprehension, but a clearer idea of what he must be like. That led him on to consider other aspects of the divine nature and then to examine the mystery of the *Trinity. Anselm's chief model at this early stage of his authorship remained the works of Augustine, and the *Monologion* shows repeated borrowing from Augustine *On the Trinity*.

Anselm initially believed that any reasonable person, presented with a clear explanation of the truths of faith, would be able to accept them. Indeed he says as much in his next book, the *Proslogion*. In the *Monologion* he had constructed "a chain of many arguments", and that had appeared to him untidy. So he began to search for "a single argument" which would prove not only that *God exists but all the other things Christians believe about him. This was the ontological proof for the existence of God. Anselm points out that everyone is able to formulate in his mind the notion of that than which nothing greater can be thought. But it is also, and equally, possible for everyone to distinguish between the "thought" of such a thing, taken simply to be an idea, and the thought of such a thing as a reality. For that than which nothing greater can be thought to exist in reality is obviously greater than for it to exist only as an idea. Anselm's controversial conclusion was that that than which nothing greater can be thought must therefore exist in reality. Though Anselm almost certainly had no direct knowledge of Plato, he was working with an idea of "reality" that was fundamentally *Platonist. To a Platonist the movement from idea to reality takes place at a level where the idea is itself more real than any particular exemplification.

Meanwhile, he was continuing with the steady teaching of his monks. An important task was grounding them in the skills they needed for the study of the Bible. Anselm taught a method that would enable the student to understand any text he was reading. Unlike the traditional commentator's patient progression through the text passage by passage, it made no use at all of extracts from patristic **auctoritates*. It was thus a quite different method of *exegesis from that which was to evolve in the 12th c. into the *Glossa ordinaria*. He composed four little treatises in this area. The first, *De grammatico*, is solely concerned with a technical question on which classical textbooks of *grammar and *logic differed: whether the word "literate" (*grammaticus*) is a *substance or a quality. The books *On Truth*, *On Freedom of Choice* and *On the Fall of Satan*, analyse one or two passages of Scripture. In the last treatise the key passage is Jn 8, 44, which describes Satan as not "standing fast in the truth". Anselm develops the themes of truth and "rightness" (*rectitudo*) progressively through the three little treatises. With the completion of this group of treatises, Anselm's period of quiet happiness as a theologian and philosopher began to come to an end. He wrote *On the Incarnation of the Word* because the controversialist Roscelin of Compiègne had accused him of teaching heresy about the Trinity. Anselm's book is not merely, or even primarily, on the issue Roscelin had raised, but on the question how it was possible for the Son to be incarnate if the Father and the *Holy Spirit were not also incarnate.

In 1093, Anselm was translated from Bec to the archbishopric of *Canterbury as Lanfranc's successor. He did not want to be archbishop. The king, *William Rufus, forced him into office and tried to invest him himself with the *ring and the *staff. Anselm had already given his loyalty to *Urban II and he strongly believed that to change it would have been a breach of "right order" (*rectus ordo*). The quarrel took him into exile and led to further disagreements with the next king, *Henry I. In exile again, Anselm came to realise that William's attempt to invest him with the ring and staff was in breach of the principle being debated during the *Investiture Contest, that the secular authority could play no sacramental part in the making of a *bishop.

This was the period of Anselm's mature writing. In the *Cur Deus Homo* he set out to show that even if Christ were taken out of the equation altogether it would be necessary to bring him back so as to give a coherent account of the manner in which the human race was able to be restored to the position and purpose for which God created it. Important here is his continuing assumption that there is a rightness to things, a *rectitudo*, a divine harmony, which is divinely ordained and cannot ultimately be frustrated, for God is omnipotent and always wills what is right. This gives an emphasis (characteristic of the period but particularly marked in Anselm) to the notion of fittingness (*convenientia*; *decentia*). Anselm points out near the beginning of the *Cur Deus Homo* that three things, "will", "power" and "necessity", are closely associated in the solutions he proposes; here too is a familiar theme of his thought brought to maturity in the *Cur Deus Homo*.

He begins by asking what problem was created by the fall of Adam and Eve. God could not simply forgive them, Anselm argues, because his own "honour" was diminished by what they had done. Something therefore had to be done to make things right again, to restore right order (*rectus ordo*). Could God himself have intervened? The objection to that is that he was not the debtor. To pay oneself a debt someone else owes is not to discharge the obligation of the other person. This patterning of "owe" and "ought" is important as an indicator that Anselm was still thinking in his earlier terms of things "having to be as they ought to be" in order for them to be "true". Could God have used an *angel? But the angel would, again, not have been the debtor. Could God have used a human being? There the difficulty was that all human beings, who were certainly debtors, were now tainted with original sin and were simply not able to do what was required. Logically, the only possibility was for a being who was both God and man to do what was needed, for only he both owed the debt and was able to discharge it. And so we come back to the incarnate Christ, who was indeed the only solution.

Anselm's last years – and the works of his maturity were written in his sixties and seventies – were taken up with two or three main themes. In 1098, while he was in exile at the papal court seeking the *pope's backing for his stand against the king of *England, he was called on by Pope Urban II to frame a rebuttal of the arguments of the Greeks attending the council of Bari. This was an important issue. In 1054 a *schism had begun, dividing the Eastern and Western Churches. The division was mainly political and turned in some measure upon Greek indignation about the claims of the bishop of Rome to primacy over the four *patriarchs of the East. There were, however, old theological disagreements, the most important of which was the debate about the inclusion of the **filioque* clause in the *creed. The original version of the creed had said that the Holy Spirit proceeded from the Father. The Western version said that he proceeds from the Father and the Son. The Greeks objected to this both because it was an addition to the creed, and because it was not correct. In their view, it created two "origins" or "principles" in the Trinity, Father and Son, and the Father should stand alone in that position. This was a notion heavily dependent on the Pythagorean and *Neoplatonist idea that unity is metaphysically better than plurality, particularly strong in the theology of the old Eastern half of the Empire, where the direct study of texts in Greek had continued to be relatively easy.

Anselm's *On the Procession of the Holy Spirit* was completed four years later. He knew nothing of the history of the dispute, either in the eleventh century or earlier. He approached the problem straightforwardly as one of reason. His argument turns on symmetry. Only if the Spirit proceeds from the Father and the Son do we have a situation in which each *Person of the Trinity has an attribute peculiar to himself and each has an attribute which he shares with the other two. Only the Son has a Father; only the Father has a Son; only the Spirit does not have a Spirit proceeding from himself. But both the Father and the Spirit do not have a Father; both the Spirit and the Son do not have Son; and both the Father and the Son have a Spirit proceeding from themselves.

In these last years of his life Anselm also went back to the subject of free will, now linking it systematically with the question of the relationship between human *freedom of choice and divine foreknowledge and *predestination and the action of *grace. On his death bed, Anselm was still hoping to complete a book on the origin of the *soul for, as he said, if he did not do so, he was not sure that anyone living would be able to.

Anselm's influence in his own time and in the period immediately after his death was perhaps greater, ironically, in the area of *spirituality than that of speculative *theology. There are many manuscripts of his *Prayers and Meditations* and a vast penumbra of spurious imitative spiritual writings attributed to him with confidence during the Middle Ages. His theological and speculative writing had the disadvantage for the next generation that its close argument made it not easy to use in short extracts or quotations. But his achievement there is not readily measured by counting the manuscripts. In the long term the importance of his ideas was recognized and philosophers and theologians in the centuries since have wrestled with his arguments not for their antiquarian interest but for their intrinsic value and importance.

*The Works of St Anselm*, F. S. Schmitt (ed.), R. W. Southern (ed.), 6 vols., Rome-Edinburgh, 1938-1968. – *Memorials of St Anselm*, R. W. Southern (ed.), F. S. Schmitt (ed.), Oxford, 1969. – Eadmer, *The Life of St Anselm*, R. W. Southern (ed.), Oxford, 1972. – *The Letters of St Anselm of Canterbury*, W. Fröhlich (tr.), Kalamazoo (MI), 1990-1994 (3 vol.). – *Anselm of Canterbury: the Major Works*, G. R. Evans (ed.), B. Davies (ed.), Oxford, 1998. – *A Concordance to the Works of St Anselm*, G. R. Evans (ed.), Millwood (NY), 1984.

A. Koyré, *L'Idée de Dieu dans la philosophie de saint Anselme*, Paris, 1923. – *Spicilegium Beccense I, Ier congrès anselmien*, Paris, 1959. – J. Vuillemin, *Le Dieu d'Anselme et les apparences de la raison*, Paris, 1971. – G. R. Evans, *Anselm and talking about God*, Oxford, 1978. – *Spicilegium Beccense I, 4e congrès anselmien*, Paris, 1984. – G. R. Evans, *Anselm*, London, 1989. – R. W. Southern, *St. Anselm and his Biographer*, Cambridge, 1963. – R. W. Southern, *St Anselm: a Portrait in a Landscape*, Cambridge, 1997.

Gillian R. Evans

**ANSKAR OR ANSGAR (801-865).** A Benedictine monk of *Corbie who became **scholasticus* of *Corvey, then first bishop of *Hamburg (831), Anskar is considered the apostle of *Scandinavia.

*The month of June.* Bas-relief in the baptistery of Parma, by Benedetto Antelami. Early 13th c.

After having been almoner to a converted Danish prince (Harald Klak) between 826 and 828, in 829 Anskar received the task of organising the Christian community of Birka, the great emporium of central *Sweden, where he built the first church in Scandinavia (830-831). *Louis the Pious gave him the new *bishopric of Hamburg, along with the revenues of the monastic *cella* of Torhout (Flanders). Gregory IV charged him with a legation to the Scandinavians and *Slavs of the North. After 840 Torhout was taken from him, and in 845 the *Vikings ravaged Hamburg. Anskar fell back on *Bremen whose vacant episcopal see he occupied. He later founded a church at Slesvig and another at Ribe (*Denmark) and, during a second misssion to Sweden, re-established a *parish at Birka in *c.*852. In 864, he received the **pallium* for the archbishopric of Hamburg-Bremen, with authority over the whole of the Scandinavian lands.

After his death, which occurred at Bremen, his work was continued by his successor Rembert († 888), but Sweden's first Christian establishments declined rapidly. In fact, Anskar's *mission affected only a minority of merchants: this was the real reason for the failure of his precocious attempt to evangelize Scandinavia. The *Vita Anskarii*, written by Rembert between 865 and 873, provides precious information on 9th-c. Sweden. Anskar himself composed some works including the *Virtutes et miracula beati Willehadi*. But the medieval Swedish liturgy ignored the missionary saint until the late 14th c., when Nicolaus Hermansson, bishop of *Linköping, dedicated an *officium* to him. In the 15th c., Anskar was honoured in Sweden as founder of the national Church, with his *anniversary feast on 4 February.

L. Musset, "La Pénétration chrétienne dans l'Europe du Nord", *SSAM*, 14, Spoleto, 1967. – *The Christianisation of Scandinavia*, B. Sawyer (ed.), P. Sawyer (ed.), I. Wood (ed.), Alingsås, 1987. – A. Dierkens, "Saint Anschaire, l'abbaye de Torhout et les missions carolingiennes en Scandinavie", *Études offertes à Pierre Riché*, 1990, 301-313.

Jean-Marie Maillefer

**ANTELAMI, BENEDETTO (*c.*1150-*c.*1235).** We have no reliable information on Antelami's life. His surname was common among the stonecutters of the Lombard Pre-Alps. His first signed and dated sculpture is a high-relief *Deposition from the Cross* in *Parma cathedral (1178). Still Byzantine in the symmetry that guides the composition and the nielloed cornice that frames the scene, the work is innovative in the distinct modelling of the figures wrapped in finely folded drapery which recall contemporary Provençal sculpture, and especially in the emotion and gravity of expression of the figures that mark the artist's work.

His real masterpiece is the cycle conceived for the *baptistery at Parma, begun in 1196, of which Antelami may also have been the *architect. Completed with the help of collaborators, it is divided into sculptures placed both outside and inside the building, and develops a complex iconographical programme relating man's destiny to the Christian mysteries. The theological emphasis on concordances between the Old and New *Testaments, converging towards the *Annunciation of the Birth of Christ* and the *Glorification of the Virgin*, does not prevent ample concession to fantastic and imaginary repertories taken from the bestiaries. In the external lunettes of the three portals are depicted the *Last Judgment, an allegory of Life taken from the well-known Oriental legend of Barlaam and Josaphat, and the Adoration of the *Magi (the other work signed by the artist).

In the period between the *Deposition* (1178) and the start of the Parma baptistery sculptures (1196) comes a series of works whose attribution is still disputed, like the most recent part of the decoration of the façade of the cathedral of Borgo San Donnino (Fidenza), where the intervention of collaborators is certain. In this interval, the master's work seems more evident in the vigorous reliefs of the marble **cathedra* in the apse of Parma cathedral and in the slightly later reliefs made for the two portals in the façade of Sant'Andrea at Vercelli (*c.*1227) as well as in the high relief with the equestrian figure of Orlando da Tresseno (1233), on the outside of the Broletto at *Milan. Many disciples and imitators of Antelami perpetuated the art of his school beyond the mid 13th century. Dependent on this current are the sculptures of the lunette depicting the Adoration of the Magi in San Mercuriale at Forlì, the cycles of the months in *Ferrara cathedral and in the church of Santa Maria della Pieve at Arezzo and the reliefs with the Dream of St Mark on the main portal of St Mark's basilica in *Venice and the lives of St *Martin and St Regulus in the atrium of *Lucca cathedral.

G. de Francovich, *Benedetto Antelami, architetto e scultore e l'arte del suo tempo*, Milan-Florence, 1952. – G. Duby, G. Romano, C. Frugoni, *Battistero di Parma*, Milan, 1992. – C. B. Verzar, "Antelami, Benedetto", *DoA*, 2, 132-133.

Monica Chiellini Nari

**ANTEPENDIUM.** The *pallium* (*pall) or *antependium* was the great *veil of *silk or rare stuff that, in late Antiquity and the first centuries of the Middle Ages, surrounded the *altar. It was also placed on the *tomb of saints, as a sign of veneration and respect. The *pallium* could also be a covering of precious metal, worked and ornamented with precious stones: the basilica of S. Ambrogio at *Milan preserves one from the 9th c. in solid *gold. The *antependium* became the precious fabric that "hung in front of" the altar and that often changed with degrees of solemnity.

J. Braun, *Die christliche Altar*, Munich, 1932.

Guy-Marie Oury

**ANTHONY OF PADUA (1195-1231).** Anthony was born at Lisbon in 1195, perhaps on 15 August. Son of the knight Martino di Afonso and his wife Maria, both descended from the city's nobility, he was baptized under the name Fernando. He received his first education at the cathedral school before 1210, after which he entered the community of Augustinian Canons of St Vincent, at the gates of Lisbon, and was later sent to the mother house of *Coimbra in 1212. The rich *library of the monastery of Santa Cruz gave the young *canon the biblical and patristic training of the future preacher. 1220 was both the year of his *ordination at Santa Cruz and of his *conversion to the Franciscan ideal, aroused by the sight of the *relics of the five friars killed at Marrakesh, 16 Jan 1220. It was indeed the dream of *martyrdom that led Fernando to the *Franciscan Order and in particular to the Franciscan brothers of the hermitage of St Anthony at Olivais, near Coimbra. On his entry into the Franciscan Order, Fernando took the name Anthony in homage to St Anthony Abbot. At the end of 1220 he left for *Morocco, where he spent the winter but had to leave in March 1221 due to the poor state of his health. On the return journey, a storm forced him to land in Sicily. From there he went to *Assisi where, from 30 May to 8 June, he took part in the order's general *chapter. Remaining in the shade and practically unknown, he accompanied the provincial minister Gratian to *Romagna and asked permission to live in the hermitage of Montepaolo near Forlì, where he remained until September 1222. It was on 24 Sept, while he was taking part in priestly ordinations at Forlì, that his confreres had the revelation of his great biblical and patristic knowledge as well as his oratorical talents. At the end of the month, he obtained the post of preacher and was sent to Rimini where, according to tradition, in 1223 he was able to convert a great number of *heretics including the heresiarch Bonomillo. But the idea of Anthony's anti-heretical commitment has been much modified by recent historiography, which tends rather to see him concerned with teaching and training future preachers, an activity to which he began to dedicate himself, with *Francis's consent, between the end of 1223 and the first months of 1224. His first school was Santa Maria

*The Twelve Apostles.* Altar-frontal from the diocese of Seo de Urgel. Catalan school, 12th c. Barcelona, Catalonia Museum of Art.

della Pugliola at *Bologna, also frequented by members of the *secular clergy and students of the university. Between autumn 1224 and the end of 1227, Anthony taught and preached in France: at Arles, Montpellier, Toulouse, Limoges (where he was *guardian of the *convent), Brive, Bourges, Le Puy (as guardian of the Minors). In 1227 he was in Italy again, for the general chapter of Assisi of 30 May. It was perhaps in that year, at the initiative of the new minister general John Parenti, that he was elected provincial minister of northern Italy. The following years (1228-1230) saw him in Milan and Vercelli (1229-1231), in *Padua and in the march of Treviso. He taught, preached and worked at perfecting his *Sermones dominicales* and composing his *Sermones festivi*, but also dedicated himself to *contemplation at the hermitage of Camposampiero. After the first daily lenten *preaching in Feb-March 1231 at Padua, Anthony died on 13 June 1231. On 30 May 1232 he was canonized by *Gregory IX in Spoleto cathedral.

Anthony's hagiographical tradition, as it developed in the 13th c., can be divided into four stages: the first (1232-1238) represents the early phase of the cult and comprises the *Vita prima* (also called *Assidua*), the *Officio ritmico* and the *Vita secunda* (*Juliana*), these latter composed by Julian of Speyer. The second stage coincides with the generalate of Fra Crescenzio da Iesi (1244-1247) and the beginnings of a Franciscan *hagiography: from this period dates the redaction of the *Dialogus de gestis sanctorum fratrum Minorum*. The third phase is that of the "Anthonian relaunch", marked especially by the recognition of the body, 8 April 1263, and by the general chapter held at Padua near the saint's tomb in 1276 during the generalate of Fra Girolamo d'Ascoli. It was the minister general himself who gave the impetus to a new *Vita*, whose redaction was entrusted to John Peckham (Franciscan ex-provincial of England) and which today seems identifiable with the *Benignitas*. To the fourth stage, at the end of the century and the beginning of the next, belong the *Raymundina* and the *Rigaldina*, fruits of the order's new commitment (sanctioned especially by the general chapters of 1292 and 1295) to recovering the *gesta* of sainted friars. Finally, late but important fruits of the hagiographical tradition are the *Liber miraculorum* (*c.*1369-1374), the *Epitome* of *Bartholomew of Pisa, the *Vita sancti Antonii* (15th-c., but revised and published by Lorenzo Surio in 1572) and the *Sancti Antonii vita* of the prehumanist Paduan notary Sicco Polentone (15th c.). On 16 Jan 1946, Pope Pius XII proclaimed Anthony a *Doctor of the Church.

*Antonii Patavini Sermones dominicales et festivi*, B. Costa (ed.), L. Frasson (ed.), G. Luisetto (ed.) and P. Marangon (ed.), Padua, 1979 (3 vol.). – *Vita prima o "Assidua"*, V. Gamboso (ed.), Padua, 1981 ("Fonti agiografiche antoniane", 1). – *Giuliano da Spira, Officio ritmico e Vita secunda (c.1235-1240)*, V. Gamboso (ed.), Padua, 1985 ("Fonti agiografiche antoniane", 2). – *Vita del "Dialogus" e "Benignitas" (1246-1280)*, V. Gamboso (ed.), Padua, 1986 ("Fonti agiografiche antoniane", 3). – Anthony of Padua, *Seek First his Kingdom*, L. Poloniato (ed.), Padua, 1988. – *Vite "Raymundina" e "Rigaldina" (1293-1300)*, Padua, 1992 ("Fonti agiografiche antoniane", 4).

*S. Antonio 1231-1981. Il suo tempo, il suo culto e la sua città*, Padua, 1981. – A. D. de Sousa Costa, *S. Antonio canonico regolare di S. Agostino e la sua vocazione francescana. Rilievi storico-storiografici*, Braga, 1982 ("Estudos e textos da idade média e rinascimento", 3). – *Le fonti e la teologia dei sermoni antoniani. Atti del congresso internazionale di studio sui "Sermones" di s. Antonio di Padova (Padova, 5-10 ottobre 1981)*, A. Poppi (ed.), Padua, 1982. – V. Gamboso, *Antonio di Padova. Vita e spiritualità*, Padua, 1995. – *"Vite" e vita di Antonio di Padova. Convegno internazionale di studio (Padova, 29 maggio - 1 giugno 1995)*, 1996, 1-2, 7-379 ("Il Santo", series 2). – *Pensamento e testemunho. Congresso internacional. 8° centenario do nascimento de santo Antonio*, Braga, 1996 (2 vol.). – *In nome di Antonio: La "Miscellanea" del Codice del Tesoro (XIII in.) della Biblioteca Antoniana di Padova. Studio ed edizione critica*, L. Frasson † (ed.), L. Gaffuri (ed.), C. Passarin (ed.), Padua, 1996.

Laura Gaffuri

**ANTHROPOLOGY, HISTORICAL.** The expression "historical anthropology" appeared in France around 1970, under the influence of the history called "of the *Annales*". Thus in 1974 the review *Annales* published a special number entitled *For an Anthropological History*, and in 1978 it devoted a number to the *Historical Anthropology of Andean Societies*. However, the discovery by historians of the works of ethnologists on "traditional societies" is much earlier. Marc Bloch and Lucien Febvre had not been unaware of it, but this attention increased when, after the Second World War, an important theoretical revival of ethnology occurred, particularly under the influence of Claude Lévi-Strauss. This favoured a rereading of pioneers like Marcel Mauss. Anglo-Saxon anthropology, or social anthropology, was equally important (E. Evans-Pritchard), as was the ethnology of traditional French societies (Arnold Van Gennep, Louis Dumont). More than just a discipline – the definition of it given in 1986 by André Burguière: "A history of attitudes and habits", is too restricted –, historical anthropology is the desire to combine the acquired knowledge, the research fields and the methods of anthropology with the historical approach.

This encounter is fertile in the study of *kinship systems, which for ethnologists is the key to their discipline: the fundamental role of the system of kinship relations in medieval society has already been brought out (G. Duby, D. Barthélemy, P. Guichard, A. Guerreau-Jalabert, S. D. White). Likewise, the contribution of anthropology is essential in the history of the *body: physical and biological history, but also the study of "body techniques" (Marcel Mauss, 1936), which fit into social systems of meaning and communication, as into the relationship of medieval people with their own bodies and those of others. Likewise, for the anthropologist, identifying systems of representation is an essential work. A history of these systems has been instituted under the label "history of mentalities". To the analysis of a "folk" culture, experienced in the rural world as in the aristocracy (J. Le Goff, J.-C. Schmitt), has been added research on complex symbolic wholes, like *heraldry or colours (M. Pastoureau). Political history (in which *politics and the sacred overlap) would in turn, in the footsteps of Marc Bloch (*Les Rois thaumaturges*, 1924), also benefit from the contributions of anthropology.

A. Burguière, "Anthropologie historique", *Dictionnaire des sciences historiques*, Paris, 1986, 52-60. – J.-C. Schmitt, *La Raison des gestes dans l'Occident médiéval*, Paris, 1990. – J. Berlioz, A. Guerreau-Jalabert, J. Le Goff, "Anthropologie et histoire", *L'Histoire médiévale en France. Bilan et perspectives*, Paris, 1991, 269-304.

Jacques Berlioz

**ANTHROPOMORPHISM.** In his *De laudibus sanctae crucis* (*c.*840), *Rabanus Maurus distinguishes the *sign (*signum*: abstract, like that of the bare *cross) from the *image (*imago*: *e.g.* that of the emperor or that of *Christ). From the 10th c., in the representation of God as in that of Christ's cross (*imago crucifixi*), the (representative) image gradually prevailed to the detriment of the simple sign: hence the anthropomorphic images of *God the Father and the *Trinity. Without ever having the theoretical coherence of a formal *heresy, this humanization of God was a fundamental tendency of the Western religious mentality, though currents of negative theology or *apophatic *mysticism continued to be well represented in the Middle Ages. This tendency triumphed especially from the 12th to the 15th c. in religious art and *theatre, and coloured the various ways of addressing God and speaking to Him. *Jews and Muslims criticized the Christians for it, but they justified it by appealing to the Incarnation.

F. Boespflug, *Dieu dans l'art*, Paris, 1984.

François Boespflug

## ANTICHRIST

**Exegesis.** Antichrist is the incarnation of the leader of the forces of *evil against the forces of *Christ during the tribulations of the end of *time. Medieval *exegesis followed the tradition of early Christianity in the description of this eschatological figure; the biblical texts are its main sources. The rare mentions of Antichrist by name (1 Jn 2, 18. 22; 4, 3; 2 Jn 7), indirect mentions of him (2 Th 2, 3-11) or the prophetic words of Christ (Mt 24, 5. 24; Mk 13, 6. 22; Lk 21, 8) all imply the key traits of the figure of Antichrist: he will appear before long, before Christ's Second Coming; denier of Christ, seducer of the Church and of Christians, he will set himself up against God and have himself worshipped in his place; after the persecution inflicted on the Christians, he will be destroyed by Christ or his agent. The other major biblical sources are the *Apocalypse and *Daniel (especially Rev 13 and Dan 11). Finally, exegesis identified in the *Bible certain types (Antiochus Epiphanes, Simon Magus) and symbols of Antichrist (especially in the Apocalypse): the most often cited being the beast with seven heads from the sea (Rev 13, 1).

Among non-biblical sources of the tradition were the *apocrypha, the *Sibylline oracles (Tiburtine sibyl, 4th c.) and Pseudo-Methodius's *Description of the Last Times* (late 7th c.). Conservative exegesis, following Augustine and Jerome, placed the coming of Antichrist just before Christ's Second Coming and the *Last Judgment: *Isidore of Seville (*c.*570-636) and the Venerable *Bede (*c.*673-735) expected him at the end of the sixth age, the age of the Church. Around 954, *Adso of Montier-en-Der synthesized the tradition in a veritable biography (*Libellus de Antichristo*), taken up and enriched throughout the Middle Ages: Antichrist appears there as a *tyrant and pseudo-Christ parodying Christ. The *Glossa ordinaria*, an orthodox exposition of biblical tradition (12th c.), insists on the imminence of the end and the violence of Antichrist.

*Joachim of Fiore († 1202) diverged from tradition: he admitted several comings of Antichrist, the main one ("great Antichrist") preceding a spiritual era. His conception was radically utilized in the numerous political and religious polemics hatched between the 13th and 15th cc.: *Frederick II and then 14th-c. popes like *Boniface VIII were successively identified as Antichrist by their enemies. The theme of Antichrist spread at the same time in all types of literature, generally conforming to the conservative exegesis: *sermons, historical works, *theatre (*Ludus de Antichristo*, *c.*1155-1160), allegorical poems (*Tournoiement Antécrist*, *c.*1234-1237); *vitae* of Antichrist multiplied in the 15th century. The iconography of Antichrist, inspired by the Apocalypse, represents him in accordance with the conservative exegesis.

M. Reeves, *The Influence of Prophecy in the later Middle Ages*, Oxford, 1969. – R. K. Emmerson, *Antichrist in the Middle Ages: a Study of Medieval Apocalypticism, Art and Literature*, Seattle (WA), 1981. – R. E. Lerner, "Antichrists and Antichrist in Joachim of Fiore", *Spec.*, 60, 1985, 553-570.

Marc Boilloux

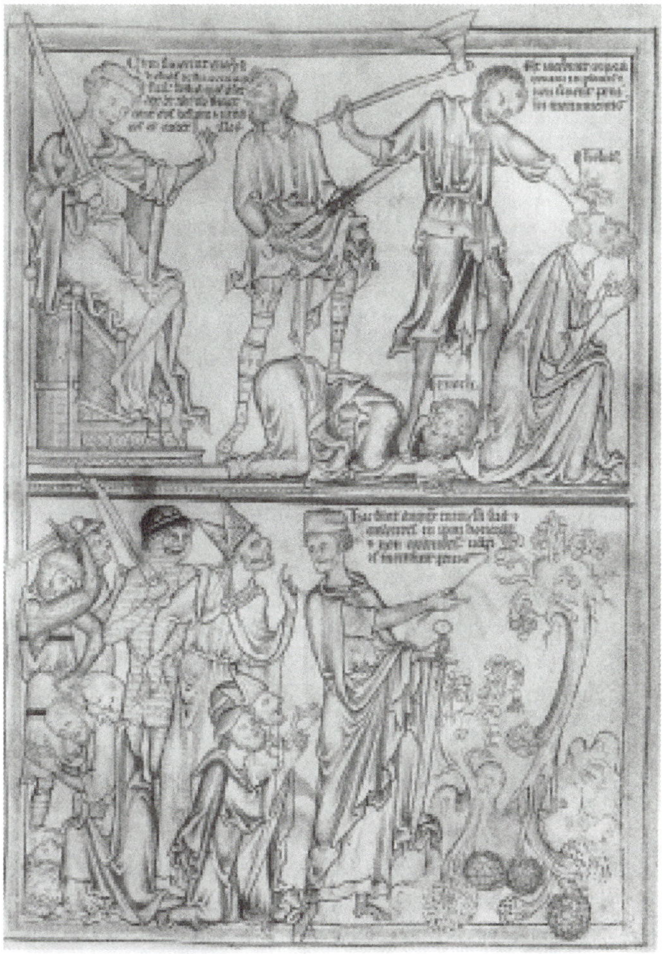

*Antichrist makes the roots of a tree flower.* Miniature from an Anglo-Norman Apocalypse. New York, Pierpont Morgan Library (Ms 524, fol. 7).

**Spirituality.** Antichrist is a character in the eschatological drama whose scenario was established from the beginning of Christianity on the margins of official theology. He is called "Antechrist" since he must appear before (*ante*) Christ's return at the end of *time, or "Antichrist" because he is an antithesis of *Christ. He appears by name in St John's two epistles (1 Jn 2, 18-22; 4, 3; 2 Jn 7) and, under various names, in *apocalyptic literature. The best description of his person and activity is in a treatise of *Adso of Montier-en-Der entitled *Of the Birth and Times of the Antichrist*, written in 953-954. His biography is presented as the antithesis of Christ's. Born at Babylon, he will be brought up at Bethsaida and Chorazin by magicians and sorcerers. He will reign in *Jerusalem whence he will launch the final persecution against the Christians and the elect. These will have been prepared for his coming by the return to earth of Enoch and *Elijah. Kept in reserve for this task by God, they will instruct and train the Christians for spiritual combat for three and a half years. The Antichrist, son of the Devil, will finally unleash the persecution and will martyr the elect with Enoch and Elijah. His reign will last three and a half years to conclude the last week of the world. Then Christ himself, or the archangel *Michael, will kill the Antichrist before inaugurating the *Last Judgment after forty days of penitence.

The outlines of this eschatological scheme had already been drawn by Hippolytus of Rome early in the 3rd c., and would remain at the forefront of the Christian mentality well beyond the end of the Middle Ages. Numerous treatises and *libelli* would perpetually strain to make out the signs of his coming, multiplying the number of precursor antichrists, chosen from among historical characters or the author's contemporaries. *Millenarian writers follow his coming with Christ's millenarian reign, while for the orthodox it precedes only the Last Judgment. The addition to the scenario of the person of the Emperor of the Last Times, whose abdication at Jerusalem must precede the opening of the last week of the world, gives the scheme a more clearly political and topical turn, particularly from the 13th cenury on.

The extreme popularity of Antichrist rested mainly on the integration into *history of the drama that he animated, and on the ease with which its precursory signs could be made out in the misery of the times.

C. Carozzi, H. Taviani-Carozzi, *La Fin des Temps*, Paris, 1982. – *The Use and Abuse of Eschatology in the Middle Ages*, W. Verbeke (ed.), *et al.*, Louvain, 1988. – *The Apocalypse in the Middle Ages*, R.K. Emmerson (ed.), B. McGinn (ed.), Ithaca, NY, 1993. – R.M. Wright, *Art and Antichrist in Medieval Europe*, Manchester, 1995.

Claude Carozzi

**ANTICLERICALISM.** The notion of anticlericalism, as well as the term, were forged in the 19th c. to designate the doctrine and movement of opposition to the influence of the clergy in public affairs. In this sense, "anticlericalism" supposes the existence of a clear distinction between *Church and State, which began to prevail in the West only from the time of the *Gregorian reform, in the second half of the 11th century. It is precisely at this moment that the first manifestations of hostility to ecclesiastical structures and personnel appear (in the documents).

Laypeople won over to the Gregorian ideals required of their priests at that time that they conform to the models of behaviour defined by the papacy. Linking the *validity of the *sacraments to the moral state of the celebrants, they went so far as to boycott the liturgical services of unworthy priests, desert their churches and refuse to pay the *tithe. But the contestants (*e.g.* the *Patarines at Milan) were soon declared "heretics" by the Church authorities. Many historians today make them "anticlerical" (though many "*clerics" appear in their ranks): indeed "anticlericalism", here defined as a rejection of the established hierarchy and its representatives, would, in the West, be the common point of most "*heresies" between the 11th and the mid 14th century.

From the 13th c., the opposition of the *laity to ecclesiastical exactions and their refusal to pay tithes, parochial rights and "offerings" attached to the administration of the sacraments undoubtedly reveal their distrust concerning the alterations to an ecclesial economy in which monetary exchanges were taking a growing place. The dispute was sometimes the cause of aggression, violence and revolts, mostly anti-episcopal but sometimes also aimed at simple priests. In some cases, the obligatory mediation of priests between this world and the next that was questioned: such an attitude could issue in a rejection of the *priesthood and the sacraments, an "antisacerdotalism" towards which the *Waldenses in particular slid. But the exasperation of the laity also found expression, in town as in the country, in a certain "scepticism", which cast doubt on fundamental assertions or institutions of the Christian religion defined by the Church, as well as in mockery: *e.g.* that of the villagers of Montaillou who, according to the records of the inquisitor Jacques Fournier, bleated to imitate the officiant or parodied the singing of the *Pater*. In social satire too: the **fabliaux* and *chansons* of the 13th c. frequently represent priests as ignorant, concubinary, seducers of married women. Bishops, monks and mendicant friars (whom the poet Rutebeuf turns to ridicule) were no better treated.

At the end of the Middle Ages, certain mystical currents preached the direct relationship of the believer with God and, heralding the Protestant Reformation, an attitude of individual improvement outside ecclesial structures.

W. L. Wakefield, "Some Unorthodox Popular Ideas", *MeH*, new series, 4, 1973, 25-35. – R. I. Moore, *The Birth of Popular Heresy*, London, 1975. – J. Chiffoleau, "Vie et mort de l'hérésie en Provence et dans la vallée du Rhône du début du XIIIe au début du XIVe siècle", *Effacement du Catharisme?*, Toulouse, 1985, 73-99 ("CFan", 20). – F. Blanchetière, "Contestation des structures ecclésiales et hérésie au XIIe siècle", *RHPhR*, 67, 1987, 241-249. – *Aspects de l'anticléricalisme du Moyen Âge à nos jours*, J. Mary (ed.), 1988 ("PHChr", 18). – *Anticlericalism in late Medieval and early Modern Europe*, P. A. Dykema (ed.), H. A. Oberman (ed.), Leiden, 1993.

Michel Lauwers

**ANTIJUDAISM.** Religious hostility towards *Jews developed throughout the Middle Ages, taking different forms in different times and places. A distinction must be made between the official attitude of the Church and that of the Christian populace. Jewish-Christian polemic was expressed mainly in treatises *adversus Judaeos*. Theologians, while affirming the necessity of the survival of the Jewish people, permanent reminder of Christ's Passion and proof of the truth of the Scriptures, ceaselessly reaffirmed the responsibility of the Jews for the crucifixion and the blindness of those who would not recognise the Messiah. From Antiquity, Church *Fathers had developed these different themes, on which the papacy leaned to define the place of the Jews within *Christendom.

From the 11th c., Jewish communities found themselves physically threatened by the pressures of popular antijudaism. The time of the first *crusade is considered the end of a relative equilibrium. The route of the crusaders was marked by attacks against German Jews in spring 1096; at the time of the preaching of the second crusade, forced *conversions and massacres affected *England and the North of the kingdom of *France. This violence reappeared sporadically in the form of accusations of *ritual murders or profanation of *hosts, made until the end of the Middle Ages especially in Northern Europe. This attitude, which was radicalized after the 13th c., had great consequences for the condition of Jews living in the West.

While renewing the *Constitutio pro Iudeis* granted by *Calixtus II between 1119 and 1124 and showing some concern for the protection of Jewish communities, the *popes nevertheless hardened their position towards them. From the 13th c., conciliar decisions multiplied, repeating former legislation and in particular certain canons of the early medieval *councils applied solely in Visigothic *Spain and aiming to isolate the Jews and limit their contacts with Christians. Several canons of the fourth *Lateran council (1215) brought together the main orientations followed from now on, which inspired civil legislation, in particular the regulation of lending to Christians, the obligation to wear a distinctive sign and the prohibition on holding public office. The condemnation of the *Talmud between 1239 and 1248 and the institution of regulated forced preaching by the *bull *Vineam Soreth* (1278) are so many signs of a marked deterioration in Jewish-Christian relations experienced first in England, France and Germany, then a century later in the Iberian peninsula and Italy.

The process culminated in the *expulsions of Jews, which affected England from 1290, France in 1394 and the *Spain of the *Catholic Kings in 1492.

B. Blumenkranz, *Juifs et chrétiens dans le monde occidental (430-1096)*, Paris-The Hague, 1960. – G. I. Langmuir, *Towards a Definition of Antisemitism*, Berkeley (CA), 1990. – G. Dahan, *Les Intellectuels chrétiens et les Juifs au Moyen Âge*, Paris, 1993. – *HChr*, 4-6, 1990-1993. – R. Chazan, *Medieval Stereotypes and Modern Antisemitism*, Berkeley (CA), 1997.

Danièle Sansy

**ANTIOCH.** A town in northern *Syria, on the Orontes, 22 kilometres from the coast, an ancient Seleucid foundation, in the 1st c. BC Antioch became the most important Roman city in Asia. A commercial city, it was also an important intellectual and theological centre. It was there that Jesus' disciples were first called Christians, and Antioch played a great role in the expansion of Christianity in the East. Attacked and pillaged several times by the Persians, it was rebuilt by Justinian (527-565). Conquered by the Arabs in 637 or 638, during the first centuries of Muslim occupation it was a key point in the organisation of the frontier defences. Resuming the offensive against the Arabs, the Byzantines recaptured Antioch in 969 and kept it until 1084, when it fell into the hands of the *Seljuks. When the Franks of the first *crusade reached *Constantinople, the Emperor Alexius *Comnenus forced them to swear to yield the city to him after they had conquered it. After a long and arduous siege, it was taken by the crusaders on 28 June 1098 and given to the Norman Bohemund.

Rising on the slopes of Mount Silpius, Antioch was surrounded by gardens, with a city wall more than 12 kilometres long and dominated by a citadel built in the 10th century. It had numerous churches such as St Peter's cathedral where the Latin princes and patriarchs were buried. It was also the seat of an Armenian *bishopric, a Greek patriarchate and a Jacobite patriarchate; when the Franks arrived they replaced the Greek *patriarch by a Latin one, but at certain periods they authorized the reinstallation of a Greek patriarch at Antioch.

Political life at Antioch in the first half of the 12th c. was marked by conflicts with the Muslims of northern Syria and Byzantine attempts to get their suzerainty recognised. From 1146, Prince Raymond of Antioch had to face the Muslim counter-offensive led by Nūr al-Dīn. In 1188, when *Saladin conquered a great many fortresses in northern Syria, Antioch itself was threatened. But a truce was concluded, and after Saladin's death conflicts with the *Ayyubids were rare, while tension with the Armenian kingdom of *Cilicia increased considerably. In 1193, while Bohemund III was held prisoner by Leo II, prince of Lesser *Armenia, the inhabitants of Antioch, to defend themselves, proclaimed a commune. In 1201, after Bohemund III's death, Leo II of Lesser Armenia and Bohemund IV of Tripoli struggled for possession of Antioch. Bohemund IV finally won in 1219, thus uniting the two States of Antioch and Tripoli. Under Bohemund V (1233-1251) and Bohemund VI (1251-1275), Antioch grew weaker; under the influence of the king of Lesser Armenia, it sided with the *Mongols. In 1268, Sultan Baybars captured the city and massacred the population to punish it for its alliance with the Mongols. Under the *Mamluks, it was a place of no great importance.

C. Cahen, *La Syrie du Nord à l'époque des croisades et la principauté franque d'Antioche*, Paris, 1940. – M. Streck, H. A. R. Gibb, "Anṭākiya", *EI(E)*, 1, 1960, 516-517. – G. Downey, *A History of Antioch from Seleucus to the Arab Conquest*, Princeton (NJ), 1961. – D.S. Wallace-Hadrill, *Christian Antioch*, Cambridge, 1982. – S.D. Campbell, *The Mosaics of Antioch*, Toronto, 1988.

Anne-Marie Eddé

**ANTIPHON.** The primary sense of "antiphon" is the chanting of alternate choirs. It is still used in this sense in the West for the psalmody of the *office. But in the Latin tradition the term has come, from at least the 7th-8th cc., to designate a formula, often very brief, chanted before and after the psalm or sometimes between the verses. By extension, the term is also employed for formulae of the same type chanted independently of the psalmody. In the *Byzantine liturgy the term "antiphon" is employed in the same senses, but further designates the 68 groups of *psalms into which the psalmody is divided and more especially the gradual psalms (*anavathmi*) and the three groups of verses with refrain and *troparia* chanted at the start of the Divine liturgy.

"Antienne" and "Antiphone", *DACL*, 1, 2, 1907. – E. Nowacki, "The Gregorian Antiphons and the Comparative Method", *Journal of Musicology*, 4, 1985-1986, 243-75. – T. Bailey, *Antiphon and Psalm in the Ambrosian Office*, Ottawa, 1994. – J. Halmo, *Antiphons for Paschal Triduum-Easter in the Medieval Office*, Ottawa, 1995.

Irénée-Henri Dalmais

**ANTIPHONARY.** The word *antiphonarius* or *antiphonale* is derived from *antiphona*, meaning an *antiphon or anthem, a sung piece. From the 8th c., it designated the antiphonary of the *mass (also called "*gradual", from the name of the chant that introduced the *Alleluia*), the antiphonary of the *office, or else manuscripts that contained both these.

The antiphonary of the mass (or gradual) contained the *incipit* of the sung pieces, often notated, that the **schola cantorum* had to perform under the direction of the choirmaster during mass (chants of the proper: *introit, *offertory and communion antiphons; and the melodies of the chants of the ordinary: the **Kyrie*, the **Gloria*, the **Credo*, the **Sanctus* and the **Agnus Dei*). The antiphonary of the office contained the *incipit* of the chants reserved for the different *hours of the liturgy of the office, pieces of biblical origin alternating with original creations.

The unification of liturgical chant in the West during the Carolingian period was possible thanks to the diffusion of the Gregorian antiphonary. In the sphere of the office, by contrast, this did not suppress local traditions. In the second half of the Middle Ages, both books were progressively integrated into the *missal and the *breviary.

R.-J. Hesbert, *Antiphonale missarum sextuplex*, Brussels, 1935. – R.-J. Hesbert, *Corpus antiphonalium officii*, Rome, 1963-1979 (6 vol.). – M. Curran, *The Antiphonary of Bangor*, Blackrock, 1984. – M. Huglo, *Les Livres de chant liturgique*, *TSMÂO*, 52, 1988.

Éric Palazzo

**ANTIPOPE.** Any person claiming to be St Peter's successor without the canonical rules of *election having been respected is called an antipope. He could be a *pope elected in an irregular way after the death or illegitimate deposition of a pope. The antipope could also enter into rivalry with a regular pope: there was then a *schism, the most frequent case in the Middle Ages. The antipope was designated by a faction to checkmate the legitimate pope; the promoters of antipopes were generally the Roman nobility, the emperor or a party of *cardinals.

The word does not appear officially until the late 14th c., though it first occurs in 12th-c. England. Indeed, a strict definition of the canonical rules of papal election had to be formulated before there could be a legal category designating one who infringed them. In earlier periods, invective, which tarnished an opponent's name, was extremely rich. Designations insisted on the diabolical character of the antipope and on the disorder his action introduced into the Church. This savour of insult persisted in the word "antipope", which doubtless owed its success to its closeness to "*Antichrist".

The notion was hence always subject to polemic: the antipopes were certain of their own right. It was thus difficult to establish a list of irregular pontiffs, all the more since the electoral norms were only gradually defined. The work of Mercati (1947) rapidly became an official list.

A. Mercati, "The New List of the Popes", *MS*, 9, 1947, 71-80. – D. MacCarron, *The Great Schism: antipopes who split the Church*, Dublin, 1982. – E. Stoller, "The Emergence of the Term *antipapa* in Medieval Use", *AHP*, 23, 1985, 43-61. – O. Guyotjeannin, "Antipape", *DHP*, 1994, 118-121.

Pierre Kerbrat

**ANTONINES.** The Hospitaller Order of St Anthony in Viennois (Isère) arose in *c.*1095. At this time there appeared in Europe a *sickness called *ignis sacer* by reason of the burning pains it caused. Only in the 17th c. was it diagnosed as ergotism (*ergotismus gangraenosus* and *ergotismus convulsivus*). The hallucinations linked to the illness and caused by the LSD contained in ergot increased people's anguish and they often sought help from their familiar saints. Crowds of *pilgrims thus appeared in a small village in the *Dauphiné where the (presumed) *relics of St Anthony Abbot had arrived some decades earlier and which had meanwhile taken the name of Saint-Antoine.

The monks of the *priory of Saint-Antoine, dependent on the abbey of Montmajour, had been entrusted with the *pastoral care of the place and the care of St Anthony's relics, while local laypeople had joined together in a *confraternity to come to the aid of pilgrims. The quality of the care expended on the pilgrims, particularly the sick, the construction and extension of a *hospital and doubtless also the first therapeutic successes soon led the confraternity to take charge of hospitals in other towns like Chambéry, Gap and *Besançon, and before it had been in existence for a century we find it in northern Italy, Flanders, Spain and Germany and soon in the Holy Land. In 1232, the Holy See obliged the brothers and sisters to adopt a religious rule. In 1247, the Antonines were recognised as an order of their own, following the Rule of St *Augustine, and in 1297 it was transformed into an order of *canons with an *abbot at its head.

The work of the Antonines in running hospitals and dispensaries and effectively combating the sickness, which from the 12th c. was called "St Anthony's fire", was considerable. As a consequence of this success the network of branches was extended ever further, as far as Portugal and the Baltic, from Scotland to Cyprus, grouping together more than 370 hospitals caring for thousands of sick and infirm. By the generalized rearing of "St Anthony's pigs" as well as by the *collections organised annually in every *parish, the Antonines were present everywhere. The exceptional popularity of the collections, whose proceeds could represent up to two thirds of the total income, was conditioned by fear of St Anthony, whose image had been transformed from that of a good-natured healer, through the avenger who punished insufficient piety towards him, to that of a "fire demon" (Huizinga) who struck indiscriminately.

The rationalistic sensibility of the *Renaissance and the religious disturbances of the 16th c., the prohibition of St Anthony's pigs and collections, and the almost total disappearance of St Anthony's fire due to the improvement of the quality of life and better medical care, meant the end of the order in its existing form. Despite a reform (1616-1634), its decline could not be stemmed. By the *bull *Rerum humanarum conditio* of 17 Dec 1776, the Order of Antonines was incorporated into the Order of *Hospitallers of St John of Jerusalem, by then known as the Order of Malta.

H. Chaumartin, *Le Mal des ardents et le Feu Saint-Antoine*, Vienne, 1946. – A. Mischlewski, *Un Ordre hospitalier au Moyen Âge: Les chanoines réguliers de Saint-Antoine-en-Viennois*, Grenoble, 1995.

Adalbert Mischlewski

**ANTONINUS OF FLORENCE (1389-1459).** Antonino Pierozzi, a Florentine, was a *Dominican friar (1406) and archbishop of *Florence (1446).

Son of a notary, he studied *canon law; but the influence of *John Dominici led him to enter the Dominican observants (1405). A *novice at Cortona, he lived successively in the *convents of Fiesole, Foligno (1409-1411), Cortona (1411-1421; prior in 1418), Fiesole (prior in 1321), Naples (prior in 1426), Rome (convent of Santa Maria sopra Minerva, prior in 1429) and finally Florence, in the convent of St Mark, recently granted to the Dominican *Observance by Pope *Eugenius IV, and of which Antonino was elected prior (1438). Other posts were entrusted to him at the same time: vicar general of the observants in *Tuscany, then of the reformed convents *citra Alpes* (1438). At St Mark's, Antoninus showed his full capacity; he directed his monks, supervised the building of the *library ordered by Cosimo de' Medici, regulated *confraternities (*penitents, children, good works), preached, confessed at length, directed consciences.

His appointment by *Eugenius IV to the see of Florence on the death of Archbishop Bartolomeo Zabarella aroused surprise, but mainly joy (Jan 1446). Once consecrated (13 March) and after his solemn entry and enthronement, the *archbishop chose his collaborators (including two nephews). We see him at work, at prayer, in charity, penance, penury.

A *synod (April) and a pastoral *visit (Aug 1446-April 1447, 149 *parishes) informed him rapidly about the material and moral situation of the *diocese. He found it mediocre, and acted to reorganise the management of temporalities: his own and that of the parishes. On the spiritual level, he took in hand the reform of the clergy, training, appointments, moral standards. Concerning the laity, he was assiduous in *preaching, which he kept clear and pedagogical and which he accompanied with a vigorous campaign to redress morals (*usury, gaming, *marriage) and faith.

Self-taught, but an immense reader (*Decretum*, Scripture, Latin and Greek *Fathers, modern authors) and a rapid writer, Antoninus soon added writing to his activities. Moral, theological, spiritual, pastoral, his work is that of a pastor. His first treatises were aimed at confessors, children (*Libretto della dottrina cristiana*), a penitent lady of the *Medici family, or addressed a precise moral theme (*Tractatus de cambiis*). Once bishop, the prelate intensified his work, writing one after another a catechism, a *Summula confessionalis*, an opusculum of *spiritual direction and especially, taking up his nights, a considerable moral *summa* on the theme of how man, *soul and *body, *intellect and *will, can, in all conditions to which he is subject, pass from *vices to virtues. A chronicle, *Summa historialis*, an apologetic compilation, completes the corpus. Hostile to *humanism, Antonino left a mark on his time, locally as a pastor, lastingly as a moralist. Canonized in 1523, he has been the main patron of Florence since 1959.

A. d'Addario, "Antonino Pierozzi, santo", *DBI*, 3, Rome, 1961, 524-532. – *SOPMA*, 1, 1970, 80-100. – P.F. Howard, *Beyond the Written Word: Preaching and Theology in the Florence of Archbishop Antoninus, 1427-1459*, Florence, 1995.

Charles-Marie de La Roncière

**ANTONIO DA BUTRIO (1338-1408).** This celebrated *Decretalist was venerated in his lifetime both for his qualities as a professor and for the example of his religious and moral virtues. His university career was essentially at *Bologna, where he attracted numerous pupils, among them future great representatives of 15th-c. canonical science, like John of Imola, Francesco *Zabarella or Dominic of San Gimignano.

Antonio da Butrio left *Commentaries* on the *Decretals and on the *Sext*, *Consilia* and various treatises. Today, his reputation as a *canonist is that of a prolix author, but his writings circulated and were not without influence, notably on *Panormitanus.

L. Prosdocimi, "Antonio da Butrio", *DBI*, 3, Rome, 1961, 541-542. – P. Ourliac, H. Gilles, *La Période post-classique (1378-1500). La problématique de l'époque. Les sources*, Paris, 1971.

Jacques Krynen

**ANTWERP.** The Merovingian citadel called Antwerp probably dates from no earlier than the 7th c.: it was built close to an earlier settlement, *Chanelaus/Caloes*, situated further south. Later the abbey of Saint-Michel would be built south of the citadel. In 836, the old citadel was completely devastated by the *Vikings; shortly after, these Vikings seem to have founded a commercial counter to the north, and erected a fortification near the *Steen*. Shortly before 980, for the first time since the Vikings, Antwerp was again fortified: *Otto II, emperor of Germany, made it a defence post along the Scheldt to protect the western frontier of his Empire. Having become the possession of *Godfrey of Bouillon, duke of Lower *Lorraine, Antwerp was sold in 1096 to count Godfrey I of Louvain and was henceforth part of *Brabant. The town's earliest privilege dates from 1221. It had been surrounded by ramparts towards the end of the 12th century. In the course of the 13th, the town on the Scheldt became an important commercial link between England and Germany: the ensuing development was such that from now on it was one of Brabant's four chief towns and twice had to enlarge its fortified wall. In 1296, Antwerp obtained rights as a depot for English wool: this would be the start of an economic boom that lasted until 1355. In the years 1337-1340, it was the most important international wool market in the world and one of the greatest financial centres in Western Europe.

The rivalry Antwerp represented for the Flemish towns suffered a setback when, after the death of Duke John II of Brabant (1355), the count of Flanders, Louis de Male, received Antwerp and part of the marquisate in *fief: from now on all social agitation would be put down in blood. Antwerp would remain under Flemish administration until 1405. The social troubles that agitated *Flanders profited it, especially when the foreign merchants left Bruges to settle there. The transition to Burgundian rule was made without difficulty: indeed, as duke of Brabant, Philip the Bold largely pursued the policy of his predecessors, in particular following a commercial policy which was favourable to Antwerp. But the situation would change with his great-grandson, *Charles the Bold, who set up a frankly absolutist and centralizing regime. For this reason he could not get himself recognised as duke of Brabant without coming up against strong opposition in the *port town. His wars, the considerable rise in *taxation, all his methods of government would lead to a grave political crisis under the government of his daughter, Mary of Burgundy (1477-1482). In this period the *corporations obtained for a time the right to sit among the **échevins* or aldermen. Under Maximilian of Austria, unlike the Flemish towns (*Bruges and *Ghent) and most of Brabant (*Brussels and Louvain), Antwerp remained faithful to its lord, in return for which it received wide economic advantages. Moreover most of the foreign merchants left Bruges, then in a state of agitation, for the town on the Scheldt which just then (1492) was granted a new depot tax, on alum.

In the 16th c., Antwerp would attain the dimensions of a world commercial metropolis.

F. Prims, *Antwerpen door de eeuwen heen*, Antwerp, 1951. – H. Van Der Wee, *The Growth of the Antwerp Market and the European Economy, Fourteenth-Sixteenth Centuries*, The Hague, 1963 (3 vol.). – *Antwerp: Twelve Centuries of History and Culture*, K. Van Isacker (ed.), R. Van Uytven (ed.), Antwerp, 1986.

Lieve De Mecheleer

**APOCALYPSE OF JOHN**

**Exegesis.** The Apocalypse was received by the Latin Middle Ages as a text on whose canonicity there was sufficient agreement, and there was no longer any significant dispute as to its attribution to the apostle John. Especially from the 6th c. the book's authority was recognised and was based on a long theological (culminating in the early 5th c. with Augustine and Jerome) and canonical tradition. The book was mentioned in the Muratorian biblical canon (2nd c.) and legitimized by Innocent I († 417), the African councils of Carthage and the decrees of Damasus and Gelasius, which brought together texts of still uncertain redaction, but which might date back to the late 4th c.: in any case, the Apocalypse was inscribed in the list of sacred books.

Although, in the Latin world, further interventions to confirm this situation were only occasionally necessary – *e.g.* that of the fourth council of *Toledo in 633 presided over by *Isidore of Seville –, a contrary tradition still continued to affect the Latin *exegesis of the Apocalypse. The Greek *Fathers had rejected the text by a large majority, and doubted its attribution to John. Perhaps the most representative case of this rejection was Eusebius of Caesarea (263-339), but until the 7th c. it was shared by nearly all Eastern authors and it characterised a theological situation destined to last much longer. Another element that continued to influence the reception of the Apocalypse among the Latins was the pressure of the *apocrypha, among which were numerous apocalypses and which, despite condemnation by Innocent I, were destined to arouse considerable interest. Among the New Testament apocrypha should be remembered particularly the *Apocalypse* of Paul (numerous medieval versions are known in English, Danish, German and Slavonic, dependent – except the Slavonic – on the Latin redaction, which is known by some 60 manuscripts and in its original form probably dates from the 3rd-4th cc.) and the *Apocalypses* of Esdras and Thomas (the latter cited as apocryphal in the Gelasian decree and known in five Latin and one English version).

The rejection of the Apocalypse by the Greek world and the problem posed for the Church by the apocrypha long favoured the prevalence of a moderate hermeneutic, in which the themes that had characterised theological debate from the early centuries, even among the Latins, persisted: to promote the inclusion of the book in the Canon, a spiritual and moral reading had been stressed which forbade the *millenarian interpretations held – on the basis of chapter 20 – particularly by the Montanists of the 3rd century. To those who awaited the beginning of a millennium of peace on earth, it was replied, in accordance with the spiritual and moral reading, that all the symbols of the Apocalypse describe the foundation of the Church by *Christ and that, thanks to this, a period of limited domination of the *demon had already opened on earth: this was the mystic millennium and no other should be expected.

Moreover, the text of the Apocalypse itself made it possible to assume this type of exegesis, thanks to the strong christological references of its signs and of eschatological works. These aspects were given greater importance by Augustine's adherence to the interpretative model laid down in the rules of the Donatist Tyconius (late 4th c.), which led, thanks to a concordist and *typological method, to a spiritual interpretation in which the character of collective subjects was attributed to the figures of the Apocalypse: Babylon the Great represented in general all the enemies of the true Church; the scenario of the whole text was the non-historical struggle between *good and *evil, with the victory of the good obtained by the coming of Christ. The persistent Alexandrian exegetical tradition, already strengthened by the teaching of *Origen (first half of 3rd c.), gave dynamism to this model, with the development of an allegorical exegesis. Later, thanks to Jerome's rereading of the first commentary on the Apocalypse to survive entire, that of Victorinus of Pettau (martyred in 304), the *Augustinian position could be received and developed, also validating a scheme by which the successive revelations of the Apocalypse (the seven letters, seven seals, seven trumpets, seven signs, seven cups, seven visions of heaven, seven visions) were to be understood as successive recapitulations, in various forms, of the same revelations.

These spiritual, existential and ecclesiological interpretations did not always imply an outright rejection of every literalist and historical reading of the book's prophetism. Augustine himself had certainly denied literal *millenarianism, but after having first accepted it – which was justified, since millenarian teaching had had illustrious representatives in the Latin tradition (Irenaeus and Justin in the 2nd c., Lactantius in the early 4th). But these tendencies remained marginal and occasional, re-emerging here or there, often in connection with popular millenarian movements led by pseudo-prophets.

In line with Tyconius and Augustine, the early Middle Ages considered the Apocalypse an account of the events that had led to the coming of Christ and the foundation of the Church, events after which history was nothing more than a long wait, in which the negative and obscure aspects grew as the founding event receded in time. Thus the 6th-c. exegeses of the Apocalypse, with Apringius of Beja, Primasius, the brief texts of *Caesarius of Arles and *Cassiodorus, as well as the exegesis of *Bede (672-735) – who, as well as a commentary on the Apocalypse, wrote *De temporum ratione* – have been considered by historiography mainly as evidence of the transition from Tyconius and Augustine, *i.e.* the ancient tradition, to the medieval tradition. The Tyconian line was confirmed in the West, notably because of the prevalence of the method of compilation in Carolingian and late Carolingian exegesis, applied to the Apocalypse in the commentaries of *Alcuin (perhaps a pseudepigraphical work), *Haimo of Auxerre (in 865: the text was long attributed to Haimo of Halberstadt) and Berengaud (a monk at Ferrières, *c.*859). After a long "exegetical silence", in the 10th-11th cc. the memory of the Apocalypse is connected mainly with *Adso of Montier-en-Der's *Liber de ortu et tempore Antichristi* (written for Gerberge, queen of Francia, *c.*968) and its adaptations, as well as with the wide circulation of the predictions of the *Sibylla tiburtina*, but up to this time there are still no elements to suggest an interruption of the Tyconian sequence in the understanding of it.

It must be remembered however that the whole exegetical literature of the early Middle Ages is still very little studied; when particular analyses have been made, motifs of individual interest have often been found. We may cite especially the case of *Beatus of Liébana, who left a commentary in three redactions (the last in 786), a text accompanied by a splendid iconographical apparatus, circulated only in the Iberian peninsula, which evokes a monastic use and an ecstatic conception of the Apocalypse. Still more significant is the case of *Ambrosius Autpertus († 784), whose exegesis referred the Apocalypse account to the story of the *love between Christ and the Church and consciously made parallel use of the *Song of Songs, with a view to obtaining the outline of a spiritual anthropology. In both cases, the Apocalypse appeared in its visionary meaning, as a book thanks to which Christians continue in *time to have visions of the eternal: a mystical reading of the book delivered and justified its exegesis from mere repetition, making it more a literary work and an *ars contemplandi.* In parallel with these experiments must be considered the well-known use of the Apocalypse in the liturgy throughout the Middle Ages.

This was the background for the 12th-c. monastic readings, which, while continuing the tradition of spiritual exegesis, cannot be superimposed on the Tyconian schema. The most important examples were those of *Rupert of Deutz († 1131) and *Richard, prior of *Saint-Victor from 1162 to his death there eleven years later. The *Gregorian reform too, with Bruno of Segni († 1123), could assume this type of reading of the Apocalypse, making it a mirror of the mystical responsibility of Christians in *history.

*Joachim of Fiore (*c.*1130-1202) is incomprehensible without reference to the monastic and mystical tradition, as well as to the spiritual sense of *Gregory VII's *reform: he achieved an inspired convergence by reading the Apocalypse as an account not just of Christ's coming into the world, but especially of the presence of the *Trinity in the world. While developing elements that may have come to him from Rupert's work, he recovered the possibility of a literal interpretation: in his theological awareness, he did not consider Christ's coming as closed once for all in time, and he made it an example of what the Trinity continually accomplishes by embracing human history. Human history unfolds a *theophany, and the appearance of Christ is not conceivable for him as the beginning of a decline, but as the unveiling and opening of a new way in history. In this sense, often reduced to a simple schema, the Apocalypse became the matrix of a literature, sometimes ideological in character, by which the 13th and 14th centuries attempted to foresee the course of events and justify a historical work: its best results are in the works of Alexander the Minorite, *Peter John Olivi (still unedited), *Ubertino da Casale and *Arnold of Villanova.

These positions were opposed by scholastic *theology, in which the Apocalypse lost its specific role. It must be borne in mind that in the tradition of the glossators of the school of *Laon, the Apocalypse was integrated into the general effort of continuous reading of the whole *Bible. In the 13th-14th cc., analogous cases of continuous reading can be cited in *Hugh of Saint-Cher, Pseudo-Albert the Great, *Thomas Bradwardine, *Nicholas of Lyra and Martin of Laon. The method of *scholasticism combined ill with the visions described in the Apocalypse; and in any case the hermeneutical method aimed still more markedly to offer a concordist vision of all Holy Scripture; the theological content of these exegetical attempts became mainly moral and ecclesiological. Although, in this context, historical exegesis began to take on a certain importance, there were as yet no signs of those readings in which the Apocalypse would be seen as an account of historical facts close to the time of its composition.

*Frogs coming from the mouths of the dragon, the beast and the false prophet.* Tapestry of the *Apocalypse*, Angers, 1373-1387, by Nicolas Bataille. Angers, Tapestry Museum.

R. Manselli, *La "Lectura super Apocalypsim" di Pietro di Giovanni Olivi*, *StSc*, 1955, 19-21. – C. Leonardi, "La Spiritualità di Ambrogio Autperto", *StMed*, 3rd series, 9, 1, 1968, 1-131. – G. Baget Bozzo, "Modello trinitario et modello cristologico nella teologia della storia di Gioacchino da Fiore e Tommaso d'Aquino", *Renovatio*, 9, Genoa, 1974, 39-50. – A. Strobel, "Apokalypse des Johannes", *TRE*, 3, 1978, 174-189. – *La Gerusalemme celeste. Catalogo della mostra. Milano. Università Cattolica del S. Cuore, 20 maggio-5 giugno 1983*, M. L. Gatti Perer (ed.), Milan, 1983. – *The Use and Abuse of Eschatology in the Middle Ages*, W. Verbeke (ed.), D. Verhelst (ed.), A. Welkenhuysen (ed.), Louvain, 1988. – M. Simonetti, "L'Apocalisse e l'origine del Millennio", *VetChr*, 26, 1989, 337-350. – *The Apocalypse in the Middle Ages*, R. K. Emmerson (ed.), B. McGinn (ed.), Ithaca (NY)-London, 1992, 428. – R. Landes, "Millenarismus absconditus. L'historiographie augustinienne et le millénarisme du haut Moyen Âge jusqu'à l'an Mil", *MA*, 98, 1992, 355-377. – D. Visser, *Apocalypse as Utopian Expectation (800-1500)*, Leiden, 1996.

Francesco Santi

**Iconography.** The iconography of John's Apocalypse was presented very differently in the East and in the West, given that the canonicity of this writing, disputed in the East until the 14th c., was admitted in the West from the 4th c., since it was attributed to *John the Evangelist.

Despite the existence of Greek commentaries on the Apocalypse (by Andrew of Caesarea and Aretas of Caesarea), the Apocalypse appears only sporadically and occasionally in Eastern art in the Middle Ages, in the form of elements existing in the Apocalypse but inserted into wholly different programmes; thus the crystal sea (Rev 4, 6) in Hagioi Apostoloi at Sinassos (9th c.) or the lake of fire (Rev 20, 15) at Egri Tas kilisesi (9th c.). Russian art also offers interesting examples. In 1422, Andrew of Caesarea's commentary would be illustrated for the first time.

Western art presented the Apocalypse in the form either of scenes, often forming sequences or complete cycles, mainly analytic in character, or of themes, sometimes organised in programmes that were mainly synthetic in character. In both cases, interpretations and commentaries could influence the general texture. Three main types of interpretation existed in the early medieval West: the political reading, the *millenarian reading and the recapitulatory reading. It was the latter that most profoundly marked the iconography of the early Western Middle Ages.

The first surviving example of a complete cycle illustrating John's Apocalypse is the manuscript of the *Trier Apocalypse* (9th c.). It is mainly literal and analytic: the surviving Carolingian Apocalypses of the 9th and 10th cc. are little different in character. This series was carried on in the 11th c. by the *Bamberg Apocalypse*, whose function was more political than religious. In Catalan Romanesque art, the cycle of the *Roda Bible* corresponds to this generally sequential pattern, though some interpretative elements come to interfere with it.

In the group of Mozarabic and post-Mozarabic *Beati* (9th-12th c.), the text of John's Apocalypse is followed, passage by passage, by a painting, followed by a systematic commentary; the illustration, while closely following John's text, is sometimes enriched or inflected with interpretative connotations, fortified by a pictorial treatment of theological and cosmic scope. In this series, the famous *Saint-Sever Beatus* (11th c.) is a particular case.

In the 12th c., the theological implications are often manifest, particularly (but not solely) in manuscripts where the Apocalypse is accompanied by a discursive commentary. This is the case in parts of the *Liber Floridus* devoted to the Apocalypse (Wolfenbüttel and Paris manuscripts), in *Haimo's Commentary on the Apocalypse (Oxford manuscript), but also in a *Bible with very interpretative illustration for the Apocalypse, made at *Verona (Vat. lat. 39). This interpretative character, theological and synthetic in tendency, is manifested particularly for those themes most dense in meaning, like the Woman of the Apocalypse (Rev 12) who can be identified with the Church (celestial and terrestrial) or the Virgin, or like the heavenly *Jerusalem, with a variety of theological values, to which in the 12th c. was added the notion of a fortified town. A fine example of this is at *Tournai cathedral.

It was in monumental art that the synthetic character of the iconography of the Apocalypse had its greatest flowering. The great *Romanesque portals give sculpted programmes fed by exegesis and reflection; tympana like those of *Moissac, La Lande de Cubzac (Gironde) and Saint-Michel d'Aiguilhe are clearly mainly apocalyptic in character. Likewise, monumental pictorial programmes deliberately group together various notions around apocalyptic themes, often mingled with other Old Testament themes or theological or liturgical themes, like that of *theophany; thus at Saint-Chef in Dauphiné, Civate in Lombardy, Sant'Elia di Nepi in Latium and Saint-Hilaire-le-Grand at *Poitiers. This does not necessarily exclude concrete and historical characters from these representations.

For the Apocalypse as for iconography in general, the 1200s saw a return to direct narrative illustration; as in the great illuminated *Bibles of Europe around 1200. The Gothic *cathedrals were often the setting of this type of sequential presentation; a clear example is that of *Reims cathedral (sculpture of the west front). In the 13th-c. West, various tendencies in the reading and illustration of John's Apocalypse would exist in parallel. Certain German or central European works show the rise of an increasingly complex conception of painted programmes, as at Matrei; by contrast, a break with the past (though not a total innovation) took place with *Joachim of Fiore, leading to a linear, and no longer recapitulatory, reading of *time, the third and last age being characterised by the presence of monsters. A tendency, already old, but which grew to a greater extent at this time (it was this tendency that would have the greatest posterity for the illustration of the Apocalypse) was that which tried to make John's narratives and *visions accessible to the *laity, not just by translating the biblical text into the vernacular, but also by a radical change in the understanding of the Apocalypse – which then became like a strange and marvellous, but concrete, tale, visualized in a transparent manner in the series of 13th- and 14th-c. Anglo-Norman Apocalypses.

In the late Middle Ages, a pictorial whole like that of Karlstein would return to a conception that was both interpretative and political. But the sequential and predominantly literal conception continued to give rise to manuscript illustrations like that of Heinrich von Hesler's Apocalypse. One of the last outbursts of the Middle Ages in the illustration of manuscripts of the Apocalypse is offered in the 15th c. by the Flemish Apocalypse in the Bibliothèque nationale de France, whose symbolic structure inaugurates a new modernity.

F. Van der Meer, *Maiestas Domini. Théophanies de l'Apocalypse dans l'art chrétien*, Paris, Rome, 1938 ("Studi di antichità cristiana, publicati per cura del Pontificio istituto di archeologia cristiana", 13). – *Allgemeine Ikonographie*, 1968, 142 ("LCI", 1). – F. Van der Meer, *Apocalypse: Visions from the Book of Revelations in Western Art*, London, 1978. – *L'Apocalypse de Jean, Traditions exégétiques et iconographiques, III^e-XIII^e siècle*, Y. Christe (ed.), Geneva, 1979 ("Études et documents publiés par la section d'Histoire de la Faculté des Lettres de l'université de Genève", 11). – M. Mentré, *Création et Apocalypse, Histoire d'un regard humain sur le divin*, Paris, 1984. – R. Barthelemy-Vogels, C. Hyart, *L'Iconographie russe de l'Apocalypse*, Paris, 1985 ("Bibliothèque de la Faculté de Philosophie et Lettres de l'université de Lièges", 241). – *The Apocalypse in the Middle Ages*, R. K. Emmerson (ed.), B. McGinn (ed.), Ithaca (NY), London, 1992. – M. Mentré, *Illuminated Manuscripts of Medieval Spain*, London, 1996. – D. Visser, *Apocalypse as Utopian Expectation (800-1500)*, Leiden, 1996.

Mireille Mentré

## APOCALYPTIC LITERATURE

**The West.** The corpus of apocalyptic literature consists of a very heterogeneous group of texts composed throughout the Middle Ages, but especially in the 10th-11th and 12th-14th centuries. They express a way of conceiving truth as an unveiling of divine perfection, narrating the presence of the eternal in or beyond *time. This literature developed largely in the form of commentary on John's *Apocalypse, as well as on the apocalypses of *Daniel and the gospel of Matthew (ch. 24). Also among its sources were the *apocryphal apocalypses, which, despite their illegitimation by Innocent I, continued to have significant popularity. During the centuries of the late Middle Ages, apart from the traditional literature of commentaries, there appeared a rich literature of treatises *de Antichristo*, whose precursor was the book of *Adso of Montier-en-Der (dating from *c.*968, its popularity continued through the 13th c.), and "prophecies" of which an important example is the *Sibylla tiburtina*, circulated from the 11th century. Prophecies of this type developed in a multitude of texts, still little studied, whose redactions intersect: a well-attested example, made particularly interesting by the rich iconographical apparatus, is the *Vaticina pontificum*, which bring together fifteen anonymous prophecies concerning the *popes from *Nicholas III (1277-1280).

For a first orientation, and in general, two intersecting lines of development can be identified. On one side, Latin medieval apocalyptic finds one of its points of greatest clarity in the work of *Hildegard of Bingen (1098-1179). In the visions of her *Scivias*, the theme of the Apocalypse joins with that of the *Song of Songs to tell of the passion between God and man in history: for her, all time is a fragment of eternity, yearning for it and at the same time mirroring in itself the whole of time. This type of apocalyptic is present mainly in monastic literature and becomes explicit in the commentaries on the Apocalypse by *Rupert of Deutz († 1131) and *Richard of Saint-Victor († 1173). The theme of a succession of times leading up to the glorious end does not emerge in it as a main theme, but the feeling develops of a relationship between *prophecy and *mysticism, which would permeate the founders of the Minorite movement (beginning with *Francis of Assisi himself) and undergo further development in feminine mysticism, with *Angela of Foligno (1248-1309) and Margaret Porete († 1310).

In *Joachim of Fiore (*c.*1130-1202), the line of *monastic theology is fully conscious, but onto it is grafted a second form of Latin apocalyptic, which awaits and foresees – last in succession of earthly times – a totally divinized time, a time of peace. It shows more interest in identifying men and situations that clarify the concreteness of this historical process. In its most schematic form, this idea would represent the main ideological resource of numerous reformist and radical movements in the 12th-14th cc., aiming firstly at ecclesiastical reform and then from the 14th c. at the legitimation of this or that national political power. At the same time, this type of apocalyptic was the essential cultural nutriment for the efforts to reconquer the *Holy Land (in the name of the promise [Rom 11, 26] of final ingathering into the Christian faith), and in the context of its assertion must also be included the foundations of new orders: apropos of the *crusades, we think of the *military orders and the Order of *Carmel or of Elijah, whose return was expected by apocalyptic; apropos of Church reform, reference is mainly to the Order of Friars Minor and the various eremitical congregations, brought together in the late 13th c. in the Order of *Hermits of St Augustine. The final time of peace was on one hand entrusted to the guidance of an elite of *perfecti* and, on the other, foresaw the full gathering of all people into the Church, restoring to the *laity a spiritual role previously overshadowed. Indeed, in the radical *ecclesiology of apocalyptic, the laity once more assumed an important role. This development also gave rise to numerous mass revivalist movements, which marked the most important dates of expectation of the end: the crusade of the *Pueri* in 1212, the music of the Alleluia processions of 1233, the **Pastoureaux* in 1251 and the *flagellations of the Disciplinati in 1260 (one of the years that most merited attention in the calculations of those who awaited the end of the world) represented the widespread conviction of living in the third age, the so-called age of the Spirit, for the Church and for the world: the age foretold by the new readings of the Apocalpyse.

The historiography of the last two centuries has studied mainly the latter aspect of apocalyptic, its project of the future, and has given it the honour and the blame for having generated various forms of contestative and revolutionary historicism, by virtue of the idea that the truth about man lies in his future and that time is the best instrument of knowledge. This conclusion is moreover – in the strict sense – opposed to that which was the starting-point of medieval apocalyptic, which was precisely a theology of the eternal.

K. Löwith, *Meaning in History*, Chicago, 1949. – B. Töpfer, *Das kommende Reich des Friedens. Zur Entwicklung chiliastischer Zukunftshoffnungen im Hochmittelalter*, Berlin, 1964. – E. R. Daniel, "Apocalyptic Conversion: the Joachimite Alternative to the Crusades", *Tr.*, 25, 1969, 127-154. – M. Reeves, *The Influence of Prophecy in the Later Middle Ages: a Study in Joachimism*, Oxford, 1969. – R. Lerner, "Refreshment of the Saints. The Time after Antichrist as a Station for Earthly Progress in Medieval Thought", *Tr.*, 32, 1976, 97-144. – *Apocalyptic Spirituality*, B. McGinn (ed.), New York, 1979. – B. McGinn, "Awaiting an End. Research in Medieval Apocalypticism 1974-1981", *MeH*, 11, 1982, 263-289. – *Les Textes prophétiques et la Prophétie en Occident (XIIᵉ-XVIᵉ siècle)*, A. Vauchez (ed.), Rome, 1990. – G. Dickson, "Carisma e revivalismo nel XIII secolo", *Poteri carismatici e informali: Chiesa e società medioevali*, A. Vauchez (ed.), A. Paravicini Bagliani (ed.), Palermo, 1992, 96-113. – R.K. Emmerson, R.B. Herzmann, *The Apocalyptic Imagination in Medieval Literature*, Philadelphia, 1992. – E.L. Risden, *Beasts of Time: Apocalyptic Beowulf*, New York, 1994. – V.P. Zimbaro, *Encyclopedia of Apocalyptic Literature*, Santa Barbara (CA), 1996.

Francesco Santi

**Byzantium.** A literary genre of Jewish origin, apocalyptic claims to reveal (*apocalyptein* in Greek) divine secrets. In the Middle Ages, it was divided into two categories, the first of which consisted in a journey through the domains of the afterlife. At Byzantium this apocalyptic genre reached its apogee in the 10th century. In the West it received a sublime literary expression in *Dante Alighieri's *Divine Comedy*.

The apocalypses of the second and more important category had a historico-political character. Events taking place at the time of the visionary were interpreted by him in the perspective of universal *history, considered as a closed system, beginning with *Creation, containing four successive empires and ending in an eschatological chaos to which the Parousia would put an end. The first complete scenario is found in Methodius's *Revelations*, written around the end of the 7th c. but whose author hid under the name of a Church Father who died in 311; this pseudonym allowed him to predict events that had already occurred, a routine procedure serving to inspire confidence in the reader ("*vaticinatio ex eventu*"). Pseudo-Methodius began with a historical sketch aiming to demonstrate that the fourth empire was the Roman, *i.e.* Byzantine, Empire. When it reached its end, this empire would be invaded by the Arabs but a liberating emperor would arise and put them to flight. Then the whole world would be devastated by Gog and Magog. *Antichrist would appear, the emperor would lay down his crown on Calvary and Antichrist would be killed by Christ. Written in Syriac but soon translated into Greek and thence into Latin and Old Church Slavonic, Pseudo-Methodius's *Revelations* had a profound influence on the whole medieval world. In the West, the fourth empire was, *e.g.*, identified with the kingdom of the *Franks.

In the 8th c., many visions circulated in the *Byzantine Empire, including *Sicily, under the name of the prophet Daniel. Here the historical sketch was omitted and the last emperor was identified with various potentates. In the 12th c., a third genre was established, that of illustrated oracles attributed to the Emperor Leo VI the Wise (886-912).

G. Podskalsky, *Byzantinische Reichseschatologie*, Munich, 1972. – C. Mango, "The Future of Mankind", *Byzantium. The Empire of New Rome*, G. Podskalsky (ed.), London, 1980, 201-217. – P. J. Alexander, *The Byzantine Apocalyptic Tradition*, Berkeley (CA), 1985. – P. Magdalino, "The History of the Future and its Uses: Prophecy, Policy and Propaganda", *The Making of Byzantine History. Studies dedicated for Donald M. Nicol*, R. Beaton (ed.), C. Roueché (ed.), London, 1993, 3-34.

Lennart Rydén

**APOCRISIARY.** The word *apocrisiarius*, which means "charged with carrying a reply", designated an ambassador, whether in the service of the emperor, the *patriarch or even an eminent citizen. Byzantium had no specialized personnel at its disposal, calling instead on officials of other services or those close to the emperor. The ambassador, provided with precise instructions, had to gather information on the wealth and military strength of the countries visited and advertise the wealth of the Empire, while sometimes carrying out his mission at his own expense. Reciprocally, foreign envoys were strictly watched during their journey and stay in the capital, where imperial audiences suggested to them the omnipotence of the emperor. In the ecclesiastical field, the apocrisiary was the representative, occasional or of long duration, of a high official (patriarch, *bishop or abbot).

*Byzantine Diplomacy. Papers from the Twenty-fourth Spring Symposium of Byzantine Studies, Cambridge, March 1990*, J. Shephard (ed.), S. Franklin (ed.), Aldershot, 1992.

Jean-Claude Cheynet

**APOCRYPHA, BIBLICAL.** The term "biblical apocrypha" covers a considerable group of writings connected with the Old or the New Testament, but which have not been received into the canonical tradition of Jews or Christians. From the 4th c., the

Western Christians gradually admitted several Jewish (intertestamentary) books that had been rejected by the compilers of the Torah. They excluded others emanating from the earliest Judaeo-Christian communities, apostolic "acts" and pseudogospels, and wavered until the 13th c. before rejecting the chapters added to the fourth book of Esdras (1, 2 = 5 Esdras, and 15-16 = 6 Esdras), a letter to the Laodiceans and psalm 151. The *Apocalypse itself long remained suspect in Byzantine Christianity. The New Testament apocrypha are the most interesting. Often of gnostic origin, they met a very difficult reception in the West: St Jerome waxed indignant at the "deliria of the apocrypha" and a celebrated decree, once attributed to Pope Gelasius I (492-496), forbade by name the use of 28 of them (the list, prohibiting 61 books in all, probably emanated from Gaul in the 5th-6th cc.). But a good many of them circulated as far as learned circles; the *Historia scholastica* made great use of them, and that work by the Parisian master *Peter Comestor (*c.*1160) is known to have quickly become the elementary manual of biblical history. The narratives, notably on the infancy of Christ and on the Virgin *Mary, translated from the 4th-5th cc. into Latin and from the 12th c. into the main vernacular languages, inspired Christian iconography. There follows a list of the New Testament apocryphal writings that were known to the Western tradition.

A first group recounts the infancies of the Virgin and of Jesus. 1) The *Protogospel of James* was a fertile source for the Marian cult, the feasts of the *Conception and Nativity of the Virgin, the *Presentation, Joachim and *Anne. 2) The *Infancy Gospel according to Thomas* (Vienna palimpsest, 5th c.). 3) The *Gospel of Pseudo-Matthew*, a Latin adaptation of the *Protogospel of James* (6th-7th c., *Liber de infantia* or *Historia de nativitate Mariae et de infantia Salvatoris*; more than 130 medieval manuscripts), revised by *Paschasius Radbertus for the needs of his christological realism. From Pseudo-Matthew come the *crib, the ox and the ass, or the eulogy of the bees at the singing of the **Exultet* in southern Italy. 4) The London *Liber de infantia Salvatoris* (London, BL, Arundel 404; another version at Hereford). 5) The Paris *Liber de infantia Salvatoris* (BNF, ms. lat. 11867, 13th c.). 6) The *De nativitate Mariae*, copied in *Jacobus de Voragine's **Golden Legend*.

A second group deals with Jesus' Passion: 1) The *Gospel of Nicodemus*, which brought together in the 5th-6th cc. some *Acts of Pilate*, two letters of Pilate, and a *Descent of Christ into Hell*; 2) the *Vengeance of the Saviour*, apparently originating in 11th-c.(?) Aquitaine; 3) The *Death of Pilate* (13th-14th c.?).

In a third group are the apostolic acts, of Paul, Peter, Andrew, John and Thomas, very widespread in 4th-c. Manichean circles. The *Acts of Paul* (account of his journeys, with the stay at Iconium which includes a passion of St Thecla) are with the *Acts of Peter* probably the oldest. The legend of Peter returned in Catholic form in the "pseudo-Clementine" writings translated in the 4th c., recopied in the Carolingian period, which relate in particular the conflict with Simon Magus. *Gregory of Tours gave publicity to the *Acts of Andrew* (*Virtutes Andreae*, or *Liber de miraculis beati Andreae*); the Westerners used several versions of this in the 10th-11th centuries. The *Acts of John* were conveyed mainly by Pseudo-Abdias (Gaul, 6th-7th c.) and Pseudo-Melito (6th c.) who vulgarized the stay at Ephesus and the conversion of Drusiana, especially in the insular tradition; the *Acts of Thomas* (his mission to *India) are summarized by Pseudo-Abdias and Gregory of Tours. The other apostolic acts were little known in the West, save in Ireland (*Acts of Bartholomew*, *Passion of Matthew*) or in the summaries of them given by Pseudo-Abdias. To these writings is added the rich tradition of *Dormitions* or Assumptions of the Virgin, which ensured the triumph of the feast of 15 Aug and the Assumption in Carolingian society.

In a fourth group we can bring together the epistles: as well as the *Letter to the Laodiceans* and the *Third Epistle to the Corinthians*, the *Letter of Pseudo-Titus* (Spain, a 5th-c. hymn to virginity, a single manuscript known). The most important are the *Letters of Christ and King Abgar* (cited by Eusebius of Caesarea and his translator Rufinus), the *Letter of Lentulus* (13th c.) which describes Christ's physical appearance and rapidly found an echo in iconography, and *St Paul's correspondence with Seneca* (fourteen 4th-c. letters claiming to prove the superiority of Christianity over the wisdom of antiquity).

The fifth group contains apocalypses, which are prophecies of the end of the world and *visions of the afterlife: the *Apocalypse of Paul* (*Visio Pauli*, 5th-6th-c. Latin version), which describes the pains of *hell, was the best-known in the West; the *Apocalypse of Thomas* lists the signs of the last days (several rival versions from the 5th to the 12th c.; one of them in the Anglo-Saxon homilies of Vercelli, no. 15). We may also cite the *Questions* (or *Gospel*) *of Bartholomew*, little known in the Latin world.

*Gli Apocrifi del Nuovo Testamento*, M. Erbetta (tr.), Casale Monferrato, 1975-1981 (4 vol.). – R. Cameron (ed.), *The Other Gospels: Non-Canonical Gospel Texts*, Cambridge, 1982. – W. Schneemelcher, *New Testament Apocrypha*, 1, *Gospels and Related Writings*, Cambridge, 1991; 2, *Writings Relating to the Apostles; Apocalypses and Related Subjects*, Cambridge, 1993. – J. K. Elliott, *The Apocryphal New Testament*, Oxford, 1993.

M. McNamara, *The Apocrypha in the Irish Church*, Dublin, 1975. – B. M. Metzger, *An Introduction to the Apocrypha*, Oxford, 1977. – Aurelio de Santos Otero, *Die handschriftliche Überlieferung der altslavischen Apokryphen*, 1, Berlin, 1978. – C. Carozzi, *Eschatologie et au-delà. Recherches sur l'Apocalypse de Paul*, Aix-en-Provence, 1994. – S. C. Mimouni, *Dormition et Assomption de Marie. Histoire des traditions anciennes*, Paris, 1995. – *Two Old English Apocrypha and their Manuscript Source*, J. E. Cross (ed.), Cambridge, 1997. – *The Medieval Gospel of Nicodemus*, Z. Izydorczyk (ed.), Tempe (AZ), 1997. – M. Clayton, *The Apocryphal Gospels of Mary in Anglo-Saxon England*, Cambridge, 1998.

Guy Lobrichon

**APOLOGETIC.** Apologetic is the reasoned justification of *faith in revealed truths. This meaning – not identifiable everywhere since it often remains banally polemical – expresses the idea of evidence supported by theological rationality. It can be seen in *Thomas Aquinas: the *articles of faith treated in debate with the unbeliever must not be made the object of a pretended demonstration by necessary reasons, since in their transcendence human *reason receives them as revealed. On the other hand, no necessary reasoning can be opposed to them without being false. The intention is to defend the faith; so St Peter says "be ready always", not to prove, but "to give good reason for" (1 Pet 3, 15) the immunity from error for what the Catholic faith confesses (*De rationibus fidei*, ch. 2, t. 40, 58, 3-22). Argument must always be modeled on the references admitted by the interlocutor, whether Scripture – with *Jews the Old Testament, with *heretics the New – or natural reason to which everyone owes assent. But reason, deficient in what concerns divine realities, offers only a certain truth which, doing away with errors, must be shown to be in accord with the Christian faith (*Summa contra gentiles*, I, 2).

To the patristic debate with Christian heresies and *Judaism, medieval apologetic added a concern with the more recent Muslim religion. At first polemical, it became a reasoned dialogue, sometimes to the point (Raymond *Lull) of giving reasoning an excessive role. The formulation of theological science in the 13th c. allowed its method and function to be defined. The Byzantine *John of Damascus not only fought against heresies but also wrote a *Dialogue of a Christian and a Saracen*. Among the Syrians or Arabic-speakers, Abū Qorra, among the Latins *Isidore of Seville, *Julian of Toledo, *Alcuin, *Rabanus Maurus, *Peter Damian and *Peter the Venerable wrote against heretics, Jews and Muslims. Peter *Abelard wrote a dialogue between a Christian, a Jew and a pagan (close to *Islam). The writings of Anselm of Havelberg, Hugh Aetherian and, on the Greek side, Nicholas of Methone and *Nicetas Choniates concern the controversy between Romans and *Orthodox (**Filioque*, procession of the *Holy Spirit), as does Thomas Aquinas's *De erroribus Graecorum* (which unfortunately uses the dubious documentation of Nicholas of Durazzo). After *Alan of Lille and Moneta of Cremona, the *mendicant orders wrote in the 13th c. against *Waldenses, *Cathars and especially Islam: *e.g.* Thomas Aquinas's **summa* called *Against the Gentiles* (exact title: *Sum of the Catholic Truth against the Errors of the Unbelievers*), an arsenal of the best theological reasons: then, before Raymond Lull, came *Raymond Martini, *Riccoldo of Monte Croce, and later *Alfonso Buenhombre. The 15th c., which knew the rationalism of the Renaissance, saw the essays of Alfonso of Zamora, *Nicholas of Cusa, Marsilio *Ficino and, in connection with the council of *Florence in 1439, the works of *Bessarion.

P. Sbath, *Vingt traités philosophiques et apologétiques d'auteurs arabes chrétiens du IXᵉ au XIVᵉ siècle*, Cairo, 1929.

G. Graf, "Apologetisch-polemische Schriften gegen Islam und Judentum", *Geschichte der christlichen arabischen Literatur. II. Die Schriftsteller bis zur Mitte des 15. Jahrhunderts*, Vatican, 1947, 472 f. – A. G. Beck, *Kirche und theologische Literatur im byzantischen Reich*, 2, 1, Munich, 1959. – B. Blumenkranz, *Les Auteurs chrétiens latins du Moyen Âge sur les Juifs et le Judaïsme*, Paris, The Hague, 1963. – L. Hagemann, "Bibliographie du dialogue islamo-chrétien. Auteurs chrétiens du monde latin des XIIIᵉ et XIVᵉ siècles", *Islamochristiana*, 6, Rome, 1980, 260-278. – J. Cohen, *The Friars and the Jews. The Evolution of Medieval Anti-Judaism*, Ithaca (NY), London, 1982. – *Christian Arabic Apologetics during the Abbasid Period (750-1258)*, S. K. Samir (ed.), J. S. Nielsen (ed.), Leiden, 1994.

Édouard-Henri Wéber

**APOPHATIC, CATAPHATIC.** Though *Dionysius the Areopagite uses them only once to designate the two ways of access to *God, these terms are borrowed from him. It was in fact *John Scotus Eriugena, the medieval translator of Dionysius, who definitively brought them together to define the two branches of *theology: one affirmative or cataphatic, the other negative or apophatic (*Periphyseon* I, 458-462).

Latin theology developed apophaticism little, except in the school of *Albert the Great, mainly with *Thomas Aquinas and Meister *Eckhart. Commentator on the *Mystical theology*, Albert was its interpreter on the level of noetic (theory of *knowledge) and *mysticism. St Thomas and Eckhart took up this point of view to explore, from Dionysius, the notion of being and the reality of union with God.

B. Krivocheine, *In the Light of Christ*, Crestwood (NY), 1986. – F. O'Rourke, *Pseudo-Dionysius and the Metaphysics of Aquinas*, Leiden, 1992.

Marie-Anne Vannier

**Historical and theological evolution.** These two concepts, apparently of little weight, are in fact of such fundamental importance that, in their historical development, they determined two different, if not opposed ways of *knowledge – especially theological – between East and West. As Christos Yannaràs has recently claimed, Western Christianity was "alienated" and "altered", and "deviated" from fidelity to the New Testament, as it had been in the first centuries; this deviation had repercussions in all the cultural forms of Western Europe (art, *music, *architecture, but also sociology, economy, etc.). This was the result of an incorrect conception, by scholastic *theology and Western *philosophy in general, of the apophatic character of knowledge. Apophatic theology signifies that which proceeds from knowledge of *God by way of negation, *i.e.* by saying what God is not. Greek gnoseological procedure (from Heraclitus to Gregory *Palamas) is based on the transition of the existent from *hiddenness* to *revelation/manifestation* and on the consequent *relationship* that comes to be formed with the knowing subject. Thus existents are not "defined" starting from subjective logico-rational requirements, suitable to determine their *essence*, so much as from the manifestations of the diversity of their *modes of existence*, which, arising out of these existents, are offered to human knowledge. When dealing with a *person, the *truth* about that person is likewise a *manifestation/revelation*, not of his *essence* (*ousia*), which is common to all persons, so much as of his mode of *personal existence* which, being unique and unrepeatable, makes knowable only the *otherness* of the "other". Turning our attention to the Person of God (indeed, the triadic God), it must be emphasized that man cannot establish a gnoseological discourse concerning God's *ousia*, which remains ineffable and incommunicable, but he can develop a discourse concerning God's *operations* (revelations); and these make knowable only his substantial otherness. So, precisely because based on an *immediate personal* experience, this relationship of the human person with the God-Person remains inexpressible and incommunicable: wholly *apophatic*. So, concludes Yannaràs, the apophaticism of the Greek East, which is a *personal apophaticism*, does not mean the impossibility of knowing God's *ousia*, but the impossibility of one who has been able to form an immediate personal relationship with God communicating to another subject the "gnoseological content" deriving from this loving personal relationship with God. The Western claim to "pose" rationally the existence and reality of God cannot fail to lead to a gradual annihilation of God, to his death, as would happen with Nietzsche or Heidegger. The *cataphatic* method, however, based substantially on the induction/*analogy that attributes to God, to the highest degree, the perfections encountered among creatures, is more or less identical in East and West.

P. N. Trempelas, *Dogmatics* [in Greek], Athens 1959, 186 f. – M. Schmaus, *Katholische Dogmatik*, 1, Munich, 1960, 306 f. – C. Yannaràs, *Heidegger e Dionigi Areopagita: assenza e ignoranza di Dio*, Rome, 1995.

Attilio Stendardi

**APOPHTHEGMATA.** The name *Apophthegmata Patrum* designates a whole set of edifying words and anecdotes of the first Christian hermits of Egypt. Handed down at first by oral tradition, these generally short pieces were soon written down and grouped into series centred on a single person or a particular theme. More abundant collections were later formed, numbering sometimes hundreds of apophthegms. Their spread was rapid, since from the

6th c. three collections were translated into Latin, one by Pelagius and John, Roman *clerics and future *popes, the other two by Paschasius of Duma and *Martin of Braga. Later appeared Syriac, *Coptic, Arabic, Armenian, Georgian and Ethiopian translations, so that from the early Middle Ages the Apophthegms of the Fathers were widespread in all parts of the Christian world, from *Syria to the ends of the Iberian peninsula.

This diffusion seems to have begun mainly from *Palestine. In the monasteries of the Gaza region, in the 6th c., the Apophthegms were particularly appreciated, as witness the numerous citations in the correspondence of Barsanuphius and John and the works of Dorotheus. They were also always in great favour in the Greek monasteries, especially on Mount *Athos. In the 11th c., Paul, founder of the monastery of the Evergetis at Constantinople, made a vast compilation of spiritual texts including more than 1500 apophthegms. This *florilegium, preserved in numerous manuscripts, was edited several times from the mid 19th century. In Russia, from the beginnings of Christianity, the Desert Fathers may be said to have made their entrance at the same time as the Gospel and monasticism.

After the biblical books, undoubtedly no works were more read and copied than the collections of apophthegms. In the manuscript stocks of our libraries, they hold a considerable place under the most varied titles: *Paterica*, *Gerontica*, *Ascetica*, *Verba Seniorum*, *Vitae Patrum*, florilegia, Paradises of the Fathers, Gardens of Monks, etc. Merely for the collection translated into Latin by Pelagius and John, Dom Colomba Battle has listed and surveyed more than 400 manuscripts, dating from the 6th to the 15th c. and from every provenance. He has also pointed out nearly 500 mentions of manuscripts of this collection in surviving medieval catalogues. Finally he has listed 120 authors who refer to them, from St *Benedict to Martin Luther. Similar inquiries about all the collections in the various languages would highlight the immense and universal influence of the Apophthegms not just in Christian history and *spirituality, but also in the fields of literature and art. To cite just one example, in Old French literature there are several dozen 13th-c. *contes*, mostly unedited, whose theme was borrowed from the Apophthegms or which are sometimes just translations, more or less close.

C. M. Battle, *Die "Adhortationes Sanctorum Patrum" im lateinischen Mittelalter*, Münster, 1972. – *The Sayings of the Desert Fathers*, B. Ward (ed.), rev. ed., London, 1981. – L. Regnault, *Les Pères du désert à travers leurs Apophtegmes*, Solesmes, 1987. – A. Solignac, "Verba Seniorum", *DSp*, 16, 1992, 383-392. – G. Gould, *The Desert Fathers on Monastic Community*, Oxford, 1993.

Lucien Regnault

**APOSTASY.** "Apostasy" originally designated the abandonment of the Christian faith after reception of *baptism. It was a grave problem in the context of the pre-Constantinian persecutions, then reappeared in another form in the 13th c., at the time of the *Inquisition's struggle against *heresy. Indeed, since "true apostasy is that by which one renounces the faith" (Thomas Aquinas, *Summa theologiae*, IIa IIae, q. 12, a. 1), those who returned to heresy after a first *abjuration (relapse) could be considered guilty of this sin. Finally, in the Middle Ages, the term "apostate" very often designated priests or monks who renounced their *vows.

"Apostasie", *DThC*, 1, 2, 1931, 1602-1612. – "Apostasie", *DDC*, 1, 1935, 640-652. – *Mittellateinisches Wörterbuch bis zum ausgehenden 13. Jahrhundert*, 1, Munich, 1959, 758-759. – F. D. Lugan, *Runaway religious in medieval England, c.1240-1540*, Cambridge, 1996.

Patrick Henriet

**APOSTLES' CREED.** The *creed, used in *baptism in the early Church, received various formulae according to times and places. That of Rome, in the 4th c., appears stable; its fixity may have been due to a particular rite, the *redditio symboli*. This public act of the catechumen presupposed an invariable text; considered original from then on, this was called the creed of the Apostles. Ambrose and Rufinus add that the Twelve, before separating, themselves composed this summary in twelve articles.

Later some imagined that each apostle, from Peter to Matthias, produced one article; an example of this personalization can be seen in two pseudo-Augustinian sermons (*PL*, 39, 2189-2190). It only remained, according to medieval *typology, to find 12 prophetic verses prefiguring the articles. The correspondence appeared in the 12th c.; thus James the Great's "born of the Virgin Mary" was coupled with *Isaiah's "behold a virgin will conceive".

This "apostolic *Credo*" quite often came into pastoral writings: *synods, rituals, books of *prayers, religious *dramas, etc. Its use declined when the apostolicity of the creed was contested: at the council of *Florence, then by the *humanists (*Valla). It was used especially in art, from the 12th to the 16th c. or even later: *enamels, "Savoyard" *stalls, mural *painting, etc. In *c.*1400, Duke John of Berry had some distinguished works ornamented with it: windows of his **Saintes Chapelles*, Great and Little Hours etc. Several hundred examples are known in Europe. This fertile theme, quite forgotten in France, was restudied after the fire in 1983 that damaged one of its finest examples, the stalls of *Saint-Claude.

É. Mâle, *Religious Art in France: the late Middle Ages*, Princeton (NJ), 1986. – H. de Lubac, *Christian Faith: the Structure of the Apostles' Creed*, I, London, 1986. – *The Sermon-Conferences of St. Thomas Aquinas on the Apostles' Creed*, N. Ayo (ed.), Notre Dame, Ind., 1988. – P. Lacroix, "Le Thème iconographique des stalles de Saint-Claude . . . et son rayonnement européen", *Société d'émulation du Jura, Travaux 1988*, Lons, 1989, 85-120. – F. Boespflug, "Autour de la traduction pictoriale du Credo . . .", *Rituels. Mélanges Pierre-Marie Gy*, Paris, 1990, 55-84. – *Pensée, image et communication en Europe médiévale (Saint-Claude et Lons, 1990)*, Besançon, 1993.

Pierre Lacroix

***APOSTOLICI.*** The movement of the *apostolici* in its first phase, *i.e.* throughout the second half of the 13th c., seems particularly Italian. The sources mentioning them are few: indeed, information comes almost exclusively from the *Chronicles* of Friar *Salimbene of Parma. When Salimbene wrote, however, the *apostolici* were facing the difficult decision imposed on them by the canon *Religionum diversitatem nimiam* of the second council of *Lyon (1274): in short, they had to decide whether to accept the norm that wished to put an end to their experiment (by ending recruitment and imposing the progressive movement of their members on other religious *orders recognised by the church authorities), or to follow the way of disobedience to its unforeseeable and dangerous end. The Franciscan chronicler thus saw what happened to the *apostolici* in the light of the Lyon measures and their tendency not to conform to them: events which were interpreted as deviant imitation of and undue rivalry towards the legitimate and authentic "mendicant" testimony of the Friars Minor and the Friars Preachers. They were also interpreted in an eschatological perspective that put their origin in 1260, year of the devotion of the *flagellants, and the year when, in line with certain Joachite visions, the "third age of the world", the era of the *Holy Spirit, was due to begin. In reality, the Statutes of Parma in the 1250s already mention the existence of a "*domus religionis Apostolorum*": *i.e.* they attest an origin of the *apostolici* chronologically earlier than that polemically fixed by Salimbene.

On the basis of this evidence, even Salimbeni's attribution of the *apostolici*'s origins to Gherardo Segarelli must be taken with caution: with no less caution must be considered the information on the beginnings of the movement and the extempore and paradoxical behaviour attributed to the "founder".

On the positive side, we know that the *apostolici*, of mixed composition, followed a pauperistic-evangelical inspiration, penitential and itinerant, that they sought contacts with the church hierarchies when they intended to go beyond their initial spontaneity and take on an institutional form, and that this intention led to disagreements and tension within their own ranks. Finally we know that between 1268 and 1296 successive papal measures declared them *heretics. Segarelli ended on the pyre in July 1300. Then opened a new phase whose most prominent figure was Fra *Dolcino of Novara and which culminated in the dramatic events in the Vercellese and Novarese Alps.

R. Orioli, *Venit perfidus heresiarcha. Il movimento apostolico-dolciniano dal 1260 al 1307*, Rome, 1988. – G. G. Merlo, *Eretici ed eresie medievali*, Bologna, 1989, 99-105, 135-136.

Grado G. Merlo

**APOSTOLIC LIFE.** The original ideal of imitation of the Apostles and the apostolic Church could insist either on the perfection of their Christian life, or on their *ministry. The former way prevailed for more than a thousand years: in the 4th c., the expression "apostolic life" appeared in Africa.

Pachomian *monasticism intended at this time to imitate the community of the Church of Jerusalem formed by the Apostles. According to Theodore of Tabennisi, the "holy community" taught the "apostolic life" or "Way". The model of the infant Church, in accordance with Acts 2, 42-47 and 4, 32-35, inspired *coenobites with the ideal of a church radiating *faith and charity. In the 5th c., John *Cassian armed it with an effective myth: *coenobitism was not the imitation, but the pursuit of the life of the infant Church, abolished everywhere else. In the West, from the late 4th c., St Augustine had discerned, in the imitation of the Apostles by "disappropriation" in the community, the means to ensure unanimity "towards *God" (*in Deum*) and the proof of charity. He realized it in his three successive monasteries of friends, laymen and finally clerics, and transmitted it by his sermons, his commentaries and his Rule, in which we read the declaration: "*Apostolica enim vita optamus vivere*". The theme of apostolic life, and even the expression, recur in the Western *Rules, which would later earn St Augustine the title of "renewer of apostolic life". The bringing together of cathedral clerics into *chapters of *canons in the 7th c. brought attention to the myth of the early common life of clerics, which survived in muted form into the 11th century.

In the 11th c., monks and canons agreed to attach themselves to the Church of the Apostles by the common life and even by each of the elements of their claustral life and their *profession. Under *Urban II, Cassian's myth was further enriched. In a bold historical move, the pope distributed the upper life of the early Church among monks and canons.

However, the *reform of clerics tended to marry the "apostolic life", drawn from Acts, with the "rule of the Apostles" or "*evangelical life", drawn from the gospel of the mission (Mt 10 and par.). This was the inspiration of itinerant preachers such as *Robert of Arbrissel and *Norbert of Xanten. If the majority of these hermit-apostles were also founders of communities of monks and regular canons, another part, often of lay origin, saw a Christian incompatibility between the life of the *cloister and the itinerant form of their commitment. Dissensions and hesitations then appeared. The synthesis was made by St *Dominic in the Constitutions of the Order of Preachers, in 1215-1220, who succeeded in enriching the theme of apostolic life with the evangelical mendicancy of the preacher, and soon of the *convent. This development was a synthesis of the ideal of the apostolic life of the infant Church with that of the "rule of the Apostles", sources of the institution of the *mendicant orders.

C. Dereine, "La vie apostolique dans l'Ordre canonial du IXᵉ au XIᵉ siècle", *RMab*, 51, 1961, 27-53. – M. Maccarone, "I papi del secolo XII e la vita comune e regolare del clero", *La vita comune del clero*, 1, Milan, 1962, 349-411. – M.-H. Vicaire, *L'Imitation des Apôtres. Moines, chanoines, mendiants (IVᵉ-XIIIᵉ siècle)*, Paris, 1963. – P. C. Bori, *Chiesa primitiva*, Brescia, 1974. – M.-H. Vicaire, *Histoire de saint Dominique*, 1, Paris, 1982, 108-111, 171-178 (2nd ed.). – J. Laudage, *Priesterbild und Reformpapsttum im XI. Jahrhundert*, Cologne, 1984, 44-46, 197-206, 236-242. – M.-H. Vicaire, "Le modèle évangélique des Apôtres à l'origine de l'Ordre de saint Dominique", *Heresis*, 13-14, Villegly, 1990, 323-350.

Marie-Humbert Vicaire †

**APPARITION.** Accounts of apparitions are common in medieval literature. Distinguished from *visions by a specific Latin or vernacular terminology (*apparere, apparitio* and their derivatives), apparitions were defined as visible manifestations of the divine world. They were characterised by the intrusion of personalities from the other world (*God, *Christ, the Virgin *Mary, the devil, *angels, saints, *ghosts, etc.) or more rarely of celestial elements (luminous signs, cosmic prodigies) in the visionary's daily environment. Unlike the man favoured by a vision, the beneficiary of an apparition retained his normal perception of the place he was in without experiencing any sensation of spatial change or loss of consciousness, though it might sometimes happen that the apparition occurred during a *dream or an *ecstasy. The absence of this type of topographical or descriptive precision makes the distinction between a vision and an apparition a difficult one.

In the classification of visions into three kinds – corporeal, spiritual and intellectual – established by St Augustine in his commentary on Genesis in the literal sense (*De Genesi ad litteram*, 12, 6-7) and later taken up by many medieval theologians (*Alan of Lille [† 1203], *David of Augsburg [† 1272], *Thomas Aquinas [† 1274]), apparitions correspond to corporeal visions. Like visions, they are usually connected with a revelation ordinarily transmitted by the voice of the appearing being, whence the name of *revelationes* sometimes taken by collections of texts which mingled accounts of visions with accounts of apparitions (*revelationes* of Agnes Blannbekin [† 1315] or of *Bridget of Sweden [† 1373], for example).

From the 12th c., accounts of apparitions became particularly numerous in hagiographical *legends and collections of *miracles or **exempla*. Apparitions, like visions, were thought to allow normal communication between the living and the *dead, contribute to the development of the cult of a saint, or support new doctrines like that of *purgatory, for example. They also had the function, in times of crisis, of making divine chastisements visible and maintaining *social order.

Apparitions also furnished the matter of a literary genre. Close to the personifications of allegorical poetry, they constituted, as fictional characters, a narrative framework *sui generis* based on the model of *Boethius's († 524) *Consolation of Philosophy*, which enjoyed a great reputation in the Middle Ages.

W. A. Christian, *Apparitions in Late Medieval and Renaissance Spain*, Princeton (NJ), 1981. – P. Dinzelbacher, *Vision und Visionsliteratur im Mittelalter*, Stuttgart, 1981. – P. Dinzelbacher, "Importanza e significato delle visioni e dei sogni per l'uomo medievale", *Schede Medievali*, 19, 1990, 253-265. – J. C. Schmitt, *Les revenants, les vivants et les morts dans la société médiévale*, Paris, 1994. – A. Vauchez, *Saints, prophètes et visionnnaires. Le pouvoir surnaturel au Moyen-Age*, Paris, 1999.

Sylvie Barnay

**APPEAL.** Appeal was a complaint formulated before a higher judge against a sentence passed by a lower judge if a person felt himself injured by the judgment pronounced. Under the influence of the False *Decretals (between 846 and 852, according to P. Fournier and G. Le Bras), a hierarchy of appeal took the place of the *provincial council (previously the first court of appeal), starting from the *bishop and going up to the *pope – who could appoint judge-delegates instructed to pronounce on these appeals – via the *metropolitan and the exarch (*primate or *patriarch). With the development of *officialities from the late 12th c., the starting-point extended further down: *archpriest or rural dean, *archdeacon, bishop. . . but it was always possible to appeal directly to the metropolitan, though in theory one was supposed to appeal from the subaltern judge to his immediate superior. Appeal was made to the higher judge by reason of his jurisdiction, which was why appeal was not made from the diocesan official to the bishop, who was considered to represent the same court.

*Appeal to the pope.* The pope, by reason of his primacy, could receive appeals, a practice affirmed from the 5th c. by Zosimus, Boniface I and Celestine I (418-432). Gratian states that any Christian has the faculty to appeal directly to the Roman Church, no matter from what part of the world (II$^{a}$ pars, causa IX, q. III, c. 17, Friedberg, I, 611). The reinforcement of the administrative centralization of the Church around the papacy entailed the development of Roman courts, and St *Bernard mentions the multiplication of appeals to the pope in a letter to *Innocent II (*Ep.* CLXXX). However it was forbidden to appeal from a judgment of the pope to another tribunal, hence the practice of appeal "from the ill-informed pope to the better-informed pope".

*Appeal to the council.* In the 14th c. was developed "*appellatio ad futurum concilium proxime congregandum*", "appeal to the future council general", a consequence of the development of the theory of the *council's superiority to the pope, expressed at the council of *Constance (1415, 4th and 5th session). But *Martin V (1417) and *Calixtus III (1457) reacted violently against this practice; finally *Pius II launched a major *excommunication against whoever appealed to the council, in the *bull *Exsecrabilis*, of 18 Jan 1459. Appeals to the council were notably formulated by kings (such as *Philip the Fair), parliaments and *universities.

*Appeal as from abuse.* This practice consisted of appealing before a secular jurisdiction against a judgment of an ecclesiastical judge suspected to be contrary to the *ordinances and laws of the realm, and to the liberties of the *Gallican Church. The practice appeared in France in the first years of the 14th c., during the reign of *Philip VI (appeal to the king against sentences of ecclesiastical judges); its legal organisation dates from the *Pragmatic Sanction of Bourges (1438). Appeal as from abuse was developed from the time of the *concordat of Bologna, passed between François I and Leo X, regulating the liberties of the Gallican Church.

A. Amanieu, "Appel", *DDC*, 1, 1935, 764-818. – R. Naz, "Appel comme d'abus", *ibid.*, 818-827. – A. Bride, "Appel", *Cath.*, 1, 1948, 738-739.

Jean-Loup Lemaître

**APPRENTICESHIP.** Apprenticeship was the time when *children and the young acquired by practice the elements of their trade; it often ended in a rite of passage: *dubbing, *ordination, university *degree, inscription in a trade. From the 12th c., the hierarchy – apprentice, journeyman, *master – appears in the regulated trades. Contracts, used for a masculine minority, specify durations, payments to the patron, or the meagre salaries conceded. Parents and tutors were guarantors of the young person who was lodged and fed. The regulations favoured entry at 14 and a duration of three years, but notarial acts show the extreme variety of situations and the drift of the 15th c. towards apprentices of 17 and over, who thus found employment at a discount.

*Les Entrées dans la vie, initiations et apprentissages*, *AEst*, 5th series, 1-2, 1982.

Françoise Michaud-Fréjaville

**APULIA.** In Roman times, Apulia covered the north of modern Puglia and the neighbouring areas: the south of the region was called *Calabria, a name that shifted during the early Middle Ages to designate the former *Bruttium*. However the name Apulia or Puglia has never ceased to be used for the south-east region of *Italy, ancient Calabria included. It consists of two great zones: to the north, the plain of the Tavoliere, bordered by the Appenines and the Gargano; and south of the Ofanto, limestone plateaux.

In Antiquity, the region was covered with a fairly dense network of small cities, a number of which had *bishops. The *Lombard invasion of the Tavoliere in the late 6th c., doubtless accompanied by an *epidemic of plague, led to the abandonment of numerous cities; southern Apulia did not come under the Lombards until the 7th century. In the 8th c., great estates, little cultivated, occupied the peripheral areas; the area of *Bari developed in the 9th c., before being occupied from 847 to 871 by a Muslim emirate. Recovered thanks to the collaboration of the *Carolingian and Byzantine emperors, Bari passed for nearly two centuries, with the whole region, under the authority of Byzantium, which founded fortified cities (serving episcopal sees) and villages there and favoured a society of small proprietors; but with the exception of the far south, which was Hellenized, the region remained Latin.

The Norman conquest (1041-1071), carried out under the authority of a duke of Apulia, created a multitude of counties and lordships which adapted to the pre-existing conditions and developed the northern plain and the peripheral areas, but led to numerous local wars. From 1127 to 1139, the region was conquered with difficulty by *Roger II of Sicily, who brought the aristocracy to heel and imposed a royal administration; thus arose in the 12th c. the provinces of Terra di Bari and Terra di Otranto, and in the 13th c. that of Capitanata (Tavoliere); these remained the institutional framework of the region until the 20th century. *Agriculture developed together with population, notably in the 12th c.: the Terra di Bari produced oil, the Capitanata corn. The 13th c. marked the limits of this development: *Frederick II's fiscal and economic policy weighed heavily; the emperor built many palaces in Capitanata, where he often resided, sometimes overstraining the small settlements. But Apulia continued to sell oil and corn to the towns of northern and central Italy; Venetians and Florentines trafficked there; and the crisis of the second half of the 14th c. (plague, civil wars) was rampant in the region. In Capitanata developed the transhumance of flocks coming from the *Abruzzi: in 1443, *Alfonso of Aragon created at Foggia the "*dohana menae pecudum*" that administered it.

Apulia housed two *pilgrimage sanctuaries: that of *Monte Sant'Angelo from the beginning of the Middle Ages, and that of St *Nicholas at Bari from the late 11th century.

S. La Sorsa, *Storia della Puglia*, Bari, 953-1962 (6 vol.). – V. von Falkenhausen, *Untersuchungen über die byzantinische Herrschaft in Süditalien*, Wiesbaden, 1967. – G. Musca (ed.), *Storia della Puglia*, Bari, 1979. – J.-M. Martin, *La Pouille du VI<sup>e</sup> au XII<sup>e</sup> siècle*, Rome, 1993 ("CEFR", 179).

Jean-Marie Martin

**AQUITAINE.** There are as many Aquitaines as there are historical periods, if not historians. For C. Higounet (1971), who approaches the subject through historical geography, Aquitaine corresponds to the Aquitanian Basin or else to the South-West, as far as the external boundaries of Aunis and Saintonge (Charente-Maritime and Charente), Périgord (Dordogne), Quercy (Lot and part of Tarn-et-Garonne), Comminges and Couserans (parts of Haute-Garonne and Ariège). M. Rouche (1979) tries to grasp the regional phenomenon through the political and religious events of the early Middle Ages in the three Roman provinces of *Aquitania Prima*, *Aquitania Secunda* and *Novempopulana*, to which he adds the city of *Toulouse which became the capital of the *Visigoths in 418. What have these different Aquitaines been, politically and administratively, since the Roman conquest?

The first known mention of Aquitaine is by Julius Caesar, for whom Aquitaine went from the Garonne to the *Pyrenees. Becoming a Roman province, Aquitaine underwent several modifications. In *c.*27 BC Augustus created a province of the Aquitani as Caesar had demarcated them, but adding 14 peoples who occupied the territory between the course of the Garonne and that of the Loire (Strabo). This Great Aquitaine was recast by Diocletian, who reconstituted Caesar's old Aquitaine under the name of Novempopulana, and divided the rest in two. From 355 to 368, these two Aquitaines between the Loire and the Garonne were joined and then separated again. From 418 to 507, the Visigothic kingdom of Aquitaine included all or part of Aquitaine as well as the present *Languedoc.

After *Clovis's victory over Alaric II in 507, the descendants of the king of the *Franks carved up Aquitaine several times. In 602, for the first time, the *chronicle of Pseudo-Fredegar employs the new term "*Gascony" to designate the old Novempopulana. In the 7th c., the expeditions and influence of the Gascons extended even beyond the Garonne. A Great Aquitaine from the Garonne to the Loire tended to be reconstituted at the end of the 7th and first half of the 8th c. under independent dukes: Lupus (659-*c.*676), Eudes (711-732), Hunald (741-746), Waifar (746-766). On *Charlemagne's return from Spain, he created a kingdom of Aquitaine, which he entrusted to his son *Louis, whom Pope *Adrian I crowned king of Aquitaine at Rome, 15 April 781. This kingdom was formed of the four ecclesiastical *provinces: Bourges (Aquitania I); Bordeaux (Aquitania II); Eauze, later Auch (Novempopulana); and *Narbonne (Narbonensis I). When Louis became emperor in 814, he was succeeded in the kingdom of Aquitaine by his younger son Pippin (817-838). *Charles the Bald kept up the fiction of a kingdom of Aquitaine, consecrating as kings his sons Charles (855) and then Louis the Stammerer (867).

At the end of the reign of Charles the Bald began the fortunes of a new *duchy of Aquitaine. Bernard Plantevelue, already in 877 count of Auvergne, Limousin, Rouergue and the Toulousain, added in 878 Gothia and Berry, then the Mâconnais and the Lyonnais. After his death powerful comital families appeared: the counts of Auvergne, descendants of Bernard Plantevelue, the counts of Toulouse and the counts of *Poitiers. From 888, Rainulf II, count of Poitiers, took the title of king in Aquitaine, but he abandoned it in 889 for that of "duke of the greater part of Aquitaine". William the Pious, son of Bernard Plantevelue, took the title of duke of Aquitaine in 909: it was he who founded the abbey of *Cluny in 911. From now on, apart from the period 936-941, when the title of duke of Aquitaine and the county of Auvergne belonged to the count of Toulouse, the title of duke of Aquitaine was borne by the counts of Poitiers. South of the Garonne, counts of *Gascony whose origin remains obscure called themselves dukes of Gascony after 977. Their duchy, enlarged to include the Agenais and the Bazadais, incorporated the county of Bordeaux after 977. But a crisis of succession in Gascony, starting in 1032, ended in the union of the duchy of Aquitaine and that of Gascony, under the dynasty of the house of Poitiers.

In 1137, shortly before his death, William X put all his domains and the person of his heiress, his elder daughter *Eleanor, under the wardship of *Louis VI. The reality of the duchy appears from now on solely in the title of Duke of Aquitaine taken by Eleanor's husbands (*Louis VII until 1152; *Henry Plantagenet, duke of *Normandy, count of *Anjou, and king of *England from 1154) and sons (William, *Richard Coeur de Lion) who successively governed her possessions with her. The duchy of Aquitaine remained until 1453 the sole continental possession of the *Plantagenet state. The territories of this "English" Gascony were sometimes swollen to almost the whole Garonne basin and part of the Massif Central, sometimes reduced to the surroundings of Bordeaux and Bayonne, sometimes occupied by the king of *France. One of its finest moments was on 19th July 1362, when *Edward III made Aquitaine a principality which he gave to his son the Black Prince for life. When in 1371 the Black Prince, sick, left the continent for England, this principality finally disappeared. After the French reconquest there remained only Gascony and Guienne (a popular form of Aquitaine), two provinces of the Ancien Régime.

Though the administrative and political framework of Aquitaine underwent important upheavals during the Middle Ages, the Church of Aquitaine preserved the administrative districts of the late Empire. Bordeaux thus became, from *c.*340, the capital of Aquitania II. On Bordeaux depended, from now on, the *dioceses of Agen, Périgueux, Saintes, Angoulême and Poitiers. Only the diocese of Buch (Arcachon basin) disappeared in the 6th century. To the *province of Eauze, then from 879, at the latest, to that of Auch which followed the boundaries of Novempopulana, were attached the cities of Bazas, Aire, Dax, Lescar, Oloron, Tarbes, Lectoure, *Saint-Bertrand-de-Comminges and Saint-Lizier-de-Couserans. From 585 at Dax, then from 675 in nearly all of Aquitania II and Novempopulana, the episcopal lists are interrupted until the 10th century. At the end of the 10th c., a *bishopric of the Gascons, bringing together the ancient *dioceses of Dax, Aire, Lescar and Oloron, later Bayonne and Bazas, had been formed for the benefit of a brother of the duke of Gascony. In the 11th c. the *archbishop of Auch, St Austinde, restored the dioceses of his province after the break-up of the bishopric of the Gascons. At the start of the 12th c., a difference broke out between Bourges and Bordeaux over the primacy of Aquitaine. Two events served as pretext to put forward the superiority of Bourges: the occupation of the see of Bordeaux by a partisan of *Anacletus during the papal *schism of 1131, and the rivalry of the *Capetians and Plantagenets.

Decorative mosaic, consisting of inscriptions, at the Great Mosque of Cordova. Islamic art, *c.*786.

It was a privilege that the archbishops of Bourges had been granted since the end of the 11th c., and which Rome had gradually recognised. It was solemnly defined by *Eugenius III in 1146 and was confirmed more than once up to the time of *Innocent III. It was the former archbishop of Bordeaux, who became pope in 1305 as *Clement V, who released the church of Bordeaux from all subordination to Bourges, putting an end to the long quarrel over the primacy of Aquitaine. In 1317-18, his successor the Cahorsin *John XXII created the new metropolis of Toulouse, as well as the bishoprics of Lombez and Montauban dismembered from Toulouse, the bishopric of Condom detached from Agen, the bishopric of Sarlat detached from Périgueux and the bishoprics of Luçon and Maillezais detached from Poitiers. These metropolises and their *suffragan bishoprics formed the framework of ecclesiastical life up until 1789. The late Middle Ages were further marked in Aquitaine by two important *foundations. In 1331, John XXII erected a *university in his home town of Cahors. Bordeaux had to wait until the mid 15th c., when Pey Berland, archbishop of Bordeaux, obtained the grant of a university in 1441.

C. Perroud, *Des origines du premier duché d'Aquitaine*, Paris, 1881. – A. Richard, *Histoire des comtes de Poitou*, Paris, 1903. – L. Auzias, *L'Aquitaine carolingienne (778-987)*, Toulouse-Paris, 1937. – F. Lot, R. Fawtier, *Histoire des institutions françaises au Moyen Âge*, Paris, 1957, 1, 157-183. – *Bordeaux pendant le Haut Moyen Âge*, C. Higounet (dir.), *Histoire de Bordeaux*, 2, Bordeaux, 1963. – *Bordeaux sous les rois d'Angleterre*, Y. Renouard (dir.), *Histoire de Bordeaux*, 3, Bordeaux, 1965. – *Histoire de l'Aquitaine*, C. Higounet (dir.), Toulouse, 1971, 153-236. – *Histoire de l'Aquitaine. Documents*, C. Higounet (dir.), Toulouse, 1973, 79-171. – M. Rouche, *L'Aquitaine. Des Wisigoths aux Arabes 418-781. Naissance d'une région*, Paris, 1979. – J. Clémens, "La Gascogne est née à Auch au XIIe siècle", *AMidi*, 1986, 98, 165-184. – *Aquitaine and Ireland in the Middle Ages*, J.-M. Picard (ed.), Blackrock, 1995. – A. Tcherikover, *High Romanesque Sculpture in the Duchy of Aquitaine, c.1090-1140*, Oxford, 1997. – J. Martindale, *Status, Authority and Regional Power: Aquitaine and France, 9th-12th Centuries*, Aldershot, 1997.

Jacques Clémens

**ARAB CULTURE AND CIVILIZATION.** The Arab world is much earlier than *Islam and indeed than Christianity, though its cultural development and geographical expansion owe much to the religious factor and above all, of course, to Islam.

**Up to the foundation of Islam.** Traces of the existence of the Aribi people, on the Western borders of Mesopotamia, date back to the beginnings of the 1st millennium BC and appear in Assyrian texts. Nomads and oasis-dwellers on the margins of the deserts and the great sedentary empires, we see them contribute auxiliary forces to the powers of the moment: Babylonians or Assyrians (9th-8th cc.), Achaemenid Persians (from the 6th c.), Romans (AD) then again Sasanid Persians or Byzantines (4th to 7th cc. AD). Because of their stock-breeding activities, especially that of the dromedary, domesticated from the 2nd millennium BC, the Arabs were closely connected with the transport and politico-military control of commercial goods between the North and South of the Arabian peninsula.

In this context arose the splendid Arab city-state of Petra, whose existence can be followed from the 4th c. BC to the first centuries AD. Further south, towards the Yemen, from 500 BC, developed the kingdom of Saba, which owed its prosperity to the *incense trade and set up a type of royal authority. These examples prove that it would be wrong to think of the Arabs exclusively as a nomadic people, split up into rival tribes. Caravan cities could be transformed into capitals and heads of tribal confederations into sovereigns of small States. This is what later happened with the Kinda dynasty (5th-6th c. AD) which was able to create an Arab political entity, dealing with Byzantium and Persia. This attempt to organise the Arab world of the peninsula, prelude to that of the prophet *Muḥammad, was accompanied by an important cultural activity. To the Kinda we owe the most illustrious of the representatives of pre-Islamic Arabic poetry, Imrū l-Qays (6th c.).

The Arabic language is part of the Semitic group of languages. Its earliest written traces are graffiti, probably of Christian origin, dating back to *c.*300 AD. Writing appeared around the 6th c., and pre-Islamic literature would be consigned to writing only from the 7th and 8th cc., *i.e.* after the major event in the history of the Arabic language, the Koranic revelation (612-632). Indeed the sacred text insists on this point: it was "a Koran in Arabic", made to be clearly understood by those who used that language.

**Expansion and apogee of Arab-Muslim civilization (7th-12th cc.).** In the 7th c., the Arab world swelled under the effect of the expansion of Islam. It spread over the shores of the Mediterranean and to the interior of the East. The ethnic Arabs remained dominant under the *Umayyad dynasty of *Damascus (7th-8th cc.) but gradually gave way, primarily to Iranians, under the *Abbasids of *Baghdad (8th-10th cc.). Then came the break, with the installation of rival caliphates, notably the *Shi'ite *Fatimids of *Cairo (10th-12th cc.). The decline and fragmentation of the classical Arab-Muslim world took place at the pivotal moment of the Christian *crusades, the arrival of the *Mongols (capture of Baghdad, 1258) and the rise of the Turkish world (the *Mamluks at Cairo in the 13th c.), prelude to the rule of the *Ottomans (16th c.).

In explaining the development of classical Arab-Muslim civilization, a place altogether apart must be provided for the Arabic language, a formidable tool of thought and a decisive factor of cultural unification, beyond the Arabic-speaking countries and peoples. Throughout the period under consideration, the literary figures and theologians, even those whose original language was not Arabic, wrote in Arabic. This was the case, to cite just one example, of the Iranian Abu Hāmid al-*Ghazālī (1058-1111), whose work, which occupies a central position for Islamic thought and practices, was written in Arabic.

Word of Allah revealed through the *Koran, the Arabic language was from the beginning anchored in the religious. Study of the Koran and of the words and life of Muḥammad formed the basis of Islamic beliefs. From this flowed works of exegesis, legislation, mysticism, but also biographies of the first Muslims, studies of genealogy, real Arab science, narrations of conquest and then of the history of Islamization. Thus one of the greatest Muslim authors, al-*Tabarī (839-923), composed both a monumental Koranic commentary and a gigantic universal history. While an uninterrupted succession of great historians won renown (al-Masūdī, 10th c.; Ibn al-Athīr, 12th-13th c.; *Ibn Khaldūn, 14th c.), the works of famous geographers would open up new horizons, within the extent of the Muslim world and the journeys that could be made in it. Alongside the works of geographers like al-Bakrī (11th c.), al-Idrīsī (12th c.) and Ibn Battūta (14th c.), we must point out the existence of a genre of travel writing (*rihla*) occasioned by the pilgrimage (**Hajj*) to *Mecca. A very lively example is provided by Ibn Jubayr (12th-13th c.) who made his way to Mecca, then of Shi'ite obedience, from his native Andalusia.

Only a passing reference can be made to the development of linguistic studies in the proper sense: grammar, lexicography, etc, but attention must nevertheless be given to an eminently Arab and Muslim art, *Arabic calligraphy, and its derivative, *illumination. Originally a pious act, the manuscript copying of the Koran was gradually beautified, giving rise, through different styles of writing (*e.g.* Kufic), to a veritable art, cultivated with fervour not just by writers but also by artisans who transported the word of Allah onto the walls of mosques and princely palaces. The word "Arabesque" remains symbolically linked to this original art.

On the level of thought, a major episode in the history of the Arab world, of Islam and of world thought occurred at Baghdad under the caliphate of the *Abbasid al-Mamūn (9th c.). This was the translation into Arabic of Greek scientific and philosophical thought, very often the work of Christian Arabs. By this channel was propagated the thought of *Aristotle, Plato, etc. The Islamic philosophical current (*falsafa*) would seize on it, the outcome being commentaries and reformulations that would often produce tensions with religious dogmatics. Al-*Kindī (9th c.), Ibn Sīnā (*Avicenna, 11th c.) and Ibn Rushd (*Averroes, 12th c.) were milestones in this movement of Arab-Islamic thought which would reach Europe through Muslim Andalusia.

The rational impulse had been given, and its impact could be measured (briefly) in *theology, with the *Mu'tazilite current that engaged in debates, *e.g.*, on the Koran: was it created or uncreated? But it was mainly in the scientific domain that the progress of knowledge and practice made itself felt. In *medicine, al-Rāzī (*Rhazes), in the 10th c., was the first to write about measles and scarlet fever. Ibn an-Nafīs (13th c.) discovered the venous circulation. Ibn Sīnā bequeathed, in his monumental *Canon of medicine*, the essentials of the Greek contribution. Muslim astronomers, at the confluence of Indian *astronomy and the heritage of Ptolemy, would multiply observations, discover new stars, establish or complete astronomical tables, spread and perfect the use of the *astrolabe and the compass. But the study of the natural sciences did not progress without *alchemy (Jābir Ibn Hayyān, perhaps 9th c.), while astronomy bordered on *astrology, especially in princely courts. The name of al-Khawārizmī (9th c.), from which the term "algorithm" is derived, illustrates the Arab contribution to *mathematics, mainly to algebra. Other treatises that deserve mention include those on *optics or, in a wholly different domain, falconry.

Finally there remains one of the bases of the Arab-Islamic identity: the architecture and decoration of the *mosque, an object indissociably religious and cultural. The architectural and aesthetic success of the mosques was attained very early (*Kairouan, Damascus, *Jerusalem), and nowhere better than in the mosques can we measure the foreign contributions that Islam was able to integrate into a multitude of buildings so diverse but so unified in their structure and intention. The mosque was often close to another original element of the Arab town, the souk or bazaar, and this is perhaps a reminder us in a symbolic way of how Islam and commerce have been linked from the beginning.

A. Miquel, *La Littérature arabe*, Paris, 1969. – M. Rodinson, *The Arabs*, London, 1981. – C.E. Bosworth, *Medieval Arabic Culture and Administration*, London, 1982. – M. Fakhry, *A History of Islamic Philosophy*, New York, 1983. – M. Arkoun, *La Pensée arabe*, Paris, 1991 (4th ed.). – A. Khatibi, M. Sijelmassi, *The Splendour of Islamic Calligraphy*, London, 1996.

Constant Hamès

**ARABIA, CHRISTIANS AND JEWS IN.** Cradle of *Islam, Arabia possesses the principal holy places of that religion, *Mecca (Makka) where the prophet *Muḥammad (*c.*575-632) was born and lived until 622, and *Medina (*al-Madīna*, "the City"), first capital of the Muslim Empire. If the latter ceased to play a notable political role from the 660s, when the first *Umayyad *caliph transferred his capital from Medina to *Damascus, it kept into our own day a prominent religious role in the Muslim world. Mecca occupied an important rank in religious and legal studies, all the more readily since the pilgrimage or **Hajj* – which each believer had to make at least once in his life – brought the most eminent scholars there.

From the time of the first caliphs, the problem was posed of whether other revealed religions apart from Islam could be tolerated in the Arabian peninsula. At the beginning of Islam, Christians were particularly numerous in the oasis of Najrān (now in Saudi Arabia, near the frontier with Yemen), in the Yemeni provinces of the Red Sea, in the Yemeni island of Socotra and on the Arabian shore of the Persian gulf.

Judaism was also strongly rooted in Yemen, not at the periphery but at the heart of the country: the royal dynasty, the aristocracy and no doubt a considerable part of the population were converted to it in the 4th-5th centuries. Jews had dominated the country until the reign of King Yūsuf As'ar Yath'ar, who had persecuted the Christians of Najrān in Oct-Nov 523, provoking an intervention from Christian *Ethiopia. They were equally well settled in the North of the Hijāz (western Arabia), notably at Yathrib (which became Medina under Muḥammad), Khaybar and Taymā': at the time of Muḥammad's arrival at Yathrib, the oasis had five tribes – two non-Jewish, the Aws and the Khazraj, and three Jewish, the Qurayza, the an-Nadīr and the Qaynuqa'. Judaism was also present in the Persian gulf.

Apparently, other religions had only a very limited influence. If Manicheeism won followers among the Arabs, notably in Lower *Iraq, it does not seem to have ever played an important role in the peninsula. As for Zoroastrianism, the conversion of Arabs remains hypothetical. It is true that Islamic sources sometimes mention Zoroastrians in Arabia, but these were Persians.

The policy of the Islamic power was to expel the numerous

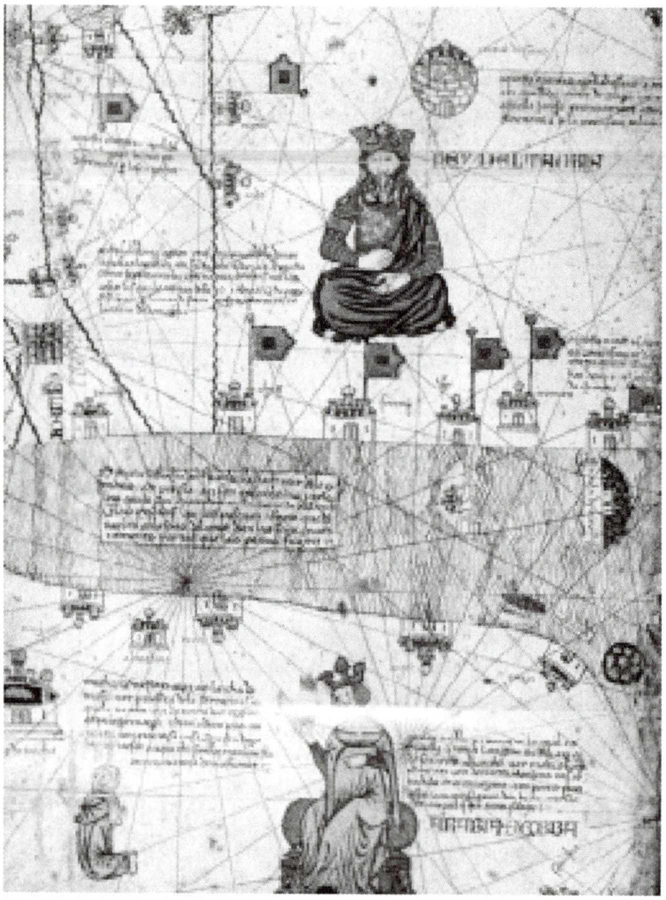

Representation of Arabia in Crescas's *Catalan Atlas*, 1375. Paris, BNF.

followers of Christianity and Judaism from Arabia. This decision, seemingly taken in 640, under Caliph 'Umar (634-644), was based on two arguments. The first was a saying (Arabic *ḥadīth*) of Muḥammad, spoken shortly before his death, of which a dozen variants exist, notably: "I would expel the Jews and the Christians from the Arabian peninsula, so as to leave only Muslims there". The second argument was that the Jews and Christians had not respected the pacts concluded with the Islamic authorities.

Learned Islamic tradition presents the expulsion of 640 as total and permanent, but this is a dogmatic conviction, not a historical fact. Several sources, Christian (*Nestorian Syrians) as well as Muslim (Yemeni Arabs) clearly indicate that Yemeni Christianity remained lively well after 640. Christianity is mentioned at Ṣan'ā' in the 830s, with an allusion to a "bishop of Yemen and Ṣan'ā'" named Peter in a Nestorian source. In the first years of the 10th c., Patriarch John IV replied to the questions of a Yemeni priest named Hasan ben Yusūf. At Najrān, the Christian community still had considerable political weight in the late 9th c.: according to a Yemeni Arab source, the first Zaydite *imām of Yemen, al-Hādī ilà l-Haqq Yahyà ben al-Husayn (897-911), concluded an accord with the Christians and Jews of the oasis, on 22 jumādā II 284 (Thursday 28 July 897), at the time of the foundation of the Zaydite principality. A second Yemeni Arab source, the *sīra* (biography) of the imām al-Mansūr bi-llāh al-Qāsim ben 'Alī l-'Iyānī (999-1003), alludes to the Christians of Najrān in muharram 390 (Dec 999-Jan 1000). In the 13th c., the oasis was still one third Christian and one third Jewish, according to the testimony of the Persian traveller Ibn al-Mujāwir.

A Nestorian Christian text written in Arabic in *c.*1700, the *Unedited statistic*, agrees perfectly with this information. Though its validity has often been suspected, notably became it mentions Christians in the Yemen in the 13th c., we must undoubtedly revise or modify the cricitisms it has been subject to. The *Unedited statistic* cites a province of Yemen, with Ṣan'ā' as metropolitan see and two bishoprics, Zabīd (with figures for the year 1210) and Najrān (for 1260). It also mentions a bishopric at Aden (curiously placed "in the province of Hijāz") that existed until 1250. On the other hand it ignores Socotra, where Nestorian Christianity was still alive right at the end of the 13th c., when *Marco Polo passed that way, and even in the 16th c., on the arrival of the Portuguese.

On the coast and in the islands of the Persian Gulf, Christianity is reliably attested only until 676. A collection of decisions taken by the synods of the Nestorian Church mentions several bishoprics in the Gulf and, in exhortations and reproaches addressed to the faithful, gives numerous details of the life of the communities. A resolution dated 676 forbids the Christians of the Gulf to drink wine on feast days in the taverns of the Jews, since there is no lack of Christian establishments where they can satisfy their desire to drink.

The strong Jewish community of Yemen resisted the pressure of Islam better. It occupied an important place in the Yemeni society and economy until the emigration of tens of thousands of people to Israel in 1949-1950.

The evident contradiction between the learned tradition of a total expulsion in the 7th c. and the much later presence of Jews and Christians in various regions of the peninsula is doubtless what caused the restrictive interpretation of the expression "Arabian peninsula": notably in Yemen, many scholars reckoned that this expression designated the Hijāz only.

J. Beaucamp, C. Robin, "L'Evêché nestorien de Māshmāhīg dans l'archipel d'al-Bahrayn (Vᵉ-IXᵉ siècle)", *Dilmun. New studies in the Archaeology and Early History of Bahrain*, D. T. Potts (ed.), Berlin, 1983, 171-196 ("Berliner Beiträge zum Vorderen Orient", 2). – G. Fiaccadori, "Yemen nestoriano", *Studi in onore di Edda Bresciani*, S. F. Bondì (ed.), S. Pernigotti (ed.), F. Serra (ed.), A. Vivian (ed.), Pisa, 1985, 195-212. – A. Ferré, "Muhammad a-t-il exclu de l'Arabie les Juifs et les chrétiens?", *Islamochristiana*, 16, 1990, 43-65. – *L'Arabie antique de Karib'īl à Mahomet. Nouvelles données sur l'histoire des Arabes grâce aux inscriptions*, C. Robin (dir.), *Revue du monde musulman et de la Méditerranée*, 61, 3, Paris, 1991. – B.-Z. Eraqi Klorman, *The Jews of Yemen in the Nineteenth Century*, Leiden, 1993 ("Brill Series in Jewish Studies", 6). – G.R. Smith, *Studies in the Medieval History of the Yemen and South Arabia*, Aldershot, 1997.

Christian Robin

**ARABIC CALLIGRAPHY.** Arabic writing, alphabetical in type, belongs to the Semitic scripts; it has 25 consonants, three semi-vowels and three long vowels. Appearing under the influence of Syriac in the Christian Arab kingdoms of Lower Mesopotamia, from the 7th c. it benefited from the creation of the immense Arabo-Islamic empire. Arabic, liturgical language and language of culture, was a sacred language since it was in Arabic that the *Koran was revealed to the Prophet. Arabic writing hence had considerable prestige, which progressed with the Islamization of the Empire, even when this did not coincide with Arabization. Such a sacralization of the script explains why Arabic characters, adapted to the Semitic languages, were also used to write Iranian (Persian and Afghan) or Turkish languages.

The calligraphy linked to this sacred script is hence both an art and a science, sometimes on the threshold of the divinatory and talismanic practices of the mystics (the "science of the lettered"). It benefited from the general use of *paper in Islamic lands from the 9th century. It was doubtless in the 10th c. that the mutual proportions of the letters began to be codified. Numerous types of script then developed according to their use (archives, charters, copies of the Koran, letters, works of erudition), their region (we observe greater sobriety in Andalusia and the *Maghreb than in the Orient) and finally their instrument and medium (*qalam* of cut rosewood sliding over paper, legends on coins, bands engraved in stone or stucco). Two great forms of writing quickly stood out from the Arabic script: an angular script for noble use, Kufic, reserved for the Koran or monumental inscriptions, and whose function became purely ornamental after the 12th c.; and a rounded cursive script (*naskhī*), more rapid, whose use spread among the scribes of the Empire or Iranian ceramicists around the 9th and 10th centuries.

It was from this cursive branch of writing that the medieval calligrapher enumerated the "six styles" illustrated by famous artists like Ibn al-Bawwāb (11th c.) or Yāqūt al-Musta'simī (13th c.) at *Baghdad. These six styles were *naskh*; *muhaqqaq* and its reduced version *rīhān*; *thulūth* used for titles and borders, and its rounded variant *tawqī'*; and finally *riqā'*, a reduced version of *tawqī'* used for epics, tales or the final pages of the Koran. After the 13th c., Baghdad took a back seat to the Persian and the Turkish calligraphers who developed the six styles and added to them *ta'līq*, used for office correspondence, and *nasta'līq* and *siyāq*, used for financial registers. After 1453, Istanbul notably became a great centre of calligraphy.

J. Sourdel-Thomine, A. Alparslan, M. A. Chaghatai, "Khaṭṭ", *EI(E)*, 4, 1978, 1113-1128 (2nd ed.). – N.F. Safwat, *The Art of the Pen*, London, 1996.

Catherine Mayeur-Jaouen

**ARABIC CHRISTIAN LITERATURE.** Each province of the *Byzantine Empire conquered by the Muslims in the late 7th c. kept (as today) a more or less numerous Christian community, with its own group language (Christian Arabic) influenced by the languages formerly spoken and written, Syriac in Greater *Syria, west and east Mesopotamia and *Iraq, *Coptic in *Egypt. These languages left traces, since for a long time there was a certain bilingualism, and some lasted as cultivated or liturgical languages.

These provinces belonged originally to four *patriarchates: *Antioch (now in Turkey), Seleucia-Ctesiphon (near *Baghdad), *Jerusalem (*Palestine) and *Alexandria (Egypt); but the doctrinal differences that appeared at various *councils led to the formation of new patriarchates. Ephesus (431) provoked the *schism of the *Nestorians, now called "Assyrians" to distinguish them from the Catholics of this branch, who are called "*Chaldeans". Chalcedon (451) saw the rise of anti-Chalcedonians in Egypt and Syria. Constantinople (680), called *in Trullo*, condemned the *monothelites, supporters of the Emperor *Heraclius's *Ekthesis* of 638, to which the *Maronites seem to have adhered for a time. Meanwhile a fraction remained faithful to the faith of the emperor, whence their nickname "Melkites" – in Syriac or Arabic, *malik* designated the emperor. Rome later created "uniates", which multiplied the number of patriarchates still further.

This article deals only with the *religious* sciences, excluding the considerable contribution of Christians, especially those of Syrian origin, in the various spheres of the secular sciences: *astronomy, *medicine, *mathematics, *philosophy, etc. We should not forget that it was mainly Christians, often via the Syriac, who transmitted the whole Greek, Persian and Indian scientific or philosophical heritage to the Arabs and – by the Latin *translations made of them – to the West. The six genres that form the whole of the religious sciences will thus be considered below: 1) *theology*, either *dogmatic*, presenting Christians with the fundamentals of the faith, or *apologetic* (when the authors expound the faith against opponents, either non-Christian or of an adverse confession); 2) *ecclesiastical history*, in which secular events often mingle; 3) *spirituality*, including asceticism and ethics; 4) *biblical studies*: this should include the versions of the Bible, but these are excluded here since they were very often earlier than the literary movement, and too often anonymous; this article will be limited to commentators, rarely to authors of hermeneutics; 5) *homiletic*, quite important, including sermons for various occasions; 6) *law*, including ecclesiastical canons and civil laws, the patriarch being regarded by the Muslims as the civil as well as religious head of his "nation" (Jacobite, Coptic, etc.).

The following divisions of Arabic Christian literary development should not be taken strictly, but very flexibly, since acculturation to Arabic culture did not take place uniformly in every community: one sometimes lagged behind another.

**Emergence of an Arabic Christian literature (8th-10th cc.).** This period, characterised by the establishment and pre-eminence of the *Abbasid caliphate of *Baghdad, is marked by theological, especially apologetic, works as well as by numerous Arabic versions transmitting the main elements of the heritage of Antiquity to *Arab culture. Works of *controversy include those of Theodore Abū Qurra, bishop of Ḥarrān, and the East Syrian Timotheus, for his discussion with Caliph al-Mahdī, and that of the Jacobite Ḥabīb ibn al-Ḥidma abū Rā'iṭa; in the 9th c., the East Syrian 'Ammār al-Basrī also wrote apologies; likewise two philosopher-doctors, the Melkite Qusṭā ibn Lūqā and the East Syrian Ḥunayn ibn Isḥāq, replied to the letter of a Muslim sage, 'Īsā al-Munaghghim; the same century saw the apology of Pseudo-Kindī (not to be confused with his Muslim homonym), a refutation of *Islam, translated in 1141 by *Peter the Venerable, and the controversy between Ibrahīm of Tiberias – a Melkite monk – and a Muslim *emir. In the 10th c., apologetic is well represented by the Melkite patriarch Sa'īd ibn Bitrīq and two eminent *Jacobite philosophers, Yaḥyā ibn 'Adī – who, in two apologies and several treatises, refuted the objections of two *Mu'tazilite philosophers – and his disciple 'Īsā ibn Zur'a, as well as by Isrā'īl, bishop of Kaṣkar, and two philosopher-doctors, the Melkite Naẓīf ibn Yumn, and the Jacobite 'Īsā ibn Yaḥyā. In Egypt, literary production began in the 10th c., with the theologian *Severus ibn al-Muqaffa' who wrote, among other things, three works expounding the dogmas of the Coptic Church and three more defending it against various Christian opponents.

Among the Melkites, history was first practised in the 10th c. by Sa'īd ibn Biṭrīq, patriarch of Alexandria, whose Annals would be used by William of Tyre in the 12th c., and by Maḥbūb (Agapius) ibn Qusṭanṭīn, bishop of Manbigh.

Among the East Syrians, spirituality developed in the 9th c. with the monk Ḥanūn ibn al-Ṣalt, inspired by the Syriac work of *Isaac of Nineveh, and the (Nestorian) bishop of Jerusalem, Elias al-Ghawharī. In Egypt, it is represented by Severus ibn al-Muqqaffa', who composed a *Treatise of remedy for sadness and treatment of suffering*. Ethics were tackled by two philosophers: the Melkite Qusṭā ibn Lūqā (9th c.), who expounded the various characters, and the Jacobite Yaḥyā ibn 'Adī (10th c.), who dealt with the correction of character.

Biblical commentaries were tackled by only two authors: the Jacobite Nonnus of Nisibis, whose commentary on John's gospel exists in an Armenian version, and the Melkite Bišr ibn al-Sirrī, who commented on the gospels and the book of Daniel; both of the 9th century.

In homiletic we must mention, for the Melkites alone, Theodore Abū Qurra, for three homilies that circulated under his name.

**The golden age (11th-12th cc.).** This epoch saw the full flowering of Arabic Christian letters, with a certain time lag in Egypt, where the rise really began in the 12th c. and was prolonged until the mid 14th. We see also the decay of the Abbasid caliphate and its disappearance with the capture of Baghdad by the *Mongols, before the Christians of Irāq were dragged into the collapse of the Mongol Empire in the 14th century.

This period saw veritable theological *summae;* for the 11th c., the works of the Melkite ʻAbdallāh ibn al-Faḍl (three dogmatic works and two apologetic treatises) and the dogmatic poems and four apologetic treatises of Sulaymān, bishop of Gaza; among the Maronites, a dogmatic book by Metropolitan David and an apologetic treatise by Thomas, bishop of Kafarṭāb; among the Jacobites (or West Syrians), the important work of Yaḥyā ibn Gharīr. But in this field the greater number of works were done by East Syrians; among these, the philosopher-doctor ʻAbdallāh ibn al-Ṭayyib wrote a book on the basis of (the Christian) religion, six treatises of apologetics, the account (a real *summa*) of the controversy of Elias bar Šināyā with the vizir al-Maghribī and seven apologetic treatises, while Elias I, *catholicos* of Baghdad, wrote a book on the foundations of religion, and the philosopher-doctor Saʻīd ibn Hibatallāh ibn Aṭradī wrote a theological compendium. Among the Copts, the 11th c. saw only an anonymous *florilegium, probably translated and adapted from a similar work in Coptic – composed to demonstrate the soundness of the anti-Chalcedonian point of view against the probable Chalcedonian work. It bears the revealing title *Confession of the Fathers.*

The 12th-c. output was mainly apologetic: among the Melkites, five treatises of this type by Paul, bishop of Sidon, an epistle dealing with the various (Christian) confessions by ʻAfīf ibn al-Makīn, and a treatise on the priesthood by Agatho, bishop of Homs; among the Jacobites, a treatise on the unanimity of the (Christian) faith by ʻAlī ibn Dāwūd al-Arfādī, and an epistle on unity and Trinity by Muḥyī al-Dīn al-Isfaḥānī; among the West Syrians, a refutation by Ibraḥīm ibn ʻAwn of a Jewish contradictor and some others; among the Copts, a defence of the particular usages of the Copts by Michael, bishop of *Damietta, a work on unity and Trinity by Simʻān ibn Kalīl ibn Maqāra, and two treatises of apologetic by Peter, bishop of Malīgh.

In the 13th c., the number of works is very large. Among the Melkites, the most important were the account of the controversy between Muslim scholars and a monk named George, and an apology by another monk called Gerasimos; among the Nestorians, a work on the authenticity of the Gospel by Īsuʻyāb ibn Malkūn, bishop of Mardin, and two treatises on the foundations of (the Christian) religion by ʻAbd-īšūʻ, bishop of Nisibis. The Copts were the most productive: two apologies by Abū ʻl-Ḥayr al-Rašīd ibn al-Ṭayyib, a treatise on faith by Peter al-Sadamantī, an apologetic epistle by Paul al-Bušī, an important *summa theologica* by Mu'taman ibn al-ʻAssāl, an apologetic exposition by Michael, bishop of Atrīb and Malīgh, and two theological books by Peter ibn al-Rāhib.

For historical works, the tradition was kept up among the Melkites with Yaḥyā ibn Saʻid of Antioch, continuing the work of his relative Saʻīd ibn Biṭrīq; among the Nestorians, the bilingual (Syriac-Arabic) chronicle of Elias bar Šināyā, with the important anonymous chronicle of Siʻirt; among the Copts, the first part of the *History of the Patriarchs* – with no equivalent in all the Christian East, it would be summarized in the 18th c. by E. Renaudot – by Mawhūb ibn Manṣūr ibn Mufarrigh, continued by various authors; in the 12th c., the Nestorian Mārī ibn Sulaymān inserted into his *summa theologica* a history of the Nestorian *catholicoi*, while in Egypt Abū Ṣāliḥ gave a description of the churches and monasteries of Upper Egypt (it is still disputed whether or not he plagiarized his 12th-c. predecessor Abū ʻl-Makārim). The 13th c. left three works (translated into Latin in the 17th c.), that of the Jacobite Gregory ibn al-ʻIbrī (*Bar Hebraeus) and those of the Copts Peter ibn al-Rāhib and George al-Makīn, also translated into Ethiopic.

In the field of spirituality, works were numerous: in the 11th c., the Melkites produced important versions of the Fathers, a florilegium of moral sentences and a work on the problem of evil by ʻAbdallāh ibn al-Faḍl, while the Nestorians produced a book on penitence by ʻAbdallāh ibn al-Ṭayyib and three works by Elias bar Šināyā: a collection of *Sentences useful to the soul and the body*, a letter on chastity, and an opusculum on the vices and virtues. The 12th c. left only a work in rhymed prose dealing with asceticism by the Copt Simʻān ibn Kalīl ibn Maqāra. The 13th c. produced more, with the treatise on the soul by the Jacobite Gregory ibn al-ʻIbrī and four works written by Copts: a treatise on the virtues by Peter al-Sadamantī, a work on confession by Patriarch Cyril ibn Laqlaq, a treatise on the soul by al-Asʻad ibn al-ʻAssāl, and a sort of Penitential by Michael, bishop of Atrīb and Malīgh, which would be plagiarized by Faraghallāh al-Aḥmīmī and translated into Ethiopic.

Exegesis was Arabized from the 11th c. with the Melkite ʻAbdallāh ibn al-Faḍl, but especially with the works of the Nestorian ʻAbdallāh ibn al-Ṭayyib, whose works would spread as far as Egypt. In the 12th and 13th cc., the majority of commentaries were by Copts: Marqus ibn Qanbar, Simʻān ibn Kalīl ibn Maqāra, Peter al-Sadamantī – author of a treatise on hermeneutics, a subject unique among the Copts –, Paul al-Bušī, Ibn Kātib Qayṣar, John al-Qalyūbī and Mu'taman ibn al-ʻAssāl.

Homiletic is well represented in the 11th c. by the Nestorian *catholicos* Elias ibn al-Ḥadīṯī, and in the 13th c. by the Jacobite patriarch John ibn al-Maʻdanī and four Coptic writers, Paul al-Bušī, John al-Qalyūbī, al-Ṣafī ibn al-ʻAssāl and his brother Mu'taman. Canon law began to be written down in Arabic from the 11th c.: among the Maronites, a collection by an anonymous author; among the Nestorians, the work of ʻAbdallāh ibn al Ṭayyib; among the Copts, the compendium of Yūnus ibn ʻAbdallāh (sometimes surnamed Abū Ṣulḥ). But we must await the 12th and 13th cc. for series of canons of the Coptic patriarchs Christodoulos and *Gabriel ibn Turayk. Later came the Nomocanons of Gabriel ibn Turayk, Michael, bishop of Damietta, and al-Ṣafī ibn al-ʻAssāl.

**The dark centuries (14th-16th cc.).** Two facts mark this period: following the Mongol invasion, literary activity diminished considerably in eastern Mesopotamia and Iraq and, consequently, in Greater Syria; while in Egypt the Christians were tending to become a minority, which had repercussions on the production and circulation of works, except in the first half of the 14th c. when several major authors emerged, such as the religious encyclopedist Abū 'l-Barakāt ibn Kabr († 1324) whose principal work, the *Lamp in darkness*, is an incomparable source. The seizure of power by the *Ottomans (1518) confirmed this diminished state of affairs.

G. Graf, *Geschichte der christlichen-arabischen Literatur*, 1-5, *StT*, 118, 133, 146-147, 172, 1944-1953. – G. Troupeau, "Arabe-chrétienne (littérature)", in *Dictionnaire des Littératures*, 1, Paris, 1985-1987, 89-90. – R.-G. Coquin, "Langue et littérature arabes chrétiennes", in M. Albert *et al.*, *Christianismes orientaux. Introduction à l'étude des langues et littératures*, Paris, 1993, 35-106 ("Initiations au christianisme ancien"). – *Christian Arabic Apologetics during the Abbasid Period (750-1258)*, S.K. Samir (ed.), J.S. Nielsen (ed.), Leiden, 1994.

René-Georges Coquin †

**ARABIC MANUSCRIPTS.** Arabic manuscripts copied between the 8th and the 15th c. (the earliest codex is datable to 843, but several fragments date back in all probability a century earlier) may number a million, or represent about a third of those we know today. Dispersed over some 40 countries and in public, private or semi-private libraries whose material is still sometimes unknown, an exact evaluation is difficult. Indeed, every year several catalogues of newly indexed material appear, and the wealth of certain public libraries is only beginning to be known with precision: it is estimated, *e.g.*, that today there are between 100,000 and 150,000 Arabic manuscripts in the city of Istanbul alone, while thirty years ago only three-quarters of this number was known.

This wealth is explained by the extent of a territory which, from the 7th c., extended from the Iberian peninsula to the frontiers of China, and where there soon circulated in the Arabic language Koranic literature, dogmatic *theology, legal treatises, translations of the products of Hellenistic science and Sasanid civilization, studies of language (grammar, lexicography, prosody, philology), the products of historical and historiographical monumental literature, and also mystical manuscripts, travel narratives or descriptions of the world, finally literary works properly so-called (poetry, stories, fanciful literature, literary "sessions"). This wealth is also due to the respect that surrounded writing and the book, symbols of knowledge and wisdom: by *c.*990, the interest showed in them by scholars or bibliophiles had led the bookseller al-Nadīm to publish his *Fihrist*, which was both the first history of Arabic literature and the oldest known bookseller's catalogue from the civilizations of the Mediterranean periphery. The illuminated Arabic manuscript was esteemed for the beauty of its paintings, those of the *Baghdad school in particular, or for the use of calligraphy as a decorative element. Muslim and learned, it could preserve certificates of "reading" or "audition", or "authorizations to transmit" delivered under the authority of an uninterrupted chain of transmitters, which represent important evidence for the specialist in the transmission of knowledge or the historian of texts and scholarship.

Christian manuscripts are much less numerous. We designate thus, not so much manuscripts of texts by Christian authors as manuscripts that contain works of religious inspiration (biblical or patristic literature, hagiography, canon law, liturgy, etc.) copied essentially from *Egypt to *Iraq. Some of these are among the oldest Arabic manuscripts preserved and we frequently find in them, alongside a *hejiran date, the equivalent in an older system of dating. From the material point of view, Arabic manuscripts are distinguished by the antiquity of the use of *paper: the oldest dated paper codex preserved in Europe – manuscript or. 298 of Leiden university library, dated 866 – is an Arabic manuscript. As for medieval Arabic literature, it is still partly unedited, and, in most disciplines, texts believed lost are periodically rediscovered.

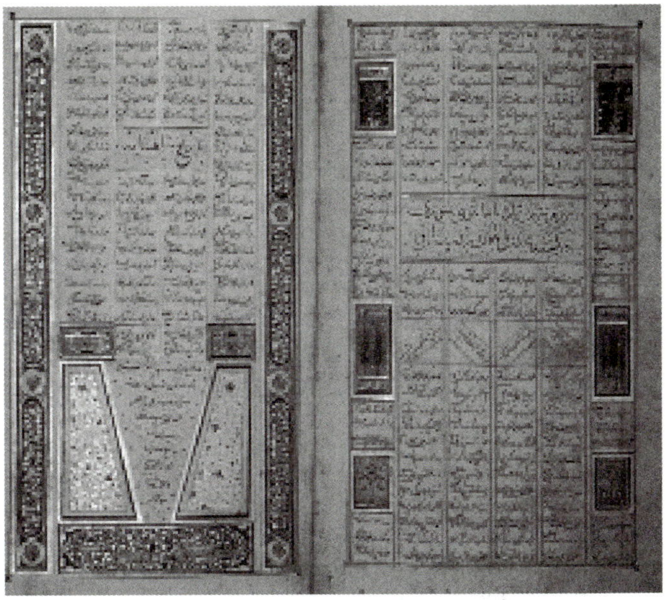

Arabic manuscripts. 14th-c. illumination from the *Book of Kings*, 1370. Istanbul, Topkapi Museum.

Al-Nadīm, *al-Fihrist*, B. Dodge (tr.), New York-London, 1970.

C. Brockelmann, *Geschichte der arabischen Literatur*, Weimar-Berlin, 1898-1902. – G. Graf, *Geschichte der christlichen arabischen Literatur*, Vatican, 1953. – F. Sezgin, *Geschichte des arabischen Schrifttums*, Leiden, 1967-1984 (9 vol. appeared). – J. Pedersen, *The Arabic Book*, G. French (tr.), Princeton (NJ), 1984 (tr. of *Den Arabiske Bog*).

Geneviève Humbert

**ARABIC PAPYRI.** Employed from at least 2000 BC in Egypt, its land of origin, the *papyrus was used by the Arabs following their conquest of that country in 640. Its Islamic utilization increased with the development of the needs of writing and long remained dominant, despite the introduction of *paper at the end of the 8th c. AD. Arabic papyrology is the science that occupies itself with texts written on papyrus. Nevertheless, it has always been normal to include in it non-literary documents written on other materials, like leather, *parchment, linen, paper, *ostraca*, bone or wood.

Despite the antiquity of papyrus as a writing material in *Arab culture, the science of Arabic papyrology is not old. Indeed, it was not until 1824 that it began to be spoken of, with the discovery of two papyri in a little sealed pot, found in a tomb or well, near the pyramids of Saqqara; A. S. de Sacy published them and became the founder of this discipline. But it did not really take off until 1877 when some papyri were found in the ruins of the former Arsinoë-Krokodilopolis (Kom Faris and Kom al-Kharyana) north of the town of al-Fayyum. In the course of the following years, excavations were continued and brought to light increasingly numerous materials.

The pieces found were sold to the museums of Berlin, the Bodleian Library at Oxford and above all the National Library of Vienna. Thus was slowly built up the famous PER (Papyri Erzherzog Rainer) collection which for the moment has the most Arabic pieces in the world and which celebrated its hundredth anniversary in 1983. Excavations continued successfully in the hills of Old *Cairo, and in other ruins including that of the necropolis of Memphis, Abusir al-Malak, Ahnas (Herakleopolis), al-Ushmunayn (Hermopolis Magna) and Kom Eshkau (Aphrodito).

Discoveries also multiplied in Upper Egypt, at Akhmim (Panopolis), Gabalayn (Pathyris) whence came a part of the Heidelberg collection, and Edfu (Apollinopolis Magna) where the Institut français d'archéologie orientale du Caire discovered important pieces including a famous codex, the only more or less complete book written on papyrus. Outside Egypt, there have been very few discoveries of papyrus, except in *Palestine.

More or less important collections have thus been formed progressively across the world. In the East, that of Cairo is the most considerable, particularly with the former Khedival Library (now Dar al-Kutub), which contains more than 2000 pieces. In America, we must mention especially the University of Chicago, whose Oriental Institute has constituted since 1929 a collection containing in particular historical, literary and Koranic texts. At the library of the University of Michigan (Ann Arbor), some pieces are preserved, as well as at the museum of the University of Philadelphia and in certain other collections that have not been catalogued or are not yet well known.

In Europe, the Vienna collection is by far the most important. It owes its origin to a collaboration between the merchant Theodor Graf (during his stays in Cairo), the director of that library, Joseph von Karabacek, himself a papyrologist, and Archduke Rainer. Today it numbers more than 50,000 pieces and fragments, including more than 10,000 papyri. In Germany, there are several collections at Hamburg, Berlin and Giessen, made up of business letters and documents. But it is at Heidelberg that there are, among letters of all sorts, some rare pieces of exceptional value, like the administrative correspondence of an *Umayyad governor of Egypt, dating from 710 AD, the earliest existing version of the life of the prophet *Muḥammad and the history of King David, and finally the only surviving papyrus roll in Arabo-Islamic culture. In France, there are several hundred papyri at the Louvre and at Strasbourg, containing various contracts and letters, including some fragments of the famous correspondence mentioned above. In England, there are small collections in the British Museum, at Manchester in the John Rylands Library, and in the Bodleian Library at Oxford.

It is needless to insist on the importance of papyrus for the study of *palaeography, orthography and the Arabic language in general. But by the fact that papyrus was for a long time the writing material *par excellence*, these documents have acquired a capital importance for the study of the private and social life of individuals (marriage, divorce, legal indictments and trials) as well as public life, administrative and economic. In these last two fields, private and official documents constitute a source often unique of its kind, transmitted in an original and authentic form, which adds to the value of the evidence it contributes.

A. Grohmann, *APEL*, 1-6, Cairo, 1934-1961. – J. David-Weill, *Le Djâmi' d'Ibn Wahb*, Cairo, 1939-1948 (2 vol.). – A. Grohmann, *Einführung und Chrestomathie zur arabischen Papyruskunde. I. Einführung*, Prague, 1954. – N. Abbott, *Studies in Arabic Literary Papyri, I. Historical texts*, Chicago (IL), 1957; *ibid., II. Qur'ānic Commentary and Tradition*, 1967; *ibid., III. Language and Literature*, 1972. – Y. Rāgib (Ragheb), *Marchants d'étoffes du Fayyoum. D'après leurs archives*, Cairo, 1982-1996 (5 vol. so far). – G. Khan, *Arabic Papyri*, London, 1992. – G. Khan, *Bills, Letters and Deeds: Arabic papyri of the 7th to 11th centuries*, London, 1993. – R. G. Khoury, *Chrestomathie de papyrologie arabe. Documents relatifs à la vie privée, sociale et administrative dans les premiers siècles islamiques*, Leiden, 1993. – R. G. Khoury, *Papyrologische Studien. . .*, Wiesbaden, 1995. – W. Diem, *Arabische Geschäftsbriefe*, Wiesbaden, 1995. – W. Diem, *Arabische Privatsbriefe*, Wiesbaden, 1996.

Raif Georges Khoury

**ARACOELI.** The church dedicated to the Virgin, situated in *Rome, at the summit of the Capitol, has been known by this name ("altar of heaven") since the 13th century. In previous centuries, the hill belonged almost entirely to the Benedictine abbey of Santa Maria del Campidoglio. In the mid 13th c., the pope obliged the monks to hand over the buildings and the church to the *Franciscans; these undertook works of enlargement and rebuilding, and commissioned for the apse a *mosaic, now lost, representing the scene of the Vision of the Virgin attributed for centuries to Augustus, after which he was supposed to have built on the Capitoline hill an altar "to the son of God". The cloister of Aracoeli, close to the seat of the Roman *commune, often housed the citizen assemblies. The image of the Virgin preserved there has enjoyed great renown from the 14th c., to the point of being invoked as protection against the plague. The grandiose marble stairway was built as a votive offering for the end of the *Black Death of 1348.

*S. Maria in Aracoeli*, Rome, 1976 (2nd ed.). – P. Verdier, *La Naissance à Rome de la Vision de l'Aracoeli*, *MEFRM* 94, 1, 1982, 85-119.

Giulia Barone

**ARAGON.** The region that bears the name of Aragon nowadays occupies 47,669 sqare kilometres, covering three natural units: the central *Pyrenees in the north, the Iberian chain in the south, and the Ebro depression, link between the two sides and element of communication and unity between the Aragonese territories. The name, borrowed from the river that flows in the Berdun channel, is, of all the Christian political entities of the Iberian peninsula, the one that appears first (828). This name, which was purely geographical to start with, was later used to define a political unit.

Early in the 8th c., at the time of their expansion in the Iberian peninsula, the Muslims conquered and occupied the lands of the Ebro valley and the central Pyrenaean regions, reaching the North of the lands of present-day Aragon in *c.*720. Their presence affected the various territorial and human entities unequally, depending on the previous degree of Romanization and the *Visigothic imprint. On the arrival of *Islam, the peoples of the North and those of the South were already Christianized, though we cannot evaluate to what degree and with what intensity. On the other hand, it is attested that *Mozarabic communities persisted in the main urban centres, where a hierarchical episcopal organisation was maintained, as well as the existence of several churches and monasteries that were part of the Visigothic tradition. However, the appearance on the political scene of important convert families or *muladies* like the Banū Qasi and the Banū Amrus testifies to the *conversion to Islam of a part of the native Aragonese oligarchy, which contributed to the religious and cultural transformation of the territory and, in a word, its Islamization.

Towards the middle of the 8th c., the upper march of Andalus was engaged in a series of struggles that broke out immediately after the *coup d'État* of Abd al-Rahman I, sole survivor of the massacre of the *Umayyads in the East, who founded an independent emirate at *Cordova and tried to impose his power on the great Muslim lords of Aragon. At this juncture, the rebels turned their gaze towards the neighbouring Carolingian Empire, asking the *Franks for protection and military aid against the new Cordovan *emir. Thus it was that, profiting from the Muslim political crisis, *Charlemagne extended his rule to the eastern Pyrenees (Hispanic March) and fixed his military enclaves in the territories of Sobrarbe, Ribagorza and Aragon. The Carolingian administration placed in these positions firstly Frankish counts, then native officials, who figure confusedly in medieval Christian historiography.

The first sources worthy of credit correspond to the very first years of the 9th c.: they mention the existence of a Count Aureolo or Oriol, who ruled the lands situated opposite Huesca and *Saragossa. Soon after appeared a local dynasty which, starting with Count Aznar I, lasted until the early 10th century. In the 9th c., the early county of Aragon was organised in the Echo valley, later extending to the valleys of Ansó, Boráu and Canfranc. In order to control and colonize Aragonese territory, the Franks leaned on monks who, commanded by St Zacharias, founded at Echo in the years 809-814 the monastery of San Pedro de Siresa as well as other monastic centres which allowed them to dominate the entrance to the nearest valleys, and the rural populations.

It was in the first decades of the 10th c. that the county of Aragon lost its independence and entered the orbit of the kingdom of Pamplona. Around 922, King Sancho Garcés I of Pamplona subjected the county to his hegemony; his son García Sánchez I married the daughter of the last count of Aragon.

The reign of Sancho Garcés III called the Great (1000-1035) was the most remarkable of this Pamplonan dynasty. The king was able to recover his territory after the devastating campaign of al-Mansūr and extend it over the whole northern fringe of Aragon. He leaned by preference on the monasteries to repopulate and reorganise his territories, thus according them a socio-economic function complementary to their religious and cultural mission. To this end, Sancho III introduced the Cluniac *reform, whose spiritual and normative elements were the most effective means of developing and modernizing Aragon.

On the death of Sancho III the Great, control of Aragon reverted to his son Ramiro, an enigmatic – perhaps illegitimate – and controversial figure. Despite this, Ramiro I (1035-1062) was the architect of the birth of the kingdom of Aragon; he was able to recover a lost independence, impose his authority over a heterogeneous territory and give the Aragonese signs of identity marked by Christianity.

His successor Sancho Ramírez (1062-1094) inherited from his father a kingdom already soundly established. To maintain its stability, he pursued a political line of openness: infeudation of the kingdom to the Holy See, replacement of the *Hispanic liturgy by the Roman rite, reform of the monasteries under the *Benedictine Rule and reorganisation of the common life of the *secular clergy. All these measures had a single aim: the religious rearmament of the realm, in cohesion with the rest of *Christendom. But the unifying reforms of Sancho Ramírez also extended to the ideological and cultural domains: the best examples being his rallying to the idea of a crusade against Islam, the adoption of the Carolingian *script, the use of the musical notation of Aquitaine and the expansion of *Romanesque art are the best examples of it. In this dynamic of openness to the outside, the pilgrimage road to Santiago de *Compostela in *Galicia facilitated the transit not just of pilgrims but also of merchandise and ideas, contributing to the demographic and economic progress of the kingdom. The creation of the town of Jaca, centre of Aragonese political life and main episcopal see, is the best illustration of this.

On this basis of material prosperity and human consensus, Sancho Ramírez's successors envisaged an advance towards the "flat land". Thus *Peter I (1094-1104) conquered Huesca and Barbastro, and his brother Alfonso I the Battler (1104-1134) undertook a campaign in the Ebro valley that culminated in the capture of Saragossa (1118), with the support of the principal nobles of the French Midi. But despite his military successes, the death of the Battler opened one of the gravest political crises recorded in Aragon, since in his testament the monarch bequeathed the kingdom to the *military orders. Faced with this vacancy of power, and at the request of the local nobility who did not accept this testamentary disposition, Ramiro II (1134-1137) abandoned monastic life to assume the government of Aragon. His departure from the monastery and subsequent marriage resulted in the birth of an heiress, the *infanta* Petronilla, who married the count of *Barcelona, Raymond Berenguer IV. Their son Alfonso II restored the reigning dynasty, completed the territorial reconquest as far as the Teruel region and inaugurated a political entity unprecedented in the history of Christian *Spain: the Crown of Aragon.

New lands were added to the Catalano-Aragonese union, either by *vassalage or by conquest. In the reign of *Peter II (1196-1213), the dream of Occitan unification faded away. The king became embroiled in the crusade against the Albigenses led by *Simon de Montfort, and was killed at the battle of Muret. The expansion of the Crown thanks to the *Reconquest was more effective and enjoyed a spectacular advance during the reign of James I the Conqueror (1213-1276): conquest of the kingdoms of Majorca and *Valencia as well as, later, *Sicily, *Sardinia, *Corsica, *Naples and the duchies of Athens and Neopatras.

After the territorial union achieved in the 15th c. by the *Catholic Kings, the Crown of Aragon gradually disappeared, first as a political entity, then as an institutional reality.

J. M. Ramos Loscertales, *El reino de Aragón bajo la dinastía pamplonesa*, Salamanca, 1961. – J. M. Lacarra, *Aragón en el pasado*, Madrid, 1972. – *Aragón en su historia*, Saragossa, 1980. – A. Ubieto, *Historia de Aragón*, Saragossa, 1981-1989. – T. N. Bisson, *The Medieval Crown of Aragon*, Oxford, 1986. – *Historia de Aragón I. Generalidades*, Saragossa, 1989. – E. Lourie, *Crusade and Colonisation: Muslims, Christians and Jews in medieval Aragon*, Aldershot, 1990. – A. Ubieto, *Los orígenes de los reinos de Castilla y Aragón*, Saragossa, 1991. – Y. T. Assis, *Jewish Economy in the Medieval Crown of Aragon, 1213-1327*, Leiden, 1997.

María José Sánchez Usón

**ARCHAEOLOGY, MEDIEVAL.** The archaeology of medieval society, which studies the imprints it has left in the soil – estiges of buildings, necropolises, fossilized field boundaries, po tery, tools, pits, culinary waste, etc. – runs separate from but parallel with the study of documentary evidence.

Three phases can be distinguished in the development of medieval archaeology. The first, from the early 19th to the mid 20th c., may be considered the prehistory of the discipline. Medieval archaeology was then an activity reserved for learned societies and was not taught at universities. It was mainly interested in prestigious monuments – churches, *castles – or *cemeteries, especially by reason of their rich funerary trappings, though some more modest sites, like early medieval earthworks, were surveyed at this time. Improvements in methods of excavation in protohistory, notably in Germany and Scandinavia, led medievalists to become aware of the fact that the soil was a historical document, leading to a second phase, the birth of medieval archaeology as a scientific discipline. This phase was marked by the beginnings of the teaching of medieval archaeology in universities and the creation of specialist reviews, a development that occurred in the 1950s in Great Britain, Germany, Scandinavia, the Netherlands and Poland, in the 1960s in France and still later in Italy and Spain. This period was characterised by a diversification of the sites excavated and the setting up of research programmes responding to historical problems defined through written sources: research was done on 11th- and 12th-c. earth and wooden fortifications to date the appearance of the first castles; on late medieval deserted villages to determine the date of their abandonment and measure the effects of the Great Plague on the *demography of the countryside; on "material culture", mainly the morphological and technical study of pottery and excavation of workshops.

From the 1970s, the development of "rescue" archaeology (or preventive archaeology) in response to the destruction caused by great works of rural development or renovation of urban centres led to a multiplication of projects from which medieval archaeology benefited greatly. This period was marked by the spread of the techniques of open-area excavation and improved recording techniques as well as the development of systematic surveys including geophysical studies. It was also characterised by increasingly frequent recourse to the soil sciences and natural sciences (sedimentology, archaeozoology, palaeobotany etc.) which trained specialists in historical periods and diversified methods of analysing the palaeo-environment. Finally, it was marked by the appearance of new fields of research: an urban archaeology that was no longer limited to the excavation of a particular monument, but sought to understand the evolution of the urban network as a whole; the birth of landscape archaeology, which strove to reconstruct the evolution of settlement patterns, the laying out of detailed surveys (field boundaries and infrastructure) and man's impact on the natural environment; also in a rural setting, interest shifted from the archaeological site to the landscape. Its capacity to apprehend space in all its chronological depth is a distinguishing characteristic of medieval archaeology in contrast with documentary history. The archaeologist has to establish his own documentation and field work, whether excavating or prospecting, which necessarily involves smaller and more defined places or spaces than those usually recognised by historians of texts. On the other hand, the chronological scale is generally much longer: the very nature of his unit of observation – site or territory – often leads the archaeologist to transgress the chronological boundaries between *Middle Ages and Antiquity, or Middle Ages and the modern period. Medieval archaeology tends more and more to dissolve into an "historical archaeology" that extends from Antiquity to the pre-industrial period.

Recent archaeological enquiry is characterised by the emergence of historical agendas that no longer arise out of written sources but from archaeological data themselves. This is the case, for example, of the question of the origins of the medieval *village, which would doubtless never even have been asked from the written sources alone, or that of the re-evaluation of the "*grands défrichements*" or *clearances of the 11th and 12th centuries, which consider what archaeology teaches us about the antiquity of rural settlement. This is also the case for studies of pottery that allow us to come to grips with the organisation of production, currents of trade and areas of distribution, as well as all aspects connected with use: culinary preparations and dietary fashions, division into fine and coarse wares as evidence of social status. Another characteristic of the recent evolution of medieval archaeology is undoubtedly an increasing tendency to encroach upon the field of neighbouring disciplines. Landscape archaeology has radically reviewed the methods of historical geography as it was traditionally practised; the archaeology of standing buildings encroaches on the field of art history to the extent that it deals with the study of buildings in elevation, though it does so with different objectives and methods: it is less a matter of studying artistic styles and influences than of identifying building campaigns through stratigraphical analysis akin to that of excavation. The ambition of medieval archaeology even extends to fields that seemed previously reserved for historians of texts, like socio-economic structures, political organisation or the expression of beliefs or attitudes through material culture.

A young discipline, archaeology is still in a phase when it must produce its own data by resorting to excavation and prospecting, and create its critical instruments. In nearly every field, the syntheses it produces are still fragile and their validity short-lasting. Correlation with written sources is revealed in practice to be much more complex than was initially thought: historians have expected archaeology to provide an illustration or complementary information that it was not always able to deliver. On the other hand, it has revealed whole sections of medieval history that often call into question the knowledge derived from written sources and invite a reinterpretation of the texts.

C. Taylor, *Fieldwork in Medieval Archaeology*, London, 1974. – M. de Bouard, *Manuel d'archéologie médiévale*, Paris, 1975. – *25 Years of Medieval Archaeology*, D.A. Hinton (ed.), Sheffield, 1983. – G. Fehring, *The Archaeology of Medieval Germany*, London, 1991. – *Medieval Europe 1992: a Conference on Medieval Archaeology in Europe*, York, 1992. – *The Study of Medieval Archaeology*, H. Andersson (ed.), J. Wienberg (ed.), Stockholm, 1993. – R. Gilchrist, *Gender and Material Culture: the Archaeology of Religious Women*, London, 1994.

Élisabeth Zadora-Rio

## ARCHBISHOP, ARCHBISHOPRIC

**The West.** Appearing at first in the East, and only in the mid 8th c. in the West, the title and dignity of archbishop manifested a superior apostolic delegation, exercised at need in several *provinces. Rapidly, in the Carolingian period, it was attached to the *metropolitan, to reinforce his prestige and the links that united him to Rome: the archbishop alone received from the pope the **pallium*, a band of ewe's wool symbolizing his office. During the period of its greatest influence, when provinces corresponded to specific territorial wholes, the archiepiscopal dignity allowed its titular to confirm the *election of the *bishops of his province, *visit their *dioceses to correct abuses, including those of the ordinary, and preside over the *provincial councils that, up to the 12th c., had an essential legislative responsibility. From the 13th c., the development of papal power considerably reduced the responsibilities of this position.

*DDC*, 1, 1935, 927-934.

Vincent Tabbagh

**Byzantium.** In the *Byzantine Empire, there were two sorts of archbishop. The archbishops of the patriarchate of Constantinople were *bishops who depended directly on the *patriarch, were chosen by him and by the permanent *synod, and participated in that synod; what differentiated them from *metropolitans was that they had no *suffragan bishoprics under their authority. The independent autocephalous archbishops (archbishops of *Cyprus or of *Ohrid in Bulgaria) did not depend on the patriarchal administration; they were elected by the bishops of their region and were like little patriarchs without the title.

H. G. Beck, *Kirche und theologische Literatur im byzantinischen Reich*, Munich, 1959, 67-68.

Marie-Hélène Congourdeau

## ARCHDEACON

**The West.** The archdeacon, immediate auxiliary of the *bishop, participated with him in the management of the *diocese. This function originated in the Church in the last centuries of Christian Antiquity: the archdeacon, first among the *deacons of the episcopal city, was mainly in charge of administering church property and supplying the needs of the destitute. From the 8th c., he became a veritable "vicar" of the bishop, commissioned to control the *clerics of the diocese. Because of the increase in the number of *parishes, many dioceses went from having one archdeacon to having several. No doubt this dignitary remained linked to the episcopal city (often he belonged to the cathedral *chapter), but the diocesan territory was divided into several areas, each of which constituted an archdeaconry. This evolution was not invariable: many dioceses in southern countries remained faithful to the model of the single archdeacon. Each Church had in fact the chance to organise itself according to its own customs and traditions.

In the 12th c., the archidiaconal function, rid of its feudal fetters, could be fully exercised. It was by the consent of the archdeacon that churches were restored and the new status of parishes defined. According to *councils and *synods, it was his job to control the situation of clerics and the state of churches. The archdeacon exercised an ordinary jurisdiction: he had his own courts. His authority was exercised notably on parish *visits and in certain circumstances he levied taxes (procurations). The archidiaconate constituted a *benefice and, in addition, parish churches were sometimes incorporated in this office.

Yet, even before the 13th c., the archdeacon's privileged situation was threatened. With the creation of *vicars general and *officiales foranei*, bishops had fully dependent auxiliaries at their disposal. Moreover, the head of the diocese kept a firm hand on *penance (reserved cases) and *marriage (prohibitions, *dispensations). Violent conflicts sometimes set bishops against archdeacons; in certain cases agreements were reached, but sometimes the archidiaconal dignity could fade away and even disappear. Yet in the late Middle Ages and later, some archdeacons correctly assumed the obligations of their office, as witness the visits of Josas or of Liège.

"Archidiacre", *DDC*, 1, 1935, 948-1004. – S. Hamilton, "Diocesan organisation in the Middle Ages. Archdeacons and rural deans", *PBA*, 19, 1943, 132-167. – R. Locatelli, R. Fietier, "Les archidiacres dans le diocèse de Besançon (fin XIe – fin XIIIe siècle)", *MSHD*, 34, 1977, 51-76. – S. Watanabe, "Les fonctions des archidiacres à Langres aux XIe et XIIe siècles" and R. Favreau, "Archidiacres et actes des évêques de Saintes aux XIe et XIIe siècles", *A propos des actes des évêques. Hommage à Lucie Fossier*, M. Parisse (dir.), Nancy, 1991, 277-294 and 265-275.

Joseph Avril

**Byzantium.** In the early centuries of the Eastern church, the archdeacon of a *diocese (who was generally the oldest of the *deacons) assumed, in addition to his liturgical functions as deacon, the direction of the episcopal administration. He was, as it were, the right hand of the *bishop, whose duties he could take over temporarily in case of a vacancy of the see. From the 7th c. the archdeacon lost this administrative role to the archons and kept only his liturgical role, in which he had precedence over the other deacons.

H. G. Beck, *Kirche und theologische Literatur im byzantinischen Reich*, Munich, 1959, 99, 114-115. – J. Darrouzès, *Recherches sur les Offikia de l'Eglise byzantine*, Paris, 1970.

Marie-Hélène Congourdeau

**ARCHITECT.** It is frequently said that the *cathedrals were built anonymously to the greater glory of God, that all the citizens took part in the collective work in witness to their faith. We now know that it was not quite like this: while it is true that the work was felt to be the result of an active collaboration between all the participants, each according to his capacity and his own role, it is also true that we know many names of medieval master *masons, sometimes inscribed on the façades of cathedrals – *e.g.* Buscheto and Rainaldo, the architects of *Pisa cathedral –, sometimes on the paving of naves in the form of *labyrinths, like Jean d'Orbais, Jean Le Loup, Gaucher of Reims and Bernard of Soissons at *Reims, or Robert de Luzarches and Thomas and Renaud de Cormont at *Amiens; and besides, the cathedrals were too complex works not to have been executed by specialists. One man, for example, *Villard de Honnecourt, has been the object of passionate discussion: known by his portfolio of sketches, actually notes taken in the course of his travels, he was no doubt more a curious man than a real architect.

Virtually nothing is known about the training of medieval master masons and their working methods. The earliest known scale models date back no further than the 16th c., like that of the façade bloc of Saint-Pierre at Louvain. The medievals were unaware of perspective, and architectural drawing appeared only in the course of the 13th century. It is probable that the choice of course to take was inspired more or less by existing works. We can see here and there, at Reims, at *Limoges, at *Clermont in particular, on walls or terraces, designs engraved in full size that constituted working documents. Master masons must have learnt their craft mainly on the job, by the empiricism of daily practice of work and also often at their own expense. Accidents were not unknown: thus at Ardenne (Calvados), in 1230, the choir collapsed on the abbot and his 25 monks while they were celebrating the office. Many buildings created too audaciously had to be consolidated later, like the choirs of *Tournai or Saint-Quentin.

In Italy, direct evidence of the activities of individual architects comes mainly from north and central Italy. Lanfranc, "mirabilis artifex, mirificus aedificator", a Lombard architect active in the 11th and 12th cc., built *Modena cathedral, a prototype of Emilian Romanesque architecture and model for the sacred buildings of *Nonantola, *Ferrara and *Verona. Guidetto da Como, sculptor and architect (12th-13th cc.), rebuilt the façade of the cathedral of San Martino at *Lucca in Pisan style in 1204 and contributed to the construction of Prato cathedral. The works at *Milan cathedral, an example of *flamboyant Gothic in Italy, were long headed by Simone di Orsenigo, chief engineer and master mason; among the German, Flemish, French and Lombard sculptors who contributed to its construction was Giovannino de' Grassi, listed in 1391 as architect and sculptor among the paid employees of the Opera del Duomo. Lorenzo Maitani designed the façade of *Orvieto cathedral and contributed to the restoration of the acqueduct at *Perugia and the castle of Castiglion del Lago; he also collaborated on the construction of *Siena cathedral. There were also working collectives formed by sculptors, builders and architects. The best known was that of the "maestri campionesi", from which emerged personalities like Anselm, active on Modena cathedral; Giovanni Seniore, author of the *baptistery at *Bergamo and, in part, the Certosa of *Pavia; or Matteo, author of the façade, ambo and baptistery of Monza cathedral. Famous at *Rome were the Cosmati, a family of marble-workers so called from the name of one of their best-known members: famous for decorations, they also ended

Overstolzen House at Cologne. 13th c.

by concerning themselves with working out architectural forms, not worrying about volumetric investigations or problems of construction but trusting to a balanced, classicizing taste. To the family of the Vassalletto in particular we owe the narthex of San Lorenzo fuori le Mura and the cloisters of *St Paul's without the Walls and *St John Lateran. Particularly important was the figure of the architect-scuptor, like Giovanni *Pisano and above all *Arnolfo di Cambio. The former worked especially at Siena, where he was master builder of the cathedral, whose original façade he designed (it was eventually done to a different design in the 14th c.); he also took part in building the cathedral of Massa Marittima and the baptistery and cathedral at Pisa. Arnolfo di Cambio, a multi-talented artist known mainly as a sculptor (his was the first crib, in *Santa Maria Maggiore at Rome), is referred to in a 14th-c. document as master builder of *Florence cathedral; recent criticism has also ascribed to him the design of the church of Santa Croce and the Palazzo Vecchio at Florence.

Medieval architects are also known in other parts of Europe: in England, Walter of Hereford was royal master of Caernarvon Castle and Vale Abbey; William of Wykeham was master builder of *Winchester cathedral and worked at *Westminster and Windsor. The names of some German master builders are also known: in particular the Parler family, who worked at *Cologne, *Prague and *Vienna.

But it was mainly in 13th-c. France that the professional figure of the architect took on a prominent role. Until the early 13th c., the master mason had shared the life of his companions on the building site, but then appeared the architect in the modern sense of the term, *i.e.* one who conceived the work but entrusted its realization to others: thus Gautier de Varinfroy, identified on the building sites of the cathedrals of Meaux, *Évreux and perhaps *Sens and Saint-Père de *Chartres. During the second half of the 14th c., Gilles Largent also supervised several building sites including the north crossing of the collegiate church of Saint-Quentin and the tower and spire of *Cambrai cathedral. At the turn of the 16th c., the Parisian Martin Chambiges worked on the transept of Sens cathedral, the façade block of that of *Troyes and the transept of Saint-Pierre de *Beauvais. The presence of the same masters in widely separated geographical places naturally played a great role in the diffusion of certain stylistic fashions.

This transformation of the very nature of the master mason's work was naturally accompanied by a rise in his social level: the annual salary of Gautier de Varinfroy gives proof of this, rising to 50 pounds, or a third of the value of a very respectable house. In a sermon preached in *c.*1261, the Dominican Nicolas de Biard railed against architects who came onto the building site in gloves with their graduated rule, and knew only how to give orders.

J. H. Harvey, *The Medieval Architect*, London, 1972. – *Les Bâtisseurs des cathédrales gothiques*, R. Recht (ed.), Strasbourg, 1989. – C. M. Radding, *Medieval Architecture, Medieval Learning*, New Haven (CN), 1992.

Jacques Thiébaut

**ARCHITECTURE, CIVIL.** Civil architecture includes public buildings and private dwellings, but excludes military constructions and rural architecture. Important public buildings comprised essentially imperial and royal *palaces, residential palaces and communal palaces, as well as towers and city gates and, to some extent, *castles. The small number of medieval civil buildings to survive – a phenomenon due mainly to the continual renewals and transformations undergone by *towns at later dates – obliges us to refer to the few remaining examples and to indirect evidence such as literary sources, *miniatures and *mosaics.

The word "palace" is derived from the Latin name of the *mons Palatinus* at Rome, on which the Emperor Augustus and his successors built the imperial residences. The word initially designated the imperial residences of the late Empire (*Constantinople, *Milan, Split, etc.) and then royal residences (*Theodoric's palace at *Ravenna, *Charlemagne's palace at *Aachen). From the architectural point of view, Western royal palaces, similar in plan to Byzantine ones, were contained in a fortified enclosure and consisted of a group of multifunctional buildings, in response to the political requirements connected with them; nearly always such buildings – such as the palace of the dukes of Burgundy at *Dijon or that of the counts of Champagne at *Troyes – were the product of stratifications of various periods. In *Italy, there are important examples of residential palaces at Ravenna (House of Droedo, with Byzantine-type decorations) and *Venice (Ca' del Mosto, with arcades of oriental type, and somewhat later the Ca' d'Oro, which sums up the typical Venetian architecture, light and perforated, with a plan that would remain unchanged for centuries). In the communal period, between the 11th and 14th cc., there developed mainly in Tuscany the model of the signorial "tower house", both a symbol of power and prestige and a military element. In the Mezzogiorno the Arab style prevailed, widespread also at Byzantium and in *Spain: *e.g.* the Zisa at *Palermo, a cubical building with a single opening and blind arcading on the outside, characterised by a complex internal structure with an air-cooling system; or the Casa dei Rufolo at Ravello, built in the 13th c. in Arab-Sicilian style, with vaults and domes and polychrome facing.

During the 12th c., the basic pattern for seats of communal authority (town hall, *palazzo comunale*, *hôtel de ville*, *Rathaus*, etc.) was established. They generally consisted of a large portico on the ground floor where the citizen assembly could meet and where the *market was often held, while on the upper floors were the council meeting-rooms and the offices of the various officials. Symbol of municipal autonomy, the tower or *belfry housed the communal clock, which served to summon the people. Among the oldest Italian *palazzi comunali* are the Palazzo della Ragione of *Verona, characterised by a large porticoed courtyard, and the *Broletto* of Como, which shows Gothic influences in the ogival arcades of the portico and the biforate and triforate windows; in a later phase were built the Palazzo Pubblico of *Piacenza, also with evident Gothic influence, and the Palazzo Chiaramonte at Palermo. Nor can we ignore the Doge's Palace at Venice, the Palazzo Pubblico at *Siena, and the Palazzo Vecchio at *Florence or, in France, the Palace of the Popes at *Avignon, considered the finest example of 14th-c. civil architecture in Europe.

Towers, tall massive rectangular structures with smooth or rusticated walls and few windows, dwellings of powerful families, markedly characterised the medieval urban landscape: some examples survive at San Gimignano, Corneto (Tarquinia), *Bologna (towers of the Garisenda and Asinelli), *Genoa (tower of the Embriaghi) and *Rome (Torre delle Milizie). Among city gates must be mentioned Porta Nuova at *Milan, Porta Vittoria at Como, San Gervasio at *Lucca and especially the Porta di Capua – built between 1240 and 1250 and demolished in 1557 – admired by Renaissance architects for its form, of clear classical inspiration.

Little is known about the town *house of the early Middle Ages, by reason of the decline of the *town during the 7th-10th centuries. Where possible, the structures bequeathed by Antiquity were reused, but the dominant trait was an impoverishment of building techniques and architectural models: houses were generally built of wood and often contained a single undifferentiated space. From the 10th and 11th cc., urban renewal entailed a considerable rise in private building. In close connection with the evolution of society, a model of domestic architecture was worked out, characterised by a single-family multifunctional house (joint properties are no earlier than the late Middle Ages). The social differentiation of domestic architecture was also accentuated. The houses of ordinary people are little known, while the dwellings of patricians and lordly residences, whose size and architectural elegance increased from the 13th c., dominated the urban landscape.

G. Chierici, *Il palazzo italiano dal secolo XI al secolo* XIX, Milan, 1952-1957 (3 vol.). – D'une *ville à l'autre. Structures matérielles et organisation de l'espace dans les villes européennes (XIII<sup>e</sup>-XVI<sup>e</sup> siècle)*, J.-C. Maire-Vigueur (ed.), Rome, 1989. – P. Garrigou Grandchamp, *Demeures médiévales, coeur de la cité*, Paris, 1992. – A. Restucci (ed.), *L'Architettura civile in Toscana. Il Medioevo*, Milan, 1995. – N. Rubinstein, *The Palazzo Vecchio, 1298-1532*, Oxford, 1995.

Étienne Hubert

**ARCHITECTURE, ECCLESIASTICAL.** Ecclesiastical architecture responds, from a purely practical point of view, primarily to the requirements of worship and secondarily to the needs of those who dedicate themselves to the religious life. It consequently comprises a great number of buildings with different purposes: churches, cloisters, baptisteries, oratories, *abbeys and monasteries, episcopal and papal palaces, as well a series of related buildings such as *colleges, seminaries, presbyteries, *libraries and *hospices. But ecclesiastical architecture has also always had a strong artistic, cultural and ideological value, capable as it is of giving form and expression to civilization and the spirit, through the medium of matter.

The Middle Ages were able to translate into art the sacrality connected with religious feeling, developing new architectural styles and reflecting in them the doctrinal vision of the Church, militant and triumphant, not just on the large scale of urban *cathedrals, but also in the more unassuming reality of villages and the countryside. Indeed the church was often the only stone building for many miles and it was an indispensable reference-point for the social life of the time. Between the 10th and 12th cc. – the period of *Romanesque art – the number of churches grew considerably, modifying the appearance of the territory. Churches were everywhere, from the village oratory to the castle *chapel; those of large or middling size – *priories, abbeys, cathedrals – were usually built by religious institutions and were more accurate in their architectural structure.

Sacred building *par excellence*, the church in the Middle Ages was much more than a place of worship: it guarded the *relics of the saint, it was a place of *prayer, but also a meeting-place. The aisles, large areas almost completely free of benches, were dedicated to the people; the division between these and the space dedicated to the clergy was evident, emphasized by the presence of a wooden or stone screen. The early Middle Ages did not erase the architectural imprint that distinguished the early Christian churches, built on the model of the Roman *basilica: the plan was still the same, with a central nave and two or four side-aisles. The Greek- or Latin-cross plan came to prevail over the rectangular pattern: thus the transept was added to divide choir from nave. Church architecture began to be the favourite site of architectural experimentation: in the 9th c., Lombard builders began a decisive rationalization of space with the vaulted roof, which allowed the development of powerful concentrated masses, a typical characteristic of Romanesque art (which enjoyed lasting popularity and numerous original developments especially in the Italian regions, from Tuscan to Apulian Romanesque). The invention of the ribbed vault laid the basis for the daring experimentalism of *Gothic art: when architects discovered that narrow ribs and slender pillars were enough, with rampant arches on the inside and flying buttresses on the outside, to support ever taller sacred buildings, it enabled them to open up of precious *stained-glass windows. This was the natural evolution of a need that had already arisen with Romanesque art: to embellish a church with paintings and sculpture created by the greatest artists of the time, so as to translate into visible form the teachings of the Church in its catechetical and pastoral activity, and at the same time to manifest its growing spiritual and temporal power.

The atrium, intended for penitents and catechumens and characteristic of all major early Christian basilicas, disappeared around the 7th c. with the diminution of the liturgical reasons for which it had been created. The *baptistery, understood as a building attached to the basilica and intended for conferring *baptism, kept its proper purpose as long as the sacrament was imparted by immersion, a ceremony that required a large pool. With the ever more frequent use of the baptismal font, the building lost its *raison d'être* and in fact disappeared during the 15th century. Architecturally important examples are found particularly in Italy, from the baptistery of Santa Severina near Catanzaro with its segmented dome set on eight columns, repeating a Byzantine pattern, to the buildings of Agliate, Biella, Ventimiglia and Cremona that follow Romanesque themes. The baptisteries of *Parma, *Pisa, *Florence and Volterra are buildings singular in their artistic individuality and rich in decorations and sculpture of considerable artistic value.

The *cloister, born of the practical needs of claustral life, was used in the Middle Ages in monasteries, cathedrals and *collegiate churches. Around the 11th c. spread a very common typology, with limited apertures supported by doubled columns on the ground floor (San Cosimato at Rome, Saint-Lizier in the *Pyrenees). Stylistic variations of some importance occur in the French cloisters of *Moissac and Saint-Cugat del Valles and in many Spanish cloisters thanks to the adoption of figured capitals, while at Rome, in the cloisters of *St John Lateran and *St Paul's without the Walls, classical reminiscences are united with pictorial striving.

Similar in structure to the church, the *oratory, square or rectangular in plan with a single *altar, could be self-standing or else joined to larger religious buildings; in the second half of the 13th c. arose the oratory with its own façade, like those dedicated to St Bernardino and set alongside Franciscan churches: *e.g.* in particular those of *Assisi and *Siena.

The monastic orders also played an important role in spreading new architectural forms: the Rule of St *Benedict codified norms and typologies of construction with extreme precision, in response to the needs of a rational, functional common life that would favour the establishment of a perfect community. The earliest plan of an abbey complex is that of *Sankt Gallen (820), and it did not vary substantially over time: the distribution of the monastic buildings next to the church (cloister, *chapter house, kitchens, dormito ies) was derived from the earliest Benedictine models, imposing a bare and functional monumentality. The subsequent Cluniac and *Cistercian reforms also conformed to the same models, while introducing innovations of some importance that had notable reflections on the ecclesiastical architecture of the time: it is unanimously acknowledged that Cistercian architecture made a significant contribution to the spread of Gothic in Italy.

Also important, at a later date, was the contribution made to artistic development by the *mendicant orders, who intended to translate their own ideals into a sober architecture: nave covered by a simple wooden roof, churches without transepts or towers; in general, elimination of ambulatories and radiating chapels, *i.e.* anything that would prevent unification of space. In reality however, the use of cross-ribbed vaults prevailed over the trussed roof, though the rule of excluding superfluous ornaments was more respected. Dominican and Franciscan architecture enjoyed their widest expansion in Italy and Germany, markedly in the Rhineland: the greatest examples are, for the *Franciscans, the churches of St Francis at Assisi, Santa Croce at Florence and San Francesco at *Bologna, and, for the *Dominicans, Santa Maria Novella at Florence, San Domenico at Bologna and Santa Maria sopra Minerva at Rome. In Germany, *Regensburg cathedral is a characteristic example.

Alongside sacred architecture, residential building too was involved in a process of structural renewal and enlargement, to coincide with its functional amplification: in dependence on the cathedral, which affirmed its predominance over other religious institutions, arose the episcopal palace, forming complexes in some respects similar to those of abbeys. Palaces of artistic value include those of *Laon, *Auxerre, *Narbonne, *Reims and, in Italy, those of *Orvieto, *Viterbo and *Anagni. Papal residences were enriched and became more sumptuous: the Vatican Palace took on the dignity of a real papal residence during the 13th c., supplanting the Lateran Palace, which had been rebuilt and enlarged during the 9th c. and was badly damaged by several fires in the 14th century. During the *Avignon period, the grandiose Palace of the Popes was built in that French city, of considerable architectural and artistic worth and rich in *tapestries and *frescos.

Medieval ecclesiastical architecture, interpreted and defined in terms of its religous meaning, coincided with the spread of Roman-rite Christianity throughout Europe and represented the crossroads of the artistic, economic and material efforts of a whole society, as well as interpreting the reality of a complex aspiration to the supernatural.

P. Toesca, *Il Medioevo*, 1, Turin, 1927; 2, Turin, 1951. – E. Lavagnino, *L'arte medioevale*, Turin, 1960. – H. E. Kubach, *Architettura romanica*, Milan, 1972. – L. Grodecki, *Architettura gotica*, Milan, 1976. – G. Duby, *L'arte e la società medievale*, Rome-Bari, 1977. – W. Sauerländer, *Le cattedrali gotiche (1140-1260)*, Milan, 1991. – *HChr*, 5, 1993, 507-516.

Lucia Velardi

**ARCHPRIEST, RURAL DEAN.** These two terms were used to designate the same subordinate dignitary of the diocesan hierarchy. The two words originally corresponded to two clearly identical types of competence: archpriestships in southern regions, elsewhere deaneries. But in some *dioceses the two names coexisted.

The dual name could well be the consequence of the historical evolution of the institution. Originally the title of archpriest was borne by the first of the priests of the episcopal city, before being given to the heads of the rural, mostly baptismal, churches. This organisation was indeed maintained in the *pievi* of Italy, and certain dioceses kept the single archpriest. Elsewhere, with the multiplication of churches and the creation of archdeaconries, *parishes were regrouped or were united into *decanatus* or deaneries. The dean must then rapidly have been identified with the archpriest of a rural district.

The more or less similar powers of these two dignitaries were defined by Carolingian legislation. They were later blurred, but one consequence of the restorations and *donations of churches was the establishment of new statutes for parishes, formulated with the consent of archpriests and rural deans. From now on these exercised direct control over the behaviour of *clerics and the conduct of the faithful; moreover they held their own court of justice.

From the 13th c., *provincial councils and especially diocesan *synods also codified the powers of archpriests and rural deans. Like the *archdeacon, these possessed an ordinary jurisdiction and designated **officiales*. Close to the *parish priests, usually dependent on the *bishop, they governed their areas more effectively than did the archdeacon. Their role appears to have been of primary importance in the declaration of *testaments and the transmission of diocesan legislation (synodal *statutes). This authority was exercised in two ways: by visitation and by meetings of the clergy (*calends).

At the time of a *visit, the archpriest or rural dean levied taxes on the church (procurations), which were added to the resources connected with his office. The archipresbyterate or diaconate was defined as a *benefice, with all the usual excesses (*pluralism, non-*residence). This does not alter the fact that in the late Middle Ages these ecclesiastics occupied an essential place in the diocesan organisation.

J. Faure, *L'archiprêtre des origines au droit décrétalien*, Grenoble, 1911. – E. Griffe, "Les origines de l'archiprêtre de district", *RHEF*, 13, 1929, 16-50. – "Archiprêtre", *DDC*, I, 1935, 1004-1026. – P. Andrieu-Guitancourt, *Essai sur l'évolution du décanat rural en Angleterre d'après les conciles des XII^e^, XIII^e^ et XIV^e^ siècles*, Paris, 1935. – F. Toussaint, "Les doyens ruraux et les assemblées synodales aux anciens diocèses de Liège et de Cambrai", *Miscellanea moralia in honorem Domini Arthur Janssen*, Louvain-Gembloux, 1948, 655-669 ("BEThL", 3). – F. Toussaint, "Élection et sortie de charge du doyen de chrétienté dans les anciens diocèses de Liège et Cambrai", *RFE*, 47, 1952, 50-80. – E. Brouette, "Les doyens de chrétienté du diocèse de Liège des origines à la fin du XIII^e^ siècle", *Leod.*, 58, 1971, 20-41.

Joseph Avril

**ARIANISM.** Arianism takes its name from a priest of Alexandria, Arius, who in the years 318-323 came into conflict with his bishop on the subject of trinitarian theology. Arius affirmed the supremacy of the Father, only true God, unbegotten, over the Son, his creature, and over the Holy Spirit. Very rapidly the quarrel spread over the whole East; so the Emperor *Constantine called the first ecumenical *council, which was held at Nicaea in May 325. An overwhelming majority condemned Arius's position: the council defined a profession of faith, the *Creed of Nicaea, which affirmed that Christ was "the Son of God begotten of the Father, begotten and not created, consubstantial (*homoousios*) with the Father". Arius and the two bishops who refused to subscribe to the Creed were exiled. But the quarrel recommenced on the pretext that the term *homoousios* was not in the Scriptures; Arianism reappeared from the end of the reign of Constantine († 337) and was upheld by the Emperors Constantius (337-361) and Valens (364-378). On 1 Jan 360, the council of Constantinople proclaimed the official faith of the Empire: "the son is like (*homoios*) the Father", an imprecise formula that did not go against Arius's position. This "moderate" Arianism, though unacceptable to the partisans of the faith of Nicaea, was transmitted to the Goths by the preaching of Bishop Ulfila († 383) who translated the Bible into Gothic. After Valens's death, the Emperor Theodosius, a convinced Nicene, held a second ecumenical council at Constantinople which restored the faith of Nicaea (381). At the end of his reign (395), Orthodox Catholicism was the official religion of the Roman world.

Apart from the *Franks who remained *pagan, the Germanic peoples who settled in the Western Roman Empire from the 5th c. were Arians. However, the coexistence of Arians with the Catholic clergy and people posed no great problems except in the Vandal kingdom of North Africa, at the start of the *Visigothic kingdom and in *Italy at the end of the reign of *Theodoric († 529) and at the time of the *Lombard invasion (from 569). Apart from these exceptions, the Catholic episcopate maintained good relations with the Arian kings, especially in the *Burgundian kingdom.

On the whole, the Arian clergy is little known and does not seem to have tended towrads proselytism; the Germans, particularly the Goths, considered Arianism a national religion and, in contrast to the Catholics, had no universalist aims. It was for this reason that Arianism disappeared quite rapidly from the whole West: at first in Africa and Italy in the wake of the Byzantine reconquest (complete from 534 in Africa and only in 554 in Italy), then in Gaul owing to the conquests of the *Merovingians (*Aquitaine in 507 and the Burgundian kingdom in 534), and finally, thanks to the conversion of the rulers, in Visigothic *Spain in 587-589, then in Lombard Italy at the end of the 7th century.

*Aristotle.* Carved high relief on the right bay of the royal (west) portal of Chartres cathedral.

F. Cavellera, "Arianisme", *DHGE*, 1, 1930, 103-113. – M. Meslin, *Les Ariens en Occident*, Paris, 1967. – H.-I. Marrou, *L'Église de l'Antiquité tardive*, Paris, 1985, 36-55, 76-78, 206-217. – W.A. Sumruld, *Augustine and the Arians*, Selinsgrove (PA), 1994. – D.H. Williams, *Ambrose of Milan and the End of the Arian-Nicene Conflicts*, Oxford, 1995.

Michèle Gaillard

**ARISTOTLE, ARISTOTELIANISM**

**The West.** The history of medieval thought coincides to a great extent with that of the reception, interpretation and utilization of the works of Aristotle. Examining this question from the point of view of Christian culture (the situation is different in the Islamic world and the Jewish world), we can schematically distinguish two periods: the first, from the 3rd to the 11th c., when Aristotle was known only as a logician, and the second, from the 12th to the 14th c., when the whole of the *corpus aristotelicum* was rediscovered.

Towards the end of the 3rd c., Marius Victorinus translated Porphyry's *Isagoge*, which had recently become the standard introduction to the *Categoriae*, into Latin; eighty years later, Albinus (or perhaps Vetius Agorius Praetextatus) drew up the *Categoriae decem*, a recast Latin version of a Greek paraphrase of Aristotle's *Categoriae*: thus began to be outlined the project of a "Latin *organon*" that would be realized more than two centuries later by *Boethius. The latter's working plan was much more ambitious: it was to put "into the Roman language" and expound all Aristotle's writings on *logic, *ethics and *nature, so as to show their substantial convergence with the dialogues of Plato. In fact, in some fifteen years (504-520) of intense work, Boethius managed to prepare versions of the *Isagoge*, the *Categoriae*, the *De interpretatione*, the *Topics*, the *Sophistical refutations*, the *Prior* and perhaps *Posterior Analytics*, accompanied by commentaries (two for the *Isagoge* and the *De interpretatione*, one for the *Categoriae* and probably the *Topics* and the *Analytics*) which summed up with no particular originality the Greek exegetical tradition of the 3rd and 4th centuries. Boethius's contemporaries were capable of profiting only in part from his vast work. Thanks to the evidence of *Cassiodorus, we know that the monks of *Vivarium had already ruled out of their working programme the *Analytics*, the *Topics* and the *Refutations*; and the situation worsened during the phase of cultural stagnation that lasted from about 650 to 750. Recovery began in the Carolingian period, when *Alcuin rediscovered the *Categoriae decem* and Boethius's version of the *De interpretatione*. Between the 9th and the 11th cc., the *Isagoge*, the authentic *Categoriae* and, at least in part, the *Topics* also began to circulate again: studied and commented on, these texts and the reading that Boethius had given of them represented until the mid 12th c. the basis of logical training, and provided the terminology, the conceptual instruments and a number of the main problems of philosophical and theological debate.

Around 1130 opened the second, decisive phase of medieval Aristotelianism: that of the true discovery of Aristotle – the whole Aristotle – and his establishment as the supreme authority. James of Venice, Henry Aristippus and other anonymous translators prepared integral Greco-Latin versions of fundamental works like the two *Analytics*, the *Physics*, the *De generatione*, the *De anima*, the *Parva naturalia*, and partial versions of the *Metaphysics*, the *Nicomachean Ethics* and the *Meteorologica*. At the same time there developed a movement of *translations from Arabic to Latin, to which we owe the first circulation in the West of the *De caelo*, the first three books of the *Meteorologica* and numerous pseudo-Aristotelian treatises, among them the very influential *De causis*. This movement continued until the early 13th c. with Michael Scot, who translated a number of commentaries by *Averroes accompanied by the Aristotelian text, thus contributing a new and more complete version of the *Metaphysics*, Philip of Tripoli, discoverer of the *Secretum secretorum* and Hermann the German, who applied himself to the *Rhetoric* and Averroes's commentary on the *Poetics*. In the middle of the century a new generation of Hellenists arrived on the scene, whose contribution would be decisive. In 1246-1247 *Robert Grosseteste produced the first complete version of the *Nicomachean Ethics*, accompanied by a vast corpus of Hellenistic and Byzantine glosses, while Nicholas of Sicily and Bartholomew of Messina tackled pseudo-Aristotelian writings like the *De mundo*, the *Problemata* and the *Physionomia*. Finally it was the turn of the greatest and most productive medieval translator, *William of Moerbeke, who between 1260 and 1280 retranslated or revised nearly all the earlier versions of Aristotelian texts, and made the first Latin translation of works like the *Politics* and the *Poetics*, as well as several Greek commentaries.

The diffusion of the new "Aristotelian library" was neither immediate nor unopposed. Though the whole *Organon* was secured in the second half of the 12th c. (*John of Salisbury made use of it in his *Metalogicon* of 1159), the non-logical texts circulated more slowly. Among the causes of this difficulty in acceptance must certainly be counted the hostile attitude at first manifested by the ecclesiastical hierarchy. A first censure fell from the synod of Paris in 1210, which forbade the teaching of "Aristotle's books of natural philosophy" under pain of *excommunication; five years later, the statute of the arts *faculty, prepared by the papal legate *Robert of Courson, prescribed the teaching of the *Organon* and eventually the *Ethics*, while avoiding "Aristotle's books of *metaphysics and natural philosophy". Intended to protect sacred science from the infiltrations of pagan thought, these interdictions were partially softened in 1231 by *Gregory IX, who maintained them while waiting for a commission of theologians to examine the Aristotelian doctrines and eliminate their errors, so that "having taken away all that is suspect, we can freely study the rest without hesitation".

*Innocent IV in 1245 and *Urban IV in 1263 still dreamed anachronistically of this project of an expurgated edition, which was abruptly halted by the death of a commissary, but which would in any case have been unachievable in the face of the growing circulation of translations, the diffusion of Averroes's commentaries and the gradual entry of the Aristotelian works into university *curricula*. The decisive turning-point was marked here by the statute of the arts faculty of *Paris (1255) which adopted as "textbooks" practically all Aristotle's writings then known. This was a permanent victory, whose significance was not confined to Paris: though he had already been favourably received at *Oxford, *Cologne and *Padua, it was only from this date that Aristotle became the foundation of philosophical teaching in all the European *universities. During the 14th c., often unjustly presented as an anti-Aristotelian century, this privileged institutional position was further reinforced, thanks to the public support now given by the ecclesiastical and university authorities who imposed, as an alternative to the risky novelties of *moderns* like *Ockham and *Nicholas of Autrécourt, fidelity to the Christian Aristotelianism of the *antiqui doctores* (*Albert the Great, *Thomas Aquinas, *Giles of Rome). The new *cursus* of studies of the university of Paris, published in 1366, reaffirmed the central character of the *corpus aristotelicum* in the programmes of the arts faculty; programmes that were to suffer no substantial modifications on this point, even with the reform promoted in 1452 by Cardinal Guillaume d'*Estouteville.

The influence exercised by Aristotelian thought on the culture of the later Middle Ages was so vast and so deep that it is impossible to define exactly its nature and its limits. Much of the philosophical literature of the 13th, 14th and 15th cc. consisted of commentaries on Aristotle, which pursued aims at once exegetical and theoretical: expounding, explaining and interpreting his works became the occasion, and the incitement, to isolate and discuss a set of problems interesting in themselves. But the heritage of the "Philosopher" was not limited to this: still more than a set of ideas and theories, he transmitted to scholastic philosophers and theologians a scientific ideal, an organic and hierarchical conception of knowledge, the principal instruments of logical demonstration and analysis, a set of principles and definitions, certain fundamental conceptual pairs (*act and potency, *form and matter, *substance and accidents) and a precise scientific terminology. It is thus erroneous and reductive to present Aristotelianism as one of the "currents" of *scholasticism. In reality, it was its intellectual strength, less defined but much more invasive than a "current of thought": it was the horizon, the form, the "language" of different or even conflicting theoretical experiments, of a multiplicity of "Aristotelianisms" related by their common subject-matter, their methods of argument and their sources, more than by the identity of their contents.

M. Grabmann, *Methoden und Hilfsmittel des Aristotelesstudiums im Mittelalter*, Munich, 1939. – M. Grabmann, *I divieti ecclesiastici di Aristotele sotto Innocenzo III e Gregorio IX*, Rome, 1941. – D. A. Callus, "The Introduction of Aristotelian Learning at Oxford", *PBA*, 29, 1943, 229-281. – M. Grabmann, "Aristoteles in zwölfen Jahrhundert", *MS*, 12, 1950, 138-150. – F. van Steenberghen, *Aristotle in the West. The Origins of Latin Aristotelianism*, Louvain, 1955. – L. Minio-Paluello, *Opuscula. The Latin Aristotle*, Amsterdam, 1972. – P. Marangon, *Alle origini dell'aristotelismo padovano (sec. XII-XIII)*, Padua, 1977. – B. G. Dod, "Aristoteles latinus", *The Cambridge History of Later Medieval Philosophy*, Cambridge, 1982, 45-79. – C. H. Lohr, "The Medieval Interpretation of Aristotle", *ibid.*, 80-98. – *Aristotle and his Medieval Interpreters*, R. Bosley (ed.), M. Tweedale (ed.), Calgary, 1992. – L. Bianchi, E. Randi, *Les Vérités dissonantes. Aristote à la fin du Moyen Âge*, Paris, 1993. – J. Marenbon (ed.), *Aristotle in Britain during the Middle Ages. Proceedings of the International Conference at Cambridge, 8-11 April 1994*, Turnhout, 1996. – C. J. Nederman, *Medieval Aristotelianism and its Limits*, Aldershot, 1997. – L. Bianchi, "Aristote à Paris, 1210-1366", *Censure et liberté intellectuelle à l'Université de Paris (XIII^e-XIV^e siècles)*, Paris, 1999, 87-162.

Luca Bianchi

**Byzantium.** The influence of Aristotle's thought was considerable in Byzantium. The manuscripts of his works occupy the fourth place after those of the New Testament, John Chrysostom and *John of Damascus. His treatises were frequently commented upon, particularly his *logic (T. Prodrome, J. Pediasimos, Michael of Ephesus). From 1165, the professor of philosophy at the imperial school had to teach only Aristotle. In intellectual circles, polemic between the partisans of the Stagyrite and those of Plato was revived in the first half of the 15th c. by *Gemistus Plethon.

M. Cacouros, "De la pensée grecque à la pensée byzantine", *Encyclopédie Philosophique Universelle*, A. Jacob (dir.), 4, *Le Discours Philosophique*, J.-F. Mattei (dir.), Paris, 1998, 1362-1384, 1377-1380 (bibl.).

Michel Cacouros

**ARLES.** In the 4th and 5th cc., Arles was the periodic residence of the emperor, an active administrative centre and the meeting-place of the council of the Seven Provinces. This central status explains why the town kept an important political function under the *Visigoths and *Ostrogoths and justifies the claims of its *bishops not to come under the authority of the *metropolitan bishop of *Vienne as well as the establishment of an autonomous ecclesiastical provice in 450. The early Middle Ages were for Arles a time of withdrawal within a town wall restored under Theodoric, the time when the town's religious topography was established (*cathedral, Saint-Étienne, monastery of Saint-Césaire). After a certain eclipse under the *Franks, the town became a capital once more when, to fight against the *Saracens, the Provençal counties regrouped under the authority of a duke residing within its walls. The dislocation of the Carolingian Empire ended in the formation of a kingdom of *Provence, then of *Burgundy, also called the kingdom of Arles; but from the end of the 10th c. this title of *caput regni Burgundie* did not correspond to any real function.

On the other hand, until the 12th c. Arles was the residence of the counts of Provence and of the *archbishop, rich and powerful by reason of a considerable *patrimony and his pre-eminence over all the Provençal bishops. In the 12th c., the powers of the *count and the archbishop were threatened by the consulate (1131), one of the oldest in Provence, which finally came to an end in 1251. The period from the late 10th c. to the mid 13th saw a real expansion: topographical expansion south and north of the city, demographic growth (around 1270-1320, with more than 2,200 hearths, Arles was the second town in Provence), economic prosperity (activity of the *port in connection with Italy), and a great deal of ecclesiastical building (cathedral of Saint-Étienne, later Saint-Trophime, establishment of a network of 15 *parishes, installation of convents of *mendicant orders and houses of *Templars and *Hospitallers, and above all the building of the abbey of Saint-Pierre de Montmajour). The existence of the cemeteries of Les Aliscamps and the situation of Arles on one of the routes leading to *Saint-Gilles and Santiago de *Compostela were the origin of legends, in which historical figures mingled with heroes of *chansons de geste*.

By contrast, the following period saw the town's decline. From the end of the 12th c., the counts got into the habit of residing at Aix, then in the 14th and 15th cc. at Tarascon. From 1251 the town, subject to the count of *Anjou, became the see of a comital *viguier*. In the 13th c., the archbishop lost his *temporal power and his pre-eminence over the Provençal episcopate; then the metropolitan see of Arles was reserved for prelates occupying high positions at the papal court of *Avignon and nearly always absent. In 1471, a *province of Avignon was created and that of Arles reduced to three *dioceses (Arles, *Marseille and Toulon). In the 14th and 15th cc., the town suffered from plagues and wars: it lost more than half its population. On the commercial level, it was now no more than an annexe of Avignon, and remained a great centre only of *agriculture and *animal husbandry. Within its walls, building was rare (building of a Gothic chevet at Saint-Trophime in connection with the cult of the Blessed Louis Aleman, archbishop of Arles from 1423 to 1450). Arles possessed one of the most important Jewish communities in Provence, destroyed in 1484. It was also the home of the author of the only vernacular Provençal chronicle, Bertrand Boysset (1365-1415).

L. Royer, "Arles", *DHGE*, 4, 1930, 231-243. – J. Hubert, "La topographie religieuse d'Arles au VI^e siècle", *CAr*, 1947, 17-27. – P.-A. Février, *Le Développement urbain en Provence de l'époque romaine à la fin du XIV^e siècle*, Paris, 1964. – J.-M. Rouquette, *Provence romane*, 1, Saint-Léger-Vauban, 1974 ("La nuit des temps"). – L. Stouff, *Arles à la fin du Moyen Âge*, Aix-en-Provence, Lille, 1986.

Louis Stouff

**ARMAGH.** Old *Irish *Ard Macha* ("the hill of Macha") in the present County Armagh, traditionally regarded as the site of St *Patrick's principal church, and later seat of the primacy, is situated about 3 kilometres from *Emain Macha*, site of the prehistoric "capital" of Ulster, one of the five great provincial kingdoms of the pre-Christian period. Although there is no mention of the site in Patrick's own writings, and although other early traditions associate him with Downpatrick (County Down), recent archaeological excavations in the city have uncovered signs of Neolithic settlement and 5th-c. burials which may be associated with the earliest Christian settlement. The first documented claims to Patrician status are in the *Vita S. Patricii* by Muirchú maccu Machtheni and the anonymous *Liber Angueli* (both 7th c.). By *c.*700 Armagh was already the centre of a strong Patrician cult and laid claim to control over a widespread confederation (*paruchia*) of monastic houses supposedly founded by the saint. Its *de facto* claims were formally recognised in the 12th c., when Armagh was established as the seat of the primacy of the Irish church.

T. Ó Fiaich, "The Church of Armagh under Lay Control", *SeArm*, 5, 1969, 75-127. – R. Sharpe, "St Patrick and the See of Armagh", *CMCS*, 4, 1982, 33-59. – N.B. Aitchison, *Armagh and the Royal Centres in Early Medieval Ireland*, Woodbridge, 1994.

Dáibhí Ó Cróinín

## ARMENIA

**History.** The strategic position of the Armenian plateau beyond the Euphrates gave Greater Armenia, caught between the classical Mediterranean world and the Iranian and then Muslim East, a turbulent, fragmented and often tragic political history. Long disputed between Rome and Persia, the first kingdom of Christian Armenia, divided between the two empires in *c.*387, was extinguished in 428 and reborn only at the end of the 9th century. Rarely mistress of its own destiny in the Middle Ages, Armenia regained its autonomy only when the balance of the opposed forces that surrounded it prevented them from dominating it. However, this same precarious situation favoured Armenia on the cultural level, opening it up to numerous influences from which it managed to create its own culture based on social, religious and intellectual institutions independent of their political framework, which they outlasted.

From the 5th to the 7th c., Armenia was governed by Persian viceroys or *marzpans* residing at *Duin, several of whom belonged to the local nobility. The efforts of the Sasanids to reimpose Mazdaism on an already Christian Armenia in 450-451 provoked a violent revolt during which the nobility, united around their hereditary military commander Vardan Mamikonean, preferred martyrdom to apostasy. Armenia rose again against *Iran in 481 and 571-572, but the Sasanid period was also the time when the fundamental institutions of Armenian culture developed and took root.

On the social level, until the end of the Middle Ages Armenia preserved an Iranian aristocratic structure categorically opposed to the Greco-Roman tradition of elective magistratures. In this system called *naχarar* (noble), the great families entrenched in their almost inaccessible fortresses held not just vast principalities, but also hereditary offices that the king himself could not revoke. The Mamikonean were from generation to generation grand marshals of Armenia, like the Sūrān in Iran. This tradition of hereditary offices was so deeply anchored that, to begin with, it even extended to the dignity of patriarch or *catholicos*, in flagrant violation of the canons of the Church. The conciliar signatures of the 6th c., such as those of Meršapuh, bishop of Tarōn, and the Mamikonean family, demonstrate that the great families were also represented in the church hierarchy. The dedication of a 7th-c. church also testifies to the rights and autonomy of the rural lords: "I, Nerseh, apo[hy]pate and patrician, lord of Širak and Aršarunik', built this church in the name of the Mother of God, and in intercession for myself, and for Šušan my wife, and for Hrahat our son."

The urban network characteristic of the Greco-Roman world remained perforce foreign to this almost feudal society. The few Hellenistic towns did not survive the Sasanid destruction of the 4th c., and when urban centres reappeared in the 9th-10th cc. it was mainly on the lands of Muslim *emirs. Philologists have long told us that the titles, names and much of the vocabulary of classical Armenian date back to Iranian antecedents. On 7th-c. Armenian steles, the figures are clothed in the trousers and side-pointed tunic

Church of the Holy Cross, Aghtamar. Lake Van (Turkey), 10th c.

of the Parthian nobility. 10th-c. donors represented on their churches wear embroidered caftans and large oriental turbans, not Byzantine costume.

The seminal event that turned this Iranian society towards the West was its *conversion to Christianity. Though we now take for granted that the new faith coming from Mesopotamia first reached southern Armenia, national tradition gives priority to the mission of St Gregory the Illuminator who came from Caesarea in Cappadocia to convert the court and people of Greater Armenia early in the 4th c. (in 314 rather than 301). The *evangelization of Armenia and the consecration of St Gregory at Caesarea detached the Armenians for ever from their oriental forebears and identified the image of Armenia with its Christianity. The Armenian patriarch residing in Sasanid territory had to recognise, at least *de facto*, the jurisdiction of the King of Kings, but the latter was obliged to tolerate the new religion after the uprising of 481. The parallel distancing of the Armenian Church from Constantinople after the council of Chalcedon in 451, whose doctrine it condemned early in the 7th c. as tainted with *Nestorianism, reinforced the autocephaly of its patriarch, who had abandoned any consecration at Caesarea. The Church replaced the vanished Crown as rallying-point of Armenian loyalties, and it victoriously resisted all Byzantine attempts to force a dogmatic reconciliation in the 6th and 7th centuries.

The final indispensable element for the creation of an Armenian identity was the invention of an alphabet under the aegis of the Church by St Maštoc‘ early in the 5th century. Rapidly provided with a version of the Bible, its own liturgy and a vigorous literature, Armenia almost immediately enfranchised itself from the Greek or Syriac intellectual tutelage to which it had been subject. Thus, on the eve of the mid 7th-c. Arab conquest, the fundamental aspects of Armenian culture, its decentralized aristocratic society of Iranian type jealously guarding its privileges, its autocephalous Church upheld by an unshakably Christian ideology and its national literature, were too solidly established to be easily uprooted by political events with which they were not connected. The country's prosperity, despite the ravages of *Heraclius's campaigns against Persia, can be measured by the multiplicity of churches with which it was covered at this time.

To begin with, the appearance of the Arabs brought few changes. The nobility, threatened in its privileges by Justinian's legislation which subjected it to Roman law, and the *catholicos*, irritated by the measures taken to force him into communion with the imperial Church, accepted Arab suzerainty in 653. For their part, the new arrivals had to respect the rights of the *naχarars* in order to obtain the support of the famous Armenian cavalry in defence of the Caucasian passes against the incursions of Byzantium's *Khazar allies. The tribute levied remained relatively modest. The Muslims' initial *toleration did not encroach on Armenia's ecclesiastical autonomy, and *Catholicos* John of Ōjun, received with respect by the *caliph, was able to hold an official council of reunion with the Syrians in 725. The country's administration united the greater part of the Armenian plateau, less the southern regions, with Caucasian *Albania and Iberia in a great province named Arminīya, whose governor replaced the Sasanid *marzpan* at Duin before being transferred in 789 to Partaw, in Albania, outside the country. The few garrisons intended to ensure the strategic points interfered very little with the local powers. The country's prosperity followed its course.

This relatively stable situation was brutally modified in the early 8th c., and even more so after the accession to power of the Muslim dynasty of the *Abbasids in 750. The augmentations of tribute, the Abbasids' growing religious intolerance, accompanied by persecutions and the establishment of Arab emirates around lake Van, in the Lower Araxes valley and as far as Tiflis in Iberia, began to modify the demography and autonomy of the Armenian plateau. Attacked in their religious institutions and their power, the *naχarars* multiplied revolts, provoking by their actions the increasingly pitiless reprisals of the caliphate. Decimated in 706 and 748-750, the Armenian nobility was almost totally annihilated on the battlefield of Bagrewand in 775. Any literary or artistic activity disappeared. Abandoned by Byzantium, all of whose forces were mobilized for its own defence against the Arab assaults, Armenia went through one of the blackest periods of its history.

The gradual enfeeblement of the Abbasid caliphate, distracted in the *Caucasus by the revolt of Babek (809-837) supported by a party of Armenian princes, inaugurated a turning-point. The almost simultaneous passing of Byzantium from the defensive to the offensive in the East led to a new equilibrium on the frontiers of Armenia. Profiting from the international situation and from a series of propitious circumstances inside the country, the Bagratid family, whose rise had benefited from the support they gave the Sasanids and *Umayyads, put themselves at the head of the Armenian reawakening. Protected from Muslim attacks by the position of his ancestral domain of Sper at the far north-west of the Armenian plateau, the Bagratid prince Ašot Msaker, the "Man-eater" (806-826), restored the Armenian State. The silver mines of Sper allowed the Bagratids to buy the neighbouring territories from the descendants of their lords, impoverished or vanished in the upheavals of the previous century, among others the fortress of *Ani in Širak which they made their capital. Posing, like his ancestors, as a loyal servant of the distant caliph, Ašot Msaker profited from this to attack the local emirs with impunity and to obtain from the Abbasids the title of "Prince of Princes" of Armenia. The Armenian Church gave him its support as to a defender of the faith.

The rise to power of the Bagratid dynasty was nevertheless slow and painful despite the successes of Ašot Msaker. The division of his domains between his sons, Prince Bagarat and marshal Smbat, weakened it. Byzantium, shaken by the defeat of Amorion in 838, was in no state to offer help against the Arabs. The disastrous campaign of the Turk Bugha the Elder, sent by Caliph al-Muttawakkil in 852, devastated Armenia and ended with the captivity of all the Armenian lords, including the Bagratid brothers, at the Abbasid court of Samarra. There they were obliged to apostatize in order to escape death, with the single exception of the marshal, Smbat the Confessor.

The assassination of the caliph in 861 and the Byzantine recovery under Basil I allowed the Armenian renaissance to resume its course. Ašot the Great, son of the Confessor, resumed his ancestor's policy. In the face of the other Armenian principalities, divided and dishonoured by the return of the apostates of Samarra, Ašot I, who was always supported by the Church, reconstituted his domains and asserted his power. In 884, he had himself crowned king by the *catholicos* with the tacit consent of the emperor and the caliph, who each sent a crown for the ceremony, which marked the reappearance of an autonomous State in Armenia after more than four centuries.

The reign of Ašot the Great inaugurated a brilliant period for Armenian culture. All over the plateau, large monastic agglomerations, some of which were royal foundations, replaced the isolated churches of previous times and served as cultural centres. Literary tradition revived in the 10th c. under the aegis of *Catholicos* John the Historian and the great mystical poet Gregory of Narek. The king, as head of the Bagratid family, extended his authority over all the branches of his house, from Tarōn in the south to Iberia in the north, where Ašot had his relation the curopalate Adernerses crowned. The marriages of his daughters to the prince of Siwnik‘ in the north-east and lord Arcruni of Vaspurakan, who held the lands surrounding lake Van, equally augmented his power. The family's prestige was raised still further by the genealogy that traced it back to the house of David and thus of Jesus. However apocryphal these claims, they were accepted by contemporaries, whether *Catholicos* John in Armenia or the Emperor Constantine Porphyrogenitus in *Constantinople.

This brilliant beginning of Ašot I's kingdom ended with a rude check immediately after his death, since it rested on nothing but the king's strong personality, as *Catholicos* John had noticed, and not on solid constitutional bases. On the international level, the autonomous status of his State was compromised by the refusal of the Byzantines and Arabs to allow him the title of king, confining him to the formulae of *archōn tōn archontōn* and *baṭriq al-baṭariqa*, equivalent to the former title of "Prince of Princes". In his own country, the king was theoretically the suzerain of all the other princes, but the centrifugal tradition of the system of *naχarars*, whose loyalty rarely went beyond the interests of their house, hampered all attempts at control or centralization. Even in his own family, the new king Smbat I (890-912/914) had to oppose the ambitions of his uncle. Interspersed with Muslim emirates, the Armenian territory presented no unity. The royal domain in the north-east offered an excellent refuge, but was too distant to dominate the entire plateau. The failure to reconquer the former capital of Duin, abandoned most of the time to Muslim emirs, divided Armenia in two and made it vulnerable to attacks from Azerbaijan. Despite all his efforts, Smbat could not simultaneously face the intrigues of his family, his abandonment by Adernerses of Iberia, the rivalry of Gagik Arcruni, who had himself crowned king of Vaspurakan in 908 by emir Yūsuf of Azerbaijan, and especially the attacks of the latter who took Duin after the devastation of the town by the earthquake of 893, which had driven out even the *catholicos*. Beaten after 20 years of struggle, Smbat the Martyr was forced to surrender to Yūsuf, who had him executed after his refusal to accept *Islam, and exposed his headless body on a cross at Duin.

The death of the martyr king brutally sobered his rivals, allowing the fortunes of his kingdom to be redressed. Gagik I Arcruni put himself at the head of the resistance against Yūsuf, while Smbat's son, Ašot II the Iron King, took refuge once more in his distant domain, resuming for the third time the Bagratids' work of reconstruction. Supported by *Catholicos* John the Historian and by a Byzantine *army, as well as by Adernerses of Iberia, who had him crowned king in 914/915, Ašot II rebuilt his power. The disgrace of Yūsuf, who had revolted against the caliph, even gained him the title of *Šahanšah*, King of Kings, which extended his authority over the Muslim emirs as well as over his Christian vassals.

This time, the king's work was more lasting. His successors Abas I (928-952/953), Ašot III the Merciful (952/953-977), Smbat II (977-989/990) and finally Gagik I (989/990-1017/1020?) succeeded each other without hindrance. Armenia's cultural development continued with renewed vigour, and the prestige of the Bagratids reached its apogee under Ašot III, crowned at Ani, which he made his capital in 961 and where the Bagratids were rejoined by the *catholicos* in 991. Even the emirs of Duin recognised his suzerainty, and the Arab sources mention that the king stopped paying any tribute to the caliphate, thus demonstrating his absolute independence. Ašot III's support of the Church against attempts at separation by the sees of Siwnik‘ and Albania, as well as against the heresy of the Thondrakians and a recrudescence of Chalcedonianism, condemned once more by the council of Ani in 969, gained him the constant support of the churchmen. The growth in international trade passing through Ani favoured Armenia's prosperity: 10th-c. Arab geographers praise its wealth of minerals and plants, its fine horses, its white falcons and its manufacture of metals, ceramics, glass and especially dyed and embroidered luxury fabrics, "whose equivalent is nowhere found [and] which are virtually unrivalled in quantity and quality". Enriched by this trade, Ani rapidly grew and was covered with monuments. When Basil II's victorious campaign led him in 1000-1001 to the gates of Armenia and all the rulers hastened to tender him their submission, only Gagik I felt sufficiently powerful to stay at home at Ani, "since he reckoned that it would be degrading for him to appear".

Two elements contributed to compromise these fine results fatally. As has already been noted, the king never succeeded in dominating the separatism of his vassals. Perhaps scenting danger, all the kings and princes of Armenia obeyed Ašot III's order to assemble in 974 in the neighbouring province of Hark‘ while the Emperor John I Tzimisces and the Byzantine army skirted the Armenian frontier. But the "assembly of Hark‘" was a unique case. Gagik I Arcruni had already taken the title of king of Vaspurakan in 908, irremediably dividing Armenia in two. The dynasty of Siwnik‘ followed his example before the end of the century. More gravely, faced with the ambitions of his brother Mušeł and his younger son Gourgēn Kiwrikē, Ašot III had to dismember his own State by creating for them the secondary kingdoms of Kars-Vanand in 961-962 in the west and Lori-Tašir in the north of the kingdom of Ani in *c.*972. Gagik I's successor, Yovhannēs-Smbat (1017/1020?-1040), spent his whole reign fighting against his brother, the anti-king Ašot IV the Brave. A century after the coronation of Ašot I, a series of Bagratid kinglets had replaced him. The same fate awaited Vaspurakan, divided into three in *c.*972, and Siwnik‘, split into two in *c.*987. The Iberian Bagratids, themselves divided between Abkhasia, Iberia-K‘artli and the principality of Tao (in Armenian Tayk‘), pursued their own interests, increasingly cut off from their Armenian kinsmen by their adherence to the Chalcedonian *Orthodoxy of their subjects. Only the prestige of Gagik I of Ani could assert his authority outside his immediate domain. Armenia, broken up into small States, was incapable of being a match for an enemy from outside.

This danger was not slow to manifest itself. The Byzantine Emperor, Christ's image on earth, could tolerate no equals, and the enfeeblement of Islam at the end of the 10th c. no longer provided him with a counterbalance. The dogmatic polemics between Constantinople and Armenia, renewed after the council of Ani and succeeding to the relative calm of the previous period, exacerbated their relations. The inexorable eastward advance of Byzantium began to eat away at Armenian lands. The first to be engulfed, Bagratid Tarōn became a Byzantine *theme from 966-967. The subsequent campaigns of Basil II saw the annexation of Tao-Tayk‘, to which the western marches of Armenia were joined, probably after the death of Gagik I, to create the theme of Iberia.

In 1021-1022, harassed by Daylamite raids from the east, the last Arcruni king surrendered Vaspurakan to Byzantium, which made it into the theme of Basprakania in exchange for vast domains in *Cappadocia. Relying on the imprudent testament of Yovhannēs-Smbat, by which he bequeathed his kingdom to the emperor in the absence of direct descendants, Michael IV claimed Ani from its last king, Gagik II, son of Ašot the Brave. The forced abdication of Gagik, also compensated by lands in Cappadocia, after his enticement to Constantinople was coupled with the surrender of Ani in 1045 by the *catholicos* to the Empire, which designated the town as capital of the theme of Iberia and Greater Armenia. Thus, before the middle of the 11th c., only the little States of Loṙi and Kars, with part of Siwnik‘, still existed in Greater Armenia, which the *catholicos* also left for four centuries. The great *Seljuk invasions that captured Ani in 1064 and Kars the following year, pushing king Gagik-Abas into Cappadocia, completed the destruction of the Armenian States. The disappearance after 1080 of all the legitimate heirs, Bagratid or Arcruni, the massive migration of the Armenian nobility into Cappadocia and *Cilicia, then into *Crimea and the Balkans – which enriched the Empire and created new centres, while impoverishing the homeland –, put an end to any dream of political autonomy.

The prosperity of Ani, sold in 1072 by Alp Arslan to the Kurdish dynasty of the Shāddādids, lords of Ganja and Duin, continued under its new masters. Some small centres persisted in Loṙi and eastern Siwnik‘ or Xac‘ēn (modern Karabagh). The isolation of the monasteries allowed them to maintain some intellectual activity. The Bagratids of Iberia reunited and consolidated their States after the fall of their Armenian kinsmen and recaptured Ani in 1199. Northern Armenia flourished briefly in the 13th c. under the Christianized Kurdish dynasty of the Zak‘arids: they tried to re-establish the *naχarar* system on the basis of old and new families, and to renew intellectual lustre by encouraging new monastic foundations. But their status vis-à-vis Iberia, of which they were probably vassals despite their show of independence, remains doubtful. This last awakening was brief. In 1236, the last Zak‘arids wisely acknowledged *Mongol rule; all trace of them is lost before the end of the century. From then on, save for some enclaves lost in the mountains, only the return of a *catholicos* to his former see of *Ejmiacin in 1441 and the monastic centres and those of the diaspora preserved the idea of an Armenian identity. The plateau of Armenia, invaded by the Timurids and by semi-nomadic Turkoman tribes, then conquered by the *Ottomans who partitioned it with the Safavids of Persia at the start of the 16th c., lost all trace of autonomy until the 20th century.

J. Laurent, *L'Arménie entre Byzance et les Turcs seljoucides* [sic] *jusque'en 1081*, Paris, 1914. – S. Der Nersessian, *Armenia and the Byzantine Empire*, Cambridge (MA), 1945. – R. Grousset, *Histoire de l'Arménie des origines à 1071*, Paris, 1947 (outdated). – V. Minorsky, "The Shāddādids of Ani", *Studies in Caucasian History*, London, 1953, 79-106. – C. Toumanoff, "Armenia and Georgia", *CMH*, 4, J. Hussey (ed.), 1962, 593-637 (2 vol.). – C. Toumanoff, *Studies in Christian Caucasian History*, Georgetown, 1963. – H. Manadian, *The Trade and Cities of Armenia in Relation to Ancient World Trade*, N. G. Garsoïan (tr.), Lisbon, 1965. – S. Der Nersessian, *The Armenians*, London, 1969. – N. Adontz, *Armenia in the Period of Justinian. The Political Conditions Based on the Naχarar System*, N. G. Garsoïan (ed., tr.), Lisbon, 1970. – K. Yuzbashyan, "L'Administration byzantine en Arménie aux X$^{e}$-XI$^{e}$ siècles", *REArm*, new series, 10, 1973-1974, 139-183. – A. Ter Ghewondyan, *The Arab Emirates in Bagratid Armenia*, N. G. Garsoïan (tr.), Lisbon, 1976. – J. Laurent, *L'Arménie entre Byzance et l'Islam depuis la conquête arabe jusque'en 886*, M. Canard (ed.), Lisbon, 1980 (new ed. revised and updated). – *Histoire des Arméniens*, G. Dédéyan (ed.), Toulouse, 1982 (uneven). – C. Cahen, *La Turquie pré-ottomane*, Istanbul-Paris, 1988. – R. Hovannirian (ed.), *History of the Armenian People*, 2 vol., London-New York, 1996. – N. Garsoïan, *L'Eglise arménienne et le Grand Schisme d'Orient*, *CSCO*, 574, subs. 1000, Louvain, 1998.

Nina G. Garsoïan

**Historians.** Historiography followed very closely on the creation of the national alphabet in Armenia at the start of the 5th c., and formed one of the main branches of its literature. It was perpetuated throughout the Middle Ages and faithfully reflects the society for which it was created. The greatest problem it poses us, that of the dating and attribution of sources, due to its late manuscripts, is a natural outcome of the country's deeply perturbed history. Thus for over a century, the date of Moses of Xoren's *History of Arm nia* has oscillated between the 5th and the 9th century.

Arising after the country's conversion, and especially after the great rebellion of 451 against the effort of the Sasanids to reimpose Mazdaism on Armenia, Armenian historiography was hostile from the start to any non-Christian society, Persian or Muslim. Its earliest monuments, the *Cycle* attributed to Agathangelos on the evangelization of Armenia by St Gregory the Illuminator, and Koriwn's *Life of Maštoc‘*, praising the inventor of the alphabet, are essentially *hagiography. The central works that form the Armenian received tradition, Agathangelos, Koriwn and Moses, followed by the panegyrics of the heroes of 451 by Lazar of P‘arpi and Elišē who liken the Armenians to the Maccabees, affirm their devotion to Christianity to the point of martyrdom and turn towards the West. Only the anonymous 5th-c. *Epic histories*, falsely attributed to Faustus of Byzantium (P‘awstos Buzand), which rest on lost oral sources, reflect the country's Iranian past. Products of an aristocratic society, the so-called "Histories of Armenia" are often limited to the praise of one of the great families, such as those of Lazar and the *Epic histories* for the Mamikonean or that of Moses for the Bagratids. However Moses, among others, also seeks to place Armenia's history in a wider context.

Historiography languished after its great flowering in the early Christian period. Only the *History* attributed to Bishop Sebēos and that of the priest Lewond menion the end of the Sasanids and the Arab conquest. The restoration of the Armenian kingdom by the Bagratids is described by Catholicos John VI Drasχanakertc‘i the Historian and, for the later period, by Stephen of Tarōn called Asołik, of whom only the last part is contemporary. The history of the rival southern dynasty, Thomas Arcruni's *History of the house of Arcruni*, gives less by way of political and chronological detail, but it paints a wonderful picture of the turbulent society of the Armeno-Arab wars. The *History of the Albanians of the Caucasus* is part of the compilation of Moses Drasχanakertc‘i or Kałankatuac‘i. The fall of the kingdoms and the *Seljuk invasions form the subject of Aristakēs Lastiverc‘i's brief *Account of the misfortunes of the Armenian nation* and the *Chronicle* of Matthew of Edessa (Uṙhayec‘i) which, despite its numerous faults, furnishes us with important and sometimes unique information on Armenian hostility to the Byzantine reconquest and on the next generation of the vanished realms.

The Zak‘arid renaissance and the intellectual activity of the monasteries produced a great new period of historiography in the 13th century. The *History* of Kirakos Ganjakec‘i is one of the main sources for the *Mongols, and Stephen (Step‘annos) Ōrbelean's *History of the province of Sisakan* clarifies the importance of Siunik‘, governed by his family, and the great monastery of Tat‘ew, of which he was archbishop. Even the brief *Historical summary* of the scholar Vardan the Great (Arewelc'i) reveals the continuation of the cultural tradition and the relations between Greater Armenia and *Cilicia in his own time. There are even some useful details in Samuel of Ani's *Chronological tables* despite their aridity. These works mark the end of the great historiographical tradition in an Armenia dismembered by the Mongol and Turkoman invasions, except for a brief reappearance in the second half of the 17th century.

Łewond the Priest, *Histoire des guerres et des conquêtes arabes en Arménie par Ghévond le prêtre*, G. Shahnazarean (tr.), Paris, 1856. – Matt'ēos Uṙhayec'i, *Chronique de Matthieu d'Edesse*, E. Dulaurier (tr.), Paris, 1858. – Kirakos Ganjakec'i, "Histoire du vartabied Kirakos de Gandzak", *Deux historiens arméniens*, M.-F. Brosset (tr.), St Petersburg, 1861. – Step'annos Orbelean, *Histoire de la Siounie*, M.-F. Brosset (tr.), St Petersburg, 1866 (2 vol.). – Samuēl Aniec'i, "Samouel d'Ani. Tables chronologiques", *Collection d'historiens arméniens*, M.-F. Brosset (ed.), vol. 2, St Petersburg, 1876, 339-483 (reprinted Amsterdam, 1979). – Sebēos [?], *Histoire d'Héraclius par l'évêque Sébéos*, F. Macler (tr.), Paris, 1905. – Asołik, *Histoire universelle par Étienne Asołik de Tarōn*, 2ᵉ partie, F. Macler (tr.), Paris, 1917. – Movsēs Drasxanakertc'i Kałankatuac'i, *History of the Caucasian Albanians*, C. J. F. Dowsett (tr.), Oxford, 1961. – Koriwn, *The Life of Maštoc'*, B. Norehad (tr.), New York, 1964. – Aristakēs Lastiverc'i, *Récit des malheurs de la nation arménienne*, M. Canard (tr.), H. Berbérian (tr.), Brussels, 1973. – Agat'angelos, *Agathangelos. History of the Armenians*, R. W. Thomson (tr.), Albany, 1976. – Movsēs Xorenac'i, *Mosēs Khorenats'i. History of the Armenians*, R. W. Thomson (tr.), Cambridge (MA), 1978. – Ełišē, *Elishē. History of Vardan and the Armenian War*, R.W. Thomson (tr.), Cambridge (MA), 1982. – T'ovma Arcruni, *Thomas Artsruni. History of the House of the Artsruni*, R.W. Thomson (tr.), Detroit, 1985. – Yovhannēs Drasxanakertc'i, *History of Armenia*, K. H. Maksoudian (tr.), Atlanta, 1987. – P. P'awstos Buzand, *The Epic Histories attributed to P'awstos Buzand (Buzandaran Patmut'iwnk')*, N. G. Garsoïan (tr.), Cambridge (MA), 1989. – Vardan Arewelc'i, "The Historical Compilation of Vardan Arewelc'i", R. W. Thomson (tr.), *DOP*, 43, 1989, 139-183. – Łazar P'arpec'i, *History of the Armenians*, R. W. Thomson (tr.), Atlanta (GA), 1991.

C. J. F. Dowsett, "Armenian Historiography", *Historians of the Middle East*, B. Lewis (ed.), P. Holt (ed.), London, 1962, 258-268. – M. Abeghian [Abełyan], *Istorija drevnearmjanskoj literatury*, Erevan, 1944-1946; re-ed. 1975.

Nina G. Garsoïan

**Cultural centres.** The aristocratic society of medieval Armenia was hostile to the towns, which were only rarely cultural centres, a role generally reserved for the monastic communities. From the late 9th c., a multitude of monasteries was established in remote parts of Armenia, among others at Hałbat, Sanahin and Hoṙomos, the Bagratid necropolises of the north, Makenoc' and Tat'ew in Siunik', Varag, Ałbak, Narek and Muš in the south. In these large agglomerations, purely religious buildings were surrounded by libraries and rooms for the translation, copying and illumination of manuscripts, and for discussions and philosophical and theological teaching which transformed them into veritable academies. Thus, the importance of Narek in the 10th c. followed the renown of its great theologian and mystic poet, Gregory of Narek.

The isolation of these cultural centres allowed them to survive the *Seljuk invasions and maintain an intellectual continuity after the fall of the Bagratid Crown in the 11th century. The Zak'arid renaissance of the 13th c. added a number of new foundations, such as Sałmosavank', Yovhannavank' and Gełard in the Araxes valley, Hałarcin, Goš, Kec'aris, Haṙichavank' and Marmašen in the north and east, and Glajor and Ganjasar in the east. The polemics aroused by their opposition to attempts at union with the Catholic Church in Cilicia, as well as with the Friars Unitors, created by Rome in the 14th c. to reconcile Greater Armenia, provoked a constant intellectual activity in all these centres. The centre of opposition was Tat'ew, housing a total of about 500 monks led by the great theologian St Gregory of Tat'ew, whose successors formed a school. Despite the troubles of the time and the distance of its see, Tat'ew's extensive connections even allowed it to bring painters "of the Frankish nation" to decorate its cathedral. Likewise, Armenian customary law received its first codification in the work of Mxit'ar Goš. Philosophy, rhetoric, calligraphy and illumination were part of the programme of the "second Athens" of Glajor. The works of the earliest Armenian historians have only survived thanks to the copies made at Bałeš (Bitlis), near lake Van. After the *Ottoman and Safavid conquests of the 15th c., the monastic centres, recognised as perpetual foundations or **waqfs* protected by Muslim law, survived and even prepared the Armenian cultural renaissance of the 17th century.

*Haghbat*, Milan, 1970 ("Documenti di architettura armena", 1). – *Sanahin*, 1970 (*ibid.*, 3). – *G(e)ghard*, 1973 (*ibid.*, 6). – *Goshavank*, 1974 (*ibid.*, 7). – *Ketcharis*, 1982 (*ibid.*, 11). – *Haghartzin*, 1984 (*ibid.*, 13). – *K'asakhi vank'er*, 1986 (*ibid.*, 15). – *Gandzasar*, 1987 (*ibid.*, 17). – *Sevan*, 1987 (*ibid.*, 18).

*Medieval Armenian Culture*, T.J. Samuelian (ed.), M.E. Stone (ed.), Chico (CA), 1984.

Nina G. Garsoïan

**ARMENIAN LITERATURE.** Armenian literature begins with the invention of an individual script by Mesrop Maštoc' (*c.*360-439). Although familiar with Greek and Syriac, Armenian church leaders needed a written form of Armenian for missionary purposes. Close contacts with Edessa, *Cappadocia and *Constantinople encouraged translation from Syriac and Greek of theological works (Bible, liturgy, patristics), followed by secular texts used in the schools of late Antiquity (philosophy, grammar, rhetoric).

The first translators also composed original works, the earliest being a *Life of Maštoc'* by his pupil Koriwn, and a treatise on the problem of *evil by another pupil, Eznik. Historical writing rapidly developed. Notable are Agat'angełos on the work of Gregory the Illuminator and the conversion of Armenia; the *Buzandaran* for the conflict of traditional and Christian mores in the 4th c.; Ełiše, for the Armenian response to Sasanian oppression in the 5th century. The most significant historian is Movsēs Xorenac'i, who shaped ancient myths and traditions into a coherent account of Armenia from its origins to the death of Maštoc'.

Theological writing gives information about the christological debates and the *schism of the Eastern churches (especially the *Book of Letters*, for correspondence between Armenians, Syrians, Greeks and Georgians, 5th to 13th c.). Much patristic literature was translated. There is an extensive original homiletic and hagiographical literature. Biblical commentaries abound; Step'anos of Siunik' (8th c.), Hamam (9th c.), Grigor Narekac'i (10th c.), Nersēs Lambronac'i, *Nersēs Šnorhali (both 12th c.), Vardan Arewelc'i, Gēorg of Skewra (both 13th c.). Canon law was first codified by Yovhannēs Awjnec'i (catholicos 717-728), and secular law by Mxit'ar Goš in 1187. Scientific subjects were rarely pursued (except for Anania of Širak, 7th c.) until the 12th c., when Arabic influence was strong, especially in *medicine. Finally, fables and gnomic sayings were a popular genre.

Armenian historians provide valuable information on the Muslim invasions, Byzantium, the *Caucasus, the *crusades and the *Mongols. Also important are 13th-c. Armenian adaptations of the *Syrian Chronicle* of *Michael the Syrian and the *Georgian Chronicles*. Following the crusades and close Roman contacts with the Armenian kingdom in *Cilicia, Latin missionaries of the *Dominican Order were active in Greater Armenia and sparked theological controversies. *Albert the Great and *Thomas Aquinas were both translated. The Latins were attacked by Grigor Tat'ewac'i (1340-1411), the last great traditional Armenian theologian.

The most famous Armenian religious poets are Grigor of Narek (945-1010?) and Nersēs Šnorhali (catholicos 1166-1173). Secular themes become popular from the 13th c., though much of the love poetry has mystical overtones (Konstantin Erznkac'i, Yovhannēs T'ulkuranc'i). Motifs of exile now appear (Mkrtich' Nałaš, 15th c.), reflecting the ever widening diaspora of Armenians.

H. Thorossian, *Histoire de la littérature arménienne. Des origines jusqu'à nos jours*, Paris, 1951. – V. Inglisian, "Die armenische Literatur", *Handbuch der Orientalistik*, 1, 7, Leiden, Cologne, 1963, 156-250. – R. W. Thomson, *Moses Khorenats'i: History of the Armenians*, Cambridge (MA), 1978. – *East of Byzantium: Syria and Armenia in the Formative Period*, N. G. Garsoïan (ed.), T. F. Mathews (ed.), R. W. Thomson (ed.), Washington (DC), 1982. – J. R. Russell, *Yovhannes T'ulkuranc'i and the Mediaeval Armenian Lyric Tradition*, Atlanta (GA), 1987. – R. W. Thomson, *A Bibliography of Classical Armenian Literature*, Turnhout, 1995.

Robert W. Thomson

## ARMY

**The West.** From its Germanic origins, the medieval military system kept the principle by which all free men capable of bearing arms could be called to serve the holder of the power of command, though, quite early on, a concern for effectiveness, then the theoretical vision of a functional tripartition of society, led to the profession of arms being reserved for a group of professional warriors.

From the 9th-10th cc., armies were formed around a core of heavy horsemen. However, this preponderance of armoured *cavalry did not cause the disappearance of more lightly armed combatants and "footmen", notably archers, whose role as auxiliaries was far from negligible.

In the 10th-11th cc., the feudal organisation of the military system made "*host" service the primary source of recruitment of armies. The knight who had to serve his lord with arms and horses, without counterpart, had himself to accompany the combatants he was in charge of recruiting, or whom he spread among his own vassals.

From the mid 11th c., Western armies were capable of launching great expeditions: the conquest of *England in 1066 and the first *crusade in 1095-1099. However, the need to increase manpower obliged war leaders to resort not just to the host-system but also to mercenaries, who developed in a significant way from the 12th century. At the same time, the rise of the *towns is revealed by the appearance, within armies, of urban militias. *Peasant communities were equally solicited: they provided the army with means of *transport and non-combatant auxiliaries.

Despite the strengthening of its manpower and the diversification of its recruitment, the 13th-c. army retained its feudal structures, though important changes took place: voluntary and mercenary service developed; the number of knights diminished while the mass of "squires", *nobles who neglected to be *dubbed, grew; moreover the perfecting of siege techniques favoured the appearance of miners, pioneers and "engine-masters" (engineers), while the importance of archers and crossbowmen grew. In the late 13th c., the custom of paying men of war, including those who served by virtue of feudal obligations, spread, particularly in France.

These characteristics were ceaselessly indicted in the 14th century. During this period, the recruitment of armies was diversified and their social composition became increasingly heterogeneous. The progress of techniques, artillery, means of transport and fortification gave rise to a personnel of specialists.

The *Hundred Years' War, by its length, led to the most profound modifications. The system of raising troops that consisted of engaging and then dismissing combatants in accordance with circumstances was both expensive and productive of disorder ("Great *Companies", "*écorcheurs*"). So King *Charles VII of France decided to lay the foundations of a permanent army by creating regular companies in 1445, then the "*franc-archers*" in 1448. He was later imitated by *Charles the Bold, duke of Burgundy.

J.-F. Verbruggen, "L'art militaire en Europe occidentale du IXe au XIVe siècle", *Revue internationale d'histoire militaire*, Paris, 1953-1955, 486-496. – C.W. Hollister, *Anglo-Saxon Military Institutions*, Oxford, 1962. – P. Contamine, *War in the Middle Ages*, Oxford, 1984. – B. Schnerb, "De l'armée féodale à l'armée permanente", *Le Miracle capétien*, S. Rials (ed.), Paris, 1987, 123-132. – M. Keen, *The Laws of War in the Late Middle Ages*, Aldershot, 1993. – M. Strickland, *War and Chivalry: the conduct and perception of war in England and Normandy, 1066-1217*, Cambridge, 1996.

Bertrand Schnerb

**Byzantium.** Byzantium inherited the military structures of the Late Empire. The central army of *comitatenses* was established in garrisons under the orders of five *magistri militum*, two at *Constantinople, two in Illyricum and one in the East. Under Justinian a *magister* was added for *Armenia. Along the frontier were installed *limitanei*, who remained to the end fighting units, charged with opposing barbarian raids. The troops were recruited from the Empire, especially from among the rude mountain peoples like the Isaurians, and from the *foederati*, barbarians established by treaty within the limits of the Empire. Troops of allies, barbarians from outside the Empire, completed the full strength. This force was however constantly diminishing. The *Notitia dignitatum* (early 5th c.) still counted on a manpower of 500,000 for the whole Empire, but under Justinian the Byzantine army numbered no more than 150,000 soldiers, of which a growing number were cavalry. A campaigning army like that of Belisarius in Africa consisted of 14,000 combatants.

The invasion of the *Slavs and *Avars, the Persian and then Arab victories, forced a complete reorganisation of military structures. In the second half of the 7th c., the *limitanei* disappeared and the troops of *comitatenses* were distributed over the whole territory still controlled by Byzantium, forming thematic armies led by *strategoi*. A new central army, that of the *tagmata*, was gradually reconstituted beginning with the garrison of the capital. Constantly under arms, composed of paid troops commanded by domestics, dukes or catapans, the *tagmata*, whose original nucleus consisted of the *scholae* to which were added in particular the *excubitores* and the *hikanatoi*, were led by the emperor in person or, from the 8th c., by the domestic of the *scholae*. They reinforced the *themata* (*themes), whether to repel a regular offensive of the Muslims or the *Bulgars, or to take the initiative in operations against these enemies.

From the 10th c., the army of the *tagmata*, better adapted to the offensive policy of the Empire, which from now on dominated the Near East, acquired pre-eminence over the declining army of the *themata*. In the next century, provincial *tagmata* appeared and units composed of foreigners multiplied: Russian infantry, Frankish *cavalry, *Saracen archers etc. The troops were massively installed on the frontiers, while the heart of the Empire, including the capital, was largely demilitarized. Nevertheless, the *Turks breached the Eastern defences. This setback did not entail great changes, the number of mercenary soldiers depending solely on the financial capacity of the State. The army of the *Comneni was still effective, and that of the Lascarids of *Nicaea permitted the reconquest of Constantinople and the ambitious policy of Michael VIII; but, from the 14th c., Byzantium gained its last successes more by diplomacy than by arms.

J. F. Haldon, *Recruitment and Conscription in the Byzantine Army c.550-950*, Vienna, 1979. – N. Oikonomides, "A propos des armées des premiers Paléologues et des compagnies de soldats", *TMCB*, 8, 1981, 353-371. – W. E. Kaegi, *Army, Society and Religion in Byzantium*, London, 1982. – J. F. Haldon, *Byzantine Praetorians, Poikila Byzantina* 3, Bonn, 1984. – M. C. Bartusis, *The Late Byzantine Army: Arms and Society 1204-1453*, Philadelphia (PA), 1992. – J. F. Haldon, *State, Army and Society in Byzantium*, Aldershot, 1995. – W. T. Treadgold, *Byzantium and its Army, 284-1081*, Stanford (CA), 1995. – E. McGeer, *Sowing the Dragon's Teeth: Byzantine Warfare in the Tenth Century*, Washington (DC), 1995.

Jean-Claude Cheynet

**ARNOLD OF BRESCIA (died 1155).** Expelled from Brescia on the occasion of a citizen revolt against the bishop, the regular *canon Arnold of Brescia went to France where he appears alongside *Abelard at the famous council of Sens in 1140. *Bernard of Clairvaux wanted him condemned to monastic reclusion; but instead he went to *Paris where, on the hill of Sainte-Geneviève, he taught *divinae litterae* to a group of poor students. We next find him passing through the *diocese of *Constance: on this occasion too the Cistercian Bernard warned the local bishop of the danger posed by any juncture between Arnold's preaching and the political initiative of the "*divites et potentes*". In 1145, thanks to the benevolence of Pope *Eugenius III, Arnold went on a penitential pilgrimage to *Rome. Here the volatile political situation – a communal organisation which had recently sprung up, reinforcing its own desire for autonomy with the imperial myth of Rome – led him into extensive preaching against the worldly power of the upper echelons of the church and their betrayal of the most authentic apostolic tradition.

From Rome, or rather from the myth of Rome as "seat of empire, fount of liberty and mistress of the world", was to have begun a reform both ecclesiastical and religious. The happy meeting between Arnold's reforming passion and the initiative for political renewal of the dynamic Roman *cives* did not last long: the latter started to distance themselves from Arnold's more extreme and radical positions, and when Pope *Adrian IV, shortly before Easter 1155, placed an inderdict on the city, only the lowest ranks of Roman society seem to have continued their support of Arnold. Expelled from Rome, he was captured by *Frederick I's men and handed over to the cardinals sent by the pope: after perhaps being hanged, his body was given to the flames and his ashes dispersed in the Tiber so that no popular cult could arise over his remains. Thus ended the extreme manifestation of that Christian radicalism whose roots were based in the *Patarine movement of the 11th c. and which had sought to transform the church not just institutionally, but also on the more strictly religious level: that of the evangelical witness of the individual Christian.

The episode of Arnold of Brescia appears as the last attempt to give designs for reform a concrete social and political form, with consequent implications for the upper echelons, lay and clerical, of "Christian society".

A. Frugoni, *Arnaldo da Brescia nelle fonti del secolo XII*, Rome, 1964 (re-ed. Turin, 1989). – G. Miccoli, "La storia religiosa", *Storia d'Italia*, 2, Turin, 1974, 616-639. – G. G. Merlo, *Eretici ed eresie medievali*, Bologna, 1989, 33-38.

Grado G. Merlo

**ARNOLD OF VILLANOVA (*c.*1240-1311).** His date and place of birth are unknown, but Arnaldus de Villa Nova called himself a Catalan and from boyhood he lived at *Valencia, in the territories recently reconquered by James I. In 1260 he was a student at the university of *Montpellier. After 1280, having left Valencia for *Barcelona, he became doctor to the royal house of Aragon-Catalonia and frequented the *Dominican *studium linguarum*. In 1282 he translated Galen's *De rigore, iectigatione et spasmo*, and from 1290 he was a master of medicine at Montpellier university. He formed confidential relations with the sons of Peter the Great, in particular James II and *Frederick III. It was during a diplomatic mission to Paris for James that he published his *De tempore adventus Antichristi* (1300). From this time on, his spiritual commitment increased: he had to sustain grave conflicts with the *masters of the University, then with the Order of Preachers. Arnold was doctor to Pope *Boniface VIII in 1300, then to the royal house of *Provence and Pope *Clement V, with whom he was connected even before he became pope. Counting on this set of relationships, he tried to assume the role of spiritual and political reformer, but his programme had some application only in *Sicily. After his death and with the accession of *John XXII, new attacks began on his work, which was condemned by a provincial court at *Tarragona in 1316, even though, since the time of Boniface VIII, the pope had reserved the examination of Arnold's writings for himself.

Arnold circulated collections of his writings, partly using his own private *scriptorium*, partly with the help of James II (at the university of Lleida) and Frederick III (at the Sicilian court). These **summae* were addressed to a wide public and brought together texts in Latin and/or the vernacular. Some of these collections, in accordance with his proposed programme of conversion, were translated into Greek. More occasional was his circulation of lectures and advice for *beguines, while his frequent writings defending himself against the ecclesiastical and civil authorities were circulated in the same way as his spiritual works. Much of his theological output was destroyed after the condemnation of 1316, and important works like the *Alia informatio beguinorum* have survived only through the documentation of notaries. His numerous medical works consist of *translations from the Arabic as well as writings on medical training, natural *philosophy, clinical practice and hygiene. They were circulated through the traditional channels of the School or dedicated to important persons, and were in great demand until the first years of the 17th century. In some cases medical concerns were joined to spiritual ones. The authenticity of many works is uncertain, including the abundant alchemical output attributed to him, which is probably entirely apocryphal.

Arnold's work was the basis of the birth of *medicine as a scientific discipline: he studied its epistemological basis and took an active part in organising its study in *universities (at Montpellier, in the name of Clement V, he dictated the curricula in 1309). He combined a precise knowledge of the Arabic scientific tradition with a conscious insistence on experiment. Of great importance was his contribution to medicines and their dosage. His spiritual doctrine was close to that of his radical *Franciscan contemporaries: imminent end of the world (1378), coming of an

*Antichrist, the problem of recognising "true" Christians. These ideas led him to advocate a direct use of the *Bible and a radical evangelism, and to give credit to new revelations and *visionary experiences, his own and others. Much of his literary output consists of "autohagiography", in which he represents his own experience as evidence of sanctity.

*Obres catalanes*, 1. *Escrits religiosos*, 2. *Escrits mèdics*, M. Batllori i Mundo' (ed.), J. Carreras i Artau (ed.), Barcelona, 1947 ("Els Nostres Clàssics"). – *Opera opera medica*, I. Garcia Ballester (dir.), J. Paniagua (dir.), M. McVaugh (dir.) *et al.* (to appear).

R. Manselli, *Spirituali e Beghini in Provenza*, Rome, 1959, 55-80. – F. Santi, *L'Obra espirituals d'Arnau de Vilanova*, Valencia, 1987. – A. Paravicini Bagliani, *Medicina e scienza della natura alla corte papale del Duecento*, Spoleto, 1991.

Francesco Santi

**ARNOLFO DI CAMBIO (1240/1250 - 1302/1310).** Architect and sculptor, born at Colle Valdelsa, died at Florence, one of the major artists of the second half of the 12th c., a contemporary of Giovanni *Pisano and parallel, in sculpture, to the young *Giotto. He is thought to have received his training in contact with the artistic milieu of the Cistercians. Later entering the studio of Nicola *Pisano, under whose direction he worked between 1265 and 1268 on the *Ark of St Dominic* in San Domenico at Bologna and on the *Pulpit* of Siena cathedral, he developed a marked interest in antique sculpture, also favoured by his stay at Rome (and perhaps in the South) and by his frequenting the house of Anjou: the honorary statue of *Charles of Anjou at Rome (Musei Capitolini) is attributed to him. His attachment to antique models, classical, Hellenistic or Etruscan, together with a terse rigour in his amply plastic and volumetric construction of figures, appears especially in his sculptures at *Perugia (Galleria Nazionale), thought to be remains of the *Fountain* commissioned by the Perugians from the "subtilissimus et ingeniosus magister" and executed between 1277 and 1281; and, for supporters of this statue's Arnolfian paternity, it also returns around 1300 in the bronze *Saint Peter* in the Vatican basilica; nor is it diminished in the *Monument to Cardinal De Braye* in San Domenico at *Orvieto (1282), a work that combines adhesion to classical art (the *Virgin enthroned* is an antique statue readapted) with a knowledge of the French Gothic art that flourished around Louis IX. Evidence of this openness are the works that Arnolfo later made at Rome: from the *Ciboria* at St Paul's (1284) and Santa Cecilia (1293) to the *Annibaldi monument* in *St John Lateran (*c.*1290), in which the architectonic setting disciplines the sculptural element; to the *Crib* of *Santa Maria Maggiore (1285-1291); to the complex structure of the *Chapel of St Boniface*, commissioned from him around 1296 by *Boniface VIII as a future funeral monument: previously in the counter-façade of *St Peter's, it is now dismembered (plastic remains in the Vatican Grottoes).

But only at Florence could this architectural vocation, updated on *rayonnant* Gothic, acquire a monumental dimension: in the other buildings partly attributed to him (Badia, Santa Croce, Palazzo Vecchio), but especially in the cathedral of Santa Maria del Fiore, for whose work, begun around 1296, he was by 1300 being praised by the city's Council of a Hundred. Arnolfo had very probably already worked out a project for the cathedral substantially close to that later carried out (radiating chapels, dome), but concentrating on the façade, whose first three levels he accomplished. Evidence of this is the design made by Bernardino Poccetti (Museo dell'Opera del Duomo) in 1587 at the time of the destruction of the façade, which was ornamented with mosaics and sculptures following a Marian iconographical programme. Many of the statues are preserved: at Florence, in the Opera del Duomo and in private collections (*Nativity*, *Madonna enthroned*, *Boniface VIII*, *Apostles and Deacons*); at Berlin, Staatlichen Museen (*Dormitio Virginis*), and at Cambridge (MA), Fogg Museum (*Angel*). They attest his plastic rigour, close to Nicola Pisano, but organised by a clearly architectonic will.

His activity as a painter has possibly been recognised (Romanini) in the *Stories of Isaac* in the upper church of St Francis at *Assisi.

H. Keller, "Der Bildhauer Arnolfo di Cambio und seine Werkstatt", *Jahrbuch der Koenigle Preussischen Kunstsammulungen*, 55, 1934, 205-228; 56, 1935, 22-45. – A. M. Romanini, *Arnolfo di Cambio*, Milan, 1969. – A. M. Romanini, "La Cattedrale gotica: il caso di Arnolfo a S. Maria del Fiore", *Storia dell'arte italiana*, 12, Turin, 1983, 5-45. – E. Carli, *Arnolfo*, Florence, 1993. – J. Poeschke, "Arnolfo di Cambio", *DoA*, 2, 480-485.

Enrica Neri Lusanna

**ARNULF OF CARINTHIA (*c.*850-899).** Arnulf, son of Carloman, was entrusted with the march of Carinthia in 876, and had managed to ensure himself a position of independence by 882. Deposing Charles III (the Fat), the magnates proclaimed him king in 887 at the **placitum* of Forchheim. With *Bavaria as the centre of his power, he had a new palace built at *Regensburg.

Arnulf favoured several families of the aristocracy who helped him fight against the Northmen and *Slavs. In 895, he entrusted *Lotharingia to his son Zwentibold. At the pope's appeal, he set out for *Italy and was crowned emperor in 896. At the end of his reign, gravely ill, he saw the power of the magnates prevail.

H. Löwe, *Deutschland im fränkischen Reich*, Stuttgart, 1970.

Geneviève Bührer-Thierry

**ÁRPÁDS.** The modern name for the native dynasty of kings of *Hungary, taking their origin from Duke Árpád († after 900), under whom the Hungarians occupied the Carpathian basin. Up to the dynasty's extinction in 1301, the 17 generations who succeeded him included 5 grand dukes and 21 kings. The first Christian king, St *Stephen, was crowned in 1000. The principle of succession within the dynasty was at first by *senioritas* (10th c.), supplemented in the 11th-12th cc. by the principle of *idoneitas*, which led the way for interference by neighbouring powers, especially the *Empire and Byzantium who more than once supported rival candidates. Succession in the female line occurred only twice, with Peter Orseolo (1038-1041; 1044-1046) and Samuel Aba (1041-1044), both sons-in-law of St Stephen, who died without male successors. The lineage that provided all subsequent Árpád kings was descended from St Stephen's cousin, Vazul, blinded and thus eliminated by the king to ensure the succession of his son St Imre († 1031) who, however, died before him. After a period of troubles and revolts, Vazul's exiled children restored the power of the Árpáds in Hungary in 1046. The dynasty's reputation for *sanctity was founded by the elevation of the relics of St Stephen and St Imre in 1083, obtained by St *Ladislas (1077-1095), who was canonized in turn in 1192 under Béla III (1172-1196). In the 13th c., two princesses were added to these saintly predecessors: St *Elizabeth (1207-1231), daughter of *Andrew II (1171-1235) and widow of Count Louis of Thuringia, and St Margaret (1242-1270), daughter of Béla IV (1235-1270), who entered the *Dominican

*The offering of the heart.* Tapestry from an Arras workshop. 15th c. Paris, Musée National du Moyen Âge et des Thermes de Cluny.

Order; subsequently, several more Árpád princesses were also venerated as *beatae*. The five sovereigns mentioned were also those who must be considered the most important historically: St Stephen as founder and first Christian legislator of the kingship; St Ladislas who restored that order after the pagan uprisings; Béla III who modernized the *monarchy by establishing a *chancery and a court according to the "modern" criteria of the time; Andrew II who led a *crusade and published the Golden Bull in 1222 to guarantee the constitutional rights of the *nobility; and finally Béla IV who rebuilt and modernized the country after the Tatar invasion of 1241. After the extinction of the dynasty, several claimants sought to win acceptance for descent in the female line: Wenceslas III Přemysl (king of Hungary under the name of Ladislas from 1301 to 1305), Otto of Bavaria (in 1305-1307) and Charles of Anjou (1309-1342) who emerged the winner from these struggles for the Crown.

*Scriptores Rerum Hungaricarum*, E. Szentpétery (ed.), 1-2, Budapest, 1938.

F. Makk, *The Arpads and the Comneni*, Budapest, 1989. – G. Klaniczay, "From Sacral Kingship to Self-Representation", *The Uses of Supernatural Power*, Cambridge, 1990, 79-128. – Gy. Kristó, *Die Arpaden-Dynastie*, Budapest, 1993.

Gábor Klaniczay

**ARRAS.** Evangelized in the late 4th c. by St Diogenes, Arras owes its rise to the settlement in 658, in the marshes of the Crinchon, of a monastic community placed under the patronage of the first bishop St Vedastus (Vaast, † *c.*540). In the Carolingian period, the *abbey, holding immense properties, became under the impetus of Abbot Rado a cultural centre, as is attested by its rich *library. At this time the **scriptorium* produced fundamental works in the Franco-insular style, which are of great importance in the history of medieval painting. After a decline due to the invasions of the Northmen, its early revival was due to the energetic monastic *reform that came from Lotharingia through the mediation of *Richard of Saint-Vanne, who ruled the abbey for nearly ten years (1009-1018). In the 11th c., the painting studios of Saint-Vaast accelerated the Romanesque renaissance by creating fertile syntheses between English art, *Ottonian art and the old local Carolingian culture. Arras later owed its fortune to the cloth industry, which developed thanks to a happy geographical situation between England and the *Champagne *fairs. The town's apogee was the 15th c. through its art of *tapestry, for which Arrageois manufacturers found an international market (cf. the English word for tapestry: "arras"): they produced works in a courtly style, of refined elegance, such as the *Offering of the heart*, preserved in the Musée de Cluny, or the *Geste de Jourdain de Blaye* (Padua, Museo Civico).

The town developed around two poles, the abbey and the *cathedral. The monastic buildings, rebuilt without scruple in the 18th c., were destroyed in the war of 1914. The Gothic cathedral, erected in 1160, was given over to the Cult of Reason under the Revolution, then sold in 1798 and finally systematically destroyed between 1799 and 1805. Hardly anything remains today but some sculpted capitals preserved in the Arras museum, the remarkable quality of which surpasses many contemporary works. Thanks to old documents and excavations, we can reconstitute the history and forms of this cathedral, whose construction was finished only in the 15th c. when the vaults of the nave were put in place, and whose façade could not be completed. The initial plan of the building was close to that of the contemporary cathedral of *Laon. The choir was short, with an ambulatory to which an axial chapel was later added, the transept abnormally long, the elevation quadripartite, a principle whose archaism was preserved by the architects of the nave in the 13th century.

P. Héliot, "Les anciennes cathédrales d'Arras", *Bulletin de la commission royale des monuments et des sites*, IV, 1953. – J. Lestocquoy, *Deux siècles de l'histoire de la tapisserie (1300-1500)*, Arras, 1978. – B. Delmaire, *Le Diocèse d'Arras de 1093 au milieu du XIVe siècle. Recherches sur la vie religieuse dans le Nord de la France au Moyen Âge*, Arras, 1994 (2 vol.).

Editorial staff

***ARS ANTIQUA, ARS NOVA*****.** Two terms used by 14th-c. theorists to distinguish between *rhythmic principles that developed in Paris during the 12th through 13th cc. and innovations that arose there in the early 14th century. The word *ars* referred to the rules and craft of musical composition. *Ars nova*, the new system, was first described in the treatises of Philippe de Vitry (*Ars nova*, *c.*1320) and Jehan des Murs (*Noticia artis musice*, 1319 or 1321, and *Compendium musicae practicae*, *c.*1322). Jacques de Liège (*Speculum musicae*, book VII, after 1323, before *c.*1330), a strident critic of the new *music, defended the 13th-c. musical genres and rhythmic style of those whom he called the *antiqui*. He called the craft of this earlier music *ars antiqua*, *ars vetus* and *ars veterum*, and the actual compositions *cantus antiquiis*. Current usage of *ars antiqua* and *ars nova* is broader than that of the early theorists, denoting in addition musical styles, repertories and epochs of composition.

The main theorists of the 13th c., Johannes de Garlandia, Lambertus, *Franco of Cologne and the Sankt-Emmeran Anonymous, described conventional patterns of long and short durations that were the rhythmic foundation of the *ars antiqua*.

Known as modes, these rhythmic patterns were organised in groups of three or six time units, called *tempora*. Six common modes can be expressed in number of *tempora* as follows: 2-1, 1-2, 3-1-2, 1-2-3, 3-3 and 1-1-1. A perfect long note contained three *tempora* and the proper breve equalled one *tempus*. Usually no more than three equal semibreves could be sung in the time of one breve. However, in a few rare cases, notably in compositions attributed to Petrus de Cruce, from four to seven semibreves were performed equal to a breve.

The rhythmic theory of the 14th-c. *ars nova* changed or eradicated many of the rules of the *ars antiqua*. The modes were eliminated, and *tempora* or breves could be grouped in twos, as well as threes. In addition, either two or three equal semibreves could be sung in the time of a breve. The semibreve, formerly the smallest unit of measure, now could be subdivided into either two or three equal minims. With the introduction of the minim, the speed of the larger note values decreased so that the *ars nova* semibreve and breve slowed to approximately the speed of the *ars antiqua* breve and long.

*Ars nova* principles first appeared in the *cantilena* and *motet, which were forms inherited from the 13th century. The earliest major source of these pieces is the manuscript Paris, BNF, f. fr. 146, copied between 1316 and 1318, which contains *ars nova* motets interpolated in the *Roman de Fauvel* and songs by Jehannot de Lescurel († 1303 or 1304). The 13th-c. genres of organum and conductus disappeared, much to the chagrin of the conservative critic Jacques de Liège, who also lambasted the rhythmic and notational complexities of the new style of music. Later in the 14th c., the *polyphonic chanson and the ordinary of the *mass reached great heights at the hands of the composer *Guillaume de Machaut. Toward the end of the century, musical style became even more rhythmically complex and is known among modern scholars as *ars subtilior*.

T. Gérold, *La Musique au Moyen Âge*, Paris, 1932, 236-287. – J. Chailley, *Histoire musicale du Moyen Âge*, Paris, 1950 (re-ed. 1984). – *Ars Nova and the Renaissance 1300-1500*, D.A. Hughes (ed.), G. Abraham (ed.), Oxford, 1960. – G. A. Anderson, "Ars antiqua", *DMA*, 1, 1982, 542-547. – G. K. Greene, "Ars nova", *DMA*, 1, 1982, 548-553. – M. Haas, "Die Musiklehre im 13. Jahrhundert von Johannis de Garlandia bis Franco", *Die mittelalterliche Lehre von der Mehrstimmigkeit*, F. Zaminer (ed.), Darmstadt, 1984, 89-159. – E. Roesner, F. Avril, N. Regalado, *Le Roman de Fauvel dans l'édition de Mesire Chaillou de Pestain: A Facsimile of Paris, Bibliothèque Nationale, Fonds Français, 146*, New York, 1990, 22-42. – A. Hodeir, *Les Formes de la musique*, 1993 ("QSJ", 478).

Mary E. Wolinski

***ARS MORIENDI.*** Very early on, the Church formulated models of the "Good Death". During the early Middle Ages, the often very detailed death-scenes of Saints' Lives or the prescriptions of monastic *customaries relating to the deaths of the brothers were part of a pedagogy of death. But the models thus proposed were for "internal use only", these texts being little read outside religious establishments. Not until the end of the Middle Ages were models for death spread among the faithful.

From the 13th c., concerned for a greater involvement of the faithful, the Church manifested a concrete desire to assist the sick and *dying. At this time, *sermons specifically devoted to death were composed, whose message was always the same: *death must be expected at any moment and in every place. These were still texts belonging to a literary genre rather than sermons actually preached, and at this time they only concerned the great. On the

*The temptation of despair.* Engraving from the *Ars moriendi.* Anepistographic Latin texts. Unsigned, *c.*1465-1470 (?). Paris, BNF (Xylo 21, fol. 7 v°-8 r°).

other hand, between the late 14th and the early 15th c., treatises of a new type began to be written: thus the *Medicine of the soul* or *Science of Dying Well*, written in *c.*1403 by Jean *Gerson. The work was in four parts, bearing respectively on the exhortations to be made to the sick, the questions to be put to him, the *prayers he was to recite, and advice for those who assisted him. Forming a precious guide for *clerics who had to accompany the dying, the *Science of Dying Well* had an immense success, attested by numerous manuscript and printed exemplars, as well as several translations.

Gerson's treatise moreover inspired two more works: the *Ars moriendi* (author and date of composition unknown) and the *Tractatus artis bene moriendi* (attributed to several 15th-c. authors), which were in turn widely circulated, giving rise to an abundant literature: numerous Arts of Dying (more or less close to their models), which circulated mainly between 1450 and 1530, in the form of little books of piety, most often written in the vernacular, which penetrated lay milieux.

The *Ars moriendi*, whose earliest exemplars date from the mid 15th c., was illustrated by woodcuts. While the text evoked the "*temptations" of the devil at the moment of the death-agony and the "good inspirations" of the angel, the images depicted opposite it represented the dying man extended on his deathbed, surrounded on one side by the Virgin, the heavenly court, the guardian *angel, and on the other by Satan and the army of *demons, all disputing his *soul.

The Arts of Dying represented a new *spirituality, more aimed towards individuals, according more importance to personal mediation and individual *conscience. The use of the vernacular and the presence of images recall their pedagogical function and explain their success. The aim of the *Artes moriendi* was dual: to provide models of dying well, but also to lead the faithful to live better while awaiting their death. In this sense, as much as an "art of dying", the *Artes moriendi* proposed to their readers an "art of living well".

A. Tenenti, *La Vie et la mort à travers l'art du XVe siècle*, Paris, 1952. – R. Rudolf, *Ars moriendi*, Cologne-Graz, 1957. – A. Tenenti, *Il senso della morte e l'amore della vita nel Rinascimento*, Turin, 1957 (2nd ed. 1989). – R. Chartier, "Les Arts de mourir, 1450-1600", *Annales*, 31, 1976, 51-75. – F. Rapp, "La Réforme religieuse et la méditation de la mort à la fin du Moyen Âge", *La Mort au Moyen Âge*, Strasbourg, 1977, 53-66. – G. Hasenohr, "La Littérature religieuse des XIVe et XVe siècles", *GRLMA*, 8, 7, 1988, 277-283. – D. L. d'Avray, "Sermons on the Dead before 1350", *StMed*, 31, 1990, 207-223. – C. Bascetta, "Art de bien vivre et bien mourir", *DLFMA*, 1992, 96-99.

Michel Lauwers

**ART, ARTIST.** The reorganisation by Martianus Capella and *Cassiodorus of the old pedagogical method, favouring the *liberal arts over manual activities, hardly favoured the position of the artist over the centuries. In the 12th c., urban growth and social and mental transformations led to other attitudes: *Hugh of Saint-Victor in his *Didascalicon*, *Honorius Augustodunensis and *John of Salisbury (*Policraticus*) attest, in their ways, these new ideas. Moreover, since the defence of the artist's activity composed by Plotinus in his *Enneads* (3rd c.), there had existed a certain tradition that conferred on the artist the capacity to surpass mere sensible realities. However, in the texts, we do not find any specific term reserved for those whom today we would call "artists": the word *artefices* serves commonly to designate artisans and artists without distinction; the word *artista* designates a person who studies or practises exclusively the liberal arts; in the late 13th c. the same term, employed in *Salimbene's *Chronicle*, designates a person possessing particular technical abilities. But distinctions appear more clearly within the artistic field: a place apart was thus acknowledged for the *architect (early in the 7th c., *Isidore of Seville describes him as at once the *mason, the *caementarius* and the author of the project; in the Carolingian period, *Rabanus Maurus repeats this definition).

Little by little, practical activity prevailed over theoretical aspects: not until the 13th c., particularly in France, did the architect regain a privileged status, as witness the signatures of architects – from now on more numerous than those of sculptors. The position of goldsmiths was also higher than that of other artisans: working with precious materials, like master glassmakers, they enjoyed general respect (the first medieval biography of an "artist" is the *Life* of St *Eligius, the great Limousin goldsmith and an important person at the *Merovingian court). We know names and figurative representations of some miniaturists of the *Romanesque period (*e.g.* the portrait of Hugo, doubtless a monk at the abbey of *Jumièges, in a text of St Jerome, Oxford, Bodleian Library, ms. 717). From the 12th c., in Italy, at *Pisa, at *Modena, the stonecutter (sculptor) saw his role increase on the building sites of those new collective patrons, the *communes. At the same time, in France and in Germany, signatures of sculptors become less rare (on the main *altar of the church of Saint-Sernin at *Toulouse, late 11th c.; in Goslar cathedral; in the choir of *Worms cathedral). The activity of painters developed in the communal period in the towns of *Tuscany: it was also in this environment that a first break occurred with the traditional conception of the "mechanical arts". In canto XI of the *Purgatorio*, *Dante mentions the names of two miniaturists (Oderiso da Gubbio and Franco Bologna) and two painters (*Cimabue and *Giotto), comparing them to those of contemporary writers. Soon after the middle of the 13th c., in *courts, at Paris, Naples, London or Prague (in the 14th c.), appeared the Court artist.

V. Mortet, P. Deschamps, *Recueil de textes relatifs à l'histoire de l'architecture et à la condition des architects en France au Moyen Âge, XIe-XIII[e] siècle*, Paris, 1911. – E. Mâle, *Art and Artists in the Middle Ages*, Redding Ridge (CT), 1986. – *Artistes, artisans et production artistique au Moyen Âge*, Paris, 1986-1991 (3 vol.). – A. Borst, *Medieval Worlds: Barbarians, Heretics and Artists in the Middle Ages*, Cambridge, 1991. – A. Erlande-Brandenburg, *De pierre, d'or et de fer. La création artistique au Moyen Âge, IVe-XIII[e] siècle*, Paris, 1999.

Daniel Russo

***ARTES PRAEDICANDI.*** These were *treatises written for preachers to explain to them the different procedures for composing a *sermon. In France, one of the first treatises was written by *Alan of Lille *c.*1200, followed soon after by those of the Englishmen Alexander of Ashby and Thomas of Chobham. Later, this literary genre took off considerably; an estimated 200 or so *Artes praedicandi* survive from before 1500. Originally, these works responded mainly to pastoral concerns. But in the 14th and 15th cc., purely technical teaching tended to prevail, and was largely influenced by *scholastic methods and *rhetoric.

Alan of Lille, *The Art of Preaching*, G. R. Evans (ed.), Kalamazoo (MI), 1981.

J. J. Murphy, *Rhetoric in the Middle Ages. A History of Rhetorical Theory from Saint Augustine to the Renaissance*, Berkeley-Los Angeles-London, 1974. – M. C. Briscoe, *Artes praedicandi*, Turnhout, 1992. – F. Morenzoni, "La littérature des *artes praedicandi* de la fin du XIIe au début du XVe siècle", *Geschichte der Sprachtheorie*, 3, *Sprachtheorien in Spätantike und Mittelalter*, S. Ebbesen (ed.), Tübingen, 1995, 339-359.

Franco Morenzoni

**ARTEVELDE, JACOB VAN (1290/1295-1345).** A Flemish politician, Jacob van Artevelde was born in *Ghent of a prosperous merchant family. He was chosen as leader in his town's struggle against the Francophile count Louis of Nevers. His ambition was to restore social concord by broadening participation in the municipal government of Ghent: for this reason he called the oppressed weavers to sit among the **échevins*, together with representatives of the small trades, the fullers and the burghers. He negotiated a federation of the three towns of Ghent, *Bruges and *Ypres. Though a regent had been appointed to replace the count who had fled to France, it was Artevelde who exercised effective power in the county. At first he followed a policy of neutrality in the *Hundred Years' War; but in 1339 he concluded an alliance with *England against *France, which allowed the restoration of commercial relations with England. Artevelde also managed to conclude an agreement between *Brabant, *Flanders and Hainaut, but the authority he held was undermined by social struggles between weavers and fullers; he was murdered during a weavers' *revolt.

P. Carson, *James van Artevelde, the Man from Ghent*, Ghent, 1980. – D. Nicholas, *The van Arteveldes of Ghent*, Ithaca (NY), 1988.

Lieve De Mecheleer

**ARTHUR.** King Arthur, a character around whom was organised, in medieval romantic literature, an ideal *court attracting marvellous adventures, is situated at the intersection of history and Celtic legends.

The historical memory of Arthur was at first that of a war leader, celebrated as a model of valour by the 7th-c. Welsh *Gododdin*; the *Historia Brittonum*, attributed to Nennius (9th c.), made this *dux bellorum* – he was not yet a king – the victor over the Saxons who had invaded Britain. The victory of Mount Badon (516), which an earlier historian, *Gildas, had attributed to the Roman Aurelius Ambrosius, was his work: Arthur had triumphed by carrying the image of the Virgin, thus freeing the Britons. According to Nennius, Arthur had won another twelve battles, most of them within the borders of Scotland; thus, from the 9th c., the victories claimed by the Britons over the Saxon invaders were associated with the hero's name. Finally, the *Annales Cambriae* (mid 10th c.) date Arthur's fall, which coincided with the death of his nephew Medraut or Mordred who betrayed him, to 537.

In parallel with these historical or pseudo-historical elements, legendary material, borrowed from Celtic folklore and sometimes inspired by local legends, made Arthur a mythical figure engaged in otherworldly adventures. The *Historia Brittonum* tells the legend of Cabal, Arthur's dog, who left his footprint on a pile of stones, Carn Cabal. A 10th-c. *Welsh poem, the *Spoils of Annwn*, describes an expedition of Arthur against the fortress belonging to the chief of Annwn: a transposition of a raid on the other world. The Welsh *romance of *Kulhwch and Olwen* (*c.*1100) already makes Arthur the king of a marvellous court whose knights have magical powers. These mixed traits recur in *Geoffrey of Monmouth's work, the *Historia regum Britanniae* (before 1139), which installed the hero for ever in the glory of a learned work divulged by innumerable manuscripts. In it we find Arthur's fabulous birth – Uther Pendragon was able to have union with Yngerna by taking on, thanks to *Merlin's sorcery, the appearance of Duke Gorlois ; his magnificent conquests – Ireland, Iceland, Gaul; the images of a courtly life in which *tournaments and *love held first place, the glorious struggle with the Romans and the felony of Mordred. The king's end was brought about by the usurpation of Mordred who united himself to Gvennuera, Arthur's unfaithful wife. The king confronted the traitor near the river Camla: Mordred was killed and Arthur, grievously wounded, abandoned the crown to his cousin Constantine, son of Cador duke of Cornwall, in the year 542 of the Incarnation, then retired to Avalon.

Popularized both by Welsh storytellers – the *cyvarwyddon* – who were themselves in contact with Irish traditions, and by learned or pseudo-learned texts, the figure of Arthur offered itself to 12th-c. romancers as a rich and malleable material. A character endowed with the prestige of history, he was conceived as the creator and defender of the kingdom of Logres (Britain), whose power rivalled that of Rome: as such, the Arthurian victory was a revenge for the Roman conquest of Britain. But the king was also connected with the other world, into which he could make expeditions; like the Irish hero Finn, central figure of the Leinster cycle, he did not know death: he lives for ever in the isle of Avalon where his sister Morgan, heiress of the Celtic Muirgen, both woman and *fairy, healed him. Finally, gathering around himself characters chosen for their valour, as in Celtic tradition, he could form an admirable court, open to chivalrous and courtly values.

The importance of Arthur in medieval literature is thus explained in two complementary ways: he is an exceptional person, author of considerable exploits and destined for universal reign, but also and even more, the assembler of mythical heroes on whom his glory partly rests. Robert de Boron's romance of *Merlin*, of which we now possess only prose versions, tells the story of the ascent of Uther's son to the conquest of Britain and the assertion of his power in the face of various enemies. Entrusted to a tutor, the young man four times passes the test that designates him for the kingship, and which consists in extracting the sword fixed in an anvil. Anointed at Pentecost, he must first withstand the rebellion of the kings who owe him obedience: thanks to the help of Gauvain and his brothers, he manages to master these rebels. Next comes the struggle against the Saxons: it is in this context that Arthur, who fights in the service of Leodagan of Carmelis, marrries Guenevere. Later, he has to fight the Romans, called in by Claudas; the motif of the struggle against the Romans reappears at the end of the prose romance of *Lancelot*.

*King Arthur and his knights set out by boat to achieve the Holy Grail.* French manuscript, 14th c. Turin, National Library.

The Arthurian romances, primarily those of *Chrétien de Troyes, see Arthur as the head of a prestigious company of knights on whom it is incumbent to achieve adventures whose glory will be reflected on the court. The king thus remains in the background, as we see in the *Chevalier de la Charrete*: having compelled him by a gift, the seneschal Keu obtains from Arthur the right to defend the queen; not up to his task, he stands aside for *Lancelot, who confronts and kills Guenevere's abductor. Similarly, in the *Conte du Graal*, Arthur is helpless against the knight with vermilion arms, who has come to defy him at his banquet and pours a cup of wine over the queen, in a sort of symbolic violation that strikes the court with sterility: it is *Perceval, in his youthful ardour, who has to attack the aggressor and put him to death. The Arthurian court is thus that of a king who "makes knights", as it says in the *Conte du Graal*, and for this reason always has a heroic phalanx at his disposal. Sometimes, however, the king's image is laughable: at the beginning of the *Chevalier au Lion*, the king abandons his knights right in the middle of a solemn court to go and pay inopportune respects to Guenevere.

The great *Lancelot-Graal* prose romance tries, as a whole, to give the king a complex image, not without tragic grandeur. Seen through the eyes of Claudas, his rival, Arthur is a powerful and chivalrous king, able to win over rich and poor by his valour and generosity of heart; but others condemn him as a feudal lord who cannot come to the aid of his vassals, since he lets Claudas disinherit Lancelot and his cousins Bohort and Lionnel. His fidelity to Guinevere is not exemplary: he lets himself be seduced by the enchantress Gamille as well as by the "false Guenevere". And more than once he is publicly humiliated by "prudhommes" who reproach him for his failings or by dictatorial knights, like Lionnel, who recalls him to his duties. Towards Lancelot, his *friendship and loyalty are admirable, but not without limits. On one hand, the king does not deal sufficiently tactfully with the pride of his knights, and the merited but too conspicuous praises he showers on Lancelot arouse the jealousy of certain companions of the *Round Table and prepare the later fratricidal struggles. On the other hand, the revelation of Guinevere's *adultery with Lancelot provokes in Arthur such hatred and then despair that his emotions forbid him to appeal for the hero's help to overcome Mordred. Fixed in the posture of the lord who refuses to listen to salutory advice – the vision of Gauvain himself cannot make him change his mind – Arthur is locked into a tragic and grandiose fate. With him disappear the majority of his companions, along with the weapon to which he owed his consecration – the sword Excalibur – which a mysterious hand receives in the lake into which it is thrown. In fact, what the romancer brings out in the history of the ruin of the Arthurian kingdom is the dramatic consequences of passion and desire: redeemed in Lancelot by the chivalrous qualities that take him to the heights of valour, in Arthur it becomes an *incestuous relationship – just as his father Uther's love for the fair Yngerna had been adulterous – that gives birth to Mordred, by whom the disaster comes.

*The Works of Sir Thomas Malory*, E. Vinaver (ed.), P. J. C. Field (revised), 3rd ed., Oxford, 1990 (3 vol.).

J. Marx, *La Légende arthurienne et le Graal*, Paris, 1952. – R. S. Loomis, *Arthurian Literature in the Middle Ages*, Oxford, 1959. – L. Alcock, *Arthur's Britain*, Harmondsworth, 1973. – J. Markale, *King Arthur, King of Kings*, London, 1977. – R. Morris, *The Character of King Arthur in Medieval Literature*, Cambridge, 1982. – *The Legends of Arthur in the Middle Ages*, P.B. Crout (ed.), Cambridge, 1983. – *The Arthurian Encyclopedia*, N.J. Lacy (ed.), Woodbridge, 1986. – *The Arthur of the Welsh*, R. Bromwich et al. (ed.), Cardiff, 1991. – O.J. Padel, "The Nature of Arthur", *CMCS*, 27, 1994, 1-31.

François Suard

**ARTICLES OF FAITH.** An article of faith is the form given to a part of *Revelation, which can be distinguished from, but is capable of being joined to other propositions. The whole constitutes the essence of what we must believe in order to reach God. *Thomas Aquinas justifies this division into articles: *faith is a participation in God's own knowledge, and uncreated wisdom has no need to distinguish in order to know, yet *man's participation in this knowledge remains, in spite of everything, imperfect and limited: the object of faith has its full force as truth and can be taught and transmitted only if it is presented in a way that is clear and precise to the mind.

The expression "articles of faith" seems relatively late. Gratian does not know it. It is used, but with discretion, by *Peter Lombard in his *Sentences* (III, 25, 2, 2); likewise by *John Beleth (late 12th c.), Gautier of Saint-Victor († 1180) and *Peter of Poitiers, a Victorine († 1217). Its use is more frequent from the 13th c.: pastoral works like Thomas of Chobham's († *c.*1236) *Summa de arte praedicandi* or various treatises of Raymond *Lull († 1315). Thomas Aquinas seems to attach great importance to the division of the faith into articles (III *Sent.* 25, q. 1, art. 1 and 2; *Summa theologiae*, II$^{a}$ II$^{ae}$, q. 1, a. 6).

"Articles of faith" can be compared with two other expressions, older and used almost constantly over the centuries: "rule of faith" (*regula fidei*), known as early as Tertullian († 220) and used by Augustine († 430) in some 60 texts (Scriptural commentaries, *Letters*, *Confessions*, etc.). The councils of Africa (345-525) and that of Orange (529) refer to it.

"Symbol of faith" is less frequent: thus Augustine uses it only four times, but Carolingian councils and *capitularies, and synodal *statutes from the 13th c. use the term when they ask priests to teach their congregation the content of the faith. If the statutes of the synod of Paris (*c.*1205), canon 84, order priests to expound the symbol of faith, distinguish their articles and strengthen the faithful in each of them, the synodal of the West (*c.*1220) does not use these terms, but specifies what must particularly be explained: faith in the *Trinity, in the Incarnation, the seven *sacraments, the *vices and the *works of mercy.

Articles and symbol of faith were related to each other as element and whole. Indeed the articles of faith were most often grouped together in symbols or professions of faith: the *Apostles' Creed, which appeared in its present form in the 6th c.; the Nicene-Constantinopolitan Creed, inserted into the Western *mass after the gospel in *c.*794; the so-called Athanasian Creed, more assuredly of 6th-c. southern Gaul, used in psalmodic form in the *office. These *creeds used by the liturgy and for pastoral ends were not exclusive: thus the fourth *Lateran council (1215) opened with a long canon *On the Catholic faith* centred on the Trinity, *Creation (against the *Cathars), the Incarnation, the *Redemption, the Church and the sacraments.

In the 13th c., theologians and *canonists often structured the *I believe in God* into 12 or 14 articles, which they related to the Father, the Son and the Spirit, or else to the Divinity in itself and the humanity of *Christ.

*Councils and *synods generally associated the *I believe in God* and the *Lord's Prayer; from the 13th c., they added the *Hail Mary* (first part): two, then three texts that had to be known, understood and recited. This grouping, the commentaries propounded and the place of the creed in the liturgy show that the *I believe in God* was considered as much a *prayer as a profession of faith.

J. de Ghellinck, *Patristique et Moyen Âge. Études d'histoire littéraire et doctrinale, tome 1. Les recherches depuis cinq siècles sur les origines du symbole des Apôtres*, Gembloux-Brussels-Paris, 1949. – H. de Lubac, *Christian Faith: the structure of the Apostles' Creed*, I, London, 1986. – J. Longère, "L'Enseignement du *Credo*: conciles, synodes et canonistes médiévaux jusqu'au XIII$^{e}$ siècle", *SE*, 32, 1991, 309-341.

Jean Longère

**ARTS OF LOVE.** From the 12th c., court literature gave a large place to the description of *love and its effects on individuals and social life. It turned on Ovid's *Ars amatoria*, translated by *Chrétien de Troyes in 1160. Though this translation has not survived, we do have several 13th-c. adaptations: in verse – those of Maistre Elie, Jakes d'Amiens, the anonymous author of the *Clef d'amors*, and Guiart – and in prose – that of an anonymous author who added to his translation a continuous commentary. They are not too concerned with literal fidelity, they abridge Ovid, transpose him, erase his paganism, eliminate mythological digressions, adapt the Roman's technical advice to life in urban and courtly France: the bath-house, the *market or the church, frequented by young people in search of encounters. These adaptations are due to *clerics who are not embarrassed by Ovid's immorality. In any case, a small group of original texts in Latin and French asks the question which, of the cleric and the knight, is best endowed for love, and in this "debate of the clerk and the knight" it is generally the former who wins.

Others were alive to the scandal to the love of God caused by extra-conjugal love of Ovidian or courtly inspiration. Hence embarrassed works or works of awkward interpretation. The most remarkable is Andreas Capellanus's *De amore* (*c.*1185), three books in Latin prose of which the first two define love, propose models of seduction dialogues which take into account the social position of the interlocutors, and cite rulings and judgments on love attributed to great ladies of the time such as Queen *Eleanor; the third is a severe condemnation of adulterous love and of *women. The author is well acquainted with Arthurian literature and the world of the courts; his treatise may have been written to instruct churchmen about the passions fashionable in the world and put them on their guard. A century later, the *Franciscan Matfre Ermengaud wrote in *langue d'oc* an important *Breviari d'Amor*, an exposition of Christian morals incorporating a "Perilhos tractat d'amor de las donas" which is like an anthology of the *troubadours.

Apart from properly didactic texts, there is hardly a fiction, *romance or *chanson d'amour* that does not have an exemplary character and does not suggest a model of amorous comportment. We must at least mention the subtle works of the canon of Amiens, Richard de Fournival, whose *Bestiaire d'amours* (*c.*1250) is an amorous letter addressed to a friend; in it he describes his sentiments, comparing them to the features of real or fabulous morals ascribed to the animals. Finally and especially, how can we ignore the *Roman de la Rose* of Guillaume de Lorris and Jean de Meung, "where the whole art of love is enclosed"?

Andreas Capellanus, *Andreas Capellanus on Love*, P.G. Walsh (ed.), London, 1982.

G. Segre, "Ars amandi classica e medievale", *GRLMA*, 8, 1, 1968, 109-116. – P.L. Allen, *The Art of Love*, Philadelphia, 1992. – P. Cherchi, *Andreas and the Ambiguity of Courtly Love*, Toronto, 1994.

Pierre-Yves Badel

**ARTS OF POETRY.** *Artes poeticae* teach how to practise the art of writing. These manuals do not ask questions about the nature of literature. They describe and prescribe effective techniques. They do not have a theoretical character, though their authors are aware that no rule can make up for the absence of vision in a writer. Though translated by *William of Moerbeke in 1278, Aristotle's *Poetics* was ignored; its title was given to a commentary by *Averroes, translated before 1256 by Hermann the German. By contrast, Horace's *Letter to the Pisos*, called *Poetria*, was well known. The main Latin arts, written in verse or prose, are Matthew of Vendôme's *Ars versificatoria* (1175), Geoffrey of Vinsauf's *Poetria nova* (1210), Gervase of Melkley's *Ars poetica* (1215), Évrard the German's *Laborintus* and Jean of Garlande's *Parisiana poetria* (1235). Their public was that of the schools: they were written by *clerics for clerics. They teach how to write literary work in verse or prose. Their sources are Horace and the *Rhetoric* attributed to Cicero. Their advice extends to the way to begin a poem, the procedures of development, the ornamentation of thought by figures and tropes, versification both metric (in the antique manner) and rhythmic (based on rhyme and number of syllables). The models cited are poets and prose writers, ancient and medieval.

In the vulgar tongue we can cite, for Occitan, the *Razos de trobar* (*c.*1200) and the *Leys d'amors* (1355); for French, Brunetto Latini's *Trésor*, *Guillaume de Machaut's *Remède de Fortune*, Eustache Deschamps's *Art de dittier* and a series of arts of "second" rhetoric that crown the treatise of Pierre Fabri (1521). These treatises were made for court poets and members of **puys* (poetry societies). Apart from that of Fabri, they are exclusively concerned with *poetry. They define rhymes and verses, strophes and combinations of strophes (*ballades*, *virelais*, *rondeaux*), they give examples. Sometimes they juxtapose this study of "tailles" with a choice of mythological narratives (or "poèteries") good to put into verse. Their references are only to earlier poets, from the *troubadours to Alain Chartier.

For the Latin manuals, the art of poetry is confused with *rhetoric. The vulgar manuals express a more complex feeling. To define poetry as a second rhetoric, the first being prose, implies that orators and poets obey the same laws; yet the idea persists that verse, with its *rhythm of which rhyme is the most obvious sign, has more to do with *music: thus for *Dante and for Deschamps, who makes the art of rhyming a "natural" music. This idea has its source less in the speculations of *Boethius than in the conditions that gave rise to lyric poetry which, from the troubadours to Machaut, was always sung.

E. Faral, *Les arts poétiques du XIIe et du XIIIe siècle*, Paris, 1924. – D. Kelly, *The Arts of Poetry and Prose*, Turnhout, 1991.

Pierre-Yves Badel

**ARUNDEL, THOMAS (1353-1414).** Son of Richard Fitzalan, tenth earl of Arundel, and brother of the eleventh earl, Thomas Arundel was among the highest English *nobility. Destined at once for the ecclesiastical life, he began a brilliant career after a period at Oriel College, *Oxford, where he obtained the *degree of bachelor of arts: archdeacon of Taunton from 1370, he was rapidly a canon of Chichester, *Hereford, *Exeter and *York before becoming bishop of Ely in 1373. In 1388 he was promoted archbishop of York and, in 1396, transferred to *Canterbury.

Arundel was a very political prelate. When the Lords opposed *Richard II and his favourite Michael de la Pole (Suffolk), he was sent by the lords and Commons to the king to obtain Suffolk's dismissal: he became *chancellor of England in his place in October 1386. But the distrust and hostility between Richard and the lords continued to grow, and when Richard tried to shake off the tutelage of the council dominated by the Lords, five of them (including the earl of Arundel) appealed against his advisers. The "lords appellant" crushed the royal levies at Radcot Bridge, and Richard's supporters were exiled or executed. Arundel was chancellor during this stirring period, but the government of the appellants was ineffective, and in May 1389 Arundel was replaced as chancellor by the veteran Wykeham, while Richard resumed control of the government.

Arundel was chancellor again in 1391-1396, but when Richard II undertook to revenge himself on the lords appellant, he was dismissed; his brother the earl of Arundel was executed, and he himself was the object of a process of impeachment in *Parliament. Richard II then obtained his transfer to the (Clementist) archbishopric of *St Andrews, and Arundel took the road of exile: he lived at Rome and Florence, where he made the acquaintance of Coluccio *Salutati, in Germany at Cologne – where he was joined by his nephew, the new earl of Arundel – and in France, at Paris, where he found another exile, Henry of *Lancaster.

He accompanied Lancaster in 1399 in his victorious ride across England: he immediately resumed possession of his archbishopric of Canterbury and became chancellor again; under these two titles, he played a key role in Lancaster's accession to power under the name of *Henry IV, preaching the sermon at the opening of Parliament in 1399 and crowning the new sovereign at *Westminster. Chancellor again in 1407 and 1412, under Henry IV he played an important role in the Council, but he was mainly concerned with combatting *Lollardy: thus in 1411 he made an armed visitation of the University of Oxford, a manifest violation of the *University's privileges. The scandal was great, but the archbishop held firm and got Pope *Boniface IX to revoke the *exemption enjoyed by the University. He thus managed to strike a fatal blow against Lollardy, permanently deprived of its university supporters. However, this control exercised over Oxford had nefarious effects on intellectual life.

*DNB*, 1885-1900. – *BRUO*, 1, 1957, 51-53. – M. Aston, *Thomas Arundel. A Study of Church Life in the Reign of Richard II*, Oxford, 1967. – R.N. Swanson, "Archbishop Arundel and the Chapter of York", *Bulletin of the Institute of Historical Research*, 54, 1981, 254-7.

Jean-Philippe Genet

**ASCENSION.** The first representations of the Ascension date from the end of the 4th century. Among the most significant evidence of these representations is an ivory tablet from northern Italy (Bayerische Nationalmuseum, Munich). Here the reference to antique apotheoses is strongly marked. *Christ climbs a mountain and passes into the sky, his wrist seized by the Father's hand coming out of the *clouds.

In the East, the first *images of the Ascension (6th c.) propose another formula. In the upper part, Christ is depicted on a *throne, in a *mandorla supported by four angels. Below are gathered the apostles (including St *Paul), the Virgin and the two angels delivering the message announcing the second coming (Acts 1, 11). It is a theophanic representation, insisting on the Son's celestial *glory, and sometimes tinged with an eschatological perspective. This type became the norm in *Byzantine art.

Though known in the West, it did not prevail there. The *Carolingian Renaissance more readily used the early Christian type, from which the mountain and the hand of God were progressively eliminated (11th c.). However, it was the formula divulged by the *Ottonian manuscripts of the *Reichenau school that spread massively between the 10th and the 12th c.: the apostles and the Virgin watch Christ rise, in frontal position, in a mandorla surrounded by four angels. These angels accompany the rise rather than cause it. Two of them lean down to earth to deliver the message of hope (Acts 1, 11); sometimes, especially in the German world, it is Christ himself who leans down to reassure his disciples.

From the end of the 12th c., the images would insist on the very instant of Christ's disappearance: all that now appears of his body are the feet and the bottom of his tunic, the rest being already lost in the clouds. On earth, the apostles and the Virgin surround the mount of Olives on which remain imprinted the marks of Christ's feet, which, according to pilgrims' accounts, still existed in the church of the Ascension at *Jerusalem. This model prevailed from the 12th c. throughout northern Europe.

Italy remained largely refractory to this representation. Faithful to the Byzantine model until the late 13th c., Italian artists later adopted the formula worked out by *Giotto in the lower church of Assisi and especially in the Scrovegni chapel at Padua. This last *fresco repeats the early Christian model, adding to it two elements inspired by the *Meditationes vitae Christi*: the ascension of the just of the Old Testament and the angels, the kneeling position of the witnesses to the scene – this element also spread into the rest of Europe. From the mid 14th c., Giotto's successors preferred to give the Christ of the Ascension a strictly facial position (Andrea di Bonaiuto in the Spanish Chapel at Santa Maria Novella, Florence).

H. Schrade, "Zur Ikonographie der Himmelfahrt Christi", *VBW*, 8, 1928-1929, 66-190. – H. Gutberlet, *Die Himmelfahrt Christi in der bildenden Kunst von den Anfängen bis ins Hohe Mittelalter*, Strasbourg, 1935. – V. M. Schmidt, "Ascensione", *Enciclopedia dell'arte medievale*, Rome, 1991, 572-577.

Pierre Kerbrat

## ASCESIS, ASCETICISM

**The West.** Ascesis consists of a number of practices (penitential exercises, privations, *mortifications, *contemplation) aiming to achieve the *soul's enfranchisement from the *body and to transcend earthly attachments in order to reach perfection. As such, ascesis is not a specifically Christian phenomenon. It is common to some Greco-Roman philosophical schools and to Oriental wisdoms. Yet the gospel message gives Christian ascesis a specific purpose: beyond *contempt for the world and hatred of oneself, it becomes a renunciation of the human being determined to consecrate himself totally and freely to God, in accordance with the precepts of Christ: "Whoever will come after me, let him deny himself, and take up his cross, and follow me" (Mk 8, 34; Lk 9, 23; Mt 16, 24).

In this context and as an alternative to *martyrdom in the absence of persecutions, *monasticism was, from the first centuries of Christianity and throughout the early Middle Ages, the chosen field of ascesis conceived as an instrument of restoration of spiritual *freedom and return to *God. Unlike eastern monasticism, western monasticism, particularly that which inspired the Rule of St *Benedict, was characterised in this sphere by *discretio*. Benedictine ascesis had two fundamental aspects: renunciation of pleasure and struggle against *temptations. Nevertheless, in the feudal context of the 11th and early 12th cc., monastic ascesis hardened under the influence of the values of heroism and struggle that guided the *spirituality of the feudal period as a whole. Moreover, the polemic that opposed lay power to religious power in this perod accentuated the temptation to flight and contempt of the world, less as a form of evasion of social life and its commitments than as a negative judgment on certain structures that were an obstacle to the flourishing of religion. So the monastic spirituality of the 11th and early 12th cc. stressed the condemnation, traditional among Benedictines, of the terrestrial world and the search for voluntary suffering, even if, in practice, contempt of the world was never applied literally. The methods used in ascesis were on one hand privation and renunciation, particularly as to *food (*fasting or doing without certain dishes), on the other hand the imposition of voluntary suffering. The bodily mortifications that ascetics inflicted on themselves were varied, but common to all: wearing of *hairshirts and other rough or painful garments, *flagellation, vigils, sleeping on the ground, etc.

But monasticism did not exhaust Christian ascesis, even if it was nearly always its model *par excellence*. Before the appearance of monasticism in the East, ascesis was practised by virgins and the continent outside any kind of monastic organisation. This current of independent lay asceticism lasted throughout the Middle Ages, in the person of hermits who peopled the *deserts of the Mediterranean lands and the mountainous and wooded regions. These lay hermits expanded and hardened the monastic model, giving themselves up to unbridled asceticism and ever more extravagant mortifications, in defiance of traditional *discretio*. The search for the ascetic exploit found its most perfect expression in Italian eremitical milieux, from the 11th c. and under the influence of *Peter Damian, milieux that produced, *e.g.*, St Dominic Loricatus, who enclosed his body in a sort of metal corset studded with nails. Indeed, this exacerbated form of ascesis is explained both by the anguish for *salvation and by the desire to imitate Christ's torments to the end. In this sense, it is a precursory sign of the evangelical reawakening, and indeed equally characterised the practices of the flagellants in the 14th century. Without going to such excesses and under less painful forms, the fascination exercised by the ascetic tendencies of reformed monastic spirituality is expressed in most of the lay spiritual movements of the 11th c., peace movements, *pilgrimages or *crusades, so many manifestations that aimed at the acquisition of salvation through the *merits of privation, or even suffering.

In the 12th and 13th cc., the development of devotion to Christ's humanity and to the suffering God expanded the mimetic character of ascesis, already being formulated by the Italian hermits of the 11th century. In the context of the spread of the apostolic ideal, from now on ascesis served an ideal of imitation of Christ by a very realistic reproduction of the sufferings of the *Passion. It thus acquired a more clearly positive aim, which was a response to the practice (judged negative) of ascesis in heretical and particularly *Cathar milieux, where it was based on the dualist conviction that the flesh was bad, as well as on hatred of the world and of man. Moreover, the search for physical suffering increasingly tended to be joined to apostolic currents of voluntary *poverty and charity to flow into an ideal of religious life compatible with the lay state: that of the groups of *penitents who multiplied in the late 12th and the 13th c. in communities of *laici religiosi* and then in the *confraternity movement. At a time when an autonomous lay spirituality was being worked out, ascesis was thus no longer the exclusive domain of monks; indeed laypeople tended to appropriate it. The Church itself required regular ascetic practices from the faithful: abstinence from meat three times a week, fasting during *Lent, *Advent, *Ember Days, *vigils of *feasts, and Fridays. But alongside these obligatory practices, laypeople began to practice a collective ascesis, not hesitating to bring out into the open mortifications previously confined to the obscurity of cloisters or cells. Thus in 1260 a penitent of Perugia organised in his town an expiatory procession of a new type, in the course of which the participants publicly flagellated themselves. This formula met with great success and the *flagellant movement subsequently gained over the whole of central and northern Italy. The main reason for this success was that, by these ascetic exercises, the penitents, including the flagellants, reproduced Christ's sufferings in their daily existence, in a familiar context and without leaving the world.

Whatever their forms, all these mortifications were behind the construction of a reputation for *sanctity. Ascesis was, for popular recognition as well as for the ecclesiastical authorities, one of the chief distinctive signs of an exceptional life in the service of God. For this reason, a person's perfection and sanctity were necessarily measured by the intensity of the ascesis he practised and the sufferings, renunciations and macerations he imposed on himself. More than any other form of sanctity, ascesis made the man who practised it a point of transition between the human and the divine, between the natural and the supernatural. Indeed, while the ascetic strove to "follow naked the naked Christ", he who saw him or venerated him recognised in him the characteristics of the suffering Christ.

The ascetic practices of the early 13th c. lasted until the end of the Middle Ages in a religious climate very sensitive to dolorist meditation and contemplation of the sufferings of the Passion. Admittedly, association with the Passion – by its reproduction in each person's flesh and life – remained a foundation of late medieval piety, oriented towards salvation by works; and yet the meditative aspect of this piety was being expanded at the very time when the liturgical part of the search for salvation was being developed to extremes.

*The Vision of God: The Christian Doctrine of the Summum Bonum,* Cambridge 1992. – "Ascèse, ascétisme", *DSp*, 1, 1937, 936-1010. – *Monks, Hermits and the Ascetic Tradition*, W.J. Sheils (ed.), Oxford, 1985. – A. Vauchez, *La Spiritualité du Moyen Âge occidental, VIII^e-XIII^e siècles*, Paris, 1994 (2nd ed.).

Cécile Caby

**Byzantium.** In Byzantine spirituality, the term "ascesis" (from Greek *askèsis*, "exercise", "training") covers all the practices by which the Christian, especially the ascetic, imitating Christ with respect to the evangelical commands and precepts, mortifies his flesh and masters his passions. In a restricted and negative sense, it can designate external practices of mortification: "asceticism" can be employed in this case, though the two terms are hardly distinct. A wider and more positive meaning is possible: ascesis then designates the intense practice of the virtues.

Ascesis is not peculiar to Christianity. The thing and the word occur in the Greek philosophers, particularly the *Neoplatonists, and among the Jews (Philo of Alexandria). In Christianity, ascetic tendencies appear from the time of the New Testament (which does not use the term) and ascesis is conceived as an imitation of Christ. The link with *martyrdom is strong, whether ascesis is a preparation for martyrdom or an equivalent to it. Though every Christian practised ascetic exercises such as fasting, vigils and chastity, from the 3rd c. there is evidence of ascetics who, without leaving their community, led a special life, in particular practising virginity.

In the 4th c., with the first developments of *monasticism, especially in its anchoritic form, ascetic life tended to be confused with monastic life. The term "ascetic" became equivalent to monk, and the place where ascesis was practised (*askètèrion*) designated the monastery. Yet in the protobyzantine period there existed non-monastic confraternities that may be considered as groupings of ascetics: *philoponoi*, *spudaeoi*. Meanwhile, asceticism penetrated society: the conduct of pious laymen (like the mother of *Theodore the Studite, in the 8th c.) or of certain emperors (Theodosius II,

Justinian, Nicephorus Phocas) or empresses (Pulcheria, Theophano) is described in the same terms as monastic life.

In monastic spirituality, ascesis was conceived as a first step: the "practical" life aimed to subdue the passions, conquering the demons who aroused them; it preceded contemplation, knowledge of God, gnosis. One of the most influential ascetic authors of the Byzantine world, Evagrius Ponticus (late 4th c.) presented the stages of the spiritual life thus: "Faith is strengthened by the fear of God, and this in turn by abstinence; this is made inflexible by perseverance and hope. Impassibility is born, which has charity for daughter; and charity is the door of natural science, to which succeed theology and, finally, *beatitude". We see that ascesis in the strict sense (abstinence, perseverance) is not separate from *faith, fear of God, or *hope, and that its object is the mastery of the passions (impassibility, *apatheia*), *charity and gnosis.

The principal ascetic practices aim at conquering the passions, and firstly the more carnal ones: abstinence combats gluttony; *continence and *chastity or, better, *virginity oppose lust. Mastery of sleep, of the tongue, the repression of all desire to possess are equally important. Withdrawal from the world, either by departure to the *desert (anachoresis) or by entry into a monastery, is the first step of monastic life. The *coenobite, or the beginner being formed in the anchoritic life under the direction of a master, learns to suppress his own will by practising an absolute obedience. The *anchorite, for his part, cut off from the world in his cell or in his desert, devotes himself to solitude and silence (*hesuchia*).

Ascetic life gave rise to specific exercises, whose practice could be moderate, but which were sometimes pushed to extremes, or even to extravagance: fasting, sometimes of a frightening austerity (fasting one day in two, or all week, or even a total fast lasting forty days); long years of solitude; reclusion in a cell; privation of sleep; sleeping on the bare ground; refusal to wash. The will to leave the world could lead the ascetic to withdraw to the top of a column (*stylites) or up a tree (dendrites). It could be accompanied by a rejection of all that belonged to civilization: refusal of all meat, or even of all cooked food; life in the open air (*hypètres*); a life of wandering in desert places (*boskoi*). The perfection of ascesis, in certain texts (*Life of Mary the Egyptian*), could include nakedness and could come close to an animal life. We also see exercises of mortification by physical suffering: *hairshirts, chains, exposure to heat and cold, to insect or plant stings. Meditation on death also engendered particular exercises: living near or in tombs.

Several attitudes towards ascetic exercises are observable. Important movements aimed to moderate the excesses of ascesis: this was the case not just in the coenobitic world, where obedience and work were favoured as against corporeal ascesis; it was also the case in the anchoritic world, where several texts remind us that ascesis must be practised with discernment (*diakrisis*). If not, it leads to pride, madness and spiritual ruin. It is not an end in itself; nor must it be practised with ostentation. Certain deviant forms, linked, *e.g.*, to the *dualist heresies, are condemned. In the 12th c. on the other hand, the movement critical of monasticism took certain aspects of asceticism as its target. Yet in many Saints' Lives or ascetic texts, the insistence on ascesis and on its extreme forms, the listing of veritable records of austerity (especially in protobyzantine *Syria), show clearly that *sanctity was often linked to the most rigorous practices, which appeared as the proofs by which the saint was elevated above ordinary mortals.

By the fact of the link between ascesis and monasticism, and the fundamental place of ascesis in spiritual life, the major part of the very abundant monastic and spiritual literature of the Byzantines may be considered as ascetic. We will content ourselves here with pointing out some particularly important authors or works of the protobyzantine period, the most fertile from this point of view. In the middle Byzantine period, we still meet with important works (*e.g.* the *Catecheses* of *Theodore the Studite, *c.*800). But, apart from the *hesychast movement, they had neither the influence nor the originality of the classical works of the 4th-7th centuries.

Among these, we may list the *Lives of the monastic saints*, which, at the same time as celebrating a memory, put forward a model: thus Athanasius of Alexandria's *Life of Anthony* (shortly after 356) or, for the great Syrian ascetics, Theodoret's *Historia philothea* (5th c.). *Apophthegms and collections of edifying histories also belong to ascetic literature: the *Apophthegms of the Fathers* hand down the essentials of the teaching of the Egyptian Fathers and, from the late 5th c., exercised an immense influence in both East and West; the *Spiritual meadow* of John Moschus (7th c.) is a collection of anecdotes set in Egypt, *Palestine and Syria. Among authors whose teaching left a mark on the Byzantine world, we must single out Basil of Caesarea (4th c.), whose ascetic writings served as charter to the coenobitic world, Evagrius Ponticus (late 4th c.) whose work, so important and original, was rediscovered in our own days; Diadochus of Photice, Nilus of Ancyra (5th c.); Dorotheus, Barsanuphius and John of Gaza, who left their mark on 6th-c. Palestine; and *John Climacus (7th c.), whose *Ladder* recapitulated the teaching of the Fathers. If, in essentials, this literature was from the beginning written in Greek, some works were translated from other languages: thus those of *Cassian (5th c.), originally written in Latin; or those of *Isaac of Nineveh, translated in the 9th c. from Syriac.

*The Vision of God: The Christian Doctrine of the Summum Bonum*, Cambridge 1992. – L. Regnault, *Les Sentences des Pères du désert*, Solesmes, 1966-1976 (3 vol.). – Evagrius Ponticus. *Traité pratique, ou le moine*, A. and C. Guillaumont (ed.), 1-2, 1971 ("SC", 170 and 171). – *Les Apophtegmes des Pères*, J.-C. Guy (ed.), 1993 ("SC", 387). – "Ascèse, ascétisme", *DSp*, 1, 1936, 936-1010. – G. Florovsky, *The Byzantine Ascetic and Spiritual Fathers*, Vaduz, 1987.

Bernard Flusin

**ASHES.** Abundantly attested in the Old Testament (Jos 7, 6-2; 2 Sam 13, 19; Ezek 27, 30; Job 2, 12; 42, 6; Jon 3, 6; Esth 4, 3), the practice of covering oneself with ashes was for Christians synonymous with penitence and grief. Practised at first in private, in the 10th and 11th c. covering oneself with ashes became a sign of public *penance. Several ritual *ordines* describe the imposition of ashes on penitents on Ash Wednesday, inaugurating the period of *Lent.

In the Middle Ages, ashes were used for other rites than penance, like the anointing of the sick and the *dedication of churches.

*DACL*, 2, 2, 1910, 3037-3044. – *DSp*, 2, 1, 1953, 403-404. – *CaP*, London, 1986-1988 (4 vol.).

Éric Palazzo

**ASS, FEAST OF THE.** The ass, which had kept the Baby Jesus warm and taken the *Holy Family to Egypt, played an important role, from the 12th and 13th cc., in the dramatic *offices and collective rejoicings that marked the Christmas cycle. Ridden sometimes by a young girl, who personified the Virgin and held a child in her arms, sometimes by a child, "bishop of fools", or wearing a *mitre, the ass could be led into the church or through the town, in a *procession that was part of the "feast of Fools" or of the "Innocents", also called "feast of the Ass". The religious chants intoned on this occason ended with a *prosa* vaunting the virtues of the ass, or with cries: at Beauvais, at the feast of the *Innocents, the participants let out "hee-haw's".

J. Heers, *Fêtes de fous et Carnavals*, Paris, 1983. – G. Cohen, "Ane (Fête de l')", and A. Ibos-Auge, "Office des Fous", *DLFMA*, 1992, 64-65, 1084.

Michel Lauwers

**ASSASSINS.** Followers of an Ismā'īlī *Shi'ite sect founded in 1094 during a crisis of succession to the *Fatimid caliphate of Egypt. Strongly entrenched around Alamut in northern *Iran, the Assassins spread to *Syria in the 12th-13th cc., where they were known under a name derived from the Arabic *Hashīshiyya* (hashish smokers). This term, which thus entered the vocabulary, does not imply that they drugged themselves, but seems to have been applied to them as a term of contempt. They were distinguished by the systematic use of assassination as a political weapon to establish their law. Their victims were *Sunnis, Shi'ites or Franks, and the sect reached its apogee under the direction of Sinān (1162-1192). The *Mongols put an end to their power in 1256 and the *Mamluks finally eliminated them from Syria in 1273.

B. Lewis, *The Assassins: Terrorism and Politics in Medieval Islam*, London, 1985.

Anne-Marie Eddé

**ASSISI.** A town in *Umbria, situated off the Via Flaminia, Assisi (Lat. *Asisium*, *Assisium*) was an episcopal see directly dependent on the apostolic see. The patron of the *diocese was St Rufinus, bishop and martyr (236?), accompanied by St Victorinus and, later, St *Francis. A Roman *municipium*, very prosperous in the imperial period, its medieval history is a succession of sacks and destructions, from Totila to *Charlemagne, from Christian of Mainz to the troops of Perugia and Niccolò Piccinino. Part of the Lombard (then Frankish) duchy of *Spoleto, from the time of *Frederick I the town became a county directly dependent on the *Empire (1160). The visible sign of this subordination was the imperial *Rocca*, the object of a popular revolt in 1198. Despite earlier scattered evidence, the existence of the *commune dates from this time, marked by loyalty to the *pope and alternation, usual for middle-sized Umbrian towns, between adherence to *Perugia and to other external powers, signorial attempts (Muzio di Francesco, 1319-1321) and internal divisions, ending in its annexation to the *States of the Church by Paul III.

In the city's traditional system, the *chapter of St Rufinus, established in the cathedral church built by Bishop Hugo between 1019 and 1028, seems (at least according to the magnificent archives, unedited) to have had more importance than the *bishop. On the Hugonian edifice arose the new cathedral, begun in 1140 but completed only in the first years of the 13th century. It was

*The Deposition from the Cross* (*c.*1320). Fresco by Pietro Lorenzetti (1280-1348) in the basilica of St Francis at Assisi.

*The Assumption of the Virgin.* Painting by Girolamo di Benvenuto, *c.*1498. Montalcino, Museo Civico e di Arte Sacra.

there that *Frederick II was baptized. In the city, the chapter of St Rufinus, the episcopal clientele and the imperial *boni homines* together set up a blocked system against which the *populus*, the rest of the population, rose up in 1198 only to end by suffering the revenge of its enemies, supported by Perugia.

Such was the situation of the town when the *Franciscan experience occurred, an experience that (after his death more than in his lifetime) gradually became the sole source of vitality and identification for local society in its architectural, institutional and spiritual significance. The concentration of all energies around the Franciscan pole, at the same time as the irremediable decline of the town in the medieval and modern periods, drained their vigour from the other components, religious and civil, of Assisi's history.

*DHGE*, 1, 1912, 1121-1124. – C. Cenci, *Documentazione di vita assisiana, 1300-1530*, 1-3, Grottaferrata, 1974-1976. – *Assisi in tempo di san Francesco. Atti del V Convegno internazionale di studi francescani*, Assisi, 1978. – A. Grohmann, *Assisi* (*Le città nella storia d'Italia*), Rome-Bari, 1989.

Attilio Bartoli Langeli

**ASSUMPTION (iconography).** Towards the end of the 13th c., the Resurrection of Mary gave way in iconography to the Assumption. But there is no question of Assumption in the Bible: the legend was late, modeled in the 6th c. on the rapture of the prophet *Elijah and the *Ascension of Christ. The old names for the feast – *Transitus Virginis*, *Dormitio*, *Depositio* – indicate that Mary died before being transfigured in glory.

Like Christ's Ascension, Mary's Assumption was conceived in the West in the form of bodily *resurrection (Notre-Dame at *Senlis, lintel of the west portal, *c.*1190). At *Autun, in the 12th c., Mary pierces the vault of her sepulchre, as *Christ goes through the lid of his sarcophagus, without breaking the seals. In this sense, the representation of Mary's death and that of her resurrection are to be conceived in the more general framework of a theology of human *death: the glorification of Mary's *body anticipates what will happen at the end of time to all the elect. This is certainly the meaning of the whole programme carved on the tympanum of the west portal of Notre-Dame at Senlis. However, unlike Christ's Ascension, Mary's Assumption is passive: angels carry the Virgin up to the kingdom of heaven. In the 13th c. and even more in the 14th, the Assumption is depicted, in cycles of monumental painting, as a mounting up to heaven and so is placed at the climax of iconographical programmes (*e.g.*, in central Italy, at *Orvieto, in the cathedral of Santa Maria della Stella, *c.*1357-1364; at *Pisa, in the church of San Francesco, Sardi Campigli chapel, 1397-1398; at *Siena, in the chapel of the Priors at the Palazzo pubblico, 1407).

The Assumption was distinguished at this time from the Immaculate *Conception, which was interpreted rather as a descent to earth: in the 15th c., contamination occurred between the two representations. The Virgin of the Assumption could appear standing on a crescent moon, her forehead crowned with twelve stars (like the Woman of the *Apocalypse) recalling the twelve apostles pressing round her bedside at the moment of her death (*e.g.* on sculpted works in Brittany after the mid 15th c., or in Bavaria, in the entourage of Hans Leinberger, at the beginning of the 16th). In the late 15th c., the Assumption tended to be transformed into an Ascension: instead of being carried by angels to heaven, Mary rises alone, arms extended upward, under the gaze of the Apostles (the *mandorla that enclosed Mary becomes a crown of angels and cherubim arranged at the base of the figure.

Connected with the iconography of the Assumption, there also developed the representation of Mary in the heavens letting fall her girdle to convince the apostle Thomas of her glory. This theme was widespread in Tuscan iconography, in particular from the second half of the 14th c. (Andrea di Cione, called Orcagna, *Tabernacle of Orsanmichele*, sculpted reverse, 1359, Florence; Agnolo Gaddi, *fresco decoration of the chapel of the Sacro Cingolo, Prato cathedral, 1393-1395).

M. Jugie, *La Mort et l'Assomption de la Sainte Vierge. Étude historico-doctrinale*, Vatican, 1944. – M.-L. Thérel, *Le Triomphe de la Vierge-Église. Sources historiques, littéraires et iconographiques*, Paris, 1984. – S.-C. Mimouni, *Dormition et Assomption de Marie. Histoire des traditions anciennes*, Paris, 1995. – *La Vierge à l'Enfant d'Issenheim. Un chef-d'oeuvre bâlois de la fin du Moyen age*, Paris, 1998 ("Les dossiers du musée du Louvre").

Daniel Russo

**ASTROLABE.** An astronomical instrument, usually of brass, offering, in the form of a flat, easily-transportable disc, a good depiction of the daily movement of the heavenly vault, the astrolabe may go back to Greek Antiquity. It was known in Christian Europe, through the intermediary of the Arabs, from the extreme end of the 10th c. and enjoyed a great vogue from the 12th; its use in *university teaching ensured it a lasting success until the 17th c., perfectly justified by its real pedagogical qualities and the facilities it procured as an instrument of calculation for the solution of all the problems, astronomical as well as astrological, connected with the daily and annual movements of the sun and the stars.

On the other hand, it is altogether wrong to see the astrolabe as a piece of equipment for observing the heavenly bodies, and consequently it had nothing to do with the movement of maritime *discoveries that marked the late Middle Ages: to connect it with them is an error often made, due to its bearing the same name as the nautical astrolabe, a relatively late instrument that typologically has nothing to do with the astronomical astrolabe.

There exist a respectable number of astrolabes, among which are distinguished oriental astrolabes (Arab, Persian, Indian) and Western astrolabes; of the latter a good hundred date from the Middle Ages (practically all of the 14th or 15th c.), but they are distinctly more numerous in the 16th and 17th centuries.

*Jordanus de Nemore and the Mathematics of Astrolabes*, R.B. Thomson (ed.), Toronto, 1978. – A. Turner, *The Time Museum, Catalogue of the Collection, 1, Time Measuring Instruments, 1, Astrolabes, Astrolabe Related Instruments*, Rockford, 1985. – E. Poulle, "L'Astrolabe", *La Recherche*, 178, Paris, June 1986, 756-765.

Emmanuel Poulle

*The Astrolabes or the Zodiac* (detail). 15th-c. Flemish tapestry from Toledo cathedral. Toledo, Santa Cruz Museum.

**ASTROLOGY.** Astrology, "discourse on the stars", based on belief in the influence of heavenly bodies on the sublunary world, played a considerable role in the mind of the Christian elites in the Middle Ages. When they were not confused with each other, astrology and *astronomy were generally considered by medieval intellectuals as the two complementary faces of one and the same discipline. Examination of astrological data was the primary purpose of astronomical calculations and an auxiliary, often considered indispensable, of the practice of *medicine. The fact that a great many doctors took astral influences into account and that *astronomia-astrologia* was part of the *quadrivium* thus allowed astrology doubly to claim a scientific status.

This scientific status went back to the Hellenistic period and was based notably on the authority of two great 2nd-c. Greek scholars, Ptolemy and Galen. The former, inspired conceiver of a mathematical astronomy in the *Almagest*, was also the author of the most famous book of astrology ever written, the *Tetrabiblion*, in which he expounded the majority of the theories that astrologers would go on using from his day to our own. The latter, in his *De diebus creticis*, directly related the movement of the humours of the human *body and the *sicknesses that result from them to the course of the Moon.

Ptolemy's work and that of several Greek authors, like Dorotheus of Sidon and Vettius Valens, later spread to Byzantium, then to the Arab world, where they were enriched by a certain number of Indian and Persian elements. The judgment of the stars (*ahkâm al-nujûm*), the act by which astrology raises itself into a judge of men's destiny, knew from then on, from the 8th to the 13th c., in Islamic lands, an authentic golden age, as witness the incredibly high number and the quality of the sages who practised it. Byzantine astrology, very dynamic in the sphere of political horoscopes from the 5th c., benefited from Islamic contributions from the 8th c. and knew good times until the fall of *Constantinople.

In the Latin West, the situation was radically different until the threshold of the 12th c., since the work of the Greek and Arab astronomers and astrologers was not yet known there. In the early Middle Ages there was hardly any true astrological theory, with the exception of the simplistic and stereotyped system of the *lunaria* and *zodiologia*, based on the position of the Moon in the course of the lunar month and in each of the signs of the *zodiac.

The reappearance in Christian Europe of a learned astrology, taking into account a great number of celestial parameters and forming a clearly organised and hierarchical system of knowledge, took place in the first half of the 12th c., at a time when *translations from Arabic to Latin were beginning to give the basic rules of astrological judgments and providing astronomical tables allowing the planets to be placed on horoscopes. The scientific status of astrology was reinforced at the same time, inasmuch as the astral determinism taught by Arab *science was inserted relatively coherently into the Aristotelian theory of natural causality, diffused from the 12th c. in the West. The considerable attraction of *Aristotle and of Arab astrology in the *university world of the 13th c. then set off several reactions on the part of the Church, of which the most important was that of the bishop of Paris, *Stephen Tempier, who in 1277 condemned 219 propositions, some 30 of which led directly to astral determinism. But the effect of these condemnations in no way slowed down the activity of the astrologers, who however accompanied their predictions with formulae that allowed them to save the appearance of respect for the divine will and man's free *will.

So we see a slow rise in the influence of astrology in the West, from the middle of the 12th c. to the beginning of the 14th, then a sudden extension of its practices from 1320, due notably to the use of new astronomical tables, the *Alfonsine tables, whose universal and systematically sexagesimal character allowed a considerable improvement in the technical possibilities of the art of prediction. Moreover the relative decline of Aristotelianism, manifested at the end of the Middle Ages, led to a partial contamination of astrology by the Jewish *kaballa* and to attempts like that of Marsilio *Ficino, aiming to integrate it into Neoplatonist thought, more clearly oriented towards esotericism.

From 1470, the spread of printing gave a new stimulus to astrological output. It was vulgarized by way of almanacs and annual predictions, which became general all over the West and were now addressed to the whole of the cultivated public. The practice of astrology nevertheless remained, on the threshold of the *Renaissance, the prerogative of a small elite of *clerics who were for the most part mainly doctors, the professional astrologer being an exception.

Medieval astrologers distinguished four main parts in the study and practice of their art: nativities, revolutions, elections and interrogations. Nativities were related to horoscopes of the birth and conception of individuals and the judgments that could be

*The Theologian and the Astrologer.* Wood-cut from Pierre d'Ailly's *Concordia Astronomiae cum Theologia*, 1490. Paris, BNF.

drawn from them. The study of the revolutions of nativities was based on the examination of the sky at the moment of the anniversary of the subject's birth. That of the revolutions of years rested on the horoscope of the spring equinox of a particular year, or even of the new and full moons immediately preceding the equinox. Election corresponded to the choice of favourable moments to undertake such or such a thing. As for interrogations, they were intended to provide answers to questions asked of the astrologer by a person who came to consult him, the practitioner having to draw up the horoscope of the precise moment when the question had been asked him.

Analysis of the conjunctions of the superior planets, as well as that of comets, was connected with annual revolutions. The Sasanid doctrine of the great conjunctions of Saturn and Jupiter, known in the *Byzantine Empire from the 8th c., standardized by the Iranian astrologer Albumasar in the 9th c. and transmitted to the Latin West in the 12th, exercised considerable influence on the whole Christian world, in the field of the interpretation of major natural, political or religious events: hypothetical tempests of 1186, linked to the presence of all the planets in the sign of Libra; *Black Death of 1348 and *Great Schism of 1378, interpreted after the event as the consequences of the conjuctions of 1345 and 1365, etc. As for comets, they usually foretold catastrophes, notably the coming death of some king or prince, and had done so since the early Middle Ages.

Medieval astrology was thus never reduced to a set of techniques of prediction. It was a comprehensive system of interpreting the world, seeking to embrace every sphere of human life. And it was as such that it aroused numerous queries and polemics as to its orthodoxy and legitimacy.

In fact, the general consensus on the reality of the influence of the heavens on the terrestrial world was broken when it came to determining the precise nature and extent of that influence. Did the stars produce their effects only on natural phenomena or did they determine to various degrees, directly or through the passions and humours, the individual and collective actions of men? Should a distinction be made between a good astrology, which would confine itself to the study and prevision of these natural phenomena, and a bad astrology, *superstitious and divinatory, whose judgments would be based on a negation of free will? The debate, immense and multiform, has had a considerable echo in East and West up to the modern period.

So attacks on astrology were very numerous, and of two kinds. A great many theologians, heirs to the Church *Fathers and in particular to St Augustine, held roughly to the idea that, the secrets of the future belonging only to God, astrologers were imposters. But this idea was far from making for unanimity among their ranks, and a man like *Pierre d'Ailly admitted the doctrine of great conjunctions to the point of making them the main object of an attempt to reconcile *theology, *history and astrology. Rare and little-heeded, by contrast, were great minds like Nicole *Oresme, *Henry of Langenstein and *Pico della Mirandola, who dared to attack the scientific foundations of astrology and managed to demonstrate the quasi-impossibility of formulating exact predictions. At the dawn of the modern period, judicial astrology, though condemned by the Church and contested by certain scholars, was in fact at the apogee of its influence and prestige in the Christian world.

L. Thorndike, *A History of Magic and Experimental Science*, vol. 1-4, New York, 1923-1934. – M. Préaud, *Les Astrologues à la fin du Moyen Âge*, Paris, 1984. – S. J. Tester, *A History of Western Astrology*, Woodbridge, 1987. – D. Pingree, A. Kazhdan, "Astrology", *The Oxford Dictionary of Byzantium*, 1, New York-Oxford, 1991, 214-216. – H.M. Carey, *Courting Disaster: Astrology at the English Court and University in the later Middle Ages*, Basingstoke, 1992. – *Medieval Lunar Astrology*, L. Means (ed.), Lewiston, NY, 1993.

Jean-Patrice Boudet

## ASTRONOMY

**The West.** The Latin inheritance in astronomy was not great: the *Dream of Scipio* and its commentary, Pliny and Martianus Capella bequeathed only an elementary *cosmology. So that medieval astronomy only really began with the *translations from the Arabic made in the 12th c. (with an exception for the *astrolabe, known since the extreme end of the 10th c.). Intimately joined to *astrology, which provided a justification for it and encouraged its development, the rise of astronomy was linked to that of *university education, which produced all its practitioners.

Astronomy was applied at three levels of knowledge. The elementary level was that of cosmology, the only one where the Latin and Arabic inheritances converged; it produced a university manual that was tirelessly copied and commented on into the 17th c., John of Sacrobosco's *Treatise on the Sphere*, in which classical reminiscences reduced the vocabulary transposed from Arabic to a bare minimum.

For astronomy of the *primum mobile*, *i.e.* of daily movement, there was a large range of documentation, made up of a great variety of trigonometrical tables or tables of spherical astronomy relating to this movement (tables of declinations, of right and oblique ascensions, lists of stars or geographical coordinates) and a range of instruments and treatises on instruments. The tables were essentially of Greek origin but, having been transmitted through the Arabs, had received notable enrichments. But their track is difficult to follow, since these sorts of tables have a very fractured manuscript tradition and were regrouped or else dispersed according to the needs of the practitioners who copied them. It is certain that the greater number were part of one or other of the two groups of Arabic astronomical tables translated into Latin in the 12th c.: the tables of al-Battani and the so-called Toledo tables, but it is equally certain that some had other origins.

The astronomical instrumentation of the *primum mobile* was essentially pedagogical in aim: its primary vocation was to explain this or that consequence of daily movement (variability of the duration of the diurnal arc according to geographical latitudes and over the year for a given latitude, difference between equatorial coordinates, ecliptic coordinates and local coordinates, etc.) and to provide a calculated evaluation of them. Chronologically, the astrolabe and then the old quadrant (11th c.) were the first Latin instrumental equipment, but this was greatly enriched in the 13th c. as a result of the development of university teaching: the new quadrant and the *saphea* were derivations of the astrolabe, the *turquet* was more original. Alone of these instruments, the astrolabe was made in exceptionally large numbers; the artisans who made them would all be anonymous if we could not, by chance, cite the name of one of the most prolific of them, Jean Fusoris, established at Paris at the beginning of the 15th century. We are very well informed about all these instruments by a technical literature as varied as it is abundant.

We should point out that all this instrumental equipment did not in any way answer the needs of astronomical observation, a marginal and little-known activity in the Middle Ages (*observare* did not mean to observe but to calculate, and even, more vaguely, to work in astronomy).

Planetary astronomy was interested in the movements of the planets; these were regulated by a complex combination of epicycles and eccentricities worked out by Ptolemy, known in the West through the channel of translations from the Arabic and which the Middle Ages never really questioned: when there was a dispute about the Ptolemaic construction, it did not go beyond the domain of philosophical generalities. This was because this construction had the decisive advantage over any rival constructions of being supported by an unassailable mathematical formulation. And the practice of planetary astronomy in the Middle Ages was primarily the utilization of this mathematical formulation that was the planetary astronomical tables.

The first tables, in the West, were translations from the Arabic, all made in the 12th c.: the tables of al-Khwarizmi, of al-Battani, and those of Azarquiel known as the Toledo tables, all of which had a properly planetary part; then, very soon (from the mid 12th and in the 13th c.), adaptations of the planetary part of the tables of Azarquiel were made using the Christian *calendar and for another meridian than that of Toledo: so-called tables of Marseille, Pisa, Toulouse, Malines, etc., according to their meridian of reference. Finally, in 1320, the *Alfonsine Tables, properly Latin tables, of unknown origin but improperly or mischievously put under the name of *Alfonso X of Castile, were established at Paris by members of the university: these gave the last two centuries of the Middle Ages a very well-performing astronomical tool.

At the same time as the astronomical tables, efforts were made to set out to the university public a more directly accessible exposition of the theory of the planets than that of Ptolemy's *Almagest*; the anonymous text known under the name of *Theorica planetarum Gerardi*, the *Theorica planetarum* of Campanus of Novara, the work of George Peurbach and Regiomontanus were assuredly responsible for the extreme vitality of high-level astronomy in the late Middle Ages.

This is why it would be erroneous to judge medieval Latin astronomy as rather unimportant on the grounds that it showed little interest in observation and remained apparently under the tow of Arab *science: the contagious enthusiasm of its adepts greatly contributed to establishing in medieval society a taste for the science of the heavens, a taste that was admittedly supported by the omnipresence of astrology, but which also strove to diffuse as widely as possible a science of quality.

E. Poulle, *Les Sources astronomiques (textes, tables, instruments)*, 1981 ("TSMÂO", 39). – J. Samso, *Islamic Astronomy and Medieval Spain*, Aldershot, 1994. – E. Poulle, *Astronomie planétaire au Moyen Âge latin*, Aldershot, 1996. – S. C. McCluskey, *Astronomies and Cultures in Early Medieval Europe*, Cambridge, 1998.

Emmanuel Poulle

**Byzantium.** Byzantine astronomy was a continuation of ancient astronomy: it rested essentially on two works by Claudius Ptolemy (*c.*130), the *Almagest* and the *Easy Tables*, and on his commentator Theon of Alexandria (*c.*364). Not until the 7th c. do we see the first properly Byzantine astronomical treatise: Stephanos of Alexandria's Commentary on the Easy tables, written *c.*617 and inspired by Theon's Little Commentary. In the 9th c., many astronomical treatises were copied in sumptuous manuscripts. Astronomy was taught in the higher schools, but it is hard to judge the astronomical knowledge of the 9th and 10th cc. for lack of evidence. We know that *astrology was practised all through this period, which presupposes at least the use of astronomical tables.

In the 11th c., the situation changed: scholia dating from 1032 compare Ptolemy's tables with those of the astronomer Alim (Ibn al-A'lam, d. 985); an important manual of *c.*1072 uses the tables of al-Khwārizmī and Ḥabash al-Ḥāsib, for the first time with trigonometric functions. Symeon Seth (*c.*1058) knew the Arab value for the precession. At the same time Ptolemy's astronomy continued to be practised. From the 11th c. dates the sole surviving Byzantine *astrolabe (in the municipal museum of Brescia), dated 1062. Arab influence continued in the 12th c., but this impetus was stopped short by the capture of *Constantinople by the fourth *crusade in 1204.

In the late 13th and all through the 14th c., astronomical studies enjoyed an unprecedented expansion. Ptolemy's astronomy was rediscovered: in *c.*1310 Theodore Metochites wrote an enormous work entitled *Elements of astronomy* in which he explained the astronomy of Ptolemy; his disciple Nicephorus Gregoras predicted eclipses of the sun with the help of Ptolemy's tables and wrote on the astrolabe; his rival Barlaam of Seminara also calculated the eclipses of 1333 and 1337 with the help of the *Almagest*. Nicholas *Cabasilas completed Theon's *Commentary on the Almagest*. Around 1368, Isaac Argyrus composed *New tables* based on Ptolemy. At the same time, from the late 13th c., Gregory Choniades imported Persian treatises on astronomy to Constantinople and *Trebizond. These were used by George Chrysococces who wrote, *c.*1347, a Persian syntaxis adapting the *Zīj-i ilkhānī* of Naṣīr ad-Dīn aṭ-Ṭūsī. In *c.* 1352, Theodore Metochites composed an astronomical *Tribiblos* in which he juxtaposed the astronomy of Ptolemy and the Persian astronomy transmitted by Chrysococces. In the late 14th and in the 15th c., astronomy at Byzantium was open to all foreign influences: Jewish, Latin, Islamic. On the whole, it was characterised by the long survival of Ptolemy and a lack of observation and creativity, though this was compensated by its receptivity to foreign influences.

A. Tihon, *Études d'astronomie byzantine*, 1994 ("CStS", 454). – E.S. Kennedy, *Astronomy and Astrology in the Medieval Islamic World*, Aldershot, 1998.

Anne Tihon

## ASYLUM, RIGHT OF

**The West.** The right of asylum was an acknowledged privilege of sacred places, putting them under protection from all lay intrusion, all secular action, where persons liable to be pursued were protected from all constraint, pursuit or seizure.

From the 4th c., churches were considered places of asylum, a practice attested by St Ambrose, St Gregory Nazianzen and Ammianus Marcellinus. A law of Theodosius I (392) tried to limit this right. The earliest recognition of asylum granted by the Church dates from a constitution of 21 Nov 419. The Theodosian code excluded from it various categories of person, such as debtors to the treasury or Jews, who tried to pass themselves off as converts in order to enjoy the privilege, armed men, whether free or slaves. Moreover, the refugee was not exempt from penalty, but this had to be negotiated by the bishop. The *Code of Justinian refused it to homicides, adulterers and ravishers of virgins. The Church requested its legalization at the council of Carthage (399) – from when it was confirmed by civil law – took on its defence (council of Orange, 441) and gave it new foundations. Ecclesiastical tradition offered original aspects compared to the ancient law: *clerics were forbidden to hand over to justice a refugee who risked death or mutilation, and had to intercede in his favour.

In the *Merovingian period, right of asylum became a heavy burden for the churches, inasmuch as great men frequently put themselves under its security. *Charlemagne tended to restrict it, the *capitulary of Heristal (779) refusing entry to asylum for those who incurred the *death penalty. In 873, *Charles the Bald confirmed the inviolability of the church, but also of its porch (*atrium*) and the presbytery belonging to it.

The development of the *cult of the saints and their *relics, offering a protection more immediate than divine protection, entailed a renewal of right of asylum, since the saint was thought to protect the places consecrated to him. Papal and royal privileges of *immunity granted to churches generally forbade officials to penetrate the domain of the immunist. The church and the monastery, with their annexes, formed a territory of variable extent enjoying a privileged status; from the 11th c., "immunity" often became synonymous with "asylum".

The *provincial councils of the 11th-12th cc. (Clermont, 1095; Reims, 1131; Pisa, 1134) supplemented earlier legislation. The second *Lateran council (1139) ended with a reminder of the right of asylum of churches and *cemeteries, and Gratian's *Decretum* brought together, without much order, the texts that would from now on be authoritative in the Church (cause XVII, q. IV, Friedberg, I, 815-828), the **Decretals* contributing some complements (book III, tit. XLIX, *De immunitate ecclesiarum, coemeteriorum et rerum ad eas pertinentibus*, Friedberg, II, 654-657). But restrictions were added from the 13th c.: highway brigands, or persons committing a *homicide or mutilations within the asylum, were excluded from it. Refugees could also be handed over to secular *justice, on condition that it did not condemn them to death or to a mutilating penalty. Right of asylum remained undisputed in the Middle Ages and was recognised by lay jurists such as Beaumanoir, but it was progressively called into question, notably by the *towns, and suffered flagrant breaches from the early 16th century.

G. Le Bras, "Asile", *DHGE*, 4, 1931, 1035-1047. – L.-R. Misserey, "Asile en Occident", *DDC*, 1, 1935, 1089-1103. – P. C. Timbal, *Le droit d'asile*, Paris, 1939 (law thesis).

Jean-Loup Lemaître

**Byzantium.** From the Greek *asylon* (a non-pillaged, inviolable place, refuge), the term "asylum" designated a place of worship covering fugitives (criminals, political and others, including slaves) with its protection, and by extension the institution by virtue of which the imperial authorities recognised the impunity accorded by the Church to those who took refuge in a sacred place. At Byzantium this meant churches and monasteries, into which the police were not authorized to go and search for a man pursued for his criminal acts or even for his debts, nor for a slave escaped from his master, and that by virtue of the sanctity of the place. It was the same mentality that forbade the sale of merchandise or cohabitation between men and women in this kind of place. Thus the beneficiary of asylum had to stay there all his life by virtue of the spiritual and legal bond that united him to the institution that had taken him in; from then on he was under the protection of the Church and outside all secular jurisdiction. In the church of Hagia Sophia, a special place was reserved for beneficiaries of asylum. Ecclesiastical *sanctions were also pronounced against those who violated this immunity, whose protection even covered dependencies of churches, like courtyards or gardens, as Theodore Balsamon tells us in the 12th century.

Thus, a great number of Christians seem to have sought and obtained refuge in churches. Imperial legislation sometimes tried to reduce this privilege of the Church by excluding from this protection homicides, thieves and those who had committed adultery, arguing that asylum should protect victims and not the guilty. In the 10th c., Constantine VII Porphyrogenitus extended the benefit of asylum to murderers, but Manuel I abolished this in 1166. Later, at least at Hagia Sophia, the ecclesiastical authorities in charge of examining supplicants were represented by the *protekdikos*, at the head of a court that had to pronounce on the matter in the name of the *patriarch.

E. Herman, "Zum Asylrecht im byzantinischen Reich", *OrChrP*, 1, 1935, 204-238. – R. Macrides, "Killing, Asylum and the Law in Byzantium", *Spec.*, 63, 1988, 509-538.

Stavros Perentidis

## ATHANASIUS I OF CONSTANTINOPLE (*c.*1230 - after 1309).

A monk of *Athos, Athanasius opposed the *Union of Lyon. His rigour impressed Andronicus II, who made him *patriarch in 1289 despite the *synod's opposition. He surrounded himself with rigorist monks and tried to reform the Church and society on the monastic model. He drew down the hostility of the intellectuals and *bishops whom he wished to send back to their *dioceses. Fearing a *schism, Andronicus II broke with him in 1293, then recalled him in 1303. He resumed his reforms, to which Andronicus gave imperial sanction. He also undertook to feed the refugees fleeing the Turkish advance. Discouraged by the growing dispute, he resigned again in 1309.

*The Correspondence of Athanasius I Patriarch of Constantinople. Letters to the Emperor Andronicus II, Members of the Imperial Family and Officials*, M.-A. M. Talbot (ed.), Washington (DC), 1975 (*CFHB*, 7).

*HChr*, 6, 1990, 178-180.

Marie-Hélène Congourdeau

**ATHOS.** 100 kilometres south-east of *Thessalonica, Athos forms the easternmost of the three peninsulas that prolong Chalcidike southwards, as well as the most mountainous and least accessible. It is a vast territory 45 kilometres long by 5-10 wide, unpropitious to agriculture, but whose wooded landscapes, dominated by the high mountain of Athos (2033 m.) and overhanging the sea, are everywhere admirable and propitious to meditation. Depopulated in the 6th c. and perhaps earlier, for at least two centuries Mount Athos was nothing but a reserve of pasture and forest, no doubt little exploited. At the end of the 8th c. or towards the beginning of the 9th, some hermits settled in this "desert", which from the end of the 10th c. was named the "Holy Mountain" (*Hagion Oros*) *par excellence*, and which has remained into our own day the main monastic centre of *Orthodoxy. This continuity, exceptional in the East, explains the wealth of Athonite documentation and its importance for the history of Byzantium.

The monasteries of Athos have been able to preserve their archives, some of them for more than a thousand years. The documents of the Byzantine period, which are the object of a systematic edition in the collection "Archives of Athos" (ArAt), begun by G. Millet and P. Lemerle, are the most important written source. Literary works, written in Athonite circles (especially Saints' Lives) or elsewhere, supplement our information particularly on the spiritual life, whose documents (especially relative to the landed possessions of the monasteries) preserve numerous medieval manuscripts, some of which were written at Athos or carry information useful to its history. The archaeological sources are on the whole less well known: the precious objects preserved in church treasuries, the *icons and *frescos are reproduced in albums but have only been partially studied; some of the churches (see *e.g. Iviron* I, 64-68, by P. Mylônas) and medieval towers have been the subject of publications.

The oldest evidence relating to Athonite *monasticism is undoubtedly earlier than 841: it is a canon, composed probably at Thessalonica by Joseph the Hymnographer, in honour of St Peter the Athonite, who was a hermit at Athos and to whom a cult was officially paid at the time in the region. Two 10th-c. texts suggest that the monks and hermits of Mount Athos already had a certain reputation in the mid 9th c.: the chronicler Genesius mentions the monks of Athos among those who came to *Constantinople in March 843 to celebrate the restoration of *images, but it is not certain that this mention is not anachronistic; the second text is more certain: the Life of Euthymius the Younger relates that the saint, then a monk in a monastery of *Olympus, decided in 859 to go to Athos, since he had heard that *ascesis was practised there. He settled there and, with Joseph the Armenian, formed the first anchoritic group that we know of. Other groupings of monks or hermits were established at Athos and in eastern Chalcidike, in

*Theotokos* (Mother of God). Miraculous icon at the Iviron Monastery on Mount Athos.

particular around a powerful character, John Kolobos, who before 883 founded a monastery (later called Kolobou) at Hierissos, on the isthmus that gave access to the Athonite peninsula. By June 883 the number of Athonites had become sufficiently important for the Emperor Basil I to agree, at the request of John Kolobos, to recognise the Athonite entity as such and to grant it privileges: he forbade any official to cause any injury to the monks of Athos and those of Kolobou (*i.e.* not to demand any rent on the lands in escheat which they occupied legally and whose proprietors they implicitly became) or local shepherds to pasture their flocks on the mountain (*Prôtaton*, no. 1); this last prohibition was ill-respected, as witness the affair of the Vlach shepherds who settled with their families on Athos at the beginning of the 12th century. No doubt very early (before 908), probably because they had to manage property in common, the Athonites provided themselves with a central organisation under the authority of a *prôtos*. From 941-942, the *prôtos* had the job of dividing among the Athonites the pension (*roga*) that the emperor began to dispense to them, at a rate of a piece of gold per person per year: originally of three pounds (hence in principle for 216 monks), it went up to seven pounds under Nicephorus Phocas. In 943, Athos, considered as a moral person, further obtained from the State authorities a part of the land in escheat that extended between Athos and Hierissos (*Prôtaton*, no. 5). It is probable that the setting up of informal groups of hermits at Athos preceded the foundation of monasteries, in which the monks followed in principle a common rule and led a communal life. But the distinction between various types of establishment was not clear, and doubtless never was, all the more since several monasteries at Athos had hermitages under their dependence. The first monasteries (apart from the mysterious "monastery of Athos", mentioned in 942) are attested in 956 (Xeropotamou), *c.*960 (Bouleuteria) and before 979-980 (Klementos). These were modest establishments, founded doubtless in the early 10th c., numbering at most some tens of monks. Each of these monasteries cultivated fields and vines on the mountain; none of them possessed property outside.

Towards the middle of the 10th c., the state of mind and the reality changed. Perhaps under the influence of Studite monasticism, not without internal conflicts, but without the other forms of monastic or eremitical life being eliminated, a new type of establishment, which we may call great monasteries, was put in place at Athos. They were founded and directed by members of the aristocracy; the monks of these establishments were numbered no longer by tens but by hundreds, the emperor entrusted them with the management of immense estates in Chalcidike and Macedonia, which made them great business concerns, within which the *oikonomos* played an essential role. Their first founder was Athanasius. An orphan raised in an aristocratic family of *Trebizond friendly with the Phocas family, Athanasius arrived at Athos as a hermit, perhaps in 957. Nicephorus Phocas, then *strategos*, persuaded him to found a monastery at Athos to which he himself would retire, and sent funds (6 gold pounds) to build the establishment, modest at the outset, which was called Lavra (the laura), doubtless because it comprised, as well as a monastery proper (*koinobion*), hermitages (*kellia*), and because the monks of the monastery had the opportunity to devote themselves on the spot to ascetic exercises. The monastery's founder, Nicephorus Phocas, became emperor in 963, and this immediately entailed the enrichment of Lavra, which received from the emperor a pension in cash and in corn, *relics and, above all, the monastery of Peristerai near Thessalonica with its estates and its tenant *peasants, or **paroikoi*, in Chalcidike (*Lavra* I, 13-77). At Athos, the praisers of times past set about vilifying those who accumulated wealth, precious objects and estates and dreamed of nothing but acquisitions and aggrandisements. The eremitical party, led by the *prôtos*, complained to the Emperor John Tzimisces of the scandals, conflicts and damage caused by the very existence of Lavra and the actions of its hegumen Athanasius. The emperor sent to Athos a mediator, a monk of *Studios, who was charged with pacifying the rancours and who gave Athos, before summer 972, a regulation accepted by all, the so-called **Typikon* of Tzimisces or *Tragos* (*Prôtaton*, no. 7). This document, invested with the imperial authority, specified, in 28 clauses, numerous regulatory or disciplinary points, safeguarded the rights of the hermits who lived in groups (kelliots) or in isolation (hesychasts), but above all ratified the particular place of Lavra within Athonite monasticism. A precedent was created. Soon afterwards, a second great monastery was founded: some Georgian aristocrats had come to settle at Athos, in hermitages dependent on Lavra, before 959; one of them, John Tornik who in 979, at the request of the Emperor Basil II, had led a victorious expedition against a usurper, came with a considerable booty (1200 gold pounds and precious objects) and received from Basil II, as well as the litle monastery of Klementos at Athos, four monasteries in Macedonia (including Kolobou) and their immense fortune in land, fiscal revenues and *paroikoi*. On the site of Klementos, the construction of the monastery of the Georgians (the laura of the Iberians), which we call Iviron, began immediately (*Iviron* I, 3-91). At the same time, other monasteries were founded, that of the Amalfitans (later absorbed by Lavra) and, among the 20 monasteries that exist today, Vatopédi, Esphigmenou, St Paul, Xenophon, Xeropotamou, Zographou. These numerous foundations meant that *coenobitism was to be the preponderant way of life at Athos from the end of the 10th century.

Relations among the Athonite establishments and with the outside world were regulated by a complex organisation, sitting at Karyes, the "capital" of Athos, situated at the centre of the peninsula. This government was directed by the *prôtos* and consisted of assemblies, a council and the officials of the Prôtaton. The assemblies (*synaxeis*) brought together the hegumens of the monasteries and in principle the heads of eremitical groupings and the hesychasts; they met three times a year, at Christmas, Easter and 15 August, in the church of Karyes, then, in the 12th c., in another building (*kreterion*). These assemblies, under the presidency of the *prôtos*, ruled on the most important affairs and chose the *prôtos*. Between times, decisions were taken by the *prôtos* assisted by some 15 hegumens forming what we call the council (*Prôtaton*, no. 8: *Typikon* of Constantine Monomachos, of 1045, which supplemented the *Typikon* of Tzimisces). The role of the hegumens of the great monasteries, Lavra, Iviron and Vatopédi, became preponderant; the retinue to which they had a right at assemblies shows that from 1045 they took precedence over the *prôtos* himself. The election of the *prôtos* was confirmed by the emperor, who sent him his bâton, then in the 14th c., when political authority seemed less stable than religious authority, by the *patriarch; the *prôtos* seems to have been elected for life (which did not rule out his dismissal in times of trouble), then at the end of the 14th c. his mandate became annual, which suggests that the institution was in decline. The *prôtos* represented the Holy Mountain before the authorities of the Empire, dispensed justice and exercised disciplinary powers within the Mountain. He was assisted by several officials, in particular an *oikonomos*, overseers (*epiteretes*) charged with police duties, and an ecclesiarch (*Prôtaton*, 111-164). The central organisation managed the property of the community. If, originally, mount Athos was collectively given to the monks, it would later seem that part of the Athonite land belonged to the monasteries that were established there, but the rest, gradually diminished by cessions granted to these monasteries (called imperial by contrast to the *kellia* dependent on the *prôtos*) but increased by recoveries from establishments fallen into escheat, belonged to the community. These common lands (whose quantity diminished with time) were let long-term to kelliots. To these revenues were added donations, made by laymen or by the monasteries of Athos, the whole permitting the subsidizing of the working expenses of the central organisation, in particular for the church of Karyes.

Other monasteries were founded in the 11th or 12th c. (among the surviving monasteries: Docheiariou, Karakalou, Philotheou, Kastamonitou, Kultumus); others date from the 14th (Dionysiou and the *Pantocrator). Certain monasteries, like those of the Georgians and Amalfitans from the 10th c., brought together monks of similar geographical origin: thus the monastery of the Russians in the 11th c., which later changed site and is now called St Panteleimon, Chilandar, the monastery of the Serbs from the 12th c., and Zographou, which in the 13th c. became a Bulgarian monastery. The majority of the monasteries mentioned above were founded by important persons and received gratuities and privileges from the emperors. They all had a similar plan: an enclosing wall, a fortified entrance and at least one tower gave them the appearance of a town; inside, the cells of the monks were built onto the enclosure wall on several levels; in the centre was the refectory (*trapeza*) and the main church (*katholikon*). These churches also had a similar plan: in an inscribed cross, they were dominated by a central dome and had three apses, two *narthexes and side-chapels. The frescos that ornamented them have usually been repainted in the modern period, but the church of the Prôtaton preserves a group of well-preserved 14th-c. paintings.

The wealth of the monasteries promised security and attracted monks, poor peasants or aristocrats looking for a peaceful retirement; some of these monasteries housed very large numbers: Lavra would have had 700 monks in 1045 (*Prôtaton*, no. 8), Iviron 300 in the same period (*Iviron* I, 39), Esphigmenou 200 monks at the beginning of the 14th c. (*Esphigménou*, 25). These *koinobia*, which were often situated on the edge of the sea or had steps leading down to the coast, possessed fishing-boats and, for the richest of them, merchant shipping, with which they went to sell, as far as Thrace or even *Constantinople, the products of Athos (wood) and those of the estates (cereals and wine). Indeed all the monasteries mentioned possessed estates outside Athos, in Chalcidike and Macedonia (including premises to let at Thessalonica), in Thrace, in the isles of the northern Aegean, in the Balkans and even in Asia Minor; the number of estates tended to increase with time, by donation (guaranteeing prayers for the salvation of the souls of well-to-do peasants, aristocrats or kings) or by purchase. The landed fortune of some of them is quite well known: N. Svoronos (*Lavra* IV, 168) has estimated at 75,000 *modioi* (750 hectares) the cultivated area held by Lavra in the 14th c.; at this time, the whole of the lands possessed by Iviron attained the same area (*Iviron* III, 14). The lands of Iviron were worked by more than 550 families of *paroikoi* (*ibid.*, 24), who owed the monastery taxes, *corvées* and rents; by comparison, the number of *paroikoi* of Esphigmenou was 120 (*Esphigménou*, table opposite p. 22), and that of the *paroikoi* of Lavra 880 in the *theme of Thessalonica alone (*Lavra* IV, 173e).

Athos certainly did not remain sheltered from the events that affected the Empire; it took part in its economic expansion, it was affected by wars and disasters (the *Black Death of 1347-1348), it suffered the repercussions of political changes, generators of insecurity (in the form of piracy), while managing on each occasion to win over the goodwill of the new regional authorities. Athos also played a role in religious movements within Orthodoxy, in the evolution of the forms of monastic life, and it exercised an influence over the whole Orthodox world. The first half of the 11th c. and that of the 14th were the periods for which the prosperity of Athos is most evident, but it seems that, in a world that was becoming politically unstable, the power and wealth of Athos, despite the confiscations decided on at the end of the 11th c. in the reign of the Emperor Alexius I *Comnenus, only grew greater, until the third quarter of the 14th century. Subsequently the emperors, to subsidize the *army, then the sultans (who permanently controlled the region from 1430), proceeded to other confiscations, which diminished its wealth. The *oikonomoi* of the *metochia* (centres of management of the monastic estates in Macedonia), by the help they could bring to the peasants and the initiatives they took among them, and the monasteries themselves, thanks to the immunities they enjoyed for their estates and the protection they ensured them, certainly played a role in the economic development of Macedonia.

The capture of Constantinople by the crusaders in 1204, which for a time entailed the submission of a party of the Athonite monks to the Roman authorities, and the *Union of Lyon in 1274 led to religious conflicts within the Holy Mountain. It was at Athos in the years 1316-1338 that Gregory *Palamas, later archbishop of Thessalonica, strove to give a theological foundation to *hesychasm (the prayer of the heart that gives grace to contemplate God) and to spread the ascetic practices associated with this form of spirituality among groups of hermits, and then at the head of a great *koinobion*, Esphigmenou. At the end of the 14th c. the coenobitic rule seems to have been weakened in certain monasteries to the benefit of *idiorrhythm, which allowed the monks, or some of them, to lead within a monastery, on the material and spiritual levels, a life disengaged from the constraints of community (see *Pantocrator*, 153). "Intellectual" life at Athos was always full of contrast: the majority of the monks, coming from a peasant background, were illiterate, but we also find men of high culture, like the Georgian George the Hagiorite at Iviron in the 11th c., or Palamas. The prestige of the Holy Mountain explains why the sojourn of a monk at Athos might be the starting-point for an ecclesiastical career leading to a *bishopric, or to the *patriarchate. Some monasteries, like Iviron or Philotheou, housed *scriptoria*, and at the end of the Middle Ages most of them had collected important libraries of manuscripts. Moreover, Iviron and the Slav monasteries contributed greatly, by translations, to the diffusion of Byzantine religious literature in the Orthodox world.

P. Lemerle *et al.*, *Acta de Lavra*, I-IV, *ArAt*, Paris, 1970-1982. – J. Lefort, *Actes d'Esphigménou*, *ArAt*, Paris, 1973. – D. Papachryssanthou, *Actes du Prôtaton*, *ArAt*, Paris, 1975 (2 vol.). – J. Lefort *et al.*, *Actes d'Iviron*, I-III, *ArAt*, Paris, 1985-1993. – V. Kravari, *Actes du Pantocrator*, *ArAt*, Paris, 1991.

S. Lampros, *Catalogue of the Greek Manuscripts on Mount Athos*, Cambridge, 1895-1900 (2 vol.). – G. Millet, *Monuments de l'Athos*, Paris, 1927. – *The Treasures of Mount Athos*, Athens, 1973-1991 (4 vol.). – *Mount Athos and Byzantine Monasticism*, A. Bryer (ed.), M. Cunningham (ed.), Aldershot, 1996.

Jacques Lefort

**ATTO OF VERCELLI (died before 964).** Of *Lombard origin, born perhaps at Ticino, Atto received a good education. He was part of the cathedral *chapter of *Milan before becoming bishop of Vercelli in 924. Close (but not archchancellor) to King *Hugh of Provence, at odds with Berengar II, he stands out mainly for his work in favour of the reform of the clergy and his struggle against political interference in Church affairs (on which he wrote, *c.*943, *De pressuris ecclesiasticis*). To support his work of reform he composed the *Capitulare*, a collection of 100 canons taken from *Theodulf of Orléans, notably opposing *simony and *Nicolaitism. As well as a commentary on St *Paul's *epistles (little studied), *letters and *sermons, he wrote the *Polypticum quod appellatur Perpendiculum*, a singular and difficult work which, not without a certain enigmatic character, tackles the problems of his time. He died before 964.

"Perpendiculum": *PL*, 134, 1853, 859-880. – *ASAW*, 37, 2, G. Goetz (ed.), 1922. – *De pressuris ecclesiasticis*, J. Baur (ed.), Heidelberg, 1975.

S. F. Wemple, *Atto of Vercelli. Church, State and Christian Society in Tenth-Century Italy*, Rome, 1979. – C. Frova, "Il 'Polittico' attribuito ad Attone di Vercelli (924-960 ca.): tra storia e grammatica", *BISI*, 90, 1982-1983, 1-75. – G. Gandino, "Cultura dotta e folklorica a Vercelli nel X secolo", *BSBS*, 90, 1992, 253-279. – L. Ricci, "A proposito della paternità attoniana del *Polipticum*", *Filologia mediolatina*, 4, 1997, 133-152.

Claudio Leonardi

***AUCTORITATES.*** In the Middle Ages, *auctoritates* (authorities) were texts recognised as worthy of credit because they gave clear witness to the truth. Holy Scripture was the *auctoritas par excellence*, as well as the works of the Church *Fathers. Their number grew in the course of the period, with the *translation of new works, Greek, Arabic or Hebrew. *Auctoritates* were used grouped together in *florilegia, which attempts were made to organise logically into collections of *Sentences (*Peter Lombard). Their importance declined from the 12th c.: though instruments of truth, they were suspected at that time of being also liable to deform it. It then became necessary to interpret them by the method of **quaestio* and *expositio*, whose model was Peter *Abelard's work, **Sic et non*.

M. D. Chenu, *La Théologie au douzième siècle*, Paris, 1966, 353-357. – *Les Genres littéraires dans les sources théologiques et philosophiques médiévales. Actes du colloque international de Louvain-la-Neuve, 25-27 mai 1981*, R. Bultot (ed.), Louvain-la-Neuve, 1982.

Jaime García Álvarez

**AUDOIN (*c.*600-684).** St Audoin (Ouen), a native of the Soissonnais, belonged to the powerful aristocratic *kinship group that supported the activities of Columbanian missionaries in *Neustria-*Burgundy. Audoin himself founded the monasteries of Rebais in Brie (*c.*635) and Fontenelle near Rouen (in 648). Educated at the court of Chlotar II among the friends of the young *Dagobert, he held important positions at the palace before becoming bishop of *Rouen in 641. Supporter of a strong Neustria, he played an active role among the kings and mayors of the palace, while opposing the rise of the Pippinids in *Austrasia. He died at a great age and his cult developed rapidly.

F. Vacandard, *Vie de saint Ouen, évêque de Rouen (641-684)*, Paris, 1902. – G. Scheibelreiter, "Audoin von Rouen", *La Neustrie*, H. Atsma (ed.), 1, Sigmaringen, 1989, 195-216.

Régine Le Jan

**AUGSBURG.** Augsburg, an episcopal see in eastern *Swabia, well situated at the meeting-place of Germany and Italy, was called on to take an important place in imperial politics, but also in the development of trade, to which it owed its flourishing mercantile society.

Though the residence of a *bishop is not attested until the 8th c., it would make the town, under the episcopate of St *Ulrich (923-973) and after the victory of the Lechfeld (955), a pole of imperial policy. *Frederick I would end by holding the position of *advocate of the bishopric and the city (1168), which allowed the middle class that had developed over two centuries to be emancipated. Thanks firstly to fustian, then, from the mid 15th c., from mining allied to high finance, Augsburg, now an imperial town, would be dominated by an active mercantile oligarchy, organised from 1368 into *guilds. It was by associating imperial politics with their affairs that the Fugger brought the town's economy to its apogee, though two thirds of the population led a precarious existence.

The urban area, imaging this evolution, was long divided between the *cathedral in the north and the church of St Afra in the south, according to a pattern frequent in the episcopal towns of southern Germany. While the continuity of Christian worship at Augsburg rested on the veneration given to the former, by the 9th c. at latest there were two *chapters. The reconstruction necessary after the Hungarian assault, and the changes at the close of the 10th c., explain the closure of St Afra, henceforth a Benedictine *abbey, and the foundation of the *collegiate churches of St Stephen (women), St Peter and St Maurice (men). The latter had pastoral responsibility for the suburb that had developed around it, south of the episcopal city, and that was gradually invested with a municipal oligarchy independent of the other chapters. The expectations of this ruling group, like those of an expanding population in which there was considerable professional differentiation, led in the late 12th c. to the development – together with the regular chapters of St George and the Holy Cross, both soon given *cure of souls of the suburbs north and west of the town – of a particularly dynamic apostolic movement, and then from the 13th c. the birth of *beguinages in working-class quarters, under the care of the *mendicant orders, as well as a multitude of foundations of a social nature (Fuggerei).

The growing awareness by the middle class of these changes and of its own role was expressed in the *chronicles of Zink or Meisterlin as well as in the editions of Peutinger. This Augsburg *humanism was also closely connected with the Emperor Maximilian, manifesting the polarization of urban politics seen in the acceptance of the Reformation, then the imposition of Catholic elites in 1548 – all the more since the bishop had been settled at Dillingen since the late 15th century.

F. Zoepfl, *Das Bistum Augsburg*, Augsburg, 1955 (diocese). – *Geschichte der Stadt Augsburg*, G. Gottlieb (dir.) *et al.*, Stuttgart, 1984, 115-241 (town).

Martial Staub

**AUGUSTINE OF ANCONA (1270-1328).** Augustinus Triumphus, a native of Ancona, *Hermit of St Augustine, studied at Paris from 1297 to 1300; he later commented on *Peter Lombard's *Sentences* before becoming *reader at the school of the Augustinians at Padua. He was master of theology from 1313 to 1315 and in 1322 chaplain to Charles, son of *Robert the Wise, king of Naples and Sicily. His *Summa de potestate ecclesiastica* (ed. Rome, 1479, 1582) was written in 1326, two years after the publication of *Marsilius of Padua's *Defensor pacis*. Augustine also wrote a *Tractatus brevis de duplici potestate praelatorum et laicorum* (ed. in R. Scholz, *Die Publizistik z. zeit Philipp des Schönen u. Bonifaz VIII*, Stuttgart, 1903; repr. Amsterdam, 1962, 484-501), *De potestate collegii mortuo papa* (*ibid.*, 501-508), *De facto Templariorum* (*ibid.*, 508-516) and *Tractatus contra articulos inventos ad diffamandum sanctissimum patrem dominum Bonifacium papam* (ed. H. Finke, *Aus den Tagen Bonifaz VIII*, Münster, 1902, LXIX-XCIX).

Augustine as a theologian was part of the 14th-c. *Augustinian school. His main work, the *Summa*, is of considerable breadth; its essential point is the unconditional defence of papal supremacy, with the help of argumments inspired by the work of *Giles of Rome, whose theocratic tradition he perpetuates. It has been claimed that he seeks in this work to refute the anti-curialist positions of Marsilius of Padua. However that may be, for him the *pope holds a power accorded directly by God; he is the highest in dignity and the most perfect, since this power is that which Christ held on earth and which he has conceded to his *vicar. The pope is the holder not just of spiritual power, but also of *temporal power, superior to the mere civil power of princes, admittedly in accordance with law, but in a purely formal way. *Kings and emperors depend on the pope for their confirmation and approval; proofs of this can be given, drawn not just from Scripture or the Dionysian principle of hierarchical subordination, but also from history, like the *Donation of Constantine or the translation of the *Empire.

For Augustine, the Church is a mystical entity really existing outside its members; it is the *populus christianus* and its supernatural end is ordered to the plenitude of papal power. The pope is the source of all power, spiritual or temporal; he is "the name of jurisdiction"; it is he who confers on the emperor temporality and power to administer. By virtue of his spiritual power, he himself rules the temporal, through the mediation of the secular princes, whose power is temporal and corporal. Successor of *Melchizedek and Christ, in his person he unites all the attributes of royal and priestly government: the pope governs in place of Christ: he is both *dux* and *rector* of the Christian people. In addition he is not just the head, but also the heart of the social body.

The temporal is derived from the spiritual: just as matter exists for the sake of form, likewise everything to do with the order of the body and the temporal is for the sake of the spiritual. The power of the emperor is derived from the papal power, which is its source, though the converse is not true. The intellectual posiiton of Augustine of Ancona marks both the summit of hierocratic thought and its most extreme form, harbinger of decline.

M. Wilks, *The Problem of Sovereignty in the Late Middle Ages. The Papal Monarchy with Augustinus Triumphus and the Publicists*, Cambridge, 1963. – Y. Congar, *L'Église, de saint Augustin à l'époque moderne*, Paris, 1970.

Jeannine Quillet

**AUGUSTINE OF CANTERBURY (died 604).** Prior of the monastery of St Andrew at Rome, St Augustine was charged by Pope *Gregory the Great with the Christian *mission to *England. Augustine and forty Roman monks arrived in England in 597 and succeeded in converting King *Æthelbert of Kent to Christianity, whereupon the Kentish kingdom adopted Christianity *en masse*. Augustine was consecrated as first archbishop of *Canterbury and, through consultation with Gregory, laid down the guidelines for the diocesan structure of the English church. He brought a number of *books to England, a few of which may survive. There also survives in his name a *Libellus responsionum* (preserved by *Bede, *Historia Ecclesiastica*, I, 27), which consists of answers given by Gregory to questions raised by Augustine concerning matters of ecclesiastical discipline.

A. J. Mason, *The Mission of St Augustine to England according to the Original Documents*, Cambridge, 1897. – N. Brooks, *The Early History of the Church of Canterbury*, Leicester, 1984, 3-14. – I. Wood, "The Mission of Augustine of Canterbury to the English", *Spec.*, 69, 1994, 1-17. – R. Meens, "A Background to Augustine's Mission to Anglo-Saxon England", *Anglo-Saxon England*, 23, 1994, 5-17.

Michael Lapidge

**AUGUSTINE, RULE OF SAINT.** "Having become a priest, he soon founded a monastery in the Church and began to live with the servants of God in the way and on the principles fixed at the time of the Holy Apostles: above all, that none should have anything of his own in this community, but that all should be common to them, and that to each should be given according to his needs. This is what he had already done himself when he returned from abroad to his own land." In these terms Possidius, disciple and biographer of Augustine († 430), describes his master's first two African experiments in community. But Possidius calls the line followed by the Christians of the apostolic age a rule (*regula*); now, we find no work under this title in the bishop of Hippo's well-known *Retractations* nor in the list of his works made out by

*Quarrel of the devils and angels over St Augustine.* Woodcut from St Augustine's *City of God.* 1486-1487. Abbeville, Municipal Library.

Possidius; hence the delicate problem, posed into our own day, of the Rule of St Augustine. A recent reconstruction has been proposed on the basis of a sound inquiry into the manuscript tradition of the main texts in question. This reconstruction remains "work in progress".

Augustine having left, in 391, the first monastery of Thagaste where he had brought together some friends in 388, the only one of those friends who remained there, Alypius, brought back from a journey to Bethlehem the disciplinary and liturgical elements of a monastic regulation (*Ordo monasterii*) which Augustine approved and, perhaps, prefaced. But, becoming a priest at Hippo, Augustine had founded another monastery of lay brothers there and drawn up for them a general directive (*Praeceptum*) that Alypius added to his monastic regulation. The combination of these two texts was immediately taken to Italy, whence it reached Gaul, Spain and even central Europe, all countries where it came to be added to the local *Rules being built up by nascent *monasticism.

By now a bishop, Augustine had had to bring peace to a women's monastery of which his sister had been superior: he sent them a severe letter (*Objurgatio*) which was combined with a female adaptation of the monastic regulation of Thagaste. Finally, Augustine held firmly to the renunciation of property by the clergy of his bishopric.

When *Benedict of Aniane was charged with reforming the monasticism of the Frankish Empire (817), he did it on the basis of the Rule of *Benedict of Nursia (6th c.), which no less than others was inspired by Augustine's monastic writings. Thus, in his collection of various Rules illustrating the Rule of St Benedict (*codex regularum*), Benedict of Aniane made the Rule of St Augustine appear in the form of male directives. But all over the West there circulated, under Augustine's name, compositions of various descriptions that conveyed, through the vagaries of manuscript transmission, the male and female versions of the regulation of Thagaste and the directives of Hippo, whether or not accompanied by the letter to the turbulent nuns.

Carolingian legislation had reduced monastic practice to the observance of the Benedictine Rule accompanied by some improvements, while allowing *clerics grouped together in the service of the great churches according to their ancient canons the freedom appropriate to their state. Now, the doctor of Hippo was venerated as a great bishop, leader and inspirer of his clergy. So it is not surprising that the more zealous of the *canons defined by the Carolingian model should have appealed to an Augustinian Rule in order to engage in a personal renunciation of *property which indeed the *capitulary of 816 left them free to do. Thus, the *Gregorian reform of the 11th and 12th cc. saw the multiplication of Canons Regular of St Augustine of various observances.

This diversity in observance (*ordo*, *order) was evidently facilitated by the variety of manuscript traditions of the Augustinian ideal. The apostolic see saw nothing inconvenient in this and liberally approved the choice of the Rule of St Augustine made by the canons of a renowned sanctuary, by groups of clergy and laity poorly settled in the countryside, by the brothers and sisters of a *hospital, or even by a *cathedral. Doubling the monastic state which *Cîteaux had somewhat stiffened into a Benedictine literalism, another religious state was formed, it too based on personal commitment to this or that observance of a rule that was reputable, if not exactly definite in its tenor. Thus the second *Lateran council (1139), which held to the Rules of St Benedict for monks and St Augustine for canons "regular", obliged those female religious who had always been *nuns to follow one or other of these two Rules, or else that of St Basil. The prevalence of the flexible directives of Hippo (*Praeceptum*) as an allowed rule (*regula recepta*) permitted the facing of new necessities that went beyond the liturgical and charitable role of monks: speculative study and *preaching.

The fourth *Lateran council (1215) applied the brakes to the teeming new forms of religious life (*religiones*) that sheltered behind the three Rules mentioned in 1139. If the sons of St *Francis and the Hermits of Mount Carmel, like *Grandmont in 1189, saw their particular rule approved shortly after by the apostolic see, it was under the Augustinian rule that the sons of St *Dominic had their formula approved at the same time. But it was the *Hermits of St Augustine who were to consecrate the name of the bishop of Hippo as legislator of religious life, to the point that, in some European languages, they were designated solely by the name of their master: Augustines or Austins.

The Roman *Curia of *Alexander IV was sufficiently well provided with experts in religious law to bring together in 1256, around some Augustinian groupings of Italian hermits, a new centralized group: the Order of Friars Hermits of St Augustine, which received the privileges of the *mendicant orders and followed them in their urban settlement, to the point that all towns of any importance soon had their four *convents of mendicants. But their eremitical tendency and their *pastoral care in the countryside remained alive, as witness the Constitutions of 1290 and the accounts of *Jordan of Saxony's *Vitae fratrum* in 1357; this tendency was encouraged by Augustinian legends and pseudo-sermons. Divided at first into four provinces, the order numbered 17 provinces in 1295 and 24 in 1329, from Poland to Portugal, from Ireland to the isles of Greece. In the 15th c., the observance of *poverty led to the appearance of congregations of observants alongside the *conventuals within the order. These congregations anticipated the Discalced and Recollect Augustinians of the modern period.

Jordan of Saxony, *Liber vitae fratrum*, 1943. – M.-T. Disdier, "Ordre dit de saint Augustin", *DHGE*, 5, 1931, 499-595. – E. Briem, "Ermites de saint Augustin", *DHGE*, 15, 1963, 787-791. – L. Verheijen, *La Règle de saint Augustin*, Paris, 1967. – A. Kunzelmann, *Geschichte der deutschen Augustiner-Eremiten*, Würzburg, 1969-1975. – B. Van Luijk, *Le Monde augustinien du XIII^e au XIX^e siècle*, Assen, 1972. – D. Guttierez, *Los Agustinos en la edad media*, 1, *1256-1356*, Rome, 1977; 2, *1357-1517*, 1980. – V. Desprez, *Règles monastiques d'Occident, IV^e-VI^e siècle. D'Augustin à Ferréol*, Bégrolles-en-Mauges, 1980. – *Nouvelle approche de la règle de saint Augustin*, 1, Bégrolles-en-Mauges, 1980; 2, Louvain, 1988. – A. Zumkeller, *Augustine's Ideal of the Religious Life*, New York, 1986. – G. Lawless, *Augustine of Hippo and his Monastic Rule*, Oxford, 1987.

Jean Becquet

**AUGUSTINIANISM.** St Augustine was born on 13 Nov 354 at Thagaste and died on 28 Aug 430 at Hippo, the town whose Catholic bishop he had been since 395 or 396.

His conversion in 386 had the benefit, among other things, of freeing his intellectual and literary vocation. When the congregation of Hippo unexpectedly chose him as their priest in 391, he already had a considerable body of work behind him; and he rapidly became the "duty theologian" of the numerous African episcopate, an honour that his colleagues manifestly did not dispute with him. At the end of 40 years of *ministry, thanks to a multitude of requests and controversies, Augustine's written work covered the whole field of Christian doctrine. Christendom rapidly became aware of this, to judge by the legend inscribed under his earliest (6th c.) effigy, in the old Lateran Library: "*Diuersi diuersa patres sed hic omnia dixit, romano eloquio mystica sensa tonans*." From copy to copy, Augustine's works, or at least some of them, enjoyed an incomparable circulation. In 1930, Dom A. Wilmart listed 258 manuscripts of the *Confessions*, 233 of *De Trinitate*, 376 of *De civitate Dei* and 368 of the *Enarrationes in psalmos*. L. Verheijen has listed 317 manuscripts of the *Rule*: so many witnesses to the great tradition of religious life in the Order of Canons Regular and the Order of Friars *Hermits of St Augustine. The systematic inquiry being made by the Vienna Academy is revealing many other pieces. In any case, the numbers have a merely indicative value, since only a small part of the output of the copyists' workshops has survived. It was here that the Latin Middle Ages found its "theological common ground", in the wide or informal sense, incorporating all the elements of Christian culture: *philosophy, *theology, law, *spirituality, *mysticism.

Augustine's "Augustinianism" was nothing but Christian doctrine; he did not have in mind the formulation of some personal system. He had faith in the Christian truth and applied himself to acquiring an understanding of it, following the principle "*crede ut intelligas*". But it was an interpretation of Christianity heavily marked by the event of conversion and the spiritual experience that followed. Augustine reflected particularly on the relationship between Platonism and Christianity; his conception of Christ as illuminating *Word, interior master, would be called the theory of illumination when the need arose to compare it, whether to oppose it or to reduce it, with the Aristotelian-Thomist theory of *abstraction. The long meditation he developed in the *Confessions* on his past, on his responsibility as a sinner and God's care for him, on *conversion as a restoration of interiority, would nourish medieval spirituality (P. Courcelle); as would the reflections in books VIII-XV of *De Trinitate* on the structure of the mind created in God's image, before it was reduced to a theory of trinitarian *analogies. The theme of *Christus totus* would greatly inspire that of the mystical body. Finally, the deeper reflection on *freedom, *grace and *predestination, provoked by Simplicianus's questions on the epistle to the Romans, would figure in the Pelagian controversy and its endemic sequels in the Christian West.

O. Rottmanner has put forward a strict and narrow definition of Augustinianism: it is "the doctrine of unconditioned *predestination and the particular saving will, as St Augustine developed it in the last period of his life . . . relaxing nothing up to his death". The formula is thus reserved to designate Augustine's particular and disputed interpretation of the mystery of salvation. Augustinianism in this sense arose either from a reaction against the monks of Provence or, even earlier, from that against Pelagius. The course of its history has been clearly summarized by E. Portalié under the name of "theological Augustinianism" in his long article in the *DThC* (1, 2, 2515 f.), which is also the best-documented overall exposition dedicated to the phenomenon of Augustinianism in all its complexity. The inconvenience of the conception advocated by Rottmanner is that it favours the reduction of Augustinianism to a series of crises and doctrinal exacerbations: the predestinationism of Godescalc in the 9th c. (*DThC*, 1, 2, 2527-2530), that of *Thomas Bradwardine in the 14th (*DThC*, 1, 2, 2535-2539), prelude to the dramas of the Reformation and Jansenism. Controversies are certainly not the best way to promote understanding of the faith.

Happily, the Augustinian spirit blows where it will. During the 11th- and 12th-c. renaissance, those strong doctrinal personalities *Anselm of Canterbury, *Bernard of Clairvaux, Peter *Abelard and *Hugh of Saint-Victor, among many others, maintained their Augustinian inspiration, each according to his own genius. This time also saw the flowering of small works of piety which their authors or readers attributed to Augustine in all simplicity of heart, while the scholastic use of Augustine's works was being prepared by the formation of collections of *Sentences, the most influential of which would be those of *Peter Lombard.

In the 13th c., *Thomas Aquinas, on the advice of his master *Albert the Great, followed Augustine in theology but preferred *Aristotle to him in philosophy. This option allowed him to discern clearly a Platonic component in Augustinian doctrine; Augustine, he considered, had followed Plato as far as the Christian faith allowed him to. "It was," said É. Gilson, "a model of the best history of philosophy, and one whose importance was capital". The Thomist discernment, indeed, laid down the principle of the division of Christian thought between the "*Platonism of the *Fathers" and the "Aristotelianism of the *scholastics"; it also permitted a disentangling of the intellectual debates of the 13th c., as would be done in the neoscholastic *belle époque* on the theme of the distinction or opposition between the "Aristotelianism" of some and the "Augustinianism" of others (see De Wulf; Ehrle). Thus was accredited the notion of a "medieval philosophical Augustinianism", which Pierre Mandonnet defined by the "absence of a formal distinction between the spheres of philosophy and theology", the corresponding tendency "to efface the formal separation of *nature and *grace" and the preference given to Plato over Aristotle (see *DThC*, 1, 2, 2503-2514). According to É. Gilson, concerning the problem of the agent *intellect we must also distinguish two forms of Augustinianism: "Avicennizing" and "Aristotelizing", both represented especially in the *Franciscan school. But, in the opinion of F. Van Steenberghen, there was here "a fund of Aristotelian doctrines quite heavily contaminated by Neoplatonist contributions from various sources". As for the distinctive traits pointed out by P. Mandonnet, they belong to theology. Put differently, Augustinianism in the 13th c., as at any other time, was part of the unitary regime of the understanding of *faith, which was no more confused than any other, as witness the reflection on theological epistemology pursued by thinkers such as *John Scotus, Anselm, Abelard, Hugh, Bonaventure, etc.

The notion of "political Augustinianism" accredited by H.-X. Arquillière is expressly modelled on P. Mandonnet's definition: "the tendency to absorb the natural law of the *State into supernatural justice and ecclesiastical law . . . which culminates in the theocratic ideas of the Middle Ages." The notion has been severely criticized by H. de Lubac.

According to Père Portalié (*DThC*, 1, 2, 2485-2499), the term "Augustinianism" designates the doctrine of grace defended by the Augustinian Order in the 17th-18th centuries. Père Cayré (*DThC*, *Tables générales*, 1, 317 and 320) extends it to the whole doctrine of the Order of Friars Hermits of St Augustine (from its foundation in 1256), whose first masters were *Giles of Rome and *James of Viterbo. This position does not seem to contribute to simplifying the problems of Augustinianism.

E. Portalié, "Augustinisme (développement historique de)", *DThC*, 1, 2, 1931, 2501-2561. – A. Wilmart, "La Tradition des grands ouvrages de saint Augustin", *Miscellanea Agostiniana*, 2, Rome, 1931, 257-315. – H.-X. Arquillière, *L'Augustinisme politique*, Paris, 1934. – O. Rottmanner, "L'augustinisme. Étude d'histoire doctrinale", *MSR*, 6, 1949, 29-48. – F. Cayré, *DThC*, *Tables générales*, 1, 1960, 314-324. – P. Courcelle, *Les Confessions de saint Augustin dans la tradition littéraire*, Paris, 1963. – L. Verheijen, *La Règle de saint Augustin*, Paris, 1967. – H. de Lubac, "Augustinisme politique?", *Théologies d'occasion*, Paris, 1984, 255-308. – G. Madec, "La Notion d'augustinisme philosophique. Essai de clarification", *Jean Scot et ses auteurs*, Paris, 1988, 147-161.

Goulven Madec

***AUSCULTA FILI.*** A letter of *Boniface VIII to *Philip the Fair, 5 Dec 1301, whose *incipit* is modeled on that of the rule of St *Benedict. Reacting to the arrest of the bishop of Pamiers ordered by the king, the pope warns the latter that he would be wrong to believe he has no superior on earth, reminds him that all disposal of ecclesiastical dignities comes from the Holy See, and summons the French bishops to Rome. The letter was thrown into the fire in full royal council and a caricatural summary of it circulated. From then on, the rupture between Boniface VIII and the French court was consummated.

A. Thomas, *Les Registres de Boniface VIII*, 3, Paris, 1907, 4424.

G. Digard, *Philippe le Bel et le Saint Siège (1285-1304)*, 2, Paris, 1936, 82-99.

Jean Coste †

**AUSTRASIA.** Of Germanic origin, the terms "Austria/Auster" and "Austrasii" appear in *Gregory of Tours at the end of the 6th c., at the moment when territorialization of power entailed the establishment in the north of the Frankish kingdom of three regional entities, the *tria regna*. Austrasia corresponded to the Frankish part of the Eastern kingdom, from *Laon to the Rhine and from the mouths of the Rhine to the Burgundian plateau. Its emergence was not linked to the definition of a cultural identity of its own, but to a regional consciousness, inscribed in a royal space that had

*The Hanging of Judas.* 12th-c. capital in the cathedral of Saint-Lazare, Autun.

been progressively determined by the partitions of the *Merovingian kingdom, the territorialization of power, and royal changes of site. The centre of gravity of this space had been resolutely anchored to the east ever since Childebert II had transferred his capital from *Reims to *Metz at the end of the 6th century. Until the victory of Chlotar II, king of *Neustria, over Queen Brunhild in 613, Austrasia was the most powerful of the three Merovingian kingdoms. In the 7th c. it submitted, directly or indirectly, to the tutelage of Neustria-*Burgundy, though without losing its autonomy. Here as elsewhere, the major phenomenon was the rise of a powerful aristocracy that combined the holding of the high civil and religious offices with the possession of vast landed *estates. The Christianization of the countryside that led at this time to the foundation of numerous monasteries on aristocratic estates, and the firstfruits of the economic revival that the northern regions would enjoy in the 8th-9th cc., increased its influence. After the death of King *Dagobert in 639, royal power was weakened, while two rival aristocratic factions, that of the Arnulfids-Pippinids and that of Wulfoald-Gundoin, struggled for control of the mayorship of the palace, which had become the main public office. Pippin II managed to prevail in Austrasia in the early 680s, before beating the Neustro-Burgundians at Tertry in 687 and putting the reunified Merovingian kingdom under Austrasian tutelage.

At this time, the peripheral provinces were practically autonomous. So *Charles Martel and his successors fought vigorously to resume control of the lost regions and extend the realm. For this, they relied systematically on the Austrasians, who became the spearhead of *Carolingian policy. They put their friends in the highest offices of the Empire, while Austrasian families were installed in the conquered provinces, to divide up the country. At the end of the 8th c., it seemed that the building of the palace of *Aachen in Austrasian territory must reinforce the leading role of Austrasia. In fact, Austrasian regional consciousness grew indistinct. The rulers had created a new royal space, which this time extended to the whole of Francia, from the Seine to the Rhine. They practised a policy of integration that effaced the old antagonisms, with such success that the partition of 843 did not follow the frontiers of the former Austrasia, and the term "Austria" came in the 9th c. to designate the regions situated beyond the Rhine, before being applied to what is now Austria.

E. Ewig, *Frühes Mittelalter, Rheinische Geschicht*, 1, Düsseldorf, 1980. – F. Cardot, *L'Espace et le pouvoir. Étude sur l'Austrasie mérovingienne*, Paris, 1987. – M. Parisse, *Austrasie, Lotharingie, Lorraine*, Nancy, 1990.

Régine Le Jan

**AUTHORITY.** By *auctoritas*, in the Middle Ages, was understood a quality by which a given being increased and enhanced his natural condition. He who had *auctoritas* ruled, governed, and conferred dignities. From a point of view close to the judicial, *auctoritas* was that quality by virtue of which a person was worthy of credit and capable of performing responsible actions; thence the term came to designate the person himself and, equally, the writing or document in which his *auctoritas* was expressed. It was in this sense that they spoke of *auctoritas Augustini* (authority of Augustine) or *auctoritas* of this or that Church *Father.

*Auctoritas* was a sort of *charism or gift conferred by God, whether by the intermediary of a certain rite – *e.g.* the *coronation of a *king – or by virtue of *consecration for *bishops, *ordination for priests, *profession for monks, swearing-in for magistrates, etc. He who had received it possessed something that made him superior. This was why *auctoritas* was manifested as a *maiestas*, which was set above others to make them better.

*Auctoritas* was manifested, *e.g.*, in the *magisterium, which was granted by means of a **licentia docendi* (authorization to teach) conferred by the bishop. It was equally manifested in the magistrature, which was authentic when its representative was invested with an *auctoritas* given by the king and, in certain cases, by the bishop. *Auctoritas*, for the monk or the religious, was *sanctitas*, while for the statesman it was *maiestas*.

In its most elevated degree, *auctoritas* was God's *providence, which guided and led everything towards a *magis* (more) that elevated and perfected. Hence the fact that *history was always considered in the Middle Ages as prophetic or sacred history.

Medieval man thus lived by authority and within a cosmic and *social order based on authority. Beings were not set on a level of equality, but in a hierarchical relationship with one another.

However, the vision of the world on which the Middle Ages closed was no longer so much founded on authority. Indeed there developed a permanent critique – sometimes explicit, sometimes subterranean – of the concept of *auctoritas*, based on a rational view of the world (libertine students). *Reason met authority on equal terms and unseated it. In the 10th and 11th cc., two radically opposed views of reality existed side by side: this was the time of polemic between *auctoritas* and *ratio*, or between dialecticians and anti-dialecticians. This opposition to *auctoritas* manifested itself still more forcefully in the 12th c., with two particularly important representatives: St *Bernard and Peter *Abelard. In the 13th c., the rationalist view of the world and society developed from *Aristotelian philosophy and, especially, through the intermediary of what was called *Averroism. The idea of a negation of *auctoritas* by reason reached its apogee in the 14th c. with *nominalism. From then on, everything was played out solely on the level of the individual, according to an egalitarian interpretation of reality. *Auctoritas* ceased to be a charism and was transformed into a mere responsibility or office: there were no more authorities, only functionaries.

S. Alvarez Turienzo, *Nominalismo y Comunidad*, 1961 ("CDios", 6). – M. D. Chenu, *La Théologie au douzième siècle*, Paris, 1966. – R. Dragonetti, "Auctor, autor, actor", *Lettres de l'École*, 1, 1979, 186-196. – R. Dragonetti, *La Vie de la lettre au Moyen Âge*, Paris, 1980. – L. M. de Rijk, *La Philosophie au Moyen Âge*, Leiden, 1985.

Jaime García Álvarez

**AUTUN.** A town in *Burgundy (now in Saône-et-Loire), Autun was the seat of a *bishopric at least from the early 4th century.

Nothing is known of the building of the *cathedral, whose name, Saint-Nazaire, and position are only attested in the early Middle Ages. Outside the town, several monasteries were founded near necropolises: Saint-Symphorien from the 5th c., Saint-Martin in the late 6th and, within the walls, Sainte-Marie and Saint-Andoche with a nearby *xenodochium* (*hospice for strangers). All these foundations existed, with several rebuildings of which we have descriptions, at least up to the late 18th century.

It was in the upper part of the city, not in the lower town originally occupied by the old forum, that religious life developed around the cathedral. In the 9th c., texts, verified by archaeology, show the installation of common buildings (dorter, refectory, galleried *cloister) which were later (12th c.?) abandoned in favour of canons' houses, of which many medieval and modern examples remain.

Immediately next to the old cathedral of Saint-Nazaire (which, rebuilt, survived into the 18th c.) was built between 1120 and 1140 the church of Saint-Lazare. Intended originally for the veneration of the saint's *relics, this jewel of *Romanesque architecture and sculpture (**Last Judgment* on the tympanum of the central portal, and capitals) was considered a second cathedral soon after its construction. In this cathedral and at several points of the town, we can also admire the effects of the *patronage of the Rolin, a family distinguished in the service of the dukes of Burgundy in the second half of the 15th c. (*Nativity* of the Master of Moulins and *Virgin* of Autun).

D. Grivot, G. Zarnecki, *Gislebertus, Sculptor of Autun*, New York, 1961. – D. Grivot, *Autun*, Lyon, 1967. – J.-C. Picard, "Autun", *TCCG*, 1986, 37-45. – *Autun-Augustodunum*, Autun, 1987 (exhibition catalogue).

Christian Sapin

*Scenes from the life of St Stephen.* Carolingian fresco in the crypt of the former abbey church of Saint-Germain d'Auxerre, 841-859.

**AUXERRE.** At Auxerre, in northern *Burgundy (now in Yonne), a *bishopric and Christian development are attested before the mid 4th c., when Bishop Valerianus appears at the council of Cologne. Though tradition gives this bishop a predecessor, the episcopal list only becomes trustworthy from the late 7th c. with the episcopate of Aunarius, who held several *synods and promoted the *cult of the saints.

Before this date, the town had only a small number of sanctuaries. Within the walls, the site of the first *cathedral is unknown. A new one was built in the 5th c. on the site of the present Gothic cathedral, under the name of Saint-Étienne. Outside the walls, the old necropolis of Montartre had a funerary basilica later known by the name of Saint-Amâtre. Opposite it, to the north-east, was the tomb of Bishop St Germanus (448). The *oratory of his **villa* gave rise to a *basilica, then to the Carolingian monastery of Saint-Germain, whose intellectual influence went beyond the limits of the region, with the presence of several generations of lettered monks known today as the School of Auxerre. From this period (mid 9th c.) date the still-surviving *crypts and their paintings devoted to the life of St Stephen.

In the following centuries, monasteries (Saint-Julien, Saint-Marien, Saint-Martin, Notre-Dame) and parish churches also developed, more than 30 sites in all, forming the Christian topography of the town. From the 12th c., it enjoyed a brisk expansion connected with the quality of its *wines, which easily reached Parisian markets via the Yonne and the Seine.

In the cathedral, the crypt dates from the great rebuilding early in the 11th c., while the upper parts belong to the Gothic stages (13th-14th cc.), as does a fine collection of *stained glass and the sculptures on the portals. Saint-Eusèbe and Saint-Pierre show the continuity of religious rebuilding between the 12th and the 16th c., dominating a civil building that hardly predates the 16th century.

C.B. Bouchard, *Spirituality and Administrations: the Role of the Bishop in Twelfth-Century Auxerre*, Cambridge (MA), 1979. – D. Denny, "A Romanesque Fresco in Auxerre Cathedral", *Gesta*, 25, 1986, 197-202. – *Abbaye Saint-Germain d'Auxerre, Intellectuels et artistes dans l'Europe carolingienne (IX$^{e}$-XI$^{e}$ siècle)*, Auxerre, 1990 (exhibition catalogue). – J.-C. Picard, "Auxerre", *TCCG*, 1993.

Christian Sapin

**AVARS.** In 570 the Avars, a people of nomad horsemen from the steppes of central Asia, settled in the Danubian bend, as the *Huns, to whom they were related, had done before them. They forced the *Lombards, led by Prince Alboin, to move into northern *Italy. Ruled by chiefs who bore the title of *khagan*, they made raids throughout central Europe and amassed the spoils of their conquests in the ring between the Tisza and the Danube. They acquainted the West with the use of the stirrup which allowed the horseman to use his lance more effectively.

Around 625, the *Slav tribes rose against the Avars and formed a sort of confederation under the direction of a Frankish merchant, Samo. But the Avars remained fixed in central Europe until the end of the 8th century. Collusion between Tassilo III of Bavaria and the Avars obliged *Charlemagne to intervene from 788. In 795, his son Pippin reached the ring and took possession of part of the treasure. Next year he returned, razed the ring and filled 15 carts with the fabulous wealth of the Avars. Then missionaries from *Salzburg sought to convert that people. *Alcuin and *Paulinus of Aquileia warned them against too great haste, advice that was not heeded. In 799 the Avars revolted again, whence a new expedition. In 805, the khagan accepted *baptism and became a vassal of Charlemagne. Part of the Avars who refused to submit to Frankish law fled eastward and settled in the Bulgar kingdom that Khan Krum was constructing. To protect his Empire, Charlemagne created the *limes avaricus* that later became the eastern *march (*Ost Mark* or *Ost Reich*: Austria).

J. Deer, "Karl der Grosse und der Untergang des Awarenreiches", in *Karl der Grosse*, W. Braunfels (ed.), Düsseldorf, 1965, 719-791. – P. Liptak, *Avars and Ancient Hungarians*, Budapest, 1983.

Pierre Riché

***AVE MARIA.*** In its initial Latin form, borrowing its words from the salutation of Elizabeth (Lk 1, 42) and that of the angel *Gabriel (Lk 1, 28), this prayer of praise intended to exalt the motherhood of the Virgin *Mary spread from the 10th c. and established itself in the devotion of the faithful at the end of the 11th century. In the 12th c., the *Ave Maria* was added with the **Credo* and the *Lord's Prayer to the number of official prayers. In the 13th and 14th cc., a great many *councils prescribed its recitation. Completed by a prayer of petition at the end of the Middle Ages, the formula of the *Ave Maria* was definitively fixed in 1568 with the adoption of the new Roman *breviary.

H. Thurston, *Familiar Prayers. Their Origin and History*, London, 1953, 90-114. – "Ave Maria", *Marienlexicon*, 1, St. Ottilien, 1988, 309-317.

Sylvie Barnay

**AVERROES (1126-1198), AVERROISM.** Abū l-Walīd Muhammad ibn Rushd (transformed in Latin into Averroes) was an Andalusian jurist, scholar, theologian and philosopher, born at *Cordova and died at Marrakesh. He was known in the West by the three latter aspects of his work. His *Generalities* on *medicine were translated and widely diffused. They aimed to make a classification of the medical knowledge of the time and were marked by an insistent logicism. In *astronomy, he took part in the movement that contested the system of Ptolemy, which culminated with al-Bitrawjī (Alpetragius). His theological work existed in the context of the rationalizing reform of *Islam undertaken by Ibn Tūmart, founder of the *Almohad Empire. This part of his work was hardly known except by *Raymond Martini and perhaps, through him, *Thomas Aquinas; but these seem to have retained of it only some particular philosophical theses. In philosophy, Averroes was above all "the Commentator" on *Aristotle. This labour of clarification of the work of the "first master", as the Arabs called him, was undertaken at the request of a ruler and took the form of three series of commentaries. Apart from a possible context of control of the work by an official commission, the reason for this gradation lay in Averroes' wish to restore the authentic Aristotle, beyond the *Neoplatonist interpolations introduced by the Arab thinkers of the East. The "little commentaries" are a simple presentation. The "middle commentaries" follow the order of the text. The "great commentaries" go into detail and – despite the charge of servility made against the author – may go so far as to complete or even correct the master's position. Most of these last are known only in Hebrew or Latin translation since Averroes' work suffered, in the Muslim

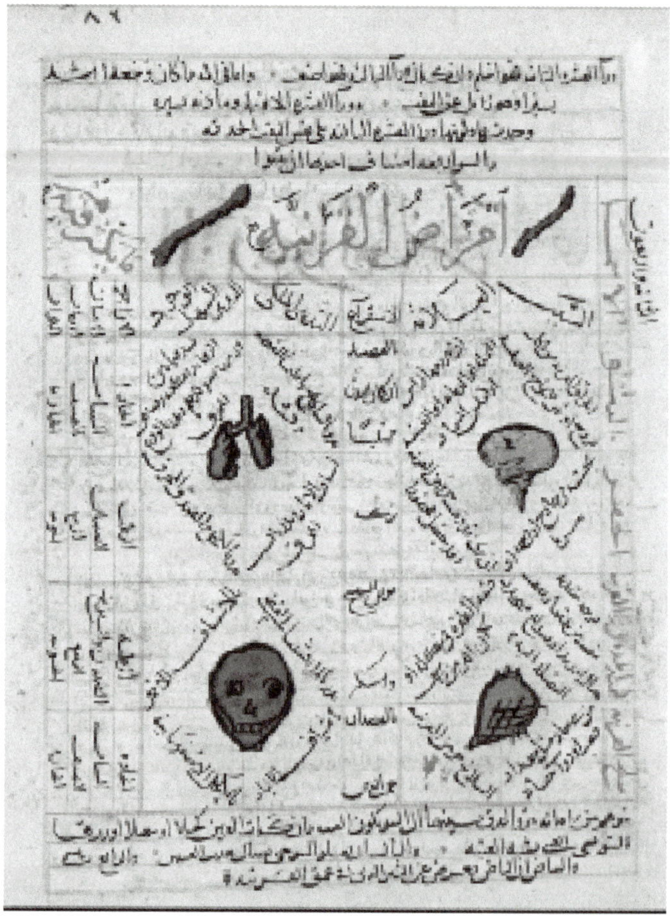

*Canon of Medicine.* Al Qanum manuscript of the works of Ibn Sina (Avicenna, 990-1037). 14th c. Damascus, National Museum.

world, first from a transitory disgrace of the author shortly before the end of his life, and especially from the disappearance of the Almohad world to which it was closely linked. But it was preserved by the rationalist current of European *Judaism.

It was only late that Averroes' work gained ground in the West, through the intermediary of Jewish authors or of translators like Michael Scot. The start of his influence seems to date from 1230; by *c.*1250, *Albert the Great was widely using him and Thomas Aquinas cites him explicitly more than 500 times. With *Siger of Brabant the tide seems to have turned, allowing the appearance of a veritable "Averroist" school. But it is to Raymond *Lull that we owe this word. Paradoxically, this Arabist did not know the Andalusian author's work directly; in his missionary project towards Islam, he asserted only the need for Christianity to unite in eliminating "a specifically Parisian paganism" (F. Van Steenberghen) in the same way that Islam rejected the "paganism" of Ibn Rushd. This perception led to a grave alteration in thought about the Arabic author, the Latins believing they found his own doctrine in his commentaries. Considered characteristic of this philosophy were the five following assertions: 1) The world is eternal. 2) *God does not know particulars and hence there is no *providence. 3) There is no free *will. 4) The possible *intellect is numerically one, as is the active intellect; consequently there is no individual *immortality nor moral responsibility of the individual. 5) *Philosophy and *theology are in contradiction ("double *truth") and the supernatural must be rejected.

*Multiple Averroès*, J. Jolivet (ed.), Paris, 1978. – M. Cruz Hernandez, *Abū l-Walid ibn Rushd (Averroes). Vida, obra, pensamiento influencia*, Cordova, 1986. – O. Leaman, *Averroes and his Philosophy*, Oxford, 1988. – P. Rosemann, "Ibn Rushd: a Catalogue of Editions and Scholarly Writings from 1821 onwards", *Bulletin de philosophie mediévale*, 30, 1988, 153-215. – D. Urvoy, *Ibn Rushd (Averroes)*, London, 1991.

Dominique Urvoy

**AVICEBRON (*c.*1022-*c.*1058).** Avencebrol, often cited in the 13th c. (by *William of Auvergne, Vitalis of Le Four, *Albert the Great, *Thomas Aquinas. . .), considered a Muslim, author of the *Fons vitae* (*Source of Life*), was identified in the 19th c. as the Jewish philosopher and poet Solomon ibn Gabirol, generally connected with the (neo-)platonising current. Born at Malaga, he died at *Valencia, after living mainly at *Saragossa, protected by the (Jewish) vizir of the king of *Granada. As well as the *Source of Life* (the Arabic original is lost; the Hebrew extracts are known under the title of *Meqor hayyim*), Solomon ibn Gabirol was the author of a great mystical poem *Keter malkhut* (Crown of Glory) and of religious and secular poetry. Translated into Latin by John of Spain and Dominic Gundisalvi in *c.*1150 (at *Toledo?), the *Source of Life* exercised a certain influence on Christian thought in the 12th c. (Gundisalvi), the first half of the 13th c. (discussions on the plurality of forms and universal *hylomorphism) and then the second half of it (*Avicebron's positions were refuted by Thomas Aquinas, but agreed by Vitalis of Le Four and certain *Franciscans).

*Avencebrolis Fons vitae*, C. Baeumker (ed.), *BGPhMA*, 1, 2-4, 1895. – Ibn Gabirol, *The Improvement of the Moral Qualities*, S. Wise (ed.), New York, 1966. – *Livre de la Source de vie*, J. Schlanger (tr.), Paris, 1970. – I. Davidson (ed.), *Selected Religious Poems of Solomon Ibn Gabirol*, New York, 1973.

J. Schlanger, *La philosophie de Salomon ibn Gabirol*, Leiden, 1968. – T. Rudavsky, "Conflicting Motifs: Ibn Gabirol on Matter and Evil", *NSchol*, 52, 1978, 54-71. – G. Dahan, "L'incontro con la filosofia ebraica", *Storia della filosofia Laterza*, 2, *Il medio evo*. – P. Rossi (ed.), C. A. Viano (ed.), Rome, 1994 ("Enciclopedia del sapere").

Gilbert Dahan

**AVICENNA (980-1037).** Abū Alī al-Husayn ibn Sīnā (Latinized to Avicenna): a Tajik philosopher and doctor who wrote in Arabic an Persian (born at Af'hana, near Bukhara, died at Hamadhān). He was a self-taught doctor and extremely precocious since he taught medicine from the age of 16. In his Autobiography he claims to have possessed all his knowledge at the age of 18 and since then to have used only his personal judgment. He was, in any case, incontestably one of the most powerful minds of all time and, in Arabic thought, one of the rare creators. Proceeding mainly from memory, he was more anxious to expound his own opinion than that of *Aristotle. As a doctor, he was attached to the concrete and extended Aristotle's logic to take it to the level of practical application. An enormous output of his survives, though an important part has been lost and the esoteric part was not transmitted to the medieval West.

The *Canon of Medicine* is his main work in that discipline. It reconciles clarity of exposition with the character of a **summa* of contemporary knowledge. While al-Rāzī (Rhazès) was considered the best clinician, the *Canon* always passed for the best synthesis, incorporating even the rules of experimentation that were not rediscovered until the 19th century. Translated entire by *Gerard of Cremona between 1150 and 1187, it underwent 86 more *translations (often partial) into Latin and Hebrew. It was the basis of teaching in all *universities up to the Renaissance, imposing the use of Arabic technical vocabulary, and was edited even in its original language at Rome in 1593.

In *philosophy he did not exercise the same authority, but his influence was more lasting. Of his great work, the Book of healing (of the soul), the introduction to the first part (on *logic), nearly all the second part (on physics and psychology) and the whole of the fourth part (on *metaphysics) were translated from the third quarter of the 12th century. At that time Aristotle was hardly known except as a logician, and Avicenna's text was taken for a mere commentary. When Aristotle was better known, the doctrine of the origin of the world, *God, the soul, the *intellect and the *angels were retained from the Muslim author's thought. Violently attacked in 1230 by the bishop of Paris, *William of Auvergne, he remained a great authority for a Franciscan tendency of English origin (*Roger Bacon, *Duns Scotus). *Thomas Aquinas made great use of him in his *De ente et essentia*, but cited him less later, while keeping great respect for him. He was increasingly rivalled by *Averroes.

By his own admission, Avicenna understood Aristotle's *Metaphysics* only through the explanation of al-*Fārābī: his thought was thus a Platonized Aristotelianism. Each *universal notion defines an essence that is a reality independent of the individual that possesses it. All that can be distinctly thought has an existence: so the *soul is distinct from the *body. Avicenna followed al-Fārābī's doctrine on the intellect and conceived of thought as the individual receiving *knowledge from the one agent Intellect. *Being is inherent to all that is thought, but being is distinguished into "possible", presupposing a *cause to bring it into being, and "necessary", existing by its own essence: all objects of experience are possible beings that hence refer to a necessary Being that is the cause of their existence. This necessary Being, *God, is one and ineffable. But possible beings can appear necessary by the fact of the necessity of the first cause: this was denounced by al-*Ghazālī, and an effort of adaptation by Duns Scotus was necessary to put at the origin of this series of causalities a sovereignly free divine *will.

R. de Vaux, *Notes et textes sur l'avicennisme latin aux confins des XII^e et XIII^e siècles*, Paris, 1934 – A. M. Goichon, *La Philosophie d'Avicenne et son influence en Europe médiévale*, Paris, 1940. – F. Rahman, "Essence and Existence in Avicenna", *MRSt*, 4, 1958, 1-16. – M. E. Mamura, "Some Aspects of Avicenna's Theory of God's Knowledge of Particulars", *Journal of the American Oriental Society*, 82, 1962, 299-312. – P. Morewedge, "Philosophical Analysis and Ibn Sina's 'Essence-Existence' Distinction", *Journal of the American Oriental Society*, 92, 1972, 425-435. – D. Gutas, *Avicenna and the Aristotelian Tradition*, Leiden, 1988.

Dominique Urvoy

**AVIGNON**

**History.** Avignon has been inhabited since the neolithic period; it developed from the *rocher des Doms* dominating the Rhône; a Marseillais counter, then a Gallo-Roman town, it had a certain importance, as witness the remains discovered in the 1970s; it received the title of Latin colony under the reign of Claudius, then of Roman city in the 2nd century. A first Christian community is attested there with the priest Rufus in the 3rd or 4th century.

After the barbarian *invasions, it was occupied by *Burgundians, *Visigoths and *Ostrogoths and ceded by the latter to the *Franks in 537; after its recapture for the Burgundians, the patrician Mummolus defended it in 581 against the Austrasian Duke Guntram Boso; the town then occupied the Rock and its immediate vicinity; we know little of its religious development, except the name of some of its bishops: the patrician Dynamius (604-625), the noble Magnus (650-660) and his son Agricola (660-700), the hermit Veredemus from Uzès (700-722), whose *epitaphs existed in the 17th c. in the church of Saint-Pierre.

Subjected under *Charles Martel, the Avignonese appealed to the Muslims of *Narbonne but the town was taken after a second siege, ravaged and burned (737). In the following century, it was incorporated in the kingdom of *Lothar, then of Louis the Blind who in 896 and 898 held the castle of Avignon, and from then on it was part of the German Holy Roman Empire. Great landed *estates, once in the hands of a southern aristocracy, passed sometimes into the ecclesiastical *patrimony and often also into the hands of the Frankish aristocracy.

After some obscure centuries under the authority of the *bishop and the *count, later of a viscount, the town began to prosper once more; admirably placed at the confluence of the Rhône and the Durance, it was disputed by the houses of *Toulouse, *Barcelona and Forcalquier, between which it remained undivided. The land was put under cultivation, urbanization increased, **bourgs* of artisans were built, a *bridge was thrown over the Rhône (*c.*1180), the town was surrounded by a double wall of ramparts; an urban patriciate was set up, composed of knights, jurists and experienced men who formed a *commune with consuls and a **podestà* and in fact governed the town.

During the Albigensian crusade, after the fourth *Lateran council, Avignon sided with Count *Raymond VI of Toulouse; in 1226 it refused passage to King *Louis VIII who descended the Rhône valley to chastise it, underwent a siege of three months and had to capitulate and accept the rigorous conditions of the papal *legate, the cardinal of Sant'Angelo: destruction of 300 strongholds and the ramparts, payment of a ransom. A new uprising was put down in 1251 by Alphonse of Poitiers and *Charles of Anjou, brothers of St *Louis, by their marriages respectively count of Toulouse and count of *Anjou; the town lost its commune, its autonomy and even its archives, which would figure among those of the counts of *Provence. In 1290 the king of France, *Philip the Fair, heir to Alphonse of Poitiers, ceded his rights to *Charles II of Anjou, count of Provence, from now on sole lord of Avignon, where he was represented by a *viguier* (*provost).

In 1309, Pope *Clement V, who led a wandering existence, being unable to go to Italy, settled provisionally at Avignon, where he lived intermittently until his death in 1314; his successor, *John XXII, who had been bishop of the town, settled there indefinitely, though without renouncing the prospect of returning to Rome; his successors *Benedict XII and *Clement VI built a grandiose palace intended to house the papal court and its administration. It was Clement VI who bought the town from Queen Joanna of Naples for the sum of 80,000 florins (1348). To protect the town, *Innocent VI decided on the construction of a new wall. *Urban V in 1367 and *Gregory XI in 1376 took the road back to *Italy, the former without being able to maintain himself there; but on Gregory's death, the troubled election of *Urban VI led to the eruption of a schism among the *cardinals who elected a second *pope, Cardinal Robert of Geneva who took the name *Clement VII. He could not remain in the peninsula and returned to Avignon. His successor, *Benedict XIII, worked doggedly to keep the tiara despite the secession of his cardinals, who supported the way of cession to put an end to the *Great Schism. He underwent a four-year siege in the papal palace and finally fled from Avignon in disguise, 11 March 1403. The Catalans, his supporters, with his nephew Rodriguez de Luna, kept control of the town until the second siege of the palace, at the end of which they had to capitulate (1411).

Provisional capital of Christendom for seventy years, Avignon had completely changed its appearance. Its surface area had tripled to house the court and all the persons gravitating round it. The population included citizens and papal officials, prelates and their *familiae*, merchants and artisans come to ply their activities in the immense market that was the town, as well as visitors and petitioners, lay and clerical (some of these last sometimes stayed long years); it attained perhaps 40,000 inhabitants in the first part of the 14th c. before being reduced by a third or a half by the Great Plague of 1348. The *laity were divided into citizens, under the jurisdiction of the temporal court and the *viguier*, and courtiers, who were under the authority of the marshal of the court, *clerics being subject to the jurisdiction of the *bishop or that of the audience of apostolic causes.

Numerous new buildings had been necessary. Benedict XII and Clement VI set the example with the apostolic palace, which for 20 years was an immense building site. The 20 or 25 cardinals, who had benefited from premises requisitioned on their behalf ("*liveries"), often replaced these with luxurious dwellings where they lived surrounded by their suite, in the image of the pope; some also built pleasure-houses outside Avignon or at Villeneuve.

Numerous constructions or reconstructions affected the already dense urban tissue of the old walled town. Within the town itself, but especially outside the original wall, then in ruins, were created building plots called *bourgs* or *bourguets* on lands belonging to Avignonese nobles, who sold out of necessity, or townspeople who made fruitful land deals: along new streets perpendicular to the main roads, the land was cut up into longitudinal parcels conceded on a long lease and on condition of building within a certain time. This development took place in virtually total anarchy, at the mercy of supply and demand, uncontrolled by the papacy which was not yet proprietor of the town, and was brutally halted by the plague of 1348. It subsequently resumed only moderately, by reason of new difficulties (renewed *epidemics, economic difficulties, threats by bands of mercenaries, successive departure of two popes, schism). The new town wall built under the pontificates of Innocent VI to Gregory XI, to a doubtless very deliberate plan, incorporated all the new buildings as well as the *gardens.

The quarters on the outskirts were inhabited by a laborious population of artisans and farm-workers, commercial activities being established within the old walled area and, more precisely for *banking and luxury *commerce, in the hands of Tuscans, in the parishes of Notre-Dame-la-Principale and Saint-Didier, near the Exchange; the papal officials lived near by in the parishes of Saint-Étienne, Saint-Agricol, Saint-Pierre and Saint-Symphorien with old Avignonese families engaged in the traditional activities of *fusterie* or the weaving and sale of hemp.

The popes led a life sometimes sumptuous (Clement VI), sometimes relatively austere (Benedict XII and Urban V), but always punctuated by religious *offices. They attracted *artists and *humanists to Avignon; numerous personages (rulers, princes, prelates, ambassadors) came to visit the supreme pontiff. The papal court could comprise from 300 to 500 persons; its services – administration (Apostolic *Camera, *chancery, audience of apostolic causes, *Penitentiary) and domestic household (*chapel, kitchen, pantry, butlery, smithy, guards and guards of honour, almonry of the *Pignotta, etc.) – spilled over from the palace into the town.

Paradoxically, this century saw few religious foundations (the *Dominicans of Sainte-Praxède outside the town, the Benedictine college of Saint-Martial and the *Celestines, under Clement VII); the parishes of Avignon increased in size but remained seven in number; three of them (Saint-Agricol, Saint-Pierre and Saint-Didier) would be erected into *collegiate churches thanks to the liberality of the pope and two cardinals. The buildings were rebuilt and enlarged. The four convents of *mendicants were very flourishing, especially that of the Friars Preachers who benefited from the generosity of cardinals and prelates of their order. A *university, created by *Boniface VIII shortly before the arrival of the papacy, was celebrated for its juristic teaching.

Avignon's prestige survived the departure of the papacy. Cardinals continued to reside there, sovereigns came to visit; *John XXIII, elected by the council of *Pisa, dreamed for a time of resettling at Avignon and did some work on the palace. But the Avignonese revolted against *Eugenius IV's nephew, Marco Condulmer, bishop of Avignon and rector of the *Comtat Venaissin; the cardinal of Foix took the town after a siege of two months and received the title of *vicar and *legate (1433). The town remained a centre of attraction and a great place of business.

At one time there was a question of transferring the council of *Basel there and holding a meeting of the Christian communities of the East to restore Church unity; the antipope *Felix V, appointed by the council, tried to rouse the town but did not succeed. Yet the Avignonese rejected the cession of the town to the Dauphin. The pope had Avignon governed by a legate, the first one being Cardinal Peter of Foix, who lived in the palace and had overall spiritual jurisdiction over the ecclesiastical *provinces of *Arles, Aix, *Vienne, Embrun and *Toulouse.

After the death of the cardinal of Foix (1464), Pope *Sixtus IV appointed as legate Charles de Bourbon and then his own nephew Giuliano della Rovere, in whose favour he had erected the bishopric into an *archbishopric. He was to live there until 1503, leaving a deep mark on the town by his administration (foundationsand university reforms) before becoming pope as Julius II.

J. Girard, *DHGE*, 5, 1931, 1121-1142. – J. Girard, *Évocation du vieil Avignon*, Paris, 1958. – B. Guillemain, *La Cour pontificale d'Avignon*, Paris, 1962. – G. Mollat, *The Popes at Avignon 1305-1378*, London, 1963. – Y. Renouard, *The Avignon Papacy 1305-1403*, Hamden, 1970. – *Histoire d'Avignon*, Aix-en-Provence, 1979, 17-312. – D. Vingtain, *Avignon. Le Palais des Papes*, La Pierre-qui-vire, 1998.

Anne-Marie Hayez

**Art.** A city of Roman origin, situated on the bank of the Rhone, chief town of the *Comtat Venaissin. The early Middle Ages left a sad mark on Avignon: amidst *invasions and sieges, the population, reduced by war and *epidemics, took refuge around the Rock that dominated the town, enclosed in its cramped, fortified Late Imperial wall. Not far from the citadel or *castrum*, along the south slope, stood the basilica of Notre-Dame, the baptistery or church of St John the Baptist and the church of St Stephen. When he died in *c.*700, Bishop St Agricol of Avignon had just founded a monastery on this side of the citadel. The *count who held the town settled with his court in his fortified castle. South of the city, a small hermitage, Saint-Ruf, was established on an early Christian site.

The 11th c. marked the economic rise, and hence the extension, of the town: Notre-Dame was rebuilt and its closeness to the episcopal dwelling earned it the name Notre-Dame-des-Doms; other churches were rebuilt or appeared: Saint-Agricol, Sainte-Madeleine whose tower stood on one of the Roman arches of the Fusterie; *extra muros*, since the town overflowed its boundaries, were Notre-Dame-la-Principale, Saint-Symphorien, Saint-Didier, Saint-Pierre. The abbey of Saint-Ruf developed into a renowned artistic centre. The period of prosperity engendered by the establishment of the *commune favoured the construction of monuments, some of which still survive. Completed in 1185, the *bridge of Saint-Bénezet, the first bridge from the sea, facilitated commercial exchanges: a *chapel and a *hospital supplemented it. A double wall protected the town, following the line of the first Roman rampart and incorporating the **bourgs* and their churches. A dozen gates pierced the walls protected by towers while the moats were fed by the waters of springs brought from the suburbs. The *bishop, whose sculpted marble **cathedra* can be admired in the *cathedral, rebuilt his palace on the south slope of the Rock. Opposite and on another rise, the commune erected its own: its high walls of small stones are still visible along the Rue Peyrolerie. The old Jewry occupied the west slope of the Rock.

Fresco by Matteo Giovanetti of Viterbo in St Martial's chapel at the Palace of the Popes, Avignon. 1344-1345.

In 1226, King *Louis VIII, on his way to the second crusade against the Albigenses, could see beyond the walls the fortified houses of the knights and the Rock crowned with defences. Defeat obliged the Avignonese to demolish part of their ramparts, most of the arches of the bridge and nearly 300 strongholds. However, despite the end of communal independence, the inhabitants put their city on its feet again. *Convents were even founded outside the walls, in particular those of the *Dominicans, *Franciscans,

Augustinians and *Carmelites, near the gates. Other houses like those of the nuns of St Lawrence, St *Clare or St Catherine, the buildings of the *commandery of St John and the hospitallers of St Anthony, and numerous hospitals arose *intra muros*.

At this time the peaceful little city – which numbered some 6000 inhabitants at the start of the 14th c. – experienced a prodigious event: the installation of the *pope and the *Curia within its walls in the years 1310-1320. The considerable growth in the population led to a housing crisis dealt with by exceptional legislation. Thus, to lodge the *cardinals and their retinues, groups of houses called "*liveries" were ceded to them. The city became a cosmopolitan, effervescent Gothic town. Pope *John XXII, former bishop of Avignon, improved the episcopal palace and built an audience hall on the south front, perpendicular to the treasury. Yet *Benedict XII felt cramped and decided to erect a new*palace. On 17 June 1336, he exchanged the episcopal palace for the cardinal's livery of Arnaud de Via built below the Rock. Building began with the Pope's tower and the transformation of St Stephen's chapel into a papal chapel dedicated to the apostles Peter and Paul. One after another arose, around the old courtyard, the Guest wing, the *Consistory wing and that of the Grand Tinel, the Familiar wing against the Belltower. The Study tower and those of the *oratories, kitchens and latrines completed the east front. The Great Gate, surmounted by the papal arms, stood at the entrance onto the Place des Cancels. The pope settled into his palace-monastery, decorated by an international team of painters. Painted furniture, oriental carpets, *tapestries from Paris or Flanders and chandeliers completed the decorations. The ostentatious *Clement VI enlarged the building. Used to the Gothic creations of his French homeland, he had recourse to the talent of a *Francilien*, Jean de Louvres, for the Garde-Robe tower above the bath-house, the great kitchen with Saracen chimney, and especially the double-bayed Audience wing surmounted by the Clementine chapel opening onto the loggia of Indulgences, and the wing of the great dignitaries pierced by the Porte des Champeaux. The Old Palace was thus succeeded by the New Palace whose luxury was expressed in the sumptuosity of the mural *paintings created by the studio of maestro Matteo Giovannetti of Viterbo. The walls of the reception rooms and chapels told the story of Sts *John the Baptist, *John the Evangelist and Martial, apostle of the Limousin, the *prophets, the *Last Judgment, the Virgin in *Majesty, on a background of gold, silver and lapis lazuli, making the palace a cultural centre from which the first Avignon school radiated. In the apartments, the secular decoration recalled the careless pleasures of lords and their taste for nature. The cardinals, settled in their magnificent fortified houses, chose their painters or their sculptors, goldsmiths, Sienese by preference, suppphers and merchants of precious fabrics, *furs and *objets d'art*. Their liberality extended to the rebuilding of the parish churches in which they were buried: Saint-Didier (Bertrand de Déaux), Saint-Pierre (Pierre des Prés), Saint-Martial (Pierre de Cros). Some of the orders – Carmelites, *cordeliers*, Augustinians, Dominicans – also rebuilt their church. Simone *Martini decorated the porch of Notre-Dame-des-Doms for Cardinal Stefaneschi. But in mid-century the threat of the Great *Companies obliged *Innocent VI hastily to establish a new fortified wall around the city enclosing the new **bourgs* and the vast *convents. Nearly 4 kilometres long, the wall, partly completed by *Urban V from 1364, was reinforced by semi-circular towers and pierced by monumental gates. Avignon, by now the centre of the Christian world, was the crucible in which literary and artistic currents mingled. Nearly 1500 students profited from the university and the colleges, artists and men of letters crowded around the pontiff or the cardinals, attracted by patronage.

Despite the terrible plague, despite the *Great Schism, the final quarter of the century saw further construction of churches (Sainte-Catherine, Saint-Martial) and convents, like the grandiose one of the *Celestines founded by King *Charles VI of France over the tomb of Cardinal Peter of Luxemburg (1394). After the papacy's final return to *Rome (1417), the liveries, convents and noble dwellings lost their inmates and the town its inhabitants, but Avignon, a brilliant business centre and strategic crossroads of Italian trade, kept its privileged position: churches were enlarged, squares created (Place de l'Horloge, du Change), liveries transformed; King *René had Nicolas *Froment and Francesco Laurana working there. The painters Enguerrand *Quarton and Pierre Villate, the sculptors Jacques Morel, Antoine Le Moiturier and Ferrier Bernard lived in Avignon. A second Provençal school was born in this climate of bourgeois and financial prosperity, which was to last until the Wars of Religion in the 16th century.

L.-H. Labande, *Le Palais des Papes et les monuments d'Avignon au XIVe siècle*, Marseille, 1925. – S. Gagnière, J. Granier, *De la Préhistoire à la Papauté*, Avignon, 1970. – A. Borg, *Architectural Sculpture in Romanesque Provence*, Oxford, 1972. – *Histoire d'Avignon*, Aix-en-Provence, 1979. – M. Laclotte, D. Thiébaut, *L'École d'Avignon*, Paris, 1985. – J. Gardner, *The Tomb and the Tiara: Curial Tomb Sculpture in Rome and Avignon in the later Middle Ages*, Oxford, 1992.

Roberte Lentsch

**AYYUBIDS.** A dynasty of independent *Sunni rulers, founded by *Saladin (in Arabic Salāh al-Dīn ibn Ayyūb), which reigned in Egypt, *Syria, Upper Mesopotamia and Yemen from 1171 to 1260, ensuring the intellectual and economic development of those regions. On Saladin's death in 1193, his domains were shared between the different members of his family. Although the sultans of *Cairo, al-Malik ad-ādil (1200-1218) and al-Malik al-Kāmil (1218-1238), managed to impose themselves for a time, the rivalries and conflicts between Saladin's descendants considerably weakened the Ayyubids, which explains their policy of coexistence with the *Latin States, their incapacity to resist the *Mongols (conquest of *Aleppo in 1260) and the seizure of power in Egypt by the *Mamluks in 1250.

C. Cahen, "Ayyūbides", *EI(E)*, 1, 1960, 796-807. – R. S. Humphreys, *From Saladin to the Mongols. The Ayyubids of Damascus, 1193-1260*, New York, 1977. – P. Balog, *The Coinage of the Ayyubids*, London, 1980. – *The Cambridge History of Egypt*, 1, *Islamic Egypt, 640-1517*, C. F. Petry (ed.), Cambridge, 1998.

Françoise Micheau

**AZYME, AZYMITES.** Traditionally, the Eastern Christians used leavened bread for the *Eucharist and the Westerners unleavened (*a-zumos*) bread. This difference in rite posed no problems until the 11th c., when it was enrolled in the polemic against the Latins and Armenians, styled "azymites". For the Greeks, the use of unleavened bread was a Jewish practice, contrary to the Gospel (the accounts of the Last Supper have *artos*, "leavened bread"), heretical (leavened bread symbolizes the union of two natures in Christ) and vain (azymes, dead bread, cannot represent the living Christ).

J. Meyendorff, *Initiation à la théologie byzantine*, Paris, 1974, 128-129. – M. H. Smith, *And taking Bread. . . Cerularius and the Azyme Controversy of 1054*, Paris, 1978.

Marie-Hélène Congourdeau

# B

**BABEL, TOWER OF.** The theme appears in patristic catechesis, in Gregory Nazianzen (*Serm.* 41, 16; *PG*, 36, 449c), John Chrysostom (Pentecost Homily 2; *PG*, 50, 467c) and especially Augustine (*Sermon* 271; *PL*, 38, 1245-1246). In iconography, the tower of Babel (in Hebrew, *Babel* means "Gate of God") is contrasted with *Pentecost. Two types of representation appear, the moment of construction of the tower proper being distinguished from that when God introduces the confusion of tongues. Often, within the representation, the two moments are separate: thus in St Mark's basilica at Venice, on the *mosaics of the narthex (13th c.), on one side is shown the labour of the *masons and other workers, on the other God, warned by the angels and descending to earth, at the foot of the tower, to put an end to the disorder. Sometimes the diversity of tongues is expressed by diversity of races. Equally, in the phase of construction of the tower, two types of buildings can be depicted: either a tower in stages that recede as they go up, or a square (or circular) tower with spiral external ramps (as on the miniature in a *Book of Hours, illuminated at Paris for the duke of Bedford, *c.*1433; London, BL). In the scene of confusion of tongues, the characters indicate their mouth with their finger. Finally, representations of the tower of Babel are so many occasions to illustrate the activities and development of a building site.

O. Casel, "Art und Sinn der ältesten christlichen Osterfeier", *Jahrbuch für Liturgiegeschichte*, 44, 1938, 1-78. – A. Parrot, *La Tour de Babel*, Strasbourg, 1941 ("Bulletin de la Faculté de théologie protestante"). – P. Du Colombier, *Les Chantiers des cathédrales*, Paris, 1953 (1973, 2nd ed.).

Daniel Russo

*Construction of the Tower of Babel.* Manuscript of Rabanus Maurus' *De Universo.* 1023. Monte Cassino. Abbey Archives.

**BAGHDAD.** Baghdad, capital of the *Abbasid Empire, was founded in 762 by the second *caliph of the dynasty, al-Mansūr, on the banks of the Tigris, in *Iraq.

It was both to get away from the popular and turbulent city of Kūfa and to create a town that was the symbol of the new regime that the caliph decided to found this new residence, which in a few decades underwent a considerable development.

The town founded in 762 on a site with both strategic and economic advantages (a place where the Tigris and Euphrates approached each other) was at first a circular fortified city bordering the Tigris and a canal. On the inner esplanade rose the caliph's palace and the adjacent Great Mosque. The markets, originally part of this group, were moved in 773 and installed in a suburb to the south named Karkh. This urban centre, which modern historians call the "round city", received the official name of "City of salvation", a Koranic expression evoking paradise.

The town was not slow to be extended. In 773, on the east bank of the Tigris, was founded the town of Rusāfa, intended for the princely heir, which enjoyed a development all the more considerable since in 812-813 Baghdad suffered a siege that saw the destruction of the old round city. Also the caliphs, when they returned to Baghdad in 892 after the interlude of Samarra, settled in a group of palaces situated south of Rusāfa. New palaces appeared under the Buyids and the *Seljuks, and **madrasas* or colleges of religious science were created in the late 11th century.

Baghdad, which was not just the seat of the Abbasid caliphate, but also a very active intellectual, literary and artistic centre, was sacked by the *Mongols in 1258. It survived, but only as a provincial capital.

A. A. Duri, "Baghdād", *EI(E)*, 1, 1960, 894-908. – E. G. Heilman, *Popular Protest in Medieval Baghdad 295-334 A.H./908-946 A.D.*, Ann Arbor (MI), 1979. – J. Lassner, *The Shaping of 'Abbasid Rule*, Princeton (NJ), 1980.

Dominique Sourdel

***BAILLI, BAILLIAGE.*** The French term *baillie* at first meant "commission", and a *bailli* designated any demesnial agent, of whatever rank, whether or not exercising judicial or financial powers. The *bayle* of the French Midi and the *bailli* of *Plantagenet *Normandy were subordinate agents of the prince, similar to the *prévôts* (*provosts) of the North.

The royal *bailli* of the late French Middle Ages was a high-flying personage, representing the king in the plenitude of his powers over a vast area, the *bailliage*. As often in France, the fact preceded the institution. In 1184 *Philip Augustus sent *baillis*, recruited among the members of the *curia regis*, to control the activity of the *prévôts* and to hold judicial sessions. The king of France might have been inspired by the justiciars of the kings of *England in Normandy, though it may be that, faced with the same needs, the two rulers reacted in the same way. The new *baillis* moved around in twos or threes. They held assizes and collected

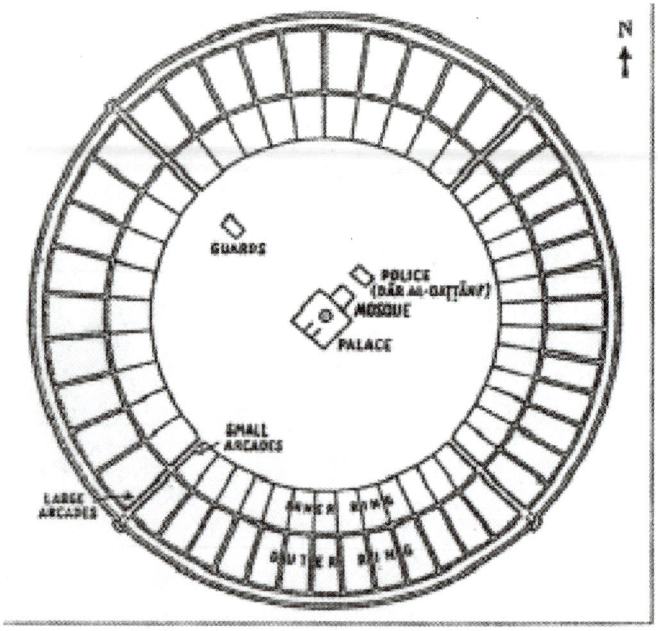


Baghdad, the Round City, 762-766. Plan reconstructed by Lassner.

the irregular revenues of the domain; they periodically rendered an account to the court. The institution gradually became established and, around 1240-1250, the *bailli* became a single agent, established in a fixed district, the *bailliage*. He was appointed by the king, salaried, and revocable at any moment; no longer belonging to the *curia*, he was subject to the control of the central institutions and the royal inquisitors (*e.g.* in 1247). The career of many of them was short; those who had long careers occupied several posts and were subject to administrative moves. Recruited from the minor *nobility and the urban middle class, they received a legal training; they could not exercise their office in the *bailliages* from which they came or where they owned property.

This model, which lasted about a century, evolved after 1350. On one hand, the growing complexity of affairs led to new agents assisting the *bailli* (general lieutenant) or exercising certain of his attributes (receivers, captains); but it would be wrong to speak of the "dismemberment" of the office. On the other hand, and this was a consequence of the wars, foreign and civil, the nature of the *bailli*'s office changed: the *bailli* became a political agent, subject to the parties in power. The rules of public office were now no longer observed: non-residence, exercise of office in the *bailliage* of origin; office now monopolized by the *noblesse d'épée*. Finally, in the second half of the 15th c., the king delegated vast powers to governors in provinces larger than the *bailliages*. At the end of the Middle Ages, the governor had supplanted the *bailli*, leaving him only an honorific title sought after by the provincial nobility. The *bailliage* continued to exist as a judicial framework, but it was rivalled by districts arising from the development of *taxation: dioceses and *élections*. Though of different origin, *seneschals and *sénéchaussées* became, from the mid 13th c., institutions similar to that of the *bailli*.

G. Dupont-Ferrier, *Gallia Regia, ou État des officiers royaux des bailliages et sénéchaussées de 1328 à 1515*, Paris, 1942-1966 (7 vol.). – A. Bossuat, *Le Bailliage royal de Montferrand*, Paris, 1957. – L. Carolus-Barre, "Les baillis de Philippe III le Hardi", *ABSHF*, 1969, 109-244. – A. Demurger, "Guerre civile et changements du personnel . . . des baillis et sénéchaux (1400-1418)", *Francia*, 6, 1978, 151-298. – J.W. Baldwin, *The Government of Philip Augustus*, Berkeley, 1986, 125-36, 220-4, 428-33. – J. Barbey *et al.*, *Histoire des institutions de l'époque franque à la révolution*, Paris, 1990 ("Droit fondamental").

Alain Demurger

**BALDWIN I OF JERUSALEM (1058-1118).** Son of Count Eustace II of Boulogne and of Ida, daughter of the duke of *Lorraine, Baldwin was originally intended for the clerical state. After studying the *liberal arts, he became a *canon at Reims, Cambrai and Liège, then renounced his ecclesiastical career. He accompanied his brothers Eustace III of Boulogne and *Godfrey de Bouillon on the first *crusade. Called in by the Armenians, he created the first Oriental Frankish state at Edessa. On Godfrey's death, he was crowned king of *Jerusalem, 25 Dec 1100. A tireless warrior, he extended his kingdom by conquering Arsuf and Caesarea, *Acre, *Beirut and Sidon. He died without heir in 1118 on his return from a campaign in Egypt. His cousin Baldwin of Le Bourcq succeeded him.

H. E. Mayer, "Études sur l'histoire de Baudouin Ier, roi de Jérusalem", *Mélanges sur l'histoire de royaume latin de Jérusalem*, Paris, 1984, 10-91.

Michel Balard

**BALDWIN II OF JERUSALEM (died 1131).** Son of Hugo, count of Rethel, Baldwin of Le Bourcq accompanied his cousin *Godfrey de Bouillon on the first *crusade. He received the county of Edessa from *Baldwin I, who had become king of *Jerusalem. On the latter's death he succeeded him (1118), leaving the county to his cousin Joscelin de Courtenay. His reign was marked by arduous campaigns in northern *Syria, to defend *Antioch and Edessa; he spent two years in prison. Once free, he tried in vain to take *Aleppo and *Damascus, in alliance with the Ismā'īlis ("*Assassins"). He strengthened the royal power at the expense of the barons and the Church (council of Naplus, 1120). At his death (1131), the kingdom of Jerusalem had attained its greatest extent.

J. Prawer, *Histoire du royaume latin de Jérusalem*, 1, Paris, 1969, 279-310.

Michel Balard

**BALEARICS.** The Mediterranean archipelago of the Balearics owes its name to the Greeks, while its islands, *Maiorica* (Majorca), *Minorica* (Minorca) and *Ebussus* (Ibiza), owe theirs to the Romans and Carthaginians. In the Middle Ages, after the Christian reconquest, the Balearics took the name of *Regnum Maioricarum*.

The installation of *Islam early in the 11th c. effaced all vestiges of the Christian presence attested by ruins of early Christian basilicas in Majorca and Minorca and by the existence of *dioceses in the 5th century.

In the 13th c., James I the Conqueror (1213-1276) inaugurated his Mediterranean policy by the conquest of the Balearics, justified by the need to defend the Catalan coast from Muslim attacks: Majorca was taken in 1229; Minorca, a tributary of *Aragon in 1231, was not occupied militarily until 1287 by Alfonso III the Liberal (1285-1291); Ibiza, in 1235.

James I's testament allowed his son, James II of Majorca (1276-1311), to organise an independent kingdom in the Balearics, which was annexed to the Crown of Aragon in 1348 by the Aragonese King *Peter IV the Ceremonious (1336-1387).

J. F. Cabestany, *Expansio catalana per la Mediterrània*, Barcelona, 1967.

María José Sánchez Usón

**BALL, JOHN (1331-1381).** John Ball was born in Essex around 1331; he seems to have belonged to a modest rural family possessing some property at Colchester. According to the chronicler Thomas Walsingham, he began his career as priest in charge of singing masses at St Mary's abbey, *York, but we can place him with certainty as *chaplain at Colchester between 1377 and 1381 at least: he was already preaching at that time in Essex and then in Kent, since he was cited to appear before the archbishop of *Canterbury in 1366 and was even excommunicated in 1379. So he was one of those "poor priests", marginal priests, uncontrollable since possessing no fixed *benefice, whose popular and often subversive preaching the episcopal hierarchy feared above all things.

In June 1381, when the *Peasants' Revolt broke out, he seems to have been thrown into *prison at Maidstone for continuing to preach despite his *excommunication, and he must have been freed by the rebels, whom he accompanied in their wanderings. The *chroniclers doubtless exaggerate his role, but we have several letters written in an obscure style and sometimes signed with borrowed names, preserved by the chroniclers Henry Knighton and Thomas Walsingham; not forgetting the account given by Walsingham and *Froissart of the celebrated sermon preached at Blackheath on the text "When Adam delved and Eve span, who was then the gentleman?", when he cried out: "What have we done to be thus held in bondage? Are we not all descended from one father and one mother, Adam and Eve?"

Much has been asked about his adherence to the *Lollard doctrine. In fact there is nothing to prove that Ball was a disciple of *Wycliffe. His "revolutionary" social ideas do not necessarily come from the latter: they can just as well be attached to the "protest literature" whose finest example is the poem *Piers Plowman* by William *Langland (himself perfectly orthodox); but, with many other "poor priests", Ball was no doubt part of that fringe of clergy inspired by Wycliffe's London preaching, if not by his learned works. His attacks on *tithes and his defence of the legitimacy of refusing to pay the tithe to an absentee or unworthy *cleric are in any case directly in line with Wycliffite positions. Certain details of his "confession", contained in the *Fasciculi zizaniorum* in which the Carmelite theologians assembled a solid dossier against Wycliffism, show that it was a fabrication, but it no less faithfully represents his views and agrees with the portrait painted by the chroniclers. Ball was present at the interview between King *Richard II and the leader of the revolt, Wat Tyler, but he fled after Tyler's murder. Imprisoned at Coventry, he was finally executed at St Albans on 15 July 1381, and the four quarters of his corpse were exposed in four cities of the realm.

R. B. Dobson, *The Peasants' Revolt of 1381*, London, 1970. – B. Bird, D. Stephenson, "Who was John Ball?", *Transactions of the Essex Archaeological Society*, 3rd series, 8, Colchester, 1976, 287-289. – A. Hudson, *The Premature Reformation*, Oxford, 1988, 66-67.

Jean-Philippe Genet

**BALTS.** The Balts, who reached the banks of the Baltic around 500 BC, are among the oldest Indo-European peoples. From the time of the departure of the Goths, Pomeranians and Pruthenians settled between the Vistula and the Niemen. The Lithuanians grouped together between the Niemen and the Dvina while the Letts (*Estes* and *Lives*) occupied the northern lands as far as the Gulf of Finland.

The Christianization of these peoples, still *pagan at the dawn of the 13th c., was slow, difficult and closely linked to German colonization eastwards: *Ostsiedlung*. The Pomeranians, divided from 1107 between Pomerelia around *Gdańsk and imperial *Pomerania west of the Vistula, were resolutely evangelized by *Otto of Bamberg between 1124 and 1128. They did not recover their unity until 1478.

By contrast, the first attempts to Christianize the Pruthenians, by *Adalbert of Prague in 997 and Bruno of Querfurt in the 12th c., ended in failure: the *Cistercians were thrown into gaol in 1178 and 1216; the crusade of Christian, bishop of Chelmno, and Philip, a monk of Olivo, was hardly more successful.

Consolidating their state organisation in the 13th c., notably under their chief Skomand, the Pruthenians gave themselves up to pillaging raids on their neighbours of Chelmno. Reckoning that *evangelization needed military support, *Gregory IX called a crusade in 1230 and handed over Kulmerland, now a land of St Peter, to Hermann of Salza, grand master of the *Teutonic Order, entrusting the conversion of the Prussians to him. The first successes were felt in 1249 but, carried away by their Lithuanian neighbours, who had returned to paganism in 1253 on the death of *Innocent IV, the Pruthenians revolted. Massacres intensified between 1260 and 1274, before the insurgents capitulated and submitted to Christianity in 1284. Teutonic force had overcome their resistance. But German colonization did not exterminate the Pruthenians, who kept their social structure, their homes and even took part alongside their conqueror in the colonization of Samland. But in order to enter the middle class, a number of them renounced their language in favour of German, henceforth the main factor in German integration. In 1285, the first Pruthenian thus entered the *Rat* of Königsberg.

The Lithuanians resisted for longer, fiercely opposing all attempts at Germanization. For this reason, at first, they refused conversion, before seeking Polish support against the common enemy. Mindaugas (1200-1263), the federate king, allowed himself to be seduced by the Gospel, doubtless in order to guarantee the western frontiers of his *duchy and allow him to continue his expansion into Russian and Tartar lands. But under pressure from his subjects, Gedymin (1316-1341), the real founder of the Lithuanian state, had to renounce the Christian faith. The *rapprochement* with the Poles finally decided the conversion of the Lithuanians. Jogaila, grandson of Gedymin and grand prince of *Lithuania (1377-1434), adopted Christianity in 1386, in which year he married *Hedwig, heiress of *Poland; by becoming King *Ladislas II Jagiello of Poland, he achieved the personal union of Poland and Lithuania, urging his Baltic subjects to conversion. Profiting from discord between Catholics and Orthodox, Grand Duke Witovdt restored Lithuania's autonomy. Nevertheless, the community of interests remained sufficiently strong for Lithuanians and Poles together to crush their old Teutonic enemy in 1410 at Tannenberg (*Grunwald). But not until 1440 was Casimir IV Jagiello able to reintegrate the Lithuanian territory into the Polish kingdom.

Teutonics, Danes and Hanseatics were, with Cistercians, the main architects of the Christianization of the Letts of Livonia (from the name of the *Lives*, established between *Estonia and the Dvina). From 1180, Meinhard, a canon of Segebert in Holstein, followed the merchants who went up the Duna and in 1184 obtained authorization from the Russian prince of *Polotsk to build his church. Thus was built, in 1186, the church of Uxhull, the first in all Livonia. In 1201, *Albert of Buxhövden founded *Riga, becoming its first bishop. But the brutal colonization of the *Knights of the Sword provoked, from 1204, resistance and revolts like those of the peasants of Oesel in 1206. In 1225, Innocent bestowed

Estonia on the Christian Danes who had occupied it from 1216 and had founded, in 1219, the bishopric of Tallinn, attached to that of *Lund.

Waldemar IV Atterdag, king of *Denmark, gave Livonia in fief to the Knights of the Sword, who were joined by the Teutonic Knights in 1228, which once more gave effective control of the territory to the Germans. The Germanic middle class, originally from the Hanseatic towns of *Lübeck, *Hamburg and *Bremen, had already established themselves in the towns, while the knights of Mecklenburg-Holstein Germanized the rural nobility. Nevertheless the clergy, who had received two thirds of the occupied territories, controlled most of the lands and kept considerable independence from the Knights of the Sword who had received only one third.

In 1346 Waldemar IV, whom the *Hanse had brought to power, ceded Estonia to the Teutonic Knights, opponents of the Hanse men, for 19,000 Prussian marks. From now on the Christianized Letts were entirely subject to German power. Nevertheless, Germanization affected essentially the urban and rural elites, only with difficulty penetrating the villages, where the traditional culture and structures were maintained.

R. Wittram, *Baltische Kirchengeschichte*, Göttingen, 1956. – M. Hellman, "Balten", *LdM*, 1, 1980, 1390-1391. – *Storia religiosa dei popoli baltiei*, A. Caprioli (dir.), S. Vaccaro (dir.), Varese, 1987. – *HChr*, 5-6, 1990-1993.

Simonne Abraham-Thisse

**BAMBERG.** A town and *bishopric of *Bavaria, populated from a very early period. At the end of the Carolingian period, the town was the property of the Babenbergs and a royal possession from 906. In 973 *Otto II offered the town as a gift to Henry the Quarrelsome, whose son, the emperor *Henry II, completed the town and erected its bishopric in 1007. In the 11th and 12th cc., Bamberg was often the seat of imperial diets and *synods. The population, composed of merchants (Rhine commerce to Bohemia and Hungary) and artisans, but also the *ministerials situated near Domberg, was throughout the Middle Ages unable to free itself from the bishop's lordship, while the immunities accorded to certain religious institutions from the 13th c. conceded more rights to their titulars than to the townsmen ("war of immunities" from 1430 to 1440).

The creation of the bishopric of Bamberg by Henry II at the time of the synod of *Frankfurt, 1 Nov 1007, was also part of a political strategy. Bamberg was at the crossroads of communications between Italy and the eastern parts of the Empire. After his victory over margrave Henry of Schweinfurt, he had to fill the political void. The new *diocese was created from parts of the dioceses of *Würzburg (conflict with Bishop Henry I) and Eichstätt. The rich endowment of the diocese with property, revenues and privileges allowed it a rapid expansion, with the creation of important churches and monasteries. The situation of this diocese was particular by reason of the *exemption it enjoyed from the metropolitan diocese of *Mainz: from Otto I (1106), the bishops were consecrated by the *pope. Pope Clement II († 1047), formerly bishop of Bamberg under the name of Suidger, as well as the emperors Henry II and Conrad IV were buried at Bamberg. The town possessed an important cathedral *school and a *library, endowed by Henry II with manuscripts that had belonged to Otto II and *Otto III. Bishop St Otto I (1102-1139, mission to *Pomerania) carried out an in-depth economic and religious reform of the diocese and monasteries. He founded or reformed some 30 monasteries in or out of his diocese. Bamberg became the centre of the memory and cult of Henry II, canonized in 1146, and his wife *Cunegund, canonized in 1200. Between 1220 and 1237, as part of the reconstruction of the cathedral, were created the famous sculptural works (porch, choir) of the "Master of Bamberg", influenced by sculptors of Reims.

H. Burkhard, "Bamberg", *DHGE*, 6, 1932, 457-471. – E. Freiherr von Guttenberg, A. Wendehorst, *Das Bistum Bamberg*, Berlin, 1937 and 1966 (2 vol.; "GermSac", 2, 1-2). – B. Schimmelpfennig, *Bamberg im Mittelalter. Siedelgebiete und Bevölkerung*, Lübeck-Hamburg, 1964 (bibl.). – K. Dengler-Schreiber, *Scriptorium und Bibliothek des Klosters Michelsberg in Bamberg*, Graz, 1979. – *Das Bamberger Stadtrecht*, H. Parigger (ed.), Würzburg, 1983.

Franz Neiske

**BAN, BANALITY.** The word "ban" (Latin *bannum*) is of Germanic origin; it was used in the first centuries of the Middle Ages to designate the power of command acknowledged to belong to the war leaders. Carolingian legislation made it one of the key concepts of the organisation of the State. Emanating directly from the emperor and committed to his officers, counts, dukes or marquises, the ban was power both to order and to punish: it designated the capacity to recruit and command the *army, to exercise *justice and levy fines. It also included the management of fiscal estates and the collection of taxes, and made its holder the local representative of imperial power in its totality. The military function predominated, and often led to the care of a public fortress being made the main attribute of the power of ban. The word "ban" appears with a new meaning early in the 11th c. to designate a new type of organisation of powers, usually designated by the name of *castellany. Its fortunes in the feudal period suggest that the first castellan lordships were built around public fortresses that had been appropriated by their guardians, with all the powers of which they were the visible sign and guarantee. Subsequently, the meaning of the word was extended to the whole of the powers enjoyed by the castellan lord over the men of his district. From then on it was not so much a public office referring ultimately to the idea of a State, as a general power of constraint, whose forms varied according to times and regions. It was firstly, in accordance with its ancient sense, the power to dispense justice, *i.e.* to summon the men of the castellany before its own *court and if necessary to condemn them. It was also power over *roads, *bridges and fords, which justified the levying of a payment, the old "toll", on all trade. The ban also included the procuring of services, sometimes of a military nature, but especially in *labour; this aspect may have been connected with the obligation to maintain the fortress but, in the event, it was hard to distinguish from a power of demesnial type, and for this reason it took on, under the name of "banality", a much more general meaning, evoking all the services, in labour, *money or kind, required by the lord from the men subject to him. It comprised the **corvées* to be performed on the lord's land and the revenues that might come from the redemption of those liable to *corvée*, but also the burdensome obligation to make use of the lord's services for a number of daily needs: the bread-oven, the *mill and the press could have *banal* status, as could collectively used resources like rivers and ponds, *forests, meadows. The variety of *banal* exactions appears limitless: only men's resistance to constraint and their capacity to keep alive an idea of law and public order constituted an obstacle to the endless extension of the powers of the ban.

*The vials of wrath.* Miniature from the *Bamberg Apocalypse* offered by Henry II and Cunegund to the abbey church of St Stephen at Bamberg. Reichenau school, 11th c. Bamberg, Staatsbibliothek (Mss. Bibl. 140, fol. 40 v°).

G. Duby, *Rural Economy and Country Life in the Medieval West*, London, 1968. – D. Barthélemy, *L'Ordre seigneurial*, Paris, 1988. – M. Bloch, *Feudal Society*, London, 1989. – J.-P. Poly, É. Bournazel, *The Feudal Transformation: 900-1200*, New York, 1991.

Mathieu Arnoux

**BANGOR.** A cathedral city in north *Wales; the church is said to have been founded by St Deiniol in the 6th c. and the *diocese dates from about 1120. It was the religious centre of the kingdom of Gwynedd, several of whose rulers were buried there. A town grew up around the *cathedral and was burned by the English in 1211; there were 53 burgesses there in 1306. In the years before the conquest of 1282, relations between *Llywelyn ap Gruffydd, the prince of Wales, and Bishop Anian of Bangor were strained and there is a reference to a plot in the cathedral against the prince. The cathedral was built in the 12th c.; it was severely damaged in the war of 1282 and again during the revolt of *Owain Glyndŵr in the early 15th century. It was extensively restored by Bishop Skevyngton (1509-1533). At Bangor in 1405 Owain Glyndŵr is said to have met Edmund Mortimer and the earl of Northumberland to divide England and Wales between them.

G. Williams, *The Welsh Church from Conquest to Reformation*, Cardiff, 1962. – M. L. Clarke, *Bangor Cathedral*, Cardiff, 1969.

Antony D. Carr

**BANKING.** Apart from the *commodatum* loans practised throughout the medieval West by religious establishments and, in certain regions, by *Jews, the functions exercised by the banker arose out of the exchange economy and the diversity of monetary types. Unknown in the early Middle Ages, the profession of banker was primarily that of a moneychanger who, installed behind a counter (*banco*), knew the types and value of the specie in circulation, checked the quality of *money and practised the manual exchange of coins.

But from the 12th c., international *commerce imposed throughout medieval Europe other methods of payment or compensation than the transporting of cash. The Genoese bankers were the first to add to the practice of changing that of deposit, reimbursable on demand, then that of clearing by transfer from one deposit to another, then by transfer between bankers "in current account" with each other.

Italian merchant bankers, natives of *Piacenza, Asti, *Siena or *Florence, took on a role that combined the service of international trade in the business towns or the *Champagne *fairs, perfectly justified in the eyes of the Church, with much more speculative practices, taking account of market fluctuations: rich *merchants and business societies, foremost among which were Italians, Flemings, then southern Germans, had available liquidities that they were ready to make fructify in all the markets.

The letter of exchange, derived from a contract authenticated by a *notary, was a convention by which a lender provided a sum of money to a borrower, who engaged to reimburse it at the appointed time (operation of credit), but in another place and another currency (operation of exchange). Originally connected with the difficulties of long-distance *commerce, the contract, then the letter of exchange, provided the lender with an interest disguised by manipulations of the rate of exchange; sometimes a re-exchange

*The finances of the commune of Siena in time of peace and in time of war.* Painting by Benvenuto di Giovanni, 1468. Siena, State Archives.

clause was sometimes stipulated, the return rate being set in advance at a price above the market price; this meant a loan with certain gain, hence one condemned by the Church as *usurial, since the interest could not be justified by the risk run.

The sums used by the bankers for their exchanging operations came from *capital put on deposit for a fixed period, sometimes at short notice, remunerated by an interest that the Church considered legitimate to the extent that the depositer remained the owner of the funds invested and thus participated in any benefits of the enterprise. The scale of these deposits was considerable: at the time of the resounding failure of 1342, the king of England owed the Bardi of Florence 900,000 florins, while their registered capital was no more than 100,000 florins.

The loans thus allowed to princes, *popes or *towns were generally accompanied by negotiated guarantees comprising either tax exemptions on merchandise exported or the collection of public revenues. Alongside the great companies were created consortiums of creditors, like the Casa di San Giorgio of Genoa, set up in 1408 by the union of the bearers of the State debt, to whom *Genoa had ceded the exploitation of its colonial domain and the farming of indirect taxes. This immense and lasting enterprise contributed widely to the perfecting of accountancy and book-keeping. At the end of the Middle Ages, the towns of northern Italy had become the places of apprenticeship *par excellence* of commercial and banking techniques.

Y. Renouard, *Les Hommes d'affaires italiens du Moyen Âge*, Paris, 1949. – J. Le Goff, *Marchands et banquiers du Moyen Âge*, 1956 ("QSJ", 699). – R. C. Mueller, *The Venetian Money Market. Banks, Panics and the Public Debt 1100-1500*, Baltimore, London, 1997.

Philippe Braunstein

**BANQUET.** The banquet took its name from the bench (*banc*), which was often one with the table used for meals. It designated a collective feast. The theme of the banquet is inseparable from medieval history. Whether public or private, lay or religious, these meals were primarily so many occasions to reinforce the ties of sociability and solidarity between members of the community. Indeed there were hardly any groups, however little organised, who did not have recourse, if only in symbolic form, to a banquet: *confraternity or *corporation meal for the *feast of the patron saint, collective Whitsun meal practised by certain Alpine village communities sometimes up to the 1930s, parish meal or *Defructus* (from the first words of an *antiphon chanted at Christmas *vespers). The surviving menus prove that these feasts were an occasion for a junket. For the banquet also appeared as an antidote to the recurrent fear of *famine. The remains of these feasts were distributed to the poor, a gesture of *alms continuing an old custom in use in monasteries.

We distinguish several sorts of banquets: political-type public banquets, princely or aristocratic meals, like the first meal taken by *William the Conqueror and his entourage on English soil in 1066, whose memory is preserved by the *Bayeux Tapestry, or the famous Pheasant Banquet offered by Philip the Good, duke of *Burgundy, at Lille on 17 Feb 1454, during which *vows were pronounced to God, the Virgin, the ladies and the bird, but also feasts organised by municipalities in honour of illustrious guests; private banquets, *e.g.* for the celebration of weddings, or burials, took place either in the family home or in churches, as did the religious banquets that served as an occasion for great feasts. The banquet marked a high point of confraternal life. Whether statutorily provided for or not, the community banquet obeyed strict rules and required for its preparation all the efforts of those responsible. It could take place in church, but most often it was held in the confraternity house or in the *hôtel* of one of the masters. These *agapes* brought together hundreds of guests or even a thousand at the confraternity of Santiago *pilgrims at Paris in the 14th century! Alongside real banquets, the great number of fictitious banquets described in medieval literature between the 12th and 15th cc. evokes a happy universe in which the cohesion of the assembled group is consolidated in a display of collective abundance and joy. In texts as in images, the dishes are invested with a meaning that goes beyond strict alimentary description to reveal the desires and fantasies of the guests. The notion of joy, indissociable from that of banquet, finds its full dimension in the symbolism of the eucharistic banquet, prefiguration of the heavenly banquet.

M. Venard, "La fraternité des banquets", *Pratiques et discours alimentaires à la Renaissance, Actes du colloque de Tours 1979*, J.-C. Margolin (dir.), R. Sauzet (dir.), Paris, 1982. – *Boire et manger au Moyen Âge. Colloque de Nice, 1982*, Nice, 1984. – B. Laurioux, *Le Moyen Âge à table*, Paris, 1989. – *La Sociabilité à table. Commensalité et convivialité à travers les âges. Actes du colloque de Rouen, 14-17 novembre 1990*, Rouen, 1992, 178.

Dominique Rigaux

**BAPTISM.** At the beginning of the Middle Ages, baptism remained the Church's most important *sacrament. It was administered according to Christ's prescription (Mt 28, 19), still quite often by the *bishop to adults but also to children, and at the end of a long cycle of preparation (catechumenate). A rite of passage *par excellence*, it marked firstly the neophyte's break with paganism and his entry into the community of Christians, then, as St Augustine came to insist, the effacement of original sin and rebirth in Christ's *Redemption (it was celebrated on the eve of *Easter or sometimes Pentecost).

Without calling into question this fundamental character of baptism, the progressive extinction of ancient paganism from the beginning of the medieval millennium entailed profound modifications, which are often impossible to date with precision. We can enumerate four main ones.

First, the generalization of baptism of small children (or paedobaptism). This came about quite early in the West, and owed its rise partly to the very pessimistic position taken by St Augustine on original sin, dooming children who died without baptism to eternal damnation. Two stages in this major evolution: at first children were baptized during their first year, always by preference at Easter. This usage is attested in any case in the 8th century. Later, more slowly, appeared baptism from birth (*quamprimum*), at first reserved for cases of urgency (danger of *death), then extended to all the new-born. It became general practice in the West in the 13th century. At this time, a softening of the position of theologians (the *scholastics; *Thomas Aquinas) on the fate of children who died unbaptized (only deprived of the *beatific vision in *limbo) did not lead to an abandonment of the practice of baptism *quamprimum*, on the contrary, for at the same time the *child had acquired a new place in society. Thus the synodal *statutes of the 13th c. very frequently remind parents that in case of urgency they must themselves proceed to baptize their child. Similarly the late Middle Ages saw a multiplication of sanctuaries of *respite to which people came to implore the resurrection of a stillborn child, time to administer baptism to it.

The uniformization of baptismal rites was also new. It affected

*Baptismal font* by Renier de Huy (detail). Mosan art, *c.*1107-1118. Liège, collegiate church of Saint-Barthélemy.

the West and was decided on by *Charlemagne, who wanted to impose on his whole Empire the *Roman liturgy with some *Gallican additions. But as he also intended to restore certain ancient practices, there was a contradiction, of which the great inquiry of 812 into the way *archbishops explained and administered baptism in their *province gives a good account. In fact, if a certain unity was established in the Frankish world, the Spanish baptismal liturgy (which practised simple – not triple – immersion) was maintained until the 11th c., and the Irish until the 12th. In the East, diversity remained the rule, with four main rites (*Coptic, *Byzantine, Syrian and Armenian).

Transformations of the ritual of baptism were another innovation. They came about essentially in the early Middle Ages, and were the consequence of the generalization of paedobaptism. They consisted firstly of a simplification: the old catechumenate had no more *raison d'être* and steadily disappeared in the 8th century. Similarly for certain postbaptismal rites: the anointing once given by the bishop (*confirmation) was now separated from baptism – except in the East – since, becoming individual, it was now conferred by a priest in the setting of the *parish. On the other hand, postbaptismal *communion still continued to exist in certain regions of the West until the 12th century. Another evolution: the substitution, in most regions of the West, of infusion or aspersion for immersion, which is partly explained by the young age of those baptized. It entailed the replacement of *piscinae* by the *fonts from now on installed in churches, and the progressive disappearance of *baptisteries (except in northern Italy where they were still being built in the 12th c.). We can also easily understand the development of the role of *godparents for the little baptizee, incapable of saying anything. Finally, we must mention the addition of a formula of Eastern origin which passed, doubtless from the 6th c., into Spain, then from there to the rest of the West, where it was at first used for baptism in case of urgency, then in all cases: "*Ego baptizo te in nomine Patris et Filii et Spiritus Sancti.*" Pronounced by the celebrant after the triple immersion or infusion, over the centuries it acquired a sacramental value of its own: it was this that had to be spoken by laymen obliged to baptize in great urgency in the absence of a priest. Thus, in the 13th c. in the West, the liturgical stages of baptism were the following: *exorcism and blessing of the baptismal *water, into which was then plunged the Paschal candle, then triple insufflation of the spirit, triple renunciation of Satan, anointing with *oil of exorcism, then triple immersion (or infusion) accompanied by profession of faith, and pronouncement of the baptismal formula. The ceremony ended with a postbaptismal anointing and reclothing in the white garment of the neophyte.

Finally, the last innovation made to baptism in the Middle Ages was in the preponderant place taken by *clerics in its administration. This was already perceptible in the Carolingian period and was naturally strengthened by the *Gregorian reform. What from now on ensured the *validity of baptism was the recital by the priest of the above-mentioned formula, much more than the profession of faith alone. And in cases of necessity when a layman had to stand in for the absent priest, the synodal statutes of the 13th c. very firmly prescribe that the infant thus baptized, if he survives, must be taken to the parish church so that the priest can celbrate the complementary rites, and, in case of doubt as to the exactness of the formula used, rebaptize him.

Finally, we should mention that baptism was often at the centre of medieval disputes about *heresy. Apart from the *Cathars who rejected it because it had recourse to a material mediation (water), others would not admit the new aspects of it mentioned above. Some, for various reasons, rejected infant baptism (heretics of Arras in 1025; Petrobrusians and Henricians in the first half of the 12th c.), while others, in the name of a certain Donatism, rose up against the clericalization of the sacrament (heretics of Orléans in 1022, of Arras in 1025; certain *Waldenses).

J. Corblet, *Histoire dogmatique, liturgique et archéologique du sacrement de baptême*, Paris, 1881 (2 vol.). – J.-C. Didier, *Faut-il baptiser les enfants? La réponse de la Tradition*, Paris, 1967. – J.-P. Bouhot, "Explication du rituel baptismal à l'époque carolingienne", *REAug*, 24, 1978, 278-301. – P. Niles, "Baptism and the Naming of Children in Late Medieval England", *Medieval Prosopography*, 3/1, Spring 1982, 95-107. – M. Rubellin, "Entrée dans la vie, entrée dans la chrétienté, entrée dans la société. Autour du baptême à l'époque carolingienne", *Les Entrées dans la vie. XIIe congrès de la SHMES*, Nancy, 1982, 31-51. – P. M. Gy, "Du baptême pascal des petits enfants au baptême quamprimum", *Haut Moyen Âge: culture, éducation et societé. Mélanges P. Riché*, La Garenne-Colombes, Nanterre, 1990, 353-365. – P. Cramer, *Baptism and Change in the Early Middle Ages*, Cambridge, 1993. – R. Cabie, *Les Sacrements de l'initiation chrétienne*, Paris, 1994.

Michel Rubellin

**BAPTISM OF CHRIST.** All four evangelists describe Christ's baptism (Mt 3, 13-17; Mk 1, 9-11; Lk 3, 21-22; Jn 1, 29-34). Jesus came from Nazareth to the Jordan to be baptized by *John. He at first refused, but Jesus insisted. After Jesus had been baptized, the Spirit of God descended from heaven like a dove and a voice announced: "This is my beloved son, in whom I am well pleased." This divine manifestation (epiphany) was commemorated on 6 January. Representations of the baptism were gradually enriched by the presence of one or more angels, and sometimes by the personification of the Jordan. After having been present with the characteristics of a child, Jesus later appears as an adult. The liturgy of the rite of *baptism comes into the illustrations: the dove pours *oil from a phial, Jesus still half-immersed receives the lustral *water on his head (*Klosterneuburg enamel by *Nicholas of Verdun, 1181). This baptism by infusion then took the lead. This theme was taken up in the iconography of the baptism of *Clovis.

L. Réau, *Iconographie de l'art chrétien*, 2, 2, Paris, 1955-1959, 295-304. – G. Schiller, *Ikonographie der christlichen Kunst*, 1, Gütersloh, 1966, 137 f. – *LCI*, 4, 1972, 247-255. – C. de Mérindol, "Le recueil de Névelon pour l'abbaye de Corbie et son modèle: quelques sources de l'art roman", *Car.*, 35, 1987, 81-112 (here 90-92, 108-109).

Christian de Mérindol

**BAPTISTERY.** The word "baptistery", of Greek origin, means "reservoir". With other terms also alluding to *water, like *lauacrum* or *tinctorium*, it was used from Antiquity to designate the monument reserved for the administration of *baptism, while keeping its original meaning until the end of the 5th century.

Because baptism was originally reserved for the *bishop, the baptistery was normally part of the episcopal group. It could be an isolated monument, as at Poitiers, but most often it was next to the *cathedral, or even linked to it by a portico as at Riez. Their plans vary even more than those of churches: while generally adopting an arrangement centred on the pool, the known examples exhaust all geometrical forms – square, circle, polygon, etc. – with no marked predilection for the octagon to which Ambrose of Milan accorded a symbolic value (the eighth day was that of the *Resurrection); size and decoration were equally variable, but baptisteries were often precious monuments, richly ornamented, which allowed churches to assert their rank.

The size, form and fittings of baptismal pools (or *piscinae*), generally sunk into the ground, varied just as much. Some had no feedpipe, some no outlet, some neither one nor the other; most were no more than 0.5 metres in depth, which reduced baptismal immersion to a symbolic dimension; and sometimes, as at Geneva, we can make out two pools (for men and women? adults and children?): such variety explains why we can only rarely reconstruct the form of the liturgy, which moreover is often ill-known for the first centuries of Christianity.

From the early Middle Ages, baptisteries, often important ones, were built near the basilicas of the *martyrs; other more modest ones flanked parish churches in which priests were now allowed to baptize, while the generalization of infant baptism gradually led to the replacement of pools by *fonts. Despite conciliar canons reiterating the prohibition against catechumens entering the building before the ceremony, at this time baptisteries lost their singular character within the cathedral group: they served as *oratories, housed *relics or even *altars or burials. This relative banalization explains the survival of certain ancient buildings, as at Aix or Fréjus; in other regions however, separate monumental edifices in the antique manner went on being built throughout the Middle Ages, as at Venasque or Valence and, at a later date, the Romanesque baptisteries of northern Italy (Parma, Padua, Florence, etc.).

A. Khatchatrian, *Les Baptistères paléochrétiens*, Paris, 1962. – J. Guyon, "Le Baptême et ses monuments", *Naissance des arts chrétiens*, Paris, 1991, 70-87. – G. Duby, G. Romano, C. Frugoni, *Battistero di Parma*, Milan, 1992.

Jean Guyon

Interior of the baptistery of Fréjus, late 4th or early 5th c.

**BAR HEBRAEUS (1226-1286).** Gregory Abū l-Faraj, the last great *Jacobite Syrian writer, contemporary with the *Mongol invasions. Born at Melitene, he lived for some time at *Antioch, then still in the hands of the Franks. Becoming a monk, he went to Tripoli where he studied medicine and philosophy. Ordained bishop of Gūbās in 1246, he was appointed metropolitan of *Aleppo in 1253, then *maphriān* of Takrīt (*Iraq) in 1264. He died at Marāgha (Azerbaijan), but his body was buried near Mosul. A fertile polygraph, he was the author of some 30 works on theology, philosophy, history, grammar, science and belles-lettres. Among them are a secular *Chronicle* and an ecclesiastical *Chronicle*, of which he made a summary entitled *Abridged History of the Dynasties* (ed. and tr. E. Pocock, Oxford, 1663), and the *Candelabrum of the Sanctuary*, a theological summa divided into 12 "bases" (see in *PO*).

Bar Hebraeus, *Chronicon syriacum*, E.A.W. Budge (ed.), Oxford, 1932.

J.-M. Fiey, "Esquisse d'une bibliographie de Bar Hebraeus († 1286)", *Parole de l'Orient*, 13, 1986, 279-312.

Gérard Troupeau

**BARBARIAN LAWS.** Until their settlement in the Roman Empire, the German peoples followed oral customary laws. The establishment of the Romano-barbarian kingdoms made necessary the revision of common *Roman law and the writing down of ancestral customs, the *Stammesrechte*. Intended to limit *violence and private vengeance, the barbarian laws were primarily codes of penal law, based on the *oath, a minute tarification of penalties, and fines of composition (*wergild). They were also codes of private law, regulating transmission of inheritance, matrimonial transfers, etc.

The first barbarian laws were those of the *Visigoths (*Lex Wisigothorum Recesvindiana*). The code of Euric was probably promulgated between 469 and 477, while collections of common Roman law were formulated (Edict of Theodoric [453-467], Breviary of Alaric [*Breviarium Alaricianum*], promulgated in 506). The law of the *Burgundians (*Lex Burgundiarum*, internationally known as *Loi gombette*, but technically called *Lex gundebada* or *gumbata*, from King Gundebald who was its author) and the Roman law of the Burgundians were drawn up in the late 5th or early 6th c. at the initiative of King Gundebald. The earliest version of the Salic law of the Salian *Franks (*Lex Salica*) dates from the last years of the reign of *Clovis (507-511). The Ripuarian law (*Lex Ribuaria*) is an abridged version of the Salic law, dating from 633/634 and intended for the Rhineland duchy of *Cologne. Among the *Lombards, the Edict of Rothari was promulgated on 22 Nov 643 at Pavia. It represents the most complete compilation of all the *Stammesrechte*. In Germany, the redaction of laws was linked to the integration of peoples into the Frankish kingdom (*Lex Francorum*). The *Pactus Alamannorum* was doubtless drawn up under Chlotar II at the start of the 7th c. and the *Lex Alamannorum* at the time of Duke Lantfrid, between 712 and 715. The law of the Bavarians (*Lex Baiuvariorum*) probably dates from 743/744. It shows great similarities with the *Lex Alamannorum*. Finally in 802, on the occasion of the great assembly of Aachen, *Charlemagne had the laws of the *Saxons, *Thuringians and *Frisians set down in writing. All these laws were written in Latin. In England, King *Æthelbert of Kent had laws drawn up in Old English at the beginning of the 7th c., followed in the 7th and 8th cc. by the laws of Wessex and Mercia.

The principle of the *personality of law was the very foundation of the barbarian laws. However, in the Carolingian period, a *de facto* territoriality was established in each of the *regna*. In this context, we should not overlook the *capitulary of 786 that instructed the **missi dominici* (royal representatives with functions of administrative control and jurisdiction) to ascertain in the various places the so-called *professiones iuris*, *i.e.* which law people wished to be subject to. This – together with the Latin compilation of the laws – is further proof of the definitive "encounter of two cultures" (Bognetti). The application of the barbarian laws also posed the problem of the limits of royal power, particularly *vis-à-vis* the aristocracy. The laws were in fact drawn up on the initiative of kings who wanted to be the guarantors of order and peace. It was for this reason that they had them revised several times, up to the 9th c., and that they were led to legislate on precise points, for the whole of their subjects, in the form of edicts or capitularies.

H. Brunner, *Deutsche Rechtsgeschichte*, 1, Berlin, 1961. – *Laws of the Alamans and Bavarians*, T.J. Rivers (ed.), Philadelphia, 1977. – C. Schott, "Der Stand der Leges-Forschung", *FMSt*, 13, 1979, 29-55. – G. Vismara, "Le Fonti del diritto romano nell'alto medioevo secondo la più recente storiografia (1955-1980)", *SDHI*, 47, 1981, 5 f. – *The Laws of the Salian Franks*, K.F. Drew (ed.), Philadelphia, 1991.

Régine Le Jan

**BARBARIANS.** For an inhabitant of the Roman world, the Barbarian was someone who spoke an incomprehensible language and whose civilization was primitive. All the peoples whom Rome had not been able to subject, the *Afri Barbari* or Berbers in North Africa, the Celts of Britain, the Germans beyond the Danube and the Rhine were Barbarians. To protect themselves from the Celts, the Romans built Hadrian's Wall in the north of conquered Britain; to protect themselves from the Germans they built the *limes* along the Rhine and Danube.

The Celts and Germans were two Indo-European groups whose civilizations had some common characteristics. The Celts on the eve of the great *invasions occupied the periphery of Great Britain and *Ireland. The Germans were divided into several peoples: the eastern Germans (Goths, Gepids, Vandals, *Burgundians, *Lombards) and the western Germans (Marcomans, *Alamanni, *Thuringians, *Franks, *Saxons and, in the lands of the North Sea, *Angles, Jutes and *Frisians). The northern Germans remained confined to *Scandinavia. The Barbarian, whether Celt or German, could not live outside the framework of his family, tribe or people. Around the leaders of the tribe was grouped an aristocracy of professional warriors. The Germans very early enjoyed a great reputation in the Roman world. If the western Germans were mainly foot-soldiers, those of the East influenced by the steppe peoples were remarkable horsemen. In the barbarian family, Celtic or German, the woman played an important role. She was the guardian of family purity and family tradition. The man could take several wives into his home, concubinage being recognised as legal (*Friedelehe* among the Germans). *Education of children took place within the wider family under the authority of the father or uncles. At the age of puberty, the young German entered the adult world. The Celts had a system of early adoption or "fosterage". Family solidarity among both Germans and Celts was very great: an offense committed against one member of a family was felt by the whole clan and had to be avenged. To limit the effects of vengeance, they thought up pecuniary compensations fixed by custom: *log n-enech*, "face money" among the Celts, **wergild* or blood money among the Germans. In case of litigation between plaintiff and defendant, if no judge could decide between them, Celts and Germans had recourse to the *ordeal: single combat, trial by red fire or boiling water. The gods of the Germans and Celts belonged to the Indo-European pantheon: the god of light and intelligence, the Lug of the Celts, corresponded among the Germans to Tiwaz, venerated alongside Wodan from whom the kings claimed to be descended; the Celtic Taranis was the doublet of Thor, the god of storms, etc. At seasonal festivals, sacrifices took place in sacred places near springs, giant trees or megaliths. To appropriate supernatural forces, the Germans had recourse to *magic in various forms. The artistic works yielded by barbarian tombs date from late Antiquity. They differ totally from classical Roman art. Barbarian jewels, belt plaques and *fibulae are ornamented with interlacings and stylized animal figures. Among the Celts, goldsmith's work continued the tradition of La Tène art.

Well before the invasions, the Romans were influenced by the barbarian world and even opened their doors to the Germans. They made them peasants and soldiers by applying the system of "hospitality". Thus the invasions were usually "migrations of peoples". Barbarian kingdoms were progressively created in the Roman Empire until the time when that Empire disappeared in 476. A great many of the Barbarians were then Christians but of *Arian confession. The *pagan Irish, *Anglo-Saxons and Franks were baptized in the Catholic rite. The Arians were converted to Catholicism in the 7th century. The conversion of the Celts and Germans was as important for the West as the "peoples' migrations". It permitted the birth of a new civilization in medieval Europe.

P. Riché, P. Le Maître, *Les invasions barbares*, Paris, 1953 (9th ed., 1996). – P. Riché, *Education and Culture in the Barbarian West, Sixth through Eighth Centuries*, Columbia, S.C., 1976. – P. Riché, *L'Europe barbare*, Paris, 1989 (2nd ed., 1992). – Y. A. Daujé, "Le Barbare", *Recherches sur la conception de la barbarie et de la civilisation*, Brussels, 1989. – A. Borst, *Medieval Worlds: Barbarians, Heretics and Artists in the Middle Ages*, Cambridge, 1991. – M. Richter, *The Formation of the Medieval West: Studies in the Oral Culture of the Barbarians*, Dublin, 1994.

Pierre Riché

**BARCELONA.** The Iberian tribe of the *Laetani* were the earliest known population of the site of Barcelona. In the 3rd c. BC, the Carthaginians founded *Barcino* there, perhaps named from the family of *Barca*. In 133 BC, the town was conquered by Scipio Aemilianus, who settled around Mount Taber the *Colonia iulia augusta paterna faventia Barcino*, part of *Hispania citerior*, whose capital was *Tarragona. Christianization was early. Cugat was martyred there under Diocletian (284-305). An episcopal see, *suffragan to Tarragona, appeared from 347: Pacianus, bishop from 360 to 390, fought paganism and Novatianist rigorism there. The *Visigoth Athaulf (410-415) made Barcelona the capital of his realm, which included the north of the Iberian peninsula, *Aquitaine and *Septimania, but it was relegated to the second rank by *Toledo at the start of the 6th century. *Provincial councils were held there in 540 and 599. Its bishops Quirtius, Nebridius and Idacius took part in the rise of Isidorian culture.

Around 715, the collapse of the Visigothic kingdom led to its conquest by the Arabs. In 801, the town was taken by the *Franks and Goths commanded by *Louis of Aquitaine: capital of a county on the frontier with *Islam, it was integrated into the Carolingian world; its *bishopric was attached to *Narbonne until the reconquest of Tarragona in the mid 12th c.; a cathedral *chapter appeared from 944. The dismemberment of the Carolingian Empire allowed the emergence of a native dynasty of *counts, founded by Wilfred I (870-897). From the 12th c., the counts of Barcelona managed to unite the Catalan counties around their town, federate their lands with the neighbouring kingdom of *Aragon and push their Mediterranean expansion as far as *Sicily and Athens. The *port of Barcelona was lively. *Merchants and weavers profited from its commercial rise. The town did not stop growing until the early 14th century. A new city wall, built in the reign of James I (1213-1276), contained the numerous dwellings that extended beyond the Roman rampart from the 11th c.: it was enlarged in *c.*1350. At that time, civil – royal *palace, *hospital, naval dockyards – and religious buildings – *cathedral, *convents of the *mendicant orders – were built in the Gothic style.

But in the 14th and 15th cc., crisis ravaged the town, prey to intestine struggles between the *rentiers* of the Busca and the merchants and craftsmen of the Biga: the joint effects of plague, *famine and wars were demographically disastrous: the hearth returns allow us to follow its population curve: from 50,000 inhabitants in 1340 to 20,000 in 1477. At the start of the 16th c., Barcelona lost its dominant position in the Catalano-Aragonese confederation to *Valencia.

A. Duran, *Barcelona i la seva història*, Barcelona, 1972. – *Història de Barcelona*, J. Sobrequés (dir.), Barcelona, 1992. – S. P. Bensch, *Barcelona and its Rulers, 1096-1291*, Cambridge, 1995.

Martin Aurell

Choir of Barcelona cathedral, 14th c.

**BARI.** An Adriatic port in *Apulia, now a regional capital; the old town occupies a low promontory. In Antiquity, it was a city of middling importance, though it had a *bishop in 465; the episcopal see still seems to have existed in the 7th c., but later disappeared until the 10th century. The town was occupied in the 7th c. by the *Lombards of *Benevento. It assumed importance in the 9th c., becoming the seat of a *gastald*, before being conquered by the Muslims and becoming from 847 to 871 the capital of an emirate that extended over central and southern Apulia. The joint action of the Carolingian Emperor *Louis II and the Byzantine Emperor Basil I enabled the expulsion of the Muslims in 871; in 876 the city passed under Byzantine control; in 895 it became the capital of a military province covering Apulia, the *theme of Langobardia, which in the 960s became the catapanate of Italy; in the 11th c., the catapan resided in a fortified *praitôrion* on the site of the present basilica of San Nicola. The rebel Melo of Bari introduced *Normans into Apulia in 1017. In the 10th c., Bari regained an episcopal, then an archiepiscopal see, housing the titular of the see of Canosa di Puglia, which had disappeared in the 9th c.; in the 11th c., the ecclesiastical *province occupied all central Apulia and extended as far as Kotor, in what is now Montenegro.

At the end of a long siege, *Robert Guiscard took Bari in 1071 and built a castle there. In 1087, sailors from Bari brought back to their city the body of St *Nicholas of Myra, an early Christian bishop of Asia Minor, in whose honour was built a basilica consecrated by Pope *Urban II; its first abbot was Elias, who later became *archbishop; in the 12th c., San Nicola was a *collegiate church, flanked by a *hospice for pilgrims. The town was the site of two *councils, in 1053 and 1098. After the death of Robert Guiscard (1085), Bari was disputed between his two sons, Duke Roger and

Cathedra or throne "of Archbishop Elias". Basilica of St Nicholas, Bari. Carved marble, *c.*1100-1105.

Bohemund; in fact it became independent under the authority of the archbishop, then that of Grimoald Alferanita (1119-1132) who in 1123 took the title of prince; *Roger II subdued the town in 1132, then in 1139. In 1156, *William I (whose chief counsellor was emir Maio of Bari) destroyed the city, which had made a pact with the Byzantine invaders: the cathedral had to be rebuilt. Becoming capital of the province of Terra di Bari, the town was rivalled by its neighbours. *Frederick II gave it a new *port and a *fair. The *Angevin period was difficult: Bari suffered wars (siege of 1349); it was infeuded to the princes of Taranto and finally to the *Sforza: the duchess of Bari, Bona Sforza, queen of Poland, is buried in San Nicola. Nevertheless the town benefited from favourable conditions: the port seems to have been active at the time of the *crusades; above all, it benefited from the 12th c. from the development of olive cultivation; in the Angevin period, Bari was a great market for oil; it traded with *Constantinople and the Balkans.

M. Petrignani, F. Porsia, *Bari*, Bari, 1982. – J.-M. Martin, *La Pouille du VI^e au XII^e siècle*, 1993 ("CEFR", 179).

Jean-Marie Martin

**BARTHOLOMEW OF PISA (died 1401).** Born at Rinonico (*Pisa), Bartholomew took the habit of the Friars Minor in 1352 and was a pupil of Bartolo da Buti, a famous *master of the Pisan *studium* and commentator on *Dante's *Divine Comedy*. He completed his training at Padua and Florence, obtaining his doctorate of theology at *Cambridge in 1376. An active preacher – we have his 88 Florentine lenten *sermons of 1390 (*De casibus conscientiae*, ed. Lyon 1519) and the 58 Pisan ones of Lent 1397 (*De contemptu mundi*, ed. Milan, 1498) – he owes his fame to the work *De conformitate vitae beati Francisci ad vitam Domini Iesu* (1385-1390) in which he exalts the sanctity of the Order of Friars Minor by evoking the lives and miracles of its main representatives.

Bartholomew of Pisa, *De conformitate vitae beati Francisci ad vitam Domini Iesu*, Quaracchi, 1906-1912.

Massimo Papi

**BASEL, COUNCIL OF (1431-1449).** After much procrastination, *Martin V convoked a *council at Basel on 1 Feb 1431 and appointed Cardinal Giuliano *Cesarini president of the assembly. The debates began on 23 July, but by the end of the year only a negligible number of Fathers had arrived in the conciliar town. *Eugenius IV, the new pontiff, saw this as a way to rid himself of the council and on 18 Dec he authoritatively pronounced its dissolution. But the ecumenical assembly, supported by the Emperor *Sigismund, continued to sit. To avert the danger of a crisis dangerous to the Church, the pope retracted (14 Feb), admitting the nullity of his decision and recognising the council's legitimacy. The superiority of the council over the *pope, theme of the *bull *Dudum sacrum* (1433), remained the fundamental problem of the ecclesiological debate: pope and council each wished to exercise supreme power. The flight of the pope, forced out of *Rome by a revolution (1434), contributed to weakening the papal party.

At Basel, the work was divided among four deputations: faith, peace, reform and common affairs. The lower clergy, enjoying the same rights as the *bishops, constituted the mass of the council and were a preponderant force, since decisions were taken by majority vote. It was this motley crowd that claimed to administer the Church. The Fathers, in defiance of the papacy, wished to add an executive role to their legislative one. The decree of 9 June 1435 aimed to divert the resources of the Apostolic See by suppressing *annates. The council tried to extirpate the *Hussite heresy and obtained a relative success by getting the **compactata* of Prague adopted (30 Nov 1433). But the Fathers got bogged down in administrative and juridical tasks. The pope profited from this. Arguing the need to hold a council of *union with the *Orthodox Greeks, Eugenius IV decided to transfer the ecumenical assembly to *Ferrara, a town preferred by the Easterners (Sept 1437). The situation was finally tipped in favour of the Roman pontiff when the legate Cesarini left Basel on 9 Jan 1438. The council then ceased to be canonical.

Cardinal Louis Aleman, a warm partisan of the conciliar theory, assumed the presidency of the minority fraction. Under his inspiration, the Basel extremists deposed Eugenius IV (25 Feb 1439) and elected *Felix V (Amadeus VIII of Savoy) on 5 Nov 1439. Having few powers and a limited obedience, the *antipope left Basel in November 1442. From then on the assembly grew continually weaker. Forced out of the town by *Frederick III (1448), it decreed its own dissolution on 25 April 1449, shortly after the abdication of Felix V (7 April). Though many of its legislative texts were followed up – particularly in France, in the wording of the *Pragmatic Sanction of Bourges (1438) –, the assembly of Basel never managed to make the council's authority triumph over that of the pope.

*DHGE*, 6, 1932, 356-362. – J.W. Stieber, *Pope Eugenius IV, the Council of Basel and the Secular and Ecclesiastical Authorities in the Empire*, Leiden, 1978. – *HChr*, 6, 1990, 117-140.

Michel Fol

***BASILEUS.*** The ruling principles of Byzantine imperial power had a dual origin: Roman, itself heir to the Alexandrian and Hellenistic tradition, and Christian. The terrestrial order being the reflection of the celestial, the Emperor held the place of God here below. Constantine Porphyrogenitus advised replying to barbarians who had the impudence to ask for imperial vestments or insignia that these had been delivered to *Constantine, founder of the Empire, by an angel. God, sole true source of legitimacy, chose whom he would call to govern, while the *army, the senate and the people ratified the divine election. This triple investiture was largely theoretical. The people, though feared for their violent and unpredictable reactions, had no effective role and we never see an emperor plead popular support. The senate, despite its prestige as an old Roman institution, had hardly more influence, as it was not a homogeneous body and, as a general rule, did not put forward a candidate. So it was the army that dominated, and more precisely, in the protobyzantine period, the palatine corps, since in the mid 5th c. the emperor settled at *Constantinople in the shelter of an invincible wall. Later the thematic armies, notably that of the Anatolikoi, successfully advanced the candidature of their *strategos*.

In reality these principles left great freedom in the choice of an emperor. Two modes of succession coexisted, apparently contradictory, but justified without difficulty by the divine origin of the imperial power: inheritance and usurpation. The emperors in place naturally inclined to favour their sons and often took the precaution of crowning them in their own lifetime so that after their death the traditional triple *acclamation was no more than a formality. This tendency to heredity in the office is perceptible from the protobyzantine period, but it was only gradually accepted by public opinion, starting with the Macedonian dynasty (867-1056) which supported without detriment several regencies, the presence of co-emperors, and even culminated in the solitary reign of an old woman, Theodora, the dynasty eventually dying out for lack of an heir. A successful usurpation justified itself by its own success: God had abandoned the bad emperor. Such overthrows were accompanied by various premonitory signs: natural catastrophes, earthquakes, *epidemics, *famines or the defeat of the imperial armies. The rebel's victory legitimized him, his defeat returned the responsibility for these evils to the people. This political system, inheritance tempered by usurpation, typical of the Byzantine spirit of *economy, explains by its flexibility the absence of dispute over the imperial office right up to the end of the Empire. Power was seized more often by arms (Phocas, Heraclius, Leo III, *Leo V) than by a palace coup (*Nicephorus I, John Tzimisces).

The titles borne by the emperor reveal the Christian ascendancy. The emperor, divine (*theios*), holy (*hagios*), equal to the apostles (*isapostolos*), holds in his right hand a globe surmounted by a cross, but he remains a mere mortal, a servant (*doulos*) of the Lord, as symbolised by the *akakia*, a little purse containing dust, reminding him of his inexorable future. Constantine had retained from the principate the old title of *semper augustus*, which lasted until *Heraclius. He, after his victory over the Persians, his sole rivals for dominion over the *oikoumene*, replaced it with the old title, Hellenistic in origin and long employed unofficially, of

Heraclius and his son Heraclius Constantine, bearing the *stemma*. Solidus from Ravenna, 613-629. Paris, BNF.

*basileus* of the Romans, his Christian character being marked by the complementary formula of *pisto en Theo basileus*. Byzantine diplomacy strove to forbid the use of the title of *basileus* by any other head of State, on the principle that the earthly Empire, image of the heavenly Empire, could not be other than unique. It was obliged to concede to the *Carolingians and *Ottonians the plain title of *basileus*, reserving for the master of Constantinople the specific title of "*basileus* of the Romans", but it could not prevent *Simeon, whose victories had brought him to the gates of the capital, from calling himself *basileus* of the Romans and *Bulgars. Several emperors simultaneously could be *basileis*, whether an emperor with his son or sons, or when a co-emperor was joined with a minor or a dominated emperor, but only one exercised plenitude of power, as *autocrator*. On coins, from the time of Phocas (608-610), the principal emperor was distinguished by his wearing a beard alongside his beardless colleagues. The emperor, whom, apart from the soldiers or the Constantinopolitans, his subjects never saw, was present in the provinces by his image, coins or actual *icons, object of a veritable cult. On great religious feasts, his icons were paraded in solemn *processions together with those of the saints. The imperial portrait on coins, whose reverse carried the Cross, Christ or the Virgin, on *seals or on punches, guaranteed that there was no fraud.

The emperor was at the head of a dual hierarchy, one concerning foreign peoples, the *ethnikoi*, by the fiction of the family of princes, and the other concerning his subjects by the treaties of precedence, the *taktika*. Christian princes could hope, according to their fortune, to be considered as brothers or sons, the more modest or pagans as friends. From the 9th to the 12th c., the emperors consented only exceptionally to unite their family with foreigners, as Basil II consented, reluctantly, to the union of his sister Anne with *Vladimir the Great of Kiev. From the 12th c., the declining condition of the Empire obliged them to use imperial marriages to procure allies.

The emperor, representing God on earth, was the source of all

View of the nave of the basilica of Sant'Angelo in Formis, near Capua (Campania), built in 1073 by the monks of Monte Cassino.

power, but this did not authorize him to behave arbitrarily, since he had to exercise to the highest degree the Christian virtues, piety, justice, philanthropy, acting for the common good of his subjects. Sole legislator with respect to custom and the legislation of previous emperors, he alone delegated his authority to officials and withdrew it from them *ad nutum*. His relations with the second personage of the Empire, the *patriarch, were complex, though there had never been room for a quarrel between the Priesthood and the Empire. On one hand the patriarch was on the same footing as an official, chosen by the emperor, as the act of nomination of the said patriarch attests; on the other he received, when necessary, the emperor's profession of *Orthodoxy, he crowned him, was his confessor and took part in the great ceremonies of his private life, *marriage, baptism of *porphyrogenete princes. The emperor exercised his power over the terrestrial Church and could, for example, modify the competence of the patriarchate of Constantinople, like Leo III who augmented it at the expense of the papacy by the transfer of Illyricum. In matters of dogma, only the *council was sovereign, but a council convoked and presided over by the emperor. Everyone knows what efforts Justinian and Heraclius made to reconcile Orthodox and monophysites and how far the *iconoclast emperors wished to define the doctrine on *images personally. Their failure did not put an end to imperial temptations: Manuel Comnenus took an active part in the dispute over "My Father is greater than I". Finally, alone among laymen, the emperor could enter the sanctuaries of churches.

Everything was in place for a veritable imperial religion, of which the Great *Palace, abandoned in the 12th c. in favour of the Blachernae palace, was the major sanctuary. The ceremonies enacted there assumed the appearance of religious services. The emperor's presence imposed silence and no dignitary could receive a gift directly from his hands without a cloth to prevent all personal contact. Foreign ambassadors, subject to the same constraint, waited long in antechambers before being admitted to one of the great reception rooms, the Magnaura or the Chrysotriklinos. In sign of veneration, they approached under the feigned restraint of the guards and saluted the sovereign by a *proskinesis*, their forehead touching the ground. At this moment the throne rose and automata animated golden lions that moved their tails and birds that sang. On the feasts of Christmas and Easter, the emperor, in imitation of Christ, received the apostles, washed the feet of the poor and welcomed to his table twelve guests, the highest dignitaries of the State.

List of the Byzantine dynasties: Constantinian (324-363), Valentinian (364-384), Theodosian (394-450), Justinian (518-602), Heraclid (610-711), *Isaurian (717-802), Amorian (820-867), *Macedonian (867-1056), *Ducas (1059-1078), *Comneni (1081-1185), *Angeli (1185-1204), Lascarids (1204-1261), *Palaeologi (1261-1453).

G. Dagron, *Naissance d'une capitale. Constantinople et ses institutions de 330 à 451*, Paris, 1974. – O. Rösch, *"Onoma basileos". Studien zum offiziellen Gebrauch des Kaisertitel in spätantiker und frühbyzantinischer Zeit*, Vienna, 1978. – M. McCormick, "L'imperatore", *L'Uomo bizantino*, G. Cavallo (ed.), Bari, 1992, 341-379. – G. Dagron, *Empereur et prêtre. Étude sur le "césaropapisme" byzantin*, Paris, 1995.

Jean-Claude Cheynet

**BASILICA.** The word "basilica", of Greek origin – it meant "royal" – was at first applied to the public buildings of Hellenistic rulers; the Romans later employed it to designate the multifunctional halls that served as courthouse and meeting place; then, because they often used this architectural type for their churches, the Christians used it in turn, even seeing these buildings, from *Isidore of Seville in the 7th c., as the dwelling of the king of heaven built in the image of an earthly *palace.

Civil basilicas often had the form of an elongated rectangle prolonged on the short side by a rounded apse where the judge sat on a dais; often with several aisles covered by a wooden roof and separated by a colonnade, they had a raised central area lit by windows. This was also the plan of many Christian basilicas in which the clergy (and often the *altar) took their place in the apse, while the people, kept at a distance by a choir barrier, stood in the nave or aisles.

But this pattern, known to the moderns by the name of "basilica plan", was far from being always followed. Firstly because it was capable of numerous variants, if only in the apse, which could be semicircular, horseshoe-shaped, rectangular, polygonal, etc. Next because additions could be made: a transverse area, or transept, in front of the apse; a vestibule, or *narthex; porticos, on the sides or in front of the façade where they formed an atrium (*St Peter's at Rome); towers, etc. Finally – and especially – because there was sometimes room for the most varied solutions: at Rome especially, we know basilicas with a circular ambulatory (*e.g.* San Sebastiano), others circular like San Stefano Rotondo, or even polygonal (like the Daurade at *Toulouse) or cruciform (thus at Milan and in northern Italy, or again in Syria), etc.

Though the usage prevailed of preferentially reserving the term *ecclesia* for the episcopal church (or *cathedral), the term "basilica" was applied throughout the early Middle Ages to all religious monuments, including the modest creations of the Roman catacombs. For this reason, it designated especially funerary edifices, whether buildings rising over the *tomb of a saint (like Sainte-Geneviève at Paris, *Saint-Martin at Tours) or *foundations holding *relics, *e.g.* *Saint-Germain-des-Prés; in the great *towns however, and in *Rome in particular, basilicas also served the usual spiritual ministry of the Christian people.

R. Krautheimer, *Corpus basilicarum Christianarum Romae*, 5 vol., Vatican, 1937-1967. – C. R. Brühl, *Palatium und Civitas*, Cologne-Vienna, 1975. – N. Duval, "L'Ecclesia, espace de la communauté chrétienne dans la ville" and "L'Architecture cultuelle", *Naissance des arts chrétiens*, Paris, 1991, 50-69 and 186-219. – S. Hill, *The Early Byzantine Basilicas of Cilicia and Isauria*, Aldershot, 1996.

Jean Guyon

***BASTIDE.*** The term "bastide" could cover several meanings in the Middle Ages. Derived from Italian *bastia* or Occitan *bastit*, *bastida*, which designated a building under construction, a building-site, the term *bastida vel bastia* appears for the first time in 1204, but the first bastide dates from 1222 (Cordes) and the last from 1373 (Labastide d'Anjou). The majority were created between 1250 and 1350. Bastides, forms of concentrated settlement deliberately implanted in a rural setting by one or more founders, existed only in the English or French Aquitanian basin, whose main urban backbone they were (they number some 350). The objectives of their founders were part of the search for profit and power. The purpose was to capture the fruits of the growth that followed on land *clearance, ensure the control of previously dispersed populations by grouping them together, and hold onto lands some of which were frontier territories.

At the origin of every bastide was an act of *paréage* and a *charter of customs: a lord (often a *Cistercian abbey) gave land to royal or comital agents who were charged with populating it; the act of *paréage* allowed both parties to share the rights and revenues of the new town. The charter attracted new inhabitants who ensured the development of agricultural land while benefiting from public security and prospects of material comfort. Some bastides were not creations *ex nihilo* but enlargement of an existing urban area (*e.g.* Villeneuve-d'Aveyron where a **sauveté* already existed).

What distinguished the bastide from the *village was its chequer-board division, the product of concerted town-planning. Dwellings and lands were squared off so as to facilitate fiscal exactions (*i.e.* at Solomiac, each plot of 14 spans by 5 had to pay a *rent of 5 *denarii*). The blocks of *houses, square or rectangular, cut through by a network of perpendicular streets, were organised around the central square reserved for the *market and surrounded with arcaded houses.

Secondly, a *bastide* or *bastille* could designate a fortified building at the entrance to a town.

Finally, in 13th-c. *Provence, the *bastide* was a two-storey tower situated in a strategic place, whose role was to assert the presence of a comital or lay power (Pélissanne, 1246). Some gave rise to hilltop villages (the bastide of Les Jourdains). In the 14th and 15th cc., the bastide had no longer an upper storey or battlements: it passed into the hands of the bourgeoisie and became, in the 16th c., the pleasure-house and centre of agricultural development well known in pre-industrial Provence.

M. Beresford, *New Towns of the Middle Ages*, New York, 1967. – C. Higounet, *Paysages et villages neufs du Moyen Âge*, Bordeaux, 1975. – *Géographie historique du village et de la maison rurale*, C. Higounet (ed.), Paris, 1979. – O. de Saint-Blanquat, *La fondation des bastides royales dans la sénéchaussée de Toulouse aux XIII^e et XIV^e siècles*, Toulouse, 1985. – B. Cursente, *Villages gersois II – Les bastides*, Auch, 1991. – J. Bentley, *Fort Towns of France*, London, 1993. – B. Gilles, *L'Aventure des bastides du sud-ouest*, Toulouse, 1993.

*The Last Supper*, by Tilman Riemenschneider. Altar of the Holy Blood, 1499-1505, church of St James, Rothenburg ob der Tauber (Bavaria).

Christine Barnel

**BATALHA.** The *Dominican convent of Santa Maria da Vitoria, founded by the first ruler of the Aviz dynasty, John I, in recognition of the victory obtained by his troops over those of the Castilian invader at Aljubarrota in 1385, was built some 15 kilometres from the field of battle. The work, begun in 1388, went on until the start of the 16th century. But most of the buildings of Batalha (church, funerary *chapels, *cloisters) predate 1438 and are in the *Gothic style; only the *Capellas Imperfeitas* (Unfinished Chapels) are Manueline.

Pantheon of the Aviz dynasty, Batalha is for the Portuguese one of the most important of their memorials, perpetuating the memory of an essential step in the emergence of the nation.

L. Grodecki, *L'Art gothique*, Paris, 1973. – R. Durand, *Histoire de Portugal*, Paris, 1992.

Robert Durand

**BAVARIA.** Bavaria, the region between the Lech, the Danube and the Alps, has a history marked by great continuity from the early 6th century. The only one of the five ethnic duchies to have survived in the form of a territorial State – if we leave out the separation of Austria in 1156 –, Bavaria owed this more to structural reasons than to its dukes, belonging successively to the Agilulfings (*c.*550-788), the Liutpoldings (947-1002), the Welfs (1070-1180), then the *Wittelsbachs (from 1180). It formed an area of transition, first between the world of the *Franks and that of the *Lombards, then in the direction of central Europe. Nor was its cohesion ever threatened by the great *towns, all situated on the margins (*Augsburg, *Nuremberg) or in decline in the late Middle Ages (*Regensburg). Though *archbishop and *bishops managed to form so many enclaves, yet on the whole the Church was an essential factor of continuity thanks to the coincidence between country and ecclesiastical provice. Moreover, the weight of *monasticism, because it was favoured by the aristocracy, was a uniting factor and had favoured the birth of a Bavarian culture.

This continuity is evident behind Bavaria's two beginnings: the two ages of the ethnic duchy and, from the 12th c., the development of a State. Just as the first duchy had ended by entering the Frankish orbit in 591, St *Boniface in 739, in the pope's name, fixed the *dioceses at the dukes' places of residence, Freising, *Passau, Regensburg and *Salzburg. The confiscation of the duchy in 788 did not threaten its unity. With the *erection of Salzburg into a metropolis in 798, a Bavarian Church was formed; the episcopal *abbeys that emerged from the reorganisation dedicated themselves, like the Benedictine and canonical establishments of the 8th c., to the care of the past. The second duchy was, like the first, kept in the *Empire, after the accession of the duke to the kingship (*Henry II). Bavaria was administered as a vice-realm to which bishoprics and old religious establishments were directly subject, which, added to the early territorial peace (1094), would constitute one of the foundations of the future State. By concentrating from the beginning, unlike the Welfs, on Bavaria and establishing the basis of a patrimonial rule, the Wittelsbachs managed to construct the largest State in *Germany, despite their engagement in imperial politics. They acquired the Palatinate in 1214; then Louis of Bavaria (1314-1347) was called to the Empire. The adoption of primogeniture in 1506 put an end to the partition of the duchy. The religious establishments that emerged from the monastic *reform and the apostolic renewal, who sat in the Estates in the place of the bishops and alongside a nobility of civil servants and territorial towns, sketched out a national history. This configuration would make Bavaria a centre of the Catholic reformation.

E. Bauerreis, *Kirchengeschichte Bayerns*, 1-5, Sankt Ottilien, 1949-1955. – *Handbuch der bayerischen Geschichte*, 1-2, M. Spindler (ed.), Munich, 1967-1969. – *Medieval Architecture and Sculpture in Europe, Part 9: West Germany: Bavaria*, A. Simpson (ed.), London, 1979. – *Handbuch der bayerischen Kirchengeschichte*, 1-2, W. Brandmüller (dir.), Sankt Ottilien (to appear).

Martial Staub

**BAYEUX.** Bayeux first appears in history as capital of a Gallo-Roman *civitas*, that of the *Baiocasses*. In the Late Empire, its old name of *Augustodurum* was abandoned in favour of that of the people of the *civitas*, following a classical process. It was then called *Baiocae*, deformed into *Bagiae* (11th c., on the *Tapestry*), then in French *Baex* (14th c.) and finally *Baieux* (15th c.).

The town was Christianized quite early, receiving its first bishop, St Exuperius, in the 4th century. In the 9th c., the town and its region were hit by the *Viking invasions. Bishop Baltfridus was even killed in 858. In 924 the Bessin, the county of which Bayeux was capital, was attached to *Normandy by the first duke, *Rollo. Subsequently, Bayeux knew a period of great prosperity in the 11th c., when its bishop was *Odo of Conteville, half-brother of *William the Conqueror, who occupied the episcopal see from 1049 to 1097. It was he who built the *cathedral dedicated in 1077, whose *crypt and west towers (restored in the 12th and 13th cc.) still remain, and commissioned the *Bayeux Tapestry (actually an *embroidery) intended to ornament the nave of that cathedral. However a grave catastrophe struck the town and the cathedral, both destroyed in 1105 during the civil war between the sons of William the Conqueror. The town lost its rank as Normandy's secondary capital in favour of *Caen, a new town developed by the duke-king. The cathedral was rebuilt from the 12th c. (pillars of the nave), but mainly in the 13th. In the 15th c., it was finished by the building of a central tower (completed in the 19th c.).

The medieval town had up to 18 *parishes, a reflection of its ancient splendour. Today there remains the church of Saint-Patrice (and its fine Renaissance-style tower). The town's suburb still had the priory of Saint-Vigor-le-Grand, restored by Odo of Conteville. The parish church has an early medieval episcopal throne in Vieux marble. Since the Middle Ages, Bayeux has suffered no massive destruction. So it has kept its network of medieval streets, several timber-framed houses of the 14th and 15th cc. and numerous stone *hôtels* of the 16th, 17th and 18th centuries.

M. Beziers, *Histoire sommaire de la ville de Bayeux*, Caen, 1773. – "Bayeux", *Art de Basse-Normandie*, 54, Caen, 1969. – S. Bertrand, M. Lecarpentier, *Bayeux monumental*, Bayeux, 1977. – *Medieval Architecture and Sculpture in Europe*, 7, *France: Bayeux and Coutances*, L. Grant (ed.), London, 1978. – "IXe centenaire de la cathédrale de Bayeux", *Art de Basse-Normandie*, 76, Caen, 1978-1979. – L. Musset, *La Tapisserie de Bayeux. Oeuvre d'art et document historique*, Saint-Léger-Vauban, 1989 ("La Nuit des temps"). – F. Neveux, *Bayeux et Lisieux, villes épiscopales de Normandie à la fin du Moyen Âge*, Caen, 1997.

François Neveux

**BAYEUX TAPESTRY.** The name of the city of *Bayeux (now in Calvados) recalls that of an ancient Gallo-Roman people, the Baiocasses. The episcopal see there has been constantly maintained; in the Norman period, it was closely controlled by the dukes. *William the Conqueror put there his half-brother Eudes or *Odo, who was bishop of Bayeux from 1049 to his death (1097). It was Eudes who took the initative in the creation of the so-called Bayeux tapestry. This "canvas of the conquest", as it was long called, is an *embroidery nearly 70 metres long by 50 centimetres wide relating Harold's journey to *Normandy, William's expedition to *England up to the battle of *Hastings and doubtless his *coronation at *London. The tapestry in its present state is incomplete, but a partial description by Baldric of Bourgueil, bishop of Dol, gives the end, which goes from Hastings to London and the royal coronation of the Norman duke. Though from the 10th to the 12th cc. it was frequent in Scandinavian and Norman lands to make narrative embroideries, it must be admitted that in its development and design the tapestry is a unique monument.

Executed probably between 1066 and 1077 in an English workshop, doubtless at *Canterbury, the narration emphasizes Harold's error and *perjury. This Saxon duke is sent to Duke William to acquaint him with King Edward's intention to leave him his throne. Taken prisoner by the count of Ponthieu and freed by William's intervention, Harold accompanies him on an expedition to *Brittany, then receives arms from him (*dubbing?) and finally swears him an *oath (of loyalty or support?). On the death of

*Edward the Confessor orders Harold to go and tell William the Conqueror that he will one day be his successor.* Bayeux Tapestry, *c.*1070-1080. Bayeux, Musée de la Tapisserie.

*Edward the Confessor, Harold has himself proclaimed and crowned king. William of Normandy assembles a great fleet, recruits soldiers from various regions, crosses the Channel in September 1066 and defeats Harold's troops at the battle of Hastings after having almost lost the fight. The tapestry shows these events, with many glimpses of daily life that add to its interest. The narrative is bordered by two margins illustrated with animals, fables and some anecdotal drawings. Historical debate centres on the name and intention of those who commissioned it. The argument that the tapestry was to ornament Bayeux cathedral for its consecration in 1077 is not convincing; another hypothesis is that of a design by Odo, William's brother and minister, to convince the English by exposing in their palaces the proofs of perjury and of William's legitimacy. The tapestry would have come back to Bayeux at the time of Odo's disgrace in 1082, with all his treasures. After that it is not mentioned until 1476 in the cathedral treasury.

*The Bayeux Tapestry*, F.M. Stenton (ed.), 2nd ed., London, 1965. – S. Bertrand, *La Tapisserie de Bayeux et la manière de vivre au XI^e siècle*, Saint-Léger-Vauban, 1966 ("La nuit des temps"); 2nd ed. L. Musset, *ibid.*, 1989. – M. Parisse, *La Tapisserie de Bayeux, un documentaire du XI^e siècle*, Paris, 1983. – D. M. Wilson, *The Bayeux Tapestry*, London, 1985. – S.A. Brown, *The Bayeux Tapestry: History and Bibliography*, Woodbridge, 1988. – *The Study of the Bayeux Tapestry*, R. Gameson (ed.), Woodbridge, 1997.

Michel Parisse

**BEATIFIC VISION.** Holy Scripture promises the elect, after their death, a knowledge of *God "as he is", "face to face", (1 Jn 3, 2; 1 Cor 13, 12). The Catholic doctrine of the beatific vision has the peculiarity of having been defined in the Middle Ages, in 1336. Pope *Benedict XII thus put an end to the controversy unleashed by his predecessor, while concluding more than a century of scholastic reflection on the question.

After several years of theological disputes, the Parisian condemnation of 1241 gave the scriptural "face to face" a metaphysical translation: the blessed see the very essence of God. But how could a finite creature know an infinite God? This essential question in turn fed important theological debates at the turn of the 13th-14th centuries. After the condemnation of the *beghards by the council of *Vienne in 1311, most theologians adopted the dispositive role of the light of glory enabling the *intellect to receive the divine essence as form and hence be in bliss. Many other questions were debated apropos of the vision of God in this period. But the one that made the greatest stir, at all levels of society, was raised by *John XXII in 1331: when do the *souls of the saints enjoy the beatific vision? Just after their death or only at the end of time, after the *Last Judgment? The pope, by pronouncing in favour of the latter solution, unleashed a controversy that shook the whole of Europe. The *spiritual Franciscans who had fled to the emperor's court drew arguments from it to try to have John

XXII deposed for *heresy. However, most of the other *Franciscan masters took his side. The *Dominican theologians almost unanimously criticized his opinion and this even earned one of their numbre, Thomas Waleys, imprisonment. Princes like John of Aragon and *Robert of Naples made their contributions. The king of France, *Philip VI of Valois, had two propositions of the Franciscan general Guiral Ot, favourable to John XXII, solemnly condemned in December 1332 by the greatest theologians of the university of *Paris. The pope retracted his opinion on his deathbed in Dec 1334. It was left to his successor Benedict XII to define, on 29 Jan 1336, in the constitution *Benedictus Deus*, that "All [souls] immediately after their death and the aforesaid expiation for those who have need of this expiation, even before the *resurrection of their *body and the general judgment, . . . are and will be in heaven, . . . they have seen, see and will see the divine essence with an intuitive and even facial vision. . .".

M. Dykmans, *Les Sermons de Jean XXII sur la vision béatifique*, Rome, 1973. – C. Trottmann, *La Vision béatifique, des disputes scolastiques à sa definition par Benoît XII*, Rome, 1995.

Christian Trottmann

**BEATIFICATION.** Until the 13th c. and even later in many cases, there was no difference, as to vocabulary, between *beatus*, "blessed", and *sanctus*, "saint". But codification by the *popes of the procedure of *canonization, early in the 13th c., ended by having repercussions on terminology: from the second third of the 14th c., there was a tendency to reserve the term "saint" for those servants of *God canonized by the Roman Church, who could be venerated by all the faithful, and to designate by the name of "blessed" those whose cult had been granted recognition by a *bishop at the level of his *diocese, as well as certain persons, not numerous, whose *sanctity the Holy See had approved while confining their cult to a religious order or a diocese (*e.g.* Robert of La *Chaise-Dieu in 1351, or the *Franciscan *martyrs of *Morocco in 1481). Only in 1662, with the decrees of Alexander VII, did beatification become an obligatory stage on the way to canonization.

A. Vauchez, *Sainthood in the Later Middle Ages*, Cambridge, 1997.

André Vauchez

**BEATITUDE, HAPPINESS.** At the beginning of the Middle Ages, *Boethius defined happiness as "the perfect state resulting from the coming together of all goods" (*Consolation of Philosophy*, III, pr. 2). In fact, happiness is generally conceived as the permanent state of rest in which all man's true desires find their fulfilment by the possession of the supreme *Good. Happiness then appears as the final end of human activity and by this fact occupies a cardinal place in medieval anthropology and morality. Thus reflection on beatitude, the theological name for happiness, inaugurates the moral part of *Thomas Aquinas's *Summa theologiae*.

The *scholastics distinguished between objective beatitude, *i.e.* the object whose possession procures happiness, and subjective beatitude, *i.e.* the act by which *man enters into possession of that object. For Christianity, objective beatitude consists essentially in the supernatural union with *God which is procured, in the Kingdom, by the *beatific vision: "We shall be like him; for we shall see him as he is" (1 Jn 3, 2). The search for happiness is thus inseparable, particularly since St Augustine, from the spiritual quest for God. But in the 13th c., certain radical *Aristotelians rehabilitated a more purely human happiness, immanent fruit of philosophical activity. It was partly against them that St Thomas formulated the theory of the natural desire to see God. He established that in the final analysis the *intellect finds its rest only in the vision of the divine essence, ultimate explicatory principle of reality. Now, this vision is a supernatural gift: only God gives God.

Concerning subjective beatitude, two tendencies appear, according as the apprehension of the beatifying object is attributed to the intellect or the *will. For St Thomas, beatitude can only be an act of the intellect. Even if it is effectively moved by *love, it is the intellect alone that can apprehend by cognitive union the divine essence, the will being a faculty of tendency and not of apprehension. This cognitive union is the feat of an intuition without intermediary, in which the intellect, raised up by the light of glory, is directly informed by the divine essence. This vision then blossoms in the will in fruition or enjoyment of the animate object finally possessed. For *Duns Scotus and the *Franciscan tradition, the will is a more noble *faculty than the intellect. Consequently, fruition, an act of will, is not a mere property of beatitude: it defines it formally, the vision being only the condition of it. Moreover, since *freedom of indetermination is essential to the will, it remains even in the face of the sovereign Good, so that it is by an altogether free act that the blessed enjoy God.

C. Trottmann, *La Vision béatifique, des disputes scolastiques à sa définition par Benoît XII*, Rome, 1995.

Serge Bonino

**BEATUS OF LIÉBANA (died 798?).** Beatus, of Asturian origin, belonged to the monastery of St Martin of Liébana (Valcavado), whose foundation is attributed to St Turibius of Astorga (mid 5th c.). According to *Alcuin, he held the position of *abbot, encouraging the monks of his community to deepen their knowledge of Scripture and surrounding himself with a small group of disciples among whom appears Etherius, future bishop of Osma.

Beatus read Greek and may have had some rudiments of *Hebrew. Several *hymns of the *Hispanic liturgy are attributed to him. But his best known work is a *Commentary on the *Apocalypse* whose first version he wrote in 774. Confining his personal contribution to some rare reflections, the author sets out a compilation of patristic texts drawn, he says, from St Ambrose, St Fulgentius of Ruspe, St *Gregory the Great, Apringius of Beja, St Augustine and Tyconius.

This text enjoyed wide circulation until the 12th century. We have 33 copies dating from the mid 10th c. to the 1200s; some survive incomplete. 22 of these manuscripts are illustrated by miniatures which give them an exceptional value. Among the best examples of this remarkable collection is the "Beatus" kept at the library of the Colegio Santa Cruz in *Valladolid. Made at the monastery of Valcavado in 970, it has no less than 87 miniatures of which 35 occupy one or even two full pages. The originality of these depictions lies in their use of very lively and strongly contrasted colours. It is not hard to recognise the influence of the techniques used by the Christian artists of Muslim Andalusia.

The manuscript of the Colegio Santa Cruz reproduces the third and last version of the *Commentary*. Dated 784, it is distinguished from its predecessors by numerous allusions to *Elipandus of Toledo and his opinions. In the early 780s, at the time of his controversy with Bishop Migetius, Elipandus formulated the doctrine of *adoptianism. What seems to have been quite an important part of the Iberian clergy rallied to it, but Elipandus also met resolute opposition, led by Beatus of Liébana and Etherius of Osma. Beatus may have been behind the doctrinal letter addressed by *Adrian I to the bishops of the peninsula to denounce Elipandus's ideas. In any case there is no doubt that, in association with Etherius, he was the author of the *Adversus Elipandum Libri II*, written in 785. While the work hardly stands out by the relevance of its theological arguments, it demonstrates a very lively sense of the controversy. Beatus does not hesitate to put the quarrel on a political level, accusing Elipandus of serving the interests of the emir of *Cordova.

M. N. Alonso Cortes, *Universidad de Valladolid. El Beato de su biblioteca*, Valladolid, 1971. – M. Mentré, "Les représentations mozarabes", *L'enluminure romane. Dossiers d'archéologie*, Jan-Feb 1976, 68-75. – *Libros y documentos en la Iglesia de Castilla y Leon*, Burgos, 1990, 57-66.

Daniel Baloup

**BEAUNEVEU, ANDRÉ (died *c.*1401/1403).** Master of the "works of cutting and painting" for Duke *John of Berry from 1386 to his death, the sculptor and painter André Beauneveu, born at Valenciennes, would have received his training in Hainaut, near *Brabant, whence the bold and supple rendering of his models. His beginnings were Parisian (tomb of *Charles V). He was primarily a sculptor (apostles and *prophets of the castle chapel of Mehun-sur-Yèvre and the *Sainte-Chapelle of Bourges), but he also decorated manuscripts (Psalter of the Duke of Berry).

M. Meiss, *French Painting in the Time of Jean de Berry*, 2nd ed., 1, London, 1969. – S.-K. Scher, "Observations sur les relations entre André Beauneveu, Jean de Cambrai et Claus Sluter", *Actes des Journées internationales Claus Sluter*, Dijon, 1992, 277-293.

Alain Girard

**BEAUTY.** Medieval considerations on beauty are the result of an overall vision of the universe for which each positive attribute of the created world finds its origin and its coherence in *God. As such, beauty is identical with God and is present in created realities only as a *participation in beauty. It is nevertheless an attribute inscribed in the *ontological structure of every being, inasmuch as this structure belongs to the order of the divine disposition: on this account everything is beautiful. Visible beauty is a vestige of God which favours our intellectual grasp of him and authorizes our symbolic return to him. The beautiful pleases by its harmony, which results from relations of proportion based on *numbers. Ideas of beauty as *light or as splendour of form obey the same logic of a dual reduction of the visible *good: first to its intelligible *reason and then to its *metaphysical principle.

E. de Bruyne, *Études d'esthétique médiévale*, Bruges, 1946 (3 vol.). – W. Tatarkiewicz, *A History of Six Ideas: an Essay in Aesthetics*, London, 1980. – U. Eco, *Art and Beauty in the Middle Ages*, New Haven, 1986.

Tiziana Suarez-Nani

**BEAUVAIS.** The history of Beauvais in Merovingian times is little known. Its rise in the 9th c., marked by the holding of a *council in 845, was soon curtailed by the *Viking invasions between 852 and 940. The assertion of episcopal power is revealed in the last years of the 10th c. by the construction of a *cathedral, called Notre-Dame-de-la-Basse-Oeuvre, which still preserves the oldest memory of Beauvais's medieval buildings. But conflicts between the bishop-count and the *commune, solidly installed from 1099, more than once disturbed the social equilibrium, in particular at the time of Bishop Milo of Nanteuil's confrontation with *Louis IX. This

Choir of the cathedral of Saint-Pierre, Beauvais, 13th c.

difference delayed the reconstruction of the cathedral of Saint-Pierre, begun by Milo after the fire of 1225. The vaults of the choir, daringly raised to a height of 47 metres, collapsed in 1284, only 12 years after their completion. At great expense the damage began to be repaired, work interrupted by the feudal wars and the English occupation. Not until 1499 could the *chapter entrust Martin Chambiges with the completion of the work. The plan of the *architecture, in which the structural research begun at *Chartres found one of its culminating points, was to be grandiose, if we imagine a nave such as Viollet-le-Duc tried to reconstruct it. The choir, with its three vertical bays bordered by double side-aisles, ended in a seven-sided apse, echoed by the seven radiating pentagonal chapels. The airy design of the triple elevation, in which narrow slender arcades were surmounted by a perforated triforium topped by tall windows occupying the whole width and height of the wall, contributed to the effect of verticality of this very nervous structure.

We must also mention the church of Saint-Étienne, the oldest Christian sanctuary in Beauvais, where *canons from Saint-Vaast in *Arras were established in 1072. Today the *collegiate church juxtaposes a nave, whose ribbed vaults, restored in the 13th c., rest on *Romanesque walls, and a majestic choir, rebuilt in the 16th c. in the *Flamboyant taste. One of the archaeological interests of Saint-Étienne is in the early date of the ribbed vaulting of the side-aisles of the nave.

A. Erlande-Brandenburg, *L'Art gothique*, Paris, 1983. – M. Bideault, C. Lautier, *Île-de-France gothique*, Paris, 1987. – S. Murray, *Beauvais Cathedral*, Princeton (NJ), 1989.

Editorial staff

**BEC, LE.** Founded *c.*1035 as a modest hermitage by the blessed Herluin, a converted Norman soldier, the abbey of Bec with its monastic *school became one of the most important *abbeys in *Normandy towards the end of the 11th century.

The school owed its renown to *Lanfranc, who directed it for 16 years. After his departure to Caen, St *Anselm succeeded him as *prior of the community and director of the monastic school. Anselm's presence at the head of the school completely changed the content and spirit of the teaching: instead of being content to teach *grammar and *dialectic and a biblical *exegesis confined to mere *glosses, Anselm led his pupils to the contemplation of the difficult mysteries of faith by the way of *reason. During St Anselm's abbacy, the abbey expanded considerably: its estates and priories multiplied everywhere in Normandy, in England, in France as far as the Île-de-France. From the time of the conquest, the abbey of Bec produced the future archbishops of *Canterbury: after Lanfranc and St Anselm, Abbot *Theobald (fifth abbot) also occupied the primatial see of England.

The school of Bec still attracted prelates in the 12th c., but above all it continued to provide a great number of *abbots and *bishops, among them the famous humanist Robert de Torigni, future abbot of *Mont Saint-Michel and author of the *chronicle of Bec, a precious source for the abbey's history. Most of the literary works by the monks of Bec at this time are anonymous, attesting their interest in *rhetoric, grammar, dialectic, *canon law or *poetry, but never again reaching the heights of thought of a St Anselm. Like the other monastic schools, that of Bec also declined with the rise of the Parisian schools and the foundation of the *university. The abbey possessed a famous *library that in the early 12th c. contained some 160 volumes, but was enriched in 1164 by 113 volumes: it was almost entirely lost during the Revolution. The same fate befell the abbey's inestimable *cartulary establishing the abbey's rights over 30 priories and 120 churches.

Over the centuries, the abbey's destiny followed the vicissitudes of history. To start with, there were only wooden buildings. From 1039 the abbey was rebuilt, but only in 1073 was the community able to establish itself on the site of the present monastery. Thanks to the generosity of Lanfranc, then archbishop, a church was built in 1077. In 1150 the church was severely damaged by a fire, and in 1263 another fire almost entirely destroyed the church and the monastery. During the *Hundred Years' War, the fortified abbey became the scene of violent fighting and was taken and sacked by the English in 1421. During the Revolution, much of it was destroyed; up to 1948 it was used as a stable.

P. Ragey, *Histoire de saint Anselme archevêque de Cantorbéry*, Paris, Lyon, 1889 (2 vol.). – A. Porée, *Histoire de l'abbaye du Bec*, Évreux, 1901 (2 vol.); re-ed. Brussels, 1980. – S.N. Vaughn, *The Abbey of Bec and the Anglo-Norman State, 1034-1136*, Woodbridge, 1981. – *Les Mutations socioculturelles au tournant des XIe-XIIe siècles*, R. Foreville (dir.), Paris, 1984 ("Études anselmiennes, IVe session").

Coloman Viola

**BEDE THE VENERABLE (673-735).** One of the great *Doctors of the Western Church, Bede lived an uneventful life as a monk and scholar at *Wearmouth-Jarrow, to which he was delivered as an *oblate in *c.*681 and where he remained until his death. Our knowledge of his life is derived solely from his own account of himself in the final chapter of his *Historia Ecclesiastica* (V, 24). In that chapter Bede also provides a full list of his writings, which embrace pedagogy, *computus, biblical *exegesis, *history, *hagiography and poetry. Bede's pedagogical writings included treatises *De orthographia*, *De natura rerum* and *De arte metrica*. The latter survives in hundreds of manuscripts and was still being used in the 16th c. as an elementary introduction to metre. His introduction to computus, *De temporum ratione*, enjoyed a similarly wide circulation. He composed many biblical commentaries, usually heavily indebted to earlier patristic authorities (Augustine, Jerome, *Gregory) but designed especially to treat those books of the *Bible that had not been the subject of earlier commentaries (such as Samuel, *Kings, Ezra, Nehemiah, Tobit, *Song of Songs, Mark, Luke, the Catholic *Epistles and the *Apocalypse). As a historian, Bede is best known for his great *Historia Ecclesiastica*, an account of the introduction of Christianity to *England and the growth of the English Church down to Bede's own day (731), but he also composed a comprehensive set of *Chronica maiora* (appended to *De temporum ratione*) and a history of the abbots of Wearmouth-Jarrow. As a hagiographer, he is best known for his lives (in prose and verse) of St Cuthbert, but his most influential work was his *Martyrologium*, the earliest historical *martyrology compiled in the West. Much of his Latin poetry has been lost, but various epigrams and *hymns survive under his name.

*PL*, 90-95, 1861-1862. – *Two Lives of St Cuthbert*, B. Colgrave (ed.), Cambridge, 1940. – *Bedae Opera de Temporibus*, C. W. Jones (ed.), Cambridge (MA), 1943. – *Bede's Ecclesiastical History of the English People*, B. Colgrave (ed.), R. A. B. Mynors (ed.), Oxford, 1969. – *CChr.SL*, 119-123, 1969-1983.

*Bede, His Life, Times and Writings*, A. H. Thompson (ed.), Oxford, 1935. – *Famulus Christi*, G. Bonner (ed.), London, 1976. – G. H. Brown, *Bede the Venerable*, Boston, 1987. – P. Hunter Blair, *The World of Bede*, Cambridge, 1990. – *Bede and his World: the Jarrow Lectures*, London, 1994.

Michael Lapidge

**BEGHARDS.** Lay *penitents, the beghards were never as numerous as their female counterparts, the *beguines. The first mentions of beghards in Flanders, northern France and Germany date from 1220-1250. The term "bégard" (sometimes "bogard") was used mainly in Flanders and the German regions, while in Romance countries "béguin" was preferred.

Itinerant or forming small communities (but never beguinages in the proper sense), the beghards sometimes lived off *alms. But many of them worked, notably in the clothing industry. At *Brussels, Louvain, *Antwerp, *Bruges, the beghards formed veritable associations of weavers, dividing their time between work and exercises of piety. Hence they were not just at odds with the ecclesiastical authorities, as were the beguines: they were also up against the pressure of the urban authorities and the trade *corporations, for whom they were direct rivals. In the course of the 14th c., they fell under the tutelage of the *guilds.

In the Empire, condemned as "sturdy beggars", the beghards were very soon persecuted. In the old Netherlands, integrated with the charitable structures of the weavers, in the 14th and 15th cc. they adopted the Rule of St *Augustine or entered the Franciscan *Third Order. But up to the 16th c. there were frequent disputes between them and the weavers' guilds.

G. des Marez, "Les bogards dans l'industrie drapière à Bruxelles", *Mélanges Paul Fredericq*, Brussels, 1904, 279-287. – J. Le Leu, "De Begarden te Antwerpen (1296-1476)", *Fr*, 34, 1979, 21-60. – W. Simons, *Stad en apostolaat. De vestiging van de Bedelorden in het graafschap Vlaanderen (c.1225-c.1350)*, Brussels, 1987, 222-223.

Michel Lauwers

**BEGUINES, BEGUINAGES.** In the late 12th-c. West, new religious experiments developed, combining a lay state with a life of *penance and *contemplation. This is the context in which we must place the beguinal movement: though consecrated to the service of God, the beguines were bound neither to monastic *vows nor to the common life nor to a rule approved by the ecclesiastical hierarchy. Living as *nuns, they remained laywomen.

The movement was mainly urban. A demographic imbalance characterised by an excess of *women, very high among the populations emigrating to the *towns, partially explains the extent of the phenomenon. From the 13th c., numerous cities harboured dozens of beguinal communities. In the 14th c., the town of Basel had at least 400 beguines, *Strasbourg at least 600, and *Cologne more than a thousand.

Some beguines lived alone, leading an itinerant existence or remaining under the family roof; others shared a house; still others lived in "courts" called "beguinages", veritable villages within a town, formed of several houses or convents, provided with a *chapel, an infirmary and other common buildings. The beguines lived off *alms, but also off the work of their hands.

At first they were designated by the expression *mulieres religiosae*, "religious women". But very soon, in the northern part of Europe, the name *beguinae* was given them. Elsewhere, the same experiments received other names: according to *Jacques de Vitry († 1240), one of the first observers of the movement, "they are called beguines in Flanders and Brabant, papelardes in France, *humiliatae* in Lombardy, bizokes in Italy, coquenunnes in Germany". "Beguine" was originally a disparaging term, used for "heretics", since the beguinal movement had numerous detractors. In 1216, the pope had admittedly approved the beguinal communities "not just in the diocese of *Liège, but in the kingdom [of France] and in the Empire" (according to a letter of Jacques de Vitry); and in 1233 a *bull had accorded them papal protection. However, many churchmen were reluctant to admit the "intermediate situation" (*Zwischenstand*) of the beguines, which implicitly blurred the distinction between clergy and *laity, reasserted by the *Gregorian reform, as well as all the social and legal classifications imagined by the Church. Because they did not know where to place them, the laity accused the beguines of "hypocrisy", while the *secular clergy were hostile to their often privileged relations with the *mendicants which often put them outside the jurisdiction of the ordinary priests. Moreover, the informal social networks of which the beguines were part could not but embarrass the institutional church: even outside their communities, the beguines met, prayed together, discussed their experiences. Above all, they read, knew how to write, took possession of the sacred texts, translated them into the vernacular. It even happened that some of them wrote *treatises, as witness the mystical works of Beatrice of Nazareth, *Hadewijch of Antwerp or Margaret Porete, or spoke in public. The immediate relationship they had with God, in contemplation and *ecstasy, accorded no role to the priests. In short, the Church's social function found itself threatened.

Faced with beguinism, the institutional church adopted two types of attitude. Sometimes, the beguinal experiments were totally rejected and likened to *heresy. This was notably the case in the Rhineland, where the beguines were persecuted from the 13th c., even before the declaration pronounced against them at the council of *Vienne in 1312 and promulgated in 1317. Sometimes, the Church strove to "integrate" the beguines. Some were made to adopt the Rule of St *Augustine or to join the *Third Order. In the diocese of Liège and in Flanders, the episcopal authorities and the civil authorities proceeded to the "*enclosure" of the beguines: those who were separate were brought together in precise places, "beguinages" (these henceforth constituting the sole authorized form of beguinism), then provided with regulations and visited regularly by priests designated for that purpose. Whilst everywhere else the beguinal movement died out, the great beguinages of the North survived the crisis of the first quarter of the 14th century.

E. W. McDonnell, *The Beguines and Beghards in Medieval Culture*, New Brunswick, 1954.– J. C. Schmitt, *Mort d'une hérésie. L'Église et les clercs face aux béguines et aux béghards du Rhin supérieur du XIV<sup>e</sup> au XV<sup>e</sup> siècle*, Paris, 1978. – R. E. Lerner, "Beguines and Beghards", *DMA*, 2, 1983, 157-162. – B. Delmaire, "Les Béguines dans le Nord de la France au premier siècle de leur histoire", *Les Religieuses en France au XIII<sup>e</sup> siècle*, M. Parisse (ed.), Nancy, 1985, 121-162. – M. Lauwers, "Paroles de femmes, sainteté féminine. L'Église du XIII<sup>e</sup> siècle face aux béguines", *La critique historique à l'épreuve*, C. Braive (ed.), J. M. Cauchies (ed.), Brussels, 1989, 99-115. – W. Simons, "The Beguine Movement in the Southern Low Countries. A Reassessment", *BIHBR*, 59, 1989, 63-105. – *Meister Eckhart and the Beguine Mystics*, New York, 1994. – H. Grundmann, *Religious Movements in the Middle Ages*, Notre Dame (IN), 1995. – S.M. Murk Jansen, *Brides in the Desert: the Spirituality of the Beguines*, London, 1998.

Michel Lauwers

**BEING, ESSENCE, EXISTENCE.** The existent (*ens*), *i.e.* the thing that is, constitutes, when considered as such, *inquantum ens*, the object of *metaphysics. Now, every existent presents two dimensions. On one hand, it is something determined and, on the other hand, it exists. Thus, on the subject of any reality whatever, the mind asks two questions: What is it (*quid sit*)? And, does it exist (*an sit*)? The first question is that of the essence (or again: quiddity, *nature). It aims to determine an intelligible structure and culminates in a definition that situates the existent in question among other existents. The second question, that of existence, took on particular prominence in the intellectual climate engendered by the great monotheistic religions. In effect, the dogma of *creation drew attention to the radical contingency of existents, whose actual existence, the proper effect of *God's creative action, could not necessarily flow from their essence. This thus led to an emphasis on the distinction between being and essence.

A whole metaphysical tradition, which favoured the formal level of essence, understood being (*esse*) as a property, essential or accidental, of essence. For *Avicenna, being is really distinct from essence, but it is an accident. For *Duns Scotus, each state of essence secretes its own form of existence, actual existence being nothing but the mode of existence proper to the individualized essence.

For St *Thomas Aquinas, by contrast, being (*esse*), irreducible to the essential order, is the act of essence, that is to say that being and essence, co-principles of the existent, mutually maintain, in each existent, a relation of *act to potency, of determinant to determined. Certainly, essence is already an act and a perfection in its order, but it is still susceptible, in another and more radical order, that of actual existence, to a further determination, that of *esse*. *Esse*, act of acts and perfection of all perfections, is thus presented as the intensive, ultimate and inclusive perfection, which gives each essence and its determinations all their weight of reality.

Despite these divergences on the nature of being, medieval thinkers readily associated the problematic of being with that of God. For some, God is the supreme essence, eternal Being (Augustine), necessary Being (Avicenna) or infinite Being (Duns

Scotus); for others, he is revealed as the plenitude of the act of being, subsistent Being itself, the source, consequently, of the being and thus of all the reality of creatures (Thomas Aquinas). Yet the *Neoplatonist tradition, present all through the Middle Ages, maintained the idea of a certain anteriority of God, the One or the *Good, to being, and apprehended him as a "nothing" richer than being.

É. Gilson, *L'Être et l'Essence*, Paris, 1948. – A.A. Maurer, *Being and Knowing*, Toronto, 1990.

Serge Bonino

**BEIRUT.** A *port on the east coast of the Mediterranean, Beirut is now capital of *Lebanon. The site has been occupied since prehistoric times. In Phoenician times, Beirut was eclipsed by Byblos. In the Roman period, as *Berytus*, it rose and became a great administrative, commercial and university centre (school of law). In 551, a violent earthquake accompanied by a tidal wave destroyed the town. The Byzantine Emperor Justinian (527-565) rebuilt the ruins, but the town never regained its prosperity and the Arabs had no difficulty in taking it in 635. The *Umayyad *caliph Mu'āwiya (661-680) brought colonists from Persia to repopulate the town and its region, and during the first centuries of *Islam Beirut was part of the province of *Damascus. At the start of the *Abbasid period, the jurist al-Awzā'ī, founder of a Syrian legal school, settled at Beirut where he died in 774. In 975 Beirut was taken, like many other towns on the Syro-Palestinian coast, by the Byzantine general John Tzimisces, but the *Fatimids of Egypt took it back shortly afterwards. It remained under their rule until the conquest of *Syria-*Palestine by the *Seljuk Turks between 1071 and 1078. The town was then part of the territories of Tutush, brother of the sultan Malikshāh.

In 1099, the crusaders made no attempt against Beirut on their way to *Jerusalem, but in May 1110 the king of Jerusalem, *Baldwin I, helped by Genoese and Pisan ships, besieged the town and took it by assault. The population was massacred by the Italians against the king's orders. Beirut was now included in the kingdom of Jerusalem, on the frontier with the county of Tripoli, and the first Latin bishop of Beirut was designated in 1112. The *Hospitallers built the church of St John the Baptist, which later became the al-'Umarī *mosque. The town was first handed over to the Flemish family of Guines before becoming part of the royal domain in 1166. In 1187 *Saladin retook Beirut, but King Aimery de *Lusignan (1197-1205) managed to recapture it in 1197 and gave it to John of Ibelin who rebuilt its fortifications and developed the activities of its port from 1220. In 1231, the troops of *Frederick II stormed the town but could not occupy the citadel, and the Ibelin family regained possession the following year. They kept it until 31 July 1291, when the town was taken by the *Mamluks shortly after the fall of *Acre. Beirut then became a governorship attached to the province of Damascus.

The environs of Beirut produced fruits, iron, and wood from a pine forest south of the town. Beirut also had commercial relations with the Syrian hinterland, Egypt and, from the time of the *crusades, the Christian West. From the 15th c., its *silk exports developed. It was in the *Ottoman period, above all in the 19th c., that Beirut really took off to become the future capital of the State of Lebanon.

C. Korolevskij, "Beyrouth", *DHGE*, 8, 1935, 1300-1340. – N. Elisséeff, "Bayrūt", *EI(E)*, 1, 1960, 1137-1138. – N. Jidejian, *Beirut through the ages*, Beirut, 1973. – J. Prawer, *Histoire du royaume latin de Jérusalem*, Paris, 1975 (2 vol.).

Anne-Marie Eddé

**BELARUS.** Belarus is formed by the land situated in the basin that marks off the middle course of the Dvina, the upper course of the Dniepr, the Beresina – a tributary of the latter's left bank – and, to the south, the Pripet. In the 7th-8th cc., the *Slavs arrived in Belarusian territory, as witness among other things the remains of burned Balt towns. Absorbing the remaining part of the Balt population, they formed three great tribes: the Krivitches (*Kriviči*), to the north the Dregovitches (*Dregoviči*), to the east the Radimitches (*Radimiči*). These divisions served as foundation for the organisation of the state or territory. In the central part of the territory of the Krivitches the principality of *Polotsk was founded early in the 9th century. Its centre, Polotsk, was one of the centres of that Eastern Slavia that was starting to be called *Rus'. The 10th-11th cc. saw three rival *imperia* there: that of *Kiev, that of Polotsk and that of *Novgorod, all three governed by princes of *Viking origin. The Vikings, called *Varangians in Rus', formed princely "trusts" whose ranks were supplemented by Slavs. In *c.*976, to avenge the refusal of the hand of the daughter of the prince of Polotsk, Prince *Vladimir (whose seat was then at Novgorod) conquered Polotsk, killed the princess's father and married her by force. He later placed Iziaslav, the son born of this union, on the throne of Polotsk, thus founding the local dynasty of the Iziaslavids. Seeking to enlarge their possessions, the Iziaslavids clashed with the grand princes of Kiev for possession of *Pskov and Smolensk. Another object of their rivalry was the wooded and partly swampy region of Polesia, situated in the Pripet basin, where the Dregovitches had mixed with a Balt population, the Iatviegs. In the 11th c. the most advanced Polesian cities – Pinsk and Turov – were centres of principalities. The prestige of the principality of Polotsk was strengthened by the foundation of a *bishopric at the end of the 11th century. Polotsk was a centre of Christianization of the lands of north-west Rus'. Later appeared the bishopric of Pinsk and Turov. Culturally, Polotsk occupied a dominant position, as witness the *Life of St Euphrosyne* (composed at Polotsk in the early 13th c. at latest) – daughter of a 12th-c. prince of Polotsk, she dedicated herself to the copying of sacred books – and the monuments of stone religious architecture dating from the 12th century. As well as Polotsk, 11th-c. sources note the existence of the cities and urban areas of Brest, Volkovysk, Vitebsk, Orcha, Minsk, Slutsk and Grodno. The first mention of *Novogrodek dates from 1212, but the existence of a town in that place seems earlier. Certain towns, such as Minsk, Grodno, Slutsk and Novogrodek, were capitals of small principalities in the 12th-13th centuries.

In the 1230s, most of the lands of Rus' fell under the yoke of the Tatars. The lands of Belarus remained out of reach of their domination. However, they were within the sphere of expansion of the Order of *Knights of the Sword, who had established themselves in Livonia early in the 13th c., threatening Polotsk and, further north, Pskov. The aggression of the Knights of the Sword was equally felt by the pagan Lithuanians, settled in the south of Livonia, who were at that time in the process of creating the organs of a State. As their moving force, they had an organisation into "trusts" commanded by dukes (*kunigas*). Defending themselves from the pressure of the orders of chivalry (*Teutonic Knights to the west), the Lithuanians turned their expansion towards the east. Faced with the dangers that threatened them, from the orders of chivalry on one side and the Tatar invasions on the other, the Russian principalities of the West, seeking military support, aimed from the 1240s to bring Lithuanian *kunigas*, whether they would or not, to their princely capitals. In 1262 Polotsk was governed by the Lithuanian Duke Tovtivil. The Lithuanian dukes who settled in the lands of Belarus (and of *Ukraine in the 14th c.), as well as their "trusts", were Slavicized. The external sign of this Slavicization was their baptism according to the Eastern rite. The Lithuanian Duke Mendog († 1263) made Novogrodek his capital. In the 14th c., Lithuanian expansion into Russian lands was continued by Gedymin (1316-1341), who governed Novogrodek (Belarus) and Kiernov (Lithuania), and by his son Olgierd (1345-1371). Reigning over the lands of *Lithuania and western Ruthenia, they gave themselves the title of Grand Dukes of Lithuania and Ruthenia. Later they added "and Samogitia". They were also called "masters" (*hospodar*), which emphasized the patrimonial character of their power. These titles mirrored the structure, both ethnic and political, of a State that from the 14th c. was commonly given the name of Lithuania. In this State, the majority of the population – in the mid 14th c. it has been estimated at more than 85 % – were Ruthenians, ancestors of the Belarusians and Ukrainians. During the Middle Ages a differentiation appeared between the Ruthenians and the Great Russians who made *Moscow their centre. In the Grand Duchy of Lithuania, the ethnic and cultural preponderance of Ruthenians led to Old Belarusian, which was a synthesis of Old Church Slavonic and the local west Ruthenian dialects, being made the official language of the whole Grand Duchy.

Conscious of the preponderance of the Ruthenians, the Lithuanians, defending their cultural and ideological identity, long retained their *paganism. They were the last people in Europe to decide, at the end of the 14th c., to adopt, via *Poland, the Christianity of the Latin rite, combining this with a political union. Grand Duke *Ladislas Jagiello (Władysław Jagiełło, 1381-1434), who became king of Poland, accompanied the establishment of a *Catholic bishopric at Vilno with discriminatory measures against *Orthodoxy. In 1387 mixed marriages between Catholics and Orthodox were forbidden, as was the building of new Orthodox churches; the privileges granted to lords and boyars were reserved for Catholics alone. The composition of the grand ducal council, too, was entirely Catholic. Jagiello's policies were opposed by his elder brother Andrew, duke of Polotsk, himself Orthodox. The resistance of the Polotskians was stamped out by force (1387). After the death in 1430 of Vitold (Vytautas), who had governed the Grand Duchy under the nominal sovereignty of Jagiello, discrimination against the Ruthenians led to a civil war. When Vitold's younger brother Sigismund, son of Keistut, became head of the Grand Duchy, Svidrigiello, a brother of Jagiello, was charged with the recognition and defence of the rights of the Ruthenians – though he himself was a Catholic. The result was that, in 1432 and 1434, edicts were issued equalizing the rights of Catholic and Orthodox lords and boyars, with the exception of access to the grand ducal council proper. While at the start of the 15th c. the proportion of Orthodox princes and lords in the elite of power was hardly 10 %, by the end of the century it had risen to 37 %, and in the 16th c. it was over 40 %. Taking into account the numerical importance of the two communities, it is evident that the Lithuanians were privileged; nevertheless, from the reign of Casimir Jagiellon (Kazimierz Jagiellończyk, 1440-1492), we can observe a closer approach of the two communities to create a common government of the Grand Duchy of Lithuania, though the last restriction on the rights of the Orthodox Ruthenians was not lifted until 1563.

After the union with Poland, the lands of western Ruthenia followed the Polish example by adopting "*Magdeburg law" as the form of organisation and legal existence of the towns. It began by reaching the most westerly town, Brest (1390), then, at the end of the 15th c., Grodno (1496), Polotsk (1498) and Minsk (1499). In the towns of the grand duchy, including the capital, Vilno (Vilnius), situated on the frontier of the Belarusian and Lithuanian lands, it was taken as a principle that the urban authorities would be composed half of Catholics (Lithuanians, Poles, Germans) and half of Orthodox (Ruthenians). In the towns of Belarus the Orthodox predominated, which made the principle of parity advantageous for the Catholics. For all that, it was an expression of the equality of rights of the two communities in urban life.

The origin of the name "Belarus" has not yet been clarified. We find it used in the 14th c. by the Rutheno-Volhynian *chronicler *Ipatievski Letopis*. The Polish chronicler Janko of Czarnków († 1384) noted that Grand Duke Jagiello (Ladislas) and his mother were imprisoned in 1381 "*in quodam castro Albae Russiae, Poloczk dicto*". The Germans also used the term *Weizzen Reuzzen* at the start of the 15th century. At that time it did not embrace Black Rus' (Black Ruthenia), situated to the south-west and comprising the towns of Grodno, Volkovysk and Slonim. Some are of the opinion that the term Belarus (White Rus') came from the fact that it was free, hence "white", Ruthenia, as opposed to Black Ruthenia which was subject much earlier to the rule of Lithuania. Others connect the term "White Rus'" to the colour of the traditional costume of the population, while explaining "Black Rus'" by the preponderance of plains and marshland in that region.

The status of the Belarusian lands in the Grand Duchy of Lithuania, the role of the Old Belarusian language in the life of the State, the development of literature, all favoured the development in the 15th-16th cc. of the Belarusian language. It is characterised by the abundance of the vowel *a* and the frequency of the syllables *ak* or *ka* (*e.g.* Polish and Russian *ovca* = Belarusian *avečka*), the replacement of *v* by *ŭ* or *u*; and the frequency of the suffix *čyn*, feminine *čyna*. A large number of Polish, German and Lithuanian terms are found in Belarusian. It was in this language that the Lithuanian statutes were written – three codifications of the Grand Duchy (1529, 1566, 1588) – as well as the Lithuano-Belarusian chronicles, in particular the oldest, the *Chronicle of the Lithuanian grand dukes* (*Latopisec velikih kniazej litovskih*), dating from the mid 15th c. or thereabouts.

The idea of a continuity of the Belarusian linguistic-cultural whole with its ethnic-cultural base, that of the Krivitches and Dregovitches, was accepted by Efim Karskij, a remarkable specialist in the Belarusian language and culture, and, following him, by the historian Vladimir Pičeta. Another view connects the formation of a Belarusian language and national identity, in the 15th-16th cc., with a differentiation in Old Russian national feeling, which was produced as a result of the expansion of Kiev (among other places, this view is expounded in Polish and English scientific literature by Henryk Paszkiewicz and in Belarusian by M. Pilipenko). At the same time we may emphasize the ethnic-cultural continuity and the continuity of forms of political existence between Belarus and the duchy of Polotsk. The Grand Duchy of Lithuania was in this sense a Lithuanian-Belarusian State. In fact, until the 19th c. the term "Lithuanian" designated, not a national identity, but membership of a State, while the distinctive sign of Belarusian (and Ukrainian) nationality was their confession, Orthodox until the end of the 16th c., then also partly Greek Catholic. The incorporation of the south Ruthenian (Ukrainian) lands into Poland in 1569 precipitated the process of differentiation and separation of the Belarusian and Ukrainian peoples.

H. Paszkiewicz, "The Three Russian Nations", *The Making of the Russian Nation*, London, 1963. – V. V. Sedov, *Slavjane verhnego Podneprovja i Podvinja* [The Slavs of the upper Dnepr and Dvina], Moscow, 1970. – E. E. Rydzevskaja, *Drevniaja Rus' i Skandinavija IX-XIV vv.* [Ancient Rus and Scandinavia, 9th-14th centuries], Moscow, 1978. – M. Jarmolovič, *Staražytnaja Bielarus. Polacki i Novaharodski peryjady* [Ancient Belarus: the Polock and Novogorodok periods], Minsk, 1990. – *Imia tvaë Bielaja Rus'* [Your name, Belarus], G. M. Sahanovič (ed.), Minsk, 1991. – M. F. Pilipenko, *Vozniknovenie Belorusi. Novaja koncepcija* [The creation of Belarus. The new conception], Minsk, 1991. – A. K. Kraŭcovič, *Stvarenne Vialikaga Kniastva Litoŭskaga* [The creation of the Grand Duchy of Lithuania].

Juliusz Bardach

## BELL, BELFRY

**The West.** Divine service had to be announced publicly to the community living near the *oratory or church; the signals used varied greatly. The use of bells comes from Italy; big bells were called *campanae* (from the province of Campania) and little ones *nolae* (from the town of Nola). The ringing of bells became popular between the 6th and the 8th c.; the first *campanili* erected to hang bells appeared in the 8th century. According to a *capitulary of *Charlemagne of 789, corroborated by contemporary texts, each parish church possessed or ought to possess its bell. Belfries multiplied in various forms – gable-belfries, tower-belfries, spire-belfries – all over the place, especially from the 11th century.

The ceremony of *consecration of bells goes back to the 8th c. and is found in sources of *Gallican origin; the ceremonial was fixed in the mid 11th c. and remained relatively stable thereafter. When bells multiplied in towers, in the 12th c., they began to be distinguished by the names of their function (vesper-bell, alarm-bell), then by nicknames.

J. D. Blavignac, *La Cloche. Études sur son histoire et sur ses rapports avec la société aux différent âges*, Paris, 1877. – H. B. Walters, *Church Bells of England*, Oxford, 1912. – H. Leclercq, "Cloche, clochette", *DACL*, 3, 1914, 1954-1977. – A. E. de Staercke, *Cloches et carillons. L'histoire folklorique des cloches*, Brussels, 1946. – G. P. E. Elphinck, *The Craft of the Bellfounder*, Chichester, 1988.

Guy-Marie Oury

**Russian Church.** Like the other *Slav peoples of Greek rite, the Russians received from Byzantium only the simander (*bilo*) – a kind of wooden or metal gong – and borrowed, apparently very slowly, the use of bells from the Latins. Chemical analysis of medieval specimens reveals a casting technique similar to that of the West. The presence of bells is attested at *Novgorod in 1066. Small in size, they must at first have been attached to convenient supports, later to belfries in the form of a wall pierced with openings at the top, the *zvonica*, of which there is an example at St Sophia, Novgorod, erected in 1439 in place of an earlier and probably identical building.

E. E. Golubinsky, *Istoriia russkoy tserkvi*, 1 (2), Moscow, 1904.

Vladimir Vodoff

**BELOOZERO.** The White Lake, situated about 500 kilometres north of *Moscow, gave its name to a region of forest and swamp which was erected into a principality from 1238 to 1485, for the benefit of the cadets of the Muscovite dynasty. It was in this land that St Cyril of Beloozero (1337-1427), son of a Moscow boyar, contemporary and friend of *Sergius of Radonezh, founded in *c.*1397 the monastery since called St Cyril's, on the edge of the little lake of Siverskoe. Close by, the abbey known as St Therapont was founded by the saint of that name, one of Cyril's companions († 1426), and numerous little hermitages arose over the following decades. This expansion was the result of a demanding spiritual search and a colonizing movement that led the Russians to populate the regions of the North, rich in *salt, game and fish, relatively spared by the incursions of the Tatars and the *epidemics of plague. 19th-century Russian historiography exalted the flowering of monastic foundations of this time and gave Beloozero, with the nearby districts of Vologda, Galich and Chuxloma, the name of the "North Russian Thebaïd".

St Cyril's of Beloozero acquired considerable landed property from the 15th c., though the abbey was distinguished from the other *coenobitic communities that arose in the wake of St Sergius of Radonezh by a stricter attachment to poverty, both individual and collective. It was moreover characterised by an intellectual life more intense and more creative than elsewhere: the library of St Cyril's was the main medieval Russian ecclesiastical repositary, together with that of the metropolitan see of Moscow; *chronicles or fragments of chronicles were written in the monastery and give proof of independence from the Muscovite versions of the facts. Within North Russian monasticism, an austere milieu sometimes brought into conflict with the ecclesiastical hierarchy, was formed in the late 15th and early 16th cc. the movement of "non-possessors" (*nestiazhateli*) that rose up against the enrichment of the Church. Their chief masters of thought were Nilus of Sora († 1508) and Bassian Patrikeev († *c.*1545), who were opposed by Joseph Volokolamsk († 1515). After having been an influential member of the court of *Ivan III of Moscow, Bassian Patrikeev suffered a disgrace and the grand prince obliged him to retire within the walls of St Cyril's at Beloozero (1499). As a monk, he was again in favour in Moscow between 1509 and 1531. He was then a fierce critic of monastic wealth until metropolitan Daniel I had him condemned for heresy.

During the modern period, despite the extension of their estates and spectacular architectural transformations that have made them both fortresses and jewels of Russian religious art, the monasteries of Beloozero have kept up a fairly strict practice of evangelical poverty and have sheltered as much as imprisoned some independent minds or high personages disgraced by the *tsar, such as Patriarch Nikon (1605-1681).

G. Fedotov, *The Russian Religious Mind*, Cambridge (MA), 1946-1966, 2 vol. – M.-J. Rouet de Journel, *Le Monachisme russe et les monastères russes*, Paris, 1952. – V. O. Ključevskij, *Drevnerusskie žitija svjatyx kak istoričeskij istočnik*, Moscow, 1988.

Pierre Gonneau

**BENEDICT XI, POPE (1240-1304).** Born in 1240, Nicholas Boccasini became a *Dominican at *Treviso, his home town. *Reader, then provincial, he was elected master of the order in 1296. He sided with *Boniface VIII against the *Colonna and negotiated peace between the kings of France and England. Cardinal of Santa Sabina from 5 Dec 1298, be became bishop of Ostia on 2 March 1300. Elected *pope on 21 Oct 1303, he took the name Benedict XI in memory of Benedict *Caetani. He created three Dominican *cardinals and revoked his predecessor's *bull *Super cathedram* as too unfavourable to the religious. He died at Perugia on 7 Jan 1304, before being able to excommunicate Nogaret.

L. Jadin, *DHGE*, 8, 1935, 106-116. – *HChr*, 6, 1991.

Agostino Paravicini Bagliani

**BENEDICT XII, POPE (*c.*1285-1342).** Jacques Fournier, son of a modest family from Saverdun in the diocese of Pamiers, had been a *Cistercian monk at Boulbonne and Fontfroide, of which he became abbot; appointed bishop successively of Pamiers (1317) where he engaged in the conversion of heretics, and of Mirepoix (1326), he became cardinal of Santa Prisca (1327); he opposed *John XXII in the quarrel over the *beatific vision. Elected *pope on 20 Dec 1334, Benedict XII was crowned on 8 Jan 1335. Continuing to reside at *Avignon, he replaced John XXII's episcopal dwelling with a palace that was both fortress and monastery, built by his compatriot Pierre Poisson.

An austere pope, he reformed the papal court: he marked out the powers of the marshal, appointed secretaries to write the secret letters, and reorganised the *Penitentiary; *chaplains called "intrinsic" (by contrast to the commensal chaplains whose role was mainly prestigious) were charged with saying the *offices daily with the pope. Minute reforms concerned the religious *orders – *Cistercians, Benedictines, *Franciscans, Augustinian Canons –, notably prescribing for the former two the regular holding of *chapters; but the pope met resistance from the *Dominicans. By the *bull *Pastor bonus* (1335), he facilitated the return of religious *gyrovagues to their monasteries of origin. He suppressed *commendation for *bishoprics and *abbeys and sent away from the papal court bishops and churchmen with *cure of souls. He revoked all *expectative graces in 1335, fought against *pluralism and imposed an examination for receiving *benefices; he ordered the registration of petitions. He extended the field of papal *reservations, but he lessened the weight of *taxation and limited the fees charged by prelates for proxies.

He supported the expansion of the Christian faith by sending Friars Minor, who were well received by the khan of south Russia; an embassy from the emperor of China came to Avignon. Transactions with the emperor of *Constantinople came to nothing.

In *Italy, he observed a pacific policy from which the tyrants profited. He agreed to negotiate with the *Visconti and raised the *interdict that weighed on Milan; but the agreement only bore fruit after the pope's death. He charged the archbishop of Embrun, Bertrand de Déaux, to pacify and reform the *Patrimony of St Peter and keep an eye on the integrity of papal officials. Benedict tried to make peace in the conflict between France and England, negotiating truces and excommunicating the Flemings, allied to *Edward III. Transactions with the excommunicated Emperor Louis of Bavaria came to nothing; at Rense, the imperial electors proclaimed that the emperor held his power only from *God (1338). In the Iberian peninsula, papal diplomacy restored peace between Portugal, Castile and Navarre, as well as between Aragon, Majorca and Genoa.

Benedict XII died on 25 April 1342 and was buried in Notre-Dame-des-Doms in Avignon. A man of duty, rigid, sometimes accused of avarice and obstinacy, in any case no diplomat, at his death he left a difficult situation in the Papal States and his attempts at reform did not survive him.

P. Fournier, *HLF*, 32, 1, 1936, 174-209. – J. B. Mahn, *Le Pape Benoît XII et les Cisterciens*, Paris, 1951. – B. Guillemain, *La Politique bénéficiale du pape Benoît XII*, Paris, 1952. – C. Schmitt, *Un pape réformateur. . . Benoît XII et l'ordre des Frères mineurs*, Florence-Quaracchi, 1959. – G. Mollat, *Les Papes d'Avignon*, Paris, 1964 (10th ed.). – B. Guillemain, *DBI*, 8, 1966, 378-384. – L. Boehm, "Papst Benedikt XII (1334-1342) als Förderer der Ordensstuden. Restaurator-Reformator – oder Deformator regularer Lebensform?", *Geschichtsdenken, Bildungsgeschichte, Wissenschaftsorganisation. Ausgewählte Aufsätze von Laetitia Boehm anlässich ihres 65 Geburtstages*, Berlin, 1996 (Hist. Forschungen, 56), 347-377.

Anne-Marie Hayez

**BENEDICT XIII, POPE (1342-1422).** The family into which Pedro de Luna was born in 1342 (not 1328) was allied to the kings of *Aragon and his mother was descended from a Moorish king of Majorca. He studied *canon law at the university of *Montpellier, became a doctor and taught there for some time in the 1370s. He was given *prebends in Spain (Calatayud, Lérida, *Valencia) and promoted cardinal in 1375, without having been a bishop. Known as the cardinal of Aragon, he followed *Gregory XI to *Rome. At the *conclave of 1378, he gave his voice for Bartolomeo Prignano (*Urban VI) but then rallied to the dissident cardinals to elect *Clement VII. *Legate of the latter in Aragon, Castile, Navarre and Portugal, he worked for twelve years to win them over to the Avignonese cause, organising dissenting meetings and inquiries. When he returned to *Avignon in 1390, only Portugal remained in the Urbanist camp.

In 1393, a new legation took him to France to follow the peace negotiations with the English. But he was in Avignon when Clement VII died suddenly in Sept 1394. The majority of the *cardinals felt that whoever was elected should, in the last resort, consent to withdraw so as to permit union, and they engaged themselves by an agreement subscribed in conclave to follow that path. As he agreed to make this commitment, his prestige got him rapidly elected: ordained priest on 3 Oct 1394, he was crowned on 11 Oct under the name of Benedict XIII.

From 1395, discord broke out between the new *pope and the kingdom of France, where the simultaneous cession of both pontiffs had been designated by the assembly of clergy as the best way to reach unity. Benedict XIII, it was thought, had only to hasten to carry out the conclave's agreement. But he did not intend to let others dictate his conduct, and in 1398 he had to face a revolt. After the proclamation of *subtraction of obedience, Benedict, in his palace of Avignon and helped by his compatriots, resisted armed troops and captivity. In 1403 he escaped, while the rebels returned to obedience.

Forced to negotiate with his opponent, in 1407 he accepted the principle of a meeting and advanced towards Savona; but the meeting was continually put off and most of the cardinals, won over to the party of union, rejoined their Urbanist colleagues at *Pisa to organise a *council of the two obediences. For his part, he convened his followers at Perpignan and refused to submit to the summons of the Pisans who pronounced his deposition. From 1409 to 1415, Spain, Scotland and the French Midi remained subject to him, until King *Sigismund of Germany managed to bring them over at the council of *Constance. Benedict took refuge at Peniscola and continued to behave as pope until his death, which occurred on 22 Nov 1422 but was kept hidden by his last followers unil 23 May 1423. His piety and intellectual qualities impressed his contemporaries, but he remains famous for his obstinacy.

*Lettres de Benoit XIII (1394-1422)*, J. Paye-Bourgeois (ed.), Brussels, 1983.

Hélène Millet

**BENEDICT OF ANIANE (*c.*750-821).** Founder of monasteries and inspirer of the religious policy of the Emperor *Louis the Pious, Witiza was the son of a count of Maguelone of Visigothic origin. Raised at the court of *Pippin the Short and *Charlemagne, he decided to leave the world and retire to the monastery of Saint-Seine after 774. Disillusioned by the laxity of morals at Saint-Seine, he settled at Aniane, near *Montpellier, on paternal property. In company with disciples soon outshone by his rigour, he sought the ways of an ascetic life, following the examples of Pachomius and Basil before returning to the more temperate model offered by the Rule of *Benedict of Nursia, of which he later became the zealous propagator to the point of adopting "Benedict" as a *conversion name. From this first experience, Benedict gained a very intimate knowledge of the different early monastic *Rules, which he tried to synthesize in his *Concordia regularum*. The example of Aniane won over numerous monasteries in the kingdom of *Aquitaine, then ruled by Charlemagne's son Louis. As an Aquitanian, Benedict took part in the struggle waged against the *adoptianist heresy and the positions of Felix of Urgel.

After 814 Louis, becoming emperor, called him to his side and founded for him, near *Aachen, the monastery of Cornelimünster (Inden), destined to be the model of the monastic *reform inspired by the sovereign. Benedict was both the inspirer and the *missus* of this reform promulgated at the synods of Aachen (816, 817, 818/819) and in a series of imperial *capitularies. Following the terms of these texts of laws, *regular clerics had to choose between two clearly distinct paths: the Benedictine model, *i.e.* the Rule of Benedict of Nursia alone, or else the canonical model. This policy of monastic unification (*una regula*) was accompanied by practical measures or customs themselves common (*una consuetudo*), intended to bring the Rule of St Benedict up to date. These customs in large part concerned liturgical life, a field in which Benedict's legacy was equally important; we owe him in particular a version of the Gregorian *sacramentary. The feast of St Benedict of Aniane is 11 February.

Benedict of Aniane, *Concordia regularum*, *PL*, 103, 1851, 703-1380. – "Vita Benedicti Abbatis Anianensis et Indensis", *MGH.SS*, 15, 1887-188, 198-220. – Benedict of Aniane, "Munimenta fidei", J. Leclercq (ed.), *StAns*, 20, 1948, 21-74. – Benedict of Aniane, "Regula sancti Benedicti abbatis Anianensis siue Collectio capitularis", J. Semmler (ed.), *CCMon*, 1, 1963, 515-536.

J. Semmler, H. Bacht, "Benoît d'Aniane", *LdM*, 1, 1980, 1864-1867. – J. Semmler, "Benedictus II: una regula – una consuetudo", in *Benedictine Culture 700-1050*, W. Lourdaux (ed.), D. Verhelst (ed.), Louvain, 1983, 1-49.

Dominique Iogna-Prat

**BENEDICT OF NURSIA, BENEDICTINE RULE.** Among the various currents that influenced *monasticism in the West, a major place must be given to the influence of St Benedict and the Benedictine Rule, which was adopted in Gaul for the first time by the monastery of Alta Ripa near Albi, *c.*620-630. Originally it was only one rule among others, but its intrinsic qualities as well as the support it obtained from the Roman Church led to its being progressively imposed on all the coenobitic groups of the West, as happened in the East with the Rule of St Basil.

We know little enough about St Benedict, who is hardly known except through what *Gregory the Great tells us of his life and miracles in the second book of his *Dialogues*. According to the most recent works, he seems to have been born *c.*490 at Norcia (Nursia) in the Umbrian Apennines, to a prosperous family. The young Benedict went early to *Rome, where he received a school education impregnated with ancient culture, still very much alive in the early 6th century. But this teaching soon aroused in him a reaction of disgust, and he lost no time in going to a mountainous region east of Rome to learn "learned ignorance". He spent three years in solitude in a grotto near *Subiaco, in the upper valley of the Aniene, practising the most extreme asceticism. After a vain attempt to join a community in the neighbourhood, he himself founded twelve small monasteries that brought together the hermits of the district. His prestige not ceasing to grow, Roman aristocrats sent him young children as *oblates, the most famous of whom were his main disciples, Maurus and Placidus. But Benedict, having come into conflict with the priest who had jurisdiction over the Subiaco region, left with a few monks and went to settle a hundred kilometres further south, on *Monte Cassino. This migration, which took place *c.*530, was followed by a definitive settlement and a monastery was built on top of the mountain, on the ruins of an old temple of Apollo. After having founded another monastery at Terracina, Benedict died in 547 or rather, according to the most recent hypotheses, around 560. He was buried at Monte Cassino with his sister St Scholastica, but the abbey was destroyed by the *Lombards in *c.*580 and tradition has it that his *relics were taken to Saint-Benoît-sur-Loire in France by a Frankish monk who discovered them in the ruins. We know from Gregory the Great that he who was later called "the father of Western monks" was in his lifetime a charismatic man to whom many *miracles were attributed. But it is probable that his memory would quite soon have been lost if he had not left a monastic rule that was to constitute his main claim to glory.

However, the genesis of this text and its sources of inspiration remained obscure until quite recently. The Benedictine Rule was composed at Monte Cassino between 530 and 560 but, apart from a brief mention by Gregory the Great, its diffusion is not attested before the early 7th c., and the oldest known manuscript (Oxford, Bodleian Library, Hatton 48) dates from *c.*700. Some forty years ago, certain authors even expressed doubts on the historical reality of Benedict and the importance of his legislative work, when it was discovered that a very long anonymous rule, known by the name of *Regula magistri*, was in fact earlier than that of the abbot of Monte Cassino. Far from being, as had previously been thought, a prolix gloss on the Benedictine Rule, that of the unknown "Master" was its source, and Benedict saw himself reduced from the role of original author to the modest rank of a mere abbreviator! Today this hypothesis which once made a great stir is accepted by everyone, and recent work by Adalbert de Vogüé, as well as his new edition and French translation of the Rule of St Benedict in the collection "Source Chrétiennes", has confirmed its validity. Far from complicating things, acceptance of this dependence simplifies them and, in particular, makes more likely the fact that the man of God celebrated by Gregory the Great and the abbot and legislator of Monte Cassino were one and the same person. If Benedict did not draw up the charter of Western monasticism but simply retouched an earlier text by adapting it to circumstances and integrating other contributions into it, we can understand better why his work produced no extraordinary impression on his contemporaries at a time when many normative works, aiming to codify the usages of monastic life, flourished throughout the West and why the author himself calls it simply "a little rule for beginners" (*RB*, 73, 8). This is not a manifestation of false humility. St Benedict was in fact aware of a decline in monastic life as compared with the golden age of the Desert Fathers and took account of the changes that had occurred since then: since the solitary life – whose full difficulty he had experienced himself – was suitable only for chosen souls and most candidates for monastic life were not capable of facing its rigours, what mattered above all was to define the rules of a solidly structured community life. Without breaking with the *anchoritism that remained for him the glorious and desirable hereafter of *coenobitism, Benedict added to the vertical relationship that united the monks to the *abbot, the spiritual master under whose authority they agreed to put themselves, a horizontal relationship based on the mutual charity that should reign between the sons of a single Father.

The same realism, inspired not by a pessimism of principle but by the state of society in his time, led the abbot of Monte Cassino to limit ascetic requirements to the strict minimum. Not content with limiting obligatory *fast days, he allowed the monks a measure of *wine at each meal, whereas those of the "great days" had only drunk *water. Likewise, his insistence on manual labour proceeded from an adaptation to new economic conditions. Written at a time when the prosperity of ancient Italy was finally vanishing, the Benedictine Rule aimed to create autonomous religious communities – with their *mill, their *forge and their **scriptorium* – adapted to times of alimentary penury and cultural regression. This is one of the reasons that explains its success when, from the 7th c., the exchange economy grew sluggish throughout the West and State structures were engulfed in turmoil, making way for a new world based on autarkic rural cells.

But there is still an element of mystery in the exceptional success encountered by the Rule of St Benedict, which the practical sense of its author is not sufficient to explain. How was this text of modest length, written for a few 6th-c. Italian monasteries, able to impose itself on all the religious communities to the point of becoming the charter of Western monasticism?

Two different reasons underlay this amazing success: the content of the Rule itself and the external support it received from ecclesiastical and lay authorities because of its qualities of balance and measure. St Benedict's text had the merit of being clear and relatively brief. It was divided into 73 short chapters, preceded by the famous Prologue beginning with the words: "Listen, o my son, to the precepts of the Master, and incline the ear of your heart"; throughout it, spiritual advice alternates with practical directives. We cannot fail to be struck by the simplicity of tone and the impression of serenity that emerges from it. For Benedict, monastic life must be accessible to all who seek God; it is presented as "a school of the Lord's service", which is contrasted with the secular school. In it we learn to attain *sanctity, not by a feverish activity or excessive efforts, but by giving ourselves up to the *grace of Christ and letting it act in us. The instruments of this return to God are silence – which allows us to hear his voice –, *obedience, in particular to the abbot, who holds the place of Christ in the community, and *humility "mother and mistress of all *virtue". These objectives once fixed, the Rule specifies the means to attain them and defines a framework of life: the monk's time is divided between *labour, *prayer and **lectio divina*, *i.e.* reading and *meditation on the *Bible. Each of these three elements is very important: manual labour is for the coenobite the most normal form of *ascesis: "If the monks live by the work of their hands, like our fathers and the Apostles, then they will truly be monks" (*RB*, 48, 5). Six hours a day in summer were devoted to laborious activities, *i.e.* three times more than to prayer. The latter was both public and private. Its communal expression was the *divine office, recital of a series of *psalms and *readings taken from holy books, at fixed *hours, from vigils to compline. But liturgy did not have to be empty formalism: "Let your mind be in harmony with your voice", says the Rule. By prayer, the monk intercedes with God for himself and for others. He implores him to push back the forces of *evil ("*Deus, in adiutorium nostrum intende*"), gives thanks to him for his benefits and praises him for having created and saved the world. As for the times given over to reading, which took place during the meal, eaten in silence, they concretely illustrate the absolute primacy recognised by the Rule to the Word of God, with which the monk must impregnate himself so as to interiorize it and subject his life to it.

The last part is devoted to communal discipline: it deals with the dormitory, where the monks sleep fully clothed, penances to be inflicted on those who do not respect the prohibition on private property ("Let this spiritual vice be cut off at the root!" "Let all be common to all") and the obligations of fraternal *charity. The early text did not anticipate – save exceptionally – that monks should receive the *priesthood or that priests should enjoy any priority within the community. The abbot was to be elected by the whole community, if possible by common agreement, if not "by the part ruled by a wiser judgment, even if it is the less numerous". A man of eclectic synthesis, St Benedict skilfully combined for the government of monasteries the three political systems known to the ancient world: monarchy, oligarchy and democracy. The Benedictine abbot was elected for life and possessed extensive powers. But he had to surround himself with the advice of the most aged and, for important decisions, consult the whole body of monks, who all had a voice in the *chapter.

Despite these intrinsic qualities and the sense of measure (*discretio*) that impregnated it, the Benedictine Rule did not impose itself at once on all the monasteries of the West. In the 7th c., it was often used concurrently with other *Rules, each community making a more or less harmonious mixture of the various observances, as we see in the abbeys founded by St *Columbanus. Indeed it was only at the end of a long detour that the Benedictine Rule managed to make a decisive breakthrough in European monasticism. The advantage it took was connected with the *evangelization of *England. That country was converted to Christianity by envoys of Pope Gregory, a great admirer, as we have seen, of St Benedict. So it was the latter's rule that the Roman missionaries propagated in the new Anglo-Saxon monasteries, where it enjoyed great success from the start. Led by both political and ethnic reasons to distance themselves from the Irish and Welsh, the English monks adopted without difficulty the Benedictine lifestyle, whose moderation contrasted strongly with the sometimes excessive austerity and chronic instability that characterised Celtic monasticism.

As the conversion of Germany was in large measure the work of Anglo-Saxon monks, it is not astonishing that the Rule of St Benedict immediately acquired a position of monopoly in that country. St *Boniface got it adopted by the great abbey he founded at *Fulda, and in 742 the first *synod of German bishops laid down that all monks should follow it. From then on, the movement spread like an oil-slick and extended, under the impulse of the *Carolingian rulers, to the whole of the West where it was already known and appreciated. The diffusion of Benedictine observances was facilitated by the close collaboration established, from the reign of *Pippin the Short, between the Frankish kings and the papacy, as well as by the rebirth of Monte Cassino, rebuilt from its ruins in 718 by Abbot Petronax. Charlemagne had the text of the Benedictine Rule recopied there and this "authentic" exemplar, kept in the imperial palace, served from now on as reference. The abbey of *Sankt Gallen in Switzerland still preserves a copy of this manuscript, made in the reign of *Charles the Bald.

The extension of the Benedictine Rule to all the monasteries of the Carolingian world was the work of Charlemagne's successor, *Louis the Pious. At the council of Aachen in 817, it was decided

*The Unbelief of St Thomas*. Miniature from the *Benedictionary of St Æthelwold of Winchester*. London, BL.

that the "holy rule" would from now on be the only one allowed. A revision was made of the text, from which prescriptions that had become inapplicable were eliminated, while efforts were made to fill the gaps concerning employment of time and the forms of liturgical prayer. These measures had been recommended by *Benedict of Aniane, a Benedictine abbot of Languedoc who played the role of ecclesiastical adviser to the emperor. They were promulgated in the form of a monastic *capitulary having the force of law, which aimed to restore in its full vigour the observance of the regular life. One of the main objectives of the *reform was to react against the tendency to secularization of monasteries. These were bidden to abandon their subsidiary activities, especially teaching which was given in *schools intended in principle for *novices but also frequented by the children of the aristocracy. But these injunctions were on the whole little followed and until the early 12th c. the abbeys remained the main places of formulation and transmission of culture both sacred and profane.

*La Règle de saint Benoît*, A. de Vogüé (ed.), J. Neuville (ed.), Paris, 1964-1972 (6 vol.). – *The Rule of Saint Benedict*, London, 1984.

E. de Solms, *La Vie et la Règle de saint Benoît*, Paris, 1977. – A. De Vogüé, *Community and Abbot in the Rule of Saint Benedict*, 2 vols., Kalamazoo (MI), 1978-88. – *Sous la règle de saint Benoît*, J. Dubois (ed.), Geneva, 1982. – M. Gretsch, "The Benedictine Rule in Old English", *Words, Texts and Manuscripts*, M. Korhammer (ed.), Cambridge, 1992, 131-58. – *Moines et religieux au Moyen Âge*, J. Berlioz (ed.), Paris, 1994.

André Vauchez

**BENEDICTIONARY.** Benedictions figure in *sacramentaries and *pontificals, of which they generally form a distinct part, or else constitute an independent book called a benedictionary. We distinguish simple benedictionaries, which appeared in the 9th c. in the form of separate booklets (*libelli*) containing episcopal benedictions for the *liturgical year, and the complete benedictionaries that were developed in the 10th and 11th cc. and whose content was broadened to include prayers and *ordines*.

The *bishop's second book after the pontifical, the benedictionary was essentially intended for the episcopal liturgy.

E. E. Moeller, *Corpus benedictionum episcopalium missae*, *CChr*, 162, 1971-1973 (4 vol.). – É. Palazzo, *Histoire des livres liturgiques. Le Moyen Âge, des origines au XIII<sup>e</sup> siècle*, Paris, 1993.

Éric Palazzo

**BENEFICES, ECCLESIASTICAL.** The practice of benefices goes back to the Carolingian period, when the habit began of granting a cleric the right to levy revenues on Church property in return for spiritual obligations, service or office. The benefice thus comprised three elements: 1) the spiritual service it imposed; 2) the right to levy the fruits of that service; 3) the fruits themselves of that service. Initially benefices were perpetual, a cleric remaining in the church to which he was attached, a practice confirmed again by the decrees of the council of Trent, but from which the *pope could derogate. The office was inseparable from the benefice.

Benefices were divided into secular and regular benefices, the former being those that could be possessed by *clerics, the latter only by religious. Secular benefices comprised the papacy, *bishoprics, dignities of *chapters, cure-priorships, perpetual vicariates, simple cures, *chapels and *chaplaincies; regular benefices were abbacies and claustral offices having revenues assigned to them (conventual *prior, *chamberlain, almoner, hospitaller, sacristan, *cellarer, etc.).

These benefices were simple or double and could be possessed in *title or in *commendation. Secular benefices were called simple when they had no *cure of souls and were exempt from administration (canonries not being a dignity, parsonages, chapels and chaplaincies), double when they were charged with administration (dignities of the Church and of chapters, cures). The pope, bishops and *parish priests always possessed correctional and penitential jurisdiction. Double regular benefices were abbacies or claustral offices in exercise (conventual or claustral priorships, etc.), simple benefices were non-conventual priorships, the monastic state and that of regular *canon.

A regular benefice was possessed in title by a religious exercising all its functions, and in commendation when it was held by a *secular cleric enjoying a *dispensation from regularity.

Benefices were called "collative" when they were at the appointment of a collator, or "elective" when they depended on the outcome of an *election, which could in some cases be confirmed by the superior (confirmative elective benefice).

Minor benefices under the tutelage of bishops, *abbots, *cathedral and conventual chapters were in general conferred by them. From the second half of the 13th c. (with *Clement IV), the popes used their right of *reservation (general and special reservation) to substitute themselves for the ordinary collators on the occasion of vacancy of benefices. Finally, benefices could be resigned by their holders.

G. Mollat, *La Collation des bénéfices ecclésiastiques à l'époque des papes d'Avignon (1305-1378) [Lettres communes de Jean XXII.* Introduction], Paris, 1921. – G. Mollat, "Bénéfices ecclésiastiques", *DACL*, 7, 1934, 1337-1370. – J. Gaudemet, *La Collection par le roi de France des bénéfices vacants en régale des origines à la fin du XIV<sup>e</sup> siècle*, Paris, 1935. – B. Guillemain, *La Politique bénéficiale du pape Benoît XII (1334-1342)*, Paris, 1952. – L. Caillet, *La Papauté d'Avignon et l'Église de France. La politique bénéficiale du pape Jean XXII en France (1316-1334)*, Paris, 1975. – M. Bégou-Davia, *L'interventionisme bénéficial de la papauté au XIII<sup>e</sup> siècle. Les aspects juridiques*, Paris, 1997.

Jean-Loup Lemaître

**BENEVENTO.** Benevento was conquered in *c.*570 by a *Lombard troop who made it the capital of a duchy, which in the 7th c. extended over the greater part of continental southern *Italy. When *Charlemagne captured *Pavia in 774, Duke Arichis II of Benevento asserted his independence by taking the title of prince. The principality was divided in 849 and 981. What remained of it was conquered by the *Normans, except for Benevento itself which was given to the *pope in 1051 and formed a papal enclave (sometimes invaded); it formed a *commune in 1128; the consulate was suppressed in 1281. Arichis enlarged the area of the city and built the monastery of Santa Sofia there; a *concordat with the king of *Sicily was concluded at Benevento in 1156; in 1266, *Manfred was killed near the town by the troops of *Charles of Anjou. The minuscule *script used in southern Italy from the 9th to the 12th c. is called "Beneventan".

S. Borgia, *Memorie istoriche della pontificia Città di Benevento dal secolo VIII al secolo XVIII*, Rome, 1763-1769 (3 vol.; repr. Bologna, 1968).

Jean-Marie Martin

**BENJAMIN I OF ALEXANDRIA (died 661).** The 38th Coptic patriarch of *Alexandria (622-661), he lived in troubled times with the end of the Persian occupation of *Egypt (617-627), the return of the Byzantines under *Heraclius, and finally the Arab conquest (637-641) and the permanent establishment of *Islam. In 631,

Heraclius instituted Cyrus as Melkite patriarch of Alexandria and governor of Egypt: Cyrus, unable to rally the monophysite *Copts to a *monothelite formula, unleashed a violent persecution against them, emptied their monasteries and seized their churches. Benjamin hid in Upper Egypt whence he returned only with the Arab conquest, restored with honour to his see by Amr ibn al-As who, at the head of a few Arab troops, counted on his authority to hold the Christian population. From then on Benjamin devoted himself to the restoration of his community and its monasteries, notably that of St Macarius.

*History of the Patriarchs of the Coptic Church of Alexandria*, *PO*, 1, 1907, 487-518. – C. D. G. Müller, "Benjamin I", *The Coptic Encyclopedia*, New York, 175-177.

Maurice Martin

***BEOWULF.*** The Old English poem known as *Beowulf* (it bears no title in the single manuscript which preserves it) is, at 3,182 lines, the longest surviving poem in any early Germanic language; it is also by general agreement the greatest poem in any early medieval vernacular language before *c.*1100, and is by any reckoning one of the great literary monuments of the Middle Ages. Its greatness lies not so much in its unprepossessing subject-matter (it concerns a hero who in his youth slays two monsters, and in old age is killed while trying to slay a dragon), as in its treatment of this subject, for it is a poem of vast and profound reflection on themes such as the transience of human life and human civilization, on the bonds which hold society together and the pressures which break them, on fate, courage, pride, duty, heroism, vengeance, and death. The action of the first part of the poem is set in Denmark, at the court of King Hrothgar. Hrothgar has just completed the construction of a magnificent hall, which unfortunately attracts the envious attacks of a nocturnal monster (whose name is given as Grendel, but whose appearance, by design, is only vaguely described). After killing and eating many of Hrothgar's thegns over a period of years, the report of the attacks prompts a young Geatish hero (the homeland of the Geats was in southern Sweden) to try his luck by challenging the monster (when first introduced, the hero is not named; subsequently, at the point he arrives at Hrothgar's hall, he gives his name as Beowulf). After presenting his credentials (and after some challenge to these credentials by one of Hrothgar's retainers), Beowulf and his men are left alone in the hall to await the approach of the monster. (This part of the narrative is told in the manner a ghost story.) After a fierce struggle, Beowulf succeeds in wrenching off the monster's shoulder; the monster flees to his dwelling in a haunted mere in order to die. Joy is restored to the hall; Hrothgar and his thegns celebrate by listening to stories (one of them, told at length, concerns the disastrous and deadly outcome of an intertribal marriage, the intention of which had been to establish peace between potential enemies). Unfortunately, the peace achieved by the killing of Grendel is short-lived: on the following night, Grendel's mother (who has not thus far been mentioned) comes to the hall to avenge her son, and carries off Hrothgar's favourite thegn. Accordingly, the following morning, Beowulf and his men, accompanied by a troop of Hrothgar's men, are obliged to follow the bloody trail to the haunted mere, which Beowulf enters alone, in order to pursue the monstrous mother to her lair. Whereas he had fought Grendel unarmed, he is heavily armed for his encounter with the mother; but in this case his weapons are of no avail, and he only succeeds in killing her by using a giant's sword which was luckily hanging on the wall. By the time he returns to the surface of the mere, the troop of Hrothgar's men have abandoned him for lost, but his own (Geatish) retainers are waiting loyally for his return. Once again peace is established in Hrothgar's hall, and the celebrations include the elaborate dispensing of gifts by Hrothgar to Beowulf. Beowulf and his men then return to their homeland, and Beowulf reports all the events of the journey to the Geatish king, his uncle Hygelac: (his report to Hygelac includes many details and reflections which were not given in the initial narrative). The narrative now switches suddenly to a time near the end of Beowulf's life, when, after succeeding to the Geatish throne, he had ruled the Geats for fifty years. Unfortunately, an unnamed Geat had stumbled accidentally upon a treasure that had been deposited many years before by a people who had subsequently vanished; the treasure was currently being guarded by a fire-breathing dragon. The man stole a cup from the treasure, and the dragon subsequently took vengeance on the Geats by flying about at night and burning their houses. It fell to old King Beowulf to deal with the dragon. He set out accompanied by a troop of retainers who were, however, too frightened to go with him to the dragon's lair (which is described in terms that suggest a Neolithic chambered tomb). Beowulf confronts the dragon and kills it, but receives a mortal wound. One of his retainers, a man of his own tribe named Wiglaf, comforts Beowulf in his last moments (the dying Beowulf utters a long speech in which he recalls many events of his earlier life, including an overseas raid that resulted in the death of his uncle, King Hygelac, supplying details which help, finally, to put the raid into perspective). The poem closes with the funeral of Beowulf, and with the sober, indeed frightening, realization that the Geats, now left without a courageous leader, will be prey to the aggressions of neighbouring peoples.

Even this simplified and abbreviated account of the narrative will indicate something of the complex structure of the poem: that all the events it describes are interlaced with reflections in such a way that their significance can only be grasped in retrospect, through contemplation. Its style is allusive and enigmatic: the poet invites meditation by avoiding explicit statement. The diction of the poem is compact and powerful, heightened by a rich poetic vocabulary, especially of compound nouns and adjectives, much of which is not attested elsewhere in Old English. The poem is preserved uniquely in a manuscript written *c.*1000 (now London, BL, Cotton Vitellius A. xv). Although, to judge from errors in the transmitted text, the surviving manuscript is evidently a copy of a poem composed earlier, there is no scholarly consensus on how much earlier: some see the poem as a product of the eighth century, others as a product of the tenth (or even early eleventh). The poem is deeply puzzling in many ways: what, for example, would be the most probable English audience for a poem wholly concerned with Scandinavian legend? But even if it is not possible to achieve scholarly consensus on such questions, opinion is unanimous that *Beowulf* is a rewarding, if difficult, poem that repays repeated reading with increased insight into the nature of human life and society.

*Beowulf and the Fight at Finnsburg*, F. Klaeber (ed.), 3rd ed., Boston, 1950.

D. Whitelock, *The Audience of Beowulf*, Oxford, 1951. – A. G. Brodeur, *The Art of Beowulf*, Berkeley, Los Angeles (CA), 1959. – E. B. Irving, *A Reading of Beowulf*, New Haven (CT), 1968. – J. D. Niles, *Beowulf: the Poem and its Tradition*, Cambridge (MA), 1983. – F. C. Robinson, *Beowulf and the Appositive Style*, Knoxville (TN), 1985. – A *Beowulf Handbook*, R. E. Bjork (ed.), J. D. Niles (ed.), Exeter, 1997.

Michael Lapidge

**BERENGAR OF TOURS (*c.*1000-1088).** Priest, **scholasticus* at *Tours, whose preaching provoked the important 11th-c. *Eucharistic controversy. Born at the start of the century, of a well-to-do family, he acquired a sound training in *grammar and *dialectic at *Chartres under *Fulbert. In 1032 he was a *canon of *Saint-Martin at Tours and *grammaticus* at the cathedral school, of which he soon became director. In *c.*1040 he also received the posts of *archdeacon and episcopal treasurer at Angers.

Beginning to teach Holy Scripture at Tours around 1048, he became enthusiastic about the eucharistic doctrine attributed to *John Scotus Eriugena and, on the eve of the Roman synod of 1050, he addressed a note to *Lanfranc, master of studies at the abbey of *Bec, reproaching him for judging John Scotus's opinion as heretical, though it had been condemned. The note was taken to *Rome where it caused a scandal. The synod presided over by *Leo IX condemned it as heretical and *excommunicated Berengar in his absence. Summoned to the synod of Vercelli the same year, he first sought support and instigated several conferences which all turned to his disadvantage. He tried to meet the king of France, Henry I, who handed him over to one of his household who held him captive to extort a *ransom, so that he was unable to appear at Vercelli, where Leo IX, likening his doctrine to that of John Scotus, once more branded him with *heresy.

Disgusted at the condemnations brought against him, he threw himself into frenetic attacks on the Church of Rome and the *pope, straining his ingenuity to prove that the eucharistic bread remained bread after the *consecration, and spreading trouble among the clergy in France and beyond. Freed late in 1050, he was defeated, humiliated and condemned at several synods. His doctrine, based on the rational evidence provided by *dialectic, caused scandal. He finally went to Rome at Hildebrand's suggestion and appeared at the synod of Lent 1059 presided over by *Nicholas II. It was his greatest humiliation. He had to throw his writings on the *Eucharist into the fire and pronounce a formula of *abjuration and a Catholic profession contrary to his own feelings. Back in France, he circulated a work *Contra Synodum*, which drew down on him a severe refutation from Lanfranc, against whom he wrote a defence of his own doctrine, vehement and injurious to his opponents, which Lessing rediscovered at Wolfenbüttel in 1770. It is there that we find the essence of his thought, rather than in the score of his *letters that survive. Summoned again to a Roman synod in 1079, he was forced to accept a Catholic formula that he could admit, and retired to Saint-Cosme where he died in apparent peace with the Church in 1088.

Beringerius Turonensis, *Rescriptum contra Lanfrannum*, R. B. C. Huyghens (ed.), *CChr.CM*, 84, 1988.

R.W. Southern, "Lanfranc of Bec and Berengar of Tours", *Studies in Medieval History Presented to Maurice Powicke*, R.W. Hunt (ed.), Oxford, 1948, 27-48. – J. de Montclos, *Lanfranc et Bérenger, la controverse eucharistique du XI^e siècle*, Louvain, 1971.

André Cantin

**BERGAMO.** Bergamo, a city in *Lombardy, strategically situated on the southernmost buttress of the Alpine foreland, between two rivers, the Adda and the Oglio, probably founded by Gauls but later a Roman *municipium*, was from the 4th c. the seat of a *bishopric and from the end of the 6th c. one of the most important duchies in Lombardy. The *Arian religion of the dominant social classes was supplanted in the 7th c. by Catholic Christianity. But the quarrel over precedence between the two *cathedrals of St

Interior of the church of San Tommaso in Limine at Almenno San Salvatore, near Bergamo. Early 12th c.

Alexander and St Vincent may well have its origin in the former coexistence of both confessions of faith. After *Charlemagne's victory over King *Desiderius (774), Bergamo became a county. However the bishop, to whom King Berengar also entrusted *temporal power in 904, maintained control of the town itself, while the interest of the counts was concentrated more on the territorial possessions adjoining the city. *De facto*, but not yet *de jure*, episcopal power ceased during the *Investiture Contest with the deposition of Bishop Arnulf, loyal to the emperor, at the synod of Milan in 1098. Then arose a *commune dominated by the aristocratic families, whose first *consules* are attested in 1108. Its traditional attitude in favour of the emperor was reversed during the conflict between *Frederick Barbarossa and the Italian towns (1154-1183). In 1167 Bergamo was one of the co-founders of the *Lombard League and no longer had privileged relations with the German Empire. Intestine rivalries appeared between Ghibelline (Suardi, Colleoni) and *Guelf (Rivola, Bonghi) families: the former favoured the landowners and the nobles; the latter supported the **popolo*, which included merchants and artisans. The rivalries were attenuated in the 1170s by the government of an external **podestà*, replaced each year. From 1230, the popular forces took power inside the town. The election in 1264 of the Milanese Filippo della Torre to this post for a duration of ten years marks the transition towards a signorial form of government, under the dependency of the powerful neighbouring town of *Milan, and marks the start of a long agony of the commune, exacerbated by an overt civil war in 1296. After the brief interlude of King John of Bohemia, elected *signore* in 1331, Bergamo was permanently under the *signoria* of the *Visconti of Milan from 1332, apart from the period of *Malatesta government between 1407 and 1419. Attempted risings by local families all ended in failure. In 1428, the rule of the Visconti was finally superseded by that of *Venice, which lasted until 1797.

The medieval extent of the town corresponded to the area of the *città alta*, surrounded on the summit of the hill by the Venetian wall built between 1560 and 1580; to it in the 13th c. were added *borghi* situated in the plain. The most important monument of the episcopal period is the Romanesque basilica of Santa Maria Maggiore. From the time of the commune dates the Palazzo della Ragione on the Piazza Vecchia. The fortress of the Rocca, east of the town, was built by John of Bohemia in 1331, while to the west the Citadel was built in 1335 by the first Visconti *signore*. A funerary chapel built between 1473 and 1476 commemorates Generalissimo Colleoni, who was in the service of Venice.

B. Belotti, *Storia di Bergamo e dei Bergamaschi*, 1-2, Bergamo, 1959 (2nd ed.). – J. Jarnut, *Bergamo 568-1098*, Wiesbaden, 1979. – C. Storti Storchi, *Diritto e istituzioni a Bergamo dal comune alla signoria*, Milan, 1984. – M. L. Scalvini, G. P. Calza, P. Finardi, *Bergamo*, Bari, 1987. – L. K. Little, *Liberty, Charity, Fraternity: Lay Religious Confraternities at Bergamo in the Age of the Commune*, Northampton (MA), 1988. – M. Blattmann, *Die Statutenbücher von Bergamo. Eine Kommune "erlernt" den Umgang mit geschriebenem Recht*, Munich, 1999.

Marita Blattmann

**BERGEN.** The town occupies a favoured *port site on the west coast of *Norway. According to the *Royal Sagas*, Bergen was founded by King Olaf Kyrri (1066-1093) at the foot of the Fløien massif, on the shore of a well-sheltered fjord, close to a royal estate (Alreksstad). There Olaf Kyrri built a first stone church destined to become the *cathedral. During the 12th c. the see of the *bishopric for West Norway (Vestland), initially fixed at Selja, was moved to Bergen. The *relics of St Sunniva were transferred on 7 Sept 1170. Before that, King Eysteinn Magnusson (1103-1123) had installed the first Norwegian monastery there (Benedictines of Munkeliv). Also established, around 1150, were two *Cistercian abbeys (monks, from *Fountains Abbey, at Lyse; *nuns at Nonneseter) and one of Augustinians (Jonsklostret, between 1150 and 1180). The rise of Bergen as a religious centre was impressive: In *c.*1200 there were already 11 churches, and in the 13th c. two new *convents (*Dominicans *c.*1230, *Franciscans in the second half of the century) and six more churches were built. In *c.*1320 there were 21 churches, five abbey churches, a chapel royal and three *hospices at Bergen. Such a concentration of religious institutions attests the importance acquired by the town. A royal residence from its origins, in the 13th c. Bergen became the real capital of the kingdom and the seat of the *chancery, under the reigns of Hákon Hákonarson (1217-1263), Magnus Lagaböter (1263-1280) and Eirik Magnusson (1280-1299). During this period were built a palace (Håkonshallen, begun in 1261) and a castle (of which the so-called Rosenkranz tower remains).

In the Middle Ages, Bergen was one of the main ports of Northern Europe for international *commerce. Norwegian navigators, especially active from the *Viking period in the direction of England, were gradually supplanted by German *merchants. The presence of the latter is discernible at Bergen from 1186 and we can see that from 1248 the supply of grain to the Norwegian West was carried on from *Lübeck. In 1250 the king of Norway granted a series of privileges to the Germans who frequented Bergen. In the 14th c. an important German establishment (Tyske Bryggen) developed at Bergen, well known to us through archaeological excavations starting in the 1950s. Situated immediately next to the port, on 400 metres of quays, it comprised some 30 concessions (*Höfen*). But the medieval *runic inscriptions exhumed at Bergen (some 350, carved on wood, many of which have a commercial character) attest that Norwegians, men and women, often organised into associations (*félag*), took part in the transactions. Bergen was one of the four counters of the *Hanse, and trade was controlled for the most part by the Lübeck *Bergenfahrer*, only a part of whom went to Bergen (*copgeselle to Bergen*) or lived there all year (*vintersittere*). In fact, in the 14th c. the habit grew up not just of coming to Norway between May and September, but of passing the winter there. Alongside the merchants, there were numerous German artisans at Bergen: many had their stalls in the main street (*Stretet*) of the town. Commerce was concentrated on four regions: England (Boston, Hull), Flanders (*Bruges), the Rhineland and the Baltic Sea (Lübeck, Rostock, *Gotland). Bergen's prosperity rested on its exports of dried cod (*skrei*) and fish-oil which represented 90 % of the total. The rest was made up of skins and butter. Imported were cereals, *textiles, *salt, *wine, beer, *spices, wax. Some practised a triangular commerce (flour from Lübeck to Bergen, dried fish from Bergen to Boston, cloth from Boston to Lübeck).

In the 14th c., the Lübeckers monopolized connections between Norway and England and the trading town of Boston depended on Bergen. Relations between the German merchants and the Norwegian monarchy were sometimes tense, particularly at the end of the 13th century. Following a royal ordinance reducing their commercial freedom (1282), the *Wend towns mounted a blockade of the Norwegian coasts (1284). In 1294, the Germans were forbidden to trade north of Bergen. Throughout the Middle Ages, the town was under the authority of a royal official (*gjaldkeri*) who presided over the local assembly (*mót*), but the authority of the municipal council was broadened in the 14th and 15th centuries. Moreover Bergen's central political role declined after 1299, the year when King Hákon V Magnusson (1299-1319) moved his chancery to Oslo. In the second half of the 15th c. the Hanseatic domination of Bergen began to be contested by the commercial aggressiveness of the Dutch, while Norwegian fish was rivalled on the European market by cod from *Iceland. Nevertheless, it is estimated that at the end of the Middle Ages, at Bergen, the value of dried cod exports reached 20,000 marks per year. At this time, the town numbered up to 7000 inhabitants (2000 of them Germans). At the time of the Reformation, most of the religious buildings were destroyed. There remains from the Romanesque period only the church of St Mary with its powerful west front.

P. Dollinger, *La Hanse*, Paris, 1964. – *Bjørgvin bispestol*, P. Juvkam (ed.), Oslo, 1968. – N. Bjørgo, "Det eldste Bergen", *Sjøfartshistorisk årbok*, Bergen, 1970, 53-130.

Jean-Marie Maillefer

**BERNARD DÉLICIEUX (died 1319).** Born at *Montpellier to an eminent family, Bernard Délicieux entered the *Franciscan Order in *c.*1284. *Reader at *Carcassonne, then at *Narbonne, he personified the broad intellectual opening up of the Languedocian milieu; he was close to Raymond *Lull and friendly with *Arnold of Villanova. Though primarily a man of action, his favourite instrument was the word. He occupied a central position in the political and religious history of *Languedoc at the start of the

14th century. From 1295 to 1304, he led the revolt of Carcassonne and *Albi against the *Inquisition. After this, for a long time he attended the *Curia to obtain his absolution, then settled at the convent of Béziers. Sensitive to Joachism and the influence of *Peter John Olivi, he adhered to the party of the *Spirituals, whom he defended at Avignon in 1317. In *John XXII he had a personal enemy who knew his earlier actions well and had him thrown in irons.

Bernard Délicieux successfully followed a pastoral policy of appealing to and meeting with the urban elites, a genuine mission field in late 13th-c. Languedoc. But in 1317, *heresy had practically disappeared, the papacy was "French" and the role of the Inquisition was to support monarchical power. New structures were prevailing in Church and in State. Condemned to close imprisonment in Dec 1319, Bernard Délicieux died two months later in the *prison of Carcassonne.

B. Hauréau, *Bernard Délicieux et l'Inquisition albigeoise*, Paris, 1877. – J.-L. Biget, "Autour de Bernard Délicieux", *RHEF*, 1984. – A. Friedlander, "Jean XXII et les Spirituels. Le cas Bernard Délicieux", *CFan*, 26, 1991. – A. Friedlander, *Processus Bernardi Delitiosi: The Trial of Fr. Bernard Délicieux, 3 September – 8 December 1313*, Philadelphia, 1996.

Jean-Louis Biget

**BERNARD GUI (*c.*1261-1331).** Born at Royère in Limousin, to a family of lesser nobility, Bernard Gui took the habit in Sept 1279 with the Friars Preachers of *Limoges and then followed the cycle of higher studies proper to the order, which he completed in 1291 at *Montpellier rather than at Paris, sign of a strong, if not creative, mind.

He became a pillar of his order, *reader at Limoges and *Albi (1291-1294), prior at Albi, *Carcassonne, Castres and Limoges (1294-1307) and preacher general from 1302, inquisitor for *Toulouse from Jan 1307 to 1324, except in 1316-1319 when he was procurer general of the Preachers at *Avignon. Between 1321 and 1324 he composed an *Inquisitor's Manual* which developed and systematized previous treatises. The *Book of Sentences* of the Toulouse *Inquisition for the years 1305-1323 allows us to see his methods. He paid as much attention to mercy as to punishment: out of 980 sentences, he handed over only 42 people to the *secular arm. He excluded from *penance and reconciliation only those who relapsed or who died hardened in *heresy.

In 1323 *John XXII made Bernard Gui bishop of Tuy in Galicia, transferred to Lodève in July 1324. Promotion, but to meagre *bishoprics: Bernard did not belong to the world of the great dynasties of bishops and cardinals of Gascony, Languedoc and Quercy. He showed himself an excellent administrator of his *diocese. He restored the spiritual discipline of his flock and his clergy by pastoral *visits, synodal *statutes and regular meetings of priests. In the temporal sphere, he showed himself anxious to assert his rights and defend his lordship over the town against the inhabitants and the king's men.

He died on 30 Dec 1331, and was buried in the church of the Preachers at Limoges near the high altar. Bernard Gui appears a man of certainties, who practised *obedience, revered *authority and judged that of the pope to be self-evident. He is a perfect example of the senior "field officers" who enabled the Church and the papacy to surmount the turbulence of the late 13th and the first third of the 14th century. A happy man too, who confided to his friends that a wise man should rejoice at least five times a day.

His originality lies in his role as chronographer, historian and hagiographer, impressive in his fecundity. He was a man of pen and book much more than of words. He built a monument to the glory of his order. After 1311, he went over to universal *history and drew up a great work which he completed in 1316 under the title *Flores chronicorum*. At the same time he established the succession of the *popes, emperors and kings of *France. He returned to local history in order to exalt the Limousin through its religious history.

His position as procurer general led him to write a life of St *Thomas Aquinas, whose *canonization trial began in 1318, and a catalogue of the great theologian's works. Then he began a *Speculum sanctorale* ("Mirror of the saints") which he finished in 1329. These major works circulated widely in the 14th and 15th centuries. *Charles V of France had some 15 of them translated.

Bernard Gui shows the qualities of a good historian, with awakened critical faculties. He believed in the progress of scholarship according to its own proper procedures and, in the *convents he passed through, he never ceased to revise the manuscripts of his own works. In this respect he left a fertile inheritance.

A. Thomas, "Bernard Gui, frère Prêcheur", *HLF*, 35, Paris, 1921, 139-232. – "Bernard Gui et son monde", *CFan*, 16, 1981. – B. Guenée, "Bernard Gui (1261-1331)", *Entre l'Église et l'État. Quatre vies de prélats français à la fin du Moyen Âge (XIII*e*-XV*e *siècle)*, Paris, 1987, 49-85.

Jean-Louis Biget

**BERNARD OF CLAIRVAUX (1090-1153).** St Bernard was born at Fontaine-lès-Dijon (some kilometres north of *Dijon). His father was a knight of modest rank, his mother, Aleth de Montbard, was of a lineage prestigious both in *Burgundy and in *Champagne. Third of seven children, he was deeply influenced in childhood by his mother, whom he lost at the age of 16 or 17. Destined to be a *cleric, he received a good literary education with the secular *canons of Châtillon-sur-Seine.

Around the age of twenty, he decided to enter the monastery of *Cîteaux, founded in 1098 by Robert of Molesme to the south of Dijon, where the most arduous monastic *ascesis was practised, in a strict return to the *Benedictine Rule, far from the turmoils of the world. He convinced his brothers and close relations to "convert" with him. In April 1112 (or May 1113), Bernard arrived at Cîteaux with thirty companions. In June 1115, he was sent to Champagne with a dozen monks to found the abbey of *Clairvaux in the Val d'Absinthe on the bank of the Aube, not far from *Troyes. Viscerally attached to his community, Bernard remained *abbot of Clairvaux all his life, refusing any other dignity in the Church. For fifteen years, Bernard dedicated himself to the development of Clairvaux. At his death, the Order of Cîteaux numbered 345 monasteries, 167 of them dependent on Clairvaux.

Thanks to his charisma and personal prestige, as well as his power of conviction and his rhetorical skill, rather than to the importance of the position he held, he widened his field of action: he arbitrated in conflicts between lords, and opposed the intrusion of lay princes (including the king of France) into the affairs of the Church. He supported the first *Templars. His influence increased at the time of the schism of *Anacletus, against whom Bernard chose *Innocent II whom he judged to be a better *pope. For eight years, from 1130 to 1138, the abbot struggled to impose him: he succeeded, at the cost of ceaseless journeys and manifold interventions. Having gained in prestige and authority, Bernard then advanced on all fronts. Where he saw a fault in the Church, he felt himself obliged to interfere: "None of God's affairs is foreign to me", he said (Letter 20). He suffered from it: "I am the chimaera of my age, neither cleric nor layman. I have abandoned the life of a monk, but I still wear the habit . . ." (Letter 250).

He was upheld by an indestructible energy, despite fragile health, and a passionate character, sometimes vehement and authoritarian. But, passing from causes to individuals, he could be tender: he recommended kindness to the countess of Blois, who questioned him about the *education of her son. He ceaselessly intervened in vacancies and episcopal elections to support the candidate whom he considered as having the better moral level; we can count 17 interventions of this type, some of them stormy, as at Langres (1137-1138) or at *York (1140-1147). He did not hesitate to give advice to prelates, encouraging them to fulfil their obligations and criticizing the luxury of their way of life. The rise of urban schools in which *logic was applied to revealed truths worried him: when he addressed the Parisian students in 1140, it was to turn them away from their studies towards Clairvaux. Soon after, he got *Abelard and his disciple *Arnold of Brescia condemned by Rome. His attempts were not all crowned with success: discovering the progress of the *Cathar heresy, he went to *Languedoc in 1145: it was a failure; in 1148, he tried in vain to obtain the condemnation of the theologian *Gilbert of Poitiers. Bernard rallied to the project of a new *crusade, for him an occasion for pardoning sins: he preached it on 31 March 1146 at *Vézelay. In the Rhine valley, a monk unleashed the people against the Jewish communities. Bernard went there and put an end to the massacres: for him, the Jewish people was the bearer of Jesus' humanity. The defeat of the crusade (which he did not accompany) affected him. He withdrew to Clairvaux and dedicated himself to Scripture and the revision of his works. In spring 1153, he set out, ill, for *Metz to restore peace there. He died in his abbey, 20 August 1153, aged 63. Canonized in 1174, he was proclaimed a *Doctor of the Church in 1830.

This man "all-powerful despite himself and condemned to govern Europe" (J. Michelet) was above all a monk, a bearer of exacting demands. Luther would praise him for it. Bernard wanted to go back to the sources of *monasticism, in a ceaseless quest for purity and rigour. Hence his wish to free his order's monasteries from the lay world and give them material independence. Hence this innovative renunciation that prevailed in Cistercian art, as witness the architectural achievement of the monasteries. Bernard was also a mystical theologian of importance. His writings (*letters, sometimes in the form of *treatises, *sermons) flowed directly from his activities as abbot and pastor; apart from the letters, whose recipients were various, Bernard wrote for monks.

Nourished by biblical, patristic and classical culture, his work is sometimes baffling, and demands attentive reading. The importance of Scripture is seen particularly in his sermons, intended to comment on a precise biblical text, as witness the magnificent collection of *Sermons on the *Song of Songs*. Bernard's style is powerful and original (it would often be copied), thanks to a mixture of spontaneity, lyricism and literary reminiscences. Bernard's mystical theology applies primarily to the monk. The aim of the monastic life is union with *God and *ecstasy; and this by a gradual process passing through two great stages: *meditation or consideration, in the gradual search for truth (purification, self-examination, struggle against sins); then *contemplation which supposes recollection, purity, *prayer and possession of all the *virtues. Foremost in this quest are the themes of self-knowledge, in a veritable "Christian Socratism" (Étienne Gilson), and *man's responsibility in his actions.

The doctrine of the *image and likeness is primary: God has made man in his image and likeness (Gen 1, 26) but, though the image remains the same, *sin has installed man in a "region of unlikeness"; but the likeness can be partially restored by man – thanks to the action of *Christ – and will be so totally in *paradise. If the union of God with man requires an intermediary, Jesus, and the support of the *Holy Spirit, it is done in the *love of God ("The reason for loving God, is God. The measure of loving him, is to love him without measure" [*De diligendo Deo*, I, 1]). If the Virgin occupies a restricted place in Bernard's work (at Lyon, the saint even opposed the institution of a feast in honour of her conception), she is evoked with fervour, as iconography would testify – notably by the theme of lactation.

The centuries that followed the saint's death remembered him as the mystical doctor and the theologian of union with God. The 16th-c. reformers praised the rigorous monk and his criticisms of the papacy. In the 18th c., the mystical vein was prolonged by a sugary iconography of the "Mellifluous Doctor" and the devotee of the Virgin; meanwhile the philosophers of the Enlightenment saw him as a fanatic urging men to massacre on the crusading routes. The 19th century gave his character an even more negative aspect: he was seen as the enemy of reason, the tormentor of Abelard. "What then was St Bernard's work? The opposition of a man of genius to the currents that swept his century along", wrote A. Luchaire severely in 1901 in Lavisse's *Histoire de France*. If recent works still insist on Bernard's conservatism ("Patron of already lost causes", wrote Jacques Le Goff in 1964, "he was the great spiritual interpreter of *feudalism"), his activities and his works appear more and more complex and still demand all the attention of historians.

*The Letters of St Bernard of Clairvaux*, B. Scott James (ed.), London, 1953 (re-ed. Stroud, 1998). – *Sancti Bernardi Opera*, L. Leclercq (ed.), H. Rochais (ed.), C. H. Talbot (ed.), Rome, 1957-1977 (8 vol.). – Bernard of Clairvaux, *On the Song of Songs*, K. Walsh (ed.), I. Edmonds (ed.), Kalamazoo (MI), 1979-1983 (4 vol.). – Bernard, *Sermons pour l'année*, P.-Y. Emery (tr.), Turnhout, 1990 (Fr. tr. under way in "SC").

A. Vacandart, *Vie de saint Bernard, abbé de Clairvaux*, Paris, 1895-1910 (2 vol.). – É. Gilson, *The Mystical Theology of Saint Bernard*, Kalamazoo (MI), 1990. – *Bernard de Clairvaux*, Paris, 1953. – J. Verger, J. Jolivet, *Bernard-Abélard ou le cloître et l'école*, Paris, 1982. – G. R. Evans, *The Mind of St. Bernard of Clairvaux*, Oxford, 1983. – M. Casey, *Athirst for God*, Kalamazoo (MI), 1988. – G. Duby, *Saint Bernard. L'art cistercien*, Paris, 1989 (1st ed. 1976). – J. Leclercq, *Bernard de Clairvaux*, Paris, 1989. – M.-M. Davy, *Bernard de Clairvaux*, Paris, 1990 (1st ed. 1945). – *Saint Bernard et le monde cistercien*, L. Pressouyre (dir.), T. N. Kinder (dir.), Paris, 1990-1992. – B. P. McGuire, *The Difficult Saint Bernard of Clairvaux and his Tradition*, Kalamazoo (MI), 1991. – *Bernard de Clairvaux. Histoire, mentalités, spiritualité*, *SC*, 380, Paris, 1992. – *Vies et légendes de saint Bernard. Création, diffusion, réception*, J. Berlioz (ed.), Cîteaux, 1993. – M. B. Pranger, *Bernard of Clairvaux and the Shape of Monastic Thought*, Leiden, 1994. – A. H. Bredero, *Bernard of Clairvaux. Culte et histoire*, Turnhout, 1998.

Jacques Berlioz

**BERNARD OF PARMA (died 1266).** This *canonist played an important role in the doctrinal promotion of pontifical law (*ius novum*). His *gloss on the *Decretals became in effect the *Glossa ordinaria*. For this work, which occupied him up to the end of his life, he used all the earlier glosses; but he referred mainly to Alan, Bernard of Compostela the Elder, *Lawrence and Vincent of Spain, as well as to Tancred, whose teaching he had followed at *Bologna.

Though this major *oeuvre* is characterised by clarity of exposition, we do not find real legal theories developed in it. That task would fall to the *Decretalists immediately following, notably *Hostiensis.

P. Ourliac, *DDC*, 2, 1937, 781-782. – G. Le Bras, C. Lefebvre, J. Rambaud, *L'Age classique (1140-1378). Sources et théories du droit, HDIEO*, 7, 1965.

Jacques Krynen

**BERNARD OF PAVIA (died 1213).** Trained at *Bologna, where he taught for some time, then bishop of Faenza and finally of *Pavia, this *canonist was one of the main architects of the classical law of the Church.

His *Breviarium extravagantium*, which brings together texts of old law omitted by Gratian and the recent *Decretals, is presented as complementary to the **Decretum*. Though never obtaining official recognition, it enjoyed considerable popularity: it held the place of *Compilatio prima*. His *Summa decretalium*, more than its title indicates, is a veritable *summa of canon law in which the Decretals do not occupy the essential place. The merit of these works consists in the methodical classification of extracts and the clear presentation of subjects. By this desire to systematize and put in order, Bernard of Pavia had in view not just the profit of students but also that of the Church, which then had a law available to it that was technically equivalent to the codifications of Justinian. Bernard of Pavia wrote other works, most of them edited entire.

G. le Bras, *DDC*, 2, 1937, 782-789. – G. le Bras, C. Lefebvre, J. Rambaud, *L'Age classique (1140-1378). Sources et théories du droit, HDIEO*, 7, 1965.

Jacques Krynen

**BERNARD OF TIRON (*c.*1046-1117).** St Bernard was born near Abbeville. A brilliant student, he entered the abbey of Saint-Cyprien at *Poitiers, then became prior of *Saint-Savin. On the death of the abbot, he refused to succeed him and fled to the forests of Maine. There he led an eremitical life, in contact with other solitaries. To escape the solicitations of his monks, he had to go to the Isle of Chausey. In turn, the abbot of Saint-Cyprien sought him out to succeed him at the head of the abbey. In 1100, Bernard was present at the council of Poitiers with *Robert of Arbrissel. *Cluny was claiming rights over Saint-Cyprien. Bernard resisted and was put under *interdict. He profited from this to rejoin the hermits of Maine and undertook great preaching tours. In a blazing sermon at Coutances, he incited *clerics to separate from their wives. At the request of his monks, Bernard went to Rome to defend the rights of Saint-Cyprien against Cluny. He obtained satisfaction, but came into conflict with his brethren because of the excessive rigour of his monastic *reform. Though supported by Rome, he abandoned his monastery. In 1109 he founded a new establishment near Nogent-le-Rotrou. Once more in conflict with Cluny, with the help of *Ivo of Chartres he created the monastery of the Holy Trinity of Tiron (now Thiron, Eure-et-Loir). Supported and richly endowed by the reigning dynasties and comital families, the congregation of Tiron experienced remarkable growth and threw off many abbeys and *priories. Bernard died in 1117.

His life, written by his disciple Geoffroy le Gros, has been the object of contradictory judgments. It is a text of exceptional wealth on the eremitical and monastic life at the turn of the 11th-12th centuries. Bernard appears in it not just as an intransigent and touchy Benedictine reformer, but also as an architect of the wider *Gregorian reform, insofar as this was also an application of the monastic model to the *secular clergy.

J. von Walter, *Die ersten Wanderprediger Frankreichs. Studien zur Geschichte des Mönchtums*, 2, Leipzig, 1906. – *L'eremitismo in Occidente nei secoli XI e XII*, Milan, 1965. – J. de Bascher, "La 'Vita' de saint Bernard d'Abbeville, abbé de Saint-Cyprien de Poitiers et de Tiron", *RMab*, 59, 1979-1980, 411-450.

Jacques Dalarun

**BERNARDINO OF FELTRE (1439-1494).** The *Franciscan preacher Martino Tomitano was born at Feltre to a well-off, cultivated family where he received an excellent education. He had begun to study law at the university of *Padua when he chose to enter the Order of Observant Friars Minor in 1456, under the name of Bernardino. Having completed his theological studies, he was ordained priest at Venice in 1463, then designated as preacher in 1469. From then on, he travelled ceaselessly through northern and central *Italy, barefoot and in the greatest privation, despite a fragile constitution. We have 23 complete sets of his lenten *sermons, between 1470 and 1494, as well as abundant *preaching for *Advent and ordinary Sundays. With vehement eloquence, he attacked luxury in *clothing and social injustice. To fight against the ravages produced among the poorest by loans at usurious rates, he founded at Mantua in 1484 the first **Monte di Pietà*, an institution that spread rapidly in the great towns of northern Italy. He died at *Pavia, where his remains are preserved in the church of San Giacomo-extra-Muros. From the first, the town and region venerated him as a saint, but his cult was only approved in 1654 by Innocent X.

*ActaSS, Septembris VII*, Antwerp, 1760, 874-983.

G. Barbieri, *Introduzione ai Sermoni del beato Bernardino Tomitano da Feltre*, Milan, 1964. – V. Meneghin, *Bernardino da Feltre e i Monti di Pietà*, Vicenza, 1974.

Dominique Rigaux

**BERNARDINO OF SIENA (1380-1444).** Bernardo degli Abizzeschi, born at *Siena, died at l'Aquila, was one of the greatest *Franciscan preachers of the Middle Ages and a dominant figure of the Observant *reform. He exercised his charitable activities and his apostolate in all the great towns of northern and central *Italy in the first half of the 15th century.

Son of a powerful family of Siena, he was orphaned very early; his paternal uncle took care to give him a sound humanist and legal education. However, his girl-cousin and his grandmother greatly developed his mystical temperament. He was part of a *confraternity of *disciplinati* (*penitents) when the plague was declared at Siena in 1400; he took over the direction of the hospital and co-ordinated the help of the sick. He subsequently decided to enter religion; on 8 Sept 1402, after some hesitations, he chose the reformed branch of the *Observance, more ascetic, of the *Franciscan Order; he was ordained priest in 1404. From the first his superiors recognised his oratorical talents and gave him a mission to preach. He preached his first lenten cycle at Siena in 1406.

From 1408 to 1427, he dedicated himself entirely to itinerant *preaching and travelled all through the Italy of the communes. Little by little, his reputation was established and his success became considerable: the citizens came by hundreds to hear his *sermons in the public square, which sometimes lasted three hours. We possess living proof in the 45 sermons which a Sienese cloth-shearer took down in 1427. The vigour of his moral teaching, expounded with vivacity, humour and sometimes asperity, aroused numerous conversions and provoked the urban authorities to issue statutes against luxury and gaming. Bernardino was always attentive to the condition of his audience when he demanded the reform of morals. He showed himself particularly subtle on the problem of *usury and commercial profits. He strove especially to restore civil peace in towns torn apart by factional conflicts.

His political influence was great; the dukes of Milan and Urbino, the Emperor *Sigismund of Luxemburg consulted him and he preached the crusade against the *Turks. The Dominican preacher Manfred of Vercelli, jealous of his success, accused him of *heresy (1423); but he managed without difficulty to justify his orthodoxy at Rome. At the same time, he continued to organise the Franciscan Observance, of which he became vicar general after having recognised the impossibility of a reunification of the order for which he had hoped. In 1444, the observants were established in 230 *convents. At his death, he was considered one of the greatest saints in Italy. His *canonization was solemnly proclaimed by *Nicholas V at Pentecost in the *jubilee year of 1450.

*Acta SS, Maii V*, Antwerp, 1685, 257-318. – *S. Bernardini Senensis Opera Omnia*, Quaracchi, 1950-1965 (9 vol.).

C. Piana, "I processi di canonizzazione su la vita di San Bernardino da Siena", *AFH*, 44, 1951, 87-160 and 383-435. – R. Manselli, "Bernardino da Siena", *DBI*, 1960, 215-226. – I. Origo, *The World of St Bernardino*, London, 1963. – *Bernardino predicatore nelle società del suo tempo*, *CCSSM*, 1976. – F. Mormando, *The Preacher's Demons. Bernardino of Siena and the Social Underworld of Early Renaissance Italy*, Chicago, 1999.

Philippe Jansen

**BERNOLD OF CONSTANCE (1054-1100).** A disciple of Bernard of Constance, the monk Bernold of Constance, probably son of a married *cleric, composed numerous works, historical, polemical and theological. His *chronicles are one of our best sources of knowledge of the pontificates of *Gregory VII and *Urban II. He remains famous for his vigorous defence of the papal prerogatives in the quarrel between the *priesthood and the *Empire. Bernold claimed that the *pope was competent to depose princes and *excommunicate them; he could also release subjects from their *oath of loyalty sworn to the penalized prince: the oath being sworn in consideration of the office held by the prince, it automatically lost its object if the prince was deprived of his office.

W. Hartmann, "Bernold von Konstanz", *LdM*, 1, 1980, 2007-2008.

Brigitte Basdevant-Gaudemet

**BERTHOLD OF REGENSBURG (*c.*1210-1272).** A *Franciscan close to the Joachites, companion of *David of Augsburg, he was the most important medieval preacher in the German language and was the object of a popular cult from his death (he bears the title of *beatus* in his order). His main work was his *sermons, preached generally in German before immense crowds, mainly in the south of the Empire and in Hungary. Resorting to anecdotes, **exempla*, proverbs, puns, dialect forms, etc., mastering innumerable rhetorical techniques, scrutinizing the techniques of heretical preaching, Berthold's sermons – many of which were transcribed – were not just particularly well adapted to their use and hence effective, but moreover constitute for the historian a remarkable mine of information on the popular culture of the time. Pope *Urban IV turned these gifts to the advantage of the crusade, instructing Berthold and *Albert the Great to preach it.

*DHGE*, 8, 1935, 980-987. – *DSp*, 1, 1937, 1532-1533. – *LdM*, 1, 1980, 2035-2036. – *NDB*, 2, 1955, 164-165.

Joseph Morsel

**BERTRAND DU POUJET (*c.*1280-1352).** Born at Castelnau-Montratier (Lot), a *familiaris* of the future *John XXII who made him *cardinal of the *titulus* of San Marcello on 18 December and appointed him *legate in Italy (1319). He did not set out until the following year; his mission took place in Lombardy (1320-1326), then in Romagna and Emilia (1327-1334). In the struggle the papacy was waging against the Ghibellines, he excommunicated Matteo *Visconti and then put Milan under an *interdict, but he could not continue military operations. Promoted bishop of Ostia (1327), in Romagna he brought back under the obedience of the Church Modena, Parma and finally Bologna where he settled his residence and where the *pope thought of establishing himself. But a project to create a kingdom for John of Bohemia alarmed the Romagnols; the papal armies were defeated and the legate had to flee in 1334. He died at *Avignon.

G. Mollat, *DHGE*, 8, 1935, 1068-1074. – P. Jugie, "Un Quercynois à la cour pontificale d'Avignon", *CFan*, 26, 1991, 69-95.

Anne-Marie Hayez

**BESANÇON.** Main *oppidum* of the Sequani, Besançon occupies a natural defensive site whose exceptional position was noted by Julius Caesar, with its citadel and the enclosed bend of the Doubs. At the time when the *civitas Vesontiensium* became, under Diocletian (284-305), metropolis of the *Provencia maxima Sequanorum*, Christianity, brought from *Lyon by Sts Ferreolus and Ferjeux, was already implanted in the town: a bishop named Pancharius subscribed to the council of Cologne in 346, while a century later the prelate held the rank of *metropolitan. Spared by the great *invasions, the city suffered more from the colonization of the *Alamanni (after 450), revealed by a discontinuity in the episcopal list. Under the Merovingians, the town kept its cramped Late Imperial appearance, with a **civitas* falling back on the slopes of Mont Saint-Étienne, and the vast *suburbium* of the bend so lightly occupied that two Columbanusian monasteries easily settled there in the early 7th c. (Saint-Paul and Jussamoutier).

Not until the Carolingian period did Besançon, then baptized *Chrysopolis*, take on more importance with an episcopal group established on the site of the present *cathedral of Saint-Jean, a quarter for the *chapter, and a mint. It seems hardly to have been affected by the political partitions, nor even by the formation of the kingdom of *Burgundy into which it was integrated. However, when this latter fell under German subinfeudation (1032), its *archbishop and then the count of Burgundy became the favoured instruments of imperial influence in Burgundy. A great reforming prelate alongside the Emperor *Henry III and Pope *Leo IX, Hugh of Salins (1031-1066) is considered a new founder of the town, whose lordship he obtained.

From this period emerged most of the institutions that would last beyond the Middle Ages: those of the *diocese with its thousand *parishes, its 15 deaneries and archdeaconries (reduced to 5 in 1253); those of the town with its half-dozen parishes, its two cathedrals (Saint-Jean and Saint-Étienne), to which were added two *abbeys (Saint-Paul, Saint-Vincent), a *collegiate church and a *priory. While the urban network intensified in the Bend from the 12th to the 14th c., while the *mendicant orders settled there early (3 *convents before 1250) and *hospital structures were consolidated with the Order of the Holy Spirit, communal agitation called in question the archbishop's *temporal power over the town. The Bisontine *commune, officially recognised by the emperor in 1290, henceforth ceaselessly increased its pressure, supported by the dukes of Burgundy. The struggles thus arising form a contrast with the town's apparent stability in other spheres: its ten thousand inhabitants divided among 7 quarters were more inclined to agricultural (*vines) than to artisanal or commercial activities; on the religious level, the sole novelty of the late Middle Ages came from the settlement of a convent of *Carmelites (1392) and the installation of St *Colette (1410), who made Besançon the centre of her reforming activities.

*Histoire de Besançon*, C. Fohlen (dir.), Paris, 1961 (2 vol.; re-ed. 1981). – *Besançon et Saint-Claude*, M. Rey (dir.), 1977 ("HDF").

René Locatelli

**BESSARION (1399/1400-1472).** Born at *Trebizond to a modest family, the young Bessarion was noticed by metropolitan Dositheus, who took him with him to *Constantinople in *c.*1415. There he studied *rhetoric and philosophy under the direction of John Chortasmenos and George Chrysococces. He took the monastic habit under the name Bessarion in 1423, and was ordained priest in 1431. From 1431 to 1436, he lived at *Mistra in the Peloponnese, where he furthered his philosophical studies with *Gemistus Plethon. He returned to Constantinople at the wish of the Emperor John VIII *Palaeologus who wanted to send him to the council of Ferrara-*Florence. He was appointed metropolitan of Nicaea in 1437, the year he embarked for Italy. He was one of the main orators of the Greek delegation, whom he led to subscribe to the *union and put an end to the schism, 6 July 1439, despite the opposition of Mark Eugenicus, metropolitan of Ephesus. After this rally, he returned to the Byzantine capital in 1440 for a brief stay, during which he learned of his elevation to the cardinalate and his appointment as titular of the Twelve Apostles, 18 Dec 1439. He was back in *Florence a year later and took part in the union of the other Eastern Churches. By now a *Catholic, he became an eminent member of the Roman hierarchy. He settled at *Rome when Pope *Eugenius IV transferred the council there in 1443, and built a house near the church of the Twelve Apostles which became one of the great centres of *humanism. Very active for the last thirty years of his life, he never forgot his Greek origin.

He multiplied diplomatic initiatives for a *crusade to be organised against the *Turks who threatened his country. After the fall of Constantinople in 1453, he obtained the meeting of a congress at *Mantua (1459-1460) in the presence of Pope *Pius II; but his project was not carried out, due to the lack of real eagerness of the princes of the West to make war in the East. In 1463, after the capture of Trebizond and his appointment as *Latin patriarch of Constantinople, he redoubled his efforts and pressed *Venice to intervene, her overseas possessions being more and more threatened. His project was on the point of succeeding and he joined the fleet of Pius II, who had put himself at the head of the crusade, when the latter died in July 1464. Bessarion made a final effort to stir up the necessary forces to save *Greece. He wrote to the princes of Italy, and Pope *Sixtus IV sent him as *legate to *Louis XI to obtain his help. On his return from this mission, he died at *Ravenna, 18 Nov 1472.

Though he had twice been an unsuccessful candidate for the pontifical see (1455, 1471), Bessarion was a precious agent of the pope, governor at Bologna from 1450 to 1455, ambassador in Germany in 1460. But, opposed to a drift of the papal power towards monarchy, he tried to limit it at the time of the election of Paul III. His position in the *Curia allowed him to attempt a reform of the Greek-rite monasteries in southern Italy and Sicily. In 1446, he was present at the general *chapter of the Order of St Basil that decided on the sending of an apostolic visitor, which was done in 1456 when he was appointed abbot of *Grottaferrata. He sought to restore discipline and the teaching of Greek.

But his greatest success was in his literary activity. Author of works of *theology in favour of the Latin thesis of the procession of the *Holy Spirit, he distinguished himself particularly in *philosophy in the *In calumniatorem Platonis*, where he defended Plato's philosophy while alleviating the polemic between *Neoplatonists and Aristotelians. In order to make known the cultural heritage of ancient Greece, he undertook, with his collaborators George of Trebizond and then Niccolò Perotti, to translate numerous texts like the works of St Basil, the *Memorabilia* of Xenophon and the *Metaphysics* of *Aristotle. With Lorenzo *Valla, he sought to establish a method of textual criticism. He was also a great collector of *books. He bought and had copied as many works as possible in Greek and Latin, and thus assembled the richest *library of his time. After his death, its thousand or so books constituted the kernel of the Bibliotheca Marciana at Venice.

H. Vast, *Le cardinal Bessarion (1403-1472)*, Paris, 1878. – L. Mohler, *Kardinal Bessarion als Theologe, Humanist und Staatsmann*, Paderborn, 1923-1942 (2nd ed. 1967, 3 vol.). – L. Labowski, *DBI*, 9, 1967. –*Il Cardinale Bessarione nel V centenario della morte (1472-1972)*, *MF*, 73, July-December 1973. – L. Labowski, *Bessarion's Library and the Bibliotheca Marciana*, Rome, 1979. – G. Fiaccadori, *Bessarione e l'Umanesimo, Catalogo della Mostra, Venezia, Biblioteca Nazionale Marciana (27 aprile - 31 maggio 1994)*, Naples, 1994. – J. Monfasani, *Byzantine Scholars in Renaissance Italy*, Aldershot, 1995.

Claudine Delacroix-Besnier

**BEVERLEY.** St John of Beverley founded the church (where he was buried in 721) at the end of the 7th c., but, destroyed by the Danes in 867, it was refounded by King Æthelstan in *c.*934. The magnificent *collegiate church that still stands was built between 1120 and 1240; at the time it was served by a dozen *canons and some 30 *clerics, ruled by a *provost. St John's tomb drew many *pilgrims, and the church exercised a great influence over the whole of northern England. But Beverley (Yorkshire) was also a town of 4000 inhabitants in 1377 (the tenth largest in England) and a centre of the wool industry, whose municipal history was very eventful (troubles of 1381-1382).

R. B. Dobson, "The Risings in York, Beverley and Scarborough 1380-1381", R. H. Hilton, T. H. Alston, *The English Rising of 1381*, Cambridge, 1984.

Jean-Philippe Genet

**BIBLE**

**History.** One of the most impressive manifestations of the Christianization of the Western world is the impregnation of space and mentalities by the Bible: medieval art (sculpture, *architecture), the "scripture of the unlettered", narrated the Bible; the stories of the Old and New Testaments gradually replaced pagan folklore and constituted a new fund of narrative from which medieval man drew rules of life, consolation and models. But above all, the Bible was a written text, constantly studied and providing the cleric not just with the basis of his *doctrine but also with an infinite repertoire of examples which served to illustrate his positions. This survey will separate the Bible of the *laity from that of the learned, giving first place to the latter, since for the people of the Middle Ages it was a "text".

**The Bible of the learned.** It was a book, or rather books: one of the terms that designated it up to the 12th c., *Bibliotheca*, clearly indicates that it continued to be the collection of *codices* (about ten) that it had been in the early centuries. Groupings gradually came about (Heptateuch), and single-volume bibles (*pandects*) appeared. The unity of the whole was felt, both in ideas and in presentation; the term *Biblia* (passing into the singular) was ultimately used. From the rich decorated manuscripts of the early Middle Ages to the "pocket bibles" of 13th-c. Parisian students, the Bible became a book (and no longer just the Book, bearer of the divine word and hence requiring to be worthy, in the richness of its appearance, of that word), object of attentive study and no longer just of sacred reading. Not that the content underwent any kind of desacralization: all through the Middle Ages it remained *holy scripture*, *pagina sacra*, terms which, as we will see, were not without ambiguity in the 13th century.

The Bible of the Christian West was a Latin bible; from the 12th c., vernacular translations were made (of the *Psalter in particular) for the use of rich laymen or the lower classes; for a moment these caused the Church some anxiety: "Romance" translations served to support heretical preaching. Though the wave of translation proceeded without causing further disquiet (when the translations incorporated the teaching of the manuals: *Peter Comestor's *Historia Scholastica*, Peter Riga's *Aurora*), for *clerics the sole text of reference was the Latin *Vulgate, due in great part to St Jerome, who, translating the Old Testament directly from the Hebrew and revising the New Testament from the Greek, brought about the abandonment of the Old Latin translations clearly present in the earlier Latin *Fathers and still in use in the liturgy (in the greater part of the West, the Psalter continued to be read in the version *iuxta LXX*, though revised by Jerome). Ceaselessly recopied, sometimes contaminated by the old translations, the text was periodically revised. At the start of the 13th c. it was stabilized: a text of middling quality was adopted by the university of *Paris, provoking the sarcasm of *Roger Bacon and leading to an important critical labour, origin of the "*correctories of the Bible".

The Bible was at the centre of teaching in the Middle Ages. On the most elementary level, the Psalter was the text from which they learned to read (the tradition continued: in the 12th and 13th cc., it was still with the *Psalms that Christians began Hebrew). But above all, on a higher level, the Bible was commented on and expounded. In the first part of the Middle Ages (up to the 12th c.), monastic (private) reading was nourished on biblical commentaries; we have but little information on the conditions in which the Bible was taught to monks. From the 12th c., urban (episcopal, chapter-) *schools gave the best of their time to the study of the Bible, as witness the examples of the Victorines, *Robert of Melun or the Parisian masters of the end of the century; the biblical text was studied for its own sake, but the masters began to develop the theological questions aroused by certain passages. With the rise of the *universities, the study of the Bible took a scientific and systematic turn; in the *faculty of theology, the Bible was the major text, before and after the **Sentences* of *Peter Lombard: at an elementary degree, the biblical bachelor devoted himself to a *cursory* reading of the text (probably with the help of Peter Comestor's *Historia Scholastica*); at a higher degree, the master of theology studied in depth one (or several) biblical book, analysing it rigorously and considering all its aspects. The study of *theology was intimately mingled with the study of the biblical text: until *c.*1260 no distinction was made between theology and Holy Scripture, and the terms *theologia*, *Sacra pagina* and *Sacra scriptura* referred equally to one or the other. In the prologues of the commentators of the *Sentences*, there gradually appears (between 1250 and 1260) a conception of the study of theology considered apart from biblical *exegesis.

University study provoked the reorganisation of the book: made more manageable in its presentation, it was divided into *chapters and sometimes accompanied by the tools that were contemporarily being worked out; the object of all these was to make consultation of the biblical text easier: collections of interpretations of Hebrew and Greek words, *concordances (*Hugh of Saint-Cher), specialized glossaries, collections of *distinctions.

**The Bible of the laity.** In the Middle Ages, "lay" often had the sense of unlettered. The mission of the clergy was to teach the Bible to the laity: they did this by images and by word of mouth. St *Gregory had said: "What Scripture presents to those who can read, the image offers to the unlettered (*idiotis*), since the ignorant see in it what they must follow and, in it, those who cannot read, read" (*Ep.* XI, 10); in various formulations (cf. *William of Bourges: "images are the letters of the laity"), this idea was taken up all through the Middle Ages and corresponds accurately to a concern of the Church and to the reality of a great part of medieval art. The capitals, sculptures and paintings of the *Romanesque and *Gothic churches provided this teaching: the depictions overlapped the major themes of learned exegesis (literal illustration of narratives, link between Old and New *Testaments, *typology, essential ideas of theology). To a lesser degree, no doubt, since intended for a smaller public, illuminated bibles contributed to this teaching. But we find a still popular visual teaching, with, on one hand, the *Biblia pauperum* ("Bibles of the poor", whose modest illustration repeats the great themes in a familiar way) and, on the other, the sermonizing Bibles, veritable comic strips which visually provided the narrative and its typological interpretation.

The layman also heard the teaching of the Bible: the preaching that was addressed to him, hence in the *vernacular, appealed ceaselessly to the Bible. Not just because it followed the order of the liturgical readings of Sundays and great feasts, but also because it utilized the biblical narrative as one of the sources from which it drew its models of edification. Likewise, the *theatre of the Christian West related the Bible: its roots were within the liturgy (of *Easter, which provided the Plays of the three Maries and of the *Resurrection; Christmas, which provided the Plays of Herod, Rachel, the *Innocents) and, though it gradually enfranchised itself, its preferred subjects remained biblical, from the first *plays (*Sponsus*, *Jeu d'Adam*, *Ordo Ioseph*, *Ludus Danielis*) to the great Passions of the 15th c. or to certain gigantic "productions" like the *Mystery of the Old Testament* which embraced the whole of the biblical narrative.

In this way, at least a fragmentary knowledge of the Bible spread in the West and ended by constituting one of the elements of Christian culture and *spirituality. This component, which would contract in the course of time and tend to disappear in the modern age, seems to explain numerous attitudes and reflexes of the people of the Middle Ages, working people or intellectuals.

F. Stegmüller, K. Reinhardt, *RBMA*, 1950-1980 (11 vol.). – *The West from the Fathers to the Reformation*, *CHB*, G. H. W. Lampe (ed.), 2, 1969. – J. Leclercq, *The Love of Learning and the Desire for God*, London, 1978. – E. Mâle, *Religious Art in France*, 3 Vols., Princeton (NJ), 1978-1986. – *The Bible and Medieval Culture*, W. Lourdaux (ed.), D. Verhelst (ed.),

Louvain, 1979. – W. Cahn, *La Bible romane*, Fribourg, 1982 (Fr. tr.). – B. Smalley, *The Study of the Bible in the Middle Ages*, Oxford, 1983 (3rd ed.). – *Le Moyen Âge et la Bible*, P. Riché (ed.), G. Lobrichon (ed.), Paris, 1984. – *The Bible in the Medieval World*, K. Walsh (ed.), D. Wood (ed.), Oxford, 1985. – A. Vernet, A.-M. Genevois, *La Bible au Moyen Âge. Bibliographie*, Paris, 1989. – *The Bible in the Middle Ages*, B.S. Levy (ed.), Binghamton (NY), 1992.

Gilbert Dahan

**Translation.** During the thousand years of the Middle Ages, the Bible of the West was of course the Latin Bible. The translation of the sacred texts into the vernacular languages of Europe gradually made headway due to obvious pastoral needs.

The regions of Germanic or Gaelic speech felt this need earliest. *Ireland was thus the first Western country to give itself a religious literature in the vulgar tongue. The first Bible in a Germanic language, that of Ulfila, dates from the second half of the 4th c. (with incomplete New Testament). The Anglo-Saxon scholar *Ælfric translated the Heptateuch into Old English prose at the end of the 10th century. After the commented translation of the Psalms by *Notker the Stammerer and that of the *Song of Songs by Willirams von Ebersberg (*c.*1060), German psalters multiplied in the 12th-13th cc., and around 1350 was published the Augsburg Bible, which gave the New Testament and the *Gospel of Nicodemus* in Middle High German.

*Psalters were also the first biblical texts established in Dutch and in Early English (9th c.). In addition to the so-called Psalters of Vespasian and King *Alfred, we can count no less than eleven surviving English psalters from the 9th to the 11th centuries. The *evangeliaries of *Lindisfarne and Rushworth (late 10th c.) also contain *glosses in Old English. But the first complete English-language Bible was the *Wycliffe, or *Lollard, Bible at the end of the 14th century.

In *Romania*, where the *Latin of the clerics was more or less understood by the Christian people up to the end of the Carolingian period, translations of the Scriptures, for *preaching purposes, came later. Yet from 813, conciliar canons (council of *Mainz and third council of *Tours) were already encouraging *bishops and priests to preach "in the popular Romance or German language so that all may understand".

From the 11th c., interest in the New Testament revived. Itinerant preachers played on the frontiers of orthodoxy and *heresy; textual communities were set up, mingling clerics, religious and laity around the *lex et disciplina* of the *apostolic life. In this context, apart from the French Psalter of Lanfranc (*c.*1100), the basis of the Gallican Psalter that would be reproduced up to the Reformation, the first "French" translations of the Scriptures were largely of the New Testament in *langue d'*oc*, and of *Cathar and *Waldensian origin.

The earliest is a complete New Testament, of Cathar origin (Lyon, Bibl. mun., Ms. PA 36) datable to the early 13th century. Four 14th-c. Waldensian Bibles containing the New Testament and *Wisdom Books, as well as some unattributable Occitan New Testaments datable to the 13th-14th cc., form a corpus of Provençal Bibles, whose family of origin has been defined by Samuel Berger as an *Old Languedocian* Latin, close to the *Vetus latina*.

The first translations of the Scriptures into Italian were made no earlier than the 13th c. by the *mendicants; Spanish Bibles are distinguished by work in common by Jewish and Christian scholars on the Old Testament, begun in the 13th c. and culminating in the first third of the 15th c. in the *Biblia de la Casa Alba*.

S. Berger, "Les Bibles provençales et vaudoise", *Rom.*, 18, 1889, 353-422. – H. R. Nuesch, *Altwaldensische Bibelübersetzung*, Bern, 1979. – "Bibelübersetzungen", *LdM*, 1983, 96-104. – M. Zink, "Prédication en langue vernaculaire", *Le Moyen Âge et la Bible*, Paris, 1984, 459-516.

Anne Brenon

**Iconography.** The illustration of biblical manuscripts began with the addition of images to the separate biblical books, such as *Genesis, the *Psalter, the Books of *Kings or the Gospels. The oldest surviving evidence dates from the 5th and 6th cc. and comes from the Byzantine and Near-Eastern world as well as the Latin world. This illustration must have been presented in the form of small images each recounting an isolated scene or a very precise moment of the biblical story (Cotton Genesis and the tables of canons of the Gospels of Rabbula), following the archaic tradition that went back to the ancient illustration of texts copied on rolls. The transition from the roll to the *codex, in a format close to the modern quarto, offered other possibilities of copying and decoration. One of the consequences was the regrouping of texts and images. With regard to the *image, the changes were profound. The surface of the page and the structure of the codex led to the creation of the frontispiece, which could refer either to the author of the text or to the content of the work. The best example of these changes in the Latin world is the famous Ashburnham Pentateuch, possibly from the 7th or 8th c. (Paris, BNF). The oldest Latin Bible in one volume is the Codex Amiatinus (Florence, Bibliotheca Laurentiana), copied in Northumbria early in the 8th c. and inspired by the *Codex Grandior* of *Cassiodorus (*Vivarium, 6th c.): the portrait of Ezra in his study at the beginning of the Old Testament corresponds to the *Maiestas Domini* at the beginning of the New Testament.

The Carolingian period was of great importance for the history of the Latin Bible, with regard to the text and to the material and spiritual presentation of the book, the latter being manifested brilliantly in the decoration. The illustration of the Bamberg Bible is binary: one frontispiece per Testament. The first depicts a *Creation cycle (from the creation of *Adam to the burial of Abel) at the beginning of *Genesis, the second represents the *Maiestas Agni* (sacrifice and *eschatology) at the beginning of the Gospels. Thereafter the number of frontispieces increases: four in the Grandval Bible (London, British Library; Genesis, *Exodus, Gospels, *Apocalypse), seven plus the dedication miniature in the Vivien Bible (Paris, BNF; St *Jerome, Genesis, Exodus, Psalms, Gospels, Paul's *epistles, Apocalypse) and finally 24 in the Bible of San Paolo fuori le Mura.

The production of Bibles was a fundamental activity of monastic **scriptoria* between the 10th and 12th centuries. Decoration underwent an essential change at this time, for from now on the image was mainly localized in the large initial at the beginning of certain books. But if more books were illustrated in the Romanesque Bibles, the content of each image was often reduced. Iconographical innovations occur, such as the creation of the universe (no longer just of man as with the Carolingians) or an interest in the *Song of Songs.

The Parisian milieu of the 13th c. was important not just for the history of the text (university Bible) but also for its decoration. The evolution begun with the Romanesque Bible was now complete: all the books, down to the shortest epistle, were now illustrated. This process was accompanied by a notable reduction in format and a spectacular growth in production resulting in a falling off in quality. We also observe a wider circulation of the biblical text. Furthermore, the development of picture bibles increases. The best witness to the latter are the extraordinary Parisian undertaking of the *Bible moralisée* (Moralized Bible) and the beautiful Maciejowski Bible (New York, Pierpont Morgan Library, ms. 638).

The iconographical tradition is further developed in the *Bible historiale*, a French translation of the Bible heavily interpolated with passages from *Peter Comestor's *Historia scholastica*. We possess numerous exemplars, some of them commissioned by royalty. These Bibles are generally well illustrated. At the same time the *Biblia pauperum* (Paupers' Bible) was being composed in Germany; its illustrations were organised following the typological method, which brought out correspondences between the Old and New *Testaments.

The *Bible moralisée* and the *Biblia pauperum* contain the seeds of the Catholic and the Protestant attitudes to the Bible: in the former, the role of the biblical text is limited, in favour of ecclesiastical *doctrine and the practice of the *sacraments; in the latter, trust is put in the text which is deemed to contain its own explanations. Admittedly, the *exegesis presented in the Paupers' Bible, entirely based on a somewhat mechanical *typology, appears naive today, while the latent antisemitism of the Moralized Bible appears shocking. But beyond these weaknesses, which bear the mark of their time, these two types of illustrated Bible reveal something very profound in the Christian approach to the Bible.

A. Laborde, *La Bible moralisée illustrée*, Paris, 1911-1929. – K. Weitzmann, "Die Illustration der Septuaginta", *MJBK*, 3-4, 1952-1953, 69-120. – J. Williams, "A Castilian Tradition of Bible Illustration: The Romanesque Bible of San Millan", *Journal of the Warburg and Courtauld Institutes*, 28, 1965, 66-85. – H. L. Kessler, *The Illustrated Bibles from Tours*, Princeton (NJ), 1977. – W. Cahn, *Romanesque Bible Illumination*, Ithaca (NY), 1982. – I. Levin, *The Quedlinburg Itala, the Oldest Illustrated Biblical Manuscript*, Leiden, 1985. – K. Weitzmann, H. L. Kessler, *The Cotton Genesis, British Library Cod. Cotton Otho B.VI*, Princeton (NJ), 1986. – G. Sed-Rajna, *The Hebrew Bible in Medieval Illuminated Manuscripts*, New York, 1987. – K. Weitzmann, H. L. Kessler, *The Frescos of the Dura Synagogue and Christian Art*, Washington, 1990. – H. L. Kessler, "Bibbia", *Enciclopedia dell'arte medievale*, 3, Rome, 1992, 468-487. – G. Schmidt, "Bibbia dei poveri", *ibid.*, 3, Rome, 487-491. – A. Bianchi, "Bibbia moralizzata", *ibid.*, 3, Rome, 491-493. – *The Early Medieval Bible*, R. Gameson (ed.), Cambridge, 1994. – J. Lowden, *The making of the Bibles moralisées*, 1, *The Manuscripts*, 2, *The Book of Ruth* (forthcoming).

Yolanta Zaluska

**BIEL, GABRIEL (*c.*1410-1495).** Gabriel Biel, the proponent of a non-speculative *theology and *mysticism, after having been trained in the *viae antiqua* and *moderna*, exercised his talents as preacher at *Mainz cathedral (1457-1465), before affiliating himself with the Brotherhood of the Common Life (before 1468) and being called to the chair of *via moderna* at Tübingen (1484-1492). His *sermons and his theological work borrow from several sources (*Duns Scotus, William of *Ockham, Jean *Gerson and *Thomas Aquinas), but show clearly his pastoral concern and his profound piety, in a synthesis that marked Martin Luther.

H.A. Oberman, *The Harvest of Medieval Theology*, Cambridge (MA), 1963. – Bubenheimer, "Biel, Gabriel", *VerLex*, 1, 1978, 853-858 (2nd ed.). – W. Dettloff, "Biel", *TRE*, 6, 1980, 488-491 (2nd ed.). – J. L. Farthing, *Thomas Aquinas and Gabriel Biel*, Durham (NC), 1988.

Martial Staub

**BIOGRAPHIES.** In a Christianized world, the importance of each individual was bound up with the chance of his personal *salvation and his role in God's plan. Up to the Carolingian period, works dedicated to an individual outside this context were very rare: there was no success but a spiritual one. But eighty per cent of historical texts were biographies of *bishops or *abbots, whose *sanctity was recognised or presumed. The ancient model, prestigious but distant, was hard put to it to maintain itself in the face of the hagiographical model, much closer and more everyday; moreover both were ethical and not properly historical genres (whence some specific marks: omission of dates, treatment of character by significant anecdotes, without chronological order). A greater degree of historicity may have pushed Saints' Lives towards the biographical genre, but this happened only under the impetus of strong motivations: the commemorative requirements of active communities, like *Cluny celebrating its first abbots; the excitement of the words spoken by saints of fascinating personality, like *Anselm of Canterbury related by Eadmer, or St *Francis of Assisi by his contemporaries, or St *Louis by Joinville, led to them bringing out the significant details of a personality, ignored by a hagiographical tradition more directed towards the exemplary and the universal.

Biographies of laypeople did not appear before the Carolingian period when, in his Life of *Charlemagne (*Vita Karoli*), imitation of Suetonius allowed *Einhard to describe the emperor in his physical and mental characteristics. They were at first exclusively biographies of rulers, especially frequent in the Ottonian Empire; from the 12th c. they tended to be merged into the *history by reign. Biographies of princes, often panegyrics testifying to a lively dynastic or ethnic awareness, arose in the 11th c. in the strong principalities (*Normandy). Interest in simple *noblemen, often fighters, appeared from the 13th c., in the vernacular (*Histoire de Guillaume le Maréchal*); in the 15th c. they became innumerable and, notably in *Italy under *humanist influence, reflected a new cult of personality and energy. *Christine de Pizan, for *Charles V of France, renewed the ethical, rather than historical, biography of kings.

Autobiography posed crucial problems, since to know oneself was perforce to acknowledge oneself a sinner. Despite the great model of St Augustine's *Confessions*, the true medieval autobiographies all arose out of an imbalance, at times when the individual in crisis needed to turn in on himself. Self-evaluation appeared in moments of violent emotion, in *Rodulfus Glaber. St *Valerius in the 7th c., *Rather of Verona, later *Abelard all felt themselves persecuted; *Otloh of Sankt Emmeran describes the traumatizing violence of his crises of doubt; *Guibert of Nogent, like Augustine, speaks directly to God of his sins. In all of them, self-criticism and pleading in self-defence are closely linked, sometimes ironically as in Rather. Shame and awkwardness in analysing oneself only receded significantly in the course of the period 1050-1200.

G. Misch, *Geschichte der Autobiographie*, Frankfurt am Main, 1949-1969; 2, *Das Mittelalter*, 1955 (3 vol.). – J. F. Benton, "Consciousness of Self and Perception of Individuality", *Renaissance and Renewal in the Twelfth Century*, Oxford, 1982, 263-295. – *Problèmes et méthodes de la biographie*, Paris, 1986. – W. Berschin, *Biographie und Epochenstil im lateinischen Mittelalter, Quellen und Untersuchungen zur lateinische Philologie des Mittelalters*, 8-10, Stuttgart, 1986-1991 (up to 920).

Pascale Bourgain

**BĪRŪNĪ, AL- (973 - after 1050).** One of the greatest scholars of the Muslim world, born in Khwārizm and died at Ghazna soon after 1050. He was interested in history, mathematics, astronomy and the natural sciences. After the conquest of Khwārizm by the Ghaznavid Mahmūd, he was taken captive to Ghazna and was from then on attached to the court of the *Ghaznavid rulers who gave him their protection. He had previously met *Avicenna (Ibn Sīnā) in circumstances unknown to us and begun a bitter polemic with him on the nature and transmission of heat and light; but the debate was cut short and their meeting had no sequel. Though living in the metropolises of eastern *Iran at the time of the renaissance of Persian literature, he wrote his work in Arabic, a language for which his praise was unbounded: "The sciences of all regions of the world have been translated into the tongue of the Arabs, have been embellished, have penetrated hearts, and the beauty of the language has circulated in the veins and arteries. . . . I judge this from my own experience; I was brought up in the language [of Khwārizm] . . . later I set myself to learn Arabic and Persian and am consequently an intruder in both languages who strives to perfect himself in them. But I avow that I prefer to be insulted in Arabic than praised in Persian."

Of all his works, the most important are the *Chronology of the Ancient Peoples*, dealing with calendars and eras, meteorology and *astronomy (Eng. tr. E. Sachau, London, 1879), the *Description of India* (Eng. tr. E. Sachau, London, 1888) in which he presents the philosophical and cosmological theories of Hinduism and which he prepared while accompanying Mahmūd on his expeditions to northern India, and finally his great encyclopedia of astronomy, *Al-Kānūn al-Mas'ūdī*, dedicated, as its name indicates, to the second Ghaznavid ruler Mas'ūd.

He composed many other works – 138 according to the list he himself drew up, 180 according to the bibliographical labours of D. J. Boilot –, in particular a treatise on mineralogy, a treatise on medicinal drugs and a work on trigonometry (Fr. tr. M-T. Debarnot, Damascus, 1985).

In all his work, he manifested great open-mindedness, a particular interest in the heritage of India (he was initiated into Sanscrit), great scientific rigour and rare qualities of observation and deduction. He rejected conjectures based on speculation and inquired into the merits of the scientific theories of his time. This is how he formulates the hypothesis of a heliocentric rather than geocentric world: "I have seen the *astrolabe invented by al-Sijzī. It pleases me infinitely and I praised it greatly because it is based on the idea, which some maintain, that the effect of the displacement we see is due to the movement of the earth, not that of the sky. Upon my life, this is a difficult problem, both to resolve and to refute. For it is all the same whether you hold that the earth is in movement, or the sky". Neither in the Muslim world nor in the Christian West has al-Bīrūnī been given the renown called for by the breadth, variety and originality of his work. None of his works was translated into Latin, unlike those of his contemporary Avicenna.

*Al-Bīrūnī Commemoration Volume. A.H. 362 – A.H. 1362*, Calcutta, 1951. – D. J. Boilot, "L'Oeuvre d'al Bêrunî: essai bibliographique", *MIDEO*, 2, 1956, 161-256; *ibid.*, 3, 391-396. – *Al-Bīrūnī Commemorative Volume*, Karachi, 1979 (papers read at the International al-Bīrūnī Congress in 1973). – A. S. Khan, *A Bibliography of the Works of Abu' l-Raihan al-Biruni*, New Delhi, 1982. – J. Samsó, "Al-Bīrūnī in al-Andalus", *From Baghdad to Barcelona: studies in the Islamic exact sciences in honour of Prof. Juan Vernet*, J. Casulleras (ed.), J. Samsó (ed.), Barcelona, 1996, 2, 583-612.

Françoise Micheau

*Study for the construction of an astrolabe*. Miniature from a manuscript of al-Bīrūnī. 14th c. Edinburgh, University Library.

## BISHOP, BISHOPRIC

**The West.** The bishop, appearing from apostolic times as leader of a city's Christian community, then defined as the successor of the Apostles and the ordinary at the head of a *diocese, was an essential element of the organisation of powers in medieval society. By his *consecration, he alone possessed the plenitude of the *priesthood, which reserved for him the conferring of holy *orders, the blessing or altars and sanctified places, the confection of holy *oils, the *absolution of reserved cases. To this power of order was added a power of jurisdiction, surveillance and punishment, which he exercised at first through the *synod and the *visit, closely connected in the Carolingian period, but which were partially voided of their significance. The one became a legislative organ, the other a rather formal exercise, entrusted to others, the *archdeacon in the *parishes, delegates in the regular establishments; the enforcement of jurisdiction was now in the hands of the *officiality. Finally, episcopal responsibility found itself limited by the extension of papal power after the *Gregorian reform, the development of a universal legislation by the great *councils, and the desire for independence of monks, *mendicant orders and then *chapters in search of *exemption. The system of *benefices gave *parish priests, proprietors of their parish, wide autonomy from the bishop, which was further strengthened in the early 13th c. by their monopoly of the instruments of salvation.

But the episcopal function went beyond the mere ecclesiastical framework. Protector of the old Roman *civitas* from the barbarian ruler, then essential cog of the Imperial Church, in the 10th and 11th cc. the bishop took comital powers in his city, conquered or received vast landed lordships and surrounded himself with a warrior clientele, thus putting himself in a strong local position. In the late Middle Ages, the development of the *State limited his influence in *Italy and *France, unless he personally entered the prince's service, but the bishops of *England sat as such in *Parliament, and their German brothers were at the head of their own principality over which they exercised a quasi-sovereign power.

The recruitment of the episcopate remained predominantly aristocratic throughout the medieval West, with nuances according to times and places. In France, the local *nobility, which dominated exclusively between the 10th and the 13th c., left some room in the 14th c. for the *parvenus* of the king's or the *pope's service, *university men and *mendicant friars, when the designation of bishops was removed from chapter *elections to become part of a game of negotiations and a system of apportionment between Paris and *Avignon. The late 15th c. saw the return of the great families to the episcopal sees, when the revenues were once more considerable.

G. Le Bras, *Institutions ecclésiastiques de la Chrétienté médiévale*, 2, 1964, 365-376 ("HE", 12). – K. Pennington, *Pope and Bishops*, Philadelphia, 1984. – E.U. Crosby, *Bishop and Chapter in Twelfth-Century England*, Cambridge, 1994.

Vincent Tabbagh

**Byzantium.** The *patriarchate of *Constantinople was divided into *provinces, themselves subdivided into *dioceses. The bishop of the provincial capital, called "*metropolitan", had jurisdiction over the bishops of his province, his *suffragans.

The bishop was chosen by the *synod of his metropolis. He had to be at least 35 years old and have been married only once; his wife had to retire to a convent because the bishop could not have a wife. The bishop was generally chosen from among the archons of the metropolis. From the 9th c., the bishops were often chosen from the monks; this practice became general in the 14th c., to the great detriment of the secular clergy.

The bishop chosen by the synod was consecrated by his metropolitan. He had to pronounce a profession of faith summing up the Nicene Creed, the seven ecumenical *councils and the canons of the holy *Fathers. According to the controversies in the Church, *anathemata were added to this profession of faith.

Canon law forbade the transfer of a bishop from one see to another. This prohibition was often circumvented, especially for the promotion of a bishop to a metropolitan or even patriarchal see. With the Arab and then Turkish conquests, such transfers multiplied, because numerous bishops, unable to rejoin their dioceses, were given others: this practice, which concerned mainly metropolises, was called *epidosis*.

The first duty of the bishop was preaching. He also carried out judicial functions: he judged clerics guilty of crimes and arbitrated in disputes between clerics and laymen: appeal could also be made to him in civil disputes. Governmental indifference, especially in the provinces outside the emperor's authority (territories under Arab or Turkish rule), contributed to extend the prerogatives of the bishop, who was often the sole authority to whom the Greek populations could appeal. He also had to take care of the poor, sick and orphans.

The bishop was helped in his various tasks by a staff of clerics, usually *deacons: *didaskaloi* for teaching, *orphanotrophus* for charitable works, *oeconomus* for administering church property, *chartophylax* and notaries for the chancery. Their number depended on the size and resources of the diocese. The latter consisted of the revenues of ecclesiastical estates, taxes on the laity and the *kanonikon*, a sum paid by the clergy at the time of his ordination. This *kanonikon*, which could give rise to abuses, was officially abolished by Andronicus II in the 14th c., but the practice was perpetuated. The revenues varied greatly from one diocese to another.

The occupation of Byzantine territories by the Muslims threw the Church's organisation into confusion. Many bishops could not rejoin their sees and resided at Constantinople. The absence of a bishop often entailed in the forsaken sees a feeling of having been abandoned, which explains numerous apostasies.

A. Guillou, "L'évêque dans la société méditerranéenne des VIe-VIIe siècles: un modèle", *BECh*, 131, 1973, 5-19. – *HChr*, 6, 1990, 155-162.

Marie-Hélène Congourdeau

**BLACK DEATH.** The first of the great *epidemics of plague that affected Europe in the 14th and 15th centuries. The plague, induced by the Yersin bacillus, endemic in certain regions, sometimes becomes epidemic. It takes the bubonic form or the primitive pneumonic form (lethality of the former 60-80 %, of the latter 100 %, seemingly independent of the subject's physical state). It is spread by fleas (bubonic plague) or saliva (pneumonic plague). Absent from the West since 767, the plague arrived at Messina in September 1347, *Marseille in November 1347 and spread along the land or sea *communication routes. In 1348 it affected a great part of France and Italy and reached England, western Germany and the Spains, in 1349 Germany and Scandinavia, part of France and the Netherlands, in 1350 northern Germany and central Spain, in 1352 Russia. Everywhere, some neighbourhoods or areas were unaffected. The epidemic may have been helped by very high densities and promiscuity in the *towns. Against it, medieval *medicine was totally helpless.

The consequences of the Black Death were considerable, under several heads.

Demographic consequences: hitting certain exposed groups more heavily (lawyers, *secular clergy, enclosed groups), but without differentiation of age or sex, it led to immediate population losses difficult to evaluate (hearth statistics, insufficiently close brackets and rapid replacement of urban hearths). We can calculate the specific loss as 53 % in Savoy, 25-55 % in England, 58 % in Sweden, 39 % in Navarre, 50-60 % at Bremen, 25-30 % at London, 50 % at Siena, 60 % at Florence. Everywhere it was followed by a flurry of marriages.

The economic consequences were so striking that the *chroniclers noted them: sudden and considerable rise in salaries, which compelled governments (England, France) to *taxation. Fall in agricultural prices. In east-central Europe, end of the *Ostsiedlung* (colonization of the East). The survivers were relatively enriched. Psychological and social consequences: fear led to persecution of the *Jews, notably in central Europe. Safety was sought in flight to the countryside or in claustration. The incentive to make a *testament increased.

Cultural consequences: the plague was understood as a manifestation of divine wrath, hence a search for the proper means to appease it, *processions and cult of healing saints, ostentatious penitence of the *flagellants.

The demographic consequences were considerably amplified by the numerous recurring plagues – 1360-1362, 1374-1375, 1382, 1399-1401, 1412, 1438-1439, 1481-1482, 1494-1503 – which prevented any recovery, though their specific mortality seems not so high as that of the Black Death itself.

J. C. Russell, *Late Ancient and Medieval Population*, Philadelphia (PA), 1958. – E. Carpentier, "Autour de la Peste Noire. Famines et épidémies dans l'histoire du XIVe siècle", *Annales*, 1962, 1062-1092. – P. Ziegler, *The Black Death*, London, 1969. – J. N. Biraben, *Les Hommes et la peste en France et dans les pays européens et méditerranéens*, Paris-The Hague, 1975 (2 vol.). – N. Bulst, "Der schwarze Tod. Demographische, wirtschafts- und kulturgeschichtliche Aspekte der Pestkatastrophe von 1347-1352. Bilanz der neueren Forschung", *Saec.*, 30, 1979, 45-67. – *The Black Death*, D. Williman (ed.), Binghamton (NY), 1982. – *The Black Death in England*, W. M. Ormrod (ed.), P. G. Lindley (ed.), Stamford, 1996.

Henri Dubois

**BLACK PRINCE (1330-1376).** Edward, called the Black Prince, was the eldest son of *Edward III of England. He achieved distinction in the *Hundred Years' War with France, particularly by his leadership of victorious English forces at the battle of *Poitiers in 1356, when King John II of France was captured. Although considered one of the greatest soldiers of his age, the early death of the Black Prince destroyed Edward III's hopes of conclusive victory against *France.

H. J. Hewitt, *The Black Prince's Expedition of 1355-1357*, Manchester, 1958. – C. T. Allmand, "The Black Prince", *History Today*, 26, 1976, 100-108. – J. H. Harvey, *The Black Prince and his Age*, London, 1976. – R. Barber, *The Life and Campaigns of the Black Prince*, Woodbridge, 1986.

Laura Napran

**BLANCHE OF CASTILE (1188-1252).** Wife of King *Louis VIII of France. Daughter of *Alfonso VIII of Castile and Eleanor of England, she married Louis in 1200. She supported him on his expedition to England (1216-1217) and gave him eleven (or twelve) children, whom she raised with rigour and trained in piety. Queen in 1223, she was widowed in 1226 and was made guardian of the young King *Louis IX with government of the realm. She was exposed to the hostility of the barons and the attacks of pamphleteers. She continued to advise her son, even when he had defined his own policy; but she was hostile to the young Queen Marguerite. Louis IX left her in charge of the kingdom and his children when he went on *crusade; she died 22 Nov 1252 and was buried at Maubuisson, which she had founded.

R. Pernoud, *Blanche of Castile*, London, 1975. – G. Sivery, *Blanche de Castille*, Paris, 1990.

Jean Richard

**BLASPHEMY.** In Greek, *blasphemia* means "wounding word". In the Bible, "blasphemy" keeps this general sense (1 Cor 10, 30), but particularly designates the word that outrages God. When *Thomas Aquinas († 1274) defined blasphemy as being "a certain derogation from the excellence of a perfection, and especially of a divine perfection" (*Summa theologiae*, II[a] II[ae], 13, 1), he showed himself still aware of a non-religious meaning of the term. However, it was insofar as it offended God that blasphemy was the object of reflection by the theologian and the legislator.

The Old Testament demands the death of the blasphemer (Lev 24, 16): "And he that blasphemeth the name of the Lord, he shall surely be put to death, and all the congregation shall certainly stone him: as well the stranger, as he that is born in the land." Jesus was himself condemned as a blasphemer (Mk 14, 64). Christ taught that "he that shall blaspheme against the Holy Ghost hath never forgiveness" (Mk 3, 29).

In the 6th c., Justinian's *Novellae* punished the blasphemer by torture, and *death in the case of backsliding. The *sanctions provided by medieval law were not generally so rigorous. In the *Capitularies of *Charlemagne and *Louis the Pious collected by Ansegisus (years 789 to 826), capital punishment is demanded only in the case of blasphemy pronounced in a church, otherwise public *penance and imprisonment is envisaged. In the 12th c., the *Decretum* of *Ivo of Chartres and Gratian's **Decretum* speak of deposition and *anathema. In 1236, Pope *Gregory IX decreed that the blasphemer should be kept seven successive weeks at the church door during high *mass, without cloak or shoes, with a cord around his neck. Joinville reports that St *Louis († 1270) put a goldsmith of Caesarea to the torture and burned the nose and lower lip of a bourgeois of Paris for blasphemy. However Pope *Clement IV (1265-1268) proscribed mutilations and capital executions for this offence. Resort was had, with a frequency hard to establish, to fines, pillory and *prison. *Philip VI de Valois, by letters patent of 22 Feb 1347, returned to corporal punishment. His *ordinance would be renewed by the kings of France until the 18th century.

Theologians applied themselves to defining the nature and gravity of blasphemy, distinguishing different sorts of it (blasphemy of mouth, of heart, accompanied or not by hatred of God, spoken directly against him or dishonouring his works, emitted in the heat of passion, with or without awareness of the words spoken, etc.) and interpreting Christ's words concerning the blasphemy against the *Holy Spirit. This consisted either of final impenitence or deliberate choice of *sin through despair, presumption, rejection of *conversion, obstinacy, opposition to known truth or envy of the *grace given to others.

A. Molien, "Blasphème", *DDC*, 2, 1937, 902-920. – R.-H. Helmholz, "Blasphemy", *DMA*, 2, 1983, 271-272.

Gilles Berceville

**BLEMMYDES, NICEPHORUS (1197-*c.*1270).** Son of a doctor, he studied philosophy and *medicine in Asia Minor. He was a doctor for seven years, then a member of the patriarchal clergy at *Nicaea (at that time capital of the Empire). In *c.*1235 he became a monk and opened a school where he trained the intellectual elite of the following decades. He was offered the *patriarchate, but refused it. Embroiled with his old pupil, the Emperor *Theodore Lascaris, he retired to a hermitage. He left an *Autobiography* and works of philosophy (commentaries on *Aristotle's Logic and Physics: *PG*, 142), science (*Universal Geography*), medicine and *theology (treatise on the procession of the Holy Spirit, commentaries on the Psalms). His commentaries on Aristotle served as manuals for the teaching of philosophy until the 18th c., and the humanist Giorgio Valla used them widely in his encyclopedia.

Nicephorus Blemmydes, *Autobiographia*, J. A. Munitiz (ed.), *CChr.SG*, 13, 1984 (Eng. tr., *SSL*, 1988).

*Nikephorus Blemmydes: a partial account*, J.A. Munitiz (ed.), Louvain, 1988.

Marie-Hélène Congourdeau

*St Columbanus presents the city of Bobbio.* Detail of the sarcophagus of St Columbanus by Giovanni dei Patriarcis, 1480. Bobbio, Abbey of San Colombano.

**BLESSED BREAD.** The custom of distributing blessed bread at the solemn Sunday *mass went back at least to the 9th c. (recommendation of Pope St *Leo IV, 847-855). At the council of Nantes (*c.*897), the term **eulogia* was used to designate the blessed bread. The formula of blessing the bread in the Roman ritual dates from that *council. The origin of blessed bread must probably be sought in the *offertory of the mass where the faithful themselves brought the material for the sacrifice: what remained over, after the *deacons had taken the bread necessary for the sacrifice of the day, was later distributed to the people, to the participants, sometimes to the poor as *alms. When the offerings ceased in their original form, blessed or non-blessed bread continued to be distributed to those who did not communicate or were not even present. The dying demanded it, travellers found in it protection from the perils of the road. Numerous *superstitions were attached to this practice. In Friuli, on 14 Feb, at the *sagra* of Prachiuso, blessed bread was distributed in a figure of eight big enough to go round the arms, called "St Valentine's bread", to which was accorded prophylactic virtues such as the healing of epileptics.

"Eulogie", *DThC*, 11, 1932, 1731-1733. – *DACL*, 5, 733. – *Cath.*, 10, 1985, 416-417.

Dominique Rigaux

**BLOOD, PRECIOUS.** The importance of the blood of Jesus in Christianity comes from the fact that it is directly included in the doctrine of the mystery of *Redemption and *Salvation. This is the basis of the eminence of the Precious Blood whose cult the Church has exalted since the 13th century. At that time we see multiplying in the figurative arts the *image of the bloody Crucified, in which angels piously collect the precious liquid spurting from the wound in his side while *Mary Magdalene – generally dressed in red – clasps his feet, her mouth pressed against the flowing blood. The devotion spread thanks partly to the *Quest of the Holy Grail*, a 12th/13th-c. *romance that brought together various legends around biblical elements: the *Grail, a cup used by Joseph of Arimathea to receive the blood from Christ's *wounds before his entombment (Mt 27, 57-60) is also the cup of the Last Supper. *Miracles of bleeding hosts and new iconographical themes such as St Gregory's *Mass, which exalted both the *Passion and the *Eucharist, reveal a growing enthusiasm for the *Holy Blood.

For the powers, and principally the therapeutic virtues, that medieval man acknowledged in blood were multiplied when it came to the blood of Christ. The Precious Blood was an infallible medicine and among the most sure as long as it was applied with faith. Among the innumerable *relics of the Precious Blood preserved by the chief towns of Christendom, that of *Mantua seems to have had authority. Pope *Pius II Piccolomini did not hesitate, in 1459, to venerate it for his own healing. But the theological and religious status of the blood shed during the Passion was not unanimous, and the same Pope Pius II found himself obliged, three years later, to intervene with all his authority in the controversy between the mendicant friars, *Dominicans and *Franciscans, on this subject.

The thirst for a purifying bath in the shed blood goes right through the 15th c. like a leitmotiv. Abundantly illustrated by the iconographical themes created at this time – the Mystical *Winepress –, we find it both in the phantoms that haunted medieval consciences and in the writings of mystics like *Catherine of Siena recalling that *Christ gave us "his Blood as a bath, so that in it we might wash away the leprosy of our iniquities". At the end of the 15th c., the Blood inundated the faithful and submerged them in the exuberant visions of the sermons and prophecies of a *Savonarola. In this atmosphere of exacerbated sensibility, the glorious blood of the *Lamb that redeemed mem's sins merged with the lurid disasters of the *Apocalypse.

Catherine de Sienne, *Le Sang, la Croix, la Verité. Treize lettres*, L.-P. Guigues (Fr. tr.), Paris, 1940.

G. Didi-Huberman, "Un sang d'images", *Nouvelle revue de psychanalyse*, 32, Paris, 1985, 123-153. – D. Alexandre-Bidon, *Le Pressoir mystique. Actes du colloque de Recloses*, Paris, 1990. – R. Grégoire, "Sang", *DSp*, 14, 1990, 319-333.

Dominique Rigaux

**BOBBIO.** In the upper Trebia valley, some 45 kilometres south-west of *Piacenza. Forced out of Bregenz by the death of his protector Theudebert, king of *Austrasia, *Columbanus was well received by the *Lombard King Agilulf and his Catholic wife Theodelinda who settled him in 612 in this mountainous and then unpopulated region. The benefactors also had a political interest: to the south was the Byzantine enclave of *Genoa. The monastery, originally dedicated to Sts Peter, Paul and Andrew, was consecrated to St Columbanus after 615.

His first successors Attalus, Bertulf and Bobolenus obtained from the *pope and from King Rothari an *exemption whose nature is disputed: the documents of 643 and 652 are known only by interpolated 12th-c. copies. It remains true that the Lombard period was very favourable to the abbey: 150 monks who had freedom of *election and considerable estates. Its apogee was in the 8th-9th centuries. This wealth attracted covetousness, the *Carolingians appointed *abbots, the monks themselves appealed to Wala of

Corbie in 834 who introduced the reform of *Benedict of Aniane. The *polyptychs of 862 and 883 offer a glimpse of the agrarian history of northern *Italy.

The decline of Carolingian power sharpened the appetites of the bishops of Tortona and *Piacenza; in 983 *Gerbert of Aurillac, appointed abbot, lamented the misery into which the monks had fallen. The creation of a *bishopric at Bobbio itself improved the situation. But in the mid 12th c. terrible conflicts set the bishop against the monastery, which entered a profound decline. Today, 11th- and 15th-c. constructions remain among the 17th-c. buildings.

Bobbio's glory is due to the exceptional *library that existed there in the Carolingian period; *Dungal left a collection of 25 manuscripts there, and a mid 9th-c. catalogue lists no less than 700 manuscripts. Some dated from the 4th-5th cc., others were produced in the **scriptorium*. 100 of them contained classical authors. One might mention in particular Cicero's *De re publica* (palimpsest), the Medici Virgil and the Bobbio Missal. This treasure began to be dispersed in the Middle Ages: an inventory of 1461 lists only 243 manuscripts. In the 17th c., some went to Milan; after 1803 (suppression of the abbey) the remaining stock ended in the National Library of Turin where part was destroyed by a fire in 1904. The misfortunes of this library inspired Umberto Eco in his novel *The Name of the Rose*.

C. Cipolla, G. Buzzi, *Codice diplomatico di S. Colombano di Bobbio*, *FSI*, 1918. – F. Bonnard, *DHGE*, 9, 1937. – W. Goez, A. Petrucci, *LdM*, 2, 1983. – *The Bobbio Missal*, E.A. Lowe (ed.), Woodbridge, 1991.

Bruno Judic

**BOCCACCIO (1313-1375).** It was probably at *Florence rather than Certaldo, cradle of his family, that Giovanni Boccaccio was born. Son of an influential businessman, Boccaccio (Boccaccino) di Chelino, he received a good intellectual education first at Florence, then at *Naples, where his father had been transferred to represent the powerful Bardi company (1327-1341). There he found a city wide open to *commerce and a brilliant, refined, aristocratic *court. The university of Naples and the rich *library of *Robert the Wise awoke in the young Boccaccio an eclectic curiosity and, with his literary vocation, a taste for erudite research. His apprenticeship in the old courtly tradition culminated in *La caccia di Diana*, a mythological fable in verse; while the narrative technique and mature style of his verse and prose romances (*Filostrato*, *Teseida*, *Filocolo*) renewed the genre. Returning to Florence (1341-42) as an attentive observer of communal life, Boccaccio inaugurated a realistic approach to society. His meeting with *Petrarch (1350) led to an exceptional *friendship and a fruitful intellectual fellowship, attested by a lively correspondence. His relations with the humanist circles of *Padua and the Augustinian milieu of Florence are notable for the transition, made in his work (poetic and narrative) and promoted in his defence of *poetry (*Genealogia deorum gentilium*), from scholastic cultural forms to Renaissance forms and ideals; from the legacy of *Dante to the moral and poetic lesson of Petrarch. His Florentine works (*Comedia delle ninfe fiorentine*, *Elegia di Madonna Fiammetta*, *Ninfale fiesolano*) attest his interest in a new public: that of the citizen elite of the *Arti Maggiori*, and in particular that of the privileged ladies who were the inspiration and dedicatees of his works (despite the misogyny of the late *Corbaccio*), particularly of his major work, the *Decameron* (1349-51): in this collection of a hundred tales, the narrative system, serving both as thematic framework and literary programme (a group of ten narrators fleeing the plague tell stories for ten days in an idyllic retreat), allows Boccaccio to put forward a **summa* of the art of narration; in the short story, by now definitively fixed, are found integrated and transformed the aesthetic and ideological options of earlier tradition

Miniature from a manuscript of Boccaccio's *Decameron*. Paris, BNF (Ms ital. 63, fol. 304 v°).

(*exempla, lais, *fabliaux, *romances, contes, fables. . .). Narrative mastery and critical awareness, forged in the emulative exercise of erudite biographies (*Trattatello in laude di Dante*, Life of Petrarch), are displayed in the collections of exemplary lives (*De casibus virorum illustrium, De mulieribus claris*), before converging in the commentary on the *Commedia*, the *Esposizioni sopra la comedia di Dante*: a final vibrant homage to Dante, and a veritable literary testament.

*Genealogia deorum gentilium*, V. Romano (ed.), Bari, 1951 (2 vol.). – *Tutte le opere di Giovanni Boccaccio*, V. Branca (ed.), Milan, 1967-1992 (10 vol.).

V. Branca, *Boccaccio medievale e nuovi studi sul "Decameron"*, Florence, 1986. – F. Bruni, *Boccaccio*, Bologna, 1990. – *Lessico Critico Decameroniano*, Turin, 1995. – F.S. Stych, *Boccaccio in English: a Bibliography of Editions, Adaptations and Criticism*, Westport (CT), 1995.

Claude Cazalé Bérard

**BOCCANEGRA, WILLIAM (died 1274).** Of a family that was "popular" but firmly established among the Genoese ruling class, he was probably born in the early years of the 13th century. The earliest certain information makes him Genoese consul at Aigues-Mortes (1249) and Acri (1249-1250), then councillor of the Commune in 1251 and 1256.

Early in 1257, following a popular riot, he was proclaimed captain of the people with supreme power for ten years, to be exercised with the assistance of a council of 32 elders. The event was part of the struggles between *Guelf and Ghibelline aristocracy and between magnates and people, at a time of economic and military crisis for the city. Despite the commercial treaty and defensive alliance signed with *Manfred, king of *Sicily, in 1257 and confirmed two years later, which re-opened the Regno to Genoese *commerce, Boccanegra's internal position in the first years of his government suffered from persistent difficulties in the war against the Pisans in *Sardinia and the unfortunate conduct of operations against the Venetians in the *Holy Land.

Meanwhile Boccanegra devoted himself to restoring the *commune's disordered finances. After a series of administrative and fiscal measures, on 16 June 1259, strong in a growing consensus, he decreed the nullity of cessions of public revenue made for a period of more than one year in violation of the laws of 1155 and 1214, converting the State's relative debt into a perpetual income redeemable at an interest of 8 per cent. That year a plot was discovered, but he forced the plotters to flee and banished them; they were recalled in 1260 under the influence of the great movement of penitence and reconciliation aroused at Genoa and elsewhere by the *flagellants. The treaty of Ninfeo, signed with Michael *Palaeologus on 13 March 1261 (ratified 10 July), crowned Boccanegra's policy, marking the end of the Latin Empire of the East, willed and sustained by *Venice; indeed it confirmed the commercial predominance of the Genoese at *Constantinople, where the Venetian settlements were occupied and destroyed.

According to the partisan account of the *Annales Ianuenses*, Boccanegra made himself odious to both nobles and people by the increasingly authoritarian and personal character of his government. On 8 May 1262, after fighting in which his brother Lanfranc was killed, a plot directed by the Grimaldi forced him into exile at Aigues-Mortes. In 1266, as vicar of King *Louis IX, he was instructed to superintend the fortification of that town; in 1270 he obtained some lands from the count of *Toulouse, and in 1272 a pension from King *Philip III. He died before January 1274.

In 1276, members of his family were back in *Genoa. His brother Marino, as *operarius portus et moduli*, directed among other things the construction of the Old Harbour. William's eldest son Nicholas (born 1257) was Genoese vicar in *Corsica in 1289 and then commanded an unsuccessful expedition to Sardinia. In 1339, Lanfranc's grandson Simon Boccanegra was elected first doge of Genoa. Simon's brother Egidio Boccanegra was a famous admiral, victor over the Moors in 1340. He beat the Portuguese in 1372 on the Tagus and the English at La Rochelle, taking prisoner their admiral John Hastings, earl of Pembroke.

J. Morize, "Aigues-Mortes au XIIIe siècle", *AMidi*, 26, 1914, 313-348. – C. Imperiale di Sant'Angelo, *Iacopo d'Oria e i suoi Annali. Storia di un'aristocrazia italiana nel Duecento*, Venice, 1930, 77-112. – R. S. Lopez, "Boccanegra, Guglielmo", *DBI*, 11, Rome, 1969, 31-35. – G. Caro, *Genova e la supremazia sul Mediterraneo (1257-1311)*, Genoa, 1974-1975, 1, 17-122 (= "Atti della Società ligure di storia patria", 88-89 [N.S. 14-15]). – V. Vitale, *Breviario della storia di Genova*, 1, Genoa, 1975, 73-81. – R. S. Lopez, *Su e giù per la storia di Genova*, Genoa, 1975, 231-240. – L. T. Belgrano, "I Genovesi ad Acquemorte", *Giornale linguistico*, 9, 1882, 326-341. – G. Petti Balbi, "Genesi e composizione di un ceto dirigente: i "populares" a Genova nei secoli XIII e XIV", *Spazio, società, potere nell'Italia dei Comuni*, G. Rossetti (ed.), Naples, 1986, 85-103.

Antonio Placanica

**BODEL, JEHAN (1165/70-1210).** Jehan Bodel, a *trouvère* of *Arras, was the author of the *Jeu de saint Nicolas* (*c.*1200), a *chanson de geste* – the *Chanson des Saisnes* – some pastorals and *fabliaux, and the *Congés*, poems of farewell written on the occasion of his retirement to a *leper-house. *Le Jeu de saint Nicolas* is a capital work which inaugurated a new genre: the dramatic miracle. The game inserts tavern and street scenes into a crusading intrigue against the *Saracens. The world of the Orient and that of Arras meet each other around the statue of St Nicholas. The *Congés* too introduce a new genre (*Adam de la Halle would later write several), and the *Saisnes* show originality by integrating elements of the chivalrous *romance into an *epic dealing with *Charlemagne's crusade against the *Saxons.

C. Foulon, *L'Oeuvre de Jean Bodel*, Paris, 1958. – T. S. Faunce, "Bodel, Jean", *DMA*, 2, 1983, 290-291.

Renate Blumenfeld-Kosinski

**BODY.** The body is part of *man forming a composition with his spiritual *soul, in common language, and, in authors more anxious for rigour, co-principle with the animating principle in every living being, *i.e.* with the spiritual soul in man. For dualists, the body is a substance distinct from the soul. Only *Thomas Aquinas prefers another definition which, using *Aristotle's *hylomorphism, professes a composition of prime matter formless in itself (not body) with a single intellective and animating substantial form. "Body" can be seen from two points of view: that of the generic corporeity of a living being, to implicitly designate its totality without specifying its complete *nature (reasonable, in man); and looking solely at its corporeal dimensions in an abstract and mathematizable way (*De spiritualibus creaturis*, 4, 14; *De ente*, 2, t. 43, 371, 105 f.). In the former sense, "body" thus refers, in man, to all human nature which is rational but in its incarnate aspect. The corporeal condition is beneficial to the soul, since it is given its intellective information through sensible images (*Summa theologiae*, I[a], q. 89, a. 1; *De malo*, 5, 5, t. 23, 141, 205 f.). The separation from the body imposed by the body's *death deprives the soul of the perfection of human nature, so that the separated soul aspires to regain, by the promised *resurrection, its animation of the body which is henceforth promoted to *immortality by a supernatural gift (*Summa contra gentiles*, IV, 79, § 413; *De potentia*, 5, 10).

In the dualist current, pessimism about the body was clarified by the theological doctrine of the falling off due to original sin. Physical suffering, death and the moral weaknesses due to sensuality (from which the Bible says that the Creator, in his plan, had exempted man) received from this a first explanation which referred to eschatological restoration. But in the 13th c., theologians henceforth brought out the positive value of the body. Though a dualiser, St *Bonaventure emphasized the excellence of its upright posture, which corresponds to the soul's orientation towards the divine, and its sexed condition, which concurs to the perfection of human nature and will be maintained in the resurrected state, not for generation but for the perfection and *beauty of the elect, since it will be enfranchised as originally from disordered inclinations (*In L. Sententiarum* IV, 43 dub. 1, 4, 918). *Thomas Aquinas freed himself further from prejudices: corporeal pleasure is an indispensable human *good and requires only to be regulated by *reason in favour of the higher pleasures of the spirit: study, *friendship, *contemplation (*Summa theologiae*, I^a^ II^ae^, q. 34, 1; II^a^ II^ae^, q. 141, 3; q. 142, 1). Taught by reason, the sensible passions contribute to the dynamism of the spiritual *will (I^a^ II^ae^, q. 24, 2-3).

Thomas Aquinas, *Summa theologiae*, I^a^ II^ae^, q. 24-48 (on the passions). – Guillelmus de Sancto-Victore, *De natura corporis et animae*, M. Lemoine (tr.), Paris, 1988.

"Chair", *DSp*, 1, 1937, 936-1010. – É. Gilson, *Jean Duns Scot. Introduction à ses positions fondamentales*, Paris, 1952. – D. Gorce, "Corps", *DSp*, 2, 1953, 2338-2378. – P. Daubercies, "La Théologie de la condition charnelle chez les Maîtres du haut Moyen Âge", *RThAM*, 30, 1963, 5-54. – W. Hiss, *Die Anthropologie Bernhards von Clairvaux*, Berlin, 1964. – É. Gilson, *Le Thomisme*, Paris, 1965 (6th ed.). – T. Schneider, *Die Einheit des Menschen*, *BGPhMA*, new series, 8, Münster, 1988 (2nd ed.). – É.-H. Wéber, *La Personne humaine au XIII^e^ siècle*, Paris, 1991. – *Medieval Theology and the Natural Body*, P. Biller (ed.), A.J. Minnis (ed.), Woodbridge, 1997.

Édouard-Henri Wéber

**BOETHIUS (*c.*480-*c.*524).** A member of the noble family of the Anicii, A. M. S. Boethius lost his father very young. The immediate protection given him by Q. A. M. Symmachus, later his father-in-law, had a determining influence on him, intellectually and politically as well as morally and spiritually. His *cursus honorum*, so far as we know it, made him successively patrician (*c.*507), ordinary consul (510) and master of the offices (*c.*522). His deep scientific erudition gained him for some time the esteem, even the admiration, of King Theodoric the Great. But he was the victim of a political conspiracy, which in all probability concealed a religious conflict, and accused of plotting and treason. Finally arrested, tortured and executed, Boethius died without having been able to complete the immense programme he had set himself.

Ambitious, by a sort of idealized mission, to be the instructor of the Latin West, for this end he had undertaken to translate, among other things, the complete works of Plato and *Aristotle, then to harmonize them in a sort of philosophical, more especially peripatetico-Neoplatonist, syncretism. The greater part of Boethius's surviving work consists of translations of treatises by Aristotle and logical monographs. To these must be added a version of Porphyry's *Isagoge* and two commentaries on it, as well as a study of Cicero's *Topics*. Until about the 1130s, part of all this formed the corpus called *Logica vetus*. In the strictly scientific sphere, Boethius also, according to *Cassiodorus, translated

*The Flight of a Soul.* Miniature from a French version of Boethius's *Consolation of Philosophy.* 15th c. Rouen, Municipal Library.

Pythagoras (music), Euclid (geometry), Archimedes (mechanics), Ptolemy (*astronomy) and Nicomachus of Gerasa (arithmetic). Today we possess only his *Institutio arithmetica* and his *Institutio musica*. On the theological level he is credited, on the basis of a document known as *Anecdoton Holderi*, with the composition of five treatises called *Opuscula sacra* (briefly: I. – *De trinitate*; II. – *De praedicatione*; III. – *De hebdomadibus*; IV. – *De fide christiana*; V. – *Contra Eutychen et Nestorium*). This pentalogy is the sole production allowing us to make Boethius an overtly Christian thinker – a character that was long disallowed him. Deliberately hermetic, his thought, which is also wholly polemical and deeply penetrated by *logic, is here in turn trinitarian and christological, a veritable orthodox bastion armed against heresy and paganism. The posterity of the *Opuscula*, from the Carolingian period to the end of the Middle Ages, was such that their author was cited as if equal to a patristic source. His philosophical testament (the *Consolation of Philosophy*), a prodigious synthesis of his thought, had a still more exceptional future. In this prose dialogue, Boethius, who knew he was condemned to death, pursued a vast metaphysical dialogue with *philosophy, taking as topics of conversation particularly fortune, free *will, *providence, divine prescience and *predestination, more suitable for consoling. In the course of this ample and lyrical meditation, prestigious Greco-Latin influences such as Plato, Aristotle, Seneca, Plotinus, Augustine and Proclus are interwoven in profusion.

Manlii Severini Boetii, *Opera omnia*, *PL*, 64, 1860. – *Philosophiae Consolatio*, L. Bieler (ed.), *CChr.SL*, 94, 1, Turnhout, 1957. – *The Theological Tractates*, H. F. Stewart (ed.), E. K. Rand (ed.), S. J. Tester (ed.), Cambridge, 1978.

Bogomil stele. Bosnia. 15th c.

M. Cappuyns, "Boèce", *DHGE*, 9, 1937, 348-380. – H. M. Barrett, *Boethius. Some aspects of his times and work*, Cambridge, 1940. – P. Courcelle, *La "Consolation de philosophie" dans la tradition littéraire*, Paris, 1967. – L. Obertello, *Severino Boezio*, Genoa, 1974 (2 vol.). – *Boethius. His Life, Thought and Influence*, M. Gibson (ed.), Oxford, 1981. – H. Chadwick, *Boethius. The Consolations of Music, Logic, Theology and Philosophy*, Oxford, 1981. – E. Reiss, *Boethius*, Boston, 1982. – *The Medieval Boethius*, A. J. Minnis (ed.), Cambridge, 1987. – N. H. Kaylor Jr., *The Medieval Consolation of Philosophy: an Annotated Bibliography*, New York, 1993.

Alain Galonnier

**BOETHIUS OF DACIA (13th c.).** Danish by origin, a *master at the arts *faculty of *Paris *c.*1270, Boethius of Dacia was, with *Siger of Brabant, one of the main targets of the condemnation promulgated on 7 March 1277 by Bishop *Stephen Tempier against the Parisian intellectuals suspected of *Averroism. We know hardly anything of his life, but his writings make him one of the greatest philosophers of the 13th century. Like all the *magistri artium* of his time, Boethius composed commentaries on the main works of *Aristotle: we still possess those on the *Topics*, the *Physics*, the *De generatione et corruptione* and the *Meteorologica*. He also wrote important *Quaestiones super Priscianum Minorem* (or *Modi significandi*) and three short but dense opuscula: *De aeternitate mundi*, *De summo bono* and *De somniis*.

Boethius made important contributions in three directions. Firstly, with the *Modi significandi* he offered one of the most representative examples of the tradition of linguistic research known by the name of "speculative *grammar". Secondly, in the *De summo bono*, he defined with great clarity the ethical ideal characteristic of medieval and Renaissance "Averroism": the supreme *good that man can attain in his earthly life consists in the full realization of his rationality, *i.e.* in the "intellectual pleasure" that the philosopher experiences in the *contemplation of *God as first *cause. Thirdly, especially in the *De aeternitate mundi*, Boethius developed a subtle analysis of the relationship between philosophical truths and religious truths, which aimed to guarantee their harmony through a clear separation of their respective levels of discourse: *philosophy embraces all that is rationally demonstrable and assumes as criterion of truth the coherence of conclusions in relation to premises, but these are only valid in the domain of natural causes; *faith, on the contrary, is the bearer of absolute truths which, referring to the action of supernatural causes, are undemonstrable in principle.

É. Gilson, "Boèce de Dacie et la double vérité", *AHDL*, 22, 1955, 81-99. – G. Fioravanti, "Boezio di Dacia e la storiografia sull'Averroismo", *StMed*, 7, 1966, 283-322. – R. Hissette, *Enquête sur les 219 articles condamnés à Paris le 7 mars 1277*, Louvain, 1977. – L. Bianchi, *Il Vescovo e i filosofi. La condanna parigina del 1277 e l'evoluzione dell'aristotelismo scolastico*, Bergamo, 1990.

Luca Bianchi

**BOGOMILS.** Members of a dualist sect founded in the 10th c. by a certain "Pop Bogomil", the Bogomils ("pleasing to God") were, according to the Greek view but not according to the Armenian evidence, influenced by the *Paulicians. In the 11th c., the sect's doctrine took root among the aristocracy of *Constantinople under the direction of Boris the Bogomil, known from the *Alexiad* and from the *Refutation* of *Euthymius Zigabenus commissioned by Alexius I *Comnenus. The sect later spread throughout the Balkans, particularly in *Bosnia where the Patarine Church was set up under its influence, in Asia Minor where the patriarch of Nicaea composed a treatise against it in the 13th c., in Italy, in Germany and above all in *Languedoc where the *ecclesiae Dragometiae, Bulgariae, Dalmatiae* are mentioned in the Acts of the council of Saint-Félix-de-Caraman in 1167, and the Bulgar *heresy (*Bulgarorum haeresis*) from the early 13th century.

Fundamentally rebels against the Orthodox hierarchy whose authority and sacraments they denied, especially that of baptism, the Bogomils tenaciously opposed the *Byzantine Empire which pursued them for centuries. Consequently, except for a "secret book" known by the name of *Interrogatio Johannis*, whose Slav original is lost, the beliefs of the Bogomils are known to us mainly through the polemic of their adversaries. According to these, the Bogomils were dualists who separated the divine world, conceived in a *cosmology spread over seven heavens, from the material world, the work of Satan. As God's *Word evidently could not have participated in *evil by assuming a flesh created by Satan, the Incarnation was therefore conceived as Docetist or illusory. In order to distance themselves as far as possible from any stain, the "elect" of the sect were kept to a severe *ascesis that forbade them the consumption of meat and wine, as well as any sexual relations. In the eyes of contemporary ecclesiastical authorities, such beliefs and practices were largely sufficient to identify the Bogomils as "neo-Manichees".

Despite the perpetual persecutions, the names of the "Churches of Bulgaria" given by the acts of Saint-Félix-de-Caraman, as well as references to Bogomil bishops and even to a *Papa Niquinta*, attest a far-reaching hierarchical structure and long-standing links with Western Europe. Nevertheless, the sect does not seem to have survived the *Ottoman conquest of the Balkans in the 14th-15th centuries.

D. Obolensky, *The Bogomils*, Cambridge, 1948. – M. Loos, *Dualist Heresy in the Middle Ages*, Prague, 1974. – L. Denkova, "Des Bogomiles: ontologie du Mal et orthodoxie orientale", *Heresis*, 13-14, Villegly, 1990, 65-87.

Nina G. Garsoïan

**BOHEMIA.** Westernmost province of the present Czech Republic; it takes its name (Latin *Boiohaemum*) from the Celtic people of the Boïes who lived there from half-way through the 1st millennium BC. Towards the end of the great migration of peoples, in the 6th and 7th cc., Slav tribes coming from the east settled in this territory, much of which was empty. They were led by the legendary patriarch Čech, who gave the country its Czech name, Čechy. Politically fragmented, Bohemia was coveted by conquerers from the west (German *Franks) and east (*Avars, then Slav Moravians), but kept its independence, except for a brief attachment to Great Moravia towards the end of the 9th century. At this time too, it received the first Christian missionaries, some Germans but mainly *Slavs, from Great Moravia. After the fall of that state in 906 and the dismantling of its ecclesial organisation created by St Methodius, Bohemia became a principality governed by the native dynasty of the *Přemyslids, and an autonomous *diocese after the foundation of the bishopric of *Prague in 973. Two local martyr-saints played a very important role in this constitution of temporal and spiritual powers independent of foreigners: Prince *Wenceslas (Václav, assassinated in 935) and Bishop *Adalbert (Vojtěch, massacred in 997). The Christianization of Bohemia would be completed in the course of the 10th and 11th centuries. The Slav liturgy, linked to the *mission of St *Cyril and his brother St Methodius, was definitively supplanted at this time by the Western Latin rite, the last Slavonic place of worship being the monastery of Sázava founded by St Procopius in 1032. Also at the same time came the regularization of relations with the Holy Roman *Empire: the Přemyslid princes agreed to recognise the emperor's suzerainty, while keeping their independence from him in practice. Several events would raise the political prestige of Bohemia: attachment of Moravia (1020), admission among the *Prince Electors of the Empire in the middle of the 13th c., and above all the elevation of the Czech principality to the rank of a kingdom (the reigning prince became king of Bohemia in 1158).

Right at the beginning of the feudal period, large parts of Bohemia became lands of colonization and, from the 12th c., the limits of inhabited territory were rapidly extended as far as the

Charles IV's castle at Karlštejn in the Berounka valley, Czech Republic. 1350

mountain chains that formed the country's natural frontiers. The most important factor of this repopulation of the countryside in the early Middle Ages was the foundation of monasteries, at first Benedictine, then *Cistercian, *Premonstratensian and others. The oldest Benedictine monasteries were installed close to the court, like the women's cloister of St George in the enclosure of Prague castle (*c.*970) or the men's abbey of Břevnov (in 993). Subsequently, monasteries founded by rulers or other illustrious persons would spread out to the edge of the inhabited territory (Opatovice, Plasy, Pomuk, Sedlec, Želiv), or even in areas still deserted (Kladruby, Teplá, Vyšší Brod), with a religious, cultural and economic influence very important for the region round about.

Another impetus was given to the further development of Bohemia by the exploitation of mining deposits and the foundation of royal towns under the Přemyslids in the 13th century. Colonists from Western Europe, mainly *Germany, played a massive part in this culminating stage of medieval urbanization. Their arrival introduced into the country a Czech-German bilingualism, but also the progressive application of the most advanced norms of Western law (feudal law, city law, mining law, lease law), from which the mass of the population also benefited. The Czech ruler, previously an absolute monarch, from now on had to reckon with the *nobility, constituted from the 13th c. as an estate, the second centre of power in Bohemia. The political emancipation of the clergy did not go forward so fast. Agent of transmission of European culture and science, the Church of Bohemia was from the beginning a solid supporter of the dynastic power; its attempts to acquire a certain political and economic independence from the king and the nobility were crowned with only partial success, in the 14th century.

After the extinction of the royal dynasty of the Přemyslids in 1306 and the period of political disorders that followed, the authority of Bohemia was restored during the reign of *Charles IV (1346-1378), of the house of *Luxemburg. Educated in his youth at the court of France, Charles founded in 1348 the first *university in central Europe at Prague; in 1344, before his accession to the throne, he had obtained the elevation of the *bishopric of Prague to the rank of an *archbishopric; elected as head of the Holy Roman Empire, in 1355 he received the crown of the king of Rome. From then on, Bohemia became the most powerful country in the Empire, and Czech one of the great literary languages of Europe. *Suzerain of the Crown provinces (*Moravia, *Silesia, Upper and Lower Lusatia), King Charles of Bohemia was the most influential monarch in central Europe.

During this time, the Czech nobility finally conquered an autonomous position within the new structures of society, which was organised into estates – and split into two distinct bodies (lords and knights). The Church, on the contrary, always remained linked to the throne. The expensive tastes of the court, the great nobility, the patrician bourgeoisie and the ecclesiastical dignitaries, compared with living conditions that never ceased to deteriorate for the lesser rural nobility, the artisans, the *peasants and the simple *clerics in this beginning of the general crisis that the medieval economy was about to suffer, led to growing tensions within the very heterogeneous feudal society. Appeals for rectification came here, as elsewhere in Europe, from ecclesiastical circles. The activities of the preachers of Prague went hand in hand with the learned *disputations of the *doctors of the university and the movement of religious renewal of the **Devotio moderna*. From the beginning of the 15th c., Czech reformers espoused very closely the views of the English theologian John *Wycliffe, considered a *heretic by the Church. Polemics on the subject of his doctrine broke out at Charles University in 1409 into an open struggle between the two camps, then the defeat of the anti-Wycliffites, who withdrew from Prague.

The condemnation by the council of *Constance of Jan *Hus, great reforming theologian and disciple of Wycliffe, followed by his death at the stake in July 1415, led throughout Bohemia to a bloody confrontation between supporters and opponents of the new religious current, hostile to Rome and symbolized by the *chalice for the communion of the laity. Not until 1434 did the victory of the moderate wing of the Hussite movement allow it to find means of reconciliation with the Catholic Church and the Emperor *Sigismund, heir to the throne of Bohemia. The Hussite majority of the Czech population remained nevertheless cut off from the cultural, religious and political development going on elsewhere in Europe. As the result of a prolonged interregnum, the royal power was voided of its substance and the country fell under the control of the great aristocratic families, Hussite or *Catholic and often rivals, the Rozhemberk, the Lobkovic, lords of Kunštát, the Hradec, etc. The royal towns, mostly Czech and Hussite, strove in vain to wring from the ruler a little more independence and a wider representation in political life. They suffered moreover from the economic rivalry of the great landed properties of the nobility and the towns newly founded by them (called "of servile tenure").

The Catholic Church took a long time to recover from its defeats and the damage suffered in the course of the 15 years of Hussite wars. The life of the monasteries resumed with great difficulty, the *parish network, once very dense, crumbled for lack of *secular clergy, and the hierarchical instances functioned only in theory (*e.g.*, the archiepiscopal see of Prague remained vacant from 1421 to 1561). The level of teaching in Catholic and Hussite schools, including the university of Prague of Hussite obedience, declined ceaselessly. The birth and rise of the *Unity of Brethren, the first Czech Church to cut its bridges with Rome, represents a very important moment on the religious and cultural level. Its founder, the great 15th-c. reformer Petr Chelčický, rejected the *temporal power of the Church and its engagement in the affairs of the world. Though resolutely hostile to the system of feudal society, the Unity did not wish to impose its views of a juster world in the existing political framework, or rise up forcibly against it. The Brethren would be persecuted to varying degrees by the two officially recognised Churches, the Hussite majority and the Catholic minority. They would nevertheless bring many positive elements to Czech religious and cultural life.

At the end of the Middle Ages, the Czech State found itself heavily handicapped on the international scene by long years of war. The links between Bohemia, with its Hussite majority, and the Crown provinces, little touched by Hus's teaching, were largely slackened. Moreover, the head of the Hussite party, *George of Poděbrady, elected king of Bohemia in 1458, waged wars unsuccessfully against his neighbours, notably *Hungary. Nor did his successors on the throne, the Catholic dynasty of the Polish *Jagiellonians, manage significantly to consolidate their positions in central Europe and thus widen Bohemia's audience abroad.

After the death of the young King Louis, who fell in battle against the *Turks in 1526, the estates general of Bohemia brought Archduke Ferdinand of *Habsburg to the throne. This choice was the prelude to the creation, in central Europe, of a supranational community of countries whose links at first were rather loose, but which were later centralized in the hands of Austria.

V. Novotný, J. V. Šimák, J. Šusta, F. M. Bartoš, R. Urbánek, *České dějiny* [Czech history], I-III, Prague, 1912-1930 (12 vol.). – *Handbuch der Geschichte der böhmischen Länder*, K. Bosl (ed.), Stuttgart, 1966. – F. Šmahel, *The Idea of the "Nation" in Hussite Bohemia*, *Hist(P)*, 16, 1969, 133-247; 17, 1969, 43-197. – J. Kadlec, *Přehled českých církevních dějin* [Outline of Czech religious history], I-II, Rome, 1987 (re-ed. Prague, 1991). – Z. Boháč, "Historical-ecological Aspects of the Bohemian Feudal State Economy", *Historická ekologie*, 1, Prague, 1988, 11-59 and charts.

Zdeněk Boháč

***BOHEMIAN PLOUGHMAN.*** *Ackermann aus Beheim*, a prose dialogue written in *c.*1400 in German but in a Czech milieu, offers a reflection on the meaning of life; the Ploughman, presented as a lettered man, disputes with Death who has just taken his young wife. Also attributed to the author, master John of Šitboř (also called John of Saaz or of Tepla, d. *c.*1415), is a Czech work, *Tkadleček* (Little Weaver), sometimes considered a mere parody of the Ploughman. The similarity of form (dialogue) and subject (loss of a loved one) has raised a good many questions about the mutual links between the two texts. It still remains to be known whether *Ackermann* was an original work of John of Tepla, inspired by the loss of his wife in *c.*1400, or whether it leaned on another, older text, which also served as model for the Czech *Tkadleček*.

Johann von Tepl, *Der Ackermann aus Böhmen*, K. Spalding (ed.), Oxford, 1950. – Johannes von Saaz, *Death and the Plowman, or the Bohemian Plowman*, E. N. Kirrmann (tr.), Chapel Hill (NC), 1958 (repr. New York, 1969).

A. Hrubý, *Der Ackermann und seine Vorlage*, Vienna, 1971. – E. Schwarz, "Johannes von Tepl", *Lebensbilder zur Geschichte der böhmischen Ländern*, 2, Munich, 1976.

Jana Zachová

**BOLESLAS I OF BOHEMIA (929-972).** Prince of *Bohemia from 935 to 972, creator of the unified Czech State, Boleslas took power in 935 by assassinating the reigning prince *Wenceslas I, his elder brother, with whom he disagreed on the subject of relations with the nascent Holy Roman *Empire. Boleslas rapidly liquidated the independent principalities in the territory of Bohemia, gave the country a centralized administration, established the levying of taxes and, towards the end of his reign, began to strike the first Czech *coinage. He enlarged his State by annexing vast territories to the east: *Silesia, Little Poland and its dependencies extending as far as the frontiers of Kievan *Rus', northern *Moravia and north-east *Slovakia. After long struggles with the German Emperor *Otto I, he nevertheless made an act of allegiance in 950 and even supported him militarily in 955 at the battle of the Lech against the Hungarians. He allied himself with *Poland, giving his daughter *Dobrava in marriage to *Mieszko I, a still pagan Polish prince who was not long in converting. Boleslas I held talks with Rome in view of creating the bishopric of *Prague (they ended in 973, in the reign of his son Boleslas II).

V. Novotný, *České dějiny* [History of Bohemia], I, 1, Prague, 1914.

Dušan Třeštík

**BOLESLAS I THE BRAVE (967-1025).** Bolesław Chrobry or Boleslas the Brave, duke (992) then king (1025) of *Poland, was the son of *Mieszko I, duke of Poland, and Princess *Dobrava. He continued his father's policy, which tended to strengthen the freshly created State and affirm its recently-adopted Christianity. He supported Christian *missions to the Veleti, the Prussians and the Iatviegs. Profiting from the goodwill of the Emperor *Otto III, he obtained the canonization of Bishop *Adalbert (Wojciech) in 999 and the creation in 1000 of an archbishopric at *Gniezno with bishoprics at *Poznań, *Wrocław, *Cracow and Kołobrzeg. He brought in the first groups of religious who observed the *Benedictine Rule. In 1002-1018, he waged wars against the Germans, which ended with the peace of Bautzen (Budziszyn, 1018), by which he obtained Milsko and Lusatia. Boleslas the Brave enlarged the frontiers of the State by annexing to Poland a part of *Slovakia and *Moravia as well as, ephemerally, *Bohemia (1003-1004): in the east, he upheld the frontiers on the Bug (1018). His reign increased Poland's importance on the international scene.

A. F. Grabski, *Bolesław Chrobry. Zarys dziejów politycznych i wojskowych*, Warsaw, 1964. – F. Dvornik, *Les Slaves*, Paris, 1970.

Zbigniew Piłat

**BOLESLAS II THE BOLD (1041/42-1081).** Boleslas the Bold or the Generous, in Polish Bolesław Śmiały or Szczodry, Polish prince and from 1076 king of *Poland, was the son of the Polish prince Casimir the Restorer and the Kievan princess Dobronega. After the tragic events of 1031-1039, the Polish State had been rebuilt in the reign of Casimir the Restorer. On the territorial level, the capital had been transferred to *Cracow; nor had Casimir managed to regain the Crown lost by Mieszko II in 1031. Such was the inheritance of Boleslas the Bold in 1058, when he took power after his father's death.

He broadly pursued his predecessor's policy in favour of centralizing power; he took care to strengthen the Church – an important element in consolidating the State – by helping to establish a *bishopric at Płock and contributing to new Benedictine foundations at Tyniec, Lubin and Mogilno. He worked to strengthen Poland's international position by following a very active foreign policy. He interposed in the dynastic quarrels of *Rus' and *Hungary. Conflicts with *Bohemia led to a deterioration in his relations with the *Empire. In 1066, he lost East *Pomerania, but recovered for Poland the territory of Grody Czerwienskie (the red Ruthenian towns). He engaged in the *Investiture Contest, joining the Gregorian camp, which gained him increased independence from *Germany. The result of this rapprochement with the papacy was the authorization, given by *Gregory VII, to restore the metropolis of *Gniezno in 1075 and have himself crowned king there in 1076.

But Boleslas's strong power and very active foreign policy had many detractors in the country. In 1079, after the discovery of a plot, the king condemned to death the bishop of Cracow, *Stanislas, who was probably connected with the opposition. The active intrigues of his opponents forced Boleslas to leave Poland and take refuge in Hungary, where he died in 1081, probably at the monastery of Eszék (now Osijek). Power passed to his brother Ladislas (Władysław) Herman, who benefited from the support of the opposition. With the death of the king and the subordination of the State to Germany and Bohemia, Poland's international position suffered a visible decline.

T. Grudzínski, *Boleslaus the Bold, Called also the Bountiful, and Bishop Stanislaus: the Story of a Conflict*, Warsaw, 1985. – J. Powierski, *Kryzys rządów Bolesława Smiałego*, Gdańsk, 1992.

Zbigniew Piłat

**BOLESLAS III WRYMOUTH (1086-1138).** Boleslas III Wrymouth, in Polish Bolesław Krzywousty (1086-1138), Polish prince, was the son of the duke of *Poland, Ladislas Herman (Władysław Herman). After his father's death (1102), he governed

Funerary monument of Rolandino de' Romanzi at the Certosa near Bologna. 13th c.

the country in common with his brother Zbigniew; then from 1108, when his brother was expelled before being blinded in 1112, Boleslas ruled alone.

In the years 1119-1124, he added East *Pomerania to Poland and subjected to his authority West Pomerania where he supported the activity of Bishop *Otto of Bamberg (1124-1128) in favour of Christianization. Thanks to his support new *bishoprics were created at Włocławek, Lubusz and Wolin. Boleslas also supported the religious *orders – essentially the Benedictines and *Premonstratensians. He strove to make Poland independent of the *Empire; one consequence of this was a rapprochement with the pope. He fought a successful war against the Emperor *Henry V in 1109. In 1129-1130 he drew closer to *Denmark, marrying his daughter Ryksa to the Danish heir Magnus. He maintained good relations with *Hungary, taking sides in the dynastic quarrels that agitated it (1132-1134). Before dying in 1138, he established a testament dividing Poland into provinces which he distributed to his sons. This was the beginning of the partitioning of Poland into duchies, which came to an end only in the early 14th century.

P. David, *La Pologne et l'Évangélisation de la Poméranie aux XIe et XIIe siècles*, Paris, 1928. – K. Maleczyński, *Bolesław III Krzywousty*, Wrocław, 1975.

Zbigniew Piłat

## BOLOGNA

**Town.** Well situated on the old *Via Aemilia* that led from the Adriatic to the Po, starting-point of two roads crossing the Apennines (to Pistoia and *Florence), Bologna, seat of the *university with the best reputation for teaching law, was among the main towns of the West at the start of the 14th century.

In the 6th c., the conquest of *Italy by the *Lombards transformed this city into an outpost of the Eastern Empire: to the west, the kingdom of the Lombards (*Langobardia*); to the east, the Byzantine lands (*Romania*, now *Romagna). The town belonged to the Exarchate of *Ravenna but was conquered by the Lombards before being included in the Carolingian Empire. Until the 11th c., it played only a minor role in the shadow of Ravenna.

The town's golden age coincided with that of communal civilization. Enriched by the systematic exploitation of fertile countyside from which *serfdom was abolished in 1256, Bologna attracted numerous students and teachers of civil law and *medicine from far away: this was the origin of its image as a prosperous and learned city (*grassa e dotta*). The town developed until it numbered about 50,000 inhabitants occupying part of the 400 hectares marked out by the third town wall (13th-14th cc.). Its architecture was marked by the use of brick and wood, while the streets were often flanked by porticos creating a transitional area between public space and the private domain. An active urban municipalism (Piazza Maggiore, successive *palazzi comunali*, palace of the Podestà and the Captain of the People) vied with religious buildings of great renown: monastery of Santo Stefano, convent of the *Dominicans housing the tomb of the order's founder.

Recognised by the Emperor *Henry V (1116), the *commune carried its institutions to a high degree of perfection. Directed by consuls, then by an outside **podestà*, in the 13th c. the commune was controlled by the people (**popolo*), a group of citizens enrolled in trade and ward associations. Directed by elders (*anziani*), then by a captain, the people played a growing political role under the influence of *notaries including the famous Rolandino Passaggeri. The object was to counterbalance the power of the great Bolognese families, vast turbulent households sometimes of feudal origin, enriched by trading activities and moneylending, reigning over a tangle of houses, towers and private courtyards (*corte de'Galluzzi, torre degli Asinelli*).

Dominated by the *Guelf party, weakened by internal struggles between the *popolari* and the magnates as well as by the defeat and expulsion of the Ghibelline families, Bologna was incapable of achieving lasting rule over Romagna and transcending the framework of the city-state. In the 14th c., it was controlled alternately by the papacy (with the legations of *Bertrand du Poujet and *Albornoz) and the *Visconti of *Milan. In the 15th c., under the *signoria* of the Bentivoglio, the town did not have the brilliance of its neighbours *Modena and *Ferrara, and under Julius II it was attached to the *States of the Church.

A. Hessel, *Storia della città di Bologna, dal 1116 al 1280*, Bologna, 1975 (It. tr. of *Geschichte der Stadt Bologna von 1116 bis 1280*, Berlin, 1910). – F. Bonnard, "Bologne", *DHGE*, 9, 1937, 645-660. – A. Ferri, G. Roversi, *Storia di Bologna*, Bologna, 1984 (2nd ed.).

Jean-Louis Gaulin

**University.** Contrary to the medieval legend that ascribed its origins to a law school founded by the Emperor Theodosius II in 423 or to modern theories that would find a precedent for it in the hypothetical episcopal schools of the 11th c., the university of

Bologna came into being spontaneously at the beginning of the 12th c. when a series of illustrious professors came to teach in that town without being appointed by any authority, civil or ecclesiastical. At its origin we find contracts made between *masters and pupils: a number of students wishing to follow the lessons of a particular master formed an association and engaged to recompense the master they had chosen; in exchange, he was obliged to teach them for a certain time.

The number of Bolognese professors tended to increase. Alongside the civilists who obtained from the Emperor *Frederick Barbarossa a privilege (*habita*) removing the students from the ordinary jurisdiction and allowing them to choose between that of their masters and that of the *bishop (1158), a school of *canon law developed. One of its representatives, Gratian, drew up in *c.*1140 his **Decretum* which became the basis for Church legislation.

The renown of these professors drew to Bologna a great number of students, Italians and foreigners. Grouped into *nations according to their country of origin, they soon formed veritable corporations which, at the end of the 12th c., constituted themselves into two *universitates scolarium*, that of the Citramontanes, *i.e.* the Italians, and that of the Ultramontanes, numbering up to twelve nations, from Germans, Poles and Hungarians through representatives of the French provinces to English and Spaniards. Each one annually designated a *rector, together with councillors who exercised administrative power and jurisdiction with him. The professors chosen by the students for a limited duration took an *oath to the rector and engaged themselves not to teach elsewhere than Bologna. They necessarily had to intervene to deliver *degrees and to co-opt titular professors. To do this, they constituted themselves into a permanent commission of examinations and formed the two colleges of *doctors, one for civil law, the other for canon law.

The apogee of this autonomous university education was around the middle of the 13th c., a time when the teaching of civil law shone most brightly there with Azo, Odofredus and Accursius. From all points of Europe, students came to follow their teaching and, on returning to their own country, propagated their method. A number of universities more particularly dedicated to law were founded on its model.

But transformations were already coming about. *Frederick II, worried by the hostile attitude of the town, a member of the *Lombard League, founded the university of *Naples in 1224 and forbade his Italian subjects to go and study at Bologna. Pope *Honorius III, on the pretext of remedying abuses, put the *archdeacon of the cathedral in charge of delivering the **licentia docendi*. The commune began to create public chairs and restricted the right of professorship to citizens of Bologna alone; from then on the masters were in the pay of the town. Moreover, the two universities of *jurists saw two more universities, of *medicine and *theology, established alongside them. Bologna thus lost its pre-eminence, and the most famous Italian jurists of the 14th and 15th cc. went to teach elsewhere, at *Pisa or *Perugia, *Padua or *Pavia.

A. Sorbelli, *Storia dell'Università di Bologna*, Bologna, 1940. – S. Stelling-Michaud, *L'Université de Bologne et la pénétration des droits romain et canonique en Suisse aux XIII^e^ et XIV^e^ siècles*, Geneva, 1955. – *Dissertationes historicae de Universitate Bononiensi*, Bologna, 1956. – C. M. Radding, *The Origins of Medieval Jurisprudence: Pavia and Bologna, 850-1150*, New Haven, 1988.

Henri Gilles

Reliquary of the Corporal of the Miracle of Bolsena (back) by Ugolino di Vieri, 1338. Sienese school. Orvieto cathedral.

**BOLSENA, MIRACLE OF.** A eucharistic *miracle that took place in 1263 in the church of Santa Cristina at Bolsena, north of Rome. At the moment of *consecration, the *host changed into flesh between the hands of an unbelieving Bohemian priest. Many miracles of bleeding hosts are known in the Middle Ages, but that of Bolsena caused a great stir because Pope *Urban IV personally verified the veracity of the prodigy and instituted the feast of *Corpus Christi (Corpus Domini) some months later. However, it remains difficult to establish a relationship of cause and effect between the two events.

The story of the miraculous host and the *corporal stained with blood is related on the enamels of the *reliquary made by the Sienese artist Ugolino di Vieri (1337-1338). This masterpiece of Italian *goldsmiths' work is preserved in *Orvieto cathedral, in the so-called chapel of the Corporal, built for that purpose between 1350 and 1361. The mural paintings by Ugolino di Prete Ilario (1357-1364) offer a florilegium of eucharistic prodigies of the time. The miracle of Bolsena also inspired one of Raphael's most famous works in the Camera of Heliodorus at the Vatican.

A. Lazzarini, *Il miracolo di Bolsena. Testimonianze e documenti dei secoli XIII e XIV*, Rome, 1952. – E. Franceschini, "Origine e stile della bolla 'Transiturus'", *Aevum*, 39, 1965, 218-243.

Dominique Rigaux

**BONAGRATIA OF BERGAMO (died 1340).** Entering the Order of Friars Minor in *c.*1310, thanks to his legal learning he became assistant *procurator of the *Franciscans at the *Avignon *Curia.

Here he initially sided vigorously against the "zealots" of the Rule. When *John XXII intervened to resolve the age-old question of *poverty, he followed the fortunes of the order's leaders, in particular *Michael of Cesena. From 1328 he was at the court of Louis of Bavaria and took an active part in the violent controversy with the Avignonese papacy, putting his great legal learning at the service of the emperor. He died at Munich in 1340 and is buried in the Franciscan church there.

H. J. Becker, "Bonagrazia da Bergamo", *DBI*, 11, 1969, 505-508. – A. Tabarroni, *Paupertas Christi et apostolorum. L'ideale franciscano in discussione (1322-1324)*, Rome, 1990.

Grado G. Merlo

**BONAVENTURE (*c.*1217-1274).** Saint and *Franciscan, born at Bagnoregio *c.*1217, died at Lyon 15 July 1274. Bonaventure (Bonaventura) came to Paris to be inscribed in the *faculty of arts in 1235. A *master of arts in 1234, he entered the Order of Friars Minor and studied theology under the teaching of *Alexander of Hales († 1245), *John of La Rochelle († Feb 1245), *Eudes Rigaud and William of Melitona. Biblical bachelor in 1248, sententiary bachelor in 1250, in 1254 he obtained his **licentia docendi* with the *Quaestiones disputatae de scientia Christi*. From this time regent master of the friars' school, he was elected minister general of the order on 2 Feb 1257 at Rome. Created cardinal bishop of Albano by Pope *Gregory X on 28 May 1273, he assisted him during the second council of *Lyon from 7 May to 15 July 1274, the date of his death.

His scriptural writings consist of the *Lecturae in Ecclesiasten*, *in Lucam*, and *in Ioannen*; his theological writings are the *Commentaria in IV Libros Sententiarum Magistri Petri Lombardi*, the *Breviloquium* and the *Quaestiones disputatae de scientia Christi*, *De mysterio Trinitatis* and *De perfectione evangelica*. Bonaventure's theological masterpiece is incontestably the *Itinerarium mentis in Deum*. His *sermons comprise: 50 *Sermones dominicales*, 265 *Sermones de tempore* brought together in a manuscript collection at Milan, 62 *Sermones de diversis* scattered among 63 manuscripts, and *Collationes de decem praeceptis* (1267), *De septem donis Spiritus sancti* (1268) and *In Hexaemeron* (1273). His spiritual writings are the *De triplici via*, the *Soliloquium*, the *Lignum vitae* and the *De perfectione vitae ad sorores*. His Franciscan writings comprise the *Legenda maior* and, for the choral office, the *Legenda minor*. Finally, the *Apologia pauperum* was intended as a reply to the attacks of the secular masters against the evangelical ideal of the *mendicants.

With Bonaventure, the first Franciscan school reached its apogee. When in 1243 the young master of arts asked to become a Franciscan, he was the first to receive his whole theological education at the *studium*. The originality of Bonaventure's teachers was developed under Francis's influence, so that Bonaventure had no difficulty in thinking "in Franciscan". The sources of his thought and the major themes of his *theology are also a testimony to the evangelical renewal inaugurated by *Francis of Assisi.

Bonaventure had in fact chosen his sources. The masters of the arts faculty, *Siger of Brabant and *Boethius of Dacia, defended an *Aristotle tainted with *Averroism. *Thomas Aquinas would use all his strength to give the Philosopher an authentic and acceptable interpretation. Bonaventure moved in another world. Aristotle was for him an authority who must be read critically and with eyes open. When in 1273 he gave his conferences on the *Hexaemeron*, he remained faithful to what he had determined in his lecture on the *Sentences or in the disputed questions. He denounced the nefarious influence of Aristotle in theology and undertook to expound what, according to him, Christian *wisdom consisted in. This Christian wisdom that he intended to expound determined the sources of his knowledge; his choice was significant, since he turned more readily to Pseudo-*Dionysius than to Aristotle. That is to say that he intended to construct a spiritual synthesis and not a rationally scientific work.

The major themes of Bonaventurian thought appear from his first works as a biblical bachelor, gain strength continually from reflection and experience and receive their finished expression in his last works. These themes are the place of *Christ as *medium*, "expressionism", and reflection on *homo imago*. The first major theme is the place Bonaventure gives to Christ as *medium*. The starting-point of Bonaventure's trinitarian theology is taken from Pseudo-Dionysius: *God is the *Good in continual diffusion. The overflowing source of life that is the Father is the origin of the eternal generation of the Son, likeness of the Father. The *Word expresses the Father and the whole of creation, at the same time as it reveals to us how we are created and how we are called to return to the unity of the Father. *Medium* within the *Trinity, Christ is thus the *medium* between God and creation. And because God is *love, God sends his son to bring the world *salvation; the cross is the supreme manifestation of God's humility, unsurpassable evidence of Christ the *medium* of our *Redemption. From the Father, Christ sends the Spirit into the hearts of believers: the Word is the *medium* of our divinization. The triad of uncreated Word, incarnate Word and inspired Word synthesizes the vision of the universe as he was able to construct it in his reflections on Scripture and on what Augustine, *Hugh and *Richard of Saint-Victor and Pseudo-Dionysius, commented on by *John Scotus Eriugena, had been able to tell him about it.

The second major theme flows immediately from the first, and is that of "expressionism". If *man's divinization, in which the Dionysian hierarchical activity consists, is effected by the divine Word by means of theophanies, "expression" takes on a noetic power of revelatory manifestation. At work in the production of the divine Word, "expression" or *theophany is manifested in the created spirit when its origin and status are revealed to it.

The third major theme intimately linked to the former two is that of *homo imago*. A central theme of biblical thought and Greek patristics, it became the fundamental element of Bonaventure's Christian anthropology. He stressed two aspects: the first demonstrates that the image can be the simple presence of elements whose conformity creates this particular relationship that makes one being the image of another; the second aspect is that of the relationship itself enclosed in the image with the underlying idea of *participation. The resulting identity between the image and the exemplar is not such that the image and the exemplar form only one between the two of them, but it does not distinguish them so far as to make them totally extraneous to each other. Augustine's word *capax Dei* thus signifies a dynamic orientation, an impetus towards the exemplar from whom it takes its whole image-being.

In the *Itinerarium mentis in Deum* Bonaventure successfully synthesized these three major themes: to know God in the creature is to know his presence and his activity; to know God by the creature is to mount up from effect to *cause, God as Being, whole and entire inside and outside all things, but also God as Good, sovereign diffusion of the Good that he is in himself, a diffusion expressed in creation.

Bonaventure is "the privileged place of convergence and confluence of all the currents and all the ideas of the world which, from all sides, irrigate and fertilize the milieu of the 13th c." (Hans Urs von Balthasar, *La Gloire et la Croix*, II, 328). It is indeed, in fact, a matter of convergence and confluence, because none of those who play their part in the construction of his thought occur there as they are in themselves, so much does the unifying power coming from elsewhere allow Bonaventure to attain to the simplicity of an original synthesis. This unifying power turns out to be Francis of Assisi.

Bonaventure was fully conscious of being the witness of two worlds, the world of the human and religious culture of his time which his 22 years at Paris studying and teaching *philosophy and theology led him to discover, and the world of Francis of Assisi's evangelical revival which, for 17 years, he had to animate in a very varied order shot through by contradictory currents, at the same time as he had to take an active part in the vicissitudes of the Church's life while keeping an attentive eye on the evolution of the controversies and disputes of the university of *Paris. His interventions in 1267, 1268 and 1273 seemed to him indispensable in the face of the peril he saw mounting in the world of culture and the world of the Church. He gave his order a balanced structure, he offered his friars a life of St Francis as a bond of unity, he also wanted to talk aloud to the teachers and students of the theology faculty.

Between these two worlds, that which allowed the germination of St Francis of Assisi and that in which "man's spirit is prostituted", Bonaventure chose. In his personal experience nourished by profound and continual thought, he found in himself the presence of God which he sought and which he could find only by opening himself up to his word in a *faith accepted and lived in *contemplation and love.

*The Works of St. Bonaventure*, 5 vol., Paterson (NJ), 1960-1970. – *Saint Bonaventure's Disputed Questions of the Mystery of the Trinity*, St. Bonaventure (NY), 1979.

É. Gilson, *The Philosophy of St Bonaventure*, Paterson (NJ), 1965. – E.W. Cousins, *Bonaventure and the Coincidence of Opposites*, Chicago, 1978. – Z. Hayes, *The Hidden Center: Spirituality and Speculative Christology in St Bonaventure*, New York, 1981. – J.-G. Bougerol, *Introduction à saint Bonaventure*, Paris, 1988. – L. Mathieu, *La Trinité créatrice d'après saint Bonaventure*, Paris, 1992.

Jacques-Guy Bougerol

**BONIFACE VIII, POPE (*c*.1235/1240-1303).** Born Benedict *Caetani, at *Anagni, to a family of the lesser nobility, he studied law and became a papal *notary. From 1264 he began a diplomatic career. *Cardinal-deacon in 1281, then priest in 1291, thanks to his *benefices he built up a considerable landed property, not without arousing resentments which help to explain his tragic end.

On 5 July 1294, in *conclave, he gave his vote to the hermit Pietro da Morrone, who became *Celestine V. When Celestine realised his own incompetence, Caetani gave him advice that facilitated his *resignation and, 11 days later, on 14 Dec 1294, was elected to succeed him.

One of his first acts was to revoke or suspend the measures taken by his predecessor and to renew the personnel of the *Curia, thus announcing an authoritarian pontificate. On the political level, the pope considered himself the arbiter of thrones. He intervened in the successions to the thrones of *Hungary and *Poland, tried in vain to bring *Sicily back into obedience to the Church, opposed Albert of Austria in the *Empire, then turned round and took his side when it became useful in his struggle against *Philip the Fair.

His difference with the king of France was one of the major threads of his pontificate. A first phase concerned the problem of the *taxation of the clergy by temporal rulers (**Clericis laicos*). Then followed a period of *entente cordiale*, marked among other things by the *canonization of *Louis IX. During this period, in May 1297, Boniface had to face the attack of the two *Colonna cardinals who maintained the invalidity of Celestine's resignation and hence the illegitimacy of his successor. The rebels were quickly removed from office and then *excommunicated. They later figured among the deceased pope's accusers.

The pontificate attained its apogee with the *jubilee of 1300 (the first in history) but, from the following year, conflict resumed with the French court. Boniface having appointed a bishop without consulting the king, Philip had the man arrested, drawing down on himself a heavy reprimand (**Ausculta fili*). Then, rising to the level of principles, in 1302 Boniface published the *bull *Unam Sanctam*, in which he claimed that everyone was subject in all things to the Roman pontiff. From then on things moved ever faster, especially when the jurist Guillaume de Nogaret became the king's adviser on religious affairs. On 12 March 1303 Nogaret accused the pope of heresy and demanded that a *council be called to judge him. The king still hesitated but, after a *Parlement held at Paris in June, gave his consent and instructed Nogaret to go and notify Boniface of the grievances against him and to oblige him to call the council. It was at Anagni, on 7 Sept, that the legate succeeded in gaining access to the pope, thanks to an armed escort. The intervention of Sciarra Colonna added violence and pillage. Boniface, who refused to consent to the demands made of him, was put under guard, but not struck. Freed after two days by his repentant countrymen, he left for *Rome where he died on 11 Oct 1303.

To legitimize his action, Nogaret tried to obtain the pope's condemnation for heresy, *simony, sodomy, etc. The trial opened in 1310 at *Avignon, but was suspended without sentence the next year.

P. Dupuy, *Histoire du différent d'entre le pape Boniface VIII et Philippes le Bel, roy de France*, Paris, 1655. – T. S. R. Boase, *Boniface VIII*, London, 1933. – G. Digard, *Philippe le Bel et le Saint-Siège (1285-1304)*, Paris, 1936 (2 vol.). – E. Duprè Theseider, *DBI*, 12, 1970, 146-170. – T. Schmidt, *Der Bonifaz-Prozess*, Cologne-Vienne, 1989. – J. Coste (ed.), *Boniface VIII en procès*, Rome, 1996.

Jean Coste †

**BONIFACE IX, POPE (died 1404).** Pietro Tomacelli, elected *pope 2 Nov 1389, succeeded *Urban VI, his Neapolitan compatriot, to whom he owed the essentials of his career. Like his predecessor, Boniface IX eluded all proposals put to him to regulate the question of the *Great Schism. Possessing more the qualities of a secular prince than of a head of the Church, he fought against the anarchy that reigned in *Italy. Already master of *Rome and the *Patrimony, in 1403 he was the most powerful man in the peninsula. The rebuilding of the Castel Sant'Angelo (1403) symbolized the triumph of apostolic power in the Eternal City and the *States of the Church. Boniface took extraordinary measures to mitigate the growing deficit of the Roman *Curia's coffers, due in part to the existence of schismatic popes at *Avignon. The failure of a projected *concordat with England (Nov 1398) illustrates a pontificate with no significant religious influence.

*DHGE*, 9, 1937, 910-922. – *HChr*, 6, 1990.

Michel Fol

**BONIFACE OF CREDITON (672/675-754).** Born *c.*672-675 in Wessex (*England), Winfrid lived and was educated at *Exeter and Nursling and became a priest at the age of 30 or slightly less. After a first attempt to settle on the continent (716), he returned to England and became abbot of Nursling. In 718 he set off again and went to *Rome, where Gregory II gave him the name Boniface and entrusted him with a *mission to the *pagans of Germany. After spending three years with *Willibrord, he settled in *Hesse (foundation of Amoeneburg, 722). Becoming a *bishop, he entered into relations with *Charles Martel, founded the monastery of *Fritzlar after having thrown down the oak of Geismar, then went to *Thuringia where he remained until 735 (foundation of Ohrdruf).

In 732, Gregory III sent him the archiepiscopal **pallium* and asked him to institute bishops, which he did in *Bavaria, after having long preached there (735-737). He came back from Rome in 738 with the title of *legate, held *synods, created the *dioceses of *Salzburg, Freising and *Regensburg, confirmed that of *Passau and added those of Eichstätt and *Würzburg. The sees of Buraburg and *Erfurt were ephemeral (741-743). In his monastic policy, he was assisted by *nuns who came from Britain and took part in his missionary activities (Tauberbischofheim, Kitzingen). Boniface worked in close liaison with Charles Martel and then Carloman, but not with *Pippin. His activity manifested itself, from 742 to 747, in the foundation of *Fulda (744) and the regular meeting of *councils (*concilium germanicum* of 743) permitting him to impose the bishops' authority and to regulate the discipline of *clerics and monks. His unifying role throughout the Frankish kingdom ended in 747. Ceasing his missionary wanderings, he settled in the archiepiscopal see of *Mainz from 746 to 754, not having obtained that of *Cologne. He was much occupied with his foundation of Fulda, directly subject to Rome. Finally, in disagreement with the policy of the Carolingian king, he set out in 754 to preach in *Frisia, where he was killed on 5 June.

*S. Bonifatii et Lulli Epistolae*, M. Tangl (ed.), *MGH.ES*, 1, Berlin, 1916 f. – The *Letters of Saint Boniface*, E. Emerton (ed.), New York, 1940.

W. Levison, *England and the Continent in the Eighth Century*, Oxford, 1946, 70-93. – T. Schieffer, *Winfrid-Bonifatius und die christliche Grundlegung Europas*, Freiburg, 1954. – *The Greatest Englishman*, T. Reuter (ed.), Exeter, 1980. – K. U. Jäschke, "Bonifatius", *TRE*, 7, 1981, 69-74. – F. Prinz, *Frühes Mönchtum im Frankenreich*, Munich, 1988 (2nd ed.). – P. Kehl, *Kult und Nachleben des heiligen Bonifatius im Mittelalter (754-1200)*, Fulda, 1993.

Michel Parisse

**BOOK.** During late Antiquity, the use and production of books declined to the point where they no longer existed except in monasteries and *cathedral churches. Copyists worked to reproduce the Holy Scriptures, *liturgical books and, in the more important centres, part of the works inherited from pagan Antiquity; they imposed the *codex at the expense of the roll. But the curiosity of some, like Abbot *Lupus of Ferrières in the 9th c., exchanges from one monastery to another and the art of copyists and illuminators ensured not just the survival of the book but its first golden age, under the *Carolingians.

It must be recognised, however, that the revolution that took place from the 12th c. tended to throw the previous step into the shade. Gradually, the book escaped from the confines of **scriptoria* and acquired an unprecedented importance. The development of the *schools, then the birth of the *universities in the 13th c., the appearance of new professional bodies specializing in the practice of writing, such as *jurists, and the progress of literacy among *nobles, *merchants and artisans multiplied the applications of the book: it became a tool of secular studies, work, leisure and private devotion. The contents changed. We see previously marginal themes assert themselves (*e.g.* law), while the traditional contents of written culture were gradually adapted to the tastes and capacities of new readers; from the 13th c., the book was open to the vernacular languages.

Unprecedented applications imposed an effort of imagination on the layout and production of tools of consultation. University books are conspicuous for their generous margins on which the *master's commentary could be inscribed. To facilitate the consultation of collections, ever more elaborate indexes and tables were perfected. The evolution of needs was also quantitative. Book production acquired an almost industrial character. Specialization of tasks led to the appearance of new skills: parchment maker or paper maker, copyist, bookbinder. *Paper, known since the 11th c., gained ground but did not truly prevail until the 15th c., when its cost was about 13 times cheaper than *parchment. The work of the copyist himself was transformed by the **pecia* system, which led to an appreciable gain in time. The invention of printing by *Gutenberg in *c.*1450 in the *Mainz region aimed to permit a new increase in production. The effect was immediate. In 1500, we can count 237 centres in the West equipped with a press or having welcomed one. But we still have to wait some years more before the introduction of printing led to a veritable revolution and gave birth to the modern book.

E. I. Eisenstein, *The Printing Revolution in Early Modern Europe*, Cambridge, 1983. – *Le Livre au Moyen Âge*, J. Glenisson (dir.), Paris, 1988. – H. J. Martin, *Histoire et pouvoirs de l'écrit*, Paris, 1988.

Daniel Baloup

**BOOKS OF HOURS.** A book of *prayers intended for the *laity, the Book of Hours succeeded the Carolingian prayerbooks and the psalters of the 12th and 13th cc., but addressed a much wider public than before, aristocratic and bourgeois. The production of Books of Hours underwent a vigorous expansion from the early 15th c.; it reached its apogee in the 16th c., with exemplars printed (the overwhelming majority at Paris) and illustrated with woodcuts. Alongside the individualized hours of bibliophile princes, which are among the masterpieces of medieval painting, went thousands of *books produced in series in great centres like *Paris, *Rouen or *Flanders, at *Bruges and *Ghent, not forgetting that more modest copies with no or few decorations must also have existed.

The genesis of this new book was connected both to the growing cult of the Virgin and to the quest for a mode of expression specific to private lay piety, yet desirous of imitating the prayer of the canonical *hours of the clergy. This culminated in the borrowing of an element attached to the *breviary: the little office of the Virgin, shorter and easier to handle, which in France followed the regional usage of a *diocese, while in Flanders and Italy the usage of Rome was almost exclusive. Added originally to the *psalter (from the second half of the 12th c.), it later formed the central core of the new book to which its eight hours lent their name. It was always most richly illustrated, very frequently with a cycle of the Infancy of Christ which was at the same time a Marian cycle, from the *Annunciation to the Coronation of the Virgin. The other essential texts of the Book of Hours (with their usual illustration) were the *calendar (signs of the *zodiac and *labours of the months), the seven penitential *psalms followed by the *litanies of the saints (scene of the life of *David), intercessory prayers to the saints (portraits or martyrdoms) and the office of the *dead (varied iconography, usually a funeral scene). Other texts were nearly always present: Hours of the Cross and the Holy Spirit (Crucifixion and *Pentecost), four gospel pericopes (portraits of the *evangelists), the Marian prayers *Obsecro te* and *O Intemerata*, which, with the *Fifteen Joys of the Virgin*, were the favourite place to include, in an image of the Virgin and Child or the *Pietà, the (generally stereotyped) figure of the book's recipient, most usually a woman. Books of Hours were written in *Latin, the vernacular being used, if at all, only for a few secondary texts, the calendar, the *rubrics and some prayers.

The majority of surviving manuscripts are of French, then Flemish (including exemplars destined for Spain and Portugal) and Dutch origin; also Italian, but these last are considerably less studied. Less numerous are those of English origin, perhaps because of massive disappearances at the time of the Anglican Reformation. The rarity of Books of Hours in German lands appears to signify a fundamentally different attitude of piety.

The prayer of the hours by the laity was favoured within institutions like the mendicant *Third Orders (recitation of the little office of the Virgin) and the *confraternities (celebration of the office of the dead). Many surviving manuscripts, however, are in a state of freshness that leads us to doubt their daily use and emphasizes their social importance as precious and prestigious objects.

V. Leroquais, *Les Livres d'heures manuscrits de la Bibliothèque nationale*, Paris, 1927 (3 vol.); suppl., Mâcon, 1943. – A. Labarre, "Heures (Livres d)", *DSp*, 7, 1969, 410-431. – R. S. Wieck *et al.*, *The Book of Hours in Medieval Art and Life*, London, 1988. – R. S. Wieck, *Painted Prayers. The Book of Hours in Medieval and Renaissance Art*, New York, 1997.

Claudia Rabel

*Jesus before Pilate*, from the *Heures de Marguerite d'Orléans* (after 1426). Paris, BNF (Ms lat. 1156 B, fol. 135).

**BORIS AND GLEB (*c.*990-*c.*1010-1015).** The first Russian saints (baptismal names Roman and David). Born of the Bulgarian wife of the first Christian ruler of Kievan *Rus', *Vladimir the Great, they were assassinated after their father's death by their older half-brother Sviatopolk. Having offered no resistance to the attackers sent by him, but instead prayed for forgiveness for their brother, they not only fell as innocent victims of the struggle for the succession to the throne, but also provided a saintly model of princely conduct. In literary texts, the description of their death follows the biblical account of Cain and Abel, the two princes being allegorically identified with Abel – prototype of Christ – while Sviatopolk is identified with Cain and systematically called "the Accursed One". They have thus become an ideal paradigm of *martyrdom and indeed of self-sacrifice in the name of God, while the history of Kievan Rus' has acquired the status of a sacred text encoded in Holy Scripture itself. At the same time, their *cult provides a specific model of perception of holiness and sainthood (the "typically Russian" model of *strastoterpets* or "Passion-Sufferer", a manifestation of "Holy Rus'").

Because of the phonetic similarity between the name Glěb (pronounced "Hlěb" in many Russian, Ukrainian and Belarusian dialects) and the Slavonic lexeme "hlěb" ("bread"), they are believed to be guardians of the fields, corn and fertility, and protectors of the harvest. This popular belief apparently embodies the archaic idea of the ruler's function as deity-protector of the fertility of his land, providing the vernacular background for a further development of their cult. The hagiographical framework of their early veneration, from the first decades of the 11th c., was a cluster of tales about the dynastic struggle after the death of Vladimir the Great. Drawing on popular tradition, these adhere equally to the conventions of the Byzantine *vita* and to the canons of the oral legend. They are: the *Russian Primary Chronicle* (*Povest' Vremennyx Let*), compiled in the Monastery of the *Caves at Kiev in *c.*1115, *Nestor of Kiev's *Lesson of the Life and Murder of the Blessed Passion-Sufferers Boris and Gleb*; the *Tale and Passion and Encomium of the Holy Martyrs Boris and Gleb* (12th or early 13th c.), etc.; as well as a 12th-c. *Sermon on the Cult of Boris and Gleb*, the *Paremejnik Reading for Boris and Gleb*, etc.

Boris and Gleb were canonized on 20 May 1072 and became the most venerated saints of Rus'. Their feasts are 24 July (day of Boris's murder) and 2 May (translation of the relics).

A. Poppe, "La naissance du culte de Boris et Gleb", *CCM*, 24, 1981, 29-53. – G. Lenhoff, *The Martyred Princes Boris and Gleb: A Socio-Cultural Study of the Cult and the Texts*, Columbus (OH), 1989 (UCLA Slavic Studies, 19). – *The Hagiography of Kievan Rus'*, P. Hollingsworth (tr., intro.), Cambridge (MA), 1992, pp. xxvi-lviii, 3-32, 97-134, 183-231. – A. Poppe, "Der Kampf um die Kiever Thronfolge nach dem 15 Juli 1015", *FOEG*, 50, 1995, 275-296. – *Russia Medievalis*, 8, 1, 1995, 5-68.

Florentina Badolanova

**BORIS OF BULGARIA (died 907).** First Christian prince of *Bulgaria (852-889). He began by making an alliance with *Louis the German, but unfavourable military circumstances obliged him to form links with Byzantium. He agreed to convert and took the

*John Hayton of the Premonstratensian Order, cousin of the king of Armenia, offers his book to John the Fearless, duke of Burgundy.* Early 15th-c. miniature by the Boucicaut Master from the *Livre de Merveilles*, a collection of accounts of the voyages of Marco Polo, Odoric of Pordenone, William of Boldensele, John Mandeville, John Hayton and Riccoldo of Montecroce. Paris, BNF (Ms fr. 2810, fol. 226).

name of Michael (the emperor of *Constantinople Michael III had been his godfather). The introduction of Christianity provoked a lively reaction from the aristocracy who considered the *conversion an act of political submission. In 869-870, the *council of Constantinople decided that Bulgaria would receive its Church organisation and its prelates from Constantinople. Boris nevertheless managed to emancipate himself from Byzantine tutelage on the cultural level by welcoming the *mission of *Cyril and Methodius, expelled from *Moravia. The capital, Pliska (later Preslav), and *Ohrid became cultural centres where a rich Slav Christian literature flourished.

V. Giuzelev, "Boris I", *Kirilo-Metodievska Enciklopedia*, 1, Sofia, 1985, 222-233 (bibl.).

Vasilka Tăpkova-Zaimova

**BOŘIVOJ (died *c.*894).** First Christian Czech prince of the *Přemyslid dynasty, Bořivoj traditionally received *baptism in 883-884 with his wife Princess Ludmila (later declared a saint) from the hands of the Moravian archbishop Methodius, at the court of Duke Svatopluk of Great *Moravia. Bořivoj's reign was contemporary with the German-Moravian conflict, which was particularly envenomed at the time of the Emperor *Arnulf; this facilitated the emancipation of the Czech tribes from the rule of the dukes of Great Moravia and made possible the creation of a State of their own. Bořivoj resided first at Levý Hradec, then he settled at *Prague, which became the capital of the new State. Bořivoj made Christian influence lasting in *Bohemia; to him is attributed the foundation, notably, of the church of Our Lady at Prague. By Princess Ludmila he had two sons, Spitigniev and Vratislav.

F. Dvornik, *Les Slaves*, Paris, 1970. – B. Chropovsky, *Les Slaves*, Prague, 1989, 225-226.

Zbigniew Piłat

**BOSNIA.** From the time of the final partition of the Roman Empire (395), the geopolitical area of modern Bosnia-Herzegovina formed part of the Western Empire. Following the treaty of Aachen between *Charlemagne and Michael Rhangabe (812), Bosnian territory remained under the protection of the Frankish kingdom.

Old Slavonic by tradition and under the dominant influence of Croat glagolitism (biblical translations, liturgical texts, religious and secular literature), Bosnian Christianity – under the jurisdiction of the Roman pontiffs – was organised around a single Catholic *bishopric, founded shortly before 1089, which included the vast territory of the *banat* (vice-kingdom) of Bosnia and the neighbouring areas.

Early in the 13th c., diplomatic sources and the writings of Latin controversialists notice a heterodox community called the "Church of Bosnian Christians": a product of the medieval evangelical movement, it was influenced by Waldensian doctrines and *Cathar hierarchical structures. Alerted, *Innocent III reacted, and in the presence of the papal *legate John of Casamare the representatives of the "Christians" abjured the "Manichaean" *heresy and promised to follow the doctrine taught by the Roman Church.

There is no doubt that the followers of the Bosnian Church sincerely sought to recover the example of the first Christians and the purity of the early Church. But because of their severe criticisms of religious institutions, they were misunderstood by the church authorities and condemned by the secular power, while they themselves, under the influence of the *Waldenses and of Cathar pessimism, began to depart from Catholicism and the fundamentals of Christianity.

From the 13th c., the *mendicant orders established in Bosnia a sort of bridgehead for meetings between East and West. *Dominicans and *Franciscans organised disputes with the Bosnian "Christians", preached the Gospel to the *Cumans and established dialogue with the Orthodox. Their missionary activity oriented them towards the study of oriental languages, more particularly Arabic, which was of great use to the Franciscans in the 15th c. in their contacts with the *Ottoman conquerors.

The Turkish invasion modified the religious map of the Balkans. Stephen Thomas, king of Bosnia (1443-1461), called on the followers of the Bosnian Church to choose between *conversion and exile. At this time numerous "Christians" chose to be expatriated to Herzegovina. Under the protection of the Ottoman invader there appeared in Bosnia a militant *Orthodoxy that later identified itself with the propagation of an aggressive Serbism. The Franciscans and, in smaller numbers, the priests officiating in Old Church Slavonic remained in place and encouraged the Catholics to remain faithful to the Church.

E. Fermendžin, *Acta Bosnae potissimum ecclesiastica ab anno 925 usque ad annum 1752*, Zagreb, 1892. – J. V. A. Fine, *The Bosnian Church*, New York, 1975. – F. Šanjek, *Les Chrétiens bosniaques et le mouvement cathare aux XII*[e]*-XV*[e] *siècles*, Paris-Louvain, 1976 ("Recherches", 20). – N. Klaić, *Srednjovjekovna Bosna* [Medieval Bosnia], Zagreb, 1989. – J. Džaja, *Die Franziskaner im mittelalterlichen Bosnien*, Werl (Westphalia), 1991. – N. Malcolm, *Bosnia. A Short History*, London, 1994.

Franjo Šanjek

**BOUCICAUT MASTER (early 15th c.).** An anonymous Parisian illuminator who owes his provisional name to his masterpiece, the illustration of the *Heures du Maréchal de Boucicaut* (Paris, Musée Jacquemart-André), and whose activity can be put roughly between 1405 and 1425. He is sometimes identified, on no firm grounds, with Jean Coene of *Bruges. He was probably an artist heading an important studio whose output was very uneven, but who personally made a decisive contribution to the evolution of French art, particularly by the care which he gradually developed for a true representation of space.

M. Meiss, *French Painting in the Time of Jean de Berry. The Boucicaut Master*, London, 1968.

Albert Châtelet

***BOURG.*** Though originally designating a fortress (*Burg* in German retains this sense), the *bourg* (*burgus*) was a built-up area with neither religious nor military function, which distinguished it from the **civitas* or the *castrum*. It seems that gradually the notion of trading activities was attached to it. From the 10th c., the phenomenon of the *bourg* manifests the beginnings of urban and commercial expansion, but also the conquest of *agriculture.

The rural *bourg* was a seignorial creation and grouped together *coloni* and dependent tenants. But it also designated the built-up areas or quarters arising out of urban and commercial development, though terms like *suburbium* or *portus* were used more in German-speaking regions. Usually not fortified to begin with, the *bourg* came into being near a centre of power or concentration of wealth. The 10th and 11th cc. saw the multiplication of castral *bourgs*, near a fortified seignorial residence, or monastic *bourgs*, near a monastery. They concentrated the activities of transformation and exchange, craftsmanship and *commerce, profiting from the needs of the *castle or monastery, especially when the latter was the object of an important *pilgrimage. Around or within the *towns, we also note the presence of one or more suburban *bourgs*, most often attesting urban growth. The building of new walls and the erection of new *parishes in the 12th or 13th c. took into account the presence of these new urban quarters.

Some *bourgs* could be the fruit of a deliberate policy of creating urban or rural centres, as in Western France, with a different meaning from the **sauvetés* of the Garonne regions, or *villeneuves*, where, provided with privileges and liberties, they were sometimes able to attract an important population. But, if *bourgs* could give rise to urban entities sometimes rivalling a pre-existing town, many disappeared or did not go beyond a limited stage of development. At any rate, the *bourg* illustrates the birth in the Middle Ages of an urban network independent of that bequeathed by Roman Antiquity and responding to new styles and currents of trade.

As for the term "bourgeois" (*burgensis*), it appeared between the late 10th and early 11th century. It originally designated the inhabitants of the *bourg*, but its spread in the course of the 12th c. shows that from now on it possessed a wider meaning. In fact it designated all the inhabitants of the town, thus showing the slow process by which the town detached itself from the rural world and acquired a specific economic character. Composed of *merchants, specialists in monetary activities, men with an income from land or political power, this new social category was very much a mixture and only slowly acquired its own individuality. Subject to the power of the lord of their town or *bourg*, the bourgeois slowly acquired the desire to participate in the government of the town, in proportion to their social rise, in the 12th and 13th centuries.

View of the ambulatory of Bourges cathedral, late 12th - early 13th c.

T. Endeman, *Markturkunde und Markt in Frankreich und Burgund von 9. bis 11. Jahrhundert*, Constance, Stuttgart, 1964. – L. Musset, "Peuplement en bourgage et bourgs ruraux en Normandie du Xe au XIIIe siècle", *CCM*, 9, 1966, 177-208. – *La Ville médiévale, Histoire de la France urbaine*, G. Duby (dir.), 2, Paris, 1980, 59-141.

Thierry Pécout

**BOURGES CATHEDRAL.** The construction, in which Henry de Sully took the initiative around 1195 to replace the old 11th-c. *cathedral, is unique in its kind, though contemporary with *Chartres, with which it is often contrasted. Its structure is of an extreme simplicity, in which the interior volume finds an unequalled coherence: neither radiating chapels nor transept break its continuity. Its size and the audacity of its elevation (the five aisles are spread out in perfect pyramidal hierarchy) reinforce the originality of a plan that would be little imitated. On the outside, a double flight of flying buttresses balances the masses.

The deployment of the five west portals confirms the ambition of this grandiose programme, whose threshold is the *Last

Judgment sculpted on the central portal. The sculptures of the *rood screen, now partly remounted in the Louvre museum, surrounded the main *altar with the story of the *Passion. Finally the *stained glass windows, among the most interesting of the 13th c., were arranged according to a learned theological programme, with complex correspondences and implications between the Old and New *Testaments. Their aesthetic value is equal to this iconographical power.

A second great phase of building opened at Saint-Étienne with the arrival of Duke *John of Berry in 1392, thanks to the *patronage of the court grandees, Jacques Coeur at their head, to whom we owe the building of the sumptuous chapel in a side-aisle of the nave.

W. Sauerländer, *La Sculpture gothique en France, 1140-1270*, Paris, 1972 (1st ed. Munich, 1970). – T. Bayard, *Bourges Cathedral: the West Portals*, New York, 1976. – L. Grodecki, *Le Vitrail gothique*, Paris, 1984. – R. Branner, *The Cathedral of Bourges and its Place in Gothic Architecture*, New York, 1989.

Editorial staff

**BRABANT.** Brabant was a territory formed from *Lotharingia, in a frontier zone between East and West Francia. In the late 9th c., favoured by the weakening of the emperor's power, the local aristocracy began to assert its claims. But only a century later did it form independent principalities. In the late 10th c., the Régnier, a powerful family of the Carolingian entourage with possessions in the Meuse region, formed a principality comprising Hainaut and a Brabant centred on the county of Louvain, between the domains of the count of *Flanders to the west and those of the bishop of *Liège protected by the emperor to the east.

The rule of the comital family of Louvain, offspring of the Régnier and belonging to the *Empire, was built up and consolidated in the 11th c. thanks to *advocacy and the usurpation of church properties it permitted, in the counties of Louvain, *Brussels, the monasteries of Nivelles and Gembloux. In the early 12th c., it obtained the ducal title of Lower *Lorraine and the marquisate of *Antwerp. In 1288, Duke John I could successfully dispute the succession of the duchy of Limbourg with the count of *Luxemburg.

The development of the cloth industry strengthened an urban network that had been forming since the 11th and 12th centuries, with Wavre, Louvain, Brussels and especially Nivelles as principal centres, while Malines was a religious centre. Admittedly the urban patriciate had to face agitations and strikes led by fullers in the mid 13th c., then early in the 14th, but its financial power allowed it to impose itself on the ducal power which asked for its help. Thus John III had to come to terms with the urban aristocracies and grant the towns numerous privileges. In 1339 he allied himself with the towns of Flanders, led by Jacob van *Artevelde, and the English. Likewise, when the duchy fell to Wenceslas of Luxemburg in 1355 after his marriage to Jeanne de Brabant, the duke had to deal with Brabant and the towns by granting numerous concessions in 1356 (known as the *Joyeuse Entrée*).

In the 15th c., Brabant increased its *textile activities. In 1430 the duchy had come by inheritance to Philip the Good and become one of the parts of the Burgundian State. While rural areas saw a rise in the manufacture of linen, Louvain, Malines and Brussels exported luxury articles like *tapestries. But it was mainly Antwerp, restored to Brabant by the count of Flanders in 1406, that profited from the decline of *Bruges to stand out at the end of the century as the duchy's main commercial and financial centre.

M. Martens, *L'Administration du domaine ducal en Brabant au Moyen Âge*, Brussels, 1954. – F. Vercauteren, "La formation des principautés de Liège, Flandre, Brabant et Hainaut, IXe-XI[e]", *L'Europe aux IXe-XI[e] siècles; aux origines des États nationaux, Colloque de Varsovie, 1965*, Warsaw, 1968, 31-42. – A. Uyttebrouck, *Le Gouvernement du Duché de Brabant au bas Moyen Âge, 1355-1430*, Brussels, 1975. – J.-L. Kupper, "Mathilde de Boulogne, duchesse de Brabant (H1210)", *Femmes. Mariages-Lignages: XIIe-XIV[e] siècles*, J. Dufournet (ed.), M. Jezierski (ed.), Brussels, 1992, 233-55.

Thierry Pécout

**BRAGA.** Braga played a prominent religious role in the early history of *Portugal: the activities of St *Martin in the 6th c. and the reformer *Fructuosus in the 7th were essential. So it was quite natural that Braga should become the religious platform for the creation of the kingdom, the *archbishops effectively seconding *Afonso Henriques in his struggle for independence. Under the influence of the Cluniac Gerard, Braga finally adopted the *Roman liturgy and was recognised as a metropolis in 1103, but obtained the primacy only in 1346. Royal *donations and *pilgrimages allowed it to increase its possessions in quantity, leading from the 13th c. to violent reactions from the Portuguese rulers, who tried to diminish its grip and its landed power.

A. Pimenta, *DHGE*, 10, 1938, 352-361. – P. David, *Études historiques sur la Galice et le Portugal du VIe au XIIe siècle*, Lisbon, Paris, 1947. – J. Marques, *Ensaios, I, Braga Medieval*, Braga, 1983. – *História de Portugal*, 2, J. Mattoso (dir.), Lisbon, 1992.

Christophe Picard

**BRANDENBURG.** A region of north-east *Germany, between *Magdeburg and the river Oder. Peopled originally by *Slavs, it was colonized from the mid 12th c. through the joint efforts of Wichman, archbishop of Magdeburg, and *Albert the Bear, founder of the Ascanian dynasty, who in 1157 took the title of margrave of Brandenburg. An electorate of the *Empire from 1220, the margravate passed in turn under the authority of the *Wittelsbachs (1323), *Luxemburgs (1373) and finally *Hohenzollerns (1417). Most of its towns were not founded until the 13th c. (Berlin *c.*1230, Frankfurt on the Oder 1253) and their growth was modest. However this region of *latifundia*, feudal in structure, profited from river tolls and the trade in cereals and *wines exported by its *ports, several of which were part of the *Hanse.

J. Schultz, *Die Mark Brandenburg*, 1, Berlin, 1961. – C. Higounet, *Les Allemands en Europe centrale et orientale au Moyen Âge*, Paris, 1989. – F. Rapp, *Les Origines médiévales de l'Allemagne moderne*, Paris, 1989.

Simonne Abraham-Thisse

**BREAD.** During the Middle Ages, bread had its primordial place and its diversity in the material and spiritual heritage of the Christian West.

Flour kneaded with water and a bit of fermented dough was turned into bread in a fixed, closed and regularly maintained oven, an investment beyond the means of most households. The obligation to resort to the onerous services of the miller relativized still more the notion of "domestic" bread and explains the early appearance in *towns of numerous manufacturers whom the authorities professionalized by according them exclusive rights of sale and sometimes the right to possess an oven.

After the 11th c., wheat, rye or a mixture of the two prevailed in bread-making, leaving barley and spelt, grains of produce grown for flour but requiring to be husked, and oats, which rise badly, to bad lands and difficult periods.

Flour made into dough "such as is milled" gave a wholemeal bread with a brown compact crumb, which kept well, basis of the diet of *peasants, poor people on assistance and monks of severe *ascesis (*Cistercians, *Carthusians). Everywhere, lay and ecclesiastical households possessed in their bakery one or more bolter-sieves that, by sifting wheat flour, gave a very white bread for the masters and a darker bread for servants, workmen and, in most monasteries, for everyday use by the monks. From the 13th c., bakers, numerous, well-equipped and well-trained, recognised as "servants of the public weal", daily supplied the population of the towns with well-sifted rye bread, appreciated in certain regions (*Brittany, *Champagne, north and central Germany), wheat-and-rye bread (*Paris, *London) and above all wheat bread which became the urban cereal *par excellence*. They offered two or three varieties with significant names: soft bread, tasty bread, provision bread made of fine flour, medium-quality bourgeois *méjean* or *biset*, trencher bread, braided or festooned bread (the ordinary quality also had culinary uses!).

These loaves, generally round and unsalted, were for a long time sold separately at a fixed moderate price, in accordance with a socio-political principle going back to the early Roman Empire. The competent municipal authorities gradually established weights in accordance with the market price of grain. Panification proofs, "bread trials" or "assays" allowed them, by considering the cost of corn, logs and firewood, milling expenses and the salary of the baker and his workers, to establish what weight should be given to pieces of each variety. During the 15th c., a number of towns started to abandon this system in favour of a system of fixed weight and variable price, just as complex in its working but responding to a new economic sensibility.

L. Stouff, *Ravitaillement et alimentation en Provence aux XIVe et XVe siècles*, Paris-The Hague, 1970. – F. Desportes, *Le Pain au Moyen Âge*, Paris, 1987. – G. Comet, *Le Paysan et son outil. Essai d'histoire technique des céréales (France, VIIIe-XVe siècle)*, Rome, 1992. – C. Dyer, *Standards of living in the later Middle Ages*, Cambridge, 1989.

Françoise Desportes

**BREMEN.** A missionary *bishopric under the direction of the Anglo-Saxon Willehad existed in the region of Bremen from 787. The *diocese of Bremen was created in 805. Under *Anskar, the bishoprics of *Hamburg and Bremen were combined into a single archbishopric (848-864) which, for reasons of ecclesiastical politics, kept the name of Hamburg until the 13th c., though the bishops chose to reside at Bremen. King *Arnulf granted the town its first *merchant privilege in 888; the statue of Roland, which has dominated the market place since 1404, symbolizes the town's independence from the *archbishop, lord of the place. Bremen did not fully become an Imperial town until the 17th century. From the late 13th c. it was a *Hanse town which quite often distanced itself from the policy of *Lübeck.

H. Schwarzwälder, *Geschichte der Freien Hansestadt Bremen*, 1, Bremen, 1975.

Gerhard Theuerkauf

**BRENDAN.** A 6th-c. Irish saint who died (according to the *Annals of Ulster)* in either 577 or 583 and was the abbot of Clonfert in Connacht. For reasons now irrecoverable (but which might have some basis in fact), Brendan was famed as a traveller; in the late 7th c., *Adomnán, in his *Vita S. Columbae* (III. 17), records a voyage made by Brendan to visit St *Columba. It was perhaps this reputation for voyaging that led to St Brendan being adopted as the central figure in a Latin adaptation of a genre of literature well attested in Irish vernacular (the *immrama):* the adaptation, known as the *Navigatio S. Brendani*, was one of the most widely read texts of the Latin Middle Ages: it survives in more than 150 manuscripts and was translated into most vernacular languages. Its author is unknown, but there are convincing reasons to think that the work was composed in the south-west of *Ireland in the last quarter of the 8th century.

*Navigatio Sancti Brendani Abbatis*, C. Selmer (ed.), Notre Dame (IN), 1965. – J. J. O'Meara, *The Voyage of St Brendan: Journey to the Promised Land*, Dublin, 1976.

C. Selmer, "The Vernacular Translations of the *Navigatio Sancti Brendani*: a Bibliographical Study", *MS*, 18, 1956, 145157. – G. Orlandi, *Navigatio Sancti Brendani: Introduzione*, Milan, 1968. – D. N. Dumville, "Two Approaches to the Dating of *Nauigatio Sancti Brendani*", *Studi medievali*, 29, 1988, 87-102.

Michael Lapidge

**BRETHREN OF THE COMMON LIFE.** The sources diverge somewhat as to the foundation of this institution in the *Netherlands in the late 14th century. But the following facts are accepted: Gerhard *Groote gathered around himself some students whom he provided with copying work, giving them at the same time a spiritual training. Meanwhile, priests and laymen came together in the vicarial house of Florent *Radewijns to lead a life in conformity with the evangelical ideal of Acts 4, 32 ff.: a common life leading to sharing of goods. In 1383, Groote assured the material basis of the foundation by accepting a donation in favour of "two or three poor priests who would live in retreat" and would be a model for the faithful who had recourse to their apostolate. An austere communal life for the priests and support for the students, such were the characteristics of this semi-religious institution whose revenues came from the copying of manuscripts.

This non-canonical mode of religious life (*status medius*) led to attacks on the brethren by the *mendicant orders. Defended by Gerard *Zerbolt van Zutphen and approved in 1401 by the bishop of *Utrecht, Frederick of Blankenheim, they were also supported by Chancellor *Gerson at the council of *Constance in 1419. Their expansion was slow and resulted more from the appeals of pious burghers than from a concerted policy. They spread into the northern Netherlands (beyond *Deventer and Zwolle, to Hoorn, Almelo, Delft, Gouda, Bois-le-Duc, Groningue, Utrecht, Nijmegen) and Germany (*Münster, *Hildesheim, *Herford, among others). In the southern Netherlands, we find them at *Brussels, *Liège, Louvain. These different houses were grouped together in *colloquia* (a sort of *chapter) – the *colloquium* of Zwolle (before 1431) and that of Münster (1431) – which tried by annual meetings to standardize the life of the communities.

The contribution of the Brethren to the scholastic education of the young and the spread of *humanism has long been debated. In fact, of the Brethren's 45 houses, only four of them (Liège, Groningue, Utrecht and Wolff-Trèves) possessed *schools. Elsewhere, however, as at Deventer, Brussels, Harderwijk or Bois-le-Duc, the Brethren worked in close accord with the urban schools. They housed the students, acted as their tutors and expounded Scripture to them in familiar colloquies. The treatises of Dirc van Herxen († 1457), director of Zwolle, bear witness to this activity. Their contribution to the nascent humanism was more devout than intellectual, marked by a certain pessimism and subordinating science to moral progress and the *salvation of the individual. More and more, their houses were oriented towards the preparation of the young for conventual life. After the Reformation and the council of Trent, their houses disappeared. Some were taken over by the Jesuits or transformed into seminaries.

C. Van der Wansem, *Het ontstaan en de geschiedenis der Broederschap van het Gemene Leven tot 1400*, Louvain, 1958. – A. Hyma, *The Christian Renaissance. A History of the "Devotio Moderna"*, Hamden (CT), 1965 (2nd ed.). – W. Lourdaux, "Frères de la Vie commune", *DHGE*, 18, 1977, 1438-1454. – R. Stupperich, *Brüder vom gemeinsamen Leben*, *TRE*, 7, 1981, 220-225.

Georgette Épiney-Burgard

**BREVIARY.** Before the 12th and 13th cc., the term "breviary" designated various miscellanies or summaries. From the 13th c., it received the technical sense of a book containing all the parts of the *divine office, usually in portable form, with lessons of *matins shorter than that of the office celebrated in church, sometimes without the *psalter, which was recited by heart. Alongside the portable breviary, whose use was spread by the *mendicant orders, there also existed the choir breviary and the chamber breviary.

P.-M. Gy, "La Mise en page du bréviaire", *La Mise en page des livres au Moyen Âge*, J. Vezin (ed.), Paris, 1990. – É. Palazzo, *Histoire des livres liturgiques, le Moyen Âge, des origines au XIII^e siècle*, Paris, 1993.

Pierre-Marie Gy

**BRIAN BORU or BÓRAMA (died 1014).** Hero of the pseudo-historical *Cogadh Gaedhel re Gallaibh* (a 12th-c. political propaganda tract written for the Uí Briain), Brian Boru was nevertheless a real historical personage.

On the death of his brother Mathgamain in 976, Brian succeeded to the kingship of the Dál Cais. Within a few years he had succeeded in bringing all Munster under his control, and he spent the following years consolidating this rule. In 984 Brian, allied with the Norse of Waterford, ravaged Osraige, Leinster and Meath; in 985 he tightened his grip on the Déisi of Waterford. But Brian's rise to power was a threat to the Uí Néill, and he and the Southern Uí Néill leader, Máel Sechnaill II, attacked and counter-attacked each other over several years until in 997, at a royal meeting near Clonfert, the two rulers came to an agreement: Máel Sechnaill would henceforth be ruler of the northern half of *Ireland, and Brian would be recognised as king of the southern half. This alliance was consolidated in 998 when Brian Boru and Máel Sechnaill joined forces for the first time against the Norse of *Dublin.

The battle of Glenn Máma, in 999, was decisive in Brian's career, when he defeated the united forces of the Leinstermen and the Norse of Dublin; this was followed by an attack on, and plunder of, Dublin. Brian now felt strong enough to break his alliance with Máel Sechnaill, and in 1001 the Southern Uí Néill were forced into submission. By 1005, Brian could claim, with much authority, to be King of Ireland, or 'emperor of the Irish' as he was titled in the *Book of Armagh*.

During the next years Brian had to contend with dissident northern and Leinster kings. When in 1012 the Ostmen of Dublin joined the Leinstermen in one such revolt, the consequent conflict, that of Clontarf on Good Friday 1014, was perhaps the most famous battle in Irish history. As recorded in *Cogadh Gaedhel re Gallaibh*, the battle ended in the victory of the Dál Cais over Dublin and Leinster, but in the course of the action Brian Boru himself was assassinated. Following the death of this powerful personality, the alliances he had forged fell apart, and it was a further half century before the Dál Cais reasserted such dominance – this time under the leadership of Brian's grandson Tairdelbach and using the surname Uí Briain, 'of the descendants of Brian'.

Donncha Ó Corráin, *Ireland before the Normans*, Dublin, 1972. – T. W. Moody (ed.), F. X. Martin (ed.), *The Course of Irish History*, Cork, 1984. – S. Duffy, *Ireland in the Middle Ages*, London, 1995.

Elin Manahan Thomas

**BRIDGE.** The medieval West inherited from the Roman Empire a limited number of stone bridges, essentially located in the Mediterranean countries, which long continued to be used. But their lack of maintenance, their situation, ill-adapted to new political and economic needs, the demands of large-scale *commerce and the rise of *towns in many regions explains the flowering, from the 11th-12th cc. to the mid 14th c., of new works arising from the initiative of lay and ecclesiastical lords and communities of inhabitants, which contributed to a restructuring of the inhabited area and the communication networks.

Among the financing used, recourse to charity in the form of *alms, *donations and *legacies developed particularly copiously from the 12th c., a movement favoured from the 13th c. by the grant of letters of *indulgence accorded by *popes and *bishops in favour of benefactions: indeed participation in the building of a bridge, which allowed travellers to avoid the perils of crossing rivers and eased the wanderings of *pilgrims, was considered a pious work. In this context arose specific institutions, "bridge works", intended to gather the sums of *money necessary for the erection and upkeep of the work and manage its use. The most dynamic of these developed in connection with the great stone bridges built over the Rhone: *Avignon, *Lyon (*c.*1180) and Pont-Saint-Esprit (1281), but also at Bonpas, *Metz, *Orléans, *Namur and in *Tuscany. Bringing together laymen and laywomen in charitable *confraternities, they mainly took charge of the service of the *collections made thoughout Christendom, as well as the upkeep of a *hospital and a *chapel built at one of the bridgeheads or sometimes on one of the piers. Completely independent from each other like the confraternities, from which they borrowed many characteristics, they kept up more or less close, indeed more or less conflictual, links with the communal authorities, who frequently interfered in the appointment of their "rectors" and in their management, in the name of the public unity associated with the bridge's existence. In any case they never constituted a religious order of "friars pontiffs", too complacently echoed by historiography from the 17th century.

The religious feeling attached to bridges gradually disappeared in the second half of the 15th c. and the first half of the 16th, when the representatives of public authority finally took charge of the management of *communication routes. The sole evidence of it today are the remaining vestiges of crosses and chapels, and the dedication (Saint-Nicolas, Saint-Esprit. . .) which some of these works still retain.

M. N. Boyer, "The Bridgebuilding Brotherhoods", *Spec.*, 29, 1964, 635-650. – D. Le Blévec, "Une Institution d'assistance en pays rhodanien: les Frères pontifes", *Assistance et charité*, Toulouse, 1978, 87-110 ("CFan", 13). – J. Mesqui, *Le Pont en France avant le temps des ingénieurs*, Paris, 1986. – N.P. Brooks, "Rochester Bridge, AD 43-1381", *Traffic and Politics*, N. Yates (ed.), J.M. Gibson (ed.), Woodbridge, 1994, 1-40.

Daniel Le Blévec

Seal of Alphonso X the Wise (1221-1284), King of Castile. Miniature from *The Index of Royal Privileges.* 12-13th c. manuscript. Archives, Santiago de Compostela Cathedral. (Photo: G. Dagli Orti)

Knight on horseback. 7th-c. Lombard object. Florence, Bargello Museum. (Photo: G. Dagli Orti)

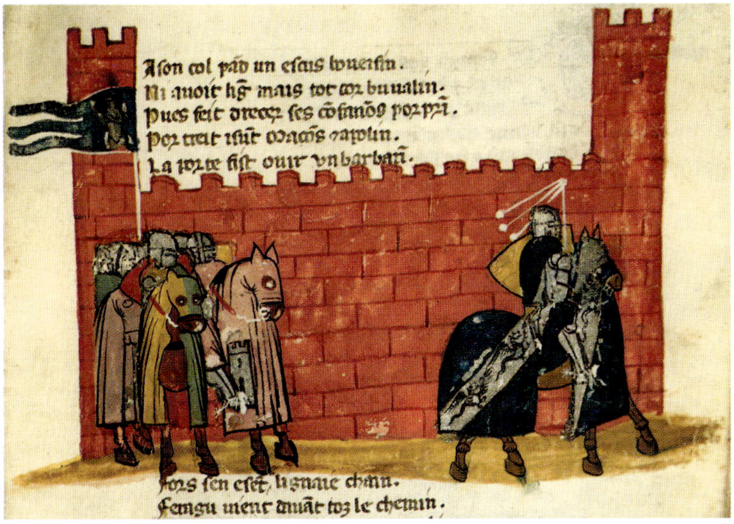

Knights leaving a fortress. Miniature from *Entrée d'Espagne,* 14th-c. French manuscript. Venice, Biblioteca Marciana. (G. Dagli Orti)

Submission of John of Anjou to Ferdinand I of Aragon, King of Naples. Miniature by J. Maio from *De Majestate.* Manuscript of 1492. Naples. (Photo: G. Dagli Orti)

Saint Louis dispensing Justice. Miniature from *Justinianum infortiatum,* 14th-c. manuscript (fol. 107v°). Library of the Escorial, Spain. (Photo: G. Dagli Orti)

Alfonso VI, King of León and Castile. Miniature from *The Index of Royal Privileges.* 12-13th c. manuscript. Archives, Santiago de Compostela Cathedral. (Photo: G. Dagli Orti)

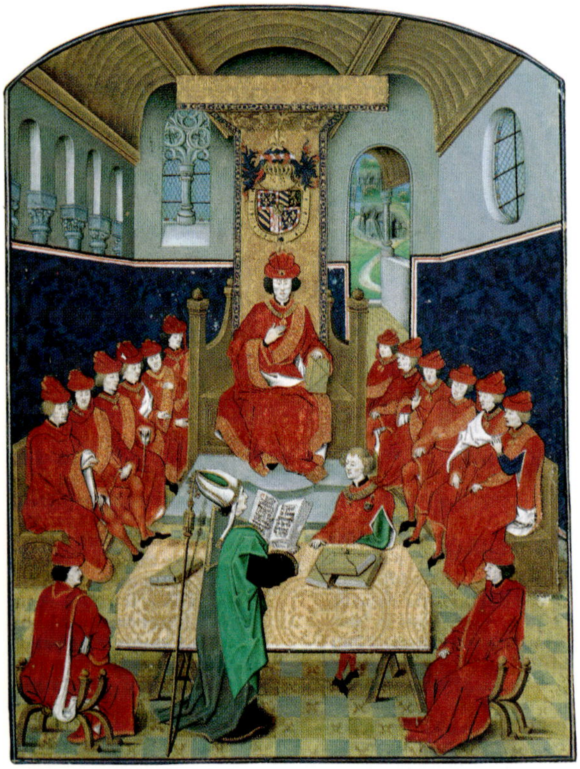

Chapter of the Order of the Golden Fleece. Miniature from the manuscript of *The Golden Fleece* by William Fillastre, Bishop of Tournai, 1473. Municipal Library, Dijon. (Photo: G. Dagli Orti)

The Cardinal Virtues: Magnanimity, Temperance, Justice. Fresco by Ambrogio Lorenzetti, 14th c. Palazzo Pubblico, Siena. (Photo: G. Dagli Orti)

**BRIDGET (1303-1373), BRIDGETTINES.** St Bridget (in Swedish: Birgitta) Birgersdotter, sprung from the ruling aristocracy, had eight children from her marriage in 1316 to Ulf Gudmarsson. After a pilgrimage to Santiago de *Compostela in 1341-1342, they retired to the monastery of Alvastra where Ulf died in 1344. The development of Bridget's prophetic gifts was due to Matthias Övedsson. These prophecies made reference to contemporary religious and political events, such as *e.g.* the war between England and France.

From 1350 Bridget lived at *Rome. The motive for this departure for Rome have been the object of several hypotheses: pilgrimage for the holy year; wish that the *pope should recognise the rule of the *order she wanted to found, received during a *vision; reform of the Church in its centre; return of the pope from *Avignon; crisis in her relations with the Swedish royal couple, Magnus Eriksson and Blanche of Namur. Her religious messages, often doctrinal in tone, addressed to dignitaries of Church and State, came from her total self-giving, often accompanied by *ecstasies, to the Saviour of the world, the husband of her soul whom she had chosen to the end of her life, to be his spouse to deliver heavenly *revelations (*celestes revelationes*) to the world.

Bridget's *spirituality is characterised by penetrating psychological analyses and a strong identification with female existence, espressed in her mariology. She died at Rome, 23 July 1373, after many pilgrimages to Italy and the *Holy Land. Her *Revelationes* were drawn up by the exiled Spanish Bishop Alfonso of Jaén and she was canonized on 7 Oct 1391 by Pope *Boniface IX for the regions under his obedience, a *canonization confirmed by Pope *Martin V in 1419 for the whole of Christendom.

Bridget's life at Rome, accompanied by her daughter *Catherine and her two confessors, was a sort of preparation for monastic life as it developed under Catherine's authority from 1374 at *Vadstena in Sweden, according to the approval given by the pope in 1370 and supplemented in 1378. By 1500 the Order of *St Saviour, *Ordo Sancti Salvatoris*, had 25 male and female *abbeys including five in Scandinavia, two in Italy, one in England and in Poland. In the German Baltic region there was only one, but founded by reigning lords and influential. By contrast, there were several groups of abbeys in Bavaria and Holland. The rule required strict *enclosure, and the order dedicated itself to its mission to the people through liturgy and *preaching in its great conventual churches, common to the *nuns and priests of the order.

*Sancta Brigitta Revelaciones*, 1, H. Aili (ed.), B. Berg (ed.), C. G. Undhagen (ed.), Stockholm, 1977; *ibid.*, 4, 1992; *ibid.*, 5-7, 1971-1991. – *Revelaciones Extravagantes*, S. Eklund (ed.), Uppsala, 1972-1991 (3 vol.).

J.A. Schmidtke, "'Saving' by Faint Praise: St. Birgitta of Sweden, Adam Easton, and Medieval Anti-Feminism", *American Benedictine Review*, 33, 1982, 149-61. – *Brigitta, hendes waerk og hendes klostre i Norden*, T. Nyberg (ed.), Odense, 1991. – *Santa Brigida profeta dei tempi novi*, Rome, 1993.

Tore Nyberg

**BRIEF, APOSTOLIC.** The apostolic brief was a category of papal letter, at first reserved for political and administrative correspondence, created to simplify the formalities required for the expedition of *bulls. The earliest example dates from 1390. The brief was written on vellum, closed and sealed with red wax, with the *pope's secret *seal, called the "*fisherman's ring"; the date was calculated according to the style of Christmas, *i.e.* by beginning the year on Christmas day. The name of the addressee did not appear in the text but outside the folded document, in the manner of an address.

A. Giry, *Manuel de diplomatique*, Paris, 1894, 699-701. – T. Frenz, *Papsturkunden des Mittelalters und der Neuzeit*, Stuttgart, 1986, 28-30.

Michel Hayez

**BRISTOL.** Bristol owed its fortune to wool: its *merchants, kept outside the "staple" monopoly of Calais, simple "merchant venturers" trading at their own risk and peril, specialized in the sale of cloth. The rise of the English *textile export trade conditioned the rise of Bristol: the third town in *England in 1377 with 9,500 inhabitants, from 1334 it was the richest after *London. Its merchants were active all over the Atlantic seabord and opened up a regular route to *Iceland: in 1497, John and Sebastian Cabot (of Genoese origin) discovered Newfoundland. A merchant city, Bristol had no *bishop in the Middle Ages; but the abbey church of St Augustine (Augustinian Canons) became a superb cathedral in 1542, and the parish church of St Mary Redcliffe, built thanks to the Canynges family, is one of the jewels of perpendicular *Gothic.

M. M. Postan, *Medieval Trade and Finance*, London, 1973. – M. Spallanzani (ed.), *Produzione, commercio e consumo dei panni di lana (nei secoli XII-XVIII)*, Florence, 1976.

Jean-Philippe Genet

**BRITTANY.** For Brittany, the Middle Ages were primarily the time of the Breton migration, that of the establishment of the people and the language. The Bretons of Britain settled in Armorica from the 4th c., pushed by the Scots of *Ireland, then by the advance of the *Angles and Saxons from 450 onwards and during the 6th century. The migration transformed the linguistic face of Armorica, where the still living Gallic substrate easily accommodated the importation of a Britonic language from which it differed little, so much that Breton covered the west and north of the country, the most densely colonized parts. New patterns of life appeared, whose memory is preserved by place-names. They testify to the strong hold of religious leaders over the migration, such as the *plou* (Latin *plebs*, Welsh *plwyf*), a primitive parish, or the *lann*, heir to the hermitages or monasteries. When, from the end of the 6th c., Armorica became Brittany, the Christian imprint was already there as a particular trait.

It was also the time of political emancipation. The time of the "kingdoms" which, from the 6th c., managed to oppose the advance of the *Franks, from whom they were separated by a march at the end of the 8th century. The time of the kings, an experience which, despite its brevity, left a deep mark (851-874). Finally the time of the dukes, who, after a long period of political obscurity, profited from circumstances to play their personal card once more. The century of the Montforts (1365-1491) marked Brittany's political apogee: the princes rejected any idea of subjection to *France and refused liege *homage, aiming to construct a sovereign principality endowed with modern means of government and legitimized by reference to past kingship. French monarchical centralization ruined these hopes of independence, and military defeat (1488) was a prelude to personal union (1491) and then permanent union (1532).

Resistance to political assimilation was not synonymous with cultural marginalization. In all spheres, Brittany was open to influences, in the 9th c. preferring Roman religious usages to Celtic ones. At the heart of a Western world that tilted towards the

Atlantic, at the crossroads of European *commerce, it was involved in the trade in *salt (Guérande, Bourgneuf), *wine (Poitou, Bordelais) and linen (Morlaix, Locronan, Vitré). The intense circulation of men diversified these influences: Bretons willingly left home to plough the seas or make a career in arms, the Church or administration, but also to escape the misery that did not spare them during the crisis of the 14th and 15th cc.; numerous foreigners landed on Armorican shores, sometimes political refugees, more often economic partners from all the nations of Europe. Breton civilization was profoundly marked by this: from techniques of naval construction (caravelle) to artistic production (*Flamboyant Gothic), it testifies to a remarkable capacity to integrate models and to synthesize, which prepared the great achievements of the early modern period.

A. Mussat, *Arts et cultures de la Bretagne. Un millénaire*, Paris, 1979. – *Histoire de la Bretagne*, Rennes, 1985, 3 vol. (for the Middle Ages, A. Chedeville, H. Guillotel and N.-Y. Tonnerre, J.-P. Leguay and H. Martin). – J. Kerhervé, *L'État breton aux XIV^e et XV^e siècles. Les ducs, l'argent, les hommes*, Paris, 1987 (2 vol.). – M. Jones, *The Creation of Brittany*, London, 1988. – W. Davies, *Small Worlds: the Village Community in early Medieval Brittany*, London, 1988. – J.M.H. Smith, *Province and Empire: Brittany and the Carolingians*, Cambridge, 1992. – *Toute l'Histoire de la Bretagne. Des origines à la fin du XX^e siècle*, J.-J. Monnier (ed.), J.-C. Cassard (ed.), Morlaix, 1997.

Jean Kerhervé

**BROGNE.** A Benedictine *abbey founded in 919 by the nobleman Gerard who gave it his patrimonial possessions and introduced monks and *relics into it from *Saint-Denis in France, the abbey of Brogne (now in Belgium) became the centre of a monastic *reform that spread through Flanders (*Ghent), Normandy (*Saint-Wandrille, *Mont Saint-Michel) and Champagne (Saint-Remi at *Reims) from 935, at the same time as reforms from other Lotharingian centres. This reform was based on the strengthening of the temporality, the choice of a regular *abbot and the strict application of the *Benedictine Rule. Brogne had a *school and a well-stocked *library, which earned it a certain influence up to the 12th century.

D. Misonne, "Gérard de Brogne", *DHGE*, 10, 1938, 829-832. – *Gérard de Brogne et son oeuvre réformatrice*, *RBen*, 70, 1960.

Michel Parisse

**BROU.** Margaret of Austria, daughter of Maximilian of Austria and Mary of Burgundy, built the church of Brou (Ain) to the plans of Jean Perréal between 1505 and 1515 to respect a vow of her mother-in-law Margaret of Bourbon, mother of Philibert II of Savoy († 1504). This church, in the *Flamboyant Gothic style, introduced several bits of Renaissance style. The columns without capitals throw out a cluster of palm-branch ribs prolonged in all the elements of the vaulting. It is known for its wealth of statuary,

*Victory of the inhabitants of Ghent led by Philipp van Artevelde outside Bruges in 1381.* Miniature from Froissart's *Chronicles* ("Breslau" manuscript), 1472. Berlin, Staatsbibliothek Preussischer Kulturbesitz.

works by Michel Colombe and Conrad Meyt, particularly the *rood screen and the tombs of the donors, but also for its *stalls by Terrasson (1530-1532), its *altarpieces and *stained glass windows. Placed in a recess, the tomb of Margaret of Bourbon represents the donor on a black marble slab; that of Philibert has a double representation of the dead man (unique example) surrounded by Virtues (or Sibyls); the third, still more ornate, also shows two recumbent figures of Margaret of Austria.

V. Nodet, *L'église de Brou*, Paris, 1928. – P. Vitry, "L'église de Brou", *Congrès archéologique (Lyon et Macon)*, 98, 1935, 261-5.

Jean-Pierre Nicol

**BRUGES.** Bruges, perhaps originally a *bridge, was built up from several urban areas situated around the *count's *castle and the church of Saint-Gilles. The region's dense rural population probably had favourable consequences for the town's early urban dynamism. Indeed the city's first commercial activities were oriented towards its hinterland. At the start of the 12th c., Bruges comprised three *parishes, Notre-Dame, Saint-Donat and Saint-Sauveur, contained within its walls the areas of the Vieux-Bourg and the Bourg, and comprised an area close to 90 hectares.

The count of *Flanders installed part of his administration there and gave his protection to *textile activities and *commerce, benefiting the cloth trade. The town seems to have enjoyed great prosperity in cloth from the late 11th c., and in May it held one of the greatest *fairs in Flanders. Until the 14th c., the *merchants of Bruges obtained their primary material, wool, from England, before being supplanted by foreign merchants; the town imported grain from France after having utilized its hinterland. The city's influence thus reached the whole West, since merchants from Germany, Italy, the *Hanse, the Iberian peninsula and the British Isles are attested at Bruges in the 13th century. In the following century, foreign merchants were represented by a dozen consulates. This important commercial traffic fed flourishing activities of exchange, brokerage and a hotel trade. However the town's maritime outlet, the gulf of Zwin, had to be dredged ceaselessly from the 9th and 10th cc. because of the silting up of the area. The out-ports of Damme in the late 12th c. and then Sluys were necessary, but they occasioned trans-shipments.

An urban patriciate developed early, but after the 13th c. it abandoned commerce to foreigners and devoted itself to landed and seignorial investments. An *échevinage* is attested in the 13th century. Bruges saw itself covered with public buildings like the town hall, St John's hospital and the cathedral of Saint-Sauveur. In the 15th c. it also housed a number of artists such as Hans *Memling or Jan *van Eyck. The town was provided with communal institutions in the 12th c., but had to wage a long struggle in the 14th c. against the count's attempts to take them over. In the late 15th c., Bruges rose up with the other towns of Flanders against Duke Maximilian of Austria. Deprived of a number of its privileges, the city then suffered a clear diminution of its already declining commercial activities.

Galbert of Bruges, *The Murder of Charles the Good*, J. B. Ross (ed.), New York, 1959 (repr. Toronto, 1982).

H. Van Werveke, *Bruges et Anvers, huit siècles de commerce flamand*, Brussels, 1944. – R. de Roover, *Money, Banking and Credit in Medieval Bruges*, Cambridge, 1948. – A. E. Verhulst, "Les origines et l'histoire ancienne de Bruges (IXe-XIIe siècles)", *MA*, 66, 1960, 37-63. – J. A. Van Houtte, *Bruges, essai d'histoire urbaine*, Brussels, 1967.

Thierry Pécout

**BRUNO OF LA CHARTREUSE (*c.*1030-1101).** Born at *Cologne, Bruno followed the teaching of the episcopal *school at *Reims. After his studies, he became a *canon of the *cathedral, then in 1056 he was chosen as *scholasticus*, an office he would exercise for nearly a quarter of a century. Some of his former pupils became *bishops or *abbots and were protagonists of the reform of the Church, among them the future Pope *Urban II.

In 1081, Bruno was proposed by the *chapter for the metropolitan see of Reims. But he had already taken the decision to abandon offices, honours and riches. A first experience of eremitic life in the forest of Sèche-Fontaine, near *Troyes, was a failure. Attracted by the reputation of the new bishop of Grenoble, Hugh, Bruno went and asked him to grant him and the six companions who had followed him a "*desert" in the mountains of his *diocese: thus were founded, in June 1084, in a clearing 1180 metres up, the first hermitages of the Chartreuse, simple wooden cabins opening onto a gallery by which the solitaries went to the church, the only stone building, for *matins and *vespers. The other offices, as well as *prayer, reading, manual labour and meals, took place in the cell. On *Sundays and feast days, the *office and the common refectory brought the hermits together. Bruno's two companions who were not priests settled a little lower down and, as the first lay-brothers, dedicated themselves to the material tasks indispensable to the life of the community, notably husbandry.

Early in 1090, Urban II, in search of competent advisers, called his former master to the service of the papacy. Obediently, Bruno left for *Rome after having taken care to designate Landuin as *prior of his community of Chartreuse. But, faithful to his contemplative vocation, he could not remain at the papal court, nor accept the archbishopric of Reggio that was offered to him. In autumn 1090, he obtained permission to retire to a new desert, in *Calabria. Given a kind welcome by Count *Roger, he installed a hermitage in a mountainous and wooded site in the diocese of Squillace (Santa Maria della Torre). Numerous companions joined him, to lead a life of prayer identical to that of the solitaries of the desert of Chartreuse. From his retreat, Bruno wrote a letter to his friend from Reims, Raoul le Verd, and another to his brothers at the Chartreuse, in which he exalted the purity and excellence of the contemplative ideal. He died on 6 Oct 1101. His *canonization took place in 1514. Without having drawn up any rule, but by his sole example, he was the model of those who, following him, would embrace the vocation of seeking God in solitude: thanks to the first *Carthusians' fidelity to the ideal to which Bruno, by his life, had given exceptional witness, the form of life he had established for them would be perpetuated into our own day.

G. Posada, *Maestro Bruno, padre de monjes*, Madrid, 1980. – A. Ravier, *Saint Bruno le chartreux*, Paris, 1981. – *La Grande-Chartreuse par un chartreux*, Bellegarde, 1984, 11-24 (14th ed.). – *The Oxford Dictionary of Saints*, Oxford, 1984, 58-9. – B. Bligny, *Saint Bruno, le premier chartreux*, Rennes, 1984. – G. Gioia, *L'Esperienza contemplativa. Bruno il certosino*, Milan, 1989.

Daniel Le Blévec

**BRUSSELS.** Brussels developed in the early Middle Ages from several centres of population. Situated in a marshy area, at a level of trans-shipment for river *navigation on the Senne, and at the crossing of the routes leading to *Antwerp and *Cologne, the town nevertheless remained small until its growth in the later Middle Ages.

In the 10th c., fortifications enclosed a *portus* doubled with a *market, and the population seems to have been concentrated around the churches of Saint-Nicolas and Saint-Véry; the latter was probably founded by a castellan. In the 12th c., the town was given a new rampart, which seems to attest a certain growth. The city, originally an agricultural centre, knew activities connected with the cloth industry from the 13th c., if not earlier. It exported cloth to the *Champagne *fairs, and from there to *Italy and *Venice. It rebuilt its *cathedral under the influence of the style that prevailed East of the Parisian basin. Commercial and industrial prosperity was doubled with demographic growth in the course of the 14th century. In fact, at this time Brussels enjoyed a clear expansion of its *textile activities due to the relative neutrality of the dukes of *Brabant during the *Hundred Years' War. The Brussels cloth industry specialized in quality articles like the violet cloth it exported to the farthest bounds of the West. The town built several halls, under the instigation of the duke of Brabant and then of its own town council.

The *échevinage* was in the hands of the great patrician families, who drew their revenues from the economic and fiscal control of *commerce and the provisioning of the urban population. In 1280, a *revolt of the fullers revealed the social tensions at work in the city. But it was the 15th c. that saw Brussels join the ranks of the great metropolises of the West, with a population probably exceeding 30,000 inhabitants. Indeed, when Philip the Good decided to take up residence there, it became a veritable princely capital and rivalled *Dijon or Nancy in the Burgundian States. The building of the town hall, completed at the end of the century, also attests the success of its urban elites. The attraction exercised by the *court over numerous *artists made Brussels an important centre of manuscript *illumination and painting, with artists such as Rogier *van der Weyden. The presence of the prince appeased social tensions somewhat. But in 1421 the urban institutions had to take into account the aspirations of the *métiers* excluded from decisions. The burgomeister was assisted by advisers in charge of overseeing the management of the towns' finances. With Antwerp, Brussels became the principal centre of Brabant.

G. Des Marez, *Bruxelles au XV^e siècle*, Brussels, 1953. – A. Henne, A. Wauters, *Histoire de la ville de Bruxelles*, Brussels, 1958. – A. Favresse, *Études sur les métiers bruxellois du Moyen Âge*, Brussels, 1961. – *Bruxelles, croissance d'une capitale*, J. Stengers (ed.), Brussels, 1979.

Thierry Pécout

**BUDA AND PEST.** Towns of central *Hungary separated by the Danube. Pest, built in the 10th c. from an old Roman fort controlling the crossing of the Danube, became from the early 13th c. a commercial crossroads animated by colonists of German origin, and benefited from the 1230s from a royal *charter of franchises. Following the ravages caused by the Tatar invasion of 1241, King Béla IV decided on the construction in 1247 at Buda (on the other bank of the Danube) of a fortress, where much of the population of Pest took refuge. Pest, henceforth considered a suburb of Buda and administered by Buda's municipal magistrate, enjoyed a rapid commercial growth from the 14th c., which allowed it to recover its autonomy in the following century. It had some 8000 inhabitants in the late 15th c., slightly less than Buda, the royal residence.

*Budapest története* [History of Budapest], L. Gerevich (dir.), 1-2, Budapest, 1973.

Marie-Madeleine de Cevins

**BULGARIA.** Bulgaria's surviving monuments still allow us to perceive the importance it had in the Middle Ages, when it extended from the Danube to the Aegean Sea and from the Black Sea sometimes to the Adriatic. Submerging the Romanized Thracians, the *Slavs (6th c.) were in turn dominated by the Protobulgars (7th c.) from the Eastern steppes.

In 865 Prince *Boris, caught between Rome and Constantinople, received baptism from Byzantine missionaries. Under Prince *Simeon (893-922), the disciples of *Cyril and his brother Methodius were welcomed at Preslav, then at *Ohrid; they multiplied biblical, liturgical and patristic translations, written at first in the Glagolitic alphabet, then in the Cyrillic alphabet which adapted Greek letters to Slav vowels. After these centuries of influence, as far as distant *Rus', Byzantium, always worried about its powerful Bulgar neighbours, crushed them in 1018 under Basil Bulgaroctonos: the Byzantine occupation would last two centuries. A second Bulgar kingdom appeared at the start of the 13th c., with Tŭrnovo as the new capital. The Assenid kings and their 14th-c. successors, of whom John-Alexander was the most outstanding, went on defending the kingdom despite Serbian, Byzantine and Turkish threats. In 1396 the *Turks finally won the day and occupied Bulgaria until the 19th century.

Among the brick-built monuments predating the *Slavs, the domed basilica of St Sophia still stands at Sofia, though often altered. But the Old Metropolis of Nessebar/Mesemvria, like the Red Church (central plan) of Peruštica, is just ruins. At Pliska, capital of the first kingdom, the fortress of fine stones still stands just clear of the ground, surrounding the remains of the palace, the noble houses and various churches, such as the great basilica. The second capital, Preslav, contains within its walls, dominating the Tica, palace and churches: the Round Church with its carved stones, the church of Patleina to which was attached the factory of glazed *ceramics, similar to those of *Constantinople. At Tŭrnovo, the palace-fortress dominates many churches built outside the walls, while other more modest buildings occupy the hill of the Trapezica.

More fascinating still, the *frescos of four churches, among others, reflect the evolution of Byzantine painting on Bulgarian soil. The monastery of Bačkovo, near Plovdiv, built through the initiative of Pakurianos, a half-Georgian half-Armenian nobleman in the service of the Byzantine emperor, preserves a two-storey funerary church, lined with portraits of saints (Apostles, bishops, deacons, monks. . .) and some Old Testament and *Last Judgment scenes (11th c.). The little church of Bojana near Sofia is covered with high-quality frescos, including the portrait of the *sebastocrator* Kaloïan, its founder, accompanied by an inscription of 1259. The restoration of the frescos of the tower of Chreljo, in the enclosure of St John's monastery at Rila, has allowed its themes of Divine Wisdom and King *David to be placed within the stylistic harmony of the 14th century. The paintings of the *Crkvata* of Ivanovo (a rock-cut chapel in northern Bulgaria), rich in architectural details and antiquizing figures in the "Palaeologan" style, attest the Constantinopolitan tradition of the 14th century.

A. Grabar, *La Peinture religeuse en Bulgarie*, Paris, 1928. – A. Božkov, *Die bulgarische Malerei von den Anfängen bis zum 19.Jahrhundert*, Recklinghausen, 1969. – K. Mijatiev, *Die Mittelalterliche Baukunst in Bulgarien*, Sofia, 1974. – I. Dujčev, "De la fondation de l'État bulgare à la conquête ottomane", *Histoire de la Bulgarie*, Roanne-Sofia, 1977, 57-244. – V. Giuzelev, *Medieval Bulgaria*, Villach, 1988. – L. Mavrodinova, *La Peinture médiévale en Bulgarie jusqu'à la fin du XIV^e siècle*, Sofia, 1993.

Suzy Dufrenne

**BULGARS.** The formation of the Bulgar nation in the Middle Ages occurred through the fusion of various ethnic elements, among which the *Slavs and the Bulgars (conventionally called Protobulgars) occupied a primary place.

The *invasions of the Slavs of the so-called "Bulgar" group, who were part of the Southern Slavs, began mainly in the first half of the 6th c., south of the Carpathians. In the 7th c., a part of these invasions took place under the aegis of the *Avars, established in *Pannonia. In the second half of the 7th c. we can speak of Slavinias, autonomous organisations within the confines of the *Byzantine Empire (in Moesia, Thrace, Macedonia and as far as Thessaly and the Peloponnese). These organisations often lived on the margins of provincial government. The authorities at *Constantinople sometimes granted them the status of *foederati*. The findings of *archaeology and linguistics confirm the information of written sources as to the numerical importance of the Slav groups established in the lands that remained waste. There the Slavs came into contact with the provincial population of the Empire, composed of Thracians and, in the western parts of the Balkan peninsula, Illyrians – both to a great extent Hellenized or Romanized.

The presence of Bulgars in the Balkans is recorded from the last two decades of the 5th c.: they served in the Byzantine *army on its campaigns against the *Ostrogoths. They came from regions beyond the northern shore of the Black Sea, and consisted of a mixture of survivors from Attila's empire and tribes of Onogurs. Later, Bulgar groups included in the khaganate of the Avars took part in the latter's raids south of the Danube. Early in the 7th c., "Bulgaria on the Volga" was formed in the north Pontic regions, but it was rapidly displaced under the blows of the *Khazars. It was then, in the 660s, that Asparukh's Bulgars left Bulgaria on the Volga and moved towards the Danube delta. Asparukh, who had penetrated Moesia and Scythia Minor, had to fight against the Byzantine armies. The military operations of 680-681 ended with the recognition of Danubian Bulgaria (681).

From this period began the symbiosis between the Slavs and the Bulgars, since the latter had occupied the former's territory. In these relations between cultivators and nomads, it was the more numerous Slav element that finally prevailed. But the Bulgars, military organisers of the State, left it their name. *Conversion and the introduction of the Cyrillic alphabet were of great importance for the affirmation of the national identity. In the late 9th and early 10th c., the term "Slavs" disappeared, and all the subjects of the Bulgar State were finally known as "Bulgars". The new elements of Turkic origin (*Pechenegs, *Cumans, etc.), who settled in small numbers in the lower Danube region in the 11th-12th cc., left only few traces and were largely integrated into the Bulgar nationality.

V. Tăpkova-Zaimova, "Genèse des peuples balkaniques et formation de leurs États", *Byzance et les Balkans à partir du VI^e siècle*, London, 1979, N. XX, 1-15. – D. Angelov, *Neugasvašto samosŭznanie (Bălgarskata narodnost prez vekovete* [Imperishable Consciousness (The Bulgar Nationality over the Centuries)], Sofia, 1991. – *Bălgarski vekova*, Tangra (ed.), 1, Sofia, 1999, 102.

Vasilka Tăpkova-Zaimova

**BULL.** The use of a lead *seal (*bulla*) was not reserved for the papal *chancery: princes and communities of inhabitants also used them. The German Roman emperor and the king of *Sicily used a golden bull after the manner of the Byzantine emperors in the most solemn documents, as the Emperor *Charles IV did in 1356 to definitively regulate the election of the sovereign by the Diet.

By extension, in the papal chancery the bull designated a letter of the *pope, less solemn than the privilege and more so than the *brief. According to the rank of the addressee, the lead bull was sealed over red silk laces or a simple hemp cord. On the inverse appeared the heads of the apostles Peter and Paul, on the reverse the name of the reigning pope. Types departing from this model are rare: thus in *c.*1465 Paul II reused a medallion representing him holding an audience. Between his *election and his *coronation, the new pope used only the reverse of the bull.

A. Giry, *Manuel de diplomatique*, Paris, 1894, 661-704. – T. Frenz, *Papsturkunden des Mittelalters und der Neuzeit*, Stuttgart, 1986. – P. N. R. Zutshi, *Original papal letters in England, 1305-1415*, Vatican, 1990.

Michel Hayez

**BURCHARD OF WORMS (*c.*965-1025).** Bishop of *Worms from 1000 to 1025, Burchard reorganised the temporal administration of his episcopal city. But he is famous mainly for his canonical work. His *Decretum* (*PL*, 140), a voluminous *canonical collection predating the *Gregorian reform, is in line with the collections of the early Middle Ages, though it already heralds some "reforming" themes (condemnation of *simony, relations of princes with the ecclesiastical powers, etc.). The *Decretum* insists on the role of the *bishop, the essential authority to preside over the *reform of local religious life. Very widely diffused, its success is also shown by the very numerous borrowings made from it by Gratian when he composed his own **Decretum*.

P. Fournier, G. Le Bras, *Histoire des collections canoniques en Occident depuis les Fausses décrétales jusqu'au Décret de Gratien*, 1, *De la réforme carolingienne à la réforme grégorienne*, Paris, 1931, 364-421. – M. Kernier, R. Kaiser, "Burchard, Bischof von Worms", *LdM*, 2, 1983, 946-951.

Brigitte Basdevant-Gaudemet

**BURGOS.** Founded in 884 by Count Diego Rodriguez Porcelos as part of the policy of repopulating the Christian kingdoms, Burgos acquired importance in the 10th c. when *Castile became a powerful and almost independent county. Situated on the route to Santiago de *Compostela, the town grew from the late 11th c. and developed commercial and artisanal activities long monopolized by foreigners – French, Lombard, English or German.

In 1068, the former *bishopric of Oca was officially transferred to Burgos and from 1104 benefited from *exemption; its *parishes were never territorial areas, but the assembly of those who, independently of their residence, chose to belong to the community of this or that church. Its role as capital – more symbolic than real – of Castile had as corollary the development of the town in the 13th c.; to the monastery of *Las Huelgas founded in 1187 by *Alfonso VIII was added, from 1221 and under the aegis of the bishop and King Ferdinand III, the construction of a Gothic *cathedral, while Burgos was given a city wall, increased its administrative area and diversified its activities, and its Jewish community enjoyed an undeniable prosperity. Burgos received the official title of "head of Castile and chamber of kings" – *cabeza de Castilla e camara de los reyes*" – and in 1255 the *Crown imposed its laws, the Fuero Real, on it; nearly a hundred years later, in 1345, the king created a "municipal council" of 16 *regidores*, royally appointed and charged with the town's government and administration.

From the late 13th c., urban life was dominated by the merchants who, joined in the *confraternity of knight-merchants of Santa Maria Real de Gamonal, devoted themselves to

View of the vault of the choir of Burgos cathedral, 13th c.

international *commerce, extending their family networks from Flanders to *Italy; supported by the Crown, they monopolized the urban magistratures, invested in the lands of the administrative area, enriched themselves through maritime insurance and adopted an aristocratic way of life, while systematicaly favouring the export of the wool that came from the flocks of the *nobility and the Church. The 15th c. was the "golden age" of the merchants of Burgos, among whom were numerous *conversos*, and the town profited from the economic prosperity of the kingdom.

From the late 14th c., the cathedral grammar schools were supplemented by the teaching of law, paid for by the town; the cultural level rapidly rose, and many *clerics and laymen passed through the universities of *Salamanca, *Valladolid or *Bologna. In the first half of the 15th c., Bishop Alfonso of Cartagena played a political and intellectual role that took him from the king's council to the council of *Basel, while the members of the municipal oligarchy surrounded themselves with *books, prided themselves on their knowledge of literature and *humanism and financed works of art or imported them from Flanders. Burgos systematically favoured the *fairs of Medina del Campo created in *c.*1420 and, at the time of the revolt of the *Communidades* in 1520-1521, sided with the king against the other towns of Castile.

C. Estepa, T. F. Ruiz, J. A. Bonachia, H. Casado, *Burgos en la Edad Media*, Burgos, 1984. – *La Ciudad de Burgos*, Burgos, 1985. – H. Casado, *Señores, mercaderes y campesinos. La comarca de Burgos a fines de la Edad Media*, Valladolid, 1987. – T.F. Ruiz, *The City and the Realm: Burgos and Castile, 1080-1492*, Aldershot, 1992.

Adeline Rucquoi

**BURGUNDIANS.** A series of age-old migrations led the Burgundians from their native Scandinavia all through Germany, from the shores of *Pomerania (late 2nd c. BC) to the banks of the Rhine and then Lac Léman, around Geneva. It was there in Sapaudia (from Chablais to Yverdon), to protect *Italy's Alpine approaches (from the *Alamanni), that Aetius transferred their most advanced detachment in 443. This military colony, established in Rhineland Gaul around *Mainz and *Worms since the breakthrough of 406, was converted to Catholicism. But its expansion was checked from 436-437 by the Romans, helped by the *Huns, who subdued the Burgundians remaining beyond the Rhine and massacred those on the left bank (20,000 warriors with their "king" Gunther, an episode taken up in the **Nibelungenlied*).

It was at most 50,000 survivors who were cantoned in 443 as federates between the *Alps and the Jura, admittedly reinforced over 15 years by the arrival of their fellows from Germany abandoned by the Huns (Burgundians fought on both sides in the battle of the Catalaunian fields in 451). Under the protection of the imperial authorities (until 517 each of their kings obtained the dignity of "*magister militum Galliarum*") and by alternating alliances with the other German kingdoms, over half a century the Burgundians took control of most of the heavily Romanized Rhone basin. Under Gundioc (*c.*457-*c.*470) and his brother Chilperic († *c.*480), at first allied to the *Visigoths (responsible for their Arianization?), they took part in imperial elevations (Avitus in Gaul in 455, Glycerius at *Ravenna in 473, promoted by Gundioc's son Gundobad, nephew-successor of the patrician Ricimer). This allowed them to extend their area of settlement in 458 to Lyonensis I (and Sequanensis?), then to Viennensis as far as the Drôme (463) and as far as the Durance in 475, the date when their kingship was officially recognised over all these territories, the principal king having his seat at *Lyon while Geneva was devolved to his successor designate (brother or son).

They subsequently prevailed against the *Visigoths on the borders of Viennensis (471-477), then under Gundobad (*c.*480-516) against the *Ostrogoths (raids in the Po valley in 491-494, then Sigismund's union with a daughter of *Theodoric) and especially the *Franks, with whom they made a common front against the Alamanni (pushed back north-eastward at this time): marriage of Gundobad's niece Clotild to *Clovis in 492-493, brief conflict (500-501) between the two kings due to Clovis's intervention in the internal quarrels of the Burgundian dynasty, finally rapprochement (marriage of a daughter of Sigismund to Clovis's eldest son Theuderic, common campaigns for the conquest of Visigothic Gaul in 507-510). The assimilation of the Burgundians to the Gallo-Roman substrate, facilitated by the measures compiled by local jurists to regulate relations between the two peoples (*Lex Burgundionum* promulgated in 502, then supplemented), was manifested in the influence of the *bishops (Avitus at *Vienne), the retreat of *Arianism (part of the royal family was Catholic from the late 5th c., including Gundobad's two sons Sigismund and Godomar), Sigismund's institution of a monastic metropolis at Agaunum (515) and the meeting of a "national" *council at Épaone (517).

These conditions explain the kingdom's resistance to Frankish takeover, effected after more than ten years of wars between Clovis's sons and Sigismund (captured and executed in 523-524) and then Godomar (battle of Vézeronce, 524) who was finally defeated in 534, and the persistence of a "Burgundian" entity well beyond that (specific political identity of Burgundia in the 6th- and 7th-c. *regnum Francorum*, "Romano-Burgundian" domain brought to light by the Merovingian *archaeology of the lands centred on Lac Léman and the Jura).

É. Demougeot, *La Formation de l'Europe et les Invasions barbares*, 1, Paris, 1969, 50, 357-358, 476-479; *ibid.*, 2, 1979, 248-251, 491-497, 649-674. – *Le Burgondes. Apports de l'archéologie. Actes du colloque international de Dijon (5-6 novembre 1992)*, H. Gaillard de Semainville (dir.), Dijon, 1995.

Gérard Moyse

**BURGUNDY.** The kingdom of the *Burgundians (late 5th - early 6th c.) comprised the region of *Lyon and Geneva, Sequania and the cities of Chalon, *Autun and Langres. Little is known about the settlement of the Burgundians: their *Arianism was not very militant, the legal regime of "*personality of law" was lasting. In 534 the *Franks conquered the region and expelled the dynasty but preserved the kingdom, from now on Frankish. King Guntram (561-592), son of Chlotar and grandson of *Clovis, resided at Chalon-sur-Saône and settled monks in the basilica of Saint-Marcel. After him, the kingdom was governed by the kings of *Neustria or *Austrasia. In the 8th c., after a Muslim raid (in 725 or 731), *Charles Martel established counts of his choice and secularized Church *property. Far from the centres of decision of the Carolingian state, power belonged more and more to the *counts.

The partition of Verdun (843) made the Saône the frontier of the West Frankish kingdom. Leading counts amassed countships. In 879 Boso, elected king, temporarily grouped together the counties of Burgundy, the Lyonnais region, the *Alps and *Provence. His death (887) and the *Viking invasions of 887-889 brought to the fore the count of Autun, Richard "the Justiciary": he ammassed personal countships and vassal countships, was called *dux* or *marchio* from 890 and defeated the Northmen (898, 911).

During the early Middle Ages and from the late 5th c., Burgundy enjoyed a precocious development of *monasticism: Réôme, Saint-Germain d'Auxerre, Dijon, Saint-Marcel, *Autun, Bèze, later Flavigny, then after the Viking invasions *Vézelay, Pothières and finally *Cluny (909), which in turn reformed Burgundian monasteries (Dijon, 989). *Jews are mentioned at Chalon in the Carolingian period.

After Richard († 921), his son Rudolf was king of France (923-936); then under Rudolf's brother Hugh the Black, western Burgundy was contested by the Robertian Hugh the Great. Unity on both sides of the Saône was restored by Hugh's sons Otto and Henry, but in 1002, on Henry's death, his nephew King Robert II abandoned the lands beyond the Saône and reconstituted a Western duchy. From the time of Robert son of King Robert II (1032), the Capetian dynasty reigned until 1361.

The dukes, loyal vassals of the kings of France, controlled neither Nevers, *Auxerre nor Tonnerre; they gained Chalon in 1237, but lost control of Mâcon in 1239. In the 11th and 12th cc. their authority came up against the growing independence of great ecclesiastical lordships, the weakening of the powers of the counts to the advantage of the castellans, and the preponderance of freeholds. The dukes used military powers to ensure control of the castellans and extended their custody of the churches. They enlarged their domain (Semur-en-Auxois, Châtelet de Chalon, county of Grignon, the whole of Dijon, *castellanies in Bresse, Auxonne and lands in the Comté) and acquired external vassalages. The ducal principality was strengthened again in the 13th c. by

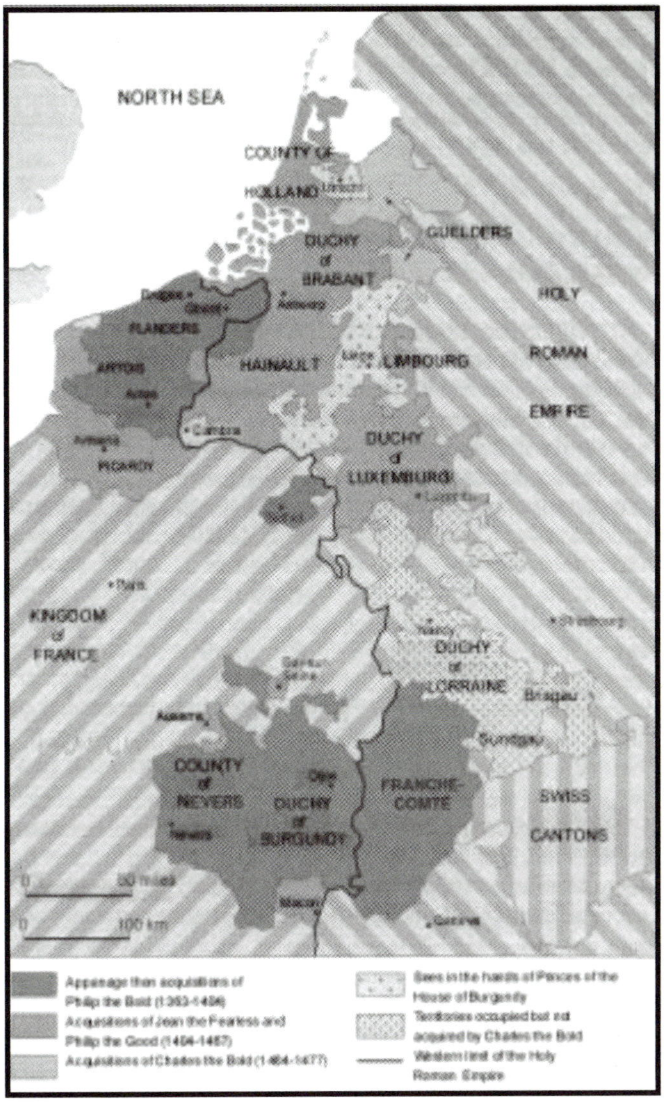


The Burgundian State in the 14th and 15th centuries.

other extensions of the domain and by subinfeudation: county of Chalon, lordships of Brancion and Montréal, lands in *Champagne, Pontailler. Ducal influence penetrated Church lands, while lay lordships were controlled by requiring an *oath for fortresses and by the resumption of freeholds. The concept of the "barony of the duchy" was based on superior justice, the right to indict, the granting of *fairs and *markets, the coining of *money, all within a coherent territory. Financial means were increased by better exploitation of the domain, the *towns, the *Jews, the Cahorsins, tolls and fairs, coining and frontier taxes. The economy profited from the revival of trade from the 12th c. and the proximity of the *Champagne fairs. The fairs of Chalon, created by the dukes in 1239 and 1280, were internationally frequented from the end of the 13th century. Ducal institutions appeared: *chamberlain, offices of receivership and general receivership, Household, distinct from the *curia* or council, court of justice, examination of accounts, **baillis* and castellans. The dukes were very active outside Burgundy: Robert I and Hugh I in Spain, Hugh III, Eudes III and Hugh IV on *crusade.

Starting from Cîteaux and *Clairvaux, *Cistercian monasticism spread in Burgundy. Among the daughters of Cîteaux (1098) were *La Ferté and *Pontigny. Five more houses were created in the duchy: notably *Fontenay.

The duchy of Eudes IV, King John and the Valois differed little from the Capetian duchy. It was enlarged in Champagne, by the Charolais (1390), the county of Nevers (1348-1404), then the Mâconnais, the county of Auxerre and Bar-sur-Seine (permanently in 1435). The duke was also count of Burgundy and Artois from 1330 to 1361 and from 1384. Also in 1384, the duchy became part of a group more and more centred on the region of the *Netherlands. The king's influence made itself felt during the lease of John II (1350-1360) and the reattachment to the *Crown (1361-1364). From 1392 to 1435, the dukes played a major role in the affairs of the realm. From 1410 to 1435 they were at war against the Armagnac, then the Dauphinal party.

Institutions were perfected. The Household, reorganised on the royal model, grew considerably. From the time of Eudes IV, the *army was paid. It contained the noble contingents of the *bailliages* and companies of professionals. Duke *Charles the Bold profoundly transformed its structures, recruitment and discipline. The higher organs of justice always required the ducal council, but a council for the Two Burgundies was created at Dijon in 1386, specifically for justice. *Jours* or *Parlement* sat at Beaune for the French part and at Saint-Laurent-lès-Chalon for the *Empire. The Council of Dijon was raised to a sovereign court by Duke Charles in 1471. From Eudes IV, there were a *chancellor and secretaries of the duke. The lower rungs of ducal justice were the *prévôts* and the *baillis*, as well as several specific jurisdictions.

For the finances, various formulae of regulating expenses and managing funds were tried, generally with a treasurer and a receiver. Eudes IV already had special auditors of accounts. In 1386 the Dijon audit-office (*Chambre des Comptes*) was created to assess accounts, control the running of the Domain, organise the *salt trade and preserve the archives. In the middle of the 14th c., a new financial system, of royal origin, was set up in the part attached to the kingdom, with meetings of State assemblies, resting on an "imposition" of 1/20 of transactions, 1/8 on the sale of *wine, and a salt tax (sea- or from Salins). To these was added, irregularly, a direct duty or hearth-tax based on real hearths. The duke got the king to give him the proceeds of these taxes. From 1384, the duke favoured the sale to the Duchy of the salt of Salins, among whose producers he was. The mints of Dijon and Chalon were royal, but ducal coin was struck in the Empire. The population, hit by numerous plagues (1348, 1360-1361, 1400-1402, 1438-1439), reached its lowest level around 1430. Society was marked by the number and weight of a very rural *nobility that was closely linked to the prince and did not hesitate to serve him outside Burgundy. A nobility of little wealth but which, despite the crisis in its revenues, succeeded in keeping its rank at the local level. The *peasants were still very largely serfs, but this *serfdom slowly retreated in the 15th century. The peasants suffered from insecurity: 1357-1375 (*Companies and troop movements), 1411-1435 (civil war), 1438-1445 (the *Écorcheurs*, a major crisis) and 1471-1475 (war against the French). Large *towns were few (the most important was *Dijon, with 2,350 hearths in 1357): they had no dominant activity and their tradesmen were organised only late. Urban society saw the traditional patriciate decline in favour of new leaders, *merchants and lawyers.

The economy was diversified. The cereal production of the plain permitted exports via the Saône. From Eudes IV, the dukes promoted the wines of the Côte d'Or, called "of Beaune", exported to *Paris, the *Netherlands and *Avignon. Cattle-raising was important in Auxois, and the sheep-farming of the Dijonnais and the Montagne supplied the export of quality wool to *Milan in the 14th century. Cloth was manufactured at Dijon, Châtillon and Semur. Burgundy was a great producer of linen and hemp cloth, exported to the Mediterranean basin. The two *fairs of Chalon-sur-Saône, an international market mainly of cloth, but also of *furs and leather, supported by the demand of the Avignon market and the purchases of the Papacy, were at their height between 1321 and 1360. From 1360 (insecurity, depopulation and overtaxation), economic activity regressed sharply. The fairs of Chalon ceased to exist in 1430 (war and rivalry of the Geneva fairs). The general impoverishment of the 15th c. led Duke Philip the Good to moderate his fiscal demands.

After the death of Charles the Bold, *Louis XI ordered the seizure of the duchy and county of Burgundy. Manoeuvred by their president Jean Jouard, the Estates of the duchy decided to rally to the king, 18 Jan 1477. Their example was followed by the Estates of the County. But the populace and part of the nobility refused to follow and, after *Dole, Auxonne and then the Charolais, Dijon rose on 26 June, followed by Chalon and other towns. Despite the favours accorded by Louis XI, notably the confirmation of the Parlement, later transferred to Dijon, and despite the treaty of Arras in 1482 which ratified by preterition the annexation of the duchy to the Crown, a Burgundian irredentism long persisted.

M. Chaume, *Les Origines du duché de Bourgogne*, Dijon, 1925-1937 (4 vol.; re-ed. 1978). – J. Richard, *Les Ducs de Bourgogne et la formation du duché du XIe au XIVe siècle*, Paris, 1954. – R. Vaughan, *Philip the Bold, John the Fearless, Philip the Good, Charles the Bold*, London, 1962-1973 (4 vol.). – O. Perrin, *Les Burgondes*, Neuchâtel, 1963. – R. Vaughan, *Valois Burgundy*, London, 1975. – H. Dubois, *Les Foires de Chalon et le commerce dans la vallée de la Saône à la fin du Moyen Âge*, Paris, 1976. – *Histoire de la Bourgogne*, J. Richard (ed.), Toulouse, 1978 (2nd ed. 1987). – *Histoire de Dijon*, P. Gras (ed.), Toulouse, 1981 (2nd ed. 1987). – M. T. Caron, *La Noblesse dans le duché de Bourgogne, 1315-1477*, Lille, 1987. – C. B. Bouchard, *Sword, Miter and Cloister. Nobility and the Church in Burgundy, 980-1198*, Ithaca (NY)-London, 1988. – J. Rauzier, *Finances et gestion d'une principauté au XIVe siècle. Le duché de Bourgogne de Philippe le Hardi*, Paris, 1996.

Henri Dubois

**BURIAL.** In the Middle Ages, inhumation in the parish *cemetery was the usual form of Christian burial. But the institutional church left the freedom to choose another burial-place. In reality, the power to depart from the common rule was a privilege that concerned only the most powerful.

The first "privileged inhumations" appeared in the 4th c., in extra-urban necropolises: convinced that a saving power emanated from the bodies of the saints, many Christians asked to be buried as close as possible to a *martyr's *tomb or a *reliquary. Because of the important number of inhumations *ad sanctos* brought to light by *archaeology, this manner of burial has been called a "mass privilege". But alongside the innumerable tombs indistinctly arranged close to the holy remains, particular monuments – private mausoleums joined to the tomb of a saint or martyrial chapels – housed the bodies of the distinguished *dead. From the 6th c., mausolea *ad sanctos* disappeared as purely funerary edifices; burials then took place inside churches, and increasingly often inside cities.

From this period, however, *councils forbade inhumation in sanctuaries. To no effect: ecclesiastical dignitaries and members of the lay aristocracy elected to be buried there. At the end of the 8th c., while lamenting to see churches transformed into cemeteries,

Bishop *Theodulf of Orléans did not rule out the burial of certain people there. A canon of the council of *Mainz (813), followed by Gratian's *Decretum*, authorized the inhumation in churches of "bishops", "abbots", "worthy priests" and "lay believers". In the 12th c., the liturgist *John Beleth admitted that of "holy fathers", "patrons" and "defenders". Thus, despite the opposition of churchmen to the hereditary transmission of this privilege (formulated from the synod of Meaux, 845), a certain funerary inequality was set up.

The (privileged) inhumation of the *laity often concerned the whole of their *family. In the churches founded or endowed by their cares, rulers and lords arranged burial places destined for the deceased members of their kin; at the moment of *death, the majority asked to join the tomb of their ancestors. Testators of the later Middle Ages expressed the same desire. The Church recognised their right: according to a rule established in 816 by Pope *Leo III (followed by *Gregory IX's *Decretals* in 1234), the dead who had expressed no other choice were to be buried with their ancestors. The principle of burial with one's ancestors, which linked up with an ancient tradition, was justified by the example of the Patriarchs (Gen 47, 30; 49, 29. . .) and the frequent mention in Scripture of *sepulchrum patrium*.

To their parish cemetery or church, many preferred inhumation in a religious institution, where the monks would keep up their memory and pray for their *salvation. By virtue of privileges emanating from papal authority, religious generally obtained the right – reserved in theory to the bishop, then to the *parishes – to bury those who had requested it, on condition of safeguarding parish rights: part of the offerings made on the occasion of the *funeral and burial was given to the priest of the parish that had lost one of its members. Yet the multiplication of burial-places was behind numerous conflicts between churches, which all strove to preserve their monopoly in matters of burial. By reserving the inhumation of the dead for themselves, ecclesiastical institutions often tried to assert their rights over a territory and its inhabitants. The parish was the ordinary place of burial of the faithful, the fact of interring someone in the places where he had resided in his lifetime allowed these places to accede to the status of "parish". Control of the land and power over men was thus for a long time the true stake in conflicts over burial. At the end of the Middle Ages, it became more material: at this time burial fees represented one of the main sources of revenue of the parish clergy.

A. Bernard, *La Sépulture en droit canonique, du* Décret *de Gratien au concile de Trente*, Paris, 1933. – J. M. Bienvenu, "Les Conflits de sépulture en Anjou aux XIe et XIIe siècles", *Actes 91e congrès national des Sociétés Savantes, BPH*, 1966, 673-685. – W. J. White, "Changing Burial Practices in Late Mediaeval England", *Ricardian*, 4/63, Dec 1978, 23-30. – D. Bullough, "Burial, Community and Belief in the Early Medieval West", *Ideal and Reality in Frankish and Anglo-Saxon Society*, P. Wormald (ed.), D. Bullough (ed.), R. Collins (ed.), Oxford, 1983. – M. Colardelle, *Sépulture et traditions funéraires du Ve au XIIIe siècle dans les campagnes des Alpes françaises du Nord*, Grenoble, 1983. – *L'Inhumation privilégiée du IVe au VIIIe siècle en Occident*, Y. Duval (ed.), J.-C. Picard (ed.), Paris, 1986. – Y. Duval, *Auprès des saints, corps et âme. L'inhumation "ad sanctos" dans la chrétienté d'Orient et d'Occident du IIIe au VIIe siècle*, Paris, 1988. – J. C. Picard, *Le Souvenir des évêques. Sépulture, listes épiscopales et culte des évêques en Italie du Nord des origines au Xe siècle*, Rome, 1988. – F. S. Paxton, *Christianising death: the creation of a ritual process in early medieval Europe*, Ithaca (NY), 1990. – H. Geake, *The Use of Grave-goods in Conversion-period England c. 600-c. 850 AD*, Oxford, 1997.

Michel Lauwers

**BURSFELD.** The *abbey of Bursfeld, founded in the 11th c. in Lower *Saxony, was the cradle of a Benedictine congregation of strict observance. John Dederoth, who reformed the monastery in 1433, had discovered the importance of this return to the sources of monastic life, both in *Italy and at *Trier, where John Rode had already restored the original discipline to Saint-Maximin. Strongly organised, the congregation, whose general *chapters met every year and whose visitors controlled the application of the statutes, managed in the 16th c. to group together more than 130 monasteries in the *Empire. The Reformation caused it to lose 40 of them, including the mother house.

P. Volk, *Fünfhundert Jahre Burfelder Kongregation*, Münster, 1950. – P. Becker, "Erstrebte und erreichte Ziele benediktinischer Reformen im Spätmittelalter", in K. Elm, *Reformbemühungen und Observanzbestrebungen im spätmittelalterlichen Ordenswesen*, Berlin, 1989, 23-24.

Francis Rapp

**BURY SAINT EDMUNDS.** Situated in a region of eastern *England subject to Scandinavian attack and settlement, *Beodricesworth* was apparently a royal vill to which was translated the body of *Edmund, the king of East Anglia killed by the Danes in 869, according to the *Passio* composed by *Abbo of Fleury in the 980s. No contemporary record survives, and later sources disagree on the date of the foundation of an ecclesiastical community, but some historians have associated another Edmund, king of England 939-946, with this translation. Reform may have come from *Ramsey in the 980s, although 11th-c. evidence ascribes Bury's refoundation in 1020 to King *Cnut (1016-1035) during whose reign a new church was built. Especially favoured by King *Edward the Confessor (1042-1066), it was among the wealthiest monastic houses in 1086. After the *Norman conquest, the monastery's struggle against the bishop of East Anglia, who attempted (without success) to take it over, led to a notorious rewriting of the past which obscures its early history. Wealthy and dynamic, it was a popular *pilgrimage site, a thriving monastic borough, and an educational and cultural centre with an impressive *library, from which grew an influential school of monastic history-writing. It was dissolved by Henry VIII in 1539.

C. Hart, *The Early Charters of Eastern England*, Leicester, 1966. – A. Gransden, "The Legends and Traditions concerning the Origins of the Abbey of Bury St Edmunds", *EHR*, 100, 1985, 1-24. – D. N. Dumville, *English Caroline Script and Monastic History*, Woodbridge, 1993, 30-48.

Lesley Abrams

**BUSCH, JOHANNES (1399/1400-*c.*1479).** Born at Zwolle, an adherent of the *Devotio moderna*, Johannes Busch was a Canon Regular of St Augustine at the convent of *Windesheim. An active reformer, he became prior at Sulta near *Hildesheim (1440-1447; 1459-1479) and prior at Neuwerk near Halle, in the archdiocese of *Magdeburg (1447-1454). In 1452, *Nicholas of Cusa appointed him papal commissary and visitor in charge of the *reform of convents. He died at Sulta.

His most important writings are historical. He composed two dissertations, *De viris illustribus ordinis canonicorum regularium monasterii in Windesem* and *De origine monasterii in Windesem*, as well as *De origine devotionis moderne*. In his *De reformatione monasteriorum*, he described his reforming activity in the convents entrusted to him.

C. Minis, "Busch, Johannes", *VerLex*, 1, 1978, 1140-1142.

Thom Mertens

**BYZANTINE AND SYRIAN LITURGIES.** The Byzantine liturgy, which, starting from the capital of the Empire, *Constantinople, had radiated out to become, from the 11th-12th cc., the common liturgy of all the Churches of Chalcedonian *Orthodoxy, drew on various sources: the tradition of *Jerusalem, those of the communities of Asia Minor, but above all that of *Antioch, at least from the start of the 5th century. It was organised in the course of the 9th-10th cc. under the predominant influence of the monasteries in and around the capital, to which – in the wake of the Arab conquests – flowed numbers of monks from *Syria and *Palestine (notably the monastery of St Sabas near Jerusalem, whose monastic rule – **typikon* – would be adopted for the ordering of the *office of the hours). This liturgy took the form in which it has survived to our own day mainly in the monastic centre of Mount *Athos, created at the end of the 10th c. on the model of the Constantinopolitan monastery of St John the Precursor, the *Studios. Elsewhere the break-up of the *patriarchate of Antioch during the 5th-6th cc. and the creation of "national" Churches of Aramaic culture and Syriac language would entail the organisation of liturgies rooted both in this culture and in the Antiochene tradition proper. Thus were constituted, alongside that of the Church officially recognised as orthodox by the imperial authorities – and for this reason often called "Melkite" –, a "*Jacobite" liturgy (from the name of the main instigator of the "monophysite" church) and, following a disagreement among monasteries of Chalcedonian confession but Aramaic culture, that of the *Maronites, formed into an independent patriarchate on Mount *Lebanon in the course of the 8th century. Their liturgy would incorporate and preserve usages and rites familiar to the Syriac-speaking communities and also, eventually, others coming from the Latin West. Some of these are found in the liturgy that was organised in Mesopotamia, starting from the cultural and commercial centres of Edessa (Urfa) and Nisibis, within the Church of the Sasanid Persian Empire, called by the Byzantines "*Nestorian" by reason of its attachment to the teaching of the Antiochene Doctors condemned by the "Orthodox" *councils: Theodore of Mopsuestia and above all Nestorius, considered to be their leading man.

In their diversification, all these liturgies, to which could be added that of the Church of *Armenia, allow us to recognise a common cultural ground, whose original home was the cosmopolitan city of Antioch, both Greek and Syrian in culture: capital of the administrative "diocese" of the East since the end of the 3rd c., a great centre of cultural and economic diffusion, it was also – and above all – in an exceptional way the seat of a Church of apostolic origin. No other, apart from *Jerusalem and *Rome, was to play a role of such importance in the elaboration of Christian liturgies. A long and complex elaboration, whose progress the surviving evidence lets us follow only incompletely. Its fundamental lines are already firmly drawn – for the eucharistic liturgy and the great sacramental rites of *baptism and *ordination of *bishops, priests and *deacons – in the collection commonly called the *Apostolic Tradition*, dating from the first third of the 3rd c., repeated and developed at the end of the 4th c. in the ample Antiochene compilation of the *Apostolic Constitutions* and the Syriac compilation of the *Octateuch of Clement*. From the same period we also possess the postbaptismal catecheses of Cyril of Jerusalem, Theodore of Mopsuestia and John Chrysostom, with numerous information gleaned from Chrysostom's preaching, during both his ministry at Antioch and his episcopate at Constantinople. To the same period we can also date the earliest redactions of eucharistic prayers: that of Jerusalem, called "of St James", which would be adopted by the Jacobite church; the Antiochene one of the Apostles, which in its most developed form would become the common *anaphora of the Byzantine liturgies, most habitually supplanting the Cappadocian Anaphora of St Basil. The same common foundation also appears for the rituals of baptism and ordination.

From the 6th-7th cc. the diversification of the liturgies became specific at the same time as new elements were introduced or intensified, at the level of ritual as well as of the texts that have come down to us and whose history we can follow. Commentaries or directories allow us to know what doctrinal and spiritual interpretation of them was proposed. This goes above all for the Byzantine liturgy which was veritably formed in the course of this period, both as regards ceremonial, which incorporated many elements of that of the imperial court, and the contribution of monastic usages. The same is true, though to a lesser degree, of the Antiochene liturgy as it took shape in the Jacobite church. For that of the Nestorian Church, on the other hand, our information is much more restricted; surviving liturgical documents are few and mostly late, going back no further than the *Mongol period. The Nestorian Church also seems, more than the other churches, to have kept faithfully to the rules of the reorganisation undertaken on the morrow of the Arab conquests by Patriarch Isho'yabh III (650-658); at the turn of the 12th-13th cc., Patriarchs Elias III Abu Halim (1176-1190) and Yahballaha II (1190-1222) would succeed in fixing the repertoire of patristic readings, chants and prayers in the *Gazza* (the Treasure).

More than in that of ritual, more or less elaborate and solemn, it is particularly in the dual field of hymnody and euchology that each of these liturgies shows specific traits. And this mainly because it was hymnody that held a place and importance in the various Eastern liturgies out of all proportion to that allowed it in the West in the *Roman liturgy. Syria, Hellenized or still Aramaic, very quickly appeared as the creative focus. The *Odes of Solomon*, rediscovered at the start of the 20th c., are our earliest evidence, given that hardly anything has survived of the abundant output of Bardesanes of Edessa in the late 2nd century. But the master whose influence would be exercised, directly or indirectly, over all the Oriental churches was St Ephrem of Nisibis (305-373). The rhythmic discourses (*memrē*) and instructions (*medressē*) which he composed were the beginning of a vast output including adaptations in Greek or Armenian that have not ceased to provide an important part of the repertoire that feeds and sustains the faith and piety of Eastern Christians. One of the most brilliant of these adaptations consists of the "Scrolls" (*Kontakia*) of a Hellenized Syrian from Emesa (Homs), Romanus the Melode, a deacon at *Beirut and then at Constantinople in the time of Justinian. Certain strophes are still in use in the Byzantine liturgy where they have given rise to a characteristic literary genre. But these long poems – often 24 strophes following the letters of the alphabet – have to a great extent been replaced by another form of hymnody, also of Syrian origin, its shorter strophes (*troparia*) intercalated between the verses of psalms or scriptural canticles and grouped together in the framework of these canticles (Odes) sung at the morning *office to form "Canons" of three, eight or nine Odes. One of their first initiators, early in the 8th c., was Andrew, bishop of *Crete, of Damascene origin, as well as his compatriots Cosmas and above all *John of Damascus, a monk of St Sabas near Jerusalem. It is doubtless largely thanks to monks of St Sabas who emigrated to Constantinople that this form of hymnody was introduced and fructified in the Byzantine liturgy with the great melodists of the monastery of *Studios: *Theodore, Theophanes, Joseph and their imitators. In the Syriac language, the Mesopotamian (Nestorian) liturgy kept, in hymnody as in other fields, a certain sobriety, incorporating alongside the Ephremian basis the compositions of Narsai and Babai. Jacobite Syriac hymnography, on the other hand, is extremely rich; its earliest representative was Bishop Jacob of Sarug, author in particular of canticles (*soghitē*), which had many imitators.

The same fertility, if not the same redundancy, is manifested by the Jacobite Church in the field of euchology. While for its most fundamental element, the Eucharistic prayer (Anaphora), the Byzantine churches kept to the formula of Antiochene origin, called that of St John Chrysostom, and to the formulary of St Basil, originally from *Cappadocia, and while the Nestorian Church faithfully preserved the very ancient Mesopotamian Anaphora of the Apostles, but added to it two formularies of Syrian origin attributed to Theodore of Mopsuestia and Nestorius, the Jacobite Syrian church never ceased in the course of time to compose new Anaphorae starting from that of Jerusalem (St James) or from the ancient Antiochene anaphora of the Apostles, or even that of St Basil.

The same goes for the other euchological formulae: few in number and sober among the Nestorians and even the Byzantines, they are manifested in the Antiochene Syrian Church by original creations, notably the *Sedro*, which was originally created to accompany the offering of *incense, evening and morning or in the framework of the eucharistic celebration, but which ended by proliferating in all the other offices. After a doxological introduction, the body of the *Sedro* takes the form of a catechetical instruction culminating in a lyrical strophe normally accompanying the offering of incense.

I. H. Dalmais, *Liturgies d'Orient*, Paris, 1980. – R. Taft, *The Byzantine Rite. A Short History*, 1992.

Irénée-Henri Dalmais

**BYZANTINE ART.** Byzantine art and its evolution are intimately linked to the politico-military and religious context of the Empire. The triumphs of Justinian's reign were offset by a period of troubles whose consequence was the *iconoclast crisis. The territorial conqests of the *Macedonian emperors went hand in hand with an artistic renaissance, while an over-elaborate art developed under the *Comneni. After the Latin occupation of *Constantinople (1204), the return of the *Palaeologi generated an artistic renaissance intended to glorify the Greek past.

**The dark centuries (7th c. to early 9th c.).** The post-Justinian period served as setting for two antithetical artistic movements. A severe hieratic style, proper to express the presence of the sacred (mosaics of St Demetrius at *Thessalonica, *c.*730), developed conjointly with an interest in the antique tradition (frescos of Santa Maria Antiqua, Rome). Mythological and secular subjects are abundantly present on silver tableware throughout the 7th century.

Iconoclasm, in force from 726 to 843 except for a brief return to *images between 787 and 815, was opposed to figurative representations, which it replaced with aniconic compositions dominated by the motif of the cross. The iconoclast polemic and the formulation of the doctrine of religious images that it entailed provided the roots of middle Byzantine iconography, which stressed the themes of Christ's Incarnation and dual nature.

**The Macedonian renaissance (867-1056).** The term "renaissance" is explained by a renewal of interest in the cultural heritage of the past which coincided with a political and economic recovery of the Empire. Imperial ideology, founded on the divine origin of power, was transmitted by means of iconographical themes such as the Offering or symbolic Crowning by Christ.

A coherent programme of monumental decoration was put in place in central-plan churches dominated by Christ *Pantocrator in the cupola, surrounded by the celestial hierarchy, and the Virgin of the Incarnation in the apse. The distribution of key episodes of the New Testament found an adequate space in the plans of Greek-cross churches with central domes. These compact edifices, with façades enlivened by offset plans, arcades, patterns of bricks, reflect a privatization of devotion and the multiplication of monastic establishments (churches of Constantine Lips and Myrelaion at Constantinople; Panagia ton Chalkeon at Thessalonica). Vast-dimensioned cupolas carried by pendentives were adopted in *Greece in edifices decorated with mosaic cycles: the *katholikon* of Hosios Lukas (after 1011), the Nea Moni of Chios (1045-1055), Daphni (late 11th c.). Groups of frescos of the same period are also attested in *Cappadocia: the Great Dovecote of Çavuşin, Tokali and Elmali Kilise at Göreme; in Russia: St Sophia at *Kiev (1037-1046); and in Macedonia: St Sophia at *Ohrid (1037-1056).

A *humanist movement reinforced by a tendency to bring together and copy ancient texts would influence the basic models of this art, which was oriented towards immaterial figures intended to express Christian spirituality. Abstract backgrounds, coloured in gold, receive hieratic bodies on a monumental scale, with impassive faces. Interest in the culture of Antiquity remained predominant in works produced for the imperial court (*ivories, manuscripts, *silks, *goldsmiths' work) up to the late 10th century. The crafts, organised into trade bodies, show a homogeneous character both in the choice of iconographical types and in techniqes of manufacture and decoration. The taste for polychromy, characteristic of goldsmiths' work (translucent *enamels, metals encrusted with niello and precious stones), recurs in sculpture or in painted and glazed *ceramics (*sgraffito*). The development of private devotion was expressed by an expanded production of objects of a prophylactic nature (crosses, *reliquaries, portable *icons), illustrating prayers of intercession (*Deêsis, military saints, medical saints).

**From the *Comneni and *Angeli to the Latin occupation of Constantinople.** The 12th c. was a decisive period in the evolution of Byzantine art. The programme of the choir was marked by the ascendancy of the liturgy and of theological discussions centring on the nature of Christ and his place in the *Eucharist: the officiating bishops, in semi-profile holding their scrolls, converge on the Amnos, Christ the *Lamb lying on the altar or in the paten. The *fresco, which supplanted the *mosaic, went down to the bottom of the walls, thus favouring a direct relationship with the congregation. The play of line and design allowed the artist to express the emotion of the protagonists, whom he placed in pathetic scenes (the Threnos or last lamentation of the Virgin over Christ's body; the descent from the Cross). The slender figures with contorted faces marked by thick lines and circles were represented in movement in floating draperies with multiple folds.

The Comnenian style is well attested in Macedonia: St Panteleimon at Nerezi (1164), St George at Kurbinovo (1191); in Greece: St Anargyroi at Kastoria (*c.*1180); Hosios David at

Thessalonica (late 12th – early 13th c.); in *Cyprus: Panagia Phorbiotissa at Asinou (1105-1106); Panagia tou Arakou at Lagudera (1192). Mosaics, though abandoned at this period, characterise the commissions of the Norman kings of *Sicily: *Cefalù (1148), Martorana (1143), *Monreale (1180-1190). At Constantinople, a major work is the votive panel of John II Comnenus and his family (1118-1122) in the south tribune of Hagia Sophia.

**Latin occupation of Constantinople (1204-1261).** The capture of Constantinople by the Latins led to a diaspora of Byzantine artists. New centres were established at *Nicaea, *Trebizond, Arta and Thessalonica, which took over from Constantinople. But the essential characteristics of 13th-c. Byzantine art are found in *Serbia, where local workshops were set up employing painters from Constantinople. Their style, stamped by monumentality, marks a break with the mannerist tendency of the 12th century. The figures, whose plasticity is accentuated, adopt measured movements expressing intimate feelings of calm. The most representative paintings are those of the churches of Studenica (1208-1209), Mileševa (before 1228) and Sopočani (1263-1268).

Despite the departure of the richest donors and the elite of Byzantine society, the workshops of Constantinople continued to produce luxury articles, icons and manuscripts. Greek artists were employed to execute the monumental works intended for the Latins (cycle of St *Francis of Assisi at Kalenderhane Camii).

**Palaeologan renaissance (1258-1453).** The Empire, reduced and weakened, was restored around its capital. The will to assert a specific national identity against the Latins and *Turks awoke a patriotic current in which the glory of Antiquity was rediscovered. The religious renewal coloured with mysticism also had its consequences for art. A humanist movement entailed a diversified artistic patronage, recruited among wider social layers than those of the imperial court and the higher clergy. Members of the aristocracy built funerary chapels on to earlier edifices which they surrounded with an ambulatory. A profusion of iconographical details borrowed from Antiquity (miniature architecture, personifications, philosophers) was integrated into traditional compositions that became more narrative. These were enriched with new subjects inspired by prayers and liturgical *hymns, psalms, *apocryphal gospels. Scenes unfolded within complex decorations filled with fantastic architecture. The voluminous treatment of bodies was achieved by a subtle graduation of tones lit by luminous highlights.

The mosaics of the church of Pammakaristos (1310-1320) and those of the monastery of Chora (1315-1321) are the finest groups in the capital, to which can be added the panel of the Deêsis in the south tribune of Hagia Sophia (1261-1262). The funerary chapel of the church of Chora, entirely covered with frescos, presents a detailed composition of the *Last Judgment. Paintings whose quality equals that of the capital are found in centres like Thessalonica: St Nicholas Orphanos (*c.*1320), church of the Prophet Elijah (after 1360); *Mistra: Peribleptos (1348-1380), Pantanassa (*c.*1428) in Greece; Dečani in Serbia (1338-1347/1348).

This glimpse into Byzantine art, as we are able to present it today, is dependent on the works that survive and their state of preservation. The commonly admitted theses and the chronology are susceptible of more accurate definition through the progress of *archaeology, associated with scientific analyses and a better exploitation of textual and epigraphical sources.

L. Rodley, *Byzantine Art and Architecture*, Cambridge, 1993. – *L'Art du Moyen Âge*, J.-P. Caillet (dir.), Paris, 1995. – A. Cutler and J.-M. Spieser, *Byzance médiévale. 700-1204*, Paris, 1996. – *Moyen Âge. Chrétienté et Islam*, C. Heck (dir.), Paris, 1996. – J. Lowden, *Early Christian and Byzantine Art*, London, 1997. – T. F. Mathews, *Byzantium from Antiquity to the Renaissance*, New York, 1998.

Brigitte Pitarakis

**BYZANTINE CHURCH.** The Byzantines did not develop a systematic *ecclesiology. For them, the Church was not a society parallel to secular society, obeying carefully codified laws. It was a spiritual reality whose most important part was in heaven with God. What constituted the Church on earth was the communion of Christians around their *bishop (local church), the bishops with their patriarch, and the patriarchs among themselves. This conception was opposed to the hierarchical structure of Western ecclesiology which presented the *pope as the source of communion.

Byzantine ecclesiology developed in opposition to the claims of Rome to incarnate the communion of the Churches. This opposition was expressed on three levels: the role of the patriarchs and that of the ecumenical councils.

The five *patriarchs: from the first centuries of Christianity, the local Churches of the universal Church were organised around five patriarchs: those of *Rome, *Antioch, *Jerusalem, *Alexandria and *Constantinople. This theory of pentarchy (five patriarchates), originally the outcome of administrative needs, in the course of time took on an ecclesiological value: the five patriarchates were the five senses of Christ's body which was the Church. Each patriarch administered the territory over which he had jurisdiction, but acted in communion with the other patriarchs. The equality of the five patriarchs, which was opposed to the primacy of the papacy, had been asserted still more vigorously by the Byzantines after the rupture of 1054. However, it was challenged by another Byzantine conception: that of the patriarch of Constantinople as ecumenical patriarch.

The ecumenical patriarch: since the 28th canon of the council of Chalcedon (a canon not recognised by Rome), the see of Constantinople held second place after Rome, as new capital of the Empire. From 595 its bishop received the title of ecumenical patriarch. This title made the patriarch of Constantinople the *primate of the East. After 1054, the Roman church being considered schismatic (or even heretical), certain patriarchs of Constantinople asserted that the primacy otherwise acknowledged to the pope now reverted to them. This title was the source of the universalist claims of the great 14th-c. patriarchs (Philotheos, *Callistus, Anthony IV) who put forward the ecumenical patriarch as the father of all the Churches, with rights of inspection over the internal affairs of the other patriarchates, and the source of the episcopate.

The ecumenical *councils: a tribunal superior to the ecumenical patriarch, the ecumenical councils (bringing together the delegates of the five patriarchs) were considered to be the ultimate source of *authority in the Church. For the Byzantines, only an ecumenical council could settle a question of dogma. Their greatest complaint against the Roman church was that she had added the **Filioque* to a formula of faith defined by a council (the *Creed of Nicaea), without the question having been examined by another council. This was one of the points on which opposition between Byzantine ecclesiology and Roman ecclesiology was strongest, since it gave the pope a role in defining the faith that the Byzantines acknowledged only to the councils. This primacy of the councils also explains why the Byzantines always, from 1054, called for the holding of a truly ecumenical council (that of *Lyon in 1274 not meeting the required criteria) to discuss the *union of the Churches: a position defended among others by Barlaam before the pope in *Avignon in 1339, and by *John VI Cantacuzenus before the legate Paul in 1347. The title of a treatise of Nilus Cabasilas, of the same period, explains "that the sole obstacle to union is the pope's refusal to call an ecumenical council".

The internal organisation of the Byzantine Church was closely bound up with the imperial power. Indeed the patriarch was considered an official (capable of exercising the regency) and the Empire was a "symphony of powers": so the law of the Church and the law of the State had to be in agreement.

The administration of the Byzantine Church was determined by a set of canons emanating from the Church *Fathers and ecumenical councils. In the 9th c., the **Nomocanon in 50 titles*, compiled under the direction of *Photius, brought together by themes the whole of the canonical and imperial legislation. Later commentators (principally, in the 12th c., Zonaras, Aristhenes and Balsamon) asked themselves what should be done if a law and a canon contradicted each other. All replied that the canons had priority over the laws. In practice however the imperial will nearly always prevailed.

It was the whole question of relations between the patriarch and the emperor that was at stake. A 9th-c. document, also due to Photius, the *Eisagoge* (or *Epanagoge*), defined the Empire as an organism directed by two equal powers: the patriarch ruled souls and the emperor ruled bodies. In practice, despite the patriarchs' claim that the soul was superior to the body, the emperor nearly always had the upper hand since he always had the possibility of dismissing recalcitrant patriarchs.

The history of the Byzantine Church was shot through by currents that disputed the official ecclesiology in the name of a return to sources and the true nature of the Church. One of these disputes concerned the role of the patriarch in relation to the *metropolitans, both in their eparchy and in the permanent *synod. The question was raised by metropolitans anxious for the independence of the Church, given that the patriarch, appointed by the emperor, was often dependent on him.

In the 10th c., there was a controversy between Euthymus, metropolitan of Sardis, and an anonymous author, on the point of whether the patriarch chose the metropolitans or merely ordained the candidate chosen by the synod. An underlying question was that of whether the patriarch administered the eparchies of his patriarchate directly or whether he was subject to his synod just as the patriarchs together were subject to the ecumenical councils. In fact, from the 7th c., the patriarch always chose the metropolitans. In the 14th c., the great patriarchs of the *hesychast movement presented the patriarch as the source of the episcopate, adopting for the Byzantine Church a pyramidal ecclesiological plan similar to that of the Roman church at the same date.

Other currents went so far as to contest the validity of the Church as a hierarchical institution. Monastic circles were always foci of opposition to the hierarchical Church. Usually, the opposition stayed within the Church and was content to appeal to the primacy of *sanctity over administration. An extreme form of this "internal" spiritual opposition was the position of *Symeon the New Theologian, in the 10th c., who claimed that without a conscious experience of the *Holy Spirit it was not possible to do *theology, and that a monk who, though not a priest, was highly spiritual, was a more suitable confessor than a cleric who did not have this spiritual experience.

There were periods in which, when the hierarchical Church seemed too servile in its obedience to the emperor's wishes, the monks held up the torch of resistance and claimed to represent the Church: this was the case, *e.g.*, during the *iconoclast crisis or the resistance to the Union of Lyon (1274) or of Florence (1439).

Opposition sometimes went as far as *schism, espousing permanent sectarian tendencies and rejecting the very notion of a hierarchical Church: the Messalians in the 4th c., later the *Paulicians and the *Bogomils, the Arsenites at the turn of the 13th-14th cc., claimed to oppose to the visible hierarchy an invisible hierarchy, dissuading the faithful from sacramental practice and accusing the visible Church of having betrayed its mission. The theologians (Diadochus of Photice against the Messalians, Theoleptus of Philadelphia against the Arsenites) responded to them by recentring ecclesiology on the theology of salvation: the visible Church, in the person of the bishops, is the source of the *sacraments, and hence of salvation. The episcopal succession is the channel of the *grace issuing from Christ, a grace independent of the personal *sanctity of the bishop and of the priests on whom he confers the priesthood.

J. Darrouzès, *Documents inédits d'ecclésiologie byzantine*, Paris, 1966. – J. Meyendorff, *Initiation à la théologie byzantine*, Paris, 1975. – C. Walter, *Art and ritual of the Byzantine Church*, London, 1982. – J. M. Hussey, *The Orthodox Church in the Byzantine Empire*, Oxford, 1986.

Marie-Hélène Congourdeau

**BYZANTINE EMPIRE.** The conversion of *Constantine, the foundation of *Constantinople in 330 on the site of Byzantium and the creation of the gold *solidus* laid the foundations of a renewed Empire, still Roman, but becoming Christian in the course of the 4th century. This Empire was to last for more than a thousand years. Its history can be divided into three phases: the protobyzantine Empire up to the 7th c., the medieval State until 1204 and finally a declining Empire falling back on the Aegean Sea, which perished in 1453 with the fall of its capital.

The protobyzantine Empire was in many respects a continuation of the late Roman Empire. From Diocletian and Constantine it inherited a powerful *army that allowed it in the East to safeguard the oriental *limes* against the powerful State of the Sasanid Persians and repulse the barbarian *invasions, despite the grave setback suffered against the Goths at Adrianople in 378. It also developed an effective palace administration in which the praetorian prefect and the *magister militum* stand out. The economy remained based on the prosperity of the cities and the vigour of trade: Antioch, Alexandria and Carthage remained regional capitals of the first order.

Christianity became the state religion under Theodosius in the late 4th c., but paganism long remained lively. Its decline is symbolically expressed by the closing of the school of Athens under Justinian. An ecclesiastical hierarchy was put in place under imperial authority. At the council of Chalcedon, the pre-eminence of certain sees was recognised, with the establishment of a "pentarchy": the *patriarchates of *Rome, *Alexandria, *Antioch, *Constantinople and *Jerusalem. Constantinople obtained the second rank, as residence of the emperor, behind Rome to which was recognised a primacy of honour. The definition of dogma and notably the question of the nature of Christ divided the faithful. In

325, at Nicaea, the first *council convoked by the emperor in person, the *Arian position was discarded. At Chalecdon, in 451, the "orthodox" definition of the dual nature of Christ was rejected by a large part of the eastern provinces won over to monophysitism and *Nestorianism.

In the 6th c., Justinian judged the moment ripe to reconstruct the Empire, badly damaged in the West by the barbarian invasions, and his generals, Belisarius and Narses, succeeded in regaining Africa, *Italy with Old Rome and southern *Spain. This reconquest has often been judged severely for having exhausted the Empire, but it allowed Byzantium to retain positions in Italy for centuries. Signs of weakness appeared. The *Slavs began to spread into the Balkans. The plague made its reappearance with grave consequences locally, as at Constantinople. Economic expansion in the countryside suffered a pause in *Syria, Antioch was ravaged by earthquakes, but at the end of the 6th c. the Empire still represented a considerable power, with no rival apart from the Sasanids.

The reign of *Heraclius (610-641) marked a turning point. Victor in a harsh civil war, the new emperor suffered terrible reverses against the *Avars in Europe and the Persians, losing the rich provinces of the East; Constantinople suffered its first great siege in 626. In a last effort, Heraclius managed to prevail over the Sasanid monarchy, which collapsed, but a new enemy – the Muslims – resumed the offensive in the East and took possession, this time permanently, of *Palestine and Jerusalem, the Holy City of the Christians, and of Syria and Egypt, long the granary of Constantinople. Doubt as to the perpetuity of the Empire protected by God gripped the population, who took refuge in the cult of *images, *relics and saints.

The century that followed Heraclius's death gave Byzantium its medieval characteristics, beginning with its retrenched frontiers. The Arabs were halted with difficulty on the Taurus, and the *Caucasus was lost, as were Carthage and Africa in the west. The Slavs and then the *Bulgars limited the Byzantine presence in the Balkans and Thrace and on the Aegean coast. The *Lombards seized the greater part of Italy, except for the *Exarchate of *Ravenna, which fell in 751, and *Sicily. The army was completely reorganised so as to find its necessary provisioning on the spot and to defend territory in depth. It was divided into great administrative areas, the *themes, governed by *strategoi* who combined military and civil powers. Demographic decline accelerated, the towns retracted into *kastra* (fortresses) and even Constantinople was depopulated to such an extent that the emperor *Constantine V had to carry out authoritarian transfers of population. Commercial transactions collapsed, gold *coinage became rarer. The sole consolation for the emperors was that the population living under their command was henceforth almost exclusively Chalecdonian, except for some heretics and *Jews.

The reforming emperors of the *Isaurian dynasty, Leo III and *Constantine V, managed to remove the Muslim threat by repelling the besiegers of Constantinople in 718 and defeating a powerful

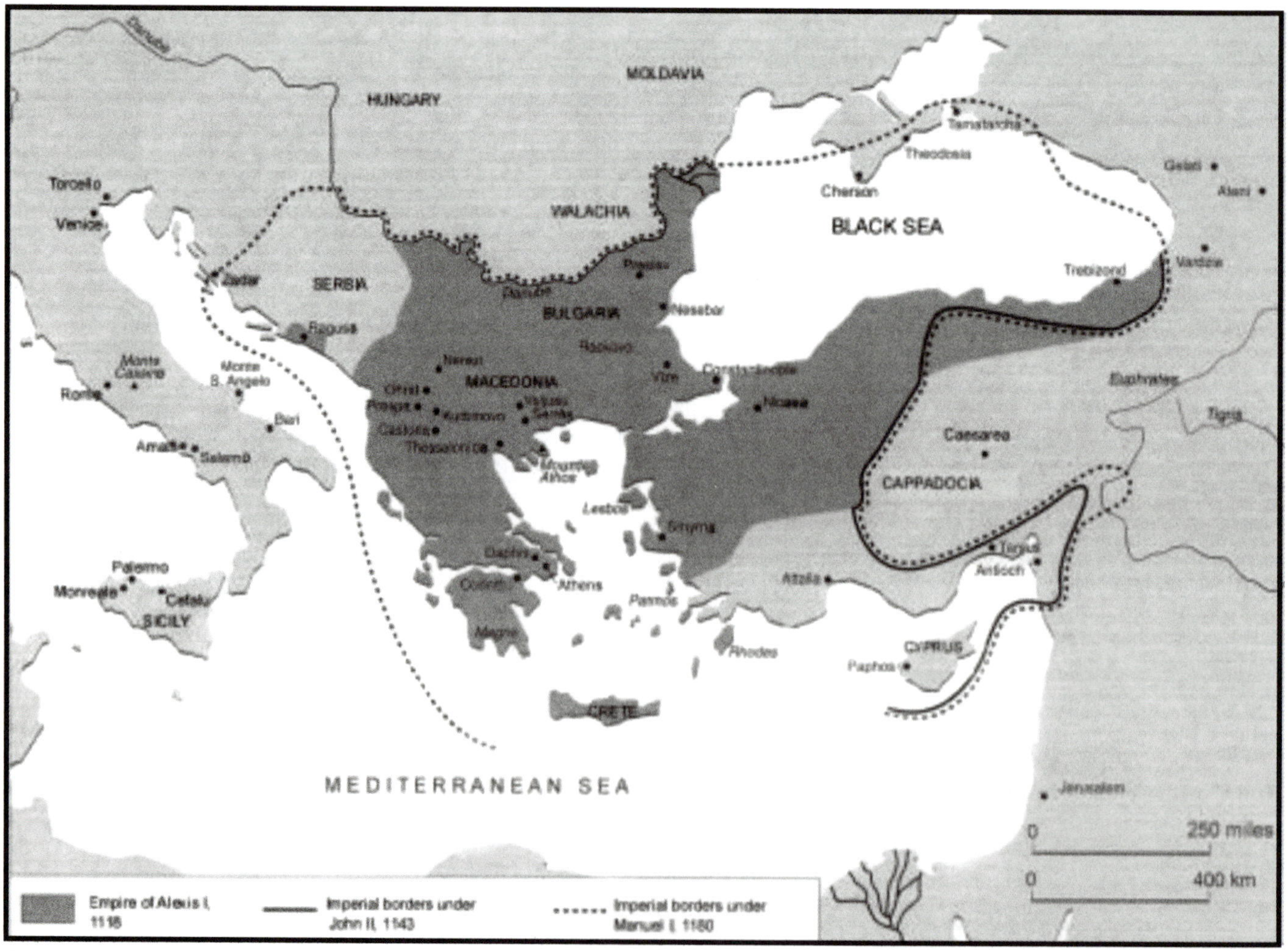

The Byzantine Empire under the dynasty of the Comneni in the 12th century.

Arab army in Asia Minor in 741. They strove to take the Church in hand and eradicate what they judged to be a return to idolatry, the cult of images, but their success was temporary.

Around 750 we see a slow reversal of circumstances. Demographic growth resumed very slowly after the end of the plague, the rural economy developed once more, the currency gradually found its place. This expansion took place in the European part of the Empire until the 14th c., while in Asia Minor there was a leveling off in the 11th c. before a resumption in the second half of the 12th. The towns revived, as witness the construction of churches and monasteries, which multiplied from the 10th c., notably at Constantinople. The artistic and cultural renaissance coincided with the coming to power of the *Macedonian dynasty which for two centuries (867-1056) ensured a certain political stability.

This regained dynamism of Byzantium expressed itself in territorial expansion from the 9th century. In the Balkans, despite the Bulgar power, the Slavs were subjugated and Christianized. In Asia Minor, the Muslims finally retreated under the pressure of generals who emerged from the military aristocracy forged in Akritic wars, their most complete representatives being the Phocas family. Melitene, Tarsus, *Crete and finally Antioch were reconquered. Basil II, breaking with the traditional military elites, chose expansion in the Balkans and in 1018 subjected *Bulgaria.

In the middle of the 10th c., the Byzantines who had regained their old frontiers of the Danube and the Euphrates, with no posible rivals, believed in a lasting peace and adopted a defensive strategy. But the end of the Macedonian dynasty provoked half a century of internal troubles before a general, Alexius *Comnenus, founded a dew dynasty. Moreover, at the same moment there apeared in the West the *Normans, who took possession of southern Italy, the *Pechenegs who invaded the Balkans, and the *Seljuk Turks who installed themselves in Asia Minor after their victory at Manzikert (1071).

Under the military dynasty of the Comneni, the Empire regained its status as a great power, but was unable to eliminate the Turks from the Anatolian plateau. It also progressively came up against the expansionist interests of the Latin world. The Byzantines had appealed to the Latins to fight against the Turks, but the *crusades rapidly engendered a feeling of mistrust between the partners, notably over Syrian Antioch. The appeal to the Italian *maritime republics, *Venice, *Pisa and *Genoa, gave Byzantium the succour of a fleet, but at the price of economic concessions whose nefarious consequences were felt only after 1204. These provoked tensions between the Greeks and the Latin merchants. Religious incomprehension was accentuated without permanent rupture after the "*schism" of 1054. All these elements culminated in the turning aside of the fourth crusade and the pillage of Constantinople, captured in 1204.

Partially reconstituted from the provinces of Asia Minor, the Empire recovered its capital in 1261 under Michael VIII *Palaeologus, founder of the last Byzantine dynasty. A State henceforth based on the values of Hellenism, Byzantium could not simultaneously confront the Westerners, who remained present in the Balkans, and the new Turkish tribes, among them the *Ottomans, pushed into Asia Minor by the *Mongol advance, all the more since its *commerce had passed into the hands of Italian merchants. The civil wars of the first half of the 14th c. doomed the sketchy Balkan State that was set up around 1340 after the Ottomans had completed the conquest of Bithynia. After that,

*The Last Judgment.* Miniature from a mid 11th-c. Byzantine manuscript. Paris, BNF (Ms gr. 74, fol. 51 v°).

Byzantium was no more than a territory disputed between the Serbs, triumphant for a time under Tsar Dušan, and the Ottomans, established in their new capital of Adrianople. Western help was tied to the *union of the Churches, which was repugnant to the natives. In the 15th c., despite some late crusades and some fine sucesses in the Morea where *Mistra testifies to the potential dynamism of Hellenism, the State was reduced to the capital and its suburbs. In May 1453, despite some Latin help, the town succumbed to the assaults of Mehmet II's Ottomans who entered Hagia Sophia, fulfilling the old dream of the Arab conquerors. Byzantium bequeathed its religion to the Slavs and its culture, transmitted by refugees, to the West, thus contributing to the *Renaissance.

G. Ostrogorsky, *History of the Byzantine State*, Oxford, 1968 (dated, but useful for the framework of events). – D. Obolensky, *The Byzantine Commonwealth*, London, 1971. – A. Ducellier, *Byzance et le monde orthodoxe*, Paris, 1986. – J. F. Haldon, *Byzantium in the Seventh Century*, Cambridge, 1990. – *The Oxford Dictionary of Byzantium*, A. Kazhdan (ed.), New York-Oxford, 1991 (3 vol.). – W. E. Kaegi, *Byzantium and the Early Islamic Conquests*, Cambridge, 1995. – M. Whittow, *The Making of Orthodox Byzantium (600-1025)*, London, 1996. – D. M. Nicol, *The Last Centuries of Byzantium 1261-1453*, Cambridge, 1993 (2nd ed.). – W. Treadgold, *A History of the Byzantine State and Society*, Stanford (CA), 1997.

Jean-Claude Cheynet

**BYZANTINE MANUSCRIPTS.** Our knowledge of the places and circumstances of copying of Byzantine manuscripts, like that of their history and circulation, is based esentially on examination of the *books themselves. Documents relating to copying centres and libraries are rare. So we must multiply approaches: study the texts from a philological point of view, their place in a *stemma*; analyse subscriptions (which sometimes contain, as well as a date, clues as to the status of the scribes or the place of their activity); identify hands and establish lists of manuscripts attributable to a single copyist; examine *codicological peculiarities from which we can establish series allowing us to infer the existence of a *scriptorium*; look at marks of possession and readers' annotations. The prosopographical study of professional scribes or scholars (copying books for themselves), like that of patrons, offers new materials to the history of scholarship at Byzantium, from the "first *humanism" of the 9th and 10th cc. to that golden age of philology, the "Palaeologan renaissance", after the reconquest of 1261.

The flow of Byzantine scholars and manuscripts to *Italy, especially after 1453, fertilized the Western *Renaissance of the 15th and 16th centuries. Among collectors and seekers of manuscripts, princes or humanists, we must mention Cardinal *Bessarion (*c.*1400-1472), a Greek won over to the Latin cause, a great bibliophile and philologist, who made a collection of manuscripts of the main texts of Greek literature, sacred and profane, in order to save the heritage of Hellenism: his legacy formed the initial basis of the Biblioteca Marciana at *Venice. *Crete, a Venetian possession and veritable hub, played a capital role in this movement from east to west, as the output of the *scriptorium* of Michael Apostolis (*c.*1420-1474 or 1486) shows. At Venice itself it was often Cretans who animated the workshop of Aldo Manuzio, participating from the 1490s in the work of preparing *editiones principes* of the Greek *classics, whose sources were Byzantine manuscripts or copies made more recently in Italy.

J. Irigoin, "Pour une étude des centres de copie byzantins", *Scr.*, 12, 1958, 208-227; 13, 1959, 177-209. – A. Dain, *Les Manuscrits*, Paris, 1975 (3rd ed.). – *Griechische Kodikologie und Textüberlieferung*, D. Harlfinger (ed.), Darmstadt, 1980 (bibliog., 657-678). – B. L. Fonkic, "*Scriptoria* bizantini. Risultati e prospettive della ricerca", *RSBN*, new series 17-19, 1980-1982, 73-118. – N. G. Wilson, *Scholars of Byzantium*, London, 1983. – L. D. Reynolds, N. G. Wilson, *D'Homère à Érasme. La transmission des classiques grecs et latins*, Paris, 1984 (Fr. tr.). – H. Hunger, *Schreiben und Lesen in Byzanz. Die byzantinische Buchkultur*, Munich, 1989. – P. Canart, *Paleografia e codicologia greca. Una rassegna bibliografica*, Vatican, 1991 ("Littera antiqua", 7).

Philippe Hoffmann

# C

**CABASILAS, NICHOLAS (*c.*1320-*c.*1398).** Inscribed among the saints by the patriarchate of Constantinople in 1983, this author of the late *Byzantine Empire recapitulates the essentials of the spiritual intuitions of the Byzantine tradition. Born at *Thessalonica, he received there a spiritual education inspired by the hesychast movement, then developing on nearby Mount *Athos, and began the substantial studies that he completed at Constantinople. When *John VI Cantacuzenus took power in 1347, he chose as counsellors the Thessalonian *Demetrius Cydones and, at the latter's suggestion, his childhood friend Nicholas Cabasilas. The legally-trained Cabasilas carried out several diplomatic missions in the emperor's service. When John VI abdicated in 1354, Cabasilas left the political scene. He dedicated himself to his private affairs, as well as writing spiritual works. He spent his last years at Constantinople, no doubt a simple layman living in the ambience of the monastic fraternity of the Xanthopouloi. His love of peace was such that, avoiding polemics, he kept up ties of friendship with the followers of Gregory *Palamas, opponents of the *union of the Churches, as well as with Demetrius Cydones, who became a Roman Catholic.

We possess secular writings by him. Most of them reflect his training as a jurist: eulogies of Anne of Savoy, mother of John VI, and of Matthew Cantacuzenus, son of John VI; treatises against *usury; pamphlets against confiscations of monastic goods by the authorities or against abuse of the right of *asylum. Others express philosophical concerns, against scepticism but also against the denigration of secular wisdom, widespread in monastic circles. We also have commentaries on mathematics and literature.

But the heart of his work is religious: explanations of the liturgy, *homilies and eulogies of saints, and above all the *Life in Christ* (*SC*, 355, 361), a treatise on the spiritual life based on the sacraments of initiation (baptism, confirmation, *Eucharist) and on meditation. In these works, he expresses the ideal of a lay *hesychasm, a mystical life in the world: *sanctity, based not on personal merits but on the grace of Christ communicated by the sacraments, is a gift of God addressed to all and which we have only to accept.

*PG*, 149-150, 1865. – Nicholas Cabasilas, "Contre les abus des autorités envers les biens sacrés", I. Sevcenko (ed.), in "Nicolas Cabasilas's Anti-zealot Discourse: a Reinterpretation", *DOP* 11, 1957, 81-171. – Nicholas Cabasilas, *A Commentary on the Divine Liturgy*, London, 1978. – Nicholas Cabasilas, *Life in Christ*, London, 1995.

M. Lot-Borodine, *Un maître de la spiritualité byzantine au XIVe siècle: Nicolas Cabasilas*, Paris, 1958. – *HChr*, 6, 1990, 450-452 and 508-515 .

Marie-Hélène Congourdeau

**CADI.** The functions of the judge (*qāḍī*) in *Islam varied at different periods. The source of jurisdiction was the *caliph; the judges acted as his delegates, but also as delegates of a governor or an independent ruler. Theoretically, their competence extended to all spheres of Muslim law (**sharīʿa*). In reality, they were limited by "rival" jurisdictions like the court (*mazālim*) presided over by a ruler, by one of the governors, or by a State apparatus responsible for criminal justice, called *shurta* (police).

E. Tyan, "Ḳāḍī", *EI(E)*, 4, 1978, 373-374. – B. G. Weiss, "Qāḍī", *EncRel(E)*, 12, 1987, 124-126. – I. Schneider, *Das Bild des Richters in der "Adab al-qāḍī" Literatur*, Frankfurt am Main, 1990. – J. Schacht *et al.*, "Maḥkama" [court], *EI(E)*, 6, 1991, 1-44.

Claude Gilliot

**CAEDMON.** A cowherd on the monastic estates of *Whitby in the time of abbess Hild († 680), he was inspired by a nocturnal vision to compose a poem in his native language celebrating the glory of God's creation; though he was illiterate, Caedmon's poem was taken down in dictation by scribes at Whitby, and accordingly he has been regarded as the earliest vernacular English poet. Our knowledge of him derives solely from a chapter in *Bede's *Historia Ecclesiastica* (IV, 24), and in two early copies of that work a nine-line poem in Old English is appended to Bede's Latin account of the poem's content. According to Bede, Caedmon also composed poems on the narratives of Genesis, Exodus, and on the Lord's Incarnation, Passion, Resurrection and Ascension; but these poems are not thought to survive.

A. H. Smith, *Three Northumbrian Poems*, London, 1933, 38-41. – C. L. Wrenn, "The Poetry of Caedmon", *PBA*, 32, 1946, 277-295. – U. Schwab, *Caedmon*, Messina, 1972. – D. K. Fry, "Caedmon as a Formulaic Poet", *Oral Literature*, J. J. Duggan (ed.), Edinburgh, 1975, 41-61.

Michael Lapidge

Chevet of the church of Saint-Étienne, Caen (men's abbey). Romanesque and Gothic art, 11th-13th c.

**CAEN.** Site of a *port and crossroad of land routes, the town of Caen does not really appear until the 11th c., despite the attested existence of settlement since the early Middle Ages. A *charter of Count Richard II for *Fécamp (1025) mentions for the first time the churches, tolls and *mills of Caen. By setting up the *castle and two Benedictine *abbeys, Saint-Étienne and La Trinité, *William the Conqueror created the conditions for the town's further development. Between 1060 and 1135, Caen was an immense building site: abbeys (built between 1060 and 1090, then rebuilt in the first third of the 12th c.), castle (fortifications, Échiquier or Old Palace, built *c.*1100, *Henry I's keep). The chapel of Sainte-Paix (*c.*1075), built on the site where the oath of the *Truce of God was sworn, commemorates one of the first Peace Councils, held in 1061. The medieval town had numerous *parishes: Saint-Nicolas and Saint-Gilles, the two parishes created near the abbeys, Saint-Jean, Saint-Pierre, Saint-Sauveur-du-Marché and Notre-Dame-de-Froide-Rue were the most important. After 1204 and the incorporation of *Normandy into the French royal domain, *Philip Augustus strengthened the keep and the wall; the town, whose trade prospered and population grew, welcomed the *Franciscans (1236), the *Dominicans, Cordeliers and *Crosiers (1275), then the *Carmelites (1278). Besieged and taken by *Edward III of England in 1346, Caen was surrounded with fortifications in 1354, but was taken again in 1417 by *Henry V, who established himself there and created a *university. It did not return to the king of *France until 1450.

Despite the depredations of the French Revolution and the bombardment of 1944, Caen still harbours a remarkable medieval architectural heritage: the abbey church of Saint-Étienne, with its Romanesque nave with high tribunes, the triforium passage going right round the building from the start, marked the culmination of half a century of architectural research in Normandy and would profoundly influence Anglo-Norman architecture; its facade with two perfectly "harmonic" towers foreshadows *Gothic facades, while the nave vaulting of intersecting ribs (*c.*1115) is the first of its kind. The abbey church of La Trinité, severely restored in the 19th c., attests a more archaic original part (mass of the nave façade with closed tribune) and more hesitations in its realization. Rebuilt from the late 11th c. (façade), the abbey church is remarkable for its columned *crypt (11th c.), its double-windowed apse decorated with sculptures akin to those of *Canterbury cathedral (*c.*1110), its system of upper triforium passage and its "six-part false vaults", an essay in vaulting of the 1130s quickly abandoned elsewhere by reason of its weight.

G. Bouet, *Analyse architecturale de Saint-Étienne de Caen*, Caen, 1868. – M. Baylé, *La Trinité de Caen*, Paris-Geneva, 1979. – M. de Bouard, *Le Château de Caen*, Caen, 1979. – *Histoire de Caen*, G. Désert (ed.), Toulouse, 1981.

Maylis Baylé

**CAESARIUS OF ARLES (470-542).** Born at Chalon, he entered the clergy at 17 and shortly afterwards the monastery of *Lérins, where the young and fervent Caesarius ruined his health. Sent to *Arles for treatment, he was there ordained priest, governed a monastery (499-502) and became *bishop. His long episcopate (502-542) shows his loyalty to the monastic life, which he made his *clerics share, as well as his pastoral zeal. The latter is attested by more than 200 *sermons. At his death, the monastery of St John at Arles, founded by him in 512, had more than 200 *nuns. For them he wrote the first monastic rule intended for *women, which he later summarized for the use of monks.

*Caesarius of Arles: Sermons*, 3 vols., New York, 1956-73. – Césaire d'Arles, *Oevres monastiques*, A. de Vogüé (ed.), J. Courreau (ed.), *SC*, 345, 1988; *ibid.*, 398, 1994.

W. M. Daly, "Caesarius of Arles, a Precursor of Medieval Christendom", *Tr.*, 26, 1970, 1-28. – W. E. Klingshirn, *Caesarius of Arles*, Cambridge, 1993.

Adalbert de Vogüé

**CAESARIUS OF HEISTERBACH (1180-*c.*1240).** A *Cistercian, Caesarius of Heisterbach was novice-master, then *prior of the monastery of Heisterbach, near Bonn. A prolific author, he composed Latin *homilies on the gospels of Sundays and feast-days, Lives of St Engelbert of Cologne († 1225) and St *Elizabeth of Thuringia (1207-1231), and *Eight books of miracles* (of which we have only fragments). But his main work is the *Dialogue of miracles*, composed between 1219 and 1223, a treatise of dialogued spiritual reading. The author depicts a novice and a monk discoursing, heavily reinforced by **exempla* (some 800), often taken from the experience of Caesarius or his brothers, on subjects embracing the militant life of the Christian and the effective way to fight against the devil.

Césaire de Heisterbach, *Dialogue des miracles, 1, De la conversion*, A. Barbeau (tr.), Oka (Quebec), 1992 ("Voix monastiques", 6).

Jacques Berlioz

**CAESARIUS OF SPEYER (died 1238/1239).** A penitential preacher at *Speyer, a student at *Paris, Caesarius of Speyer followed the fifth *crusade to *Syria, where, thanks to Brother *Elias, he entered the Order of Friars Minor in 1219-1220. On his return to Italy, he supplemented the *Regula non bullata* with biblical texts. As provincial, he headed the first mission to Germany; but he was obliged to retire to a hermitage in the *Spoleto Valley. Having rallied to the Friars Hermits opposed to the new tendencies of the *Franciscan Order, whose ideas were expressed in the *Sacrum commercium*, he was put under house arrest by Elias and accidentally killed in 1238-1239.

A. Gattucci, "Cesario da Spira", *I compagni di Francesco e la prima generazione minoritica*, Spoleto, 1992, 119-165.

Michael Cusato

**CAETANI.** Attested at *Rome from the late 11th c., the Caetani appear in the 13th c. at *Anagni, *Pisa and *Naples. Benedict Caetani, *cardinal from 1281 and *pope from 1294 to 1303 under the name of *Boniface VIII, made the Caetani one of the most influential families of Rome and *Latium. His father Roffredo I had married Emilia Patrasso of Guarcino, whose family connections with *Gregory IX and *Alexander IV opened the doors of the Roman *Curia to the young Benedict.

Benedict Caetani managed to assign prestigious titles of *nobility to his relatives (his nephew Pietro became marquis) and round off his possessions in the kingdom of *Sicily. His nephew Francis and his cousin Benedict received the cardinal's hat. The crusade led by Boniface VIII against the two *Colonna cardinals, whom he deposed and declared heretics, ended favourably for the Caetani on the territorial level. In *c.*1300 their possessions extended, in the south, from Ninfa to Terracina and as far as the kingdom of Sicily, where in 1299 Roffredo II had married the heiress of the county of Fondi. In the Roman Campagna, the

Caetani dominated the Via Appia and the Via Latina. The acquisition of the monumental tomb of Cecilia Metella allowed them to build a fortified complex at the gates of Rome, the *civitas caietana*. At Rome itself, from 1302 the Caetani possessed the Torre delle Milizie, an indispensable springboard for any expansion towards the Quirinal. At the other end of the town, they controlled the access road to the Isola Tiburina (the *ponte Fabricio*). To the north, an agreement with the Sienese (1303) allowed them to take possession of a large part of the possessions of the Aldobrandeschi.

After the death of Boniface VIII, a quarter of a century of contention with the Colonna, eager to recover their rights, reduced their estates in the North, but left intact their dominant position in the South. From the mid 14th c., the Caetani were divided into four branches: the palatine Caetani, heirs to the former Aldobrandeschi possessions; and the three branches descended from Roffredo III, who shared the county of Fondi and the *fiefs of the South.

The expansionist policy of Onorato I († 1400) was an obstacle to *Urban V's return to Rome; but the help he gave to *Gregory IX was decisive. Disappointed by the election of *Urban VI (1378), he allowed the French cardinals to meet at Fondi to elect *Clement VII. A conflict broke out within the family, the palatine Caetani remaining loyal to Urban VI; it led to the partial destruction of Ninfa (1380).

A new division of property (1418) split the Caetani into two new branches: those of Sermoneta allied themselves particularly with the Roman Curia, while the Caetani of Fondi were subinfeudated to the kings of *Aragon.

G. Caetani, *Domus Caietana. Storia documentata della famiglia Caetani*, Val di Pesa, 1927 (2 vol.). – G. Marchetti-Longhi, *I Caetani*, Rome, 1942. – *DBI*, 16, 1973. – L. Fiorani, *Ninfa: una città, un giardino*, Rome, 1990. – B. Arnold, "Caetani", *Die Grossen Familien Italiens*, Stuttgart, 1992, 116-128.

Agostino Paravicini Bagliani

**CAFFA.** "A Genoese city on the edge of Europe", the ancient Greek colony of Theodosia, on the Crimean coast, was occupied by the Genoese in *c.*1275. In a few decades it became the flower of the Genoese counters in the Black Sea, handling most of the trade between the West and the Mongol East. A Franciscan *mission settled there in 1287; thirty years later, Friar Jerome obtained from the *pope the creation of a vast *diocese extending from the mouths of the Danube to the Volga. Caffa became the starting-point for mendicant friars sent to evangelize the *Mongol lands. The presence of strong Greek and Armenian communities also made it an active centre of the Eastern Churches. The town was taken by the *Ottoman fleet in 1475.

J. Richard, *La Papauté et les missions d'Orient au Moyen Âge (XIII^e-XV^e siècles)*, Rome, 1977. – M. Balard, *La Romanie génoise (XII^e – début du XV^e siècle)*, Genoa-Rome, 1978 (2 vol.). – C. Delacroix-Besnier, *Les Dominicains et la chrétienté grecque aux XIV^e et XV^e siècles*, Rome, 1997.

Michel Balard

**CAIRO.** The name "Cairo" comes from the Arabic *al-Qāhira*, "the Victorious", the name given to their foundation by the Shi'ite Fatimids in 969.

Pharaonic precursors, whether Memphis, the capital of Lower Egypt situated on the left bank of the Nile, or the settlements to the north of the town, need not be considered, the discontinuity between these early sites and the medieval city being too manifest. Fusṭāṭ, on the other hand, founded in 641 on the right bank of the Nile at the foot of a Byzantine fortress (Egyptian Babylon) by the Muslim conquerors from Arabia, is the original town. It is so both historically and geographically since there was continuity in the subsequent foundations regularly displaced northwards on the occasion of political changes: after Fusṭāṭ, the most southerly, al-'Askar was founded by the Abbasid governor in 750, then al-Qaṭā'i by Ibn Ṭūlūn in 879, and Qāhira, the last and northernmost, in 969.

The continuity is also symbolic since Fusṭāṭ – whose site, now called "Old Cairo", is part of the present town – was, for the Muslims of the Middle Ages, the first Muslim town on African soil before the conquest of the *Maghreb. At first, in fact, it was a camp-town (*misr*), the conquerors having divided up the terrain, at the time of the siege of Babylon, into lots (*khitta*) assigned to the tribes who set up tent there. Only the centre had an urban appearance with the construction of the first *mosque in the West, the Jāmi' 'Amr, the governor's house and the dwellings of some notables; this urban part was rapidly developed. The *Copts, employed especially for administrative tasks, settled there (Coptic was spoken at Fusṭāṭ in the 8th c.).

Qāhira was something else altogether. It was a true foundation (following a ritual involving astronomers) with a political design: the *Shi'ite *Fatimid *caliphs coming from Tunisia hoped, after Egypt, to conquer the whole of the *Abbasid *Sunni Muslim East. It was a reserved princely town, with walls and monumental gates, two gigantic palaces, mosques (including al-Azhar) and a centre for the teaching of Shi'ite doctrine, the "house of wisdom", some souks indispensable for the life of the court and some particularly prestigious industries such as the *tiraz*, a workshop for the weaving of official fabrics, and, here too, lots (here called *hāras*) assigned to the different ethnic groups that made up the army.

During this period Fusṭāṭ became an industrious town (*port, sugar refineries, grain warehouses, trading quarters. . .) profiting from the international trade that the Fatimids succeeded in attracting to the Red Sea and Egypt. It was also a period of great *toleration for Jews and Christians, and numerous churches were built. The urban fabric became continuous from Fusṭāṭ to Qāhira until the terrible crisis of 1020 when entire quarters of the town were ruined.

The return to Sunnism with the *Ayyubid dynasty (1171-1250) had direct consequences for the town. The new sultans, beginning with *Saladin, opened up the reserved city of Qāhira, destroyed the gigantic Fatimid palaces and built, between Qāhira and Fusṭāṭ, on the model of the military architecture of *Syria, the Citadel, which became the centre of power, and walls enclosing the three constitutive elements of what became modern Cairo: Qāhira, the Citadel and Fusṭāṭ. It was around these three poles that the Egyptian capital would develop once more under the next dynasty, that of the *Mamluks (1250-1517). These princes, cut off from their lands of origin, fervent Sunnis and living in a town of considerable landed revenues, multiplied religious, economic and palatine foundations. From these they drew a legitimacy in the eyes of the Muslims whom they governed, an effective anchorage in this country where they were not born and a not inconsiderable financial profit. The city conquered by the *Ottomans in 1517 was, despite the crises that affected it throughout the 14th c., one of the greatest cities in the world.

M. Clerget, *Le Caire, étude de géographie urbaine et d'histoire économique*, Cairo, 1934. – J. Abu Lughod, *Cairo, 1001 Years of the City Victorious*, Princeton, 1971. – C. F. Petry, *The Civilian Elite of Cairo in the later Middle Ages*, Princeton, 1981. – J.-C. Garcin *et al.*, *Palais et maisons du Caire*, 1, *Époque mamelouke (XIII^e-XVI^e siècle)*, Paris, 1982.

– D. Behrens-Abouseif, *Islamic Architecture in Cairo, an Introduction*, Leiden, 1989. – S. Denoix, *Décrire Le Caire: Fusṭāt-Miṣr d'après Ibn Duqmāq et Maqrīzī*, Cairo, 1993. – B. Shushan, *Popular culture in medieval Cairo*, Cambridge, 1993. – A. Raymond, *Le Caire*, Paris, 1993.

Sylvie Denoix

**CALABRIA.** Before designating the former land of the *Bruttii*, the western extremity of the Italian peninsula, the word "Calabria" applied only to the Salento (*terra d'Otranto*). At first used by simple geographical extension in the mid 7th c., the expression very soon settled on Bruttium, the modern province of Calabria, under the effect of the conquest of the Salento by the *Lombards (670-680). Bruttium itself had not been exempt from earlier invasions, from the incursion that saw the death of Alaric near Cosenza in 410, through Vandal raids, to the Greco-Gothic war. Nevertheless the 6th c. was a period of prosperity; *Cassiodorus, rallying to Theodoric, favoured his home province and founded monasteries there.

The arrival of the Lombards in 591 provoked a grave crisis, marked not just by the provisional depopulation and episcopal vacancy of many cities, which progressively moved from the coast inland, but also by the fracture of the territory, into a northern half attached to *Benevento and then Salerno, and a southern half that remained Byzantine, dependent at first on the *Exarchate of *Ravenna, then on the *theme of *Sicily, created shortly before 700. After the conquest of that island by the Arabs (from 827), *Saracen incursions multiplied on the coasts, where fixed colonies even settled (the emirates of Amantea, Tropea and Santa Severina). A first attempt by the Emperor *Louis II to reduce them was completed by the Byzantines themselves, as part of their reconquest of the whole Italian South in the late 9th century. The former Bruttium then became the theme of Calabria, dependent from 975 on the catapan residing at *Bari. Hellenization, already very marked, was reinforced, discernible alike in language, law, settlement, civil (notably fiscal) and religious institutions (Basilian *monasticism, clergy dependent on the *patriarchate of Constantinople).

In the mid 11th c., the *Normans took the fortified towns one by one, obliging the last Byzantine officials to leave Squillace, the last Greek redoubt on the gulf of Catanzaro, in 1059. They immediately set up a system of feudo-vassalic relations and a policy of religious Latinization, based on the attachment of *bishoprics to Rome and the creation of Benedictine *abbeys (Santa Eufemia at Lamezia, the Trinity of Milet, Santa Maria della Matina in the Crati valley, etc.). At the turn of the 12th and 13th cc., Calabria passed with the rest of the Norman possessions into the orbit of the Swabian Empire. Apart from the foundation of Monteleone Calabro, *Frederick II left a less deep mark on Calabria than on *Apulia. After the war of the *Sicilian Vespers, the country was no more than a colonial appendage of the kingdom of *Naples where the rivalry between *Angevins and Aragonese took a particularly harsh form.

V. von Falkenhausen, *Untersuchungen über die byzantinische Herrschaft in Süditalien vom 9. bis 11. Jahrhundert*, Wiesbaden, 1978 (It. tr., Bari, 1978). – *Storia del Mezzogiorno*, 2, Naples, 1991. – P. de Léo, "Kalabrien", *LdM*, 5, 1991, 861-864.

Ghislaine Noyé-Bougard

The al-Azhar mosque, Cairo, 10th c.

**CALATRAVA, ORDER OF.** The Order of Calatrava was one of the first native *military orders founded in the Iberian peninsula, in the 12th century. Its origins go back to the recovery of a frontier enclave, which the Castilian King Alfonso VII had given in 1147 to the *Templars to defend against the *Almohads. After the monarch's death, the Templars lost interest in it. Faced with the inaction of the lay nobility, Raymond, abbot of Fitero, a Navarrese *Cistercian monastery, went to Calatrava where in 1158 he founded a religious fraternity composed of voluntary monks and knights. The new order adopted the Cistercian Rule; it was approved firstly in 1163 by the chapter general of Cîteaux, then in 1164 by Pope *Alexander III, who took it under his protection. In 1186, Calatrava was affiliated to *Morimond.

J. F. O'Callaghan, *The Spanish Military Order of Calatrava and its Affiliates*, London, 1975. – D. W. Lomax, *Las Ordenes militares en la peninsula ibérica durante la Edad Media*, Salamanca, 1976.

María José Sánchez Usón

**CALENDAR.** The calendar that prevailed in the Latin West at the beginning of the *Middle Ages underwent several revisions. Under the Roman Empire, several chronological reference-points succeeded each other: the first Olympiad, the foundation of Rome, the beginning of the Julian era. These different datings were challenged, early in the Middle Ages, by the first Christians who adopted as reference 29 August 284, beginning of the era of the Martyrs, also called the era of Diocletian. As for dates, these were always calculated, as in the Roman calendar, by taking as reference the reign of the last serving consul.

Not until 532 did the monk Dionysius Exiguus fix the starting-point of the Christian era at the birth of Christ. He situated this event, whose calculation was quickly shown to be inexact, on the eighth day of the *calends of January of the year 754 *ab Urbe condita*, *i.e.* 25 December of the year 1. To establish this date, he based himself on the gospel of St Luke according to whom Jesus was about 30 years old at the time of his baptism, which took place in the 15th year of Tiberius.

In adopting the chronology of Dionysius Exiguus, the Church clearly indicated that a new period of mankind was beginning, that announced by the Old Testament prophets. This dating was at first used only for events later than the birth of Christ; everything before that was dated from the creation of the world, so far as it could be determined by an analysis of the Bible. After having received the decisive agreement of the Venerable *Bede, the fixing of dates from the Christian era passed slowly into general use. It was first adopted by the Anglo-Saxons, then in France in the late 8th c., in Germany in the 9th and by the papacy in the 10th century. It appeared regularly in the acts of the pontifical *chancery only from the time of *Eugenius IV, in 1431. Not until the 17th century did the birth of Christ become the sole chronological reference-point.

Julius Caesar had fixed the duration of the year at 365 days and six hours, divided into 12 months. Every four years, a day was added after 24 February. This rule was maintained in the Middle Ages, the insertion taking place between 23 and 24 February. The beginning of the year varied according to region. The Roman civil year, in agreement with the Julian calendar, began on 1 January; but the Roman military had kept the old date of 1 March. The Christian Church put into competition three more dates: 25 December or Incarnation style, 25 March or Annunciation style, or *Easter day, which was movable; in the end the Church gave a Christian meaning to the date of 1 Jan, which coincided with Christ's *Circumcision. But it was not until 1564 that an edict of Charles IX of France put an end to these variations by officially fixing the beginning of the year on 1 January.

In the Roman calendar, three days in each month served as references to specify the dates: the first day of the month marked the calends, the nones fell on the fifth or seventh day from month to month, and the ides on the 13th or 15th day. This Roman tradition still prevailed in 1300 in some official documents. However, from the 8th c., the West had adopted the seven-day week which introduced a regular framework. The Babylonians had classified seven "stars" in a fixed order: Saturn, Sun, Moon, Mars, Mercury, Jupiter and Venus; a day was consecrated to each of them, according to a cycle which began anew every seven days. The names, recalling these "stars", were for the most part kept by the Christians: in France, the moon's day became *lundi*, Mars's day *mardi*, Mercury's day *mercredi*, Jove's day *jeudi*, and Venus's day *vendredi. Samedi* (from *sabbata*) and *dimanche* (from *dominicus*) replaced the days dedicated to Saturn and the Sun, a designation retained in the Anglo-Saxon countries. *Sunday would be the first day of the week instead of Saturn's day or Saturday.

Christianity brought out the close connection between the week and the divine model revealed in Genesis. In consequence, man would work for six days and rest on the seventh. This seventh day, the Lord's day, was substituted for the Jewish Sabbath and an edict prohibiting work on that day was issued by the council of Nicaea in 325. In thus getting its hands on time, the Church was well backed up by the royal political authority. In 802, *Charlemagne forbade work on Sundays and on the *feast-days fixed by the Church.

Though it had adopted the pagan astrological terminology, the Catholic Church built on this septenary structure its own system of concordances. The history of mankind was divided into six eras, related to the six days of *creation and the six *ages of life. In this periodization conceived by St Augustine, the first era, from *Adam to *Noah, corresponded to infancy, the second, from Noah to *Abraham, to childhood, the third, from Abraham to *David, to adolescence, the fourth, from David to the fall of Babylon, to youth, the fifth, from the Babylonian captivity to the birth of Christ, to maturity, and the sixth, from the birth of Christ to the end of time, to old age. "Then the Lord will come and the everlasting Sunday will begin." As J. Le Goff notes, "linear eschatological Christian time was directed towards eternity not as in an ascending line, but on the contrary in a descending line, a decline." This pessimistic conception of human *time, widely adopted by the Church, in particular by monastic circles, would be maintained during the Middle Ages, though, from the 12th c., the idea emerged of a process of amelioration and growth.

A.A. MacArthur, *The Evolution of the Christian Year*, London, 1953. – J. Le Goff, "Calendario", *Enciclopedia Einaudi*, 2, Turin, 1977, 501-534. – C. Frugoni, "Chiesa e lavoro agricolo nei testi e nelle immagini dalla tard'-antica all'età romanica", *Medioevo rurale. Sulle tracce della civiltà contadina*, Bologna, 1980, 321-341. – G. Perpes, *Les Colonnes du temps. Histoire du calendrier*, Cuers, 1987. – F. Maiello, *Storia del calendario*, Turin, 1993.

Perrine Mane

## CALENDS

**Liturgy.** *Calendae* (from *calo*, "I call") designated the first day of the month among the Romans, where the *pontifex maximus* summoned the crowd to notify it of *ferial days. *Calendarium*, at first designating an account-book, was used only late to mean "calendar". The Roman calendar, regressive (the second half of the month being counted backwards from the first of the following month), was in use in the Western liturgy until Vatican II: in calendars, *martyrologies, *necrologies. There was also a habit, at the chapter *office following prime, in monasteries or among *canons, before beginning the reading of the martyrology and the necrology, of recalling the day of the month and the age of the moon, a practice often designated by its first element: "reading the calends", *calendas legere*, or *pronuntiare*.

H. Grotefend, *Zeitrechnung des deutschen Mittelalters und der Neuzeit*, Hanover, 1891. – F. Cabrol, "Circoncision (fête de la)", *DACL*, 3, 2, 1948, 1718-1728 (2nd ed.). – H. Leclercq, "Kalendae", *DACL*, 7, 1, 1928, 623-624. – P. Couderc, *Le Calendrier*, 1988 ("QSJ", 203; 6th ed.). – A. Borst, *Die karolingische Kalenderreform*, Hanover, 1998 (*MGH.Scriptores*, 46).

Jean-Loup Lemaître

**Ecclesiastical institution.** This institution, also called "*chapter" (*capitulum*), "assembly" (*conventus*), "meeting" (*convocatio*), "congregation" (*congregatio*) or even "council" (*concilium*), designated the meetings of the priests of a single territorial area (archpresbytery or deanery). The name (*calendae* or *kalendae*) came from their frequency: according to Carolingian legislation, the priests met on the first day of each month to deal with the affairs of their *parish and give an account of the exercise of their *ministry. The calends do not seem to have been organised everywhere: their working was linked to the strength of deans on the ground and the generalization of the synodal system. Moreover, their monthly rhythm was not kept up.

Originally these meetings had a primarily judicial and administrative function, but this was modified in the 13th century. The priests were now no longer solely occupied with problems of common interest, but under the direction of the *archpriest or rural dean they studied the episcopal directives (synodal *statutes). Each assembly kept its working rules; some even codified their customs (records). Thus the calends, when they were regularly convened, contributed to strengthen solidarity among the deans, even giving rise to confraternities of priests (calendary priests).

J. Burklé, *Les chapitres ruraux des anciens évêchés de Strasbourg et de Bâle*, Strasbourg, 1935. – H. Wagnon, "Les 'records ecclésiastiques' des assemblées décanales de l'ancien diocèse de Liège", *Proceedings of the Second International Congress of Medieval Canon Law, Boston College, 12-16 August 1963*, 1965, 473-483 ("MIC.S", 1). – J. Gaudemet, *Le gouvernement de l'Église à l'époque classique*, 2, *Le gouvernement local*, 1979, 309-312 ("HDIEO", 8, 2).

Joseph Avril

**CALIPH.** The term "caliph", in Arabic *khalīfa*, is the name given to the head of the Muslim community.

The first caliph, Abū Bakr, called himself *khalīfa rasūl Allah*, "successor of God's messenger", and this expression was abridged to *khalīfa* or caliph. But the official title of the caliphs, from the second caliph, 'Umar, was *amīr al-mu'minīn*, "*emir of the faithful", a title indicating that the caliph was both the spiritual and temporal head of the Muslim community.

The caliph, charged with applying Islamic law and suppressing doctrinal innovations, had to lead the prayers and the pilgrimage (*Hajj*) to *Mecca and wage legal war or *jihād*. According to the theory of *Sunni jurists, he was designated following the free choice of the members of the community, who then swore an oath of allegiance to him. In practice, the caliph got into the habit of designating his heir by the procedure of anticipated election, and consultation took place only when there was no heir designate. The dynastic usage was thus established at the time of the *Umayyads (660-749) and maintained at the time of the *Abbasids (749-1258). It was also practised by the *Fatimids (909-1171), who made their sovereignty rest on a designation by the Prophet, not on the choice of the community.

D. Sourdel *et al.*, "Khalīfa", *EI(E)*, 4, 1978, 937-953 (2nd ed.).

Dominique Sourdel

**CALIXTUS II (*c.*1060-1124), POPE.** Guy was one of the sons of William the Great, count of *Burgundy, a territorial prince allied to the Burgundian and imperial high aristocracy. Two of his brothers followed an episcopal career, Hugh at *Besançon (1085-1101) and Octavian at Savona (1119-1128); another distinguished himself in the *Reconquest, becoming count of *Galicia and then marrying the heiress to the kingdom of *Castile, while the first *crusade saw three of Guy's brothers die in the *Holy Land. After receiving an intellectual and religious education at the chapter school of Besançon, in 1088, though he had not reached the required age, Guy was elected archbishop of *Vienne, where his family possessed an important *honour. The young prelate was soon marked out by the ardour with which he defended the *patrimony of his church, not hesitating to clash with Bishop Hugh of Grenoble over material interests, justifying the means employed by the end sought. Spokesman of the reformers in the kingdom of Burgundy, he was appointed papal *legate (1107) and showed himself, in the *Investiture Contest, hostile to any papal concession to the emperor: he denounced *Paschal II's capitulation at Ponte Mummolo (11 April 1111) and thus drew down the hatred of *Henry V. The papacy's situation not ceasing to deteriorate, the *cardinals present at *Cluny at the death of *Gelasius II chose to succeed him the archbishop of Vienne, who had a reputation for firmness (2 Feb 1119). Once elected, Calixtus II abandoned this intransigence for a more realistic policy, while preserving the essentials of the *Gregorian reform: he strengthened his ties with Cluny, confirmed the Charter of Charity (1119) and sought to mobilize the French episcopate to defend the papal cause. Strong in this support, he could renew negotiations with Henry V and, after some vain attempts (including the meeting at Mouzon, 18 Oct 1119), he and the emperor signed the celebrated *concordat of *Worms (23 Sept 1122), called the pact of Calixtus, which put an end to the Investiture Contest by a compromise safeguarding the elective principle, while sparing the material interests of the German ruler. His reforming and peacemaking activity found its culmination and its confirmation in the ecumenical council of *Lateran I (1123), which updated the essentials of the measures adopted locally in the course of a century of reform. So Calixtus, who died on 13 Dec 1124, deserved this dedication engraved on an altar of Peter in Santa Maria in Cosmedin: "to Calixtus II, pope of peace".

U. Robert, *Histoire du pape Calixte II*, Paris-Besançon, 1891. – G. Miccoli, "Callisto II, papa", *DBI*, 26, 1973, 761-768. – M. Stroll, "Calixtus II: A Reinterpretation of his Election and the End of the Investiture Contest", *SMH*, 3, 1980, 3-53. – I. S. Robinson, *The Papacy, 1073-1198*, Cambridge, 1990.

René Locatelli

**CALIXTUS III (1378-1458), POPE.** Alfonso Borgia (Borja) was born at Xativa near *Valencia. He studied *canon law and civil law. After graduating, he became secretary of *Alfonso V, king of Aragon and Naples, bishop of Valencia (1429), was created *cardinal by *Eugenius IV (1443) and finally elected *pope on 8

April 1455 (crowned 20 April). He had to face various problems: peace between the Italian princes, made precarious by the expansionist policies of the king of *Naples; maintenance of Christian doctrine in *Bohemia, whose ruler was an *Utraquist; and especially the *Turks, who had occupied *Constantinople in 1453. To confront them, he appealed for a crusade (*bull of 15 May 1455), an appeal coolly received by the European powers. He was neither a patron of the arts nor a *humanist, being too much taken up with the Turkish problem and the protection of his numerous nephews, who came to Rome at the head of groups of Catalans.

S. Schüller-Piroli, *Die Borgia Päpste: Kalixt III und Alexander VI*, Vienna, 1979. – J.-F. Alonso, *DHP*, 1994, 264-266.

Anna Esposito

**CALLISTUS I OF CONSTANTINOPLE (died 1363).** A disciple of Gregory the Sinaite and partisan of Gregory *Palamas, Callistus was hieromonk at Iviron when he was elected *patriarch of Constantinople in 1350. He got the doctrine of Gregory Palamas confirmed by the *council of Blachernae in 1351. A friend of *John VI Cantacuzenus, Callistus nevertheless refused to crown Matthew Cantacuzenus in 1353 and was deposed. After the return of John V to the throne and the abdication of John VI Cantacuzenus (Dec 1354), he regained his office (1355-1363).

Callistus left hagiographical works (Lives of Gregory the Sinaite and Theodosius of Tŭrnovo, Eulogy of John the Faster), liturgical works (13 prayers) and homiletic works (more than 60 *sermons).

J. Darrouzès, *Les Regestes de 1310 à 1376*, 1977, 2311-2346 and 2373-2460 ("RAPC", 5). – *PLP*, 5, 1981, 44, no. 10478.

Albert Failler

**CAMALDOLESE ORDER.** Established from the hermitage of Camaldoli founded by *Romuald of Ravenna in 1023-1027 north of Arezzo, the Camaldolese Order as such only came into being in 1113 when, sanctioning a period of foundation and aggregation of establishments gradually put under Camaldoli's jurisdiction, *Paschal II formally recognised the congregation and put it under the protection of the Apostolic See. At this date the area of Camaldolese influence covered mainly *Tuscany and, through *Pisa, *Sardinia. In the second half of the 12th c. it extended throughout central Italy (Emilia, *Romagna, the *Marches), reaching *Veneto in the 13th century.

Camaldolese observance was defined by the *Benedictine Rule and the customs of the order. The first customs (1074-89), very brief, influenced by *Peter Damian, legislated on the eremetical life. They were supplemented by long constitutions, of disputed date (doubtless mid 12th c.), which prefigured the organisation of the nascent order. From the mid 13th to the mid 14th c., an official legislative corpus was promulgated (five books *de Moribus*) primarily concerning *coenobites. These statutes were supplemented and amended by the general *chapters (annual or triennial), as well as by local constitutions. They regulated the details of the observance of hermits, monks, *nuns, lay brothers and sisters, as well as the relations of the Camaldolese establishments among themselves and with Camaldoli.

The order brought together communities associating hermitages and coenobite houses (*e.g.* Camaldoli and Fontebuono), monasteries and various dependencies (*hospitals, parish churches, etc.), all subject to the *prior of Camaldoli (as such, prior general), elected for life by the general chapter, at first exclusively from within the eremitic community of Camaldoli, then also from the coenobites. His manifold prerogatives and the centralization of government that followed from them were maintained until the 1490s, barely tempered by the general chapter, by the institution in 1271 of a Definitory (4 coenobites, 2 hermits and the prior general) taken from the chapter general, and by tendencies to local autonomy.

Camaldolese dynamism, long nourished by Tuscany (Camaldoli, Pisa, *Florence), was ensured in the second half of the 15th c. by the Venetian establishments that pursued the work of spiritual restoration, led at first by Prior Ambrogio *Traversari († 1439), in the setting of a congregation of Camaldolese observance that arose at San Michele di Murano (Venice) and was confirmed by *Sixtus IV in 1476.

A. des Mazis, "Camaldoli", "Camaldules", *DHGE*, 2, 1949, 509-510, 512-536. – P. Robert, "Camaldules", *DSp*, 2, 1, 1953, 50-60. – G. Cacciamani, "Camaldolesi", "Camaldolesi (monache)", "Camaldoli", *DIP*, 1, 1974, 1718-1725, 1725-1726, 1726-1777. – G. Penco, *Storia del monachesimo in Italia dalle origini alla fine del Medioevo*, Milan, 1983 (2nd ed.). – C. Caby, *de l'érémitisme rural au monachisme urbain: les Camaldules en Italie à la fin du Moyen Âge*, Rome, 1999 ("BEFAR").

Cécile Caby

**CAMBRAI.** The town of Cambrai (*Cameracum*), now a sub-prefecture of the département du Nord, appears in sources in the 4th c., replacing Bavay as capital of the *civitas* of the Nervians. At the end of the 6th c., Cambrai became the seat of the *bishopric installed at *Arras by St Vaast. The town developed from the *Merovingian period to the 11th c. (successive ramparts of the 4th, 9th and 11th cc.). Most of its *parishes and religious establishments predate 1100. Its medieval population is unknown (10,000 inhabitants in the 15th c. has been suggested).

From the 10th c., the lord of Cambrai was the bishop, count of Cambrésis. In fact the *pagus* of Cambrai, allotted to *Lothar I in 843, had gradually passed over to East Francia and Cambrai became the most westerly bastion of the imperial Church: the bishop was count of the Cambrésis (some 150 places) from 1007 by concession of the emperor. His *diocese, Francophone in the south, Dutch-speaking in the north, was the most extensive in the *province of *Reims.

The bishops had to sustain long struggles against the castellans of the town (d'Oisy family), the counts of *Flanders and then Artois and finally the townspeople. *Revolts (from 958) and a *commune (1077) obliged them to accept these last (1107-1226); in 1227 the *lex Godefridi* left the townspeople extensive rights. In the 15th c. the town entered the sphere of influence of the dukes of *Burgundy, but remained imperial until 1677 (annexation by Louis XIV).

Apart from its function as a religious capital, Cambrai was a rich agricultural *market and a prosperous *textile centre: the famous *mulquinerie* goes back to the *mollequins* (light linen fabrics) of the late Middle Ages.

Cambrai had 12 parishes, nine territorial (Saint-Vaast, Saint-Géry, Sainte-Croix, Saint-Martin, Saint-Georges, la Madeleine, Saint-Nicolas, Saint-Sauveur de Cantimpré, Sainte-Élisabeth) and three personal (Saint-Sépulcre, Saint-Aubert, Saint-Gengoul), three secular *chapters (cathedral chapter, Saint-Géry, Sainte-Croix), the abbey of Saint-Sépulcre, two chapters of regular *canons (Saint-Aubert, Cantimpré), a convent of *Franciscans, the *beguinage of Cantimpré and some ten *hospitals and *leper hospitals.

Cambrai has lost nearly all its medieval monuments: the fine Gothic *cathedral (1150-1250) was demolished after 1796. The

Church of the Holy Sepulchre, Cambridge.

municipal archives were burned in 1918, but there is still a wealth of hospital archives at Cambrai and a great wealth of material from ecclesiastical establishments in the *Archives départementales du Nord* at Lille.

W. Reinecke, *Geschichte der Stadt Cambrai bis zur Erteilung der Lex Godefridi (1227)*, Marburg, 1896. – H. Dubrulle, *Cambrai à la fin du Moyen Âge (XIIIe-XVIe siècles)*, Lille, 1903. – R. Branner, "The Transept of Cambrai Cathedral", *Gedenkschrift Ernst Gall*, M. Kuhn (ed.), Berlin, 1965, 69-85. – H. Platelle, "Cambrai et le Cambrésis au XVe siècle", *RNord*, 1976, 349-382. – *Les Diocèses de Cambrai et de Lille*, P. Pierrard (dir.), Paris, 1978. – *Histoire de Cambrai*, L. Trenard (dir.), Dunkirk, 1981. – R. Fossier, "Cambrai", *LdM*, 2, 7, 1983, 1407-1408.

Bernard Delmaire

**CAMBRIDGE UNIVERSITY.** Like many medieval *universities, Cambridge dates its existence from no formal act of *foundation and from no certain date. It is usually thought to take its origins from a settlement of scholars from *Oxford when that university went into voluntary suspension in 1209. Among the leaders of the migrating scholars was one John Grim, Master of the Schools at Oxford in 1201, and it is likely that Cambridge was chosen because it was his native town, although the influence of the entourage of Eustace, bishop of nearby Ely, was significant.

In 1225, by which year the *studium* of Cambridge was of sufficient status to have a *chancellor, with powers delegated by the *bishop, the number of potential scholars was increased by the establishment in the town of a house of *Franciscans, and in 1238 by a *Dominican house also. An *indult of *Gregory IX, dated 14 June 1233, recognised the university with a grant of *ius non trahi extra*, but its security as a corporation derived more immediately from its recognition by the *Crown with three writs granted by *Henry III in 1231. A compilation of statutes found in ms. Angelica 401 dating from *c.*1250 shows the university with a chancellor, proctors, bedels, regent masters and formal arrangements for assemblies, judicial procedures and commemoration of benefactors. From the late 14th c., the business of the assemblies of *masters was drawn up by a *Caput Senatus* consisting of one *doctor from each of the senior *faculties and one representing the religious houses, with one regent and one non-regent master under the presidency of the chancellor or vice-chancellor.

An assault on university property and personnel during the *Peasants' Revolt of 1381 provoked royal grants increasing the scholars' rights in the town and in 1401 a papal grant removed the bishop's interest in the election of the chancellor. In 1433 *Eugenius IV freed the masters from all ecclesiastical jurisdiction. Tension between the university masters and the friars was endemic.

Like Oxford, Cambridge soon developed a number of *colleges, the first, Peterhouse, being founded in 1278. Five others followed in the 14th c., and by 1500 they numbered twelve, each with a dining hall and arrangements, if not buildings, for communal worship. The founders were predominantly lay persons anxious to secure both *masses for their souls and an increase in the supply of educated men to Church and State. Founded as societies of masters, supported by endowments, the colleges came to admit younger scholars, either supported by endowments or paying for their own maintenance and tuition. Many students, however, were accommodated in unendowed hostels, and it was not until the 16th c. that college membership became obligatory. The largest and richest of the colleges was the King's Hall, an annexe of the Chapel Royal established by *Edward II and refounded by *Edward III.

In the earliest years the faculties of divinity and *canon law were dominant, although civil law was to flourish in certain colleges. Medical studies were pursued by relatively few and were commonly supplemented by study overseas. Although it is possible that both *Robert Grosseteste and John *Duns Scotus taught briefly there, at no time in the Middle Ages did Cambridge produce a scholarly tradition to rival that of the Merton school at Oxford, and, in spite of papal and royal favour, its alumni in this period seldom competed in number, and never in eminence in Church and in State, with those of its mother university.

A.B. Emden, *A Bibliographical Register of the University of Cambridge to 1500*, Cambridge, 1963. – C. Brooke, R. Highfield, *Oxford and Cambridge*, Cambridge, 1988. – A.B. Cobban, *The Medieval Universities: Oxford and Cambridge to c.1500*, Aldershot, 1988. – D.R. Leader, *A History of the University of Cambridge*, I, Cambridge, 1988. – *Medieval Cambridge*, P. Zutshi (ed.), Woodbridge, 1993.

Elizabeth Leedham Green

**CAMERA, APOSTOLIC.** Financial organ of the papacy, the Apostolic Camera collected the revenues, saw to the expenditure and judged any litigations. Its usefulness was recognised in the 11th c. and it was developed under *Urban II with reference to the administration of *Cluny. After 1120, the Apostolic Camera was independent. Cencius (the future *Honorius III) completed the recapitulation of its revenues (**Liber censuum*) in 1192.

The *camerarius* – in the 15th c., *cambellanus* – whose function absorbed several ancient offices of the Roman *Curia, was chosen by the *pope from among the *archbishops or *bishops; in the 13th c., he was a *cardinal; from 1319, he was no longer part of the *Sacred College. He was the pope's main collaborator. The *camerarius* appointed the papacy's financial agents at the curial see and in *Christendom (treasurers of the *States of the Church, commissioners and *collectors). He controlled their accounts, and all the quittances delivered to the papacy's debtors were made out in his name. His function did not cease on the pope's death. He was helped in the 13th c. by two treasurers, who kept the precious objects and liturgical ornaments. After 1343-1344, there was only one: designated by the pope, he administered the papal coffers and if necessary replaced the *camerarius* to whom he was subordinate. Drawn from the pope's entourage, he remained at his post for a shorter time than the *camerarius* and subsequently received an episcopal see.

The clerks of the Camera ensured the functioning of the service: they prepared contracts and "cameral" letters, examined the collectors' accounts and carried out missions. They were *notaries of the apostolic authority. Of seven at the end of the 13th c., only three remained under the Avignon popes; *Eugenius IV went back to seven in 1438 and published their statutes in 1444. With the *camerarius*, the treasurer and if necessary some advisers, the council of the Camera was thus constituted.

On the Camera depended a particular jurisdiction, the audience of the Camera, which employed an auditor (from 1277 at least), a vice-auditor, a *procurator fiscal introducing cases in which the Roman Church was implicated, *advocates fiscal who pleaded the briefs, a sealer, a gaoler and notaries.

The issuing of papal *money was done under the responsibility of the Camera. A guard and a *provost were the sole permanent personnel, residing at *Rome, at Sorgues in the *Comtat Venaissin until 1354, at *Avignon and again at Rome.

From the mid 13th c., the pope's *letters were prepared in the Camera; they were entrusted to scribes of the pope, different from the scribes of the apostolic letters of the *chancery. Their competence was extended, embracing notably the diplomatic field; the most important missives were then drawn up by specialists (secretaries) from 1341. Men of high culture, often of Florentine origin, they took part in the *humanist movement of the 15th century.

Finally, couriers (*cursores*) carried part of the correspondence, also making purchases, delivering writs and keeping the treasure. There were about 50 of them in the 14th century.

Receipts and expenses were put down in books of *Introïtus et exitus* or in *Collectorie*, whose first surviving examples date from *Boniface VIII (1299 and 1302). The series becomes almost regular from *John XXII (1316). These precious account-books do not reflect the whole of the financial activity of the Roman Church, but only the movement of funds at the central level of the papal treasury. In the 14th c., the annual budget varied from 235,000 to 500,000 florins. In deficit from the 1360s, it was supplied by borrowing. These sums were lower than those known at the same period for England, the kingdom of Naples or France. From the second third of the 13th c., the Camera established relations with the great commercial and *banking societies of *Siena, *Lucca, Pistoia and *Florence. After the crashes of the second quarter of the 14th c., it had recourse to less powerful companies.

J. de Loye, *Les Archives de la Chambre apostolique au XIV*[e] *siècle*, Paris, 1899. – C. Samaran, G. Mollat, *La Fiscalité pontificale en France au XIV*[e] *siècle*, Paris, 1905. – Y. Renouard, *Les Relations des papes d'Avignon et des compagnies commerciales et bancaires de 1316 à 1378*, Paris, 1941. – G. Mollat, *Les Papes d'Avignon, 1305-1378*, Paris (10th ed.), 1964. – B. Guillemain, *Les papes d'Avignon, 1309-1376*, Paris, 1998.

Bernard Guillemain

**CAMPIDANO.** The largest plain in *Sardinia, not without features and hills. It extends over the whole central-south part of the island between the gulf of Oristano and that of Cagliari. It is important for the production of cereals. In the Middle Ages the word Campidano did not have its modern meaning, which indicates the entire geographical extent of the plain. The term was applied to only four of the *curatoriae* (legal-administrative divisions) into which the *judicates were divided. These were: the Campidano of Cagliari (in that judicate, it extended around the city towards the east of the island), of Simaxis, of Milis and of Maggiore (these three *curatoriae* were in the judicate of Arborèa and were concentrated in the central-west zone around the capital, Oristano).

R. Pracchi (ed.), A. Terrosu Asole (ed.), *Atlante della Sardegna*, Rome, 1974-1980.

Mauro Sanna

**CAMPIN, ROBERT (1379/1380-1444).** A painter working at *Tournai. His activity is attested from 1406. Between *c.*1415 and 1432 he headed a very important studio. During the tradesmen's uprising which gave the town a democratic regime between 1425 and 1428, he engaged in local politics, which later earned him two successive condemnations on secondary pretexts, which led him to dissolve his studio in August 1432. At least two famous painters, Jacques Daret and Rogier *van der Weyden, worked with him between 1427 and 1432, in principle as *apprentices, in reality as companions. His personal work has been identified with the group of pictures brought together under the provisional name of "Maître de Flémalle".

Of remarkable originality, he evolved rapidly in the course of his career and very soon developed a realism tending to representation of the everyday world. The triptych of the *Entombment* (London, Courtauld Institute) combines characters still close to International Gothic with a precision of rendering objects as if in imitation of sculptures, which suggests probable contacts with Klaus *Sluter. Three panels, claimed by their 19th-c. seller to have come from a non-existent abbey of Flémalle, are the surviving elements of a great *altarpiece (Frankfurt, Staedelinstitut). Two of them show large solemn figures, standing on a carpet of flowers rendered with precision, in front of a standard, and the third a grisaille evoking with singular plastic force a sculpted group of the *Trinity. The same museum preserves the fragment of a volet representing the *Bad Thief*, remnant of a large altarpiece of the *Deposition from the Cross*, known by a copy (Liverpool, Museum), perhaps made for the Bruges mansion of the duke of *Burgundy: the *wounds of the crucified Christ are depicted with an almost sadistic precision. His most revolutionary creation, probably in 1422-23, is the *Triptych of the Annunciation* or *Mérode Triptych* (New York, the Cloisters) painted for Jean Imbrechts of Malines and his wife: it evokes the gospel scene in a bourgeois interior and St *Joseph in a carpenter's shop with a surprising precision of details. The objects seem to be simultaneously elements of daily reality and allegorical attributes of the qualities of the Virgin or of divine realities. Close to it in spirit are a *Nativity* (Dijon, Museum) and a triptych wing, the *Marriage of the Virgin* (Madrid, Prado).

After the dispersal of his studio, Robert Campin painted at least two more works, a memorial tableau of a bishop, a *Hermit of St Augustine, presented to the Virgin of the Immaculate Conception by Sts Peter and Augustine (Aix-en-Provence, Musée Granet) and two wings from a triptych finished in 1438 for the

*The Nativity* by Robert Campin, known as the Maître de Flémalle, 15th c. Dijon, Musée des Beaux-Arts.

Franciscan minister of the province of Cologne, Heinrich Werl (Madrid, Prado). His influence was considerable, not just in *Flanders but all over northern Europe, in the development of the new style that prevailed at the start of the 15th c., in providing solutions rougher and sometimes more monumental than those of Jan *van Eyck.

E. Panofsky, *Early Netherlandish Painting*, Cambridge (MA), 1953. – M. Davies, *Rogier van der Weyden*, London, 1972.

Albert Châtelet

**CANON.** The term "canon" became usual only in the *Carolingian period, when the rule of Aachen was drawn up (817) for religious communities which refused to follow the example of St *Chrodegang's *clerics at *Metz and adopt a monastic lifestyle. Canons were subject to common life in praying, eating and sleeping, but unlike monks they could have possessions, and a part of the community's revenues, the *prebend, was assigned to them personally.

From the mid 11th c., certain communities of canons came closer to the monastic ideal. Reformed houses had a tendency to form associations: *Saint-Victor at Paris, the Val-des-Écoliers, Sant-Ruf, etc., thus became heads of *orders. There were also new *foundations, such as those of the *Premonstratensians, which, under the impetus of St *Norbert, spread throughout Europe. To the requirements of life in community, these *canons regular added pastoral concerns that took them out of their *cloister.

The canons who remained *secular were grouped into a *chapter around the church they served collegially. Each chapter was regulated by its own statutes. Generally, men became canons by the will of the church's patron and on condition of having received one of the major *orders. Each canon had a stall in the choir, a voice in the chapter and received the fruits of a prebend. The dignitaries held particular offices that earned them supplementary emoluments and a more elevated hierarchical position.

In the *cathedrals of France, liturgical service was generally performed by secular canons, except in the Midi where several communities (*e.g.* *Toulouse or Maguelone) followed the Rule of St *Augustine. Still more rare were chapters arising out of *abbeys which, like that of Montauban, were erected into cathedrals. Much coveted *benefices, the prebends of cathedrals and great *collegiate churches gave rise to acute struggles for influence. By means of *reservations, from the 13th c., the *popes interfered more and more in the composition of chapters; they often became the stake of secular princes wishing to set up the clerics who served them.

Distinguished for their merits or their nobility, canons formed a well-rewarded elite. Skilful in procuring *dispensations of all kinds, they got ahead in clerical society by accumulating prebends. Either between the *hours of prayer or on days when they were not obliged to keep *residence, canons had time that they were free to occupy in their own way. The management of the estate or the chapter institutions (*school, *hospital. . .) offered a multitude of occupations on the spot. But many personalities had an intellectual, cultural or political influence that went far beyond the limits of their city.

H. Millet, *Les Chanoines du chapitre cathédral de Laon (1272-1412)*, Rome, 1982. – *I Canonici al servizio dello Stato*, Modena, 1992.

Hélène Millet

**CANON LAW, CANONISTS**

**The West.** Under the name of canonists we designate more particularly the *jurists who, in the Middle Ages, formulated or commented on the texts of the Church's law, called canon law.

Canon law was formulated slowly in the course of the first centuries of the existence of the ecclesial institution; it was born of the need to ensure the discipline necessary for the life of any social body and the obligation to give coherent order to the many texts emanating from very varied sources (writings of Church *Fathers, conciliar canons, papal legislation) whose accumulation had made apprehension of the essential rules of this law difficult.

The first canonists appeared in the Carolingian period; they drew up treatises on particular points of discipline, such as the famous *De divortio Lotharii* of *Hincmar, archbishop of Reims. For two centuries, the efforts of the canonists tended to offer users a compendium of the essential texts of the new law, which became more and more detached from *theology. Thus were born the works of *Burchard of Worms (*c.*1010) and *Ivo of Chartres († 1117). But it was the composition of the *Concordia discordantium canonum* by the Bolognese monk Gratian, in *c.*1140, that led to a first flowering of canonists.

Becoming official Church law under the name of Gratian's **Decretum*, this work became the basis of teaching in the *universities, at *Bologna, *Paris and *Oxford. The numerous authors who wrote on the *Decretum* formed the school of *Decretists. Rolando Bandinelli – the future *Alexander III –, Rufinus and Stephen of Tournai were the authors of the first *summae on the *Decretum*. Around 1190, *Huguccio of Pisa completed the *Summa* that constituted the first synthesis of the works of the Decretists, and shortly afterwards *John Teutonicus composed the *Glossa ordinaria* on Gratian's treatise.

The legislation of the *popes of the second half of the 12th and the early 13th c., commented on by *Bernard of Pavia, Tancred of Bologna, Richard the Englishman, *Lawrence and Vincent of Spain, led quite naturally to the compilation by the Dominican *Raymond of Peñafort of the famous *Decretals of *Gregory IX which constituted the second part of the *Corpus juris canonici* (1234). Applying to this new text the same methods as the Decretists to the *Decretum*, a new school appeared, that of the *Decretalists. This was the classical age of canon law; the first great *apparatus* on the Decretals was composed by Sinibaldo *Fieschi, the future *Innocent IV. At the same time, Henry of Susa (*Hostiensis) was teaching at Paris before becoming archbishop of Embrun and cardinal of Ostia and publishing in 1271 his *Lectura Decretalium*, "the first colossal monument of legal science" (G. Le Bras). Ecclesiastical *procedure was at the same time the object of the Languedocian Guillaume *Durand's *Speculum judiciale*.

While the last quarter of the 13th c. reveals no exceptional talent, *Boniface VIII, himself a canonist, gave new impetus to canon law studies by promulgating the *Liber Sextus*, brilliantly interpreted by three talented Frenchmen, *Jean Lemoine, Bérenger Fredol and Guillaume de Mandagout, and at Bologna by Gui de Baysio, nicknamed the Archdeacon († 1313), whose disciple *Johannes Andreae († 1348) undisputably dominated his time.

The Clementines stimulated the works of the Toulousain Guillaume de Montlauzun, the Montpellieran Josselin de Cassagnes and Cardinal Pierre Bertrand. At the same time, the Breton Henri Bohic perfected a new method that originated in the genre of *distinctiones*.

The following generation was marked especially by the Italians Giovanni da Lignano († 1383) and Baldo († 1400). While the *Great Schism, like the *Hundred Years' War, was unfavourable to university studies, it did lead to the writing of numerous treatises like those of *Gilles Bellemère, Pierre Bohier and Martin of Zalva. The councils of *Constance and *Basel, then the *Pragmatic Sanction in France were the occasion to multiply memoirs and treatises. 15th-c. Italy continued to produce powerful works, like those of Cardinal *Zabarella, Pietro da Ancharano and *Antonio da Butrio, and around 1425 a new generation began its career with Tartagnus, Andrea Barbatia and especially Nicola de Tudeschis or *Panormitanus († 1445) who edited the last complete commentary on the Decretals before the council of Trent.

But what characterised the 15th century was the internationalization of the science of canon law, more marked than in previous centuries. Alongside the Italians, the Frenchman Bernard de Rosier and the Spaniard Juan de *Torquemada left considerable work. The creation of new universities in Germany, Flanders, Switzerland, the Iberian peninsula and even in France gave occasion for a multiplicity of talents to manifest itself: Jacob Radewitz at *Leipzig, Henry of Odendorp at *Cologne, Guillaume Bont at *Louvain, Peter of Andlau at Basel, John Alfonso of Benavent at *Salamanca and Guillaume Benoît at Cahors trained numerous pupils and left writings many of which can still be consulted, though they have been accused of being unable to renew the methods of their predecessors. Not until the champions of the Reformation and Counter-Reformation would this renewal be accomplished.

*HDIEO*, 7, 1965. – *HDIEO*, 13, 1971. – R. H. Helmholz, *Canon Law and the Law of England*, London, 1987. – S. Kuttner, *History of Ideas and Doctrines of Canon Law in the Middle Ages*, 2nd ed., Aldershot, 1992. – S. Kuttner, *Medieval Councils, Decretals, and Collections of Canon Law*, 2nd ed., Aldershot, 1992. – J. Brundage, *Medieval Canon Law*, London, 1995.

Henri Gilles

**Byzantium.** Under the name of canonists are designated the Byzantine jurists who, from the 12th to the 15th c., commented on the canons or drew up practical manuals of ecclesiastical law.

The Church's corpus of canons was confirmed by the council called "Quinisext" or *in Trullo* (691-692) but only as to the authenticity of the source, not fundamentally, and later supplemented by three further *councils. Thus was established a very heterogeneous set of official norms, sometimes superseded or even contradictory, decreed by councils very distant from each other in time and space, or attributed to the 4th-c. *Fathers. This complexity of the canonical corpus thus imposed the writing of commentaries to clarify the text. This task was carried out in the 12th c. by Alexius Aristenos, mandated by the Emperor John II *Comnenus († 1143), then later, *c.*1159, by the jurist and imperial official John Zonaras, and finally by Theodore Balsamon, archivist of the *patriarchate, future patriarch of *Antioch and author of a commentary on the **Nomocanon* in 14 titles. All worked in more or less the same way, drawing up a commentary for each canon separately, placed after the original text, without making modifications to the text itself.

Later, in the 14th c., utilitarian redaction was preferred: the monk Matthew Blastares drew up his *Syntagma* in alphabetical order of matter (1335), and his work was translated and circulated in the Slav world. His contemporary Constantine Harmenopoulos, a judge by profession, preferred systematic classification for his *Epitome of the holy canons* (1346). These two even retouched the text and simplified or modified its expression. Other collections did not have the same success as their predecessors: the systematic *Syntagma* of the hieromonk Macarius (perhaps Metropolitan Macarius of Philadelphia, mid 14th c.) and the *Synopsis* (summary) of the canons by Arsenius, a monk at the monastery of Philotheos on Mount *Athos.

N. Van der Wal, J. H. A. Lokin, *Historiae iuris graeco-romani delineatio. Les sources du droit byzantin de 300 à 1453*, Groningen, 1985, 108-112, 116-117. – *To Byzantio kata ton 12o aiôna. Kanoniko dikaio, kratos kai koinônia*, N. Oikonomides (ed.), Athens, 1991.

Stavros Perentidis

## CANON OF THE MASS

**The West.** From the Carolingian period to the 20th century, there were in the *mass three elements, called respectively the *preface, **Sanctus* and canon, to which modern liturgical vocabulary gives the overall name of "eucharistic prayer". The *canon actionis*, or simply the canon, is the rule of the sacred action, the text of the prayer that, in the *Roman liturgy of the mass, goes from the *Sanctus* to the *Lord's Prayer.

The text of the canon was immutable from the time of St *Gregory the Great, except on three points: the generalized use, from the Carolingian period, of the *Memento* of the dead, which seems previously to have been reserved for masses specially offered for the *dead; a small number of redactional variants for the main *feasts of the year; and finally, rare local pecularities, *e.g.* in the list of saints. A first redaction of the canon was cited in the 4th c. by St Ambrose; several modifications were later made by 5th- and 6th-c. *popes. Its text was marked by the style of ancient Roman prayer. It differed from the prayers that, in the *Gallican liturgy before *Charlemagne and the *Hispanic liturgy up to St *Gregory VII, occupied the same place in the mass, in that the latter were formed of sections that varied from one mass to another. Compared with the Greek "*anaphorae", which have a similar function in the liturgy of the mass, the Roman canon says much less about thanksgiving and insists more on the sacrifical aspect of the *Eucharist.

From the Carolingian period, the canon was spoken by the priest in a low voice, with the sole exception of the words "*Nobis quoque peccatoribus*", the priest not raising his voice again until just before the *Pater*, to say "*per omnia saecula saeculorum*". At the beginning of the 13th c., under the influence of Christian piety, in order to show them to the congregation the priest elevated first the consecrated *host, immediately after the words of *consecration spoken over the bread, then likewise the *chalice, after the words over the wine. This great *elevation (so called to distinguish it from the little elevation that accompanied the conclusion of the canon) was from then on accompanied by a silent *adoration and, in certain cases, chants addressed to the Blessed Sacrament.

Following St Gregory the Great (*Ep.* 9, 26), the medievals saw in the canon a prayer developed from the consecratory words instituted by Christ. Unlike the liturgical science of our own time, they were unaware of the importance of the eucharistic prayer in early Christianity and its roots in Jewish prayer.

J.-A. Jungmann, *The Mass of theRoman Rite*, London, 1959.

*CaP*, 2, *The Eucharist*, London, 1986. – P.-M. Gy, *La Liturgie dans l'histoire*, Paris, 1990, ch. 10.

Pierre-Marie Gy

**Byzantium.** The Western terms "canon" or, more commonly nowadays, "eucharistic prayer", correspond to the Byzantine term **anaphora*. With a basic meaning of "leading up to something higher", it early became an overall term for the eucharistic liturgy, while in later Byzantine use it was reserved to the central part of the liturgy, during which the bread and wine are consecrated. There were two versions: that attributed to St Basil, to whom, according to his *Life* by Pseudo-Amphilochius, it was revealed by Christ in a vision; and that attributed to St John Chrysostom. Both are Antiochene in origin but, at least by the 12th c., the latter predominated.

In the 9th-c. text, the earliest to survive, after the dismissal of the catechumens, the prayers of the faithful, the carrying of the offerings to the *altar and the recitation of the *Creed, the anaphora begins with a dialogue (as in the Latin rite). There follows a text equivalent to the Latin *preface, culminating in the **Trisagion* (again as in the Latin rite). There was some controversy as to whether the *Trisagion* was directed only to Christ or to all the members of the Trinity. Then there is an account, much longer in Basil's liturgy, of the events that led up to the Last Supper, culminating in the recital of Christ's words: "This is my body. . . This is my blood." Only after this is the Epiclesis prayer recited. This prayer (reintroduced into the Latin liturgy in the reforms subsequent to Vatican II, but placed *before* the recital of the Last Supper) invokes the Father to send down the *Holy Spirit, in order to change the bread and wine into the body and blood of Christ. This central act of the anaphora, known in Western theological language as *transubstantiation, was the subject of controversy in the Middle Ages – and subsequently – between the Eastern and Western Churches. *Epiclesis* (invocation) was a term in general use with reference to *sacraments for an appeal to the Holy Spirit to consecrate. The disputed question in the *Eucharist was: at what moment precisely did Transubstantiation take place? The Western view was that it took place when the priest recited the words attributed to Christ at the Last Supper. The Eastern view was that it took place when the Holy Spirit was invoked. On the whole Western theologians, at least, now hold that the two texts are complementary. There follow (again as in the Latin rite) prayers for the living and the *dead. This included readings from the *diptychs of specific names of living and dead people by the *deacon, a practice which dates back at least to the 5th century. The anaphora ended (once more as in the Latin rite) with the recital of the *doxology, to which the laity replied: *Amen*.

N. Cabasilas, *A Commentary on the Divine Liturgy*, London, 1978.

F. E. Brightman, *Liturgies Eastern and Western*, Oxford, 1896, 321-337, 373-390. – S. Salaville, "Épiclèse eucharistique", *DThC*, 5, 1, 1924, 194-300. – R. Taft, *OrChrP*, 49, 1983 f.

Christopher Walter

**CANONESSES, SECULAR.** From the Merovingian period, certain *nuns were attached to the group of *canons, and before 816 the early medieval *councils thus distinguished between *abbesses of nuns and abbesses of canonesses. In his reforming activity, *Benedict of Aniane in 816 devoted a very long *capitulary to those who lived "canonically", giving his instructions to nuns as well as to monks in 817. Certain womens' abbeys still refused to apply the *Benedictine Rule strictly and hence remained *chapters. From then on, there existed in German countries (particularly Saxony), in northern Italy and Lotharingia many communities of canonesses, whose regime of life was often very close to that of nuns, but who kept many freedoms: relations with their *family, leave from the monastery, possession of an individual lodging, personal *property, right to receive inheritances and make *testaments. Recruited exclusively from the highest *nobility, the canonesses limited the number of their *prebends, maintained a small group of canon-priests for *mass and to administer the *sacraments, practised co-optation and lived comfortably.

In the late 10th and in the 11th c., there were some conversions to the Benedictine life, but then the canonesses, in contrast to the many nuns of the various *orders, hardened their institutions, imposed nobiliary exclusivism in their texts and refused to comply with the orders of a papacy mistrustful of them. In the later Middle Ages, secular canonesses maintained their "chapters of noble ladies", claimed to belong to the Benedictine Order without following its Rule, and remained very close to their families or to the ruler; some abbesses even became princesses of the *Empire. Among the best-known houses were Remiremont, Mons, Maubeuge and Andenne in *Lotharingia, Baume and Château-Chalon in the county of *Burgundy, *Essen and Neuss in the Rhineland, *Gandersheim and *Quedlinburg in *Saxony, and many others. The secular canonesses represented a religious way of life very specific to the imperial lands.

K. H. Shäfer, *Die Kanonissenstifter im deutschen Mittelalter*, Stuttgart, 1907. – M. Parisse, "Canonisse secolare", *DIP*, 2, 1975. – M. Parisse, "Les chanoinesses dans l'Empire germanique (IXe-XI[e] siècles)", *Francia*, 6, 1978, 107-126. – P. Heidebrecht, C. Nolte, *Leben im Kloster*, 1988, 79-115.

Michel Parisse

**CANONICAL COLLECTIONS.** A canonical collection is a compilation bringing together a more or less considerable number of fragments of texts each possessing a certain value in *canon law, drawn from various sources. Each fragment, called an **auctoritas*, is normally preceded by an indication of its source.

This definition is vague, because the notion of canonical collection covers a multiplicity of things. They constituted the usual manner of knowledge and transmission of canon law from the first centuries to the 15th century.

As to the nature of the texts used, the authors drew indifferently on various sources of canon law, the main ones being scriptural writings, patristic or other later doctrinal writings, texts for the most part without normative value, but capable of acquiring the authority of a legal ruling by their inclusion in a canonical collection. We also find canons of *councils, general or provincial, as well as extracts of papal *Decretals, the fundamental sources of canon law. The compilers also had recourse to secular law, Carolingian *capitularies or *Roman law, used mainly from the second half of the 12th c., the time of the discovery in the West of Justinian's compilations. Canonical collections also contained apocryphal texts, fakes made up of bits and pieces to bolster the thesis of an author, and put under the authority of a famous person in the Church (*e.g.* the group of "false Isidorians" composed in the 9th c. and attributed to the *popes of the first centuries). Moreover, the redactors made various interpolations, often deliberately, sometimes resulting from a predecessor's error which they faithfully copied. Once incorporated in a collection, all the texts, whatever their origin, author or date of production, acquired the same general legal value, *i.e.* the authority recognised for the whole collection.

To compose their collection, the authors referred sometimes, though rarely, to the actual source from which they took an extract. More often, they used earlier canonical collections, copying passages, keeping or modifying the order in which their predecessors had presented the texts. Hence a repetition of errors, which imposes on the historian the important work of searching for the manner of transmission of the collection as a whole, and of each text composing it. If the author wanted to develop a personal *doctrine, the choice of texts, the way they were cut up and their order of presentation brought out his own doctrine. The presentation of many collections, especially among the earlier ones, does not seem to respond to any concern for methodical classification, by dealing with themes. This is the case of numerous works recapitulating conciliar series *en bloc*; this legislation is habitually drawn up without any plan. Gradually, "systematic" collections became more frequent. They drew on more diversified sources and tried to group *auctoritates* by subjects dealt with.

The legal authority of these collections also varied considerably. Generally a private work, the value of a collection corresponded to the moral or doctrinal authority of its author (usually a *bishop or *abbot). However, from the extreme end of the 12th c., the pope sometimes – rarely – gave one of his household the task of drawing up a collection; or else he confirmed a work by promulgating it. These works acquired official value; they were required to be put into practice throughout the Latin Church. The apogee of the classical law of the Church is marked by the *Corpus juris canonici*, a compilation bringing together five great collections produced between the mid 12th and the mid 15th century. This group remained in force in the Latin Catholic Church until the Code of Canon Law was drawn up in 1917.

G. Fransen, *Les Collections canoniques*, *TSMÂO*, 10, Turnhout, 1973. – J. Gaudemet, *Les Sources du droit canonique VIII^e-XX^e siècles*, Paris, 1993. – *Archbishop Wulfstan's Canon Law Collection*, J.E. Cross (ed.), A. Hamer (ed.), Woodbridge, 1998.

Brigitte Basdevant-Gaudemet

**CANONICAL INSTITUTION.** At the creation of rural churches or annexes, the newly designated *cleric received his spiritual authority from the *bishop together with his *priesthood. These two elements were closely joined. But from the Carolingian period, this practice consonant with traditional *ecclesiology deteriorated. In effect, incumbents were too often designated and ordained independently of the bishop's intervention. This was the result of the situation of churches that had become the property of laymen and of *regulars.

The council of *Clermont (1095) initiated a reaction, establishing a strict separation of the temporal and the spiritual within the parochial institution. From now on the incumbent, responsible for the church to its patron, was responsible to the bishop for the government of souls. Designated by the titular of the church, he was presented by him to the head of the *diocese or his representative who entrusted him with the church to rule (**cura animarum*).

The practical procedures of canonical institution were fixed according to the customs proper to each diocese. In general, the cleric declared under *oath that he had been regularly designated, promised obedience to the prelate and engaged himself to reside and to receive *orders. After having been admitted by the bishop, the newly-elect took an oath to the patron of the church for the temporality.

Furthermore, any priest brought in to replace the titular of a *parish had to be accepted by the bishop. In fact, at the end of the Middle Ages, many ecclesiastics who were titulars of churches were dispensed from *residence and reception of orders, while clerics recruited without any episcopal recognition performed the pastoral *ministry.

J. Avril, "Église, paroisse, encadrement diocésain aux XII^e-XIV^e siècles", *La paroisse en Languedoc (XIII^e-XIV^e siècles)*, *CFan*, 24, 1990, 23-49. – J. Avril, "Quelques aspects de l'institution paroissiale après le IV^e concile du Latran", *Église et réformes dans l'Église de la Réforme grégorienne à la Préréforme, Actes du 155^e Congrès national des Sociétés savantes, Avignon 1990*, Paris, 1991, 93-106.

Joseph Avril

## CANONIZATION

**The West.** During the first millennium, the organisation of Christian cults and the recognition of *sanctity were within the competence of local Churches. But the growing success of the cult of *relics and the desire of each religious community to possess some led to an anarchic proliferation of devotions which imperial legislation, in the Carolingian period, strove to limit by reserving to *councils or assemblies of *bishops the right to order the translation of saintly bodies. But these measures were hardly applied after the 9th c., by reason of the prolonged crisis suffered at that time by the West. The reaction came from the papacy which began to regain a certain prestige. In 993, Bishop *Ulrich of Augsburg († 973) was proclaimed a saint at Rome by Pope John XV, at the request of the German clergy. In 1020, for the first time we meet the word "canonize" in the sense of official authorization of a cult, in a papal document ratifying the cult rendered to St Simeon of *Polirone, an Armenian hermit who died near *Mantua in 1016. This was not a novel procedure but, as the *pope was the highest *authority in the Church, his guarantee gave a particular lustre to the cult of a servant of God and was hence particularly sought after.

Up to the early 13th c., regional councils and *bishops

continued as in the past to institute cults, but the use spread in the course of the 12th c. of having new saints proclaimed in the presence of the pope or of a papal *legate. From *Alexander III (1159-1181), this custom tended progressively to become a rule, the papacy striving to bring the cult of saints under its control in order to eliminate the risks of error and to ensure that, in this sphere, figures of Catholic sanctity capable of providing models of behaviour for *clerics and *laity and supporting comparison with the *Cathar *perfecti* should prevail. Little inclined to entrust this to the bishops, too subject to local pressures and sometimes lacking in critical spirit, the popes of the late 12th and early 13th cc. instituted, at first *de facto*, then *de jure* (1234), the principle of papal reservation of the right of canonization: the traditional prerogatives of prelates in this sphere were not formally abolished, but from now on only the pope possessed the right to proclaim a dead person a saint and allow him the honours of a liturgical cult celebrated by the whole Church, by reason of the universal character of his power of jurisdiction.

At the same time, the Holy See set up a procedure of inquiry in legal form into the life and *miracles of the "candidate for the altars", soon designated under the name "canonization trial", which would allow him to make a pronouncement in full knowledge of the case. When he had passed a favourable sentence, the pope proceeded to the liturgical ceremony of canonization, following which the inscription of a new name in the Roman Church's "catalogue of saints" was notified to *Christendom by one or more *bulls. These authorized the solemn translation of the saint's relics and indicated the texts of the *office that were to be used at the celebration of his *feast.

A. Vauchez, *Sainthood in the Later Middle Ages*, Cambridge, 1997.

André Vauchez

**Byzantium.** In the early Eastern church, the recognition of *sanctity was very informal: after his death, a holy person was recognised as a saint by his entourage, his community, his monastery; his memory was celebrated on the *anniversary of his death; *miracles took place at his tomb; a disciple wrote his Life and his liturgical *office; his name was inscribed in his Church's calendar of saints; his *image was painted and venerated. This procedure (popular cult, celebration, *hagiography and iconography, inscription in the liturgical calendar) bore the name *anagnôrisis* (recognition). Its extension to other churches, which could go as far as inscription in the patriarchal calendar, was exceptional. This weak control of the Church over the *cult of the saints explains the profusion of local cults.

From the late 13th c., under the influence of the West whose practice had long been much more structured, Byzantium adopted a more rigorous procedure that resulted in veritable canonizations.The first saints who seem to have benefited from this process were Patriarch Arsenius and Patriarch *Joseph I, two contested *patriarchs whose official canonization undoubtedly had political reasons. Some twenty canonizations followed under the *Palaeologi, while many other saints continued to have just a local cult. Among the saints recognised by the patriarchate of Constantinople at this time were Meletius the Confessor, Peter of Kiev, three martyrs of Lithuania, Patriarch *Athanasius I and, above all, Gregory *Palamas.

The case of Gregory Palamas is exemplary: when he died at *Thessalonica in 1359, the Thessalonians immediately began to venerate him; miracles took place at his tomb; Patriarch *Callistus demanded a report on these miracles. Meanwhile his disciple Philotheus Kokkinos, a former patriarch, wrote his *Eulogy* and a liturgical office. His cult spread at Thessalonica and Mount *Athos: this was the first stage, that of the local cult. Becoming patriarch of Constantinople again in 1363, Philotheus began by officially authorizing his cult on Mount Athos and in a monastery at Constantinople, then in 1368 he presided over a *synod that instituted the cult of Gregory Palamas at Hagia Sophia: this proclamation in synod, after inquiry, entailing integration into the patriarchal calendar, bore the name *anakèruxis* and was the equivalent of our Western canonization.

*HChr*, 6, 1990, 563-564. – *The Oxford Dictionary of Byzantium*, A. P. Kazhdan (ed.), New York, 1991.

Marie-Hélène Congourdeau

**The Russian Church.** As at Byzantium before the Palaeologi, canonization was long done in an informal way: certain dead people were venerated at their place of burial. Three canonizations were an exception: in 1072 at the latest, those of *Boris and Gleb (the two princes murdered in 1015), in 1108 that of Abbot *Theodosius, founder of the monastery of the *Caves († 1074) – three models of sanctity, princes and monk, that remained popular in Russia. To find other general canonizations, we must probably wait until 1448 (Metropolitan *Alexis and *Sergius of Radonezh). But only in 1547-1549 were all locally-venerated saints made the object of an official canonization.

E. E. Golubinsky, *Istoriia kanonizatsii sviatyx v russkoy tserkvi*, Moscow, 1903. – É. Behr-Sigel, *Prière et sainteté dans l'Église russe*, Paris, 1950.

Vladimir Vodoff

**CANONS, REGULAR.** At the end of Christian Antiquity, *clerics admitted to the service of the great churches – *cathedrals or *basilicas – were subject to regulations, the "canons", so that we may speak in this context of a canonical or canons' life. These *canons could obviously perform their duties more or less regularly, in the more general sense of the term. In the wake of monastic asceticism, bishops like Diodore of Antioch or Eusebius of Vercelli had tried to group the clerics of their entourage into a sort of monastery, the better to control their disinterestedness and their morality. The most remarkable of these bishops was assuredly Augustine of Hippo, whose writings on the subject would have the success of a rule throughout the Latin Middle Ages.

With the Merovingian period, the spread of the *priesthood among monks and the basilica or missionary service of some of them would lead to a rapprochement between the monastic and the canonical state, though the former involved the personal *profession of a strict rule and the second merely obliged the traditional usages of a church. *Gregory the Great, while distinguishing monks from canons, made quite clear that common life in the tradition of the early Church remained the ideal of the clergy, but the multiplication of basilicas raised in honour of the *martyrs and the generosity of the faithful towards them further facilitated the confusion between the two states, all the more since the monastic title of *abbot was often given or taken to honour the superiors of communities of canons.

That is why Carolingian legislation, following *Chrodegang of Metz, aimed at distinguishing clearly between the two states. In 816, a *council met at Aachen and confirmed under the name of *Canons or Institutions of the Fathers* the essence of the old canonical regulations: though the canons of the great churches were held to a certain claustral life in these churches, they could eat meat and possess inherited or casual *property. The Rule of Aachen had a success comparable to the Rule of St *Benedict assigned to monks the following year; the cathedrals and basilicas followed it, but also the *collegiate churches that multiplied in the first feudal age. This success was especially visible in the German Empire, but also at *Lyon or *Reims. In practice, common life was generally reduced to the celebration of the *office and the administration of property; particular houses were built in the claustral enclosure and the revenues were divided into individual *prebends whose number depended on the church's resources. The parochial service, even that of the great church, was left to ordinary clerics. By its balance and flexibility, the Carolingian formula for canons would cross the centuries into our own time.

The period of *invasions once passed, Western *Christendom rediscovered the Carolingian norms, but a general renewal – the *Gregorian reform, in the 11th-12th cc. – tended to purify and precisely define those norms, both for the respective role of clergy and *laity in the life of the Church and for the role of monks and canons in the service of the churches. On this second point, a more rigorous disinterestedness towards material goods would lean on the traditional theme of the *apostolic life, *i.e.* the life and times of the apostles, when all was common to all, according to the Acts of the Apostles. Among monks, the exact practice of the Rule of St Benedict sufficed; for canons, the Rule of St *Augustine was sought out, and those who freely made *profession of it were called *regulars in this strict sense, the others being assigned the pejorative name of *seculars. Ecclesiastical legislation would confirm this terminology.

The basis of this regularity was the individual renunciation of property by clerics advocated by Augustine, but left by the Roman council of 1059 to those alone who were willing. The common life of the *cloister, with dorter and refectory after the monastic model, was the means of recruiting this new profession whose rights and duties were detailed by various local *customaries. This too was a great success, due to various factors such as rising population or the effective attention of the apostolic see. Canons' churches adopted Augustinian regularity in an isolated way, regulars replacing seculars by extinction; others grouped themselves together in diocesan association as at Halberstadt, others again gave rise to centralized organisations on the *Cistercian model, either by association or by foundation of daughter houses. In this last category, the *Premonstratensian Order was the major success due to its European expansion and its internal structure, but we must also mention *Saint-Victor at Paris and its doctrinal influence. Cathedral and collegiate churches generally escaped the Rule of Aachen, but even in this case some had regular daughter houses in which their members could make profession.

The Gregorian reform inviting the laity to disseize themselves of churches in favour of the *bishops, some ceded them to monks, others to canons, regular or otherwise. For certain regular orders founded by hermit-clerics who had more or less held the role of popular preachers, the service of these churches was possible and desirable; in return, the monks had to subcontract the parish service. However, the risk of dilution of regular communities in cure-priories was real, despite the precautions taken by Rome to preserve in these *priories a minimum kernel of three or four religious.

Regular canons made use, like other orders, of the services of lay-brothers and sisters, and some new communities consisted of juxtaposed male and female communities; the latter comprised *nuns of the Carolingian type or lay-sisters, or both. Monasteries of these nuns, especially in the lands of the *Empire, adopted Augustinian rather than Benedictine regularity: thus we find *abbeys and priories of regular canonesses of St Augustine, controlled by the diocesan bishop or by the *chapter general of a new order.

In the 14th c., the *Avignon papacy concerned itself with revising the working of the religious *orders on the lines of the *Lateran councils, the most important of which was in 1215. After having regulated in 1336 the question of Benedictine monks not yet brought into a central organisation of Cluniac or Cistercian type, the "religion of the black monks", *Benedict XII did the same in 1339 for the "religion of the regular canons of St Augustine . . . the religion established by Christ's disciples in the early Church". The system of regional chapters and canonical *visits was cited as an indispensable remedy for a regrettable dispersal of manpower. The personal status of the religious was carefully emphasized, notably in their training, and great attention given to the organisation of studies: one subject in twenty had to be sent away to study.

Despite these directives, the canonical world kept Augustinian regularity the less in proportion as its churches were more isolated from the traffic of *benefices and *commendation, especially in times of penury engendered by the wars and *epidemics. Founders of the Gregorian period had been well able to envisage the possible suppression of deserted houses, but as the churches served by a regular community had acquired a legal personality, the very absence of candidates for profession made the disappearance of their ministers difficult. Secularization, sanctioned by the apostolic see, was the only solution, *i.e.* return to the Carolingian usages which, allowing secular canons to keep their own resources, made their upkeep by the community less burdensome. The process is very visible for the rare regular cathedrals, which, being obviously unable to disappear, were all secularized at the start of the 16th century.

C. Dereine, "Chanoines", *DHGE*, 12, 1953, 353-405. – J. Hourlier, "Les Religieux", *L'Age classique, 1140-1378*, *HDIEO*, 10, 1974, 82-87. – *Istituzioni monastiche e istituzioni canonicali in Occidente. 1123-1215*, Milan, 1980. – J. Becquet, *Vie canoniale en France aux X<sup>e</sup>-XII<sup>e</sup> siècles*, London, 1985. – *Le Monde des chanoines (XI<sup>e</sup>-XIV<sup>e</sup> s.)*, *CFan*, 24, 1988.

Jean Becquet

**CANOPY.** The Latin word *discus* meant a disc or plate: it was essentially a light roof borne by columns or suspended, intended to protect and honour a holy place or an important person, to make them conspicuous.

It could also be a *pallium* (English "*pall"), a *baldacchino* (a costly fabric made in Baghdad), in the form of a tester. It was akin to the **ciborium* that was customarily erected above the *altar, but generally instead of being of hard material (wood, stone, marble, metal), it was of fabric.

When the *ciborium* over the altar disappeared, it was often replaced by a canopy, lighter and taking up less room; the altar had to be protected from above against any material accident.

The canopy seems to have served to protect *relics or *reliquaries, the chair of the *bishop or other great men. When the Blessed Sacrament *procession developed (14th c.), it was protected by a mobile canopy that was borne above it. Great men were often treated in the same way for solemn entries.

J. Braun, "Das Altarciborium und der Altarbaldachin", *Der christliche Altar*, Munich, 1924, 185-275.

Guy-Marie Oury

**CANOSSA.** A place in the Apennines in the province of Reggio Emilia, occupying a dominant position over the Po valley, Canossa was the seat of the Attonid dynasty.Seat of a community of *canons (975), it was transformed by Beatrice of Lorraine into a Benedictine monastery (1075) in which lived the monk Donizone, author of the *Vita Mathildis* (1114). Canossa had its hour of glory at the time of the famous meeting on 28 Jan 1077 between Pope *Gregory VII and the Emperor *Henry IV – though this meeting marked no more than a pause in the *Investiture Contest.

After the extinction of the dynasty with the death of Countess *Matilda (1115), Canossa became the seat of a local *castellany and, following factional struggles, was largely destroyed.

A. Fliche, "Canossa", *Cath.*, 2, 1949, 479-480. – P. Golinelli, *Matilde e i Canossa nel cuore del Medioevo*, 3rd ed., Florence, 1996. – H.E.J. Cowdrey, *Pope Gregory VII, 1073-1085*, Oxford, 1998.

Paolo Golinelli

**CANTERBURY.** The Roman town of *Durovernum* was abandoned by *c.*400; it was resettled in about the second half of the 5th c. as the capital of the Jutish kingdom, *Cantwaraburh*. King *Æthelbert's queen Bertha used the nearby church of St Martin even before *Augustine had been sent by Pope *Gregory the Great in 597 on a *mission to convert the people of *England. Recalling the Roman basilicas of *St John Lateran and *St Paul without the Walls, Augustine built or adapted a church which he dedicated to the Saviour (hence subsequently called Christ Church) as his *cathedral and, just outside Canterbury and to the west of St Martin's church, he founded the monastery of Sts Peter and Paul. Augustine was the first *archbishop, and his four successors in this office were Roman monks who had been members of his original mission. Under Augustine and his successors, Canterbury achieved the primacy which it retains to the present day; and its primacy was consolidated later in the 7th c. by the prestige and planning of the great *Theodore of Tarsus, who was archbishop 668-690. Canterbury's enduring strategic significance was that it lay on the route from *London to the Continent; by the same token, it was open to attack by *Vikings from the 8th c. to the 11th. With the end of the kingdom of Kent and the rise of the kingdom of Mercia, the supremacy of the church of Canterbury over the southern *province of England was questioned, though confirmed by papal privilege (802) and a *provincial council (803). The Vikings devastated some of the minster churches that had been set up in Kent in the 7th c. and later, and parts of their estates were acquired by Christ Church. The national revival of the church gained a particular impetus in Canterbury from the archiepiscopate of *Dunstan (960-988); his cathedral was made into a wholly monastic community shortly after his death. Dunstan rededicated the monastery of Sts Peter and Paul to Sts Peter, Paul and Augustine, and it was subsequently known as St Augustine's.

St Augustine's abbey was the *burial place of the Kentish royal dynasty until the later 8th c., and of the first ten archbishops of Canterbury; some of their *tombs were revealed when the *abbey site was excavated in the early 20th century. In 1993 archaeological investigations inside the present Christ Church cathedral revealed the footings of the pre-Conquest church and confirmed the early 12th-c. recollections written by the monk Eadmer: it was bipolar, with both an eastern and a western apse and altars. At the east end were the tombs of the archiepiscopal saints Ælfheah (martyred by the Vikings in 1012) and Oda († 958), to either side of the *altar of Christ, with another altar, containing *relics of St Wilfrid, to their east; at the western end was the *oratory of St Mary, which apparently was used for archiepiscopal masses and for rites that involved the *laity. Oda had restored the church, heightening its walls, but the final form of the west end is likely to have been an early- to mid-11th-c. creation.

It was four years after the Normans had conquered England before they replaced the Anglo-Saxon archbishop of Canterbury, Stigand, with *Lanfranc (1070-1089), a former monk and *prior of the Norman abbey of *Bec and *abbot of Duke *William's *foundation of Saint-Étienne at *Caen. The cathedral church and most of the monastic outbuildings of Christ Church had been destroyed by fire in 1067, and Lanfranc set about rebuilding them on a grand scale, with accommodation planned for over 100 monks; he also commenced the process of separating the monks' community from his own household, with distinct estates being allotted to each. The process of rebuilding continued under his successors *Anselm (1093-1109) and, later, *Theobald (1139-1161), both of whom had also been monks at Bec. The creation of a **scriptorium* and a large and influential *library of patristic and other texts was initiated by Lanfranc but owed more to another ex-monk of Bec, Ernulf of Beauvais, prior from 1096 to 1107.

St Augustine's abbey benefited from a major building campaign under Abbot Scolland or Scotland (1079-1087; formerly a monk of *Mont Saint-Michel) and subsequently. At the same time the liturgical and domestic lives of the monks in both houses were overhauled: a version of the Cluniac Rules was prepared by Lanfranc for the governance of Christ Church and very possibly also of St Augustine's (today commonly called his *Monastic Constitutions*), with major alterations to their calendar and general liturgical practices.

Also at the end of the 11th c., a continental monk, *Goscelin, who spent a few years at St Augustine's abbey, prepared accounts of some of the principal saints of whom there were relics there. At Christ Church, two precentors were active hagiographers: Osbern († *c.*1093) and Eadmer (*c.*1060-*c.*1130). Osbern was an Englishman, and Lanfranc early in his archiepiscopate sent him to Bec for about two years as a disciplinary measure: he wrote *Vitae* of Dunstan and Ælfheah (Alphege). Eadmer, of a Canterbury family, spent much of his life as the companion of Archbishops Anselm and Ralph d'Escures (1114-1122), and wrote a *biography of the former, while he later wrote *Vitae* of Bregowine, Dunstan, Oda, *Oswald, *Audoin and Wilfrid.

But the entire future history of Canterbury was to be dominated by the murder of Archbishop *Thomas Becket on 29 Dec 1170, before the altar of St Benedict in his own cathedral, by four knights of *Henry II. Just one *secular cleric was with him when he died; his relations with the monastic community had not been close. But the *miracles attributed to him from very soon after his death transformed his cathedral into a centre of *pilgrimage on an international scale, while the fortuitous destruction of the choir by fire in 1174 gave the monastic community the opportunity to rebuild the choir. First under a French architect, William of Sens, and then under the more innovative William the Englishman, the choir was reconstructed in the *Gothic style (1174-1183; the corona to its east was completed in *c.*1200). In both the main and clerestory windows, a major programme of *stained glass was effected, with *typological scenes of the life of Christ, Saints' Lives and, a little later, scenes of Becket's miracles. In 1220 Becket's remains were translated to a new shrine in the chapel of the Holy Trinity to the east of the choir – an occasion marked by the first of the 50-year

Jubilees of St Thomas. The pilgrims' offerings this year totalled the vast sum of 1142 pounds.

The first half of the 13th c. was marked by uneasy relations between the monks of Christ Church and their archbishop, especially in the time of *Edmund Rich (archbishop 1233-1240; canonized 1246), when Prior John Chetham was forced to resign and enter the *Carthusian Order (1238) and all the brethren were *excommunicated. Thereafter, the cathedral community enjoyed a quieter prosperity, with some capable priors – notably Henry of Eastry (1285-1331) and Thomas Chillenden (1391-1411), both men of a legal cast of mind but also active as builders; most of the major work of rebuilding the nave, probably to the designs of Henry Yevele, took place during the latter's priorate.

Archiepiscopal involvement was reduced, as the see was ruled from Lambeth Palace, across the Thames from the royal *palace of Westminster, or from one of the archbishop's other residences. Archiepiscopal appointments to monastic offices became a mere formality. Intellectually the most distinguished prior of the late Middle Ages was William Sellyng or Tyll (1472-1494), who made three long visits to Italy, became fluent in Greek, and made Christ Church a centre for the dissemination of Italianate learning in England. In 1540 the priory was suppressed and most of the monks pensioned off; a year later the 28 remaining monks were appointed *canons or minor canons of a refounded cathedral establishment.

St Augustine's abbey in the late medieval period is best known for its historical writing, especially the *chronicles compiled by William Thorne and Thomas of Elmham. The abbey was suppressed in 1538, some of its buildings being adapted as a royal palace.

The archbishop of Canterbury was head of the province of Canterbury, which extended over central and southern England (though all *Great Britain and *Ireland were sometimes claimed), and which in the late 11th and 12th cc. claimed precedence over the northern province of *York with varying degrees of success; a compromise finally ended the wrangling in 1353. During archiepiscopal vacancies, the spiritual jurisdiction of the province was exercised by Christ Church Cathedral Priory: these *sede vacante* powers greatly enhanced its political standing even though they were not particularly lucrative. The archbishop of Canterbury was also head of the *diocese of Canterbury, which covered eastern and part of central Kent; from the 12th c. onwards, he ran this through the *archdeacon of Canterbury, making the latter office peculiarly important.

J. W. Legg (ed.), W. H. St J. Hope (ed.), *Inventories of Christchurch, Canterbury*, London, 1902. – *The Monastic Constitutions of Lanfranc*, D. Knowles (ed.), London, 1951.

C. S. Phillips, *Canterbury Cathedral in the Middle Ages*, London, 1949. – C. R. Dodwell, *The Canterbury School of Illumination, 1066-1200*, Cambridge, 1954. – M. H. Caviness, *The Early Stained Glass of Canterbury Cathedral, circa 1175-1220*, Princeton (NJ), 1977. – M. H. Caviness, *The Windows of Christ Church Cathedral, Canterbury*, London, 1981, "Corpus Vitrearum Medii Aevi. Great Britain", 2. – *Medieval Art and Architecture at Canterbury before 1200*, N. Coldstream (ed.), P. Draper (ed.), London, 1982. – N. P. Brooks, *The Early History of the Church of Canterbury*, Leicester, 1984. – M. Sparks, *St Augustine's Abbey, Canterbury, Kent*, London, 1988. – D. Kahn, *Canterbury Cathedral and its Romanesque Sculpture*, London, 1991. – B. Bischoff, M. Lapidge, *Biblical Commentaries from the Canterbury School of Theodore and Hadrian*, Cambridge, 1994. – P. Collinson, N. L. Ramsay, M. Sparks, *A History of Canterbury Cathedral*, Oxford, 1995. – K. Blockley et al., *Canterbury Cathedral Nave*, Canterbury, 1997.

Nigel Ramsay

*Scenes from the life of Thomas Becket.* Stained glass at Christ Church, Canterbury, 12th-13th c.

**CANTOR.** From the 4th c., the Syrian collection of the *Apostolic Constitutions* mentions psalmists or cantors; they are considered as lower ministers, on the same level as lectors, doorkeepers, *acolytes and exorcists. But it was in *Syria that they formed a special grade of the hierarchy. In the *Byzantine liturgy, their position is less clear. In the West, the *Statuta ecclesiae antiqua* (Gaul) give a place to cantors in the Church organisation, under the inspiration of Eastern canons; these rules influenced later *liturgical books, but they do not rigorously reflect lived reality.

By contrast, *Rome gave an important place to the **schola cantorum*, whose origins are little known but whose place in the celebration is very marked, as witness, *e.g.*, the arrangement of the choir of the Romanesque church of San Clemente (*cancelli* and ambos dating from the 12th c.).

Elsewhere in the West, the cantor and his assistants had an important role in canonical and monastic communities. They ensured the good performance of the chants of the *office and the *mass, and the performance of ceremonies in general. The precantor was in fact the old master of ceremonies. He wore the cope and his badge was the cantor's baton which sometimes took the form of a *tau, but which was traditionally surmounted by a small statue of the church's patron saint.

M. Andrieu, "Les ordres mineurs dans l'ancien rite romain", *RSR*, 5, 1925, 233-239. – E. Josi, "Lectores, schola cantorum", *EL*, 44, 1930, 282-290.

Guy-Marie Oury

**CAPETIANS (987-1328).** The name of the third dynasty to reign over *France comes from the *cappa* (*cloak) of St *Martin of Tours, in the keeping of Hugh Capet. The dynasty reigned for just over three centuries. In a direct line succeeded Hugh Capet (987-996), Robert II the Pious (996-1031), Henry I (1031-1060), *Philip I (1060-1108), *Louis VI (1108-1137), *Louis VII (1137-1180), *Philip II Augustus (1180-1223), *Louis VIII (1223-1226), St *Louis IX (1226-1270), *Philip III the Bold (1270-1285), *Philip IV the Fair (1285-1314), then his three sons Louis X the Stubborn (le Hutin) (1314-1316), *Philip V the Tall (1316-1322) and Charles IV the Fair (1322-1328).

Probably of Saxon origin, the Capetians entered history in the 9th c. with Robert the Strong who made his name against the *Vikings. The accession of Hugh Capet came at the end of a troubled century in which Capetians and *Carolingians had alternated on the throne. Robert's two sons and his son-in-law Rudolf of Burgundy had reigned over the *Franks in place of under-age or absent Carolingians. Hugh was elected in preference to Charles of Lower Lorraine as more capable and more acceptable to all. Some spoke of usurpation, but it was quickly forgotten. Nevertheless it became necessary at the start of the 13th c. to invent a filiation between Carolingians and Capetians to conceal this awkward hiatus (*reditus regni ad stirpem Karoli*). The Capetians possessed only a minute domain between *Paris and *Orléans and had powerful rivals. But they could count on the Church, controlled a score of *bishoprics and plenty of *abbeys and had the support of *Cluny and the papacy. The prestige of anointed royalty remained great, even if it brought few concrete powers. At first, the dynasty was preoccupied mainly with surviving.

Hardly was he anointed when Hugh associated his son Robert with himself on the pretext of an expedition. Association of the heir on the throne and his *consecration in his father's lifetime were rituals until the time of Philip Augustus who was able to dispense with them, the inheritance being then no longer contested. But that supposed luck: always, for ten generations, to have a grown-up and capable son. The Capetians had them and sometimes forced the matter by multiplying hasty remarriages to produce the necessary heir. The birth of Philip Augustus was presented as a *miracle. Many kings reigned for long periods, which allowed minorities to be avoided.

However, if the Capetians skilfully made play with consecration in order to institute a hereditary royal succession to the eldest male, we need not believe that they thought of the kingdom differently from other princes. Cadets received their portions and important appanages, like the brothers of St Louis. The idea that the blood of *kings merited rules of its own does not really date before the 1300s. In 1316, for the first time, Louis X left only a small daughter of legitimate ancestry. Circumstances made Philip V king. *Women could not mount the throne, the blood of kings was definitively different. The greatest success of the Capetians was to have involuntarily, down the generations, constituted a dynasty and defined clear rules of succession to the throne.

E.M. Hallam, *Capetian France 987-1328*, London, 1980. – A.W. Lewis, *Royal Succession in Capetian France*, Cambridge (MA), 1981. – P. Contamine, "Le Royaume de France ne peut tomber en fille. Fondements, formulation et implications d'une théorie politique", *Perspectives médiévales*, 13, 1987, 67-81. – E.A.R. Brown, *The Monarchy of Capetian France and Royal Ceremonial*, London, 1991. – *Le Roi de France et son royaume autour de l'an mil. Colloque Hugues Capet, Auxerre, 1987*, Paris, 1992. – J. Krynen, *L'Empire du roi*, Paris, 1993.

Colette Beaune

**CAPITAL, CAPITALISM.** Widely diffused from the 18th c. by political economy and then, after the mid 19th c., by social philosophy and militant discourse, the terms "capital" and "capitalism" have entered the historical vocabulary to describe and interpret fundamental structures of contemporary economies and societies.

Their retrospective use has been the object of a debate between medievalists and modernists ever since W. Sombart's celebrated thesis on the origins of capitalism: the premonitory symptoms of this phenomenon can be sought in the long term, it can also be discovered as constitutive of all organisation of social life. The use of the terms "capital", "capitalism" can be justified as an analogical convenience of vocabulary, or as the use of a tool adequate to analyse relations of production and the social relations that flow from them in any form of human society.

The term "capital" was coined in the 17th c. to designate *property and *wealth, from an older adjective indicating "that which is at the head" (*caput*), *i.e.* first. If we admit that no wealth can be produced without the help of pre-existing wealth, we will concur with the idea that capital results from previous work: it is accumulated work.

Between the 10th and 13th cc., within a system called "*feudal" whose structures it would gradually ruin, profit played a growing role and mobilized wealth. On the theme "new wealth, or son of wealth?" the origin of the capital invested in enterprise is still being discussed, and the part taken in the revival of mobility of property by mining investment has undoubtedly been underestimated: from the late 12th c., this considerably increased the mass of coinable *metal in circulation. But it is unanimously agreed that the concentration of productive capital was an essentially urban and mercantile phenomenon.

It was in the towns of *Italy that, thanks to the quality and abundance of surviving written sources, historians first established the "laboratory" where they could observe capitalist exploitation: the setting up of business societies, urban *rent, the power of credit on household life and on public life were accompanied by a control exercised by a narrow group over the salaried work of the greater number.

Proudhon stressed the alienating effects of capitalism, defining it as "an economic and social regime in which capital, the source of revenue, does not generally belong to those who put it to work by their *labour". From this point of view can be interpreted the contrasts of medieval society and the *violence that flowed from this in the *towns and countryside of the West. However, though the spirit of profit permeated the old society of orders, the power of the models and ultimate ends proposed by the Church put a brake on the power of *money, even among the richest. All the same, capitalism was far from having invaded every sector of economic life, though the businessmen of the Middle Ages, international *merchants, financiers of princes and towns, held a growing place in society.

G. Fourquin, *Histoire économique de l'Occident médiéval*, Paris, 1969 (collection "U"). – R. Fossier, *La Société médiévale*, Paris, 1991 (collection "U"). – C. Dyer, "Were there any capitalists in fifteenth-century England?", *Enterprise and individuals in fifteenth-century England*, J. Kermode (ed.), Stroud, 1991, 1-24.

Philippe Braunstein

**CAPITAL SINS.** When the popular expression "capital sins" appeared in the 1270s, it designated seven terms that were the same as the "vices" of the theologians. They were pride, envy, anger, accidie, avarice, gluttony and lust. This list of *vices went back to *Gregory the Great († 604) [*Moralia in Job*, XXI, 87]. It owed its diffusion to the influence of *Peter Lombard's *Book of *Sentences* (1139) and its modifications to *Hugh of Saint-Victor, who also invented the term "capital" vices (1141).

Totally absent from theological or learned writings throughout the Middle Ages, the expression "capital sins" was used only in short works for simple priests and in didactic, narrative or poetic literature. It was the consequence of the choice made in 1215 to order *confession by the framework of the vices, a concept unknown to the majority of priests as well as to their flocks. By the vices, theologians distinguished seven great involuntary tendencies, outcome of original sin, that led men to sin consciously and repeatedly. From each vice arose *sins linked to the same end. Gregory had also fixed their list. Neglecting the involuntary aspect of the vices, penitential confession concerned only the actual sins that flowed from them. Since the interrogation of the faithful was based on a timeless model of the characteristic manifestations of each vice, the technicians of confession, especially the *mendicants, reworked them and designated new sins in order to respond better to the mission of catechesis to reform morals. This was what was taught by **summae* and *Confessors' Manuals. Each vice thus quickly acquired a variable sinful content, adapted to audiences and times.

The appearance of the expression "capital sins" in 1270 confirmed this updating. When a new order of recital of the vices, supported by the mnemotechnic term SALIGIA – forged with the first letter of each of the names *superbia*, *avaricia*, *luxuria*, *ira*, *gula*, *invidia*, **acedia* – arose in the 1270s, it set out in reality a new hierarchy of sins based on the gravest of the social disorders denounced by *clerics. The replacement in the late 14th c. of "acedia" by "sloth" belonged to the same movement of adaptation. This order of recital, which distorted the original meaning of the system of vices, was generalized in numerous learned works even while their authors rejected the term "capital sins". Did they understand this expression in terms of capital punishment, suggesting the false idea that all the sins springing from a vice are mortal, a theory opposed by *Thomas Aquinas in his *De malo*? Was it because the disappearance of the word "vice" hid the influence of original sin? Yet the totally erroneous designation of seven mortal ("deadly") or criminal sins lasted throughout this period. This was the most elementary level of the Church's teaching, since it addressed the most ignorant priests as well as *children. It is present especially in English literary texts. When laymen in the late 14th c. began to take pleasure in the seven names of the capital sins in order to judge, censure or accuse others, this at least proved that they knew how to recite them.

Jean Gerson, "Examen de conscience selon les sept péchés capitaux", and "A.B.C. des simples gens ou Alphabetum puerorum", *Oeuvres complètes*, 7, 1, P. Glorieux (ed.), Paris, Tournai, 1966, 393 f. and 154 f. – Thomas de Aquino, *Q. D. De malo*, Rome-Paris, 1982, Q. 8 a. 1, Q. 9 a. 2 ("Leonine edition", 23). M. W. Bloomfield, *The Seven Deadly Sins. An introduction to the history of a religious concept, with special reference to Medieval English Literature*, East Lansing (MI), 1952. – P. Michaud-Quantin, "Sommes de casuistique et Manuels de confession au Moyen Âge (XII^e-XVI^e siècle)", *AMNam*, 13, 1962. – S. Wenzel, *The Sin of Sloth: Acedia in Medieval Thought and Literature*, Chapel Hill (NC), 1967. – M. Vincent-Cassy, "L'Envie au Moyen Âge", *Annales*, 1980, 253-271. – A. Solignac, "Péchés capitaux", *DSp*, 12, 1, 1984, 853-862.

Mireille Vincent-Cassy

***CAPITULA EPISCOPORUM.*** These were the episcopal decisions intended for the clergy of the parish churches. Often ill known, they are nevertheless part, like the *councils and *capitularies, of Carolingian legislation. They appear under the form of simple, precise prescriptions intended to recall the main essentials of priestly *ministry and clerical life. Among the most iportant are the *capitula* of *Theodulf of Orléans, Raoul of Bourges, Gerbald of Liège, Roger of Trier and Herard of Tours. These little collections theoretically remained in force until the end of the 13th century. One of them, the last to be written (*Admonitio synodalis*), would be included in the synodal liturgy and transcribed until the 13th century.

*Capitula episcoporum*, 1, P. Brommer (ed.), 1984 ("MGH.F"; with a list of manuscripts and old editions on pp. IX-X). – *Capitula episcoporum*, 2, R. Pokorny (ed.), M. Stratmann (ed.), 1995 ("MGH.F"). – *Capitula episcoporum*, 3, R. Pokorny (ed.), 1995 ("MGH.F"). – *Ordines de concilio celebrando*, H. Schneider (ed.), 1996 ("MGH.F").

Joseph Avril

**CAPITULARIES.** Capitularies were legislative acts promulgated after the Carolingian general assemblies that met every year. Before the high officials, dukes, *counts, *bishops, *abbots and vassals, the *king submitted questions that were to allow the reform of the kingdom. *Clerics on one side, *laity on the other gave their advice and the replies were formulated in a series of articles named "chapters" (*capitula*) that together formed the capitulary. The king presented them orally, then promulgated them in writing so that his officials should have a sort of memorandum. There are some 200 capitularies of the Carolingian period. In 789, after a general assembly, a capitulary of 82 articles called *Admonitio generalis* was promulgated. It gave a programme of administrative and religious reforms to bishops, priests, clerics and everyone. Chapter 72 was on the teaching of *children in *schools; the final chapter, 82, was a sort of sketch of a *sermon that the priest had to preach. Capitularies subsequently multiplied. It has been reckoned that there were three important capitularies before *Charlemagne's *coronation in 800 and 17 between 800 and 814.

Different sorts of capitularies are distinguished. There were capitularies entrusted to **missi* (*capitula missorum*), which the *missi* had to reread and apply in the territory entrusted to them. Others corrected old laws (*capitula legibus addenda*), supplementing or modifying existing laws like the Salic law, the Bavarian law in 801 or the Ripuarian law in 803. There were capitularies concerned with general questions (*capitula per se scribenda*); thus the capitulary *De villis*, promulgated between 770 and 800, reformed the administration of the royal *estates. This capitulary in 70 chapters looked at everything: upkeep of buildings, furnishing of rooms, womens' workshops, exploitation of woods, making of *wine, preparation of salted *foods, down to the plants that the ruler wanted to see cultivated in kitchen *gardens and orchards. Another series was devoted to ecclesiastical affairs (*capitula ecclesiastica*). Finally, capitularies were promulgated for *Italy by Pippin, king of Italy, between 782 and 813.

Charlemagne's successors continued this legislative work. Ecclesiastical capitularies multiplied under *Louis the Pious. The capitulary of Quierzy promulgated by *Charles the Bald before his departure for Italy in 877 is famous. The last capitularies date from 884 in the time of Carloman.

In the reign of Louis the Pious, the capitularies were grouped together in collections. In 827, Abbot Ansegisus of *Saint-Wandrille edited the existing capitularies in four books. In the mid 9th c., in order to defend Church property, attempts were made to fabricate false capitularies. Thus a collection attributed to Benedict the Levite contains authentic and apocryphal texts. It was part of the collection of False Isidorians fabricated in *c.*850 either at *Le Mans or at *Reims.

F.L. Ganshof, *Recherches sur les capitulaires*, Paris, 1958. – C. de Clercq, *Neuf capitulaires de Charlemagne concernant son oeuvre réformatrice par les "missi"*, Milan, 1968. – H.R. Loyn, J. Percival, *The Reign of Charlemagne: Documents on Carolingian Government and Administration*, New York, 1975. – R. McKitterick, *The Carolingians and the Written Word*, Cambridge, 1989.

Pierre Riché

**CAPITULATIONS, ELECTORAL.** From the 12th c., at episcopal elections, certain colleges of *canons imposed a "capitulation" on the elect, obliging him to follow a certain policy and renounce certain rights. This custom was especially frequent in the lands of the *Empire, in *Germany, where seignorial interests were closely linked with those of the church authorities. The first case known in Germany dates from 1216 (*Hildesheim). In 1204 *Innocent III imposed a *penance on the bishop of Todi for having accepted commitments on *oath before his *election. But the case of Todi was exceptional for *Italy. In *France too, the papacy's power of intervention in the election of *bishops and the regalian right of the sovereign were such as to curb the *chapters' freedom of negotiation.

The system of capitulations ended by affecting the election of the supreme pontiff. On 24 Dec 1350, *Clement VI borrowed 16,000 florins from the college of *cardinals. This was the first time the papacy had come into such a position of dependence on the cardinals. On Clement VI's death, the college of cardinals even managed to get all its members to sign a capitulation. The newly-elect would commit himself to curb *nepotism; the number of cardinals, fixed at 16, could only be brought up to 20 with the consent of at least two thirds of the cardinals; the *consistory's right to freedom of expression was guaranteed; the constitutions of *Gregory IX (1234) and *Nicholas IV (1289), concerning the alienation of Church property and the beneficial policy of the papacy, would be confirmed; the pope's nephews were excluded from the office of marshal of the *Curia and the rectorates of the Papal States; transfers of *tenths to a lay ruler or to the *Camera could not be done without the approval of two thirds of the cardinals. The demands were thus of a financial nature; they in no way aimed at any sharing of the *pope's power. All the cardinals present at the *conclave took the oath; but some of them, including Stephen Aubert, the future *Innocent VI, did so under reservation of the legal *validity of the action. Six months after his election, Innocent VI, after having taken the cardinals' advice, declared this capitulation illegitimate and incompatible with the pope's "plenitude of powers". The capitulations of 1394, 1404 and 1406 were no longer of a financial nature: they obliged the elect to work for the unity of the Church.

The system of capitulations was used in 1519 at the election of the Emperor Charles V. Such a contract later became traditional. It served to guarantee the "freedom" of the German States against imperial power.

J. Lulvès, "Die Machtbestrebungen des Kardinalats bis zur Aufstellung der ersten päpstlichen Wahlkapitulationen", *QFIAB*, 13, 1910, 73-102. – *Sachwörterbuch zur deutschen Geschichte*, Munich, 1958, 1357.

Agostino Paravicini Bagliani

**CAPPADOCIA.** Cappadocia was the central region of the Anatolian plateau. Rich and populous, at the heart of the Roman and then *Byzantine Empire, it suffered Persian and Arab invasions. From 863, the Byzantine reconquest brought peace and prosperity; its apogee was the 10th and 11th cc., up to the arrival of the *Turks. The rebirth of Turkish Anatolia in the 13th c. also affected the Christian communities, which were endangered in the *Ottoman period, until the 17th century.

Converted early, Cappadocia had numerous Christians in the 2nd century. *Origen taught and stayed at Caesarea (235-238). Gregory, the Illuminator of *Armenia, was enthroned there in 314. In 370, the bishopric of Caesarea had 50 **chorepiscopi* and the Church of Cappadocia was made famous by Basil the Great, his brother Gregory of Nyssa and his friend Gregory Nazianzen.

Traditional cults persisted, like that of celestial Zeus at Venasa (modern Avanos, 8 km from Göreme). Religious syncretism explains heresies, including a popular iconoclasm condemned again in *c.*900 by Aretas of Caesarea.

Some protobyzantine and medieval ruins remain, but very few in comparison with rock-cut monuments. The complexity of the geography favoured *eremitism, but *coenobitism, preached by Basil and Theodosius, was early. Monasteries, situated in or near villages, were part of the village landscape.

The evidence of the rock-cut monuments is important because of their abundance and continuity (6th-13th cc.). Though the chronology of the paintings has no support from dated inscriptions before the 10th c., the earliest churches, *iconoclast and pre-iconoclast, are identifiable by their programme, iconography and ornamentation, to which equivalents can be found in the Mediterranean and transcaucasian art of the early Middle Ages.

This material allows us to judge the evolution of the cult of the Cross and of *images. It fills the gaps in *Byzantine art, *e.g.* for the blanket decoration of the 7th and 8th cc., Greco-oriental in style, and for many 10th-c. formulae, prototypes or abortive attempts at later imagery (Virgin of tenderness, *Dormition, Prophetic visions, *Last Judgment, appearance of the archangel *Michael to Joshua, St Eustace's vision of the cross between the antlers of a stag, etc.). Finally, the decoration of the New Church of Tokali (950-963) can be considered the masterpiece of the mural *painting of the time. Its foundation was due to the Phocas, a powerful family that ascended the throne in the person of Nicephorus (963-969), whose victories over the Arabs were commemorated 3 kilometres from there, in the Dovecote of Çavuşin.

N. Thierry, M. Thierry, *Nouvelles Églises rupestres de Cappadoce. Région du Hasan dagi*, Paris, 1963. – F. Hild, M. Restle, *Kappadokien*, *TIB*, 2, Vienna, 1981. – "La Cappadoce aux surprenantes richesses", and "L'Art religieux de la Cappadoce", *Histoire et Archéologie, Les Dossiers*, 63, Paris, 1982; *ibid.*, 121, 1987. – N. Thierry, *Haut Moyen Âge en Cappadoce. Les églises de la région de Çavusin*, Paris, 1983, 1994. – C. Jolivet-Levy, *Les Églises byzantines de Cappadoce: Le programme iconographique de l'abside*, Paris, 1991.

Nicole Thierry

**CAPREOLUS (died 1444).** John Capreolus, a *Dominican from the Rouergue, studied at *Paris in 1407-1411. Received as master of theology, he was appointed regent at the *studium generale* of *Toulouse; he ended his career at the convent of Rodez (1426-1444). His four *Libri defensionum theologiae divi doctoris Thomae de Aquino in libris Sententiarum* are a systematic defence of Thomism against all the criticisms made against it since the early 14th century. In this, Capreolus anticipated the Italian Thomist school of the 16th c., notably Cardinal Cajetan (1468-1534).

*Johannis Capreoli Defensiones Theologiae Divi Thomae Aquinatis*, C. Paban (ed.), T. Pègues (ed.), Frankfurt am Main, 1967 (7 vol.).

M. Grabmann, "Johannes Capreolus o.p., der *Princeps Thomistarum* (gestorben 1444) und seine Stellung in der Geschichte der Thomistischen Schule", *Mittelalterliches Geistesleben*, 3, Munich, 1956, 370-410. – T. Kaeppeli, *SOPMA*, 2, 1975, 395.

Jacques Verger

***CAPUCIATI* OF LE PUY.** In 1182, a group of laymen established themselves into a militia under the authority of the bishop of *Le Puy-en-Velay, to restore peace to a region deprived of a prince since the 10th c. and infested with **routiers*. Its members bore a white hooded garment, decorated with an image of the Virgin and Child with the inscription "*Agnus Dei qui tollis peccata mundi, dona nobis pacem*". Last avatar of the peace movements active at Le Puy since the council of 994, after a first success the rising turned into a *revolt against the *seigneurs banaux*; it was soon brought down by the king allied to the feudal barons. The militia was then replaced by a Marian *confraternity whose pious and moral obligations recall those of *penitents.

G. G. Meerssseman, *Ordo fraternitatis, confraternite e pietà dei laici nel medioevo*, Rome, 1977, 196-201.

Catherine Vincent

**CARCASSONNE.** The Old City that overlooks the town of Carcassonne is one of the finest groups of medieval *architecture in Europe. *Oppidum* of the Volcae Tectosages, then a Roman colony under the name of Julia Carcaso from the 1st c. BC, the town was at first a centre of commercial exchange on the road between the Mediterranean and *Aquitaine. Its military vocation took over at the time of the barbarian *invasions. In the 4th c. the place was fortified. Its first wall – Roman and not Visigothic as romantic historiography was pleased to imagine – was provided with 38 towers, of which some 20 still exist.

Despite the successive occupations of *Visigoths (6th-7th cc.) and Arabs (8th c.), the early Middle Ages hardly altered the Romanized substratum of the region, any more than it left any architectural evidence at Carcassonne. After a first comital dynasty of *Carolingian origin, from the late 11th c. the Viscounts Trencavel united in their own hands Carcassonne, Béziers, *Albi and Razès: the vast viscountcy thus created was at the centre of the rivalries between the counties of *Toulouse and *Barcelona, which would mark its history throughout the 12th century.

Carcassonne was the seat of a *bishopric from *c.*570, and the Romanesque *cathedral of Saint-Nazaire had been built within its walls. In 1167 the *Cathar communities of the Carcassès were sufficiently numerous and tolerated by the comital authorities to organise themselves into a Church, with an ordained bishop. In August 1209 the stronghold was taken by the crusading army. Its young viscount, Raymond Roger Trencavel, whom the *pope had described as a protector of the *heretics, died in a dungeon. After the failure of the attempt by *Simon and Amaury de Montfort to establish a new dynasty, the crusade of *Louis VIII burned the Cathar bishop of Carcassès, Pierre Isarn, at Caunes-Minervois in 1226 and led to the attachment of the Trencavel viscountcies to France in 1229: Carcassonne became the capital of a **sénéchaussée* and the royal administration gave the *cité* its definitive appearance, encircled at that time with a second wall.

After Raymond Trencavel's attempt to retake the town in 1240, the suburbs, too exposed, were destroyed, and from the middle of the century a **bastide* of repopulation was built on the other side of the Aude and provided with a consulate. This Lower Town became a prosperous centre of drapery, while the Upper *Cité*, around its Gothic-choired cathedral, remained the episcopal see and inquisitorial seat. Within its walls, it kept its military and political function.

Under *Philip the Fair, the *rage carcassonnaise*, a popular *revolt against the Dominican *Inquisition, supported by the Franciscan *Bernard Délicieux, ended tragically. Despite its burning by the *Black Prince in 1355, the ravages of the plague, the revolt of the Tuchins in 1382 and the decline of its cloth industry, by the end of the *Hundred Years' War the Lower Town of Carcassonne had finally taken the lead, politically and economically, from the Old *Cité* on the heights.

*Histoire de Carcassonne*, P. Wolff (dir.), Toulouse, 1984, 43-107. – J. Blanc *et al.*, *La Cité de Carcassonne, des pierres et des hommes*, Paris, 1999.

Anne Brenon

**CARDINAL.** Three groups of cardinals existed at *Rome. First the cardinal-bishops (*episcopi cardinales*), present at Roman *synods before the middle of the 11th c., titulars first of seven, then of six *dioceses situated in the immediate neighbourhood of Rome: Ostia, Albano, Palestrina, Porto, Silva Candida, Gabii (later Labicum, then *Tusculum) and Velletri (later Sabina). Their main task was to perform, once a week each, a liturgical service at the basilica of *St John Lateran. The cardinal-priests (*presbyteri cardinales*), responsible for the titular churches attested at Rome since the 4th c., were so called because they lent their liturgical services to the four patriarchal basilicas of *St Peter's (Vatican), St Lawrence Without the Walls, *St Paul's Without the Walls and *Santa Maria Maggiore. Around 1100, they numbered seven for each *basilica, making a total of 28. The cardinal-deacons (*diaconi cardinales*) – divided into seven palatine *deacons and 12 regional deacons – read the Gospel at the Lateran and in the stational churches of Rome. The seven palatine deacons were descended from the seven earliest regional deacons, who originally performed charitable duties in the seven regions of Rome. The 12 regional deacons are attested from the mid 10th c., following the new subdivision of Rome into 12 regions. The number of cardinal-deacons was fixed in *c.*1100 at 18.

On the origin of the term *cardinalis* itself, opinions are divided. *Cardinalis* seems, according to some (M. Andrieu, S. Kuttner), to be an attribute given to *bishops, priests and deacons who lent their service to a foreign church for which they had not been consecrated, but in which they had been incardinated. On the other hand, this term might have designated all those who offered their service to the episcopal church (C. G. Fürst). This last interpretation is based on the fact that, up to the 11th c., the cardinal *clerics present in the many dioceses of Italy, France, Germany and England took part in liturgical worship alongside the bishop. The title of *cardinalis* would hence refer to their belonging to the cathedral clergy.

A fundamental evolution took place from the mid 11th c., from

Choir of Carcassonne cathedral, 1270-1320.

which time the cardinals of the reforming papacy were at the disposal of the *pope, *cardo et caput* of the universal Church. Between *Leo IX (1049-1054) and *Paschal II (1099-1118), the three groups of cardinals, representing the clergy of the city of Rome and the *suburbicarian bishoprics, became the main instrument of government of the universal Church.

Leo IX decided soon after his election to appoint persons he could trust as cardinal-bishops. From this pontificate and for half a century, the cardinal-bishops (whom some sources call "Lateran bishops") were the most important group in the pope's immediate entourage. They abandoned the weekly liturgical service at the Lateran to take an active part in the government of the Church.

In April 1059 *Nicholas II promulgated a decree concerning the *election of the pope, which laid down a procedure in three phases: the cardinal-bishops would begin the discussion and later bring in the cardinal-priests, while the rest of the clergy and the people would acclaim. In case of fundamental limitation of freedom of election by the Romans, the papal election could take place outside the *Urbs*. The decree of 1059, which likened the cardinal-bishops to *metropolitans, to whom tradition acknowledged a right of interference in the election of the bishop, accorded the cardinals alone the exclusive right to elect the pope.

The decree of 1059 established a real pre-eminence of the cardinal-bishops. But the participation of the cardinal-priests was already complete by the time of the election of Paschal II (1099). The cardinal-deacons appear in the signatures to pontifical privileges from 1095. From the early 12th c., the college of cardinals was definitively organised into three groups. At the time of the *schism of 1130, their belonging to different ranks posed no problem. Between 1123 and 1153, the position of cardinal underwent considerable developments. Already under *Calixtus II (1119-1124), the cardinals had become the pope's privileged collaborators in the sphere of the administration of justice. The signing by cardinals of pontifical privileges, which originally bore only the signature of the pope, became the rule under the pontificates of Honorius II and *Innocent II: this reflected an active participation of the cardinals in the government of the universal Church. The old liturgical functions of the cardinals were progressively transferred to the papal *chapel. From now on the cardinals took on judicial and governmental responsibilities. The *consistory, already attested under *Urban II (1088-1099), met regularly from the pontificate of Innocent II (1130-1143). It replaced the former synod of the clergy of Rome.

In papal letters, the participation of the cardinals in decisions taken by the pope in consistory is manifested by the use of the formulae "*de communi fratrum nostrorum consilio*", "*de fratrum nostrorum consilio et voluntate commune*" and other analogous ones. Frequent from the 12th c., these became altogether traditional in the next century.

The cardinals had not the right to convene a *council: this is stated by Gratian's **Decretum*, then by the principal *canonists (*John Teutonicus, *Huguccio). This right belonged to the pope alone.

Was the pope obliged to consult the cardinals? Some canonists claimed that a pope could not promulgate a general law for the universal Church without the cardinals; for others, recourse to the cardinals was not obligatory. The question was put again, in these terms, in the early 14th century.

*Innocent III (1198-1216) had defined the cardinals as being the *membra capitis*, the *membra magna ecclesiae romanae*. He applied to the cardinals for the first time a metaphor of Pauline origin (Eph 5, 30), appropriating the corporative ideas of his time. This metaphor became traditional from the mid 13th century. According to *Hostiensis († 1271), the universal Church was a body whose "general" head was the pope, while the cardinals were its "particular" members. The cardinals were *pars corporis domini papae*. This image, which the canonists preferred because it was derived from the *Code of Justinian (9, 8, 5) which defined the Roman senators in an analogous way, emphasized the ecclesiological intimacy between pope and cardinals: together, they constituted the universal Roman Church. The metaphor of the body implied recognition of the cardinals' right to participate in the jurisdictional power of the head of the Church, but also their subordination to the supreme power of the pope.

The authority of the cardinals during the vacancy of the apostolic see was clarified in the course of the 13th century. Many canonists (Huguccio, John Teutonicus, Bartholomew of Brescia) acknowledged extensive powers for the cardinals during the vacancy of the apostolic see. Because the pope's authority was exercised in agreement with the cardinals, during the vacancy of the Roman Church that authority could only be exercised by the cardinals, who could *e.g.* depose a bishop.

Though generally favourable to the extended powers of the cardinals, Hostiensis was more restrictive concerning their rights during a vacancy. The cardinals could only take decisions "in case of grave necessity and immediate danger". The "corporative" image of the Church limited their actual powers. Again according to Hostiensis, the pope's death made the Church acephalous: the cardinals, though called to act in place of the *caput*, were not the head itself.

S. Kuttner, "Cardinalis: the History of a Canonical Concept", *Tr.*, 3, 1945, 129 f. – M. Andrieu, "L'origine du titre de cardinal dans l'Église romaine", *Miscellanea G. Mercati*, Vatican, 1946, 113-114. – J. Leclercq, "'Pars corporis papae'. Le sacré collège dans l'ecclésiologie médiévale", *L'Homme devant Dieu. Mélanges offerts au Père H. de Lubac*, 2, Paris, 1964, 183-198. – C. G. Fürst, *Cardinalis: Prolegomena zu einer Rechtsgeschichte des römischen Kardinalskollegiums*, Munich, 1967. – A. Alberigo, *Cardinalato e collegialità. Studi sull'ecclesiologia tra l'XI e il XIV secolo*, Florence, 1969. – M. Dykmans, "Les pouvoirs des cardinaux pendant la vacance du Saint-Siège d'après un nouveau manuscrit de Jacques Stefaneschi", *ASRSP*, 104, 1981, 119-145. – D. Jasper, *Das Papstwahldekret von 1059. Überlieferung und Textgestalt*, Sigmaringen, 1986, 98-119. – A. Paravicini Bagliani, *HChr*, 5, 1993.

Agostino Paravicini Bagliani

**CARLISLE.** In the Roman period *Luguvallium* had been the rear base of Hadrian's wall. Devastated by the Danes, under the Normans it regained its military role: from 1092 they built a powerful *castle there, and the town, capital of Cumberland, commanded the western part of the "border", the Anglo-Scottish frontier: *Parliament sat there in 1307. But in the 14th and 15th cc. it was constantly exposed to Scots raids and its prosperity suffered; the town was never very heavily populated. It was also an ecclesiastical capital, though the *bishopric of Carlisle was rather poor by English standards. The *cathedral, rebuilt at the end of the Middle Ages, was served by a *priory, at first of the Order of Arrouaise, then of Augustinian Canons.

M.R. McCarthy, "Thomas Chadwick and Post-Roman Carlisle", *The Early Church in Western Britain and Ireland*, S.M. Pearce (ed.), Oxford, 1982, 241-56. – M.R. McCarthy, "The Origins and Development of the Twelfth-Century Cathedral Church at Carlisle", *The Archaeology of Cathedrals*, T. Tatton-Brown (ed.), J. Munby (ed.), Oxford, 1996, 31-45.

Jean-Philippe Genet

**CARMELITES.** A religious family whose origin traditionally goes back to the prophet Elijah and the settlement of his disciples on Mount Carmel. In any case, the presence of hermits on the site is attested from Antiquity. In the 13th c., evidence multiplies, given the existence of a group of Latin hermits who arrived with the first *crusades and whom the Limousin Aymeric de Malifaye, *patriarch of *Antioch (1141-1193), first federated around a church dedicated to the Virgin *Mary. *Albert, patriarch of *Jerusalem, drew up a first rule of Carmelite life for them in *c.*1209 (confirmed by *Honorius III in 1226), wholly oriented to continual *prayer and solitary life.

After a first expansion in *Palestine (which it finally abandoned for five centuries in 1291, with the end of the Latin kingdom of Jerusalem), the order was transported to Europe in *c.*1235, from which date it enjoyed a rapid development. In 1247, the election of a first *prior general (*Simon Stock, or more probably a certain Godefroid) opened the phase of consolidation of the order throughout the West over the centuries. Its increasingly urban settlement, the development of a common life among its members, the softening of the rule of silence and *fasting, the acceptance of pastoral charges, put it from now on among the *mendicant orders, and it would gradually assert itself, not without resistance from the *secular clergy, alongside the young and prestigious families of St *Francis and St *Dominic. This new orientation culminated in a first mitigation of the rule, made official by *Innocent IV in 1247 and 1252. To this delicate period would be referred the tradition of the appearance of the Virgin Mary, Carmel's protectress since its birth in the *Holy Land, to Simon Stock, handing him the *scapular to which the spiritual privileges of the Carmelite family would be attached.

Throughout the 13th c., the Carmelites would have to cope with a troublesome canonical problem, that of a certain hesitation on the part of the Holy See to acknowledge their existence in the face of the *Lateran council of 1215, which had forbidden the creation of new *orders. However, a clear decision of *Boniface VIII in 1298 would permit Carmel a new expansion in the next century, the century of the masters of theology John Baconthorp († 1348) and Michael of Bologna († 1400) and especially St Peter Thomas (1305-1366), theologian, diplomat, defender of the faith, and finally *Latin patriarch of Constantinople.

Carmel's very prosperity would cause it to suffer the full blow of the dramas of the second half of the century: the *Black Death decimating its *convents, the *Great Schism cutting the order in two, the beginning of the *Hundred Years' War destroying a third of its houses, recruitment too easily and too young leading to numerous defections and the multiplication of regular *dispensations. From then on the pursuit of the Carmelite life would oscillate between inevitable mitigations of the original observances, accorded by *Eugenius IV in 1432 and *Pius II in 1459, and the return to the sources desired from the time of Nicolas le Français (prior general from 1268 to 1271) by a whole current that had never resolved to abandon the *eremitism *pur et dur* of the beginnings: in 1413 began the so-called reform of Mantua, followed by that of Albi in 1499, and especially that imposed on the whole order by the blessed John Soreth, prior general from 1451 to 1471. Under his priorate we see – the first time this can be ascertained – the organisation of a female Carmelite life and a *Third Order, both destined for a brilliant future.

F. de Sainte-Marie, *Les Plus Vieux textes du Carmel*, Paris, 1944. – "Carmel", *DHGE*, 2, 1949. – J. Smet, *The Carmelites*, Chicago, 1975. – J. Smet, *I Carmelitani*, 1, Rome, 1989.

Max Huot De Longchamp

***CARMINA BURANA.*** A collection of poetic compositions dating from the first decades of the 13th century. The codex containing them, Munich 4660, was discovered in 1803 in the library of the monastery of Benediktbeuern; hence the name given to the collection. Its geographical origin is still disputed: some scholars suggest Styria, in particular the town of Seckau, while other interpretations identify a line further north passing through *Klosterneuburg, Neustift and Benediktbeuern. The manuscript is divided into four thematic sections: moral-satirical compositions; amorous compositions; playful and hedonistic compositions; and spiritual dramas. The authors are largely unknown; but the themes and tones suggest a milieu directly linked to the *Goliards. So the authors would have been *clerici vagantes*, rather marginalized from *university circles; the prevalently individualistic aspect of the poems confirms this. The compositions knew forms of musical accompaniment, resembling the *Minnesänger, whom they also resemble by affinities of style and especially content. The phenomenon of multilingualism, also typical of preaching and medieval *poetry in general, is a characteristic element of the collection; the Carmina Burana show an extremely rich linguistic *mélange*, largely Latin-German, but with evidence of Romance and even Greek elements. Their poetry is equally rich in the use of metaphor and wordplay and the parodic use of the classical and biblical **auctoritates*. Among the *classics, a particular place belongs to Ovid: Ovidian metaphors on the theme of *amores* recur, often used satirically, as do *exempla* and linguistic and metrical artifices that make this, in the final analysis, a decontextualized poetry. To the theme of *love – predominant in the collection – are added moralistic intentions in satires against the clergy and a delicate feeling for nature; some compositions refer to a refined medieval Epicureanism, like a Bacchic-Goliardic universe contrasted with the Christian universe.

B. K. Vollmann (ed.), *Carmina Burana*, Frankfurt, 1987. – P. Rossi (ed.), *Carmina Burana*, Milan, 1989. – *Love Lyrics from the Carmina Burana*, P. G. Walsh (ed.), Chapel Hill (NC), 1993.

*Carmina Burana: Facsimile Reproduction*, B. Bischoff (ed.), Brooklyn, 1967. – J. Mann, "Satiric Subject and Satiric Object in Goliardic Literature", *Mittellateinisches Jahrbuch*, 15, 1980, 63-86. – O. Sayce, *Plurilingualism in the Carmina Burana*, Göppingen, 1992. – T.M.S. Lehtonen, *Fortuna, Money and the Sublunar World*, Helsinki, 1995.

Lucia Velardi

**CARNIVAL.** A cyclical feast of variable date linked to the lunar calendar, carnival took place 40 days before *Easter. Its first possible date, 2 Feb (the day the bear emerged, according to popular belief), was also a fixed *feast, Candlemas, *Purification of the Virgin in the Christian calendar. Heir to the ancient Saturnalia and Lupercalia and perhaps to the Celtic feast of Imbolc, carnival was based on popular traditions which the Middle Ages integrated to create a custom that flourished in the *towns. Its name, which appeared in the 12th c., was already an interpretation: *carnelevare*, in Latin, suggests abstention from meat, or *Caramantran*, entry into *Quadragesima* or *Lent. The carnival season began at Christmas and culminated in the three days preceding Ash Wednesday, and constituted the fat period with its values and its symbolic objects. It was the temporary subversion of the temporal and *social order, the reign of the wild man, of all kinds of excesses and follies.

Carnival was a set of customs rather than an organised feast, whose *games were based on inversion and antithesis. Combats were moralized in the context of the Christian Middle Ages, and all these rites had a propitiary character. Despite prohibitions of masques by church *councils, ceremonies parodying the liturgy (feast of Fools, *Asses, *Innocents) took place in churches with the participation of the lower clergy.

Realm of *youth, laughter and joyous brotherhood, the street was the sphere of the carnival, traversed by burlesque or sumptuous processions thanks to the support of the *corporations and municipalities at the time of their domination. Financed by collections, its leaders exercised social control over *marriages and deviant behaviour. Carnival became a costly spectacle. *Farces multiplied on the boards, while, in the courts, masquerades appeared from the 14th century. The people were more and more dispossessed by the urban middle class, the aristocrats or the princely authority.

Bear, stag, cock, bull, pig, ass or cat constituted a bestiary whose popular symbolism was interpreted in terms of Christian values. Masks of animals or men dressed as women played a thousand pranks and danced in the streets to the sound of infernal music. It was the triumph of the body and overeating, with an abundance of fat and flatulent *foods propitious to the circulation of wind and souls.

The judgment and execution of the Carnival effigy, burned at the stake at the end of winter, were necessary for life to begin again in the spring.

J. Caro Baroja, *El Carnaval*, Madrid, 1965. – M. Bakhtine, *L'Oeuvre de François Rabelais*, Paris, 1970 (Fr. ed.). – J. Heers, *Fêtes, jeux et joutes dans les sociétés d'Occident à la fin du Moyen Âge*, Paris, 1971. – C. Gaignebet, *Le Carnaval*, Paris, 1974. – P. G. d'Alaya, M. Boiteux, *Carnavals et Mascarades*, Paris, 1988.

Martine Boiteux

**CAROLINGIAN RENAISSANCE.** In the Frankish kingdom, the first intellectual springtime flourished under *Charlemagne, guardian and protector full of understanding of all that was humanly beautiful and great. He not only showed in his person a lively desire for culture, he also worked with breadth of view to raise the cultural level of the clergy and people, since this task appeared to him one of the main duties of the State and the Church. His first *capitulary (769) already prescribed that ignorant priests should be suspended and, if they did not improve, deposed, since "those who do not know the Law of God cannot preach to others". A series of positive measures supplemented this prescription. All the *cathedrals and all the monasteries had to create *schools (*Admonitio generalis* of 789), which were intended primarily to prepare *clerics and monks for their vocation, but which also profited many others. In certain monasteries, alongside the *schola interior* for young monks (*oblates), there was a *schola exterior* or *publica* for future *secular clerics and for laymen. Country priests also received orders to maintain elementary boys' schools (synod of *Mainz, 813), though in practice this could only be done in particularly favourable conditions. Before *ordination, candidates for the *priesthood had to be examined on their intellectual state (capitulary of 803).

Charlemagne brought scholars, poets and artists from various countries, notably England and Italy, and with them formed a sort of learned academy. At their head was *Alcuin of York, who became (from 782) director of the palace school and abbot of *Saint-Martin at Tours. Others included the Lombard *Paul the Deacon, a monk of *Monte Cassino († *c.*799), author of an esteemed collection of *homilies and historian of his people (*Historia Langobardorum*); the grammarians *Peter of Pisa († before 799) and *Paulinus of Aquileia († 802 as patriarch of Aquileia); the theologian *Ambrosius Autpertus († *c.*781); the poet *Theodulf, a Spanish Goth who became bishop of *Orléans († 821); the Frank *Einhard, with a lively artistic sense, later – though a layman and married – *abbot of Seligenstadt am Main († 840), who wrote the Life of Charlemagne in the manner of Suetonius (*Vita Karoli Magni*) and built several famous churches. The *Empire's most renowned centres of culture were the palace school (*Schola palatina*) which had already existed for some time, but which first and foremost was to train future high officials and princes of the Empire, and the episcopal school of Tours which served as model for similar establishments in the monasteries of *Fulda, *Reichenau, *Sankt Gallen, *Corbie, *Corvey, Werden, etc.

Intellectual activity in the Frankish Empire, supported by a lively literary output, found its main expression in the theological sphere. It slowed down at the end of the 9th c., when political conditions in Francia became worse. By reason of its close dependence on classical Antiquity and the Church *Fathers (especially *Gregory the Great and Augustine), this cultural flowering presents a character that is backward-looking, anthologistic, imitative and largely lacking in personality and originality. Nevertheless the "Carolingian Renaissance" and later the "Ottonian Renaissance", as it is customarily called, present one of the finest pages of the history of the early Middle Ages. They herald the fertile union of the Christian spirit with the cultural heritage of Antiquity.

W. Ullmann, *The Carolingian Renaissance and the Idea of Kingship*, London, 1969. – *Poetry of the Carolingian Renaissance*, P. Godman (ed.), London, 1985. – R. McKitterick, *The Carolingians and the Written Word*, Cambridge, 1989. – *Carolingian Culture*, R. McKitterick (ed.), Cambridge, 1993. – P. Riché, *HChr*, 4, 1993, 738-754. – R. McKitterick, *The Frankish Kings and Culture in the Early Middle Ages*, Aldershot, 1995.

Editorial Staff

**CAROLINGIANS.** The Carolingian family left its direct mark on history from the early 7th c. until 987. In a first stage, it had acquired the political responsibilities that gradually made it a princely dynasty. With *Pippin the Short, in 751, it acceded to royalty, and in 800 *Charlemagne became emperor. These successive titles both supposed and founded a dynastic legitimacy. Unlike the other old Germanic royal families, this legitimacy did not rest on a very ancient acquisition, but was on the contrary the fruit of a slow advance. What is more, it was never totally incontestable, doubtless because it was acquired and because those who had allowed its acquisition, the aristocracy and the Church, could always contest its exercise before finally eliminating it.

The first two members of the family who emerge into history are Arnulf, bishop of *Metz around 614, and Pippin I the Old. It was the union of Arnulf's son Ansegisel with Pippin's daughter Begga that formed the stock of the future dynasty. This union was also that of two considerable patrimonies situated in *Austrasia, two groups of alliances and two clienteles; in short, of all that made up the strength of a great aristocratic family. Arnulf and Pippin having taken the part of Chlotar II and contributed to the fall of Brunhild and Theuderic II, they were rewarded, the former by the bishopric of Metz, capital of the kingdom of Austrasia, the latter by the Mayoralty of the Palace of the same kingdom. After an eclipse in the time of *Dagobert I, Pippin the Old returned to the forefront before dying in 640. His son Grimoald then tried to make up for lost time. Mayor of the Palace in his turn, he had his son adopted by King Sigebert III of Austrasia under the Merovingian name of Childebert. But soon after the king's death, in 656, Grimoald and Childebert were killed by the *Neustrians. Pippin II, son of Ansegiselus and Begga, later came to the fore, from 679. After numerous setbacks, he finally defeated the Neustrians in 687 at Tertry. From then on, he governed the whole of the Kingdom of the *Franks by accumulating the palace mayoralties, while Theuderic III nominally ruled. Up to 714, he exercised the powers of a *princeps* as the documents call him. This title designates a form of power assuming the royal prerogatives without bearing the title; and without being mandatorily hereditary. In 714 a form of heredity seems to have taken shape, as witness the bargaining carried out by Pippin's widow Plectrude to ensure the succession to one of her small sons, Theodoald, aged six. But the Neustrians rejected this solution. However one of Pippin II's sons, *Charles (much later called Martel), who had been set aside, took up the challenge and regained the positions held by his father. In his turn *princeps* and Mayor of the Palace, he governed until 741.

It was under his quasi-reign that the second stage of the acquisition of dynastic legitimacy began. In the first place Charles initiated the *dilatatio regni*, the expansion of the realm, notably towards the south; *Aquitaine, *Septimania and *Provence. To attain this end, he considerably augmented his clientele by the generalizing of vassalic *recommendation. He could thus bring together men beyond the limits of his clientele and alliances. Moreover, the ritual respect and obedience (*obsequium*) traditionally owed to the king by his officials and domestics were by this expedient transferred to the *princeps*. The aristocracy were then either held in check or tamed. We know that he was only able to follow this policy by acting to the detriment of the Church. *Abbots and *bishops were laymen assuming and accumulating political offices; vassals were installed on church lands. But Charles favoured *missions to northern and eastern Europe in conjunction with the papacy; his conquests to the south were made at the expense of *Islam. The foundations of a future alliance with the papacy were laid, even if the *princeps* refused to aid the papacy against the *Lombards. On his death, the realm was partitioned between two of his sons like an inheritance, with no other protests than those of a son who was set aside. Princely legitimacy was acquired by the family in the forms that prefigured royal legitimacy.

But that legitimacy could not be obtained except through an external contribution, providing a sacrality that the family did not hereditarily possess. This was the *consecration by the bishops in 751 and by the *pope in 754. To reach this point, two Mayors of the Palace, Pippin and Carloman, princes of the Franks, had to make the alliance with the papacy effective. For this they had to reform the Frankish church with the help of the Anglo-Saxon missionary *Boniface. In the midst of a series of general *councils, they undertook to purge the episcopate, which could no longer be held by quasi-laymen. They also made their vassals enfoeffed on church lands recognise the superior property rights of those lands. Without ceding anything important of what formed the foundation of their power, they had settled the main disputes with the Church. Carloman retired in 747, and the papacy explicitly allowed Pippin to be consecrated by Boniface and the Frankish bishops in 751, after having been elected by the Franks. In 754 Pope *Stephen II came to Francia and again consecrated Pippin, as well as his two sons Carloman and Charles. A text, doubtless written at *Saint-Denis early in the 9th c., specifies that the pope had forbidden a king to be chosen from outside Pippin's descendants. Royal dynastic legitimacy was thus acquired, without being innate like that of the *Merovingians; which explains the efforts made to attach themselves to the latter by false genealogies, and the introduction of Merovingian names into the family: Louis and Lothar, born in 778 (only Louis survived).

Charlemagne originated a third stage, undoubtedly not sought at the outset: accession to the *Empire. He was sole king from the death of his brother Carloman in 771, and from then on he initiated a considerable amplification of the *dilatatio regni*. In 774 he became king of the Lombards and thus released the papacy from their grip. The establishment of a sort of papal state became possible, and the alliance of the Franks with *Rome was sealed. But at the same time Charlemagne put the Holy See under his tutelage. While this tutelage did not affect the spiritual sphere, it did confine the pope to this sphere. The Church, as an institution established in the *saeculum*, had as its head in reality the king of the Franks. Head of the Christian people, Charlemagne attacked the Muslims of *Spain in 778, with little success, but between 772 and 797 he conquered pagan *Saxony and thus completed by force the missionary work begun by St Boniface. Some expeditions agains the pagan *Slavs and *Avars completed his portrait as defender and propagator of *Christendom. In fact, at that moment, apart from the British Isles and Byzantium, the kingdom of the Franks and Lombards coincided with Christendom. The papacy, which thought it had received from the time of Constantine the disposal of the imperial insignia for the West, could consider itself within its rights in transferring them to Charlemagne, and this is what took place in 800.

An imperial legitimacy had thus entered the Carolingian family: it too was acquired, but was it hereditary? In 806, *Charlemagne partitioned his kingdom into three for the benefit of his sons then living, but did not hand over the imperial title. But in 813, Louis being the sole survivor, his father crowned him at *Aachen before dying.

Starting from this apogee, we can discern the stages of a slow and gradual decline. The reasons for this have less to do with incapacity of persons than with the return of traditional constraints, which gradually demolished the acquired legitimacy. In the first place, the custom of family partitions continued, but the imperial title was indivisible. In 817 *Louis the Pious (817-840) associated his eldest son Lothar in the Empire and gave his other sons, Pippin and Louis, subordinate kingdoms. The birth of a fourth son, Charles, by his second wife provoked family conflicts which lasted until their father's death. By that time Pippin was dead, but Louis and Charles leagued themselves against the emperor, *Lothar I. In 843 the treaty of Verdun created two kingdoms, one on each side of a central band consisting of *Italy, the future kingdom of Provence-Burgundy and *Lotharingia, all of which formed Lothar's share. But on the latter's death (855), a subsequent partition confined the Empire to Italy (*Louis II, 855-875), while Charles got the kingdom of Provence, and *Lothar II (855-869) the area that would later be called Lotharingia. *Charles the Bald (840-877) and *Louis the German (840-876) respectively governed West Francia and East Francia, first adumbrations of the future kingdoms of *France and *Germany.

Another traditional constraint resulted from the Carolingians' mode of government. The territory was entirely cut up into counties, whose holders, the *counts, received an almost total delegation of royal power, with no other *quid pro quo* than to enter into royal *vassalage. The envoys (*missi dominici*) charged with watching over them belonged to the same imperial aristocracy, and their control could not be very effective. In the kingdoms, which were immense in view of contemporary means of communication, a localization of real power was inevitable. At the end of the 9th c. it was an established fact. But meanwhile, at a higher level, the greater aristocratic lineages were starting to cut out principalities for themselves. The kings had in fact had to entrust frontier *marches or military *duchies to dukes or counts in order to face external *invasions. Thus old divisions with foundations as much ethnic as administrative, which had never been truly suppressed, came back to life: *Aquitaine, *Burgundy, *Saxony, *Bavaria, etc. Others were created: *Flanders, *Normandy, *Swabia. At the turn of the 10th c., a new political configuration was thus created, placing the kings at the summit of an aristocratic hierarchy that controlled them. But these kings themselves had in this evolution lost the greater part of the substance of their real power. The branches of the Carolingian family had distributed a great deal of their property in *benefices for their vassals, and had also given much of it away. The rest had fallen into the hands of the counts and princes who were by now hereditary holders of local powers. In fact the traditional hold of the aristocracy over the royal power had returned to the foreground, under different forms but with the same intensity as in Merovingian times. From there to choosing kings from among themselves was only a single step, seeing that one of the foundations of Carolingian legitimacy, the consensus of the magnates, could appear to have been overturned.

At the same time as the aristocracy, the other political force of the time, the Church, had resumed its autonomy. It too got round to imposing the weight of a traditional constraint. Firstly, the bishops, who consecrated the kings, thought that in the framework of a Christian empire it was for them to define the royal power and mark its limits. Secondly, the papacy resumed the disposal of the imperial insignia after the death of Louis II, and sought to impose a primacy of jurisdiction over the bishops. The latter, who from 826 (council of Paris) sought to moralize the royal power, did not, for all that, intend to weaken its legitimacy, only to keep it within a Christian framework. Archbishop *Hincmar of Reims (845-882) played a great role in this evolution, but at the same time as he enumerated the duties of the king, he was likewise contributing to sacralizing his function by drawing up ever more complete rituals of *consecration. This dual tendency would continue until the 11th century. However the bishops also acted to ensure the autonomy of the churches, to get their rights and privileges respected; this resulted in the formation of independent units of local power, religious but also political. *Archbishops and bishops, appointed by the kings and then also by the princes, vassals of the sovereigns, sat like lay princes at the summit of the hierarchy of power. Alongside the princes, they too determined royal legitimacy. It was these bishops who deposed Louis the Pious in 833. Boso, the first non-Carolingian king, was elected and consecrated king of Provence in 879 by a council of bishops. In 987 it was Archbishop Adalbero of Reims who set aside the last Carolingian claimant and presided at the election and consecration of Hugh Capet. All the changes of dynasty that came about from 888, both in Germany and in France, found bishops to stand surety for them. The popes likewise made emperors up to the imperial consecration of *Otto I at Rome in 962.

It was not the extinction of the family that led to the final setting aside of the Carolingians. In 987, Louis V's uncle was capable of reigning and had sons to succeed him. It was rather a gradual loss of the substance that formed the basis of this capacity to reign, what we term "legitimacy", a term that is ultimately hard to define.

B. W. Scholz, *Carolingian Chronicles*, Ann Arbor (MI), 1972. – *Charlemagne: Translated Sources*, P. D. King (ed.), Kendal, 1987. – *The Annals of St-Bertin*, J. L. Nelson (ed.), Manchester, 1991. – *The Annals of Fulda*, T. Reuter (ed.), Manchester, 1992.

R. McKitterick, *The Frankish Kingdoms under the Carolingians, 751-987*, London, 1983. – K. F. Werner, "Les origines", *Histoire de France*, J. Favier (dir.), 1, Paris, 1984. – P.J. Geary, *Before France and Germany*, Oxford, 1988. – S. Lebecq, *Les origines franques*, Paris, 1990. – L. Theis, *L'héritage des Charles*, Paris, 1990. – P. Riché, *The Carolingians: a Family who Forged Europe*, Philadelphia (PA), 1993.

Claude Carozzi

***CARTA DE LOGU.*** The code of laws of the *judicate of Arborèa (in *Sardinia) issued, perhaps in 1392, by *Eleonora, judge-regent of the kingdom. The *Carta*, written in the local language, is divided into 198 chapters, of which the first 132 belong to the civil and penal code and the other 66 to the rural code (drawn up to safeguard the fields, devastated by livestock left in the wild state). Promulgated in the wake of the similar codes drawn up between 1355 and 1365 by Eleonora's father, Mariano IV, the *Carta* contains norms of Roman, Byzantine and customary law. It survived until the end of the kingdom (in 1420), indeed from 1421 it was used by the Aragonese to regulate justice in the enfeoffed countryside. The original of the Code has not survived, but there are nine printed editions and a damaged paper manuscript of the 15th century.

E. Besta, *La Sardegna medievale*, 1908-1909. – E. Besta, *Il diritto romano come diritto consuetudinario*, 1934. – E. Besta (ed.), "Carta de logu", *Studi sassaresi*, 3, 1903, fasc. I, in collaboration with P. E. Guarnerio. – B. Pitzorno, *Le leggi spagnole del Regno di Sardegna*, Sassari, 1919. – F. C. Casula, *La 'Carta de Logu' del regno di Arborèa*, Cagliari, 1994.

Mauro Sanna

**CARTHUSIANS, CHARTERHOUSE.** The foundation of the first hermitages of the Chartreuse by St *Bruno and his six companions in June 1084 marks the starting-point of a development unprecedented among all the religious movements that emerged from *eremitism. The Carthusian Order was only truly constituted under the priorate of *Guigo I (1109-1136), after the writing of the *Customs of Chartreuse*, which were adopted by several communities of hermits in the *Alps and the Jura. After the meeting of the first *chapter general, under the priorate of Antelm, in 1140, the supreme legislative and judicial authority of a centralized *order was put in place, under the pre-eminence of the *prior of the Grande Chartreuse.

The rigour of the solitary life, the need for a fervent and carefully tested vocation, and finally the law of small numbers that limited each "Chartreuse" to 12 choir fathers and 16 lay brothers, ruled out an expansion analogous to that of the other monastic orders. Progress was regular but slow, gradually gaining all Eastern France, Spain, Italy and England. At the beginning of the 13th c., there were still only 40 Charterhouses, all situated in isolated, mountainous and forested places, propitious to the flourishing of the life of solitude and contemplation desired by the founder.

Every Charterhouse was surrounded by its "*desert", a vast domain whose exclusive occupants were the monks, bounded by limits they were forbidden to cross, and to which access for the outside world was carefully controlled by the "lower house" or "correrie", residence of the brothers in charge of exploiting the lands. The "upper house" was the monastery proper, the fathers' individual cells meeting around the great *cloister, and the buildings housing the few activities for which the monks met – church, refectory, chapter house – shared between the sides of the little cloister. The cell was like a veritable house, composed of several rooms: the first, serving as vestibule, was called the "Ave Maria", by reason of the presence of an image of the Virgin before which the Carthusian inclined himself when he entered his hermitage; the second, larger, was the *cubiculum*, at once *oratory, study, dining-room and bedroom; a third, situated at a higher level, served as woodshed and workroom. A gallery and a little *garden completed this dwelling where the Carthusian passed the main part of his existence, shared between spiritual exercises and manual *labour (craftsmanship, gardening).

The isolation of the Carthusian in his hermitage at the heart of the monastery, of the monastery in the middle of its "desert" and of the desert from the world guaranteed solitude and silence, indispensable for the accomplishment of his contemplative vocation, *i.e.* the spiritual journey he must follow in order to speak with *God alone. This journey took place in stages, of which the four main ones were compared by Prior Guigo II, at the end of the 12th c., to the rungs of a ladder, which the religious must climb one after the other. The first is reading, intended to feed the mind and favour *meditation, which is the second: an effort of thought to understand the sacred text properly. The third step is *prayer, a personal manifestation of fervour, leading to *contemplation, last rung of this ladder of monks which allows the *soul to rise from earth to heaven, to fuse with God and from now on to be one with Him.

But the Carthusians, following Bruno himself, considered that perseverance in the life of solitude could only be effectively accomplished with the help of the balance contributed by some moments of communal existence shared with their brethren: in church for the celebration of certain *offices (*mass, *vespers, *matins), in the refectory (*Sundays and *feast days), in chapter to deal with the affairs of the house, and on their weekly walk (*spaciementum*).

To realize their vocation fully, the Carthusians had to be free from all material care: the brothers took charge of the exploitation of the lands, the upkeep of the buildings and the artisanal activities in the workrooms, in a concern for autarky intended to limit contacts with the outside world. The brothers were no less religious, obliged to perform a number of spiritual exercises, and were under the authority of the bursar. The prior was the elected superior of the community and its spiritual guide: all owed him *obedience, but he himself had to give proof of *humility, in conformity with the prescriptions of the Customs.

The order's expansion continued with regularity in the course of the 13th c. and it took off in an extraordinary way in the 14th, a time when more than a hundred houses were founded, divided among all the countries of Europe, attesting to the attachment of certain social elites, notably urban, to an order symbolizing an ideal of high *spirituality. Increasingly Charterhouses were implanted close to *towns: the first was that of Vauvert near *Paris, founded in 1257 by St *Louis. Many became the necropolis of princely families. For the construction and decoration of the new *foundations, the powerful of this world (*Innocent VI at Villeneuve-lès-Avignon, the duke of *Milan at *Pavia, the king of *Aragon at Miraflorès, the duke of *Burgundy at Champmol, others elsewhere) appealed to the greatest *artists, who deployed their talents on the communal parts, notably the church, the little cloister, the external façades. This concern for ostentation, intended to perpetuate the glory of the founders, was very far from the original austerity and the tradition of rusticity proper to the order. Only the cells, changeless setting of the Carthusian's everyday life, and the intangible respect for the statutes now symbolized fidelity to the spirit of the desert and allowed the monks, despite the sumptuosity of the décor that clothed their houses, to remain those athletes of Christ, "soldiers under the Lord's tent" that *William of Saint-Thierry had seen them as in the 12th century. Privileged intercessors because, like *angels, they were in direct contact with the realities of *heaven, the Carthusians remained at the end of the Middle Ages a reference-point of authentic religious vocation and enjoyed a real influence in the religious thought of the West thanks to the writings of two of them, *Ludolf of Saxony (*c.*1295-1377), author of a *Vita Christi*, and Denys of Rijkel, called *Denis the Carthusian (*c.*1402-1471), an outstanding figure in the spiritual literature of his time.

The origins of the first women's community attached to the Order of St Bruno, Prébayon in Provence, are obscure. It was undoubtedly only after its transfer to Saint-André-de-Ramières near Orange in the mid 12th c. that the *nuns manifested their desire to join the Carthusian current. The prior of the Grande Chartreuse, Antelm, got John of Spain to draw up an adaptation of the Customs, which was adopted by the houses founded later.

Like that of the fathers, the nuns' day was divided between prayer, meditation and work. But solitude was less insisted on: meals were not taken in cells but in the refectory. The lay sisters and *oblates were charged with the material tasks.

The relations of the womens' houses with the order posed numerous problems, due to the reluctance of the Carthusians to take charge of their *spiritual direction. A spirit of insurrection frequently blew among the nuns. The material difficulties faced by many womens' Charterhouses in the late Middle Ages, the stretching of the statutes that the nuns were often guilty of, served as pretexts for the chapter general to separate itself from some of them, notably in Provence.

The female branch of the Carthusian Order was illustrated by some engaging personalities whose edifying life or mystical *graces had an influence outside their cloisters: Béatrice d'Omacieu, a nun at Prémol in the late 13th c., Marguerite d'Oingt, prioress of Poleteins (1286-1311), Roseline de Villeneuve, prioress of La Celle-Roubaud in the first third of the 14th c. († 1329).

Guigo I, *Coutumes de Chartreuse*, *SC*, 313, 1984.

C. Le Couteulx, *Annales ordinis cartusiensis*, Montreuil-sur-Mer, 1887-1891 (8 vol.). – S. Autore, "Chartreux", *DThC*, 2, 1905, 2274-2318. – Y. Gourdel, "Chartreux", *DSp*, 2, 1953, 705-776. – M. Laporte, *Aux sources de la vie cartusienne*, La Grande Chartreuse, 1960-1977 (8 vol.). – J. Dubois, "Quelques problèmes de l'histoire de l'ordre des Chartreux à propos de livres récents", *RHE*, 63, 1968, 27-54. – J.-P. Aniel, *Les Maisons de Chartreux, des origines à la chartreuse de Pavie*, Paris, 1983. – *La Grande Chartreuse par un chartreux*, Bellegarde, 1984, 11-24 (14th ed.). –

Daniel Le Blévec

**CARTULARY.** Mainstay of numerous *charter-rooms, the cartulary was a collection of copies of documents, compiled in the form of a volume or sometimes a roll, on the initiative of the holder of the documents. The spread of this practice in the central centuries of the Middle Ages, essentially among ecclesiastical proprietors of all types and all orders, the mass of documentation thus transmitted to historians, the convenience of its arrangement, all explain why from the 18th c. the cartulary gained the status of a favourite source of medieval scholarship. Inexhaustible collections of facts about medieval societies, cartularies were the object of an interest that was never denied: careful preservation under the French Revolution, with public libraries as natural depositaries; massive and sometimes hasty publication promoted by romantic historiography.

Indirect heir to the *libri traditionum* in which certain *abbeys registered *donations (*traditiones*) as they were received, the cartulary appeared in the 9th and 10th centuries. It then consisted mainly of the organised transcription of small groups of documents (dossier-cartulary). It was progressively enriched by a desire for exhaustiveness and an assertive glance back at the glorious past and the rights acquired by an ecclesiastical establishment. These motivations went hand in hand with a desire for restoration and often (late 10th-12th cc.) with a more literary form, mingling narrative and transcription of documents (chronicle-cartulary). In the 12th and 13th cc., the custom spread, to the *secular clergy but also to the great urban communes and lay princes, whose *chanceries made the cartulary, before the existence of chancery registers and business records, a sort of administrative directory. We even find them among various lay lords and proprietors, particularly in *Great Britain. This was the time of ordered and exhaustive compilations, often enriched by non-diplomatic pieces (**censuaria*, inventories) and tools of reference (tables). Less numerous in *Italy (great abbeys affected by the *Gregorian reform, *communes), cartularies were common in the Iberian peninsula.

The new legal requirements developed in the 13th c. put the cartulary, as a collection of copies, in a position of inferiority vis-à-vis the original titles: display cartularies can be found (authentification of copies by *notaries or scriveners), and cartularies were produced up to the end of the *Ancien Régime*, but in declining number and always more with an eye to the scholar than that of the administrator. Attention and innovations progressively moved towards classification of the originals, leading to the birth of modern archive-keeping and the concurrent development of the inventory of archives, which grew during the decline of the cartulary.

H. Stein, *Bibliographie générale des cartulaires français*, Paris, 1907 (reorganisation in progress at IRHT). – G. R. C. Davis, *Medieval Cartularies of Great Britain: a Short Catalogue*, London, 1958. – A. Rucquoi, "La invención de una memoria: los cabildos peninsulares del siglo XII", *Temas medievales*, 2, Buenos Aires, 1992. – Les *Cartulaires*, O. Guyotjeannin (ed.), L. Morelle (ed.), M. Parisse (ed.), Paris, 1993 ("Mémoires et documents de l'École des chartes", 39).

Olivier Guyotjeannin

**CASAMARI.** The foundation of the *Cistercian abbey of Santa Maria di Casamari in the diocese of Veroli, on the road from Sora to Frosinone, in the shelter of a hill lapped by the river Amaseno and marking the border between Erici and Volsci, dates from 1140, on an original *Benedictine monastery erected between 1005 and 1035 on the ruins of the Roman Cereas. The name is generally accepted as deriving from *Casa Marii*, the villa of Gaius Marius, the famous general and statesman (157-86 BC). The Benedictine church was dedicated to the martyrs Sts John and Paul. Between 1149 and 1151, by direct intervention of St *Bernard and Pope *Eugenius III, the Cistercian reform was introduced.

In 1203, in accordance with the rigid *canons of the order, began the imposing construction of the *abbey complex: church, *cloister, *chapter house and dorter. The first stone was blessed by *Innocent III. The basilica, consecrated by *Honorius III on 5 Sept 1217, was dedicated to the Virgin, like all the order's abbeys, and to Sts John and Paul. By their cultural activity, fervent studies and an innate capacity for politico-religious mediation suited to the times, the monks of Casamari attracted the favour of kings, princes, emperors and *popes, whose esteem and friendship they often enjoyed. Important names include those of the Blessed John, first Cistercian *abbot of Casamari; Luca Campano, preacher of the fourth *crusade, able *architect, abbot of Casamari and then of Sambucina, later archbishop of Cosenza, where he was responsible for building the *cathedral; and Abbot John IV, papal *legate in France, England and Bulgaria. The emperor *Frederick II stayed there repeatedly and may even have been affiliated to the abbey.

In the 12th and 13th cc., Casamari founded various daughter houses in Italy. The first, Santa Maria della *Sambucina, had previously been a foundation of *Clairvaux, which, at the request of *Roger II in 1139, sent a first colony of monks in 1140. This failed to take off, so in 1160 Casamari sent a considerable number of monks. In 1180, Casamari founded Santa Maria della Mattina in the diocese of San Marco Argentano (Cosenza), on a pre-existing Benedictine monastery of 1066. By a series of negative events, this new abbey would eventually absorb Sanbucina, which was reduced to its *grange. The next foundation was San Galgano (1201) in the diocese of Volterra, on the site of a small hermitage where the saintly hermit had died in 1181. San Galgano itself made five *foundations. Then followed Sagittaria in Lucania (1216), Santi Giusti e Pastore (1217) near Rieti; San Domenico di Sora (1222); San Pietro di Paliano (1243) in the diocese of Palestrina; and finally Santa Maria di Ustica (1257) on the island of that name.

Casamari's period of expansion was blocked and the abbey suffered a rapid decline due to events such as the transfer of the papacy to *Avignon (1305-1378) and the *Great Schism (1378-1417). In *c.*1450 *Martin V gave the abbey in *commendation to Cardinal Prospero *Colonna. All this reduced it to a role of secondary importance. After various vicissitudes, it is now the head of the Cistercian congregation of Casamari, with its own dependent houses, part of the Cistercian Order of Common Observance.

The abbey church is preceded by a portico with three arcades, the side ones pointed. Within are three aisles divided by cruciform pillars with rounded arches; the ribbing of the vaults rests on inverse conical corbels. At the crossing of the nave and the transepts is a lantern-campanile. The Burgundian Gothic forms eliminate the need for flying buttresses and other complex systems to balance the thrust of the vaults. Casamari thus represents a more evolved form of Gothic than does *Fossanova. Here and there, especially in the portal, we note the contribution of local artists. The cloister is simple, with two-light groups. The elegant chapter house and other rooms are all vaulted, with an ingenious and complex system of supports. These characteristics made Casamari an *ad hoc* centre for the spread of *Gothic.

P. F. Kehr, *Regesta Pontificum Romanorum, Italia pontificia*, 2, *Latium*, Berlin, 1907. – B. C. Bedini, *Le abbazie cistercensi d'Italia*, Casamari, 1966. – A. M. Romanini, "Le abbazie fondate da S. Bernardo in Italia e l'architettura cistercense primitiva", *Studi su S. Bernardo di Chiaravalle nell'ottavo centenario della canonizzazione*, Rome, 1975. – G. Duby, *San Bernardo e l'arte cisterciense*, Turin, 1982. – F. Farina, B. Fornari, *Storia e documenti*

John Cassian, *Collationes*. Top right, Cassian holds his book, of which the monks of Saint-Amand offer an exemplar to the superior of their abbey. Below, the scribe writes the first word of the text on a sheet of parchment. Mid 11th c. Valenciennes, Municipal Library (Ms 169, fol. 2 r°).

*dell'abbazia di Casamari, 1036-1152*, Casamari, 1983, 21. – F. Farina, B. Fornari, *L'abbazia di Casamari nella storia dell'architettura e della spiritualità cistercense*, Casamari, 1990. – M. Bernabò Silorata, *Federico II a Casamari. Lettura simbolica degli elementi figurativi dell'abbazia*, Jesi, 1995. – I. Gobry, *Il secolo di Bernardo. Cîteaux e Clairvaux (sec. XII)*, Rome, 1998, 168, 453.

Attilio Stendardi

**CASIMIR (1458-1484).** Casimir Jagiello, in Polish Kazimierz Jagiellończyk, prince and heir, saint (feast 4 March), patron of *Poland and *Lithuania, was the second son of the king of Poland Casimir Jagiellończyk. In 1471, as a claimant to the throne of *Hungary, he took part in an unfortunate expedition to try to obtain the crown. He took part alongside his father in the political life of the State; in 1481-1483 he exercised power in the kingdom of Poland as regent of the grand duke, then he went to Lithuania, where he died. He was buried in Vilnius cathedral. Casimir's personality was formed under the equal influence of John *Długosz and Filippo Buonacorsi (called Callimachus), the former still belonging to the medieval period, but the latter to the *Renaissance. Casimir's piety was characterised by an ardent Marian cult, summed up in the watchword: "*omni die dic Mariae mea laudes anima*" ("Daily, daily, sing to Mary. . ."); he was closely connected with the sanctuary of Jasna Góra. He was canonized in 1521 by Pope Leo X, but the *bull concerning him disappeared in 1522; so in 1602 Pope Clement VIII confirmed his *canonization.

K. Górski, "Kazimierz Jagiellończyk", *Polski Słownik Biograficzny*, 12, Wrocław, 1966-1967, 286-288. – *Oxford Dictionary of Saints*, Oxford, 1984, 68-9. – J. Kłoczowski, "Casimir", *Une Église éclatée: 1275-1545*, A. Vauchez (dir.), *HSSC*, 7, 1986, 91-95.

Leszek Wojciechowski

**CASIMIR THE GREAT (1310-1370).** Casimir III the Great, in Polish Kazimierz Wielki, king of *Poland in 1333, was the son of the king of Poland Ladislas the Short (Władisław Łokietek) and Princess Hedwig of Kalisz; he was Poland's last ruler of the *Piast family. When Casimir the Great came to power in 1333, Poland's international situation was very difficult. The king followed a skilful foreign policy. He established peaceful relations with the *Teutonic Order by the provision of Kalisz of 1343. By a treaty dating from 1348, the Luxemburgs renounced their rights over the Crown of Poland, and Casimir recognised their position in *Silesia. Good relations with *Hungary bore fruit in an alliance in 1339. In the years 1340-1366, Casimir expanded eastward, annexing Galician Ruthenia (Red Ruthenia) to Poland.

The measure of Poland's importance at the time of Casimir the Great is given by the congress of *Cracow of 1364, in which the monarchs of central Europe took part. Casimir the Great supported the country's economic development, contributing to the creation of 500 villages and 70 towns as well as the expansion of *commerce. He reformed the judicial system, the administration and finances, and strengthened the system of defence by building 50 new fortresses. Founded in 1364, the *university of Cracow had great importance for the whole of central Europe, especially in the 15th century. The great economic, cultural and social advance of the State that took place during Casimir's reign, as well as the deepening of the process of Westernization, contributed to give Poland a primary role in that part of Europe.

P. W. Knoll, *The Rise of the Polish Monarchy. Piast Poland in East Central Europe, 1320-1370*, Chicago (Ill), 1972. – J. Wyrozumski, *Kazimierz Wielki*, Wrocław, 1982.

Zbigniew Piłat

**CASSIAN, JOHN (*c.*360-*c.*435).** Since the end of his life, St John Cassian's *Institutions* and *Conferences* have been used all over the Christian world. These works occupied a privileged place in the catalogues of medieval libraries. Their influence would persist into the modern world through the writings of St Ignatius of Loyola and St Teresa of Avila.

Cassian, introducing the customs of anchoritism to the West thanks to a long experience of Eastern monastic practices, became one of the models of *coenobitism. So we should not be surprised if, according to the *Vita* of Fulgentius of Ruspe, the latter undertook a pilgrimage to Egypt after reading the *Institutions* and *Conferences*. Later, from St *Bernard to St *Thomas Aquinas, numerous authors would find food for thought in his writings. But it is in monastic legislation that the real significance of his work can be measured. The reading of Cassian is recommended in chapters 42 and 73 of the Rule of St *Benedict, together with that of the Lives of the Fathers and the Rule of "Holy Father Basil". His influence was felt in numerous monastic *Rules such as those of *Caesarius, the Master, Eugippus, Benedict, *Columbanus and *Fructuosus. The highest expression of this dependence was the *Rule of Cassian*, a literal summary of the mid 7th c. taken from the first four books of the *Institutions*.

In another connection, from the 5th c., his theories would circulate and then pass on to posterity. A long list of citations of his works has been established by M. Olphe-Gaillard and M. Cappuyns. The idea of *tradition was developed by his contemporary Vincent of Lérins in his treatise *Commonitorium*, but his arguments depend on book IV of *De incarnatione*. So it was natural that later on *Rabanus Maurus describing the four kinds of *prayer (*De clericorum institutione*), *Peter Damian justifying the clothing of hermits or *Rupert of Deutz establishing the monastic origin of the "*apostolic life" (*De vita vere apostolica*) should use Cassian as an **auctoritas*. Cited for his theories on the "two ways" and the "two ends" of man, he was used especially for his doctrine of *vices and virtues, itself re-examined by *Gregory the Great in his *Moralia in Iob*, then amalgamated with *Alcuin's *Liber de virtutibus* at the end of the 8th century.

Cassian's literary success during the Middle Ages is indisputable. For proof, the *collatio*, the reading during the evening meal in monasteries, takes its name from the habit of reading his *Conferences* at that time.

M. Olphe-Gaillard, "Cassien (Jean)", *DSp*, 2, 1937, 214-276. – M. Cappuyns, "Cassien (Jean)", *DHGE*, 11, 1939, 1319-1348. – J.-C. Guy, *Jean Cassien. Vie et doctrine spirituelle*, Paris, 1961. – O. Chadwick, *John Cassian*, 2nd ed., London, 1968. – P. Rousseau, *Ascetics, Authority and the Church in the Age of Jerome and Cassian*, Oxford, 1978.

Pierre Bonnerue

**CASSIODORUS (before 490 - after 580).** Born in Odoacer's *Italy – his father was praetorian prefect at the time –, Cassiodorus opened his *cursus honorum* by a eulogy of the *Ostrogothic king *Theodoric. Quaestor (507-511), ordinary consul (514), *magister officiorum* (523), praetorian prefect (533), he held the essential position of royal chancellor for thirty years. His project of establishing a Christian university at Rome, with the support of Pope Agapetus, was interrupted by the beginnings of the Byzantine reconquest. After a stay at *Constantinople, in *c.*550 he retired to his estates in Bruttium, near *Vivarium, where he founded a monastery. He then engaged in a new task as private administrator, ascetic guide and professor of Christian science, which he fulfilled until his death.

His secular works comprise a *Universal chronicle* (enumeration of consulates); a *History of the Goths* (commissioned by the king) in 12 books, lost save for fragments, but known from the clumsy summary of the Ostrogoth Jordanes; *Variae* (*Varieties*), and a *compendium* in 12 books of his chancery work. His religious works comprise a memorandum *On the soul*; *On orthography*, intended for the copyists of Vivarium; *Commentaries on the Psalms*, a preparation for the psalmody; the *Institutiones divinarum et humanarum litterarum* which deal with sacred reading and the *liberal arts: a clear and well organised summa, which would be a reference for the intellectuals of subsequent centuries; and his *Tripartite History*, a mosaic of extracts translated from the Greek historians of the Church, a best-seller of the early Middle Ages.

*PL*, 69 and 70, 1847-1848. – "De orthographia", *Grammatici Latini*, H. Keil (ed.), 7, Leipzig, 1880, 143-210. – *MGH.AA*, 12, 1894. – *Institutiones*, R. A. B. Mynors (ed.), Oxford, 1961 (1st ed. 1937). – *CChr.SL*, 96-98, 1958-1973.

M. Cappuyns, *DHGE*, 11, 1949, 1349-1408. – H. Wolframm, *History of the Goths*, Berkeley, 1988. – F. Brunhölzl, *Histoire de la littérature latine du Moyen Âge*, 1, Turnhout, 35-49 and 240-243.

Michel Banniard

**CASTELLANY.** Between the mid 11th and the 12th c., in numerous regions, a new organisation of powers replaced the institutions inherited from the Carolingian administration. A new territorial division was put in place, its names varying according to region: "*châtellenie*", "*viguerie*", "*sauvement*", "*mandement*", "district", etc. The sources often allow us to perceive only one aspect of the alteration: the monopolizing of public powers and judiciary *authority (right of *ban), imposition of new and unaccustomed rights on productive activities (customs and bad customs, exactions, *tallage) and usurpation of church estates. The setting up of castellan power was accompanied by an unleashing of *violence, which left the *peasants with no choice but to resign themselves to oppression and dependence.

The expression "castellan lordship", forged by historians to designate the new power, emphasizes an essential element of the institution, the *castle. This could be, especially in the 10th c., a public fortress whose guardian had become autonomous, but archaeologists have also shown that in nearly every region of Europe the building of castles or fortified residences was the important moment of the construction of a lordship. Often consisting of a simple tower (the *rocca* of the Mediterranean regions) or an earthen *motte supporting a wooden building, the castle housed the lord's *family, as well as the knights that constituted his armed force. The change was not restricted to the form or the consistence of power. The lordships were in effect new types of organisation of space and productive functions. The castral **bourg* established at the foot of the castle concentrated artisanal activities and places of trade, while a new hierarchization of dwellings sometimes entailed a reorganisation and extension of cultivated lands. Numerous lordships were thus established in areas of land *clearance, but they could also specialize: in Italy or Germany, castellan lordships appeared in mining districts to control the production of precious *metals more closely. Most often, however, it was *fairs and *markets that aroused the covetousness of castellans confident of benefiting from the taxes imposed on transactions and from the revenues induced by the concentration of movable wealth.

Some have seen this new managerial cell of society as the very motor of the growth of the West, and its establishment as a revolutionary phenomenon. However the study of castellan lineages shows that this new type of power perpetuated the domination of a small number of families already in place sometimes since the Carolingian period. Innovative in its form of organisation of power, the castellan lordship was not, for all that, the instrument of a subversion of the *social order established in the early Middle Ages.

D. Barthélemy, *L'Ordre seigneurial*, Paris, 1990. – J.-P. Poly, É. Bournazel, *The Feudal Transformation*, New York, 1991.

Mathieu Arnoux

**CASTILE.** Castile – "land of *castles" –, first mentioned in documentation of *c.*800, east of the kingdom of Oviedo in the Cantabrian cordillera, was a frontier zone opposite the Vascones. Under the impetus of the local *comites* the region was populated, bishops "of Castile" appeared from 804, residing at Oca, Muñó or Valpuesta, and in 884 Count Diego Rodriguez founded the town of *Burgos. In the 10th c., the county of Castile came into being through the union of several small counties by Count Fernán González (930-970), who increased the extent and independence of his territory, fought victoriously against the Muslims, fixed the southern frontier along the Duero and followed a princely policy: foundation of monasteries, appeal to *Mozarabic *populatores*, matrimonial alliances with the kings of *Navarre and *León, and palace intrigues which more than once earned him imprisonment at the hands of the kings of León. Count Fernán González's descendants continued his policy and, without breaking officially with the *Crown, acted completely independently. The county was then characterised, in contrast to the kingdom of León which was dominated by great seignorial proprietors and had preserved the written law, by the presence of a population of free *peasants, grouped in village communities, to whom the possession of a horse and arms offered the possibilities of social ascent, which observed a customary law and spoke a slightly different language – Castilian appears for the first time in late 10th-c. glosses from the monastery of San Millán de la Cogolla.

At the death of Fernán González's last male descendant in 1029, Castile passed into the orbit of the kingdom of Navarre; Ferdinand, second son of Sancho III of Navarre and Mayor of Castile, became count of Castile, defeated his brother-in-law the king of León in 1037 and, anointed at León, took the title of king of Castile and León. But the union of the two "kingdoms" remained unstable until 1230, date of their definitive union under Ferdinand III; it was cemented in 1302 when the **Cortes* became general and no longer specific to each kingdom. From the second half of the 11th c., an intense propaganda, organised from monasteries like Silos or San Pedro de Cardeña, exalted Castile at the expense of León: *epic poems celebrated the exploits of Rodrigo Díaz de Vivar, the *Cid (1040-1099), the mythical founders – the "Judges of Castile" – and Count Fernán González; a hagiographical literature interested itself in local saints such as St Dominic of Silos (*c.*1000-1073) and St *Dominic Guzmán (1170-1221); and around 1224-1226 Bishop Juan of Burgos wrote a *chronicle of the kings of Castile beginning with Count Fernán González. In *c.*1180, King *Alfonso VIII of Castile founded the peninsula's first *university at Palencia – soon imitated by the king of León at *Salamanca (*c.*1218) – shortly before winning, against the Muslims, the decisive battle of Las *Navas de Tolosa which opened the doors of Andalusia; *clerics trained at Palencia appear to have quickly opted for the vernacular language, whether dealing with theological, historical or hagiographical themes, while King Ferdinand III (1217-1252) had the code of laws, the Fuero Juzgo, translated. The choice of Castilian as official language of the realm by *Alfonso X (1252-1284), who had legal codes, universal and national chronicles, scientific texts, notarial acts and chancery acts written in that language, crowned a movement that had begun nearly two centuries before, in the course of which the county of Castile had finally prevailed over the kingdom of León. Heraldic emblems, repeated to satiety from 1230 – from royal garments to horses' harnesses, wall ornaments, *seals and coins –, gave the arms of Castile precedence over those of León. In the mid 13th c., *Burgos, Castile's historic capital, whose bishopric had enjoyed *exemption from 1104, received the title of "head of Castile and chamber of kings" – "*cabeza de Castilla e camara de los reyes*" – and began a merciless struggle against *Toledo over the right of speech in the *Cortes*.

Despite a multitude of common traits in the history of the two kingdoms, Castile had thus finally won and, from the second half of the 12th c., "Castile" and "Spain" became interchangeable terms. The first general chronicles of the kingdom, in Latin like that of Rodrigo Jiménez de Rada or in the vernacular like the *Primera chronica general de España* (1260-1270), related a *history in which *Spain, lost by the last *Visigothic kings – from whom the kings of León were descended – had been "restored" by the kings of Castile.

Thus, from the 12th c., the characteristics of medieval Castile merged with those of the Crown of Castile, whose holder was king of Castile, León, Toledo, *Galicia, *Seville, *Cordova, Murcia, Jaén and the Algarve and lord of Molina and Viscaya. The

Fortifications of Avila (Castile). 12th-c. ramparts.

*Reconquest, a military undertaking likened by Pope *Paschal II in 1102 to a crusade, favoured the development of a society of free men liable to military service, at once peasants, *merchants or artisans, and men at arms. The repopulation of the conquered territories south of the Duero – the *extrema Durii* or first Estremadura – in the course of the second half of the 11th c., then of "New Castile" and Estremadura during the 12th, and finally of Andalusia from the third decade of the 13th, was done under the aegis of the Crown, which, by the concession of *fueros* (franchises) to communities of *populatores*, encouraged the development of a network of towns, endowed with ample areas that they administered, developed and defended and with which they served the king militarily and financially. Moreover the extent of the territory and its demographic weakness favoured the development of *animal husbandry and *commerce.

The political life of the Crown of Castile from the end of the 12th c. thus turned around three poles: the king, the urban oligarchies and the landed *nobility, and the *Cortes* were often turned to account to reaffirm the alliance of the king and the towns. The permanence of war and the existence of urban militias enabled the maintenance of a social mobility that made the very concept of nobility fluid, and, apart from theoretical treatises, it was difficult to distinguish between the *hidalgo* and the *caballero*, since both defended their realm and their faith by force of arms, and as such enjoyed fiscal exemptions. On the other hand the Visigothic tradition, preserved at León and copied by Castile, gave the kings particular powers, further strengthened by the introduction of *Roman law in the 13th century. The king of Castile, holder of the *imperium*, was moreover "defender of the faith", *i.e.* responsible for orthodoxy of doctrine and the eradication of *heresy and ignorance; so the Church of Spain was subject to the royal power, while the clergy never managed to form an "order" within society, and the foundation of universities long remained the privilege of a Crown that associated *scientia* with *potestas*.

The glorious period of the Reconquest suffered a setback after the incorporation of the greater part of Andalusia between 1230 and 1270. The troubled period that followed, marked by *famines, various calamities, plague and a state of endemic civil war and generalized insecurity, had as corollary a "reflection" of the political and social actors: the representatives of the towns meeting in the *Cortes* worked out a programme of government and preserved their urban autonomy, the *monarchy completed the judicial labours begun under Alfonso X, and the nobility used letters to legitimize itself. From 1370, Castile enjoyed a new and very brilliant period under the aegis of the new dynasty of the Trastámara. A higher nobility, born out of internal struggles, formed immense "States" at the expense of the royal or ecclesiastical domain, obtained concessions of revenues and struggled to impose its power within the royal council; titles of nobility, previously unknown, made their appearance, while the great aristocratic families lived in town, patronizing the arts and imposing an ideal that combined the spirit of *chivalry with antique "virtue". The development of large-scale international commerce played a role in the many Castilian attempts to control the straits of Gibraltar and in the support given to *France in the *Hundred Years' War against another maritime power, *England. The merchants of Burgos, organised into a "university of merchants", controlled the export of wool, encouraged the creation of *fairs, and imported cloth, *silks and works of art. The alliance between the Crown and the urban oligarchies was unfailing and often came into play even within the great "States" of the higher nobility. Prosperity and the management of large-scale commerce were accompanied by an intense cultural and artistic life, which mingled Hispanic roots – *Mudejar art, literary, historical and epic themes – with influences from Italy – *humanism, Renaissance art – and Northern Europe – themes of chivalrous literature, court etiquette, fashions, table manners. Theologians and *doctors of law took an active part in the councils of *Constance and *Basel and the papal *Curia soon contained a number of Castilian prelates.

At the end of the 15th c., the kingdom of Castile was undoubtedly the best-populated state in the Iberian peninsula, that whose commerce was most brilliant and whose king possessed the greatest powers. Its centre remained fixed in the region that had seen it develop in the 11th and 12th cc., around *Burgos, *Valladolid, Medina del Campo and Segovia. But on the marriage of the *Catholic Kings – both descendants of King John I of Castile –, Castile kept its autonomy: it conquered *Granada, America belonged to it, and in 1512 *Navarre was attached to it. And in the "Crown of Spain" reunited by the *Habsburgs from 1516, its name and its arms retained the primacy.

J. Pérez de Urbel, *Historia del condado de Castilla*, Madrid, 1945. – J. A. Maravall, *El concepto de España en la Edad Media*, Madrid, 1954. – S. de Moxó, *Repoblación y sociedad en la España cristiana medieval*, Madrid, 1979. – J. Valdeón, *Aproximación histórica a Castilla y León*, Valladolid, 1982. – P. Iradiel, S. Moreta, E. Sarasa, *Historia medieval de la España cristiana*, Madrid, 1989. – T.F. Ruiz, *The City and the Realm: Burgos and Castile, 1080-1492*, Aldershot, 1992. – S. Barton, *The Aristocracy in Twelfth-Century León and Castile*, Cambridge 1997.

Adeline Rucquoi

**CASTLE, FORTIFICATION.** One of the major phenomena of medieval society was the proliferation of castles and fortifications: involving the *ban and the warrior class, it affected one of its foundations. The traditional definition of the castle (*castrum*, *castellum*. . .) as the fortified residence of a powerful man and his entourage is inadequate to express the complexity of its functions and the evolutions that affected this complex organism at different times and places.

The fortifications of the early Middle Ages were generally undertaken by the public authorities in charge of locally ensuring the protection of a group, whether rural, pre-urban or urban. These vast collective works, temporary or permanent, were limited in number and as yet played a minor role. Morphologically, they were derived from earlier models and gave a dominant place to wood and earth.

The 10th and 11th cc. marked an important turning-point with the appearance and multiplication of true individual castles best symbolized by the *turris* and the *motte, and the development of collective rural *castra* of settlement. The evolution was more or less uniform. The right to fortify had at all times been a regalian privilege. The proliferation of castles at the initiative of aristocrats encouraged the weakening or even the failure of public authorities in favour of princes and then lords of lesser rank, in a territorial framework that was ceaselessly reduced in size, from principalities to castellan lordships. The castle was at the heart of the reorganisation of powers and lands that affected Europe. It was a residence of the *nobility and a centre of political, social, economic, military and sometimes even religious command, where seignorial protection and exploitation were exercised in concert.

From *c.*1150, princes and *kings began to recover their powers at a time when economic expansion was freeing greater resources, while validating new partners and other modes of government. They resumed the initiative in castral matters. The consequences of this were many. Castles and residences were more and more clearly distinguished. Fortresses, generally of stone, lost in surface area what they gained in practical and symbolic efficacity. This was the time of keeps (*donjons*), then of castles with reduced surfaces and highly developed curtain walls, while the noble dwelling tended to be demilitarized. At the same time, a more effective control of the spread of defensive attributes and the installation, among an already dense settlement, of intercalary dwellings and residences of knights or lords of little importance led from the late 12th c. to the development of fortified houses, simple moated enclosures, residential or demesnial in purpose, whose fortified elements were much reduced.

Urban communities started on a new phase of collective fortifications and began to acquire more autonomy in the matter. A phenomenon that became patent with the later Middle Ages and occasionally affected certain *villages.

M. W. Thompson, *The Decline of the Castle*, Cambridge, 1987. – *Le Château en France*, J.-P. Babelon (dir.), Paris, 1989 (re-ed.). – N. J. G. Pounds, *The Medieval Castle in England and Wales*, Cambridge, 1991. – H. Kennedy, *Crusader Castles*, Cambridge, 1994.

Annie Renoux

**Historical and political evolution.** The weakening of central power and the development of *agriculture enlarged the role and function of the castle, making it the very symbol of feudal society. The explicitly military connotation of castles was no more important than their political and social significance. Begun as a movement of self-defence by landed lords and the populations connected with them, the phenomenon known to historians as **incastellamento* gradually assumed a wider function, with a meaning of legal and social cohesion and political renewal. It corresponded, in fact, to the tendency to autonomy inherent in the landed power of the aristocracy, both military and ecclesiastical. Thus, while being connected to the traditional public order – by virtue of direct royal authorization to build castles, granted either to private individuals or to ecclesiastical entities, or to whole collectives –, in reality the phenomenon of fortress-building ended by becoming a benefit with a hereditary tendency, in which the castle itself was the central element of small local lordships. The transformation of the typology of settlement and of the very appearance of the landscape brought with it a transformation of the structures of power: in exchange for the protection he ensured, the lord had a right to exercise power, judging and punishing, and could ask the population to contribute economically through services and tribute. In this way, the castle became for the powerful, nobles or churchmen, an efective indirect method of imposing their own rule on the *peasant population. The castellan lord was the possessor and administrator of a whole fortified village, made up of a walled enclosure for external defence, the keep – the highest part of the stronghold, which dominated its entrance and served to sustain the final defence of the whole complex – and the inhabited nucleus, with the lord's residence, lodgings for domestics and the armed force, a *chapel and shelters for livestock and food, indispensable in case of a siege.

From the architectural point of view, the medieval castle was a progressive reworking and enrichment of the *castra* of Roman times, which were simple redoubts, rectangular enclosures fortified with embankments and ramparts or surrounded by crenellated walls. The fortifications of the early Middle Ages were initially isolated forts, rising alone in a high or at least dominant place, in which the feudatory's dwelling was limited to a few rooms cut into the towers and walls. Later the castle increasingly took on the structure of a fortified village, with the ample circle of walls strengthened on the outside by enscarped walls called barbicans. The walls were provided with lookout turrets linked to each other by passages inside or outside the crenellations, which formed the "beat" of the sentinels. In case of siege, between the fortress's crenellations were placed bartizans, mobile shelters that could be raised and lowered and served to protect the defenders; with the appearance of artillery, castles were provided with bastions, a polygonal ring of walls totally without crenellations or loopholes. If surrounded by a moat, the castle was linked to *terra firma* by the drawbridge, which was drawn up at night or in case of danger.

Within this general architectural typology can be distinguished

Castle of La Loarre, near Huesca, Aragon.

different structures and styles, linked to the different geographical areas. The French *château*, whose origins go back before the 10th c., stood on the *motte, an earth mound linked to an enclosure within which were dwellings and services; in later centuries there appeared on the motte the *donjon*, a main tower of stone, fortified and strengthened. Typical in German lands was the *Wasserburg* (water-castle), usually in a plain or defended by a moat, or placed on a small island – like the famous castle of Pfalzgrafenstein, built on a small island in the Rhine; in the Swabian period the plan was simplified and concentrated, with the appearance of the *donjon*, together with an independent external defensive system erected at the weakest points. The British style was typologically extremely varied, but had the common character of a very strong defence, with ramparts, palisades and keeps, the equivalent of the French *donjon*. At the end of the 12th c., buildings became polygonal or were erected encircled with towers and reinforced entrances. In *Spain, the encounter between Western and Eastern elements led to the birth of the **mudejar* style, with walls with projecting turrets, pentagonal towers and crooked gates.

Prevalent in *Italy was the castle naturally situated in a high place, sometimes – as in the case of Colle Casale (Viterbo) – projecting over a ravine, but the so-called "spur site" was also in demand. The castle was surrounded by a strong circle of walls, usually with a single gate giving access to the inhabited part, above which rose the tower, quadrangular or pentagonal, less often round. There was a clear geographical differentiation: in central Italy – particularly in *Latium, cradle of the phenomenon of *incastellamento* –, given the scarcity of economic means available, easily-defendable natural positions were particularly exploited. In the North (*e.g.* Castelfranco Veneto, Marostica), the design of the *architecture and the quality of execution and materials used speak rather of a precise need to consolidate the dominant image of *Communes and Signorie. Finally, in southern Italy, alongside the preponderant role played by local religious potentates, we should mention the series of castles built in *Apulia by *Frederick II, whose most original and balanced product is Castel del Monte, with its octagonal plan, octagonal towers and a portal in the form of a triumphal arch; to it explicitly refer the Ursino castle at Catania, Castel Maniace at Syracuse and the Emperor's Castle at Prato.

F. Cusin, "Per la storia del castello medievale", *Rivista storica italiana*, 1939. – R. von Uslar, *Studien zu frühgeschichtlichen Befestigungen zwischen Nordsee und Alpen*, Cologne-Graz, 1964. – G. Fasoli, "Castelli e signorie rurali", *Atti della XIII settimana di studio sull'Alto Medioevo*, Spoleto, 1966. – G. Vismara, "La disciplina giuridica del castello medievale", *Studia et documenta historiae et iuris*, 38, 1972. – P. Brezzi, *La civiltà del Medioevo europeo*, 2, Rome, 1978, 475-504. – G. Fournier, *Le château dans la France médiévale. Essai de sociologie monumentale*, Paris, 1979. – P. Toubert, *Feudalismo mediterraneo. Le strutture del Lazio medievale*, Milan, 1980 (It. tr.). – A. A. Settia, *Castelli e villaggi nell'Italia padana. Popolamento, potere e sicurezza fra IX e XIII secolo*, Naples, 1984. – R. Luisi, *Scudi di pietra. I castelli e l'arte della guerra tra Medioevo e Rinascimento*, Rome-Bari, 1996.

Lucia Velardi

**CASTRACANI, CASTRUCCIO (1281-1328).** Born in 1281 to Ruggero di Castracane and Puccia degli Streghi, in 1300 he left *Lucca following the clashes that brought the "black party" to power. After having been in arms in the service of the Scaligeri and of *Venice, he joined Uguccione della Faggiuola and militarily re-entered his city, where on 12 June 1316 he was acclaimed Captain and Defender. In 1320 *Frederick the Fair granted him the title of imperial vicar of Lucca, Valdinievole and Lunigiana, confirmed by Louis of Bavaria (1324); in 1327, Louis made him duke of Lucca. In 1324 and 1328, he was *excommunicated by *John XXII. He died of malarial fever on 3 Sept 1328. Machiavelli saw in him the ideal figure of the Prince.

L. Green, *Castruccio Castracani. A Study on the Origins and Character of a Fourteenth-Century Italian Despotism*, Oxford, 1986. – "Castruccio Castracane e il suo tempo", *Actum Luce*, 13-14, Lucca, 1986, 1-450.

Antonio Romiti

**CASUISTRY.** The word "casuistry" comes from the Latin *casus* (*cause): a legal or canonical situation, a human action, a case of conscience whose moral value one seeks to establish since it does not appear very clear: this is the task of the casuist. This latter term was vulgarized by Pascal in the *Provincial letters*, but not until the mid 19th c. did the *Dictionnaire de l'Académie française* admit "casuistry" (*casuistique*). Following the criticisms and attacks of Pascal, a restrictive and pejorative sense was added to, even when it did not, as often, replace the former sense; casuistry then designated a disposition to complacent subtlety which weakened the import of the laws and could lead to laxism. However, it must be appreciated that casuistry did not begin in the 17th c., though it enjoyed a sort of apogee then. In a spontaneous form, everyone practises it sometimes, if he is concerned to make his life agree with some moral requirements. In a more or less elaborate and detailed way, philosophical or religious ethics often propound interpretative rules that aim to make them immediately practical. Thus *Aristotle included casuistical developments in his *Nicomachean Ethics*; likewise Seneca in his *Letters to Lucilius*. Two authors among others, and two works appreciated and used in the Middle Ages.

The rabbis contemporary with or later than Christ discussed and resolved real or fictitious cases with great care for fidelity to the Law. Primarily concerned to teach the principles that ruled the life of his disciples, Christ did not hesitate to resolve the cases that his interlocutors, pharisees or doctors of the law, submitted to him to embarrass him: adulterous woman (Jn 8, 3-11), sabbath rest (Lk 6, 1-11; 14, 1-6), taxes due to Caesar (Lk 20, 20-26).

The admission of gentiles into the young Church raised the question of whether to maintain certain Jewish observances: decisions of the council of Jerusalem (Acts 15, 23-29) and of the apostle Paul concerning meat consecrated to idols (1 Cor 8). Contemporary with the formation of the New Testament, the *Didachè* specifies the behaviour of the disciple in the domain of ritual and liturgy (VI, 3 - X). A work of the mid 2nd c., the *Shepherd of Hermas*, contains a series of precepts relating to almsgiving, backbiting, lying, conjugal chastity, and penitence. The reconciliation of *lapsi* and baptism given by heretics posed difficult practical problems to the Church of the first centuries.

On the level of legislation, the *councils of the early Middle Ages or the Carolingian period promulgated series of canons, used by the *canonical collections of the 10th-12th cc. and Gratian's **Decretum* (*c.*1140): Church *property, status of *clerics, exclusion from the community, relations with *Jews, engagement and *marriage, reconcilation of *penitents, lending at interest. In the 12th and 13th cc., councils such as *Lateran III (1179) and Lateran IV (1215), synodal *statutes like those of Paris (*c.*1205) or the Synodal of the West (*c.*1220) took decisions in the sacramental sphere and that of family or economic ethics (*e.g.* restitution) that would orient the Church's pastoral teaching and law.

In a less elaborate way, *Penitentials (6th-13th cc.) nearly all appealed to a minimum of casuistry. Indeed, the list of sins and their tariffed sanctions (*e.g.* seven days of fasting on bread and water for a calumny) were most often accompanied by an invitation to the priest to examine the penitent's situation with solicitude, to adapt the satisfaction if necessary, or to commute it (recital of 100 *psalms in place of two days' fasting).

Towards the end of the 12th c., the *confessors' manuals that replaced the Penitentials sought mainly to instruct the priest, to facilitate the judgment he passed and the appreciation of the *penance he imposed. By the *Liber casuum conscientiae* included in his *Summa de sacramentis*, *Peter Cantor († 1197) prepared and clarified this pastoral inflection on the level of doctrinal and moral reflection. Some decades later *Raymond of Peñafort († 1275) compiled a legal and moral documentation (*Summa de paenitentia*, *Summa de matrimonio*). He issued judgments and advice that tried to help pastors and people in matters of civil and ecclesiastical legislation (morality of *commerce, war, peace, inheritances, etc.). The writings of Raymond of Peñafort would serve as a basis in the following centuries for many treatises of similar inspiration. The best known work is the *Summa moralis* of St *Antoninus, Dominican archbishop of Florence († 1459), concerned in his writings and preaching to favour examination of conscience with a view to *confession.

The propositions upheld by the Franciscan William of *Ockham († 1348) and the *nominalists would exercise great influence in the late Middle Ages and the early modern period, *e.g.* the difficulty of the *reason in attaining the universal, God's will as source of determination of *good and *evil, the value of obligation as foundation of morality, interest in concrete cases. Practical consequences: the importance accorded to the law and the various commandments, the permitted and the forbidden, each person's problems and doubts. In the 16th c., the practice of confession would be renewed and intensified, partly in reaction to Protestantism.

Casuistry certainly helped in the formation of consciences and in a *pastoral care attentive to the family, social and economic situation of individuals, but, too cut off from moral theology, it ordinarily left aside what related to the exercise of the virtues and evangelical perfection. This would go to establish the material of ascetical and mystical theology, for which there developed another science of individual cases: *spiritual direction.

R. Brouillard, "Casuistique", *Cath.*, 2, 1949, 630-636. – J. Longère, "L'influence de Latran III sur quelques ouvrages de théorie morale", *Le troisième Concile de Latran (1179). Sa place dans l'histoire*, Paris, 1982, 91-103. – J.-M. Aubert, "Probabilisme", *Cath.*, 11, 1988, 1064-1076.

Jean Longère

**CATALONIA.** Catalonia came into being, like the other Christian principalities of the northern Iberian peninsula, after the Arab-Berber conquest of the 8th century. The expeditions made by the *Franks and *Visigoths of *Septimania in the name of *Charlemagne ended in the annexation to the *Empire of the lands that would one day be Catalan: Gerona fell in 785, *Barcelona in 801; at Barcelona's south gates, beyond the Llobregat extended the *marca hispanica*, the Carolingian frontier with al-Andalus (Andalusia). The Catalan *bishoprics, once dependent on *Tarragona, were attached to *Narbonne: Roman ritual and the *Benedictine Rule were imposed, to the detriment of *Mozarabic practices. The kings of West Francia soon lost control of Catalonia. In 878, at the time of the assembly of Troyes, Louis the Stammerer for the last time appointed a *count, Wilfred I (870-897), member of a native family that received most of the Catalan counties. Heredity was imposed: his dynasty monopolized the countships until 1410. Wilfred I founded or restored the main monasteries in his lands – *Ripoll, Sant Joan de les Abadesses, Sant Gugat del Vallés, *Saint-Michel-de-Cuxa – and organised the reconquest and repopulation of central Catalonia. On his death, he distributed his counties among his children: the eldest, Wilfred II Borrell (897-911), received Barcelona; his successors acquired supremacy over the other counts, their kinsmen, holders of Empúries, Roussillon, Besalú, the Cerdagne and Urgell. In the course of the 10th c., links with the king of France gave way: Wilfred of Besalú (927-957) was the last Catalan count to do him *homage; to the journey between Seine and Loire, his relations preferred the *pilgrimage to *Rome, where they obtained many privileges from the *pope for their *cathedrals and monasteries; they did not hesitate to submit to the *caliph of *Cordova to avoid the attacks of his troops. In 987, the joint effect of the sack of Barcelona by al-Mansur and the usurpation of Hugh Capet finally consummated the break: the new king of France was incapable of coming to the help of the Catalan counts, whose Carolingian legitimism rejected the Robertian *coup d'état*. Ramon Borell of Barcelona (992-1017) was the first count to strike coins with his own effigy; from the break-up of the Umayyad caliphate of Cordova at the start of the 11th c., he imposed his law on the Muslim *emirs. A Catalan identity appeared, steeped in Gothicism and obsolete attachment to the *Carolingians (M. Zimmermann).

In the 11th c., the higher aristocracy took the lead in Catalonia, revolting against the authority of the counts. It occupied previously public *castles. Freeholders, well-do-do *peasants, became knights in its service: *oaths and *homages ratified their loyalty to the great men. The peasantry lost their *freedom: humiliating tolls, the *mals usos*, sanctioned their servitude. Historians dispute the nature of this change. For P. Bonnassie, this "*feudalism" descended on Catalan society in the short period of a sudden change, in the years 1030-1060; it was the bitter fruit of the economic growth encouraged by the massive consignments of *gold coming from al-Andalus, now tributary to the Christians. J.-M. Salrach prefers to speak of a long process of "feudalization", spreading the rise of the aristocracy and the subjection of the peasantry between the 3rd and the 12th centuries. In response to private wars and *revolts against the prince, the clergy, over whom whistled the spirit of the *Gregorian reform, tried to pacify society: *Oliba, bishop of Vich (1018-1046) and abbot of Ripoll and Saint-Michel-de-Cuxa, allied to Ermessende of Carcassonne, countess of Barcelona, invented the *Truce of God. Culture, particularly scientific culture, shone out in Pyrenean monasteries in contact with the knowledge conveyed by the Arab world. On the building sites of *cathedrals and churches, the techniques of *Romanesque art spread, imported from *Lombardy and al-Andalus.

From the 1060s, Raymond Berenguer I of Barcelona and his wife Almodis de la Marche restored the count's authority. They subdued the old aristocracy whom they attached to themselves by rites of feudality; a legislative code, the *Usatges de Barcelona*, promulgated in 1068, regulated the new relations between the prince and the *nobles. In 1067, the count used the tributes levied on the neighbouring emirs to buy *Carcassonne. The family of the counts of Barcelona continued its expansion under Raymond Berenguer III (1093-1131) who annexed to his domain the counties of Besalú (1111), *Provence (1112) and Cerdagne (1117). The conquest of *Tarragona (1118) allowed him to restore its *archbishopric and detach the Catalan *dioceses from the ecclesiastical *province of *Narbonne. Raymond Berenguer IV (1131-1162) completed the conquest of New Catalonia, between the Llobregat and the Ebro, taking Tortosa (1148) and Lérida (1149). By his marriage with Petronilla, he federated his principality, with respect to its native institutions, with neighbouring *Aragon and obtained the royal title for his successors. To differentiate these two territories, *charters increasingly employed the word "Catalonia", the land of *castlans*, members of castle garrisons. Catalan already displayed its own dialectal traits within the Occitan group, as witness the *Homilies of Organyà* (*c.*100), the first known literary text in this language.

The count-king *Alfonso I (1162-1196) took over the counties of Roussillon (1172) and Pallars Jussà (1192) and fought on the Occitan and Muslim fronts. He composed *chansons* in *langue d'*oc* and attracted numerous *troubadours to his court. He encouraged the settlement of *Cistercians on his lands: their monastery of *Poblet became the new royal necropolis. His son *Peter II (1196-1213) was killed during the Albigensian crusade. James I (1213-1276) by the treaty of Corbeil (1258) renounced his rights over the Midi, in exchange for emancipation from the sovereignty of the king of France. He conquered the *Balearic islands (1229-1235) and the kingdom of *Valencia (1232-1245). In the 14th c., his successors pursued expansion in the Mediterranean: *Sardinia, *Sicily, the duchies of Athens and Neopatras, conquered by the Almogávares, came under their rule. Barcelona and the other *port towns of the confederation enjoyed unprecedented growth. Their *merchants and craftsmen were particularly susceptible to the *preaching of the *mendicants. Among the *Dominicans, the canonist *Raymond of Peñafort took part in 1218 in the foundation of the *Mercedarian Order for the redemption of captives. Among the *Franciscans, Raymond *Lull (1235-1315), a fervent missionary, was the first to use the vernacular in philosophical works; Francesc *Eiximenis (*c.*1340-1409) drew up his great *encyclopedia *Lo Chrestià*, and the renegade Anselm Turmeda (1352-1423) *La disputa de l'Ase*. The *Spirituals were numerous despite the persecutions of *John XXII; the personality of *Arnold of Villanova (1235-1311) presided over the birth of several communities of *beghards; King *Peter IV (1336-1387) protected them and profited from the spread of Joachite themes exalting the messianism of his house. Official *historiography, represented by *chroniclers like Ramon Muntaner or Bernat Desclot, equally served the interests of the *Crown.

The 15th c. marks the decline of Catalonia. The Castilian dynasty of Trastámara ascended the throne of Aragon in 1412 after the compromise of Caspe, in which *Vincent Ferrer and Benedict XIII ensured the triumph of the candidature of Ferdinand I (1412-1416). The pursuit of Mediterranean imperialism under *Alfonso V (1416-1458) attached *Naples to the confederation, while exhausting the human and financial resources of the Catalan population, ravaged by *famine and *epidemics. The power of John II (1458-1479) was contested by the Catalan aristocracy in revolt: during the civil war, the *remences*, enslaved peasants of Old Catalonia, took up arms. They obtained their freedom through the Sentencia Arbitral de Guadalupe, given in 1486 by Ferdinand II the Catholic (1479-1516) who united the Catalan-Aragonese confederation with *Castile by his marriage with Queen Isabella. Under the Trastámara, Italian *humanism penetrated Catalan letters, as witness *Lo somni* of Bernat Metge (1340-1413) or the poems of Ausiàs March (1397-1459). The chivalric *romance reached its apogee with *Tirant lo Blanc* by Joanot Martorell (1413-1468). *Flamboyant Gothic prevailed in religious and civil *architecture. At the start of the 16th c., Castile, strengthened by a precocious demographic recovery, took over the leadership of Iberia from a Catalonia in crisis.

*Histoire de la Catalogne*, J. Nadal (dir.), P. Wolff (dir.), Toulouse, 1982. – T. N. Bisson, *The Medieval Crown of Aragon*, Oxford, 1986. – P. Freedman, *The Origins of Peasant Servitude in Medieval Catalonia*, Cambridge, 1991.

Martin Aurell

## CATENAE, BIBLICAL

**The West.** The title of *catena* appeared for the first time in the West in 1321 apropos of *Thomas Aquinas's *Catena aurea*, composed between 1261 and 1268 and called by its author *Expositio continua*.

The *Glossa ordinaria*, which was progressively established in the 12th c. and appeared in a uniformized version in the mid 13th, borrowed most of its explanations from the works of the *Fathers, but these were usually known in their original version, and from this point of view the *Gloss does not have the interest of the Eastern *catenae*.

Thomas Aquinas, in the dedicatory epistle to Pope *Urban IV that opens the *Catena aurea*, defines the aim of his work thus: to comment on the Gospel in a sustained way by compiling the teachings provided by various books of "*Doctors". His work is remarkable for the wealth and novelty of its documentation, as well as the care with which it selects and arranges its sources. It was part of the effort of *rapprochement* between East and West in the late 13th c. and had a great influence on later *exegesis of the gospels.

R. Devreesse, "Chaînes bibliques grecques", *DBS*, 1928, 1084-1233. – M. Geerard, *CPG*, 4, 1980. – C. Curti, "Catenae, Biblical", *EEC*, 1, 1992, 152-153.

Gilles Berceville

**Byzantium.** The expression "Biblical catenae" designates a literary form of Scriptural interpretation that appeared in the 6th c. in the Greek church of Palestine. It gradually spread to the whole Byzantine world and beyond, by translation or adaptation, into the Latin – *Thomas Aquinas's celebrated *Catena aurea* on the four Gospels –, Syriac, Armenian, *Coptic, Arabic and *Ethiopian realms. It remained productive until the end of the *Byzantine Empire and even later, in 16th-c. Italy and the monasteries of Mount *Athos.

The term *catena* comes from the medieval Latin for "chain". Early terminology speaks of "exegetical extracts" or "collection of exegeses": catenae are compilations of extracts, either from literary forms of interpretation of Scripture (commentaries, *homilies and scholia) or from non-exegetical works commenting occasionally on biblical verses. These exegetical extracts, generally preceded by their author's name, are set down in the same order as the verses of the *Bible. So a catena consists of a "concatenation" of one or more exegetical extracts borrowed from various authors, whose order is strictly determined by the "chain" of biblical verses.

The inventor of the catena was probably the famous Christian sophist Procopius of Gaza, of whom only some *Epitomes* (abridgments) survive. Around 540, an anonymous author, doubtless a pupil of Procopius but working at Caesarea in Palestine,

*Cathar at the stake.* Minute-book of Alfaro de France (adviser of Simon de Montfort). Pen-and-ink sketch drawn by a clerk in the margin of an interrogation report.

made a catena on the *Psalms, the "Palestinian catena", essentially from the commentaries of Didymus, Eusebius, *Origen and Theodoret, as well as the homilies of Basil, Cyril and John Chrysostom. Several dozen more catenae on the Psalms would subsequently be composed, firstly in Palestine, then, from 650-700, at *Constantinople and in its dependencies. The catenae on the New Testament seem to date from this second period.

Not every book of the Bible gave rise to catenae: no historical book from Ezra onwards; neither Wisdom nor Ecclesiasticus; not Mark. This absence is not deliberate, but corresponds to the non-existence of Greek exegesis on these books.

The catenae are revealing of the importance given in the Middle Ages to the tradition of the Fathers, and they allow us a knowledge of numerous exegetical works that would otherwise have disappeared: thus, in the case of the Psalms, the interpretations of Apollinaris, Athanasius, Cyril of Alexandria, Didymus (in part), Eusebius of Caesarea (except Ps 51-95, 3), Evagrius, Hesychius of Jerusalem (in part), Origen (in part) and Theodore of Mopsuestia.

G. Dorival, *Les chaînes exégétiques grecques sur les Psaumes*, 1, Louvain, 1986; 2, 1989; 3, 1992; 4, 1996. – F. Petit, *La chaîne sur la Genèse*, 1, Louvain, 1992; 2, 1993; 3, 1995. – G. Conticello, "San Tommaso ed i Padri: la Catena aurea super Ioannem", *AHDL*, 57, 1989, 31-92.

Gilles Dorival

**CATHARS, ALBIGENSES.** From the 10th c. in the *Byzantine Empire, from the 11th in Western *Christendom, there appear a number of heretical communities sharing common characteristics that distinguish them from other contemporary movements of religious criticism and renewal. The texts know them under various names, including Albigenses in the French Midi. We will follow the convention of calling them Cathars. The Church also called them, more simply, the *heretics. They themselves used no other name than Christians in the West, or Christopolitans and *Bogomils ("loved by God") in the East.

By their reading of the Scriptures, which was both literal and critical, by their opposition to the superstitious practices of the Roman Church, its dogmatic innovations and the framework of its institutional domination, by their constant reference to the ideals of *apostolic life and the practices of the early Church, these communities broadly form part of the great evangelical and *anticlerical movement of the 11th century.

Though the peasant Leutard, in *Champagne in the year 1000, may have confined himself to breaking crosses, insisting on *chastity, denouncing *tithes and preaching the Gospel, the lettered *canons burned by King Robert the Pious at *Orléans in 1022 seem already to have been conferring the Holy Spirit by *laying on of hands. Analogous groups are found from Piedmont to *Flanders; but it is in the Rhineland, in the first half of the 12th c., that indisputable Cathar communities are described with precision.

Those who were called the heretics did not merely reject the practice of infant *baptism by a rationalist critique, they rejected all the *sacraments of the great Church as not based on Scripture, including the *Eucharist, out of docetism; they did not believe in Christ's human incarnation and they practised their own sacrament, a baptism in the Spirit, by laying on hands: dressed as religious, they lived in communities of men and women and worked with their hands; organised and structured into clergy, higher clergy and ordinary believers, they had the dual character of regular monks and *secular clerics: in his letter to St *Bernard in *c.*1145, Énervin, provost of Steinfeld, likens them to a counter-church. He also indicates that their bishop and his companion, brought before the archbishop of *Cologne before being burned, "defended their heresy with the words of Christ and the Apostle"; that they claimed to be apostles themselves, and knew that they had brothers as far away as Greece.

At the end of the 12th c., we also learn that they were dualists (*Ekbert of Schönau) and that their communities were sufficiently numerous and influential in France, Italy, Albigeois, Toulousain, Agenais and Carcassès to be organised into Churches administered by an episcopal hierarchy in the manner of the Eastern Churches (mission of the Bogomil Nicetas to the meeting of Saint-Félix-Lauragais in 1167). In the 13th c., the massive supply of specific documents provides precise information on Catharism: most of the sources are admittedly of *Catholic origin (*Summae* of anti-heretical polemic and archives of the *Inquisition), but they do not contradict what we learn from Cathar documents (treatises and rituals), which gives us original glimpses into the heretical religious sensibility.

At the start of the 13th c., Catharism managed to implant itself lastingly in four parts of Europe: *Bulgaria, *Bosnia, northern *Italy and *Languedoc, perhaps for the simple reason – but a reason that remains to be analysed region by region – that the feudal authorities there left the "good Christians" to preach more or less openly and set out to populations in need of pastoral teaching their simple, reassuring and *a priori* Christian response.

Organised and structured into a Church, resting on a whole network of overt and dynamic religious houses, Cathar preachers presented themselves as "good Christians", claiming apostolic filiation against the "usurping" Roman Church. A single sacrament, baptism in the Spirit and in fire, abundantly based in Scripture, combined for them all the sacred functions of Catholicism. They called it "baptism of Jesus Christ" or *consolamentum*: as baptism, this sacrament conferred the character of a Christian; it remitted *sins just as Catholic *baptism remitted original sin and *penance mortal sins; it could thus ensure *salvation, even on one's deathbed as final penance or *extreme unction; as *marriage, it achieved the mystical union of the human *soul, of divine origin, with the *Holy Spirit, since, equivalent to a *confirmation, it supplemented baptism in water by the outpouring of the Spirit: "Except a man be born of water, and of the Spirit, he cannot enter into the kingdom of God" (Jn 3, 5) – or, in the Baptist's words: "But he that cometh after me . . . shall baptize you with the Holy Spirit, and with fire" (Mt 3, 11).

On the level of practice, the *consolamentum* was equivalent to the pronouncement of monastic *vows (life in community, according to the Rule of the evangelical precepts, ritual prayers, *continence and abstinence) that made Cathar Christians, both men and women, into religious; but it was also equivalent to an *ordination, since it conferred on Christian men and women the right to preach and the power to bind and unbind sins by conferring this sacrament in their turn. Much more than the *dualism of their interpretation of the Scriptures, it was the practice of this single Christian sacrament that created the identity and unity of Cathar Churches across Europe. This explains why the members of this regular-secular Cathar clergy were generally considered, by witnesses before the Inquisition of the Midi, as "Good Men and Good Women, and Good Christians, who had the power to save souls".

Thanks to inquisitorial sources, the sociology of the overt establishment of Catharism in the French Midi is particularly well known. Catharism was accepted there as an ordinary Christianity, particularly favoured among the prosperous classes: small aristocracy, commercial and skilled bourgeoisie of the **bourgs* and *castra*. The crusade against Count *Raymond of Toulouse, the viscount of *Carcassonne and *Albi and their vassals (1209-1229) decimated the Cathar Church on its great collective pyres before depriving it of its natural protectors; the establishment of a French, Catholic power and the setting up of the Inquisition condemned it to a clandestinity that became desperate after the fall of Montségur and the ruin of the last political and military hopes of the count of Toulouse (1244). A policy of proscriptions, delation and terror among the population of believers ended, in the first third of the 14th c., in the elimination of the Cathar Church from its Languedocian territories, which became royal **sénéchaussées*, despite that Church's last and impressive burst of energy under the brothers Authié between 1300 and 1310.

In Italy, the Inquisition only showed itself truly effective after the victory of the *Guelfs, and repression was retarded by some decades. Depositions of dualist tendency are still found in the archives of the Italian Inquisition at the very beginning of the 15th century. In Bulgaria and Bosnia, it was the Muslim Turkish invasion that drew a veil of silence over Christians and Bogomils in the second half of the 15th century.

Catharism, unlike *Waldensianism, was totally eliminated from history. The causes of its disappearance were many: an archaic Christianity, it showed itself less well adapted to the new *spirituality of the Gothic and *Franciscan period than it had been to the world of Romanesque *monasticism; a Church closely organised around a sacrament and a clergy, it would prove less capable of renewing itself in clandestinity than a simple movement of spontaneous revolt; and above all, the Roman Church, backed by the political authorities, marshalled against it a repression of rare efficiency.

After its disappearance from memory and a whole series of attempts at religious, literary and even esoteric recovery, Catharism is just beginning to be disengaged from its matrix of myths; the problem of its origins is not definitively resolved. It may, like its Bogomil counterpart, have represented the updating, in the climate of the medieval reforms, of an early Christian tradition of Scriptural exegesis and sacramental practice; the dogmatic character of its dualism has probably been exaggerated: it was much more certainly by its rejection of the sacrament of the altar, of the incarnation of the Son and of an eternal *hell that it was opposed to the Catholic Church. In any case it would be wrong to go on pretending today that it was a foreign body within medieval *Christendom.

J. Duvernoy, *La Religion des cathares*, Toulouse, 1989. – *Bibliographie de l'Histoire médiévale en France*, 1965-1990, Paris, 1992, 149. – J. R. Strayer, *Albigensian Crusades,* Ann Arbor (MI), 1992. – Y. Hagman, "Le rite d'initiation chrétienne chez les cathares et les bogomiles", *Heresis*, 21, Carcassonne, 1993, 13-31. – A. Brenon, *Les Cathares, vie et mort d'une Église chrétienne*, Paris, 1996. – M. D. Costen, *The Cathars and the Albigensian Crusade,* Manchester, 1997. – M. Lambert, *The Cathars*, Oxford, 1998.

Anne Brenon

***CATHEDRA.*** *Liturgical objects and ornaments played a precise emblematic and allegorical role in the Middle Ages, and certain elements like the faldstool or, more importantly, the episcopal throne, which were part of the furniture of the church, were charged with precise symbolic values. The *cathedra* or episcopal chair was particularly important because it was placed at the end of the apse, the point on which the congregation's attention converged. Despite its name, it was not derived from the Greek *cathedra*, but rather from the *thronos* with which it had in common the arms and high back. Not only was it part of the instruments of worship, it tended to qualify the sacred building: it was from the presence of the episcopal cathedra that the *cathedral, where the *bishop, with the *chapter, celebrated religious functions with particular solemnity, took its name. Among early Christian examples are the *cathedra* of the Euphrasian basilica of Parenzo (*Istria), that of Santa Sabina at *Rome, or the ivory *cathedra* of Bishop Maximian at *Ravenna, with episodes from the Old and New Testaments. The "*chair of St Peter", enclosed by Bernini in his celebrated bronze cover, actually dates from the 8th-9th centuries. And it is in the Romanesque period that we see an increase in the production of *cathedrae*, with a wide variety of iconographical and symbolic elements making use of various *typologies and materials. Thus we pass from the Cosmatesque *cathedrae* ornamented with *mosaic in the churches of San Clemente, San Lorenzo and Santa Sabina at Rome, or that of the Vassalletto at *Anagni, to the sculpted *cathedrae* especially prevalent in southern *Italy, with decorations rich in variants taken from various sources. Often supported by real or imaginary animals (elephants in the *cathedra* by the sculptor Romuald in the cathedral of Canosa, lions

Cathedra of San Barbato at Benevento cathedral. 12th c.

in that of Calvi, caryatids or atlantes in that of the basilica of San Nicola at *Bari), they generally refer to the struggle between *good – represented by the person of the bishop who, by his presence alone, subjects demonic and negative forces – and *evil. From the Gothic period, *cathedrae* were made of wood, which has made their preservation into our own time difficult. Moreover the importance of the *cathedra* gradually diminished, in proportion to the prevalence of a new arrangement with the *altar attached to the end wall of the church and the consequent displacement of the episcopal throne to one side.

C. Frugoni, "L'Ideologia del potere imperiale nella 'Cattedra di S. Pietro'", *BISI*, 86, 1976-1977, 67-182.

Monica Chiellini Nari

**CATHEDRAL.** However unimportant it may be, these days a church is easily called a "cathedral"; this is because a cathedral nowadays is hardly distinguished from a parish church any more, indeed it often performs the same functions, and as such it has an ordinary priest at its head, even if from time to time the *bishop comes there to celebrate a solemn *office. But on the juridical level, a cathedral cannot be confused with a religous edifice possessing another status. At the time of Christianization, bishoprics were set up. At their head were designated bishops whose task was to administer the *sacraments. Cathedral groups were constructed in the capital towns of **civitates*, inside their fortifications. These buildings comprised the *domus* of the bishop and the *clerics attached to his person and often three near-by churches: one, dedicated to the Virgin, was reserved for the bishop, the second for the cathedral clergy, the third, bearing the name of St John, was the place where the bishop administered *baptism, which was done by immersion until the Carolingian period. Annexed buildings, connected with the bishop's charitable *foundations, completed this group. Thus veritable holy towns developed within cities.

After the period of crisis of ecclesiastical institutions that corresponded to the end of the *Merovingians and the "reign" of *Charles Martel, a reorganisation was imposed. Under *Charlemagne and *Louis the Pious, the function of *metropolitan *archbishop regained a lost lustre, and the reform conceived by *Chrodegang, bishop of Metz, to regulate the life of his cathedral clerics by making them live in community according to the Rule of St *Benedict, was extended to every *diocese. So everywhere new buildings had to be created to ensure this common life, a refectory, a dormitory and a chapter house organised around a *cloister, the whole surrounded by an *enclosure wall. At the same time, the bishop was sometimes entrusted with new tasks, notably that of the civil administration of the town he lived in. Numerous cathedral churches were rebuilt or modernized: thus at *Reims, *Noyon and *Cambrai. In the 9th and 10th cc., the last *invasions upset the existing organisation, as interruptions in the lists of bishops indicate, but few episcopal sees disappeared at this time.

From the late 11th c., however, we see a rebirth of the *towns, and at the same time the *Gregorian reform gave back the clergy its prestige and dignity. *Romanesque art was the artistic expression of this new climate. Then began a great movement that found its culminating point in the Gothic period: the reduction of the number of buildings by their fusion, even if partitions within the new edifice imposed on everyone his allotted place – like the *rood screen and the *choir enclosure that separated the clergy from the congregation. This anxiety to isolate themselves from the *laity to celebrate the many offices of daily life in quietude is particularly clear in cases where the cathedral also had to accommodate numerous *pilgrims come to venerate the *relics housed there. It was to ease their circulation that the formula of the ambulatory with radiating chapels was worked out: from the 11th c., the cathedrals of *Rouen, *Chartres and *Auxerre, whose dimensions were already considerable, were among the buildings with this plan. On each side of the church developed buildings intended for the bishop and the *canons. The episcopal palace contained a *chapel, while the canons could have a cloister, but, the majority of cathedral *chapters having refused the discipline of the common dormitory, individual houses were allotted to the *canons. The renown of certain episcopal *schools, like those of Chartres or *Laon, supposes the existence of particular buildings, but nothing is known of them.

From 1140 began the *Gothic period; over a dozen decades, the majority of the cathedrals were renewed in considerable dimensions. These formidable building-sites did not fail to pose great problems of *town planning, even though a great part of the terrain occupied by the new buildings already belonged to the sacred enclosure. The creation of these gigantic edifices entailed demolitions and transfers of buildings. We are very ill-informed about the solutions found for the practical problems posed by these enormous building-sites: the decision to construct a new edifice could be taken conjointly by the bishop and the chapter; in other cases, the former might take no interest in the affair and leave the direction of operations and its financing to the latter; it was the revenues of the bishop and the canons (the latter's share becoming more and more important over time, as the role they played in the administration of the fabric also indicates) that – at least to begin with – procured the necessary funds; it was later necessary to appeal to other sources of finance like alienations of properties, *collections linked to *processions of relics, *indulgences; it is certain that the fiscal exactions entailed by these constructions were sometimes a source of discontent, or even of rebellion, as can be seen at Reims and *Amiens. The accounts corresponding to the years of construction proper are unfortunately lost. Often building-sites started off well, then activity had to be slowed down, resources dwindling when more costly works were reached (erection of scaffolding, more delicate cutting of stones in the upper parts). Generally the site was open to the east, a new ambulatory enveloping the old one, but it was otherwise at Cambrai, Chartres or Amiens. The need to ensure daily worship obliged the old building to be retained for decades, it being demolished bit by bit as the new work advanced. We can only be surprised at the rapidity with which these buildings were created, when we consider the technical means available at the time; we forget, *e.g.*, that to ensure their stability it was necessary to put down foundations going very deep, as far as the solid rock. To speed up the work, new techniques were perfected, like the cutting of stones in series.

At the end of the 13th c., architectural activity slowed down as economic and demographic circumstances deteriorated; the *Hundred Years' War and its financial consequences (taxes levied in one form or other by rulers, non-return of dues owed by peasants) further aggravated the situation; people then confined themselves to minor works, like the embellishment of interiors with furniture and *tapestries. *Confraternities or *corporations were authorized to build chapels dedicated to their patron saints between the piers of the flying buttresses, which increased the surface of the buildings often to the great prejudice of the external or internal effects intended by their first creators. It can thus be claimed that no cathedral was really finished: it was the towers and spires that suffered most from this halt in building enthusiasm.

The modern period (especially the 18th c.) neglected the upkeep of the cathedrals, and the French Revolution destroyed some, like those of *Arras and Cambrai, which were among the finest. Favoured by the renewal of Catholicism and the rise of Romanticism, the 19th c. undertook the restoration of the buildings, a task to which the public authorities – who in France have been in charge of the upkeep and repair of cathedrals since 1905 – now devote considerable sums.

J. Gimpel, *The Cathedral Builders*, London, 1993. – A. Erlande-Brandenburg, *The Cathedral*, Cambridge, 1994. – *La Cathédrale (XII^e^-XIV^e^ siècle)*, *CFan*, 30, Toulouse, 1995. – *The Archaeology of Cathedrals*, T. Tatton-Brown (ed.), J. Munby (ed.), Oxford, 1996.

Jacques Thiébaut

Reims cathedral, 11th-12th c.

**CATHERINE OF BOLOGNA (1413-1463).** Caterina Vigri, born at *Bologna of a diplomat father, was introduced to the ducal court of Niccolò III d'Este where she received a *humanist education. On her father's death, in *c.*1427 she entered a community of *Franciscan tertiaries who, under the influence of Friars Minor of the *Observance, evolved towards a religious life with *vows. In 1432 she adopted the Rule of St *Clare, but with revenues and *property. In 1456, with some companions, she founded the monastery of *Corpus Domini* at Bologna, becoming its *abbess. Catherine is known mainly thanks to her major work, many times re-edited, *The Seven spiritual weapons*, in which she traces the stages of return to God the Father with *Christ the Spouse. Despite traditional aspects of medieval piety, her work denotes an interiorization of the spiritual life. Catherine was canonized in 1712 (feast 9 May).

Catherine of Bologna, *Le Sette Armi Spirituali*, Bologna, 1981. – A. Van den Wyngaert, *DHGE*, 11, 1949, 1505-1506.

Élisabeth Lopez

**CATHERINE OF GENOA (1447-1510).** Caterinetta *Fieschi, born at *Genoa, belonged to a family that gave the republic doges and the Church *popes and *cardinals. Married in 1463 against her will, she suffered the infidelities of her husband, Giuliano Adorno. On 20 March 1473, while preparing for *confession, she had a decisive experience of the saving presence of God and of her own miseries. Her intense mystical life was joined to tireless charitable activity among the sick of the Genoa *hospital. Until 1499, she underwent many supernatural experiences and physical penances in the absence of any *spiritual direction. The source of her activity and her *doctrine was the experience of the presence of *Christ in her. She lived a "mystical purgatory", a purificatory stage necessary in her eyes in order to respond to God and know him. Patron saint of Genoa, Catherine Fieschi was canonized in 1737 (feast 15 Sept).

St Catherine of Siena gives her heart to Christ. Painting by Guidoccio Cozzarelli, 1450-1516. Siena, Pinacoteca Nazionale.

*Libro de la Vita mirabile e Dottrina santa de la Beata Caterinetta da Genova. Nel quale si contiene un utile e catholica dimostratione e dichiaratione del purgatorio*, Genoa, 1551.

P. Debongnie, "Catherine de Gênes", *DHGE*, 11, 1949, 1506-1515. – F. von Hugel, *The Mystical Element of Religion as Studied in St. Catherine of Genoa and her Friends*, 2 vols., 1961. – *Oxford Dictionary of Saints*, Oxford, 1984, 70.

Élisabeth Lopez

**CATHERINE OF SIENA (*c*.1347-1380).** Catherine Benincasa, born at *Siena, died at *Rome, was canonized by the Sienese Pope *Pius II in 1461 and numbered among the *Doctors of the Church by Paul VI in 1970.

Catherine was the last-born of the numerous family of Lapa and Jacopo, a dyer at Siena. At the age of six, a *vision of *Christ revealed her mystical vocation to her; she chose *virginity and marriage to Christ. Around 17, against her family's will and contrary to custom, she was admitted by the *Dominican *Third Order, continuing to live in her parents' house. Her spiritual formation was guided by the friars of the convent of San Domenico. Catherine constructed her *mysticism of union with Christ through the systematic destruction of her body and through partaking of the *Eucharist; she assisted the poor and sick and created around her a spiritual family of which she was the *mamma*.

Though she wished to enjoy Christ in *contemplation, he pressed her to fight for the Church. The objectives of Catherine's "public life" (from 1370) were the *crusade, the return of the *pope from *Avignon to Rome, and the reform of the Church. These projects requiring peace in *Christendom, Catherine gave herself up to political activity, by an intense correspondence and several journeys. A general *chapter of the Dominicans at Florence in 1374 recognised the religious quality of her life and gave her as confessor *Raymond of Capua, who was later her biographer (*Legenda major*, finished in 1395). In 1375, at Pisa (1st April), she received Christ's *stigmata, invisible unlike those of *Francis of Assisi. From June to September, she lived at Avignon and managed (no doubt) to see Pope *Gregory XI; she also wrote to him and with others convinced him to return the Church's government to Rome (Jan 1377). Back in Siena, she intervened in the *politics of the Italian towns and *signorie*. She stayed for a time in Florence (1377-1378) to reconcile that town with the pope. But her political interventions were not well informed and were far from convincing the Florentines, and Catherine at one time found herself seriously threatened. In 1378, when the *Great Schism began, Catherine, called to Rome by *Urban VI, devoted herself to the cause of the Roman pope and the reform of the Church, until the death that allowed her total union with Christ.

Catherine's written work is considerable. The *Dialogue on divine providence*, or *Book of divine doctrine* (1377-1378), dictated by Catherine to her secretaries in her moments of *ecstasy, defined, in an affective and vivid way, her theology of union between *man and *God through Christ. The *Letters* were copied into collections by her disciples in order to spread her cult. The cult of Catherine was promoted by the Dominican Order; it proposed a model of feminine *spirituality face to face with the world and confirmed a great mystical experience.

Catherine of Siena, *The Dialogue*, S. Noffke (ed.), London, New York, 1980. – *The Letters of Catherine of Siena*, Binghamton (NY), 1988-.

R. Fawtier, L. Canet, *La Double Expérience de Catherine Benincasa*, Paris, 1948. – E. Dupré-Théseider, "Caterina da Siena", *DBI*, 22, 1970, 361-379. – *Atti del Simposio internazionale cateriniano-bernardiniano (Siena 1980)*, D. Maffei (ed.), P. Nardi (ed.), Siena, 1982. – *Catherine de Sienne*, Avignon, 1992 (exhibition catalogue).

Odile Redon

**CATHERINE OF SWEDEN (*c*.1331-1381).** Daughter of St *Bridget of Sweden and the knight Ulf Gudmarsson, at the age of 19 Catherine became the widow of the knight Eggard van Kyren, whom she had made promise, according to the *Vita Katherine*, that their marriage would remain chaste.

In the Holy Year 1350, when her husband was still alive, she set out to *Rome to join her mother and her group of devout companions. She was then a dreamy and introverted young woman, completely submissive to her mother's authority. After her mother's death in 1373, she revealed quite another personality and worked energetically to complete her mother's work both at Rome and in *Sweden. Inspiring confidence and respect, she successfully pleaded the interests of the Swedish Church and the *Bridgettine Order. She gave active support to Pope *Urban VI against the *Avignon pope, *Clement VII. In 1380 she returned to Sweden, where she died the following year at the monastery of *Vadstena, aged 49. Her order considers her a saint and venerates her as such. Her cult spread in the Nordic countries, but the *canonization process was interrupted when Sweden broke with the Church of Rome in the 16th century. The spiritual collection *Siælinna thröst* has wrongly been attributed to her.

*Vita Katherine*, Stockholm, 1487 (repr. Uppsala, 1891; *BHL*, no. 1710). – J. F. de Pavinis, *Faciem tuam illumina super seruum tuum domine*, Rome, *c.*1480 (*BHL*, no. 1714). – *Processus seu negocium canonizacionis b. Katerine de Vadstenis*, Uppsala, 1942-1946 (*BHL*, no. 1714b).

*VSB*, 3, 1949, 528-532. – "Sainte Catherine de Suède", *Cath.*, 2, 1949, 700. – H. Gillingstam, "Katarina Ulfsdotter", *Svenskt biografiskt lexikon*, 21, Stockholm, 1975, 3-7. – C. Krötzl, *Pilger, Mirakel und Alltag*, Helsinki, 1994.

Anders Fröjmark

**CATHOLIC.** Received in the early Middle Ages in the sense of Augustine and Vincent of Lérins, as a qualitative expression of the Church's mission, this adjective would evolve, especially after 1054, in a more and more confessional direction. For the Churches of the East, Catholicity designated trinitarian development in history, and its dimension was manifested in the *Eucharist. For the West, "catholic" more and more signified *ecclesia* (or even **curia*) *romana*. For *Innocent III, all was Catholic that proceeded from and acknowledged itself within the *plenitudo potestatis* of the *pope. In *scholasticism, the Eucharist, the universal *sacrament, was the basis of the project of the *ecclesia universalis*. By its reinforcement of the Petrine ministry in the West, the adjective "catholic" had a tendency to pass from a horizontal dimension to a vertical dimension.

Y. Congar, "L'Eglise est catholique", *MySal*, 15, 149-179. – P. Steinacker, *TRE*, 18, 1969, 72-80.

Michel Deneken

**CATHOLIC KINGS.** Isabella, queen of *Castile from 1474 to 1504, and her husband Ferdinand, king of *Aragon from 1479 to 1516, each enjoyed a long reign that allowed them to pacify and reform their countries. This duration was one of the major reasons for their success. The young *infanta* Isabella was recognised as heiress to the throne by her half-brother Henry IV, at the expense of his daughter Joan (1468). Despite her promise not to marry without royal consent, in 1469 she clandestinely married the heir to the *Crown of Aragon. After the brutal death of Henry IV in 1474, Isabella was hastily proclaimed queen. The delegates of the towns of Castile had confined Ferdinand's power within strict limits; but, taking into account the civil troubles and the Portuguese invasion, Isabella soon granted her husband nearly all powers, for the needs of pacification. Becoming king of Aragon in 1479, he did the same for his wife. However, each Crown kept its autonomy, its frontiers and institutions, having in common only a royal couple, as well as a similar foreign and religious policy. The marriage of Isabella and Ferdinand did not mean the union of their kingdoms, but a bicephalous government, or conjoint government. So they were not tempted, and perhaps never had the idea, to call themselves kings of *Spain, nor ever envisaged dividing their kingdoms among their children. When their only son and then their eldest daughter Isabella died, their daughter Joan, wife of Philip the Handsome, was recognised as heiress to the two Crowns.

From her accession to power, Isabella had to follow a policy of pacification and pardon towards a numerous *nobility whose power was not counterbalanced by any middle class. The majority of the great nobles rallied. In 1489, a Castilian victory put an end to the Portuguese invasion. But calm was longer in returning than has been claimed, despite the decisions taken at the **Cortes* of Madrigal in 1476 and those of *Toledo in 1480. The kings very soon ceased to call assemblies, desiring as partners only members of the middle and lesser nobility, true support of the regime. As for Ferdinand, hardly had he ascended the throne of Aragon than he had to confront the problem of the *remensa* (very heavy banal rights weighing on the Catalan peasants). He put an end to the quarrel by the sentence of Guadalupe in 1486, which suppressed these "bad customs" on condition that the peasants redeemed them and indemnified their lords. But it remained to redress the economic situation, particularly worrying at *Barcelona, which was hardly possible before 1492.

Isabella and Ferdinand undertook an offensive foreign policy in the Mediterranean, then against the Muslim kingdom of *Granada (which fell in 1492 and was incorporated in the Crown of Castile) and finally at *Naples, a private preserve of the Crown of Aragon. Isabella entrusted Christopher *Columbus with the discovery of the Indies (12 Oct 1492), which earned her and her husband the title of Catholic Kings in 1494. Finally, in 1512, *Navarre was reattached to Castile.

The religious policy of the Catholic Kings was more questionable. Admittedly, they achieved the *reform of the monastic orders, already well advanced, and imposed the transition to the *Observance with satisfactory results. But their obstinacy in putting an end to the "Spain of three religions", probably in a desire for unification, leaves us perplexed. If the States of the peninsula had tolerated the *Jews on their territory throughout the Middle Ages, it was certainly not out of disinterest. The kings had quickly become aware of the services the Jews could render them. Apart from the nobility, the other social categories were envious and antisemitic. In 1391 a terrible antisemitic riot broke out. Some rich Jews preferred to leave the peninsula, while among those who remained many judged it more prudent to convert. These *conversos* or new Christians aroused mistrust and hatred, out of fear of insincere *conversions. From the middle of the 15th c., incidents multiplied and the idea gradually prevailed of resorting to the *Inquisition as the only way to verify purity of faith.

The kingdom of Castile possessed no inquisitorial tradition. So much so that, from 1460, Castilians were numerous in demanding that the old Aragonese inquisition be extended to Castile. In 1478 Isabella and Ferdinand finally obtained from Pope *Sixtus IV the setting up of a wholly new organism, an ecclesiastical Inquisition associated with the lay authorities, under royal control but independent of the papacy and the episcopate. In 1480, the sovereigns established the first tribunal of the Inquisition at *Seville, an active centre of *Judaizers. From January 1481, the first sentences passed were stupefying in their harshness: executions numbered hundreds and *prison sentences thousands. The *chroniclers vary as to the figures, but all emphasize the characteristics of this tribunal which spread terror: the essential role of delation, the suspect's ignorance of his fault, the absolute secrecy. All over the country, public opinion was severely shaken. Isabella and Ferdinand found in Tomás de *Torquemada the man of the situation. Of Jewish-Christian origin, a *Dominican, he militated very young in favour of a return to observance. Brought into contact with court circles, he gained the esteem of the king and queen and was appointed inquisitor in 1482. The Catholic Kings wished to obtain from the *pope the generalization of the Inquisition to the whole of the Crown of Castile, and in particular the reform of the old Aragonese Inquisition on the Castilian model. In 1483 Sixtus IV, despite his disapproval of the Inquisition's brutal ways, designated Torquemada inquisitor general for the States of the Crown of Aragon. In 1484 at the latest, Torquemada added to these functions those of inquisitor general of the kingdom of

Stone slab-crosses (*khatchk'ars*) in the cemetery of Noradouz (Armenia), 11th-13th c.

Castile. This choice of a single person to head the Inquisition in the two Crowns symbolized in a remarkable way the common religious policy of the two sovereigns. Torquemada left his mark on the new institution: centralization and efficiency. The *conversos* were rapidly eliminated.

As for the Jewish question, it was posed in very different terms. As non-Christians, the Jews were not subject to the tribunal of the Inquisition. Three months after the conquest of Granada, on 31 March 1492, Isabella and Ferdinand decreed the *expulsion before the month of July of all Jews who would not convert. The chroniclers of the time estimate that the majority of the Jews preferred exile to conversion. This is no longer the opinion of historians, who think that only an important minority had the courage to launch themselves into an exile full of adventures, and propose to evaluate the number of exiles at about 40,000 to 50,000 persons out of the 70,000 or 80,000 that the two Crowns could count. The Jews at first embarked for nearby destinations: *Provence, some Italian towns, the *Maghreb. Others reached *Navarre and *Portugal on the way. But for the majority, this refuge was only provisional. In fact, the expulsion from the Crowns of Castile and Aragon was part of a distressing decade for the Sephardic Jews, since little by little those States that were still tolerant closed their frontiers, expelled them or forced them into conversion. So much that, for many, a second Exodus had to be envisaged.

Finally, the *Mudejars (Muslims) posed a yet different problem. Not numerous in the Crown of Castile (save at Granada), they were densely established in certain lands of the Crown of Aragon (in particular the *Huertas*). After the conquest of Granada in 1492, where freedom of worship had been guaranteed them, began the enterprise of conversion that made them *Moriscos*. The first bishop of Granada, the *Hieronymite Hernando de Talavera, who attached the greatest importance to sincerity of faith, did not make many new Christians and was rapidly replaced by Cardinal Cisneros, charged with forcing them into baptism. The clergy tried to entice them by certain advantages, but used mainly threats and ill-treatment, which led to a rebellion in 1500. On 11 Feb 1502, a decree obliged all the Muslims of Castile (with the exception of the Moors of Aragon and *Valencia, who would have been irreplaceable in the fields) to choose, before 30 April, between exile and baptism. We do not know the number of those who left.

*Los Trastámaras y la unidad española (1369-1517)*, *Historia General de España y América*, L. Suárez Fernández (ed.), 5, Madrid, 1981. – J. Perez, *Isabelle et Ferdinand, rois catholiques d'Espagne*, Paris, 1988. – M. A. Ladero Quesada, *Los Reyes Católicos: la corona y la unidad de España*, *La Corona, los pueblos americanos*, 1, Madrid, 1989.

Marie-Claude Gerbet

**CAUCASUS.** By Caucasus is generally understood Subcaucasia, *i.e.* the territories situated south of the Great Caucasus chain as far as the Taurus and the steppes of Azerbaijan, hence including the historic *Albania, *Armenia and *Georgia. We must also include in it the Caucasian populations north of the chain, in particular the Circassian group, which remembers having been once (partially) Christianized, before its late Islamization from the 15th century.

The Caucasus could not fail to be – and still is – a coveted region. A place of refuge, since an important part of it is made up of valleys isolated from each other for many months of the year, it is also a place of transition, from the great steppes of the north to the south, and from east to west from Persia to Anatolia. It is still a rich and coveted plain, from the Black Sea to the Caspian Sea.

At the meeting-place of great empires, Subcaucasia – Caucasian Albania, Armenia and Georgia – was protected, colonized or conquered by the Byzantines and Persians, invaded by the Arabs, devastated by the *Khazars, *Turks and *Mongols. In the late Middle Ages, it became the battleground of the *Ottoman Turks and the Persians. Only the high mountain regions, difficult of access and of little economic interest, such as Svaneti, remained autonomous and kept a strong substrate of pre-Christian religion.

In the 7th c., the Arabs conquered the region and imposed annual tribute and military service. At first they were quite well received, since they interfered little with internal political or religious life and seemed to bring unity and peace to regions long agitated by rivalry between Byzantines and Persians. But from the early 8th c. the civil administration of Caucasian Albania passed directly into Arab hands, while its patriarch was made subject to Armenia. Keeping its language, culturally Armenized, it was gradually absorbed by the Arab and then Turco-Mongol Muslims.

In the 8th c., only western Georgia (the kingdom of Abkhasia) remained independent, the rest forming the province of Arminiya. But in Armenia as in Georgia, despite the rivalries of the great families, the unified State slowly emerged.

In 884, Ashot Bagratuni was crowned king of Armenia. The kingdom lasted less than two centuries. In 888 Adarnasses, another Bagratid prince, became king of the Georgians, but not until 1008 did Bagrat III reign over a truly unified Georgia. The king controlled a highly-structured feudal system. It was a time of political power, economic prosperity and cultural flowering for Georgia: it culminated in the reign of Queen Tamar (1184-1213). The *Mongol invasion in the 13th c. brutally interrupted this great century. The repeated attacks of *Timur, between 1386 and 1401, were catastrophic for Georgia: in the course of the 15th c., it split into three kingdoms and five principalities.

In Armenia, no kingdom survived the 11th c.: the greater part of the country was broken up into emirates dependent on the sultan of Persia. But commercial exchanges continued, corporations were created. From the late 11th c. a powerful and brilliant Armenian State developed in *Cilicia, an important meeting-place with the Greek and Latin West. The Armenian Church, non-Chalcedonian in tendency, kept its independence, despite the efforts of Byzantine emperors and attempts at Church union. The main influence of the Friars Unitors, Latin missionaries, was the introduction of the *scholastic method in *theology.

The Georgians, who had rallied to the formulation of the council of Chalcedon, hence to Byzantine *Orthodoxy, did not espouse the quarrels between Byzantines and Latins: in the 13th c., their relations with the papacy were good.

Literature enjoyed a great flowering at this time. The Armenian language spoken in Cilicia became a literary language for legal works, scientific treatises and fables; the Church continued to celebrate and compose in its classical language. The foundation in 980 of the monastery of Iviron (which means "of the Georgians") on Mount *Athos inaugurated a splendid period of Georgian literature in translation. In the 12th c. a secular literature and a poetry in Middle Georgian developed, whose masterpiece is Shota Rustaveli's *The Knight with the Panther Skin*. Architecture, sculpture, with the special art of the *khatchk'ars* – Armenian stone slabs engraved with crosses –, miniatures and chased metalwork reached the heights.

The capture of *Constantinople, then the fall of the Empire of *Trebizond, closely linked with Georgia, cut Armenians – but many had emigrated – and Georgians off even more from Western Europe. Only in the late 18th c. were contacts, only distantly recalling those of the crusading period, revived. Subcaucasia remained no less the eastern bastion of European *Christendom.

A. Sanders, *Kaukasien. Geschichtliches Umriss*, Munich, 1943. – *Histoire des Arméniens*, G. Dédéyan (dir.), Toulouse, 1982. – K. Salia, *History of the Georgian Nation*, Paris, 1983. – *HChr*, 4, 1993, 457-596.

Bernard Outtier

**CAUCHON, PIERRE (1371-1442).** Born to a rich family of *Reims, Pierre Cauchon studied at the university of *Paris from which he graduated in law and later became *rector. His positions in favour of Church reform led him into the Burgundian camp from 1407. He defended *Jean Petit's *Apology* at *Constance and negotiated the treaty of Troyes. A very influential adviser of the duke of Bedford, he accumulated canonries. As bishop of *Beauvais, the diocese where *Joan of Arc had been captured, he presided over the court that condemned her at *Rouen with zeal and incomprehension. Count-bishop of Lisieux in 1432, he was one of the negotiators of the treaty of Arras. Dying, he left his fortune to poor scholars.

F. Neveux, *L'Évêque Pierre Cauchon*, Paris, 1987.

Colette Beaune

**CAUSE.** The legal term "cause" (Latin *causa*) can be understood firstly as a term of *procedure, likened to a demand or question (main cause, incident cause). In fact, the term was much wider; it meant the whole of the affairs submitted to a jurisdiction: it was synonymous with legal proceedings. In this sense, *canon law distinguished minor or simple causes, within the competence of the ordinary judge (the *bishop), from major causes reserved exclusively for the *pope. Likewise there were civil causes and criminal causes. Within a single set of affairs, the habit grew up of reserving important developments in particular causes, such as causes of *beatification or *canonization, beneficial causes and especially matrimonial causes. The former dealt with the procedure to be followed in order to have someone recognised as a *beatus* or saint. The history of these causes followed the evolution of the *cult of the saints. From earliest Christian Antiquity, *martyrs and then mere confessors were honoured; great freedom was left to the recognition of local cults. Faced with a number of abuses and a great anarchy, the papacy gradually imposed official recognition. The pontificate of *Alexander III was essential in this respect. In the 13th c., canonization may be considered the business of Rome.

Under the general term "beneficial causes" were grouped all disputes raised about ecclesiastical *benefices and submitted to a judge. It could be a difference arising over the *title by whose virtue the benefice had been obtained, or about simple possession. The competence of the Church was exclusive until the 13th c.; but the lay power intervened on the occasion of right of *patronage, then more generally in matters of possession. One point was gained in the late Middle Ages: lay *courts, essentially *parlements*, were competent in possessory law. The benefice-holder had to give proof of peaceable possession and at least the colour of a title, *i.e.* emanating from one who had the right to confer the benefice, even if he could not exercise that right in the case in question. Possessory law was in fact considered a temporal question; the Church, it was said, had no territory. Petitory law, *i.e.* discussion about title and canonical *investiture, remained the competence of the *officiality.

Matrimonial causes were about the different procedures connected with *marriage, the most important ones tending to annul unions contracted in violation of the numerous prohibitions.

The word "cause" could also be understood as one of the determining elements of contracts, that without which the contractants would not be committed. *Roman law did not know unity of cause; this was confused with final aim. This pertained to the very conception of the Roman contract, which remained very attached to formalism. Canon law brought to the theory of contract the notion of respect for one's given word and the more general principle by which only consent obliged (*solus consensus obligat*). The cause then appeared as a limit to the sole force of consent; hence this logical consequence: liability based on an illicit cause was nul. From canon law, the notion was taken up by the Romanists and thence passed into the French tradition of the general theory of contracts.

G. Chevrier, *Essai sur l'histoire de la cause dans les obligations*, Paris, 1929. – "Cause", *DDC*, 3, 1942. – J. L. Gazzaniga, *Introduction historique aux droits des obligations*, Paris, 1992.

Jean-Louis Gazzaniga

**CAUSE AND EFFECT.** Cause is defined as the positive principle which is at the origin of the *being of a thing which is called its effect. Cause denotes more than principle. The latter means only a relation of origin, like that of the line to the point that engenders it, while cause implies an influx relative to the very being of the effect. Causality, first datum of human experience, seems for *Thomas Aquinas a manifestation of the radiating generosity of the act of being. Integrating, in effect, the Aristotelian tradition by which the *sign of a being's perfection is its capacity to produce another itself and the Platonic tradition of the fecundity of the *good (*bonum diffusivum sui*), St Thomas declares that any act or perfection tends to communicate itself, to make others participate in its own *ontological richness.

Following *Aristotle, the *scholastics ordinarily distinguish four types of cause, which between them account for the existence of the effect. The material cause and the formal cause are intrinsic causes, in the sense that they enter into the essential structure of the effect. Attached to the formal cause, but as extrinsic cause, is the exemplary cause: idea or model. The efficient cause and the final cause are extrinsic causes. The efficient cause, whose divisions are many (principal cause and instrumental cause, first

*The Last Judgment.* Detail: *two apostles.* Wall-painting by Pietro Cavallini, *c.*1250-*c.*1350, in the church of Santa Cecilia in Trastevere, Rome.

cause and second cause . . .), is the agent that communicates being to an effect distinct from itself. The final cause is the good pursued: both that which motivates the agent and that gained by the effect. It is called the cause of causes, because, by the attraction it arouses in the agent, it sets going the whole causal process.

Beyond its interest for the understanding of *metaphysical dynamisms, the theme of causality plays an important role in medieval *theology, since it provides the basis for the possibility of a discourse on the existence and perfections of *God. The mind mounts up from the perfections discovered in creatures and whose imperfection manifests their dependence, their status as effect, to their cause, and apprehends something of the perfection of God, in accordance with the Aristotelian principle that the effect resembles its cause in such a way that the cause precontains in its own mode the perfection it communicates to the effect. The *Neoplatonist tradition by which the cause gives only what it does not have led rather to a certain *apophaticism.

The evolution of medieval thought from *Duns Scotus tended to eclipse the Aristotelian model of a reciprocal causality of total causes in favour of a concurrent causality of partial causes. This new model, which marginalized the formal cause and the final cause in favour of matter on one hand and the productive efficient cause on the other, ushered in the mechanistic model of causality, characteristic of modern thought.

A. de Muralt, *L'Enjeu de la philosophie médiévale*, Leiden, 1991. – L. Elders, *The Metaphysics of Being of St. Thomas Aquinas in a Historical Perspective*, Leiden, 1993, ch. 19 and 20.

Serge Bonino

**CAVA DEI TIRRENI.** Early in the 11th c. a nobleman of Salerno, Alferius, was been sent to Germany by his prince. He met Abbot *Odilo of Cluny, received his monastic training at *Cluny, returned to Salerno and retired to a cave north-west of the town; in 1025 the prince offered him the surrounding territory; thus was founded the *abbey of Santissima Trinità di Cava. Its success was rapid in the 11th and 12th cc.: it received *immunity from *Urban II and founded a congregation that extended as far as *Apulia and *Sicily (*Monreale). Cava developed Cluniac *spirituality in southern Italy. Difficulties began in the second half of the 13th c., aggravated by wars, then by the general crisis. In 1394, *Boniface IX made the *abbot a *bishop; in 1431, the abbey passed under the regime of *commendation; in 1497, it was integrated into the congregation of St *Justina of Padua.

P. Guillaume, *Essai historique sur l'abbaye de Cava d'après des documents inédits*, Cava dei Tirreni, 1877.

Jean-Marie Martin

**CAVALLINI, PIETRO (*c.*1250-*c.*1350).** Formed in the Byzantine culture omnipresent in Italy, like all the *artists of the time, the painter and mosaicist Pietro Cavallini worked at first at *Rome in the most important churches and for renowned patrons, and was able to assimilate the experiments of *Cimabue, who stayed at Rome in 1272. The mosaic decoration of the apse of Santa Maria in Trastevere, 1291, remains Byzantinizing in both style and iconography. Amid six episodes of the life of the Virgin, Cavallini introduces the presentation by St *Peter of the *donor, Pietro di Bartolo Stefaneschi, to the mother of Christ. The *Last Judgment scene of Santa Cecilia in Trastevere, *c.*1293, already shows an evolution: these are majestic figures, thrown into relief by intense shadows and isolated by empty spaces which create an effect of depth. Cavallini uses colour to give great autonomy to each form and to confer a solemn calm on his bold and placid figures. The expressive power that emerges from his solid compositions does not alter their poetic richness, marked by religious fervour. In 1308, he settled at *Naples and worked notably for *Charles II and *Robert the Wise (fresco of Santa Maria Donna Regina), then returned to Rome around 1315. He then escaped from the Byzantine manner and his art became more sensitive, under the dual influence of Antiquity and the *Gothic models of his time. While Rome experienced a great artistic activity, Cavallini played an important role in the Italian painting of the late *duecento* and early *trecento*. His place in the formation of *Giotto should not be minimized. Head of a studio, he appears in the course of his long career as an initiator in the history of painting at Rome, by the attention he paid to the last known examples of ancient sculpture and *mosaic.

P. Hetherington, *Pietro Cavallini, A Study in the Art of late Medieval Rome*, London, 1979.

Alain Girard

**CAVALRY.** In Roman military tradition, cavalry played a secondary role consisting essentially of lightening the march of the troops, carrying out flanking manoeuvres on the battlefield and pursuing the enemy in flight.

In Germanic military usage, notably among the *Franks, the place of the cavalry was hardly more important. Only slowly, from the 7th and 8th cc., did the cavalry's role begin to evolve. From the reign of *Charlemagne, the heavy cavalry was the most solid part of the Frankish *army. From then on the horsemen formed an elite, both social and military, within the troop. The evolution of the role of the heavy cavalry has often been compared with the development from the 8th c. of the beneficial system: the Frankish man of war whose services the ruler wanted to ensure needed from now on an important endowment in land and revenues sufficient to equip, arm and mount himself.

From the 10th c., certain technical improvements, notably the almost universal adoption of the stirrup and the high saddle, as well as the perfecting of a particular technique that allowed the horseman to "couch the lance", made possible the use of heavy cavalry as a mass formation to break the opposing line by a frontal charge. This allowed *Otto the Great to win the decisive victory of the Lechfeld over the Hungarians in August 955, and *William the Conqueror to win that of *Hastings in 1066.

However, combat on horseback demanded the choice of an offensive tactic that was often opposed to the prudence of medieval war leaders. The use of the impetuous charge favoured by the French was more and more often opposed, in the 12th and 13th cc., by combat on foot combined with the defensive option, chosen by the English and Germans. Thus at Bouvines the bulk of the imperial army dismounted at the moment of confronting the *host of *Philip Augustus.

The 14th c. saw the decline of the role of the heavy cavalry on Western battlefields: the rude experiences of the French *nobility faced with the infantry of the Flemish communes (Courtrai, 1302) and especially the bloody lesson of Crécy (1346) had the effect of generalizing foot-combat. Cavalry was then used only for outflanking manoeuvres and pursuit, which even gave rise to the equipping of a light cavalry.

Not until the late 15th c. do we see the duke of *Burgundy, *Charles the Bold, advocate a new tactical system in which the breaking force of the heavy cavalry was to be combined with the use of powder artillery. But this tactic was a failure against the Swiss infantry, sufficiently mobile to be able to take the initiative even against cavalry.

J.-F. Verbruggen, "La tactique militaire des armées de chevaliers", *RNord*, 29, 1947, 161-180. – C. Gaier, "La cavalerie lourde en Europe occidentale du XIIe au XIVe siècle: un problème de mentalité", *Revue internationale d'histoire militaire*, Paris, 1971, 385-396. – P. Contamine, *War in the Middle Ages*, Oxford, 1984. – B.S. Bachrach, "'Caballus et Cabellarius' in Medieval Warfare", *The Study of Chivalry*, H. Chickering (ed.), T.H. Seiter(ed.), Kalamazoo, 1988, 173-211. – B.S. Bachrach, "Charlemagne's Cavalry: Myth and Reality", *Military Affairs*, 47, 181-7.

Bertrand Schnerb

**CAVES, MONASTERY OF THE.** The monastery of the Caves (Kievo-Pečerskii monastyr') appears to be the first Kievan monastic foundation not due to a lay initiative. So at least it is presented by the texts that describe the beginnings of this community, traditionally attached to the *monasticism of Mount *Athos. According to them, a Russian monk, Anthony, returning in 1051 from Athos where he had taken the habit, retired to a cave situated on the heights of the right bank of the Dniepr, south of *Kiev. The hermit brought together a few disciples (including *Theodosius) and then left their direction in the hands of a hegumen, Barlaam. Under Barlaam's hegumenate, the community grew; a church, consecrated to the Dormition, rose on the site of Anthony's cave, and the prince of Kiev, Iz'yaslav Iaroslavich, granted the monastery lands and authorization to build. In 1062, Theodosius was elected hegumen by his brethren. He may be considered the true founder of the monastery and, more widely, of Russian monasticism, to which he bequeathed a communal discipline and a model of monastic *sanctity. Theodosius applied the Studite Rule to the monastery, in a version that he seems to have had directly from a Greek monk who came from Constantinople. Whatever the rigour with which this rule may have been followed (it was subject to various mitigations under Theodosius and again after him), its aim was to break with the practice of *eremitism and promote *coenobitic life. The superior's role of *spiritual direction was strongly affirmed, though in actual fact only Theodosius seems to have exercised a true pastorate.

Under Theodosius's influence, the monastery's relations with the authorities were marked by signs of independence. The monastery sought to pose as the moral adviser of princes and, on the occasion of various conflicts between it and them, its voice came to fill the silence of a submissive secular Church; it thus made itself the echo of the aspirations of the aristocratic milieu that fed its recruitment.

Up to the *Mongol invasion, the influence and power of the monastery of the Caves was manifested by the importance of its building programme; the church of the Dormition, rebuilt in stone between 1073 and 1076, was ornamented with *mosaics and *icons by artists from Byzantium. The *Paterikon* of Pečersk insists on the links that united the community to Constantinople and the Greek clergy. But the monastery was not a place of scholarship, nor of translation of Greek literature into Slavonic. It was a more particularly Russian intellectual centre and the centre of an important historiographical and hagiographical activity.

R. Casey, "Early Russian Monasticism", *OrChrP*, 19, 1953, 372-423. – V. Vodoff, *Naissance de la chrétienté russe*, Paris, 1988, 163-185. – M. Heppel (tr.), *The Paterik of the Kievan Caves Monastery*, Cambridge (MA), 1989.

Irène Sorlin

**CEDD (died 664).** Bishop of the East Saxons, he and his brother Chad (first bishop of Lichfield) were trained at *Lindisfarne under the Irish bishops Aidan and Finan. When the kingdom of Essex was converted to Christianity through King Sigebert (Sigeberht), Cedd became its first *bishop (654). He founded monasteries at Bradwell-on-Sea (some of whose fabric survives) and Tilbury, as also at Lastingham in Northumbria, where he was subsequently to die of the plague. Nearly everything known of Cedd derives from *Bede's *Historia Ecclesiastica* (III, 21-23).

*Bede's Ecclesiastical History of the English People*, B. Colgrave (ed.), R.A.B. Mynors (ed.), Oxford, 1969.

Michael Lapidge

**CEFALÙ.** First of the royal *foundations of *Sicily, on the sea route between *Palermo and Messina, clinging to the Monti delle Madonie, Cefalù, a small new town founded in 1130, was laid out in a geometrical plan at the foot of the old acropolis that had held the Norman *castle. Its *cathedral was dedicated to the Saviour and Sts Peter and Paul and was to become the mausoleum of *Roger II and his family. The first stone was laid at Pentecost 1131; its *bishop was Jocelin, Augustinian prior of Bagnara in *Calabria, who set up a regular *chapter twinned with his *priory. Two porphyry sarcophagi were installed in 1145, the apse completed in 1148, but the church was still not consecrated at Roger II's death, and the bishopric was not recognised by Rome until 1166.

The plan of the basilica (west towers, narrow transept, raised tripartite sanctuary) was modeled on *Cluny II and in turn inspired *Monreale and the Norman Sicilian style; its construction remained largely unfinished. The decoration also bore the mark of political

Christ Pantocrator in the apse of Cefalù cathedral. 12th c.

uncertainty and interruptions: it comprised a royal cycle of *frescos on the façade and a cycle of *mosaics in the central apse (Virgin, archangels, apostles), continued in the lower registers of the presbytery (*prophets and saints) and in the vaults (cherubim and seraphim). An adaptation of a Byzantine programme for a domed church, it put Greek and Latin *Fathers face to face, insisting on the presbyterial elements, and thus well expressed the dual reality of the Sicilian church in Val Demone (from Cefalù to Taormina): the Latin Church, episcopal, rested largely on a Hellenic and Arabo-Christian base, presbyterial and monastic.

A funerary rather than a royal and triumphal basilica, Cefalù had a narrow *diocese cut out of the diocese of Messina-Troina, but this territorial poverty was compensated by the granting of exceptional political privileges, jurisdiction over the city and Pollina, fiscal rights over the export of salted tuna in particular; moreover vast *donations (the church of Santa Lucia of Syracuse, churches and *casalia*) constituted an estate scattered all over Sicily. The town, a simple fishing port with little room for viticulture, and its nobility of knights and *notaries, lived in the 12th and 13th cc. essentially on the profits of the management of this dispersed landed fortune. From the *Sicilian Vespers of 1282, in the logic of the general process of secularization, the authority of the counts of Ventimiglia, installed at Geraci, was extended over the diocese and then over the bishopric, from which it wrenched its jurisdiction and its *fiefs (the old *casalia* now depopulated), while the town fell back on marine activities largely financed by its clergy.

G. de Stefano, *Il Duomo di Cefalù*, 1960. – I. Peri, *Uomini, città e campagne in Sicilia dall'XI al XIII secolo*, Bari, 1978. – M. Gelfer-Jurgensen, *Medieval Islamic symbolism and the paintings of Cefalù cathedral*, Leiden, 1986.

Henri Bresc

**CELESTINE III, POPE (1105/1106-1198).** Hyacinth Boboni came from a powerful Roman family allied to the *Orsini. He became a *cardinal in 1144. For 47 years Cardinal Boboni established his influence within the *Sacred College. He was very early involved in the discussions between the Holy See and the *Empire. In 1158, sent by *Adrian IV, he met *Frederick I Barbarossa before Augsburg. Then he played an essential role in the organisation and progress of the interview of Venice in 1177.

This long experience of the *Curia and of temporal affairs led to him being designated at the age of 85 to succeed Clement III (1191). While the Sacred College proceeded to his *election, *Henry VI marched on *Rome. He went there to seek the imperial crown promised by Clement. Negotiations took place: Celestine deferred his *consecration in order not to have to concede too early to the demands of the adverse party. Agreement was finally reached at the expense of *Tusculum: crowned on 15 April 1191, the day after the consecration of the new pontiff, Henry handed Rome's detested rival over to the pope; Celestine abandoned the town to the Romans; Tusculum was devastated.

Celestine III's pontificate was wholly dominated by tensions between the Holy See and the Empire. With prudence or pusillanimity, the new *pope always avoided confrontation. Despite the *concordat of Gravina concluded in 1192 with Tancred, Celestine never overtly opposed the imperial manoeuvres against *Sicily. The murder of Albert of Louvain, designated bishop of *Liège by the supreme pontiff against the emperor's candidate, brought no reaction. The imprisonment of *Richard Coeur de Lion, taken hostage by Leopold of Austria with the tacit complicity of Henry VI, aroused only late recriminations which spared the emperor. But the rapprochement of the years 1195-1196 marked a certain strengthening of the papal position. Not that Celestine III had decided to react, but Henry needed him: to give the Empire a hereditary character, he had to ensure the co-operation of the pope. Henry VI tried to seduce the pontiff by proposing a collaboration to achieve one of his greatest projects: the *crusade. Faced with Celestine's hesitations, he decided to force his hand and launched the expedition on Easter day 1195. The pope now hardly had a choice; on 1st August, he promulgated a *bull to endorse the undertaking. But the emperor's efforts came to nothing. During the autumn of 1196, on his way to Sicily, he failed to reach a compromise with Celestine. Timidly, the supreme pontiff encouraged Italian resistance against Henry. But his state of health deteriorated, and only the chance of a fever that surprised the emperor at Messina allowed him to survive his adversary. He died on 8 Jan 1198 after having tried to impose Cardinal Giovanni *Colonna as his successor.

R. Foreville, *HE*, 9, 2, 1953, 216-227. – R. Mols, *DHGE*, 12, 1953, 62-77. – I.S. Robinson, *The Papacy, 1073-1198*, Cambridge, 1990. – L. Vones, "Célestin III", *DHP*, Paris, 1994.

Daniel Baloup

**CELESTINE V, POPE (1209/1210-1296).** Peter of the Morrone was born in late 1209 or early 1210 in the region of Molise, central Italy, probably at Sant'Angelo Limosano, a small agricultural town. After an introduction to monastic life, he became a hermit in the early 1230s, living in Abruzzo, notably on Monte Maiella and Monte Morrone. His fame as a *thaumaturge drew constant visitors; likewise, his holiness attracted many followers, obliging him to obtain ecclesiastical approval for the group; this was granted in 1263 by *Urban IV, who incorporated Peter's disciples into the Benedictine Order. To ensure the stability of the new congregation, Peter went to *Lyon and obtained a privilege from *Gregory X in 1275. In 1293 he established the seat of the congregation at the new abbey of Santo Spirito del Morrone, near Sulmona; he himself lived in a hermitage on the mountainside overlooking the monastery.

This move occurred during the interregnum following the death of Pope *Nicholas IV on 4 April 1292. The *cardinals, divided between the *Orsini and *Colonna factions, could not agree on a new *pope. But pressure exerted by *Charles II of Anjou and others helped break the impasse, and on 5 July 1294 in Perugia the octogenarian Peter was unexpectedly and unanimously elected pope. Although Peter was known to some important clerics and secular leaders, he was probably selected not for his leadership potential but for his usefulness as a compromise candidate, whose reign would not be long. Peter was crowned pope under the name of Celestine V at L'Aquila on 29 August 1294; he established an unusual *indulgence that granted plenary *absolution to those who visited, under certain conditions, the church where he was crowned. Celestine appointed twelve new *cardinals, accommodated the Franciscan *Spirituals in his hermitages and granted many favours to his monastic congregation, but it was soon apparent that he had little talent or inclination for his new tasks. When the *Curia moved to *Naples in November, Celestine considered renouncing the papacy and returning to the eremitical life; and he did so on 13 Dec 1294, after consultations with Cardinal Benedetto *Caetani. This same prelate was elected Pope *Boniface VIII eleven days later and, fearing that Peter might change his mind about his abdication, the new pope sent emissaries to bring his predecessor to him. Peter was arrested trying to flee to Greece and was brought to Fumone, where he was confined until he died on 19 May 1296. Under pressure from the French King *Philip IV the Fair, Pope *Clement V canonized Peter on 5 May 1313 at *Avignon.

Celestine has often been identified as *colui che fece per viltade il gran rifiuto*, "he who through cowardice made the great refusal" (Dante, *Inferno* 3, 59-60), but it is not certain that this was the poet's intention.

*AnBoll*, 16, 1897, 365-487. – F. X. Seppelt, *Monumenta Coelestiniana*, Paderborn, 1921. – A. Frugoni, *Celestiniana*, Rome, 1954 (2nd ed. 1991). – P. Herde, *Cölestin V (1294) (Peter vom Morrone)*, Stuttgart, 1981. – *HChr*, 5 and 6, 1990-1993.

George Ferzoco

**CELESTINES.** The name of the monastic Order of Celestines comes from its founder, St Peter Celestine. Pietro Angelieri, called "da Morrone", was born at Isernia in the kingdom of *Naples in *c.*1215. He became a Benedictine monk and chose to live as a hermit on Monte Morrone in the *Abruzzi. Small communities formed around him; they were officially recognised in 1274 by Pope *Gregory X at the second council of *Lyon, but were organised as a new Benedictine congregation. Pietro da Morrone, becoming *pope in 1294 under the name of *Celestine V, established the constitution of those who were henceforth called Celestines.

The rule they followed was that of St *Benedict, to which they added long periods of *prayer and *fasting as well as harsh *mortifications. The ordinary habit was a white tunic and a black cowl and *scapular. The *abbot general, elected every three years by a general *chapter, sat at Morrone. Everywhere they settled, the Celestines enjoyed numerous spiritual and temporal privileges.

The order rapidly extended throughout Italy. It was introduced into France in 1300 by *Philip the Fair, who obtained the *canonization of the founder from *Clement V, the first *Avignon pope. The order drew immense prestige from this, and at the start of the 15th c. it numbered 96 houses in Italy and 17 in France. But relations between the two congregations were difficult and, under cover of the *Great Schism, Pope *Clement VII created a French province; it obtained its autonomy in 1417 and, a little later, even got two Italian houses put in its charge.

The links between the Celestines and the political authorities in the different Italian States are still little known, but in France most of the monasteries were founded by *kings and princes. The Paris monastery was particularly distinguished by the royal family, who interred the hearts and entrails of the sovereigns there. Throughout the kingdom, the Celestines received numerous *donations; their benefactors were wealthy bourgeois, but also King *Charles V and Duke Louis of Orléans, the latter making them his main testamentary beneficiaries.

In France as in Italy, the Celestines possessed a rich temporality, which they managed without parsimony. But they were known less for their prodigality than for their religious fervour, and prayers and masses for the *dead were requested from them. Celestine *spirituality was traditional; in the 14th c., it conquered the strong personality of *Philippe de Mézières, counsellor of Charles V. At the end of the 15th c., although open to *humanism, it had no understanding of the spirit of the Reformation.

C. Telera da Manfredonia, *Historie sagre degli huomini illustri per santita della congregatione de Celestini, dell'ordine di S. Benedetto*, Naples, 1689. – A. Becquet, *Gallicae Coelestinorum Congregationis Ordinis Sancti Benedicti Monasterium Fundationes virorumque vita aut scriptis illustrium elogia historica*, Paris, 1719. – C. Sustrac, *Les Célestins de France (1300-1789)*, Paris, 1889. – J. Duhr, "Célestins", *DSp*, 2, 1953, 377-385.

Françoise Gadby

## CELIBACY, ECCLESIASTICAL

**The West.** Faced with a 4th-c. legislation imposing *continence on the higher clergy, without forbidding them all matrimonial ties, and practices that varied according to region but were often doubtless very free, the *Gregorian reform, impregnated with monastic asceticism, constructed from the 11th c. an arsenal of texts that prescribed the total *chastity of major *clerics: it vigorously attacked what appeared to it an essential lapse, if necessary aligning the faithful against concubinary clerics. The first *Lateran council, in 1123, declared *marriage contracted by a major cleric after his *ordination invalid, and accepted the *consecration of married men only if they abandoned all relations with their wife; this legislation, later followed and spread by numerous local *councils and *synods, was the foundation of medieval *canon law on the question. But the *validity of *sacraments delivered by a concubinary priest was always reaffirmed, against many heterodox currents of the 12th century.

A continuity of authors and milieux expressed themselves against the rule of celibacy. In 1074, the members of a Parisian synod judged it insupportable and hence unreasonable. The late 13th and early 14th cc. saw particularly lively debates on the subject: men of letters like Jean de Meung, royal *legists like Pierre du Bois, even bishops like Guillaume *Durand the Younger were hostile to it. In the 15th c., *Lollards, radical *Gallicans and followers of Nature took up positions against it with fundamental arguments, and official canonists like Cardinal *Zabarella or *Panormitanus with arguments of expediency. In a treatise of 1413, *Gerson clearly asserts that sacerdotal incontinence is a lesser evil than a shortage of priests.

In practice, the law does not seem to have ever been wholly respected, but always owing to a minority. If at the end of the 15th c. freedom of morals had largely won over the papal court, and if the registers of *officialities show the unbridled sexual activity of certain priests, prolonged marital life had become the exception. The views of the faithful about the incontinent priest were doubtless ambiguous: in one place, he was a victim of *denunciations to the official and nocturnal expeditions by groups of young people to discover him in a delicate situation and hold him to ransom; in another, on the contrary, such a priest could live openly before his whole village with his housekeeper and his children for many years. In short, the problem of celibacy must be seen in a wider perspective, that of the adhesion to or rejection of the break imposed by the *Gregorian reform between the cleric and the rest of society.

*DDC*, 3, 1942, 133-136. – *Cath.*, 2, 1954, 756-763. – *Le Clergé délinquant (XIII^e-XVIII^e siècle)*, B. Garnot (dir.), Dijon, 1995.

Vincent Tabbagh

**Byzantium.** The Greek equivalent of the Western term "celibacy" is *agamía*, which literally means "non-marriage". This was essentially a canonical state. The virtues associated with it were discussed rather under the terms "virginity" (*parthenía*) and "chastity" (*agnótēs*).

The writings of the Greek *Fathers on the notion of virginity are numerous. They were directed primarily to *women, not necessarily *nuns, to whom were extolled the spiritual riches available to the *virgo intacta*. Pope Clement may already have written letters on the subject as early as the 2nd century. Methodius of Olympus's *Banquet of the ten virgins* (3rd c.) includes an important discourse attributed to Thecla, the apocryphal disciple of the apostle Paul. The Cappadocian Fathers and John Chrysostom also wrote about virginity.

The theme of chastity for men was treated more particularly by ascetics and hermits, who put the accent less upon the gloriousness of the virtue than upon resistance to *temptation. The notion of celibacy developed, in Eastern tradition, as an aspect of the monastic state. Basil of Cappadocia (4th c.) wrote that men who made a religious *profession tacitly accepted the celibate life. Those whose behaviour was subsequently libidinous or voluptuous were subject to the *sanctions applied to the fornicator. In due course celibacy was taken for granted as a constituent element of the monastic state. A matter upon which Western and Eastern tradition differ is that of the celibacy of the clergy. In the early Church, no objection was raised to the *marriage of priests and *bishops. The first general *councils did not pronounce on the subject. Discipline varied according to regions, the imposition of celibacy on bishops developing earlier in the West than the East. In 528 the Emperor Justinian forbade married bishops, not because he considered celibacy to be necessary to their spiritual condition but because he esteemed that their property should be inherited by the Church and the poor rather than by their families. However, it was only at the council *in Trullo* (Quinisext, 692) that rules for the celibacy of the clergy were definitively codified. Henceforth bishops were obliged to observe celibacy. Widowers were eligible for the episcopacy, but a married priest, if appointed bishop, had to send his wife to a distant nunnery. A married man could be ordained a priest or a *deacon. However, it was forbidden for a priest or deacon to marry after *ordination. Consequently, if his wife died, he automatically became a monk and committed to celibacy. The legislation of the *Byzantine Church has not been modified since the council *in Trullo*.

G. Bardy, I.-H. Dalmais, "Célibat des religieux et des clercs", *Cath.*, 2, 1954, 756-760, 761-762. – F. Vernet, "Célibat ecclésiastique", *DSp*, 2, 1954, 386-387.

Christopher Walter

**CELL.** In *monasticism, the term *cella* originally designated any kind of enclosed space, a cell as well as a monastery, or even a gatehouse, a hostelry, an infirmary, a dormitory or a place of reclusion. Gradually, under the enrichment of the monasteries and the diversification of topographical vocabulary, *cella* came to correspond to the "centre of management" of an *estate at some distance from the monastery. Placed under the direction of an *abbot or a *prior, a few religious were settled there to oversee the exploitation of the *villae*, store the harvests in the *granges and collect the tenants' *rents for the *abbey.

G. Marié, "Celle", *Cath.*, 2, 1949, 771-772. – "Cella", *DIP*, 2, 1975, 744-747. – P. Bonnerue, "Eléments de topographie historique dans les règles monastiques occidentales", *Studia Monastica*, 37, 1995, 57-77.

Pierre Bonnerue

**CELLARER.** From the time of his entry into a monastic community, the *novice gave up all his property, consequently the *abbot had to provide for all his needs. This was the function of the cellarer (from the Latin *cellerarius*), a steward or bursar. He, of whom St *Benedict said that "he must be like a father to the whole community" (32, 2), was charged with the preservation and distribution of the monastery's goods, principally *food. From his cellar, he drew the produce necessary for *alms and for preparing meals, and had to receive all who asked (*children, the sick, guests, the poor). He was expected to be neither "avaricious" nor "spendthrift" of the monastery's property.

G. Marié, "Cellérier", *Cath.*, 2, 1949, 773. – J. Řezáč, "Cellario", *DIP*, 2, 1975, 747.

Pierre Bonnerue

**CELTIC LITURGY.** The term "Celtic liturgy" broadly describes the Christian rite which was practised in the British Isles from the time Christianity was first introduced, perhaps during the 2nd c. AD, when Britannia constituted several provinces of the Roman Empire, until such rite was eventually superseded by Roman rite as a result of contacts between the Celtic countries (mainly *Wales and *Ireland) and the Romanized English church, from the 7th c. onwards, and ultimately as a result of the Norman conquest of Wales and Ireland during the 12th century. For this large period the evidence is uneven and fragmentary, consisting primarily of a few surviving *liturgical books and material remains of various kinds (churches recovered by excavation; ecclesiastical furniture such as *chalices, etc.). Because of the unevenness of the evidence, it is not possible to form a comprehensive view of "Celtic" liturgy (in contrast with Roman rite), and few scholars today would be prepared to speak, as did Mabillon, of a *liturgia hibernica*. Nevertheless it is possible to ascertain that, in some respects, the Celtic (especially Irish) rite differed from that of *England and the Continent: aspects of the monastic *office (especially its collects and *hymns) are known from the late 7th-c. "Antiphonary of *Bangor", and the 8th-c. "Stowe Missal" contains various features, including the ordinary of the pre-Gregorian (Roman) *mass, which had by then been superseded elsewhere in Europe. In the case of private *prayer, represented in several surviving Irish prayerbooks, the idiosyncratic intensity of Irish *litany-like petitions for protection and *absolution were to prove influential on English prayer.

*The Antiphonary of Bangor*, F. E. Warren (ed.), *HBS*, 4 and 10, London, 1893 and 1895. – G. F. Warner, *The Stowe Missal*, *HBS*, 31-32, London, 1915. – L. Gougaud, "Celtiques (liturgies)", *DACL*, 2, Paris, 1925, 2969-3022. – F. E. Warren, *The Liturgy and Ritual of the Celtic Church*, J. Stevenson (ed.), Woodbridge, 1987. – J. P. Mackey, *An Introduction to Celtic Christianity*, Edinburgh, 1989.

Michael Lapidge

**CEMETERY.** Two peculiarities characterise medieval cemeteries. First, their location: while ancient necropolises were always situated far from inhabited places, in open country or next to roads, medieval burial places were at the heart of towns and villages. The approach of the burial-ground to the inhabited area (from the 7th c.), then their coincidence (complete at the end of the first millennium) are a social and cultural phenomenon of the first importance, which attests a profound change in the relations between living and *dead. Moreover, if the necropolises of Antiquity accepted all the deceased without distinction, Christian cemeteries were reserved for believers only: the bodies of *pagans, *Jews, unbaptized infants, the *excommunicated, all those who did not belong (or no longer belonged) to the Christian community were excluded from it.

As well as parish churches directly subject to episcopal jurisdiction, other places of worship were provided with a cemetery. Ecclesiastical communities, in particular, obtained the right to inter their dead on the spot and often to give *burial to believers who requested it. Indeed monastic cemeteries often served as family necropolises for members of the aristocracy. Alongside the friars' cemetery, some *abbeys also possessed a *cimiterium nobilium* (cemetery of the nobles) or *populare cimiterium* (as it is called by an 11th-c. *customary of *Cluny), reserved for the *laity.

In the Middle Ages, the cemetery was also a place for the living. Blessed, consecrated and marked out by the *bishop, it was a place of *asylum. The building of protective perimeter walls around churches goes back to the 5th century. The *capitularies of the 9th c. were already presenting cemeteries as places of refuge and peace. But it was the movement of the *Peace of God, around the year 1000, that reinforced their particular status: more than any other place, the circular sacred area that surrounded the church, where the dead were buried, had to be exempt from *violence.

In the parish cemeteries rested, collectively, the ancestors of the community. Buried often in the bare ground, the bodies of the deceased were quickly lost in anonymity. Regularly (ritually), the soil of the cemeteries was turned over, the bones of the dead removed. Thus was formed the ancestral community. Points of anchorage and rallying-points, cemeteries favoured the coming together of people and the concentration of dwellings: around the year 1000, sometimes earlier, *villages were fixed at the places where the dead were buried. In some regions, in the 11th and 12th cc., cemeteries were even "colonized" and progressively parcelled out, when they were not created from scratch to receive burials and dwellings. Elsewhere, they harboured seignorial *donjons*. Sometimes fortified, they formed reliable retrenchments. And everywhere, in the country and in the *towns, up to a late date, cemeteries were used for meetings, assemblies, festivities; *markets and *fairs were held in them, accords and treaties concluded in them, justice dispensed in them. Centre of attraction to the living, guarantee of the cohesion of the soil, seat of collective memory and customary practices, such did cemeteries appear in the Middle Ages. From the 13th c., however, the Church systematically condemned, through synodal *statutes, all secular activities that took place in burial grounds. But folklore long retained the traces of the presence of the ancestors and their collective intervention in the cemeteries.

L. Musset, "Le Cimetière dans la vie paroissiale en Basse-Normandie (XI^e^-XIII^e^ siècles)", *CLD*, 12, 1963, 7-27. – P. Duparc, "Le Cimetière, séjour des vivants (XI^e^-XII^e^ siècles)", *BPH, 1964*, Paris, 1967, 483-504. – J. Chiffoleau, *La Comptabilité de l'au-delà. Les hommes, la mort et la religion dans la région d'Avignon à la fin du Moyen Âge*, Rome, 1981, 155-165. – E. Zadora-Rio, "Les Cimetières habités en Anjou aux XI^e^ et XII^e^ siècles", *Actes 105^e^ congrès national des Sociétés Savantes, Caen 1980, Études archéologiques*, Paris, 1983, 319-329. – *L'Église, le terroir*, M. Fixot (dir.), E. Zadora-Rio (dir.), Paris, 1989. – *Anglo-Saxon Cemeteries*, E. Southword (ed.), Stroud, 1990. – *L'Environment des églises et la topographie religieuse des campagnes médiévales*, M. Fixot (dir.), E. Zadora-Rio (dir.), Paris, 1994. – A. Ducloux, *"Ad ecclesiam contingere". Naissance du droit d'asile dans les églises (IV^e^-milieu du V^e^ siècle)*, Paris, 1994. – G. Halsall, *Early Medieval Cemeteries,* Skelmorlie, 1995. – C. Treffort, *Christianisme, rites funéraires et pratiques commémoratives à l'époque carolingienne*, Lyon, 1996.

Michel Lauwers

The "Lille" censer. France, second half of 12th c. Lille, Musée des Beaux-Arts.

**CENSER.** The censer (*acerra, thymiamaterium, turibulum, incensorium, encensier*) was a liturgical vessel used for burning *incense, formed of two "boats" one above the other, linked by small chains that also served to suspend and balance it; the lower boat, resting on a short foot, held the incense; the perforated upper boat let the smoke out.

Censers of the *Romanesque period were usually approximately spherical (censer of Renier, Lille Museum), but the upper cup sometimes took on a more important development, being enriched with more or less stylized architectural forms in which we must doubtless see an evocation of the heavenly *Jerusalem (censers of *Trier cathedral treasury). In the *Gothic period, this architectural decoration became general, the upper cup frequently having a decoration of Gothic arcades one above the other (group of 14th-

11th-c. pottery. Vessels, lamps. Workshop of Le Molay Littry.

and 15th-c. Tuscan censers in the Museo dell'Opera del Duomo at Siena; censer from *Ramsey abbey, London, *c.*1350, V & A, London). In the 15th c., the openings and other architectural elements evolved, adopting *Flamboyant forms.

H. Leclercq, "Encensoir", *DACL*, 5, 1, 1922, 21-35. – É. Taburet-Delahaye, *L'Orfèvrerie gothique – XIIIe-début XVe siècle – au musée de Cluny. Catalogue*, Paris, 1989.

Élisabeth Taburet-Delahaye

**CENSURES.** Censures were ecclesiastical *sanctions depriving Christians (clerical or lay) of certain spiritual benefits. "Medicinal" penalties, they lasted only until the amendment of the guilty. There were three: 1) *Excommunication, which led to exclusion from the community of the faithful and in particular prevented *burial in consecrated ground. 2) *Interdict, which suspended religious services; it could be applied to places (town, kingdom, etc.) or persons. 3) Suspension, which concerned only *clerics. It deprived them of an office, a *benefice, or both.

Up to and including the 12th c., "excommunication" was more or less synonymous with "censure". It was *Innocent III (1198-1216) who specified the meaning of the terms.

"Censures", *DThC*, 2, 2, 1923, 2113-2136. – "Censures", *DDC*, 3, 1942, 169-223.

Patrick Henriet

***CENSUS, CENSUARIUM.*** The *census* was a *rent, generally in *money, exacted by the tenant-in-chief of an estate from his own tenant in seisin or investiture of a plot. After the 15th c., the word came to designate various rights arising from lordship; it was then ranked among "feudal rights".

The origin of the *census* may go back to the "canon" required of *coloni* in late Antiquity, when it was the object of a written contract. Its extension between the 6th and 10th cc. resulted from the diminution of *slavery, hence the need to have recourse to "enfeoffed", *i.e.* installed, manpower, at the time of the establishment of a bipartisan system of exploitation on the great estates. It then most often consisted of some small coins and a rent in kind, and was accompanied by service in *labour, this latter practice subsisting here and there until the 12th century. After the year 1000, the *census* slid down to the level of a rent in kind; it became the normal form of land tax, either with a written document or by oral *custom, sometimes "avowed" before a seignorial jurisdiction (England). The amount was fixed by custom and hence very difficult to increase, so that the devaluation of money in the 14th c. tended to make it almost recognitive (from 1 to 5 % of the revenues of an estate) and thus useless and even unjustified in the eyes of the *peasants, in contrast to payments in kind (*champart, terrages*) or the heavier and more alienating rents. It was payable in money generally once a year, after the harvests, practically hereditary (the *lods et ventes* of transfer were modest and unquestioned), transferable and divisible. Its amount appears to have differed extraordinarily from one piece of land to another without discernible cause: nature of the soil, legal status of the holder, ancient customs, alteration?

The *censuarium* was a register or collection of pages on which were entered, as well as services, the rents due from each plot of an estate; in its ideal structure it involved the location and description of the plot, the obligations incumbent on the holder, and his name. The origin of these – simple administrative documents, hence very often destroyed when no longer needed – goes back to Antiquity (3rd c.). The two great periods of their drafting, or sometimes their gradual appearance, were the 8th-10th cc., during the setting up of the bipartisan system of reserved lands and allotted parcels on the great estates, and the 14th-15th cc. when the administrative difficulties of landowners forced them to keep a precise statement of their requirements.

R. Boutruche, *Seigneurie et féodalité*, Paris, 1968-1970. – G. Fourquin, *Lordship and Feudalism in the Middle Ages*, New York, 1976. – *Censiers et terriers*, Rome, 1977 ("Informatique et histoire médiévale"). – R. Fossier, *Polyptiques et censiers*, *TSMÂO*, 28, Louvain, 1978. – *Les revenus de la terre, complant, champart, métayage en Europe occidentale . . .*, Auch, 1987 ("Flaran", 7).

Robert Fossier

**CENTO.** A cento is, strictly speaking, a text entirely composed of literal borrowings from one or more other texts. The 4th and 5th cc. were the golden age of the cento: the Roman patrician Faltonia Proba and the Greek empress Eudoxia were authors of sacred histories in verse exclusively made up of hemistichs, Virgilian for the one, Homeric for the other, in order to confer a prestigious literary expression on the sacred account, perhaps also to Christianize revered authors; on another level, Ausonius's scabrous *Nuptial cento* was entirely made from verses of Virgil ironically taken out of their original context. Medieval writers were happy to adopt the same attitudes of reverence and distance towards the ancient texts: from Carolingian *homilies, sometimes pure collages of extracts of exegetical works of the *Fathers, to encyclopedic **summae*, compilations of earlier writings, to *poetry in metrical verses, which playfully associated sentences and formulae borrowed from *auctores*, learned literary output often, without avowing it, comes under the heading of the cento.

O. Delepierre, *Tableau de la littérature du centon chez les anciens et les modernes*, London, 1874-1875 (2 vol.).

Jean-Yves Tilliette

**CERAMICS.** The term "ceramic" is applied to terracotta products and includes pottery, architectural terracotta (tiles, bricks, paving tiles) and objects such as lamps and statues.

After the 5th c., we see a great dispersal of pottery production. The forms derive from the usual antique forms. The decoration, when it exists, consists of a series of applied horizontal bands pricked out with multiple geometrical motifs. The firing, ill controlled and at quite a low temperature (about 800°), gives colours varying from beige to red and dark grey. Glazes, thick and brownish, are extremely rare. On the whole ceramics circulated little.

In north-west Europe, from the 9th to the 11th c. production essentially consists of *ollae* (cooking pots, globular in form), pitchers, rare small bowls, sometimes large mortars. We note the frequency of applied bands decorated with a rowel or with thumbprints, and the presence of prominent striations caused by turning. Notable among others is the output of the Meuse region called "Andenne" ware. Glazing becomes less rare: leaded, greenish, often speckled, it rarely covers the whole of the vase. From the 11th to the 13th c. types diversified.

In southern Europe, Byzantine and Islamic influences are reflected in a wider range of forms and an important development of polychrome decoration which reaches its apogee in maiolica with painted decoration and tinned glaze, and particularly in "metallic lustre" ceramic with its play of iridescent colours. Another decoration obtained by incisions and enhancement of colours also developed, notably the Italic "*sgraffito*".

In north-west Europe at the start of the 14th c., a type of ceramic intended for the table and overloaded with decoration was widely used. It is called "highly decorated". At the same time and in the same geographical area appeared a pottery fired at more than 1200°: stoneware. Its degree of impermeability is remarkable. Its manufacture supposes a progress in kiln technique and control of firing. Its production was confined to regions possessing suitable clays: Beauvaisis, Normandy, Alsace, the Rhineland, south-east England.

Architectural ceramics were little made in the early Middle Ages, but their production intensified later. Yellow and brown decorated paving tiles had a tremendous vogue from the 13th to the 16th century.

*La Céramique médiévale en Méditerranée occidentale. Colloque: Valbonne, 1978*, Paris, 1980 (*"Colloques internationaux du CNRS"*, 584). – *La céramique (Ve-XIXe siècle), fabrication, commercialisation, utilisation. Actes du 1er congrès d'archéologie médiévale*, Caen, 1987. – M. MacCarthy, C. M. Brooks, *Medieval Pottery in Britain AD 900-1600*, Leicester, 1988.

Anne-Marie Flambard Héricher

**CEREMONIAL.** The *Ceremoniale* was the typological culmination of the ordinaries, at the meeting of the Middle Ages and the Renaissance (15th-16th cc.). Like the *Ordinary, the Ceremonial was a book descriptive of the liturgy, but unlike the former it contained no reference to liturgical texts, preferring to increase the indications describing the rites. The Ceremonial developed in the 15th c., essentially at the papal court, at a time when the desire arose for a codification of the papal liturgy, which had become more and more sumptuous. At the request of Innocent VIII (1484-1492), Agostino Patrizi Piccolomini and Jean Burckard put together a Ceremonial, first published in 1516 and often reprinted subsequently.

A.-G. Martimort, *Les Ordines, les ordinaires et les cérémoniaux*, *TSMÂO*, 56, 1991, 89-106. – É. Palazzo, *Histoire des livres liturgiques. Le Moyen Âge, des origines au XIIIe siècle*, Paris, 1993.

Éric Palazzo

**CESARINI, GIULIANO, SENIOR (*c.*1398-1444).** Of modest origin, he began his studies very young and commenced in law at the university of *Perugia, then at *Bologna. He gained his doctorate in civil and *canon law at *Padua and had *Nicholas of

*Danse macabre.* Minstrel, student and peasant. 15th-c. fresco (detail) in the abbey church of Saint-Robert, La Chaise-Dieu.

Cusa among his pupils. *Martin V promoted him *cardinal-deacon (1430), then appointed him *legate in *Bohemia for the *Hussite question (1431). President of the council of *Basel (1431), he was among the most fervent partisans of the *conciliar theory. But in 1438, out of loyalty, he rejoined the council transferred to Ferrara, then to *Florence, where he played an active role in the *union of the Eastern Churches. He was also legate in the Danubian countries, where he died in 1444. A man of acknowledged integrity, this *jurist was one of the main figures in the Church of his time.

*DHGE*, 12, 1953, 220-249. – *HChr*, 6, 1990.

Michel Fol

**CHAIR OF SAINT PETER.** From the 4th c., the *feast of the Chair of St Peter celebrated *Peter's Roman episcopacy on 22 February. The term itself referred to the papal office and the stone **cathedra* that *Gregory I had put in the apse of *St Peter's basilica. From the 13th c., it designated a wooden throne situated near the high *altar and venerated as a *relic. This was undoubtedly the throne of *Charles the Bald, given to *John VIII and preserved since the 17th c. beneath Bernini's *Cattedra* in the apse of the basilica.

*La Cattedra lignea di s. Pietro in Vaticano*, Rome, 1971. – M. Maccarrone, "La 'Cathedra Sancti Petri' nel Medioevo: da simbolo a reliquia", *Romana Ecclesia Cathedra Petri*, 2, Rome, 1991, 1249-1373.

Agostino Paravicini Bagliani

**CHAISE-DIEU, LA.** The abbey was founded in the mid 11th c. by Robert of Turlande, son of a middle-ranking noble family with possessions in Brivadois, Margeride and on the borders of Rouergue. Nephew of Rencon, bishop of *Clermont, Robert was entrusted very young to the illustrious *chapter of Brioude. After many years of life as a *canon, during which he acted as treasurer, Robert was drawn to the monastic life, but the "laxity" that he saw in Cluniac houses led him to look rather to the stricter Benedictine abbeys, like that of *Monte Cassino where he made a *pilgrimage in *c.*1040.

On his return, he settled in a lonely spot in the Livradois on 28 Dec 1043, in a place belonging to two churchmen who donated it to him. The canon became a hermit while continuing to seek a new mode of monastic practice. This step was not original: John

Gualbert, founder of *Vallombrosa, a bit later *Stephen of Muret or St *Bruno did much the same. But Robert remained within the Benedictine tradition.

The new abbey was rapidly built, and Bishop Rencon consecrated the abbey church which, following the original title of Clermont cathedral, was dedicated to Sts Vitalis and Agricola. Unlike the Cluniac houses, the new *foundation, which took the significant name of *Casa Dei* – the house of God –, was put resolutely under episcopal authority.

Robert's most striking subsequent action was the creation of some 50 *priories, all centres of religious life, spread through all the *dioceses of the Massif Central. He died at La Chaise-Dieu on 17 April 1067 and was buried on the 24th, date of his feast.

The end of that century and the course of the next saw the apogee of La Chaise-Dieu. The founder's successor, Durand, a priest of Clermont, combined his office with that of *bishop of his home town. The next *abbot, Adelelm, was called to Spain by *Alfonso VI and the reforming clergy to eliminate the last practitioners of the *Hispanic liturgy. Under Seguin (1078-1094), La Chaise-Dieu was closely mixed up in the foundation of the Chartreuse: by a donation of 1090, the Auvergne abbey contributed to the temporalities of the hermits installed by St Bruno. From the *crusade preached in 1095, La Chaise-Dieu received numerous donations, which the crusaders had to concede to it in order to obtain financial help. The most important beneficiary of this exchange was one of the expedition's leaders, Count Raymond of Toulouse. Pons (1094-1102) was then head of the monastery, which attained its greatest territorial power with Stephen of Mercoeur († 1146). Many Spanish and Italian possessions were added at that time to its impressive network of influences and revenues in France.

The domestic feudal struggles of the Auvergne and the wars between *Capetians and *Plantagenets contributed to sending La Chaise-Dieu into a slow period of stagnation, which cannot quite be called decline. In the 13th c., the abbot of La Chaise-Dieu headed a congregation comprising 11 abbeys: Borzone, Brantôme, Faverney, Frassinoro, Caillac, Montauban, San Marino at *Pavia, San Sesto at *Piacenza, La Valdieu and Saint-André at *Vienne, not counting tens of priories.

Thanks to the election of one of its monks to the papacy under the name *Clement VI (1342-1352), and then that of his nephew (*Gregory XI, 1370-1378), the prestige of La Chaise-Dieu was maintained, albeit rather artificially. At the moment of the worst crises suffered by the kingdom in the 14th c., the abbey, thanks to the subsidies of the Avignon popes, offered the world the spectacle of sumptuous rebuilding works whose results are still admired today, as well as the famous mural painting depicting the **danse macabre*. Early in the 16th c., the abbey founded by Robert of Turlande fell under the regime of *commendation which put it – institutions, privileges and immense revenues – into the hands of the king.

P. R. Gaussin, *L'Abbaye de La Chaise-Dieu (1043-1518)*, Paris, 1962. – A. Erlande-Brandenburg, "L'abbatiale de la Chaise-Dieu", *Congrès archéologique (Velay)*, 133, 1975, 720-55. – P. R. Gaussin, *Le Rayonnement de la Chaise-Dieu*, Brioude, 1981.

Michel Aubrun

**CHALDEANS.** Oriental Christians. The Church that called itself "Oriental" and which the Middle Ages called "Nestorian", in reference to the *christological doctrine of Nestorius that it had adopted in the 5th c., has been called "Chaldean" since the council of Florence. The *Nestorians had spread as far as *Egypt and *Syria thanks to those countries' commercial links with Mesopotamia; but contacts with the Chalcedonian Churches remained limited. However, Latins who settled in the *Holy Land, such as Oliver of Paderborn, questioned the reality of their adherence to the "Nestorian" doctrine. On the occasion of the council of *Lyon (1245), *Innocent IV exchanged professions of faith with their prelates, who had already been approached by the *Dominicans of the Jerusalem convent. The arrival of the *Mongol bishop Barsauma in Rome in 1287 was the occasion for conversations, at the end of which he declared himself in union of faith with the *pope, who sent Catholicos Yahballaha III a *mitre and a *ring as a sign of acknowledgment of his primacy. Barsauma himself sealed some letters of indulgence with his – Latin – *seal, and Yahballaha welcomed Dominicans to his residence, Maragha.

But *Riccoldo of Montecroce noted in 1289 that the adhesion of the catholicos to the Roman profession of faith left reservations existing among the faithful: a church in which he had preached against Nestorius was purified with rosewater. The preaching of Latin missionaries, *e.g.* in Persia or in *China, had created an awareness of the dogmatic and ritual differences between the two Churches, while elsewhere (*India, *Cyprus) these same Nestorians made no difficulties about accepting help brought to them by Latin religious or practising an intercommunion that failed in other places, where the Chaldeans who rallied to Rome separated from their Church. At the council of *Florence, *Eugenius IV sought to achieve with the other Oriental Churches the *union he had concluded with the Greeks. The apostolic representative sent to the catholicos of the Orientals, Anthony of Troia, does not seem to have reached him. It was the metropolitan of Tarsus, Timothy – who may have lived at Cyprus –, who came to Florence and there adhered to the council's decisions, accepting the christological doctrine proposed to him (1445). It was then that Eugenius IV promulgated the *Decretum pro chaldaeis* that proclaimed the union of the two Churches. But this document was unable to reach the heart of the Chaldean Church, which remained Mesopotamia, nor its dependencies in India, those in Central and East Asia being then in the process of disappearing. The union thus proclaimed had still to be achieved in reality, and the state of the Orient at this time was not favourable to closer contacts.

J. Gill, *The Council of Florence*, Cambridge, 1959. – J. Richard, *La Papauté et les Missions d'Orient au Moyen Âge*, Rome, 1977.

Jean Richard

**CHALICE.** A vessel used for the *consecration of the wine in the course of the *mass. Conciliar or synodal canons prescribed that they were to be made of precious materials, usually *gold or silver, though copper, tin and lead were tolerated. Texts and some rare surviving work attest that hard stones, *ivory, *glass, wood and horn were also used. When a metal other than gold was employed, the inside of the cup had to be gilded.

"Ministerial" chalices, reserved for the *communion of the congregation which seems to have been practised until the 13th c., were larger: the *calices maiores* described in Carolingian texts doubtless belonged to this type.

The form of medieval chalices was derived primarily from that of the two main types of ancient drinking vessel: the goblet, with a tall narrow cup, and the cantharus, with a wide-mouthed cup and two handles. Thus the chalice of St *Eligius († 659) formerly preserved at *Chelles and known by a 17th-c. drawing, that given

Chalice with the name of the emperor Romanus II (959-963). Byzantine art, 10th c. Venice, treasury of St Mark's basilica

by Duke Tassilo of Bavaria (749-788) to the abbey of *Kremsmünster, and a group of Carolingian chalices, less precious but close in form, belong to the "goblet" type, while the very small gold chalice discovered at Gourdon (early 6th c.), the silver one found at Ardagh (first half of 7th c., Dublin, National Museum of Ireland) and the gold chalice of Bishop St Gauzlin of Toul († 962, Nancy cathedral treasury) are related, more or less directly, to the example of the ancient cantharus. Original forms also appear, notably in Spain (chalice of San Domingo de Silos, *c.*1063, and chalice of San Isidoro de León, *c.*1101), distinguished in particular by the development of the hemispherical foot.

In the 12th c., the forms usually seem to conform to a type characterised by an approximately hemispherical cup – with or without handles – a more or less flattened spherical joint and a foot in the shape of a truncated cone with a concave curve, a type perhaps derived from Byzantine examples. By contrast, there is great diversity in their decoration. In the 13th c., forms evolve from this type: the cup is shortened to form only a third- or a quarter-circle, and the joint is frequently ornamented with a ribbed motif.

In the late 13th c., at first in Italy, a new type appeared, characterised mainly by the form of the cup, with a wide "corolla" mouth, while the joint is often bossed and the contour of the foot is frequently polylobate (chalice offered by Pope *Nicholas IV [1288-1292] to the treasury of the basilica of Assisi). These forms spread rapidly north of the Alps and were continued sometimes until late in the 15th century. At this time, the cup evolved towards a less wide and more deep "tulip-shaped" form (the chalice dated 1411 offered by *Charles VI of France to St Catherine's monastery on Mount *Sinai or that made in *c.*1420 by the da Sesto workshop and preserved in the treasury of St Mark's, Venice).

C. Rohault de Fleury, "Calices", *La Messe. Études archéologiques sur les monuments*, 4, Paris, 1888, 45-153. – J. Braun, *Das Christliche Altargerät in seinem Sein und in seiner Entwicklung*, Munich, 1932. – *Trésors des églises de France*, Paris, 1965. – J. M. Fritz, *Goldschmiedekunst der Gotik im Mitteleuropa*, Munich, 1982.

Élisabeth Taburet-Delahaye

**CHALICE FOR THE LAITY.** The use of the chalice for the communion of the *laity in both kinds, attested from the origins of the liturgy of the Roman Church, gradually fell into disuse. With the mystical renewal of eucharistic piety, in late 14th-c. *Bohemia Matthew of Janov began to revive the desire for a frequent communion for all the congregation – which does not necessarily prove that he practised it under both kinds. This would only come about under the impetus of another great figure of the Czech reform movement, *Jacobellus of Stříbro, who in 1414 launched the battle of the chalice. Having assembled for this purpose a whole arsenal of arguments drawn from authoritative texts such as Gratian's **Decretum*, he then exploited it thoroughly in his polemic over the chalice with the Catholic master Ondřej (Andrew) of Brod. He moreover felt himself backed up by the personal experience of *Jerome of Prague, who returned in spring 1414 from a stay in Orthodox circles in *Poland and *Lithuania. Jacobellus, an advocate of the chalice, was also the first to use it towards the end of 1414 for the communion of the laity, with the support of the eminent German specialist in *canon law, Nicholas of Dresden. They are both considered authors of the theology of the chalice, otherwise called co-founders of Czech *utraquism.

It is not clearly established that the practice of the chalice for the laity began to become general before Jan *Hus's departure for Constance; but once arrived in that town, he expressed his agreement with *communion in both kinds for all. In the eyes of Rome, admission of the laity to the chalice was absolutely unacceptable, since it compromised the liturgical unity that existed at the time. That is why, faced with the situation in Bohemia, the council of *Constance pronounced an avalanche of *interdicts against certain ministers of the Church, at all hierarchical levels. The university of *Prague reacted in March 1415 in the name of all the components of the movement, in a solemn declaration by which the Czech Hussites adhered publicly to communion with the chalice, thus braving the authority of the Roman Church. This official act marked one of the essential differences between Hussites and *Catholics in matters of dogma and liturgy. Becoming the symbol of the Czech reform movement and then hoisted on the standards of Hussite warriors, the chalice announced to all contemporaries a programme of reforms that went well beyond the particular problem of sacramental rites. It would have a great moral effect, helping weld together the community of the faithful in a profound spirit of belonging to the same cause. Perfect harmony between the different currents of Hussitism, united in veneration of the *Eucharist under two kinds, knew no false notes until the polemic over the communion of children (from 1417); only once did it fall apart, in the case of the *Taborite "Picarts", despisers of the holy sacrament (1420-1421).

The serious problem of the chalice was at the centre of the laborious and complicated negotiations between the Utraquist and Catholic parties, both during the Hussite revolution and after the defeat of its radical wing at the battle of Lipany (1434). In the end, the chalice was the sole point of their programme that the Catholic Church would concede to the moderate Hussites in the set of accords concluded with them between 1433 and 1436 (called **compactata*). From the international point of view, the legalization

Reims, interior of the basilica of Saint-Remi, 12th c.

of two confessions in the Czech lands created a situation unprecedented in Western *Christendom: in effect, for the first time in the history of the Middle Ages now ending, the hegemony of the Catholic Church found itself lastingly breached on a precise territory. In the course of the following decades, some threats would certainly hover over the *compactata*, but it was only the lost battle of the White Mountain (1620) that opened the way to the final liquidation of the chalice, as part of the forced return of Bohemia and *Moravia to Catholicism.

A. Molnar, "Theologie husitského kalicha [Hussite theology of the chalice]", *TPKR*, 1965, 1-9.

B. Kopičková

**CHAMBER OF CARDINALS.** The organ of the *Sacred College for the administration of its revenues, which consisted essentially in a half-share, with the Apostolic *Camera, of common services, or a third of the gross annual revenues of an episcopal or abbatial income on the occasion of the appointment in *consistory of a new prelate. The *cardinals' *familiares* and officials also levied a fifth of the lesser services, the major part going to those of the *pope. The succession of *chamberlains of the College, appointed by the pope for life, is established from the last quarter of the 13th c.; they were assisted by two *clerics. The College more often found itself granting loans to the pope and the Apostolic Camera than the other way round.

P. M. Baumgarten, *Untersuchungen und Urkunden über die Camera collegii cardinalium für die Zeit von 1295 bis 1437*, Leipzig, 1898.

Michel Hayez

**CHAMBERLAIN.** The chamberlain (*camerarius*) was a financial administrator. He was one of the main officials of the king's entourage after *Pippin the Short's abolition of the dignity of Mayor of the Palace. His function was to watch over the king's valuable objects, jewels, plate, wardrobe. The chamberlain was assisted in his task by *cambellani* in the palace of the *Capetian king. This office declined from the 13th c. in favour of the financial and fiscal organs that grew out of the *curia regis*. Likewise, within the administrative institutions of the papal monarchy, the *camerarius* was the guardian of the *popes' fiscal receipts from the late 11th c. and directed the Apostolic *Camera whose role increased in the 14th century.

J. Raffali, "Caméria", *DDC*, 2, 1937, 1273-1275.

Thierry Pécout

**CHAMPAGNE.** In ecclesiastical geography, Champagne has no unity: *Reims, former metropolis of Belgica Secunda, became in the 8th c. the seat of an *archbishopric that brought together the northern *dioceses of the realm (including Châlons), while *Sens subordinated *Troyes and Meaux, and Langres depended on *Lyon. In feudal Champagne, the ecclesiastical countships of the north (Reims and Châlons) contrasted with the principality formed in the 11th-12th cc. by the Thibaudian family. To give structure to estates accumulated by the luck of inheritance, this family exploited the currents of international trade that crossed them, creating poles of attraction capable of unifying them along an axis. An efficient organisation in four towns (Troyes, Provins, Lagny and Bar-sur-Aube), following a calendar that ensured a revolving continuity, allowed southern Champagne to become the meeting-place of *merchants and a financial centre of the first importance. The count was able to shine by his liberality, surround himself with a brilliant *court which was the cradle of French literature (*Chrétien de Troyes) and hold his own against the Capetian before joining his own dynasty to his. The last countess, Jeanne († 1305), became queen of *France and brought her domain to the *Crown.

Champagne was a thoroughfare, but it was also a march, ever since the partition of Verdun (843) had made the Meuse the frontier between the kingdom of France and the *Empire. This situation led to it playing host in particular to a whole series of great reforming *councils that aimed to redress the morals of *clerics and make the German ruler relax his grip in the *Investiture Contest: Reims, 1049 (*Leo IX), Troyes, 1107 (*Paschal II), Reims, 1119 (*Calixtus II), 1131 (*Innocent II), 1148 (*Eugenius III). From the mid 12th c., the *bishops were worried about the progress of the Manichaean *heresy among the mass of *textile workers. The tragic epilogue was the massacre of Mount Aimé (near Vertus) in 1239, in which 143 *Cathars perished.

At the end of the 13th c., Champagne had 164 *abbeys, including 66 *Cistercian ones mostly founded before the death of St *Bernard of Clairvaux (1153); the same saint supported the introduction of the "new knighthood", the Order of *Templars (founded by the Champenois Hugues de Payns), whose rule he had commended at the council of Troyes (1128). To the Benedictines the region owes its most beautiful 11th-c. buildings, Saint-Remi at Reims, Notre-Dame at Montier-en-Der, and Saint-Étienne at Vignory. Their *architecture is especially marked by the Carolingian tradition, and up to the mid 12th c. the *Romanesque art of Champagne favoured simple volumes beneath visible roof-timbers, with limited sculptural decoration. Langres cathedral is a late offshoot of the art of *Cluny II at the moment when the influence of the Île-de-France was expressed in the flowering of *Gothic. In addition to the quest for light that gave Champagne an exceptional wealth of *stained glass (12th-16th cc.), we note the smiling elegance of a Champenois statuary that gave its masterpieces to Notre-Dame at Reims around 1250, then to Troyes at the end of the Middle Ages, with more gravity.

M. Crubellier, M. Bur *et al.*, *Histoire de la Champagne*, Toulouse, 1975 (2nd ed. 1980). – T. Evergates, *Feudal Society in the Baillage of Troyes under the Counts of Champagne, 1152-1284*, Baltimore, 1975. – M. Crubellier, P. Demouy *et al.*, *Champagne Ardenne*, Paris, 1981 (2nd ed. 1987). – *Feudal Society in Medieval France: documents from the county of Champagne*, T. Evergates (ed.), Philadelphia, 1993.

Patrick Demouy

**CHANCELLOR, CHANCERY.** The term "chancellor", always a little vague and out of focus, served to designate the head of the writing office of a lay or ecclesiastical *authority, *pope or *bishop, prince or *commune.

In the Late Roman Empire, the *cancellarius* was a mere usher, posted at the *cancellus* (door) of the court; the officers in charge of writing down and validating the documents of the *Merovingian king were called "referendaries", as in the 5th-c. Empire. The "chancellor", head of the notaries, appears around the beginning of the 9th c. in the Carolingian *palace, where the milieu was clericalized – another break with the old traditions. The position was soon divided between an "archchancellor", political head before becoming a distant ecclesiastical dignitary (archbishops of *Reims, *Mainz, *Trier), and an actual chancellor, whose links with the royal *chapel were reinforced. It was doubtless in imitation of the *Empire that the papal palace provided itself with a chancellor (first attested in 1005), a simple adjunct of the *bibliothecarius* who himself secured the monopoly on delivery of documents; the two offices were united from 1037, then the title of chancellor was exclusive from 1144. The last three centuries of the Middle Ages saw the institutionalization of more stable, specialized writing offices (acts ceasing to be established by their beneficiaries), adorned with the name of chancery and provided with a regular personnel: undifferentiated and mutually competing (*notaries, *abbreviators and writers of the *pope's *bulls, who left the drawing up of *briefs to the secretaries and that of the numerous *letters to other organs, Apostolic *Camera or *Penitentiary Office). Evolution took place by fits and starts, generating dysfunctions that were periodically regularized in the 14th-15th cc., but left largely personal relationships, private forms (valets of notaries) and uncertain margins (*procurators of benefice-holders) still in existence.

The prince's chancellor quickly became a key figure in the administration: controlling the output of writing, at least in its most solemn form, he oversaw the mechanisms of decision-taking, in matters of finance and still more of diplomacy, justice or appointment of officials. By a paradox that is only apparent, the periods of growth of chanceries were also those of long vacancies of a too invasive office (in *France for most of the 13th c., in the pontifical *chancery from 1216 to 1908); the function was then allocated to another person, keeper of the king's *seal, papal vice-chancellor, who quickly gained in importance. The institution of episcopal chancellors was still more complex: the title did not exist everywhere and, like the *archdeacon, this collaborator of the bishop was a member of the cathedral *chapter. His role in the writing of documents overflowed into the preservation of archives and, when there was no **scholasticus*, teaching: he played an often essential role in the 12th c. when the cathedral *schools flourished, thus at *Paris where the *university soon challenged his direction of the schools.

M. Richardson, "Henry V, the English Chancery, and the Chancery English", *Spec.*, 55, 1980, 726-50. – C.W. Smith, "Some Trends in the English Royal Chancery, 1377-1483", *Medieval Prosopography*, 6/1, Spring 1985, 69-94. – B.-M. Tock, *Une Chancellerie épiscopale au XIIe siècle: le cas d'Arras*, Louvain-la-Neuve, 1991 ("Publications de l'Institut d'études médiévales", 12). – O. Guyotjeannin, P. Pycke, B.-M. Tock, *Diplomatique médiévale*, Turnhout, 1993 (2nd ed., 1995; "L'Atelier du Médiéviste", 2).

Olivier Guyotjeannin

**CHANCERY, PONTIFICAL.** The office in which the acts of the papacy were drawn up, sealed and sent off, the chancery appeared necessary from the 4th c., in proportion as Roman primacy was asserted. The *notaries or *scrinarii* who drew up the acts and kept the archives were put under the authority of the **primicerius* and *secundicerius*, offices inspired by the Byzantine court. After the confusion of the 10th c., a reorganisation was gradually carried out under the direction of a chancellor (*cancellarius* in 1005), who was confused with the librarian and who was often a *bishop of a see near Rome before being a *deacon. The term "chancery" (*cancellaria*) is not attested until 1182. Western influence then prevailed.

Two sorts of acts were delivered: privileges and mandates, the latter representing the *pope's correspondence. Great precautions were taken to discourage forgers. *Papyrus was used until the early 11th c., before being replaced by *parchment. The original was drawn up in a particular *script (*littera romana*) difficult to decipher; it was accompanied by a certified copy in cursive minuscule. The text, checked by the pope who inscribed *benevalete* or two S's (*subscripsi*), mentioned the personage by whom the act was given and bore a date. At the bottom, a lead *bulla* was appended by hemp cords, bearing the name of the reigning pope. Few pontifical acts have been preserved, and nearly always thanks to their recipients (some 900 between 888 and 1054).

From the 12th c., the chancery grew with the increase in interventions by the papacy. The *chancellor was a cardinal-priest or deacon; but from 1187 the head of the service only had the title of vice-chancellor, and was a *cleric of quite modest rank. *Boniface VIII reintroduced a *cardinal, still bearing the name of vice-chancellor. Several bureaux were established. That of petitions received requests for graces: conformable to formularies, they were countersigned by the pope (*Fiat*, *Fiat ut petitur*), or passed only before the vice-chancellor. The *datary put a date on the agreed petition. Registers of petitions are preserved only from *Clement VI (1342), not without lacunae. The bureau of the minute prepared an abridgement of the act; in the 13th c., it numbered seven notaries, who ended by being concerned only with important acts; they were then called protonotaries and came into competition with the secretaries, who belonged to the Apostolic *Camera. The number of scribes (*scriptores*) was around 100. The bureau of the corrector, which employed only a small number of specialists, verified the form and content of the letter, had it begun again if necessary, taxed it and directed it either to the pope before whom it was read, or to the auditor of contradicted letters where the attorneys of the contending parties had a chance to oppose it. The bureau of the *seal, where engrossed and agreed acts were brought three times a week, was held by two Cistercian lay-brothers who could neither read nor write, appointed by the pope himself. The bureau of register recopied the acts in a simplified form to be put in the archives; but

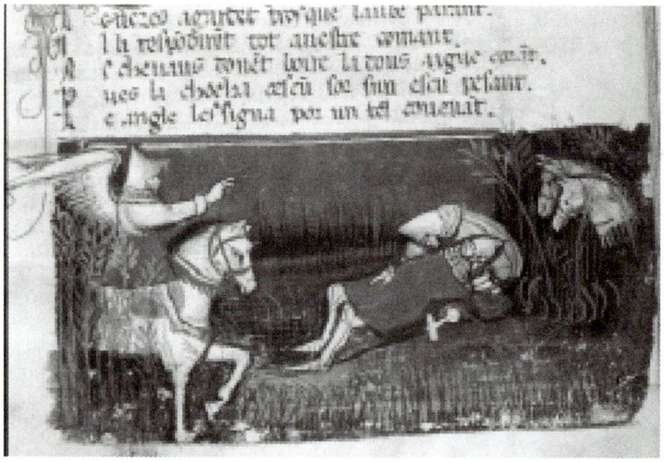

*The Death of Roland.* Miniature from a 14th-c. manuscript of the *Chanson de Roland.* Venice, Bibliotheca Marciana

the series preserved are far from being complete. *Letters were progressively classified by subject-matter in three great divisions: secret letters, curial letters, common letters.

The importance of the chancery diminished in the 15th century. From *Martin V, an apostolic secretariat appeared necessary for a more rapid and more secret correspondence; from it developed the secretariat of briefs to princes and the secretariat of Latin letters. It was one of the origins of the Secretariat of State.

R. Fawtier, *Les Registres de Boniface VIII*, 4, Paris, 1939 (introduction). – A. Dumas, "L'Église au pouvoir des laïques (888-1057)", *HE*, 7, 1948 (ch. IV). – G. Mollat, *Les Papes d'Avignon. 1305-1378*, Paris, 1964 (10th ed.). – C. R. Cheney, *The Study of the Medieval Papal Chancery*, Glasgow, 1966. – R. Fawtier, *Le Fonctionnement administratif de la Papauté d'Avignon*, Rome, 1988-1990. – P. N. R. Zutshi, *Original Papal Letters in England, 1305-1415*, Vatican City, 1990. – B. Guillemain, *Les papes d'Avignon, 1309-1376*, Paris, 1998.

Bernard Guillemain

***CHANSON DE GESTE.*** "*Chanter de geste*" was, according to 13th-c. theoreticians, to celebrate the exploits of heroes and kings, but also those of Fathers in faith: so there would be no difference between epic narratives and Lives of saints. The reality was different, since the object of *epic poems was warlike action waged either against the *Saracens or against the enemies of the king or lord. But the religious dimension is evident, since it is for God that heroes fight when they confront the infidel, and again it is with the high deeds of God that their courage and self-denial are compared, even when their struggles are secular.

Inspired by the value systems of the Middle Ages – *feudalism, with the necessary loyalty in observing the vassalic contract, *chivalry, with the defence of the Church – the *chanson de geste* becomes known to us only when it starts to be written down: the first surviving text (the **Chanson de Roland*) dates from the last 40 years of the 11th century. In it we recognise an elaborate art, which associates lyric procedures – versified strophes of unequal length called *laisses* – and narrative procedures: the poet has recourse to stereotyped motifs, a sort of framework that guides inspiration without curbing it. As its name indicates, the epic poem is really a song, performed by a **jongleur* to unobtrusive *music: thus, from its beginnings, the epic art was essentially oral and linked to direct communication with the public. We find evidence of its existence from 1030, but we may suppose an older epic activity, in unknown forms, since songs in honour of the former kings were known to *Charlemagne, who wanted them transcribed to prevent them falling into oblivion. The output of epics (some hundred poems) developed over the 12th and 13th cc., then the songs progressively lost their links with lyricism and oral recitation: in the 14th c., the poems had become voluminous works, intended for reading.

A thematic classification allows us to distinguish epics dominated by the crusading ideal (*Chanson de Guillaume*), "songs of revolt" opposing the vassal to the lord or rival families (*Raoul de Cambrai*, *Les Lorrains*) and "songs of adventure" (*Huon de Bordeaux*). But texts can also be arranged around founding persons or events. Guillaume d'Orange, his brothers and relations thus form a *geste*, at once a heroic family and a group of epic narratives, while numerous poems were created from the memory of the battle of Roncevaux and its heroes. Finally, historic events that marked an era – the first *crusade, the struggle of Du Guesclin against the English – could find in epic song the fitting vessel for the commemoration of a deep emotion.

J. Rychner, *La Chanson de geste. Essai sur l'art épique des jongleurs*, Geneva, 1955. – M. de Riquer, *Les Chansons de geste françaises*, I. Cluzel (Fr. tr.), Paris, 1957. – S. Kay, *The Chanson de Geste in the age of romance: political fictions*, Oxford, 1995.

François Suard

***CHANSON DE ROLAND.*** Preserved in a manuscript (Digby 23) in the Bodleian Library, Oxford, the oldest version of the *Roland* (between 1120 and 1150) is the first and one of the finest of the **chansons de geste*. Constructed like an antique drama, it tells of the annihilation of *Charlemagne's rearguard, commanded by the emperor's nephew Roland: Ganelon, the hero's stepfather and jealous of his valour, betrays him and his companions to the *Saracens. Warned by the call of Roland's horn, Charlemagne returns to Roncevaux to mourn for his nephew and avenge him, in a gigantic confrontation with the infidels. Learning of her fiancé's death, the fair Aude dies of grief, but the traitor is cruelly punished.

The *chanson* is based on the crusading ideal and the exaltation of the vassal's loyalty: this is why Ganelon, though he has some reasons for opposing Roland, can only be a traitor since he strikes a blow, through his champions, at his lord's power. With the figure of Roland, the text also brings out the lack of moderation inseparable from the epic character: refusing to call Charlemagne to his help while there is still time, Roland makes an *apologia* for a heroism that neglects the result of the mission entrusted to him in favour of the exaltation of risk and valour considered as absolutes. Alongside him, Oliver defends his lord's interests, in order to see his cause defended effectively. From the first known work, the epic poet thus poses the dilemma essential to *epic, which oscillates between a heroism detached from all connection with the real and the exaltation of victories effectively won. *Roland* honours both parties: To Charles's nephew belongs the palm of glory in arms and *martyrdom suffered for the faith – the angels of the Lord come to gather his soul –; to the emperor belongs the decisive revenge over the Saracen people.

As well as the characteristic values, the essential historical and aesthetic traits of the epic are already in place. The poem has a substrate of identifiable fact, the ambush laid for Charlemagne's army in the Pyrenean defiles on 15 Aug 778 by Basque or Gascon highlanders, which caused quite serious losses. The legend has notably transformed these facts: the *Franks' opponents are now enemies of the faith, whom the Christians confront in a gigantic struggle. As for the literary procedures of the epic, these are already perfectly mastered, with pairs of friendly (Roland and Oliver) or inimical characters (Roland and Ganelon), which allows a distinction to be made between the variants of the heroic type, and especially the alliance between lyricism (parallel strophes, used notably for the scenes of lamentation) and narrative.

The *Chanson*'s success was astonishing. As well as a learned adaptation (Pseudo-*Turpin), it was rewritten many times, in French as well as other European languages (Spanish, Italian, German, Norse, Welsh), while several epic poems took it as their model.

J. Bédier, *La Chanson de Roland commentée*, Paris, 1923 (re-ed. 1968). – *La Chanson de Roland*, I. Short (ed.), Paris, 1990. – *The Song of Roland*, Woodbridge, 1990.

J. Horrent, *La Chanson de Roland dans les littératures française et espagnole au Moyen Âge*, Paris, 1951. – P. Haidu, *The Subject of Violence*, Bloomington, 1993.

François Suard

**CHAPEL.** The term "chapel" is probably derived from *cappa* (*cloak or cape), an allusion to the relic of St *Martin preserved in the *oratory of the first kings of France, which followed them when they moved around. It was applied to the set of objects necessary for celebrating eucharistic worship, and those that were attached to it. By extension, "chapel" ended by designating the oratory itself.

We must differentiate between a chapel and a *chaplaincy. The latter was a *benefice attributed to a *chaplain who was charged with a specific service laid down in the act of *foundation. In general, the chaplaincy entailed no architectural expression of its own and was accommodated in existing buildings.

By contrast, a chapel always involved an *altar of its own. It could be integrated in the general plan of a church (chapel of the Ursins in Notre-Dame, Paris) or built as an annexe (chapel of the Virgin at Saint-Germer-de-Fly). It could be housed in a public establishment like a *college, a *prison or a *hospital (chapel of the Quinze-Vingts), in a *castle where it could be integrated, isolated or built next to the door in a symbolic defensive role, in an urban palace or a private *hôtel* (chapel of the *hôtel de Cluny*). It could be established in a building of its own in town or in the country.

Generally possessing neither baptismal *font nor regular service, the chapel did not play the role of a parish church. But it could be the home of a trade *confraternity (Saint-Julien des Ménétriers, Paris).

By extension, "chapel" designated the body of ecclesiastics serving this building. From the 13th c., the travelling chapel of the king of France comprised a confessor, an almoner, a first chaplain, three then six chaplains, four clerks and subordinate personnel.

The same term characterised the group of adult musicians, lay and professional, who sang there under the direction of a chapel-master. It was different from the cathedral choir composed of alb-boys (or choirboys) and staffed by masters of *music and *grammar.

In medieval texts, a silver-gilt or vermilion "chapel" can designate the set of *liturgical objects indispensable for the celebration of *mass (*chalice and paten, cruets and their tray). Likewise we find mentioned, according to their material or liturgical colour, *silk, satin, crape or damask "chapels", or white, red, variegated or black "chapels", the set of priestly *vestments and ornaments necessary for the service.

*Trésors des églises de France*, Paris, 1965 (exhibition catalogue). – *L'Eglise et le Château Xe-XVIIIe siècle, Cahiers de Commarque*, Bordeaux, 1988.

Claudine Billot

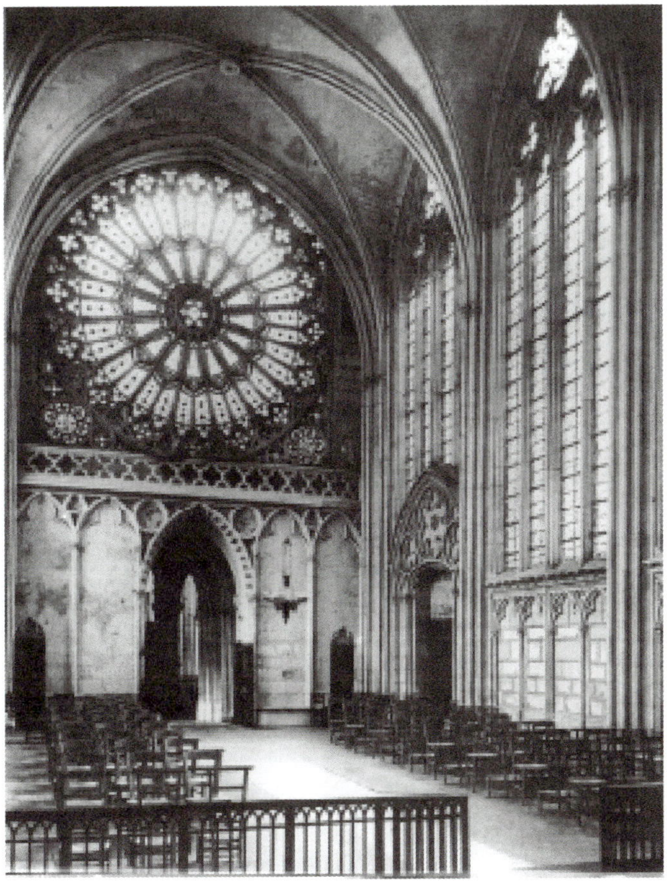

The chapel of the Virgin, Saint Germer-de-Fly. 13th c.

**CHAPLAIN.** In the later Middle Ages this term covered a number of churchmen occupying subordinate posts: replacements of *parish priests, priests serving charitable institutions, confraternity priests. In particular it was applied to *secular priests serving *foundations properly called "*chaplaincies". Like that of any parish priest, his appointment was subject to the approval of the diocesan hierarchy, whose control he was subsequently under: so he had to possess the qualities required of any cleric aspiring to a *benefice. The chaplain's function consisted essentially of liturgical obligations, viz. the celebration of masses. The chaplain also had to respect the privileges of the *parish. He could not keep payments intended for the parish priest; moreover, he was obliged to respect the *hours of the *offices, sometimes he even had to assist at the hours or at the parish high *mass. In certain cases, *e.g.* that of a private *oratory, the chaplain could escape the authority of the *diocese and become a rival to the parish priest. In return, he was required to help the latter in the exercise of his *ministry. In the end the multiplication of foundations in certain churches was to entail the creation of communities of chaplains, sort of priestly confraternities.

A. Derville, "Les chapelains de Saint-Géry de Cambrai au XIVe siècle", *MA*, 95, 1989, 255-278. – J. Avril, "Les chapelains de chapellenies", *Le Clergé séculier au Moyen Âge*, Paris, 1993, 113-125. – B. Delmaire, *Le diocèse d'Arras de 1093 au milieu du XIVe siècle*, Arras, 1994 (2 vol.).

Joseph Avril

**CHAPLAINCY.** Up to the 12th c., *capellania* corresponded to "incumbency", *i.e.* the exercise of pastoral government at the head of a *parish; from the 12th c., this term was applied to an institution created to say *prayers for the intention of the *dead or sometimes for the living. Any *foundation of a chaplaincy supposed three conditions. First an incumbent, the *chaplain, usually a *secular priest charged with celebrating masses. Then a place of worship, viz. an *altar or a *chapel in a parish, *abbey or *collegiate church. Finally an endowment intended to provide for the incumbent's upkeep. So this institution constituted a *benefice, and it would experience all the vicissitudes of one (*pluralism, non-*residence, *reservation). For all that, it was for some of the faithful the expression of a certain personal piety: as the *testaments of the late Middle Ages prove.

J. Queguiner, *Recherches sur les chapellenies au Moyen Âge*, Paris, 1950 (thesis, École des chartes). – K. L. Wood-Leigh, *Perpetual Chantries in Britain*, Cambridge, 1965. – N. Beriou, "Les chapellenies de la province ecclésiastique de Reims", *RHEF*, 57, 1971, 255-278.

Joseph Avril

**CHAPLET.** The chaplet or *rosary is a devotional object made up of pieces of bone or wood on a thread, moved along as vocal *prayers are said. Its use is not confined to Christianity and is found in the Hindu and Muslim traditions. The Middle Ages called it a "paternoster", a deformation of the invocation *Pater noster*. A custom of uncertain date organised its recitation into five tens of *Ave*s separated by a *Pater*, the whole preceded by a *Credo*, a *Pater* and three *Aves*; this, recited three times, constituted the rosary. Around the 15th c., the term "chaplet" came in, by analogy with the crowns or *chapes* of flowers that were worn as a sign of rejoicing or ornamented the heads of statues, including that of the Virgin.

A. Duval, "Rosaire", *DSp*, 12, 1988, 937-967.

Catherine Vincent

**CHAPTER.** This word covers several monastic and canonical practices and institutions, which all have a single origin, the celebration from the late 8th c., in the setting of the common life, in a particular room outside the choir, of a brief *office following prime, where was read notably a "chapter" (*capitulum*) of the monastic or canonical *Rule. One read or listened to a chapter in that room, one went *ad capitulum*, "to the chapter"; the place took the name of the passage read: "chapter room", or simply "chapter". The specific book used for the celebration of this office combined the Rule, the *martyrology, the *necrology and the homiletic *capitula* and was likewise called the "chapter-book". The "chapter" (room) being the place where the (professed) monks or *canons met daily, where decisions about the community's life were taken and *professions and admissions into its confraternity were made, by metonymy the word "chapter" designated all the professed religious or canons who took part in it ("had a voice in the chapter") and this meeting of capitulants itself.

Hence "chapter" designated: 1) a room where a monastic or canonical community met; 2) the eminent members of that community (the professed among monks and the prebendaries among canons); 3) the meeting that brought together the choir-monks and where important decisions were taken. By extension, it also designated: 4) all the regular or secular canons composing the clergy (*presbyterium*) of a *cathedral church, as well as the lower choir (*clerics not holding a canon's *prebend): the "cathedral chapter"; and 5) the prebend-holding canons forming the clergy of a *collegiate church, as well as the lower choir: the "collegiate chapter".

The "general chapter" originated in the conventual chapter: it was the meeting, generally annual but sometimes triennial, of religious under the common authority of an *abbot. Created at the instigation of *Cîteaux, its practice was quickly adopted by the new *orders: Arrouaise, Prémontré, the *mendicant orders, the canons of *Saint-Victor and the *Hospitallers, then the black monks and *canons regular, who were grouped by province. The *Dominicans propagated among certain orders – *Carmelites, *Servites, *Mercedarians – a modified form of annual general chapter. But in fact the general chapter brought together only the representatives of the religious: abbots, *priors or specially designated delegates. Holding sittings in accordance with a procedure well defined by the statutes, it entrusted the preparation of dossiers to a commission consisting of the *definitors, whose decisions had to be approved by the *sanior pars* of the assembly. The general chapter had mainly a legislative role concerning the order, but also controlled administration, persons and property, acting on the houses through the intermediary of the visitors.

The term "rural chapter", met in certain historians, designated in reality a community of priests (*prêtres-filleuls*, obituary priests, *méparts* ["half-shares"], etc) without any *benefice or jurisdiction, whose sole role was the celebration of foundation masses.

J. Hourlier, *Le Chapitre jusqu'au moment du Grand Schisme: origine, développement, rôle juridique*, Paris, 1936. – J. Hourlier, *L'Age classique (1140-1378). Les religieux, HDIEO*, 10, 1974, 345-354 (conventual chapter), 375-392 (general chapter). – R. Schieffer, *Die Entstehung vom Domkapitel in Deutschland*, Bonn, 1976. – J. Dubois, "Le Rôle du chapitre dans le gouvernement du monastère", *Sous la règle de saint Benoît. Structures monastiques et sociétés en France du Moyen Âge à l'époque moderne*, Geneva-Paris, 1982, 21-37. – B. Dobson, "Cathedral Chapters and Cathedral Cities: York, Durham, and Carlisle in the Fifteenth Century", *Northern History*, 19, 1983, 15-44. – J.-L. Lemaître, "Aux origines de l'office du chapitre et de la salle capitulaire. L'exemple de Fontenelle", *La Neustrie. Les pays au nord de la Loire de 650 à 850*, Sigmaringen, 1989, 365-369. – H. J. Becker, J. Dubois, *LdM*, 5, 1990-1991, 938-942. – R. Gane, *Le chapitre de Notre-Dame de Paris au XIVe siècle . Étude sociale d'un groupe canonial*, Saint-Étienne, 1999 (CERCOR, Travaux et recherches).

Jean-Loup Lemaître

**CHAPTERS, BIBLICAL.** The present division of the *Bible into chapters probably goes back to *Stephen Langton; he will have perfected it at *Paris early in the 13th c. (*Robert of Courson used it in his *Summa*, *c.*1204-1208). It replaced older divisions, non-homogeneous (*e.g.* *Alcuin's Bible) and less well-balanced. However, the old system of titles and subtitles (*tituli*, *breves*) was sometimes conjointly maintained. Division into verses took place in the 16th c.; in the 13th c., the chapters were divided into sections identified by the letters A to G.

A. Landgraf, "Die Schriftzitate in der Scholastik um die Wende des 12. zum 13. Jh", *Bib.*, 18, 1937, 74-94. – A. d'Esneval, "La Division de la Vulgate latine en chapitres. . .", *RSPhTh*, 62, 1978, 559-568.

Gilbert Dahan

**CHARACTER.** Medieval *theology gave the term "character" the technical sense of a spiritual mark made indelibly in the *soul by the three *sacraments of *baptism, *confirmation and *orders. Before St *Thomas Aquinas, theologians saw the character of baptism and the other two as anticipated sacramental marks of the coming kingdom of God. St Thomas rather saw the character of orders and the other two as deputations to the sacramental worship of the Church in the present world. For the priest, it was the sacramental character that made him capable of consecrating the *Eucharist and remitting sins.

H. Moureau, "Caractère sacramentel", *DThC*, 2, 1923, 1698-1708.

Pierre-Marie Gy

**CHARISM.** Often used in the sense popularized by M. Weber as an exceptional quality that makes someone a leader in the group, for Christians the word "charism" has a wider meaning. From the Greek *charisma* (same root as *charis*, "*grace"), it means a supernatural gift granted for the common good in order to build up the Body of Christ (Rom 12, 6; 1 Cor 12, 4 f.; 1 Pet 4, 10-11). Sometimes restricted to the extraordinary spiritual gifts (glossolalia, *miracles, *prophecy, *visions. . .) that shed lustre on the nascent Church, in fact the word coveres all the *gifts of the Spirit (see Vatican II, *LG*, 12).

In the Middle Ages, the word was seldom used; it is not in the index of St *Bonaventure's *Opera omnia* and it is used only rarely in the plural (*charismata*) in the works of St *Thomas Aquinas, to signify spiritual gifts in general. However, the reality was well known, but it was designated by the expression "*gratia gratis data*" ("grace freely given") to distinguish it from "*gratia gratum faciens* ("grace that makes agreeable [to God]", sanctifying grace; see Thomas Aquinas, *Summa theologiae*, I$^{a}$ II$^{ae}$, q. 111, 1, 4-5). This means that the subject who receives a charism is not internally transformed by it (it is sanctifying grace that works this transformation), but is merely its provisional holder for the benefit of the ecclesial community; the *Holy Spirit uses him as an instrument in the broad sense. Whether ministerial or personal, all charisms come under this law of instrumentality (prophecy is in the service of *faith, as is papal *infallibility); all are ordered to the only value that is an end in itself, the grace that is the anticipation of *eternal life in this life.

This subordination, in the ecclesial *economy, of freely given graces to sanctifying grace is heavily emphasized by St Thomas when he distinguishes between the two types of gifts of the Spirit cited above, notably at the end of the *Secunda Secundae* where he integrates the consideration of charisms into the wider perspective of the diversity of states of life and *ministries. He thus deals with: 1) charisms (qq. 171-178); 2) forms of life, active or contemplative (qq. 179-182); offices or states (what St *Paul calls ministries; qq. 183-189). In this place Thomas studies only the main charisms attested by the New Testament (prophecy, rapture, tongues, speech, miracles), but for all that the list is not restrictive.

The approach is completed by his treatment of *Christ: His plenitude of grace and His mission imply that He must have been endowed with all the charisms, in particular prophecy and the gift of miracles (III$^{a}$, q. 7, a. 7-8; q. 13, a. 2, ad 3).

J.-V.-M. Pollet, "Charisme", *Cath.* 2, 1949, 956-959. – "Charisma", *TRE*, 7, 1981, 681-698. – J.-P. Torrell, "Les Charismes au service de la révélation", *Thomas d'Aquin, Somme théologique*, 3, Paris, 1985, 961-1012. – *Recherches sur la théorie de la prophétie au Moyen Âge, XII$^{e}$-XIV$^{e}$ siècle, Études et textes*, Fribourg, 1992 ("Dokimion", 13).

Jean-Pierre Torrell

**CHARITY.** The first centuries of the Middle Ages followed the teaching of the *Fathers on charity. The works of St Augustine and St *Gregory, themselves nourished by St John and St Paul, exercised an influence attested by numerous *florilegia, like Defensor of Ligugé's *Liber scintillarum* (second half of 7th c.). *Paschasius Radbertus († 859), in his treatise *On Faith, Hope and Charity*, was the first to present a systematic exposition, using a method that would blossom only in the 12th century. That time saw the appearance of spiritual authors who testified to their own experience, but also a more speculative current that tried to define a problematic of charity. To the first group belongs St *Bernard, whose doctrine on charity is expounded in his *Letter* to *Guigo the Carthusian, his *Treatise on the Love of God* and his *Commentaries on the *Song of Songs*, where we read the formula: "the reason why we must love God, is God; its measure, to love without measure." Bernard describes four degrees leading from natural *love to the almost inaccessible level of the love of *God for himself, passing through the love of God for his benefits, then for his goodness. The new *orders – *Carthusians, Victorines, *Cistercians – expounded the same ideas. *William of Saint-Thierry († 1148) in *The Nature and Dignity of Love*, or *Ælred of Rievaulx († 1167) in *Spiritual Friendship*, insist on the role played by *grace in the love of God and hence on its disinterested character. The theologian Peter of Blois († 1204) affirms, on the contrary, the interested character of charity (*dilectio*), which he sees as a *faculty of desire of the rational *soul and, as such, of natural origin. William of Saint-Thierry identifies it with the *Holy Spirit. This opinion, which recurs in *Peter Lombard, led to an impasse. The author of the **Sentences* would come to define charity as a **habitus*. St Thomas *Aquinas reconciles the natural and supernatural dimensions of this *virtue. It is, between man and God, a *friendship in *Aristotle's sense, *i.e.* a community. Under the circumstances, the object of sharing is none other than *beatitude. St Thomas also takes up the notion of order of charity, which depends on the various objects to which it is applied. *Duns Scotus insists on the disinterested character of the love we must, above all things, feel for God. He clarifies earlier positions by making the necessary distinctions. Natural love applies to what can be known without *faith. Charity applies to what is known only by faith. As much as *knowledge by faith surpasses natural knowledge, so much does charity possess a dignity superior to that of natural love.

Thomas Aquinas, "Charity", *Summa theologiae*, II$^{a}$ II$^{ae}$, 23-46.

P. Rousselot, "Pour l'histoire du problème de l'amour au Moyen Âge", *BGPhMA*, 6, 1908. – M.G. Newman, *The Boundaries of Charity*, Cambridge, 1996.

Michel Lemoine

**CHARIVARI.** A discordant concert given by young people, generally bachelors, the medieval charivari was reserved for *marriages considered irregular, particularly remarriages. One of the earliest references to it is in the revised *Roman de Fauvel* (*c.*1320). This ritual based on inversion developed along with the self-assertion of the village community and the grouping together of young men charged with defending the natural order. It ended with a drinking-bout, paid for by money given by the couple to the participants.

*Le charivari. Actes de la table ronde organisée par l'EHESS et le CNRS, Paris, 1977*, J. Le Goff (dir.), J. C. Schmitt (dir.), Paris-The Hague, 1981. – *Masques et déguisements dans la littérature médiévale*, Montreal-Paris, 1988.

Claude Gauvard

**CHARLEMAGNE (747-814).** Charles was born in 747 into the most powerful family of the *Austrasian aristocracy, which ruled the kingdom of the *Franks from 751. His father *Pippin III, allied by his wife Bertrade to the *Merovingian high aristocracy, took care to have his son consecrated by the *pope in 754 at the same time as himself. On his death in 768, Charles and his brother Carloman each inherited part of the kingdom. Carloman's death made Charles the sole heir in 771.

Charlemagne surrounded by philosophers. 12th-c. tapestry. Halberstadt (Saxe-Anhalt), cathedral treasury.

The king of the Franks then undertook military operations on the marches of the kingdom: a long campaign against the Saxons began in 772. It was interrupted by a war against the *Lombards under *Desiderius, whose ambitions in *Italy threatened Pope *Adrian I. The capture of *Pavia in 774 was the occasion for Charles to proclaim himself king of the Lombards. In 778 he led a raid on the borders of Muslim *Spain, failing before *Saragossa. The resumption of the war in *Saxony occupied him again until 785, then he annexed *Bavaria and reduced the *Avars in 796.

The vast territorial group thus constituted by conquest also underwent an administrative reorganisation. The margins of the kingdom were governed by margraves who concentrated between their hands military commands over territories called "*marches". Francia was subdivided into **pagi* governed by delegates of the king, *counts, overseen by imperial envoys, the **missi dominici*. *Bishops and *abbots, belonging to the high aristocracy, were agents of the monarch. The aristocracy was attached to the *king by a private network of *vassalage and by the granting of *benefices, often fiscal domains, in exchange for its services. In fact, all free men were linked to the authorities by an *oath of loyalty and came under the *justice of the count.

The influence of *romanitas* and of the concept of power coming from Byzantium made itself felt from the end of the 8th c.: the construction of the *palace of *Aachen around 790 and the activity of scholars like *Alcuin or *Paul the Deacon attest this. The weakening of the authority of the Eastern emperor and the appeal of Pope *Leo III, threatened by the Roman aristocracy, raised Charles to supreme arbiter, a position confirmed by his imperial *coronation at *Rome in December 800. Presenting himself as a new Augustus and a new David, at the risk of coming into conflict with Byzantium, he legislated in all his domains, intervening in the definition of dogma, getting the main legal texts of the nations of the *Empire set down in writing. He maintained diplomatic relations with the British Isles, the Asturian princes, the *patriarch of *Constantinople and the *caliph of *Baghdad. On his death in Jan 814, his son *Louis succeeded him. In the Middle Ages, Charlemagne remained the figure of the Christian prince, unifier of *Christendom, alongside *Constantine, and the symbol of the imperial idea, as his *canonization by *Frederick I Barbarossa in 1165 confirmed.

Einhard and Notker the Stammerer, *Two Lives of Charlemagne*, L. Thorpe (tr.), Harmondsworth, 1969. – *Charlemagne: Translated Sources*, P. D. King (ed.), Kendal, 1987.

J. Fleckenstein, *Karl der Grosse*, Göttingen, 1962. – *Karl der Grosse. Lebenswerk und Nachleben*, W. Braunfels (dir.), P. E. Schramm (dir.), Düsseldorf, 1965-1968. – L. Halphen, *Charlemagne and the Carolingian Empire*, Amsterdam, 1977. – W. Ullmann, *The Carolingian Renaissance and the Idea of Kingship*, London, 1969. – R. Folz, *Le Couronnement impérial de Charlemagne*, Paris, 1989 (2nd ed.). – P. Riché, *The Carolingians: a Family who Forged Europe*, Philadelphia, 1993. – S.E. Farrier, *The Medieval Charlemagne Legend: an Annotated Bibliography*, New York, 1993.

Thierry Pécout

**CHARLES IV, EMPEROR (1316-1378).** Wenzel, son of John of Luxemburg, king of *Bohemia, and Elizabeth of Bohemia, was sent in 1323 to the court of King Charles IV of France. The latter imposed his own name on him, had him given an education unusually advanced for a lay prince and married him to Blanche of Valois (1329). In 1331 he became his father's lieutenant in northern *Italy, in 1334 marquis of *Moravia. Wounded at *Crécy where his father was killed, he was elected king of the Romans on 11 July 1346 and crowned at Bonn in 1347, king of Italy in 1355 and emperor soon after, and finally king of *Burgundy in 1365.

Charles set himself to consolidate his family's patrimony, notably in Bohemia and Moravia, which ensured him real power. On the other hand, he widely distributed royal properties to rally supporters to himself; in fact his election had not been easy. His opponent had been the controversial Louis IV of Bavaria. It was thanks to the support of the archbishop of *Trier (his great-uncle), the new archbishop of *Mainz and the *pope that he managed to win; he had himself elected and crowned a second time in 1349. The last great German emperor to have such political standing, in 1356 he published at *Metz the Golden Bull that definitively organised the proceedings of the imperial election. A politician rather than a ruler, he maintained good relations with most of his neighbours, tried to gain *Poland by marriage, watched over the destiny of *Hungary and Austria and had close relations with *France.

Charles IV was a very well educated man, knowing five languages (Czech, German, French, *Italian, *Latin). He had a programme of grandiose achievements that favoured Bohemia: he got the papacy to erect *Prague into an *archbishopric in 1344 and undertook to make that town a great capital by founding a *university (1346) and building the new cathedral of St Vitus (Sankt Veit) where he was buried and a *bridge that bore his name (Karlsbrücke) and linked the town to the "castle"; he favoured the development of the arts (sculpture and painting) and the decoration of *books.

*Kaiser Karl IV, Staatsmann und Mäzen*, F. Seibt (ed.), Munich, 1978.

P. Moraw, "Kaiser Karl IV, 1378-1978", *Politik, Gesellschaft, Geschichtsschreibung, Giessener Festgabe für František Graus*, Cologne, 1982, 224-318. – P. Moraw, "Karl IV", *LdM*, 5, 1991, 971-974.

Michel Parisse

**CHARLES THE BALD (823-877).** King of West Francia (843-877) and emperor (874-877), Charles the Bald was the son of *Louis the Pious and his second wife Judith of Bavaria. By the imperial ordinance of 817, Louis the Pious had established that his eldest son *Lothar would become sole emperor while his other sons, Pippin and Louis, would receive secondary kingdoms. The birth of Charles and his mother's insistence that he be well endowed broke these arrangements. From 829 (diet of *Worms) to the death of Louis the Pious in 840, the brothers' conflicts among themselves and with their father were almost continuous: projects to partition the *Empire followed each other without ever creating unanimity.

After the death of Louis the Pious, Charles the Bald and *Louis the German formed an alliance against their elder brother Lothar, whom they defeated at the battle of Fontenoy-en-Puisaye (841). On 14 Feb 842, they confirmed their alliance by the *oaths of *Strasbourg. Next year, the partition of Verdun divided the Empire into three kingdoms and gave West Francia to Charles the Bald.

The king was then aged 20. He belonged to the generation that had benefited from the first *Carolingian Renaissance and had received a good education. At his court, in particular in his palace at Compiègne, the arts, letters, *dialectic and *theology were cultivated. From 845 to 867 the famous *John Scotus Eriugena, the only original thinker of the Carolingian period, taught there.

Charles the Bald's reign was occupied by many struggles to impose his authority in *Aquitaine, against the Bretons and Northmen, and against the magnates of the kingdom in general who profited from the circumstances to behave like princes.

From 845, he had had to abandon Aquitaine to his nephew Pippin II. But in 848 he had himself crowned king of Aquitaine at *Orléans and resumed control of the region, which he entrusted to his own son in 855. In 846 he had been forced to accept the *de facto* independence of *Brittany under Nominoë, who was succeeded by Erispoë and then by Duke Salomon. The raids of the Northmen on the Seine and the Scheldt becoming ever more intense, Charles was obliged to entrust a great command in *Neustria (region between Seine and Loire) to Robert the Strong, ancestor of the *Capetians.

Meanwhile, the magnates of Neustria and Aquitaine had revolted and appealed to Louis the German, who penetrated Charles's kingdom in 858. But the resistence of Archbishop *Hincmar of Reims and the clergy grouped around him obliged Louis to withdraw. Other revolts broke out, led by Charles's own sons Louis the Stammerer and Charles the Child. Despite this, Charles the Bald bore up and continued to govern in the manner of the first *Carolingians, notably by publishing *cartularies.

On the death of *Lothar II in 869, he took possession of *Lotharingia and had himself crowned king at *Metz by Hincmar. He reached *Aachen but, threatened by Louis the German, had to withdraw to Western Lotharingia. In 875, on the death of the Emperor *Louis II, he received *Provence, and Pope *John VIII crowned him emperor on 25 December. He made himself master of the kingdom of *Italy but, when he wanted to take possession of Eastern Lotharingia on the death of his brother Louis the German, he was defeated at Andernach by his nephew Louis the Younger (876).

Pope John VIII called him to his aid in Italy and, following his duty as emperor despite the opposition of the aristocracy and Hincmar, Charles crossed the Alps. A greatly superior German army obliged him to retreat and he died on the way back at Avrieux, in the Maurienne valley.

*Charles the Bald.* Miniature from the Sankt Emmeran *Codex aureus.* Munich, Bayerische Staatsbibliothek (Ms lat. 14000, fol. 5 v°).

His reign, culturally brilliant, was marked by the wish to maintain the Carolingian structures whatever the cost. But in order to disarm the opposition of the magnates on his departure for Italy in 877, Charles had had to recognise the heredity of *fiefs (capitulary of Quierzy), and to fight against the Bretons and Northmen he had had to create great commands that were destined to become almost autonomous principalities.

*Charles the Bald, Court and Kingdom*, M. T. Gibson (ed.), J. L. Nelson (ed.), Oxford, 1981 (2nd ed. 1990). – P. Riché, *The Carolingians: a Family who Forged Europe*, Philadelphia, 1993. – J. L. Nelson, *Charles the Bald*, London-New York, 1992.

Michel Sot

**CHARLES I OF ANJOU (1227-1285).** Born in 1227, Charles of Anjou was king of *Naples from 1266 to his death in 1285. A younger brother of St *Louis, he was less open and more harsh than his elder brother. Very early he demonstrated the qualities of a head of State: thoughtful, clear-headed, strict, bold and tenacious, beneath a chivalrous exterior praised by the poets of his time, but which concealed a very strong ambition. From his father *Louis VIII he had received in appanage the counties of Maine and *Anjou. From 1246, *Blanche of Castile persuaded her son Louis IX to conclude Charles's marriage with the countess of *Provence, of the royal family of *Aragon. The influence of the French *monarchy thus reached the Mediterranean, which offered itself to Charles of Anjou's political dreams. He peopled Provence with French administrators, trained in the monarchical feudal law that regulated the county of Anjou: a régime hostile to the municipal liberties traditional in Mediterranean lands. Provence could thus serve as a base for St Louis's *crusade in Egypt, in which Charles took part. On his return to France, he was solicited by the French popes *Urban IV and his successor *Clement IV to assume the Crown of *Sicily. The Holy See wanted to take southern *Italy away from the Hohenstaufen, heirs of the great Emperor *Frederick II who had animated the Ghibelline party against Rome.

Charles at first refused, entirely occupied in subjecting Provence and extending his influence over Piedmont. Once he was master of the Alpine passes, he accepted the repeated offers of the two French pontiffs. In 1265, he embarked at *Marseille for Ostia. Well received at *Rome, he was there crowned king of Sicily by five *cardinals in *St Peter's basilica. Joined by a numerous army that crossed northern Italy, he attacked Frederick II's illegitimate son *Manfred, who had been proclaimed king by the barons of the kingdom of Sicily in 1258. Manfred joined battle near *Benevento and met his death there (1266). His partisans regrouped around the young *Conradin, Frederick II's legitimate grandson, who had come from Germany: but he was beaten soon after his entry into the kingdom, near the defile of Tagliacozzo (1268); the defeated prince was captured, judged as a rebel to the Holy See and beheaded at Naples.

Rich in men and money, Charles organised his conquest by establishing a French-style feudal hierarchy there, to the detriment of the towns; he reinforced the sound bureaucracy inherited from the Byzantines, *Normans and Swabians; he developed the fiscal system, whose comfortable returns were ensured by a very strong administration, which controlled a multitude of economic activities directly encouraged by Charles I. He could thus give free rein to his ambitions outside the kingdom. He profited from a twenty-year vacancy in the *Empire – the "great interregnum" (1254-1273) – to extend his influence over central Italy, as head of the *Guelf party enjoying the favour of the *popes and financed by Florentine *bankers. *Florence was traditionally Guelf. Charles likewise used the support of Venetian *merchants to attack the *Byzantine Empire through *Greece. But he had to interrupt this offensive to take part in the crusade of his brother Louis IX against Tunis (1270); when Charles arrived in Tunisia, his brother was already dead of plague. Charles saved the remnants of the Christian army by making an agreement with the *emir of Tunis. Finally, he returned to the Balkans, conquering Albania, of which he was proclaimed king (1272).

He was prevented from pursuing his plans against *Constantinople by Ghibelline intrigues in northern Italy, revived by the election of a new German emperor, *Rudolf of Habsburg (1273). Papal diplomacy prevented a conflict breaking out between Rudolf and Charles: the papacy wished to pacify Europe in order to prepare a new crusade. Charles then decided to buy the title of king of *Jerusalem from the French princess who held it (1277) and recommenced military and naval preparations against Constantinople. But the Ghibellines of Sicily reached an agreement with the king of Aragon, *Peter III, a plot favoured by the hatred of the Sicilians for the rigorous administration of the *Angevin agents; while the Crown of Aragon dreamed of dominating the western Mediterranean. On 30 March 1282, the Angevin agents were massacred all over Sicily (rising called the "*Sicilian Vespers"). Peter of Aragon came to succour the rebels: so Charles wanted to take him in the rear by organising a crusade against him in agreement with his nephew *Philip III, king of France, and the pope. But Peter III defeated the French army and the Angevin fleet: Charles I finally died defeated in 1285.

The loss of rich Sicily was an irremediable handicap for the kingdom of Naples, and led to it falling more and more under the thumb of the great Florentine merchants. Such was the price of the too extensive ambitions of Charles I of Anjou. However, thanks to his good administration, the kingdom still remained sound: monarchical power dominated the towns and the feudalized barons. If expansion in the direction of Africa was now ruled out by the loss of Sicily, Angevin foreign policy kept the paths opened up by Charles I towards the Balkans and *Hungary, for he had married his son Charles to a daughter of the Magyar ruler of the time; by thus aiming at the control of the Adriatic, he wanted to oppose the rivalry of *Venice, at sea and in the Byzantine Empire.

L. Cadier, *Essai sur l'administration du royaume de Sicile sous Charles Ier et Charles II*, Paris, 1891. – G. Yver, *Le Commerce et les Marchands dans l'Italie méridionale aux XIIIe et XIVe siècles*, Paris, 1903. – E. G. Léonard, *Les Angevins de Naples*, Paris, 1954. – J. Huré, *Histoire de la Sicile*, Paris, 1957. – *Gli angioini di Napoli e di Ungheria*, Rome, 1974 ("Problemi di scienza e di cultura", 210).

Georges Peyronnet

**CHARLES II OF ANJOU (1254-1309).** Born in 1254, son and successor of *Charles I, Charles II was king of *Naples from 1285 to his death in 1309. He is the least-known king of the Angevin family, between such marked figures as his father and his son *Robert the Wise. And his reign was marked by no salient event. His *court was less brilliant than that of his father, but his policy was less bellicose and more realistic.

On the death of his father, Charles II was a prisoner of the Sicilians who had put themselves under the rule of the Crown of *Aragon in 1282. The young prince had been captured in a naval battle fought off Naples and lost by him. The *pope, nominal *suzerain of the kingdom of Naples, steadied the interregnum there by reorganising the fiscal system, developed excessively by Charles I. At the same time the Holy See carried on negotiations with the new king of *Sicily and his brother the king of Aragon to get Charles II freed. He was released in return for a heavy *ransom and a promise to abandon Sicily. Returning to Naples in 1289, he prepared peace by abandoning the counties of Maine and *Anjou to Charles de Valois, brother of *Philip the Fair. Pope *Boniface VIII got a treaty concluded putting an end to the conflict between Naples and Aragon (1295), then, halting confused military operations, another treaty between *Frederick (III) of Aragon, second king of independent Sicily, and Charles II (1302): the king of Naples recognised *de facto* this independence of the "kingdom of Trinacria" while himself keeping the title of "King of Sicily".

After this laborious compromise, hardly brilliant but realistic, Charles II directed his diplomacy to other horizons. His father had married him to a daughter of King Béla IV of *Hungary, whose Magyar dynasty came to an end without heirs in 1301. Pope Boniface VIII, suzerain of the Crown of St Stephen, then supported the claims of Charles Robert (Carobert) of Anjou, a descendent of Béla IV in the female line and grandson of Charles II, who supported this candidature among the Hungarian magnates charged with electing the king, while a party of those magnates preferred the son of the king of *Bohemia, who was also descended from Béla IV. This second candidate stood aside, transmitting his rights to the duke of *Bavaria, another descendent of Béla IV; this duke finally renounced the Crown of St Stephen in 1307: Carobert was then proclaimed king (1308) and solemnly crowned in 1310.

In the Balkans, Charles II lost Albania, conquered by the Serbs in 1292. He kept Corfu, plus certain rights of succession in the

Greek principalities. Thus it was that a son of Charles II became prince of Achaia (the North and West of the Peloponnese) in 1294. Charles II also succeeded in getting another of his sons recognised as count of Piedmont by the feudal lords of that province (1304), which from then on was administered regularly on the model of neighbouring *Provence, with which Charles II was occupied in person, in an effective and beneficial way, in 1306 and 1307.

He had discharged the administration of the kingdom onto his younger son Robert, appointed vicar general of the realm after the death of Charles's eldest son in 1296; next year, Robert was designated heir in agreement with the pope and the principal communities of the kingdom. Charles II let him occupy himself with home affairs and Angevin policy in central *Italy, where *Florence appointed Robert captain general of the Guelf League of Tuscany in 1305. Charles II cared from now on only to administer Provence. Returning to the kingdom when he felt his end near, he died in his palace near Naples in 1309, but was buried, according to his wishes, in a convent at Aix-en-Provence. Thus passed away modestly, standing aside for his son Robert, this pious and unostentatious king, who was able to compensate for the loss of Sicily and Albania by the installation of an *Angevin dynasty in Hungary and another in *Greece, while consolidating the influence of the *Angevins of Naples in northern and central Italy and making the administration of the kingdom and Provence more just and more respected.

L. Cadier, *Essai sur l'administration du royaume de Sicile sous Charles Ier et Charles II*, Paris, 1891. – G. M. Monti, *La Dominazione angioina in Piemonte*, Turin, 1930. – G. M. Monti, *Da Carlo I a Roberto d'Angiò*, Trani, 1936. – B. Hóman, *Gli Angioini di Napoli in Ungheria (1290-1403)*, Rome, 1938. – E. G. Léonard, *Les Angevins de Naples*, Paris, 1954. – *Gli angioini di Napoli e di Ungheria*, Rome, 1974 ("Problemi di scienza e di cultura", 210).

Georges Peyronnet

**CHARLES V OF FRANCE (1338-1380).** Born at Vincennes, 21 Jan 1338, son of King John II the Good and Bonne of Luxemburg, daughter of King John of Bohemia, he was the first dauphin of the house of *France (1349). Duke of *Normandy in December 1355, he was at the battle of *Poitiers (19 Sept 1356) when the royal army was beaten and King John taken prisoner by the English. As the king's lieutenant, he faced the opposition of the estates general, the agitation led by the king of *Navarre and the Parisian *revolt of Étienne Marcel († 31 July 1358). The treaty concluded at Brétigny and sworn at Calais in October 1360 gave *Edward III, king of *England, Guyenne enlarged by the neighbouring provinces: Poitou, Saintonge, Agenais, Limousin, Périgord, Quercy, Bigorre, Angoumois, as well as Ponthieu, Calais and the county of Guines. The king's *ransom was fixed at 3 million gold écus. Becoming king on his father's death (8 April 1364), Charles V inherited a realm amputated of a third of its territory and ravaged by the "companies" of unemployed mercenaries. The first objective of his reign was to rid the kingdom of the *Companies and reconquer the lost provinces. A small army of professionals, under the leadership of the Constable Bertrand du Guesclin, carried out the reconquest while avoiding fixed battles. The negotiations of Bruges (1374) led only to truces. By the time of the king's death, the English held only Calais, Guyenne and certain places in *Brittany, but peace was not concluded. New difficulties appeared in 1378: conflict with Brittany, the *Great Schism. Charles V had close relations with his maternal uncle, the Emperor *Charles IV of Luxemburg, king of *Bohemia, who visited him at Paris in 1378.

*Charles V*, 14th c. Paris, Louvre.

Charles V's government was dominated by the requirements of the war: organisation of the *army (ordinances of 1374-1375), ship-building in the arsenal of Clos de Galées at *Rouen. He marked a decisive step in the growth of the *State: *taxation, direct (hearth tax) and indirect (custom dues, *salt tax), set up to pay King John's ransom, was accepted as a means of defending the country against the companies and obtaining peace, but led to revolts at the end of the reign. Charles V and his counsellors wished to strengthen the basis of the State by *ordinances specifying the functioning of the various institutions. Adopting election for the choice of *chancellor and president of the *Parlement, they contributed to the formation of the circle of royal officials and of the Parlement, first great body of State. The system of appanages to establish a certain decentralization and the holding of great assemblies to promote communication complete this picture of a thoughtful policy. Charles V was the king of the intellectuals. Those of his entourage represented the two tendencies of political thought of the time, the jurists and the philosophers (Nicole *Oresme, Raoul de Presle, *Philippe de Mézières). He founded the royal *library of the Louvre, ordered translations of *Aristotle (*Politics*, *Ethics*, *Economics*) and St Augustine (*The City of God*) and had a political *encyclopedia compiled (*Le *Songe du vergier*) demonstrating the superiority of royal power. He was behind numerous constructions at Paris and thereabouts (Louvre, Bastille, hôtel Saint-Pol, *Sainte-Chapelle de Vincennes) and commissioned many works of art to the glory of royalty (*Grandes chroniques de France* and their illustration). He died aged 42 on 16 Sept 1380. On his deathbed, he abolished the hearth tax that was beginning to cause the revolt of the Midi. Married to Jeanne de Bourbon, he had eight children of whom only *Charles VI and his brother Louis, duke of Orléans, survived. Charles V left in the national consciousness the memory of a wise king and a restorative reign.

R. Cazelles, *Société politique, noblesse et couronne sous les règnes de Jean le Bon et Charles V*, Geneva, 1982. – F. Autrand, *Charles V le Sage*, Paris, 1994.

Françoise Autrand

**CHARLES VI OF FRANCE (1362-1422).** Born at Paris 3 Dec 1368, son of *Charles V and his queen Jeanne de Bourbon, he became king of *France in 1380. Despite the *ordinance of 1374 fixing the majority of *kings at 14 years, he was consecrated on 4 Nov 1380. For eight years, power belonged to his uncles the dukes of *Anjou, Berry and *Burgundy. In 1381-1383 they faced *revolts all over the kingdom: *Languedoc, *Flanders, urban revolts (Maillotins at Paris, Harelle at *Rouen). The victory of Roosebeke over the Flemish (1382) restored royal authority. To preserve the German alliance and consolidate the influence in the *Netherlands of the duke of Burgundy, heir to the county of Flanders, the dukes negotiated the king's marriage with Isabeau of Bavaria (1385). In November 1388 Charles took power. He governed with the team of "marmousets" who adapted and continued the policies of Charles V. They perfected the State service and laid the basis of a statute of public office. Anxious to gain the hearts of his subjects, they organised great *fêtes* in 1389, a *fête* of *chivalry in May, a Parisian *fête* for the solemn entry of Queen Isabeau. A journey by the king to Languedoc (1389-1390) brought the king's grace, but also his *justice, to the Midi. After the attempt on the life of the Constable de Clisson, Charles and his council decided to make war on the duke of *Brittany.

While crossing the forest of Le Mans with his army, Charles, after an encounter with a strange person, had an attack of madness in which he tried to kill his brother (1392). His illness lasted 30 years, with alternating manic and depressive fits separated by intervals of lucidity. As he aged, his attacks grew ever longer and depression overcame him with ideas of death, loss of identity and refusal to eat or care for his body. At each remission, Charles went back to work. After Agincourt (1415), his reason gave way permanently.

Favoured by the king's "absences", the princes wrangled for power. Their interests were divergent. Duke *John of Berry and especially the king's brother Louis, duke of Orléans, pushed without circumspection for the development of the State, the duke of Burgundy championed reforms, and all quarrelled over the product of an increased fiscal burden. In 1407, the duke of Burgundy had Louis of Orléans assassinated. The crisis grew worse: civil war between Armagnacs and Burgundians, Parisian revolt of the Cabochiens (1413), resumption of the English war, defeat of Agincourt (1415). In 1418 the Burgundians took *Paris. The dauphin *Charles, aged 15, led astray by the Armagnacs, organised a dissident government in his appanage of Berry and Poitou. The assassination of John the Fearless, duke of Burgundy, on the bridge of Montereau by the dauphin's supporters (1419) cut France in two. By the treaty of Troyes, the king and queen disinherited their rebellious son in favour of *Henry V, king of *England, who married their daughter Catherine. Charles VI died after Henry V, on 21 Oct 1422. At his *funeral, for the first time, the coffin was surmounted by an effigy representing the king, with the insignia of royalty, and over his tomb was pronounced the formula: "The king is dead, long live the king!" Charles VI had twelve children by Queen Isabeau, of whom six survived. By Odette de Champdivers he had a daughter, Marguerite de Valois. The reign of Charles VI passed for disastrous, yet it was an important time in the development of national feeling. Identifying their own sufferings and those of their king with Christ's *Passion, the French of the 15th c. called him Charles *le Bien-Aimé*.

F. Autrand, *Charles VI. La Folie du roi*, Paris, 1986. – R.C. Famiglietti, *Royal Intrigue*, New York, 1986.

Françoise Autrand

**CHARLES VII OF FRANCE (1403-1461).** Born on 22 Feb 1403, fifth son of *Charles VI of France and Isabeau of Bavaria, betrothed in 1413 to Marie of Anjou, daughter of Duke Louis II and Yolande of Aragon, he was raised at the court of *Anjou and became dauphin after the death of his brothers. On the entry of the Burgundians into *Paris, the Armagnacs took him away to his appanage of Berry-Poitou where he organised a government. The assassination of the duke of Burgundy, John the Fearless, at Montereau (10 Sept 1419) long weighed on his conscience. The treaty of Troyes (21 May 1420) between the duke of Burgundy and the king of *England, accepted by the demented king and the powerless queen, recognised *Henry V as heir to the *Crown of *France: he married Catherine, daughter of the king and queen. Charles was disinherited and banished on account of the murder at Montereau. The dauphin's pretended bastardy was just a later argument of Anglo-Burgundian propaganda. From 1420, the treaty was attacked on grounds of law: the king could not dispose of the Crown.

On the death of Charles VI (1422), Charles took the title of king. The years 1422-1429 were marked by struggles for influence between Armagnacs, Angevins and "Richemonts" (Arthur of Brittany, earl of Richmond, Constable of France in 1425). Charles VII's army, defeated at Verneuil in 1424, could hardly defend the approaches to the Loire. *Joan of Arc, after delivering *Orléans from the besieging English, took Charles to *Reims where he was consecrated on 17 July 1429. The French were now sure that the "true king of France" was Charles VII and not *Henry VI, whom the English consecrated at Paris in 1431 after the execution of Joan of Arc. Clan struggles around the king and poor military results did not prevent Charles VII from negotiating his reconciliation with the duke of Burgundy (treaty of Arras, 1435), followed by the recapture of Paris (1436). Paris was once more the capital of the kingdom, but Charles VII, after making a solemn entry (1437), did not reside there. For more than a century, Paris would be a capital without a king. After eight years of fighting in the Île-de-France, Guyenne and especially *Normandy, Anglo-French negotiations ended in the truce of Tours (1444). After the resumption of combat, the battles of Formigny (1450) and Castillon (1453) ensured the reconquest of Normandy and Guyenne. The reform of the *army in 1445 was primarily a remedy for the scourge of the *Écorcheurs* (mercenary companies). 15 regularly paid military companies were created. The Scots company who formed the king's guard, the artillery organised by the Bureau brothers and the *franc-archers* (reserved infantry) completed this system which was the origin of the permanent army. The military effort required an enormous fiscal effort, for which the consent of his subjects, at first requested from the provincial Estates, was later the object of bargaining between towns and royal officials. Only *Languedoc kept its Estates, whose function became administrative. The restoration of royal authority after the years 1440-1445 was spectacular. Supported by the mass of war-harassed French, especially *nobles and towns, and by the institutional framework of royalty inherited from previous reigns, Charles VII triumphed over princely revolts: Praguerie (1440), plots around the count of Armagnac or the duke of Alençon, who was judged at a *lit de justice* at Vendôme in 1458 (see *Fouquet's miniature). These rebellions were supported by the dukes of *Brittany and *Burgundy, whose principalities were heading towards independence, supported by the dauphin Louis, who was hostile to the Angevin party and to Agnès Sorel, the mistress flaunted by the king.

Charles VII, called *le Victorieux* but also *le Bien Servi*, governed with devoted counsellors and officials. The statute of Montils-lès-Tours (1454) re-established the constitutional State and restored its institutions. It prescribed the writing down of different customs. The creation of provincial *parlements* (*Toulouse, 1443; Bordeaux, 1451; Grenoble, 1457) established a decentralization that put royal *justice within reach of subjects. The *Pragmatic Sanction of Bourges (1438) organised the autonomy of the *Gallican Church. Economic reconstruction after thirty years of wars, disorder and depopulation (the population of the kingdom is reckoned as ten million, half what it had been in 1328) was only just beginning. The towns were the first to recover their prosperity. The renewal of large-scale international *commerce began from the lands of the Loire with the activity of Jacques Coeur, the king's treasurer. The last years of the reign were darkened by the disaffection of the dauphin and by fear of conspiracies. Of Charles's children by Queen Marie of Anjou, *Louis XI and Charles (1446-1472) survived, as did three daughters, married to the duke of Bourbon, the duke of *Savoy and Gaston de Foix.

G. de Fresne de Beaucourt, *Histoire du règne de Charles VII*, Paris, 1881-1891. – M. Vale, *Charles VII*, Oxford, 1974.

Françoise Autrand

**CHARLES VIII OF FRANCE (1470-1498).** Son of *Louis XI and Charlotte of Savoy, Charles VIII was born at Amboise, 30 June 1470. Sickly and very small, he passed his childhood in the castle of Amboise where his father kept him under heavy guard, fearing the poisoning, abduction or illness of his only son. Before dying, Louis XI solemnly gave him instructions, made him swear to continue his policy and keep his counsellors, and designated

*Portrait of Charles VII* by Jean Fouquet, 1420-1470. Paris, Louvre.

his daughter Anne of France and his son-in-law Peter of Bourbon, lord of Beaujeu, to govern. After the king's death (30 Aug 1483), the Beaujeu faced the revolt of the princes (Bourbon, Albret, Dunois and especially Louis, duke of Orléans, heir to the infant king). They convoked the estates general at *Tours in 1484. For the first time the deputies of the three estates came together, elected throughout the realm by assemblies of **bailliages* and **sénéchaussées*. Condemned by public opinion, the *Guerre folle* of the princes was ended by the battle of Saint-Aubin-du-Cormier where Orléans was taken prisoner (1488). Renouncing the king's planned marriage to Marguerite of Burgundy, the Beaujeu forced on *Brittany the union of its duchess Anne with the king. The treaty of Rennes (15 Nov 1491) put an end to Breton independence.

Emerging from tutelage, Charles VIII undertook the conquest of the kingdom of *Naples, which was part of the *Angevin succession. He obtained peace with his neighbours by the treaties of Étaples with *England (1492), Barcelona (restitution of Roussillon and the Cerdagne to *Aragon) and Senlis (restitution of Artois and the county of *Burgundy to the *Habsburgs) in 1493. Crossing *Italy without hindrance, the French army entered Naples where Charles was crowned (May 1495). Against the invasion, the Italians formed the League of Venice. At the battle of Fournoue, the *furia francese* cleared a way back for the French army. Charles VIII died at Amboise, 8 April 1498, after having hit his temple on a door-lintel. His policy reflects the atmosphere of the time: attachment to rights acquired by succession, myths and dreams expressed by legends, *romances and prophecies (*crusade, conquest of *Constantinople, restoration of the Eastern Empire), but also the ideal of moral, political and religious reform that inspired the king, converted after the death of his two sons.

Y. Lalande-Mailfert, *Charles VIII*, Paris, 1986.

Françoise Autrand

*Charles the Bold, duke of Burgundy.* Miniature from the manuscript of the *Statutes of the Golden Fleece*, 15th c. Madrid, Instituto de Valencia de Don Juan.

**CHARLES MARTEL (684-741).** The Mayor of the Palace Charles Martel is known mainly for his victory over the Arabs at Poitiers and his secularizations of Church property. He deserves better than that.

He was the son of Pippin II, called Pippin of Herstal, and a concubine named Alpaïde. On his father's death in 714, he managed to gain possession of the Mayorship of the Palace of *Austrasia, then three years later that of *Neustria, but he had to struggle against Duke Eudes of Aquitaine who had formed a sort of principality, against the bishops of *Lyon, *Orléans and *Auxerre who had made themselves independent, and against the Bavarians, *Alamanni and Frisians who threatened the frontiers. To consolidate his rule in Neustria, Charles installed his friends and relations wherever he could. He used in his own favour the advantages of *vassalage which, since the 7th c., had been one of the foundations of Western society. He gave his vassals, on a tenure of **precaria*, lands that belonged to the Church. Charles was then able to regain a footing in the peripheral principalities thanks to his warriors and the missionaries. He supported the efforts of the Anglo-Saxons *Willibrord in *Frisia and *Boniface in *Thuringia and *Bavaria. South of the Loire, *Aquitaine was outside his authority. Charles profited from the Muslim invasion in this region to intervene. Indeed Duke Eudes appealed for his help. Charles managed to defeat an Arab-Berber army on 25 Oct 732 between *Poitiers and *Tours at Moussais. This victory was of great importance for the destiny of Charles and the Carolingian family. Profiting from his victory and the death of Duke Eudes in 735, Charles Martel descended as far as the Garonne, took the town of Bordeaux and obliged the new duke to promise fidelity to him. He also intervened in the Rhone valley and in *Provence not just to beat the Arabs, but also to subject the aristocrats who were independent. But he was unable to take *Narbonne. In *Burgundy, he installed his sons and distributed estates and *abbeys to Bavarian aristocrats who put down roots.

The mayor of the palace felt strong enough not to have a king elected as successor to the Merovingian Theoderic IV who died in 737. But he did not take the title of *king himself. In 739 Pope Gregory III, threatened by the *Lombards who wanted to take *Rome and unite *Italy, appealed to the man whom he appointed "vice-king". But Charles needed the Lombards for his struggle against the Arabs and did not intervene in Italy.

So Charles Martel governed the Frankish kingdom. Unlike his father, he usually resided in Neustria. He was surrounded by the *clerics of his "*chapel" which preserved a piece of St *Martin's cape. He was a friend of the monks of *Saint-Denis to whom he entrusted the education of his son *Pippin. In his lifetime, he allotted Austrasia, Alamannia and Thuringia to his eldest son Carloman, and Burgundy, Neustria and Provence to Pippin. He died on 22 Oct 741 at the palace of Quierzy and was buried at Saint-Denis among the *Merovingian kings. By his warlike virtues and political skill, Charles put an end to a period of uncertainty and prepared the success of the family that received his name: the *Carolingians.

P. Riché, *The Carolingians: a Family who Forged Europe*, Philadelphia, 1993. – K. F. Werner, *Les Origines*, Paris, 1984, 342 f. – *Karl Martell in seiner Zeit*, J. Jarnut (ed.), U. Nonn (ed.), M. Richter (ed.), Sigmaringen, 1994.

Pierre Riché

**CHARLES THE BOLD (1433-1477).** Eldest son of Philip the Good and Isabella of Portugal, born at *Dijon on 11 Nov 1433, Charles called "the Bold" (*le Téméraire*) was duke of *Burgundy from 1467 to 1477. Though count of Charolais, he rarely lived in his Burgundian dominions. His "fiery" temperament, allegedly much influenced by his mother, led him to engage in the War of the Public Good against King *Louis XI of France. After the indecisive battle of Montlhéry, which threatened *Paris, he obtained the restoration of the Somme towns (1465).

Heir to an amalgam of principalities, his policy aimed at unifying his States with the help of a strong administrative structure and trying to link up the two parts of the Burgundian State, *Flanders and Burgundy. He aroused many fears among his neighbours, in the kingdom of *France as well as in *Lorraine and *Switzerland. To provide himself with the means for such a policy, between 1471 and 1473 he organised a modern *army, partly permanent, consisting in particular of regular companies provided with a strong artillery, which burdened the finances of his States.

Very soon he clashed with *Ghent and especially with *Liège, which was supported by *Louis XI; but Charles obliged the king to help him in the repression and to sign the treaty of Péronne in 1468. Subsequently invading *Picardy, he failed before *Beauvais whose defence was organised by Jeanne Hachette, then before *Rouen, in 1472. From 1469, the duke laid hands on the margravate of *Alsace. In 1473 he aimed at Lorraine, obliging Duke René II to sign the treaty of Nancy, which opened its gates to him, but he increased fears at Bern, Basel and *Strasbourg: these towns feared the creation of a new *Lotharingia, all the more when in January 1474, at Dijon, the duke revealed his ambition of restoring the kingdom of Burgundy. So Sigismund, the Swiss and the towns of

Alsace joined together against him; and in May the Burgundians had to leave Alsace. Soon, Louis XI formed an alliance against him with the Swiss, René II and the Emperor *Frederick III. Despite the reconquest of Lorraine in 1475, the year 1476 was fatal to him: he was beaten by the Swiss at Grandson (2 March) and Morat (22 June). In October 1476 he left Franche-Comté for Lorraine and laid siege to Nancy, a siege during which he died, 5 Jan 1477. His ashes were transferred to *Bruges in 1550.

If Werner Paravicini saw Charles's thirst for glory as the cause of his failure, still we must not forget the military reasons for it – a heterogeneous army as well as a lack of resources to pay enough mercenaries – and still more, the lack of cohesion among the peoples and territories constituting this "middle State" of which he dreamed. Moreover, the discrepancy between Charles's military means and his ambitions is evident. On his death, the last great Western duke left an heiress, Mary of Burgundy, who married Maximilian of *Habsburg in August 1477: the destiny of Western Europe would be profoundly modified by this marriage.

R. Vaughan, *Charles the Bold*, London, 1973. – W. Paravicini, *Karl der Kühne: Das Ende des Hauses Burgund*, Göttingen, 1976. – K. Schelle, *Charles le Téméraire*, Paris, 1979. – P. Contamine, "Charles le Téméraire, fossoyeur et/ou fondateur de l'État bourguignon", *Des pouvoirs en France (1300-1500)*, Paris, 1992, 87-98. – P. Gresser, *Le Crépuscule du Moyen Âge en Franche-Comté*, Besançon, 1992.

Jacky Theurot

**CHARTER, CHARTER-ROOM.** The term "charter", in its meaning of a written document constituting a title, is derived from the Greek word *kartè* (*papyrus leaf). It has been in current use since *Merovingian times, when it designated the private document as opposed to the sovereign's document (*carta pagensis / preceptio regalis*). It gained a more general meaning in the central centuries of the Middle Ages, in rivalry and sometimes in opposition to "privileges" and "letters" (at the French royal *chancery, the charter maintained itself, in solemnity, between these two extremes). The term was restored to honour by the scholarship of the *Ancien Régime* and still more by romantic historiography, which made the charter one of the great categories of sources of medieval history. Drawn up in a proper form to confer validity and authenticity on it, the charter is thus defined in our eyes, not without anachronism, by a dual contrast with *letters in the modern sense and with other archival documents, drawn up for internal use (accounts, inventories, documents of estate management, etc.). From the Middle Ages, it engendered the word *cartarium* ("charter-room"), a depositary and collection of the titles of a proprietor, lay or ecclesiastical.

The preservation, almost exclusive up to the 12th c., of ecclesiastical *cartaria*, favoured by the place of writing in the clerical world but also by the greater stability of the *patrimony of religious establishments, favours the historian at the same time as it unbalances his gaze. Indissolubly linked to temporal possessions, and hence to the cares of the world, charters attracted all the attention of ecclesiastical proprietors anxious not to let slip the rights of their establishment; belonging to the sphere of Martha, they were symbolically rejected only in extreme cases, like the *eremitism of *Grandmont. Crystallizing information about *property and transactions of land or movable goods, drawn up in a local context, charters indirectly give a mass of information about the surrounding society. This set of facts is indissolubly linked to the form and formalities implemented at the time of its redaction: forming a screen, they also constitute in themselves a complex of information about medieval societies and cultures, which the science of diplomatics has hardly begun to decipher.

Too much linked to the central centuries of the Middle Ages, a time when the use of writing was sufficiently developed for numerous transactions to be entrusted to it and sufficiently rare for a strong charge of symbolism, and hence power, to be attached to its production and preservation, the charter subsequently declined: though the rules of study and criticism defined for its study retain their validity, the written titles of the late Middle Ages and the modern period go under another terminology and through other channels of production, in which the *notariate, producer of public instruments, and its northern substitutes (acts of gracious jurisdiction) occupy centre-stage.

O. Guyotjeannin, J. Pycke, B.-M. Tock, *Diplomatique médiévale*, Turnhout, 1993 (2nd ed., 1995; L'Atelier du Médiéviste", 2). – *Graphische Symbole in mittelalterlichen Urkunden*, P. Rück (ed.), Sigmaringen, 1996.

Olivier Guyotjeannin

**CHARTRES.** It was doubtless to *Charles the Bald's gift of the *relic of the Virgin's veil in 876 that Chartres owed its glory after the *Viking invasions of 858 had destroyed the essentials of the first cathedral. Among other dates that mark its history, one may single out 1007 when *Fulbert acceded to the episcopate, stimulating a very innovative architecture, of which the *crypt remains, and inaugurating a brilliant intellectual tradition, which continued all through the 12th c. with the great thinkers *Ivo, *Bernard and Thierry of Chartres, *Gilbert of Poitiers, *William of Conches and finally *John of Salisbury. This century was prosperous, as witness the construction of new ramparts in 1181, under Bishop *Peter of Celle.

In 1134 the fire that destroyed part of the town served as a pretext for restoring Fulbert's cathedral, which was given a new façade. The grave deterioration suffered by the façade of the abbey church of *Saint-Denis gives this Royal portal an exceptional interest for the history of art. Still *Romanesque in the mystical rigidity of its forms, it inaugurates the *Gothic in the breadth of its programme: processions of kings and Old Testament *prophets form the columns that support, on the tympana, the triple mystery of the Incarnation, *Last Judgment and *Apocalypse.

A new fire in 1194 occasioned a reconstruction that brought Gothic techniques to their apogee. Of unusual width, the cathedral nevertheless carries its vaults to a height of 37 metres. The revolutionary use of flying buttresses authorizes the suppression of the tribunes, a cause of gloom, and the piercing on the upper storey of double bays surmounted by a rose. These innovations permit the blossoming of the *stained glass windows, whose essentials have survived intact: three *rose windows dedicated to the Last Judgment, the Apocalypse and the Genealogy of Christ, lower windows enumerating biblical or hagiographical stories, higher windows exalting the great figures of sanctity. Though painting on *glass is dominant at Chartres, it does not eclipse sculpture, which displays on the north and south portals a new humanism, by which the project of the *Redemption is expressed, in an range of motifs never yet attained.

Chartres in the Middle Ages also included, within the ramparts, the six parish churches surrounding the cathedral, outside them the abbeys of Saint-Jean-en-Vallée and Saint-Martin-au-Val, and finally Saint-Père, which preserves one of the largest collections of 14th-c. stained glass.

The *Châsse* of St Maurice, 9th-11th c. Saint-Maurice, abbey treasury.

A. Katzenellenbogen, *The Sculptural Programs of Chartres Cathedral, Christ, Mary, Ecclesia*, Baltimore (MD), 1959. – *The Contractors of Chartres*, 2 vols., London, 1979-1981 (2nd ed.). – *Histoire de Chartres et du pays chartrain*, A. Chédeville (ed.), Toulouse, 1983. – C. Manhes-Deremble, *Les Vitraux narratifs de la cathédrale de Chartres*, Paris, 1993.

Colette Deremble

**CHARTRES, SCHOOL OF.** Since the pioneering studies of R. L. Poole and A. Clerval in the late 19th c., the expression "school of Chartres" has been used ambiguously to refer both to the cathedral *school at *Chartres and to a group of 12th-c. thinkers associated with Chartres who share common humanist and, in particular, Platonizing intellectual preoccupations. In studies published in 1970 and 1981, R. W. Southern has argued that the reputation of the school of Chartres has been exaggerated over the last hundred years, that after the death of Bernard of Chartres in *c.*1126 there is no evidence for a particularly distinctive intellectual tradition at Chartres, that it is illusory to speak of Chartrian *Platonism, and that *Paris had outstripped Chartres as an educational centre from the early 12th century. Southern's arguments have been valuable for encouraging renewed critical attention on its historical and intellectual importance.

The reputation of the school of Chartres rests on the fame of three *chancellors of the cathedral who were themselves celebrated as teachers: Bernard of Chartres (active there as *magister* from 1112 to his death in *c.*1126), his pupil *Gilbert of Poitiers (chancellor 1126-*c.*1137/1142), and Thierry of Chartres (archdeacon of Dreux in the 1130s, chancellor from 1142 and still alive in 1149). Southern's argument that even in the early 12th c. Paris was much more dominant than Chartres as an educational centre has not been seriously challenged. Everard of Ypres reports that he had heard Gilbert lecture in Chartres to a class of four, in Paris to one of nearly 300. Häring's detailed study of teachers at Chartres has not been able to refute Southern's observation that, while Thierry definitely taught in Paris in the late 1130s, his signature is not found on any Chartres cathedral *charters prior to becoming its chancellor. Whether Thierry was a brother of Bernard of Chartres is uncertain, though not impossible. While there is equally no firm evidence that *William of Conches taught at Chartres, allusions to the town in his commentary on Priscian suggest it likely that he taught there at least early in his career. *John of Salisbury does not make it clear in the *Metalogicon* where William was teaching when he studied under him in the early 1140s.

While Southern is right to emphasize the greater size of Parisian schools in the 12th c., his comments about the lack of a distinctive intellectual tradition at Chartres need to be revised in the light of recent research. Its *library was exceptionally rich in the 12th century. The recent discovery of Bernard's commentary on Plato's *Timaeus* confirms what John of Salisbury says about his Platonic interests. William of Conches, certainly his pupil, is interested not just in Platonic tradition, but in elaborating a scientific vision of *language and the physical world of undoubted originality. Gilbert's reputation rests on the speculative subtlety of his commentaries on *Boethius's *Opuscula sacra*, while Thierry became famous as a learned expositor both of Boethius and of all the *liberal arts. An *epitaph praises Thierry as a successor to *Aristotle, the first to study the *Analytics* and *Sophistici Elenchi*, texts which he incorporated into his *Heptateuchon*. The school of Chartres in the first half of the 12th c. became home to a vision of Christian humanism based on all the liberal arts, which would be overtaken by an increasingly exclusive interest in *logic and *theology in the schools of Paris.

A. Clerval, *Les Écoles de Chartres au Moyen Âge*, Paris, 1895. – P. Dronke, "New Approaches to the School of Chartres", *AEM*, 6, 1969, 117-140 (published in 1971). – É. Jeauneau, "Lectio philosophorum", *Recherches sur l'école de Chartres*, Amsterdam, 1973. – R. Giacone, "Masters, Books and Library at Chartres according to the Cartularies of Notre-Dame and Saint-Père", *Vivarium*, 12, Leiden, 1974, 30-51. – N. Häring, "Chartres and Paris Revisited", *Essays in Honour of Anton Charles Pegis*, Toronto, 1974, 268-329. – R. W. Southern, "The Schools of Paris and the School of Chartres", *Renaissance and Renewal in the Twelfth Century*, R. L. Benson (ed.), G. Constable (ed.), Cambridge (MA), 1982, 113-137.

Constant Mews

***CHÂSSE.*** The French word *châsse*, from *capsa*, "box" (*capsa, urna, casse fierte*), means a casket enclosing *relics, whose use probably derives from the ancient funerary urn. In the Middle Ages, this casket usually took a form resembling a church or a small monument. Frequently of *goldsmiths' work, these *châsses* could also be made of other precious materials or of painted wood.

A group of early medieval *châsses*, made between the 6th and 10th cc., designated by the expression "purse reliquary", is distinguished by a very simple form – parallelepipedal box surmounted by a double-sloping roof – small size, height greater than the width, and execution in precious materials – *gold or silver, sometimes ornamented with cloisonné *enamel (Mortain *châsse*, Altheus *châsse* from the Sion treasury, *châsse* of Pippin from the *Conques treasury).

From the 11th and 12th cc., the most common type of medieval *châsse* was diffused, characterised by the longitudinal development of the rectangular casket, surmounted by a simple double-sloping roof that could also evoke a sarcophagus (silver *châsse* of San Isidoro at *León, 11th c., numerous great Rheno-*Mosan *châsses* of the late 12th and early 13th cc., like those of St Maurinus and St Albert at the church of St Pantaleon, *Cologne) or sometimes a more developed roof, trapezoidal in section (Ambazac *châsse*, from the *Grandmont treasury, *c.*1189, *châsse* of the Three Kings in Cologne cathedral, *c.*1180-1230), of very large dimensions.

In the *Gothic period, these forms were perpetuated – the parallelepiped surmounted by a double-sloping roof was the type of most 13th-c. Limousin *châsses* – but tending to more compact proportions and greater height, thus more closely resembling architecture. *Châsses* were also frequently enriched with the decorative vocabulary of contemporary architecture: gables, pinnacles, trilobate arcades, crocketed ridge, etc. Though none of the great 13th-c. Parisian *châsses*, known from documents, has survived, some provincial examples such as the *châsses* of St Taurinus of Évreux (*Évreux, Saint-Taurin, between 1240 and 1255) and St Romanus of Rouen (*Rouen cathedral, *c.*1260-1280) demonstrate this evolution. In the 14th and 15th cc., the forms and decoration of *châsses* evolve with those of architecture, but the taste for this type of *reliquary seems to fade away, in favour of a great variety of other forms.

J. Braun, *Die Reliquiäre des christlichen Kultes und ihre Entwicklung*, Freiburg-im-Breisgau, 1940. – M.-M. Gauthier, *Émaux du Moyen Âge occidental*, Fribourg, 1972. – J. M. Fritz, *Goldschmiedekunst der Gotik im Mitteleuropa*, Munich, 1982.

Élisabeth Taburet-Delahaye

**CHASTITY.** Chastity is a *virtue that makes one capable of subjecting the movements of *concupiscence to the authority of *reason. Chastity, which far surpasses *continence, is also an evangelical counsel. According to St *Thomas Aquinas, it is one of the counsels that Christ gives as a friend, a means he suggests to bring the mark of *salvation to human relationships. Though some Christians make profession of chastity in religious *vows, all are called to understand this counsel and put it into practice in their way of life.

Thomas Aquinas, *Summa Theologiae*, Iª IIªᵉ, q. 108, a. 4; IIª IIªᵉ, q. 151.

R. Plus, A. Rayez, "Chasteté", *DSp*, 2, 1, 1953, 777-797.

Jean-Marie Gueullette

**CHAUCER, GEOFFREY (1343?-1400).** The founder of modern English poetry, Chaucer is also an example of the rise of the middle class and a critical witness of his times. He led a very active professional life among princes and kings: financial controller, charged with missions abroad, member of *Parliament, responsible for royal estates.

His true vocation, however, was poetry. His grandfather and father had imported *wines from the continent; he himself adapted into English the themes, procedures and vocabulary of the French and Italian poets. His *Book of the Duchess* comments on the death of Blanche of Lancaster, *The House of Fame* deals lightly with the mystery of literary creation, *The Parliament of Fowls* unites praise of *love with social satire. *Troilus and Criseyde* is a magnificent hymn to love, despite the sorrows of Troilus. To atone for having portrayed Criseyde's disloyalty, Chaucer wrote the *Legend of Good Women*. Death prevented the completion of the *Canterbury Tales*, his masterpiece. The pilgrimage to *Canterbury blends selfish ambitions – pursuit of marriage, power, money – with the journey to the heavenly *Jerusalem. Chaucer mixes up literary genres (chivalric *romance, Saints' Lives, animal *fable, etc.), portraits of upwardly-mobile bourgeois and debates on current topics (role of *women, power of *money, religious hypocrisy). His characters, whether *pilgrims or protagonists of the tales, are steeped in vices and qualities – in short, humanity. Chaucer narrates their adventures with humour and charity.

Chaucer avoids all extremism. He carefully avoids following *Wycliffe in his opposition to Church institutions and dogmas. And yet, with Wycliffe's "*Lollard" disciples he denounces those who "parasitize" the truth of the Gospel and forget or, worse, exploit God for selfish ends. The saintly characters of the *Tales* are the humble and pacific: patient spouses, martyred little boy, country priest and his peasant brother. These characters, it is true, do not stand out as much as their less virtuous companions: the hunting Monk, the smirking *Prior, the truculent Wife of Bath, the insinuating Friar, the rich *Doctor, the Pardoner, etc. Chaucer, who exalts simplicity, practises an oblique art. He adopts several points of view, uses several spokesmen. He offers the reader an open-minded work, with pluralistic and often contradictory readings.

Interested in the rigour of the *sciences as well as in literary sophistications, Chaucer wrote a *Treatise on the *Astrolabe* and an *Equatorie of the Planetis*. He was inspired by *Boethius and meditated on his *Consolation*, which he translated and which pervades his *Troilus*, many of his *Tales* and his *Ballade of Good Counsel*: "Lift your eyes to your heavenly homeland, go, pilgrim. He who is the Truth will give you freedom".

*The Riverside Chaucer*, L. D. Benson (ed.), Boston (MA), 1987 (Oxford, 1988).

C. Muscatine, *Chaucer and the French Tradition*, Berkeley (CA), 1957. – J. Mann, *Chaucer and Medieval Estates Satire*, Cambridge, 1973. – H. Cooper, *The Structure of the Canterbury Tales*, London, 1983. – P. Strohm, *Social Chaucer*, Cambridge (MA), 1989. – H. Cooper, *Oxford Guides to Chaucer: The Canterbury Tales*, Oxford, 1989. – J. Mann, *Geoffrey Chaucer*, Hemel Hempstead, 1991. – B. Windeatt, *Oxford Guides to Chaucer: Troilus and Criseyde*, Oxford, 1992. – D. Pearsall, *The Life of Geoffrey Chaucer: a Critical Biography*, Oxford, 1992. – D. Wallace, *Chaucerian Polity*, Stanford, 1997.

André Crépin

**CHELLES.** A royal *abbey situated in the Marne valley. In *c.*511, *Clovis I's wife Clotild founded a church dedicated to St George in this royal **villa*. Clovis II's wife Balthild founded a women's monastery there in 658/9, at first under the Columbanian *Rule, then the *Benedictine; she retired there in 664/5 and died there *c.*680; she was canonized by Pope *Nicholas II. A 7th-c. chasuble attributed to her is preserved in the museum. Under the abbacy of *Charlemagne's sister Gisela, the monastery enjoyed a new expansion; some 20 manuscripts survive from its **scriptorium*. King Robert II presided in his palace of Chelles over the *synod of 994 and the *council of 1008. A *charter of 1128 accorded communal franchises to the town, but the seignorial rights of the *abbess were reaffirmed in 1320. The abbey was dissolved in 1792.

C. Torchet, *Histoire de l'Abbaye Royale de Notre-Dame de Chelles*, Paris, 1889.

David Coxall

**CHERNIHIV.** Chernihiv (Chernigov), a historic town in *Ukraine, is situated on the right bank of the Desna. In the 9th c., it was the political centre of the tribal union of the Severiani. From the 9th c., it was put under the authority of the princes of *Kiev. In 1024, under Prince Mstislav Vladimirovich, son of *Vladimir Sviatoslavich (the Great), it became the capital of a separate principality. After Mstislav's death in 1036, the territory of Chernihiv was reintegrated in the State of Kiev. From 1054, the principality of Chernihiv became an autonomous region of Kievan *Rus'. Its most important rulers were Princes Sviatoslav Iaroslavich (1054-1073), Vsevolod II Olgovich (1127-1139) and Michael Vsevolodovich (murdered by the Tatars in 1246). Chernihiv's local dynasty, the Olgovich, contested with other branches of the *Rurikid dynasty, in particular that of the Monomakhovich, the right of supremacy over Kiev. In 1239, Chernihiv was taken and devastated by the *Mongols. From the second half of the 14th c., it was attached to the grand duchy of *Lithuania, and from 1503 to 1618 to Russia.

Chernihiv's most important monuments of medieval architecture are the cathedrals of the Saviour (*c.*1036), Sts Boris and Gleb (*c.*1123), the Annunciation (*c.*1186), the Dormition at the monastery of Ielets (mid 12th c.), and the Good Friday Church (12th-13th c.).

Iaroslav Isaievych

**CHICHELE, HENRY (1362-1443).** Born to a middle-class London family – his brother Robert was sheriff and mayor of *London – Henry Chichele studied at *Winchester, then at New College, *Oxford. Doctor in civil law (1396), he was an *advocate at the *Court of Arches, sent to the Roman *Curia (1404-1408), then delegated to the council of *Pisa in 1409. Bishop of St David's in 1407, he became archbishop of *Canterbury in 1414. Close to *Henry V, whom he accompanied to France (1419, 1420), he was an experienced diplomat. Continually a member of the Council during the minority of *Henry VI, he generally opposed Cardinal Beaufort, but was mainly concerned with preserving the independence of the English Church against a papacy in full revival.

*DNB*, 1885-1900. – E. F. Jacob, *The Register of Henry Chichele, 1414-1443*, Oxford, 1937-1947 (4 vol.). – E. F. Jacob, *Henry Chichele and the Ecclesiastical Policy of his Age*, London, 1951. – *BRUO*, 1, 1957, 411-413.

Jean-Philippe Genet

**CHILD, CHILDREN.** Contrary to what certain historians have claimed, the Middle Ages were interested in children and did not consider them small adults: this is attested both by texts and by images depicting the child, alone or in the *family (pedagogical treatises, numerous illustrations especially from the 12th c., excavated objects that belonged to children).

Childhood was divided into three periods. From birth to the age of two, *infantia* was the time when the child did not speak. From two to seven years, the child learned to speak and walk, but was still incapable of reflective acts. The third part of childhood, *pueritia*, was from seven to twelve years. This was the age of *reason. Boys were distinguished from girls and learned their letters. Around twelve, they became pubescent and reached "legitimate age": for *canon law, girls could marry at twelve and boys at fourteen.

The idea of the child held by medieval man differed according to times and temperaments. For some, following St Augustine, the child was sinful from conception, since marked by original sin; so he had to be baptized from birth. Besides, the child was an infirm being, comparable to the madman deprived of reason; he unsettled adults and prevented parents from being generous to the poor since he monopolized all their resources. For others – the majority – at a very young age the child had exceptional qualities, above all innocence, so much that for them the word *puer* should be connected with "purity". This theme marked monastic literature: thus St *Benedict, writing his Rule in the 6th c., gave an important place to the child, who had a "voice in the *chapter" of the monks (ch. III) "since from childhood Samuel and Daniel judged the elders" and "not without reason did Christ draw the children to himself" (ch. LXIII). The pure innocent child was like an intermediary between God and man. From his mouth "issued truth". One child denounced a criminal, another gave advice on the *election of a bishop.

Being innocent, the child was gratified by heavenly *visions, like the little Benedict, Benezet, to whom during an eclipse of the sun God gave orders to build the *bridge of *Avignon. Children could step in where adults had failed. Thus, in the early 13th c., "children's crusades" were organised to deliver the *Holy Land: Stephen of Vendôme, a shepherd boy to whom Christ had appeared, or the German Nicholas led towards the Mediterranean bands of children and adolescents, who were captured and sold as slaves (see *Popular Crusades).

The model of the child was the Child Jesus, whose cult spread in the 12th c., especially in *Cistercian circles. *Ælred of Rievaulx, in his *De Jesu puero*, evokes the first years of Christ's life, giving each one a symbolic significance. Thus took shape the concept of "spirit of childhood" dear to many mystics, from St *Bernard to St Thérèse of Lisieux.

However, optimism diminished towards children who reached the age of puberty: "Childhood is succeeded by adolescence, a sensual and undisciplined age, which believes that *virtue is painful and difficult and which is set on pleasure", wrote Julian of Vézelay in the 12th century.

S. Shahar, *Childhood in the Middle Ages*, London, 1990. – P. Riché, D. Alexandre Bidon, *L'Enfance au Moyen Âge*, Paris, 1994. – B. A. Hanawalt, *Growing Up in Medieval London*, Oxford, 1995. – J. A. Schultz, *The Knowledge of Childhood in the German Middle Ages, 1100-1350*, Philadelphia, 1995. – D. Lett, *L'enfant des miracles. Enfance et société au Moyen Âge (XII^e-XIII^e siècle)*, Paris, 1997. – D. Alexandre-Bidon, D. Lett, *Les Enfants au Moyen Âge, V^e-XV^e siècles*, Paris, 1997 ("La vie quotidienne").

Pierre Riché

**CHINA, CHRISTIANITY IN.** The circumstances of the appearance of Christianity in China are related in the inscription in Syriac and Chinese characters engraved at Si-ngan-fu (Sian) by the **chorepiscopus* Adam in 781 and rediscovered in 1625. In 635, a religious from Persia, A-lo-pen, presented a request to the Emperor T'ai-tsung of the T'ang dynasty, who had the Scriptures translated and authorized the propagation of the "radiant religion"; A-lo-pen built a monastery. Other edicts followed; the Christians had to suffer vexations from the Buddhists and Confucians; their church was even confiscated. In 724, they obtained the designation of an official protector; the *catholicos* of *Baghdad erected their church into a metropolis. Yet in 781 Bishop John bore only the title of "bishop of the two capitals" (Si-ngan and Lo-yang); he came from outside, but the two *archdeacons and the four *chorepiscopi* were Chinese; Syriac was the liturgical language, but Christian texts in Chinese have been found at Tuen-huang, notably a hymn to the Trinity. But in 845 Christianity was caught up in the proscription of foreign cults, which aimed primarily at the Manichaeans.

Christianity reappeared in Northern China with the Turko-Mongol dynasties (Liao and Kin) from the 11th century; but it developed mainly under the *Mongol dynasty; the metropolis was then fixed at Khanbaliq and *bishoprics are met with in other towns. At the same time, merchants were frequenting the ports of Southern China: Canton (where they were massacred in 878) and especially Zaytūn (Ch'üan-chou): in the late 13th c. we find a bishop there as administrator of the Manichaeans and Christians. It has been admitted without proof that these had made no recruits among the Chinese; the use of Chinese characters in funerary inscriptions permits us to doubt this.

Latin missionaries appeared in 1293 with *John of Montecorvino who founded convents at Khanbaliq (Beijing), Zaytūn and Lin-tsin and, becoming *archbishop in 1306, created a *suffragan bishopric of Khanbaliq at Zaytūn; Armenians, Alans, Turkish and no doubt Chinese converts appear with Italian merchants among its flock. Tombstones with Latin inscriptions have been found at Zaytūn.

It is not certain whether Christianity was proscribed once more under the Ming; a text of 1400 still speaks of the Christians of Cathay who were asking for the arrival of a new archbishop. But the Christians of Turko-Mongol origin, the Alans and other elements brought by the Mongols had been pushed back onto the steppe and contacts with the West had become impossible. Chinese Christianity must have died out in the first decades of the 15th century.

*The Mission to Asia*, C. Dawson (ed.), London, 1955. – K. Enoki, "The Nestorian Christianism in China in Mediaeval Time", *L'Oriente cristiano nella storia della civiltà*, Rome, 1964, 45-82. – J. Richard, *La Papauté et les Missions d'Orient au Moyen Âge*, Rome, 1977. – P. Pelliot, J. Dauvillier, *Recherches sur les chrétiens d'Asie centrale et d'Extrême-Orient, II, 1. La Stèle de Si-ngan-fou*, Paris, 1984. – S. N. C. Lieu, *Manichaeism in the Later Roman Empire and Medieval China*, Manchester, 1985.

Jean Richard

**CHIVALRY.** The concept of chivalry covers two realities, one socioprofessional, the other cultural. These realities themselves evolved between the 11th and the 15th century.

**The 11th century: birth of chivalry.** The *seigneurie* was the most characteristic trait of the society that was established shortly before the year 1000 in the western part of the dislocated former Carolingian Empire. At that time the power of the castellans increased to the detriment of the more or less extinct central authority. It rested on two main complementary elements: the *castle, symbol of the former public power in process of privatization; and the *milites*, armed vassals or servants of the lords, who exercised the power of coercion, enforced order (or disorder) and were free from the seignorial exactions that they imposed by force on the *peasants. The majority of these warriors were descended from the free men of the Carolingian period, but not all were. In the German Empire in particular, we find numerous serf-knights (**ministeriales*), whom the emperors used in their service to counter the power of the great *nobles. They came to form a sort of nobility whose function was linked to their status (*Ritterstand*). The western regions were little acquainted with this situation, but there we find numerous *milites* originating in the upper levels of the free peasantry, while others were armed servants of lords or princes, living in their house, *mesnie* or *familia* and constituting their guard. A single word unites them: they formed the *militia*, an ambivalent term inheriting the nuances both of public service and of armed force. All the *milites* (sing. *miles*) were indeed warriors, but up to the mid 11th c. this word could still include those who fought on foot, *pedites*, or on horse, *equites*. Increasingly however, the *milites* were the *cavalry, elite warriors *par excellence*.

Their equipment, condition *sine qua non* of their status, distinguished them: one or more horses trained for combat; offensive arms: broad-bladed sword, lance-javelin or pike; the bow was left to the foot-soldiers. Their defensive arms consisted of a metal helmet soon provided with a nasal, the helm, and an interlaced coat of mail, the hauberk, relatively supple and light (12-13 kg.). A shield or buckler completed the equipment that was handed over to the new knight at a ceremony of which we still know little, *dubbing. A technical innovation appeared towards the middle of the 11th c. and was widespread in France before 1100: the long lance, held under the arm in fixed horizontal position, gradually replaced the javelin and pike for the elite

*Battle between knights and enemies.* Miniature from the *Life and miracles of St Edmund, king and martyr, c.*1130. New York, The Pierpont Morgan Library (Ms 736, fol. 7 v°).

warriors. This new method of fighting bound the lance solidly to the knight, made fast to his horse thanks to the deep saddle and stirrups widespread by the 9th century. It transformed equestrian combat into a frontal onslaught whose aim was to unsaddle the knight, now better protected by his defensive arms from sword or javelin blows, but more vulnerable to the powerful impact of the frontal onslaught generated by the speed and mass of the projectile (lance plus knight plus horse).

Chivalry properly so-called may have arisen out of this new method which, from now on, spread and prevailed. From the mass of ordinary warriors, it isolated the elite of knights who practised it: the *milites* and their teachers who became their companions in arms in combat but also in the training exercises, quintains, jousts and *tournaments that appeared in the same period. From now on the *milites* were professional equestrian fighters and the professional contrast between *milites* and *inermes* (the unarmed) tended to be transformed into a social gulf separating the knights from the subordinate mass. This gap was only in its preliminary stages in the 11th c., at a time when the trifunctional arrangement of society, preached by bishops like *Adalbero of Laon or Gerard of Cambrai, distinguished three orders in the ideal society: those who prayed, those who worked with their hands, and those who fought. This last order, designated by the term *bellatores*, included the knights, but did not yet designate them; their rank was still too subaltern. Chivalry was not yet an *ordo*.

The Church, however, took note of the invasive presence of the knights. All over France, the distant power of the *king declined and that of the princes, closer to home, was sometimes disparaged by castellans and even by knights who confronted each other in private wars and transformed themselves into pillagers to the detriment especially of ecclesiastical establishments. The bishops of *Aquitaine, supported by the local aristocracy, attempted there, from the end of the 10th c., to extract from the *milites* solemn *oaths pronounced in public assemblies on the *relics of saints who, at that time, enjoyed great popular fervour. The movement of the *Peace of God, launched at Charroux (989), was spread by many other *councils in France in the 11th century. The knights who took the oath (not all did so!) engaged themselves essentially to direct their *violence only against other warriors and not against *inermes*, particularly the Church, its personnel, its servants and its property. At the start of the 11th c., the Truce of God tried to impose an *ascesis on warriors: to abstain from their sport – war – on holy days commemorating Christ's *Passion and *Resurrection: Friday, Saturday and *Sunday.

These purely negative limitations were not yet an ethic; they rather defined taboos, restrictive prohibitions. Private war between Christians was not even forbidden: it was merely regulated, circumscribed. But in 1054 the council of Narbonne clearly declared that "he who kills a Christian undoubtedly sheds the blood of Christ". This would tend to the canalization of the warlike forces of *Christendom against the infidels outside it. The idea of war took root, leading to the *Reconquest in *Spain and the *crusade preached by *Urban II in 1095 at *Clermont, during a peace council. So the crusade was a continuation of the Peace of God movement and joined the *pilgrimage, whose privileges it shared. By it, hardened pillagers were invited to repent and gain their *salvation by becoming soldiers of Christ: *milites Christi*.

Holy war thus sanctified the crusaders, but not knighthood as such, which, on the contrary, was likened, in a play on words, to malignity: *militia - malitia*. But it placed before the eyes of the knights a moral *duty proper to them, an ideal of Christian chivalry that would persist all through the Middle Ages, and whose emblematic hero could be the Roland of the **chanson de geste*.

**The 12th century: rise of chivalry.** Several elements came to modify the status of knights in the 12th century. They tended to favour the progressive fusion of the knights with the nobility, which took shape at the end of the 12th century.

– A political factor: the recovery of royal power in France. The castellans bore the costs of this, but not the knights, who sometimes managed in turn to take the title of *sire* without actually possessing any *castellany. They dominated the villagers from their strongholds.

– A demographic factor: to limit the breaking up of estates by inheritance, the aristocracy, imitated by the knights, tended to restrict *marriage to one of their sons and then established primogeniture. Noble younger sons thus joined the majority of knights' sons as *errants*. Together they formed the category of "bachelors", *juvenes*, unmarried and ill-provided with lands, in contrast to the *seigneurs* (*seniores*) who were married and held lands.

– A social factor: the rise of the middle class who, in the second half of the century, became influential at *court, threatened to rival the nobility and created among it a feeling of fear that exacerbated the assertion of its privileges.

– A psychological factor: the companionship of warriors, forged on battlefields and still more at court and in tournaments, created a "class" solidarity that brought knights and nobles together.

– A legal factor: the growing cost of the knightly equipment and pace of life and of the sumptuous festivities that marked entry into knighthood (dubbing) led the aristocracy to filter this entry more narrowly and reserve it for its own sons. Thus, the knights tended to form a caste.

– The military function of the cavalry was not yet attenuated. It remained, with little technical evolution, the "queen of battles". But the word "cavalry" or "chivalry" was coloured by increasingly clearcut supplementary nuances, social, honorific and ideological.

The ideology of chivalry, indeed, was enriched. We can perceive it better thanks to the abundance of sources, by now no longer just monastic or even ecclesiastical.

In the domain of the *langue d'*oc*, the poetry of the *troubadours (themselves sometimes knights) exalted *fin' amors*, usually adulterous *love, through the carnal veneration that the knights of the court bore for the Lady, the wife of the *seigneur*. Interpretation of this is difficult and controversial, and its realism is disputable. We can at least say that *courtly love, spread in the second half of the century in northern France by the **trouvères* and in Germany by the **Minnesänger*, originally expressed the sexual frustration of poor knights, *juvenes* and bachelors, without wife or lands, reduced to looking for adventure, as well as the growing importance of *women in society and in mental attitudes.

Following the poet Jehan *Bodel (late 12th c.), we generally distinguish three "matters" of *romances: 1) the *matière de France* which included and prolonged the epics, still sang of purely warlike chivalry and the joy of exchanging blows, exalted the sense of lineage and *honour and the duty of a vassal. 2) The *matière antique* expressed the growing taste for the East and introduced new themes like the shimmering of colours, the taste for luxury and ostentation manifested at feasts, tournaments and dubbings. 3) The *matière de Bretagne*, even more popular, flourished in the second half of the 12th c. in the Arthurian romances: Love and Adventure developed their interlaced motifs to infinity and were set up as the proper knightly values. The romances also preached other values like *largesse*, the taste for giving gifts and ostentatious spending, virtues by which the knights who benefited from them lived, witness to a new *rapprochement* between knighthood and nobility. Here the defence of the weak takes on a form more courtly than religious: women, "damsels in distress" (without protection), attract the attention of the knight errant much more than do the poor, the orphan or the churchman, and the aim of the knight's intervention is mainly to prove his valour to himself and his peers at court, and to increase his "price" in the eyes of his Lady.

The irruption of these secular values into works of chivalry led the Church to react. It did so by infusing its ideology into the ceremonies of dubbing and by Christianizing literary works in its turn, as witness the evolution of the theme of the *Grail and the transition from the courtly hero (Yvain or *Lancelot) to the mystical hero (*Perceval and Galahad in France, Parzival or Lohengrin in Germany) at the turn of the century. In the 13th century, the knighthood reached its apogee; its military function was maintained (feudal *host), its fusion with the nobility accelerated and its ideology triumphed. At the start of the century, the *Prose Lancelot* projected the image of a knighthood instituted by God since the rupture of the equality of the original times; at that time, knights were divinely invested with the mission to govern the people whom they ruled by right, and to protect Holy Church, *widows and orphans. An allegorizing tendency then developed which attributed to each piece of knightly equipment a particular mission or a necessary *virtue. There was a veritable mystique of chivalry tending to diffuse the idea of a "chivalry by divine right". *Treatises on chivalry amplified and popularized these elements (*Ordene de chevalerie*, Raymond *Lull), visually affirmed by the liturgical rites of dubbing which became ever later and rarer in the course of the century. Many sons of nobles were no longer "armed knights", and remained pages or squires all their lives. Knighthood tended to become a supplementary decoration to which nobles had a right by birth, but which not all could attain.

**The 14th-15th centuries: decline and mythologization of chivalry.** The 14th century accentuated the decline of the knighthood but exalted its ideology. The evolution of armies in the course of the *Hundred Years' War led to the weakening of its function, despite its attempts at adaptation: the buckler was pared down and would disappear; the helm was closed and provided with a visor; the rigid articulated armour was strengthened and completed by greaves and gauntlets; the very horse was protected, and the knight thus became a sort of heavy ironclad, invulnerable (but slow) when on horseback, but easy prey when on the ground. The battles of *Crécy (1346) and Agincourt (1415) betrayed the ill-adaptation of the French knighthood to new forms of war and revealed the growing superiority of infantry, archery and soon artillery; at the same time there was an aceleration in the evolution that led from the old feudal host to the paid *army of professionals of all arms recruited by contract, then to permanent national armies (*Charles V). National feeling developed, weakening at the same time the values, at once universal and individual, of chivalry.

Chivalry, however, did not die, but changed more and more into ideology. It was expressed in the crusading idea that occupied all minds in the 14th and 15th cc., but which never came to anything concrete; in single combats regularly offered, but generally declined; in the mad temerity of chivalrous heroes, often in vain; in tournaments whose popularity grew ceaselessly, but which became more and more of a spectacle, a ritualized confrontation of two knights in armour, recognisable only by their armorial bearings. The idealization of chivalry is tinged with nostalgia in *Froissart or Malory, at the moment when, in reality, its effectiveness was decreasing, when armies numbered fewer and fewer knights and were even led by squires (Du Guesclin). It continued with the creation of lay orders of chivalry (1348: Order of the *Garter) which multiplied in the 15th c. and attested both the prestige of chivalry as an ideal and its decline as an institution.

At the end of the Middle Ages, there existed a set of virtues, a code of honour, an aristocratic behaviour made up of generosity and haughtiness, ostentation and good manners, gloryseeking and respect for the weak. A code that inspired the "laws of war" and moulded mental attitudes through the idea that "*noblesse oblige*".

E. Köhler, *L'Aventure chevaleresque*, Paris, 1974. – M.H. Keen, "Chivalrous Culture in Fourteenth-Century England", *Historical Studies*, 10, 1976, 1-24. – G. Duby, *The Three Orders: Feudal Society Imagined*, Chicago, 1980. – *Knighthood in Medieval Literature*, W. H. Jackson (ed.), Woodbridge, 1981. – F. Cardini, *Alle radici della cavalleria medievale*, Florence, 1982. – J. Flori, *L'Idéologie du glaive, préhistoire de la chevalerie*, Geneva, 1983. – P. Contamine, *War in the Middle Ages*, Oxford, 1984. – M. Keen, *Chivalry*, London, 1984. – C. Harper-Bill, R. Harvey, *The Ideal and Practice of Medieval Knighthood*, Woodbridge, 1984; *ibid.*, 2, 1986; *ibid.*, 3, 1988. – G. Duby, *William Marshal*, London, 1986. – J. Flori, *L'Essor de la chevalerie, XIe-XIIe siècles*, Geneva, 1986. – A. Barbero, *L'Aristocrazia nella società francese del medioevo*, Bologna, 1987. – A. Scaglione, *Knights at Court*, Berkeley (CA), 1991. – J. Flori, *La Chevalerie en France au Moyen Âge*, Paris, 1995. – M. Keen, *Nobles, Knights and Men-at-Arms in the Middle Ages*, London, 1996.

Jean Flori

Nave and choir of the church of Santa Sabina at Rome, 5th c. (restored in 1919).

**CHOIR ENCLOSURE.** Limit of the space reserved for the clergy and the main celebrations, the choir enclosure was materialized to begin with by low barriers, often perforated, of wood, metal, marble or stone. In the course of the Middle Ages, these enclosures took on more monumental forms in some cases.

The designation of these barriers by the name of *cancelli* (hence "chancel") repeats the ancient word and usage that can already be found in pagan monuments when it was desirable to limit access to the public. Rediscovered often in fragmentary form in the early Christian sites of Italy (Rome, San Lorenzo), these barriers can be more easily reconstructed for the churches of Greece, Syria or Africa, for the 5th-6th centuries. In these cases the choir enclosure, the trace of whose posts and the slabs fixed in them can be found in the soil, marks out precise areas of celebration occupying from one to three bays with the *synthronos*, the episcopal **cathedra*, the *altar and the link with the *ambo. In other cases, as in Africa, there was no ambo.

With the conciliar decisions and *capitularies of the Carolingian reforms, the boundaries between congregation and clergy were reasserted. We find proof of this in the new architecture of *abbey churches or *cathedrals altered after the councils of Aachen (816-817). Lapidary proofs are numerous from the late 8th c. (*Metz), in particular in south-eastern France, northern Italy (Aquileia) and at Rome (Santa Sabina, 824-827).

When important architectural modifications appeared, such as the lengthening of choirs, the appearance of ambulatories in the 11th c. or the monumental assertion of the sanctuary on a podium very often surmounting the *crypt, the enclosure lost its meaning or was modified. In some cases the success of the formula with ambulatory favoured the redeployment of decorated choir enclosures in the *Gothic period; these, combining with the old ambo, gave rise to monumental groups like the *rood screen (Notre-Dame at Paris, *Bourges – reduced or mutilated – *Albi, Auch, *Toledo). In these cases, the canons' *stalls and the high altar were concealed in order to create a privileged space for the prayer of the community. Constructions of this type that escaped the destruction of the Wars of Religion often disappeared in the 17th and 18th centuries.

"Cancel", *DACL*, 2, 2, 1910; "Iconoclaste", *ibid.*, 7, 1, 1926; "Jubé", *ibid.*, 7, 2, 1927. – J. Hubert, "La vie commune des clercs et l'archéologie", "La place faite aux laïcs dans les églises monastiques et dans les cathédrales aux XI^e^-XII^e^ siècles", *Arts et vie sociale de la fin du monde antique au Moyen Âge*, Geneva, 1977, 125-192. – "Chorschranken", *LdM*, 2, 1983.

Christian Sapin

**CHOIR SCHOOL.** Choir schools arose out of the *scholae lectorum* that, from the late Empire, employed very young children for the readings and for singing the *psalms. In the 4th c., the churches of Rome and Milan were surrounded by these young children, chosen sometimes from the age of three. Their participation in the liturgical chant is well attested in the 6th c. in the Churches of East and West where these little *clerics performed the functions of *reader and *acolyte. In the 7th c., the **schola cantorum*, whose creation John the Deacon attributes to *Gregory the Great, replaced the *schola lectorum*. After a decline, at the end of the 7th c., the *scholae cantorum* of the Empire were restored by *Pippin and then *Charlemagne on the Roman model; they brought masters from Rome who could teach the chant that was the product of Gregory's reform. *Schools, dependent on the *cathedrals, were created at *Sankt Gallen, *Metz, *Rouen, *Soissons. For them were selected, for their pure voices, very young children who, until their voice broke, were maintained there and received a literary and musical education. Their number generally varied from four to twelve, according to times, revenues of *chapters and importance given to worship. In *Spain, they were called *seises* because there were originally six of them, as there would remain at *Toledo throughout the 16th century. These *pueri cantores*, still called *clerici* or *clericuli* – "little clerics" – were obliged to take part in the canonical *hours, the psalmody and the responsorial chant, but it is probable that, very early on, they could be entrusted with the upper voice of the descant and of the later forms of *polyphony.

The organisation of the choir schools varied little throughout the medieval West. Reponsibility for them was incumbent on the *cantor, the second dignitary, but it was the whole chapter who governed the choir school, financed it with the revenues of the **fabrica* and the refectory, chose the masters, supervised the teaching and took disciplinary measures. It designated *canons – the commissioners – to oversee the education and daily upkeep of the children, denounce any abuses and seek out gifted children, when they were lacking. Originally, there was only one master who taught both *Latin, from *liturgical books and patristic texts, and liturgical chant. Later, two masters, that of *grammar and that of *music, would share these functions. At the end of the Middle Ages, because of the enlargement of the polyphonic repertoire, the place of the music master was preponderant; he became the chapel-master. He lived with the children of the choir school in a house allotted by the chapter, saw to their upkeep and provided their musical education and their singing training.

Choir schools were seedbeds of musicians; many composers of the late Middle Ages began their musical career in the shadow of a cathedral as *pueri cantori*.

A. Collette, *Histoire de la maîtrise de Rouen, depuis les origines jusqu'à la Révolution*, Paris, 1892. – J.-A. Clerval, *L'ancienne maîtrise de Notre-Dame de Chartres, du V^e^ siècle à la révolution*, Paris, 1889. – C. Wright, *Music and Ceremony at Notre-Dame of Paris, 500-1550*, Cambridge, 1989.

François Reynaud

***CHOREPISCOPUS.*** The word *chorepiscopus* is Greek and means "rural bishop". These bishops existed in the East from the 3rd or even the 2nd century. The 4th-c. Eastern *councils mention them usually to limit their competence. They acknowledged a certain jurisdiction for them, but under the authority of the bishop of the town. In the West, the first mentions of *chorepiscopi* date from the 5th-6th cc., and they disappeared in the 11th-12th cc. Rare in England, unknown in Italy, they were found mainly in Germany (especially Bavaria) and the Frankish countries.

The *chorepiscopus* held his mission from the *bishop. He taught, oversaw the clergy and had a certain coercive power. He could ordain *clerics, confer major *orders, give *confirmation, reconcile *penitents and consecrate churches. But his authority and the exact extent of his powers are contested. The false Isidorians, very severe towards them, contributed to the disappearance of a hierarchy that counted for little in the history of the Western clergy.

J. Leclercq, "Chorévêque", *DDC*, 4, 1942, 686-690.

Jean Gaudemet

**CHRÉTIEN DE TROYES (*c.*1135-*c.*1183).** Active in the last 30 years of the 12th c., the writer Chrétien de Troyes, whose name, place of origin and patrons – Marie de Champagne and Philippe d'Alsace, count of *Flanders – are known, was the true founder of the medieval *Arthurian romance. With five *romances that can certainly be attributed to him, he confirmed the "matter of Britain" as the domain *par excellence* of narrative fiction, associating in a unique way the knightly search for glory in combat, the other-worldly adventure, and *love. The transition from earlier romantic tradition, using sources derived from antiquity, to the Arthurian domain did not occur all at once: Chrétien's second work, *Cligès*, still reminds us of the romance of Antiquity. However, from the start, essential conquests were made. Firstly in the domain of prosody and the use of poetic rhetoric: Chrétien uses the octosyllable of his predecessors with flexibility and makes use of all the figures of *rhetoric; he intervenes at his own will in the narration, questioning his reader about problems of *casuistry, which he debates with finesse. Above all, he gives the structure of the tale an essential role in the production of its meaning: this "conjointure", this subtle architecture of the romance, builds the meaning of the text in the relationship of each episode to all the others. Finally, using a variety of sources, tales handed down orally or already written down, Chrétien sets before his hero a complex itinerary in which outer adventure and inner adventure are indissociable. Such is already *Érec et Énide*, an adventure of a love won by knightly prowess, but which exclusive desire risks destroying. *Le Chevalier de la Charrete* is the triumphant association between amorous adventure – *Lancelot's passion for Queen Guinevere – and "marvellous" adventure: through his quest, the hero delivers the queen and frees the prisoners of Gorre, a realm conceived in the image of the other world. *Le Chevalier au Lion* is a narrative meditation around the motif of the *fairy at the fountain: this *allegory of amorous bliss, which can also cause loss of identity – Yvain, repudiated by Laudine, goes mad –, engenders the theme of the double: it is thanks to the lion that the hero, becoming the "Knight of the Lion", gives himself the chance to receive the pardon of his *amie*. But the masterpiece, creator of an endlessly fertile myth, is the *Conte du Graal*. Image of life and the times, where the hero's questions, if he dared ask them, could halt the procession that passes before his eyes, the *Conte* turns an other-worldly adventure intended to restore a sterile king to power and fertility into a personal adventure offered to every reader: through testing, the hero discovers his identity, linked to awareness of transgression, renews his links with a family he was unaware of and encounters the need for *conversion; he then enters into communion with the *Grail king and can succeed him.

Chrétien de Troyes, *Arthurian Romances*, W. W. Comfort (tr.), London, New York, 1914 (repr. 1967). – Chrétien de Troyes, *Perceval. The Story of the Grail*, N. Bryant (tr.), Cambridge, 1982.

J. Frappier, *Chrétien de Troyes*, Paris, 1957 (re-ed. 1968). – *The Legacy of Chrétien de Troyes*, N. J. Lacy (ed.), D. Kelly (ed.), K. Busby (ed.), Amsterdam, 1987-1988 (2 vol.).

François Suard

## CHRIST

**Spirituality.** We must ask whether the figure of Christ in the Middle Ages was different from that forged at the the beginning, in Christian Antiquity, and then in the modern and contemporary period. The reply is positive: the figure of Christ fashioned by culture has a history and, like all history, it has known both continuity and innovation.

In the Byzantine Middle Ages, the continuity of the Christ-figure formulated by Cyril of Alexandria (370-444) and confirmed at the council of Ephesus (431) prevailed. Predominant in this figure was the Logos, *Word of the Father, in the fullness of his divinity: the humanity was, as it were, absorbed into the Logos; the sole subject was the Word, and his humanity, the humanity of Jesus, was left in shadow. Christ, then, was the revelation of the Father. Man was enlightened by him and could enter this light if he entrusted himself to the Spirit of God: the revelation of *God by Christ provoked in man a *deificatio*, an entry into the Father. Byzantine christology was a theological reflection within the trinitarian *mystery, but a reflection in which Christ, whose humanity played only a minor role, assumed a glorious and regal aspect, like that of the Father.

The Latin West referred not to Cyril but to Leo the Great and the council of Chalcedon (451), where the christological formula of a single divine *person in two distinct *natures, divine and human, was fixed. The limitation of Chalcedon lay in the fact that the human nature was in some way separate from the divinity, while its strength came from the fact that Christ's humanity necessarily had to be assumed, given the fact that it was neither engaged nor quasi-incorporated in the divinity, which was what resulted from Cyril's formulae. In the East, forms of theopaschism were possible: the *Deus patiens* meant that not just humanity but suffering and death were attributed to the divinity; and could lead to a form of docetism, *i.e.* the denial of Christ's bodily substance. In the West, the theopaschite formula could not be used, because only Christ's human nature suffered and died, not the Word. This conception was combined with Augustine's conception of original sin, which considered man to be deeply soiled by *sin, calling for a *salvation that he could not give to himself. Christ was not, as in the East, the light of the Father that enlightened man and led him to union with his God; Christ was rather the Word that assumed the sinner's humanity and saved him by his divine being. The problem was not so much man's divinization (*deificatio*) as his liberation from sin, his *redemption (*redemptio*). Christology in the West thus involved a very obvious soteriological component. This aspect favoured (and the model was again Augustine, the Augustine of the *Confessions*) a personal relationship between the sinner and Christ, an intimate dialogue, a call for help by one who, in abjection, discovered his own *soul and offered it to Christ. Behind the dominant Christ-figure of the Middle Ages, that of Christ crucified, was thus the choice of Chalcedon, and it is here that we see the novelty of medieval christology as compared to patristic or Eastern christology: the image of Christ that prevailed was that of a suffering and dying man, who precisely in his death revealed the divine face and, by offering himself as victim to the Father, saved all humankind.

But we must bear in mind that after the conflict with *paganism had ended, during the early Middle Ages, between the 6th and 9th cc., Christ became the sole social horizon and the Christian faith was incarnated in *Christendom or, to put it differently, assumed a historical reference. While, at the end of the 6th c., *Gregory the Great could think of Christ as the spouse of the soul (in line with Augustine's *Confessions*), in the course of these centuries, dominated politically by new Germanic populations, a christological sentiment prevailed that saw in the Son of God both a saviour and a powerful lord. At a different level and with different tonalities, we see the hegemony of political power over religious power, characteristic of the Christian East, which took on a universal value at the end of the 8th c. with *Charlemagne; Christ was then considered especially as the one who saved from the wrath of the Father, stronger than any possible Germanic hero, mediator and king, indeed mediator because king.

In the Carolingian period, we encounter a plurality of christological attitudes and formulations, the most important of which were those of *Alcuin and *John Scotus Eriugena. The former took up the theme of Christ's humanity. From now on, any form of *Arianism seems set aside, and, against the *adoptianist ferment, active in *Catalonia and Arab *Castile, according to which Christ was the Father's natural son by divinity and adoptive son by humanity (by these terms they wished to emphasize Jesus' full humanity, his imperfection as man), Alcuin repeated the formula of Chalcedon and reaffirmed the full humanity of Christ, whom he considered, against these adversaries, perfect from conception. By contrast, it was not the theme of Christ's humanity that interested John Scotus: heir to the mystical tradition of Gregory the Great, but even more aware of the Greek theological and spiritual tradition (Gregory of Nyssa, Pseudo-*Dionysius, *Maximus Confessor), he reintroduced the notion of *deificatio*, since for him man was co-son of the Father's divinity in Christ; Christ was the medium between God and the cosmos, just as Christ was both creative wisdom and created wisdom: that is why Christ was the very archetype of *man.

But the Eriugenian position remained a minority one, while the Chalcedonian tradition prevailed: the dominant figure became that of Christ redeemer and crucified. The classic work of medieval *christology was *Anselm of Canterbury's *Cur Deus Homo* (1099). His analysis, which claimed to be rational, based on *rationes necessariae*, started from man considered as marked by a sinful condition; man could not remedy the offence he had committed against God, only God himself, insofar as he was also man; a God-man who freely accepted death; the Son was the victim of the Father. Thus Christ was no longer a glorious king, but a king wearing a crown of thorns, a crucified king. Christ's humanity was put in the foreground, because it was the humanity that suffered, not his divinity. The symbolic efficacity of this figure was enormous: Christ's suffering assumed an infinitely redemptive value in the eyes of the Father and gave all human suffering a divine value. This *theology allowed a singular mystical development: the theme of the *cross (and almost immediately the eucharistic theme, which renewed the event of the cross) became the theme of compassion and *love: sinful man saw on the cross both his own death and his own life and knew that, in the *Eucharist, he could touch the Man-God, could even incorporate him into himself for his own regeneration.

The Chalcedonian heritage of Christ the redeemer thus found itself overtaken: the love demanded by the Crucified had as its consequence not salvation, but rather union. The *mysticism of love that developed from the 12th c. was one of the christological novelties of the Middle Ages (*Bernard of Clairvaux, *Isaac of Stella, *William of Saint-Thierry). Christ was neither exclusively nor principally redeemer and saviour, he was master, friend, lover of the man who loved him. Thus the figure of Christ invaded the West, not that of the Word, as in the East, but that of a man-Jesus who had an existence of his own. Mysticism told a story of love between like beings, not an act of salvation between unlike beings. The Middle Ages did not yet manage to perceive the suffering of God in Christ: they saw only the suffering of his humanity; so they did not perceive the human dimension of God and the divine dimension of man; the Middle Ages did not formulate a theology of this type: in other terms, mysticism did not become a theological topic, and there was a dichotomy between theological reflection and mystical experience.

This did not prevent mysticism and a few isolated theological reflections from perceiving this christological plenitude. In *Francis of Assisi (13th c.), the disfigured face of man revealed the splendour of God's face, as he declared in his *Testament*, though he did not see that the face of God was also the poor face of man. In *Gertrude of Helfta (13th-14th c.) there took place an exchange of man's heart with the divine heart, and Gertrude went so far as to see herself as the mother of Jesus. *Angela of Foligno (13th-14th c.) asociated the plenitude of love (Bernardine theme) with the plenitude of nothingness (Dionysian theme) and thus attained the heights of mystical consciousness (she considered herself beyond Francis's testimony). Meister *Eckhart, whose theology remained isolated (and in part condemned by the papacy), formulated a mystical theology in which man was God in nothingness; but nothingness was not the negation of God, it was a moment of God, by which man (whose archetype was Christ) was not enclosed in his creaturely nature, but went beyond it. By contrast, an exclusively soteriological christology was continued in Lutheranism, while the Middle Ages transmitted to the modern Roman Church a christology that, with the theme of love (which wants not to save, but to communicate itself) and that of nothingness (where God and man meet), goes beyond that of Chalcedon. In the Middle Ages, Jesus of Nazareth was truly born alongside the Word of God, united to it but visible and comprehensible in himself.

J. Pelikan, *The Christian Tradition. A History of the Development of Doctrine*, 1-4, Chicago (IL)-London, 1971-1984. – *Il Cristo*, C. Leonardi (ed.), 3, *Testi teologici e spirituali in lingua latina da Agostino ad Anselmo di Canterbury*, Milan, 1989; *ibid.*, 4, *Testi teologici e spirituali in lingua latina da Abelardo a san Bernardo*, Milan, 1991; *ibid.*, 5, *Testi teologici e spirituali da Riccardo di San Vittore a Caterina da Siena*, Milan, 1992. – C. Bynum, *Jesus as Mother. Studies in the Spirituality of the High Middle Ages*, Berkeley (CA), 1992.

Claudio Leonardi

**Iconography.** The information provided by the gospels on Christ's earthly appearance is sparse and wholly hypothetical; the divine form revealed by the Transfiguration – face shining like the sun and garments white as snow – is described as contrasting markedly with Jesus' ordinary appearance, from which it may be deduced that his physical characteristics and dress were not seen as extravagant in the contemporary Jewish context. Yet very rarely did medieval Christian depictions try to be faithful to Christ's historical prosopography by giving him the physiological characteristics of the people of the Near East, with the possible exception of the Jewish Christian sect of Nazarenes, accused by Epiphanius of Salamis (3rd c.) of representing the Saviour as one of themselves, and a Syrian artist who, according to a 6th- or 7th-c. source, made a portrait of him "with the appearance of a Galilean".

Originally giving little attention to depiction, early Christianity neither encouraged nor explicitly prohibited the representation of Christ, first attested in allegorical and symbolic images of the 1st and 2nd cc. in the catacomb cycles. The earliest iconographical themes, like the *Good Shepherd, were introduced as metaphorical illustrations of gospel parables and messages, and not with the aim of documenting the earthly appearance of Jesus of Nazareth. Likewise, in the centuries between late Antiquity and the early Middle Ages, the formation of a more or less standard iconography of Christ was heavily conditioned by the desire to express themes and dogmatic concepts. The Saviour was imagined less in what must have been his actual features than in an idealized type that, even in representations of gospel episodes, alluded to his dual divine and human nature.

Following Is 53, 3 ("When we shall see him, there is no beauty that we should desire him"), some currents of thought of the early Church (Celsus) attributed to Christ an ugly and deformed apearance, but this was not followed up in artistic representations; on the contrary, the passage of Isaiah was considered a reference to the divine humiliation in Christ's passion, and the contrary idea prevailed, based on Ps 44, 3 ("the light of thy countenance"), that exalted the superhuman beauty of the Saviour, imagined as a youth with hair infused with white luminosity. The type of the adolescent, beardless Christ was widespread in many representations of the kind, whether narrative or portrait, but in time it was used mainly to emphasize the universal and ahistorical nature of the pre-incarnate Christ (the *Emmanuel* of Is 7, 14 and Mt 1, 23). The mature, bearded type, common from the 4th c., echoed ancient representations of Zeus and the tradition of portraits of famous philosophers, considered ideals of humanity; the choice of white or gold-veined garments – in accordance with a typology already linked to eschatological themes in Jewish tradition – was likewise determined by the gospel information on Christ's aspect in his celestial glory (Mt 17, 2; Lk 9, 29), no less than the characterisation of his hair as "blond" or "white as snow" and circumfused with light (Rev 1, 14). His usual dress, worked out from the 3rd c., consisted of a tunic decorated with vertical stripes (*clavi*) and a pallium or cloak; among his more frequent attributes were the *rotulus*, perhaps derived from the iconographical type of the ancient philosopher, and the book, sometimes closed, sometimes open and bearing gospel passages insisting on Christ's divinity (Jn 8, 12; 14, 6).

The images of Christ that formed during the early Middle Ages came to interpret various aspects of christological doctrine. To magnify Christ's divinity and majesty, schemes were used such as that of the **Transfiguration*, in which he was manifested within the Old Testament *kabod* or "glory of light" (cf. Ezek 19, 16-25), anciently rendered by *clouds, then by a luminous circle later stylized into a *mandorla. Contaminations between the visions of Isaiah (6, 1-4), Ezekiel (1, 1-28) and John (Rev 4, 1-11) fed the representation of the so-called *Maiestas Domini* (*Majesty), in which Christ, seated – on a throne, a globe or a rainbow – within the *kabod*, appeared surrounded by the four symbols of the *Tetramorph. This scheme, whose earliest appearance is in a mosaic in Hosios David at *Thessalonica (5th c.), thus associates an eschatological note with the glorification of the Lord in his divinity. The representation of the *Last Judgment, however, does not seem to have been introduced before the post-iconoclastic period (Torcello mosaic, 9th c.): Christ, contained in the mandorla and surrounded by the various celestial hierarchies, prepares to distinguish the blessed from the damned, while the Virgin and *John the Baptist, with whom a soteriological nuance is introduced, address a prayer of intercession to him in favour of mankind. The image of the *Madonna and Child, rendered as an ahistorical person characterised by the attributes of Christ in *glory (*e.g.* the *rotulus*), illustrated the dogma of the Incarnation.

In the Carolingian West, the beardless type continued to be repeated in association with representations of Christ in glory, but it was progressively supplanted by the mature, bearded representation. From the 9th c., the theme of the majesty of Christ was combined with that of the Crucifixion, in order to express his victory over death and *sin and emphasize how the *Passion, as the condition of mankind's *redemption, reveals the glory and power of *God; the Catalan wooden statues known as *majestates* illustrate the paradoxical distinction between the instrument of torture (the *cross), reinterpreted as a triumphal symbol, and the superhuman and atemporal aspect conferred on Christ with his thick beard, fixed and terible look and long tunic (sometimes enriched with references to sacerdotal symbology). In the absidal programmes of *Romanesque churches, the stress is put mainly on eschatological doctrine and the most frequently recurring themes are the *Maiestas Domini* and, in this case in the 13th c., the **Deêsis*, in which Christ appears enthroned next to the Virgin and John the Baptist (then *John the Evangelist, by contamination with the scheme of the *Crucifixion*) in the act of interceding for mankind; analogous subjects are carved above main doors, particularly in northern Europe and Spain. The association of these themes with the area of the liturgy makes clear the close connection between the Passion – and its repetition in the *Eucharist – and the Redemption of mankind.

Especially from the 12th c., the introduction of eschatological, soteriological and eucharistic allusions seems to have had an increasingly central importance in christological subjects. On the basis of the context of their exposition and their intended use, *images were called on to express an aspect of dogma, though trying at the same time to convey the theological complexity of the figure of Christ. Into representations insisting on the eschatological theme were progressively introduced iconographical elements alluding to the Sacrifice of Christ, so much that in the 14th c. the most common rendering of the **Last Judgment* would consist of a half-naked Christ showing his *wounds and flanked by the cross and the other instruments of torture, while in the *Deêsis* the enthroned Christ was replaced by an emblematic image of the Passion, the *Imago Pietatis*.

Parallel to the illustration of theological concepts, images of Christ also met more concrete devotional needs. Subjects like the scenes depicting the miracles of Jesus were repeated, from the 3rd to the 6th c., in sarcophagus sculptures and in embroidery on articles of clothing, since the Saviour's thaumaturgical quality was interpreted as a way of exalting, sometimes in a *magic or apotropaic sense, his role as healer *par excellence*. Portrait images of Christ spread especially in the East in association with private worship, and their iconographical schemes were developed in the tradition of *icon painting, which had a Western outpost at *Rome, where a panel with Christ enthroned, anciently considered **acheiropoietos* or "not made by human hand" and later (11th c.) a work of St Luke, enjoyed vast fame throughout Europe; the iconic imitation of Christ in devotional painting was relatively widespread in Italy in the 13th c., though favouring the themes that alluded to the Passion. In the last centuries of the Middle Ages, it was mainly themes like the *Imago Pietatis* and the *Crucifixion* that were repeated in images intended for private worship, while the humanized representation of the Infant in Marian schemes was preferred, with ever greater intensity, to the portrait of Christ in glory.

F. Van der Meer, *Maiestas Domini*, Paris-Rome, 1938 ("SAC", 13). – C. Ihm, *Die Programme der christlichen Apsismalerei vom vierten Jahrhundert bis zur Mitte des achten Jahrhunderts*, Wiesbaden, 1960. – R. Sanfaçon, "La Tradition symbolique de la deuxième vision de l'Apocalypse et les débuts de l'art gothique", *Mélanges R. Crozet*, Poitiers, 1966, 993-1001. – *L'Apocalypse de Jean. Traditions exégétiques et iconographiques (IIIe-XIIIe siècle)*, Geneva, 1979. – H. Belting, *Das Bild und sein Publikum im Mittelalter*, Berlin, 1981. – G. Schiller, *Ikonographie der christlichen Kunst*, 5, 1-2, Gütersloh 1990-1991. – T. F. Mathews, *The Clash of Gods. A Reinterpretation of Early Christian Art*, Princeton (NJ), 1993. – P. Skubiszewski, "Cristo", *Encyclopedia dell'Arte Medioevale*, 5, Rome, 1994, 493-521.

Michele Bacci

**CHRISTENDOM.** The term "Christendom" began by designating the community of Christians, with a sense close to that of *ecclesia*, then it took on a greater density of connotations. Christendom was defined not just geographically by boundaries or frontiers, but above all by its members' awareness of belonging to a single group whose common cultural source was the Christian religion. Medieval Christendom was more of a project, an ideal, than a political or geographical reality.

After the political disappearance of the Roman Empire in the 5th c. and the dislocation of the Carolingian Empire in the 10th, there no longer existed any *authority transcending the frontiers of increasingly cramped political frameworks, from the German national duchies to the **seigneuries* of West Francia. The unity of the Western world was restored from the 12th c., starting from allegiance to a single source of religious authority whose centre and content were provided by the papacy since the German emperor could no longer rally to himself the whole of the Christian peoples. The awareness of belonging to a community was effected thanks to frictions, with the world of *Islam in the Mediterranean, with the Slav peoples, but also with Eastern Christendom – the *schism of 1054 being merely an epiphenomenon hardly perceived by contemporaries. The papacy was the architect of this new self-awareness.

*Court of women dressed in the fashion of Charles VI.* Miniature from Christine de Pizan's *Book of the City of Ladies*, 15th c. Chantilly, Musée Condé.

In proportion as the doctrine of papal supremacy was built up, whether with regard to the local powers of the Church held by *bishops, *canons or *abbots, or to the *temporal powers, the papacy was conceived as the head of a body all of whose members owed it obedience. After the assertion by *Gregory VII of the papacy's autonomy from the emperor, then the defence of the Church by *Alexander III, *Innocent III and *Innocent IV conceived Christendom as an ordered and hierarchized edifice in which the *pope, as depositary of the divine will, held all sovereignty. More than the Church conceived as the assembly of the faithful or as administrative machinery, Christendom was the field of exercise and incarnation of the terrestrial Church. The Christian lands, in full expansion, whether in Eastern Europe among *Slavs or *Balts or in the South and East against the Muslims, provided the geographical setting of that power.

However, as a concept with a universal vocation, Christendom came into conflict with the national particularisms of *States in process of formation. The Roman Church itself aserted itself in the same way as these, thanks to an increasingly structured administrative and fiscal machinery and papal States that made the papacy a political power among others. The contesting of this state of affairs by movements within Roman Christianity, then cast out into dissidence and *heresy, prepared the dissolution of Christendom as a whole united by a single faith. Thus Christendom, even before being dislocated in the 16th c. by the multiplication of Christian confessions setting themselves up against the claims of the papacy, was undermined by the appearance and affirmation of national States in Western Europe in the 14th and 15th centuries.

J. Rupp, *L'Idée de Chrétienté dans la pensée pontificale des origines à Innocent III*, Paris, 1939. – W. Kölmen, *Regimen Christianum*, Berlin, 1973. – "The Concepts of 'Ecclesia' and 'Christianitas' and their Relation to the Idea of 'Plenitudo Potestatis' from Gregory VII to Boniface VIII", G. Ladner, *Images and Ideas*, 2, Rome, 1983, 487-515.

Thierry Pécout

**CHRISTIAN OF DENMARK (1425-1481).** Count of Oldenburg. King of *Denmark from 1448 under the name of Christian I, king of *Norway in 1449, duke of Schleswig in 1460 and of Holstein in 1474, he was also king of *Sweden from 1457 to 1464. Starting from the county of Oldenburg, the dynasty of counts entered, for centuries, the history of *Scandinavia and Schleswig-Holstein. In fact Christopher, king of the union of Denmark, Norway and Sweden, died childless in 1448. Christian was then able to impose himself as king of Denmark and Norway, but was unable to do so lastingly in Sweden. On the death of Adolf VIII, duke of Schleswig and count of Holstein, in 1459, the line of the Schauenburg died out; Schleswig and Holstein, which were to remain "eternally united", were attached by personal union to Denmark.

A. von Brandt, "Die nordischen Länder von 1448 bis 1654", *Handbuch der europäischen Geschichte*, 3, Stuttgart, 1971, 962 f.

Gerhard Theuerkauf

**CHRISTINA OF MARKYATE (*c.*1100-*c.*1155/1166).** *The Life of Christina of Markyate* (published entire in 1959 from a single much-damaged Latin manuscript) is a *biography by a monk of St Albans, a confidant of the virgin, of exceptional interest for our knowledge of an exceptional female destiny and of English society in the first half of the 12th c., at the particular time when the *Gregorian reform defined the *sacrament of *marriage. In the transhistorical category of virgins who want only Christ for spouse, Christina has nothing of the timeless and conventional about her. This middle-class girl born at Huntingdon was married by force, escaped and lived hidden in two successive reclusories including that of Markyate near St Albans before directing there a female community dependent on St Paul's, London.

*The Life of Christina of Markyate. A Twelfth Century Recluse*, C. H. Talbot (ed.), Oxford, 1959 (*OMT*).

Paulette L'Hermite-Leclercq

**CHRISTINE DE PIZAN or PISAN (1364-1429).** The biography of Christine de Pizan is essentially contained in her works. This quest for herself is inseparable from the high conception of writing held by this author, one of the foremost writers of French literature.

Born in Italy in 1364, she came to France in 1368 with her father Tommaso Pizzano, a celebrated Bolognese doctor and astronomer who entered the service of *Charles V (*L'Avision Christine*). She considered her childhood a golden age, and the king served as her main political model (*Livre des fais et bonnes meurs du sage roy Charles V*). At 25, she was the *widow of Étienne Castel, a *notary of the *chancery by whom she had three children. After this happy marriage which she evokes in her ballades, she had to face material difficulties, which a polished and, for a woman, exceptional culture enabled her to surmount (*Livre du chemin de long estude*, *Libre de la Cité des dames*). From 1400, she chose to live by her pen and, consequently, "to become a man" (*Livre de la mutacion de fortune*). Her first writings took her into the debate over the *Roman de la Rose*, in which she defended the honour and position of *women (*Livre des trois*

Unnamed king. Stained-glass window from the west front of Reims Cathedral. (Photo: G. Dagli Orti)

Eternal Consolation. Christ blessing dignitaries of Church and State (including Frederick III, John II the Good, Philip the Good and Charles the Bold). Manuscript of 1462. Municipal Library, Valenciennes.

Francis of Assisi healing a wounded man. Fresco by Giotto in the Basilica of St Francis at Assisi. c. 1300

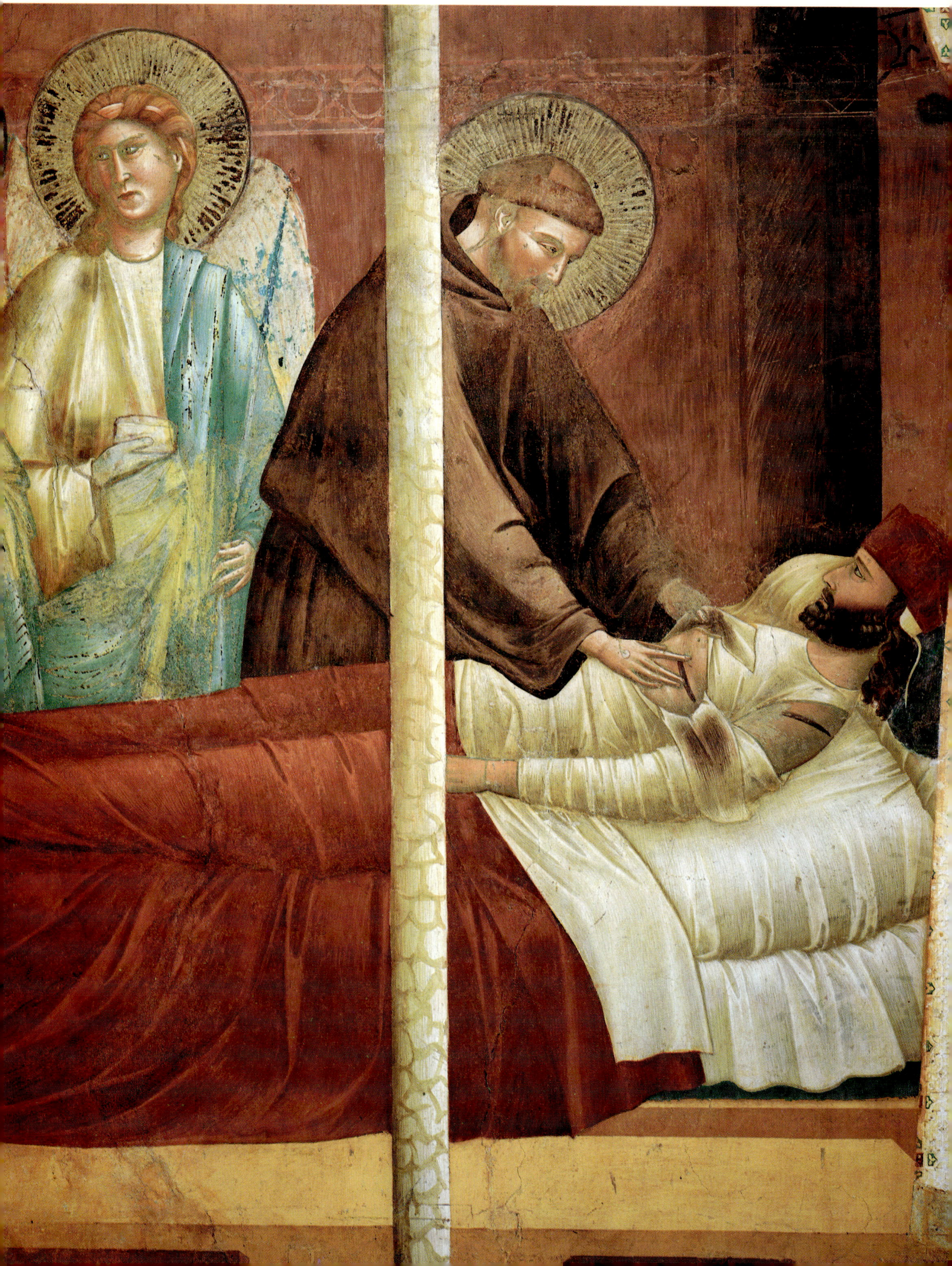

*vertus*). Her work is impregnated with the texts of Antiquity, which she knew in French and doubtless in Latin. She adapted them to Christian morality (*Epistre d'Othea*) and made a creative compilation in which she touched on every field, including the art of war (*Livre des faits d'armes et de chevalrie*). Her recourse to princely protectors, mainly the dukes of Orléans, Burgundy and Berry, was a necessity which she accomplished without concession, since, as the successive dedications and the contents of her works show, Christine wished to play the role of a critical and constructive political adviser to them (*Epistre à la reine Isabeau*, *Livre de prod'ommie*). She took part in the reflections of political theorists on the reform of the realm (*Livre du chemin de long estude*, *Livre de policie*). A woman, she lent her voice to incite the great to peace (*Lamentation sur les maux de la France*, *Livre de la paix*).

A committed writer without belonging to a political party, by her actions she tended, according to a recovered Ciceronian ideal, to seek among the princes the mentor who could give help to the successive dauphins, palliate the king's madness and resolve the civil war. But from 1418 Christine de Pizan shared the failure of the first *humanists: her writing had not succeeded in reforming the world. Doubtless retired to Poissy, she broke her silence on 31 July 1429 to celebrate *Joan of Arc (*Ditié de Jehanne d'Arc*) and died soon after.

Christine de Pisan, *the Treasure of the City of Ladies*, Harmondsworth, 1985. – Christine de Pizan, *The Book of the Body Politic*, K. Langdon Forhan (ed.), Cambridge, 1994. – *Christine de Pizan's Letter of Othea to Hector*, J. Chance (ed.), Woodbridge, 1997.

C. C. Willard, *Christine de Pizan: her Life and Works*, New York, 1984. – E. Yenal, *Christine de Pizan: a Bibliography*, London, 1989 (2nd ed.). – "Christine de Pizan", *Revue des langues romanes*, 92, 1988, 2 (special no.). – "Christine de Pizan", *DLFMA*, 1992, 280-287. – *Politics, Gender, and Genre: the Political Thought of Christine de Pizan*, M. Brabant (ed.), Boulder (CO), 1992. – R. Brown-Grant, *Christine de Pizan and the Moral Defence of Women*, Cambridge, 2000.

Claude Gauvard

**CHRISTOLOGY.** Christology is the name given to that part of *theology whose object is *Christ, *i.e.* the study of the Incarnation of the *Word (christology in the restricted sense) and of his saving work (soteriology).

The council of Chalcedon (451) defined the fundamental principle of all Orthodox christology: there is in Christ one sole *person (contrary to the doctrine of Nestorius, condemned in 431 at Ephesus) and two *natures (contrary to the doctrine of Eutyches, "monophysitism"): "One and the same Son, Our Lord Jesus Christ, complete as to divinity and complete as to humanity, truly God and truly man . . . . One and the same Christ in two natures, without mixture, without transformation, without division, without separation: because the union has not suppressed the difference of natures, each one has preserved its manner of being, and has come together with the other in a single person or hypostasis."

For Byzantine theology, the coherence and implications of the dogma emerged in the first centuries of the Middle Ages. The various christologies were worked out in a constant oscillation between the two points of view both equally justified by Chalcedon: divine penetration of the humanity by the Word ("theandrism" on which the Alexandrian tradition insisted), and the wholeness of the human assumed by the Word (on which the Antiochene tradition insisted).

Leontius of Byzantium († 541), by distinguishing hypostasis and *enhypostaton* (that which exists in a hypostasis), and his contemporary Leontius of Jerusalem, by asserting that the one hypostasis of Christ was that of the pre-existing Word ("one of the holy Trinity suffered in the flesh"), contributed to a better understanding of the dogma. *Maximus Confessor († 662) opposed *monothelism by identifying human *will and divine will in Christ: both of them, proceeding from the same Word, are in harmony, but they each keep their specific identity. Monothelism was condemned by the third ecumenical *council of Constantinople (680-681).

*John of Damascus († 749) made a synthesis of the East's previous theological gains. He would be the classic author in every period of the Byzantine Middle Ages, and it was mainly through his intermediary that Western *scholasticism became aware of the Greek tradition. John emphasized that the Word had the initiative in the Incarnation ("we do not speak of a man divinized but of a God who was made man"); the divine hypostasis, archetype of humanity, individualized the human nature of Christ who, for this reason, is the new Adam, recapitulating all humanity in him for the sake of its deification; we must exclude from Christ all ignorance and, among the passions, all those that, owing to sin, are contrary to nature and would taint its perfection. After *Germanus of Constantinople († *c.*733) and before *Theodore the Studite († 826) and *Nicephorus Confessor († 828), John defended the cult of *images against *iconoclasm, monophysite in tendency.

After the final defeat of iconoclasm ("triumph of *Orthodoxy" in 843), theological controversies in the Byzantine world concerned only a few isolated individuals and were quickly concluded. The work and authority of Gregory *Palamas († 1359) favoured in the Orthodox world a spiritual and doctrinal christocentrism: in Christ and in him alone, a real participation in the very life of God was offered to man, hence the insistence of his disciples on the sacramental life (Nicholas *Cabasilas's treatise, *Life in Christ*).

For the Latin Middle Ages, *Anselm of Canterbury († 1109) showed why it was necessary for the Son to be incarnated, rather than the Father or the Spirit. His theology of *satisfaction should not be reduced to the comparison of *God to an offended lord whose *honour demands an infinite reparation, which can only be accomplished by an innocent man-God whose sacrifice is credited to the account of the guilty and exempts them from the merited punishment. *Justice, for Anselm, is an aspect of the divine goodness desirous of making man capable "of setting himself to rights and picking himself up by himself". If it had to be a man-God who ransomed man, it was so that he might be "the slave of God alone and equal in everything to the good angels".

Innumerable monastic and especially *Cistercian writings were devoted to Christ. Without ignoring dogmatic speculations, their aim was mainly to favour a *meditation savouring of *mystery and intimacy with the Saviour. We wish to know him in order to imitate him and be transformed into him: "May the Son of God, already formed in you, grow in you until he becomes, for you and in you, measureless" (*Isaac of Stella). Attention was concentrated on this or that aspect of Jesus's humanity, and a multiplicity of devotions gradually developed: to Christ's infancy (*Ælred of Rievaulx's treatise on the Infant Jesus at twelve years, mid 12th c.), to the various scenes of his *Passion, to his *Name (hymn, *Jesu dulcis memoria*), to his Heart (St Lutgarde's [† 1244] experience of exchange of *hearts), to his *Blood or to his *Wounds.

Scholastic reflection was primarily to do with the manner of union of the two natures in Christ. The different positions were brought down to three opinions in *Peter Lombard's **Sentences* (before 1152): the first, called "assumed *suppositum*", distinguished two *supposita* in Christ, one created, a composite subsisting of *soul and *body ("this man"), and the other uncreated, the Word that

*Saint Christopher carrying the Child Jesus.* Late 13th-c. fresco at Pernes-les-Fontaines, Tour Ferrande (France).

subsists only in its divine nature, while being substantially united to the first *suppositum* ("this man is the Word"). The second was called "composite person": there is only one uncreated *suppositum*, the Word that subsists in the divine nature and in the human nature. The third came from *Abelard († 1142) and was called "Word clothed in humanity": the human body and soul were assumed by the Word separately, and in an accidental manner (thesis condemned by Pope *Alexander III in 1177). *Thomas Aquinas († 1274) identified the first opinion with Nestorianism and the third with the heresy of Photinus ("the man is made God"). According to him, only the second was compatible with the *Catholic faith.

In his *Summa theologiae*, Thomas presents Christ as he by whom man, departing from God, concretely effects his return to God. He studies first the mystery of the Incarnation in itself, the *ontology and psychology of Christ. As to the reason for the Incarnation, he prefers to hold to the teaching of Scripture: it was to free man from *sin that the Word was incarnated; each of the three divine persons has by right an equal power to subsist in the human. Thomas then comments on what Christ did and suffered on earth in order to bring out its saving significance. In the Incarnation, Thomas considers mainly the descent of the Word into the human which it took to itself, and conceives Christ's humanity as the "conjoint instrument" of his divinity.

The mystical experience of *Francis of Assisi († 1226), culminating in the stigmatization of *Alverna, was entirely dominated by Christ on the cross. For his disciple *Bonaventure († 1274), all knowledge must be related to Christ, whom he calls the *medium*, centre and mediator, of God and creation, being and knowledge. Christ is our only teacher, the way in that he gives us belief, the truth in that he gives us understanding, the life in that he gives us *contemplation. The Franciscan John *Duns Scotus († 1308) insists on the historical aspect of the Incarnation, on the wholeness of the humanity assumed by the Word, which for him possesses an "existence in itself", without for all that constituting a person in itself alone. Duns Scotus moreover asserts that the Incarnation, whose first aim was the fulfilment of the created order in the person of the Man-God, would have come about even if man had not sinned. Finally, Scotists and Thomists (*e.g.* the Dominican *Capreolus, † 1444, identifying person and existence) clashed on the two questions of the unity of being in Christ and the reason for the Incarnation.

J. Meyendorff, *Le Christ dans la théologie byzantine*, Paris, 1969. – E. H. Wéber, *Le Christ selon saint Thomas d'Aquin*, Paris, 1988. – J. Leclercq, *Regards monastiques sur le Christ au Moyen Âge*, Paris, 1992. – J. Pelikan, *The Christian Tradition*, Chicago, 1977. – J. P. Torrell, *Le Christ en ses mystères. La vie et l'oeuvre de Jésus selon s. Thomas d'Aquin*, 1, Paris, 1999.

Gilles Berceville

**CHRISTOPHER.** A saint martyred in Lycia, Christopher was undoubtedly one of the most venerated saints in the Middle Ages. According to the Eastern legend, Christopher, who was called Reprobus before being baptized, was a dog-headed cannibal. He was converted to the Christian faith. Arrested, he refused to apostatize and perished amid frightful torments. This is a hagiographical fable, but evidence of a cult goes back to the 5th c.: an inscription found in Bithynia mentions the consecration of a church in his honour in 452, and in the 6th c. a monastery dedicated to his name existed at Taormina (*Sicily).

The Western legend was rather different. It made Christopher a giant who wanted to use his strength in the service of the most powerful master: first a king, then the *demon, finally *Christ. Once taught by a pious hermit, he settled near a river to help travellers across. One night a child turned up. As he crossed, the weight became so heavy that the giant had difficulty in reaching the other bank. This child, who was none other than Christ, told him of his coming *martyrdom. Christopher then went to Lycia to preach. He made numerous *conversions and died by beheading.

*Jacobus de Voragine's *Golden Legend* (13th c.) made the story of Christopher famous in the West. But images of the good giant carrying the Child Jesus on his shoulder, examples of which are known from the 12th c., preceded the *legend. Christopher's very name, which means "Christ-bearer", could have inspired this legend which in turn became a source of inspiration for the saint's later iconography, in the East as well. The evolution of the legend which overlaps with other known stories like that of Julian the Hospitaller and the "crossing of the water of the winter darkness" fed an abundant folklore.

Among numerous attributions, Christopher was thought to protect against an evil particularly feared in the Middle Ages, *death without *confession, called "bad death". It was enough to have seen his *image to be preserved from that danger for the day. This was why the custom spread through the West of painting the saint's gigantic effigy on church façades or on town gates (Bern). It was accompanied by formulae to be recited, of the type: "Look at Christopher and go your way reassured". These wall paintings, which could reach a height of eight metres (cathedral of Spilimbergo [Friuli]), were designed to be seen by all and from a distance. They flourished in those crossing places, the Alpine and sub-Alpine regions, where St Christopher, patron of travellers, was invoked by *pilgrims in difficulty. He was also invoked against the plague and eye diseases, which is why he often appears in company with anti-plague saints. Moreover, the vision of the Christ-child on his shoulder corresponded to the vision of the *host. By associating devotion to St Christopher with the desire to see the host, whose *elevation had at that time acquired the same apotropaic value as the *image of the saint, collective belief reinforced the legitimacy of these practices. Though for the *humanists, like Erasmus, this devotion represented the very type of the "superstitious cult", it was not until after the council of Trent that the saint's images were systematically destroyed.

*ActaSS*, July, VI, 125-149.

H. F. Rosenfeld, *Der heilige Christophorus, seine Verehrung und seine Legende*, Leipzig, 1937. – *BSS*, 4, 1964, 349-364. – G. Benker, *Christophorus Patron der Schiffer, Fuhrleute und Kraftfahrer. Legende, Verehrung, Symbol*, Munich, 1975.

Dominique Rigaux

**CHRODEGANG OF METZ (*c.*715-766).** A native of the district of *Liège, if Chrodegang was not the grandson of *Charles Martel as an unfounded tradition has it, he still belonged to the high Frankish *nobility. After studying at the monastery of Saint-Trond, he made a career at the court of Charles Martel, then at that of his son Carloman who appointed him to the bishopric of *Metz (741). There he energetically pursued the *reform begun by St *Boniface and played a preponderant role in *councils. He acted in liaison with the mayor of the palace, then king, *Pippin the Short and with the *pope. Sent on an embassy to Rome in 753, he brought back *Stephen II, who was threatened by the *Lombards. The pope consecrated Pippin a second time – it had already been done in 751 by Boniface – at *Saint-Denis (28 July 754).

Chrodegang introduced at Metz a certain number of *Roman liturgical customs, particularly concerning chanting and the order of offices. These Roman customs spread through Gaul and Germany from Metz. After the death of St Boniface, he received from the pope the **pallium*, usual badge of the archiepiscopal or *metropolitan dignity. In 762, at Attigny, he figured among the 44 prelates who concluded an association of prayer for the *dead (100 *masses and 100 *psalters at the decease of each member). He died on 6 March 766 and his body was buried at the abbey of *Gorze, which he had founded in 748 and considerably developed.

But Chrodegang's name is especially associated with his *Rule for Canons* in 34 or 86 chapters, composed for the clergy of his church between 751 and 755 in order to reform it. A compilation of extracts from the *Fathers, councils and especially from the Rule of St *Benedict, it imposed on *clerics the common life, with recitation of the *office, refectory and dorter in common, in an *enclosure. The *canons had to donate their property to the community, but they kept the usufruct and could exceptionally obtain authorization from the *bishop to live outside the enclosure. This rule, initially intended just for the clergy of Metz, was an immense success. It was included in the *Rule imposed on all the canons of the Carolingian Empire by the council of Aachen in 816.

*The Old English Version of the Enlarged Rule of Chrodegang Together with the Latin Original*, A.S. Napier (ed.), London, 1916.

T. de Morembert, "Chrodegang", *DHGE*, 12, 1953, 781-784. – *Saint Chrodegang. Communications présentées au colloque tenu à Metz à l'occasion du douzième centenaire de sa mort*, J. Schneider (ed.), Metz, 1967.

Michel Sot

**CHRONICLES, CHRONICLERS**

**The West.** In the Middle Ages, "chronicle" served to designate a historical work, as did "*annals" or "*histories". For a long time there was ambiguity about these different terms.

Merovingian and Carolingian authors, from *Gregory of Tours in the 6th c. to John of Saint-Arnoul in the 10th, indifferently employed the three terms, which thus designated any account of what had actually happened. But from the 4th c., Eusebius of Caesarea's *Ecclesiastical History* and *Chronicle*, which possessed authority throughout the Middle Ages in their Latin translations, had established a distinction between "history", which favoured narrative, and "chronicle", which favoured chronology. This distinction was not perceived as fundamental, and even in the 12th c. *Otto of Freising could entitle his work *Chronica sive historia de duabus civitatibus*. "Annals", which appeared only in the 7th-8th cc., confined themselves to noting year after year, very briefly and without more elaboration, the events whose memory was intended to be retained. Hence they were not the work of a historian, but they sometimes furnished him with his primary materials. The historian's labour could thus transform "annals", which disappeared totally in the 12th and 13th cc., into "chronicles": in *c.*1200, the chronicler *Gervase of Canterbury wrote that "chronicle is another name for annals".

In the 14th c., there were only "chronicles" and "histories": the former were, in theory, succinct and followed chronology step by step, the latter more developed, grouping facts by reign and by subject. These questions of definition that occupied a very narrow circle of specialists were often ignored by the majority of medieval historians. For them the important thing was strictly to respect chronological order, *ordo temporum*, and to explain the causes and circumstances of events. It remains the case that the word "chronicle" passed to posterity as the common form of medieval historical narrative, covering texts of very different natures.

Among chronicles, the most ambitious were the universal chronicles that related the history of the world from its creation to the time of their author or to the end of time, such as *Vincent of Beauvais's *Speculum historiale* whose success is attested by the hundred or so manuscripts still surviving. But there were also more modest works – modest in their ambition, not in their success – such as *Martin of Opava (Troppau)'s *Chronicle of the Popes and Emperors*. Finally, others were the expression of a more official history. Thus the *Capetians maintained a historian from the reign of *Philip Augustus. For instance, the anonymous Religious of Saint-Denis wrote a chronicle of the reign of *Charles VI, and in 1437 Jean Chartier became "chronicler of France" with the mission of writing a chronicle of the reign of *Charles VII.

B. Guenée, "Histoires, annales, chroniques. Essai sur les genres historiques au Moyen Âge", *Annales*, 1973, 997-1016. – K. H. Krüger, *Die Universalchroniken*, Turnhout, 1976. – A. Gransden, "The Chronicles of Medieval England and Scotland", *JMH*, 16, 1990, 129-150. – E.M.C. Van Houts, *Local and Regional Chronicles*, Turnhout, 1995.

Isabelle Heullant-Donat

**England.** England has a long tradition of historical chroniclers, writing in both the vernacular Old English and in *Latin. The most important works in Latin of the Anglo-Saxon period include *Gildas' *The Ruin and Conquest of Britain*, a history of Christian Britain written in the 6th c.; Nennius' *History of the Britons* (*c.*830), which includes material on King *Arthur; and *Bede's *Ecclesiastical History of the English People* (completed 731). The

*Anglo-Saxon Chronicle*, an important work in annalastic form, written in the vernacular, was begun in the late 9th c. and continued by many authors.

Important historical works produced after the *Norman Conquest by English and *Anglo-Norman authors, written in Latin, include Simeon of Durham's *History of the Church of Durham*; Eadmer's *History of Recent Events in England*, an account of St *Anselm's public acts and the relations of *Church and State in England; *Orderic Vitalis' *Ecclesiastical History of England and Normandy*, a history of *Normandy up to the mid 11th c., of the Norman Conquest, and of England during the reigns of *William I, *William II and *Henry I; *William of Malmesbury's *Deeds of the Kings of the English*, a history of English monarchs through Henry I, using Anglo-Saxon sources which are now lost, and his *Deeds of the Archbishops and Bishops of the English*, a valuable work on the history of episcopal sees and religious buildings in England; Henry of Huntingdon's *History of the English*, an ambitious history extending to the accession of *Henry II; "Benedict of Peterborough's" *Chronicle of the Reigns of Henry II and Richard I*, an insightful history of the English government and of national and European affairs; Roger of Howden's *Chronicle*, which includes an eyewitness account of the third *crusade; Ralph Diceto's *Epitome of Chronicles* and *Images of History*, which chronicle both English political affairs and Church history; Richard of Devizes' *Chronicle of the Time of Richard I*, a heavily biased work concerning *Richard I and his military exploits; Gervase of Canterbury's *Chronicle*, which includes much material on the history of *Canterbury, and his *Deeds of Kings*, a political history of England from the earliest times; Robert of Torigny's *Chronicle*, a reliable history containing detailed information on the continental campaigns and politics of Henry II and his sons; William of Newburgh's *History of English Affairs*, which contains valuable biographical information on Richard I; and Roger of Wendover's *Flowers of History*, a compilation of historical authorities up to 1202, as well as original work up to 1234.

A. Gransden, *Historical Writing in England*, London, 1974-1982 (2 vol.). – J. Taylor, *English Historical Literature in the Fourteenth Century*, Oxford, 1987. – A. Gransden, "The Chronicles of Medieval England and Scotland", *JMH*, 16, 1990, 129-150; 17, 1991, 217-243. – D. E. Greenway, "Authority, Convention and Observation in Henry of Huntingdon's Historia Anglorum", *Anglo-Norman Studies XVIII*, C. Harper-Brill (ed.), Woodbridge, 1996, 105-121. – E. J. King, "Benedict of Peterborough and the Cult of Thomas Becket", *Northamptonshire Past and Present*, 9, 3, 1996, 213-220.

Laura Napran

**Byzantium.** At Byzantium, the chronicle was an important genre whose identity can be perceived even if, at certain periods, it tends to be confused with history.

The most recognisable variety is the universal chronicle which, juxtaposing or mixing sacred and secular history, begins with the creation of the world and goes on to the period contemporary with the writer. Often, the chronicle is a learned "chronography" that tries to measure *time: date of Creation, of the Incarnation, of Easter. The language of the chronicles and their conception of history are marked by popular elements. The link between events is tenuous. Interest tends towards the isolated and salient fact. Prodigies, presages and legendary motifs are not rare. These traits and the relative abundance of manuscripts suggest that certain chronicles were intended for a less learned public than the histories. The education and social position of the chroniclers vary. Sometimes, they are mere compilers. In other cases, the chronicler, continuing a predecessor, does the work of a historian in the original part of his work. As well as universal chronicles or their continuations, there are also abridged chronicles and "brief chronicles", of which the most important are regional (Epirus, *Trebizond) or relate to the arrival of the *Turks. The fact that, in all essentials, the history of the Byzantines was centred on *Constantinople is what gives such informatin its value.

From the protobyzantine period, the genre of the universal Christian chronicle is well represented. It rests on the works of Sextus Julius Africanus (3rd c.) and Eusebius of Caesarea (4th c.). The first surviving chronicles are the *Chronography* of John Malalas (6th c.), written in popular language by an official, and the *Chronicon Paschale*, a learned work dating from the reign of *Heraclius, concerning itself particularly with Easter cycles.

In the second part of the 7th c. and in the 8th c., the situation is obscure. The history of the genre becomes possible to grasp once more with the learned *Chronography* of George Syncellus, from Adam to Diocletian. Written in *c.*806 by a man close to Patriarch Tarasius, it witnesses to the cultural revival at Byzantium. On his death, George left the task of completing the work to his friend Theophanes. He, a monk of aristocratic origin, a confessor of *Orthodoxy under *Leo V, wrote before 815 one of the major chronicles of Byzantium, our main source for the 7th and 8th centuries. The work of George the Monk, written around 866-867, is the other important chronicle of the 9th century.

In the 10th c. was published a *Continuation of Theophanes*, from 813 to 961; it was written in the entourage of the Emperor Constantine VII Porphyrogenitus by several authors. In *c.*976, Symeon Magistros or the Logothete composed a universal chronicle whose original part concerns the reigns of Constantine VII and Romanus Lecapenus. At the end of the 11th c., John Skylitzes compiled a *Historical Abridgement* (811-1057) which is a continuation of Theophanes, but which is a history of reigns rather than a chronicle.

Under the *Comneni, we owe two interesting works (from the creation to 1118) to John Zonaras, a senior official, and Michael Glykas, an imperial notary. In the same period, Princess Irene Comnena commissioned a versified universal chronicle from Constantine Manasses. Output decreased after that: the chronicles of Joel and Ephrem, the latter versified, are of no great interest. Only the work of Theodore Skutariotes (late 13th c.), from Adam to 1261, has the dignity of the chronicles of the previous centuries.

H. Hunger, *Die hochsprachliche profane Literatur der Byzantiner*, 1, 1978, 243-504 ("HAW").

Bernard Flusin

**West Slavs.** The production of historical literature among the West *Slavs appeared from the time of the State of Great *Moravia with the Lives of Sts *Cyril and Methodius, written in the 9th century. Later, this activity was concentrated essentially in Bohemia and Poland. Among the chroniclers writing about the West Slav lands in the 10th and 11th cc., many were of Byzantine, Arab or German origin.

A properly Slav output developed in a remarkable way in 12th-c. *Bohemia. We have an exceptional chronicler in the person of Cosmas (*c.*1045-1125), a *canon of *Prague who had studied at *Liège; his *Chronicle of Bohemia* (*Chronica Boemorum*), written in the years 1110-1125 in rhymed rhythmic prose, contains information going up to 1125; it is the most precious source for the early history of Bohemia. Cosmas had as continuator a canon of

Vyšehrad of whom nothing is known except that he wrote his chronicle in the years 1126-1142. Great importance must also be given to the Sázava chronicle whose author was an unknown monk of that Benedictine abbey, and which was written in the years 1173-1177. Later continuators of Cosmas were the Prague canon Vincenty and especially Jarloch (*c.*1165-*c.*1228), superior of the *Premonstratensian monastery of Milevsk, who had studied at *Würzburg. His work, going up to 1198, is a very important source for Czech history in the last quarter of the 12th century. In the following period, historiographical output in Bohemia increased dynamically; among others appeared the *Chronicle of Zbraslav*, the so-called Chronicle of Dalimil – the first to be written in Czech –, the *Styrian Chronicle*, the Chronicle of Přibík of Radenín called *Chronicle of Pulkava*, the Chronicle of Beneš Krabice of Veitmíle as well as the extraordinarily interesting autobiography of *Charles IV.

The first chronicle written in *Poland was the *Polish Chronicle*, by an author of whom nothing more is known: since he probably came from France, he was later known as Gallus Anonymus; this chronicler was probably brought from *Hungary to Poland by Duke *Boleslas Wrymouth; this source sheds light on the first period of Poland's history up to 1113; Gallus's *Chronicle* was a source of information for his successors. Another interesting literary vestige, the *Carmen Mauri*, was written soon after 1153 by an unknown Benedictine monk who came from the Romanesque cultural area; it describes the life and acts of the Palatine Peter (Piotr) Włostowicz, and has survived only in fragmentary form. The next Polish chronicler was Master Vincent (Wincenty) called Kadłubek (*c.*1150-1223), a priest of the *collegiate church of Sandomir, appointed bishop of *Cracow in 1207. He had probably studied at *Paris and *Bologna, and his *Polish Chronicle* (*Chronica Polonorum*), which goes up to 1202, is of great value as a source, particularly in the part not dealt with by the chronicle of Gallus Anonymus; it has the character of a political treatise and possesses great artistic qualities.

In the 13th and 14th cc., many chronicles appeared relating the history of Poland, *e.g.* the *Chronicle of Dzierzwa*, the *Polono-Silesian Chronicle*, the *Chronicle of Great Poland*, the Chronicle of Janko of Czarnków, the *Chronicle of the Princes of Poland* and the *Chronicle of Oliwa*. The crowning activity of the chroniclers of medieval Poland was, in the 15th c., the immense work of John (Jan) *Długosz.

Bachman, *Beiträge zu Böhmens Geschichte Geschichtsquellen*, Innsbruck, 1900. – P. David, *Les Sources de Pologne à l'époque des Piasts (963-1386)*, Paris, 1934. – J. Dąbrowski, *Dawne dziejopisarstwo polskie (do roku 1480)*, Wrocław, 1964. – D. Třeštík, *Kosmas. Odkazy pokrových osobnosty naši minulosti*, Prague, 1966.

Zbigniew Piłat

**East Slavs.** Historiography is probably the field in which Christian culture bore most abundant fruit among the East *Slavs.

Among the texts translated from Greek (usually in *Bulgaria) that circulated in *Rus', we find the chronicles of John Malalas, George Hamartolos, Simeon the Logothete and others, generally recast into universal chronicles (*khronografy*). On this basis, from the 11th c., developed an original historiography. It is preserved in late compilations (the two earliest manuscripts date from the 14th c.), the *letopisi* (sing. *letopis'*, literally "*annals", though the usual translation is "chronicle"). They usually bear fortuitous titles, reflecting more the history of the manuscript than its content. Philological and historical analysis of these texts allows us to make out several *svody*, earlier compilations that we can manage, well or badly, to identify and date. For example, the first Russian historiographical work, the Narrative of Bygone Years (*Povest' vremennykh let*), known as the *Russian Primary Chronicle*, forms the beginning of numerous *letopisi*, of which the Chronicle of the monk Lawrence (*Lavrent'evskaia letopis'*), that of the monastery of St Hypathius at Kostroma (*Ipat'evskaia letopis'*) and that of Radziwiłł (illuminated) give the earliest versions. The different *svody* were often written by churchmen, sometimes in monasteries, but nearly always commissioned by political or religious authorities, which affects their exposition of the facts. The Narrative of Bygone Years, with its grandiose vision of the history of Rus' placed in the context of salvation-history, is an undoubted masterpiece, due perhaps to the monk *Nestor who, according to the Paterikon of the *Caves, devoted himself to historiography, or to Abbot Silvester of Vydubicki who recast the work early in the 12th century.

Unfortunately, the horizon later contracted and many chronicles are often no more than rather dry princely deeds, though with some exceptions: the chronicles of *Novgorod or of *Pskov describe meteorological phenomena, natural calamities, social movements, etc. The abundance of materials from the second half of the 15th c. allows interesting comparisons between the versions emanating from the court of *Moscow, the metropolitan see or the political centres then disappearing (*e.g.* Tver') or that of an independent compilation written by the monks of St Cyril at *Beloozero. In the 15th c., all this material was recast in the huge historical encyclopedias of the Muscovite State.

I. Sorlin, *TMCB*, 5, 1973, 385-408. – H. J. Grabmüller, *JGO*, 24, 1973, 394-416; *ibid.*, 25, 1977, 66-90. – Papers by D. Bulanin, J. Luria, V. Vodoff in *Histoire de la littérature russe, des origines aux Lumières*, Paris, 1992.

Vladimir Vodoff

**CHRYSOBULL.** The imperial chancery of *Constantinople, then of *Nicaea and *Trebizond, gave the name "chrysobull" to various types of documents bearing the emperor's golden *bull. The most solemn was the *logos* chrysobull, normal form of treaties and important privileges. The earliest surviving originals date from the 11th century. The chrysobull with its many codified formal nuances was particularly representative of imperial power.

F. Dölger, J. Karayannopoulos, *Die Kaiserurkunden*, Munich, 1968. – N. Oikonomides, "La chancellerie impériale à Byzance du XIII$^{e}$ au XV$^{e}$ siècle", *REByz*, 43, 1985, 167-195.

Bernadette Martin-Hisard

**CHRYSOLORAS, MANUEL (*c.*1350-1415).** Manuel Chrysoloras, Byzantine diplomat and promoter of Hellenic culture among the first *humanists, was born at *Constantinople. Professor at *Florence from 1397 to 1400, he trained the first Hellenizing humanists. He composed a famous manual of *grammar entitled *Erotèmata*. From 1400, he devoted himself to diplomacy. As ambassador of Manuel II *Palaeologus (1391-1425), he went round the European courts to implore their help against the *Turks. In 1408, he composed a *Comparison* between Constantinople and *Rome to illustrate the unity of the two civilizations. In 1414, in the *Exhortation in the Name of the Nation*, the last part of a *treatise, he encouraged the emperor to reorganise education. He died at *Constance in 1415.

E. Gamillscheg, "Chrysoloras Manuel", *LdM*, 2, 1983, 2051-2052. – G. Dagron, "Manuel Chrysoloras: Constantinople ou Rome", *ByF*, 12, 1987, 280-288.

Sophia Mergiali

**CHUR.** Chur, undoubtedly an episcopal city from the 4th c., was governed by its *bishops until 807, then was the seat of the counts of Upper Raetia. From 831 the bishops recovered part of their rights, and in the 10th c. the privileges and immunities conceded by *Otto I formed the basis of the episcopal lordship extending over the town and the Alpine passes. In 1282 the middle class and the municipal council appeared, but the transmission of the episcopal rights to the townspeople took place only in the 15th century. The episcopal domain then retained its own administration.

The bishop of Chur was a prince of the *Empire who owed *servitium* to the king and kept his loyalty to him, particularly at the time of the *Staufen.

C. Simonett, *Geschichte der Stadt Chur*, 1, Chur, 1976.

Geneviève Bührer-Thierry

**CHURCH AND STATE.** The paired terms Church and *State designate abstract notions moulded by the evolution of the conditions of life and mental attitudes. Hence the extreme complexity of the relations between what the Middle Ages called *sacerdotium* and *imperium* or "the two *swords", comparing their respective places to those of the sun and the moon. Here we will only consider two "stages", separated by a sort of vacancy of thought, which ended in a grave crisis.

The "barbarian monarchies" had not ignored the Church, often better organised and more powerful than themselves. They had enriched it, sometimes assisted it, receiving in return the support of its *authority and sometimes thus exposing themselves to rather heavy interventions in their management of secular affairs. The Carolingian idea was one of collaboration. Did the authorities thus hope to forget their spoliations, the former confiscations of Church lands by *Charles Martel (714-741)? There were many others.

Following the example of the biblical kings (Saul, *David), *Pippin had himself consecrated, first by his *bishops, then with his sons by Pope *Stephen II when the latter came to Gaul (754). The new dynasty was thus put under *God's protection and in His service. Next year, appealed to by the pontiff, Pippin crossed over to *Italy, delivered the papacy from the *Lombard peril and established its first elements of *temporal power by laying the basis of the *Patrimony of St Peter. *Charlemagne strengthened the alliance, showing himself generous to the Church. The collaboration was not without dangers. The emperor, "God's elect", wanted to rule his Church. He intervened in trinitarian *theology and, in 809, had the **Filioque* inserted into the **Credo*, after having imprudently taken sides in the *iconoclast quarrel. Assemblies of "magnates", in which bishops figured, mingled political problems with ecclesiastical discipline, as attested by the *capitularies. Charles's strong personality maintained the balance. Under his successor, *Louis the Pious (814-840), Pope Gregory IV intervened in family disputes over power, since for him "the government of souls, which belongs to the pontiff, is more important than temporal government, which belongs to the emperor" (833). The episcopate controlled power and soon disposed of it. *Archbishops such as *Agobard of Lyon and *Ebbo of Reims reminded them that a king who betrayed his charge was nothing but a *tyrant and should be deposed. There followed Louis's humiliation at Saint-Médard in Soissons and his condemnation to perpetual penance (833). There was now a duality of powers, with the balance in favour of the Church. The collaboration was short-lived, though it left a more fortunate mark on teaching and the arts. The *Carolingian family kept some semblance of power until 987, but the death of *Charles the Bald (877) marked the end of its real power and the support it could represent for the papacy.

For nearly two centuries (up to the second half of the 11th c.), we can hardly speak of relations between Church and State, or of a doctrine of such a thing. If there was no longer any State worthy of the name, the Church too was going through a difficult time, with an often weakened papacy and mediocre episcopates. But the memory of the Carolingian Empire was revived in a **Renovatio imperii* by *Otto I, crowned emperor at *Rome in 962 by John XII. The Roman synod that met on that occasion decided to concern itself "with the state and government of all *Christendom". That of 981 condemned *simony "throughout the world". Was the alliance of Church and Empire for the government of the world being reborn? It was very imperfect. In fact, with the three Ottos (962-1002) and their successors, the emperor dominated the Church. This was the time of the "Imperial Church" (*Reichskirche*). St *Henry II (1002-1024) watched over this Church (earning him his *canonization in 1146), while his son *Henry III (1039-1056) deposed three *popes and chose five.

The *Gregorian reform, the restoration of Roman *authority and, on the other side, the consolidation of the monarchies made dialogue between Church and State once more possible and necessary, but often difficult. We can trace its vicissitudes throughout Christian Europe. Opposed to monarchs anxious for their independence and sovereignty stood a restored and hierarchized Church, led by a papacy sure of its rights and determined to have them respected. There was no lack of crises: in the *Empire, the *excommunication of *Henry IV and *Canossa (1077), that of *Otto IV (1210), the long conflict between *Frederick Barbarossa and Rome, which led him to oppose an *antipope to *Alexander III (1059), the deposition of *Frederick II at the council of *Lyon (1245), the conflict with Louis of Bavaria (1314-1346) and his excommunication by *John XXII. In *England, the conflict with *Thomas Becket, archbishop of *Canterbury (1170), the revolt of King *John against *Innocent III, the regulation of relations between the two powers by the Constitutions of *Clarendon (1164). In France, the "matrimonial crises" with *Philip I and *Philip Augustus, the conflict between *Boniface VIII and *Philip the Fair, and a multitude of less spectacular difficulties with the papacy and the episcopate. On the other hand, the Church could count on supporters and the "vassal" kingdoms of the Holy See, which paid it tribute. But as *Gregory VII made clear in a letter to King Géza of *Hungary, "they are not subjects, as if they were slaves; they are sons". Aroused by these crises and nourishing them, contrary theories developed (Gregory VII, 1095), claiming that the pope could depose the emperor and release his subjects from their loyalty. Early in the 12th c., by contrast, Hugh of Fleury claimed the divine origin of royal power and denied the pope the faculty of deposing *kings. At about the same time, St *Bernard accorded the pope the "two swords", but forbade him to use the temporal sword, Christ having told Peter to "put the sword back in its scabbard".

In the middle of the century, Gratian's **Decretum* avoided engaging in the doctrinal debate of the two powers. He preferred to deal with more concrete questions, in particular the use of the temporal sword by the Empire. For him, there existed a triple dualism: that of law (natural law and customary law), that of *laity and clergy, that of the *auctoritas* of pontiffs and the *potestas* of kings.

From the 1160s to the mid 13th c., the *canonists envisaged relations between what they called *sacerdotium* and *regnum*. The *Decretum* did not offer them a compulsory model, but gave the essential texts, from Gelasius to Gregory VII, and history showed them the acuteness of the problem. Early in the 13th c., three *Decretals of Innocent III (*Per venerabilem*, *Novit*, *Venerabilem*) invited them to put Roman authority in first place. There was no overall theoretical exposition in their writings, only *glosses or passages from their **summae*. On essential points, their opinions often differed.

Their analyses rested on a certain conception of power, that of the pope and those of the princes. The former came from *God, whose *vicar the pope was. He availed himself of the "*Tu es Petrus*". The Roman pontiffs were *Peter's successors. For princes, things were more complex. For Simon of Bisignano (*c.*1177-1179), the power of kings was "attributed" by *election; the *consecration given by the pontiff "confirmed" it. Was this putting it "below" the pontifical power? Or, as *Marsilius of Padua would do in the 14th c., asserting its independence from religious authority? The analysis was pushed further with *Huguccio, followed twenty years later by *Lawrence of Spain. All power comes from God (*omnis potestas a Deo*), that of the emperor as well as that of the pope. But the former exercises it *in temporalibus*, the latter *in spiritualibus*. This is what the vocabulary of the time calls *jurisdictio divisa*, a notion in frequent use among the 13th-c. *canonists (*Hostiensis), but ignored by theologians. It appears again in the 14th c., in the writings of the Bonifacian quarrel (John of Paris [*Jean Quidort]). By the fact of this common origin of their powers, the pope cannot claim to be "greater than the emperor". For Lawrence, a chronological argument confirms this deduction: "There were emperors before there were popes." The two swords are not identical and do not have the same use. By reason of its spiritual character, the pope's sword can intervene indirectly in temporal matters. But, in the temporal, the pope is not *iudex*, except in a subsidiary way, in case of negligence or vacancy of the secular power. Alan (*c.*1210) is moderate: the pope has the two swords, because "there is only one head". But he cannot "keep the temporal sword for himself" (Christ said to Peter: "put the sword back in the scabbard"). He leaves it to the prince, who thus holds it from him, but it is not at his disposal.

There remained jurisdiction, the right for the pope to depose the emperor, to release his subjects from their loyalty. Before *Innocent IV replied affirmatively to this question by deposing *Frederick II (1245), the point was debated between the canonists. In favour of this right, Rufinus and some others availed themselves of a passage from Gregory VII's letter to *Hermann of Metz (1081), recalling that Pope *Zacharias had deposed Chilperic, the last *Merovingian king. The text was taken up into Gratian's **Decretum*. The *Decretists took possession of it. In the mid 13th c., following the writings and acts of Innocent III and Innocent IV, theocratic doctrines progressed. Hostensius, while distinguishing the two jurisdictions, firmly defended the superiority of the pope, without limiting it to *ratio peccati* (reason of *sin).

Among theologians, the major contributions were those of St *Thomas Aquinas († 1274) and *Albert the Great († 1280). The former's *De regimine principum* (finished by his disciple *Ptolemy of Lucca) proposed a middle position. The two powers come from God, but the spiritual end is the higher. The two spheres must remain distinct and their competences respected: "In questions that concern the civil good, we must obey the secular rather than the spiritual power." The former, for all that, is inferior to the latter. It is subject to it *ratione peccati* (by reason of sin). The unworthy king can be deposed by it.

The Bonifacian quarrel gave occasion for the opposing theses to be asserted loudly. The Romanists engaged in the debate. By a subtle analysis, Cino da Pistoia († 1336) sought a compromise: "*Imperium a Deo, Imperator a populo* (The Empire comes from God, the emperor from the people)". *Marsilius of Padua and William of *Ockham insisted on the independence of the *kingdoms, preparing new times, while the canonists defended the omnipotence of a papacy that was no longer able to get it respected.

S. Mochi Onory, *Fonti canonistiche dell'idea moderna dello Stato*, Milan, 1951. – M. Maccarrone, *Papato e impero dall'elezione di Federico I alla morte di Adriano IV, 1152-1159*, Rome, 1961. – Y.-M. Congar, "L'Église et l'État sous le règne de saint Louis", *Actes du Colloque du 7e centenaire de saint Louis, 1970*, Paris, 1976, 257-271; reprinted in *Droit ancien et structures ecclésiastiques*, London, 1982. – Y.-M. Congar, "Orientations de Bonaventure et surtout de Thomas d'Aquin dans leur vision de l'Église et celle de l'État", *1274 Année charnière: mutation et continuités*, Paris, 1977, 691-711 ("Colloques internationaux du CNRS", 558). – P. G. Caron, *Corso di storia dei rapporti fra Stato e Chiesa*, 1, Milan, 1981. – M. Maccarrone, "La Papauté et Philippe Auguste. La décrétale 'Novit ille'", *Philippe Auguste*, Paris, 1982, 385-408 ("Colloques internationaux du CNRS", 602). – H. Bielefeld, "Von der Päpstlichen Universalheerschaft zur autonomen Bürgerrepublik", *ZSRG.K*, 73, 1987, 70-130. – H. Vidal, "Aspects montpelliérains de la Bulle 'Per venerabilem'", *Recueil de Mémoires et travaux publié par la Société d'Histoire du droit des aanciens pays de droit écrit*, 15, Paris, 1991, 49-65.

Jean Gaudemet

**CHURCH AND SYNAGOGUE.** On either side of the crucifixion, medieval image-makers loved to set, to the right a woman with *crown and *nimbus, brandishing the standard of victory and collecting *Christ's blood in a *chalice, and to the left another woman turning away, eyes bandaged, standard broken, crown falling. These are allegories of the Church, born at Christ's death and destined to perpetuate his sacrifice in the *Eucharist, and the Synagogue which, refusing to acknowledge Christ as the expected Messiah, lost its precedence. This scheme finds its literary source in the rhetorical dialogues called *Altercatio Ecclesiae contra Synagogam*, a genre that flourished all through the Middle Ages, in particular from the pen of *Isidore of Seville, to oppose the Jewish and Christian arguments.

The earliest medieval *images appear in *Carolingian times: in the **Sacramentary* of Drogo, a woman with a nimbus elevates a chalice while, to the left of the crucified, an old man symbolizes the Old Law. The constraints of symmetry rapidly generalized the contrast of two female allegories, one on each side of Christ, expressing the medieval taste for antitheses. The iconographical formula had many variants, according as the wish was to multiply the signs of the Synagogue's fall from grace (a serpent blinds her, elsewhere she is mounted on the ass of obstinacy, lets fall the broken Tables of the Law, or is trampled under foot) or to show on the contrary, but this is more rare, how the coming of Christ leads her out of night. Sometimes the axis of their antithesis is not the crucifixion, and we see Christ enthroned crowning the Church and dismissing the Synagogue. Finally the allegorization of the two figures can borrow more indirect renderings, that of the live and the dead *tree, or be accompanied by the combat of the *vices and virtues.

With some rare theologians, *Suger, in a *stained glass window of *Saint-Denis, distinguished himself by putting into images the Pauline doctrine of the unveiling of the Synagogue: the Incarnation allows the *Jews to contemplate the *mysteries previously hidden. Thus antisemitic hostility can be replaced by demonstration of the harmony of the two *Testaments, represented by the Gospel in the

*Church and Synagogue.* Miniature from the *Lambeth Bible.* London, Lambeth Palace Library (Ms 3, fol. 307).

hands of the Church and the phylactery of the Old Law in the hands of the Synagogue, and the Synagogue, unveiled, can allow itself to be led by the *prophets towards the plenary *revelation of the latter times. But from the 13th c. their evolution reveals a hardening of the images, in part influenced by the *crusades, and confirmed by the measures of exclusion taken against the Jewish communities.

W. Seiferth, *Synagoge und Kirche im Mittelalter*, Munich, 1964. – B. Blumenkranz, "Géographie historique d'un thème de l'iconographie religieuse: les représentations de Synagoga en France", *Mélanges R. Crozet*, 2, Poitiers, 1966, 1141-1157. – W. Greisenegger, "Ecclesia und Synagoga", *LCI*, 1, 1968, 570-578.

Colette Deremble

**CHURCHING.** This term designates a religious ceremony solemnly marking the return of a woman to the Church after childbirth. Its origins go back to Lev 12, 2-7, which forbade young mothers all contact with the sacred after their confinement and imposed on them a ceremony of purification and expiation. In the Middle Ages, *clerics wondered about the *validity of this prescription. *Gregory the Great, the first to pronounce, then Herard of Tours and *Nicholas I no longer accorded it any value. However, certain *Penitentials still condemned women who did not respect the old law. Not until *Innocent III was the statute of women in childbed definitively fixed in the canons: ritually pure, she could nonetheless, out of devotion, deny herself access to the holy places: but no ceremony was necessary after this privation.

In the lay mentality, however, churching seemed indispensable and all *women, without social distinction, submitted to it. In the course of the later Middle Ages, some Penitentials prolonged, in accordance with Leviticus, the duration of purification for the birth of a daughter, but from the 13th c. the delay became the same for both sexes. Generally, the Church fixed it at forty days, but in practice women shortened it, since, following lay custom, they could not take up their customary occupations before their churching. The *parish was the unit responsible for the ceremony. The *parish priest thus assured himself that the young mother was guilty neither of concubinage nor of *incest, nor of other crimes which would prevent the ceremony. The rite followed essentially two liturgical forms: according to the region concerned, the mother submitted to "purification" (France, England) or to "introduction" (Empire). To both, the woman came with a candle in her hand. Purification took place after *mass, which the mother attended apart from the congregation: after the final reading of the Prologue to John's Gospel, the priest offered her some *blessed bread (she was formally forbidden to communicate unless she had confessed beforehand), sprinkled her with holy *water, then she rejoined the rest of the congregation. Introduction took place at the church door: received by the officiating priest who recited *psalms and *prayers, the woman was sprinkled with holy water, then invited to enter the church holding the stole or the hand of the priest, who recited more prayers.

Although, from the mid 16th c., churching was conceived as a blessing and a thanksgiving, the medieval liturgy remained impressed with purificatory symbols and rites of reinstatement, as if the woman, by her lying-in, had been excluded from the Christian community.

A. Franz, *Die kirchlichen Benediktionen im Mittelalter*, Fribourg, 1909. – W. von Arx, "La Bénédiction de la mère après la naissance, histoire et signification", *Conc (F)*, 132, 1978.

Emmanuelle Caillier

**CHURCHWARDEN.** The term *matricula* meant a "list" or "register". Later, *matricularius* was used to designate the servant of a church, a cleric or layman doing the duties of a modern sacristan, and was sometimes applied to the administrators of vestry funds. But originally the *matricularius* had his name transcribed on a list, either that of the *clerics attached to a church, or more frequently the **matricula* of the poor receiving their subsistence from a religious establishment (parish or monastic church).

From the Carolingian period, a change took place: *matricularii* were no longer the poor, but auxiliaries of the clergy employed in the service of the sanctuary, concerning themselves with the *sacristy and the upkeep of the buildings (**fabrica*). Then *matricularii* gave way to churchwardens, and the documents show with relative precision what their duties were. The churchwarden rang the *bells, guarded the church, was responsible for the upkeep of the sacred *vessels and liturgical *vestments. If he was a cleric, he was allowed to serve at the *altar, even to perform the reading of the epistle at *mass. The office involved resources, sometimes substantial ones, constituting a *benefice. Because he was concerned with the buildings, the churchwarden was sometimes chosen to manage the *fabrica*. Finally, the duties of churchwarden seem to be confused with those of the beneficed cleric, guardian of the church in certain *dioceses, the *costarius*.

P. Adam, *La vie paroissiale en France au XIVe siècle*, Paris, 1964, 80-86. – M. Rouche, "Le matricule des pauvres. Évolution d'une institution de charité du Bas-Empire jusqu'à la fin du Haut Moyen Âge", *Études sur l'histoire de la pauvreté (Moyen Âge-XIVe siècle)*, Paris, 1974, 83-110. – B. A. Kumin, *The Shaping of a community: the rise and reformation of the English parish, c.1400-1560*, Aldershot, 1996.

Joseph Avril

**CIBORIUM.** Vessel in which the consecrated hosts are kept. The word is derived from the Latin *ciborium*, a term designating the *aedicula* or baldachin placed above the *altar. This word itself comes from the Greek *chiborium*, with a dual meaning of *aedicula* and drinking goblet.

It seems to have been in the Carolingian period, around the mid 9th c., that the custom appeared of putting the eucharistic *reservation on or above the high altar: from then on, it was frequently hung from the baldachin (*ciborium*) sheltering the altar, as numerous descriptions or illuminated depictions attest. The object was then usually in the form of a covered cup, but it remained generally designated either by a very general name (*custodia*, *pyxis*, *capsa*, *capsella*, *vas*, *cuppa*) or by a term indicating its form: "tower" (*turris*), "dove" (*columba*), "ship". The terms "*tabernacle" (*tabernaculum*) and "ark" (*arca*) were reserved for *aediculae* placed above the altar.

One of the characteristics of medieval eucharistic reservation was hence the variety of forms and dimensions it could have. If today the term "ciborium" is reserved for a definite type, of dimensions sufficiently important to receive quite a large number of hosts, with two hemispheres linked by a hinge and resting on a base, it does not seem to have been the same in the Middle Ages. When we meet it, the word can in fact designate objects with no base or hanging above the altar.

As with *chalices, the conciliar canons and liturgical texts frequently mention the materials that can be used to make eucharistic reservations. These are in the first place precious materials, *gold, silver, *ivory, rock crystal, but also copper and *enamelled copper – "Limoges work" is sometimes specifically mentioned –, *glass, tin, wood.

C. Rohault de Fleury, "Ciboires", *La Messe. Études archéologiques sur ses monuments*, 5, Paris, 1888, 57 f. – J. Foucart-Borville, "Les tabernacles eucharistiques dans la France du Moyen Âge", *BM*, 148, 4, 1990, 348-381.

Élisabeth Taburet-Delahaye

**CID, THE (1043-1099).** Born into a family of the higher *nobility, Rodgrigo Diaz de Vivar, the Cid, was educated with Sancho II, future king of *Castile, who made him his *alférez* (leader of the army). In Jan 1072, at Golpejera, he defeated *Alfonso VI of *León, who thus lost the war against his brother Sancho II. Some months later, the king of Castile was assassinated at Zamora; Alfonso VI, suspected of having ordered the crime, inherited the *crown, becoming king of Castile and León. Rodrigo Diaz then imposed on him the humiliating *oath of purgation. But the new king could not dispense with his services: he sent him to levy tribute on the *emir of *Seville whom he defended in his war against *Granada.

Castle of Vagha, Cilicia, 11th-12th c.

On his return to Castile he fell into disgrace: Alfonso VI exiled him in 1081. Departing with his followers, he entered the service of al-Mu'tamim of *Saragossa: in 1082, he took prisoner Raymond Berenguer II, count of *Barcelona; two years later, he defeated Sancho Ramirez, king of *Navarre. In 1097 Alfonso VI, whose kingdom was threatened by the *Almoravids, recalled him. This reconciliation was most precarious: a second banishment forced Rodrigo, whose lands were expropriated by the king, towards *Valencia. He took the castle of Polop from the emir of Lérida, from where he held to ransom the petty *Saracen kings of the Levant. The count of Barcelona, who saw with displeasure this diversion of Muslim tribute, raised an army against him: he was beaten again at Tévar in 1090 and renounced his interests in the region. The Cid defended Alcadir, emir of Valencia, from Almoravid attacks. But in 1093 his protégé was assassinated during a revolt of the Valencians; Rodrigo laid siege to the town, which he took next year. With the help of *Peter I of Aragon, he stopped the Berber advance at the battles of Cuarte (1094) and Bairén (1097). After putting down the rebellions of the Muslims of Valencia, he favoured the Christians, turning the *mosque into a *cathedral; at his elbow the new *bishop, Jerome of Périgord, propounded the crusading spirit to counterbalance the **jihād* preached by the Almoravids. *Toleration in relations between Christians and Muslims, once allies against their own co-religionists, disappeared. In 1098 the Cid married his daughters to the king of Navarre and the count of Barcelona. He died next year. Despite the help brought by Alfonso VI, his widow Ximena was unable to hold Valencia, which fell under Almoravid rule in 1102. Rodrigo, called *Sayyid* or *Sid* ("lord") by his Arab allies, is hardly the incarnation of the swashbuckling hero, loyal defender of *Christendom, vulgarized by his fine **chanson de geste*, written down in 1207; still less does he represent the romantic spokesman of a great unitary *Spain. He was primarily the frontier adventurer, strong in his military skill and his following of young bachelors, leading an errant life in the service of the highest bidder.

M. D'Epalza, S. Guellouz, *Le Cid, Personnage historique et littéraire*, Paris, 1983. – D. Nicolle, *El Cid and the Reconquista: warfare in medieval Spain, 1050-1492*, London, 1988.

Martin Aurell

**CILICIA.** Situated at the north-east extremity of the Mediterranean, Cilicia is separated from *Syria by the Amanus to the east, and from Anatolia by the Taurus to the north. The eastern part is a triangular plain watered by three rivers, flowing past the three historic cities: Misis (alias Mopsuestia), Adana and Tarsus,

*The Virgin in Majesty with angels and four prophets, c.*1280-1285, by Cimabue. Florence, Uffizi.

St *Paul's city, while the West is a compact mountainous massif. Christian Cilicia was dependent on the *patriarchate of *Antioch.

From the middle of the 7th c., the expansion of *Islam made Cilicia a buffer zone between Arabic Syria and Byzantine Anatolia, constantly ravaged by military expeditions. Gradually, the frontier between the two empires stabilized along the river Lamos, which cuts Cilicia in two and on which prisoners were exchanged. The Cilician plain thus passed under Arab control and Caliph Mamūn, who died in the Taurus in 833, was buried at Tarsus. To defend its eastern frontier, Byzantium was happy to use its Armenian generals, thus creating a *de facto* demographic state around Cilicia. From 868 to 905, the region was included in the domains of the Tūlūnids, a Turkish dynasty of Egypt. But the 10th c. would mark the Byzantine reawakening, the "*Macedonian dynasty" possessing exceptional generals, often Armenians like John Tzimisces and Mleh. Under Nicephorus Phocas, Cilicia became Byzantine once more (965), as did Antioch. These successes were soon compromised, in the 11th c., by Turkish penetration: Byzantium lost the whole interior of Anatolia, and had no more than a theoretical power over Cilicia where Armenian dynasts came to the fore, often having emigrated from the destruction of their States.

The arrival of the first *crusade at the end of the century added a new element: during the 12th c., Cilicia was disputed between Byzantium (its official suzerain), the Norman princes of Antioch, the *Seljuk sultans of Anatolia, Syrian *emirs and local Armenian lords. Gradually, the Armenian dynasty of the Rupenids prevailed, and one of its barons managed in 1198 to get the German *Empire to grant him a royal crown: Lewon I imposed his authority by adopting Frankish customs and legislation, creating a Western-type feudal State. During the 13th c., this kingdom would play a key role in the Near East. Lewon's son-in-law and successor, Het'um I, successfully played the card of the *Mongol alliance, continued by his son Lewon II. This golden age was reflected in several spheres: artistic, with its marvellous Cilician illuminations, architectural, through impressive fortresses, and commercial, the *port of Ayas (or Lajazzo) becoming a hub of east-west exchanges.

After Lewon II (1289) began the decline, marked by a dialogue of the deaf with the Avignon papacy, intransigent in its demands for religious submission. In 1375, the Egyptian *Mamluks took the capital, Sis, leading the last king, Leo V de *Lusignan, into captivity. Cilicia then went through 150 years of anarchy under various Turkoman tribes, until its incorporation into the *Ottoman Empire early in the 16th century.

E. Alfoldi-Rosenbaum, *A Survey of Coastal Cities in Western Cilicia*, Ankara, 1967. – S. Der Nersessian, "The Kingdom of Cilician Armenia", *A History of the Crusades*, K. H. Setton (ed.), Madison, 1969, 2, 630-659. – T. Boase, *The Cilician Kingdom of Armenia*, Edinburgh, 1978. – C. Mutafian, *La Cilicie au carrefour des empires*, Paris, 1988. – H. Hellenkemper, F. Hild, *Kilikien und Isaurien*, Vienna, 1990. – C. Mutafian, *Le royaume arménien de Cilicie*, Paris, 1993.

Claude Mutafian

**CIMABUE (died *c.*1302).** Cenni di Pepo, called Cimabue, is documented from 1272 to 1302. In canto XI of the *Purgatorio*, *Dante writes of him (vv. 94-96): "He had thought to hold the field, and now Giotto is the favourite". Vasari opened his series of *Lives* with him: "Cimabue was in a way the initial cause of the renewal of painting." There is little documentary evidence of his life and work: he is mentioned at *Rome in 1272; in 1301-1302 he received payments at *Pisa for the mosaic of *St John* in the cathedral apse and a *Maestà* at the hospital of Santa Chiara. He must have died soon after.

His work departs from Byzantine ways of painting, without wholly breaking with them. We see this, *e.g.*, in the evolution of his great painted wooden crucifixes: that of Arezzo (*c.*1265-1268), strongly expressive, that of Santa Croce (*c.*1272) at *Florence, of a new sensibility, or those of his last years. Likewise, he gives proof in the Santa Trinità *Maestà* (*c.*1285-1286; now in the Uffizi, Florence) of a new intensity of expression, a new sense of space, of bodily volumes. His participation in the *fresco decoration of the basilica of San Francesco at *Assisi is very important: between 1277 and 1280, he did the painted Crucifixion in the north arm of the transept of the upper church, as well as the four *evangelists on the vault: on this occasion, he undoubtedly directed the first Italian "team" working on the Franciscan building. Among his other works are the painted fresco in the lower church of the Assisi basilica (a *Virgin with angels and St Francis*), the *St Francis* he painted for Santa Maria degli Angeli at Florence, The Bologna

*Maestà* (church of the *Servites of Mary) and that of the church of San Francesco at Pisa (now in the Louvre). His *St Francis* at Florence broke with the late Byzantine clichés of earlier masters and influenced *Giotto.

J. Strzygowski, *Cimabue und Rome. Funde und Forschungen zur Kunstgeschichte und Topographie der Stadt Rom*, Vienna, 1888. – E. Sindona, *L'Opera completa di Cimabue e il momento figurativo pregiottesco*, Milan, 1975. – L.-C. Marquès, *La Peinture du Duecento en Italie centrale*, Paris, 1987. – R. Gibbs, "Cimabue", *DoA*, 7, 314-319. – L. Bellasi, *Cimabue*, Paris, 1998 (Fr. tr.).

Daniel Russo

**CIOMPI, UPRISING OF THE.** The best known of the urban *revolts of the late Middle Ages broke out in *Florence in 1378 and was so called from the name assigned to its main protagonists, the *ciompi* or wool-carders, the less qualified paid workers of the woollen industry. While recognising the weight of circumstantial factors such as the difficulties created in the city by the divisions among the *Guelf oligarchy and the protraction of the war with the *pope, the most recent historiography has tended to link the uprising with structural characteristics of Florentine society such as the great polarization of *wealth, the iniquity of the fiscal system, the harshness of the corporative legal institutions, and the political, social and even urbanistic marginalization of the citizen population. The textile workers had supported the artisans of the lesser *corporations in the revolt that broke out in June against the dominance of the "popolo grasso". In July, they decisively accelerated the struggle against the merchant *bankers in power by coming out armed into the streets and besieging the palaces of the *Podestà and the Priors. They managed to impose the formation of a friendly government presided over by the carder Michele di Lando and the creation, in favour of the workers without rights, of the new Arts of Woolcarders, Dyers and Doublet-makers. This "revolutionary" experiment lasted only six weeks, during which the grave economic sitatuation, partly due to the blocking of wool production by the proprietors of the workshops and the radicalization of the insurgents' programme, led to their progressive isolation. Di Lando himself abandoned his old companions. The extreme reponse of the Ciompi, at the end of August, was a new insurrection, which was drowned in blood through the intervention of groups of wool-workers, butchers and tavern-keepers. Then began the executions and espulsions of the leaders of the revolt, while most of the gains they had made – first of all the creation of the Art of Woolcarders – were annulled.

P. Wolff, M. Mollat, *Ongles bleu, Jacques et Ciompi*, Paris, 1970. – *Il Tumulto dei Ciompi. Un momento di storia fiorentina ed europea*, Florence, 1981. – A. Stella, *La révolte des Ciompi. Les hommes, les lieux, le travail*, Paris, 1993.

Franco Franceschi

**CIRCUMCISION.** The excision of the foreskin is a custom widespread in the Semitic world and elsewhere; it signifies membership of the community and is considered a rite of integration into it. Among the Jews, circumcision took place on the eighth day and was the physical sign of the alliance with God, entry into the life of the people of the covenant, depositary of the promises. Jesus was circumcised on the eighth day and received his name on that day, as we see in Luke's infancy gospel.

1 Jan, feast of the Circumcision, which came eight days after Christmas, was the Roman feast of the new year; the principle was

Representation of the Trinity in the *Commentary on the Sentences of Peter Lombard*. Brussels, Royal Library (Ms 470, p. 4).

to begin the year well and hence to make it a day of rejoicing, which impressed its mark on the following months. It was necessary to dispense lavishly, give lavishly, eat lavishly; it was a sort of *carnival. At Rome, in certain Christian circles, 1 Jan was made a day of penitence, in reaction to the disorders involved in the pagan festivities in honour of Janus *bifrons*.

But the Christianization of the *feast does not predate the mid 7th c.; a *mass at Santa Maria dei Martiri (the old Pantheon) celebrated the octave of Christmas. In Gaul, in the 8th c., 1 Jan was turned into a Marian feast. Subsequently, numerous new year customs (*guilanée*, forcible *collections, etc.) passed into Christian folklore or were tolerated by the Church, without being assumed by it, but it often had to intervene to regulate them.

G. Frenaud, "Le culte de Notre Dame dans l'ancienne liturgie latine", *Maria*, 6, 1961, 157-211. – C. A. Miles, *Christmas Customs and Traditions, their History and Significance*, New York, 1976. – J. M. Guilmard, "Une antique fête mariale au 1er janvier dans la ville de Rome?", *EO*, 11, 1994, 25-67.

Guy-Marie Oury

**CIRCUMINSESSION.** The Greek concept of *perichoresis* (found in Gregory Nazianzen, then in *John of Damascus) was first translated into Latin by *circumincessio* (*Bonaventure) and then, in the 12th c., by *circuminsessio* (*Thomas Aquinas), and sometimes by *circumpermeatio*, these different terms introducing more static or more dynamic nuances to describe the mutual indwelling of the three *persons of the *Trinity ("The Father is in me, and I in him": Jn 10, 38 and 14, 10-11) from the fact of their consubstantiality and their relations of origin (Nicaea, 325, and Chalcedon, 451). Put differently, the eternal *Word which is "in the bosom of the Father" (Jn 1, 18) does not "leave" it by becoming the Word incarnate in *time: "In *God alone is specifically and

*Monks cutting wood.* Decorated letter Q. Miniature from Gregory the Great's *Moralia in Job* from the abbey of Cîteaux, 12th c. Dijon, Municipal Library (Ms 170, fol. 59).

perfectly realized a unity of essence with distinction of Persons" (Bonaventure). Attested very early in tradition (Irenaeus, *Adversus haereses*, III, 6, 2), called in question by various heresiarchs in Antiquity, this property was explored by the learned *theology of the central Middle Ages, notably by *scholasticism (Thomas Aquinas, *Summa theologiae*, I$^{a}$, q. 42, a. 5: the Son is in the Father, and *vice versa*, by essence, by relation and by origin; the same goes for the *Holy Spirit, who is in the Father and in the Son, and *vice versa*), and continued to function as a rampart against *tritheism and modalism. The visualization of this property absent from creatures gave rise, in Western medieval art, to curious anthropomorphic figures (persons covered by a single cloak, more or less entwined in each other, like twins or Siamese twins, with three heads), many of which would be condemned by the Church at the Renaissance.

A. Deneffe, "Perichoresis, Circumincessio, Circuminsessio", *ZKTh*, 47, 1923, 491-532. – L. Prestige, "Périchoréô and Périchôrèsis in the Fathers", *JThS*, 29, 1928, 242-252. – L. Prestige, *God in Patristic Thought*, London, 1977. – F. Boespflug, Y. Zaluska, "Le Dogme trinitaire et l'essor de son iconographie en Occident, de l'époque carolingienne au concile de Latran IV (1215)", *CCM*, 4, 1994, 181-240.

François Boespflug

**CISTERCIANS, CÎTEAUX.** Founded on 21 March 1098 as a result of conflicts between two parties in the abbey of *Molesmes over the obervance of the *Rule of St *Benedict, the New Monastery (a name kept until 1119) was to have unforeseeable influence thanks to the entry in 1113 of the knight Bernard of Fontaine (St *Bernard) and his companions.

Originally some monks of Molesmes, wishing to observe the Rule of St Benedict in its purity, in contrast to the customs that had been imposed on them, sought to live more harmoniously in *prayer, manual *labour and reading. They were thus part of the general current of "return to the sources" in every sphere that went through monastic life: simplicity of dress, possessions and liturgical ornamentation. In 1100, Pope *Paschal II accorded them his protection and the privilege of not depending on any authority but his own. In doing so, the pontiff exhorted them to introduce no modification into their rule of life and to keep far from the world in a life of holy austerity. The first statutes stressed this point, as well as the rejection of revenues tied to the possession of churches with curial rights (oblations, mortuaries) or the possession of seignorial rights (communal ovens, *mills). The main characteristics of the *reform were handed down in the *Charter of Charity* or statutes, and in the monastic Usages (*Ecclesiastica officia, Usus conversorum*). We possess several redactions, which reveal the evolution of these documents and the currents that went through the new *order. The founders' essential concern was authenticity and rejection of all superfluity, keeping a distance from the world and obtaining the means of subsistence by *labour. This state of mind was the main factor in the choice of sites for new *foundations (on the borders of *dioceses and lordships on lands still uncleared) so as to be able to establish an estate without inconveniencing any neighbours. Disputes very soon arose with these, however. Uniformity of observance was controlled by the annual visitation of the immediate father-*abbot, and faults punished at the annual general *chapter. Other new monastic groups drew on the legislation of Cîteaux for themselves (Prémontré, Arrouaise, etc.) or were affiliated with it due to lack of recruitment (*Savigny and Obazine in 1147).

The rapid success of Cîteaux and its order was manifested particularly in the very important acquisition of *property, rights and *exemptions of all sorts obtained from *popes, *kings and lords, which aroused jealousy and conflicts. Less than 25 years after their origin, the *abbeys were engaged in the commercial expansion that the world is familiar with and there were few that did not invest in the purchase of lands or town houses, the rebuilding of their church and monastic buildings, and the establishment of a good *library, as witness certain 12th-c. catalogues that still survive. The craftsmanship took various forms, but the quality of the work was always the same, marked originally by rigorous ascetic principles that became more flexible from the 13th century. The creation of **conversi* was not, properly speaking, Cistercian, but their systematic organisation to live the religious life with a state other than monastic status was Cistercian. Many monks were chosen to be *bishops, *cardinals, *legates, even a *pope (*Eugenius III, 1145-1153). They took an active part in the Church's life, in its schismatic conflicts (against *Anacletus in 1130, for *Alexander III in 1159) and dogmatic conflicts. St Bernard distinguished himself in the struggle against heterodoxy, opposing the Henricians and Albigenses. In the 13th c., the popes readily appealed to the Cistercians particularly against the *Cathars and for the *evangelization of the lands of northern Europe. A reading of the registers of *Innocent III reveals several hundred transfers of debt addressed to abbots and monks. Sometimes they were judged too heavy and the abbot of Cîteaux applied for them to be discharged. However the order, considered a powerful and devoted auxiliary of papal policy, was the object of papal benevolence. Thus, *Innocent IV supported Stephen of Lexington, abbot of *Clairvaux, in his foundation of St Bernard's College at *Paris (1245). A serious higher education movement began from 1237. The general chapter gave its endorsement for several *clerics to live in Paris. In 1256, Guy de l'Aumône was instructed to teach them. In the following years, *colleges were founded at *Montpellier, *Toulouse and *Oxford. The general chapter even imposed the sending of one monk for every abbey of 20 monks and so on in proportion. But Clairvaux was obliged to sell the Paris college in 1321.

Within the order, the 13th c. was marked by grave conflicts of authority between Cîteaux and its first four daughters: a non-concerted deposition of the abbot of one of the four daughter houses by the abbot of Cîteaux in 1215 and the *election of the abbot of Cîteaux without the participation of the four daughters after Guy of Burgundy's election to the cardinalate (1262) obliged Pope *Clement IV to diminish the power of the four immediate abbots by the *bull *Parvus fons*. The legislation established in 1152 was revised in 1204 and promulgated in 1240 and 1256 in 15 distinctions, including one established for *nuns. Indeed this period saw numerous requests by women's monasteries to be attached to the order. Incorporated under the control of an immediate father, the nuns were to have a general chapter by country. The inclusion of houses of nuns represented such a burden on the order that in 1228 any new foundation was forbidden. Strict *enclosure being imposed in 1220, they had to be able to be materially self-sufficient. A male personnel was provided for them: a confessor, *chaplains and lay-brothers brought from a men's abbey or recruited on the spot. The sisters dedicated themselves to manual labour, the transcription of manuscripts and soon the *education of *children.

Many monasteries benefited from royal generosity, particularly that of St *Louis, who frequently exchanged letters with the general chapter of Cîteaux. Royaumont (1228) and Maubuisson where *Blanche of Castile was buried in a Cistercian habit (1253) are the best-known. The Cistercians supported the *crusades in the *Holy Land by their prayers and finances, and thus obtained a privileged position. But under *Philip the Fair and his jurists, Cîteaux was a particular target of royal repression and seizures.

The *Hundred Years' War (1337-1453) ruined numerous abbeys, and during the *Great Schism (1378-1417) there were so many abuses connected with the personal enrichment of monks holding office that in 1390 the abbot of Cîteaux received the power to reform the monasteries of both sexes in the name of the general chapter. Many abbots were invited to the councils of *Pisa, *Constance, *Basel and Ferrara-*Florence. Nevertheless, despite the efforts of one of them who had become pope (*Benedict XII, 1334-1342) to reform the order, it was a far cry from the original orientations of Cîteaux. In 1317-1318 Jacques de Thérinnes, abbot of Chaalis, described the *vows of the order addressed to *John XXII: solemn celebration of the *offices, holy reading, *meditation, strict enclosure, very frugal nourishment, sometimes manual labour. While Benedict XII strove against *nepotism in offices and honours at the heart of the order, forbidding the study of law and favouring the legations of the *mendicants at the expense of Cîteaux in order to incite Cistercian monks to live in retreat, study centres multiplied, as did the number of bachelors and *doctors in the order.

The early 15th c. saw a diminution in the number of monks and the birth of congregations that gradually distanced themselves from the order's mother abbey to the point of complete secession. The general chapter insisted on *reform of the observances and on keeping faithful to the Rule (in 1439, return to the common dormitory and insistence on rising at night). However the practice of *commendation gained ground, despite the efforts of popes and general chapters to hold back the movement and despite the attempts of Jean de Cirey, abbot of Cîteaux (1476-1501), to persuade some 40 abbots to adopt the articles of Paris recapitulating the earlier statutes establishing the obligations of the monks. The act was published at the next general chapter. After the medieval period, several reforms brought new life to this great *order.

*DHGE*, 12, 1953, 874-980. – L. Lekai, *Les Moines blancs*, Paris, 1957. – J.-B. Auberger, *L'unanimité cistercienne primitive. Mythe ou réalité?*, Achel, 1986. – *DSp*, 13, 1988, 738-814. – J. B. Lefèvre, "Histoire des institutions des abbayes cisterciennes", *Monastères bénédictins et cisterciens dans les albums de Croy*, Brussels, 1990. – *L'Architecture cistercienne*, Paris, 1995, no. 8000-8003 (CD-I).

Jean-Baptiste Auberger

**In Italy.** *Italy's first contacts with Cistercian monasticism occurred in the second decade of the 12th c., following the initiative of *Stephen Harding, abbot of Cîteaux, who – as part of the liturgical reform promoted by his predecessor *Alberic with the aim of recovering the full observance of the *Benedictine Rule – had sent some monks to *Milan to learn the authentic way of singing the Ambrosian *hymns, recommended by Benedict to his followers. But the diocese of Milan was not the first place of Cistercian settlement, perhaps because of the city's difficult situation, involved politically and militarily in the struggle against Como and Lodi and torn religiously by the internal divisions that set part of the clergy and the laity against Archbishop Grosolano. From the original stock of French foundations, the Cistercian order spread first to north-west Italy from 1120, when a monastery arose at Tiglieto in the diocese of Acqui, the first to be established outside the borders of France. In 1124 a new community was formed, again in Piedmontese territory, at Lucedio in the diocese of Vercell. In 1131, at Sestri in Ligurian territory, the Benedictine abbey of Sant'Andrea went over to the Cistercian Rule, opening a decade characterised by a great fervour of initiatives. The flowering of Cistercian abbeys in the 1130s was connected with the work done by *Bernard of Clairvaux to end the *schism between *Innocent II and the *antipope *Anacletus II, the latter supported mainly by *Roger II of Sicily. Bernard's efforts to bring the Church back under a single recognised leadership aimed at creating a climate of religious ardour around Innocent II, as well as concrete support, of which the rise of Cistercian abbeys supported by various political forces favourable to the legitimate *pope was a significant factor.

In 1134 a monastic community related to one of Cîteaux's first daughter houses, *Morimond, was established in the diocese of Milan, at Coronate near the Ticino, nearly on the border with Pavian territory. Two years later the new community was moved a short way off, to a place that took the name of Morimondo. In 1135 arose Chiaravalle della Colomba in the Piacentino, Chiaravalle Milanese (the first Italian foundation expressly willed by St Bernard), *Fossanova in southern *Latium and Staffarda near Saluzzo.

In 1139 Pope Innocent II entrusted Bruno, *abbot of Chiaravalle, with the delicate task of reforming, spiritually and temporally, a Benedictine monastery belonging to the Roman Church, San Pietro di Cerreto (in the diocese of Lodi), which thus went over to the Cistercian Rule. In 1140, a similar change affected the great abbey of *Casamari, in Frusinate, destined to become one of the most illustrious Cistercian houses. In some areas the new foundations had very intense relations with the urban world from the start (*e.g.* in the areas of Milan and *Piacenza); in others – as in south-west Piedmont – the period of origins was marked by the protection and *donations of illustrious dynasties of *counts and marquises: the counts of *Savoy, the marquises of Galuzzo, Gavi and Monferrato. In any case the Italian experience of the white monks – where rejection of the world in search of the *desert was accompanied by a strong impulse to work among the people – represented a high degree of adaptability to the different social and political situations in which the various houses developed, combining religious ardour with active participation in earthly things. Bernard's activism also opened the way to Cistercian expansion in southern Italy. Against Roger II of Sicily, supporter of the antipope Anacletus, Bernard invoked the intervention of the emperor *Lothar III; but after the failure of military operations and after the agreement concluded in 1139 between Roger and Innocent II, a rapprochement took place between Bernard and the Norman ruler, which opened the doors of the kingdom of *Sicily to the white monks. Thus the order's growth in the southern areas had an eminently political significance, rather than a religious or economic one as elsewhere, and the Cistercian foundations that followed can be considered an expression and a guarantee of the agreement reached between the Norman State and the Church.

The great leap forwards of the 1130s (a period of great development for the order in general) continued with intensity in the following decades. Between the 12th and 13th cc., nearly all the Italian Cistercian monasteries of the Middle Ages were founded: here were represented all the five lines that went back to the French mother monasteries. The majority were related to *Clairvaux, a strong nucleus to *La Ferté, fewer to Cîteaux, *Morimond and *Pontigny. Geographically, Cistercian abbeys were distributed in every area of the peninsula and in the islands. In general the *abbey complexes consisted – following the typical plan of the order – of various buildings arranged around a central *cloister and answering the many needs of the monastic communities: religious-spiritual, economic, representational. During the 12th c., the Italian foundations rapidly acquired considerable prestige both in the religious-ecclesiastical sphere and in the civil-political sphere, as witness, among others, two episodes: the task entrusted by the superior of Clairvaux to the abbots of Chiaravalle Milanese, Casamari and Fossanova in 1174 and successfully performed, to obtain Bernard's *canonization (after the order's first request had been rejected by Pope *Alexander III in 1163); and the presence of the abbot of Chiaravalle Milanese, the only non-member of the college of *cardinals, in the papal delegation that in 1153 took part in the negotiations of *Constance that specified the respective obligations of the *pope and the emperor in view of *Frederick I's first Italian expedition.

The prestige and the spiritual concerns that animated the communities of reformed *monasticism attracted large donations from laymen and churchmen, who contributed to making those foundations not just centres of *spirituality, but dynamic nuclei of economic activity, in various directions from *agriculture to *animal husbandry, craftsmanship and *commerce. In addition to donations, shrewd plans of acquisition contributed to forming large landed *patrimonies, into which were introduced rational models of organisation of labour (an orientation confirmed by the fact that, where it was not possible to acquire, the Cistercians sought to lease the lands bordering on their possessions under long-term contracts, so as to extend their own control over large continuous extents of land).

As in other European regions characterised by settlements of ancient origin, the Cistercian *granges tended to arise where a *village (which the monks reorganised in the form of a grange) or a farm already existed, though there were also cases of villages created *ex novo*. In any case, Cistercian intervention tended to profoundly renew models of settlement, modify property relations and their relative legal forms, rationalize the use of the land and the collection of the rights weighing on it and augment the productivity of agricultural *labour.

In the first half of the 12th c., the Cistercian experience, originally restricted to male monasticism, was broadened to include women's monasteries. Reforming ferments favoured the birth of some houses of *nuns that adhered to the rigid principles of the Cistercian rule or the crossing over of pre-existing houses to the new rule, often incorporating or empowering charitable centres that arose in the wake of the reforming movements. Like the men's houses, the women's *coenobia* inspired by the rule of Cîteaux soon attracted wide approval thanks to the austerity of their life, their moral rigour, their organising abilities, their commitment to charity and the economic advantages offered by the work of the nuns.

C. E. Boyd, *A Cistercian Nunnery in Medieval Italy. The Story of Rifreddo in Saluzzo, 1200-1300*, New York, 1943. – R. Manselli, "Fondazioni cisterciensi in Italia settentrionale", *Monasteri in alta Italia dopo le invasioni saracene e magiare* (secc. X-XII), III Convegno di storia della Chiesa in Italia (Pinerolo, 6-9 settembre 1964), Turin, 1966. – R. Comba, L. Chiappa Mauri, E. Occhipinti, M. Bellero, "Economia monastica: I cisterciensi e le campagne", *Studi storici*, 26, 1985, 237-251. – *Chiaravalle. Arte e storia di un'abbazia cisterciense*, P. Tomea (ed.), Milan, 1992. – *I cisterciensi nel mezzogiorno medioevale*, H. Houben (ed.), B. Vetere (ed.), Galatina, 1994.

Elisa Occhipinti

**CIVIL OFFICE IN FRANCE.** "To our officials is given, under our authority, the direction of the acts by which are policed and maintained the public affairs of our realm of which they are the essential ministers as members of the body of which we are the head": thus was defined, in an *ordinance of 1467, the function of the officials who for more than two centuries had permitted the growth of the French State by serving it in the sphere of *justice and administration. From the mid 13th c., the organisation of institutions required a specialized and competent personnel. Agents of the progress of the modern *State, officials were targets for grievances, implicated in every political crisis of the 14th or 15th centuries. After a rapid development of bureaucracy, the requirements of economy and reform restricted the number of officials. Institutions and personnel were in place around 1350: their numbers remained fixed for a century. Growth did not resume until after the *Hundred Years' War. In all, the ordinary central administration in the capital numbered hardly more than 200 persons in the 14th and 15th centuries. In 1505, there were no more than 12,000 royal officials in the whole of *France.

Originally *clerics, officials remained attached to the Church by their studies, by the ecclesiastical *benefices that rewarded some of them and by the influence of ecclesiastical institutions, which provided in the benefice a model for the code of office. The action of the *Parlement in the second half of the 14th c. laid the first stones of a code of public office. Acting "in the exercise of their duties", officials were placed under the special safeguard of the king and the authorization of the king's servants limited their responsibility. First articulated in 1359, the principle that an official could not be removed from office "without being heard", *i.e.* without recourse to justice, gradually prevailed. The ordinance of 1467 on the stability of offices, after the disordered beginnings of *Louis XI, merely confirmed a recognised custom. To be the holder of an office, it was necessary to have a letter confirming the appointment, to have it registered and finally to be inducted into the office, often by taking an *oath. The donation of offices by the king was dependent on royal favour, thus on "impetration by prayers and importunity of petitioners". To this system was preferred, from the reign of *Charles V, that of election, which guaranteed the choice of officials who were "good and sufficient", "fit and proper", *i.e.* competent. Adopted under the influence of the model of the Church, the ideas of *Aristotle and democratic pressure, election peaked in 1413 and retreated after the *Hundred Years' War.

At that time, in the well-organised milieu of royal officials, appeared the private venality of office. Prepared by the practice of farming out certain offices and that of designating one's successor to office (*resignatio in favorem* of benefices), venality, though not well thought of, was not forbidden except for offices of justice and counsel. It was sufficiently widespread in the 15th c. for there to be a right price for the office of *notary and secretary to the king. Officials' wages, fixed in money of account at the end of the 13th c., did not change in the 14th and 15th centuries. They were supplemented by pensions and royal gifts and by more or less licit appended revenues. These revenues, together with the prestige of royal service and the privileges allowed by the king to officials, gave them an eminent place in society, to the point of allowing some of them to enter the *nobility and get their social group recognised as a "fourth estate", which later became the *noblesse de robe*.

F. Autrand, "Offices et officiers royaux en France sous Charles VI", *RH*, 242, 1969, 285-338. – *Histoire des fonctionnaires et de la fonction publique en France*, 1, Paris, 1993.

Françoise Autrand

***CIVITAS*, CITY.** In Antiquity the term *civitas* designated the territory put under the authority of a capital town. In Gaul, in Germany, in Britain, this territory usually corresponded to that occupied by a people at the time of the Roman conquest. The town that dominated this territory could have various kinds of status: *colonia*, *municipium*, free town, etc.

From the late Empire, the term no longer designated the territory but the town itself. The seat of authority took precedence over the space it controlled. The *towns thus designated under the name *civitas* show common characteristics. They were provided with a rampart, were always the seat of a *bishopric, often the seat of a lay power in the early Middle Ages. Thus the map of the cities, *e.g.* in Gaul, transcribes very faithfully that of the bishoprics. A town that rose to the rank of bishopric would be called a city, a town whose bishop settled elsewhere changed its designation.

Gradually the term "city" (*cité* in French) took on a still more restricted meaning. From the *Carolingian period, it now designated only the part of the town within the ramparts. The immediate outskirts could bear various names, but always names that distinguished them. Medieval texts give the name *cives* only to the inhabitants of the *civitas*.

In the Middle Ages the use of the word **villa* spread, and the duality between the city and its surroundings was perpetuated. The use of the formula "city and town" became general in the 14th c., and the panoramas of the 16th c. are eloquent in this respect.

Behind the wall of the enclosed city were a number of components, expression of its three functions, religious, political and military, civil. In Gaul, from the beginnings of Christianization, the bishop and his *clerics were established in the city. Recent works have shown that the transfer of the *cathedral to the city was the exception, not the rule as historiography had led us to understand. This is to say that very early, often from the 4th c., but rarely before the edict of Constantine which recognized Christianity in 314, the Church found its place alongside the lay authorities, whose incapacity it often palliated. The reform carried out in the 8th c. by Bishop *Chrodegang of Metz, whose object was to recover the ideal of common life, was expressed by the delimitation of *canons' quarters which became one of the elements of the landscape of all medieval cities. The public buildings that took the place of the former municipal institutions – comital or royal *palace, courthouse, *castle or residence of territorial princes or the king – succeeded each other, often on the same site. By contrast, it was often outside the original walls, in the "town", that the communal palace or town hall was established. The area of cities varying from two or three hectares to several dozen, the place reserved for the inhabitants varied in the same proportions. As a place where authority was exercised from the late Empire, the city jealously preserved this prerogative which distinguished it from the rest of the built-up area throughout the medieval millennium.

*Histoire de la France urbaine*, 1, Paris, 1980. – *Naissance des arts chrétiens*, Paris, 1991.

Henri Galinié

**CLAIRVAUX.** Third daughter of *Cîteaux, founded on 25 June 1115 by the 25-year-old Bernard of Fontaine on lands belonging to his family in the diocese of Langres, the community of Clairvaux enjoyed an extremely rapid rise. The modest *monasterium vetus*, whose square *chapel survived until the French Revolution, was succeeded after 1133-1135, despite St *Bernard's misgivings, by a great *abbey situated some hundreds of metres to the east. The church built on that occasion probably had a flat chevet; it was replaced shortly after St Bernard's death (1153) by a vast choir with ambulatory and radiating chapels.

At that date, the family of Clairvaux was already the most important in the *Cistercian Order: around 175 houses, 90 of them in France and some 50 in the British Isles, out of a total of 345 to 350. The rise continued in the second half of the century, especially abroad. Until the 13th c., recruitment was largely international (Flanders, England). Clairvaux also furnished the Church with *bishops and *cardinals.

The first community had lived in strict *poverty, but the abundance of *donations, the rational exploitation of resources (flocks, *mills, *forges, woods) and a deliberate policy of purchases, even the acquisition of serfs, took it in the way of riches. The economic and demographic crisis of the 14th c., as well as the wars, later dealt a perceptible blow to this prosperity.

This policy of prestige and power should not make us forget that Clairvaux was also a centre of spiritual and intellectual life, as witness its *library, one of the most important in Christendom. From the 12th c., the abbey accumulated a precious stock of patristic texts (about 300 volumes), among which – something extremely rare for that time – were the complete works of St Augustine. Later, under the impetus of Abbot Stephen of Lexington (1242-1255), Clairvaux played a decisive role in the opening up of the Cistercian Order to *university culture (foundation of St Bernard's College at *Paris in 1245). The library's monumental catalogue, drawn up in 1472 at the time of the accession of Abbot Pierre de Virey, offers a very precise reflection of this intellectual wealth. Even today, with more than 1400 existing manuscripts, mostly preserved at Troyes, the stock of Clairvaux is the most abundant of all French medieval stocks.

R. Fossier, "La vie économique de l'abbaye de Clairvaux des origines à la fin de la guerre de Cent-Ans", *Positions des thèses . . . de 1949, École nationale des chartes*, Paris, 1949, 57-63. – J.-M. Canivez, "Clairvaux",

*Saint Clare.* Fresco by Simone Martini, 1283-1344. Assisi, basilica of St Francis, lower church.

*DHGE*, 12, 1953, 1050-1061. – A. Vernet, J.-F. Genest, J.-P. Bouhot, *La Bibliothèque de l'abbaye de Clairvaux du XIIe au XVIIIe siècle*, 1, Paris, 1979; 2, Paris-Turnhout, 1997. – *Histoire de Clairvaux. Actes du colloque de Bar-sur-Aube/Clairvaux (22-23 juin 1990)*, Bar-sur-Aube, 1991.

Jean-François Genest

**CLARE OF ASSISI (1194-1253).** Chiara Offreducio di Favarone, born at *Assisi, had the childhood and adolescence of a young noblewoman. In *c.*1211 occurred her meeting with *Francis of Assisi, recently installed with his first companions at the *Portiuncula. It was there that she received the habit from his hands on the eve of Palm Sunday 1212. After staying for some months with the Benedictines of San Paolo di Bastia and Sant'Angelo, she finally settled at *San Damiano where some young girls joined her. Calling herself "the little plant of our father St Francis", she struggled until her death to get recognition of the specific character of her order: to live without revenues or *property and to remain under the jurisdiction of the Friars Minor.

A small nascent community, the Damianites observed the *formula vivendi* given by St Francis. The original is lost, but this document is summarized in chapter 6 of the Rule. After the *Lateran council's decision (1215) to forbid any new congregations, the Poor Ladies had to attach themselves to an existing order. The title of *abbess was then imposed on Clare. Moreover, in 1218 the enlarged community received the Benedictine-inspired Constitutions of Cardinal Ugolino, protector of the order. From 1215, the *privilegium paupertatis* was nevertheless granted; this right to possess neither revenue nor property was renewed several times by *Honorius III and *Gregory IX, but only for San Damiano. At the same time, the *bull *Quoties cordis* of 14 Nov 1227 granted *spiritual direction to the First Order. In order to harmonize the legislation, in 1247 *Innocent IV imposed a new rule that maintained property in common. From this date, Clare began drawing up her Rule, finished in 1253, in order to safeguard the fundamental points. This first rule written by a woman and for *women was approved for the monastery of San Damiano, the papacy reserving the right to apply the Rule of Innocent IV, modified by *Urban IV (1264). The future of the order was bound up with this complex problem.

The *spirituality of the foundress is known by her *Writings* (*letters to *Agnes of Bohemia, testament, Rule), the evidence of her companions at the *canonization trial, and the *Vita* of *Thomas of Celano. Her interior life belonged to medieval spirituality: centred on *Christ the Spouse, it was drawn by *contemplation of the Son suffering his *Passion. A large place was given to *ascesis as privileged means of the nuptial encounter with Christ. Clare of Assisi wrote little; she was a model in her lifetime and after her death; however, the opportunity for the *nuns to possess revenues and property would notably modify their conditions of life and their spiritual vitality.

Clare was canonized on 15 Aug 1255 by Pope *Alexander IV; her feast is on 11 August.

*Francis and Clare: the Complete Works*, R.J. Armstrong (ed.), I.C. Brady (ed.), London, 1982. – Claire d'Assise, *Écrits*, *SC*, 325, 1985.

Thomas of Celano, "Legenda sanctae Clarae virginis", *Acta SS*, 11 Aug, Antwerp, 1735, 754-767. – G. Lazzeri, "Procès de canonisation de sainte Claire", *AFH*, 13, 1920, 403-507. – M. Bartoli, *Clare of Assisi*, London, 1993. – W. Maleczek, *Klara von Assisi, Das 'Privilegium paupertatis' und der Testament*, Rome, 1995. – *Claire d'Assise et sa posterité. Actes du colloque international de l'UNESCO (1994)*, Paris, 1995.

Élisabeth Lopez

**CLARE OF MONTEFALCO (1268-1308).** Entering as a child the girls' *hospice founded by her father, Clare grew up in a small religious community which followed no rule, but consecrated itself to an austere life of penitence and absolute *poverty (to the point of mendicancy). In 1290, following probable pressure by the church authorities, the community adopted the Rule of St *Augustine, but it was always followed by *Franciscans, probably *Spirituals. In 1291, Clare became *abbess of the monastery. All through her life she had *visionary gifts: she opens one of the first chapters of Italian *mysticism. At her death, Clare's heart was opened and it was thought that the instruments of Christ's *Passion could be seen represented in it. An inquiry into her virtues and *miracles was authorized by the Holy See in 1318, but Clare was not canonized until 1881.

*Il processo di canonizzazione de Chiara da Montefalco*, E. Menesto (ed.), Perugia-Florence, 1984. – C. W. Bynum, *Holy Feast and Holy Fast*, Berkeley (CA), 1987. – G. Barone, "Problemi ancora aperti intorno a Chiara da Montefalco", *Movimento religioso e mistica femminile nel Medioevo*, P. Dinzelbacher (dir.), D. Bauer (dir.), Milan, 1993, 248-257.

Giulia Barone

**CLARENDON, CONSTITUTIONS OF.** The 16 "customs of the realm", whose formal recognition *Henry II demanded at Clarendon in January 1164, restricted ecclesiastical rights in a number of key areas: punishment of criminous clerks (3); *excommunication or *interdict of tenants-in-chief (7); *appeals (8); and episcopal *elections (12). Becket's refusal to ratify them led to his exile and murder, after which Henry conceded freedom of appeal to the papal *Curia and the jurisdictional *immunity of the clergy.

*Councils and Synods with other Documents relating to the English Church*, 1, 2, D. Whitelock (ed.) *et al.*, Oxford, 1981, 852-893. – R. Foreville, *L'Église et la royauté en Angleterre. . .* , Paris, 1943, 125-127. – *NCE*, 3, 1967, 914-915. – *TRE*, 5, 1980, 394-397.

Anne J. Duggan

**CLASSICS.** Thus are conventionally designated the Greek and Latin writers of pagan Antiquity. The reading of their works posed from the outset a serious problem for Christian scholars in that, while necessary for learning the language and transmitting scientific knowledge, they also conveyed propositions considered untruthful or scandalous. The contradiction was magistrally resolved by Augustine who, in his *De Doctrina Christiana*, showed how the resources of classical *rhetoric could and must be put in the service of propagating the Christian message. In a vivid image, Jerome (*Ep. 70 Ad Magnum*) compared pagan literature to the captive of Deuteronomy 21, 10-13, whose nails and hair had to be cut before she could be admitted to one's bed. In the East, the Cappadocian Fathers, notably Basil of Caesarea, professed the same principles. It was they who governed, with some nuances, the attitude of medieval scholars to the classics, both in the Latin West and in the Byzantine world.

**The West.** The period of intellectual low tide, the dramatic decline of written culture linked to the quasi-disappearance of the *school system between the 6th and 8th cc., nevertheless saw the maturing of essential undertakings in the history of the survival of the classics in the Middle Ages: the Italian aristocrat *Cassiodorus († 580) had works useful for learning the seven *liberal arts transcribed in his Calabrian monastery of *Vivarium, while his contemporary *Boethius, "the last of the Romans" († 524), worked out a synthesis between *Platonism and Aristotelianism and translated the Stagyrite's logical works into *Latin; bishop *Isidore of Seville († 636) compiled a monumental *encyclopedia in 20 books, the *Etymologies*, intended to replace that of Pliny; the Anglo-Saxon monk *Bede († 735) wrote, among other works, treatises on *grammar and natural history. These scholars have rightly been called the "founders of the Middle Ages". However, such efforts of synthesis allowed people to save themselves the trouble of a direct return to the sources: the very rare classics of which a manuscript trace dating from the dark ages has been preserved are technical treatises (on grammar, *medicine, land-surveying, strategy).

The situation changed with the "*Carolingian Renaissance": no-one is unaware that we owe the preservation of the immense majority of Latin classics to the zeal of 9th-c. scribes. The most popular authors at that time were the poets: Virgil, whose study had never completely been abandoned, Horace, the epics of Lucan and Statius, the satires of Persius and Juvenal, the comedies of Terence, on which Abbess *Hrotswith of Gandersheim composed moralizing pastiches for her *nuns. The sole prose-writers to benefit from the same enthusiasm were Cicero, for his manuals of rhetoric, and the historian Sallust. All these texts were studied at school, as prove the great number of glossed manuscripts and the flourishing of commentaries of an essentially grammatical tenor: the monumental work of the great pedagogue *Remigius of Auxerre († after 908) formed a link with the techniques of text explanation worked out during late Antiquity. These facts indicate the scope, but also the limits, of the Carolingian Renaissance: though the classics were now read – and indeed they formed a small minority of the school canon by comparison to the Christian writers of the 4th and 5th cc. –, it was mainly to find in them models of writing and fine style. The aim of this study was primarily to guarantee linguistic correctness; aesthetic pleasure remained suspect. Even in the middle of the 11th c., the ascetic cardinal *Peter Damian († 1072), though a distinguished stylist himself, fulminated against the *auctores* the same furious condemnations as had Jerome and *Gregory the Great.

Perhaps this was because at this time they began again to constitute a danger to Christian *faith and morals. The relative secularization of teaching, which came out of the monasteries where it had been entirely oriented towards the praise of God, and developed in urban centres (*Reims, *Chartres, *Angers, *Orléans), the access of a ceaselessly growing public to written culture, meant that people's attitude towards the classics began to be modified. Thus Ovid, the scandalous author of libertine poems and especially of that encyclopedia of paganism, the *Metamorphoses*, was rediscovered with enthusiasm. The conquering optimism of the 12th c., enamoured of *beauty and ready for any speculative boldness, was incarnated in the work of the masters of the cathedral school of *Chartres, flourishing around 1150: Bernard and Thierry of Chartres, Bernard Silvestris and *William of Conches – whose lessons have been preserved for us by their pupil *John of Salisbury († 1180), the perfect model of the medieval humanist – thus undertook to apply to the classics the method of reading previously reserved for the sacred text, allegorical *exegesis. They taught that under the veil (*integumentum*, *involucrum*) of the frivolous or shocking letter lay a sense that was not in contradiction with revealed Truth; by using these principles, Ovid himself could be Christianized. For other authors, the exegetical effort was less forced: Seneca, whose Stoic ethic and taste for introspection had such Christian resonances ("*Seneca saepe noster*", said even the severe Tertullian), to whom had long been ascribed an apocryphal correspondence with St *Paul, fed the reflections of moralists.

The other great discovery of the 12th c. was Greek philosophy and *science, particularly that of *Aristotle. The Western Middle Ages had been very largely ignorant of Greek: *John Scotus Eriugena († *c.*877), translater of Pseudo-*Dionysius, was the exception that confirmed the rule. Things did not start to change until the 13th century. Yet not all Aristotle's works were translated directly; some went through an Arabic intermediary, in the frontier zones of *Spain and southern *Italy. Their reception by the West was quickly triumphal: the role they played in the history of the development of *scholastic thought needs no comment. The 13th c. was also the age of *florilegia, encyclopedic *summae* that took over from that of *Isidore. Like the *Speculum majus* of *Vincent of Beauvais († 1264), they formed veritable patchworks of **auctoritates*. Symbolic in this respect is the immense success enjoyed at this time by Valerius Maximus, considered less as historian than as the author of the first collection of **exempla*.

However, this culture of the **summa* (both sum and summary) based on choice morsels, as well as the technicality of scholastic *philosophy, a great producer of abstruse neologisms, soon aroused the hostility of enlightened amateurs who wanted to recover an unmediated contact with the ancient authors. *Petrarch and *Boccaccio were great discoverers and great readers of rare texts (Cicero's letters, Livy, Apuleius's *Golden Ass*). But these atypical geniuses were not isolated cases. The mercantile middle class, which conquered power in the young communal States of Italy, needed to establish the legitimacy of its government, which it did notably by reviving the memory of Roman grandeur. The old, rich *libraries of *Verona, *Bobbio and *Monte Cassino were laid under contribution. From the late 13th c., the Paduans Lovati († 1309) and Mussato († 1329) brought their illustrious compatriot Livy, herald of republican freedom, out of the oblivion into which he had fallen to begin a new and triumphant career. The earliest *humanism thus had a clear political colouring. But there was still a dazzled fascination with Antiquity and an inextinguishable thirst for discoveries. During the interminable council of *Constance, the Florentine *Poggio Bracciolini († 1459), papal secretary, occupied his leisure in exploring the stocks of old monastic libraries, *Cluny, *Sankt Gallen, *Fulda, *Hersfeld, etc. He exhumed treasures: Lucretius, Tacitus, Petronius, a dozen unknown orations by Cicero and many more texts besides. By *c.*1450, the essentials of Latin literature as we know it had been made available.

**Byzantium.** The history of the survival of the Greek classics is more or less symmetrical to that just outlined. Thanks to the work of scribes and the zeal of *humanists of all epochs, the development of classical culture in the West appears punctuated by a succession of rediscoveries: we today, at the end of this process, possess more or less the texts known to the scholars of the Late Empire. In the East, on the other hand, there is more the impression of a gradual dwindling. There is something surprising about this: imperial continuity, the political and cultural centralism of *Constantinople, the immobilism of the written language would suggest the existence of not too discontinuous traditions. But they are quite hard to retrace in detail, given the dearth of ancient manuscripts. Thus it is often accepted that the scholarly canon, excluding the great majority of the plays of Aeschylus and Sophocles, was fixed from late Antiquity; but there is no formal proof that tragedies now lost did not survive for several centuries more.

At the time of the permanent partition of the Roman Empire in 395, the periphery of the East Mediterranean was peopled with flourishing higher schools. A century and a half later, only two remained, those of Constantinople and *Alexandria. In 529, Justinian had closed the philosophical school of Athens – a highly symbolic gesture! – which exhaled whiffs of paganism too strong for his taste. So here too the 6th, 7th and 8th cc. would be "dark ages", not so much by reason of the external threat of *Islam as because of the brutality of the ceaseless theological quarrels, which sometimes degenerated into civil wars.

*Iconoclasm was only finally liquidated in 843. The second half of the 9th c. immediately enjoyed a spectacular cultural renaissance, dominated by the exceptional figure of Patriarch *Photius († *c.*893). His famous *Library* listed and commented on some 280 works, more than 120 of them by secular authors. These were mainly historians (many of them now lost), but also orators, romancers and grammarians. Poetry however was absent. Its hour would come in the 10th c., in the course of which the *Greek Anthology* was compiled and the existing comedies of Aristophanes collected. Under the dynasty of the *Comneni, Archbishop Eustathius of Thessalonica († *c.*1192) wrote an enormous commentary on the *Iliad*, making wide use of the methods of allegorical exposition. With his correspondents and friends John Tzetzes, master of the school of Constantinople, and Michael Choniates, bishop of Athens, he had a passion for rare and difficult authors, Pindar, Callimachus, Hipponax.

The interlude of the Latin Empire (1204-1261) was disastrous, much more so than the *Ottoman victory of 1453 would be. It was probably then that a number of the works known to Photius or Eustathius were destroyed. While the teaching of the great classics – Homer, the tragedians – enjoyed a remarkable rise in the peripheral zones to which Constantinopolitan intellectuals were exiled (Asia Minor and apparently the *terra d'Otranto*), many rare texts were lost for good. After this dramatic episode, the empire of the *Palaeologi, which politically was no more than the "sick man" of Europe, was yet the scene of a vigorous cultural recovery. Here must be cited the name of the great Maximus Planudes († 1305), a man of tireless curiosity who, not content with promoting the study of authors not inscribed on the school programme, such as Plutarch and Nonnus, and publishing the most complete version of the *Anthology* (which bears his name), translated Augustine, Boethius and even Ovid into Greek. From now on, exchanges between East and West intensified: Italian scholars flowed into Constantinople to learn Greek, while Byzantine scholars, to ward off the imminent catastrophe, removed their libraries to *Venice. In 1397, a chair of Greek was created at the *studium* of *Florence for the Byzantine scholar Manuel *Chrysoloras. In 1500, all the Greek and Latin classics were widespread in Italy.

E. R. Curtius, *European Literature and the Latin Middle Ages*, W.R. Trask (tr.), London, 1953. – B. Munk Olsen, *L'étude des auteurs classiques latins aux XI^e et XII^e siècles*, Paris, 1982-1989 (4 vol.). – *Texts and Transmission. A Survey of the Latin Classics*, L. D. Reynolds (ed.), Oxford, 1983. – N. G. Wilson, *Scholars of Byzantium*, London, 1983. – L. D. Reynolds, N. G. Wilson, *Scribes and Scholars. A Guide to the Transmission of Greek and Latin Literature*, Oxford, 1992 (3rd ed.). – *The Classics in the Middle Ages*, A.S. Bernardo (ed.), S. Levin (ed.), Binghamton (NY), 1990. – B. Munk Olsen, *I Classici nel canone scolastico altomedievale*, Spoleto, 1991. – C. Villa, "I classici", *Lo Spazio letterario del Medioevo. I: Il Medioevo latino, vol. I, La produzione del testo*, 1, Rome, 1992, 479-522. – C. Baswell, *Virgil in Medieval England*, Cambridge, 1994. – N. Rudd, *The Classical Tradition in Operation*, Toronto, 1994. – *The Classical Tradition in the Middle Ages and the Renaissance*, C. Leonardi (ed.), B.M. Olsen (ed.), Spoleto, 1995.

Jean-Yves Tilliette

**CLAUDIUS OF TURIN (died 827).** Claudius, a native of Spain, arrived at *Lyon in *c.*800, probably with Felix of Urgel, exiled for his *adoptianist views. Esteemed for his exegetical commentaries, he became *chaplain to *Louis, son of *Charlemagne and king of *Aquitaine. On Louis's accession in 814, he followed him to *Aachen to teach Scripture there. In 817, Louis got him elected bishop of *Turin. Continuing to pursue his exegetical activity, *Augustinian in inspiration, he stood out by his great rigorism. In *c.*825 he wrote a treatise, the *Apologeticum et rescriptum adversus Theodemirum abbatem*, which harshly attacked the cult of *images, the *cross and *relics, as well as *pilgrimages. This text, known only from a summary made by his enemy *Jonas of Orléans, must be understood in the context of Carolingian hostility to the cult of images, accentuated by the influence of the circle of *Agobard of Lyon.

G. Italiani, *La tradizione esegetica nel commento ai Re di Claudio di Torino*, Florence, 1979.

Alain Boureau

**CLEARANCES.** The vast medieval movement of extension of cultivated land at the expense of wasteland, *forest or swamps varied in forms and importance according to times and regions. From the late 10th c., we see signs of it in Mâconnais and *England, and from the year 1000 the Flemings gained land from the sea. Expansion culminated in the 12th c. and continued in the 13th, but ran out of breath before the middle of the century, except in some valleys of mountainous areas, or in Eastern Europe beyond the Elbe. We distinguish three great forms that succeeded each other in time.

Firstly, clearance by extension of cultivation: cultivated lands grew more or less by stealth. A field was slowly enlarged, a border lengthened, some plough lines were gained from the waste. This entailed no new settlement and left few traces in texts, but we can cite a *village of the Milanese whose wastes declined from 45% to 16% of the administrative area over 80 years of the 13th century.

A second phase culminated between 1150 and 1200: important undertakings settled new villages on lands gained for cultivation. This generally resulted from political acts of territorial development, decided by the lords (lay, religious or even urban communities). Often two lords joined forces to found a *villeneuve*. They had to provide the waste land, find the labour, advance the seed. In order to attract men, they granted them advantages, material or legal, and were not always very particular about their origin. Some were fugitives, but the majority were poor tenant farmers or small freeholders.

Finally came a third stage, viz. individual initiatives of intercalated settlement outside the villages: these often gave rise to single-tenant holdings directed towards *animal husbandry. This form seems to multiply around 1220-50.

Clearances were behind the economic growth of the Middle Ages, but opinion is divided as to their origin. They were concomitant with demographic growth and, for some, it was the increase in the number of people that led them to clear lands to feed themselves. Others think the transition to generalized cereal cultivation that accompanied the clearances improved nutritional conditions, leading to an increase in the population. Progress in technical equipment does not seem to have been a determining factor. On the other hand, it is possible that a stabilization of the *climate in an oceanic phase favourable to cereal cultivation favoured the settlers.

Clearances left numerous traces in the landscape (field divisions), as well as in place-names, with numerous "Essarts", "*Bastide", "*Sauveté" . . .

G. Duby, *L'Économie rurale et la vie des campagnes*, Paris, 1962. – *Histoire de la France rurale*, G. Duby (ed.), 1, Paris, 1975. – G. Sivéry, *Terroirs et communautés rurales dans l'Europe occidentale au Moyen Âge*, Lille, 1990. – *Medieval Farming and Technology. The Impact of Agricultural Change in Northwest Europe*, G. Astill (ed.), J. Langdon (ed.), Leiden-New York-Cologne, 1997.

Georges Comet

**CLEMENT IV, POPE (died 1268).** Born at *Saint-Gilles-du-Gard, Guy Foucois studied law at *Paris. A married lay jurist, he wrote a treatise on the *Inquisition (*Quaestiones quindecim ad inquisitores*). Widowed, he was elected bishop of *Le Puy in 1256 and archbishop of *Narbonne in 1259. *Urban VI created him cardinal-bishop of Sabina in 1261 and entrusted him (1263) with the *Penitentiary. *Legate in England (1263), he was unable to set foot on the island. In his absence, he was elected *pope, 5 Feb 1265. He never entered Rome and created no *cardinals. He recognised *Charles of Anjou as king of *Sicily (1265). By reserving ecclesiastical *benefices for the papacy, he opened the way to the system of *expectative graces.

A. Paravicini Bagliani, *HChr*, 5, 1993.

Agostino Paravicini Bagliani

*Pope Clement IV invests Charles, count of Provence, with the kingdom of Sicily.* Fresco of *The History of Charles of Anjou's conquest in Sicily* (detail) at Pernes-les-Fontaines, Tour Ferrande (France). Late 13th c.

**CLEMENT V, POPE (died 1314).** Bertrand de Got was born at Villandraut (Gironde) around the middle of the 13th century. He studied law at *Orléans and *Bologna. A Gascon, he soon entered the service of the king of England. In 1287-1288 he seems to have been *Edward I's *procurator at the Roman *Curia. The cardinalate (1294) of his brother Béraud, archbishop of *Lyon, opened the doors of the papal court more widely to him. *Boniface VIII appointed him bishop of Comminges (1295), then archbishop of Bordeaux (1299). Under this pope, he maintained a position of balance in the conflict with *Philip the Fair. In 1302, he was at Rome to take part in the council that was to condemn the king of France, and became *chaplain to Cardinal Francesco *Caetani.

His *election to the pontificate took place at *Perugia on 5 June 1305. Bertrand was then on a pastoral *visit to Lusignan. Philip the Fair had the papal coronation celebrated at Lyon (14 Nov 1305). On 15 Dec 1305, Clement V created ten *cardinals, all French and Gascons save one Englishman. The Italian cardinals were thus put in a minority from the beginning of the pontificate. Later the pope created ten more cardinals, all French. In April-May 1307, at Poitiers, Philip the Fair demanded from the pope the suppression of the Order of *Templars and the condemnation of Boniface VIII. Proceedings against that pope's memory were opened on 13 Sept 1309. Clement V managed to bring them to an end without pronouncing a condemnation. The sentences unfavourable to the king were annulled and struck off the registers of the *chancery. Clement V finally ordered inquiries against the Templars, and brought the question before the council of *Vienne, which decided (22 March 1312) to abolish the order, not for legal reasons but for the "general good". Its properties were transferred to the *Hospitallers of St John of Jerusalem, while a commission was charged with judging the grand masters of the order.

Apart from this, Clement V entrusted the *universities of *Rome, *Paris, *Oxford, *Bologna and *Salamanca with the responsibility of teaching *Hebrew, Greek, Arabic and Syriac; he also brought together a series of constitutions promulgated before and after the council of Vienne, called *Clementines.

Choosing from 1308 to establish himself at *Avignon, in the heart of the *Comtat Venaissin, which was the property of the Holy See, he was content to live in the Dominican convent there. He does not seem to have wanted to live permanently in France.

Clement V was not totally subject to Philip the Fair. By canonizing *Celestine V (1311), he implicitly recognised Celestine's renunciation of his pontificate in favour of Boniface VIII. Nearly always ill after the council of Vienne, the pope was unable to react to the execution of Jacques de Molay, last grand master of the Templars. Death overtook him at Roquemaure (Gard) on 20 April 1314.

B. Guillemain, *Les Recettes et les Dépenses de la Chambre apostolique pour la quatrième année du pontificat de Clément V (1308-1309)*, Rome, 1978. – A. Paravicini Bagliani, "Clemente V", *DBI*, 26, 1982, 202-215. – S. Menache, *Clement V*, Cambridge, 1998.

Agostino Paravicini Bagliani

**CLEMENT VI, POPE (1291-1352).** Pierre Roger, born in the castle of Maumont in the parish of Rosiers-d'Égletons, entered La *Chaise-Dieu aged ten and studied theology at *Paris. He became abbot of *Fécamp (1326), bishop of *Arras (1328), archbishop of *Sens (1329), then of *Rouen (1330), then *cardinal of SS. Nereo e Achilleo (1338). A distinguished orator, he defended the rights of the episcopate at the assemby of Vincennes and enjoyed royal favour.

Elected *pope on 7 May 1342 and crowned on 19 May, the new pontiff was known for his generosity, kindness and affability. He considerably increased the number of collations conceded by apostolic authority and distributed *expectative graces without counting. He showered favours on his many relations (six *cardinals were appointed in his family) and his Limousin compatriots. With his pontificate began the series of volumes in which petitions were registered (22 for his reign).

Centralization was reinforced and *taxation increased (*annates, *spoils, proxies) while the collection of taxes was organised better.

His court was sumptuous, though charity was not neglected (17 % of expenses dedicated to *alms and the service of the *Pignotta). He completed the palace begun by *Benedict XIII and added to it a second building in a wholly different style, remarkable for its ornamentation. He bought *Avignon from Queen Joanna of Naples for 80,000 florins (1348).

The end of his reign was saddened by the plague that ravaged all Christendom (1348-1349) and gave rise to excesses in the Rhineland against the *Jews and to the extravagances of penitents, the *flagellants, condemned by the pope (1349).

Despite his political gifts, Clement VI met many difficulties in *Italy where the Church was no longer mistress of her *States. The pope resumed the bellicose policy of *John XXII, but money was lacking and, after some successes, the rector of *Romagna, Astorge de Durfort, was unable to pay his troops and had to dismiss them. It was necessary to treat with Giovanni *Visconti, lord of *Milan, who had laid hands on *Bologna and received its vicariate (1352). The *Patrimony of St Peter was effectively ruled by Giovanni di Vico, prefect of Rome, while at *Rome itself a man of humble origin, the tribune *Cola di Rienzo, had seized power (1347); but he was soon expelled by the Roman nobility (1347), handed over to the pope and imprisoned at Avignon.

In the kingdom of *Naples, vassal of the Holy See, Clement VI sent Cardinal Aimery de Châtelus to the young Queen Joanna who had to promise obedience (1344); after the murder of her husband, Andrew of Hungary, she fled before the arrival of a Hungarian army; taking refuge at Avignon, she sold the town and obtained from the pope the regularization of her union with her cousin Louis of Taranto, who took over the administration of the kingdom.

The Emperor Louis of Bavaria negotiated to obtain his *absolution but, because of the draconian conditions imposed, ended by abdicating (1343); a little later the pope pronounced his deposition (1346). The electors proposed the candidature of *Charles of Luxemburg, son of King John of Bohemia, who had known Clement VI well at the French court. Elected emperor at Rense (1346), he did not keep his promises of submission and the pope did not authorize his coronation at Rome.

Clement VI several times negotiated truces in the Anglo-French conflict; but he was more favourable to *Philip VI, to whom he allowed important loans and the collection of *tenths. The English deplored the collation of their country's *benefices to foreigners (notably cardinals) and in 1346 *Edward III confiscated all the revenues of benefice-holders who were neither English nor resident, while in 1351 *Parliament decreed the Statue of Provision, hostile to all interference.

Despite his intelligence and his diplomatic qualities, Clement VI obtained only precarious results; the papal treasury had been emptied. He died on 6 Dec 1352; in accordance with his wishes, his body was buried at the monastery of La Chaise-Dieu which he had rebuilt.

P. Fournier, *HLF*, 37, 1938, 209-238. – G. Mollat, *DHGE*, 12, 1953, 1129-1162. – B. Guillemain, *La Cour pontificale d'Avignon*, Paris, 1962. – G. Mollat, *Les Papes d'Avignon*, Paris, 1964 (10th ed.). – B. Guillemain, *DBI*, 26, 1982, 215-222. – D. Wood, *Pope Clement VI. The Pontificate and Ideas of an Avignon Pope*, Cambridge, 1989.

Anne-Marie Hayez

**CLEMENT (VII) (1342-1394).** In the absence of official recognition by the Roman Church, Clement VII remains in the eyes of history the first of the Avignon *popes to inaugurate the period of the *Great Schism, in 1378. A deep fracture took place at that time within *Christendom, which rapidly divided into two obediences. After having proclaimed, 9 Aug, the nullity of the *election of *Urban VI which they had carried out themselves several months earlier, the *cardinals (mostly French), entrenched at Fondi, brought Robert of Geneva to the throne of St Peter on 20 Sept 1378.

Born in the castle of Annecy in 1342, the youngest son of Amadeus III, count of Geneva, he was also, through his mother, a nephew of Cardinal Guy of Boulogne, a house related to the *Valois. Robert was the last to bear the title of count in direct line (1392-1394). With him was extinguished one of the most illustrious families of the Savoyard aristocracy. *Chancellor of *Amiens cathedral, canon of Paris, bishop of Thérouanne (1361) and archbishop of *Cambrai (1368), he received the cardinal's purple from *Gregory IX in 1371. A brilliant mind and polyglot, the "cardinal of Geneva" showed himself also an energetic man of war. At the head of the papal armies, the legate of Italy subjected *Bologna and *Romagna, in revolt against the Church (March 1378).

Elected pope, he fixed his residence at *Avignon (May 1379) and attempted at great expense to establish his legitimacy: by force, deliberately neglecting a way of regulating the conflict by the method of *conciliarism; by diplomacy, following a vain policy of winning over adherents. In fact, Clementist obedience was never to go much beyond *France and her satellites. Clement VII overwhelmed the French clergy with taxes to replenish the exhausted papal coffers. Under his pontificate, fiscal policy underwent a notable development, as did its corollary, beneficial practice. But his sumptuary policy did not save him from having to resort to expedients. He died on 16 Sept 1394.

*DHGE*, 12, 1953, 1162-1175. – P. Duparc, *Le Comté de Genève (IX$^{e}$-XV$^{e}$ siècles)*, Geneva, 1955. – R.-C. Logoz, *Clément VII (Robert de Genève), sa chancellerie et le clergé romand au début du Grand Schisme (1378-1394)*, Lausanne, 1974. – *Genèse et débuts du Grand Schisme d'Occident (1362-1394)*, Paris, 1980. – *DBI*, 26, 1982, 222-237.

Michel Fol

**CLEMENTINE COLLECTION.** The Clementines are one of the *canonical collections composing the *Corpus juris canonici*. In 1314, *Clement V had ordered their composition in order to bring together the main legislative texts promulgated since the Sext (1298). They were published in 1317 by *John XXII who sent them to the universities of *Bologna and *Paris and thus gave them official and universal value. The Clementines repeat some constitutions and *Decretals published since the Sext, but reproduce mainly the canons of the council of *Vienne (1311-1312) which have not come down to us directly and are known essentially through this collection. Numerous uncertainties remain as to what modifications the redactors of the Clementines made to the canons of this ecumenical *council (in particular the arrangements relating to the *mendicant orders). The Clementines are divided into five books, on the same plan as the Decretals of *Gregory IX; they contain 52 titles and 106 chapters.

G. Mollat, "Corpus Juris Canonici", *DDC*, 4, 1949, 635-639. – C. Lefebvre, in G. Le Bas, C. Lefebvre, J. Rambaud, *L'Age classique, les sources et la théorie du droit (1140-1378)*, Paris, 1965, 252-254.

Brigitte Basdevant-Gaudemet

**CLERICAL ORDERS.** From the 3rd c., *clerics formed an ordered hierarchy, and the different tasks of the service of the *altar were confided to specialized corps: porters, lectors, exorcists, *acolytes, *subdeacons, *deacons and priests, which were entered, at least from the acolytate up, by a public and ritualized ceremony. For a long time, only the last two formed the major or holy *orders, and it was only in the late 12th c. that the subdeacons joined them. In the later Middle Ages, the minor orders were in fact brought together in the acolytate, though Guillaume *Durand's **Pontifical* describes rites of specific *ordination for each of the seven ranks. These now appeared no more than stages, often rapidly crossed, on the way to the *priesthood; exceptionally, among *canons, some deacons remained in that order all their lives.

J. Tixeront, *L'Ordre et les Ordinations*, Paris, 1925.

Vincent Tabbagh

***CLERICIS LAICOS.*** A *Decretal of *Boniface VIII (24 Feb 1296) reminding lay powers that they had no right to submit *clerics to *taxation and forbidding the clergy to provide any contribution to their rulers without authorization from the Holy See. The measure aroused reactions in England and especially in France. *Philip the Fair replied by forbidding any sending of coin out of the realm without his consent. By a series of letters of Feb 1297, Boniface then mitigated his prohibition.

G. Digard, *Les Registres de Boniface VIII*, 1, Paris, 1886, 1567. 2308-2312.

G. Digard, *Philippe le Bel et le Saint-Siège (1285-1304)*, 1, Paris, 1936, 257-272 and 295-297. – J. McNamara, "Simon de Beaulieu and Clericis Laicos", *Tr*, 25, 1969, 155-170.

Jean Coste †

**CLERICS.** Patristic tradition designated by the Greek term *cleros* those who, as successors to the Levites of Israel, were devoted to the service of the altar. In the classic period of the Middle Ages, the term "clerics" covered all those individuals whose hair had once been cut by a barber in the form of a crown in the presence of their *bishop, and who had received a written attestation of this. This entry into the clergy by *tonsure could be done from the age of seven, but also much later, beyond 20; the candidate, presented by his *parish priest, had to be of legitimate birth, free, and to have assimilated the rudiments of school learning. It opened up certain possibilities, but also comprised obligations. The cleric came under the *justice of the Church courts, he could possess an ecclesiastical *benefice, without *cure of souls, if he remained celibate, and took *orders at the requisite age; he sat in the closed choir of his parish church and there took part in singing the divine service. But he had to have his head shaven so that the tonsure remained visible, wear a long, modest habit, which *synods described regularly for each *diocese, marry a virgin if he married, not remarry if he were widowed, and continue to be able to read and write. Those at least were the rules that jurisprudence progressively fixed in 14th-c. France, where lawsuits and debates on the clerical state were numerous.

Faced with royal courts that sought to restrict as far as possible a milieu that fell outside them, the Church reacted only clumsily, caught between the broad definitions of local *officialities and papal texts, marked by the Gregorian desire to establish a firm distinction between clergy and *laity. It was commonly admitted in the late Middle Ages that the status of cleric was lost by those who did not live "clergily". At this time, virtually every boy who had gone to *school received the tonsure, clerics making up an important proportion of the male population, something like a third, even in the countryside. Those who did not enter an ecclesiastical career by receiving orders exercised a great variety of professions, even butchers and moneychangers, and lived with wife and children. Medieval society hence contained an important group with an ill-defined status, midway between priests and laymen.

R. Genestal, *Les Procès sur l'état de clerc aux XIV$^{e}$ et XV$^{e}$ siècles*, Paris, 1909. – G. Le Bras, *Institutions ecclésiastiques de la Chrétienté médiévale*, 1, 1959, 150-171 (*HE*, 12).

Vincent Tabbagh

**CLERMONT.** A town of the Auvergne (Puy-de-Dôme), in the Middle Ages Clermont was a provincial capital and episcopal see. It is perhaps best known as the location of the famous church *council of 1095, where Pope *Urban II preached the first *crusade. Known as *Nemossos* by the indigenous Celtic peoples

*God comes to chastise Adam.* Capital in the church of Notre-Dame-du-Port, Clermont-Ferrand. 12th c.

and *Augustonemetum* in Gallo-Roman times, it became the capital of the Arverni tribe after the fall of Gergovia and was given the name of Clermont from the 7th century. 5th- and 6th-c. writers like Sidonius Apollinaris and *Gregory of Tours mention Clermont as a commercial, ecclesiastical and cultural centre, a role it continued to play throughout the Middle Ages. Essential to Clermont's lasting importance as a commercial town was its situation at the junction of several Roman roads. Linked to *Limoges and Saintes to the west, Bourges and the Loire valley to the north, *Lyon to the east and from there to the Mediterranean, the site was always a vital commercial centre, attracting *merchants from many regions, including Arabs from the Iberian peninsula and Syrian and Jewish traders from the Middle East. Until 1317 Clermont was the sole episcopal see of the Auvergne. The area's geographical unity contributed to the administrative strength of the *diocese, which contained more than 800 *parishes. Many of the bishops of Clermont were outstanding leaders. Several, such as Stephen II (*c.*945-976), Begon II (980-1010) and Aimeri (1111-1150), were former monks or superiors of *abbeys like La *Chaise-Dieu or *Conques, and used their close links with these powerful monastic centres to reinforce their episcopal authority. The influence of its bishops and their communication with cultural centres like La Chaise-Dieu may help to explain Clermont's precocious artistic achievements. In 946 the *cathedral of Clermont was dedicated. This building, of which only the *crypt remains, was rebuilt in the 11th c. and destroyed in 1218 to make way for a Gothic structure. The probable creator of its innovative design, which incorporated an ambulatory with radiating chapels, was the cleric Aléaume, a sculptor and goldsmith who also fashioned the cathedral's renowned golden statue of the Virgin. The *Romanesque cathedral seems to have served as prototype for various 11th-c. architectural monuments such as Saint-Aignan at *Orléans and the famous Romanesque churches of Orcival and Issoire in the Limagne. The 12th-c. sculpted capitals of Notre-Dame du Port at Clermont prove the astonishing creativity of the medieval Auvergnat artists, and the *stained glass windows of the apse form a remarkable 13th-c. group.

A. Tardieu, *Histoire de la ville de Clermont-Ferrand*, Moulins, 1870-1871 (2 vol.). – A. Bossuat, "Clermont", *DHGE*, 12, 1953, 1435-1458. – M. Vieillard-Troiekouroff, "La Cathédrale de Clermont du Ve au XIIIe siècle", *CAr*, 2, 1960, 199-247. – A.-G. Manry, *Histoire d'Auvergne*, Clermont-Ferrand, 1965. – *Histoire de l'Auvergne*, A.-G. Manry (ed.), Toulouse, 1974. – R. Sève, "La Seigneurie épiscopale de Clermont des origines à 1357", *RAuv*, 94, 1980, 85-268. – *Le Concile de Clermont et l'appel à la croisade. Actes du colloque de Clermont-Ferrand (juin 1995)*, Rome, 1997.

Priscilla Baumann

**CLIMATE.** The history of climate has been seriously considered only as an adjunct of prehistory, by German or Russian scholars (Bogolepov, 1908), in the early 20th c. and especially after 1955 (*Anglo-Scandinavian Review*; P. Pédelaborde, *Le Climat du Bassin Parisien* [1957]; E. Le Roy Ladurie, *Le Climat depuis l'an mil* [1967]). But it is especially the scientists who, having understood that the construction of present and future models can only be based on the past, and hence on history, have provided and still are providing certainties, from new sources.

The texts give us people's points of view and feelings (faced with rain, drought, cold, harvest. . .), their interpretations and also information and series of scientifically interpretable data: proclamation of grape harvests, pannage of pigs, length of freezing of rivers or lakes (the Rhone at *Avignon frozen for 15 weeks in 1364; the *barbarians crossing the frozen Rhine *en masse* on 31 December 406), first appearance of this or that flower or fruit. Many documents accompanied and dated by a *seal allow us, thanks to pollen in the wax, to detect its distant or local origin and to study the flowers thus gathered, their blossoming and the micro-climate. *Archaeology has provided trees datable by the annual double ring in the wood, the relative thickness of the spring and autumn rings, their compactness and density. To these can be added the study of animal or vegetable remains, the sequences of fossil pollens, "varves" or bi-annual sedimentary layers at the bottom of glacial lakes (Lac Léman, Lake Constance), moraines, peat. The decisive contribution has been provided by the study of ice sheets.

The general tendency for the thousand years of the *Middle Ages is given by the Greenland core (1972, W. Dansgaard). Temperatures rose during the early Middle Ages, especially from 900 to 1100; supplementary sources seem to indicate a greater rainfall before *Charlemagne; from about 1200 there was a sharp fall; then, despite some increases (mid 13th, mid 14th, late 15th cc.), temperatures remained cold and got colder until the mid 18th century. By and large the Alpine glaciers give comparable results. However, local conditions as attested by tree rings, pollen, texts, etc., reveal the thousand nuances that must be added, according to geography, to the widely confirmed general pattern. The consequences were a slight northward shift of habitable zones. The fertile volcanic lands of *Iceland and *Greenland welcomed Norwegian settlers. The icepack must have receded: L'Anse aux Meadows, excavated and reconstructed, proves the voyage to *Vinland suggested by the *sagas (*Leif the Fortunate*). We should not too much exaggerate the concomitant advance of the deserts as the root of Islamic expansion from Arabia. Likewise, the remarkable growth of the West must certainly be placed in a context of more regular harvests, with faster and ampler plant growth, together with a sharp increase in population, less ill-nourished; but climatic evolution cannot "explain" the feudal peace, the organisation of production and society. The glorious 13th c. was a cooler period, and the reversal of circumstances in the 14th had many causes other than climatic ones! The influence of climate must not be neglected, but it should not figure as the sole or even principal cause among all the natural and human factors that make history.

P. Alexandre, *Le Climat en Europe au Moyen Âge*, Paris, 1987. – R. Delort, *Pour une histoire de l'environment*, Paris, 1993. – C. Lorius, *Glaces de l'Antarctique*, Paris, 1993. – *Les Catastrophes naturelles dans l'Europe médiévale et moderne*, B. Bennassar (ed.), Flaran, 1996.

Robert Delort

**CLOAK.** The crisis of the ancient world and the advent of medieval societies coincided with the progressive establishment of and growth in the function of emblems, as always happens in periods of scarce literacy during which the depicted image is invested with a mnemonic, symbolic or didactic function. This appears clearly in the rich decorum of the costumes and ornaments of the Empire, where every element, from *clothing to attributes, performed an allegorical function that alluded to the universality and plenitude of power. The same happened in the papacy where, *e.g.*, the symbolic value of the *tiara was such that with *Boniface VIII it represented the totality of papal power, both spiritual and political (*triregnum*). Even before the formation of genuine heraldic systems, there must have existed distinctive non-figurative signs of grade and class, as demonstrated by, *e.g.*, the costumes of the officials in the Byzantine mosaics of San Vitale at *Ravenna: alternation of bands or stripes and particular types of material performed this function.

Colour itself played an important function in distinguishing grades and persons; thus purple, sometimes doubled with squirrel *fur, was always reserved for the cloaks of *kings and emperors and, at the other extreme, the *mendicant orders were distinguished more by the colour than the cut of their robe, while a white *silk or ermine cloak was reserved for papal garments, and colour, with its symbolic and emblematic value, performed a precise ritual function in liturgical *vestments.

Though the use of the cloak as a practical garment is very old, from remotest times it was invested with a particular sacral and lay dignity. In ancient Greece, *e.g.*, the *chlamys* was a rectangular cloak worn mainly by warriors, while classical antiquity knew various types of cloak. But of these it was certainly the **pallium* that was invested with the greatest authority, to the point of being employed as an imperial cloak. The *pallium* also entered the Catholic liturgy, where it became a sacred vestment, symbol of the episcopal dignity and powers reserved solely for the *pope, *archbishops, *patriarchs and *primates. But it was *feudalism that established various types of cloak related to degrees of *nobility, by fixing the cloak among the elements given to the knight at his *dubbing. Among cloaks invested with a high sacral authority was that attributed to *Charlemagne, preserved in the imperial treasury at Vienna and used for the *coronations of the Holy Roman *Empire, though in reality, as the text embroidered on the hem makes clear, it was woven only later at *Palermo under the kings of *Sicily and went to Germany with *Constance of Hauteville, wife of the Emperor *Henry VI. A royal badge of office, the cloak also accompanied kings to *burial, thus *e.g.* the body of Charlemagne's grandson Bernard, king of Italy from 810-818, exhumed in 1639 in the church of Sant'Ambrogio at Milan, was wrapped in a large cloak of white damasked silk with a border interwoven with *gold and coloured silk.

It was not rare for cloaks, whether royal or pontifical, to be enriched with figured motifs, embroidered or woven: animals, fabulous beings, symbols of terrestrial or spiritual power that extended to the whole cosmos.

C. Frugoni, "L'ideologia del potere imperiale nella 'Cattedra di S. Pietro'", *BISI*, 86, 1976-1977, 67-182.

Monica Chiellini Nari

Romanesque cloister at the monastery of Santo Domingo de Silos (Spain): two bas-reliefs in a corner of the gallery, *The Pilgrims at Emmaus* and *The Unbelief of St Thomas*.

**CLOISTER.** The term "cloister", though common, can be ambiguous, since the Middle Ages did not employ it exclusively in the sense that it has today. While the cloister often designated a building adjoining a church – *abbey, *cathedral or *collegiate –, it could also qualify the whole territory marked out by the monastic or canonical *enclosure.

Before signifying a courtyard of geometrical form, surrounded by galleries opening onto it by arcades, the earliest monastic texts employ the word *claustrum* to refer to the monastery precincts, which the brothers, bound by their enclosure, could not leave without the *abbot's authorization. This is so in the *Rules of St Pachomius and St Basil in the 4th c. and St *Benedict in the 6th, as in the majority of Carolingian *councils. The word "cloister" then symbolized all the buildings, generally surrounded by a wall, within which the common life of the monks took place and beyond which they could not circulate freely. In this sense must be understood expressions such as: "to enter the cloister" or "the customs of the cloister".

This same meaning was also used to designate canons' quarters. Rules for *canons, like those of St *Chrodegang (*c.*751) and of Aachen (817), or that of St Augustine rediscovered by the *Gregorian reform of the 11th and 12th cc., recommended canons to follow a regular common life within a cloister so as to fulfil the ideal of *apostolic life proposed by the Scriptures (Acts 2, 42-47). Its organisation answered the same demands as those of the monastic life (dormitory, refectory, etc.). But with the gradual relaxation of discipline, common life was abandoned in favour of individual houses belonging to the *chapter and conceded personally to each *canon on his entry into a *benefice. The cloister (or "close") then designated not just the canons' buildings but the quarter in which these houses were situated around the cathedral. It was sometimes bordered by a fence (Viviers), a ditch (Neuvy-Saint-Sépulcre) or a system combining both (*Autun).

It was probably in reusing ancient *villae* that the builders of the first monasteries understood the benefit of an organisation around a central peristyle courtyard: the atrium. This open yard, surrounded by a gallery at first timbered, then vaulted, was the heart of the monastery. Being at the centre of the regular buildings, it was the obligatory crossing point that joined them. Place of *meditation, reading and repose, this cloister was, with the church, the centre of religious life. It was usually square or rectangular in form, though rare monasteries preferred oval (Abington), triangular, symbolizing the *Trinity (*Saint-Riquier), or trapezoidal forms (Le Thoronet).

H. Leclercq, "Cloître", *DACL*, 3, 2, 1914, 1991-2012. – J. Carron-Touchard, *Cloîtres romans de France*, Saint-Léger-Vauban, 1983 ("La Nuit des temps").

Noëlle Deflou

**CLOTHING.** Little medieval clothing survives; like finds from archaeological digs, it tells us about primary materials, techniques of cutting and sewing and metallic accessories. Most of our information comes from illustrated sources and archive documents whose facts usually concern only aristocratic circles.

*Textiles held first place among primary materials: linen for undergarments or summer clothing, woollen cloth of variable quality for overgarments, *silk for religious *vestments and princely pomp. Leather had a more limited employment: shoes, cases and bags or whole garments sometimes reinforced with metal plaques for the military, since armour entirely of *metal was very costly. Long held in disrespect, *furs enjoyed great favour in the late Middle Ages; kid and rabbit or squirrel and sable were usually worn with the fur inwards.

Popular costume evolved little. The considerable value of its primary materials in comparison with the standard of living forbade width, length or frequent replacement. But it was sometimes adapted to the seasons, to bad weather, to activities; apart from the apron, specific working clothes were rare.

The male costume of the warrior aristocracy was that which evolved most. The arrival of the "*barbarian" peoples relegated the clothing of ancient tradition, tunic and mantle or cape, to the domain of religion and dignity. But from the 11th c. Frankish or German warriors copied the long, flowing garments of the Mediterranean. In the 14th c., it is among them that we find the group of young people who launched the fashion of clothing adapted and composed of different pieces to cover the upper and lower parts of the body (doublet and hose). Quality of materials, intensity of colours, fullness, wealth of ornamentation emphasized hierarchies. With a long delay, the middle class of the *towns, then the *peasants adopted and adapted aristocratic fashions.

Female clothing evolved less spectacularly. Yet village *women adopted the colour blue earlier than peasant men. The female imagination expressed itself in headwear: the simple veil of early days was replaced among peasant women by the black or red hood in the late Middle Ages, while noble ladies invented extraordinary constructions of linen or silk.

Sign of belonging to a group, a social category or an age group, costume gave a positive distinction to dignitaries and a negative distinction to the excluded (*Jews, outcasts, *prostitutes) or those who had voluntarily renounced the world (members of religious *orders or hermits). Laws and regulations, issued by *kings or urban authorities, imposed on everyone a clothing or distinctive signs related to his status. Social pressure relaxed only at princely or popular feasts which authorized cross-dressing.

*Actes du premier congrès international d'histoire du costume (Venise 1952)*, Milan, 1955. – R. Levi-Pisetzky, *Storia del costume in Italia*, 2-3, Milan, 1964-1966. – E. Piponnier, *Costume et vie sociale. La cour d'Anjou (XIV^e-XV^e siècle)*, Paris, 1970. – S. M. Newton, *Fashion in the Age of the Black Prince. A Study of the Years 1340-1365*, Woodbridge, 1980. – *Cloth and Clothing in Medieval Europe*, N.B. Harte (ed.), K.G. Ponting (ed.), London, 1983. – G. R. Owen-Crocker, *Dress in Anglo-Saxon England*, Manchester, 1986. – *Le Vêtement. Histoire, archéologie et symbolique vestimentaire au Moyen Âge*, Paris, 1989 ("Cahiers du Léopard d'Or", 1). – E. Piponnier, P. Mane, *Se vêtir au Moyen Âge*, Paris, 1995.

Françoise Piponnier

**CLOUD.** The cloud is the quintessential divine *sign, whether it opens to allow the elect to perceive the object of his contemplation (St John the Evangelist, in the 9th-c. Gospels of Lothar: Paris, BNF, ms. lat. 266) or whether it appears as the immediate manifestation of the sacred, suggestng the opening of secular space over the other space that gives it its truth (*Giotto, *The Ecstasy of St Francis*, Assisi, upper church, *c.*1297-1299). In this case, the cloud serves as an attribute of any form of ascent and transport. More generally, it is associated with the irruption of the sacred: it marks, as a sign of *theophany, the person whom it isolates from the rest of the composition (*Christ and *Mary in the scene of the *Foundation of *Santa Maria Maggiore* by *Masolino da Panicale, now at the Museo Capodimonte, Naples). From a *typological point of view, it follows the pillar of cloud that served as guide to the people of Israel in their exodus from Egypt.

K. Keyssner, "Nimbus", *PRE*, 17, 1, 1936, 591. – G. Van der Leeuw, *La Religion dans son essence et dans ses manifestations*, Paris, 1948, 54-65 (Fr. tr.).

Daniel Russo

**CLOVESHO.** The (unidentified) site of a series of English church *councils, first established by Archbishop *Theodore (668-690), and intended by him to be annual, which are known to have taken place through the 8th and into the 9th c. (the last being attested in 825). The promulgations of several of these councils, notably those of 747 and 803, have been preserved. Recent scholarly opinion inclines to the view that *Clovesho* was located in Mercia, perhaps near Leicester, perhaps at Brixworth; but the identification cannot yet be proved.

*Councils and Ecclesiastical Documents relating to Great Britain and Ireland*, 3, A. W. Haddan (ed.), W. Stubbs (ed.), Oxford, 1869-1878, 3, 360-385, 541-548 (3 vol.); repr. 1964. – S. Keynes, *The Councils of Clovesho*, Leicester, 1994. – C. Cubitt, *Anglo-Saxon Church Councils c. 650-c. 850*, London, 1995.

Michael Lapidge

**CLOVIS (*c.*466-511).** Our knowledge of Clovis is of the scantiest. Indeed, with the exception of rare contemporary sources whose transcriptions have been preserved (in particular the letters of St Remigius and St Avitus), it rests essentially on the few pages devoted to him by *Gregory of Tours († 594) in the *Decem libri historiarum*. Writing more than half a century after the ruler's death, the author seems to have found difficulties in bringing together sufficient documentation, notably by reason of the rapid attrition of oral evidence. Thus he was led to fill out the account of undeniable historical facts (several are supported by other sources) with unverifiable anecdotes and details, as well as with moral or religious considerations, the real object of his work. The succession of the main stages of Clovis's reign have always been the object of controversy among historians, as has their quinquennial rhythm, calculated from the king's accession (their exact date cannot be fixed since we do not know whether Gregory counted in ordinal or cardinal numbers).

According to Gregory of Tours, Clovis was aged 45 when he died in 511, which would allow us to date his birth to 466. His father Childeric then reigned between Somme and lower Rhine over a part of the Western *Franks (wrongly called *Salians until recently). Allied with the last representatives of Roman authority in Gaul – Aegidius, Count Paul, then Syagrius son of Aegidius – he fought several times on their behalf against the *Visigoths and the Saxons on the Loire. As the letter addressed by St Remigius to Clovis on his accession in 481-482 attests, he administered in the name of the Roman authorities the vast province of Belgica Secunda, whose northern half had in fact already been in the hands of the Franks for several decades. Clovis's mother Basina was the former wife of King Bisinus of Thuringia whom Childeric had seduced when his people had forced him into temporary exile. We know of at least three sisters: Audefleda, Albofleda and Lantechilde. Though Childeric's tomb was discovered by chance at *Tournai in 1653, it is not certain that this Roman town was the king's permanent residence, where Clovis might have spent his childhood.

The silence of the sources on the first years of his reign suggests that Clovis, administrator of Belgica Secunda in his turn, at first kept up good relations with Syagrius. But in the fifth year of his reign (486-487), a veritable military *putsch* allowed the Frankish king to defeat the *magister militum* of the Gauls and throw off Roman tutelage.

Though the so-called victory of Soissons (we do not know the place) allowed Clovis to extend his rule as far as the Loire, the pacification of the lands between Seine and Loire seems to have been only gradual. In the tenth year of his reign (491-492), the Frankish king was induced to fight a campaign against the Thuringians who had reached the lower Rhine and threatened the Frankish kingdoms on its left bank (though the kingdom of *Thuringia in central Germany was not conquered by the Franks until the 530s). In the years that followed, Clovis pursued a policy of matrimonial alliances, giving his sister Audefleda in marriage to *Theodoric, king of the *Ostrogoths, and himself marrying a Catholic Burgundian princess (though her people practised *Arianism), Clotild, in 492-494. This was in fact a second union, since Clovis already had a son, Theuderic, whose mother, according to modern historiography, came from the royal family of the Eastern (later called Ripuarian) Franks (not a concubine, as Gregory claims): as witness his name and the fact that on his father's death he inherited the old Frankish kingdom of *Cologne. Clotild gave Clovis at least five children: Ingomer (born and died 494), Chlodomir (495-524), Childebert († 558), Chlotar (500-561) and finally Clotild (who married the Visigothic King Amalaric, successor to Alaric II).

In the fifteenth year of his reign (495-496), Clovis had to intervene against the *Alamanni, whose advance threatened the Frankish kingdom of Cologne as well as that of the *Burgundians. He was the victor, not without difficulty according to Gregory of Tours, in an unknown place traditionally but wrongly situated at Tolbiac (now Zülpich, in Germany), site of another battle between Franks and Alamanni. Still according to Gregory of Tours, it was this victory, obtained after having implored the God of Clotild, which decided the Frankish king to convert. In fact, a favourable climate for this already existed, prepared by the relations Childeric had formed with St Remigius and St Geneviève and upheld by Clotild. Though the place is not specified, the royal *baptism certainly took place at *Reims, Remigius's episcopal see, one 25 December. Its date has always been keenly disputed by historians. If we subordinate the event, as a later source suggests (*letter of St Nicetius of Trier to the *Lombard Queen Clodoswind, Clovis's grand-daughter, in 567-568), to a preliminary visit of Clovis to St *Martin's tomb at *Tours, it could only have taken place on the occasion of one of the campaigns against the Visigoths, of which we know three: in 496, 498 and 507. The baptism being also consecutive to a campaign against the Alamanni, of which two are known, in 496 and 506, it must thus be put in 496 (traditional date, but plausible), 498 (or 499) or 508, a date that seems to prevail nowadays.

In 500-501, internal dynastic quarrels led Clovis to an intervention with no sequel in Burgundy. This would definitively mark the beginning of a solid alliance between Franks and Burgundians, directed against their common neighbours the Alamanni and Visigoths and reinforced by the *conversion of the Burgundian King Gundobad to Catholicism. Not mentioned by Gregory of Tours, a second war against the Alamanni is indicated in 505-506 by *Cassiodorus. It would allow Clovis finally to eliminate their advance on the left bank of the Rhine. But the main enemy remained the Visigothic kingdom of *Toulouse, which controlled the regions between the Loire and the *Pyrenees. The support of the Eastern Roman Emperor Anastasius, which kept Theodoric in *Italy, allowed Clovis, supported by the Ripuarian Franks and Burgundians, to beat Alaric II at Vouillé in 507. This victory, presented by Gregory as a crusade against the Arian Visigoths (while a part of the Gallo-Roman and Christian aristocracy supported them), was in reality the logical pursuit of a conquest that had practically marked time for twenty years. But it was not total, since Vasconia (future *Gascony) and *Septimania (future *Languedoc-Roussillon, kept by the Visigoths who reformed their kingdom in *Spain with *Toledo as capital) escaped the Franks.

It was at Tours, doubtless in 508, that Clovis celebrated his triumph in the purest antique tradition, clad in purple and crowning himself with a diadem. Envoys of Anastasius conferred on him the codicil of the honorary consulate, an honorific distinction that sanctioned his victory and confirmed his pre-eminence over the other *barbarian kingdoms of the West. Nothing remained for Clovis, a "new Constantine" as Gregory of Tours was pleased to write, but to provide himself with a capital. His choice fell on *Paris, not for strategic reasons (other towns had greater military importance), but probably because of the burial-place of St Geneviève († doubtless in 502), whose links with the nascent Frankish dynasty had been so close. This is what led Clovis and Clotild to build over her tomb the basilica of the Holy Apostles (future Saint-Geneviève), in an annexe of which they placed their dynastic mausoleum.

If we may trust Gregory, the last years of Clovis's reign saw the bloody annexation of the still-existing Frankish kingdoms of northern Gaul, which finally allowed him to be called "King of the Franks". The king also legislated, notably having the first version of the Salic Law drawn up. Some months before his death, he held at *Orléans in July 511 a *synod of the *bishops of Gaul that presided over the birth of the Merovingian Church. The king died at the end of the year, doubtless 27 November. He left as an inheritance to his sons, who shared it out in accordance with Germanic tradition, the most powerful barbarian kingdom of the West (its "natural space" having to be completed by the annexation of Burgundy in 534 and of Provence in 536) and, what was more, its first Catholic State.

Of all the Germanic kings of the West, Clovis thus appears as the one whose work was both most successful and most lasting. In this we must definitely see the political and military genius of a king whose personality the sources hardly permit us to discern, but also the capacity for acculturation of a people who, as an active minority (some tens of thousands as compared with several million Gallo-Romans), was able to preserve the antique and Christian cultural heritage of Gaul, while enriching it with Germanic contributions (laws, customs, vocabulary). So Clovis, whose people gave their name to *France, justly deserves to be considered its distant founder and its first *king.

G. Kurth, *Clovis*, 1896 (re-ed. Paris, 1978). – J. M. Wallace Hadrill, *The long-haired kings and other history*, London, 2nd ed. Toronto, 1982. – K.-F. Werner, *Les origines*, Paris, 1984 ("Histoire de France", 1). – I. Wood, "Gregory of Tours and Clovis", *RBPH*, 63, 1985, 249-272 (*Histoire médiévale, moderne et contemporaine*, fasc. 2). – S. Lebecq, *Les origines franques (Ve-XIe siècle)*, Paris, 1990. – P. Périn, "The undiscovered grave of King Clovis", M. Carver (ed.), *The Age of Sutton Hoo. The seventh century in north-western Europe*, Woodbridge, 1992, 255-264. – I. Wood, *The Merovingian Kingdoms (470-751)*, London, New York, 1994. – W. M. Daly, "Clovis: how barbaric, how pagan?", *Speculum*, 69, 3, July 1994, 619-664. – M. Spencer, "Dating the baptism of Clovis (1886-1993)", *Early Medieval Europe*, 3, 2, 1994, 97-116. – M. Rouche (dir.), *Clovis. Histoire et mémoire*, Paris, 1997, 2 vol. (Actes du Colloque international d'histoire de Reims, 1996). – L. Theiss, *Clovis. De l'histoire au mythe*, Paris, 1996. – D. Shanzer, "Dating the baptism of Clovis: the bishop of Vienne vs the bishop of Tours", *Early Medieval Europe*, 7, 1, 1998, 29-57.

Patrick Périn

**CLUNY.** On 11 Sept 910 (or 909), William III, duke of *Aquitaine and count of Mâcon, later called "the Pious", made a gift to Berno, abbot of Baume-les-Messieurs and of a group of monastic establishments situated in Berry and in the Jura, of a **villa* near Mâcon in order to found there a Benedictine monastery put under the patronage of the apostles *Peter and *Paul. In the *charter of foundation, William renounced any rights over the establishment, left the free *election of the *abbot to the community and put the monastery directly under the protection of the papacy. These arrangements (infrequent but not truly exceptional in the early 10th c.) provided Cluny with the conditions for the emergence and rise of a *monasticism independent of the spiritual and *temporal powers up to the 1200s.

In 926, Berno's *testament assigned Cluny to his disciple *Odo, under whose abbacy (927-942) the monastery really got under way. Odo marked Cluny lastingly with his learning, his *ecclesiology and his reforming ideas. In 931, a privilege of Pope John XI accorded Cluny a right of *reform that allowed its abbot to take charge of any monastery at the request of a lay abbot and to accept any monk whose monastery refused to be reformed. Odo was thus called to *Rome, *Fleury-sur-Loire and Aquitaine, and launched the Cluniac tradition of reform that remained, until the end of *Maiolus's abbacy, a personal undertaking of the abbot.

After the abbacy of Aymard (942-954), important for the growth of the temporality, Cluny experienced a major turning-point in its history under Maiolus (954-994) and *Odilo (994-1049). On the occasion of the *consecration of its second church (Cluny II) in 981, the monastery acquired *relics of the apostles Peter and Paul and was transformed into a sort of "little Rome". In those same years, Cluny became an autonomous sanctuary thanks to the privilege of *exemption delivered by Gregory V (998) and extended by John XIX (1024) to all Cluniacs "wherever they may be". This latter arrangement marked the true birth of the *Ecclesia cluniacensis* as an ecclesiastical network (*abbeys and *priories) centred on the Burgundian sanctuary and especially on its abbot, who was usually on his travels. The autonomy of the *Ecclesia cluniacensis* was materialized by the drawing up of the customs; the first known customs (*Consuetudines antiquiores* contemporary with Maiolus) were strictly liturgical; the second, *Liber tramitis aevi Odilonis*, regulated both the monastery's internal life and the community's relations with external powers (*bishops, *kings, emperors, etc); the last known customs (called those of Bernard and Ulrich, from the name of their redactors, contemporaries of the sixth abbot, *Hugh of Semur) were of the same nature and applied themselves to giving a legal form to the monastery's sovereignty. The Cluniacs were in effect, from about the year 1000, sovereign lords who had secured for themselves, like other lay or ecclesiastical castellans of that period when *seigneurie banale* was being established in Southern Francia, the former prerogatives of royal power (in particular *justice). This **seigneurie* had the characteristic of defending its prerogatives by ways that were primarily ecclesiastical, such as the prohibition of ecclesiastical enclosures at the time of the movements of the *Peace and Truce of God or, a little later, the establishment of the Cluniac "sacred *ban" under the (Cluniac) Pope *Urban II; thus it was that, at the time of the *Gregorian reform, Cluny became the little laboratory of an important historical process: the territorialization of the *libertas ecclesiae*.

Under Maiolus and Odilo, Cluny was primarily a regional power implanted in *Burgundy, Auvergne, *Provence and *Italy, on the route to *Rome. With the abbacy of Hugh of Semur (1049-1109), Cluny was extended to the four corners of Europe. To the north, the Cluniacs installed important dependencies in the *Capetian kingdom (in particular the priory of Saint-Martin-des-Champs at *Paris). After the conquest of *England by the duke of *Normandy in 1066, the Cluniacs took part in the effort of monastic reconstruction undertaken by *William the Conqueror. Despite the existence of ancient and close links with the *Empire from the time of the Ottonian and *Salian rulers, the Cluniac push to the east was more difficult. The spirit of independence of the Burgundian monks came up against the logic of the imperial system in which the emperor and his supporters, particularly the bishops, had the upper hand over the monastic establishments; so it was not until late (second half of 11th c.) and often through the intermediary of monasteries adopting the Cluniac customs while remaining legally independent (Saint-Blaise, *Hirsau, *Siegburg) that Cluny penetrated the imperial world. At the appeal of Sancho III of *Navarre and especially *Alfonso VI of *León-Castile, the Cluniacs took part in the entreprise of political and religious reconquest of the Iberian peninsula and contributed to the establishment of the *Roman liturgy in place of the *Hispanic liturgy. The rulers and aristocracy of the peninsula found in Cluny both an instrument of ecclesiastical policy and a "Roman" sanctuary, placed under the patronage of Peter and Paul, on whose assistance in the next life the ministering monks were, from the abbacy of Odilo (founder of the *feast of All Souls, 2 Nov), great specialists. Conversely, the Cluniacs considered *Spain a tributary land whence came the *gold necessary for their economy. Thus it was Spanish *rent that financed the construction of Cluny III, the largest church in the medieval West (until St Peter's in Rome), begun by Hugh of Semur.

The development and progressive structuring of the *Ecclesia cluniacensis* under the abbacy of Hugh of Semur were contemporary with the great reform of the Church and the confrontation between the Empire and the papacy in a politico-religious quarrel known as the *Investiture Contest. These events marked the history of Cluny. Cluniacs were directly involved in the reform movement as instruments of the papacy: legations of Hugh of Semur, then of his successor *Pons of Melgueil; integration into the papal entourage as cardinals; participation in the establishment of a chamber of accounts (**Camera*) by Pierre Gloc on the model of Cluny; and finally the accession of a Cluniac to the papacy as *Urban II, the pope of the first *crusade. In return, Cluny's destiny at that time depended very largely on the papacy. The Cluniac network is often represented as a sort of autonomous ecclesiastical State, hierarchically structured pyramidally from the head (the mother abbey) down to the members (abbeys, priories). This is to reckon without the obligatory intermediary represented by the pope, who, from *Gregory VII, disposed of the right to create or suppress a religious institution and to go back on the privileges formerly conceded by his predecessors. Cluniac history in the 11th, 12th and 13th cc. thus consisted of interminable quarrels between the Burgundian monastery and one or other of its rebellious dependencies, in particular prestigious former abbeys (*Saint-Gilles-du-Gard, *Vézelay, Baume-les-Messieurs. . .) that did not accept subjection to an "arch-abbot". In these disputes between establishments all put directly under the jurisdiction of Rome, the pope arbitrated in accordance with his needs of the moment, which did not necessarily correspond to those of Cluny.

The fragility of the *Ecclesia cluniacensis* appeared under the abbacy of Pons of Melgeuil (1109-1122), marked by a severe internal crisis that can only be understood when situated in the context of the rise (late 11th - early 12th cc.) of new religious movements, eremitic or monastic in expression, which, after the manner of *Bernard of Clairvaux and the *Cistercians, defined themselves in opposition to the Cluniac model. In response, the abbacy of *Peter the Venerable (1122-1156) marked the time of change. A series of statutes came to supplement or even correct the customs and changed the orientation of Cluniac life (whose lordly pomp and liturgical splendour were criticized) towards greater austerity. With the help of *Henry of Blois, bishop of *Winchester, Peter tried to re-orient the monastery's economy, structurally dependent on *donations, towards a direct and more rational exploitation of its estates. Like Hugh of Semur and to a lesser degree Pons of Melgueil, Peter was heavily involved in the affairs of his century. But, unlike his predecessors (except for the already very distant Odo), he was the only one to be equally involved on the doctrinal level, writing works against *heretics such as *Peter of Bruys (*Against the Petrobrusians*), mingling his voice with the *antijudaism contemporary with the second crusade (*Against the Jews*) and diabolizing *Islam in *Against the Saracens*. In his *Treatise on miracles*, which, in the manner of *Peter Damian, mingles edifying stories and theological or ecclesiological teachings, and his collection of *letters, which are often veritable small *treatises, Peter the Venerable set himself to describe Cluny as a little *Ecclesia* in itself, *catholica, casta, libera*, refuge of the *laity and bringing together the various forms of belonging to the sacred order (priests, *bishops, *cardinals, *popes; *recluses [Marcigny-sur-Loire], monks and hermits).

In 1132 Peter called a general *chapter, generally considered the first step towards less abbatial monarchism and more collegiality within the *Ecclesia cluniacensis*. But it was only with the statutes of Hugh V (1199-1207) that the practice of the annual general chapter became, in imitation of Cistercian usages, an institutional mechanism. From then on we can speak of an "Order of Cluny" structured into provinces whose establishments were periodically visited. Cluny continued to play a role within Benedictine *monasticism until the end of the Ancien Régime, but with nothing like the influence attained in the 10th, 11th and 12th centuries. This "Cluny after Cluny" still needs to be better studied, as the recent works of G. Melville, P. Racinet and D. Riche have shown. The *order, falling back more and more on the kingdom of *France, was – a paradox of history – from now on doubly under tutelage. Tutelage of the king, to whom custody over many of the Cluniac establishments was conceded in the 13th c. and who in 1281 integrated Cluniac seignorial justice into the judicial organisation of the kingdom (with possible appeals from the judgments of the abbot to the *Parlement of Paris); tutelage above all of the pope who, from the late 12th c., acted within the order as a superior authority, deposing the abbot at need. This control was radicalized still further in the 14th c. with the system of *commendation, by virtue of which the pope appointed the abbot of Cluny and the abbots and principal *priors of the order.

*Cluniac Monasticism in the Central Middle Ages*, N. Hunt (ed.), Hamden (CT), 1971. – *Cluny in Lombardia. Atti del Convegno storico celebrativo del 9 centenario della fondazione del priorato cluniacense di Pontida (22-25 aprile 1977)*, *ItBen*, 1, 1979-1981. – G. Constable, *Cluniac Studies*, London, 1980. – B.H. Rosenwein, *Rhinoceros Bound: Cluny in the Tenth Century*, Philadelphia (PA), 1982. – "Cluny", *LdM*, 2, 1983, 2172-2193. – A. H. Bredero, *Cluny et Cîteaux au XII*[e] *siècle. L'histoire d'une controverse*, Amsterdam, 1985. – M. Pacaut, *L'Ordre de Cluny*, Paris, 1986. – D. Poeck, *Cluniacensis Ecclesia*. – E. M. Wischerman, "Grundlagen einer cluniacensischen Bibliotheksgeschichte", *MMAS*, 62, Munich, 1988. – B. H. Rosenwein, *To Be Neighbor of Saint Peter. The Social Meaning of Cluny's Property 909-1049*, Ithaca (NY), 1989. – G. Melville, "Cluny après 'Cluny'. Le treizième siècle: un champ de recherche", *Francia*, 17, 1990, 91-124. – P. Racinet, *Les Maisons de l'ordre de Cluny au Moyen Âge*, Louvain-Brussels, 1990. – D. Riche, *L'Ordre de Cluny, de la mort de Pierre le vénérable à Jean III de Bourbon. "Le vieux pays clunisien"* (Doctoral thesis. Université Lumière-Lyon II, 1991), to appear. – "Cluny", *DLFMA*, 1992, 311-316. – G. Constable, "The Abbot and Townsmen of Cluny in the Twelfth Century", *Church and City 1000-1500*, D. Abulafia (ed.), M. Franklin (ed.), M. Rubin (ed.), Cambridge, 1992. – D. Iogna-Prat, "Les coutumiers et les statuts de Cluny comme sources historiques (v.940-v.1200)", *RMab*, new series, 3, 1992, 23-48. – J. Wollasch, "Cluny und Deutschland", *SMGB*, 103, 1992, 7-32. – J. Wollasch, *Cluny, Licht der Welt*, Düsseldorf, 1996. – *Der cluniacensische Klosterverband (10.-12. Jahrhundert)*, Munich, 1997. – D. Iogna-Prat, *Ordonner et exclure. Cluny et la société chrétienne face à l'hérésie, au judaisme et à l'islam*, Paris, 1998. – *Die Cluniacenser in ihrem politisch-sozialen Umfeld*, G. Constable (ed.), G. Melville (ed.), J. Oberste (ed.), Münster i. W., 1998.

Dominique Iogna-Prat

**CNUT (994?-1035).** A celebrated king of *Denmark, Cnut (Canute, Knútr inn Mikli, Knútr the Great) reigned as king of *England from 1016 to 1035. He fulfilled the dream of his father, Sveinn Tjugguskegg (Forkbeard), to unite *Norway, Denmark and England under his *crown. To do this, it was probably he who built the famous circular fortified camps (as at Trelleborg) that were doubtless barracks or training camps for the conquest of England. He married Emma, the widow of an *Anglo-Saxon king. He systematically developed Christianity in Denmark, building churches, setting up monasteries and installing numerous Anglo-Saxon *clerics who left a deep mark on the Christian religion in Denmark.

P. Stafford, "The Laws of Cnut and the History of Anglo-Saxon Royal Promises", *Anglo-Saxon England*, 10, 1982, 13-90. – M.K. Lawson, *Cnut*, London, 1993. – *The Reign of Cnut*, A.R. Rumble (ed.), London, 1994.

Régis Boyer

**COADJUTOR.** When a titular of a *benefice, major or minor, was no longer able to carry out his duties, he was replaced by a coadjutor, designated by the *bishop in the case of a *parish priest, by the *metropolitan or the cathedral *chapter, with papal authorization, in the case of a bishop. The coadjutor did not possess the *title and enjoyed only a part of the revenues, but he received *consecration and held the plenitude of jurisdiction.

Somewhat similar situations, though in which the term "coadjutor" does not appear, muliplied in the later Middle Ages, with the *resignation of certain aged bishops in favour of *e.g.* their nephew. Until his death, the bishop kept the title and part of the revenues, and, generally installed in one of the castles of his **mensa*, he sometimes continued to exercise certain rights, the collation of benefices among others. The resignatary also bore the title and performed the duties that the bishop had resigned to him.

G. Le Bras, *Institutions ecclésiastiques de la Chrétienté médiévale*, 2, 1964, 402 and 422 ("HE", 12).

Vincent Tabbagh

**CODE OF JUSTINIAN.** The Code of Justinian represents the main part of the "Corpus iuris civilis", the codification established by the Emperor Justinian (reigned 527-565). In 528, worried about the great disparity and discordances of ancient Roman law, he appointed a commission of jurists to select from among all the norms of *Roman law those that were to remain in force and to classify them in thematic order, excluding all that had expired or fallen into disuse. After a year the codification was ready, and on 16 April 529 it came into force. All reference before the courts to former sources was then prohibited. However, immediately after this promulgation, the need appeared for a revision of the material and a new formulation, especially in order to integrate the imperial constitutions promulgated in the meanwhile. So, early in 534 the emperor ordered this new work, and the *Codex Justinianus repetitae praelectionis*, the second edition of the Code, compiled like the former under the presidency of Tribonian, came into force on 16 Nov 534.

The reasons that led Justinian to undertake this work show his conception of the monarch's legislative role: without abrogating the old law, it had to be invested with the formal force that the imperial will conferred on it. The problem of discordant norms was resolved by the application of the principle that the later law abrogated the earlier. Moreover the constitution *Cordi*, the law by which the Code was introduced in 534, provided for the later publication of other laws to supplement the codification. Indeed Justinian promulgated a great number of these during his reign, called "New constitutions after the Code" (*Novellae*). To ensure that the authentic text was respected and to preserve it from any outside alteration, the emperor forbade the composition of commentaries in the margin of the text of the Code, and even its translation (except word for word), which would risk making marginal notes a non-authentic added part.

P. Krueger, *Corpus iuris civilis*, 2, Berlin, 1877. – P. E. Pieler, "Byzantinische Rechtsliteratur", in H. Hunger, *Die hochsprachliche profane Literatur der Byzantiner*, 2, Munich, 1978, 400-419. – N. Van der Wal, J. H. A. Lokin, *Historiae iuris graeco-romani delineatio. Les sources du droit byzantin de 300 à 1453*, Groningen, 1985, 31-38.

Stavros Perentidis

**CODEX, CODICOLOGY**

**The West.** In Antiquity, the image of the *book was that of a roll of *papyrus leaves pasted to each other side by side to form a long strip on which writing was arranged in columns juxtaposed from left to right, and rolled round a stick. A rather impractical procedure, which did not easily permit turning back in the text. However, the *volumen* (from Latin *volvere*, to roll up) or rolled volume prevailed for long centuries until the appearance in the 1st century AD of another form of book: the book formed of a collection of leaves held together at one side and allowing easy access to any part of the text.

The book appeared from now on in this form of the *codex*, a collection of leaves folded in two and grouped in one or more small fascicles or quires, formed usually of four sheets folded in two, or eight leaves. These quires were then sewn together along the fold and joined to the binding. A *codex* could contain one or more works; conversely, a single work could be divided among several *codices*. On the other hand, it frequently happened in the Middle Ages that books or fragments of books of different provenance might be bound into a single binding: in this case the *codex* thus formed is said to represent so many codicological units.

Codicology is the name given to the discipline relating to the material study of the book. It originally included the history of manuscripts, the history of collections, the present situation of books, their conservation, catalogues and repositories, and finally the manuscript trade. But since the 1960s the work of certain researchers has led this discipline to evolve into narrower confines: how, when and where was such a book made? by who, for whom and for what purpose was it used? Today, some codicologists extend their researches to all written documents in whatever material form they may be, emphasizing the conditions, milieu and purposes of their production. In 1934, J. Destrez opened the way to a more concrete orientation, with a study of the production of university manuscripts. More recently, the work of F. Masai, the publications of L. Gilissen and the researches of C. Bozzolo and E. Ornato have led to an "experimental" codicology, while more recent manuals of *palaeography give a large place to the codicological study of written documents.

L. Gilissen, *Prolégomènes à la codicologie*, Ghent, 1977. – J. Vezin, "La Fabrication du manuscrit", *Histoire de l'édition française, I, Le Livre conquérant: du Moyen Âge au milieu du XVII^e^ siècle*, Paris, 1982. – C. Bozzolo, E. Ornato, *Pour une histoire du livre manuscrit au Moyen Âge*, Paris, 1983 (2nd ed.). – J. Lemaire, *Introduction à la codicologie*, Louvain-la-Neuve, 1983. – A.G. Weiler, *Codex in Context*, Nijmegen, 1985. – *The Role of the Book in Medieval Culture*, P. Ganz (ed.), Turnhout, 1986. – B.

Shailor, *The Medieval Book*, New Haven, 1988. – D.H. Banks, *Medieval Manuscript Bookmaking: a bibliographical guide*, London, 1989. – M. Maniaci, P.F. Munafo, *Ancient and Medieval Book Materials and Techniques*, Vatican, 1993. – *Making the Medieval Book*, L. Brownrigg (ed.), London, 1995.

Françoise Gasparri

**Byzantium.** Codicology is the material study of the manuscript *book. The form of the *codex* appeared in the 1st c. AD and supplanted the *volumen* from the 4th century. The only rolls produced at Byzantium were intended for the liturgy (writing parallel to the "short side", contrary to the ancient usage). But great biblical *codices* copied in the 4th c., almost square in format, still offered a page layout (in several parallel columns) similar to that of a *volumen*. Medieval manuscripts were copied on *parchment or *paper (whose use was known from the second half of the 11th c.). Byzantium seems never to have made paper – a material always imported from the Mediterranean East, the *Maghreb, Muslim and Christian *Spain and, from the 13th c., *Italy. The Italian invention of watermarking is of great utility in dating. The *codex* was a collection of "quires", often quaternions (8 folios), though other types (ternions, quinions, senions. . .) are not rare. In parchment quires, the "flesh" and "flower" sides alternated so that the quire began with a "flesh" side and two sides of the same type always faced each other (Gregory's law).

The writing was guided by rulers applied in each quire according to determined systems, which, by the play of horizontal and vertical lines, created patterns (or "types") that were counted by hundreds. It was generally done with compasses or dividers, and we also observe – rarely – reinforcements in blacklead or brown ink. The quires were numbered with the help of letters, or "signatures", the possible locations (on the first recto and/or the last verso) allowing a multiplicity of combinations. The use of catchwords was exceptional, and the rare known cases are explained by "Latin" influence.

Binding was not done until after the copy had been completed: sewn to each other, the quires were fixed to wooden press-boards covered with a linen cloth and then with a piece of leather decorated with punches using the technique of cold stamping; the Byzantines did not employ gold leaf decoration. The binding could be protected by metal "bolts" fixed to the press-board: the book was laid flat, the smooth back being invisible, and the cut edges sometimes bore a painted decoration and even a brief title. The "Western" usage of the chain, to fix the book to a support, is unknown.

J. Leroy, "La Description codicologique des manuscrits grecs de parchemin", *La Paléographie grecque et byzantine*, Paris, 1987, 27-44. – J. Irigoin, "Typologie et description codicologique des manuscrits de papier", *Paleografia e codicologia greca*, D. Harlfinger (ed.), G. Patro (ed.), 1, Alessandria, 1991, 275-303 ("Biblioteca di scrittura e civiltà", 3). – P. Hoffmann, "L'Art de la reliure à Byzance sous les Paléologues", *Byzance. L'art byzantin dans les collections publiques françaises*, Paris, 1992, 467-471.

Philippe Hoffmann

**COENOBITE, COENOBITISM.** Composed of two Greek terms (*koinos*, "common"; *bios*, "life"), the Latin word *coenobium* (monastery of communal life) appears for the first time in a *letter written by St Jerome in 384 (*Ep.* 22, 34-35). Forty years later, John *Cassian in turn used it (*Conferences*, 18, 4-5) and drew from it the derivative *coenobiota* (monk living in a *coenobium*), whence our term "coenobite". Coenobitism, then, is the monastic life led in community, as opposed to the solitary life of *anchorites or hermits. These two ways of being a monk, while opposed to each other, are intimately linked. The founder of coenobitism in Egypt, St Pachomius, had been formed in the school of the anchorite Palamon, and the early coenobitic life remained strongly marked by its eremitical origins: during the greater part of the day, the coenobite remained alone in his cell. Conversely, the common life was conceived by Jerome and Cassian as an indispensable preparation for those who wished to embrace the solitary life: true hermits emerged from *coenobia*. This fundamental relationship of the two types of *monasticism gave rise, nevertheless, to divergent views: while the greater number, with Jerome and Cassian, considered exodus to the *desert legitimate in certain conditions and saw in the solitary life the summit of monastic renunciation, some, following Basil (*Rule*, 3), rejected all anachoresis and advocated a common life closed on itself. In the former point of view, which was that of the Master and St *Benedict (*Rule*, 1, 2), the two ways of life were often made to relate to another dichotomy: the "*active life " (ascetic purification), led in the *coenobium*, was succeeded by the "contemplative" life, whose ideal setting was solitude.

The inspiration for Christian coenobitism must be sought in Scripture. Pagan (Pythagoreans) or Jewish antecedents (Essenes) played an altogether secondary role. For the founders of the 4th c., the principal model was the early Church of Jerusalem, where all were "of one heart and one soul" in the sharing of goods and in obedience to the Apostles (Acts 2-4). This example of the Acts was even considered by Cassian and others to be the true historical source of coenobitism, which had lasted from the apostolic period alongside secular Christianity. However, in this imitation of the early Church, there were different emphases. For a certain Egyptian tradition, represented by Jerome, Cassian and the Master, the coenobitic pact rested above all on *obedience. For Augustine, on the contrary, the primordial idea was the union of hearts in charity. Benedict brought the two points of view together. From the *Rule of the Master* he also inherited the image of the "school of Christ", which referred implicitly to the group of twelve disciples assembled around Christ, their master, whose place was taken in the monastery by the *abbot.

In the ancient history of coenobitism, the most important evolution was the change of dwelling that came about in *c.*500: from individual cells to the common dormitory.

H. Leclercq, "Cénobitisme", *DACL*, 2, 2, 1910, 3047-3248. – A. de Vogüé, "Vita comune", *DIP*, 19, 2000.

Adalbert de Vogüé

**COIMBRA.** Coimbra is a town in the centre of *Portugal. Its name comes from the Latin *Conimbriga*, the name of a Roman town situated about 15 km south of the river Mondego. Conimbriga was devastated by the *Suevi (in 465 and 468) and fell into decline. For this reason, over the following decades most of the inhabitants together with their institutions, including the episcopal see, moved to the nearby village of *Aeminium*. According to Avelino J. Costa, the bishop of Conimbriga settled at Aeminium between 580 and 589, without altering his title. Under *Visigothic rule, the new Coimbra enjoyed a certain prosperity. Worship was given to Christian *martyrs like St Comba, St Pelagius or St Goldofre. There were also prelates known for their *sanctity. From the 7th to the 11th c., the *bishops of Coimbra temporarily administered the neighbouring *dioceses of Viseu and Lamego. Under Muslim rule (711-1064), Coimbra had an important *Mozarabic social component. Before the 11th c., churches were built in the town and dedicated to St *Mary, St *Peter, the Saviour, St *Michael, St John (of Almedina), St *Christopher, St Cucufat and St Vincent. In the outskirts of the town, important Mozarabic monasteries were established, some of which followed a double rule, such as Lorvão, Vacariça and St George of Coimbra; these had active *scriptoria*, among others of lesser importance. After a period of crisis, the bishopric was restored in 1080 during the episcopate of Paterno. In that year, the council of *Burgos decided to suppress the *Hispanic liturgical rite. Coimbra resisted this obligation over a long period and did not feel the effects of the adoption of the Roman-Gregorian rite until the episcopate of the Frenchman Maurice (1099-1109).

In the first half of the 12th c., after several trials against the bishopric of Porto, which were judged at Rome, the long frontiers of the diocese of Coimbra were confirmed, and at the same time it was defined as a *suffragan of the archdiocese of *Braga. Despite this, during the following decades there were regularly prolonged litigations against other neighbouring prelates, like those of Guarda, Viseu and Lisbon. In the same period, Coimbra saw a series of ecclesiastical *foundations, especially of parish churches, thus accompanying the process of formation of Portugal, under the reign of King Dom *Afonso Henriques († 1185). This king chose Coimbra as capital of the new kingdom. The reforms for *canons reached Coimbra through the foundation of the powerful monastery of the Holy Cross (1132), which followed the Rule of St Rufus of Avignon, under the orientation of Theotonius († 1162), a friend of St *Bernard of Clairvaux and the first Portuguese saint. This monastery possessed a rich *scriptorium* and a very active school of canons, where St *Antony of Padua received his training. The capitular *scriptorium* and school were no less active and possessed one of the largest *libraries in medieval Portugal. Not until 1210 were the capitular and episcopal jurisdictions separated.

A whole set of new monastic institutions would continue to arise up to 1250, the most eminent examples, besides the temporarily Benedictine monasteries of Lorvão, Vacariça and St Mary of Seiça and those of the *canons regular of St Augustine (St George of Coimbra, St Peter of Folques and St Romanus of Seia), being the *Cistercians. These annexed Benedictine institutions like St Mary of Seiça and Lorvão or created others such as St Mary of Estrela and St Paul of Almaziva. Women's monasteries were also established, like that of St Mary of Semide, O.S.B., those of regular canonesses (St John of Donas and St Anne, C.R.S.A.), or those of Cistercian *nuns: Lorvão (1205), Celas (1214), etc. The *mendicant orders reached Coimbra with the *Franciscans (1217) and *Dominicans (1219). In 1286 was founded the first monastery of *Poor Clares, to which Queen Isabella of Aragon would retire (she died in 1336 and was canonized). In the Cistercian monasteries indicated, we find the blessed Sancha, Teresa and Mafalda, connected with the Portuguese royal family (13th c.). The Dominicans went through a phase of prosperity in the 15th c. and founded new convents in the diocese of Coimbra: Jesus of Aveiro, Our Lady of Mercy of Aveiro, Our Lady of Victory of *Batalha. A Dominican nun was even beatified: the blessed Joanna the Princess († 1490).

In 1279 and 1338, Coimbra went through a period in which the bishops were Languedocians: Aymeric of Éberard, Raymond of Éberard I and Raymond of Éberard II, Jean des Prés of Montpezat. This corresponded to a Portuguese political and cultural tendency favourable to Occitania, stimulated by the kings themselves. At this time devotions such as *Corpus Christi and the Immaculate *Conception of Mary were established in the diocese, certainly under the pastoral influence of the Franciscans. To this can be added the important role that the *laity themselves played in local religious expression. Thus forms of socio-religious association developed, beginning as early as the 13th c., with a proliferation of *confraternities, *hospitals and benevolent institutions.

In 1320, the diocese included four archdeaconries (Coimbra, Vouga, Penela and Seia), among which were distributed some 230 churches under its jurisdiction, besides the ten monasteries that performed important parochial activities. The conflicts with the royal authorities – especially on account of the polemical laws of disamortizement, royal approval, or prohibition of episcopal lordships – that were occasionally repeated, did not prevent relations between the bishops and the *Crown being marked overall by mutual solidarity. In 1472, on account of the bishops' collaboration in Portuguese maritime expansion, the king conceded the title of *count to the prelates of Coimbra.

P. A. Nogueira, *Livro das Vidas dos Bispos de Coimbra*, A. R. Madahil (ed.), Coimbra, 1942. – *Liber anniversariorum ecclesiae cathedralis Colimbriensis (Livro das kalendas)*, P. David (ed.), T. S. Soares (ed.), Coimbra, 1947-1948 (2 vol.). – *Livro Preto da Sé de Coimbra*, A. J. Costa (ed.), L. Ventura (ed.), M. T. Veloso (ed.), Coimbra, 1977-1979 (3 vol.; 2nd ed., Coimbra, 1999). – *O Cartulário de S. Paulo de Almaziva*, M. J. A. Santos (ed.), Coimbra, 1981. – *Synodicon Hispanum*, 2, *Portugal*, A. García y García (dir.), Madrid, 1982. – *Bulário Português. Innocêncio III (1198-1216)*, A. J. Costa (ed.), M. A. Marques (ed.), Coimbra, 1989. – *Livro Santo de Santa Cruz de Coimbra (Cartulário do Séc. XII)*, L. Ventura (ed.), A. S. Faria (ed.), Coimbra, 1990.

M. R. Vasconcelos, *Notícia histórica do mosteiro da Vacariça . . . e da serie chronologica dos bispos desta cidade desde 1064*, Lisbon, 1864. – A. Vasconcelos, *A Sé-Velha de Coimbra (Apontamentos para a sua história)*, Coimbra, 1930 (2 vol.). – I. P. David, "Français du Midi dans les évêchés portugais (1279-1390)", *Bulletin des Études Portugaises et de l'Institut Français au Portugal*, 9, Lisbon, 1942, 16-17. – *A Sé Velha de Coimbra. Das origens ao século XV*, Porto, 1947. – I. P. David, *Études historiques sur la Galice et le Portugal du VI^e au XII^e siècle*, Paris, 1947. – A. N. Gonçalves, *Inventário artistico de Portugal, Cidade de Coimbra*, Lisbon, 1947. – I. P. David, "Coïmbre", *DHGE*, 13, 1956, 204-221.

Saul Gomes

## COINAGE

**The West.** Instrument of an exchange economy, as standard of values and principal means of payment, *money was not in exclusive use, everywhere and always, in the Middle Ages. On the margins of *Christendom there long existed a natural economy, based on barter and ignoring monetary tokens. Elsewhere we distinguish real money that circulated – coins of *gold, silver or *billon* (base silver) – from money of account, which took as its basic unit an old real specie.

Medieval money was defined by its type and its legend, the *metal of which it was composed, its weight, its value and its currency. The type was the principal image-motif that the coin bore and which gave it its name: cross, shield (*écu*), *lily, *crown, throne, *lamb or sheep. Minting was normally a royal prerogative, and the ruler's effigy adorned the piece, which thus became a symbol of power, at the same time as carrying a significant religious iconography – *e.g.* the Byzantine gold *solidus* of the *iconoclast period. The legend consisted of the ruler's name and titles, generally accompanied by a religious invocation. Only the weight of precious metal of which it was composed determined the value of the piece, while the *titre* or degree of fineness determined the proportion of precious metal, if it was an alloy. Gold money was more specifically reserved for international exchanges and the bounty of rulers, silver and *billon* for the needs of everyday life. The theoretical weight resulted from the fact that the same number of pieces were cut from ingots of the same titre and definite weight: 240 silver *denarii* to the pound under the *Carolingians, 72 gold *solidi* to the pound in the *Byzantine Empire. The value, not indicated on the pieces, depended on the weight of fine metal they contained. It varied according to monetary changes, which, being caused by the chronic lack of precious metal and the profit taken by the ruler from his rights over minting, could affect the titre, weight or currency of specie in relation to money of account. Crises resulted, important in the West especially at the end of the 13th c. and the time of the *Hundred Years' War.

Monetary history shows a constrast between East and West. At Byzantium, from the 4th c., there circulated concurrently the gold solidus (*nomisma*), the silver *milliaresion* and the copper *follis*, in a system that remained unchanged until the 10th century. The *Abbasid caliphate imitated its powerful neighbour, with the gold *dinar* and the silver *dirhem*, but the disintegration of caliphal power led to a multiplication of devalued coinage minted by the *emirs. In the West, the gold *solidus* disappeared under the *Merovingians in favour of *thirds* and especially of barbarian coins, inaccurate copies of Roman prototypes. The reforms of *Pippin the Short and *Charlemagne introduced a silver monometallism, whose sole coin was the *denarius*, rapidly devalued by reason of usurpations of the mints by feudal lords. In the 13th c. the rise of a merchant economy obliged a return to good money: silver *gros* at *Venice and in the Italian towns, gold florin and ducat, imitated all through the West (*gros* and *écu* of St *Louis). After the monetary crises engendered by the Hundred Years' War, the West did not recover sound money until the second half of the 15th century.

E. Fournial, *Histoire monétaire de l'Occident médiéval*, Paris, 1970. – P. Grierson, *Monnaie et monnayage*, Paris, 1976. – P. Grierson, M. Blackburn, *Medieval European Coinage 1*, Cambridge, 1986. – P. Spufford, *Money and its Use in Medieval Europe*, Cambridge, 1988. – C.E. Blunt, B.H.I.H. Stewart, C.S.S. Lyon, *Coinage in Tenth-Century England*, Oxford, 1989. – P. Grierson, *The Coins of Medieval Europe*, London, 1991. – C. Morrisson, *La Numismatique*, 1992 ("QSJ", 2638).

Michel Balard

**Byzantium.** The creation of the *solidus* by *Constantine in 312 marks the beginning of the Byzantine coinage. Various periods can be distinguished: from 312 to 720, a hierarchized system with several denominations in the three metals: *gold, silver and bronze; from 720 to *c.*900, only one denomination per metal, a reflection of the diminished role of *money; from 900 to 1092, expansion and crisis of the *nomisma*; from 1092 to *c.*1350, period of the gold *hyperpyron*; from 1367 to 1453, period of the silver *hyperpyron*. The purity and stability of the gold coinage made it, with the *dinar*, an international currency in the Middle Ages. Its reputation long resisted the various crises that affected it: after the moderate devaluation of the years 950-1060, connected with the territorial and economic expansion of the Empire, and the grave fall in fineness between 1068 and 1091, Alexius restored it and the *hyperpyron*, known in the West under the name of "besant", remained widespread in Mediterranean *commerce until the mid 13th century. But an irremediable weakening, due to the collapse of the imperial finances and the flight of gold to the West, led around 1350 to its abandonment in favour of silver. This had previously had a variable share of the issue. At first marginal, it supplemented gold in the Middle Byzantine period, with a more favourable ratio of 1 to 8. Issues of gold and silver were, most of the time, of real money whose intrinsic value was equal to its nominal value. The bronze coinage (called *follis*, from 498 to 1092), often manipulated and a source of inflation, was a largely fiduciary currency, something unknown to the West before the 16th century.

Money was an essential instrument of *taxation and finances; the State demanded taxes in gold and paid its expenses in one of the three metals according to the case. The production of money, at first in numerous mints, at *Alexandria, *Ravenna, Carthage or Syracuse, was centralized at *Constantinople and secondarily at *Thessalonica from the 9th c. to 1387. After the partition of 1204, various coinages of Byzantine type were struck in the Balkans, at *Nicaea (1204-1261) or at *Trebizond.

The Byzantine coinage is an original source for the political and economic history of the Eastern Empire. Its iconography reflects the progressive Christianization of the imperial ideology, completed in the course of the 7th c., and the vicissitudes connected with *iconoclasm: its structure evolved in accordance with the contemporary financial and economic context and its complexity contrasts with the long monopoly of the *denier* in the West. Progress in our knowledge of its metallic composition and its circulation has shed light on the causes of devaluations as well as on the role and the spread of money inside and outside the Empire, one of the most monetarized of the Middle Ages.

T. Bertelè, *Numismatique byzantine*, Wetteren, 1978. – P. Grierson, *Byzantine Coins*, London-Berkeley (CA), 1982. – M. F. Hendy, *Studies in the Byzantine Monetary Economy*, Cambridge, 1985. – C. Morrisson *et al.*, *L'Or monnayé*, 1, *De Rome à Byzance*, Paris, 1985. – P. Grierson, *Byzantine Coinage in its International Setting*, Cambridge, 1990. – C. Morrisson, *Monnaie et finances à Byzance: analyses, techniques*, 1994 (repr. "CStS", 461).

Cécile Morrisson

**COLA DI RIENZO (1313-1354).** Son of artisans, Cola di Rienzo frequented a school for *notaries and acquired from youth a wide classical culture (his direct knowledge of prose writers, notably Livy, and poets has been demonstrated). This culture later earned him the esteem of *Petrarch, who had an intense but brief epistolary relationship with him. Cola was sent to *Avignon in 1342 as representative of the new popular regime, to ask the *pope to celebrate a *jubilee in 1350; in the minds of the applicants, this jubilee was to contribute to the recovery of the citizen class. Cola was well received there, made friends with Petrarch, made the acquaintance of influential persons and got himself included in the "pontifical family", a group of well-placed people in the pope's service and possessing privileges. On his return to *Rome he was given the post of notary of the Capitoline chamber, which allowed him to perceive the city's problems, first among which was the excessive power of the *baroni romani*, the representatives of the great aristocratic families, holders of great properties in the countryside, but solidly rooted in town. For decades their members had monopolized the highest communal offices. The reforming programme that Cola set out after his return from Avignon (1344) found enthusiastic support among the "productive classes" of the town, landed proprietors, *merchants and artisans, as attested by a participant in the *Chronicle* of Anonymus Romanus. This programme envisaged first of all the submission of the barons, the restoration of peace, in town and in the country, so as to permit the resumption of *commerce and a more rapid and impartial administraton of justice. Cola saw the possibility of creating a consensus around his ideas not just by his own refined culture, but also by a propaganda that was effectively expressed in images placed at the most central and important parts of the town.

He succeeded in taking power on 20 May 1347. The first implementation of his programme, which also envisaged the creation of a citizen militia to counter the forces of the barons, obtained the support of the papal *vicar and met no organised resistance from the barons, some of whom rallied to him. His partisans showed themselves more sceptical about his project of a grand union between the Italian cities: these were to be allied on the basis of a common political choice and to claim the right to designate the emperor. Cola had taken this idea from the *lex de imperio*, going back to Vespasian, to the detriment of the German princes who had ruled the *Empire for centuries. Although the great celebrations of 1 August 1347 brought together the representatives of 27 cities at Rome and marked the apogee of Cola's power, he was quickly abandoned by the pope, tied as always to the interests of the barons and threatened in his prerogatives in the choice of emperor. Stripped of power and imprisoned, Cola left Rome at the end of 1348 and took refuge with the **fraticelli* of La Maiella, whose eschatological expectations left a mark on him. Between the end of 1350 and 1352 he lived at *Prague, where he sought to involve *Charles IV in his dreams of universal renewal. Sent by Charles under escort to Avignon, Cola defended himself against accusations of *heresy and ended up in the employment of Pope *Innocent VI, who was trying to regain control of central *Italy through the activities of Cardinal *Albornoz. The *Curia sought in effect to make use of the credit they supposed Cola could still enjoy at Rome to reassert their own power in the town. But the return of Cola, now a puppet in other hands, disillusioned the Romans, who allowed the thirst for vengeance of the barons whom he had so ill-used in 1347 to be unleashed against him. On 8 Oct 1354 Cola, seeking to escape the uprising fomented against him, was fleeing in disguise when he was murdered on the steps of the Capitol.

*Briefwechsel des C. di Rienzo*, K. Burdach (ed.), P. Piur (ed.), Berlin, 1913-1929. – Anonymus Romanus, *Cronaca*, G. Porta (ed.), Milan, 1979.

P. Piur, *C. di Rienzo*, Vienna, 1934. – J.-C. Maire-Vigueur, *Cola di Rienzo*, *DBI*, 26, 1982, 662-675.

Giulia Barone

**COLETTE OF CORBIE (1381-1447).** Long in search of a form of religious life, Colette Boylet was one of the best-known *recluses of the 15th century. But her reputation is due to her reforming activity in the *Franciscan Order, particularly the Second Order. Her life, woven of supernatural phenomena and marvels, was fixed in its major elements by her confessor, Pierre de Vaux, and one of her companions, Sister Perrine. These two *Vitae* present a figure of *sanctity that later biographers would enrich without modifying.

Born 13 Jan 1381 (or 1382) at *Corbie in *Picardy, she spent her childhood and youth in a carpenter's shop dependent on the powerful *abbey. The only daughter of an elderly couple, she was orphaned at about 15 years. Early marked by devotion to the *Passion and by the graces of *prayer and ascetic life, she wished to become a *nun. She seems at first to have been a *beguine, then, disillusioned by brief stays with the Benedictines and the Urbanist *Poor Clares of Moncel near *Beauvais, she entered the Franciscan *Third Order and became a recluse, 17 Sept 1402, under the influence of Father Pinet, *guardian of the convent of Hesdin.

During four years of intense spiritual life and *mortifications, she had a *revelation of her mission: to reform, say her biographers, "the order of *monsieur* St Francis". Her new confessor, friar Henri de Baume (1367-1439), future collaborator and author of spiritual treatises, persuaded her to go to *Benedict XIII at Nice (Oct 1406) to obtain permission to follow the Rule of St *Clare. Papal documents prove that, from April 1406, Colette obtained permission to found a monastery. The main effect of her stay at Nice was to transform the recluse into a professed nun of the order, with the chance of becoming abbess. In 1410, after various changes of place, Colette, joined by a few companions, was able to take possession of the monastery of the Urbanist Poor Clares of *Besançon.

From this date until her death at *Ghent, *foundations or community reforms followed each other: Auxonne (1412), Poligny (1417), Seurre and Moulins (1421-1423), Decize (1419-1423), Aigueperse (1423-1425), Vevey (1424-1426), Orbe (1426-1428), *Le Puy-en-Velay (1425-1432), Castres (1426-1433), Lézignan (1430-1436), reform of the monastery of Béziers (1434), Heidelberg (1437-1443), Hesdin (1437-1441), Ghent (1441-1444), Amiens (1442-1445), Mont-à-Mousson (1444-1447). The predominance of foundations in Burgundian territory suggests a network of influential laypeople and a tacit agreement of the great houses independently of their political quarrels; the role of the duchesses of *Burgundy and Bourbon was not negligible.

An adaptation of the rule culminated in 1434 in the Constitutions, a major work of the *reform. Colette showed her originality in strengthening the power of the *abbess and the penitential aspect of the nuns' life. The papacy progressively imposed these Constitutions on the majority of Poor Clares who wished to return to *observance of the founding rule.

Colette was canonized in 1807 (feast 7 Feb).

*La Règle de sainte Claire et les Statuts de la Réforme de sainte Colette*, Bruges, 1892. – P. de Vaux, Sr. Perrine, *Les Vies de sainte Colette Boylet de Corbie, publié par Ubald d'Alençon*, Paris, 1911. – E. Lopez, *Sainte Colette. Aspects culturels d'une forme de sainteté au Moyen Âge*, Saint-Étienne, 1994.

Élisabeth Lopez

**COLLECTARY.** The *collectarium* was the book of the celebrant of the *office; it contained the *capitulae* (brief *readings) and collects (*prayers) pronounced at each hour of the day. From the 11th c., the collectary enjoyed, together with the *psalter, a central role in the process of establishing a single book for the office, the *breviary. The first collectaries made their appearance in the 9th c., when they contained only the collects of the different *hours of the office. From the 10th c., the work was enriched by other pieces (*hymns, *psalms, benedictions), forming composite collectaries. In the 11th and 12th cc., a part of the *ritual, in particular for the books used in the monasteries, was joined to the collectary.

P.-M. Gy, "Collectaire, rituel, processional", *La Liturgie dans l'histoire*, Paris, 1990, 91-126. – *The Durham Collectar*, A. Correa (ed.), *HBS*, 107, London, 1992. – É. Palazzo, *Histoire des livres liturgiques. Le Moyen Âge, des origines au XIII^e^ siècle*, Paris, 1993.

Éric Palazzo

**COLLECTION, COLLECTOR.** A systematic collection of *alms, exercised personally among a great number of persons, the *quaestua* in the strictly legal sense was contrasted to other forms of gift, such as the offering for the celebration of *mass, or alms deposited in the church chest.

While the *monasticism of the early centuries renounced the possession of individual *property, the Order of *Grandmont forbade all possession, lived in total *humility and practiced a controlled mendicancy: in the collection, only the strict minimum was allowed, *i.e.* what was necessary for one day. The *mendicant orders too renounced the possession of property, both for the individual and for the community. From then on, collection became the necessary way for the order to ensure its subsistence. *Quaestuatio* as a principle of existence was justified by the *Franciscans in their desire to follow the *poverty assumed by *Christ and thus give proof of a profound humility. For the *Dominicans, the collection was intimately connected with *preaching. The preacher obtained from others a sort of compensation corresponding to the service he rendered. *Quaestuatio* as sole means of subsistence was violently criticized in the mid 13th c. at the time of the quarrel between the *mendicants and seculars at the university of *Paris. Opponents (*e.g.* *William of Saint-Amour) saw it as failing to respect the ruling laid down by St *Paul and followed by Gratian's **Decretum* which obliged every *foundation to be endowed. The second council of *Lyon (1274) limited the number of mendicant orders and thus sought to pacify the conflict. As well as collections, the mendicant orders envisaged other forms of revenue; burials in *cemeteries and churches, construction of funerary *chapels, celebration of masses for the *dead, etc.

*Quaestuatio* as a means of humiliation held a great place in the devotion of certain 13th-c. saints, *e.g.* *Angela of Foligno or *Clare of Montefalco.

As well as the collections organised by the mendicant orders to ensure their subsistence, the Middle Ages knew another type of collectors (*quaestores*). Sent by the Church, they were charged with collecting funds to enable the construction or repair of churches, the organisation of the *crusade, the distribution of *indulgences, etc. On the occasion of the fourth *Lateran council (1215), the papacy sought to limit the abusive activities of certain collectors by demanding greater control over their activities.

R. Naz, "Quête", *DDC*, 7, 1965, 440-444. – M. Dufeil, *Guillaume de S. Amour et la polémique universitaire parisienne*, Paris, 1972. – A. Carpaneto, "Questus", *DIP*, 7, 1983, 1154-1160.

Véronique Pasche

**COLLECTORS, PAPAL.** From the late 13th c., in its fiscal effort, the papacy divided Christendom into zones of contribution, allocated to itinerant exactors; they were usually called "collectors" and their zone a "collectory". In the 14th c., France, fiscally very important, was divided into a dozen collectories. The collectors were designated by the *pope or the *chamberlain and put under the latter's authority. They were mostly churchmen of modest rank, with a legal training that allowed them to make the most of their important powers and apply papal fiscal law in its complexity.

J. Favier, *Les Finances pontificales à l'époque du Grand Schisme. . .*, Paris, 1966, 93-163.

Jean-Daniel Morerod

**COLLEGE.** In the Middle Ages, *collegium* designated any society of individuals meeting for a common aim. Only gradually was the word's present meaning fixed. Previously people just said "the house (*domus*) of the poor students [of *Sorbonne, Navarre, Merton]".

The first colleges appeared at *Paris even before the birth of the *university, modest *foundations housing a few poor scholars. The institution did not really get off the ground until after 1250, with the full rise of the University. Pious benefactors instituted colleges to provide poor students with board and lodging, plus a weekly grant for current expenses. The founder provided a building and revenues; he drew up the statutes, which imposed a strict discipline on the members. The colleges had a certain autonomy and elected their heads, but recruitment (often among the compatriots or relatives of the founder) and supervision of discipline were in the hands of external visitors. The colleges were most numerous at Paris. In all, nearly 70 colleges, secular or monastic, were founded there before 1500. Colleges were also numerous in England (18 at *Oxford, 14 at *Cambridge). In southern Europe, the institution took root hesitantly; the only large college was the College of Spain at *Bologna (1367). Colleges also multiplied in the 15th c. in *Germany and *Poland.

The college was progressively transformed. Some remained simple houses for poor students, but others became teaching institutions. Some, enjoying vast buildings or fine libraries, took on large numbers. Regents were engaged to give teaching "exercises" distinct from those of the *faculties and, though in 1500 the colleges still held no more than 10 to 20 % of the students, their diffuse type of teaching (it was there that *humanism first penetrated), the discipline imposed on their members and the influence they had over the rest of the university meant that they tended to become the dominant institutions within it. In the recruitment of members, the requirement of *poverty gave way to the search for intellectual capacity or social standing. Finally, colleges began to be created outside universities, as establishments preparatory to higher studies.

All this heralded the triumph of the college in the modern period when it became the keystone of the European educational system.

H. Rashdall, *The Universities of Europe in the Middle Ages*, F. M. Powicke (ed.), A. B. Emden (ed.), Oxford, 1936 (3 vol.; 2nd ed.). – A. L. Gabriel, "The College System in the Fourteenth-Century Universities", *The Forward Movement of the Fourteenth Century*, F. L. Utley (dir.), Columbus, 1961, 79-124. – A.B. Cobban, "The Role of Colleges in the Medieval Universities of Northern Europe", *Bulletin of the John Rylands University Library*, 71, 1989, 49-70. – *I collegi universitari in Europa tra il XIV e il XVIII secolo*, D. Maffei (dir.), H. de Ridder-Symoens (dir.), Milan, 1991. – *A History of the University in Europe*, I, H. de Ridder Symoens (ed.), Cambridge, 1992.

Jacques Verger

**COLLEGIATE CHURCH.** A collegiate church was a church comprising a certain number of priests forming a *chapter, the *canons, living on the *prebends assigned to them – whose revenues formed the "great fruits" – and distributions, and who were charged with celebrating *mass and the *office regularly. A collegiate church would be founded with the agreement of the *pope by a layman or a churchman who provided its endowment, with the aim of augmenting divine service. Collegiate churches multiplied, favoured by Frankish legislation (St *Chrodegang's *Rule for canons; council of Aachen of 817), then especially in the 11th c. with the rise of the seignorial regime which led to the foundation of numerous collegiate churches in fortified **bourgs*.

J.-J. Légier, *Les Églises collégiales en France, des origines au XVe siècle*, Paris, 1955 (law thesis). – J.-F. Lemarignier, "Aspects politiques des fondations de collégiales dans le royaume de France", *La Vita comune del clero nei secoli XI-XII*, Milan, 1959, 19-49. – J.-L. Lemaître, "Les Créations de collégiales en Languedoc par les papes et les cardinaux avignonnais sous les pontificats de Jean XXII et Benoît XII", *La Papauté d'Avignon et le Languedoc (1316-1324)*, Toulouse, 1991, 157-198.

Jean-Loup Lemaître

**COLMAR.** Attested from 823, not far from the mother-parish of Horburg, Colmar (*Columbarium*) was the chief town of a fisc given by *Louis the Pious to the abbey of *Münster (founded *c.*675 some 15 kilometres from Colmar). In *c.*965 one of the two urban centres, the *Oberhof*, belonged to the abbey of Payerne (Switzerland, canton of Vaud), while the other, the *Niederhof*, belonged to the *bishop, then in *c.*975 to the cathedral *chapter of *Constance. The church of the *Oberhof*, whose patrons were the family of Eguisheim Dabo, was dedicated to St *Peter, that of the *Niederhof*, whose patron in the 12th c. was *Frederick Barbarossa, to St *Martin.

It was around St Martin's that the town developed; the present church was built in the 13th c. on the site of an earlier, no doubt Ottonian, church. St Martin's became *collegiate in 1234 and numbered 16 *canons in 1245. At the same time the *mendicant orders were settling in Colmar: Dominican *nuns (the monastery of *Unterlinden, existing from 1230 and integrated into the order in 1245; Catherinettes in 1311), *Dominicans (1278), *Franciscans (church dedicated in 1292, now the Protestant temple of St Matthew), Augustinians (1316), Knights of St John. The buildings still attest the importance of the communities: Unterlinden (a museum with celebrated collections including the Issenheim altarpiece), Dominicans (municipal library, which preserves important remnants of the conventual and monastic libraries).

14th-c. Colmar is marked by the historical work of the Dominicans, mainly the *Chronicle* and the *Annals of the Dominicans of Colmar*, and by the mystical centre that developed at Unterlinden, made famous by Catherine of Gueberschwihr's *Vite sororum* (before 1350). The *reform of the Dominican province of Teutonia began from Colmar. Among important works of art of this period are the *stained glass of the Dominicans (inspired by the **Speculum humanae salvationis*) and *altarpieces (including that of St Martin's by Gaspard Isenmann). In the late 15th c., the Marian cult manifested itself in a confraternity of the *rosary attested in 1484 and in Martin *Schongauer's famous picture, the *Virgin of the Rose-hedge* (1473). Colmar went over to the Reformation in 1575.

*Histoire de Colmar*, Georges Livet (dir.), Toulouse, 1984.

Jean-Luc Eichenlaub

**COLOGNE.** Cologne, a Rhineland city founded in AD 49 by the Romans (*Colonia Agrippina*), enjoyed immense prosperity in the Middle Ages, linked to the political importance of its *bishops and its role as a commercial crossroads.

An episcopal see from the 4th c., Cologne was an important centre of Frankish kingship, capital of the Ripuarian *Franks, then capital of the *regnum* of *Austrasia from the time of Chlotar II (614-629). Linked to the *Merovingian kings, from the mid 7th c. the bishops of Cologne also had favoured relations with the Pippinids.

After a vain attempt in the 740s, *Charlemagne managed to transform Cologne into an archiepiscopal see in 794-795. But it was especially under the pontificate of Bruno (953-965), son of *Otto I and archduke of *Lorraine, that the archbishop of Cologne became one of the first men of the realm, with full seignorial rights over the town and the county. In 1052, Pope *Leo IX made the archbishop of Cologne *primate of *Germany, which did not prevent his successors siding with the emperor in the *Investiture Contest.

Attempts by the town's middle class to gain autonomy from the archbishop are visible from 1074, but it was mainly in the 12th c. that a true patriciate developed; the town hall was built between 1114 and 1119, and the council was using its own *seal in 1149.

The archbishop of Cologne, Prince-Elector of the Holy Roman *Empire from the 13th c., was also head of a principality called the Electorate of Cologne, which developed mainly under Conrad of Hochstaden (1238-1261). Its extent varied considerably and its capital was Bonn, since Cologne, a free town from 1212, was outside the prince's authority. Implicated in various political struggles for supremacy over the region, the Electorate was relegated to the rank of a second-class power following the defeats of Soester (1444-1449) and *Münster (1450-1456).

The town's economic wealth rested on long-established craftsmen who worked a great deal for export: they made cloths (the wool weavers formed the most important *corporation), all sorts of *metal objects, *goldsmiths' work. The town also enjoyed a remarkable situation as crossroads between the north-south route brought into being by the Rhine and the east-west route linking *Saxony to *Flanders. Finally Cologne is remarkable for the number of its churches: the *cathedral, rebuilt from 1248 in a *Gothic style close to that of *Amiens cathedral, became an international *pilgrimage centre from 1164 thanks to the *relics of the Three Wise Men; the church of St Pantaleon, founded by Bruno in 957, is among Germany's oldest monuments.

L. Ennen, *Geschichte der Stadt Köln*, Cologne, 1863-1880 (5 vol.). – F. Irsigler, *Die wirtschaftliche Stellung der Stadt Köln im 14. und 15. Jahrhundert*, Wiesbaden, 1979. – F. R. Erkens, *Der Erzbischof von Köln und die deutsche Königswahl*, Siegburg, 1987.

Geneviève Bührer-Thierry

*Martyrdom of St Ursula outside the city of Cologne.* Painting by the Master of the Little Passion, 1411. Cologne, Wallraj-Richartz Museum.

**COLONNA.** The first Colonna are attested from the early 12th century. Cardinal Giovanni Colonna († 1244) gave his family a Ghibelline political orientation, which introduced a permanent element of conflict into Roman political life. Cardinal *legate at *Constantinople (1204), he brought back to *Rome, for his church of San Praxede, a column considered to be that of the *Flagellation. The *cardinal's three brothers, Landolfo, Oddone and Giordano, founded the branches of Riofreddo, Gallicano and Palestrina. At Rome, the family seat was the quarter of SS. Apostoli. The family's dominant branch, that of Palestrina, possessed a key position in the *commune and in the *Curia. After the defeat of the Hohenstaufen, the Colonna went over to the side of the *Angevins and thus received *fiefs in the *Abruzzi. The relations maintained by Giovanni († 1291) and Jacopo († 1318) with the kings of France and Popes *Nicholas III and *Nicholas IV were to show themselves very useful: Giovanni was senator for a long time; Jacopo became a cardinal (1278). In 1288, when his nephew Pietro also entered the *Sacred College, the Colonna had reached a sort of apogee. It was precisely against this importance that *Boniface VIII fought. When in 1297 Sciarra sequestrated the papal treasure, the *Caetani pope launched a crusade against the Colonna and had Palestrina destroyed. The two Colonna cardinals then replied with a political manifesto and sought support from the king of France.

At *Avignon, Cardinal Giovanni († 1348) and his brother Giacomo († 1341) played a not inconsiderable role. Both kept up close relations with *Petrarch, who was long the cardinal's *chaplain. Another Colonna, the *Dominican Giovanni († 1343-1344), influenced the poet with his *De viris illustribus*, a collection of 330 *biographies of famous men. At Rome, the Colonna fell under the political influence of *Cola di Rienzo (1352). Niccolò († 1410) and Giovanni († 1413) tempted fortune as *condottieri* in the service of the king of *Naples. On 11 Nov 1417, Oddone Colonna, of the Genazzano branch, was elected *pope at *Constance under the name of *Martin V. Entering Rome in 1420, this pope (the only one of his family), tried to restore life to the *Urbs*, then in an anaemic state. His brother Giordano († 1424) was made duke of *Amalfi and Venosa in 1419, as well as prince of Salerno. Martin V appointed his nephew Prospero († 1463) cardinal, and his nephews Antonio († 1472) and Odoardo († 1462) lords of Paliano, Serrone, Nettuno and Astura. *Eugenius IV momentarily stopped the family's expansion, but from the mid 15th c. cardinals Prospero and Giovanni secured a permanent place for the Colonna among the Roman families that would take control of the papal court at the *Renaissance.

P. Paschini, *I Colonna*, Rome, 1955. – P. Partner, *The Papal State under Martin V*, London, 1958. – *DBI*, 27, 1982, 253-457. – A. Rehberg, "Colonna", *Die Grossen Familien Italiens*, Stuttgart, 1992, 171-188.

Agostino Paravicini Bagliani

**COLOURS, LITURGICAL.** The origin and establishment of liturgical colours remain misunderstood problems. In the early days of Christianity, the officiant celebrated worship in his ordinary garment; whence a certain unity at the level of *Christendom; whence also a predominance of white or undyed *vestments. Then, progressively, white seems to have been reserved for the feast of *Easter and the most solemn *feasts of the liturgical calendar. The other colours appeared only quite slowly. At any rate, by the end of the Carolingian period, the practice that consisted of associating a colour and a feast or a season of the calendar is attested in numerous *dioceses. But usages were controlled by the *bishops and varied greatly from one diocese to another.

Then came Cardinal Lotario, the future *Innocent III. In *c.*1195, while still only a *cardinal-deacon, he wrote several treatises including one on the *mass: *De sacrosancti altaris mysterio.* In this youthful work, the author compiled and cited much, but in the matter of liturgical colours he described the usages of the *diocese of *Rome on the eve of his own pontificate. Until then, in this field, Roman usages could be taken as reference (this was what *liturgists and *canonists recommended), but they had no real normative scope at the level of Christendom; bishops and congregations often remained very attached to local traditions. Thanks to Innocent III's immense prestige, things began to change in the course of the 13th century. The idea increasingly imposed itself that what was current at Rome had an almost legal scope. And especially the writings of this *pope, youthful works though they were, became obligatory authorities. This was the case of the treatise on the mass. The long chapter on colours was not just taken up by all the 13th-c. liturgists, it also began to be put into practice in numerous dioceses.

There is no room here to describe in detail the distribution and symbolism of colours throughout the *liturgical year as Lotario set them forth, but we will point out their main elements. White, symbol of purity, was used for the feasts of *angels, virgins and confessors, for Christmas and Epiphany, Holy Thursday and Easter Sunday, Ascension and *All Saints. Red, recalling the blood shed by and for *Christ, was used for the feasts of apostles and *martyrs, for those of the *Cross and for *Pentecost. Black, connected with grief and penitence, was used for masses of the *dead, as well as during the season of *Advent, the feast of the Holy *Innocents and from Septuagesima to Easter. Finally, green was required on days when neither white, red or black were suitable.

More descriptive than normative, Lotario's text on liturgical colours moved in the direction of a unification of liturgical practices. The troubles of the Church in the 14th and 15th cc. delayed the institution of this unification. But in the next century, the decisions of the council of Trent and the Missal of St Pius V (1570) made the Roman usages, *i.e.* those described at the end of the 12th c. by the future Innocent III, obligatory throughout the Catholic Church.

Innocent III, "De sacrosancti altaris mysterio", *PL*, 217, 1855, 799-802.

G. Haupt, *Die Farbensymbolik in der sakralen Kunst des abenländischen Mittelalters*, Leipzig, 1944. – M. Pastoureau, "*Ordo colorum.* Notes sur la naissance des couleurs liturgiques", *LMD*, 176, 1989, 54-66.

Michel Pastoureau

**COLUMBA OR COLUM CILLE (521-597).** Known by a *Vita* written in *c.*690 by *Adomnán, *abbot of *Iona. Offspring of an Irish royal family, he became a monk and founded numerous monasteries. In 563, by now a priest, he left *Ireland for *Scotland as a missionary *pilgrim, settled on the little island of Iona at the limit of the Scottish and Pictish kingdoms, converted the king of the Picts and in 574 consecrated the new king of the Scots. Without being a *bishop, he exercised jurisdiction over all his *foundations both in Ireland and in Scotland. His disciples founded the monastery of *Lindisfarne (in north-eastern *England). After his death, his cult, very popular in Ireland and Scotland, was equally widespread in Gaul and Germany. His feast day is 9 June.

*Adomnán's Life of Columba*, A. O. Anderson (ed.), M.O. Anderson (ed.),

Oxford, 1991. – R. Sharpe, *Adomnán of Iona: Life of St Columba*, Harmondsworth, 1995.

F. O'Briain, *DHGE*, 13, 1953. – D. W. Rollason, *LdM*, 3, 1986. – *Studies on the Cult of St. Columba*, C. Bourke (ed.), Dublin, 1997.

Bruno Judic

**COLUMBANUS (*c.*540-615).** Irish, known by a *Vita* written in the 7th c. by *Jonas of Bobbio. He became a monk at Bangor under the direction of St Comgall. He received a sound *Latin training and a monastic education marked by asceticism. The Christendom descended from St *Patrick († 461) was original: spared by the *barbarian *invasions, it developed a *monasticism ruled by powerful abbot-bishops and based on the practice of *mortifications and the seeking of exile to preach the Gospel.

Pioneer of Irish missionaries on the continent, Columbanus landed in Gaul in 590. Welcomed by King Guntram, he settled south of the Vosges in the frontier *forest between *Burgundy and *Austrasia, founded Annegray and then, given the influx of disciples, *Luxeuil and Fontaines. With no official mandate to exercise his apostolate, it was simply by the strength of his personality and the conviction of his *faith that he imposed on rulers, clergy and inhabitants. Scandalized by the state of the Gallic clergy, unworthy *bishops not up to their jobs, the façade of Christianity ill-concealing a lively *paganism, he wanted to preserve Irish usages absolutely: *Easter *computus, and independence of monasteries from bishops.

But the real conflict broke out with Brunhild; her grandson Theoderic had several bastards whom the astute grandmother wanted to have blessed by Columbanus, who refused categorically. In 610, Brunhild had him expelled, but at Nantes his boat was pushed up onto the bank by the tide. Columbanus then went to the kingdom of Chlotar II. In Brie, he made a deep impression on the family of Authar, whose son St *Audoin was to found Rebais while in 630 another son, Ado, founded *Jouarre. Via the Moselle and the Rhine, he reached the present Lake Constance where he left his disciple Gall to establish a hermitage that became the abbey of *Sankt Gallen. He crossed the Alps and the *Lombard Queen Theodelinda procured him the means to found *Bobbio in the Ligurian Apennines; it was there that he died, 23 Nov 615.

Of him we preserve *letters, *homilies and poems, but especially a monastic *Rule, or rather a collection of spiritual counsels, and a *Penitential presenting a new discipline of *penance, from now on based on lists of sins to which corresponded tariffed sanctions; this discipline propagated by Columbanus would enjoy a growing success during the early Middle Ages and in the long term modify the practice of the Roman Church.

*PL*, 80, 1863. – G. S. M. Walker, *Sancti Columbani Opera*, Dublin, 1957 (*SLH*, 2). – *Le Pénitentiel de saint Coloman*, J. Laporte (ed.), 1958.

*Mélanges colombaniens, congrès de Luxeuil*, Paris, 1951. – F. O'Briain, *DHGE*, 13, 1953. – *Colombano pioniere. . ., Atti del convegno internazionale di studi colombiani*, Genoa, 1974. – *Columbanus and Merovingian Monasticism*, H.B. Clarke (ed.), M. Brennan (ed.), Oxford, 1981. – H. Haupt, *LdM*, 3, 1986. – *Columbanus. Studies on the Latin Writings*, M. Lapidge (ed.), Woodbridge, 1997.

Bruno Judic

**COLUMBUS, CHRISTOPHER (1451-1506).** Born at *Genoa in 1451 to a family of weavers, Columbus there acquired the practical education of 15th-c. merchants and sailors. He first went to sea in the service of Genoese businessmen, to Lisbon from 1476, then along the *African coast, to Madeira, the Canaries and Azores. His reading, his experience of the sea and the information he gathered persuaded him that it was possible to "reach the Levant [*China and Japan] via the Ponant". Early in 1484, he put his project to the king of *Portugal, who treated him as a crank. Columbus then left for Palos in *Spain where he gained the support of the *Franciscans, some nobles and Genoese and Florentine businessmen established at *Seville. He completed his reading and was introduced to court, but had to wait for the capture of *Granada before Queen Isabella would accept his project: the capitulations of Santa Fé (17-30 April 1492) specified the conditions of the expedition, financed by Italian *bankers and "*Marranos" in favour at court.

With two caravelles and a *nao* (ship) manned by sailors from Palos, Columbus put to sea on 3 August 1492; he made for the Canaries in order to profit from the trade winds favouring travel westward. After a long voyage on unknown seas, on 12 October he reached the little island of Guanahani in the Bahamas. He thought he had reached the lands of the Great Khan, or Cipango (Japan), which he sought from island to island, as far as Cuba and Hispaniola (Haiti). He took possession of the new lands in the name of the *Catholic Kings and was ecstatic over the nature and corporeal characters of the peoples of the New World, whom he dreamed of converting easily to Catholicism. His obsessive search for *gold and *spices came less from the desire to enrich himself than to increase the resources of *Christendom to enable it to beat the *Turks. The theme of crusade underlay his search for the Indies and the East and the outlines of a project of colonization. His dramatic return to the Iberian peninsula was followed by a triumphant reception (March-April 1493), which encouraged him to undertake new expeditions.

His three further voyages (1493-1496, 1498-1500, 1502-1504) brought him more failure than glory. He explored the Antilles, the larger islands, the gulf of Mexico, the Orinoco delta where he thought he had found one of the rivers of *Paradise, the coasts of central America. But he came up against the ill will of the colonists he had settled at Isabela in Haiti, and the hostility of the Indians to the colonial exploitation they were beginning to suffer. He was replaced as governor of the Indies and lost some of his rights. Returning from his fourth voyage, he got the *Book of privileges* established and died on 20 May 1506 at *Valladolid, without having fully benefited from the glory and wealth that his discovery of the New World deserved.

J. Heers, *Christophe Colomb*, Paris, 1981. – M. Mahn-Lot, *Portrait historique de Christophe Colomb*, Paris, 1988. – P. E. Taviani (ed.), *Nuova Raccolta Colombiana*, 19 vol., Rome, 1988-. – J. B. Russell, *Inventing the Flat Earth: Columbus and Modern Historians*, New York, 1991. – V. I. J. Flint, *The imaginative landscape of Christopher Columbus*, Princeton (NJ), 1992. – M. Balard, *Christophe Colomb. Journal de bord 1492-1493*, Paris, 1992. – J. Dotson, A. Agosto, *Christopher Colombus and his Family: the Genoese and Ligurian Documents*, Turnhout, 1998.

Michel Balard

**COMMANDERY.** The basic territorial division of a *military-religious order, directed by a commander (the term "preceptor" exists only in the Latin form of *praeceptor*). It comprised a headquarters, with dwellings and farm buildings, a *chapel (round chapels are the exception) and dependant houses (or members). The fortifications, often late (*Hundred Years' War), were those of a fortified house rather than a *castle, except where in contact with the Infidel (*Spain, Prussia) and in the great centres (*Paris).

The commandery was a place of recruitment and training, a centre of economic development and often a retreat house for old soldiers.

G. Marié, *DHGE*, 11, 1949, 1339. – A. Demurger, *Vie et mort de l'ordre du Temple*, Paris, 1989.

Alain Demurger

**COMMENDATION.** Commendation was the *provision, for a cleric provided with a permanently-held *benefice, of another provisional benefice, which was a way of getting round the prohibition on *pluralism of benefices.

In the early Middle Ages, commendation was the giving of a benefice entrusted provisionally and in its interest to someone other than its titular: a bishopric when the *bishop was sick or performing a penance; an *abbey entrusted to another *abbot in the absence of its superior. So it had primarily a provisional, temporary aspect. It could also be applied to parish churches, though it was forbidden to any holder of a benefice with *cure of souls, who had to resign any supernumerary churches he possessed. Canon 14 of the second council of *Lyon (1274) forbade multiple commendations.

From the 13th c., it tended to be prolonged indefinitely, to become perpetual, and was granted in the interest of the commendatory, no longer in that of the church. If the old commendatory was bound to the administration of the benefice (but not always to the temporality), from now on commendatories confined themselves to collecting the revenues of the temporality. *Innocent IV, in his commentary on the *Decretals* (*c.*1245), was the first *pope to be disturbed about the abuses of commendation, which had to remain the exception: the commendatory had to have a *dispensation and did not have true jurisdiction over the church. While Guillaume *Durand pointed out that plurality of benefices was contrary to the old law, *Clement V (*c.*1306-1307) acknowledged that he had given way to the importunate and multiple appeals of kings, princes and prelates. An excellent way of keeping up good relations with the temporal powers, it was also a source of revenues for the *Avignon papacy, popes like *John XXII multiplying them without shame, and *cardinals also taking possession of conventual *priories and regular benefices. In 1335, *Benedict XII revoked all commendations made under his predecessors, save those of *cardinals. This practice particularly encumbered monasteries and priories, who tried to escape from it, sometimes by buying it back. The commendatory could also resign the benefice obtained in commendation, against an annual pension.

At the time of the *Great Schism, it was a way of recruiting partisans in violation of canonical rules. A new effort was made at the council of *Constance (40th session, 30 Oct 1417): *Martin V notably suppressed, in return for compensation, commendations of monasteries and conventual priories with more than 10 religious, and of parish churches, with an exception in favour of cardinals or patriarchs with insufficient resources; it was forbidden for *hospitals, almonries and *leper-houses. Leo X (1513-1521) tried a final reform: bishoprics and abbacies could no longer be given except to persons who fulfilled the conditions laid down by *canon law, vacant monasteries would no longer be given in commendation, all commendation in favour of cardinals was forbidden, save that of monasteries, where they had to appoint suitable *vicars or *suffragans. In France, the *concordat of 1516 no longer spoke of commendation, but it entailed the king's hold over the major benefices (right of presentation) to the benefit of the great families of the kingdom. From then on it became the provision of a regular benefice granted to a *secular, with dispensation of regularity.

*View of the market at the Ravenna gate, Bologna.* Miniature from a 15th-c. Italian manuscript. Bologna, Museo Civile.

G. Mollat, *La Collation des bénéfices à l'époque des papes d'Avignon [Lettres communes de Jean XXII*, "Introduction"], Paris, 1921. – R. Laprat, "Commende", *DDC*, 3, 1942, 1029-1085. – G. Mollat, "Le Roi de France et la collation plénière des bénéfices ecclésiastiques", *MAIBL*, 14, 2, 1951, 107-286.

Jean-Loup Lemaître

**COMMERCE.** It is traditional to distinguish three great periods in Western commercial venture in the Middle Ages: a time of contraction of trade between the period of the *invasions and the 11th c.; an age of expansion from the 11th to the 13th c.; and finally a trading "crisis" in the late Middle Ages, between 1350 and the early 16th century.

H. Pirenne thought that the Arab invasion of the Near East and North Africa had led to the halting of trade beteen Western *Christendom and the Oriental world. The research provoked by his thesis, without leading to the total revision of M. Lombard who saw the West glutted with Muslim gold, has shown that there was no closing of the Mediterranean. Admittedly, the Christian West, even before the Arab advance, lacked *gold and had slowed down its trade with the areas of the Eastern Mediterranean. However, *merchants from southern Italian towns (*Amalfi, *Gaeta, Salerno) frequented the markets of *Alexandria and

*Constantinople, as did the Venetians. The merchants of these towns, which all belonged to the Byzantine world, brought to the market of Pavia in the 10th c. precious stuffs and luxury products, which they traded with merchants from the Nordic countries.

The most active commercial traffic in the West was concentrated in the Meuse valley and around the North Sea in the Carolingian period. Frisian and *Viking merchants, weakly tied to working the soil, would seek distant products, which they stored in "*ports" like Duurstede and Tiel. The trade they organised via the three great rivers, Scheldt, Meuse and Rhine, led to the creation of *portus*, which were not ruined by the Norman invasions. Often established in places where land routes met rivers, they were the expression of a limited but certain expansion of urban life based on trading activities. Without denying the importance of the role played by the *Frisians, historians have shown the fundamental part taken by town-country commercial links, notably in the Meuse region. It was not just in the Meuse region that what M. Postan could call "commerce without merchants" could flourish, so active were certain *fairs, notably at the gates of *abbeys (*Foire du lendit*, Saint-Vaast Fair).

The West at this time had little merchandise to export, not to mention its poverty in gold, for trafficking with the two worlds, Byzantine and Muslim, where a gold *coinage reigned. The development of the trade in *slaves (procured from the Slav world) through the intermediary of *Verdun merchants or Venetians provided the Westerners with a medium of exchange, much of which they used to obtain leather articles, precious fabrics or Arab coins from the Muslims. The traffic in highly-priced objects should not make us forget that in the Po valley or at the heart of the Parisian Basin a traffic in foodstuffs flourished. "The transition from the agricultural economy predominant in the 10th c. to the stage of the urban economy predominant from the 11th c. represents not an evolution, but the amplification of a pre-existing phenomenon" (R. Doehaerd).

On the morrow of the year 1000, the West multiplied its commercial links both with the East Mediterranean world and with the lands of central and northern Europe, not counting the internal traffic that was developing in it. The Genoese and Pisan "viscounts" built fleets with which they drove the Muslims out of the Tyrrhenian and even carried the fight into Africa (pillage of Al Mahdya in 1087). The first *crusade gave the Westerners important bases in the East Mediterranean, by the concession of quarters in the ports of *Syria. But Constantinople and Alexandria remained the most important points of convergence for Westerners in search of *spices and precious stuffs, for which from the 12th c. they could trade cotton and woollen cloth, while continuing to provision the Muslim world with wood, various *metals, arms and slaves. The development of trade rested on contracts generally limited to one voyage, devised at *Genoa or *Venice: "commendations" (sharing of benefits, 3/4 for the sedentary associate and 1/4 for the traveller), *colleganza* (contribution of *capital equal to 1/3 for the sleeping partner and 2/3 for the active partner, with profit-sharing in variable proportions), *societas maris*. Merchants, who became businessmen in the 13th c., created companies in which family capital and clients' deposits were invested. At Constantinople, the Venetians obtained important customs privileges; and their rivals, Genoese and Pisans, tried to obtain the same advantages from the **basileus*. To secure the domination of traffic within the *Byzantine Empire and eliminate their rivals, the Venetians did not hesitate to divert the fourth crusade.

If the Venetians took an essential part in the rise of Western traffic in the East Mediterranean, the Genoese for their part were able to develop links with the Northern world. Merchants from the hinterland of *Lombardy (*Milan, Cremona, *Pavia and especially *Piacenza) Piedmont (Asti) and then *Tuscany (*Siena, *Lucca, and later *Florence) gave the Ligurian port a cosmopolitan aspect. From Genoa, in the second half of the 12th c. these merchants crossed the Alpine passes to quicken the fairs of *Champagne, where they met Flemish and German merchants. In order to avoid large transfers of *money they devised the contract of exchange, a notarial act permitting the concealment of interest by exchange of moneys of Genoa against moneys of the French mint of Provins, then of *Paris and *Tours in the 13th century. The Champagne fairs thus became a sort of great permanent *market among the four towns that shared their meetings: Bar-sur-Aube, Provins, *Troyes and Lagny. But it should not be forgotten that demographic growth, accompanied by a slow improvement in the level of life and the development of a money economy, contributed widely to the progress of trade throughout the West.

A double colonial movement accompanied Western commercial expansion. In the north, along the Baltic, German merchants took part in the "push to the East", and their frequenting of the great market of *Gotland, then that of *Novgorod, put them in a position to provide the West with *furs, honey, wood and dried fish, which they brought to the ports of *London and *Bruges. In the Mediterranean, the movement that began with the quarters in the Syrian ports took shape with the establishment of the Venetians in *Crete and certain ports of call on the route to Constantinople (Modon, Euboea), as well as in the Black Sea. The treaty of Nymphaea, concluded in 1261 between Genoa and Michael *Palaeologus, gave the Genoese after the restoration of the *Byzantine Empire a privileged position at Constantinople and in the Black Sea (colonies of Péra and *Caffa). Starting from Caffa, but also from Ajaccio, Italian merchants, profiting from the "*Mongol peace", went to *India and *China, from now on bypassing the Muslim intermediary to procure *spices, *silk and precious stuffs, which they exchanged for Western woollen fabrics. The opening of a regular *navigation line between Genoa and Bruges in 1277, then between Venice and Bruges in 1314, welded Europe to Asia. The Champagne fairs lost much of their commercial importance when Italian merchants went directly to *England to look for wool which they would work in the workshops of their own country.

The late 13th and especially the first half of the 14th c. saw the failure of the greater part of the Italian companies, notably at Florence between 1343 and 1346. These societies then revealed the weakness of their structures as well as the clumsiness of their managers, subject to the pressures of rulers. This was the prelude to more important economic difficulties after 1350: demographic depression connected with *epidemics of plague, insecurity of certain regions due to conflicts, monetary instability, and Turkish pressure in the East.

Important innovations allowed greater flexibility in the development of commercial affairs. Companies with multiple branches adopted less rigid structures, which heralded the holding system in the autonomy of the various daughter-houses. The best-known example is that of Francesco *Datini, but none of the new companies attained the size of those of the 13th c. in volume of capital and investments at stake, number of agents, breadth of commercial activity and influence. The letter of exchange, "a cheque drawn on a foreign place, drawn up in a coin different from that of origin" (G. Fourquin), put in touch at least three people: beneficiary, drawer, drawee. It was doubled by the use of the cheque, a written order to pay a sum to a third party; endorsing the cheque could bring in a fourth person. These two new forms of fiduciary money contributed greatly to the transformation of *banking activities, in which speculation on the exchanges was widespread. At the same time, double-entry book-keeping, also called *alla veneziana*, simplified the keeping of accounts, thanks to the entering of debit and credit articles from the "daily" book into the "great book". Ships of ever higher tonnage for long-distance *transport: Hanseatic *kogges*, galleys *a mercato* and *nefs*, carried up to 1000 metric tonnes around 1460.

Merchants met each other especially at the great fairs that multiplied, spreading round the kingdom of *France (Chalon, *Lyon, Geneva, *Bruges, *Antwerp, Bergen op Zoom) or in the *Empire (*Frankfurt, *Leipzig, Nördlingen). While the fairs of Chalon-sur-Saône disappeared in the 15th c., those of Geneva and Lyon – the "silk fairs" (J. Heers) – thrived, becoming with Bruges the rendezvous of Italian finance. *Hanseatic merchants, whose apogee was in the 14th c., flocked to the quays of Bruges. Opposite *Flanders, *England became a great maritime power, thanks to the "Merchant Adventurers" who trafficked in woollen cloth, manufactured from this time forward on British soil. From *Italy to the North Sea the old maritime lines were perpetuated, but the land routes, by the St Gotthard and the Rhine valley, attracted a large share of overland trade, though the Italian merchants who went from Lombardy to *Burgundy or to Geneva and Lyon circulated by the Simplon.

If the Venetians long remained attached to their positions in the Eastern Mediterranean despite the *Turks, the Genoese for their part turned back towards the West, despoiled as they were of their Eastern colonies. The members of the Genoese merchant colonies of the Iberian peninsula lent their help to the Portuguese rulers in their expeditions along the *African coasts and it was with the support of the Genoese colony at Lisbon and then that of *Seville that Christopher *Colombus prepared his *journey that led to the *discovery of the American continent. Between Italy and Flanders, the magnet of southern Germany gradually emerged in the course of the 15th century. Supported by the Fondaco dei Tedeschi at Venice, an imitation of the commercial and customs system of the Muslim lands, German merchants imposed their fustians and began to practise trading in money. The Fugger family of *Augsburg took a large share in the second half of the 15th c., together with other families of *Nuremberg, in the great commercial and banking traffic. Thanks to Venice and Genoa, the Mediterranean still remained the centre of gravity of international commerce, but the strength of the Iberian lands was already appearing, supported by their new ship, the caravelle, better suited than galleys and *nefs* to face the Ocean. The end of the 15th c. heralded a new age of international commerce.

M. Lombard, *L'Islam dans sa première grandeur*, Paris, 1971. – R. Doehaerd, *The Early Middle Ages in the West*, Amsterdam, 1978. – G. Fourquin, *Histoire économique de l'Occident médiéval*, Paris, 1979 (2nd ed.). – H. Pirenne, *Mohammed, Charlemagne and the Origins of Europe*, London, 1983. – J. Heers, *L'Occident aux XIV<sup>e</sup> et XV<sup>e</sup> siècles. Aspects économiques*, Paris, 1990 (5th ed.). – P. Contamine, *L'Économie médiévale*, Paris, 1993. – J.H. Munro, *Textiles, Towns and Trade*, Aldershot, 1994. – D. Nicholas, *Trade, Urbanisation and the Family*, Aldershot, 1996. – E.S. Hunt, J. Murray, *A History of Business in Medieval Europe, 1200- 1550*, Cambridge, 1999.

Pierre Racine

## COMMUNE

**Italy.** Between the late 11th and early 12th cc. – following the long and profound crisis of public order that had struck what remained of the Carolingian State structure from the 10th c. – there emerged in vast areas of Western Europe a wholly new institutional phenomenon, a new form of organisation of public life in its legal, political and economic aspects, which took the name of "commune" and which took shape essentially as a form of self-government of urban and, in many cases, rural communities.

The communal movement shows far from uniform lines of development, which makes any attempt to force it into a general interpretative model arduous if not impossible. Indeed, the impossibility of reducing *ad unum* a phenomenon that escapes any kind of simplification has, from a methodological point of view, stimulated more recent historiography to study its origins and development, looking again at its events over culturally homogeneous and geographically compact areas. In *e.g.* southern Italy, the *universitates* of city populations never reached the point, in the intersecting relations between *monarchy and noble potentates, of creating organisms with a strong political connotation.

In north-central Italy, the communal phenomenon had its roots in the crisis of public order of the *Regnum Italiae*; a crisis caused by the lack of co-ordination betwen political power and social forces, exacerbated in the Ottonian period and manifested in its full gravity on the occasion of the *Investiture Contest. The real need for a stable organisation of society was most felt in *Italy, where the continuity and liveliness of city life, the survival of a coherent and variegated class of free men, the complex economic and political links that united the urban centres with their respective rural districts and the important presence of *bishops in public life contributed to give the communal phenomenon characteristics wholly different from the communal movement in the rest of Europe.

From the 11th c., thanks to a considerable demographic and economic recovery, the *town recovered an important role as a meeting-place, a centre of production and marketing, a reference-point for the peasants who flowed into it giving new life to crafts and retail trade. Within it emerged the new forces of *mercatores*, artisans and professionals, but at the same time it was guaranteed and motivated by feudatories and lords. The power of *counts and marquises – which in an urban context had never been feudal in nature, since the cities, where they represented public power, had never been enfeoffed to them – remained restricted to the subjects who lived and worked on their allodial or feudal properties, while a considerable part of the *comitatus* ended up in the hands of bishops and vassals. The diminution of the power of the various dynasties of counts and marquises was counterbalanced, in the urban world, by an increasing power of the bishop who, independently of his more or less prolonged exercise of public powers, assumed within the urban consciousness a unique capacity to represent it and attract its social forces and political components. All this came about independently of any imperial political will: the intervention of the emperors of the Saxon dynasty was dictated by the need to define the episcopal power in order to include it in a general political framework and not by a conscious desire to promote it.

In a situation like the Italian, where nearly all the cities were seats of *dioceses, the figure of the bishop, who very often came from among the citizens, became a precise reference-point for the whole body of citizens, a figure closer to the interests, needs and expectations of the *cives* than the count could be: the latter gradually lost importance and power in the urban centre and ended by abandoning it and withdrawing to one of the *castles situated in the extra-urban part of his area of government. Nor should we ignore the fact that the bishop, independently of his exercise of public functions within the city, extended his personal power over the *contado* where his personal *property was immune from the jurisdiction of public officials. These immune areas, scattered like spots on a leopard, on one hand reinforced the links between city and *contado* and on the other made the territory subject to the count's jurisdiction far from compact. Obviously, in this case too, the phenomenon did not affect the whole of north-central Italy equally: in *e.g.* *Tuscany, the solidity of the marquis's power considerably limited the development of any such episcopal power.

Around the figure of the bishop there slowly crystallized a socially composite group – made up of vassals, lawyers, *notaries and *merchants – from which were chosen the officials who collaborated with the prelate in the management of military, civil and judicial tasks (*vicedomini*, *advocates, *consiliarii*). This group, made up of people of high social rank, but not exclusively of *nobles, increasingly succeeded in limiting the bishop, in some cases to the point of almost completely ousting him from the management of public affairs. The weakening of episcopal power occurred at the same time as the grave institutional crisis known as the *Investiture Contest: at a certain point, not always identifiable by the historian and in any case not the same for every situation, this socially identifiable group, formed of the main elements of the city, entering into a sworn association (*coniuratio*, *societas*, *concordia*), began to govern the urban world not just in their own interests but in the name of the entire urban community and with the awareness of representing a political entity holding public powers. It must be borne in mind that the commune came into being as a public organisation, an association of groups of citizens tending on one hand to guarantee peace within the city and on the other to work out functional and efficient forms of self-government, and not as a private association of nobles aiming at the conquest of local power. The private origin of the commune is also denied by the fact that the holders of public power, whether laymen or churchmen, were ineluctably implicated, as actors or as opponents, in the communal phenomenon.

Though the social extraction of the elements that promoted the formation of the commune was not substantially homogeneous, it would not be wrong to say that this new organisation came into being as an aristocratic formation: the ruling class appears a real ruling aristocracy made up of a collection of allied groups bound together both by blood-relationships and by a community of economic interests. Yet the commune's prosperity also appears closely linked to the less prominent social groups, the *mercatores*, *negotiatores* and artisans who, as well as representing the economic skeleton of the new organism, were always ready to take up arms in defence of its autonomy and its institutions (*libertas et consuetudines*). Indeed, the pre-eminent position of an aristocratic class was legitimized precisely by the fact that it managed to guide the rest of the citizens, who felt no difficulty in being represented by that social group.

Formally the birth of a commune came about at the moment when a magistrature, nearly always collegiate in character, consciously assumed the political representation of the inhabitants of a whole community. This qualitative leap, which marked the transition to the commune properly so-called, did not come about at the same time in every urban situation, and the appearance of a magistrature that represented the citizens did not necessarily imply the immediate elimination of other public powers such as those of the bishop, the count or the marquis.

The magistrates placed at the summit of the commune took various names: in Italy they were usually called consuls, though important exceptions are not lacking, such as the senators of the Roman commune. The *consules* made their first appearance in Pisan documents of the years 1081-1085 and later appeared at Biandrate (1093), Asti (1095), *Milan (1097), Arezzo (1098), *Genoa (1099), Pistoia (1105), *Ferrara (1105), *Lucca (1115), Cremona (1112-1116), *Bologna (1123), *Piacenza (1126), *Modena (1135) and *Parma (1149). Elected under systems that differed from place to place, the consuls, whose number seems to have varied from two to more than 20, with discrepancies not just between one commune and another but also within the same commune, held directly in their hands or through their representatives a large part of the civil and military powers, administered the city's finances, organised the armed forces, led military campaigns, directed the commune's "foreign" policy and administered civil and penal justice. The duration of their mandate also varied considerably according to time and place: at *e.g.* Genoa, the initial mandate was of four years and was reduced to a single year in 1122; while at *Perugia it changed from a duration of two months to that of a year.

The need for the *cives* to take part in the management of the *res publica* found a satisfactory answer in their presence at an assembly (*parlamentum*, *concio*, *conventus*, *arenga*, *colloquium*), composed of all the members of the communal association, whose main function was the election of the consuls with consequent delegation of power and the solemn *oath of the elect.

In the first half of the 12th c., nearly all the cities of north-central Italy were given communal institutions, profiting appreciably from the crisis that, between the *Concordat of *Worms (1122) and the ascent to the throne of *Frederick I Barbarossa (1152), more or less simultaneously affected the two universal institutions: the *Empire and the papacy. Precisely in this space of time, the city commune proceeded with greater effectiveness to the conquest of the *contado*, subjecting the signorial forces, lay and ecclesiastical, who ended by moving to the cities and being integrated into the commune's ruling class.

At the moment when Frederick I set his hand to the restoration of imperial order, the political situation of north-central Italy appears clearly defined: the communes were transformed into genuine territorial powers that, while formally recognising imperial *authority, enjoyed a wide degree of administrative autonomy not very far from real independence. At the same time, however, the Italian communes did not formulate a unitary political line, even one of a defensive character, and they were often engaged in a struggle among themselves for the control of *commerce and the conquest of regional supremacy: *e.g.* the lacerating conflicts between Milan and Cremona, *Pisa and Genoa, Bologna and the communes of *Romagna. The emperor's policy, initially aimed at reducing the economic and military power of the commune of Milan, in the wake of the formulation of *Roman law made by the *jurists of the Bolognese *Studium*, acquired precise features at the second Diet of Roncaglia (Nov 1158) when, together with an unequivocable wish to relaunch the universal role of the Empire, the basis was laid for a precise design, economic and fiscal even more than political, aimed at recovering all the royal rights and all the fiscal revenues assumed by the communes. Thus we see on one hand the tendency to reduce the magistrates elected by the *cives* to the rank of officials of the emperor with the obligation to swear loyalty to the sovereign, and on the other the demand for the **regalia*, the rights and payments of a permanent or occasional character reserved exclusively for the person of the emperor, with particular attention to the exercise of justice and the exaction of the *fodrum*, an imposition in kind, subsequently transformed into a money tax, received when the sovereign was present in a particular territory of the Empire. The imperial demands profoundly affected those practical activities that were the basis of the communal economy: the right to collect taxes, to appropriate pecuniary fines imposed as well as the goods of those who died without heirs, to coin *money, to build fortifications, *ports and canals, to elect magistrates, to establish political relations with other communes. But at Roncaglia, Frederick did not limit himself to claiming regalian rights (*iura regalia*) with a patrimonial content, which indeed the sovereign was disposed in large part to regrant to the communes in return for the payment of a rent; the emperor went further, ordering the rebuilding of imperial palaces in the cities and promulgating a law in feudal matters, with retroactive effect, that forbade the alienation of *fiefs, thus calling in question a large part of the possessions that the city communes had acquired in the previous decades.

The Italian communes, rightly seeing the imperial policy as an attempt to curb their political autonomy and strike at their economic prosperity, joined in an alliance whose boundaries were not always well defined, known as the *Lombard League (*Societas Lombardiae*), and found themselves opposed to Barbarossa in a harsh military conflict that also involved the papacy and the *Norman kingdom. Its salient moments were the destruction of Milan (1162) the vain siege of Alessandria (1174-1175) and the defeat of the imperial troops by Milanese infantry and Lombard cavalry near Legnano (1176). After a six years truce, agreed in 1177 at the Peace of Venice between Frederick I and Pope *Alexander III, the conflict between the Empire and the allied communes of the Lombard League ended in 1183 with the Peace of *Constance. With the peace treaty "conceded" by Frederick I, a compromise was reached on the basis of which the communes were included in the institutional structure of the Empire as being subject to public law in the same way as the great vassals and received recognition of their *consuetudines* and the faculty of electing their own magistrates and administering justice. Moreover, in exchange for a rent, many of the regalian rights denied at Roncaglia were recognised to the communes, not least those of building fortifications and renewing intercommunal alliances. For their part, the communes swore fealty to the Empire, accepted that the consuls were invested by the emperor, consented to the payment of the *fodrum* and the other occasional contributions and offered a sum of 16,000 imperial pounds as indemnity for war damages. Finally, they acknowledged the emperor's role as the highest legal authority, to which appeal could be made.

With the full political success of the communes brought about by the Peace of Constance, the consulate, the institution that had represented the unifying moment of communal politics, tended to become the expression of a restricted power-group, until it was replaced by a figure more appropriate to the needs of an oligarchical structure, the citizen **podestà*, holder of a power characterised by a considerable strengthening of executive and judicial functions and by a considerable margin of discretion: he could be made answerable only after his period of office had ended.

The citizen *podestà*, whose mandate varied in length between six months and a year, alternated with the consuls at the head of the commune over an interval of time from the Peace of Constance to the first decade of the 13th c. when it gave way to the "foreign" *podestà*. Consequently the citizen *podestà*, who nearly always came from the circle of families of the consular aristocracy, while representing the symptom of a crisis within the communal phenomenon, did not constitute a break with the past but was fully part of the experience of the aristocratic regime.

With the appearance of the *podestà*, *i.e.* the replacement of a plural magistrature, as the consulate had been, by an almost dictatorial figure who concentrated a large share of power in his hands, the assembly of *cives* also disappeared, giving way to conciliary organisms (*consilium maior* or council of the bell, *consilium minus* or *consilium credentiae*), more or less numerous but always an expression of restricted groups, which were expected to control the activities of the commune and the *podestà*, while the need for participation of the *habitatores civitatis* found an outlet in the networks of clienteles that, vertically pervading urban society, bound large segments of the population to the ruling groups. Another important characteristic of the period of transition from the consular-aristocratic commune to the podestarial-oligarchical commune was the breaking up of the tendency to unanimity characteristic of the first phase and the division into factions, not so much social as political: the nobility and the people, where by *populus* must be understood the mercantile and artisan classes, *i.e.* the whole of the *cives* who took part in political life but belonged neither to the nobility nor to the mass of poor and salaried workers. Obviously the people, understood as a conscious political faction, did not arise suddenly but had its historical roots in the *corporations of arts and *métiers*, the neighbourhood associations and the military organisations of the *pedites*.

The bitterness of the intestine struggles and the situation of serious instability that characterised the second phase of communal history led to the appearance of the "foreign" *podestà*, a figure who, at least in theory, being outside the citizen factions, seemed the bearer of an otherwise unhoped-for impartiality in the management of power. In reality, the foreign *podestà* was chosen by the prevalent faction from a circle of politically allied families and ended by being himself an instrument of the dominant party.

At the moment when the clash between the noble factions broke the balance over which the communal government had presided in the consular phase, the people erupted onto the scene as an autonomous socio-political subject giving rise to an organisation parallel to the aristocratic commune, the *societas populi*, led by a *podestà* of its own or by a captain (*capitaneus populi*). The conquest of the commune by the **popolo* was slow and gradual: initially it functioned as a pressure group with the objective of defending the interests of its own members, later it was organised as a political party that shared power with the consular aristocracy, finally it occupied the commune's centres of power and assumed its government. The people, as a unitary organisation whose objective was the management of power, while presenting itself as a social and political alternative to the noble commune, had no choice but to entrust its own leadership to elements of noble extraction capable of directing a politico-military organisation, as in the case of the Della Torre at Milan. With the appearance of elements of the aristocratic class at the head of the popular movements, we begin to discern those authoritarian solutions that would lead to the birth of the *signoria*. Moreover, the division into internal factions was visibly reflected in the commune's "foreign" policy, since every party in the city had links and affinities with the similar parties of other communes.

The political rise of the people and the consolidation of the rule that the *podestà* had to be an outsider were a direct consequence of the struggle that had lacerated the noble framework of the original commune. But the access of the people to the management of power was reduced, in the final analysis, to the prevalence of its richer members in continual tension not just with the nobles but also with the lower layers of the population. At the end of the 13th c., this tension would inevitably lead to an institutional change characterised by the delegation of an almost absolute power (*balia, arbitrium, dominium*) in favour of a single individual, the *signore*, naturally keen to transform a power determined by extraordinary circumstances into a lifelong and, eventually, hereditary power.

H. Pirenne, *Medieval Cities: their Origins and the Revival of Trade*, F. D. Halsey (tr.), New York, 1925. – G. Fasoli, *Scritti di storia medievale*, Bologna, 1974. – G. Volpe, *Origine e primo svolgimento dei comuni nell'Italia longobarda. Studi preparatori*, Rome, 1976. – J. K. Hyde, *Società e politica nell'Italia medievale*, Bologna, 1977. – G. Rossetti (ed.), *Forme di potere e struttura sociale in Italia nel Medioevo*, Bologna, 1977. – G. Tabacco, *Egemonie sociali e strutture del potere nel Medioevo italiano*, Turin, 1979. – G. Chittolini (ed.), *La crisi degli ordinamenti comunali e le origini dello stato del Rinascimento*, Bologna, 1979. – D. Waley, *Le città-repubblica dell'Italia medievale*, Turin, 1980. – O. Capitani, R. Manselli, G. Cherubini, A. I. Pini, G. Chittolini, "Comuni e Signorie: istituzioni, società e lotte per l'egemonia", G. Galasso (ed.), *Storia d'Italia*, 4, Turin, 1981. – *Le città in Italia e in Germania nel Medioevo: cultura, istituzioni, vita religiosa*, Bologna, 1981. – R. Bordone, *La società urbana nell'Italia comunale (secc. XI-XIV)*, Turin, 1984. – *La pace di Costanza 1183*, Bologna, 1984. – K. Bosi, *Il risveglio dell'Europa: l'Italia dei Comuni*, Bologna, 1985. – A. I. Pini, *Città, comuni e corporazioni nel Medioevo italiano*, Bologna, 1986. – *Storia della società italiana, 6: La società comunale e il policentrismo*, Milan, 1986. – R. Bordone (ed.), G. Sergi (ed.), *Progetti e dinamiche nella società comunale italiana*, Naples, 1985. – A. M. Nada Patrone, G. Airaldi, "Comuni e Signorie nell'Italia settentrionale: il Piemonte e la Liguria", G. Galasso (ed.), *Storia d'Italia*, 5, Turin, 1986. – O. Capitani, *Storia dell'Italia medievale*, Rome, Bari, 1986. – G. Cracco, A. Vasina, M. Luzzati, "Comuni e Signorie nell'Italia nordorientale e centrale: Veneto, Emilia-Romagna, Toscana", G. Galasso (ed.), *Storia d'Italia*, 7, 1, Turin, 1987. – G. Arnaldi, D. Waley, R. Manselli, "Comuni e signorie nell'Italia nordorientale e centrale: Lazio, Umbria e Marche, Lucca", *ibid.*, 7, 2, Turin, 1987. – R. Bordone (ed.), J. Jarnut (ed.), *L'evoluzione delle città italiane nell'XI secolo*, Bologna, 1988. – E. Sestan, *Italia comunale e signorile*, Florence, 1989. – M. Sanfilippo, *Medioevo e città nel Regno di Sicilia e nell'Italia comunale*, Messina, 1991. – F. Opll, *Federico Barbarossa*, Genoa, 1994. – H. Keller, *Signori e vassalli nell'Italia delle città (secoli IX-XII)*, Turin, 1995.

Berardo Pio

**France.** The commune was the association of the inhabitants of a town united by *oath to guarantee the maintenance of peace. Recognised by the seignorial authorities, it could be given a *charter comprising various privileges.

In the 11th c., the urban milieu was marked by instability. The lay and ecclesiastical lords could not contain the formation of rival aristocratic clans, who, by their confrontations and their arbitrary exactions, created insecurity and disorganised the market. The population, divided into groups dependent on the lords, was composed of a kernel of landowners' families, well acquainted with customary law, practicing *commerce, managing lordships (**ministeriales*), providing the second-rank clergy and the men at arms of the garrison. This elite emerged from a populace of artisans, *peasants and servants.

Forms of professional (*guilds) or religious association (*confraternities) preceded the sworn peace associations and communal associations encouraged by the Church to bring order and protect citizens from arbitrariness and *violence.

In northern France, the communes were widespread especially in the ecclesiastical province of *Reims, at Saint-Quentin (1081), *Beauvais (1099), *Noyon (1108-1109). The *revolt of *Laon (1111-1112) created suspicion of the movement. From 1120, the clergy emphasized derogations from the rights and goods of the Church caused by the ambition of the townspeople, rose up against the profanation of the peace oath and opposed the setting up of communal jurisdictions. The king, who appreciated the military and financial support of the communes, supported them or broke them according to his interests.

The commune was confirmed by a charter that established sworn peace, fixed military obligations (militia) and accorded various privileges (franchises). These were fiscal alleviations or recognition of the citizens' administrative and jurisdictional autonomy. The magistrates (mayor, jurors or **échevins*) were elected by the townspeople or designated by the lord. Communal power fell into the hands of a minority of influential families (patriciate). From the mid 12th c., the original sworn commune disappeared. The lords confined themselves to the granting of franchises. In the 13th c., undermined by financial difficulties (*Noyon), *jurisdictional quarrels (Laon) and social conflicts (*Beauvais), the communes declined. Many were put under tutelage or suppressed by the king (early 14th c.). In the French Midi, it was the Italian model of the consulate that prevailed (12th c.).

C. Petit-Dutaillis, *The French Communes in the Middle Ages*, Amsterdam, 1978. – *Les Origines des libertés urbaines. Actes du 16e congrès de la Société des historiens médiévistes de l'enseignement supérieur (1985)*, Rouen, 1990.

Alain Saint-Denis

**COMMUNICATION ROUTES.** Up to the 7th c., the West's system of communications remained indebted to the Roman inheritance in its main orientations and its structures. From the *ports of the western Mediterranean basin, which, despite an obvious decline in traffic, remained in close contact with the East and the *Maghreb, its main axes diverged towards the Danube and Rhine frontiers, the Channel ports and Britain, *Aquitaine and *Spain. The question is what type of route was most used: it was long considered that the early Middle Ages gave its preference to waterways because of the lack of upkeep of the public road system inherited from Rome. In reality, the latter continued for some centuries to play the role for which it had been conceived, viz. rapid communication for military and administrative purposes. Communications connected with economic activity preferred to use all the ramifications of the pre-Roman road network for short-distance or light *transport, and the navigable network for long-distance or heavy transport.

The improvement of land transport techniques and the renewal of the *road network, associated with the great growth of a West whose centre of gravity had tipped northwards from the 7th and 8th cc., undoubtedly led to an intensification of continental traffic and, from the 12th c., authorized the development of *fairs in places (*e.g.* *Champagne) situated at the crossroads of land routes and not waterways. But this was possible only at the price of the development of an indirect *taxation that continued to hamper mercantile circulation. For tolls, which the feudal system had multiplied on land more easily than on *water, justifying them by the necessity of guarding and maintaining the roads, were always offputting.

This was doubtless why the medieval communications system continued to favour waterways and, as far as possible, sea-routes – especially from the 12th c., when part of the *crusades and the Genoese and Venetian attempts at hegemony over the Mediterranean stimulated maritime traffic between West and East, while German expansion eastwards and the development of the *Hanse reanimated the northern seas, from the Baltic to the Atlantic. The arrival, from the end of the 13th c., of Hanseatic boats at the Bay of Bourgneuf and the exactly contemporary arrival of Italian boats at *London and *Bruges were the prelude to the opening up of the great ocean route. But, after a century and a half of slackening activity, it was not until the second half of the 15th c. – with the return of continental peace, the rising power of the *States and the adumbration of a first mercantilism – that not only did the Atlantic route flourish, but land routes reawoke, in particular between *Italy and the transmontane lands, and a new generation of *fairs came into being at the foot of the Alpine passes.

R. S. Lopez, *The Commercial Revolution of the MiddleAges*, Prentice Hall (NJ), 1971. – *Les Transports au Moyen Âge. Actes du Congrès de Rennes, ABret*, 85, 1978. – A. C. Leighton, *Transport and Communication in Early Medieval Europe (500-1100)*, Newton Abbot, 1980. – P. Contamine, M. Bompaire, S. Lebecq, J.-L. Sarrazin, *L'Économie médiévale*, Paris, 1993.

Stéphane Lebecq

## COMMUNION

**The West.** In the Middle Ages, eucharistic communion, always received after *fasting (except in the case of the *viaticum), was at first given to small children, as earlier and still today in the East, from the time of their *baptism, with consecrated wine, and this until about the 12th century. From then on, the communion of small children gradually fell out of use (as did, in a general way, communion of the *chalice) and first communion was postponed until the age when *children became capable of confessing, communion being henceforth always preceded by *confession.

Before the fourth *Lateran council (1215), the most common rhythm of communion was, for all Christians, on the two or three main *feasts of the year, for religious approximately once a month. Canon 21 of the acts of Lateran IV (Denz.-Sch. 812) fixed the Church's double commandment that all were to communicate at *Easter after having confessed, the question being theoretically debated among theologians of whether a believer not conscious of having committed a mortal *sin was bound to confess at that time. From the 13th c., the practice of rather more frequent communion developed slowly among more pious persons, but remained distinctly less frequent than the practice of confession.

The medieval *theology of communion attached great importance to St *Paul's statement that he who communicates unworthily eats his own condemnation (1 Cor 11, 27-29) and St Augustine's distinction between the two ways of communicating, the sacramental way (common to the good and the bad) and the spiritual: the latter is reserved for the good, and can be practised even if one does not materially receive the *sacrament.

Saint Augustine, *Sermons*, 71, XI, 17. – J. A. Jungmann, *The Mass of the Roman Rite*, London, 1959.

*The Last Supper*. Paten, 6th-7th c. Washington, Bliss Collection.

P. Browe, *Die häufige Kommunion im Mittelalter*, Münster, 1938. – P. Browe, *Die Pflichtkommunion im Mittelalter*, Münster, 1940. – *CaP*, 2, *The Eucharist*, London, 1986.

Pierre-Marie Gy

**Byzantium.** *Bishops, by concelebrating at the same liturgy, and lay people, by eating the consecrated bread (leavened in the Greek Church), proclaimed their fraternal communion. An *excommunicated person was barred from receiving the *sacrament. Representations in art of the Communion of the Apostles show them receiving the bread in their hands and drinking the wine from the *chalice. This practice probably went out of fashion as, during the Middle Ages, the liturgy became progressively more "sacralized". Now lay people in the Greek Church receive from the priest, in a spoon, a morsel of bread steeped in wine directly in the mouth.

R. Taft, "Communion", *The Oxford Dictionary of Byzantium*, 1, Oxford, 1991, 491.

Christopher Walter

**COMMUNION OF SAINTS.** The expression "communion of saints", contained in the *Credo*, designates the spiritual union between all Christians as well as their union with Christ; the union of those in *heaven (Church triumphant) with those on earth (Church militant) and those in *purgatory. It thus expresses the *mystery of the communion of the just across time and space.

The redactions of the early creeds did not possess this expression, which is equally absent from the Eastern creeds, but the notion is in the New Testament (1 Cor 12, 4 -6. 12-13. 26-27; Col 1, 24). The communion of saints probably entered the Latin *Credo* early in the 5th century. It is first mentioned in the baptismal catechesis of Niceta of Remesiana: "From the beginning of the world . . . all the saints who have been, who are, who will be, form but a single Church . . . . Believe, then, that it is in that one Church that you will obtain the communion of saints". At the end of the century, the communion of saints is mentioned in the usual creed of the Churches of southern Gaul (treatise of Bishop Faustus of Riez, † *c.*490).

But who (or what) were these saints? Several exegeses could be put forward, for grammatical reasons. The reference to communion with sacramental realities, chosen by *Thomas Aquinas (*Expositio super symbolum apostolorum*, 10), was not the earliest. For Cyprian and Augustine, it meant communion among the faithful; in an anonymous 5th-c. exposition of Gallic origin, the communion of *hope of the living with those who died in *faith. These three meanings would be taken up by the Catechism of the Council of Trent (I, 10).

On the substratum inherited from late Antiquity, the Western Middle Ages created, together with purgatory, a gigantic system of solidarities. The community of life of the just implied the interdependence and solidarity of a body, common participation in the same means of *sanctity and the pooling of the *merits of all the saints. It was up to the Church to manage this *treasure of the works accumulated within its communion. It disposed of them by way of *indulgences, granted to Christians living and *dead, by *masses and *prayers that alleviated the pains of purgatory for the dead, by masses and votive prayers that ensured the support of the Church triumphant in human activity. In the 15th c., priests specialized in managing *foundations that manifested this sense of solidarity. The 16th c. would be the golden age of *ad hoc* communities of priests, particularly in southern *Italy and in a swathe of land going from the Jura to the *Pyrenees, where they established themselves for two centuries under the name of communities, universities, confraternities, *méparts* of chantry-priests or obituary priests, creating a relationship between the priest and the congregation very different from the pastoral ideal promoted by the reforms.

"Communion des saints", *DThC*, 3, 1, 1923, 429, 480. – *VSAM*, 4-5, Paris, 1945. – "Communion des saints", *Cath.*, 2, 1949, 1391-1393. – *Les Quatre fleuves*, 25-26, Paris, 1988.

Nicole Lemaître

**COMMYNES, PHILIPPE DE (1446/1447-1511).** Lord of Argenton. If he were not the author of the famous *Mémoires*, one of the great texts of French political literature, whose reputation inside and outside France has never been in doubt since the 16th c., Commynes would be for specialists a statesman among many others, having put his perspicacity and, more specifically, his talents as a diplomat at the service of *Louis XI and, to a lesser extent, *Charles VIII and Louis XII. Indeed in 1476 he was undoubtedly Louis XI's main adviser.

Born of a French-speaking Flemish family both *noble and patrician, Commynes received a first-rate aristocratic education and entered young into the service of the dukes of *Burgundy, Philip the Good and *Charles the Bold. He first bore arms, on the Burgundian side, at the battle of Montlhéry (1465). In 1468 he was present at the famous interview of Péronne between Charles of Burgundy and Louis XI, and had to make approaches to the latter. He changed sides in 1472 and was from then on a faithful servant of the king of *France, whose intelligence, courage and realism he admired, while Charles appeared to him as tending more and more towards an almost insane megalomania, Moreover Louis received the defector with favour, making his marriage and his fortune. In a few years Commynes had become one of the richest men in the realm, thanks to his lordships in Poitou, thanks also to the wages, gifts and pensions he received. After the death of Charles the Bold in 1477, he had more reservations about Louis's policy over the Burgundian inheritance. Doubtless he would have liked more circumspection. From then on his favourite home was *Italy, on which he became one of the best authorities.

In 1484 he thought to make good by drawing closer to Louis, duke of Orléans, brother-in-law – and rival – of Anne of France and *Charles VIII. Whence his disgrace, followed by a period of imprisonment (1487-1489). He finally obtained his freedom, but recovered only a small part of his fortune and his credit. His opposition to the conquest of the kingdom of *Naples did not prevent him from being entrusted with a long and important diplomatic mission to *Venice (1494-1495). Later on, Louis XII had to use his services again in Germany (1506) and Italy (1507).

He began to write his *Mémoires* with the aim of providing first-hand information for Angelo Cato, archbishop of Vienne, who was keen to write a Latin *biography of Louis XI. That part of the *Mémoires* concerning the reign of Louis XI (from 1464-1483) was written in 1489-1490, soon after his release from prison, while his account of the Italian expedition was composed between the end of 1495 and the end of 1498.

Commynes was not content to relate the events he had lived through, in close-packed, direct language. A man of experience and cultivation, he intended to make judgments, often balanced ones, to make something of his wide experience and to express the results of his reflections, both political and moral. His admiration for his "master" Louis XI does not prevent him criticizing him more than once. He shows himself expert in matters of war and attentive to public finances. His information is usually exact. Careful of truth and wisdom, he is not too flagrant in his biases. The major paradox of the man Saint-Beuve called "our Machiavelli in mellowness" is that he served without reservations a king of manifestly absolutist tendencies, while the political philosophy expressed in his *Mémoires* is in favour of a moderate government and an organic dialogue between the king and his subjects, notably through the institution of the States General. Commynes became a writer after the harsh experience of *prison: his vision of the world, sincerely Christian, bears the trace of this.

Philippe de Commynes, *Mémoires*, J. Calmette (ed.), G. Durville (ed.), Paris, 1924 and 1925 (3 vol.). – Philippe de Commynes, *Mémoires*, P. Contamine (ed.), Paris, 1994.

J. Dufournet, *La Destruction des mythes dans les* Mémoires *de Philippe de Commynes*, Paris, 1966. – J. Dufournet, *La vie de Philippe de Commynes*, Paris, 1969. – J. Liniger, *Philippe de Commynes*, Paris, 1978. – J. Blanchard, *Commynes et les Italiens. Lettres inédites du mémorialiste*, Paris, 1993.

Philippe Contamine

**COMNENUS.** Name of a Byzantine dynasty that reigned from 1057 to 1059 and from 1081 to 1185. The first famous Comnenus, Manuel, distinguished himself in 978 under Basil II by his defence of Nicaea against the rebel Bardas Skleros. His son Isaac came to power after a military coup but, a sick man, relinquished the Empire to his accomplice Constantine *Ducas. In April 1081 his nephew Alexius, encouraged by his mother Anna Dalassena and served by brilliant and numerous family alliances, seized the throne from Nicephorus Botaniates. Whatever his daughter, author of an *Alexiad*, may say, the new emperor was a rather mediocre general, suffering heavy defeats at the hands of the *Normans at Dyrrachium in 1081 and the *Pechenegs at Dristra in 1087, but he had in his favour a long reign and a remarkable capacity to thwart internal and external intrigues. In 1118, he left his son John an Empire purged of the Normans and Pechenegs, after the victory of Lebunion in 1091, while in the East the *Turks were pushed back to the central plateau. Indeed Alexius had been able to make skilful use of the passage of the first *crusade, though Bohemond's refusal to hand back the reconquered *Antioch opened up a quarrel with the Latins that lasted nearly a century.

John II (1118-1143), the family's best general, continued his father's work so well that all the coasts of Asia Minor were once more Byzantine. John's son Manuel (1143-1180) tried simultaneously to set foot in southern *Italy, counteract the projects of the Hungarians and subject them, and impose his sovereignty on the *Seljuks and Danishmends, but saw his ambitions annihilated in 1176 by the bloody defeat of Myriokephalon, which ended all hope of a complete reconquest of Asia Minor. Manuel's son Alexius II being a minor, his mother Maria of Antioch became regent. In 1182, they could not oppose the usurpation of a cousin of Manuel, Andronicus, who put them to death some time after having entered *Constantinople at the price of a general massacre of the Latin colony. The tyrannical character of Andronicus, who physically eliminated his potential rivals, and his powerlessness to stop the Norman army that took *Thessalonica on 15 August 1185, led to the emperor's downfall and murder in September, leaving a free place to his relative Isaac *Angelus.

Once peace had returned, the period of the Comneni was a period of economic expansion, as witness the growth of towns in Europe (Thebes, Corinth, Athens), despite the Norman raid of 1147. In western Asia Minor, the construction of a network of fortresses gave back life to this region, Turkoman raids being almost controlled. The ascendancy of Italian *commerce was as yet more a source of conflict with the natives than a serious cause of financial weakening for the State.

*The Alexiad of Anna Comnena*, E. R. A. Sewter (tr.), Harmondsworth, 1969.

M. Angold, *The Byzantine Empire 1025-1204*, London-New York, 1984. – A. Harvey, *Economic Expansion in the Byzantine Empire 900-1200*, Cambridge, 1989. – J.-C. Cheynet, *Pouvoir et contestations à Byzance (963-1210)*, Paris, 1990, 337-425. – P. Magdalino, *The Empire of Manuel I Komnenos, 1143-1180*, Cambridge, 1993. – M. Angold, *Church and Society in Byzantium under the Comneni, 1081-1261*, Cambridge, 1995.

Jean-Claude Cheynet

***COMPACTATA* OF JIHLAVA.** The negotiations over a compromise between Czech *Catholics and *Hussites, the normalization of their relations with the Church, represented by the council of *Basel, and the rights of the Emperor *Sigismund of Luxemburg, claimant to the throne of *Bohemia, intensified during the years 1433 and 1434. They finally ended on 5 July 1436, thanks to the signing of the *compactata* of Jihlava, during the diet of the provincial estates meeting in this town in western *Moravia. By this document, the Church accepted the programme of the moderate Hussites and authorized *communion in both kinds for the *laity of Bohemia and Moravia, as well as the *ordination of *Utraquist priests; thus was legalized the coexistence of two confessions in a single country. Having joined himself to the pact signed between the diet of Jihlava and the council of Basel, the Emperor Sigismund thus opened his way to the throne of Bohemia.

F. M. Bartoš, *The Hussite Revolution 1424-1437*, J. M. Klassen (ed.), New York, 1986.

Miloslav Polívka

***COMPACTATA* OF PRAGUE.** At the diet of the *Hussite estates (nobility, towns and clergy) at *Prague, a delegation of *Utraquist priests signed with the representatives of the council of *Basel, 30 Nov 1433, the *compactata* of Prague – an accord aiming to create the conditions for a compromise between the *Catholic Church and the Hussites and put an end to the wars that set them against the opponents of the *chalice, local and foreign. The council had promised to show understanding and recognise the essential points of the Hussite programme (the "Four Articles of Prague"), but in their moderate version and to the exclusion of the claim that would have made *communion in both kinds obligatory for all the subjects of the kingdom of *Bohemia. This accord, which clearly weakened the position of the radical Hussite currents, political and military, was a prelude to their defeat and the opening of new negotiations at Jihlava.

P. Čornej, *Lipanská křižovatka* [The crossroads of Lipany], Prague, 1992. – W. Eberhard, "Der Weg zur Koexistenz", *Bohemia*, 33, Munich-Vienna, 1992, 1-43.

Miloslav Polívka

**COMPANIES OF FORTUNE, GREAT COMPANIES.** The Companies, or Great Companies (so called for self-glorification, intimidation or propaganda) were militias of mercenaries led by their own captain or *condottiero*. Formed in Europe after the year 1000 with the disintegration of the feudal *armies, they were composed of elements of various nationalities (originally Spaniards, Germans and Flemings) and continued to be involved in nearly every war up to the 16th century.

**In Italy.** From the 14th c., the Companies were particularly widespread in *Italy, where communal and signorial autonomies made necessary the presence of armed troops whom it was not convenient to recruit and train within the urban framework. But in the 14th c., together with the mercenarism that was now the prevalent form of military service, feudal and citizen armies still existed. In *e.g.* Italy, armies of feudal type were enrolled in Piedmont, the *States of the Church and the kingdom of *Naples. Citizen armies were formed in 1356 by the Signoria of *Florence and in the same period by the Commune of *Rome.

Mercenarism arose in the 13th c. and prevailed decisively in the 14th, organised into so-called companies in France and especially Italy, real corporations that were later supplanted by companies organised and led by private individuals, who put themselves in the service of princes. They were formed by a leader, often a younger son of a feudal family who gathered around himself men of the most varied origins, coming generally from poor regions, but determined to make their fortune by the profession of arms, who put themselves in the service of the belligerent who offered them most. The captain was also called the *condottiere* since it was he who dealt with the employment or *condotta* of the company. Germans, English, Swiss, Bretons and Gascons were among the first to form companies. The first mercenary soldiers entered Italy in the train of the emperors *Henry VII and Louis of Bavaria and remained there, giving rise to the first companies, whose soldiers and leaders were thus nearly all foreigners. Among the most famous leaders were the German duke Werner of Urslingen, whose company took part in the civil wars that devastated the kingdom of Naples after the death of King *Robert of Anjou, and then went through *Romagna and *Veneto; the Breton John of Montreal, called Fra Moriale, who organised a great

Cathedral of Santiago de Compostela. Portal of Glory (detail), 11th-12th c.

company composed of 6000 French, German, Hungarian and Italian soldiers, with which in 1353-1354 he sacked Romagna, *Umbria and *Tuscany, and who was taken and killed by *Cola di Rienzo; the German count of Landau, or Conte Lando; and the Englishman John Hawkwood, known as Giovanni Acuto. Towards the end of the 14th c., Italian companies also arose, the first of which was that "of St George", commanded by Alberico da Barbiano. During the *Great Schism, in the pay of *Urban VI, he came into prominence in 1379 by defeating the Breton bands of the *antipope *Clement VII. From the school of Alberico da Barbiano emerged two more Italian captains, Muzio Attendolo called "lo Sforza" and Braccio da Montone called Fortebraccio, protagonists of Italian military affairs over the following decades. They in turn formed two schools of captains: the Sforzesca, based mainly on manoeuvring capacity, and the Braccesca, based mainly on striking force.

While the mercenary militias formed an element of reinforcement for the European monarchical States, making rulers independent of the military support of their feudatories, in Italy they were elements of disturbance and instability. The companies, condemned in 1179 by the first *Lateran council and in 1366 by a *bull of *Urban V, produced highly successful captains among whom were Federico da Montefeltro, Francesco Bussone called "il Carmagnola", Niccolò Piccinino, Bartolomeo Colleoni and Erasmo da Narni called "il Gattamelata". The *condottieri* quickly aspired to play an ever greater role in the political life of the various States and to become themselves heads of state, contributing, by their rapid and alternating fortunes, to creating a situation of uncertainty, crisis and disintegration in Italian political life. In the first half of the 15th c., the *condottiero* Facino Cane became lord of a vast territory between Piedmont and *Lombardy and practically lord of the duchy of *Milan; Braccio da Montone obtained the lordship of *Perugia and numerous cities in Umbria; Francesco *Sforza, son of Muzio Attendolo Sforza, became marquis of *Ancona and then, in 1450, lord of Milan.

M. Del Treppo, "Gli aspetti organizzativi, economici e sociali di una compagnia di ventura italiana", *Rivista storica italiana*, 85, 1973. – G. Ancona, "Milizie e condottieri", *Storia d'Italia*, 5, *I documenti*, Turin, 1973. – M. E. Mallet, *Mercenaries and their Masters. Warfare in Renaissance Italy*, London, 1974.

Attilio Stendardi

**In France.** In 1360, the conclusion of the peace of Brétigny-Calais between the king of *France, John II, and the king of *England, *Edward III, had as its immediate consequence, after five years of war, a massive redundancy of combatants. Part of these then grouped together under the orders of captains determined to continue the war on their own account.

In his *Chronicles*, Jean *Froissart describes this composite troop in which warriors from all quarters fought alongside each other, notably mercenaries "d'estrange nations", Germans, Brabantines, Flemings, Hainaulters, Bretons, Gascons, as well as "mauvais Français" impoverished by the wars and determined to enrich themselves by pillage and *ransom. From 1360 to 1362, they successively attacked *Champagne, the Barrois and *Burgundy, then reached the Rhône valley, ravaging the Lyonnais and the Forez. They later spread through the whole of the kingdom, with a clear predilection for the southern regions.

From 1360 and for about twenty years, the intensity of the companies' activities varied in accordance with the evolution of the wars: as soon as truces expired, the "gens de compagnies" rejoined the royal or princely armies, and as soon as hostilities ceased they began to make war again on their own account.

Faced with this peril, at the local level, measures of defence within the **bailliage* or the **sénéchaussée* were combined with the payment by towns or States of heavy sums intended to purchase the departure of the "*routiers". For their part, the papal, royal and princely authorities strove to get rid of the Great Companies by engaging them, with more or less success, to take part under the orders of prestigious captains in distant expeditions: to *Italy (in 1362), "outre-mer" (in 1365), even to *Spain (in 1367) or the *Empire (in 1375). However, these various measures were far from being effective.

In the end, it was the quasi-permanence of a state of war between 1369 and 1380 and the decision of King *Charles V to maintain a standing *army that led the Great Companies to disappear. Subsequently, though the military system that consisted of engaging troops and then dismissing them according to circumstances and needs led once more to the appearance of uncontrolled bands comparable to the Great Companies (thus the *écorcheurs* of the years 1430-1440), the phenomenon no longer had the extent that the disorganisation of the State had allowed it to attain in 1360.

P. Contamine, "Les compagnies d'aventure en France pendant la guerre de Cent Ans", *MEFRM*, 87, 1975, 365-396. – P. Contamine, *War in the Middle Ages*, Oxford, 1984.

Bertrand Schnerb

**COMPOSTELA.** Around 820-830, in the place called the Field of the star (*Campus stellae*), site of an old Visigothic necropolis, lights and *apparitions indicated to Bishop Theodemir of Iria the existence of the *tomb of the apostle St James. The marble-lined *domuncula – arcis marmoricus* – was soon covered by a sanctuary, then by a more sumptuous building begun in 899. As the urban centre grew, the *bishops of Iria settled at Compostela, whose *dominium* they assumed. Despite the wall built in *c.*960 against the Northmen, the town was taken and pillaged by the troops of al-Mansur in 997 and a new wall had to be erected.

The influx of *pilgrims in the 11th c. transformed Compostela into an urban centre with a multitude of activities, able to take advantage of the prosperity of the 12th century. Under Bishop Diego Gelmírez (1100-1140), a fervent supporter of the *Gregorian reform and *chancellor of Queen Urraca, the bishopric was declared exempt (1104) and made an *archbishopric (1124) and, as an apostolic see, allowed cardinal *canons. While ordering the building of a fourth sanctuary, a masterpiece of *Romanesque art, Diego Gelmírez transformed Compostela into a brilliant intellectual centre open to French influences. The church's documents were compiled into a *tumbo*, while various authors drew up the *Historia compostellana* to the greater glory of the archbishop; the policy he followed as lord of the town led in 1116-1117, then in 1136, to a *conjuratio* of the inhabitants, *merchants, goldsmiths and various artisans, who finally obtained greater autonomy for their *concilium*. In *c.*1138-1140 the **scriptorium* of Compostela produced the *Liber sancti Iacobi* or Codex Calixtinus, intended to increase the fervour of pilgrims, and a treatise *De consolatione rationis* by Master Peter of Compostela.

Between 1157 and 1230, Compostela played an increased role in an independent kingdom of *León: its archbishops were chancellors of the realm and in 1197 King Alfonso IX was dubbed a knight there; in the late 12th c., the royal *notary, master Bernard of Compostela the Elder, was called to *Rome where he compiled the *Collectio romana*. In the 12th c., favoured by episcopal vacancies during which the king usually charged the inhabitants with protecting the *roads, Compostela tried to shake off the yoke of ecclesiastical lordship, but in 1320 the new archbishop, the *Dominican Berengar of Landorra, drowned a new Compostelan rebellion in blood. The crisis of the 14th and 15th cc., the general insecurity and "absence of justice" led the inhabitants to form themselves into an *irmandade* (fraternity) against the archbishop in 1458, then to take part in the general uprising of 1467-1469. The creation of the *Audiencia* of *Galicia by the *Catholic Kings (1480) restored peace, and the construction of the royal *hospital from 1501, followed by the destruction in 1505 of the Romanesque cloister, considered too small, marked the beginning of a new and glorious period for Compostela.

L. Vásquez de Parga, J. M. Lacarra, J. Uria Riu, *Las Peregrinaciones a Santiago de Compostela*, Madrid, 1948-1949 (3 vol.). – "Gelmírez, Diego", "Santiago" and "Santiago de Compostela, diócesis de", *DHEE*, 1972-1975. – *Santiago de Compostela. 1000 ans de pèlerinage européen, Catalogue de l'exposition Europalia*, Ghent, 1985. – F. López Alsina, *La Ciudad de Santiago de Compostela en la alta Edad Media*, Santiago de Compostela, 1988.

Adeline Rucquoi

**The cult of St James and the pilgrimages.** In Spain a real cult of St James existed even before the discovery of his tomb, though there are no traces of it until after the Muslim invasion. To begin with, it did not have a general character, but from the time of the discovery of the tomb the cult enjoyed a real "explosion", at first locally and very soon in all the Christian kingdoms of *Spain and Europe. It was told how the saint appeared at the battle of Clavijo in 834 and put the Moors to flight. A knight of the Pimentel family and his horse, passing a stretch of sea while the Apostle's body was being translated, were covered with shells, and the shell of St James thus became the emblem of pilgrims.

Around 1075, Bishop Diego Peláes began to build the great Romanesque *basilica that still exists, with later additions such as the famous *Portico of Glory* (1188). From the first years, the kings showered donations on the sacred place. The tomb and the town formed around it were called *sancti Jacobi*, in Spanish *Sant-Yago* and then Santiago.

One of the most typical manifestations of this universal veneration was the *pilgrimages that, from the beginning, began to flock to Compostela along the roads of the Spanish Christian kingdoms and very soon of all the European States, following the propagation by the *Martyrologies of information about the discovery of the apostolic tomb. By the beginning of the 11th c., the movement had acquired great importance: many pilgrims came from Catalonia, France, Germany and Flanders, and in the latter countries Spain was soon named *Jacobsland*. The ever-growing number of pilgrims entailed the need for a thorough highway, assistential, legal and liturgical organisation. The *iter, via, caminus s. Jacobi* that linked *Barcelona to Padrón on the Atlantic is mentioned by documents from the late 10th c.; in organising this "way", the actions of the kings were effectively backed up by the initiatives of individuals and especially of *bishops and religious *orders, who built numerous hospices and *hospitals in the service of pilgrims. Saints like St Dominic of Calzada and St John of Ortega, dedicating their lives and their foundations to the assistance of wayfarers, demonstrate how much spiritual value was put on the pilgrimage to Compostela. The great initial impetus was due to Bishop Diego Gelmírez, with the support of the kings of Spain and the blessing of the *popes, who showered the see with prerogatives and privileges, declaring it first *exempt and then *metropolitan and granted further *indulgences and spiritual graces to anyone who made the pilgrimage to the tomb of St James. *Alexander III granted the jubilee indulgence, declaring every year in which the saint's feast (25 July) fell on a *Sunday a Compostelan Holy Year. This jubilee is still regularly celebrated and is regarded as equal to the Roman *jubilee; it is the only case of an indulgence that has never been suspended, not even when the Compostelan jubilee year coincided with that of Rome (see J. Guerra, *Roma-Santiago. La bula "Deus omnipotens"*, Santiago, 1954). Indeed, until after the 15th c., the tomb of St James in Spain was venerated and visited as much as those of the princes of the Apostles at *Rome. This is confirmed by the innumerable churches, hospitals and confraternities of St James that sprung up everywhere. The protection of the apostolic sanctuary and the pilgrims that went there was, together with the war against the Muslims, the fundamental aim of the military order of *St James of the Sword created in 1163. During the Middle Ages, this uninterrupted flow of European pilgrims to Spain was the most continuous and effective link between the Iberian peninsula and the rest of *Christendom. Along the pilgrim routes developed an intense *commerce with Europe, undertaken by elements extraneous to Spanish society, especially *Jews and Franks, who settled along the roads to Compostela and , in the 11th and 12th cc., created flourishing *markets in the towns along them (Pamplona, Jaca, Sanguesa, Puente la Reina, Estella, Los Arcos, Logrono, Nàjera, Belorado, *Burgos, Sahagun, *León), which had considerable colonies of foreigners devoted to commerce. They even founded some *towns and constituted special boroughs (*burgos*) in others, to which the kings granted special privileges. The presence of these populations and their activity made a profound change to the Spanish economy, previously mainly agricultural; at the same time appeared municipalities and municipal freedoms, together with institutional forms of feudal European type. Similar groups of immigrants settled all over the place and fused with the native element everywhere, but more rapidly in the centres crossed by the pilgrim routes.

Through these roads the new Christian art, *Romanesque, also spread in Spain, coming to replace the strongly Arabic-influenced Visigothic art. It started perhaps from *Saint-Martin at Tours and culminated in the cathedral of St James, the most grandiose and inspired example of a pilgrimage church (see works by E. Male, A. Kingsley Porter and E. Lambert).

The old city is still entirely medieval in appearance; the famous *cathedral replaces the old one, sacked and burned by *Saracens in 997. It is a great Latin-cross basilica with three aisles in Byzantine Romanesque style, a transept, ambulatory and apse chapels; it has a series of important sculptures in the *Portico of Glory*, while the *cloister is in the *flamboyant Gothic style (16th c.); other notable buildings are the Royal Hospital (1511, Plateresque) and the bishop's palace (12th-13th c.).

A. Lopez Ferreiro, *Historia de la Santa A. M. Iglesia de Santiago de Compostela*, Santiago, 1898 f. (12 vol.). – L. Duchesne, "Saint Jacques en Galice", *AMidi*, 12, 1900, 145-180. – "La catedral de Santiago de Compostela", *Archivio esp. de Arte y Arqueología*, 31, 1926, 155-156. – Z. García Villada, *Historia ecclesiastica de España*, 1, 1, Madrid, 1929, 27-104. – A. López, "Bibliografia del Apóstol Santiago", *Nuevos estudios crítico-históricos acerca de Galicia*, L. Gómez Canedo (ed.), 1, Santiago, 1947, 3-130. – C. Sánchez Albornoz, "La auténtica batalla de Clavijo", *Cuadernos de Hist. de España*, 9, 1948, 94-139. – *Historia compostellana*,

Flórez (ed.), 20, 1-598 and then *PL*, 170, 889-1236 (Sp. tr., Santiago, 1950). – T. D. Kendrick, *Saint James in Spain*, London, 1960. – J. M. Lacarra, "Espiritualidad del culto y de la peregrinación a Santiago antes de la primera Cruzada", *Pellegrinaggi e culto dei santi in Europa fino alla prima crociata*, CCSSM, 4, Todi, 1963, 113-144. – R. Oursel, *Pèlerins du Moyen Âge*, Paris, 1978. – *Saint Jacques de Compostelle: la quête du sacré*, A. Dupront (ed.), Turnhout, 1985.

Maria Cristina Buschi

## COMPUTUS, ECCLESIASTICAL

**The West.** The Latin *computus* means calculation, counting. *Computi* were the tables used to establish the church calendar, from the feast of *Easter, which was movable. The Jewish Passover, determining the anniversary of Christ's death and *Resurrection, was celebrated on 14 Nisan; from the 3rd c., the Christians reached an agreement to celebrate Easter on the following *Sunday, but divergences arose in calculating the day when the Jewish 14 Nisan fell. In 325, at the council of Nicaea, the *Fathers invited all the Churches to rally to the Alexandrian computus and celebrate Easter on the Sunday following the full moon that began after the spring equinox (hence between 22 March and 25 April). The possible variation was five weeks. The rules for calculating the feast of Easter are the object of ecclesiastical computus.

The Middle Ages inherited the labours of Dionysius Exiguus, a Scythian monk who came to *Rome in *c.*500 and died in *c.*540, who won acceptance for the Alexandrian cycle of 19 years and established a count of years from the birth of Christ (or what he believed to be the year of Christ's birth).

The Venerable *Bede's *Liber de temporibus*, finished in *c.*703, explained the different divisions of *time and the seasons. A little later (725) he composed a more thorough book on chronology, *De temporum ratione*. These two books were subsequently much studied and inaugurated a particular genre of medieval literature. Several treatises *De computo* exist, such as that of *Rabanus Maurus and especially that of Heric of Auxerre, one of the most widespread. The two great initiators of scientific studies in this field were *Abbo of Fleury (*c.*954-1004) and *Gerbert of Aurillac, *pope under the name of Silvester II († 1003), who considerably enlarged the field of vision of the usual authors of *computi*, whose preoccupations were mainly liturgical.

W. W. Rouse Ball, *A Short Account of the History of Mathematics*, London, 1919. – B. Krusch, *Studien zur christlich-mittelalterlichen Chronologie*, 2 vol., Berlin, 1938. – C. W. Jones, *Bedae Opera de Temporibus*, Cambridge (MA), 1943. – M. Noirot, "Comput", *Cath.*, 2, 1954, 1430-1431. – P. S. Baker, M. Lapidge, *Byrhtferth's Enchiridion*, London, 1995.

Guy-Marie Oury

**Byzantium.** The calculation of the date of Easter, on which the movable feasts of the *liturgical year depended, took on particular importance at Byzantium due to the fact that it was closely associated there with the establishment of a system of dating starting from a world era.

The calculation of the date of Easter was based first on respect for a biblical prescription (Ex 12, 2 and 12, 18) that fixed the Passover on the 14th day of the first (lunar) month of the year, and then on the wish to differentiate the Christian feast from the Jewish feast. The rule of Sunday observance, which extended to all the Churches from the 3rd c., did not suffice to make this distinction, and the computists sought to give the first lunar month a stable definition, adapted to the (solar) Julian *calendar. Very soon, the first moon of the year was attached to the spring equinox, symbolic date of the *Creation and Incarnation. Thus, in the Christian Church, the date of Easter was fixed at the Sunday following the full moon after the spring equinox. From the 3rd c., Alexandrian and Roman computists sought to work out a cycle that would allow them to forecast the date of Easter over several years. The first attempts were based on the lunar cycle which, every 19 years, brought the 14th day of the moon back to the same day of the month of March or April. But the Alexandrian computists also sought to determine in advance the weekday of the Easter moon. Thus they worked out the Easter cycle of 532 years, which resulted from the multiplication of the 19-year lunar cycle by the 28-year solar cycle.

The Alexandrian computists tried particularly to make the symbolism of the week-days in the book of Genesis coincide with the main events of the gospel. The cycles thus worked out did not coincide with the dating systems in use and did not permit the elements of Christ's chronology to be linked to the chronology of world *history. This preoccupation appeared at Byzantium at the end of the 6th century. The prologue of the *Chronicon paschale* connected the Easter cycle of 532 years with the world era in such a way as to give the events of Christ's life a date adapted to the civil chronology and compatible with the symbolism of the days of the liturgical calendar. Thus arose the protobyzantine era, which fixed the creation of the world at minus 5509. More utilitarian treatises, composed under *Heraclius, attest the research done to put the Easter cycle and the world era in harmony with the cycle of *indictions; this desire resulted in the Byzantine era of 5508, which had the advantage of making the indictional cycle of 15 years begin at the same time as the lunar and solar cycles, so that the division of any world year by 28, 19 or 15 allowed the position of that year in each of these cycles to be found directly.

V. Grumel, *La Chronologie*, Paris, 1958. – J. Beaucamp, R. Bondoux *et al.*, "Temps et histoire: le Prologue de la *Chronique pascale*", *TMCB*, 7, 1979, 223-301.

Irène Sorlin

**COMTAT VENAISSIN.** The *Comitatus Venassinus*, or marquisate of Provence – the county of *Provence being south of the Durance – was a product of the treaties of 1125 between the count of *Toulouse and the count of Provence, and of 1195 between them and the count of Forcalquier. Its territory covered Mont Ventoux, some places in the Delphinal Baronies, the plateau of Vaucluse, the north of the Petit Luberon, as far as the outskirts of *Avignon. Its capital was Pernes-les-Fontaines, seat of the *seneschal and then of the rector before his installation at Carpentras (1320).

After the Albigensian crusade and the dispossession of the count of Toulouse, the treaty of Paris (12 April 1229) allotted the country to the *pope, but the administration of the king of *France and the restorations to the count of Toulouse altered the effect of this. Alphonse of Poitiers, brother of *Louis IX, deployed his talents there from 1251 to his death (1271) as count of Toulouse, while having an inquiry made into his rights.

In 1274, Pope *Gregory X obtained from *Philip III the Bold the right to directly administer his State, which consisted of about 80 towns and castles. The three orders met together in local Estates. *Clement V arrived at Avignon in 1309, but continued his itinerant existence like his Roman predecessors. Only in 1348 did *Clement VI buy Avignon from Queen Joanna of Naples, but *John XXII had already taken advantage of the return of the suppressed property of the Temple by the *Hospitallers of St John to round off the State to the north and buy *fiefs from the dauphin of Viennois. Under John XXII, local wars, then the passage of the Great *Companies and the devastations of Raymond de Turenne at the time of the *Great Schism, would lead to the fortification of towns and villages.

The *Jews, witnesses to the popes' relative *toleration towards them, remained in their ghettos or "carrieros" at Avignon, Carpentras, Cavaillon and L'Isle-sur-la-Sorgue.

The rector had endlessly to defend his prerogatives from his powerful neighbour, the *legate of Avignon. At the time of the legate Peter of Foix (1433-1464), who skilfully moderated the conquering policy of the dauphin, future *Louis XI and heir to the county of Provence (1481), most of the rectors were French. Pope *Sixtus IV, before imposing his nephew Giuliano della Rovere as legate, made him the first *archbishop of Avignon (1475), a see detached from the *province of *Arles, with the bishops of Carpentras, Cavaillon and Vaison as *suffragans.

J. Girard, *Les États du Comtat Venaissin*, Paris, 1908. – C. Faure, *Études sur l'administration et l'histoire du Comtat Venaissin du XIII<sup>e</sup> au XV<sup>e</sup> siècles*, Paris, 1909. – *Atlas historique de Provence, Comtat*, Paris, 1969. – H. Dubled, *Histoire du Comtat Venaissin*, Carpentras, 1981.

Michel Hayez

## CONCEPTION OF THE VIRGIN MARY

**The West.** The conception of the Virgin has two meanings in theology: we speak of the active conception of *Mary for the virginal conception of Jesus by the action of the *Holy Spirit; the passive conception of Mary designates her begetting by her parents. While the virginal conception of Jesus is attested by the Infancy gospels (Mt and Lk), no scriptural text refers to the passive conception of Mary. It is the *apocrypha, such as the protogospel of James, that mention it. The birth of Mary is presented there as miraculous: Joachim and *Anne were sterile; one day, the high priest refused Joachim's offering, attributing his sterility to his sins. Joachim then left town, but an *angel appeared separately to husband and wife to promise them posterity. They met at the Golden Gate of Jerusalem, and later saw the promise fulfilled in the birth of Mary.

These apocrypha favoured the progressive spread of the *feast of the Conception of Mary in the East, then in the West starting from *England, which celebrated it from the 11th century. Theologians were not slow to react. In a letter addressed to the canons of Lyon in *c.*1137, St *Bernard rose up against this innovation. He held to the following reasoning: Mary was conceived according to the ordinary ways of human procreation, but the procreative act is always stained with *concupiscence; so the conception of Mary cannot be declared holy or celebrated by the Church because this would be to honour *sin. As for Mary's immunity from original sin, the West could not at first admit it, being too much marked by *Augustinian doctrine (according to which parents, because of concupiscence, transmit original sin at the same time as life). Finally, the 13th-c. *doctors invoked the universality of the *redemption worked by *Christ to refuse this privilege to Mary, who would otherwise have had no need to be redeemed.

A decisive turning was taken by John *Duns Scotus early in the 14th century. He suggested that Mary was able to benefit from a perfect redemption, while being preserved from original sin from the time of her conception. From then on, the doctrine of the Immaculate Conception prevailed and only the *Dominicans refused to rally to it, creating confusion among the faithful who heard contradictory preaching. In 1439 the council of *Basel promulgated a decree that made the Immaculate Conception a dogma. But at that date the council was *schismatic and its decision took no effect. To pacify feelings, in 1476 Pope *Sixtus IV forbade public controversies; but the debate was resumed from the end of the 15th century. So the Middle Ages ended without the doctrine of the Immaculate Conception having been clarified to the satisfaction of all.

X. le Bachelet, "Immaculée Conception", *DThC*, 7, Paris, 1927, 845-1218. – P. Robert, "L'Immaculée Conception au Moyen Âge", *La Vierge Immaculée. Histoire et doctrine*, Montreal, 1954, 117-151. – E. D. O'Connor (ed.), *The Dogma of the Immaculate Conception. History and Significance*, Notre Dame (IN), 1958. – J. Galot, "L'Immaculée Conception", *Maria*, 7, 1964, 9-116.

Marielle Lamy

**Byzantium.** A feast of the Conception of Mary, also called feast of the Conception of Anne, existed in the East from the 8th c. (see the canon of this feast by St Andrew of Crete). In the 11th c., it was among the public holidays at *Constantinople. But the notion of an original stain transmitted from Adam, from which *Mary was preserved from her conception (a notion that was behind the dogma of the Immaculate Conception in the West), was foreign to the East. Mary was the all-pure, without speculation as to the moment of her "purification". At the end of the Middle Ages, favoured by polemics between Greeks and Latins, positions hardened, leading to the present opposition (the *Orthodox reject the idea of an immaculate conception of Mary).

M. Jugie, *L'Immaculée Conception dans l'Écriture sainte et dans la tradition orientale*, Rome, 1952.

Marie-Hélène Congourdeau

**CONCILIARISM.** The term "conciliarism" designates a body of *doctrines formulated between the late 14th and mid 15th cc., which assigned a fundamental place to the *council in the life of the Church and wanted to make it an instrument of permanent reform of the institutions and morals of *Christendom.

The rise of conciliarist principles was linked to the failure of all attempts to end the *Great Schism, which had broken out in 1378 and led to the division of the Church into two camps: the partisans of the pope of *Rome and those of the pope of *Avignon. The idea of resorting to a general council to rule on the major problems of Christendom had already been suggested several times since the late 13th century. It regained a certain actuality when it became evident that the schism of 1378 would be prolonged. To put an end to the bad will of the rival obediences, two German clerics of the university of *Paris, *Conrad of Gelnhausen and *Henry of Langenstein, proposed in 1380 to bypass the apparently insurmountable obstacle created by the *pope's supreme power of jurisdiction by referring to Christ's intention: if he had entrusted a particular *authority to *Peter, it was because he wanted the Church to remain always one. His successors could not create an obstacle to this fundamental law without becoming unfaithful to their mission. In this case, the council representing the universality of believers was empowered to put them back on the right path. For the moment these ideas had little echo, so new were they, but they became influential after 1400 when a new generation of theologians and *canonists, among them the Frenchmen *Pierre d'Ailly and Jean *Gerson and the Italian Francesco *Zabarella, awoke to the scandal created by the permanence of the schism and undertook to put an end to it by formulating a veritable ecclesiological doctrine adapted to those times of crisis. The conciliarists recognised that the pope was the head of the Church, but were opposed to his exercising an unlimited hegemony. The supreme pontiff was nothing without the universal Church and possessed no power that did not already belong to it. Hence the council could judge the pope if he went astray, for it held its authority directly from Christ.

These ideas triumphed at the council of *Constance, which proclaimed the deposition of Pope *John XXIII and restored the unity of Christendom by electing his successor, *Martin V, in 1415. But the conciliarists also wanted to prevent such grave events happening again. To this end, they adopted in 1417 the decrees *Haec sancta* and *Frequens* which affirmed the council's superiority over the pope and the latter's obligation to summon it frequently in order to proceed to the reform of the Church "in head and members". But at the council of *Basel (1431-1449), the upholders of conciliarism came into conflict with the pope and his supporters and hardened their pretensions, going so far as to maintain, with *Panormitanus and John of Segovia, the doctrine of the infallibility of the council, which was not only competent in times of *schism or crisis but in all circumstances, and whose decisions could prevail over those of the pope. Although the papacy finally triumphed after 1450, conciliarist ideas, which had enjoyed great favour in *university circles, long remained influential in certain parts of Christendom, such as the German lands or *Poland.

B. Tierney, *Foundations of the Conciliar Theory*, Cambridge, 1968. – A. Landi, *Il papa deposto (Pisa, 1409). L'idea conciliare nel grande Scisma*, Turin, 1985. – *HChr*, 6, 1990, 293-298.

André Vauchez

**CONCLAVE.** The term "conclave" means literally "under lock and key", the *cardinals having to be locked up in order to elect the *pope. The conclave properly speaking did not exist until the constitution of *Gregory X (1271-1276) *Ubi periculum*, promulgated in 1274 by the second council of *Lyon, which fixed at ten days the delay after which the *election had to be begun and ordered the reclusion of the cardinals. In the first three days, the cardinals were to receive only two meals a day, then only *bread, *wine and *water. The pope met with strong resistance from the cardinals and had to lean on the *bishops to get his constitution published (1 Nov 1274). *Ubi periculum* was suspended, perhaps even revoked, by Popes Adrian V (1276) and John XXI (1276-1277); it was later established by *Celestine V (28 Sept 1295). It was respected at the election of *Boniface VIII (1294-1303).

The actual idea of shutting up the cardinals at papal election time was inspired by the election procedure of the doges of *Venice and the **podestà* of a number of Italian *communes. In 1241, Senator Matteo Rosso *Orsini shut the cardinals up in the Roman palace of the Septizonium to force them to put an end to their divisions. In 1270, after a vacancy that had already lasted a year and a half, Raniero Gatti, captain of the people at *Viterbo, also locked the cardinals in the bishop's palace and removed the roof. This did not prevent the cardinals building little wooden cabins inside and adding several more months to the longest vacancy of the apostolic see. The controversialist Cardinal John of Toledo had advised opening the roof to let in the Holy Spirit. It was thus under the pressure of the lay authorities of *Rome and Viterbo – too long a vacancy was harmful to their city's interests – that a type of papal election arose in the 13th c. that would become the papacy's invariable procedure and would last into our own day.

After Gregory X's *Ceremonial (1272-1273), the conclave was described again in the ceremonial books of the late 14th c. (Pierre Ameilh, François de Conzié). The innovations were secondary and confirmed the principles of the constitution of 1274, veritable "constitutional charter" of the papal conclave.

E. Petrucci, "Il problema della vacanza papale e la costituzione 'Ubi periculum' di Gregorio X", *Atti del Convegno di studio per l'VIII Centenario del 1° Conclave (1268-1271)*, Viterbo, 1975. – M. Dykmans, *Le Cérémonial papal de la fin du Moyen Âge à la Renaissance*, Rome, 1977-1985 (4 vol.). – B. Schimmelpfennig, "Papst- und Bischofswahlen seit dem 12. Jahrhundert", *Wahlen und Wählen im Mittelalter*, Sigmaringen, 1990, 173-196.

Agostino Paravicini Bagliani

**CONCORDANCES.** Directories conceived in the 13th c. by theologians to facilitate the labours of *exegesis, containing words and expressions of the *Bible and indicating, by means of cross-references, all the places in which they are found. Two types of concordances can be distinguished, real or verbal, based on the content and arrangement of the articles.

Real concordances grouped together words and expressions by theme. The Irish theologian *Thomas Gallus († 1246), a *canon at the abbey of *Saint-Victor in *Paris, used concordances of this type, but based on an alphabetical division of the *chapters of the Bible, to write his commentaries on Pseudo-*Dionysius the Areopagite. *Robert Grosseteste, bishop of *Lincoln († 1253), composed real concordances on Holy Scripture and the Church *Fathers, but also on secular authors. The references were grouped around nine subjects (*De Deo*, *De verbo*, etc.). Each subject comprised a certain number of subdivisions (thus, for the chapter on *God: *De unitate Dei*, *De trinitate Dei*, *De iusticia*, etc.), designated by conventional signs. These signs recur in the margins of the manuscripts that Grosseteste and his collaborators read and indexed.

Verbal concordances were veritable dictionaries of words and expressions, arranged in alphabetical order. These concordances were produced in three stages by the *Dominicans of Paris between 1235 and 1285.

In the first concordance, composed undoubtedly with the help of *Hugh of Saint-Cher, a *master of theology at the convent of Saint-Jacques (1230-1235), the words were arranged in alphabetical order, followed by references established according to a system of division of the Bible into chapters. The chapters were in turn divided into seven parts designated by letters of the alphabet (*a* to *g*). Thus *Aaa* (Jer 1, 6) was followed by the cross-references: *Je: Ic, XIIId; Eze. IIIIf*, indicating that the passage in question would be found in the book of *Jeremiah (Je), the first chapter (I), in the part designated by the letter *c*, and in the 14th chapter (XIV), in the part designated by the letter *d*. The same passage was found in the 4th chapter (IIII) of the book of *Ezekiel (Eze) in the part designated by the letter *f*.

The "English" concordance, also produced at Paris around 1252 under the direction of an English Dominican, Richard Stavensby, set out to improve on the previous system by completing the cross-references: the biblical passage was cited *in extenso* alongside the reference. For the passage indicated above, we thus have *Aaa. Jerem. Ic : Aaa domine deus ecce nescio loqui quia puer ego sum.* But these directories, in which the citations took up too much space, did not succeed in replacing the first, more manageable concordance.

So it was judged necessary to work out a third solution.

The third concordance, attested from 1275, reduced these citations to a more reasonable proportion. Its success was due to a better conception, but above all to the fact that this version profited from a very wide circulation in intellectual circles, thanks to the rise of the system of reproducing university *books by sections (*pecie*).

C. Spicq, *Esquisse d'une histoire de l'exégèse latine*, Paris, 1944, 172-178. – M. A. Rouse, R. H. Rouse, "La concordance verbale des Écritures", *Le Moyen Âge et la Bible*, Paris, 1984, 115-122. – A. Vernet, A. Genevois, *Bibliographie de la Bible*, Paris, 1990, 60-61.

Donatella Nebbiai-Dalla Guarda

**CONCORDAT.** The term "concordat" designates an agreement between the Holy See and a secular authority. A once widespread doctrine saw the concordat as a concession made by the Church to the temporal power. Such an interpretation does not correspond to the reality of the facts. In reality the concordat was the culmination of a negotiation, sometimes long and difficult, in which the two parties were called to make reciprocal concessions in order to obtain recognition of what they considered essential. So the concordat was, in its judicial nature, if not in its content, closer to an international agreement than to a concession of the spiritual power. While concordats were numerous in the 19th and 20th cc., they were exceptional in the Middle Ages. Neither the political conditions nor the dominant ideas on relations between *Church and States were favourable to any such formulation of their relations.

To try to put an end to the *Investiture Contest in the German Empire, the envoys of *Paschal II proposed an agreement that was rejected by the German episcopate (concordat of *Sutri, 1111: *MGH.Const*, I, 140) because it would have involved abandoning all their temporal domains. On 23 Sept 1122, by two constitutive declarations of the concordat of *Worms, *Calixtus II and *Henry V put an end to this conflict, the emperor renouncing *investiture by *ring and *staff and guaranteeing freedom of *elections (*MGH.Const*, I, 159). This "common-sense solution" (A. Fliche), inspired by the ideas of *Ivo of Chartres, could "with a bit of good will" have ended a conflict that had gone on too long. But the imprecision of the texts, their equivocations and their gaps left the door open to new debates.

In *France, a concordat was concluded on 2 May 1418. It bore essentially on the election of *bishops and *abbots and the collation of *benefices. It was made obligatory in "Burgundian" France by an *ordinance of 9 Sept 1418, but from 1423 it was no longer observed. It had not been ratified by the Dauphin's France. A projected concordat was negotiated between *Charles VII and *Eugenius IV in 1442-1444. It came to nothing, the *pope having refused to give way to the demands of an assembly of clergy. After the abrogation of the *Pragmatic Sanction of Bourges (1467), a precarious concordat was concluded between *Sixtus IV and *Louis XI in 1472.

In the *Empire, concordats were concluded in 1448 with *Frederick III and in 1449 with the German princes. Concordats were also concluded in 1198 between the Holy See and the kingdom of *Sicily and in 1243 between the papal *legate and the *commune of Vercelli.

H. Wagnon, *Concordat et droit international*, Louvain, 1935 (thesis). – J. Juig, *L'Église et les États, Histoire des concordats*, Paris, 1990.

Jean Gaudemet

**CONCUPISCENCE.** Concupiscence designates any movement of desire towards a material good, contrary to *reason. For this reason, many authors saw it as a consequence of the *sin that gave *man a rebellious flesh. For St Augustine it was the direct and major consequence of original sin, exemption from concupiscence being one of the preternatural gifts. The medievals remained more or less faithfully attached to this conception, but insisted on the fact that what is sinful is not the mere existence of desire, but the fact that it becomes disordered and is no longer subject to the authority of the higher powers of the *soul. For St *Thomas Aquinas, concupiscence is applied to all desires of the senses, but his thought subsequently usually limits it to sexual desire.

Thomas Aquinas, *Summa Theologiae*, I$^{a}$ II$^{ae}$, q. 30.

C. Baumgartner, "Concupiscence", *DSp*, 2, 2, 1953, 1356-1373.

Jean-Marie Gueullette

**CONFESSION.** In theological terms, confession is, with *contrition and satisfaction (or reparation), one of the three elements of the sacrament of *penance. In the strict sense, it consists in the avowal of faults made by the sinner to a priest; in the broad sense, confession is synonymous with the sacrament of penance and covers the three elements distinguished above.

In the history of the Church, penitential discipline underwent a considerable evolution. During the first six centuries, the Church knew, for grave faults, the penance called canonical, accorded once in a lifetime, non-reiterable, sometimes joined to permanent prohibitions concerning certain professions or conjugal life. For this reason, it was not often received except by aged Christians or those in danger of *death.

From the 6th c., Irish monks would practise and make known another form of penance, called private or tariffed penance, based on the avowal of the guilty party and the imposition of a satisfaction established by booklets (*Penitentials) available to the confessor, reiterable as often as necessary. This new discipline was quite quickly accepted on the continent. In the 8th and 9th cc., the Carolingian *councils and *capitularies tried to put order into the penitential commutations (redemption of years of *fasting by *almsgiving) and the satisfactions imposed, often differing from one book to another. A council held in 813 at Chalon-sur-Saône went further; it tried to abolish tariffed penance and impose a return to the canonical form, but this could not be done. In fact a compromise was established and, from the 9th c., there would be two ways of doing penance: one according to the Irish, tariffed model for secret faults, the other according to a public process for faults that had caused scandal. This public penance, which had the character of a coercive penalty, had few things in common with the canonical penance of the first centuries. Introduced in the so-called Gelasian *Sacramentary, it later passed into the Roman *Pontifical.

From the late 12th c., there were no longer two penitential processes but three, according to the distinction formulated by *Peter Comestor († 1179) (*De sacramentis: de paenitentia*, 24-25) and repeated by *Alan of Lille († 1203), Robert of Flamborough (before 1234), *Peter of Poitiers († *c.*1216) and Thomas of Chobham (*c.*1235) in their *confessors' manuals. 1) Solemn public penance, whose imposition was reserved for the *bishop: it was begun on Ash Wednesday, and reconciliation took place on Holy Thursday. *Clerics could not be subjected to it, and it was not reiterable. It was inflicted for particularly scandalous public sins (*parricide, *sacrilege, etc.). 2) Non-solemn public penance, which any *parish priest could impose. It consisted of a penitential *pilgrimage and it was reiterable. Laypeople received it for public sins considered less scandalous (murder, *theft of Church property); major clerics (*bishops, priests, *deacons) – not subject to solemn penance, as we said – for their scandalous faults. This penance-pilgrimage, launching repentant (in principle) criminals onto the roads, gave rise to exactions and scandals that may be imagined. 3) Private penance was imposed for hidden sins of all kinds. It was reiterable and accessible to clerics and *laity. The third form of penance was admittedly the one most commonly received by Christians in the Middle Ages.

*Councils and *synods insisted on confession and the care that pastors must bring to it. Penance was the sacrament dealt with at greatest length by the synods of the 13th c.; in *c.*1220, the synodal of the West did not hesitate to introduce canons of tariffed penance that would help the priest in his questioning of the sinner and the choice of satisfaction to impose.

When did people confess? There were three favoured liturgical *feasts that associated eucharistic *communion and confession beforehand: Christmas, *Easter and *Pentecost. But preachers lamented that clerics and laypeople hardly confessed once a year, and that more out of habit than contrition (Alan of Lille, *Ars praedicandi*, 31). Easter confession and communion would take a growing place in pastoral directives and in the life of the faithful: a tendency that would be recognised and confirmed as law for the universal Church by canon 21 of the fourth *Lateran council (1215), insisting that every Christian confess "at least once a year to his parish priest" and receive communion at Easter. What use was made of solemn penance? By the reserved cases that multiplied from the 13th c., the bishops seem to have ensured their own right of control over the administration of penance at least for the gravest faults, since in these cases sinners had to be sent to them for *absolution. Reserved cases appear to have been a substitute form of solemn penance.

The lists of sins or models of interrogation in the confessors' manuals focus the attention of the modern reader on the avowal: this allowed the confessor to evaluate the culpability and inflict the corresponding penalty; by the *humility it required, it was already a form of expiation: theologians insisted more and more on this aspect.

Penitential tariffs strongly emphasized another component of the *sacrament: the need to satisfy, *i.e.* to make reparation for the offence committed against *God by *sin, the wrong inflicted on one's neighbour. We may find the penances inflicted heavy or excessive: but for peoples whose morals were still crude, in times marked by *violence, they favoured a certain education of *conscience and contributed to the improvement of behaviour.

A final element often ignored by historians of penance: the presence of *prayer in this sacrament. Admittedly this was by way of satisfaction, a substitute penalty, but from the 9th c. the *Rituals show that, apart from the questioning, it was all prayer by the priest and the penitent: prayers multiplied before and after, *psalms, *litanies, kneeling, *prostration, churchgoing.

C. Vogel, *Le Pécheur et la pénitence au Moyen Âge*, Paris, 1969. – J. Avril, "Remarques sur un aspect de la vie religieuse paroissiale: la pratique de la confession et de la communion du Xe au XIVe siècle", *L'Encadrement religieux des fidèles au Moyen Âge et jusqu'au concile de Trente*, Paris, 1985, 345-363. – J. Longère, "Prière et pénitence", *Prier au Moyen Âge. Pratiques et Expériences (V[e]-XV[e] siècles)*, Paris-Turnhout, 1991, 175-200. – J. Longère, "La pénitence selon le *Repertorium*, les instructions et constitutions et le pontifical de Guillaume Durand", *Guillaume Durand, évêque de Mende (v. 1230-1296)*, Paris, 1992, 105-133.

Jean Longère

**CONFESSORS' MANUALS.** The first medieval confessors' manual is generally considered to be *Alan of Lille's *Liber paenitentialis* at the end of the 12th century. Chronologically, confessors' manuals followed the *Penitentials which, from the end of the patristic age to the 12th c., fixed the nature, importance and length of *penance imposed for grave sins: this was the so-called tariffed system of penance. However, the application of the sentence was not automatic: in fact several penitential collections contain a canon attributed to Jerome, but in fact by Halitgar, bishop of *Cambrai (817-831), which already appeals to the initiative and personal judgment of the priest.

Though they do not entirely set aside the fixed scale of the preceding period (such a sanction for such a fault), which were sometimes recopied until the 15th c. (*Burchard of Worms's *Corrector et medicus*), the new manuals have a much wider aim. Valuing the active and personal role that the priest has in the administration of penance, they emphasize the demands this entails and try to help him respond to them. To this end, they teach him or remind him of the moral and spiritual qualities, the personal example of life and the attitude of acceptance that facilitate the confidence and avowal of the penitent. Moreover, these works try to improve the pastors' knowledge of moral theology (restitution, *usury), sacramental theology (celebration, *validity) and *canon law. Thus the priest will be more able to exercise a ministry of judgment, stimulate the contribution of the sinner and choose a satisfaction adapted to the capacities of the penitent and the gravity of the fault.

In various proportions, all the manuals study the three elements of penitence: *contrition, *confession or avowal, satisfaction or reparation, the first being considered the indispensable disposition for making the other two. Interest in the *absolution given by the priest grew with the development of so-called reserved cases that obliged the penitent to be sent before the higher authority for certain grave faults. Another element took a growing place: the examination of concrete situations, cases that might be presented, which the priest had to know: What to do if. . . ? Has someone sinned when. . . ? Growing attention to these cases of *conscience would lead, towards the end of the Middle Ages, to vast **summae* of *casuistry in which practical directives aiming at the administration of the *sacrament would have only a rather small place.

By contrast, confessors' manuals proper would examine only a minimum of concrete situations and would study essentially the actions of the penitent and the priest during the reception of the sacrament.

It is certain, however, that the authors of confessors' manuals contributed to the development of casuistry by their anxiety to make known and apply the divine and ecclesiastical precepts in the numerous acts of human life. Their morality may appear negative: it was more of a law not to be transgressed than an ideal to be pursued; however, unlike some of their modern successors, the medieval authors of penitential or casuistical *Summae* did not aim at minimizing or overturning the law.

The Penitentials of the previous period concentrated on the external and social aspect of the fault. Manuals of confession benefited from the progress of theological reflection: elements of *sin, nature and *faculties of the *soul, penetration and progressive adaptation of *Aristotelian *ethics. This would lead to attention being put not just on the actual act of sinning, but also on everything that could surround and influence its realization: the age, disposition, consent and especially intention of the penitent; the contrition shown; the circumstances of time, place and, where appropriate, complicity; the range and consequences of the fault. What was judged in the penitential tribunal was not just a bad deed, a sin, but the whole of its components and, above all, the author of the act, a responsible person.

Confessors' manuals permit an excellent approach to medieval *pastoral care, its profound tendencies, its evolution. They demonstrate the privileged relationship that the Church wanted to establish between the priest and each member of his flock through the sacrament of penance, its wish to personalize the *cure of souls.

P. Michaud-Quantin, *Sommes de casuistique et manuels de confession au Moyen Âge (XII^e-XVI^e siècles)*, Louvain-Lille-Montreal, 1962. – P. Michaud-Quantin, "Les Méthodes de la pastorale du XIII^e au XV^e siècle", *Miscellanea Mediaevalia . . . herausgegeben von Albert Zimmermann*, Berlin, 1970, 76-91. – J. Longère, "Quelques *Summae de paenitentia* à la fin du XII^e et au début du XIII^e siècle", *La piété populaire au Moyen Âge*, Paris, 1977, 45-58.

Jean Longère

**CONFIRMATION.** In Antiquity, Christian initiation in the West involved a bath in *water, the post-baptismal rites (later called "confirmation") and the *Eucharist; it was celebrated under the presidency of the *bishop, usually at *Easter, sometimes at *Pentecost or Epiphany, except in cases of urgency. This is what we still find in the 7th-c. *Ordo romanus XI.*

From the end of Antiquity, this ritual unit would be dismembered. In view of the numbers of catechumens, it was no longer possible for the bishop to preside over every initiation, and this gave rise to two different disciplines: the East delegated the presidency to the priest and preserved the unity of the three *sacraments; the West kept confirmation for the bishop, which entailed breaking the initiation into three stages. In the episcopal towns, the old tradition was kept up longer; in the country, the priest conferred *baptism and the child was confirmed when (and if) the bishop came by. By the 12th c., baptism *quam primum* had become the general practice, and thus the succession of the three sacraments was restored: baptism by the presbyter, no longer linked to Easter, confirmation by the bishop on his pastoral *visit, and first *communion at the age of reason. Confirmation then became an autonomous sacrament, counted as such in the septenary (*c.*1150); it could eventually be postponed to the age of seven.

The term "confirmation", *Gallican in origin, made its appearance at the council of Riez in 439. At Rome, it would not become a technical term until the 7th century. In *theology too, the influence of Gaul was decisive; in his Pentecost homily *Advertamus* (460-470), Faustus of Riez answered the (new) question: what did confirmation add to baptism? Using a military analogy, he compared baptism to birth and confirmation to growth. His views were ascribed by the 9th-c. False *Decretals to the authority of Pope "Melchiades", whence they passed to Gratian and the *scholastic theologians. The discussions of the latter concerned notably the institution of this sacrament, its possible superiority over baptism since it was conferred by the bishop (*e.g.* *Hugh of Saint-Victor: *PL*, 176, c. 461) and, above all, the essential rite, whether anointing with *oil or *laying on of hands as in the Acts of the Apostles.

The celebration of confirmation remained sober and simple throughout the Middle Ages; the sacramental formula varied, finally taking the form "*Signo te signo crucis et confirmo te chrismate salutis in nomine Patris et Filii et Spiritus sancti. Amen* (I mark you with the sign of the cross and confirm you with the chrism of salvation in the name of the Father, the Son and the Holy Spirit. Amen)". Guillaume *Durand's late 13th-c. **Pontifical* gave it a fuller form, notably adding the *alapa* or blow by the bishop on the confirmand's cheek, with the formula *Pax tecum* (Peace be with you).

P.-M. Gy, "Histoire liturgique du sacrement de confirmation", *LMD*, 58, 1959, 135-145. – G. Kretschmar, "Firmung", *TRE*, 11, 1983, 192-204. – P. De Clerck, "La dissociation du baptême et de la confirmation au haut Moyen Âge", *LMD*, 168, 1986, 47-75.

Paul De Clerck

**CONFRATERNITIES.** Prayer unions and mutual aid societies arising from the initiative of ordinary believers, confraternities played a major role in the medieval period, alongside more constrictive structures such as the *parish. The confraternity was put under the invocation of one or more patron saint, whom it celebrated at an annual feast by manifestations both religious (*procession, *vespers and *mass) and convivial (*banquet), suitable to weld together the group's identity.

The origins of confraternities are connected with the various forms of associative movement, both Roman and Germanic in tradition, that co-existed in early medieval society. They are attested in the Carolingian period by the episcopal interdictions they were subject to, but it is difficult to make out their content at this time. It can be better discerned in the late 11th c., when groups designated by the unspecific words *confraria*, "fraternity" or "confraternity" can be identified under the jurisdiction of Benedictine monasteries, where they might undertake to illuminate the *altar of their patron saint. With other communities and individuals, they were associated in the spiritual benefits of the place, in prayer *fraternities. Then, in the late 12th and in the 13th c., confraternities of *clerics were founded in cathedral *chapters to help poor priests. Simultaneously, the *laity, anxious to contribute personally to their *salvation, were attracted by ways of life marked by certain renunciations and a fraternal dimension (fraternities of *penitents, *Humiliati, *Third Orders among the mendicant friars). The confraternal movement found its place in this group, but the formulae it proposed to its adherents were less demanding, though animated by the same ideal.

But the apogee of the confraternities was in the last two centuries of the Middle Ages when they proliferated both in *towns and in the country. In the cities, each one had up to several hundred members, neither the poorest nor the richest; in *villages, the confraternity could incorporate the whole community of inhabitants, like the confraternities of the Holy Spirit in the Alpine regions. Groups were formed in accordance with geographical (parish, quarter, village), professional (*métiers*) or even religious criteria (former *pilgrims); but they remained for the most part open to any loyal adherent who respected the statutes and paid his entry dues and his annual contribution, high or lower according to the company's policy.

The aim of medieval confraternities had nothing corporatist about it, with some few exceptions. It was primarily religious, and depended on the *communion of saints and the virtue of *charity to contribute to the individual salvation of the *confrères*. Each company applied itself to weaving, on behalf of each of its members, a network of heavenly protectors, its patron saint or saints, and earthly intercessors, the poor whom it gratified and who prayed for it in return and the *confrères* themselves who prayed for one another. To this it added a treasure of intercessory *prayers: regular masses celebrated for the group over the year, each day, week or month according to its means, *alms and other pious works. In consequence, it is not surprising to find that help among *confrères* concentrated on the last moments of life and on *funerals: visits to the sick and prayers for them, organisation of a decent funeral celebration which all the members of the confraternal family were often bound to attend alongside those of the *family in the flesh, then inclusion in the prayers for all the group's deceased. From the 13th c., the spread of the notion of *purgatory put into concrete form the saving value, recognised well before, of prayer for the *dead. Indeed this preoccupation was behind the foundation of the earliest companies, which owed nothing to the *epidemics of plague that reappeared in the West in 1348. However, the profound economic and social changes of the late Middle Ages, which entailed the dislocation of traditional solidarities (communities of inhabitants or families), as well as the evolution of behaviour towards a more marked individualism, sharpened the fear of dying alone, which was behind the success of the confraternities. But it would be unjust to limit their mutual aid to the funerary aspect alone; confraternities were able to bring help to those of their members who fell into *poverty (who then became the "uncomplaining poor") or were tried by severe illness, such as *leprosy.

Some companies broadened their charitable activities beyond the limits of the group, for the benefit of all the destitute, in a perspective that was not totally disinterested, since these were so many "good works". Apart from the punctual distributions of money or provisions that they nearly all went in for, the more powerful applied themselves to supporting the *foundation and management of a *hospital, maintaining the poor regularly or organising gifts of provisions in times of shortage. Some of them acquired a specialization in funerals, burying the local poor, which they kept beyond the medieval period. So confraternities were not strangers to their city. On occasion, they became propagators of cults connected with local history: choice of the town's protecting saint as titular, celebration of a striking victory, participation in festivities organised by the town. And more than one future municipal leader was initiated by them into collective management. Moreover, they contributed to the maintenance of social concord, bringing members of different origins into contact with each other at the annual meeting. Finally, they involved their members in peaceful behaviour, trying to regulate the conflicts that broke out among them through the authority of the elder members before resorting to justice. But they could come to espouse partisan causes, notably in the kingdom of *France during the *Hundred Years' War, and become a leaven of division.

Because of this, the political and ecclesiastical authorities had an ambivalent attitude towards them. Autonomous groups bound by *oath, a counter-power feared by the ruling classes, they aroused suspicion and were regularly but ineffectively condemned. From the Church, they gained official recognition on condition of confining themselves to charitable and liturgical activities. In accordance with principles that heralded those of the Catholic Reformation, they were subject to the authorization of the *bishop and were progressively integrated into the life of the parish, to whose renown they contributed by the maintenance and decoration of *chapels allotted to them. The *mendicant orders did not hesitate to use them as elements of *pastoral care, *e.g.* in northern Italy in their struggle against *heresy.

Based on intercessory prayer and charitable practices, medieval confraternities were thus part of the religion of works denounced by the Protestant reformers. But it would be unjust to deny them any role in religious education. They gave it a place on the annual feast day by reading the company's statutes with edifying preambles, by listening to a *sermon or taking part in some literary game, *tableau vivant* or even *mystery, to the glory of the holy patron. Moreover, they invited their members to a minimum of personal prayer, most frequently by accumulating *Paters* and *Aves*. Finally, towards the end of the period, some of them cultivated individual devotion (Marian confraternities of the *Laudesi* in Italy or or the *Rosary in the Rhineland), sometimes in demonstrative forms inherited from the *flagellants (*Disciplinati*, confraternities of "*penitents"); insistence on more regular frequenting of the *sacraments pointed in the same direction. Singing and musical forms in general also had great importance for the extra-liturgical spiritual expression of the confraternities, especially the penitential ones; particular mention should be made of the *Laudario* of Cortona, precious for the history of *music.

By their voluntary and massive adherence to the confraternal movement, the faithful manifested their desire to work personally towards their salvation, a sign of the awakening of a Christian *conscience which, while remaining aware of the saving solidarity of the *communion of saints, gradually opened up to the glow of private devotion.

G. Le Bras, "Les confréries chrétiennes: problèmes et propositions", *RHDF*, 1940-1941, 310-363. – G. G. Meersseman, *Ordo fraternitatis, confraternite e pietà dei laici nel medioevo*, Rome, 1977. – O. G. Oexle, "*Conjuratio* et *ghilde* dans l'Antiquité et dans le haut Moyen Âge", *Francia*, 10, 1982, 1-19. – B. A. Hanawalt, "Keepers of the Lights: Late Medieval English Parish Gilds", *JMRS*, 14, 1, 1984, 21-37. – *Le Confraternite romane*. . ., L. Fiorani (ed.), Rome, 1984. – *Le Mouvement confraternel au Moyen Âge: France, Italie, Suisse*, Rome, 1987. – J. R. Banker, *Death in the Community*. . ., Athens-London, 1988. – L. K. Little, *Liberty, Charity, Fraternity: lay religious confraternities at Bergamo in the age of the commune*, Northampton (MA), 1988. – *Cofradias, gremios, solidaridades en la Europa Medieval*, Pamplona, 1993. – C. Vincent, *Les Confréries médiévales dans le royaume de France (XIII^e^-XV^e^ siècle)*, Paris, 1994. – V. Bainbridge, *Gilds in the medieval countryside: social and religious change in Cambridgeshire, c.1350-1558*, Woodbridge, 1996.

Catherine Vincent

**CONFRATERNITIES, MUSLIM.** The phenomenon of confraternities (*ṭarīqāt*) arose out of *Sufism or *taṣawwuf*, of which it was an institutionalization that became generalized especially from the late Middle Ages. At the origin of every confraternity was a sheikh around whose personality assembled disciples (*murīd*) who submitted to a discipline of prayer and a more or less original doctrine. After the master's death, his teaching was handed down orally and through a hagiographical literature. The mother house was generally near the founder's tomb, to which pilgrimages were organised. The different orders varied in structure and hierarchy. Each one had its particular discipline which represented a "way" (*tarīqa*) leading to God, with a chain of initiation (*silsila*) formed of an uninterrupted succession of sheikhs going back to the Prophet. Life in a confraternity was organised round vigils, fasts, sessions

*Majesty of St Faith.* 10th-c. reliquary-statue.Treasury of Conques Abbey (Aveyron).

of *dhikr* (invocation of the names of God) and spiritual concerts (*samā*) for certain orders. The novice entered the confraternity by initiation and, after a period of apprenticeship, had the right to wear the cloak of the Sufis and the headwear of the order. The members of the *tarīqā* were called, according to the case, dervishes, *fuqarā*, *bābā*, etc. The Sufi's aim was to obtain contemplation of truth and divine reality (*haqīqa*) by means of mystical states (*hāl*) and spiritual "stations" (*maqām*). The classic personalities to whom the majority of Sufis were attached were celebrated mystics, poets and theologians, as different as Hasan Basrī, Bistāmī, Junaid, al-*Hallāj, al-*Ghazālī, Suhrawardī, Ibn Arabī, Attar, *Rūmī, etc. Among the most outstanding of the old confraternities, we may cite: in *Iraq, the order of the *Qādiriyya* founded by Abd al-Qādir al-Jīlānī († 1166) and that of the *Rifāiyya* named after Ahmad Rifāī († 1175), the latter made famous by their spectacular practices (walking on fire, absorption of ground glass, etc.); in Egypt, the *Ahmadiyya* or *Badawiyya* founded by Ahmad al-Badawī († 1276); in central Asia, the *Kubrawiyya* and *Yasawiyya*, created in the 12th c., and the *Naqshbandiya* in the 14th. In North Africa, the confraternities were organised around personalities like Abū Madyan († 1197) and Shādhilī († 1256). *Iran claimed great mystics and poets like Abū Saīd († 1049) and Attar († *c.*1230), and the majority of *Shi'ite congregations were attached to Shāh Nimatullāh Wālī († 1431). Among the *Ottoman Turks, confraternities were strongly developed and structured (*Mevlevī* and *Bektashī* in particular, the latter playing a political role as chaplains to the janissaries). Certain popular confraternities or extremist branches of the official orders affected an open contempt for social and religious conventions: wandering dervishes and *Malamatiyya* using paradox and syncretism were very active, from the later Middle Ages, in the flexible Islamization of certain regions of the Balkans, the *Caucasus, central Asia and black Africa.

M. Molé, *Les Mystiques musulmans*, Paris, 1960. – G. Anawati, L. Gardet, *Mystique musulmane*, Paris, 1976. – *Les Voies d'Allah. Les ordres mystiques dans le monde musulman des origines à aujourd'hui*, A. Popovic (ed.), G. Veinstein (ed.), Paris, 1996.

Michel Balivet

**CONQUES.** The little village of Conques in the Rouergue has a past that coincides with a prestigious page of medieval history, beginning at the time of the *Saracen invasions, with Dado, a solitary to whom is attributed the building of a church dedicated to the Saviour. The favours of *Louis the Pious and, in 838, Pippin II, king of *Aquitaine, who granted Figeac to the abbey, contributed less to its glory than the romantic arrival in *c.*865 of the *relics of St Faith, a young girl martyred at Agen at the end of the 3rd century. The reputation of her *miracles, amplified in the 11th c. by Bernard of Angers's "Book of the Miracles of St Faith", and its privileged position as a major stop on the *pilgrimage route to Santiago de *Compostela contributed to the wealth of the *abbey, whose possessions grew ceaselessly and whose power was sufficient to preserve its freedom from *Cluny.

This expansion legitimized the rebuilding by Abbot Odolric (1031-1065) of a church capable of containing crowds. But, to complete the original plan, several campaigns were needed, in particular that led by Abbot Bego (1087-1107). The short nave, bordered by simple side-aisles, contrasts with the ample development of the transept, crowned on each arm by two staggered absidioles. To this Benedictine characteristic is added an ambulatory with radiating chapels, proper to pilgrimage churches, whence the imposing complexity of the volumes of the chevet. Inside, the nave with powerful slender piers receives indirect light from spacious tribunes, whose quarter-circle vaults shoulder the main semicircular barrel vault.

Outside, the monumental façade shelters one of the most original portals in *Romanesque sculpture: *Christ the King passes sentence of *Judgment, separating on the left a chaotic *hell where monstrous devils make the convulsed damned pay the price of their sins, and on the right the serene procession of the elect, led by the Virgin, St *Peter, Dado and *Charlemagne, in memory of the Carolingian benefactions.

Conques has the exceptional luck of having preserved part of its treasure, the richest surviving from the medieval period. In it are the disparate contributions of gifts of every provenance and the marks of the local output of a *goldsmith's workshop, including the portable *altar of St Faith, in the form of an "A", called "Charlemagne's A" or Bego's "lantern". The strangest piece, in its fierce and composite art, precursor of statues in the round and bearer of a spirituality bordering on idolatry, is the *reliquary that enclosed the saint's skull in the chased silver mask of an Emperor of the Late Empire. The *Majesty, enthroned in a seat of goldsmiths' work, gleams with antique gems, precious stones set in filigree, fragments of jewelry from every period, taken from Carolingian *crowns and Byzantine jewels. It was offered to the fascination of the faithful behind the main altar, in the silky shimmer of *gold and the uncertain light of candles.

J. C. Bonne, *L'Art roman de face et de profil. Le tympan de Conques*, Paris, 1985. – J. C. Fau, *Rouergue roman*, Saint-Léger-Vauban, 1989 (3rd ed.).

Colette Deremble

**CONRAD OF GELNHAUSEN (died 1390).** *Provost of *Worms and professor of the university of *Paris, Conrad of Gelnhausen, though German, belonged to the English "*nation". He owed his renown in the 14th c. to a treatise on conciliar theory. Dedicated to *Charles V of France, the *Epistola concordiae* (1380) laid the foundations of what would become the doctrine of *conciliarism: the thesis of a recourse to the *council in order to regulate the major problems of the Church. Since the legitimacy of the two *popes was in doubt, it was up to an ecumenical council – an emanation of the Church – to restore supreme law. These innovative ideas, inspired by those of William of *Ockham, found no application. Conrad retired to Germany and became the first *chancellor of the university of Heidelberg, founded in 1386. He died 13 April 1390.

*DHGE*, 13, 1956, 484. – *HChr*, 6, 1990.

Michel Fol

**CONRAD OF GROSSIS, also called OF PRUSSIA or OF BRUSSIA (died 1426).** A *Dominican from 1370, a great promotor in Germany from 1388 (after a *pilgrimage to the *Holy Land) of the Dominican *Observance supported by the order's general master *Raymond of Capua, who appointed him his *vicar. From the *convents of *Colmar and Schönensteinbach (a women's convent near Basel), which he reformed respectively from 1389 and 1395, he spread the Observance all over the Rhine valley, in southern Germany and *Switzerland. But Raymond of Capua's death dealt a severe blow to the Dominican *reform, and Conrad could do nothing but retire and finish his life at Schönensteinbach.

A. Barthelmé, *La Réforme dominicaine au XV<sup>e</sup> siècle*, Strasbourg, 1931. – *DHGE*, 13, 1956, 496-498. – *NDB*, 12, 1980, 540. – *LdM*, 5, 1991, 1364.

Joseph Morsel

**CONRAD OF MARBURG (died 1233).** Already a famous preacher, instructed by *Gregory IX in June 1227 to pursue *heretics as part of a project of "reform" of the Church in Germany, Conrad of Marburg managed to obtain the collaboration of two other figures, Conrad Dorso and John called the Blind, who had "spontaneously" undertaken an activity of anti-heretical repression. Thus was created a sort of "triumvirate" which from 1231 to 1233 acted with cruelty – adopting the curious practice of shaving the hair of repentant "heretics" above the ears – mainly in the regions of the Rhine valley, in liaison with the directives of the papacy. But local opposition to Conrad of Marburg and his associates soon arose within the Rhineland episcopate and among the German lords. In 1233, he was killed with Conrad the Franciscan near *Marburg, while Conrad Dorso was killed at *Strasbourg and John the Blind hanged near Friedberg.

A. Patchovsky, "Zur Ketzerverfolgung Konrads von Marburg", *DA*, 37, 1981, 641-693.

Grado G. Merlo

**CONRAD OF MAZOVIA (*c.*1187-1247).** Conrad of Mazovia, in Polish Konrad Mazowiecki, duke of Mazovia of the *Piast dynasty, was the son of Prince Casimir the Just (Kazimierz Sprawiedliwy) and Princess Helena. He governed Mazovia from 1202. The main problem of his reign was caused by the invasions of *pagan peoples, Prussians, Iatviegs and *Lithuanians. The attempts he made to resolve this situation by his own means and with the help of the rulers of other Polish duchies were unsuccessful. An order of *chivalry was organised for this purpose, the Dobrynian Order or Fraternity of the Knights of Dobrzyń, which disappointed the hopes that had been put in it.

So in 1226 Conrad made contact with the *Teutonic Knights, promising the order the land of Chełmno as a home base to attack the territory of Prussia, while all the lands conquered in Prussia were to revert to the duke of Mazovia. Conrad's objective was to make himself master of *Cracow, which was the symbol of power over the whole State. He attained this end transitorily in 1229-1231 and in 1241-1242. He also followed an active policy on the Russian side. Moreover, he showed a profound understanding of the reform then being carried out by the *Catholic Church. Despite these positive aspects, his reign has been evaluated mainly in the light of the fatal consequences of the introduction of the Teutonic Knights into *Poland.

J. Mitkowski, "Konrad Mazowiecki", *Polski Słownik Biograficzny*, 13, Wrocław, 1967-1968, 584-586. – H. Boockmann, *Der Deutsche Orden. Zwölf Kapitel aus seiner Geschichte*, Munich, 1981.

Zbigniew Piłat

**CONRAD OF URACH, also called OF ZÄHRINGEN (died 1227).** A Cistercian from 1199, papal *legate from 1215 and *cardinal of Porto and Santa Rufina from 1219.

A member of the illustrious Zähringen dynasty, to which belonged the bishop of *Liège whose *canon and dean he became (1195), Conrad abandoned the world and, like two of his brothers, joined the *Cistercian Order, where he climbed the ladder of honours until he became *abbot of *Clairvaux (1215), then of *Cîteaux (1217).

His diplomatic efforts as papal legate earned him the cardinal's purple, without putting a stop to his activities as legate, notably in southern France against the Albigensian *heresy, then in the *Empire to prepare a *crusade, whose failure must be seen in the context of the growing opposition between the papacy and the Emperor *Frederick II.

*DHGE*, 13, 1956, 504-507. – *NDB*, 12, 1980, 551.

Joseph Morsel

**CONRADIN OF SWABIA (1252-1268).** Orphan son of Conrad IV and heir to the kingdoms of *Sicily and *Jerusalem, Conradin was unable to impose his rights either in *Germany or in southern *Italy, where he was opposed first by the presence of his paternal uncle *Manfred, then from 1263 by that of *Charles of Anjou, invested with that kingdom by the *pope. Becoming on his uncle's death (1266) the sole focus of the Ghibellines in Italy, he went there in 1267. Encountering the *Angevins at Tagliacozzo, 23 Aug 1268, he was forced to flee; captured and sent to Charles, he was beheaded at *Naples on 29 Oct. Symbol of innocence crushed by the cynicism of power, Conradin became the object of contemporary imperial nostalgia and the romantic emblem of neo-Ghibelline nostalgia.

R. Morghen, *Il tramonto della potenza sveva in Italia*, Rome, 1936.

Anna Benvenuti Papi

**CONSCIENCE.** The word *conscientia*, among the medievals, was limited to the ethical sphere and was never used in the sense of "consciousness". The term is taken from St *Paul (Rom 9, 1; 2 Cor 1, 12: Greek *suneidêsis*), Augustine (*Enarrationes in Ps. 53*, 8, 5 f.: *CChr*, 39, 652) and *John of Damascus who defines it as the Divine law in our understanding: "The Law of God that supervenes in our intellect exercises there an attraction towards God and pricks our conscience. This is what is meant by the conscience that is in our intellect" (*De fide orthodoxa*, c. 95, no. 2: ed. Buytaert, 1955, 359).

According to *Thomas Aquinas, the word "conscience" is understood on three levels: 1) In priority, it means the activity applying a cognition held according to a universal mode to a free operation calling for regulation in accordance with the *good. Identifiable in the prefix "con-", which means a bringing together, the application of the rule of the good to the operation or possible operation (case of abstention) earns the *will its ethical excellence, because the evaluation thus formulated is a "verdict of *reason" ("*conscientia [est] quodammodo dictamen rationis*" [*Summa theologiae*, Iª IIªᵉ, q. 19, 5]). Like *Peter Lombard and St *Bonaventure, Thomas explains regulation applied to the activity under consideration by reference to the notion of synderesis, explained as a "spark" of the *soul and defined as a natural and hence inamissible **habitus* of evaluation in accordance with the good. Even in the very human case of erroneous reason, conscience obliges the subject and assures the freeedom of his will from moral fault. Obviously, this applies to invincible error, since ignorance by negligence does not excuse (*ibid.*, a. 5-6; *De veritate*, 17, 3-4).

2) "Conscience" means the *habitus* of synderesis, the principle that presides over the evaluation-in-accordance-with-the-good thus applied. Inherited from St Jerome (*In Ez.* 1, 6: *CChr*, 75, 12, 218 f.), the word "synderesis" designates this natural (since in accordance with the *nature of the reasonable and voluntary agent) moral *habitus*, which has its seat in the practical reason according to Thomas (*ibid.*, a. 12) and in the affective power according to St *Bonaventure (*In L. Sententiarum*, II, 39, 2, 1 and II, 909).

3) Finally "conscience" is that cognitive power (the *intellect) which, as seat of the aforesaid *habitus*, is the mediate source, through synderesis, of the act of applying the rule of the good to the operation.

Bonaventure, *In L. Sententiarum*, II, d. 39 a. 1-2. – Thomas Aquinas, *Summa theologiae*, Iª, q. 79, a. 12-13; Iª IIªᵉ, q. 19, a. 5. – Thomas d'Aquin, *Questions disputées du De veritate: Raison supérieure et raison inférieure (q. XV); De la syndérèse (q. XVI); De la conscience (q. XVII)*, J. Tonneau (ed. and tr.), Paris, 1991 ("Bibliotheque des textes").

R. Carpentier, "Conscience", *DSp*, 2, 1953, 1548-1575. – C. Spicq, "Suneidèsis", *Notes de lexicographie néotestamentaire*, Fribourg-Göttingen, 1978, 854-858.

Édouard-Henri Wéber

**CONSECRATION.** The term "consecration" was one of the words used in the Middle Ages to devote a person or an object to a religious use, by invoking God's intervention in its favour; it was used synonymously with "*ordination", "benediction" and other terms. Thus in the *Gelasian *Sacramentary*, we find the *ordinatio* of priests (Book I, XX) and *deacons (XXII), the *benedictio* of *salt (XXXI-XXXII), *oil (XL), baptismal *water (XLIIII), the *altar and the *chalice, as well as other objects (LXXXVIII) and *orders (XCV-XCVI), the *consecratio* of a *basilica and a paten (LXXXVIII), of the deacon (XCVII), the priest (XCVIII) and a virgin (CIII), but also the *confectio* of oil (XL) and the *dedicatio* of places (XCIII) and of a *baptistery (XCIIII); the term *sanctificatio*, on the other hand, does not appear in this list.

It was this word, however, that would become the technical term to designate, at *mass, the conversion of the bread and *wine into the body and blood of Christ, in accordance with the word of Jesus at the Last Supper (Mt 26, 26-29 and par.). Medieval theologians understood consecration in line with a text of Ambrose (*De sacramentis* IV, 14-17: *SC* 25a, 109-111) stating that it was by the repetition of the creative word of Christ that consecration took place (*conficere*). Carolingian theologians, however, would encounter philosophical difficulties in giving an account of the conversion of the eucharistic elements (debates of *Paschasius Radbertus with *Ratramnus and *Rabanus Maurus): these would return in the 11th c. with *Berengar of Tours, who had to make a "*realist" profession of faith at the council of Rome in 1059.

Thus eucharistic *theology would often be reduced to the explanation of the consecration and the justification of the priest's power to confect the *sacrament. In the 13th c., popular piety was manifested in the "desire to see the *host", which culminated in the ostension of the consecrated *species (the *elevation); theologians, for their part, defined substantial conversion (*transubstantiation) with the help of *Aristotelian categories. These precisions were ratified at the council of *Florence in the Decrees for the Armenians (1439) and for the Jacobites (1442) and repeated at the council of Trent.

In the 14th c., discussions took place with the Greeks (Nicholas *Cabasilas, *Explanation of the Divine Liturgy*: *SC*, 4a, XXVII ff.) concerning the moment of consecration. The Latins, partisans of Ambrose's theology, were astonished to find that the Easterners attributed the consecration not to the words of Christ, but to the invocation for the coming of the *Holy Spirit (epiclesis); *Benedict XII rejected this theology in his *Libellus ad Armenios* of 1341.

Thomas Aquinas, *Summa theologiae*, IIIª, q. 75-77.

H. de Lubac, *Corpus mysticum. L'eucharistie et l'Église au Moyen Âge*, *Theol(P)*, 1949.

Paul De Clerck

**CONSECRATION OF KINGS.** The origin of consecration must be sought in the Old Testament. In the eyes of the people of Israel, kingship was an attribute of God and belonged properly to God. When a king appeared for the first time in their history, he was chosen by God through the intermediary of the prophet Samuel and received royal anointing from God through him. From then on, the legitimate king (Saul, *David, then *Solomon) was God's lieutenant, his vicar. Jesus, the Messiah, was to belong to the line of David and be king for ever.

The first attestation of a royal anointing in the West of the Christian world seems to come from *Spain. In the late 7th c., the legitimate descendant of the *Visigothic kings received unction from the bishop of *Toledo on his accession to the throne. The earliest evidence concerns the anointing of King Wamba in 672. The attestations of *Gildas in early 6th-c. Britain lack clarity, like nearly all his work. In the *Anglo-Saxon part of the island, a "benediction" *mass for the royal *coronation seems to have appeared from the 8th century.

The first *Carolingians, whose legitimacy was disputable, wanted to make it inviolable by a religious rite. *Pippin had himself crowned by St *Boniface, the papal *legate, in 752, then again in 754 with his wife Bertha and his sons Charles and Carloman, at *Saint-Denis, by Pope *Stephen II; he seems to have received unction at this time, as did *Charlemagne at *Rome on Christmas Day 800, when he was crowned emperor.

From then on, the *kings at their accession did not just receive from the *bishop's hands the insignia of their dignity, notably the

*The coronation of Charles VI by the bishops and barons.* Miniature from the *Grandes Chroniques de France*, *c.*1375-1379. Paris, BNF (Ms fr. 2813, fol. 3 v°).

*Pope Martin V at the council of Constance.* Miniature from the *Chronicle of Ulrich of Richental*, 15th c. Prague, University National Library.

*crown; they were "anointed", like David and Solomon. This unction conferred a sacred character on them, particularly when the law of succession by primogeniture was not yet soundly established. The ceremony of handing over the insignia, *ring, sword, standard and diadem, later had parallels in the great principalities (*Normandy, *Brittany), but the unction of consecration was a royal privilege.

In the Carolingian Empire, the ceremonial was soundly established in 848, at the time of the consecration of *Charles the Bald by the archbishop of *Sens; the *oil of consecration was the holy chrism. *Reims became the town of consecration in the 11th c., and the oil used by the archbishop was that contained in the holy **ampulla*, which had been brought by St Remigius for the *baptism (not consecration) of *Clovis. This legend contributed to augmenting the prestige of the kings of *France and the *cathedral of Reims.

M. Bloch, *Les Rois thaumaturges*, Strasbourg, 1924. – J. Jackson, *Vive le roi!: a History of the French Coronation from Charles V to Charles X*, Chapel Hill (NC), 1984.

Guy-Marie Oury

**CONSECRATION OF VIRGINS.** In the 3rd and 4th cc., in both East and West, there existed groups of Christian virgins (*virgines Deo dicatae*), who practised perfect and perpetual *continence and devoted themselves to *prayer. They gradually constituted an *ordo*, and *bishops and *councils were concerned with regulating them. By the solemn imposition of the veil, done by the bishop alone, and the recital of suitable prayers, they were consecrated to God. In the service of the clergy, they stood in lieu of deaconesses, especially at the time of *baptism of women by immersion. As well as *virginity, they adopted *humility, simplicity and devotion to the poor, and instructed catechumens.

R. Metz, *La Consécration des vierges dans l'Église romaine*, Paris, 1954. – "Les Vierges chrétiennes en Gaule au IVe siècle", *Saint Martin et son temps*, *StAns*, 46, 1961, 109-132.

Michel Parisse

**CONSISTORY.** Under the Roman Empire, the term *consistorium* designated the place where the emperor's advisers held their deliberations, then the imperial council itself. *Urban II (1088-1099) strengthened its role, reserving important questions for it. The role of this solemn judicial assembly increased along with that of the *cardinals as exclusive collaborators of the *pope. And it was during the consistory that the pope announced the creations of cardinals. The private consistory consisted of pope and cardinals meeting together in the pope's **Camera*.

J. Sydow, "Il 'consistorium' dopo lo Scisma del 1130", *RSCI*, 9, 1955, 165 f. – W. Maleczek, *Papst und Kardinalkolleg von 1191 bis 1216*, Vienna, 1984.

Agostino Paravicini Bagliani

**CONSTANCE.** The episcopal see of Constance was founded in the 7th century. Its *bishops were often *abbots of *Sankt Gallen and *Reichenau. Endowed with privileges, the city developed under Salomon III (890-919), then in the 10th c. under Conrad (934-975) and *Gebhard (979-995), especially with the foundation of a second urban core around the abbey of Petershausen. It enjoyed a second apogee in the reign of *Frederick I who concluded a treaty there with Pope *Eugenius III in 1153 and a peace with the Lombard towns in 1183.

In the early 14th c., the town appeared to be the most important in the region and extended its jurisdiction over the Thurgau. But the successes of the Swiss confederates finally made it a frontier town, whose influence declined in the 15th century.

H. Maurer, *Konstanz im Mittelalter*, Constance, 1989.

Geneviève Bührer-Thierry

**CONSTANCE, COUNCIL OF (1414-1418).** Though it cannot be numbered among the great dogmatic *councils, the council of Constance, called in order to end the *Great Schism (1378), holds an important place in the history of the Church. Convoked on 5 Nov 1414 by the *antipope of *Pisa, *John XXIII, at the insistence of the king of the Romans, the future Emperor *Sigismund of Luxemburg, this 16th ecumenical assembly brought together nearly 400 prelates and dignitaries of the Church, surrounded by a crowd of *clerics and laymen. Alongside *bishops and *abbots, the presence of *doctors of the *university, ardent defenders of the doctrine of *conciliarism, was an innovation. On the council's programme, as well as the extinction of the schism, were the defence of the faith against the ideas of *Wycliffe and Jan *Hus and the reform of the Church.

From the start *John XXIII, who considered himself the sole legitimate pontiff, came into conflict with the conciliar assembly, in particular with Cardinal *Pierre d'Ailly, but he quickly had to give way. The council adopted voting by *nation: Italian, French, English and German, then Spanish in 1416, and by the decree *Haec sancta* (1415) affirmed its sovereign *authority to which all, including the *pope, had to submit, since it was held from Christ. The Fathers of Constance deposed Pope John XXIII (May 1415) and the *Avignon pope, *Benedict XIII, who had no influence from December 1415, and also accepted the abdication of the Roman pontiff Gregory XII (July 1415). The council, now the Church's sole instrument of government, restored the Church's unity.

The assembly was dominated by the moderates, among them the *canonist *Zabarella and the *chancellor of the university of *Paris, Jean *Gerson, partisans of a system in which pope and council would govern the Church in complementary association. Thus, the decree *Frequens* provided for conciliar meetings at fixed intervals to ensure the maintenance of the institution and limited the prerogatives of the Apostolic See (Oct 1417). The council then decided on the holding of a *conclave in which was incorporated an extraordinary college composed of six members of each nation to elect a new pope. On 11 Nov 1417, the choice fell on Otto *Colonna who took the name *Martin V, thus putting a final end to the Great Schism. He closed the assembly on 22 April 1418 by pontifical decree.

Having condemned two *heresies and burned two heretics, Jan Hus (1415) and *Jerome of Prague (1416), the council of Constance did not manage to accomplish the great moral reform of the Church or make the Church's government evolve from a monarchy to a democracy.

*DThC*, 3, 1938, 1200-1224. – R. Baumer, *Concilium Constanciense (1414-1418). Das Constanzer Konzil (Wege der Forschung)*, Darmstadt, 1977. – *HChr*, 6, 1990.

Michel Fol

**CONSTANCE OF HAUTEVILLE (1154-1198).** Daughter of *Roger II, king of *Sicily, in 1186 she married the future emperor *Henry VI, son of *Frederick Barbarossa. After the death of her nephew *William II in 1189, she worked with her husband to assert her rights over the kingdom of Sicily, whose rule was contested by Tancred of Lecce, by whom she was captured in 1191. After the conquest of the Kingdom, the day after her husband's *coronation as king (1194) she became the mother of the future *Frederick II. On Henry's death in 1197, she kept the title of empress, but concerned herself solely with Sicily. She died before concluding an agreement with *Innocent III to define the problem of Sicily's feudal dependence on the Holy See; but she had time to recommend her son to the pope's protection.

G. Baaken, "Konstanze", *Neue deutsche Bioographie*, 12, Berlin, 1980.

Mauro Sanna

**CONSTANTINE, CULT OF.** First Christian emperor (306-337), founder of *Constantinople, Constantine was rapidly heroized and considered a saint. Imperial ideology, represented by Eusebius of Caesarea's *Life of Constantine*, and the care with which the emperor organised the mausoleum where he was to rest amidst the cenotaphs of the apostles, contributed to ensure him a special place. From the protobyzantine period, the main elements of the legend were in place: vision of the cross; finding of the True *Cross by Constantine's mother Helena; *baptism by Pope Silvester. However, more critical currents coexisted. It was in the 8th and 9th cc. that the legend became popular. It took various forms and was enriched by romantic or hagiographical motifs. After the 10th c., it ceased to evolve. We know 25 Lives or eulogies of St Constantine. At Constantinople, several sanctuaries or monasteries were put under his name: the imperial mausoleum and the chapel near the Holy Apostles; the chapel under the column in the Forum. St Constantine, the thirteenth apostle, was celebrated with his mother Helena on 21 May.

A. Kazhdan, "Constantin imaginaire: Byzantine Legends of the Ninth Century about Constantine the Great", Byz., 57, 1987, 196-250.

Bernard Flusin

**CONSTANTINE V, EMPEROR (718-775).** Byzantine emperor (741-775) of the *Isaurian dynasty, associated in power by his father Leo III from 720. He defended the Empire against the Arabs and *Bulgars (victory of Anchialos, 763), conducted an active diplomacy with the *Carolingians, reorganised the *army, rebuilt the aqueduct of Valens at *Constantinople; he called a *council forbidding the worship of *icons (Hiereia, 754) and, from 766, persecuted the monks who had refused to take an oath against icons. The valour of the man, around whom a legend was constructed, doubtless explains the violence with which he was rejected after the restoration of icons (843): his tomb was opened and his corpse burned; the sources presented him as a mad and sanguinary tyrant and gave him the surname "Copronymus".

A. Lombard, *Constantin V, empereur des Romains*, Paris, 1902. – S. Gero, *Byzantine Iconoclasm during the Reign of Constantine V with Particular Attention to the Oriental Sources*, *CSCO*, 384, *Sub.* 52, Louvain, 1977. – I. Rochow, *Kaiser Konstantin V. (741-775)*, Frankfurt am Main, 1994 (Berliner Byzantinische Studien, 1).

Marie-France Auzépy

**CONSTANTINE THE AFRICAN (11th c.).** The Middle Ages gave several versions of the biography of Constantine the African. According to Peter the Deacon, monk and librarian at the abbey of *Monte Cassino from 1110 to 1153, he was born at Carthage and made distant journeys in his youth, to train himself in various disciplines, including medicine: *Cairo, *India, *Ethiopia. Returning to his own country, he aroused jealousy by his knowledge, had to flee and thus arrived in southern *Italy. According to other evidence, about a century later, Constantine was a Muslim merchant. Through commercial exchanges, he had ascertained that Italian doctors lacked technical works. After having learned medicine in his own country, he came back loaded with manuscripts, part of which were damaged by the wreck of his ship, then he converted to Christianity in order to enter Monte Cassino and work there as a translator.

It is difficult to prefer one or other of these biographies. All that seems certain is that Constantine was born in north Africa, that he mastered Arabic and *Latin, knew medicine and lived at Monte Cassino as a monk under the abbacy of *Desiderius, *i.e.* between 1058 and 1086. The milieu that accepted him offered conditions favourable to his undertaking: while the abbey of Monte Cassino was the centre of a renaissance of letters and arts, the nearby school of *Salerno gave a medical teaching that had already acquired some renown. The reputation of these two institutions favoured the rapid spread of the texts thus translated into Latin.

Constantine the African's *translations freely adapt their Arabic models. They give an account of the *medicine worked out at *Kairouan in the 9th and 10th cc. (in particular the celebrated *Viaticum* of Ibn al-Jāzzar) and the doctrine of Galen, a Greek doctor who lived at Rome in the 2nd c. AD. One of the major works translated by Constantine, the *Royal book* of the scholar of Persian origin Alī ibn al-Abbās al-Majūsī, was a synthesis of Galenism as

Interior of the church of Sts Sergius and Bacchus. Istanbul.

it had been formalized at *Alexandria in the 5th-6th cc. and transmitted in Arabic. Dedicated to the abbot of Monte Cassino, under the title of *Pantegni* ("The Whole Art"), this imposing work was abundantly cited, even by non-medical authors, in the 12th and 13th centuries. It rested on a subdivision of medicine into "theoretical" medicine and "practical" medicine which gave that discipline the status of a *science and provided its practitioners with a rationally based step forward. Constantine himself translated only the theoretical part and certain chapters of the practical part. This was probably completed by his disciples.

V. Von Falkenhausen, "Costantino Africano", *DBI*, 30, 1984, 320-324. – H. Bloch, *Monte Cassino in the Middle Ages*, 1, Rome-Cambridge (MA), 1986, 93-110, 127-134. – D. Jacquart, F. Micheau, *La Médecine arabe et l'Occident médiéval*, Paris, 1990, 96-129. – *Constantine the African and ‘Alī ibn al-Abbas al-‘Mağūsī, The* Pantegni *and Related Texts*, C. Burnett (ed.), D. Jacquart (ed.), Leiden, 1994.

Danielle Jacquart

**CONSTANTINOPLE.** Throughout the Middle Ages Constantinople remained the prestigious town it had become in late Antiquity, even though, after a certain point, its reputation was not matched by the reality. Its position on the Bosphorus kept its importance alive, and only a very particular historical and political situation led it to suffer depopulation and impoverishment before it became once more, under the name of Istanbul, a megalopolis and the capital of a new Empire.

**History.** The history of Constantinople is intermingled with that of the *Byzantine Empire. It did not cease to be its capital through all its vicissitudes, to the point where, in the 15th c., territory and capital were practically identical. The sole notable exception to this situation was the interlude of the Latin conquest, when it became the capital of an ephemeral and virtually powerless Latin Empire that ceased to exist in 1261, while the living forces of the Byzantine Empire took refuge in Asia Minor.

The threats that weighed on the Empire in the 7th c., the power regained from the second half of the 9th c., the difficulties that, from the mid 11th c., led to a long decline ending in the capture of the town and the end of the Empire in 1453, necessarily had repercussions on the appearance and image of the capital. We will content ourselves with marking the events and evolutions that weighed particularly on the destiny of the town itself.

A place apart must be given to the sieges it suffered several times, which had heavy repercussions on the people of the capital, though for long centuries it remained invulnerable. Thus the Avar danger culminated in 626 in a siege that was the occasion for a spectacular rise in the cult of the Virgin, considered the protectress of the town. The Arab threat was particularly lively in the late 7th and early 8th c. (last "great" siege in 717-718). The *Bulgars succeeded it in the 9th and first half of the 10th century. In 1090, Constantinople was again attacked, this time by the *Pechenegs. But the great rupture, in the history of the town as in that of the Empire, was obviously the double capture of July 1203 and April 1204, when the Westerners of the fourth *crusade used the pretext of dynastic quarrels to attack Constantinople. The town never recovered from the fire and pillage of 1204. Admittedly, the treaty of 1261 with the Genoese permitted the development of Pera on the other side of the Golden Horn, a Genoese colony soon surrounded by ramparts. But Constantinople from now on was no more than a lightly-populated town, whose ramparts could not resist the new weapon of artillery. It was taken by the *Turks on 29 May 1453, after a short siege.

**Population.** In the 7th c., the town's most flourishing period was already in the past; its inhabitants had become less numerous both because of the plague that wrought havoc from the mid 6th c. (when the population fell by 50 %) and because of the general political situation. The loss of Egypt, Constantinople's main source of grain, led to difficulties in provisioning, which from now on had to be done from less distant regions. But the absence of information on *famines in the 8th and 9th cc. suggests that a balance was established between the resources of the hinterland and a sufficiently sparse population. The long interruption in the functioning of the main aqueduct, destroyed in 626 and repaired only in 768 under *Constantine V, also suggests a heavily reduced population. This repair, for which it had been necessary to bring abundant manpower from other regions of the Empire, was perhaps connected with a certain recovery of population, manifest in any case at the end of the 9th century. The disorders of the 14th c. once more accelerated the depopulation of the town, especially when to the civil wars was added the *Ottoman threat, becoming more visible and more concrete after the capture of Gallipoli in 1354.

What else is known about this population? Its composition changed: in the 9th and 10th cc., an important influx of Armenians was added to the traditional population. Later appeared Italian *merchants, coming at first from *Amalfi and *Venice, from the 10th century. The Venetians and Pisans formed the most important groups in the 11th and 12th cc., soon followed by the Genoese.

Numerous treaties linked the Empire and various Italian cities, by which these obtained commercial advantages. The Italians settled in the quarters of Constantinople, in particular towards the Golden Horn, where the main commercial traffic was concentrated at the time. The tensions that this situation entailed were one of the causes of the massacre of the Latins in 1182, at the time of the seizure of power by Andronicus Comnenus. But in the 14th c. a great part of the petty commerce, even in foodstuffs, seems to have fallen into the hands of Italian merchants, who resettled at Constantinople quite rapidly after the recapture of the town by the Byzantines.

**Economy.** Some privileged sources give indications about the activities of artisans and merchants as well as their organisation. The Book of the Prefect, a 10th-c. text of regulations, allows us to envisage the organisation of certain professions in the form of what we might call corporations, though this term is not to be understood in the precise sense it took in the West. A manuscript, also of the 10th c., allows us to elucidate another aspect of the organisation of petty commerce and the artisanate. It contains information on the purchase of some shops at Constantinople. Here we discover a middle class of persons who were well off, but not part of the world of the powerful connected with the court and known through traditional historical sources. They included perhaps some merchants or artisans, but mainly officials or dignitaries who rented out purchased shops and drew a stable and substantial revenue from them.

Constantinople remained prosperous during a great part of this period thanks to the presence within its walls of the emperor and representatives of the Empire's most powerful families. Their revenues came from lands they possessed in the provinces, particularly in Asia Minor, until the advance of the *Seljuk Turks after the battle of Manzikert (1071) gave new importance to the western provinces. A great part of these revenues was spent at Constantinople where a luxury artisanate developed, but where it was also invested in buildings and religious foundations. The artisanate devoted to the needs of everyday life is paradoxically the least well known. We do not even know for sure whether the production of ceramics should be ascribed to Constantinople or to its immediate neighbourhood. After the loss of the eastern provinces, the majority of luxury products were manufactured at Constantinople, though workshops also existed at *Thessalonica. In particular the proof-marks that guaranteed the quality of the metal on 7th-c. silver vessels suggest Constantinopolitan production. The Life of Theodore of Sykeon shows the saint buying silver liturgical vessels at Constantinople for his church. Finally we may recall a particular output, that of *books, illuminated or not, well known at Constantinople and linked to the importance of local intellectual life: *scriptoria* are attested from the 9th c., and are still found in the 14th. There was an imperial *scriptorium* and a patriarchal *scriptorium*; others were attached to monasteries, *e.g.* the monastery of *Studios.

**Town planning and monuments.** The most important change in the town's appearance came about with the abandonment of the great monuments characteristic of the ancient town. As everywhere in the Empire, these monuments were no longer maintained or repaired. *Nymphaea* and great public baths disappeared very quickly. The church of St Euphemia is a former hall of the palace of Antiochus. The monumental road system, with its porticos and its great streets lined with colonnades, was no longer kept up. Pigs and lambs were sold in the forum of Theodosius, sheep and donkeys in other squares. In the Book of the Prefect, fines were threatened against merchants who, to sell their livestock clandestinely, hid them in noble houses. For Constantinople as for the other towns of the Byzantine Empire, some would speak of ruralization. This term essentially conveys the fact that no further interest was taken in a certain monumentality of the city: not that there were no longer important, if not grandiose, monuments, but they were no longer integrated into the urban fabric. Reading the legends that circulated from at least the 8th c. about the ancient buildings or antique statues still numerous in the town, we become aware that all real contact with Antiquity was lost. And it was not just the great ancient buildings that were abandoned: archaeology has shown irrefutably that one of the largest and most richly decorated churches of the early Christian period, St Polyeuctus, was abandoned in the 12th century. Nevertheless considerable expense, on the part of the emperor as well as the aristocracy, went into the construction of monuments, which never stopped for long throughout the medieval history of Constantinople, at least before the beginning of the 14th century. In the 8th and early 9th cc., we must mention essentially repairs to the ramparts, especially after the earthquake of 740, but the years that followed the *iconoclast crisis, in particular the reign of Basil I (867-886), saw a rise in the number of new buildings as well as restorations of older buildings. It has been remarked that, even more than for new buildings, the word "new" (*neos*, *nea*) was systematically used for renovations: this practice corresponds well to an ideology that ran very deep in the Byzantine world, which valued return to the old order much more highly than innovation. Was not the *salvation of the whole human race a restoration of man's situation close to God, as it had been before the fall? It was in the name of this same ideology that Michael VIII, after having recaptured Constantinople from the Latins, erected a triumphal column in front of the church of the Holy Apostles.

Foundations and restorations concerned buildings different in nature and function from those that distinguished the towns of Late Antiquity. Apart from utilitarian works (repair of ramparts, improvement of *ports), architectural activity was oriented in three directions: buildings for the use of the emperor, residences of great dignitaries, construction of churches and, more generally, religious buildings. Constantine's great *palace, with the improvements that had been made to it, long remained the centre of the Empire's political life, the "eye of the world" to use a Byzantine expression, and the main residence of the Byzantine emperors. In the 7th and 8th cc., we know from written sources only a few relatively unimportant works, which hardly modified the nature of that immense complex, situated between the hippodrome and Hagia Sophia.

Much more considerable improvements and notable enlargements took place in the reigns of Michael III (842-867) and especially Basil I (867-886), who thus marked his wish to restore the Empire. Throughout this period, the Great Palace remained not just the scene of the emperor's private life, but even more that of part of the ceremonies that punctuated his public life. Lists of precedence acquaint us with the dignitaries admitted on each occasion to share his table, and the different dining-rooms used according to circumstance, the most solemn being that "of the Nineteen Beds", where meals were still taken reclining, following the Roman tradition.

With the *Comneni, the Great Palace began to lose its importance. It still kept an administrative function and its function as official residence. Some great ceremonies, such as *coronation, the *marriage of an emperor or his son, great receptions particularly of ambassadors, if not of foreign rulers, took place there. It was characteristic that the Great Palace remained an essential target in attempts to take power by sedition. Pillaged at the time of the Latin occupation, it was hardly used by the *Palaeologi and slowly fell into ruin before the capture of Constantinople by the Turks. It had been replaced as the emperors' preferred residence, from the reign of Alexius I Comnenus (1081-1118) but especially under Manuel I (1143-1180), by the Blachernae palace, situated in the north-west of the town on the site of a palace attested from the 5th c., associated with an important sanctuary of the Virgin. The installation in this new palace can be considered the symbol of a new way of governing in which powers were increasingly concentrated around the family and clientele of the emperors.

While aristocratic residences are very little known, the most important expenditure, both by the emperors and the aristocratic families, went on the construction of churches and monasteries as well as the charitable foundations connected with them. The decoration was sumptuous and the rare surviving vestiges show that Constantinople was also the crucible of Byzantine painting. The great monasteries stand out as an essential element of Constantinople's urban landscape. Some have been preserved, thanks to their transformation into *mosques, others are known only through written sources. Perhaps the most important imperial foundation was the monastery of the Pantocrator (Zeyrek Cami), dynastic monument of the Comneni, where those emperors were buried. But only a tiny part of its decoration survives. A prestigious example of a private foundation was the renovation early in the 14th c., by Theodore Metochites, of the monastery of Christ of Chora (Kariye Cami). The mosaics and frescos of its main church are privileged witnesses to the last flowering of *Byzantine art under the Palaeologi.

But a few exceptional monuments were not enough after 1261, despite the efforts of Michael VIII Palaeologus (1259-1282), after he had reoccupied the town, to mask its weakness and depopulation. The descriptions of visitors and travellers in the 14th and 15th cc. give evidence of a very loose urban fabric. The ramparts gave the impression of enclosing a series of villages separated from each other by fields, gardens and vineyards.

**Intellectual life.** Throughout the duration of the Empire, Constantinople remained the essential scene of the Byzantine Empire's intellectual and theological debates and, more generally, its cultural life. These were rarely unrelated to power struggles. In the 7th c., the last episodes of the christological disputes that played such an important role in Late Antiquity came to a head at Constantinople. Later, it was also at Constantinople that the debates around *iconoclasm developed. On this occasion began the progressively greater attention paid to the texts of the past, their authenticity, which was the origin of what is called the Macedonian renaissance. The activity of the monks of the monastery of Studios at the urging of their hegumen *Theodore, the intellectual activity of Patriarchs Tarasius and *Nicephorus, played a precursory role. Later we see the figure of Leo the Mathematician, also called the Philosopher, one time archbishop of *Thessalonica under the Emperor Theophilus, hence suspect of iconoclasm, but to whom, after he had been deposed, was entrusted the direction of the school of the Magnaura, which may be considered a sort of imperial *university. Patriarch *Photius and Aretas were the most striking witnesses to the renewal of intellectual life and the most active editors of ancient texts.

More generally, around the 9th c. we see the development of intermediate teaching, limited essentially to Constantinople and reserved for a restricted social group, from which emerged those who, around the emperor and the *patriarch, exercised power and administered the State.

A more profound attempt to make use of ancient thought took place in the mid 11th c. with Michael *Psellus. But above all we must cite Psellus's pupil John Italus, whose teaching was condemned in 1082, essentially no doubt because he had tried to apply philosophical reasoning, *Aristotelian in particular, to the sphere of religion. This episode, which had echoes and repercussions into the 12th c., was essential, since it shows the impossible position Byzantine intellectuals were in, unlike their homologues in the Western world, in developing a thought that was original and enfranchised from *tradition. The concentration of intellectual life at Constantinople, in proximity to the centres of power, represented by the emperor and the patriarch, who in these circumstances joined forces, made this repression possible. Even the final flowering of Byzantine intellectual life under the Palaeologi, contemporary with the last rise of the arts, did not issue in a real revival.

R. Janin, *La Géographie ecclésiastique de l'Empire byzantin. Le siège de Constantinople et le patriarcat oecuménique: 3. Les églises et les monastères*, Paris, 1953. – S. Runciman, *The Fall of Constantinople 1453*, Cambridge, 1965. – P. Lemerle, *Le premier humanisme byzantin*, Paris, 1971. – W. Müller-Wiener, *Bildlexikon zur Topographie Istanbuls*, Tübingen, 1977. – G. Dagron, *Constantinople imaginaire. Études sur le recueil des Patria*, Paris, 1984. – C. Mango, *Le Développement urbain de Constantinople (IVe-VIIe siècle)*, Paris, 1985. – C. Mango, *Studies on Constantinople*, Aldershot, 1993. – C. Mango (ed.), G. Dagron (ed.), *Constantinople and its Hinterland*, Aldershot, 1995. – P. Magdalino, *Constantinople médiévale. Études sur l'évolution des structures urbaines*, Paris, 1996.

Jean-Michel Spieser

***CONSTITUTIONS OF MELFI.*** Code of laws of the Kingdom of *Sicily issued in 1231 by *Frederick II. Also known as the *Liber Augustalis* (though their true title is *Liber Constitutionum Regni Siciliae*); *Pietro della Vigna collaborated in drawing them up. The *Constitutions* are divided into three parts: public law, penal law and feudal law. They express the theory of a government that could do without the saving action of the *pope. Inspired by *Roman law, Byzantine, Lombard, Norman and *canon law, they are marked by pragmatism. They are of particular importance for their lucid exposition of Frederick's fiscal programme, their attempt to strengthen royal power and their desire to limit particularistic forces. Without the organic unity of Roman legal texts, they confine themselves to facing the problems of reconstruction of the *Regno* weakened by wars. Though lacking in organic unity – a defect common to all ancient and medieval legislative compilations – they have rightly been judged the greatest lay legislative monument of the Middle Ages, not just in *Italy but in Europe.

F. Calasso, *Medioevo del diritto*, 1, *Le fonti*, Milan, 1954, 441 ff. – S. Gensini (ed.), *Politica e cultura nell'Italia di Federico II*, Pisa, 1986.

Mauro Sanna

**CONTEMPLATION.** The word "contemplation", inherited from the philosophers of Antiquity, Holy Scripture and the Church *Fathers, meant, in the tradition of the Western Middle Ages, not seeing, but looking at, directing the attention of one's mind towards *God and his *mysteries. This state of *prayer, difficult to define, was often evoked by means of symbolic terms such as "rest", "leisure", "sabbath", "vacation" and other biblical images. It presupposed *ascesis, self-control, a certain interior silence; it was considered a sort of anticipation of what total union with God in vision would be. It was prepared by activities like spiritual reading, *meditation, prayer, the study of *theology. It was not in any way incompatible with the occupations proper to each state of life, like *labour and the pastoral *ministry. It required the keeping of a just balance between action and contemplation. The exposition of the contents of contemplation evolved throughout the Middle Ages: at first, in *monasticism, mainly under the influence of St Augustine, *Cassian, St *Gregory the Great; then, partly under the influence of the texts of Pseudo-*Dionysius, in *scholastic theology, especially that of St *Bonaventure and St *Thomas Aquinas and their school; finally among the 14th- and 15th-c. mystics, several of whom were saints. There was increased analysis of the psychological aspects of contemplation, its degrees and manifestations. When contemplation fixed its orientation on a form of life, this was designated the contemplative life, and St Thomas formulated the aim of the apostolate that derived from it: "*contemplata aliis tradere*", "share with others the realities you have contemplated".

"Contemplation", *DSp*, 2, 1953, 1311-2034. – J. Leclercq, *Otia monastica. Études sur le vocabulaire de la contemplation au Moyen Âge*, Rome, 1963 ("StMon", 51).

Jean Leclercq †

**CONTEMPT OF THE WORLD.** The question posed by *contemptus mundi* in the Christian Middle Ages is vast and complex. *Contemno* means to hold negligible, to disdain. The appeal of moralists and Spirituals was all the more insistent as the seduction of the world became stronger in the Church and threatened to invade everything.

The attitude towards the world was not simple, on account of that word's plurality of meanings in the New Testament. By *sin, the world created *good by *God became bad, since it fell into the power of the prince of this world. By all its being, it proclaimed God; but, by its *de facto* orientation, it set itself up against God, opposing its own values to those of the Gospel.

Thus, the world appeared under two aspects, apparently opposed, according to the point of view one looked from. *Ontologically, there could be no contempt of the world, since it was God's *creation, and the great *cathedrals were seen as presenting a "mirror of the world", to use Émile Mâle's expression. On the moral level, it was absolutely necessary to keep one's distance and adopt the difficult attitude that consisted in placing oneself above the seductions of the world. One had to free oneself from the world, while working for the *redemption and *salvation of the world. *Contemptus* insisted on the aspect of enfranchisement and freedom by renunciation.

The doctrine was fundamentally the same within the Church (it was not the same in the heterodox currents that manifested themselves from the 12th c.), but its applications varied considerably from one author to another, one tradition to another, one epoch to another. In general, *Augustinianism and *Cistercian *monasticism insisted on the negative aspects of the world and the danger it could present. The philosophers of the 12th c. exalted the positive values more; as did the *Aristotelian current of the following century.

*Le Mépris du monde*, Paris, 1967. – P. Grelot, É. Pousset, "Monde", *DSp*, 10, 1980, 1620-1646.

Guy-Marie Oury

**CONTINENCE.** In the broad sense, the object of continence is temperance in the sphere of the search for nourishment and the desires of the flesh. Its seat is in the *will where it behaves as a *virtue since it is applied to a *vehement* passion, as St *Thomas Aquinas says, *i.e.* one that urges to action. To contain oneself is in fact not moral *per se*, everything depends on the act that is thus regulated. Here we find the antique conception of virtue, which is primarily moderation of what, in *man, could be too animal and instinctive. Affirming that the seat of continence is in the will, St Thomas situates it outside the *reason, which allows him to say that the incontinent knows what he is doing, he knows what is bad in principle. It is unmastered passion that makes him do what he would otherwise reject.

In a more restricted but more common sense, continence designates abstinence from all voluntary sexual pleasure. It would even come to designate merely the abstention from *marriage imposed on *clerics in major *orders. St Thomas demonstrates that, in this sense, it is necessary to the religious state since this requires the putting away of everything that prevents the human will from turning to *God. Sexual union prevents this total consecration to God by the increase in desire and the dispersal of energies that it entails.

Following the first *Lateran council (1123), pontifical texts and the acts of numerous *provincial councils and diocesan *synods insisted on a renewal of ecclesiastical discipline concerning *celibacy. The aim of these texts was on one hand the struggle against the existence of a married clergy, going as far as the *excommunication of clerics who contracted marriage, and on the other the obligation of continence for the celibate clergy. It was thus that *sanctions were envisaged against clerics who kept a concubine at home, and that they were forbidden to draw up a *testament in her favour.

Thomas Aquinas, *Summa Theologiae*, IIª IIªᵉ, q. 155-156.

A. Sertillanges, *La Philosophie morale de saint Thomas*, Paris, 1922, 486-496.

Jean-Marie Gueullette

**CONTRACEPTION**

**The West.** Our notion of contraception depends on what idea we have of conception. In the Middle Ages, abortion before 40 days (generally procured by drugs) was perceived as contraception, and the *Penitentials punished it by only a year of *penance – as against three years for abortion after 40 days, and seven years (the same as for *homicide) after the animation of the foetus. This perception recurs in the lists of reserved cases of the later Middle Ages and the modern period.

As for contraception in the sense in which it is understood now, the Middle Ages knew *coitus interruptus* – probably little practised outside court circles – and the tampons of herbs or wool used by *prostitutes. We may also recall the elaborate flirtations, characteristic of prenuptial relations in the countryside, that normally procured pleasure without risk.

J.-L. Flandrin, *L'Église et le contrôle des naissances*, Paris, 1970. – P. Biller, "Birth-Control in the Medieval West", *PaP*, 94, 1982, 3-26. – J.T. Noonan, *Contraception: A History of its Treatment by the Catholic Theologians and Canonists*, Cambridge (MA), 1986. – J.-L. Flandrin, *Sex in the Western World*, Reading, 1991. – J.M. Riddle, *Contraception and Abortion from the Ancient World to the Renaissance*, Cambridge (MA), 1992.

Jean-Louis Flandrin

**Byzantium.** In Byzantine popular *medicine, drugs facilitating conception were more numerous than contraceptives. Sterility was the great evil; abortion and infanticide were the contraception of the poor. Learned medicine was nevertheless aware of contraception (periodical abstinence, *coitus interruptus*, pessaries, magic), which it preferred to abortion, but reserved for "risky" pregnancies.

The Church primarily condemned abortion and infanticide. But contraception, which usually aimed at preventing an illegitimate pregnancy, is mentioned in the *Penitentials, such as the *Kanonikon* of Pseudo-John the Faster (9th c.). Likened to a monthly murder, it was judged more severely than abortion, because the woman did not know how many children she had "eliminated".

E. Patlagean, "Sur la limitation de la fécondité dans la haute époque byzantine", *Annales*, 1969, 1353 f. – J. Riddle, "Oral Contraception and Early Term Abortifacients during classical Antiquity and the Middle Ages", *Past and Present*, 132, 1991, 23-32.

Marie-Hélène Congourdeau

**CONTRITION.** Since the council of Trent, it has been standard to group together under the term "contrition" the two movements of the *soul that are sorrow for having sinned and detestation of *sin with the firm purpose not to sin again. This is what is expressed by the standard "act of contrition". But these two facets of contrition are a summary of the reflections of medieval theologians in the wake of the *Fathers. The latter insisted on one or the other aspect. The *scholastics debated, as was their custom, as to what was the most important dimension of contrition: detestation of the fault, sorrow for having committed it, repulsion from sin or the will to annihilate it. Each *master, in his commentary on *Peter Lombard's fourth book of *Sentences*, gave his opinion on the question. St *Thomas Aquinas proposed a diachronic and synthetic view of the question. He considered that contrition had to begin by a disengagement from sin, which required its perception. Sorrow of the soul was thus first, and it necessarily entailed the desire to free oneself from sin. Hatred of sin was not properly part of contrition since it existed perfectly in *God. Likewise, the firm purpose not to sin again was not absolutely required for pardon. These theologians were unanimous in affirming the necessity for contrition in order to obtain from God pardon for sins. Sin being an injury done to God, a voluntary choice of what distances us from Him, it is necessary that the sinner deny this attitude of rejection of God before He can pardon the offence (commentary on *IV Sent.*, book IV, by St Thomas and St *Bonaventure).

Contrition was traditionally distinguished from attrition or imperfect contrition. Perfect contrition was sorrow and detestation of sin due not to the evil it caused the sinner, but to the injury against God. Attrition, on the contrary, had as its motive not the *love of God but the ugliness of sin and especially the fear of punishment. Debate on these questions was violent at the time of the Reformation; it had its roots in the attempts at distinctions that were put in place from the 14th century. The classical scholastic doctrine, which made the love of God manifested by contrition the heart of the sacrament of *penance, had in fact been breached in particular by *Duns Scotus and by *nominalists like *Durand of Saint-Pourçain, who insisted on the authority and power of *absolution.

Thomas Aquinas, *Summa Theologiae*, III, q. 90, a. 2.

J. Delumeau, *L'Aveu et le pardon*, Paris, 1990, 51-78.

Jean-Marie Gueullette

**CONTROVERSY BETWEEN JEWS AND CHRISTIANS.** From the beginnings of Christianity, there had been a debate with the *Jews: it developed throughout the Middle Ages in the form of familiar conversations or learned discussions, spontaneous meetings or organised debates in which the champions of the two religions faced each other before an attentive public. Narrative literature provides numerous evidence of this, bringing together the most varied interlocutors. For the early Middle Ages, there was the discussion between King Chilperic and his Jewish supplier Priscus (Gregory of Tours, *History of the Franks* VI, 5) or that in 1031 between Conrad II's Jewish doctor and *Wazo, future bishop of *Liège (Anselm of Liège, *Gesta* 44: *PL*, 142, 735). In the 12th c., these spontaneous conversations multiplied, sometimes involving such considerable persons as *Abelard, *Gilbert of Poitiers or the Jewish exegete Joseph Qara. From the 13th c., however, the church authorities, emphasizing the dangers presented by such discussions, reserved them for experienced *clerics.

This debate gave rise to a polemical literature, Christian (in Latin and the vernacular) and Jewish (in Hebrew). It took the form of the dialogue or the *treatise (sometimes also an exchange of *letters). The dialogues were allegorical (*Church/Synagogue) or claimed to be an account of actual discussions; among the most successful were, on the Christian side, *Gilbert Crispin's *Disputatio Iudei et Christiani* (1092-1093) and Inghetto Contardo's *Disputatio contra Iudeos* (1286); on the Jewish side (where the dialogue form was less used), Joseph Kimhi's *Sefer ha-berit* (Book of the covenant) (*c.*1150). Three fictional works, dialogues in several voices, also brought in pagans or Muslims: Peter Abelard's *Dialogue*, *Judah ha-Levi's *Sefer ha-Kuzari* and Raymond *Lull's *Book of the Gentile and the Three Sages*, a work exceptional for its serenity and the breadth of its views. The treatises were constructed around Old Testament texts considered as witnesses to Christ and the Church (*Isidore of Seville, *William of Bourges, Judah ben Reuben) or centred on a restricted number of themes, notably those of the coming of the Messiah, the *Trinity and the Mosaic laws.

In general, the controversy turned on the interpretation of Scripture (the Christians reproaching the Jews with their blindness or deafness, the Jews accusing the Christians of interpreting the Old Testament arbitrarily), the stake being evidently to define who was the *Verus Israel*, the "true *Israel", repositary of the divine message. The argument claimed to appeal to *reason (*ratio*) and to recognised texts (*auctoritates*); it dealt above all with scriptural arguments, certain verses (Gen 49, 10; Is 7, 14, etc.) being constantly cited.

In the Latin works, the genre underwent an important evolution in the 13th c., with an increasingly sure knowledge of *Hebrew and of Jewish literature: the works of *Raymond Martini and then the opuscula of *Nicholas of Lyra used rabbinic texts in abundance. Likewise, works of this period in Hebrew show a better knowledge of Christian dogmas.

From the 13th c., when relations between Christians and Jews became tense in the West, spontaneous debates on religious subjects gradually gave way to solemn *disputations before a numerous audience. The first of these public disputations was in fact a legal action against the *Talmud and *rabbinic literature: held at *Paris in June 1240, it followed the *denunciation in 1239 by a converted Jew, Nicholas Donin of La Rochelle, of the "blasphemies" and "follies" contained in the Talmud. On the orders of *Louis IX, a great deal of Jewish literature was seized in northern France and the disputation was organised in the presence of the Queen Mother, *Blanche of Castile; Nicholas Donin faced four of the most eminent Jewish scholars, including *Yehiel of Paris and Moses of Coucy. Several high-ranking churchmen (including the archbishop of *Sens, the king's chaplain and *William of Auvergne) made up a sort of jury. The debate took place in a very heavy atmosphere. A dossier of extracts of rabbinic texts (Talmud, commentaries of *Rashi, liturgical texts) was compiled, but, even before the pope had pronounced sentence, an important number of Jewish books were burned at Paris, in the Place de la Grève (1242 or 1244).

The climate of the second great 13th-c. disputation was less tense: at *Barcelona in 1263, the Jewish-born Dominican Pablo Cristiani faced Moses ben Nahman (*Nahmanides), the highest rabbinic authority in Spain; the debate took place in the presence of King James I the Conqueror and numerous notables; the discussion turned on the coming of the Messiah, the Christian representative using rabbinic texts in support of his demonstrations. Despite some moments of *détente* (notably an exchange between the king and Nahmanides), the debate was cut short. We possess an account in Hebrew (*Vikuah* [Disputation] by Nahmanides) and a shorter report in Latin.

The Jewish polemist Meir ben Simeon's Hebrew work *Milhemet mizva* (Holy war) describes a public debate with the archbishop of *Narbonne, Guillaume de la Broue (1245-1257). In 1336, Alfonso XI instigated a public disputation between the convert *Alfonso of Valladolid (Abner of Burgos) and the Jews of the town; the main theme was that of the *Birkat ha-minim* (Blessing of the heretics), a liturgical text constantly targeted by Christian polemists.

The disputation of Tortosa (1413-1414), presided over by the antipope *Benedict XIII, took place in a tense climate; once more, rabbinic literature was at the centre of the debates, simultaneously used by the Christian representatives (including Jerome of Santa Fé) as an arsenal of arguments and denounced for its blasphemies and stupidities; the Jewish side was represented notably by *Joseph Albo and several other scholars. Several public disputations took place in Italy in the 15th century.

B. Blumenkranz, *Les Auteurs chrétiens latins du Moyen Âge sur les Juifs et le judaïsme*, Paris-The Hague, 1963. – D. J. Lasker, *Jewish Philosophical Polemics against Christianity in the Middle Ages*, New York, 1977. – H. Schreckenberg, *Die christlichen Adversus-Judaeos Texte*, Frankfurt-Bern, 1982-1988 (2 vol.). – R. Chazan, *Daggers of the Faith. Thirteenth century Christian Missionizing*, Berkeley (CA), 1988. – G. Fioravanti, "Polemiche antigiudaiche nell'Italia del Quattrocento", *Ebrei e Christiani . . . Atti del VI Congresso dell'Associazione italiana per la studia del giudaismo*, Rome, 1988, 76-91. – G. Dahan, *La Polémique chrétienne contre le judaïsme au Moyen Âge*, Paris, 1991. – *Contra Iudaeos: ancient and medieval polemic between Christians and Jews*, O. Limor (ed.), G. G. Strouma (ed.), Tübingen.

Gilbert Dahan

## CONTROVERSY BETWEEN MUSLIMS AND CHRISTIANS

**The East.** It was with the development of Muslim *theology and the criticism of Christianity by *Mu'tazilite theologians, from the second half of the 8th c., that Islamo-Christian controversy arose. On the Muslim side, the themes of the controversy turned essentially on the dogma of the *Trinity, incompatible with that of the divine Unicity on account of its three hypostases: Father, Son and *Holy Spirit; and the dogma of the Incarnation, *i.e.* the union of divinity and humanity in the person of Jesus, his divine sonship, crucifixion and *Resurrection being unacceptable to *reason. On the Christian side, the main disputed points were the prophetic character of *Muḥammad, the inimitable character of the *Koran, the prediction of Muḥammad by the Scriptures and their falsification by the Christians.

From the 8th to the 12th c., Islamo-Christian controversy gave rise to a number of literary works belonging to three genres: debate, correspondence and refutation. The debate (*disputatio*) which took place between two interlocutors, one Christian and the other Muslim, in the course of one or more "sittings", seems to be the earliest genre of controversy. Of these debates, set down in writing after they had taken place, we possess four, which took place between: the *Nestorian *catholicos* Timothy († 823) and Caliph al-Mahdī (775-785) [written first in Syriac, it was translated into Arabic and survives in four different redactions]; the Melkite bishop of Harrān, Theodore abū Qurra († *c.*830), and Caliph al-Mamūn (813-833); the Melkite monk Abraham of Tiberias and three Muslim doctors, before the governor of *Jerusalem, *emir Abd al-Rahmān al-Hāshimī (*c.*820); the Nestorian metropolitan of Nisibis, Elias ibn Shināyā († 1046) and the vizir al-Maghribī († 1027).

The second genre of controversy, correspondence, is represented by two exchanges of letters between Muslim and Christian correspondents, the Muslim beginning his epistle by inviting the Christian to convert, by virtue of the Islamic precept of "good counsel". The first exchange consists of the brief epistle addressed by the Muslim Abd Allāh al-Hāshimī to the Christian Abd al-Masīh al-Kindī, and the latter's long reply. This correspondence, which took place at the time of al-Mamūn, became very famous and was translated into Latin in the 12th c. by *Peter the Venerable. The second exchange comprises the epistle addressed by two members of the Banū l-Munajjim family to two Christian scholars: the Nestorian ibn Ishāq († 873) and the Melkite Qustā ibn Lūqā († *c.*912), and their replies.

Refutation is illustrated in the late 9th c. by two Mu'tazilite theologians: al-*Kindī († *c.*870) and al-Warrāq († 909) who composed, the former a *Refutation of the Christians*, the latter a *Refutation of the three Christian sects* entitled the *Principles of proofs*. In the next century, the *Jacobite philosopher Yahyā ibn Adī († 974) replied to al-Kindī by a short epistle and to al-Warrāq by a voluminous treatise, in which he took up each of his objections (150 on the Unicity and 125 on the Incarnation) and refuted them. Likewise, his pupil 'Isa ibn Zur'a († 1008) replied to the Mu'tazilite theologian al-Balkhī († 931), author of a refutation of Christianity entitled the *Sources of proofs*.

H. Putman, *L'Église et l'Islam sous Timothée I*, Beirut, 1975. – Kh. Samir, P. Nwyia, *Une correspondance islamo-chrétienne*, *PO*, 40, 1981, 521-723. – G. Tartar, *Dialogue islamo-chrétien sous le calife al-Mamūn*, Paris, 1985.

Gérard Troupeau

**The West.** With the development of theology, polemical works on the Muslim side aimed primarily to convince their Christian rivals of the altogether innovative contribution of *Islam, which the latter long considered a *Nestorian sect. Even in the 15th c., Cardinal *Nicholas of Cusa (1401-1464) considered it a Christian *heresy. Thus he undertook to examine the *Koran attentively, in his *Cribratio Alkorani*, in terms of its supposed conformity to the Gospel, which for him constituted the norm of perfection.

The first centuries of Islamo-Christian controversy were marked by a spirit of extravagant and injurious polemic. *Peter the Venerable (1092-1156), a man quite tolerant for the time, tried to engage in a more pacific dialogue with Islam, but this was unable to get a footing. As abbot of *Cluny, he was the founder of Islamic studies in Europe: indeed it was he who first had the Koran translated into Latin, at his own expense, in 1142-1143. We owe him also the famous collection of Latin *translations of Arabic texts that bears the name *Corpus Toletanum* or *Collectio Toletana* since it was made at *Toledo. In it are four titles, including the *Summa totius haeresis Saracenorum* and the *Epistola de translatione sua* – two brief texts that were to serve as introduction to the reading of the *Corpus Toletanum* – and the *Contra sectam Saracenorum* which is the longest of these writings. If on the whole the attitude of the abbot of Cluny remained polemical and subjective with regard to Islam, he did not fail to expound its ideas correctly. However he cites the Koran only sporadically, for lack of having studied it well, a task he perhaps wished to accomplish later, *i.e.* after a detailed analysis of the teachings of the Muslim religion.

With the help of these writings, the Christian West was later able to participate more effectively, alongside Eastern Christian theologians, in the apologetic task that consisted in assembling rational and Koranic proofs in favour of the truth of the dogmas of the Church. Subsequent controversies bore mainly on the following themes: the dogma of the unity of *God and the *Trinity; the person of *Christ and its dual *nature, divine and human; the authenticity of the *Bible. On the Islamic side, on the contrary, the stress was put on the following points: *Muḥammad as seal of the prophets; the Koran as divine revelation; Islam as religion of justice and morality. The two camps were thus bent primarily on showing the veracity of their own religion and its superiority to others, which did not allow them to engage in a true dialogue. Moreover, the climate of relations between the Christians and Islam, already very disturbed by the *crusades, deteriorated still further in the 14th c. with the growing threat held over *Christendom by the progress of the *Ottoman Turks in eastern and central Europe.

L. Gardet, G. Anawati, *Introduction à la théologie musulmane. Essai de théologie comparée*, Paris, 1948. – D. Norman, *Islam and the West*, Edinburgh, 1960. – A.-T. Khoury, *Les Théologiens byzantins et l'Islam, textes et auteurs (VIII$^e$-XIII$^e$ siècle)*, Leiden, 1969. – A.-T. Khoury, *La polémique byzantine contre l'Islam (VIII$^e$-XIII$^e$ siècle)*, Leiden, 1972. – P. Khoury, *Matériaux pour servir à l'étude de la controverse théologique islamo-chrétienne de langue arabe du VIII$^e$ au XII$^e$ siècle*, Würzburg-Altenberge, 1989, 1991, 1997 (3 vol., bibliography).

Raif Georges Khoury

**CONVENT.** It is very difficult to unravel from medieval texts the primary meaning of the Latin word *conventus*, translated into English as "convent". The original meaning seems to be "assembly". In Epistle 255, n. 2 (*PL*, 182, 463 B), St *Bernard employs the word in that sense. *Peter the Venerable uses the same word in the *Statutes of the Congregation of Cluny*, VI (*PL*, 189, 1027 D). *Peter of Celle exhorts his monks thus: "*Vos, fratres carissimi, conventum facite, sed conventum apostolorum, sed conventum sanctorum, sed conventum virtutum; non ventum, sed conventum. Ventum facit qui seminat inter fratres discordias; conventum facit qui discordes pacificat* (You, dearest brothers, make a convent, but a convent of apostles, a convent of saints, a convent of virtues; not wind (*ventum*), but convent: he makes wind who sows discord among the brothers; he makes convent who reconciles quarrelling brothers)" (*PL*, 202, 698 D).

To this first sense must be added the very different one of public agreement, session, where the Latin *conventus* joins *mallus*. Hence the medieval university meaning, attested by texts which, while confirming the original sense, synonymous with *congregatio*, "assembly of teachers" (*Chartularium univ. Paris*, I, 20: text of 1215) at *Paris and *Montpellier, meant at *Bologna and in the southern *universities the private examination required to obtain the *degree of *doctor and the public examination conferring this degree (*Padua 1259; Bologna 1288).

In the Middle Ages, the use of the Latin word *conventus* no longer designated what it had meant for St Ambrose or St Augustine, both the union of human and divine *natures in *Christ (Faustus of Riez, *Epist.* 7) and carnal union (Ambrose, *Ps. 37*, 8; Augustine, *Contra Iul.* 4, 8, 39) or even conjugal union (Augustine, *De nupt. et conc.*, 2, 27, 44).

In the religious sphere, the word "convent", as we employ it today, appeared only very rarely in the 13th century. For example, in all the biographies of St *Francis by *Thomas of Celano, *Bonaventure, etc., out of eight incidences of *conventus*, four have the meaning of assembly, two designate the friars' convent at Naples and one the monastery of *San Damiano. Only in the 14th c. with the *Actus beati Francisci*, a Latin version and source of the *Fioretti*, do we find eight incidences of the word *conventus* in the modern sense of convent.

The word most used in the 13th c. to signify "convent" is *domus*. This term appears both in papal documents, *bulls, etc., and in *chronicles. For example, the word *domus* is given 125 times in Thomas of Celano's biographies and 41 times in Bonaventure's *Legenda maior* and *Legenda minor*. But it is rare to find the word *domus* designating a convent of *nuns. Rather we find the word *monasterium*.

D. Du Cange, *Glossarium...* [*Du Cange*], Paris, 1845. – A. Blaise, *Lexicon latinitatis medii aevi*, Turnhout, 1975. – O. Weijers, *Terminologie des Universités au XIII$^e$ siècle*, Rome, 1987.

Jacques-Guy Bougerol

**CONVENTUALS.** One of the three branches of the Order of Friars Minor, founded in 1517. Conventualism began in the 1230s, when in Italy many friars left their hermitages to settle in *convents, in cities, to be closer to the people and to sources of *alms. Conventualism suggests the style of life peculiar to these friars: immense convents, landed *property, engagement of *clerics in apostolate and study. This move to the cities necessitated a certain relaxation of the austere *poverty enjoined by the Rule, and the papacy accepted these changes.

Resistance to this adaptation of the way of life of the Friars Minor took two main forms in the course of history; the first, led by the *Spirituals of the Order of Friars Minor, culminated at the council of *Vienne (1312), where *Clement V made a distinction between the adherents of literal poverty (the Spirituals) and the "conventual friars" (the community). Discontent aroused by the liberties taken by conventualism with regard to poverty (recognition of property, collection of revenues, circulation of *money), which was spread by the fact of the disintegration of the Spirituals, resurfaced during the 1360s among the friars called "observants". Attempts at appeasement authorizing them to obey only their own superiors were simply a prelude to the separation that took place in 1517, at a "very" general *chapter (*capitulum generalissimum*) called by Pope Leo X. After having declared, on 31 May, in *Ite vos* that the observants would from now on constitute the Order of Friars Minor, and that individual and collective property would be recognised, on 12 June in *Omnipotens Deus* he formed the conventuals of the Order of Friars Minor into a separate branch of the *Franciscan family, empowered to elect its general and its provincial, while keeping the right to possess common property.

R. Huber, *A Documented History of the Franciscan Order from the Birth of Saint Francis to the Division of the Order under Leo X*, Milwaukee (WI), 1944. – G. Odoardi, "Conventuali", *DIP*, 3, 1976, 1-37. – *HChr*, 6, 1990, 528-530.

Michael Cusato

***CONVERSI.*** During the Christian Middle Ages, *conversio* was the consecration of a life to God, withdrawal from the world. Hence it designated the commitment of the lay adult who decided on a life of *ascesis, in solitude as a hermit or within a community. The layman could entrust his *children to a monastery (*oblatio*) for their *education and so that they should become monks, but he also had the possibility of freely entering a monastery himself. The advantages and inconveniences of these two ways of entering a monastery were known in the Middle Ages and were openly discussed (*Epistola nuncupatoria* of Udalric of Regensburg, at Cluny). According to their cultural level and the professions they had previously exercised, *conversi* could perform various functions within the monastery. Those who had no education (*illiterati*) devoted themselves to manual *labour, the others could be engaged in administration. As lay-monks, both groups were excluded from numerous forms of liturgical celebration, but belonged to the number of monks. Former *clerics or other cultivated persons became monk-priests.

Within present-day research, there is continual discussion about the thesis asserting the existence of an old (just described) and a new institution of *conversi*, whom some think to recognise in the 11th c. in the *reform movements of Camaldoli, *Vallombrosa, *Cluny and *Hirsau. These lay brothers had no chance of becoming priests and were competent only for simple tasks, with the aim of lightening the burden of the monk-priests. This form of life was especially prevalent among the *Cistercians; they had a distinct appearance (*fratres barbati*) and a separate lodging from the other monks (*fratres exteriores*) and followed their own form of life (*regula conversorum*). Such a separation is not attested at Cluny until the 12th c. and came from the social differentiation very marked in society and reproduced in the monastery. By contrast, in the *memento* of the *dead, lay brothers were always cited as monks in the full sense.

J. Dubois, "L'institution des convers au XIIe siècle. Forme de vie monastique propre aux laïcs", *I laici nella "societas christiana" dei secoli XI e XII. Atti della terza settimana internazionale di studio, Mendola, 21-27 agosto 1965*, Milan, 1968, 183-261. – W. Teske, "Laien, Laienmönche und Laienbrüder in der Abtei Cluny. Ein Beitrag zum 'Konversen-Problem'", *FMSt*, 10, 1976, 248-322; *ibid.*, 11, 1977, 288-339. – *Ordensstudien, Bd I: Beiträge zur Geschichte der Konversen im Mittelalter*, K. Elm (ed.), Berlin, 1980. – C. Davies, "The Conversus at Cluny. Was He a Lay Brother?", *Benedictus. Studies in Honour of St Benedict of Nursia*, Kalamazoo, 1982, 99-107. – J. Wollasch, "A propos des *fratres barbati* de Hirsau", *Mélanges Georges Duby*, Aix-en-Provence, 1993. – *Les Mouvances laïques des ordres religieux*, Saint-Étienne, 1996.

Franz Neiske

**CONVERSION.** A fundamental element of religion and philosophy, conversion had different expressions at different times. If in the first centuries it designated essentially the personal reversal of feeling that led to *baptism, in the Middle Ages it took on a more clearly social meaning and applied either to entry into a monastic order, or to the conversion of peoples, or to a change of religion. When it expressed a return to interiority, it had the nuance of *paenitentia*, "penitence", since medieval theologians saw it mainly as the renunciation of *sin that so marked the thought of the time.

So we can note a lexical shift between the Hebrew term *shub* which expresses the idea of conversion in the Old Testament, those of *epistrophe* and *metanoia* which are the Greek transcription of it, and the Latin term *paenitentia* which takes on more of a moral sense, already implied in the term *metanoia*.

The idea of return to unity, of change following an encounter with God, remained, but with different accents, sometimes more theatrical, as with *Bernard who arrived at *Cîteaux with part of his family. But in the Middle Ages, conversion could no longer have the dramatic character of *e.g.* Augustine's, since in the West the *Empire was Christian and all were baptized. Its radicality was manifested, then, by entry into an order, a company of *flagellants, etc. It was, for the mentality of the time, the sole way of *salvation, that of the Church militant. Already St *Benedict described the beginnings of monastic life from the vocabulary of conversion, thus giving it an institutional dimension.

In the Middle Ages, conversion also and especially designated that of peoples (*Anglo-Saxons, *Scandinavians, *Slavs. . .) to Christianity. This conversion, which had not only a religious dimension but also a political one, came about through the intermediary of missionaries: *Columbanus, Gregory the Illuminator, *Cyril and Methodius, etc., who announced the Gospel and co-operated to establish ecclesial structures once the rulers were baptized. This conversion of peoples was not without its excesses and sometimes gave rise to mass conversions between 900 and 1050.

Add to this the forced conversion of *Jews in *Spain in the late 14th c. (before the episode of the **Marranos*).

With another objective, that of the salvation of all, and without political aims, St *Dominic worked for the conversion of all and chose *preaching to prepare people for conversion, re-using in his own way the **exempla*, those "anecdotes of a historical character presented as arguments of a discourse of persuasion" (J. Le Goff, *L'Imaginaire médiéval*, Paris, 1985, 99), and aiming at an immediate conversion.

Less existential than at the time of the *Fathers, unless among the *Rhineland mystics, though *Eckhart added to it the notion of detachment, conversion played a decisive role in the formation of medieval civilization.

C. Vogel, *Le Pécheur et la Pénitence au Moyen Âge*, Paris, 1969. – *Rhétorique et histoire. L'exemplum et le modèle de comportement dans le discours antique et médiéval*, *MEFRM*, 92, 1980-1981. – A. Angenendt, "The Conversion of the Anglo-Saxons considered against the Background of the Early Medieval Mission", *SSAM*, 32, 1986, 747-92. – J. Muldoon, *Varieties of religious conversion in the Middle Ages*, Gainsville (FA), 1997.

Marie-Anne Vannier

**CONVERSION TO ISLAM.** In the Muslim Empire, there could only be conversion of a Christian or a Jew to *Islam, Muslim law forbidding, under pain of death, the conversion of a Muslim to Christianity or the return of a convert to his religion of origin, those two acts being considered apostasy.

By virtue of the treaties of capitulation signed by their ancestors with the Arab conquerors, the "covenanted" Christians (**dhimmī*) had the right to live in "Islamic territory" and to remain in their infidelity, on condition of paying the capitation and the land tax. Despite this option given to the Christians to retain their religion, it is observable that at all times and in all countries there were individual or collective conversions to Islam. So we must look for the reasons why these Christians, of all confessions and all conditions, converted. These reasons seem to have been much more economic and social than religious. Economic reasons came first, since conversion allowed the Christian to escape fiscal oppression when it became intolerable; indeed, the Christian who was unable to pay the capitation and the land tax because of their excessive rate had no other resource than to convert, in order to pay the legal Muslim taxation, whose rate was infinitely lower; indeed, since payment of the land tax, much heavier than the *tithe, was collective, entire villages converted. In second place came social reasons, since conversion gave the Christian the chance to come out of the ghetto in which the status of *dhimmī* enclosed him; it allowed him, in fact, to escape the humiliation and abasement that the distinctive signs caused him; it also allowed the Christian official to keep his position during the measures of dismissal of *dhimmī* that periodically occurred, and to reach the highest posts of the Muslim administration, as did the *Nestorian scribes, ancestors of the Banū Wahb, the Banū Makhlad and the Banū l-Jarrāh, under the *Abbasids; finally, it allowed the Christian to divorce his wife – which his religion forbade – and marry one or more Muslim women. In third and last place came religious reasons: these concerned a small number of intellectuals who, for philosophical reasons, decided to embrace Islam. This was the case, *e.g.*, of the *Jacobite philosopher Ibn Suwār († *c.*1043), the Nestorian physician Ibn Jazla († 1100), who composed a *Refutation of the Christians* after his conversion, or the Melkite physician Ibn al-Mutrān († 1192). On the circumstances of Ibn Suwār's conversion, we have the interesting testimony of his biographer, al-Bayhaqī († 1169): "Ibn Suwār one day passed a school where a master endowed with a fine voice was reciting the Sura of the Spider. He stopped, wept a moment, then went on. That night he saw in a dream the Prophet, who said to him: 'O Abū l-Khayr, it is a shame that one like you, despite your knowledge, should deny my prophetic character'. In his dream, Ibn Suwār was converted between the hands of God's Messenger. When he awoke from his dream, he publicly manifested his conversion. He studied law despite his great age, learned the *Koran by heart and his conversion was good".

D. C. Denett, *Conversion and the Poll Tax in Early Islam*, Cambridge (MA), 1950. – R. W. Bulliet, *Conversion to Islam in the Medieval Period*, Cambridge (MA), 1979. – *Conversion and Continuity*, M. Gervers (ed.), R. J. Bikhazi (ed.), Montreal, 1990.

Gérard Troupeau

**CONVERSIONS TO CHRISTIANITY AND JUDAISM.** Conversions to *Judaism and Christianity always posed problems in a society in which it was difficult to change status, social or religious. However, the medieval West long remained a more open society than is generally thought: *Jews and Christians lived together, sharing dangers but also festivals. If the communities separated more and more sharply in the 13th c. in northern Europe, conviviality was maintained in the south (Spain, Languedoc, Provence, Italy), involving numerous social relationships, which the church authorities condemned. Whether the reasons for conversion were social, psychological or genuinely religous, they constituted a fairly constant phenomenon (taking into account the nuances just stated) and one always keenly denounced by the religous authorities.

The mission to the Jews, with a view to converting them to Christianity, was not truly defined until the 13th century. Even then, the Church's official attitude remained ambiguous, hesitating between the desire to bring the Jewish people into the house of God and the wish to let it continue to assume its role of privileged witness to Christian truth (forcible conversion being constantly condemned). The miserable condition of converts (rejected by their original community, deprived of their goods by the secular power, not always welcomed by the Christians) was an obstacle to conversion. Gradually however (second half of 13th c.), preaching to the Jews became a real institution (protested against by those concerned), notably in *Spain (*Nicholas III, *bull *Vineam Soreth*, 1278); meanwhile the reception of converts was organised, with the creation of specialized establishments (*domus Iudeorum*) or the adoption of proper measures to ensure proselytes the means of subsistence (council of Valladolid, 1322). It seems that in several cases Jews were converted, seduced by the intellectual development of the Christian world (*mendicant orders). Some of these proselytes in turn became missionaries to lead their old co-religionists to the Christian faith; thus *William of Bourges, *Thibaud of Sézanne, Pablo Cristiá, *Alfonso of Valladolid. Conversions affected all social levels.

Conversions of Christians to Judaism were doubtless more rare, but still real, even during the most sombre periods for the Jews; converts encountered immense difficulties, which obliged them to emigrate. *Baptism being indelible, conversion to Judaism was likened to a *heresy and punishable by *death. *Clement VI's bull *Turbato corde* (1267) posed the problem of returnees to Judaism, but implied that there were also conversions of cradle Christians; it charged the *Inquisition with this problem, aiming not just at individuals but also at Jewish communities who favoured conversions or sheltered proselytes. Motivations were varied: besides conversions of slaves or domestics (constantly curbed by the church authorities), we know of a love story (an English cleric was converted and married a Jewess, around 1220), but the most frequent reason was doctrinal; the Church never ceased to warn against the seduction exercised by Judaism and the Jews' knowledge of the Scriptures, susceptible of exercising a too potent attraction on the faithful. Among the best known cases of conversion to Judaism were, in the 9th c., the deacon Bodo (who became Eleazar), in the 11th c. Andrew, archbishop of *Bari, and John, priest of Oppido (who became Obadiah), and the affair of the German converts who took refuge in Aragon at the start of the 14th century.

B. Blumenkranz, *Juifs et chrétiens dans le monde occidental, 430-1096*, Paris-The Hague, 1960. – G. Dahan, *Les Intellectuels chrétiens et les juifs au Moyen Âge*, Paris, 1990.

Gilbert Dahan

**CONVOCATION, ENGLISH.** The clergy was not represented as such in the English *Parliament: admittedly, the *bishops and the main *abbots were convened as barons, and the bishops, notably, played a role of the first importance; but the representation of the lower clergy declined rapidly and practically disappeared at the end of the 14th century. Another institution developed in the mean time: Convocation. This consisted of assemblies of clergy for each of the two *provinces of *York and *Canterbury, which, from *c.*1340, became totally independent of Parliament, with which they had at first been linked.

From the point of view of the State, Convocation had primarily a financial function: it allowed it to obtain the clergy's consent to its fiscal demands. The basic unit was the *tenth, generally payable in two halves, on ecclesiastical *benefices and the temporalities attached to them; the tax base was dependant on the scale established by Pope *Nicholas IV in 1291. As with Parliament, the vote of *taxation gave rise to animated debates, and several months were sometimes needed to obtain the agreement of the clergy's representatives. Convocation designated the *collectors (usually *regulars) responsible for levying the sums and handing them over to the *Exchequer. The contribution of the Convocation of the South (Canterbury) was between about 13,000 and 16,000 pounds, that of the province of the North (York) 1800 pounds in principle, the devastations caused by the Scots being frequently invoked as an excuse for paying less. To reach the benefices not counted in 1291 and the unbeneficed *secular clerics, capitation-type taxes were created (*clerical poll tax*), which could reach 4000 pounds. We must add however that a part of the goods of the Church and of clerks was also subject to parliamentary taxation, and that a part of the papal revenues in *England was also levied by the king.

But Convocation was not purely and simply a fiscal machinery; the meeting of Convocation, like that of Parliament, was opened by a solemn *sermon, preached by the *archbishops or an eminent churchman, often dealing with current problems (political or doctrinal). The discussion of *gravamina*, the ills suffered by the clergy and whose assorted list of demands for reparation was sometimes presented to Parliament in the form of an ecclesiastical petition, gave rise to animated debates that made Convocation a sort of little ecclesiastical parliament.

W. Wake, *The State of the Church and Clergy of England in their Councils, Synods, Convocations . . .*, London, 1703. – D. B. Weske, *Convocation of the Clergy: a Study of its Antecedents and its Rise . . .*, London, 1937. – F. M. Powicke, C. R. Cheney, *Councils and Synods . . .*, 2, 2, Oxford, 1964. – R. N. Swanson, *Church and Society in Late Medieval England*, Oxford, 1989.

Jean-Philippe Genet

**COOKING.** Limited in the 1960s and 1970s to discussions of rations and provisioning, the history of *food has recently been widened to include cooking, *i.e.* the concrete way in which food is prepared and consumed. In this matter there is no lack of medieval documents, though they are more numerous for the 14th and 15th centuries. Apart from account-books, too little used, the only ones to form a series are cookery books.

Preserved in more than a hundred manuscripts, medieval collections of culinary recipes arose out of the practice of master cooks in the service of prelates or princes. As such, they reflect aristocratic cooking, although certain treatises like the late 14th-c. *Menagier de Paris*, exceptionally, addressed the middle class and although culinary manuscripts, constantly augmented and modified, were gradually opened up to more common practices.

One of the more striking traits of medieval cooking, which we find as much in account-books as in recipes, was the variety and abundance of *spices. There were more than 15 exotic products judged necessary for the production of dishes: never had the Western aromatic palette been so broad. But not all spices had the importance of ginger, cinnamon or saffron (whose exorbitant price did not at all hinder its use): thus nutmeg, mace or cubeb, latecomers to Europe, remained secondary. Variety, in this case, was accompanied by abundance, at least at the higher levels of society, and it has been calculated that the *court of the *Dauphiné in the early 14th c. had an annual consumption of over a kilogram of spices per person. But for all that, medieval cooking was not a hotchpotch of pungent and haphazard flavours: analyses have shown that the spices were used in precise associations (among themselves and with other ingredients), sometimes indicative of regional tastes.

The other great characteristic of medieval cooking was its duality, imposed by religious obligations that were, for rich tables, an occasion for tasting costly products (fresh sea-fish or fine fresh-water fish) often presented in imitation of those served on meat days. It is not impossible that this use of disguised dishes may have arisen in the *abbeys, where the meatless was the rule and the whole art of the cook consisted in giving the illusion of what could not be consumed. But not all adaptations were possible and so *canon law imposed a strict division of fats, *e.g.* between lard and oil, obliging cookery books to present meatless variants on the meat-day recipes. But meat-day cuisine did not mean a fatty cuisine. Comprising few fried dishes – except in the Mediteranean countries – medieval recipes drew, on the contrary, on a light cuisine in which sauces contained neither oil, butter nor even flour.

The minimal equipment attested by inventories hardly permitted *peasants to eat anything but boiled dishes or those stewed for a long time in a pot. The presence of a spit was a sign of luxury and the consumption of roast fowl functioned as a sign of social distinction. It is precisely between these two poles, that of "soup" and that of "roast", that the majority of surviving recipes are distributed. It was also their succession that defined the fundamental core of the medieval meal, at least as it was practised in French court circles.

14th- and 15th-c. collections of recipes thus reveal an already well-established cuisine, breaking cleanly with that practised in Roman Antiquity. The break seems to have come about during the early Middle Ages, with the enrichment of the stock of spices and the abandonment of *garum*, a fish condiment much used by the contemporaries of Apicius. At the same time, the fact that the eater was no longer lying on his side but sitting at a table doubtless better enabled him to taste roast meats, which, as we have seen, would become the pivot of the meal.

If the broad outlines of medieval cooking seem well in place from the 10th-11th cc., it did not cease to evolve subsequently, less under Arab influence, often invoked by historians but in the end of little effect, than by a slow internal maturation. Thus, in the domain of spices, the late Middle Ages were marked by the disaffection manifested by the aristocracy for pepper, widely consumed among the populace. The 14th and 15th centuries belonged to ginger, whose tart flavour was often combined with that of cinnamon. This period also saw a first breakthrough for sugar, previously considered simply as a medicament.

Over and above well-marked common traits, there existed medieval cuisines, certainly adjusted to the diversity of local conditions but also to the reality of national or regional tastes. Not all these tastes are explained and it is, *e.g.*, quite difficult to account for the French taste for nutmeg, while across the Channel they preferred the aril of the nutmeg tree, *i.e.* mace. The association of cinnamon, considered a sweet spice, with pepper was equally characteristic of English cooking – much attached in general to mixed flavours, like bitter-sweet – while in Mediterranean countries this sweetness was, on the contrary, reinforced by that of sugar.

The taste for sugar, and for sweeteners in general, was another line of fracture between the various European cuisines. Already well-marked in the English and Italian collections of the 14th c., it grew ceaselessly during the following century, which saw, in response to this heavy demand, a spectacular sugar boom in Sicily and the Spains. Long remaining resistant to this substance, French palates too were converted in the 15th c., though to a much lesser degree.

*Winged genius bearing a medallion.* Fragment of Coptic hanging, 6th c. London, V&A.

While some Europeans already doted on sugar – whose culinary uses were not limited to sweetmeats served at the end of a meal – there was also a butter-eating Europe. Travellers and doctors describe a heavy consumption of butter in the north-west of the continent, from Flanders to Brittany, passing through England. However, cookery books do not entirely reflect this division. Thus we discern an upsurge of butter in the Italian courts during the 15th c., even in the south of the peninsula. No doubt butter served to distinguish these courts from the southern peoples, great consumers of oil; in England, on the contrary, butter was so widespread that aristocratic cooks made it a point of honour not to use it, preferring olive oil.

But, from the 16th c., butter would invade the cookery books, in France as in England: was this the reflection of a new taste for "fat", or greater openness to common practices? Unless, as Jean-Louis Flandrin has supposed, these were the first effects of the Reformation. But for all that, medieval cuisine did not disappear. Repertoire and seasonings were perpetuated in the books of the 16th c., though important evolutions can be discerned in them. The real break came about in the second half of the 17th c., with the emergence of a French "*nouvelle cuisine*" which overturned the European gastronomic landscape. In culinary matters as in others, we must speak of a "long *Middle Ages".

*Manger et boire au Moyen Âge. Actes du colloque de Nice (1982)*, Paris, 1984 (2 vol.). – B. Laurioux, *Le Moyen Âge à table*, Paris, 1989. – O. Redon, F. Sabban, S. Serventi, *The Medieval Kitchen. Recipes from France and Italy*, Chicago-London, 1998. – *Du manuscrit à la table. Essais sur la cuisine médiévale*, C. Lambert (dir.), Paris-Montreal, 1992. – J.-L. Flandrin, *Chronique de Platine. Pour une gastronomie historique*, Paris, 1992. – M. Montanari, *The Culture of Food*, Oxford, 1994. – *Histoire de l'alimentation*, J.-L. Flandrin (dir.), M. Montanari (dir.), Paris, 1996. – B. Laurioux, *Les livres de cuisine mediévaux*, Turnhout, 1997.

Bruno Laurioux

**COPT, COPTIC.** The word "Copt" designates one of the Egyptian Christians, pure descendants of the Pharaohs; the Greek word *Aiguptios* being a somewhat deformed transcription of the old Egyptian: *'Hwt k3 Ptḥ* (the house of the spirit [*ka*] of [the god] Ptah); this word having been Arabized (keeping only the consonants) into *qibṭī*, plural *Aqbāṭ*, it was employed by the Arabs to designate the Christian Egyptians. These formed the Coptic "nation": they were the majority in that country from the 7th to the 11th century. Between the 12th and 14th cc., Islamization turned them into a minority, the present proportion (estimated at 8 to 10 %) being reached around the 14th century. The period between the 14th and 18th cc. marked the blackest period of the Christian community; at the start of the 19th c. the status of *dhimmī* (second-class citizen, non-Muslim) was abolished, at least theoretically (since attitudes did not follow), under the influence of the Enlightenment and, with the establishment of a veritable "democracy", equality was proclaimed for all citizens, whatever their religion.

The Coptic language is the last stage of the old Egyptian language; true, the Arabic language was imposed for administrative acts in 705 (Christian era), but we have dated bilingual *papyri (Greek-Arabic or Coptic-Arabic) up to 996, and a festal letter (*i.e.* announcing the date of *Easter) written in Greek by an early 8th-c. Coptic *patriarch. In short, the Coptic language seems to have maintained itself all over *Egypt up to the 10th c., though even in the 14th c. we have literary work that is really bilingual (Coptic and Arabic) and many Coptic manuscripts were copied in the 11th and 12th centuries. Moreover, there exist many Coptic "islands" (as in Berber lands, not long ago, there were villages where women and children understood only Berber), but Arabic advanced ineluctably – the golden age of *Arabic Christian literature was, in Egypt, the 12th and 13th cc. – which supposes great progress in the Arabization of the country. There were important works in Coptic in the 7th c., but literary output went on diminishing; there was only recopying (in monasteries, where Coptic culture was kept up): they lived on what they had and produced nothing new. All new work was in Arabic. This Coptic language is still that of liturgical texts, even today, at least in books, since only the cantors, often blind, repeat by heart and uncomprehendingly the chants handed down orally, composed in Coptic, while the priest usually reads or chants the prayers using the Arabic translation; some books of more recent composition, such as the *Synaxarion or the Difnar (*antiphonary), are written entirely, or very nearly so, in Arabic.

In the 13th and 14th cc., scholars, realizing that Coptic was in a fair way to becoming a dead language, composed, for Arabic-speaking readers, grammars (following the structure of Arabic grammars) and lexicons (called *salālim*, "ladders", since they were arranged like ladders, the two columns of Coptic words and their Arabic equivalents suggesting the rungs of a ladder), in order to perpetuate the language of their ancestors.

P. du Bourguet, "Copt", *Coptic Encyclopedia*, 2, New York, 1991, 599-601. – R. Kasser, "Language(s), Coptic", *Coptic Encyclopedia*, 8, New York, 1991, 145-151.

René-Georges Coquin †

**CORBIE.** In *c.*657, Queen Balthild, widow of Clovis II, chose the estate of Corbie (now in the *département* of the Somme) to found an *abbey into which, some years later, she introduced several monks from *Luxeuil. Under the leadership of Valbert, they followed the Rule of *Columbanus. From 664 the abbey was removed from episcopal jurisdiction, and the *charter of *immunity granted in 661 by Balthild thus took on its full dimensions. The rise of Corbie at that time was very rapid, stimulated by several factors: the adoption of the Rule of St *Benedict in the 8th c., the personality of Abbot *Adalard and the development of an important **scriptorium* whose products remain among the most sumptuous of the Carolingian schools. A cousin of *Charlemagne, Adalard's long abbacy at Corbie was marked by intense political activity at the Carolingian court, recounted in the *Life* written by his contemporary *Paschasius Radbertus. Abbot from 771, he was sent to *Italy by Charlemagne to help his son Pippin in his government (781-805). Disgraced by *Louis the Pious in 814, he had to go into exile and only in 822 returned to Corbie which he directed until his death. The statutes he gave the monastery are an early example of the practical adaptation of the Rule to the imperatives of the *coenobitic life of several hundred monks.

It was during his exile that he set out with his brother Wala to found *Corvey, the new Corbie, on the banks of the Weser. This abbey, whose architecture still gives evidence of the Carolingian period, has often been taken as a model for what Corbie might have been. But only the personality of Adalard allows us to suppose a common inspiration between the two buildings, since the absence of vestiges above ground or architectural excavations reduces any parallel to conjectures. We do know however that, from the beginning, Corbie possessed two sanctuaries (Sts Peter and Paul and St Stephen) to which a third was added before the middle of the 9th c. (St John the Evangelist). This ternary organisation, present at *Saint-Riquier and Saint-Vaast, is an explicit homage to the Holy *Trinity, as Angilbert explains in his *ordo* of Centula. Of the abbey church we know only, thanks to the *Lives* of Adalard, that a tower marked a transept crossing in front of a developed choir. From the end of the 9th c., the monastery was regularly devastated by pillages or fires which obliged the monks to abandon Sts Peter and Paul's in *c.*1026 in favour of St John's, to which they transferred the *relics and *tomb of Adalard. The *Romanesque abbey church, rebuilt in the middle of the 11th c., was razed in 1502 to be replaced by the present *Flamboyant church.

*Corbie abbaye royale, XIII*[e] *centenaire*, Lille-Paris, 1962. – C. Heitz, *L'Architecture religieuse carolingienne. Les formes et leurs fonctions*, Paris, 1980. – D. Ganz, *Corbie in the Carolingian Renaissance*, Sigmaringen, 1990. – C. de Merindol, "Dans la topographie de Corbie d'après les textes", *CAr*, 41, 1993, 63-90.

Noëlle Deflou

**CORBINIAN (died *c.*730).** St Corbinian was, with Rupert and Emmeran, one of the Frankish missionaries who, working like their Anglo-Saxon brethren in close connection with Rome, were invited by the dukes of *Bavaria to organise the Bavarian Church before *Boniface. He divided his activity between Freising, where he exercised his position as *bishop, and the Bavarian-Lombard frontier, where he founded the *collegiate church of Kuens and where he was buried. He is known to us from the *Vita* composed from oral testimonies in *c.*770 by one of his successors, Arbeo, on the occasion of the *elevatio* of his body at Freising.

*Der heilige Willibald*, H. Dickershof (dir.) *et al.*, Regensburg, 1990, 29-142. – W. Störmer, "Korbinian", *LdM*, 5, 1991, 1443.

Martial Staub

**CORDOVA.** The *bishopric of Cordova, whose origin is little known, amidst an abundant and often suspect *martyrology, was *suffragan to the archbishopric of *Seville. Despite this, the town occupied a particular place during the Muslim period (711-1236) and especially during the three centuries of the Umayyad dynasty (756-1031) whose capital Cordova was. Indeed, if the episcopal hierarchy remained officially the same, the bishop of Cordova was recognised by the Umayyad authorities as the representative of the *Mozarabs of Andalus. The legal status of the Christians was quite close to that of the protected or **dhimmī* throughout the medieval Muslim world, with their officials (the bishop and the count or *kūmīs*, the *exceptor* in charge of collecting the taxes that

Cordova: interior and mihrāb of the mosque, 8th-10th c.

fell on the *dhimmī*, and the "*cadi of the Christians"); but the situation of the Mozarabs evolved in the 9th century. This century marked a profound crisis in Andalusian society, in particular through the reduction in the number of Christians and the *conversion of their elites. Numerous *clerics were exiled to the north, but others, like *Eulogio in 859, chose *martyrdom – at least 58, according to hagiographies – faced with a power that could not permit the proclamation of *Christ's superiority to *Muḥammad without undermining its own legitimacy. In the 10th c., by contrast, the definitive triumph of *Islam allowed the Umayyad caliphs to surround themselves with the most brilliant Christian intellectuals such as Recemundo (Rabū b. Zayd), ambassador of Abd al-Rahmān III (913-961) to *Otto I or to *Constantinople and, under al-Hakam II (961-974), author of the famous *Cordova Calendar*, one of the rare large-scale Christian works of this time. Thus the Christians could profit, like the other communities, from the advantage procured by the presence of a strong power and from its patronage.

From the 11th c., the history of the Mozarabs of Cordova differed little from that of the Christians of Andalus in general, marked by the descent of Alfonso I the Battler in 1125-1126, the departure of the Mozarabs to *Saragossa or their deportation, the suppression of the Christian officials under the *Almohads. Now the recovery of Cordova would pose no problem of relations between *Catholics and Mozarabs. Later on, Cordova, formed of 14 *parishes, occupied a secondary place between the two archbishoprics of *Toledo and Seville in the history of *Castile. The movement of exclusion of non-Christian communities was followed by the establishment of the *Inquisition in 1482.

E. P. Colbert, *The Martyrs of Cordoba*, Washington (DC), 1962. – F. J.

*Coronation of a Byzantine emperor* in the *Byzantine chronicles of John Scylitzes.* 14th-c. Greek codex. Madrid, National Library.

Simonet, *Historia de los Mozárabes de España*, Madrid, 1983 (4 vol.; 1st ed. 1897). – E. Levi-Provencal, *Histoire de l'Espagne musulmane*, 3, Paris, 1950-1967, 214-226. – F. Pérez, *DHGE*, 13, 1956, 837-871. – K. B. Wolf, *Christian Martyrs in Muslim Spain*, Cambridge, 1988.

Christophe Picard

## CORONATION

**The West.** The ceremony of coronation appeared for the first time in the Christian West in 800, when Pope *Leo III handed over the imperial *crown to *Charlemagne, and at that time it conformed to the Byzantine ritual. From 816, *consecration, which had appeared earlier, was linked to coronation in the ceremony of ascending the throne, and this usage lasted all through the Middle Ages.

At the same time, the liturgical aspect of the ceremonial developed and the ritual was specified, strictly defined in the *Ordines* that multiplied from the 10th century. They brought to perfection a ceremony that had important similarities among the main European powers, *France, *England and the *Empire. The *king or emperor firstly swore an *oath to protect the Church and safeguard the peace before being anointed by a prelate. He then received his insignia, principally the crown and the sceptre, handed over by the archbishops of *Reims in France, *Canterbury in England or, for the emperor, by the *pope. The coronation was gradually fixed in one place: Reims, *Westminster or *Rome.

Yet certain monarchs ignored anointing and were content with sumptuous coronations. Thus in *Castile, from 1135, the kings received only the crown and none of them was anointed, with the single exception of Alfonso XI in 1332. Moreover, that monarch was one of three Castilians who practised self-coronation: after having been anointed, he took the royal diadem and placed it on his head alone.

Coronation was an important constitutional act for any *monarchy since, up to the 13th c., the new king did not really acquire the plenitude of his powers until after this ceremony. The crown proved the royal or imperial dignity of its holder and invested him with his rights. However, from 1270 in France or 1272 in England, the heir took the title of king on the death or burial of his father and from then on exercised all the royal prerogatives. Thus, though the mystico-liturgical aspect of this ceremony was developed at the end of the Middle Ages, this ritual gradually lost its constitutional values; the true legitimacy was now dynastic, the king's eldest son automatically becoming the new monarch.

For the papacy, on the contrary, during the same period, coronation gained in importance and magnificence. It took place at *St Peter's in Rome and the bishop of Ostia was its principal officiant. It conformed to a precise ritual: consecration or benediction of the pope, then handing over of the **pallium* and the *tiara.

Thus, while at the end of the Middle Ages coronation was no longer for the Empire and the Western monarchies a determinative constitutional act, the papacy made it the symbol of its new princely power.

P. E. Schramm, *Kaiser, Könige und Päpste*, Stuttgart, 1970 (4 vol.). – T. F. Ruiz, "Une royauté sans sacre: la monarchie castillane du bas Moyen Âge", *Annales*, May-June 1984, 429-454. – J.L. Nelson, *Politics and Ritual in Early Medieval Europe*, London, 1986. – B. Schimmelpfennig, "Couronnement impérial", "Couronnement pontifical", *DHP*, 1994, 483-484. 484-486.

Murielle Gaude

**Byzantium.** The way the emperors were crowned varied over the centuries. It was never the decisive moment of the promotion of a new emperor, since his reign began after the traditional triple *acclamation by the *army, the Senate and the people: the man who received the crown was already emperor. Constantine VII Porphyrogenitus's *Book of Ceremonies* (10th c.) preserves the description of some imperial coronations. The emperor left the Great *Palace, still dressed in a *sagion* and *scaramancum* (silk robe), with no *chlamys* and no crown. In his walk towards Hagia Sophia, close to the Palace, he met successively the senators and then the demes, who acclaimed him, and crossed the barracks of the palatine guard (the *Scholia*). Before entering the church, he changed clothes in the *metatorion* (*mutatorium*), then, accompanied by the *patriarch, he was led to the *ambo, after the senators, the demes and the dignitaries had taken their places in the church. The patriarch handed the chlamys and *fibula to the emperor after having blessed them, then took the crown in both hands and placed it on the sovereign's head, saying "in the name of the Father, Son and Holy Spirit", while the congregation sang the **Trisagion*. In the case of the coronation of a co-emperor, it was the full emperor who gave the crown. The emperor, once crowned, either followed the ordinary liturgical *office or communicated with the presanctified bread, then he descended from the ambo and, seated on a small throne, received the dignitaries. Unlike the emperor, the empress was not crowned in Hagia Sophia, but in the Great Palace in two rooms, the Augusteus and the Tribunal of Nineteen Beds. The empress was not necessarily crowned at the same time as her husband, but could wait *e.g.* until the birth of a *porphyrogenete prince.

This ritual was established gradually after the foundation of the new Rome. Valens, the first emperor to be enthroned at *Constantinople, received a crown in 364 at the Hebdomon, a place of troop concentration seven miles from the town. The religious ceremony of a coronation by the patriarch appears only in the 5th c. when Marcian or more certainly Leo I, having no dynastic legitimacy, wished to put more emphasis on the divine origin of their power. This ceremony, at first accessory, took on growing importance as an element of legitimation of a new emperor, but the *Great Church, Hagia Sophia, did not become the usual setting of the coronation until 641. The material anointing seems to have constituted the last important modification, the date when this gesture appeared being still debated. For a long time the emperors were considered as being anointed by the Lord, but it is not until the coronation of *Theodore Lascaris in 1208, perhaps under Latin influence, that anointing is clearly attested: it would continue until the end of the Empire.

A. Vogt, *Constantin VII Porphyrogénète. Le Livre des Cérémonies, Commentaire*, 2, Paris, 1935, 1-30. – D. M. Nicol, "Kaisersalbung: The Unction of Emperors in Late Byzantine Coronation Ritual", *BMGS*, 2, 1976, 37-52.

Jean-Claude Cheynet

**CORPORAL.** The corporal is the sacred cloth on which the eucharistic body (*corpus*) of Christ rests directly. At *mass, it is spread on the *altar and, at an early date, it could serve to cover the offerings to protect them, so that the "*pall" that could cover the *chalice was just a duplication of it. Its dimensions were reduced from the time when the custom of consecrating non-fermented unleavened bread was adopted, in the Carolingian period: it then sufficed that it should be big enough to hold the chalice, the pyx containing the *hosts for *communion and the great host for the celebrant. It was spread on the altar at the moment of the *offertory. It folded into nine equal squares.

"Corporal", *DACL*, 3, 2, 1914, 2986-2987. – "Corporal", *Cath.*, 3, 1954, 203-204.

Guy-Marie Oury

**CORPORATION.** An association bringing together within itself all the members of a single trade: *masters, *apprentices and employees. From the late 19th c., the term has been systematically applied to all the former communities of arts and trades, whether corporate bodies or not.

Originating in an associative movement with many forms, but not directly connected with the artisans' colleges of Antiquity, they were originally as much fraternal peace unions as professional groupings controlled by a political authority or coalitions formed to defend common interests. In northern and central *Italy, unions of merchant-manufacturers (the future *Arti maggiori*) were formed from the 12th c. and aimed early at a share or even a monopoly of power in the *commune, as at *Florence after 1293. Analogous situations are observed in the Flemish and Rhenish towns, but rather later. Elsewhere however, trade communities were under the control of the local political power, whether seignorial, communal or even royal; the statutes regulating them, very rare before the 13th c., were a mixture of ratification of professional customs, police measures and confirmation of banal rights, and were modelled on communal *statutes, the best example being the famous *Livre des métiers* made for 101 of them in *c.*1268 on the initiative of the provost of Paris, Étienne Boileau.

In the 14th and especially the 15th c., the interests of the nascent modern *State converged with those of the masters of trades or of the increasingly numerous professionally recruited confraternities, who wished to escape the burden of feudal powers; hence the great abundance of those statutes of public order that made them into bodies with a legal personality and policing rights, monopoly of exercise and recruitment, free choice of their officials, but with no jurisdictional or political powers. The fact is patent in the kingdoms of *France, *England and *Castile, but also in the towns of *Italy or *Germany, where the arts and trades were confined to a purely corporative role. Everywhere, this new regime based on the family workshop reinforced the position of the masters, who closely controlled apprenticeship and regulated access to the trade to the detriment of their paid workers whose economic dependence became irreversible. However, class conflicts were very sporadic and the corporative monopoly, nowhere general, was still very far from having the sterilizing consequences attributed to it in the 18th century.

S. L. Thrupp, "The Gilds", *Economic Organization and Policies in the Middle Ages*, M. M. Postan (ed.), E. E. Rich (ed.), E. Miller (ed.), Cambridge, 1963, 230-280 ("The Cambridge Economic History of Europe", 3). – E. Coornaert, *Les Corporations en France avant 1789*, Paris, 1968. – B. Chevalier, *Les Bonnes Villes de France du XIV^e au XVI^e siècle*, Paris, 1982, 76-83. – A. I. Pini, *Città, comuni e corporazioni nel Medioevo italiano*, Bologna, 1986.

Bernard Chevalier

***CORPUS CHRISTI* or *CORPUS DOMINI*.** The expression "body of Christ" has designated both the *Eucharist and the Church since the time of St Paul, but the expression "mystical body" has gradually been reserved for the latter. From the mid 11th c., theological discussions on the nature of the *sacrament led to the affirmation of the dogma of Christ's Real Presence in the sacred *species. Christ's body became the object of an intense devotion that culminated in the institution of the *feast called Corpus Christi. It originated around *Liège, home of great theoreticians of eucharistic dogma such as *Alger of Liège and Renier of Saint-Laurent, and also the cradle of *beguinage, associated with the practice of frequent *communion. It was a pious laywoman connected with the *Premonstratensians, *Juliana of Mont-Cornillon, who was behind its institution, because of a *vision she received in 1208, which was kept secret by the bishop of Liège, Robert de Turlotte, until 1246. But not until the *archdeacon of Campines, Jacques Pantaleon, became *pope under the name of *Urban IV was the feast instituted at *Rome, in 1264. And the celebration was not truly established until 1317, date of the *Decretal published by his successor *Clement V. The institution of the new feast was the occasion for the papacy to affirm its pre-eminent role in the liturgical sphere. Indeed the *bull of 1264 contained in an appendix the texts of the *office and the *mass that the pope wanted to see used for this feast throughout *Christendom and which are said to have been composed at his request by St *Thomas Aquinas.

The success of this festivity in the late Middle Ages clearly appears in the multiplication of *preaching and *plays, the proliferation of *confraternities devoted to the holy sacrament and especially the importance of public *processions. The eucharistic procession, which constructed or confirmed hierarchies and developed an "iconography of power" that inspired the ceremonies of royal entries in the late Middle Ages, played a real social role. A whole language was created around the Corpus Domini, integrating a wide range of practices such as expositions of hosts, Easter burials, and the appearance of new iconographical formulae. The image most common from 1320, notably in Italian painting, revived a theme of Byzantine iconography: the Communion of the Apostles. In French manuscripts, artists preferred to illustrate Corpus Christi by a subject that has too often been confused with the Last Supper: the Institution of the Eucharist, or by the representation of the procession, which made its appearance from the mid 14th c. and prevailed during the 15th. A third formula was used very early to illustrate Corpus Christi: the *elevation of the *host, following different variants. But this

Saint-Florent (Corsica). Chevet of the former cathedral of Nebbio, *c.*1125-1140.

enthusiasm for celebrating the body of Christ also led to the development of paraliturgical or even *magical practices, a source of numerous abuses, and aroused accusations of *heresy.

P. Browe, *Die Verehrung der Eucharistie im Mittelalter*, Munich, 1933 (repr. Freiburg im Breisgau, 1967). – E. Dumoutet, *Corpus Domini. Aux sources de la pieté eucharistique médiévale*, Paris, 1942. – M. Rubin, "Corpus Christi Fraternities and Late Medieval Piety", *Voluntary Religion*, W.J. Sheils (ed.), D. Wood (ed.), Oxford, 1986, 97-109. – M. Rubin, *Corpus Christi. The Eucharist in Late Medieval Culture*, Cambridge, 1991.

Dominique Rigaux

**CORRECTORIES OF THE BIBLE.** Though the term *correctorium* is reserved for the critical revisions of the 13th and 14th cc., the text of the Latin *Vulgate was revised at several times in the Middle Ages. Under *Charlemagne, *Alcuin and *Theodulf worked on the task of improving Jerome's text; Theodulf, with the help of (converted?) *Jews, made use of the Hebrew. *Stephen Harding, abbot of Cîteaux, "astonished by the discordances presented by the Latin manuscripts" of the *Bible, worked on a comparison with the Hebrew and the Aramaic, which he completed in 1109 (Dijon Bible, BM 1-4). Another *Cistercian, Nicholas Maniacoria († *c.*1145), accomplished an important textual labour, calling on the Hebrew (*Suffraganeus Bibliothece*, revision of the *psalter. . .). In the 13th c., the university of *Paris imposed a text (taken from the Alcuinian recension) established without this critical effort; it seemed unsatisfactory and was criticized by *Roger Bacon. Groups of *Dominicans and *Franciscans set to work to revise it; their labours produced the biblical correctories; except in the case of the great correctory of Saint-Jacques (Paris, BNF, ms. lat. 16717-16722), where the critical annotations enclose the biblical text, these were *opuscula* giving verses followed by critical remarks. The main correctories, apart from that of Saint-Jacques (between 1250 and 1260 ?), were: that of *Hugh of Saint-Cher; the *Correctorium Sorbonicum*; the correctory of *William de la Mare; and that of Gerard de Huy.

Though some authors (William le Breton) were content with second-hand material, borrowed in particular from the commentaries of Jerome and *Andrew of Saint-Victor, the majority of correctories were the product of a very careful comparison between the basic text (Parisian), the Hebrew, Aramaic and Greek originals, the ancient versions (Septuagint, Vetus Latina) and different families of Vulgate manuscripts (generally divided between *antiqui* and *moderni*). The knowledge they show of *Hebrew and Greek is generally remarkable.

In the 14th c., this task continued and was more of a personal work: thus *Nicholas of Lyra brought together the critical notes of his **Postilla* for use by students.

H. Denifle, "Die Handschriften der Bibel-Correctorien des 13.Jh.", *ALKGMA*, 4, 1888, 264-311, 471-601. – L. Light, "Versions et révisions du texte biblique", *Le Moyen Âge et la Bible*, Paris, 1984, 55-93 ("Bible de tous les temps", 4). – G. Dahan, "La Connaissance de l'hébreu dans les correctoires. . .", *RTL*, 23, 1992, 176-190.

Gilbert Dahan

**CORSICA.** Christianized very early, Corsica was taken in hand at the end of the Vandal *invasions by Pope *Gregory the Great who restored the Church hierarchy there and encouraged the development of *monasticism. After the *Lombard invasions that affected the island in the 7th c., Corsica became part of the *patrimony of the papacy. Until the mid 9th c., Corsica resisted *Saracen incursions partly thanks to the protective measures of the *Carolingians (appointment of the marquis of Tuscany as *tutor Corsicae*), but from that date the island became a base for Saracen raids into the Tyrrhenian basin, and the centre of important migrations, mainly to *Rome. The island was liberated in the course of the 11th c. by the joint efforts of *Pisa, *Genoa and *Aragon, who remained the main competitors in the island for the rest of the Middle Ages. In the late 11th c., Pisa took the advantage: in 1077, to affirm his *suzerainty over the island, *Gregory VII delegated to it Pandulf, bishop of Pisa, whose successors never ceased thereafter to extend their privileges. For this reason and because of the elevation of the Pisan *bishopric to *metropolitan status, Corsica became the stake of a war between Pisa and Genoa, provisionally ended in 1133 by Pope *Innocent II (then a refugee in Pisa) at the cost of dividing the island's jurisdiction between the *archbishoprics of the two powers. The Pisan government proved very beneficial to the island, whose civil and religious administrations were restored. The monasteries of Pisa and Genoa exercised a decisive influence there both by reason of the importance of their insular possessions and by their support for religious reform, as attested by the diffusion in Corsica of a typically Tuscan architectural style.

The weakening and then defeat of Pisa at Meloria (1284) opened Corsica up to the Genoese. At the same time the island became a pawn in the papal manoeuvres to settle the *Angevins in southern *Italy, against the Aragonese claims. It then went through a phase of disorder marked among other things by disorganisation of the *parish structures and monastic decline, compensated only by the introduction of the *mendicant orders (especially the

*Franciscans) and the hospitallers of the *Misericordia of Pisa. Uprisings multiplied, whether religious like the penitential movement of the Giovannali, starting in the late 1340s and annihilated on the orders of *Urban V, or social like the uprising led in 1358 by Sambucuccio d'Alando. At the end of this revolt, Corsica submitted to Genoa in exchange for the granting of *statutes, but the application of these put an end neither to the rule of the traditional lords nor to a general situation of anarchy. In the late 14th c., following a baronial uprising supported by the king of Aragon, Genoa ceded its rule in Corsica to a group of financiers to whom it was in debt, while the traditionally competing powers worked in vain to enforce their rights; *Alfonso V of Aragon in 1420 or Pope *Eugenius IV in the following decade. Finally, in 1453 Corsica was ceded by the Republic of Genoa to the Bank of St George, which immediately promulgated the *Capitula Corsorum* guaranteeing a regular administration and economic and penal rules propitious to the return of a certain prosperity.

*Histoire de la Corse*, P. Arrighi (dir.), Toulouse, 1971. – S. P. P. Scalfati, *La Corse médiévale*, Ajaccio, 1994.

Cécile Caby

***CORTES.*** Arising directly out of the extraordinary *curia regis*, the *Cortes* came into being in 1188 at *León, when for the first time the representatives of the *towns were called to sit with the noble and ecclesiastical counsellors. The *Cortes* of the kingdoms of *Castile and León, called together from 1302 and always on royal convocation, had to vote taxes and swear an *oath to the heir to the throne; 100 towns sent delegates and grievances to it in the early 14th c., only 17 in the 15th. The *Cortes* of *Portugal were convened from the mid 13th century. In the domains of the Crown of *Aragon, the *Cortes* of Aragon, *Catalonia, *Valencia and the *Balearics always met separately, and their four "arms" – upper *nobility, middle nobility, clergy and towns – managed to impose a control on the king within what has been called "pactism".

E. Sarasa Sánchez, *Las Cortes de Aragón en la Edad Media*, Saragossa, 1979. – *Las Cortes de Castilla y León en la Edad Media*, Valladolid, 1988 (2 vol.). – J. F. O'Callaghan, *The Cortes of Castile-León, 1188-1350*, Philadelphia (PA), 1989.

Adeline Rucquoi

***CORVÉE.*** This was the obligation to provide *labour, which the lord levied from his men. It could be required on various grounds. It developed in the early Middle Ages on the great *estates, whose proprietors mobilized the manual labour of their subjected tenants. Performed primarily in agricultural work for the lord on his reserve, it also applied in the master's house and *textile workshop or for the *transport of produce. Being the main charge of servile tenure, which was habitually encumbered with an arbitrary service or a service of three days a week, the *corvée* could be heavier than the dues of the free tenant, who was most often subject to a seasonal service (in general twice fifteen days a year) or a *lot-corvée* (the complete cycle of cultivation of a plot).

Following the disintegration of the domanial régime, *corvée* was generally reduced to less than ten days per holding after the year 1000. The levying of statute labour by the *seigneur justicier* or the territorial prince developed in this period, without reaching the level of the early Middle Ages.

Yoshiki Morimoto

*The Evangelist Matthew.* Miniature from an evangeliary of Corvey abbey, 10th c. Paderborn, Diocesan Museum.

**CORVEY.** A monastery on the Weser, near Höxter (Westphalia), founded in 822 by *Adalard of Corbie (Corvey was *Corbeia nova*) and his brother Wala. In 836, the *relics of St Guy (Vitus) were brought there from *Saint-Denis. Corvey was an important centre for the Christianization of *Saxony, for *missions to the lands of the North (*Anskar) and historiographical works: *Translatio sancti Viti*, Rembert's *Vita Ansgarii*, Widukind of Corvey. The monastery possessed a *library of classical authors (Cicero, Tacitus, Pliny) and a manuscript of **Heliand*. The church was built in the 9th c. (the westwork, decorated with *frescos, still survives). Corvey also possessed much property in northern Germany as far as Holland, as the *Traditiones corbeienses* (822-877 and 965-1023) attest. On the initiative of *Henry II, the monastery accepted the reform of *Gorze. Apart from the *Investiture Contest, Corvey was always on the side of the king. In 1090, the monastery adopted the reform of *Hirsau. Under the abbacy of Wibald (1146-1158), it was restored and enjoyed a time of late apogee (composition of the *Liber Vitae*). In 1501, it was attached to the congregation of *Bursfeld.

H. H. Kaminsky, *Studien zur Reichsabtei Corvey in der Salierzeit*, Cologne, 1972. – K. Honselmann, L. Schütte, *Die alten Mönchslisten und die Traditionen von Corvey*, Paderborn, 1982-1992 (2 vol.). – K. Schmid, J. Wollasch, *Der Liber vitae der Abtei Corvey*, Wiesbaden, 1983-1989 (2 vol.). – T. Vogtherr, "Die Reichsklöster Corvey, Fulda und Hersfeld", *Die Salier und das Reich, Bd. 2, Die Reichskirche in der Salierzeit*, S. Weinfurter (ed.), Sigmaringen, 1991, 429-464. – M. Sagebiel, "Corvey", *Westfälisches Klosterbuch*, K. Hengst (ed.), Münster, 1992, 215-224.

Franz Neiske

**COSMOLOGY.** In the Middle Ages, the cosmos was never conceived in purely physical terms. Various theological or *metaphysical notions always marked the frontiers of the field studied by scholars, or called into question certain doctrines received from Antiquity. Thus we find cosmological discussions in the theological context of commentaries on *Peter Lombard's **Sentences* (12th c.), a treatise that students of *theology had to study and comment on. At an earlier time, it was Plato's *Timaeus*, read through Calcidius's translation (fragmentary) and Commentary (4th c.), that provided the essential principles of the physical explanation of the universe, which scholars strove to reconcile with the *Genesis account, notably in works called *Hexaemeron* that dealt with the work of the six days of *creation. Created by divine *providence, the four *elements (earth, *water, air, fire) were the material of the *heaven and the earth. It was by their movement that these elements found their consistency and their place, and they were the origin of the various things in the world and their organisation. In the course of the 13th c., the medieval conception of the world was decisively influenced by *translations of *Aristotle's treatises, mainly the *Physics* and *De caelo*, with the commentaries of *Averroes, translations made in the late 12th and early 13th centuries. The cosmos, finite and spherical, was composed of two clearly distinct parts: the celestial world, composed of 9 spheres bearing the planets (moon, Mercury, Venus, sun, Mars, Jupiter, Saturn) and the sphere of the fixed stars, which were incorruptible and moved in a uniform, eternal, circular movement; and the so-called sublunary world, of beings subject to generation and corruption, formed of the four elements. This cosmos was provided with an ordered structure, involving six *a priori* directions, up and down, right and left, before and behind, which provided simple movements with their condition of possibility: circular movement around the centre, straight movements from or towards the centre. Combined with a theory of the elements that attributed to them natural movements upwards or downwards, and a theory of natural places according to which the earth was immobile in the centre of the world, this ordered structure provided a conceptual framework that explained all the movements produced in the world. The detail of the celestial movements was the object of *astronomy, which took its methods from Ptolemy and his continuators, Arabs and then Latins. But cosmology, understood as a general conception of the universe, depended rather on *philosophia naturalis* whose problems were studied in commentaries and collections of questions bearing on various points of Aristotle's treatises. Among the most discussed subjects in the 13th and 14th cc. was the question of the *eternity of the world (admitted by Aristotle, but rejected by theology), that of the possibility of a plurality of worlds, that of the *nature of the celestial movers, of the influence of celestial movements on the sublunary world, the possibility of the void, or of an infinite space outside the world (*i.e.* beyond the last celestial sphere enveloping the Aristotelian cosmos), or that of the number of celestial spheres, *i.e.* the spheres of the planets and the spheres necessary for the machinery of the world or required by theology (motor sphere with no stars, empyrean, sphere of the celestial waters, etc.). The discussion of questions of this sort did not lead to a questioning of the principles of Aristotelian cosmology (the eternity of the world excepted), but it allowed, by the play of opinions *pro* and *contra*, the production of a detailed analysis of the physical and metaphysical notions that combined to form the cosmological theories. In the 14th c., the discussion of such questions showed great virtuosity on the part of authors who appealed to the newly acquired resources of *logic and the philosophy of *language in the exploration of physical problems.

P. Duhem, *Medieval Cosmology*, Chicago, 1987. – E. Grant, *Planets, Stars and Orbs. The Medieval Cosmos, 1200-1687*, Cambridge, 1994. – R. Simek, *Heaven and Earth in the Middle Ages*, Woodbridge, 1996. – M.-P. Lerner, *Le monde des sphères*, 2 vol., Paris, 1996-1997.

Henri Hugonnard-Roche

## COUNCIL

**The West.** Councils go back to the first years of the Church (council of Jerusalem). From the 3rd c., conciliar activity was important in both East and West. It reached its apogee between the 6th and the 15th c., a period during which councils largely dominated church life, especially by their legislation. A typology is impossible. Terminology is uncertain. The Latin *concilium* and the Greek *synodos* (*synod) were employed interchangeably. Qualifying adjectives are imprecise: universal, general, grand, plenary, perfect, provincial. The number of participants, their qualifications, the presidency were not fixed by law. The aim (and hence the nature) of councils was not always the same, and often one council had several aims. The term "ecumenical" was used from ancient times, but was not always applied to councils that rank as "ecumenical councils" in Bellarmine's list (*Controversiae*, 1586): *e.g.* the council of *Frankfurt (794) was called ecumenical. Up to Constantinople IV (869-870), the councils that figure in the list of ecumenical councils were Eastern in their meeting-place and the great majority of their members. Since that date and up to Vatican II, they have been Western from both points of view.

The ecumenical councils from the 7th to the 15th c. are successively: Constantinople III (680-681), *Nicaea II (787), Constantinople IV (869-870), *Lateran I (1123), *Lateran II (1139), *Lateran III (1179), *Lateran IV (1215), *Lyon I (1245), *Lyon II (1274), *Vienne (1311-1312), *Constance (1414-1418), *Basel-Ferrara-*Florence-Rome (1431-1445), Lateran V (1512-1517).

Our knowledge of the councils is imperfect. Usually, their legislative provisions have come down to us only through *canonical collections. At the price of what modifications, suppressions, interpolations? We do not know. We know at least that the canons of the council of Vienne underwent revisions before being inserted into the "*Clementines" and published in 1317, four and a half years after the end of the council. Of the holding of councils, the debates or silences that punctuated them, the votes and the way voting was carried out, the number and qualifications of the participants, we know little, sometimes nothing, before the great debates of Constance and Basel.

According to times and places, from the 7th to the 15th c., the frequency of councils was very uneven. Besides, how can we make a single "countability" fit the Roman synods of the late 10th c. at which *pope and emperor debated the "status and government of all *Christendom" (962), modest *provincial councils attended by three or four *bishops, and general councils at which hundreds of bishops, *abbots, *canons and laymen judged, legislated, decided on *crusades or deposed unworthy princes? In France, between 1074 and 1215, some 140 councils were held, eleven in the province of *Reims, nine in that of Bordeaux, one each for *Tours and *Arles, none for four provinces. Over a period of a century (888-987), we know of 35 provincial synods in western France, 28 in Germany and imperial Italy (eight for the province of *Mainz, one each for those of *Cologne and *Salzburg). In Capetian France, we count 76 councils between 1100 and 1150 (22 in the province of Reims, 15 in that of *Rouen, one for Tours); only nine in the province of *Toledo between 1257 and 1498 (with a total halt between 1380 and 1472, relating to the crisis of the *Great Schism and local difficulties). We observe as many differences in the number of participants (800 to 1200 at Lateran IV, 300 to 500 at Lateran I, 300 at Lateran III or at Vienne) and in their qualifications. *Archbishops and bishops were in a majority (some 300 at Nicaea II, Lateran I and III, Lyon II; but 150 at Lyon I, about 100 at Vienne), but also abbots, other *clerics, laymen representing princes (at Lateran IV, ambassadors of *Frederick II of Hohenstaufen the young king of *Sicily, the emperor of *Constantinople and the kings of *France, *Hungary, *Aragon, *Cyprus and *Jerusalem) and towns; also barons, princes (Baldwin II of Constantinople and *Raymond VII of Toulouse at Lyon II); sometimes *women, queens, *abbesses or mere laywomen. But from various testimonies it would seem that only the bishops voted. Convocation was up to the archbishop for metropolitan synods. Great meetings were called by archbishops and bishops, or by the papacy in liaison with the emperor or the king.

The council was a religious act. The liturgy fixed its manner of celebration (*ordo ad synodum* of the *Pontifical, *De modo generalis concilii celebrandi* of Guillaume *Durand). The presidency of the provincial council belonged to the archbishop. For the others, it was *metropolitans, sometimes papal *legates (for 22 councils in France between 1110 and 1150) or the pope himself (eight times in France in the same period).

There were no limits to the competence of the conciliar assembly. It was all a matter of circumstances. The council defended the faith and condemned novelties (*Aristotle's physics and metaphysics at Paris in 1209-1210). It judged culpable clerics and hostile princes (deposition of *Otto IV and *excommunication of *Raymond VI of Toulouse at Lateran IV; deposition of Frederick II at Lyon I). Its judicial function was sometimes more important than its legislative activity (in 23 councils out of 76 in France between 1100 and 1150, as against ten that took legislative measures). Other councils imposed peace (Soissons, 1155; Pont-Audemer, 1199) or preached crusade (*Clermont, 1095; Paris, 1185, 1188), opposed the Tartar invasion or struggled against the Albigenses.

We know little of the conditions in which voting was carried out. The official texts speak of "unanimous" decisions when we sometimes know from other sources that there were debates and a persistent minority of dissidents! But, as *Panormitanus wrote in 1442, "what is done by the greater and better part, the law considers as done by the whole body", or again: "Where the majority is, there we presume the Church is."

The relations between councils and popes varied. Leaving aside the tumultuous times of Constance and Basel and, at the other extreme, small provincial councils, "great" councils were not always called by the pope or presided over by him or his legates. The pope's *authority over the council was affirmed from the Gregorian period. **Dictatus papae* XVI (the "dictate of Avranches") states: "Only the pope can call universal councils. No synod can be considered valid without his consent." Gregorian *canonists developed this thesis. At the Lateran council of 1215, it was the pope who legislated, "the sacred council giving its approval". Conciliar legislation could not go against that of the *Decretals.

*Mansi*, 1759-1789 (1st ed.); 1901-1927 (t. 31 to 35 for the councils from 1439 to 1720). – *Concilia aevi carolini*, A. Werminghoff (ed.), *MGH.Conc*, 2, 1-2, 1906-1908 (re-ed. 1979). – K. J. Hefele, H. Leclercq, *A History of the Christian Councils*, 5 Vols., Edinburgh, 1871-1896. – *HCO*, G. Dumeige (dir.), 3-11, 1962-1981 (Constantinople II and III to Lateran V). – J. Vives, T. Martin, G. Martinez, *Concilios visigoticos*, Barcelona-Madrid, 1963. – *COD*, 1973 (3rd ed.); Fr. ed. Paris, 1994. – I. Schröder, *Die westfränkischen Synoden von 888 bis 987*, *MGH.H*, 3, 1980. – *Die Konzilien der Karolingischen Teilriech, 843-859*, W. Hartmann (ed.), *MGH.Conc*, 3, 1984. – *Die Konzilien Deutschland und Reichsitalien, 916-1059, t. 1, 916-960*, E. D. Hehl (ed.), *MGH.Conc*, 6, 1, 1987. – J. Gaudemet, B. Basdevant-Gaudemet, *Les Canons des conciles mérovingiens*, *SC*, 353-354, 1989 (2 vol.). – G. Alberigo, A. Melloni, L. Perrone, *Storia dei Concili Ecumenici*, Brescia, 1990. – B. Basdevant-Gaudemet, *Les Évêques, les Papes et les Princes dans la vie conciliaire en France du IVe au XIIe siècle*, *RHDF*, 69, 1991, 1-16. – *KonGe.D*, 11, W. Brandmüller (ed.), 1991. – C. Cubitt, *Anglo-Saxon Church Councils c.650-c.850*, London, 1995.

Jean Gaudemet

**Byzantium.** Councils or *synods are assemblies of *bishops and other Christians dealing with questions of doctrine and discipline. We distinguish ecumenical, episcopal, metropolitan and patriarchal councils. The *Byzantine Church recognised seven ecumenical councils: Nicaea I (325), Constantinople I (381), Ephesus (431), Chalcedon (451), Constantinople II (553) and III (680-681), *Nicaea II (787). Metropolitan councils, composed of the bishops of a *province under the presidency of a *metropolitan, met twice a year (after the 7th c., once a year). They were the courts of appeal of the episcopal councils. Among patriarchal synods, the most important was that of *Constantinople. We must distinguish the *Synodos endemousa*, a permanent assembly of bishops who advised the *patriarch, from the occasional patriarchal councils, whose decisions, sometimes, were registered in the **Synodikon* of Orthodoxy.

A. Papadakis, A. Cutler, "Councils", *The Oxford Dictionary of Byzantium*, P. Kazhdan (ed.), New York, 1991, 540-543.

Bernard Flusin

**COUNT.** The count (*comes*) was originally a palace official of the Roman emperors of the Late Empire or a military leader. Under the *Franks, from the second half of the 8th c., the Germanic institution of *Grafen* was fused with that of the Roman *comites*, giving rise to a complex system of counties. Under the *Merovingians, the count palatine was a great officer of justice, assessor of the royal court. The count was also a representative of the *king in the *towns, alongside the *bishop.

The *Carolingians preserved and enlarged the administrative structure of the Frankish kingdom, making the counts their representatives in the administrative areas (**pagi*) of the *Empire. In Italy the change came around 814, with the transformation of the Lombard dukes into Frankish or Alammanic counts.

For the most part they had royal powers and dispensed *justice in the name of the monarch, summoning free men to the comital *mallus* (*court). They had the duty of leading to war the contingent they had to raise in their administrative area, and the delegated power to impose dues, taxes and tolls. They were seconded by viscounts, *viguiers* and centenars when the extent of their jurisdiction necessitated administrative subdivisions of the *pagi*; certain counts held authority over several *pagi*, especially in the north of the Empire. The emperor recruited these trusted men, whom he could revoke, from among the upper *Austrasian aristocracy, in other words usually among his kinsmen. The counts were the king's vassals: they were linked to him personally. In return for their responsibilities (*comitatus*), the emperor conceded them fiscal lands (the comital *honour) and a share in taxes and fines, which increased their patrimonial revenues.

Despite the tutelage of the imperial envoys (bishops or **missi dominici*), the count profited from the weakening of royal power towards the end of the 9th c. to multiply his local clienteles and transform his position and his remuneration into a hereditary property. After the 10th c., the principal comital families dominated territories often more extensive than the *pagi*, and their heads behaved like independent princes, especially in the western part of the Empire. There the term "count" then became a title whose content lost its precision. Counts reigned over veritable *territorial principalities after having accumulated a number of regalian rights, like the count of *Barcelona or those of *Provence, *Anjou, Blois, *Poitiers, *Normandy or *Flanders. Lesser lords also arrogated the title by usurping the rights of *ban. In Saxon England (the *ealdorman*), in Germany or in the *Regnum Italicum*, the count still kept a function as an agent of public *authority. The title's fortunes suffered a decline from the late 11th c., and its ambivalence can be seen in the hierarchy of the 12th-c. imperial *nobility. With the autonomy of the cities, the counts ended up confined to their *castles and to the countryside, and theirs became essentially a noble title transmitted from father to son, but without political powers. Meanwhile the great ducal houses asserted themselves (*Aquitaine, Normandy, *Burgundy, *Savoy, duchy of *Milan) from the 12th, at the time of the revival of royal authority in the West.

K.F. Werner, "Missus, Marchio, Comes. Entre l'administration centrale et l'administration locale de l'empire carolingien", *Histoire comparée de l'administration (IVᵉ-XVIIIᵉ siècle), Actes du XIVᵉ colloque historique franco-allemand, Tours, mars-avril 1977*, W. Paravicini (ed.), K. Werner (ed.), Munich, 1980, 191-239. – J. L. Harouel, J. Barbey, E. Bournazel, J. Thibaut-Payen, *Histoire des institutions de l'époque franque à la Révolution*, Paris, 1987. – B. Arnold, *Count and Bishop in Medieval Germany*, Philadelphia (PA), 1991.

Thierry Pécout

**COURT OF ARCHES.** The Court of Arches was the highest ecclesiastical court of the province of *Canterbury; it developed in the second half of the 13th c., notably under the archbishopric of *John Peckham. Judging on *appeal from the various ecclesiastical courts of the *dioceses of the *province, it was in fact the supreme ecclesiastical jurisdiction in *England. It was installed in the church of St Mary of the Arches in *London, not at Canterbury; the dean of St Mary le Bow, an enclave of eleven London *parishes directly dependent on the *archbishop, presided over it and thus exercised a jurisdiction distinct from that of the *official of Canterbury. The court played a determining role in problems of *benefices; it also had a mission to protect the parties while appeals to the court of Rome were pending.

B. L. Woodcock, *Medieval Ecclesiastical Courts in the Diocese of Canterbury*, Oxford, 1952.

Jean-Philippe Genet

**COURT OF LAW.** The court was necessary for the establishment of judgment, since the medieval judge did not act alone. The word "tribunal", however, was hardly used in the Middle Ages, which is indicative of the fluidity of the content to which it refers.

As defined in the *barbarian laws and the Carolingian period, the court was public; it consisted of all free men, and the fact of sitting in the *mallus publicus* of the county and that of the *viguerie* or hundred was a constitutive element of *freedom. *Boni homines* were charged with saying what the law was. From the 10th c., *justices were diversified, the number of courts grew and they acquired a private character. These were "courts" or "councils", unstable in composition, itinerant and unspecialized. In the *castle, *familiares* peopled the seignorial court, and added to them were vassals summoned by virtue of their duty of counsel, to such an extent that the seignorial court tended to be confused with the feudal court. Men cognizant of *custom could be consulted to say what the law was and to ensure that the formalism of the accusatory procedure was respected. Judicial actions were particularly slow there, and they could be a means for lords to dominate their vassals. But, in a way, the ignorance of the courts was also a guarantee of equity. Only the ecclesiastical courts or *officialities, reserved for *clerics and for certain offences, stand out by their organisation.

The nature of lay courts changed with the teaching of law in the *universities, the requirements of inquisitorial procedure and the rise of administrative centralization. In the late Middle Ages, both in the system of *castellanies and in that of **bailliages* in France or counties in England, courts became public and were stabilized. They were then the province of a restricted group of professionals: lawyers. From now on, officials judged alone, assisted by counsellors who were professional practitioners, *advocates and attorneys, who had no part in pronouncing sentence and hence no responsibility. Sergeants charged with maintaining order and executing the judge's decisions were auxiliaries of the court. The legal education of lawyers varied according to the degree of importance of their jurisdiction. For subordinate officials, it could be mediocre. Despite an ever more rigorous definition of their composition – that of the *Parlement of Paris was fixed by the *ordinance of 1345 – and an effort to define by what majority of those present sentences should be passed, until the end of the Middle Ages courts retained the flexibility of a council, and the majority of them remained itinerant.

Y. Bongert, *Recherches sur les cours laïques du Xᵉ au XIIIᵉ siècle*, Paris, 1949. – B. Guenée, *Tribunaux et gens de justice dans le bailliage de Senlis à la fin du Moyen Âge (vers 1380-vers 1550)*, Paris, 1963. – J. Bellamy, *Crime and Public Order in England in the Later Middle Ages*, London-Toronto, 1973. – F. Autrand, *Naissance d'un grand corps de l'État. Les gens du Parlement de Paris 1345-1454*, Paris, 1981. – J. Chiffoleau, *Les Justices du Pape. Délinquance et criminalité dans la région d'Avignon au XIVᵉ siècle*, Paris, 1984.

Claude Gauvard

**COURT, ROYAL.** The prince's entourage, who give him help and advice in taking his decisions, administer *justice and rule his domains, are traditionally called the "court". In the 11th and 12th cc., the courts of the Western princes constituted a familiar and changeable group in which the great officials stand out: the steward or *seneschal (Fr. *sénéchal*, Ger. *Truchsess*) directed the provision of services; the butler (*bouteiller* or *échanson*; *Schenk*) was concerned with *wine and *food; the *chamberlain (*chambrier* or *chambellan*; *Kämmerer*) with *clothing and furnishings; the constable (*connétable*) with horses. The *chancellor directed the accounts department and the use of the *seal. From the 13th c., the unity of the *curia regis* disappeared. The prince's domestic service was separated from the State service, for which specialized institutions were created. Princes retained trusted advisers, waged and sworn in, who assisted them in the exercise of power: they formed the Council. It evolved first in *England, followed by *France. To these remote origins goes back the title of councillor given to all those who exercise powers delegated by the *king, especially his justice, while the assembly they form, met together, was always called a "court". The royal or princely residence was also called a "court". In the 14th and 15th cc. it was both a place for living in and a place of power, and served as setting for the *mise en scène* of power and for the spectacle of social hierarchy. The aim of the *ordonnances de l'Hôtel* (for France, the earliest is 1261) was both to curb expenses (100,000 francs a year in France under *Charles VI) and to assign, in this crowd of several hundred persons, a place to each according to his rank. *Chroniclers made precise records of *banquets, events and ceremonies, as well as of models of protocol for the future that served to establish "ceremonial". Court customs were more a matter for living memory, a speciality of old princesses. At the court of *Burgundy in the late 15th c., the countess of Namur (first cousin of Charles VI, born Jeanne d'Harcourt) "was the person most knowledgable about all estates in the realm of France and had a great book in which everything was written". These "court honours" were the origin of etiquette. In 1336, an ordinance of the dauphin Humbert II fixed the customs (menus, duties, costume), as well as everyone's rank and ceremonial, on the model of the court of *Naples. King *Peter IV of Aragon did the same in 1344, which earned him the surname "the Ceremonious". The equivalent existed for France before the middle of the 15th century. *Christine de Pizan describes the order of *Charles V's court, the retinues of royal journeys, the official banquets and the visits of foreign princes. She adds that two lords of the court served as veritable masters of ceremonies. This model, with that of the brilliant court of *Edward III of England, was transmitted to the court of Burgundy, splendidly ordered in the 15th c., which bequeathed its organisation and etiquette to the *Habsburgs, while in the late 15th c. the court of England fixed its very ancient ceremonial. The chief cultural centre of the 12th c., the court of *Henry II *Plantagenet, where courtly culture blossomed, saw the rebirth of the old theme of court satire. Among the *clerics of the royal entourage, the court, with its restlessness so inimical to study and *virtue, was compared to *hell and to the diabolical "*mesnie Hellequin*". The infernal vision of the court was toned down by the moralists of the 14th and 15th cc., though criticism of courtiers did not stop. But, as the scene of royal grandeur, the court was finally recognised as the "school of all courtesy".

*L'État et les aristocraties, XII*ᵉ*-XVII*ᵉ *siècle, France, Angleterre, Écosse*, Paris, 1989.

Françoise Autrand

**COURTLY LOVE.** A fact of literature and a fact of civilization, courtly love (*amour courtois*) appeared as a critical term – and received its first definition – in Gaston Paris's article on *Chrétien de Troyes's *Le Chevalier de la Charrete* (or *Lancelot*) in 1883. Paris emphasized the illegitimate character of the love between *Lancelot and Guinevere, the wife of King *Arthur; the inferior position of the lover vis-à-vis his lady; the fact that such a love made the lover more valiant and that *love was an art with a code, as also were courtesy and *chivalry. This definition led a certain number of scholars astray because they took it in a too universal sense, while it applied almost exclusively to a single *romance. In the same Chrétien's *Érec et Énide*, for example, "courtly" love is deployed in a matrimonial context in which Énide sees herself as Érec's wife as well as his *amie*.

So it is important to see what courtly love – or *fin'amors* for the *troubadours – can signify in different genres, different regions and at different times. There seems to be general agreement that a new conception of love, which seemed to value the woman much more than in previous epochs, began to blossom in the 12th century. A more refined way of life, a court life where amorous ideals that gave more importance to individuals began to mingle with older ideals of a warriors' collective, aroused new modes of thought and literary expression. This revolution marked the *courts of the French Midi as well as those of northern *France and *England. It may perhaps also be connected with family incidents: in 1152 Henry of Anjou had married *Eleanor of Aquitaine, grand-daughter of the first known troubadour, William IX of Aquitaine, after she had divorced *Louis VII of France the same year. *Henry became king of England in 1154. Moreover it was Eleanor's daughter, *Marie of Champagne, who had commissioned the *Le Chevalier de la Charrete* from Chrétien de Troyes.

Social as well as cultural facts were behind the origin of courtly love. As G. Duby has shown (1964), a class of "*youth" was formed in the 12th c. and grew because of the laws of primogeniture. Though these "youths" sought an advantageous *marriage, they often had to be content to admire and desire the wives of their lords: this is the classic situation of the troubadours' *chansons*. Moreover, the Church's growing hold over marriage might have provoked a reaction in literature, which sang of *adultery and sexual pleasure as if the constraints of morality and lineage did not exist. J. Frappier adds other social facts: "the expansion of the economy and of commercial exchanges, the tendency of the *nobility and the knights to close ranks and turn themselves into a hereditary class and codify their rules of conduct". The codification of conduct, in particular amorous conduct, already appears in Ovid whose works, especially the *Ars amatoria* and the *Remedia amoris*, circulated widely in the 12th century. The "12th-c. Renaissance" marked northern France and England much more than the Midi, with the result that courtly love there was more impregnated with Latin culture. Ovid's amorous psychology as well as his amorous stratagems entered Francophone literature but, in doing so, often lost their ludic character. The sufferings of lovers, love as sickness or war, secret love, love at first sight, the (so-called) idealization of woman, these themes constitute the repertoire of amorous fiction up to our own time. By contrast, two other traits of courtly love, the ennobling function of love and the possible sublimation of *sexuality, seem to come rather from Plato, through the Arabic poetry of medieval *Spain.

For troubadours such as Bernard de Ventadour, Jaufré Rudel or Marcabru, the lady is the *donna* or *midons* (lord) to whom they address their desires, often giving her a code name or *senhal*. In fact, in the majority of the poems the lady is effaced, transformed into a projection of masculine desire which generally remains unassuaged. Is the lady a lure of her lord, who uses her to "keep a tight rein on the young men of his household" (G. Duby), or is she rather the pretext used by poets in search of a patron (Bornstein), or indeed is she really the beloved woman who inspires the *mezura* and *cortezia* sung by the troubadours? All these scenarios seem plausible and doubtless apply to individual cases. The *poetry of the troubadours plays with a repertoire of themes: love from afar, *joi*, the sexual dream, spiritual exaltation before the lady, the threat of *losengiers*, that group of scandalmongers who lie in wait for lovers. Also mixed up in this game are the *trobairitz*, the poetesses of the 12th century. Are their voices more natural and more authentic than those of the men? As the corpus of their poems is much smaller (a score of poems) than that of the troubadours, we are less aware of a possible uniformity in their themes. In any case, we find in them frank expressions of feminine desire as well as an awareness of the dangers of masculine behaviour, real or poetic.

In the romances of northern France and England (*e.g.* the romances of antiquity, created in an *Anglo-Norman milieu), courtesy was at first deployed without being connected with the *fin'amors* of the troubadours. A little later, Chrétien de Troyes offers, in his five great romances, an exploration of love outside marriage (*Lancelot*), within marriage (*Érec et Énide*, *Yvain*) and in an almost sacred setting (**Perceval ou le Conte du Graal*). After Chrétien, the romancers embroider variations on the themes of the valour aroused by love, service of the lady (in the form of *tournaments or adventures), the obedience owed to her, etc. Towards 1186 we find a codification of what today would be called courtly love in Andreas Capellanus's *De arte honeste amandi*. Essentially in the form of dialogues and debates held at "courts of love" (peopled by fictional transpositions of real people like Marie de Champagne), books I and II emphasize the fundamentally adulterous character of that love. The third book offers an altogether conventional condemnation of love and exalts the spiritual life. Conceived as a game in the Ovidian manner, this text has often been interpreted as a wholly serious scholastic discussion, which seems rather to falsify its ludic character.

Love as a game with its rules and linked to a refined court life also stands out in the allegorical literature of the 13th c. (above all in the *Roman de la Rose* of Guillaume de Lorris and Jean de Meun) and the 14th c., where poets like *Guillaume de Machaut and Jean *Froissart (in his amorous "dits") play with the traditional roles of poet, lover and patron, and offer us a new equation of love and poetry as art.

Towards the end of the Middle Ages, *Christine de Pizan and Alain Chartier put the problem of courtly love on a new basis. For Christine, such a love is dangerous: *women too easily let themselves be caught in the snare of courtly language which, as she demonstrates in her *Épistre au Dieu d'Amour* (1399) and the *Livre des trois vertus* (1405), is only words and does not attest a true love. Far from being at the service of woman, courtly love is revealed here as an abuse of women intended to satisfy masculine vanity. But when in Alain Chartier's *La Belle Dame sans merci* (1424) the lady refuses the knight – exposing the lying character of the courtly code and language – the latter dies: thus the problem of courtly love eluded any facile resolution, even on the threshold of the *Renaissance.

Andreas Capellanus, *Andreas Capellanus on Love*, P.G. Walsh (ed.), London, 1982.

J. Frappier, "Vues sur les conceptions courtoises dans les littératures d'oc et d'oil au XIIe siècle", *CCM*, 2, 1959, 135-156. – R. Nelli, *L'Érotique des troubadours*, Toulouse, 1963. – G. Duby, "Dans la France du Nord-Ouest au XIIe siècle: les "Jeunes" dans la société aristocratique", *Annales*, 19, 1964, 835-846. – M. Lazar, *Amour courtois et* fin amors *dans la littérature du XIIe siècle*, Paris, 1964. – G. Duby, "La femme, l'amour et le chevalier", *L'histoire*, 1, 1978, 6-13. – D. Bornstein, "Courtly Love", *DMA*, 3, 1983, 668-674. – P. L. Allen, *The Art of Love*, Philadelphia, 1992. – P. Cherchi, *Andreas and the Ambiguity of Courtly Love*, Toronto, 1994.

Renate Blumenfeld-Kosinski

**CRACOW.** The town of Cracow is situated in Little Poland, on the left bank of the Vistula, in a place where the eponymous founder (Krak/Krok) traditionally defeated a *dragon. Tumuli and other sites studied by *archaeology allow us to date the first human settlements on these fertile valley terraces to the 7th and 8th centuries. Later, a first *castrum* was established in the 8th c., then an occupied fortified site (Okół) at the foot of the *castrum*, in the 10th c., where a cache of four tonnes of axes was found: not properly tools, rather a sort of money for barter. Cracow must then have been the centre of power of the Vislani who extended to the borders of *Rus': it is cited by Ibrahim ibn Laqub in 965-966. In the first half of the 10th c., the Vislani passed under Czech rule and, from 973, were included in the diocese of Olomouc in *Moravia. The first *bishop dependent on the metropolitan see of *Gniezno was installed at Cracow around the year 1000. The town was then part of the Polish State of *Mieszko I, and under Casimir the Restorer in the 1140s it became the capital of *Poland.

On the hill of Wawel remain several vestiges of 10th-c. churches. The cathedral of St Wenceslas (a title betraying Czech influence) was begun early in the 11th c. and continued on a plan of Rhenish type. It was dedicated secondly to St *Stanislas after the *canonization of that martyr bishop in 1254, and became the main cult-centre of the saint who was, with St *Adalbert, the patron of Poland. In 1320 King Ladislas the Short, then all his successors, were crowned there, near the tomb of St Stanislas. Thanks to the care the bishops lavished on their *school and the establishment of a rich *library, the cathedral became a brilliant intellectual centre, particularly in the sphere of *historiography (John *Długosz, d. 1480). On the east part of the hill rose the ducal, then royal *palace, whose foundations date from the 11th c. and which was the object of great works under *Casimir the Great in the 14th century.

The built-up area also numbered 18 churches, and a Jewish colony is attested there from the 11th century. Al-Idrisi presents Cracow as a flourishing town "with many houses as well as many inhabitants, *markets, vineyards and *gardens". The communal movement manifested itself there in the early 13th c., a time when the *Dominicans and then the *Franciscans came to settle there. After the *Mongol incursion of 1241, a new town plan was defined by Boleslas the Chaste (1257) who also granted the town numerous legal and commercial privileges. A revolt in 1311-1312 led to the reduction of urban autonomy, but this prevailed once more in the 14th and 15th centuries, favoured by a spectacular development of local crafts and *commerce as well as international trade with Italy, Hungary and the Black Sea regions. A *university was founded in 1364 and quickly enjoyed a vast influence; the arts also shone there (high altar of Veit *Stoss in St Mary's church) and the town was surrounded by satellite cities, one of which, Kazimierz, housed a particularly prosperous Jewish community in the 15th c., after its eviction from the metropolis.

A. Gieysztor, "La Pologne médiévale", *Histoire de la Pologne*, Warsaw, 1971. – *Histoire religieuse de la Pologne*, J. Kłoczowski (dir.), Paris, 1987. – J. Wyrozumski, *Dzieje Krakowa. Kraków do schyłku wieków średinch* [History of Cracow, Cracow up to the decline of the Middle Ages], Cracow, 1992.

Aleksander Gieysztor †

## CREATION

**Theology.** A fundamental inquiry into origins, the question of Creation came down through the ages and took on particular acuteness in the Middle Ages, with the theme of Mirrors of the world, the controversy over the *eternity of the world and, more generally, the problem of *being.

This reflection on Creation had already been one of the poles of patristic thought. But while the *Fathers opted for a commentary on *Genesis in the framework of the *Hexaemeron*, medieval authors preferred the form of **quaestiones*, which set out a fundamental discussion of the problem.

St Augustine, who synthesized patristic thought on the Creation and left his mark on the Middle Ages, had already turned, in the *De Genesi ad litteram*, to the genre of *quaestiones*. More radically, the transition was made by several authors: *John Scotus Eriugena who championed the rights of *reason and interpreted Creation in a speculative way, St *Anselm who deployed all the resources of reason to understand Creation and *Redemption, *Abelard who inaugurated a systematic use of *dialectic.

With the great syntheses of the 13th c., which combined *philosophy and *theology, the theology of Creation was clarified: *Hugh of Saint-Victor used the two "books" of Scripture and Creation to give his school his intellective theology, and Thierry of Chartres interpreted Creation in terms of *God's universal causality. *Platonism remained a reference, largely reformulated in their work.

This reference tended to disappear with the difference established by *Peter Lombard between *facere* and *creare*, producing and creating, *i.e.* creating *ex nihilo*. This last specification of *ex nihilo* was taken up and systematized at the fourth *Lateran council, before being made explicit by St *Thomas Aquinas.

From before the dawn of the 13th c., the influence of *Aristotle became decisive with the development of Latin *Averroism and the controversy over the eternity of the world, introduced by *Siger of Brabant; against it St *Bonaventure and St Thomas were led to take up a position, the former replying in the negative, the latter specifying that the assertion of a beginning was a matter of faith.

In the *Summa contra gentiles* (book II) and the *Summa theologiae* (I[a], q. 44-48), St Thomas disengaged the ontological dimension of creation, by showing that God was the *Ipsum esse* or the *actus essendi* that gave being to creatures. So Creation was defined essentially as a relation between created being and the Creator. St Augustine had already specified this, St Thomas disentangled its theological implications.

In the 14th c., *Eckhart returned to the results of the Thomist synthesis, but after a Dionysian rereading of the problem he introduced negativity into his understanding of Creation. *Ontology, *ethics and *mysticism interfere in his work, where he makes detachment the condition of accomplishment of created being.

A. D. Sertillanges, *Les grandes thèses de la philosophie thomiste*, Paris, 1928. – C. Fabro, *La nozione metafisica di partecipazione secondo san Tommaso d'Aquino*, Milan, 1939. – C. Fabro, *Dall'essere all'esistente*, Brescia, 1965 (2nd ed.). – L. Scheffczyk, *Création et Providence*, Paris, 1967. – R. C. Dales, *Medieval Discussions on the Eternity of the World*, Leiden, 1990. – A. De Muralt, *Néoplatonisme et aristotélisme dans la métaphysique médiévale. Analogie, causalité et participation*, Paris, 1995.

Marie-Anne Vannier

**Iconography.** Of the Creation account in the book of *Genesis, what concerns us here is the first account, the Hexaemeron, (Gen 1, 1-24), which describes *God's creative work over six days, the ordering of the world that succeeded the original chaos. On the first day, God created *light (Gen 1, 2-5); on the second day he separated the waters and the *heaven (Gen 1, 6-8); on the third day, he separated the waters and the Earth (Gen 1, 9-13); on the fourth day, God set in the firmament the Sun, the Moon and the stars (Gen 1, 14-19); on the fifth day, he created the birds and the fish (Gen 1, 20-23); on the sixth day, the animals that would inhabit the dry land (Gen 1, 24-25), and finally man "in his image": "Man and woman he created them" (Gen 1, 27). On the seventh day, God rested (Gen 2, 3): this day was blessed and sanctified.

*The Six Days of Creation and the story of Adam and Eve.* Mosaic in the cupola of the west narthex, St Mark's basilica, Venice. 13th c.

Depictions of the first verses of Genesis abound both in the Byzantine world and in the West, and are of great richness: they draw their essence from the biblical text, but may also be inspired by Christian *exegesis and sometimes by the scientific and philosophical ideas of Antiquity.

All-powerful God presides over the creative act. He is generally seen in action, in contrast to the repose of the seventh day. Thus, the *Logos* can be seen tracing out the world with a compass: the architect's tool was then the attribute of creative activity. God appears with the characteristics of *Christ with the *nimbus, or from the 14th c. as an old man, sometimes wearing a *tiara.

Despite the diversity and complexity of depictions of the first creation narrative, it is possible to separate some procedures that translate the works of the six days into images. These are often surrounded by disks suggesting the circularity of the universe. For the first day, while the creation of light can be identified with that of the *angels, the juxtaposition of two areas, one light, the other dark, can illustrate the separation of light and darkness. A single formula also suggests the separation of the waters and the heaven. For the third day, the emerging land can be inscribed in a circle surrounded by the sea which appears in undulating chevrons; *trees can also materialize the creation of the Earth and its fertile flora. The stars are commonly represented to illustrate the work of the fourth day. Birds, fishes, quadrupeds, of which several species are sometimes discerned, as well as *man, are the constant figures of the activity of the fith and sixth days.

Two main types of iconographical programme can be distinguished. Many cycles set out an inventory of the successive acts of Creation ordered in clear and separate visions. This interpretation of the stages of the formation of the world appears *e.g.* in the Byzantine Octateuchs of the 11th and 12th cc., on the *frescos of the abbey church of *Saint-Savin-sur-Gartempe (12th c.), or in sculpted groups. On the south window of the west front of *Laon cathedral (1200), the figure of the *Logos* is reproduced on each of the ten archstones of the second arch moulding, six of which refer literally to the first account of Creation. For the first four days, God holds disks in which are emblematically inscribed the cosmic works; on the fifth day he holds a bird and a fish; on the sixth he is accompanied by some goats and by man.

By contrast, other depictions insist on the immediacy of God's creative activity: the works of the six days are integrated into a harmonious composition, forming an organised and coherent whole. In a German Bible of Anton Koberger (15th c.), the world is ordered into concentric spheres, in line with medieval scientific ideas on the ordering of the universe. In the outermost circumference are God and the angels; then comes the circle of the heaven constellated with stars, then the circle of the oceans peopled with fishes, and finally in the centre the verdant and well-stocked Earth, where the incarnate *Word extracts the woman from the side of the sleeping man, this last episode coming from the second Creation narrative.

While many iconographical cycles make clear choices, others combine different perspectives. In a 15th-c. historiated Bible (Paris, BNF, ms. lat. 9471), God blesses the man and the woman surrounded by birds and quadrupeds who people the Earth's surface; but four disks are integrated into this setting in order to recall the cosmic works of the first days.

Finally, some representations offer very complex Creation structures. The two lower registers of an *illumination of *Honorius Augustodunensis's *Clavis physicae* (12th c.) provide an example: the works of Creation are associated with the four *elements that make up the universe, while Christ holds six bunches ending in *fleurs de lys* representing the six days of Creation. More than an illustration of the Genesis account, this symbolic depiction sets out a scientific and theological synthesis of medieval ideas on the *order of the world.

Fanny Caroff

**Italy.** The medieval iconography of creation appears in illuminated *codices, cycles of paintings and *mosaics and in sculpture. In early medieval sculpture, interesting depictions of the creation cycle occur on an 8th-c. relief in Terracina cathedral, the altar-frontal of Salerno cathedral (1100), where there are also writings referring to the division of light from darkness, the capitals and reliefs of the façade of *Modena cathedral, carved by Wiligelmo in 1106, contemporary ones on the façade of Cremona cathedral, the bronze panels of the doors of San Zeno at *Verona and those by Bonanno Pisano at *Monreale cathedral. Particularly important mosaics are those of Monreale cathedral and the Palatine Chapel at *Palermo (12th c.), and those in the cupola of the atrium of St Mark's at *Venice (13th c.), derived from earlier manuscript depictions. In basilica paintings, the cycle appears with important depictions at *Rome, in the frescos of San Giovanni a Porta Latina (1191-1198), those of the abbey of San Pietro at Ferentillo and others of the grotto of San Lorenzo in the crypt of *Anagni cathedral. In the lower church at *Assisi, a late 13th-c. fresco shows the creation with *Christ in majesty at the centre enclosed in a *nimbus of cherubim. In the Gothic period, apart from miniatures, the episodes of the creation often appear in the ornamental sculptures of Northern cathedrals (Notre-Dame at *Paris, *Amiens, *Chartres, *Auxerre, Fribourg) and in *stained glass, among which that of Ulm cathedral has an original iconography. In Italy, there are important reliefs by Lorenzo Maitani on the façade of *Orvieto cathedral and by Andrea da Pontedera and *Giotto on the Florentine campanile. In the *Renaissance, depiction of the whole episodic narration was abandoned in favour of single scenes from the cycle, in sculpture or painting.

M. Mentré, *Création et Apocalypse: histoire d'un regard humain sur le divin*, Paris, 1984. – A. Grabar, *Le vie della creazione nell'iconografia cristiana. Antichità e Medioevo*, Milan, 1986. – *Enciclopedia dell'arte medievale*, Rome, 1992.

Maria Cristina Buschi

**CRÉCY, BATTLE OF.** The battle of Crécy, 26 Aug 1346, was the first major land battle of the *Hundred Years' War between England and France. English troops, led by *Edward III and the *Black Prince, defeated the numerically superior French forces of *Philip VI of France. The success of the English longbowmen (firing more than half a million arrows from a good defensive position), combined with a lack of coherent leadership on the French side, resulted in more than 10,000 French losses, compared with approximately 500 English losses. Philip VI was forced to retreat, while the English forces proceeded to the siege of Calais.

C. Allmand, *The Hundred Years War*, Cambridge, 1988. – R. Neillands, *The Hundred Years War*, London, 1990.

Laura Napran

***CREDO*, CREED.** Four creeds had referential value in the Middle Ages, both as texts for personal and liturgical *prayer and as confession of faith and norm of orthodoxy. The core of the *Apostles' Creed went back to the 3rd c. and arose out of the liturgy. Its definitive text, with the addition of the **Filioque*, was later. It was long learnt by heart to be "given back" at *baptism (*redditio symboli*). Throughout the Middle Ages, learning it was one of the main objectives of catechesis. Pastors and theologians composed many commentaries on it. From the 11th c., the Creed of Nicaea-Constantinople was introduced into the liturgy, to be sung by the congregation on *Sundays and *feast days. A rampart against the *Arian heresy, charged with greater dogmatic precision and serving as touchstone in relations with *schismatics and *heretics, this Creed was forged in the East, where many other creeds were current – though not the Apostles' Creed. The Nicene-Constantinopolitan Creed reached the West through Spain and England. *Alcuin seems to have played a role in its "importation" into the Frankish Empire. It was another two centuries (Benedict VIII in 1014) before the Church of Rome adopted it and prescribed its singing *ad publicam missam*, at least on the feasts that it mentions (Christmas, *Easter, *Pentecost . . .). Its use was then ceaselessly extended. This was the first creed to be set to *music, soon very sumptuously, which led to its gradual confiscation by the choir.

Two other texts stand out in the well-stocked library of medieval confessions of faith. The *Quicumque vult*, still called the Athanasian Creed, longer than the other two, remained a matter for theologians and *clerics, who had it in their *breviaries. The fourth referential creed was the canon *Firmiter* of *Lateran IV (1215), promulgated against the Albigensian heresy, and reproduced at the head of the *Decretals. From the late 14th c., the idea of the four creeds was abandoned. In the 15th c., *Denis the Carthusian mentions only the first three.

J.-A. Jungmann, *The Mass of the Roman Rite*, London, 1959. – J. N. D. Kelly, *Early Christian Creeds*, 3rd ed., London, 1972. – J.-C. Schmitt,

"Du bon usage du Credo", *Faire croire. Modalités de la diffusion et de la réception des messages religieux du XIIe au XVe siècle*, Rome, 1981, 337-361 (for the inculcation of the Credo in pastoral care). – F. Boespflug, "Autour de la traduction pictorale du Credo au Moyen Âge (XIIe-XVe siècle)", *Rituels*, P. de Clerck (ed.), É. Palazzo (ed.), Paris, 1990, 55-84. – *Pensée, image et communication in Europe médiévale*, Besançon, 1993.

François Boespflug

**CRESCAS, HASDAI (died 1412?).** A Jewish philosopher, he died at *Saragossa after having held important positions (spiritual and secular) at the head of the communities of *Spain, notably during the persecutions of 1391. His main work (in Hebrew), *Or Adonai* (The Light of the Lord), is theological; it aims to demonstrate the veracity of the main dogmas of *Judaism and contains a rigorous critique of *Aristotelianism (notably of its physics). We also owe him a work of anti-Christian polemic (written in Catalan, preserved in a Hebrew translation of 1451), *The Refutation of Christian Dogmas*, in ten chapters.

S. Fischer (ed.), *Or Adonai*, Jerusalem, 1990. – *The Refutation of Christian Principles by Hasdai Crescas*, D. J. Lasker (tr.), Albany (NY), 1992.

H. A. Wolfson, *Crescas' Critique of Aristotle*, Cambridge (MA), 1929. – E. Schweid, "The Religious Philosophy of Hasdai Crescas", *Or Adonai*, Jerusalem, 1970. – C. Sirat, *La Philosophie juive médiévale en pays de chrétienté*, Paris, 1988, 176-189. – M. Tobiass, *Crescas: un philosophe juif dans l'Espagne mediévale*, Paris, 1995.

Gilbert Dahan

**CRESCENTII.** A Roman family prominent in the 10th and 11th centuries. The name Crescentius appears for the first time in Roman documents among the signatories to a sentence passed by the Emperor Louis III in 901, in the portico of the imperial palace built by *Charlemagne near *St Peter's. This Crescentius was one of the citizen judges who assisted the emperor in discussing the case brought before the sovereign: so he must have been a prominent person and enjoyed a certain reputation in the city.

Not until 40 years later, when *Rome was ruled by the *princeps* *Alberic, does another Crescentius appear, again present at a sentence, passed this time by the *princeps* himself. At the Roman synod of 963, presided over by the Emperor *Otto I to judge the deeds of Pope John XII, there appears, among the various notables of the city, Crescentius *caballi marmorei*. This nickname very probably derives from his residence in the area of the Quirinal, where were the famous statues of the Dioscuri and their horses, originally from the baths of Constantine. After the death of Otto I (972), various characters of this name begin to play a high-profile role in Roman political life. In June 974, a certain Crescentius *de Theodora*, thought to be the son of the brother of Crescentius *de caballo marmoreo*, led a revolt in Rome against the legitimate *pope, Benedict VI, which led to the election of an *antipope (Boniface VII). The revolt failed thanks to the intervention of *Otto II, but Crescentius suffered no direct consequences, which suggests a well-rooted and respected power. Certainly his family even then had large possessions in Sabina and was extending its interests to the territory of Velletri.

Up to the death of Otto II, the family remained in the shade, to re-emerge at the time of the difficult succession to Benedict VII (the years 984-985). Pope John XV (985-996) had been elected thanks to pressure from John, son of Crescentius *de Theodora*, who managed to obtain the patriciate of the Romans (985), corresponding to the responsibility, received from the pope, for the secular affairs of Rome and its territory. John's death in *c.*990 saw the emergence of his brother, called Crescentius II, who held the county of Terracina and the rectorate of Sabina. In 988 he took the title that had been *Alberic II's, that of *senator omnium Romanorum*. In the 990s he manifestly controlled papal policy and, notwithstanding the interventions of *Otto III, resisted until 998 when the sovereign took armed possession of the city and had him killed. The family's fortunes only recovered after Otto's death, with Crescentius's son John who held the patriciate again between 1001 and 1012 and ramified the presence of his *familiares* in control of positions in Rome and its territory. His death decreed the end of the predominance of his family group in Rome, supplanted by the house of *Tusculum, who for the next 30 year perpetuated the same political line, aiming at a papacy that was essentially an expression of the city's aristocracy.

G. Bossi, "I Crescenzi di Sabina stefaniani e ottaviani", *ASRSP*, 41, 1918, 111-170. – P. Brezzi, *Roma e l'Impero medioevale*, Bologna, 1947. – P. Brezzi, "Aspetti della vita politica e religiosa di Roma tra la fine del sec. X e la prima metà del sec. XI", *Bollettino della badia greca di Grottaferrata*, 9, 1955, 115-126.

Federico Marazzi

**CRETE.** Occupying a key position at the heart of the Mediterranean, the island of Crete was greatly coveted. A Byzantine possession, it suffered *Slav incursions early in the 7th c. and raids by Mu'awiya's Arab fleet in 651, before being occupied by the Arabs between 823 and 828. For Byzantium the event marked the loss of one of the most strategic points in the east Mediterranean and a consequent weakening of the Byzantine thalassocracy. For a century and a half, the island became an emirate, a haven for Arab corsairs, against which Byzantine attempts at reconquest (844, 865, 949) failed. But in 961 Nicephorus Phocas, at the head of a great expedition, retook Candia and brought the island under Byzantine rule again. Crete was then a "*theme", under the authority of a *strategos*. It was repopulated by transplanting Greeks and Armenians there, and rechristianized under the direction of a *metropolitan assisted by twelve *suffragan bishops.

At the time of the fourth *crusade, Boniface of Montferrat obtained from the **basileus* Alexius IV *Angelus the right to occupy Crete. Deprived of means, he ceded the island to *Venice in August 1204 for 1000 silver marks. The occupation of Crete was made difficult by the resistance of the Greeks led by their *archontes* and by the intervention of the Genoese. Venice decided to send military colonists; from 1208, she divided the island into six *sestiers*, themselves divided into *turms* and castellanies. She reserved the lands around Candia for herself and divided the rest of the territory between the Latin Church and the Venetian feudatories. She set up a strong administration led by a "duke of Candia", favoured the Latin Church and forbade the installation of *bishops of *Orthodox obedience. The Greek *archontes*, excluded from government, rose up several times: the Cortazzi between 1264 and 1278, the Kallergis between 1282 and 1299 and again between 1364 and 1367. The Venetian feudatories, oppressed by the demands of the metropolis, also took up arms against her in 1363. After this date there was a rapprochement between the two ethnic groups that allowed Venice to hold the island as an enclave in the *Ottoman world until 1669.

Crete played a great role in the international economy of the late Middle Ages. Considered the granary of the Venetian empire, it was the primary provider of agricultural produce (corn, wine and oil) for the metropolis. Each year two convoys of Venetian galleys (*mudae*), those of *Cyprus and *Alexandria, passed through her *ports. She was also the natural base for the hulls and unarmed ships of Venetian businessmen who came to ship from her warehouses (Canea, Candia, Retimo) the most precious products: *spices, Brazil wood, *silk and cotton from Egypt or *Syria, *salt and sugar from Cyprus, horses, slaves and alum from Asia Minor. In the medieval world, Crete was in many respects another Venice.

F. Thiriet, *La Romanie vénitienne au Moyen Âge*, Rome, 1959. – J. Tulard, *Histoire de la Crète*, Paris, 1962 ("QSJ", 1018). – D. Tsougarakis, *Byzantine Crete. From the Vth Century to the Venetian Conquest*, Athens, 1988. – M. Gallina, *Una società coloniale nel trecento, Creta fra Venezia e Bisanzio*, Venice, 1989. – D. Stöckly, *Le système de l'Incanto des galées du marché a Venise (fin XIII*e*-milieu XV*e *siècle)*, Leiden, 1995.

Michel Balard

**CRIB.** The manger for animals in which Jesus was placed at his birth (Lk 2, 7-13). The crib of Bethlehem was a very frequent place of *pilgrimage from the 2nd century. In the Middle Ages, pretended *relics of it were preserved in several sanctuaries, notably at *Rome, at *Santa Maria Maggiore where the little *oratory of Sancta Maria ad Praesepe, cut into the side of the basilica in imitation of the Bethlehem grotto, contributed greatly to propagating devotion to the crib. Comparison between the crib and the *altar, frequent in medieval art, was part of a long scriptural tradition which, since the *Fathers, had associated the image of the Child Jesus with that of the *host. The analogy also recurs in the liturgy and seems to be the origin of the temporary construction in churches of three-dimensional representations, memorials to the *Nativity. The invention of this is attributed to St *Francis of Assisi who instituted the first living crib during the celebration of Christmas *mass at Greccio in 1223.

The presence in representations of the crib of the ass and the ox, not mentioned in the gospel, led to many commentaries by medieval authors. The liturgy definitively confirmed the usage by mentioning the two animals in a *response of the feast of Christmas. Fixed cribs, as we know them today, appeared in churches in the 15th c. at the same time as the rise of the cult of the Infancy, while figurines of the Child Jesus multiplied, especially in Italy.

*DACL*, 3, 1914, 3021-3029. – *Cath.*, 3, 1952, 288-291. – *DSp*, 2, 1953, 2520-2526.

Dominique Rigaux

**CRIMEA.** Called Gazaria in Western sources, Crimea saw Venetian *merchants establish themselves on its shores (at Soldaia), followed by Genoese (at *Caffa). For Latin missionaries it became the normal route to the *Mongol khanate of the *Golden Horde. From 1280, friars minor settled at Soldaia, in 1287 at Caffa, in the 14th c. at Cembalo, then at Solgat and Illice. In 1317 the papacy erected a *bishopric at Caffa, another at Soldaia before 1393, while in 1333 the ecclesiastical *province of Vosporo was created and before the 14th c. that of Solgat, in the heart of Tartar Crimea. The network of mendicant provinces and bishoprics in Crimea was modelled on that of the Genoese "counters" north of the Black Sea, and did not survive their disappearance in 1475.

J. Richard, *La Papauté et les missions d'Orient au Moyen Âge (XIII*e*-XV*e *siècles)*, Rome, 1977. – M. Balard, *La Romanie génoise (XII*e*-début de XV*e *siècle)*, Genoa-Rome, 1978 (2 vol.). – C. Delacroix-Besnier, *Les Dominicains et la chrétienté grecque aux XIV*e *et XV*e *siècles*, Rome, 1997.

Michel Balard

**CROATS.** The Croats (in Croatian *Hrvati*), an ancient people whose ethnic origin is not completely explained, left their original home north of the Carpathians (White Croatia, near *Cracow, in the upper Vistula basin) to settle between the 6th and 7th cc. in Illyricum, a part of Southern Europe under Byzantine rule, between the Eastern Adriatic (Roman *Dalmatia and *Istria) and the Drava and Danube (Roman *Pannonia). At this time, they presented Slav characteristics and formed, with other *Slav peoples, the historical area of the South Slavs.

The region that from the 7th c. became the political and cultural area of the Croats saw the appearance of written culture and Christian civilization in late Antiquity. The Greeks, entering the Eastern Adriatic in the 4th c. BC, had founded colonies there (Issa, Pharos, Tragurion, Epetion), witnesses to Hellenic culture. The Romans, attaching Istria to the Dalmatian coast, had conquered the interior of the Illyrian lands and the Pannonian countries at the beginning of the Christian era. Romanization and early *Christendom homogenized the territory between the Adriatic and the Danube into a cultural entity that would be decisive for the coming centuries. The centres of development were Salona, Siscia, Sirmium, Parentium, Pola, Iadera, Narona, Epidaurum, Mursa. The *basilicas and *cemeteries of Christian antiquity, the saints and *martyrs of early Christian *hagiography, destined to become the patrons of Dalmato-Croatian cities, trace a continuity between Antiquity and medieval Croatian Christian culture.

In the 7th and 8th cc., the Croats have no written sources, but Christianization had already begun, as had the formation in the central Adriatic of the core of the Croatian State, which took the name of *Regnum Croatorum* in the mid 9th century. The adherence of the Croats to medieval Christian civilization, and their political history at the time of the rulers of Croatian blood, were largely determined by the Croatian area where the political, state, ecclesiastical and jurisdictional interests of *Franks, Byzantium and papal *Rome intersected and where two European cultural spheres met each other: the Greek East and the Latin West. With the peace of Aachen (812), Croatian territory fell under the authority of the Franks, while the towns of Krk, Osor, Rab, Zadar, Trogir, Split, *Dubrovnik and Kotor remained the Byzantine "*theme" of Dalmatia. Christianization from Friuli and Aquileia (added to the earlier Christianization from the Dalmatian towns) was completed under Prince Borna in the early 9th century. Adriatic or Dalmatian Croatia, governed by the Trpimirović dynasty, became a principality of Carolingian type, then a kingdom (925). The most powerful Croatian rulers – Trpimir, Domagoj, Branimir, Tomislav, Petar Krešimir IV, Zvonimir – united the Croatian territories over a period of three centuries: in the south-east, Dalmatia, the territories as far as the rivers Vrbas, Usora and Neretva; in the west, part of Istria; in the north, Pannonian Croatia as far as the Drava and Danube. In *c.*1102, when the Croatian dynasty died out, the Croats joined the Hungarians in a personal union, under the *crown of the Árpád dynasty (the *Angevins of Naples reigned from 1301 and the *Habsburgs from 1527), but the Croatian State kept its political individuality with its ban and its assembly. *Venice coveted Istria and Dalmatia from the 12th c. and, when the Hungarian-Croatian King Ladislas the Magnanimous sold it "his rights" over Dalmatia (1409), the Most Serene Republic finally consolidated its position on the east coast of the Adriatic.

The Christianized Croats, integrated into Latin *spirituality, entered on the scene of history in the 9th century. Their first written expression was *Latin, issuing from Antiquity and the Roman tradition in Dalmatia, but also the Frankish *missions. From the 9th to the 12th c., beginning with Trpimir (*dux Chroatorum*) in 852 and Branimir, princes, kings and Church dignitaries confirm the existence and ecclesiastical organisation of the Croatian State by *epigraphy, documents of rulers, their correspondence with the Roman *Curia, and sacred buildings. Religious and cultural life flourished thanks to the Benedictines who settled at the invitation of Prince Trpimir (845-864), at whose court worked one of the most learned Benedictines of the 9th c., Gottschalk (Godescalsus Fuldensis). The Croats were instructed in Latin, as Pope John X recommended to King Tomislav in 925, dignitaries were trained at Cividale, Croatian princes wrote their names in the famous Codex Aquileiensis (5th-6th c.). Prince Branimir gained independence and put the Croat principality and its Church, with Nin as *bishopric, permanently beneath the wing of the Roman Church and Western Christian civilization (879). The Dalmatian bishops, enfeoffed to *Constantinople until 923, were brought under the jurisdiction of Rome by Pope John X (councils of Split, 925 and 928). He re-established the antique metropolis of Salona for them at Split and, after having suppressed the bishopric of Nin, accorded the *archbishop of Split *metropolitan rights over the Dalmato-Croatian Church. Thus was formed a single Croato-Dalmatian ecclesiastical area which gradually became ethno-cultural, comprising Byzantine Dalmatia and the lands of the Croat rulers and determining for the coming centuries the territory, extent and history of Croatian culture.

Medieval Croatian Latinism, the richest in the Slav world, issuing from late Antiquity, later drew on the sources of contemporary European Latin literature. The first hagiographies and texts on the history of the Church of Split appeared in the Dalmatian towns. Following the *Evangeliarium Spalatense* (6th-7th cc.), liturgical manuscripts were written in numerous Benedictine **scriptoria* and cathedral *chapters (at Split, Trogir, Osor, Zadar – the "Croatian Monte Cassino"), in the spirit of the *Carolingian Renaissance and the Ottonian Renaissance. They shine by their literary riches, the beauty of their lettering (with the particular form of the Dalmatian Beneventan *script), their *illuminations (traces of Byzantine, but also Italian and French, influence) and the refinement of their written expression. The Croatian Latinists also produced legal, philosophical, scientific, and in particular historiographical works, creating a supra-regional Croatian culture. In Pannonian northern Croatia, the beginnings of the written expression and ecclesiastical and cultural life of the Croatian people are linked to the bishopric of Zagreb, founded in 1093-1094 when the Árpád dynasty was extended to the Croato-Dalmatian kingdom under King *Ladislas I Árpád, brother-in-law of the Croatian King Zvonimir (re-establishment of the antique and medieval bishopric of Sisak). The earliest *liturgical books of Zagreb drew their roots, through *Hungary, from the Benedictine *scriptoria* of northern France (archbishopric of *Rouen); but contact was also rapidly established with the Dalmatian *scriptoria* of southern Croatia. The bishopric of Zagreb possessed its own rite until 1788, when it adopted that of the Roman Curia. In the 13th and 14th cc., it was a great centre of written culture and teaching. In the 13th c. the *chapter of Čazma was created, becoming the new cultural centre of medieval Slavonia. The Benedictines, *Cistercians, Paulians, *Franciscans and *Dominicans were the promoters of this development.

Medieval Croatian written culture was trilingual (Croatian, Latin, Church Slavonic in Croatian redaction) and presents three

Church of St Donatus at Zadar (Dalmatia), seen from the south-west. Mid 8th c.

scripts (Latin, Glagolitic, western-type Cyrillic). The Croatian principality and the bishopric of Nin saw, probably from the 8th and 9th cc., the beginnings of a missionary literature in the Slav language. It received new strength in the second half of the 9th c. with the culture of Cyrillo-Methodian tradition – works in Old Church Slavonic written in Glagolitic characters, liturgy in the Slav language – that conquered Istria, Kvarner and the Dalmatian coast and penetrated deeply into the continental hinterland. Thus, Latin and Old Church Slavonic in Croatian redaction – the latter very early replaced by the vernacular in non-liturgical texts – remained traditional in the Croatian Catholic Church and in medieval Croatian literature. In the early Middle Ages, Croatian literature, genetically linked to the Cyrillo-Methodian tradition and to Byzantine and Slav sources (biblical, liturgical, *apocryphal and hagiographical texts), was an integral part of Slav literature. But from its beginnings, and in particular at the apogee of the Middle Ages, it was open to Western Europe. Biblical texts, translated from the Greek Septuagint, were adapted to the Latin *Vulgate, the Franciscan redactions of the plenary *missal and the plenary *breviary were adopted, as well as new subject-matter and new literary genres. The Benedictines, then the Franciscans in particular, wrote pious works but also secular texts, belonging to the European culture of *chivalry. Latin and Italian literature, French themes and Franco-Italian literature furnished models directly; indeed, all of Western European literature exercised its influence indirectly. The Croatian *editio princeps* of the Glagolitic

Missal (first South Slav incunabulum) was published in 1483. Medieval Croatian culture was an important intermediary between Latin Europe and the Slav literatures of the South and East.

Medieval Croatian sacred art, born from the antique and early Christian heritage, was enriched by contact with the European arts (Byzantine through *Ravenna, Frankish, Italian, central European) and developed its own styles and schools. In Adriatic Croatia, from the 8th to the 11th c., early Christian basilicas were rebuilt, and at the same time were built small rustic churches illustrating a "Palaeocroatian" architecture unique in its genre and pre-Romanesque monuments with motifs of "Palaeocroatian" interlacing and inscriptions mentioning the Croatian *župans* and princes. *Pre-Romanesque, *Romanesque and *Gothic monuments show all the European forms in Istria, in the Kvarner, in the Dalmatian towns, in particular at Zadar, Šibenik, Trogir, Split, Dubrovnik and Kotor, as do *codex miniatures, *frescos, paintings on wood, mural *paintings and the Dalmatian school of painting, unique in its genre (late Gothic and Renaissance). These styles flourished particularly thanks to the Benedictines and Franciscans and reveal Italian influences, from the school and styles of *Monte Cassino to those of *Venice. The great builders, sculptors and painters of medieval Croatia were master Radovan, Andrija Buvina, Juraj Dalmatinac, Nikola Firentinac, Blaž Jurjev, Vincent of Kastav; some of these already made the transition from the Middle Ages to the *Renaissance. Julius Clovio Croata, born at Grižane, was the greatest European miniaturist of the Renaissance. The development of continental Croatia, with Zagreb as centre, was more akin to that of Central Europe. It knew Romanesque art (influence of French sculpture) and went through a very long period of Gothic style. By reason of Venetian rule over the coast and the presence of the *Turks on the Croatian frontiers in the 15th c., northern Croatia remained somewhat isolated from Adriatic Croatia and its great literary and artistic Renaissance, particularly brilliant at Dubrovnik. The tragic battle of Krbavsko Polje against the Turks (1493) saw the old Croat nobility perish; in the 16th c., Croatia became *antemurale christianitatis* and lost part of its lands in defending Western civilization, while Zagreb finally became the metropolis.

The universities of *Bologna and *Paris and the European "university renaissance" made their influence felt in Croatia from the early 13th century. Croatians studied and worked in European cultural centres, where they were designated by the epithets *Dalmata*, *Croata*, *Slavus*, *Illyricus* (Hermanus Dalmata Slavus, Janus Pannonius at the *court of the Hungarian king *Matthias I Corvinus, Georgius of Sclavonia or "de Sorbonna" among others). The precocious Latin and Glagolitic *humanism marked out the way in Croatia for humanist and Renaissance currents coming from *Italy. Marko Marulić of Split (1450-1524), king of medieval Croatian literature and father of Renaissance Croatian literature, became one of the greatest names of European culture. His *De institutione bene vivendi* was the only book, apart from his breviary, that St Francis Xavier took with him to India.

V. Štefanić, *Hrvatska književnost srednjega vijeka* [Croat literature in the Middle Ages], Zagreb, 1969. – E. Hercigonja, *Srednjovjekovna književnost* [Medieval literature], Zagreb, 1975. – R. Katičić, "Die Literatur des frühen kroatischen Mittelalters in ihren slawischen und europäischen Zusammenhängen", *WSlJb*, 28, 1982, 27-52. – I. Petrović, "Prvi susreti Hrvata s ćirilometodskim izvorištem svoje srednjovjekovne kulture", [First encounters of the Croats with the Cyrillo-Methodian sources of their medieval culture], *Slovo*, 38, Zagreb, 1988, 5-54. – N. Klaić, *Povijest Hrvata u srednjem vijeku* [History of the Croats in the Middle Ages], Zagreb, 1990.

Ivanka Petrović

**CROSIERS.** Several religious *orders (military or hospitaller) bore the name "Crosiers", due to their particular devotion to the Holy *Cross: the Canons Regular of the *Holy Sepulchre ("Jerusalem Crosiers"), founded in 1114; the canons regular of the Holy Cross of Coimbra ("Portuguese Crosiers"), founded in 1131; the hospitallers of Bologna ("Italian Crosiers"), founded in 1169; the canons regular of the Holy Cross with the red star ("Crosiers of Bohemia"), founded at Prague in 1237-1252; the canons regular of the Holy Cross of Clairlieu ("Belgian Crosiers"), organised in 1248; the canons regular of the red heart, founded in 1256, a *mendicant order suppressed at the council of *Lyon in 1274, but which maintained itself in Bohemia and especially Poland (whence the name "Polish Crosiers"). Crosiers are also attested in Ireland, but remain little studied.

*DSp*, 2, 2, 1953, 2561-2576 (Belgian C.). – *DHGE*, 13, 1956, 1042-1062 (Belgian C.). – G. Q. Reiners, "A Survey of European Crosier Historiography in the last 50 Years", *Clair-lieu*, 46, 1988, 99-113. – "Kreuzherren", *LdM*, 5, 1991, 1500-1502.

Joseph Morsel

**CROSS, CRUCIFIX, CRUCIFIXION.** In the Christian art of the West, the representation of the cross seems at first sight preponderant in every period. But on examination, the situation is more complex and a number of markers allow us to propose a fairly precise periodization. In the 2nd and 3rd cc., we generally see bare crosses; from the 4th to the 12th c., crucifixes and Crucifixions also celebrate the *Majesty of Christ; after the first third of the 12th c., representations evolve towards the anecdotal genre of the story of Christ's *Passion, the idea of his kingship giving way to that of Redemption by the sacrifice on the cross.

Over the centuries, crosses were represented alone, with no other iconography. Thus, in the apse of St Irene, the Emperor Constantine set a great cross that did not bear Christ. In these cases, he was depicted either on the ceiling, between the sun and the moon (*St John Lateran), or in a medallion (San Stefano Rotondo). Surviving crosses from the time of Justinian are equally bare. In the first centuries of Christianity, the Cross was thus more of a *sign than a concrete reminder of the events of the Passion. In some chosen scenes, it was depicted in preference to *Christ. A sort of shame seems to have dictated this reluctance to show the suffering of God on an ignominious instrument of torture (among the Romans, crucifixion was reserved for bandits and thieves). This attitude long prevented the development of the iconography of the Crucified and, in consequence, favoured triumphal forms such as the Majesty of Christ and the *Ascension, which effaced the suffering and the shame. The *Doctors of the Church played on the contradiction between the sign and its deep interpretation. St Paul already noted: "It is true that the Cross is a scandal to the Jews and folly to the pagans, but for those who are called, both Jews and Greeks, it is Christ the power of God and the wisdom of God" (1 Cor 1, 23-24). Later commentaries do not depart from this line: St Leo († 461), *Ivo of Chartres in the 11th c. and others, all see in the Cross the sign of Christ's glory, by very reason of the abasement it supposes.

When in the 4th c. the peace of Constantine put an end to the great persecutions, the representation of the Cross replaced living *icons of Christ's Passion. In the late 4th c., a cross was put at the summit of the *mosaic decorating the apse of the church of Santa Pudenziana at *Rome: as instrument of victory, the Cross surmounted a seated Christ, enthroned amidst his Church and preserving it. The same conception is found in the general design of churches, notably in the adoption of the cruciform plan: in 382, St Ambrose interpreted the cross plan he had just traced out for the church of the Holy Apostles at *Milan as a sign of the triumph of Christ and his Cross. In the 7th and 8th cc., in Ireland, Scotland or England, a great carved stone cross was erected outside the church (*e.g.* the Bewcastle Cross) or inside it, between the nave and the choir (the Ruthwell Cross, *c.*731). It was decorated with a whole iconography, ordered, as at Ruthwell, by a double programme: on the south face, towards the nave, is exalted the *Ecclesia Christi*, while on the other face is celebrated the *Vita monastica*. At the base of the south face, the sculptors put a Crucifixion directly related to the habits of *prayer of the congregation, who at that time knelt at the foot of the cross and prayed facing east. Traces of these practices are also found in monastic buildings, since a monumental cross was ordinarily painted on the east wall. From the late 10th c., under the influence of *Cluny, elaborate crucifixes were placed on the *altar, of lesser dimensions but still making use of these conceptions. Then, during the 11th and 12th cc., great crucifixes of painted wood were suspended from the vault of the choir, above the high altar (thus, in *Spoleto cathedral, the great crucifix painted in 1198 by Alberto Sozio). The Cross and the crucifix were also cosmic signs: they indicated the four cardinal points (Cassiodorus, *In Psal.* 21, 18; Sedulius, *Carmen paschale*, V, 190-194); in their upright part, they reveal the secret dispositions that God has made for the *redemption of mankind (Venerable Bede, *Commentary on the Song of Songs*, 5, 15). The two great Christian *mysteries of the Incarnation and Passion are thus seen as God's eternal designs, which, in the image of the Cross and the crucifix, emerge from the ground.

In accordance with this overall conception, Christ is represented quite young, raised up on the wood of the cross, upright, eyes open or closed, depending on workshops and fashions. Under his feet is set the triumphal footstool, the *suppedaneum* cited by the Psalms (Ps 99, 5; 110). Up above is shown the hand of God crowning the head of his Son (*Crucifixion*, *ivory panel, *c.*1050, Brussels, Musées royaux). But around the 11th c. a quantitative and qualitative change took place: the Crucifixion increasingly prevailed in iconography. To a very great extent, Cluny was behind these innovations: within a broader framework of Church reform and anti-heretical struggle, Cluny made the crucifixion one of the bases of the new liturgy it was promoting. The *feast of the Invention of the Cross, 3 May, and that of the Exaltation, 14 Sept, took on a particular brilliance. Based on the Gregorian ideal, a mode of depiction soon prevailed: it was dual, since in monumental programmes it associated the Majesty of Christ enthroned, in the centre of the apse or the tympanum, with the Crucifixion represented close by (*e.g.* the painted decoration of the priory church of Saint-Sylvain at Chalivoy-Milon [diocese of Bourges], *c.*1130-1138). There was thus greater insistence on the moral aspect of *Revelation, less on its theological aspects: the way was open to the reinterpretation of the crucifixion as the crowning of Christ's earthly life.

Towards the middle of the 12th c., the representation of the Crucified insinuated itself into compositions previously reserved for Christ in Majesty: at Saint-Julien de Jonzy, at the centre of the tympanum is Christ in Majesty surrounded by a *mandorla, and below it on the lintel the Last Supper with Christ and the Apostles (mid 12th c.); on the carved tympanum of *Champagne churches,

*The Crucifixion.* 9th-c. ivory plaque, surrounded by a border of spun copper garnished with precious stones and oriental cloisonné enamels. Upper binding of an evangeliary, Metz school, first half of 9th c. Paris, BNF (Ms lat. 9383).

Christ in Majesty was replaced by Christ crucified at the centre of the tympanum, set above the Last Supper depicted on the lintel. This is one indication among others of the part from now on taken by the Crucifixion in the iconography of Christ. A century later, around 1250, the representation of the Crucified became more and more that of the suffering Christ: on one of the folios of the Evesham Psalter (fol. 6 v°; London, British Library, Add. ms. 44874), the cross is now made of the knotty wood of the dead *Tree and Christ lies extended upon it; the body is dislocated under the effect of pain; the chest is lifted in a final spasm; finally, on a lower level, a small kneeling devotee, hands joined, contemplates the scene and, more particularly, Christ's two feet crossed one over the other. This last element of the representation is a reference to Christ's *mercy as it was seen by monastic milieux, from the 10th-11th cc. (*e.g.* St Anselm, *Tenth Meditation on Christ's passion*). In this way, an older theme is taken up and transferred into the milieu of the new religious *spirituality that formed in the course of the 13th century.

With the *mendicant orders, especially the *Franciscans, the dolorist interpretation prevailed, encouraging a relative appropriation of the iconography of the Crucifixion. Borrowing numerous arguments from St *Bernard, St *Francis preached "Christ Lord and God", but also "Christ the servant, true God and true man": he insisted on the movement of descent accepted by the Father's *Word, abandoning the divine glory to become a poor man among men. After the 1260s in central Italy, notably in *Umbria, St Francis of Assisi was represented at the feet of the Crucified, contemplating the single *nail or the bleeding *wounds:

on the *Crucifixion* painted in *c.*1325 (now at Siena, Pinacoteca Nazionale, no. 34), Ugolino di Nerio presents him curled up at the foot of the Cross, ready to receive the last breath of Christ who bends his head towards him. In the 14th c., and still more in the 15th, other religious *orders and certain fringes of the *laity took up this overall schema, whether to magnify a particular vocation (the *Crucifixion* painted by Fra *Angelico in the former chapter room of the Dominican convent of San Marco at *Florence, *c.*1441-1442), or to accompany a personal piety (thus in folio 15 of the Psalter of Jeanne de Laval, *c.*1470-1480; now at Poitiers, BM, ms. 41).

E. Sandberg-Vavala, *La Croce dipinta nell'arte italiana*, Verona, 1924. – P. Thoby, *Le Crucifix des origines au concile de Trente*, Nantes, 1959. – D. Russo, "Saint François, les Franciscains et les représentations du Christ sur la croix en Ombrie au XIIIe siècle", *MEFRM*, 90, 1984, 647-717. – B. Raw, *Anglo-Saxon Crucifixion Iconography and the Art of the Monastic Revival*, Cambridge, 1990 ("Studies in Anglo-Saxon England", 1). – M.-C. Sepière, *L'Image d'un Dieu souffrant (IXe-Xe siècles). Aux origines du crucifix*, Paris, 1994.

Daniel Russo

**CROSS, RELIC OF THE.** Of all the *relics of the *Passion, the True Cross was by far the most widespread and the most highly prized. It consisted of the pieces forming the cross on which Jesus was crucified on Good Friday: the post, the beam (the *patibulum* that would have been the only part Christ carried), the support, the pedestal and the title. Yet there is no certain evidence of this relic before the mid 4th century. Indeed while, from the 1st century of the Christian era, St *Paul and the Apostolic Fathers of the East recognised the symbol of the *cross as the distinctive form and, as it were, synonym of Christianity, the attention of the first disciples seems to have been concentrated solely on the holy tomb and the Mount of Olives.

The earliest mentions of the relic of the Holy Cross go back to the *Catecheses* of St Cyril, bishop of Jerusalem, who in *c.*348-350 mentions the True Cross "which we see among us today". The following decades saw the progressive elaboration of the *legend of the finding of the relic by St Helena, the Emperor *Constantine's mother, destined to become one of the most popular edifying stories of the Middle Ages; in the late 4th c., St Ambrose of Milan (395) and St John Chrysostom (398) are still unaware of any supernatural episode in the finding of the relic but, from the first years of the next century, with Rufinus, Paulinus of Nola, then Sulpicius Severus, commenced the cycle of miraculous explanations (a sign from heaven indicated the place where the relic was buried, the empress healed or raised a dead woman). The legend of the "invention" was thus primarily a literary motif intended, three centuries after Christ's Passion, to justify the exposition of a relic of the Cross at *Jerusalem.

Jerusalem was in fact a major centre of expansion of the cult of the True Cross from the 4th century. The travel narrative of Etheria, who visited Jerusalem in 395, attests the attraction exercised on *pilgrims by the Holy City, but also illustrates the priority of the *Holy Sepulchre in the genesis of the principal *feasts of the Cross (Adoration on Good Friday or Invention). From the 5th c., Jerusalem played the role of centre of diffusion of the cult of the Cross, since at this time fragments of the oriental relic ended up in countries as diverse as *Georgia, North Africa, *Italy or Gaul. But after the temporary disappearance of the Cross after the capture of Jerusalem by the Persians in 614, we find it at *Constantinople from 635, and the role of Jerusalem declined; accounts of gifts or divisions become rarer, without totally disappearing, and from the 10th c. pilgrims who came to the Holy City had to be shown the stump of the *tree from which the Cross was said to have been cut. Penetrating into the *Holy Sepulchre on 5 Aug 1099, the crusaders found no holy relic there and had to wait patiently for a week before a new "invention".

By this date, Constantinople had for several centuries been the major centre of diffusion of the relic and its cult. Ever since the discovery of the Cross by St Helena, its division had allowed an important part of it to be sent to Constantine in his capital; this first gift was soon supplemented by new fragments (such as the piece that Justin II brought back from Apamea of Antioch in 574) and by the Jerusalem relic in 635. As at Jerusalem, the Holy Cross gave rise to the formation of liturgical solemnities (on 30 July and 14 August in the Orthodox calendar) and the development of political practices. From the 7th c., Constantinople became the essential starting-point for traffic in the True Cross. The *iconoclast crisis (8th c. - mid 9th c.) entailed a momentary slowing down, but the restoration of *Orthodoxy in the Byzantine capital allowed devotion to the Cross to flourish fully and pilgrimages of Westerners to develop. Henceforth Constantinople was the source from which the relic-treasuries of the West were fed (*Regensburg in the 9th c., *Orléans in the 10th, *Cologne, Toul or Aniane in the 11th), but it was with the fourth *crusade that the Eastern capital became a prodigious warehouse of relics for the West; in his account of the capture of Constantinople in 1204, Geoffrey de Villehardouin wrote that "since the world was created, there has never been so much booty in one town". Thanks to the pillage organised by the new rulers, the West enjoyed a veritable influx of relics of the Holy Cross: Pope *Innocent III (though he had blamed the crusaders for the sack of 1204) found himself being offered four *staurothecae*; Baldwin I, having become emperor, offered *Philip Augustus in 1205 a gold cross containing a fragment a foot long; later, Baldwin II ceded to St *Louis the Crown of Thorns (1238) and a sumptuous box-*reliquary containing several fragments of the Cross (1241) for which the French king built the *Sainte-Chapelle at Paris, not neglecting to distribute portions of the Cross to several churches in his kingdom (*Sens, Royaumont, *Vézelay...). The development of the cult of the Cross thus enjoyed an apogee between the 11th and the 13th c., which the accelerated circulation of the relic after 1204 merely amplified.

Ever since the earliest testimonies, it is remarkable that the relic's area of expansion included the whole of the Christian world. But it was in the West that the devotion reached its greatest development. The choice of the Holy Cross as a name for churches, *chapels or *oratories is a prime proof of it; while no church at Constantinople was dedicated to the Cross, *Rome had one from the 5th c. (built by Pope Hilarus, 461-468), and France nearly 600 before the 15th c., the majority appearing between the 12th and 14th centuries. The degree of solemnization of feasts of the Cross (Invention on 3 May, Exaltation on 14 Sept) in calendars and *liturgical books also attests, from before the year 1000, the importance of this devotion. But it is inventories of relics that best illustrate the extent of the cult of the True Cross in the West; in the order of classification, which indicates the hierarchy of relics, portions of the Cross always appear at the head; moreover, inventories of the 14th and 15th cc. generally mention several reliquaries containing fragments of the Cross (16 at *Laon cathedral, nine at that of *Bayeux, 12 in the treasury of *Charles

V of France).

In the West as in the East, the True Cross had from the earliest centuries of its history a political function that no other relic could equal. In the Byzantine area, the *basileis* thus used the "precious imperial wood" as a guarantee of treaties or for the swearing of oaths (as in 1097 Alexius I *Comnenus asked the crusaders to guarantee the integrity of the Empire); likewise, a portion of the Cross always accompanied the emperor on his military campaigns. In the West, the relic of the Cross served similarly to sanction an agreement or a treaty; its *image even appeared in diplomatic texts or on the frontispieces of illuminated manuscripts of the *Bible as a sign of alliance between the Lord and the ruler. Certain relics also served to guarantee the veracity of an *oath, like the Cross of Saint-Laud d'Angers on which King *Louis XI (1461-1483) sent numerous turbulent great lords to commit themselves to a fidelity that heralded the subjection of modern times.

The devotion with which the Westerners surrounded the True Cross explains why it was at the centre of the polemics of the 16th century. For John Calvin, the relics of the Cross were enough to freight a large ship, while Henry Kipping claimed that 300 gibbets could have been erected with all that wood . . .

C. Rohault de Fleury, *Mémoire sur les instruments de la Passion de Notre Seigneur Jésus-Christ*, Paris, 1870. – A. Frolow, *La Relique de la Vraie Croix. Recherches sur le développement d'un culte*, Paris, 1961. – P. Jounel, "Le culte de la Croix dans la liturgie romaine", *LMD*, 75, 1963, 65-82. – C. Moulin, "Les églises et chapelles Sainte-Croix en France", *RHEF*, 62, 1976, 349-361. – M.-M. Gauthier, *Highways of the Faith: Relics and Reliquaries from Jerusalem to Compostela*, London, 1987. – J.-M. Matz, "Religion et politique à la fin du Moyen Âge: la Vraie-Croix de Saint-Laud d'Angers", *ABret*, 95, 1987, 241-263. – S. Borgehammar, *How the Holy Cross was Found*, Stockholm, 1991.

Jean-Michel Matz

**CROSS, SIGN OF THE.** The sign of the cross is *par excellence* that of the Christian *mystery: the wood of ignominious punishment which by the *Resurrection became the instrument of glorification, as exalted by St John, is the foundation of the Pauline theology of *salvation. A *sign of Christian identification from the apostolic period – signing on the forehead (*sphragis*) accompanying *baptism – it was both the seal of divine mastery over the world and the way of interior exploration for the believer in his quest for *Christ. The liturgy gave it a fundamental place in the administration of the *sacraments, in *exorcisms and blessings. The very organisation of the liturgical calendar, which attests the development of devotion to the cross by the *feasts of the Invention (3 May) and Exaltation of the cross on 14 Sept (7th c.), stimulated the manifestations of piety whose expression the sign accompanied.

In the representation of which it was the object, in the *gesture that traced it out, it was perceived, by the supernatural power that emanated from it, as the manifestation of God's saving presence. The sign of the cross put the Enemy (the devil) to flight, it sacralized space and marked out the place protected for the living and the *dead. In *prayer, in the *litanies whose invocations it punctuated, it had a value at once imploring and imperative, by the fact of unshakeable certainty in its efficacity. But beyond that, for a very narrow elite among those who chose to make it the focus of their existence and who wished to be *cruce signati*, like the *Crosiers of the 13th c., it could become the culmination of an existence itself crucified, like that of *Francis of Assisi, who became by his *stigmata the living image of the sign graven in his very flesh.

M. Olphe-Galliard, "Croix (mystères de la)", *DSp*, 2, 2, 1953, 2607-2623. – M. J. Picard, "Croix (chemin de)", *ibid.*, 2576, 2606. – M. Vinken, "Croisiers", *ibid.*, 2561-2576. – E. Dinkler, *Signum Crucis*, Tübingen, 1967. – A. Rayez, "Humanité du Christ", *DSp*, 7, 1, 1969, 1063-1096. – J. Kopec, A. Rayez, "Instruments de la Passion", *DSp*, 7, 2, 1971, 1820-1831. – *CaP*, London, 1986-1988 (4 vol.). – V. Grossi, "Cross, Crucifix", *EEC*, 1, 1992, 209-210.

Pierrette Paravy

## CROWN

**History.** The word "crown" had two meanings in the Middle Ages. The crown was firstly a material object, a state head-dress worn by *kings and queens as an attribute of their power on *feast-days. The diadem or crown was used by Roman emperors and *barbarian kings. From 816 in the West, anointing (if anointing there was) and crowning took place in a single ceremony called *consecration or *coronation. The new king committed himself to the Church and the people, then he received anointing and the *insignia regni*. Finally, the crown was put on his head by an ecclesiastical dignitary. Coronation preceded *acclamation. In *France, coronation took place at *Reims from the 11th c.: it was a monopoly of the *archbishop; after the ceremonies, the insignia went back to *Saint-Denis. The crown used, held by the twelve *Peers during the ceremony, was attributed to *Charlemagne; it disappeared in 1590. This was the great imperial crown, a very heavy crown (3.7 kg), open, with a bandeau and four fleurons, whose date of fabrication is uncertain (12th or 13th c.). From the time of John II, the *reliquary crown of St *Louis, which enclosed a splinter of the true *cross, also came to be used. It was melted down in 1793. In the lands of eastern Europe, the crown as an object was conceived as sacred (crown of the founding saint-king), and to hold it was a strong argument for conquering the throne. The crowns of princes should not be confused with that of the king.

But the Crown was also an immaterial entity, timeless, distinct from the royal person and from the realm. The idea appeared in the 12th c., in *England earlier than in France. It was theorized in the 14th c., when the question of the right of *women to the Crown was concretely posed. This led to the justification of an instantaneous male succession. The Crown, like the king, never died. This fiction allowed a madman or a child to reign. But the king had duties towards the Crown. He had to defend it and augment it, *i.e.* to increase its lands, its rights or its prestige. The domain and rights of the Crown were inalienable. France was the last country to have the inalienability of the Crown sworn to, in the reign of *Charles V. The king was the administrator of the Crown, which was sometimes imposed on him as a burden. Conversely, subjects also had duties to the Crown. In France, this idea had few consequences, and the Crown remained *corona regis* more than *corona regni*. But in England, the barons revolted in the name of the rights of the Crown, which the king was bound to respect. In the kingdoms of the East, the *corona* could also escape from the king and the *nobles could depose the king in the name of the Crown. So the notion of a Crown could just as much reinforce *monarchy as threaten it.

M. Hartung, *Corona regni. Studien über die Krone als Symbol des Staates im späten Mittel Alter*, Weimar, 1961. – D. Gaborit-Chopin, "Les couronnes de sacre des rois", *BM*, 133, 1975, 165-181. – R. Cazelles, *Société politique, noblesse et couronne sous Jean le Bon et Charles V*, Paris, 1982.

Colette Beaune

Votive crown of precious stones. Treasury of Guarrazar, 621-672. Madrid, Archaeological Museum.

**Art.** The term "crown" designated a wide range of things in the Middle Ages, while the head-dress to which we now give that name received several names at that time. In the strict and most frequent sense of an ornament for the head, the medieval crown had various aspects: secular, private, official, symbolic, sacred.

The use of crowns of flowers and foliage, inherited from antique *mores*, was frequent in the Gothic period: "chaplets of flowers" or leaves were commonly offered (courtly iconography of the Crowning of the lover). At the same time there existed precious "chaplets" or "head circlets" of *gold, enhanced by pearls or precious stones and intended for the heads of the richest. The form of crowns varied considerably and, in any one period, very different types could be used: solid or perforated bands, generally composed of plates held together by hinges, rosettes or bouquets of foliage that, in the 14th c., opened out at the top of long thin stems. The modern classification of crowns according to the rank of persons was not current in the Middle Ages. The wearing of crowns was not reserved for kings, queens and princes, and in France in 1283 an *ordinance was necessary to forbid the wearing of gold or silver crowns by the middle class.

But the crown remained primarily the symbol of *authority. Distinct from the papal *tiara, it was the royal attribute *par excellence*. Very different from the bay- or oak-leaf crowns of classical antiquity, medieval royal crowns went back to Byzantine models: those of Constantine and his sons, in the form of a diadem, a golden circlet loaded with precious stones and underlaid by rows of pearls. The "iron crown" or crown of the kingdom of *Italy, of uncertain date, kept at Monza and traditionally donated by Theodelinda, was a gold circle composed of six rectangles joined to each other by hinges, inside which was a strip of wrought iron (hence the name) made, according to tradition, from one of the *nails of the holy *Cross; the crown was enriched with diamonds, *enamels and precious gems. Also at Monza was the so-called crown of Theodelinda, similar to the 7th-c. crowns of Guarrazar near Toledo, which recall the crowns of the pre-Carolingian period. In the 9th c., several portraits of rulers show a crown provided with a sort of pendants and surmounted by a transverse arch, but this "stirrup" was not general. Elsewhere, portraits of *Charles the Bald and the bronze *Charlemagne* in the Louvre attest a crown with rosettes with stems of varying length. The crown of the Holy Roman *Empire (Vienna, Schatzkammer) is a good example of the imperial crown, formed of tall articulated plates whose curved form is inspired by Byzantine models, held together by hinges and surmounted by a great golden stirrup. In contrast to this type of "closed" crown is the "open" crown of the kings of France. The treasury of *Saint-Denis kept the two similar crowns "the king's" and "the queen's" (smaller), made of four plates, each surmounted by a great rosette and ornamented with precious stones (13th c.?). By contrast, the "holy crown" kept in the same treasury was also ornamented with four rosettes, but had a single supporting band. A tall rich lining of fabric enriched with pearls and precious stones occupied the centre of these "open" crowns, evoking somewhat the aspect of a tiara. The king's crown and the holy crown were used for *coronations, but from at least the 13th c. the king of France had a second, personal crown made for himself for this ceremony.

In early medieval texts it is sometimes hard to distinguish descriptions of votive crowns from those of "crowns of light". The latter, inspired by *polykandela*, were often of a form that evoked the ramparts of the heavenly *Jerusalem (crowns of light of Hildesheim, 11th c.; Aachen, *c.*1166; Gross Komburg, *c.*1130). Votive crowns were suspended above the *altar, under a **ciborium*, following a custom attested by depictions from the 4th c. and still in force at the end of the Carolingian period. Crowns worn by princes were offered and suspended from chains in churches, but the crowns suspended from chains at Guarrazar (Madrid, Archeological Museum) are too small ever to have been worn. The same seems to be true of the Carolingian crown of Monza.

The existence of reliquary crowns must be explained by reference to the instruments of Christ's *Passion, notably the holy crown of thorns. After buying the holy crown in 1239, St *Louis had it enclosed in a *reliquary in the form of a gold crown, kept in the *Sainte-Chapelle. The crown of Namur (early 13th c., Diocesan Museum), with a band of articulated and rosetted plates, had likewise been made for the holy thorns, while the crown of the Dominicans at Liège (*c.*1270-1280, Louvre Museum) and that of the Paraclete (*c.*1320-1330, Amiens treasury) housed a wide selection of *relics.

"Couronne", V. Gay, *Glossaire archéologique du Moyen Âge et de la Renaissance*, 1, 1929 (1st ed. 1887). – A. Twinning, *A History of the Crown Jewels of Europe*, London, 1960. – P. Lasko, *Ars Sacra 800-1200*, Harmondsworth, 1972. – H. Pinoteau, *Vingt-cinq années d'études dynastiques*, Paris, 1982. – D. Gaborit-Chopin, *Regalia*, Paris, 1987-1988 (exhibition catalogue).

Danielle Gaborit-Chopin

**CROZIER.** The crozier (*baculus, crocia, crossa*) was a pastoral *staff, emblem of *authority and dignity, badge of office of the *bishop or *abbot. He received it at the moment of his *consecration, as *Isidore of Seville describes early in the 7th c., so that he could "direct or correct, or support the weakness of the faithful".

In the first centuries of the Middle Ages, the tip of the staff sometimes took the form of a crutch-handle which, from its resemblance to the Greek letter, was called a "*tau"; this form tended to disappear after the 12th century. More often, the tip was curved, either to describe a circular arc reminiscent of a walking-stick (croziers of Delémont, 7th c., and Montreuil-sur-Mer, 11th c., which extend Irish examples – Clonmacnoise crozier – into the 12th c.), or to coil up into a volute with several revolutions. This latter type became preponderant in the West from the 13th century. This tip – or head – was set on top of a great staff.

The coils of the volute frequently ended in a serpent's head, doubtless recalling Araron's rod and the bronze serpent. This serpent could be associated with another animal – *lamb, ram, ibex, more rarely a deer (*e.g.* the Rouen crozier from Saint-Georges de Boscherville): the meaning was then enriched by the recollection of the struggle of *Good against *Evil. The serpent was also sometimes associated with a vegetable decoration (example in Amiens museum, from *Corbie) or a human figure, notably to form the group of St *Michael fighting the *dragon (numerous Limousin croziers, *e.g.* that from *Fontevraud, Angers museum). There might also be other scenes within the volute (*e.g.* the Deposition in the Tomb on the ivory example in the Arles museum).

In the Gothic period, the outer curve of the volute was enriched by more or less developed crockets, and the inside frequently held a figured group or scene: *Annunciation, Virgin and Child or glorious Virgin, Coronation of the Virgin, Crucifixion, Christ in *Majesty, more rarely a saint (*e.g.* St Galgano, Siena, cathedral museum); the object's possessor was sometimes represented in prayer before one of these scenes (*e.g.* Cologne, cathedral treasury).

Though the staff seems usually to have been of wood, sometimes of metal or *ivory, the head was executed in various materials: *gold or silver for the more precious, often copper or bronze, these different metals being frequently *enamelled, but also ivory, rock crystal, and more rarely other hard stones.

H. Leclercq, "Crosse", *DACL*, 3, 2, 1914, 3145-3149. – D. Gaborit-Chopin, *Ivoires du Moyen Âge*, Fribourg, 1978. – J. M. Fritz, *Goldschmiedekunst der Gotik im Mitteleuropa*, Munich, 1982.

Élisabeth Taburet-Delahaye

**CRUSADES.** "Crusade" is a rare, late word (mid 13th c.) derived from the cross that the participants sewed onto their clothing. Before that the phrase used was "journey to Jerusalem" (*iter hierosolymitanum, via Sancti Sepulcri*), then "passage" or "voyage *d'outre-mer*". In the strict sense, this was a *pilgrimage in arms directed to Christ's tomb at Jerusalem and decided by the *pope, who granted spiritual and temporal privileges to the crusaders, whom texts call *peregrini* more often than *crucesignati*. In the broad sense, we sometimes understand by this term any war waged by the Church against *heretics and other enemies of the papacy, a confusion contested by historians like H. E. Mayer.

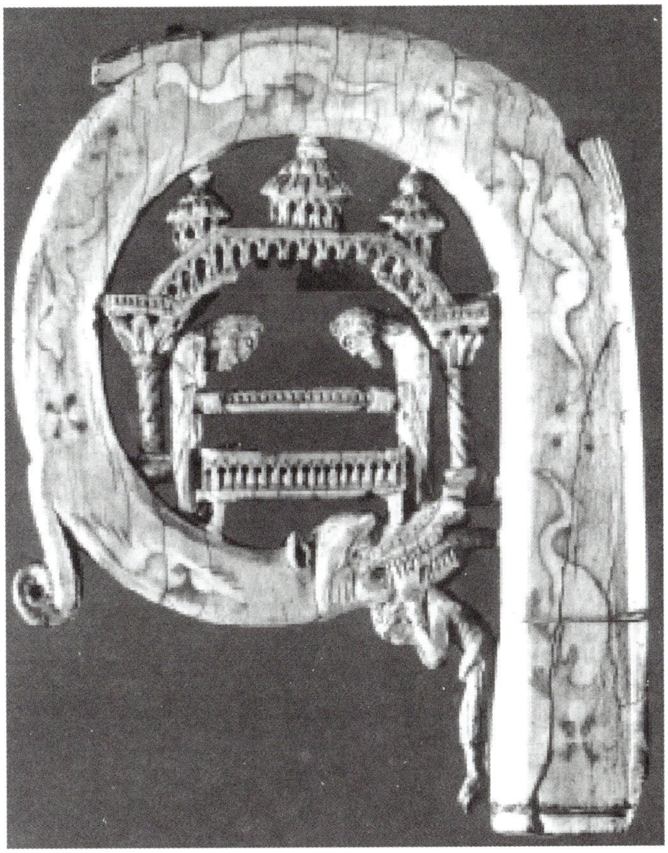

*The Deposition in the Tomb*. Fragment of an ivory crozier. Arles, Musée Réattu.

At the origins of the crusade, the combination of economic and social circumstances of the 11th c. (demographic growth, shortage of lands, "*Peace of God" movement, beginning of expansion of Italian *commerce) was not the determining cause but only a context favourable to its launching. The crusade in fact resulted from a conjuncture of slowly-evolving factors and immediate causes. These factors were the ideal of pilgrimage to the *Holy Land, conceived from the 7th c. as a means of *penance and imposed in the 11th c. on breakers of the peace, and the gradual transition from the idea of legitimate war to the idea of sacred war waged for the defence of Christians against the infidel, applied notably in 11th-c. *Spain. The immediate causes were the advance of the *Turks in Asia Minor (victory of Manzikert, 1071) and the appeals to the pope for help by the Byzantines (embassies of Michael VII in 1074 and Alexius I in 1095) who spoke of the misfortunes of the Christians of Anatolia and the persecutions, more supposed than real, in the *Holy Land. But while Byzantium dreamed more of reinforcements or the sending of Western mercenaries like those the Empire had long employed, the popes (*Gregory VII, then *Urban II), whose power was growing, envisaged an expedition directed by the Church.

At the council of *Clermont (Nov 1095), Urban II called on the Christians of the West to cease their fratricidal wars, succour their brethren in the East and liberate *Jerusalem. The success of the appeal, taken up by numerous preachers including *Peter the Hermit, rapidly went beyond France and the class of men capable of bearing arms to whom the pope wished to limit it. Ill-equipped bands set out, massacring *Jews in Germany, pillaging on their way in Hungary and Byzantium, before themselves being massacred by the Turks in Asia Minor. The "barons' crusade", four armies that set out from northern (*Godfrey of Bouillon), central or southern France (Raymond of Toulouse) and southern Italy (Bohemund), joined forces in Asia Minor in May 1097 after having promised Alexius I to restore the lands they reconquered from the Turks. The crusaders took Nicaea and handed it over to the Empire; they then occupied Edessa and took *Antioch after a long siege (1098) and finally Jerusalem (15 July 1099). The "after-crusades" (Lombards, French, Bavarians), numerically as important as the former, were defeated in Anatolia by the Turks. But Genoese and Venetian help, arriving by sea, contributed effectively to the installation of the crusaders. The *Latin States of the East were born: the county of Antioch (Bohemund), the county of Edessa (Baldwin of Boulogne), the county of Tripoli (Raymond of Toulouse), the kingdom of Jerusalem (*Godfrey of Bouillon, then his brother *Baldwin I). Profiting from a constant but minor flow of pilgrims and especially from the religious and political dissensions of the Muslim world, playing off *Damascus against Mosul, they extended and maintained their conquests, not without difficulty.

In 1145, the loss of Edessa led to the second crusade: the king of France, *Louis VII, and the Emperor Conrad III travelled separately and lost three quarters of their forces in Anatolia. Moreover, instead of attacking *Aleppo, they besieged Damascus in vain; it was the patent failure of a princely pilgrimage. The pressure of the atabegs of Mosul (Zengi, Nur ad-Dīn, Salah ad-Dīn) grew: they restored to honour the themes of the *jihād* against the Franks and unified the Muslim world, taking Damascus in 1154, then Egypt in 1169.

Appeals for a crusade and requests for help remained without effect until the annihilation of the Frankish troops by *Saladin at Hattin and the capture of Jerusalem (1187) set in motion the third crusade. The greatest rulers took part in it: *Frederick I Barbarossa, *Philip Augustus, *Richard Coeur de Lion; the emperor was drowned in *Cilicia and his army dispersed. The kings of France and England concluded the siege of *Acre (1191). Richard I never managed to advance as far as Jerusalem, but imposed on Saladin a treaty guaranteeing freedom of pilgrimage and respect for the "kingdom of Acre", that coastal fringe from Tyre to Jaffa kept by the crusaders.

In 1198, *Innocent III launched the fourth crusade: purely papal, it obtained the adhesion of Champenois and Flemish contingents led by Boniface of Montferrat. Unable to pay the sum agreed on for transporting the army, the crusaders agreed, despite the pope's prohibition, to help *Venice take the Christian town of Zara in *Dalmatia (1202) and then, in exchange for a promise to support the envisaged expedition against Egypt, to restore the young Alexius IV and his father Isaac II *Angelus to the throne of Byzantium (1203). But the latter were unable to meet their commitments, tension mounted between the Greek population and the army, and an uprising brought a convinced anti-Latin to power. So, after having signed a treaty of partition of the *Byzantine Empire (*partitio Romaniae*) with Venice, the crusaders took *Constantinople on 13 April 1204, giving themselves up to violence and pillage. Innumerable treasures or *relics were destroyed or taken to the West.

The early 13th c. was marked by many more expeditions endowed with the status of a crusade: in the Baltic lands, against the Albigenses from 1209, in Spain (victory of Las *Navas de Tolosa, 1212). But the Holy Land remained the primary aim, both in the popular mind – as shown by the Children's Crusade in 1212 – and for the Church. At the fourth *Lateran council (1215), Innocent III organised a fifth crusade in which German contingents predominated. It captured *Damietta, because, since 1169 and the unification – *de facto* or *de forma* – of Egypt and *Syria, it was on Egypt that pressure had to be put in order to loosen the stranglehold on the Holy Land. But the legate Pelagius intransigently refused the sultan's offer to give back the crusaders the former territory of the Latin kingdom of Jerusalem. The march on *Cairo was a failure and the encircled army had to return to Damietta (1221) and withdraw.

The Emperor *Frederick II who, engrossed in the problem of putting his own States in order, had been unable to take part in it, promised to direct a sixth crusade, which preceded him to Syria and which he finally joined in 1228. But the pope, irritated by his delays and wishing to attack southern Italy, excommunicated him. King of Jerusalem by his marriage to the heiress of the Crown (1225), Frederick II concluded with the sultan the treaty of Jaffa (1229) which gave the town of Jerusalem and the *Holy Sepulchre back to the Christians while leaving the Temple to the Muslims. Internal conflicts, which had been undermining the Latin States since the end of the 12th c., were aggravated by this conflict between the pope and the emperor, between the emperor and the Frankish nobility, and would henceforth be ceaseless, even in the face of the gravest dangers. The results gained by Frederick II were consolidated for a time by the "barons' crusade" (the count of Champagne, the duke of Burgundy, *Richard of Cornwall, brother of *Henry II of England) following which the cession of several regions (Sidon, Tiberias, Jaffa, Ascalon) was obtained from the sultan: the kingdom recovered its pre-1187 frontiers.

A reversal of alliance decided on by the Frankish barons led to the capture of Jerusalem by the Khwarizmians and the annihilation of the army at La Forbie near Gaza (1244). The news provoked the departure of the seventh crusade: at the head of the contingents of France, Morea and Cyprus, St *Louis took Damietta but failed at *Mansura in his project of conquering Egypt. Taken prisoner (1250), he was freed in return for an enormous *ransom and then spent four years in *Palestine, negotiating truces, restoring *entente* between the Latin princes, putting the coastal places back in a state of defence (Jaffa, Caesarea, Acre, Sidon).

But the *Mamluks who came to power in Egypt (1250) were victorious over the *Mongols at Ain Jalut (1260). Their sultan, Baybars, took possession of Syria and encircled the Latin States, taking from them between 1263 and 1271 all the places still held in the interior (Nazareth, Bethlehem, Beaufort, Krak des Chevaliers), as well as Jaffa, Caesarea and Antioch. The Frankish States were reduced to a few enclaves. The eighth crusade was marked mainly by the failure of St Louis's expedition, probably directed against Egypt but turned aside by *Charles of Anjou to the siege of Tunis, where the king died (1270). The Aragonese and English contingents who reached the Holy Land could obtain nothing but a ten-year truce and access to the Holy Places. It was the last of the great crusades. Later projects failed under the intrigues of the princes, while the suicidal division in the Latin States continued. Acre was taken in May 1291 and the last places in Palestine were evacuated the same year.

The shock caused by the capture of Acre was considerable. Throughout the 14th c. crusading projects flourished, dreaming of restoring the unity of an increasingly divided West, breaking down

Egypt by a blockade and exploiting the Mongol alliance or that of the mythical *Prester John. These undertakings were aimed primarily at ensuring security in the Mediterranean: in 1310, *Rhodes was conquered and entrusted to the Hospitallers; in 1344, a naval league captured Smyrna; in 1390, Louis of Bourbon took Mahdia in Tunisia. The *Ottoman advance later shifted the priority towards helping the Byzantine Empire and then Eastern Europe (in 1366, Amadeus of Savoy recaptured Gallipoli; 1396, failure of *Sigismund at *Nicopolis; in 1399, Boucicaut landed at Gallipoli; 1444, Hungarian and Polish failure at Varna. . .). After the fall of Constantinople, new "holy leagues" were organised, the most famous of them culminatng in the victory of Lepanto (1571) and one of the last in the lifting of the siege of Vienna (1683).

The organisation of the crusade as it will be outlined here was a multiform and evolving reality. It was always decreed by the pope, who generally preached it himself before delegating the task to authorized clerics, often his legates. Alongside official preachers (St *Bernard in 1145) there also acted popular preachers (Peter the Hermit, the monk Ralph in 1145, Fulk of Neuilly in 1202) whose influence and excesses (notably antisemitism) were sometimes dangerous. From the 13th c., the *mendicant orders played a growing role and preaching manuals were written.

The crusader pronounced a *vow that committed him, on pain of *excommunication, to go to Jerusalem on a provided "passage". He enjoyed temporal privileges that put his family and property under the protection and jurisdiction of the Church and dispensed him from paying interest on his debts, themselves suject to a moratorium. He enjoyed spiritual privileges: the crusading indulgence, remission of penalties incurred for his sins. The spirit of penitence and moderation had to reign in the army, generally controlled in this respect by the *legate who accompanied it and who often also played a political role (*e.g.* *Adhemar of Le Puy, Pelagius).

The financing of the crusade was at first purely private: the first crusaders sold their goods or pledged them to the religious establishments who alone were capable of providing the necessary *money. Then lords and *kings demanded *aid* from their vassals for their departure on crusade and pressed the churches to contribute to these heavy expenses. After 1150, a system of general *taxation was gradually put in place in *England and *France. The *Saladin tithe* was levied in 1188 with the pope's authorization on all the subjects of both kingdoms and increased to 25 % on the Jews. The Church too passed from the *collection of gifts to the imposition of *clerics: **tenths* of variable rate and duration were common in the 13th c. and were at the origin of the *papal financial administration of the 14th century. The gifts of the *laity were augmented by authorizing the redemptions of vows and extending, by means of finances, the crusading indulgence to "unfit" believers, a system that ended by linking the preaching of the crusade to the sale of *indulgences.

Indeed the cost of expeditions went on mounting: the land route followed by the first two crusades, through the Balkans and Asia Minor, less onerous but not safe, was gradually abandoned at the end of the 12th c. in favour of the sea route. The construction or location of a fleet for the transport of numerous troops (thus the 15,000 men of 1248, including 3000 knights with their mounts) was a heavy expense which the crusaders of 1202 could only honour by lending their services to Venice.

At the same time, strategy was refined; better informed of the situation in the East than in 1099, the crusaders several times

*Crusaders of the Minutolo family.* 14th-c. fresco in the cathedral of San Gennaro, Naples.

attacked Egypt to make it relax its pressure on the Holy Land, or sought Eastern alliances (Byzantium, princes of Damascus, Mongols) more or less judiciously. Tactics had to take account of the vulnerability of heavy *cavalry faced with the mounted archery and light cavalry of the Turks and a constant numerical inferiority. Hence the prudence of the Franks, for which they were often blamed by the crusaders who came out from Europe, and the importance given to the construction of fortresses.

The creation of Latin States in the East, "colonies" often without any definite metropolis, was one of the most tangible consequences of the crusades: the Holy Land was held for only two centuries, but the kingdom of *Cyprus, a product of the third crusade, remained independent until 1489 and Venetian until 1571, while the various Latin possessions that emerged from the fourth crusade, Venetian or Frankish, then Catalan, continued to exist until the 15th and sometimes the 17th c. (Venetian *Crete, up to 1669). The governing population of these colonies – mainly French or Italian – was always a minority, and was essentially but not exclusively urban. The need to protect pilgrims and defend these States gave rise to the *military orders (*Hospitallers, *Templars, *Teutonic Knights). They provided a permanent but also independent and often intractable army, whose role was essential in the maintenance of fortresses and the defence of *Palestine, then in policing the Mediterranean. Their possessions in East and West made them from the 12th c. the *bankers of the crusade.

The role of the crusades in the development of trade with the East has often been exaggerated, but it is undeniable. In the commerce of the Levant, alongside Egypt and Constantinople, Syria came to occupy a far from negligible place: the products of Damascus, Mosul or further Asia provided a return freight for the ships that transported pilgrims and provisioned the Holy Land. The crusades brought to the West, to an extent hard to determine, new techniques (*e.g.* of *navigation) and new products (*glass, *silk, camlets, brocades, sugar-cane, cotton, apricots, etc.). They also brought to the East a constant flow of men and silver. This drain stimulated the monetarization of the Western economy, but also impoverished part of the *nobility, while contributing to the return to a gold *coinage in the West (1252) and certainly to the development of the Italian towns.

In the history of civilization, the oriental influences transmitted through the crusades were stronger on the material level (habits of dress, taste for luxury that penetrated via *Italy to Northern Europe in the Gothic period) than on the cultural level. The "colonial" art of the Latin States borrowed little from local traditions, despite exceptional examples like the Psalter of Queen Melisende or the Resafa Chalice. Intellectual contacts with the Orient were rare, save with Greek milieux between the 13th and 15th centuries. And it was mainly on the "frontiers" of *Spain or *Sicily that knowledge of *Islam progressed, while preaching persisted in conveying a denatured image of the enemy, despite efforts at greater understanding by some missionaries. On the Muslim side, the crusades aroused no comparable unitary movement, though the Frankish presence revived the **jihād*, used rather as an instrument of middle-eastern policy, and led to the creation of a military State in Egypt increasingly intolerant towards the Oriental Christians (*Maronites, Armenians) who had compromised with the Franks and Mongols in the 13th century.

The local Christian communities, at first favourable to the crusaders, gave little support to the Latin Church's claims to hegemony, and only the Maronites agreed in 1182 to recognise Roman primacy. Above all, the crusades were the main cause of the rupture with Orthodox Christendom. The *schism of 1054 long remained an affair of clerics, and an awareness of unity had continued to exist throughout the 12th c., despite the difficulties and misunderstandings that never ceased to accompany the passage of the crusading armies, and despite the conflict of interests of Byzantium and the Latins in the East or in Italy. The events of 1204 were decisive in anchoring in the Byzantine national consciousness, inseparable from *Orthodoxy, a hatred of the Latin stronger than that of the Turk. This explains the repeated failures of attempts at a *union of the Churches, undertaken to ensure Byzantium the aid of the papal crusades.

The crusading indulgence was accorded not just to expeditions to Jerusalem or for the defence of the Christians of the East. From the 12th c., it was given to expeditions made in Spain or *Portugal against the Muslims, which in the end benefited from an automatically renewed *bull. It was also used in analogous situations against the *pagans of the Baltic lands. From the 13th c., it was extended to wars against heretics (the *Cathars, then the *Hussites), schismatics, or enemies of the Roman Church in Italy (*Frederick II, *Manfred, *Peter III of Aragon), or during the *Great Schism.

But this indulgence was not as plenary as that accorded for expeditions against non-Christians, and its use for such purposes aroused lively criticism even at the time, propagated mainly by *trouvères* and *troubadours and whose importance should not be minimized. Such criticisms were all the more favourably received as failures aroused growing doubt, starting with the second crusade, and as the taxation that flowed from them was increasingly ill-supported by an opinion whose enthusiasm declined without altogether disappearing.

In fact the crusading ideal continued to exist: individual *conversion and penitence of the believer, but also a common enterprise, capable – as it sometimes showed – of surmounting divisions and rifts, a decisive element in the formation of medieval *Christendom and its *spirituality.

S. Runciman, *A History of the Crusades*, 3 vol., Cambridge, 1951. – *A History of the Crusades*, K. M. Setton (ed.), Philadelphia (PA), 1955-1989 (6 vol.). – P. Alphandéry, A. Dupront, *La Chrétienté et l'Idée de croisade*, Paris, 1954-1959. – E. Sivan, *L'Islam et la Croisade*, Paris, 1968. – J. Prawer, *Histoire du royaume latin de Jérusalem*, Paris, 1969. – J. Richard, *L'Esprit de la croisade*, Paris, 1969 (selected texts). – *CStS*, 49, 69 and 182, 1976, 1979, 1983. – K. M. Setton, *The Papacy and the Levant (1204-1571)*, 1976-1984 (4 vol.). – J. Richard, *The Latin Kingdom of Jerusalem*, Amsterdam, 1979. – F. Gabrieli, *Arab Historians of the Crusades* (selected texts), London, 1984 (1st ed. 1969). – E. Delaruelle, *L'Idée de croisade au Moyen Âge*, Turin, 1980. – C. Cahen, *Orient et Occident au temps des croisades*, Paris, 1983. – E. Siberry, *Criticism of Crusading: 1095-1294*, Oxford, 1985. – J. Riley-Smith, *The Crusades*, London-New Haven (CT), 1987. – H. E. Mayer, *The Crusades*, London, 1988 (2nd ed.). – C. Morrisson, *Les Croisades*, 1994 (7th ed.; "QSJ"). – C.T. Maier, *Preaching the Crusades*, Cambridge, 1994. – *The Oxford Illustrated History of the Crusades*, J. Riley-Smith (ed.), Oxford-New York, 1995. – J. Richard, *Histoire des Croisades*, Paris, 1996. – J. Riley-Smith, *The First Crusaders, 1095-1131*, Cambridge, 1997. – *Montjoie: Studies in Crusade History in Honour of Hans Eberhard Mayer*, B.Z. Kedar (ed.), J. Riley-Smith (ed.), R. Hiestland (ed.), Aldershot, 1997.

Cécile Morrisson

**CRYPT.** A crypt is an architectural structure situated beneath the choir and sometimes the transept of churches, reached by steps inside the building. These constructions were intended for the cult of *relics as well as the *burial of important people.

The term at first designated underground caverns or galleries dug in the rock, on which places of worship were built in the Constantinian period (basilica of the Nativity at Bethlehem, of the *Holy Sepulchre at Jerusalem, *St Peter's or *St Paul's without the Walls at Rome). *Gregory of Tours uses the word to designate funerary *hypogea or underground *oratories created in direct relation to the cult of relics. In the 6th and 7th cc., this type of architectural structure became widespread. *Gregory the Great built a semi-circular crypt under St Peter's basilica: on each side, the circular passage ended in steps that allowed the faithful to circulate. It was crossed in the centre by a corridor via which they reached the apostolic *tomb under the high *altar. The monument responded to the growing influx of *pilgrims and the wish to keep them away from the place of liturgical celebration.

This architectural solution had a wide and enduring success. Outside Rome, it was adopted at *Saint-Denis (775), *Saint-Maurice d'Agaune (late 8th c.), Sankt Emmeram at *Regensburg (after 791), etc., and commonly occurs up to the 10th century. The 9th c. was particularly inventive in conceiving these sacred spaces: circular at St Michael's, *Fulda (820-822); rectangular (818-819), then with a U-shaped corridor opening onto a space with three aisles at Saint-Germain, *Auxerre (841). The designers of Carolingian crypts tended to create relatively extensive and articulated spaces to respond to the habit of burying important people there and the need to have well-defined spaces for their monuments. The Ottonian period saw a uniformization of architectural models, with a marked preference

Crypt of the church of Saint-Laurent at Grenoble, 6th c.

for spaces with several aisles, punctuated by columns, and ending in an apse. This enlargement of the space, going so far as to create a veritable lower church, was caused by a new liturgical need, the crypt becoming an oratory intended for the *offices. Several types of crypts are found: crypt with one room and apse, very widespread in central Europe up to the 13th c., crypt with room surrounded by an ambulatory onto which could open chapels corresponding to those of the choir, external crypts backing on to the apse of the choir but slightly lower (Meuse region), transepted crypts like those influenced by the first construction at *Speyer (1024-1041), etc. The fittings of the choir in the Gothic period – notably the creation of chapels radiating around the ambulatory, capable of housing relics and important burials – made crypts less indispensable. The rare constructions are explained by architectural necessities of foundation and not by liturgical imperatives.

F. Deshoulières, "Les cryptes en France et l'influence du culte des reliques sur l'architecture religieuse", *Mélanges en hommage à la mémoire de Fr. Martroye*, Paris, 1940, 213-238. – A. Grabar, *Martyrium. Recherches sur le culte des reliques et de l'art chrétien antique*, Paris, 1943-1946. – J. Hubert, "*Cryptae inferiores et cryptae superiores* dans l'architecture religieuse de l'époque carolingienne", *Mélanges d'histoire du Moyen Âge en mémoire de Louis Halphen*, Paris, 1951, 351-357. – *Le monde des cryptes*, C. J. Nesmy (ed.), Saint-Léger-Vauban, 1973 ("La nuit des temps"). – M. S. Burke, "L'uso e la diffusione delle cripte nell'Europa carolingia", *Roma e l'età carolingia. Atti delle giornate di studio*, Rome, 1976, 319-323. – D. De Bernardi Ferrero, "Cripte presbiterali romane e cripte carolingie", *ibid.*, 325-330. – C. Heitz, "Cryptes pré-romanes", *Du VIII^e^ au XI^e^ siècle: édifices monastiques et culte en Lorraine et Bourgogne*, Paris, 1977, 31-34. – G. Binding, M. Restle, "Krypta", *LdM*, 5, 1991, 1554-1557. – F. Guidobaldi, M. T. Gigliozzi, "Cripta", *Enc. dell'arte medievale*, 3, Rome, 1992, 472-487.

Pierre Kerbrat

## CULT OF THE SAINTS

**The West.** The first believers whose memory the Church commemorated were the *martyrs, *i.e.* Christians who had been executed by persecutors because of their *faith. Their cult is not attested in the Latin Church before the 3rd c., but it later spread throughout the Roman Empire from Africa. The saint was a particular dead person, since the *anniversary of his death was celebrated by the Christian community – and not just by those close to him – as that of his birth into *heaven (*dies natalis*). He was considered to enter immediately into a blessed eternity, by reason of his fidelity to Christ with whose sacrifice he was united by his sufferings. No procedure of *canonization existed at that time, but the cult of the saints was under the control of local *bishops.

From the 4th c., the cult of the saints became one of the fundamental aspects of Christian piety. Transposing to the religious domain the system of human relations that characterised the society of Late Antiquity and the early Middle Ages, Christians considered their saints as "patrons" capable of interceding in their favour with the Divinity, as did members of the aristocracy close to the prince. Their protection could be invoked on every occasion, but their miraculous power was manifested in all its plenitude in the place where their body or their *relics rested. The *virtus* that emanated from holy bodies procured health for the living and eternal *salvation for the *dead. It also counteracted *demons and could deliver the possessed. The desire of believers to benefit from their protection rapidly led to a multiplication of relics, and churches often took the name of the saint whose body, or one of its fragments, they housed. Though each local church was anxious to possess its own saints, a certain number of them were the object of a cult throughout Christendom, in particular the Apostles, the Virgin *Mary, *John the Baptist, St Michael and some particularly prestigious martyrs like St Stephen or St Lawrence. Contrary to a widely credited idea, phenomena of cultual continuity between pagan gods and Christian saints are relatively rare. The cult paid to the saints was originally more of an urban phenomenon, since it was in the necropolises of the cities that the martyrs and bishops rested. It later spread into the countryside, as this was Christianized.

The growing success of the cult of the saints led to the redaction of passions of martyrs or *legends of confessor saints, which described in a stereotyped way and a heroic mode the exploits of God's servants, as well as collections of *miracles, often linked to a particular sanctuary. These texts were only integrated into the liturgical *offices recited by *clerics at a relatively late date (8th c. at *Rome). Monastic communities began from the 7th c. to draw up lives of their founding or reforming saints and devote a cult to them. From all this resulted a certain anarchy which the ecclesiastical hierarchy sought to end by strengthening episcopal control, as witness a series of prescriptions that appear in the *capitularies of *Charlemagne and *Louis the Pious. These texts expressly forbade the veneration of new relics without the consent of the local ordinary and reserved to the emperor or to a *synod the right to order the translation of saints' bodies, *i.e.* their transfer from a *tomb to a *reliquary or an *altar. Up to the early 13th c., this liturgical ceremony presided over by a prelate constituted an act sufficient to guarantee the licitness of the cult paid to a servant of God. But these disciplinary rules were far from being respected everywhere, which explains why the promoters of new cults addressed themselves increasingly frequently to the papacy from the 12th c., and why the papacy finally affirmed, under *Innocent

III and *Gregory IX, its exclusive privilege of canonizing saints, *i.e.* of authorizing the celebration of their liturgical cult all over the Christian world or in a given country. This new procedure in no way diminished the enthusiasm of the faithful for the cult of the saints, which enjoyed considerable growth all over the West between the 13th and 15th cc., both in the domain of liturgical worship and in the framework of the civic religion promoted by the public authorities.

P. Jounel, *Le Culte des saints dans les basiliques du Latran et du Vatican au XII^e siècle*, Rome-Paris, 1977. – P. Brown, *The Cult of the Saints: its Rise and Function in Latin Christianity*, London, 1981. – T. Head, *Hagiography and the Cult of Saints*, Cambridge, 1990. – B. F. Abou-El-Haj, *The Medieval Cult of Saints*, Cambridge, 1994. – *La Religion civique à l'époque médiévale et moderne (chrétienté et islam)*, A. Vauchez (dir.), Rome-Paris, 1996. – A. Vauchez, *Sainthood in the Later Middle Ages*, Cambridge, 1997.

André Vauchez

**Byzantium.** Christian Antiquity transmitted to the Byzantine world the cult of the *martyrs with its practices and its theology which made the holy martyr one of the glorious dead who was honoured and an effective intercessor who was prayed to. The great persecution followed by the peace of the Church led to major developments. Numerous Eastern Churches maintained their saints, and the rallying of *Constantine to Christianity allowed the cult paid to them to become public.

Though they were the saints *par excellence*, the martyrs were not alone. The *prophets and apostles had preceded them, the holy *bishops and, especially, the ascetics and monks joined them. The choir of saints was not a closed group with defined limits. Private or local devotion led to numerous cults. Particular Churches played a major role, but very soon certain saints were honoured more widely. The first *martyrology we possess (Syriac martyrology of 411, translated from a Greek document) was already a learned compilation. The great centres were provided with an abundant *sanctoral that went beyond the list of local saints. In the 9th and 10th cc., *Constantinople continued this movement and it was there that the instrument was formulated that sought to bring all the saints together: the **Synaxarion* of Constantinople.

The date or memorial of a saint inscribed in the calendars was in principle the *anniversary of his death. It was then that the saint's feast took place, modest (commemoration in the *office) or splendid: celebration resembling a fair, vigil, *procession. Secondary feasts were possible and personal piety could be continual.

The most splendid feasts took place at the tomb of the saint sometimes enshrined in a *martyrium*, a central-plan building conceived to facilitate the devotions of pilgrims. *Martyria*, at first outside the towns, later made their way inside. Martyrium and church, in principle distinct, could be confused, and from the 5th c. we see churches bearing the name of a saint. Certain cities honoured a particular saint (Demetrius at *Thessalonica). Great sanctuaries (St Menas, St Sergius, St Theodore. . .) saw an influx of pilgrims, and the cult of the saints could change the nature of a place: Rešaina, from a village, became a city (Sergiopolis). Cults spread and led to secondary places of worship. We must also take private devotion into consideration.

The *relic played an important role. The devout sought to be in contact with it by kissing it, touching it, sleeping near it (incubation), receiving a liquid in which it had been bathed. It could be translated or divided, each part having the same virtue as the whole.

Also venerated was the saint's *image, to which was paid, especially from the 6th c., a cult whose abuses provoked a reaction: *iconoclasm (8th-9th cc.). The image prevailed with the restoration of *Orthodoxy (843), but it did so in the novel form of the *icon, at once revered and guarded.

H. Delehaye, *Sanctus, Essai sur le culte des saints dans l'antiquité*, 1927 ("SHG", 17; repr. 1970). – A. Grabar, *Martyrium, Recherches sur le cult des reliques et l'art chrétien antique*, 1-2, Paris, 1946. – P. Brown, *The Cult of the Saints. Its Rise and Function in Latin Christianity*, London, 1981. – H. Delehaye, *L'ancienne hagiographie byzantine*, Brussels, 1991.

Bernard Flusin

**CUMANS.** The Cumans (more properly Kumans) were a nomadic Turkic people. Called "Kun" by the Hungarians and "Polovtsy" by the Russians (these names suggest a "pale" colour), they had been forced out of Mongolia by the Kitan and had absorbed the Qipchaq of eastern Siberia; in 1054, they appeared on the frontiers of the Russians. In 1091, they had crushed the *Pechenegs, pursued their remnants as far as *Hungary and occupied their territory. Those who remained north of the Aral Sea formed relations with the Khwarizmian Muslims. Defeated in 1109 by *Vladimir Monomakh, Khan Otrok fled to *Georgia with 40,000 warriors, received baptism and helped King David II, now his son-in-law, against the Muslims (1122); he later returned to the steppes.

The Cumans who settled north of the Black Sea and the Caspian formed two confederations that fused together in the late 12th century. Their conflicts with the Russians, marked by reciprocal razzias, one of which is celebrated in the *Story of Prince Igor*, did not rule out family ties: several of their princes bore Russian names. And it was with the Russian princes that they confronted the *Mongols who defeated them on the Kalka (1223). Their bands passed into the pay of the Hungarians and of German princes, and took advantage to pillage them; Hungary even called in the *Teutonic Knights to contain their raids. It was with the Cumans that Tsar Kalojan defeated Emperor Baldwin of Constantinople, whose successor managed to stem them in 1208. But in 1239, those who lived nomadically in *Bulgaria went into the service of Baldwin II. The defeat of the Kalka allowed the king of Hungary to extend his protectorate over their country (he entitled himself *rex Cumanie*) and *Dominican missionaries to make sufficient *conversions for the pope in 1229 to create a bishopric "of the Cumans". The Mongols reappeared in 1238 and, because they carried out copious massacres, the Cumans asked permission to enter Hungary, offering to become Christians; but the Hungarians killed numbers of those whom the king had thus welcomed. Béla IV persisted in establishing them in his kingdom and married his son to the daughter of their chief. Hardly Christianized, the Cumans remained troublemakers; King Ladislas the Cuman, who favoured them, had to repress their revolt in 1280. *Evangelization made no headway; the pope had to create a *mission of Friars Minor for the Cumans of Hungary (1348) and allow a diminution of *tithes for those who became Christians. They do not seem to have been permanently Christianized until the late 14th c.; but the Cumans kept their individuality within the Hungarian kingdom.

An important Cuman element continued to exist under the power of the Mongols: 13th-c. travellers found Christian Cumans as far as Mongolia, and Ibn Batuta considered the "Qipchaq" of *Crimea to be Christians. They gradually became absorbed into the Tatar population.

A. Palóczi Horváth, *Petchenegs, Cumans, Iasians: Steppe Peoples in Medieval Hungary*, Budapest, 1989. – P. Golden, "The Cumans", *Cambridge History of Early Inner Asia*, Cambridge, 1990, 277-284.

Jean Richard

**CUNEGUND, EMPRESS (*c.*978-1033).** Born into the family of the counts of *Luxemburg, in *c.*998 Cunegund (Kunigunde) married Duke Henry of Bavaria, who became king in 1002. As queen, then empress (1014), she enjoyed great influence. But her image and posthumous glory were marked by the sterility of her marriage, which, exceptionally, did not lead to her repudiation. Keeping her close to him, *Henry II associated her especially in the creation of the bishopric of *Bamberg. Widowed in 1024, she retired to her *foundation of Kaufingen, where she died on 3 March 1033. Her body was transferred to Bamberg, where a reputation for *sanctity arose late, in the wake of that of her husband who was canonized in 1146. Nourished by legends of her celibate marriage and *ordeal revealing her fidelity and *virginity, this reputation culminated in her *canonization, 29 March 1200. Her cult, enriched with Marian themes, was fervent in the late Middle Ages.

R. Folz, *Les saintes reines du Moyen Âge*, Brussels, 1992, 82-93.

Patrick Corbet

***CURA ANIMARUM*, CURE OF SOULS.** In the Middle Ages this expression designated the authority entrusted by the *bishop to a churchman who received a *benefice involving the charge of souls. We can discover the distant origin of *cura animarum* in the Church *Fathers and the Carolingian authors. The formula was applied at first to any pastoral function whatever, before being restricted to that of the *parish priest. The use of *cura animarum* became general in acts relating to the status of churches, before being recognised by the council of *Clermont (1095). This assembly specified that in parish churches the priests were instituted by the bishops, to whom they were answerable for the *cura animarum*.

This prescription, ceaselessly repeated, made *canonical institution the essential act of designation of the incumbent. In fact, the situation was more complex, since the parish church constituted a benefice, *i.e.* a group of revenues intended to provide for the needs of its holder. Now, by *cura animarum*, *clerics acceded to a parish benefice independently of the reception of holy *orders, from which they could in any case be dispensed. Thus was set up a dissociation between the benefices and the exercise of the pastoral *ministry (office). In fact, the holder of the benefice arranged a substitute in the person of a stipendiary cleric (*vicar, *chaplain).

We must not confuse *cura animarum* and jurisdiction. This latter notion, originating in *Roman law, made its reappearance in the 12th c. and described the spiritual power of any cleric ordained to the *priesthood. In short, jurisdiction consisted of the execution of sacerdotal powers (*executio ordinis*). So a cleric could hold the *cura animarum* of a church without exercising the priesthood. Conversely, the priest recognised by the bishop exercised a spiritual jurisdiction, but did not possess the benefice and thus the *cura animarum* of the church he served. However *cura animarum* was always applied to the government of souls, since from this expression was drawn the term *curatus*, which later became a noun and, from the 13th c., designated the head of the *parish, the French *curé*.

J. Avril, "Quelques aspects de l'institution paroissiale après le IVe concile du Latran", *Église et réformes dans l'Église de la réforme grégorienne à la préréforme, Actes du 115e congrès national des Sociétés savantes, Avignon 1990*, Paris, 1991, 93-106. – J. Avril, *Pastoral Care, Clerical Education and Canon Law (1200-1400)*, London, 1981.

Joseph Avril

**CURIA, ROMAN.** In ancient Rome, the term *curia* had designated a group of important families, then the seat of the Senate. From the beginning of the 11th c., the revival of this word caused the term *palatium*, which had defined the court over the centuries, to fall into disuse. The Roman Church, taking inspiration from royal and imperial *courts, adopted it towards the end of the 11th c. under the impetus of the reforming papacy. Referring to lay and French, notably Cluniac, models, *Urban II (1088-1099) laid the foundations of a "curial" organisation. Under this pontificate the terms *curia*, *camera* and *cappella* are attested for the first time. A Frenchman and former Cluniac, Urban II not only borrowed from *Cluny a new term to designate the financial organ of the apostolic see, he also seems to have used the Cluniac *camera* for the reception and transfer of *rents, revenues and *donations. Under *Paschal II (1099-1118) and *Calixtus II (1119-1124) again, Cluny controlled the Roman financial administration.

Urban II also reorganised the *chancery, deciding to abandon the old Roman curial *script in favour of chancery minuscule, and introduced a new date for the beginning of the year.

A college of papal *chaplains is attested after the pontificate of Urban II. The importance of this *chapel, whose model was certainly of German origin, increased considerably under Paschal II. Its rise confirmed the decline of the old *scriniarii* (secretaries).

After the victory of the *Gregorian reform and the end of the *schism of 1130, the Roman Church had become a veritable high court of justice to which flowed increasingly frequent *appeals of all kinds, which required new competencies. The recruitment of *cardinals felt the effects of this. The first half of the 12th c. records an increased presence of *magistri* among the cardinals as well as eminent *jurists (*Peter of Pisa) and theologians (*Robert Pullen).

At the time *Innocent III became pope (1198), the chancery and the *Camera were – since 1194 – under the authority of a single cardinal, Cencius, the future *Honorius III. Innocent III returned to the earlier situation, and even Honorius III made no attempt to reunite these two traditionally distinct organisations. Innocent III's three cardinal chancellors and his five vice-chancellors came from them, as did the *scriptores*. The vice-chancellor was helped by *notaries, *abbreviators, correctors, distributors and "rescribendaries", as well as by the clerics in charge of keeping the registers. Vice-chancellors and notaries were generally men of experience, trained in the great new schools of law (*Bologna, *Paris). As with the old *notarii regionarii*, the number of the pope's notaries was limited to seven. Some of them were charged with important diplomatic missions (legations). At the beginning of the 13th c., the *scriptores* were relieved of their liturgical duties and devoted themselves more particularly to the drawing up of acts. They formed a college, whose first traces go back to the pontificate of Innocent III. It was only from the time of Innocent III that the *scriptores* set their signature (in the form of a *sigla*) to the cover (*plica*) of the documents, which served as a basis for their fees.

Until the end of the 13th c., very few cardinals directed the Camera. The new pope generally appointed a confidential person to this post. The head of the Camera became undoubtedly the most important curialist in the 13th century. The way had been prepared in the 12th c. by men like Boso or Cencius. The *camerarius* lived in the Lateran, close to the pope. The camerlengo was responsible for the reception of the revenues of the Roman Church, administered the pope's palace as well as the churches dependent on the papacy, and had charge of the administration of the landed *patrimony of the *States of the Church. Towards the end of the century, the office of *camerarius* was no longer exclusively connected with the person of the pope. The council of *Vienne (1311) decided that in case of the pope's death, the cardinals were to appoint a new *camerarius* for the whole duration of the vacancy of the apostolic see.

From the pontificate of *Innocent IV (1243-1254), the pope's treasury, comprising *library, archives and jewels, gold and silver *vessels, furniture, carpets, *liturgical objects and ornaments, was put under the responsibility first of one, then of two treasurers, who generally belonged to the college of the pope's chaplains.

The first traces of *bankers officially residing at the Roman curia goes back to the *ordo* of Cencius, who speaks of *officiales camerarii* and mentions a *cambiator*. The title of *campsor camerae* (moneychanger of the Camera) appears under *Gregory IX (1227-1241). Under *Urban IV appeared the title of *mercatores camerae* or *mercatores domini papae*. For a long time the company of the Buonsignori (of *Siena) occupied a position of monopoly. *Gregory X (1271-1276) brought to the curia the bankers of his home town (*Piacenza), the Scotti. Towards the end of the 13th c., the most important companies were those of the Mozzi, Spini and Chiarenti. These bankers were in charge of regulating all the payments of the Camera, even those intended for the curialists.

The complexity of the procedures made indispensable the presence at *Rome of attorneys, Italian *jurists with stated competencies. Their work was controlled by the *audientia litterarum contradictarum*, a sort of court for attorneys.

During the first half of the 13th c. appeared a new type of legal personnel composed essentially of the papal chaplains called in to replace the cardinals, previously his sole collaborators in the administration of justice. Innocent III was the first to use as auditors, much more systematically than in the past, members of his chapel enjoying his confidence.

Under Innocent IV, within the relatively large group of the pope's chaplains emerged a more restricted number of *auditores (generales) sacri palatii*. The constitution of this specialized legal body gradually took the administration of justice away from the other papal chaplains residing at the Roman curia.

The organisation of the *Penitentiary Office was in place from the beginning of the 13th century. The only curial organisation apart from the almonry to have purely spiritual tasks, it was also the only one in the 13th c. to be presided over by a cardinal. The first attestation of a curial cardinal charged specifically with looking after penitential affairs coincides with the pontificate of Innocent III. Recruited almost exclusively among the two main *mendicant orders (*Dominicans and *Franciscans), the *penitentiaries had the power to give *absolutions and to commission ordinary *bishops to give *dispensations.

Under Innocent III, the official distribution of *alms by the pope and the Roman curia appears a well-established tradition. In the course of the 13th c., a specific organisation was created: the almonry, whose origins escape us. Every day, poor people assembled – generally in the refectory of the basilica of Theodore – to receive food, money and clothing. At the pope's death, the members of the almonry had to wash the dead man's body, dress it in papal *vestments and then entrust it to the penitentiaries. The almonry was also in charge of the annual *procession from *St Peter's to the hospital of the Holy Spirit where the curialists were cared for when the curia was at Rome.

E. Göller, *Die päpstliche Pönitentiarie*, Rome, 1907-1911 (2 vol.). – B. Rusch, *Die Behörden und Hofbeamten der päpstlichen Kurie des 13. Jahrhunderts*, Königsberg, 1936. – R. Elze, "Die päpstliche Kapelle im 12. und 13. Jahrhundert", *ZSRG.K*, 36, 1950, 171-175. – P. Rabikauskas, *Diplomatica pontificia*, Rome, 1964. – J. Sayers, "Canterbury Proctors at the Court of 'Audientia litterarum contradictarum'", *Tr.*, 22, 1966, 311-345. – G. F. Nüske, "Untersuchungen über das Personal der päpstlichen Kanzlei 1254-1304", *ADipl*, 20, 1974, 39-240; 21, 1975, 249-431. – P. Classen, "Die römische Kurie und die Schulen", *Studium und Gesellschaft im Mittelalter*, J. Fried (ed.), Stuttgart, 1983.

Agostino Paravicini Bagliani

**CURSE.** Cursing, calling upon God or the gods to punish or destroy the accursed, and on mankind to exclude the accursed from society, entered Christian tradition as an integral part of Jewish, Roman and Greek cultural traditions. In addition to religious curses, Greek and Roman custom included curse formulae in legal transactions to add urgency to the execution of contractual obligations. In the Old Testament, the effects of a curse are death or exile. In the New Testament, curses, such as Peter's curse which struck dead Ananias and Sapphira (Acts 5), or that with which Paul threatens false preachers (Gal 1, 8-9) are understood to kill. Thus cursing tradition enters the Middle Ages in a wide spectrum of religious and worldly instances in which supernatural sanctions are intended to change behaviour or enforce social obligations.

Medieval curses are closely linked with the tradition of *excommunication. The exact nature and degrees of excommunication differed considerably across time, as did the role of curses in it. Excommunication was intended as a corrective, not as a punishment, and thus implied temporary exclusion either from the sacramental life of the community or from the community as a whole. From the 9th c., some churchmen sought to define *anathema as a more severe form of excommunication meaning eternal damnation, in effect a curse. This form of curse was reinforced by the use of curse formulae reminiscent of pagan curses in declarations of anathema as well as the assimilation of the anathematized with various biblical victims of curses. In the early Middle Ages, anathema curses were used to strengthen the sentence of excommunicates who did not seek *absolution.

Again in the tradition of classical usage, curse formulae also appear frequently in the penalty clauses of *charters, particularly in monastic documents. Here, in addition to stipulating a payment of a fine for breaching the terms of a *donation, exchange or sale, malefactors are threatened with a curse of eternal damnation. Such curse formulae, as well as the generally unrealistic and thus symbolic sums named as fines, presumably added solemnity to private transactions. Although such formulae appear from at least the 8th c., they become particularly frequent in the 10th and 11th centuries. This frequency is attributed to the decline of formal Carolingian institutions of justice and the need to replace public enforcement with the fear of divine retribution. In general, the use of such curse formulae declines in the later 11th and 12th cc., perhaps in response to the development of other, more effective means of enforcement.

A third curse tradition, closely related to both the anathema and the penalty clause in charters, is a formal ritual of malediction developed in monastic communities between the 9th and 11th centuries. These liturgies, which comprised part of the liturgical *Clamor*, drew on both biblical and liturgical traditions to censure publicly monastic enemies. The ritual itself is presented as a blessing should the individual mend his ways. Only if he does not is he to incur the impressive list of disasters and punishments the ritual announces. Such rituals presumably grew from a monastic desire to exercise a public ritual punishment similar to excommunication, which was the sole prerogative of *bishops. However, like the diplomatic penalty formula, the monastic curse disappeared in the course of the 12th century.

"Malédiction", *Cath.*, 8, 1979, 260-263. – E. Vodola, *Excommunication in the Middle Ages*, Berkeley (CA), 1986. – L. K. Little, *Benedictine Maledictions: Liturgical Cursing in Romanesque France*, Ithaca (NY), 1993.

Patrick J. Geary

***CURSUS.*** We call "cursus" the types of rhythmic structures, based on the place of the tonic accent of the words, that characterised the ends of phrases in artistic *Latin prose. This system was substituted in the Middle Ages for the classical one of metric *clausulae* based on the alternation of short and long syllables. Three types of cursus were favoured by medieval theoreticians: *cursus planus* (*"íllum dedúxit"*), *cursum tardus* (*"íre tentáverit"*) and *cursus velox* (*"hóminem recepístis"*). Infrequent during the first millennium, the practice of the cursus was codified in the 11th c. by the masters of the school of *Monte Cassino. From then on, it was systematically set to work first by the papal *chancery, then by men of letters: in *Dante, the three types mentioned above represent more than 98 % of *clausulae*. The Italian *humanists of the trecento progressively abandoned the cursus, but its use was perpetuated in papal documents up to the beginning of the 16th century.

M. Nicolau, *L'origine du cursus rhythmique et le début de l'accent d'intensité en latin*, Paris, 1930. – T. Janson, *Prose Rhythm in Medieval Latin from the IXth to the XIIIth Century*, Stockholm, 1975.

Jean-Yves Tilliette

**CUSTOM.** Understood as a source of law, custom was the whole of the legal usages observed by the population of a given place or a particular social group; it was imposed on institutions, especially legal ones. It had its basis in the memory and consensus of the people and not in a promulgation and redaction, differing in this from law. In the Middle Ages, custom formed an essential part of the law throughout Western Europe, but with great regional differences of evolution. For a long time, it was not clearly separated from the whole of the usages of a group or a place; it is not invoked in texts as a source of law until the mid 12th c. in France, and the expression "customary law" appears in the *summa Trecensis*, a learned Italian work of slightly earlier. Custom is among the sources of law distinguished by Gratian's **Decretum* in *c.*1140. We should not imagine that it was then, as a principle, very old: it took over from more conventional practices, often but not necessarily ancestral. In principle, custom rested on antiquity; but, being oral and consensual, it could suffer adaptation and innovation; some of the most famous customary institutions – exclusion of dowered daughters or lineal repurchase – seem no earlier than the late 12th century. Furthermore, custom was territorial and not personal, unlike the law of the early Middle Ages; moreover the word "custom" (*consuetudo*) and its equivalent "usage" (*usus* and its derivatives) also covered the rights and dues of lords or of the Church, which were not particularly old. This semantic link between legal usages and the obligations of subjects reveals a close connection between the formation of principalities, lordships or *towns and the recognition of custom as the law of a given territory. *Charters of franchises also often mingled customary arrangements and determinations of the lord's rights; the customary territory – the jurisdiction – evolved in accordance with the political construction of each region. In the 14th- and 15th-c. "Europe of States", regional customs unified or supplanted local ones, as is shown by the increasingly frequent use of the expression "general custom", designating that of a whole province.

Memory was the repositary of custom and the judge was surrounded by assessors considered to know it; their advice was binding on him as long as it was unanimous. Indeed, procedures kept alive its memory or allowed its content to be ascertained. Entry of rulers into office or the meeting of assemblies, such as general **placita*, were the occasion for a recital or a public reading of the custom, which also allowed it to be amended or supplemented. While knowledge of custom was easy in a restricted area, it became difficult to measure as administrative evolution entailed the organisation of procedures of appeal, which put general customs in competition with other more local ones: we see this with the immense jurisdiction of the *Parlement of *Paris. Moreover, the political and administrative edifice put in place officials (**baillis*, castellans, etc.) often foreign to the region they served. It was hence increasingly necessary to make proof of custom, whether the judge proceeded to an inquiry or whether those being judged procured witnesses. The kingdom of *France (and some neighbouring regions) knew in particular the inquiry by *turba* (usually a group of ten persons), regulated by an *ordinance of 1270 and abolished in the 17th century. Other procedures existed, such as recourse to *chef de sens* (consultation of a higher or well-informed institution), or the production of legal precedents in court. The – so frequent – request not to be subject to foreign judges must be understood in connection with anxiety about knowledge of custom. A whole literature of practitioners developed, especially in the 13th and 14th cc.: *styles* – court procedures – collections of cases, and especially *customaries, which brought together and commented on the usages of a region, supplemented and clarified by recourse to learned rules or to the customs of neighbouring regions. Ordinarily, these dealt with the law of the land and the law of *fiefs; this was the case of Philippe de Beaumanoir's *Coutumes de Beauvaisis*, Jacques d'Ableiges's *Grand Coutumier de France* (understood as Île-de-France) or Eike von Repgow's *Sachsenspiegel*. Private compilations, these customaries came nevertheless to serve as proof of custom. Finally, the official redaction of customs, imposed by *Charles VII in 1454, aimed, perhaps primarily, to dispense the judge from having to establish it and those judged from having to prove it.

Custom was made precise by contact with learned law; it was defined with the help of *Roman law and dealt with by civilists and *canonists; they defined its characteristics, its connections with *mores* and usages, with municipal statutes, with written law. They asked whether oral character was determinative, whether consensus or popular usage was the basis of custom, to what extent custom supplied what was lacking in the law or could be opposed to it, and to what extent custom derived from the people could be valid against the power of the prince. Through their variety, the learned theories and the political exigencies they reflected gradually led custom to lose its flexibility, by specifying the requirement of antiquity (custom had to be *immemorial*), sometimes modified in terms of the conformity, or not, of custom with Roman law. Its autonomy went the same way, theoreticians defending the principle of its conformity to *reason, which allowed the prince to attack "bad customs", and culminating in the principle that the validity of custom depended on the – at least tacit – acquiescence of authority, on its official redaction or on the sanction of jurisprudence.

In 13th-c. France, the South of the kingdom recognised the superiority of written law; even sanctioned by a charter of franchises, local customs were hardly invoked any more from the 14th century. The North, by contrast, was recognised as customary and the writing down of customs was late there. This division of the realm is difficult to explain; perhaps it reflected the pre-eminent role in the Midi of jurists specializing in Roman law and having doctrinal reservations about custom, while in the North, Church jurists – especially *officialities – prevailed, whom *canon law made more accommodating towards custom. However, since law was studied through notarial practice, the frontier of principle did not prevent the existence of local usages in the South (a custom of practitioners), nor a learned evolution of legal institutions in the North, the will of *notaries and the learned formulary not being without repercussions on the law itself. In the 16th c., Roman law was reaffirmed in the Midi, while the North remained customary; yet custom there was increasingly written down, verified by legal authority, controlled by the ruler and rivalled by the resumption of legislative activity; attested mainly through jurisprudence, the redactions and usages of the courts, custom tended to merge with them. From the 14th c., what was alive and autonomous in custom had mainly to do with commercial or professional practices.

Philippe de Beaumanoir, *The Coutumes de Beauvaisis of Philippe de Beaumanoir*, F. R. P. Akehurst (ed.), Philadelphia (PA), 1992.

J. Gilissen, *La Coutume*, 1982 ("TSMÂO", 41). – G. Van Dievoet, *Les Coutumiers, les styles, les formulaires et les "artes notariae"*, 1986 ("TSMÂO", 48). – P. Ourliac, "Réflexions sur l'origine de la coutume", *MSHD*, 45, 1988, 341-354. – *La Coutume-Custom*, 2, 1990 ("RSJB", 52). – *Law, Custom, and the Social Fabric in Medieval Europe*, B.S. Bachrach (ed.), D. Nicholas (ed.), Kalamazoo (MI), 1990. – R. C. Stacey, *The Road to Judgment*, Philadelphia (PA), 1994. – R. Fleming, *Domesday Book and the Law: Society and Legal Custom in early Medieval England*, Cambridge, 1998.

Jean-Daniel Morerod

**CUSTOMARY, MONASTIC.** A monastic customary was a document indicating a monastery's way of life, from day to day, generally in a particular house. This document could bear various names: *regula*, *ordo*, *usus*, *institutio*, *consuetudines*, *liber consuetudinum*, *statutum*, *breviarium caeremoniarum*.

From the time when monks became numerous, monastic life in a laura or a *coenobium* involved certain norms, accepted by all. A first, fundamental point concerned the spirit in which life had to be lived in the monastery. Then it was necessary to organise daily life and prayer life, liturgy and private *prayer, insofar as it interfered with the common life, and fix the timetable. It was necessary to regulate the organisation of the community, the way of designating the superior, the various offices, the reception of postulants, the training of *novices, relations with the world, visitations, reception of guests (and which guests?), journeys, relations with neighbours and the church hierarchy, and the indispensable economic life. Finally there were disciplinary measures for the amendment of offenders. In the period of the beginnings of monastic life in the West, from the 5th to the 7th c., we know some 30 documents of this type, called "monastic *Rules", more or less developed. In them we find these two main elements, principles of religious life and usages permitting life to be lived according to these principles from day to day, what would later be called "customs". The Rules of *Augustine, Basil, Pachomius and "the four Fathers", were the "source Rules". Subsequently, founders were inspired by them to compose the norms of their house.

At the time of a *foundation, a rule was adopted, either composed by the founder-superior himself, or one coming from another monastery. In the latter case, the imported rule was modified so as to adapt it to local conditions. The same thing was done by the superior who composed his own rule inspired by a pre-existing text. Each monastery thus had its particular norms, the "custom of the place", of which the *abbot was guardian and authorized interpreter. A rule was followed, but by adapting it, *i.e.* adding particular usages to it. These particular usages would take the name of "customs" as opposed to acknowledged rules. A typical example is that of *Monte Cassino where, at the end of the 8th c., the Rule of St *Benedict was followed, but on certain points the usages practised at the monastery differed from those of St Benedict (liturgy, food, work, clothing). These customs, called *usum*, were observed "*per consuetudinem, sicut a maioribus nostris utiliter instituta sunt*". Note the appeal to the elders: it was they who guaranteed particular usages. The characteristic tendency of the customs was their practical side, which distinguished them from the rule, foundation of the monastery's life. The rule of the founder (in this case St Benedict) was still followed some two hundred years after his death, but with adaptations, renewed usages. So we see the working of the relationship between "rule" and local traditions or "customs". This corresponded to a still very free stage of monastic life.

*Charlemagne, then his son *Louis the Pious, helped by St *Benedict of Aniane († 821) tried to organise and unify the increase in monastic life. After an austere training in the Egyptian style at Saint-Seine in Burgundy, Benedict of Aniane founded a monastery in Languedoc, where he adopted the Rule of St Benedict, the only rule suitable for monks and summing up all other rules. But in choosing the Rule of St Benedict, he added "salutary" customs to it, since there were things of which the rule did not speak and which were necessary for daily life, and moreover some prescriptions had to be omitted in order to safeguard propriety (otherwise called the progress of lifestyle, hygiene, etc.) or out of consideration for human weakness, as indeed the Rule of St Benedict wishes. The domain of custom was thus clearly delimited in relation to that of the rule: it was everything that was changing, linked to external conditions. While the rule expressed the ideal, principles had to orient the life of the monastery and the monk. Under the influence of Benedict of Aniane, in accordance with the decisions of the monastic synod of Aachen (817), the Rule of St Benedict officially became the sole rule of the monasteries of the *Empire. So in the monasteries of the West this rule was followed, but at the same time, no less voluntarily, other norms and customs were always being added to it, which modernized or adapted it to times and places. To observe the rule, from the 10th c., was to receive a set of norms, of which the Rule of St Benedict was the first but not the only one. Thus we see the close link between what was called "rule" and the matter that was put into the customaries. No monastery without a rule, and also no rule lived without customs and hence a customary.

Normally the custom was simply lived, and had no need to be

written down. The circumstances of its codification also explain the literary genres encountered.

There were customaries of *ordinary type. They were written to fix liturgical usages, when the period of creation was over. Their genesis is explained by monastic liturgical practice. To remind the community of what had to be sung, or what ceremonies had to be observed, the *cantor read in *chapter the "brief" where they were written down. Bringing together the pages of the brief formed the basis of a collection of these customs. Thus the original Cluniac documents, then later the great customaries of the 12th-13th cc. (*Bec, *Fleury).

Then there was the customary of daily usages, which were put down in writing when there was a need to transmit an *ordo*, a way of living, to another house. This house could be either a new foundation in search of a rule, or a house that needed to be reformed. Such a need was manifested at first particularly in periods of expansion, when new monasteries were founded, and later at times of restoration, when abandoned houses were restored or refounded. Often the two phenomena were concomitant, particularly in the Carolingian period (Benedict of Aniane), in the 10th-11th cc. and, later, in the 14th-15th centuries. Examination of the chronological table of customaries verifies that these centuries were also those of the appearance of customaries.

**Geography of customaries.** The study of customaries and the differences of usage they attest (comparative method) shows us, in the 9th-10th cc., two great groups, that of *Cluny and its related houses, in the Aquitanian world, and the "Frankish" group, extended over a broad band, from *Fleury to the banks of the Danube (*Regensburg). In this more traditional Frankish group, usages predating the *reform of Benedict of Aniane, before the introduction of the Rule of St Benedict, seem to be better preserved. The English world borrowed from both groups. Later the influence of Cluny, and exchanges between monasteries, led to a certain unification of daily usages, while liturgical customs on the contrary kept their singularity more easily.

*CCMon*, 1, 1963, 59-74 (list of known customaries and their editions). – L. Donnat, "Les Coutumiers monastiques, une nouvelle entreprise et un territoire nouveau", *RMab*, new series, 3, 1992, 5-21.

Lin Donnat

**CYNEWULF.** The majority of Old English poetry that has come down to us has been transmitted anonymously. There are four religious poems, however, which have embedded within them the name CYN(E)WULF, spelled out in *runic script, and it is a reasonable assumption that these poems are the product of a single poet named Cynewulf, though it is impossible to identify any vernacular poet of this name in surviving Anglo-Saxon records. The four poems in question are: *The Fates of the Apostles* (a poem apparently based on a version of a Latin *Breuiarium apostolorum,* and which treats in order the ways in which the apostles were martyred); *Elene* (an account of the finding in Jerusalem of the true *cross by St Helena, the mother of Constantine the Great); *Juliana* (a poetic rendering of the *Passio S. Iulianae*, concerning the martyrdom of St Juliana); and *Christ II* (loosely based on an Ascension Day homily of *Gregory the Great). On the basis of the language of these poems, it has been suggested that Cynewulf was a 9th-c. Mercian poet; there is agreement among students of Old English that the modest corpus of poems shows Cynewulf to have been a poet of religious intensity and considerable literary skill.

K. Sisam, *Studies in the History of Old English Literature*, Oxford, 1953, 1-28. – D. G. Calder, *Cynewulf*, Boston, 1981. – E. R. Anderson, *Cynewulf: Style, Structure and Theme in his Poetry*, Rutherford (NJ), 1983. – A. H. Olsen, *Speech, Song and Poetic Craft: the Artistry of the Cynewulf Canon*, New York, 1984. – *Cynewulf: Basic Readings*, R. Bjork (ed.), New York, 1996.

Michael Lapidge

**CYPRIAN OF KIEV (died 1408).** *Metropolitan of *Kiev and all Rus' (1375-1408), this Bulgarian monk, in the service of the ecumenical *patriarchate of *Constantinople, sought to make the Church's interests triumph amidst the antagonism created by the appearance of two powers, *Moscow and *Lithuania, on the ruins of Kievan *Rus'. Installed at the head of the Lithuanian *dioceses, exposed to the hostility of Moscow, he could not reunite the two parts of his province until 1390. At the same time, this learned and cultivated prelate worked to reform the liturgy, propagated *hesychast writings among the East *Slavs and contributed to the revival of Slavonic literature.

D. Obolensky, *DOP*, 32, 1978, 79-98.

Vladimir Vodoff

## CYPRUS

**Political and economic history.** A Byzantine province in the forefront of the reconquest from *Islam, Cyprus profited from the disintegration of the Empire at the end of the 12th c. to gain autonomy from *Constantinople under the rule of its governor Isaac *Comnenus. *Richard Coeur de Lion profited from these separatist tendencies to conquer the island in 1191, during the third *crusade. He gave it to the Order of the Temple, then sold it to Guy of Lusignan, former king of *Jerusalem. Of Poitevin origin, Guy was the founder of a dynasty that would hold Cyprus until *Venice took control of the island in 1474. The local population, Greek and *Orthodox, accepted Latin rule without great resistance, though the *Lusignans introduced a Latin ecclesiastical hierarchy and reduced the Greek churches to no more than coadjutors of their Latin colleagues.

During the 13th c., the island's history was closely linked with that of the States of the *Holy Land: Cyprus put up a fierce resistance to the power of *Frederick II and supported the Ibelins infeoffed in the island. Its kings more than once exercised the regency of the kingdom of Jerusalem and opposed *Charles of Anjou who had bought Mary of Antioch's rights to the Crown. The island took in an important number of Latin refugees from *Syria after the *Mamluk conquests and from 1291 it was the outpost of Christendom against Islam. Famagusta, Nicosia and Limassol housed a growing cosmopolitan population and became the privileged depots of Levantine trade in the first half of the 14th century. The crusading projects then being worked out gave the island an essential role, to the point that in 1365 Peter I tried to reconquer *Alexandria, with no lasting result.

Brawls between Genoese and Venetians at the time of the coronation of Peter II led in 1373 to the intervention of *Genoa, which subjected the king to the payment of heavy tributes and took over the town of Famagusta. Impoverished and discredited, the Lusignans could prevent neither the Mamluk invasion in 1426 nor the takeover of the island by Venice, which pushed Queen Catherine Cornaro to abdicate in 1489. A century later (1571), this Venetocracy was reversed by the *Ottomans.

Michel Balard

**Religious and cultural history.** In Byzantine times, the island of Cyprus was peopled by Eastern Christians, the majority Greek, to whom were added the Latins from the end of the 12th century. The Greek Church of Cyprus, which asserted its autonomy from the *patriarchates of *Antioch and *Constantinople, comprised 14 *bishoprics, including one metropolis, and several monasteries. The Frankish conquest led in 1197 to the creation of an archbishopric of Nicosia and three bishoprics, and the *concordat of 1223 aligned the structure of the Greek episcopal sees on that of the Latin *dioceses, imposing on them a subordination that aroused grave difficulties, resolved only by the *Bulla cypria* of 1260. From now on the two rites appear to have coexisted without too many clashes, in return for an acceptance by the Greeks, as by the Armenians, "*Jacobite" Syrians, "*Nestorians" and *Maronites, of Roman primacy. All had their churches and their monasteries. The council of *Florence favoured the Greeks. Several Latin monasteries were transferred from *Syria to Cyprus because of the Muslim conquests. The island enjoyed a certain intellectual life attested by legal and historical works in Greek and French, the latter language being that of the court and administration. The symbiosis between the various populations led to the gradual penetration of Syrian and Greek elements firstly into the middle class, then into the nobility, both originally Frankish, and even into the Latin clergy.

G. Hill, *A History of Cyprus*, 2 and 3, Cambridge, 1948. – C. Mango, "Chypre carrefour du monde byzantin", *Rapports et co-rapports du XV^e Congrès international des études byzantines*, 5, Athens, 1976. – C. P. Kyrris, *History of Cyprus*, Nicosia, 1985. – J. Richard, "The Institutions of the Kingdom of Cyprus", *A History of the Crusades*, 6, K. M. Setton (ed.), Philadelphia (PA), 1989. – P. W. Edbury, *The Kingdom of Cyprus and the Crusades 1191-1374*, Cambridge, 1991. – *Historia tès Kuprou*, 4, *Mesaionikon Basileion Enetokratia*, 1, T. Papadopoulos (dir.), Nicosia, 1995 (in Greek). – N. Coureus, *The Latin Church in Cyprus, 1195-1312*, Aldershot, 1997.

Jean Richard

**CYRIL AND METHODIUS (826/827-869 and *c.*820-885).** Byzantine missionaries, often called "apostles of the Slavs". Natives of *Thessalonica, the two brothers were Byzantine but connected with Slav circles and bilingual from infancy. Originally archon of one of the Sclavinias, the elder brother, Methodius (monastic name), later embraced the religious life and became hegumen of the Polychron monastery on Mount *Olympus in Bithynia. Constantine, the younger (named Cyril only shortly before his death, after having entered a monastery at Rome), was part of the intellectual circle of the future Patriarch *Photius and was later professor of philosophy. No works of Cyril survive from this period save some extracts translated into Old Slavonic. In 860-861, the two brothers were charged by the emperor to undertake a diplomatic mission to the *Khazars, in the course of which Cyril found the alleged mortal remains of St Clement at Cherson in *Crimea. In 863 they were sent to Great *Moravia, whose prince, Rastislav, had written to the emperor of Byzantium asking for missionaries, though the region had already been Christianized before by Latin missionaries from the German *Empire and the patriarchate of Aquileia.

Cyril and Methodius combined their religious and political mission with a vast cultural programme: that of creating for the *Slavs a written literature in their mother tongue. It was an original step for the time since, even in the *Byzantine Church, Greek was considered the sole and unique cultural and religious language. Cyril, himself an excellent philologist knowing several languages, was inspired by models from the East at the time of early Christianity, when many peoples living in the Empire as well as outside its borders possessed written literatures in their own languages, which they used sometimes even as liturgical languages. Probably at the time of his stay on Mount Olympus, Cyril created for the Slavonic language a special script, the glagolitic alphabet (the Cyrillic characters, basically representing an adaptation of the Greek alphabet, were created only later in *Bulgaria), and with Methodius and some pupils began to translate extracts from the Scriptures into the Slavonic language. But this activity could only fully be carried on in Moravia, where the two brothers completed the translation of the four gospels and the epistles, translated selected passages from the Old Testament and – their most revolutionary innovation – went so far as to translate into Slavonic the whole ceremony of the *mass, as well as other liturgical texts.

In the space of three and a half years, Cyril and Methodius trained numerous disciples in Moravia as well as in the Slav principality of Kocel in *Pannonia, but they rapidly perceived that this country was entering the orbit of the Western *patriarchate. So they obeyed the invitation of the pope and set out for *Rome in winter 867-868. Pope Adrian II, having approved what they had done, made Methodius and some of his pupils enter *orders and, after Constantine's death on 14 Feb 869, designated Methodius *legate of the Holy See for the Slav lands and archbishop of Pannonia and Moravia, which had been a part of the former archdiocese of Sirmium. This appointment, which in the end applied only to Moravia, was solemnly confirmed in 880 by *John VIII in his *bull *Industriae tuae*, in which he expressly ratified the use of the Slavonic liturgy. Methodius and his pupils continued with their intense literary activity. A complete translation of Scripture is attributed to him (though it has not survived), as well as of numerous theological works. He also established the first Slav Codes (civil as well as religious rules), adapting Byzantine models.

The work of Cyril and Methodius was characterised not just by great originality, but also, despite the first great *schism between the Eastern and Western Churches which broke out just at that time, by a spirit of universalism inherent in early Christianity as well as by great impartiality and great *toleration; it was mainly thanks to this that a good part of the Slav peoples were converted to Christianity, and for this reason Pope John Paul II rightly proclaimed the two brothers, with *Benedict of Nursia, patrons of Europe.

F. Grivec, *Konstantin und Method, Lehrer der Slaven*, Wiesbaden, 1960. – F. Dvorník, *Byzantine Missions among the Slavs*, New Brunswick, 1970. – V. Vavřínek, B. Zástěrová, "Byzantium's Role in the Formation of Great Moravian Culture", *BySl*, 43, 1982, 161-188.

Vladimír Vavřínek

**CYRIL OF TUROV (died before 1182).** Rus' monk, bishop of Turov, consecrated before 1169, a talented theologian endowed with remarkable force of literary expression, Cyril was surnamed the "second Chrysostom". A master of symbolico-allegorical exegesis, he was an accomplished connoisseur of Greek homiletic. A long list of works, preserved in manuscripts from the 13th to the 16th c., is attributed to him. Certainly his are eight *homilies, three monastic discourses of which the best known is the *Discourse on the Soul and the Body*, a liturgical canon, a *confession of sins and a cycle of 33 *prayers for the *hours of the whole week. Cyril corresponded with the prince of Suzdal', Andrei Bogoliubski, and opposed the heretic Theodore, bishop of Suzdal'.

G. Podskalsky, "L'évêque Cyrille de Tourov, le théologian le plus important de la Rus' de Kiev", *Irèn.*, 61, 1988, 507-522. – *Sermons and Rhetoric of Kievan Rus'*, S. Franklin (tr., intro.), Cambridge (MA), lxxv-xciv, 55-157, 169-170.

Andrzej Poppe

# D

**DADISHO QATRAYA (second half of 7th c.).** This Syro-oriental monk, a native of the Qatar region of the Persian gulf, composed numerous ascetic writings, in particular a *Commentary* on the Syriac recension of the 15 treatises of Abba Isaiah of *Scetis (Egyptian monk, first half of 5th c.), a translation of the *Paradise of the Western Monks* (perhaps the *Lausiac History*), one or more works on the solitary life, in particular *Seven Weeks of Solitude*, and *letters. He thus gives us a description of the religious state of the time, in particular that of the daily life of a hermit.

R. Draguet, *Commentaire du livre d'abba Isaïe, par Dadisho Qatraya*, *CSCO*, 326 (Syriac text), 327 (Fr. tr.), Louvain, 1972.

A. Guillaumont, *DSp*, 3, 1957, 2-3.

Micheline Albert

**DAFYDD AP GWILYM (fl. 1315/1320 – 1350/1370).** The most famous of Welsh poets. Born, it is said, in the parish of Llanbadarn Fawr, and reportedly buried in Ystrad Fflur, few other details are known of Dafydd's life. His family seems to have included in its history several officials of the English Crown, among whom Dafydd's uncle, Llywelyn ap Gwilym († 1346?), the Constable of Newcastle Emlyn, played a large part in the poet's life. It was through his uncle that Dafydd received instruction and gained his awareness of cultural influences from the Anglo-Norman world, influences that drew Welsh poetry and the bardic tradition into the mainstream of European literature, as well as introducing European elements in turn into the Welsh repertoire.

The Welsh Casanova, Dafydd is famous for his love-poetry, in which he plays the principal role of wounded, rejected, and occasionally triumphant lover. The object of his affection, Morfudd, Dyddgu, or some other of a host of girls, is almost always unattainable, and Dafydd is constantly frustrated by "Yr Eiddig", the jealous husband, or other obstacles. The poet's failures are mostly recounted with tongue in cheek, however, and indeed self-deprecation is the chief purpose of many of Dafydd's comic poems, for example *Trafferth mewn Tafarn*.

Characteristic of Dafydd's imagery is that of nature. A forest, or a house of branches, are the settings for his trysts, and the nightingale and lark his companions, whom he personifies and imagines as being messengers, "llateion", to the poet's beloved. Such personification and flight of imagination were most novel in Welsh poetry; and no less innovative was Dafydd's choice of verse-form. Dafydd used both the older metres of *englyn* and *toddaid*, but it was his development of the seven-syllabled lines in rhyming couplets, the *cywydd*, that led to this metre's increasing flexibility and popularity.

Not entirely caught up in his loves and failures, Dafydd also contributed to the less personal aspects and genres of the Welsh bardic tradition. Among the corpus of his work, seven praise-poems survive to Ifor Hael, Dafydd's generous patron; and several amusing debate-poems attest his acquaintance with his contemporaries, such as Madog Benfras and Gruffudd Gryg. But these more rigid genres, too, bear the strong imprints of a personality who has survived the centuries as *Wales's best-loved poet.

Thomas Parry (ed.), *Gwaith Dafydd ap Gwilym*, Cardiff, 1952. – R. Bromwich (tr.) *Dafydd ap Gwilym:A Selection of Poems*, Llandysul, 1982.

R. Bromwich, *Dafydd ap Gwilym* ("Writers of Wales"), Cardiff, 1974. – R. Bromwich, *Aspects of the Poetry of Dafydd ap Gwilym*, Cardiff, 1986. – H. Fulton, *Dafydd ap Gwilym and the European Context*, Cardiff, 1989.

Elin Manahan Thomas

**DAGOBERT I (*c.*608-639).** Son of Chlotar II, Dagobert continued the work of reconstruction of the kingdom of the *Franks begun by his father. Delegated king in *Austrasia from 623, in 629 he inherited the whole kingdom after having excluded his half-brother Charibert from the succession. Installed from now on in *Neustria, he governed with counsellors recruited as much from the old Gallo-Roman families of the Midi, such as *Eligius or Desiderius, as from the Frankish aristocracy of the north, such as Dado or Wandrille. He made tours of pacification in the *regna*, kept in check the Bretons, the Gascons and the Germans beyond the Rhine and gratified the churches with gifts and privileges, especially *Saint-Denis, where he was buried and where after his death the legend of the good king would begin to develop. However, if he did much for Gallo-Frankish unity, he could not obliterate the old regionalisms and had to share out the kingdom between his sons Sigebert and Clovis.

*The Fourth Book of the Chronicle of Fredegar with its Continuations*, J. M. Wallace-Hadrill (ed.), London, 1966. – L. Theis, *Dagobert, un roi pour un peuple*, Paris, 1982. – S. Lebecq, *Les Origines franques (Ve- IXe siècle)*, *Nouvelle Histoire de la France Médiévale*, 1, Paris, 1990. – I. Wood, *The Merovingian Kingdoms (450-751)*, London-New York, 1994.

Stéphane Lebecq

**DALMATIA.** Dalmatia, a historical province of Croatia, extends from Rijeka in the north-west Adriatic to Kotor in the south-east. The Dalmatian archipelago consists of six hundred islands separated from the continent by the mountain chain of the Dinaric Alps. The inhabitants of the Roman province of Dalmatia, harassed by *Ostrogoths, *Avars and *Slavs (5th-6th c.), returned to their devastated towns when the *Croats occupied the north-west of the Balkan peninsula in the 7th century. Dalmatia had already accepted Christianity and the city of Salona preserved important vestiges of it: in the first half of the 6th c., two important *councils had been held there under the presidency of its *archbishop. After the *invasions, Pope John IV (640-642), a Dalmatian by origin, erected the city of Spalato into an archbishopric, transferring to it the title of Salona, under Byzantine tutelage though it was in a territory formerly under the jurisdiction of the Roman Church. Indeed, problems had begun around 538 with the new Byzantine presence in Dalmatia during the war waged by Justinian to recover Italy, in that economic, political and cultural life moved ever further towards the coastal strip and the islands. At this point, the Dalmatian Church too became part of the politics of the Empire, which even after the fall of *Ravenna (751) maintained its presence in the Adriatic.

When the *Franks occupied imperial Dalmatia in 805, Byzantium reacted, intervening again in 810. With the peace of

Cathedral of Split (Dalmatia), seen from the north-east.

Aachen (812) between the **basileus* Michael I Rhangabe and *Charlemagne, the Frankish Empire obtained *Istria, Liburnia and Dalmatia except for the maritime cities, which remained under nominal Byzantine sovereignty. This created problems for the Croats, who had meanwhile been converted to *Catholicism and were conscious of belonging to the Roman *patriarchate and not that of Constantinople.

Meanwhile the city of *Venice, which had been in the Byzantine sphere, consolidated its own political and economic organisation and gradually managed to assert its autonomy. Becoming the hinge of commercial exchanges between the European West and the Byzantine-Islamic East, from the 10th c. Venice came to have a strong presence in the vast area of the East Mediteranean. For this reason the inhabitants of the Dalmatian coasts decided to ask for their help against pirate raids. In 1000, at the invitation of the Dalmatians, Doge Peter Orseolo II headed a fleet that defeated the Narentine pirates, earning the title of *dux Dalmatiae et Croatiae* but creating a precedent for a Venetian presence in Dalmatia. For three centuries Venice engaged in a struggle with the kingdom of *Hungary for rule over the Dalmatian coast. The region long remained divided into two spheres of influence: the northern, as far as Zara, that of Venice; the southern, as far as Almissa, that of Hungary. King Tomislav (910-928) incorporated the Dalmatian coast into the kingdom of Croatia. After Stefan Držislav (969-997), Peter Krešimir IV (1058-1074) and Demetrius Zvonimir (1075-1089), the kingdom of Croatia, Dalmatia and Slavonia was united with Hungary in 1102. Subsequently, the development of *feudalism put real authority into the hands of the great families, while the towns enjoyed wide communal autonomy before their final submission to Venice. In 1409, in exchange for a payment of 100,000 ducats to King Ladislas of Hungary, the Republic of Venice obtained the cession of all rights over Dalmatia, which thus became a Venetian province. During the 15th c., a new impulse was given to the region's administrative reorganisation: the communal system gradually disappeared – it had flourished for a season in some coastal cities, which around the mid 13th c. had given themselves statutes in which Latin legal traditions and Slav customs converged – and Dalmatia's main centres were each governed by a Venetian noble. At the same time the popular classes came forward, with a general development of production and the arts, which increased throughout the *Renaissance.

Christianity played an important role in Dalmatian history. From the liturgical point of view, while a *Slavonic liturgy in glagolitic script existed, the region underwent both Byzantine and Latin influence, because of its political vicissitudes; but neither the use of Slavonic nor the glagolitic liturgy disappeared with the Gregorian reform. The religious establishments were nurseries of Latin and Slav culture and their propagation. The Benedictines and the *mendicant orders (*Dominicans and *Franciscans) contributed to the evolution and propagation of the scientific and artistic rebirth, as witness the precious manuscripts of their *libraries, from Zadar to Kotor. Nor should we forget art and architecture, in particular the churches, whether *pre-Romanesque (church of the Holy Cross at Nin, rotunda of St Donatus at Zadar), *Romanesque (cathedrals of Rab, Zadar and Kotor), *Gothic (tower of Split cathedral, municipal palace at Trogir) or Gothic-Renaissance (cathedral of St James at Šibenik). The Turkish advance in the 15th c. did not arrest this development, favoured by maritime activity and by the genius of a people who managed to survive the contests between Venice and the *Ottoman Empire that ended only in the 18th century.

A. Ivandija, D. Kečkemet, *L'Art sacré en Croatie*, Zagreb, 1971. – F. Dvornik, *Gli Slavi. Storia e civiltà dalle origini al secolo XIII*, Padua, 1974. – J. Ferluga, *L'amministrazione bizantina in Dalmazia*, Venice, 1978. – F. Šanjek, *Crkva i kršćanstvo u Hrvata*, 1, *Srednji vijek* [The Church and Christianity among the Croats in the Middle Ages], Zagreb, 1988 (2nd ed. 1993). – F. Conte, *Gli Slavi. La civiltà dell'Europa centrale e orientale*, Turin, 1991. – T. Raukar, *Hravatsko srednjovjekovlje. Prostor, ljudi, ideje* [Croatia in the Middle Ages. Territory, People, Ideas], Zagreb, 1997.

Franjo Šanjek

**DALMATIC.** The Dalmatic was a garment used in Roman high society in Late Antiquity; its name indicates its origin (*Dalmatia). At *Rome, among *clerics, only the *pope and his *deacons had a right to wear it. The same was true in other Italian cities, *e.g.* *Milan and *Ravenna. In the Carolingian period, the dalmatic had become the liturgical *vestment of *bishops, whoever they were, and their deacons. As the bishop also wore the chasuble for the solemn celebration of *mass, the dalmatic became for him a sort of light, short robe (or *dalmaticella*), while the dalmatic of the deacons was ornate and made of precious stuff. The dalmatic began to lose its original form of a robe in the 12th c. and become more of an ornament. From having been white, it conformed to the various liturgical *colours (gold, white, red, green, violet, black), according to celebrations.

L. Duchesne, "Le costume liturgique", *Origines du culte chrétien*, Paris, 1920, 399-419. – P. Salmon, *Étude sur les insignes du pontife dans le rit romain*, Rome, 1955, 24 f.

Guy-Marie Oury

Mosque of the Umayyads at Damascus. Detail of the west portico decorated with mosaics: rivers, palace. Byzantine art, *c*.708.

**DAMASCUS.** In Arabic Dimashq al-Chām, Damascus was created in the middle of the 2nd millennium BC by Aramaeans on the east slope of Anti-Lebanon, in Ghouta, an oasis irrigated by the canalized arms of the Baradā. Situated on the edge of the steppe, it constituted a unique crossroads between Egypt, Arabia, Mesopotamia and Asia Minor; to the west, a pass opened the way to the Mediterranean. The city enjoyed a major role in the political structures of the Syrian area, the Bilād al-Chām of the Arabs, the whole of the usable lands east of the Mediterranean. Damascus was conquered in 635 by the Arabs, retaining a Christian quarter at Bab Touma and a Jewish quarter at Bab Charqī. Under the *Umayyad caliphate (660-750), Damascus was the capital of the first Arab-Muslim empire, from the Atlantic to the borders of China and *India. At its centre, occupied in turn by Aramaean, Hellenistic and Roman temples, then by a Byzantine church, Caliph al-Walīd built the celebrated *mosque in 705. From 750 to 860, under the direct rule of the *Abbāsids of *Iraq, Damascus exercised only a reduced influence in central *Syria. Later it defended dynasties established in Egypt (Tulunids, Ikshīdites). Finally, from 969 to 1075, the *Shi'ite *Fatimid *caliph of *Cairo exercised intermittent rule there. The city then suffered numerous troubles (Christian churches destroyed on the orders of al-*Hākim, mosque of the Umayyads burned down in 1069). Depopulated and miserable, it regained its prosperity and a certain autonomy after 1076 under the *Seljuks and the Burids. The town, centre of art, crafts and commerce, developed rapidly. The philosopher al-*Ghazālī lived at Damascus in 1095-1096. The Franks, installed at *Jerusalem in 1099, tried unsuccessfully to occupy the city in 1147, though allied to it. Nūr al-Dīn ibn Zankī, a Turkish prince of northern Syria, reunified Muslim Syria and made Damascus his capital in 1154, constructing superb buildings including a hospital. On his death in 1174, the Kurd Salāh al-Dīn (*Saladin), sultan of Syria and Egypt, assembled at Damascus the army which, at Hattīn in 1187, swept the crusaders out of *Palestine. In 1240, the great Andalusian mystic Ibn 'Arabī died at Damascus. In 1260 the *Mongol army, fresh from taking *Baghdad, occupied *Aleppo and Damascus. It was defeated at 'Ayn Jālūt in Palestine by the *Mamluks of Egypt, who took the place of the *Ayyubids, Saladin's successors, in Syria. Certain Christians having profited from the Mongol presence to victimize the *Sunnis of Damascus, the condition of the minorities was more difficult under the Mamluks, who made Damascus their second capital. The town suffered further Mongol descents, notably in 1300. Ibn Taymiyya began his teaching at Damascus in 1284 and died there in prison in 1328 for having opposed those whom he considered a threat to Sunnism: *Sufi followers of Ibn Arabī, Shi'ites, Mongols, Christians of western obedience. In 1400-1401, Tamerlane made a pact there with *Ibn Khaldūn, massacred part of the population and took the craftsmen to Transoxiana. The town once more went through a difficult period.

N. Elisséeff, "Dimashk", *EI(E)*, 2, 1965, 277-291 (new ed.). – *Damas*, Paris, Jan 1993 ("Autrement").

Thierry Bianquis

*Daniel in the lions' den.* Capital from the former church of Sainte-Geneviève, Paris, 11th c. Paris, Louvre.

**DAMIETTA.** A town of Lower Egypt, in the eastern part of the Nile delta, on the Mediterrranean. Important from Byzantine times, it was conquered by the Muslims with the rest of Egypt in 641. Surrounded by walls, it was defended especially by a powerful tower, built in the middle of the Nile, called the Tower of the Chain. Apart from its strategic importance, Damietta was also a great centre of textile production. At the time of the *crusades, the Franks made several attempts to take it. They ocupied it from 1219 to 1221, during the Fifth Crusade. *Louis IX took it in June 1249, but had to hand it back when he was taken prisoner, in April 1250. The *Mamluks, who then came to power, dismantled it and put an end to its prosperity.

P. M. Holt, "Dimyāṭ", *EI(E)*, 2, 1965, 292.

Anne-Marie Eddé

**DANCE.** What we know of dances in the Middle Ages, we owe essentially to condemnations of them. Acts of *councils, episcopal statutes and *Penitentials, though they often repeat condemnations in the same terms, give sufficient information for us to have some idea of these ludic manifestations. In the early Middle Ages, the *calends of January gave rise to festivities of all sorts, as happened in Antiquity. To these dances and masquerades of antique type were added those celebrated by the Germans at the time of the winter solstice. The summer solstice was also a time of dances: "diabolical" songs, dances and round dances. Any rite of passage – *marriage, *burial – was inevitably accompanied by dances. The Church not only warned the *laity who indulged in such events, it condemned *clerics who took part in marriage feasts and all those who danced not just in front of the church but in the church. The Roman councils of 826 and 853 forbade these practices.

To uproot the popular taste for dancing, the Church, in conformity with its pastoral principles, sought to utilize dancing by incorporating it into the liturgy or the paraliturgy. At the translations of *relics that multiplied in the Carolingian period, the clergy and people testified to their joy by *tripodia* which were religious dances. In some accounts of translations, the word *chorea* was also used, which had the same sense. At *Corvey, nocturnal dances took place around the relics of St Guy, a saint reputed to cure demoniac possession. At Sainte-Foy at *Conques, at *Saint-Martial at *Limoges, in the 11th c., clerics and laity danced. We can point to other manifestations, such as the Easter dance at *Auxerre around the *labyrinth on the *cathedral floor, the round dance of the *chapter at each appointment. At Gournay, the clerics danced on St *Nicholas's day. In his commentary on Isaiah, St *Thomas Aquinas writes: "Dancing is not bad in itself: according as it is ordered to various *ends and takes place in certain circumstances, it comes to be an act of *virtue or *vice". Excesses were doubtless committed, so much that throughout the Middle Ages the Church denounced the abuses of choreography in places of worship. Eudes of Sully († 1208) forbade dances in churches and *cemeteries. The councils of Avignon (1209), Paris (1212) and Rouen (1231) repeated the same condemnations. This did not prevent dances, and a *bull of *Eugenius IV in 1439 even accepted the dances of the *seises* of *Seville to celebrate the Immaculate *Conception.

*Chorea*, round dances and *tripodia* enjoyed great popularity until the council of Trent. They survived even to our own day in the famous dancing procession of *Echternach in Luxemburg on Whit Tuesday.

E. Bertaud, "Danses religieuses", *DSp*, 3, 1957, 22-37. – P. Riché, "Danses profanes et religieuses dans le haut Moyen Âge", *Mélanges Robert Mandrou*, Paris, 1985, 159-167. – J. Horowitz, "Les danses cléricales dans les églises au Moyen Âge", *MA*, 1989, 279-292.

Pierre Riché

**DANIEL.** With *Isaiah, *Jeremiah and *Ezekiel, Daniel belongs to the group of the four major *prophets. However, his legendary character cannot be disputed. The biblical book that relates his exploits and visions is not by his hand. The popularity of the character of Daniel and the iconographical riches that flowed from it are explained by the fact that, like *Joseph, Daniel in the lions' den was considered by theologians as prefiguring Christ in the sepulchre, and that he was also the symbol of the soul saved, the man protected by God.

The iconographical type of Daniel is fairly stable: he was generally represented beardless and wearing a Phrygian cap. Two types of animal could accompany him, lions by reason of the episode of the lions' den and the ram connected with his apocalyptic vision. Daniel is rarely represented alone, but most frequently put in the group of prophets, as in the *Well of Moses* made by Klaus *Sluter between 1396 and 1405 for the Chartreuse of Champmol, at *Dijon. Iconographical cycles illustrating different episodes of the story of his life could also be consecrated to him.

The themes that Christian art borrowed from the book of Daniel are divided into three groups. The first and most developed is the narrative cycle consisting of the episodes of Susanna, the three Children and Daniel spared by the lions. If the judgment of Daniel is illustrated early in Christian art, representations of the episode of Susanna bathing did not really develop until the 15th c., the *Bible offering in this case a pretext for the depiction of a sensual female nude. The story of the Three Children in the furnace, illustrated from the 2nd c. at Rome, also appears on a capital of the cloister of *Moissac and on bas-reliefs at Saint-Lazare d'Autun.

But the best-known scenes belonging to this cycle are undoubtedly those of Daniel in the lions' den. The limited space of capitals, where the figure of Daniel is very familiar in the 12th c., as *e.g.* at *Autun, allows only the representation of Daniel between two lions. The miniatures of manuscript books allow the development of other details of the story, like Daniel fed by Habakkuk (miniature in the *Mirror of human salvation* dating from the 15th c. and preserved in the Musée Condé at Chantilly).

The second narrative cycle, consecrated to the explanation of *dreams, and the third, which relates to apocalyptic *visions, are less frequently shown.

E.G. Tasker, "Daniel", *Encyclopedia of Medieval Church Art*, J. Beaumont (ed.), London, 1993.

Frédérique Trouslard

**DANIEL OF HALYCH (1201-1264).** Daniel of Halych (Galicia) (Danylo Romanovich Halytskyi) was prince, then king (from 1253) of *Galicia and *Volhynia. After the death in 1205 of his father Roman Mstislavich, Daniel and his mother spent some time in exile in *Poland and *Hungary. Helped by devoted boyars, he managed to establish his authority in Volhynia in 1229 and in Galicia in 1238. In 1239, he annexed *Kiev to his principality and sent his army leader (voivode) Dimitri (Dmytro) to defend Kiev against the *Mongol (Tatar) armies of Batu Khan, who inflicted a defeat on him in Dec 1240. Daniel triumphed over a coalition of Hungarians and revolted boyars in the spectacular battle of Iaroslav (Jaroslaw). He was obliged to acknowledge the sovereignty of the *Golden Horde, but continued to assemble forces to regain his independence. With this intention, he built several strongholds, among them his capital Kholm (Chelm), and *Lviv (Lvov, Lemberg), named after his son, Lev Danilovich. In 1253, he accepted the royal *crown offered him by Pope *Innocent IV. The rapprochement with the papacy was of short duration, since the *pope could give him no real help against the Mongols. In 1254-1255, Daniel defended his principality against the Mongol troops under the command of Kuremsa; subsequently, however, he was forced to dismantle the fortifications of several towns to avoid provoking the Tatars. The *Chronicle* of Galicia-Volhynia salutes Daniel as a courageous warrior, a prudent diplomat and the protector of the inhabitants of the towns.

S. Kieniewicz (ed.), *Histoire de la Pologne*, Warsaw, 1971. – N. L.-F. Chirovsky, *An Introduction to Ukrainian History*, 1, New York, 1981.

Iaroslav Isaievych

**DANIIL THE HEGUMEN (12th century).** A 12th-c. Russian abbot, sometimes identified with Daniil, bishop of Jurev (1114-1122). He wrote the account of a journey from *Constantinople to the *Holy Land, usually dated to 1106-1108, which is part of the genre of *itineraries of pilgrimages to the Holy Places. Leaving Constantinople by sea, he stopped at Ephesus and in some islands before reaching *Jerusalem. He stayed sixteen months in the Holy Land, during which time he lived for a long time in the Laura of St Saba in the *desert of *Palestine. His account is exceptionally rich and detailed and contains various information on distances, countries visited and on the relations between Latins and *Orthodox.

Daniil Egumeno, *Itinerario in Terra Santa*, M. Garzaniti (ed.), Rome, 1991.

J. Glušakova, "O putešestvii igumena Daniila v Palestina", *Problemy obšcestvenno-politiceskoj Rossii i slavjanskich stran*, Moscow, 1963, 79-87.

Adele Cilento

**DANILO II OF SERBIA (14th c.).** *Archbishop of the Serbian church, eminent theologian, man of letters and connoisseur of the arts, monk then hegumen of Chilandar, Danilo II courageously defended his monastery against the Catalans (1307-1309). A gifted diplomat, he carried out several missions for his friend King Milutin. He left a large literary *oeuvre*, including six *Lives of Serbian Kings and Archbishops* of great historical value. Danilo himself worked out architectural plans and *fresco programmes for his foundations, in particular at *Peć and Jelašci. He also oversaw the construction of Banjska and Dečani, two great royal foundations.

*L'Archevêque Danilo II et son époque, Colloque scientifique international à l'occasion du 650e anniversaire de sa mort, décembre 1987*, V. J. Djurić (ed.), Belgrade, 1991 (in Serbian).

Gordana Babić †

***DANSE MACABRE*.** Just as the Middle Ages were ending, the theme of the *danse macabre*, that procession of couples from various strata of society, formed of a living person swept along by his dead double, was expressed in literature, iconography and *music. It combined two themes present in French *poetry from the 12th c. (Hélinand de Froidmont): the estates of the world, and ineluctable *death. The adjective employed at the time, "*macabré*", of disputed etymology, might refer to the book of Maccabees, extracts of which were used in the liturgy of the *dead.

The first traces of *Danses macabres* date from the late 14th c.: a Spanish poem, *La dança general de la Muerte*, and a paraliturgy recorded at Caudebec-en-Caux in 1393 (mimed sermon?). But the version that would ensure the theme's popularity well beyond the Middle Ages was the set of paintings with versified *legenda* made in 1424 at the cemetery of the Innocents at *Paris. These showed a hierarchical succession of 30 male couples representing all estates of society, from the *pope, the emperor and the king to the labourer and the *child. They developed, for the benefit of those who passed by this much-frequented place, the lesson of the future that awaits everyone, this death generative of decay – corpses, not skeletons, lead the *dance – whose role as social leveller should not make us forget its too sudden appearance. The work's success was such that in 1485 the Parisian printer Guy Marchant published a first version of it (text and image), followed in 1486 by a supplemented edition. Throughout the 15th c., the sinister merry-go-round occurs in the form of *frescos or wood-carvings in France (La *Chaise-Dieu, Haute-Loire; *La Ferté-Loupière, Yonne; Kermaria-an-Isquit, Côtes-d'Armor), in England and Germany where it still inspired painters and engravers in the 16th c. (Hans Holbein the Younger). Only Italy stayed away from this theme, preferring that of the Triumph of Death whose cavalcade sweeps away everything in its path (*Pisa, Clusone in *Lombardy).

The echo awoken by these works used to be attributed to the sombre tones of the final centuries of the Middle Ages, cast into gloom by recurrent *epidemics, the *Hundred Years' War and the difficulties of economic recession. Death had by then become more familiar, to the point of arousing a fascination that went hand in hand with a strong appetite for life. It now appears that this crisis should be situated at a wholly different depth. Beyond surface accidents, contemporaries found themselves confronted with the break-up of traditional structures (*village, *family) and a questioning of authorities (Church shaken by the *Great Schism, local powers overturned by the construction of the modern *State). Through their taste for the macabre, would they not express their anguish faced with the loss of their roots and the new solitude of the individual?

V. Dufour, *La danse macabre des Saints-Innocents de Paris . . .* , Paris, 1874. – "Danse macabre", *DLFMA*, 1992, 367-368.

Catherine Vincent

**DANTE ALIGHIERI (1265-1321).** A Florentine, the greatest poet of medieval Europe, and one of the greatest of mankind. The profound inspiration of his religious work also makes him Christianity's greatest poet. Born in *Florence in 1265, to a family of the lesser nobility, he took part in the lively intellectual and political life of that city at the end of the 13th c., playing a prominent role in both spheres. In literature, he and Guido Cavalcanti were the creators of the poetic movement that he himself named the "Dolce Stil Nuovo", which was to renew Italian love *poetry, previously linked to the forms inherited from the Provençals. In Italian *politics, then dominated by the struggle between the White and the Black *Guelfs (the former representing the newly emerging mercantile middle class, the latter the landed nobility, openly supported by the Roman curia as part of the theocratic policy of *Boniface VIII), he sided with the Whites and in 1300 attained the position of Prior, *i.e.* a member of the governing college of the city. When the Blacks prevailed with the *pope's support in 1301, his commitment to the city's independence from curial interference led him to that exile from which he would never return.

To the Florentine period belongs his poetry inspired by the "Stil Nuovo", most of which he collected in a small book entitled *Vita Nuova*, written in the form of *prosimetrum*, a prose narrative alternating with verse compositions. In this juvenile work he celebrated his love for a young woman, Beatrice, inaugurating the theme of disinterested *love: the object and end of poetry was the praise of the beloved woman, so that no event, not even her death, could in any way condition it. Towards the end of the book Beatrice in fact dies, and in the last sonnet the poet describes a vision in which he contemplates her glorious in paradise, and promises himself that he will no longer speak of her until he can do so in such a way as to "say of her what was never said of any woman".

Also attributed to Dante's youth nowadays is an anonymous work of comic realism, strongly erotic, the *Fiore*, an adaptation of the *Roman de la Rose* in the metrical form of a necklace of sonnets. Critics have long doubted and still doubt this attribution, but most now accept it: it would considerably enlarge the comic dimension of Dante's poetry in the period before the exile.

After leaving Florence, Dante wandered through various friendly courts, first in *Tuscany (as long as he hoped to return to his city), then more permanently at *Verona with Cangrande della Scala (between about 1313 and 1318) and finally at *Ravenna, with Guido da Polenta, where he found an honoured hospitality until his death, on 14 Sept 1321.

To the first part of his exile belong new love songs, which reveal a different, powerfully realistic style (called "petroso" from the Donna Pietra of whom they sing), and other great, committed songs on doctrinal subjects, as well as the so-called "canzoni morali" and two of his three prose works, doctrinal in character, differing in subject but similar in intention, the Latin *De Vulgari Eloquentia* and the vernacular *Convivio*, datable with fair approximation between 1305 and 1307, before the beginning of his poem.

The use of the vulgar tongue for a philosophical *treatise like the *Convivio* was a revolutionary act consciously performed by Dante, who gave his reasons for it in book I: the intention of spreading *science – true source of happiness for man, created rational – even among the unlettered (hence the title of *Convivio*, banquet, in which the author breaks the bread of knowledge for those who are not in a position to taste it); and at the same time the challenge of demonstrating the intrinsic possibilities of the new vulgar tongue, as capable as *Latin of expressing any concept, however elaborate, and destined to supplant, like the "new sun", that "spent" sun now heading for its setting.

The subjects of the treatise – broken off after book IV – are various: the order of the heavens and the *angels (a sort of *cosmology, of Neoplatonist origin) in II, the praise of *philosophy as dispenser of happpiness in III, the definition of nobility as not due to blood but to the value of the individual person in IV, the latter a treatise that outlines Dante's political ideal in the providential figure of the single emperor placed by *God at the forefront of history. The work's philosophical sources – *Aristotelian, *Neoplatonist, *scholastic – reveal the cultural patrimony acquired by Dante in his Florentine studies, a patrimony that would be the basis for his major work, the *Divine Comedy*.

The book's importance lies on one hand in its definition of a strong conceptual structure centred on the person of *man, especially in his cognitive and ethical aspects, a structure with Aristotelian foundations but strong Christian connotations; and on the other in its extraordinary linguistic operation, which created the vernacular philosophical language, both in terminology and in the complex, prolix literary style, Latin in structure, that laid the basis for Italian prose, scientific as well as narrative, as would soon appear in Giovanni *Boccaccio' s *Decameron*.

The other treatise, *De Vulgari Eloquentia*, written in Latin since it was aimed specifically at men of letters, was intended in turn to give the "vulgar eloquence" the same dignity as Latin, establishing for it the same norms that regulated the older language, and thus making it capable of singing the most elevated subjects, reserved for the tragic style. But the newest part of the treatise was the first book, introductory in character, which discussed human *language in general, its origin and history, showing its subdivisions in the various lineages of the European languages, and finally reaching the various spoken languages of *Italy, with a singular anticipation of modern linguistic science. This treatise too, like the *Convivio*, remained unfinished.

It almost seems that Dante, having laid the essential bases of his thought and of the instrument necessary for expressing it, could no longer bear to enlarge on it, urged on by a different project that replaced all others in his mind, as if that alone could fulfil his deep inner aspiration: to write a work that would offer firstly himself, but also all mankind, the way to reach full and perfect happiness, the fulfilment of every desire.

Dante's third important prose work, the only one complete and organically concluded, the treatise *De Monarchia*, has not yet been given a unanimous date. Most now tend to assign it to the time of the writing of the *Paradiso*, but a minority of critics think it was composed at the time of the election of *Henry VII and his descent into Italy.

The treatise expounds Dante's political doctrine, which turns wholly on what was then the central problem of the relations between Church and Empire. Written in Latin, as being doctrinal in character and on a subject that went beyond Italian boundaries, the work was divided into three books. In the first, theoretical in plan, he demonstrates that for people to live together in harmony a

*Portrait of Dante Alighieri.* Fresco by Andrea del Castagno (1410-1457). Florence, Uffizi.

monarchical government is necessary, *i.e.* the leadership of a single person. In the second, that such a task falls by right to the Roman people, who have been entrusted with it by divine *providence. Finally, the third confronts the problem of the relations between the *pope and the emperor, maintaining by a multitude of arguments that the latter's *authority depends directly on God and is not subject to that of the former, except out of reverence. The fundamental ideas of this treatise are the same that, in prophetic form, govern the historico-political structure of the poem. In it we can make out two main cultural components: on one hand, the influence of the *Franciscan tradition, aimed at the spiritual revival of the Church, against the moral corruption and attachment to temporal power then dominant; and on the other, that of the philosophical current of Latin *Averroism, as regards the autonomy recognised to philosophy, *i.e.* *reason, from *faith, an autonomy on which the Empire's independence of the Church was based.

But the work in which Dante's genius found its true and complete expression, that for which his name is known throughout the world, from a few years after his death until today, is the great poem of the afterlife, the "Divine Comedy" as it was named in the 16th c., adding to the title its author gave it the adjective "divine" that has remained with it, as if by tacit universal acknowledgement of its deepest meaning.

In this poem Dante intended to relate, in the form of a journey to the realms of the other world, man's eternal destiny as Christianity set it out, *i.e.* that of a being of supreme dignity, created by God in his image and called to unite himself with him in the fulness of divine life, by virtue of the freedom allowed him and the intelligence and love given to him, precisely the three qualities that make him similar to the creator.

The journey through the three realms, a journey of purification from *sin and ascent to the divine world, is depicted on one hand as a redemption of the author-protagonist from the dark wood of his juvenile aberrations, on the other as a prophetic indication of the way of salvation for all mankind. Its model should be sought not so much in the various medieval accounts of *visions, with which its narrative and dramatic plan and its cosmological structure have nothing in common, as in the great classical poem that, with similar prophetic intent (though on the historical plane, while the *Comedy* moves on the metahistorical plane), describes a descent into the world of the dead, the *Aeneid* of Virgil, whom Dante indicates from the beginnng as "his master and his author".

The character of the work is in fact not religious, but highly literary; it is a work of poetry, which thus required pains from its author, and of experimental technique, as is declared and emphasized many times throughout the poem. Dante wished to speak to men with an essentially ethical intention (cf. *Ep.* XIII, 39-40), through the language of poetry, which he considered capable of acting on souls (as Orpheus and his singing had tamed the wild beasts) making "cruel hearts" mild (*Conv.* II I, 3).

But the poem that he created, while inspired by the ancients, bore a radical innovation: the *Comedy* is an epic poem, the only one of its kind, that celebrates not the heroes of myth and legend, but historical man in his particular individuality, one in which kings and emperors have the same role as the unknown common man. Historical facts break into the poem from the beginning (*nacqui sub Iulio*, says Virgil, *Inf.* I, 70); of each person met, we know the geographical homeland, the mountains, the rivers, the city where he lived. Not only this: the great story – another absolute innovation – is told in the first person, the hero-protagonist is the author himself, secure only in his historical name, and around him crowd obscure people, his friends, acquaintances, even relatives, almost as if he has just left them on the paths of this world, which seem to merge with those of the next.

But each of them – the humble and the powerful – has an equal, absolute dignity; for this historical man is endowed with freedom, with which he chooses his eternal destiny: his deeds done in time remain in eternity, deciding his fate. The kiss of Francesca, the tears of *Manfred, the self-stripping of *Francis on the piazza at Assisi, all assume, in the dramatic force of Dante's *terzine*, an absolute value, which reverberates from history to eternity. The dignity and freedom of the individual, time and history as bearers of eternal values: these are the great innovations that Christianity brought to the culture of Greco-Roman Europe, and of which Dante's *Comedy* is the voice.

The journey to the three realms (Inferno, Purgatory, Paradise) is told in three great parts or "canticles", each of 33 chapters or "cantos", plus one of prologue, making 100 in all. Its metre is the concatenated terzina, Dante's own invention. The ternary structure thus recalls the central mystery of Christianity, that *Trinity that, from the inscription on the gate of Hell to the vision of the final canto of the Paradiso, seems to enclose the whole poem.

Each realm is imagined with its particular characteristics, but each is subdivided into various degrees, of punishment or beatitude. Their arrangement is structured so as to traverse the whole universe vertically, according to the geocentric figure of the then-known cosmos, the Ptolemaic. *Hell opens beneath the city of *Jerusalem, like an abyss in the form of a funnel, subdivided into crags or rings, down to the centre of the earth where Lucifer is fixed. At the antipodes of the holy city there rises in the ocean the mountain of *Purgatory, also subdivided into cornices, and on its summit is the Garden of Eden, or Earthly *Paradise. From here Dante, after descending to the bottom of Hell and ascending through a narrow passage to the beach of Purgatory and thence from crag to crag to its summit, rises towards the Empyrean and, having crossed the nine Ptolemaic heavens, finally attains the direct vision of God. This structure, solid and harmonious, holds the great poem in figurative and narrative unity, so that it reflects the order and harmony of creation impressed on it by its creator.

Within the homogeneity of the whole, the characters of the three realms are very different. The very subdivision into different degrees of punishment or glory is done in the *Inferno* according to classical ethics, in the *Paradiso* according to the Christian *capital sins, in the *Paradiso* according to the different models of *sanctity in history.

Also profoundly different is the quality of the landscape and the human connotation of the inhabitants, to which a different stylistic timbre corresponds. In the end, the three realms of the afterlife are nothing but figures of the different forms of human life in *time, seen in reference to God: separation from him in sin, return to him in repentance, union with him in sanctity.

The greatness of Dante's poetry, which has always fascinated his readers, lies precisely in its profound penetration of the reality of the human condition, as well of that of nature, in all its forms, from the most abject to the most sublime. Every motion or aspect of man's *soul seems intimately known to him, as does every gesture, look or smile that reveals it, and the same may be said of every aspect of the creation, from the humble burning of a firebrand to the great celestial phenomena.

This absolute realism, which enables his verse to draw with supreme clarity the sad love of Francesca, the tragic death of *Ugolino, the lament of the dying *Manfred or the ardour of Francis on *Alverna, makes him – as T. S. Eliot writes – the most universal European poet. To this maximum range of values corresponds the range of style and language, from the comic and stony of the *Inferno* to the sublime of the *Paradiso*.

Man appears in the *Inferno* with a stronger and more prominent personality, since he has nothing but himself, which indeed is what he wants. His model is *Farinata, who raises himself in his tomb of fire as if defying God himself. His human greatness is left to him: gentleness to Francesca, loyalty to *Pietro della Vigna, magnanimity to Farinata, thirst for knowledge to Ulysses. But they are immersed in a profound darkness of solitary desperation. Here violence, wailing and darkness reign.

Man in the *Purgatorio* appears meek, aware of his weakness and trusting not in himself, but in that God who gratuitously saves him. His model is Manfred, the powerful prince who, mortally wounded, turns weeping to the merciful God who accepts him. Mildness encompasses the *Purgatorio*, from the colour of the sky to the songs intoned by the souls in the various cornices, to their actions marked by patient *hope and nostalgia, feelings proper to exiles from their homeland, as they are.

In the *Paradiso* the scene changes: in the seven heavens of the planets, the blessed appear only as lights or flames. Dante has boldly renounced the forms proper to earthly experience, landscape and the human figure, creating a world of light, music and word alone, to signify the life of the spirit, that of divine eternity. The personality of the individuals, while remaining intact in its historical particularity, is here subordinated to a harmonious blending, expressed by the songs, dances and celestial figures that the blessed lights compose from heaven to heaven. The life of the blessed in Dante can be defined in the words spoken by the first of them, Piccarda: "*e 'n la sua voluntade è nostra pace* (and in his will is our peace)" (III 85). The great speeches of the *Paradiso* are not individual in character: either they expound in lofty theological poetry the great truths of faith, or they present in prophetic language the historical condition of humanity in its dolorous aberration and the providential model to which it must be brought back (thus for the *Empire in canto VI, the city in cantos XV-XVI, the religious orders in cantos XI-XII).

But in the Empyrean, which is reached in the final cantos, historical humanity and man's *body find their glorification: the great rose imagined by Dante, whose white petals are the blessed themselves clothed in their glorious body, replaces with daring inventiveness the biblical city of the *Apocalypse. This flower, germinated from the womb of *Mary where the incarnation of the Word took place (*Par.* XXXIII 7-9), concludes the imagery of the poem with supreme beauty. But in the final vision, where Dante remains alone in front of the light of *God himself, the mystical component that pervades the whole canticle prevails and, in the *contemplation of the two great Christian mysteries, the Trinity and the Incarnation, consummates the final possibility of the sublime language created by a poet to express the experience of the divine.

There also remain by Dante: a collection of thirteen *Epistles*, especially important being the three written on the occasion of Henry VII's descent into Italy, and that with which he offered the third canticle to Cangrande della Scala; two Latin *Eclogues*, composed on the Virgilian model in his last years at Ravenna; and finally a scientific treatise, the *Questio de aqua et terra*, a dissertation given at Verona in 1320 on the problem of the different level of the surface of the waters and of the land that emerges from them.

*Le Opere di Dante*, critical text by the Società Dantesca Italiana (Florence, 1921, 2nd ed. 1960). The Società Dantesca Italiana's "Edizione Nazionale", includes: *Monarchia* (Milan, 1965), the *Commedia* (Milan, 1966-1967; 2nd ed. Florence 1994), the *Fiore* and the *Detto d'Amore* (Milan, 1984) and the *Convivio* (Florence, 1995).

Commentaries: Dante Alighieri, *La Divina Commedia*, N. Sapegno (ed.), Milan, 1957 (3rd ed. Florence 1985). – Dante Alighieri, *The Divine Comedy*, with commentary by C. Singleton, Princeton (NJ), 1970-1975. – H. Gmelin, *Die Göttliche Komödie* (commented ed.), Stuttgart, 1955-1957. – Dante Alighieri, *Commedia*, with commentary by A. M. Chiavacci Leonardi, Milan, 1991-1997. – The best commented edition of the *Opere minore* is that of the collection *Letteratura Italiana, Storia e Testi*, vol. 5, Milan-Naples, 1979-1988.

B. Nardi, *Dante e la cultura medievale. Nuovi saggi di filosofia dantesca*, Bari 1942 (3rd ed. 1983). – M. Barbi, *Problemi fondamentali per un nuovo commento della Divina Commedia*, Florence, 1956. – E. Auerbach, *Dante, Poet of the Secular World*, Chicago (IL), 1961. – A. M. Chiavacci Leonardi, *Lettura del Paradiso dantesco*, Florence, 1963. – R. Guardini, *Studi su Dante*, Brescia, 1967. – G. Contini, *Un idea di Dante. Saggi danteschi*, Turin, 1970. – C. S. Singleton, *La Poesia della Divina Commedia*, Bologna, 1978. – G. Petrocchi, *Vita di Dante*, Bari, Rome, 1985. – *Dante Now: Current Trends in Dante Studies*, T.J. Cachey (ed.), Notre Dame (IN), 1995.

Anna Maria Chiavacci

**DATARY, APOSTOLIC.** For the Middle Ages, it is more exact to speak of a single official, the *datarius*, than a true service of *dataria*. Even the first known *datarius* does not predate 1417, under *Martin V, and his function was to give the date to petitioners and to submit them to registration, as could be done from the 13th c. (*data communis*) and even in a collegial way, among *notaries in front of the *pope. Paul II confined him to this role (1464). *Sixtus IV (1475) authorized the *datarius* to associate with himself a *Franciscan master of theology.

L. Célier, *Les Dataires du XV^e^ siècle et les origines de la daterie apostolique*, Paris, 1910. – T. Frenz, *Papsturkunden des Mittelalters und der Neuzeit*, Stuttgart, 1986, 57-60.

Michel Hayez

**DATINI, FRANCESCO (*c.*1335-1410).** Born at Prato, son of an obscure family of shopkeepers, orphaned by the plague of 1348, Francesco di Marco da Prato soon went to *Avignon, where he climbed the ladder of commercial success. He fulfilled the migrant's classic dream by returning to settle in *Tuscany in 1383, but could not resolve to disengage from his activities, which he extended and diversified until *c.*1400, gaining a foothold in *Florence. Lacking an heir, he left his fortune to a lay charitable institution, an arrangement that allowed, centuries later, the preservation of a singularly rich private fund of archives.

I. Origo, *The Merchant of Prato*, London-New York, 1957. – F. Melis, *Aspetti della vita economica medievale*, Siena, 1962. – M. Luzzati, "Datini, Francesco", *DBI*, 33, 1987, 55-62.

Jérôme Hayez

**DAUPHINÉ.** The principality of the Dauphiné, part of the *Empire but destined to become the possession of the heir to the French Crown after the "transfer" of 1349, was created from the 11th c. in a territorial area extending from the Rhône valley to the Grésivaudan and the High *Alps of the Briançonnais, Embrunais and Gapençais, containing seven *bishoprics (*Vienne, Valence, Die, Grenoble, Viviers, Gap, Embrun) belonging to three metropolises, two local, Vienne and Embrun, and the third, Aix, external. Over three centuries, three dynasties of counts and then dauphins – families of Albo (1029-1162), Burgundy (up to 1182) and La Tour (up to 1349) – worked to unite this land in the heart of the former kingdom of *Burgundy, itself a product of Lotharingian vicissitudes after the partition of 843. The political role of the archbishop of Vienne seems to have been decisive at two moments: in 879, with the choice of Boso, king of *Provence, the first non-Carolingian ruler, then in Bouchard's decision to infeudate to Guigo of Albo the Southern Viennois, which he himself had received before 1029, in the last years of the Rodolphian dynasty that died out in 1032; he thus opened up a future to the first of those who bore the name "Dauphin" from the time of Guigo IV (1133-1144).

The legacy of the Viennois past was important in the religious history of the Dauphiné. It was characterised by a strong tradition going back to the very beginnings of Christianization, as *Ado's **Martyrology* (third quarter of 9th c.) attests: from the 4th c. it rested on the memory of the great bishops, builders and evangelizers or instigators of practices destined to be a model of religious behaviour for a long time to come, such as *Rogations (established by St Mamertus, *c.*475), which remained a favourite manifestation in Western rural tradition of the appeal for God's protection on the fruits of the earth; it also rested on the extent of restoration after the secularizations of the Carolingian period, in favour of the important religious centres of the Rhône valley that were to furnish solid roots for the *Gregorian reform (Saint-Pierre, Saint-André, Saint-Ferréol). Much later, when diocesan structures predominated, the work of the provincial council of Vienne (1289), which served as disciplinary reference in each of the *suffragan bishoprics until the end of the Middle Ages, then that of the general council of *Vienne in 1311-1312, at a time of difficult negotiations between the French Crown and the new *Avignon papacy, confirmed the importance of the region's oldest *dioceses.

The period of progressive structuring of the Dauphiné was also that in which the reform of the Church underwent new developments, well-documented insofar as it concerned bishops and monks. The activity of the *legate *Hugh, bishop of Die from 1073, energetic here and throughout the kingdom of Burgundy, favoured a precocious renewal of the episcopal body in favour of men won over to his views. Restoration of cathedral *patrimonies and *restitution of *tithes and *patronages held by laymen were accompanied by new monastic and canonical *foundations. From the time of the establishment of the abbey of Bonnevaux (diocese of Vienne, 1117), then those of Léoncel (diocese of Valence, 1137) and Valcroissant (diocese of Die, 1188), the *Cistercians settled next to the old Benedictines of the lowlands and the Cluniacs, possessed of numerous *priories. The priories dependent on the Augustinian Canons of Saint-Ruf (nearly 30 from the mid 12th c.) reinforced the density of centres in the lowlands, while in the upper Dauphiné the *collegiate church of Saint-Laurent d'Oulx, founded in the mid 11th c. and soon patron of numerous parish churches, was a centre of regular life in a region previously unprovided with it. The destiny of those foundations of purely Dauphinois origin was uneven. The Order of Chalais (diocese of Grenoble, first quarter of 11th c.) had only an ephemeral existence and was attached to the neighbouring Chartreuse in 1304. Only two centres were to have a brilliant future as heads of *orders: the Grande Chartreuse and Saint-Antoine en Viennois. The former was established in 1084 by St *Bruno with the decisive support of Bishop St Hugh (1080-1132) on the Delphino-Savoyard boundary of the diocese of Grenoble, in a forested "*desert" propitious to the eremitic life chosen. Possessed from 1201 of 39 houses, seven of them in Dauphiné, the order was to enjoy continuous expansion throughout the Middle Ages and have nearly 200 houses on the eve of the Reformation. In exact antithesis of *Carthusian solitude, the hospitaller foundation of Saint-Antoine en Viennois (*Antonines, 1070), which became head of an Order of Canons of St Augustine detached from the Provençal Benedictines of Montmajour in 1297 and by the end of the Middle Ages had 192 *commanderies forming a dense network all over Middle and Germanic Europe, was to attract crowds to the renowned *pilgrimage centre that it became.

A land of tradition, inherited from the early Middle Ages and still alive, a land of monastic renewal in the 11th and 12th cc., the Dauphiné was also a land of conflict, to judge by the southern preaching of *Peter of Bruys (diocese of Gap, 11th c.) and especially by the *Waldensian presence after the migration of the disciples who had clustered round *Waldes at Lyon in the late 12th century. A manifestation of aspirations to reform in a *laity soon opposed to the Church hierarchy, since the latter condemned the free expression of the evangelical ideal by those whom it had not trained for it, the movement initially began to take root in the valley refuges of the upper Dauphiné, where it was at first able to prosper freely, sheltered from the inquisitorial initiatives of the

*Scenes from the life of David.* Miniature from the *Bible of Stephen Harding*, from the abbey of Cîteaux, *c.*1109. Dijon, Municipal Library (Ms 14, fol. 13 r°).

*mendicant orders active in the Rhône region. So it was not individuals but whole communities that came to light when, in the Avignon period, from 1330, the papacy undertook to pursue them actively in the valleys of Vallouise, L'Argentière and Fressinières and in the Valcluson, itself linked to the wider world of Piedmontese heterodoxy. Very violent in the years 1360-1380, the endemic pursuits reached a paroxysm at the time of the crusade of 1488, which had the effect of reinforcing the new Provençal diaspora but, for all that, failed to eradicate the germs of the conflict, which was to lead, in nearby Piedmont, to a fusion with the new Reformation in whose service Guillaume Farel of Gap was active (Chanforan, 1532).

The existence of dissidence on such a scale stimulated the orthodox determination to redress the balance. In terms of repression, this was manifested in the upper Dauphiné by vigorous pursuits against peasant *magic, condemned as *sorcery from the second quarter of the 15th c. in the name of a militant Christianization.

From a positive point of view, it led to a new effort of attentive training of Christians, which was indeed recommended by the whole reformist current. By pastoral *visits – only those of the bishops of Grenoble are preserved, but they were carried out by every bishop in the region –, by synodal *statutes propagated, by missions (St *Vincent Ferrer, 1399-1403) and the establishment of mendicant centres that came to supplement a first patchy settlement, the Dauphiné was worked by the forces of renewal. Their uneven efforts were perceptible among the faithful, both in the nerve-centres (diocese of Embrun) and in those regions that harboured open milieux attentive to the new currents of sensibility (Grenoble, Vienne).

Thus the Dauphiné of the years 1520-1530, time of the first preaching of the Reformation at Grenoble (Pierre de Sébiville, 1524), manifests a situation that anticipates the 16th c. by the evident presence of two religious sensibilities equally alive and exacting, a situation propitious to the explosion of violent acts linked to their confrontation and, in the end, to the fact that both were rooted in reformist currents.

B. Bligny, *L'Église et les Ordres religieux dans le royaume de Bourgogne aux XI^e et XII^e siècles*, Grenoble, 1960. – *Histoire du Dauphiné*, B. Bligny (dir.), Toulouse, 1973. – L. Boisset, *Un concile provincial au XIII^e siècle, Vienne, 1289. Église locale et société*, Paris, 1973. – *CAF, 130^e session, 1972, Dauphiné*, Paris, 1974. – *HDF*, B. Bligny (dir.), 12, 1979. – *Dauphiné roman*, Saint-Léger-Vauban, 1992 ("La nuit des temps"). – P. Paravy, *De la Chrétienté romaine à la Réforme en Dauphiné. Évêques, fidèles et déviants (milieu du XIV^e siècle-vers 1530)*, Rome, Paris, 1993.

Pierrette Paravy

**DAVID.** The figure of David (*c.*1000-961 BC), king and prophet, reputed author of the *Psalms, enjoyed incontestable popularity in the Middle Ages, due to his close link with the person of the Messiah. Type of the figure of the Christ-king, he was also his prophet and forebear. We can differentiate between a juvenile David, shepherd or warrior, and an older David, king and psalmist.

David could be represented beardless, wearing a simple tunic (exomis, leaving one side of his chest bare, in early Christian art; short peasant tunic in medieval art). He also often carried a shepherd's crook. Surrounded by his flock, he was the *Good Shepherd. This *image sometimes recalls the ancient model of Orpheus. The shepherd's youth could equally apply to the warlike vigour of the conqueror of Goliath: statues of Donatello (Florence, Bargello) and Michelangelo (Florence, Academy).

The second type is by far the most common. We find it on numerous frontispieces of *psalters, but also of *Bibles and *Books of Hours or of liturgical chants. David, bearded, is seated on a *throne. He is crowned and wears royal vestments. He holds a harp or a psaltery; rarely, he is given a phylactery designating his song. Around him sometimes appear four musicians, dancers or scribes. Steger calls these representations *Majestas David regis*.

David was the model of the Christian prince and his images often served to legitimate their power: thus, he is dressed as a Frankish king in the Bible of *Charles the Bald, grandson of the *novus David* *Charlemagne. Scenes in which Samuel anoints the young David for the first time (*e.g.* in the *Sankt Gallen *Psalterium aureum*, 9th c.) had, in the West, an obvious political significance. In psalters of the 13th and 14th cc., the anointing often gives way to a *coronation.

Cycles of the life of David have existed ever since the paintings in the synagogue of Dura Europos (244-245). We find them at *Cologne (St Gereon, second half of 11th c.), *Vézelay (capitals), *Chartres (north front), *Reims (west front), etc. The most complete cycle consists of the 60 miniatures of *Stephen Harding's Bible (Dijon, BM, 12-15, early 12th c.). Apart from the anointing mentioned above, the most popular scenes of David's life were those that referred *typologically to *Christ's victory over *Evil (David and Goliath, David overcoming the bear or the lion).

Finally, figures of King David occur among those of the *prophets and those of the Nine Worthies (late Middle Ages).

H. Steger, *David Rex et Propheta. König David als vorbildliche Verkörperung des Herrschers und Dichters des Mittelalters, nach Bilddarstellungen des achten bis zwölfsten Jahrhunderts*, Nüremberg, 1961. – G. Suckale-Redlefsen, *Die Bilderzyklen zum Davidleben von dem Anfängen bis zum Ende des 11. Jahrhunderts*, Munich, 1972. – M. Philonenko, "L'histoire du roi David dans l'art byzantin. Nouvel examen des plats de Chypre", *Les Pays du Nord et Byzance. Actes du colloque nordique et international de byzantinologie, Upsal 1979*, R. Zeitler (ed.), 1981 ("AUU. Figura", new series, 19). – S. Maser, "L'Image de David dans la littérature médiévale française", *MA*, 99, 1993, 423-448. – M. Mihályi, "Davide", *Enciclopedia dell'arte medievale*, 5, Rome, 1994.

Pierre Kerbrat

**DAVID OF AUGSBURG (*c.*1200-1272).** German *Franciscan, itinerant preacher (like his companion *Berthold of Regensburg), anti-*Waldensian inquisitor in *Bavaria and mystical theologian.

David was one of the chief spiritual authors of the 13th c. and his chief text, *De exterioris et interioris hominis compositione*, was one of the most widely-read manuals of methodical *meditation (nearly 400 *Latin manuscripts survive); it had a decisive influence on the **Devotio moderna* and was for several centuries the standard manual of monastic asceticism.

*DThC*, 4, 1924, 153-157. – *DSp*, 3, 1957, 42-44. – *NDB*, 3, 1957, 533-534. – *DHGE*, 14, 1960, 116. – *LdM*, 3, 1986, 604.

Joseph Morsel

**DAVID OF DINANT (13th c.).** A native of Dinant (Belgium), David was *chaplain to *Innocent III in 1206. He was the author of *Problemata* addressed to *Frederick II. Of his *Quaternuli* and a treatise on anatomy (which suggests a sojourn in the South), we possess only fragments. Having professed *pantheism, he was condemned in 1210 by the council of Sens, and in 1215 by *Robert of Courson. The *council ordered his works to be burned; the *legate forbade them to be read. *Albert the Great cites and refutes several of his theses.

M. Kurdzialek, "Anatomische und embryologische Äusserungen Davids von Dinant", *SAGM*, 45, 1961, 1-22. – M. Kurdzialek, "L'idée de l'homme chez David de Dinant", *Symbolae Facultatis litterarum et philosophiae Lovaniensis*, series A, 1, Louvain, 1976, 311-322.

Agostino Paravicini Bagliani

## DEACON, DIACONATE

**The West.** The term "deacon" designated the penultimate in dignity of the major *orders, just beneath the *priesthood. From the 2nd c., deacons were found in every Christian community. Up to the 10th c., the functions of the deacons underwent a great development; they were later restricted, as is already attested by Gratian's **Decretum*. The Roman *Pontifical of 1485 sanctioned this evolution by limiting their role in the *mass to that of preparing the offerings and reading the Gospel, as well as the administration of *baptism. The widespread opinion that the deacon could administer the sacrament of *penance was regularly condemned from the 11th century. *Clement V fixed the minimum age of diaconal *ordination at 20; it was normally just a step towards the priesthood.

"Diacre", *DThC*, 4, 1924, 703-731. – "Diacre", *DDC*, 4, 1949, 1198-1206.

Bruno Galland

**Byzantium.** The diaconate was the first of the major orders. The deacon had to be at least 25 years old and could not marry after his *ordination. Originally his functions were liturgical (he served as intermediary between the celebrant and the people), social (he seconded the *bishop in his charitable works) and administrative. From the 6th c. his importance grew in the administration of the patriarchate of *Constantinople, where the offices were reserved for him: as such, he sat on the permanent *synod. This role grew until the 14th c., then declined, most of the *patriarchs of the final centuries preferring to choose their collaborators among the monks.

J. Darrouzès, *Recherches sur les Offikia de l'Église byzantine*, Paris, 1970.

Marie-Hélène Congourdeau

## DEAD, PRAYERS FOR THE

**The West.** The first allusions to a Christian *prayer for the dead go back to the 2nd century. But not until the 4th c. were prayers of thanksgiving, recited in honour of the *martyrs, clearly distinguished from prayers of *intercession, intended to help the ordinary dead. According to Augustine († 430), the dead who merited it could benefit from supplications made on their behalf by the living, through prayers, eucharistic celebrations and *alms. Until the end of the Middle Ages, prayers, masses and alms were the three main types of intercessions for the dead recognised by the Church. To these, many added *fasting (*Ivo of Chartres, Gratian, *John Beleth. . .), some *tears (the Venerable *Bede) or the discipline (*Peter Cantor).

The custom of interceding for the dead was based only on a single passage of Scripture: on the morrow of his victory over Gorgias, Judas Maccabeus had organised a collection to make a "sacrifice" intended to wipe away the sins of his soldiers dead in battle: "all resorted to prayer" (2 Mac 12, 41-45). But as well as this scriptural text, frequently cited, Christian authors justified intercessory prayers for the dead by referring to the "custom of the universal Church".

In the 7th and 8th cc., prayer for the dead flowed into the mould of the monastic *office, *hours recited in common. The Christians had replaced the traditional lamentations at mortuary *vigils and *funerals by the singing of *psalms, *hymns and biblical readings: these texts were arranged to form the office of the dead. Between the 9th and the 10th c., the recital of the office of the dead became common and generally of daily occurrence in monasteries and *chapters. It was even advised for the *laity: the noblewoman *Dhuoda recommended her son to pray regularly for the dead members of his family "especially in company with many others, during nocturnes, *matins, *vespers and the other hours". As for masses, while it was customary to evoke the dead at each eucharistic celebration (at the *Memento* of the dead), from the 6th and 7th cc. the habit caught on of celebrating "private masses" for the intention of particular deceased. Also, the number of *masses celebrated in religious communities underwent a considerable increase, which necessitated augmenting the number of altars in the churches and the number of priests among the monks. Finally, alms were usually distributed through the intermediary of religious communities, which received the gifts of the faithful.

In the 11th and 12th cc., prayers and masses for the dead, the organisation of which was one of the main activities of ecclesiastical communities, took the form of commemorations. The Pauline expression "*memoria in orationibus*" (memory by or through prayers), recurrent in documents, well characterises the liturgical customs of this time. In order to preserve the memory of the dead, lists of names were drawn up: at first written down on *diptychs or in the margins of *sacramentaries, then in the Carolingian *libri memoriales*, they were transformed into necrologies, organised in order of the *calendar, in which appeared the names of the deceased members of monasteries and chapters, as well as those of their lay benefactors. Performed by churchmen in exchange for gifts (or "alms"), the commemoration of the dead was very closely linked to the functioning of seignorial society.

In the late Middle Ages, the eucharistic celebration was considered the most efficacious help for the dead: by *testament, the faithful started to demand masses for their *salvation by tens, hundreds or even thousands. At the same time, funerary prayer was "laicized": from now on it was performed by lay *confraternities and groups of *penitents; moreover the text of the office of the dead, often illustrated by miniatures, appeared in the 14th and 15th cc. in all books of private devotion.

J. Ntedika, *L'Évocation de l'au-delà dans la prière pour les morts (IVe-VIIIe siècles)*, Louvain-Paris, 1971. – D. Sicard, *La Liturgie de la mort dans l'Église latine des origines à la réforme carolingienne*, Münster, 1978. – J. Chiffoleau, *La Comptabilité de l'au-delà. Les hommes, la mort et la religion dans la région d'Avignon à la fin du Moyen Âge*, Rome, 1981. – A. Angenendt, "Missa specialis: Zugleich ein Beitrag zur Entstehung der Privat-Messen", *FMSt*, 17, 1983, 153-221. – R. E. Reynolds, "Dead (office of the)", *DMA*, 4, 1984, 117-118. – J. Chiffoleau, *L'Église et la mémoire des morts dans la France médiévale*, Paris, 1986. – P. A. Fevrier, "La Mort chrétienne", *Segni e riti nella Chiesa altomedievale occidentale*, 2, Spoleto, 1987, 881-942. – J. L. Lemaitre, *Mourir à Saint-Martial. La commémoration des morts et les obituaires à Saint-Martial de Limoges du XIe au XIIIe siècle*, Paris, 1989. – F. S. Paxton, *Christianizing Death. The Creation of a Ritual Process in Early Medieval Europe*, Ithaca (NY), London, 1990. – E. Rebillard, *"In hora mortis". Évolution de la pastorale chrétienne de la mort aux IVe et Ve siècles*, Rome 1994.

Michel Lauwers

**Byzantium.** The notion that prayers offered by the living for the dead could hasten their attainment of eternal rest developed slowly in the early Church, as did the reciprocal notion that the dead could intercede for the living. The belief became stabilized in the 11th c. that the dead could benefit from the *intercession of the saints, notably at the moment of the *judgment of the *soul. Intercessory prayers were addressed particularly to the Virgin and St *John the Baptist, who were represented in scenes of the *Last Judgment interceding for mankind at the throne of Christ. Intercession for the dead was introduced into the liturgy in the prayer of intense supplication recited after the reading of the Gospel. After petitions in favour of the living, there was one in favour of the deceased founders of the church and for all orthodox who piously reposed in this and other places. It also became the practice to cut particles from the *prosphora* (bread offered for *consecration at the liturgy) and to offer them in commemoration of dead people (rather like a Western mass intention). There were also special days in the year consecrated to prayer for the dead. On the Saturday eight days before the beginning of *Lent, the Canon for the Dead was read at the *office of *Orthros*. In the case of individual deaths, besides the prayers for the *dying and the rites of *burial, there were celebrations on the third, ninth and fortieth day after *death. It has been maintained that the forty days of mourning were based on the Israelites' mourning for Moses, although this, in fact, only lasted thirty days (Dt 34, 8). Subsequently a liturgy could be celebrated on the *anniversary of the death of the deceased.

Aristocratic and imperial patrons of monastic foundations expected the monks of the community to pray for the repose of their souls. Instructions were given in the **typikon* of their foundation. For example, in the *Typikon* of the Pantocrator, precise instructions are given for commemorations to be made in favour of deceased members of the family of John *Comnenus, the founder. These consist mainly of *prosphora* offered at the liturgy, together with three baskets of *kolyba* on Saturdays. The emperor also laid down what prayers were to be said for him after his death: commemoration on the *diptych of the dead, a **Trisagion* to be chanted each day and a *pannychis* (a short office for the dead, not an all-night vigil) at *Orthros*. Dispositions were also given for the lights to be lit at his tomb. The *kolyba*, a cake made of boiled wheat and variously flavoured, was (and still is) regularly distributed at funerals and anniversary or other commemorations of the dead. Its origins and symbolic meaning are obscure. Most probably it derives from the ancient practice of eating a meal at the tomb of a deceased person.

P. de Meester, *Ritual-Benedizione Bizantino*, Rome, 1929, 73-148. – M. Arranz, "Les prières presbytérales de la 'Pannychis' de l'ancien Euchologe byzantin et la 'Panikhida' des défunts", *La Maladie et la mort des chrétiens dans la liturgie*, A. Pistoia (ed.) *et al.*, Rome, 1975, 31-82.

Christopher Walter

**DEAD, THE.** According to a common opinion, the dead in the Middle Ages played no role in the affairs of the living: Christians honoured their dead, prayed for them, offered a cult to some of them, the saints, but never maintained an "ancestor cult" analogous to that encountered in many traditional societies.

In reality, things were much more complex. It is true that in *c.*421-422, in his treatise *De cura pro mortuis gerenda* (On the care due to the dead), which was the first Christian codification of the cult of the dead, Augustine denied any utility to the majority of funerary rites. More exactly, he dissociated funerary rites, which formed part of the customs of the various peoples, from the Christian practice of intercessory *prayers for the dead, inspired by faith in the *Resurrection: while funerary customs (the ceremony of obsequies, the rites performed over the mortal remains, *burial, upkeep of *tombs) could in no way help the deceased, intercessory prayers for the dead (prayers, masses and *alms) could, on the contrary, comfort and deliver those who merited to benefit from them.

At any rate, during the very early Middle Ages, the institutional church does not seem to have shown much interest in the rites surrounding the decease of ordinary Christians. For a long time, the *funeral ceremonies and burial even remained "private" ceremonies, though this did not imply the absence of a priest. At most, churchmen condemned manifestations of grief that were too explicitly opposed to the Christian faith (lamentations at funerals, meals on the tombs, etc.). Thus, for a long time, two ways of envisaging relations between the living and the dead coexisted in the West. According to a traditional model, shared by the majority of the *laity, the living had to attend to their dead mainly in the setting of the relations of carnal *kinship. And only when the rites of passage had been performed, in a *family setting, could the deceased join the community's "ancestors". At this point other ritual procedures, involving no longer just his relatives but all the members of the community, marked the entry of the deceased into the world of the "ancestors". According to the other, ecclesiastical model, the "cares due to the dead" were the business of all Christians. The faithful interceded for each other, and all Christians, in communion, prayed for all the departed. In this perspective, it was thus the Church, instead and in place of families and communities of inhabitants, that took charge of the deceased. Thus, to the familial and customary cult of the dead, churchmen gave a spiritual character. The *Eucharist, celebrated at funerals and on the *anniversaries of *deaths, the evocation of all the dead at each *mass (at the *Memento* of the dead), as well as the veneration of those deceased freed from carnal ties who were the saints, contributed to "spiritualize" the cult of the dead.

From the 8th and 9th cc., the institutional church set up a whole series of liturgical institutions and customs, capable of taking concrete charge of deceased believers. Founded on spiritual ties, monastic groups were the first to establish the relations between living and dead which the churchmen preached. In the 8th c. were formed the first associations, bringing together *bishops and *abbots, whose members engaged themselves, on the death of one of them, to celebrate the memory of the deceased, by having *psalters and "special" masses recited for their intention. Religious houses also exchanged lists of names (those of their members and benefactors, living and dead together), which each institution wrote down in its "book of life" (*liber vitae* or *liber memorialis*). Reforming *monasticism spread these usages: the memory of deceased brothers remembered by the assembly of monks allowed the *abbeys to reinforce their cohesion, forge links, extend their influence. The Carolingian authorities also exploited the rites of remembrance of the dead: from ecclesiastical establishments founded or endowed by their cares, the rulers required prayers for their *salvation and the safety of the realm, as well as the celebration of anniversary services for the deceased members of their family and their predecessors. The lists of dead of these "family monasteries" reflect the networks of friendship and alliance that constituted the *Empire.

Towards the year 1000, while communities of inhabitants were coming together around *cemeteries, forming *villages and *parishes, the two funerary models met: the relationships connecting the living to their deceased relatives found themselves incorporated in the spiritual community forged by churchmen. The latter became, at least for the aristocracy, obligatory intermediaries between the living and the dead. Local potentates, masters of *castles, holders of the "*ban" and dispensers of justice in effect demanded for themselves and their deceased relatives the liturgical services of the ecclesiastical communities; they set up veritable family necropolises in the religious houses. If the lords connected their *salvation with that of the "ancestors", it was because they owed them their name, their status and their rights. Thus by keeping up the memory of their ancestors, they legitimized their own power. Recalling the memory of the dead was one of the main tasks of ecclesiastical communities: every day, monks and *canons celebrated the memory of the deceased members of their community, but also of the relatives of local lords, whose names were written down in their "*necrology". In exchange, ecclesiastical establishments received numerous gifts and saw an eminent social role acknowledged to them: in the 11th and 12th cc. the cult of the dead was "the pump of the system of monastic domination" (D. Iogna-Prat).

The great particularity of the cult of the dead in Western medieval society lay in the role played by the Church: to evoke the dead, to lean on "ancestors" – which is characteristic of any customary society – it was necessary to pass through the ecclesiastical rites and institutions, to adopt the spiritual models defined by the clergy. The institution of a *feast of all the dead, on 2 Nov, in the 1030s at the latest, at the abbey of *Cluny, represents a decisive step in the long process of "spiritualization" of the cult of the dead: from this moment on, not a single deceased person escaped, at least ideally, from the grip of the Church.

Towards the end of the 12th c., while practices of remembering the dead that had previously been limited to some social groups spread through society, particularly in the *towns, and preachers propagated the doctrine of the Church, notably its ideas on *purgatory (which theologians had just defined as the third place of the afterlife), the dead lost the structuring social function they had had in the seignorial period. Maintenance of the memory of the ancestors was replaced by the concern of individuals for their salvation and that of those close to them. The privileged ties that united religious communities at a local level with neighbouring aristocratic families progressively gave way to a sort of "funerary market". Institutions charged with interceding for the dead multiplied, pious *legacies fragmented: from now on, individuals bought intercessory prayers and masses "retail", now here, now there. The new religious orders, particularly the *mendicants, posed as veritable "specialists" in intercessory prayers for the dead. *Testaments, which made a massive reappearance in the West from the 13th c., were the main vehicle of the new customs. By acknowledging a certain autonomy to individuals, by authorizing them to derogate from *custom, testamentary practice attests that society rested less on ancestral rules and more on institutions based on law.

By definitively cutting individuals off from their ancestral attachments, *epidemics, together with the increase in mortality and the crises of the 14th and 15th cc., amplified the transformations begun by urbanization and rural exodus. Many had left the land of their ancestors; when their time came to die, it was impossible for them to join their fathers. They palliated this absence by flamboyant funerary pomp: theatricality of funerals, minutely organised *processions, use of mourning dress, etc. The truly obsessional accumulation of masses for the *soul's salvation, demanded by testators, also reflects, as J. Chiffoleau has shown, the disarray of uprooted and orphaned populations. The repetitive, almost uninterrupted, celebration of masses for the dead had no other end than to forge innumerable new links with the afterlife, to bring the living and the dead closer together. In the urban churches, the clergy doubled: alongside *parish priests and *canons proliferated a whole population of *chaplains, living off pious *foundations and testamentary legacies and whose function consisted in celebrating, all day long, masses for the dead. Convents of mendicants also drew great profit from this new "market of *death": an essential part of their revenues came from the funerary services they provided in their convents. At the same time new types of solidarity were formed: lay *confraternities charged with concerning themselves with the dead and praying for their salvation multiplied. Fearing to die alone and be unable to benefit from decent funeral celebrations, the inhabitants of towns and villages grouped together in what were in effect mutual aid associations.

The "flamboyant piety" of the late Middle Ages, part of which was the profusion of funerary rites and macabre themes, was the sign of a growing distance between the living and the dead. In the 16th c., the protestant reform movement would call into question this ritual exacerbation.

K. Schmit, J. Wollasch, "Die Gemeinschaft der Lebenden und Verstorbenen in Zeugnissen des Mittelalters", *FS*, 1, 1967, 365-405. – O. G. Oexle, "Memoria und Memorialüberlieferung im früheren Mittelalter", *FMSt*, 10, 1976, 70-95. – J. Chiffoleau, *La Comptabilité de l'audelà. Les hommes, la mort et la religion dans la région d'Avignon à la fin du Moyen Âge*, Rome, 1981. – P. J. Geary, "Échanges et relations entre les vivants et les morts dans la société du haut Moyen Âge", *Droit et cultures*, 12, Nanterre, 1986,

3-17. – J. L. Lemaître, *Mourir à Saint-Martial. La commémoration des morts et les obituaires à Saint-Martial de Limoges du Xe au XIIIe siècle*, Paris, 1989. – D. Iogna-Prat, "Les Morts dans la comptabilité céleste des Clunisiens de l'an Mil", *Religion et culture autour de l'an Mil*, Paris, 1990, 55-69. – P.J. Geary, *Living with the Dead in the Middle Ages*, Ithaca (NY), 1994. – C. Treffort, *Christianisme, rites funéraires et pratiques commémoratives à l'époque carolingienne*, Lyon, 1996. – M. Lauwers, *La Mémoire des ancêtres, la souci des morts. Fonction et usages du culte des morts dans l'Occident médiéval*, Paris, 1997. – J.-C. Schmitt, *Ghosts in the Middle Ages: the living and the dead in medieval society*, Chicago, 1998.

Michel Lauwers

**DEAN (UNIVERSITY).** The dean in medieval *universities was the *doctor who presided over the college of doctors of a *faculty and exercised a certain authority over it, though limited by the higher authority of the *chancellor and the *rector. The dean was generally elected. He appears at the university of *medicine at *Montpellier in 1220, in the higher faculties of *Paris (*theology, *canon law, medicine) after 1250. He is later found in the university foundations that followed the Parisian model (especially in France and the Empire). However, in these cases, even the faculty of arts now had a dean.

H. Rashdall, *The Universities of Europe in the Middle Ages*, F. M. Powicke (ed.), A. B. Emden (ed.), Oxford, 1936 (3 vol.; 2nd ed.).

Jacques Verger

**DEATH**

**The West.** As the end of earthly life, death in the Middle Ages was profoundly marked by the Christian note that was dominant in society. Associated with the *Last Judgment, it aroused fear and anguish in the Christian; yet the Judgment was also the day of liberation, entry into eternity. So it was between these two poles that the history of Christian attitudes to death oscillated.

In the Middle Ages, death could affect an important part of the population, on the occasion of *famines or plague. It could even reduce the population of an entire region to nothing, as demographic studies of the *Black Death attest. Death could also be the result of a punishment following a sentence. In this case, it was exposed before the eyes of everyone to serve as an example.

The death of the individual could take on a dimension of plenitude: for monks, this instant represented the last act of a life devoted to God. *Bernard of Clairvaux expressed this happiness in describing the death of his brother Gerard: he "died singing and singing he died". What is promised is not an anguished *judgment, but a time of light: "Great luminary, light shining in darkness . . . . Morning star more clear than the others because closer to the day, more like the Sun . . . . Dawn that becomes day on our earth". To this joy is opposed the sorrow aroused by this "bitter" and "horrible" separation, provoking fear among those who remain: "I have a horror of my death and that of those close to me" (in J. Leclercq).

Hagiographical accounts also describe the last earthly moments of the saints, occasion for *miracles: a perfume wafts from the tomb, a sweet music is heard. Perfume issuing from the lifeless body of the saints emphasizes the impossibility of putrefaction of their flesh: divine *grace offers *immortality to the *body.

The liturgy gave death an important place. From the time of the Gelasian *sacramentary, the Church guided the Christian in his journey to death: after recommending the *soul, it accompanied the preparation of the body with *prayers and organised prayer vigils in church, before the tomb and after the *burial. At the time of *Gregory the Great is attested the *Memento mortuorum* whose aim was to recommend to God all the deceased who were named, either mentally or aloud. The deceased were thus evoked at the end of the *office. In the early Middle Ages, whether in the prayer of Gelasius or *Alcuin or in the Anglican prayer, prayers interceded for the *redemption and *salvation of the soul.

Commemoration of the *dead was intensified in the course of the Middle Ages. From the 7th c., in *Ireland, appeared rolls on which were written the names of the community's dead. In the Carolingian period, living and dead were inscribed on registers and would be recommended in the *canon of the *mass: these were "books of life". To these were added necrologies, lists of the deceased read at the *office, and obituaries, which listed the *anniversary services founded by the deceased. The Carolingian reform played a preponderant role in this liturgy of the dead by introducing the notion of "individual death". In the mid 11th c., *Cluny introduced an annual commemoration of the *dead on 2 November, close to the feast of *All Saints celebrated the day before. This "feast of the dead" was destined to have great success.

The development of belief in *purgatory as an intermediate place between earth and *paradise increased still further the fundamental role of intercessory prayers in preparation for death. Already St Augustine had emphasized the virtues of intercessory prayer to attenuate the purifying fire (*City of God*, XXI, 24). In effect, medieval man sought to anticipate the circumstances surrounding his death, thanks to the practice of the *testament which allowed him to fix his material and spiritual succession. He would thus envisage the place of his *burial and *funeral, the masses celebrated in his memory, the division of his various properties, not forgetting his choice of heir. The funeral was an occasion for the deceased to be surrounded by churchmen – regular and *secular clergy could be present together – who, thanks to their prayers, would diminish the pains he had to endure in purgatory. The organisation of anniversary masses and eucharistic celebrations also held a preponderant place in the organisation of his soul's salvation ensured by the Christian. In the course of the later Middle Ages, and more precisely in certain regions such as southern France, an extreme multiplication of this type of intercessory prayer developed.

As to choice of burial, the early Middle Ages favoured proximity to the *martyrs and saints (*ad sanctos*), which was supposed to guarantee the salvation of the soul. But the *cemetery that extended around the church remained the usual place. It was also a place of sociability and exchange, where feasts and *banquets were organised. From the 12th c., the inside of the church became a favourite place for the deposition of bodies, especially near the *altar. Though *canon law sought to limit this evolution, it developed and even led to the construction of individual and family funeral *chapels. In the 13th c., the *convents of the *mendicant orders were added to the parish church which had so far taken the majority of burials; the success of the new orders led to innumerable conflicts with the *secular clergy.

Burial was the occasion for rulers – the emperor, the *pope, *kings, as well as local rulers – to manifest their dynastic and individual awareness in the organisation of funerals marked by an often highly developed ceremonial. These ceremonies were as much the expression of continuity and transmission of power as of family and collective grief.

While funerary statues generally represented the deceased in attitudes of eternal rest, funeral monuments from the late 14th c. revealed the torments that death could inflict on the body: the corpse gnawed by worms and toads reminded everyone of the nothingness with which he would one day be confronted. From the first half of the 14th c., the art of the macabre (cemetery of *Pisa) attests the success of the theme of death that was enriched in the final centuries of the Middle Ages. The portrayal of every class of society – emperor, pope, king, knight, prince and princess, *merchant, mendicant, monk, servant – faced with the figure of death emphasized both the ineluctability of death and the equality of all before it. The **Ars moriendi*, which enjoyed a very considerable development in the second half of the 15th c., offered the Christian a means of preparing himself for the assaults of death. The combination of text and very evocative images thus reminded the dying person of all the *temptations he would have to face. The success of the *Ars Moriendi* became even greater with the development of the printing-press.

A. Tenenti, *Il senso della morte e l'amore della vita nel Rinascimento (Francia e Italia)*, Turin, 1989 (1st ed. 1957). – K. Schmid, J. Wollasch, "Die Gemeinschaften der Lebenden und Verstorbenen in Zeugnissen des Mittelalters", *FMSt*, 1, 1967, 365-405. – N. Huyghebaert, *Les Documents nécrologiques*, 1972 ("TSMÂO", 4). – J. N. Biraben, *Les Hommes et la Peste en France et dans les pays européens et méditerranéens*, Paris, 1975. – R. Chartier, "Les arts de mourir", 1450-1600, *Annales*, 31st year, 1976, 51-75. –D. Sicard, *La Liturgie de la mort dans l'Église latine des origines à la Réforme carolingienne*, Münster, 1978. – J. Chiffoleau, *La Comptabilité de l'au-delà. Les hommes, la mort et la religion dans la région d'Avignon à la fin du Moyen Âge*, 1980 ("CEFR", 47). – J. L. Lemaître, *Répertoire des documents nécrologiques français*, P. Marot (dir.), Paris, 1980 ("Recueil des historiens de la France, Obituaires", 7). – *Death in the Middle Ages*, Louvain, 1983. – *Memoria, Der geschichtliche Zeugniswert des liturgischen Gedenkens im Mittelalter*, K. Schmid (ed.), J. Wollasch (ed.), Munich, 1984. – J. Chiffoleau, *Les Justices du pape: délinquance et criminalité dans la région d'Avignon au XIVe siècle*, Paris, 1984. – J. Leclercq, "La joie de mourir selon saint Bernard de Clairvaux", *Dies Illa. Death in the Middle Ages, Proceedings of the 1983 Manchester Colloquium*, Manchester, 1984, 200-204. – P. Ariès, *Images of Man and Death*, Cambridge (MA), 1985. – J.-P. Albert, *Odeur de sainteté. La mythologie chrétienne des aromates*, Paris, 1990. – N. Ohler, *Sterben und Tod im Mittelalter*, Munich, 1990. – *Tod im Mittelalter*, A. Borst (ed.) *et al.*, Constance, 1993. – P. Binski, *Medieval Death: Ritual and Representation*, London, 1996. – C. Daniell, *Death and Burial in Medieval England*, London, 1997.

Véronique Pasche

**Byzantium.** Departure from this life, in the Byzantine world, was not done without preparation: alerted by preaching on the last ends, a theme very present in monastic thought, some Byzantines chose renunciation of the world and monastic life; many drew up their testament, in which appeared gifts to the poor and, for the richer, foundation of monasteries, in order to repair their faults and gain their salvation.

Thus Michael Attaleiates founded the hospice of the All-Merciful in 1077. They also provided for the different forms of future commemoration, rightly ensured by the monks who were the beneficiaries of donations or foundations.

Funerary beliefs were manifold. From his death pangs, the terrified dying person saw himself surrounded by *angels and *demons with their account-books, and the *soul resisted to avoid being snatched from the *body; moreover, the soul was not supposed to leave the body until three days after death, when the viscera tore apart; on the ninth day, the soul was examined by angels, while the body fissured; finally, on the fortieth day, the soul underwent a first *judgment, before the *Last Judgment, and the joints of the body came apart. This schema of decomposition of the body, and its variants, was, according to G. Dagron, elaborated from the funerary liturgy and not the latter from a physiological examination. After having crossed the *teloniai* (customs turnstile), the soul reached *paradise or was thrown into *hell.

The funerary rites naturally began with the preparation of the body: the eyes and the mouth were closed, a piece of money was sometimes put in the mouth (this ritual of pagan origin long survived in the Byzantine Empire); the body was then washed, clothed in a *shroud, put on a bier and exposed. During the wake, weepers were present: this pagan ritual, though sharply criticized by the *Fathers, was perpetuated throughout the Empire; it was even encouraged at imperial *funerals. Prayers for the *dead, heirs to the antique prayers to the dead, took place originally near the tomb, then at the church. These prayers took place at the funeral, on the third day after death, on the ninth, sometimes the twelfth, the fortieth, finally on the *anniversary of death. A year of mourning was recommended by the Church.

M. Alexiou, *Ritual Laments in the Greek Tradition*, London, 1974. – G. Dagron, "Troisième, neuvième et quarantième jour dans la tradition byzantine: temps chrétien et anthropologie", *Le Temps chrétien de la fin de l'Antiquité au Moyen Âge*, Paris, 1984, 429-430.

Anne-Françoise Loué

**DEATH PENALTY.** In Late Antiquity, the death penalty was common and was accompanied by more or less refined *tortures (Theodosian code). At the beginning of the Middle Ages, the various national laws of the Germanic peoples favoured pecuniary composition: capital punishment seems to recede at this time. It still struck at offences against public order (*lèse-majesté*, desertion, treason, etc.), but spared those guilty of private crimes, in particular murderers, at any rate to the extent that they were able to pay. This system of reparatory fines disappeared in the feudal period: in the second half of the Middle Ages, capital punishment was a daily commonplace.

Legal documents show the low value put on human life, but also the variety of situations according to region. Thus at *Paris, out of the 107 sentences passed by the criminal chamber of the Châtelet (royal law *court) between 1389 and 1392, 98 were capital executions. The gravity of the penalties seems unrelated to the nature of the offences: 66 % of those executed were thieves, often occasional ones. In *Provence at the same period, the death penalty seems much rarer: a hundred executions for the *Comtat Venaissin between 1320 and 1418 (but the evidence is much more lacunose). But all regions have in common the variety of punishments and their spectacular character. Apart from hanging, by far the most common, we must cite beheading (followed by hanging), burying alive (for women), burning, drowning, or even scalding for coiners. Many of these penalties had a symbolic value which was no longer always understood by the medieval population (with the exception of purifying fire). The sanctions were exemplary and aimed to make an impression on the spectators: the prolonged exposition of the bodies, sometimes cut in pieces, had the same aim.

The Church never questioned the right of the civil powers to use capital punishment. St *Thomas Aquinas reminds us that it is legitimate to put to death the individual who threatens the common good. In acting thus, the civil power is the "vicar of God". In the Middle Ages, only the *Waldenses (late 12th c.) opposed the death penalty: they were undoubtedly the first to do so in the history of mankind. Their evangelical arguments were evidently fought and reduced to nothing by the Church, which expressed itself in particular through the mouth of *Alan of Lille.

*Moses on Mount Sinai receives the tables of the Decalogue.* Miniature from a 9th-c. Bible. Perugia, Chapter Library of San Giuliano.

J. Iimbert, *La Peine de mort. Histoire, actualité*, Paris, 1967 (2nd ed. 1972). – J. Chiffoleau, *Les Justices du pape. Délinquance et criminalité dans la région d'Avignon au XIV*[e] *siècle*, Paris, 1984, 234-242. – B. Geremek, *The Margins of Society in Late Medieval Paris*, Cambridge, 1987. – J. M. Carbasse, *Introduction historique au droit pénal*, Paris, 1990.

Patrick Henriet

**DECALOGUE.** The term "Decalogue" (the Ten Commandments) designates the ten words revealed in the Old Testament (Ex 20, 2-17; Dt 5, 6-21) and cited here and there in the New Testament (see Lk 18, 2; Rom 13, 9). It was taken up in *ethics, especially following *Peter Lombard's **Sentences* (III, dist. 37), as an expression of natural law, following St Augustine's classification. From the 13th c., an abundant literature of expositions of the Decalogue developed, notably in manuals of *pastoral care expounding the whole of Christian *doctrine starting from the group of the Decalogue, **Credo*, *Pater* and *sacraments. We also find self-sufficient expositions, the first commandment expounding *faith, the others morality.

E. Mangenot, "Catéchisme", *DThC*, 2, 1910, 1895-1907. – E. Dublanchy, "Décalogue", *DThC*, 4, 1911, 161-176. – M. W. Bloomfield *et al.*, *Incipits of Latin Works on the Virtues and Vices, 1100-1500 A.D.*, Cambridge (MA), 1979.

Bertrand-Georges Guyot

**DECRETALISTS, DECRETISTS.** A proper distinction must be made between Decretists and Decretalists. The former were *canonists, commentators on Gratian's **Decretum*, the latter commentators on the collections of *Decretals that multiplied from the 1180s.

The Decretists inaugurated the doctrinal work of the canonists, which rapidly, and until the 15th c., enjoyed a remarkable expansion. Gratian's *Decretum* furnished them with an abundant mass of texts concerning all aspects of canon law. Stimulated by the renaissance of studies of *Roman law, whose centre from the early 12th c. was *Bologna, canonists commented on the *Decretum* in the lessons they gave in a nascent *university.

These commentaries were handed down in written works of various types: *glosses of texts, often subsequently compiled into *apparatus*, **quaestiones* expounding a concrete case and proposing answers, following the method of *scholastic teaching, or "practical exercises" of contradictory expositions (*quaestiones* systematic exposition following the order of the texts of the *Decretum*; later (from the 13th c.), commentaries (often *Lecturae*) recapitulating the teaching of the *masters. As well as Bologna, always considered the main centre of canonical science, other centres of study appeared, at *Paris, *Oxford, *Cologne, *Coimbra, *Salamanca, etc. Bolognese, French, Rhenish and Anglo-Norman schools gave evidence of originality. Not all the Decretists are known, and much of their work is unpublished. Among the famous names were Paucapalea, the earliest known Decretist, whose *Summa* remained the object of discussions; Rolando, a Bolognese canonist, not to be confused with Rolando Bandinelli, the future *Alexander III; Rufinus († 1190); the *Summa coloniensis* (*c.*1169), witness to the brief rise of the Rhenish school; John, bishop of Faenza (*c.*1170-1171); *Huguccio, master of the future *Innocent III; and Bazianus.

The Decretalists, late 12th-c. commentators on the first collections of Decretals (*Compilatio I*[a]), give lustre to 13th-c. canonical science, with the great names of *Bernard of Pavia, Alan the Englishman, Vincent and *Lawrence of Spain († 1248), *John Teutonicus († 1245?), *Raymond of Peñafort († 1276), *Innocent IV, *Hostiensis († 1271), the author of the *Summa aurea*, and many others. The diversity of their origins attests the "European" influence of 13th-c. canonical science. Much remains to be done to edit their works, analyse their methods and evaluate their knowledge.

A. van Hove, *Prolegomena, Commentarium lovaniense in codicem iuris canonici*, Malines-Rome, 1928 (2nd ed. 1945). – S. Kuttner, *Repertorium der Kanonistik*, Vatican, 1937 (re-ed. 1973). – A. Stickler, *Historia fontium*, Turin, 1950. – C. Lefebvre, *L'Age classique, 1140-1378. Sources et théorie du droit*, Paris, 1965, 266-328 ("HDIEO", 7). – A. Garcia y Garcia, *Historia del derecho canonico, I, El primo millenio*, Salamanca, 1967. – *BMCL*, 1970. – K. W. Nörr, "Die kanonistische Literatur", *Handbuch der Quellen und Literatur der neueren europäischen, Privatrechtsgeschichte, Bd. I, Mittelalter*, Munich, 1973, 365-382. – A. Garcia y Garcia, *Estudios sobre la canonistica portuguese medievale*, Madrid, 1976. – A. Gouron, "Une école ou des écoles? Sur les canonistes français (v. 1150-1210)", *Proceedings of the VIth International Congress of Medieval Canon Law, Berkeley, 1980*, 1985 ("MIC.S", 7), 223-240. – R. Weigand, "Die anglonormanische Kanonistik in den letzten Jahrzenten des 12. Jahrhunderts", *Proceedings of the VIIIth International Congress of Medieval canon Law. Cambridge, 1984*, 1988, 249-263 ("MIC.S", 8). – R. Weigand, "Frühe Kanonisten und ihre Karriere in der Kirche", *ZSRG.K*, 76, 1990, 135-155.

Jean Gaudemet

**DECRETALS.** At the end of the 12th c., the *canonist *Huguccio, probably inspired by *Sicard of Cremona, defined the Decretal as a reply given by the Roman pontiff on an uncertain point of law to someone (most often a *bishop, sometimes an *abbot, a *canon or a layman) who had asked him to clarify it. Inspired by the example of the rescripts of the Roman emperors, such replies were given from the 4th century. They multiplied and gained more authority after the consolidation of papal omnipotence and Roman centralization in the second half of the 12th century. With the conciliar canons, which they quickly overtook in number and authority, they became the essential sources of canon law. The **summa "Et est sciendum"* (*c.*118?-1185) held the *pope to be the "master of law". He could go against existing positive law (but not against natural law or divine law). If the pope went against the canons by a Decretal, it was because he wanted to depart from them, "*quod ei licet* (which he was authorized to do)". As a reply given for a particular case, the Decretal should in principle have obligatory force only for that case. In fact, however, it emanated from the omnipotence of the pontiff, who "made the law" and who, as supreme judge, could annul any legal decision that did not respect the rule laid down by the Decretal. So in reality the Decretal laid down a general rule of law.

The abundance of Decretals, their dispersal and the difficulty of knowing their tenor and authority led to the composition of Collections of Decretals from the years 1177-1179 (*Coll. parisiensis I^a^*). At first private works, some of these collections took on an official character in the 13th c. (the first being the *Compilatio V^a^* in 1226).

G. Fransen, *La Décrétale et les Collections de décrétales*, *TSMÂO*, 1972. – P. Landau, "Die Entstehung der System. Dekretalensammlungen", *ZSRG.K*, 66, 1979, 120-149. – W. Holtzmann *et al.*, *Decretales ineditae saec. XII*, 1982 ("MIC.C", 4). – S. Kuttner, *Medieval Councils, Decretals, and Collections of Canon Law*, 2nd ed., Aldershot, 1992. – J. Gaudemet, *Les Sources du droit de l'Église en Occident*, Paris, 1993.

Jean Gaudemet

**DECRETALS, FALSE.** The False Decretals are part of a group of four collections, abounding in interpolations and false texts. The other three are: the Autun *Hispana*, a reworking of the *Hispana* collection in its Gallic form (*Hispana Gallica*), with a single known manuscript (former manuscript of Autun), not widely circulated or published; the *Capitula Angilramni*, 71 chapters claiming to have been sent by *Adrian I to Angilram, bishop of *Metz (769-791); and the false capitularies, claimed to be the work of one Benedict the Levite, and whose three books supplement Ansegisus's four books of capitularies. In them we find authentic *capitularies from 569 to 829, sometimes rewritten, and three quarters of fabricated texts.

The False Decretals, which are attached to this group dominated by fakes, are said to be the work of one Isidorus Mercator (whence the name of False Isidorians often given to the group). The collection is in three parts: false *Decretals attributed to the *popes from Clement (88-97) to Miltiades (311-314); the canons of 54 *councils from Nicaea to Seville II (619), plus Toledo XII (683), with interpolations, corresponding to the first part of the Autun *Hispana*; Decretals from Silvester (314-335) to Gregory II (715-731), generally authentic (including the richest known collection of Leo I's Decretals). The whole is framed by borrowings from the *Dionysio-Hadriana* (at the start, a Preface; at the end, the synod of 721). In total, it numbers more than 10,000 fragments. The collection had a considerable circulation. More than 100 manuscripts of it are known. Its dominant tendency, which was that of all fakes of this kind, was to remove the Church from lay control and its consecutive disorders. For that, it was necessary to restore discipline and *authority, firstly that of the Roman pontiff, but also that of the *bishops, by attacking the excessive power taken by the *metropolitans. An important place was given to judicial *procedure (borrowing much from *Roman law) and the struggle against *violence. The collection was composed after 847 (it uses the False capitularies) and before 852 or 857 (it is cited at that date by *Hincmar of Reims). Its place of composition is uncertain: *Le Mans (P. Fournier), the province of *Reims (W. Goffart, S. Williams), perhaps *Corbie (Fuhrmann?).

Brought to *Rome in 864, it seems to have fallen into oblivion, but it enjoyed great success from the late 10th c. and was widely used in the *canonical collections and Gratian's **Decretum*.

*Decretalium collectio*, J. Merlin (ed.), *PL*, 130, 1853 (1st ed. 1524; 2nd ed. 1530). – P. Hinschius, *Decretales-Pseudo-isidorianae*, Leipzig, 1863. – H. Fuhrmann, *Einfluss und Verbreitung der Pseudo-isidorischen Fälschungen*, *SMGH*, 24, 1972-1974 (3 vol.).

Jean Gaudemet

***DECRETUM* OF GRATIAN.** Many studies of Gratian's *Decretum* have dealt with its creation, and the exceptional wealth of its canons, which cover a thousand years of history, but uncertainties still remain. A venerable but ill-supported tradition makes Gratian a *Camaldolese of *Bologna, expert in law, active in the 1140s. The date of the *Decretum*, whose true name is the *Concordia discordantium canonum*, is uncertain, but probably around 1140. Several clues to its composition suggest that the *Decretum* was not composed "at one go". Major additions were made to it before it had attained a wide circulation.

The *Decretum* is divided into three parts, themselves subdivided in different ways: first 101 "distinctions", then 36 "causes", subdivided into "questions"; finally, five more "distinctions", dealing in particular with Churches, *baptism and *confirmation. Every question concerning the life of the Church is dealt with by the *Decretum*, from the status of the *cleric to *marriage, from the hierarchy to Church *property, from the theory of law to monastic life, etc. It is difficult to make out a rigorous plan in the order given to this multiplicity of questions. This is undoubtedly the consequence of the "manufacture" of the collection, staggered over a certain time and probably made by the contribution of many "teams" working under the direction of a master.

The *Decretum*'s exceptional wealth would itself have sufficed for its success. But it offered more. Firstly a choice, out of the thousands of texts offered by the *canonical collections that multiplied from the 11th century. This choice made the collection manageable, sufficient, and its manuscripts not too heavy. At the same time the *Decretum*'s author wanted to reconcile the often contrary texts that had multiplied over the centuries, emanating from different authorities, sometimes with opposed opinions and responding to different situations. To achieve this *Concordia discordantium canonum*, the *Decretum* accompanied the texts it cited with short commentaries (the *dicta Gratiani*), which tried to explain and resolve the opposing solutions of the **auctoritates*. The *Decretum* was thus both a very rich collection of texts and a doctrinal work that, for the first time, tried to help the users of a disparate legal collection.

*Spiritual Power and Temporal Power.* Miniature from Gratian's *Decretum* with gloss by Bartholomew of Brescia, 1314. Paris, BNF (Ms lat. 3893, fol. 1).

The *Decretum*'s success was immense. It eclipsed previous canonical collections. The commentaries made of it in the schools gave rise to the first *faculties of *canon law, the "faculties of Decretum". From the years around 1145, **summae* recorded these first explanations. They went on multiplying and growing. As for the *Decretum*, though it never received official endorsement from the papacy, it became the first of the collections that contributed to the formation of the *Corpus Iuris Canonici*, which remained until 1917 the code of the Roman Church.

E. Friedberg, *Decretum Magistri Gratiani*, Leipzig, 1879 (re-ed. 1955; only modern crit. ed.).

J. Rambaud-Buhot, "L'Age classique, 1140-1378, Sources et théorie du droit", *HDIEO*, 7, Paris, 1965, 49-129. – S. Kuttner, *Gratian and the Schools of Law 1140-1234*, London, 1983. – T. Reuter, *Wortkonkordanz zum Decretum Gratiani*, Munich, 1990. – J. Gaudemet, *Les Sources du droit de l'Église en Occident*, Paris, 1993. – A. Winroth, *The Two Recensions of Gratian's Decretum*, *ZSRG.K*, 83, 1997, 22-31. – C. Larrainzar, "El Decreto de Graciano del codice F di Firenze, BN Centrale, Conventi soppressi, A.I. 400", *Ius Ecclesiae*, 10, 1998, 421-489.

Jean Gaudemet

**DEDICATION.** Greco-Roman civilization, as well as Jewish tradition, knew rites of dedication. A temple was solemnly consecrated, a civic building (theatre, civic *basilica) was opened. The specific meaning of *dedico* was that of dedicating, consecrating, officially declaring the appurtenance and intention of a thing of public interest. The Old Testament mentions the dedication of steles, altars, houses, temples. For Christian churches, dedication was at first the solemn celebration of the *Eucharist for the first time in a new building, sometimes accompanied by the deposition of *relics of *martyrs under the *altar or, in the case of the use of a pagan place of worship for Christian worship, purification by lustration.

In Frankish Gaul, onto this original background were grafted developments recalling the rites of Christian initiation: "baptism" of the church by aspersion, blessing, unction. The celebration of dedication was enriched with new additions and became, from the 11th c., the most sumptuous rite of the Western liturgies.

A.-G. Martimort, "Le rituel de la consécration des églises", *LMD*, 63, 1960, 86-95. – C. Vogel, R. Elze, *Le Pontifical romano-germanique du Xᵉ siècle*, 2, Vatican, 1964, 82-180. – P. Jounel, "Dédicace", *Dictionnaire encyclopédique de liturgie*, 1, D. Sartore (ed.), A. M. Triacca (ed.), Turnhout, 1992, 261-271 (Fr. tr.).

Guy-Marie Oury

***DEÊSIS.*** The Greek word *deêsis* means petition. There was a functionary at the imperial court whose job was to transmit petitions to the emperor. The word also figures in ecclesiastical inventories to denote *icons, no doubt votive, whose precise subject is not normally indicated. Since the 19th c. the word has been current among art historians to denote a specific composition: the Mother of God and St *John the Baptist placed either side of *Christ with outstretched arms. Sometimes the Mother of God holds a roll inscribed with a petition in her hand, which invites comparison with the functionary responsible for petitions at the imperial ocurt. However she may appear like this before Christ without St John the Baptist (the so-called *Paraklesis*). Furthermore art historians apply the term Deêsis to similar compositions, in which other saints may be substituted for the Mother of God or St John the Baptist. These ambiguities favour confusion in the use of the word.

In Byzantine iconography, the typical Deêsis *gesture of outstretched arms may signify *adoration as well as petition. It is likely that in the earliest "Deêsis" compositions the Mother of God and John the Baptist are represented adoring Christ as the two principal witnesses to his divinity. However a new connotation of *intercession may have been added as early as the 6th c., when the Mother of God saved *Constantinople from invaders and became the principal patron of the city. In medieval *Byzantine art, the Deêsis as a specific composition was widely represented. It was a popular funerary subject, placed in the apse of votive chapels to invite the two saints to intercede in favour of the *souls of those buried there. Such chapels are particularly common in *Cappadocia. It also appears on icons for private devotion, often with the person who commissioned it prostrate before the celestial group. John Mavropous, in an epigram, describes such an icon, in which an emperor begs for intercession on the Day of Judgment. From the 11th c., the figures of the Deêsis were represented on the beams of iconostases, sometimes with angels and other saints, notably apostles. In this case the composition was probably intended to remind the laity, whose view of the liturgy was blocked by the iconostasis, of their need to address prayers to intercessors. Also in the 11th c., when the *Last Judgment iconography was established, the Mother of God and St John the Baptist were introduced on either side of Christ, interceding for mankind before Christ enthroned, who, flanked by the apostles, appears as supreme judge.

*Deêsis and saints.* "Harbaville Triptych". Constantinopolitan ivory work, mid 10th c. Paris, Louvre.

T. von Bogyay, "Deêsis", *RBK*, 1, Stuttgart, 1966. – C. Walter, "Two Notes on the Deêsis", "Further Notes on the Deêsis", *Studies in Byzantine Iconography*, London, 1977. – A. Cameron, "The Theotokos in 6th-Century Constantinople", *JThS*, 29, 1978, 79-108. – C. Walter, "Bulletin on the Deêsis and the Paraclesis", *REByz*, 38, 1980, 261-269. – C. Jolivet-Lévy, *Les Églises byzantines de Cappadoce*, Paris, 1991.

Christopher Walter

**DEFINITOR.** The *Cistercian general *chapter elected four "definitors" who legislated in its name and became the permanent council of the *abbot of Cîteaux. In the 12th and 13th cc. this became general, with variants, in the *orders that possessed such chapters. The *Dominicans used it in their provincial chapters, and had "general definitors" elected by the provinces, who, two years out of three, formed the general chapter. The alternation of these chapters with the chapter of provincials produced a bicameral system.

L.-R. Misserey, "Chapitres de religieux", *DDC*, 3, 1942, 595-601. – L. Moulin, "Le pluralisme dans l'ordre des Frères prêcheurs", *Res publica*, 2, Brussels, 1960, 50-66.

Marie-Humbert Vicaire †

**DEGREES, ACADEMIC.** In the *schools of the 12th c. and at the beginning of the creation of the *universities, there was only a single degree, that of *licence to teach (*licentia docendi*).

With the development of university studies and the organisation of studies in the *faculties, a preliminary phase was put in place, viz. bachelorship. The bachelor was a student who had reached the second phase of his studies and had obtained the right, by examination or otherwise, varying according to university, to give certain courses. Bachelorship existed in all the faculties. In the faculty of arts, a scholastic exercise, the *determinatio*, was necessary to obtain this degree. In the faculty of *theology, there were three categories of bachelors: *baccalarii biblici*, who lectured on the *Bible, *baccalarii sententiarii*, who taught *Peter Lombard's **Sentences*, and *baccalarii formati*, who took part in *disputations.

The *licentia* involved an examination by the *masters of the faculty, meeting as a commission of examiners, subsequently making a deposition of their opinion. Originally implying merely authorization to teach, the *licentia* had a different character from the other degrees by the fact of being conferred by the ecclesiastical authorities (the *chancellor at *Paris and the *archdeacon at *Bologna), while the other university degrees were accorded directly by the masters. After the examination of the *licentia*, one was licensed, but not yet a master.

To obtain the master's degree (or doctorate), it was necessary to submit to a ceremony called *inceptio*, by which one officially entered the corporation of masters. One first had to ask for authorization to accede to the ceremony, for which a deposition by the masters and a series of *oaths were necessary. The ceremony itself consisted of two parts, *vesperie* or *vespers and, next day, *inceptio* proper or *principium*, the session of *investiture by which the new master solemnly began his teaching. The essential part of these two sessions was a disputation (*disputatio*). After *inceptio*, the candidate was thus a master (or *doctor). He normally committed himself to hold disputations for the next forty days and to teach in his university for one to two years (obligatory regency). If he shirked these obligations, he was considered as perjured and struck off from the University.

O. Weijers, *Terminologie des universités au XIII^e siècle*, Rome, 1987. – *Universities in the Middle Ages, A History of the University in Europe*, H. de Ridder-Symoens (ed.), 1, Cambridge, 1992.

Olga Weijers

**DEMETRIUS CYDONES (*c*.1324-*c*.1398).** A native of *Thessalonica, he became *mesazôn* (prime minister) of *John VI Cantacuzenus in 1347. Having learnt Latin for the needs of Byzantine diplomacy, he discovered western *theology; he then undertook to translate *Thomas Aquinas. After the abdication of John VI in 1354, he entered the service of John V. He preached alliance with the West against the *Turks and opposed the followers of Gregory *Palamas. In 1357 he became a *Catholic and accompanied John V when John did likewise in 1369. After the death of John, he served Manuel II, but left him because of the hostility of the Palamites. He died in *Crete. Many of his disciples became *Dominicans.

F. Tinnefeld, *Dèmètrios Kydonès. Briefe*, 1, 1, Stuttgart, 1981; 1, 2, 1982; 2, 1991.

Marie-Hélène Congourdeau

**DEMIURGE.** The term "demiurge" had various meanings: it designated firstly the architect of the world in Plato's *Timaeus*, then the world-soul in Plotinus and, for the gnostics, the lower gods who made the world.

Of these different meanings, the Middle Ages took up that of Plato, known to it from Calcidius's translation and commentary on the *Timaeus*. Thus the medievals, from *Boethius to the school of *Saint-Victor, in some sense Christianized Plato's demiurge in order to identify him with the creator *God of the book of *Genesis, which provoked criticism from *Simon of Tournai. In the 13th c., this identification was refuted and the unique action of the creator defined, following the controversy over the *creation of matter and the appeal to "*creatio ex nihilo*".

A. E. Taylor, *Platonism and its Influence*, London, 1925.

Marie-Anne Vannier

**DEMOGRAPHY.** Demography was at first "the statistical study of human communities" (Robert), aiming to enumerate the people in a given place at a given time. To it was later added the study of the biological and sociological mechanisms controlling the reproduction, increase or decrease and equilibrium of populations. Historical demography concerns the study in time of these two orders of phenomena; it is both a statement and an explanation of ancient populations.

The Roman tradition of taking general censuses of the population was not kept up in the Middle Ages, which, in general, had no effective registration of births, marriages and deaths. Any study of medieval demography must supply this dual absence by making the best of the sources.

**Sources.** These are primarily statistics. General statistics was the business of the *State or, at least, of the authorities. A knowledge of the number of his subjects provided an indication of the prince's power. It was probably in this spirit that, in *William I's Anglo-Norman kingdom from 1086, a census of the king's tenants and members of the clergy, the **Domesday Book*, was made. The kingdom of *France does not seem to have known a general statistical inquiry before that of *c*.1328 called "State of *parishes and hearths", which answered a dual purpose, fiscal and statistical. More clearly fiscal in nature were the *collectae* of the kingdom of *Naples and *Sicily in 1277 and 1282, the reckoning of the 1377 "Poll Tax" in *England or, in the *Empire, Maximilian's *Gemeiner Pfennig* of 1495. Other medieval statistics were more restricted (*dioceses, principalities, mainly *towns) and were generally fiscal. Statistics of "parishioners" exist for dioceses (*Peter's Pence in England or *Scandinavia, debit accounts of the Norman dioceses, **pouillés* at *Chartres and *Rouen). The financial system often provided statistical data in the form of censuses of taxpayers or taxation accounts (*e.g.* principalities of the *Netherlands [*Brabant, Hainaut], of *Germany, *Burgundy, *Dauphiné, duchies of *Spoleto or *Urbino). Very frequently, statistics were established in an urban setting or in that of a city-state. The towns of *Italy had lists of citizens summoned to swear to a treaty, or of men capable of bearing arms (Poggibonsi, from 1226). Some (Fribourg in *Switzerland, *Reims, *Nuremberg, Nördlingen, *Strasbourg) preserved censuses of mouths and grain, or just mouths, or accounts of the *salt-tax, based in Italy on *bocche* ("mouths"). Another setting was the landed *estate (the English "manor"). Statistical returns survive from certain Carolingian *polyptychs (*Saint-Germain-des-Prés, Saint-Rémi at Reims) or, at a later date, from the manorial inquests of England ("extents"), from **censuaria* or terriers. These documents all inform us, directly or indirectly, about the size of the population. But except for censuses of mouths, they do not directly tell us the total number of souls, and they require appropriate treatment. One problem is to evaluate, in the fiscal documents, the proportion of taxpayers to the total population (as in *e.g.* the Paris *Livres de la Taille*) and to estimate the number of the exempt or indigent. When only those over a certain age are listed (as in the 1377 Poll Tax in England: over 14 years), or those between two ages (men of military age), we must likewise get back to the total population. Many documents give only hearths or heads of families: so these must be modified by a multiplier, or hearth coefficient, which should always be fixed by reference to the true composition of hearths (which is not often known). The determination of this coefficient is frequently discussed by demographic historians. For Domesday Book, 3.5, 4.5 and 5 have all been proposed. For the state of affairs in *c*.1328, the proposed coefficients of 3.5 (*Paris) and 5 have been disputed. Another difficulty is that the mean composition of the hearth varies at different times (*Ypres, Reims, *Verona or *Florence), which forbids the use of fixed coefficients.

Next come sources for demographic mechanisms. To define

the demographic pattern of a population, we must know its differential rates of birth, *marriage, fertility and mortality by ages, its ages at marriage and *death, intervals between births, the calendar of conceptions. The absence of registrars makes this very difficult. In France, registration of baptisms began in *Brittany (Nantes) at the start of the 15th century. At Florence, baptisms of boys and girls were made accountable from the 14th c. (their number is preserved from 1450) and *burials are known from approximately 1385. Tax registers note deceases (*Dijon). The *post mortem* inquests of England, inventories after decease and, to a certain extent, *testaments (Lyon) tell us about the composition of the *family, matrimonial status, age at *marriage, mortality, coefficient of masculinity. *Post mortem* inquests help us establish, in England, tables of mortality based on mortality at different ages, and calculate life expectancy and mortality rates at different periods (at least among the *nobility).

The most complete, as well as accurate, source of knowledge of the demographic pattern of a medieval society is certainly the Florentine *catasto* (wealth tax) of 1427-1429, which gave rise to a census, in principle exhaustive, of the families of Florence and its *contado*, based on individual declarations giving the composition of families, the sex and age of their members and the constituents of their *wealth. The practice of the *catasto*, going back to imperial Rome, had been abandoned with the fall of the Empire and resumed only on the initiative of the *Communes. We should particularly mention the *catasti* of Siena (1202), Milan (1208) and Genoa (1214); after 1250 the practice of the *catasto* became general. During the 15th c., the responsibility for the description of property shifted from the community to individual heads of families.

**Results.** Evaluations of the population of a State have been obtained: for England in 1086, between 1.1 and 2.3 million inhabitants. For the same kingdom in 1377, after three plagues, from 2.5 to 3 million. The population of the kingdom of France in *c.*1328: of the order of 16 to 17 million (before the plagues). The Angevin kingdom of Naples and Sicily in 1277: 1.6 million. Evaluations for regions or districts, *e.g.* four Norman *dioceses in the 12th c., *Normandy in 1221, Dauphiné in 1338, the English counties in 1377. For towns or city-states, examples are more numerous: Paris in *c.*1328 (probably 200,000), Reims, Ypres, Nuremberg, *Augsburg, Basel, Strasbourg, Überlingen, Prato, Pistoia, Florence (110,000 in 1338), etc.

The knowledge of populations, in hearths or in inhabitants, allows us to calculate densities, notably rural densities. These reveal their tremendous variety in time and place. France in 1328 shows a mean density of 7.9 hearths per sqare kilometre, going from 22 per square kilometres for the Valois to less than 6 for the mountains of the Auvergne. England in 1377 had counties numbering more than 21 inhabitants per square kilometre and others numbering less than 4. In *c.*1470, in the Burgundian Netherlands, *Flanders had 77 inhabitants per square kilometre and *Luxemburg 6. Urbanized regions were regions of high rural density, but there were also high densities in mainly rural areas.

Comparison between successive estimates of population allows us to sort out the trend for Western Europe: maximum population in the late 13th c. and, locally, the early 14th c.; high tensions and food crises in the early 14th c.; catastrophic evolution under the blow of the plague from 1348; recovery starting at a variable date after 1430 and culminating only in the 16th c., often at a lower level than that of 1347.

The demographic pattern has been studied mainly in England and Italy. In England, "extents" of manors and *post mortem* inquests allow us to follow the growth and decline of the population, to calculate the coefficient of masculinity, matrimonial status, age at marriage, rates of birth, fertility and mortality at different ages and to construct mortality tables and calculate life expectancies. In *Tuscany, the Florentine *catasto* provides information of the same type on the composition and evolution of the "hearth", as well as on the cycle of evolution of families. Elsewhere, the rare record books do not allow such extensive conclusions.

K. J. Beloch, *Bevölkerungsgeschichte Italiens*, 1, Berlin, 1937; *ibid.*, 2, 1939; *ibid.*, 3, 1961. – J. C. Russell, *British Medieval Population*, Albuquerque (NM), 1948. – R. Mols, *Introduction à la démographie historique des villes d'Europe*, Louvain, 1954-56. – J. C. Russell, *Late Ancient and Medieval Population*, Philadelphia (PA), 1958. – D. Herlihy, *Medieval and Renaissance Pistoia. The Social History of an Italian Town*, New Haven, 1967. – M. A. Arnould, *Les Relevés de feux*, *TSMÂO*, 18, 1976. – D. Herlihy, C. Klapisch-Zuber, *Tuscans and their Families, a Study of the Florentine Catasto of 1427*, New Haven, 1985. – J. and M. Dupaquier, *Histoire de la démographie*, Paris, 1985. – D. Herlihy, *Medieval Households*, Cambridge (MA), 1985. – J. C. Russell, *The Control of Late Ancient and Medieval Population*, Philadelphia, 1958. – M. Ginatempo, L. Sandri, *L'Italia delle città. Il popolamento urbano tra Medievo e Rinascimento*, Florence, 1990. – *Histoire de la population française*, J. Dupaquier (ed.), 1, Paris, 1991 (2nd ed.). – C. Klapisch-Zuber, *La Maison et le nom. Stratégies et rituels dans l'Italie de la Renaissance*, Paris, 1991.

Henri Dubois

## DEMON, DEMONOLOGY

**The West.** In his manifold appearances and under his various names – Satan, Lucifer or the Devil could designate the chief obeyed by the troop of devils or demons, sometimes named Baal, Beelzebub, Belial, Behemoth – the devil was omnipresent in the medieval universe. He was the "prince of this world" (Jn 12, 31); down here, "he led the dance" (J. Le Goff). While the Old Testament largely ignores him, the New Testament, following popular Judaism and apocryphal literature, multiplies references to the devil (notably Mt 4; 13. 19 and 39; Jn 8, 44; 1 Pet 5, 8; Rev 12, 9-10). Federating the multitude of demonic spirits of popular Judaism, and at the same time proceeding from the dissociation of the ambivalent figure of Yahweh, he counts among the most original creations of Christianity.

Largely following the *Fathers, notably Augustine and *Gregory the Great, medieval theologians gave great attention to the devil. Important things were at stake: it was necessary, despite the recognised power of Satan, to make a distinction from true *dualism (doctrine of Mani, *Catharism). In this respect, the conception of the devil's origin was decisive. Though resting on a very narrow scriptural basis, the fall of the *angels became an essential story. If the *Book of Enoch*, a Jewish apocryphon attributing the fall to the angels' carnal desire for women, enjoyed considerable credit up to the 4th c., medieval authors based their explanation on the pride of Lucifer, the first of the angels, and his wish to equal *God. Lucifer and his followers were then expelled from the celestial *paradise and condemned, for their greater suffering, to dwell eternally on earth and in the infernal depths. Such was the origin of *evil; such was the first act of the history of the universe, which was linked, from the year 1000 (Aelfric of Eynsham), to the creation of *man, willed by God to replace the fallen angels in heaven. Whatever the variations in the story, the devil was not an independent principle of evil; he was a creature of God who, after his fall, remained subject to the divine will.

*Hell.* Detail of the fresco *Heaven and Hell.* School of Bologna, 15th c. Bologna, Pinacoteca Nazionale.

Nevertheless, the Creator did not will evil: as St *Thomas Aquinas makes clear, the demons were created good; they are bad not by *nature, but by *will, by virtue of the bad use of their free will.

The second important point concerns the devil's powers over man and the world. The original sin of *Adam and Eve is the devil's revenge. By virtue of that fault, he acquired a real right of possession over man, what theologians called *ius diaboli.* They undoubtedly emphasized that Satan was truly the "prince of this world" only until the coming of the Redeemer, who redeemed that right by his sacrifice. The episode of Christ's *Descent into Hell, to free the just who died before the Incarnation, strikingly demonstrates the end of the devil's omnipotence. Yet Gregory the Great notes bitterly that, to look at the world, his power does not seem to have been visibly diminished. We find in all our authors this balance between the formidable strength of Satan, perhaps emphasized more in the early Middle Ages, and the limits imposed on him by the Incarnation, undoubtedly given more value after the year 1000. In fact, *Anselm of Canterbury, at the end of the 11th c., was one of the first theologians radically to contest the theory of *ius diaboli*, acknowledging only the *ius Dei*. Yet the devil by no means disappeared from the intellectual scene, and we see in the final centuries of the Middle Ages a development of learned demonology, or even a satanic obsession, as witness the evolution of clerical ideas on the witches' *sabbath.

Every aspect of the life of demons aroused reflection: their incorporeal, aerial nature; their capacity to act on the human *body or *soul; the impossibility of their returning to God; their sexual activity (*e.g.* *William of Auvergne or Thomas Aquinas admit that, in the form of incubi and succubi, they transmit a human seed, but are not able to procreate by their own nature). Devils keep certain advantages of their angelic nature, in particular a knowledge superior to that of men. In his treatise *On the divination of demons*, Augustine admits that they can foretell to men events of which the latter are ignorant, notably thanks to the rapidity of their movements. But St Thomas emphasizes that this power, very different from the gift of *prophecy received from God, rests only on a knowledge of natural causalities and is, when all is said and done, only a conjecture drawn from present facts.

Beliefs, stories and *images declined to infinity the facets of the power of the Evil One. He inspired all the enemies of the just, the *pagans (whose gods were mere demons, and whose idols were effigies of the devil), the *Jews and the Muslims. The *heretics of the 11th, 12th and 13th cc. were held to be envoys of Satan, when they were not credited with a veritable cult of the devil, prefiguring belief in the witches' *sabbath. Antithesis of the body of the Church, all formed a body of which Satan was the head

(*Adso of Montier-en-Der). Between these two bodies, combat raged, until the final unchaining foretold by the *Apocalypse and sometimes felt to be imminent. The weapons available to the devil to extend his hold over men were manifold. By possession, he beleaguered bodies; by *temptations, notably sexual, he aimed most particularly at exceptional souls, beginning with Christ and the saints (Athanasius's *Life of Antony*, **Golden Legend*). By imposture, he disguised evil as *good, as when, having taken on the appearance of St James, he induced a pilgrim to castrate himself and commit *suicide. The motif of the diabolical pact was spread through the legend of Theophilus, known in the texts and in an abundant iconography from the 9th c. and especially from the 12th century. Finally, there were many who, particularly in the monasteries of the 11th and 12th cc., felt the continuous, obsessing, agonizing presence of the devil (*Rodulfus Glaber, *Guibert of Nogent, *Peter the Venerable).

But the power of the devil was kept under control. Faced with the heavenly forces – the angels, the saints, the Virgin, Christ – his defeat was certain. In hagiographical accounts, temptations – which he could only inflict with God's permission – appear as a trial necessary for the manifestation of *sanctity; the devil was the foil of the saintly hero who necessarily triumphed over him. Men could thus resort to the protection of the heavenly powers, like that of the Church: *sacraments (primarily *baptism and *penance) and rites (*exorcism, *consecration, benedictions, funerary liturgy) repulsed the devil or effaced the mark of his power. Finally, other *gestures or objects were particularly effective against the devil, some prescribed by the Church (*fasting, *prayer, sign of the *cross, *relics, etc.), others not (amulets, etc.).

Until the 9th century, iconographic treatment of the devil developed only very slowly. In the Carolingian period, depictions of him multiplied, but the manifestation of his evil nature remained unobtrusive: his negative traits were confined to his partial nakedness, his dark colour or his hirsute locks; in the scene of the Temptation, he is often as handsome and well dressed as Christ. At the turn of the *millennium, the iconography of the fall of the angels appeared and a specific depiction of the demon was diffused, insisting on his animal and monstrous characteristics. Between the entirely human appearance he donned in order to deceive and his numerous animal manifestations (serpent, *dragon, insect, black bird, lion. . .), one representation was dominant: the devil kept an anthropomorphic silhouette, but this appearance – veritable *imago Dei* according to Gen 1, 26 – was perverted, by deformity and tension (ugliness, curved posture, gesticulations, thinness or obesity) and above all by the addition of animal traits (animal snout, horns, tail, paws and claws, hairy body, bat's wings from the 13th c. . .).

If iconography more and more vigorously emphasized the evil nature of the devils, it also insisted more on the power of their leader, the "*imperador del regno doloroso*" described by *Dante. Sometimes from the 12th c., but especially from the 14th and 15th cc., there developed a veritable representation of the Majesty of Satan, emphasizing his authority by his sometimes gigantic size, his frontal and seated position, the insignia of power (throne, sceptre, crown) and the order he imposed on his court.

In all, the undoubtedly reinforced presence of Satan in the medieval universe can be understood only if we consider also the powers that controlled him: divine and saintly figures, but also authorities, of Church and of State, of whom Satan's body was the negative reflection, and who strengthened their power in the victorious combat they waged against absolute Evil.

A. Graf, *Il diavolo*, Rome, 1980 (1st ed. 1889). – *Satan. EtCarm*, 1948. – "Démon", *DSp*, 3, 1957, 141-241. – *Le Diable au Moyen Âge*, *Senefiance*, 6, 1979. – J. B. Russell, *Lucifer. The Devil in the Middle Ages*, Ithaca (NY), 1984. – *Santi e demoni nell'alto medioevo occidentale*, 1989 ("SSAM, 1988", 33). – *L'Autunno del diavolo*, E. Corsini (dir.), E. Costa (dir.), Milan, 1990 (2 vol.). – J. Baschet, *Les Justices de l'au-delà. Les représentations de l'enfer en France et en Italie (XII^e-XV^e siècle)*, *BEFAR*, Rome, 1993. – N. Cohn, *Europe's Inner Demons*, London, 1993. – J. Baschet, "Diable", *Dictionnaire raisonné de l'Occident médiéval*, J. Le Goff (dir.), J.-C. Schmitt (dir.), Paris (in preparation).

Jérôme Baschet

**Byzantium.** The wealth of vocabulary that served to designate demons at Byzantium attests the importance attributed to these maleficent forces that surrounded human beings. But traditions about demons vary according to the type of text concerned, and we can distinguish a popular demonology, a clerical demonology and a learned demonology, not ignoring the mutual relations and influences that united these categories.

Behind the popular *superstitions, attested mainly by *exorcisms and talismans, were perceptions much older than Christianity and common to various peoples of the Mediterranean and Near East. They were to do with *death and the world of the *dead, whence the chthonian character of the often female figures that emerged from them (subterranean or submarine dwelling, monstrous physique, infirmities such as blindness or lameness). Intervening at those moments when the human being is most vulnerable (birth, *marriage, *sickness, travel), these baleful divinities were moved by jealousy and envy, symbolized on amulets by the image of the owl and the evil eye.

These widespread beliefs and the apotropaic practices they engendered were fought by the Church, which tried to replace them with a demonology that conformed to the Old and New Testament traditions: as fallen *angels, the demons sought to turn people, particularly monks and ascetics, away from the faith and take possession of their *soul, whether by possessing it in this life or by disputing it with angels in the afterlife. These Christianized demons, who borrowed a number of traits from pagan demons, are well represented in hagiographical literature.

Learned demonology is illustrated by two 12th- or 13th-c. treatises wrongly attributed to Michael *Psellus. The aim of these texts was to give a synthesis of *Neoplatonist ideas (Porphyry, Iamblichus, Proclus) and the teaching of the Church *Fathers. They pose the theoretical problem of the "nature" of demons and propose a classification and a hierarchy based on the abode and specific activities of the various spirits. Furthermore, they are interested in magical practices intended to conciliate or exorcize demonic forces. An apocryphon of Jewish origin dating from the 1st c. AD, the *Testament of Solomon* (ed. MacCown, Chicago, 1922), presented as a treatise on practical demonology, also exercised great influence, both on learned literature and on the tradition of exorcisms.

A. Delatte, C. Josserand, "Contribution à l'étude de la démonologie byzantine", *AIPh*, 2, 1934, 207-232. – P. Joannou, *Démonologie populaire, démonologie critique au XI^e siècle, la vie inédite de saint Auxence par Michel Psellos*, Wiesbaden, 1971. – P. Gautier, "Le *De daemonibus* du Pseudo-Psellos", *REByz*, 38, 1980, 105-194; *ibid.*, 46, 1988, 85-107. – R. P. H. Greenfield, *Traditions of Belief in Late Byzantine Demonology*, Amsterdam, 1988. – I. Sorlin, "Striges et géloudes, histoire d'une croyance et d'une tradition", *TMCB*, 11, 1991, 411-436.

Irène Sorlin

**DENIS THE CARTHUSIAN (*c.*1402-1471).** Denis, born *c.*1402, resolved early to be a *Carthusian. Rejected on account of his youth, he set off to wait patiently at the university of *Cologne, where he took his mastership of arts in 1424. In 1425, he finally entered at Ruremonde, where he lived until his death in 1471. In 1451-1452 he accompanied *Nicholas of Cusa, papal *legate in *Germany, and between 1465 and 1469 he held the post of rector of the new Charterhouse of Bois-le-Duc.

He was one of the most prolific and erudite authors of religious literature of the late Middle Ages. His philosophical and theological output spans the whole of the Christian tradition, from the Church *Fathers to his own time, and earned him the title of Ecstatic *Doctor. Unfortunately, there are few surviving original manuscripts of this theoretician of mystical experience.

*Opera omnia in unum corpus digesta ad fidem editionum Coloniensium cura et labore Monachorum sacri Ordinis Cartusiensis favente Pont. Max. Leone XIII*, Montreuil-Tournai-Parkminster, 1896-1935 (44 vol., in 4°).

A. Stoelen, "Denys le Chartreux", *DSp*, 3, 1957, 430-449.

Benoît Goffin

**DENMARK.** The Danish Middle Ages began in the 8th c., at the time when the great commercial centres, which would soon be called on to undergo considerable extension by reason of *Viking activities, developed: *e.g.* Hedeby, which would be one of the great rallying points of the celebrated pirate navigators. It was the Middle Ages too, according to the Scandinavian definition of this historical term, that saw on one hand the Christianization of the country, with Haraldr Gormsson (*c.*940), and on the other the great expeditions of Sveinn Tjugguskegg and his son Knútr inn Mikli (*Cnut the Great) to *England (*c.*1030), whose declared aim was to obtain total supremacy not just over the three *Scandinavian countries, but also over Great Britain: ambitions soon reduced to nothing, but which left deep and lasting traces in the Danish consciousness. It remains clear that this period (around the *millennium) was glorious for Denmark: King Godfred had found the means, around 800, to put an end to Carolingian ambitions by laying out the impressive Danevirke (a defensive wall that completely closed off Jylland and whose ruins still exist), and Christian missionaries such as St *Anskar, who made several journeys in this country, attest the vitality of this culture. At the same time, the Danes were probably the most active of the Vikings, at least in the western sector of their incursions; it was they who settled down permanently in England (in the region that bore their name: the Danelaw) and in *Normandy. Particularly gifted and tireless *merchants, they certainly left their mark on the whole of the Viking phenomenon, if only for immediate cultural reasons: the *runic alphabet bore their imprint, notably in its simplified version, the new *fuþark*.

With King Svend Estridson (1047-1074) was outlined what would be the major characteristic of this country's history: collusion or collision between *Church and State. For the moment, we see an *entente* between the two powers, but the rest of the medieval history of this country would be that of a long struggle between the two powers, a struggle concluded by the victory of the Church, a victory that would finally be the cause of the success of Lutheranism in the early 16th century. Svend had five sons whose contentions for the succession to the throne took up the country's attention, to the benefit of the Church, which had just founded an *archbishopric at *Lund (then in Danish territory) with very powerful prelates like Bishop Asser (1104) or his nephew Eskil (1137). The epoch of the Valdemars (1157-1241), which marks

Gold altar-frontal from Lisbjerg (Jutland), 1125-1150.
Copenhagen, National Museum.

the most glorious period of the Danish Middle Ages despite the hard struggles against the *Wends (Slav tribes), established Denmark's supremacy in the realm of *commerce (visible in the exansion of towns like Ribe or Copenhagen) and the rise of royal power. At the same time, the Church acquired a power that would end by provoking its loss. But monastic life enjoyed an unprecedented expansion (Benedictines notably at Ringsted, *Cistercians at Soro, not to speak of the *mendicant orders: Greyfriars Streets and Whitefriars Streets still exist in most of the great Scandinavian towns, attesting the success of these orders at the time). A time of solid religious settlement, also attested by innumerable wooden and stone churches built all over the country, the time of the Valdemars can pass for one of the high points of Danish history, since the country, which had acquired a quasi-supremacy over all its neighbours, was then considered the most important in Northern Europe.

Yet the period 1241-1387 introduced elements that would considerably weaken the power of the sovereigns: rise of the power of the Church, growing power of the upper middle class which obliged the *kings to conclude *charters with it, threat of the duchies of Schleswig and Holstein and the great towns of the *Hanse. Towards the end of the 14th c., the Danish *monarchy was in such bad shape that the kingdom was more than once without a ruler. It needed the political energy of Valdemar Atterdag, around

1360, and then the combination of circumstances that made his daughter Margrete the heiress to the three Scandinavian kingdoms (union of Kalmar in 1389), for Denmark to recover the position it had held for so long. Augmented by *Norway, *Iceland and the Faeroe islands, not counting the southern provinces of *Sweden (Scania, Blekinge, Halland, etc.) that it had possessed from time immemorial, the country long remained the most important in the North, whence incessant and often bloody quarrels with Sweden.

*Denmark Medieval History*, N. Skyum-Nielsen (ed.), N. Lund (ed.), Copenhagen, 1981. – E. Roesdahl, *Viking Age Denmark*, London, 1982. – B.P. McGuire, *The Cistercians in Denmark*, Kalamazoo (MI), 1982. – *The Birth of Identities: Denmark and Europe in the Middle Ages*, B.P. McGuire (ed.), Copenhagen, 1996.

Régis Boyer

**DENUNCIATION.** The obligation laid on Christians to denounce the sins of their fellows was based on Mt 18, 15-17. It was with the development of inquisitorial procedure that delation entered fully into judicial practice, not just ecclesiastical but also lay. According to Nicholas Eymerich (late 14th c.), the population had six days after the arrival of the inquisitors to denounce *heretics, after which they risked *excommunication. If the inquisitor considered that the delator's security was threatened, he kept his name secret, which happened more often than not.

Nicolas Eymerich, *Manuel des inquisiteurs*, L. Sala-Molins (ed.), Paris-The Hague, 1973, 110, 117 and 219-220.

J. Guiraud, *L'Inquisition médiévale*, Paris, 1928, 98-101. – "Dénonciation", *DDC*, 5, 1953, 557-569.

Patrick Henriet

**DESCENT INTO HELL**

**Doctrine.** Only implicitly and by allusion do the Scriptures speak of Christ's Descent into *Hell (or into *Limbo) and of his purpose (notably in the Psalms, Acts 2, 24-31 and 1 Pet 3, 18-20). The **Credo* affirms it, but the formula never appears in the creeds before the 4th century. In the West, its first mention (*c.*404) appears in Rufinus, in the baptismal creed of the Church of Aquileia (*Expositio symboli*, 12, 15, 26: *PL*, 21, 352-355). In the *theology and liturgy of the Eastern Churches the formula appears early, in a paschal and baptismal context, and is contained in the formularies of some *councils, including the first *Arian ones (359, at Sirmium). The main narrative source, the *apocryphal *Gospel of Nicodemus*, whose second part is devoted to the Descent into Hell, probably does not go back beyond the 4th century.

From the 7th c., the formula spread more and more. In the West it was notably promulgated by a series of councils of *Toledo and renewed in the 9th c. by the sixth council of *Arles, assembled under *Charlemagne. Later, the dogma was confirmed at the fourth *Lateran council (1215) and the council of *Lyon (1274). The explanations given by *Thomas Aquinas (*Summa theologiae*, III[a], q. 52) would be retained until their challenge by the Protestants in the 16th century.

From the late 4th c., the *Fathers affirmed that it was Christ's *soul ("the divine soul united to the *Word") that descended into Hell, while his *body remained shrouded in the tomb; *scholasticism confirmed this (Thomas Aquinas, *Summa theologiae*, III[a], q. 52, a. 3).

Likewise, the Fathers concurred in stating that the Descent into Hell took place during the three days between his death and the *Resurrection. Only Augustine commented on the first epistle of

*Christ of the Anastasis tramples on death in chains.* Mosaic in the church of the Dormition, Daphni (detail). 11th c.

Peter (3, 18-20) in a figurative sense: it was not after his death, but before his incarnation, at the time of the flood, that Christ came in spirit to preach to *Noah's contemporaries, *i.e.* the sinners and pagans, in order to dissipate the darkness of their unbelief (*Epist.* 164, *ad Evodium*: *PL*, 33, 714-718). Augustine's metaphorical interpretation was taken up notably by *Bede (*In primam Petri*, III, 19: *PL*, 93, 58 f.) and *Walafrid Strabo (*PL*, 114, 686).

As for the work accomplished by Christ during his Descent into Hell, there were two main theories: preaching to the imprisoned spirits and the defeat of the *demon, followed by the deliverance of souls. The earliest Fathers, like Clement of Alexandria (*Stromata* VI, c. 5: *PG*, 11, 865) and *Origen (*Contra Celsum*, II, 43: *PG*, 11, 865), believed in the possibility of universal *salvation, affirming that the preaching offered the light of the gospel to all the imprisoned spirits, on the sole condition that they be of good will. But opinion changed with John Chrysostom, who stated that it was a heresy to believe in universal salvation after death and that only the just under the old Law were delivered, with the gentiles who had neither knowledge nor hope of the Redeemer, provided they had not worshipped idols and had known the true *God (*In Matth.*, hom. 36, n. 3: *PG*, 57, 416-417). *Gregory the Great held the same opinion: it could only be the just (*Epist.* 1, VII, *Ep.* 15, *ad Georgium presbyterum*: *PL*, 77, 869-870).

Christ's Descent into Hell was also presented as a victory of *Christ over *death and the demon, a trap into which the devil fell himself (Augustine, *Sermo* 130: *PL*, 38, 726; taken up by Peter Lombard, *Sent.*, 1, III, dist. XIX: *PL*, 192, 796).

*DACL*, 4, 1, 1921, 682-693. – *DThC*, 4, 1, 1924, 565-620. – *DBS*, 2, 395-431. – M. R. James, *The Apocryphal New Testament*, Oxford, 1924, 117-146.

Anca Bratu

**Iconography.** In *Byzantine art, the *image of Christ's Descent into Hell replaced the *Resurrection. Christ returns from Hell (in Greek *anastasis*, "ascent"), seizing *Adam by the wrist and drawing Eve after him. The iconography of the *Anastasis* developed in the East (*c.*700), but the earliest surviving examples are at *Rome (*frescos of Santa Maria Antiqua), dating from the pontificate of John VII (705-707).

From the 9th c., representations multiplied, at Byzantium and in the West, in manuscripts and in monumental art. They put the stress on Christ triumphant over death and the infernal powers: armed with a cross, he treads down Hades and tramples underfoot the broken gates of hell; later, strewn locks, keys and bolts are added to the doors signed with a cross. The West emphasized Christ's struggle against the devil and the infernal character of the place, in the form of a monster's throat or an architecture in flames. In the 10th and 11th cc., more of the liberated just were depicted: *David and *Solomon crowned, *John the Baptist; later other *prophets and patriarchs were added (*Isaiah, *Jeremiah, Abel; Enoch and *Elijah), as well as the good thief.

The illustration of Jacob Kokkinobaphos's *Homilies* (12th c.) shows Christ preaching: surrounded by a *mandorla of light and bearing a scroll, he brings light and the good news to the patriarchs and the just of the Old Testament.

L. Réau, *Iconographie de l'art chrétien*, 2, 2, 531-537. – *LCI*, 2, 1970, 322-331. – A. Kartsonis, *Anastasis: the Making of an Image*, Princeton (NJ), 1986.

Anca Bratu

**DESERT.** From the beginning of Christian literature, the notion of "desert" was religious: it evoked *John the Baptist and *Christ himself. John the Baptist, nourished on the products of the desert where he exhorted to *conversion and proclaimed the coming of the Lord, drew the inhabitants of Judaea to himself. The solitary could thus attract crowds, desert life being characterised by detachment from possessions and striving for conversion. Christ's testing in the desert, a fast of forty days, culminated in complete destitution: the devil, to tempt him, tried to make him turn stones into bread to appease his hunger.

In the East, extreme practice of the evangelical precepts was accomplished by flight into solitude. In *c.*270, Anthony distributed his property and retired to the Egyptian desert. In the late 4th c. at *Marmoutier – a place, according to Sulpicius Severus, as good as any desert – Bishop *Martin of Tours and his 80 disciples led, in huts and troglodytic cells, a life of penury characterised by personal renunciation of property and the chance for each to dispose of the meagre possessions of the group; they must thus be distinguished from the first Christians of Jerusalem, who practised community of property. This lack of patrimonial organisation was accompanied by an absence of hierarchy. The extreme *poverty of the desert life is emphasized by *Gregory of Tours: Eusicus, retired far from men, detested riches like dung. For *Isidore of Seville, the life of hermits is retreat to the desert, renunciation of all possessions, abandonment to God: their living consists of wild herbs or, Isidore probably thinking here of *recluses, bread and water brought to them. He distinguishes the solitary life from that of *coenobites, characterised by community of property.

This model, illustrated by Martin, seems to survive in monastic tradition continuously until the 11th century. Thus at *Conques, in the late 8th c., where Dado, having abandoned everything, retired to the desert with a companion. Their reputation drew to both of them disciples wishing to imitate their example. When the group was raised into a community and a *patrimony set up, Dado retired to a more solitary place. At the time of the formation of the eremitical group that surrounded him at the abbey of La *Chaise-Dieu, Robert, who had retired to the desert in *c.*1043, indicated that he had wanted a solitary life with a few companions and had decided to receive nothing from anyone. Having been unable to do this, he founded an *abbey. The reformers of religious life in the 12th c., like *Bernard of Clairvaux, preferred solitude within a community isolated from the world to the older forms of desert life. For them, the ideal of solitude culminated in a strengthened coenobitism. From the 13th c., the notion of "desert" was still aired, but was often weakened: solitaries and communities of hermits belonging to the Order of *Hermits of St Augustine were subsidized by *Siena. These communities were at the town gates in the next century.

G. Constable, "Eremitical Forms of Monastic Life", *Istituzioni monastiche e Istituzioni canonicali in Occidente (1123-1215)*, La Mendola, 1977, 239-264. – *L'Eremitismo in Occidente nei secoli XI e XII*, La Mendola, 1962. – J. Heuclin, *Aux origines monastiques de la Gaule du Nord. Ermites et reclus du Ve au XIe siècle*, Lille, 1988. – H. Oudart, "L'érémitisme dans les actes de la pratique au diocèse de Bourges (XIe-XIIe siècles)", *RMab*, 61, 1988. – O. Redon, "Les ermites des forêts siennoises (XIIIe-début XIVe siècle)", *RMab*, new series, 1, 1990, 213-240. – "Le choix de la solitude", *Médiévales*, 28, Saint-Denis, 1995.

Hervé Oudart

**DESIDERIUS (died 774).** Last king of the *Lombards (757-774) before the Frankish conquest. Doubtless from Brescia, he owed to *Aistulf's favour the title of duke of *Tuscany. He obtained the throne against the last partisans of the former King Ratchis, who had become a monk, with support from the papacy and the *Franks.

His reign was occupied with containing the suspicion of *Rome and the Franks. By restoring royal authority in the duchies of *Spoleto and *Benevento, attempting a rapprochement with Byzantium to regain the territories given to Rome by *Pippin the Short and allying himself with Tassilo of *Bavaria, he managed until 771 to preserve Rome's goodwill and Frankish neutrality. But after Carloman's death, he supported the latter's sons against *Charlemagne and invaded Roman territories. Solicited by *Adrian I, Charlemagne conquered the kingdom of the Lombards in 774 and deported Desiderius to Francia where he died.

P. Delogu, "Desiderio", *DBI*, 39, 1991, 373-381.

Huguette Taviani-Carozzi

**DESIDERIUS OF MONTE CASSINO (*c.*1027-1087).** Born at *Benevento, *abbot of *Monte Cassino from 1058 to 1087, *pope under the name of Victor III in 1086-1087. This member of a princely Lombard family became a monk at *Cava dei Tirreni, then at Santa Sofia in Benevento. In 1056 he chose Monte Cassino and became *provost of the Cassinese monastery of Capua. When Frederick of Lorraine, abbot of Monte Cassino from 1055, became Pope *Stephen IX, he chose Desiderius as his successor and in 1059 made him *cardinal-priest of the *titulus* of Santa Cecilia.

The activities of this abbot concerned the abbey of Monte Cassino, southern *Italy and the reform of the Church. Monte Cassino, restored in the mid 10th c. and still extending its temporality, was a sufficiently important monastery for Victor II in 1057 to grant its abbot precedence over all others. Having decided to rebuild it, Desiderius brought artists and *objets d'art*

*Abbot Desiderius offers a model of the church.* Fresco (detail) in the choir of the basilica of Sant'Angelo in Formis (Campania). Second half of 12th c.

from *Constantinople and imported columns, capitals and early Christian models from *Rome. He completed the construction of the palace, built a *library, a lodging for the abbot, a dorter, a *chapter house and a *cloister; in 1066 he began the construction of a great church, solemnly consecrated on 1 Oct 1071. Desiderius's work was destroyed by an earthquake in 1349; little remained of the church but its bronze doors. Desiderius's activities also extended to Sant'Angelo in Formis, whose *frescos still exist. Under his abbacy, Monte Cassino was a first-rate intellectual centre, housing the poets Alfanus of Salerno and Guaifer, the *chronicler Leo Marsicanus, the historian *Amatus, the doctor and *translator of Arab origin *Constantine the African; the monastery's *scriptorium* was full of activity; Desiderius himself wrote dialogues on the *miracles of St *Benedict, on the model of *Gregory the Great.

Desiderius strove to ally the papacy, in frequent conflict with the emperors, to the *Normans of southern Italy; he organised the council of Melfi (1059) at which *Nicholas II invested Richard of Capua and *Robert Guiscard with their conquests; in 1061 he appealed to Richard to guarantee the *election of *Alexander II; in 1084, Robert Guiscard sacked Rome to save *Gregory VII. Under his influence, Monte Cassino supported the great ideals of Church reform and provided monks to occupy episcopal sees. After the death of Gregory VII, he was elected pope and held a reforming *council at *Benevento shortly before his death (1087).

H. E. J. Cowdrey, *The Age of Abbot Desiderius*, Oxford, 1983. – H. Toubert, *Un Art dirigé. Réforme grégorienne et iconographie*, Paris, 1990.

Jean-Marie Martin

**DEUTEROCANONICALS.** A recent term (16th c.: Sixtus of Siena, council of Trent), it designates several Old Testament books absent from the Jewish canon but preserved in Greek, whose canonicity could be doubted by Christian authors (Jerome), but was admitted in the Middle Ages. *Hugh of Saint-Victor listed them in *Didascalicon* IV, 2: Tobit, Judith, Wisdom, Sirach, 1 and 2 Maccabees, Baruch, to which were added the Greek parts of *Esther and *Daniel; likewise for several books of the New Testament, though the question was not asked in the Middle Ages. Medieval exegetes did not question their inspired character. In controversies, the *Jews rejected their use (see *William of Bourges). Among their commentators were *Albert the Great (Bar), *Andrew of Saint-Victor (Macc), Dominic Grima (Jdth, Macc). Baruch 3, 38 was used as a *testimonium* on the Incarnation. 1 and 2 Maccabees and Judith provided a repertoire of warlike themes in *preaching and history.

C. Spicq, *Esquisse d'une histoire de l'exégèse latine au Moyen Âge*, Paris, 1944. – J. Dunbabin, "The Maccabees as Exemplars. . .", *The Bible in the Middle Ages. . . Essays B. Smalley*, Oxford, 1985, 31-41.

Gilbert Dahan

**DEVENTER.** A town in the *Netherlands, on the Ijssel (province of Overijssel), Deventer is one of the Netherlands' oldest and prettiest inland towns. A small church was built there in *c.*770 by Lebuin († 772); destroyed shortly after by the pagans, it was rebuilt by Liudger (*c.*742-809). In *c.*800, a *chapter was attached to it, which made Deventer an important religious centre of the eastern Netherlands. Shortly before 895, at the time of the *Viking invasions, the town offered temporary refuge to the bishop of *Utrecht. *Henry III offered it in 1046 to the *patrimony of that *diocese as an imperial town, with *temporal power over the city and its environs, a situation that lasted until 1528. Very powerful in the 13th and 14th cc. as a *Hanseatic town, Deventer was still an important commercial centre in the 15th century.

Here arose in *c.*1375 the movement of religious reform called the **Devotio moderna*; thanks to Deventer's position as a commercial centre and second episcopal town, it spread rapidly. Its founder Gerhard *Groote (1340-1384) lived there: in his writings and *preaching, he stressed interior *conversion and the experience of each Christian, while combatting the deviations of the Church. He was the (co)founder, at Deventer, of houses for the Brothers and Sisters of the Common Life: a movement that allowed the *laity too to exercise their piety without having to choose the religious state. As copying manuscripts was a source of revenue for these communities, the *spirituality of the *Devotio moderna* reached a numerous public of readers. After Groote's death, the movement continued at Deventer under the direction of Florent *Radewijns (1350-1400), Jan Brinckerinck (*c.*1359-1419) and Gerard *Zerbolt van Zutphen (1367-1398), all *Brethren of the Common Life and known as writers. The pupils, who frequented the celebrated *school attached to the chapter of Saint-Lebuin, received their spiritual formation from the Brethren. Among these pupils were *Thomas a Kempis (1379/1380-1471) and Gerlach *Peters († 1411) of Deventer, the greatest mystical writer of the *Devotio moderna*. In 1387, on the initiative of Radewijns, the convent of Canons Regular of St Augustine was founded at *Windesheim. During the 15th c., the Windesheim chapter (1395) had a great influence on the reform of conventual life in north-west Europe. In 1400, Johann Brinkerinck founded the convent of regular canonesses of St Augustine at Diepenveen (near Deventer):

this was the basis of the female branch of the Windesheim chapter.

At the end of the 15th c., Deventer became a centre of *humanism: this was the time when the humanist Alexander Hegius (*c.*1433-1498) taught at the chapter school; among his pupils was the young Erasmus (1469-1536).

P. Debongnie, "Brinckerinck, Jean", *DSp*, 1, 1937, 1959-1960. – C. Van der Wansem, *Het ontstaan en de geschiedenis der Broederschap van het Gemene Leven tot 1400*, Louvain, 1958. – R. R. Post, *The Modern Devotion. Confrontation with Reformation and Humanism*, Leiden, 1968. – G. Epiney-Burgard, *Gérard Grote (1340-1384) et les débuts de la Dévotion moderne*, Wiesbaden, 1970.

Mikel M. Kors

**DEVOTIO MODERNA.** The *Devotio moderna* was a *reform movement that developed during the late Middle Ages; preaching a "spirituality for today", it aimed at an evangelical and apostolic way of life for laypeople, semi-religious and religious as well as among the clergy. It began around 1375 in reaction to ecclesiastical abuses (*simony, lapses from monastic *poverty and *celibacy, unjust *taxation). The *Devotio moderna* had its roots in the women's religious movement of the early Middle Ages and was closely related to the institution of the *beguines. It flourished mainly after the *Great Schism (1378-1419), was propagated especially in the towns and was able to develop rapidly throughout the *Netherlands and *Germany thanks to the network of commercial routes (German *Hanse).

In *c.*1374, Gerhard *Groote (1340-1384) of *Deventer, a *master of the university of *Paris (1357), underwent a "*conversion"; he began by founding an autonomous community of "religious women" (1374), lived nearly three years at the Charterhouse of Monnikhuizen (Arnhem) and from 1379, as a *deacon, devoted himself to *preaching and penitence. The Meester-Geerthuis of Deventer was the first house of the Sisters of the Common Life, composed of unmarried *women and *widows who consecrated themselves to the service of God and men and live in simplicity by the work of their hands. A friend of Groote's, Florent *Radewijns (*c.*1350-1400), *vicar of the *collegiate church of St Lebuin, took an analogous initiative for men in his vicarage. The Heer-Florenshuis of Deventer was the first house of *Brethren of the Common Life, bringing together priests, *clerics and laymen. One of the most prominent brothers of the first generation was Gerard *Zerbolt van Zutphen (1367-1398), who gave solid theological and legal foundations to the devout common life.

Starting from the Meester-Geerthuis and with its help, there developed many communities of semi-religious women who, within existing *parishes, set out to lead an austere and retired life, without *vows, without monastic rule, without religious habit, but on the basis of a voluntary poverty, celibacy and *obedience in *charity. Analogous communities of semi-religious men also developed on the model of the Heer-Florenshuis. An important house of brothers was opened at Zwolle, with small communities (convicts) for boys who attended the municipal *school, directed by Johann Cele (*c.*1345-1417), which quickly acquired an international reputation. This semi-religious current of the *Devotio moderna* spread from the Ijssel region westward (Holland), eastward (Guelder, Westphalia) and southward (*Brabant, *Flanders, Rhineland).

After Groote's death, the direction of the brotherhood fell to Radewijns, that of the women's community to Johann Brinckerinck (*c.*1359-1419). It was difficult for autonomous religious communities to get recognition from the church authorities: only in 1401 did the Brotherhood of the Common Life obtain episcopal approval. Then again, the *Devotio moderna* had as its main objective the restoration of monastic life, which was in decline. This was why in 1387 the Brethren of the Common Life of Deventer founded an autonomous convent at *Windesheim, living according to the reforming spirit of their movement. This was the first of a great number of convents that appeared under the influence of the *Devotio moderna*: they were inhabited by regular *canons who followed the Rule of St *Augustine. For their part, around 1400 the Sisters of the Common Life of Deventer also founded their own monastery (of regular canonesses) at Diepenveen. It was the first of hundreds of women's convents to be marked in the course of the 15th c. by the spirit of the *Devotio moderna*. The monastic movement was its most visible manifestation; Windesheim was its heart after becoming in 1395 the seat of a new autonomous *chapter within the Order of St Augustine. On its example were formed the closely connected chapters of *Groenendaal and Neuss which were later (in 1413 and 1429) completely integrated with the Windesheim chapter. At the time of its greatest extension, this consisted of 86 men's convents and 16 women's convents. Some hundreds of women's convents founded in the 15th c. remained autonomous, while adopting the Constitutions of Windesheim. The chapter contributed to a number of monastic reforms in the course of the 15th c.; in *Germany, this was mainly thanks to Johannes *Busch (1399/1400 – after 1479). All this meant that Windesheim enjoyed special attention and protection from the papal *legate for Church reform, Cardinal *Nicholas of Cusa (1401-1464). Between 1496 and 1500, Jean Mombaer (*c.*1460-1501) introduced the Windesheim reform into convents in northern France, but with only partial success.

Following the example of Windesheim, the semi-religious houses of Brothers and Sisters of the Common Life formed unions (colloquium of Zwolle, after 1410; colloquium of *Münster, after 1431). A number of communities that followed the *Devotio moderna* found a model of life in the *Franciscan *Third Order. By following this, they resembled religious more than did the Brothers and Sisters of the Common Life, but less than the regular *canons and canonesses. They formed houses of tertiaries, men and women, which in turn founded unions (chapter of *Utrecht in 1399, chapter of *Cologne in 1427, chapter of Zepperen in 1443). From the chapter of Utrecht emerged the chapter of Sion of Holland (1418), composed of regular canons and canonesses. In the 15th c., many semi-religious houses became convents. The *Devotio moderna* rapidly lost its importance in the 16th century, largely because of the success of the Reformation and Counter-Reformation.

The *Devotio moderna* drew its inspiration from the *Carthusian monastic tradition, the Brabantine *mysticism of Jan van *Ruysbroeck and the convent of Groenendaal, the *Rhineland mysticism of Meister *Eckhart, Johann *Tauler and Henry *Suso and the monasteries of *Dominican *nuns. This current was also related to monastic reform movements such as those of the Friars Minor (observants) and Friars Preachers (congregation of Holland); it exercised a great influence on contemporary and future reform movements, such as the Union of *Bursfeld (Benedictines) and the congregation of Sibculo (*Cistercians). It also gave a strong impetus to the *humanism of the southern (Val Saint-Martin at *Louvain) and northern Netherlands (Johannes Wessel Gansfort).

It seems to have had less influence on Luther's Reformation than was long thought.

At the centre of its *spirituality was the model of the early Church (Acts 2, 41-47 and 4, 23-35) and life as a personal following of *Christ, in poverty and silence, *humility and service. Its devotees, especially the Brothers of the Common Life, developed "collation", biblical sharing, to which they also invited other parishioners and young people. In their "convicts" (small communities), they contributed greatly to the religious and intellectual formation of the youth who attended the municipal school. Their pedagogical principles, developed mainly by Jan Cele, rector of the school of the town of Zwolle, led to a considerable revival of teaching which, after the Middle Ages, would continue its evolution in the Jesuit colleges. Furthermore, the "modern devotees" laid the bases for methodical *meditation.

With the Carthusians, who were warm partisans of the *Devotio moderna*, the devotees were responsible for the greater part of the manuscript *books produced in the 15th c. in Germany and the Netherlands. Thanks to the widespread habit of the *rapiarium* (personal collection of reading notes), a rich and varied spiritual literature arose, which is still largely unedited. Gerhard Groote's *Book of Hours was a best-seller: it was written in the language of the people and intended for a wide public. *The *Imitation of Christ* belongs to world literature: its contents were assembled by *Thomas a Kempis (1379/1380-1471), who was their editor. As well as those we have cited, there were other influential actors in the Windesheim circle: Hendrik Mande (*c.*1360-1431), Gerlach *Peters (*c.*1378-1411), Jan Scutken († 1423) and Jan Van Schoonhoven (1356-1432), as well as Dirc Van Herxen (1381-1457), rector of the Zwolle fraternity.

*Devotio moderna: basic writings*, J. Van Engen, New York, 1998.

P. Debongnie, "Dévotion moderne", *DSp*, 3, 1957, 727-747. – R. R. Post, "The Modern Devotion. Confrontation with Reformation and Humanism", *SMRT*, 3, 1968. – G. Epiney-Burgard, "Gérard Groote (1340-1384) et les débuts de la Dévotion moderne", *VIEG*, 54, 1970. – W. Leesch, E. Persoons, A. G. Weiler, *Monasticon Fratrum Vitae Communis*, *Archief- en Bibliotheekwezen in België*, special no. 18 and 19, Brussels, 1977-1979. – A. G. Weiler, "Recent Historiography on the Modern Devotion: some Debated Questions", *AGKKN*, 26, 1984, 161-179. – "Geert Groote & Moderne Devotie. Voordrachten gehouden tijdens het Geert Groote congres, Nijmegen, 27-29 september 1984", *OGE*, 59, 1985, 111-505. – G. Rehm, *Die Schwestern vom gemeinsamen Leben im nordwestlichen Deutschland. Untersuchungen zur Geschichte der Devotio Moderna und des weiblichen Religiosentums*, *BHSt*, 11, *Ordenstudien*, 5, Berlin, 1985. – *La Dévotion moderne dans les pays bourguignons et rhénans, des origines à la fin du XVIe siècle. Rencontres de Colmar-Strasbourg (29 septembre au 2 octobre 1988)*, *Publications du Centre européen d'études bourguignonnes (XIVe-XV[e] siècle)*, 29, Neuchâtel, 1989.

Rudolf T. M. Van Dijk

**DEVOTION, LITERATURE OF.** If by "devotion" is meant the will to perform service to God (see Thomas Aquinas, *Summa Theologiae*, II[a] II[ae], q. 82) and the complex of feelings this service entails, then the literature of devotion comprises texts and works that explicitly guide the reader in cultivating such devotion or that express it in *prayer or *meditation. The focus on devotion itself rather than on achievement of extraordinary contact with God distinguishes this literature in principle from that of *mysticism (*contemplation) proper, though the two may overlap. Likewise, the individual rather than collective character of prayer in this literature distinguishes it in principle from liturgy, even though the latter sometimes assimilated prayers of an originally private nature (*e.g.* those of preparation for the *Eucharist) and, conversely, often lent itself to private use.

Individual, mostly anonymous, devotional prayers (*preces*) survive from at least as early as the 7th c., and collections for devotional use, which include such prayers along with *psalms and liturgical texts, appeared in the Carolingian period. Later, collections of texts by two 11th-c. authors – the *Meditationes* of John of Fécamp and the *Meditationes* and *Orationes* of *Anselm of Canterbury – were to exert wide influence. John's work anticipated, and Anselm's displayed outright, a fresh sensitivity to the *soul's affections and to *Christ's humanity and *Passion, which was to be the dominant characteristic of devotional works in the centuries to follow. Noteworthy 12th-c. works are the respective *Meditationes* of the *Carthusian *abbots *Guigo I and Guigo V and the *De institutione inclusarum* of the *Cistercian *Ælred of Rievaulx, who pioneered the technique of guiding meditation on the life of Christ to elicit affective response. In the 13th and 14th cc., christocentric and affective themes abounded in writings by *mendicants, particularly *Franciscans, *e.g.* St *Francis's highly affective prayers and the *Meditationes vitae Christi* of Pseudo-Bonaventure, which continued the tradition of guided meditation on gospel scenes.

The literature of devotion in the late Middle Ages reached audiences beyond the ranks of the religious. The Franciscan poet *Jacopone da Todi, for instance, wrote *laude* (praise-songs) enormously popular among the *laity. In the 14th and 15th cc., the *Devotio moderna* produced works that gave the themes of christocentricity and affectivity wide readership, *e.g.* the *Rosetum* of John Mombaer, an extremely methodical work of guided meditation; the movement also accorded devotion itself a newly exclusive importance by avoiding theological speculation and discussing contemplation only reticently, as *e.g.* in the *Imitatio Christi* of *Thomas a Kempis. Other works that had enormous popularity with the literate laity by the 15th c. were the so-called **Ars moriendi*, which included both exhortations and prayers, and the *Horae* or "*Books of Hours", which contained, in addition to the *Office of the Virgin, an assortment of other prayers for devotional use.

A. Wilmart, *Auteurs spirituels et textes dévots du Moyen Âge latin*, Paris, 1932. – D. Jeffrey, *The Early English Lyric and Franciscan Spirituality*, Lincoln (NE), 1975. – A. C. Bartlett, *Male Voices, Female Readers: Representational Subjectivity in Middle English Devotional Literature*, Ithaca (NY), 1995.

John Coakley

**DEVOTIONAL PRACTICES.** *Thomas Aquinas defined devotions as external manifestations of devotion, an (inner) relationship between the believer and *God. "The devotions we have for God's saints, dead or living", he wrote, "do not stop with them, but, going beyond them, reach God whom we revere in his representatives" (*Summa theologiae*, II[a] II[ae], q. 82, a. 2, ad 3). Stressing one aspect of the divinity (*e.g.* devotion to *Christ's infancy or *Passion), bearing on particular persons (the Virgin, the saints) or objects (the *host, the *cross, the *altar, *images), devotions are expressed by *prayers, attitudes and practices.

The forms of devotional practices, forged for the most part in monastic milieux, evolved but little in the course of the Middle Ages. However the end of the period saw a dual transformation: an increase in private devotional practices, and their appropriation by the *laity. From the 12th c. there developed in effect, at first in the treatises of monks and regular *canons, a reflection on personal and interior prayer. The community dimension of prayer persisted, but a sort of fracture appeared between prayer of *intercession (often collective) and devotional prayer (more individual). Now it was at this moment that two new bodily attitudes spread: prayer with hands joined and kneeling. Such a contraction of gestuality, signalling a turning-in of the individual in prayer on himself, must be put in relation to the search for an individual, more interiorized devotion. Meanwhile, in well-to-do circles, numerous believers set up private places of worship within the domestic space. Many lay *penitents also adopted practices that were previously mainly limited to religious, like *fasting and the discipline. Their appropriation by the laity often entailed variations from the original model: the recital of *psalms (in Latin) was sometimes transformed into prayers chanted (in the vernacular) in the form of singsong; the visitation of *altars, performed in the great monastic churches by the religious in *procession, gave way, notably among certain *beguines, to the devotional kissing of the altars on which the *Eucharist had just been celebrated. The devotional practices of the laity were favoured, at the end of the Middle Ages, by new media: private *images, *contemplation of which supposed an emotional participation in the *mysteries represented, *Books of Hours and works of piety, often written in the vernacular, whose solitary reading aroused *meditation.

If it is difficult to establish a chronology of Christian devotions (these varying according to social groups as much as according to times), all the same it seems that some of them acquired a growing importance over the centuries: thus, devotion to the Virgin, prayer for the *souls in *purgatory, the cult of Christ's humanity and of the host. The religious experiences adopted by the laity at the end of the Middle Ages referred to devotions that were then held in honour. The desire to communicate frequently and to see the host, for example, were part of a new devotion to the Eucharist, going back to the 13th c. and also manifested by the establishment of the feast of *Corpus Christi and the multiplication of Corpus Christi *confraternities. And while, at the same period, the cult of Christ's humanity and Passion developed, *fasts, *flagellation and ascetic practices permitted the laity to associate, in a sort of *imitatio Christi*, their martyred bodies with that of the suffering Christ.

The "privatization" and "laicization" of devotional practices was accompanied by a certain ecclesiastical control. Just as the institutional church favoured the diffusion of a "minimal" model of devotion (consisting in the recital of three prayers: the *Pater*, the **Credo* and the **Ave Maria*) and kept an eye on the contents of the prayerbooks used by the laity, it imposed restrictions on ascetic practices judged excessive, limited certain devotions and reined in local cults. But at the same time, at the end of the Middle Ages, the devotional practices of the laity were used by the religious *orders involved in dogmatic controversies. Thus in the 14th and 15th cc., supporters and opponents of the Immaculate *Conception put out propaganda among the faithful, forcing them to take sides. Preachers organised public disputes and encouraged or denounced certain devotional processions, as well as the celebration of certain *feasts. In the final centuries of the Middle Ages, the devotional practices of the laity, more or less manipulated by the clergy, could put pressure on dogmatic proceedings.

L. Gougaud, *Dévotions et pratiques ascétiques au Moyen Âge*, Paris, 1925. – E. Bertaud, A. Rayez, "Dévotions", *DSp*, 3, 1957, 747-778. –J. Chiffoleau, "La Religion flamboyante", *Histoire de la France religieuse*, J. Le Goff (ed.), R. Rémond (ed.), 2, Paris, 1988, 109-127. – J. C. Schmitt, *La Raison des gestes dans l'Occident médiéval*, Paris, 1990. – R. M. Dessì, "La Controversia sull'Immacolata Concezione e la 'propaganda' per il culto in Italia nel XV secolo", *CrSt*, 12, 1991, 265-293. – L. Gougaud, *Prier au Moyen Âge. Pratiques et expériences (Vᵉ-XVᵉ siècles)*, Turnhout, 1991. – M. Rubin, *Corpus Christi. The Eucharist in Late Medieval Culture*, Cambridge, 1991. – A. Vauchez, *The Laity in the Middle Ages*, Notre Dame (IN), 1993. – R.N. Swanson, *Religion and Devotion in Europe, c. 1215-c. 1515*, Cambridge, 1995.

Michel Lauwers

***DHIMMĪ.*** An Arabic word meaning "covenanted", applied by Muslim law to the "people of the Book" ("*ahl al-Kitāb*"), *i.e.* Jews and Christians, allowed to live in "Islamic territory" ("*dār al-Islām*") as the result of a "covenant" (*dhimma*) made between their ancestors and the Arab conquerors. This covenant guaranteed Christians and Jews the safeguard of their persons and property, on condition of payment of a tribute comprising capitation (*jizya*) and land tax (*kharāj*). The capitation was an annual tax on persons, from which certain "covenanted" could be exempted, and whose tariff varied. The basis was Sura IX, verse 29 ordering Muslims to fight the "people of the Book" who do not practise the true religion, until they pay the capitation "of their hands and by making themselves small". Land tax was an annual due which the "covenanted", who kept property over their lands, paid to the Muslim treasury. The rate of this tax varied according to the capacity of the land, and it was payable at harvest-time.

Theoretically, payment of the capitation and the land tax should have guaranteed the "covenanted" individual freedom and religious freedom. In fact, these freedoms were limited by three kinds of restrictions. The first consisted of a set of signs on clothing intended to distinguish Christians from Muslims, like the wearing of the belt (*zunnār*) on clothing and bands of yellow material (*ghiyār*) on the shoulder. These distinctive signs had no Koranic basis and seem to have been first prescribed by the *Umayyad *caliph 'Umar II (717-720). The second series of restrictions comprised barriers put in the way of Christian worship and its public manifestation, like the prohibition on building new churches or restoring old ones, exhibiting crosses or banners at processions, beating simanders outside certain hours or singing loudly during burials. These barriers had no more Koranic basis than did the distinctive signs. The third sort of restriction was the eviction of the "covenanted" from public office. Basing themselves on a dozen Koranic verses enjoining believers not to take Christians as "affiliates", most Muslim jurists thought that the "covenanted" should be excluded from public office. Yet certain jurists admitted the possibility of a Christian holding public employment, on condition that he had no power of decision. It was also Caliph 'Umar II who first decreed the dismissal of "covenanted" officials; but his decree does not seem to have been rigorously applied, since the number of these officials was judged still too high by Caliph Hishām (724-743). All these periodical measures of dismissal did not prevent there being, at all times, Christian officials in the Muslim public service, from the tax-collector to the secretary of the chancery. At the end of a certain time, these restrictive measures had a tendency no longer to be applied rigorously, but they could be brought back into force at any moment, as they were several times by the *Abbasid caliphs and especially by the Fatimid caliph al-*Hākim.

A. Fattal, *Le Statut légal des non-musulmans en pays d'Islam*, Beirut, 1958. – C. Cahen, "Dhimma", *EI(E)*, 2, 1965, 227-231.

Gérard Troupeau

**DHUODA (9th century).** This *Austrasian aristocrat is known only by the *Manual* she left for her son. On 29 June 824 she had married Bernard of Septimania, son of William of Toulouse, first cousin of *Charlemagne. While Bernard had became a counsellor to the Emperor *Louis the Pious and friend to the empress Judith, Dhuoda had settled at Uzès and it was there that this somewhat forsaken woman had decided to render her sons a service by giving them advice for their *education. The elder, William, was then 15, the other still very young. When William entered the service of *Charles the Bald, Dhuoda wrote between 30 Nov 841 and 2 Feb 843 a manual of education for the young man. She called her book a "manual" because she wanted her son to be able to hold the volume in his hand so that, by dipping into it and reading it, he would make a serious effort to put it into practice. This manual was also a Mirror in which he could contemplate the *salvation of his *soul and suppress its faults.

At the beginning, Dhuoda affirms the greatness of *God who is omnipresent and rules the whole universe; in the face of this greatness, man's misery merely stands out further. But life is a perpetual combat in the course of which the young man must fight against the *vices and acquire the *virtues. He must tend towards the eight beatitudes combined with the seven *gifts of the Holy Spirit which allow him to mount the fifteen steps that lead to perfection. As a good aristocrat, proud of her origins, Dhuoda reminds her son that he must remember his paternal and maternal ancestors and pray for them. Several chapters of the book are devoted to the duties of a son towards his father, then after the father comes the lord King Charles the Bald to whom William has been recommended. He must be loyal to him and help him with his advice. Amid the bustle of worldly life, William must avoid the habitual faults of the aristocracy, especially pride, and he must materially help the most disadvantaged. Finally, to acquire these virtues, William must read and pray. Books will provide him with models of good deeds he can perform to fulfil his dual *duty to God and his lord. He must also pray for *bishops, priests, *kings, great men, his father. Dhuoda develops this chapter on *prayer by giving examples of prayers which she takes from booklets of private prayers in use at the time. From these booklets come the prayers the young man must say evening and morning. Dhuoda wants her son to imitate the monks and doubtless does not forget that her father-in-law ended his days at Gellone, later called Saint-Guilhem-du-Désert.

We know nothing of Dhuoda after she wrote her *Manual*, but we know what happened to her sons. William, who had betrayed Charles the Bald, was captured and beheaded in 849, Bernard surnamed Plantevelue played an active political role from the mid 9th c., and his son William surnamed the Pious founded the abbey of *Cluny in 909.

*Handbook for William*, Lincoln (NEB), 1991. – Dhuoda, *Manuel pour mon fils*, P. Riché (intro., crit. text, notes), B. de Vrégille (tr.), C. Mondésert (tr.), Paris, 1997 (*SC*, 225a). – Dhuoda, *Handbook for her Warrior Son: Liber manualis*, M. Thiebaux (ed., tr.), Cambridge, 1998.

Pierre Riché

**DIALECTIC.** Taken in its earliest meaning, which remained the most common in the Middle Ages, the word "dialectic" designated one of the seven *liberal arts, and more precisely one of the three "arts of language" (*artes sermocinales*) that made up the *trivium*. But this abstract designation linked to a didactic schema is not enough; we must take into account the variety of functions that were attributed to this art, simultaneously or successively, in the course of the Middle Ages. In the beginning, more or less from the mid 11th to the mid 12th c., this word had a complex, not to say confused, sense. On one hand, it kept the meaning of "science of discussion" (*disputationis disciplina*) handed down by St Augustine (*De doctrina christiana*, II, 31, 48), which was largely what it had had for *Aristotle; but, by metonymy, it also designated *logic: it is not rare for these two terms to be taken for one another, or even juxtaposed in one and the same context. Now logic at this time had as its basic texts the first two treatises of Aristotle's *Organon* (*Categories*, *Interpretation*) plus Porphyry's *Isagoge*, with their commentaries by *Boethius and some treatises by the same author: this was what was called the "old logic", *logica vetus*. *Abelard, composing a *Dialectic* in *c.*1120, divided its contents into five treatises corresponding respectively to the elements of this corpus: thus he studied predicables (or *universals; this first part is lost), predicaments, categorical propositions and syllogisms, topical argumentation, hypothetical propositions and syllogisms, divisions and definitions. Dialectic also had a propaedeutic or, one could even say, epistemological function, vigorously affirmed by Augustine, for whom it was "the science of sciences, which teaches how to teach, teaches how to learn; only this will and can make people who know" (*De ordine*, II, 13, 38). Abelard, who cited this text and applied dialectic, like semantics and logic, to *theology, gathered bitter fruits from it ("logic has made me odious to the world"), this method having encountered keen resistance from the traditional and spiritual side of the Church. But others took part in the same current or learned its lesson.

Meanwhile the logician's library was enriched, too late for Abelard really to profit from it. The part of the *Organon* lacking to him had been rediscovered: *Prior* and *Posterior Analytics*, *Topics*, *Sophistical Refutations*; this was the "new logic" (*nova logica*). The study of its content and notably of the last cited of these treatises led to the "logic of the moderns" (*logica modernorum*), of which an important novelty consisted in shifting the analysis of terms and considering no longer just their meaning but also, or even mainly, that whose place they held in the proposition and the way in which they did so: this was, from the 12th c., the beginning of the logic of *suppositio*. From the epistemological or simply didactic point of view, such a classification of the *sciences reflects the contribution of new texts: logic was divided into "demonstrative, dialectical, critical [*temptativa*], sophistical". Soon after 1150, *John of Salisbury in his *Metalogicon* divided logic into "demonstrative, probable and sophistical"; the "probable" was subdivided into dialectic and *rhetoric, both being concerned with persuading without worrying about the truth of the arguments produced. These various traits of dialectic found a new place in the reconstituted structure of Aristotelian logic and a more specific role alongside the encyclopedic whole consisting notably of the corpuses of Aristotle and *Avicenna.

M. Grabmann, *Die Geschichte der scholastischen Methode*, 1-2, Freiburg-im-Breisgau, 1909-1911. – L. Jardine, "Humanism and the Teaching of Logic", *The Cambridge History of Later Medieval Philosophy*, Cambridge, 1982, 797-807. – M. M. Tweedale, "Logic (i): from the Late Eleventh Century to the Time of Abelard" and K. Jacobi, "Logic (ii): the Later Twelfth Century", *A History of Twelfth-Century Philosophy*, Cambridge, 1988, 196-226 and 227-251.

Jean Jolivet

***DICTATUS PAPAE.*** Under the title *Dictatus papae* (which means "text written by the pope"), in the register of *letters of *Gregory VII (3-4 March 1075), appear 27 propositions concerning the privileges and duties of the papacy. It seems not so much a real programme as the index of a small *canonical collection, unfinished or later lost, whose aim is to bring together texts from tradition referring to the rights of the *pope and his prerogatives vis-à-vis the Churches of Latin *Christendom. The majority of these propositions in fact correspond to chapters of the canonical collection called "of the 74 titles" (1051-1073).

The *Dictatus papae* is nevertheless a "new, unusual and very effective platform of action and intervention" (G. Miccoli). It surely bears Gregory's personal mark: the incisive formulation of the sentences and their inclusion in his register of attests an acute awareness of the extent of the competencies of the bishop of *Rome. The first sentence stipulates that "the Roman Church was founded by the Lord alone"; hence it cannot err (XXII: "The Roman Church has never erred; and according to the testimony of Scripture, it will never err"), and "he who is not with the Roman Church is not considered catholic" (XXVI). The pope himself "must not be judged by anyone" (XIX), his sentences are not revocable (XVIII), he alone has a universal jurisdiction (II) and can "create" new law (VII); he can depose or absolve even absent *bishops (III) and send *legates to preside over *councils, even if their hierarchical grade is below that of the bishops present (IV). He has a right to a whole series of "privileges of honour" (II, IX, X, XI, XXIII); "he alone can use the imperial insignia" (VIII). "The Roman pontiff, canonically ordained, is indubitably by the *merits of St *Peter established in *sanctity" (XXIII). The pope can depose the emperor (XII) and release subjects from the *oath of loyalty (XXVII).

A series of sentences (*He sunt proprie auctoritates Apostolice Sedis*) presents an astonishing analogy with the *Dictatus papae*: produced in central Italy before 1123-1124, this so-called *Dictatus papae* of Avranches excludes the articles (5, 8-9, 23) on the emperor; its statements are fuller and possess a different vocabulary, which suggests that it is not a product of the papal *chancery.

*Das Register Gregors VII.*, E. Caspar (ed.), *MGH.ES*, 2, 1920-1923, II, 55a, 202-208 (re-ed. 1990; 2 vol.). – *HChr*, 5, 1993, 79-80 (Fr. tr.).

G. Miccoli, "Gregorio VII, papa", *BSS*, 7, 1966, 361. – J. T. Gilchrist, "Gregory VII and the Juristic Sources of his Ideology", *StGra*, 12, 1967, 3-37. – H. Fuhrmann, "Papst Gregor VII., und das Kirchenrecht. Zum Problem des Dictatus papae", *La Riforma gregoriana e l'Europa*, 1, Rome, 1989, 123-149 (*SGSLE*, 13).

Agostino Paravicini Bagliani

**DIEGO OF OSMA (died 1207).** Diego of Acébès was bishop of Osma (province of *Toledo) from 1201 to 1207. As *prior of Osma, he received St *Dominic into the *chapter which he had just, with the *bishop, restored to full regularity (1199). As bishop, he was sent by his king to *Denmark with Dominic (1203 and 1205). *Innocent III, whom they visited, did not consent to discharge them to evangelize the *pagans. On their return, in 1206, they were engaged in *preaching against the Albigenses by the papal *legates, whom Diego persuaded to preach in evangelical mendicancy. In 1207, he founded the house of *Prouille for Dominic's converts, opening the latter's way to the Order of Preachers (*Dominicans). He died 30 Dec 1207 at Osma.

A. Lambert, *DHGE*, 5, 1931, 1343. – M.-H. Vicaire, *Histoire de saint Dominique*, 1, Paris, 1982, ch. 3-8 (2nd ed.).

Marie-Humbert Vicaire †

***DIES IRAE.*** The *Dies irae* was a very popular *sequence, sung at masses for the *dead (between the *tract and the gospel), that was long attributed to *Thomas of Celano, disciple and biographer of St *Francis of Assisi. In fact, earlier evidence of it exists. The poem is a great appeal for mercy on the Day of *Judgment, a sort of speech for the defence starting from the rights that *Christ acquired over *souls by the sufferings of his *Passion, and examples of pardon given by him.

F. Ermini, *Il Dies irae*, Geneva, 1928. – A.-M. Kurfesse, "Dies irae", *HJ*, 77, 1958, 328-338.

Guy-Marie Oury

**DIETRICH OF NIEM (1340-1418).** Dietrich of Niem, or Theodoricus von Nieheim, concentrated his literary activity on the problems caused by the *Great Schism. The essential themes of his work were the *council and criticism of the papacy. As a partisan of the *Empire, he thought the emperor had a role to play in the Church. As a *conciliarist thinker, he was inspired notably by the conciliar doctrine developed in the 14th c. by *Marsilius of Padua in his *Defensor pacis*.

Dietrich distinguished the Catholic Church, comprising all Christians (Greeks, Latins, barbarians, men and women, rich and poor) from the apostolic Church, composed of the *pope, the *bishops and the clergy.

Dietrich also followed the Marsilian theses on the Church: he made the Emperor Constantine the founder of the Roman Church; indeed, up to Constantine, the pope had no *prioritas* except by the consent of the bishops; it was the emperor who then gave him a definitive *prioritas*. It is striking that the great majority of German theologians favourable to the conciliar solution to bring an end to the Great Schism were partisans of the Empire, and favourable to an intervention by the imperial power.

For Dietrich of Niem, the emperor had a number of prerogatives in the Church, notably that of convening the council. Dietrich was also inspired by William of *Ockham and took up his "multitudinist" thesis, according to which "the papacy is the totality of believers legally associated in view of their common utility".

Though, as Marsilius of Padua had formerly maintained, the Church was composed of all the faithful who believed in Christ, the ecclesiastical hierarchy was of a purely human order. Thus Dietrich wrote that "believers can very well die in charity and go to heaven without there being any pope". For him as for his predecessors, who inspired him, the Church was infallible in its universality. But this infallibility in matters of *faith was expressed through the council.

The doctrines of Dietrich of Niem found a not inconsiderable echo in the formulation of the texts of the council of *Constance, notably in the decree *Haec Sancta*, which marked a turning-point in the doctrinal development of the Great Schism.

H. Heimpel, *Dietrich von Niem (1340-1418)*, Münster, 1932. – W. Ullmann, *Origins of the Great Schism: A Study in Fourteenth-Century Ecclesiastical History*, Cambridge, 1948. – *HChr*, 6, 1990, 292-293.

Jeannine Quillet

**DIJON.** The origin of Dijon was the Roman *castrum* (perhaps 3rd c.) established in the Suzon valley near its confluence with the Ouche, at the crossing of two great commercial routes, amid fertile countryside near wine-growing country (Gregory of Tours, *Historia Francorum*, III, 18-19). Dijon housed the bishops of Langres from the 5th to the late 9th century. The *suburbium* comprised basilicas established in the western necropolis, where the the cult of the pseudo-martyr Benignus was introduced in the 6th century. Richard the Justiciar, first duke of *Burgundy, lived there. King Lothar took Dijon in 958, and in 1016 King Robert gave it to the duke, who henceforth shared power there with the monastery of Saint-Bénigne, the *cathedral of Saint-Étienne and the viscount. In 989, Saint-Bénigne received reforming monks from *Cluny, among them *William of Volpiano.

Economic growth led to the formation of two urban areas in the *suburbium*: first the Bourg, to the west, then the Ville, to the north-east. After Saint-Médard and Saint-Jean, five other *parishes were established in the 12th c. and were later largely included, after the fire of 1137, within the town wall built by Duke Hugh II. Urbanization continued inside and outside the walls. In 1183 and 1187, Hugh III conceded to Dijon the communal institutions of Soissons and ceded his rights in the town, notably the *justice of his *prévôt*, in exchange for an annual payment. In the late 13th c., the *commune comprised nearly all the inhabitants. The mayor's jurisdiction extended over a vast suburb of 12 villages. A ducal *castle at Talant overlooked Dijon. Dijon society was dominated by the "knights of the castle" and the moneychangers who constituted a patriciate. Dijon had *Jews, and moneylenders from Asti settled there in the 13th century. To the two ancient *abbeys were added, at the end of the 13th c., the *collegiate churches of the Chapelle au Riche and the richly endowed ducal *chapel. *Dominicans and *Franciscans settled there in 1237 and 1241.

The return of the duke, begun under Eudes IV (1315-1349), was confirmed under King John and the first three Valois dukes: establishment of auditors, restoration and then partial rebuilding of the ducal palace, return of a (royal) mint, institution in 1386 of the Audit Office and Council, creation and proliferation of ducal *notaries. The population was sorely tried by the plagues of 1360-1361, 1375, 1399-1400 and 1438. In 1357 it comprised 2350 families, most of them poor. Activities were diversified, none of them dominant: urban *vine growers, small cloth-merchants, coppersmiths, pewterers, drapers. The middle class financed the rearing of sheep for wool, and the active export of wool to *Milan led to the settlement of Milanese families at Dijon in the 14th century. An urban *nobility shared the municipal offices with the *merchants and ducal officers. The arts developed in connection with the great ducal project of the Chartreuse of Champmol. In the 15th c. the Dijonais schools were a veritable *studium generale* teaching the *liberal arts.

At the meeting of the Estates of the duchy on 25 Jan 1477, the notables handed the town over to the representatives of *Louis XI. Part of the population rose up against this annexation on 26 June (the *mutemaque* during which President Jean Jouard was killed). Repression was carried out by the municipality under the control of Georges de la Trémoille. In 1480 the king fixed the seat of the new Parlement of Burgundy at Dijon (effective from 1494), but built a new castle to overlook the town.

P. Gras, "Dijon", *DHGE*, 14, 1960, 466-480. – *Histoire de Dijon*, P. Gras (ed.), Toulouse, 1981, (2nd ed. 1987). – B. Beaujard, "Dijon", *TCCG*, 4, 1986, 55-63. – J. Richard, "Dijon", *LdM*, 3, 1986, 1047-1051.

Henri Dubois

**DIOCESE.** For a long time the diocese was the only ecclesiastical unit: modelled on the **civitas* in Romanized areas, it was centred on the *bishop, the episcopal church and the *baptistery, before a smaller territory, the *parish, was slowly detached from it. Throughout the Middle Ages, dioceses made their appearance, whether drawn in the vast newly Christianized areas, or by cutting up older units. Pamiers was thus created in 1295, and in 1317 *John XXII founded 13 new *sees in the southern half of France, transforming *abbeys into *cathedrals and elevating **bourgs* into cities; he renewed the operation next year for three more bishoprics. From the 11th c., it was in fact a papal act that brought them into being, modified them or suppressed them, but princes also played their role in the undertaking. Around 1400, Latin *Christendom had some 800, of all sizes; the microdioceses of central or southern Italy contrasted with the immense bishoprics of Germany or England, and the Scandinavian or Slav regions. Northern France, Scotland and Spain presented an intermediary situation. But their size did not reflect the date of their creation, since numerous small dioceses in southern Italy were later than the year 1000.

Diversity also reigned in the internal organisation of dioceses. The model built by the *Carolingians, with its division into archdeaconries, rural deaneries or archpresbyteries and parishes, occurred only in areas where they were able to have a strong influence. Elsewhere, *e.g.* in Italy or southern France, one or two layers were absent: the former large parish and its annexed places of worship largely continued to exist. Whatever their size, their organisation or the development of institutions that left no place for them, like the monastic *orders or the *mendicant orders in the 13th c., dioceses were living entities. Every *cleric was aware of belonging to one and mentioned it in his written acts; the cathedral was the mother church of all the churches in the diocese, and the annual offerings of the parishes still sometimes marked this connection in the 15th c.; twice a year the *synod brought together *abbots and *parish priests around the bishop; the episcopal court was an administration with which several hundred diocesans had business every year; the cathedral *chapter ensured continuity and permanence over and above the succession of titulars to the see, and the cult of the first founding bishops was in full development. The weakening of the provincial structure, from the 12th c., largely profited the dioceses.

*Histoire des institutions françaises au Moyen Âge*, 3, *Les Institutions ecclésiastiques*, Paris, 1962.

Vincent Tabbagh

**DIONYSIUS BAR SALĪBĪ (died 1171).** James, son of Salībī, who became bishop of Mar'ash (Germanicia in Euphratesia) under the name Dionysius, was a fertile Syro-occidental author who has preserved for us, if only partially, the thought of earlier authors whose works are lost. He wrote a double *Commentary on the Old Testament*, material and spiritual – a vast compilation (unedited) – and a *Commentary on the New Testament* (less Paul's epistles): these two works form the most developed exegetical whole left by the Syrians; their expositions introduced the thought of Theodore of Mopsuestia († *c.*428) to the West.

I. Sedlácek, J. B. Chabot, then A. Vaschalde, *Dionysii bar Salibi commentarii in Evangelia*, *CSCO*, 15, 77, 95 and 113 (Syriac text) and 16, 85, 98 and 114 (Lat. tr.), Paris, 1906, 1915-1922, 1931-1933 and 1919-1940. – I. Sedlácek, *Dionysius bar Salibi, In Apocalypsim, Actus et Epistulas catholicas*, *CSCO*, 53 (Syriac text), 60 (Lat. tr.), Paris, 1909-1910. – *Kohelet-Kommentar des Dionysius bar Salibi*, W. Strothmann (ed.), Wiesbaden, 1988.

F. Graffin, *DSp*, 8, 1974, 29-30.

Micheline Albert

**DIONYSIUS OF TELL MAHRĒ (died 845).** *Jacobite patriarch of *Antioch and 9th-c. historian. Born at Tell Mahrē near Callinicum, he studied at the monastery of Qinnasrīn and, after its destruction in 815, that of Kaysūm. Elected patriarch in 818, he died in 845 after a pontificate troubled by his struggles against his opponents and the Muslim governors and agitated by numerous journeys, including one to *Egypt in company with the Caliph al-Mamūn in 830. His main work is a *History* (two parts in sixteen books, covering a period of 260 years, from 582 to 842). Only one chapter survives of this work important for the history of the Jacobite Church; but it was widely used by *Michael the Syrian († 1199) in his *Chronicle* and in an anonymous 13th-c. *chronicle.

Dionysius I of Tell-Mahre, *Berattelse om Alexander den Store*, Lund, 1868. – *The Seventh Century in the West-Syrian Chronicles*, A. Palmer (ed.), Liverpool, 1993.

R. Abramowski, *Dionysius von Tellmahre, Jakobitischer Patriarch von 818-845*, Leipzig, 1940.

Gérard Troupeau

**DIONYSIUS THE AREOPAGITE, PSEUDO-.** The author of the *Corpus Dionysiacum* presents himself as St *Paul's disciple, converted by his preaching on the Areopagus (Acts 17, 16-34). This false identity was generally admitted and gave him great authority all through the Middle Ages until, at the *Renaissance, the objections of Lorenzo *Valla were taken up by Erasmus. However *Thomas Aquinas pointed out the similarity between various passages in the *Liber de causis* and the *De divinis nominibus*. At the end of the 19th c., the work of H. Koch and J. Stiglmayr showed the dependence of Dionysius's thought on that of Proclus and established that he was a Christian contemporary of the last philosophers of the school of Athens.

The *Corpus* was cited for the first time in a letter of Severus of Antioch in *c.*510 and then at the synod of Constantinople of 533, where *Orthodox and monophysites opposed each other. Attempts to identify this mysterious author have been numerous (Synesius, Dionysius of Alexandria, Severus of Antioch, Peter the Fuller, Peter the Iberian, Sergius of Resaina [the first Syriac translator, d. 536]), but none of them backed up by evidence.

The authentic Areopagitic writings that form the *Corpus* are *The Divine Names*, *The Celestial Hierarchy*, *The Ecclesiastical Hierarchy*, *The Mystical Theology* and the *Letters*.

The *Corpus Dionysiacum* came to the West in the 8th century. In 758, Pope Paul I sent *Pippin the Short the whole of Dionysius's writings. In 827, at Compiègne, *Louis the Pious received from the emperor of *Constantinople, Michael the Stammerer, a complete Greek *codex of Dionysius's writings (Paris, BNF, ms. gr. 437). In *c.*832 he asked Abbot *Hilduin of *Saint-Denis for a translation of it. Then *Charles the Bald asked *John Scotus Eriugena to make a clearer translation of Dionysius's writings. The work was finished in 862. In *c.*1140, the monk John Sarrazin and *Hugh of Saint-Victor studied Scotus's translation of the *Celestial Hierarchy* with marginal and interlinear notes by the scholiasts John of Scythopolis, *Maximus Confessor, Anastasius the Librarian and some others. Hugh wrote two commentaries on the *Celestial Hierarchy*. In 1167, at the request of *John of Salisbury, John Sarrazin made a new translation of the whole *Corpus*. In 1238, *Thomas Gallus, abbot of Vercelli, published an *Extractio* of the *Corpus* and, in 1241-1244, *Explanationes* on Sarrazin's version. In 1239-1243 came a new translation by *Robert Grosseteste, bishop of Lincoln. The two great Renaissance translators were the Camaldolese monk Ambrogio *Traversari (1436) and Marsilio *Ficino (1492).

The *Corpus Dionysiacum* was commented on throughout the Middle Ages, and it is through the different religious *orders that Dionysius's influence in the West can be followed.

For the Victorines, Hugh of Saint-Victor, who commented twice on the *Celestial Hierarchy*, was interested mainly in Dionysius's symbolic *theology, while the *Mystical Theology* was at the centre of *Richard of Saint-Victor's interests.

The Dominican *Albert the Great began his commentary on the *Celestial Hierarchy* and the *Ecclesiastical Hierarchy* in 1246-1248 at *Paris. He used the *vetus translatio* of the *Corpus* by John Scotus until he discovered the *nova translatio* by Sarrazin.

*Thomas Aquinas began his *Commentary on the Divine Names* in 1260-1261 (according to Walz) or 1265-1266 (according to Pera). "St Thomas here sets himself in the tradition inaugurated by Maximus Confessor, which tried to make Dionysius intelligible to the Western world", says Chenu. Thomas's is the last of the great Western commentaries on the *Divine Names*. He returned to the "question of the divine names" in the *Summa theologiae* ($I^a$, q. 13), dealing also with the question of the *Good ($I^a$, q. 5), that of the three movements of the *soul: circular, straight and spiral ($II^a$ $II^{ae}$, q. 180, a. 6) and that of *love as unitive power ($I^a$, q. 20, a. 1).

The influence of the *Corpus Dionysiacum* made itself felt in *Rhineland mysticism. Meister *Eckhart was inspired by Dionysius to speak of the "superessential Deity" who transcends every "name" and every "property" and offers himself to the purified soul only as "darkness" and "ignorance", and to describe this interior "unification" and interior "simplification" that lead to *exstasis amoris*, apropos of which he refers his readers to the *Divine Names* (712 A).

*Tauler speaks of the superessential Deity (*überweselichen über alle ding*), the nameless (*ungenante, namlos*) God, the "superformation" of the soul in "divine Darkness", the "loss of self" in a nothingness by which the creature is united to that "which one can neither seize nor comprehend".

We may say that a change took place between the 13th and 14th cc.: from John Scotus Eriugena to Thomas Aquinas, the great medieval commentaries were on the *Hierarchies* and the *Divine Names*; from the 14th to the 17th c., from *Gerson through *Denis the Carthusian to Bérulle, it was the *Mystical Theology* that was, as we shall see, at the heart of the Dionysian current.

If in the 13th c. this Dionysian current was *Dominican, in the 14th and 15th cc. it was mainly *Carthusian. Hugh of Balma wrote a *Mystica theologia* and *Denis the Carthusian composed *Commentaria in libros S. Dionysii Areopagitae* from 1465 (vol. 15 and 16 of the *Opera omnia*). In *De contemplatione*, he made a synthesis of the Areopagite's mystical doctrine and the Thomist doctrine of the gift of *wisdom.

Finally, in the late 14th c. the anonymous English author of the *Cloud of Unknowing*, who may have been a Carthusian priest, translated Dionysius's *Mystical Theology*.

Dionysius's influence has been more important in the West than in the East. The Dionysian conception of hierarchy marked medieval thought, both theological and political. On *God and the *angels, Dionysius's contribution has been considerable. The *Mystical Theology* was the origin of the debate on learned ignorance between Gerson and the Carthusians. Finally, by the great images of darkness and the superessential ray or ray of darkness that won over Carmelite mysticism in 16th-c. Spain and

17th-c. France, from the Victorines to the Carmelites, passing through the Franciscans, Dominicans and Carthusians, Dionysius the Areopagite has influenced the whole of Western mysticism.

*Dionysiaca*, P. Chevalier (ed.), 1937, 249-262 (2 vol.) (repr. Stuttgart, 1989). – *Dionysius the Areopagite on the Divine Names and the Mystical Theology*, C. E. Rolt (ed.), 5th imp., London, 1971. – *Pseudo-Dionysius: the Complete Works*, C. Luibheid (ed.), London, 1987. – Pseudo Dionysius the Areopagite, *The Armenian Version of the Works Attributed to Dionysius the Areopagite*, R.W. Thomson (ed.), Louvain, 1987. – *Thesaurus Pseudo-Dionysii Areopagite: versiones Latinae cum texto Graeco*, P. Tombeur (ed.), Turnhout, 1995.

G. Théry, "Recherches pour une édition grecque historique du Pseudo-Denys", *NSchol*, 3, 1929, 353-422. – H.-F. Dondaine, *Le Corpus dionysien de l'université de Paris au XIIIe siècle*, Rome, 1953. – R. Roques, *L'Univers Dionysien. Structure hiérarchique du monde selon le Pseudo-Denys*, *Theol(P)*, 29, Paris, 1954. – A. Louth, *Denys the Areopagite*, London, 1989. – F. O'Rourke, *Pseudo-Dionysius and the Metaphysics of Aquinas*, Leiden, 1992. – P. Rorem, *Pseudo-Dionysius*, Oxford, 1993. – Y. De Andia, *Henosis. L'union à Dieu chez Denys l'Aréopagite*, Leiden, 1996 (Coll. Philosophia antiqua, 62). – Y. De Andia (ed.), *Denys l'Aréopagite en Orient et en Occident. Actes du Colloque internationale, Paris, 21-24 sept 1994*, Paris, 1997.

Ysabel de Andia

**DIPTYCHS.** These were lists of names, proper to each *diocese, proclaimed by the *deacon during the liturgy. They were inscribed on double tablets, whence their name. The list of the *dead included the *bishops of the diocese and other eminent deceased. That of the living included the hierarchs on whom the community depended (the *patriarch, the *metropolitan, the bishop. . .) as well as the secular authorities. The diptychs reflected the conflicts and dogmatic differences between Churches: when a Church considered that a bishop was no longer in communion with it, it suppressed his name from its diptychs.

R. F. Taft, *A History of the Liturgy of St John Chrysostom*, 4, *OrChrA*, 238, Rome, 1991.

Marie-Hélène Congourdeau

**DISCOVERIES.** A movement of exploration and conquering expansion from Europe in the direction of the other continents, beginning in the early 14th c., the discoveries involved a great number of factors that came into play unequally at different times.

Europe was fascinated by a fabulous East, a reservoir of riches which they thought they knew thanks to largely imaginary descriptions. *Prester John, a Christian sovereign supposed to reign in Asia, led to dreams of an alliance against *Islam from the rear. The combination of circumstances brought on by the great crisis of the late Middle Ages entailed the search for *gold and servile labour, the hope of importing the luxury products of Asia more cheaply.

Scientific curiosity and technical progress accumulated in the southern peninsulas a mass of knowledge and methods that made distant voyages possible. From the early 15th c., *humanists speculated on the renewal of the image of the world. Commercial *navigation benefited from methods tried out by the Italians in the Mediterranean (mariner's compass, nautical charts) and the Iberians in the Atlantic (the light, manageable Portuguese caravelle). Techniques were perfected in the 15th c., the invention of *voltas* turning the system of winds in the Atlantic to advantage.

The first initiatives were isolated. From the first half of the 14th c., the future sugar archipelagos of the Atlantic (Canaries, Madeira, Azores) were found. But systematic, and hence costly, undertakings did not begin until the following century, benefiting in the Iberian peninsula from State help and the impetus of the *Reconquest. Under the impulse of the *infante* Henry the Navigator († 1460) and then of King John II, annual expeditions went beyond Cape Bojador (1434), Senegal and Cape Verde (1444), and finally the equator (1471). The attempt to encircle Islam later led to the reaching of *India in two steps: Bartholomew Diaz doubled the Cape of Good Hope in 1488, and Vasco da Gama landed at Calicut in 1498, establishing the foundations of the Lusitanian empire.

The voyages of *Columbus began in the enthusiasm of the completion of the Reconquest and, at least to start with, his aim was to bring back gold. His undertaking did not demonstrate the roundness of the earth against an obscurantist scholarship: indeed the scholars called together to judge the idea of reaching Asia by circumnavigation, commonplace and based on a series of fertile geographical errors, opposed it with good reason. On his first voyage, touching Cuba after the Bahamas, Columbus thought he had reached Japan. After having landed on the American continent in 1498 and again in 1502, he never ceased to think he had reached the Indies. But from now on the pursuit of discovery went hand in hand with colonization.

P. Chaunu, *European Expansion in the Later Middle Ages*, Amsterdam, 1979. – F. Fernandez-Armesto, *Before Columbus: Exploration and Colonisation from the Mediterranean to the Atlantic, 1292-1492*, London, 1987. – *Lisbonne hors les murs 1415-1580: l'invention du monde par les navigateurs portugais*, M. Chandeigne (dir.), Paris, 1990.

Patrick Gautier Dalché

**DISPENSATION.** Dispensation was a particular measure that exempted, in a particular case, from a legal obligation. It was thus a source not of a rule of law, but of a subjective right. The individual character of this concession, the diversity of situations in which it was accorded, as well as the time, explain why it long resisted any systematization. The notion remained imprecise, or even ignored or misunderstood until the mid 13th century.

"Dispensations" from the law were, from all time, accorded for various reasons. *Ivo of Chartres (in the *Prologue* to his *Decretum*: *PL*, 161, 47) emphasizes *mercy to the sinner or the needs of the Church.

The rigour of the legislation issued by the *Gregorian reform made necessary a certain easing. The difficult search for a balance between general law, with its prohibitions and obligations, and the need to consider particular situations occupied *Bernold of Constance, Ivo of Chartres and *Alger of Liège. Given at first "for the needs of the Church", dispensation in the sense of "distribution" appeared in the language of Gratian, opposed to the "rigour of law" and associated with *relaxatio* and mercy. With Rufinus's *Summa*, the notion became precise. Dispensation was "an occasional derogation from the rigour of the law, accorded for a just cause, by the competent authority". *Canonists and theologians repeated the elements of this definition.

The Roman pontiff had a general power to dispense. Having power to make the law, he could dispense with its application in a particular case. In favour of this right, the doctrine also invoked *Roman law, which recognised this faculty for the emperors. The power of *bishops was more disputed. Ivo of Chartres and Gratian admitted it and, following them, the *Decretists. For them, bishops could dispense not just with their own laws, but also with universal law, by *custom or concession of the *pope, or with law itself. *Alexander III and *Innocent III introduced certain reservations and the doctrine of the *Decretalists contained all shades of opinion.

We should also mention the debates on laws from which dispensation could not be accorded: natural law, the Mosaic law and the Gospel, certain moral precepts, the opinions of the *Fathers, the canons of the first eight "general *councils". But on all these points, doctrinal shades of opinion abounded.

In any case, dispensation could only be accorded for reasons of necessity or utility duly justified. The *doctrine was abundant, but far from unanimous. But practice often – too often, according to some – had recourse to dispensation. It was even seen as "a means of government" (Le Bras). But "frequently, dispensation was granted in order to avoid *sin, and the Church wished to take account of the sometimes painful situation of the Christian faced with certain rules which it believed it had to impose on principle" (C. Lefebvre).

J. Brys, *De dispensatione in iure canonicio*, Bruges, 1925. – A. Van Hove, *De privilegius et dispensationibus*, Malines-Rome, 1939. – C. Lefebvre, "L'Age classique, 1140-1378, Sources et théorie du droit", *HDIEO*, 7, 1965, 514-532.

Jean Gaudemet

***DISPUTATIO*, DISPUTATION.** The *disputatio* was, with the *lecture (*lectio*), the main pedagogical method used in the Middle Ages, especially in *universities. The early Middle Ages had, in the antique manner, used the "dialogue" (of master and disciple). The 12th c., leaning on the resources of Aristotelian *logic, then in full revival, perfected the question (**quaestio*). This consisted in the professor disengaging, from the text on which he was commenting, a general problem which he discussed for himself according to the principles of *dialectic. The "question" was adopted in all the disciplines (*philosophy, law, *medicine, *theology). In the late 12th c., it gave rise to the disputation proper, *i.e.* an autonomous exercise, presided over by the *master, in which a theoretical or practical problem was debated; the arguments for and against, taken from authorities or from *reason, confronted each other according to the rules of the syllogism, *i.e.* of logically correct reasoning; finally the master "determined", in other words proposed his personal solution, which might be put down in writing.

With the coming of the universities, the rules of the exercise were specified: there were private disputations within each school and public or "ordinary" disputations in which masters and students of other schools could take part; the theme of the disputation was chosen by the master who organised it, but we also see the appearance of disputations *de quolibet* in which the questions were asked by the audience. The roles were shared out: the *respondens*, a bachelor designated by the master, defended a thesis; an *opponens*, also a bachelor, undertook to oppose it; the master himself presided over the debate before "determining", some days later. In every *faculty, each master had to organise several ordinary disputations a year.

In scholastic pedagogy, the disputation was a way of bringing out the truth dialectically. It was also an indispensable exercise for training students. Examinations (baccalaureate, **licentia docendi*) took the form of disputations maintained by the candidates, who prepared for them by having already taken part in several disputations organised by their master.

The 13th c. was the golden age of university disputations. They gradually fell into disuse after 1350, at least in magistral teaching; their heuristic value was increasingly contested, though bachelors continued to practice them among themselves as practical exercises.

B. C. Bazan, J. W. Wippel, G. Fransen, D. Jacquart, *Les Questions disputées et les Questions quodlibétiques dans les facultés de théologie, de droit et de médecine, TSMÂO*, 1985, 44-45. – B. Lawn, *The Rise and Decline of the Scholastic "Quaestio disputata" with Special Emphasis on its Use in the Teaching of Medicine and Science*, Leiden, 1993. – O. Weijers, *La "Disputatio" à la faculté des arts de Paris (1200-1350 environ)*, Turnhout, 1995.

Jacques Verger

**DISTINCTIONS, BIBLICAL.** The literary genre of "distinctions" had its root in the annotated reading of the books of the *Bible in the schools, and was then widely used in the structuring of *sermons. At first, it was a matter of classifying the different meanings that a biblical term could take, notably according to the four traditional *senses of Scripture; tables of these different meanings began by appearing in commentaries at passages where words could make difficulties. This procedure was maintained throughout scholastic *exegesis, *e.g.* in *Hugh of Saint-Cher in the first half of the 13th c. or Nicholas of Gorran in the second half.

The next step was to group these distinctions together by putting them in the order of the biblical text. The best known distinctions of this type are the *Distinctiones in Psalterium* of *Peter of Poitiers (late 12th c.), then those of Eudes of Châteauroux (mid 13th century).

Towards the end of the 12th c. appeared collections of distinctions classified in alphabetical order, composed by *Peter Cantor, *Alan of Lille and Garnier of Saint-Victor (or Adam of Dryburgh: Pseudo-Rabanus Maurus). These compilations seem to have been intended primarily for students of *theology. The enormous work of Peter of Capua marks the transition from the students' manual to the preachers' manual.

The intended purpose of distinctions as a working instrument for the composition of sermons becomes clear with Maurice of Provins (*c.*1250), Nicholas of Biard and Nicholas of Gorran (second half of 13th c.). Their works were no longer content to "distinguish" the biblical senses, but tended to become small dictionaries of moral theology, which is notably the case of the *Summa de abstinentia* (different from the *Distinctiones*), also often attributed to Nicholas of Biard.

The use of *distinctiones* in *preaching became the rule from the second half of the 13th century. Certain sermons, such as those of Évrard du Val des Écoliers, were now hardly more than a series of distinctions put end to end.

In the 14th and 15th cc., the compilations of Arnauld Galiard and Bindo of Siena returned to the original design of simple enumeration of biblical meanings.

R. H. and M. A. Rouse, *Biblical Distinctiones in the Thirteenth Century*, *AHDL*, 41, 1974, 27-37. – L. J. Bataillon, "Les Instruments de travail des prédicateurs", *Aspects culturels et méthodes de travail au Moyen Âge*, Paris, 1981, 197-209. – L. J. Bataillon, "Intermédiares entre les traités de morale pratique et les sermons: les *distinctiones* bibliques alphabétiques", *Les Genres Littéraires dans les sources théologiques et philosophiques médiévales*, Louvain-la-Neuve, 1982, 213-226. – J. Longère, *La Prédication médiévale*, Paris, 1982, 189-193.

Louis Jacques Bataillon

***DIT.*** A poem recited rather than sung, of great thematic variety, the *dit* developed from the mid 12th century. It accepted both the serious (*Les Vers de la mort* by Hélinand de Froidmont) and the burlesque (*Dit d'Aristote* by Henri d'Andeli), *allegory (*Le Livre des manières* by Étienne de Fougères) and the *jongleur's patter (*Dit du mercier*). It evolved from religious and satirical inspiration towards personal expression. In the 13th c., the major author of *dits* was Rutebeuf: he deals with university *disputations, pleasant subjects (*Dit de l'herberie*), daily miseries (*Griesche d'hiver*, *Mariage Rutebeuf*). In the 14th c., Baudouin de Condé, his son Jean de Condé and Watriquet de Couvin composed allegorical, moral, religious and courtly *dits*. The *dit* could also recount an amorous intrigue based on an autobiographical fiction: thus it was practised by *Guillaume de Machaut, Jean *Froissart and *Christine de Pizan.

Rutebeuf, *Oeuvres complètes*, M. Zink (ed.), Paris, 1989-1990.

*Écrire pour dire. Études sur le dit médiéval*, B. Ribemont (dir.), Paris, 1990.

Michel Stanesco

**DIURNAL.** The diurnal was the *liturgical book that contained the daytime *office, the *diurnale officii*, *i.e.* the *hours of *lauds, prime, terce, *sext, *none and *vespers, but excluding the night office, vigils or *matins and compline. The diurnal thus differed from the *breviary, which contained all the hours of the office, day and night. It was an extract from the breviary.

Manuscript diurnals exist in libraries, but catalogues, often confusing diurnals, breviaries, *psalters and *antiphonaries, cannot be trusted. Distinctions are rarely easy to make, as medieval scribes made no distinction between the genres.

É. Palazzo, *Histoire des livres liturgiques. Le Moyen Âge*, Paris, 1993.

Anselme Davril

**DIVINE OFFICE.** Divine office was the whole of the solemn *hours of prayer in common that the Church celebrated each day. It comprised the night office (vigils or *matins), *lauds, prime, terce, *sext, *none, *vespers and compline, the object of each office being to consecrate by *prayer a particular moment of the day: night, sunrise, beginning of work, mid-morning, mid-day, mid-afternoon, sunset, time of going to rest. In the 7th c., this whole became stable, with all its elements in place. Divine office was celebrated by monks and *clerics living in community; it was also partly celebrated in all churches, with a significant participation of the *laity. But the specialization of functions and the tripartite division of society, which appeared around the turn of the *millennium, into prayers, fighters and workers (the cleric, the soldier and the labourer) made the divine office the proper duty of clerics.

Carolingian legislation put the office of clerics and that of monks on exactly the same footing, as to frequency and solemnity of celebration. It insisted at the same time on the personal obligation of clerics to take part in the office of their church, but those who had a *cure of souls tended to relinquish a public office that had become too long and got into the habit of reciting their hours in private. The *councils ratified this practice and made it obligatory for all clerics in major *orders (from the subdiaconate up).

*DSp*, 11, 1981, 686-707. – R. Taft, *The Liturgy of Hours in East and West*, Collegeville (MN), 1986. – V. Raffa, "Liturgie des heures", *Dictionnaire encyclopédique de la liturgie*, 1, D. Sartore (ed.), A. M. Triacca (ed.), Turnhout, 1992, 641-658 (Fr. tr.).

Guy-Marie Oury

**DIVORCE**

**The West.** The term "divorce" (Latin *divortium*), in medieval language, was equivocal. It could designate any voluntary cessation of conjugal union, whether the pronouncement of a case of nullity, a repudiation or a genuine divorce, and whether or not pronounced by a legal authority.

Antiquity had known these various causes of rupture of the matrimonial bond; while Christianity demanded its permanence until the decease of one of the partners. But the Middle Ages, taking advantage of the existence of prohibitions on *marriage (particularly forbidden degrees of *kinship), widely allowed the cessation of a union demanded by one or both partners. At the same time, an unconsummated marriage being considered "imperfect", they also admitted that such unions could be brought to an end. Finally we must not forget that, since the original union was not necessarily a public act, a "clandestine marriage" could be ended by the simple cessation of cohabitation.

J. T. Noonan, *Power to Dissolve*, Cambridge, 1972. – J. A. Brundage, *Law, Sex and Christian Society in Medieval Europe*, Chicago (IL), 1987. – J. Gaudemet, *Le Mariage en Occident*, Paris, 1987. – B. Basdevant-Gaudemet, "Le Principe de l'indissolubilité du mariage et les difficultés de son application", *La Femme au Moyen Âge. Actes du Colloque de Sceaux 1991*, Sceaux, 1991, 35-46. – P. Landau, *Ehetrennung als Strafe*, *ZSRG.K*, 81,1995, 148-188.

Jean Gaudemet

**Byzantium.** In the tradition of *Roman law, the Byzantine mentality admitted that *marriage was not indissoluble. The *Ecloga*, a codification of 741, listed the possible reasons for divorce: *adultery, if one of the spouses threatened the other with death or neglected to warn him or her of a grave danger, if the wife was convicted of prostitution or the man was shown to be impotent. They were repeated in the *Zakon sudnyi liudem*, its 9th- and 10th-c. Slav version. To these can be added divorce by mutual consent in order to embrace the monastic life, introduced by Justinian I. In 1085, judicial sentence was instituted as the sole way of dissolving a marriage. Thanks to archives, a great number of divorce proceedings have come down to us.

J. Zhishman, *Das Eherecht der orientalischen Kirche*, Vienna, 1864. – K. E. Zachariae Von Lingenthal, *Geschichte des griechisch-römischen Rechts*, Berlin, 1892 (3rd ed.).

Stavros Perentidis

**DŁUGOSZ (1415-1480).** John (Jan) Długosz, a *canon of *Cracow in 1436, was appointed archbishop of Lwów (*Lviv) in 1480. He was the most remarkable Polish historian of the Middle Ages, author of the *Annales seu Cronicae incliti Regni Poloniae*. From 1428 to 1431 he studied at the Cracow, then entered the service of its bishop, Zbigniew Oleśnicki. After the latter's death (1455), he carried out tasks entrusted to him by King Casimir Jagiellończyk; from 1467, he taught the king's sons, among them St *Casimir. He travelled much, in *Italy, *Germany, *Palestine and *Bohemia. He established many *foundations, notable among his objectives being the promotion of the cult of St *Stanislas.

*Dlugossiana. Studia historyczne w pięćsetlecie śmierci J. Długosza*, 1-2. Cracow, 1980-1985.

D. Turkowska, *Études sur la langue et sur le style de Jean Długosz*, Wrocław, 1973.

Leszek Wojciechowski

**DOBRAVA (died 977).** Dobrava, first Christian princess of *Poland, daughter of *Boleslas I the Cruel (Srogi), duke of *Bohemia, was from 965 the wife of the Polish Prince *Mieszko I, then the mother of *Boleslas the Brave (Bolesław Chrobry) and Sventoslava-Sigrid (Świętoslawa-Sygryd), queen of *Sweden and *Denmark. The marriage of Mieszko and Dobrava was the prelude to the Christianization of Poland (966) and contributed to the establishment of good Polish-Czech relations. Medieval chroniclers credited her with supporting the young Polish Christendom; she is supposed to have founded numerous churches, notably those of the Holy Trinity and St Guy (Vitus) at *Gniezno, as well as Notre-Dame at *Poznań. Polish and German *chronicles (Gallus Anonymus, Thietmar) see her as a Christian princess-apostle converting her *pagan husband, while Czech chronicles (Cosmas) judge her more negatively, reproaching Dobrava for having married a pagan ruler.

F. Dvornik, *Les Slaves*, Paris, 1970. – A. Witkowska, "Dobrawa", *EnzKat*, 3, 1985, 1367-1368.

Zbigniew Piłat

**DOCTOR.** From Antiquity, a doctor was a professor or a *master; the word was frequently applied to *Doctors of the Church. At *Bologna, the title originally designated *jurists, *legis* (or *legum*) *doctores*. "Doctor" became one of the terms for professors, notably of law, alongside *magister*, *professor* and *dominus*. In the course of the 13th c., the word also became equivalent to a university *degree and designated one who had obtained the degree of the doctorate. At *Paris, "doctor" was especially the title of the professors of the higher *faculties.

O. Weijers, *Terminologie des universités au XIII*e *siècle*, Rome, 1987.

Olga Weijers

**DOCTORS OF THE FAITH, OF THE CHURCH.** The Middle Ages ascribed great authority to the religious teaching of the first centuries of Christianity, to those called the Church *Fathers. Among these stood out, in the Latin tradition since the Venerable *Bede (*PL*, 92, 304), in imitation of the four *evangelists, the group of the four great Doctors: St Ambrose, St Augustine, St Jerome and St *Gregory the Great. In the last years of the 13th c., Pope *Boniface VIII prescribed that the feast of each of these should be celebrated under the double rite, like those of the apostles and evangelists (Decretals, Sext, III, 22; Friedberg II, 1059). Meanwhile, from the Middle Ages, the liturgical tradition of *Cluny honoured the symmetrical group of the four great Doctors of the Greek Church: St Athanasius, St Basil, St Gregory Nazianzen and St John Chrysostom, though they were to have no place in the Roman *calendar until much later. Apart from the four great Latin Doctors, the medieval liturgical calendars did not yet know the category of the holy Doctors of the Church, which developed after the proclamation (1567) of St *Thomas Aquinas as Doctor of the Church. But from the time of his *canonization he was described as confessor and doctor, in an implicit comparison with the group of the four great Doctors.

*Cath.*, 3, 1952, 933-938.

Pierre-Marie Gy

**DOCTRINE.** The Middle Ages were the time of the **summae*. The *scholastic method, the encounter with the *Aristotelian and Arab philosophies, gave birth to intellectual enterprises of which St *Thomas Aquinas's *Summa* is the most complete and most imposing example. The notion of doctrine inherited from Augustine, signifying a unified vision of *history, was received by a Middle Ages that would give this notion a more personal sense. The rise of the *universities, encounters with other philosophies and cultures, entailed difficulties connected with the clarification of the Christian faith. Each great medieval thinker, each school, wanted to elaborate its *doctrina christiana*: the monastic model of *Anselm or *Bonaventure, the university model of *Abelard and Thomas Aquinas, etc. Each attempted to formulate what was not yet systematically called dogma, but Christian doctrine. The typically medieval literary genre of the *Sentence or the **Quaestio* lent itself particularly to this type of enterprise.

Doctrine in the Middle Ages was also the thought of a *master. The first use of the term *magister* in the modern sense is attested at *Melk in 1103. The *magister* was one who had a *doctrina*. Appeal was made to these masters to give, alongside the *Fathers of the Church, qualified advice on this or that question. These *magistri in sacra doctrina* would often emancipate themselves from episcopal tutelage. For Thomas Aquinas, he who has to instruct others in a *science must first possess a perfect certainty of the principles of that science and the *faith that is the certainty of invisible realities. The master who teaches must be faultless in what concerns the different implications of the science (*Summa theologiae*, $I^a II^{ae}$, q. 111, a. 4). Likewise, reception of science or understanding is done by teaching and by discipline. They are prescribed by the Law (Dt 6, 6). Doctrine appeals to memory, because it is right to preserve and meditate on what one has received ( $I^a II^{ae}$, q. 16, a. 12).

At the end of the 12th c. we pass from *sacra pagina*, which was a commentary on Scripture, sometimes using the methods of the school, to *sacra doctrina*. In fact, commentary on the sacred texts culminated in a problematization in which external elements (*metaphysics, physics, anthropology) would intervene. This fact explains why the Middle Ages and their notion of doctrine also saw the appearance of an ever more important dogmatization, since the papal *magisterium progressively had to decide and give solutions which were doctrine to be believed (this was the case with the *soul and its form, *nature, *homo assumptus*, *purgatory). The compilers of *summae* who desired their writings to become *doctrinae* referred to **auctoritates* (it was in the 12th c. that this word "authority" was applied to theologians) such as St Augustine, St Jerome or St *Gregory. The masters officially charged with teaching sacred doctrine relied on authors considered authentic (Fathers, *councils, *Decretals, etc.) with the reverence that was due to them (*exponere reverenter*).

M.-D. Chenu, *La Théologie au XII*e *siècle*, Paris, 1957. – J. P. Resweber, "La pensée médiévale", *Les Chrétiens et leurs doctrines*, Strasbourg, 1987, 101-169.

Michel Deneken

**DOLCINO, FRA.** Perhaps the most famous medieval *heretic, especially since he is mentioned by *Dante in *Inferno*, XXVIII, 55-60 ("Tell Fra Dolcino . . . if he does not wish to join me here soon, so to arm himself with provisions that pressure of snow may not give the Novarese a victory that would else be hard to win").

Probably a native of Novara or the Novarese, he emerged among the **apostolici* after the death of Gherardo Segarelli at the stake. The first of his encyclical letters is dated 1300: its text is handed down in a small treatise composed by the inquisitor *Bernard Gui in 1316. Dolcino enriched the simple religious intuitions of his predecessor within an eschatological schema that foresaw, with Segarelli, the beginning of the fourth of the *status sanctorum*, during which the *Holy Spirit would descend once more on the apostles, and which would last until the end of *time.

The "spiritual congregation" of the *apostolici*, which lived in *poverty in conformity with the model of Christ's first disciples and according to an inner bond, would gather up "all the spirituals of all the other religious orders", while for all those who belonged to or supported the corrupt Church (being "carnal"), a period of punishment and extermination was announced.

To *Frederick III of Aragon, "king of Trinacria" (to whom the composite Ghibelline front looked as heir to the Emperor *Frederick II in the struggle against the papacy), was entrusted the task of bringing the divine plan to completion: an era of peace would follow, during which an "*angelic pope" would be put by God at the head of the "*spirituals".

Early in the 14th c., Dolcino, perhaps at the suggestion of his eschatological visions, withdrew to the mountains of northern Piedmont, where he was gradually joined by other followers. Eschatological expectation then seems to have been translated into militant and military chiliasm (so much that Marxist historians in particular have spoken, wrongly, of "peasant struggle" connected with a "class ideology"). *Clement V immediately proclaimed a crusade. This was successful in forcing the Dolcinians to spend a harsh winter (1306-1307) in the mountain solitudes. In March 1307 the survivors (few, we may imagine) were forced to surrender. Dolcino was captured and, with Margherita di Trento (his presumed companion) and Longino di Bergamo, ended his days amid terrible *tortures, according to the anonymous *Historia fratris Dulcini heresiarche*. Thus dramatically ended a dream of spiritual regeneration. The episode was not, as some have seen it, a socio-political utopia.

R. Orioli, *L'Eresia a Bologna fra XIII e XIV secolo, I: L'eresia dolciniana*, Rome, 1975. – R. Orioli, *Venit perfidus heresiarcha. Il movimento apostolico-dolciniano dal 1260 al 1307*, Rome, 1988. – G. G. Merlo, *Eretici ed eresie medievali*, Bologna, 1989, 119-128.

Grado G. Merlo

**DOLE.** Situated in the county of *Burgundy, Dole does not appear in history until the late 11th c., in the form of a comital *castle controlling a crossing of the Doubs, not far from the frontier between *France and the *Empire, which gave rise to a *bourg*. This rapidly developed (*priory, seat of a rural deanery, *parish) and in the 13th and 14th cc. became an important *bourgade* which attracted various religious foundations: *Templars, *Cistercians, a *hospital of the Holy Spirit, a *collegiate church (1304), a *Franciscan convent (1382) which adhered to the *Observance propagated by St *Colette. By establishing the seat of the Parlement (1389) and a *university (1422) there, the dukes of Burgundy made it the capital of the province to the detriment of *Besançon, an imperial town. Dole numbered some 4000 inhabitants when the armies of *Louis XI burned it entirely down at the siege of 1479. It was reborn with the attachment of Franche-Comté to the *Habsburg possessions (1493) and regained its place as capital of a small, nearly autonomous State until the conquest of the province by Louis XIV.

J. Theurot, D. Bienmiller, M. Marmet, A. Gay, J. C. Vienot, *Histoire de Dole*, Roanne, 1982.

René Locatelli

**DOMESDAY BOOK.** *Domesday Book* is the name of a large medieval manuscript, now preserved in the Public Record Office in London, containing a description of a survey of *England dating from the 1080s. A "national" document like this one is unique in European medieval history. There also exist several related surveys like the *Exon Domesday* (covering the south-west of England), the draft return for Cambridgeshire, a (fuller) copy of the Domesday entry for Ely, and the so-called *Little Domesday* (the draft for East Anglia).

*Domesday Book* is a survey of land listed according to two different organising principles. On one hand the land of the king is listed geographically according to vill, shire and hundred, the Anglo-Saxon administrative and legal units according to which tax was levied and law was dispensed. On the other hand, the land of tenants is listed tenurially by shire, where each tenant is listed with all his properties in that shire. Generally for each property three dates are given: the owner at the time of King *Edward's death (Jan 1066), at the time of the *Norman Conquest (autumn 1066) and at the time of the compilation (1080s). Many cases of disputed ownership can be found, which form crucial evidence for the large-scale change in land ownership in the two decades following the conquest.

Any interpretation of *Domesday Book* needs to distinguish between the actual *Domesday* book, containing the description of the land, and the inquest on which the description is based. Traditionally the inquest is seen as the survey carried out in 1086, and mentioned in the *Anglo-Saxon Chronicle*, when King *William the Conqueror was faced with the threat of an imminent invasion from Denmark. Needing an assessment of his (military) resources, he ordered a full survey of the land held by his tenants-in-chief. Commissioners were sent round the country to enquire who owned what land and under what obligations. They also collected information about geld (taxes). Draft surveys were made, amalgamated and compressed under the guidance of William of Saint-Calais, bishop of Durham (1080-1096). The final result, compiled not later than 1088, is the present *Domesday Book*. A new interpretation claims a sharper divide between the original enquiry of 1085 and the *Domesday Book* in its present form. The *Domesday* enquiry was meant in the first place to establish the lands of the king and their revenues. In the course of this enquiry, other information of a subsidiary nature about tenurial and disputed lands was collected. *Domesday Book* was compiled not under William the Conqueror († 1087), but under his son *William Rufus (1087-1100) who faced a revolt in 1088. The compiler was Rannulf Flambard, the most hated medieval administrator of England. He had *Domesday Book* drawn up as a geographically arranged register listing first the land and revenues of the king. The subsidiary information collected from tenants-in-chief and the information about disputed land was added. Hence the two-pronged geographical and tenurial arrangement.

*Domesday Book seu Liber Censualis Wilhelmi primi regis Angliae*, A. Farley (ed.), 2 vol., London, 1783 [Latin text], J. Morris (ed.) with Eng. tr., 40 vol., Chichester, 1974-1986.

D. Bates, *A Bibliography of Domesday Book*, Woodbridge, 1986. – *Domesday Book: a Reassessment*, P. Sawyer (ed.), London, 1985. – R. Fleming, *Domesday Book and the Law. Society and Legal Custom in Early Medieval England*, Cambridge, 1998. – D. Roffe, *Domesday. The Inquest and the Book*, Oxford, 2000.

Elisabeth van Houts

**DOMINIC (after 1170 -1221).** Founder of the Order of Preachers (*Dominicans), born at Caleruega (Old Castile), Dominic Guzmán studied at Palencia and in *c.*1195 entered the cathedral of Osma, where in 1199 he took part in the establishment of full regularity of the *chapter, of which he was sub-prior in 1201. In 1203 and 1205, he accompanied his bishop *Diego to Scandinavia. They visited *Innocent III, who discouraged their project of evangelizing the pagans. But from 1206 Dominic was drawn into *preaching against the Albigenses by the Cistercian *legates, whom the bishop persuaded to preach in evangelical mendicancy (Mt 10), practised from then on by Dominic and then by his friars. From 1207, despite the Albigensian crusade, he continued to preach almost alone, around *Prouille, then at *Toulouse with Bishop Fulk from 1209 to 1211. When the council of Montpellier (Jan 1215) reorganised the Church of the Midi, Dominic took the head, at Toulouse, of a perpetual "*praedicatio*", a community of friars bound to him by *profession (before 25 April 1215). Bishop Fulk approved their purpose to "go, in evangelical *poverty, on foot, as religious, to preach the word of evangelical truth", gave them a mission in his *diocese and granted them a revenue. Innocent III, from whom Dominic and Fulk asked for "confirmation of an order that would be and would be called Preachers", promised this, provided they attached themselves to a regular tradition. They opted in 1216 for that of St Augustine; *Honorius III gave confirmations in 1216, 1217 and 1219.

In 1217, Dominic universalized his order. Half his friars founded a convent at Paris, others in Spain and at Bologna; he himself went to *Rome. The order already had its own traits. It preached in mendicancy, its convents were exclusively urban, it had support at Rome and was articulated on the universities of *Paris and *Bologna, where the friars were instructed and recruited. At the end of the visitation of his convents in 1219, Dominic went to Rome, then held the first general *chapter at Bologna in May 1220. At his urging, the order extended mendicancy to convents and drew up its constitutional legislation; in 1216 it had been given conventual Customs of strict observance. In 1221, Dominic was at the height of his generosity as preacher and master. He founded many new convents, held the second chapter, organised the first provinces and sent to found others, founded the women's monastery of *San Sisto and drew up its Rule; he received from the pope a preaching mission in northern Italy analagous to that of the Cistercians in *Languedoc. He died on 6 Aug 1221 at Bologna and was canonized in 1234.

His traits of *sanctity were: intense *prayer, commitment to the *salvation of his neighbour, *mercy. His genius as a legislator: the art of synthesis, achieved first in himself, of the contemplative life and preaching, "*apostolic life" and the "rule of the Apostles", study and *ministry, community between equals and *authority; openness to his times, by an acute sense of the needs of the Church and its modern values: evangelism, Roman primacy, law, the *university, urban vitality.

*MOFPH*, 1, 16, 22, 24 and 25, 1896-1966.

B. Altaner, *Der Heilige Dominikus. Untersuchungen und Texte*, Breslau, 1922. – H. C. Scheeben, *Der hl. Dominikus*, Freiburg-im-Breisgau, 1927. – M.-H. Vicaire, *Histoire de saint Dominique*, 2 vol., Paris, 1982 (Eng. tr. *Saint Dominic and his times*, London, 1964). – G. Bedouelle, *Saint Dominique ou la grâce de la Parole*, Paris, 1982. – I. W. Frank, "Dominikus", *LThK*, 3, 1995, 319-320 (3rd ed.).

Marie-Humbert Vicaire †

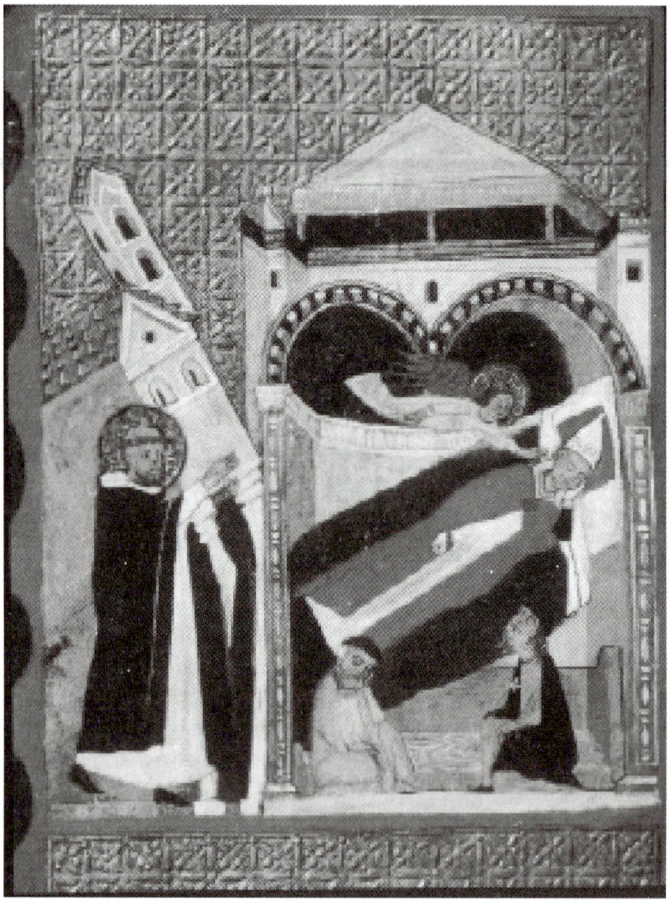

*The pope dreams that Dominic saves the Church.* Story of the life of St Dominic, anonymous Campanian painting, 14th c. Naples, Capodimonte Museum.

**DOMINIC OF FLANDERS (1425-1479).** Philosopher, *Dominican, one of the protagonists of Thomism in the 15th century. A master of arts at *Paris (before 1452), he entered the order at *Bologna in fully regular form (1461). He taught his brethren there, then at the universities of *Florence and *Pisa (1470-1474), finally the brethren at Bologna and Florence, where he died in 1479. Competent in *theology, he taught and published only in *philosophy and militated against a certain *Platonism and a secularized *Aristotelianism, for the Christian Aristotelianism of St Thomas. In date and in spirit, he is half-way between *Capreolus and Cajetan.

U. Schikowski, "Dominikus de Flandria o.p.", *AFP*, 10, 1940, 169-221. – L. Mahieu, *Dominique de Flandres. Sa métaphysique*, Paris, 1942. – T. Kaeppeli, *SOPMA*, 1, 1970, 315-318.

Marie-Humbert Vicaire †

**DOMINICANS.** The Order of Friars Preachers or Dominicans, first of the apostolic orders called "*mendicant", was founded in 1215 at *Toulouse by St *Dominic. The purpose of this clerical community was to "preach, on foot, as religious, the evangelical word of truth in evangelical *poverty". It devoted itself to the diocese and region of Toulouse. In 1217, Dominic made it a universal, centralized order of *evangelization. Three *bulls successively confirmed the Rule of St *Augustine (1216), the name and office of Preachers (1217) and *preaching in mendicancy (1219). At the founder's death (1221), the order numbered 25 *convents; there were 404 in 1277, 554 in 1303 and 631 in 1357, grouped into 12 provinces (1228), 18 (1303), 23 (late 15th c.), in Europe and Asia. It numbered 9000 friars in 1256 and 12,000 in 1337, as well as *nuns and lay *penitents.

The common work of Dominic and his friars, the Customs of 1216 and the Constitutions of 1220-1221 were until 1932 the basis of the two "distinctions" of Dominican legislation, periodically revised by the *chapters. Put in order by St *Raymond of Peñafort in 1239-1241, it was edited in 1505 with Declarations.

The institution was characterised by strength of synthesis, wealth and balance of parts, power of inspiration. The order was never divided. The immediate *profession of all religious to the master general ensured unity, stability within the order and the mobility of each friar. The *election by the friars, for a short term, of authorities whom the superior confirmed, the legislative monopoly of the chapters and their alternation, gave the order a democratic character. The annual meeting of the chapters gave it its flexibility. If the chapters governed and controlled, between whiles the masters possessed executive plenitude and the power to grant *dispensations in accordance with the needs of preaching and the *salvation of souls.

Government was assumed at all levels by the pairing of a *prior and a chapter, who took their inspiration from the most recent law. The general chapter, alternately formed of provincials and elected *definitors, was more democratic than at *Cîteaux. Annual, then biennial in 1270, it would be triennial from 1455. The order, which was represented to the *pope by a *procurator, did not ask for confirmation either of its legislation or of the master it had elected. The cardinal protector dates from 1378. The provincial chapter was an organ of decentralization that stimulated ministry and studies and controlled regularity. The prior of the convent, with his chapter, stimulated ministry and regular life.

The order's observance was a common life, unanimous and contemplative, in imitation of the Apostles, the *vita apostolica* (Acts 4, 32-35). Its austerity was increased by perpetual abstinence. St Dominic wished, and the order decided in 1236, that these obligations would be *ad poenam*, not *ad culpam* (each lapse was the object of a sanction, but was not considered a *sin), and subject to dispensation for the sake of the ministry. The original practice was mendicancy in preaching according to the "rule of the Apostles", or "*evangelical life" (Mt 10, 5-10). It gave the brothers a spirit of generosity that reached its climax in 1220 when the convents also committed themselves to daily mendicancy. These apostolic and evangelical inspirations fashioned the Preachers' *spirituality, synthesized the elements of their life and made the order the prototype of the mendicants.

*Prayer and ministry alternated in the Preachers' balance of life. They followed the liturgy of the local churches. After various attempts, in 1254-1256 the master *Humbert of Romans fixed the Dominican liturgy for the next eight centuries in the 14 books of the Prototype (1254), which *Clement IV approved in 1267. Its general note, even at the *mass, was brevity. It was a Romano-Gallican liturgy. The **cursus* was that of Rome, but simplified. The calendar, certain pieces and seven rhymed *offices were proper to the order. The chant was Parisian and had to be performed "*breviter et succincte*". It resembled that of the *Cistercians, which cut short the vocalizations. The office of the *dead was recited only once a week.

The Preachers had a devotion, full of evangelical freshness, to the Virgin, whose *office they recited going into choir. They promoted her *confraternity, which became in 1408 at Douai and in 1475 at *Cologne the confraternity of the *Rosary. Other confraternities – St Dominic, St *Peter of Verona, Holy *Name of Jesus (1274) – actively supported their ministry.

The preaching of salvation, the order's *raison d'être*, received from the start the same scope as that of *bishops: dogmatic and moral, positive and defensive. Bulls declared the friars "totally deputed to preaching" by the fact of their profession, and to *confession if they were priests. The preacher was by definition a *cleric and a priest, because preaching, which supposed Holy Writ, was crowned by the *sacraments. Devolution of the right to preach, to friars trained by study and practice, was the responsibility of the conventual prior assisted by a council. A year of *theology and the age of 25 were the conditions for "mission" outside the convent by the superior. Each convent had its "diet" of preaching and *collection. The "preacher general" himself organised his ministry in the province. Some had wider powers, in the manner of the itinerant preachers of the 12th century. The kinds, instruments and products of preaching never ceased to diversify throughout the Middle Ages. The whole group of convents of the mendicant orders superimposed on the *parish network of *Christendom a second pastoral network, which had its echo among the *seculars. The foundation of chairs of preaching multiplied in the 15th c. in *cathedrals and town churches, in parallel with those of mendicant *chapels.

Dominic's decisions in 1217 and 1220 led the order to create an efficient instrument of theological study and teaching, which the chapters developed, notably in 1259, 1305 and 1405. At the base of this centralized organisation were all the convents; a "*doctor", helped by a "master of students", taught theology in them. Its head was at the *faculty of *Paris, in which Saint-Jacques possessed two chairs, and it trained *masters whom it gave the "*ius ubique docendi*". Each province possessed one or two *studia solemna* that trained the conventual *readers; the most important of them, called *generalia*, had, like Paris, the obligation to receive from every province two or three advanced students, products of specialized schools whose diversity ceaselessly increased. This educational organisation gave the Preachers an incomparable scientific influence; it ensured an efficient decentralization of theological teaching, previously concentrated at Paris, and in the mid 14th c. allowed numerous faculties of theology to be established in the *universities.

From the beginning, the order's convents were founded exclusively in *towns, places of concentration and expanding human activity, centres from which to act on the countryside. The Preachers preferred their convents to be few, but large and in the great cities. Founded at the gates, around 1240 they moved into the centre, where their church was the main instrument of their activity. From then on, all towns aspired to possess a convent of mendicants within their walls, and the *laity attached to the friars' ministry tried to institutionalize this link. Following the example of Dominic and his successor *Jordan of Saxony, Teutonia founded numerous convents of *nuns, chief centres of Dominican *mysticism. Elsewhere the Preachers were long reluctant (1227-1259) to take charge of religious women, fearing for their studies and their poverty. Thanks to the popes and their general Humbert of Romans, the nuns received a common Rule based on that of *San Sisto (1259) and were definitively incorporated into the Preachers (1269). In the North-West, the Preachers took an interest in *beguinages, which remained outside the order. In the South, especially in northern Italy, the laity entered the fraternities of the

*Ordo de poenitentia* respectively supported by the Minors and the Preachers. In 1285, master Munio de Zamora offered them the Rule of the *Ordo de poenitentia S. Dominici* which incorporated them into the Preachers. Fraternities multiplied in the 15th c., as did secular and regular *Third Orders, in the light of St *Catherine of Siena († 1380) and after the confirmation of the Rule by the pope (1405, 1439).

The Preachers' presence in the world, their competence and morality, made them suitable for all sorts of office in the Church. The episcopate, which Dominic, wishing to preach only in *humility, had refused for himself and his sons, penetrated the order under pressure from Rome. Action against *heresy, an element of the preaching of Dominic and his first friars, did not define the order; neither the Constitutions nor Humbert of Romans's *De officiis* mention it. The office of inquisitor, instituted for the Empire in 1231, was entrusted to the Preachers in France (1232) and Languedoc (1234), where it was extended to the Minors in 1236. The inquisitor lived apart from the order. He performed his duties conscientiously, according to the procedure laid down by *canon law and the *councils, fixed in writings such as *Bernard Gui's *Practica* (1321-1324). The quality of its information, the soundness of its theology and its positive preaching of the faith gave the order its effectiveness against heresy.

The evangelization of non-Christians responded to the oldest and deepest vocation of St Dominic. Inaugurated from 1220-1221 by the sending of friars to central and nordic Europe, it had its bases in Spain, Hungary, Poland, Scandinavia, Byzantine Greece and the Holy Land. Urged on by the installation of the Latin Empire at Constantinople and the opening up of new fields in *Morocco, Persia and Central Asia, Prussia, the Baltic lands and certain regions of Russia, their apostolate in the North and East gave the friars fruitful contacts with the Greeks, the separated Christians of the East, *Jews and Muslims. It culminated in Asia with the erection of the ecclesiastical province of Sultanieh (1318), the original grouping of "Friars Peregrine" in 1300, which brought together missionaries in *Crimea, then in *Armenia, Persia, *Georgia and, in the 15th c., Ruthenia, and two Armenian societies: the Order of Preachers Unitors, created in 1336 and attached to the order in 1356, and the Armenian Friars *citra mare* from 1356. It led finally, in Europe as in Asia, to extensive linguistic and theological studies, especially in the *studia linguarum* of *Barcelona, *Valencia and Tunis, at the heart of which was the Arabist *Raymond Martini († *c.*1284).

The order was installed in 12 provinces, the first eight of which dated from 1221 and the other four from 1228: Spain, Provence, France, Lombardy, province of Rome (Patrimony, Tuscany, kingdom of Naples), Teutonia, England, Hungary, Dacia (Scandinavia), Poland, Greece (Latin Empire), Holy Land; the last four, at a distance, did not obtain all their rights until 1241. Becoming very large, they were subdivided into "*nations" in 1275, then split into two. In 1294, the province of Rome gave rise to that of Naples or *Regnum*; in 1301, Spain gave rise to Aragon and Poland to Bohemia; in 1303, Provence to Toulouse and Teutonia to Saxony; finally Lombardy was divided into Upper and Lower. In 1378, Naples gave rise to Sicily; in 1380, Hungary to Dalmatia; in 1426, Spain to Portugal; in 1481 and 1484, England to Scotland and Ireland. At this date, the order possessed 23 provinces.

Intensity and variety of apostolic ministries characterised the period. Reginald of Orléans († 1220), Jordan of Saxony († 1237), John of Vicenza (active from 1233 to 1247), *Stephen of Bourbon († 1261), Meister *Eckhart († 1327), *Giordano of Pisa († 1331), Venturino of Bergamo († 1345), St *Vincent Ferrer († 1419) were among the greatest preachers of their time. Of all the treatises on and auxiliaries to preaching, those of Humbert of Romans were the most important.

The order's doctrinal and literary activity surpassed that of all other bodies. It created two theological schools, Albertism and Thomism, to which must be added the *Rhineland mystical tradition. In *exegesis, *Hugh of Saint-Cher († 1263) and the friars of Paris procured basic instruments, such as *correctories of the text, *concordances and even *translations. *Theology saw the appearance of the *Summa* of St *Thomas Aquinas († 1274), the *Compendium* of Hugh Ripelin of Strasburg († *c.*1270) and, for *doctrine and moral practice, the *Summae on penitence* of Paul of Hungary (1220-1221) and St *Raymond of Peñafort (1235), the *De virtutibus et vitiis* of Guillaume Peyraut († 1271), the *Summa confessorum* of John of Fribourg († 1314) and the *Summa casuum* of *Bartholomew of Pisa (1338). The Friars also published in *canon law – St Raymond of Peñafort edited the *Decretals in 1234 –, catechesis, pedagogy and *apologetics. They studied ceremonies, sacred arts and *music. Their encyclopedic Mirrors also appeared in the vernacular. Their historical output, including numerous universal *chronicles, reached the level of modern *history with *Bernard Gui († 1331).

At the same time we find the order in all the services of the Church and the Christian State, so that in 1248 *Innocent IV was not afraid to call it the Church's "public horse" or providential "staff of old age". In one century, it provided two *popes, Innocent V (*Peter of Tarentaise; † 1276) and *Benedict XI († 1304), several *cardinals, 450 *bishops, all the masters of the Sacred Palace, *penitentiaries and inquisitors and innumerable papal commissaries. Counsellors and confessors of kings, they carried out all sorts of missions for them. In evangelizing the towns, they agreed to be their "*paciarii*" or conciliators and to correct their *statutes religiously. Their mendicant itinerance made them the best spreaders of *rumores* (public news) in the West, whose horizon was singularly broadened by their missionary experience.

The extent and effectiveness of the ministry of the Preachers led to clashes with earlier institutions. In the towns, cathedral chapters that possessed a monopoly on *pastoral care and important territorial rights could delay or even prevent the installation of convents of the order. There were frictions with *parish priests over their rights of *burial and their monopoly of *confession, increased by canon XXI of *Lateran IV (1215); later, over *legacies received by the order from their flock (1261). To disarm these opponents, who could prevent them celebrating their offices publicly and never called them to preach, the Friars only made a *foundation in a town after having gained the consent of all the clergy and signed pacts with them in which they renounced certain of their rights. They enlarged their chapels and appealed to bishops and especially popes. It was at Paris in 1252 that the worst quarrel broke out with the university men (see *Mendicants and Seculars, Quarrel of), on account of the growing success of the mendicants and the chairs they occupied. In 1254, scholastic conflict was combined with an attack on the Friars' ministry. After the death of Innocent IV, who had given way on some points (1254), *Alexander IV decided in favour of the mendicants (1256). The quarrel resumed in 1266-1271 and 1281, relaunched by certain bishops apropos of the Friars' privileges of hearing confession. Allayed in 1290 and then in 1300 by *Boniface VIII's bull *Super cathedram*, it resumed in the 14th and 15th centuries. But the Preachers' clashes with the civil authorities in defence of rights or decisions of the Church, such as the conflict with Louis of Bavaria (1325-1346), ended in true persecutions. In these conflicts, the Preachers overcame their temptation to rivalry with the *Franciscans and other mendicants to form a common front, and these "concords" led in the 14th and 15th cc. to lasting pacts interspersed with periodic meetings.

In the 14th c., the multiplication of common properties by dispensation and the development of "private life" among numerous religious led to attempts at *reform. They culminated with *Raymond of Capua (1380-1399) in the form of reformed convents, then reformed congregations of Lombardy, Holland, Teutonia, Spain, etc. In the 15th c., certain provinces such as Spain or Scotland would be reformed in their entirety. Despite some efforts to recover full mendicancy, especially in Italy, the order finally accepted, with the approval of *Sixtus IV (1478), certain conventual common properties, provincial and general, but largely succeeded in getting rid of private life. But the duality of reformed congregations and non-reformed provinces, which alone enjoyed constitutional rights, broke the legislative unity of the order. This was restored, however, when Bandello († 1506) and Cajetan († 1518) erected the congregations into provinces and reduced the non-reformed to vicariates. And the split of the order between two obediences, caused by the *Great Schism, which long paralysed reform, eventually disappeared. In the 15th c., the role of preaching reached a sort of apogee in Western Christian society and soon in the New World, while in the order, from England to Italy, from the Rhineland to Spain, there developed currents of interiority and return to the sources that would be expressed in the 16th c. in the Catholic and Protestant Reformations and their crises, profoundly modifying the order's situation in the world.

L. Moulin, "Une cathédrale du droit constitutionnel: l'organisation dominicaine", *Le Monde vivant des religieux*, Paris, 1964, 114-132. – W. A. Hinnebusch, *The History of the Dominican Order (to 1500)*, New York, 1966 and 1973 (2 vol.). – A. Cortabarria, "L'étude des langues au Moyen Âge chez les Dominicains. Espagne, Orient, Raymond Martin", *MIDEO*, 10, 1970, 189-248. – M.-H. Vicaire, "Les origines de la pauvreté mendiante des Prêcheurs", *Dominique et ses Prêcheurs*, Fribourg, 1977, 222-279. – M.-H. Vicaire, A. Duval, "Frères prêcheurs", *DHGE*, 18, 1977, 1369-1426. – M.-H. Vicaire, "Sacerdoce et prédication aux origines de l'ordre des Prêcheurs", *RSPhTh*, 64, 1980, 241-254. – M.-H. Vicaire, *Histoire de saint Dominique*, 2 vol., Paris, 1982 (Eng. tr. *Saint Dominic and his times*, London, 1964). – W. A. Hinnebusch, *The Dominicans: a Short History*, Dublin, 1985. – F. J. Felten, "La mendicité pour les Prêcheurs du XIVe siècle", *CFan*, 26, 1991, 307-333.

Marie-Humbert Vicaire †

**DONATION OF CONSTANTINE.** In the course of the conflict of the years 498-505, which set Pope Symmachus against the *antipope Lawrence, some *apocrypha (called "Symmachian") were composed in favour of the pontiff.

Among them was a *Constitutum Silvestri*, an embellished account of the pontificate of Silvester I (314-335). *Constantine took a prominent place, in an account where legend counted for more than history. Following this, a *Constitutum Constantini*, commonly called "Donation of Constantine", was composed around 750. The text appears in the False *Decretals, composed before 852-857. Its author is unknown and its place of composition uncertain. Perhaps it had an original element composed at *Saint-Denis with Roman complements in the years 766-796.

The text relates the legend of Constantine, suffering from *leprosy and miraculously cured, who asks the pope to explain a *dream. After penance, the emperor is baptized and so purified. There follow passages of a politico-legal nature: recognition of Roman primacy by Constantine, donation of the Lateran palace to the pope, Constantine's concession to Silvester of the imperial insignia and symbols of power, donation of the West to the pope, Constantine withdrawing to the East. These explain the text's success, the polemics and arguments it aroused. To start with, prudence prevailed. A diploma of *Otto III in 1001 denied its authenticity and attributed the *forgery to the papacy. *Leo IX used it in a letter of 1053 on the occasion of his conflict with Byzantium. The 8th-c. *Dictatus papae* allude to it. The Gregorian *canonical collections cite it, and so, following them, do the collections of *Ivo of Chartres. Gratian's **Decretum* in its first form makes no mention of it, but it was subsequently inserted. The first *Decretists were prudent, but the "Donation" became an argument of papal policy from the 13th century. It was used in both camps in a contrary sense during the Bonifacian quarrel and in the 14th century. To invoke it was not without danger for the papacy, since what the Roman emperor had given another emperor could take back. Moreover its authenticity was not unanimously accepted. Contested from 1001, it had its opponents in the entourage of *Frederick Barbarossa in 1152 and among the Bolognese glossators (Accursius). *Dante, *Marsilius of Padua and John of Paris (*Jean Quidort) followed them. The learned *Nicholas of Cusa judged it apocryphal. The *humanist Lorenzo *Valla, engaged in the conflict between *Alfonso of Naples and *Eugenius IV, demonstrated its falsity in 1440 (*De falso credita et emendata Constantini donatione declamatio*). In the late 15th and early 16th cc., some voices contested Valla's demonstration without refuting it, but acerbically criticizing him.

*The Treatise of Lorenzo Valla on the Donation of Constantine*, C. B. Coleman (ed.), Toronto, Buffalo, London, 1993. – *Das Constitutum Constantini*, H. Fuhrmann (ed.), *MGH.F*, 10, 1968, 55-106.

*Die frühmittelalterliche Papsttum und die konstantinische Schenkung*, Spoleto, 1972, *SSAM*, 1973, 257-329. – *Verbreitung der pseudo-isidorischen Fälschungen*, 2, Stuttgart, 1979, 354-407. – D. Menozzi, "La Critica all'autenticità della Donazione di Costantino in un manoscritto della fine del XIVe secolo", *CrSt*, 1, 1980, 133-154. – G. Antonazzi, *Lorenzo Valla e la polemica sulla donazione de Costantino*, 1984. – O. Guyotjeannin, "Donation de Constantin", *DHP*, Paris, 1994, 581-583. – D. Maffei, "The Forged Donation of Constantine in Medieval and early Modern Legal Thought", *Fundamina*, 3, 1997, 1-23.

Jean Gaudemet

**DONATIONS.** For the total, gratuitous and irrevocable transfer of goods as defined by Roman law, the medieval West substituted another form of liberality: the gift for the salvation of a soul (*pro anima*), whose beneficiaries were ecclesiastical institutions. Based on the redemptive value of almsgiving, justified by Scripture (Sir 3, 30; Lk 11, 41; Mt 19, 21) and the Church *Fathers (for Augustine, *alms given by the living could even purify the *dead), the practice of the gift *pro anima* became current from the 7th century. In exchange for goods ceded (mainly lands, during the early Middle Ages), churchmen pledged themselves to pray for the salvation of the donor and sometimes to receive his *burial. Thus a spiritual counter-gift corresponded to the material gift. Very soon, the spiritual benefits resulting from the gift could be extended to the relatives and "ancestors" of the donor, or even to all the faithful.

Around 1000, the gift *pro anima* became the preponderant mode of land transfer in the West, often indeed the only one in monastic *cartularies. A religious practice, referring to the expiatory character of almsgiving, it was also a social practice. For one thing, a part of the goods given to ecclesiastical institutions was redistributed to the poor. And then, in seignorial society, the gifts, as well as the disputes, confirmations and exchanges they entailed, were behind a multitude of encounters, transactions, rivalries and alliances, which contributed to form a social tissue and establish links between donors (essentially members of the aristocracy) and between them and the ecclesiastical communities.

The prestige of the aristocracy was measured by its generosity and by the privileged relations it maintained with the churches. But the game of giving was not limited to an exchange between two partners: it frequently included the "ancestors" of the donors, since these associated those in their salvation. In this way, while acquitting themselves of a debt towards their predecessors, from whom they held a name, properties and rights, the lay lords recalled the origin of their power. Religious institutions profited from gifts *pro anima*, which allowed them firstly to build up important estates, then to compensate for the pillages of which they were victims, and finally ensured them an eminent role in society: that of redistributing and transforming goods. In short, more than just a legal act "of pious motivation", as historians once defined it, the gift in the Middle Ages was a complex social process.

By provoking a movement of permanent "*restitutions" with no counterpart, the *Gregorian reform undoubtedly represented a first failure in the system of the gift. But it was above all the reappearance in the West of the *testament, linked to the renaissance of *Roman law, from the 12th-13th cc., that marked the end of the gift *pro anima* and the return of the classical donation, by testamentary *legacy.

M. Falco, *Le Disposizioni "pro anima". Fondamenti dottrinali e forme giuridiche*, Turin, 1911. – P. Jobert, *La Notion de donation. Convergences: 630-750*, Paris, 1977. – P. J. Geary, "Échanges et relations entre les vivants et les morts dans la société du haut Moyen Âge", *Droit et cultures*, 12, Nanterre, 1986, 3-17. – S. D. White, *Customs, Kinship and Gifts to Saints. The Laudatio Parentum in Western France (1050-1150)*, Chapel Hill (NC)-London, 1988. – B. H. Rosenwein, *To Be the Neighbour of Saint Peter: The Social Meaning of Cluny's Property, 909-1049*, Ithaca (NY)-London, 1989. – M. C. Miller, "Donors, Their Gifts, and Religious Innovation in Medieval Verona", *Spec.*, 66, 1991, 27-42. – *Actes à cause de mort, t. II, Europe médiévale et moderne*, Brussels, 1993 ("RSJB").

Michel Lauwers

**DONOR.** The representation of the donor, *i.e.* of him, her or them who ordered and paid for a given work, is a characteristic of the religious art of the Christian West: it is an effect much less frequent in the world of *images of *Orthodox Christendom.

Examples are rare for the earliest times, and are always to do with great men of the lay or ecclesiastical world represented on the occasion of costly gifts made to the Church, notably manuscripts. While these depictions obey the common rule of hierarchy of size between heavenly and earthly persons, they take very varied forms: the donors appear standing, kneeling or prostrate, full-face or in profile, hands joined, or presenting an object, or hands raised like antique *orantes*. They are defined primarily by the relationship that the sacred persons establish with them: benediction, presentation, or simple regard uniting donor and heavenly protector. Until the end of the 12th c., the depiction of donors in a given work is linked with exceptional circumstances

*The donor Garabet and his wife Esougan offer the manuscript to the Church.* Miniature from the *Armenian gospels*, 1236. Ispahan, Armenian Museum.

and individuals, like *Suger who insisted on marking with his image the innovative work he had carried out at *Saint-Denis by having himself represented there several times (see the window of the Life of Christ).

From the 13th c., the history of the depiction of donors in Western art is that of a constant development, under the influence of new forms of devotion. *Franciscan *spirituality emphasized the humanization of relations between *God and men, and urged the updating of these relations with the help of devotional objects which might be pictures. Meanwhile, obsession with *salvation and fear of the afterlife led people to multiply gifts in all forms for the remission of sins. At the same time, painting – crucifix, *altarpieces or polyptychs – took off in an extraordinary way and became the favourite place for the depiction of donors.

Such depiction invaded every medium in the course of the 14th and 15th cc.: sculpture (portal of the Chartreuse of Champmol by Klaus *Sluter), jewellery (ex-voto of *Charles the Bold, Liège cathedral treasury), *stained glass (that of Raoul de Ferrières in *Évreux cathedral). The multiplication of these depictions was accompanied by a standardization of forms. Donors were now depicted according to a stereotyped iconography; in profile, kneeling, hands joined, to the right of the heavenly personage, an indirect way of being depicted among the Elect. By contrast, hierarchy of size among the characters was no longer respected, and gradually donors and heavenly protectors came to be depicted on a level of equality. This iconographical scheme asserted itself vigorously and stepped outside the setting of "grand painting" to develop on votive tablets, which appeared in Italy in the 14th century. While in Flanders the heavenly characters seem to descend to earth, in Italy it is the donor who is transported to *heaven, whether by the mental representation of his *prayer or by the future vision of what he will find after his *death.

The Middle Ages saw a multiplication of such representations, effecting a dual change: on one hand the social range of the donors was broadened, on the other the purpose of the gifts was modified: originally to commemorate a *foundation or a costly gift, the object offered often also became an aid to personal devotion, a witness to an act of *grace or a gift for the sake of the soul's salvation.

E. Castelnuovo, "Il significato del ritratto pittorico nella società", *Storia d'Italia*, 5, 2, Turin, 1973. – P. L. Garson, "Suger as Iconographer: the Central Portal of the West Facade of Saint-Denis", *Abbot Suger and Saint-Denis. A Symposium*, New York, 1986, p. 183-198.

Élisabeth Antoine

**DORIA.** The legendary origin of the noble Genoese family goes back to the 10th c., when a certain Arduin, count of *Narbonne, is supposed to have married Oria, daughter of Corrado della Volta, and moved to *Genoa. By the end of the 11th c., the Doria – perhaps named from the *Porta aurea* (Portoria) – were settled in the southern zone of the city, where in 1125 Martino Doria erected the family church of San Matteo, which became a *priory of the abbey of *San Fruttuoso di Capodimonte, demonstrating the increasingly close relations with this important monastic settlement on the Riviera di Levante. In the 12th c., Ansaldo Doria, several times consul of the Commune, was among the commanders of the Genoese expedition that in 1147 defeated Almeria and Tortosa. His son Simone was the city's ambassador to *Frederick I Barbarossa in 1162 and took part in the third *crusade. In the fifth, Pietro Doria commanded the fleet that besieged *Damietta (1219).

In the civil strife of the 13th c., the Doria – who had meanwhile acquired great possessions and economic interests in *Sardinia – adhered to the Ghibelline faction (the *Mascherati*), taking part in the unsuccessful conspiracy of 1241. Percivalle Doria, **podestà* in various *communes in Italy and southern France, captain and vicar of *Manfred, combined political activities at home and abroad with an original poetic output, in vulgar Italian and Provençal, in the tradition of the Sicilian school. Also a *troubadour in the Provençal language in the first half of the century was Simone Doria, in poetic communication with Lanfranco Cicala and Giacomo Grillo, the main representatives of contemporary Genoese poetry.

In 1265, Niccolò Doria and Guido Spinola were invested with the function of *podestà* at a time of great political confusion. With the "popular" revolution of 1270, a dyarchy, composed of Oberto Doria (replaced in 1285 by Corrado) and Oberto Spinola, *capitanei Communis et populi*, ruled the city until 1291. From 1296 to 1299, the restored harmony between the two families associated them once more in the government of Genoa, with Corrado Doria – replaced by Lamba after his appointment as admiral of *Sicily (1297) – and Corrado Spinola. It was in this period that the Doria attained their greatest power: Oberto commanded the Genoese fleet that inflicted the defeat of Meloria on *Pisa (1284); his brother Lamba defeated the Venetian fleet at Curzola (1298); Jacopo Doria performed important military and diplomatic tasks for the Commune, of whose archives he was appointed *custos*; he was part of the commission charged with revising the *Annales Ianuenses* up to 1279 and was the final continuator (from 1280 to 1293) of the work begun nearly two centuries earlier by Caffaro. In 1311, on the occasion of the coming of the emperor *Henry VII, the family assumed the emblem of the eagle.

In the 14th c., the Doria were briefly in power in 1306-1309 with Bernabò and in 1335-1339 with Raffaele, still associated with members of the Spinola, Opizzino and Galeotto families. Though excluded from institutional office under the perpetual dogeship of Simone Boccanegra (1339-1344), they retained an important position in city politics. In 1351-1352, at the end of a successful naval campaign against the Venetians, Pagano Doria forced the Byzantine emperor *John VI Cantacuzenus to make peace. Luciano and, after his death in battle, Pietro Doria commanded the fleet in the war of Chioggia in 1378-1379. Other Dorias were in the service of the king of France in the *Hundred Years' War, including Aitone, admiral in various campaigns and commander of the Genoese crossbowmen in 1346 at *Crécy, where he lost his life. A branch of the family settled in the next century at *Marseille and *Avignon.

With their political influence diminished, military glory remained to the Doria in the 15th century. When Genoa rose up against the *Visconti (1455), Tommaso Doria fought at Albenga against Niccolò Piccinino, a *condottiero* of the Milanese armies. Andrea Doria, born at Oneglia in 1466 to a branch of the ancient stock, now widespread even outside Italy, ensured the Republic's independence and consolidated its institutions through the constitutional reform of 1528.

J. D'Oria, *La chiesa di San Matteo in Genova*, Genoa, 1860. – L.-H. Labande, *Les Doria de France*, Paris, 1899. – C. Imperiale di Sant'Angelo, *Iacopo d'Oria e i suoi annali. Storia di un'aristocrazia italiana nel Duecento*, Venice, 1930. – C. Fusero, *I Doria*, Milan, 1973. – W. Schäfer, "Il quartiere dei D'Oria", *La storia dei Genovesi. IX Atti del Convegno internazionale di studi sui ceti dirigenti nelle istituzioni della Repubblica di Genova, Genova 7-10 giugno 1988*, Genoa, 1989, 79-92. – G. Oreste, "I Doria", *Dibattito su quattro famiglie del grande patriziato genovese. Atti del Convegno. Genova, 15 novembre 1991*, G. Pistarino (ed.), Genoa, 1992. – Individual entries in *Dizionario biografico degli Italiani*, 41, Rome, 1992.

Genealogy: K. Schoppe, *Doriarum Genuensium genealogia et ex iis Imperatorum et Regum origo*, Augustae Vindelicorum, 1631. – N. N. Battilana, *Genealogie delle famiglie nobili di Genova*, 1, Genoa, 1825, with supplements in vol. 2 and 3, Genoa, 1826-1833 (anastat. repr., Bologna 1971). – L. L. Brook, R. Pavoni, "Doria (genealogia)", *Genealogie medievali in Sardegna*, Cagliari-Sassari, 1984, 110-115, 282-306.

Antonio Placanica

**DORMITION (*KOIMÈSIS*).** Until the 5th c., theologians avowed their uncertainty as to the fate of *Mary: did she die or not? Nobody knew. In the 5th c. there began to develop in *Palestine, starting from the feast of the Dedication of a Marian church, a feast of the Memory of Mary on 15th August. At the same period, under the influence of the controversies over the divine motherhood, apocryphal accounts began to assert Mary's death, while differing as to her posthumous fate: some claimed that she was dead and awaited the general *resurrection in *paradise; others, that on the third day her *soul was reunited with her *body.

In the 6th c., the Emperor Maurice extended to the whole Empire the Marian feast of 15th August, which was specified as the feast of the Dormition (thus affirming her death). At the same time, there spread at *Constantinople (particularly in the church of the Blachernae) the cult of the garments of Mary, using *relics in default of a body that had disappeared: belief in the Assumption of Mary (*i.e.* her being taken up to *heaven) was precisely stated, leaning on the *apocrypha and the *homilies for the feast of 15th August. From the 7th c., theologians and preachers seem by preference to have given credit to accounts that affirmed Mary's resurrection, *i.e.* the reunion of her soul and her body; this evolution is explained by theological reflection on Mary's divine motherhood and the parallel with the death and Resurrection of her Son (see *Germanus of Constantinople and *John of Damascus in the 8th c.). However, in the 10th c., the theory of so-called double assumption (separate assumption of her soul, taken to heaven with Christ, and body, buried in the earthly paradise and awaiting the general resurrection uncorrupted) enjoyed new success, thanks perhaps to the credit of the Emperor Leo VI who supported it. This theory provoked a reaction, faith in Mary's resurrection (raised to heaven with her body and soul reunited) being affirmed once more and predominating in the *Byzantine Church during the last

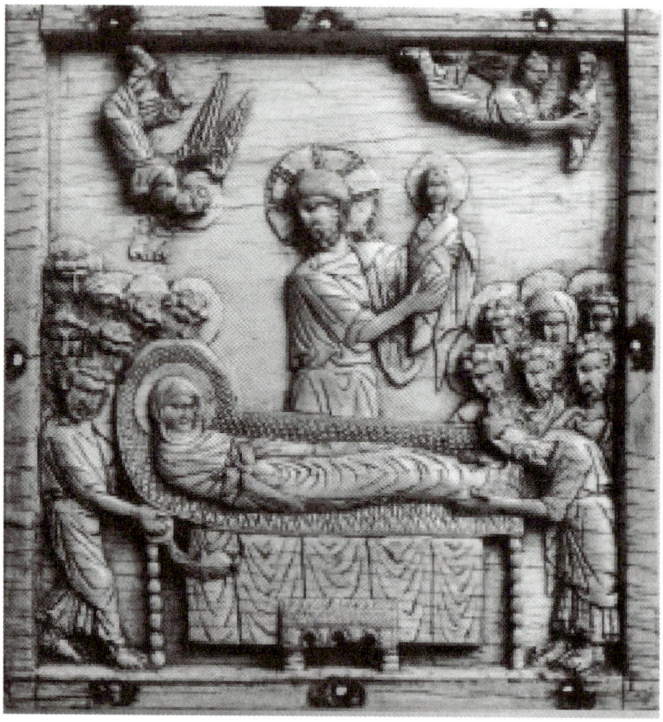

*Dormition of the Virgin.* Ivory, 11th c. Darmstadt, Hessisches Landesmuseum.

centuries of the Empire.

The feast of the Dormition (a name that did not prejudge her posthumous fate) was one of the most important of the *liturgical year, particularly in the East, preceded by a *fast like the great feasts of Christ. In the 14th c., the Emperor Andronicus II extended its solemnity to the whole month of August. But this faith in the Marian resurrection was never proclaimed as a dogma, and there has been no controversy between the Eastern and Western Churches on this question.

A. Wenger, *L'Assomption de la Très sainte Vierge dans la tradition byzantine du VI^e au X^e siècle*, *AOC*, 5, Paris, 1955. – M. van Esbroeck, *Aux origines de la Dormition de la Vierge*, 1995 ("CSts"). – S. C. Mimouni, *Dormition et assomption de Marie: histoire des traditions anciennes*, 1995 ("ThH", 98).

Marie-Hélène Congourdeau

**DOROTHEA OF MONTAU (1347-1394).** Married in 1363, she very soon aspired, following the example of *Bridget of Sweden, to lead a religious life based on an *ascesis not devoid of *mortification before leading to ecstatic experiences and feeling the presence of God, nourished by the desire for frequent eucharistic *communion. Eight of her nine children died, as did her husband in 1387. Her passionate love for God and *Christ led her, after a *pilgrimage to Rome in 1390, to have her mystical link with God openly recognised and to live as a *recluse in East Prussia from 1393. She learned the way of purification, which alone makes man capable of great *love. She died on 25 June 1394 and was canonized only in the 20th century.

*Die Aktendes Kanonisations prozesses Dorotheas von Montau von 1394 bis 1521*, R. Stachnik (ed.), A. Triller (ed.), Cologne, 1978. – E. Schraut, "Dorothea von Montau: Wahrnehmungsweisen von Kindheit und Eheleben einer spätmittelalterlichen Heiligen", *Religiöse Frauenbewegung und mystische Frömmigkeit im Mittelalter*, P. Dinzelbacher and D. R. Bauer, 1988, 373-394.

Tore Nyberg

**DOUBLE MONASTERY**

**The West.** The joint presence of men and women in the same monastic institution is attested in the history of *monasticism since its Oriental origins. In the West, these experiments rapidly became the object of warnings by the civil and religious authorities. New creations of communities grouping together both sexes appeared with the monastic and canonical *reform movement in the 11th-12th centuries.

The juxtaposition of a male and a female community, the sharing of the fruits of a single *patrimony, the presence of a group of men directing female religious or responding to their spiritual or material needs, or the creation of a female branch or establishment within an originally male congregation are not sufficient conditions to identify a double monastery. It is really in the precepts of the founder, as at *Fontevraud, Sempringham or Obazine, that we must seek the motor of a cohabitation that had spiritual value, before finding its traces in the rule or in monastic architecture. The founder once departed, it then remained to live out this project from day to day, and that was another matter.

E. Jombart, "Cohabitation", *DDC*, 3, 1942, 972-975. – M. Parisse, "Doppelklöster", *LdM*, 3, Munich-Zurich, 1986, 1257-1259. – *Doppelklöster und andere Formen der Symbiose männlicher und weiblicher Religiosen im Mittelalter*, K. Elm (dir.), M. Parisse (dir.), Berlin, 1992.

Jacques Dalarun

**Byzantium.** Double monasteries brought together monks and nuns living in separate buildings but having common *offices and the same (male or female) hegumen. The church looked on them with suspicion: Justinian's novella 123 (546) prohibited them. Canon 20 of *Nicaea II (787) forbade their creation and regulated those that existed. Patriarch *Nicephorus (9th c.) formally forbade them and suppressed those already in existence. Patriarch *Athanasius (14th c.) reiterated this prohibition.

The practice was nevertheless constant, from St Jerome's monastery at Bethlehem in the 5th c. to the monastery of the Philanthropic Saviour at *Constantinople in the 14th. Despite his own prohibitions, Patriarch Athanasius seems to have founded one on Mount Ganos and another at Constantinople (Xerolophos) which would be split in two by Patriarch Nilus in 1383, on account of wrangling between monks and nuns.

J. Pargoire, "Les monastères doubles chez les Byzantins", *EOr*, 9, 1906, 21-25. – *The Oxford Dictionary of Byzantium*, A. P. Kazhdan (ed.), vol. 2, New York, 1991, 1392.

Marie-Hélène Congourdeau

**DOUCELINE OF DIGNE.** Born at Digne in 1214, sister of the *Franciscan Hugh of Digne. She lived in turn at Digne, Barjols and Hyères. After a stay with the *Poor Clares at *Genoa, she founded, between 1240 and 1243, a *beguinage at Hyères, then at *Marseille (Roubaut). She remained there until her death, 1 Sept 1274. Her advisers were her brother Hugh of Digne until his death in 1254 or 1255, then Friar Joscelin, *guardian of the convent of the Friars Minor at Marseille. Her *Life*, written in 1297, was revised between 1312 and 1320. Its author is unknown, though it has been attributed to Phelippa de Porcellet who succeeded her as head of the beguinage. The text is in the Provençal of Marseille, and describes with great realism her *ecstasies and levitations. It is a first-rate witness to the feminine *mysticism of the Middle Ages.

Douceligne de Digne, *Vie*, J. H. Albanes (ed.), Marseille, 1879; R. Gout (tr.), Paris, 1927.

C. Carozzi, "L'Estamen de sainte Douceline", *ProvHist* 93-94, 1973, 270-279. – C. Carozzi, "Une béguine joachimite", *CFan*, 10, 1975, 169-201. – C. Carozzi, "Douceline et les autres", *CFan*, 11, 1976, 251-267.

Claude Carozzi

**DOXOLOGY (GLORIFICATION).** A fundamental element of any relationship between *man and *God, doxologies, usually in trinitarian form ("Glory be to the Father and to the Son and to the Holy Spirit"), have been recited, at least since the 4th c., at the conclusion of the psalmody, whose Christian interpretation they emphasize. In the *Byzantine liturgy and other Eastern liturgies, the *Lord's Prayer ("Our Father") ends with a doxology and, more generally, the celebrant concludes all diaconal (*litany) or sacerdotal *prayer, especially the eucharistic prayer, in the same way. The custom was later introduced of opening every celebration with a doxology.

A more developed doxology appeared very early, notably at morning prayer, developing the angelic doxology of Lk 2, 14: "Glory to God in the highest (**Gloria*)". In the *Roman liturgy, it was recited from the 6th c. at the Christmas *mass and, from the 8th c., at *Sunday and feast-day masses. On those same days, the Roman liturgy knew a still fuller doxology, the *Te Deum laudamus*.

A. Stuiber, "Doxologie", *RAC*, 4, 210-226.

Irénée-Henri Dalmais

**DRAGON.** The dragon is an animal of polyvalent symbolism, outcome of several cultural inheritances and contributions.

In the Old Testament, the dragon is a being hostile to man; identified with *Leviathan, with the serpent, it incarnates the forces of *evil that God alone can master (Job 40-41; Is 27, 1 and 51, 9). The *Apocalypse assimilates it to the serpent-tempter of Genesis, the devil and Satan (Rev 12, 9); a dragon with seven heads attacks the Woman who has just given birth (Rev 12, 1-17) and hands over his power to the Beast (Rev 13). Medieval commentaries imposed on Christendom this image of the dragon as symbol of the devil, incarnation of Satan and the forces of evil (Augustine, *Enarratio in Psalmos*, 103, 27: *PL*, 36-37, 1381-1383, the dragon "our old enemy"; Gregory the Great, *Moralia in Job*: *PL*, 76, 680; Bede, *Explanatio Apocalypsis*: *PL*, 93, 166-167).

The combat of the archangel *Michael against the dragon (Rev 12, 7-9) provided the model of the saint triumphant over the forces of evil. The theme was a commonplace of *hagiography (*e.g.* St George crushing the dragon). In the period of Christianization of the West, the saint triumphant over the dragon was an image of the victory of Christianity over *paganism (St Athanasius's *Vita Antonii*: *PG*, 26, 849). Under this same model, the story of the dragon subdued by St Marcellus, a 5th-c. bishop of *Paris, conceals the foundation-story of a medieval town, situated at the convergence of the clerical image – the saintly bishop, subduer of the forces of evil – and the folklore image, for which the dragon incarnated the hostile forces of nature, which were subjugated (*Vita sancti Marcelli* by Venantius Fortunatus, ch. X: *MGH.SRM*, IV/2, 1902, 53-54; see Le Goff).

At the turn of the 12th/13th c., the dragon (alone or crushed by St Michael) became the protective emblem of a town, the standard of a *family or a *corporation. It was probably at around the same time that the dragon appeared borne in *Rogation *processions, its tail being deflated on the third day, when it was "defeated by Christ" (John Beleth, *Rationale divinorum officiorum*: *PL*, 202, 130; Jacobus de Voragine, *The Golden Legend*, Princeton [NJ],

*Vision of St John. The beast with seven heads and ten horns.* Miniature from the *Apocalypse* of the abbey of Saint-Amand, 9th c. Valenciennes, Municipal Library.

1993, II, 23-24). The celebrated "Tarasque" of St Martha (Pseudo-Marcella's *Life of Saint Martha*, v. 1187-1212) also supposes the existence of a "ritual effigy" (see L. Dumont).

The processional dragons of the later Middle Ages show even more clearly its ambiguous image in folk culture: the offerings in kind made to them were perhaps intended to coax them, in order to render beneficent the natural forces that they incarnated.

*DACL*, 4, 2, 1921, 1537-1540. – L. Dumont, *La Tarasque. Essai de description d'un fait local d'un point de vue ethnographique*, Paris, 1951. – *Dizionario dei concetti biblici del Nuovo Testamento*, Bologna, 1976, 544-545. – J. Le Goff, "Culture ecclésiastique et culture folklorique au Moyen Âge: saint Marcel de Paris et le dragon", *Pour un autre Moyen Âge*, Paris, 1977, 236-279. – J. Simpson, *British Dragons*, London, 1980.

Anca Bratu

**DRAMA, LITURGICAL.** The Church *Fathers, notably St Augustine, had strongly condemned the theatre for its indecency and its pagan attachments. Dramatic art (essentially mime, in late Antiquity) disappeared from the 5th or 6th century. In the setting of the monastic liturgy, between the 9th and the 12th c., it revived in the form of liturgical drama. This consisted of more or less developed representations, integrated into the course of the *offices, during which clerics played different persons and held dialogues. They wore costumes and sometimes moved on a stage. The first liturgical drama was the *Visitatio Sepulchri*, otherwise called *Quem quaeritis*, known through a *troparion of *Saint-Martial at Limoges dating from 923-934 (Paris, BNF, ms. lat. 1240) and another from *Sankt Gallen, of the mid 10th c. (Sankt Gallen, Stiftsbibliothek, ms. 484). These two monasteries are generally considered the places of origin of the liturgical drama that would spread all over Europe in the course of the century, though certain *tropes seem to have been of Italian origin. The *Quem quaeritis* found its place in the *Easter liturgy, at the end of the office of *matins. Three monks advanced towards the place where, on Good Friday, the cross had been buried in a shroud. They represented the Three Maries and mimed the act of searching for something. A short dialogue then took place with another monk, dressed in white and holding a palm, representing the angel. Having learnt of the *Resurrection, the three monks returned to the community and announced the news. The angel then recalled them to show them that the shroud was empty. The monks, leaving the *censers in the sepulchre, took the cloth and showed it to the assembly, then went to lay it on the high *altar. After the *Te Deum*, the office of *lauds began. The novelty of this sequence was the appearance in the liturgy of the notion of an actor.

The exploitation of these first elements gave rise to the *Ludus pascalis*, of which complete versions from the 13th c. have been preserved (northern France). Other dramas developed at the time of the Easter feasts (the *Peregrinus* and the *Descensus ad Infernos* and, in Italy, the *Planctus Mariae*). Christmas was also an occasion to organise liturgical dramas: first the *ordo prophetarum*, then the *officium pastorum*, modelled on the *Quem quaeritis* and the *ordo Rachelis* (massacre of the Holy *Innocents). The most successful was the *officium stellae*, which put on the stage the Three Kings at Epiphany. Originally in *Latin, these dramas rapidly contained passages in the vernacular.

The history of liturgical drama is still an object of polemics between those who analyse it as a regular linear development of tropes gradually enriched (Young) and those who show that the simplest forms are not necessarily the earliest (Hardison).

K. Young, *The Drama of the Medieval Church*, Oxford, 1953 (2 vol.). – O. B. Hardison, *Christian Rite and Christian Drama in the Middle Ages. Essays on the Origin and Early History of Modern Drama*, Baltimore (MD), 1965. – W. Tydeman, *The Theater in the Middle Ages*, Cambridge, 1978. – S.E. Berger, *Medieval English Drama: an Annotated Bibliography of Recent Criticism*, New York, 1990. – E. Lalou, "Le Théâtre et les spectacles publics en France au Moyen Âge. États des recherches", *Actes du 115e congrès national des societés savantes (Avignon 1990)*, Paris, 1991, 9-33.

Pierre Kerbrat

**DREAMS.** A double tradition was imposed on the Church *Fathers concerning dreams. Although the *Bible gave many examples of dreams inspired by Yahweh, Judaism generally adopted an attitude of mistrust towards oneiric reality. By contrast, Greco-Roman culture gave them a very important place. The majority of dreams were considered to be true, capable of announcing the future when they were interpreted correctly by specialists in oneiromancy. Late Antiquity saw a strengthening of interest in dreams, notably within *Neoplatonist philosophy: for the philosophical tradition that went from Plato through Stoicism and Cicero to Plotinus, dreams were privileged means for the *soul to communicate with the deity. In the sanctuaries of the therapeutic gods Serapis and Asclepios, the rites of incubation, known through Aelius Aristides's *Sacred discourses*, were based on oneiric practice, since it was in dreams that the god appeared and prescribed a therapy for the sick person. Two fundamental treatises recapitulate the oneiric knowledge of Antiquity: Artemidorus's *Oneirocriticon* (2nd c. AD) and above all Macrobius's *Commentarius in Somnium Scipionis* (late 4th c.).

The triumph of Christianity marked a profound break in this oneiric tradition. First of all, the early prohibition of oneiromancy at the council of Ancyra in 314 deprived individuals of access to their dreams. At the same time, a new typology of classifying dreams prevailed. Whereas previously the main criterion had been their divinatory pertinence, the new framework of analysis rested on their origin: *man, *God or the devil. However, the difficulty of distinguishing these essential categories made the dream suspect to the Fathers. Their distrust was increased still more when they considered the place taken by oneiric knowledge in certain heretical sects or the libidinous character of numerous dreams. This movement of diabolization created a "society with blocked dreams" (Jacques Le Goff). Good dreams were rare and reserved for a small elite: the Christian emperors of the 4th c. were rapidly succeeded by saints and monks as privileged dreamers. It was during the early Middle Ages that the knots that joined oneirism and *hagiography were tied. Dreams punctuated the lives of the saints but also their cult (inventions of *relics, healings near their *tomb by means of rituals similar to that of ancient incubation). From the 12th c., the dream was rehabilitated. The rediscovery of ancient texts was one cause of this, though doubtless less profound than the part taken by dreams in the literature of the afterlife that flourished at this time. There was an insistence on the neutrality of numerous dreams which were a matter for physiology, psychology and finally *medicine (*Hildegard of Bingen, *Albert the Great, *Arnold of Villanova).

J. Le Goff, "Les rêves dans la culture et la psychologie collective de l'Occident médiéval", *Pour un autre Moyen Âge*, Paris, 1977. – T. Gregory (ed.), *I sogni nel Medioevo*, Rome, 1989. – L. Pressouyre, *Le rêve cistercien*, Paris, 1991. – S. F. Kruger, *Dreaming in the Middle Ages*, Cambridge, 1992.

Pierre Kerbrat

**DRINKING STRAW.** For reasons of hygiene, when *communion was given in both kinds, the eucharistic bread and the wine, communion with the *chalice was sometimes given with a drinking straw, generally of *gold. At that time great two-handled chalices, more easy to hold firmly, were used.

The straw received different names in Latin: *sipho*, *arundo*, *cannula*, *pugillaris*, *fistula*: it was a hollow cylindrical tube whose larger end, terminating in a small knob, was immersed in the chalice. It is mentioned from the 6th century. In 1415 the council of *Constance reduced its use, which was maintained in some monasteries.

J. Corblet, *Histoire dogmatique, liturgique et archéologique du sacrement de l'Eucharistie*, Paris, 1865-1866 (2 vol.). – W. S. Stoddard, *Monastery and Cathedral in France*, Middletown (CT), 1968, 366-367.

Guy-Marie Oury

**DRUZES.** The Druzes are followers of an initiatory sect derived from Isma'ili *Shi'ism. It was in Egypt, in the reign of the *Fatimid *caliph al-*Hākim (996-1021), that a movement was organised round a Turk, al-Darazī, who claimed that al-Hākim was the incarnation of the divinity, *i.e.* of the ultimate One, whence the name the Druzes give themselves, *muwahhidūn* (unitarians). In the year 408 AH (AD 1017-1018), the public announcement of this doctrine by al-Darazī provoked riots, which led the *caliph to give his support to another person of Iranian origin, Hamza b. 'Alī. When al-Hākim disappeared in 411 (1021), Hamza proclaimed that he had withdrawn in order to test his followers, but would come back one day to impose his law. The representative of the divinized al-Hākim was Hamza himself, the **imām* or supreme guide. He too disappeared shortly after the caliph, and al-Muqtanā took over the direction of the movement. It was doubtless he who brought together a number of letters emanating mostly from al-Hākim, Hamza or himself, to constitute what would be the canonical work of the Druzes, entitled *Letters of Wisdom*. After al-Muqtanā's death (after 1042), the community closed itself off, tolerating no new conversions, save a few exceptions, and keeping its doctrine secret.

After al-Hākim's death, the Druze movement declined in Egypt and propagated itself in *Syria through peasant revolts, particularly in the mountainous regions of southern *Lebanon (Gharb and Shūf), in the Wādī al-Taym, at the foot of Hermon, in the Jabal Summāq, south-west of *Aleppo, and, later, south of *Damascus in the Jabal of Haurān that still bears their name. They gradually provided themselves with a system of original religious practices and a new organisation. The community was divided into "sages" or initiates and the "ignorant" or non-initiated Druzes, though this differentiation did not do away with the social distinction between peasants and ruling families, of Arab origin. Any Druze, man or woman, could be initiated if judged worthy, but thenceforth had to lead an exemplary religious life. Following the prescriptions of Hamza and al-Muqtanā, the Druzes rejected the five pillars of the Muslim faith (in particular the *Ramadān fast and the *shahāda* or profession of faith) to emphasize submission to al-Hākim, the importance of mutual aid and sincerity towards believers (lying to unbelievers was authorized), the necessity of religious dissimulation on certain occasions, and the reincarnation of souls after death.

The Druzes maintained themselves in Syria and the Lebanese mountains under the *Mamluk dynasty, then played an important political role under the *Ottomans, when some of their families (Tanūkh, Ma'n, Shihāb) established small local dynasties.

S. De Sacy, *Exposé de la religion des Druzes*, Paris, 1838 (2 vol.). – M. G. S. Hodgson, "al-Darazī" and "Durūz", *EI(E)*, 2, 1965, 136-137 and 631-637. – T. Bianquis, *Damas et la Syrie sous la domination fatimide (969-1076)*, Damascus, 1986, 353-373 (2 vol.). – N. M. Abu-Izzeddin, *The Druzes. A New Study of their History. Faith and Society*, Leiden, 1993.

Anne-Marie Eddé

**DUALISM.** The term dualism, as opposed to monism, defines all religious doctrine that posits as independent and antagonistic the principle of all *good and the principle of all *evil (absolute dualism), or at least their manifestations (semi-dualism or mitigated dualism). In Greek and Latin medieval *Christendom, there were heterodox communities that professed a certain dualism: in the East, the *Bogomils (attested from the 10th c.), who remained mitigated dualists; in the West, the *Cathars, whose dualism (attested only at the end of the 12th c.) was, for the vast majority, absolute in the 13th.

The medieval dualisms are situated within Christianity and probably owe nothing directly to ancient Oriental dualisms. In a historical period rich in upheavals (around the year 1000) which saw Christendom define this world as a closed field in which the champions of God faced the agents of evil, they were largely inspired by a stock of gnostic traditions to develop – gradually and diversely – the latent dualism contained in germ in the New Testament: God is good / the world is evil (John's gospel and epistles), using no other authority than the canonical books. They discerned a deep-seated antagonism between the Old and the New Law, between God the Father, announced by Christ, whose "kingdom is not of this world", and the Yahweh of Genesis, author of the visible world.

For them, therefore, this dubious creator was a *demiurge. All theorized on the *Origenian myth of the fall of Lucifer or the theme, omnipresent in the 11th c., of the fall of the *angels, swept away by the tail of the "old serpent" of the *Apocalypse, but mitigated dualists also made use of a Slav apocryphon, the *Interrogatio Johannis*, to liken the demiurge to a fallen angel of God. Absolute dualists tried to resolve the internal contradiction of the system, which still attributed the origin of evil indirectly to God. Developing the internal logic of the parable of the good and corrupt *trees ("the tree is known by his fruit", Mt 12, 33), they attributed evil to an independent principle co-eternal with God.

Among the wealth of surviving sources on Western Catharism, the so-called Anonymous Cathar treatise and the **Summa* of the *Dominican Moneta of Cremona are particularly explicit as to the scriptural foundations of dualism. The *Book of the Two Principles* by John of Lugio, an Italian Cathar bishop, pushed the debate onto the ground of *scholasticism (universals of good and evil) and set out a total refutation of free *will: for the absolute dualists, human *souls were divine creatures fallen into servitude to material *bodies, but were responsible neither for their fall nor for the irruption of evil into this world. Unscathed by original sin, these souls were thus all "good and equal among themselves"; freed from evil by the baptism of the Spirit (*consolamentum*), "all will be saved". Thus preached the Cathar "good men" in the 13th century.

*Christian Dualist Heresies in the Byzantine World, c. 650-c. 1450: Selected Sources*, J. and B. Hamilton (ed.), Manchester, 1998.

M. Loos, *Dualist Heresy in the Middle Ages*, Berkeley, 1972. – S. Runciman, *The Medieval Manichee: a study of the Christian dualist heresy*, Cambridge, 1982. – J. Duvernoy, *La Religion des cathares*, Toulouse, 1989, 39-76. – R. Poupin, "Esquisse d'une histoire de la théologie du catharisme", *Heresis*, 19, Carcassonne, 1992, 31-39.

Anne Brenon

**DUBBING.** Dubbing, conferring the characteristic weapons of knighthood, made a man a knight. At the time of its appearance in the 11th c., it had only a utilitarian character and was not, for knights, an occasion for honorific or liturgical ceremony. "To dub" was synonymous with "to equip". The need the Church felt to protect itself by recruiting warriors or by confiding this task to a protective lay lord led to the creation of liturgical rituals which have been thought of as intended for the dubbing of knights, but which are in fact only the rituals of *investiture of these *defensores* (*Ordo* of Cambrai, 11th c.). The blessings were borrowed from rites of royal *consecration and, as such, were impregnated with the ideology, formerly royal but later princely, of protecting the country, the churches and the weak. This ideology thus approximated to knighthood, without yet being identical with it.

In the 12th c., dubbing took on a more aristocratic tone. Liturgical texts of this time are rare, but narrative and literary texts enlighten us on the evolution of dubbing. The Church did not yet play the principal role: this was played by a lay lord who gave the new knight the characteristic weapons of his estate: hauberk, shield, helm, lance, spurs and especially sword, symbol of the power of coercion, placed on the *altar and blessed by the officiating priest. Towards the end of the century, the custom of the bath (utilitarian? initiatory? ritual?) and the vigil of arms became widespread. The accolade, that blow given to the dubbed man to prove his physical resistance, was not a fundamental element, nor was it old: it appeared only at the end of that century, and suggests a rite of passage. The social rise of the knightly class and its aspiration to *nobility entailed a rise in the importance attached to dubbing, which became a nobiliary rite; by it, the nobility controlled entry

*Dubbing of a knight.* Miniature from a *Collection of old French poems*, *c.*1280-1290. Paris, Bibliothèque de l'Arsenal.

to the knighthood and limited access to it to its own sons.

In the 13th c., the fusion between knighthood and nobility accelerated: dubbing, reserved for nobles, became more costly and thus more rare. The knightly ideology that prevailed was expressed in the formulae pronounced at the time of dubbing and in the symbolic significance which treatises of *chivalry gave to each piece of armament; aristocratic and religious elements mingled to make the knight a defender of churches and of the weak (principally *women), but also a member of the ruling class, a governor of the people. Liturgy amplified these ideological aspects, brought together in the *ordo* of Bishop William *Durand (late 13th c.).

In the 14th and 15th cc., dubbing became rarer, later, still more costly and more sumptuous. It departed from its first meaning and was tinged with increasingly aristocratic and ideological values, finally becoming a sort of honorific nobiliary "decoration".

J. Flori, "Sémantique et société médiévale: le verbe *adouber* et son évolution au 12e siècle", *Annales*, 1976, 915-940. – J. Flori, "Chevalerie et liturgie", *MA*, 84, 1978, 247-278, 409-442. – J. Flori, "Pour une histoire de la chevalerie: l'adoubement chez Chrétien de Troyes", *Rom.*, 100, 1979, 21-53. – M. Keen, *Chivalry*, New Haven, 1984. – J. Flori, "Du nouveau sur l'adoubement des chevaliers, XIe-XIIIe siècle", *MA*, 91, 1985, 201-226. – D. Barthélémy, "Note sur l'adoubement dans la France des XIe et XIIe siècles", *Les Ages de la vie au Moyen Âge (Actes du colloque de Provins, 16-17 mars 1990)*, Paris, 1992, 108-117.

Jean Flori

**DUBLIN.** Old *Irish *Áth Cliath* ("ford of the wattles"), now *Baile Átha Cliath*, capital of the Republic of Ireland. Probably a small settlement in the early medieval period, its prominence is due mainly to it being the site of the first and most important *Viking settlement in *Ireland, established in 841 near the *dub linn* ("black pool") from which derives its modern name. The first Viking *longphort* (fortified landing-site) was at Islandbridge/Kilmainham, 2 miles upriver from the mouth of the river Liffey. This site was abandoned in 902, after defeat by the Irish. A second settlement was established in 919, after victory over Niall Glúndub mac Aédo, high-king of Ireland, at the present site of Woodquay. Around 1000, the wattle ford was replaced by a wooden *bridge, and a century later a stone fortification was erected. The wealth of the Viking inhabitants, from warfare, trading activity and the hiring out of their fleet, soon surpassed that of most Irish kings, so Dublin became a prize for would-be claimants to the high-kingship of Ireland. It also attracted the attention of the Anglo-Norman invaders, who captured the town in 1170. It passed under the direct control of *Henry II in 1171-1172 and became the administrative capital of Ireland.

A. P. Smyth, *Scandinavian York and Dublin*, Dublin, 1975-1979 (2 vol.). – C. Haliday, *The Scandinavian Kingdom of Dublin*, 1981. – P.F. Wallace, *The Viking Age Buildings of Dublin*, 2 Vols., Dublin, 1992.

Dáibhí Ó Cróinín

**DUBROVNIK (RAGUSA).** Dubrovnik (Rausium, Ragusium, Ragusa) was founded by refugees from the Greco-Roman colony of Epidaurus (Cavtat). Destroyed during the *Avar and *Slav invasions in the 6th-7th cc., the city was repeopled by *Croats, who retained its Slav identitywhile adopting Romanized culture and institutions.

Dubrovnik was subject first to Byzantium (9th c.), then to the kingdom of Croatia (10th-11th c.). From the 13th c., it formed a small aristocratic Republic and was infeudated to *Venice (1205) then recognised the authority of the kings of *Hungary and Croatia (1358), but remained independent. In the 15th c. it paid tribute to the *Ottoman empire, but kept its autonomy. Ragusan territory extended north to Ston and south to the bay of Kotor, and owed their prosperity to their merchant marine as well as the sale of industrial products in the Levant.

Ragusan bishops recognised the *metropolitan authority of the archbishop of Split, "*primate of *Dalmatia and all Croatia". In the pontificate of Gregory V (996-999), the *diocese of Dubrovnik became an *archbishopric, with the dioceses of Ston, Kotor (Dalmatia), Trebinje (Zachumliea) and Bar (Dioclea) as *suffragans. After a long conflict with the latter, which in turn became an archbishopric (1082), the archbishopric of Dubrovnik kept its rights over the dioceses of Ston-Korčula and Trebinje. St Blaise, a *martyr of Sebaste in Armenia (3rd-4th c.), was the uncontested patron of the town and protector of the Republic. For the *feast of their saint, 3 Feb, the Ragusans enfranchised slaves, restored freedom to *prisoners and practised beneficence.

Medieval travellers admired the fortifications of the town of Dubrovnik, which seemed to them "one of the finest towns ever seen and the strongest with its new walls, its avenues and its round-bottomed moats" (Fabri).

From the first millennium of Christianity, the Ragusans escorted Western travellers going on *pilgrimage to *Jerusalem, their representatives in the *Byzantine Empire watching over their safety. Later their ships transported the crusaders to the *Holy Land.

Medieval Ragusa presents monuments of all periods and all styles. Its *Romanesque, *Gothic and Gothic-Renaissance churches and palaces (former *cathedral, churches of the Friars Preachers and Minors, of the Saviour, palace of the Rectors, etc.), are the masterpieces of Italian (Paolo Veneziano, Onofrio della Cava, Salvi di Michiele) and Croatian artists (George the Dalmatian, the Andrijić brothers, Nicholas Božidarević, etc.).

V. Foretić, *Povijest Dubrovnika do 1808* [The History of Dubrovnik to 1808], 1-2, Zagreb, 1980. – J. Lučić, *Dubrovačke teme* [Selection of articles on medieval Ragusa], Zagreb, 1991. – S. M. Stuard, *A State of Deference: Ragusa/Dubrovnik in the Medieval Centuries*, Philadelphia, 1992. – B. Krekić, *Dubrovnik: a Mediterranean Urban Society, 1300-1600*, Aldershot, 1997.

Franjo Šanjek

**DUCAS.** Constantine Ducas, of a family famous since the 9th c., was among the generals who brought Isaac *Comnenus to power in 1057, and was his successor (1059-1067). After the reign of the co-emperor Romanus IV Diogenes, betrayed by the Ducas family at Manzikert (1071), Michael VII Ducas (1071-1078), a former pupil of *Psellus, reigned but, incapable of opposing external enemies, succumbed to the revolt of Nicephorus Botaniates. The reign of the Ducas family marked a broad retreat of Byzantium, the Balkans and Asia Minor being invaded respectively by *Pechenegs and *Turks. The marriage of Irene Ducaina to the future Emperor Alexius Comnenus allowed the family to retain a high rank.

D. Polemis, *The Doukai. A Contribution to Byzantine Prosopography*, London, 1968.

Jean-Claude Cheynet

**DUCCIO DI BUONINSEGNA (*c.*1255-1318/1319).** Born at *Siena, Duccio must have begun to paint around 1279, though little remains of his work before 1285: he decorated chests intended to preserve the archives of the commune of Siena and the book-covers of the Biccherna, tasks that would occupy him until 1295. The only work that can be attributed to him with certainty is the little *Virgin* of Crevole (prior to 1285; now at Siena, Museo dell'Opera del Duomo) in which the tender severity of the Byzantine Virgins survives. In 1285, he painted a *Maestà* for the confraternity of the Laudesi in the Dominican church of Santa Maria Novella at *Florence (now in the Uffizi). Starting with this work, called the *Rucellai Madonna* as the confraternity met in the

*Christ washing the apostles' feet.* Detail of *La Maestà* by Duccio di Buoninsegna, 1308. Siena, Museo dell'Opera Metropolitana.

*chapel of that family, Duccio synthesised the solemnity of the Byzantine style and the new ostentation of *Gothic. He also managed to integrate the formal orientation that *Cimabue represented at Florence.

It is possible that Duccio worked alongside Cimabue on the building-site at *Assisi (*c.*1279-1280). In 1302, we find a trace of a predella painted by Duccio for the chapel of the Novices in the Palazzo Pubblico at Siena; the work is now lost. Between 1308 and 1311, he conceived and created the great double-sided *altarpiece intended for the high altar of Siena cathedral: on the front part he painted the *Maestà* surrounded by choirs of angels and saints (among them the 40 protectors of the town); on the other face, he told the story of the *Passion, in 26 compartments. At the time it was made, the great altarpiece was decorated with a predella on which were shown scenes from the infancy and life of *Christ, as well as a coronation in the Gothic style, with scenes from the life of *Mary and scenes of the risen Christ. Once finished, the work was borne in great solemnity to the *cathedral on the day of the Assumption of Mary (patroness of Siena) in the year 1311. Duccio also composed the cartoons for the cathedral windows (*Deposition in the tomb*, *Assumption*, *Coronation of the Virgin*; *c.*1288), the *Virgin with Franciscans* (Siena, Pinacoteca Nazionale, no. 20) and the polyptychs of the Virgin and Child (Siena, Pinacoteca Nazionale, no. 28 and no. 47): these last two have a place in the history of the altarpiece in central Italy, as they are the very first great polyptychs of the Tuscan trecento.

Duccio thus dominated Sienese painting and, to a great extent, that of central Italy. He was the master of Simone *Martini and in the 1300s directed a vast studio in which his collaborators included Ugolino di Nerio (active from 1317 to 1327), Segna di Bonaventura (active between 1298 and 1327), the Master of Badia a Isola (late 13th c.) and the Master of Città di Castello (early 14th c.).

J. H. Stubblebine, *Duccio di Buoninsegna and his School*, Princeton (NJ), 1979 (2 vol.). – J. White, *Duccio. Tuscan Art and the Medieval Workshop*, London, 1979. – D. Gordon, "Duccio (di Buoninsegna)", *DoA*, 9, 341-350.

Daniel Russo

**DUCHY.** In the Byzantine world the *dux* was the military head of the provinces, especially the peripheral ones more exposed to external dangers. Once *Italy had been recovered – the other regions of Western Europe being now irremediably lost to the "Romans" – after the interminable Greco-Gothic war (554), Justinian tried to reconstruct the dual form of provincial administration, civil, entrusted to judges, and military, entrusted to dukes. For a brief period a return to the old order seemed possible, but the invasion of the *Lombards in 568-569 made it impossible for that form of government of territory to continue unchanged in those regions that resisted the invaders, in some cases for a long time. Indeed the needs of defence imposed a unification of supreme responsibility, so that the military commander, the duke, was often known by the name once applied to the higher grades of the civil administration, *magister militum*, and sometimes as *iudex*. He was an official ever more autonomous and ever more burdened with generally political responsibilities, who in turn made use of minor officials chosen locally from the clergy and the *optimates*. Thus in the north of Italy the office tended to become hereditary, particularly in the lagoon regions, while in the Byzantine territories of the south, where a more or less direct rule of *Constantinople survived, military logic, to oppose the offensive of the Arabs, led to the diminution of the importance of the duke in favour of the *theme* led by the *strategos*.

As in so many other cases, the word *dux*, together with the generic respect for the function of command, passed into the German world in general covering two different traditions, in this case to indicate those whom tradition recognised as heads of the various groups of warriors, and "dukes" soon appeared in all the new kingdoms established within the Roman *limes*. In particular the "duchy" became a typical institution of the Lombards, not in the sense that the victors took the place of the defeated in every way, simply assuming their honorific titles: after the violence of the invasion, very little of the Byzantine administrative framework remained in Lombard Italy. The kingdom was strong in the north, with its centre at *Pavia, but equally strong and substantially independent were the two duchies of *Spoleto and *Benevento, the latter destined long to survive the kingdom. While the Byzantine duke was a high official, appointed and accountable, the Lombard duke was so because of the esteem in which he was held by his people, within his *fara*. The dukes, far from being collaborators of the king, were rather his antagonists – only very rarely did the king appoint a duke – so much so that the history of the Lombard kingdom in Italy can be called the history of the conflicts between the kings and the dukes, as may be seen from *Paul the Deacon's *History of the Lombards*. But the powers of the dukes themselves were not homogeneous. The northern duke, generally settled in a city, accepted and honoured the royal legislation; the two great duchies of the centre and south legislated on their own account, while that of Benevento took the title of *dux gentis Langobardorum*, enjoyed a relatively efficient bureaucratic apparatus suggested by the contiguous Byzantine teritories, and had his own mint. In general the dukes of the border territories enjoyed wider powers than those settled in the internal areas. Moreover the powers of the dukes underwent great changes in the course of the kingdom, from the first years, when they moved largely independently of the royal sphere, to the last years, when the *monarchy was strengthened and could exercise a certain control over the actions of the dukes through *ad hoc* officials. Some made use of *gastalds* and counts in administering their territory, some enjoyed particular closeness to the kingdom, others enjoyed important family support; some quickly showed dynastic characteristics, others were imposed by personal gift, regardless of the merits of the lineage. All this deeply marked the nature of the relations between dukes and kings, contributing to a general fluidity and weakness of the kingdom. It also happened that some territories were not in the hands of a duke, but subject to a royal gastald with powers wholly analogous to those of a duke, without the complications caused by family ties, but perhaps obliged to act in partnership, if not in rivalry, with another gastald, in charge of administering the property of the royal fisc. What distinguished the duke from the gastald was the former's autonomy of decision, not the exercise of power, and it could happen that a gastald, becoming particularly illustrious, might become a duke, or a duke become a king. And when we consider that personal or tendentially dynastic ambitions allowed a duke to act militarily against a neighbouring duchy with the aim of enlarging his own region of rule, and that the title of duke in some cases suggested to the king the use of the holder as a prestigious ambassador inside or outside the Lombard borders, we have a clear idea of the fluidity of the value of that position throughout the duration of the kingdom.

Outside Italy, in the other Germanic kingdoms, as mentioned, the governors of provinces had titles taken from Roman tradition:

*patricius, dux, comes*. They too were in the long term largely autonomous from the royal power, and with increasingly marked hereditary characteristics. But the Carolingian systematization of Europe made the *count and the marquis (*duces* in sources may also be counts or marquises) the public official *par excellence*, and even the dukes that remained, in the defeated Lombard kingdom as elsewhere, were totally assimilated to the counts and especially to the marquises – we even find the alternation of the titles *dux* and *marchio* – *i.e.* the officials in charge of a *march: the largest provinces, generally those on the borders (in the case of Italy: *Istria, Friuli, Spoleto and Tuscia). Within the European framework, however, the duchy more clearly took on the characteristics of a large terrritory, comprising within itself several counties, with unequivocal "national" features: *Bavaria, *Brittany. To this were added the complications due to the spread of the relationship of personal loyalty to the sovereign, a model "exported" by the *Carolingians to all Europe under their rule, so that the public official was at one and the same time the holder of a State position and responsible to his lord, the possessor of his own property and the administrator of property pertaining to his office, with the well-known mingling of private and public that characterised those centuries of the Middle Ages, and with the tendency to exercise delegated power patrimonially. As later occurred with the disintegration of the *Empire.

An analogous tendency also characterised the vicissitudes of the Byzantine duchies. The duke, especially the duke of Rialto, made himself increasingly autonomous of Byzantium, but emphasized his links, and his legitimation, with the local *optimates*, but without the problems of *vassalage. At *Gaeta in the mid 10th c. appeared the title of *hypatos et dux, consul et dux*. Social stratification, becoming more complex, increased the need for the consent of the notables, and strengthened the tendency to the exercise of a new power, civic or territorially well characterised, so that it could happen that the duke was also the *bishop, as at *Rome, *Naples or *Amalfi. As at Byzantium, the duke associated his son in power and worked for his recognition.

Everywhere there was a slow move towards the constitution of dynastic territorial apparatuses, sometimes on a vast scale. With the formation of city *signorie* and then regional *signorie*, with the characteristics of principalities, the duchies would keep their original name, but would profoundly change their appearance, stressing their autonomous character, as real states, perhaps within a "national" State, surviving into the modern period.

G. Ostrogorsky, *History of the Byzantine State*, New Brunswick (NJ), 1969. – S. Gasparri, *I duchi longobardi*, Rome, 1978. – P. Delogu, A. Guillou, G. Ortalli, *Longobardi e Bizantini*, Turin, 1980 ("Storia d'Italia", 1). – V. Fumagalli, *Il Regno italico*, Turin, 1978 ("Storia d'Italia", 2). – A. Guillou, F. Burgarella, F. von Falkenhausen, U. Ritizzano, V. Fiorani Piacentini, S. Tramontana, *Il Mezzogiorno dai Bizantini a Federico II*, Turin, 1983 ("Storia d'Italia", 3). – R. Manselli, "Il sistema degli stati italiani dal 1250 al 1454", *Comuni e Signorie: istituzioni, società e lotte per l'egemonia*, Turin, 1981 ("Storia d'Italia", 4), 177-263.

Gabriele Zanella

**DUEL.** The duel was a way of resorting to the judgment of God, comparable to the *ordeal: in certain legal cases, the right of the plaintiff's case had to be demonstrated by his triumph on the field of battle. The practice was ancient and widely attested in the Germanic societies of the early Middle Ages. It is frequently encountered in Carolingian society, where its field of application was vast, in criminal as in civil law. Its growing success from the 10th c. seems to respond to the multiplication of proceedings by *oath, and the high number of perjuries resulting from it. Resort to the duel, or more often the mere threat of it by one of the parties, enabled the avoidance of the collective false oaths or unverifiable testimonies that interfered with the proper functioning of justice. The principle of representation, which allowed any person physically or socially unfit to fight (*woman, *child, *cleric, *Jew) to resort to the services of a champion, ensured the "equity" of the procedure, thus made accessible to all plaintiffs: in the 12th c., proof by duel was even open to *serfs. Though often used as a guarantee or a means of pressure to force the adversary to conclude a compromise, the duel was not just a legal contingency: sources give accounts of fights in the lists, which in certain cases degenerated into a brawl between all participants. The event, ritualized, could be of great *violence, favoured by the use of mercenary duellists expert in foul play; the kings of *England thus resorted to the services of condemned men who bought their pardon at the price of their contribution to justice. Unlike the ordeal, the duel did not disappear in the course of the Middle Ages. It is still encountered in the 15th c., especially in political conflicts. Indeed it was particularly adapted to cases of *felony or treason, which in principle ruled out recourse to the testimony or oath of the accused, whose word was tainted with falsehood. Also, the confrontation of champions bearing arms appeared perfectly adapted to the resolution of litigations amongst the *nobility. For this reason it served, in its extreme form, the battle, to decide conflicts between rulers once and for all. For all the *chroniclers, in a society where war was a normal form of relationship between States, battle was in rare cases a decisive recourse to the judgment of God. This legal conception of confrontation explains the importance accorded to certain battles: *Hastings, Bouvines, *Crécy. These great military confrontations, infrequent in the Middle Ages, often included, at the very heart of the engagement, real single combats between heroes of both armies. They were seen as procedures of judicial duels between two plaintiffs, the opposed rulers.

R. Bartlett, *Trial by Fire and Water. The Medieval Ordeal*, Oxford, 1986.

Mathieu Arnoux

**DUIN.** Capital of early Christian *Armenia, Duin (in Greek Doubios or Tibin, in Arabic Dabil) is on the left bank of the Azat, some 20 kilometres from Erevan. Probably founded in the 5th c., Duin replaced Artašat as capital a century later. After the fall of the Arsacid dynasty in 428, Duin became the seat of the Persian and then Arab governors and the residence of the *catholicos* or patriarch until 923. In the Bagratid period, Duin lost its status as capital and remained mainly in the hands of Arab *emirs despite Armenian and Byzantine attempts to recapture it. Recent excavations as well as the testimony of Procopius and the 10th-c. Arab geographers attest the importance and commercial wealth of Duin even after the great earthquake of 893. Recaptured from the Muslims by the Zak'arid viceroys of Queen T'amar of *Georgia, who made it her winter residence after 1203, Duin continued to prosper. The *Mongol conquest of the 14th c. was the beginning of its decline.

K. Kafadarian, "Les Fouilles de la ville de Dvin (Duin)", *REArm*, new series, 2, 1965, 283-301, 459-460. – H. Manandian, *The Trade and Cities of Armenia in Relation to Ancient World Trade*, N. G. Garsoïan (tr.), Lisbon, 1965, 81 f., 87, 133 f., 137, 143 f., 148 f., 152, 154 f., 169 f., 179, 184, 198. – A. Ter Ghewondyan, "Chronologie de la ville de Dvin (Duin) aux IXe et XIe siècles", *REArm*, new series, 2, 1965, 308-318.

Nina G. Garsoïan

**DUNGAL (9th c.).** An Irish scholar who spent his career on the Continent during the reigns of *Charlemagne and his successor *Louis. Dungal is first mentioned in a letter by *Alcuin (hence before 804); he was residing at that time at the abbey of *Saint-Denis in Paris, from where, in 811, he addressed to Charlemagne a letter concerning eclipses of the moon. He was apparently still in Paris in 814-815, if a poem addressed to *Hilduin, the newly-appointed *abbot of Saint-Denis, is by this Dungal. By 825, however, Dungal was resident in *Pavia. A *capitulary of that year stipulates that scholars of *Milan, *Bergamo and Vercelli should convene in Pavia to attend the teaching of Dungal ("*in Papia conveniant ad Dungalum*"). In 827 Dungal composed a treatise on the *iconoclast controversy. In addition to this treatise, there survives a small corpus of *letters (not counting that addressed to Charlemagne) and five poems. The date of his death is unknown, but he bequeathed his *library to *Bobbio; a number of manuscripts containing his handwriting have been identified.

*PL*, 105, 1851, 447-458, 465-530. – *MGH.PL*, 1, 1881, 406-407, 411-413 (re-ed. 1979); *ibid.*, 2, 1884, 664-665.

M. Ferrari, "In Papia conveniant ad Dungalum", *IMU*, 15, 1972, 1-52. – J. Vezin, "Observations sur l'origine des manuscrits légués par Dungal à Bobbio", *Paläographie 1981*, G. Silagi (ed.), Munich, 1982, 125-144.

Michael Lapidge

**DUNS SCOTUS, JOHN (*c.*1265-1308).** John Duns Scotus, *doctor subtilis*, studied at *Oxford between 1288 and 1301, where he was lecturing on *Peter Lombard's **Sentences*. He lectured on the *Sentences* at *Paris in 1302-1303, and he may have done so yet again at *Cambridge in 1303-1304. In 1304 he returned to Paris. He probably became Master in 1305. From 1307 until his death he lectured in theology in the *Franciscan study house in *Cologne. A substantial proportion of his writings consist of commentary upon *Aristotle. In his use of the Arabic tradition, Scotus frequently contrasts the positions of *Avicenna and *Averroes, usually favouring Avicenna. It is also of importance to the development of his thought that he worked among the Oxford mathematicians of the day, and was encouraged to use a number of mathematical examples and demonstrations.

Duns Scotus has both a deserved and an undeserved place in the history of late medieval thought as a pioneer. His writings do not form an altogether coherent system, and in many respects he was simply reflecting piecemeal on issues current in his time, returning to them as they arose in the interconnected discussions in which he was engaged. His name became attached to ideas for which he was not in every case responsible. So any summary of his thought and influence begins from that difficulty. For example, *Ockham's terminist epistemology may owe something to Scotus, but Ockham disagrees with Scotus on universals. It may be that he even exaggerated the difference for purposes of polemic, and that would be a sign of Scotist influence consciously resisted. In natural theology, Ockham develops one side of Scotus's teaching. Nevertheless, Scotus pressed things forward at a number of points.

Duns Scotus's *metaphysics begins from what *being is, its "quiddity". Metaphysical being, for him, is the most universal of these "quiddities". It simply is. *God is "being as being" in this way. His individuating attribute of infinity distinguishes him from all other being. Thus everything else is infinitely separate from God. But finite beings derive their cause from this infinite being. The evidence for this, Scotus holds, lies in Scripture, which describes God bridging the infinite gulf between our being and that of God, not in *reason. So Scotus envisages an infinite Being who is sufficient to himself, but has chosen by an act of free will to create finite being. The only possible motive for that creation is *love.

He asserts that the universe is not static. In the Scotist world, the forms are dynamic. The forms are active as formal causes and also, Scotus argues, as efficient causes. He says that it is possible to prove by necessary (demonstrative) arguments the existence of a being so perfect that his existence is itself necessary. Such perfection of being implies omnipotence, and omnipotence must underlie all "efficient causation". It is therefore possible to argue, as Scotus does, that each causal being receives from the first Being a causal efficaciousness proportional to its own degree of being. Thus, the finite being of each creature can be seen as the basis of its capacity to "cause" other beings. In that lies its own perfection. Matter is the passive power (*potestas*) in this. *Substance (seen as "*form") is the active *potestas*. He considers that efficient causes are always substances or qualities. Some primary acts are of a sort that makes them bring about secondary acts.

God provides three "real *sciences" with which the natural light of the *intellect may comprehend this universe (Scotus regards *logic as an instrument or tool only). These are drawn from the classical system which *Boethius relays in his *De Trinitate*. The first is metaphysics (Boethius's *speculativa*). Metaphysics has as its object "being as being". It is a speculative science, which seeks pure *knowledge of quiddities, things as they are, and not their accidents. *Mathematics studies material substance quantified (*quanta*), thus asking "how much of it" there is. Physics studies material substance as mobile (*mobilia*).

The philosopher studies the universe as it can be observed and reasoned about. The theologian studies what God's *Word has revealed about the way in which *man is to be saved, and thus goes beyond the range of *philosophy (Scotus also takes *theology to be essentially practical because it is concerned with *salvation). Scotus's metaphysics serves the purpose of preparing the student for theology. Scotus thinks that theological questions cannot all be resolved by reason alone. The acceptance of divine omnipotence and *immortality of the *soul, for example, rests ultimately upon *Revelation. Truths of faith cannot be shown to be false by logic, even if reasoning cannot of itself prove them true. The philosopher ought not to mingle Scriptural evidences with what can be learned by the light of the intellect. The theologian must. Scotus is fond of speaking of "necessary reasons" (*rationes necessariae*) in this connection, but with a different force than that with which the phrase is used by *Anselm of Canterbury. For example, when he asks how far we can know God, he answers that it is possible for man to have a conception of God that includes most of the necessary truths about his Being, by which he means the knowledge of the attributes that belong to his essence. But we cannot know these by reason alone. We do not have an innate idea that God exists. It is not a self-evident truth. Like Aquinas, Scotus cannot accept Anselm's ontological argument. We can know only *a posteriori*, from the nature of the universe that God has made. So we can argue only from effect to *cause.

Duns Scotus was much a man of his time in his interest in questions of *freedom and necessity. He argues that God's infinity is the ground of his freedom. Within the Godhead (**ad intra*), God's acts are governed by his infinity; this manifests itself outwardly (**ad extra*) in what we perceive as his liberty. But if God is omniscient and omnipotent, it also seems that what he knows and does must be necessary. Aristotle worked with a two-edged possibility. He believed possibility to be incompatible with both impossibility and necessity. On that understanding, what is always true is necessarily true. Scotus proposed a way round the logical possibilities that arise when modal propositions are expressed in different tenses, and thus seem to refer to what happens in the actual world at different times. The truth of a proposition in the past or present tense is a different matter from the truth of a proposition in the future tense. In the *Tractatus de primo principio*, IV, Scotus criticizes the Aristotelian *cosmology at this point. He argues that what is possible or contingent is not what is "not necessary" or "not always", but is "that of which the opposite could have happened at the very time it actually did". So contingency involves the consideration of the possibility that at a given time several different states of affairs could have obtained. Scotus applies this to free will. He holds that at any given time the *will is free with respect to the act of willing. This he applies in the particular case of God's will, emphasizing that God's will is his primary *faculty and governs his knowledge, as it does his acts. There is an essential *order of causes for every effect in the universe. These are all subordinated in order to one cause, who is God. Contingents can therefore exist only if God "causes contingently". Scotus's solution is to say that in the eternal present the divine intellect offers all possible states of affairs to the divine will to choose from. The divine will chooses and the divine intellect then grasps what it decides. So God knows and acts upon what he freely chooses from among the possibilities that were simultaneously available. In this way there is contingency in what the divine will brings about, because it could bring another of the possibilities into existence by will. Scotus, like many of his contemporaries, takes there to be an objective difference between past and future, a difference which exists for God as well as for us. So when the divine intellect contemplates the possibilities and makes one of them true by asserting it, it is choosing between simultaneously possible opposites, and in that way making one of them the future fact or truth.

On *universals, Duns Scotus believed that only that which is itself distinct can individuate. Thus universals cannot be thought to exist wholly independently of the particulars whose natures they are. The *nature of a given thing cannot be wholly universal, or it would not be possible for it to be predicated of the numerically one and particular. Yet individuating principles must have some sort of actuality. In some way the nature of each thing must be common in reality, even though it can have no existence apart from each particular.

C. Balic (ed.), *Opera Omnia*, Vatican, 1950-. – E. Gilson, *Jean Duns Scot: introduction à ses positions fondamentales*, Paris, 1952. – W. Lampen, *Joannes Duns Scotus et Santa Sedes*, Quaracchi, 1929. – D. C. Langton, *God's Willing Knowledge*, University Park (PA). – B. de Saint-Maurice, *Jean Duns Scot*, Montreal, 1944. – O. Schafer, *Bibliographia de Vita, Operibus et Doctrina Johannis Duns Scotus*, Rome, 1967. – *John Duns Scotus: Metaphysics and Ethics*, L. Honnefelder (ed.), R. Wood (ed.), M. Dreyer (ed.), Leiden, 1996. – M. Sylwanowicz, *Contingent Causality and the Foundations of Duns Scotus' Metaphysics*, Leiden, 1996.

Gillian Evans

**DUNSTAN (died 988).** Archbishop of *Canterbury. Born in the West of England (precise date unknown), Dunstan served as a young man in the household of King Æthelstan (924-939), before being appointed abbot of *Glastonbury in 940. Glastonbury was then the only Benedictine monastery in England, and from there Dunstan, with *Æthelwold (later abbot of Abingdon and bishop of *Winchester) laid plans for the *reform of Benedictine *monasticism that was later implemented with the support of King Edgar (959-975) and *bishops such as Æthelwold and *Oswald of Worcester and York. With Edgar's patronage, Dunstan was appointed bishop of Worcester (957), then bishop of *London (959) and subsequently archbishop of Canterbury (959). Dunstan was an austere man, much given to *visions, but was also a scholar of some standing, as is clear from the small corpus of his surviving *letters and poems. After his death he was venerated as a saint (feast day: 19 May).

*Portrait of Duns Scotus* by Joos van Gent, 15th c. Urbino, Ducal Palace.

*Memorials of St Dunstan*, W. Stubbs (ed.), London, 1874. – M. Lapidge, "St Dunstan's Latin Poetry", *Anglia*, 98, 1980, 101-106. – D. Dales, *Dunstan, Saint and Statesman*, Cambridge, 1988. – *St Dunstan. His Life, Times and Cult*, N. Ramsay, M. Sparks, T. Tatton-Brown (eds), Woodbridge, 1992.

Michael Lapidge

**DURAND OF MENDE, GUILLAUME, THE ELDER (died 1296).** Bishop of Mende from 1286 to 1296, called the *Speculator*. Born in the diocese of Béziers, he studied law at *Bologna and had a career in the Roman *Curia (from *c.*1265) and in the papal government of *Romagna (1280-1286 and 1295), while writing important works of *canon law, particularly the *Speculum iudiciale*, *c.*1271-1272 (Basel, 1574), the *Repertorium aureum* (Frankfurt, 1592) and the commentary on the constitutions of the second council of *Lyon (Fano, 1569), to which we can add, from the time of his episcopate at Mende, the *Instructions and Constitutions* for the church of Mende (ed. Berthelé-Valmary, Montpellier, 1905).

Around the time he became a *bishop, Durand wrote mainly on liturgy, first the *Rationale*, the most widely read treatise on liturgy and its symbolism until the 17th c., whose first redaction was finished in 1286 (a scientific edition of the *Rationale* is being published), then a revision of the *pontifical of the Roman Curia (ed. Andrieu, Vatican, 1940) and a book of episcopal blessings (ed. Moeller, *Questions liturgiques et paroissiales*, 1968). He also either revised or wrote the *liber ordinarius* (still unedited) of the Church of Mende. He was a practical-minded *canonist and *liturgist, capable of organising a vast mass of material rather than contributing new ideas to it.

A. Davril (ed.), T. M. Thibodeau (ed.), B. Guyot (ed.), *Rationale Divinorum Officiorum*, *CChr.CM*, 140, 140A, 140B, 1995-2000.

L. Falletti, "Guillaume Durand", *DDC*, 5, 1953. – *Guillaume Durand, évêque de Mende (v. 1230-1296)*, P.-M. Gy (ed.), Paris, 1992.

Pierre-Marie Gy

**DURAND OF MENDE, GUILLAUME, THE YOUNGER (died 1330).** Nephew of Guillaume *Durand (or Durant) the *Speculator*, he was *archdeacon of Mende when his uncle died, and succeeded him on 17 Dec 1296. In 1306, he was instructed by *Clement V to hold an inquiry in England with a view to the *canonization of Thomas of Cantelupe, bishop of *Hereford. In 1307, on return from a mission to Italy, he concluded the *pariage* of Mende with the king of France, sharing with him his authority over the Gévaudin, erected into a county of which the *bishop was *count. He wrote notably additions to his uncle's *Instructions and Constitutions*, a treatise on the way to celebrate a *council (*Tractatus de modo celebrandi concilii*), a memoir on the preparation of the *crusade, addressed to *Philip the Fair on the occasion of the assembly of 1313, and a *Directorium chori* for the church of Mende. Put in charge of a mission by *John XXII and *Philip VI de Valois, he set out for the *Holy Land and died on the journey in July 1330 at Nicosia, where he was buried in the church of the Cistercians of St Mary of Beaulieu.

P. Viollet, "Guillaume Durant le jeune, évêque de Mende", *HLF*, 5, 1921, 1-139. – G. Mollat, *DBF*, 14, 1960, 1171-1173.

Jean-Loup Lemaître

**DURAND OF SAINT-POURÇAIN (1270/5-1344).** Durand taught *theology at *Paris to the *Dominicans between 1307 and 1312, then at *Avignon as master of the Palace (1312-1317). He was later bishop of Limoux (1317), *Le Puy (1318) and finally Meaux (1326). His teaching, often rather critical of the positions of *Thomas Aquinas, was the object of numerous polemics, especially from the order's master, Hervé Nédellec. He left a *Commentary on the *Sentences*, several times revised, **quaestiones* and *quodlibets, *sermons and *treatises including one against the theories of *John XXII on the *beatific vision.

J. Koch, *Durandus de S. Porciano O.P. Forschungen zum Streit um Thomas von Aquin zu Beginn des 14. Jahrhundert*, *BGPhMA*, 26, 1907. – T. Kappeli, *SOP*, 1,1970, 339-350, n. 927-960.

Louis Jacques Bataillon

**DURHAM.** Situated on a spectacular site in a bend of the river Wear, the *cathedral and city of medieval Durham owed their fame, and indeed their very existence, to St Cuthbert of *Lindisfarne († 687), whose body and *relics were brought here in 995. The serious

Durham cathedral, interior elevation of the nave, 1093-1133.

danger that the extraordinary popularity of this northern saint might then be used as a focus for Northumbrian political separatism was eventually dispelled by *William I; and from the episcopate of William of St Calais (1080-1096) onwards, a long sequence of bishops of Durham nearly always used their great power in the interests of the English *Crown. It was Bishop St Calais too who in 1083 transformed the community of St Cuthbert into a Benedictine monastic cathedral, which it always remained until the *prior and monks there were replaced by a dean and *canons in 1540. Although the city of Durham itself enjoyed little economic significance, the Benedictine monks of Durham (still numbering 70 in the 15th c.) held vast estates and presided over the largest centre of institutionalized religion, *pilgrimage and learning in the north of *England.

C. M. Fraser, *A History of Antony Bek, Bishop of Durham, 1283-1311*, Oxford, 1957. – G. V. Scammell, *Hugh du Puiset, Bishop of Durham*, London, 1961. – R. L. Storey, *Thomas Langley and the Bishopric of Durham, 1406-1437*, London, 1961. – R. B. Dobson, *Durham Priory, 1400-1450*, Cambridge, 1973. – M. Bonney, *Lordship and Community: Durham and its Overlords, 1250-1540*, Cambridge, 1990. – *Anglo-Norman Durham: 1093-1193*, D. Rollason (ed.), Woodbridge, 1994.

Barrie Dobson

**DUTY.** The notion of duty as it developed especially with Kant did not exist with that meaning in the Middle Ages. Following the Ancients and the Stoics, medieval Christianity presented duty in relation to a higher law, always linked in fact to the notion of the *Good, hence to *God. In his fictitious dialogue with Boso in *Cur Deus Homo?* (1099), St *Anselm writes: "What is the due that we owe to God? Any *will belonging to a reasonable creature must be subject to the will of God" (I, 11). Duty can only be accomplished by a life led in *rectus ordo*. Thus, for St *Thomas Aquinas, the notion of duty can never be separated from the intrinsic nature of *being, in which its explanation must be sought: *ethics and its demands can be derived from *ontology and its properties. To know what each thing or being must be or do, it is sufficient to give its definition and ask it to fulfil it. The Thomist notion of duty is also linked to that of divine government, outside which the reasonable and free creature would not be able to find the perfection of its being or the *beatitude that must result from this. The *debitus* is always connected with the *justus* and the *necessarius*. It is incumbent on the creature to respond to *justice and to the ontological necessity of its *nature. Human relations are ruled by ties of debt, "to each being due what belongs to him" (*Summa theologiae*, I[a], q. 21, a. 1). There is a dual due: one regulated by *reason, the other by the determination of law (I[a] II[ae], q. 99, a. 5). Moral due can be guided by reason or necessity. But we should note that for Thomas, among the *virtues, "only justice is based on the idea of due".

The notion of duty is also connected with that of *conscience, which would undergo a remarkable evolution in the course of the Middle Ages. Duty is what man's reasonable conscience commands him to do. In the 12th c., *Alexander of Hales, theoretician, among other things, of *indulgences, asserts that *reason and *intellect naturally tend towards the good, and that conscience is the superior instance that determines the modes of action that must answer this purpose. Later on (14th c.), for *e.g.* *John Buridan, duty is dictated by the *intellectus practicus*. Duty, in mystical sensibility, is dictated by conscience by reason of the divine *love (*Latin sermons*, *Jacob autem*).

The aim of the literary genre of the Mirror (*Mirror of Princes, of saints, of the knight, etc.) was always to show the way of duty in connection with God's plan in the world. The *ordo universi* is willed by God: to do one's duty is to enter into that order and hence into the will of God. Many authors, St Thomas particularly, do not confine the notion of duty to subordinates, but emphasize the duty of the rich towards the poor, the prince towards his subjects.

J. Tonneau, "Devoir et morale", *RSPhTh* 38, 1954, 233-252. – G. Ermecke, "Pflicht", *LThK*, 8, 1963, 426-428 (2nd ed.).

Michel Deneken

**DYING, PRAYERS FOR THE.** Medieval *liturgical books contain *prayers to be recited, at least in monasteries, from the beginning of a sick person's *death agony to his expiry. Some of these prayers (or "*recommendations of the soul") go back to Christian Antiquity, in particular *Depart, soul, from this world* (*Proficiscere*), others are compositions of the early Middle Ages. The general theme is of asking the *angels to accompany the dying person to *paradise.

A. G. Martimort, "L'*Ordo commendationis animae*", *LMD*, 15, 1848, 143-160.

Pierre-Marie Gy

# E

**EASTER.** The Christian *feast of Easter was at first celebrated on *Sunday, prepared by a *fast of one or two days and prolonged by the Paschal fifty days (Greek *pentecostè*). The original object of the feast, and especially of the Easter *vigil, was the *Passion of *Christ and his *Resurrection, not separated from it. Progressively, the various events of the Passion and Resurrection were made the object of celebrations extending over several days, especially Holy Thursday (last supper, with evening *mass; Jesus betrayed by *Judas) and Good Friday (Jesus' death on the cross), the latter at first forming with Saturday and Sunday the *triduum* (three days) of the Passion and Resurrection, before this term came to be applied to the *triduum* before Easter.

In the Middle Ages, the main characteristics of the Easter feasts were the following. The three days before Easter had in common the solemn celebration of the night office, called **tenebrae* because the candles were extinguished one after another, with, during these three nights, the chanting of the Lamentations of *Jeremiah, understood as a sort of advance echo of the Passion. Meanwhile, the liturgical timetable of these days was gradually anticipated, until the Holy Thursday mass and the main *office of Friday were celebrated in the morning instead of the evening and the Easter vigil was also anticipated on Saturday morning.

On Holy Thursday, while the *hours of the office turned attention mainly to the beginning of the Passion, two celebrations prepared more directly for the Easter festivity, viz. the chrismal mass, proper to the *bishop (in which he consecrated the holy *oils, used mainly at *baptism and *confirmation); and the reconciliation of public *penitents by the bishop, whose disuetude in the course of the Middle Ages is ill known, while, since canon 21 of the fourth *Lateran council (1215), private *confession was obligatory before Easter *communion. Above all, no longer just in *cathedrals but in all churches, on the evening of Holy Thursday, mass was celebrated at the hour when Jesus instituted the *Eucharist at the Last Supper. In the final centuries of the Middle Ages there developed, after the Thursday mass, the *adoration of the Eucharist, preserved until Easter in an "Easter *sepulchre". At the same hour, the altars were despoiled of their cloths and ornaments, and this action was affected by a double symbolism: that of the interrupted *sacraments and that of the Passion. Meanwhile, at least in the great churches, a priest performed, like Jesus at the supper, the *washing of feet, also called *mandatum* (commandment) because of an anthem beginning with that word, which evoked the new commandment of charity.

On Good Friday and Holy Saturday, up to the Easter vigil, neither mass nor any other sacramental actions were celebrated and, on Friday, communion with the Eucharist consecrated the day before became more rare. On Friday, instead of mass, the main liturgical activity comprised *readings, especially that of the Passion according to St John; solemn *orations (the oldest Roman form of universal *prayer); and the adoration of the *cross by all the faithful, with the singing of the **Improperia*, *i.e.* Jesus' reproaches to his people, and the hymn **Pange lingua*.

After the day of Holy Saturday, a day without any liturgy other than that of *divine office, the Easter vigil, which was originally just the celebration of the death and resurrection, had a complex structure. It began with the blessing of the fire and that of the Easter candle, which symbolized the risen *Christ (this blessing, sung by a *deacon, was called from its first word **Exultet* [Let the host of angels exult]). Then followed the *readings, twelve or four in number according to place, accompanied by orations, attributable to St Leo and St *Gregory the Great, showing that they were chosen as prophecies of Christ the Saviour, of the Church and of Christian initiation. Then came the blessing of the baptismal *water, which in the Middle Ages was followed, at least at the papal mass, by the baptism and confirmation of some *children. Finally was celebrated the mass of the Resurrection, in which the singing of the **Gloria in excelsis* was accompanied by the ringing of the *bells, followed soon after by the singing of the *Alleluia*, the song *par excellence* of Paschal joy. The mass of Easter day, though much more solemn and more popular, comprised only two peculiarities: in many places, before mass (or at the end of the night office), the (Carolingian) chant of the *Quem quaeritis* (Whom do ye seek?), a sort of dialogue between the *angels and the women coming to the tomb, the origin of liturgical *drama; and the *sequence **Victimae paschali* (To the paschal victim).

Easter week (following the feast of Easter), which was originally a sort of retreat for the newly baptized, kept a particular importance in the Middle Ages (each day having a proper mass), and the first two days at least were holidays.

P. Jounel, "The Paschal cycle", *CaP*, 4, *The Liturgy and Time*, London, 1986. – H. Auf Der Maur, *Feiern im Rhythmus der Zeit I*, Regensburg, 1983 ("Gottesdienst der Kirche", 5). – R. Amist, *La veillée pascale dans l'Eglise latine*, 1, *Le rite romain*, Paris, 1999 ("Liturgie", 11).

Pierre-Marie Gy

**EBBO OF REIMS (775-851).** Born in *Germany, died at *Hildesheim. Ebbo became archbishop of *Reims in 813 when his foster-brother *Louis the Pious mounted the throne, but he made the mistake of intervening, with varying success, in the quarrels between Louis and his son *Lothar (he was finally deposed by *Charles the Bald in 841). In 822 he was appointed by Pope *Paschal I as *legate to the lands of the North with a *mission to Christianize them. He had the support of a protégé of the *Franks, a certain Haraldr, but, as the latter was expelled and never managed to re-establish himself, the mission that Ebbo had personally undertaken to *Denmark remained without sequel (823).

*The Gospel Book of Ebbo* (now in the Municipal Library at Epernay, is one of the finest works of the Caroloingian period. Its dramatic representation of man and its vibrant penmanship make it unique of its kind.

E. Lesne, *La Hiérarchie Episcopale en Gaule et en Germanie*, Paris, 1905.

Régis Boyer

**EBNER, CHRISTINE (1277-1356).** Christine Ebner was the dominant personality of the *convent of *Dominican *nuns at *Engelthal, one of the centres of mystical life in her time. Daughter of a patrician family of *Nuremberg, from her earliest youth she had *visions and extraordinary spiritual experiences which she wrote down in various works. Alongside the description of experiences of *ascesis and the life of *prayer, Christine Ebner's main care was to elucidate a representation of the image of *God, essentially experienced as He-who-loves. The form of this encounter is primarily dialogue. In a work that she devoted to the mystical experiences of deceased sisters of her convent, the world appears as a universe of *grace. By her life and work, in which she developed a religiosity not based on fear, Christine Ebner was among the most important *women of her time.

U. Peters, "Das 'Leben' der Christine Ebner", *Abendländische Mystik im Mittelalter*, K. Ruh (ed.), Stuttgart, 1986, 402-422. – S. Ringler, "Christine Ebner", *Mein Herz schmilzt wie Eis am Feuer*, J. Thiele (ed.), Stuttgart, 1988, 146-159.

Siegfried Ringler

**EBNER, MARGARET (1291-1351).** Born in 1291, died 20 June 1351 at Maria Medingen, Margaret came from a patrician family, the Ebner of Donauwörth, and in 1305 entered the *convent of *Dominican *nuns at Maria Medingen (Medingen, near Dillingen on the Danube). Through *Henry of Nördlingen, Margaret came into sustained epistolary contact with places where the Friends of God were settled, such as Basel and *Strasbourg, as well as with the convents of *Unterlinden at *Colmar, *Adelhausen at *Freiburg im Breisgau and St Agnes at *Cologne. Her meeting with Henry of Nördlingen, which was to determine her life, led to a spiritual *friendship. Through him, she became the central figure of the movement known as the Friends of God.

The peculiarity of Margaret's situation was that over long years of instability and psychological and spiritual illness, which went so far as to provoke paralyses and trigger off depressions, she was nonetheless endowed with exceptional interior gifts. The understanding spiritual accompaniment of Henry of Nördlingen allowed Margaret to take upon herself both her sufferings and weaknesses and the mystical experiences that disconcerted her. On the advice of her spiritual director, she began from 1344-1348 to write down an account of her mystical experiences, the *Revelations*. Reading this work as well as Henry's *letters and Margaret's one surviving letter, we remark the notable influence of *Mechthild of Magdeburg's *Flowing Light of the Godhead*. Henry had that work copied and sent to Medingen and, in an accompanying letter dated Basel 1345, presented it to the friend whom he directed in enthusiastic terms as a "linguistic miracle full of love written by the virginal organist", advising her to reread it ceaselessly (Strauch, 246, 128 f.). Admittedly, Henry long played the role of *spiritus rector*, but the *revelations evolved and Margaret became for him a teacher and prophet.

Henry believed that Margaret had a vocation. For him, she was not just a "visible road to *God" (Strauch, 235, 12), he also ascribed to her a prophetic mission to the whole Church. He went beyond the simple stage of intersubjective relationship with Margaret Ebner and added to his *preaching all the experiences she delivered to him.

By profound *contemplation of the joys and sufferings of *Mary, it was revealed to her that no-one has ever known the true humanity and true divinity of Jesus as intimately as Mary and John. Margaret wished to bear the divine child spiritually in her very womb, which led Henry to designate her a disciple of Mary and a "God-bearer" (Strauch 204, 1; 195, 43). Alongside the great veneration she bore for the Childhood and *Name of Jesus, she interiorized *Christ's sufferings in her *meditation. Mary was the mediator of the five *wounds called "signs of love" (*Minnezaichen*), which were "impregnated" into her following the example of the "great lord St *Francis" (Strauch, 63, 14 f.; 144, 13 f.; 157, 7 f.).

Externally, her life was largely a path of suffering. However, the predominant impression on rereading the *Revelations* is of joy and inner peace. Her accounts always speak of God's *love, goodness and *mercy, by which she knew herself to be carried. What also strikes us is the spiritual freedom that presided over her adoption of personal positions on certain questions and her manner of behaving. She died in the odour of *sanctity. Soon after her death, her *tomb was erected in the *chapter house, which was later transformed into the Margaret Ebner chapel in view of a cult. This secular veneration of Margaret Ebner received official ecclesial recognition on 24 Feb 1979, when she was declared blessed. Her feast is 20 June.

P. Strauch, *Margarethe Ebner und Heinrich von Nördlingen. Ein Beitrag zur Geschichte der deutschen Mystik*, Freiburg im Breisgau, 1822 (re-ed. Amsterdam, 1966; "Revelations and letters"). – *Der seligen Margarethen Ebners Offenbarungen und Briefe*, H. Wilms (tr.), Vechta in Oldenburg, 1928 (Anthology).

M. Schmidt, *DSp*, 10, 1980, 338-340. – *VerLex*, 2, 1980, 303-306 (2nd ed.). – *TRE*, 9, 1982, 245 f. – T. Schneider, *Die seligen Margaretha Ebner*, Sankt Ottilien, 1985. – *Marienlexikon*, 4, Sankt Ottilien, 1992, 276. – M. Schmidt, "Introduction", *Margaret Ebner*, L. P. Hindsley (ed. and tr.), New York, 1993, 9-59.

Margot Schmidt

***ECCE HOMO.*** After the crowning with thorns, Pilate showed Jesus to the crowd amassed before the praetorium and said: "Behold the man!" And the crowd cried: "Away with him, away with him, crucify him" (Jn 19, 14-15). In iconography, the theme is represented mainly in the 15th c.: before that, we meet it on *ivories and in illuminated manuscripts of the *Ottonian period. Jesus is depicted on a rostrum, or at the top of a staircase; he wears a crown of thorns, a purple *cloak, and holds a reed sceptre in his bound hands. On his bared breast, we see traces of the blows given at the *flagellation. A cord is knotted around his neck (as on the *Bamberg altarpiece, *c.*1429; Munich, Picture-Gallery). *Tears sometimes run down his cheeks.

E. Panofsky, "Imago Pietatis. Ein Beitrag zur Typengeschichte des Schmerzensmannes und der Maria Mediatrix", *Festschrift für Max J. Friedländer zum 60. Geburtstage*, Leipzig, 1927, 261-308. – H. Belting, *Das Bild und sein Publikum im Mittelalter*, Berlin, 1981. – H. Belting, *Likeness and Presence. A History of the Image before the Era of Art*, Chicago, 1994. – E. Panofsky, *Peinture et dévotion en Europe du nord à la fin du Moyen Âge*, Paris, 1997.

Daniel Russo

**ECCLESIOLOGY.** The concept of ecclesiology is late: as such, ecclesiology hardly appears in the Middle Ages, unless as an appendix to *canon law, *christology or the treatise on the *sacraments. So we are being anachronistic when we deal with the medieval Church in the framework of ecclesiological thought; we do not find, *e.g.* in St *Thomas Aquinas, any special treatise devoted to the Church. For the medievals, the Church was, in the Pauline formula, the body of *Christ (1 Cor 12, 12-14; Rom 12, 4 f.).

From the early Middle Ages, in the West, *ecclesia* indistinctly designated the Church, as the community of priests and people, and the *Empire or Christian society, *respublica christiana*, particularly after the death of *Charlemagne. The Church was a "quasi-person", supra-individual; it was mother, spouse, body, as we have seen; it was also holy and universal; it was the "people of *God". Christ was the head of this body, though whether in his humanity or his divinity is hard to determine precisely.

The Church was not just the body of Christ; it gradually became a "mystical" body (*corpus mysticum*). At the end of this evolution, we find the formula of Pope *Boniface VIII: "*Unam sanctam catholicam . . . quae unum corpus mysticum repraesentat, cuius caput Christus*" (*bull *Unam sanctam*, 18 Nov 1302). This transition from sacramental body to ecclesial body took place between the mid 12th and the early 14th century. To the notion of *corpus mysticum*, rich in spiritual matter, was progressively added, thanks to the contribution of the *Decretists, a legal and social dimension. The *corpus mysticum* – the Church – was one; its head, *Christ, was one; the *pope, as successor of *Peter to whom Jesus had entrusted the mission of building the Church (*Petrus petra*), was the vicar of Christ; he was the supreme head of the *respublica christiana*; thus the *doctrine of the Church joined up with arguments for papal *theocracy. St Thomas, or rather his continuator *Ptolemy of Lucca, said in his *De regimine principum* that "the supreme pontiff is the head of a mystical body of all believers". As mystical body, visible body, the Church contained all human reality; it still had to be shown that the Roman Church was holder of the primacy, which was claimed by *James of Viterbo and *Giles of Rome in their respective treatises, on the basis of the succession to the apostolic see.

Within a Church thus enlarged to the dimensions of *Christendom, papal *authority, from being purely spiritual, gradually became a power of legal or even political authority, which was a major ecclesiological turning-point: relations between the Churches and that of *Rome, *a fortiori* with the *laity, were one of subordination, which theologians expressed with a copious supply of organic or organicist metaphors, or by evoking father-son relations, etc.

*Gregory VII was the true inventor of papal monarchy, enjoying, in the name of the *freedom of the Church, an autonomy on the legal level, justified by Mt 16, 19, concerning the power of the keys, *i.e.* that of binding and loosing. It was not until *Dante, early in the 14th c., that the pontiff's moral and spiritual supremacy was affirmed over an emperor considered to be his equal. For the author of the *Commedia*, Church and *Empire were, in their universality, one and the same reality. It was this inclusive vision of the Church that would long be an "epistemological obstacle" to the formation of a *doctrine or a group of doctrines favourable to what Georges de Lagarde has called the "birth of the lay spirit in the decline of the Middle Ages" (*La Naissance de l'esprit laïque au déclin du Moyen Âge*, 5 vol., Paris-Louvain, 1956-1963), *i.e.* the demand for autonomy and independence of political power in a human community or society that no longer identified with the Church as such, whose institutions were different from ecclesiastical institutions themselves. For the opponents of papal theocracy fought the doctrine of the Church, either discussing step by step the interpretation of arguments taken from Scripture or of another nature, or proposing their own vision of ecclesiology.

Marsilian ecclesiology was of this type: it is a good example of what could be considered a sort of *compendium* of the ecclesiology of the declining Middle Ages, especially in the *Defensor pacis* (tr. A. Gewirth, Toronto, 1980). The *corpus mysticum* was then losing its legal-political coherence, if we believe the definition of it given by *Marsilius of Padua. To begin with, the priests form a part of the city; they are not the whole of it: the Church-Christian society definition is crumbling. Next, the Church is "the whole of the faithful who believe in Christ and invoke his name, and all the parts of that whole in each community, even domestic" (*Defensor pacis*, II, II, 4; see J. Quillet, *La Philosophie politique de Marsile de Padoue*, Paris, 1970, p. 167-181). Such a definition, specifies Marsilius, conforms to the sense that the Apostles conferred on the Church. In his rejection of the papal ecclesiology, Marsilius demands a return to apostolic times, to the early Church, the *poverty of Christ: admittedly, the Church as he defines it, *i.e.* a group of believers transcending the institutions of the earthly city, retains the power of order, power of the keys, to administer the *sacraments, to exhort and advise the Christian; its members still have charge of **cura animarum*; but they have no coercive power, nor must they have their own jurisdiction. At the beginning, the Church comprised the Apostles and the people of believers; so the Church must be "democratic" in its basis, representative in its functioning; it should not be governed in an oligarchical or monarchical way; in all that concerns its institutional and social life, it must be subject to the civil authorities.

In no case is the Church identified with the Roman Church. Admittedly, the papacy is of divine institution; but the designation of the *pope is a human affair. In all cases where a pope might be *heretical, a *council must be called to make a ruling, whether in matters of *faith, or to depose the heretical pope. For Marsilius of Padua, since the Church is the whole of the faithful (*universitas fidelium*), the general council is its most representative, most authentic and most appropriate tribunal: it is the council that is, in the proper sense, universal. It is the emperor who calls it, as in the earliest times of the Church; in this perspective, the pope is no more than, as *Nicholas of Cusa put it in the 15th c., *primus inter pares*. The council is composed of laity and priests, all equally Christ's faithful. Though the *priesthood is of divine origin, only essential *authority has been entrusted to it by Christ; this is the power of order or sacramental power. William of *Ockham takes up the criticism of curialist ecclesiology, from a different point of view to that of Marsilius; he defines the Church as *congregatio fidelium*, an admittedly traditional expression, but he gives it a "*nominalist" sense: it is the "sum of believers". These positions would influence the conciliar debates (*Constance and *Basel) that followed the *Great Schism (1378-1417), but in the end the papalist arguments would prevail in the mid 15th century.

H. de Lubac, *Corpus mysticum. L'eucharistie et l'Église au Moyen Âge*, Paris, 1944. – W. Ullmann, *The Growth of Papal Government in the Middle Ages. A Study in the Ideological Relation of Clerical to Lay Power*, London, 1955. – Y. Congar, *L'Ecclésiologie du haut Moyen Âge. De saint Grégoire le Grand à la désunion entre Byzance et Rome*, Paris, 1968. – Y. Congar, *L'Église, de saint Augustin à l'époque moderne*, Paris, 1970. – *HChr*, 6, 1990, 271-297.

Jeannine Quillet

***ÉCHEVIN.*** Deliberating member of a town council. Heirs of the *scabini* of the Carolingian period, charged with expounding the law to the *count's *court, in the 12th c. the *échevins* became, in the communes of *Flanders and northern France, the advisers of the mayor in the exercise of all his powers. This model later spread to the West and gradually, from the 14th c., in parallel with that of the *consulat* of the Midi, became the type of regime of all the *bonnes villes* endowed with municipal officials.

A. Giry, *Les Établissements de Rouen*, Paris, 1883, 13-23. – A. Luchaire,

*Les communes françaises*, Paris, 1890, 151-175. – L. Halphen, *Charlemagne et l'empire carolingien*, Paris, 1947, 187-192 – B. Chevalier, *Les Bonnes Villes de France du XIV^e au XVI^e siècle*, Paris, 1982, 198-202.

Bernard Chevalier

**ECHTERNACH.** The abbey of Echternach, in modern Luxemburg not far from *Trier, was founded in the 7th c. on an *estate belonging to the Pippinid family. Irmina, mother-in-law of Pippin II (Pippin of Herstal), mayor of the palace of *Austrasia, gave the *villa of Echternach to *Willibrord. This *Anglo-Saxon had come to evangelize *Frisia and made Echternach a training centre for missionaries. On 13 May 706, Pippin II and his wife Plectrude increased the *abbey's territory by *donation. Thus Echternach became a family abbey of the Pippinids. Willibrord retired there at the end of his life and died there in 739. From his time, the **scriptorium* of Echternach was quite active. The so-called *Martyrology and Calendar of St Willibrord, in Anglo-Saxon *script, seem to have been written between 700 and 710 by a scribe named Laurentius. But Echternach's most celebrated manuscript is the famous gospel-book, now in Paris (BNF, ms. lat. 9389), which must have been written and painted by monks of Insular origin.

Willibrord's successors, Abbots Adalbert († *c.*775) and Deornrad were also Anglo-Saxons. Deornrad welcomed Willihad during the revolt of the Saxon *Widukind and sheltered him between 782 and 785. A friend of *Alcuin, Abbot Deornrad became archbishop of *Sens where he died in 797. Under Abbot Ado (795-818), the **scriptorium* was still active. The *abbey was rich thanks to the *pilgrims who came to honour St Willibrord's *tomb and to the numerous landed possessions that surrounded the monastery. This *wealth aroused envy, and soon lay *abbots were put at the head of the monastery. The counts of *Luxemburg considered it a part of their properties. In the late 10th c., the monastery was reformed thanks to the actions of Count Sigefroid and the monks of Saint-Maximin at Trier. In 973, the Rule of St *Benedict was restored and the *canons were replaced by 40 monks ruled by Abbot Ravengar († 1007). The *scriptorium* and the *school were once more very active. We still possess a dozen manuscripts of authors of Classical Antiquity, particularly *Boethius, that were copied at Echternach to be used in the school. This followed the programme established by *Gerbert at the school of *Reims.

A new decadence necessitated a new *reform under the influence of *Cluny. Abbot Urold was deposed in 1028 and replaced by a monk from Saint-Maximin, Humbert. Under his abbacy (1028-1058), the *scriptorium* became very active again. The Emperor *Henry III commissioned *de luxe* manuscripts from it, such as his *Book of Hours and the celebrated Codex Aureus. The abbots continued to receive privileges from the emperors throughout the Middle Ages. In 1496, Abbot Burchard Poszwin reformed the abbey once more and built a tomb in the choir of the church to house the *reliquary of St Willibrord. The abbey was secularized in 1793. But *pilgrimages to St Willibrord continued. The pilgrims had the custom of moving towards the sanctuary in a sort of *dance, five steps forward and three steps back. This dance, which appeared in the 15th c., is still performed on Whit Tuesday.

The rich *library, which in 1761 numbered 160 manuscripts, was dispersed at the French Revolution. Part was sold to the duke of Saxe-Gotha-Altenburg and part was taken to the National Library in Paris, which still preserves 85 manuscripts.

C. Wampach, "Echternach", *DHGE*, 14, 1960, 1365-1375. – J. Schroeder, *Bibliothek und Schule der Abtei Echternach um die Jahrtausendwende*, Luxemburg, 1977. – C. Rabel, É. Palazzo, *Les Plus Beaux Manuscrits de l'abbaye d'Echternach conservés à la Bibliothèque nationale de Paris*, Paris, 1989. – N. Netzer, *Cultural Interplay in the Eighth Century: the Trier Gospels and the Making of a Scriptorium at Echternach*, Cambridge, 1994.

Pierre Riché

**ECKHART, MEISTER (1260-1328).** Eckhart was born in *Thuringia. He entered the *Dominican *convent of *Erfurt and in 1277 studied the *liberal arts at *Paris. He studiwed at the Dominican *Studium generale* at *Cologne (possible meeting with *Albert the Great); then, as a bachelor at Paris, in 1293 he read the **Sentences* of *Peter Lombard. In 1294, he was *prior at Erfurt and *vicar in Thuringia. From 1302 to 1303 he was "*magister actu regens*", *i.e.* professor at Paris, then from 1303 to 1311 provincial of the Dominican Order for *Saxony, and from 1307 also vicar general for *Bohemia. From 1311 to 1313 he was professor at Paris, from 1314 to 1322 vicar of the order's general at *Strasbourg, and from 1323 head of the *Studium generale* of Cologne. In 1326 he was accused of professing *heretical *doctrines by the archbishop of Cologne. There ensued an investigation of his case by the *Inquisition. Meister Eckhart died probably at *Avignon or Cologne.

According to Eckhart, "the being and life of every creature depend only on the search for *God and his ceaseless pursuit [literally *hunt*]" (*German works*, III, 368, 7 f.). All that is has all its *being from God. Being itself has no other foundation than himself, immediately. For Eckhart, being is dual: 1. *esse absolute*, the being of God, which exists of itself, gives itself to itself, is permanent; 2. *esse hoc et hoc*, *esse rerum*, which cannot exist by itself, but is essentially a being that is received. Every creature receives its being uninterruptedly from God, in such a way that this being in it does not cease to flow out and become. The variable *esse rerum* represents the external reality of things determined by their proper form.

But being is only God's antechamber, his temple is *reason (*Vernünftigkeit*). *Intellectus* is for Eckhart the key to gain access to pure, limpid being. It does not stop at images, but goes to the root and recognises the *principia substantiales*. *Incredibilitas intellectus* results from the fact that God is at the same time *intellectus* and *intelligere*, since the *creator* is not *creabile*. Thus, *knowledge is never more than a limited knowledge. *Unitas* is the root of all knowledge but *unitas intellectus* subsists solely in the *deus unus*.

But how can man arrive at the knowledge that is essential for him? Following the epistemological tradition of Empedocles and *Aristotle, which Eckhart accepts, a thing can only be known by its identical, so that God can only be known by God himself. By the birth of God in his *soul, *man is made capable of becoming "son of God" by God. Insofar as he is born in the human soul, God can be recognised by God in man. Man, who by the birth of God in his soul can know God as God, is also capable of understanding the christological dimension of the word of God as that of the Son responding to the Father. God as unique is acting in the soul. "The whisper of God . . . draws the soul towards itself, towards unity with God and forms it according to God" (*German works*, III, 569, 1 f.). At the bottom of the soul shines the light of God which spreads out and is exteriorized. But finally, the birth of God in the soul is a *mystery that cannot be explained adequately: "What the soul is at bottom, no-one knows. What we can know of it must be of a supernatural order, given by *grace: there, God acts in *mercy"

(*German works*, I, 124, 4-6).

The man who corresponds to God, *i.e.* who is cognizant by reason of the birth of God in his soul, is a being apart, withdrawn. He progressively leaves behind his enslaving images and thus becomes free and can live in quietude. The withdrawn man is the poor in spirit vaunted by the beatitudes, "he is a poor man who wants nothing, knows nothing, possesses nothing" (*German works*, II, 488, 5 f.). The poor (see *Latin works*, III, 337, 1 f.) insofar as they are *nihil habentes* can know "*esse nudum et indistinctum*". The *una dispositio* of the poor for which nothing can be substituted, which puts him in relation with the one God, is *relinquere omnia*. So the poor man is the free man, because free of all desire for possession, of knowing or having. He is free of his own thoughts and images which are deformed by the mode of having, so that he does not desire God, the *creation and himself in an egoistical way. But in this retreat, in this *freedom, he is open to God as creature and as "me". Since he can leave behind the possessive personal God, he can encounter the true living God. By letting God be God, he finally knows God, the creature and his "me". Hence this freedom is fertile.

According to Eckhart, there is only one *justice: the justice of God. God is creator and dispenser of *love, since he is love itself. Hence there is only one love (whose origin is God). By his birth in the human soul, God makes man capable of loving. In becoming son of God, I become loving. The man who loves is essentially moulded by the divine love. God "himself is the love by which we love" (*Latin works*, IV, 63, 11). Who loves God, truly loves God, himself and his neighbour. In loving these last two in God, he frees himself from a love of self and neighbour that can be destructive.

The man born of God becomes also a man of peace, since "what is born of God seeks peace and goes towards peace" (*German works*, I, 118, 5 f.). Everything has need of divine peace. Where this peace is introduced, anarchy, fruit of the absence of peace, disappears. The peace of God creates a pacific *order of things and of human beings. The man to whom God is present becomes "a countenance of peace" (*German works*, II, 352, 1 f.).

Meister Eckhart, *Die deutschen und lateinischen Werke*, Stuttgart, 1936 f.

N. Largier, *Bibliographie zu Meister Eckhart*, Fribourg (Switz.), 1989. – U. Kern, *Die Anthropologie des Meister Eckhart*, Hamburg, 1994 (bibl., 207-253). – N. Largier, "Meister Eckhart. Perspektiven der Forschung", *Zeitschrift f. deutsche Philologie*, 114, 1995, 29-98. – A. de Libera, *Eckhart, Suso, Tauler et la divinisation de l'homme*, Paris, 1996.

Udo Kern

**ECONOMY AND *TAXIS*.** In Byzantine thought, the two words *taxis* (*order, hierarchy) and *oikonomia* (management, arrangement, compromise or measure of "economy" in the technical sense of the term) served to convey two fundamental aspects of reality and action, whether in the spiritual universe, in human society or in the whole cosmos.

The concept of *taxis* indicates the primary quality of a whole, which is the happy arrangement of the parts, united by relations of superiority and subordination and constituting a hierarchy of *creation, as expounded by *Dionysius the Areopagite. Thus the term *taxis* covers various senses, going from the abstract to the concrete, which can be summed up under the four following points: 1. good ordering of the elements in a whole, order; 2. disposition of troops, corps of troops; 3. tables of classification of administrative units (civil or ecclesiastical districts) and of titles and positions (civil or ecclesiastical dignities); 4. place or rank of each unit or each person in these hierarchies (order of precedence).

As image of *God, in whom order is perfect and immutable, the material and human world must reproduce its model, the celestial order, as well as it can. *Sin has broken the order (*taxis*) and breathed disorder (*ataxia*) into the *creation. Restoration, at least virtual, of order was obtained by the incarnation of the Son of God, which constitutes the "economy" of *salvation in the sense that it is the measure adopted by God to save man. Here is how this notion fits logically into the various meanings of the word *oikonomia*: 1. conduct of domestic affairs (economy in the etymological sense); 2. God's conduct in obtaining man's salvation thanks to the incarnation of the Son (economy of salvation); 3. the general spirit in which the Church acts to ensure man's salvation as well as it can, short of derogating from the rigour of the laws (*akribeia*), and concrete measures dictated by this general principle (ecclesiastical economy); 4. economic or fiscal revenues allocated to a person to provide for his needs (fiscal economy, in the sense of *pronoia*).

*Taxis* remained the rule and the ideal model. *Oikonomia* was a means to recreate order, whether by a return to the old order or by setting up a new order. Thus *oikonomia* did not constitute a destruction of order and did not authorize a revolution (*kainotomia*), merely an evolution. The **basileus* was at the summit of the human pyramid and reproduced on earth the image of God, from whom all things proceeded. If he was no longer capable of maintaining order, which was his primary *duty, the emperor could be legitimately and legally deposed.

H. Kotsonis, *[Problems of ecclesiastical economy]*, Athens, 1957 (in Greek). – H. Ahrweiler, *L'Idéologie politique de l'Empire byzantin*, Paris, 1975, 129-147.

Albert Failler

**ECSTASY.** A mystical state characterised by the fact that the *soul feels *God's presence very strongly, to the point of experiencing the feeling of being one with him. This supreme degree of the relationship between man and God was first described by St *Bernard in his commentary on the *Song of Songs, an Old Testament book interpreted in the *Cistercian spiritual milieu as a dialogue between God, identified with the lover, and the soul presented as the beloved of the All-Powerful. To attain that state, which the *abbot of *Clairvaux considered exceptional, the soul must divest itself of carnal *love – which consists of loving oneself – and rise above love of neighbour and love of *Christ's humanity to be capable of loving God for himself. At the end of this spiritual ascent, the soul becomes worthy of receiving God, who makes it his bride.

Ecstasy remains inferior to what will be the face-to-face vision of God in the afterlife, but it conforms the soul to some degree to the beloved object with which it is united spiritually. The man or woman who benefit from it do not become God, but they restore in themselves the divine image cast down by *sin. *William of Saint-Thierry goes further, emphasizing that ecstasy makes the creature participate in this life in the glory of the *resurrection by restoring the *soul to the rhythm of the uncreated and creative *Trinity.

In the 13th and 14th cc., in particular among the numerous laywomen and *nuns who at that time attained a high-level spiritual experience, the search for mystical ecstasy became a major preoccupation. The majority of them sought to reach this by an intense *meditation full of compassion on the various stages of the *Passion and on the body of *Christ, instrument of *salvation as well as guarantee of eternity through the *sacrament of the *Eucharist. In this perspective, the ultimate objective was not so much union with God, which could only be partial and temporary in this life, as the search for a deification by assimilation to God's very being, following the way recommended by Meister *Eckhart, in order to permit the soul to become by *grace what God is by *nature. At the mystics' level of experience, ecstasy was distinguished from *raptus*, characterised by loss of bodily feeling, by the fact that the soul, having attained the plenitude of loving union with God, benefited from "spiritual consolations" that were reflected on the bodily level by sensations of heat, sweetness, drunkenness, lightness or liquefaction, which were described and analysed at length by the great 14th-c. mystics, particularly St *Catherine of Siena and St *Dorothea of Montau, or by their biographers.

"Extase", *DSp*, 4, 2, 1961, 2045-2189. – P. Dinzelbacher, *Dictionnaire de la mystique*, Turnhout, 1993.

André Vauchez

**EDDAS.** The name "Eddas" designates two very different though complementary Old Icelandic works.

The first, called the *Poetic Edda* or *Elder Edda* or, by virtue of a tenacious error, *Edda of Saemundr*, is a collection of mythological, gnomic, ethical, magical and heroic poems discovered in *Iceland in 1646 by Bishop Brynjólfr Sveinsson, and called the Codex Regius. The thirty or so poems it contains, of differing length, age and provenance, to which are customarily added some similar texts preserved by certain *sagas, represent the whole of the literary documents available to us for our knowledge of the Scandinavian religion. No-one knows who their authors were, but in general, in the state in which we now have them, they were written by Icelanders, probably towards the end of the 12th c., though the Codex Regius is a century later. They may hand down an immemorial oral tradition, though their elaborate form, which respects the great canons of *scaldic poetry (alliterations, stress and play of longs and shorts), requires caution on this point. They are, in any case, very *Scandinavian, some possibly originating in *Norway, others (notably the heroic ones) in *Denmark, some more expressly in Iceland. Some of them seem, by the archaism of their form (*e.g.* Hamdismál), to go far back in time, to the first stage of this culture (8th c.); others are contemporary with the redaction of the Codex. At all events the traditions they hand down, which are supported by all sorts of other witnesses, are certainly authentic and mostly concern, as well as *Germany (the Sigurdr-Siegfried cycle) or even the whole area of Indo-European expansion (the history of the marvellous Smith or *Völundarkvida*), the Scandinavian North in its entirety, though *Sweden appears to be less present.

It is convenient to classify them according to the god they celebrate: Odinn (Hávamál), Thórr (Thrymskvida), Freyr (Skirnismál), Freyja (Hyndluljód), etc. Standing apart is the heroic cycle concerning Sigurdr slayer of the *dragon Fáfnir and his prototype or archetype Helgi, himself present under two different figures. The mark of these texts is concision, rapidity, attachment to facts, to immediate data, with no concession to lyricism, *contemplation or *meditation. The major law is dynamism: gods and heroes march unflinchingly towards the consummation of their destiny, which they know in advance and make it a point of *honour to fulfil since such is their condition and since they see in it a *sign of the incarnation of the sacred. The learned form, the play of sonorities and *rhythms communicate a strange strength of conviction to these poems. As a general rule, they are gnomic in character, but the great heroic elegies in which proud lovers (Brynhildr, Gudrún) deplore their tragic loves in an almost rarefied atmosphere can attain an almost intolerable intensity. The two jewels of the collection are incontestably the *Hávamál* and the *Völuspá*. The former is a long composite poem which, in its first part, the most famous, brings together what seems to have been the wisdom of the *Vikings: prudence, mistrust, a sense of practical realities, but also a cult of *friendship and a sense of human value. The latter is a group of Dantesque visions in which a seer retraces, in searing images, the mythical history of gods and men from the beginnings (golden age) to the universal regeneration, passing through the end of *time or Consummation-of-the-destiny-of-the-Powers (*Ragnarök*).

It is clear that, without the poems of the *Poetic Edda*, we would be reduced to stammering on the subject of Germanic mythology in general and Scandinavian in particular. The vision of *man, life and the world that they set out rejects all affectation, but in no case favours brute force. The texts of the *Edda* testify firstly to a poetic science of extreme elaboration, a pronounced taste for the fine formula and for *savoir-faire* used as technique. Secondly, they are the expression of men of action (who would one day be called Vikings) in love with the values of action: digression is not the rule, any more than dullness. But it is not as an exercise in martial strength that we must read them; they testify to a love of order, a sense of organisation that fits in very well with what we can know of the Scandinavian peoples of the Middle Ages. Thirdly and especially, these beautiful texts are bathed in a magical atmosphere that is also revealed by the intense thirst for more or less esoteric knowledge evidenced by all the gods. It is even justifiable to state that the religion that springs from these witnesses is one to which the third Dumézilian function is eminently applicable.

Very different is the so-called *Prose Edda* or, more properly, *Edda of Snorri*. This is a work that the great Icelandic writer, "historian", scald (poet) and saga-writer Snorri Sturluson (1178-1241) wrote in *c.*1220. A scald himself and hence familiar with the extremely sophisticated techniques without which it was impossible to compose scaldic strophes, Snorri grieved to see this science disappear under the effect of Christianity, which had been adopted by Iceland in 999. In fact, it was impossible to compose correct *scaldic poetry without a perfect knowledge of the old religion and its myths. So Snorri set himself to divulge these techniques. His work, after a Prologue of euhemeristic character (the gods are nothing but divinized men), is divided into three parts. The first or *Gylfaginning* (Fascination of Gylfi, a mythical king) gives with magisterial elegance an overall picture of the old Scandinavian religion: by a play of questions and answers, the Swedish King Gylfi obtains the satisfaction of all his curiosity, which is as much about the gods as about the origins of all things and certain great myths. This ordered exposition is the only one available to us on this subject. It constitutes a remarkable effort of organisation of the facts at the author's disposal and, even if it does not escape visible attempts at *interpretatio christiana* (or classical), it certainly echoes respectable traditions: all the same, Snorri overtly bases himself on the poems of the *Poetic Edda* which he often cites, just as it clearly appears that he had other sources, now lost, at his disposal. In consequence his work, even if it imitates the genre of *clavis metrica et rhythmica*, banal in the Europe of its time, and even if it is visibly reminiscent of other ordered tableaux bearing on related subjects, merits respect.

Secondly comes the *Skáldskaparmál* (properly: "poetics"). Scaldic poetry was forbidden to call beings and things by their name: it proceeded by metonymies or *heiti* (as saying "sail" for "boat") and periphrases or metaphors, or *kenningar* ("the rider of the sea-king's stallion", for "the sailor"). In this part, consequently, Snorri enumerates the various *heiti* and *kenningar* that can be used to designate all sorts of creatures – the gods included – and objects. On occasion he does not hesitate, to justify what he says, to relate a myth, the principle being to say nothing that is not rationally intelligible. A lightly dashed-off anecdote (why is *gold called Sif's hair?) or, on the contrary, a long ordered exposition (on the fortunes and misfortunes of Sigurdr Fáfnisbani, on the death of Baldr) are solicited in the appropriate place to justify this image or that type of formulation. There remains the *Háttatal* or Enumeration of metres, which was indeed the first part composed: in it Snorri praises a great Norwegian dignitary and his son-in-law, the king of Norway, thanking them for the hospitality they have given him. He does this by using and justifying the rules of workmanship, the hundred or so different metres that scaldic poetry has at its disposal. The whole of the *Edda of Snorri*, in its four parts, is an irreplaceable document for us. Apart from its intrinsic value – Snorri excells in the art of rapid, lively narration, enhanced by an altogether characteristic humour very strongly evocative of English understatement; his sense of composition and his art of dialogue make him one of the greatest Icelandic narrators or *sagnamenn* – the *Edda of Snorri* has a dual value for us: it clarifies and completes the often obscure texts of the *Poetic Edda*, especially inasmuch as it connects isolated fragments into a general presentation, and it represents the sole comprehensive picture available to us of a rather disparate mythology.

*Edda Snorra Sturlusonar udgivet efter Handskrifterne*, Kobenhavn, 1931. – *Edda. Die Lieder des Codex Regius nebst verwandten Denkmälern*, G. Neckel (ed.), Heidelberg, 1962 (4th ed. revised by H. Kuhn). – *The Poetic Edda*, U. Dronke (ed.), 2 vol., Oxford, 1969-1997 [in progress].

J. de Vries, *Altgermanische Religionsgeschichte*, 1-2, Berlin, 1956-1957 (2nd ed.). – E. O. G. Turville-Petre, *Myth and Religion of the North*, London, 1964. – F. Ström, *Nordisk Hedendom. Tro och sed i förkristen tid*, Göteborg, 1967 (2nd ed.). – P. Hallberg, *Old Icelandic Poetry*, Lincoln (NE), 1975. – *Edda: a Collection of Essays*, R.J. Glendinning (ed.), H. Bessason (ed.), Winnipeg, 1983. – *Old Norse-Icelandic Literature. A Critical guide*, C. J. Clover (ed.), J. Lindlow (ed.), *Islandica*, 45, Cornell, 1985 (the first three sections). – J. Kristjánsson, *Eddas and Sagas*, Reykjavik, 1988. – R. Boyer, *Yggdrasill. La religion des anciens Scandinaves*, Paris, 1992 (2nd ed.).

Régis Boyer

**EDINBURGH.** Established as the undisputed capital of the kingdom of *Scotland during the 15th c., Edinburgh has a history of occupation from the Iron Age. The genesis of the city was a hill-fort on what is now Castle Rock. The site, a rocky outcrop, and intensive later building development make it difficult to determine the plan of this fortification or of any associated settlement that may have existed there in the early Middle Ages.

In the 6th c., *Din Eidyn* was possessed by the native British Gododdin (the Romano-British *Votadini*). In 638 it fell to the *Angles and thereafter represented the northern limits of the kingdom of Northumberland. In the 10th c., it fell to the Gaelic Scots. For the next hundred years or so, Edinburgh was a frontier fortress under the control of the kings of the Scots, whose preferred residence was Dunfermline. Edinburgh's location became more secure when Malcolm III († 1093) extended his authority south to Berwick. Nevertheless, being in the extreme south-east of the kingdom rendered the city permanently vulnerable. It was attacked by the English, razed and changed hands several times during the conflicts of the late Middle Ages.

Edinburgh first appears as more than a royal fortress in the early 12th century. This is certainly due to lack of documentation for the earlier period. By the time David I founded Holyrood abbey, around 1128, at the foot of the ridge sloping eastward from Castle Rock, there was already a settlement on the ridge outside the castle gate (Castle Hill) which could be described as a burgh (*burgum*). Focused on a marketplace, now Lawnmarket, it probably existed in the 11th c. if not earlier. David I gave the new *abbey of Holyrood permission to found its own burgh (Canongate) between the abbey and the older, royal burgh.

Despite the damage suffered in recurrent English invasions, Edinburgh enjoyed great commercial success. From the nearby port of Leith on the Firth of Forth, the city could trade with the rest of Scotland, with *England and with the Continent. Its principal exports were wool and hides, with the addition of woollen cloth and fish in the 15th century. The loss of Berwick in 1333 made Edinburgh the chief *port of Scotland. Around the same time, in 1329 Robert Bruce issued Edinburgh's first borough *charter, granting the burgesses rights over the port of Leith and other privileges for a relatively low *feu-ferme* of 52 marks per annum. In 1376, the burgh contained about 400 houses, and had at least one suburb, at Cowgate in the valley south of the ridge where the *Dominican friars had been established around 1230.

Edinburgh's emergence as a political capital city dates from the accession of the Stewart dynasty. Holyrood abbey became the dynastic mausoleum. James II (1430-1460) was born, married and buried at Holyrood, where the royal apartments had grown to dominate the abbey. He granted Edinburgh a city wall and permitted royal land below the north side of Castle Rock to be flooded for defensive purposes. By 1483, Edinburgh was the permanent seat of government and justice and, as the principal royal residence, the centre of a flourishing late medieval court-culture. Further cultural advances such as the foundation of a *university and Scotland's first printing press did not occur until the 16th century.

I. MacIvor, *Edinburgh Castle*, London, 1983. – E. Ewan, *Townlife in fourteenth-century Scotland*, Edinburgh, 1990. – S. T. Driscoll, P. A. Yeoman, *Excavations within Edinburgh Castle in 1988-91*, Edinburgh, 1997.

Judith Everard

**EDMUND (*c*.840-869).** King of East Anglia (855-869). Little is known of St Edmund's life and reign. He is remembered chiefly because he was murdered by a Danish army led by Ívarr and Ubbe, and because this murder was commemorated by *Abbo of Fleury in his *Passio S. Eadmundi* (*BHL*, 2392). His body was translated in the 10th c. to the monastery of *Bury St Edmunds, which became the centre of his cult.

*Three Lives of English Saints*, M. Winterbottom (ed.), Toronto, 1972, 67-87 (*Passio S. Eadmundi*).

A. P. Smyth, *Scandinavian Kings in the British Isles, 850-880*, Oxford, 1977, 201-213. – M. Mostert, *King Edmund of East Anglia († 869)*, Ann Arbor (MI), 1986.

Michael Lapidge

*Earl Harold gives Edward the Confessor an account of his embassy to Normandy.* "Bayeux tapestry", 11th c.Bayeux, Musée de la Tapisserie.

**EDMUND RICH (*c.*1170-1240).** Born at Abingdon, educated at *Oxford and *Paris, Edmund Rich was treasurer of *Salisbury cathedral 1222-1234 and archbishop of *Canterbury 1234-1240 (elected in 1233). Although he reconciled King *Henry III and Richard the Marshal, his short episcopate was marred by *jurisdictional disputes. He died at Soissy (Seine-et-Marne) on 16 November 1240, *en route* to *Rome, and was buried in the *Cistercian monastery of *Pontigny, whose monks promoted his *cause as a second *Thomas Becket. Canonized by Pope *Innocent IV, 16 Dec 1246; feast day, 16 November.

*DHGE*, 14, 1960, 1441-45. – C. H. Lawrence, *St Edmund of Abingdon: A Study in Hagiography and History*, Oxford, 1960. – *NCE*, 5, 108-109.

Anne J. Duggan

**EDUCATION OF CHILDREN.** In the Middle Ages, the education of *children and adolescents took place in ways that depended both on the idea people had of the nature of childhood and on social milieu, and which varied over the centuries.

In aristocratic families, the young *child was educated by his mother who gave him some initial religious instruction and taught him his *prayers. From the age of seven, the boy was taken in charge by a tutor or by his father. As he grew, he submitted to physical exercises intended to make him a good knight. Around the age of twelve, he was entrusted to a friend or a neighbouring lord to prepare for his *dubbing. Girls remained in the family *castle, where they learned to embroider, to make *music and even to read. *Christine de Pizan, in the 14th c., wished that girls were well educated. A number of works could serve as guides to parents, like the *Father's instruction to his son*, Raymond *Lull's *Doctrina pueril* or the *Instructions of St Louis to his son Philip*.

Outside the *family, until the development of *schools and *universities, education took a variety of forms. During the early Middle Ages, in Celtic lands, fosterage consisted of entrusting one's child to a monk up to the age of puberty, before sending him, provisionally or permanently, to a monastery. Until the 11th c., this form of oblation committed the child for his whole life; then the child's freedom began to be taken into account and it was accepted that he could leave the monastery at adolescence. Oblation fell into disuse, but was not officially abolished until the end of the Middle Ages. We know the life of these little monks from monastic *customaries or from scholastic colloquies like that of Ælfric Bata (early 11th c.). Girls could also be entrusted to monasteries, but generally never to leave them.

Children of the people were brought up in their family. In the country, they took part very early in the work of the fields. In *towns, they were *apprenticed around the age of ten or twelve. We possess contracts between parents and *master that specify its conditions: the boy provides clothes, the patron bed and board. Some texts attest abuse by masters or accidents at work. Manuals were composed in preparation for trades, such as the *Manual of Commercial French* written in *England in 1415.

Religious education of children took place in the family or in church through the liturgy. It was especially from the 12th c. that *clerics attended to the religious instruction and the *sacraments received by children. While at the start of the Middle Ages *confirmation and *communion were given with *baptism, later these sacraments were not administered until the age of twelve. Children were recruited to become part of choirs; others, in monasteries, occupied a privileged place in the liturgical ceremonies. December, the month of St *Nicholas and the feast of the *Innocents, was the month of childhood, marked by the feast of Christmas which brought children together around the *crib.

Finally, we must not forget that the Church came to the aid of unhappy childhood. From the 8th c., orphanages received abandoned children. The Order of the Holy Spirit specialized in this charitable work, whose beneficiaries were often destined to become clerics.

N. Orme, *Education in the West of England, 1066-1548*, Exeter, 1976. – J.A.H. Moran, *Education and Learning in the Ciity of York, 1300-1560*, York, 1979. – N. Orme, *From Childhood to Chivalry: the Education of the English Kings and Aristocracy, 1066-1530*, London, 1984.

Pierre Riché

**EDWARD THE CONFESSOR (*c.*1005-1066).** Edward was the son of King Æthelred "the Unready" († 1016) and Emma, daughter of a duke of *Normandy. Because of this Norman connection and perhaps because, after the death of his father, Emma had married the Danish King *Cnut whose dynasty ruled *England until 1042, Edward was sent to Normandy to be educated (1017). He remained there in a sort of exile for 24 years until, following the deaths of Cnut (1035) and his two sons, Edward was rather surprisingly chosen to be king (1042). However, in order to retain royal control, Edward was obliged to rely on the support of the ruthless earl Godwine (whose daughter Eadgyth/Edith he married in 1045 and whose son Harold was to be Edward's short-lived successor).

Edward's reign was peaceful on the whole, marred only by power struggles among the English *nobility. He was physically strong, a keen hunter and a shrewd diplomat, who exploited his own childlessness by making promises of the succession to, among others, *William duke of Normandy. As a result of his contacts on the Continent, Edward surrounded himself with foreign advisers and appointed many Norman and Lotharingian *clerics to English *bishoprics, which in itself proved a source of friction with the English nobility. His reputation for holiness was based on generosity to the poor, his allegedly unconsummated marriage to Eadgyth/Edith, as well as his munificent endowment of *Westminster Abbey. He rebuilt the *abbey on a lavish scale; the new building was consecrated shortly before his death, and he was buried there. It was principally Westminster Abbey that promoted the cult of the holy King Edward "the Confessor" (feast day: 5 Jan; translation: 13 Oct).

*The Life of Edward who Rests at Westminster*, F. Barlow (ed.), Oxford, 1992 (2nd ed.).

F. Barlow, *Edward the Confessor*, London, 1970 (re-ed. New Haven, 1997). – F. Barlow, *The English Church 1000-1066*, London, 1979 (2nd ed.). – P. A. Clarke, *The English Nobility under Edward the Confessor*, Oxford, 1994.

Michael Lapidge

**EDWARD I OF ENGLAND (1239-1307).** Born 17 June 1239, the eldest son of *Henry III and Eleanor of Provence, during his father's life Edward had painful experience of the perils of a weak *Crown. His own reign can be interpreted as a response to that experience, especially in his determination to improve the position of the Crown. In all aspects of government, Edward was active and forceful, and particularly effective as a military leader and strategic planner, aspects in which his father had singularly failed. He was on *crusade when his father died (1272), and returned to *England two years later with the renown of a crusader and military experience which he put to excellent use in wars against the Welsh, the Scots and *Philip IV of France, although final victory eluded him in *Scotland and *Gascony. He conquered and fortified *Wales relatively easily (1276-1277, 1282-1283), but his attempted conquest of Scotland (begun 1297) was ultimately an expensive failure, and the unpopular Gascon war (1294-98), provoked by Philip IV, achieved nothing except a return to the *status quo ante bellum*. His domestic policy was dominated by concern for good law and the maintenance of royal rights. A series of statutes and legal definitions, many drafted by his *chancellor, Robert Burnell, reformed mercantile law (*Acton Burnell*, 1283), regulated feudal law and *custom (statute of Westminster I, 1275; II, 1285), restricted the alienation of *property to the Church (statute of *Mortmain, 1279), defined the jurisdiction of ecclesiastical courts (writ of *Circumspecte agatis*, 1285), and recognised the principle of "long user" (statute of *Quo warranto*, 1290). At the same time, his constant need of *money for warfare led to the consolidation of *Parliament as an institution, containing elected representatives of town and county communities, as well as the *nobility and the Church: the so-called "Model Parliament" (1295), for example, comprised the lords (*bishops, *abbots, barons, summoned by individual writ) and the commons (two burgesses from every borough and two knights from every shire, elected in response to writs issued to the sheriffs). But his popularity dwindled as the financial strains of his government increased, culminating in 1294-1297, when he faced opposition on all sides – *merchants, the nobility, and the Church – from which he extricated himself only by re-issuing *Magna Carta and the Forest Charter (1297). He died exhausted and bankrupt, but the achievements of his reign – conquest of Wales, reform of the law, consolidation of Parliament, strengthening of the Crown – marked him as one of the greatest English kings, though he bequeathed a difficult legacy to his son.

T. F. T. Plucknett, *The Legislation of Edward I*, Oxford, 1949. – *NCE*, 5, 181-182. – E. L. G. Stones, *Edward I*, Oxford, 1968. – J. M. Prestwich, *War, Politics and Finance under Edward I*, London, 1972. – J. M. Prestwich, *Edward I*, Berkeley (CA), 1988 (re-ed. New Haven, 1997). – *DMA*, 4, 1984, 395-397. – *Edward I and Wales*, T. Herbert (ed.), G. Elwyn (ed.), Cardiff, 1988.

Anne J. Duggan

**EDWARD II OF ENGLAND (1284-1327).** King of *England, fourth son of Edward I, born at Carnarvon in *Wales in 1284, he became Prince of *Wales in 1301 and reigned from 1307 to his deposition in 1327. He inherited a series of difficult problems which included a debt of about £200,000, a war with *Scotland and a climate of mistrust between king and magnates which had characterised the closing years of the reign of Edward I. In addition, the deficiencies in Edward's character contributed substantially to the troubles of the reign. The king proved to be incompetent in the business of government, and gave little indication that he would ever devote himself consistently to affairs of the realm. His suitability for kingship was further undermined by unkingly pursuits such as acting, *music and rustic crafts. Edward was also obsessed by a number of favourites, the earliest of whom was the Gascon Piers Gaveston, whom he made earl of Cornwall. Hatred for Gaveston provided the rallying point for a group of magnates who confronted the king with a show of military force in 1310. Allied to these defects was Edward's military incompetence, demonstrated in a decisive English defeat at Bannockburn by the Scots in 1314.

Following the *revolt of 1310, a group of lay magnates and senior ecclesiastics, led by Thomas of Lancaster, the king's cousin, forced Edward to accept the Ordinances, an elaborate set of proposals for the reform of royal household government. Many of the problems of this complex and turbulent reign stemmed from the long-drawn out struggle to enforce the Ordinances, a movement that ended in failure with their repeal in 1322. The tensions of the reign led to progressive political instability and a breakdown in the rule of law, as evidenced by a series of political murders which claimed the lives of Piers Gaveston, Thomas of Lancaster, the elder and younger Despenser – Edward's two favourites in the latter years of his reign – and his treasurer Walter Stapeldon, who carried through important reforms at the *Exchequer in the 1320s. Modern historians tend to reject older notions that the reign ought to be viewed in constitutional or ideological terms, that is, as a clash between royal autocracy and opposing parties who fought for a limited *monarchy. Rather it is increasingly argued that the core of the problem lay in the competition for access to the king and to the immense sources of patronage in the royal household.

Although Edward enjoyed a partial restoration of royal power from 1322, he was finally deposed in 1327 in favour of his son, the future Edward III. His reign is clearly one of the most troubled and unsuccessful in English history.

*Vita Edwardi Secundi*, N. Denholm-Young (ed.), London, 1957 (*OMT*).

J. C. Davies, *The Baronial Opposition to Edward II*, Cambridge, 1918. – J. R. Maddicott, *Thomas of Lancaster 1307-1322: A Study in the Reign of Edward II*, Oxford, 1970. – N. M. Fryde, *The Tyranny and Fall of Edward II 1321-1326*, Cambridge, 1979. – M. Buck, *Politics, Finance and the Church in the Reign of Edward II: Walter Stapeldon, Treasurer of England*, Cambridge, 1983.

Alan B. Cobban

**EDWARD III OF ENGLAND (1312-1377).** Edward III was 14 when he became king in 1327 so the country was ruled by his mother, Isabelle of France. After seizing power from her in 1330, Edward made war against *Scotland. He proclaimed himself king of *France in 1340, won a victory at Crécy (1346) and took Calais (1347). In 1356, his son the Black Prince took John II of France captive at Poitiers. The treaty of Brétigny (1360) which gave Edward sovereign control over *Aquitaine was never properly fulfilled so war broke out again in 1369. Although he was active in domestic government for most of his reign, Edward's control of politics weakened in his last years.

W. M. Ormrod, *The Reign of Edward III*, London, 1990. – S. L. Waugh, *England in the Reign of Edward III*, Cambridge, 1991.

W. Mark Ormrod

**EDWARD IV OF ENGLAND (1442-1483).** Son of the duke of *York killed at Wakefield (Dec 1460), Edward earl of March was proclaimed king of *England in March 1461 at *London after having crushed the Lancastrians (Mortimer's Cross, St Albans). He was suppressing Lancastrian uprisings until 1464, but remained under the thumb of his Neville (*Warwick) allies. But he did build up a personal clientele, notably by his secret marriage with Elizabeth Woodville, and he allied himself with *Charles the Bold of *Burgundy who married his sister Margaret. The break with Warwick, who favoured an alliance with *Louis XI and was supported by Edward's brother Clarence, occurred in the summer of 1469; Edward was arrested. But in 1470 Warwick and Clarence had to flee to Louis XI, who reconciled them with Margaret of Anjou, wife of *Henry VI: they invaded England with French help in order to restore Henry VI of *Lancaster. Betrayed, Edward fled to Charles the Bold who gave him troops to return to England (1471): victor over Warwick at Barnet and over Margaret at Tewkesbury, he reconquered his kingdom, and Warwick, Henry VI and his son Edward were put to death (Clarence was executed in 1478). From now on sure of his power, in 1475 he mounted an expedition against Louis XI: but, Charles the Bold not joining him, he left Louis XI to buy his retreat by the treaty of Picquigny. Peace brought back calm and prosperity, but on his death his sons were mere children.

K. Dockray, *Edward IV. A Source Book*, Stroud , 1999.

*DNB*, 1885-1900. – C. Ross, *Edward IV*, London, 1974 (re-ed. New Haven, 1997). – M. K. Jones, "Edward IV and the Beaufort Family", *Ricardian*, 6/83, Dec 1983, 258-63. – A. Allan, "Royal Propaganda and the Proclamations of Edward IV", *Bulletin of the Institute of Historical Research*, 59, 1986, 146-54.

Jean-Philippe Genet

**EGBERT OF YORK (died 766).** *Archbishop of *York (732-766) and an effective Northumbrian churchman, Egbert (*Ecgberht*) was apparently able to implement various recommendations concerning instruction of the *laity and episcopal *visits made to him in a *letter by *Bede the Venerable (the *Epistola ad Ecgberhtum*) shortly before his death in 735. In implementing these recommendations, which were endorsed by the council of *Clovesho in 747, Egbert had the support of his brother Eadberht, king of Northumbria (737-758). Egbert established a *school at York, which numbered *Alcuin among its alumni; he also composed a *Dialogus ecclesiasticae institutionis* on matters of ecclesiastical discipline (including observance of embertide *fasts), but other works attributed to him (the *Excerptiones Egberti*, the *Confessionale Egberti* and the so-called "Egbert *Pontifical") are English compilations of a much later date.

*Councils and Ecclesiastical Documents relating to Great Britain and Ireland*, A. W. Haddan (ed.), W. Stubbs (ed.), 3, Oxford, 1869-1878, 403-413 (3 vol.); repr. 1964. – *Venerabilis Bedae Opera Historica*, C. Plummer (ed.), 1, Oxford, 1896, 405-423; 2, 378-388 (2 vol.).

Michael Lapidge

**EGYPT, CHRISTIANS IN (7th-15th centuries).** The 7th c. marked a decisive turning-point for Christian Egypt. After the storm of the Persian conquest (617-627) which destroyed a number of its monasteries, then the temporary return of the Byzantines who plunged into violent persecutions of the monophysite *Copts and their patriarch *Benjamin, the Arab conquest under Amr ibn al-As, completed in 641, seemed at first to open up an era of freedom and prosperity. In Coptic historiography, Amr ibn al-As enjoys great renown: by expelling the Byzantine Melkites, he restored to honour the Christians of Egypt under the authority of their legitimate head Benjamin who recovered his churches and restored the monasteries. Indeed, the Arabs at that time were few and had to lean on the loyalty of the Church, at enmity with Byzantium, in order to maintain the country, but the euphoria was short-lived. The Arab Empire, in full expansion under the *Umayyads and *Abbasids, organised itself and had immense needs which the richest part of its provinces had to satisfy. So the fiscal pressure became heavy. Alexander II (705-730) was the first *patriarch imprisoned and subjected to a heavy fine, for which he had to raise the amount by travelling the country under the surveillance of a mistrustful Muslim official. Under his patriarchate are mentioned the first *conversions to *Islam, those of provincial governors and numerous congregations with their priests, while in 725 the first of the Coptic revolts broke out. These followed each other sporadically for more than a century, despite a harsh repression accompanied by massive conversions to Islam. Thus it is generally estimated that by the mid 9th c. the Muslims were already a majority in Egypt.

Though we cannot speak of a systematic religious persecution, a process of Islamization of Coptic Egypt had been launched at the same time as that of the Arabization of the administration. Everything worked in its favour: legislation that surtaxed the Christian and forbade him access to positions of authority, the Islamic grip on social life, the superiority of an Arab civilization then at its apogee over a poor, isolated and fading Coptic culture, finally the legitimate desire of the native Christian to participate in the direction of his country. So the various political regimes that followed each other in Egypt, practically independent under the Tulunids, then for two centuries centre of the Empire of the Fatimid caliphs (969-1171), hardly affected the situation of the Christians, whose minority status was accentuated.

We must however point to a slackening of the pressure of Muslim power under the *Fatimids, more favourable to the Christians (some of their vizirs were of Christian origin) because, as *Shi'ites, they wished to counterbalance the *Sunni resistance of the population, but the latter showed itself more and more intolerant: the external manifestations of worship could no longer take place freely and, above all, destructive popular riots took place, in the course of which churches were burned. This last trait is important, as showing that a veritable hostility to Christianity had appeared among the mass of Muslims: it was supported by the growing influence of the *'*ulamā'*, and the period of the *crusades that was just beginning (capture of *Jerusalem in 1099, occupation of *Cairo by Amalric of Jerusalem in 1168) could only encourage it. And the Sunni regime of the *Ayyubids (1172-1250), inaugurated by Salah al-Din who recaptured Jerusalem, reacted harshly against the Copts.

The prostration of the community led to many modifications in ecclesiastical structures. First, the dominant function of the patriarch, now a hostage of the authorities, was weakened: he left his seat at *Alexandria and wandered in the towns of the Delta for 200 years before settling at *Cairo in the late 11th century. Famous monasteries became impoverished and then disappeared: thus Saqqara, Bawit, Balaiza and the Ennaton. Numerous bishoprics died out for lack of congregations, notably in the Delta which was dechristianized faster than the rest of the country since it was at the heart of the communications of the Arab Empire. Highly-placed laymen close to power became the real representatives and protectors of their community. Finally the Church dignitaries themselves were treated as civil servants and bought their position. Thus in 1240, after a 17-year vacancy of the patriarchal see, Cyril III had to consecrate 40 *bishops in order to fill the gaps in the eparchies and recover the sums dispensed for his *election!

Another consequence, cultural this time, of the enfeeblement of the Christian community was the Arabization of its literature (see "Arabic Christian literature"). Admittedly, in villages, recent Muslim converts could still speak *Coptic and out-of-the-way monasteries remained the conservatory of the language – as witness the production of numerous Coptic manuscripts up to a late date. But, among cultivated Christians in the towns, the Arabic language ended by prevailing. The first Copto-Arabic author was, typically enough, a bishop, Severus of Ashmunein, in the 10th century. The liturgy was translated into Arabic in the 12th c. and Mawhūb ibn Mansūr's *History of the Patriarchs* at the turn of the 11th-12th centuries. In the 13th c. appeared Ibn al-Rahib and al-Makīn, two chroniclers in the best vein of their contemporary Arab historians, as well as the three brothers Ibn al-Assal, canonists, exegetes and grammarians. A Copto-Arabic grammar and dictionary were now necessary to gain access to the ancient Christian tradition. Finally, early in the 14th c., as well as a great dictionary, Abū l'Bakarat ibn Kanbar published *The Lamp in Darkness*, a religious encyclopedia that brought together everything a Copt ought to know.

The 13th c. saw a final effort to salvage the Arabized Coptic culture, before the community entered a state of hibernation and quasi-silence under the chaotic regime of the *Mamluk sultans (1250-1517). The *History of the Patriarchs*, continued by various authors and almost dumb about contemporary events, confined itself most of the time to a simple list of names of successive pontiffs, with the date of their election and death and some edifying lines on their trials and virtues. Arab historians are more explicit. They relate for example what they call the "affair of the churches": in 1321, in one day, the populace stirred up by the Muslim *confraternities destroyed more than 60 parish and monastic churches in various towns across the country. The rigorist Muslim jurists of the time, such as Ibn Taymiyya, ordered these destructions or justified them by decree (**fatwā*) and forbade rebuilding.

Another source of precious information appears in Arabic dictionaries of biographies, which give the name and *cursus* of persons who carried out important actions. In Egypt, the name and qualifying adjective reveal whether they were of Christian origin and descent, though actually Muslim: these were "Coptic" Muslims, which meant that the genuineness of their adherence to Islam, personal or family, was often considered suspect by their co-religionists. Not numerous in positions of military and provincial command or in religious posts, they were abundant in the administrative positions of intendant, secretary or scribe, to the point of representing 50, 60 or even 75 % of the individuals given in these dictionaries for the Mamluk period. This means that no-one could accede to or keep these socially envied posts except by going over to Islam: the Christian community was thus regularly decapitated of its notables, Copts of a certain education. Hence the modest level and unobtrusiveness of the religious personnel, reduced to the performance of the liturgy. In towns, the Copts were generally merchants or artisans; the greater number of them survived in the isolated villages of Upper Egypt.

Finally there is a very explicit indicator of this withering of the community at the end of the Middle Ages: out of 200 or so monasteries listed in the 13th c. by Abū Saleh the Armenian and Abū l-Makarim, no more than 80 existed according to Maqrīzī towards the middle of the 15th c., a good half of which were in ruins or heading for complete depopulation. No doubt it was to obtain urgent help from abroad that the Coptic Church, on appeal from *Rome, signed the act of *union at the council of *Florence in 1442, but this remained without sequel or effect. And it is a miracle of a tenacious popular faith that Egypt still had 150,000 Copts and seven monasteries when Napoleon's expedition opened it up to the modern world.

*History of the Patriarchs of the Coptic Church of Alexandria*, *PO*, 1, 1907, fasc. 2 and 4; 5, fasc. 1; 10, fasc. 5. – A. S. Atiya, "Kibt", *EI(E)*, 5, 1986, 90-95 (2nd ed.). – *History of the Patriarchs of the Egyptian Church*, 2, 3 and 4, Cairo, 1943-1974. – R. Bulliet, *Conversion to Islam in the Medieval Period*, Cambridge (MA), 1978. – M. M. Martin, "Une lecture de l'Histoire des Patriarches", *POC*, 35, 1985, 15-36. – S. I. Gellens, "Islamization of Egypt", *The Coptic Encyclopedia*, New York, 1991, 936-942.

Maurice Martin

**EINHARD (*c*.770-840).** Einhard or Eginhard is known mainly as the biographer of *Charlemagne. But his activities and writings were not limited to that.

He was born in the Main valley, near Odenwald. Around the age of ten, his parents sent him as a pupil to the famous abbey of *Fulda where St *Boniface had been buried. Abbot Baugulf taught him letters and utilized his talents as a scribe. Before 796, he was sent to the Carolingian *court and admitted among the young people who formed the palace *scola*. He completed his *education with the help of some scholars, including *Alcuin. When Alcuin retired to *Saint-Martin at *Tours, he recommended Einhard to Charlemagne for the explanation of Latin *classics and the solving of arithmetical problems. The emperor made him "director of royal buildings" and sent him on various diplomatic missions. In the reign of *Louis the Pious, he lived in the sovereign's entourage and saw to the education of *Lothar, Louis's eldest son. He founded the abbeys of Seligenstadt and Steinbach in Franconia, and the emperor appointed him lay *abbot of Saint-Pierre on Mount Blandin, Saint-Bavon near *Ghent, Saint-Servais at *Maastricht, *Saint-Wandrille and Saint-Cloud. Einhard was able to exploit these lands methodically, as some of his 70 surviving *letters attest. He died at Seligenstadt in 840, at an advanced age.

Einhard is famous mainly as the author of the *Vita Karoli Magni imperatoris*, written *c*.826, in which he sought to imitate Suetonius's *Life of Augustus*, but used mainly his memories, those of his contemporaries and the Royal *Annals. The *Vita* had great success, surviving in more than 80 manuscripts. In 849 the abbot of *Reichenau, *Walafrid Strabo, published it with an introduction on the author; he divided the work into chapters to facilitate its use.

*Vita Karoli*, L. Halphen (ed.), Paris, 1947. – Einhard, *Two Lives of Charlemagne*, Harmondsworth, 1969. – *Vita Karoli*, C. Bianchi (ed.), C. Leonardi (intr.), Rome, 1980 (It. tr.). – *Charlemagne's Courtier: the Complete Einhard*, P. Dutton (ed.), Peterborough (ON), 1998 (Eng. tr.).

A. Kleinclauz, *Éginhard*, Paris, 1942. – F. Brunhölzl, "L'Époque carolingienne", *Histoire de la littérature latine au Moyen Âge*, 1, 2, Turnhout, 1991, 280-281 (Fr. tr.).

Pierre Riché

**EINSIEDELN.** Einsiedeln, a Benedictine *abbey in *Switzerland, was founded in 934 by Eberhard, a *canon of *Strasbourg cathedral, on the site where St Meinrad, a monk of *Reichenau, had retired and been murdered in 861. In 947, *Otto I conceded the abbey the privilege of *immunity, while considerably augmenting its initial endowment. Controlling one of the crossings to *Italy, Einsiedeln became one of the most privileged royal monasteries of the 10th c., as well as an active centre of monastic *reform up to the 11th century. Its **scriptorium* and its *school were developed by Wolfgang (964-971), future bishop of *Regensburg. The abbey declined from the 13th century.

H. Keller, *Kloster Einsiedeln in ottonischen Schwaben*, Freiburg, 1964.

Geneviève Bührer-Thierry

**EIXIMENIS, FRANCESC (*c*.1340-1409).** The *Franciscan Francesc Eiximenis, born at Gerona *c*.1340, studied at *Paris, *Cologne, *Oxford and *Toulouse, where he obtained his mastership of *theology, a discipline he taught at the *university of Lérida. *Guardian of the *convent of *Barcelona, he was the confessor of the royal family of *Aragon. He became the adviser of King Martin I (1395-1410) over the *Great Schism. In 1408 he was, with *Benedict XIII, the instigator of the council of *Perpignan, where he was appointed patriarch of Jerusalem and bishop of Elne, shortly before his death. His numerous works include *Lo Chrestià*, a vast moral and theological *encyclopedia. His thought, tinged with Joachite *eschatology and full of admiration for the *merchant oligarchies, reflects the spiritual traditions of Catalan Franciscanism.

D. J. Viera, *Bibliografia anotada de la vida i obra de Francesc Eiximenis (1340?-1409?)*, Barcelona, 1980.

Martin Aurell

**EJMIACIN.** Cradle of Armenian Christianity, the town of Ejmiacin was founded under the Arsacid King Vagharch (117-140); it bore the name Vagharshapat until 1945, when it took that of its principal monument: the *cathedral of Ejmiacin. At the start of the 4th c. it was the theatre of activity of St Gregory the Illuminator, evangelizer of *Armenia, who established the primatial see of that country there. After a flowering engendered by the *conversion and lasting until the 7th c., the town declined under the invasions.

Transferred to various places during the Middle Ages, the see of the Armenian church returned to Ejmiacin in 1441 and remains the residence of the *catholicos* or supreme patriarch of this autocephalous Church. A Persian possession in the late Middle Ages, Ejmiacin benefited from the 17th-c. renaissance and was one of the centres of Armenian intellectual activity in the 18th and 19th cc., notably after the conquest of eastern Armenia by Russia in 1828.

The cathedral takes its name from a *vision of St Gregory (*Ejmiacin*, "Descent of the Only Son"). Founded in the early 4th c., then destroyed by the Persians, it was rebuilt in *c*.485 and restored in the 7th century. Excavations carried out in the 1950s under the four pillars supporting the cupola and at the foot of the walls have shown that the present composition of the cathedral (taking account of additions to front and rear) is very early: its tetraconch tetrapylon square plan probably goes back to the end of the 5th century. In turn, important works executed in the 17th c. have left a strong imprint, since the high cupola on Iranizing pendentives and the lateral lanterns were rebuilt at that time, while a richly sculpted clock was added to the west.

Apart from the cathedral, some other early monuments are preserved at Ejmiacin. Built over 4th-c. *martyria*, the domed churches of Saint-Hripsimé (618) and Saint-Gayané (630) are precious witnesses to Armenian civilization during the golden age of the 7th century.

Cathedral of Ejmiacin, Armenia, 4th-17th c. General view from the south-west.

A. Khatchatrian, *L'architecture arménienne du IV^e au VI^e siècle*, Paris, 1971, 67-108. – V. M. Haroutiounian, *Etchmiadzine*, Yerevan, 1978-1985 (several editions in Armenian, Russian and French). – J. M. Thierry, P. Donabédian, *Les Arts arméniens*, Paris, 1987, 516-519. – P. Cuneo, *Architettura armena*, Rome, 1988, 88-101.

Patrick Donabédian

**EKBERT (or EGBERT) OF SCHÖNAU (*c*.1120-1184).** Born to a noble and devout Rhineland family, Ekbert studied at *Paris and became a *canon of the *chapter of Saints Cassius and Florent at Bonn. Under the influence of his sister, the famous *visionary *Elizabeth of Schönau (1129-1165), he became a monk at Schönau, in the *diocese of *Trier, and was from then on her secretary and spiritual director, noting the mystical phenomena whose privileged witness he was and propagating her message after writing it down. It is generally agreed that to a great extent he interpreted his sister's *visions, giving them a logical and learned character. Moreover, he was the author of 13 discourses against the *Cathars, whom he had met at *Cologne and in other local towns. Here we find very interesting developments on the beliefs of the *heretics, which he describes with precision before refuting them. Various *sermons and exegetical works have also been attributed to him.

*PL*, 195, 1855, 11-102.

"Egbert de Schönau", *DHGE*, 14, 1960, 1472-1475. – R. Manselli, *L'Eresia del male*, Naples, 1963, 161-165. – A. L. Clark, *Elisabeth of Schönau: a twelfth-century visionary*, Philadelphia (PA), 1992.

André Vauchez

**EKKEHARD.** Ekkehard was the patronym borne by the margraves of Merseburg and then of Misnie (968-1046) and the fourth bishop of *Prague († 1023), as well as by four monks, three of them at *Sankt Gallen (five in reality, but Ekkehard III, nephew of the first, is only mentioned by the fourth, while the *Vita* of *Notker the Stammerer is no longer attributed to an Ekkehard V).

Ekkehard I of Sankt Gallen (early 10th c.-973) carried on the tradition of liturgical poetry of Notker the Stammerer. More problematic is the understanding of his *Vita Waltharii Manufortis*, behind which is sometimes envisaged the *Epos Waltharius*, sometimes a *Vita*.

Ekkehard II of Sankt Gallen († 990), whose work was partly confused, in the *Casus sancti Galli*, with that of his uncle, Ekkehard I. Like Ekkehard IV, he taught at the monastery and outside it (as tutor to *Otto II) and was connected also with the Church of *Mainz. But his liturgical output is a continuation of the activities of his elder.

Ekkehard IV of Sankt Gallen (late 10th c.–after 1056) left a poetic work which, though composed at various times of his life (his training at Sankt Gallen, his teaching with Archbishop Aribo at Mainz, then at Sankt Gallen), has a unity not just by the fact of its being brought together by the author in the *Liber benedictionum*, but also by its clearly pedagogical rather than liturgical intention, and its interest in *biography. As such, it joins his continuation of Ratpert's *Casus sancti Galli* up to 975, a work less historical than biographical and attached to a cultural

*Isabelle of Angoulême and Eleanor of Aquitaine.* Royal hunting scene, fresco in St Radegund's chapel, Chinon. 12th-13th c.

point of view which finds only a local echo in the 13th c. in the *Vita* of Notker the Stammerer, but gives us information on Ekkehard I and II.

*Casus sancti Galli*, H. F. Haefele (ed. and tr.), Darmstadt, 1980. – *MGH* (ed. of the chronicle under way).

E. Lechner, *Vita Notkeri Balbuli*, Sankt Gallen, 1972. – P. Stotz, "Ekkehard I. von Sankt Gallen", *VerLex*, 2, 1980, 447-453 (2nd ed.). – P. Stotz, "Ekkehard II. von Sankt Gallen", *VerLex*, 2, 1980, 453-455 (2nd ed.). – H. F. Haefele, "Ekkehard 8", *LdM*, 3, 1986, 1767-1768. – G. Morgan, "Ekkehard's Signature to Waltharius", *Latomus*, 45, 1986, 171-177. – P. Stotz, "Ekkehard 5", "Ekkehard 6", *LdM*, 3, 1986, 1766-1767.

Martial Staub

**EKKEHARD OF AURA (died after 1125).** Ekkehard, *abbot of Aura, was, as a historian, loyal to the ideas of reformed *monasticism with which he was in contact at *Tegernsee (1102-1103?), then at St Michael's, *Bamberg (1105). The attention he gives to the emperor's understanding with the papacy explains, with the use of an anonymous imperial *chronicle, the differences of tone perceptible in the four successive versions of his continuation of Frutolf's *chronicle. Fixing his attention mainly on the experience he gained from his participation in the *crusade of Welf I of *Bavaria, with whom he was connected, he conferred on his chronicle that eyewitness character that made it successful (*Otto of Friesing). His *Vita* of the first bishop of *Würzburg, Burkard, is a source of great importance for the history of the town in the 8th c. thanks to the (lost) sources used.

F. J. Schmale, "Ekkehard von Aura", *VerLex*, 2, 1980, 443-447 (2nd ed.). – F. J. Schmale, "Ekkehard 4", *LdM*, 3, 1986, 1765-1766.

Martial Staub

**ELEANOR OF AQUITAINE (*c.*1122-1204).** Eleanor (Aliénor) of Aquitaine, whose misconduct has been exaggerated, was a woman of exceptional beauty, dynamism and longevity, but led a chequered life. Prematurely duchess of *Aquitaine on the death (April 1137) of her father William X, she soon became queen of *France by marrying *Louis VII (July 1137). She probably inspired the temporary disgrace (1140-1144) of *Suger and a vain expedition against *Toulouse (1141); the marriage of her sister Petronilla to Ralph of Vermandois, arranged by her (1141), led to a conflict with Thibaut IV of *Champagne. But she only gave Louis two daughters and, after their return from *crusade – which she was the first queen to accompany (1147-1149) –, the *council of Beaugency (21 March 1152) separated her from the king, who was too monkish for her taste and yet jealous. Remarried on 18 May to

Henry *Plantagenet, count of *Anjou-Maine-Touraine and duke of *Normandy, she brought him, as previously to Louis, Aquitaine as dowry – which made her more powerful than the king – and received with him the *crown of *England, 19 Dec 1154. She gave him eight *children, five of them sons, but all save the last, John, and a daughter, Aliénor, queen of *Castile, died before her. A dominating woman, she was in fact dominated by her authoritarian and unfaithful second husband. Inspirer with his sons of a vast but vain *revolt against him in 1173, she was imprisoned at Chinon, then in England from late November 1174 to July 1185 and again from spring 1186 to July 1189, date of her widowhood. Later, the rivalry between her two surviving sons – *Richard Coeur de Lion, her favourite, and John – Richard's captivity in *Germany (1192-1194) on his return from crusade and his death (1199), and *Philip Augustus's growing designs on Normandy which culminated in his capture of Château Gaillard (6 March 1204) after the forfeiture of John's continental *fiefs (28 April 1202) were further trials to her. But she faced them unshaken.

Imposing her will in Aquitaine, she had got her dear Richard proclaimed its duke (1169). *Henry II being detained on the continent, she governed England in 1160 and 1162-1164 – not without hostility towards *Thomas Becket – and in 1170 instigated the association on the throne of her eldest son, Henry the Young King († 1183). But it was after 1189 that she showed her full capacity. In 1191, meeting on the way the Emperor *Henry VI on his return from Pope Clement III, she went as far as Messina to hand over to Richard, on his way East, his fiancée Berengaria of *Navarre, chosen by herself. With Richard in captivity, she safeguarded his throne against John and collected his *ransom before bringing him back from Germany and then reconciling him with his brother. Though grand-daughter of the *troubadour Duke William IX and herself passionately fond of courtly *poetry and amorous casuistry, having welcomed Bernard de Ventadour and many others and had more than one secular poetic work dedicated to her, she retired to *Fontevraud in 1194. But, situated in contact with the two halves of the Plantagenets' continental lands – north and south of the Loire –, the *abbey, which she provided with a defensive wall, was a base of activity for her. In 1199 we see her at Châlus near the dying Richard, riding against the Angevins who had elected her grandson Arthur of Brittany count at John's expense, crossing Poitou, paying *homage at *Tours to Philip Augustus (of whom John was thus now only the under-vassal), staying at *Rouen and in *Gascony. In midwinter 1200, she brought her grand-daughter *Blanche, promised to the future *Louis VIII, from Castile. In 1202, she rode to Mirebeau where Arthur, allied to the king of *France, failed to capture her. On 31 March or 1 April 1204, shortly after John's murder of Arthur (3 March 1203), she expired at Fontevraud, which she had overwhelmed with favours. She had taken the veil there *in extremis*, but the effigy on her *tomb represents her as queen. Her posthumous eulogy by the *nuns was dithyrambic.

A. Kelly, *Eleanor of Aquitaine and the Four Kings*, New York, 1950 (3rd ed.). – E. R. Labande, "Pour une image véridique d'Aliénor d'Aquitaine", *BSAO*, 2, 4th series, Poitiers, 1952, 175-234 (re-ed. *Histoire de l'Europe occidentale, XIe-XIVe siècles*, 2, London, 1973). – R. Lejeune, "Rôle littéraire d'Aliénor d'Aquitaine et de sa famille", *CNL*, 14, 1954, 5-57. – M. Meade, *Eleanor of Aquitaine: a Biography*, London, 1978. – J.-M. Bienvenu, "Aliénor d'Aquitaine et Fontevraud", *CCM*, 29, 1-2, Poitiers, 1986, 15-27. – D. D. R. Owen, *Eleanor of Aquitaine: Queen and Legend*, Oxford, 1993.

Jean-Marc Bienvenu †

**ELECTION.** Election, from the Latin term *eligere*, "to choose", was the procedure of designating the titular of certain major ecclesiastical posts or *benefices.

In the medieval Church, *electio* was distinguished from an election in the modern sense by several characteristics. It was a choice, emanating from competent *authority; which could be, according to the case, a single individual, a community or a crowd, more or less numerous, within which no need would be felt to count the number of votes in favour of each candidate. This choice reflected the divine will; *God's choice alighted on the worthiest candidate, he whom the better part of the electoral body had selected; but that better part was not necessarily the more numerous; for most of the Middle Ages, the majority principle did not automatically prevail in election procedures. Election was only the first phase of a procedure of appointment to ecclesiastical office; it permitted the designation of a candidate who would exercise his powers only after canonical *investiture and *consecration.

Election was essentially for the titulars of major *benefices: *abbots, *bishops, Roman pontiff; it underwent an evolution in the course of the Middle Ages. For abbots and bishops, election was originally entrusted in principle to the community concerned: monks of the monastery, people and clergy of the episcopal city. The role of the people was often limited to an *acclamation, ratification of a choice not its own; bit by bit it almost disappeared, leaving the responsibility for choosing the future bishop to the cathedral *chapter alone. Moreover, the practice left plenty of room for the intervention of the "great", lay or ecclesiastical, who presented a candidate in such terms that freedom of elections was considerably reduced. Canonical legislation tried to restore more clarity in electoral procedures (fourth *Lateran council, 1215, canon 24). However, a count of the electors' voices was always refused, illustrating the idea that these elections had to be unanimous, a reflection of the Church's unity. Or again, a minority sought to impose its candidate, claiming that it constituted a *sanior pars*, capable by its dignity of overruling a *major pars*. But abuses and disorders were numerous, justifying ever more frequent papal interventions, which followed varied procedures. Imperceptibly, and without any acknowledgment, the elective system gave way to that of appointment by the pontifical power. By the *Pragmatic Sanction of Bourges (1438), *Charles VII tried to restore elections in *France. But this unilateral act of monarchical power was never accepted by Rome and functioned badly. It was expressly abrogated by the *concordat of Bologna (1516) which finally ended the electoral system practised by the Latin Church since Antiquity.

The Roman pontiff was also designated by election. The *pope, bishop of the city of *Rome, was in principle designated by the same procedure as any bishop, by the clergy and people of his city. However, from the early Middle Ages, intrigues, more frequent and more serious than elsewhere, multiplied, coming both from the Roman nobility and from the imperial entourage. To try to put an end to them, in 1059 Pope *Nicholas II promulgated a decree entrusting the election of the bishop of Rome to a college of *cardinals. The third *Lateran council (1179, canon 1), supplementing the arrangements of the Decree of 1059, required that the new pope be elected by a two-thirds majority of votes. For the first time a canonical text imposed a count of voices. In its broad outlines, this procedure is still in force.

J. Gaudemet, *Les Élections dans l'Église latine, des origines au XVIe siècle*, Paris, 1979.

Brigitte Basdevant-Gaudemet

**ELEMENTARY INSTRUCTION.** Christianity being a religion of the book, it was necessary for everyone, *laity, *clerics and monks, to have at least an elementary instruction. From the beginning of the Middle Ages, monastic *Rules insisted on learning to read: "Let all *nuns learn to read, let no monk be ignorant of letters", demand the Rules of *Caesarius of *Arles, Aurelian and Ferreolus. According to the *Rule of the Master*, small *children in groups of ten should spend three hours a day studying letters under the direction of a lettered monk, while *Benedict made provision for the use of *books, stylets and tablets for all. After having learned the alphabet, the monks read the *psalter.

To be able to read was to know one's psalter. The *master had verses copied onto tablets which the child had to learn by heart, rocking backwards and forwards as in the Rabbinic schools or, later, the Muslim schools. The use of the psalter passed into the presbyterial and episcopal *schools and was even the method of elementary reading for the laity. Children were thus impregnated with the *psalms, ruminated on them and retained them all their life. To be *psaltaratus*, "to know your psalms", meant being able to read. The acquisition of a psalter was encouraged. For those who did not want to learn *Latin, psalters were translated into the vernacular from the 12th century. The *Waldenses and *Cathars, whom chroniclers treat as illiterate since they did not know Latin, used in their schools psalters translated for both pedagogical and religious ends. The same was true of the *beghards and *beguines of northern France.

The psalter, even translated, was not the only reading book used. Distichs attributed from late Antiquity to Cato and giving a moral teaching to the young pupil were also translated into French in the 12th and 13th cc. under the name of "*chatonets*". Other collections of moral sentences, the *fables of Aesop and Avianus, were also put into the hands of beginners. Reading could be studied independently of writing. One might be able to read without ever being able to write and be content to learn to sign one's name. But in the course of the Middle Ages, the written act took on such importance in political and social life that masters encouraged pupils to acquire this technique.

The third kind of elementary teaching was counting. Reckoning on the fingers, an old technique from Antiquity, was still learned. This method was often supplemented by the study of the abacus, a sort of chessboard whose compartments had a conventional value: unit, ten, hundred. Pupils might also be invited to solve small arithmetical problems like those handed down under the names of *Bede and *Alcuin. When *Charlemagne gave his teaching programme in the *Admonitio generalis*, he wanted the child to learn the psalter, *i.e.* reading, *computus*, *i.e.* counting, but also singing and *grammar as well as notes, *i.e.* the Tironian notes that were the ancester of modern stenography. Singing was learned from psalms, *hymns and canticles and was increasingly reserved for specialists instructed by the *cantor. Grammar began the study of Latin with the treatises of Donatus. To encourage pupils to speak Latin, some *Anglo-Saxon masters such as *Ælfric wrote bilingual conversations that were the ancestors of our "Assimil" methods.

During the early Middle Ages, elementary teaching was given essentially to clerics and monks. Only a few laity of the aristocracy were instructed. From the 11th c. in aristocratic courts and in *towns, the laity wanted their children to learn something other than fighting and *hunting. People remembered that "instruction does no harm to one destined for the military life and is not just the privilege of the clerk". At the end of the 12th c., the burghers of *Ghent opened a school directed by a *canon so that their children could learn the rudiments and later help them in their trading. The *Mirrors of Princes and of the Laity that multiplied in the 13th c. attest the progress of instruction of the laity. Instruction of girls was not exceptional. If some authors, like Philip of Novara, dreaded lettered women, *Vincent of Beauvais on the other hand recommended that *women know how to read and write. It is doubtless difficult to know whether the wishes of pedagogues were really fulfilled, but we can state that books and especially religious books for the laity multiplied up to the end of the Middle Ages. *Gerson wrote the *ABC of Simple Folk*, which had a great success.

P. Riché, "Apprendre à lire et à écrire dans le haut Moyen Âge", *BSNAF*, 1978-1979, 193-203. – P. Riché, *Écoles et enseignement dans le haut Moyen Âge*, 3rd ed., Paris, 1999, 221 f. – *The Uses of Literacy in Early Mediaeval Europe*, R. McKitterick (ed.), Cambridge, 1990. – J. K. Hyde, *Literacy and its Uses*, Manchester, 1993. – M. T. Clanchy, *From Memory to Written Record*, 2rd ed., Oxford, 1994. – D. H. Green, *Medieval Listening and Reading*, Cambridge, 1994. – H. Pryce, *Literacy in Medieval Celtic Societies*, Cambridge, 1998.

Pierre Riché

**ELEMENTS, THE FOUR.** The theory of the four elements constitutive of matter (earth, *water, air and fire) had roots in Greek thought (Empedocles, Plato). Antique culture made out correspondences between these groups and the gods, the winds, the seasons, the *ages of life, the temperaments, etc. Medieval thought received this heritage through the work of the early medieval encyclopedists and the texts of the *Fathers and created two new correspondences, the four elements being referrable to the four rivers of *Paradise or the four living beings of *Ezekiel's vision. Medieval iconography inherited from Antiquity the representation of the four elements under an allegorical form. After a period of latency, the *Carolingian Renaissance once more gave a wide place to this *image, in images of crucifixion, *Christ in *Majesty, *illuminations of *Genesis ("Book of Pericopes of Henry II", *Majestas Domini* of the Cologne Gospels preserved at *Bamberg), etc.

J. Seznec, *The Survival of the Pagan Gods*, New York, 1953. – *Les quatre éléments dans la culture médiévale (Amiens, 1982)*, Göttingen, 1983.

Pierre Kerbrat

**ELEONORA OF ARBORÈA (died *c.*1404).** Daughter of the judge Mariano IV and wife of Brancaleone *Doria. In 1383, after the death of her brother, the judge Hugo III, she began to judge the *judicate of Arborèa in place of her under-age son Frederick, as queen-regent. Because of her son's death and the absence of her husband, held prisoner by King *Peter IV of Aragon, she retained the complete lieutenancy of the kingdom in place of her second son, the future Mariano V. In 1388, she concluded a first peace agreement with the new king of Aragon, John. In 1391, a year after her consort's liberation, war recommenced and the Arborese gained possession of nearly all of *Sardinia. After John's death, in 1395, she concluded a peace agrement with his successor, Martin I of Aragon. One of the judge-regent's most important acts was the promulgation, perhaps in 1392, of the collection of laws known as the **Carta de Logu*, in the Logudorese language.

*Il mondo della Carta de Logu*, Cagliari, 1979.

Mauro Sanna

**ELEVATION.** Elevation is the *gesture of ostension by which the celebrant raises the *host and then the *chalice, after having pronounced the words of *consecration of the *mass. The elevation of the host appeared early in the 13th c. and corresponded to the "desire to see the host". A decree of the archbishop of *Paris, in 1210, forbade it before Christ's words had been pronounced over the bread. It spread during the course of the 13th c., accompanied by the sound of handbells; the 14th c. saw the spread, less universal, of the elevation of the chalice. A gesture of monstration and not of offering, it did however reduce the oblation at the end of the canon to the rank of "little elevation". A characteristic trait of the new eucharistic piety, the elevation provoked *miracles and *apparitions.

E. Dumoutet, *Le désir de voir l'hostie et les origines de la dévotion au saint sacrement*, Paris, 1926. – H. B. Meyer, "Die Elevation im deutschen Mittelalter und bei Luther", *ZKTh*, 85, 1963, 162-217.

Paul De Clerck

**ELIAS OF CORTONA (died 1253).** Entering, at an unknown date, the community gathered around *Francis of Assisi, which still had an uncertain status, Elias of Cortona was sent by Francis to direct the province of the *Holy Land in 1217, and accompanied the saint to *Italy on his return from the fifth *crusade in 1220. Becoming Francis's second *vicar in 1221 after Francis had renounced the direction of the order, Elias encouraged studies, the expansion of the Friars Minor throughout Europe and the drawing up of a second Rule, approved by Pope *Honorius III in 1223. At Francis's death, he was the first to communicate to the world the miracle of the *stigmata. From 1227 to 1232, he was engaged in the construction of the basilica of *Assisi to which Francis's remains were transferred in 1230. From 1232 to 1239, he was general of the order. By his heavily centralized direction and the favour he showed to the *laity of the order, he drew down the hostility of the *clerics, scholars and representatives of the provinces most distant from Assisi. His reputation and importance are attested by the letter of *Frederick II on the occasion of the translation of the *relics of St Elizabeth in 1236, the esteem of *Clare of Assisi and the mission that Pope *Gregory IX entrusted to him in 1238 to try to reach an agreement with the emperor. Deposed in 1239 as the result of a plot orchestrated by the representatives of the provinces at the papal court to denounce his despotic government of the order, Elias went to Frederick II. Frederick having meanwhile been excommunicated, Elias equally incurred *excommunication. After the failure of all attempts to rally large sections of the *Franciscan Order to the ex-minister general, the emperor entrusted Elias with an important mission to the Byzantine emperor. Back in Italy, he retired to Cortona where he built a fine church dedicated to St Francis. Absolved of excommunication at the hour of his death (1253), Elias no less continued to represent an element of scandal and contradiction within the order, condemned by some for his "abuses" as general, considered by others, especially the *Spirituals, as the very symbol of the decline of the Minors, particularly in matters of *poverty and *humility.

D. Berg, "Elias von Cortona. Studien zu Leben und Werk des zweiten Generalministers im Franziskanerorden", *WiWei*, 41, 178, 102-126. – G. Barone, "Frate Elia: suggestioni di una rilettura", *I compagni de Francesco e la prima generazione minoritica*, Spoleto, 1992, 61-80. – S. Vecchio, "Elia di Assisi", *DBI*, 1993, 450-458.

Giulia Barone

**ELIGIUS OF NOYON (*c.*588-660).** Eligius (Éloi) was born into a Gallo-Roman family of the Limousin. He learned the goldsmith's craft and entered the service of the treasurer of King Chlotar II, who made him his master of the mint and also entrusted other missions to him (notably to the Bretons). He left the court after the death of *Dagobert I (639) and became bishop of the diocese of *Noyon-*Tournai. He died 1 Dec 660. He encouraged missions to the pagan peoples in the north of his diocese (Flemings and *Frisians), founded three monasteries (including Solignac in 632), but it was above all his reputation as a goldsmith that led to the development of his cult, thanks to the rise of craft confraternities, in northern France and Belgium.

E. Brouette, "Éloi", *DHGE*, 15, 1963, 260-263. – H. Vierck, "L'oeuvre de saint Éloi, orfèvre, et son rayonnement", *La Neustrie*, P. Périn (ed.), L.-C. Feffer (ed.), Rouen, 1985.

Michèle Gaillard

**ELIJAH.** Though medieval theologians devoted few works to Elijah (essentially a treatise by St Ambrose and a *sermon of St *Caesarius), his life often served as a reference by the wealth of its subject-matter. The hatred with which Ahab and Jezebel pursued him made him the symbol of the *martyr, his ascetic life elevated him to a mystical hero, his discouragements nourished the argument of the importance of *grace in the anti-Pelagian struggle, his pitiless repression of idolatry conferred on him the role of patron of the *Inquisition. Exegetes saw in him the figure of *Christ: pointing to the multiplication of loaves, he multiplied the flour of the widow of Zarephath; like Jesus in the Garden of Olives, he despaired under the juniper tree; his ascension in the flesh points to that of Christ, and the fire that descended from *heaven on his holocaust prefigures the Spirit of *Pentecost. If his cult prospered in the East, its sole liturgical vestige in the West is found at *Auxerre in the 6th c., and not until the fervour of the 16th-c. *Carmelites did he attain a true veneration.

Artists celebrated him in the *Transfiguration, selecting significant attributes: the raven that fed him in the desert, the wheel of the fiery chariot, the flaming sword of Mount Carmel, etc.; they exploited his *typological affinities with *John the Baptist, clothing him in a hair tunic, and especially with Christ: the raising of the son of the widow of Zarephath is rarely absent from typological versions of the *Passion.

L. Réau, "L'iconographie du prophète Elie", *Elie le prophète*, 1, 1956, ("EtCarm"). – E. Lucchesi Palli, *LCI*, 1, 1968, 607-613.

Colette Deremble

*Elijah.* Detail of the wooden door of the west front of the church of Santa Sabina, Rome. 5th c.

**ELIPANDUS OF TOLEDO (717-800).** It was in the early 750s, when the old *Visigothic capital had fallen under Muslim rule, that Elipandus became archbishop of *Toledo. His actions at the head of the Morazabic church aroused very diverse reactions. Accused by some of compromising with the *emir of *Cordova, for others he was the buckler of the Church of *Spain against the hegemonic manoeuvres of *Rome or *Aachen. Around 870, Elipandus laid the basis of the *adoptianist doctrine which he subsequently defended with the help of Felix of Urgel. Although his position was officially condemned in 785 by *Adrian I, and despite the efforts of *Alcuin who never lost hope of convincing him, Elipandus obstinately refused to retract.

*DHEE*, 2, 1972, 782-783. – *HChr*, 4, 1993.

Daniel Baloup

**ELISHA.** The name Elisha is a sort of diminutive of *Elijah, and many events of their lives are doublets, though Elisha does not incarnate asceticism as his master does. *Typological *exegesis loved to see in him a prefiguration of *Christ, and drew up equivalences between the ovation at Jericho and the *Entry into Jerusalem, the multiplication of the widow's oil and *Pentecost, the inheritance of Elijah's mantle and the *traditio legis* to the apostles, the healing of Naaman the leper in the waters of the Jordan and *baptism, the raising of the son of the Shunammite woman and that of *Lazarus, the miracle of the axe floating on the water and the *Resurrection of Christ.

The plurality of these figures fed the inspiration of *artists, who often inserted them in typological configurations. Indeed we often find the motif of the healing of the Shunammite's son, used conjointly with Elijah's raising of the son of the widow of Zarephath, to clarify paschal scenes. The parallel with Elijah is brought out in the prophetic series, as in the sculptures of the north transept of *Chartres. Elisha is recognised by his baldness, the vase of oil or the axe symbolizing his miracles, and by the two-headed dove of the double spirit that Elijah bequeaths to him.

L. Réau, *Iconographie de l'art chrétien*, 2, 1, Paris, 1956, 359-364. – E. Lucchesi Palli, L. Hoffscholte, "Elisäus", *LCI*, 1, 1968, 613-618.

Colette Deremble

**ELIZABETH OF HUNGARY or OF THURINGIA (1207-1231).** St Elizabeth was the daughter of King *Andrew II of *Hungary and Gertrude of Andechs-Meran, who herself belonged to a particularly prestigious line since it provided Europe with several queens and princesses at that time. For diplomatic reasons, she was betrothed at the age of four to the eldest son of landgrave Hermann I of Thuringia († 1217) and sent to the latter's *court to be raised there. The scene of her childhood and adolescence was the *castle of the Wartburg, in *Thuringia, where a courtly atmosphere reigned. Her fiancé meanwhile having died, at the age of 14 she married his brother Louis IV, by whom she had three *children. Under the influence of the preacher *Conrad of Marburg, the young married couple soon adopted a pious and ascetic lifestyle and Elizabeth, while conforming to the duties of her princely state, was conspicuous for her *charity to the poor. In Sept 1227, the landgrave died at Brindisi as he was about to embark for the *Holy Land in the train of the Emperor *Frederick II. His widow, aged 20, refused to remarry and, to escape the pressure of her family-in-law, left the Wartburg with two servants to retire to a cottage near Eisenach, then in 1228 to *Marburg. There she renounced all her property, which she distributed to the poor for whom she founded a *hospital dedicated to the recently-canonized St *Francis of Assisi. There she dedicated herself to the service of the most underprivileged and died of exhaustion on 17 Nov 1231, aged 24. She was canonized on 27 may 1235 by *Gregory IX.

In the last part of her existence, she had come under the influence of the first German Friars Minor and, though after her widowhood she had simply adopted the lifestyle of the **conversi* or lay *penitents who gave themselves to the service of the sick and *lepers, she was later venerated as patroness of the *Franciscan *Third Order, as her iconography attests. Her renunciation earned her great popularity, particularly in the Germanic world. Numerous *miracles took place in the splendid church built at Marburg by the *Teutonic Knights, where her remains were transferred in 1236 in the presence of Frederick II and which became a much frequented place of *pilgrimage.

C. de Montalembert, *Histoire de sainte Élisabeth de Hongrie*, Paris, 1836. – J. Ancelet-Hustache, *Sainte Élisabeth de Hongrie*, Paris, 1947. – *Sankt Elisabeth, Fürstin, Dienerin, Heilige*, Sigmaringen, 1981.

André Vauchez

**ELIZABETH OF SCHÖNAU (1129-1164).** A mystic and ecstatic visionary, Elizabeth lived from 1141 at the monastery of Schönau in the canton of Sankt Goarshausen, which had a men's house and a women's house. From 1157 she was *magistra* of the women's house under the authority of the *abbot. Under the influence of her brother *Ekbert, a monk at the men's house of Schönau from 1155, the *apparitions she witnessed from 1152 became visionary responses to the worries of the time, about which she wrote in her *letters. The harsh corporeal punishments she inflicted on herself, recurrent illnesses and numerous ecstatic experiences rapidly exhausted what strength she had. She died aged 35 of an illness accompanied by *visions.

Elizabeth of Schönau's most important work was the *Liber visionum*, composed of three books written by her brother Ekbert which at the same time provide a sort of *biography of Elizabeth. The *Liber viarum Dei* contains exhortations and *sermons intended for *clerics and *laity alike; in particular it sets out a mirror of truth for the clergy. Elizabeth may be compared with *Hildegard of Bingen in the moral elevation and evocative power of her work, though without attaining her universal grandeur. The influence attested by the circulation of her work is only the more remarkable. In 1493, Schedel's famous *Universal chronicle* mentions that in 1160 the "holy nun Elizabeth in Saxon lands was enlightened by miraculous signs and revelations [. . . transmitted by angels] which she herself described". The wide circulation of her book of visions is also attested by more than 150 manuscripts, and there are partial *translations of it in the Germanic and Scandinavian languages. Around 1370, King *Charles V of France had the *Liber viarum Dei* translated into French and illustrated by miniatures.

Elizabeth's most influential work was indisputably the *Revelationes de sacro exercitu virginum coloniensium* (1156-1157). This phantasmagorical version of the story of St Ursula and her eleven thousand virgins, based on a Latin lapidary inscription of the 4th-5th c. attesting their *martyrdom, played a determining role in propagating the *legend of St Ursula. In her revelations, in reply to a question put to her Elizabeth confirmed the authenticity of the *relics discovered at the foot of the walls of *Cologne: they were those of the 11,000 virgins who accompanied Ursula from England to Germany. Thus this vision became the basis for numerous other legendary elaborations, like that of St

Hermann Joseph of Steinfeld (1241-1252) in his *Revelationes*, or that in the very widespread **Golden Legend* of *Jacobus de Voragine († 1298). We also possess 23 of Elizabeth's *letters in reply to questions by *abbots or *nuns, among them two letters to Hildegard of Bingen. The cycle of six visions *De resurrectione beatae Mariae matris Christi* is an important contribution to the mariology of the time, notably by developing the theme of *Mary's bodily *assumption, at this time a widely debated dogmatic question. Her visions attest the assumption and her explanations recur in the arguments of 13th-c. theologians.

*PL*, 195, 1855, 119-194; 197, 1855, 214-216. – F. W. Roth, *Die Visionen der heiligen Elisabeth und die Schriften der Äbte Ekbert und Emecho von Schönau*, Brünn, 1884-1886 (2 vol.). – F. W. Roth, *Das Gebetbuch der heiligen Elisabeth von Schönau*, 1, Augsburg, 1886; *ibid.*, 2, 1886 (commentary). – W. Oehl, *Deutsche Mystikerbriefe des Mittelalters*, Munich, 1931 (repr. Darmstadt, 1972), 113-151.

K. Köster, *DSp*, 4, 1960, 585-588. – P. Dinzelbacher, "Die Offenbarungen der heiligen Elisabeth von Schönau: Bildwelt, Erlebnisse und Zeittypisches", *Studien und Mitteilungen aus den Benediktiner- und Zisterzienserorden*, 97, Sankt Ottilien, 1986, 462-482. – M. Schmidt, *Marienlexikon*, 2, Sankt Ottilien, 1989, 328 f. – A. L. Clark, *Elisabeth of Schönau: a twelfth-century visionary*, Philadelphia (PA), 1992. – S. Flanagan, "Die Heiligen Hildegard, Elisabeth, Ursula und die elftausend Jungfrauen", *Tiefe des Gotteswissens, Schönheit der Sprachgestalt bei Hildegard von Bingen*, M. Schmidt (ed.), Stuttgart-Bad Cannstatt, 1995, 209-222.

Margot Schmidt

**ELLWANGEN.** Ellwangen, a Benedictine *abbey that played an important religious and political role in Southern *Germany, was founded in 764. Intended to demarcate the borders of the *dioceses of *Augsburg, Eichstätt and *Würzburg and to establish Frankish influence on the frontier of *Swabia and *Bavaria, it would be ceded to the king and see its *abbots occupy an important place, notably in the expansion in the direction of central Europe. It reappeared with the rise of the Hohenstaufen, a context that favoured the development of the town of Ellwangen and the formation of a veritable principality. In 1460, the abbey became *collegiate, a form doubtless better adapted to this situation.

F. B. Fahlbusch, "Ellwangen", *LdM*, 3, 1986, 1849-1850.

Martial Staub

***ELUCIDARIUM.*** A *treatise composed in the form of a dialogue in question-answer form in about 1100 by the Benedictine monk *Honorius Augustodunensis for the fellow-members of his monastery. The work sets out in three books the main elements of Christian doctrine, structured according to the plan of the economy of *salvation, starting from the *creation of the world and ending with the *Last Judgment.

The Latin text, which later served essentially for the training of the lower clergy, is found widely diffused between the 12th and 16th cc. throughout the European area, no less than 380 manuscript copies having circulated in Western Europe. *Translations were made into nearly all the European languages (French, Provençal, English, Welsh, Italian, Spanish, German, Danish, Swedish, Icelandic, Czech, Russian). In French alone, five prose versions and a versified version by Gilbert of Cambres appeared, all independently of each other, not forgetting the versified transposition included in the scholastic work *Lumière as lais* by Peter of Peckham. The *Second lucidaire* adapted the text of the *Elucidarium* by reference to St *Thomas Aquinas to make it correspond to the evolution of ideas and of the Church; it also included additions connected with *pastoral care (the problem of *superstition, a *confessor's manual, the "fifteen signs", catechetical texts. . .), and was printed up to the 17th century.

The German version, made from the 12th c. under the title *Lucidarius*, had an extraordinary success with its 68 manuscripts and its 80 printed editions. This version was enriched by contemporary sources (*William of Conches, *Philosophia mundi*; *Rupert of Deutz, *De divinis officiis*; Honorius Augustodunensis, *Imago mundi*) to do with natural *science, *philosophy and *theology. The most successful Italian version (27 manuscripts) was established from the first Old French version.

Y. Lefèvre, *L'Elucidarium et les Lucidaires*, Paris, 1954. – H. Düwell, *Eine altfranzösische Übersetzung des Elucidarium*, Munich, 1974. – M. Degli Innocenti, *L'Elucidario. Volgarizzamento in antico milanese dell'Elucidarium di Onorio Augustodunense*, Bologna, 1984. – E. Ruhe, *Himmel und Hölle – Heilswissen für Zisterzienser. Der "Lucidaire en vers" des Gillebert de Cambres*, Wiesbaden, 1991. – D. Ruhe, *Gelehrtes Wissen, "Aberglaube" und pastorale Praxis im französischen Spätmittelalter. Der "Second Lucidaire" und seine Rezeption im 14.-17. Jahrhundert. Untersuchung und Edition*, Wiesbaden, 1993. – *Elucidarium und Lucidaires. Zur Rezeption des Werks von Honorius Augustodunensis in der Romania und in England*, E. Ruhe (ed.), Wiesbaden, 1993.

Doris Ruhe

**EMBER DAYS.** By "ember days" are understood a *fast on Wednesday, Friday and Saturday, placed in the liturgical *calendar at the start of each of the four seasons. The spring ember days were celebrated during the first week of *Lent, those of summer during the octave of *Pentecost, those of autumn in the third week of September and those of winter during the first week of *Advent.

"As each season is composed of three months", comments *Durand of Mende in his *Rationale*, "that is why we fast four times three days, fasting one day for each month, and thus we repair in one day the harm committed in one month" (*Rat.* V, 4, 4).

*CaP*, 4, *The Liturgy and Time*, London, 1986.

Anselme Davril

**EMBOLISM.** The term "embolism", meaning an intercalation, was already used in the 9th c. by the *liturgist *Amalarius. Other medieval liturgists, *e.g.* *Innocent III and *Durand of Mende in his *Rationale*, applied it both to the *Libera nos*, the *prayer following the *Pater* in the *mass, and to the passages of the *canon of the mass that varied for certain *feasts, *e.g.* in the *Communicantes*.

Amalarius, *Opera liturgica omnia*, 3, J. M. Manssens (ed.), Vatican, 1950, 387.

*CaP*, 2, *The Eucharist*, London, 1986.

Pierre-Marie Gy

**EMBROIDERY.** The art of embroidery consists of adding a *textile design onto a pre-existing fabric with the aid of a needle. The thread may be of different materials (*gold or *silk) and there are several types of stitch. Embroidery is of oriental origin. It spread in Europe with the taste for rich fabrics imported into, then manufactured in, *Spain and *Sicily, between the 8th and 12th centuries. Its apogee was in the 13th c. with *opus anglicanum*, English embroidery, known throughout Europe. Almost the whole

*The Crucifixion.* 12th-c. embroidery. León, Treasury of San Isidoro.

demand came from the Church for the decoration of liturgical *vestments (*mitres, chasubles. . .). But the masterpiece of medieval embroidery is undoubtedly the 11th-c. "*Bayeux tapestry".

D. King, *Opus Anglicanum: English Medieval Embroidery*, London, 1963. – M.Swain, *Scottish Embroidery: Medieval to Modern*, London, 1986. – *Autour du fil. L'encyclopédie des arts textiles*, E. Poyet (ed.), Paris, 1989. – L. Von Wilckens, *Die textile Künste von der Spätantike bis zum 1500*, Munich, 1991.

Juliette Callies

**EMIR.** Emir, in Arabic *amīr* or "chief", was the name borne in Islamic lands by any military chief, though in the *Abbasid Empire it often designated a provincial governor. At the time of the dismemberment of that empire, the emir came hierarchically below the king (*malik*), himself situated below the sultan, delegate of the *caliph. The title of emir then often designated the head of a principality, but any military leader also bore it.

The title of emir of the faithful (*amīr al-mu'minīn*) was proper to the caliph. In the 10th-11th cc., there was also a "grand emir" (*amīr al-umarā*), who was the delegate of the Abbasid caliph.

A. A. Duri, "Amīr", *EI(E)*, 1, 1960, 438-439 (2nd ed.).

Dominique Sourdel

**EMMAUS, ROAD TO.** After his *Resurrection Jesus appeared to two disciples on their way from Jerusalem to Emmaus. He walked with them, expounding the things concerning himself in the Scriptures, but they recognised him only at the breaking of the bread (Lk 24, 13-35). Only one of the two is named: Cleophas. In medieval art, two scenes illustrate this account: the walk to Emmaus, represented for the first time on the *mosaics of the basilica of Sant'Apollinare Nuovo at *Ravenna, and the meal.

From the 12th c., iconography was influenced by the liturgical *dramas played during *Holy Week. Under the impetus of eucharistic devotion, the theme of the meal was then developed, but the subject, which primarily incarnated the reality of the Lord's resurrection, was rivalled by other representations of meals, mainly the Last Supper. It even suffered an eclipse from the early 14th to the mid 15th century. In the late 15th c., images of the meal at Emmaus, once more in favour, insisted less on the breaking of the bread than on the attributes of the *pilgrim: staff, scrip, hat, often reserved for *Christ, "the only true pilgrim".

L. Rudrauf, *Le Repas d'Emmaüs*, Paris, 1955. – G. Schiller, *Ikonographie der christlichen Kunst*, 3, Gütersloh, 1971, 99. – D. Rigaux, *A la table du Seigneur. l'Eucharistie chez les Primitifs italiens 1250-1497*, Paris, 1989, 178-182.

Dominique Rigaux

**EMMERAM (7th c.).** Emmeram, bishop of *Regensburg, was *martyred in the second half of the 7th c.; he is buried at Sankt Emmeram, Regensburg.

Of Aquitanian origin and perhaps bishop of *Poitiers before his *mission to *Bavaria, he was given by Duke Theodo the task of organising the Church of his *duchy. Accused of having seduced the duke's daughter Uta, he was murdered after long torments by her brother Lantpert while he was going to *Rome. His cult spread with the writing of his *Vita* by Bishop Arbeo of Freising in *c.*772, then at the end of the 9th c. when *Arnulf of Carinthia proclaimed him patron saint of his kingdom, and finally, thanks to Bavarian missionary activity, as far as *Bohemia and *Slovakia.

K. Balb, *Emmeran und Regensburg. Legende und Kult*, Regensburg, 1973.

Geneviève Bührer-Thierry

**EMPIRE IN THE WEST.** The word "empire" translates the Latin *imperium* and designates both the power exercised by the emperor and the territory over which that power is exercised. In the course of the Middle Ages and for modern historians, it was applied to the lands governed by the German king from 962 and it progressively lost the universal significance that was attached to it. The history of the Empire is inseparable from that of *Rome, where imperial *coronation long and exclusively took place, and from that of the papacy, without which there could have been no coronation.

The Roman Empire, partitioned between East and West, disappeared, in its Western form, from Rome in 476. But the idea that it theoretically continued to exist was kept up. It gained strength at the *court of *Charlemagne, who as king of the *Franks governed nearly all the area formerly covered by the Western Empire. The circulation of the false *Donation of Constantine, composed *c.*760, spread the tradition of a division of the world between two rulers, one temporal and one spiritual. In 800, at Christmas, Pope *Leo III, who had called Charlemagne to his help, crowned him emperor, thus reviving the vanished institution. The Frankish Empire lasted hardly a century. With *Louis the Pious the idea of a single emperor predominated, reigning over *kingdoms subject to him; the title of *imperator augustus* gave substance to the idea of continuity. In reality the successive emperors, *Lothar I, *Louis II, *Charles the Bald, Charles the Fat, bore a title, defended an idea, but did not truly reign over an empire. From 908, the title was disputed between Italian kinglets without influence.

His accession to the kingdom of *Italy (952) and his victory over the Hungarians (955) made King *Otto I an *imperator* in the old style, who was invited by Pope John XII to wear the imperial *crown in default of heirs. Otto I confirmed the *Patrimony of St

*Christ and the Pilgrims to Emmaus*. Miniature from the *Psalter* of Ingeborg of Denmark, *c.*1210. Chantilly, Musée Condé (Ms 9/1695, fol. 30 v°).

Peter and sealed his understanding with the papacy. The marriage of *Otto II to a Byzantine princess emphasized the dynasty's imperial ambtions. *Otto III went further. In full agreement with the theoretician *Gerbert of Aurillac, who became *pope under the name of Silvester II, he wished to make Rome the capital of a restored universal Empire. However, the claim to control the kingdoms remained an illusion, even if the emperor governed the kingdoms of *Germany, *Italy and *Lotharingia (while awaiting that of *Burgundy), even if he made kings in *Poland and *Bohemia. This universal ambition was only a flash in the pan.

With *Henry III (1039-1056), the adoption of the title *rex Romanorum* made more visible the fact that the king elected by the German princes was considered *ex officio* as emperor designate, which led to the confusion of the Empire with the kingdom of Germany. A little later, the emperor's position lost much of its strength with the papacy's assertion of power under *Gregory VII (1075). The emperor saw his right to intervene in papal *elections contested, while the bishop of Rome claimed to control the choice of emperor. It was true that imperial coronation depended solely on the *pope. *Henry IV had to have himself crowned by his *antipope Clement III (1084), and *Henry V literally snatched his coronation from *Paschal II.

The personality of the two great *Staufen princes, *Frederick I and *Frederick II, and that of the contemporary popes *Alexander III, *Innocent III and *Gregory IX, explain the harsh conflicts that set "the *priesthood and the Empire" against each other, each contesting the other's claims to be sole master of the universe. Frederick I failed because of his Italian defeats. Innocent III, master of the situation, imposed his choices; his importance grew as he received princely *homages (*England, *Aragon). Frederick II pushed his imperial claims, supported by his titles of king of *Sicily and *Jerusalem, beyond the bounds of the reasonable. In his time, theoreticians did not contest the necessity of universal Empire and historians considered that the history of the world was continued by the uninterrupted Roman Empire, but kings took no account of any imperial power, St *Louis knowing better than most that he was "emperor in his realm". From 1250 and during the interregnum, the Empire had neither territorial existence nor theoretical definition; there was nothing more than a coveted title.

During the last two centuries of the Middle Ages, the Holy Roman Empire of Frederick Barbarossa was confirmed as the Holy Roman Empire of the German nation (commonly called the German Holy Roman Empire). The house of *Luxemburg, with *Henry VII and *Charles IV, gave it a certain lustre, but the latter of those two rulers impoverished it considerably by generously distributing royal property in order to set up a clientele loyal to himself, and he finally detached imperial election from Rome by instituting, with the Golden Bull of 1356, a college of seven *Prince Electors, three *archbishops (*Mainz, *Cologne, *Trier) and four lay princes (Palatinate, *Brandenburg, *Bavaria, *Bohemia). The confrontation between Louis IV of Bavaria and the papacy weakened imperial influence still more. *Sigismund gave it grandeur by the role he played in regulating the *Great Schism. Paradoxically, the emperor and the Empire represented a person and a notion important in the eyes of the Germans, who could not conceive a world-order without them, and at the same time they had no legal force, no means of existence other than the personal assets of their holder, no capital. When Maximilian took the imperial crown, it was to bear an ambitious title, not to acquire any power. The German Holy Roman Empire of the 16th c. no longer had anything in common with the Empire restored by Charlemagne.

P. E. Schramm, *Kaiser, Rom und Renovatio. Studien und Texte zur Geschichte des römischen Erneuerungsgedankens vom Ende des Karolingischen Reiches bis zum Investiturstreit*, Darmstadt, 1957 (2nd ed.). – R. Folz, *The Concept of Empire in Western Europe from the Fifth to the Fourteenth Century*, London, 1969. – R. M. Herkenrath, *Regnum und Imperium in den Diplomen der ersten Regierungsjahre Friedrichs I*, Vienna, 1969. – *Les Grands Empires*, *RSJB*, 31, 1973. – E. Schubert, *König und Reich. Studien zur spätmittelalterlichen deutschen Verfassungsgeschichte*, Göttingen, 1979. – *Le Concept d'Empire*, M. Duverger (ed.), Paris, 1980. – P. Moraw, "Reich", *GGB*, 5, 1984, 430-456. – R. Rapp, *Les Origines médiévales de l'Allemagne moderne. De Charles IV à Charles Quint (1346-1519)*, Paris, 1989.

Michel Parisse

**ENAMELS.** The art of enamelling originated in the east Mediterranean basin around the 14th c. BC. The word *enamel* comes through Old French *esmal* from Latin *smaltum*, used in the 9th c., which is derived from the Old German *smelzan*, to melt or smelt. It was in northern *Germany, in Lower *Saxony, that a 12th-c. monk named *Theophilus wrote a treatise on the "various arts" (*Schedula diversarum artium*) in which the technique of enamelling occupies a privileged place; this collection of recipes is the oldest surviving text on the subject. By associating a *metal, often precious, with a coloured vitreous mineral substance, the enameller seeks to rival nature, in particular to imitate her rare and precious stones.

Five fundamental technical processes allow a metallic backing to be permanently associated by fire, at temperatures that may reach 800° or 900°, with the enamels: *fonte en creux*, chasing, cloisonnage, bas-relief and painting. The first procedure was practised during the early Middle Ages: the next three were used from the *Romanesque period to the end of the *Gothic period when they enjoyed their apogee, and the last made its appearance in the middle of the 15th century. In the case of the first three procedures, a web of partitions forming a design was laid out on the surface of the metal: if the partitions of the design were obtained by melting down bronze or silver, we speak of *encrusted* enamel; if thin strips of metal were added by soldering, it was *cloisonné*, nearly always worked in *gold; if the partitions were made by scooping out cells in the metal with the help of a burin, "raising the field", it was chased or *champlevé* enamel, generally practised on copper or bronze and associated with opaque enamels. If sheets of gold or silver were engraved in light bas-relief and covered with transparent enamels that left the underlying decoration visible, one obtained translucent *basse-taille* enamels. Finally, by covering a very thin copper surface with a decoration obtained just from successive layers of opaque and translucent enamels, one obtained a painted enamel.

In Europe, from the 8th to the 15th c., the art of enamelling developed and prevailed in one or other of these techniques according to the styles proper to each civilization, from the Celtic and *Anglo-Saxon world to the Byzantine, from *Denmark to the Iberian peninsula. While Celtic civilization, in its late insular phase from the 5th to the 8th c., reached in *Ireland the highest mastery of the art of encrusted enamels on bronze and silver, an enamelling on cloisonné gold, precious and refined, of an astonishing richness of colour, developed at *Constantinople and in the Byzantine area. Precious objects of small dimensions, intended as commodities, Byzantine enamels took the form of jewels, vases, objects for secular or religious use; numbers of them passed into the ecclesiastical and princely treasuries of Carolingian and Ottonian Europe where they were imitated and interpreted by Western *goldsmiths from the 9th to the 11th century. To them we owe the origin of *Romanesque enamelling, which was directly inspired by them while transposing them onto *champlevé* copper. Romanesque enamels appeared in the first half of the 12th c. almost simultaneously in, *Aquitaine starting from *Conques, in northern *Spain and at *Limoges, and in the Meuse and Rhine valleys. At Limoges, from the early 13th c., workshops turned out in an almost industrial way, and for a wide European clientele, all the objects useful for the liturgy: shrines for the *relics of saints, crosses, *croziers, manuscript bindings, boxes for hosts or pyxes, etc. It was at *Siena in *Tuscany that translucent enamelling appeared, mainly on silver, at the end of the 13th c.; in the 14th c., at *Paris, on both gold and silver, it enjoyed an exceptional development in court circles. Midway through the 15th c., enamellers became veritable painters. The development of this last technique of enamel, at the end of the Gothic period, seems to have made its way from *Flanders to northern *Italy and *Venice. At the end of the 15th c., this new way of enamelling prevailed at *Limoges, where it was henceforth to enjoy unequalled success.

Theophilus, *The Various Arts*, C.R. Dodwell (ed.), Oxford, 1986 (*OMT*).

E. Rupin, *L'Oeuvre de Limoges*, Paris, 1890. – M.-M. Gauthier, *Émaux du Moyen Âge occidental*, 1973 (2nd ed.). – M.-M. Gauthier, *Medieval Enamels*, N. Stratford (ed.), London, 1981. – M.-M.Gauthier, G. François, *Émaux méridionaux. Catalogue international de l'Oeuvre de Limoges, t. 1, L'Époque romane*, Paris, 1987. – G. Haseloff, *Email im frühen Mittelalter. Frühchristliche Kunst von der Spätantike bis zu den Karolingern*, Marburg, 1990. – N. Stratford, *Catalogue of Medieval Enamels in the British Museum*, London, 1993.

Geneviève François

***ENCELLULEMENT.*** The French term *encellulement* designates that important phenomenon in European history, the consolidation and takeover of the countryside by men, basis of the setting up of lordships. It was accompanied by an alteration of dwelling patterns through abandonment or selection of former sites, which still marks the countryside of Europe, an organisation or reorganisation of lands with a fixing of the circulation network and the pattern of land-holding, the definitive setting up of the network of *parishes and the beginnings of self-awareness among villagers (common interests, collective mentality). The essential effect was the creation of localities within which men's lives would be confined until the disappearance of the *Ancien régime*.

The origin of this powerful mutation is still not very clear. We may see it as the effect of groups of warriors falling back on the *villages after the halting of the Carolingian pillaging raids and in the face of the dangers presented by the Norman, *Saracen and Hungarian *invasions of the 10th century. We may also invoke the disintegration of a public *authority unable to dispose of adequate means to control men, leading to the delegation or usurpation of public rights, notably of *justice, at the village level. The erection of *mottes and *castles evidently arises from these two causes. Demographic pressure accompanied by better climatic conditions may, by multiplying hands and mouths, have favoured a class of artisans and more active trade and have unleashed a market economy, to the benefit primarily of the owners of the soil and of workshops. The decline of *slavery may also have stimulated rivalry between the small communities of free men and the possessors of force, finally in favour of the latter. All these phenomena are discernible after 950 in Mediterranean Europe, towards the year 1000 in middle France, fifty years later north of the Loire and the Danube, shortly before 1100 over the Channel and beyond the Rhine, according to the degrees of resistance of the former structures, notably royal or comital ones.

The aspects of the movement are equally varied: the essential trait is the concentration of men around fixed points, parish or castral church, *cemetery, fortress of the master. **Incastellamento*, the Italian, Provençal and Iberian form of the movement, is characterized by the brutality of lords and the perching of sites on hilltops. Southern France and middle *Germany are marked by appeal by persusion to manorial workshops and the *sauvement* (protected place) in case of danger. The enclosed **bourg* with its advantageous franchises is the form of the Atlantic zones. Spontaneous gathering round the ecclesial group, sometimes without a castle, is typical of north-west continental Europe. All these nuances of *encellulement* do not hide the fact that the essential result was the seizure of the public *ban by private authority.

J. P. Poly, E. Bournazel, *The Feudal Transformation 900-1200*, New York, 1991. – R. Fossier, *Enfance de l'Europe . . .*, *NC(C)*, 17 and 17a, 1982. – *Les Communautés villageoises du Moyen Âge aux temps modernes*, Auch, 1984 ("Flaran", 4). – W. Rösener, *Peasants in the Middle Ages*, Oxford, 1992. – *Villages et villageois au Moyen Âge*, Caen, 1992.

Robert Fossier

**ENCLOSURE.** From Latin *claudere*, the term designates a material obstacle around a property; enclosure was also made up of all the ecclesiastical laws that fixed, within the reserved space, the incomings and outgoings of both outsiders and religious. From a spiritual reality, a retreat for the monk in search of *God, the notion passed to a codification by authority. Doctrine, legislation, facts and justificatory theories were influenced by various cultures. Moreover, theory and practice appear on examination to be different for monks and *nuns. The monks of St Pachomius (290-346) could receive visits from their relations and, with the superior's permission, visit them in case of *sickness. For St Basil (329-379), journeys had to possess a pastoral dimension.

From the beginnings, avoidance of contacts between monks and *women, even religious ones, was a preoccupation of legislators. The East, despite the decisions of the council *in Trullo* (692) and of *Nicaea II (787), was generally less severe on this point. From the 5th c., under the influence of the monasteries of *Cassian at *Marseille and St Honoratus at *Lérins, the West was oriented towards a greater stability of monks. The Rule of St *Benedict (480-543) required from the aspirant a commitment to *stabilitas*. But the various *councils or episcopal admonitions denote a certain difficulty in halting the wanderings of monks. This problem, endemic throughout the Middle Ages, became acute in periods of decadence; from the recommendations of St *Peter Damian (1007-1072) to the complaints of St *Anselm (1033-1109) and the letters of Pope *Innocent III (1198-1216) to the archbishop of Auch, the ecclesiastical hierarchy tried to obtain the observance of active and passive enclosure.

Though the notion of strict and perpetual enclosure appears only rarely for monks, nuns, who at the beginning benefited from notable exceptions, would see perpetual enclosure applied to them in a general way. St *Caesarius's (470-572) *Regula ad virgines*, arguing from the insecurity of the times, stipulated for nuns an enclosure without exemption. Until the 8th c., two types of monastery coexisted in the West: one with strict enclosure, the other with more flexible enclosure. From the 8th to the 10th c., various councils fixed the cases of exit for *abbesses in a more restrictive way. Active and passive enclosure tended to become general from the 11th century. The *Poor Clares were the first to pronounce a fourth *vow, that of enclosure, after the *Decretal *Periculosa* of *Boniface VIII (1298) which extended it to all nuns. Spiritual justifications frequently likened it to Christ's tomb, thus reinforcing its penitential aspect. The extension of enclosure entailed the creation of a category of external lay sisters in charge of relations with the outside world. For centuries, this primary universal law would rule the life of nuns and make their status depend on its observance.

E. Jombart, M. Viller, "Clôture", *DSp*, 2, 1953, 979-1007. – M. de Fontette, *Les Religieuses à l'âge classique du droit canon*, Paris, 1967.

Élisabeth Lopez

**ENCYCLOPEDIAS, MEDIEVAL.** No medieval work bore the title *Encyclopedia*. But many attempted to order the whole of knowledge and could claim an encyclopedic status, starting with the *Etymologies* of *Isidore of Seville, undisputed model until the irruption of *Aristotelian thought into Western thought. For Christian thought, by reason of the original sin of knowledge, there was always tension between desire for and mistrust of knowledge of the world. Following Scripture (Wis 7, 16-21; Rom 1, 20), St Augustine, in his *De doctrina christiana*, established the programme of Christian knowledge and thus authorized encyclopedic labour.

The encyclopedic work took a great variety of titles, contents and forms. Some constants can be disengaged: it was always a work of compilation, which accumulated ancient knowledge and had no vocation to innovate; it was a "book of books", which offered the reader the best of all that had been written by all known ancient authors, patristic and medieval authors and, as far as they were in circulation, the great Judaeo-Arabic and Aristotelian texts. Its organisation was always logical, in line with cosmological (four *elements, days of *creation) and philosophical classifications (*liberal arts, parts of *philosophy in the Neoplatonist, Chartrian, Victorine or Aristotelian traditions, etc.). The primary aim sought or avowed was nearly always to permit a reading of Holy Scripture on its different levels of meaning, literal, allegorical, moral; then came aids to *preaching and, in a veiled form, sometimes "scientific curiosity".

In this common framework, there were numerous differences between one work and another. First, the extent of the project itself: we can separate encyclopedias that limit the totality to natural things (*De natura/naturis rerum*, *De proprietatibus rerum*, *Das Buch der Natur*, etc.) and those that, as well as *nature, include the arts and *sciences, *ethics, *history and, at least partially, *theology (*Speculum maius/universale*, *Imago mundi*, *Trésor*, etc.). From this point of view of extension, as well as that of presentational technique, the greatest success is that of the *Speculum maius* *(naturale, doctrinale, historiale)* by the mid-13th-c. *Dominican *Vincent of Beauvais. Next, even when the project was clearly universal, particular attention favoured this or that view of the world: grammatical (Isidore), medical (*Hildegard), dogmatic and psychological (Raoul Ardent), astrological (Sydrac), political (Brunetto Latini), mystical (Giovanni da San Gimignano), moral (Pierre Bersuire), etc. Material presentation varied considerably: divisions into books and chapters, tables of contents, illustrations – sometimes important –, tables facilitating access to selective information; the size of the works goes from the simple to the centuple (30 to 40 folios for Honorius's *Imago mundi*, seven or eight large volumes of 200 to 300 folios each for the *Speculum maius*).

Up to the 13th c., these encyclopedias were written in *Latin; there then appeared, for different publics, firstly *translations and adaptations, then new compositions in *vernacular languages. Bartholomew of England's *De proprietatibus rerum* illustrates the maximum success of an encyclopedic work: it enjoyed an immense learned success in Latin (it was inscribed in the list of *books taxed by the university of *Paris in 1286) as well as in translations or adaptations into French, Provençal, Italian, English, Flemish, *Anglo-Norman, Spanish and German. Finally, in time, encyclopedias multiplied with the 12th-century renaissance and reached their apogee in the 13th century.

The following list is indicative: *Isidore of Seville, *Etymologiae rerum sive origines libri XX*; *De natura rerum* (before 621); the Venerable *Bede, *De natura rerum* (before 731); *Rabanus Maurus († 856), *De naturis rerum (De universo)*; Lambert of Saint-Omer, *Liber floridus* (1090-1120); *Hildegard of Bingen, *Liber subtilitatum diversarum naturarum creaturarum* (*c.*1150); *Honorius Augustodunensis († after 1153), *Imago mundi*; *William of Conches († after 1154), *Philosophia mundi*; *Apex physicae* (after 1153); *Richard of Saint-Victor, *Liber exceptionum* (1153-1172); Herrad of Lansberg, **Hortus deliciarum* (1175 f.); Raoul Ardent, *Speculum universale* (after 1193); Alexander Neckam, *De naturis rerum* (late 12th c.); Arnoldus Saxo, *De finibus (floribus?) rerum* (*c.*1225); Bartholomew of England, *De proprietatibus rerum* (*c.*1230-1240); *Thomas of Cantimpré, *Liber de natura rerum* (1230-1240); Gossuin of Metz, *L'Image du monde* (1246 f.); *Vincent of Beauvais, *Speculum maius* (*c.*1250); Brunetto Latini, *Trésor* (*c.*1266-1267); *Compendium philosophiae* (after 1277); Giovanni da San Gimignano († 1333), *Summa de exemplis et similitudinibus rerum*; Pierre Bersuire, *Reductorium morale* (*c.*1340); Henry of Herford († 1370), *Catena aurea entium vel problematum series*.

M. de Gandillac, "Encyclopédies pré-médiévales et médiévales", *Cahiers d'histoire mondiale*, 9, Neuchâtel, 1965, 483-595. – C. Meier, "Grundzüge der mittelalterlichen Enzyklopädik. . .", *Literatur und Laienbildung im Spätmittelalter und die Reformationzeit. . .*, L. Grenzmann (ed.), K. Stackmann (ed.), Stuttgart, 1984, 467-500. – M. T. Beonio-Brocchieri Fumagalli, *Le Enciclopedie dell'occidente medievale*, Turin, 1981. – E. M. Jonsson, "Le sens du titre Speculum aux XIIe et XIIIe siècles et son utilisation par Vincent de Beauvais", *Vincent de Beauvais. Intentions et réceptions d'une oeuvre encyclopédique au Moyen Âge*, S. Lusignan (ed.) *et al.*, Montreal, Paris, 1990, 11-32. – C. Codoner, S. Louis, M. Paulmier-Foucart, D. Hüe, M. Salvat, A. Llinares, *L'Encyclopédisme. Actes du Colloque de Caen. . .*, A. Becq (dir.), Paris, 1991. – *L'Enciclopedismo medievale 8-10 ott. 1992*, San Gimignano, 1994. – C. Meier, "Illustration und Textcorpus. Zu kommunikations- und ordnungsfunktionalen Aspekten der Bilder in den mittelalterlichen Enzyklopädiehandschriften", *Frühmittelalterliche Studien* (Münster), 31, 1997, 1-31 and tables I-XXVIII.

Monique Paulmier-Foucart

**END, FINALITY.** The end, *i.e.* that in view of which something is and acts, is a determination intrinsic to every reality, which it orders in two ways: to the perfection inherent in its form, and to the final end common to the whole of the real. In realities that are not endowed with *reason, determination towards the end results from a natural inclination, while in rational beings it is dictated by the *will. Voluntary acts, according to St *Thomas Aquinas, are the only properly human ones. The end plays the role of the final *cause, *i.e.* the first cause of action. Now, since each end is sought as a *good and since there is only one good (*God) capable of fulfilling the human desire for happiness, God represents the final cause of action of men and of all creatures, which find their fulfilment only in a return to the first principle.

*Causalità e finalità*, M. Gentile (ed.), Florence, 1959. – H. Voigt, *Das Gesetz der Finalität*, Amsterdam, 1961.

Tiziana Suarez-Nani

**ENERGIES.** The term "energies" which, in *Aristotle, designates being (*esse*) at work (as distinct from *dunamis*, which is its potency), is connected with Gregory *Palamas and Palamism. This Eastern theologian (1296-1359) was at the heart of theological controversies concerning his *doctrine of the divine. Not without references to *Dionysius the Areopagite, Gregory Palamas had recourse to the *analogy of the sun and its rays to describe the levels of knowledge of *God accessible to man. The centre cannot be known, but certain points on the surface (hypostases) can open up to man paths of knowledge, just like the rays of the sun. These rays are the divine energy, *i.e.* the whole of the operations of the attributes of God that are realized in *theophanies. Thus, at the *Transfiguration, the *light that radiated from *Christ was the divine energy. The divine energies are also realized in the Incarnation and by the gift of the Spirit. The *Synodal tome* of Constantinople in 1351 adopted the doctrine of energies. However, many criticized this doctrine for its polytheistic tendency, since the energies could be confused with a multitude of divinities.

V. Lossky, "La théologie de la lumière chez saint Grégoire Palamas", *A l'image et à la ressemblance de Dieu*, Paris, 1959. – J. Meyendorf, *Saint Grégoire Palamas et la mystique orthodoxe*, Paris, 1959. – O. Clément, *Byzance et le christianisme*, Paris, 1964.

Michel Deneken

**ENGELTHAL.** In the region of *Nuremberg. At its *foundation, it was at first a *beguinage. After being taken over by a community of *Dominican *nuns in 1248, the *convent became a centre of spiritual life and in the course of the first half of the 14th c. it developed an intense literary activity, perhaps partly under *Cistercian influence (monastery of *Helfta?). The mystic Christine *Ebner was its foremost figure. Alongside her works we also find Lives of Grace (*Gnadenviten*) and Revelations by Adelheid Langmann, sister Gertrude (in a fragmentary state) and Friedrich Sunder, the convent's *chaplain. In these works is developed a *theology that emphasizes the possibility of personal encounter with *God and the infinite plenitude of divine *grace. Devotion to the *Eucharist is particularly emphasized. The Engelthal writings are of great importance for the study of female *mysticism in the 14th century.

S. Ringler, *Viten- und Offenbarungsliteratur in Frauenklöstern des Mittelalters*, Munich, 1980. – U. Peters, *Religiöse Erfahrung als literarisches Faktum*, Tübingen, 1988.

Siegfried Ringler

## ENGLAND

**Anglo-Saxon England (to 1066).** After the collapse of central Roman government in the early 5th c., Britain, which as *Britannia* had constituted several provinces of the Roman Empire, was settled by substantial numbers of Germanic-speaking peoples from what is now *Frisia and Jutland in *Denmark. The progress of these settlements is known from archaeological and onomastic evidence (no written sources survive from this period); by the mid 6th c., the Briton *Gildas could imply that large parts of what is now England were occupied by the Germanic settlers, with the native Britons relegated to *Wales, Devon/Cornwall and several smaller enclaves. Although the 5th and 6th cc. are the darkest in the historical record, it is clear from later written sources (genealogies; Bede; the "Tribal Hidage") that the Germanic settlements existed as small independent kingdoms which, by the end of the 6th c., had begun to be absorbed into the larger kingdoms (Kent, Wessex, East Anglia, Mercia, Northumbria) which were known to *Bede in the early 8th century. During the 7th c. these emerging kingdoms contended for power (in Bede's opinion, a small number of kings were thought to have exercised *imperium* over all the other kingdoms); during the 7th c., too, the Christian *mission introduced by *Augustine (597) but followed by other Italian missionaries (such as Birinus in Wessex) succeeded in converting the various kingdoms to Christianity, as a result of the personal commitment of kings such as *Æthelbert of Kent, Sigebert of East Anglia and Edwin and *Oswald of Northumbria.

By the late 7th c., most of England was Christian; from this time onwards, England played a vital role in Christian learning and *education, witnessed in the influence of Archbishop *Theodore († 690), *Aldhelm († 709) and *Bede († 735), but also in the work of Anglo-Saxon missionaries to the Continent, such as *Willibrord († 739), who succeeded in converting the Frisians, and Wynfrith/*Boniface († 754), who became the apostle of *Germany, with his archbishopric at *Mainz. For most of the 8th c., Mercia, under two powerful kings, Æthelbald (716-757) and Offa (757-796), was able to achieve dominance over Kent and Wessex.

At the end of the 8th c., a new threat to English political security appeared in the form of *Viking raiders, who sacked *Lindisfarne in 793, and who for most of the 9th c. caused havoc throughout England. By the middle of the 9th c., much of eastern England had been settled by Danish immigrants (the immigration is still reflected in the large number of Scandinavian place-names) and came to be known as the "Danelaw"; *York was captured by Viking armies in 866 and thereafter became the capital of a new Anglo-Scandinavian kingdom. One result of the Viking attacks was that monastic life ceased to function in much of England (in Northumbria, the monasteries of *Wearmouth-Jarrow, Lindisfarne and *Whitby were deserted), with a corresponding cessation of all aspects of educational and cultural activity. King *Alfred later recalled that, when he ascended the West Saxon throne in 871, there was no-one north of the Thames who could understand *Latin.

It was Alfred himself, through the strategic fortification of crucial English cities and through a brilliant military campaign, who finally succeeded in conquering the Viking armies, and in establishing a truce (at Wedmore in 878) with the Scandinavian settlers of the Danelaw. During the reigns of Alfred's successors, Edward the Elder (899-924) and Æthelstan (924-939), Alfred's gains were consolidated; Æthelstan defeated the armies of the Scandinavian king of York at *Brunanburh* in 937, and became in effect the first king of all England. The reign of King Edgar (959-975) was characterised by his patronage of the church, in particular the monastic reformers *Dunstan, *Æthelwold and *Oswald, through whom Benedictine *monasticism was securely established throughout England, with the result that, even into the 11th c., most of those appointed to *bishoprics were monks.

Dedicatory miniature: *King Edgar between the Virgin and St Peter, the two patrons of the New Minster* (New Minster monastery, Winchester). New Minster Charter, 966. Winchester School.

In the reign of Æthelred "the Unready" (978-1016), England experienced a new and more formidable threat from Danish armies. The English were ultimately defeated by Swein Forkbeard, who placed his son *Cnut on the English throne (1016-1035). Cnut's dynasty soon petered out in 1042 and Æthelred's son, *Edward the Confessor (1042-1066), became king with the support of the powerful earl Godwine. Edward died childless in 1066, and although Godwine's son Harold briefly occupied the English throne in that year, the throne was claimed by *William duke of *Normandy (because it had allegedly been offered to him by Edward at an earlier period) and won at the battle of *Hastings on 14 October 1066.

*English Historical Documents, c.500-1042*, D. Whitelock (ed.), London, 1979 (2nd ed.). – *The Anglo-Saxon Chronicle*, M. Swanton (ed.), London, 1996.

C. Godfrey, *The Church in Anglo-Saxon England*, Cambridge, 1962. – F. M. Stenton, *Anglo-Saxon England*, 3rd ed., Oxford, 1971. – F. Barlow, *The English Church, 1000-1066*, 2nd ed., London, 1979. – P. Stafford, *Unification and Conquest: A Political and Social History of England in the Tenth and Eleventh Centuries*, London, 1989. – H. Loyn, *Anglo-Saxon England and the Norman Conquest*, 2nd ed., London, 1991. – H. Mayr-Harting, *The Coming of Christianity to Anglo-Saxon England*, 3rd ed., London, 1991. – S. Keynes, *Anglo-Saxon History: A Select Bibliography*, 3rd ed., Binghamton (NY), 1998.

Michael Lapidge

**Medieval England (1066-1500).** The *Norman Conquest of England had little effect on governmental institutions there, excepting only the language of government, which quickly changed from Old English to *Latin. The *Domesday Survey (1086), the greatest administrative achievement of the entire Middle Ages in England, was made possible by the existence of the sworn inquest, the writ as a means of communication between the king and the localities, and the hundred, and these were *Anglo-Saxon institutions. However, the effects on every other aspect of life were profound. To the newly formed Anglo-Norman realm, England contributed the *crown that gave the king-duke a prestige in Europe he would otherwise never have enjoyed, and remarkable economic resources. The latter enabled *William I (1066-1087), *William II (1087-1100) and *Henry I (1100-1135) to fight the intermittent wars in France that were necessary to maintain their hold on Normandy itself. The distribution of lands in England to the new French, mainly Norman, aristocracy was carefully planned so as to spread its influence as widely as possible, whilst preserving much of the existing infra-structure of landholding and allowing many Englishmen to continue to hold lands, though now of Norman lords. The colonization of England in this sense was completed only in *Henry I's reign. Feudal tenures were, as a rule, heritable, but could be forfeited for misconduct, and lands also escheated to the king when, as frequently happened, male heirs were lacking. Therefore, although the aristocracy developed a clear sense of social identity in the course of the 12th c., it never became a caste. Its political ambitions always centred on local affairs. There it was the king's natural partner, though, as such, to be sharply watched. In the first half of the 12th c., control of the sheriffs, who were in principle the king's agents in the counties, and the growth of a bureaucracy of professional servants around the king, were sensitive issues. On Henry I's death in 1135, the succession to the Crown was disputed between his daughter *Matilda, wife of Geoffrey of Anjou, and his nephew *Stephen of Blois. By swift action to secure the royal treasure, and with the support of some leading churchmen, Stephen obtained the throne. This, however, was almost his last success. He lacked the innate authority and ruthless determination that had enabled Henry I to maintain effective royal control at the centre and in the counties, and there was, in a real sense, anarchy in the 1140s. Moreover, Stephen lost control of Normandy to the Angevins. By the treaty of Winchester (1153), Stephen recognised Henry of Anjou as his heir.

*Henry II (1154-1189) ruled *Anjou and Poitou as well as England and Normandy, and acquired *Gascony through his marriage to *Eleanor of Aquitaine in 1152. *Taxation and demands for military service to defend their continental possessions were to complicate the relations of *Richard I (1189-1199) with the lay and ecclesiastical magnates and fatally undermine those of John (1199-1216). Henry II himself enjoyed the great political advantage of being the pacifier of a realm that did not wish for a return to civil strife. Already, at the end of the Anglo-Saxon period, all important criminal pleas belonged in principle to the Crown, and Henry I had begun to intervene in civil actions in baronial courts involving litigants who were not of the highest status.

Henry II's great achievement was to transform these beginnings into a system of common law which quickly proved more attractive to litigants than baronial *justice. Writs initiating actions in royal courts were made available to all freemen, jury procedure of various kinds replaced the archaic procedures of trial by battle and *ordeal, and justices went from the king's *court to hear cases locally. The losers by the new arrangements were the villeins who, not being free, were denied access to the new royal remedies and continued to be entirely dependent on their lord's court in civil actions and all matters relating to their lands.

Henry II's quarrel with *Thomas Becket, archbishop of *Canterbury (1162-1170) and formerly the king's *chancellor (1155-1162), is to be seen in the context of the king's determination to have a well ordered realm. The main issues in the quarrel were the king's claim to subject clerks found guilty of *felony in church courts to a secular punishment imposed subsequently in a royal court, and to regulate *appeals from church courts to the papal *Curia at *Rome. Angevin government, being more powerful than anything hitherto in operation, gave rise to more questioning than any previous government had experienced of the way in which royal power was exercised. John's loss of Normandy in 1204 to *Philip Augustus of France (1180-1224) and his quarrel (1205-1213) with Pope *Innocent III (1198-1216) over the appointment of *Stephen Langton to the see of Canterbury made him politically vulnerable. *Magna Carta, the *charter of liberties that the barons won from the king in 1215, represented an attempt – paralleled elsewhere in Europe – to find a practical basis in written *custom, a form of positive law for the principle, itself universally accepted, that the king was under law.

*Henry III (1216-1272) was only nine years old at his accession, and much of England was in the hands of Louis, son of the French king (later *Louis VIII, 1223-1226), to whom a group of barons had offered the crown before the end of John's reign. The mature Henry, now in possession of the whole country, combined a high view of kingly *authority with a poor political judgment which expressed itself in favours for his *Lusignan half-brothers and the Savoyard relatives of his queen, Eleanor of Provence (whom he married in 1236), and neglect of the counsel of the English baronage. A quarrel among the aliens in his household precipitated the main political crisis of his reign. In the Oxford Parliament (1258), he was forced to accept a council dominated by barons and having large executive powers, of a kind very unusual except during a minority. The barons, among whom Simon de Montfort soon emerged as leader, found many allies among the knightly and gentry classes, and for a time made common cause with the latter in an attempt to bring about a reform of local government and feudal relations between lord and free tenant. The practical reforms were enacted in the Provisions of Westminster (1259) and, after the collapse of the baronial movement, in the Statute of Marlborough (1267). The Provisions of Oxford (1258), which contained the political programme, proved too radical to win widespread support, and De Montfort's obstinate adherence to them brought about civil war (1263-1265) and his own death at the battle of Evesham (1265). By summoning knights from every county, and burgesses from selected *towns, to the parliament that met at Westminster in January 1265, De Montfort anticipated the future representative character of the English *Parliament. Henry III's monument is *Westminster Abbey, whose rebuilding in the *Gothic style began under his inspiration and with his material support in 1245.

As legislator and administrator, *Edward I (1272-1307) dealt with many of the problems taken up by the barons in 1258-1259, when, indeed, he was briefly of their party. Among his statutes, *De donis conditionalibus* is especially noteworthy because, as interpreted by judges, it was the foundation of the later law of entail and so influenced the history of a great many noble families and their estates in the later Middle Ages. Like his father, but with much greater success, Edward I tried to preserve royal rights and recover those that had been lost. The Hundred Rolls (1279) and Quo Warranto pleas of his reign (1278 onwards) are important fruits of such work. However, war became the dominant theme of his reign. He conquered *Wales in 1277-1284, began in 1291 a long and ultimately unsuccessful attempt to assert a claim to superior lordship in *Scotland, and was, from 1294, involved in war in France in defence of English interests in *Gascony. His position in Gascony was adversely affected by the fact that Henry III had agreed, in the Treaty of Paris (1259), to hold the *duchy as a *fief of the king of France. Direct taxes on the moveable goods of ordinary people, and indirect taxes on trade, were levied to pay for the wars, and on several occasions representative Parliaments were summoned to assent to these. By 1297, royal demands for taxes and military service were found excessive, and Edward was obliged to confirm Magna Carta with additional clauses restricting his rights in these and other respects for the future. At Edward's death in 1307, many of the ingredients of the political crises of the next forty years were in existence: the king's involvement in intermittent wars in Scotland and France, and a baronage with political grievances. The levying of taxes more frequently than in the past stimulated a new interest in the king's management of his hereditary revenues and in the efficiency of royal administration in general. To a combustible situation, *Edward II (1307-1327) added personal ineptitude and a fatal predilection for favourites, especially Piers Gaveston († 1312), who were unacceptable to the magnates. Like the Provisions of Oxford in 1258, the Ordinances imposed on the king in 1310-1311 obliged him to accept councillors whom he had not chosen, and greatly limited his freedom of action. They were revoked only in 1322, after the defeat of Thomas, earl of Lancaster, the king's most formidable opponent, at Boroughbridge in 1321, and his execution shortly afterwards. But Edward II's political ineptitude again showed itself in his renewed favour for Hugh Despenser the Elder († 1326) and his son, also called Hugh, both highly rapacious and unscrupulous men, and by his conferment on the latter, in 1322, of the important office of *chamberlain. Edward was deposed in 1327, by a committee of estates representative of the whole realm and probably appointed in Parliament. The deposition was made easier than it would otherwise have been by the existence of an acceptable heir, the young *Edward III. Even so, the fact that a way had been found of removing a crowned and anointed monarch exercised a profound influence on English political life in the later Middle Ages.

For a great part of his reign, Edward III (1327-1377) satisfied the chivalric ambitions of the English *nobility, and some of their economic ambitions too, by military successes in France. Here, he paid the wages of the military contingents of his captains, including the nobles serving in this capacity, and divided with them the spoils of war. He waged war in France, not as duke of Gascony and therefore as a contumacious vassal of the king of France, but as a claimant to the throne of France. *Charles IV, last of the *Capetians, died in 1328 without a direct heir. Edward's claim rested on the fact that he was nearer in blood to Charles than *Philip VI, first of the *Valois rulers of France. However, in the Treaty of Brétigny (1360), Edward renounced his claim to the throne of France in return for sovereign rights in an enlarged Gascony.

Edward III's wars were financed by lay and clerical subsidies and by a subsidy on the export of wool, English wool being the country's principal export and essential to the cloth industry of the *Netherlands. Parliament controlled the lay subsidy and, from 1362, the wool subsidy. Although it recognised a duty to grant taxes when the king demonstrated a need for them for the expenses of war, it could, and often did, scrutinise the character of the need. It became less the organ of royal government that it had been earlier and more a political assembly with a mind of its own. The Commons' impeachment of some of the king's ministers on charges of corrupt practices in the so-called Good Parliament of 1376, when Edward III himself was in his dotage, is a landmark in Parliament's history.

The political tensions of the last ten years of Edward III's reign characterised much of *Richard II's reign (1377-1399). Complaints against Richard, who was only ten years old at his accession, focused on the extravagance of his household, his failure to consult outside a narrow circle of favoured ministers and friends, and the patronage he was believed to confer on these people. In 1386, a commission of government was imposed on the king, and in 1388 five of his most intimate advisers were appealed of treason – a new procedure – in the so-called Merciless Parliament by a group of nobles who included Thomas of Woodstock, duke of Gloucester, the king's uncle. Other ministers and servants of the king, including some of his judges, were impeached in this Parliament. The accused, other than the judges, who had not managed to escape before the proceedings began, and who were found guilty, were executed. The Appellants were motivated as much by their dislike of peace in France – perceived as Richard's own policy – as by other aspects of his government. Richard's revenge was long delayed but extreme. In 1397 the acts of the Merciless Parliament were annulled, proceedings instituted in Parliament against the earls of Arundel and *Warwick, who had been Appellants, and the duke of Gloucester murdered, in all probability at Richard's instigation.

Richard II's actions in the last two years of his reign amounted to a tyranny, in that he ruled to a considerable extent without consent and for his own ends. Nevertheless, he might have kept his throne but for his political miscalculation in confiscating the vast Lancastrian estates when John of Gaunt, duke of *Lancaster, died early in 1399 and sentencing Henry Bolingbroke, Gaunt's heir, to banishment for life. When Henry landed at Ravenspur in July 1399, it was with the intention of deposing Richard and taking the crown himself. This he achieved, after careful preparation of the ground and the capture of Richard himself, in a meeting of estates gathered for a Parliament on 30 Sept 1399.

As king, *Henry IV never threw off the disadvantage of having reached the throne by a crooked path. His need for taxes also weakened his position. Parliament, especially the unusually long Parliament of 1406, took a close interest in the quality of government, and in particular the conduct of royal councillors. It thus continued, though in a calmer spirit, the moves made in the late 14th century to curtail corruption in government. This changing perception on the part of the Commons, as representatives of the estates of the realm, of what practices in government were permissible, forms an essential part of the background to political life in 15th-c. England.

The recipe of *Henry V (1413-1422) for political recovery was, in a broad sense, Edward III's: war abroad and peace at home. "Peace" comprised justice, in which Henry took a personal interest, encouraging, for example, the settlement of disputes by conciliation and arbitration. It also included the suppression of the *revolt of the *heretical *Lollards, led by Sir John *Oldcastle, in 1414. The resumption of the war in France on a major scale, and in particular Henry V's reassertion of a claim to the throne of France, was made possible by the fact that the Treaty of Brétigny had never been formally ratified. It was also encouraged by the existence of civil war in France between the Armagnac and Burgundian factions. Henry succeeded in conquering Normandy, and his claim and that of his heirs to succeed to the throne of France on the death of *Charles VI was recognised in the Treaty of Troyes (1420), which also arranged his marriage with Catherine de Valois. On Henry's death in 1422, his infant son succeeded to the throne, as *Henry VI, and the Lancastrian dynasty proved capable of surviving, in his person, a minority of 15 years.

The throne of any king would have been shaken by the losses sustained by the English in France during Henry VI's mature years. The surrender of Maine in 1445 represented a decision of the king himself, taken, some said, under pressure from Margaret of Anjou, whom he married in that year. Normandy was lost to the French in 1449-1450, and by 1453 only Calais was left in English hands. But Henry was personally weak and unstable, and from 1453 subject to recurring bouts of incapacitating mental illness. He was unable to prevent some leading nobles, and especially William de la Pole, duke of Suffolk († 1450), steward of the king's household (1433-1446) and for several years the dominant figure in the Council, from profiting unduly by their service as councillors, or to keep corruption within acceptable limits in local administration. The rebellion of many of the commons of south-east England under Jack Cade in 1450 was a protest against corruption in government, especially local government. In these circumstances, an interest developed, as it had scarcely done at the beginning of the century, in legitimist claims to the throne – in this case, those of Richard duke of *York († 1460) and his son Edward, later *Edward IV (1461-1483), who were descendants of Lionel of Clarence, second son of Edward III. The dynastic issue became a magnet for quarrels between noble families, of which the most notorious was that between the duke of York and Edmund Beaufort, duke of Somerset († 1455). Where this happened, the noble practice of keeping armed retainers made a resort to *violence all too easy. The battles of the civil war, later known as the Wars of the Roses, beginning with the first battle of St Albans (1455), at which the Yorkists captured the king, made a profound impression on contemporaries and posterity, but represent only a part of the disturbance to government, at the centre and locally, caused by Henry VI's inability to fulfil the duties of a king.

Edward IV was crowned king after the battle of Towton (29 March 1461), where he defeated forces loyal to Margaret of Anjou and the Lancastrians, and he reigned, with only a short interruption in 1470-1471, when Henry VI was restored, until 1483. He left an heir, offspring of his marriage in 1464 to Elizabeth Woodville, but Edward V, as he became, reigned for less than three months. Richard, duke of Gloucester, brother of the late king, who was appointed Protector, usurped the throne himself in June 1483 and reigned as *Richard III (1483-1485). It is likely, though it cannot be proved, that he caused Edward V and his brother Richard, whom he imprisoned in the Tower of London, to be murdered soon after his usurpation. In government, the reigns of Edward IV, Richard III and *Henry VII (1485-1509), first of the *Tudor monarchs, possess a unity. A high priority was given, first, to the financial recovery of the *monarchy after the long period of indebtedness under Henry VI, and secondly, to the restoration and preservation of law and order. Edward IV, like Henry VII, was an excellent man of business: he brought to royal finance skills that had been honed in the administration of the extensive family estates of the Yorkists. By using the council as a court for cases involving nobles whom it proved hard to discipline in other ways, Edward IV anticipated the Tudor Court of Star Chamber. Those who, like Sir John Fortescue († 1479), Chief Justice and author of *The Governance of England*, feared the political consequences of the impoverishment of the king in comparison to the resources of his leading subjects, could now begin to feel confident that the danger had receded.

M. H. Keen, *England in the Later Middle Ages*, London, 1973. – W. L. Warren, *Henry II*, London, 1973. – C. D. Ross, *Edward IV*, London, 1974. – E. B. Graves, *A Bibliography of English History to 1485*, Oxford, 1975. – R. A. Griffiths, *The Reign of King Henry VI*, London, 1981. – B. McFarlane, *England in the Fifteenth Century*, London, 1981. – J. C. Holt, *Magna Carta and Medieval Government*, London, 1985. – M. Chibnall, *Anglo-Norman England, 1066-1166*, Oxford, 1986. – M. C. Prestwich, *Edward I*, London, 1988. – I. M. W. Harvey, *Jack Cade's Rebellion of 1450*, Oxford, 1991. – M. T. Clanchy, *From Memory to Written Record: England 1066-1307*, 2nd ed., London, 1993. – J. R. Maddicott, *Simon de Montfort*, Oxford, 1994. – J.T. Rosenthal, *Late Medieval England (1377-1485): a Bibliography of Historical Scholarship 1975-1989*, Kalamazoo (MI), 1994. – H.M. Jewell, *Women in Medieval England*, Manchester, 1996. – *Medieval England: an Encyclopedia*, P.E. Szarmach (ed.), M.T. Tavormina (ed.), J.T. Rosenthal (ed.), New York, 1998.

Barbara F. Harvey

**ENTRY OF JESUS INTO JERUSALEM.** The four gospels, with some differences, recount Jesus' entry into *Jerusalem (Mt 21; Mk 11; Lk 19; Jn 12). Jesus, followed by the apostles, came down from Bethany to Jerusalem, mounted on an ass. "And a very great multitude spread their garments in the way; others cut down branches from the trees, and strewed them in the way" (Mt 21, 8). The entry into Jerusalem was commemorated by *Palm Sunday which preceded *Easter Sunday. This episode was represented from the early Christian period. *Processions reconstructed *Christ's entry, notably in the Carolingian world (*Metz, *Saint-Riquier) and in the *Romanesque period (*Cambrai). The entry became the reference for royal and princely entries.

L. Réau, *Iconographie de l'art chrétien*, 2, 2, Paris, 1955-1959, 396-401. – *LCI*, 1, 1968, 593-598; *ibid.*, 3, 1971, 364-365. – H. Platelle, "L'éloge des villes au Moyen Âge, Cambrai, une autre Jérusalem", *Mélanges Jean Dugnoille et René Sansen*, Athens, 1986, 65-80; repeated in "Un idea di città. L'imaginaire de la ville médiévale", Institut italien de Paris, sept. 1992. – C. de Mérindol, "Théâtre et politique à la fin du Moyen Âge. Les entrées royales et autres cérémonies. Mises au point et nouveaux aperçus", *Théâtre au Moyen Âge, 115ᵉ Congrès national des Sociétés savantes*, Avignon, 1990, 179-212.

Christian de Mérindol

**EON OF STELLA.** A small *nobleman from the region of Loudéac in Brittany, a semi-literate layman, Eon of Stella lived at first as a hermit in the *forest of Paimpont. He broke with the Church after persuading himself that he was the Son of *God, that *eum* (understood as Eon) who would come to judge the living and the dead. From then on he gave himself to rural banditry at the expense of the clergy. Brought before the council of *Reims in

*The Deeds of Ogier of Denmark, meeting of two armies.* Miniature from the *Chronicles of Bertrand du Guesclin*, 15th c. Chantilly, Musée Condé.

1148 to be judged, Eon provoked the Fathers' mirth by reasserting his divine sonship! Imprisoned, we soon lose trace of him and his few disciples. His movement was part of the *millenarian current of popular *eremitism, revived by the disastrous news from the East and the appearance of Halley's comet in 1145; his following is explained by the difficulties of a time of *famine. Eonism appears to have been an autochthonous movement, unconnected with any known sect or *heresy and without posterity, of a very poor level, if any, of intellectual conceptualization, but revealing of the common anguish nourished by constant references to the text of the *Apocalypse.

J.-C. Cassard, "Eon de l'Étoile. Ermite et hérésiarque breton du XIIe siècle", *MSHAB*, 57, 1980, 171-198; 67, 1990, 297-301.

Jean-Christophe Cassard

**EPACT.** The epact was one of the means perfected by medieval computists to palliate the difficulties arising out of the coexistence in the *calendar of a pagan Roman base (solar year, duration of the month) and oriental (week) and Jewish elements (date of *Easter dependent on the moon). Grafted onto a 19-year cycle (the number of solar years after which lunations recur in the same order) and a succession of lunar months (theoretically fitting exactly into the cycle) of 29 and 30 days, the epact was a figure, varying from one year to another, that gave the (theoretical) age of the moon on 22 March (the moon being considered full on the 14th day; to indicate the 30th day, the term used was not "epact 30" but "epact zero"). For a given year, it was thus sufficient to know the epact and the disposition of the week (indicated by the dominical letter) to determine the date of Easter.

O. Guyotjeannin, J. Pycke, B.-M. Tock, *Diplomatique médiévale*, 1993 (2nd ed., 1995; "L'Atelier du Médiéviste", 2).

Olivier Guyotjeannin

**EPIC LITERATURE.** Cradle of all literature, epic allows a community to place itself in relation to its cultural or mythical origin; rediscovering, by singing and then by recital, a word of foundation, it cultivates, in stylization, incantatory repetition and hyperbole, a strength that stimulates and justifies.

In Europe, it was the Germanic, Scandinavian and Irish literatures that turned to mythological and religious epic: exploits of heroes, interventions of gods and conquests of marvelous talismans outdid each other in intricacy. Elsewhere, notably in the romantic epic, the genre kept up essential links with *history. It had as starting-point, close or distant, one or more definite events: the Byzantine epic *Digenis Akritas* refers to facts that took place between the 7th and 12th cc., and the *Cantar de Mio *Cid* evokes the conflicts between Christians and Muslims in the late 11th century. But epic literature tells us mainly about the systems of representing the world current in the community at the actual time of the work's composition: *Digenis Akritas* celebrates the institution of the Akrites, farmer-soldiers, from a point of view critical of the proprietory aristocracy; the French epic associates nostalgia for imperial unity with a celebration of feudal, chivalric and courtly values. Certain works, more faithful to historical reality, appear as the lyrical *chronicle of an event: the *Chanson d'Antioche*, first epic of the *crusade, is close to the accounts set down by eyewitnesses, and the *Vie de Bertrand du Guesclin* celebrates in the manner of a lyrical history an episode – glorious for France – of the *Hundred Years' War.

Like other medieval literary forms, epic narratives are displaced from one cultural area to another, which allows us to reconstruct, from vestiges surviving in a given domain, legends that have disappeared elsewhere. These displacements also allow us to observe phenomena of reappropriation and transformation, like the anti-French deeds of Bernardo del Carpio, worked up in *Spain

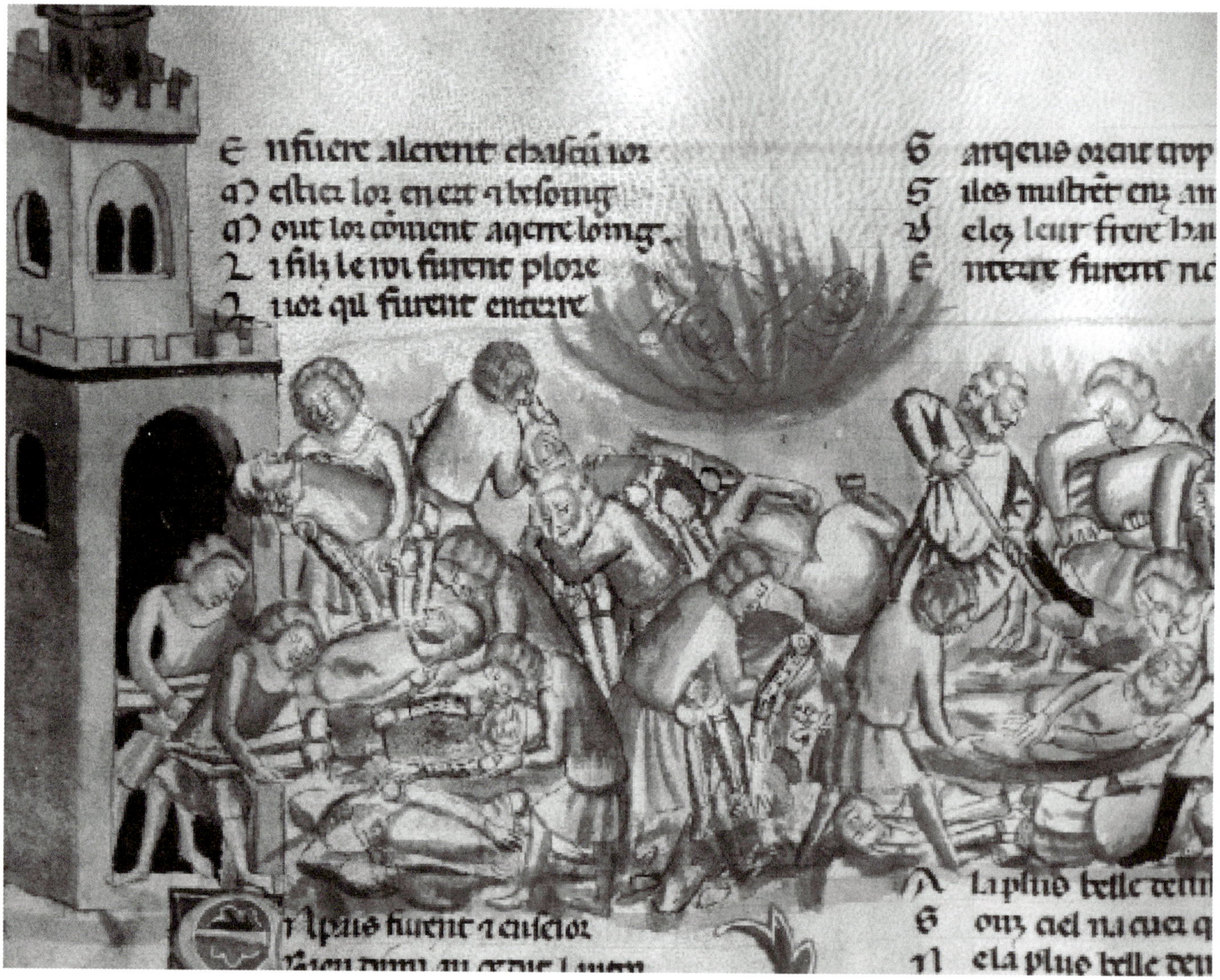

*Episode of the plague.* 14th-c. Venetian manuscript. Venice, Bibliotheca Marciana.

from the tradition of the *Roland*, or the chivalric poetry of the Italian *Renaissance, which transfigures themes and heroes of Carolingian epic. Just as a learned form of epic, which celebrated events important for the community in *Latin – the language of culture – coexisted in the Middle Ages with epic poems in the vernacular, so in the late Middle Ages the epic tradition followed two opposite directions: pedlars' chapbooks broadcast, especially in France, the *Netherlands and *Germany, the exploits of warriors of former days handed down by prose versions of modest quality, while the romances of Pulci, Ariosto and Tasso, relayed by other theatrical pieces and soon by the opera, immortalized – under the name of paladins – heroes apparently born recently, but who were none other than the Roland, Rinaldo or *Godfrey de Bouillon of the Carolingian **chansons de geste* or the crusading epics.

D. Madelenat, *L'Épopée*, Paris, 1986. – *L'Épopée*, *TSMÂO*, 49, 1988.

François Suard

## EPIDEMICS

**The West.** Our knowledge of medieval maladies is limited by the imprecision of description of clinical signs and the insufficiency of vocabulary. Endemic maladies (but susceptible to longer or shorter outbreaks) were tuberculosis (mainly described in its ganglionic or scrofular manifestations), malaria, with seasonal outbreaks, responsible in *Italy for shifts in settlement, and *leprosy, the medieval endemic *par excellence*, present in the early Middle Ages but increasing in the 12th and 13th cc., in conjunction with urban and demographic growth.

An epidemic malady very often mentioned is dysentery or "belly flux", which might correspond to typhoid fever or to bacillary or amoebic dysentery. It was rife in human groups huddled together in poor hygienic and alimentary conditions: besieged populations, armies. St *Louis and Pope *John XXII died of it.

Influenza, often confused with colds, was called "catarrh" or "influence". Epidemics of 'flu are mentioned by *Flodoard and *Orderic Vitalis and again in the 13th and 14th centuries. *Paris suffered 'flu epidemics in the 15th c., like the "*dando*" of 1427, but the "*toux*" of 1414 may have been an epidemic of whooping-cough. Smallpox raged violently, remaining endemic between epidemics. It is cited in the 6th, 8th and 10th cc., but its description by al-Razi was not known in the West (unlike one of his descriptions of measles); it particularly attacked *children. Ergotism or sacred fire, St Anthony's fire, intoxication by the ergot in rye, was not a contagious malady, but its development in cold wet weather made it seem like an epidemic. Its gangrenous form (dessication and dropping off of members) allowed mutilated subjects to survive. It seems to have been particularly rampant in France in the 11th and 12th cc. and to have become scarcer at the end of the Middle Ages (regression of rye cultivation?). Its virulence explains the cult of St Anthony, established in the Viennois in 1070, and the foundation of the hospitaller order of the *Antonines (1095).

The plague engendered great medieval pandemics, and it is this that the word "epidemic" generally designates. The first great medieval plague was the plague "of Justinian", starting in Egypt in 541, reaching *Constantinople through *Syria and Asia Minor, and entering the West by *Marseille and *Genoa. Between 541 and 767 we find fifteen epidemics of plague, ten of which affected the West, mainly in 542-543, 558-561, 570-571, 580-582, 588-591 and 599-600, generally arriving through Marseille, Genoa or *Rome. We have famous descriptions by Procopius and *Gregory of Tours. These epidemics favoured expectation of the *Last Judgment, explanation by collective *sin and divine anger, deployment of *pilgrimages, *processions and new liturgical practices (*Rogations, St Sebastian as a specialized intercessor). Their demographic impact, though undoubtedly important, particularly in Anatolia, Greece and Italy, cannot be evaluated.

The second pandemic was that of 1348-1352, called the "*Black Death"; again introduced through Marseille and Genoa, it struck at very dense and relatively very close-packed populations.

Hardly less important was the plague of 1357-1363, which came from central and eastern Europe. Like that of the early Middle Ages, the plague continued to strike through a series of epidemics at short intervals: 1373-1375 (Mediterranean), 1399-1402 (European), 1412, 1438-1439, 1479-1482, 1494-1502. The terror aroused by the impossibility of averting (unless by flight) or treating it, and by its appalling lethality in the case of the pulmonary form, profoundly modified the Western sensibility.

Syphilis, or the "great pox", did not appear in the West until the very end of the 15th century. It is mentioned from 1493-1494 and described from 1495, its sexual transmission being quickly recognised.

J. N. Biraben, J. Le Goff, "La peste dans le haut Moyen Âge", *Annales*, 1969, 1484-1510. – J. N. Biraben, *Les Hommes et la peste en France et dans les pays européens et méditerranéens*, Paris-The Hague, 1975. – R. S. Gottfried, *Epidemic Disease in Fifteenth Century England*, Leicester, 1978. – J. C. Russell, *The Control of Late Ancient and Medieval Population*, Philadelphia (PA), 1985. – D. Jacquart, F. Micheau, *La Médecine arabe et l'Occident médiéval*, Paris, 1990. – J. N. Biraben, *Histoire de la population française*, 2, Paris, 1991, 421-462 (2nd ed.).

Henri Dubois

**Byzantium.** The *Byzantine Empire suffered several epidemics, whose traces we find in *chroniclers and hagiographers or in correspondence. Particularly severe was the plague of Justinian, first appearance of the bubonic plague, which affected the whole Empire from 542, left many dead over the next two centuries and lowered morale (see Procopius, *De bello persico* II, 22; Evagrius, *Ecclesiastical History* IV, 29; *Chronicle* of *Michael the Syrian, IX, 28, etc.). In the 14th and 15th cc., recurrences of the *Black Death affected most towns in the Empire, darkening still further the last Byzantine decades (see John Cantacuzenus, *Hist.* IV, 8).

M. W. Dols, *The Black Death in the Middle East*, Princeton (NJ), 1977. – P. Allen, "The Justinianic Plague", *Byz.*, 49, 1979, 5-20. – M.-H. Congourdeau, "Pour une étude de la peste noire à Byzance", *Eupsychia. Mélanges offerts à Hélène Ahrweiler*, Paris, 1998, 149-163 ("Byzantina Sorbonensia", 16).

Marie-Hélène Congourdeau

**EPIGRAPHY.** The term "epigraphy" comes from the Greek *epigráphein*, "to write on". It designates what is written to be brought to public knowledge in a lasting way. To ensure this publicity, inscriptions were mostly written in capitals; to guarantee duration, a durable medium was used (stone, marble, *ivory, *enamel, *metal, etc.). But the nature of the medium was indifferent: stone, metal, wall-painting, *stained glass, *tapestry, etc.

In medieval epigraphy, following the work of J.-B. de Rossi and E. Le Blant, "Christian" inscriptions predating the 8th c. are sometimes discovered (Italy, France, Spain); they are very important at Rome (more than 30,000 have been published). Over the last 30 years, general collections of medieval inscriptions have been in course of publication for Germany and Austria (48 volumes), France (20 volumes), Switzerland (4 volumes) and Poland (few medieval inscriptions).

*Epitaphs form numerically the most important series of inscriptions; they preserve the memory of the deceased, request *prayers for him, exhort to a change of life. From the 13th c., they include many endowments of masses or feasts; in the 14th and 15th cc., biographical information is highly developed in them. They form an important source for knowledge of attitudes towards *death.

Numerous inscriptions are intended to ensure the publicity of public or private acts, commemorating events, passing on to posterity the names of those who commissioned or carried out the work.

*Dedications of churches, *consecrations of altars, grants of *indulgence, endowments of *anniversaries, inscriptions on *reliquaries or on the various objects associated with worship, are closely linked to the liturgy and the *cult of the saints. Then again, inscriptions identify persons and scenes, comment on iconographical programmes or sometimes offer remarkable exegetical or theological epitomes. Some can constitute a veritable *sermon addressed to the ordinary people.

All these texts enlighten us as to the *education – secular, biblical, patristic, etc. – of their authors, and provide material for the history of ideas, *spirituality and *faith. They illustrate the evolution of *Latin, the change to the *vernacular languages, the transition from classical Latin verse to assonantal or rhymed verse. By the study of writing they provide supplementary chronological references. On all these points they have the advantage of offering localized and – if only approximately – dated documents. For the medievalist, inscriptions form a documentary source that is original and precious for numerous reasons.

R. Favreau, *Les Inscriptions médiévales*, *TSMÂO*, 35, Turnhout, 1979. – R. Kloos, *Einführung in die Epigraphik des Mittelalters und der frühen Neuzeit*, Darmstadt, 1980. – W. Koch, *Literaturbericht zur mittelalterlichen und neuzeitlichen Epigraphik (1985-1991)*, 1994 ("MGH.H", 14). – R. Favreau, *Études d'épigraphie médiévale*, Limoges, 1995 (2 vol.). – R. Favreau, *Epigraphie médiévale*, Turnhout, 1997 ("L'Atelier du médiéviste", 5).

Robert Favreau

**EPIPHANY.** Emerging from Roman triumphal art, a first composition of linear type developed in early Christian art and remained until the *Romanesque period: in oriental dress, the three *Magi advance in line towards the Virgin enthroned with the Child on her knees. From the 10th c., the *crown begins to replace the Phrygian cap; in the 11th c., long tunic and mantle progressively prevail. In the 12th c., the attitudes and *gestures of the Kings diversify, their walking movement tails off before gradually coming to a halt: the first King is on his knees before the Child, while the second turns and points out the star to the last. Adoration is thus only truly signified by a single wise King. This composition was definitively adopted in the 13th century. In the 14th c., numerous secondary personages and decorations confer a theatrical aspect on the scene.

G. Vezin, *L'Adoration et le cycle des Mages dans l'art chrétien primitif*, Paris, 1950.

Véronique Guilhaume

**EPISTLES, CATHOLIC.** The non-Pauline Epistles have been described as "Catholic epistles" (since Eusebius of Caesarea and St Jerome) or "canonical epistles" (James, 1 and 2 Peter, 1, 2 and 3 John, Jude). Playing a less fundamental role in medieval *theology than the Pauline epistles, they were used on various subjects (*sacraments, *justification by works and by *faith, papacy, etc.). The most widespread commentary was that of *Bede (used in the *Glossa ordinaria*). They were commented on (in whole or in part) notably by *Peter Cantor, *Stephen Langton, Martin of León, *Peter John Olivi, Nicholas of Gorran (?), *James of Lausanne and *Augustine of Ancona.

A. Vernet, M.A. Genenois, *La Bible au Moyen Âge. Bibliographie*, Paris, 1989.

Gilbert Dahan

**EPISTLES, PAULINE.** A collection of 13 or 14 letters attributed to the apostle *Paul (Romans, 1 and 2 Corinthians, Galatians, Ephesians, Philippians, Colossians, 1 and 2 Thessalonians, 1 and 2 Timothy, Titus, Philemon and Hebrews, generally considered Pauline in the Middle Ages). Of great thematic wealth, these texts founded the *theology of Christianity. The reflection worked out in the commentaries "exercised the greatest influence . . . on the development of the *theology of the nascent *scholasticism. For it is in these commentaries that we find a great number of passages bearing on *grace, *Christ, *Redemption, the *Trinity and the *sacraments" (A. Landgraf). More rapidly than in the other biblical texts, *exegesis of the epistles often took the form of *quaestiones*, mainly theological. The commentaries of the patristic period were read throughout the Middle Ages (*Origen translated by Rufinus, Ambrosiaster, Augustine, Jerome). Among the most important medieval commentaries were, for the early Middle Ages, *Cassiodorus, *Bede, *Claudius of Turin and *Rabanus Maurus; for "pre-scholasticism", *Lanfranc of Bec, Anselm of Laon (*Glossa ordinaria*), Pseudo-Bruno the Carthusian, *Abelard and his school, *Gilbert of Poitiers and his school, *Robert of Melun and *Peter Lombard; and for "scholasticism", *Hugh of Saint-Cher, *John of La Rochelle, *Thomas Aquinas and *Peter Aureoli.

Apart from properly theological themes, certain verses or passages were particularly popular: Gal 4, 21-31, for a theory of allegorical exegesis; Rom 9, 27 and 11, 16-27, for the attitude towards the *Jews. The place of the epistles in the liturgy obviously ensured a wide diffusion of the themes they contained (lectionaries).

A. Landgraf, "Untersuchungen zu den Paulinenkommentaren des 12. Jh", *RThAM* 8, 1936, 253-281 and 345-365. – W. Affeldt, "Verzeichnis der Römerbriefkommentare. . .", *Tr.*, 13, 1957, 369-406. – A. Landgraf, *Introduction à l'histoire de la littérature théologique de la scholastique naissante*, Paris, 1973 (Fr. tr.). – H. Freytag, "Quae sunt per allegoria dicta. . . (Gal 4, 21-31)", *Festschrift F. Ohly*, Munich, 1975, 27-43.

Gilbert Dahan

**EPITAPH.** The Middle Ages inherited from Antiquity the custom of engraving in stone a commemorative inscription in honour of the deceased. But Christian ritual, like belief in *eternal life, entailed substantial formal modifications in the genre of the epitaph: rather than the length of the dead person's life, it now indicated the date of his decease, *i.e.* his entry into celestial *beatitude; the classical apostrophe to the reader ("*siste viator*": "stop, passer-by") was accompanied by a request for *prayers ("*orate pro anima mea*"); and above all, since the funerary inscription now ornamented a *tomb, it nearly always comprised an indication of place ("*hic iacet*", "here lies", "*in hoc antro*", "*sub hoc tumulo*". . .).

We can very summarily distinguish two categories of epitaph in the Middle Ages: prose epitaphs, whose traces are abundantly preserved by monuments, add to the dead person's name a rapid evocation of his career or at least a mention of his place in society. Verse epitaphs, usually in elegiac distichs, sometimes Leonine (*i.e.* with interior rhyme), more frequently found transcribed in manuscripts than actually engraved, bring out mainly the moral, intellectual or spiritual qualities of the dead person. Due to the severe constraints of metric and the relative narrowness of the semantic field of lamentation, these versified inscriptions rapidly acquired a formulary character. Their style is elliptical, "lapidary" in every sense of the term, and studded with recurrent metaphors (*e.g.* "*spiritus astra colit*", "his spirit dwells in the stars", or "*pausat in arce poli*", "he rests in the heavenly citadel"). Hence mannerist poets, virtuosi of the "variation on a given theme", like Venantius Fortunatus († 600) after whom the genre hardly evolved, excelled in writing epitaphs. We may hence legitimately suspect that not all were intended for stone or marble: the poet Baldric of Bourgueil († 1130) dedicated no less than six epitaphs to Cicero! . . . The genre, thus become autonomous, enjoyed its most perfect and most complex expression in the "tombs" of the 15th-c. French poets.

The ultraconservative character of the formulary was manifested even in inscriptions really engraved: they were hardly composed in the vernacular before the mid 13th c. (a bit earlier for the French Midi). So they are doubtless not the best monuments for judging the evolution of mental attitudes towards *death.

G. Bernt, *Das lateinische Epigramm in Uebergang von der Spätantike zum frühen Mittelalter*, Munich, 1968. – P. von Moos, *Consolatio. Studien zur mittellateinischen Trostliteratur über dem Tod und zum Problem des christlichen Trauer*, Munich, 1971-1972 (4 vol.). – R. Favreau, *Les Inscriptions médiévales*, *TSMÂO*, 47, 1979. – I. Kajanto, *Classical and Christian: Studies in the Latin Epitaphs of Medieval and Renaissance Rome*, Helsinki, 1980.

Jean-Yves Tilliette

**ERECTION.** Creation of a new dignity in the Church, usually the creation of an ecclesiastical office to which an ecclesiastical *benefice was attached, erection could consist in giving the *title and character of a benefice to a place that had not previously been one. More frequently, it meant conferring a higher title on a pre-existing benefice (*e.g.* a *chapel erected into a cure, a parish church erected into a *cathedral).

The procedure of erecting a benefice obeyed strict rules, differing according to the benefice in question. The *authority was not the same (*pope, *bishop, etc.); inquiries had to precede erection; if a pre-existing benefice found itself broken up by this erection, its titular had to be consulted. The congregation concerned could also sometimes be called to give their opinion, though that did not give them the opportunity to oppose an erection.

P.-T. Durand de Maillane, "Érection", *Dictionnaire de droit canonique et de pratique bénéficiale*, Lyon-Paris, 1770, Lyon-Paris (2nd ed., 4 vol.).

Brigitte Basdevant-Gaudemet

*Carmelite hermits at Elijah's well* by Pietro Lorenzetti (1280-1348). Carmelite altarpiece (detail), 1329. Siena, Pinacoteca Nazionale.

**EREMITISM.** Eremitism is etymologically the action of going into the *desert, *i.e.* far from the world and its temporal ambitions, alone or in a group. The aim might be to recollect oneself in order to live in *contemplation of *God, or to do *penance, either for one's own sins or for those of mankind, or again to witness to one's *faith by a particularly harsh *ascesis: *fasting, vigils, *hairshirts and other *mortifications. Eremitism gave freedom of movement for mission, itinerant *preaching or *pilgrimage. It raised up reforming vocations in the Church, but was also exposed to the suspicion of *heresy.

Very early, the meaning of the word "hermit" centred on solitaries or *anchorites, who were contrasted with *coenobites. In the 6th c., the Rule of St *Benedict called eremitism the highest form of *monasticism, which was prepared for in community. The eremitism of *Palestine, *Syria and Lower Egypt, well known through the *Apophthegms of the Desert Fathers, the *Life of St Anthony* (*c.*250-356) and archaeological excavations in the Near East, are attested from the 3rd century. They provided models for the West through the channel of the *Latin translations of Athanasius's *Life of St Anthony* (which was already read in *Trier in 336-337), the *biographies of Paul of Thebes, Malchus and Hilarion published by St Jerome in 375 and 391, the example of Eusebius of Vercelli on his return from the East (363) and, in the 5th c., the intermediary of John *Cassian's *Conferences* and *Coenobitic institutions*. Others referred to Old Testament (*Elijah) or New Testament models (*John the Baptist).

Throughout its history, eremitism oscillated between solitude and life in community. And again we remark, at all periods, that hermits were sought out to serve as spiritual guides or to take part in the *foundation or direction of coenobitic institutes.

In Egypt and *Palestine, the eremitism of the Desert Fathers continued to exist until the victory of *Islam. It took refuge in the *Lebanon or on Mount *Athos, where the monastic Republic, very markedly coenobitic, goes back to a few hermitages founded in the 8th and 9th cc. and coexists to this day with anchoritic establishments. The influence of St Basil was strong there and led more in the direction of coenobitism, but the techniques of *hesychasm, introduced in the 14th c., originating in *Sinai and perhaps *India, were better adapted to solitary life.

In the West, the example of St *Martin, founder of *Ligugé in 361 and bishop of *Tours in 371 where he created the *abbey or rather "laura" of *Marmoutier, and that of the Jura Fathers (5th c.) and St Severinus († 482), apostle of Noricum, led to vocations that played a role in the Christianization of the countryside. From the 5th c., the monks of *Lérins practised "lauriot" eremitism, *i.e.* living in *laurae*, individual cells dug in the rock, and came together only for divine service, a lifestyle midway between anchoritism and coenobitism.

The same can be said of the Irish monks, notably the disciples of St *Columbanus who, in the 7th c., supported by the *Merovingian dynasty, then by the dukes of *Alamannia and finally by the *Lombards, penetrated into northern *France, *Austrasia, the Swiss and Austrian *Alps and northern *Italy (*Bobbio). Of eremitism, the Irish monks had the itinerant character and the particularly rigorous ascesis. But they travelled in a group and owed strict *obedience to their superior. The case of St Gall, evangelizer of Alamannia, poses a problem: having disobeyed, refusing to follow his leader Columbanus to Italy, he remained permanently in the place where the *abbey bearing his name later arose. From this some have concluded that he was not Irish. But it is possible that the different versions of his life were influenced by the ideas of stability conveyed by the Rule of St Benedict, which was imposed on Western monasticism from the 9th century.

The Benedictine model led to the disappearance for two centuries, at least from the essentially hagiographical documentation, of the image of the hermit, as an anarchic vagabond without hearth or home and above all without master. The 9th and 10th cc. knew only a few hermits, especially *recluses, living in dependence on a monastery and in obedience to an *abbot.

In the course of the 11th c., perhaps under the influence of Greek monasticism, eremitism made a massive reappearance in the West, at first in Italy. St *Nilus (*c.*910-*c.*1004), a Calabrian hermit, founder of the monastery of *Grottaferrata and other establishments, was a Greek monk. St *Romuald (*c.*950-1027) stood out by his virtues of patience and ascesis. Though he wrote no Rule, he had numerous disciples and was behind the eremitical groupings of Fonte Avellana and Camaldoli. In its turn, Fonte Avellana produced St *Peter Damian (1007-1072), reforming hermit and then *cardinal, architect of the *Gregorian reform.

The eremitical movement of the 11th-12th cc. was defined more by *poverty than by solitude in the desert. It was in certain respects the result of the demographic and economic expansion of that time. The development of *towns caused the religious to flee them, while demographic development provided a public for itinerant preachers. The hermit who went into the desert was in reaction, or even in protest, against the materialism and corruption of his milieu. It is true, however, that the sources mention mainly those who came from privileged backgrounds, *nobles or churchmen. The tendency to group together was strong, whether by reason of the attraction exercised by a spiritual master, or for a simple question of survival. Several monastic congregations in the broad sense came out of this movement.

*Peter the Hermit (*c.*1050-1115), who preached with an apostolic licence, led behind him irregular crowds and, in 1096, a *popular crusade that failed lamentably, while *Robert of Arbrissel (*c.*1047-1117), founder of *Fontevraud, *Stephen of Muret (*c.*1048-1124), founder of the Order of *Grandmont, and *Norbert of Xanten (*c.*1080-1134), also with an apostolic licence, founder of the *Premonstratensians, managed to discipline and even organise their troops.

Among the eremitical creations of this time, we must also mention the *Carthusians, a semi-coenobitic, semi-anchoritic *order founded in the Alps of the *Dauphiné by *Bruno (*c.*1030-1101) with the help of Hugh, bishop of Grenoble. Although *Bernard of Clairvaux regarded eremitical solitude only as inconvenience and a sign of levity, the origins of the *Cistercians incorporated aspects of eremitism, such as poverty and desert life.

The *mendicant orders, also created from eremitical groups in the 13th c., benefited from papal approval. This marginalized those hermits who would not or could not, for economic or social reasons, put themselves under their discipline. Often threatened by the *Inquisition, exposed to accusations of heresy, they grouped together in order to survive and to obtain authorizations that would free them from pursuit.

Of those hermits who remained independent, late medieval sources mention mainly the saints or blessed, such as *Nicholas of Flüe, or high-born hermits such as Amadeus VIII, duke of *Savoy, a hermit in his castle of Ripaille near Thonon with some companions from 1434 to 1439; or those associated with *kings or princes of the Church, like the Calabrian hermit *Francis of Paola (*c.*1416-1507, defector from the *Franciscans and founder of the *Minims, something of whose *sanctity *Louis XI sought to catch.

To this vein of mystical essence or appearance, partly influenced by the *Rhineland Spirituals and the "Friends of God" movement, was added in the late Middle Ages a more utilitarian eremitism that developed especially under the Ancien Régime. In the countryside, parish communities engaged hermits as guardians of *chapels: these envisaged their activity as a job rather than a spiritual vocation. It was to discipline and organise them and to prevent false hermits from causing scandals that, from the 17th c., the Church took care to organise them into congregations and give them rules of conduct.

"Anachorètes", *DThC*, 1, 1909, 1134-1141. – R. M. Clay, *Hermits and Anchorites in England*, Oxford, 1912. – L. Gougaud, *Ermites et reclus. . .*, Ligugé, 1928. – "Ermites", *DDC*, 5, 1953, 412-429. – "Ermites", *Cath.*, 4, 1956, 391-396. – "Érémitisme", *DSp*, 4, 1, 1960, 935-982. – "Ermites", *DHGE*, 15, 1963, 766-787. – *L'eremitismo in Occidente nei secoli XI e XII. Atti della seconda Settimana internazionale di studio, Mendola, 30 agosto – 6 settembre 1962*, Milan, 1965. – "Eremita", *DIP*, 3, 1976, 1153 f. – H. Leyser, *Hermits and the New Monasticism. A study of Religious Communities in Western Europe 1000-1150*, London, 1984. – G.-M. Oury, *Les Moines*, Paris, 1987.

Catherine Santschi

**ERFURT.** A *Thuringian town situated at a crossing-point (*furt*) on the river Gera, populated since prehistoric times. Conquered by the *Franks, Erfurt was Christianized by St *Boniface, who made it the seat of a *bishopric (742-743). The town grew from the Carolingian period and attained its greatest medieval extent from 1168 (second wall). Erfurt's commercial functions lasted until the end of the Middle Ages (woad trade, a source of prosperity).

A prestigious *studium generale artium* drew students there from all over central Europe, to the detriment even of the university of *Prague, which Erfurt decided to supplant by transforming the *studium* into a *university (1379, opened in 1392). It became the second largest university of central Europe, after *Vienna, and thus trained a considerable proportion of the German *bishops, university teachers and especially *humanists of the 15th century.

*DHGE*, 15, 1963, 699-715. – H. Patze, *Bibliographie zur thüringischen Geschichte*, Cologne, 1965, 495-532. – *LdM*, 3, 1986, 2131-2138. – *Hessen und Thüringen von der Anfängen bis zur Reformation. Eine Austellung*, Marburg, 1992 (exhibition catalogue).

Joseph Morsel

**ERIK IX OF SWEDEN (*c.*1150-1160).** The short hagiographical account entitled *Vita sancti Erici* and written in the last quarter of the 13th c. provides little verifiable information on this obscure-reigned Swedish prince, who was considered a saint in *Sweden from the late 12th century. The *Vita* presents Erik as a noble Swede of royal origin, but his father Edvard is unknown. By contrast, his wife Christine was descended from Ingi the Old whose family had reigned over Sweden from 1060 to 1118. In the 1150s, Erik succeeded King Sverker the Elder (*c.*1135-1156) and founded a dynasty that occupied the throne of Sweden intermittently for a century, until 1250. His son Knut reigned from 1167 to 1196; one of Erik's daughters, Margareta, married King Sverrir of *Norway. The *Vita* makes Erik responsible for a crusade organised to convert *Finland, still *pagan. But no contemporary document corroborates this claim. However two Swedish expeditions to Finland are mentioned in 1142 and 1164 by Russian sources. The first was directed by a Swedish prince and a *bishop (St Henrik?). So it is probable that Erik took part in an operation organised at the instigation of his predecessor Sverker the Elder.

The *Vita* also vaunts Erik's generosity to the Church. In reality, his religious policy was ambiguous. While it is likely that he founded the first cathedral *chapter of *Uppsala, he also supported the patrimonial claims of his wife that culminated in the provisional expulsion of the *Cistercians freshly installed at Varnhem. On 18 May 1160, Erik met his death at Uppsala (Östra Aros), under the blows of a rival claimant to the *Crown, Henrik Magnusson. *Miracles occurred at the place of his *martyrdom. From the late 12th c. appeared the first tangible signs of a cult, reinforced perhaps by the memory of an 11th-c. martyr in the region, also named Erik, whose existence is mentioned by *Adam of Bremen (book III, ch. 54). The *calendar of the church of Vallentuna (1198) inscribes the feast of St Erik on 18 May. Around 1220, the *Saga of Sverrir* shows the king's bones resting in a shrine at Old Uppsala. In 1268, a papal *bull recognised Erik as patron of Uppsala cathedral, alongside St Lawrence. The translation of the *relics took place on 24 Jan 1273. Soon a *Vita sancti Erici* and a collection of miracles were compiled in the entourage of the archbishops of Uppsala, attesting the labours preparatory to a *canonization that would never be official. Nevertheless the figure of St Erik allowed the archbishopric of Uppsala to give importance to its new *cathedral.

Though the cult dedicated to Erik was originally restricted to the *diocese of Uppsala, by the end of the Middle Ages it extended throughout Sweden. In the 15th c., Erik became the symbol of national resistance to foreigners, notably against the policy of union preached by the partisans of *Denmark. St Erik's sword appeared in the sky at the battle of Brunkeberg (1471), ensuring the victory of the anti-Danish party, and during a war against the Russians in 1495 the banner of St Erik was borne at the head of the Swedish troops. At this time St Erik took on the figure of *rex perpetuus* of the realm. Iconography represents him as a king, with the attributes of royalty: *crown, globe, sceptre and sword. The shrine preserved in Uppsala cathedral is not the original, which was melted down in the 16th c., but it encloses a royal crown of gilded copper, the oldest in Sweden. With St Knut of Denmark and St *Óláfr of Norway, St Erik belongs to the series of *Scandinavian saint-kings.

T. Nyberg, "Erik Jedvardsson", *LdM*, 3, 1986, 2143-2144. – J. M. Maillefer, "Saint Éric de Suède: une mythologie politique et dynastique. Étude critique d'une hagiographie royale", *RAZO. Cahiers du Centre d'Études médiévales de Nice*, 8, 1988, Nice, 87-101.

Jean-Marie Maillefer

**ERLEMBALD (died 1075).** Head of the Milanese *Patarines, Erlembald succeeded his brother Landulf Cotta in the armed leadership of the movement, partly thanks to official recognition by Pope *Alexander II. On the death of Ariald (1066), he became leader of the Patarines at a time when the struggle was at its most violent. He fought the simoniac archbishop Guido da Velate to recover St Ariald's body, then struggled against the simoniac *bishops (he trampled on the baptismal chrism brought by the Lombard *suffragans at Easter 1074), but he was killed on 14 April 1075. Buried secretly at San Sesto, his body was solemnly transferred to San Dionigi by *Urban II in 1095, which was equivalent to his *canonization.

G. Miccoli, "Erlembald", *DHGE*, 15, 1963, 730-732. – P. Golinelli, *La Pataria. Lotte religiose e sociali nella Milano dell'XI secolo*, Novara-Milan, 1984.

Paolo Golinelli

**ESCHATOLOGY.** Eschatology, literally "teaching about the last things", has been understood both individually and generally, that is, insofar as it relates either to the final realities to be experienced by each Christian (the *de novissimis*, the four "last things" of *death, *judgment, *heaven and *hell), or insofar as it concerns Christian understandings of the events of the end of time which give structure and meaning to history as a whole. In the early medieval period, following the lead of patristic authors as summarized in Augustine's *De civitate Dei* 18-22, the two aspects of eschatology were treated together. Beginning with the scholastic differentiation of *theology in the 12th c., questions of individual eschatology began to receive separate consideration as a part of the *scientia consequentiarum*, or "science of conclusions", rather than as embedded in the traditional *ordo salutis*, or story of *salvation. *Hugh of Saint-Victor's *De sacramentis* (*c.*1135) considered the last things at the end of a summary of Christian teaching still based on the salvation-historical scheme of the "order of creation" and the "order of recreation". But a few decades later *Peter Lombard's *Libri sententiarum* (book 4, dist. 43-50) already treated the last things largely apart from systematic concern with *history. The triumph of the a-historical Aristotelian method in 13th-c. *scholasticism resulted in the separation of individual and general eschatology by many theologians, with the *De novissimis* being treated according to issues raised more by Aristotelian physics (*e.g.*, the status of the separated *soul, the question of the end of motion and time) than by the *mystery of *God's *revelation in history. A good example can be found in the thought of *Thomas Aquinas, though he did not live to complete the third part of his *Summa theologiae* where these issues would have received his final treatment. Some scholastic authors, especially *Franciscans like *Bonaventure and *Peter John Olivi, reacted against this trend by emphasizing the historical dimensions of Christian eschatology; but it is significant that they could not do this within the confines of systematic theology (*i.e.*, commentaries on Lombard's **Sentences*), but only through scriptural *exegesis, such as Bonaventure's *Collationes in Hexaemeron* and Olivi's *Lectura in Apocalypsim.*

Scholastic isolation of individual eschatology had advantages as well as disadvantages. A number of issues of significance could be debated with a subtlety hitherto unavailable. Among these were questions pertaining to the existence and nature of *purgatory, the *resurrection of the *body, the qualities of the risen body, and especially the nature of the *beatific vision. The last was an especially lively area of discussion under two headings: first, whether the final goal of the vision of God pertained more to the *intellect or to the *will (the *Dominicans favoured the former position, while the *Franciscans adhered to the latter); and second, whether final "face-to-face" vision was granted the redeemed soul immediately after death or only after the resurrection. Pope *John XXII went against *tradition by defending the latter view, a position that was condemned by his successor *Benedict XII in the *bull *Benedictus Deus* of 1336. Scholastic discussion provides a detailed but narrow perspective on issues of the understanding of *death, resurrection and the afterlife in the Middle Ages, topics that have been of special concern to medievalists in recent years.

Scholastic treatment of the last things forms a parenthesis in the wider history of eschatology understood as the way in which medieval Christians viewed history as a progression of divinely predetermined ages culminating in the final reward of the just and punishment of the unjust at the end of time. In this sense, all medieval understanding of history was eschatological, though some theories of history were also apocalyptic because they believed the divine plan was evident in current events and that the final triple drama of crisis-judgment-vindication was imminent. Some apocalypticists announced the date of the end; others adhered to the scriptural texts which taught that no one could predict that time, while insisting that the events leading to the end were already under way.

Three strands can be distinguished in the historical eschatology of the Middle Ages. The first or main tradition is that of non-apocalyptic eschatology. The major figure is Augustine who taught that the world was now in its sixth and final age, but that this age was of unknown duration. (The "World-Week" schema according to which history was to last for six days, or ages, to be followed by a seventh era of eternal peace was the most common medieval historical periodization.) Augustine provided the standard account of the last things, but he insisted that current events had no real relation to the true meaning of history, which remained hidden until the end, buried in mystery of *predestination to glory or damnation. Following the Donatist exegete Tyconius, he removed the apocalyptic content from the biblical texts, especially the *Apocalypse of John, by interpreting them as moral messages about the struggle of *good and *evil in the Church and in the life of each believer.

A second approach to general eschatology grew out of the imperial apocalyptic eschatology connected with the extra-biblical *Sibylline tradition found in texts such as the *Sibylla Tiburtina* (whose Greek original may date from the 4th c.; the Latin text became popular after 1000), the Pseudo-Methodian *Revelationes* (a 7th-c. Syriac work translated into Greek, Latin and many vernaculars), and *Adso of Montier-en-Der's *Epistola de Antichristo* (*c.*950). This view provided hope in time of trouble by prophesying that the current political difficulties of *Rome (the "Last Empire" according to traditional interpretations of Daniel 2) were merely a prelude to an imminent pre-Antichrist millennial period under the rule of a Last World Emperor.

The third strand of medieval historical eschatology was also apocalyptic in its belief in the predictable imminence of the last events. The context within which this final version of general eschatology appeared was that of the great *reform movement beginning in the 11th century. By holding out hope for earthly improvement of the Church (something Augustine would have doubted), the reformers laid the ground for an explosion of apocalyptic eschatology in the later Middle Ages. The key figure was *Joachim of Fiore (*c.*1135-1202), who broke with the *Augustinian tradition by creating a new historical-prophetic reading of the *Bible, especially of the Apocalypse. The Calabrian abbot believed that Scripture revealed the trinitarian structure of history according to which Father, Son and *Holy Spirit each had a proper *status* – the Father's being that of the Old Testament, the Son's that of the New, while the Spirit would be especially evident in the coming *tertius status* after the defeat of the imminent *Antichrist evident in the crises of the late 12th century. Joachim's revival of early Christian apocalyptic *millenarianism, that is, the sense of a coming better age on earth after Antichrist, was rejected by Augustinians like *Thomas Aquinas, but was widely influential on many late medieval thinkers. Some pushed it in overtly *heretical directions, like the Apostolic Brethren and the radical *fraticelli; others, like *Bonaventure, attempted to combine Joachim's new apocalyptic eschatology with more traditional forms. The split between the treatment of individual eschatological questions among the scholastic summists and the wider debate over the eschatological significance of history reflects the crisis of late medieval culture.

T. Gregory, "Escatologia e Aristotelismo nella Scolastica medievale", *GCFI*, 10, 1961, 163-174. – M. E. Reeves, *Prophecy in the Later Middle Ages*, Oxford, 1969. – B. McGinn, *Visions of the End*, New York, 1979. –W. Verbeke, D. Verhelst, A. Welkenhuysen, *The Use and Abuse of Eschatology in the Middle Ages*, Louvain, 1988. – J. Le Goff, *The Birth of Purgatory*, Aldershot, 1990. – L. Ott, E. Nabb, *Eschatologie in der Scholastik. Band IV. Faszikel 7b. Handbuch der Dogmengeschichte*, Freiburg im Breisgau, 1990. – J. J. Collins, B. McGinn, S. J. Stein, *The Encyclopedia of Apocalypticism*, New York, 1998 (3 vol.).

Bernard McGinn

## ESCHEAT

**France.** The word *aubain*, perhaps meaning "from another *ban", is attested from the 9th c. and was used especially in France to designate the foreigner as subject to law. Individually or collectively, the foreigner had to have authorization to reside and his *property rights were limited; especially, he could not transmit his property on his death, except by grace, whence the name *droit d'aubaine* given to the reversion of his property to the lord. In the kingdom of France, *droit d'aubaine* became royal from the 14th c., while the principle was asserted – without great effect – of the foreigner's incapacity to hold civil or ecclesiastical offices.

M. Boulet-Sautel, "L'aubain dans la France coutumière du Moyen Âge", *L'Étranger*, 1958 ("RSJB", 10). – C. Billot, "L'assimilation des étrangers dans le royaume de France aux XIVe et XVe siècles", *RH*, 270, 1983, 273-296.

Jean-Daniel Morerod

**Italy.** The right of escheat that weighed on the goods of foreigners was first opposed by the Church and then weakened by *Frederick II and then by the *jurist Bartolo of Sassoferrato, who determined its legal evolution by the distinction between "personal status" and "real status", *i.e.* that the "human person has his own status, in all that affects his legal status and his capacity (personal status), and this he has a right to see observed everywhere; while he will obey the status of the place as regards his property (real status). A principle still valid in international private law" (F. Calasso).

F. Calasso, *Medioevo del diritto*, Milan, 1954, 577.

Attilio Stendardi

**ESSEN.** A town in Westphalia, it came into being in 850 around a Benedictine women's monastery founded by Bishop Altfrid of *Hildesheim, near the Benedictine monastery of Werden. The monastery soon became a *foundation of *canonesses for aristocratic ladies under the protection of *Mary and Sts Cosmas and Damian. A house of canons devoted to pastoral work was founded in parallel. Free *election of the *abbess, *immunity, royal protection and free choice of ecclesiastical *advocate, such were the prerogatives of Essen, confirmed in the mid 10th c. by Pope *Agapetus II and *Otto I. Daughters of the (Ottonian) royal family and of families close to the king were elected abbesses. There were frequent quarrels with the bishop of *Cologne, notably in the 13th c. by reason of immunity and the right of free choice of *bailli*. From 1228, the abbess became at the same time a princess of the *Empire. Essen became an imperial town in 1377.

E. Wisplinghoff, *Beiträge zur Geschichte des Damenstifts Essen*, *ADipl*, 13, 1967, 110-132. – *Das Jahrtausend der Monche: Klöster-Welt Werden 799-1803*, J. Gerchow (ed.), Cologne, 1999.

Franz Neiske

**ESTATE, MANOR.** The power of the lord in the Middle Ages was based on various forms of possession of lands and domination of persons. By "estate", we understand a local unit gravitating around the landed **seigneurie*, *i.e.* around the development of the lord's lands by various forms of utilization of his men. Domestic or personal lordship and banal or justiciary lordship supplemented landed lordship in the estate to make coercion more effective. The term "estate" in the Middle Ages designated essentially the reserve (lands retained for seignorial use); this is why its modern scientific usage mainly concerns the unit whose development was centred on the direct farming of the reserve by the lord. The work force for this operation being found most often on family farms, an important part of the estate had to be divided into holdings. Thus the expression "manorial regime", particularly with the qualifying term "classic", applies mainly to the bipartite estate, cemented by the **corvée* furnished by the holdings to the reserve.

The importance of the estate was overestimated by 19th-c. scholars who considered it the almost exclusive basis of economic and social life in the early Middle Ages. Since the retreat of this classical doctrine, the place of the estate has been revised and certain specialists have minimized its extent and its influence. Today it is commonly recognised that the estate always coexisted with other forms of landed farming-properties, including those of independent *peasants. If specialists in the rural history of the early Middle Ages are now trying to re-evaluate the role of the great estate, it is from a new dynamic point of view, which wants to find in it not an omnipresent entity, but a pivot of the socio-economic development of the time. It remains no less true that the estate represented an important framework of life. Organised by seignorial initiative, it did not necessarily form a single block, but it always gave its inhabitants, servile or free, occasion for concerted activities, or sometimes even resistance. The activity of the estate comprised not just an agricultural aspect, but also an artisanal one. Always open to exchanges, it could be extended as far as the urban sphere.

Despite the succession of Roman properties in rural areas, notably arable lands, inherited by the Germans and the persistence of grand proprietorship in the early Middle Ages, the great latifundiary estate of the Late Empire did not survive the confusions of late Antiquity. In the very early Middle Ages, a period characterised by a far from brilliant economy, the typical estate was small in size (at most 200 hectares of arable land). It was cultivated mainly by slaves attached to the lord's court and did not have many holdings. Burdened with dues and with a *lot-corvée*, the holdings were not well integrated into the domanial structure, whose limited extent allowed the continued existence of a mass of independent peasants. A demographic and economic growth that began in the 7th c. subjected this small estate to an evolution towards the great bipartite estate. Thanks to important *clearances, the extent of a estate in the 9th and 10th cc. could exceed 1000 hectares of arable land, not counting the often very large wooded area. The reserve too grew, but the holdings achieved a proportionately greater enlargement. Becoming more numerous (frequently 30 or more holdings per estate), they were normalized into *manses, each of which was considered able to feed a peasant family. The manses were occupied either by former slaves established on small holdings (servile manses) or by former independent peasants (ingenuile manses). These two categories of occupants, thus transformed into tenant farmers of more or less uniformized status within the estate, had to furnish the lord with variable and heavy *corvées*, which altogether could represent three days per week. The great estate generally belonged to a powerful lord, in possession of numerous estates, which were linked by a circulation network using *transport services provided by the tenant farmers. Mixed with the exchanges that developed at this time, mainly thanks to the rise in agricultural output, this network maintained at its important points establishments of an urban character that allowed the lord to dispose of his produce; these places proved at the same time to be centres of seignorial power.

This evolution of the form of the estate represents an essential aspect of the socio-economic change that took place between the 7th and 9th cc. in the Frankish kingdom on the basis of the decline of *slavery and the generalization of the peasant family farm. The rise of servile elements was a decisive motor force in this, seignorial initiative playing an important role in the creation of the framework of economic growth. We discern in Carolingian documents, whether normative like *capitularies or descriptive like *polyptychs, a desire, shared by Crown, Church and great aristocracy, to structure rural life as far as possible according to the model of the great bipartite estate. To organise the population effectively, lords extended domestic lordship not just over the unfree but also over the free who constantly sought the protection of the powerful. The rule of the lord over his *familia* could be sanctioned by the privilege of immunity. The great estate of the Carolingian period as an entity of landed farming-property admittedly did not cover the greater part of the land. The archaic type of small estate was often maintained on the property of the petty lord, and independent peasants remained numerous. But the great estate could draw the greater part of the population into its orbit, through its extended networks and its politico-social influence.

Developed at first between the Loire and the Rhine, the great estate spread following Carolingian expansion. East of the Rhine, the manorial regime was installed in the course of the 9th c. despite a persistence of servile *labour. In northern and central *Italy, the estate took its classic form with the Frankish conquest, though it did not succeed in establishing itself as it did in the centre of the Empire. In southern France and northern *Spain, the spread of the great estate was still more limited. In *England, evolution towards the great manor existed, but has left few traces.

From the apogee of its classic form in the Carolingian period, the estate was subject to a transformation expressed mainly by the dwindling of the reserve. Its apportionment into holdings was frequent, but the lord continued to keep a good part for himself, especially around his court. Sometimes the former reserve was farmed out *en bloc* to a capable cultivator, *e.g.* an ex-manorial agent, as in north-west *Germany. At the same time, direct seignorial farming showed a tendency to contract, but exceptions abounded. Petty lords, with no domestic *seigneurie* around their lands and no *seigneurie banale* over a compact territory, maintained a small direct farm managed locally. Some ecclesiastical lords, the *Cistercians among others, practised a largely commercialized agriculture or *stock-raising, using the labour of monks and **conversi*. In certain regions stimulated by demographic and economic growth, as in 13th-c. England, seignorial farming, based on *corvées* of tenant farmers and linked to the market, became general.

The reduction of the *corvée*, another major aspect of the transformation of the estate, took place in a more radical way. Many peasants no longer performed it in the way specified in several *charters of franchises. Where the obligation to provide labour still existed, it only exceptionally exceeded ten days a year per holding. The *corvée* no longer greatly troubled the peasant farm, all the more since it was formally performed outside the great agricultural seasons. The most important burden on tenant farmers at this time took the form of *rents. Those in kind were mainly paid in grain. Handing over a quota of the grain produced could be heavy when a quarter or even half of the harvest had to be given to the lord, as was the case of the share-cropping particularly widespread in the Mediterranean area. But with the payment of a fixed quantity, the lord could not seize the surplus yield arising from an increase in productivity. Alongside rents in kind, rent in *money gradually took on importance, sometimes through the redemption of old obligations. Rent in money, in principle a fixed sum, constantly lost value along with monetary erosion.

This new system of dues, advantageous to the peasants, was linked to the strengthening of their right over their holdings. Practically hereditary from the early Middle Ages, this was so well consolidated in the central Middle Ages that peasants could fairly freely dispose of the components of their holdings. The better to work his estate, the lord resorted to tenant farming, which allowed him to adjust the rent regularly, or to the settlement of an annuity, but these procedures could not become dominant. On their holdings, though smaller than before the year 1000 (in some regions, a quarter-manse was the most common), the peasants were less subject to the constraints of the estate. The main framework of their control went more and more through the *seigneurie banale* or the nascent *State (principality, *kingdom), whose *taxation began to play a major role in the burdens on its inhabitants.

With the economic difficulties of the late Middle Ages, some lords too dependent on landed lordship lost their fortune. Others, effectively participating in social control, enrolled their peasants better. They then often re-established direct farming, based on commercialization, using a newly enlarged reserve cultivated by means of ever heavier *corvées*. This restructuring, no longer based on the archaic type of domestic lordship, was widespread east of the Elbe, an area of German immigration in the central Middle Ages. But in the majority of western regions, the estate continued to exist, more and more separate from the *seigneurie*, without being able to make substantial use of the labour of its tenant farmers.

G. Duby, *L'Économie rurale et la Vie des campagnes dans l'Occident médiéval (France, Angleterre, Empire, IXe-XVe siècles). Essai de synthèse et perspectives de recherches*, Paris, 1962 (2 vol.; 2nd ed. 1978). – *The Agrarian Life of the Middle Ages*, M. M. Postan (ed.), Cambridge, 1966 (2nd ed.); "The Cambridge Economic History of Europe", 1. – E. Ennen, W. Janssen, *Deutsche Agrargeschichte vom Neolithikum bis zur Schwelle des Industriezeitalters*, Wiesbaden, 1979. – B. Andreolli, M. Montanari, *L'Azienda curtense in Italia. Proprietà della terra e lavoro contadino nei secoli VIII-XI*, Bologna, 1983. – M. K. McIntosh, *Autonomy and Community: the Royal Manor of Havering, 1200-1500*, Cambridge, 1986. – E. Klingelhofer, *Manor, Vill, and Hundred*, Toronto, 1992. – *Medieval Society and the Manor Court*, Z. Razi (ed.), R. Smith (ed.), Oxford, 1996.

Yoshiki Morimoto

**ESTHER.** Heroine of a book in the *Bible, Esther was a beautiful Jewess living at the court of King Ahasuerus of Persia. She married the king and obtained grace for the Jews threatened by the vizir Haman, then got her cousin Mordecai promoted to the latter's place.

The interpretation of her intercession by Christian commentators led to her being considered a prefiguration of the Virgin interceding with her Son on the day of the *Last Judgment. Esther is frequently represented as a beautiful, richly-dressed young woman. The art of the 15th c. in *France and *Germany offers us numerous occurrences of this character. Though different episodes could be used by *artists, the most common scene is Esther's prayer before King Ahasuerus. This episode, present *e.g.* in the 13th c. on an arch moulding of the north portal of *Chartres cathedral, also appears on a *tapestry in the treasury of *Siena cathedral.

B. D. Walfish, *Esther in Medieval Garb*, Albany (NY), 1993.

Frédérique Trouslard

**ESTONIA.** In 1200, Pope *Innocent III gave a *bull to the clergy charged with the Christian *mission on the territory of the Livs (a Finno-Ugrian people in the process of disappearing, living on the territory of the present Republic of *Latvia). This document proves that a *crusade was undertaken against the *pagans of the east coasts of the Baltic Sea. The *cathedral erected at *Riga early in the 13th c. was consecrated to St *Mary. From now on the whole territory inhabited by the Livs, Letts and Estonians and occupied by Germans in the course of the crusade directed from Riga, was called the Land of St Mary (*Terra beate Virginis*), but also Livonia, after the name of the first people subjected. The subjection of the land of the Estonians, the "mission by the sword", began in 1208. It was commanded by *Albert of Buxhövden, a *canon of *Bremen, thenceforth bishop of Livonia. In his time was created the *military order of the *Fratres militiae Christi* (Order of *Knights of the Sword). Immediately after the bloody subjection of the whole territory of Estonia to the Christian faith and foreign administration, the new masters began to share it out.

On the territory that fell into the hands of the *Fratres militiae Christi*, William, bishop of *Modena, *legate of Popes *Honorius III and *Gregory IX, tried to form on the example of *Italy an ecclesiastical State directly dependent on the *pope. Formally, the order was subjected by Gregory IX to the *bishops; in fact, the words *obedientia, reverentia et subjectio* hid a simple spiritual submission. The order became the most powerful military force in Livonia and aimed to obtain the right of direct *suzerainty over the occupied territories. In 1233, the attempt to found a pontifical State was fiercely suppressed by the order. In 1237, the *Fratres* became a Livonian branch of the *Teutonic Order which remained in existence until 1562, totally independent after the dissolution of the Teutonic Order. In the first half of the 13th c. were founded the bishoprics of Tartu and of western and insular Estonia, with their respective cathedrals at Tartu and Haapsalu. The bishops received the lands of their *dioceses in *fief from the emperors of the Holy Roman *Empire. Though this subordination remained essentially formal (relations with the papal *Curia nevertheless remained dominant), the local *nobility and the citizens who came mainly from the regions of the northern Rhineland and Westphalia, but also from other parts of *Germany, considered themselves inhabitants of an autonomous province of Germany.

In 1238, through the intermediary of the pope's representative, northern Estonia was incorporated in the domain of the king of *Denmark by the treaty of Stensby, concluded between the king of Denmark and the Teutonic Order. The spiritual life of that region was directed by the bishop of Tallinn, a suffragan of *Lund.

As the order sought to incorporate local dioceses, from time to time there were quarrels with the prelates. During these conflicts, both parties tried to obtain support from the *pope; thus the whole political life of Livonia was open to the influence of the Roman Curia – especially during the "*Avignon captivity", when most of the Estonian bishops actually lived close to the Curia.

At the end of the 14th c., Dietrich Damerow, bishop of Tartu, directed an extended coalition against the order. He had studied at

*Paris and *Bologna and had been a familiar of the Emperor *Charles IV. In 1397, the international congress of *Gdańsk was organised to regulate this difference. In the years 1420-1430, inspired by the councils of *Constance and *Basel, the prelates of the territory of Estonia became active once more and, in collaboration with the other states, obtained the convocation of an important *representative assembly – the diet (*Landtag*) of Livonia.

One of the greatest oppositions was that between the order and Johannes Blankenfeld, successively bishop of Tallinn, Tartu and Riga, who, living in Italy, had belonged to the circle of the celebrated *humanists. The Livonian Order profited from Protestantism, widespread in Livonia in the 1520s, to diminish ecclesiastical influence and seize its property. In 1527, released from the order's *prison and on his way to join the Emperor Charles V, Bishop Blankenfeld died suddenly for obscure reasons. Though the Reformation, in Estonia too, led in 1524-1525 to the pillage of all the great churches and monasteries, the centres of the Catholic bishoprics and some great monasteries retained their importance until the beginning of the Russo-Swedish war in 1558.

Medieval institutions in Estonia were analogous to those of Europe in general. Thus, from the mid 13th c., the government of the bishoprics was organised in the traditional form of a collaboration between bishop and *chapter. On the arrival of the first German *merchants and artisans in the great commercial centres of Estonia, life there was judicially organised on the model of *Lübeck and German towns. As the mentality of the clergy after the crusade was more devout than in most of Europe, even in the 13th-14th cc. the *vita canonica* remained the basis of capitual life.

Successively, *Cistercians, *Dominicans, *Franciscans and Augustinians founded convents in Estonia (likewise the female branches). Several of these convents also became places of *pilgrimage frequented by believers from other countries. In the 13th-14th cc., remarkable works of sacred architecture were created, *e.g.* the cathedral of Tartu, in brick (the largest church in Estonia); the church of St John, influenced by French architecture, decorated with numerous sculptures in terracotta; and the *Gothic churches of Tallinn in limestone. The group of churches at Saaremaa (Oesel), with stone sculptures and mural *paintings, also has great artistic value. The bishops often brought architects from central and western Europe.

In the 15th-16th cc., the secularization of the clergy was dominant in Estonia too. To become a bishop or a *canon, it was necessary to have studied at *university. Among the *faculties, that of law had preference. In the 14th c., they made their way mainly to the universities of *Paris, *Bologna and *Prague; later, they preferred those of Rostock, *Leipzig and *Erfurt. As Estonia possessed no establishment of higher education, several gifted Estonians occupied academic or ecclesiastical posts in the great centres of Europe; this was the case from the second half of the 14th c. for most of the clergy of Livonia, of Estonian origin.

It may be supposed that only a few *subdeacons, *deacons or priests can have been of Estonian nationality and that these had to Germanize themselves. Among them, the only known member of the higher clergy was Johannes Pulck who had been **scholasticus* of the bishopric of western and insular Estonia. From the first half of the 13th c., most Estonians were baptized, but the content of their Christianity is little known. While the rites and forms of worship of the saints resembled the natural religion of the Estonians, Christianity nevertheless considerably influenced the mentality of the people and the popular *calendar. The *feasts of the saints were accepted and linked with the *pagan religion. This fusion was stimulated by the missionary Church which had founded its churches on the sites of pagan sanctuaries.

Portal of the church of St John at Tartu in Estonia.

E. Unstalu, *The History of the Estonian People*, London, 1952. – A. Vööbus, *Studies in the History of the Estonian People*, 1, Stockholm, 1969; 2, 1970. – J. Paulson, *The Old Estonian Folk Religion*, Bloomington, 1971. – *Storia religiosa dei popoli baltici*, A. Caprioli (dir.), L. Vaccaro (dir.), Sarrada, 1987.

Tonis Lukas

**ESTOUTEVILLE, GUILLAUME D' (1403-1483).** Born in *Normandy to a noble family related to the royal house of *France, he was created *cardinal by *Eugenius IV in 1439, and spent most of his life at *Rome, except for brief journeys in the entourage of the pontiffs and two missions to France, the first (1451-1453) to obtain the abrogation of the *Pragmatic Sanction of Bourges (and to reform the university of *Paris and open the proceedings for the rehabilitation of *Joan of Arc), the second (1454-1455) to convince King *Charles VII to take part in the *crusade launched by *Nicholas V. Indicated in the sources as "Cardinal Rotomagense" because of the archbishopric of *Rouen which he held in *commendam from 1453, in 1454 he became bishop of Porto, then in 1461 bishop of Ostia and Velletri, while continuing to enjoy many lesser *benefices. For 37 years he was protector of the Augustinian Order, but he was equally generous to the Benedictine Order. As a cardinal, he was often present in the *consistory and was several times appointed *chamberlain of the *Sacred College, whose dean he became in 1472. He came very close to the papal throne after the death of *Calixtus III in 1458, but fear of too marked a French influence in *Italy led to the election of Aeneas Sylvius Piccolomini (*Pius II) and of Pietro Barbo (Paul II) in 1464. *Sixtus IV appointed him chamberlain of the Holy Roman Churchin 1477 and which notably increased his influence in the *Curia and Rome.

Contemporary Roman *chroniclers notice him mainly for his exceptional *wealth, the luxury with which he surrounded himself and his *patronage of the arts: this included, at Rome, the works undertaken for *Santa Maria Maggiore, his *palace near the piazza Sant'Apollinare, the church of Sant'Agostino totally rebuilt by the famous *architect Giacomo da Pietrasanta; for Ostia and Velletri, the fortification of the walls and episcopal palaces; for Frascati, a subterranean aqueduct. His great wealth allowed him to make numerous loans to various *popes and many members of the Roman *nobility, to whom he also linked himself by an adroit matrimonial policy for the three daughters he had by a noble Roman lady, Girolama Tosti. For the benefit of his two sons, he arranged in his lifetime to set up a homogenous territorial group in the area of the Alban hills, by the acquisition of *castles and *towns with their dependencies. He died at Rome on 23 Jan 1483 and was buried in the church of Sant'Agostino.

X. Barbier de Montault, *Le Cardinal d'Estouteville bienfaiteur des églises de "Rome", Oeuvres complètes*, 1, Poitiers, 1889, 5-29. – G. Mollat, "Guillaume d'Estouteville", *DHGE*, 15, 1963, 1082-1083. – F. Gaeta, *Il Primo libro dei Commentari di Pio II*, L'Aquila, 1966, 68-77. – R. Darricau, "Guillaume d'Estouteville", *DBF*, 13, 1975, 126-127.

Anna Esposito

**ESZTERGOM.** The town of Esztergom (in Slav languages, Ostryhom) in the kingdom of *Hungary was the favourite residence of the Magyar kings until the mid 13th c., metropolis of the ecclesiastical *province of Esztergom since its foundation by *Stephen I and then see of the *primate of Hungary. In the 11th and 12th cc., it was also a town very active in the field of craftsmanship and *commerce. During the Tatar invasion of 1241, the royal part of the town suffered such damage that King Béla IV decided to transfer his residence to *Buda; from then on Esztergom suffered a demographic and economic decline, and only the ecclesiastical establishments continued to prosper. In the late 15th c., archbishops John Vitéz and then Thomas Bakócz nevertheless made it a great centre of the artistic and intellectual *Renaissance.

L. Zolnay, *A középkori Esztergom* [Medieval Esztergom], Budapest, 1983.

Marie-Madeleine de Cevins

**ETERNAL LIFE.** Belief in eternal life, which concludes the **Credo*, corresponds to one of the deepest desires of the human being, the desire for eternity. This desire was particularly acute in the Middle Ages, since it was thought that eternity was very close, which explains the numerous works dealing with what happened between *death and *resurrection, as well as the establishment in the 12th and 13th cc. of a geography of the afterlife with three essential places: *hell, *paradise and an intermediary place, *purgatory, as *Innocent IV named it in 1254. Jacques Le Goff makes clear that this introduction of purgatory was connected to a profound transformation of society and a theological systematization, realized, before *Dante, by *Peter Cantor and *Simon of Tournai. Despite its frightening character, purgatory in fact enlarged the *hope of eternal life by showing that those to whom the *beatific vision was not immediately given could benefit from it after a passage through purgatory.

More radically still, *Peter Lombard played a decisive role in medieval reflection on eternal life, in that he ended his **Sentences* with a systematic treatise on the last ends. As the commentary on the *Sentences* rapidly became an indispensable stage in the career of every medieval theologian, treatises on eternal life multiplied and thus reflected the representation that the Western Middle Ages made of themselves. A corner was thus turned between the patristic period, which was interested mainly in the resurrection, and the Middle Ages which put the stress more on eternal life. However, the medievals did not omit the resurrection, but they oriented their researches mainly towards the Parousia, whence the numerous apocalypses, some of a political character, that came into being in this period.

Through eternal life, it was in fact the Kingdom of God that was sought. As St *Thomas Aquinas emphasizes in book IV of his *Commentary on the Sentences* (d. 49, q. 1, a. 2, q. 5, sol. 5): "The expression 'Kingdom of God' is understood in two ways: sometimes it is the assembly of those who journey in *faith, and in this sense the Kingdom of God designates the Church militant; sometimes it is the college of those who are already established in their last end, and in this sense the Kingdom of God designates the Church triumphant." In both cases, the Kingdom of God is none other than the Church.

Here again, a change was brought about in relation to the patristic period, which did not accord such a place to the Church in its journey towards *salvation. This transformation was linked to the birth of the religious *orders, *confraternities, etc., and was widely influenced by St *Bernard who defined monks as inhabitants of the City of God. It had the corollary of situating reflection on eternal life not simply in the sphere of *eschatology, but of joining to it (with the exception of the mystics who put the stress on union with *God) a study of the *sacraments and *grace.

C. J. Peter, *Participated Eternity in the Vision of God*, Rome, 1964. – J. Le Goff, *The Birth of Purgatory*, Aldershot, 1990.

Marie-Anne Vannier

**ETERNITY OF THE WORLD.** The concept of the eternity of the world, often discussed by the philosophers and theologians of the Middle Ages, notably in the 13th and 14th cc., was inspired by the Greek thought of Plato, *Aristotle and Plotinus as well as the Muslim thought of *Averroes, who leaned on his precursors al-*Fārābī, *Avicenna and al-*Ghazālī, themselves influenced by the Greeks. It was not just a matter of distinguishing eternity from *time and duration (Plotinus) or identifying absolute Being (*Boethius, al-Jurjāni), but, *e.g.*, of resolving consequential questions, like the problem, posed by the gospels and the *Koran, of an eternal *God who knows the *salvation of the elect and the damnation of sinners, or that of whether Christian *predestination or Muslim destiny (*qadar*) call human *freedom into question.

L. Branchi, *L'Inizio dei tempi. Antichità e novità del mondo da Bonaventura a Newton*, Florence, 1987. – R. C. Dales, *Medieval Discussions of the Eternity of the World*, Leiden, 1990.

Edgard Weber

**ETHICS.** The term *moralis* in medieval *Latin can be applied either to a human action or to a theological or philosophical discipline. In the first sense, it means that a human action is qualified by the rules of human conduct; in the second sense, the notion designates a part of *theology (that which deals with human actions) or *philosophy. Only the latter sense is envisaged here:

morals (synonymous with ethics) is that part of philosophy that, in dealing with human actions, tries to set up a coherent theory concerning the end of human action and the value of *man's acts. Following an ancient tradition, Augustine divided philosophy into three main parts: "[Plato] divided philosophy into three parts: moral philosophy which relates especially to action; natural philosophy which is reserved for *contemplation; rational philosophy which distinguishes the true from the false" (*City of God*, VIII, 4). According to the Aristotelian doctrine known also to the Middle Ages, a distinction was to be made between theoretical philosophy, practical philosophy and technique (art; *Metaphysics*, VI, 1). In the latter case, the artisan produced an external object, while the theoretician studied, or more exactly contemplated, an object that he had not produced; and practical philosophy dealt with human activity in which the agent was the principle of the action, which, as such, was the end itself.

According to *Thomas Aquinas, who manifests the state of knowledge once *Aristotle became known in the West between 1150 and 1250, the proper business of moral philosophy was to study human operations ordered among themselves as well as to an end (*Commentary on the Ethics*, I). But since not all man's operations depend on *reason, it must be specified that only human actions "that proceed from the *will according to the order of reason" are studied by ethics. To circumscribe still better the object of this part of philosophy, Thomas adds, in perfect harmony with the Aristotelian tradition, that man as a "social animal" is a part of two groups, viz. the domestic multitude that helps man to live (or survive) and the civil multitude that allows man to live *well*. Consequently the study of human action comprises three parts: the medievals called that section of ethics dealing with the study of man's actions as an individual, *monastica*; economics examined man's operations as a member of a *family (in the medieval sense); the third part of ethics was called "*politics" and considered the activities of the civil multitude, which, in Thomas's own terms, is the most perfect whole that human reason can constitute (Prologue to the *Commentary on the Politics*).

*Hugh of Saint-Victor's *Didascalicon*, which is a good reflection of the state of knowledge in the first half of the 12th c., is aware of the Aristotelian tripartition of practical philosophy, but at the same time attests the indigence of moral philosophy at that time. Before the *translations of Aristotle's *Ethics* and *Politics*, moral reflection was generally directly linked to theological progress, as clearly appears in the case of the *Ethica* of Peter *Abelard, who discovered in the context of an inquiry into the nature of *sin that the morality of an act was constituted by the intention: "It is good intention that makes a good action." Aristotle's *Ethics*, the first commentaries on which appeared well before its complete translation by *Robert Grosseteste in 1246-1247, posed new problems: firstly, that of the final end of all human action, happiness. But the Aristotelian text also contained important developments on the *virtues and on *friendship whose influence cannot be neglected. Among the most celebrated commentators on the *Ethics* were *Albert the Great, *Thomas Aquinas and *John Buridan, not forgetting the important French translation that Nicole *Oresme made for King *Charles V. The discovery of the *Politics*, whose first complete translation was produced by *William of Moerbeke in 1260, was no less decisive for moral reflection in the West. In effect, the Stagyrite's text gave medieval commentators (among them Albert the Great, Thomas Aquinas and Nicole Oresme) the opportunity to ask questions about the city, the law and especially the social nature of *man described as a "political animal". The second part of Thomas Aquinas's *Summa theologiae* can be considered one of the most important and influential medieval treatises on morals. Establishing a synthesis between theology and philosophy, it fully integrated the recently discovered Aristotelian heritage. Thomas considered man "the principle of his own acts because he possesses free will" (prologue), and, since any agent acts towards an end, Thomas based his ethics on the establishment of a final end of man, which is *beatitude, which will consist in the vision of the divine essence. Hence all human activity is a means to attain the true end. The virtues, defined as a **habitus* of action, are its means *par excellence*, hence the capital importance of the *theological (*faith, *hope and charity) and cardinal virtues (prudence, *justice, fortitude and temperance) – the inner principles of right human action. Thomas distinguishes two external principles of good action, viz. *grace and law, which can be defined as an "ordering of reason with a view to the common good, promulgated by one who has charge of the community" (*Summa theologiae*, I$^{a}$ II$^{ae}$, q. 90, a. 4). The precepts of natural law constituting the ultimate basis of all human legislation are based on a triple natural inclination, viz. self-preservation; union of man and woman (and *education of *children); "thirdly, we find in man an attraction towards the *good in conformity with his *nature as a reasonable being, which is proper to him; thus he has a natural inclination to know the truth about *God and to live in society" (q. 94, a. 2). For Thomas Aquinas, the general principles of natural law are universal and known to all.

In a strictly Aristotelian context, it was asked whether the happiness of which the Philosopher spoke in his *Ethics*, particularly book X, could be attained by man and in a purely natural way. Aquinas replied negatively to this question, while some philosophers known as *Averroists, like *Boethius of Dacia, believed in the possibility of a full "mental felicity" obtained by philosophical *contemplation. John *Duns Scotus and William of *Ockham represented another step in medieval morals, in which *freedom played a more fundamental role. What counts is not so much conformity to a natural, *ontologically based *order as free obedience to a precept emanating in turn from free will. Hence the basis of ethics is the meeting of two freedoms, that of God and that of man, rather than an order of reason. The celebrated Ockhamite thesis of the hatred of God that God himself could prescribe is an eloquent example of the price which that *Franciscan attached to this dual freedom, that which prescribes and that which responds.

R.-A. Gauthier, *La Morale d'Aristote*, Paris, 1957. – R. Blomme, *La Doctrine du péché dans les écoles théologiques de la première moitié du XII^e siècle*, Louvain-Gembloux, 1958. – J. Jolivet, *Arts du langage et théologie d'Abélard*, Paris, 1969. – R.-A. Gauthier, *Introduction, Aristote, l'Éthique à Nicomaque*, 1, Louvain-Paris, 1970. – É. Gilson, *Saint Thomas moraliste*, Paris, 1974. – C. Flüeler, *Rezeption und Interpretation der Aristotelischen "Politica" im späten Mittelalter*, Amsterdam, 1992 (2 vol.). – A. de Libera, *Penser au Moyen Âge*, Paris, 1991. – I. Kantola, *Probability and Moral Uncertainty in Late Medieval and Early Modern Times*, Helsinki, 1994. – C. J. Nederman, *Medieval Aristotelianism and its Limits*, Aldershot, 1997. – I. T. Eschmann, *The Ethics of Saint Thomas Aquinas*, Toronto, 1997.

Ruedi Imbach

**ETHIOPIA.** Formerly Abyssinia, the East African State of Ethiopia has its capital at Addis Ababa. For 14th-c. Europe, the king of Ethiopia was confused with the legendary *Prester John, evidence of the fame attained at the time by this mysterious Christian kingdom on the edge of the universe, lost among *pagans and *Saracens. In the same period, historiographers charged with celebrating the restoration of the Solomonid dynasty wrote the legend of King Menelik I, son of *Solomon and the Queen of *Sheba, the founding myth of Ethiopia.

The history of the fascinating and enigmatic Abyssinian civilization, still little known today because, by reason of its original culture and religion, the country has nearly always lived turned in on itself, covers about three thousand years. Axum was the cradle of the Ethiopian nation, probably the outcome of a federation of Cushite and Semitic tribes. There, in this venerable capital, in the 4th century AD the emperor Ezana embraced Christianity after the welcome at court of a young shipwrecked Syrian, Frumentius, who was to become the country's first *bishop. In the following century, monks from *Antioch carried out the definitive *conversion of the people, at the same time introducing the Axumite Empire to monophysitism, which was to keep the Church of Ethiopia under the tutelage of the *Coptic *patriarchate of *Alexandria until its recent emancipation in 1959.

The only Christian kingdom of black *Africa, Axum was immediately able to open itself up to Greco-Roman influence and, thanks to commercial exchanges, enjoy a rapid economic, political and cultural rise. But this prosperity was ephemeral. Decline set in with the 6th c., when the Sasanid Persians expelled the Axumites from the Arabian peninsula, where they had extended their power under Ezana, and forced them to fall back on the western shore of the Red Sea. The coming of *Islam would soon isolate Ethiopia by preventing its access to the sea, thus cutting Axum off from Byzantium and the Mediterranean world. Previously turned essentially towards Arabia, in order to survive Ethiopia had to extend itself southwards. It then entered a long period of decline from which it would only really emerge in the 13th century. Meanwhile a new dynasty, that of the Zagué, had made its appearance in the Lasta. Its greatest ruler, Lalibela (?1190-1225), built himself a capital there, Roha, modelled on the Holy Places; the 11 monolithic churches we still admire there today are the sole vestiges of this new Jerusalem to which the name of this mystical king remains attached.

The usurping dynasty was overthrown by Yekuno Amlak (1270-1285), who thus restored the lineage of the Solomonid kings. With him truly began the Ethiopian Middle Ages, a brilliant period of about two and a half centuries during which the Empire would enjoy unprecedented prosperity. Restored to the throne of his ancestors with the help of the monks, notably the celebrated *Takla Haymanot († 1312), founder of the monastery of Dabra-Libanos, Yekuno Amlak knew how to show his acknowledgment. The monasteries benefited from royal favours and enjoyed a considerable increase. Ethiopian monks even established themselves at *Jerusalem. But this grip of monasticism on the court and on society as a whole was not slow to arouse conflicts. Theological disputes broke out between certain monastic communities and the *metropolitans sent from Alexandria. Then again, the Church, which had enjoyed a sudden rise in the wake of the Empire's expansion, showed itself generally unequal to the task required of it. So it was necessary to reorganise and reform it. This was the role arrogated to himself by King *Zara Yaqob in the 15th century. This champion of orthodoxy, like his illustrious predecessor *Amda Sion (1314-1344), contributed not a little to the kingdom's reputation in Europe. Both also made a name for themselves in the bitter struggle they waged against Islam. But the Empire remained no less heterogeneous on the eve of the disastrous conflict with Imām Grañ. Many recently conquered and annexed territories had only superficially felt the influence of the Church, and certain tribes, notably those of the eastern frontier provinces of Ifat, remained Muslims at heart. They were not slow to rise up on the arrival of Grañ, who devastated Ethiopia for twenty years (1523-1543). Fascinated by the wealth and splendour of the Ethiopian churches and monasteries, his troops pillaged frenziedly, thus ravaging the material and spiritual culture of Ethiopia's Christian Middle Ages.

Church of St George, Roha (Ethiopia). 13th c.

The literary and artistic masterpieces that survived these depredations, while making us regret the loss of a great part of the heritage, nevertheless enable us to imagine the degree of refinement Ethiopia had then attained.

The general state of dilapidation that the great majority of churches and monasteries find themselves in today should not deceive us. All the evidence agrees: the Byzantine and oriental travellers of the golden age and decline of Axum, the Portuguese and Spanish missionaries of the 16th c., all were struck with admiration on discovering the sumptuousness of the court and the magnificence of the religious buildings that covered the country. As custodians of culture, priests and monks enjoyed immense prestige from the start. Apart from *prayers and *hymns, intended to heighten the splendour of religious ceremonies, we owe them a translation of the *Bible made from the Greek and containing several *apocrypha, such as the *Book of Enoch* and the *Book of Jubilees*, mystical writings contemporary with Lalibela, *Miracles of Mary*, an Ethiopic version of a collection of 12th-c. French *legends, which had got there through the Latin East and Egypt, as well as Saints' Lives written in the 14th and 15th centuries. All these works were written in Ge'ez, or classical Ethiopic, which remains the language of the liturgy. From this same period of revival dates an original literature represented first by the celebrated *Kebra Nagast* (The Glory of the Kings), explaining the Solomonid origin of the rulers of Ethiopia, then by the first royal chronicles, the earliest of which sings in *epic style the victories of Amda Sion. King Zara Yaqob himself took up the pen in the 15th c.; he composed hymns, wrote treatises and regulated the customs of the Church, thus taking literally his role as defender of the faith.

J. Doresse, *L'Empire du Prêtre-Jean*, Paris, 1957 (2 vol.). – B. Velat, "Éthiopie", *DSp*, 4, 1961, 1453-1477. – J. Doresse, *Histoire de l'Éthiopie*, Paris, 1970. – S. Hable Sellassié, *Ancient and Medieval Ethiopian History to 1270*, Addis Ababa, 1972. – T. Tamrat, *Church and State in Ethiopia, 1270-1527*, Oxford, 1972. – J. Leroy, *L'Éthiopie. Archéologie et culture*, Paris, 1973. – A. Hidaru, *A Short Guide to the Study of Ethiopia: a General Bibliography*, Westport (CT), 1976. – C. Prouty, E. Rosenberg, *Historical Dictionary of Ethiopia*, Metuchen-London, 1981. – J. Doresse *et al.*, "Éthiopie", *Encyclopedia universalis*, 8, Paris, 1990, 952-971. – R. Pankhurst, *A Social History of Ethiopia*, Addis Ababa, 1990. – S. Munro-Hay, *Aksum: an African Civilisation of Late Antiquity*, Edinburgh, 1991. – S. Munro-Hay, R. Pankhurst, *Ethiopia*, Oxford-Santa Barbara, 1995. – R. Pankhurst, *The Ethiopians*, Oxford-Malden (MA), 1998.

Yvan G. Lepage

**ETYMOLOGY.** Etymology is a grammatical discipline whose object is the origin and filiation of words. But what for us is only an auxiliary science of historical linguistics was in the early Middle Ages the preferred tool of the knowledge of beings. Medieval thought was here indebted to a double tradition: that of Hellenistic scholarship, which established a connection of *cause and effect between things and the naming of them, and that of *exegesis, notably biblical, which had it that the name of every being bore in itself the *sign of its *metaphysical essence (see Jerome, *Liber interpretationis Hebraicorum nominum*). It thus postulated the existence of a necessary and primordial relation between words and things ("*nomina sunt consequentia rerum*"). *Isidore of Seville, in his monumental *encyclopedia impartially entitled *Etymologies* or *Origins*, "the fundamental book of the Middle Ages" according to Curtius, generalized and transmitted this *doctrine and its applications, by which the correspondence in sound between two or more signifiers enlightens us as to the reality of the signified. Thus, *Paul owes his name (Latin *paulus*, "little") to the fact that he is "the least of the Apostles" (1 Cor 15, 19), and the forename Agnes connotes the proverbial purity of the *lamb (*agnus*). Such phonetic comparisons became the basis of explanation, whether scientific – according to *Marbod's *Liber lapidum*, the stone called *dionysia* was a precaution against the evils of drunkenness –, historical – according to Rigord, *Paris was once called Lutetia because its streets, before being paved by order of *Philip Augustus, were all muddy (*luteae*) – or even theological – the comparison between *homo*, "*man", and *humus*, "earth", is commonplace.

It would be wrong to consider such reasonings as belonging to the childish logic of the pun. To the extent that the universe was conceived as a universal harmony whose elements analogically echoed each other, in which Adam, the first namer, was thought to have taken his linguistic knowledge from divine inspiration itself, etymology could rightly be considered, in the primary sense of the term, "discourse on truth". This conception was damaged by the *nominalist philosophy of *language that, from Peter *Abelard to William of *Ockham, postulated the conventional character of the linguistic sign, by the speculative *grammar of the 13th-c. "modists", for whom the meaning of words was the product of their syntactical interrelations, and by the progress of the physical and natural *sciences entailed by the rediscovery of the work of *Aristotle. Writers nevertheless continued, up to the 16th c. and beyond, to draw poetic effects from these plays on the form of words. Modern etymological science, based on the analysis of the genetic relationships betwen them, did not really attain its full growth before the 17th century.

Isidore of Seville, *Etymologiarum sive Originum Libri XX*, W. M. Lindsay (ed.), Oxford, 1911 (2 vol.).

R. Klinck, "Die lateinische Etymologie des Mittelalters", *MAe*, 13, 1970, 93-145. – E. R. Curtius, "Etymology as a Category of Thought", *European Literature and the Latin Middle Ages*, W. R. Trask (tr.), Princeton (NJ), 1953, 495-501. – R. Howard Bloch, *Etymologies and Genealogies*, Chicago, 1983. – M. Amsler, *Etymology and Grammatical Discourse in Late Antiquity and the Early Middle Ages*, Amsterdam, 1989.

Jean-Yves Tilliette

## EUCHARIST

**The West.** From the beginnings of Christianity, a commemorative ritual re-enacted *Christ's sacrifice in the form of an offering of bread and wine which was also a ritual of fellowship. It became part of the liturgy and community worship, and used Christ's words at the Last Supper which represented the approaching *Passion: "This is my body. . ." (Mt 26, 26). In the works of the Church *Fathers, the Eucharist is discussed as a commemorative *sign, but there is not much discussion of its precise philosophical or doctrinal workings and implications. In the early Middle Ages this was considered in monastic circles, but only from the 11th c., and with the intellectual engagement with the grammatico-logical underpinnings of the biblical phrases, did a debate begin to establish contrasting interpretations: first in the debate between *Berengar of Tours and *Lanfranc, and then in discussion in the university of *Paris throughout the 12th century. By 1140 *Peter Lombard's sacramental *theology listed the Eucharist as one of the seven *sacraments of the Church, and by the 1180s the term *transsubstantiatio* was in current use, designating the substantial change that occurred in the bread and wine of the *mass, which made them into Christ's flesh and blood by force of the words of *consecration uttered by the priest at the *altar. At the fourth *Lateran council of 1215, the theology of the Eucharist was linked unambiguously to the notion of *transubstantiation, and Christians were required to participate and partake of *communion at least once a year, after proper preparation, *confession and *penance.

The Eucharist thus became the central ritual of Christian life in religious houses and in *parishes. Participation was not limited to communion, the reception of Christ's body; it could also be experienced through attendance at mass with the intention of seeing the Eucharist at the moment of its *elevation in the hands of the priest after the words of consecration. A wide range of practices and regulations were created to safeguard the consecrated *hosts within churches with the intention of according them suitable veneration: precious receptacles, cloths and hangings, and lights around them.

Eucharistic teaching made strong claims which required incessant instruction and persuasive teaching to reach parishioners throughout Europe and to make its complexities intelligible. It always encountered difficulties, as what were perceptibly unchanged discs of baked dough were taught to be Christ's own historic, suffering and saving body. A variety of dissenting and doubting responses is evident in a wide range of sources, and continuous efforts attempted to counter these. Eucharistic doubt was in some cases coupled with a more fundamental critique of the institutions of the Church, and when this occurred ecclesiastical authorities reacted swiftly. *Cathar anti-materialism rejected all notions of sacramentality (the working of *grace through material *signs), popular *Lollardy derided the claims made for a piece of bread often consecrated by sinful *clerics, and *Hussite criticism approached the Eucharist from an anti-clerical direction which was opposed to clerical exclusivity in handling the Eucharist and receiving Christ's body in both forms, consecrated bread and consecrated wine, while the *laity customarily received only the bread. Criticism and discusssion emanated not only from popular movements but also from scholarly quarters. There was a *nominalist criticism of the theory of transubstantiation; *Ockham identified difficulties with the theory of miraculous action in the host *ex opere operato*, as did *Wycliffe later in the 14th century.

Yet the promise of union with Christ offered by bodily reception of that which was his body also offered occasion for devotional participation and mystical transcendence. Eucharistic devotion was very widespread in female communities (particularly the *beguines), and eucharistic *processions became an important form of lay participation, culminating in the town-wide processions that developed around the feast of *Corpus Christi in the 14th and 15th centuries. Whereas frequent communion was discouraged, as it required a high level of preparation, viewing the Eucharist was encouraged and churches offered frequent occasions for eucharistic display, in response to popular demand. As the most powerful substance available, the Eucharist was sought for healing and comfort, just as it was manipulated and used for potions and amulets. As the simplest object offering the most direct access to the divine, the Eucharist features powerfully and in various and divergent ways in the medieval picture of the world.

E. Dumoutet, *Le Désir de voir l'hostie et les origines de la dévotion au saint-sacrement*, Paris, 1926. – J. Bossy, "The Mass as a Social Institution, 1200-1700", *PaP*, 100, 1983, 29-61. – G. Macy, *The Theologies of the Eucharist in the Early Scholastic Period*, Oxford, 1984. – C. W. Bynum, *Holy Feast and Holy Fast*, Berkeley (CA), 1987. – M. Rubin, *Corpus Christi: the Eucharist in Late Medieval Culture*, Cambridge, 1991. – G.J.C. Snoek, *Medieval Piety from Relics to the Eucharist*, Leiden, 1995.

Miri Rubin

**Byzantium.** Although the word *eucharistía* was in current use in the Early Church for the principal act of Christian worship, the Greeks preferred (and still prefer) the word *leitourgía* (literally: service). A composite structure, which was developed and modified over the centuries until the set of *rubrics drawn up by the 14th-c. patriarch of Constantinople Philotheus was standardized by printing, its origins can be traced from New Testament texts. The first surviving manuscripts date from the 9th century. The liturgy always retained the character of a social meeting of Christians (*agapè*). It was also an occasion for instruction and the communication of news.

In its 9th-c. form, the liturgy began with the preparation of the offerings. This was at first executed outside the sanctuary, to which the offerings were then carried in *procession. Later a more elaborate prothesis rite took place in a chapel to the north of the central apse. After introductory *prayers, the Lectionary was carried in at the Little Entrance. The prayer of the **Trisagion* was recited, followed by the Bible *readings prescribed for the day. The catechumens were then dismissed. After the prayers of the faithful, the Great Entry with the offerings took place. This procession, when the offerings were carried from the chapel of the prothesis through the holy doors to the *altar, took on great solemnity. In late Byzantine painting a representation of the Great Entry symbolized the Celestial Liturgy. After the recital of the *Creed, the **Anaphora* or *Canon). After the *doxology that ended the Anaphora, the *Lord's Prayer was recited (as in the Latin rite *mass), followed by prayers of preparation for *communion. A prayer of thanksgiving was said after communion, the *laity were

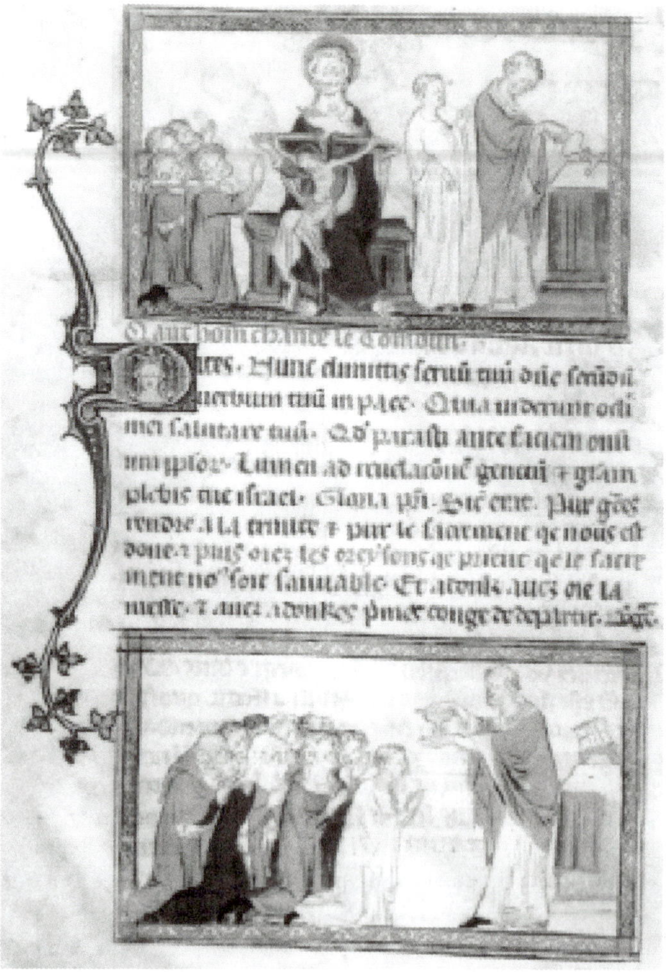

*The Eucharist. Mélanges théologiques*, 14th-c. manuscript. Paris, BNF (Ms fr. 13342, fol. 48 v°).

dismissed and the celebrant recited the so-called "prayer behind the *ambo".

The Eucharist was regularly celebrated on *Sundays – the so-called Lord's day – and *feasts, but celebrations on ordinary weekdays was not general. Of its nature, the Eucharist had a festal character. It was forbidden on *fast days, when it was replaced by the Mass of the *Presanctified. The real presence of Christ in the consecrated *species does not seem to have been questioned, although there were internal controversies from the 11th c. as to the nature of the participation of other members of the *Trinity than Christ, as well as with the Latins, notably over the use of leavened or unleavened bread. Under the form of the communion of the Apostles, the Eucharist was regularly represented in the apse of churches from the 11th century, as well as other liturgical themes.

F. E. Brightman, *Liturgies Eastern and Western*, Oxford, 1896, 307 f. – G. Kretschmar, "Abendmahl", "Abendmahlsfeier", *TRE*, 1, 1977, 59-89, 229-278. – R. Taft, *The Great Entrance*, Rome, 1978 (2nd ed.). – C. Walter, *Art and Ritual of the Byzantine Church*, London, 1982.

Christopher Walter

**EUCHARISTIC CONTROVERSY.** During the first millennium of the Christian era, the Church does not seem to have been deeply troubled by controversies relating to the *Eucharist. Admittedly, the writings of two 9th-c. monks of *Corbie have commonly been seen as evidence of a dispute in which the real presence was called in question, *Paschasius Radbertus asserting the identity of the eucharistic body of *Christ and his historical *body, and *Ratramnus insisting on the difference between the two. But recent studies clearly demonstrate Ratramnus's orthodoxy, and the author of one of these studies even doubts the existence of a controversy between Raschasius and Ratramnus, their opposition not appearing evident, nor their points of view contradictory.

It was this supposed opposition that, in the mid 11th c., triggered a controversy that profoundly influenced the development of sacramental *theology. In *c.*1048, *Berengar, a *canon of *Saint-Martin at *Tours, discovered Ratramnus's treatise on the Eucharist (attributing it to *John Scotus Eriugena), and saw in it a radical symbolism inspired by the patristic tradition – which he opposed to the ultra-*realism of *Paschasius. It cannot be denied that in thus siding with "John Scotus" (*i.e.* Ratramnus) as he understood him, Berengar was disintegrating the eucharistic belief, even if his intention was to free the Church of his time from primitive ideas. Did not the profession of faith imposed on Berengar at Rome in 1059 state that at the *mass the body of Christ was physically and really ("*sensualiter in veritate*") handled and broken by the hands of the priest and crushed by the teeth of the faithful? Did not *Lanfranc, Berengar's main adversary, see these rites as an authentic immolation of Christ's flesh ("*ipsa carnis ipsius immolatio*")? In speaking of a "substantial" presence of Christ's body in the Eucharist, the author of the profession of *faith in 1079 did not distance himself from these views, *substantia* in this text being understood physically and not metaphysically.

To justify his symbolist position, Berengar appealed to patristic *tradition, especially to the *Augustinian definition of the *sacrament, understood as a "holy sign", the *sign being for Augustine a "reality which, over and above what appears to the eyes, calls to mind something else". Was the Eucharist then just a sign and not the reality of Christ's body? In the 11th c., the defenders of the real presence, *e.g.* Lanfranc, tried to escape this difficulty by applying this notion of sign to the eucharistic flesh already constituted, which, by its real immolation, became the sign of Christ's body immolated on the cross. As the Roman professions of faith of 1059 and 1079 show, real presence and sacramental or symbolic presence were distinguished in the Eucharist at that time – far from the "*sacramentaliter praesens*" to which the council of Trent would hold.

Such representations created an impasse. Works by theologians allowed the Latin Church gradually to disentangle itself by exploring the distinction that existed in the Eucharist between "what is seen" and "what is not seen" (a distinction that was already the *leitmotiv* of Lanfranc's treatise on the Eucharist, though he could not have foreseen the developments it implied) and to this distinction applying the distinctions of "accidents" and "*substance" borrowed from the vocabulary of the School and progressively explored along the lines of the peripatetic *philosophy, whose influence increased in the 12th and 13th centuries. So there slowly appeared the *doctrine of *transubstantiation confirmed by the councils of *Lateran IV and Trent, according to which, by *consecration, the substance of bread and wine is converted into the substance of the body and blood of Christ, the species or appearances (the accidents) of bread and wine playing their role as a sacramental sign, a doctrine developed by *Thomas Aquinas, allowing the eucharistic belief of the Western Church to go from the "*sensualiter frangi*" of the council of Rome of 1059 to the "*signi tantum fit fractura*" of the Angelic Doctor.

The "Berengarian" controversy itself (1048-1080) did not go beyond the bounds of ultra-realism, though it prepared later developments. Punctuated by some 13 *councils or *synods, five of them presided over by a *pope and three by papal *legates, it comprised two great periods each terminated by a Roman council before which Berengar found himself obliged to read a profession of faith contrary to his convictions (1059 and 1079). Before 1059, Berengar had expounded his *doctrine in the *Purgatoria epistola contra Almannum*. After 1059, he attacked the council that had just condemned him in an opusculum known as *Scriptum contra synodum*, refuted by Lanfranc's treatise on the Eucharist (*c.*1066). Berengar replied to Lanfranc in a work discovered in 1770, which was certainly not circulated. Arbitrarily named *De sacra coena*, we have restored its exact title, *Rescriptum contra Lanfrannum*.

While he had some influence in his time, especially on the schools, Berengar did not found a school. We know only a single text by a "Berengarian", while a number of 11th- and 12th-c. theologians devoted works to refuting the master of Tours, notably Hugh of Breteuil, Durand of Troarn, Lanfranc, Guitmund of Aversa and *Alger of Liège.

J. De Montclos, *Lanfranc et Bérenger. La controverse eucharistique du XI^e siècle*, *SSL*, 37, 1971. – J.-P. Bouhot, *Ratramne de Corbie. Histoire littéraire et controverses doctrinales*, *EAug*, 1976. – M. Gibson, *Lanfranc of Bec*, Oxford, 1978. – P. Ganz (ed.), R.B.C. Huygens (ed.), F. Niewöhner (ed.), *Auctoritas und ratio. Studien zu Berengar von Tours*, Wiesbaden, 1990. – J. de Montclos, "Lanfranc et Béranger, les origines de la doctrine de la transsubstantiation", *IS*, 51, 1993, 297-326.

Jean de Montclos

**EUDES RIGAUD (*c.*1215-1275).** Sprung from the petty *nobility, Eudes Rigaud entered the Friars Minor in 1236. He became one of the "four masters", who in 1242 wrote a commentary on the Rule; his works herald those of the great *scholastics. Head of St Mark's *convent in *Rouen, in 1247 he was elected archbishop of Rouen with *Louis IX's support. Conscientious in his duties, he regularly visited his *dioceses, as he relates in his Register. A familiar of the king, he followed him on *crusade in 1270 and gathered the earliest information with a view to his *canonization. He took part in the council of *Lyon II shortly before his death in 1275.

J. O'Sullivan, *The Register of Eudes Rigaud*, New York, 1964. – L. Sileo, "Eudes Rigaud", *DSp*, 13, 1988, 670-674.

Catherine Vincent

**EUGENIUS III, POPE (died 1153).** Descendant of a family of Montemagno (*Pisa), Bernardo Paganelli became a monk at *Clairvaux in 1138. Hesitant at the *election of this first *Cistercian *pope (15 Feb 1145), *Bernard of Clairvaux wrote *De consideratione* for his use. *Arnold of Brescia prevented him entering *Rome until the end of 1152. In France from 1147, he held a *synod at *Paris. At *Trier, he approved the revelations of *Hildegard of Bingen. At *Reims (21 March 1148), he confirmed the reforms of *Innocent II, condemned *Eon of Stella and closed the debate on *Gilbert of Poitiers. He died on 8 July 1153 at Tivoli.

B. Jacqueline, *Épiscopat et papauté chez saint Bernard de Clairvaux*, Saint-Lô, 1975. – I.S. Robinson, *The Papacy, 1973-1198*, Cambridge, 1990. – A. Paravicini Bagliani, *HChr*, 5, 1993.

Agostino Paravicini Bagliani

**EUGENIUS IV, POPE (1383-1447).** Born to a noble Venetian family, in his youth Gabriel Condulmaro founded a community of *secular clerics practising an austere form of the Rule of St *Augustine. Bishop of *Siena (31 Dec 1407), curial *cardinal

1408-1420, he became *legate in the *march of Ancona (7 Feb 1420). On the death of *Martin V he was elected *pope, 3 March 1431. His pontificate was very troubled. In conflict with the great Roman feudal lords, he had to flee his city from 1434 to 1443. He fought against the council of *Basel which claimed to be superior to the pope, transferring it to *Ferrara (1438), then *Florence, where the treaty of *union with the Greeks was signed on 5 July 1439. A fraction of the *council remained at Basel and claimed to depose him and replace him in 1439 with *Felix V (Amadeus VIII of Savoy).

A man of acknowledged moral integrity and exemplary purity of life, Eugenius goes down as the pontiff who ensured the victory of papal monarchy over the conciliar tendency. A friend of *Nicholas of Cusa and *Bernardino of Siena, he favoured the *Renaissance and employed illustrious *artists (Fra *Angelico, *Pisanello, Donatello, Ghiberti . . .). He died on 23 Feb 1447.

J. Gill, *Eugenius IV*, London, 1961. – *DHGE*, 15, 1963, 1355-1359. – J.W. Stieber, *Pope Eugenius IV, the Council of Basel and the Secular and Ecclesiastical Authorities in the Empire*, Leiden, 1978. – *HChr*, 6, 1990.

Michel Fol

**EUGENIUS OF TOLEDO (died 657).** Trained in the Aragonese monastery of San Engracio, Eugenius was a disciple and close friend of Braulio. In 646 he was chosen by King Chindaswinth as archbishop of *Toledo. A cultured man, poet and musician, familiar with secular authors as well as Scripture, Eugenius gave particular attention to the problem of training the clergy. He was also one of the architects of the formulation of the theocratic *monarchy whose basis had been laid by *Recared and *Leander of Seville. The eighth *council of Toledo, convened by him in 653, made the sovereign the natural defender of the faith. To him are attributed liturgical *hymns, some hundred poems and a lost treatise on the *Trinity.

*DHEE*, 2, 1972, 882-883. – *HChr*, 4, 1993.

Daniel Baloup

**EULALIA.** The *martyrdom of St Eulalia at Mérida (in modern Estremadura) on 10 Dec 304 is described by Prudentius (*Peristephanon*). According to a Barcelonan Life (*c.*700) followed by *Bede, Eulalia was not burned but beheaded. The *inventio* of the tomb at *Barcelona in 878 gave new impetus to the *cult of the saint, whose name was borne by Carolingian princesses. Eulalia owes her fame to the *Sequence* copied soon after 881 in a manuscript of Saint-Amand. This poem, the oldest preserved in French, relates in 29 verses the passion and martyrdom of the saint, who refused to "serve the devil" and "lose her virginity" and who, insensible to fire, had to be beheaded. Her soul took on the appearance of a dove.

*La Cantilène de sainte Eulalie*, M.-P. Dion (ed.), Valenciennes, 1990.

Jean-Pierre Bordier

***EULOGIA.*** Literally a blessing, the word had a wide extension in early Byzantine use. It was used for gifts of a sacred nature, *e.g.* bread, consecrated or merely blessed, sent to absent persons. Later the word was used in a more restricted sense notably for pious souvenirs brought away from shrines by *pilgrims. They were often stamped with the word *eulogia*. Discs made from the soil at the shrine of St Symeon the *Stylite the Younger were considered to have therapeutic powers, as was the water or oil contained in flasks brought away from other shrines. These flasks could be decorated. Countless *eulogiae*, stamped with his portrait, were brought away from the shrine of St Menas in Egypt.

K. Wessel, "Eulogia", *RBK*, 2, 1971, 427-433.

Christopher Walter

Pope Eugenius IV at the council of Basel. Miniature from the *Chants royaux sur la Conception couronné du Puy de Rouen*, 1519-1528. Paris, BNF (Ms fr. 1537, fol. 73 v°).

**EULOGIO OF CORDOVA (*c.*800-859).** Eulogio was born at *Cordova early in the 9th c., a difficult time for the Christian community of the south Iberian peninsula. In exchange for the payment of a capitation, the Muslim authorities allowed the Christians to remain loyal to their faith; but these **dhimmī* saw numerous constraints imposed on them. The Arab-Berber occupiers took particular care to limit the number and activity of the churches and forbade all proselytizing activity. Faced with these interferences and vexations, attracted by a brilliant and dominant civilization, more and more Christians chose *conversion to *Islam. More generally, by the multiplication of mixed marriages and the gradual adoption of the customs of the conquerors, the first half of the 9th c. saw a discernible "Arabization" of the native population of al-Andalus.

This evolution aroused a deep malaise among certain Christians who saw it as an unacceptable treason; Eulogio was among them. Trained at the parish *school of San Zoilo, under Abbot Speraindeo, he became a priest and, with his friend *Alvaro, one of the foremost figures of the radical Christian movement. The journey he made to the kingdoms of the north in 845 fed his commitment to a restoration of Christianity. The crisis broke out in 851 when the monk Isaac was beheaded for having publicly denounced the errors of Islam and defended the truth of his faith. Between 851 and 859, some 40 persons followed his example. To bring an end to the disorders aroused by these voluntary *martyrdoms, emir Abd al-

Romanesque crypt in the Church of St Eutropius
at Saintes, France

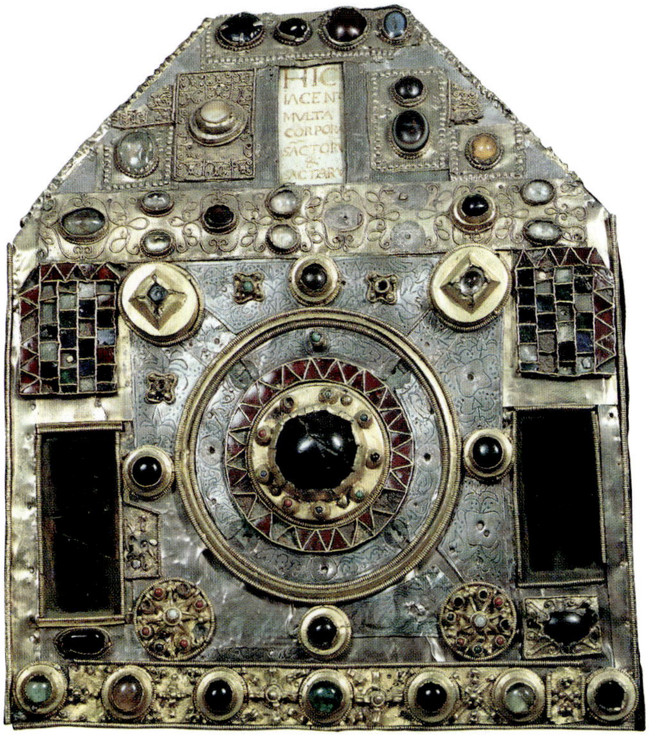


Reliquary of gold, silver, precious stones and
enamelling. Carolingian, 9th c.
Treasury, Benedictine Abbey of Conques, France

Procession by Michael Ximénez,
15th c. Prado Museum, Madrid

Martyrdom of St. Adalbert.
15th c. Gallery of Hungarian Art, Budapest

Gilt bronze crucifix from the Church of Aby (Jutland).
Mid 11th c. National Museum, Copenhagen

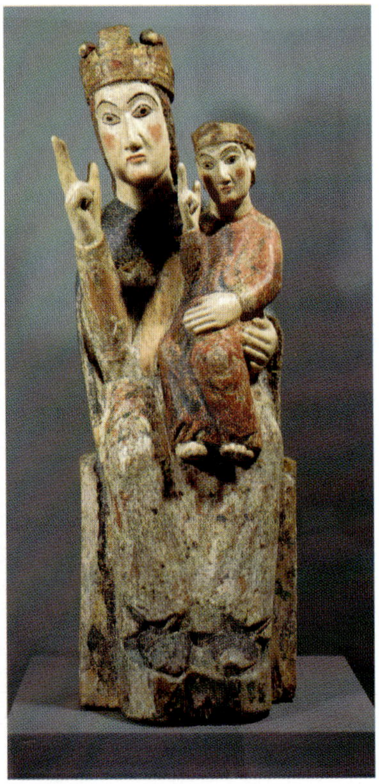

Virgin and Child.
c. 1200, polychrome wood. Diocesan Museum,
Bressanone, Italy

Rahman II put pressure on the bishop of *Seville, Recafred, who condemned the instigators in 852. The next *emir, Muhammad, intensified the repression. He purged the administration, then the army, and considerably increased the obligations and restrictions that weighed on the Christians. Eulogio became the *chronicler of these bloody episodes. He wrote the *Documentum martyriale* (851), the three books of the *Memoriale martyrum* (851-857) and the *Liber apologeticus martyrum*. These works, in which he harshly attacked Islam and exalted martyrdom, led to his arrest and execution, 11 March 859.

The drama of the martyrs of Cordova, while revealing the malaise of the Christians of al-Andalus, also marked a break. In the 850s, hundreds of *dhimmī* left Muslim *Spain to find refuge in the kingdoms of the north. Those who chose to remain lived in conditions more difficult than those that had prevailed immediately after the conquest. The movement of Arabization continued, creating a hybrid civilization, called "*Mozarabic". The role of Eulogio in these events gives rise to very varied interpretations. A hero of Christianity to some, a dangerous hothead to others.

E. P. Colbert, *The Martyrs of Cordoba*, Washington (DC), 1962. – *HChr*, 4, 1993. – K. Wolf, *Christian Martyrs in Muslim Spain*, Cambridge, 1988.

Daniel Baloup

**EUTHYMIUS I OF CONSTANTINOPLE (*c.*834-917).** Born at Isaurian Seleucia, the monk Euthymius allied himself with the future Leo VI who, on his accession, made him hegumen of a monastery of Psamathia (a quarter of *Constantinople), *syncellus*, a member of the senate and his own spiritual director. At the time of the affair of the *Tetragamy, Leo banished Patriarch *Nicholas Mysticus, whom he replaced (Feb? 907) with Euthymius. His patriarchate, agitated by *schism, was interrupted when Leo, on his deathbed, recalled Nicholas (May 912). After Leo's death, Euthymius was brutally deposed and banished to the monastery of Ta Agathou on the Bosphorus, where he died. His name was restored to the *diptychs in 956 by Patriarch Polyeuctes.

*Vita Euthymii patriarchae CP*, P. Karlin-Hayter (ed.), *BByz.*, 3, 1970.

Bernard Flusin

**EUTHYMIUS OF TURNOVO (*c.*1320/1330-*c.*1402).** The last Bulgarian patriarch before the liquidation of the autocephaly of the *Orthodox Church in *Bulgaria following the *Ottoman conquest at the end of the 14th c., Euthymius occupied the patriarchal throne in the capital of the second Bulgar Empire, Tŭrnovo, from 1375 to 1393. He died in exile, probably at the monastery of Bačkovo in the Rhodope mountains. Euthymius contributed to the spread of *hesychasm in Bulgaria and thus continued the work of his master, the monk Theodosius of Tŭrnovo. By his writings, eight hagiographical texts consecrated in part to saints of Bulgar origin, and by his philological reforms (orthography and principles of translation from the Greek) which his disciples, especially Gregory Camblak and Constantine of Kostenec, developed, he contributed to bring the Bulgar culture of his time to its apogee.

E. Kałužniacki, *Werke des Patriarchen von Bulgarien Euthymius*, Vienna, 1901. – E. Turdeanu, *La Littérature bulgare du XIVe siècle et sa diffusion dans les pays roumains*, Paris, 1947. – M. L. Hébert, *Hesychasm, Word-Weaving, and Slavic Hagiography: the Literary School of Patriarch Euthymius*, Munich, 1992. – K. Kabakčiev, *Evtimievata reforma- Chipotezi i fakti*, Plovdiv, 1997.

Christian Hannick

**EUTHYMIUS ZIGABENUS (12th c.).** Euthymius Zigabenus was a monk at *Constantinople when the Emperor Alexius I *Comnenus commissioned him to write a work refuting all the *heresies, on the model of Epiphanius of Cyprus's *Panarion* (4th c.). He compiled the *Panoplia dogmatica* (PG 130) in 28 books. The first seven are an exposition of the Christian faith from patristic citations. The next fourteen recapitulate the ancient heresies without originality. The last five deal with contemporary heresies, which Euthymius refutes himself (Armenian "*azymites", *Paulicians, Messalians, *Bogomils, Muslims). We also owe him some exegetical writings.

M. Jugie, "La vie et les oeuvres d'Euthyme Zigabène", *EOr*, 15, 1912, 215-225. – A. N. Papabasileiou, *Euthymios-Iôannès Zigabènos. Bios. Suggraphai*, Athens, 1977.

Marie-Hélène Congourdeau

**EVANGELIARY.** With *prayer and singing, reading is one of the three essential actions of the liturgy. Its roots go back far into the religious practices of the first Christians. From the beginnings of Christianity, the *Bible was read at the different meetings of the faithful. In order to meditate on the Scriptures as a whole, the biblical text was read then according to the principle of *lectio continua*, throughout the year. Very early, around the 2nd c., the annual recurrence of the main events of Christian history led to the making of a selection of *readings whose themes corresponded to the significance of the *feasts or of the liturgical season (*e.g.* the readings for *Easter, Ascension, *Pentecost). Thus it rapidly became habitual to read a given pericope (passage of the Bible) on a particular day, but before the 5th and 6th cc. no strict rule existed in this matter. Allowing plenty of room for improvisation, the early Christian centuries allowed the *bishop (or another community leader) to choose the readings of the *mass. In Antiquity and then in the Middle Ages, the number of readings in the course of the mass varied according to rite – the Roman rite and the other Western Latin rites. In the latter, the common usage consisted of three readings (Old Testament, Epistle and Gospel), with pericopes that varied from one rite to another. The Roman rite by contrast had a system of only two readings, the Epistle and the Gospel.

Before becoming a *liturgical book in the proper sense, the *evangeliarium* was at first a list of gospel pericopes distributed according to the *liturgical year. The progressive fixing of this list in the course of the early Christian centuries acquired great stability in the 7th c. and allowed the development, especially at *Rome, of systems of readings for the mass (gospels, but also epistles) that in the same period were fixed in the lists of pericopes. St *Gregory's homilies *in evangelia*, preached in 590-592, are the first written evidence of a systematic list of readings. Each *homily is preceded by the pericope commented on and the list concerns the cycle of readings in use at that time in the Church of Rome.

In the 7th c., the *Roman liturgy was reorganised and lists of gospel pericopes (*capitularia evangeliorum*) were put together on the spot. At that moment, we may say that the evangeliary did not yet exist as a book, but in the form of a liturgical list indicating the passages that had to be sought in manuscripts of the Bible or of the four gospels. The *capitulare evangeliorum* ascribes to a large part of the *liturgical year a pericope for the mass, taken from one of the four gospels. The earliest "evangeliary" (or capitulary) is the π type created around 645 and defined by T. Klauser. Each gospel pericope is indicated by the number it bears in the Eusebian numbering, as well as by its *incipit* and *explicit*, and preceded by

*Evangeliary with enamels and cameo.* Ottonian art, 10th c. Church of Gannat (Allier, France).

the day of the year. In the temporal framework of the Julian *calendar, this "evangeliary" set out a classification of feasts and their pericope on the basis of the liturgical year, in which the *temporal and the *sanctoral were mingled. The π type of 645 had great success and circulated in much of the West at the time of the Romanization of the liturgy in Gaul and elsewhere from the 8th century. It gave rise to the Romano-Frankish capitulary (*c.*750), which throughout much of the Middle Ages was imposed on all the regions of the West (if we do not take into account the multitude of local adaptations, notably for feasts of saints).

As a codicological entity, the first evangeliaries appeared in the late 8th c., but not until the late 10th c. did they prevail in mass books to the detriment of books of gospels provided with a capitulary. Between the 8th and 10th cc., the use of the latter was broadly in the majority. On the level of *codicology, the evangeliary was nothing but the "putting into *book form" of the lists of pericopes. Its practical side and the pre-eminent place it progressively occupied in the hierarchy of liturgical mass books meant that it easily prevailed before being supplanted in the course of the 11th c., at first by the lectionary of the mass (bringing together the epistolary and the evangeliary), then by a *missal incorporating the lectionary together with the *antiphonary.

The internal and external decoration of evangeliaries, and in a more general sense of books of gospels with *capitulare evangeliorum*, was one of the summits of the history of medieval art (*illumination, *goldsmiths' work, *ivory work). Especially noteworthy is the evangeliary of Godescalc, made between 781 and 783 for *Charlemagne and sumptuously painted by the scribe-artist who gave his name to the manuscript, as well as the series of evangeliaries decorated in the **scriptorium* of *Reichenau in the 10th and 11th cc. to satisfy the commissions of the Ottonian emperors and the dignitaries of the *Empire.

T. Klauser, *Das römische capitulare evangeliorum. I. Typen*, *LQF*, 28, 1935. – A.-G. Martimort, *Les Lectures liturgiques et leurs livres*, *TSMÂO*, 64, 1992. – A. Chavasse, *Les Lectionnaires romains de la messe au VIIe et au VIIIe siècle*, *SFS*, 22, 1993. – U. Lenker, *Die westsächsische Evangelienversion und die Perikopenordnung im angelsächsischen England*, Munich, 1997.

Éric Palazzo

**EVANGELICAL COUNSELS.** The vocation of the rich man (Mt 19) and St *Paul's advice on virgins suggested to the Church *Fathers the distinction between precept and counsel in the path of spiritual progress. One, an act of *authority, obliged all Christians; the other, a friendly proposition, oriented freedom without imposing it. From then on, two counsels appeared clearly: *poverty and *chastity. St *Benedict did not define monastic *profession by reference to the counsels, because he was reluctant to distinguish it from the Christian life itself; but the formula of this profession expressed three values: "*stabilitas, conversio morum et obedientia*". Ascetic writings, especially those of *Cassian, developed the theme of the counsels. During the 11th c., the clerical state, considered as a sacred commitment, was subjected to far-reaching *reform at *Rome. The *popes imposed on their *clerics a promise of *chastity and *obedience. Finally they asked them, by renouncing individual property, to commit themselves to the common life. This ended by dividing clerics into *seculars and *regulars and, at the end of the century, multiplied *chapters and orders of regular *canons who, with monks, formed the "religious". Formulae of profession for canons insisted on the unicity of the *vow of profession, with the expression "*offerens trado meipsum Deo et ecclesiae sancti N.* [patron of the chapter]". But the *Premonstratensians added to their profession the Benedictine triad, "*stabilitas, conversio morum, obedientia*".

In 1148, a new triad appeared in the *profession of the reformed canons of Saint-Geneviève: "*castitas, communio, obedientia*". It added *obedience to the two original counsels and reappeared among the *Trinitarians in 1198. While the Customs of the *Dominicans remained faithful to "the unicity of the vow of profession" (1216, Prologue), joined to a promise of obedience to the superior and his successors, St *Francis's two Rules (1221, 1223) defined the life of the friars by the triad "*paupertas, castitas, obedientia*". This very soon became general during the 13th c. as a summary of the evangelical counsels and the specific characteristics of the religious life. Among theologians and *canonists, it ended in the theory of the three vows of religion.

From 1257 to 1269, in his three polemical works, St *Thomas Aquinas used the new triad against the opponents of the mendicants. He derived from it (1270) the treatise on the evangelical counsels in the *secunda secundae* (q. 184 and 186). He legitimized the *mendicant orders by their eminent practice of these counsels, whose place in the acquisition of *salvation and Christian progress he determined. The counsels are not ends, but means. One and the same end, a single perfection, is proposed to all by the dual precept of charity, which knows no measure. The counsels, proposed in *grace, respect the *freedom proper to the New Law. By freeing the Christian from his main obstacles, such as the triple *concupiscence (1 Jn 2, 16), they favour his ascent to the perfection of charity.

L. Hertling, "Die professio der Kleriker und die Entstehung der drei Gelübde", *ZKTh*, 56, 1932, 148-174. – A. I. Mennessier, "Conseils évangéliques", *Dsp*, 2, 1953, 1592-1609. – J.-M. Van Cangh, "Fondement évangélique de la vie religieuse", *NRTh*, 95, 1973, 635-647.

Marie-Humbert Vicaire †

**EVANGELICAL LIFE.** At the beginning of the 12th c., St *Norbert, itinerant preacher turned founder of an *order of exemplary common life, declared that he had chosen "to live purely the evangelical and apostolic life". "*Apostolic life", "evangelical life", the two expressions go back to the long effort of the *Gregorian reformers to bring *clerics and religious back to the ideal of life transmitted by *Christ to the Apostles. While the apostolic life took from the life of the Twelve within the infant Church (Acts 2, 42-47; 4, 32-35) an ideal of common life, the evangelical life was inspired by Christ's instructions to the Apostles when he sent them two by two into Galilee. The ideal was in keeping with an "evangelism" that put attention not just on the teachings, but on the words and *images of the holy text.

A line of founders, from St *Stephen of Muret and St Norbert to St *Francis of Assisi, affirmed that they had no other Rule than the Gospel. This evangelism is visible in the themes of "penitence" and "flight from the world" of the Italian hermits, of "return to the infant Church" that inspired the *reform of *clerics and monks, of "walking in Christ's footsteps" and "mendicant preaching" of the hermit-preachers of the West and South of France. These latter themes were expressly related to Christ's directives to the missionaries of Galilee: "Carry neither gold nor silver", "Eat what you are given" (Mt 10, 1-16 and par.). The whole formed a sort of rule: the "rule of the Apostles" or "evangelical life". This comprised an express mission – "how shall they preach, except they be sent?" (Rm 10, 15) – an itinerancy in search of the neighbour, uncertainty of lodging, mendicancy of the preacher, an evangelical preaching of *salvation. Although, to express their ideal, the reformers deliberately combined the texts of the Acts and the Gospel, others were aware that the "rule of the Apostles" diverged from the "*apostolic life" on the levels of stability (itinerancy or *enclosure), *poverty (mendicancy or disappropriation in community), relations with the world (seeking out or separation from men), *ministry (pastoral administration of the *sacraments or cloistered *prayer) and sources (direct instructions of Christ or patristic institutions).

Some went further and declared the evangelical life incompatible with the life of *coenobites. Thus, some preachers, often of lay origin, criticized and rejected, in the name of the Gospel, common property of monks, their stability in an assured lodging, their authoritarian hierarchy. Among the *Waldenses and *Cathars, the reaction could end in *schism or *heresy. However, the hermit preachers of the early 12th c. did not accept in their life the incompatibility of the two calls. Above all, between 1215 and 1220, St *Dominic achieved in the Order of Preachers an authentic synthesis of the apostolic models of the Acts and the Gospel, creating the regular type that was progressively extended to all the *mendicants.

M.-D. Chenu, *La Théologie au XII^e siècle*, Paris, 1957, 225-273. – M.-H. Vicaire, *L'Imitation des Apôtres*, Paris, 1963, 67-90. – J. Paul, *L'Église et la Culture en Occident*, 2, Paris, 1986, 746-792 (bibliog. 1, 48-49). – "Le modèle évangélique des Apôtres à l'origine de l'Ordre de saint Dominique", *Mouvements dissidents et novateurs*, 1989, 323-350.

Marie-Humbert Vicaire †

**EVANGELISTS.** The iconographical popularity of the evangelists was at first connected with the place held by the *book in Christian worship: prized book, sacred book. Moreover, decoration and writing were not separated, as had been the case in classical Antiquity: in the 7th c., the *Book of Durrow* (Dublin, Trinity College, ms. 57) reproduced on some of its pages the ornamentation found on **fibulae* and carved stones, though it does not exclude the human figure (the *homo*, symbol of the evangelist Matthew, appears on fol. 21 v°). From the 8th c. and particularly in the 9th, in relation to ancient Roman models, the figures of the evangelists were represented, sitting on a *throne, in *evangeliaries, following the – already old – iconographical type of the author's portrait (the evangelist Matthew, on fol. 9 v° of the Canterbury Codex Aureus, first quarter of 8th c.: Stockholm, Royal Library, ms. A 135). In the Gospels of Godescalc (between 781 and 873), the throne becomes the explicit attribute of the evangelist himself; there is a clear distinction between the evangelist and his symbol: he turns his head and his gaze towards the latter, as if somehow writing at its dictation. At the same time, the evangelist drew closer to human representation (costume, insignia, writer's instruments). *Illumination from the 9th to the 11th c. rediscovered the iconographical tradition of King *David inspired by the divine voice dictating his *Psalms to him. In the Ottonian period, under *Otto III in particular, the four evangelists were represented in *majesty at the head of their gospel (*St Luke*, Gospels of Otto III, fol. 139 v°, Reichenau, late 10th c.: Munich, Bayerische Staatsbibliothek, Clm. 4453). The evangelists thus began to be represented in series. At the same moment began the disintegration of the idea of *Empire.

From the 10th c., the figure of the evangelist was assimilated to that of the *bishop: *Rather, bishop of Verona, saw in the holder of the episcopal office the image of *God and *Christ and, in consequence, the living expression of all the manifestations of the divine substance – *angels, patriarchs, *prophets, evangelists – (*Praeloquia*). The *St Mark* of the Codex Aureus of *Echternach (fol. 108: *Nuremberg, Germanisches Nationalmuseum, ms. 15642) wears a bishop's costume, since his position as archbishop of Alexandria is insisted on (*c.*983-991). In 11th-c. *Spain, in the Beatus of Ferdinand I (*c.*1047), the symbol of Matthew holds an episcopal *crozier to emphasize the character's dignity. From now on the evangelist represents the established Church. This moment of exaltation having passed, the figure lost its evocative power: in 11th-c. England, it risked being absorbed into the marginal decoration; in the 12th and 13th cc., it tended towards hybridization with the symbol (*St Luke*, Dover Bible, fol. 19, third quarter of 12th c.: Cambridge, Corpus Christi College, ms. 4). The spread of anecdotal painting contributed to its further marginalization: in the 13th c., in the 14th, in the decorative programme of churches, in monumental painting, in sculpture, the Evangelists found a reduced place on the pendentives of vaults. On *altarpieces, they maintained their presence only in their quality of saints or apostles (St Mark in the Venetian area, from the 13th c.; St John on Tuscan altarpieces, in the 14th c.). St Luke painting the Virgin enjoyed a success of its own.

A. Grabar, *Les Voies de la création en iconographie chrétienne*, Paris, 1979.

Daniel Russo

**EVANGELIZATION.** The history of the evangelization of the West from the 5th to the 11th cc. can be broken up into five stages.

When the Roman Empire in the West disappeared to give way to the *barbarian kingdoms, the evangelization of the regions occupied by Rome was far advanced. In the *towns, the populations were Christian. In the North of the West, *bishoprics had been created; in Gaul, they went from 28 in 325 to 54 in *c*.375. *Martin of Tours († 397) and Victricius of Rouen, *c*.385, evangelized the countryside; on the banks of the Danube in the 5th c., St Severinus concerned himself with the *salvation of the pagans. But the Germanic *invasions compromised these promising results. Numerous bishoprics disappeared. Moreover, the barbarians were either Arians, *i.e.* Christians but *heretics, like the Goths, *Burgundians and *Lombards, or pagans like the *Franks. No doubt the misfortunes of the time gave occasion for the bishops to replace the defaulting Romans and defend the population, like St Nicasius at *Reims, St Aignan at *Orléans, St Exuperius at *Toulouse, St *Caesarius at *Arles and Pope Leo I at *Rome. It was they, with women like Geneviève of Nanterre, who defended the populations threatened by Attila in 451.

In the late 5th c., the Frankish King *Clovis chose to cross over from *paganism to *Catholicism rather than to *Arianism. His *baptism in *c*.496 at Reims was one of the great stages of evangelization. In the letter of congratulations he sent him, Bishop Avitus of Vienne hoped that "sharing the treasures of his heart, he may spread the seed of faith among [the] more distant peoples who, until now remaining in their natural ignorance, have not been corrupted by the miasmas of depraved doctrines", here alluding to the Arian doctrines still honoured by the Burgundians. If he did not succeed in converting King Gundobad, at least the latter's son Sigismund went over to Catholicism.

Clovis's successors did nothing to promote evangelization, except to fight against paganism in their kingdom. The bishops installed in Gaul were more occupied with political quarrels than with religious problems. In *Italy, on the contrary, Pope *Gregory the Great was the first "pope of the *missions". Knowing of the existence of these pagan lands through the Anglo-Saxon slaves being sold at *Rome and *Marseille, he decided to send a mission of Roman monks to *England. Led by *Augustine, these monks managed to convert King *Æthelbert of Kent and implant a Church, when the Celts of the neighbouring countries had refused to intervene because of their hostility to the Germans. Thus, the Church of England was for centuries in close contact with Rome, whence it continued to receive support. Gregory I also sought to convert the Arian Lombards. In fact, Arianism was beginning to disappear in Burgundy and *Spain, since King *Recared was converted in 585, but the Lombards remained faithful to it until the mid 7th century.

In the late 6th c., Irish monks led by *Columbanus settled at *Luxeuil in Burgundy. In leaving their country, they did not just wish to withdraw from the world, but also to convert the pagans. "My desire", wrote Columbanus, "was to visit the pagan peoples and preach the Gospel to them". Expelled from Luxeuil by Queen Brunhild, he went to Italy. At Bregenz, he wished to preach the Gospel to the *Slavs. His disciple St Gall worked among the *Alamanni. At *Bobbio in Italy, Columbanus tried to convert the Lombards. The *abbot of Luxeuil, Eustasius, converted the Varasci in *Bavaria. His disciple Omer, helped by St Bertin and Mommelin, evangelized *Flanders and the regions of the lower Scheldt. St *Eligius, becoming bishop of *Noyon, began the evangelization of his diocesans, who received it badly. With St Amand, an Aquitanian installed in the *Ghent region and Hainaut, all three founded monasteries that became seedbeds of missionaries. But Amand wanted to go further, to the Basques, as well as pushing on in a completely different direction towards the Slav countries.

Independently of the Columbanian movement, another Irishman, St *Kilian, setting out with twelve companions, began to evangelize *Thuringia where the bishops of *Mainz had not penetrated. St Rupert settled at Juvavum, the future *Salzburg, and St *Emmeran at *Regensburg. The *Anglo-Saxons too were urged on by the desire to evangelize the pagan world. Around 680, Wilfrid, future bishop of *York, was in *Frisia. Shortly after, *Willibrord, helped by the mayor of the palace of *Neustria, Pippin II, and with the blessing of Rome, established the first bishopric in this region. Finally Winfrid, better known as *Boniface, spent some years in Frisia before engaging in a mission in *Germany. The so-called apostle of Germany was asked by Pope Gregory II in 719 to evangelize the pagans. He worked in Thuringia and *Hesse with the help of *Charles Martel and the collaboration of monks and *nuns coming like him from *England. He founded monasteries and, thanks to a fairly tolerant policy – he followed the advice given to him by Daniel of Winchester – succeeded in converting numerous pagans. In 731 Pope Gregory III conferred on him the **pallium*, *i.e.* the dignity of *archbishop for Germany, charging him to reform the Bavarian Church and then the Frankish Church. Boniface would have liked to end his days at the monastery of *Fulda, which he had founded, but in 754 he set out again for Frisia where he was put to death by obdurate pagans.

Boniface had been unable to penetrate *Saxony. *Charlemagne, an anointed king, charged with defending the Church and propagating Christianity, managed after 30 years of war to subjugate this region. Missionaries followed the soldiers, imposing *baptism and the *tithe on the population. *Alcuin was distressed by this and reproached the king and his *clerics for these brutal methods: "We must preach before baptizing", he said, "we must be preachers, not depredators". When it came to evangelizing the *Avars, subjugated after the expedition of 795, he and *Paulinus, archbishop of Aquileia, gave counsels of moderation to the Bavarian clergy who undertook to create a Church in *Pannonia.

Early in the 9th c., the first bishoprics were created in Saxony: these were *Bremen, *Münster, *Paderborn, Verden and Minden. Under Charlemagne's successor *Louis the Pious, *Hildesheim, Halberstadt and then Osnabrück completed this set. Monks from *Corbie established an annexe, *Corvey, in the heart of Saxony. The archbishopric of *Salzburg, created in 798, took charge of the creation of Churches in Pannonia and Carinthia, the first Slav country to be Christianized.

The *Slav world was vast and diverse, since we must distinguish the South Slavs (Serbs, *Croats, *Slovenes, Carinthians), the West Slavs (*Wends, Czechs, *Slovaks, Moravians) and the East Slavs (*Poland). The first Slav bishopric created was that of Nin in Croatia, a country put, like Carinthia, under the influence of the Bavarian clergy. However, Byzantine missionaries aimed at evangelizing the Central Slavs. Patriarch *Photius sent two Thessalonian brothers, *Cyril and Methodius, to *Moravia. They created a liturgy in the Slavonic language and met with great success, to the point where the *popes took an interest in their activities and Methodius and Cyril were summoned to *Rome in 868. Cyril died there and Methodius was anointed archbishop of Pannonia by Pope Adrian II. But on his return to Moravia, the missionary was persecuted by the Bavarian clergy who held onto their monopoly of evangelizing the Slavs. Pope *John VIII then accepted Methodius's liturgical innovations and gave him his support: in a letter to Prince Svatopluk, John VIII authorized the use of *Slavonic in the liturgy. But after the death of the pope (882) and the archbishop (885), Methodius's disciples were persecuted by the German clergy and fell back on *Bulgaria. There they were welcomed because Prince *Boris, who had long hesitated between Rome and *Constantinople, had finally chosen Byzantine *clerics to organise his Church. It was then that the *Scandinavians began to invade the West and that Louis the Pious sought to stabilize them by *conversion. In 826, King Harald of Denmark received baptism at *Aachen. A monk of *Corvey, *Anskar, was charged with organising the mission to the Danes and was installed in the new bishopric of *Hamburg (831). Gregory IV granted him the *pallium* in 832. But, faced with Scandinavian attacks, he fell back on Bremen where he died in 865.

Contrary to what has too often been said, the 10th c., or at least its second half, was a great century for evangelization. Under *Otto I, three bishoprics were created in Jutland and attached to the metropolis of Hamburg. The Danish leader *Harald Bluetooth was converted in 960, and on the Jelling Stone, which he erected to commemorate the event, he had a representation of the Crucifixion engraved. (A copy of this stone is installed in the square of Saint-Ouen at *Rouen). The first Norwegian Christian prince, *Óláfr Tryggvason, installed clerics from northern England in *c.*995 and took the Gospel to the Orkneys and *Iceland. *Bohemia, which had resisted the Hungarian invasions, became Christian under St *Wenceslas, then under *Boleslas. In 976, the archbishop of *Mainz consecrated the first bishop of *Prague, Dietmar. His successor was Vojtěch, also called *Adalbert. Keen on monastic life, he lived for a time at Rome in a monastery on the Aventine Hill. There he made the acquaintance of *Otto III and obtained a mission to Prussia, where he was massacred in 997. In the lands of the North Slavs, *Otto I had created the bishoprics of *Brandenburg, Havelberg, Merseburg, Zeitz and Meissen, attached to the archbishopric of *Magdeburg in 968. But the Slavs found it hard to accept the Germanization of their Church, and this led to revolts in 983. Otto III had to resume his grandfather's work and counted on the help of the Poles. In *Poland, Otto III and Pope Silvester II (*Gerbert of Aurillac) created a national Church. Its metropolitan see was *Gniezno, where St Adalbert was buried. The bishoprics dependent on it were those of *Cracow, *Wrocław and Kołobrzeg. We observe the same innovation in *Hungary, which the Bavarians on one side and the Byzantines on the other both wanted to evangelize. After the conversion of Vajk (*Stephen I) and the installation of monks at *Pannonhalma, supposed birthplace of St *Martin of Tours, Otto III and Silvester II created a national Church of which *Esztergom was the metropolis and on which several bishoprics depended.

Thus, at the start of the 11th c., the frontiers of Western *Christendom extended to the Baltic Sea and the banks of the Danube and the Vistula. Churches of Roman rite were installed, for centuries, opposite Eastern Churches. *Catholic Europe was born.

*L'Épopée missionnaire*, R. P. Millot (ed.), Paris, 1956. – S. Delacroix, *Histoire universelle des missions catholiques*, Paris, 1956, 105-141. – E. Ewig, K. Schäferdiek, "Christliche Expansion im Merowingerreich", 2, *Die Kirche des früheren mittelalters*, K. Schäferdiek (ed.), Munich, 1978, 116-145 ("Kirchengeschichte als missionsgeschichte", 2, 1). – *HChr*, 4, 1993. – P. Pierrard, *La Christianisation de la France, IIe-VIIIe siècle*, Paris, 1994.

Pierre Riché

**EVIL.** Medieval thought, like that of late Antiquity (especially Plotinus), had a marked interest in the problem of evil. The era usually asked itself what evil consisted in. By this mere wording, the problem took on a fundamental character that it had not had in the *dualisms that were satisfied to ask whence evil came. The manner of answering the question also shows that the *Platonist *metaphysic still had strength in it. Historically, this metaphysic was the basis of the theory that evil was not an autonomous entity. Among those generally put forward to illustrate this position was the argument that nothing that exists is altogether evil. Evil is a corruption and hence is detrimental to the *good, by which alone it can exist. Blindness is not the same type of reality as sightedness. Starting from this principle, Augustine had already taken issue with the Manichaean doctrine that good and evil have the same mode of existence. In fact, everything that exists, by the very fact of existing, is good. That which can exist autonomously can become the object of an intention, a desire, and can hence be considered desirable (*i.e.* good). Every living thing seeks to maintain itself in life, hence it considers this life worthy of desire. The statement of every good would thus be equivalent to the statement of every reality. We should note that the specific existent (*natura*) is the measure of all that is. Not all that is lacking to an oject is always an evil, but only that by which the specific existent and its manifestation can be corrupted.

This solution to the question of evil, already sketched out by the Greek *Fathers, was powerfully developed by St Augustine – and up to Pascal and Descartes – and, thanks to Aristotelian philosophy, clarified and developed in *scholasticism. With Augustine, scholasticism sought to take account of the fact that if all that is not *God exists by him, God's perfection could no longer be affirmed if he had thought the foundation of a thing while putting evil into it. In the formulation of evil as a privation of good (*privatio boni*), an Aristotelian term was introduced. *Privatio* designated a particular form of negation, what was missing representing a real detriment. Yet the thinkers of the Middle Ages (St *Anselm, St *Bonaventure, St *Thomas Aquinas, *Duns Scotus) ceaselessly emphasized that this determination implied no negation, not even an attenuation, of evil. *Privatio* is in fact the concept designating the parasitic form in which evil appears in the world, and does not in any way exclude evil from being really manifest. As such, nothingness radically expresses the ill-naturedness of evil. The absurdity of an ungrounded fear that would take possession of one who became aware that in truth evil may well not exist would itself be an evil (St Augustine). *Sin too is a privation. To deny the reality of sin never tempted the theologians. Yet all this is valid only if we suppose an understanding of reality that considers it not as a mere given object, but as having a qualitatively positive character. It was only when this metaphysic of *being was no longer comprehensible and had lost its power of persuasion that the theory of privation was understood as an absurd negation of evil.

But evil, as Thomas Aquinas has shown, can however be the object of a true proposition that affirms the existence of its reality. However, it does not have the autonomy of an existent and hence cannot be described without reference to a *nature.

The incommensurability of corruption gave metaphysical reflection an occasion to join itself to a historical reflection. The doctrine of original sin must give us to understand that the concrete state of reality that is man's no longer directly reflects the integrity of the divine *creation. As Augustine had shown, there can be no basis to the reality of evil, there can only be a possibility of evil. Things, in that they are created from nothing, are exposed to the corruptibility of their perfection, but this corruptibilty is not produced perforce. There is no necessity of evil. If evil appears, it is solely for historic reasons. It is to do with the *will, which is dissatisfied with the *freedom that has been conferred on it and seeks to extend its omnipotence. The historic and historically-acting origin of evil resides in the fact that the will is, in its pure spontaneity, the fruit of its own willing, that it makes its original character into its object, which it nevertheless possesses only as a condition of its willing. Medieval thought, Christian in source and orientation, thus imagined in the concept of creation a power whose sovereignty resided in the capacity, among other things, to produce a finite spontaneity. The will, which, as such, wills good, can also decide against God. But this enmity is not total, since any bad action brings its own punishment on itself (as *virtue brings its reward): "The disordered mind becomes its own punishment" (St Augustine).

The historic origin of evil, the essence of original sin and the form of its transmission were the object of a long quarrel in late scholasticism. Together with apocalyptic, the doctrine of the historic origin of evil was certainly the most potent stimulant for a critical reflection on the constricting character of philosophical doctrines concerning human nature. In this field, it was especially *Duns Scotus who contested the fact that human nature could be presented in a way as innocent and as little corrupted as is suggested by, *e.g.*, *Aristotle's *Ethics*. It is only by taking into account the fact that contemporary man is a fallen man that we can, according to *Bonaventure, formulate a precise concept of human nature, which is valid both for his original nature and for that of his fall and for nature brought to its perfection. Thus appears the opposition between *nature and state, one of the conditions allowing us to think of the original state as a state of nature.

If evil is not the characteristic of specific objects, but consists in an inadequate relationship with created things, it results from this that neither matter nor the perceptible can be considered as the place where evil resides. In treatises on the sins of the *angels – *e.g.* St *Anselm's *De casu diaboli* – it appears that at this point there was a deformation of spirit. To what extent the thought of Antiquity saw evil in an aversion to, and a weakening of, *reason still remains obscure. But it was only with the breakthrough of medieval Christian thought that the turning-away of the mind from the supreme good found its explanation in the mind itself, as St Augustine and Pseudo-*Dionysius emphasized, as did the scholasticism that accepted the explanation: evil may very well have no foundations in the true sense of the term. That which in itself is nothing does not exist through a real and efficient *cause. If such an efficient causality of evil existed, it would itself have to be evil, which, instead of producing an explanation, would merely occasion an infinite regression.

Medieval *mysticism proposed an autonomous *doctrine, closed in on itself, but particularly radical, of union between the divine will and the human will. Meister *Eckhart was always tormented by the idea of the solely conditional good. Good is not desired in its right measure, if it is only desired under the condition that it correspond to my own will. The subjectivity of willing must be totally overcome. As long as I still differentiate between what gives me pleasure and what gives me pain, I am still, according to Eckhart, a prisoner of my subjectivity. The will of God, then, has for man no absolute significance, but only a conditional and partial significance. The will created by God's will becomes its own reference and the condition of its own approval. For this reason, Eckhart preaches abandonment of one's own will, *i.e.* of any will that, in that it is a desire to possess, is already by its form an evil (but also because it desires this or that). Conformation to God's will becomes immediate: that God desires a thing is sufficient reason for it to be good. In this answer, which is very close to *nominalism, Eckhart explains why all that happens (*Geschehen*) is, as such, the result of the divine will and hence worthy of approval. This world – and here Eckhart meets *Nicholas of Autrécourt – is also the best of possible worlds. The best must produce the best, but, in reference to its origin, this world is an evil. Eckhart also meets up with *nominalism when he affirms that exterior action can add nothing in perfection or in evil to interior action.

A. D. Sertillanges, *Le Problème du mal*, Paris, 1949. – F. Billicsich, *Das Problem des Übels in der Philosophie des Abendlandes*, Vienna, 1952-1954. – G. Siewerth, *Thomas von Aquin. Die menschliche Willensfreiheit*, Düsseldorf, 1954. – C. Journet, *Le Mal. Essai théologique*, Paris, 1961. – R. Schönberger, "Die Existenz des Nichtigen. Zur Geschichte der Privationstheorie", *Die Wirklichkeit des Bösen*, F. Hermanni, P. Koslowski, Munich, 1998, 15-47.

Rolf Schönberger

**ÉVREUX.** The Roman *civitas* of *Mediolanum Eburovicorum* became the town of Évreux, one of the seven *bishoprics of *Normandy, under the jurisdiction of the archbishop of *Rouen. St Taurinus was its evangelizer and first bishop, at the end of the 4th century. The medieval *cathedral, dedicated to Our Lady, was rebuilt in the *Gothic style in the 12th and 13th cc. and completed in the 15th by a lantern-tower. The abbey of Saint-Taurin housed the saint's *relics in a *châsse*, a masterpiece of 13th-c. French *goldsmith's work.

Évreux was also one of the important political centres of medieval Normandy, in which a family of counts, related to the dukes, was established from the 10th century. After the union of Normandy with the French Crown, Évreux was an important *fief, sometimes an appanage. Under Charles II († 1387), king of *Navarre and count of Évreux, the county became the theatre of military operations of unaccustomed importance.

J. Fossey, *Monographie de la cathédrale d'Évreux*, Évreux, 1898. – E. Meyer, *Charles II roi de Navarre, comte d'Évreux, et la Normandie au XIVe siècle*, Paris, 1898. – G. Bonnenfant, *Histoire générale du diocèse d'Évreux*, Paris, 1925.

Emily Zack Tabuteau

***EX VOTO.*** An object offered to a heavenly intercessor in order to obtain a *grace (propitiatory *ex voto*) or in thanks for a grace received (gratulatory *ex voto*). This practice, which predates the Christian era, was very common in the Middle Ages, though the term *ex voto* was not employed at that time.

The important number of *ex votos* in the Middle Ages is an illustration of the development of the *cult of the saints during this period, and the habit of resorting to an intercessor in case of difficulties of all sorts: *sickness, livestock *epidemics, possession, war, shipwreck, natural catastrophe, etc. *Ex votos* were generally deposited in places of *pilgrimage (most have now disappeared, and they are known essentially by written evidence). They were thus the material proof of a grace received, a witness to the divine power or the efficacity of a saint and his cult, and consequently an encouragement to the devotion of the faithful.

The term *ex voto* covers objects of various kinds, which can be divided into three categories:

1) *Ex votos* without visual reference to the *miracle: gifts in *money, gifts of agricultural produce or livestock, candles or wax (the most frequent), but also liturgical vases, precious cloth, jewels to adorn the *altar or statue of the saint.

2) Material evidence of the miracle or its circumstances:

*Châsse* of St Taurinus, 13th c. Évreux cathedral.

crutches, staffs and orthopaedic apparatus left by the healed persons, the chains or manacles of prisoners delivered after a *vow (particularly to St Leonard, their patron), model ships brought by sailors after escaping shipwreck. Chains hanging from the wall or forests of suspended canes and staffs encumbered the most celebrated sanctuaries, like the basilica of St *Ulrich at *Augsburg or the church of St Leonard at Noblat.

3) *Ex votos* representing the sick person or the sick part of his body. One type of *ex voto* very frequent in the Middle Ages expressed this link in a symbolic way: offerings of the same weight as the person (in corn, *bread or wax) or in his dimensions (silver or wax wire, candle). These objects were most often offered as a propitiation, as it were a rite of substitution. The link with the subject of the miracle is shown still more clearly in the case of anatomical *ex votos*: in wood, in wax (most numerous), sometimes in precious metals, they represent the part of the body healed or to be healed (hand, foot, leg, etc.) or the sick person (or *animal) in his entirety. This practice, considered too *pagan, was condemned during the early Middle Ages, but became very common from the 11th century.

The late Middle Ages (14th-15th cc.) saw the appearance of a new form of *ex voto*, that of votive tablets (*tabellae votivae*), small pictures depicting the miracle or the request for *intercession. These generally obeyed the same compositional schema: the *donor was depicted kneeling, in surroundings expressing the circumstances of the miracle or of his request, while the intercessor was on his own in the upper register. These tablets appear essentially innovative in the relationship they depict, on a single support, between the earthly and the heavenly world.

L. Kriss-Rettenbeck, *Das Votivbild*, Munich, 1958. – L. Kriss-Rettenbeck, *Ex voto. Zeichenbild und Abbild im christlichen Votivbrauchtum*, Zurich, 1972. – A.-M. Bautier, "Typologie des ex voto mentionnés dans des textes antérieurs à 1200" *Actes du 99e congrès des Sociétés savantes*, Besançon, 1974.

Élisabeth Antoine

**EXARCHATE.** A new administrative area, the exarchate, appeared in the *Byzantine Empire at the end of the 6th c., reserved for the government of Africa and *Italy, outlying territories peopled by Latin-speakers and hard pressed by the enemy. The main innovation, the union of civil and military powers in the hands of the exarchs, allowed greater autonomy. But this reform had the disadvantage of facilitating rebellions. The most famous of these put *Heraclius, son of the exarch of Africa, on the throne in 610. The exarchate of Africa disappeared in 698 after the final capture of Carthage by the Muslims, and that of *Ravenna in 751 when the town fell into the hands of the *Lombards.

T. S. Brown, *Gentlemen and Officers. Imperial Administration and Aristocratic Power in Byzantine Italy A.D. 554-800*, Rome, 1984.

Jean-Claude Cheynet

**EXCHEQUER.** The Exchequer undoubtedly existed from the reign of *William Rufus († 1100), but is not known to our sources until the start of the 12th century. Despite a series of reforms between 1323 and 1326 under the impetus of the treasurer, Bishop Walter Stapledon, the Exchequer continued to function essentially according to the same procedures throughout the Middle Ages. The *Dialogus de Scaccario* written by Richard FitzNigel around 1179 shows how it funcctioned. At that time it consisted of two departments, the "lower Exchequer" or "Receipt", which received and disbursed sums of *money, and the "upper Exchequer" which was in fact a sort of chamber of accounts, where the accounts were controlled and where calculations were made on a table covered with a cloth resembling a chessboard, using a method derived from the abacus, whence the name of the institution; it was also a court of justice. The head of the Exchequer was the treasurer, a churchman until the end of the 14th c., increasingly a layman in the 15th. The upper Exchequer was directed by the four (or five) barons of the Exchequer, the lower Exchequer by the two deputy *chamberlains.

The nature of the accounts and the archives varied considerably in the course of the Middle Ages. At first there was just a single series of archives, the Pipe Roll or Great Roll; a fragment survives for 1130, but from *Henry II the series is continuous. The accounts were at first mainly those of the sheriffs (in the 12th c., the "shires" were farmed out; moreover, they had to return the fines and penalties imposed by the *chancery or the judges) and bailiffs; but, progressively, with the appearance of new administrative departments (notably the "household", the king's house), the intensification of military operations and especially the development of State *taxation, new "foreign accounts" were opened, each having their own archives: tax collectors and captains thus came to render their accounts to the Exchequer. The movements of funds were registered by two series of Memoranda, that of the "king's remembrancer" and that of the "lord treasurer's remembrancer"; after auditing of accounts and verification, the accounts were entered on the Great Roll. There was also a distinct series for outgoings, the Issue Rolls.

Receipts and payments were made according to a complex procedure, involving the issuing of wooden tallies on which were inscribed either the sums received or the sums due by the king: usually, they could not be paid directly for lack of liquidity and were assigned to a specific royal revenue; it was up to the debtor to get his tally paid by the official designated by the Exchequer. The ponderousness of its procedures and its incapacity to pay in liquid cash earned the Exchequer a bad reputation; however it was

*Council of Clermont. Excommunication of Philip I of France by Urban II.* Miniature from a 15th-c. manuscript of Vincent of Beauvais's *Miroir Historial.* Chantilly, Musée Condé.

one of the earliest and, for a long time, one of the most sophisticated of the administrations created by the Western monarchies.

Richard FitzNigel, *Dialogus de Scaccario*, C. Johnson (ed.), London, 1950 (re-ed. Oxford, 1983; *OMT*).

T. Madox, *The History and Antiquities of the Exchequer 1066-1327*, London, 1711. – A. L. Brown, *The Governance of Late Medieval England*, London, 1989.

Jean-Philippe Genet

**EXCOMMUNICATION.** Excommunication, exclusion from the community of the faithful (*separatio a communione fidelium*), grew out of biblical texts (Mt 18, 15-19) and Greek and Roman *curses. It is attested from the beginings of *Christendom. During the early Middle Ages (6th-11th c.), excommunication followed an evolution parallel to that of *penance: it became renewable, and less and less public. *Anathema, "condemnation to eternal death", was theoretically more serious, but *excludere*, *excommunicare* and *anathematizare* generally had the same meaning.

From the late 11th c., the *Gregorian reform gave new life to this *sanction, which became for the Church a weapon against recalcitrant lay powers. Thus, from the time of *Gregory VII, the subjects of an excommunicated ruler were relieved of their *oath of loyalty. But excommunication soon struck at any attack on Christian order: thus it was incurred by those who broke the *Truce of God or those who rejected an ever better-defined ecclesiastical morality (King *Philip I of France was excommunicated in 1094, 1095 and 1099 for having repudiated his wife and contracted a marriage with the wife of the count of *Anjou). From 1139, at the second *Lateran council, the papacy gave itself the means to excommunicate *en masse* those who would not respect this or that injunction: this was the procedure called *latae sententiae*, which would be much used from the end of the 12th c. to combat *heretics. So excommunication was already taking on a routine appearance: *Peter Damian, in a *letter to Pope *Alexander II, protested against this banalization, but he was not listened to.

This evolution accelerated in the late Middle Ages. Excommunication became so common that it lost a good deal of its force. For the Church, in its intense effort of control and encirclement, it was a "pedagogical" weapon (Chiffoleau). Any illicit act could fall under the blow of this once terrible sanction: those excommunicated for debt were particularly numerous. Every *Sunday, at *mass, the priest read out the list of bad Christians, obliged to leave church before the *consecration. In the little Provençal village of Moustiers-Sainte-Marie (200 hearths) in the early 15th c., in twenty years 328 persons were excommunicated or threatened with it. Such abuses would be heavily criticized by Luther before being acknowledged and reformed by the council of Trent (1563, 25th session).

R. Collier, "Excommunications à Moustiers-Sainte-Marie (Basses-Alpes) au début du XV^e siècle", *BPH*, 1965, 565-579. – J. Chiffoleau, *Les Justices du pape. Délinquance et criminalité dans la région d'Avignon au XIV^e siècle*, Paris, 1984, 265-266. – E. Vodola, *Excommunication in the Middle Ages*, Berkeley (CA), 1986. – L. Little, *Benedictine Maledictions. Liturgical Cursing in Romanesque France*, Ithaca (NY), London, 1993, 30-44.

Patrick Henriet

**EXEGESIS OF THE BIBLE.** At the centre of life and teaching, the *Bible was read, heard and commented on throughout the Middle Ages. Its exegesis underwent an evolution and aroused reflection. We will trace the outlines of the history of medieval exegesis and try to define its major characteristics.

Medieval exegesis naturally carried on from that of the *Fathers. This had arisen under the joint influence of Hellenistic exegesis (pagan: exegesis of Homer; Jewish: Philo of Alexandria) and the Jewish exegesis called *midrash*. While it integrated elements taken from both of these, Christian exegesis affirmed its originality by the place it gave to *allegory (as opposed to the myth of midrashic and pagan exegesis) and by the centrality accorded to the fact of *Christ (the whole Old Testament announced him, the New developed his message). Eastern authors preserved the mythical element (cf. Pseudo-*Dionysius), while pouring Christian exegesis into the moulds of Greek philosophy (Origen). Westerners favoured "rational" elements (including allegory, a hermeneutical advance conscious of the distance between the text and its commentary), but insisted on the importance of the "spiritual" or "mystical" interpretation. Medieval authors ceaselessly appealed to the exegesis of the *Fathers, whose interpretation was authoritative; they put themselves in relation to it in order to concur with it or contradict it. Certain names recurred constantly: *Gregory the Great favoured a spiritual approach that accorded first place to moral reflection; his commentaries on *Job and *Ezekiel broached numerous themes used for other books. Augustine was the master of thought for the Christian West: his *sermons and commentaries provided the authoritative interpretation of numerous verses; his theological *treatises illustrated the expositions of the exegetes. Jerome played an authoritative role for several biblical books (especially the *prophets); his critical work gained new favour from the 12th century. To these Latins was added a Greek, *Origen, whose writings were available to the Latin West in the translations of Rufinus and Jerome; he exercised a keen influence on philosophical reflection as well as on the mystical approach (exegesis of the *Song of Songs). The presence of other Fathers was less, but the names of Ambrose, Tertullian and John Chrysostom were frequently cited.

Although there had been a distancing from Jewish exegesis, this did not cease to be used, indirectly (through Jerome or Pseudo-Jerome, a converted Jew of the early 9th c.) or directly (oral contacts, especially in the 12th c.; reading of texts, from the 13th c.). Jewish interpretations were cited both positively ("*Hebraei dicunt*") and negatively ("*Iudaei fabulantur*"); they were supposed to clarify the literal sense, but very often it was a non-literal (midrashic) exegesis that was used, hence the disapproval of those who cited it. The Jewish exegesis of northern France contributed to the revival of Christian exegesis. In the 13th c., the translation of *Maimonides' *Guide to the Perplexed* (he wrote no biblical commentaries) furnished Christian exegetes with several themes (*creation, *prophecy, *providence) and was used for the book of Job. *Nicholas of Lyra cited rabbinic texts abundantly, particularly those of *Rashi.

From the early Middle Ages (notably commentaries on *Genesis), the secular *sciences were laid under contribution in exegesis; in the 13th c., this movement was amplified by recourse to *Aristotle and his Arab and Hellenistic commentators.

Certain medieval authors became authorities in their turn. Firstly, the authors of the early Middle Ages, such as *Isidore of Seville, the Venerable *Bede, *Rabanus Maurus or *Remigius of Auxerre, of whom numerous passages were incorporated in the *Glossa ordinaria*. This played a considerable role before being rivalled in the 13th c. by *Hugh of Saint-Cher's **Postilla* and then that of *Nicholas of Lyra; the influence of these three texts, each of which covered the whole Bible, lasted until the end of the Middle Ages. The commentaries of *Andrew of Saint-Victor were also much used from the 13th c. for the literal approach. On the other hand, some authors played a particular role for specific books: Raoul de Flay (Leviticus), *Bernard of Clairvaux (*Song of Songs).

Until the 11th c., commentators lived mainly on the patristic heritage; their works were essentially anthologies of texts of the Fathers. Yet the most important of them provided a contribution of their own. The biblical works of *Isidore of Seville comprised theoretical *opuscula* and *Quaestiones*. In the Venerable *Bede, we remark several important developments of historical or scientific themes. Anthological commentaries continued to flourish under the *Carolingian Renaissance (notably Rabanus Maurus); the personal share was more important in Remigius of Auxerre and Angelome of Luxeuil; the Jewish interpretations present in these three authors may imply contacts with *Jews. *Paschasius Radbertus was more personal still. Moreover the biblical text was revised (*Alcuin and *Theodulf). After this brilliant epoch we observe a falling-off; output remained very meagre in the 10th and 11th cc.; it was mainly monastic. The turn of the 11th/12th cc. was marked by the personalities of *Anselm of Canterbury (who did not comment on the Bible) and *Abelard (who commented on the Hexaemeron and the epistle to the Romans); Anselm's *Fides quaerens intellectum*, which laid down the principles of a *theology based on *reason, and Abelard's **Sic et non* played a decisive role in the evolution of Christian thought (and through it, on exegesis).

The 12th c. gives an impression of abundance and variety. For the history of exegesis we can distinguish three main tendencies (which grew and mingled). Anthological commentaries, after having developed in various ways, ended by acquiring a fixed form, with the *Glossa* (later called *ordinaria*), which became the standard commentary; this was elaborated firstly at *Laon, around Anselm and Ralph, then at *Paris, with Gilbert the Universal, *Gilbert of Poitiers and *Peter Lombard; its redaction for the whole of the Bible must have been completed in the 1160s. The presentation was that of more or less extensive *glosses surrounding the text commented on (*glossa marginalis*) and very brief glosses between the lines (*glossa interlinearis*). The majority of the texts came from the Fathers and the early Middle Ages, but the contribution of the redactors was sometimes important. Secondly, monastic commentaries developed; with the Benedictine revival and the founding of the *Cistercian Order, the 12th c. was a golden age of monastic culture; some commentators carried on the "anthological" tradition (Rainald of Saint-Éloi), others innovated, on various levels, like *Rupert of Deutz or St Bernard. All possessed a particular flavour and accorded a place, generally a large one, to mystical exegesis, notably tropology. The third current was linked to urban growth, with the development of scholastic centres attached to *cathedral churches. Their approach to the sacred text was more technical, more "scientific"; research into history and archaeology was more important, contacts with Jews multiplied. Meanwhile, works of textual criticism took on new vigour: at first among the Cistercians (*Stephen Harding at Cîteaux, Nicholas Maniacoria at *Rome), then in the cities, especially with Hugh and Andrew of Saint-Victor. Finally, the different elements that would permit the blossoming of a theological science were incorporated into exegesis, involving, together with the gloss and the sustained commentary, the birth of the **quaestio*, *i.e.* the development of a theme connected with the text commented on, but treated independently of it (notably in commentaries on the Pauline *epistles). Among the important schools, that of *Laon and that of *Saint-Victor at Paris (*Hugh, *Richard, *Andrew) held first place; the main Parisian *masters of the end of the century (*Peter Comestor, *Peter Cantor, *Stephen Langton) are grouped together under the name "moral-biblical school", but this was more a convergence of interests than a common membership.

The 13th c. was marked by new institutional frameworks (the *university) and the founding of the *mendicant orders. *Theology gradually (from *Alexander of Hales to *Thomas Aquinas) asserted its autonomy from the study of Scripture, but the terms *theologia* and *sacra pagina* applied to both of them for much of the century. The Bible was a fundamental text at the university, at an elementary level (biblical bachelor) and at a superior level (teaching of the master of theology). Though monastic exegesis was still alive, new forms appeared, culminating in what was called the "*scholastic method", a process of exposition that opposed contradictory opinions, established the author's opinion and resolved the problems posed by contrary opinions. Exegesis took on a more systematic and more scientific appearance; various tools were created: *concordances (*Hugh of Saint-Cher), collections of *distinctiones* and interpretations of Hebrew names; a uniform text was imposed at the university of *Paris, with a division into *chapters (due to Stephen Langton); small-format manuscripts multiplied ("pocket bibles"). While innovating, 13th-c. exegesis prolonged certain aspects that had already been favoured by the 12th century. Textual research culminated in admirable biblical *correctories, criticized, with the Parisian text, by *Roger Bacon; meanwhile, the use of Greek or *Hebrew (through the intermediary of Andrew of Saint-Victor, then of the correctories) became common. The exposition of theological problems gained in importance with the multiplication of *quaestiones*; an ever larger place was also given to questions of "physics" and *politics. Among the innovations, we remark the frequent recourse to philosophers (*Aristotle, the Arabs, *Maimonides) and the attentive study of the structure of the texts commented on, with introductions giving an overall presentation of the book to be studied, as well as a subdivision of texts that culminated in an extreme fragmentation; this may appear artificial, but it allowed a more comprehensive approach, with research into the connections between the different parts of the same book, whether cells composed of a single verse (or even smaller units) or vast passages. Reflection on exegesis itself was also developed. The spiritual interpretation, though still alive, no longer held first place.

The 14th and 15th cc. continued these tendencies; renewal came more from currents on the margin of orthodoxy (from the late 13th c.), notably in commentaries on the *Prophets, Gospels and *Apocalypse. But the general tendency remained consonant with the orientations of the previous century: development of doctrinal considerations, recourse to original texts (Nicholas Trivet). *Nicholas of Lyra's *Postilla* on the whole Bible played a major role; it aroused controversies in the 15th c., notably by its massive use of Jewish commentaries.

All this exegetical practice was accompanied by a theoretical, hermeneutical reflection, which was obviously developed in the 13th c., but was present all through the Middle Ages. Some ancient texts played a founding role. Tyconius's († *c.*400) *Liber regularum*, which was known mainly through Augustine, defined seven rules, particularly concerning typological exegesis (they were repeated by Hugh of Saint-Victor). St Augustine's *De doctrina christiana* was the essential text: it has been seen as giving birth to Western semiotics and, in fact, it situated the interpretation of the Bible in the wider domain of the interpretation of *signs. Less widespread, Junilius's *Instituta regularia divinae legis* (*c.*542) were an adaptation of a Greek text heavily influenced by Theodore of Mopsuestia; they provided various considerations on the levels of reading. *Cassiodorus's († 580) *Institutiones divinae litterarum* constituted a manual of introduction to exegesis.

*Isidore of Seville contributed to this reflection with his *Allegoriae*, which provided a list of typological interpretations. More important, the Venerable *Bede's *De schematibus et tropis* proposed an application of the figures of classical *rhetoric to the Bible. Two works by Hugh of Saint-Victor contained a theory of exegesis: the *Didascalicon*, an introductory treatise to the study of Scripture, affirmed the exegete's need for a knowledge of the *liberal arts, and emphasized the primacy of the literal sense, foundation of the hermeneutical edifice; *De scripturis sacris* was a true treatise on exegesis, which, while recalling that the study of the *littera* was of primary importance, defined the rules of spiritual interpretation. At the end of the 12th c., *Peter Cantor's *De tropis loquendi* constituted an elucidation and an investigation of *Bede's treatise, linking exegesis to the study of *language. The prefaces of several commentaries also contained theoretical reflections; for example, the preface of Rainald of Saint-Éloi's commentary on the *Pentateuch, a veritable introduction to the study of Scripture. This hermeneutical reflection intensified from the 13th century. The opening lessons of biblical courses (or *principia*) are interesting; we possess, for example, those of *John of La Rochelle and *Thomas Aquinas. The commentaries were sometimes preceded by important methodological prefaces (Dominic Grima). Certain biblical passages (especially Gal 4, 24) called for considerations on exegesis. Prologues to commentaries on *Peter Lombard's *Sentences* delivered important analyses (on the nature of biblical language, on the work of the interpreter. . .) at the moment when *theology was defining itself as an autonomous *science and enfranchising itself from biblical exegesis. From these works and from the practice of the exegetes, we can disengage a certain number of characteristics specific to medieval exegesis.

The most specific trait is surely the possibility of a plural reading: different levels of meaning were superimposed, whose veracity was admitted. Alexandrian exegesis (allegorical interpretation of the Homeric narratives, works of Philo of Alexandria) provided the starting-point; rapidly, Christian exegesis (as well as Jewish exegesis) posited the plurality of meanings of the sacred texts: as the divine word, they were of an infinite richness that man's hermeneutical efforts did not exhaust. Rabbinic exegesis distinguished between the study of the literal meaning (*peshat*) and the search for another dimension (*derash*, "research in depth"). From the patristic period, Christian exegesis took a similar step; in basing itself on the Pauline opposition between letter and spirit, it separated the literal sense from the spiritual (or "mystical") sense, sometimes with a tendency to undervalue the former, a tendency against which there were periodic warnings (sometimes from a spiritual commentator like *Gregory the Great). Gradually, without any rigorous codification taking place, various levels of reading were defined, culminating in lists of three or four *senses. The list of four levels became canonical at the start of the 13th c.: 1) the letter or history (*littera, historia*), *i.e.* the literal sense; 2) *allegory (*allegoria*), allegorical interpretation, with a variant, *typology (the persons or events of the Old *Testament prefigure or are types of, those of the New); 3) tropology (*tropologia*) or moral interpretation (persons and events designate the fluctuations of the human *soul, its qualities, its *vices, its journey), with a variant, monastic tropology (relating to the life of the monk); 4) anagogy (*anagoge*), which related the data of the biblical text to the end of the ages. Alongside this quadripartition, in the 12th c. we frequently meet a three-level list (Hugh of Saint-Victor): letter, allegory and tropology; anagogy is included in allegory, which equally concerns the past (christical allegory), the present (ecclesial allegory) and the future (the end of *time, *eschatology; hence anagogy). Indeed, in Hugh and in numerous authors, the ambivalence of the term allegory (which denoted not just allegory proper, but any move in the direction of a spiritual interpretation) indicates that in fact the plurality of readings boiled down to two fundamental levels: literal or historical sense, and spiritual or mystical sense, the one being as important and as rich as the other. To the complexity of the spiritual sense, generally received (entailing allegory proper, tropology and anagogy), corresponded the complexity of the literal sense, which does not give the impression of being a poor relation, since in it the exegetes distinguished the *littera* proper (establishment of the text, its grammar), the *sensus* (the meaning: semantic, historical, archaeological study) and the *sententia* (theological study).

The second characteristic trait is that commentators started from the fact that Holy Scripture is a divine Word expressed in human *language (cf. the Talmudic adage: "the words of the Torah are like the language of men"). Being human, the biblical text was subject to the contingencies of all texts: it could be altered (hence critical research was legitimate); it could be an object of study, using the explanatory techniques worked out for other texts; it was placed in its own time, taking account of the distance that separated its human redactors from the period of the commentator; its history was studied; its language analysed; it was expounded using the resources of *grammar and *rhetoric (early Middle Ages, 12th c.) and later those provided by *philosophy and natural *science (13th c.). But this text contained a divine message, which transcended human thought and expression. The labour of the exegete aimed at rediscovering, beyond the clothing of the words of man's language, the wealth of teaching coming from *God. So he dedicated himself to a work of deciphering, whose rules, provided by Tyconius or Augustine, were constantly reformulated. The notion of *translatio* played a capital role; a transfer of the transcendent message to the field of man's intelligence, but also a hermeneutical act that allowed the divine word to be rediscovered in the words of our own language.

The third trait is that there was a constant play of correspondences between the sacred text and the world (*nature). This was perceived as a *creation of God which, like the Bible, spoke of God. The exegete incorporated into his work a veritable decoding of nature, God's language (whence the importance of the meaning of stones, plants, animals and *numbers). To the decoding of the text, perceived as *allegoria in verbis*, corresponded the decoding of nature, *allegoria in factis* (with or without the intermediary of the sacred text).

Finally, exegesis was part of *history. It was a matter of understanding a book of life in relation both to the history that it recounted and to the history in which the exegete was plunged. Holy Scripture was not a collection of mythical accounts of facts that came about in an absolute time, but narrated events that were part of a history that had a beginning and would have an end and whose centre was marked by the coming of *Christ. Furthermore, in a movement that went from the reader to the book, exegesis was enriched in each generation: it was a perpetual search, conscious of the progress it could contribute and of the fact that it could itself enrich the text (Gregory). In this way, however important the truth transmitted by the text, the contribution of the commentator also acquired a recognised value.

C. Spicq, *Esquisse d'une histoire de l'exégèse latine au Moyen Âge*, Paris, 1944. – F. Stegmüller, K. Reinhardt, *RBMA*, 1950-1980 (11 vol.). – J. Leclercq, *Initiation aux auteurs monastiques du Moyen Âge*, Paris, 1956. – M.-D. Chenu, *La Théologie au XII^e siècle*, Paris, 1957. – H. de Lubac, *Exégèse médiévale. Les quatre sens de l'Écriture*, Paris, 1959-1964 (4 vol.). – *The West from the Fathers to the Reformation*, *CHB*, G. W. H. Lampe (ed.), 2, Cambridge, 1969. – H. Brinkmann, *Mittelalterliche Hermeneutik*, Darmstadt, 1980 . – B. Smalley, *The Study of the Bible in the Middle Ages*, Oxford, 1983 (3rd ed.). – *Le Moyen Âge et la Bible*, P. Riché (ed.), G. Lobrichon (ed.), Paris, 1984 ("Bible de tous les temps", 4). – A. Vernet, *La Bible au Moyen Âge. Bibliographie*, Paris, 1989. – P. C. Bori, *L'interprétation infinie*, Paris, 1991 (Fr. tr.).

Gilbert Dahan

***EXEMPLA.*** The Latin term *exemplum* (plural *exempla*) had three main meanings in the Middle Ages. The most usual, inherited from Antiquity, was that of an example to follow, a model of behaviour or *virtue. In the technical language of the Middle Ages, it also designated a rhetorical function and a particular type of narrative. The "rhetorical" *exemplum* was a product of Antiquity. According to the definition proposed in the *Rhetoric to Herennius* (IV, 49, 62), attributed in the Middle Ages to Cicero, this was a fact or a word belonging to the past, cited by a trustworthy person; this *exemplum* was used with intent to persuade, as in Cicero's judicial discourses. This figure of *rhetoric was employed throughout the Middle Ages; it generally took the aspect of the citation of a fact or a saying borrowed from ancient history, in works such as *Mirrors of Princes, or in treatises on government (like the *Policraticus* of *John of Salisbury, † 1180).

The *exemplum* understood as a narrative intended to "serve as proof in support of a doctrinal, religious or moral exposition" (J.-T. Welter) was systematically developed only in the context of the revival of *preaching in the 12th and 13th cc., though its use went back to the earliest times of Christianity. That is why it is given the name "homiletic *exemplum*". In 1982, Jacques Le Goff defined this type of *exemplum* thus: "A brief narration given as truthful and intended to be inserted into a discourse (generally a sermon) to convince an audience by a salutory lesson."

The spread of this *exemplum* was due mainly to the *mendicant orders. To be better understood by the masses whom they undertook to convert, preachers aimed to stuff their *sermons with exemplary narratives. Hardly having the time to research each of the anecdotes that suited them, they wanted to have fresh narrations at their rapid disposal. Hence the production of collections especially intended for their use. The first in date and the most important was that of the *Dominican *Stephen of Bourbon († *c.*1261), the *Tractatus de diversis materiis predicabilibus* (*Treatise on various Matters for Preaching) which grouped together nearly three thousand narratives and comparisons, not to speak of biblical citations (*similitudines*), patristic citations (**auctoritates*) and *scholastic reasonings (*rationes*). Before Stephen of Bourbon, the Augustinian canon *Jacques de Vitry († 1240) had drawn up collections of model sermons including a great number of exemplary narratives. And *Cistercians – *e.g.* *Caesarius of Heisterbach – had already composed collections of *exempla*, though mainly for internal use. The collections were organised primarily according to a logical order (the *gifts of the Holy Spirit for Stephen of Bourbon's treatise), or in the form of a dialogue (Caesarius of Heisterbach's *Dialogue of miracles*, composed between 1219 and 1223). But their use remained very inconvenient for the preacher who wanted to procure narrative matter rapidly. That is why, from the late 13th c., they were constructed according to the alphabetical order of their *rubrics: in *c.*1275, the *Liber exemplorum ad usum praedicantium* (Book of Exemplary Narratives for the use of Preachers), composed by an English *Franciscan, made partial use of this order; in 1277, the *Tabula exemplorum* (Table of Exemplary Narratives), also by a Franciscan author, was entirely composed according to the Latin alphabet. This procedure was perfected by the Dominican Arnold of Liège, thanks to a sophisticated system of reference from keyword to keyword in his *Alphabetum narrationum* (Alphabet of Narrations), composed between 1297 and 1308.

Though most collections were composed in *Latin (the language of preservation, but not of transmission), they also existed in the *vernacular: in *Anglo-Norman, like the *Contes moralisés* of Nicole Bozon, an English Franciscan of the first half of the 14th c.; in French, like the *Ci nous dit*, a book of Christian instruction on the basis of *exempla* (it must originally have been a book of images) composed between 1313 and 1330, doubtless by a religious belonging to a mendicant order and coming from the region of Soissons; in Italian, like the *Assempri* of the Sienese Fra Filippo degli Agazzari († 1422). Indeed, numerous Latin *treatises were translated into the vernacular, especially in the 15th c., usually – rather paradoxically – to win an aristocratic public. This was *e.g.* the case of the *Alphabetum narrationum*, translated into Catalan and English, the *Fabulae* of Eudes of Cheriton, translated into Spanish between 1350 and 1400 (*Libro de los Gatos*), the *Dialogus creaturarum* (14th c., attributed to the Milanese Mayno de'Mayneri), translated into French (1482) and English (*c.*1530), or the *Gesta Romanorum* (mid 14th c.), translated into French (*Le Violer des histoires*), English, German and Dutch.

*Exempla* are not found only in collections intended for preachers: they also appear in the aftermath of preaching, in sermons transcribed after the event and usually translated into Latin. The *exempla* may equally well have been apprehended in the course of the sermon itself by the transcribers: the best-known are those of *Bernardino of Siena, though they may not all have been picked up by the shorthand writers. Likewise, many exemplary narratives used by preachers recur in moral works written in the vernacular, as, in Italy, Jacopo Passavanti's *Lo specchio di vera penitenza* (1350-1354). Some of these works were specially intended for *women, like the *Livre pour l'enseignement de ses filles* by the Angevin knight Geoffroy La Tour-Landry (*c.*1330-*c.*1405) or the *Ménagier de Paris* composed in *c.*1393 for his young wife by a Parisian bourgeois.

The sources of *exempla* are very varied, including the *Bible, saint's lives, historical narratives, *fables, *legends and folklore traditions, and sometimes even the personal experience of the redactor (especially in the 13th c.). But often the *exempla* can be considered as marking, if not the absolute starting-point, at least a remarkable milestone in the evolution of a theme of *contes merveilleux*.

The *exempla* are precious for studying the beliefs imposed on the faithful and for apprehending the models that were supposed to lead to a change in behaviour. They also provide – involuntarily – fascinating information on the culture of the *laity and daily life. And they are particularly useful for studying medieval folklore traditions. The preacher, in fact, found himself constrained by the necessities of his "exemplary" pedagogy to immerse himself in the manifold layers of oral narrativity – notably folklore – in order to draw forth narratives and reintroduce them in the form of *exempla*, vernacular **dits* (even if transcribed in Latin) supported by a set of gestures calculated to ensure their reception.

J.-T. Welter, *L'Exemplum dans la littérature religieuse et didactique du Moyen Âge*, Paris-Toulouse, 1927 (repr., Geneva, 1973). – F. C. Tubach, *Index exemplorum. A Handbook of Medieval Religious Tales*, Helsinki, 1969 (5,400 *exempla* listed). – *Rhétorique et histoire. L'exemplum et le modèle de comportement dans le discours antique et médiéval*, Rome, 1980. – C. Bremond, J. Le Goff, J.-C. Schmitt, *L'"Exemplum"*, Turnhout, 1996 (1st ed. 1982). – *Prêcher d'exemples. Récits de prédicateurs du Moyen Âge*, J.-C. Schmitt (dir.), Paris, 1985. – C. Delcorno, *Exemplum e letteratura tra Medioevo e Rinascimento*, Bologna, 1989. – *Formes médiévales du conte merveilleux*, J. Berlioz (dir.), C. Bremond (dir.), C. Velay-Vallantin (dir.), Paris, 1989. – *Exempel und Exempelsammlungen*, W. Haug (ed.), B. Wachinger (ed.), Tübingen, 1991. – *Les* exempla *médiévaux. Nouvelles perspectives*, J. Berlioz (dir.), M. A. Polo de Beaulieu (dir.), Paris, 1998.

Jacques Berlioz

**EXEMPTION.** Exemption was the privilege removing a church or community (secular or regular) from the bishop's jurisdiction.

Every Christian was subject, spiritually and temporally, to *authority usually that of the diocesan bishop, the "ordinary". Exemption, as distinct from *dispensation, essentially concerned religious, but other persons could benefit from it. It could affect physical persons, but also places and the persons in them, and moral persons, constituted by monasteries. The person was always removed from the authority of his superior, whereas *dispensation supposed the exercise of power by that superior. Exemption accorded to monasteries could also be extended to the whole population comprised in their domains (*sacrum bannum*).

In 511, the council of *Orléans decided that all churches would be subject to the bishop of the place in which they were situated and that the bishop had the right of correction over *abbots. In 525, the second council of Carthage reiterated that only the bishop of the place where the monastery was situated could ordain *clerics and consecrate *oratories, the monastery being otherwise free from episcopal authority. The diocesan bishop preserved his right of jurisdiction over the monastery and certain liturgical acts were reserved for him: *ordinations, *consecrations, certain benedictions. *Gregory the Great (590-604) clearly repeated that the bishop had the right and the duty to survey the monasteries of his *diocese, to authorize *foundations, that he enjoyed right of *visit, that he had to confirm the *election of the abbot and control his administration. But he must not abuse his rights nor get mixed up in the temporal administration of the monastery. The settlement of Irish monks on the continent accelerated the movement, since they came from monasteries having jurisdiction over a determined territory, whose abbot functioned as bishop and exercised the power of ordination. From the 7th c., a privilege granted by the *pope allowed a monastery to be removed from the temporal and spiritual jurisdiction of the ordinary. The privilege granted by Honorius I in 628 to *Bobbio, a foundation of St *Columbanus, went beyond anything that had been granted before, forbidding any bishop – except the pope – to exercise jurisdiction there or even to celebrate *mass without having been invited to do so by the abbot. The *Carolingians reacted against this movement, and *Charlemagne proclaimed the subjection of monasteries to episcopal jurisdiction, allowing only free election of the abbot and administration of the temporality, returning to St Gregory's conception. With the weakening of royal power in the second half of the 9th c., monasteries left his protection and again sought papal protection. The belonging of monasteries to the Holy See, which appeared in Italy, at *Lucca, at the end of the 8th c., did not systematically imply exemption. By this means, the papacy multiplied points of support capable of supporting its actions. *Cluny, founded in 910 by William of Aquitaine on his lands, was given from its foundation to the *Patrimony of St Peter, while remaining subject in spiritual things to the ordinary, the bishop of Mâcon.

The *reform movement that began in the late 10th c. saw exemption as an effective way to combat the influence of bishops who were more political than religious. Only the abbot had power over the men and women dependent on the monastery; only he could penalize the monks. He was not subject to a general *interdict and, in case of accusation, could *appeal against it to the apostolic see and go to *Rome whenever he judged it useful. The bishops opposed such privileges, but the papacy had found them an effective means of ensuring the support of the monks and thus gaining privileged auxiliaries for its political as well as religious activities. Privileges of exemption spread very rapidly from then on, and from the mid 11th c. the papal *chancery formulated a new clause of submission "*nulli nisi nostrae apostolicae sedi*", tightening the links established between monasteries and the Holy See. This independence was also accorded to *priories and lands whose abbot, as temporal lord, had charge of the spirituality only; these territories were then qualified by "exemption", but were often reintegrated into the dioceses after the council of Trent.

One of the consequences of the development of the privilege of exemption was the formation of the notion of a religious *order, grouping together monasteries affiliated to a house directly dependent on the pope, independently of diocesan geographical structure; this is what happened very early with Cluny. While exempt abbeys were rare in *England and *Germany, they were much more numerous in France and *Italy and, for some monasteries, affiliation to a congregation was a way of benefiting from the fact of exemption.

The new orders founded in Italy and France in the late 11th and early 12th c., seeking a way of life close to an idealized *apostolic life, were hardly anxious for exemption. Cîteaux's *Charter of Charity* left a far from negligible place to the bishop, who alone could authorize the foundation of a monastery or bless its abbot, though he did not have the right of visitation. Though the *Cistercians avoided using the word "exemption", they managed to obtain privileges progressively removing from the bishops all authority over them. In the 13th c., their exemption was fully acknowledged. The same went for the *Carthusians, the order being placed by *Alexander III under his protection in 1176.

From their origins, the *mendicant orders were faced with the problem of exemption. The religious way of life they had chosen led them to take the form of centralized orders, made dependent on a general superior. From 1231, *Gregory IX accorded an exemption to the Friars Minors and Preachers. Exemption became personal, no longer local. Exemptions accorded to the mendicants multiplied throughout the Middle Ages, to the point of arousing protests at the council of *Constance.

A similar phenomenon developed in the late Middle Ages when, to escape *commendation and the beneficial system, stability in the monastery was replaced by stability in the congregation, suppressing all connection with the local clergy, as in the congregation of St *Justina of Padua, which was united with *Monte Cassino in 1504, and whose influence went beyond the frontiers of Italy. From 1434, the abbots, who were elected no longer for life, but for a fixed time, were dispensed from receiving the blessing of the bishop and, from 1435, the congregation received a wide exemption, later supplemented by other *bulls completely detaching the monks from their links with the local Church.

G. Schreiber, *Kurie und Kloster im 12. Jahrhundert. Studien zur Privilegien, Verfassung und besonders zum Eigenkirchenwesen der Vorfranziskanischen-ordens (1099-1181)*, Stuttgart, 1910. – G. Letonnelier, *L'Abbaye exempte de Cluny et le Saint-Siège. Étude sur le développement de l'exemption clunisienne, des origines jusqu'à la fin du XIII^e siècle*, Ligugé-Paris, 1923. – J.-F. Lemarignier, *Étude sur les privilèges d'exemption et de juridiction ecclésiastique des abbayes normandes depuis les origines jusqu'en 1140*, Paris, 1937. – J.-F. Lemarignier, "L'Exemption monastique et les origines de la réforme grégorienne", *A Cluny. Congrès scientifique. . ., 1949*, Dijon, 1950, 288-340. – E. Fogliasso, "Exemption canonique", *DDC*, 5, 1953, 637-646. – E. Fogliasso, "Exemption des religieux", *ibid.*, 646-665. – J. H. Denton, *English Royal Free Chapels, 1100-1130, a Constitutional Study*, Manchester, 1970. – J. Dubois, "Esenzione monastica", *DIP*, 3, 1976, 1298-1306. – V. Pfaff, "Die päpstlichen Klostersexemtionen in Italien bis zum Ende des zwölften Jahrhunderts", *ZSRGK*, 103, 71, 1986, 76-114. – L. Falkenstein, "Alexander III und die Abei Corbie. Ein Beitrag zum Gewohnheitsrecht exemter Kirchen in 12. Jahrhundert", *AHP*, 27, 1989, 85-195. – L. Falkenstein, *La papauté et les abbayes françaises aux XI^e et XII^e siècle. Exemption et protection apostolique*, Paris, 1997 (BEHE).

Jean-Loup Lemaître

The west front of Exeter cathedral. 13th c.

**EXETER.** A former Roman city, prosperous under the *Anglo-Saxons but ravaged by the Danes early in the 11th c., Exeter was for a long time mainly a religious and political centre: the superb *cathedral built essentially between 1112 and the late 14th c. attests the role of its *bishops, of whom some like Walter Stapledon (1308-1326) and John Grandisson (1327-1369) were remarkable figures. In the late Middle Ages, its economic functions intensified and it profited from the rise of the *textile industry, to the point of rivalling *Bristol for regional *commerce: the twenty-second town in *England for population (2300 inhabitants) in 1377, Exeter went from twenty-sixth to fifth in wealth between 1334 and 1524.

*Medieval Art and Architecture at Exeter Cathedral*, F. Kelly (ed.), [s.l.], 1991. – P. W. Conner, *Anglo-Saxon Exeter*, Woodbridge, 1993. – M. Kowaleski, *Local Markets and Regional Trade in Medieval Exeter*, Cambridge, 1995.

Jean-Philippe Genet

**EXODUS.** Several passages in the book of Exodus had particular importance in medieval thought. The attempt to define *God (Ex 3, 14, *Ego sum qui sum*) fertilized the thought of Christian and Jewish thinkers, becoming the basis of an "Exodus metaphysic" (Gilson). The declaration of the *Decalogue (ch. 20) prompted deeper reflection on the notion of law, the relationship of the ceremonial laws to the New Covenant, the permanence of the Ten Commandments (notably St *Bonaventure). The personality of Moses, central to the book, was the object of various *exegeses, notably of a widespread *typological interpretation (Moses as figure of *Christ). Finally, the passage about the Golden Calf fed the *controversy with Judaism. Apart from commentaries on the whole *Pentateuch, Exodus was commented on notably by *Peter of Poitiers, Nicholas of Tournai and Meister *Eckhart.

*Dieu et l'être. Exégèse d'Ex. 3, 14. . .*, Paris, 1978. – *Celui que est. Interprétations . . . d'Ex. 3, 14*, A. de Libéra (ed.), E. Zum Brunn (ed.), Paris, 1986.

P. C. Bori, *Il Vitello d'oro*, Turin, 1983.

Gilbert Dahan

**EXORCISM.** Exorcism was a summons addressed to the powers of *evil in the name of *Christ. The aim of this summons was to force them to recognise the omnipotence of *God and hence to vacate places. In the Middle Ages we no longer find with the same

*Scene of purification of knights.* 12th-c. bas-relief. Modena, Museo Civico.

frequency the direct *ministry of exorcism among those possessed or thought to be so, as St *Martin had practised it. At *Rome from 416, Innocent I had already limited the ministry of exorcism to priests and *deacons acting with the express authorization of the *bishop, and the discipline limiting the exercise of this power had thereafter merely to be confirmed.

But everything that was to be blessed and consecrated was the object of exorcisms, to be removed from the influence of the *demon, "prince of this world" since the original sin, and regained for God. The formulae used in these rituals were on the whole very old; the more recent ones appeared in the 11th and 12th centuries. On this point the liturgy reflected numerous popular beliefs, Christian or pre-Christian, blaming demons for all the catastrophes that had dramatic consequences for men: unleashing of the elements, tempests, storms, floods, hail, tidal waves, or simply the proliferation of animals causing great damage to man (rats, mice, mites, insects attacking harvests, etc.). There were even exorcisms and incantations concerning *epidemics or contagious diseases. So exorcism was in common use in the medieval centuries, though it was now only occasionally applied to cases of diabolical possession or suchlike things. The most frequent exorcisms were obviously those that preceded the *baptism of the very small Christian, the rites of which were modelled on those of adult baptism and hence summed up the stages of the catechumenate. There are numerous collections of exorcisms printed in the 16th c., when they were tending to be reduced by the liturgical reform of the council of Trent, or collected by scholars such as Dom Martène in volume II of his *De antiquis Ecclesiae ritibus*.

*Satan*, 1948 (bibl.; "EtCarm"). – E. Bartsch, *Die Sachbeschwörungen des römischen Liturgie, eine liturgietheologische Studie*, Münster, 1967. – A. Vergote, "Exorcismes et prières de délivrance", *LMD*, 183-184, 1990. – C. Chène, *Juger les vers. Exorcismes et procès d'animaux dans le diocèse de Lausanne (XVe-XVIe siècles)*, Lausanne, 1995.

Guy-Marie Oury

**EXPECTATIVE GRACES.** Expectatives were pontifical graces issued to petitioning *clerics and enjoining the ordinary collators to deliver to them the first *benefice of a certain nature and value that should be vacated; the cleric took his place in the line of waiting candidates, according to the date that had been put on his petition and on the apostolic letter resulting from it; sometimes a considerable time was necessary before obtaining satisfaction. The *Avignon popes multiplied concessions of expectative graces, but they generally lapsed on the *pope's death. A special category, graces *in forma pauperum*, conceded only on a few days of each pontificate, concerned "poor clerics", *i.e.* those who had no benefices.

G. Mollat, *La Collation des bénéfices ecclésiastiques sous les papes d'Avignon*, Paris, 1921. – C. Tihon, "Les expectatives *in forma pauperum* particulièrement au XIVe siècle", *BIHBR*, 1925, 51-118.

Anne-Marie Hayez

**EXPOSITION OF RELICS.** The exposition of *relics was practised from the beginning of the *cult of the saints; it happened in exceptional circumstances (inventions and translations). From the 9th c., ordinary expositions developed on precise dates of the *liturgical year (feast of a saint, feast of the translation of his relics. . .). They involved the ritual *gesture by which the relics were exposed to the faithful who, usually, were allowed to kiss them and received a blessing in return. Canon 62 of the fourth *Lateran council (1215) regulated expositions by forbidding the removal of relics from their shrines and the practice of itinerant *collections with exposition of relics, often suspected by contemporaries of fraud.

Pierre Kerbrat

**EXPULSION OF JEWS.** A royal warrant ordering an entire segment of a population of distinct confession to leave the territorial limits of the kingdoms (or to embrace the dominant religion). The medieval West experienced two waves of expulsions. The first happened very early in northern Europe, and the second affected the Jewries of southern Europe at the end of the 15th century.

The first expulsion of *Jews promulgated in *France in 1182 by *Philip Augustus affected a comparatively small royal domain (*Paris, the Paris region, the Orléanais, the Île-de-France), and did not last for ever: in 1198, the Jews were recalled. The banishment from *England in 1290 was more decisive. Irreversible, it assailed an important number of victims in a State where the authority of the *Crown extended over the entire country. In those places where the accusation of *ritual murder originated (*Norwich, 1144), where the rigorous decrees of the Lateran were respected (marginalization at all levels), *Edward I had tried, by his *Statutum de Iudaismo*, to remedy the status of his Jews, but in vain. Having infringed prohibitions and especially practised fraud by coining *money, they were condemned to exile (18 July 1290) with a respite of three months. 16,000 persons left; a handful submitted to the "house of converted Jews" (*Domus conversorum*) founded in 1232 at *London. Arriving in great numbers on French and even Provençal soil (Reillanne, Manosque), these exiles were to make a brief halt in the kingdom of France.

The expulsion of Jews decreed on 22 July 1306 by *Philip the Fair for the kingdom of *France this time affected provinces with a strong Jewish population such as *Champagne, *Normandy and *Languedoc. This measure, quite different in extent (100,000 exiled?), accompanied by confiscation of the property of the banished, mentioned by Jewish chroniclers, is also described by Christian sources which mention some *conversions and a devaluation. Iconographical sources – a precious mirror of the time – speak of profanation of the *host by a Jewish pawnbroker. The expulsion of 1306 was a financial expedient. The routes taken by the exiles reveal their cultural affinities: those of the North would not feel out of place in the Rhineland, while the Jews of Languedoc would have no difficulty integrating themselves in the area of *Perpignan, in *Catalonia and of course *Provence.

After the expulsion of 1306, two provisional returns were heavily paid for: only the most wealthy came back. The return allowed by Louis X in 1315 was limited to 12 years but never reached that term, ruined by outbreaks of popular *antijudaism (*pastoureaux* and rumours of well-poisoning). When in 1361 *Charles V, beset with external difficulties, envisaged a new return of the Jews to his kingdom, he granted them a length of stay of 20 years. From prolongation to prolongation (six years in 1364, ten in 1374, a term lengthened by five years by Louis of Anjou), always subject to higher rates of payment for entry, the Jews who returned to the French domains were not in fact numerous (some hundreds at most) and were always obliged to wear the circle and dwell together. Finally, on 17 Sept 1394, *Charles VI gave them the order to leave. Their refuges would be mainly Franche-Comté, *Switzerland, Savoy and northern Italy.

In *Spain, the Jews had just endured the worst riots ever known in the Iberian lands. The massacres of 1391 that stained especially *Catalonia with blood, part of a climate of economic troubles and incendiary preaching, shook Spanish *Judaism, engendering a marginal society of *conversos* soon reviled and exposed to the *Inquisition that was established after 1449. The transgressions they were accused of – notably the affair of the "holy child of La Guardia" – seem to have prepared opinion for the policy of expulsion. In 1492, on the morrow of the conquest of *Granada that crowned the unity of Spain and the triumph of the Cross, Ferdinand and Isabella issued a warrant that sanctioned 100,000 to 150,000 exiles, while the "new Christians" played the same role of foil in Spanish society as the vanished Jewish community had before. The Jews of *Sicily, *Sardinia and other Aragonese possessions shared the fate of their Spanish co-religionists, like those of Roussillon-Cerdagne exiled in 1493. Those of the kingdom of *Naples – except 200 rich families – would be banished later (1510).

In *Portugal, the arrival of the Spanish exiles (20,000 families?) and the pressure of the *Catholic Kings precipitated King Manuel's decision to expel them on 5 Dec 1496. In fact, this was the starting-point for a massive conversion of Jews forcibly dragged to the baptismal font, resulting in a lively crypto-Judaism. Occasional outbursts of *violence culminated in the "Killing of the New Christians" in Lisbon in April 1506 (2000 victims). During this period, despite prohibitions, there was a constant and furtive emigration of *conversos* or **Marranos*, who, beyond the seas, declared their allegiance to the faith of their fathers.

French *Provence (1500-1501) was a land of welcome for English, Languedocian (especially in 1306), Catalan (at *Arles) and Iberian Jews (boatload of Spanish exiles at *Marseille in 1492). Becoming French in 1481, the county of Provence too ended by expelling a Jewish minority that had known good times (18,000 individuals at the start of the 14th c.) but had already been much reduced by the *Black Death of 1348 (riots of Toulon and Haute-Provence). In the 15th c., urban communities resurfaced and, under King *René, remained zealous and diligent communities. The series of socio-economic troubles of the years 1484-1488 that affected the *Jewish quarters of the Rhône region ended by precipitating local edicts of exile (Arles-Tarascon, 1493-1496) that spread in 1500-1501 to the whole of Provence (edict of *Charles VIII, reiterated by Louis XII). The roads of exile led to Franche-Comté, Italy, the *Maghreb and the Balkans, as for their Spanish brothers. Many Provençal Jews opted for *conversion. Called "neophytes" (*neofiti olim judei*), adopting the patronyms of godfathers coming from the best Christian society, these Provençal converts whom Louis XII taxed in 1512 ended – with a prompt and dizzying social rise, and despite marranic behaviour to begin with (notably endogamic marriages) – by founding families and grafting themselves onto the highest lineages in the land.

Though *Germany never proceded to a general eviction of its Jews, it is there that we find, throughout the Middle Ages, the most dramatic expressions of intolerance in the form of massacres and local or regional expulsions. In the 15th c., princes and town councils adopted the formula of eradication that would mark the end of the "great German Jewish Middle Ages". This process culminated in the expulsion of the old communities of Rothenburg (1519) and *Regensburg (1520). Isolated handfuls of Jews remained here and there. More numerous nuclei were found in the half-Slav territories of the eastern frontiers. In Germany proper, no Jewish colony was able to survive except those of *Worms and *Frankfurt am Main, mother towns of German Judaism.

The Marranos were expelled from Venice, seat of the Marrano diasporain 1540. The duchies of *Milan, Piedmont-*Savoy and *Tuscany would pursue independent Jewish policies. Despite numerous moments of friction and occasional riots, *Italy as a whole had a relatively untroubled past, compared to the bloody annals of Jewish history in most other European countries.

Decrees of eviction, by and large, followed a similar pattern: obstacle to the reigning order, fomentor of troubles, agent of *usury, bearer of plague, maker of *heresies, the medieval Jew, in his difference, was synonymous with all these evils. Hence the necessity to exclude him. This was a convergence of grievances, his denunciation at all levels (verbal attacks as much as actual attacks) leading to a fatal conjuncture of popular *desiderata* and initiatives by the authorities.

D. Iancu, *Les Juifs en Provence (1475-1501). De l'insertion à l'expulsion*, Marseille, 1981. – W. C. Jordan, *The French Monarchy and the Jews*, Philadelphia, 1989. – D. Abulafia, *1492: the Expulsion from Spain and Jewish Identity*, London, 1992. – *Les Juifs d'Espagne. Histoire d'une diaspora 1492-1992*, H. Mechoulan (dir.), Paris, 1992. – N. Roth, *Conversos, Inquisition, and the Expulsion of the Jews from Spain*, Madison (WI), 1995. – D. Iancu, *Être juif en Provence au temps du roi Réné*, Paris, 1998. – R. R. Mundill, *England's Jewish solution: experiment and expulsion 1262-1298*, Cambridge, 1998.

Danièle Iancu-Agou

## EXTREME UNCTION

**The West: theology.** The *sacrament of anointing the sick, by which the priests of the Church are aware of performing for the sick the rite prescribed by the epistle of James (5, 13-16), was called extreme unction by theologians when the list of seven sacraments was fixed in the mid 12th c., the first witness to the expression being, apparently, *Peter Lombard (**Sentences*, IV, d. 2, ch. 1; Brady, 239), then, later, by official Church documents (council of *Florence, decree to the Armenians; Denz.-Sch., 1324; *Thomas Aquinas, *De articulis fidei et Ecclesiae sacramentis*). The name "extreme unction" distinguishes the anointing of the sick from that of catechumens and that of *confirmation, and it goes with the fact that, from the early Middle Ages, it was given to the sick after their last *confession and, towards the end of the Middle Ages, sometimes after the *viaticum communion. The *oil of the sick was blessed by the *bishop on Holy Thursday. With this oil, the priest anointed the sick person's body, usually on the

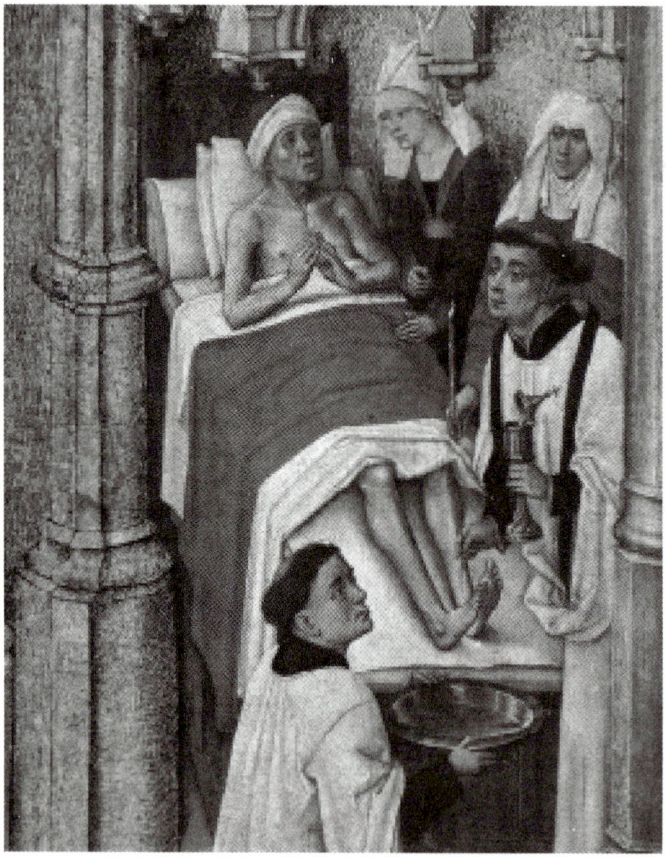

*Extreme Unction.* Triptych of *The Redemption* (detail) by Roger van der Weyden, *c.*1400-1464. Madrid, Prado Museum.

places of the five senses, with formulae (which appeared in the Carolingian period and were most widespread in the last centuries of the Middle Ages) asking for pardon for the different kinds of sins. The other, older *prayers that surrounded anointing, as well as the prayer for blessing the oil, asked for bodily healing and strength in illness for the sick person.

Scholastic theologians, seeking to specify the difference between the sacrament of unction and that of *penance, reckoned that the proper effect of extreme unction was to take away the remains of *sin (*reliquiae peccati*). They also saw sacramental anointing as the sacrament of those who left this life (*sacramentum exeuntium*), symmetrical with *baptism (of small *children), the sacrament of those entering life (*sacramentum intrantium*) (*Peter of Poitiers, *PL*, 211, 1229); the sacrament intended to efface the last sins, which for that reason should only be given to those who could sin no more (*Bonaventure, *Sent.* IV, d. 23, a. 1, q. 1; *Duns Scotus, *Report. IV Sent.* d. 23, n. 3; Vivès 24, 344); or again the sacrament that prepared man for the glory of *God (Thomas Aquinas, *Summa theologiae*, III[a], q. 65, a. 1).

H. Weisweiler, "Das Sakrament der Letzten Ölung in den systematischen Werken der ersten Frühscholastik", *Schol.*, 7, 1932, 321-353, 524-560.

Pierre-Marie Gy

**The West: practice.** Extreme unction was one of the seven sacraments, the sacrament of the sick, which, because of the rapid and inexorable evolution of serious illnesses, became the sacrament of the *dying, whence its name of *extrema* (last), the other anointings being those of baptism and *confirmation for all Christians, that of episcopal or presbyterial *ordination for *bishops and priests, that of *consecration for *kings, as well as anointings of places and objects consecrated to God (churches, altars, sacred *vessels).

On Holy Thursday, the bishop blessed the oil of the sick which was subsequently used by the priests. For a long time the people seem to have had access to it and to have used this oil themselves for (non-sacramental) anointings, since Carolingian legislation insisted on the priest's duty to keep it out of reach, under lock and key, to be faithful in giving the sacrament when asked for it, and not to let his flock die without having received it. The theological thought of the 12th and 13th cc., having unilaterally insisted on its aspect of final complement of *penance ("if he have committed sins, they shall be forgiven him", Jas 5, 15), led to the sacrament being deferred to the last moment, becoming the sacrament of the dying, administered by the priest at the same time as the viaticum.

A. Chavasse, *Étude sur l'onction des infirmes dans l'Église latine du IIIe au XIe siècle*, 1, Lyon, 1962. – P. Rouillard, "Le ministre du sacrement de l'onction des malades", *NRTh*, 101, 1979, 395-402. – A. G. Martimort, "Prayer for the sick and sacramental unction", *CaP*, 3, *The Sacraments*, London, 1988.

Guy-Marie Oury

**Byzantium.** The reference in Jas 5, 13-15 to a sacramental unction for the sick ascribes its conferment to "elders" (plural) of the Church. The Byzantine ritual originally required the participation of at least seven priests. The celebration was long, beginning with *prayers during the *vigil and ending with the actual anointing after the morning liturgy. When the rite was standardized in the 16th c., it took place after the morning office. New Testament *readings were followed by blessings, the unction and a penitential prayer. The Gospel Book was held over the sick person.

E. Mélia, "Le sacrement de l'onction des malades", *La Maladie et la mort des chrétiens dans la liturgie*, A. M. Triacca (ed.), A. Pistoia (ed.), Rome, 1975, 193-228.

Christopher Walter

***EXULTET.*** *Exultet* is the first word of the eulogy (though, with its *preface, dialogue and thanksgiving, it had the appearance of a *consecration) of the Easter candle, sung by the *deacon during the *Easter *vigil. This custom, Jewish in origin, passed into the Church and coincided with the beginning of the *Sunday vigil, but it had no uniform character before the introduction at *Rome of the blessing of the Easter candle by Pope Zosimus (417) and is first mentioned at Rome in the late 6th or early 7th c. (*Ordo* II). On the basis of style, vocabulary and the eulogy of the bee, inspired by Virgil, its paternity can be attributed to St Ambrose.

In the Roman *Missal, in the course of this chant, the *deacon fixed five grains of incense in the form of a cross and lit the candle and the lamps. During the *office, the illustrations of *Exultet* scrolls could be presented to the faithful back to front, so that they would see them the right way round.

*DACL*, 5, 1, 1922, 1559-1574. – B. Botte, C. Mohrmann, *L'ordinaire de la Messe*, Paris, 1953. – A. Guny, "Exultet", *Cath.*, 4, 1956, 1014-1016.

Guy Lanoë

**EZEKIEL.** The activity of Ezekiel, third of the major *prophets after *Isaiah and *Jeremiah, took place between 592 and 570 BC, among the Jews exiled to Babylon. From the biblical book that bears his name, it is possible to take three episodes relating trials undergone by the prophet: Ezekiel devouring the scroll (Ezek 2, 9), lying alternately on his left and right side (Ezek 4, 4-8) and cutting his beard and hair and weighing them in a balance. The book of Ezekiel also includes three major visions: the vision of the Lord in a chariot with wheels of fire (Ezek 1, 1-28), that of the dry bones brought back to life (Ezek 37, 1-11) and that of the closed door (Ezek 44, 1-4). In the same way as the prophet Isaiah, Ezekiel benefited in the Middle Ages from the development of the Marian cult, by reason of his vision of the closed door interpreted as a symbol of *Mary's virginal motherhood. That is why he is generally recognisable by the presence of the phylactery bearing the phrase: "*Porta clausa est, non aperietur*". He also has for attributes the fiery chariot of his vision and the double wheel, or else, more rarely, the scroll that he has to devour, held out by the divine hand.

Three episodes were specially used by *artists: the vision of the Lord, the dry bones and the closed door. Representations of the vision of the Lord in a chariot with wheels of fire are infrequent before the 12th century. The early Middle Ages tended to associate this scene with representations of the visions of Isaiah and St John; later, the so-called Bible of John XXII, dating from the 15th c. (library of the faculty of medicine at *Montpellier) provides an illustration.

The vision of the dry bones is interpreted as a prefiguration of the *resurrection at the *Last Judgment. This scene is represented, *e.g.*, in a miniature of the *Homilies of Gregory Nazianzen dated *c.*880 (Paris, BNF): the prophet is led by an *angel into a valley filled with bones.

The prophetic vision of the closed door, *sign of Mary's virginal motherhood and symbol of the Virgin as door of *heaven, is evoked on the prophet's phylactery; it is associated with Marian representations, as witness the statue of the prophet Ezekiel on the Portal of the Virgin at *Laon cathedral.

Frédérique Trouslard

*The Vision of Ezekiel.* Miniature from the *Missal* of the abbey of Saint-Denis, 11th c. Paris, BNF (Ms lat. 9436, fol. 15 v°).

**EZZELINO III DA ROMANO (1194-1259).** Son of Ezzelino II da Romano, called the Monk, and Adelaita of the counts of Mangona, born 25 April 1194.

By the 12th c., the family of the lords of Romano (previously called of Onara), rooted in the territory between Vicenza and *Treviso, specially at Bassano del Grappa, were playing a prominent role in the politics of the nearby cities, taking part in the struggles of city factions in the early 13th century. Ezzelino played an autonomous political role from 1223, when his father's inheritance – property, *castles, *masnade* – was divided between him and his brother Alberic. Aiming at local power and confronting the other great *domus* of the region (like the Estensi and the San Bonifacio, supporters of *Frederick II), Ezzelino first inserted himself into the political life of the commune of *Verona (**podestà* in 1226-1227). From 1232, however, he sided with the emperor while keeping control of Verona in the confused events of the following years. Between 1236 and 1237, supported by the imperial army, he took power at Vicenza and *Padua. Thus began a "pre-signorial" regime, not without some consent – especially at Verona and Vicenza –, which would last for another 20 years.

Without any formal delegation by the emperor, whose natural daughter Selvaggia he had married, Ezzelino supported Frederick's policy in *Italy; he governed using the fiscal and military resources of the city *communes, whose constitutional development was interrupted and suspended, and of his own *masnade*. Particularly after Frederick's death in 1250, Ezzelino's rule became one of pitiless harshness: repression of plots, confiscation of property (of laymen and churches), executions. Such actions justified the creation – partly through the image of Ezzelino given by chroniclers hostile to Padua – of an extraordinarily negative stereotype: Ezzelino was the prototype of the *tyrant.

*Excommunicated for his Ghibellinism, an object of resentment by those banished and exiled, Ezzelino's political fortunes decline from 1256 (crusade for the reconquest of Padua proclaimed by *Innocent IV). His reconciliation with his brother Alberic, lord of Treviso (1257) availed him little. He died at Soncino during a military expedition against *Milan (Sept 1259); Alberic was slaughtered with his family in the castle of San Zenone.

G. Cracco (ed.), *Nuovi studi ezzeliniani*, Rome, 1992 (2 vol.).

Gian Maria Varanini

# F

**FABLE, *FABLIAU*.** The hypothesis that the fable gave birth to the *fabliau* is not very convincing. The *fabliau* is fable only if we give this word the broad sense of "fiction". With no obvious genetic relationship, the two genres have a very different structure. The fable is deliberately allegorical: what it says of animals makes sense only when applied to humans. The *fabliau* is without depth, it settles directly into the "human, too human".

The 150-odd surviving French *fabliaux* are comic tales written mostly in the 13th century. Most have less than 300 verses. Their plot is borrowed from narrative tradition, written or oral, popular or learned: thus the same story independently inspired the *fabliau* of the *Vilain Mire* (the peasant doctor) and Molière's *Le Médecin malgré lui*. The setting of the *fabliaux* is that of everyday life; their pleasure is that which we get from seeing aggressive tendencies satisfied by violence or cunning and obscene tendencies by defecation or sex. The only point is to enjoy the lubricity of spouses, the false candour of girls, the ingeniousness of students, the outrages inflicted on avaricious and debauched priests, the malice of peasants. The narrators have an unequalled talent. The best handle the techniques of the literary art of their time cleverly. Some have a strong personality (Gautier Le Leu, author of the *Prêtre taint*) and are known for more ambitious works: Jehan *Bodel of Arras (*Le Vilain de Bailleul*, *c.*1200), Rutebeuf (*Le Pet au vilain*, *c.*1260), Jean de Condé of Hainaut (*La Nonnette*, *c.*1330). The *fabliau* had its contemporary equivalent in the German *Versschwank*; it disappeared with Jean de Condé, but lived again in Italian collections of novels (including *Boccaccio's *Decameron*) and their imitations, English (*Chaucer, *Canterbury Tales*) or French (anonymous *Cent nouvelles nouvelles*, Marguerite de Navarre's *Heptaméron*).

The medieval Latin collections of fables and their French verse adaptations (Marie de France, *c.*1175) are reworkings of collections from late Antiquity. The *Avionnets* go back to the adaptation of the Greek Babrius by Flavius Aviannus; the *Isopets* to a prose compilation deriving from Phaedrus and attributed to a supposed Emperor Romulus! In accepting stories from folklore and, through the intermediary of Arabs, *Jews and Spaniards, stories of oriental origin, the Middle Ages enriched an already complex tradition. The fable was a respected genre. Fables have an ample place in collections of **exempla* for the use of preachers (*Parabolae* of Eudes of Cheriton, *c.*1225; *contes moralisés* of the *Franciscan Nicole Bozon, *c.*1335): their moral lesson came auspiciously to strengthen the authority of the *sermons.

P. Menard, *Les Fabliaux, contes à rire du Moyen Âge*, Paris, 1983. – D. Boutet, *Les Fabliaux*, Paris, 1985. – P. Carnes, *Fable Scholarship: an Annotated Bibliography*, New York, 1985. – G. Dicke, K. Grubmüller, *Die Fabeln des Mittelalters und der frühen Neuzeit: ein Katalog*, Munich, 1987. – J. Hines, *The Fabliau in English*, London, 1993.

Pierre-Yves Badel

***FABRICA*.** The *fabrica* can be defined as an institution intended to provide for the construction and maintenance of sacred buildings, in particular *cathedrals, *collegiate and especially parish churches; it also took charge of *liturgical objects, *vestments and *liturgical books. The term *fabrica* went back to Christian late Antiquity at a time when church revenues were divided into four parts, one of them being reserved for the "work" of the *fabrica* (*opus fabrice*). Later, at the time of *feudalism, the *patrimony of churches would be divided up before being turned into a *benefice, *i.e.* into revenues collected by the *cleric who performed divine service. In the new situation created by the *Gregorian reform, no provision was made for buildings. They were doubtless the province of the patron or the incumbent. But the construction of cathedrals and churches made it indispensable to create an organisation that would both collect and manage the funds.

Such foundations were particularly necessary in cathedral and *chapter churches because of the decline of common life and the creation of *prebends: part of the temporality was reserved for the *opus fabrice*, and one or more *canons, called workers (*operarii*) or treasurers (*thesaurii*), were charged with maintaining the buildings. The impulse given by the cathedrals was rapidly followed by parish churches; but during the 13th c. the *fabrica* often came under the control of the parishioners. This was the time when communities of parishioners and inhabitants, entitled to representation according to the norms defined by *canonists, were organised. For the needs of buildings and liturgical objects, the parishioners designated delegates sometimes called "procurators", sometimes "providers", "receivers", "rectors", "masters", "treasurers" or "workers". The term *matricularius* (*churchwarden), also used, came from the name given during the early Middle Ages to a servant of a church. The members of the *fabrica* were generally elected for a duration fixed by the assembly of parishioners. Yet, for the *fabrica* as for the *parish, we cannot advance universal rules: statutes varied from one region to another.

From the early 13th c., the autonomy of the *fabrica* was recognised by the Roman pontiffs, and this institution constituted a benefice distinct from that of the church and the other benefices that the church could count on. It drew resources, sometimes abundantly, from its own endowments, from *tithes, gifts and *legacies of the faithful. And in case of financial difficulty, impositions were laid on the parishioners.

The history and evolution of *fabricae* in the last centuries of the Middle Ages is not always easy to follow. Records of accounts show the power and wealth of the institution that had become an important part of parish life. However, it sometimes escaped the control of the parish community and fell under the tutelage of the local bourgeoisie or the municipal authorities, the two often being identical. So the *fabrica* could lose its autonomy and its representative character: moreover, in certain regions, the *fabrica* was replaced by the village community which took over the maintenance of the church. The *fabrica* can thus be considered one of the manifestations of the vitality of communal organisations in the late Middle Ages.

P. Adam, *La vie paroissiale en France au XIV^e siècle*, Paris, 1964, 80-86. – J. Gaudemet, *Le gouvernement de l'Église à l'époque classique: le gouvernement local*, 1979, 279-281 ("HDIEO", 8, 2). – B. Delmaire, *Le diocèse d'Arras de 1093 au milieu du XIV^e siècle*, Arras, 1994 (2 vol.).

Joseph Avril

**FACULTY.** A faculty is a power of the *soul, a *potentia* ("potency") or *virtus* ("virtue" in the old sense of "manly strength", the Greek *dunamis*), its capacity to produce operations by itself. Its sources are the biblical theme of the soul as the image of *God (Augustine: triad of "memory-intellect-will") and *Aristotelian psychology read through *Avicenna. The third of the Augustinian triad and the revealed doctrine of the divine *Trinity raised the question of the unity proper to the essence of the soul and of God. Augustine added a qualification: these three powers "are not three lives but one life, not three minds but one mind, hence not three essences but one essence" (*De Trinitate*, X, 11; *BAug*, 16, 154). *Alcuin offered a modalist explanation: they were just different names (*De animae ratione*, 11: *PL*, 101, 644 B). The 13th c. saw two antagonistic solutions: strict identity (*William of Auvergne, *Bonaventure with nuances, the traditionalists); or real distinction, following *Dionysius and *William of Auxerre, *Thomas Aquinas. The debate between the latter and the Augustinianizers arose in *c.* 1270.

Affirming their real distinction, Thomas started from operative potency: on one hand, what belongs to the essence of the human subject, the higher powers of *intellect and *will ("memory" designates the intellect in its retention of irreversibly acquired intelligibles), identical to the essence of the soul in *man; on the other, the causal influx that proceeds from the object of operation (intellective, volitional) which dynamizes the intellect and the will and activates their proper receptivity. *God alone acts by his essence since he does not have to find outside himself either his intelligibles or his *good or his end to will. Hence a restatement of the notion of the trinitarian image, which is a trio not of faculties, but of cognitive and charitable operations in involution and bearing on the essence of the soul referred to its known or willed objects. Augustine's formula "one essence" designated the essence of the soul as the object of reflexive operation, hence, with a view to emphasizing the dynamic meaning of both the trinitarian image and the procession of divine Persons in eternal *circuminsession, a break with *Peter Lombard who relegated the Augustinian triad to three organ-faculties (*vires*). Later writers would ignore this restatement and confine themselves to subtleties called "formal reasons". Descartes would return to the bare modalism of Alcuin.

Fidèle d'Eysden, "La distinction de la substance et de ses puissances d'opération d'après saint Bonaventure", *EtFr*, 4, 1954, 5-23, 147-171. – John of La Rochelle, *Tractatus de divisione multiplici potentiarum animae*, P. Michaud-Quantin (ed.), Paris, 1964.

A. Schneider, *Die Psychologie Alberts des Grossen nach den Quellen dargestellt*, *BGPhMA*, 4, 5-6, 1903/1906. – E.-H. Wéber, *Dialogue et dissensions entre saint Bonaventure et saint Thomas d'Aquin à Paris (1252-1273)*, Paris, 1974. – E.-H. Wéber, *La Personne humaine au XIII*[e] *siècle*, Paris, 1991.

Édouard-Henri Wéber

**FACULTY (UNIVERSITY).** Towards the middle of the 13th c., the word "faculty" (*facultas*) took on the meaning it still has today, viz. the administrative subdivision of a *university organising the teaching of a discipline. At *Paris, there were from the start four faculties, the faculty of arts, which gave a preparatory teaching, and the three higher faculties, those of *theology, law and *medicine. The number of faculties was not fixed: some universities, especially those recently founded, had only two or three. The function of the faculties was to regulate teaching, examinations, collation of *degrees and recruitment of *masters.

O. Weijers, *Terminologie des universités au XIII*[e] *siècle*, Rome, 1987.

Olga Weijers

**FAIRIES.** The fairy is a creation of the medieval West, born out of the fusion of two fantastic figures. Towards the year 1000, Bishop *Burchard of Worms, in his *Penitential, simultaneously pummeled two *superstitions: one attached to the Parcae, goddesses of destiny; the other to the "women of the forest" (*sylvaticae*) who sometimes gave themselves to mortals. "You have done what certain women are accustomed to do at certain periods of the year: in your house, you prepare a table and set out food and drink that you have prepared, together with three knives, to allow those three sisters whom an ancient and ceaselessly perpetuated foolishness has named the Parcae to refresh themselves, if they come." The Parcae, also called *Fata* and *Fatae*, gave the fairies their name and a good part of their attributes. Their cult, inherited from Greco-Roman mythology and associated with that of the Celtic tutelary triads, remained lively for a long time. Thus was drawn in the collective imagination the figure of the fairy godmother, mistress of men's destinies, but also linked to the cult of fertility and abundance. It is she whom Burchard evokes, with the tradition of the fairies' meal. But the bishop of Worms was aware of other fantastic women who, according to a universal theme of folklore, made a gift of their love to fortunate mortals: "You have believed what some are accustomed to believe, that there exist rustic feminine creatures who are called women of the forest, of whom it is claimed that they are creatures of flesh, that they show themselves to their lovers when they wish and take (it is said) their pleasure with them and, when they wish, hide themselves and vanish". Well before the 12th c., in all likelihood, the two figures had been joined together in folklore. In the 12th c., with the birth of a new culture, secular and aristocratic, and a new vernacular literature, marvellous tales (in particular Celtic tales) were sucked into literature, where we see two types of fantastic women arise: the fairy godmother and the supernatural lover, also called the fairy. Our fairies were born out of this interpenetration of written and oral culture. From the early Middle Ages, theologians included *fata* and *sylvaticae* among the growing troop of *demons. Then, around the 13th c., the fairy became, by rationalization, a mere mortal who practised white or black *magic and was confused with the *witch or enchantress. The mythical figure tended towards the literary type. The end of this evolution was the birth of the fairy story as a literary genre in the late 17th century.

Burchard of Worms, "Decretorum libri viginti", *PL*, 140, 1853, 538-1066. – A. Maury, *Croyances et légendes du Moyen Âge*, Paris, 1896 (re-ed. 1974). – L. Harf-Lancner, *Les Fées au Moyen Âge, Morgane et Mélusine ou la naissance des fées*, Paris, 1984. – F. Dubost, *Aspects fantastiques de la littérature médiévale*, Paris, 1991. – P. Gallais, *La Fée à la fontaine et à l'arbre*, Amsterdam, 1992.

Laurence Harf-Lancner

**FAIRS.** The fair (Lat. *nundinae*) was a meeting of buyers and sellers, at more widely-spaced intervals than the *market. It was at first linked to the rhythms of rural life, to habits of purchase at winter's end, summer's end and the *feasts of certain saints. With the economic progress of the 11th, 12th and 13th cc., certain fairs acquired a function in long-distance *commerce. The right to authorize the creation of fairs and markets was a royal right, eventually usurped by princes. The possession of a fair was considered a factor in economic activity and repopulation, hence the great number of demands in *France after the *Hundred Years' War.

The fair was a Peace institution and, as such, could benefit from privileges: protection, "safe-conduct", accorded to *merchants at fairs and and on *roads by territorial princes and *kings; often, partial or total exemptions from fairground taxes, tolls or duties. A time of exceptional jurisdiction, the fair was provided with a specific court (fair-guards in *Champagne, fair-master at Chalon-sur-Saône), judging according to an exceptional procedure that aimed to give the maximum safeguard to the rights of creditors. Each fair was a time organised into successive regulated periods (entry, display, sale, *hare*, payment, exchange, taking of letters).

Chronologically, several generations of fairs can be distinguished. Those of *Flanders: Messines and Thourout at the end of the 11th c., *Ypres and Lille in 1127 and *Bruges founded in 1200, constituted an annual cycle serving the sale of local cloth, but Bruges developed a financial market of the first importance. The five fairs of *England specialized in the sale of indigenous wools. Those of *Champagne and Brie were the meeting-place, doubtless from the early 12th c., of sellers of cloth and linen from the north, and southern merchants buying cloth and linen and selling *spices, *silks, horses, jewelry, perfumes, dyes, *gold. Constituting an annual cycle, with organisations of merchants (Provençal, Italian. . .), they also developed considerable activity in the sphere of credit.

The fairs of Champagne declined in the late 13th c. and lost the cloth market after 1320. Their functions were taken over by other fairs, those of the Parisian cycle including the Lendit, those of the duke of *Burgundy at Chalon-sur-Saône (founded *c.*1239 and *c.*1280), those of *Languedoc, *Frankfurt am Main and *Brabant (*Antwerp and Bergen-op-Zoom), while the fairs of Flanders continued their activity. The apogee of the fairs of Chalon was between 1320 and 1360; after 1410, the civil war hit the French centres . After 1417, the trade of the Chalon fairs was captured by those of Geneva (mentioned from 1262). The apogee of the Geneva fairs was between 1415 and 1450: four meetings, a considerable market for the Milanese, Florentines, French, Burgundians, Swiss and south Germans, links with the Iberian economy.

In the 15th c., France was largely excluded from the international circuits, but the fair economy remained flourishing. The main centres of fairs were Antwerp (two) and Bergen-op-Zoom (two), based in part on the activity of the English and southern and western Germans. To them were added the fair of *Deventer and those of *Leipzig in *Saxony, at the meeting-point of Eastern and Western commerce. The fairs of *Lyon, much favoured by the kings of France from the 1440s, captured part of the financial functions of Geneva after 1462; their apogee was after 1489 and in the early 16th century. They were the site of an active trade in merchandise (silk, silk goods, cloth, *furs, linen, *metals, drapery, spices) and the seat of considerable financial activities (great Florentine houses of *Medici, *Pazzi, Capponi). The displacement of fairs reflected changes in economic geography. The fairs were shop-windows, centres of financial and monetary regulation and places of big business, and the fair economy complemented the urban economy.

H. Laurent, *La Draperie des Pays-Bas en France et dans les pays méditerranéens (XII^e^-XIV^e^ siècles)*, Paris, 1935. – E. Chapin, *Les Villes de foires de Champagne, des origines au début du XIV^e^ siècle*, Paris, 1937. – "La Foire", *RSJB*, 5, 1953. – J. F. Bergier, *Genève et l'économie européenne de la Renaissance*, Paris, 1963. – R. Gascon, *Grand commerce et vie urbaine au XVI^e^ siècle. Lyon et ses marchands*, Paris-The Hague, 1971. – H. Dubois, *Les Foires de Chalon et le commerce dans la vallée de la Saône à la fin du Moyen Âge (v.1280 – v.1430)*, Paris, 1976. – *Frankfurt im Messenetz Europas, Erträge der Forschung*, H. Pohl (ed.), Frankfurt, 1990, ("*Brücke zwischen den Völkern. Zur Geschichte der Frankfurter Messe*", 1). – *A commercializing economy: England 1086 to* c.*1300*, R. H. Britnell (ed.), B. M. S. Campbell (ed.), Manchester, 1995. – M. Rothmann, *Die Frankfurter Messen im Mittelalter*, Stuttgart, 1998.

Henri Dubois

**FAITH.** The theme of faith is one of those that bring out with greatest clarity the problematic underlying the whole Middle Ages. It is a veritable sounding-box, in which the most varied problems find an echo in the medieval mentality.

In the Carolingian period, we encounter two different attitudes to faith: one sought to base itself on St Augustine, the other on Pseudo-*Dionysius. The former was represented particularly by the work of *Paschasius Radbertus (790-859) entitled *De fide, spe et caritate* (*PL*, 120, 1387-1490). This was a work more pedagogical than original, in which the author sought to adapt Augustine's thought to the mentality of the time. It was one of the works that transmitted Augustine's thoughts on faith to the whole Middle Ages. To confront the subject of faith, he takes as his starting-point the definition of the epistle to the Hebrews (11, 1): "*Fides est substantia rerum sperandarum, argumentum non apparientium* (Faith is the substance of things hoped for, the evidence of things not seen)". By *substantia*, he understands the eternal, and thus the very reality of *God. In analysing *argumentum non apparientium*, he opposes "what we see" to the "invisible", *i.e.* the relation betwen faith and vision. Faith disappears where there is "vision", and that is why faith will always be provisional, proper to this life. The analysis of *argumentum* introduces it into the subject of the relationship between faith and *reason; he finds no opposition between the two, but a simple complementarity. Faith, moreover, puts *man in relationship with God, binds (*religat*) him to God, and, as such, is identified with religion: "*unde et religio nominatur* (whence it is called religion)". But faith is, above all, God's *grace and gift: "*sed donum Dei est fides* (but faith is a gift of God)". The second orientation of the *theology of faith was that based on Pseudo-Dionysius. He stressed more the reflective than the pastoral aspect. Its most important representative was *John Scotus Eriugena (810-870). Admittedly Eriugena never wrote any treatise on faith, but in his works he speaks of it ceaselessly. He approaches this subject of faith mainly in the light of knowing: man is essentially *knowledge, and faith comes precisely to satisfy this radical desire of man. In this perspective, it encounters reason, and the relationship between faith and reason would be the theme developed throughout his work. But faith and reason are not opposed since both have their foundation in God, who is One; they are two sources of knowledge, certainly independent, but between them exists a very close relationship. Faith is the principle and source of knowledge, but at the same time it is the principle of *salvation: "*Salus autem nostra ex fide inconcoat* (for our salvation comes from faith)". Faith heals reason of its ignorance. Certainly God created man as a rational being, but *sin has wounded reason. And God comes to the aid of human reason, precisely by faith: faith heals reason. But without reason there is no faith. God permits faith, but we must not stop there. Faith is truly the principle of life, a principle that tends to develop into an ever more perfect knowledge. And faith grows, develops by the intermediary of reason. Reason develops faith, prolongs the effort of faith. With Eriugena there arises in all its strength and intensity one of the key themes of the whole Middle Ages: the relationship between faith and reason.

The same theme of faith as knowledge is developed at length

and in depth by St *Anselm (1033-1109). Better still, his way of confronting this subject of faith determined to a great extent all further medieval thought. St Anselm thought about faith and gave his successors something to think about. That said, his reflections on faith are not reduced solely and exclusively to the relationship between faith and knowledge; he also studied, and in depth, the relationship between faith and *love. The foundation of his theology of faith is found in the nature of man, wounded by original sin. Before man's sin, there was no need for faith in order to know God or to live in knowledge of God. After sin, faith would be the moral condition for knowing God: it is faith that purifies the eyes of the spirit to see God. And it is in this perspective that St Anselm situates, in the first place, the relationship between faith and reason. Reason judges the value of faith: to accept faith requires a certain understanding of its content. Admittedly, to accept faith requires, beyond this understanding, the grace of God, and this because faith is not just a work of reason; it is, above all, the work of God. But faith, for him who believes, is a force that leads him to understand what he has accepted by *freedom and grace. It is a *virtue, a dynamic force that leads to "vision" and, as such, it induces reason to understand the content that it offers it. *Intellectus fidei* (understanding of faith) starts from faith and journeys towards "vision". Furthermore, faith is a transforming force, *operosa fides*, which changes or modifies all man's behaviour and, in particular, reason. Faith without works, but especially without works of reason, is a dead faith. For St Anselm, faith requires to be thought about, to be reasoned about.

In the course of the 12th c., reflection on faith changed its perspective. Certainly, the earlier themes continued to be studied, but from now on the main emphasis would be on the pastoral dimension of faith. On one hand, the problem was posed of faith among Christians who lacked all training, the "simple". These must base their faith on that of the theologians, but their faith is often reduced to a simple repetition of formulae totally incomprehensible to them. On the other hand, "infidels" are sometimes encountered, and with them arises the theme of *conversion. In both cases, the problem posed is that of the communication of faith. To proclaim the faith is in no way to transmit it by incomprehensible formulae. Man is a reasonable being and, as such, he must accept faith reasonably. Communication of faith requires, in the first place, an effort to make it comprehensible. The theme of communication of faith is the central theme of all 12th-c. theology.

Peter *Abelard (1079-1142) reflected on faith while keeping in mind the "simple", but also *Jews and infidels. Believers must be helped to make their faith explicit, just as it is necessary to bring the Christian faith to Jews and infidels. But, in both cases, this calls us to develop the rational dimension of faith, since only reason can make faith comprehensible. Abelard's problem is certainly that of the relation between faith and reason, but not in a theoretical or abstract form: it is posed in terms of communicability of faith. A faith that cannot be communicated on account of its obscurity or its incomprehensibility is not a true faith. He who lives in and by faith must know how to communicate it, and its communication needs to have *virtus praedicationis*; if we lack this *virtus* inherent in faith, communication is reduced to a simple repetition of empty formulae. The communication of faith must awaken conviction, and conviction is rooted in reason. Rational knowledge is a *divina inspiratio* similar to that of the Old Testament and that of the Jews; but this rational knowledge will never arrive at the *mystery of the Incarnation, a specifically Christian mystery. To accept the mystery of the Incarnation, we need the help of grace. *Ratio* certainly prepares us for faith, but faith is not *ratio* but *existimatio*. No more is faith *visio* or experience; it prepares us for *visio* and, as such, faith is a provisional thing.

St *Bernard (1090-1153) approached the subject of faith in a very different context from that of Abelard. His was primarily a monastic context, one of *prayer and *contemplation. It is not in the light of reason that faith acquires all its meaning, but in the light of *love. At the moment of reflection on faith, the important thing is not so much the study of its rational character as that of *pietas*, and *pietas* sets aside understanding to enter fully into love.

*William of Saint-Thierry (1085-1148) opened up a new perspective on the study of faith: the psychological perspective, or its subjective dimension. He analysed in detail and in depth the psychological process of adherence to faith. In this process, we find firstly a voluntary adherence to what is believed; by analysing this adherence, we go on to study a theme of considerable importance for the theology of faith: the co-operation between *will and grace. But faith attains its perfection only when it is communicated. And the communication of faith requires that it be thought about: and to think about it is, in the first place, to enter into communication with *tradictio*, with the Church community. Faith can only truly be thought about within and from the Church. William of Saint-Thierry distrusts individual reason, its autonomy; faced with the *nominalism of his time, he stresses the communal, ecclesial *tradictio*. The function of *ratio* will be precisely to follow *auctoritas*. The perfection of faith is found in mystical experience or in the simplicity of heart that gives itself up totally to the grace of God. Hence it is necessary to approach the content of faith through love: love illumines faith. That is why faith has no need of arguments; arguments or rational proofs are even a danger to faith, because we then accept the contents of faith by reason of rational certainty and not by the authority of divine *Revelation.

The school of *Chartres, and more precisely *Gilbert of Poitiers (1080-1154), took a different attitude to the theme of faith. The school of Chartres was a school open to scientific knowledge. As we know, *Aristotle's scientific works began to be translated from the 12th c., and in them was found a new way of approaching the study of *nature. A confrontation very soon arose between this new conception of scientific knowledge and that of faith as knowledge. For Aristotle, *knowledge had its origin in the senses, while theology situated it in faith; *science was knowledge of visible things, faith that of invisible realities. And faith, in this perspective, was presented as superior to opinion, but inferior to science. It is certain that faith and opinion are not based on necessary things, but probable ones. However there is in faith a *firm* assent; it is *perceptio veritatis rerum cum assentione sine causarum cognitione* (perception of and assent to the truth of things without knowledge of causes). It is by this that faith is distinguished from opinion. But faith is different from science. It is admittedly a knowledge, but a knowledge different from scientific knowledge: faith is perception and assent. This perception proper to faith requires a labour, an intellectual effort, since Revelation offers a whole collection of truths that reason must explore. But these contents of faith have a coherence in themselves, they are *substantia* (substances). Faith is, at the same time, *perceptio invisibilium* (perception of invisible things) and, as such, a certain vision of realities to come. This *perceptio fidei* (perception of faith), moreover, is not a theoretical, abstract knowledge; faith is an affective apprehension of divine mysteries.

The school of Chartres posed many other problems to do with faith: the relationship between the faith of the "simple" and that of theologians, the difference between human faith and divine faith, the relationship between faith and community, the dialogue of faith with Jews and infidels. In this school we encounter all the problems that the 12th c. posed about faith.

In the 13th c., the problematic of faith was fundamentally joined to that of *theology as a science. The *translation of the *Logica nova*, like that of Aristotle's scientific works, radically transformed the scientific mentality of the time. Henceforth, the problem was whether theology was really a science, on a level with Aristotelian science, and whether the *articles of faith occupy a place in theology similar to that of first principles in Aristotelian science. Until then, *intellectus fidei* (understanding of faith) had been considered as a development of the content of faith; from now on, it would be considered as the foundation of theology, and of theology as science. This is why, throughout the 13th c., little was said of faith as experience of God; it was discussed primarily in the light of scientific knowledge. The articles of faith were considered as the foundation of *argumentatio*, as scientific principles. And the perspective of faith as illumination was emphasized in line with this: faith is a divine light that discovers to us the *prima Veritas*.

*Alexander of Hales (1186-1245), for example, compares the certainty of faith with scientific certainty: the certainty of science is a speculative certainty, that of faith is an affective certainty. This affective certainty of faith is expressed in the definition of the epistle to the Hebrews (11,1 ): *substantia rerum sperandarum* (the substance of things hoped for); speculative certainty, on the contrary, is expressed in the second part of this definition: *argumentum non apparientium* (the evidence of things unseen). And his problem is precisely that of linking or uniting these two parts of the definition or these two certainties. Faith is not a purely theoretical or scientific knowledge; it exists in direct relation to life: for this reason, the conception of faith must be, above all, an affective knowledge. This is the orientation followed by St *Bonaventure (1220-1274). The central theme of his thought is that of the relationship between scientific knowledge and faith, and he analyses this relationship in the light of illumination. Reason and faith have one and the same origin, one and the same foundation: illumination. Admittedly reason, on account of sin, is weakened and sick as to knowledge of the truth; it is faith that comes to its help. That is why *philosophy, fruit of reason, is a pre-Christian state, preparatory to faith. It does not oppose it. Moreover, it is faith that gives strength and security to philosophy itself. The certainty of faith is not that of *scientia* as *visio Dei in patria* (vision of God in *heaven), any more than it is the *certitudo speculationis* (speculative certainty) proper to human science; its certainty is a *certitudo affectionis* (affective certainty), or a *veritas secundum pietatem* (truth according to piety). Faith is admittedly a knowledge, but a knowledge that is not purely speculative, but affective. Then again, faith unites us with *Christ and, as such, it is that light that allows us to understand Holy Scripture, since everything in Holy Scripture speaks to us of Christ. Faith, moreover, permits us to understand *nature itself in depth, since nature is a book that speaks to us of God. Finally, faith is the light that permits us to contemplate the very reality of God, who introduces us to his *contemplation.

The attitude of St *Albert the Great (1206-1280) was quite close to that of St Bonaventure. In his theology of faith, he develops practically the same themes: faith directs reason to God and directs it by charity: *fides operans per dilectionem* (faith acting through love). *Veritas intellectiva* (intellective truth) is proper to science, while what is proper to faith is *veritas affectiva* (affective truth). And between the two truths there is a true relationship, though the foundation of science and that of faith are totally different. In fact science, like philosophy, is *manuductio fidei* (allurement to faith), but not faith; faith is of another order, that of *assensus fidei* (assent to faith), which is the fruit of grace.

The attitude of St *Thomas Aquinas (1225-1274) to this theme of faith was different. Thomas did not build his theology of faith starting from *abstraction, but from life and, more concretely, from the different problems posed for him by infidels and *heretics. Faced with infidels, the first problem is that of reason's capacity to accept the Word of God. He is sure that faith is necessary for *salvation. But there are, and have been, many pagan and infidel philosophers who, by the effort of their reason, have come to the knowledge of God, and of God as man's final end. Their rational effort has for St Thomas a certain saving efficacity, but he never confuses faith with reason; both have different foundations. Then again, the certainty of faith is not the certainty of reason. The certainty of faith proceeds from *veritas divina*. Faith unites us to God, *prima Veritas*, but this union is not purely intellectual, it is existential, vital. In faith, *freedom, moved by *grace, always has a hand: the *intellect consents through the *will, which is moved by the grace of God. We believe *non per rationem humanam sed propter auctoritatem divinam* (not by human *reason but because of divine authority). In analysing the definition of the epistle to the Hebrews (11, 1), Thomas attributes to the word *substantia* the sense of *inchoatio gloriae* (beginning of glory) and, by that fact, he establishes a clear relationship between faith and glory. Faith is certainly light, but infused light. Thanks to it we can contemplate the truths of faith and these are presented to our mind as evident. *Argumentum*, on the contrary, is that by which the *intellect is united to truth: by faith, the intellect is united in full security to the truth of Revelation. Then again, faith belongs primarily to the speculative order; its object is *verum* (the true). That is why St Thomas does not pay much attention to the affective dimension of faith. Against heretics, Thomas vigorously emphasizes the logical unity of faith. Faith is a whole and, as such, is systematic, logical; it is indivisible, just as *prima Veritas* is indivisible. All the articles of faith are so joined to each other that to reject one of them leads to rejecting all the others. The heretic is an infidel who does not know himself. To clarify this union, or this logical coherence between the different articles of faith, is the proper task of *theology.

John *Duns Scotus (1265-1308) gave reflection on faith a new orientation: for him, the human contribution to the act of faith came into the foreground. In fact he left faith as gift or *fides infusa* (infused faith) slightly on one side, to give his attention to *fides acquisita* (acquired faith). In reality, it is man who believes, though his act of faith necessitates the action of God or of grace. Faith is admittedly assent to God's Revelation, but to make this assent real we must be certain of its credibility. And it is reason that prepares the assent of faith. Scotus strongly emphasizes the credibility of reason, but without ever forgetting *fides infusa*. This is a light from God which, from outside our mind, leads the intellect to accept Revelation. In it, it is not the will that moves the intellect, but God's truth. *Fides acquisita*, on the contrary, resides in the will and is what leads the intellect to give its assent. *Fides acquisita* is the human or anthropological dimension of faith. But Scotus makes sure that no-one can accuse him of Pelagianism: what leads the intellect to give its assent is not *fides infusa*, but the object of faith, *i.e.* the truth of God. He also has important reflections on the faith of the "simple" and that of the theologians, on faith and the knowledge of God, as well as on faith as foundation of the *social order.

William of *Ockham (1285-1347) developed and perfected Scotus's theological reflection on faith. He, too, established a clear distinction between *fides infusa* and *fides acquisita*, always seeking the relationship between them. This distinction allowed him to explain the case of the *pagan who lives in a Christian setting and who knows and admits the truths of the Christian faith, or that of the Christian who lives and acts like a pagan, as well as the relationship between the believers of the Old Testament and the faith of the members of the Church. *Fides acquisita* requires and demands an intellectual education in the faith; but faith is not just assent to revealed truths; it must be translated into works; without works faith is dead.

*Nicholas of Cusa (1401-1464) based his theology on a totally different anthropology from that of previous theologians. The intellect is radically oriented towards *God: it finds its perfection in God. And it is faith that introduces the intellect into an intimate union with God. In faith, the intellect finds its perfection: faith is peace and the serenity of reason. Certainly God is a hidden God, and faith never claims to reveal or manifest the mysteries of God in full clarity. And yet in a certain way *maxima fides* approaches *visio*.

The medieval theology of faith is extremely rich. It is envisaged under its manifold aspects: faith and charity, faith and science, faith and contemplation of God, faith and society, etc. But medieval reflection on faith is not a cold, abstract reflection: it always responds to living, concrete problems. The solution to these problems depends on the concrete situation in which the different theologians lived. That is why their theology of faith is in large part a pastoral theology, though still based on extremely profound theological reflections rooted in the Church's *tradition.

H. Ligeard, *Le Rationalisme de Pierre Abélard*, *RSR*, 11, 1911, 384-396. – J. de Ghellinck, *Le Mouvement théologique au XII<sup>e</sup> siècle*, Paris, 1914. – P. Rousselot, *L'Intellectualisme de saint Thomas d'Aquin*, Paris, 1924. – J. Cattiaux, *La Conception de la théologie chez Abélard*, *RHE*, 26, 1932, 247-295, 533-571, 788-828. – M.-D. Chenu, *La Psychologie de la foi dans la théologie du XIII<sup>e</sup> siècle*, *Études d'histoire littéraire et doctrinale du XIII<sup>e</sup> siècle*, Paris-Ottawa, 1932, 163 f. – É. Gilson, *La Théologie mystique de saint Bernard*, Paris, 1934. – M. M. Davy, *La Psychologie de la foi d'après Guillaume de Saint-Thierry*, *RThAM*, 10, 1938, 5-35. – A. M. Macaferri, *Le Dynamisme de la foi selon Albert le Grand*, *RSPhTh*, 29, 1940, 278-303. – J. de Wolf, *La Justification de la foi chez saint Thomas d'Aquin et le Père Rousselot*, Paris, 1946. – R. Guelluy, *Philosophie et théologie chez Guillaume d'Occam*, Louvain, 1947. – R. Aubert, *Le Problème de l'acte de foi. Données traditionelles et résultat des controverses*, Louvain, 1950. – M.-D. Chenu, *Introduction à l'étude de saint Thomas d'Aquin*, Paris, 1954. – M. M. Davy, *Théologie et mystique de Guillaume de Saint-Thierry*, Paris, 1954. – R. Aubert, "Le Traité de la foi à la fin du XIII<sup>e</sup> siècle", *Theologie in Geschichte und Gegenwart*, M. Schmaus (ed.), Munich, 1957, 349-370. – M. Grabmann, *Geschichte der Scholastische Methode*, 1, 2, Graz, 1957. – A. Van den Bosch, "L'Intelligence de la foi chez saint Bernard", *CitN*, 8, 1957, 85-108. – M.-M. Labourdette, *La Vie théologale selon saint Thomas d'Aquin. L'affection dans la foi*, *RTh(P)*, 60, 1960, 364-380. – B. Duroux, *La Psychologie de la foi chez saint Thomas d'Aquin*, Tournai, 1963. – L. Villette, *Foi et sacrement*, 2, Paris, 1964, 13-82. – G. Babaglio, *Fede acquisita e fede infusa secondo Duns Scoto, Occam e Biel*, Brescia, 1968. – M.-D. Chenu, *La Théologie comme science au XIII<sup>e</sup> siècle*, Paris, 1969. – E. Gössmann, *Glaube und Gotteserkenntnis im Mittelalter*, *HDG*, 1, fasc. 2, 1971. – J. M. Lecea, *Fe y justificacion en Tomas de Aquina*, Madrid, 1976. – J.C. Hirsh, *The Boundaries of Faith*, Leiden, 1996.

Jaime García Álvarez

***FAMILIA.*** "In the Middle Ages, the *familia* of a church designated all the secular persons attached to its service, whether within the monastery or in its dependencies or rural *estates" (Berlière).

The word does not appear in the Rule of St *Benedict, though it mentions the servants (*servitores*) who care for the sick. The evolution of monastic life entailed a change in the organisation of the community, though Carolingian texts, like the *synod of Aachen (817), suppose all material activities to be exercised by the monks. Well before the institution of lay-brothers in the 12th c., we find in attendance on the monks various categories of persons who, under various names, contributed to the material life of the monastery and formed its *familia*.

The earliest were *matricularii*, initially poor people inscribed in the **matricula*, who performed modest tasks, doorkeeping, bellringing; they were replaced by servants from the 10th century. In the 9th c. appeared *clerici* or *canonici*, not *clerics assigned to the service of parish churches, but to domestic tasks, genuine servants under the orders of the *abbot. *Servientes* and *famuli* were free or unfree men, essentially craftsmen ensuring the daily functioning and upkeep of the house (tailors, bakers, cooks, *masons, farrier, etc.), personnel maintained by the monastery, but sometimes salaried (from the 13th c. at Silos), and who could appear as witnesses in *charters. The great numbers of guests received by some monasteries made this domestic staff necessary.

From the 9th c., prebendaries (*prebendarii*), lodged in the monastery or in its dependencies, received their material subsistence or a life pension from the abbot, in return for *donations *in *precaria*, the *prebend (*praebenda, provenda*) being originally the daily portion of provisions given to those to whom the monastery guaranteed subsistence. **Ministeriales* were, from the 10th c., veritable officials, mayors, tax-collectors, officers of justice, as well as tradespeople, who occupied a higher rank within the *familia* and sometimes managed to transform these posts into hereditary *fiefs or honorific lay offices, with the inconveniences this represented for sound management of the community's budget.

*Oblati*, *donati*, *redditi* were also part of the *familia*. *Oblates were persons (who could be married), who offered themselves to a monastery to serve it, and put themselves under the jurisdiction of the *abbot, renouncing all property, the monastery then providing for their upkeep. The term *donatus*, which goes back to the Frankish period, covers practically the same thing, as does *redditus*, which appeared in the 13th century.

Finally, from the 12th c., **conversi* or lay brothers formed an important element of the *familia*. They must be distinguished from *monachi conversi*, monks who entered late without having received a real training. At *Hirsau we see the appearance of lay *conversi* charged with helping the monks, who directed them spiritually, laymen observing religious practice outside the *cloister, not bound by *vows, but just by a promise of *obedience. The *Cistercians, the *Carthusians, the Order of *Grandmont, the *Camaldolese, admired such laymen leading a quasi-religious life, and discharged onto them all the material tasks and the working of the land, though they did not totally replace waged servants.

U. Berlière, *La* familia *dans les monastères bénédictins du Moyen Âge*, Brussels, 1931. – J. Dubois, "L'Institution des convers au XII<sup>e</sup> siècle, forme de vie monastique propre aux laïcs", *I laici nella "Societas christiana" dei secoli XI e XII*, Milan, 1965, 193-261. – *Les Mouvances laïques des ordres religieux*, CERCOR, "Travaux et recherches", 8, Saint-Étienne, 1996.

Jean-Loup Lemaître

**FAMILY.** The term "family" has undergone a circuitous semantic evolution. Here we will define it as a group of persons united by recognised links of consanguinity and *marriage, *i.e.* a "*kinship group"; in this sense, our "family" corresponds quite well to the words used in the Middle Ages: *cognatio* and *parentela*, or relationship and lineage. The way in which the members of a network of this nature are distributed in space has to do with residence. The relationship between family organisation and manner of residence is neither automatic nor constant: in one and the same society, the composition of residential units, domestic groups, varies according to *social class – the *ménage* of an aristocrat is not that of an artisan or *peasant; and the nucleus formed by those linked by kinship is itself subject to various transformations in time, caused by births, marriages and deaths.

Confusion between order of kinship and order of residence has nourished a fruitless debate on broad family, narrow family, extended family, notions based on considering only the number of relatives dwelling under the same roof. In reality, in medieval society, as in our own, the networks of relatives that constituted families went far beyond residential units, whatever their size: "the family appears the tightest knot of solidarity, and the community inhabited does not make much change in things. Links are of flesh and blood rather than of stone and hearth" (C. Gauvard).

In its maximal theoretical extension, fixed by *canon law, an individual's family comprised all his blood-relatives (paternal and maternal), as well as all his connections by marriage (relatives of his wife or those married to his blood-relatives) within limits that increased from the 5th c. to reach the seventh canonical degree in the 11th and 12th cc., decreasing to the fourth canonical degree at the *Lateran council. This maximal extension had two main functions, whose actual practice is not always easy to measure: to define the set of those who, being already relatives, could not marry each other under pain of *incest; and to delimit the circle of those who, being relatives, were capable of inheriting from each other.

For the family was the primary and ordinary setting of the transmission of *property, status, or even a name or symbol of belonging. But, for everyone, the family also and primarily consisted of this network of effective mutual acquaintance, formed of the close and less close, within which preferential relationships were formed in daily life and on extraordinary occasions. Family solidarity was not an empty word in medieval society; it has long been perceived through the intermediary of regulations on vengeance or the waging of private wars among the aristocracy; we have an inkling of its role in the cohesion of dominant groups; it was at work, in various milieux, as much when crime was afoot as in the tutelage of minors or in the activities of production and *commerce. Yet it is indispensable to emphasize, as well, the development of nuclei of organisation and solidarity that were moulded on another form of kinship, spiritual kinship; we may cite baptismal kinship, *confraternities and parish communities.

J.-M. Turlan, "Amis et amis charnels d'après les actes du Parlement de Paris au XIV^e siècle", *RHDF*, 47, 1969, 645-698. – A. Guerreau-Jalabert, "Sur les structures de parenté dans l'Europe médiévale", *Annales*, 1981, 6, 1028-1049. – C. Lévi-Strauss, "La famille", *Le Regard éloigné*, Paris, 1983, 65-92. – A. Guerreau-Jalabert, "La Désignation des relations et des groupes de parenté in latin médiéval", *ALMA*, 46, 1988, 65-108. – C. Gauvard, *"De grace especial". Crime, État et societé en France à la fin du Moyen Âge*, Paris, 1991 (2 vol.). – D. Herlihy, *Women, Family and Society in Medieval Europe*, A. Molho (ed.), Providence (RI), 1995. – M.M. Sheehan, *Marriage, Family and Law in Medieval Europe*, J.K. Farge (ed.), Toronto, 1996.

Anita Guerreau

## FAMINE

**The West.** Famine has always lain in wait for man, from the *Bible to the contemporary world, but it was present all through the Middle Ages to the point of being a veritable "structure of everyday life" (Braudel). Men's imagery reveals the place of hunger: *miracles of feeding were numerous, and lands of Cockayne with feasting and revelry filled literature and images.

The first cause of famine was insufficiency of production: very poor yields would scarcely feed a rural population that had to hand over the surplus demanded by its masters and to feed the town-dwellers. Reserves were ill-protected and tiding-over was often a problem; and the smallest hazard had dramatic consequences. A climatic event (drought, storms. . .) led to a bad harvest, a dearth, an increase in the price of grain from which the poorest suffered. Then people ate spoiled foods, grass, earth; anthropophagy and necrophagy appeared; *epidemics ensued. Such was the pattern of "mortalities" well described by *Rodulfus Glaber around 1032. The Roman world had limited the damage by its political infrastructure and transport system: the *princeps* could send here the grain produced there. Medieval political fragmentation removed this palliative.

Famine was not socially neutral. The demand for grain being incompressible, the market was very sensitive: the least variation in supply entailed a wide variation in prices, and eating one's fill was then for those who could pay. The others begged or paid with what they had. It is probable that during the early Middle Ages a fair number of freeholders paid with their liberty for nourishment in a time of famine.

Though some writers presented famine as "one of the results of original sin" (*Honorius Augustodunensis, 12th c.), people did not sit there with their arms crossed: they cleared land. Augmenting the cultivated area allowed an increase in the overall quantity produced.

During the early Middle Ages, hunger seems to have been very severe. This is attested both by texts and by *archaeology, which uncovers the rickety skeletons of young people dead of undernourishment and malnutrition. Thanks to land *clearances and to some extent by a revival of collective administration, famine diminished in intensity in the 12th and 13th centuries. This does not mean an abundance of *food: right into the 13th c. there was severe famine in *Poland, Austria, *Aquitaine, *Paris, etc.

But the limit of colonizable land had been reached; no more could be produced; land was even allowed to revert to waste. With the great famine that raged in northern Europe in 1315-1317, the result of an unlucky succession of two years of bad harvests, famine and its faithful companion disease returned to centre-stage to cause the catastrophic mortality of the late Middle Ages.

F. Curschman, *Ungersnöte im Mittelalter*, *Leipziger Studien*, 6, 1, Leipzig, 1900. – G. Duby, *L'économie rurale et la Vie des campagnes*, Paris, 1962. – W. C. Jordan, *The Great Famine. Northern Europe in the early fourteenth century*, Princeton (NJ), 1996.

Georges Comet

**Byzantium.** The *Byzantine Empire, having a subsistence agricultural economy, necessarily suffered frequent famines, related primarily to climatic disturbances. These could be over-long and over-rigorous winters, like that of 927-928, which was the origin of the "great famine"; droughts, like that which raged numerous times from the late 5th c. to the 7th c.; excessive rains, invasions of locusts (in 516-517 around *Jerusalem). But an occasional climatic disturbance did not generally cause real famine. For this to be the case, the loss of the main harvest had to be aggravated by the loss of the secondary harvests and bad conditions had to be prolonged for at least two years, entailing the exhaustion of all the reserves. So it was only in the second year that famine settled in, as at Edessa which suffered grasshoppers in the spring of 599, then a drought in the spring of 600. Crises of production could also have human origins. Thus in 1307, when the Catalans crossed Macedonia, they pillaged the region in order to provide themselves with reserves for the winter, forced the *peasants to flee and provoked a famine.

The crises of production that developed in the countryside were transformed, in the towns that the countryside was supposed to provision, into market crises. Insufficiency of supplies led to a surge in the price of cereals. We can even see market crises, hence urban famines, without there having been any crisis of production, but simply because provisioning was deficient, as in *Constantinople disorganised by the plague in 542. The consequences of severe famines were manifold: demographic losses naturally, but also disruption of the rural population and exodus to the towns; however, famines were often confined to a single region.

Faced with this recurrent catastrophe, remedies were few. At Constantinople, the multiplicity of supply regions allowed the effects of a localized crisis of production to be attenuated. Moreover, *Constantine had established distributions of bread there on the Roman model: regular distributions limited to a small number of beneficiaries drawn by lot, and exceptional distributions from which everyone could benefit; this practice ceased with the loss of Egypt, save for the proprietors of landed property. The emperors also attempted more than once to set up a grain monopoly. Distributions of rations in time of shortage were also a very frequent theme of hagiographical literature; it was also one of the roles taken by those who had the task of almsgiving, *i.e.* essentially the monasteries.

The main famines that affected the Byzantine Empire were those of 383-385 at *Antioch, 443 at *Constantinople, 499-502 at Edessa, 516-521 in *Palestine, the 540s, 580s and 600-603 in *Syria, 927-928 and 1032 in *Cappadocia, 1037 in Thrace and Macedonia. Later, the Byzantine famines are less well known, but we can still point to that of 1306 due to the "scorched earth" policy followed by Andronicus II against the Catalans.

É. Patlagean, *Pauvreté économique et pauvreté sociale à Byzance, IVe-VIIe siècle*, Paris, The Hague, 1977. – "Famine", *The Oxford Dictionary of Byzantium*, New York, Oxford, 1991.

Anne-Françoise Loué

***FANON.*** A fanon (from an Old French term meaning a piece of material), used in the singular, designates the ornamented *amice, worn by the *pope, which at a late date took the form of a sort of silk liturgical collarette or *mozetta*, ornamented with stripes.

In the plural, *fanons* designate lappets, the two silk bands, often trimmed with fringes, that hang behind the *mitre of *bishops or *abbots. They are a memory of the circular galloon, a sort of cloth diadem, which surrounded the lower border of the early mitre and hung down behind the head.

P. Salmon, *Étude sur les insignes du pontife dans le rit romain*, Rome, 1955.

Guy-Marie Oury

**FĀRĀBĪ, AL- (*c.*870-950).** Abū Nasr (in Latin, Avennasar) Muhammad ibn Tarkhān al-Fārābī(in Latin, Alfarabius); Turkish philosopher and scholar who wrote in Arabic (born at Wasīj, near Fārāb, died at *Damascus). After the groundwork of al-*Kindī, he was the true founder of the *falsafa*, a name given by the Arabs to that one of their schools of thought that claimed kinship with the Greek heritage. So he was called the "second master", *Aristotle being the first. Though a Muslim, he owed his formation to Christian authors, and several of his disciples were Christians: his thought was marked by the 6th-c. Alexandrians' interpretation of Greek *philosophy. Only a small part of his important output was translated into Latin: the *De intellectu et intellecto*, the inventory of *sciences, the *Fontes quaestionum*, the book on Plato's philosophy and works on *ethics and *politics such as the *Recall to the Way of Happiness* or the *Compendium legum Platonis*. A larger part was translated into Hebrew. His influence also made itself felt through *Ibn Bāja and especially *Averroes, who both made great use of his commentaries on Aristotle's *Organon*. He defined the essentials of the *metaphysical world which became that of 13th-c. *scholasticism.

Étienne Gilson considered Fārābī's metaphysical adaptation of the logical distinction made by Aristotle between essence and existence "a capital date in the history of philosophy". From a dialectical analysis of the notion of essence, he concluded that the notion of existence was not included in it, that subsequently essence did not include actual existence and hence that existence was an accident of essence. There is a first *cause both of the existence of the world and its movement and of its logical structure and hence of the *knowledge we have of it. This *ontological and gnoseological architecture is given by the distinction of the functions of the *intellect, which extends the levels of human activity (potential, actual and acquired intellects) by the assertion of a transcendent Agent Intellect always in *act. It is this that has produced by "emanation" (*fayd*) the *forms that inform matter, and gives knowledge of these to human intellects. But it is not *God, who is the inaccessible One, the indefinable and self-necessary being (monotheism is hence a corollary of the divine essence), from which it itself emanates by a series of intermediaries. The end of *man is to seek to unite himself with the Agent Intellect. The prophet is endowed from the outset with this *grace, which allows him to express by imagination what the philosopher attains by *abstraction.

Fārābī's thought is essentially logical and systematizing. It depends on the maintenance of *Platonism (quasi-transcendent character of essences) within Aristotelianism. Being closely linked to monotheism and affirming the necessity of prophets, it was able to circulate freely between *Islam, Christianity and Judaism within the Arab world. But it later suffered from comparison with the great intellectual construction of *Avicenna, who owed a great deal to it.

R. Walzer (tr.), *Al-Farabi on the Perfect State: Abu Nasr al-Farabi's Mabadi' Ara Ahl al-Madina al-Fadila*, Oxford, 1985.

É. Gilson, "Les sources gréco-arabes de l'augustinisme avicennisant", *AHDL*, 4, 1930, 27-28 and 115-126. – I. Madkour, *La Place d'al-Fārābī dans l'école philosophique musulmane*, Paris, 1934. – J. Jolivet, "L'intellect selon al-Fārābī, quelques remarques", *BEO*, 19, 1977, 251-260. – M. Galston, *Politics and Excellence: the Political Philosophy of Alfarabi*, Princeton (NJ), 1990.

Dominique Urvoy

**FARCE.** A dramatic genre that developed mainly between 1450 and 1550, farce is a brief comic piece (300 to 500 verses) with a small number of characters (generally two to six). Of the 130 or so surviving pieces, half are constructed on the theme of conjugal conflicts and the trio of husband-wife-lover. The others depict, often coarsely, the themes of folly, malice, trickery. Farce is thus close to the spirit of the **fabliau*. Its characters are types: the ridiculed husband, the cunning wife, the resourceful valet, the foolish peasant, the shady advocate, the lewd monk, the grasping merchant, the swaggering soldier, etc. The masterpiece of the genre, the *Farce de maître Pathelin* (*c.*1465), longer than usual (1600 verses), brings together several themes in an elaborate action, while retaining the motif of the deceiver deceived. Entertainments of farces were still much appreciated in the 17th century.

B. Rey-Flaud, *La Farce ou la Machine à rire. Théorie d'un genre dramatique (1450-1550)*, Geneva, 1984. – J.F. Veltrusky, *A Sacred Farce from Medieval Bohemia: Mastickar*, Ann Arbor (MI), 1985. – A. Tissier, *Recueil de farces (1450-1550)*, Geneva, 1986-1989.

Michel Stanesco

**FARFA.** According to the only source on its foundation, the 9th-c. *Constructio monasterii Farfensis*, the first monastery of Farfa in Sabina was founded by the most holy Lawrence and devastated after his death by the *Lombards. A recent hypothesis has identified this person with a bishop of Sabina in the 560s and 570s. In the 12th c., a *legend attributed the foundation of the monastery to an Eastern monk, St Lawrence the Syrian, confused from then on with the bishop of Sabina. Archaeological excavations have confirmed the establishment of a religious community in the 6th century. Destroyed at the time of the Lombard invasion, the monastery was rebuilt in the late 7th c. by Thomas, a holy monk from the Maurienne valley in *Savoy, to whom the Virgin appeared in a *vision during a *pilgrimage to the *Holy Land, telling him to rebuild the church dedicated to her in Sabina.

Early in the 8th c., Faroald II, duke of *Spoleto, took under his protection the monastery situated on the border of the *Patrimony of the Roman Church and the *duchy of Spoleto. From that date, the *abbey's landed *patrimony grew considerably thanks to ducal *donations and those of the aristocratic families of Rieti. In the second half of the 8th c., the abbey abandoned its Lombard protectors to range itself alongside *Charlemagne. In the 9th c., the abbey reached its greatest splendour. But this rise was to be reduced to nothing by the *Saracens who destroyed it in 898. The partial destruction of Farfa, the attempts of Prince *Alberic to impose Roman rule and the Cluniac *reform implemented at the abbey from 936 provoked resistance from the monks, which led to an abbatial *schism. The reforming Abbot Hugh (997-1038) managed to restore monastic discipline. His successor Berard I (1048-1089) applied himself particularly to reconstructing the abbey's patrimony and incorporating the numerous fortified *villages that had multiplied in Farfa's vicinity. On the political level, Berard I always sided with the emperors against the *popes and was a loyal ally of the Emperor *Henry IV. The end of the *Investiture Contest and the *concordat of *Worms in 1122 entailed a modification of the role played by the powerful imperial abbey and, in the end, its decline.

The abbey became directly dependent on the apostolic see during the pontificate of *Innocent III (1198-1216) and from then on lost its political, social and economic weight. The great expansion of the Roman baronial families in the 13th c. entailed the fragmentation of the abbatial patrimony, whose undynamic management was further burdened by the weight of the past and the customary practice of very long-term tenancies. To try to bring a remedy to the crisis that the abbey went through over nearly two centuries, *Boniface IX appointed his nephew Francesco Tomacelli commendatory *cardinal. In the 15th c., the *Orsini asserted their hegemony over the abbey. A new *basilica was built, perpendicularly to the old, to break with the structures of the past and open it up to the outside world. It was consecrated in 1496.

I. Schuster, *L'Imperiale abbazia di Farfa. Contributo all storia del ducato romano nel Medio Evo*, Rome, 1921. – P. Toubert, *Les Structures du Latium médiéval. Le Latium méridional et la Sabine du IXe siècle à la fin du XIIe siècle*, Rome, 1973. – *Monasticon Italiae*, 1, *Roma e Lazio*, F. Caraffa (ed.), Cesena, 1981, 139-141. – L. Pani Ermini, "L'Abbazia di Farfa", in *La Sabina medievale*, M. Righetti Tosti-Croce (ed.), Rieti, 1985, 34-59. – C.B. McClendon, *The Imperial Abbey of Farfa*, New Haven (CT), 1987. – T. Leggio, *Da Cures Sabini all'abbazia di Farfa*, Passo Corese, 1992. – M. Stroll, *The Medieval Abbey of Farfa*, Leiden, 1997.

Étienne Hubert

**FARINATA DEGLI UBERTI (died 1264).** A Ghibelline of the powerful Uberti family of *Florence, long head of its own faction, Farinata became prominent when, after the expulsion of the Ghibellines from Florence after the discovery of a conspiracy (1258), they were forced to go to *Siena. Farinata with some astuteness secured the help of *Manfred, king of *Sicily; thanks to this alliance and the support of a group of exiled Florentines, Farinata and the Sienese Ghibellines were victorious at the battle of Montaperti (1260). Farinata decisively opposed the proposal advanced by the Ghibelline confederates at Empoli to raze the city of Florence to the ground.

Farinata is known mainly for the space devoted to him in the *Divine Comedy* (*Inferno*, X) by *Dante, who put him among the damned for *heresy; he was indeed condemned posthumously as a heretic together with his wife Adaleta in 1283.

Lucia Velardi

**FASTING AND ABSTINENCE.** Fasting consists in eating nothing at all, abstinence in not eating certain *foods. The one is a matter of time: you defer your meal for several hours or several days. The other is a matter of menu: you forbid yourself this or that dish or drink. To these modes of timetable and quality is added rationing, which has to do with quantity. These three types of renunciation often interfere in practice, but must be carefully distinguished.

Christian fasting has its roots in the *Bible. The Mosaic Law prescribed only an annual fast, the day of Atonement, but the historical and prophetic books often mention occasional fasts, provoked by some grave event or dolorous commemoration, and observed either by individuals or by the whole people. At the beginning of the Christian era, *Judaism shows cases of habitual fasting, ascetic in purpose, like that of the widows Judith and Anna. One of these regular practices consisted in fasting twice a week (Lk 18, 22). Primitive Christianity appropriated this custom, changing only the days, so as to link the fast to the memory of *Christ's *Passion: on Wednesdays and Fridays, only a single meal was taken in the middle of the afternoon. This observance was perpetuated in the fast of the *Ember Days. As for *Lent, it had its origin in the *Easter fast, observed by the whole Church on Holy Saturday, in union with the future baptizands. From there, the fast was extended to the previous forty days, in memory of Christ's fast in the desert. It consisted in taking the sole daily meal in the evening.

Nor is the practice of abstinence absent from Scripture. The interdictions of the Law of Moses were allowed to lapse from the start of Christianity (Acts 12 and 15), but we see certain believers rejecting meat and *wine (Rom 14, 21). Rightly or wrongly, St *Paul's views on this subject have often been interpreted as incitements to such abstinence, which became habitual in ascetic milieux and in *monasticism. In its communal form however, monasticism, after a few generations, knew the habitual use of wine or barley beer ("half a pint a day", says St *Benedict). Paul's advice to Timothy (1 Tim 5, 23) played a decisive role in this matter, though at first it was understood in a restrictive sense: wine was reserved for the sick. No less important was the Apostle's condemnation of those who rejected certain foods as impure (1 Tim 4, 1-5). Christian abstinence had other motives: it was about mastering the passions.

L. Thomassin, *Traité des jeûnes de l'Église*, Paris, 1680. – P. Régamey, *Redécouverte du jeûne*, Paris, 1959. – C.W. Bynum, *Holy Feast and Holy Fast*, Berkeley, 1987. – A. de Vogüé, *To Love Fasting. The Monastic Experience*, Petersham (MA), 1994.

Adalbert de Vogüé

**FATHERS OF THE CHURCH.** The distinction established by St *Thomas Aquinas between Scripture and *Tradition (the latter being mainly represented by the Fathers), though fundamental, can not take fully into account the complex and multiform relationship between the Middle Ages and the Fathers: indeed, that was not its intention. Moreover, the Middle Ages (apart from the 13th c.) made no synthesis on this point. As for monographs on the place of the Fathers in the Middle Ages, they are absent nowadays, hence the complexity of the subject.

The definition of the term "Fathers" of the Church can, by contrast, provide some information. It was at the Lateran council of 649 (can. 18 and 20) that the term "Fathers" was in some sense canonized to designate the *auctoritates*, the "holy Fathers recognised and received" by the Church, whose teaching was consonant with that of the *council.

The Fathers, then, were defined as masters of life, those who, by their life, showed the value of their writings and sometimes witnessed to their *faith by *martyrdom. This is why *William of Saint-Thierry, in his *Letter to the brothers of Mont-Dieu*, wished "to implant in the darkness of the West and the coldness of Gaul the light of the East and the ancient fervour of the religious life of Egypt", in order to make the life of the Desert Fathers a present reality. More generally, St Anthony was presented as the model of monastic life. The works of St Basil, St John Chrysostom, St Efrem, Evagrius, *Cassian, etc., were proposed as so many exhortations to *sequela Christi*.

Meanwhile, the Fathers were valued as *expositiones*, commentators on Scripture, as *e.g.* *Lupus of Ferrières emphasizes. Their commentaries, clarified the biblical text and helped in its reading. This appears clearly for the *Song of Songs, where the *exegesis of *Origen and Gregory of Nyssa served, in a sense, as a norm for medieval authors.

So we understand why, from the early 6th c., the Fathers were defined in the *Decretum gelasianum* as the representatives of orthodoxy, alongside the canonical writings of the Old and New Testaments, councils and apostolic sees. Six Fathers were retained for the East and six for the West; to them was added St Leo the Great, by reason of the *Tome to Flavian* which played a great role in the council of Chalcedon. Later, the list of Fathers was considerably extended.

Yet a difficulty remained: that of language, since medieval authors hardly knew Greek. This problem was rapidly alleviated. From the 9th c., *John Scotus Eriugena translated the writings of St Gregory of Nyssa and *Dionysius the Areopagite into *Latin. Then, in the 12th c., Latin monks translated the texts of the Greek Fathers, especially the Cappadocians, while benefiting from translations already made, such as those of Rufinus and those that existed in Italy and England. From then on, most of the texts were accessible.

But some authors, mainly Latin, remained in the shade: St Irenaeus, whose writings were forgotten, Tertullian, of whom only the *Apologeticum* circulated, etc. This selection made in the patristic writings went back, in fact, to *Alcuin, to St *Benedict of Aniane, *i.e.* to the *Carolingian period which acted as a filter for the writings of the Church Fathers. Thus the two authors most recopied by Carolingian **scriptoria* and most read in the Middle Ages were *Origen and St Augustine.

The different sources enabling us to know the place of the Fathers in the Middle Ages attest this. These two authors were the most frequently cited in manuscripts, lecture notes (*marginalia*), summaries, *florilegia, *capitulae*, tables, citations of Fathers and literary history (like that of *Sigebert of Gembloux who called himself the continuator of Jerome's and Gennadius's *De viris illustribus*).

Among these sources, lecture notes are very instructive. Often left over, they show what was and what was not read in the patristic texts. They may be compared with the florilegia or the *Catena aurea*, which propose a selection of extracts, scraps of texts of the Fathers, mainly with a view to *ruminatio*. These passages were not chosen by chance, but were in keeping with an overall perspective: *e.g.* to meditate on the Incarnation. On their own, the florilegia do not give all the citations of the Fathers. These citations are numerous in medieval texts, but they are not always exact. They were not products of a precise corpus (the Middle Ages not having a library of Church Fathers, as the 17th century did), but rather introduced from memory in this or that work, and, when several references are given for a single text, we are forced to conclude that none is valid.

In fact, the medievals had their own way of referring to the Fathers. They rarely commented on them, since they saw the Fathers mainly as commentators on Scripture. On the other hand, they brought them into their *sermons or, like St *Bernard, preached in the manner of the Fathers. From time to time, they referred to their theological treatises, but in that case they avoided polemical developments and often reinterpreted their conclusions, as was the case for St Augustine's *De Trinitate*. More widely, the texts of the Fathers constituted spiritual nourishment. So they were more used by *monastic theology than by *scholastic theology and they had their greatest influence in the 12th c., that time of renewal, rebirth, the very heart of the Middle Ages. Their fertilizing influence reached its full measure at this time, since the Fathers really induced the 12th-c. renewal, as witness the school of *Saint-Victor. In the 13th c., the Fathers still had an important place, but a different one. They kept the status of **auctoritates* that they had had for *Peter Lombard and Gratian, but, in the **summae*, they were put in perspective and brought in as arguments to resolve this or that theological difficulty. It was the same in the 14th c., though the *Rhineland mystics took up their ideas in their sermons, without necessarily evoking them explicitly, but opting rather for the formula: "a master has said".

In reality, the Middle Ages were deeply marked by the thought of the Fathers, to such a point that we may ask what they would have been without Origen or St Augustine. Origen's influence mainly marked the reading of Scripture, that of St Augustine was decisive, but to different degrees. The *Enchiridion* functioned as a general introduction to *Augustinian thought, the *De haeresibus* as the catalogue of *heresies, the sermons were used for pastoral purposes. *De Genesi contra manichaeos* and *De gestis Pelagii*, rediscovered in the 12th c., together with other commentaries on *Genesis and works of the Pelagian controversy, changed the direction of medieval *theology in its interpretation of *creation and *salvation. The *Confessions* had a lasting posterity and even found an echo in works like John of Fécamp's *Theological confession* and *Confession of faith*. The *canons of St Augustine, among them the representatives of the school of Saint-Victor, played a great role in this propagation of Augustinian thought, expecially for trinitarian *theology. They also modifyied and clarified it. Thus *Richard of Saint-Victor took up the basic intuition of St Augustine's *De Trinitate*, added to it a relevant inquiry into *logic and transposed it onto the mystical level.

What the medieval authors proposed was a complete rereading of the Fathers. They undoubtedly considered the Fathers as *auctoritates*, especially in the biblical sphere, but they were selective, suppressing circumstantial developments relative to the construction of communities, difficulties of the time, etc., choosing this page rather than that and, above all, integrating the Fathers into *ontological speculation. Thus they oriented them in the direction of *philosophy and the relationship between philosophy and theology, which was not necessarily their original perspective. Monastic theology maintained more of the dynamism of their writings, essentially considering the Fathers as masters of life and chosing to meditate on their writings. Thus Cassian's *Collationes* were one of the reference-points of monastic life in the Middle Ages.

We should also mention Dionysius the Areopagite who was situated at the turn of the patristic and medieval periods and who, in his guise as a disciple of St *Paul, transmitted the essence of the *Neoplatonist heritage to the Middle Ages and exercised a lasting influence on medieval authors, while being commented on by St *Albert the Great, St *Thomas Aquinas, *Eckhart, etc.

H. de Lubac, *Exégèse médiévale*, Paris, 1959. – J. Leclercq, *The Love of Learning and the Desire for God*, London, 1978. – C. Moreschini, "I Padri", *Lo spazio letterario del Medioevo, 1. Il Medioevo latino*, 1, 1, E. Menesto (ed.), Rome-Salerno, 1992.

Marie-Anne Vannier

**FATIMIDS.** The accession of the Ismā'īlī *Shi'ite dynasty of the Fatimids had been prepared by the mission of Abū 'Abd Allāh al-Shī'ī to the Kutāma, a tribe of the Berber confederation of the Sanhāja. 'Ubayd Allāh b. al-Husayn, Sherif of Salamiyya in *Syria, claiming to descend from al-Husayn, son of *'Alī and Fāṭima, the Prophet's daughter, was recognised as *caliph under the *laqab* of al-Mahdī, in Ifrīqiya (Tunisia) in 910. Exposed to the opposition of the Malikites, *Khārijites and Zanata, supported by the Umayyads of *Cordova, the dynasty failed to succumb to the revolt of Abū Yazīd (943-947). But, in 959, Jawhar victoriously led the Fātimid armies to the Atlantic. Thanks to their naval victories over the Byzantines, the Fatimids installed Kalbite dynasts in *Sicily. In 969 Jawhar occupied Egypt and founded *Cairo, where the Caliph al-Mu'izz established himself in 973, leaving Ifrīqiya under the command of the Zīrīds, Berber vassals. Wishing to put an end to the *Abbāsid caliphate of *Baghdad, The Fatimids tried to conquer Syria and got themselves recognised at *Mecca. Al-'Azīz (975-996), son of al-Mu'izz, seconded by his active vizir Ibn Killis, enjoyed a brilliant reign. The fertility of the Nile valley and Egypt's control of the trade between *Spain, North Africa, the Red Sea, Yemen, Syria and Iranian Asia, conducted by Jewish or Ismā'īlī merchants, ensured a considerable revenue, while Baghdad suffered a severe decline. Fatimid art reached its apogee in this period, as witness the objects preserved in museums like the al-Azhar and al-Hākim *mosques at Cairo. Al-*Hākim (996-1021), son of al-'Aziz, led a bloody persecution against Ismā'īlī Berbers, Christians and Jews, in a dominant position at court. After his disappearance, his successors no longer personally exercised power, which was confiscated by coteries based on private interests and communal solidarities. The Zīrīd having broken his Fatimid allegiance in 1051 in favour of the Abbāsids, the vizir al-Yāzūrī launched against him the Banū Hilāl, tribes of marauders. From 1065 to 1072 Egypt suffered a terrible crisis, combining military troubles and a murderous famine; power was assumed in 1073 by Badr al-Jamālī, a military vizir of Armenian origin. The establishment of Frankish states in *Palestine after 1099 saved the Fatimids from the threat of the *Seljuk Turks, *Sunni masters of Muslim Asia. Syria was finally abandoned except for a few ports; the last one – Ascalon – was lost in 1153. For a century and a half after the death of the Caliph al-Mustansir in 1094, an anti-Fatimid Ismā'īlī party centred on Alamūt in *Iran launched *Assassins against the Muslim princes of the East. In the 12th c., political life was difficult under the rule of military vizirs, but prosperity reigned thanks to the agricultural production of the Nile valley and to dues levied in the ports on Italian ships. Relations with the Frankish states were often good. In 1171, Salāh al-Dīn (*Saladin) designated no successor to the last caliph, bringing Egypt back to Sunnism.

M. Canard, "Fāṭimids", *EI(E)*, 2, 1965, 850-862 (new ed.). – H. Halm, *The Empire of The Mahdi: the Rise of the Fatimids*, Leiden, 1996. – *The Cambridge History of Egypt*, 1, *Islamic Egypt, 640-1517*, C. F. Petry (ed.), Cambridge, 1998.

Thierry Bianquis

***FATWĀ.*** A *fatwā* (plural *fatāwā* or *fatāwī*) is a consultation on a point of law in *Islam. Given the complexity of the law and the variety of cases and new facts that present themselves in life, the need was soon felt in Islam to have recourse to jurisconsults (*faqīh*, plural *fuqahā*, either jurisconsults or theologian-jurists) known for their knowledge, who gave *responsa prudentium* at the request of magistrates (cadis) in the exercise of their office, of theologian-jurists or of ordinary Muslims.

The specialist in Muslim law, who gave an authorized opinion on points of doctrine, was called a *muftī*. His authority was based on his reputation as a scholar. His role may be compared to that of the *prudentes* in *Roman law, while not forgetting that Muslim law was more extensive. In classical doctrine, the conditions required for the exercise of this position were: Islam, respectability and the ability to work out the solution to a difficulty (*ijtihād*) by personal reasoning. In his *responsa*, the *muftī* expounded what should be, in his opinion, the correct procedure with regard to divine law (**sharī'a*). He had to be versed in the literature of "divergences between learned jurists". Magistrates or those in religious or political authority were recommended to have recourse to him. This was the more necessary since it was not always easy even for a jurist to conclude from the examination of legal works what was allowed or forbidden in this or that circumstance. At a later period, Muslim governments sometimes appointed official muftis, but the custom of consulting private scholars continued.

Muslim law having a "totalitarian" aspect, in including every aspect of existence, it did not just play a role within a law court. It told the Muslim what were his religious duties, what was pure and impure, what he could eat and drink, what he could legitimately acquire or possess, what type of music was allowed. . . It covered conjugal and domestic ethics, transactions and sales, political ethics, the laws of war, etc. All these fields could be the object of legal consultations in case of doubt or necessity. There was no-one, up to the higher authorities of the State, the *caliph, governors and high officials, who did not solicit such advice.

With time, collections of fatwās, some of which took up several large volumes, were made in each of the four schools of *Sunni law. The most prestigious of these *summae* continued to be authoritative for later generations, such as the *Fatāwā* of the Shāfi'ite Taqīddīn al-Subkī (d. 1355), which comprised notably some 50 pages on the prohibition on building or repairing churches and synagogues in Muslim countries. New decisions are rarely found in them; but the clarifications and specifications contributed by these fatwās were often taken into consideration by the authors of new legal works. Many of these collections are precious documents for the history of mentalities, since they enable us to see what was the social and religious situation of a town or a region at a given time, while the great treatises of practical law are confined within a certain timelessness.

T. W. Juynboll, *Handbuch des islāmischen Gesetzes*, Leiden-Leipzig, 1910, 54-56. – J. Schacht, *An Introduction to Islamic Law*, Oxford, 1964. – E. Tyan, "Fatwā", *EI(E)*, 2, 1965, 866. – N. J. Coulson, *A History of the Islamic Law*, Edinburgh, 1978, 142-144. – M. K. Masud *et al.* (ed.), *Islamic Interpretation. Muftis and their Fatwas*, Cambridge (MA), London, 1996.

Claude Gilliot

**FEAST.** Very early, Christianity gave a radical critique of the festivals, spectacles and games of ancient society. According to Tertullian, the circus exploited ferocity, while the theatre lived off shamelessness: and the Christian should not be attached to any other spectacle than that of the *Last Judgment. But for all that, not every kind of festival disappeared from *Christendom.

On the question of festivals, the Christians inherited two very different theories from ancient philosophy. For some, festivals, established by the gods, were events foreign to the normal course of life, which allowed men to refrain from work, regenerate their sensibilities, and consequently enter into communication with the gods. For others, the authentic festival should take place daily; purely intellectual, it could do without rites and games. From this dual tradition was borrowed the definition of the Christian feast given by the first Church *Fathers: for the true Christian, every day was a **feria* or feast, since it was entirely dedicated to God; however, the visible and concrete elements of festive manifestations helped the less-formed or imperfect Christian to direct his attention to God.

During the first centuries, the Christian feasts were put in place: *Sunday, which commemorated the Resurrection and allowed the weekly meeting of the Christian community; the feasts of *Easter, *Pentecost, Christmas and Epiphany. Towards the end of the 4th c., the *temporal cycle was set up and the *calendar of Christian feasts substituted for that of Rome. Yet many "pagan" festivals (family, seasonal, local) were in fact kept up, despite the repeated condemnations of the church authorities. Dissuaded from "pagan" festivals, the faithful were also put on guard against the dangers they ran from the "excessive" rejoicings that marked Christian festivities: pastors denounced, *e.g.*, the *banquets, considered too sumptuous, that often took place on the occasion of the celebration of the *martyrs. Until about the 6th c., "fear of feasts" seems to have been a major worry of the Church. At most, a serene and joyful atmosphere could preside over the meetings and celebrations of Christians. Moreover, the fear of festive excesses, spectacles and rejoicings, which the institution of a "ferial" day might have encouraged, seems to explain why the Sunday rest took several centuries to take hold.

Towards the 6th c., the Christian West underwent a "ritualist revolution", which seems to have been mainly the affair of "*barbarian", rural Europe (G. Philippart): the proliferation of prohibitions (accompanied by the setting up of a system of propaganda and coercion), the institution of a day of rest (Sunday), the development of the *sanctoral (which supplemented the Christian calendar) and finally the importance given to worship as a means of activating the beliefs of the faithful and an instrument of control over the populace, led the Church to distinguish more clearly between feast days and ordinary days.

This taking account of the festive by churchmen was to a great extent a product of the pastoral method they adopted: rather than suppressing "pagan" festivals and places of worship, missionaries preferred to "Christianize" them. Thus, several Christian celebrations took the place and function of older festivals.

In the following centuries, churchmen found themselves confronted by deeply rooted folk traditions; studies have shown the vigour of these traditions throughout the Middle Ages in rural communities, *towns and the world of *chivalry. Clerical culture and folk culture fought for the mastery of *time. In parallel with the Christian calendar, a "folk time" determined the rhythm of life of most of the *laity. The period corresponding to the Easter cycle and Pentecost – during which the Church organised *processions, *pilgrimages and *crusades – was dedicated in folk culture to *youth, *dances, *tournaments and *dubbing. J.-C. Schmitt even advances the idea of a folk festival of the *dead corresponding to the Christian Pentecost. In the case of the autumn feasts which, for the populace, seem to have represented the most important reference-points of the year, the liturgical cycle (St Michael, 29 Sept; St Luke, 18 Oct; *All Saints, 1 Nov; St Martin, 11 Nov) was perfectly superimposed on the agrarian cycle (ploughing, seedtime, the opening of the fields to flocks and herds, payment of *rents) and coincided with rural *fairs at which the products of the soil were sold and exchanged.

Liturgy and folklore thus met. The feast of *Rogationtide, which took place each year at the beginning of spring during the three days before Ascension, is a perfect illustration of this. Instituted in Gaul between the 5th and the early 6th c., the main function of the Rogation days was to ensure the growth of the new crops. The communities of inhabitants who took part in this feast invoked the saints in order to obtain aid and protection, then perambulated ritually across the consecrated places and the fields, following the boundaries of the cultivated land, to sacralize the earth and stimulate its fertility. Thus the liturgy enabled the institutional church to mark out time and space, while responding to the essential needs of traditional societies: from this point of view, feasts often represented the striking of a compromise.

Medieval feasts gave proof of great elasticity. In the 13th c., Rogation days, adapted to country life, were also celebrated in *towns, at the cost of a few transformations; notably the introduction of a processional *dragon which, for the urban community, symbolized the wild beast vanquished by the city's patron saint at the time of its foundation, while churchmen saw the taming of the monster as a victory over *evil. In town, the course of the ritual perambulation followed the outline of the ramparts, drawing a sort of sacred circle around the inhabited area. Many processions of this sort were organised in the Middle Ages in order to obtain an end to an *epidemic or natural catastrophe. Repeated on a fixed date over the centuries, these celebrations allowed communities to reinforce their cohesion.

While Christian feasts were capable of evolving and being transformed, the calendar remained open to innovations; in the late Middle Ages, new feasts were instituted, such as that of *Corpus Christi. In the body of Christ, one and indefinitely divided, urban society found an ideal model. Processions, accompanied by spectacles, liturgical *dramas, *tableaux vivants*, floats depicting the main episodes in the sacred history and the great stages of the Church's life, offered the urban population an oportunity to manifest its unity at the same time as the great diversity of its components, since the different professional associations and *confraternities took part in the procession. In Italy, the feasts of local saints were taken in charge by the municipal authorities: urban authorities launched devotions, organised processions, inscribed the feast of this or that patron saint in the list of ferial and *fast days. In short, liturgy and good citizenship joined hands.

In most late medieval towns, a veritable culture of feasts developed, which permitted the expression of social tensions and authorized an – at least symbolic – questioning of the established order. From the 12th c., in cathedral *chapters, the feasts of the Christmas cycle – St Stephen, 26 Dec; the Holy *Innocents, 28 Dec; the *Circumcision, 1 Jan; Epiphany, 6 Jan – gave rise to liturgical parodies in which *canons, *deacons and choirboys overturned the hierarchy for a day and ritually contested the power of their *bishop or their elders. These festive practices were later extended to other social groups, associations of artisans and urban *guilds, and taken in charge by youth groups. The *carnival, originally connected with the liturgical cycle, was also an urban festival. It corresponded to the final days preceding *Lent, the last days of licence. In the 13th c., the tradition of the "*Bataille de caresme et charnage*" exalted the ephemeral victory of Carnival, fat and laughing, over Lent, emaciated and sinister.

P. Parent, O. Bouchay, *Fêtes médiévales en Flandre wallone*, Lille, 1952. – J. Hild, "Fêtes", *DSp*, 5, 1964, 221-247. – W. E. Mead, *The English Medieval Feast*, London, 1967. – J. C. Schmitt, "'Jeunes' et danse des chevaux de bois. Le folklore méridional dans la littérature des 'exempla' (XIII^e-XIV^e siècles)", *CFan*, 11, 1976, 127-158. – N. Coulet, "Processions, espace urbain, communauté civique", *Liturgie et musique (IX^e-XIV^e siècles)*, Toulouse, 1982, 383-397, *CFan*, 17. – J. Heers, *Fêtes, jeux et joutes dans les sociétés médiévales d'Occident*, Montreal, 1982 (2nd ed.). – J. Heers, *Fêtes des fous et Carnalvals*, Paris, 1983. – M. James, "Ritual, Drama and Social Body in the Late Medieval English Town", *PaP*, 98, 1983, 3-29. – A. Vauchez, "Liturgie et culture folklorique: les Rogations" and "Patronage des saints et religion civique dans l'Italie communale", *Les Laïcs au Moyen Âge*, Paris, 1987, 145-155, 169-186. – *Fiestas y Liturgia*, Madrid, 1988. – M. T. Lorcin, "Le Temps chez les humbles: passé, présent et futur dans les testaments foréziens (1300-1450)", *RH*, 566, 1988, 313-336. – C. Zika, "Hosts, Processions and Pilgrimages: Controlling the Sacred in Fifteenth-century Germany, *PaP*, 118, 1988, 25-64. – G. Philippart, "Temps sacré Temps chômé. Jours chômés en Occident de Caton l'Ancien à Louis le Pieux", *Le Travail au Moyen Âge*, J. Hamesse (ed.), C. Muraille-Samaran (ed.), Louvain-la-Neuve, 1989, 23-34. – P. Walter, *La Mémoire du temps: fêtes et calendriers de Chrétien de Troyes à "La Mort Artu"*, Paris, 1989. – *Feste und Feiern im Mittelalter*, D. Altenburg (ed.), J. Janut (ed.), H. H. Steinhoff (ed.), Sigmaringen, 1991. – I. Taddei, *Fête, jeunesse et pouvoirs. L'Abbaye des Nobles Enfants de Lausanne*, Lausanne, 1991. – A. Dihle, "La Fête chrétienne", *REAug*, 38, 1992, 323-325. – J. Dumoulin, J. Pycke, *La Grande Procession de Tournai (1090-1992)*, Tournai-Louvain-la-Neuve, 1992.

Michel Lauwers

**FÉCAMP.** A first *abbey founded at Fécamp by *nuns in 658 was destroyed by *Vikings in the mid 9th century. From *c.*950, the dukes of *Normandy had installed their palace in its ruins and in 990 Richard II restored the abbey to make it the sanctuary of the ducal dynasty. *William of Volpiano, called in 1001 to subject the establishment to the Benedictine obedience, made it the first among the Norman monasteries. The *relic of the *Holy Blood there made it a renowned *pilgrimage centre, ensuring the establishment's prosperity after the dukes had ceased to be buried there in the mid 11th century. The *chronicles and poems composed at Fécamp played an important role in the literary history of the *duchy.

A. Renoux, *Fécamp. Du palais ducal au palais de Dieu*, Paris, 1991.

Mathieu Arnoux

**FELIX V, POPE (1383-1451).** Amadeus VIII, born at Chambéry, became head of the county of *Savoy in 1391 on the death of his father Amadeus VII, but only really began to govern in 1398. In 1416, the Emperor *Sigismund raised Savoy to the rank of a *duchy for him. Aged 51, the widowed father of nine children, he decided to leave the world and attend solely to his *salvation. So in 1434 he handed over the lieutenancy general to his eldest son Louis, created the knightly Order of San Maurizio and retired with six companions to the comfortable hermitage of the castle of Ripaille, on the shores of Lac Léman.

His story might have stopped there without the aggravation, in 1439, of the crisis that continued to oppose the council of *Basel to Pope *Eugenius IV. Only the representatives of the popular party now remained at Basel, among them a very small number of prelates. On 16 May, the *council proclaimed its superiority over the *pope and, on 25 June, deposed him. To replace him, the council appealed to Amadeus. It was expected that he would rally to the conciliar cause the princes who had sent no embassy to *Ferrara, and pay the debts of the assembly. On 17 Dec, the duke accepted the *tiara offered him by the delegation led by Cardinal Aleman, president of the council. A week later he received minor *orders and, on 6 Jan 1440, abdicated in favour of his son.

He made his entry into Basel only on 24 June 1440 and was crowned pope (*i.e.* *antipope) there under the name of Felix V on 24 July, after having been ordained priest three days earlier. But the hopes of the conciliar *clerics were quickly disappointed. Obedience to Felix V remained very limited: partisans in some French, German and Polish *dioceses, a few *universities (*Vienna, *Leipzig, *Erfurt and *Cracow), the *Carthusians, the *Teutonic Knights and some *Franciscans and *Dominicans. The princes, on whom they had been counting to save the council, remained neutral or loyal to *Eugenius IV. Moreover, relations between the antipope and the council were soon strained. The former duke certainly intended to act in its best interests. Admittedly he consented to abandon his name and shave his beard;

but on 29 Jan 1442 he obtained the right to dispose in *commendation of vacant *bishoprics, *abbeys and *priories and to levy a tax on *benefices in the States of *Savoy . This measure was against the spirit of the council, which had abolished *annates.

After many disagreements, Felix V left Basel with his court in Nov 1442. He resided at Geneva and Lausanne. With Eugenius IV dead (1447), *Nicholas V asked the king of *France to negotiate an end to the *schism. On 7 April 1449, Felix V publicly renounced his claims in the Franciscan convent of Lausanne before the last session of the council of Basel – dissolved on the following 25 April. Amadeus was appointed *cardinal-bishop of Sabina and *vicar in the lands of his obedience; he received a pension of 6000 florins. He died at Geneva and was buried at Ripaille.

M.-J. de Savoie, *Amédée VIII: le duc qui devint pape*, Paris, 1962 (2 vol.). – E. Mongiano, *La Cancellaria di un antipapa. Il Bollario di Felice V (Amedeo VIII di Savoia)*, Turin, 1988. – B. Andenmatten, A. Paravicini-Bagliani, *Amedeo VIII – Felice V*, Lausanne, 1992.

Pierre Kerbrat

**FELONY.** Felony, attested mainly in the feudal system of north-west Europe, was the breaking of the link that united the vassal to his lord. It could be the vassal's failure to meet the obligations due to the lord, military or financial aid, participation in his council, or a deficiency in the protection given by the lord to his vassal. A ceremony seems to have taken cognizance of the breach of sworn faith which was settled by the withdrawal of the *fief conceded (forfeiture), which often meant an armed engagement. The proliferation of *homages owed to several lords from the 10th c. multiplied the risks of felony. Liege *homage was a means of counteracting this tendency.

M. Bloch, "Les formes de la rupture de l'hommage dans l'ancien droit féodal", *Mélanges historiques*, 1, Paris, 1963, 189-209.

Thierry Pécout

**FERIA.** The Christian liturgical *calendar was reluctant to use the names of the weekdays inherited from *pagan Antiquity (day of the Moon, of Mars, of Mercury, of Jupiter, of Venus), while biblical names had prevailed for Saturday (the Sabbath day) and *Sunday (the Lord's day). So the days were given a number in order, Sunday counting as the first day of the week (following the habit of the Jews): there were thus II (Monday), III (Tuesday), IV (Wednesday), V (Thursday) and VI (Friday). And as all Christian days were feasts and a celebration of the *mystery of the Lord, they were given the name "feria", from the Latin *feria*, feast day and hence a public holiday. This liturgical usage never passed into common use, and the days of the week kept their old pagan names, except in Portuguese.

F. Cabrol, "Fêtes chrétiennes", *DACL*, 5, 1922, 1403-1412. – M. Righetti, *Manuale di storia liturgica*, 2, Milan, 1955, 27-32 (2nd ed.).

Guy-Marie Oury

**FERRARA.** A Byzantine *duchy in the mid 8th c., a local tradition makes Ferrara the seat of a *bishop from the mid 7th century. Equally traditional, and early, is the hypothesis of the town's origin as an 8th-c. Byzantine "castrum" against the Lombard peril. This hypothesis has recently been contradicted, but all the reasons put forward by scholars, historians and archaeologists seem fragile: there is no sure documentary evidence of a Ferrarese *castrum* until the 10th century. Held by the *Lombards, donated by *Pippin to the *Patrimony of St Peter, then part of the of the *Carolingian kingdom, the city was substantially ruled in the 10th and 11th cc. by the bishop – since the presence of a *count is very doubtful – though the county was not formally attributed to him.

In the late 10th c., Ferrara came into the hands of the *Canossa family and remained there through the age of *reform, until the early 12th c., when the germs of the communal phenomenon were being heralded, unusually early at Ferrara. The *commune was soon disputed by rival factions led by the Adelardi and Torelli, and then by the Estensi, who replaced the Adelardi. In 1240 the marquises d'Estetriumphed, and they ruled the city first *de facto* and then, from 1264, formally as lords: *Italy's first city *signoria*. Except for a brief period, the city remained permanently in the family's hands throughout the Middle Ages. In 1329 the marquises obtained the Apostolic Vicariate, after having probably held the imperial vicariate. In 1335 Obizzo II became lord also of *Modena, and in 1344 also of *Parma. Ten years later it was the turn of the county of Rovigo, which had always been in the d'Este orbit, and Comacchio (conceded by the emperor). Soon after the middle of the century began the penetration into "Estense" *Romagna, established and maintained until 1598. The d'Este dominion finally extended over a vast region, as far as Reggio Emilia and the Garfagnana (1430-1433). The imperial duchy of Modena and Reggio in 1452, and the papal duchy of Ferrara in 1471, conferred on Borso, confirmed the unanimous recognition of the new State and its titulars. The *court, among the most princely and celebrated in Europe in the 14th and 15th cc., with an enlightened and stimulating artistic *patronage, generated a splendid artistic and literary life and gave Ferrara a wholly avant-garde town plan, suggesting its definition as the "first modern city".

Riccobaldo da Ferrara, *Chronica parva Fèrrariensis*, G. Zanella (ed.), Ferrara, 1983 (Dep. prov. ferr. di st. pat., Monumenti, 9).

*I ducati padani, Trento e Trieste*, Turin, 1979, 1-211. – *Storia di Ferrara*, 4, *L'alto Medioevo VII-XII*; 5, *Il basso Medioevo XII-XIV*, Ferrara, 1987. – A. Vasina, "L'area emiliana e romagnola", *Storia d'Italia*, 7, 1, *Comuni e signorie nell'Italia nordorientale e centrale: Veneto, Emilia-Romagna, Toscana*, Turin, 1987, 359-559. – A. Benati, A. Samaritani, *La Chiesa di Ferrara nella storia della città e del suo territorio. Secoli IV-XIV*, Ferrara, 1989. – L. Marini, "Lo stato Estense", *Storia d'Italia*, 17. – S. Gelichi, "I castelli bizantini ai confini dell'Esarcato: Ferrara, Argenta e Comacchio", G. P. Brogiolo, S. Gelichi, *Nuove ricerche sui castelli altomedievali in Italia settentrionale*, Florence, 1996, 49-62.

Gabriele Zanella

**FERULE.** Unlike the *bishop's *crozier, that of the *pope, called *ferula*, was straight. On receiving the *ferula*, the new pope took possession of the Lateran *palace, and hence of all the rights, privileges and properties connected with his office. For Cencius (1192), the ferule was the symbol "of power and correction" (*regiminis et correctionis*). Used for infeudations within the Papal State, it was a symbol of the pope's *temporal power. Attested from the 9th c., it use was lost in the 13th and 14th centuries.

P. Salmon, *Mitra und Stab*, Mainz, 1960, 67-73. – G. B. Ladner, *Die Papstbildnisse*, 3, Vatican, 1980, 309.

Agostino Paravicini Bagliani

**FEUD.** In the "*barbarian" Germanic societies, the blood-tie was formidable. The *faida* or "feud" (the word seems to be of Germanic origin: see German *Fehde*, "quarrel", "contention") was based on this tie. It was vengeance, or rather the right and especially the sacred duty of vengeance, which was passed on from generation to generation, decimating *kinship groups. It strongly recalls the *lex talionis* of ancient oriental societies. In the earliest historical times of Germanic societies, not yet Westernized, the feud appears in *epic poetry, woven out of a tangle of revenge-stories, such as the famous legend of the *Nibelungen. In an attempt to put an end to these perpetual conflicts and halt the chain of revenges, the barbarian kingships caused blood-money, **wergild*, to be paid by the murderer to the victim's family, *i.e.* a certain sum assessed according to a very precise catalogue of physical damage suffered. This system of pecuniary composition reveals the transition of the Germanic societies to the archaic State and the penal system, at the same time as their gradual acculturation to the structures of the late Empire, more or less adapted.

The system for regulating social *violence was thus put in place, supplemented by the mutual *oaths of surety, *securitates*, *treuwa* (or *treuga*, an old vernacular word, of Germanic origin, implying fidelity [*treue*], and from which "truce" derives), that we find in Frankish formularies; because often compositions pronounced as *wergild* were not enough to stop the murderous concatenations, since the *family, wounded in its *honour, might refuse them out of piety towards its *dead. And indeed, most of the time, everything continued to be regulated outside the legal institutions: the return to calls for blood was incessant and feuds would persist throughout the early Middle Ages and even beyond. The State intervening to stop them was powerless: in *England, despite the interventions of King *Alfred, they were still there in the 11th c.; in Gaul, after the *Merovingian kingship had in vain imposed *wergild*, going so far as to execute the leaders of feuds, the *Carolingian emperor, who claimed to be the "avenger of crimes and corrector of those who are mistaken", resumed the programme of "devindication". But the great aristocratic families were always throwing themselves into interminable vendettas, with which the *chronicles are strewn: the Pippinids themselves, Etichonids, Welfs of *Bavaria, Rorgonids, Guilhelmids, Goths and Toulousains, all without exception indulged in them. The old blood-ties or sworn bonds were stronger than the universalist dreams of emperors still tied by their Germanic kinships or the Christian morality of a *Benedict of Aniane or an *Agobard. Two worlds and two mentalities were opposed, with the family as stake.

In the 10th c., when the agony of the Carolingian structures was consummated, the feudal crisis would relaunch *faidae*, engendering new private wars, between aristocratic and then knightly kinships of *Burgundy, *Flanders, Auvergne or elsewhere. As in the heroic era, the feud could be appeased only by the truce: shortly after the year 1000, on the initiative of the monks of *Cluny and to the benefit of a Church soon to be Gregorian and capable of punishing contraveners, the Truce of God – heir to the *Peace – gradually put an end to feuds, both in northern France and in the Midi, on the basis of oaths sworn on *relics.

*La Vengeance. Vengeance, pouvoirs et idéologies dans quelques civilisations de l'Antiquité*, R. Verdier (ed.), J.-P. Poly (ed.), Paris, 1981-1984 (3 vol.). – J. M. Wallace-Hadrill, "The Bloodfeud of the Franks", *The Long-Haired Kings*, Toronto, 1982, 121-47. – W. I. Miller, *Bloodtaking and Peacemaking*, Chicago, 1990. – P. R. Hyams, "Feud in Medieval England", *Haskins Society Journal*, 3, 1991, 1-21.

Christian Lauranson-Rosaz

**FEUDALISM.** The use of the term "feudalism" (used by jurists only from the 17th c.) to characterise medieval society can be justified as long as we adopt a number of reservations that limit its range in space and time. Between the feudalism of Marxist historiography, which characterised a socio-economic system based on *serfdom and seignorial revenue, constituting an intermediary between a slave system and *capitalism, and the "feudal system", that superannuated and reactionary world lambasted by the Enlightenment and the French Revolution, the vicissitudes undergone by this notion have been mainly ideological. As a working concept for the historian, it still remains ambiguous, evoking now a mode of personal relationships structuring the aristocratic group, now the nature of medieval society as a whole.

Feudalism was a form of organisation of social ties specific to the Western Middle Ages and based originally on personal ties. The term is derived from "*fief" and thus puts the emphasis on what has been called the real element of man-to-man relationships, generally a landed property accompanied by rights and revenues attached to it. While *vassalage emphasized personal ties and the ritual that surrounded and codified them, feudalisn seems to have been a social system based on the holding and circulation of fiefs, and which bound the lord to his vassal. Admittedly, the feudo-vassalic relationship concerned essentially the aristocratic group, but its ideological and economic substructures were so complex that directly or indirectly it embraced the majority of social ties from the 10th and 11th centuries on.

This definition does not prevail in a field vigorously renewed by research, which has shown that the notion was far from being the essential element of medieval social relationships, whether in time or space. Thus, the fief was not the pivot of relationships between the aristocracy in the Mediterranean regions (except the kingdom of *Sicily), where we may even talk of feudalism without fiefs. The notion lost its vigour in the course of the Middle Ages and the rites of *investiture with the fief shade off somewhat, particularly after the 14th century.

Generally, feudalism was primarily that period between the 10th and 13th cc. in which Western Europe experienced the result of a weakening of the *State, the *res publica* and public *authority, products of the Greco-Roman world and utilized by the *Carolingian monarchy. The dislocation of public authority and of the prerogatives attached to it, like the holding of fortresses, the power to constrain, to impose, to administer *justice and to coin *money, all those rights known as "*regalian", made the fortune of the emperor's former agents, who asserted their autonomy from the late 9th c. and during the 10th century. This was manifested in the erection of local dynasties in principalities with fluctuating contours, such as *e.g.* *Aquitaine, *Burgundy, *Provence, the county of *Flanders, that of *Catalonia, or the German grand-duchies.

With the exception of *Germany up to the 13th c., this disintegration proceeded at much more elementary levels when castellans and lords in turn took over the powers of constraint (the *ban) in their region, their canton, their lordship. Likewise, the Lombard or Tuscan towns asserted themselves as independent entities: the assertion of communal power was thus an integral part of feudalism. What has been called the castellan crisis for the kingdom of *France continued throughout the 11th c. and through part of the next. It saw the aristocratic group asserting itself, consolidating its positions by taking over public rights and making the *benefice, that gift granted by the lord and the king to his vassal, a proper and hereditary property. The fief – the term spread in the 11th c. – illustrated and supported this rise in power. Thus, relations of authority were dependent on private ties and practices of cohesion prevailing within *family or clan groups, like *recommendation by hands and *homage. Feudalism came into being in a climate of dispersal of powers that favoured competition, rivalries and hence wars and the military. These emerged from social groups rich enough to arm themselves and fight on horseback. Feudalism was that moment when the aristocracy militarized themselves and gave themselves a morality and a system of values based on war and the fellowship of fighting men.

So feudalism rested on an apportionment of powers. Its economic foundation was the lordship within which were levied the fruits of the countrymen's labours. These found themselves enclosed by rigid structures, legal and fiscal constraints: they put themselves, especially in times of internal troubles, under the protection of the powerful in exchange for the fruits of their *labour. This disappearance, total or partial according to regions, of the freeholder (one who could inherit and transmit his property) also marked the setting up of feudalism, according to modes and a rhythm that are the objects of controversy. While it long seemed to be a disorder, feudalism appears today as the setting up of a *social order and an ideology (that of the three orders) that subtended it. More than that, it also provided the framework and the instruments of the rebirth of the notion of the State.

Feudalism seemed to have been toned down in proportion to the rebirth of a public authority. This was to forget that the feudal institutions and the law of fiefs established in customs from the 11th c. were widely laid under contribution by *monarchies, in *Catalonia, *Flanders, *England after 1066, *France or the kingdom of *Sicily. Elements such as liegedom and forfeiture allowed the king of France to assert his claims against the lords of Blois, or against the king of England for example. The notion of sovereignty and that of *suzerainty nourished the assertion of princely power. In the kingdom of Sicily, the fusion of feudal and Roman elements, as well as the contributions of *Islam, gave rise in the 13th c. to a structured power endowed with efficient and rational administration. To this extent, feudalism does not appear today as the antithesis of the State, the synonym of anarchy, but the contrary. The feudal order that guaranteed the power of potentates and territorial princes provided a framework and basis for the revival of States from the 12th c., as did *Roman law, each in a different way according to the regions concerned.

However, feudalism lost its strength to the new State structures that it had allowed to be put in motion. In the 14th and 15th cc. it no longer played such a fundamental role for political authority. The States invented new types of solidarities based on the contract, new sorts of paid fighters or administrators. Feudalism maintained itself within private relationships, the fief survived while practices of homage tended to decline in France and England. The means provided by the feudal relationship were thus rivalled by modern forms permitted by the rebirth of urban economies based on monetary exchange. On the other hand, the type of levying of revenue set up in the feudal period within the *seigneurie* continued to exist with considerable modifications up to the modern period. Thus, what the revolutionaries of 1789 overthrew was the economic and legal foundation of feudalism, the *seigneurie*, rather than forms of social relationship that had already largely disappeared, in fact if not in mentality, in Western Europe.

G. Duby, "La féodalité? Une mentalité médiévale", *Annales*, 1958, 765-771. – M. Bloch, *Feudal Society*, London, 1962. – R. Boutruche, *Seigneurie et féodalité*, Paris, 1968-1970. – *Les Structures sociales de l'Aquitaine, du Languedoc et de l'Espagne au premier âge féodal, colloque de Toulouse, mars 1968*, Paris, 1969. – G. Duby, *The Three Orders: Feudal Society Imagined*, Chicago, 1980. – *Structures féodales et féodalisme dans l'Occident méditerranéen (X^e-XII^e siècles), colloque de Rome, octobre 1978*, Rome, Paris, 1980. – A. Guerreau, *Le Féodalisme, un horizon théorique*, Paris, 1980. –F. L. Ganshof, *Qu'est-ce que la féodalité?*, Paris, 1982 (5th ed.). – G. Bois, *The Crisis of Feudalism*, Cambridge, 1984. – P. J. Geary, "Vivre en conflit dans une France sans État: typologie des mécanismes de règlement des conflits (1050-1200)", *Annales*, 41, 1986, 1107-1133. P. Bonnassie, *From Slavery to Feudalism in Southwestern Europe*, Cambridge, 1991. – J. P. Poly, E. Bournazel, *The Feudal Transformation: 900-1200*, New York, 1991. – D. Barthélemy, "La mutation féodale a-t-elle eu lieu? (note critique)", *Annales*, 1992, 3, 767-777. – S. Reynolds, *Fiefs and Vassals*, Oxford, 1994.

Thierry Pécout

**FEZ.** A town in the north of the far *Maghreb (*Morocco), Fez (*Fās*) is situated on the wadi of the same name. Twice, under the *Idrīsids and then under the *Merinids, Fez played an important role as capital and residence of the prince. When Marrakesh supplanted it as state capital in the *Almoravid and *Almohad periods, Fez retained its key function as the great commercial metropolis of the north and a centre of Arabic and Islamic culture.

The origins of Fez go back to the beginning of the *Idrīsid dynasty; in fact, it had a double foundation. In 789, Idrīs I founded a first town on the right bank of the wadi, Madīnat Fās, doubtless a simple military camp; then, in 809, his son Idrīs II founded on the other bank a new town, al-āliya (the Alid), which he peopled with Arabs and made his capital. The two establishments had a separate and often hostile destiny for nearly two centuries, but they very quickly acquired an urban character. Indeed, Madīnat Fās received 800 families who left *Cordova after the revolt of 817, while the *Kairouanis fleeing the *Aghlabids were welcomed at al-āliya, where they were soon joined by a Jewish community. The two "banks", that of the Andalusians and that of the Kairouanis, were provided with *mosques; Fez spread *Islam and *Arab culture into the Berber lands; moreover, enjoying a favourable position on the Sudanese *gold route, the town became a prosperous commercial centre. This momentum was not broken by the *Fatimids of Ifrīkiya, nor by the Umayyads of *Spain who disputed the place in the 10th and early 11th centuries.

Around 1070, the Almoravid conquest profoundly marked the history of Fez; the two towns were united and provided with a fortress (*kasba*) to the west. Moreover, the establishment of the Almoravid and then Almohad Empires, incorporating the far Maghreb and Andalusia in a Hispano-Moorish area, favoured expanded links with the Iberian peninsula to the detriment of Fez's previous links with Ifrīkiya and the East. When the Almoravids rebuilt the mosque of the Kairouanis (the *Karawiyyīn*), they called in Andalusians to decorate it.

In 1276, Fez regained its position as capital; indeed Abū Yūsuf, the Merinid sultan, founded west of the old town (Fās al-Bālī) a new town surrounded by a double wall, Fās al-Jādid, in which he built palaces, a mosque-cathedral and administrative buildings for his government. The Merinids opposed the religious particularism of the Almohads and preached a strict return to orthodoxy. They made Fez a centre for the study of Malikism and built numerous mosques and *madrasas* which attracted masters and students; these colleges, with buildings arranged around a square courtyard, represent the apogee of Hispano-Moorish ornamental art, characterised by delicate and harmonious decorative motifs. Fez kept its political, economic and cultural primacy until the 16th c., despite the popular revolt that overthrew the last Merinid in 1465.

H. Terrasse, *Histoire du Maroc*, Casablanca, 1949-1950 (2 vol.). – R. Le Tourneau, *Fez in the Age of the Marinids*, Norman (OK), 1961. – "Fās", *EI(E)*, 2, 1965, 818-823.

Philippe Gourdin

***FIBULA.*** Unlike the Roman usage, the wearing of *fibulae* was specifically female during the greater part of the *Merovingian period (mid 5th c. - mid 8th c.), as funerary *archaeology attests. The wearing by men of the cruciform fibula fixing the *paludamentum* to the shoulder disappeared with King Childeric († 481-482), *Clovis's father, whose grave was discovered at *Tournai in 1653. Not until the threshold of the Carolingian period do rare archaeological discoveries and then manuscript *illuminations attest the reappearance, connected with the return to classical taste, of male shoulder fibulae, usually discoid.

Until *c.*600, Merovingian women generally wore two pairs of fibulae. The first, small in size (zoomorphic, discoid), closed the neck of the garment or kept a veil closed over the breast. The second, asymmetrical in type (one of the ends usually bearing characteristic digitations), closed or ornamented the dress (which stopped just below the knees) at the hip. These different types of silver or bronze fibulae (milled or in sheet metal inlaid with garnets or glass beads) reflect the decorative arts of the first part of the Merovingian period.

Under the influence of Mediterranean fashion, the wearing of a single fibula at the neck (circular or quadrilobate) prevailed in the 7th c., high-quality examples being decorated with a *gold or silver leaf (sometimes embossed) set with filigree and coloured stones mounted in *bâtes* (metal settings).

P. Périn, "Art de la Gaule mérovingienne", *Encyclopaedia Universalis*, Paris, 1984 (new ed. 1989). – P. Périn, "Le haut Moyen Âge occidental", *Grand Atlas de l'archéologie Universalis*, Paris, 1985, 108-113. – P. Périn, "Les styles colorés", "Les styles animaliers", *Grand Atlas de l'art Universalis*, Paris, 1993. – M. Klein-Pfeuffer, *Merowingerzeitliche Fibeln und Anhänger aus Pressblech*, Marburg, 1993 (*Marburger Studien für Vor- und Frühgeschichte*, 14). – M. Martin, "Tradition und Wandel der fibelgeschmückten frühmittelalterlichen Frauenkleidung", *Jahrbuch des Römisch-Germanischen Zentralmuseums Mainz*, 38, 2, 1991 (1995), 629-680.

Patrick Périn

**FICHET, GUILLAUME (*c.*1433-*c.*1480).** Guillaume Fichet, born in *Savoy, studied arts and then *theology at *Paris. In 1461, he became bursar of the *Sorbonne *college. A traditional theologian, an important man at the *university (*prior of the Sorbonne in 1465, *rector in 1467, *master of theology in 1468), he was also a *humanist, one of the first to teach *rhetoric at Paris. With his friend Jean *Heynlin, he favoured the creation of the first Parisian printing press (1470) and published some 20 volumes on it (*classics and Italian humanists). We have several *treatises of his, especially a *Rhetoric*. In 1472, he left Paris for *Rome where he died.

*Humanistes français du milieu du XVe siècle*, E. Beltran (ed.), Geneva, 1989.

"Guillaume Fichet", *DLFMA*, 1992, 620-621.

Jacques Verger

**FICINO, MARSILIO (1433-1499).** Born at Figline to a medical family, Marsilio Ficino studied the humanists, *philosophy and *medicine. His interest in *Platonism also led him to learn Greek. In 1462, Cosimo de' Medici gave him a house at Careggi near *Florence, where he installed a fairly informal "Platonic academy". In 1463, he completed the translation of the *Corpus hermeticum*

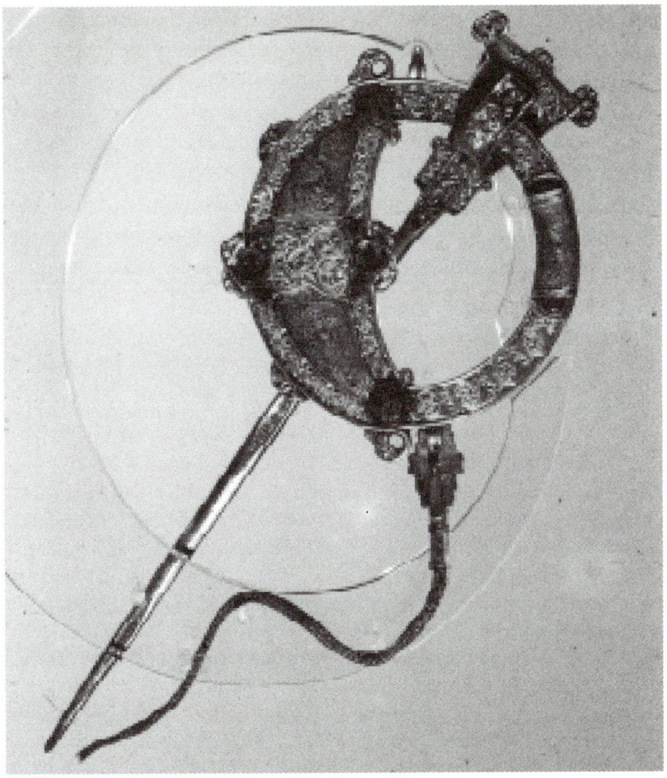

The "Tara brooch", 8th c. Dublin, National Museum of Ireland.

(the *Poimandres*), which his benefactor had asked him for and which, published in 1471 and again in 1472, was to enjoy wide circulation (for Ficino, this work expressed the "old theology" from which Platonism derived!). He also undertook to translate Plato's dialogues – which he completed before 1469. It was the first complete translation of the Greek philosopher's work (published in 1484). Among other things, Ficino wrote two great works expressing his own philosophical thought: the *Commentary on Plato's Symposium* (1469), and the *Theologia platonica* (1474; published in 1482). Consecrated a priest in 1473, he later became a *canon of Florence cathedral. In 1476 appeared his *De christiana religione*, in 1489 his *De vita*. In 1492 was published his translation of Plotinus's *Enneads* (begun after 1484); other translations of Neoplatonists appeared later. In 1495 he published his *letters (compiled from 1473). Closely linked to the *Medici (Piero, then Lorenzo de' Medici had succeeded Cosimo in their *patronage), he judged it best to leave Florence when the Florentine people expelled Piero II in 1494.

Impregnated with *Neoplatonism, Ficino's philosophy, which he himself presents as a revival of Platonism (but which was also fed from other sources), works out a complex discourse with a certain independence. His *cosmology asserts the unity of a hierarchized universe (in which the *soul occupies a central place between *God and the angelic *intellect above, and quality and the *body below), based on a continuity (permitted by the principle of mediation), and dynamic (thanks to the principle of affinity). The soul must proceed to an ascent to attain the *contemplation of God, end of human life. Exceptionally realized during earthly life, this contemplation takes place in *eternal life thanks to the *immortality of individual souls, defended throughout the *Platonic theology*. In the *Commentary on the Symposium*, Ficino also explains his conception of "Platonic love" which unites human beings by raising them up to the love of God. This identification between Platonic *love and Christian love rests on the certainty of a perfect harmony between Christianity and Platonism (true religion and true philosophy).

Leaning on his cosmology, Ficino develops in the third book of *De vita* the theory of a largely natural and astrological *magic, which constitutes a historic turning-point in this field.

A major figure of the philosophy and *humanism of the Florentine **Quattrocento*, famous in his lifetime even outside *Italy, Ficino had considerable influence on *Renaissance thought.

M. Ficino, *Opera Omnia*, Basel, 1576 (repr. Turin, 1959). – *The Letters of Marsilio Ficino*, London, 1975-1988 (4 vol. to date). – M. Ficino, *Sulla vita*, A. Tarabachia Canavero (intro., tr., notes and apparatus), Milan, 1995.

R. Marcel, *Marsile Ficin*, Paris, 1958. – D. P. Walker, *Spiritual and Demonic Magic from Ficino to Campanella*, London, 1958. – M. J. B. Allen, *The Platonism of Marsilio Ficino*, Berkeley, 1984. – *Ficino and Renaissance Neoplatonism*, K. Eisenbichler (ed.), O.Z. Pugliese (ed.), Ottawa, 1986. – *Marsilio Ficino e il ritorno di Platone*, G. C. Garfagnini (ed.), Florence, 1986 (bibliog.). – P. O. Kristeller, *Marsilio Ficino and his Work after Five Hundred Years*, Florence, 1987. – M. M. Bollard, "Marsilio Ficino and the Medici. The Inner Dimensions of Patronage", *Christianity and the Renaissance*, T. Verdon (ed.), J. Henderson (ed.), New York, 1990, 467-492. – P. Zambelli, *L'Ambigua natura della magia*, Milan, 1991. – U. Oehlig, *Die philosophische Begrundung der Kunst bei Ficino*, Stuttgart, 1992. – C. Vasoli, "Ficino, Marsilio", *DBI*, 47, 1997, 378-395 (bibl.). – *Marsile Ficin, 1499-1999 (Actes du XLIIe Colloque International d'Études Humanistes, 7-10 juillet 1999)*, S. Toussaint (dir.), forthcoming. – *Marsile Ficin et la doctrine des Anciens (Table ronde, Paris, École Supérieur, 29 novembre 1997 et 28 novembre 1998)*, 2 vol., S. Toussaint (ed.), P. Hoffmann (ed.), forthcoming.

Nicolas Weill-Parot

**FIEF.** The fief, a term of Germanic origin, designated a gift sanctioning the resumption of relations between clan groups after a conflict. It seems we must dissociate it from the term *feo*, present in the southern regions and which was perhaps of Roman origin. The fief was a gift that supposed a counterpart, hence it linked the donor and the recipient and constituted an element of social bonds. In the 11th c., the term "fief" seems to have supplanted that of "*benefice", employed since the *Carolingian period and designating the gift granted to a vassal.

The fief, important especially in north-western Europe and the kingdom of *Sicily, was most often a landed property to which were sometimes attached rights and revenues: it was a tenure. But, unlike the case of *peasant tenures, its holder did not have to pay taxes as counterpart to his enjoyment. The fief pertained to the aristocracy, but we also meet fiefs conceded to servants or specialized artisans (**ministeriales*). Save in the Mediterranean regions, the fief gradually became the principal object of vassalic relationships, the obtaining of a fief being one of the main causes for the conclusion of personal relationships. The ceremony of *investiture, which followed the *oath of *homage and fidelity, was accompanied by the handing over of objects symbolizing the land conceded and by the "*monstrée*" of the property. In the 12th c., the fief conceded was described in an act (avowal and enumeration). Finally, from the obtaining of the fief flowed the vassal's obligations of aid and counsel to his lord. The withdrawal of the fief, forfeiture, sanctioned the breaking of the personal bond following a *felony.

But between the late 9th and the 10th c. the fief tended to be considered by its holder as a patrimonial property, all the more since the practice of the "resumed fief" spread: this meant having a former patrimonial property conceded to oneself in fief in exchange for the lord's protection. In addition, the son kept the father's fief on condition of a new oath of homage and a right of relief levied by the lord. Inalienable, the fief was sometimes held by the heirs in co-lordship, a phenomenon present in the Mediterranean regions.

The importance of the circulation of fiefs in social relationships at every level of the aristocratic group nourished a reflection and a dense legal codification of customs from the 11th c. on; a veritable law of fiefs was established. The mentality that emerged from this type of exchange also impregnated ecclesiastical institutions in which the investiture of a *bishop, *e.g.*, was sometimes comparable to that of a *féal*. Finally, when the monetary economy regained its vigour in the 13th c., we see the development of the practice of the *fief-rente*, a sum of *money replacing the landed property conceded.

B. D. Lyon, *From Fief to Indenture. The Transition from Feudal to Non-feudal Contract in Western Europe*, Cambridge (MA), 1957. – G. Tabacco, "Fief et seigneurie dans l'Italie communale: l'évolution d'un thème historiographique", *MA*, 75, 1969, 5-32 and 203-234. – G. Fourquin, *Seigneurie et féodalité au Moyen Âge*, Paris, 1970. – G. Giordanengo, *Féodalité et droits savants dans le Midi médiéval*, London, 1992. – S. Reynolds, *Fiefs and Vassals*, Oxford, 1994.

Thierry Pécout

**Legal and historical evolution.** All historians agree that the fief was the institution *par excellence* of the Middle Ages, which characterised an epoch and whose traces lingered until the 18th century. An institution that structured medieval society, overturned and subverted to the core the very concept of the State as it had come down from the Roman world, and at the same time, through its intrinsic charge of legal custom, showed itself such as to remodel the fundamental fabric that would be at the basis of modern legal systems. It is also agreed that the fief was the culmination of a work of centuries, during which disparate elements of different origin met and fused, at the same time marking the decline of those original elements, their moment of involution, since they were accepted into the new at the price of their deformation and dissolution. So we should speak not so much of an institution as of a historical fact, which, because of its roots lost in time and because of the proportions of a phenomenon that gave life and a name to a society and an era, does not lend itself to easy definition. "The fief was truly the greatest customary creation of the Middle Ages: to contemplate its essential historical formation, rapidly fixing the reasons that led it to dominate the legal life of those centuries, may help us understand the spirit of the times as well as those profound transformations that were occurring in the concept of the State and the system of the sources of law and that the following period would inherit in full" (F. Calasso). For one thing, this custom was not limited, as might be expected from its definition, to the sphere of private laws but – perhaps partly under the influence of the advancing conception of the Germanic view of the State and of law – concerned the sphere of public law. We will briefly analyse the elements that came together to form the fief. Substantially, it resulted "from the conjunction of a personal relationship, *vassalage, with a real basis, the *benefice; a union supplemented by a third element of negative character, *immunity", three institutions of very different origin.

Vassalage was of German derivation and is mentioned by Caesar (*De bello Gallico*, VI, 25) and more clearly by Tacitus (*Germania*, 13-14). It provided for the voluntary subjection of an adolescent capable of bearing arms to a prince, to whom he swore loyalty and devoted every work in peace and in war – while keeping his freedom intact – in exchange for the prince's formal obligation to provide him with weapons and maintenance. In the 8th c., among the *Franks, this custom would be designated by the term *vassaticum*; it immediately became so widespread that it attracted the attention of the ruler, anxious to ensure that such a relationship, entered into among his subjects, should never be detrimental to the State. Hence the ruler himself made abundant use of it, using it as a chosen instrument to bind the great men of the Kingdom to him with a double chain – subjecthood and *vassaticum*.

At the same time, vassalage took on more definite legal outlines as a genuine bilateral contract: on one hand the lord (*senior*), who promised defence and maintenance; on the other the vassal (*vassum*), who promised loyalty and services. The ritual that presided at the contract was called *commendatio*: the *vassus*, on his knees, put his hands between the hands of the *senior* (*districtio*) and, by swearing loyalty (*homagium*), became his *homo* (*fidelis*). As in all bilateral contracts, there were two essential elements: the personal one, *vassaticum*, and the real one constituted by the *beneficium*. The singular kind of real right resulting from these two elements was called by a name of Gothic derivation, *feudum*.

The third element, which "perfected the feudal relationship as a negation of the authority of the State" (Calasso), was immunity. Together with the fact that feudal relationships were also formed between the ruler and people charged with public services, so that these no longer appeared as an emanation of public power but as a prerogative of the feudal relationship itself, it was the element of immunity that began and accelerated the degeneration and ultimate decline of the State.

Even during the Roman Empire there had been *immunes*, those exempt from *munera personalia et patrimonalia*: imperial properties and privileged categories of person immune from fiscal and personal burdens. In the 4th and 5th cc., these exemptions, by concession and still more by abuse, led to the proprietors of immune lands exercising within their borders those public powers of policing, finance and jurisdiction that otherwise belonged to the officials of the State. One consequence was that, when such lands were broken up to be granted in benefice, especially in the Carolingian period, the privilege of *immunitas* was consolidated, together with the related exercise of sovereign rights and the prohibition of *introitus*, *exactio* and *districtio*, *i.e.* entering, levying taxes and executing sentence. Thus "between ruler and subjects was interposed the barrier of the feudatory, imposing obligations on the inhabitants of his territory not as the holder of related public powers, but simply as feudal possessor of that territory".

This contamination of the two great branches of law that Rome had clearly distinguished – public law and private law – was the most typical characteristic of the feudal State. But the connotations of the fief were not always and everywhere the same. Firstly, benefices, though not originally hereditary, became so with the *Edictum de beneficiis* issued by Conrad the Salian in 1037, which also gave minor vassals the privilege of being judged by a *court of their peers. Then, the rise of *customs, partly for lack of laws, was particularly striking in this period. And it is obvious that political and economic particularism would generate legal particularism. "Moreover, in the feudal material, alongside general customs, particular customs were created, marking profound differences between fief and fief. In *e.g.* *Italy, the different conditions of environment and tradition meant that the fief, imported from France, differed in vital points from what it had been in its land of origin. For one thing, while the Frankish fief was indivisible and inalienable, the Italian fief (usually called Lombard) was divisible in accordance with the rules that governed any other kind of patrimony and could be totally or partially alienated, with or without the consent of the *senior*". This was because, in crossing over to Italy, the fief had lost its political connotation and appeared solely as an economic form.

The period of the fief's greatest flowering in Italy – the 11th and 12th cc. – was also that of the greatest development of customary law: not that "this law arose then for the first time, but more in the sense that only in this singular historical period did those conditions mature that could allow custom to prevail over law: primarily, the progressive disintegration of the State". From Liutprand to *Charlemagne, to *Pippin and the *Capitulare Italicum*, to *Isidore of Seville's *Etymologies*, there were numerous confirmations of what has been said above: "the roots of the phenomenon of custom were by now too deep for the will of the legislator to imagine he could prune them at his pleasure". Meanwhile the Carolingian Empire was falling to pieces and all the anti-State forces were exploding, and the imperial laws, ever less frequent, were in no state to follow a movement of exorbitant breadth.

R. Schröder von Künssberg, *Lehrbuch der deutschen Rechtsgeschichte*, Berlin-Leipzig, 1932, 339, note 207. – E. Besta, *Storia del diritto italiano. Il diritto pubblico*, 2, Milan, 1945, 31 f. – F. Calasso, *Medioevo del diritto*, 1, *Le fonti*, Milan, 1954, 188-197. – F. Calasso, *Gli ordinamenti giuridici del Rinascimentale medievale*, Milan, 1965, 72 f. (2nd ed.). – G. Tabacco, *Egemonie sociali e strutture del potere nel Medioevo italiano*, Turin, 1979. – F. Ganshof, *Qu'est-ce que la feodalité?*, Paris, 1982 (5th ed.). – L. Gatto, *Il Feudalismo*, Rome, 1997, 47-59.

Attilio Stendardi

**FIESCHI.** Of the stock of the counts of Lavagna, whose founder was probably a Ugus Fliscus mentioned in the second half of the 12th c., the Fieschi family of *Genoa, initially imperial supporters and then strenuously *Guelf, played an important role in the city's agitated political life and had a special importance in the history of the Church. To it belonged a great number of *bishops and *cardinals and the ascetic and mystic *Catherine of Genoa (1447-1510), as well as Ottobono Fieschi, who became *pope in 1276 with the name of Adrian V, and Sinibaldo, an eminent *jurist, cardinal and then pope (1243) under the name of *Innocent IV.

A. Sisto, *Genova nel duecento. Il capitolo di San Lorenzo*, Genoa, 1917 (9th ed.).

Franco Franceschi

**FILELFO, FRANCESCO (1398-1481).** The Italian *humanist Francesco Filelfo played an important role in the preservation and promotion of Greek culture in *Italy. Living at *Constantinople from 1420 to 1427, he learned Greek at the same time as holding official positions with the Venetian *baylo* and then with the Byzantine emperor. Back in Italy, he divided his time between teaching, writing and translating Greek authors like *Aristotle, Xenophon and Plutarch. Passionately fond of *philosophy, he took part in the debates between *Platonists and *Aristotelians, taking, with *Bessarion, the side of reconciliation.

*Francesco Filelfo nel Quinto Centenario della morte, Medioevo e Umanesimo*, 58, Padua, 1986. – *Dictionnaire des auteurs grecs et latins au Moyen Âge*, Turnhout, 1991, 664-665. – D. Robin, *Filelfo in Milan: writings 1451-1477*, Princeton (NJ), 1991.

Claudine Delacroix-Besnier

*Canterbury Psalter*, 13th c. Paris, BNF (Ms lat. 770, fol. 142).

**FILIOQUE**

**Theology.** Over the expression *Filioque*, which refers to an addition made to the *Creed of Nicaea-Constantinople of 381, designating the procession of the *Holy Spirit from the Father and the Son, a controversy developed from the 9th c. between the Greek and Latin Churches. The quarrel was both about the content of the doctrine and the legitimacy of adding to the creed.

The doctrine of the *Filioque*, later so controversial, is attested from the 4th c. (Ambrose, *De spiritu sancto*; Augustine, *De Trinitate*; *Fides Damasi*). In the East, there were divergent opinions between *Antioch and *Alexandria. Patriarch Cyril of Alexandria was accused by his opponents of having defended the *Filioque*. At *Rome, Pope Martin I included the formula in a synodal letter addressed to *Constantinople in 649, when *Maximus Confessor tried to calm the emotions aroused (*Ep. ad Marinum*). In Gaul and *Spain, the *Filioque* was included from the 4th and 5th cc. in different *regulae fidei*, intended to oppose the Priscillianist and *Arian errors. At the second council of *Nicaea in 787, the Ecumenical Patriarch Tarasius spoke of the procession of the Spirit "from the Father through the Son", which earned him a stinging reply in the **Libri Carolini* and at the synod of *Frankfurt in 794. After *Charlemagne's integration of the creed including the addition of the *Filioque* into the liturgy, it was propagated, by the intermediary of Latin monks, as far as *Jerusalem (807). Because of the opposition of the Greeks, in 809 the Latins put the matter in the hands of Pope *Leo III, who approved the doctrine of the *Filioque* while contesting its introduction into the creed. For this reason, he set up opposite St Peter's *confessio* at Rome two silver steles reproducing in Latin and Greek the text of the old creed without the *Filioque*. The *Filioque* was introduced to Rome by Pope Benedict VIII only in 1013 at the request of the Emperor *Henry II.

From 867, the addition and the very doctrine of the *Filioque* was for *Photius the main grievance against the Church of Rome. Since then, the Greek Church has considered the *Filioque* the main cause of the *schism of 1054. At the second council of *Lyon in 1274, three delegates of the Byzantine Emperor Michael VIII sung the creed with the *Filioque*, an attitude that was very controversial at Constantinople. Later, *John XI Beccus, *patriarch of Constantinople, at first imprisoned for his opposition to the *Filioque*, recognised, by studying the *Fathers in his detention, the legitimacy of the addition and from then on defended the agreement of Lyon against its opponents. His successor and opponent Gregory II attempted a formulation reconciling the temporal sphere and the eternal sphere, but full of contradictions. The reconsideration of the Latin position begun by Gregory and Beccus, which had met a favourable echo in the pro-Latin minority at Byzantium, reached fulfilment at the council of Ferrara-*Florence in 1439 (*Laetentur caeli*), which recognised the equality of the formulae "from" (the Son) and "through" (the Son), on condition that the unity of the principle of origin and of exteriorization (insufflation) was guaranteed. Even this formulation found only a very momentary and mitigated welcome at Constantinople. After the fall of Constantinople in 1453, a local *synod put an end to the *union in 1484. Setting aside a few rare attempts at mediation, as *e.g.* that of Maximus Margunios, there has been no further change of position.

Since Florence, the Greeks (Mark Eugenicus) had insistently recalled a provision of the council of Ephesus of 431 stipulating that no-one could profess a "different faith" from that of the council of Nicaea. There was room for discussion whether "faith" and "creed" could be treated purely and simply as synonyms. In fact, even after Ephesus, Greek patristics remained open to the *Filioque*.

A. Palmieri, *DThC*, 5, 1924, 2309-2343. – L. Lohn, *Graecorum et Russorum de proc. Spiritus S. a solo Patre, pars I: Photii temporibus*, Rome, 1934. – M. Jugie, "Origines de la controverse sur l'addition du 'Filioque' au Symbole", *RSPhTh*, 28, 1939, 369-385. – V. Grumel, "Photius et l'addition du Filioque au Symbole de Nicée-Constantinople", *REByz*, 5, 1947, 218-234. – M. J. Le Guillou, *Cath*, 4, 1956, 1279-1286. – J. Gill, *NCE*, 5, 1967, 913 f. – A. Papadakis, *Crisis in Byzantium: The "Filioque" Controversy in the Patriarchate of Gregory II of Cyprus*, New York, 1983; cf. B. Schultze, *OrChrP*, 51, 1985, 163-187. – J.-M. Garrigues, "A la suite de la clarification romaine: le Filioque affranchi du 'filioquisme'", *Irén.*, 69, 1996, 189-212.

Gerhard Podskalsky

**Iconography.** Following St John, St Hilary and St Augustine, the Latin expression *filioque* signifies that the third *person of the *Trinity proceeds "from the Father *and the son*" as from a single principle. The addition of this formula to the *Creed of Nicaea-Constantinople, decided by the council of *Braga (675) and welcomed in Gaul under *Charlemagne, was accepted by the Roman Church in 1013 and became an apple of discord between *Rome and Byzantium.

From the 12th c., *i.e.* at the time when an iconography of the Trinity was becoming established in the West, numerous depictions (Throne of grace, Trinity of the psalter, Coronation of the Virgin) gave particular attention to translating visually this element of doctrine, particularly by representing the *Holy Spirit in the form of a dove situated between the Father and the Son, whose wings joined the faces (Lothian Bible, *c.*1220; Tennenbacher Güterbuch, first half of 14th c.) or, more often, the centre of the respective mouths of the first two persons (miniature of the Cambrai Missal, *c.*1120); sometimes the dove was inside a *mandorla held by Father and Son (Canterbury Psalter, *c.*1210), or the Holy Spirit, depicted as a young man, rose up between the hands of the Father and the Son (Urschalling *fresco, 14th c.). Another pictorial echo of this doctrine was offered by certain *images of *Pentecost, notably in the 15th c.: they show the Father and the Son conjointly sending forth the Spirit on the disciples ("missions", theologians say, "reflect processions").

F. Boespflug, Y. Zaluska, "Le Dogme trinitaire et l'essor de son iconographie en Occident, de l'époque carolingienne au concile de Latran IV (1215)", *CCM*, 3, 1994.

François Boespflug

***FILLES-DIEU.*** This name was given to *women brought into semi-religious communities by *clerics or laymen, who appeared in the northern half of France around 1230. Some were undoubtedly reformed *prostitutes, but for others this has not been demonstrated.

The first of the 15 recorded communities was created in 1226 in *Paris by *William of Auvergne for the prostitutes whom the future *bishop had converted by his *preaching. It resembled a *hospice more than a religious congregation: its inmates took no *vows and were free to leave and get married. From 1346, only irreproachable women could enter, to be replaced in 1495 by *nuns from *Fontevraud.

Most of the communities of *Champagne, like that of Mont-Notre-Dame at Provins (before 1236), Notre-Dame-des-Prés at *Troyes (*c.*1230), la Piété-Notre-Dame-lès-Ramerupt near Arcis-sur-Aube (1229) and Val-des-Vignes at Ailleville near Bar-sur-Aube (*c.*1230), quickly adopted the *Cistercian constitutions and, while admitting that they had previously accepted penitent women, ceased to do so from then on. The Filles-Dieu of Saint-Martin-ès-Vignes at Troyes (before 1301), perhaps like those of *Reims (before 1249), were **repenties*. The presence at Troyes of two communities created at different times can be explained by the need to procure, in the second, an asylum for the *penitents now excluded from the first.

*Tournai also had two communities. Founded around 1230 for penitents by Bishop Gautier de Marvis, the Filles-Dieu of Les Prés-Porcins were replaced in 1234 by *nuns from Haspres. In 1336, a citizen founded a second community for fallen women at the Quai Taille-Pierres, which soon adopted the Rule of St *Augustine, as did the Filles-Dieu of *Arras (*c.*1228) and *Rouen (before 1246). We do not know if these last two were created for penitents. The Augustinians of Arras reappeared after the Revolution and in 1819 established themselves in the Rue Pasteur, where they still are today.

The Filles-Dieu of *Chartres (*c.*1232) probably stopped accepting *repenties* from the mid 13th c., unlike those of *Le Mans (before 1256), who, like them, professed the Rule of St Augustine, but remained faithful to their first vocation until the 15th century. Those of *Orléans (before 1235) adopted the *Cistercian constitutions and modified their recruitment before being transferred in 1249 to the *priory of Saint-Loup. We know practically nothing of the Filles-Dieu of *Tours or Angers (before 1230).

The initiative for the foundation of these communities was not taken by a single person, nor even determined by the concerted will of several. However, there is practically no doubt that the example given at Paris by William of Auvergne led to their creation.

F. Chaube, "Les Filles-Dieu de Rouen aux XIII$^{e}$-XV$^{e}$ siècles. Étude du processus de régularisation d'une communauté religieuse", *RMab*, new series, 1, 1990, 205-211.

Fabienne Chaube

**FINAL ENDS.** The notion of final ends was defined in the Middle Ages. Undoubtedly the patristic period had a *millenarian tendency (a tendency later widely reinforced around the year 1000), but it saw life's ultimate horizon mainly in the *resurrection. The medievals did the same: however, they developed various apocalyptic doctrines and, after the various natural catastrophes they suffered – *Black Death (1348-1351), *Great Schism, etc. – which were so many sources of anguish for them, they were interested mainly in *eschatology, the last things, of which they put forward a symbolic interpretation while still seeking to give them conceptual expression. How could they do otherwise when the reality they strove to define escaped experience and referred them to the final horizon of life? By the symbolism of *Judgment used in their *preaching and iconography, they evoked the last things, though usually with an *apologetic aim. In the *Divine Comedy*, *Dante sums up the various representations of the last things, thus showing the importance they had in the popular mind.

Meanwhile, the treatise on eschatology in *Peter Lombard's **Sentences* formulated the question theologically. Widely commented on, this treatise gave rise to various interpretations before the solution given by *Thomas Aquinas in the *Summa theologiae* (I$^{a}$ II$^{ae}$, q. 1-5). The notion of "*end" had a precise connotation. It came from *Aristotle and referred to teleology. It was thematized after the rediscovery of Aristotle, in order to give eschatology a conceptual form. St Thomas played an important role in this conceptualization with his treatise on the final end, the shortest but perhaps the most important in the *Summa theologiae*, in that it commands the whole of the *Secunda Pars*. In this treatise, St Thomas explains the criteria to which the final end must respond: "A man must take as final end", he writes, "what he desires as the perfect *good and as completion of his being . . . . Hence the final end must so fulfil all man's desire that nothing remains to be desired outside it, which cannot be the case if something extraneous to its perfection is still required" (*Summa theologiae*, I$^{a}$ II$^{ae}$, q. 1, a. 5). The final end that fulfils the deepest desire of the human being is none other than *beatitude (a. 7-8).

It may appear astonishing that St Thomas reduces final ends to a single one: beatitude. In fact, he tries to show by this that beatitude is the fulfilment of the human being, since it is synonymous with the vision of *God (q. 3, a. 8) and implies union with God. Several realities are hence comprised in beatitude. Moreover, beatitude shows by itself that the final end of the created being is God. Thus the solution provided by St Thomas and then by *Benedict XII's Constitution *Benedictus Deus* takes into account the other final ends.

J. G. Bougerol, *La Théologie de l'espérance aux XII$^{e}$ et XIII$^{e}$ siècles*, Paris, 1985 (2 vol.). – A. Vauchez, *The Spirituality of the Medieval West*, Kalamazoo (MI), 1993.

Marie-Anne Vannier

**FINLAND.** Finland's geographical situation, at the meeting-place of influences from West and East, was decisive for the evolution of this region from the Middle Ages. At this time, sedentary occupation still affected only the Åland archipelago and the coastal and southern zones, which passed progressively under the control of *Sweden between the 11th and early 14th centuries. Originally, the term "Finland" designated only the south-west of the country (modern Varsinais Suomi or Finland proper). This region's connections with Sweden were ancient. The toponym is attested by Swedish *runic inscriptions, notably those of Söderby Karl (Roslagen, early 11th c.) or the church of Rute (*Gotland, 12th-13th c.). Around the year 1000, however, the population appears concentrated into three areas of settlement: the south-west (regions of the Eura and Åbo/Turku), the interior (around lake Päijänne) and, further east, Karelia which extended as far as Lake Ladoga. In the 14th and 15th cc., the whole area, then integrated into the kingdom of Sweden, was called *Finlandia et partes orientales* or *Österland*. The *Scandinavians called the interior the land of the Tavasts. Mentioned in the 11th c. by a *runic inscription of Gästrikland, Tavastland was, according to Russian sources, inhabited by the Jemi (corresponding to the modern name Häme). The rest of the territory was traversed by nomads, essentially Lapps or Samelats whom Norse texts call *finnar* (whence the term Finmark to characterise the north of the Finno-Scandinavian peninsula). *Saxo Grammaticus (*c.*1200) was the first to use the word *Lappia*. The Finns (*suomalaiset*) penetrated into Finland around the beginning of the Christian era, crossing either the isthmus of Karelia or the gulf of Finland. These populations of Finno-Ugrian tongue came into contact, at the latest during the period of the great *invasions, with a Scandinavian rural colonization settled in the west of the country, as is shown by linguistic borrowings of Finnish from common Germanic.

Little is known of the organisation of the Finns before Christianization. Toponymy attests that there were sacred places (*hiisi*) and farms larger than others (*Moisio*). But excavations of necropolises seem to indicate that social differentiations were relatively little marked. Yet tradition has preserved the memory of local chiefs (Kullervo, Väinämöinen in the *epic poem *Kalevala*) or even "kings" (Faravid in *Egilssaga*). The Finns possessed war-fleets and fortified villages like those of Rapalo (in Tavastland/Häme) or Vanhalinna (near Åbo), which suggests the existence of a centralized power, at least at regional level. Archaeologists have ascertained that currents of exchange were established at an early date between Finland and its neighbours: Swedes, Russians and *Balts. During the *Viking period, the Swedes got into the habit of sending military or commercial expeditions into Finland, and *merchants from central Sweden or Gotland hugged the country's southern coasts as far as the Neva, before reaching the counters of Russia. In the 11th c., the kings of Sweden sought to impose tribute on the coastal zones, the first step of their policy of conquest. This Swedish expansion eastward went hand in hand with the progress of *conversion, whose outlines can be followed thanks to *archaeology. The *pagan practice of funerary offerings disappears from the end of the 11th c. at Åland, then ceases in the 12th c. in the region of the Eura and later around Åbo. In the interior, it was kept up in the 13th c. and, in Karelia, into the 14th. The *evangelization of Finland was the result of many interventions: Russian, English, German and Scandinavian missionaries crossed tracks there. Finland was the object of a struggle of influences between the Latin Church and the Eastern Church, but the first milestones of Christianity came from the east: the Greco-Russian origin of part of the liturgical vocabulary testifies to *Orthodox penetration. Thus the Finnish words *risti* (*cross) and *kummi* (godfather) come from Russian *krest* and *kum*, and *Raamatu* (*Bible) is derived from Greek *grammata*.

In the mid 12th c., the Swedes organised a series of operations against Finland (1142, 1156?, 1164). A bishop of *Uppsala of English origin, St Henrik, accompanied one of these (abusively presented as a "crusade"), directed by King St *Erik, in the south-west of Finland. The legend of the saint-bishop tells that Henrik found *martyrdom in Finland, killed by a Finn named Lalli. St Henrik was buried at Nousis. Between 1171 and 1237, several papal *bulls and Russian sources show that *Novgorod also waged an active policy to control Finland. The Roman Church denounced "the enemies of the *Cross" (*i.e.* the *Orthodox Russians). In 1198, Åbo was destroyed by the Russians, and the *Catholic bishop of Finland, Folkvin, had to flee. In 1237, Prince Iaroslav of Novgorod invaded the country and carried out massive baptisms in Häme. In 1216, however, the papacy had recognised Swedish sovereignty over Finland, and in the 13th c. the Swedes struck a blow at Russian expansion. Some years before, the Danes had tried in turn to set foot in Finland: in 1202 Andreas Sunesen, archbishop of *Lund, led an expedition in the south of the country and even received papal authorization to consecrate *bishops for Finland (1209). Danish rule was short-lived. Around 1240, the Swedish Duke Birger Jarl directed a "second crusade" which ended in the annexation of Tavastland/Häme. Control of this region was completed by the building of a *castle (Tavastehus/Hämeenlinna). At the end of the 13th c., Torgils Knutsson, marshal of Sweden, undertook a "third crusade" that permitted the conquest of Karelia (1293-1300) and the building of the stronghold of Viborg. Around 1300, the Swedes erected an outpost on the Neva (Landskrona) but it was taken by the Russians in the following year. In 1323, Sweden and the principality of Novgorod divided Karelia by the peace of Nöteborg (Pähkinäsaari). This ensured Sweden strategic control of the Karelian isthmus between the gulf of Finland and

Lake Ladoga. From then on, the boundary between Latin and Greek Christianity was fixed at Finland, which was permanently attached to the Western cultural sphere. But the frontier was not clearly established in the still hardly-inhabited north. The Swedes waged a new campaign against the Russians in Karelia (1348-1350), then peace reigned for about a century.

The *Dominicans played a preponderant role in the religious organisation of the country, accomplished in the course of the 13th century. The energetic Bishop Thomas (who opposed *Alexander Nevsky in 1240) was a Dominican who retired in 1245 to the convent of Visby. One of his successors, Johannes, also belonged to the Order of St Dominic (he died archbishop of *Uppsala in 1291). Finland formed a single *diocese, dependent from *c.*1220 on the archbishopric of Uppsala. Installed originally at Räntämäki or at Nousis, the episcopal see was later moved to Korois, then in the late 13th c. to Åbo. Until 1286, the bishops were buried at Räntämäki. At first called *episcopus Finlandensis*, they took the title of *episcopus Aboensis* from 1270. A cathedral *chapter was set up around 1275. In the Middle Ages the bishopric of Åbo had 125 *parishes. Many of them were created on the basis of the territorial divisions the Swedes had found at the time of the conquest: the Finnish word *pitäjä*, which means "parish", is derived from a root referring to the right of lodging. The Dominicans were also the first to settle in Finland. A Dominican *convent existed at Åbo from 1249, another was created at Viborg in Karelia (1392). In the 15th c., the *Franciscans also settled at Viborg (1403), at Raumo (1449) and at Kökar in the Åland archipelago (1472). In 1438, the council of the realm decided to found a monastery of the Order of St *Bridget in Finland, despite the resistance of the bishop of Åbo who feared competition for the revenues of his *cathedral. It was inaugurated at Nådendal/Naantali (*Vallis gracie*) in 1462.

Politically, Finland was integrated into Sweden and assimilated to a province of the kingdom. From the end of the 13th c., the habit grew up of considering the country an appanage, given to a member of the royal family who received the title of *dux Finlandie*. The first was Bengt, brother of King Magnus Ladulås. The administration was entrusted to governors. Called *advocatus* or *prefectus Finlandie* (the earliest is cited in 1278), they lived at Åbo, Tavastehus or Viborg. The country's defence was ensured by a network of fortresses: as well as Kustö (near Åbo) which belonged to the bishop, Åbohus and Tavastehus were built in the second half of the 13th c. and Viborg in 1293. In the 14th c. appeared Raseborg (Nyland) and Korsholm (Ostrobothnia), and in 1475 Olofsborg/Olavinlinna on the eastern frontier. Their guard was entrusted to a *capitaneus*. At Åland, a royal agent resided in the castle of Kastelholm (mentioned in 1388 but going back to the 13th c.). New administrative entities, detached from Tavastland, appeared after the conquest: Savolax (Savo) in 1323), Nyland (Uusimaa) in 1326, Satakunta in 1331, Ostrobothnia. In 1347, Swedish law was introduced into Finland, but legal particularism continued to exist. Indeed various customs existed in Finland in the Middle Ages: we hear of *jus helsingonicum* (the law that applied in the north of the kingdom) and in the 14th c. there was a "*legifer parcium orientalium iuris finnonici*", which indicates that a specific local law was recognised. In 1362, the king granted Finland the right to participate in the royal election, like all the other provinces.

In the late Middle Ages, notably during the period of the Union (1389-1523), Finland enjoyed considerable autonomy and played an important role in the affairs of Sweden. Those who opposed the Danish kings of the Union made it a base of resistance. In 1434, an insurrection against King Erik of Pomerania shook Finland. The possession, as *fiefs, of Finnish citadels – especially Viborg – was a decisive trump card in the struggles for power in the 15th century. It became an additional advantage when hostilities resumed against the Russians (1363-1504): thus the prestige of Sten Sture the Elder, regent of Sweden, was raised by his victory over the Muscovites in Karelia. In 1521, Finland rallied to the revolt of Gustavus Vasa against the Danes. These were expelled from Finland in 1523. From 1520, the Reformation was preached by a *canon of Åbo, Peter Särkilahti, a former pupil of Luther, and Bishop Mikael Agricola († 1557) translated the New Testament into Finnish (1548), making him the father of the written Finnish language.

In medieval Finland, the land remained essentially in the hands of the free *peasantry. The *nobility was numerically weak and mainly of foreign origin (Swedes and Germans). It was concentrated in the southern part of the country, and certain regions, such as Ostrobothnia, had no nobles at all. A middle nobility (*knapadel*) was created in the frontier marches: of native origin and enjoying fiscal privileges in exchange for defence service, it was contested in the 15th and 16th cc. by the "true" Swedish aristocracy. The distribution of the population and the difficult climatic conditions limited the extension of agriculture. In western Finland, cereals were cultivated (barley, rye, oats, but the sown areas were not large). Elsewhere agriculture was practised on patches of burnt land. On the Church estates, tenants possessed on average two oxen, two to six cows, two to ten sheep. *Hunting and fishing were essential economic activities. The most favoured region seems to have been the Åland archipelago: the construction of eleven churches on this little territory gives an idea of the wealth of its rural communities.

From the Viking age, Åland had been a hub of long-distance *commerce; during the Middle Ages, enterprising merchant-peasants (like Peter Ålänning in the late 14th c.) plied their ships to Stockholm and Reval. Other *merchants, the *Birkarlar*, criss-crossed the north of Finland from the coasts of the gulf of Bothnia. By royal privilege, they held the monopoly of trade and the right to levy tribute on the Lapps, at least from the end of the 13th century. Their trade was in *furs (beaver, marten, reindeer) which they bartered for cloth, *salt and butter. A few urban centres developed in Finland in the Middle Ages. Two may be considered towns: in the west Åbo/Turku, the episcopal city, and Viborg, administrative centre of the military march of Karelia, whose commercial activity grew in the 15th century. By contrast, Ulfby, Borgå/Porvoo, Raumo and Nådendal/Naantali remained insignificant. The presence of German merchants was decisive for the creation of these urban establishments. But German influence, very strong in Finland in the 14th c., was not generally exercised directly, but through the intermediary of the *ports of Visby, Stockholm and Reval.

E. Kivikoski, *Finland*, London, 1967. – J. Gallén, "Nöteborgsfreden och Finlands medeltida östgräns", *Skrifter utg. av Litteratursällskapet i Finland*, 427, Helsinki, 1968-1991. – E. Anthoni, *Finlands medeltida frälse och 1500-tals adel*, Helsinki, 1970. – S. Suvanto, "Medieval Studies in Finland: a Survey", *Scandinavian Journal of History*, 4, 1979, 287-304. – E. Orrman, "The Progress of Settlement in Finland during the Late Middle Ages", *Scandinavian Economic History Review*, 1981, 129-43. – *Suomen historia*, Y. Blomstedt (ed.), 2, Espoo, 1985. – H. Edgren, *Mercy and Justice: miracles of the Virgin Mary in Finnish Medieval Wall-Paintings*, Helsinki, 1993.

Jean-Marie Maillefer

***FIQH.*** The primary meaning of the Arabic word *fiqh* is: "knowledge", "understanding of". It also became the technical term designating jurisprudence, the science of Muslim law. While Muslim law (**sharī'a*) is the immutable, all-inclusive, transcendent divine law, *fiqh* is the understanding of that law that jurists (*faqīh*, plural *fuqahā*) acquire by "pious" study. It includes not just stipulations regulating ritual and religious practices (*ibādat*, including rules on ritual purity, menstruation, etc.), but also provisions concerning social life or *muāmalāt* (marriage, repudiation, family law, inheritance, law of property, contracts and obligations), political law, the laws of war – in a word, all aspects of public and private life. It divides human acts into five categories: obligatory, recommended, indifferent, disapproved and forbidden.

Since this understanding of divine law, as formulated by the jurists, governs the daily life of Muslims, the *fiqh* can be considered a law on its own. As such, it is the closest thing to positive law that Muslim tradition has provided. The need to distinguish between divine law, which by its essence cannot be derived from anything else, and human understanding of that law appears in cases where the jurists differ as to the rules.

The various stipulations must have a methodical basis derived from the sources of positive law (*usūl al-fiqh*). According to classical *Sunni doctrine, there are four sources of law: the *Koran, the **sunna* (the practice and declarations of the Prophet), the consensus of the community (*ijmā'*) and analogical reasoning (*qiyās*). The first three consist of texts or are included in texts; they are the source-material of positive law. By virtue of their inspired character, the Koran and the *sunna* (the latter handed down in the **hadīth* literature) have a particular status: they have been compiled into textual *corpus* classified as *nusūs* (plural of *nass*), *i.e.* "texts" containing precepts of law. Consensus, while not having the status of *nass*, is expressed by verbal formulations that have a textual character. It is preserved in the literature of Muslim jurisprudence. As for the fourth source, analogical deduction (*qiyās*), unlike the other three it is a method that consists in deriving from the texts legal rules that are not contained *expressis verbis*. *Qiyās* can be considered a "formal source" of law.

The jurist who established the theory of the four sources was al-Shāfi'ī († 820), though the movement of theorization was already under way before him. J. Schacht has shown that al-Shāfi'ī was seeking in this way to find a solution to the debate that existed between two movements that were disputing the supremacy over Muslim law. The first was represented by the "old schools of law" established in the first Muslim metropolises, notably Kūfa and *Medina. These had a tendency to identify the *sunna* of the Prophet with the consensus of the jurists. In reaction to this, the second movement, represented by the partisans of the *hadīth*, professed that the *sunna* of the Prophet was found in the express declarations of *Muḥammad and in his acts. So they distinguished absolutely between the *sunna* of the Prophet and the consensus of the legists. Al-Shafi'ī felt closer to the second current, but as an expert jurist he also knew that a legal edifice worthy of the name could not be content with a simple adherence to texts (the traditions of the Prophet and his companions) if it was to respond to the needs of a historical community. So he affirmed the validity of the analogical deduction practised by the old schools of law, though the jurists of this current mainly practised personal judgment (*ray*). He also firmly distinguished between analogical deduction and the personal judgment of the legists, which the old schools of law had authorized in certain cases. He excluded personal judgment and the consensus of the jurists, replacing the latter by the general consensus of the Muslim community. With him, the principles of law thus became: the Koran, the *sunna* of the Prophet (understood here as represented in the formal traditions held to go back to Muḥammad), the consensus of the community and analogical decision on the basis of one of the previous three sources.

By his insistence on the formal traditions, al-Shafi'ī gave Muslim law a heavily textual basis that it had not been obliged to have before. This evolution corresponded historically more or less to the transition from the oral to the written, from local and still very customary laws to a greater "Islamization" of the law. It was in this same period, that of the birth of the "imperial moment" of *Islam, that other branches of knowledge were codified, including literature and poetry, where the canons of taste were fixed. As for Muslim tradition, it considered its law as having proceeded directly from the Prophet and his companions. It was a classic spectacle, each human group readily describing itself, in the imagery it produced, as proceeding in a direct line from the constitution allegedly established by its founder or its fathers. Some researchers like H. Motzki have recently questioned Schacht's theory, placing the birth of Muslim law at an earlier date, though without wholly espousing the views of Muslim tradition.

During the 9th c., the old schools, which were essentially regional, gave way to schools of law (*madhhab*, plural *madhhāhib*, sometimes translated "rites") whose name was derived from authoritative jurists whom they considered their founders. The school of Abū Ḥanīfa († 767), the Hanifites, came mainly from Kūfa; that of Mālik Ibn Anas († 795), the Mālikites, from Medina. At the beginning of the 10th c., there were seven schools. Four still exist among the Sunnis: the two just named, the Shāfi'ite school and the Hanbalite school (following Ibn Hanbal, d. 855). The differences between these four schools on the theory of law are to do with its "supplementary principles", notably two of them: "preference" (*istihsān*, or discretionary opinion as distinct from strict analogy) and "consideration of common interest" (*istilāh*). The former, recognised by the Hanifite school, allows the jurist to prefer to a rule analogically deduced from a text another rule which is less obvious but which, in his opinion, allows a more equitable solution to be found for the case in question. The latter, which originated among the Malikites, but was accepted by the Shafi'ites and Hanbalites, allows the jurist to formulate a rule in terms of the common good.

The Shi'ite theory of law, notably that of the twelvers (or imamites), like that of a now-vanished Sunni school, the Zahirites, one of whose eminent representatives was the Andalusian theologian and jurist *Ibn Hazm († 1064), rejects analogical deduction. Yet the dominant current in twelver *Shi'ism (the *usūliyya*, literally "those who lean on the sources") considers *reason (*aql*) a fourth source. Some of these rational operations are mainly interpretative and depend on the texts; others are autonomous, *e.g.* the rational perception of good and evil, which came to them from the *Mu'tazilites but is totally rejected by the Sunnis. The other three sources are accepted by the Shi'ites, but with great differences. The *sunna* of the Prophet is extended to that of the infallible authority (*masūm*) of the *imāms, *i.e.* the first spiritual leaders of the community, descendants of *'Alī. As for the consensus of the community, it is reduced to being the mouthpiece of the doctrine of infallible authority written down in the Shi'ite collections of traditions. Between the period of the occultation (*ghayba*) of the twelfth imām (in 876) and that of his

*Flagellant brothers of the Fraternity of Santa Maria della Carità at Venice.* Gradual. Venice, Bibliotheca Marciana.

return, the community leans on the spiritual guidance of *mujtahid* (qualified jurists who apply their reasoning to the data of tradition). Shi'ite jurists, unlike the Sunnis, take their authority only from a single school of law, that of the "imāms and the Prophet"; it is called the Jafarite school.

J. Schacht, "Fiḳh", *EI(E)*, 2, 1965, 886-891. – G. H. Bousquet, *Le Droit musulman*, Paris, 1963. – J. Schacht, *Introduction to Islamic Law*, Oxford, 1982 (1st ed. 1964). – M. Muranyi, "Fiqh", *Grundriss der arabischen Philologie*, 2, Wiesbaden, 1987, 299-325. – B. G. Weiss, "Uṣūl al-fiqh", *EncRel(E)*, 15, 1987, 155-159. – N. Calder, *Studies in Early Muslim Jurisprudence*, Oxford, 1993. – W. B. Hallaq, *A History of Islamic Legal Theories: an Introduction to Sunni usul al-fiqh*, Cambridge, 1997. – C. Melchert, *The Formation of the Sunni Schools of Law*, Leiden, 1997.

Claude Gilliot

**FIRE, PENALTY OF.** It is well known that the greatest penalty reserved for medieval *heretics was the stake. The practice is old, and there is evidence of capital executions by fire from the 11th century. A value of just vengeance was attributed to the flames. The move from practice to legal formalization came with the anti-heretical legislation of *Frederick II, which laid down the stake for the heretic; but this had to be at the request of the Church authorities. In inquisitorial documents this request is expressed by the formulae *relinquere iudicio saeculari* or *animadversio debita*. The grave decision to subject heretics to the penalty of fire must be considered, on one hand, in the light of the tradition of intolerance that clerical culture had inherited from Antiquity, and on the other, as part of an attitude of the church hierarchy determined by requirements of a pastoral nature. Apart from its role as supreme punishment, the stake had a deterrent function: *metus mortis*, *timor penae* were to dissuade people from error and lead them to remain or return to the "unity of faith", the "true faith". Whence sometimes paradoxically tragic situations, as in the case of the *Waldensian Pietro di Martinengo (late 13th c.): already *semi combustus*, he had given signs of repentance; he was then taken out of the fire, cared for in vain and finally buried at the inquisitor's expense.

On the other hand, condemnation to the stake and execution by fire could produce effects quite different from the intentions of the Church hierarchy: if the condemned, by his firm and consistent behaviour, appeared a "martyr" or a "saint", this extreme and dramatic *torture could strike spectators as arbitrarily violent. In several places, uprisings and revolts ensued against the friars who ran the *Inquisition. The possibility of such rebellions did not escape those *clerics who at *Rome in 1155, condemned *Arnold of Brescia to the stake and decided to disperse his ashes in the Tiber to prevent a popular cult coming into being around the burned heretic's body.

J. Ficker, "Die gesetzliche Einführung der Todesstrafe für Ketzerei", *MIÖG*, 1, 1880, 177-226. – L. Paolini, "L'eresia catara alla fine del Duecento", *L'Eresia a Bologna fra XIII e XIV secolo*, 1, Rome, 1975. – G. G. Merlo, *Valdesi e valdismi medievali*, Turin, 1984, 86-92. – G. G. Merlo, *Contro gli eretici*, Bologna, 1996.

Grado G. Merlo

**FISHERMAN'S RING.** The use of a secret *seal is attested under *Clement IV in 1265. It is known by the name of *piscatoris anulus*, because it represents St *Peter casting a line from his boat. The oldest known imprint dates from 1390, associated with the first surviving *brief, and this little seal of red wax was always used for briefs.

A. Giry, *Manuel de diplomatique*, Paris, 1894, 701. – T. Frenz, *Papsturkunden des Mittelalters und der Neuzeit*, Stuttgart, 1986, 44. – P. Zutschi, "The Political and Administrative Correspondence of the Avignon Popes, 1305-1378: a Contribution to Papal Diplomatic", *Le Fonctionnement administratif de la papauté d'Avignon*, Rome, 1990, 372-384.

Michel Hayez

**FLAGELLANTS.** Medieval flagellant movements were collective, itinerant enthusiasms of a paraliturgical and "popular" character, mostly initiated by the *laity. The flagellants processed from city to city like *pilgrims, performing their penitential rite, ceasing as soon as blood began to flow down their backs. Their behaviour included chanting *acclamations and religious lyrics, carrying banners and crosses, barefootedness, semi-nakedness (1260 in Italy) or wearing religious costumes (in Italy, 1399; in northern Europe, 1261, 1348-1349, etc.). The dramatic ritual of the flagellants created converts who then took the rite to new cities. These "revivals" originated during periods of social and religious crisis – war or plague – in response to eschatological *prophecy, under the stimulus of christocentric piety. Such movements created new *confraternities, at times threatened orthodoxy and the *Jews, and had an impact on art, *drama and the sensibility of Christian pathos. The most notable movements occurred in 1260-1261 and 1349; others included the Roman pilgrimages of Fra Venturino da Bergamo (1355) and the Bianchi (1399).

The "devotio" or revival of 1260 began in *Perugia, in *Umbria, where *Camaldolese and *Franciscan influences were strong. The movement occurred at a time of papal-imperial conflict, *heresy, communal *violence and Joachite speculation about the year 1260. Winning over many northern Italian cities, the flagellants crossed the Alps, visited *Provence and *Strasbourg, and traversed *Germany, *Hungary, *Bohemia and *Poland. The Perugian flagellants were inspired by the *penitent Raniero Fasani. *Jacobus de Voragine stressed their peacemaking role: "Many enmities and strifes in *Genoa and almost everywhere in Italy were turned to peace and concord". *Women performed the rite separately, in private. In Italy, all social groups participated; north of the Alps the flagellants gradually lost clerical support, becoming marginalized socially and increasingly developing heterodox practices.

Large numbers were attracted to the flagellant enthusiasm of 1349, which took place against the background of the *Black Death and chiefly affected Germany and the *Netherlands. *Philip VI stopped its diffusion in *France. Condemned by Pope *Clement VI and the university of *Paris, the flagellants indulged in *anticlerical and antisemitic violence. These flagellant bands were strictly ruled by a lay Master or Father and practised the discipline for 33½ days in Christocentric "martyrdom". The ritual exercised an intense emotional power over the spectators.

G. Alberigo, "Flagellants", *DHGE*, 17, 1971. – E. Delaruelle, *La Piéte populaire au Moyen Âge*, Turin, 1975, 277-327. – F. Graus, *Pest-Geissler-Judenmorde*, Göttingen, 1987, 38-59. – G. Dickson, "The Flagellants of 1260 and the Crusades", *JMH*, 15, 1989, 227-267. – G. Dickson, "Revivalism as a Medieval Religious Genre", *JEH*, 51, 2000.

Gary Dickson

**FLAGELLATION OF CHRIST.** In medieval iconography, the flagellated *Christ was preceded by Old Testament types: Lamech, *Job, King Achior. Compared to the text of the gospels (Mt 27, 30; Mk 15, 15; Lk 23, 16. 22; Jn 19, 1), representations of the scene are richer. As in the Crucifixion, Christ is, at first, clothed in a long tunic, then, from the 12th c., in a simple cloth around his loins, in such a way that the blows of the rods mark lines of blood on the naked flesh. In the 15th c., following the *visions and writings of the mystics, the cruelty of the punishment is stressed (the *Revelations* of St *Bridget of Sweden). The other characteristic is the attribute of Christ, the column, generally represented as a slender shaft (Master of the Narbonne Frontal, 1377; Paris, Louvre). From the late 13th to the 15th c., the *confraternities of flagellants, especially in *Italy, popularized this type of representation (as frontispiece of their statutes; Rule of the School of S. Giovanni Evangelista, second half of 14th c.; Paris, musée Marmottan, Wildenstein collection).

C. Ginzburg, *Indagini su Piero. Il Battesimo, il Ciclo di Arezzo, la Flagellazione di Urbino*, 2nd ed., Turin, 1981 ("Microstorie", 1).

Daniel Russo

**FLAGELLATION, PRACTICE OF.** In the Middle Ages, flagellation was both imposed as a punishment and freely self-administered as an act of *penance. Penitential self-flagellation evolved out of, though continued to co-exist with, punitive flagellation. From an individual *devotional practice, flagellation became a collective, confraternal rite. Various kinds of whips and scourges were employed in what became known as the "discipline".

Flagellation was a method of correction employed by Benedictine and especially Irish monks. Early medieval Celtic *penitentials often name flagellation as a penalty for *sin. Later, in solemn public penance, the church imposed it upon the *laity for serious offences of a public nature (*e.g.* *parricide, depravity and *sacrilege). The *Inquisition also meted out the discipline amongst its less severe sentences.

Within *monasticism, flagellation developed into a voluntary penance, becoming prominent in *Camaldolese tradition with St Dominic Loricatus († 1060). St *Peter Damian († 1072), in his *De laude flagellorum*, recommended it to both monks and laymen. Pious laymen appropriated it during the 12th and especially the

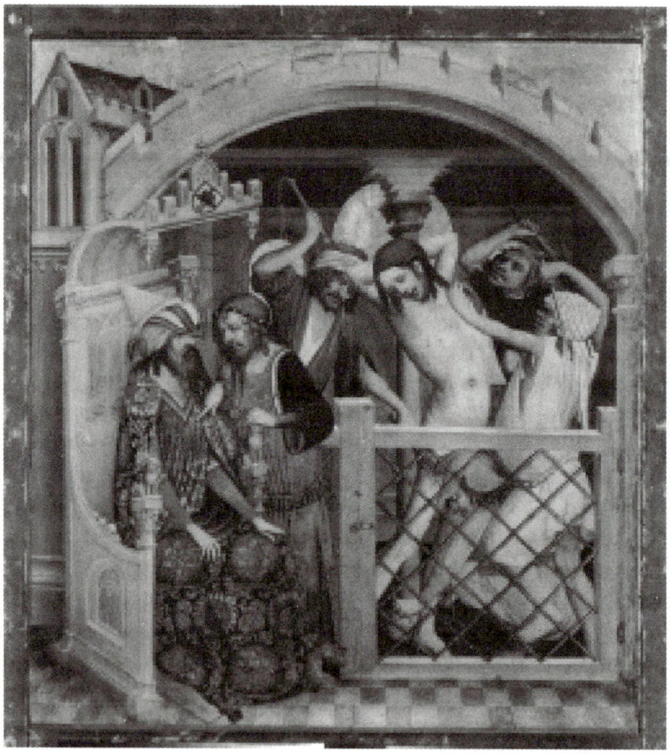

*The Flagellation of Christ* by Meister Francke, 1415-1420. Hamburg, Kunsthalle.

13th century. Devotional motives for the practice included a desire to share in the sufferings of Jesus, the apostles and the *martyrs who had been scourged. The *Flagellation of Christ was a devotional subject of medieval Christian art. Use of the discipline also figured in the piety of numerous saints and *beati* (*e.g.* *Hedwig of Silesia, Margaret of Hungary, Charles of Blois).

Extremely important for the diffusion of penitential culture amongst the *laity was the proliferation of *flagellant confraternities, attributable to the impulses awakened by the revival of the *disciplinati* of 1260. It has been calculated that as many as 1,890 penitential confraternities within *Italy and 42 in other European countries can be traced back to the stimulus of this movement. Of course, not all these confraternities were founded in its immediate aftermath, although a number were (*e.g.* in *Bologna). Flagellant confraternities, and such pious groupings as *Franciscan and *Dominican tertiaries, utilized the discipline as a collective rite of penance, but usually practised it away from the public gaze. These *confraternities were significant social and civic organisations, often in touch with mendicant *spirituality. Amidst their activities – *charity, liturgy, *prayers for the *dead, performances of Christian *drama, etc. – ritual flagellation played a part, even if it came to lose its centrality. Such confraternities remained a feature of later medieval Europe.

P. Bailly, "Flagellants", *DSp*, 5, 1964. – G. Alberigo, "Flagellants", *DHGE*, 17, 1971. – G. G. Meersseman, *Ordo fraternitatis*, 1-3, Rome, 1977. – G. Constable, *Attitudes toward self-inflicted suffering in the Middle Ages*, Brookline (MA), 1982.

Gary Dickson

**FLAMBOYANT GOTHIC.** When, early in the 19th c., A. de Caumont classified medieval architecture, dividing it into different chronological phases, he called the period covering the 15th and early 16th cc. "tertiary Gothic", giving as synonyms "perpendicular style", "prismatic style" or "flamboyant Gothic". This last expression, borrowed from the amateur A. Le Prévost, was unanimously retained by his continental successors. Nowadays the last phase of the *Gothic style is held to have appeared in France early in the reign of *Charles VI. But these first experiments slumbered from *c.* 1400, when the country was torn by grave internal conflicts, especially the resumption of the *Hundred Years' War.

Flamboyant architecture did not really flourish until around the middle of the 15th c., once peace was restored. Its last great achievements hardly seem to go beyond the 1520s. One of the traits common to all the monuments is the use of window tracery in the form of flames, by reason of the curves and countercurves at the basis of the ornamental repertoire, motifs called *soufflets* and *mouchettes*. French archaeologists have long favoured the analysis of bays and mullions to classify the different stages of Gothic architecture, which explains the success of the term "flamboyant". But historians of the architecture of the years 1380-1520 use with caution the term "flamboyant", which is incapable of accounting for the evolution and multiple, sometimes even opposed, aspects of a style that developed over nearly a century and a half and included buildings as different as Notre-Dame de Cléry and Saint-Wulfran d'Abbeville.

One of this style's major innovations was perhaps the desire to question architecture as it had previously been defined. Ribs, *e.g.*, were not always used to carry the vault: their function was mainly expressive. Or, as in the chevet of Saint-Séverin at *Paris, supports were no longer necessarily set on bases and surmounted by capitals, as had always been the case since Antiquity.

R. Sanfaçon, *L'Architecture flamboyante en France*, Laval (Quebec), 1971. – R. Recht, A. Châtelet, *Automne et renouveau*, Paris, 1988 ("Univers des formes").

Philippe Plagnieux

Axial pillar of the ambulatory of the church of Saint-Séverin, Paris, its spiral opening out into ribs. 15th c.

**FLANDERS.** Flanders, a Carolingian **pagus* on the shores of the North Sea, belonging to West Francia after 843, was raised into an autonomous principality by a comital family. Related to the *Carolingians, Count Baldwin I († 879) and his son († 918) profited from the Scandinavian *invasions and the collapse of royal power to assert themselves and found a local dynasty. The principality subsequently expanded until the 11th c., to the south where it came up against *Normandy and the king of *France, notably for domination of the abbey of *Corbie, then to the east where it took possession of lands belonging to the *Empire, Imperial Flanders.

Apart from counties held by followers like the count of Boulogne, the *count of Flanders commanded a domain firmly kept in hand, and the heart of his county ceaselessly expanded towards the German lands. He was able to profit from agricultural growth and the gain of new lands, whether on the shore of the North Sea thanks to drainage or in the *forests of the interior. From the 9th c., Flanders was in fact the scene of considerable rural expansion. It is probable that increasing human density in the countryside, mainly in the valleys of the Scheldt and the Lys, provided one of the bases of urban growth. Moreover, unlike other princes of the kingdom of France, the count kept the fortresses scattered through his domain firmly in his own hands. Flanders very soon appeared as one of the most coherent principalities in the kingdom. The count's peace also favoured the growth of *bourgades* established near a comital *castle, *e.g.* *Ghent or *Bruges, and many *towns had a similar origin. The counts favoured this beginning of urban expansion from the 11th c. by founding new centres like Lille or *Ypres and installing *fairs. They knew how to organise the management of the revenues of their domain and in the late 11th c. had an exchequer that supervised the comital finances. The revenues were increasing also by reason of commercial growth.

At first in the rural areas, then in the towns, Flanders produced *textiles that were exported ever further. Supplanting the Moselle region, it asserted itself as the main industrial centre of northern Europe in the 12th and 13th centuries. The production of Flemish cloth, after having drawn its primary material from the hinterland, turned to the wool producers of *England with whom the Flemish towns had old commercial relations. Moreover, the urban growth that accompanied the growth of *commerce and industry led to an increase in demand for the provisioning of towns that were among the most populated in the West. Towns like Bruges, Ghent and Ypres turned to importing grain from northern France and the German lands. Thus, in its own original way, Flanders entered large-scale commerce and maintained relations not just with northern and eastern Europe, but also, through the intermediary of Italian merchants, with the Muslim countries.

Centres of production, export and re-export, the Flemish towns enjoyed a prosperity that at first profited the count. But this development provoked two phenomena that nourished each other: the rise of the urban patriciate and the cupidity of the rulers of the great neighbouring principalities, like the king of England or the king of France. In fact, the development of commerce and textile activities profited a part of the inhabitants of the towns. A small number controlled the wool trade and cloth exports, as well as financial activities. To these merchant bankers must be added the drapers who mastered the different stages of textile production with its highly specialized phases. Opposite this patriciate was a mass of specialized artisans as well as all the other trades charged with ensuring the provisioning of the town. Probably very early on, the patriciate controlled the revenues taken from commerce and from the provisioning of the towns. Its aspiration to greater autonomy was equally precocious. During the crisis of succession in 1127 when the king of France tried to impose his candidate William Clito as count, this patriciate showed itself very active, not just in the towns but at a county-wide level. It managed to make the king withdraw and imposed Thierry of Alsace: meanwhile it had been able to profit from the rivalries of both candidates to get itself granted a number of privileges concerning *guilds and *communes, and guarantees against comital *taxation. Within the *échevinage* of towns like *Saint-Omer, Bruges, Douai or Ghent, the patricians asserted their preponderance during the 12th c., while benefiting from the protection of a count whose powers were always expanding. The **échevins* disposed of most of the offices of municipal administration and especially concerned themselves with commercial regulations. A *parlement*, mentioned in 1279, associated the count and his court with the *échevins* of the great towns; the Full Parlement added tradespeople and representatives of the *castellanies: it was the embryo of the Estates of the county. French influence was preponderant and the communes of Flanders were capable, like Furnes, of supporting King *Philip Augustus with their militias against Ferdinand, count of Flanders.

The 13th c. saw a diversification of Flemish society, riven by rifts between rural world and urban world, between rival towns and, within the towns where the urban patriciate faced the tradespeople, between weavers and fullers. Social tensions combined with international tensions when the patriciate and the aristocracy moved closer to the king of France. Thus, in the 14th c., Flanders was an important stake between the king of France and the king of England. As the outlet for the export of English wool, the Flemish *merchants and *bankers kept up close relations with the British Isles. The *Capetians, for their part, tried to integrate the county into the royal domain and led several military expeditions to Flanders between 1296 and 1328. From the time of Louis of Nevers, the patriciate and the count leaned on the king of France, *Philip the Fair, who tried to keep the county in his own hands. He had to send an *army to neutralize urban agitation and was beaten at Courtrai in 1302, but managed to impose a heavy tribute on the county in 1305. The count had to appeal again to King Charles IV during the revolt of maritime Flanders in 1323, before *Philip VI crushed its militias in 1328. The hostility between France and England provoked an economic crisis in Flanders in 1337. At Ghent, Jacob van *Artevelde, supported by the revolted artisans, allied himself with *Edward III, who received the *homage of the county in 1339. The *authority of the king of France was gradually worn away by the *Hundred Years' War, despite repeated interventions. Ghent asserted its political preponderance within the county under the tutelage of the merchant draper Jacob van Artevelde († 1345) and then of his son Philip, who leaned on the English alliance.

The political troubles and the rallying of the weavers to England affected commercial activities in the course of the 14th c., marked by numerous economic recessions. Flanders lost its central position in large-scale commerce and textile production. In 1419, the county of Flanders escheated to Philip the Good and was integrated into the Burgundian State. The region saw its commercial decline accelerate. When the *port of Bruges silted up, the economic centre of gravity shifted northward over the century, towards *Antwerp and *Brabant. The duke of *Burgundy's efforts at centralization came up against the resistance of the main towns, Bruges, Ghent and Ypres, which in 1477 imposed on him the "great privilege" preserving their power of decision in matters of *taxation.

Belfry-porch of the abbey church of Saint-Benoît-sur-Loire.

J. Lestocquoy, *Aux origines de la bourgeoisie: les villes de Flandre et d'Italie sous le gouvernement des praticiens, XI^e-XV^e siècles*, Paris, 1952. – F. L. Ganshof, "La Flandre", in F. Lot, R. Fawtier, *Histoire des institutions françaises au Moyen Âge*, 1, Paris, 1957, 343-426. – A. Verhulst, *Histoire du paysage rural en Flandre de l'époque romaine au XVIII^e siècle*, Brussels, 1966. – E. Vercauteren, "La Formation des principautés de Liège, Flandre, Brabant et Hainaut, IX^e-XI^e", *L'Europe aux IX^e-XI^e siècles; aux origines des États nationaux, Colloque de Varsovie, 1965*, Warsaw, 1968, 31-42. – D. Nicholas, *Town and Countryside: Social, Economic and Political Tensions in Fourteenth-Century Flanders*, Bruges, 1971. – E. Warlop, *The Flemish Nobility Before 1300*, 4 vol., Courtrai, 1975-6. – T. de Hemptine, "Aspects des relations de Philippe Auguste avec la Flandre au temps de Philippe d'Alsace", *La France de Philippe-Auguste*, R.-H. Bautier (ed.), Paris, 1982, 255-62. – *Histoire de la Flandre*, E. Witte (ed.), Brussels, 1983. – A. Verhulst, "Les origines urbaines dans le Nord-Ouest de l'Europe: essai de synthèse", *Francia*, 14, 1986, 57-81. – D. Nicholas, *Medieval Flanders*, London, 1992. – E. Panofsky, *Les Primitifs flamands*, Paris, 1992 (Fr. tr.). – P. Stabel, *Dwarfs among Giants: the Flemish Urban Network in the late Middle Ages*, Louvain, 1997.

Thierry Pécout

**FLEURY-SUR-LOIRE.** According to the tradition related in the 9th c. by the "Fleurisian" monk Adrevald, the monastery of Fleury was founded by Leodebod, *abbot of Saint-Aignan at *Orléans, on an *estate he had obtained from the *Merovingian King Clovis II: the abbot's "testament", which its editors have dated to 27 June 651, places the *foundation in time. Under the abbacy of one of its first abbots, probably Mommolus (632-663), an expedition made in common with envoys of the bishop of *Le Mans culminated in bringing from *Monte Cassino, abandoned since the *Lombard invasion, *relics claimed as those of St *Benedict of Nursia, whose patronage and *Rule would be imposed on this Loire valley monastery.

Fleury possessed a **scriptorium* (centre of manuscript copying) doubtless from the late 7th or early 8th c. and a *school – soon renowned – at the time of Bishop *Theodulf of Orléans, a contemporary of *Charlemagne. After a short eclipse partly due to the *Viking invasions – it was burned in 865 –, it was reformed by Abbot *Odo of *Cluny in the 930s: this was the starting-point for a religious and cultural revival of exceptional breadth. Centre of intense monastic life, relay of Cluniac *reform particularly in the direction of *England, the *abbey benefited from the protection and liberality of the first *Capetians – *e.g.* *Philip I, who was later buried in the monastery –, thanks to which it was able to provide itself with a temporal basis sufficient to support great buildings – a monumental porch-tower to the west of the church of Saint-Marie in the time of Abbot Gauzlin (1004-1030) – and rebuildings (the new abbey church), which have made its artistic reputation. It was able to form one of the richest medieval *libraries, alas dispersed in 1562. But Fleury's intellectual apogee was especially the period between the mid 10th c. and the first decades of the 12th, the time of Abbot *Abbo († 1004), undoubtedly the greatest literary figure of the year 1000 (with *Gerbert of Aurillac), and his successor Gauzlin, surrounded by a constellation of scholars, rhetors and poets. Fleury shone particularly in *hagiography and *history: the collective work of the *Miracula* in honour of the monastery's patron saint; the numerous Lives of saints and persons renowned for their piety (the monk Helgaud wrote that of King Robert). And with works like Aimoin's *Gesta Francorum* and the historical works of Hugh of Fleury, even before *Saint-Denis the abbey held a place in "the genesis of the official historiography of the realm" (R.-H. Bautier).

The religious and cultural brilliance was intense, but relatively short-lived: from the mid 12th to the end of the Middle Ages, while awaiting the convulsions of the 16th c., it was a story of slow decline, aggravated, despite the initatives of a few zealous abbots, by financial difficulties, then by the consequences of the *Hundred Years' War.

J. Laporte, "Fleury", *DHGE*, 17, 1969, 441-476. – J.-M. Berland, *Val de Loire roman*, Saint-Léger-Vauban, 1980, 55-148 (3rd ed.; "La Nuit des temps"). – E. Vergnolle, *Saint-Benoît-sur-Loire et la sculpture du XI<sup>e</sup> siècle*, Paris, 1985. – M. Mostert, *The Library of Fleury*, Hilversum, 1989.

Charles Vulliez

**FLIGHT INTO EGYPT.** The traditional scene, sometimes preceded by the appearance of the *angel to *Joseph, was fixed at least from the 6th c., partly inspired by the type of the *adventus* of antique art. *Mary and *Christ have the frontal position proper to theophanic revelations. Joseph holds the ass's bridle while, for reasons of symmetry and again under the influence of imperial art, the march is halted by St *Michael. In the course of the Middle Ages this solemn composition was softened, humanized and accompanied by apocryphal anecdotes, the *miracle of the corn that ripened after the passing of the *Holy Family, attack by brigands, fall of the idols at Sotinen, the palm-tree that bent down to give its fruits.

*The Flight into Egypt*. Miniature from *The History of the New Testament and the saints*. 13th-c. Anglo-Saxon manuscript. Venice, Bibliotheca Marciana.

H. Hommel, "Profectio Mariae", *ThViat*, 9, 1964, 95-112. – C. Schweicher, G. Jazai, *LCI*, 2, 1970, 43-50. – G. Schiller, *Iconography of Christian Art*, 1, London, 1971.

Colette Deremble

**FLODOARD (*c.*893-966).** A *canon of *Reims, Flodoard lived through a particularly troubled period of the history of the kingdom of West Francia and of the Church of Reims. From 919 to his death in 966, he noted the events he witnessed year by year in his *Annales*, an important source of knowledge of this poorly-documented time.

For 10th-c. readers, Flodoard's most important work was *The Triumphs of Christ*, a monumental *epic poem in 20,000 verses demonstrating how, from the origins of Christianity, in *Palestine, at *Antioch, at *Rome and all through the West, *Christ "triumphed" through his saints. This work, composed between 925 and 937, attests the immense culture of its author and his perfect mastery of metric.

Between 948 and 952, Flodoard also composed a *History of the Church of Reims*, from the origins of the city to 948. It combines the rigour of the annalist and the breadth of view of the epic poet to show how, throughout the first millennium, the Church of Reims was spiritually and institutionally built up, following the major steps – its Roman origins, the episcopate of St Remigius († 533) and the archepiscopate of the prestigious *Hincmar (845-882).

H. Platelle, "Flodoard", *DHGE*, 17, 1971, 501-503. – P.C. Jacobsen, *Flodoard von Reims*, Leiden, 1978. – M. Sot, *Un historien et son église au Xᵉ siècle: Flodoard de Reims*, Paris, 1993.

Michel Sot

**FLORENCE.** Coming into existence at the foot of Etruscan Fiesole, Roman *Florentia* (Ital. *Firenze*) was a typical colonial foundation. Little is known of the early medieval city, whose memory is attested in the legends elaborated by late medieval *chroniclers and in sporadic archaeological finds. It is also hard to identify a Florentine nucleus in Lombard *Tuscia,* the Carolingian "reconstruction", or the period of the marquisate.

When, from the 10th c., information starts to become more abundant, Florence appears only on the margin of events concerning the lay and religious *signorie* that surrounded it, not least that of the *Canossa family who bore the title of marquis from 1027 to 1115, the year Countess *Matilda died. The town went through an important period during the years of the *Gregorian reform and the *Investiture Contest, when reforming urgency was joined to the birth of communal institutions. The premises of political and administrative development laid in the 11th c. would reach maturity in the 12th, when it experienced a real refoundation, as witness the construction of a new city wall. The city's society became more composite, with a rich element of *merchants and artisans alongside the urbanized rural aristocracy. Florence was evolving her political institutions: the transition from consular to podestarial *commune, between the 12th and 13th cc., brought together the extremes of an associative dynamic animated by profound internal tensions very soon destined to explode in the form of conflict. The progressive participation of the people in civil life from the central years of the 13th c. (1251: government of the *Primo Popolo*) prepared the political advent of a business bourgeoisie characterised by strong anti-aristocratic impulses expressed politically in the choice of Guelfism, guarantor of republican liberties.

A decisive turn towards populism came in the late 13th c. with the Ordinances of Justice (1293), intended to marginalise the aristocratic and magnate class politically. This reform which gave control of the *res publica* to the **popolo* – and to the corporative system of the *Arti* in which its productive organisation was expressed – also expressed its ideological values in civic building: this was the period of the building of the Palazzo Vecchio, whose tower was higher than all others, emblems of the arrogant power of the factions. At the end of this century, *Guelf and artisan Florence also undertook its most ambitious town-planning project by building its third circle of walls. This expansion corresponded to the gradual extension of its rural territory: the need to ensure the city's strategic control of *roads and riverways had led in 1125 to the conquest of Fiesole, an episcopal city whose strategic position was a thorn in the side of Florentine security. Numerous other military enterprises conducted against the rural feudal *nobility (Guidi and Alberti) enlarged the city's area of influence and, by the end of the century, with the conquest of Empoli, the intention of imposing lasting control over the lower Arno basin was evident.

Expansion led to conflicts with the neighbouring *communes, progressively bringing Florentine external policy into the

Florence, interior of the church of San Miniato al Monte, 12th c.

framework of regional and national coalitions. In 1197, the town furthered the league of Tuscan communes against *Henry VI (league of San Ginesio) by their choice of the anti-Swabian camp, a choice that would be reaffirmed at the time of *Frederick II and *Manfred. By their financial support, the Florentine *bankers, supported by the papal *Curia, favoured the *Angevin descent on *Italy and the defeat of the Ghibellines (1266). Under the vermilion *lily and the Virgin's mantle, the Guelf city kneeling at the feet of St *John the Baptist gained a leading role in the region through a ceaseless succession of military campaigns.

Between the 13th and 14th cc., despite the unstable balance of its regime, it reached its greatest splendour, supported by a sound financial and commercial position guaranteed by its strong *gold coin, the florin. Populist and corporative, the Florence of the *Arti* and *Mercanzia* was not just one of the richest cities in Europe, but also one of the most cultivated, characterised by a very high level of literacy that for some time had allowed the development of a wide lay culture led by the ruling classes of the urban bourgeoisie, among whom *notaries and *jurists held a prominent place. In the age of *Dante, the process of consolidation of communal institutions continued, not without crises and lacerations; like many other cities of north-central *Italy, Florence was rent by intestine struggles, but these did not interrupt the tendency of the lower classes to political self-assertion, as is amply revealed by the constitutional changes of 1325, when the two councils of the People and the Commune were set up, proceeding in parallel with the reformulation of the city *statutes (Statutes of the *Podestà and Statutes of the Captain). With some pauses, territorial expansion continued (conquest of Pistoia in 1331, Arezzo in 1337 and other minor centres). Thus in the early 14th c. the city reached its greatest splendour: Giovanni *Villani, its main *chronicler, testifies to an extraordinary demographic growth (around 100,000 inhabitants) and a great financial reach ensured by the productive activities of the city *corporations or *Arti*. Of these the most important was that of Calimala, which specialized in the working of imported cloth, followed by that of Wool which gave work to about a third of the population. The Art of Exchange was conspicuous for the breadth and specialization of its turnover, its banks ensuring a highly modern business system in Europe's principal *markets. This financial capacity made the Florentines agents of exchange *par excellence*, mediators of *money and culture all over Europe.

But the city's opulence was now threatened by the great recession of the mid 14th c.: anticipated by a series of bankruptcies of the major banking companies (1342), the crisis reached its height in the years 1347-1348, when a period of *famine was followed by a virulent plague. The uncertainties and instabilities of the 1340s had also produced grave political crises, as in the years 1342-1343, when the city was offered in *signoria* to Walter de Brienne, duke of Athens. Republican liberties once restored, the financial difficulties caused by the wars with *Pisa and *Milan remained severe, and attempts to modernize the public debt by the institution of the *Monte Comune* in 1345 did not serve to restore administrative serenity. There were new moments of tension in 1378, at the height of the "war of the Eight Saints" which opposed Florence to Pope *Gregory XI, when the Florentine common people rose up demanding participation in the government. The revolt of the *Ciompi (1382) was followed by a vigorous oligarchical restoration, whose programme included a reform of the fiscal system (institution of the land register in 1427), now oriented towards a proportional method. But the commune's financial resources remained burdened by the military requirements imposed by the expansionism of the *Visconti and the expenses of the conquest of Pisa (1406) which finally gave Florence an outlet on the sea. The new oligarchical stability opened a period of prosperity marked by the development of public and private building, both urban and rural. This turn towards aristocracy, while keeping the city's Guelf connotations unchanged and leaving intact its democratic and republican structures – which indeed received their first cultural theorization in this period from the hands of the "civil humanists" – restricted to a few powerful families the conflictual character that had always marked the city's life.

These were the premises for the establishment of the *signoria* of the *Medici, who ruled the city from 1434 to 1494. During the 60 years of their rule, the Medici infiltrated their power into the republican structures of the Florentine constitutional system without modifying their forms; they accentuated the oligarchical character of institutions, controlling them through a political class of supporters and clients, intervening directly in the constitutional sphere only in extraordinary circumstances. Their external policy was also aimed at the maintenance of the *status quo*: based on the political and social "establishment", the Medici *signoria* devitalized the civil and cultural tensions of early *humanism, imposing the formal and static characteristics of *Neoplatonism. The death of Lorenzo the Magnificent (1492) ended the medieval period of Italian history and the golden age of Florentine history.

R. Davidsohn, *Storia di Firenze*, Florence, 1973. – *City States in Classical Antiquity and Medieval Italy: Athens and Rome, Florence and Venice*, A. Mohlo (ed.), K. Raaflaub (ed.), J.Emlen (ed.), Stuttgart, 1991. – J. Henderson, *Piety and Charity in Late Medieval Florence*, Oxford, 1994. – A. Molho, *Marriage Alliance in Late Medieval Florence*, Cambridge (MA), 1994.

Anna Benvenuti Papi

**FLORENCE, COUNCIL OF (1439-1443).** A continuation of the council of *Basel, canonically closed in 1438, the *council continued the fruitless work of the ecumenical assembly, transferred first to *Ferrara (1438-1439) and then to *Florence (1439-1443). Presided over by Pope *Eugenius IV (1431-1447), it ended in *Rome, where it was transferred for the last time (1443-1447). The question of Roman primacy was the essential subject of its long and laborious sittings.

The Emperor John *Palaeologus, for whom *union of the Churches was his last hope of obtaining the support of the Latin princes against the *Turks, chose to deal with Rome, preferring to acknowledge the legitimate *authority of the *pope rather than the more debatable authority of the council. Despite some reservations, he ended by authorizing the official discussion of the procession of the *Holy Spirit. The Greek theologians decided to commence the problem with the prejudicial question of the addition of the *Filioque* to the *Creed by the Latins. Following *Bessarion, the majority of the Greek delegation ended by giving way to the evidence: the Latins shared the same belief as them. In his still celebrated discourse, the *Oratio dogmatica*, pronounced 13 April 1439, Bessarion expounded that, moved by the same *Holy Spirit, the *Fathers, Latin as well as Greek, could not teach different or opposed doctrines. Of the same *nature as the Father, the Son is the same and sole principle of the Spirit.

Speed also presided over the resolution of the dogmatic difficulties touching on *purgatory, the *Eucharist and the primacy of the Apostolic See. Purgatory was affirmed as being the place of expiation for the *souls of those who, while not having been admitted immediately after *death to eternal *beatitude, were not condemned to *hell. *Transubstantiation was accomplished by the words of eucharistic institution, not by the *epiclesis* that followed *consecration in the *Byzantine liturgy. Finally the Greeks acknowledged the superiority by divine right of the Roman pontiff, successor of *Peter, head of the universal Church and *Doctor of all Christians. The *bull of union, *Laetentur coeli*, signed 5 July 1439, was solemnly proclaimed in the *cathedral of Florence.

Attempts at reconciliation with the various fractions of *Orthodoxy, though without real success, multiplied relations between East and West. The defeat at Varna (1444) of the crusaders who had set out to help the emperor weakened the union concluded at Florence; the capture of *Constantinople (1453) confirmed its failure. Finally and paradoxically, the main result of the council of Ferrara-Florence was not so much the effective reunion of the Eastern and Western Churches as the consolidation of the sovereign power of the bishop of Rome in the Latin Church and his victory over conciliarist pretensions, a victory that would eventually be revealed as permanent.

J. Gill, *The Council of Florence*, Cambridge, 1959. – DHGE, 17, 1971, 561-568. – H. Jürgen Marx, *Filioque und Verbot eines anderen Glauben auf dem Florentinum*, Bonn, 1977. – *HChr*, 6, 1990.

Michel Fol

**FLORILEGIUM.** "Collections of choice pieces" were among the major instruments of diffusion of knowledge in the Middle Ages, Greek as well as Latin. But criticism has long set aside their study in favour of that of the original texts. It is only in the last few decades that work has begun on cataloguing and systematically describing them. By their very structure, they reflect the organisation of knowledge at a given time while also informing us about methods of intellectual work.

Florilegia were as varied in their nature as they were diverse in their functions. Some were devoted to purely didactic uses: thus, the prosodic florilegia, numerous in the Carolingian period, intended to teach the rules of ancient versification to young pupils by examples. Others listed, apropos of this or that biblical verse, the patristic commentaries they provoked – these were "exegetical *catenae", in circulation from late Antiquity. Following the same principle, some undertook to regroup the authorities relating to a problem of *doctrine (dogmatic florilegia) or a point of law (canonical florilegia). But most often, these compilations answered a moral or spiritual purpose: they brought together proverbs and *sentences, extracts of authors either Christian (the most numerous), or solely pagan (see the *Florilegium gallicum*) or pagan and Christian mixed (see the *Collectaneum Sedulii Scotti*). The typology of the genre, difficult to establish, so numerous are particular cases, also has to take into account the organisation of citations among themselves: sometimes they follow each other in an apparently arbitrary order, more frequently they are regrouped by authors, by literary form (prose/verse), methodical plan (*e.g.* *virtues/*vices) or even, from the late 12th c., alphabetically.

The contents of the moral florilegium also vary in accordance with the public it was intended for: we do not find the same extracts in a collection created by an individual for strictly private devotional purposes, composed for monks or elaborated in *university circles. Thus, in the course of 13th-c. *scholasticism – and this seems original to the Western Middle Ages – appear very rigorously structured systematic florilegia, like the *Manipulus florum* of Thomas of Ireland, intended less to nourish solitary *meditation than to serve as working tools for preachers, who drew references and arguments from them. So the analysis of florilegia provides information on the sources of medieval culture (rare authors like Tibullus or Petronius were then hardly known except through their intermediary), on certain aspects of scholarly apprenticeship, but also on techniques of reasoning and methods of literary composition.

H.-M. Rochais, P. Delhaye and M. Richard, "Florilèges spirituels", *DSp*, 1964, 435-512. – R. H. and M. A. Rouse, *Preachers, Florilegia and Sermons: Studies on the Manipulus Florum of Thomas of Ireland*, Toronto, 1979. – B. Munk Olsen, "Les classiques latins dans les florilèges médiévaux antérieurs au XIIIe siècle", *RHT*, 19, 1979, 47-121; *ibid.*, 20, 1980, 115-164.

Jean-Yves Tilliette

**FLORUS OF LYON (late 8th c.-*c.*860).** Trained at the cathedral *school of *Lyon which had been founded by Archbishop Leidrad in 799, Florus, who remained a *deacon for most of his life, was above all the great master of the school of Lyon and the valued counsellor of a series of Archbishops *Agobard, Amolo and Remigius.

A representative writer and theologian of the *Carolingian Renaissance, he left numerous works of *canon law on the *election of *bishops, the privileges of *clerics and against the *Jews. In the liturgical sphere, he left a commentary on the *mass and a *martyrology. He was also an ardent theologian who notably confronted *Amalarius, Godescalc and especially *John Scotus on the question of *predestination. Some poems and a few *letters of his also survive.

M. Cappuyns, "Florus de Lyon", *DHGE*, 17, 1971, 648-654.

Michel Sot

**FOLIOT, GILBERT (*c.*1105/1110-1187).** Successively a monk at *Cluny, *prior of Abbeville, *abbot of *Gloucester (1139-1148), bishop of *Hereford (1148-1163) and of *London (6 March 1163-18 Feb 1187), Gilbert is remembered chiefly for his fierce opposition to *Thomas Becket. But he was a well-educated and distinguished English churchman and a fine *Latin stylist, although his part in the Becket controversy and his manifest *nepotism at Hereford and London cast a shadow over his reputation.

*The Letters and Charters of Gilbert Foliot*, A. Morey (ed.), C. N. L. Brooke (ed.), Cambridge, 1967.

A. Morey, C. N. L. Brooke, *Gilbert Foliot and his Letters*, Cambridge, 1965. – *NCE*, 5, 1967, 984-985. – *DHGE*, 18, 1977, 768-770.

Anne J. Duggan

**FOLLY IN CHRIST (*SALOS*).** The word *salos* designates in Greek the fool, the spiritually simple. The originality of the Eastern Church is to have made it a distinct type of *sanctity. The reference in 1 Cor 3, 18-19 – the wisdom of this world is foolishness with God – seems to appear only *a posteriori* in order to justify an *ascesis that sought *humility above all things. The sources show that madmen were only rarely locked up or tied up, and circulated freely among the towns, at once innocent butts of the community and objects of superstitious fear; indeed madness was ordinarily likened to demonic possession, and we see madmen consulted like mediums of an ambiguous supernatural, perhaps more demonic than divine. In Egypt, the **Apophthegmata* already show us *anchorites temporarily feigning mental debility in order to mask their *virtue (Or, Ammonas); from the 5th c., Palladius's *Lausiac History* mentions a *nun miming madness all her life in order to gain *merits by submitting to the bullying of her sister nuns. In Syriac milieux, this suffering humility quickly combined with the acquisition of the impassibility (*apatheia*) that characterised Adam before the Fall, and with an exuberance of provocative play-acting that allowed the *salos*, by suggestions demented in appearance but supernaturally wise in reality, to point out to contemporaries their spiritual imperfections; thus the *salos* often sought abjection by miming animality and scandal by feigning debauchery. The most consummate example is that of Symeon Salos at Emesa in the 6th c., known through the 7th-c. *Vita* by Leontius of Neapolis; but the beginnings of this evolution can be seen in the *Lives of Eastern Saints* by John of Ephesus (Hala), and even in the 4th-c. *Book of Degrees*. Already in his *Ecclesiastical History*, Evagrius placed above the *boskos* – the holy "browser" who returned to the Adamic state by living naked in the *desert and eating raw food like the animals – the *salos* who, *apatheia* once obtained, returned among men to guarantee his *humility by permanent opprobrium; the madman free from all social attachment completed the regression to animality by the subversion of "normal" human life. The imaginary saint Andrew Salos of Constantinople reproduced this type with some nuances.

The break was marked by canon 60 of the Quinisext Council of 692 which condemned voluntary imitation of madness, as risking a real demonic possession as a result of feigning it. The line of *saloi* nevertheless continued until the end of Byzantium and provided the starting-point for the Russian *yurodivi*, or even perhaps for the *malamati,* mad saints of *Islam; but several late sources are purely pejorative, and the hagiographers emphasize that their heroes are either as nothing compared to the great ancients (by remaining dumb like Sabas the Younger, or by remaining *saloi* only for a time like Athanasius the Athonite) or, like Cyril the

Phileote, condemn the majority of their confrères.

E. Benz, "Heilige Narrheit", *Kyrios*, 3, 1938, 1-55. – G. Grosdidier De Matons, "Les Thèmes d'édification dans la Vie d'André Salos", *TMCB*, 4, 1970, 277-328. – L. Ryden, "The Holy Fool", *The Byzantine Saint*, London, 1981, 106-113. – G. Dagron, "L'Homme sans honneur ou le saint scandaleux", *Annales*, 1990, 929-939.

Vincent Déroche

**FONT, BAPTISMAL.** Though the expression "baptismal font" is derived from the Latin *fons* (spring), it is applied to arrangements unconnected with the administration of *baptism by running *water, as was frequently the case at its origin. Though the great *Romanesque *baptisteries of *Italy contain monumental fonts that reproduce, above ground, an arrangement comparable to that of the ancient *piscinae*, their dimensions are often modest by reason of the generalization of infant baptism from the early Middle Ages; they are in general small basins, variable in form, often resting on or joined to a stand; some were of *metal: bronze, copper or lead.

R. de Lasteyrie, *L'Architecture religieuse en France à l'époque romane*, 1929, 697-709 (2nd ed.). – J. de Mahuet, "Fonts baptismaux", *Cath.*, 1956, 1433-1434. – F. Nordstrom, *Medieval Baptismal Fonts,* Umea, 1984. – A. E. Nichols, *Seeable signs: the iconography of the seven sacraments, 1350-1544*, Woodbridge, 1994.

Jean Guyon

**FONTENAY.** Founded by *Clairvaux in 1119 in a valley in *Burgundy, Fontenay is one of the finest European examples of a 12th-c. *Cistercian abbey: Bernardine church, *cloister, *chapter, dorter, calefactory and remarkable *forge. The construction of the buildings, financed by the English bishop Ebrard of *Norwich, was carried out at the cost of great drainage works. The *abbey prospered rapidly during the 12th c., then hardly recovered from the various sacks it suffered during the *Hundred Years' War. Its use as a paper mill saved the whole and an exemplary restoration gave it its present appearance. Fontenay was classified as "world heritage" by Unesco in 1981.

L. Bégule, *L'Abbaye de Fontenay et l'architecture cistercienne*, Paris, 1912. – A. Dimier, "Fontenay", *DHGE*, 18, 1977, 902-905. – P. Benoit, "Un site industriel médiéval: l'abbaye de Fontenay", *Mémoires de la Commission des antiquités du département de la Côte-d'Or*, 34, Dijon, 1984-1986, 219-247. – P. Benoit, *Moines et métallurgie dans la France médiévale*, Paris, 1991, 269-330.

Benoît Chauvin

**FONTEVRAUD.** The result of the settlement between Saumur and Chinon (1101) of the wandering and heterogeneous troop that from 1098 had accompanied the itinerant preacher *Robert of Arbrissel (*c.*1045-1116), the community of Fontevraud, after difficult beginnings in chance huts, saw a rapid and prodigious rise. Accepting men and *women of all conditions – including *lepers and *prostitutes – and especially favoured by Fulk V of Anjou (his daughter Matilda was *abbess from 1149 to 1155), Henry *Plantagenet and *Eleanor of Aquitaine, it soon attracted growing numbers of noble female recruits who came to dominate the other elements. In 1104, the founder put a prioress, Hersende of Montsoreau († *c.*1112), at its head. This confirmed, in this *conventus* egalitarian in origin but always intended by Robert to be double, the penitential subjection of the brethren to women who had the right of corporal correction over them. This humiliation of the male sex responded to a desire for *ascesis, and the order remained double until the French Revolution.

Baptistery of patriarch Callistus, 8th c. Cividale (Friuli), Museo Cristiano del Duomo.

The 12th c. was its first great epoch. With its monasteries of Saint-Jean-de-l'Habit (brothers, priestly and lay), Saint-Lazare (*lepers), the Madeleine (penitent prostitutes) and Saint-Benoît (infirmary) grouped around the "Grand Moutier" (choir nuns), before 1200 the mother *abbey threw off a hundred *priories from the Somme to the *Pyrenees and as far as *Champagne, plus three in *Spain and four in *England. From that time remain the abbey church with its row of cupolas, the Plantagenet necropolis, the great refectory, the curious kitchen, and Saint-Lazare.

The subsequent period, from the 13th c. to the end of the Middle Ages, was much less brilliant, though the generosity of the kings of *France took over from that of the Plantagents and, from 1224, the papacy declared the order "immediately subject to *Rome". Whereas in the mid 12th c. *Suger had spoken of four or five thousand *nuns, there were no more than 360 in 1297, when *Boniface VIII limited their number to 300. In the 14th and 15th cc., difficulties increased further. Though the *abbey escaped the pillages of the *Hundred Years' War, its surroundings were devastated several times and a number of *priories ruined. But even before the end of the Middle Ages, a revival had begun. Marie of Brittany (1457-1477) and then Anne of Orléans (1477-1491) undertook a *reform, declared applicable to the whole order by *Sixtus IV in 1479. Slowly but surely, it would be accomplished under the *abbesses of the house of Bourbon who followed each other from aunt to niece from 1491 to 1670. Having passed through new crises at the time of the Wars of Religion, the 17th c. would be a new *grande époque* for Fontevraud.

J.-M. Bienvenu, *L'Étonnant fondateur de Fontevraud, Robert d'Arbrissel*, Paris, 1981. – J. Dalarun, *L'Impossible sainteté. La vie retrouvée de Robert d'Arbrissel (v. 1045-1116) fondateur de Fontevraud*, Paris, 1985. – J.-M.

Bienvenu, "Aliénor d'Aquitaine et Fontevraud", *CCM*, 29, 1-2, 1986, 15-27. – S. Tunc, *Les Femmes au Pouvoir: deux abbesses de Fontevraud aux XIIe et XVIIe siècles*, Paris, 1993. – J.-M. Bienvenu, "Henri II Plantagenêt et Fontevraud", *CCM*, 37, 1-2, 1994, 25-32. – J.-M. Bienvenu, "Les comtes d'Anjou et Fontevraud lors du premier demi-siècle de l'Ordre (1101-1151)", *Fontevraud, histoire, archéologie*, 3, Fontevraud, 1995, 7-17.

Jean-Marc Bienvenu †

**FOOD.** In recent times, our knowledge of the typical Mediterranean diet has enjoyed a revaluation, linked to the discovery by historians and ethnologists of diet as a coherent cultural system, which, with its specific codes and its hierarchy of "alimentary values", mirrors to some extent the hierarchy of social groups and the spheres of production and exchange. In this sense, it is also closely connected with the study of the mechanisms of production in *agriculture and *animal husbandry.

The medieval diet – at least for the poorer layers of the population –, while varied, was not particularly sumptuous. Its alimentary base was *bread: not by chance was agricultural production centred on "grain", cereals of every type. The noblest cereal was wheat, immediately followed by spelt; but the most common was rye, resistant and easy to cultivate at all latitudes. Other cultivated products were barley, oats and hops; the introduction of rice and buckwheat – from the *Quattrocento used for polenta – was rather late. In particular, peasants and labourers fed on black bread, made of three parts of spelt and one of beans, but also of millet, chickpeas or chestnuts; sometimes it was consumed in the form of soup, rich in every sort of grain. White bread was reserved for lords and high ecclesiastics. In general, the medieval menu was vegetarian and frugal, made up of soups, porridges, mushes of millet and oats, vegetables, fish, bread, cakes and pies, and domestic fowl. Hospital accounts, inventories of foods given to workers and domestic accounts give the impression that the consumption of meat, eggs and cheese was gradually increasing with time, probably reflecting an improvement in mechanisms of production and more widespread prosperity. Not by chance do 14th-c. French and Italian recipes, including the famous *Viandier* of Taillevent, document a cuisine that assigns the primacy to meats. Among these, mutton was considered the food of the *poor, while pork was consumed in abundance both fresh and preserved; during the Middle Ages, moreover, the rearing of swine – beasts slightly different from today's pigs, products of a cross with wild boars – enjoyed very ample proportions, and the killing of a porker was considered a very serious crime. Beef was very little eaten, since oxen were used mainly as a work-force. Medieval *hunting had a clear entertainment value, but its economic aspect was not secondary: game was considered *res nullius*, and consequently anyone could take possession of it and eat it. Fish, especially freshwater fish, for well-known religious reasons, but also for economic reasons – given the price of meat – was one of the most common foods. Eating habits linked to religious motives included frequent *fasting; equally frequent, in line with poor frugality, was the skipping of the evening meal. In the Middle Ages, sumptuary laws regarding food were very severe, though ineffective, since those concerned denied all charges.

Legumes (chickpeas, chicklings, lupins, beans, peas, lentils) were food for all, rich and poor, and vegetables like chicory, cabbage, turnips, carrots, beets and onions were very common. Fruit too represented a well-known and widespread food: apples, pears, plums, medlars, chestnuts, peaches, quinces, hazel-nuts, almonds, mulberries, figs, walnuts, cherries; citrus fruits, however, were little cultivated. Fruit also represented a useful primary material: from apples was made cider, from quinces and other fruits, jam.

Abbey church of Fontevraud, 12th c.

Condiments were much used: *spices, often exotic and imported, enriched the tables of the wealthy; those who could not afford costly spices fell back on herbs (like basil, mint, parsley, paprika) and on garlic and onions. Olive oil was known and used mainly in Mediterranean countries, while lard was characteristic of northern latitudes. The great medieval Benedictine monasteries had a *lardarium*, a place especially for the preparation and preservation of lard; the first days of winter were known as *tempus de laride*, in reference to the slaughtering of pigs. Lard was employed both in sauces and as a dish on its own, spread on bread or buns; in *Provence and *Brittany, it was also immersed in pea-, bean- or cabbage-soup. Butter, on the other hand, was a rather expensive product: for this reason it was used uncooked or as a melted condiment on dishes, but not as a basis for *cooking. In *Italy it is possible to distinguish two different culinary traditions: a continental area, with widespread lard and animal fats in general, and a Mediterranean area, with a prevalence of olive oil. The late 14th-c. Tuscan *Libro della cocina* attests a prevalence of olive oil in condiments, while lard was used for frying and for the preparation of cakes and pastries. The Venetian *Libro per cuoco*, on the other hand, shows a preponderance in the use of animal fats, while the use of olive oil is very rare.

As for drinks, they consisted of *water, *wine, beer and milk. Wine was considered indispensable as a strengthening and nutritious drink, and its use knew very few limitations. Liqueurs were subject to very severe laws and were produced by monks mainly for medicinal purposes; the only well-known and widespread liqueur was *aqua ardens* or *aqua vitae*, a rough brandy.

Finally, as regards systems of cooking, it must be stressed that the course of the Middle Ages saw their progressive impoverishment: cooking in an oven or at moderate heat were abandoned in almost exclusive favour of cooking over a live flame; only around the end of the 13th c. was there a return to cooking in an oven and stewing.

M. Montanari, *L'alimentazione contadina nell'Alto Medioevo*, Naples, 1979. – E. Faccioli, "La cucina", *Storia d'Italia*, 5, 1, Turin, 1973, 983-1030. – J. Ferniot (ed.), J. Le Goff (ed.), *La cucina e la tavola. 5000 anni di gastronomia*, Rome-Bari, 1987. – M. Montanari, *Alimentazione e cultura nel Medioevo*, Rome-Bari, 1988.

Lucia Velardi

**FOREST.** The word *foresta* applied in the *Merovingian period to spaces – wooded or not – subject to protective regulation in the interest of the landholder, king or lord. The landholders exercised their right to hunt without restraint, rendering cultivation and settlement very difficult. The term "forest" thus came to designate exclusively the wooded zones.

During the Middle Ages, any economically viable *estate necessarily comprised wooded areas. *Towns and lords thus strove to ensure the supervision of forests, which provided firewood for domestic and industrial purposes, and indispensible material for buildings, ships, tools and *furniture. At the same time, forests offered the population a variety of plant and animal resources (honey, mushrooms, medicinal plants, berries, game) and places of pasturage for domestic *animals. A refuge for inhabitants threatened by the incursions of Normans, Hungarians and *Saracens, but also a resort for outlaws, brigands or opponents of established powers, the forest was equally a place where certain *pagan traditions were preserved and which was suspected of harbouring strange supernatural or diabolical beings, to which, by striving to combat them, the Church accorded a warrant of credibility.

Within the territory of modern France, in the early Middle Ages, wooded surfaces occupied about thirty million hectares. Invasions during the 9th and 10th centuries led to a decline in cultivated surfaces. Then, beginning in the 11th c., the relative security and improved climatic conditions allowed a rapid growth in population. But since the yield of food crops was quite low, the need for cultivable lands expressed itself principally in terms of expansion at the expense of woodlands. The great *défrichements* or land *clearances, pursued up to the 13th c., reduced the forests to some thirteen million hectares and modified their structure. The decreased availability of timber had consequences even for monumental *architecture. In the 14th c., the *Hundred Years' War and the Black Death cut back the population by nearly one third and the forest developed once again.

M. Devèze, *Histoire des forêts*, Paris, 1965. – E. M. Yates, *The Landscape of the New Forest in Medieval Times*, London, 1985. – R. Bechmann, *Trees and Man. The Forest in the Middle Ages*, New York, 1990.

Roland Bechmann

**FORGE.** Abundance of ferrous resources and widespread use of iron characterised the West from the first centuries of the Middle Ages: its extension towards central Europe gave it possession of considerable resources of wood and *metal, while the reception and acculturation of *barbarian peoples procured it the mastery of technical procedures more refined than those known in the Roman Empire. Thus, despite a less elaborate material culture, the West had a much more important, and much better distributed, iron production: while the Empire was dominated by some very important iron deposits, from the 9th c. there was hardly any region that did not possess several places where *metal was extracted and worked. This wide diffusion explains the important place given in medieval society to the blacksmith. His magical role and his social power, very marked in the Germanic epics, should not be exaggerated: the profusion of iron objects did not allow him to preserve the aristocratic position occupied in the **Nibelungenlied* by the smith Wieland, who in the French **chansons de geste* becomes the metalworker Galland. But his place was no less important in the *village community, where he was essential for the shoeing of horses and oxen, the repair of ploughs and waggons, the sharpening of tools, etc. Possessor of the necessary tools and a veterinarian by trade, he could when necessary let blood and extract teeth. So it is not surprising to see him appear as witness to numerous *charters: a technical middleman, he was also a social mediator, and from the Middle Ages his smithy was doubtless the meeting-place and information centre described by Lucien Fèvre in modern times. His particular competence gave him a special place in the manorial system where, in exchange for maintaining the tools used on the reserve, he was granted a holding. He was also one of the principal persons on the great building sites and mining sites, one of the best paid among salaried workers.

The profound evolution of techniques and economy in the course of the Middle Ages entailed a progressive specialization among metalworkers: whereas the 11th and 12th cc. had usually known just one sort of metalworker, veritable "mechanics" of *labour according to Robert Fossier, people in the late Middle Ages distinguished between ironfounders, who reduced the ore and marketed the metal, nailsmiths and locksmiths, tinkers (itinerant workers who repaired metal objects), farriers, etc. Technical evolution in the treatment of the ore and the gradual perfecting, during the 14th and 15th cc., of the indirect procedure of metal production, with blast furnaces and refineries, entailed the most profound transformation, making the reduction of ore into an autonomous activity: in the "heavy forges" was a specific population of highly specialized workers, "smelters", "finers" or "hammersmiths", mutually related and practising a very strict endogamy. But they were not so much the heirs of a caste of artisans, which seems never to have existed in Western society, as the first representatives of a new group, technicians in the service of industrial production.

G. B. Depping, F. Michel, *Veland le forgeron. Dissertation sur une tradition du Moyen Âge*, Paris, 1833. – R. Sprandel, *Das Eisengewerbe im Mittelalter*, Stuttgart, 1968. – L. Karlsson, *Medieval Ironwork in Sweden*, Stockholm, 1988. – M. Arnoux, *Mineurs, férons et maîtres de forge. Études sur la production, le commerce et le travail du fer en Normandie (XI$^{e}$-XV$^{e}$ siècle)*, Paris, 1993.

Mathieu Arnoux

**FORGERY.** Forgeries and falsifications were endemic in the Middle Ages. Not only were *charters, diplomas and other legal instruments commonly forged or interpolated, the most famous being the *Donation of Constantine, but so too were collections of secular and *canon law such as the Pseudo-Isidorian *Decretals, theological treatises, historical, *biographical and *hagiographical writings, liturgical texts, *letters, *relics, *tombs and inscriptions. The ubiquity of forgery in the Middle Ages was in a sense an inheritance from Antiquity. Forged literary works appeared already in circulation in the 4th c. BC. *Apocryphal texts, including portions of what became incorporated into the Christian *Bible, were common in the 1st and 2nd centuries.

Medieval works deemed falsifications by modern scholars fall into a variety of categories based on the nature of the falsification and the intention of the forger. Texts may be termed forgeries simply because of the false identification of their authors, done intentionally or unintentionally. Some documents have been deemed forgeries because their original purpose, *e.g.* a rhetorical exercise, was forgotten). Others, particularly charters, may have been formal or material forgeries intended to replace genuine lost documents or to provide the kind of documentation needed to prove rights that had indeed been granted, but at a time when such grants were not confirmed by the kind of documentary evidence later required. Other narrative documents were compiled in order to reflect an appropriate past, understood as a model for understanding the present and determining the proper direction of the future. Still other forgeries, such as hagiographical and devotional texts, were created in order to inspire what was considered a true and proper devotion on the part of listeners or readers. Finally, many other forgeries were undertaken with the intention of deceiving in order to obtain material benefit for the forger's own community or party.

Forgeries intended for personal gain, when uncovered, were severely punished. Other forgeries, particularly those intended to provide the written documentation demanded by contemporaries of real or supposed traditions, were treated much less harshly. This suggests that particularly at the height of forgeries, the 11th and 12th centuries, medieval people had a particular understanding of truth that varied according to the subject and the person. Thus a correct statement made by a person who intended to deceive was considered a *lie, while a false statement sincerely believed was deemed true. Forgeries made with the intention of conveying truth, not in the sense of what had been but rather what ought to have been, were thus more true than bare statements of an exact but disordered past. Moreover, because the deep institutional and communal loyalties of medieval forgers left them little or no doubt about the fundamental correctness of furthering the cause of their community against all others, then forgeries, interpolations and invented accounts of rights and privileges were deemed morally true.

Nevertheless, clashes between such communities created increasingly more sophisticated means of detecting diplomatic forgeries and guarding against forged letters and documents through the use of *seals, special scripts and authentification formulae, as well as through careful comparison of witness lists in charters with the dates of episcopal reigns in order to uncover anachronisms. Likewise, intellectuals developed the critical skills necessary to uncover anachronisms, falsifications and interpolations in literary, historical and hagiographical texts. In this manner, the ubiquity of forgery led to advanced critical skills in dealing with evidence of the past.

C. N. L. Brooke, "Approaches to Medieval Forgery", *Medieval Church and Society*, London, 1971. – G. Constable, "Forgery and Plagiarism in the Middle Ages", *ADip*, 29, 1983, 1-41. – *Fälschungen in Mittelalter*, *SMGH*, 33, 1-5, 1988. – A. Grafton, *Forgers and Critics: Creativity and Duplicity in Western Scholarship*, Princeton (NJ), 1990.

Patrick J. Geary

**FORM AND MATTER.** Plato held the possibility of *knowledge, movement towards repetitive forms and the univocity of the meaning of words to be comprehensible only if the existence of atemporal and immutable forms (ideas) were admitted. *Aristotle criticized this position, considering it a useless doubling of the world: separately existing forms cannot give structure to concrete things, nor do they make them recognisable, which can only be done by forms inherent in objects. So forms do not exist in themselves, but are always "forms-of-something". The form is that determination by which an object receives its essential characteristics. But only that can be determined which is as yet undetermined with respect to that determination: this is the matter which is in correlation with the form, but in such a way that the matter receives its reality only with the form, just as the form can only manifest itself separately through the matter (matter understood as principle of individuation). Matter is the condition permitting the same form to appear repeatedly and unrestrictedly. In this way, matter itself is not a thing (even a material thing), but a principle that is needed to make mutability and multiformity intelligible.

On this Aristotelian doctrine were based two positions at first opposed, but which in fact reveal two convergent tendencies. According to St *Thomas Aquinas, the concept of *creation implies that forms do not exist by themselves and are not eternal, but take their reality from a principle. Thus, form passes through a passive phase with respect to the ground of its reality. While the form merely makes the essence of things explicable, it is the *causa essendi*, to be distinguished from the form, that makes the thing exist. Form and matter above all constitute the unity of an essentiality that still necessitates an external principle of reality. While, for followers of the doctrine that distinguished "being" from "a being", form became a passive element, the *Augustinianism professed by *Franciscan circles made matter an entity whose reality was at least minimal. *God could also create matter *per se* (*Duns Scotus). The unity of the concrete being no longer resided, as for Aristotle, in a duality of two complementary principles, but also authorized a plurality of forms. This was needed to make identity through different phases of ontogenesis comprehensible. In St *Bonaventure's theology of history, salvation-history too was interpreted in accordance with the concept of form: *formatio-deformatio-reformatio*. Meister *Eckhart envisaged the link between the *soul and God as analogous to that which united matter and form. Finally, there appeared in *nominalism a strong tendency to reification, form and matter becoming objects *per se*.

A. Forest, *La Structure métaphysique du concret selon saint Thomas d'Aquin*, Paris, 1956 (2nd ed.). – F. Brunner, *Platonisme et aristotélisme. La critique d'Ibn Gabirol par saint Thomas d'Aquin*, Louvain-Paris, 1965. – A. Goddu, *The Physics of William of Ockham*, Leiden-Cologne, 1984. – T. Schneider, *Die Einheit des Menschen. Die anthropologische Formel "anima forma corporis" im sogenannten Korrektorienstreit und bei Petrus Johannis Olivi*, Münster, 1988 (2nd ed.).

Rolf Schönberger

**FORMOSUS, POPE (*c.*816-896).** Pope from 6 Oct 891 to 4 April 896. Before becoming *pope he had been bishop of Porto. In the previous decades Formosus had acted as a "bridgehead" of the papacy among the Slav peoples, mediator in the search for an agreement that would formalize in Rome's favour the evangelistic initiative of *Cyril and Methodius. But his dynamism in this field cost him firstly the recall of his *mission by *Nicholas I in 867 and then the refusal of Adrian II to elevate him to the dignity of *archbishop of the *Bulgars: a decision that, according to some historians, determined the defeat of the Roman Church in the drive to evangelize the Bulgars. Opposed to *John VIII as candidate for the papacy in 872, Formosus still continued under this pope to insist on being sent to Bulgaria at the head of that Church.

Given these premises, his relations with a particularly energetic pontiff like John VIII could not have been of the easiest. Two fronts opened up between Formosus and the pontiff: that of the line to be followed with the Bulgars and hence with Byzantium, which Formosus probably interpreted in a rather more aggressive way than did the pope, wishing to put a "weighty" candidature like his own at the head of the Bulgarian Church and professing greater rigidity in evaluating the occupant of the patriarchal see of *Constantinople; and, in consequence of these differences, that concerning Formosus's direct competition for the occupation of the papal see. The pope's feelings towards Formosus cannot have been of the kindest, but he must have enjoyed sufficient prestige for the pope to be obliged to accept him, since in autumn 875 he was sent as *legate to the king of France, *Charles the Bald, to sound out his availability to be crowned as emperor. This climate of confrontation finally degenerated into a real breach: Formosus fled from *Rome with some of his supporters early in 876 and took refuge with Lambert of Spoleto. He was then *excommunicated and deprived of his *orders. Pope Marinus (883-884) rehabilitated him and thus made possible his return to the Roman scene.

His *election, though officially sustained by a wide consensus, did not placate internal dissention. Politically, Formosus at first supported the Spoletans Guido and Lambert as emperors; then, fearing their excessive closeness to Rome, he supported against them the Carolingian *Arnulf, whom he crowned emperor in Feb 896. This procured him the hatred of the adverse faction. At his death, his successor Stephen VI, instigated by the Spoletans, had his corpse exhumed and subjected it to an outrageous trial. Until the first years of the 10th c., the Church of Rome remained divided among "Formosans" and "anti-Formosans", before falling under the control of the *signoria* of the family of *Theophylact.

G. Domenici, "Il papa Formoso", *La civiltà Cattolica*, 75, 1924, 1, 106-120, 518-530; 2, 121-135. – *DEP*, 120-121. – A. Lapôtre, *Études sur la papauté au IX^e siècle*, 1, Turin, 1978.

Federico Marazzi

**FORNICATION.** Applied originally to relations with *prostitutes, the term "fornication" rapidly designated any sexual union between two consenting persons free from any ties, as distinguished from *adultery, rape, lust and debauchery. In classical theology, it was considered a breach of natural law, since it activated sexual relations that were not oriented towards the conception and bringing up of a child. The notion of conformity to *nature, so important in this type of moral thought, also entailed a greater gravity for certain forms of fornication such as onanism and sodomy.

Thomas Aquinas, *Summa theologiae*, IIa IIae, q. 154, a. 2-3.

B. Dolhagaray, "Fornication", *DThC*, 6, 1, 1924, 600-611. – P.J. Payer, *Sex and the Penitentials*, Toronto, 1984. – J.A. Brundage, "'Allas! That Evere Love Was Synne': Sex and Medieval Canon Law", *CHR*, 72, 1986, 1-13. – J.A. Brundage, *Law, Sex and Christian Society in Medieval Europe*, Chicago, 1987.

Jean-Marie Gueullette

**FOSSANOVA.** By a concession of *Innocent II to the *Cistercians in 1133, concerning an 8th-c. Benedictine monastery founded from *Monte Cassino, on the southern margin of the Pontine Marshes in the territory of Priverno (diocese of Terracina), the *abbey of Santa Maria di Fossanova was founded in Oct 1135. The monks began by building a canal to carry off stagnant water (*fosso novo*, whence the name *Fossanova*). In 1173, they began to construct a new church. The old Benedictine church had been dedicated first to the Saviour and later to St Pudenziana. In accordance with the canons fixed by St *Bernard for the Order, the new abbey church was dedicated to the Virgin and St Stephen. It was consecrated by *Innocent III in 1208, the first abbey church in the Cistercian style in *Latium, a model for all the others that would follow. Its first *abbot was Gerard (1135-1170), later elected abbot of *Clairvaux.

During the 12th c., Fossanova founded three daughter houses in *Italy. First, in 1150, San Sfefano di Bosco in the diocese of Squillace (*Calabria), on a monastery founded by *Roger I in 1097. San Sfefano would in turn found Santa Trinità del Legno (*Sancta Trinitas de ligno Crucis*) in 1158, in the diocese of Rossano Calabro, previously inhabited by Greek monks. Then, in 1154, Marmosoglio (*Marmosolium*) in the diocese of Velletri, not far from *Rome. Destroyed by *Frederick Barbarossa in 1165, it was rebuilt in 1167 at Valvisciolo (*Anagni) as Nuovo Marmosoglio. Finally, in 1171, Farraria, south of Volturno, in the diocese of Teano.

According to Gobry, in 1173 Fossanova founded the abbey of Corazzo in the diocese of Martirano, on a monastery of the counts of Martirano founded in 1160. More reliable sources make Santa Maria di Corazzo derive directly from Santa Maria della *Sambucina in 1160. *Joachim of Fiore prepared for the priesthood at Corazzo from 1168 and was abbot there ten years later.

The church of Fossanova has a simple façade, enriched by a portal with Cosmatesque decorations and a great *rose window. The inside is marked by simplicity and clarity: three aisles, the central one rather high with ribbed vaults and transept arches. An octagonal lantern surmounts the presbytery. A portal with a trilobate arch, of singular design, gives onto the cloister, three sides of which are original, with round-headed arches in groups of five; the fourth side was rebuilt (*c.*1300) in Gothic forms by Roman marble-workers. The whole appears to be "a confluence of foreign artists with local, especially southern, workshops" (Giovannoni). In a cell of the convent, now transformed into a chapel, *Thomas Aquinas died on 7 March 1274 on his way to the council of *Lyon.

A. Serafini, *L'abbazia di Fossanova e le origini dell'architettura gotica nel Lazio*, Rome, 1924. – R. Bonanni, *Monografie storiche*, Isola del Liri, 1926. – M. A. Dimier, "Fossanova", *DHGE*, 17, 1209. – I. Gobry, *Il secolo di Bernardo. Cîteaux e Clairvaux (sec. XII)*, Rome, 1998.

Attilio Stendardi

**FOUNDATION.** The perpetual assignment of *property, by *donation or *testament, for the creation and upkeep of an institution or a religious service, was called a "foundation". The great foundations of churches, monasteries, *hospitals and *schools were at their apogee around 1080. They were the fundamental constituents of an ecclesiastical *patrimony and signs of *authority and *wealth for the donors, whether king or lord. Pious *legacies were encouraged at this time by the Church (council of Tours, 1163), and mass-foundations multiplied, often attached to an *altar where *chaplains celebrated *anniversary *offices. In the 13th c., the term "royal foundation" took on a very broad sense and found favour with churches and *abbeys wishing to escape seignorial tutelage. In the 14th c., paraliturgical foundations corresponded to the evolution of religious feeling, but the generosity of the faithful also posed the problem of the autonomy of foundations vis-à-vis donors and royal authority.

R. Naz, "Fondations pieuses", *DDC*, 5, 1953, 862-863.

Gérard Guyon

**FOUNTAINS ABBEY.** Fountains Abbey arose out of the secession of a group of monks from the Benedictine abbey of St Mary's in *York who, led by their *prior, Richard, settled late in 1132 in a *desert site not far from *Ripon; the example of Rievaulx, founded in 1131 not far away, persuaded them to adhere to the *Cistercian Order. After difficult beginnings, the *abbey prospered until it became the richest of the English Cistercian abbeys, with a revenue of more than 1115 pounds in 1535, derived from immense estates stretching from Cumberland to Lancashire, on which pastured a flock of more than 15,000 sheep. Destroyed in 1147, the abbey church was rebuilt essentially between 1150 and 1247 (15th-c. *bell-tower) on a plan of unusual breadth and splendour.

*The Fountains Abbey Lease Book*, D. J. H. Michelmore (ed.), Leeds, 1981. – J. Wardrop, *Fountains Abbey and its Benefactors, 1132-1300*, Kalamazoo (MI), 1987.

Jean-Philippe Genet

**FOUQUET, JEAN (*c.*1415/1420 - *c.*1477/1481).** Sources on the life of the painter Jean Fouquet, born at *Tours, are allusive and incomplete. The illuminated manuscript of the *Antiquities of the Jews* is his only certain work, authenticated by a contemporary inscription. As a young man, he travelled to *Italy and lived at *Rome between 1444 and 1446; the *portrait of Pope *Eugenius IV that he painted made him known and appreciated in Italy. Returning to *France, in 1461 he made the mortuary effigy of *Charles VII and prepared the entry of *Louis XI into Tours. His career can be followed through several commissions: an *altarpiece in 1463, pictures for the Order of St Michael in 1470, two *Books of Hours for Mary of Cleves and Philippe de *Commynes in 1472 and 1474 and, the same year, the project for the king's *tomb. In 1475 he bore the title "king's painter", but he had long worked for him. He left two sons, Louis and François, also painters.

Fouquet was trained in a *Gothic milieu: for some, at *Paris, in the studio of the "master of Bedford" or that of Haincelin of Hagueneau, for others at Bourges in the tradition of the de *Limbourg brothers. It is now considered that his *Portrait of Charles VII* (Louvre) was painted in *c.*1440, before his Italian tour. Its lack of spatial layout makes this picture still very medieval in spirit. The portrait is arranged in a confined space with no depth. In it Fouquet affirms his knowledge of Flemish art; the king is represented in a realistic way without flattery. It is the first independent portrait in French painting, taking from Gothic statuary its monumental authority and its composition on the basis of simple, ordered geometrical elements, characteristic of Fouquet's art.

The *Hours* of Étienne Chevalier (Chantilly and Louvre), before 1461, show the effects of his Italian stay, which brought solutions to his concerns about representation in three-dimensional space and a linear perspective. During the decade 1450-1460, he completed the Melun diptych, again for the treasurer of France (Berlin-Dahlem, Antwerp and Louvre), the Nouans *Pietà* (Nouans, church) and the *Portrait of Guillaume Jouvenal des Ursins* (Louvre). We also owe him several illuminated manuscripts: *Cases of noble men and women from Boccaccio* (Munich, Library),

*Caesar crossing the Rubicon.* Miniature by Jean Fouquet (1420-1477) from *L'Histoire ancienne jusqu'à César et faits des Romains, c.*1475. Paris, Louvre.

the *Grande Chronique de France* (Paris, BNF). In the *Antiquities of the Jews* (Paris, BNF), the interest in mass movements gives the history epic sense, in keeping with the subject. In these great miniature paintings, the balance between *man and *nature is always maintained by means of misty or sunny backgrounds. This work gives Fouquet's measure: he was the precursor of the *Renaissance in France, but he was not immediately followed.

N. Reynaud, *Jean Fouquet*, Paris, 1981.

Alain Girard

**FRACTION.** Fraction, that action of the *mass that consists of breaking the consecrated bread before *communion, even if the priest is the only one to communicate, had less prominence in the medieval mass than in the eucharistic celebrations of the first Christians – in the Acts of the Apostles, 2, 42, the name "fraction" is even given to the eucharistic action as such (see Lk 24, 35) –, but it remained one of the important *gestures of the mass, accompanied by the singing of the **Agnus Dei* (or, in the Milanese liturgy, by a variable chant called *confractorium*) and charged by *liturgists with various symbolic meanings related to the *Redemption, which took the place of the fundamental communal significance of the broken bread.

J. A. Jungmann, *The Mass of the Roman Rite*, Westminster (MD), 1986. – *CaP*, 2, *The Eucharist*, London, 1986.

Pierre-Marie Gy

**FRANCE.** The term "Francia" had a complicated history. In the early centuries, the present French territory was called Gaul, and the settlement of the *Franks in Gaul in the 4th and 5th cc. did not change that. The extent of the *Regnum Francorum* had no other limit than the conquest of various geographical regions. Though the treaties of 843 created three different groups of some stability (the kingdoms of *Charles the Bald in the west, the Emperor *Lothar in the centre and *Louis the German in the east), Francia could at any time designate the whole of the Frankish lands, the kingdom of Louis or that of Charles, or again a rather imprecise geographical region north of the Seine which would become the Île-de-France.

Nevertheless, a slow separation was created between France and the *Empire, and early in the 10th c. it became usual to designate the one by *Imperium* and the other by *Regnum Francorum* or *Francia*. This France had as its approximate limits the four rivers (Scheldt, Meuse, Saône and Rhône), *i.e.* a surface area of about 330,000 square kilometres. In the course of the 13th c., the progress of *Capetian power gave the realm territorial stability, and the king was now the direct or indirect master within regularized frontiers. At this time, the term "France" designated the whole of the royal domain and its subinfeudation (the *fiefs that depended on the king). From 1254, the *chancery replaced the old formula *rex Francorum* by *rex Franciae*. The *kings no longer reigned over a people but over a territory. Within it, all were subjects, and the extension of *justice and royal *taxation contributed further to specifying the frontiers in the 14th century.

This territory was idealized from the 13th century. Already people spoke of "pleasant" or "noble" or "fair France"; they began to draw pictures of it that insisted on its cultural prestige, its awareness of independence (Frank = free). In the 14th c., the realm was most often represented as a *tree or a verdant garden, symbol of all the merits of the "most Christian realm". Around 1350, France appeared as a voice deploring the evils of war, and this voice was incarnated at the very beginning of the 15th c., *e.g.* in Alain Chartier's *Quadrilogue invectif*, as a princess dressed in *lilies, tearful or triumphant, addressing her children. Indeed, if dying for one's country had long had no meaning in the Middle Ages, the sole conceivable *patria* being *paradise and the sole desirable *death that of the crusader who was taken there, everything slowly changed with the *Hundred Years' War. A lively anti-English xenophobia developed, while the king's war was presented as a *just war or a crusade. To avoid combat became shameful, and the years 1420-1430 rediscovered the duty of dying for the country. But the idea encountered strong resistance among the clergy and the Burgundians. Nevertheless, around 1500, France had become a stable territory (a bit smaller than at present), a sovereign realm and a value.

P. Contamine, "Mourir pour la patrie" *Les lieux de mémoire*, 2, 3, Paris, 1986, 11-43. – B. Guenée, "Des limites féodales aux frontières de la France", *Les lieux de mémoire*, 2, 1, Paris, 1986, 5-30. – C. Beaune, *The Birth of an Ideology: Myths and Symbols of Nation in late-medieval France*, Berkeley, 1991. – C. R. Bruhl, *Naissance de deux peuples. Français et allemands au Moyen Âge (IXe-XIe siècles)*, Paris, 1995. – *Medieval France: an Encyclopedia*, W.W. Kibler (ed.), A. Zinn (ed.), New York, 1995.

Colette Beaune

**FRANCES OF ROME (1384-1440).** Born at *Rome to a noble family, Francesca Bussa de' Leoni was married, aged twelve and against her will, to the descendant of a rich family of livestock *merchants, Lorenzo de' Ponziani, by whom she had three *children. She always practised austere *penance, gave *alms widely and devoted herself to the care of the sick, obtaining many cures (mostly considered *miraculous). She also had frequent mystical *visions. Her merits were known well beyond the limits of Rome and her gifts were praised by contemporaries such as *John of Capestrano and *Bernardino of Siena. In 1425 she founded a community of *oblates, whom she put under the spiritual guidance of the *Olivetans, who officiated in the church of Santa Maria Nova, now called Santa Francesca Romana. Frances's companions initially lived with their *families and performed works of *charity among the people, but in 1433 they formed a community. After her husband's death, Frances entered the community she had founded, for which she also dictated a Rule. On her death, 9 March 1440, her body was followed by a great crowd. Many *miracles were confirmed, but, although an inquiry was immediately authorized into her virtues and her cause was supported by the most illustrious Roman families, she was not canonized until 1608.

G. Matteotti, *Santa Francesca Romana*, A. Bartolomei Romagnoli (ed.), Vatican, 1995.

*I processi inediti per Francesca Bussa dei Ponziani (1440-1453)*, P. T. Lugano (ed.), Vatican, 1945. – *Una santa tutta romana*, G. Picasso (ed.), Monte Oliveto Maggiore, 1984. – M. L. Valenti Ronco, *Francesca Romana – la "poverella" di Trastevere*, Rome, 1985. – "Francesca Romana", *BSS*, V, Rome, 1991 (3rd ed.), 1567-1569.

Giulia Barone

**FRANCIS OF ASSISI (1181/1182-1226).** St Francis of Assisi is undoubtedly one of the major religious figures of the history of the Middle Ages and, more widely, the history of humanity. He was behind the foundation of the Order of Friars Minor as well as that of the *Poor Clares, which enjoyed a rapid expansion throughout *Christendom from the 1220s and 1230s, and his example inspired numerous laypeople who attached themselves in various forms to his spiritual ideal.

**The biographical data.** Francesco di Bernardone was born at *Assisi in *Umbria (*Italy) in late 1181 or early 1182. He was the son of a cloth-*merchant and would normally have succeeded his father in his business. But, from adolescence, he was more interested in the festive life of the gilded *youth of his city than in commercial activities. His *wealth allowed him to frequent the sons of *noble families and, through contact with them, he was impregnated with the ideas of courtly culture that were deeply to mark his mentality and behaviour. In 1202, he took part as a knight in the war between Assisi, which became an autonomous *commune in 1198, and *Perugia, and for some months he suffered the experience of captivity. Tempted by the profession of arms and chivalrous adventure, in 1205 he joined a military expedition organised by Pope *Innocent III against the partisans of the *Empire in southern Italy, but he was held up by illness at *Spoleto where a *vision ordered him to return to Assisi. He then sought his way for several years, dedicating himself to solitary *meditation, *prayer and the practice of charity.

After having broken with his father who criticized his prodigality to the poor and to churches, Francis renounced his property and put himself under the protection of Bishop Guido of Assisi as a *penitent, *i.e.* a layman engaged in the religious life. In February 1208, he became conscious of his true vocation while hearing a priest read the passage of St Matthew's gospel (Mt 10, 7-16) in which the apostles are sent out on a mission, bare-foot and without money, and he decided to live in evangelical *poverty. Keeping only a single tunic and replacing his belt by a simple cord, he called his fellow-citizens to *conversion and was soon followed by a few inhabitants of Assisi and the neighbourhood with whom he formed a small itinerant community. In 1209, he went to *Rome with his companions to get the *pope to approve his way of life, which was *a priori* suspect, so close did it seem to that of various *heretical movements. Innocent III contented himself with authorizing them orally to pursue the experiment, but obliged Francis to have himself *tonsured and to attach himself to a church, that of the *Portiuncula near Assisi.

Reassured by this relatively favourable reception, the friars, who now took the name of "minors" (*i.e.* very small, humble), developed their *preaching in central Italy and attracted numerous recruits, fascinated by Francis's personal radiance and the novelty of their way of life. Among them were *women, the first of whom, in 1212, was a young noblewoman of Assisi, *Clare, who was to originate the Order of Poor Recluses of *San Damiano, later called Poor Clares. In 1217, at the general *chapter which met at the Portiuncula, the decision was taken to send friars north of the Alps and overseas. Francis himself wanted to set out on *mission, but Cardinal Ugolino persuaded him to remain in Italy to watch over the community, in full expansion but still fragile, whose leader he was. In 1219 however, he managed to reach Egypt in the hope of going to the *Holy Land and sought to establish a religious dialogue with the Muslims besieging *Damietta.

The troubles affecting his movement caused him to return to Italy in 1220 and soon to abandon the direction of it. He had to confront the grave problems posed by the transformation of the evangelical fraternity of the first years into a religious *order regulated by a rule. Gravely ill, ill at ease in the face of an evolution that was moving ever further beyond his control, Francis alternated preaching campaigns with prolonged stays in hermitages, in particular that of *Alverna where he received the *stigmata in Sept 1224. By now almost blind, he composed the *Canticle of Brother Sun* or *Of the Creatures*, the founding text of Italian religious literature. Feeling his end approach, in 1226 he drew up his *Testament*, in which he strove to define for his friars an ideal of *evangelical life in conformity to his original project. Brought back to Assisi, he died at the Portiuncula on 3 Oct 1226 and was canonized on 16 July 1228 by Ugolino, who in 1227 had become Pope *Gregory IX.

**The sources.** These few chronological details should not delude us: the knowledge we can have of the life and personality of Francis of Assisi still includes large areas of shadow. The Poverello (poor little man) in fact hardly attracted much attention from his contemporaries during his lifetime and, with the exception of some testimonies like that of the French bishop *Jacques de Vitry and brief mentions in various Italian *chronicles, sources outside the *Franciscan Order in which he is mentioned are rare. Moreover, he himself did not leave an important *oeuvre*: two fairly short Rules (that of 1221, which best attests his intentions but was not accepted by the papacy, and the *regula bullata* of 1223), some notes, *letters and *prayers; and, while some of his writings like the *Canticle of the Creatures* and the *Testament* are rightly celebrated, they refer mainly to the last years of his existence. Essentially, we know Francis of Assisi through *legends. It is normal that it should be so since he was neither a theologian nor a legislator, but a man inspired by *God who was considered even in his own lifetime as a saint. And the memory he left to his hearers was transmitted

*Scenes from the life of St Francis* by Bonaventura Berlinghieri, 1235. Pescia, church of St Francis.

both through oral traditions some of which were not written down until long after his death – *e.g.* the *Actus beati Francisci* and their Italian adaptation known as the *Fioretti*, which date from the 14th c. – and through numerous hagiographical texts, often marked by the stylistic conventions and a preconceived idealization inherent in this literary genre.

Furthermore, the life of St Francis became a considerable prize after his death, since the Order of Friars Minor immediately experienced considerable internal tensions and was oriented by the papacy in directions that its founder had undoubtedly not foreseen. From then on, each of the interpretations given of his message sought to find a starting-point in this or that of his words and to offer a reading of his life in harmony with the option that was required to prevail. From 1228, at the request of Gregory IX, the Franciscan *Thomas of Celano wrote an official *biography, the *Vita prima*, which banalized the saint's image and contained numerous gaps, while stressing his role as founder of the order, which the *pope had already onesidedly emphasized in the *bulls of *canonization. The insufficiencies of this text led the order's authorities, in 1244, to ask for the testimonies of those who had shared his existence to be collected and written down. Part of the dossiers established in the following years by his closest companions (in particular Brothers Leo, Angelo and Rufino) was used by the same hagiographer in 1246 to draw up a *Vita secunda*, better informed, but which rewrote the story of the Poverello in the light of the crises that the order had just gone through, which had led to the elimination of Brother *Elias from its direction. It was supplemented in *c.*1250 by a collection of his *miracles

(*Tractatus de miraculis*). Other traditions, more local and closer to the ground, were expressed from the 1240s by the Anonymous of Perugia and in the Assisi Compilation, also known as the *Legend of the Three Companions*, or in poetic form (*Sacrum commercium sancti Francisci cum Domina Paupertate*), and came to contradict the official version on certain points.

In 1260, *Bonaventure of Bagnoreggio, minister general of the Friars Minor, wished to put an end to these discordances once and for all by himself writing a new biography of the Poverello, the *Vita major*, soon followed by a *Vita minor*, an abridged version of the former, and in 1266 he gave orders for all earlier biographies to be thrown in the fire. But this authoritarian measure did not regulate the problem, and when in the late 13th and early 14th cc. the conflict within the order between the majority of the community and the *Spirituals, followers of an uncompromising rigorism, became envenomed, new texts (*Legend of Perugia*, *Speculum Paupertatis*, etc.) were written by the latter in support of their positions, on the basis of earlier *florilegia. Finally, art played a great role in the *a posteriori* construction of the figure of St Francis. *Giotto in particular, with the pictorial genius that marked his Franciscan cycles at *Assisi, *Padua and *Florence, powerfully contributed to spreading the image of a *thaumaturgical saint, zealous collaborator of the papacy and eschatological hero, which was the image his patrons within the order and the ecclesiastical hierarchy wished to promote, to the detriment of other more concrete readings, like that of the Tavola Bardi at Santa Croce in Florence, which put the emphasis on his love for the poor and infirm.

**"To live according to the holy Gospel".** We cannot understand the success obtained by the *preaching of Francis of Assisi – at his death, there were already more than a thousand friars distributed among most of the countries of *Christendom and in the East – without going back to his message. When we attempt to define this, it confines itself to a few formulae that may appear banal, since he was neither a great *Doctor nor a theoretician of the spiritual life. This layman, who wrote a rough *Latin full of Italianisms, essentially left a witness: that of a man who wished to live the gospel message in its entirety. "To live according to the holy Gospel", to adopt the expression used by Francis, was a new idea at the dawn of the 13th c., at least within the Church, though various contentious religious movements like that of the *Waldenses had already advanced this claim before being condemned as *heretics by the papacy in 1184. The Poverello was right in line with this popular evangelism which he strove to live and acclimatize within the institutional Church, towards which he manifested *obedience and respect throughout his life. From the time of his *conversion, he strove to "follow naked the naked Christ" by voluntarily putting himself in concrete situations that had been known to "the Son of Man who had nowhere to lay his head". With him, for the first time in the history of Christianity, the religious life was no longer conceived just as a *contemplation of the infinite *mystery of *God – though *prayer occupied a central place in his spiritual experience – but as an imitation, or still better as a search for an ever closer conformity to the poor, humble and suffering *Christ, whose sacrifice was the source both of our divine filiation and of human brotherhood.

*Poverty was, as is well known, at the centre of the Franciscan message. For the Poverello, it was not primarily a moral *virtue or a legal status – *e.g.* absence of property, as his spiritual sons would interpret it from the 1270s – but an altogether new, concrete programme of individual and collective existence. In his time, the most austere monks, though individually without resources, remained great landed proprietors included in the seignorial and feudal system. With Francis, the demand for destitution increased since he required that those who followed him should possess nothing, neither individually nor in common, and should content themselves with what *labour and begging brought them. Living according to the Gospel implied in his eyes accepting economic precariousness and a daily dependence on others to ensure survival. It was also a condition for being on a level footing with the poor and the excluded. Francis of Assisi did not idealize poverty: for him it was a disease of society, as *leprosy was of the *body. So it must be fought by depriving oneself of superfluities and even necessities, when one met someone poorer than oneself, and it must be sought in order to rejoin suffering humanity and, through it, *Christ who loved it and espoused it.

The other pole of the Franciscan message, closely linked to the former, consisted of *humility, as witness the name of "Minors" given to his fraternity. Within this, Francis wanted equality and mutual affection to reign. The rapid growth in the number of friars and the intervention of the papacy obliged him to institute a hierarchy in it. So the Rule of 1223 stipulated that the order would be directed by a minister general, the provinces by ministers and the *convents by simple *guardians. But all these offices were elective and temporary, and the important role assigned to the annual general *chapter, in which originally all the friars took part, attests the founder's concern to create a religious community resting not on vertical relationships of *authority but on freely consented *obedience and fraternal correction. Likewise, in their relations with ecclesiastical institutions and civil society, Francis asked his friars to adopt an attitude of deferent submission, while refraining from claiming privileges or protections for themselves. His ambition was not to reform the Church, still less to attack it, but to give witness to an uncompromising fidelity to the Gospel lived in the midst of the world and among people, while proposing the alternative model of a brotherhood freed from the power of *money and from *violence and at the same time fully consecrated to the worship of *God and the service of the poor.

**The origins of the *Franciscan movement.** Francis of Assisi certainly did not set out with the intention of founding a religious order. But from the outset his project of *evangelization had a universal dimension in that it was addressed to all Christians – *clerics and *laity, men and *women – and even to *pagans. Despite his aversion to structures and institutions, the very success of his preaching involved it in a process of progressive institutionalization, under the watchful tutelage of Cardinal Ugolino who became the order's protector. The original community in which "friars minor and sisters minor" lived in symbiosis on the periphery of towns – as *Jacques de Vitry described it on the occasion of his stay at Perugia in 1216 – rapidly evolved towards more standard forms: the process of "regularization" of the movement began with the women, who were "cloistered" in the monastery of *San Damiano near Assisi, and had to adopt a Rule and a lifestyle of monastic type. Francis does not seem to have done anything to oppose this, either because he was convinced of the danger presented to his friars and himself by frequenting women or because he considered the battle lost in advance and preferred to safeguard the specific character of the the more numerous male branch.

For the Friars Minor, indeed, the question of the Rule was soon posed. Referring to the divine inspiration he had received (see *Testament*, 14: "Nobody showed me what I should do, but the Almighty himself revealed to me that I had to live according to the holy Gospel"), he refused to adopt the monastic or canonical usages proposed to him and, at the end of three years of discussions with his companions and negotiations with the papacy, managed to get the Rule of the Friars Minor approved by Pope *Honorius III in November 1223. This allowed certain original characteristics of his foundation to remain: absolute prohibition of possessions individually or in common, recourse to mendicancy to ensure daily life, and, within the community, coexistence on an an equal footing of *clerics and laymen, each reciting the *office in their own way. But Francis had to accept the institution of a noviciate and the creation of hierarchical structures, as well as the replacement of the term "fraternity" by "order".

The last years of his existence were darkened by the conflicts between certain of his companions, primarily concerned for immediate apostolic effectiveness and for this sake inclined to renounce certain requirements of the *evangelical way of life which appeared to them useless or embarrassing. Fixed establishments, the building of *convents and churches, introduction by some of ascetic or liturgical customs of monastic type, abandonment of manual *labour, growing interest in studies and theological science, recourse to *bishops and especially to the papacy to avoid the persecutions that these newcomers to *Christendom had to suffer here or there, all these distortions of the original ideal were felt by Francis as so many betrayals. Faced with these deviations, he reacted by an intensification of his personal witness of absolute destitution as he had wished to institute it, alongside the administrative government of the order, entrusted to Brother Elias after the death of Pietro Cattani, a sort of parallel hierarchy based on *sanctity, an intention attested by the blessing given to Brother Bernard on his deathbed. This process of doubling is also illustrated by the contents of his *Testament*, which aimed to provide the friars with a spiritual interpretation of the Rule by rereading it in the light of the original Franciscan experience.

The impact of Francis's message was also considerable among laypeople of both sexes. He was long attributed with the institution of a "*Third Order" which would bring together believers, married or single, who had been converted by him to a better life. Today this seems unlikely, but on the other hand it is perfectly true that, under his influence and that of his friars, the penitential lifestyle, which he himself had practised in the first years of his religious life, enjoyed a wide diffusion and that numerous laypeople put themselves under the *spiritual direction of the *Franciscans; two *Letters to the Faithful* by St Francis, defining for their use the fundamental characteristics of a fully Christian life lived in the world, attest this influence.

Francis of Assisi died on 3 Oct 1226 at the Portiuncula, cradle of the fraternity. He was canonized on 16 July 1228 by Pope Gregory IX, who intended that his reputation for sanctity should profit the Roman Church and that the Friars Minor should become the spearhead of a pastoral reconquest of the Italian cities and the struggle against *heresies. Brother *Elias, minister general of the order, also undertook the construction of a great *basilica in the *Gothic style, situated on an escarpment close to the town of Assisi, for which he appealed to the best architects and painters of the time. The founder's remains were transported there with great pomp in 1230. This was the second death of Francis of Assisi.

M. A. Habig (ed.), *St Francis of Assisi, Writings and Early Biographies: English Omnibus of the Sources for the Life of St Francis*, 3rd ed., Chicago (IL), 1977. – *Francis and Clare: the Complete Works*, R.J. Armstrong (ed.), I.C. Brady (ed.), London 1982. – *The Writings of St. Francis of Assisi*, H. Bockhouse (ed.), London, 1994.

K. Esser, *Origini e valori autentici dell'ordine dei frati Minori*, Brescia, 1972. – R. Manselli, *Saint François d'Assise*, Paris, 1982. – T. Desbonnets, *De l'intuition à l'institution: les Franciscains*, Paris, 1983. – R.D. Sorrell, *St. Frances of Assisi and Nature*, Oxford, 1988. – G. Miccoli, *Francesco d'Assisi. Realtà e memoria di un esperienza cristiana*, Turin, 1991. – C. Frugoni, *Francesco e l'inventione delle stimmate*, Turin, 1993. – *Frate Francesco d'Assisi. Atti del XXI Convegno internazionale*, Assisi, 1994. – J. Dalarun, *Francesco: un passaggio. Donna e donne negli scritti e nelle leggende di Francesco d'Assisi*, Rome, 1994.

André Vauchez

**FRANCIS OF PAOLA (1416-1507).** Founder of the *Minims. Francesco d'Alessio, also called Martotilla after his father's surname, was born at Paola in *Calabria to a prosperous *peasant family. After having spent a year of his adolescence in a *Franciscan *convent and made a *pilgrimage to *Assisi which made a great impression on him, while still young he became a hermit. His piety and austerity, pushed to the point of observing a perpetual *fast, drew to his retreat a number of disciples who formed the little fraternity of hermits of Paola; others arose in the neighbourhood. They were approved by the archbishop of Cosenza in 1470 and in 1474 by Pope *Sixtus IV, who attached them to the Franciscan family. The renown of the cures worked by the holy man extended from Calabria to *Naples.

*Louis XI, struck by a first attack of paralysis, heard tell of the Calabrian *thaumaturge and wanted him at his side to heal him. Responding to the appeals of the *pope, who counted on him to obtain the support of *France and the king of Naples, the old man, at first very reluctant, agreed to go and arrived at Plessis-lès-Tours in May 1483. Though he did not heal the king, he helped him to die well (31 August 1483). The man of God, now an unofficial diplomat despite himself, decided to remain in France with *Charles VIII.

His life now changed its orientation completely. He became the head of a *coenobitic community established in the convent built for him at Plessis in 1491, which was not slow to make daughter houses. From the court and the town, numbers came to him for healing or *spiritual direction, which was all the more remarkable in that he understood very little French and, not being a priest, did not hear *confessions. While changing nothing of his ascetic life, he was the inspired prophet whom the king consulted with respect on all his great political problems: the question of *Brittany, the return of Roussillon to *Aragon, the *reform of the French Church and the expedition to Naples, which he wanted to give the character of a crusade.

The foundation of the new Order of Friars Minims, on which he was so bent and for which he counted on the support of the French court, was granted by the Holy See on 22 Feb 1493 and confirmed on 28 July 1506.

Francis of Paola died at Plessis on 2 April 1507. The *canonization of the Calabrian peasant who became the protector of the French Crown, whose process was opened at Tours and in Calabria in 1512, was proclaimed by Leo X on 1 May 1519.

*ActaSS, 2 aprilis...* 1, Paris-Rome, 1865 (new ed.). – *I codici autografi dei processi consentino e turonense per la canonizzazione di Francesco di Paola*, Rome, 1964.

G. M. Roberti, *San Francesco di Paola. Storia della sua vita*, Rome, 1915. – R. Fiot, "François de Paule", *DSp*, 5, 1964, 1040-1051. – A. Galuzzi, *Origini dell'ordine dei minimi*, Rome, 1967. – A. Galuzzi, "François de Paule", *DHGE*, 18, 1977, 742-745. – *San Francesco di Paola. Chiesa e società del suo tempo. Atti del convegno . . . Paola, 20-24 maggio 1983*, Rome, 1984.

Bernard Chevalier

**FRANCISCANS, FRANCISCANISM.** Several religious families claiming kinship with the life and teaching of *Francis of Assisi, considered their common founder, are still present in the Church and in society. The problem of Franciscan origins is the object of a ever-open debate, given the rarity of contemporary witnesses, internal and external, at least until 1216. During the next decade they are still limited to the text of the Rules (1221 and 1223) and some brief writings of Francis himself. It is certain in any case that Francis of Assisi did not intend to found a religious *order, but rather a *fraternitas*, a group of *penitents, lay and clerical, united by the desire to serve their neighbour in *poverty and *humility. Such was the form of life that Francis observed after his *conversion when, as he describes himself in his *Testament*, his meeting with *lepers, the *love and pity he felt on contact with them, provoked in him a total reversal of values. But it is also the first image we have preserved of the Friars Minor, as it is fixed in the testimony of *Jacques de Vitry: he made the acquaintance of their new way of life during his stay in Italy in 1216, and praised their spirit of charity and their absolute poverty (associated in this first phase with manual *labour, and only exceptionally with mendicancy).

Francis's first companions were engaged in *preaching with a moral content, verbally authorized by Pope *Innocent III in 1209; but for them the true preaching was the example of Christian life that they proposed to the faithful. Very quickly, the *fratres poenitentiales* multiplied not just in *Umbria but all over central *Italy: however, in the name of their commitment to poverty, they neither possessed nor wished to possess their own establishments and lived as guests in private and religious institutions (*e.g.* *hospices to which they gave assistance). From a canonical point of view, their status was still ambiguous, the more so in that the fourth *Lateran council had forbidden the proliferation of new forms of religious life and decided that new *foundations must be referred to one of the already existing *Rules. But the Roman Church had every interest in supporting this experiment which, in perfect orthodoxy and perfect obedience to the Holy See, seemed in a position to canalize a great part of the religious disquiet and *heretical ferment then present to some extent throughout Europe, but expecially in Italy and France. So it favoured expansion of the Franciscans, whose institutional reality was unclear, by recommending them to the authorities of the local Churches (1219).

Meanwhile, Francis had organised proper "*missions" in various European countries (*France 1219, *Germany 1221), which immediately had great success, while in *Syria, the land where the Lord had lived and died, a province was created in 1217. Francis's desire to visit the *Holy Land and attempt the *conversion of the infidels led him to join the fifth *crusade (1219-1220), then uselessly engaged in the siege of *Damietta. From this journey to the East (a failure from the missionary point of view, though Francis was treated with respect and heard benevolently by the Muslim authorities), Francis returned seriously ill. His physical weakness, but still more his awareness that he could not (nor wished to) rule a great religious family that was rapidly being transformed into an order, led the saint to renounce the direction of his brethren, to retain only a role as spiritual and charismatic guide. His successors (first Giovanni Parenti, then Elias) accelerated the process of institutionalization already under way.

In 1220, the Holy See had prescribed a year of noviciate for anyone wishing to adhere to the new religious family. In 1221 came the redaction of a first Rule, not approved by the Holy See; Rome did however confirm the second version, shorter, less rich in evangelical content, more "functional", at least in appearance (*Regula bullata*, 29 Nov 1223). After this last stage of Francis's life, two tendencies seem to have taken shape among the friars: a party among them wished to remain faithful to the initial spirit of *fraternitas*, while a majority, prevalent among whom were the *clerics and more educated who increasingly adhered to Franciscanism from the 1220s, looked with favour on the transformation into an order, acquisition of new permanent urban residences, full incorporation into ecclesiastical structures and an ever-more resolute engagement in preaching, not just moral but doctrinal, as well as *pastoral care.

Evidence of these new tendencies and the suffering they caused Francis can be seen in the saint's *Testament*, an autobiographical document of painful intensity, dominated by the desire to prevent this "denaturing" of his creation. But the movement was by now inexorably launched and the *canonization of Francis in 1228, only two years after his death, provoked a new acceleration. The notable influence exercised at that time by Franciscan preachers appears in the great campaign of *penance and pacification that they waged, in collaboration with the *Dominicans, in the cities of the Po valley during the summer of 1233. But their dimension was now European: in 1224 they reached *England, where they immediately benefited from the support of the more "enlightened" *bishops engaged in the *reform of the local Church. A few years saw a multiplication in the number of those who, at *Paris or *Oxford, had received a complete theological training: from 1236-1237 they also had a regent master at Paris when *Alexander of Hales, an illustrious theologian, entered the order. The very high number of friars and the now variable situation from one province to another posed a problem, around 1235, of "internal democracy" and fully showed up the insufficiencies of a Rule that Francis had wished to see applied to the letter and without commentaries. From 1230, several friars had pointed out the difficulties of interpreting certain chapters and had obtained an intervention from *Gregory IX: he had notably decreed that the *Testament* had value only as pure moral exhortation, and that only the Rule had normative value. Especially grave was the silence of the 1223 text on the powers and forms of *election of the provincial ministers, and this text left too much latitude to the action of the minister general.

The year 1239 saw the deposition of the second general, *Elias, and the redaction of a first corpus of Constitutions, which were integrated in the following years, re-examined and reconstructed by the Narbonne *chapter of 1260, and from then on formed a reliable legislative base alongside the Rule. But the deposition of Elias had grave consequences on the external image of the order, and seemed to threaten its internal cohesion: the deposed general embraced the cause of the excommunicated Emperor *Frederick II, and sought to involve a part of the Franciscans in the great battle between the Roman church and the *Empire that tore Italy apart, especially the Centre and North, from 1239 to 1250. Firm supporters of the *pope, the Franciscans took an active part in anti-imperial propaganda and also agreed to become bearers of messages to those who, in the *regno*, aimed at the elimination of the emperor, going so far as to take part in certain insurrectional episodes.

But even after Frederick's death, the Franciscans knew no peace: in the 1250s they had to face the attacks of a part of the *secular clergy, whose spokesman was a Parisian master in theology, *William of Saint-Amour. The immediate causes of the conflict were typical of the *universities and can, in a slightly simplistic way, be reduced to the fear felt by the seculars in the face of the proliferation of chairs of *theology given to *masters coming from the ranks of the religious and hence not bound to be incorporated in the corporative structure of the university. But the roots of the dispute went much deeper. Though they had only one chair of theology as against two for the *Dominicans, the Franciscans nevertheless provided William of Saint-Amour with his main target: he had a fine time denouncing the heterodox character of the work of an Italian friar minor, *Gerard of Borgo San Donnino, markedly Joachite in character, who foretold the imminent coming of the era of the Spirit and assigned the Franciscans an essential role in the Church.

Thus the eschatological ferments present in the order from the middle or late 1240s, to which even great persons like the then minister general *John of Parma were no strangers, came to maturity. The crisis once overcome, thanks especially to the intervention of the new pope, *Alexander IV, who had been the *cardinal protector of the Minors, the Franciscans felt the need of a reliable and prestigious leader, capable of resolving the order's internal problems and giving it an external credibility. Thus was elected *Bonaventure of Bagnoregio (1257-1274): he had been a very young master of theology at Paris, had collaborated in the defence of the order against the *seculars, and was animated by a sincere reforming zeal. His legislative activity, the ideological justification finally assigned to the study of *theology, brought into close relation with the apostolic function of the Franciscans, who were called to *preaching by their vocation, and finally the new *biography of the founder, in which Francis was presented as an *alter Christus* with a large place given to the *stigmata, all contributed to the work of pacification and consolidation of the Friars Minor during Bonaventure's generalship.

During these years, Franciscanism took on the characteristics that it was long to retain: the communities of Minors were now permanently incorporated in *towns, in often vast *convents, and they began to build or rebuild their churches, often departing from the original precepts of *poverty. By now aware that study was a necessary condition for carrying out the tasks of pastors and guardians of orthodoxy that the papacy had assigned them (tribunals of *Inquisition were quite soon entrusted to Franciscans, though in lesser numbers than to Dominicans), the Friars Minor organised a scholastic system analogous to, though less meticulous than, that of the Dominicans. By contrast, the hierarchical structure of the order remained unchanged from the situation of the 1230s, but the respective powers of the ruling authorities were better defined: at the head of the order, the minister general, elected and assisted by the general *chapter; at the second level, the provincials, in analogous relation to their respective chapters; the provinces were in turn divided into custodies. As can be seen, it was a system at once structured and supple, in which the limited duration of offices was to guarantee the rapid correction of possible abuses.

However, a few years after Bonaventure's death, internal dissentions about poverty and more generally about fidelity to the founder's intentions exploded with a new violence. This time the dissidents had well-defined characteristics and assured references. Though their spiritual master was the theologian *Peter John Olivi, the best-known among the "militants" were *Angelo Clareno and *Ubertino da Casale. After alternating phases of persecution and tolerance, the *Spirituals managed to find a sure support from *Celestine V, the ex-hermit of Maiella, who was sympathetic to their aspirations to a life of total poverty detached from the world.

Thus were born the *pauperes heremitae domini Coelestini*, who could observe *Francis's Rule and *Testament* in their integrity within the *Celestine congregation. But the experiment lasted only for the time of Celestine's pontificate: *Boniface VIII, annulling all the acts of his predecessor, intended to recall the Spirituals to *obedience to their superiors. Part of them escaped by fleeing to *Greece: this episode had a lasting influence on Clareno, who became aware in that country of certain sources of Eastern *spirituality (St *John Climacus), which he even got translated. Others, like the poet *Jacopone da Todi, took the side of Boniface's political enemies, the *Colonna, whose defeat and condemnation they shared. Subsequently, the Spirituals could still count on the protection of Cardinals Colonna and Napoleon *Orsini; with Boniface dead and the papacy transferred to *Avignon, they were able to make their voice heard at the council of *Vienne, which tried to arrive at a solution satisfactory to the community (the majority of the order) and to the Spirituals. Certain convents were designated in which the latter could lead a life in accordance with their interpretation of the Franciscan Rule. From these years dates the production of certain works (*e.g.* the *Speculum perfectionis*) in which biographical material on Francis going back to the tradition of his earliest companions was reworked to forge an image of the founding saint more in accordance with the ideas of the Spirituals than that of Bonaventure's biography.

Some years later, Clareno wrote a history of the Friars Minor envisaged as a series of seven tribulations inflicted on the faithful lovers of poverty and true disciples of Francis by the laxist fraction. This time too, the compromise solution did not ensure lasting peace to Francis's sons: the pontificate of *John XXII marked a new resumption of persecutions, the abolition of all privilege and the definitive condemnation of their ideas. Clareno fled once more and died in a Calabrian hermitage, in an aura of *sanctity. All trace of Ubertino, who had accepted the habit of a Benedictine, is lost. But John XXII, by condemning in 1323 the theory of the absolute poverty of *Christ and the apostles, a theory that was at the bottom of the Franciscans' conception of poverty and was the basis of their identity as an order, also embroiled himself with the hierarchy of the Minors. *Michael of Cesena, the general, refusing to bow to the papal decisions, declared himself in favour of the Emperor Louis of Bavaria (*excommunicated by the pontiff) and attached himself to his cause for several years.

Once more, as at the time of Elias, pro-imperial dissidence was not much followed, but the crisis undergone by the order was still profound. Not by chance do we see in the mid 14th c., especially in central Italy, a resumption of ferments of renewal, concentrated in some hermitages of the Apennines. This time the reformers tried not to come into conflict with the hierarchy, by invoking recognition from the Holy See. Thanks to the indefatigable activity of Friar Paoluccio Trinci, from 1380 what is known as the Franciscan *Observance was able to enjoy official recognition. Despite that, the relations of the observants with the order's hierarchy were neither simple nor always peaceful, to such a degree that in 1517, after a long series of useless attempts to make the two tendencies within the order live together, a formal division was reached between observants and *conventuals. But in the 15th c., the "great" Franciscans all belonged to the reforming branch of the order, from *Bernardino of Siena to *John of Capestrano. Characterised initially by their aversion to urban life (considered a *temptation and an obstacle to perfect observance of the Rule) and studies, from the time of Bernardino the observants were often educated and, especially, famous preachers. The whole population was present at their *sermons, held in the great squares of the towns; the themes of observant preaching (struggle against *usury, vain luxury, factional animosity) had a great, though ephemeral, success and were in some cases accepted into the legislation of cities.

*Fonti francescane*, Assisi, 1978 (writings of Francis, first pontifical documents, external evidence and first chronicles of the Order). – *Francis and Clare: the Complete Works*, R.J. Armstrong (ed.), I.C. Brady (ed.), London, 1982.

R. Brooke, *Early Franciscan Government. Elias to Bonaventure*, Cambridge, 1959. – R. Manselli, *Spirituali e Beghini in Provenza*, Rome, 1959. – M. D. Lambert, *Franciscan Poverty*, 1961. – L. Landini, *The Causes of the Clericalisation of the Friars Minor (1209-1260) in the Light of the Early Franciscan Sources*, Toronto, 1968. – J. R. Moorman, *History of the Franciscan Order from its Origins to the Year 1517*, Oxford, 1968. – J.R. Moorman, *The Franciscans in England*, London, 1974. – *Franciscains d'oc. Les Spirituels*, Toulouse, 1975. – *Chi erano gli Spirituali*, Assisi, 1976. – *Francesco d'Assisi e Francescanesimo dal 1216 al 1226*, Assisi, 1977. – J.V. Fleming, *An Introduction to the Franciscan Literature of the Middle Ages*, Chicago (IL), 1977. – *Espansione del Francescanesimo tra Oriente e Occidente nel secolo XIII*, Assisi, 1979. – *Francescanesimo e vita religiosa dei laici nel '200*, Assisi, 1981. – P. Gratien, *Histoire de la fondation et de l'évolution de l'ordre des Frères Mineurs au XIIIe siècle*, Paris-Gembloux, 1982. – T. Desbonnets, *De l'intuition à l'institution. Les Franciscains*, Paris, 1983. – L. Pellegrini, *Insediamenti francescani nell'Italia del Duecento*, Rome, 1984. – *Il rinnovamento del Francescanesimo: l'Osservanza*, Assisi, 1985. – D. Nimmo, *Reform and Division in the Medieval Franciscan Order*, Rome, 1987. – *I Francescani nel Trecento*, Assisi, 1988. – *Francescanesimo e cultura universitaria*, Assisi, 1990. – *Eremitismo nel Francescanesimo medievale*, Assisi, 1991. – *I Compagni di Francesco e la prima generazione minoritica*, Spoleto, 1992. – M. Sensi, *Dal movimento eremitico alla regolare osservanza francescana. L'opera di fra' Paoluccio Trinci*, Santa Maria degli Angeli, 1992.

Giulia Barone

**FRANCO OF COLOGNE or OF PARIS (13th c.).** A musical theorist of the second half of the 13th century. Evidence concerning his life and activities is scarce. He is described variously as *Franco de Colonia* ("Franco of Cologne"), *Franco Teutonicus* ("Franco the German") and as a papal *chaplain and *preceptor* of the *Cologne house of the *Hospitallers of St John of Jerusalem. The appellation *Parisiensis* ("of Paris") comes from a 15th-c. Italian copy of his treatise. Regardless of his whereabouts, his treatise *Ars cantus mensurabilis* (The Craft of Measured Composition) concerns *music and theoretical concepts current in *Paris, in particular the University of Paris. His treatise is a practical description of *rhythmic patterns and notation, consonance and dissonance and the various musical genres, with some instructions about how to compose them. He is famous for an innovative system of rhythmic notation that was relatively simple and unequivocal. It continued to be used with additions and modifications through the 16th century.

W. Frobenius, "Der Musiktheoretiker Franco von Köln", *Die Kölner Universität im Mittelalter*, A. Zimmermann (ed.), Berlin, 1989, 345-356.

Mary E. Wolinski

**FRANKFURT AM MAIN.** A royal *palace is attested at Frankfurt am Main in 794, when *Charlemagne stayed there and held a general **placitum* and an important *council. In the 9th and 10th cc., the kings readily lived there, but the town's true rise, supported by the rulers who wished thus to counterbalance the development of great lordships in the region, dates only from the 12th century. The town remained under the direct jurisdiction of the king. The Golden Bull of 1356 made Frankfurt the place where the sovereign had to be elected.

The Frankfurt *fair is mentioned from 1160, but profited especially from the decline of the *Champagne fairs from the 14th century.

*Frankfurt am Main. Die Geschichte der Stadt*, Frankfurter Historischen Kommission (ed.), Sigmaringen, 1991.

Geneviève Bührer-Thierry

**FRANKS.** The origin of the Franks, who gave *France its first royal dynasty and its name, has been the object of many controversies ever since the *Merovingian period. For the 6th-c. historian *Gregory of Tours, these Germans established at the mouth of the Rhine had come from *Pannonia (middle Danube). From the *Carolingian period to the 18th c., mythological considerations situated their original homeland in Phrygia and more precisely at Troy, as Ronsard sings in his celebrated *Franciade*. At the same time, other scholars considered the Franks as originating in *Scandinavia, a theory that still had followers even recently. Only in 1714 did Fréret put forward the idea that this people originated in the federation of Germanic tribes that had fought the Romans on the Rhine. Judged "an attack on the dignity of the French monarchy" (abbé de Vertot), this less seductive theory only finally prevailed with Fustel de Coulanges (1891).

Belonging to the family of West Germans and its most westerly sub-group (called "Rhine-Weser"), the Franks appeared in history under that name only late. They appear from the mid 3rd c. as a military league which, in imitation of that formed some decades earlier by the *Alamanni (from *alle*, *ala*, "all", and *man*, "men"), progressively grouped together a number of tribes from the right bank of the lower Rhine: Chamavi, Chatti, Bructeri, Usipetes, Tencteri, Tubantes and Ampsivarii. The late addition – mid 4th c. – of the Salii to this warrior league is today considered doubtful, the very existence of this tribe being questioned (see "Salians"). Their federation took its name from *frekkr*, *fri*, which in Old Norse meant "bold", courageous".

Up to the great *barbarian *invasion of 406-407, the greater part of the Franks remained outside the Empire. While the Rhineland tribes, alongside the Alamanni, confronted Rome on land, the coastal tribes made themselves illustrious by acts of piracy in the same way as their *Frisian and *Saxon neighbours. From the late 3rd c., the Western Frankish tribes from the mouths of the Rhine who were to engender the *Merovingian dynasty abandoned their maritime activities and infiltrated Batavia (modern *Netherlands), profiting from the poor defence or abandonment of these marshy territories. However the Roman defence stabilized them in the 4th c. in Toxandria (modern North *Brabant). As far as we can judge from *archaeology, the Franks did not at this time have a really specific material culture, unlike *e.g.* the Elbe Germans, and they are known to us on the right bank of the Rhine only by incinerations with modest funerary furnishings and by the diffusion of a type of pottery called "proto-Frankish".

Other Franks also lived in the Empire from the second half of the

3rd c., as written sources attest. Some of them, defeated, were installed in Gaul as *laeti* or *dediticii*, *i.e.* "unconditionally subject": liable to hereditary military service, they were entrusted with cultivation of lands on behalf of the State or the great proprietors. Others were collectively engaged as auxiliaries in the Roman army in Egypt or the Near East. Others still, in an individual capacity, had often remarkable military careers, like Merobaudes, generalissimo of Valentinian in 375, or Bauto, military tutor of Valentinian II (380-387).

Unlike the Western Franks, the Eastern or Rhineland Franks, (later known as "Ripuarians"), continued to harass the Roman garrisons of upper Germany. Carried away by the pugnacity of their Alaman neighbours, they also several times took possession of *Cologne, *Mainz and *Trier, though without ever effectively controlling the left bank of the middle Rhine. Shortly before the middle of the 5th c., however, according to Gregory of Tours, King Clodio beat the Romans and took possesion of *Arras before being beaten and repulsed in his turn. This ancestor of Clovis seems to have concluded a *foedus* (or treaty, hence the name "federates" given to Rome's barbarian allies) with the *magister militum Galliarum*, Aetius. This was doubtless why the Western Franks joined the coalition mounted by the Roman general in 451 against Attila, thus prefiguring the alliance of Childeric († 481-482) and his son Clovis (r. 481/482-511) with the last representatives of Roman authority in Gaul, Aegidius, Count Paul and then Syagrius.

The conquest of Gaul, undertaken by Clovis from 486-487, was not accompanied, as was long maintained, by massive colonization. In fact, with the exception of the regions on the left bank of the Rhine where the progress of the German language was the consequence of a majority Frankish settlement, *Latin remained the common language of the rest of Gaul where the Franks, while imposing their rule, were in a minority. This is confirmed by funerary *archaeology (furnishings and anthropology) since, from the completion of the conquest under Clovis's sons (536), the identification of the population of Frankish stock becomes problematic. Besides, from the second half of the 6th c., all the inhabitants of the northern half of Gaul were recognised as *Franci*, in contrast to the *Romani* of the southern half of the country, proof of the achievement of "progressive fusion" between Gallo-Romans and Franks and the birth, to use the expression of Ferdinand Lot (*La Naissance de France*, 1948), of a "Gallo-Frankish patriotism".

Gregory of Tours, *The History of the Franks*, L. Thorpe (tr.), Harmondsworth, 1974.

E. Zöllner, *Geschichte der Franken bis zur Mitte des 6. Jahrhunderts*, Munich, 1970. – E. Demougeot, *La Formation de l'Europe et les Invasions barbares. I. Des origines germaniques à l'avènement de Dioclétien*, Paris, 1969; *ibid., II. De l'avènement de Dioclétien au début du VI*[e] *siècle*, Paris, 1979 (2 vol.). – L. Musset, *Les Invasions. Les vagues germaniques*, Paris, 1969 (2nd ed.). – *The Laws of the Salian Franks*, K. F. Drew (ed.), Philadelphia, 1991. – I. Wood, *The Merovingian Kingdoms 450-751*, London, 1994. – R. McKitterick, *The Frankish Kings and Culture in the Early Middle Ages*, Aldershot, 1995. – C. R. Bowlus, *Franks, Moravians, and Magyars*, Philadephia, 1995. – *Die Franken, Wegbereiter Europas*, Mainz, 1996 (2 vol.; Catalogue of the Mannheim and Berlin exhibitions, 1996-1997). – P. Périn, L.-C. Feffer, *Les Francs*, 2nd ed., Paris, 1997 (2 vol.). – M. Springer, "Gab es ein Volk der Salier?", D. Geuenich (ed.), W. Haubrichs (ed.), J. Jarnut (ed.), *Nomen et gens, Ergänzungsbände zum Reallexikon der Germanischen Altertumskunde*, 16, Berlin-New York, 1997, 58-83. – P. Périn, "La progression des Francs en Gaule du Nord au Ve siècle. Histoire et archéologie", D. Gueunich (ed.), *Die Franken und die Alemannen bis zur "Schlacht bei Zülpich" (496/97)* (Actes du colloque de Zülpich, 1996), Berlin-New York, 1998, 59-81.

Patrick Périn

**FRATERNITIES, MONASTIC.** The bond of confraternity granted by a religious community allowed the beneficiary (an isolated individual or all the members of an ecclesiastical establishment) to be associated in perpetuity with all the spiritual benefits that emanated from it, in the name of the dogma of the *communion of saints.

Thus, from the 8th c., doubtless under the influence of Irish missionaries, unions were established whose associates committed themselves to praying for each other on the decease of one of them. The earliest one identified was set up at the synod of Attigny in the Ardennes in 762; it grouped together various religious, *abbots and *bishops. Rapidly, these agreements were not confined to dignitaries but extended to all the members of the contracting houses. At each *death, the news was passed on by one of the brothers, bearing a "*roll of the dead", to the various associated establishments. The names of the deceased were preserved in each community in the form of lists written down in *Libri vitae* or *Libri memoriae*, then in *obituaries which brought together all the acts of pious *foundations.

Entry into the fraternity was granted by the abbot with the consent of the *chapter. It guaranteed the beneficiary various liturgical *prayers at the moment of his decease, then at the regular commemoration of the *dead, at the *office of prime, or even individual *anniversary services which, faced with the increasing weight of the burden, tended to become collective, for the general intention of the members of a single establishment, in accordance with a usage introduced by the *Cistercians. Frequently there was the added privilege of being able to take the habit before dying. Finally, the agreement was sometimes accompanied by the allocation of a food surplus in compensation for the effort of psalmody it engendered, or even forms of temporal solidarity (mutual hospitality of members or material aid).

Each monastery or *chapter, according to its particular devotions, its interests, the requirements of neighbourliness and its leader's links of *kinship or *friendship, was thus led to weave a web of associated churches generally numbering several dozen, but which could exceed a hundred (442 at *Cluny, on a recapitulative list from the first half of the 16th c.). Following the example of *Saint-Martial at *Limoges, these unions, at first mostly concluded in the Benedictine world and that of the cathedral chapters, were opened up to the new *orders in the course of the 12th c. and evolved in the 13th into individual concessions for *clerics and the *laity.

The desire to unite the memory of the dead in a collective prayer, which presided over the constitution of the monastic fraternities and with them the flowering of the *confraternities, ensured its prolongation well beyond the Middle Ages.

N. Huyghebaert, *Les Documents nécrologiques*, 1972 ("TSMÂO", 4); J.-L. Lemaître, *ibid., Mise à jour du fasc. n° 4*, 1985. – *Répertoire des documents nécrologiques français*, J.-L. Lemaître (ed.), Paris, 1980-1982 (4 vol.). – J.-L. Lemaître, *Mourir à Saint-Martial*, Paris, 1989.

Catherine Vincent

**FRATERNITY.** Fraternity means belonging to a group whose members are equals. Rooted in the bond between parent and *child, the desire to enter into relationship with others extends to the inhabitants of the same town, the same country, to humanity itself. Cicero distinguished the ideal of human solidarity (*humanitas*) from the bonds connecting people who share the same spiritual disposition (*caritas*). Jesus revealed a human fraternity, based on the universal paternity of *God: "anyone who does the will of my Father is brother and sister to me" (Mt 12, 50). This universal fraternity had its microcosm in the Church, whose members expressed their *love (*agape*) by sharing "all things in common . . . according to need" (Acts 2, 44-45). Christian fraternity demanded mutual aid in this life (charity) and help in the after-life (*prayer).

Remnants of this attitude survived in the early Middle Ages. Despite its hierarchized structure, Western *monasticism saw itself as a fraternity: sharing a common vocation, bound by a common Rule. "Prayer *fraternities" or "commemorative societies of the dead", attached to monasteries, united people in prayer and charity. Tripartite society, hierarchized and unequal, united by charity not fraternity, was shaken by the commercial revolution. A new middle class appeared, organised into groups of equals, called "*guilds".

But as the gap between rich and poor widened in the 12th c., the prayer *confraternities, increasingly lay, detached themselves from the monasteries and devoted themselves to works of *charity in the cities. Awareness of these inequities prompted the rediscovery of human fraternity, typified by the *fraternitas* founded by *Francis of Assisi. Francis's essential insight flowed from his encounter with the *lepers: he realized that no one, not even the most despised, is excluded from bearing the presence of *Christ. All are creatures of the same God: all are *fratres et sorores*. The Friars Minors and *Poor Clares were its microcosm.

P. Michaud-Quantin, *Universitas*, Paris, 1970. – R. Manselli, *Saint François d'Assise*, Paris, 1982. – C.M. Barron, "The Parish Fraternities of Medieval London", *The Church in Pre-Reformation Society*, C.M. Barron (ed.), C. Harper-Bill (ed.), Woodbridge, 1985, 13-37. – M. David, "Sur les traces médiévales de la fraternité", *Histoire et société. Mélanges offerts à Georges Duby*, 1, Aix-en-Provence, 1992, 113-123.

Michael Cusato

***FRATICELLI.*** Following the severe conflicts that set the Order of Friars Minor at variance in the 13th and 14th cc., the generic term *fraticelli* was applied in the 14th and 15th cc. to a crowd of dissidents, directly or indirectly linked to that religious order and to the *Franciscan movement; one school of historiography goes so far as to see them as a *heretical "sect". In the documents of the Roman Catholic Church, various appellations serve to indicate those who were later so called: "brothers of the poor life", *bizzocchi*, "*beghards", "little brothers of opinion"; all these groups were persecuted by the inquisitors in several countries of Western *Christendom, and even in the East where numerous dissidents of the Franciscan world had voluntarily exiled themselves or been forced to flee. It was these inquisitors, on the basis of papal decisions and their own legal culture, who gave a uniform image of a great diversity of religious experiences with little or no links among themselves.

C. Schmitt, *Introduzione allo studio degli spirituali e dei fraticelli*, Falconara, 1974 ("Picenum Seraphicum", 11). – G. Tognetti, "I fraticelli, il principio di povertà e i secolari", *BISI*, 90, 1982-1983, 77-145. – G. L. Potesta, *Angelo Clareno dai poveri eremiti ai fraticelli*, Rome, 1990.

Grado G. Merlo

**FREDERICK I OF HOHENSTAUFEN (1122-1190).** Frederick of Hohenstaufen (called Barbarossa) came from the family of the dukes of *Swabia, one of the most powerful families of the German aristocracy, which also had possessions in *Alsace. His father Frederick the One-eyed, a close relative of the last *Salian Emperor *Henry V, held important positions in the latter's entourage, guarding the imperial insignia on the monarch's death. His uncle Conrad, emperor in 1138, fought against the pretensions of the dukes of *Bavaria, of the Welf family. He designated his nephew to succeed him in 1152.

The new emperor had the intention of restoring all the prerogatives of his dignity. In the first place this meant imposing himself on the magnates of *Germany and especially on his kinsmen and rivals, the Welfs, led by his cousin *Henry the Lion, heir to the dukes of Bavaria and then *Saxony. Once elected king in March 1152 and after having pacified Germany, Frederick Barbarossa went to *Italy in 1154 to receive anointing and be consecrated emperor by the *pope, thus reviving on his own account the imperial idea as the *Ottonians or the Salians had conceived it. In addition he benefited from the revival of legal studies and the fruits of a reflection led by the *jurists of the *university of *Bologna from around the middle of the century and continued by the emperor's great counsellors, such as Rainald of Dassel, his *chancellor, or *Otto of Friesing, his historiographer. Notions such as imperial sovereignty, the autonomy of his power vis-à-vis the papacy and the universal vocation of his *authority gave Frederick's claims a solid theoretical justification. The *canonization of *Charlemagne in 1165, putting the Hohenstaufen in continuity with the great princes and saints of *Christendom, thus reminded everyone of the supremacy of his power which he held only from God, which earned him the enmity of the emperor of *Constantinople.

Against the papacy, he profited at first from the weakness of Pope *Adrian IV, in conflict with the king of *Sicily, and who moreover had been expelled from the City by the *revolt of the commune and senate of *Rome led by *Arnold of Brescia. Barbarossa was thus able to impose his conditions, bringing the *pope back to his city while obtaining imperial *consecration on 18 June 1155 from the pope's hands. But the restoration of imperial power in the kingdom of Italy also took the form of challenging the new powers of the *communes of *Lombardy, over which Frederick wished to recover all his sovereign rights, the *regalia*. Indeed he considered that the communes had usurped his rights, that any magistrate could only be an administrator of the emperor, and he called into question the principle of their institutions. Moreover, against the communes he preferred to support their lords, who were often the *bishops whose fidelity he hoped to receive as he had done in Germany. So during his reign Italian problems occupied a fundamental place, since it was from the peninsula that he took the main sources of his power: his ideological and legal backbone and the legitimacy conferred by his Roman consecration.

On his second expedition to the Italian peninsula, Frederick convoked a diet at Roncaglia in 1158 in order to dictate the conditions of the restoration of his *regalia* by the communes, but also by the pope, and to pose as arbiter of the rivalries of the Lombard communes, a way of imposing his authority through the medium of his arbitration. Responding indirectly to the request of the towns threatened by *Milan, whose expansionism in central Lombardy was at the expense of its neighbours such as Cremona, Lodi and *Pavia, the emperor ordered sanctions against the main ally of the Milanese, Tortona. Moreover, the fragile compromise established with Adrian IV was wrecked at the diet of *Besançon in 1157 when the pope's *legate suggested that the emperor was subordinate to the *pope, raising an outcry among Barbarossa's followers, who expelled him from the assembly. So when the new pope, *Alexander III, elected in Sept 1159, tried to contest the tutelage of the German emperor, the latter, at the instigation of his chancellor, opposed to him his own candidates, Victor IV in 1159 and Paschal III in 1164. Alexander III then excommunicated the emperor. The crisis between pope and emperor thus culminated in a *schism that lasted until 1177. From then on, the supreme pontiff, after having moved closer to *William II of Sicily, also found allies in Lombardy among the communes who, around Milan, rejected the right of Frederick and his agents to supervise the appointment of their principle magistrates. The *Lombard League, thus formed in 1167 with the pope's approval, brought together interests that the emperor had tried at the outset to dissociate by isolating Milan, which he had razed to the ground in 1162. We can see the same intransigence in Germany, where in 1163 the Hohenstaufen razed *Mainz which had risen against its bishop. However, after his defeat at Legnano in May 1176 by the Lombard League, Frederick had to come to terms with the pope and sign a truce at Venice in 1177. The peace also put an end to the schism. But Barbarossa did not give way to the communes until 1183, at the peace of *Constance where he recognised the specific character of the communal institutions, while exercising a theoretical control over the elections of magistrates, who promised fidelity to him. Thus the emperor's struggle against the towns of Lombardy favoured the birth of a *Guelfism that found in the papal alliance a means of imposing its conception of political authority on the emperor and asserting its local particularity.

In Germany, Frederick was supported by a clergy that rallied to him without too many difficulties, the diet of *Würzburg in 1165 having laid down the principle of obedience to the *antipope Paschal III. The emperor placed his relations and his family's allies on episcopal and abbatial thrones, *e.g.* Christian of Mainz, Otto of Freising or Rainald of Dassel, who received the archbishopric of *Cologne. On the other hand, the magnates distributed their help to Frederick parsimoniously. The archbishop of *Salzburg had to be subdued. The Welf *Henry the Lion, first cousin to the emperor, supported by European matrimonial alliances since he was son-in-law to the king of *England, was often restless. He was the main spokesman for the magnates' discontent with Frederick's Italian undertakings. Frederick had to eliminate his power, though it was founded on solid alliances in Bavaria and Saxony. In 1179, Henry the Lion was dispossessed of his properties mainly in favour of the *Wittelsbachs, who obtained Bavaria, and was banished from the *Empire. In his struggle against the magnates, Barbarossa could count on the support of the knights of the Empire, eager to have the heredity of their *fiefs recognised by a distant emperor rather than by too powerful dukes. The Empire was provided with institutions and the *nobility hierarchized into vassalic "shields" (*Heerschildordnung*).

Frederick's power was admittedly the product of a series of compromises that hardly survived his disappearance in 1190. But the Empire in the second half of the 12th c. enjoyed considerable influence in the West. In 1155 the emperor married the heiress to the county of *Burgundy. On the margins of the Empire, the king of *Denmark had to gain Frederick's approval in 1152 to receive his throne. The same tutelage was exercised over Duke Boleslas of *Poland, who had to acknowledge himself a vassal of Frederick. In southern Italy, Frederick negotiated an alliance with King William II of Sicily, who had long been his enemy as a supporter of the papacy. He married his son *Henry to *Constance of Hauteville, daughter of *Roger II, and had him consecrated in his lifetime as king of the Romans in 1169, attempting thus to keep the imperial dignity in his family. Reconciled with the pope, he promised to take part in the *crusade preached after the fall of *Jerusalem in 1188. Setting out from *Regensburg with an *army of crusaders, he was drowned in the Cydnos, in *Cilicia, in 1190.

M. Maccarrone, *Papato e impero dalla elezione di Federico I alla morte di Adriano IV (1152-1159)*, Rome, 1959. – M. Pacaut, *Frédéric Ier Barberousse*, Paris, 1967. – R. Folz, *The Concept of Empire in Western Europe form the Fifth to the Fourteenth Century*, London, 1969. – P. Munz, *Frederick Barbarossa. A Study in Medieval Politics*, London, 1969. – P. Munz, *Frederick Barbarossa*, Ithaca (NY), 1969. – J.-P. Cuvillier, *L'Allemagne médiévale. 1. Naissance d'un État*, Paris, 1979. – O. Capitani, "Federico Barbarossa davanti allo scisma: problemi e orientamenti", *Federico Barbarossa nel dibattito storiografico in Italia e Germania*, Bologna, 1982, 83-130.– W. Georgi, *Friedrich Barbarossa und die auswärtigen Mächte. Studien zur Aussenpolitik (1159-1180)*, Frankfurt am Main, 1990. – A. Haverkamp, *Medieval Germany, 1056-1273*, Oxford, 1992.

Thierry Pécout

**FREDERICK II, EMPEROR (1194-1250).** Frederick of Hohenstaufen was born on 26 Dec 1194. At the death of his father, *Henry VI (28 Sept 1197), he was four years old. On 28 Nov of the same year, his mother *Constance of Hauteville died, having, in her *testament, handed over the regency of the kingdom of *Sicily and the tutelage of her young son Frederick to the *pope.

*Innocent III's regency came to an end on 26 Dec 1208: Frederick had then completed his fourteenth year. To avoid a marriage with a German princess and to link Sicily to another of the papacy's vassal countries, Innocent III had projected a marriage between the young Frederick and Constance, sister of King *Peter II of Aragon and widow of King Emerich of *Hungary. The marriage was celebrated on 15 Aug 1209 at *Palermo.

In 1209 a first conflict broke out with the papacy, on account of the appointment of a new archbishop of Palermo. Next year Frederick dismissed the *chancellor Walter of Palearia, bishop of Catania and trusted agent of the Roman *Curia.

In the German question, Innocent III had initially taken the side of Otto of Brunswick, who had declared himself ready to recognise the territorial and legal claims of the Church. But immediately after the imperial *coronation, celebrated at *Rome on 4 Oct 1209, *Otto IV made a volte-face: on his way back, he stopped at *Pisa to organise the reconquest of the kingdom of Sicily, which the young Frederick II would have been incapable of resisting. Otto IV met fierce opposition from the pope, determined to prevent the union of the kingdom of Sicily with the *Empire. When the emperor crossed the frontiers of the *regno* (Nov 1210), the pope pronounced a solemn *excommunication against him. Reluctantly and urged on by *Philip Augustus, the pope fell in with the idea of getting Frederick elected king of *Germany (*Nuremberg, Sept 1211). The chancellor Walter of Palearia, who enjoyed the pope's confidence, was reinstated. Frederick II himself set out for Germany in March 1212.

The conflict with Otto IV was sealed by Philip Augustus, who managed to defeat the imperial *army on 27 June 1214 at Bouvines. The king of France sent the imperial eagle to Frederick II, who had himself crowned king again at *Aachen by the archbishop of *Mainz. He was then aged 21. To general surprise, he publicly committed himself to organising a *crusade. The presence of a papal *legate at Aachen suggests that Frederick had taken his decision in agreement with the pope. A month later, he asked the general *chapter of the *Cistercians to admit him into their community of prayer.

The fourth *Lateran council (Nov 1215) confirmed the election of Frederick II; but on 1 July 1216, Innocent III made him promise that immediately after the imperial *coronation he would renounce the government of the kingdom in favour of his son Henry. Freed from his promise by the pope's death (15 July 1216), Frederick got the young Henry elected king of Germany (*Frankfurt, April 1220). On 22 Nov 1220, Frederick II was crowned emperor according to tradition at *Rome by Innocent's successor *Honorius III (1216-1227). He took the cross from the hands of the *cardinal-bishop Hugh of Ostia, acknowledged the legal separation of Sicily and the Empire and engaged to support the Church in its struggle against *heretics. For its part, the Church accepted the personal union between the two kingdoms.

His wife, Constance of Aragon, died in 1222; falling in with the pope's wishes, in Nov 1225 Frederick married Isabella, daughter of *John of Brienne and heiress to the kingdom of *Jerusalem, then aged 14. He then committed himself to fulfilling his crusading *vow in August 1227 at the latest, but at that date an *epidemic was raging among the thousands of crusaders assembled at Brindisi, ready to set out for the *Holy Land. Even the emperor fell sick shortly after his departure and turned back in order to have himself cared for at the baths of Pozzuoli, near *Naples. He sent a messenger to Rome to explain to the pope that the crusade could not be organised in such conditions. *Gregory IX, who had had good relations with the emperor when he was *legate in *Italy, declared that the emperor's illness was faked and proceeded to excommunicate him on 29 Sept 1227, in *Anagni cathedral. In June 1228, the emperor finally embarked with forty galleys. On 7 Sept he arrived at *Acre. The imperial army comprised no more than a thousand knights. Excommunicated, the emperor could not count on the help of the Christians established in the East. The *Hospitallers of St John and the *Templars were hostile to him. He could rely only on the knights of the *Teutonic Order, as well as the Sicilians, Genoese and Pisans.

On 18 Feb 1229 he managed to reach a settlement with Sultan al-Kamil of Egypt, who was more impressed by his personality and his Arabic culture than by his military strength. A month later, in the church of the *Holy Sepulchre at Jerusalem, he took the *crown of the kingdom of Jerusalem that was laid on the altar and crowned himself. This gesture emphasized the divine immediacy of his new royal power. Frederick II then addressed a manifesto to *Christendom; for the first time, he dared to apply the words of Holy Scripture to his own person. On his return to Italy, he was saluted as a new *David.

Exasperated, the pope released all the emperor's subjects from their *oath of fidelity to Frederick. He even allied himself with the Lombard towns and tried, though without success, to organise the election of a counter-king in Germany. At the urging of Cardinal Thomas of Capua and the grand master of the Teutonic Order, Hermann of Salza, and with the collaboration of the German princes, an agreement between the papacy and the emperor was nevertheless concluded in summer 1230 at San Germano (*Monte Cassino) and at Ceprano. The price paid by the emperor was high: the Sicilian clergy were freed from royal jurisdiction; the king even renounced his right of confirmation at the appointment of *bishops.

A year after the peace of San Germano, Frederick promulgated the *Constitutions of Melfi, which he himself entitled *Liber Augustalis*. He considered himself the legitimate successor of Justinian, the great legislating emperor of late Antiquity. In March 1233, Frederick II reinforced the imperial laws against heretics. In June 1234, he asked for the pope's help against his own son. Indeed Gregory IX pronounced an excommunication against Henry (VII) on 5 July 1234. But Frederick's policy towards the Italian towns led the pope to appoint (Aug 1238) one of the emperor's worst enemies, Gregory of Montelongo, as legate for *Lombardy. On 20 March 1239, the pope for the second time pronounced an excommunication against the Emperor. Frederick's reaction to this new excommunication was not slow in coming. The *mendicants had to quit the kingdom. Appointments of bishops were subjected to the *authority of the king alone. The town of *Benevento, a papal enclave within the kingdom, suffered a blockade; the town's walls and towers were destroyed (1241).

Pope Gregory IX had convoked a *council at Rome for Easter 1241. To prevent it taking place, the emperor resorted to force. The Genoese fleet in charge of bringing the prelates to Civitavecchia was attacked by Sicilian and Pisan boats in front of the island of Montecristo (Giglio) south-west of the isle of Elba. Two *cardinals, three *archbishops and a hundred prelates were imprisoned, to the shock of all Christendom.

Gregory IX died the same year (22 Aug 1241). During the vacancy, the emperor kept up very heavy pressure on Rome and even approached dangerously close to it (July 1242, May 1243). From the *election of *Innocent IV (Sinibaldo *Fieschi, 25 June 1243), Frederick resumed negotiations. But the capture of *Viterbo by Cardinal Raniero Capocci (8 Sept) risked calling everything into question. Thanks to St *Louis and the German princes, however, a peace project was concluded on 31 March 1244. Some months later, on 28 June, determined to break definitively with the emperor, the pope fled in disguise to his home town, *Genoa. In October, he took the road to *Lyon to hold a council there that confirmed the emperor's deposition.

The struggle against Frederick had entered its final phase. There was no longer any possibility of agreement between the Papacy and the Empire. On the emperor's death (Fiorentino, 13 Dec 1250), the pope was able to return triumphantly to Italy.

E. Kantorowicz, *L'Empereur Frédéric II*, Paris, 1987 (1st ed. 1927). – *Stupor mundi: Zur Geschichte Friedrichs II. von Hohenstaufen*, G. Wolf (ed.), Darmstadt, 1966 (2nd ed. 1989). – H.-M. Schaller, *Kaiser Friedrich II. Verwandler der Welt*, Frankfurt, Zurich, 1971. – *Die Zeit der Staufer*, Stuttgart, 1977 (4 vol.). – *Federico II e l'arte del Duecento italiano*, Galatina, 1980. – A. C. Willemsen, *Bibliographie zur Geschichte Friedrichs II. und der letzten Staufer*, Munich, 1986. – D. Abulafia, *Frederick II: A Medieval Emperor*, London, 1988. – J. P. Lomax, "A Canonistic Reconsideration of the Crusade of Frederick II", *Proceedings of the Eighth International Congress of Medieval Canon Law*, Vatican City, 1992, 207-25. – *Federico II e il mondo mediterraneo*, A. Paravicini Bagliani (ed.), P. Toubert (ed.), Palermo, 1993 (3 vol.). – *Intellectual Life at the Court of Frederick II Hohenstaufen*, W. Tronzo (ed.), Washington (DC), 1994.

Agostino Paravicini Bagliani

**FREDERICK III, EMPEROR (1415-1493).** Duke of Austria of the *Habsburg dynasty, elected king of the Romans in 1439, consecrated emperor at *Rome (the last in German history to be so) in 1452, promoter of the international dimension of his dynasty. His long political career (the longest reign of the medieval *Empire) developed concurrently in three dimensions: Austria, the *Empire and Europe, leaning on each in order to progress in the others.

Frederick III represents the finished type of the late medieval German ruler, primarily a territorial prince: the Habsburg possessions monopolized an essential part of his activities, oriented towards reassembling properties that had been divided among several lineages or confiscated by the Swiss or the princes of southern *Germany. This patrimonial reassemblage was achieved at the price of monopolizing the tutelage of his young cousins and a long conflict with his brother Albert VI. Against the Swiss, Frederick III successively turned to Zurich (1442), to the *Armagnaken* (bands of "free companies" responsible for the *Alter Zürichkrieg* of 1443-1444) and then to Duke *Charles the Bold of Burgundy, before acknowledging his losses as permanent in 1474 (*Ewige Richtung*). To make up for this, the other territories of upper Germany were recovered more easily, from the 1440s. The end of his reign was also marked by the rise of the Turkish peril.

Internally, Frederick III gradually managed to master the political disorder. The imperial *consecration of 1452 and the other reciprocal arrangements with the papacy (increased control by Frederick over the Austrian Church) obtained from the *concordat of *Vienna gave his reign an appreciable ecclesiastical guarantee, which he reinforced by monumental propaganda.

As emperor, Frederick III left a mixed balance-sheet by reason of his long absence from Germany and the priority he gave to his princely interests, which threatened to turn the Electors against him and led to the election of his son Maximilian as king of the Romans in 1486. On one hand he contributed to liquidating the conciliar hypothesis by restoring the Empire to papal obedience, a return sanctioned by the concordat of Vienna (1448) guaranteeing the Roman *Curia control of the German Church. On the other hand he was preoccupied with the judicial and administrative modernization of the Empire (*Reformatio Friderici*, laws of imperial peace, etc.).

Of the imperial office, Frederick III retained mainly the universalist dimension, expressed in his reference to the two previous Fredericks (Hohenstaufen) and especially in his device *AEIOU* (*Austriae est imperare orbi universo* or, in German, *Alles Erdreich ist Österreich unterthan*: "the whole world is subject to Austria") created in 1437, but also in his wife Leonora of Portugal's change of name on the day of their marriage at Rome (shortly before his consecration): she became Helena, like *Constantine's mother.

Frederick III's wish to go beyond the limits of the German Empire was manifested notably in his Hungarian policy, which confronted him with *Matthias Corvinus (before whom he had to bend) but finally assured him the reversion of the crown of *Hungary (1463, then 1491). In the West, skilful negotiations with Charles the Bold allowed him to obtain the hand of Charles's heiress Mary for his son Maximilian, who set himself after 1477 to take possession of the Burgundian, Flemish and Netherlandish properties of his dead father-in-law.

*NDB*, 5, 1961, 484-487. – *LdM*, 4, 1989. – P. J. Heinig, *Kaiser Friedrich III. in Seiner Zeit*, Vienna, Cologne, 1993. – K. F. Krieger, *Die Habsburger im Mittelalter*, Stuttgart, Berlin, 1994.

Joseph Morsel

**FREDERICK III OF ARAGON, KING OF SICILY (1272-1337).** Third son of *Peter III of Aragon and *Manfred's daughter Constance, the infant Frederick was destined for *Sicily as part of the logic of a partition. Lieutenant of his brother James in the island (1291-1296), he was elected king by the Sicilians and crowned on 25 March 1296, Easter Day and feast of the Annunciation, in a messianic atmosphere that supported an unequal struggle against the *Angevins and the papacy. An unfaltering Ghibellinism, devoted to the cause of the *Spirituals, extracted a provisional peace in 1302 at Caltabellotta, which Frederick broke in 1314, joining the camp of *Henry VII, then that of Louis of Bavaria. In 1321 he crowned his son Peter II in order to guarantee the dynastic future; at his death, he bequeathed the county of Modica to the poor.

E. G. Leonard, *Les Angevins de Naples*, Paris, 1954, 183-195 and 218-254. – C.R. Backman, *The Decline and Fall of Medieval Sicily*, Cambridge, 1995.

Henri Bresc

**FREDERICK THE FAIR (1289-1330).** Son of the king of the Romans Albert I, Duke Frederick III of Austria was elected king in 1314, one day before Louis of Bavaria (four electors each). The neutrality of Pope *John XXII and Louis's care to avoid any decisive battle prolonged the uncertainty, which seemed about to turn in Frederick's favour due to his diplomatic efforts (supported by his father-in-law, the king of *Aragon), when the defeat of Mühldorf (1322) against Louis – whose captive he became – reversed their relative strength. Though freed in 1325, assured by Louis of the co-regency and urged on by his brother, Frederick was abandoned by the *pope and henceforth concentrated on his patrimony.

*NDB*, 5, 1961, 487. – J.-P. Cuvillier, *L'Allemagne médiévale*, 2, *Échec d'une nation*, Paris, 1984, 162-171. – B. Hamann, *Die Habsburger. Ein biographisches Lexikon*, 1988. – *LdM*, 4, 1989, 939-940.– K. F. Krieger, *Die Habsburger im Mittelalter*, Stuttgart, Berlin, 1994. – J. Berenger, *A History of the Hapsbourg Empire*, London, 1997.

Joseph Morsel

**FREE SPIRIT.** In 1311-1312, the council of *Vienne denounced in its 28th canon (*Ad nostrum*) a new *heresy that had recently spread in *Germany and whose followers, putting themselves on a high level of perfection and in freedom of spirit, "claim not to be subject to human obedience or obliged to follow the precepts of the Church since, according to them, where the spirit of *God is, there is *freedom". This condemnation hit at the *beghards and especially the *beguines, whose doctrinal deviations were also denounced in the 16th canon (*Cum de quibusdam mulieribus*). In fact, after the promulgation of the conciliar decrees by Pope *John XXII in 1317, a violent persecution broke out against those lay circles and certain of their *Franciscan or *Dominican spiritual directors, particularly in the German lands and in central *Italy. But, in 1310, Parisian theologians had burned the beguine Margaret Porete, author of the *Mirror of simple and annihilated souls* in which they had already detected the same errors, while in 1307 St *Clare of Montefalco denounced the friar minor Bentivenga and his companions to the Umbrian *Inquisition as followers of "the spirit of freedom". These accusations were repeated and amplified throughout the 14th c. by inquisitors engaged in a merciless struggle against the "brothers and sisters of the Free Spirit", in which they saw a well-organised sect with ramifications all over *Christendom.

The most recent historians, particularly R. Lerner, have shown that this was to a great extent a view of the spirit or a convenient pretext to strike at more or less informal groups of pious laypeople, particularly *women, who sought direct contact with God and expressed their spiritual experiences in the vernacular. Likewise, the accusations of moral irregularity and antinomianism hurled at the time against these men and women must be considered with the greatest reservation: objective witnesses generally agree in emphasizing their austerity of life and attachment to *poverty. Also attributed to them, perhaps more seriously, were *pantheistic beliefs ("God is all that exists and man can become God by nature"), a rejection of religious practices – in particular the *sacraments – and ecclesiastical institutions, considered useless in the perspective of a *salvation identified with an individual search for divinization. Various statements heading in that direction certainly appear in the texts emanating from these circles, like the treatise entitled *Schwester Katrei*, falsely attributed to Meister *Eckhart. But, all in all, it seems rather that a number of prelates and theologians of the time, frightened by the woolliness or ambiguity of formulation of the mystical language used by an elite of devout laypeople, harshened – isolating them from their context – expressions that strove to give an account, in a vocabulary less subtle and nuanced than that of *Latin, of the profoundest realities of the inner life, and thus conferred on them a frankly heretical character.

J. Orcibal, "Le miroir des simples âmes et la secte du Libre Esprit", *RHR*, 88, 1969, 35-60. – R. Lerner, *The Heresy of the Free Spirit*, Berkeley (CA), 1972. – R. Guarnieri, "Fratelli del Libero Spirito", *DIP*, 4, 1979, 633-652. – G. L. Potestà, *Storia e ecclesiologia in Ubertino di Casale*, Milan, 1980, 224-251. – F. J. Schweitzer, *Der Freiheitsbegriff der deutsche Mystik*, Frankfurt, 1981 (ed. of "Schwester Katrei").

André Vauchez

## FREEDOM

**Philosophy.** Without being a decisive turning-point, the condemnation of 7 March 1277 by *Stephen Tempier remains a useful landmark in the history of freedom in the Middle Ages. The bishop of Paris's condemnation threatened the freedom of thought of philosophers, and even that of theologians, in that it tried to forbid, under threat of *excommunication, any *doctrine that was too much inspired by *Aristotle and *Averroes.

Tempier's authoritarian action was aimed directly at the *masters of the arts *faculty, who had reactivated the ideal of the Aristotelian sage; the *syllabus* of the bishop of Paris thus revealed the fear of that ideal preached even by a corporation whose revenues were quite modest and whose social situation was very precarious: "Though there may be errors in *philosophy", said an anonymous master, "it is indispensable that these errors be taught and heard, not so that people may believe them, but so that they may know how to oppose them by following the way of *reason (*via rationis*), making use of philosophical methods."

The year 1277 could not fail to arouse a decisive reaction in favour of freedom of thought. Condemnation came also from theologians. Around 1290, *Godfrey of Fontaines († *c.*1306-1309) was still complaining of the harmful effects of the condemnation: "What a scandal to unbelievers and even to believers is the ignorance and naivety of these prelates who consider erroneous and contrary to the faith that which is opposed neither to *faith nor to morals."

While avoiding reference to the mid 14th c. or the claims of *John Buridan († after 1358), the exactingness of William of *Ockham († 1349-1350) can be pointed to: "Statements, especially those that are to do with the philosophy of *nature and do not concern *theology, should neither be condemned nor forbidden by anyone, because in these matters everyone should be free to say freely what he pleases".

Thus between 1250 and 1350 there was an extremely firm current of thought that echoed the vigorous judgment of *Albert the Great († 1280); in his *Commentary on Aristotle's Politics*, Albert complains of the narrow, petty obscurantism of the enemies of freedom in his time. He describes these people so fiercely opposed to Aristotle's philosophy as men for whom the reading of texts has no interest unless they can find something to condemn in them; they take pleasure, he says, in their intellectual dullness and seek to paralyse others in order to reduce them to their own inertia. It was people of this type who put Socrates to death, who forced Aristotle to leave Athens saying that he would not give the Athenians a second occasion to sin against philosophy. Bitter, "they try to inject their own bitterness into others, forbidding others to devote themselves to the search for truth in the pleasant atmosphere of a fraternal community" (*Epilogue*).

Several of the 219 articles condemned in 1277 deal with the doctrine of freedom and reveal the way in which contemporaries tackled the question: the main concern of the *syllabus* was to fight against any form of determinism (astral or theological). Consequently the aim of this text was to show that the *will gives rise to its own act (*voluntas a seipsa movetur*) and is in no way determined by external influences.

To demonstrate this freedom of the will (since psychological experience was not enough), *Henry of Ghent († 1293) emphasized, on the eve of the condemnation, that the will is the highest *faculty "in the whole inner universe of the *soul", and that it is the will that directs the intellect (as a master directs his servant), while the intellect is content to clarify the free act (as the servant directs the master by carrying a lantern for fear that he may hurt himself). What was at stake was no less than the role of *love in the totality of human experience. This is why the majority of *Franciscan thinkers from *Bonaventure on († 1274) drew on this idea.

They were thus opposed to *Thomas Aquinas († 1274) who, claiming superority for the intellect, established the basis of free will: since human will tends naturally to happiness and has for object the *Good in all its amplitude, no particular object or human reality reaches the level of the Good; while not having to make the choice of the universal good, man must however choose (*eligere*) the means to attain it among all the contingent goods that the intellect presents to him: "The root of freedom is the will as subject, and reason as *cause".

Thus we see the dawning of an opposition between what would later be called the freedom of indifference, meaning that the will is free to follow or not to follow the good presented to it by the practical judgment (a position confirmed in 1277), and the doctrine of Thomas which, leaving no room for "this lowest degree of freedom", gives itself the means to maintain both an inalienable free will (in the order of exercise) and the possibility for man to order his life by choices with a view to happiness or to the final end that shapes and directs its architecture (in the order of specification).

Before *Duns Scotus († 1308), the "voluntarist" doctrine found an ardent defender in the person of the Franciscan *Peter John Olivi († 1298) who, a fierce enemy of Greco-Arab determinism, identified man's dignity with his freedom: given the choice between losing one's freedom or crumbling into nothingness, one should prefer the second solution. Similarly, for William of *Ockham († 1349-1350), freedom consists of being able to admit acts in such a way that, without determination of the object external to it, the will can indifferently produce or not produce an effect; thus it could come about *de potentia absoluta dei* (by the absolute power of God) that God's hatred would merit eternal *salvation.

These audacious 13th-c. debates, revived by the entry of Aristotle into the West, drew in reality on a centuries-old tradition.

Defined at first as *liberum arbitrium*, freedom was conceived at first as an absence of external constraint: thus men spoke of *libertas a coactione*, or *libertas a necessitate*. In other terms, and at least from the time of Augustine of Hippo († 430), free will was presented as the aptitude of the will to determine itself from within, without any extrinsic necessity coming to limit, thwart or, *a fortiori*, determine the voluntary act. Thus the act of willing could be identified with that of disposing of free will: the will is self-possessed, and this is why the act of will is always free, otherwise it does not exist; a will can always act or not act.

From this point of view, the philosophical question of freedom boils down to the question of free will, of which *Peter Lombard († 1160), by defining it as the "faculty of reason and will," bequeathed an equivocal formula to posterity (Thomas Aquinas, *Summa theologiae*, I[a], q. 83, 1-4). We can understand the condemnation of the council of Sens (1140) which thought to read in Peter *Abelard († 1142) a reduction of freedom to the free will held to guarantee to itself alone the human capacity of doing good.

But free will is not yet freedom. To say that *man is free by himself to exercise his own acts, even if they are bad acts, is to consider the free act independently of any moral qualification. Now the epistle to the Romans (6, 20-23) says that believers are no longer servants of *sin but that, as servants of righteousness, they are free from sin; we may imagine that medieval thinkers would insist on this moral aspect of human life; they knew that Augustine had already shown the multiple meanings of the term "freedom", which sometimes signifies "free will" (*libertas a coactione*) and sometimes designates the *liberation* consecutive to the free act, or liberation from all servitude: *libertas a peccato* and *libertas a miseria*.

The use of a single term (*libertas*) to designate one or other of these two aspects of freedom lent itself – and still lends itself – to continual misunderstandings. In Augustine, or later in *Anselm of Canterbury († 1109) and especially *Bernard of Clairvaux († 1153), we find an attempt to favour the second sense of freedom: if man is free, it is essentially in that he is *freed* from the power to do ill, in that he "prefers the good". Restored by *grace, man can from now on effectively will the good. This is why there are degrees of freedom: the more man will seize and realise his true good, the more he will be free.

O. Lottin, *Psychologie et morale aux XIIe et XIIIe siècles*, 1, Louvain, Gembloux, 1942. – E. Stadter, *Psychologie und Metaphysik der menschlischen Freiheit, Die Ideengeschichtliche Entwicklung zwischen Bonaventura und Duns Scotus*, Munich, Paderborn, Vienna, 1971. – F.-X. Putallaz, *Insolente liberté, Controverses et condamnations au XIIIe siècle*, Fribourg, Paris, 1995.

François-Xavier Putallaz

**Law.** The medieval period saw the fading away in Western Europe of the legal distinctions inherited from the classical world, which distinguished between freedom and servitude. As long as a strong public *authority was maintained, freedom could be recognised by military service due to the Carolingian emperor or by capacity to belong to the count's *court of law. Later, the free man was one who remained exempt from seignorial levies, but this definition was not very precise. Thus, freedom was mainly a negative notion, and it is by analysing the status of the non-free that we attempt to discern it.

We observe in the first place that the old type of *slavery did not disappear during the medieval period. The slave trade fed markets that were not all outside *Christendom, and currents of trade from *Verdun to the Iberian peninsula were known in the 9th century. *Merchants procured slaves on the margins of Christendom, in the Slav or Baltic lands or in Eastern *Germany.

While the demand from *Islam nourished important currents of trade, *Provence and *Catalonia also used this servile *labour. However, unlike ancient slavery, these were domestic slaves, providing for the needs of an urban market. *Barcelona and *Marseille were still important pivots of it in the 13th century.

Moreover, the West knew forms of dependence within its social relationships. *Serfdom was primarily a legal notion and concerned rural society. It does not seem to have been as widespread and as generalized as was once thought, numerous *peasant freeholders falling outside the label. The ignominious taxes of *formariage*, **mortmain* and *chevage* are no longer considered as certain signs of servility. The peasant freehold seems to have endured up to the 10th c., especially in areas of agricultural gain where certain forms of appropriation were possible, such as *aprision* in Catalonia. Little present in sources, it is the object of numerous controversies. Its decline seems to have marked the rise of a military aristocracy and of *seigneurie banale*, putting pressure on isolated freeholders who were gradually put under their protection and thus became tenants. Finally, the honourable dependence present in vassalic relationships shows the social place of the notion of dependence.

The conquest of new freedoms thus came about mainly through franchises, exemptions granted by lords to communities, such as urban communities, or snatched by them from the 12th century.

M. Bloch, "Liberté et servitude personelles au Moyen Âge", *Mélanges historiques*, 1, Paris, 1963, 286-355. – J. Heers, *Esclaves et domestiques au Moyen Âge dans le monde méditerranéen*, Paris, 1981. – R.M. Karras, *Slavery and Society in Medieval Scandinavia*, New Haven, 1988. – *Les Origines des libertés urbaines. XVIe congrès des historiens médiévistes de l'enseignement supérieur public, Rouen, 1985*, Rouen, 1990. – P. Bonnassie, "D'une servitude à l'autre: les paysans du royaume", *La France de l'An mil*, R. Delort (dir.), Paris, 1990. – P. Bonnassie, *From Slavery to Feudalism in Southwestern Europe*, Cambridge, 1991. – P. Freedman, *The Origins of Peasant Servitude in Medieval Catalonia*, Cambridge, 1991. – D. Barthélemy, "Qu'est-ce que le servage en France, au XIe siècle?", *RH*, 116, 1992, 233-284. – *The Work of Work: Servitude, Slavery, and Labor in Medieval England*, A.J. Frantzen (ed.), D. Moffat (ed.), Glasgow, 1994. – D.A.E. Pelteret, *Slavery in Early Mediaeval England from the Reign of Alfred until the Twelfth Century*, Woodbridge, 1995.

Thierry Pécout

**FREEDOM OF THE CHURCH.** The freedom of the Church was one of the key words of the *Gregorian reform in the 11th-12th cc., in close association with that of Roman primacy. *Libertas Ecclesiae*, however, experienced a progressive affirmation to the extent that it was formulated both as a theoretical edifice and under the grip of the necessities of the reforming practice that unleashed the *Investiture Contest (1075-1122).

The idea of Christian *freedom, at first, according to St *Paul, a personal faculty of man's submission to *God's order and union with him, was later applied to things, churches and monasteries benefiting from *libertates* indispensible to divine service. The formation of the Carolingian *Empire, conceived as a mystical entity unifying within itself the notions of *Church and State, abolishing all division between *temporal power and spiritual power, accentuated the phenomenon. *Libertas* became synonymous with *privilegium*, usually granted by the sovereign. The imperial Church benefited from franchises, more or less wide, of a political, legal or economic nature. The major demand by the generation of

*Humbert of Moyenmoutier and Hildebrand for *libertas ecclesiae*, no longer just the mere concession of freedoms, produced a decisive break with the sacralized order of the Carolingian and Ottonian worlds. For them the "charter of freedom sealed by the Redeemer on the cross", modelled on the heavenly *Jerusalem (Gal 4, 26-32) and on the early Church, whose deposit had been left to the Roman mother Church, its herald and defender. After the liberation of the papacy from lay influence in 1059, *Gregory VII (1073-1085) decisively enfranchised the Church from the tutelage of the temporal powers by condemning lay *investiture of both *bishoprics and *abbeys. It was thus a question of restoring a real distinction between the temporal and the spiritual, a veritable overthrow of the ecclesiological structures of *Christendom.

With *Urban II (1088-1099), in the context of the *schism arising from the Investiture Contest, the theological aspect of the freedom of the Church was clarified according to the *Augustinian schema of the two bodies, that of the Church and that of the devil. Freedom meant the irreducible separation that opposed the *saeculum*, "living under the yoke of *sin and Satan", to the Church, "freed by the blood of *Christ". The secularization of churches by *investiture not only annulled all distinction between temporal and spiritual but restored, in opposition to it, the rule of the Prince of this world. Freedom fixed the defensive frontier of the Church, the missionary zone in which it confronted the *demon; the princes, according to their ecclesial attitude, thus passed from one universe to the other. The *concordat of *Worms, in 1122, ended in a compromise but left a crucial problem: the Church's inability to acknowledge that the temporal power had an end of its own, one of natural law, distinct from cooperation in the *salvation of the world. This explains the formulation of the theory of the two *swords, in which the temporal remained at the service of the spiritual which directed it, and the affirmation of papal *theocracy.

*MGH.LL*, E. Dümmler (ed.) *et al.*, 1891-1897 (3 vol.).

A. Fliche, *La Réforme grégorienne*, Paris, 1924-1937 (3 vol.). – G. Tellenbach, *Libertas, Kirche und Weltordnung im Zeitalter des Investiturstreites*, Stuttgart, 1936. – B. Szabö-Bechstein, *Libertas Ecclesiae*, *SGSLE*, 12, 1985. – J. Paul, *L'Église et la culture en Occident, IXe-XIIe siècles*, Paris, 1986 (2 vol.).

Jean-Hervé Foulon

**FREIBURG IM BREISGAU.** At the crossroads of a number of routes and *roads between the Rhine and the Black Forest, on the site of a *market-emporium of the bishop of Basel, the town of Freiburg was founded in 1120 by Konrad of Zähringen. The city enjoyed a rapid commercial rise based on a fertile soil (*vines), active crafts, trade between *Italy and the Rhineland and silver mines in the Münstertal. From 1200, its wealth allowed the construction and completion of the *cathedral, as well as the settlement of the *mendicant orders. The decline of the first half of the 14th c. was manifested by a decrease in population (from 9000 to 6000 inhabitants) and in 1368 the Fribourgeois allied themselves to the *Habsburgs. The creation of the *university as well as the attachment of the Emperor Maximilian to the town of his youth prepared the new prosperity of the 16th century.

*The Medieval Statutes of the Faculty of Arts of the University of Freiburg im Breisgau*, H. Ott (ed.), J.M. Fletcher (ed.), Notre Dame (IN), 1964. – *Freiburg im Mittelalter. Vorträge zum Stadtjubiläum*, W. Müller (dir), Bühl i. Baden, 1979. – *Freiburg 1091-1120, Neue Forschungen zu den Anfängen der Stadt*, H. Schadek (dir.), T. Zotz (dir.), Sigmaringen, 1995.

Odile Kammerer

*The Raising of Lazarus*, 12th-c. fresco in the nave of the basilica of Sant'Angelo in Formis (Campania).

**FRESCO.** The term "fresco" designates one of the techniques of mural *painting in which, following the etymology derived from the Italian "*pittura a fresco*", the pigments, usually of mineral origin and diluted in water, were applied to still fresh (*fresco*) plaster, composed of a mixture of sand and slaked lime (calcium hydroxide). A chemical reaction with the carbon dioxide contained in the air led, during the drying of the plaster, to the formation of a skin of calcium carbonate in which the pigments were fixed. This technique was especially used in *Italy from the *trecento*. Before that, painters also used mixed techniques.

O. Demus, *La Peinture murale romane*, Paris, 1970. – A. Prache, F. Avril, *La Peinture monumentale en Europe hors de l'Italie au XIIIe et au XIVe siècle*, Geneva, 1979. – *La Pittura italiana delle origini*, E. Castelnuovo (ed.), Milan, 1986. – H. Toubert, "Peinture murale romane. Les découvertes des dix dernières années", *Arte medievale*, 2nd series, 1, 1-2, Rome, 1987, 127-162. – C.L. Connor, *Art and Miracles in Medieval Byzantium*, Princeton (NJ), 1991.

Hélène Toubert

**FRIARS OF THE SACK.** The Order of Penitence of Jesus Christ, also called Friars of the Sack by reason of their coarse clothing, was founded in 1248 by a knight of Hyères connected with the *Franciscans. Duly approved, it followed the Rule of St *Augustine and resembled the *mendicant orders in the practice of strict *poverty and *preaching, notably among the infidel. Present from *England to the *Holy Land, it had up to 122 houses, nearly half in *Provence and *Languedoc, but had no female branch. It was the most important of the orders suppressed by the second council of *Lyon (1274), a decision slowly followed by effects in the South where the Friars of the Sack were very popular.

R. I. Burns, K. Elm, "Penitenza di Gesù Cristo", *DIP*, 5, 1980, 1398-1404. – L. J. Simon, "The Friars of the Sack. . .", *JMH*, 18, 1992, 278-296.

Catherine Vincent

**FRIDOLIN (7th c.).** Fridolin, a missionary in southern Alemannia, doubtless in the second half of the 7th c., was a native of the region of *Poitiers. He developed (with the support of King Clovis II?) the cult of St Hilary in the upper Rhine valley. He retired to end his days on the Rhine island of Säckingen, where he subsequently formed a community of *canons attested in the 9th century. The cult of St Fridolin developed in *Alsace, southern Baden and

*Switzerland: he is the patron saint of Glarus. Fridolin's activities are known only by a *Vita* written around 970-980, doubtless by the bishop of *Speyer.

I. Müller, "Balther von Säckingen und seine Fridolinsvita", *FDA*, 101, 1981, 20-65.

Geneviève Bührer-Thierry

**FRIENDSHIP.** A fundamental reality of human life and more specifically of Christian life, an expression of *love of *God and neighbour, friendship is one of the treasures of life. Celebrated and profoundly lived by St Gregory Nazianzen, St Augustine, St *Dominic, St *Francis, St *Bernard . . . , friendship had an important place in *monastic theology, mainly in the 12th century.

Very early on, *Aristotle (*Nicomachean Ethics* VIII-IX) and Cicero (*De amicitia*) defined it as agreement on all human things, accompanied by benevolence and affection, and explained that, to arise and develop, friendship supposes *virtue and considers the other as an *alter ego*.

With some exceptions (*Alcuin, *Rabanus Maurus, *Benedict of Aniane), the Carolingian period remained tied to the rhetorical form propounded by Cicero. By contrast, St *Anselm gave in his *letters (to *Lanfranc in particular) a much more personal expression of friendship.

But it was above all *Ælred of Rievaulx, with the two works that he wrote at the request of St Bernard while he was staying at *Clairvaux: *Spiritual Friendship* and the *Mirror of Charity*, who set out a sort of charter of friendship for the 12th century. This charter was the same that gave the monasteries their coherence and made them an expression of the famous Augustinian *cor unum*. Without ignoring the difficulties, occasional ambiguities and tribulations of friendship which he had confronted and which he evokes in his letters, Ælred studies the various other forms of friendship before coming to spiritual friendship, which plunges "those whom it has united into *contemplation" (*Spiritual Friendship*, 677 C). Thus he reformulates the Ciceronian definition in these terms: "A friend is in some sort the guardian of the very soul; my friend will be the guardian of my love or of my soul itself, he will keep all its secrets in loyal silence, as far as he can he will correct the faults he perceives or else he will support their imperfections; he will share its joys and sorrows; all that concerns his friend, he will feel as his own. In consequence, friendship is that virtue that binds souls by a sweet alliance of predilection and makes of several a single one" (663 C), until the unity of all in *Christ (672 D).

Going even further than Ælred of Rievaulx, *Richard of Saint-Victor and then *Henry of Ghent see the archetype of all friendship in the life of the *Trinity itself. The originality of their viewpoint is that they do not reduce friendship to a bipolarity but emphasize that, by its very nature, it implies a third who objectifies, shares and develops that friendship.

Doubtless human friendship has no common measure with the life of the Trinity but, as St *Thomas Aquinas showed (*Summa theologiae*, $I^{a}$ $II^{ae}$, q. 36, a. 3-4), it represents the highest form of *love. Medieval authors strove to live it.

B. P. McGuire, *Friendship and Community, The Monastic Experience 350-1250*, Kalamazoo (MI), 1988. – M. Stone, *Marriage and Friendship in Medieval Spain*, New York, 1990. – R. Hyatte, *The Arts of Friendship*, Leiden, 1994.

Marie-Anne Vannier

**FRISIA.** According to Latin authors of the 1st c. AD, the Frisians occupied the shores of the North Sea beyond the Rhine frontier: it was in the coastal fringe of the present Dutch province of Friesland that they appear to have developed their earliest culture, whose special features were dwellings perched on artificial mounds intended to protect them from the strongest seas, and the pastoral exploitation of the salt marshes. From there they spread, between the 5th and the 8th c., along the coasts from *Zealand to the western shores and islands of Schleswig-Holstein and began to play a role as mercantile intermediaries between *England, the Rhineland and *Scandinavia. While the *Franks were able, not without trouble, to subjugate them between the 7th and early 8th cc., only the Anglo-Saxon missionaries (in particular *Willibrord, first bishop of the Frisians from 695, whose see was established at *Utrecht; and *Boniface, *martyred in Frisia in 754) managed to rally them to the Christian faith.

The period of their integration into the political and cultural orbit of the West (late 8th-early 9th c.) was also that of the apogee of large-scale Frisian *commerce: from Dorestad, its pivot at the head of the Rhine delta, Frisian *merchants went upriver as far as *Alsace, frequented the *markets of *London, *York or *Saint-Denis, and above all opened up the first regular line of *navigation between the West and the Baltic via Haithabu, carrying there not just the products of their Rhenish hinterland, but also the first evangelizers of Scandinavia. While it is possible that the lure of their cargoes (*wine, arms, silver pence) motivated the unleashing of *Viking piracy, it is certain that, placed in the front line, the Frisians were their first victims.

Because of piracy, the pillage and partial occupation of Frisia by the Danish Vikings, hydrological movements that modified the Rhine delta and compromised the privileged position of Dorestad, and political troubles that agitated its hinterland, by the end of the 9th c. Frisia had lost the central place it had held in the communications system of northern Europe in the early Middle Ages. Integrated in 843 into Lower *Lotharingia, then in 870 into the German kingdom (soon *Empire), Frisia was from now on split among several principalities, among them those of the bishops of Utrecht and the counts of Holland, whose ambitions were often contradictory. At least the initiative of both of these contributed to turn the population away from distant horizons and harness them, from the late 10th c., to the great work of draining the coastal swamps. But the success of polderization confirmed the communities of inhabitants in their demand for a peasant *freedom that would not agree to submit to any seignorial power, and culminated in the final medieval centuries, at least in what would become the Dutch province of Friesland, in the rejection of any princely *authority whatever.

J. J. Kalma, *Geschiedenis van Friesland*, Leeuwarden, 1973 (2nd ed.). – *Algemene geschiedenis der Nederlanden*, 1-2, *Middeleeuwen*, D. P. Blok (ed.) *et al.*, Haarlem, 1981-1982. – S. Lebecq, *Marchands et navigateurs frisons du haut Moyen Âge*, Lille, 1983 (2 vol.). – E. Knol, *De Noordnederlandse Kustlanden in de Vroege Middeleeuwen*, Groningen, 1993.

Stéphane Lebecq

**FRITZLAR.** A monastery and town in northern *Hesse, on the Eder, 25 kilometres south-west of Cassel, founded by St *Boniface in 723-724. In 732-733, a monastery was founded there (St Peter's) that became a *mission centre until the foundation of *Fulda in 744. *Charlemagne raised it to the rank of an Imperial monastery.

*Henry I was made king there; many kings stayed there and many sessions of the diet were held there. In 1005 the monastery, now a *foundation of *canons, was put under the tutelage of the archbishopric of *Mainz. It was almost entirely destroyed by the anti-king Rudolf of Rheinfelden in 1079. In the late Middle Ages, it became an institution of canons for the *children of the *nobility and upper middle classes. It possessed an important treasury and *library. The town was developed by the archbishops of Mainz, especially from the 12th c., and became an important centre of *commerce (grain, linen). Despite the development of its own organs of government, the city nevertheless remained under the influence of the archbishop of Mainz.

K. E. Demandt, *Die Chorherren St Peter zu Fritzlar*, Marburg, 1985.

Franz Neiske

**FROISSART, JEAN (*c.*1337 - after 1404).** The latest research on the most famous – and most prolix – of the French-speaking *chroniclers of the late Middle Ages insists on the literary quality of his work and makes him a writer in a category of his own, both sympathetic and discerning. Born at Valenciennes in Hainaut, Froissart, future painter and singer of *chivalry, came from a *merchant background. He embraced a clerical career, but everything suggests that his religious concerns and feelings were, if not tepid, at least conventional: he was firstly *curé* of Lessines, then *canon of Chimay, two places in what is now the Belgian part of Hainaut. Like many contemporary writers, his literary activity depended on the mediation of a protector, who could guarantee him an income, connections and a public. His first such was a protectress, one of the daughters of William I, count of Hainaut, Philippa, married to *Edward III of England. In her service from 1361 to 1369, he multiplied his contacts with several great military figures of the times and travelled a great deal: *England, *Scotland, *Aquitaine, *Savoy, *Milan, *Rome. Other protectors followed: Robert of Namur, Philippa's brother-in-law, Wenceslas of Luxemburg, duke of *Brabant, Guy of Blois. All his life he loved to move around in order to be present as a well-placed witness at great events and to "interview" (because Froissart was in a sense a journalist and even a reporter) the people capable of faithfully explaining political and military vicissitudes to him. He died in or around 1404, after having pursued his literary labours almost to the last.

Even though the chronology of his *Chronicles* is imprecise or inexact and their geography hazy or fantastic, even though he gives too little room to official documents, even though he is too sensitive to the political and mental environment he is writing in, even though his love of the picturesque often leads him to dwell on the surface of things and present a onesided view of reality, even though he is hopeless at figures, Froissart, whose vision was incontestably wide, human and European, tried above all to be faithful to historical truth, which he affected to pursue with obstinacy and scruple. Innumerable aspects of social life (the *court, war, noble entertainments, but also urban conflicts, even the condition of the *peasants) appear in the thread of his four books of *Chronicles* in the form of a savoury recital studded with real gems of expression, artistically composed, concrete, vivid, often anecdotal – the objective being to retrace, for the sake of the noble public, the "great wars" engaged in by *France, *England and the neighbouring countries from 1327 to 1400. Up to 1360, his text is derived very closely from the *Chronicle* of Jean le Bel. There are several redactions of the first two books, differing quite widely in

*The author offers his book to the duchess of Burgundy.* Miniature from Froissart's *Chronicles*, 15th c. Chantilly, Musée Condé.

form and substance. Froissart's *Chronicles* had an immense and lasting success, as attested, among other things, by the large number of manuscripts (often brilliantly illuminated) dating from the 15th century.

Endowed with a fine literary education, prompt to pick up and take in all sorts of influences (among them that of *Chaucer), Froissart, lauder of arms, was also a love-poet, of the lineage of *Guillaume de Machaut: in this vein may be cited *L'horloge amoureuse* (a very interesting poem, if only for the technical history of the first mechanical clocks) and above all *Meliador*, a poetic saga of more than 30,000 verses, in the Arthurian style.

*Chroniques*, Kervyn de Lettenhove (ed.), Brussels, 1867-1877 (28 vol.); *ibid.*, Paris, 1869-1875 (15 vol. appeared). – G. T. Diller, *Froissart. Chroniques. Dernière rédaction du premier livre, éd. du ms. de Rome, Reg. lat. 869*, Geneva, 1972. – Jean Froissart, *Chronicles*, G. Brereton (tr.), Harmondsworth, 1978. – G. T. Diller, *Froissart. Chroniques, Le ms. d'Amiens, livre I*, Geneva, 1991.

J. Picoche, *Le Vocabulaire psychologique dans les* Chroniques *de Froissart*, Paris, 1976. – *Froissart historian*, J. J. N. Palmer (ed.), Woodbridge and Totowa, 1981. – G. Jäger, *Aspekte des Krieges und der Chevalerie: Untersuchungen zu Jean Froissarts Chroniques*, Bern, 1981. – P.F. Ainsworth, *Jean Froissart and the Fabric of History*, Oxford, 1990. – G. T. Diller, *Attitudes chevaleresques et réalités politiques chez Froissart...*, Geneva, 1984. – *DLFMA*, 1992, 775. – K.M. Figg, *The Short Lyric Poems of Jean Froissart*, New York, 1994.

Philippe Contamine

**FROMENT, NICOLAS (1435?-1484?).** A painter active in *Provence from 1465 to his death, first at Uzès, then, from at least 1468, at *Avignon. A triptych of the *Raising of Lazarus* (Florence, Uffizi), painted for Francesco di Guccio di Tommaso Coppini, bishop of Terni, probably in *Flanders or *Picardy, where he must have trained, is signed and dated 18 May 1461. He is known especially for his triptych of the *Burning bush*, painted in 1475-76 for

King *René and destined for St Saviour's *cathedral, Aix-en-Provence, where it still is. His art was strongly marked by Flemish formulae, but acquired a certain hardness of modelling which tautened the forms and drapes in a more typically Provençal taste.

M. Laclotte, D. Thiébaut, *L'École d'Avignon*, Paris, 1983.

Albert Châtelet

**FRUCTUOSUS OF BRAGA (died 665).** The life and work of Fructuosus of Braga, essentially handed down in the *Vita Fructuosi* written soon after his death, are hard to make out. His role as a monastic organiser was such that in the late 11th c., to counter Braga's autonomy, Diego Gelmirez had his *relics transferred to Santiago de *Compostela. This renown was at first bound up with the creation in the South and West of the Peninsula of an important monastic network served by the redaction of his *Regula monachorum* in *c.*640. At the head of the *diocese of *Braga from 656, he continued the organising work of St *Martin and, as *abbot of Dumium, his cultural work.

*PL*, 87, 1087-1131. – M. C. Díaz y Díaz, *La Vida de São Frutuoso de Braga*, Braga, 1974. – S. Valério, *Vida de São Frutuoso Arcebispo de Braga*, J. Cardoso (tr.), Braga, 1978. – Valerius, *Vita*, F. C. Nock (tr.), Washington, 1946.

J. Mattoso, *Religião e Cultura na Idade Média Portuguesa*, Lisbon, 1982, 11-27, 355-393.

Christophe Picard

**FRUTTUARIA.** A former Benedictine *abbey in Piedmont (province of *Turin), founded in 1003 by *William of Volpiano, *abbot of Saint-Bénigne at *Dijon, benefiting from royal and papal privileges such as free *election of the abbot, *exemption and papal protection. Monastic life there was marked by William's reforming thought, as well as by the spirit of *Cluny, of which written traces were handed down in the *Consuetudines fructuarienses*. In the 11th c., this abbey became the centre of reforming *monasticism in northern *Italy, where more than 50 monasteries claimed kinship with it. Through *Siegburg near *Cologne and through Sankt Blasien in the Black Forest, the *reform of Fruttuaria also spread to *Germany.

*Consuetudines fructuarienses-sanblasianae*, L. G. Spätling (ed.), G. Dinter (ed.), *CCMon*, 12, 1, 1985. – M. Dell'Omo, "L'abbazia medievale di Fruttuaria e i centri della riforma fruttuariense", *Monastica V. Scritti vari*, 1985, 185-201 ("MCass", 52).

Franz Neiske

**FULBERT OF CHARTRES (*c.*960-1028).** Born in *Italy, Fulbert studied at *Reims, then at *Chartres where he became *bishop in 1006. A renowned scholar, he played an important role in contemporary *politics and theological debate, trained numerous disciples, including *Berengar of Tours and Bernard of Angers, to whom he did not always transmit his Platonizing tendencies, and from his death in 1028 was honoured as a saint. His *portrait exists, dated 1028, in an *illumination of an *obituary at Chartres, precious evidence that shows him preaching to his people in front of the *cathedral he had built. Indeed he stands out not just for his influential writings, in particular on Marian theology, but as an ardent builder, to whom the cathedral *crypt still testifies.

*The Letters and Poems of Fulbert of Chartres*, F. Behrends (ed.), Oxford, 1976 (*OMT*).

A. Clerval, "Fulbert de Chartres", *DThC*, 6, 1, 1924, 964-967.

Colette Deremble

**FULDA.** A Benedictine *abbey in *Hesse, on the Fulda, a tributary of the Weser, founded on 12 March 744 by Sturm, a disciple of St *Boniface, to serve as a point of support for the *mission to *Saxony. From 751, he obtained from the mayor of the palace Carloman and from Pope *Zacharias the *donation of the lands surrounding the abbey and *exemption from episcopal jurisdiction, to which *Charlemagne added *immunity in 774.

Fulda's rise was favoured by the presence of the *relics of St Boniface, killed in *Frisia in 754. To respond to the development of the cult, on his return from exile at *Jumièges, in 765 Sturm undertook the enlargement of the first church around the saint's burial, placed in the western part of the building. Then, in 791 began the construction of a new edifice, more ambitious and innovative, entrusted to the monk-*architect Ratgar who took the Roman basilica of *St Peter's as model. The church was "occidented", with a wide semicircular apse at the west end opening onto a transept of 77 metres. To the two choirs, east and west, corresponded two columned *crypt-halls, one of which housed the relics of the saint. To the east was added a "paradise" reached by a triple portal. The new *basilica was consecrated on 1 Nov 819 by the bishop of *Mainz, and soon thereafter a new four-winged *cloister, as well as a cemeterial rotunda, in imitation of the *Holy Sepulchre. Fulda housed 600 monks at this time and its *patrimony was increased thanks to donations, despite the weight of building costs which entailed some internal troubles. Its *manses – 15,000 in the 12th c. – were scattered from Frisia to northern *Italy, and its filiation was numerous. Fulda's expansion reached its apogee in the late 11th c., covering a territory vast enough to be recognised as an ecclesiastical principality in 1220.

From the 13th c., the abbey entered a long decline, incapable of resisting the appetites of its powerful neighbours, such as the landgrave of *Hesse. Its spiritual and intellectual influence was curtailed after the abbacy of *Rabanus Maurus (822-842), *Alcuin's former pupil, whose brilliant mind and pedagogical qualities had attracted monks from all over western France (*Lupus of Ferrières, *Einhard, *Walafrid Strabo) and made Fulda one of the greatest centres in *Germany. But the abbey *school preserved a remarkable *library and a renowned **scriptorium*.

M. F. Fischer-Foswald, "Zur Baugeschichte des Fuldaer Klosterkirchen, Litteratur und Ausgrabungen in Christlicher Zeit", *Beihefte der Bonner Jahrbücher*, 28, *Rheinische Ausgrabungen*, 1, Cologne, 1968. – K. Schmid, *Die Klostergemeinschaft von Fulda im früheren Mittelalter*, Munich, 1978. – C. Heitz, *L'architecture religieuse carolingienne, les formes et leurs fonctions*, Paris, 1980. – *Kloster Fulda in der Welt der Karolinger und Ottonen*, G. Schrimpf (ed.), Frankfurt am Main, 1996.

Sylvie Allemand

**FULMINATION.** Fulmination was the act by which the ecclesiastical authorities enforced a *censure, in particular *excommunication, which struck like a thunderbolt (Latin *fulmen*). The term was taken from classical (Jupiter) but also biblical vocabulary. Though little used before the late Middle Ages, it appeared early: Ferrandus of Carthage († 546-547) speaks of the right of priests to combat *heretics "by the thunderbolt of *anathema [*fulmine anathematis*]".

Ferrandus of Carthage, "Ep. 3", *PL*, 67, 1848, 889B.

"Fulmination", *DDC*, 5, 1953, 915. – *Lexicon latinitatis nederlandicae medii aevi*, O. Weijers (ed.), M. Gumpert-Hepp (ed.), fasc. 28, Leiden, 1987, 423-424. – J. F. Niermeyer, *Mediae latinitatis Lexicon minus*, Leiden, 1993, 456.

Patrick Henriet

**FUNERAL**

**The West.** In Christian Antiquity, funerals (except those of a *bishop or a priest) were not the concern of the ecclesial assembly, but of the deceased's *family, from the time of his *death to his *burial, which took place quickly, cremation (practised by the pagans) being excluded as opposed to hope in the *resurrection of the *body, and the prayer of the *Psalms replacing the funeral lamentations of the pagans. As the Middle Ages advanced, more recourse was had to the priest, especially for *mass to be offered for the deceased, and, in many cases, to the *prayer of the clergy or of religious, so that funerals became liturgical in the proper sense.

The course of the funerary liturgy comprised the *office of the dead, the mass, the rite after mass called **absolutio*, the transfer of the body to the place where it would be buried (a *cemetery attached to the church, or in some cases a *tomb within the church itself), and burial.

D. Sicard, *La Liturgie de la mort dans l'Église latine des origines à la réforme carolingienne*, Münster, 1979. – B. Nilsson, *De Sepulturis*, Stockholm, 1989 (funerals in medieval canon law; in Swedish with German summary). – *CaP*, 3, *The Sacraments*, London, 1988. – C. Daniell, *Death and Burial in Medieval England, 1066-1550*, London, 1997.

Pierre-Marie Gy

**Byzantium.** Byzantine civilization inherited from both Greek and Israelite tradition a great respect for the *dead. However the inspiration of Byzantine funerary ritual was different in that the *resurrection of the dead had become an *article of faith. Thus a funeral, besides being a ritual farewell to the deceased and an occasion of praying for the repose of his *soul, was also, as it were, a celebration of his "birthday" in *heaven, a theme that is picturesquely represented in *Byzantine art by an *angel receiving from the deceased person's mouth his soul under the form of a baby sometimes wrapped in swaddling clothes.

The sources for Byzantine funerary ritual are abundant, but particularly important is the 15th-c. text due to *Symeon of Thessalonica (*PG*, 155, 669-696). However it should be noted that, as Symeon himself complained, funerals were not always conducted as he prescribed. After being washed and anointed, the body was clothed. *Bishops and priests were dressed in liturgical *vestments, monks in their religious habit and laypeople either according to their station in life or in a white *shroud. An *icon was placed on the dead body, which was then carried to the church. The **Trisagion* was sung, because the dead person's soul was now with the angels. A priest's body was to be placed before the Holy Doors of the sanctuary, a layman's body in the nave. Symeon was critical of the fact that, for the sake of convenience, bodies were invariably placed in the centre of the nave. The *akolouthia* (ritual *prayers and *psalms) was then performed. It seems to have developed from the *office of *Orthros* (morning office). After the body had been censed, the ritual *aspasmós* (farewell *kiss) took place. The body was then taken to the *cemetery for *burial. Symeon complained of disorder at funerals. Certainly, graphic accounts have come down to us of the funeral cortège, with torchbearers, trumpet players, flute players and professional mourners.

Funerary scenes were often represented in Byzantine art. At first it was the custom to show the dead body being lowered into a sarcophagus. Later the lying-in-state was preferred. Possibly the model for this was the *Dormition of the Virgin, but in due course it was regularly taken up particularly for the death of saints. Mourners stand around the laid-out body. The last kiss may be given. Some participants make mourning *gestures. A bishop may be represented reading from a book on which are inscribed the first words of Psalm 118, regularly recited at funerals.

*La Maladie et la Mort des chrétiens dans la liturgie*, A. Pistoia (ed.) *et al.*, Rome, 1975. – C. Walter, "Death in Byzantine Iconography", *ECR*, 8, 1976, 113-127. – C. Walter, *Art and Ritual of the Byzantine Church*, London, 1982, 137-144.

Christopher Walter

**FUR.** Furs are animal skins, lined with their hair and usable as *clothing; they are distinct from skins of leather, feathers, *parchment or wool (except light skins with very fine lambswool, or kids' hair). While the early German Middle Ages, up to the time of *Charlemagne, traditionally used furs as protection from the damp cold or in war, the influence of luxury, not so much Byzantine as Islamic, gained on "feudal" society, mainly between the 13th and the early 15th century.

"Domestic" skins broadly predominated, especially in rural areas, but in the Mediterranean world stillborn lambs (or killed very young) gradually captured the luxury market. The whole West provided them. Italian *merchants were their main transporters or sellers. Less important in terms of fur-bearing surface, but much more precious and infinitely varied were wild animal skins provided either by Western *hunting or, in rare qualities, by the lands of the South and North-East. The South provided leopards, sand foxes (fennecs) or deer, civet-cats, small lynxes, martens, dormice and especially the innumerable rabbits of Iberia, then of *England after their introduction there early in the 13th century.

The great *forest, from *Scandinavia and *Poland to the Urals, provided great numbers of very precious pelts: sables, arctic foxes, martens, beavers, ermines and white weasels (*létisses*) and above all squirrels (*vairs*) of changing hues carefully identified according to their provenance or aspect: moulting, spring-summer or autumn-winter, etc. Their hierarchy was essentially due to fashion, sometimes to tradition, above all to their rarity and their price.

For the South, the trade in precious pelts was in the hands of Italians; from the 13th to the 15th c., they resold part of them to Turkish Islam, the Near East or Egypt, where they met Catalans or Provençals. But the greater part came from deepest Europe and especially the *Hanseatic world.

Some two million pelts annually were transported and negotiated by a few large commercial societies but mainly by small non-specialist merchants, and treated by fur-merchants who sold them on in bales to Western courts, where they were made up by tailors and especially by skinners. The profession of skinner enjoyed a remarkable expansion from the 13th to the early 15th c.; specialized professions appeared (lamb-furriers, squirrel-furriers, wild game furriers, old-furries for reused pelts, etc.). The number of their members was considerable. Collectively rich and powerful (from the 13th c. they sponsored the finest *stained glass windows at *Chartres and *Bourges), they formed part of the *arti maggiori* at *Florence and *Magdeburg and of the "*six corps*" at *Paris.

The consumption of (especially luxury) furs was augmented throughout the 14th c. under the effect of the system of liveries worn by the entourages of lords and also because of the constant increase in furred surface required by the new types of garment (surcoats).

From the 11th and 12th cc., the importance of furs was

considerable in the West; it is echoed in the language of *heraldry (sable, vair, ermine), in iconography ("royal" ermine, even though anyone could wear it and though *kings used the humble squirrel until 1390, then martens, black lambs or sables). The balance of payments surplus in favour of the Baltic was largely due to furs. Western consumption depopulated the Russian forests of precious species and pushed adventurers and trappers towards the Pacific: sable practically paid for the conquest of Siberia, as across the Atlantic, it was the beaver (and the fur trade) that were to push English and French trappers towards the Pacific. The two greatest States in the world were initially born out of the overconsumption of the medieval West.

E. M. Veale, *The English Fur Trade in the later Middle Ages*, Oxford, 1966. – R. Delort, *Le Commerce des fourrures en Occident à la fin du Moyen Âge*, Rome-Paris, 1978-1980 (2 vol.). – J. Martin, *Treasure of the Land of Darkness: the Fur Trade and its Significance for Medieval Russia*, Cambridge, 1986. – "Pelze", *LdM*, 6, 1993, 1866-1868. – *Leather and Fur. Aspects of Early Medieval Trade and Technology*, E.A. Cameron (ed.), London, 1998.

Robert Delort

**FURNITURE.** Taken in its most common sense, the term "furniture" designates movable objects used in dwellings. Few medieval examples survive, essentially church or *sacristy furniture or exceptional objects, hardly representative. Iconographical sources still privilege the more favoured milieux, but they reveal the appearance and manner of use of the furniture cited in archive documents, registers of accounts and inventories, which offer a precise overall view of medieval furnishing from the 13th century.

Storage units *par excellence*, chests of all dimensions, made of quality wood (oak, walnut) or mediocre wood (beech, conifers), could be provided with locks and bolts. Sometimes painted or carved, they served to store linen, *clothing, utensils and a great variety of merchandise, as well as stocks of *food. Caskets enclosed the more precious goods: jewels, silver, property deeds. Wall cupboards were more rare. Shelves figure in kitchens, to store household utensils, or in shops.

Three-legged stools and backless benches appear in the late Middle Ages in the most modest dwellings. Fixed or folding chairs and individual armchairs are already less difficult to find. Thrown onto these chairs, cushions or hangings increased their comfort. Only the chairs of princes were surmounted by a *canopy, and early in the 15th c. we see the appearance of upholstered furniture in royal courts. Benches with pivoting backs allowed people to sit either facing the chimney or with their back to it. They were often associated with tables, still largely consisting of a plank laid on trestles, set up and removed at every mealtime. Yet, in modest settings, this type of table was exceptional and the crockery was set on a small rudimentary piece of furniture called a "buffet", or perhaps on the ground. The bed is sometimes the sole piece of furniture mentioned among the poorer people, composed of a mattress, a blanket, sheets and a simple bedstead. Even when it was sumptuously draped with hangings, it comprised only a framework and sometimes a wooden head. Testers and curtains were simply held up by iron rods planted in the walls or suspended from the ceiling. Cradles, masterpieces of sculpture, painted and gilded among princes, had only a restricted distribution.

This was also the case of sideboards. Used originally as auxiliary furniture on which the cup-bearers and other squires arranged the crockery and the courses next to the seignorial table, they were enriched with a lower compartment, closed by doors, and rows of shelves on which silverware or tinware were permanently on show.

H. Havard, *Dictionnaire de l'ameublement et de la décoration depuis le XIIIe siècle jusqu'à nos jours*, Paris, 1838-1921 (4 vol.). – V. Gay, H. Stein, *Glossaire archéologique du Moyen Âge et de la Renaissance*, Paris, 1883-1928. – E. Eames, *Furniture in England, France and the Netherlands from the Twelfth to the Fifteenth Century*, London, 1977. – C. Tracy, *English Medieval Furniture and Woodwork*, London, 1988. – P. Thornton, *The Italian Renaissance Interior (1400-1600)*, New York, 1991.

Françoise Piponnier

**FURSEY (died 649).** An Irish monk, he left *Ireland to go on *pilgrimage for the love of God. With the permission of King Sigebert, he settled at first in East Anglia (*c.*630) at a former Roman camp called *Cnobheresburg* (now Burgh Castle, Suffolk). According to *Bede (*Historia Ecclesiastica*, III, 19), Fursey (Fursa) was devoted to the study of sacred books and monastic disciplines; he was also vouchsafed a number of *dream-visions which Bede records (*ibid.*). Fursey subsequently went to Francia; with the patronage of King Clovis II, he built a monastery at Lagny, where he died in 649. After his death, his remains were translated to Péronne, which subsequently became a focal point for Irish pilgrims. St Fursey's feast day is 16 Jan.

*MGH.SRM*, 4, 1902, 423-449 (re-ed. 1977).

J. Hennig, "The Irish Background to St Fursey", *IER*, 77, 1952, 18-28. – P. Ó Riain, "Les Vies de Saint Fursey: les sources irlandaises", *RNord*, 69, 1986, 405-413.

Michael Lapidge

# G

**GABRIEL, ARCHANGEL.** In the book of *Daniel (8, 15-27; 9, 20-27) appears the archangel Gabriel whose name means "man of God", "man in whom God confides". He comes to tell Zacharias of the future birth of *John the Baptist (Lk 1, 11-20). He announces to *Mary that she will give birth to Jesus (Lk 1, 26-37). According to apocryphal texts, he holds the position of guardian and protector of church doors. Usually he is represented as a young man; he has wings and a *nimbus. In Italy, from the 14th c., he is given female characteristics. He appears sometimes with Zacharias and most often in the *Annunciation scene, bearing the angelic salutation: "*Ave Maria gratia plena*".

"Gabriel", *LCI*, 2, 1970, 74-78. – "Annonciation", *LCI*, 4, 1972, 422-437.

Christian de Mérindol

**GABRIEL II (IBN AL-TURAYK) (12th c.).** Coptic *patriarch from 1131 to 1145. Named Sa'īd and surnamed Abū 'l-'Alā', he was a simple layman (an exception among Coptic patriarchs).

Born to a family of high officials, he was ordained *deacon of the church of St Mercurius, in Old *Cairo; he was a scholar, and renowned for his generosity to the poor, whether strangers or not. After the death of Patriarch Macarius, in 1127 or 1128, the patriarchal see was vacant; finally the notables of *Alexandria took the advice of the monks of the monastery of Abū Maqār, at *Scetis, and chose as candidate for the patriarchate Sa'īd abū 'l-'Alā'.

He was consecrated at Alexandria; then, according to tradition, he went to the monastery of Abū Maqār. Ancient and modern biographers and historians agree in praising this patriarch for his spiritual *wisdom, his piety, his struggle against *simony (plague of the Coptic church), his reforms and his *virtue.

Among his most important works, we must cite his series of 32 canons: his *Nomocanon*, first of its kind among the *Copts, in which he tried to classify systematically, according to the theme being treated, all the legal texts that had force of law in his Church.

The drawing up of the *Lectionary of Holy Week* has been attributed to him, though without proof.

S. Khalil, "Gabriel II", *DHGE*, 19, 1979, 528-539 (abundant bibliography). – S. Labib, "Gabriel II, ibn Turayk", *Coptic Encyclopedia*, 4, New York, 1991, 1127-1129.

René-Georges Coquin †

**GABRIEL BARLETTA (died after 1480).** This *Dominican preacher was perhaps born in Aquino or Barletta (but Barletta seems rather to be a surname). Probably a disciple of *Antonino Pierozzi, archbishop of *Florence, Barletta was a recognised orator whose reputation was such that there was a saying "*nescit praedicare qui nescit barlettare*". (Documents from the *faculty of theology at the *university of *Bologna show a license in *theology at *Parma in 1472 for a Gabriel de Brunis de Barletta.) Barletta was the author of *Sermones quadragesimales et de sanctis* (Sermons on *Lent and on the saints) including 52 *Sermones dominicales*, 28 *De sanctis*, 3 *Extravagantes* and 4 *De adventu*, first published at Brescia in 1497. His *sermons packed with **exempla* are of particular interest by reason of their composite style.

A. Derville, "Gabriel Barletta", *DSp*, 6, 1967, 3-4. – L. Lazzerini, "Per latinos grossos, studio sui sermoni mescidati", *Studi di Filologia italiana*, 29, Florence, 1971, 219-339.

Rosa Maria Dessì

**GADDI, TADDEO (1295/1300-1366).** According to Cennino Cennini (*Libro dell'Arte*), Taddeo Gaddi (born at *Florence) was a disciple of *Giotto for 24 years before becoming, in the last years of his master's life, his main collaborator in the creation of important works (Bologna polyptych, now in the Museum of Medieval Art; polyptych of the Baroncelli chapel in the church of Santa Croce, Florence). Among his personal works, dating from 1315-1320, are the *Virgin and Child enthroned* in the church of San Francesco at Castelfiorentino and the same subject in the Museo Comunale at Castiglion Fiorentino, as well as the great *fresco cycle of *Legends of the Virgin Mary* in the Baroncelli chapel. Other commissions, carried out after 1334-1337, witness to the evolution of his style towards a softer, more nuanced model and an attenuation of spatial composition: thus, on the Berlin Triptych (Staatliches Museum; 1334), on the quadrilobate panels of the doors of the presses in the *sacristy of Santa Croce at Florence (now at the Gallerie dell'Accademia, Florence; the Munich Picture Gallery; and the Staatliches Museum, Berlin). Some of his works are influenced by the art of Maso di Banco (documented at Florence, from 1341 to 1346): these are, *e.g.*, the *Deposition from the Cross*, the *Entombment* in the Museo dell'Opera di Santa Croce, and the decorative scheme of the Bardi di Vernio chapel in the same church.

On Giotto's death (1337), Taddeo Gaddi was considered his most direct successor and received many commissions. Thus he painted figures of saints in the *crypt of San Miniato al Monte (1341); he was called to *Pisa to paint the *Story of Job* in fresco in the Camposanto; he completed a great polyptych for the high *altar of the church of San Giovanni Fuorcivitas at Pistoia. After 1350 and a disturbing combination of political, economic and social troubles, he remained rather isolated. He painted further Virgins and Child (*c.*1355) in the churches of Santa Felicità and San Lorenzo delle Rose. He finished the frescos of the refectory of Santa Croce. He conceived and realized two Crucifixions in fresco, one in the church of Ognissanti, the other on the walls of the sacristy of Santa Croce.

R. Longhi, "Qualità e industria in Taddeo Gaddi", *Paragone*, 3, 1959, 1-20; *ibid.*, *Opere Complete*, 7, Florence, 1974, 85-101. – A. Ladis, *Taddeo Gaddi*, Columbia, London, 1982.

Daniel Russo

**GAETA.** On the whole, Gaeta's medieval history was that of continental southern *Italy in general and northern Campania in particular. But from the 9th to the 12th cc., it enjoyed a period of autonomy from the great political formations of its hinterland, including the papacy.

Gaeta's history first began to differ from that of its neighbours with the descent of the *Lombards into Italy in the 6th c.; this Germanic people occupied only the northern and inland parts of the peninsula, leaving much of the South and the coasts to the Byzantines. The 9th c. saw an important change in Gaetan political life: in the 860s and 870s, the *hypatos* Docibile (in some documents also called *prefecturius* – the title *hypatos*, of Byzantine origin, corresponded to the Latin *consul*) arrogated political authority to himself and his family; in the mid 880s, Pope John VIII conferred the title of papal rector on him. Docibile I strengthened his family's power especially through marriage alliances, with the aim of putting his relatives in powerful positions in the hinterland, and associated his son John I with him on the throne. In 914 at the latest, John did the same with his son Docibile II. These operations began to make political power hereditary. In *c.*930, Docibile II assumed the title of *dux*, duke: no mere formal change, this directed the evolution of Gaeta's political institutions along the same path as that of other "Byzantine" territories like *Naples and *Amalfi. Docibile II's son John II (associated in 933) is attested as duke from 957 to 959, while his other son Marinus held the *duchy of Fondi. But neither John nor his brother Gregory (died 981) associated any son with themselves. Their other brother Marinus, previously duke of Fondi, associated on the throne his own son John III, in 984.

In 992, while John III was exercising ducal authority in Gaeta and had associated John IV with himself on the throne, his brother Leo had become duke of Fondi and his other brothers Daufer and Gregory were counts respectively of Traetto and Castro d'Argento. Bernard, a fifth son of Marinus, was bishop of Gaeta in 997. The process of evolution led to increased autonomy for certain areas within the duchy, especially Traetto, which claimed a political authority of its own, almost separate from the Gaetan duchy. In the 990s, following this splitting up, the duchy's political unity began to be heavily undermined.

Despite this, social life developed substantially in the 10th and 11th cc.: geopolitical expansion was accompanied by an increase in crafts and *commerce. John III, a farsighted politician, maintained excellent relations with the emperor *Otto III. John's wife Emilia played an important role in Gaetan politics, ruling the State in an exemplary way after her husband's death, first on behalf of her son John IV, then of her grandson John V, attested around 1023. The great dynamism and vigour of the role of *women in Gaetan society around the year 1000 was a real exception to the general picture of southern medieval society. In the 11th c., Gaeta was firmly at the centre of a flourishing commercial system: its *merchants took a leading role in the East (*Constantinople) and in Italy, especially the north and centre (particularly *Rome and *Pavia). A strong Gaetan mercantile presence is attested *e.g.* at Naples, in which "*maiores et minores*" citizens were involved. In this period Gaeta played an important part in Italian events: in 849 its ships fought at Ostia against the *Saracens, while its army played the major part in the victory of the Garigliano in 915, which marked the final defeat of the Saracens in Italian territory.

Despite its robust mercantile characteristics, from the 1020s the duchy and its territories were affected by the phenomenon of **incastellamento*. Factors contributing to this were the requirements of defence and the need to bring together the dwellings of the rural population, who could thus engage in, or at any rate make use of, greater opportunities for commerce and trade; the role of the *nobility in building *castles appears less certain. The first *castra* on Gaetan territory were Traetto and Castro d'Argento, then Suio from 1023; later Itri, Spigno and Castrum Garilianum. The autonomous evolution of socio-political structures was abruptly interrupted by an external event: in 1032, Docibile I's last descendant was deposed by Pandulf IV, prince of Capua, who took possession of Gaeta; never again would ducal power return to the hands of a Gaetan. It was conquered soon after, perhaps with the support of the local *nobility, by Pandulf's enemy Sergius IV of Naples, who kept it until 1038; he in turn was expelled by the emperor Conrad II, who assigned the duchies of Gaeta and Capua to Sergius's greatest enemy, Guaimar IV of Salerno.

But Guaimar's rule met considerable resistance. In 1041 he allowed a *Norman leader closely connected with him, Rainulf of Aversa, to take the title of duke. But Rainulf died before 1045, and this strengthened the political hold of Gaetan society, which managed to prevent Guaimar resuming the crown. Athenulf, count of Aquino and son-in law of Pandulf IV of Capua, was made *consul et dux*, though he had to be ransomed, through the diplomatic intervention of Abbot Richerius of *Monte Cassino, from the imprisonment in which Guaimar was holding him after capturing him in battle.

All these complex events incontrovertibly demonstrate that, by the mid 11th c., Gaeta was part of the political and economic evolution of the areas on both sides of the Garigliano, partly because its *port was a very important means of access and provisioning for the regions of the hinterland. Particularly aggressive was Richard Quarrel of Aversa, who replaced the princes of Capua between 1053 and 1058 after the death of Pandulf V. But, partly through the diplomatic help of the abbot of Monte Cassino, Athenulf was able to prevent the Normans conquering Gaeta. He died in 1062, leaving his son Athenulf II a minor with his mother Mary as co-ruler. From 1063, however, the evidence attests Norman supremacy in the city: having expelled Mary, Richard associated his son Jordan on his throne and maintained the little Athenulf as a subordinate associate, probably a mere local emanation of his own authority. The other members of the ramified ducal family soon came to terms with Quarrel, whose vassals they became: John of Maranola obtained Castro d'Argento; Lando married one of Quarrel's daughters and obtained Traetto; Mary herself was betrothed to the heir to the throne, Jordan. Thus, by the 1050s, Gaetan autonomy was at an end. The duchy was transformed into a multitude of lordships independent of each other, all vassals of the prince of Capua. Gaeta itself was soon allotted to a follower of Richard, Count Lando of Traetto, who took the traditional title of consul and duke.

Around 1130, the year of *Roger II's coronation as king of *Sicily, southern Italy was in an uproar due to the clash between Roger and much of the southern Italian feudal nobility, who violently opposed the conquest and the desire of the former count of Sicily to make himself sole ruler of a unified State. Richard, son of Count Bartholomew of Carinola, had become duke of Gaeta in 1121. He modelled his attitude to the Hauteville on that of the prince of Capua, whose vassal and blood-relative he was (his father Bartholomew was a brother of Prince Jordan, who died in 1090), and thus came into collision with Roger.

In 1135, after years of bloody war, Roger II granted the principality of Capua to his son Anfusus who, according to Chalandon, also took the title of duke of Gaeta. The city found an institutional place in the Regno as defined by King Roger at the two great general assemblies of Ariano in 1140 and Silva Marca in 1142. In place of the duchy, the monarch instituted the new county of Fondi and put at its head the Norman Goffredo of Aquila. The territory's other *fiefs were also granted to feudatories of Norman origin, nearly all dependent on the count of Fondi. A document of 1141 attests that the consuls and people of Gaeta had taken an *oath "*salva tamen fidelitate domini Roggerii*" to a certain Athenulf, holder of the fief of Spigno-Saturnia.

Despite this new situation, the city enjoyed important privileges during the Norman kingdom. Its citizens could elect the holders of the old magistrature of the consulate "*sine licentia curiae*", and have an autonomous mint; but above all they were allowed to practise commerce "*pro communi utilitate*". The city had flourishing relations with *Genoa, *Pisa, *Sardinia and *Venice, and within the walled city an eminent group of citizens continued to survive, having adapted themselves to the duchy's annexation to the Regno in 1135. Towards the end of the 12th c., in the declining years of the Norman dynasty, a *charter rich in exemptions and privileges was granted to the city by King Tancred of Hauteville, formerly count of Lecce. This was the stormy time of the struggle for the succession to the throne, which broke out after the death of *William II and in which Taancred, the representative of the pro-Norman party, opposed *Henry VI of Hohenstaufen, emperor of Germany, who was determined to conquer the Regno (he had married Roger II's daughter *Constance). Tancred sought to exploit to his advantage the existing excellent relations between Gaeta and the *Crown, and in exchange for support against Henry he granted the city the right to belong to the Crown, with the following privileges: exemption from the jurisdiction of the royal justiciars; subjection to the curia of Palermo alone; choice of judges from among its own citizens; respect for local usages and *customs; and exemption from payment of certain taxes connected with commercial activities. This is attested by the *Statutes of Gaeta*, confirmed by Tancred in 1191, an authentic monument to *iurisdictio*, that local autonomy that knew how to fuse compelling local administrative necessities with the heritage of *Roman-Byzantine law. The *Codex diplomaticus cajetanus* was a living memory of it.

Tancred's death and the passing of the Regno under the Swabian dynasty changed the institutional framework of which Gaeta and the former duchy had become part in the second half of the 12th century. Thereafter Gaeta would follow the political vicissitudes of the southern kingdom, in particular its changes of dynasty, from Swabians to *Angevins in 1266 and from Angevins to Aragonese in the mid 15th century.

F. Chalandon, *Histoire de la domination normande en Italie méridionale et en Sicilie*, Paris, 1907. – A. Maerores, *Gaeta im frühen Mittelalter (VIII bis XII Jahrhundert)*, Gotha, 1911. – F. Schupfer, "Gaeta e il suo diritto", *Rivista italiana per le scienze giuridiche*, 59, 1914, 82-92. – A. Leccese, *Le origini del ducato di Gaeta e le sue relazioni coi ducati di Napoli e Roma*, Gubbio, 1941. – F. Calasso, *Medio Evo del diritto*, 1, *Le fonti*, Milan, 1954. – F. Calasso, *Gli ordinamenti giuridici del rinascimento medievale*, Milan, 1965, 158, 171, 225-226. – P. Delogu, "Il ducato di Gaeta del IX all'XI secolo. Istituzioni e società", *Storia del Mezzogiorno*, 2, 1, *Il Medioevo*, Naples, 1988, 189-236. – P. Fedele, *Scritti storici sul ducato di Gaeta*, L. Cardi (ed.), Gaeta, 1988. – P. Skinner, "Politics and Piracy: the Duchy of Gaeta in the Twelfth Century", *JMH*, 21, 1995, 307-319. – E. Cuozzo, "L'annessione del ducato di Gaeta al Regno di Sicilia", *Normanni. Feudi e feudatori*, Salerno, 1995, 217-233.

Edoardo D'Angelo

**GALICIA (SPAIN).** A former Roman province, from 411 to 585 Gallaecia was an independent kingdom ruled by the *Suevi, converted to Christianity by *Martin of Braga in the mid 6th century. The *Visigothic province, administered from the towns of *Braga and Lugo, was temporarily occupied by Muslims in the early 8th c. before entering the orbit of the Christian kingdom of Oviedo in *c.*750-760. The discovery at *Compostela in 820-830 of the *tomb of the apostle James, soon proclaimed patron of the monarchy and of *Spain, closely associated the region with the Christian kingdom of Oviedo-*León.

In the profoundly rural Galicia of the 9th-11th cc., divided into districts or *commissa* comprising several **villae* belonging either to one or more *domini* or to the *peasants, the bishops of Iria-Compostela reorganised the network of *parishes following the *Parrochiale Suevorum*. The efforts of *bishops and *counts did not always prevent the devastations of the *Vikings, then those of al-Mansur in the late 10th c., while between 950 and 1035 the *comites* of Galicia, always ready to revolt, played a predominant role at the court of *León where, in rivalry with the *comes* of *Castile, they made and unmade kings. In 1065-1070, Galicia was again an independent kingdom, before being permanently incorporated into the *Crown of Castile-León. In 1139, the *portucalense* territory south of the Miño, entrusted by king *Alfonso VI to his son-in-law Henry of Burgundy, became independent when Henry's son *Afonso was proclaimed king of *Portugal.

Increasing agricultural yields and the lure of the route of St James in the 12th c. contributed to Galicia's prosperity; a network of *towns covered the region, notably along the coasts, where fishing and *commerce brought life to numerous *ports. There were conflicts between the inhabitants of the towns and their ecclesiastical lords, at Compostela in 1116-1117 and 1136, at Lugo around 1157-1161, at Tuy after 1170. During the second half of the 12th c., the kings of León reorganised the *merindad mayor* of Galicia and gave *fueros* (franchises) to numerous towns, while, following the example of the monastery of Sobrado in 1142, numerous communities adopted the *Cistercian rule. In 1232, the *Franciscans created the province of Santiago, before the *Dominicans too chose to install themselves at Compostela.

From the 1300s, the decline of the *pilgrimage, the remoteness of political centres and various calamities created a critical situation from which the lay *nobility profited to increase their possessions and revenues at the expense of ecclesiastical institutions and towns, holding *pilgrims, travellers and *merchants to ransom. Insecurity became general and, in the years 1467-1469 and in the name of the king, Galicia was the theatre of a general uprising, called the *Irmandiños*, against the local lords who terrorized the population.

J. C. Bermejo *et al.*, *Historia de Galicia*, Madrid, 1980. – F. López Alsina, *La Ciudad de Santiago de Compostela en la alta Edad Media*, Santiago de Compostela, 1988. – E. Ferreira Priegue, *Galicia en el comercio marítimo medieval*, Corunna, 1988. – C. Barros, *Mentalidad justiciera de los Irmandiños, siglo XV*, Madrid, 1990.

Adeline Rucquoi

**GALICIA (UKRAINE).** Galicia (Halychyna), a historical province in south-western *Ukraine, comprises the regions of *Lviv (Lvov, Lemberg), Ternopil and Ivano-Frankivsk. The Austrian province of Galicia (Galizien or, its official name, "Königreich Galizien und Lodomerien") was a political entity from 1772 to 1918, consisting of the essentially Ukrainian territory of the former Galicia (East Galicia for the Austrians) and south-eastern *Poland (West Galicia for the Austrians).

In the late 10th c., the territory of the future Galicia was part of Kievan *Rus'. In the late 11th and early 12th cc., it included the principalities of Zvenyhorod, Terebovlia and Peremyshl (Przemysl), governed by the brothers Rostislavich, grandsons of

Prince *Iaroslav the Wise of Kiev. In 1141, Vladimirko Volodarevich united these principalities under his authority and made Halych (Halicz, in Latin *Galicia*) his capital. Under the reign of Iaroslav Osmomysl (1153-1187), the principality of Galicia enjoyed a period of economic and cultural expansion. In 1199 the prince of *Volhynia, Roman Mstislavich, created the united principality of Galicia-Volhynia. Its most celebrated rulers were kings *Daniel of Halych (1238-1264) and George (Iuri) I (1301-1308). After the assassination of the last prince, Iuri II Boleslav, *Hungary, *Lithuania and Poland began to dispute Galicia among themselves. It was finally incorporated into the kingdom of Poland in 1387 and remained under Polish rule until 1772. The greater part of Galicia (which took the name of Red Ruthenia) was integrated with the palatinate of Ruthenia, while its northern part was incorporated into the palatinate of Belz. Lviv was the political and economic capital of Galicia. Polish law replaced Ruthenian law in the administration of the province, while the *towns and certain *villages were administered according to German law. The majority of the rural population of Galicia remained Ukrainian, while in the towns, as well as Ukrainians, lived a number of Poles, Germans and *Jews. In some urban centres, colonies of Armenians played an important role in economic life.

P. R. Magocsi, *Galicia: a Historical Survey and Bibliographic Guide*, Toronto, 1983.

Iaroslav Isaievych

**GALLICAN LITURGY.** It would be more accurate to say "Gallican liturgies", since there was no unified liturgy for the whole of Frankish Gaul (except the Narbonnaise, where the *Hispanic or "Visigothic" liturgy was practised). At any rate, the term "Gallican liturgy" covers all the liturgical usages regulating public worship in the Frankish kingdoms. These lasted until the introduction of Roman usages by the *Carolingian rulers between the middle of the 8th c. and the first decades of the 9th. In many cases the liturgy of Roman type included many earlier elements, both in the chants and in the rites, thus ensuring their survival.

Gaul, progressively converted to Christianity by the Latins (except *Lyon), received the basic elements of its liturgy, as to the structure of its rites, from *Rome; but this liturgy developed on the spot, undergoing various influences from *Milan, Byzantium and elsewhere. In fact, we know the liturgy used by the Gauls only partially, through the canons of the Merovingian *councils (mainly of the 6th c. and the following decades), or through the work of some Gallic *bishops like St *Caesarius of Arles († 543) and St *Gregory of Tours († 594). But in the absence of a great unifying centre, usages seem to have varied considerably from Church to Church.

The first part of the *mass (liturgy of the Word) ended by presenting many analogies with the *Byzantine and Syrian liturgies, but mainly in the secondary rites. The eucharistic prayer remained variable, longer than at Rome where a "*canon" appeared very early (in this case in a fixed eucharistic prayer, which was "the rule", with some variable elements: *preface, *Communicantes*, *Hanc igitur*).

The liturgical *office had the same canonical *hours as at Rome, but its extent and duration were much more important, each office comprising a greater number of *psalms, especially the night office. Many vigils were practised in the course of the year on major *feasts or the *anniversaries of local *martyrs. But the distribution of the *psalter was not homogeneous in every *diocese.

As for ritual and feasts, the liturgy was much less sober than at Rome, and the use of multivalent symbolism presented an air of kinship with the practices of the Eastern Churches. It was in this sphere that survivals were most numerous after the disappearance of the Gallican liturgies as such. The amalgam created by the Carolingian *liturgists reintroduced many usages, generally marked by an exuberant lyricism.

H. Leclercq, "Gallicane (liturgie)", *DACL*, 6, 1924, 473-593. – E. Griffe, "Aux origines de la liturgie gallicane", *BLE*, 1951, 17-43. – A. Davril, "France (la liturgie en)", *Dictionnaire encyclopédique de la liturgie*, 1, D. Sartore (ed.), A. M. Triacca (ed.), Turnhout, 1992, 462-464 (Fr. tr.).

Guy-Marie Oury

**GALLICANISM.** Gallicanism corresponded to a status of the Church of France, under the protection of the king considered as the guarantor of its "liberties". It entailed a rejection of interventions by the *pope in the functioning of the Church of the realm, and it originally presupposed the superiority of the general *council to the pope. Its main characteristics appeared gradually, justified in theory by the *Parlement and the university of *Paris. Its champions tried to take its origin back to *Charlemagne or, less audaciously, to St *Louis on the grounds of a regulation which was in fact a *forgery made around 1450.

In the kingdom of *France, the king, a sacred personage, exercised prerogatives not just over ecclesiastical *property in his quality as temporal lord, but also as protector of the Church of the realm and as special guardian of several Churches whose revenues he collected in case of vacancy of the episcopal see (temporal **regalia*) and in which he even appointed to *benefices dependent on the *bishop (spiritual *regalia*). He also conferred certain benefices of which he was the patron. St Louis confined himself to informing *Innocent IV in 1247 of the discontent aroused by papal interventions considered unwarranted. The notion of the "liberties of the Gallican Church" took shape, while in legal affairs the ecclesiastical *justices increasingly suffered the encroachments of royal justice and the lay jurisdictions.

In 1302, at the time of the conflict between *Philip IV the Fair and *Boniface VIII, Pierre Flote vigorously denounced the pope's policy of interference. Under the *Avignon popes, *entente* reigned because the French *clerics and the royal finances profited from the liberality of the *Curia. The *Great Schism changed matters. From 1380, the **Songe du vergier* exalted the king as "ordained and established by God". The crisis would incite him to take measures of safety himself. Following the Parisian *councils of 1396 and 1398, at which the orators denounced the taxes and collations of *benefices decided by *Benedict XIII, the kingdom withdrew from the Avignonese obedience: the former regime of *elections to *bishoprics and *abbeys and collation of minor benefices "by those to whom collation belongs" was theoretically restored, and any papal claim in beneficial, fiscal or legal matters was suppressed. An orator commented: "It is for the king to act in such a way that the Church of his realm may not be subject to the pope, except within proper and reasonable limits [in matters of *faith]."

As the council of *Basel was severely restricting the rights of the pope, *Charles VII called an assembly of the clergy at Bourges at which he promulgated the *Pragmatic Sanction on 7 July 1438: this document recapitulated the conciliar provisions about the periodic meeting of *councils and clerical discipline, and instituted the beneficial, legal and financial regime of the Church of France

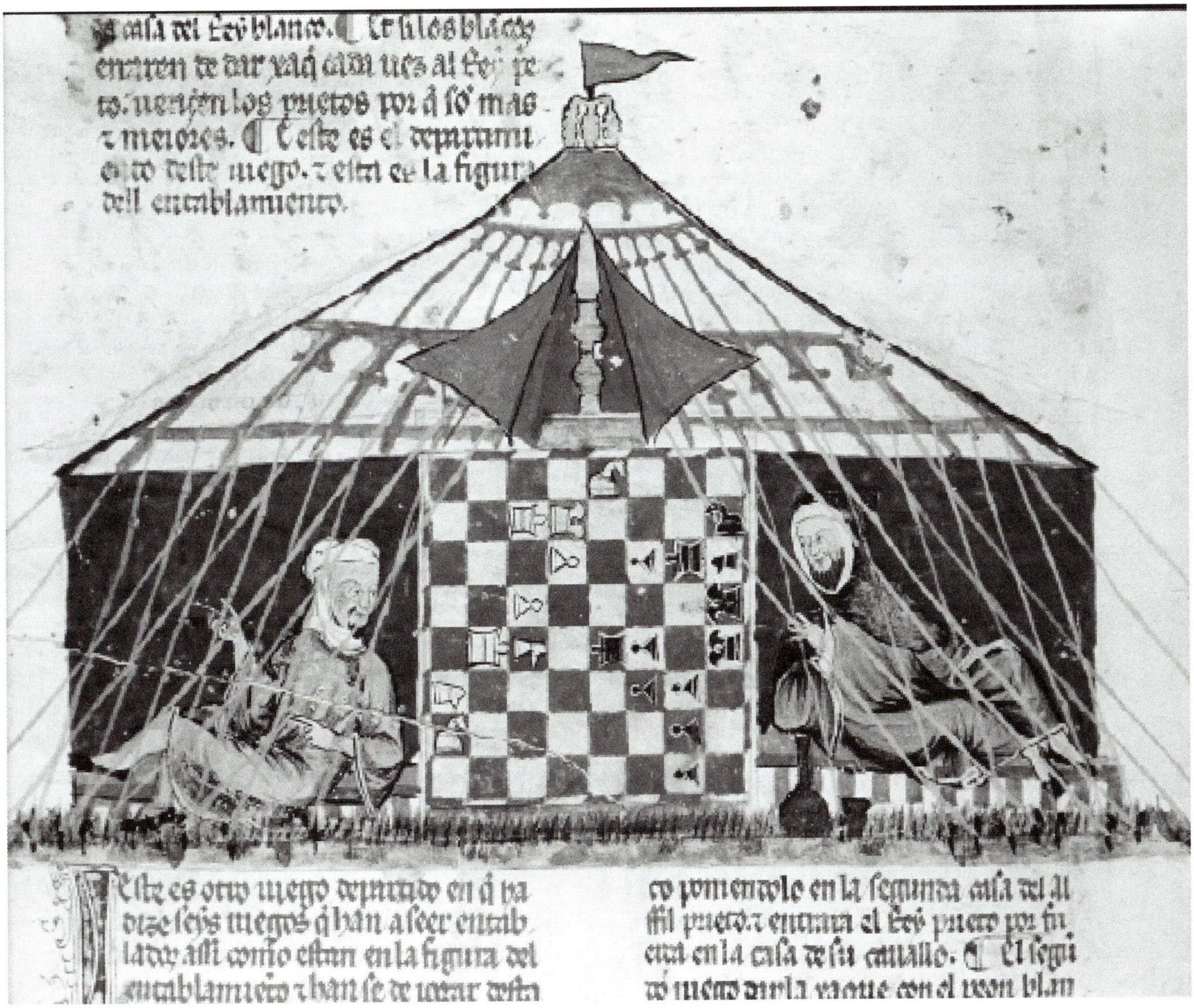

*Two Arabs playing chess.* Miniature from the *Book of Games* by Alfonso the Wise, 1282. Madrid, Escorial Library.

as sketched out in 1398 and 1407. The application of the Pragmatic Sanction revealed lasting gulfs. The Paris Parlement made itself the intransigent defender of the regime of "liberties". The king did not renounce intervention in the elections of prelates; he desired to come to an arrangement with the pope, who had refused to recognise the act of 1438; this was the policy of *Louis XI, and in 1516 it culminated in the *concordat of *Bologna. But the Church of the Midi, led by the archbishop of *Toulouse and the bishop of Périgueux, showed its hostility; it was attached to the power of the pope, "sovereign of this world, having the principal cure of all the Churches and spiritual things".

At the end of the Middle Ages, differences appeared between royal Gallicanism, "parlementary" Gallicanism and university Gallicanism, all claiming to safeguard the "liberties" of the Church of France.

H. X. Arquillère, "Gallicanisme", *DAFC*, 2, 1911, 193-274. – V. Martin, *Les Origines du Gallicanisme*, Paris, 1939, 2 vol. – E. Delaruelle, E.-R. Labande, P. Ourliac, *L'Église au temps du Grand Schisme et de la crise conciliaire (1378-1449)*, Paris, 1962, 329-368. – J.-L. Gazzaniga, *L'Église du Midi à la fin du règne de Charles VII (1444-1461)*, Paris, 1976.

Bernard Guillemain

**GAMES.** The Latin term *ludus*, "game", has a wide range of meanings covering a variety of fields, from *theatre to *dance, from childish diversions to gaming with dice. The present article is limited to what can be covered by the English term "game".

The Middle Ages played a lot, though its games often escape the historian's perception by reason of the allusive character of the sources and their dispersal. Some medieval games were inherited from the Greco-Roman world, like all games of arms, throwing, balls, bowls, marbles. One of them, honed and perfected, the game of tennis, enjoyed its apogee in the early 16th century. Also inherited from Antiquity were all games of chance, among which the game of dice may be considered the medieval game *par excellence*. Other games were imported, like chess which came from Asia to Europe around the year 1000, simultaneously from the north and the south. A final category seems specifically medieval, though the question of origins is far from settled. These were the card games that arose during the last quarter of the 14th c., as well as collective games like the *jeu de la soule* ("Shrove Tuesday Football"), games that arose out of ceremonial practices linked to the *calendar.

The rules of these games can sometimes be reconstructed. For the most part, they are close to the modern rules. However, their evolution reveals a growing complexity (*e.g.* the introduction of trumps into the game of cards). Chess was radically transformed at the dawn of the 16th c. with the possibility offered to noble pieces of taking from a distance and the Queen's increased powers.

The whole world played, and most games gave rise to stakes, from a few small coins risked in the tavern on Sunday to the enormous sums gained or lost at a time by a Louis d'Orléans (1372-1407) or a Philip the Bold (1342-1404). Some social or professional categories showed a more marked penchant for games. Thus the *nobility made them an element of distinction, in which ostentation played the primary role. **Chansons de geste* and courtly literature made chess an attribute of noble life. Men of war, royal officials, domestics and clerics let themselves be seduced by the game.

Faced with this "ludic invasion", the response of the authorities was not uniform. Heirs to Roman legislation, anxious to maintain order, the civil powers tried to prohibit these practices; then for the sake of peace and quiet, they preferred to profit from them and regulated the conditions and course of games. A penal phase was succeeded by a fiscal phase. The Church, which saw games as an activity that could turn to contempt of *God, neighbour or self, soon confined its prohibitions to *clerics alone, distinguishing between athletic games (authorized), intellectual games (tolerated) and games of chance (forbidden).

J. J. Jusserand, *Les Sports et les jeux d'exercice dans l'ancienne France*, Paris, 1901. – J. Huizinga, *Homo ludens. Essai sur la fonction sociale du jeu*, Paris, 1951 (Fr. tr.). – H.J.R. Murray, *A History of Board Games other than Chess*, New York, 1978. –J. M. Mehl, *Les Jeux au royaume de France du XIIIe au début du XVIe siècle*, Paris, 1990. – J. M. Carter, *Medieval Games*, New York, 1992.

Jean-Michel Mehl

**GANDERSHEIM.** Situated in what is now the town of Bad-Gandersheim (Lower *Saxony), the *abbey of Gandersheim was founded in 852 by the Saxon Count Liudolf and his wife Oda, ancestors of the *Ottonian dynasty. In the early Middle Ages, this *chapter of noble ladies, typical of ancient Saxony, engaged in ceaseless conflicts with the bishop of *Hildesheim to guarantee their privileges of direct attachment to the authorities of the *Empire and the Holy See. Its political and cultural prestige, most strikingly that of *Hroswitha, continued through the Middle Ages. The establishment finally disappeared in 1810.

H. Goetting, *Das reichsunmittelbare Kanonissenstift Gandersheim, Die Bistümer der Kirchenprovinz Mainz. Das Bistum Hildesheim*, 1, 1973 ("GermSac", new series, 7). – "Gandersheim", *DHGE*, 19, 1981, 1066-1081.

Monique Goullet

**GARDEN.** The garden held an essential place in medieval religious thought and imagery. The two paradigms of gardens in the Middle Ages were the earthly *paradise and the enclosed garden (*hortus conclusus*) of the *Song of Songs (Song 4, 12-5, 1), an image used to symbolize the *virginity of the Virgin. Earthly paradise and *hortus conclusus* were often confused in medieval iconography, showing both as fortified gardens.

Gardens had an important role in the life of monastic establishments, where to frequent them was conceived as a spiritual *ascesis. The plan of the *abbey of *Sankt Gallen, in the 9th c., provided for three gardens: a kitchen garden, a medicinal garden and an orchard which was also the abbey's *cemetery. These three types of garden recur in later monastic establishments. Likewise, the geometrical order of flower-beds, the origin of "French" gardens, and the mixture of vegetables, aromatic plants and flowers remained characteristic of medieval gardens.

Gardens are omnipresent in courtly literature. The most famous of all literary orchards is that of the *Roman de la Rose* whose central theme develops the sexual symbolism of the enclosed garden; the application of the sacred metaphor of the *hortus conclusus* to profane *love caused a scandal that for over two centuries, from the 13th to the 15th c., fed a controversy in which the theologian Jean *Gerson took part.

Late medieval account-books show that aristocratic gardens comprised the same elements as the allegorical gardens known through iconography or literary texts: fortified enclosure, monumental fountain, arbours or pleasure pavilions. They also contained "wonders" like the automata moved by hydraulic machines in the park of the counts of Artois at Hesdin, in northern France.

Interest in gardens manifested itself in the importance of the hydraulic irrigation or drainage works that were sometimes created to improve them. Marshes, like that of *Paris or *Saint-Omer, were widely exploited for horticulture from the 12th c. (hence the term *maraîchage*, "market gardening"). Gardens played an important role in supplying *food and in the production of industrial plants (flax, hemp, dye plants, saffron) or the acclimatization of new species. They seem to have multiplied from the 13th c. inside town walls as well as on the periphery of *towns, around which they formed a halo.

M. Stokstad, J. Stannard, *Gardens of the Middle Ages*, Lawrence (KS), 1983. – J. Harvey, *Mediaeval Gardens*, London, 1981. – *Medieval Gardens*, E.B. MacDougall (ed.), Washington (DC), 1986. – *Jardins et vergers en Europe occidentale (VIIIe-XVIIIe siècle), Flaran*, 9, Auch, 1989. – T. McLean, *Medieval English Gardens*, London, 1989. – W. Janssen, "Gartenkultur im Mittelalter", *Wieviel Garden braucht der Mensch*, G. Bittner (dir.), P. L. Weinacht (dir.), Würzburg, 1990, 59-84.

Élisabeth Zadora-Rio

**GARTER, ORDER OF THE.** Founded in 1348 by *Edward III, king of *England, in homage to the myth of the *Round Table and, more prosaically, to bind to his own person the best available military talents, including Sir John Chandos and the earl of Northampton. To begin with, the order seems to have been based on the cameraderie typical of the world of *tournaments, to create a group of knights with a strong common identity. The limited number of members, only 25 until the 17th c., has made the Garter one of the most exclusive honours in the world. The order's motto is *Hony soit qui mal y pense* (shame on him who thinks ill of it).

E. Ashmole, *Institutions, Laws and Ceremonies of the most noble Order of the Garter*, London, 1672. – J. Vale, *Edward III and Chivalry: Chivalric Society and its Context, 1270-1350*, Woodbridge, 1983.

Niccolò Capponi

**GASCOIGNE, THOMAS (1403-1458).** A native of Yorkshire (his father Richard was a gentleman from near Leeds), Thomas Gascoigne studied at *Oxford where, though a *canon of *Wells, he lived all his life at Oriel College. He was *chancellor of the *university in 1444-1445. A renowned preacher, this *doctor of *theology, an enthusiast for St Augustine, wrote several works (collection of *sermons, Saint's lives), but is celebrated today mainly for his *Liber veritatum*, in principle a theological dictionary on which he worked from 1434 until his death; in fact the two great manuscript volumes contain many commentaries and digressions on contemporary events which make it a veritable mine for the university and ecclesiastical history of this period.

J. E. T. Rogers, *Thomas Gascoigne: Loci e Libro Veritatum*, Oxford, 1881, 225-232. – *DNB*, 1885-1900. – *BRUO*, 2, 1958, 745-748. – W. Pronger, "Thomas Gascoigne", *EHR*, 53, 1938, 602-626 and 54, 1939, 20-37.

Jean-Philippe Genet

**GASCONY.** The word "Wasconia" or Gascony appears in 602 in a Frankish *chronicle to designate the region situated between the *Pyrenees and the Garonne. It was the part of the territory of Romanized *Aquitaine that had suffered the infiltration of the Vascones. This people, of very ancient and disputed origin, had resisted both Roman civilization and Christianity, between the upper Ebro valley and the western Pyrenees. Pressed by the *Visigoths who had founded a kingdom in *Spain, around 578 it had begun to shift northwards. Remaining numerous on both sides of the Pyrenees as far as the middle and lower Adour valley where it kept its language and its traditions (Basque country), to the north it fused with the earlier population to whom it gave leaders, warriors and linguistic elements that occur in the Gascon language which is part of the Occitan family. Gascony never had precise limits; it might have extended as far as Bordeaux, gone slightly beyond the Garonne and included the Ariège valley, but it never reached the Toulousain. Its history is little known before the end of the 11th c. by reason of the rarity of sources or the difficulty of interpreting them. It can be held that neither the *Merovingians nor the *Carolingians permanently subdued it, that the Arabs merely went through it, that it was Vascones who surprised *Charlemagne's rearguard at the pass of Roncevaux (778). After 816, Gascony enjoyed a *de facto* independence. In the mid 9th c., Sancho Mitarra established a dynasty which, not without territorial changes, held Gascony until 1058 as a principality, rather like *Normandy in the same period. The *Vikings went up the Garonne and the Adour; they were defeated at Taller in 982.

At the time the Vascones penetrated it, the country was provided with Christian institutions: from 314, Eauze had a *bishop; in 506, at the council of Agde, the *metropolitan of Eauze, the bishops of Bazas, Dax, Aire, Oloron, Beneharnum (Lescar), Auch, Lectoure, le Comminges, le Couserans and la Bigorrre were present or represented. Parish churches had been planted. *Monasticism seems to have been represented only by a few groups of hermits. We know nothing certain of Sts Luper, Lizier, Orens or Quitterie. An old fund of beliefs in the forces of *nature and the effectiveness of *magical practices faded slowly. The rule of the pagan Vascones shattered these still fragile structures: when Carolingian *clerics drew up lists of bishops, they left sees vacant for the 7th and early 8th centuries. Laymen, great proprietors and local potentates, probably took possession of them. Hardly had the hierarchy been restored than the *Vikings, by destroying Eauze, provoked the transfer of the metropolitan see to Auch (*c.*879). The consolidation of the Gascon principality allowed Gomdaud, brother of Duke William Sancho, and then Arsieu to extend their episcopal *authority over most of the Gascon sees confused into a "bishopric of Gascony" (after 977).

Around the year 1000, history clears up. Monasteries were founded at Sorde, Saint-Sever and Condom. *Cluny attached Saint-Mont to itself in 1075. In the 12th c., the *Cistercians, *Premonstratensians, *Templars and *Hospitallers settled there. *Pilgrims to Santiago de *Compostela crossed the region; the famous *Guide* describes the inhospitable moor where the walker risked sinking up to his knees. But, in central and eastern Gascony, land *clearances expanded around *castelnaux* – fortified *villages attached to a *castle – and **sauvetés* – villages protected by a religious establishment. Bayonne (the Basque name of Lapurdum) became a bishopric. Under the impetus of St Austinde, archbishop of Auch (1050-1065), the secular Church became part of the *reform movement coordinated by Amatus, bishop of Oloron and then of Bordeaux, *legate of *Gregory VII. In the 13th c., the *mendicant orders settled, while new population groupings were organised through the **bastides*.

In 1058, the union of Gascony and *Aquitaine under the Poitevin duke Gui-Geoffroi, who took the name William VIII, and then the passing of this territorial group under the authority of the kings of *England after the marriage of duchess *Eleanor with *Henry II, brought Gascony into the long and complicated vicissitudes of the conflict between the kings of England and *France that ended with the capture of Bayonne and Bordeaux by *Charles VII (1451 and 1453). At the margins of this long war, there were innumerable confrontations between the Gascon lords: viscount of Béarn, count of Armagnac, sire d'Albret. Gascony was untouched by the *Cathar religion. It gave the Church a *pope: *Clement V (1305-1314), but the *Great Schism divided it.

C. Higounet, *Histoire de l'Aquitaine*, Toulouse, 1971. – M. Bordes, *Histoire de la Gascogne des origines à nos jours*, Saint-Étienne, 1977. – M. Rouche, *L'Aquitaine des Wisigoths aux Arabes. Naissance d'une region (418-781)*, Paris, 1979. – M.W. Labarge, *Gascony, England's First Colony, 1204-1453*, London, 1980. – R. Mussot-Goulard, *Les Princes de Gascogne (768-1070)*, Marsolan, 1982. – M. Beresford, *New Towns of the Middle Ages*, Gloucester, 1988. – M.G.A. Vale, *The Angevin legacy and the Hundred Years' War, 1250-1340*, Oxford, 1990.

Bernard Guillemain

**GAUTIER DE COINCY (1177-1236).** The monk Gautier de Coincy was the author of the most important collection of *miracles (58), several pious songs and *sermons in verse. The *legends told by Gautier de Coincy concern the Virgin *Mary. From the *council of Ephesus (431), veneration for the Holy Virgin Mother of God had begun to develop, first in the East, then in the West. In the 12th-13th cc., Marian piety enjoyed its greatest extension in the West, both in monastic circles and among the *laity. More than 2000 miracles in *Latin and 1100 in French survive from the Middle Ages, in verse as well as prose.

The Marian miracle is strongly structured: Mary acts as consoler of the *penitent or as mediator with her Son; she saves the believer who vows fervent devotion to her. The *salvation is sometimes *thaumaturgical, as in the miracle where she wipes a monk's sores and gives him the breast to save him from a grave illness. More often, the Virgin confounds the devil or saves the sinner's *soul, even if he repents at the last moment.

The sources of Gautier's miracles are the Latin legends, most of which come from the East. One of the miracles tells the story of the monk Theophilus, who made a pact with the devil, but was saved by the intervention of the Virgin; this Greek legend must have spread to the West through the intermediary of an abundant literary and iconographical tradition. Another famous legend tells the story of a young man who puts a ring, a present from his *amie*, on the finger of a statue of the Virgin, promising to serve her all his life. But he forgets his promise and marries. On the wedding night, the Virgin interposes herself between him and his wife, reproaching him for his faithlessness. The young man retires from the world to a hermitage. Gautier expresses his edifying lesson in a verbal play that heralds the preciosity of late medieval rhetoricians: "Let us leave Marots and Marions and marry Mary who marries her *maris* (husbands) in heaven".

Gautier de Coincy, *Miracles of the Virgin*. Manuscript, second third of 14th c. Paris, BNF (N.a.f. 24541, fol. 235 v°).

In his poems, Gautier imitates – not without pathos – the "chanson" of the **trouvères*: however, the "sweet sickness of *love" that fills him finds its source not in the courteous lady, but in the "heavenly queen". He expresses an intimate alliance of *poetry and religious experience.

F. Koenig, *Les Miracles de Nostre Dame. Par Gautier de Coinci*, Geneva, 1955-1970. – B. Cazelles, *La faiblesse chez Gautier de Coinci*, Saratoga, 1978. – *Vierge et Merveille. Les miracles de Notre-Dame narratifs au Moyen Âge*, P. Kunstmann (ed. and tr.), Paris, 1981. – *Gautier de Coinci: le texte du miracle, Médiévales*, 2, Paris, May 1982.

Michel Stanesco

**GDAŃSK.** Gdańsk (Danzig) is the chief town of East *Pomerania, a historical province of *Poland. City and *port were founded at the mouth of the Vistula, on the Baltic, in *c.*980; the earliest information on it dates from 997. From the late 10th c., Gdańsk was within the frontiers of Poland; lost in 1066, it came back under the power of Poland in 1119. In the 12th c., Gdańsk was the seat of the local dynasty of Pomerania, which depended on the senior Polish princes. In the years 1227-1231, it gained complete independence; from 1294, after the extinction of the Pomeranian dynasty, the prince of Great Poland Přemysl II (king of Poland from 1295) took possession of Pomerania and Gdańsk; after his death in 1296, Gdańsk passed for a short time into the hands of Ladislas the Short (Władysław Łokietek), then of the *Přemyslids, who from 1300 were at the same time kings of *Bohemia and Poland. From 1306, Pomerania was once more a possession of Prince Ladislas the Short (king of Poland in 1320). The *Brandenburger invasion of 1308 obliged Ladislas to turn for help to the *Teutonic Knights who, after having expelled the Brandenburgers, themselves occupied Gdańsk and Pomerania by force of arms in 1308-1309. Gdańsk remained in their possession until 1454, when the inhabitants expelled the Teutonic Order; in 1466, by the treaty of Toruń, Gdańsk was recovered by Poland.

In 1257-1263, the suburbs of Gdańsk received the law of *Lübeck; the centre-town received its urban law (law of Chełmno, or Kulm) only in 1343. In the 14th c., Gdańsk was already an urban area composed of an old town, a centre-town and a new town as well as several **bourgs* of lesser importance. The population of Gdańsk grew from a few thousand inhabitants in the 13th c. to 40,000 in the 16th. Alongside the local Polish population, German colonists settled there from the late 13th c., then colonists notably from Holland, *Flanders and France. The main source of *wealth and power for the patriciate was *commerce; from the 11th, 12th and 13th cc., Gdańsk was an important Baltic port, a member of the *Hanse from 1361. In the late 14th and early 15th cc., its role increased rapidly, as it became the main port of the vast Polish-Lithuanian State; after 1454, Gdańsk received very important privileges from King Casimir Jagiello, which led to a great development of commerce and of the town's importance. It possessed its own considerable commercial fleet – nearly 600 vessels in the mid 15th c.; it maintained commercial links with, among others, the *Netherlands, *Germany, Western France, *England, *Denmark, *Sweden, *Novgorod and even *Portugal. Gdańsk's artisanate also developed; in the 14th c., it had between ten and twenty *corporations.

In the Middle Ages, Gdańsk was an important centre of religious life, attached to the ecclesiastical *province of Poland: it had numerous churches – *e.g.* St Nicholas, St Catherine, Our Lady which later became the town's chief sanctuary; *hospitals, parochial *schools and numerous religious *confraternities appeared; lastly the religious *orders settled there: *Cistercians at Oliwa close by, *Dominicans, *Carmelites, *Bridgetines and *Franciscans, as well as a few *beguinages. An intellectual milieu formed in the 15th c., hundreds of inhabitants of Gdańsk going to study at *university, essentially at *Leipzig, *Vienna or *Cracow. Medieval Gdańsk also saw a development of artistic life: artistic influences from the Netherlands and other regions of Western and northern Europe passed through there on their way to Poland. In the 16th c., Gdańsk was the largest and richest of the towns of the Polish "Republic" (the *Rzeczpospolita*), it had immense political and military importance and it was at the same time the largest port in the Baltic.

P. Simson, *Geschichte der Stadt Danzig bis 1626*, 1, 2, 4, Gdańsk, 1913-1918. – *Historia Gdańska*, E. Cieślak (ed.), 1-2, Gdańsk, 1978-1982. – *History of Gdańsk*, Gdańsk, 1988.

Zbigniew Piłat

**GEBHARD OF CONSTANCE (died 995).** A member of the powerful *Alamannian family of the Udalrichinger, Gebhard became bishop of *Constance in 979; he received the *ring and *staff from the hands of *Otto II. Very close to the royal family and to Hadewig, duchess of *Swabia, he took part in the Roman expedition of 981, then acted as adviser to the empress Theophano. From 990, he administered the *bishoprics of *Padua and *Pavia.

In 983 he founded the church of St Gregory at Petershausen, for which he brought back from *Rome in 989 *relics of St

*Gregory and a privilege from Pope John XV. His successor Ulrich II proceeded to the elevation of his relics on 27 August 1134.

*Die Bischöfe von Konstanz, Geschichte und Kultur*, E. Kuhn (ed.), Friedrichshafen, 1988.

Geneviève Bührer-Thierry

**GELASIUS II, POPE (*c.*1060/1064 - 1119).** Born at *Gaeta, John was educated at *Monte Cassino at the time of Abbot *Desiderius and the monk Alberic. From 1088, he began a brilliant career at *Rome. In 1101, he was made *cardinal-deacon of Santa Maria in Cosmedin and was put in charge of the pontifical *chancery which he helped reorganise. Loyal to *Paschal II, he defended his policy at the *Lateran council (1116), then retired to Monte Cassino. On Paschal II's death, he was elected *pope under the name of Gelasius II (24 Jan 1118). The Frangipani family and the presence of the Emperor *Henry V prevented him from holding on to Rome. The opposition of the two camps was exacerbated when Henry V got the *antipope Gregory VIII elected. After an exile at Gaeta and a brief return to Rome, Gelasius II left for France (autumn 1118) where he met *Louis VI. He died at *Cluny (28 or 29 Jan 1119) and was buried there.

R. Krohn, *Der päpstliche Kanzler Johannes von Gaeta (Gelasius II)*, Marburg, 1918. – I.S. Robinson, *The Papacy, 1073-1198*, Cambridge, 1990. – G. Schwaiger, "Gélase II", *DHP*, 1994, 723-724.

Pierre Kerbrat

**GEMISTUS PLETHON (*c.*1360-1452).** Georgios Gemistos, surnamed Plethon, was certainly the most remarkable figure of 15th-c. Greek culture. He was born at *Constantinople. After following the traditional studies (he was a pupil of *Demetrius Cydones), he stayed at the court of Adrianople with Elisha, a Jewish scholar living among Ottomans and a follower of the *falsafa*. Returning to his home town, he taught *philosophy. His subversive ideas let loose an ecclesiastical intrigue; the Emperor Manuel II, with whom he remained on good terms, sent him to the court of *Mistra, as counsellor to his son the despot Theodore II. In 1438-1439, he took part in the council of Ferrara-*Florence; on this occasion, he met a circle of Western scholars whom he instructed in the interpretation of Platonic texts; for them he wrote the treatise *On the Differences between Plato and Aristotle*, starting-point of a long controversy between *Platonists and *Aristotelians. He spent the end of his life at Mistra where he worked for the restoration of Hellenism.

For Plethon, Christianity was reponsible for the decline of Greece. The Oracles of the magi of Zoroaster (the *Chaldaean Oracles* transmitted by Michael *Psellus), considered pre-Platonist and pre-Pythagorean, were to serve as text of reference in the *metaphysical and religious sphere. In the *Treatise on the Laws*, only part of which survived the *auto-da-fé* decided by *George Scholarius, Gemistus Plethon worked out a *theology to support the political system he advocated. The divine world (the Platonic Ideas) forms a strictly structured and centralized hierarchy; any idea of divine *trinity is rejected. *Apophatic theology is excluded. Zeus, the supreme god, is distinguished from all other beings because he alone is self-subsistent, but he is neither inexpressible nor unknowable; he is father, *demiurge and king; his activity and will are rational and necessary (there is no divine arbitrariness). A multiplicity of gods is needed to produce the world and govern it (a *basileus* could not directly administer each individual citizen). *Man links the intelligible and the sensible worlds. Then, in the *Treatise on the Virtues*, Plethon deduces from these foundations a morality inspired by Platonic-Stoic rather than Christian ideas, capable of restoring Greece.

C. M. Woodhouse, *George Gemistos Plethon*, Oxford, 1986. – B. Tambrun-Krasker, *Georges Gémiste Pléthon, Traité des vertus*, Athens-Leiden, 1987. – W. Blum, *Georgios Gemistos Plethon, Politik, Philosophie und Rhetorik im spätbyzantinischen Reich*, Stuttgart, 1988. – B. Tambrun-Krasker, *Magika logia... Oracles chaldaiques. Recension de Georges Gémiste Pléthon*, crit. ed. with intro., Fr. tr. and commentary, Athens-Paris-Brussels, 1995.

Brigitte Tambrun-Krasker

**GENESIS**

***Exegesis.** The first book of the *Bible was one of the most commented on: its narrative richness and the number of problems it raised aroused the interest of exegetes. The beginning (*Hexaemeron*) was the object of separate commentaries, which testify to the great contemporary doctrinal currents (Ambrose, *Bede, *Abelard, Thierry of Chartres, *Honorius Augustodunensis, *Robert Grosseteste, St *Bonaventure, *Henry of Ghent). More generally, the commentaries of the early Middle Ages and 12th c. make long *excursus* on questions of natural *science, while those of the 13th and 14th cc. develop *metaphysical and philosophical considerations. The stories are often treated allegorically, but many commentaries give equal room to the different "*senses". Among the most important are those of Jerome, Augustine, *Remigius of Auxerre, *Hugh and *Andrew of Saint-Victor, *Peter John Olivi, Thomas Waleys, Meister *Eckhart and Dominic Grima.

A. Borst, *Der Turmbau von Babel*, Stuttgart, 1957-1967. – *In principio. Interprétations des premiers versets de la Genèse*, Paris, 1973. – G. Dahan, "L'histoire de Caïn et Abel...", *RThAM*, 49, 1982, 21-89; *ibid.*, 50, 1983, 5-68.

Gilbert Dahan

**Iconography.** Many iconographical cycles devoted to the book of Genesis in the Christian East as well as in the West (*Saint-Savin-sur-Gartempe) exist, but they usually retain just one or other of the edifying episodes: the account of *creation or the stories of *Noah, *Abraham and his descendants around the figures of *Isaac, *Jacob or *Joseph.

K. Weitzmann, H. Kessler, *The Cotton Genesis*, Princeton (NJ), 1986.

Fanny Caroff

*Genesis. The Creation of Adam.* Miniature from the so-called *Bible of St Bernard* from the abbey of Clairvaux, 12th c. Troyes, Municipal Library (Ms 458, fol. 6 r°).

Portrait of Genghis Khān. China, Yuan period, 13th-14th c.

**GENGHIS KHĀN (1167-1227).** Founder of the *Mongol Empire. Temujin, son of a clan chieftain, Yesugei, who was murdered by the Tatars when he was nine, had been abandoned by his father's vassals and had survived grave dangers. Thanks to the help of the khan of the Keraït, he grouped together the Mongol clans, disposed of his rivals and wiped out the Tatars; he had taken the title of khan. In 1203, he turned against his ally, destroyed the organisation of the Keraït people and then that of the Naïman and the Merkit, two other peoples penetrated by Christianity, and made of all these elements a new people, the "Blue Mongols", divided into military units, the "thousands", in charge of which he put his followers who formed a new aristocracy. Marriages with the daughters and wives of the defeated reinforced this unity. In 1206, the Teb-Tengri (the shaman Kököčü) proclaimed him *qaghan*, giving him the name Genghis Khān (universal khan) and investing him with a heavenly mandate that subjected the entire world to him. Genghis promulgated rules that formed a code, the Yassa, notably prescribing respect for all cults and their ministers.

In 1211 he attacked the Kin Empire of Northern China, whose submission was not completed until after his death; in 1218 he turned against the Naïman Küčlüg, who had taken possession of the empire of the Kara-Khitaï (established in the Ili and Chou basins). Having eliminated him, he crossed the Syr-Daria to attack Sultan Muhammad of Khwarizm and, at the cost of bloody massacres, occupied Transoxiana, Khorassan and Afghanistan while his generals sacked northern *Iran, Azerbaijan and *Georgia and defeated the coalition of Russians and *Cumans (1219-1223). Genghis, returning to Mongolia, attacked the kingdom of the Tangut (south of the Hwang-Ho loop). In the course of this campaign he died, in 1227.

Before his death, he had given an embryonic administration to the empire he had formed and to which were added a number of kingdoms and tribes – notably those of the Siberian forest – who had accepted his sovereignty. Contemporaries were struck by the contrast between the massacres and pillages, the deportations and exactions that had marked his campaigns, and his care to make his subjects live in peace and to ensure order where his authority was recognised. He himself was accessible to the influence of scholars, like the Kitan Ye-liu Chou-Tsaï, knew how to use the Muslims who rallied to his cause and to whom he entrusted governments, and willingly heard religious of different beliefs, while remaining attached to the cult of Eternal Heaven (the Tengri) revered by the nomads of the steppe. Moreover, he had kept the way of life of his ancestors, not renouncing it to adopt the customs of the sedentary peoples whose usefulness as tributaries he had ended by acknowledging.

R. Grousset, *L'Empire mongol (Ier phase)*, Paris, 1940. – P. Ratchnevsky, *Genghis Khan: his Life and Legacy*, Oxford, 1991.

Jean Richard

**GENOA.** "A city thrown at the sea" and backed by the arid slopes of the Apennines, Genoa built its fortune on the exploitation of the sea. The site, occupied from the 5th c. BC, retains few traces of a Romanization that was undoubtedly slow and difficult. A first Christian community was set up in the 3rd c. under the leadership of *bishops, the most famous of whom was San Siro (*c.*360). Passing in turn under the power of Goths (early 6th c.), Byzantines (537), *Lombards (*c.*640) and *Franks (774), in 958 the city gained recognition of an independence that it asserted in the 11th c. under the leadership of its bishops and families of viscounts. The struggle against the *Saracens in the Tyrrhenian sea (1016), in Tunisia (1087) and in *Spain (1092-1093) procured it a booty that nourished *commerce and allowed it to take part in the first *crusade with powerful fleets.

Urban autonomy favoured the organisation of the citizens into a voluntary mercantile and military association, the *Compagna*, which ended by representing the city's collective interests and converged into a single representative organism, the *commune. In exchange for its help to the Frankish barons of *Syria-*Palestine, Genoa obtained "counters" and customs privileges that gave a great impetus to its commercial activities in the *Holy Land, but also in Egypt, the *Byzantine Empire, *Sicily, the *Maghreb and Spain. From the 12th c., Genoa commanded the direct routes between the *fairs of *Champagne and the Levant. In the course of its territorial and economic expansion, it clashed with *Pisa, which it defeated at Meloria in 1284, and *Venice, which it opposed in long "colonial" wars caused by commercial rivalry in the Byzantine area; despite the Genoese victory of Curzola in 1298, hostilities were prolonged with no decisive result. These economic successes had their reversals. Fiercely individualist, this people of *merchants could not give their town political stability. Power passed initially from consuls to *podestà*; the popular and middle-class revolt of 1257 brought to power the captain of the people William *Boccanegra, removed after only five years by the dyarchy of the Ghibelline families of *Doria and Spinola. Genoa's great families disputed with each other in continual factional struggles: the Ghibellines were replaced by the *Guelf families of *Fieschi and Grimaldi, supported by *Robert of Anjou and Matteo Visconti. Genoa finally attained a certain institutional stability in the regime of *perpetual doges* (1339-1528), inaugurated by the election of Simone Boccanegra as life doge.

The 14th c. saw the apogee of the network of Genoese counters in the Mediterranean: *Caffa and Genoese Gazaria (*Crimea) in the Black Sea, Pera in the suburbs of *Constantinople, Chios and Mytilene in the Aegean sea, Cadiz, *Seville, Lisbon, *Bruges and *Antwerp, *London and Southampton in the West. There the Genoese sold Mediterranean products and exported local produce in a vast traffic that did not necessarily pass through Genoa. They were also *bankers, ship-owners, discoverers of unknown lands, from the Vivaldi brothers in 1291 to Christopher *Columbus, born Genoese but in the service of Spain during his great *journey of 1492. In the 15th c., the rise of *Ottoman power led to the gradual loss of Genoese establishments in the East and obliged the centre of interest to move westward. This weakened the city's political structures. Threatened by creditors grouped together in the bank of St George (1417), the Republic was unable to resist French rule (1396-1409), followed by the *signoria* of the *Visconti (1421-1436). Only in 1528 did admiral Andrea Doria, allied with Spain, give it constitutional laws (biennial doges) that inaugurated an aristocratic republic, which survived until the 1790s..

Genoa's medieval artistic output shows the strong influence of French *Gothic: characteristic are the *case Doria*, with a façade of alternating rows of black and white stone, the church of San Matteo and the *Cathedral; also medieval was the famous Lantern of Genoa, built at the entrance to the *port in 1139, but rebuilt in its present form in 1543.

E. Bach, *La Cité de Gênes au XII^e siècle*, Copenhagen, 1955. – J. Heers, *Gênes au XV^e siècle*, Paris, 1961. – L. Balletto, *Genova, Mediterraneo, Mar Nero (secc. XIII-XV)*, Genoa, 1976. – M. Balard, *La Romanie génoise (XII^e-début du XV^e siècle)*, Genoa-Rome, 1978. – L. Grossi-Bianchi, E. Poleggi, *Una Città portuale del Medioevo: Genova nei secoli X-XVI*, Genoa, 1980. – G. Airaldi, *Genova e la Liguria nel Medioevo*, Turin, 1986. – G. Pistarino, *La capitale del Mediterraneo: Genova nel Medioevo*, Bordighera, 1993. – S. Epstein, *Genoa and the Genoese, 958-1528*, Chapel Hill (NC), 1996.

Michel Balard

**GENTILE DA FABRIANO (*c.*1370-1427).** Gentile di Niccolò, called "da Fabriano", was born at Fabriano and died at *Rome. His training and early activity are for the most part rather obscure. During these years, however, he evolved into one of the influences of International *Gothic, well represented in central *Italy, between *Siena, *Orvieto and *Perugia, by local studios of miniaturists, engravers and *goldsmiths. These precious and courtly forms of art seemed adapted to a society that was experiencing a return to *feudalism (at Fabriano, at Montefano). Around 1390, he did the small *altarpiece of *The Virgin and Saints* (now in Berlin). He later left Fabriano to travel and visit the main artistic centres of north-central Italy: *Venice, Brescia, *Florence, Siena, Orvieto and finally Rome; he painted at this time, for persons of high rank, wooden panels and *frescos that would exercise their influence on the Lombard and Venetian painters of late Gothic.

The few works that survive of Gentile da Fabriano's activity nevertheless give us a good picture of his technical and stylistic capacities: thus he passed from the sumptuous and fragile

*The Adoration of the Magi*, 1423, by Gentile da Fabriano (1370-1427). Florence, Uffizi.

arabesque of the Valle Romita polyptych (a *Coronation of the Virgin and Saints*; now at Milan, Brera gallery) to the more geometrical composition of the Quaratesi polyptych (*c.*1425; now dismembered and shared between London, Florence, Rome and Washington), in which he shows his knowledge of the questions of volume and perspective that were being asked at Florence. Between these two polyptychs, he painted the Virgins of *Pisa (Museo Nazionale San Matteo) and Washington (National Gallery), then that of Orvieto cathedral, which seems later. He was chosen by Palla Strozzi shortly before 1423 to paint, in his *chapel in the church of Santa Trinità at Florence, an *Adoration of the Magi* (signed and dated; now in the Uffizi). As the outcome of that choice by which the too old, and too Florentine, Lorenzo Monaco (1370-1423/1424) found himself supplanted, Gentile took the lead as one of the leading painters of the town of Florence, particularly appreciated by the governing oligarchy.

K. Christiansen, *Gentile da Fabriano*, London-Ithaca (NY), 1982. – R. Jones, "Palla Strozzi e la sagrestia di Santa Trinità", *RArte*, 4th series, 37, 1, 1984, 9-106. – *Gentile da Fabriano. Il polittico di Valle Romita*, Milan, 1993. – H. Wohl, "Gentile da Fabriano", *DoA*, 12, 298-303.

Daniel Russo

**GENUFLECTION.** Genuflection is one of the attitudes of *prayer, mentioned in the New Testament: Stephen at the moment of his *martyrdom (Acts 7, 60), *Peter at the moment of raising Tabitha-Dorcas (Acts 9, 40), *Paul making his farewells to the believers of Miletus and Tyre (Acts 20, 36; 21, 5). The aim is to intensify prayer: "I bow my knees unto the Father . . that he would grant you, according to the riches of his glory, to be strengthened with might by his Spirit" (Eph 3, 14-16).

It may be an attitude of penitence, *humility, repentance, as well as intensity of prayer; it is also the attitude of individual, secret, personal prayer. Genuflection expresses veneration, respect, submission. The medieval usage was genuflection on both knees. Genuflection on one knee comes from secular usage: it is mentioned in chivalric and courtly literature.

M.-J. Bidot, "Somatique et liturgie, ou le sens sacré des attitudes et des gestes", *ParLi*, 1963, 218-228. – E. Bertrand, "Génuflexions et métanies", *DSp*, 6, 1966, 213-226. – G.-M. Oury, *Les gestes de la prière*, Paris, 1998, 95-104.

Guy-Marie Oury

**GEOFFREY OF MONMOUTH (*c.*1100-1155).** Born *c.*1100, probably at Monmouth in *Wales, Geoffrey played an essential role in the spread of the Arthurian "matter" among men of letters. From 1129 to 1151 he was a secular teacher at St George's College, Oxford; in 1151 he was elected bishop of St Asaph and died in 1155. His literary activity dates from the period when he taught at *Oxford, and its major work is the *Historia regum Britanniae* (*History of the Kings of Britain*), finished before 1139. This essentially uses three earlier works: *Gildas's *De excidio et conquestu Britanniae* (6th c.), *Bede's *Historia ecclesiastica* (8th c.) and the *Historia Brittonum* (9th c.) attributed to Nennius; but it also has recourse to Welsh or Breton legends.

The work begins with the story of the ruin of Troy, then tells of the birth of Brutus, great-grandson of Aeneas, and his settlement in Britain. Like all medievals, Geoffrey was susceptible to the myth of Trojan origins: the Britons too had those glorious losers as models. The history then shows the establishment of kingship in Britain, the royal genealogies up to Caesar, then relations with Rome: at the moment when the country, devastated by successive wars, was a prey to the barbarians, appeared the prophecies of *Merlin. Then came the British recovery, with the reigns of Ambrosius, Uther and finally *Arthur, who unified Britain under their power; with Merlin's help, they bore down on the Saxon invaders and laid low the pretensions of the Romans. But Arthur was himself betrayed by his nephew, to whom he had entrusted the regency of the kingdom: the decline of the Britains, many of whom left the island, was then inevitable.

The *Historia* professed to be primarily a literary work; it set out a brilliant, picturesque and tragic fresco of the vicissitudes of a people destined for destruction, but also for memory, like that of Troy. It enjoyed immense success – 200 manuscripts – and was quickly adapted into French. Geffrei Gaimar used it from 1140 for his *Estoire des Angleis*, but it was the Norman Wace who, by his paraphrase of *Brut* (1155), dedicated to Queen *Eleanor, confirmed it as the *summa* of the Arthurian stories. The elements contributed by Geoffrey – the story of Arthur's conception, the first version of the destruction of the kingdom – were doubtless relatively unimportant compared to the burgeoning legends that appeared in romantic works from the second half of the 12th c.; but Geoffrey contributed the necessary impetus by giving it the guarantee of the scholar. Geoffrey, who in 1134 had published prophecies of Merlin detached from the *Historia*, returned for his last work to his favourite hero: his *Vita Merlini* (1148) in hexameters added new traits to the figure of the prophet, but it had much less success than the prophecies and the *Historia*.

*The Historia Regum Britanniae of Geoffrey of Monmouth*, A. Griscom (ed.), London, 1929. – Geoffrey of Monmouth, *The History of the Kings of Britain*, Harmondsworth, 1976. – *The Historia Regum Britanniae of Geoffrey of Monmouth*, N. Wright (ed.), Cambridge, 1985. C. Brooke, "Geoffrey of Monmouth as a Historian", *Church and Government in the Middle Ages*, C. Brooke (ed.), D. Luscombe (ed.), G. Martin (ed.), D. Owen (ed.), Cambridge, 1976, 77-91. – W.R. Leckie, *The Passage of Dominion: Geoffrey of Monmouth and the Periodization of Insular History in the Twelfth Century*, Toronto, 1981. – A.G. Rigg, "Geoffrey of Monmouth", *A History of Anglo-Latin Literature 1066-1422*, Cambridge, 1992, 41-51. – M.J. Curley, *Geoffrey of Monmouth*, New York, 1994. – S. Echard, *Arthurian Narrative in the Latin Tradition*, Cambridge, 1998.

François Suard

**GEOMANCY.** Geomancy was a divinatory technique that aimed at knowledge of the past, present and future by the interpretation of sixteen figures formed of four formations of points, odd or even in number, placed in compartments called "houses". The whole of this arrangement was called a geomantic theme. Luck came into it only during the throwing of the points, which was originally done on the ground, whence the name geomancy, divination on the earth, used in the Latin West. The geomantic theme was formed following strict rules, starting from the first four figures obtained by cancellation of the points traced on the ground. Each one of the sixteen figures and the sixteen houses possessed a principal meaning and derivative meanings, particular qualities and values, some of which were drawn from associations with the humours, the temperaments, the seasons, the signs of the *zodiac or the planets. The interpretaton of the theme by the geomancer rested on the adaptation of the meanings and values and qualities of the figures to those of the houses, according to the question asked. It was complicated by the introduction, from the 13th and 14th cc., of numerous astrological notions.

The more or less legendary origins assigned to it by geomancers made geomancy originate with the Mesopotamians or the Indians. It was certainly practised in the Arab world from the 10th c., and in the 12th c. it penetrated almost simultaneously into the Latin West and the Byzantine East through the *translation of Arabic treatises. In the Latin West, the first treatise known in the 12th c. is that of Hugh de Santalla (*Ars geomancie*), who also translated Arabic astrological texts. The treaty *Si quis per artem astronomicam* is attributed to *Gerard of Cremona, another known translator of Arabic texts. A third 12th-c. treatise, *Estimaverunt Indi*, is anonymous. Other texts of the 13th, 14th and 15th cc. survive. The most important are those of Bartholomew of Parma, *William of Moerbeke, Jean de Murs and Roland l'Écrivain. Texts in *Hebrew, Greek, French and Provençal attest the diffusion of this technique in both time and space. The personality of the authors, like that of the recipients of the works or the possessors of manuscripts, gives some indications as to the intellectual and social milieu in which geomancy developed. The condemnation of geomancy in anti-divinatory writings and the mentions made of it in a number of literary works or *chronicles from the second half of the 13th c. attest the breadth of its its diffusion. Certain authors, like *Dante in the *Divine Comedy* or Jacques de Guise in the *Annales du Hainaut*, even show a thorough knowledge of geomantic technique, which, though it never enjoyed the success of *astrology, held an important place in the medieval divinatory sciences.

T. Charmasson, *Recherches sur une technique divinatoire: la géomancie dans l'Occident médiéval*, Paris, 1980.

Thérèse Charmasson

**GEORGE OF PODĚBRADY (1420-1471).** Jiří z Poděbrady, son of one of the great noble families of *Bohemia, became the main political representative of Czech utraquism after 1440. In 1452 he was elected regent of the kingdom (with the title of administrator of the country), then king of Bohemia in 1458 after the death of the young Ladislas Posthumous. He made meritorious efforts to restore peace in his country ravaged by the *Hussite wars and to consolidate the authority of the State. He won renown by numerous diplomatic initiatives, notably the project (1462-1464) of founding a league of Christian rulers, led by the king of *France and charged with resolving international differences amicably. In Bohemia, he practised a policy of peaceful coexistence of the "two peoples" with equal rights, *Utraquists and *Catholics. That is why the *pope declared him a *heretic and deposed him in 1466. Despite the military actions brought against him by the Czech opposition, the German crusaders and *Matthias Corvinus, king of *Hungary, George of Poděbrady maintained himself on the throne until his death, at the price of severe losses and numerous diplomatic concessions.

E. Denis, *Georges de Podiébrad. Les Jagellons*, Paris, 1890. – F. G. Heymann, *George of Bohemia. King of Heretics*, Princeton (NJ), 1965. – O. Odložilík, *The Hussite King. Bohemia in European Affairs 1440-1471*, New Brunswick (NJ), 1965.

Jaroslav Boubín

**GEORGE OF THE ARABS (died 724).** Syro-occidental bishop of the Arab tribes of the Euphrates. He completed the *Hexaemeron* of *Jacob of Edessa († 708), an encyclopedic work in the service of the theological, philosophical and cosmographical science of the time, a genre that was in honour from Ephrem († 373) to the 9th century. But his main work was the Syriac translation of Aristotle's *Organon* (*Categories* and *Prior Analytics*).

J. B. Chabot, *Jacobi Edesseni Hexaemeron seu in opus creationis libri septem*, *CSCO*, 92 (Syriac text), Paris, 1928, 278-357. – A. Vaschalde, *CSCO*, 97 (Lat. tr.), Paris, 1932, 237-306 (the seventh treatise is by George, on "the man whom God created in his image"). – K. Georr, *Les Catégories d'Aristote dans leurs versions syro-arabes*, Beirut, 1948 (ed. of the Syriac and Arabic versions).

Micheline Albert

**GEORGE SCHOLARIUS (GENNADIUS II) (*c.*1403-1472).** Patriarch of Constantinople. Fired by *Aristotle and the Latin theologians, he opened a school of *philosophy and translated or summarized *Thomas Aquinas, from whom he differed only on the **Filioque*. In 1439 he took part in the council of *Florence, then stood aside from the polemics over the *Union, dedicating himself to the defence of Aristotle against *Gemistus Plethon.

Under the influence of Mark Eugenicus, he became the leading champion of opposition to the Union and became a monk. Captured by the *Turks in 1453, the Sultan made him *patriarch of *Constantinople (as Gennadius II).

He resigned several times and ended his days in a monastery. We owe him some works of philosophy, *translations from Latin and polemical *treatises.

C. J. G. Turner, "The Career of George Gennadius Scholarius", *Byz.*, 39, 1969, 420-455.

Marie-Hélène Congourdeau

**GEORGIA.** Before the 12th c., no kingdom or principality bore the name of Georgia (Sakartvelo), but on the south slopes of the *Caucasus were a number of regions whose inhabitants were aware that they differed from their neighbours, firstly by their language and writing, attested from the 5th c., and later by their Church; they were divided, one on each side of a secondary chain of the Caucasus, into two great areas: western Georgia (in Georgian: Egrisi and Apxazeti; in Greek: Lazica and Abasgia) and eastern Georgia (in Georgian: Kartli; in Greek: Iberia).

What we know of the medieval Georgian world, little known to its great neighbours, rests mainly on Georgian sources: historiographical and hagiographical texts mainly clarifying the history of eastern Georgia, manuscripts, evidence of *archaeology and art history.

Up to the 7th c., the two parts of Georgia evolved relatively distinctly. In the west, in contact with the Roman world through the garrisons maintained on the coast, the kingdom of Lazica oscillated between Sasanian and Byzantine alliances; the latter prevailed in the 5th c. before evolving in the 6th towards an annexation pure and simple, which favoured a certain unification of all western Georgia. Christianity, linked by national traditions with the apostolate of St Andrew, developed there, starting from the coast, in the framework of a few Greek *bishoprics dependent on the *patriarchate of *Constantinople. Byzantium was taking an interest in these regions at the time, mainly because of the access they permitted through the Caucasus to the world of the steppes whose seething instability worried the Empire. However, it had neither the means nor the time to really carry out the political incorporation of too distant Lazica into the imperial system. At the time of the expansion of *Islam, the territory was in fact independent and had returned to its old divisions.

In eastern Georgia ,where the weight of the mountainous and trans-Caucasian peoples was a constant fact of history, various regions linked by their evolution now to *Armenia, now to *Albania, gravitated around a central core, dominated by the town of Mcxeta, then by Tbilisi. At that place was a kingdom of ancient origin, ruled from the 4th c. by a partly Iranian dynasty, but integrated into the Christian world since the *conversion of its king at the time of *Constantine. The *bishopric of Mcxeta became in the 5th c. the metropolis of a developed *province, attached to the patriarchate of *Antioch which conferred on its head the title of *catholicos*, thus laying the basis of the future national Church of Georgia. Christianity developed under the influence of Syro-Palestinian monasteries; but the religious authorities anchored their Church in Chalcedonian orthodoxy at the start of the 7th century. No-one can say for sure exactly what were the power and the real degree of independence of the Christian kings of Kartli; the kingdom disappeared in the course of the 6th c. under the actions of the Sasanians, and it was the fragmented territories that the Arabs brought under their rule in 643-645 and subsequently tried to integrate with others in the province of Arminiya. Here again, it was the Caucasus and its defiles that interested the Arabs, as they had interested the Persians.

A single *emir was established in Georgian territory, at the important crossroads of Tbilisi (Tiflis in Arabic), but his authority could never extend to the whole of Kartli and the emirs subsequently tended to escape the control of the *caliph and the governor of Arminiya. On the periphery of their area of activity, new political powers were being formed from the 8th c., in the hands of Christian Georgian families who gave themselves princely or royal titles. In the 9th and 10th cc., a branch of the Bagratid family, also active in Armenia, consolidated its hold on the south-west, in the region of T'ao-K'lardzheti, with the support of a powerful monastic movement; but it was weakened by internal quarrels between two branches, one of which had taken the title of king of the Kartvelians while the other, bearer of the dignity of *curopalates*, played an active role in the nearby Byzantine and Armenian territories. At the same time, another line of kings, of little-known origin, working from Kutaisi, unified western Georgia, under the name of Apxazeti; remaining attached to the Empire, they nonetheless contributed to their progressive removal from the authority of the patriarchate of Constantinople and developed the liturgical use of the Georgian language. Early in the 11th c., the inheritance of the kings of the Apxazi and the whole Bagratid family was concentrated in the hands of a single man, Bagrat', first of a line of "kings of the Apxazi and Kartvelians"; throughout the 11th c., this new line strove to establish its power over central Kartli which it disputed with the emirs of Tbilisi and the Armenian kings on one hand, and with another great Georgian family settled in the most easterly part of Georgia, K'axeti, with the title of **chorepiscopus*, on the other. The activity of aristocratic families, whose rise coincides with the arrival of groups of *Seljuk Turks in the second half of the century complicated the political map. The unification of the Georgian world made decisive progress at the turn of the 11th and 12th cc. under King David (1089-1125) who annexed K'axeti, reconquered Tbilisi in 1122 and led a long expansionary movement towards the Caspian sea and Armenia. The expansion of economic life seems to have accompanied and followed the establishment of this vast domain. This movement continued under David's descendants, notably the prestigious Queen Tamar (1184-1215). The power of these kings was contemporary with the massive arrival of Latins in the East; they were happy to encounter a nation they had previously been unaware of, and they appreciated their military strength all the more since it depended on a people whose Christian qualities they also discovered. Religious contacts with the West were formed from then on.

From the 9th c. especially, the Church had in fact been the solid support of the Georgian group of countries. The institution of the *catholicoi* had never suffered an eclipse and their national role was strengthened by their obtaining – doubtless by stages and always in the framework of the patriarchate of Antioch – autocephaly, which seems to have been acquired in the mid 11th c., just as the extension of the powers of the *catholicos* to the whole of the Georgian world, the west included, seems to have been acquired at that time. The number of church buildings multiplied along with that of bishoprics, often founded by the princes. We must especially emphasize the role of the monasteries which developed on Georgian soil, but also in *Palestine, in *Syria, at Constantinople and its environs (thus the monastery of Iviron on Mount *Athos). The activity of numerous monks in translating Greek texts gave the Church a complete corpus of fundamental texts around which it unified dogma, canon law and the liturgy, thanks to which it undertook to reform the practice and moral life of Christians, as attested by the acts of the national *council of Ruisi-Urbnisi held under the presidency of the king in 1103.

But these cultural contacts did not cause the Georgian nation to lose its specific identity; this was expressed through the progressive redaction of the historiographical corpus of national traditions, through the cult of its own saints, particularly that of St Nino, apostle of the Kartli in the 4th century. We can still follow the setting up of political institutions which allow us to see the originality and complexity of this Caucasian society, which was regulated by its own legal practices, foreign to Romano-Byzantine law, and remained culturally close to Iranian models; this is shown in the 12th c. by the epic work of Shota Rustaveli, *The Knight of the tiger-skin*.

*Mongol attacks in the 13th c., the repeated invasions of *Timur between 1386 and 1405 and the first *Ottoman actions in the 15th c. hit the Georgian territories hard. These attacks were combined with bitter internal rivalries which from the 15th c., caused the Bagratid edifice to split lastingly into several kingdoms and principalities.

C. Roustaveli, *Le Chevalier à la peau de tigre*, S. Tsouladzé (tr.), Paris, 1964.

A. Alpago-Novello, V. Beridze, J. Lafontaine-Dosogne, *Art and Architecture in Medieval Georgia*, Louvain-la-Neuve, 1980. – B. Martin-Hisard, "Christianisme et Église dans le monde géorgien", *HChr*, 4, 1993, 549-603. – B. Outtier, "Langue et Littérature géorgiennes", M. Albert *et al.*, *Christianismes orientaux*, Paris, 1993, 263-296.

Bernadette Martin-Hisard

**GERALD OF WALES (*c.*1146-1223).** Son of an English lord and a Welsh noblewoman, Gerald of Wales (Giraldus Cambrensis) was educated at *Gloucester abbey before studying at *Paris, where he was a pupil of *Peter Comestor. A master of arts, he later studied *canon law there. A royal clerk from 1183 to 1208, *archdeacon of St David's (1175-1203) and *canon of *Hereford, he was elected bishop of St David's in 1199 but, as he wished to obtain the transformation of this see into a metropolitan archbishopric, the English clergy blocked his appointment after a long procedure at *Rome. As well as one of the first medieval autobiographies, he left works on *Ireland (*Topography* finished before 1186 and *Expugnatio*) and *Wales (*Itinerarium* and *Descriptio*), several Saints' Lives, a manual for the Welsh clergy (*Gemma ecclesiastica*), several treatises dealing with ecclesiastical affairs, numerous *letters and *sermons, and a *Mirror of Princes, the *De principis instructione*.

Gerald of Wales, *The Journey through Wales and The Description of Wales*, L. Thorpe (tr.), Harmondsworth, 1978. – *Gerald of Wales: the Jewel of the Church*, Leiden, 1979. – Gerald of Wales, *The History and Topography of Ireland*, J. O'Meara (tr.), Harmondsworth, 1982. – Gerald of Wales, *Concerning the Instruction of Princes*, Felinfach, 1991.

*DNB*, 1885-1900 – *BRUO*, 1, 1957. – J. Mann, "Giraldus Cambrensis and the Goliards", *Journal of Celtic Studies*, 3, 1981, 31-9. – R. Bartlett, *Gerald of Wales, 1146-1223*, Oxford, 1982. – R. Bartlett, "Rewriting Saints' Lives: the case of Gerald of Wales", *Spec.*, 58, 1983, 598-613.

Jean-Philippe Genet

**GERARD OF ABBEVILLE (died 1272).** *Archdeacon of *Brabant (*diocese of *Cambrai), then of Pontieu (diocese of Amiens), theologian, regent master at the university of *Paris from *c.*1261. He took part in the quarrel between the *mendicants and the *seculars from 1256 by attacking *Thomas of York's *Manus que contra omnipotentem*; the writing of this *Contra aduersarium* was interrupted by the condemnation of *William of Saint-Amour and the work was not published until 1269, when Gerard had relaunched the controversy by a *sermon (31 Dec 1268) followed by *quodlibetical disputes and a *Liber apologeticus* in which he had to defend himself against the mendicants. His role was not limited to controversy; his work, largely unedited, reveals him as an *Augustinian theologian open to *Aristotelianism, very typical of the secular university tradition. In his *testament, he left his rich *library to the *Sorbonne College.

A. Pattin, *L'Anthropologie de Gérard d'Abbeville. Étude préliminaire et édition critique de plusieurs "Questions quodlibétiques" concernant le sujet, avec l'édition complète du "De cogitationibus"*, Louvain, 1993.

P. Grand, "Gérard d'Abbeville", *DSp*, 6, 1967, 258-263. – *DHGE*, 20, 1984, 714-715 (bibliography).

Louis Duval-Arnould

**GERARD OF BORGO SAN DONNINO (died 1276/1277).** A *Franciscan, born at Borgo San Donnino (now Fidenza, in Emilia). In 1248 he came to *Paris to finish his studies, in 1252 he was promoted to *reader in *theology and in 1254 he published his *Liber introductorius in Euangelium aeternum* as well as a glossed edition of *Joachim of Fiore's *Concordia noui et ueteris testamenti*. Using Joachim's thought but going beyond it, he divided the *history of the world into three eras: that of the Father, under the law; that of the Son, under *grace; that of the Spirit, under a better grace; from the year 1200, the eternal Gospel (the work of Joachim) had supplanted the gospel of *Christ, and in 1260 would begin the great tribulation of *Antichrist, while the work of the Spirit would be accomplished by the new mendicant orders. Denounced by the secular *masters of the *university of Paris, then in the midst of their struggle against the *mendicant orders, these works were condemned by *Alexander IV in 1255 and again in 1256. Gerard, exiled to *Sicily, was recalled to Paris in 1258 by St *Bonaventure, minister general, there to be judged canonically. Condemned to life imprisonment as a *heretic, he died obstinate in his beliefs.

P. Péano, "Gérard de Borgo San Donnino", *DHGE*, 20, 1984, 709-721.

Louis Duval-Arnould

**GERARD OF BROGNE (died 959).** Born in the late 9th c. near *Namur, Gerard used his family property to found a monastery at *Brogne where he made religious *profession in 919. Having obtained *relics of St Eugenius from the abbey of *Saint-Denis and brought together a few monks, he became its *abbot in 923. The quality of the monastic observance he imposed there drew the attention of the great men of this world, who appealed to him to restore regular life in numerous communities. Personally or through the intermediary of his disciples, Gerard introduced the *reform at *Ghent (Saint-Bavon), in Hainaut and *Picardy (Saint-Bertin) and in *Normandy (Fontenelle, *Mont Saint-Michel). It operated on the basis of an understanding between the monks of Brogne, the *bishops and the rulers of the nascent feudal principalities, in the form of a return to the Rule of St *Benedict in the interpretation of it given by *Benedict of Aniane in the Carolingian period. The three principles on which it was based were the re-establishment of an abbot chosen by the monks, a strict respect for discipline and a sound management of the monastery's temporality. Gerard of Brogne was canonized by Pope *Innocent II in 1131.

"Gérard de Brogne", *DHGE*, 10, 1938, 829-832.

André Vauchez

**GERARD OF CREMONA (died 1187).** Among the most fundamental achievements that marked the intellectual renewal of the 12th c., Gerard of Cremona's *translations from Arabic to Latin nourished the *university teaching of the following centuries. Nearly 80 works were thus put into Latin, in the most varied fields: *philosophy, *mathematics, *astronomy, *medicine, *alchemy, divinatory science. He introduced the authors of Greek Antiquity who had been translated into Arabic (*Aristotle, Ptolemy, Archimedes, Euclid, Galen, etc.) and the philosophers or scientists of the Muslim world, eastern and western (*Avicenna, al-*Fārābī, al-*Kindī, the Sevillian of the first half of the 12th c., Jābir ibn Aflāh and his critique of Ptolemy, etc.). Born at Cremona in *Lombardy, in *c.*1145 Gerard went to *Toledo, where he remained until his death in 1187. The wealth of *Arabic manuscripts offered by the town, some 70 years after the Christian reconquest, as well as the presence of scholars from different backgrounds, explains its intense translating activity, unique in the history of medieval culture.

*The Latin Translation of the Arabic Version of Euclid's Elements: commonly ascribed to Gerard of Cremona*, H.L.L. Busard (ed.), Leiden, 1984. – Claudius Ptolemäus, *Der Steinkatalog des Almagest, Die arabisch-mittelalterliche Tradition*, 2, *Die lateinische Übersetzung Gerhards von Cremona, herausgegeben und bearbeitet von Paul Kunitzsch*, Weisbaden, 1990.

R. Lemay, "Gerard of Cremona", *Dictionary of Scientific Biography*, 15, suppl. 1, New York, 1978, 173-192. – D. Jacquart, "L'École des traducteurs", *Tolède XII^e-XIII^e siècles*, L. Cardaillac (dir.), Paris, 1991, 177-191 ("Autrement Série Mémoires"). – *Gerardo da Cremona*, P. Pizzamiglio (ed.), Cremona, 1992.

Danielle Jacquart

**GERBERT OF AURILLAC (*c.*945/950-1003).** The life and work of Gerbert of Aurillac, who became *pope under the name of Silvester II, are known to us through the 220 *letters he wrote before his pontificate, *charters promulgated at *Rome, his philosophical and scientific treatises and some pages of the *History of France* written by his disciple Richer, a monk of Saint-Remi at *Reims.

Born in *Aquitaine, Gerbert was a monk at Saint-Géraud d'Aurillac, then spent three years in *Catalonia learning the *mathematical sciences: arithmetic, geometry, *music and *astronomy. Going to Rome in 970, he astonished Pope John XIII and the Emperor *Otto II by his scientific knowledge. In 972, he went to *Reims and directed the *school there with great success. Otto II asked him to reform the abbey of *Bobbio which possessed a very rich *library, but Gerbert spent only two years there and in January 984 returned to Reims. He then helped Archbishop Adalbero first to support the three-year-old King *Otto III, then to bring about the triumph of Hugh Capet over the *Carolingians (June 987). After Adalbero's death, Gerbert hoped for the succession, but Hugh Capet preferred to appoint Arnulf, nephew of the Carolingian claimant Charles of Lorraine, in order to disarm his opponents. In fact Arnulf rapidly betrayed the king and was replaced by Gerbert (June 991). But the papacy refused to recognise the "intruder", whence a conflict from 991 to 997 between Gerbert and Rome. As long as Hugh Capet lived, Gerbert could resist and defend his "Gallican" ideas, but after the king's death he was abandoned by Robert the Pious and retired to *Germany, where he became the preceptor of Otto III. The emperor compensated him for the loss of Reims with the archbishopric of *Ravenna (April 998), where he undertook some reforms.

After the death of Pope Gregory V, the emperor appointed Gerbert to the succession. The former schoolmaster took the name of Silvester II, since he wished to collaborate closely with Otto whom he considered a "new Constantine". Under their impetus, Rome became the capital of the Christian West. The pope encouraged Otto to create a Church in *Poland independent from that of Germany (foundation of the archbishopric of *Gniezno in the year 1000). He sent a *crown to *Stephen, king of *Hungary, who also established a national Church with the consent of the pope and the emperor. Roman *Christendom thus extended its frontiers as far as the Vistula and the middle Danube. In February 1001, because of a *revolt by the Romans, Otto III and Silvester II left the City and settled at Ravenna. After the emperor's death in Jan 1002, the pope returned to Rome. He died there on 12 May 1003 and was buried at the Lateran.

In the late 11th and the 12th c., legend seized on this learned man, who was presented as a magician who had made a pact with the devil. Then Gerbert was forgotten, before being rediscovered in the 16th c. by protestants and *Gallicans who saluted him as a precursor of theirs, by reason of his anti-Roman policy during the Reims affair.

*Gerberti postea Silvestri II papae Opera mathematica*, N. Bubnov (ed.), Berlin, 1899. – Gerbert, *Correspondance*, P. Riché (ed.), J.-P. Callu (ed.), Paris, 1993 (2 vol.; "Les Belles Lettres").

*Gerberto, scienza, storia e mito, Atti del Gerberti symposium*, Archivum Bobiense, Studia, 2, 1985. – P. Riché, *Gerbert d'Aurillac, pape de l'an mil*, Paris, 1996 (3rd ed.). – *Autour de Gerbert d'Aurillac, le pape de l'an mil.* Album de documents commentés reunis sous la diréction de O. Guyotjeannin e E. Poulle, Paris, 1996. – *Gerbert l'Européén*, Actes du Colloque d'Aurillac (Mémoires de la société "La Haute Auvergne", 3), Aurillac, 1997.

Pierre Riché

**GERHOH OF REICHERSBERG (*c.*1092/1093 - after 1167).** Gerhoh of Reichersberg, theologian and reformer, was born in *c.*1092-1093 at Polling and died 27 June (year unknown) at Reichersberg (*Bavaria). After having studied in various *schools at Polling, Freising, Moosburg and *Hildesheim, Gerhoh became **scholasticus* at *Augsburg in 1117, then retired *c.*1120 to the *canons of Rottenbuch. From 1126 to 1132 he lived at *Regensburg, violently attacked the corrupt and feudal clergy, then was offered the provostship of Reichersberg at the request of Pope *Innocent II. There he ended his life, after having satisfactorily held the office of *prior for the profit of his community.

Gerhoh was a very virulent reformer. At Rottenbuch, he failed to lead the canons in the way of strict discipline, on account of a demanding and excessive rigorism. During his stay at *Regensburg, he stigmatized the secularization of the clergy, which he held responsible for its enrichment, mingled with feudality (*De aedificio Dei*, 1128). He considered *clerics guilty of irregular life *heretics and *schismatics and composed the *Dialogus inter saecularem et regularem*, which drew the papacy's attention to him. His violence ended by alarming *Rome and the *cardinals, who stopped putting confidence in him (1156). At first neutral in the *schism of 1159, he rallied to *Alexander III in 1163.

Theologian and canon, he was particularly alive to the importance and sacred aspect of the *priesthood. He ardently defended the unity of the divine person and the human *person in *Christ, to such a degree that he was nearly accused of monophysitism; but he also defended the thesis of the equality of Christ and the Father, like the *adoptianists. In 1142, he wrote a *Libellus de ordine donorum spiritus sancti* in which, in liaison with *Rupert of Deutz, he developed a historical *theology linked to an *exegesis of the *Bible. He always relied on the complete text of Scripture, as we see in his commentary on the *Psalms. He took violently against the christological teaching of the Frenchmen *Abelard, *Gilbert of Poitiers and *Peter Lombard, since he held that there was a connection between *dialectic and the secularization of the clergy. His last works attest a profound pessimism: *De investigatione antichristi* (1160-1162), *De quarta vigilia noctis* (1167). His work had no influence in his time, unless at Reichersberg, since it was circulated only late.

*PL*, 193, 1854. – *Letter to Pope Hadrian about the Novelties of the Day*, N.M. Haring (ed.), Toronto, 1974.

E. Meuthen, *Kirche und Heilsgeschichte bei Gerhoh von Reichersberg*, Leiden, 1959. – P. Classen, *Gerhoch von Reichersberg. Eine Biographie*, Wiesbaden, 1960. – A. Lazzarino del Grosso, *Armut und Reichtum im Denken Gerhohs von Reichersberg*, Munich, 1973.

Michel Parisse

**GERLACHUS (12th c.).** A lay glass-painter from Lower *Saxony or the middle Rhine, active around 1150-1160, Gerlachus is known by five *stained-glass panels from the church of the *Premonstratensians at Arnstein-am-Lahn (*Hesse), preserved at the Westfalisches Landesmuseum of Münster (scenes from the story of Moses and fragments of a **Tree of Jesse*). He is identified by an inscription – REX REGU(M) CLARE GERLACHO PROPICIARE (Illustrious king of kings, have mercy on Gerlachus) – which accompanies the *portrait of the *artist at work, inserted at the bottom of the scene of the Burning Bush. This signature and this portrait of a glass-painter are the earliest known to this day.

L. Kalinowski, "Virga versatur. Remarques sur l'iconographie des vitraux romans d'Arnstein-sur-Lahn", *Revue de l'art*, 62, 1983, 9-20.

Anne Granboulan

**GERMANUS I OF CONSTANTINOPLE (634-733).** Patriarch of *Constantinople (11 Aug 715 - 17 Jan 730) and saint (feast 12 May). Son of a great Byzantine family, he was castrated in 679 when his father was executed. As bishop of Cyzicus, he approved the Emperor Philippicus's return to *monothelism in 711, then returned to *Orthodoxy after the latter's death. Appointed *patriarch, he played a key role in the troubled period preceding the accession to power of Leo III (717). At an unknown date, he negotiated a treaty with the *Bulgars. He did not oppose Leo III's *iconoclasm before 730, but at that date he refused to sign the official declaration forbidding devotion to *icons: he was then deposed. He was author of *homilies important for Marian piety, of a *Treatise on Heresies* and perhaps a *Commentary on the Divine Liturgy* put under his name and known under the name of *Mystical History of the Church.*

*CPG*, 3, 1979, 8001-8033. – P. Meyendorff, *On the Divine Liturgy*, Crestwood (NY), 1984 (Eng. tr.).

L. Lamza, *Patriarch Germanos I von Konstantinopel (715-730)*, *Das Östliche Christentum*, new series 27, Würzburg, 1975.

Marie-France Auzépy

**GERMANY, KINGDOM OF.** It is a delicate matter to fix the date of Germany's birth. The term "Deutschland", used in the singular, did not appear until 1500. Of course the German language is much older (8th-9th cc.), though the consciousness of being German was not forged at that time among the various peoples, Bavarians, Saxons, *Alamanni, etc. This feeling of identity was doubtless not collectively felt before the 12th c., though German historians reckon that there were national rulers from the time of *Henry I (919-936). So there were German *kings from the 10th c., who bore the title of "king of the Romans" or "of the Teutons", a Latin term translating the German *diutisch*. By contrast, there was no German State before the 12th or even the 13th c., and the strength of regional feelings remained extreme throughout the Middle Ages.

The kings of medieval Germany were closely dependent on the higher *nobility, never having been able to free themselves from the encumbrance of an elective *monarchy. Hereditary succession came about only fortuitously, always with the consent of the princes, thanks to the temporary superiority of a king. Even *Frederick II (1215-1250) had to make concessions to obtain the election of his sons Henry (VII) and then Conrad IV.

Though originally the *Prince Electors represented all the princes of the *Empire, lay and especially ecclesiastical, their number was progressively reduced in the 13th c.: from 1257, only seven of them had the right to elect the king (archbishops of *Trier, *Cologne and *Mainz, margrave of *Brandenburg, prince palatine of the Rhine, king of *Bohemia and duke of *Saxony).

This elective monarchy, with no fixed capital, saw the succession of several dynasties, from the *Ottonians of the 10th c. to the *Habsburgs of the 15th. Admittedly, each ruler made his personal mark, more or less strong, on events, but all had to suffer similar conflicts.

Major conflicts opposed them to the more powerful of the territorial princes: *Otto the Great (936-973) against the dukes of *Saxony and *Bavaria, *Henry V (1106-1125) against *Lothar of Supplinburg who succeeded him on the throne, *Frederick Barbarossa (1156-1190) against *Henry the Lion, *Frederick III (1438-1493) against *Matthias Corvinus, king of Bohemia. No defeat was irredeemable, no success final. But from the 13th c. (the "Great Interregnum" of 1250-1273), the power of the German nobility and its autonomy from royal power increased considerably. Episodically, rulers like *Rudolf of Habsburg (1273-1291) or *Charles IV (1346-1385) gave weight to the royal *authority (Golden Bull of 1356, which confirmed the exclusion of any papal intervention in the election of the king of the Romans). Never, in fact, were the kings able to dispose of sufficient resources to assert their authority: their finances were limited and fleeting, the *army at the mercy of the goodwill of the vassals, the administration hardly effective except in the regions close to the king and his patrimonial lands. From the end of the 13th c., the principalities were formed into veritable States (*e.g.* Bavaria).

For a time, the alliance with the Church (*Reichskirchensystem*) allowed the royal power to establish itself, from the reign of Otto the Great to that of Frederick II, the apogee being under *Henry III (1039-1056), but confrontations with the papacy (the long *Investiture Contest from 1056 to 1122, marked by the humiliation of *Canossa and concluded by the *concordat of *Worms) left lasting traces. Relations with the Church were finally fixed by the concordat of 1448, in force until 1808.

The efforts made by the rulers to ensure the help of the "third Germany", that of the *towns and knights, were largely a failure. The towns were bridled by the Statute of 1231 and suffered from continual private wars between the lords; their political ascent was brought to nothing by the defeat of Döffingen in 1389. As for the knights, they were a group both too incongruent and too turbulent to serve as a prop for royal policy.

But the life of Germany was also marked by a great expansion, the *Drang nach Osten*, inaugurated from the time of Henry I and pursued vigorously until the 13th century. The territory of the Reich was extended as far as the Oder, vast principalities were set up (Brandenburg), an original civilization came into being, made up of borrowings from the German and Slav worlds. This movement transformed the face of central Europe, so true is it that the Germans had their gaze turned more to the east than to the west, despite the incorporation of the county of *Burgundy into the Reich in 1033. Under the reign of *Rudolf of Habsburg, in 1282, Austria and Styria were integrated into the family patrimony, a decision whose implications began to be understood at the very end of the 15th c. when Maximilian came to power.

Germany's incontestable vitality was also manifested in the development of the *Hanse from the 13th c. under the impetus of *Lübeck, followed by its flowering in the 14th and 15th centuries. The *merchants and towns of North Germany made their wealth and power felt at this time. German expansion and dynamism can be measured by the agricultural growth visible from the 10th c., with the establishment of the *villicatio*, the great *estate, where the proportion of non-free *peasants was greater than in *France; and by the spatial extent to which the *seigneurie* took root in the 13th c., accompanied by the spread of technical progress and *money and the multiplication of *villages and towns. Admittedly the *Black Death of 1348-1351, with its numerous recurrences, and the grave crisis that was prolonged until about 1450 considerably affected German society: deserted villages (undoubtedly one in four), population dropping from more than 15 million souls to 8 million, loss of liberties for numerous peasants. Yet the towns maintained or even diversified their activities (*textiles, mines, arms and *commerce), the financial companies affirmed their importance (the Fugger; the Welser, the Ravensburg company). Germany, politically divided, was a real economic power in the middle of the 15th century.

The Church of the kingdom of Germany was distinguished by the considerable political role played by the prelates in political life: *Willigis, archbishop of *Mainz, under *Otto II and *Otto III, Engelbert, archbishop of *Cologne, at the time of *Frederick II, Baldwin, archbishop of *Trier, under *Charles IV, among many others. If the episcopate was influential, the *regulars were no less so, benefiting from the *reform of *Gorze in the 11th c. and the rise of the *Cistercians and *mendicants in the 12th and 13th centuries. The troubled period of the late Middle Ages saw criticisms heaped against the monks, but reform was put in place through the efforts of *Nicholas of Cusa and the regular *canons of *Windesheim, as well as the return to strict *obedience among the Benedictines and *Dominicans. By contrast, German animosity towards the papacy continued growing. The theme of devouring papal *taxation, expressed by the Church's highest dignitaries and repeated by *chroniclers, was incontestably one of the foundations of German nationalism in the second half of the 15th century.

Simultaneously, both inside and outside the Church, the expression of religious feelings attained great heights. It is enough to evoke the names of several *women, from *Hildegard of Bingen to *Gertrude the Great, or men, from the poet *Walther von der Vogelweide to Meister *Eckhart, to grasp the breadth of the contribution of German civilization to the culture of medieval Europe. Though *universities developed late (the first was founded at *Prague in 1348), they quickly acquired remarkable influence, accompanied by a wide circulation of *books, as "the appetite for

*The Ark of the Covenant.* Mosaic in the apse of the chapel of Germigny-des-Près (Loiret). 9th c.

the divine was recognised in many cases as the appetite for reading" (F. Rapp). But religious life was marked by sudden "disturbances", from the Rhineland *Cathars of the 12th c. to the *Hussite wars of the 15th c., and the pogroms of which the *Jews, accused of *ritual murder of Christian children, were victims from the late-13th century.

Occupying a vast territory, the kingdom of Germany could attain political unity only fictitiously or episodically, but even if the State could not impose its *authority apart from the principalities, economy, religion and culture developed; sometimes outstripping the rest of Europe, sometimes inspired by it (e.g. the spread of courtly *poetry from *France). The German nation was forged despite the vicissitudes of *politics, cemented by its religious and cultural vitality.

*Deutsche Geschichte*, 2, Göttingen, 1983 (2nd ed.); *ibid.*, 3, 1973. – J. P. Cuvillier, *L'Allemagne médiévale*, t. 1, *Naissance d'un État*, Paris, 1979; *ibid.*, t. 2, *Échec d'une nation*, 1982. – H. Thomas, *Deutsche Geschichte des Spätmittelalters, 1250-1500*, Berlin, 1983. – *Propyläen Geschichte Deutschlands*: 2, Berlin, 1986; 3, 1985. – H. Fuhrmann, T. Reuter, *Germany in the High Middle Ages*, Cambridge, 1986. – J.W. Zophy, *An Annotated Bibliography of the Holy Roman Empire*, 1986. – H. Boockmann, *Stauferzeit und spätes Mittelalter. Deutschland 1125-1517*, Berlin, 1987. – P. Dollinger, *La Hanse*, Paris, 1988. – C. Higounet, *Les Allemands en Europe centrale et orientale au Moyen Âge*, Paris, 1989. – F. Rapp, *Les origines médiévales de l'Allemagne moderne*, Paris, 1989. – B. Arnold, *Princes and Territories in Medieval Germany*, Cambridge, 1991. – T. Reuter, *Germany in the Early Middle Ages 800-1056*, London, 1991. – *Die neue Deutsche Geschichte*, 2, 1992 (2nd ed.). – W. Spiewok and D. Buschinger, *Histoire de la littérature allemande au Moyen Âge*, Paris, 1992. – F. Krieger, *Die Habsburger im Mittelalter*, Berlin, 1994. – *L'Allemagne au XIII^e siècle*, M. Parisse (dir.), Paris, 1994.

Sylvain Gouguenheim

**GERMIGNY-DES-PRÉS.** The *oratory of Germigny-des-Prés was built inside the sumptuous *villa of *Theodulf, a supporter of *Charlemagne, bishop of *Orléans and *abbot of *Fleury. Dedicated to the Saviour, it was finished in 806. Its similarity to the palatine *chapel of *Aachen is limited to the existence of a central plan. The oratory is a square, each side of which possessed an apse. It was lighted by a three-storey lantern-tower. The *mosaic that decorates the eastern apse represents the Ark of the Covenant surrounded by two cherubim. The choice of this theme is to be related to the iconophobe ideas of Theodulf, one of the redactors of the **Libri Carolini* and responsible for the effacement of the *image of *Christ in painting between 780 and 810.

J. Hubert, "Germigny-des-Prés", *CAF, 93^e session. Orléans... 1930*, Paris, 1931, 534-568. – C. Heitz, *L'Architecture religieuse carolingienne*, Paris, 1980, 82-85.

Pierre Kerbrat

**GERSON, JEAN (1363-1429).** Jean Le Charlier, theologian, preacher, *chancellor of the *university of *Paris, studied *philosophy and *theology at the *Collège de Navarre*, partly under the direction of *Pierre d'Ailly, whose protégé he was. He succeeded him in 1395 as chancellor. *Doctor of theology in 1393, he taught, with a brief interruption when he retired to *Bruges, until he left for the council of *Constance in 1415. After the *council and a long journey across the *Empire, unable to return to Paris for fear of the duke of *Burgundy, Gerson finally settled at *Lyon and carried on a great literary activity.

Gerson was one of the most celebrated and best-read authors of the later Middle Ages, and editions of his works were innumerable. His influence on Christian *spirituality and thought undoubtedly lasted into the 19th century. In theology, he borrowed some general principles from Pierre d'Ailly and he criticized speculation, especially when it mixed theology with physics and *logic; he postulated a language and a set of problems proper to theology, which he saw as linked to the rules of *rhetoric and on which he imposed a moral preoccupation and an almost moralizing tone; while leaning discreetly on *Ockhamite theology, he opposed all forms of Scotism. In morals, he gave great attention to *women, the couple, the *education of *children. For spirituality, he would always remain under the influence of Pseudo-*Dionysius, at first through the intermediary of some commentators, later in direct and continuous contact with the text. It was then that he became more favourable to *John Scotus Eriugena.

His ecclesiological and political thought was dominated by a concern for doctrinal orthodoxy and Church *reform. His desire for orthodoxy led him to oppose the doctrine of *tyrannicide, to insist that the council condemn Jan *Hus and *Jerome of Prague, to write about the way to recognise *heretical opinions and about the superiority of the theologian to the *jurist. His aspiration to reform committed him to the path of *conciliarism, a doctrine that would later estrange him from the new generation of theologians, *e.g.* Francisco de Vitoria.

Jean Gerson, *Oeuvres complètes*, P. Glorieux (ed.), Paris-Tournai, 1960-1973 (10 vol.; bibl. vol. 1).

D. C. Brown, *Pastor and Laity in the Theology of Gerson*, Cambridge, 1987. – M.S. Burrows, *Jean Gerson and 'De consolatione theologiae' (1418)*, Tübingen, 1991. – Z. Kaluza, "Jean Gerson", *Encyclopédie philosophique universelle*, 3, Paris, 1992, 547-549. – G. Ouy, "Jean Gerson", *DLFMA*, Paris, 1992, 782-785.

Zénon Kaluza

*Monk preaching*. Miniature from Jean Gerson's *Mirror of humility*, 15th c. Valenciennes, Municipal Library (Ms 1462)

**GERSONIDES (1288-1344).** Levi ben Gershom (or RaLBaG), Jewish exegete, philosopher and scholar of southern France, was born perhaps at Bagnols-sur-Cèze (whence his name, Master Leo of Bagnols). He lived mainly at Orange and stayed at *Avignon, where he was in touch with the papal court. In the field of *philosophy, Gersonides' contribution is remarkable: his *Sefer milhamoth Adonai* (Book of the Wars of the Lord) is an attempt to analyse essential themes of *theology (*immortality of the *soul, *prophecy, *providence, *creation) using the conceptual tools provided by Aristotelianism (and *Averroes); his thought is rigorous and, by virtue of this, his positions more audacious than those of *Maimonides. The fifth part of the "Book of the Wars of the Lord" is a treatise on *astronomy, often copied separately (and translated into Latin). His astronomical work also includes a treatise (dedicated to Pope *Clement VI) on Jacob's Staff, an instrument invented by him to determine the angular distance between the stars; translated into Latin, it exercised a certain influence in the 14th century. We also owe him a treatise, *De numeris harmonicis* (preserved in Latin). Gersonides also commented on *Aristotle's *logic; his super-commentaries (on the commentaries of Averroes), translated in the 16th c., were incorporated in the celebrated Venetian editions of Aristotle by the Giunta. His biblical commentaries (*Job, *Song of Songs, Ecclesiastes, *Esther, Ruth, *Pentateuch, historical books, *Daniel, Proverbs) rapidly became classics of Jewish exegesis and were incorporated in the great annotated *Bibles.

Gersonides (Magister Leo Hebraeus) presents the example of a Jewish scholar in constant touch with his Christian colleagues, notably astronomers. His work on harmonic *numbers was written at the request of Philippe de Vitry and he seems to have been in contact with Jean des Murs. The translation of his treatise on astronomy was the fruit of a collaboration with a member of the Order of *Hermits of St Augustine, Peter of Alexandria.

Levi ben Gershom, *The Book of the Wars of the Lord*, S. Feldman (tr.), Philadelphia (PA), 1984-1987 (2 vol.; vol. 3 in preparation).

A. Combes, *La théologie mystique de Gerson. Profil de son évolution*, 2 vol., Paris, 1963-1964. – C. Touati, *La pensée philosophique et théologique de Gersonide*, Paris, 1973 (2nd ed. 1992). – B. Goldstein, *The Astronomical Tables of Levi ben Gerson*, Hamden, 1974. – J.J. Staub, *The Creation of the World according to Gersonides*, Chico (CA), 1982. – *Gersonide et son temps*, G. Dahan (ed.), Louvain-Paris, 1991. – *Studies on Gersonides*, G. Freudenthal (ed.), Leiden, 1992. – R. Eisen, *Gersonides on Providence, Covenant, and the Chosen People*, New York, 1995.

Gilbert Dahan

**GERTRUDE THE GREAT (1256-1302).** A native of *Thuringia and an orphan, Gertrude was entrusted at the age of five to the monastery of *Helfta, where she received a sound cultural and spiritual training under the direction of *Mechthild of Hackeborn. In the course of her studies in the *artes liberales*, she suffered a profound crisis following her first *vision of *Christ, 27 Jan 1281: "From a grammarian, she became a theologian", her sisters later said, and she then devoted herself exclusively to the study of Holy Scripture and the works of the *Fathers, particularly St Augustine, and St *Bernard of Clairvaux. She left two works: the *Legatus divinae pietatis*, translated into German early in the 15th c., and the *Exercitia spiritualia*. These are written accounts of her visionary experiences, established according to her on God's advice during Holy Week 1289. The accounts of these meditative and ecstatic encounters with Christ show a intense sponsal *mysticism in veneration of the Sacred Heart of Jesus. Behind Gertrude's life of *grace was, like that of Mechthild of Hackeborn, an intense life entirely devoted to liturgy, *contemplation and reading of Scripture, which nourished her language and her universe of representations. Of the five books of the *Legatus*, only the second was written by Gertrude herself, the others having been dictated by her or compiled after her death by the sisters.

Love of *God and a disposition to suffering determined Gertrude's life and thought. She wanted to signify God's love for men, whose highest symbol was the Sacred Heart of Jesus, by her earthly solicitude for others in order to awaken the love of God in others. The signs of *grace were the *stigmata of Christ borne by Gertrude's heart, at the end of an exchange of her own *heart with that of Christ. The comparison with St *Francis's stigmata suggests itself here, especially in the link with his dream face.

The description of the state of *unio* ends with Gertrude, as with Mechthild of Magdeburg, in the acoustic representation of *music as a symphony emerging from the total loving harmony between God and man. It becomes the expression of the "sweet melody" of a spiritual music that grasps the complexity of that state, in order to sensibilize it by a synaesthetic description.

St Gertrude's feast day is 16 November.

*Sanctae Gertrudis Magnae virginis ordinis Sancti Benedicti Legatus Divinae Pietatis accedunt ejusdem Exercitia Spiritualia. Opus ad codicum fidem nunc primum integre editum Solesmensium O.S.B. Monachorum cura et opera*, Paris-Poitiers, 1885. – *Gertrud die Grosse, Gesandter der göttlichen Liebe*, J. Lanczkowski (tr.), Heidelberg, 1989. – Gertrude the Great of Helfta, *Spiritual Exercises*, G. J. Lewis (ed.), J. Lewis (ed.), Kalamazoo (MI), 1989. – Gertrude the Great of Helfta, *The Herald of God's Loving-Kindness: Books One and Two*, A. Barrett (ed.), Kalamazoo (MI), 1991. – Gertrude of Helfta, *The Herald of Divine Love*, M. Winkworth (ed.), New York, 1993. – *Exercitia spiritualia*, S. Ringler (ed.), forthcoming.

*DSp*, 6, 1967, 331-339. – *VerLex*, 3, 1980, 7-10 (2nd ed.). – *TRE*, 12, 1984, 538-540. – G. Jaron Lewis, *Bibliographie zur deutschen Frauenmystik*, Berlin, 1989, 196-223. – *Marienlexikon*, 3, Sankt Ottilien, 1989, 629; 4, 1992, 567. – M. J. Finnegan, *The Women of Helfta*, Athens (GA), 1991.

Margot Schmidt

**GERVASE OF TILBURY (after 1150 - after 1221).** Born in *England, but educated at *Bologna in *Italy, Gervase was attached to the young Henry (son of *Henry II) until his death in 1193, then entered the service of *William II of Sicily and then that of the Emperor *Otto IV, a relation and ally of King *John of England. For him he composed in *c.*1210 the *Otia imperialia*, which had a tremendous success: the first part of the work told the story of *Genesis, the second was a sort of historical geography, the third a collection of "marvels" revealing the most curious beliefs of his time. Though in Otto's service, Gervase had a moderate political attitude. He died in England after 1221.

*DNB*. – *DLF*. – A. Duchesne, *Gervais de Tilbury, Otia Imperialia*, Paris, 1993 (3rd part).

Jean-Philippe Genet

*The Kiss of peace.* Miniature from the *Missal and Pontifical of Stephen, bishop of Luçon*, 14th c. Paris, BNF (Ms lat.8886, fol. 300 v°).

**GESTURE.** The study of gestures is a bit of a wager, since all direct observation is excluded. But the sources are manifold: normative texts, liturgy, iconography. In the Middle Ages, gestures were ambivalent: "Thus the gesture was at once exalted and deeply suspect, omnipresent and yet subordinate" (J.-C. Schmitt). Antiquity bequeathed to medieval thought the abstract vocabulary of the gesture, an ethical reflection on the gesture (through *modestia* and *temperantia*) and the link between *language and gestures within *rhetoric. With Christianity there began a fundamental ambiguity towards the *body: the "prison of the *soul", it remained nonetheless exalted, by the fact of the *mysteries of the Incarnation and *Redemption.

Though, with monastic asceticism, the "antiquizing" tradition was broken – all the gestures of the monk having to merge into the uniform movements of a community – from the 11th c. and especially in the 12th c., in vocabulary and imagery, the notion of *gestus* returned in strength: *Hugh of Saint-Victor made a veritable virtue of the ideal gesture, realized through the discipline of the body, which, if well-governed, could become the place and one of the means of man's *salvation. In the world of the *laity, the Church sought to subject the "gesticulations" of play-actors, *women and impulsive young folk to the rules of morality. According to the case, the Church knew how to condemn or integrate into its own values behaviour such as singing, dancing or dramatic games.

In medieval society, numerous gestures (like the sign of the *cross) were thought to transform matter or beings by the effect of an intrinsic power bringing about the action of invisible forces. In *vassalage, the role of symbolic gestures (like *kissing on the mouth) was essential. The gestures of *prayer demonstrated a veritable relationship of vassalage between *man and *God; in the 11th and 12th cc., two gestures of prayer imposed themselves: hands joined at the height of the breast with fingers elongated, and *genuflection. The efficacity of gestures, notably apropos of the *sacraments, suffered from harsh ecclesiastical criticism which sought to return the gesture to the rank of a *sign and not of an efficient *cause; but at the same time the liturgy of the *mass was dramatized, made more theatrical: the gesture of *consecration was amplified, the exaltation of the body of *Christ going hand in hand with that of the priest.

Gestures were also revealing of power, establishing a distinction between orders or estates. The laity had their own code of gestures: table manners developed from the 12th century. With the progressive recognition of manual *labour and its productive value, technical gestures were legitimized: from the 13th c., Christian iconography (calendars) managed to give a precise and objective account of them.

J. Le Goff, "Le rituel symbolique de la vassalité", in *Pour un autre Moyen Âge*, Paris, 1977, 349-420. – R.G. Benson, *Medieval Body Language*, Copenhagen, 1980. – J.-C. Schmitt, *La Raison des gestes dans l'Occident médiéval*, Paris, 1990 (Bibliothèque des Histoires). – Y. Carré, *Le Baiser sur la bouche au Moyen Âge*, Paris, 1992.

Jacques Berlioz

**GHAZĀLĪ, AL- (1058-1111).** Abū Hāmid Muhammad al-Ghazālī (in Latin Algazel): Persian jurist, theologian and mystic who wrote mainly in Arabic (born at Tūs, near Meshhed). A complex personality, who circulated all through the Middle East and had a turbulent career, he was called the "proof of Islam". But he was hardly known to the Latin Middle Ages except by a very particular aspect of his work: his confrontation with Arab *philosophy of Hellenic inspiration (*falsafa*). And even this aspect was itself distorted. In fact, Ghazālī's work was essentially a search for synthesis, aiming to bring together around *Sunni orthodoxy the maximum number of intellectual and spiritual aspects of the Muslim world. He excluded only what seemed to him absolutely irreconcilable with *Islam. In the *falsafa* of *Fārābī and *Avicenna, he distinguished three parts: *logic, physics and *metaphysics. He considered the former fertile and, with two works of introduction to that discipline, he contributed to annexing it to Muslim teaching and giving it a place alongside the old Semitic method of reasoning with two terms (*qiyās*). But physics seemed to him useless, since he was a theologian attached to the vision of a world formed of atoms in discontinuous *time, where all was directly dependent on the will of *God. And metaphysics seemed to him frankly heretical since it ended in a denial of *creation, *providence, *miracles, the *resurrection of the body, *paradise and *hell, and was unable to establish the incorporeality of God or the *immortality of the *soul. To carry out his task of selection, Ghazālī proceeded in two stages: in the first, he expounded with great competence and objectivity the "Intentions of the philosophers" (*Maqāsid al-Falāsifa*); then he refuted these in his "Destruction of the philosophers" (*Tahāfut al-Falāsifa*). The latter was written not from the philosophical but from the religious point of view; it was also able to incorporate technical arguments, such as a penetrating critique of the idea of natural causation.

Dominic Gundisalvi's Latin *translation (*Toledo, 1145) contained only the first of these two works, whose apparent neutrality (the introduction and exordium having been omitted) and Latin title, *Logica et philosophia Algazelis Arabis*, led to a belief that Ghazālī himself was of the party of the *falāsifa*. The confusion was further compounded by the fact that Ghazālī had been (wrongly) presented by *Almohad propaganda as the master of that movement's founder, Ibn Tūmart, and that the Almohad power had been favourable to *falsafa*, giving official positions to Ibn Tufayl and *Averroes. But Averroes would nevertheless reject this partisan presentation and take Ghazālī as his main target in his "Destruction of the Destruction" (*Tahāfut al-Tahāfut*). And his work was equally misunderstood by the Latins, who neglected his personal work and only followed up his commentaries on *Aristotle. Raymond *Lull, though he knew Arabic, followed the common error: he dealt with the original text of the logical part of the *Haqāsid*, of which he made a very free adaptation in *Latin and Catalan, but went no further. Only *Raymond Martini had access to other important texts by Ghazālī; he cited in particular the *Tahāfut*, which enabled him to situate Averroes's reply more correctly. But not until Cajetan, in the late 15th c., would this broadening of perspective be assimilated by *scholasticism.

Al-Ghazali, *Freedom and Fulfilment*, Boston, 1980. – Ghazzali, *The Ninety-nine Beautiful Names of God*, Cambridge, 1992. – Al-Ghazali, *The Incoherence of the Philosophers*, M. E. Marmura (tr.), Provo (UT), 1997. – Al-Ghazali, *The Niche of Lights*, D. Buchman (tr.), Provo (UT), 1998.

A. Wensinck, *La Pensée de Ghazzālī*, Paris, 1940. – M. Alonso-Alonso, "Influencia de Algazel en el mundo latino", *And.*, 17, 1958, 371-380. – C. Lohr, "Logica Algazelis: Introduction and Critical Text", *Tr.*, 21, 1965, 223-290. – M. Sharif, *Ghazali's Theory of Virtue*, Albany (NY), 1975. – M.H. Zuberi, *Aristotle, 384-322 B.C. and Al Ghazali, 1058-1111 A.D.*, Karachi, 1986. – *Ghazali: la raison et le miracle, table ronde Uesco, 9-10 decembre 1985*, Paris, 1987. – R. M. Frank, *Al-Ghazali and the Ash'arite School*, Durham (NC), 1994.

Dominique Urvoy

**GHAZNAVIDS.** A dynasty of rulers of Turkish origin who reigned in eastern *Iran and what is now Afghanistan from 977 to 1187. Founded by Subuk Takīn, a general and governor of the *Samanids, its capital was Ghazni, whence it took its name. This important commercial centre enjoyed two centuries of prosperity and a brilliant intellectual life: the scholar al-*Bīrūnī worked there, and there Firdawsī (932-1020) composed the *Book of Kings*, an epic of the rulers of ancient Persia and the first masterpiece of Persian literature. The palaces and *mosques the Ghaznavids built there, as well as at Lashkar-i Bāzār, have been the object of important excavations. The Ghaznavids made themselves famous particularly by the conquest of northern *India, carried out by Mahmūd (999-1030). But they came up against the power of the *Seljuks, to whom they had to abandon Iran after the defeat of 1040, as well as the rivalry of the Ghorids, who sacked Ghazni in 1150 and took possession of the Ghaznavid territories in 1187.

B. Spuler, "Ghaznawids", *EI(E)*, 2, 1965, 1050-1053 (2nd ed.). – C. E. Bosworth, "The Early Ghaznavids", *The Period from the Arab Invasion to the Saljuqs*, *CHIr*, 4, 1975, 162-197. – C.E. Bosworth, *The Later Ghaznavids*, Edinburgh, 1977.

Françoise Micheau

**GHENT.** Ghent began to develop from the 7th c. near the confluence of the Scheldt and the Lys: the Celtic place-name Ganda means "confluence". It was populated around two centres of settlement, both religious centres founded in the first half of the 7th c. and having agricultural functions: the abbeys of Saint-Bavon and Saint-Pierre. A *portus* is attested under the Carolingians, and Ghent was the capital of a *pagus*. Having several times suffered the depredations of the *Vikings, the urban area was recreated around the keep built by Count Baldwin II († 918) from the late

9th century. A church of Saint-Jean was present in 941, but it was now the comital *castle that attracted the creation of a compact agglomeration.

The protection of power favoured the presence of a produce market and trading activities on a local scale, and the *counts' support for the town's economic dynamism was unfailing. A *market developed and the *merchants of Ghent are attested in the other towns of *Flanders from the early 11th century. We see them buying back rights at the abbey of Saint-Bavon in order to be able to transmit their landed properties. In 1127-1128, they had an *échevinage* at their disposal and intervened in the struggles between the candidates for the comital succession while getting privileges granted to them. They invested in the *commerce of corn and especially of cloth and flax.

The growth of the town accompanied the development of the cloth trade. Ghent was at the heart of vast currents of trade, between the *Hanse, *England which provided its main raw material, wool, its outlets to the West and its connections with the great Mediterranean commerce that fed the cloth trade with mordants and the *fair with luxury products. In the 13th c., Ghent was one of the greatest towns in the West. Linked to the sea and to its *ports of Aardenburg and Damme by a canal, in the 13th and 14th cc. it raised buildings (the *belfry, the town hall, numerous markets, the church of St John) attesting its industrial and commercial dynamism,

The *échevinage*, in the hands of the most powerful patrician families, governed the city. In the 14th c., social tensions opposed the patricians to the tradesmen among whom the weavers and fullers, excluded from power, occupied a considerable place. These crises echoed Anglo-French rivalries. Hit by the economic crisis arising from those rivalries, Ghent plunged into depression and agitation in the 14th century. In 1336, the patrician Jacob van *Artevelde († 1345) expelled the count with the support of the English and, in the count's absence, Ghent tried to follow a policy on a county-wide scale, rallying the other cities as well as *Brabant and Limburg. In the late 15th c., after its conflict with the Burgundians, Ghent like the rest of Flanders suffered a clear economic recession.

V. Fris, *Histoire de Gand, depuis les origines jusqu'à 1913*, Brussels, 1930. – H. Van Werveke, *Gand, esquisse d'histoire sociale*, Brussels, 1946. – D. M. Nicholas, "The Population of 14th c. Ghent", *HMGOG*, 24, 1970, 97-111. – D. Nicholas, *The Domestic Life of a Medieval City: Women, Children and the Family in Fourteenth-Century Ghent*, Lincoln (NE), 1985. – D. Nicholas, *The Metamorphosis of a Medieval City: Ghent in the Age of the Arteveldes, 1302-1390*, Lincoln (NE), 1987. – P.J. Arnade, *Realms of Ritual: Burgundian Ceremony and Civic Life in late Medieval Ghent*, Ithaca (NY), 1996.

Thierry Pécout

**GHOSTS.** Antiquity held to a widespread belief that the *dead could come back to the living and torment them, in particular when the conditions of their passing away or the conduct of members of their *family did not satisfy them. The cult of ancestors, the celebration of *parentalia*, the sacrifices offered to the *lares* all aimed to keep the dead at a distance, to give them rest, in order to preserve the peace of the living. Faced with such beliefs, the Christian Church at first adopted a very restrictive position. Augustine († 430) denied the possibility of any relations between the living and the dead: with the exception of the saints, the dead were not concerned with the living and did not intervene in their affairs. *Apparitions of the dead were nothing but *dreams or diabolical illusions. The sole duty of Christians towards the dead was to pray for their *salvation.

Nevertheless, belief in ghosts did not disappear from the West. Alongside the new ideas imposed by the Church, the traditions were often kept up. In the Germanic and Scandinavian countries, "Christianized" later, legislative texts took measures intended to avoid the return of certain deceased, such as criminals. Archaeological discoveries attest such practices, while the *sagas of the early Middle Ages mention dead people who return to revenge themselves or punish the living.

Christian texts themselves were not totally unaware of ghosts. In order to illustrate the effectiveness of *intercession for the dead, *Gregory the Great († 604) had composed little stories about dead people who spoke to the living to request their *prayers. Then, from the 11th and especially the 12th c., ghosts made a massive entry into ecclesiastical literature. The seignorial society established around the year 1000 had entailed a profound rearrangement of the links between the living and the dead. Being based on *custom, handed down in aristocratic families, seignorial power presupposed that the memory of the ancestors was maintained. When their successors failed to do this, the dead "came back" to denounce them: the ghosts presented in the stories of the 12th c. demand that their last wishes be respected, and torment those who intended to throw off their memory. The Church set itself to record and compose ghost stories, because it drew the maximum profit from the relationship with the dead that these stories intended to re-establish: it was, in fact, the ecclesiastical communities who carried out the celebration of the memory of the dead, in particular that of the lay lords, and who received their gifts. In the collection of *miracula* composed towards the mid 12th c. by *Peter the Venerable, abbot of *Cluny, ghosts demanded the prayers of the monks, confirmed the gifts made in their lifetime to the *abbey, and put pressure on descendants. In the 13th c., after *purgatory had been defined as the third place of the afterlife, preachers composed **exempla* intended to spread the doctrine of the Church among the faithful: ghosts, most often *souls purging their pains in purgatory, asked the living for prayers in order to shorten the length of their trials, and in particular taught them about their "state" in the afterlife.

The Church had "Christianized" ghosts, but its role in this sphere was rivalled. The inhabitants of *e.g.* the village of Montaillou communicated with the dead through the intermediary of a layman, the "*armier*", messenger of souls: he met the dead and took charge of their commissions to the living. In Friuli, it was the *benandanti* who, in the manner of shamans, served as intermediaries between the village community and the world of the dead, who had to be invoked to guarantee domestic abundance and fertility. In the late Middle Ages, churchmen often diabolized the collective apparitions of the dead, the troops of ghosts, known since the 12th c. as "*mesnie Hellequin*"; they also established complex procedures for questioning the dead who appeared individually, involving at once *exorcism, disputation and inquisition, and aiming to win them over, and domesticate them. Several accounts (*Gervase of Tilbury in the 13th c., John Gobi in the 14th) recount long dialogues between the ghost and the churchmen present at its appearance. It was a matter of "making the dead talk" the better to control them. The information provided by the ghosts thus interrogated sometimes formed veritable *treatises, in which doctrinal questions were touched on.

But at the same time, the ghost stories of the late Middle Ages, less stereotyped, longer and more detailed, were symptomatic of the crises of that time, the breaking of traditional links. More than ever, the return of the dead (which certain historians interpret as a "return of what was repressed") signalled that the "work of mourning" was no longer being carried on.

Recently, Jean-Claude Schmitt has emphasized that ghost stories, often the result of a chain of testimonies, by being repeated throughout the Middle Ages, "produced" the belief in the return of the dead (despite Augustine's authority) and led to all sorts of social practices. For the appearance of a dead person, set down in writing and then reproduced, was "not just a single supernatural event" but "a cultural object that was socially constituted according to its circulation".

E. Le Roy Ladurie, *Montaillou: Cathars and Catholics in a French village 1294-1324*, Harmondsworth, 1980. – J. Chiffoleau, *La Comptabilité de l'au-delà. Les hommes, la mort et la religion dans la région d'Avignon à la fin du Moyen Âge*, Rome, 1981, 399-408. – R. Finucane, *Appearances of the Dead. Cultural History of Ghosts*, London, 1982. – C. Ginzburg, *The Night Battles,* London, 1983. – C. Lecouteux, *Fantômes et revenants au Moyen Âge*, Paris, 1986. – *Le Retour des morts*, Paris, 1987 ("Études rurales", 105-106). – H. Bresc, "Culture folklorique et théologie. Le revenant de Beaucaire (1211)", *Razo*, 8, Nice, 1988, 65-74. – J. C. Schmitt, *Ghosts in the Middle Ages,* Chicago, 1998.

Michel Lauwers

**GIFTS OF THE HOLY SPIRIT.** The use of a sevenfold list of gifts to describe the gratuitous and benevolent action of the *Holy Spirit by which *souls are sanctified is observed mainly in the Latin Church. Its scriptural basis is Isaiah 11, 2-3 in the *Vulgate translation, which lists "the spirit of wisdom and understanding, the spirit of counsel and might, the spirit of knowledge and piety, the spirit of the fear of God". St Augustine was inspired by this to organise the *theology of the gifts, applying to the spiritual progress of the Christian this verse initally referred to *Christ at his *baptism. According to him, the seven gifts of the Spirit accompany the soul's ascent towards *God by degrees, from fear to wisdom, in reverse order to that given by the scriptural text. He also compares this list to that of the seven requests of the *Pater* and that of the first seven beatitudes according to St Matthew. His influence, joined to that of *Gregory the Great, for whom the gifts co-operate in the struggle against *evil, had a profound influence in the 12th and 13th cc. on *Cistercian monks (St *Bernard, Adam of Perseigne), then on theologians, to whom, from *Philip the Chancellor to *Thomas Aquinas, we owe a more conceptual approach to the subject. From the 12th c., the gifts were opposed to the seven *capital sins which they contributed to combatting, or associated with the stages of the *active life and the contemplative life. The three pairs named in the verse (wisdom and understanding, counsel and might, knowledge and piety) called for reflection on the particular affinities of the gifts and their reciprocal influences. Around 1235, especially, was affirmed the distinction of the gifts from the *virtues and, as a corollary, their mutual hierarchization. This led to a differentiated appreciation of the human way of behaving, based on the virtues, and the "ultrahuman" way of behaving, characterised by the use of the gifts, according to the distinction made by Thomas Aquinas.

Rare were the theologians who, like *Duns Scotus, did not rally to these views. Outside learned circles, the opposition between the gifts and the capital sins became a *topos* of medieval hagiographical literature. *Jacques de Vitry used the sevenfold division of gifts to structure part of the *Life* of *Marie of Oignies (1216), and *Stephen of Bourbon to organise the whole treatise he wrote for preachers (*De septem donis*, *c.*1250-1261). And in the main *canonization procedures of the early 14th c., intellectual capacities and culture, considered the consequence of a divine gift, occupied a privileged place. However, apart from *Ruysbroeck and *Denis the Carthusian, the mystics made little use of the classical list of gifts in translating their spiritual experience.

O. Lottin, *Psychologie et morale aux XII^e et XIII^e siècles*, 3, Louvain, 1942-1960, 329-344; *ibid.*, 4, 667-736. – F. Vandenbroucke, "Dons du Saint-Esprit. II: Le Moyen Âge", *DSp*, 3, 1957, 1587-1603. – J. Berlioz, "La Mémoire du prédicateur. Recherches sur la mémorisation des récits exemplaires (XIII^e-XV^e siècles)", *Temps, Mémoire, Tradition au Moyen Âge, Actes du XIII^e Congrès de la S.H.M.E.S.P.*, Aix-en-Provence, 1983, 157-183. – A. Vauchez, *Sainthood in the Later Middle Ages*, Cambridge, 1997.

Nicole Bériou

**GILBERT CRISPIN (*c.*1046-1117).** Abbot of *Westminster, Benedictine, author of works of controversy and theological opuscula, he entered the monastery of *Bec at the age of 15 and was taught there by *Lanfranc, then by *Anselm of Canterbury, with whom he remained friends; he was elected *abbot of Westminster in 1085. We owe him notably a *Life* of Herluin, founder of Bec, and various small *treatises (*De simoniacis*, *De casu diaboli*, *De anima*, etc.). His main works are to do with *controversy: a *Disputatio Iudei et Christiani*, dating probably from 1092-1093, doubtless relies on real discussions with a *Jew of *Mainz who had business dealings with the *abbey, but it was written after conversations with St Anselm and intended to constitute a practical application of the principles stated by Anselm in his *Cur Deus Homo*, an argument resting on necessary reasons; in fact the work, remarkable for its serenity, brings into play mainly scriptural **auctoritates*. The *Disputatio Christiani cum gentili* is pure fiction.

*The Works of Gilbert Crispin, abbot of Westminster*, A. Sapir Abulafia (ed.), G. R. Evans (ed.), Oxford, 1986.

J.A. Robinson, *Gilbert Crispin, Abbot of Westminster*, Cambridge, 1911. – B. Blumenkranz, "La *Disputatio Judei cum Christiano* de Gilbert Crispin", *RMAL*, 4, 1948, 237-252. – R. W. Southern, "St Anselm and Gilbert Crispin", *MRSt*, 3, 1954, 78-115. – A.G. Rigg, "Gilbert Crispin", *A History of Anglo-Latin Literature 1066-1422*, Cambridge, 1992, 31.

Gilbert Dahan

**GILBERT OF POITIERS (after 1085-1154).** Gilbert of Poitiers, also called Gilbert de la Porrée (*Porreta*), was doubtless born in that town. He studied the *liberal arts at *Poitiers under a certain Hilary, then under Bernard of Chartres. He later went to study Scripture and its glosses under Anselm of Laon and his brother *Ralph. He was a *canon at Poitiers, then at *Chartres where he became *chancellor. In *c.*1140, he went to teach at the cathedral *school of *Paris. In 1142 he was made bishop of Poitiers and stopped teaching. In 1148, at a *council held at *Reims, he was accused by St *Bernard of having upheld *heretical positions on the *Trinity; but he was not condemned. Renowned for his great learning in the liberal arts and his astonishing knowledge of the Church *Fathers, he commented on biblical texts (*Psalms, St Paul's *epistles, *Apocalypse) and on *Boethius's *Theological opuscula*. A *Book of Six Principles*, much studied in the 13th c., was wrongly attributed to him.

Gilbert's own *doctrines are expounded in his commentaries on Boethius; here he supports the Catholic positions notably in trinitarian theology and *christology, within a conceptual system

*Gilbert, bishop of Poitiers, and his three disciples Jourdan Fantosme, Ivo of Chartres and John Beleth.* Miniature from Gilbert of Poitiers's *Commentaries on Boethius*, mid 12th c. Valenciennes, Municipal Library (Ms 197, fol. 4 v°).

of rare strength and depth, expounded in a scattered way, as results from the very genre of the *gloss: in every being we distinguish "what it is" (*quod est*) and "that by which it is" (*quo est*); in *God alone are these two instances identical; *quod est* is also called "*substance"; *quo est*, "subsistence". To this composition corresponds a dual significance in the name: *pro substantia* and *pro qualitate*, which are, in brief, respectively its reference and its signification. Each being participates in several subsistences which range from the most general to that closest to the individual.

Individuals are thus ranged under *species and genera because they are "conformable" among themselves according to their various subsistences, but an individual cannot be reduced to the collection of its subsistences: each has its "property" which makes it what it is individually, thus, for *e.g.* Plato, his "Platonity" (*platonitas*). There are three principles: God, the idea, and matter (a view that goes from Plato via Calcidius to Bernard of Chartres); the divine essence is the "first form", being; the idea does not mix with matter, and what we call the "forms" of matter are nothing but the reflections of ideas.

In *metaphysics and *logic as in *theology, Gilbert originated the school of "Porretans" (*porretani*), of which some evidence has survived. The two main options of his *philosophy – the rigorous sense of individuality, and the Platonizing doctrine of the efficacity of form – were not without consequences for theology and its controversies. He himself and/or his disciples were attacked for having allegedly distinguished God from the divinity "by which he is", and having thus replaced the *Trinity of Persons with a "quaternity", and for having insisted on the distinction between the Persons and the divine essence.

*The Commentaries on Boethius by Gilbert of Poitiers*, N. M. Häring (ed.), Toronto, 1966 (*PL*, 64 should be avoided).

H. C. van Elswijk, *Gilbert Porreta, sa vie, son oeuvre, sa pensée*, Louvain, 1966. – B. Maioli, *Gilberto Porretano. Dalla grammatica speculativa alla metafisica del concreto*, Rome, 1979. – A. Berthaud, *Gilbert de la Porrée, évêque de Poitiers, et sa philosophie (1070-1154)*, Frankfurt am Main, 1985. – T. Gross-Diaz, *The Psalms Commentary of Gilbert of Poitiers*, Leiden, 1996.

Jean Jolivet

**GILBERT OF SEMPRINGHAM (*c.*1088-1189).** Born before 1089 at Sempringham (Lincolnshire) to a noble family, Gilbert was destined very young for the clerical state and received a good education in *Normandy. After his return to *England, his father had ecclesiastical *benefices conferred on him and he occupied various posts in the service of the bishops of *Lincoln. But he soon turned towards the religious life and created in the parish church of St Andrew at Sempringham a community of cloistered *women with whom he associated *conversae*, charged with domestic tasks, and lay brothers who tilled the land. The success of the experiment stimulated the generosity of donors, which allowed the creation of other similar establishments (there were thirteen in 1189) at first in that region, then all over England. Much marked by *Cistercian influence, Gilbert tried to have the white monks take charge of his *foundations, but in 1147 he met with a refusal from the *chapter general of *Cîteaux. Encouraged by Pope *Eugenius III, he then added little groups of regular *canons to the three branches that his communities already comprised, in order to carry on their government.

From these initiatives resulted a double order, original in structure since women held a considerable place in it and lived in symbiosis with *clerics in the setting of close but separate monasteries, sharing with them a common church, divided by a middle wall, where religious *offices were celebrated. Austere and demanding to himself and others, in 1164 Gilbert had to face a revolt of the **conversi*, who would not put up with being supplanted by regular canons in the administration of the houses and brought complaints against him before Pope *Alexander III. After several inquiries, the founder had to consent to some alterations in the *order's discipline so as to restore peace, but the status of the Gilbertine *priories was finally confirmed by *Rome in 1178. Gilbert died aged over 100 in 1189 and the *miracles that immediately multiplied over his *tomb attested his reputation for *sanctity. A *canonization trial, carried out in a exemplary way for the time, was organised by the papacy at the unanimous request of the English Church, and *Innocent III officially instituted his cult in 1202.

*The Book of St Gilbert*, R. Foreville (ed.), G. Keir (ed.), Oxford, 1987 (*OMT*).

R. Foreville, *Saint Gilbert of Sempringham. His Life and Achievement*, Honeywood, 1986. – B. Golding, *Gilbert of Sempringham and the Gilbertine Order, c.1130- c.1300*, Oxford, 1995.

André Vauchez

**GILDAS.** Gildas is known as the author of the *De excidio Britanniae,* a lengthy and impassioned diatribe, addressed to five Romano-British princes, concerning the evils that have befallen the British (including the invasion of their island by *Anglo-Saxons) as a result of their sins. Although nothing is known of Gildas outside the *De excidio,* the work itself permits various deductions about the dates of Gildas's literary activity and the state of Latin culture in late Roman Britain. Identifications (though they are conjectural) of the five princes point to a date in the early 6th c.; and the form of the *De excidio*, which is conceived as forensic oratory and is structured according to the principles of late antique *rhetoric, suggests that Gildas was trained as a rhetor in a late antique Romano-British school. Furthermore, his extensive quotations from the Old Testament permit various deductions about the text of the *Bible that was known in Roman Britain. In any event his picture of the advent of Anglo-Saxon invaders in 5th-c. Britain (the *adventus Saxonus)* has influenced all subsequent historiography, including notably the account given by *Bede in Book I of his *Historia ecclesiastica.*

*Gildas: the Ruin of Britain*, M. Winterbottom (ed.), Chichester, 1978. – *Gildas: New Approaches*, M. Lapidge (ed.), D. Dumville (ed.), Woodbridge, 1984. – F. Kerlouégan, *Le De excidio Britanniae de Gildas. Les destinées de la culture latine dans l'Isle de Bretagne au VIe siècle*, Paris, 1987. – N. Wright, "Gildas's Reading: a Survey", *Sacris Erudiri*, 32, 1991, 121-162. – N. J. Higham, *The English Conquest: Gildas and Britain in the Fifth Century*, Manchester, 1994.

Michael Lapidge

**GILES OF ROME (1243-1316).** Giles of Rome (Egidio *Colonna, Aegidius Romanus), a *Hermit of St Augustine, was doubtless a pupil of St *Thomas Aquinas at the theology *faculty of *Paris from 1269 to 1272, after having studied for his mastership of arts. Was he perhaps the preceptor of the future *Philip the Fair, to whom he dedicated his *De regimine principum*? He taught *theology at Paris in 1285. First regent master of the Augustinians, then general of his order from 1292 to 1295, at that date he was appointed archbishop of Bourges by *Boniface VIII, with whom he retained strong links. He was one of the main theoreticians of the supremacy of spiritual and papal power over *temporal power in the 13th c., a position he developed in his *De ecclesiastica potestate* (ed. R. Scholz, Weimar, 1929, repr. 1961).

For him, the papal power was in fact the supreme doctrinal power. The *pope could be judged by no-one, but was judge of all things, through the perfection, *sanctity and *spirituality of his state (*status*). As such, his jurisdiction extended over all things and no-one could be compared to him. Spiritual *authority was, by its nature, above all human authority.

Taking up the argument of the two *swords (from Lk 22, 38: "And they said, Lord, behold, here are two swords. And he said unto them, it is enough"), Giles makes the first sword, the temporal, depend on the second, the spiritual, by virtue of the principle of *order that presides over the universe: things would not be ordered if one of the swords were not subordinate to the other; it is the temporal sword that is so, by virtue of the *dialectic governing the relationship of the inferior to the superior. In general, sacerdotal power is superior to all human power. In political society, everything must be ordered to the will and reverence of the ecclesiastical power, whether arms, temporal goods possessed by *kings, or laws promulgated by them; earthly power has only to judge the just and the unjust, unless insofar as it is inspired by the spiritual power; the laws of the *Empire are to be ordered under the canons of the Church, whence they draw their force and their firmness; they must not contradict ecclesiastical laws, but must rather be confirmed by the spiritual, *i.e.* ecclesiastical power.

One of the most thorny problems of power was that of *property: what were the rights of the Church in the matter of temporal goods? Against the *Franciscan "*Spirituals", followers of meritorious *poverty, Giles of Rome recalls that property is a right for the Church: it has *dominium* over all temporal goods. What does this mean? Temporal goods serve spiritual goods and are ordered to them; it is on this condition that they are true goods; the pope is their master, since he rules *souls and consequently the *bodies that are at their service, and in consequence also temporal goods. The natural order is not, of itself, just; it needs the Church's warrant in order to be justified. The Church and its head, the *pope, is at the centre of the law, though without suppressing the sphere of exercise of *temporal power, which is an auxiliary of the Church. Giles of Rome is hence one of the most representative theologians of the hierocratic current at its apogee.

Giles of Rome, *Errores Philosophorum*, J. Koch (ed.), J. O. Riedl (tr.), Milwaukee (WI), 1944. – *Giles of Rome on Ecclesiastical Power*, R.W. Dyson (ed.), Woodbridge, 1986. – *Aegidii Romani opera omnia*, F. Del Punta (ed.), G. Fioravanti (ed.), Florence, 1987 f.

M. Pacaut, *La Théocratie*, Paris, 1957. – M. J. Wilks, *The Problem of Sovereignty in the Later Middle Ages*, Cambridge, 1964. – W. Ullmann, "Boniface VIII and his Contemporary Scholarship", *JThS*, 27, 1976, 58-87. – C. Trifogli, "Giles of Rome on Natural Motion in the Void", *MS*, 54, 1992, 136-161. – "Egidio Romano", *DBI*, 42, 1993, 319-341.

Jeannine Quillet

**GILLES BELLEMÈRE (1342-1407).** Born at Château-du-Loir in 1342, Gilles Bellemère was one of the greatest *canonists of his time. After graduating in civil law at the *university of *Orléans (1364), in 1367 he entered the **familia* of Cardinal de Beaufort, the future *Gregory XI. He accompanied him to *Rome when *Urban V took the papacy back to the Eternal City. After studying at the pontifical university, he received his doctorate *in utroque jure* (civil and canon law) in 1374. The same year, he became auditor of the Sacred Palace and was charged with compiling the conclusions of the **Rota*. On the death of Gregory XI, he rallied on 22 June 1378 to the *cardinals who had withdrawn to *Anagni, who sent him to *Avignon to expound the Church's situation to the cardinals remaining in that town. That autumn he returned to *Italy to give the newly elected *Clement VII the funds collected in France by the papal treasurer. On his arrival at Fondi, he learned of his appointment as auditor of contradicted letters; at the same time, he was given the position of regent of the pontifical *chancery, which he held until the papacy's return to Avignon.

On 8 Oct 1383 he was promoted bishop of Lavaur. An influential adviser of Clement VII, he carried out several missions in *Brittany (1382) and *Flanders (1386) to try to detach the clergy of those provinces from Urbanist influence. Becoming bishop of *Le Puy in 1390, he was transferred to the episcopal see of Avignon in 1392.

Clement VII's death ended to his ascendancy. He failed in the two missions entrusted to him by *Benedict XIII to rally the king of France and the university of Paris to the solution advocated by the Avignon pope to end the *Great Schism (1394 and 1395). By then he was no longer one of the *pope's intimate advisers. He adhered with some delay to the *subtraction of obedience and then adopted a prudent attitude, confining himself to the administration

*The pope approves the order of St Francis.* Predella (detail) of the altarpiece of *St Francis receiving the stigmata* by Giotto (1267-1337). Paris, Louvre.

of his *diocese and devoting himself to writing his canonical work. He rallied easily to Benedict XIII at the time of the restoration of obedience in 1403. He died in March 1407 after reforming the statutes of the university of Avignon.

As a canonist, Gilles Bellemère left a considerable work. Apart from circumstantial works such as the *Decisiones rotae* of 1374, 1375 and 1377 and the *Consilia* in which he collected the consultations given by himself and other Avignonese jurists on various legal cases, notably on the affairs of Clement VII's family, or particular memoirs on the question of the schism (*De ostensione veritatis, Opus novum in facto Scismatis*), he devoted 25 years (1381-1404) to drawing up an imposing commentary on the whole of the *Corpus juris canonici*, of which only part has been printed, in the 16th century. The author wished to provide a complete panorama of the legal literature of his time by inserting into his collection whole passages of *jurists then considered authoritative in order to spare the reader the trouble of resorting to the originals.

H. Gilles, "Gilles Bellemère, canoniste", *HLF*, 40, 1974, 211-281.

Henri Gilles

**GIORDANO OF PISA (*c.*1260-1310).** Giordano of Pisa, also called of Rivalto from his presumed birth-place, entered the *Dominicans in 1280. While teaching *theology, he was a very popular preacher, mainly at *Florence and *Pisa, and the first by whom we have *sermons written entirely in Italian. He preached sometimes four or five times a day, on liturgical texts, on the **Credo* or on *Genesis. Sent to teach at the university of *Paris, he died on the way.

Giordano da Pisa, *Sul Terzo Capitolo del Genesi*, Cr. Marchioni (ed.), Florence, 1992.

C. Delcorno, *Giordano da Pisa e l'antica predicazione volgare*, Florence, 1975. – *SOPMA*, 3, 1980, 52. – D. R. Lesnick, *Preaching in medieval Florence: the social world of Franciscan and Dominican spirituality*, Athens (GA), 1989.

Louis Jacques Bataillon

**GIOTTO (1267-1337).** A Florentine, born at Vespignano, Vicchio di Mugello, died at *Florence. Giotto doubtless served an *apprenticeship in the studio of *Cimabue, *c.*1280-1290. At *Rome itself, or on the international building-site of the basilica of St Francis at *Assisi, he familiarized himself with the classicizing tendencies of contemporary painting. His earliest works have been recognised at Assisi and dated to the late 1280s (Old and New Testament scenes in the upper part of the nave of the upper church of St Francis). Two scenes of the *Legend of Isaac* in the third bay of the nave (upper part) are also attributed to him. Shortly afterward, Giotto revived the theme of the great crucifix with the work carried out for Santa Maria Novella at Florence.

Between 1295-1296 and 1300, helped by numerous collaborators, Giotto worked on the *Legend of St Francis* on the lower part of the wall of the nave of the upper church of St Francis at Assisi (28 panels). In 1300 he was called to Rome by Pope *Boniface VIII, on the occasion of the *jubilee: he had to decorate the *loggia* of the Lateran palace (now in *St John Lateran); he had to do in *mosaic the *Embarkation of the Apostles led by St Peter*, of which only fragments now survive (vestibule of the present *St Peter's basilica). Some works, like the polyptych of the Badia (Florence, Uffizi) or the *Virgin Enthroned* of San Giorgio della Costa, witness to his stay at Florence right at the beginning of the 14th century. According to the information of the chronicler Riccobaldo Ferrarese, his stay at Rimini must be situated at the same dates (1300-1303, *Crucifix* of the *Malatesta temple). From 1304 to 1306, Giotto worked on the decoration of the Scrovegni chapel, in the church of Santa Maria della Carità at *Padua. Soon afterward, he painted the *Maestà* of the church of Ognissanti at Florence (now in the Uffizi). He was later at Assisi again, where he decorated in *fresco the chapel of the Maddalena, in the lower church of the basilica of St Francis.

He stayed at Padua, perhaps around 1317, where he worked on the *Crucifix* of the Scrovegni chapel (perhaps also on frescoes with astrological themes, now disappeared, in the town hall). We find him again at Florence, in the Peruzzi chapel, where he began to paint the *Histories of the two St Johns* (church of Santa Croce), as well as the Raleigh polyptych (Museum of Art, North Carolina), doubtless the *altarpiece designed for the *altar of the same chapel. The frescos he did in the Bardi chapel, in the church of Santa Croce, can be dated to 1325-1328 at the latest. From 1329 to 1333, Giotto worked at *Naples, with his studio: remaining at Florence, Taddeo *Gaddi did the polyptych of the Baroncelli chapel. In 1334, Giotto returned to Florence: on 12 April, the Signoria appointed him master of works for the *cathedral building-site. He designed the first plans for the campanile of Florence cathedral, perhaps also sketches for the hexagons of the first course. Around 1335, Giotto stayed at *Milan, called there by Azzo *Visconti for works that have now disappeared.

G. Previtali, *Giotto e la sua Bottega*, Milan, 1967. – F. Bologna, *I Pittori alla corte angioina di Napoli*, Rome, 1969. – L. Bellosi, *La Pecora di Giotto*, Turin, 1984. – M. Barasch, *Giotto and the Language of Gesture*, Cambridge, 1987. – L. Bellosi, *Giotto: Complete Works*, Florence, 1989. –

F. d'Arcais, *Giotto. Gli affreschi di Assisi et di Padova*, Milan, 1994. – E. Lunghi, *The Basilica of St. Francis of Assisi: the Frescoes of Giotto, his Precursors and Followers*, London, 1996. – C. E. Gilbert, "Giotto", *DoA*, 12, 681-696. – *The Arena Chapel and the Genius of Giotto: Padua*, A. Ladis (ed.), New York, 1998. – *Giotto, Master Painter and Architect: Florence*, A. Ladis (ed.), New York, 1998.

Daniel Russo

**GLASGOW.** Seat of a *bishopric from at least the 11th c., the church was probably founded by St *Kentigern († *c.*612). Its history is obscure before the 12th c., when King David I (1124-1153) revived and endowed the bishopric. The *cathedral, built over St Kentigern's shrine, dates from the 12th-16th centuries. The *diocese was the second largest and wealthiest in *Scotland, and its bishops men of national importance. The episcopal burgh or town of Glasgow grew up around a crossroads about 0.5 kilometres south of the cathedral. In 1451 Bishop William Turnbull obtained *bulls from Pope *Nicholas V founding a *university at Glasgow. In 1492 Bishop Robert Blackadder secured the *erection of an *archbishopric with metropolitan jurisdiction over Argyll, Galloway, Dunblane and Dunkeld. At the Reformation (1560), Archbishop James Beaton fled to France, taking with him many documents from the archives of the church of Glasgow, which were destroyed during the French Revolution.

*Registrum Episcopatus Glasguensis*, Edinburgh, 1843. – J. Durkan, J. Kirk, *The University of Glasgow, 1451-1577*, Glasgow, 1977.

Alan Macquarrie

**GLASS.** The manufacture of glass in the Middle Ages is known to us by some *treatises, of which the most pertinent are by religious scholars: the *Schedula diversarium artium* of the monk *Theophilus, composed in *Germany early in the 12th c., is one of the best sources of information. Not by chance was glass-making, like most other arts, dependent from the 7th c. on the monasteries. There was preserved the experience inherited from Antiquity, and there were put into practice the technical innovations of the time. Religious centres, being great landed proprietors, had the means (raw material and fuel) for this art. *Archaeology has revealed glassmakers' workshops from the early Middle Ages, close to the cathedral of Maguelone and the basilica of Torcello (7th c.) or, still in *Italy, near the monastery of *San Vincenzo at Volturno (9th c.). Very numerous workshops are known from the 12th c., through texts or archaeology, in the enclosures of religous communities or on their landed *estates.

A small number of glass objects from late Antiquity and the early Middle Ages have decorations and/or inscriptions of Christian inspiration. These symbols (labara, crosses) and these figured representations, borrowed from the biblical world, were obtained by various procedures: *gold leaf cut out and put between two transparent glass layers (a technique called *fondi d'oro*, 4th c.), engraving (4th-5th cc.) and moulding. This last technique, the latest, lasted until the 8th c.; the use and significance of this glassware, which we find in *tombs as well as on inhabited sites, remains uncertain. Its presence is rarely linked to the existence of a religious site and its liturgical character remains to be shown.

On the *enamelled glassware (traditionally called Syro-Frankish) of the late 13th and early 14th cc., probably from the workshops of Murano, Christian iconography, drawn in particular from the *Legend of the Saints*, reappears and occupies an important place, alongside armorial bearings and scenes of court life. The most frequent inscription, *Ave Maria Gracia Plena*, attests the persistence of the Marian cult.

Excavations in churches often lead to the discovery of glassware. Under the pavement, hidden in a trench or carefully laid in a previously or specially constructed tank, glass objects, out of use, but formerly used in worship, are preserved. The most common are lamps or cruets for serving *water and wine at *mass or to contain holy *oils.

In altars, glassware of every form was turned aside from its first function (table vessels) to be reused as *reliquaries. Among the earliest examples are the Catalan finds dating from the 11th c. which are naturally, for the most part, Islamic glassware. In certain cases antique glassware may have served this purpose. But the most abundant discoveries are the late medieval glassware from the *altar-tables of churches in *Germany and Belgium.

Ritual deposits in tombs from the 11th to the 16th c. sometimes include glass. Our knowledge of this glassware rested for a long time solely on funerary discoveries, which do indeed reproduce the forms of domestic crockery. But these are not funeral offerings intended to contain nourishment for the afterlife, as in Antiquity – though we may ask whether such practices do not also contain a reminiscence of *pagan customs – but Christian rites. The typology and position of these objects in burials enable us to study the symbolism of these vases. The flasks (phials or other recipients) doubtless had the same role as earthenware pots, to contain holy water to protect the deceased from *demons, in accordance with the information of the 13th-c. *liturgist *Durand of Mende. As for the symbolism of lamps found in burials, it refers to various texts of the New Testament, and we can also see here a reference to the "light of the world" (Mt 5, 16), especially for pieces deposed in bishops' tombs. The identification of this glassware with lamps is not always evident: the form is only sometimes explicit, but any other object may also do duty as a lamp. Similarly *chalices, signs of the deceased's ecclesiastical dignity, can be identified only by their position on the breast or between the hands. For these are not glassware that was really used for the liturgy in the priest's lifetime, but *simili*, mere drinking vessels evoking the eucharistic vessel of precious metal. The custom of placing a chalice on the dignitary's body, sometimes accompanied by a paten, is mentioned in numerous texts which also make clear that these insignia will be made from a common material, base metal or glass.

F. Rademacher, *Die deutschen Gläser des Mittelalters*, Berlin, 1933. – A. Dasnoy, "Coupes en verre ornées de symboles chrétiens", *ASAN*, 48, 1956, 360-373, pl. 13-28. – D.B. Harden, "Glass Vessels in Britain, A.D. 400-1000", *Dark Age Britain*, D. B. Harden (ed.), London, 1956. – E. Baumgartner, I. Krueger, *Phönix aus Sand und Asche, Glas des Mittelalters*, Munich, 1988. – D. Foy, G. Sennequier, *A travers le verre, Moyen Âge et Renaissance*, Rouen, 1989. – D. Foy, "Les Coupes à décor chrétien moulé: une aire de production provençale", *Annales du 12e Congrès de l'Association Internationale pour l'Histoire du Verre (Vienne, août 1991)*, Amsterdam, 1993, 207-224.

Danièle Foy

**GLASTONBURY.** Despite the claims of later historians, no archaeological or literary evidence exists to support the presence of a religious community at Glastonbury before the late 7th c., and the identity of its founder is unknown. Closely associated with royalty throughout its history, it is linked with the monastic *reform of the 10th c. (through the figure of its abbot, *Dunstan, *c.*940-956, later archbishop of *Canterbury), and by 1066 was the richest religious house in England. There was violent resistance to the first Norman abbot, and later a protracted dispute with the bishop of Bath (who attempted unsuccessfully to annex Glastonbury to his see), which lasted until 1234. From the 12th c., the efforts of historians such as *William of Malmesbury and the "discovery" of King *Arthur's bones in 1191 began the process of mythologizing which culminated in the identification of Glastonbury as the *fons et origo* of Christianity in Britain and as Arthur's Avalon. Its consequent standing as a *pilgrimage centre served to increase its wealth and status, and it was a rich prize in 1539 when the abbot and two monks were hanged, the abbey dissolved, the massive *library dispersed, and the site sold for cash.

J. A. Robinson, *Somerset Historical* Essays, London, 1921. – *The Early History of Glastonbury*, J. Scott (ed.), Woodbridge, 1981. – L. Abrams (ed.), J. P. Carley (ed.), *The Archaeology and History of Glastonbury Abbey*, Woodbridge, 1991. – P. Rahtz, *Glastonbury*, London, 1993. – L. Abrams, *Anglo-Saxon Glastonbury*, Woodbridge, 1996.

Lesley Abrams

***GLORIA.*** *Gloria in excelsis Deo* is a *hymn of praise sung by the Latin Church during festive masses, suppressed at *ferial masses and during times of penitence. It is the second chant of the ordinary, after the **Kyrie*. It is also called the "great *doxology" in contrast to the little doxology that concludes the recital of all the *psalms, or again the "angelic hymn" because its first words, "Glory to God in the highest and peace to men of good will", are those by which the angels announced the birth of Christ to the shepherds of Bethlehem (Lk 2, 14).

Originally, it was a hymn for the *office of *matins in the Greek Church. In the 4th c. it passed into the Latin Church, perhaps through the intermediary of Hilary of Poitiers. In the 6th c., Pope Symmachus generalized its use at *mass. The first version, comparable to the present text, goes back to the late 7th century. This text is a continuous composition, without recapitulation, vestige of a genre cultivated at the beginnings of Christianity, the *Psalmi idiotici*, modelled on the Old Testament *psalms; and the *Gloria XV*, one of the oldest to survive, is composed in a style very close to psalmody.

At the earliest times, the *Gloria in excelsis Deo* was probably sung by the whole assembly, before coming into the sphere of the *schola*. Its style is neither melismatic nor very ornate. Some 50 different medieval melodies have come down to us, some of which have often been *troped.

The *Gloria, laus et honor* is a hymn not to be confused with the preceding; its text is attributed to *Theodulf of Orléans. It was sung on *Palm Sunday during the *procession.

Finally, the *Gloria Patri et Filio et Spiritui Sancto...*, or little doxology, is a sort of supplementary *verse that ends the recital of all psalms, canticles and the final response of each nocturne.

H. Leclercq, "Doxologies", *DACL*, 4, 1921, 1525-1536. – D. Bosse, *Untersuchung einstimmiger mittelalterlicher Melodien zum "Gloria in excelsis Deo"*, Erlangen, 1954 (typed document).

Claire Maître

**GLORY.** According to theologians, glory is the visible manifestation of the *majesty, omnipotence and holiness of *God, as these are reflected in *creation. In iconography, it is rendered by any form of aureole that surrounds the representation of *Christ, then, from the last quarter of the 10th c., representations of the *evangelists and *Mary. Not until towards the end of the 13th c., more certainly in the 14th and 15th cc., does glory surround the figures of saints.

*Saint Luke*, miniature from the *Gospels of Otto III*, Reichenau school, late 10th c. Munich, Bayerische Staatsbibliothek (Ms lat. 4453, fol. 139 v°).

In the West, the glory is the circle or oval painted around Christ's *throne: at the beginning of Christian art, as later, the motif came from the circular medallions (*imagines clipeatae*) around the effigies of the heroized *dead. The formula was at first followed as it stood: Codex Amiatinus I (fol. 796 v°, *c.*700, Northumbria; Florence, Biblioteca Laurenziana); Gospels of Gondoin (fol. 12 v°, *c.*751-754; Autun, Municipal Library, ms. 3); or in the illuminated manuscript at Lorsch (*c.*800, Bucharest, National Library). From the mid 9th c., Christ was put within an aureole that had the form of an almond, oval or broken (*e.g.* in the illuminated manuscripts at *Tours). Towards the middle of the century, at *Saint-Martin at Tours, the almond is broken above and below; the globe on which Christ sits is put at the base of the *mandorla, just touching its border. At the same period, the oval of the mandorla may be framed by a lozenge whose corners hold the evangelical symbols (Moutier-Grandval Bible, called Arundel Bible, Tours, mid 9th c.; London, BL, Add. 10546). This iconographical type is the origin of the *tetramorph as represented in Western art. In the 10th and 11th cc., rainbows fringed with whisps of *cloud are added to the composition: in the *Codex Aureus* of Saint-Emmeran, they separate the places of the evangelists from the area of the celestial vision. In the 11th c., the mandorla, in the form of an almond, and the globe are changed into two circles interlaced in a figure-of-eight, supporting Christ seated in the middle (Bible of Saint-Aubin d'Angers, Angers, Municipal Library, ms. 4, fol. 208) or, in 12th-c. mural *painting, in a rainbow attached to the sides. At the same moment, at the height of his power in art, the evangelist too appears in a glory, seated on a rainbow (*St Luke* in the *Gospels of Otto III*, fol. 139 v°, Reichenau, late 10th c.: Munich, Bayerische Staatsbibliothek, Clm. 4453). On Adorations of the *Magi of *Ottonian date, *Mary appears in majesty within an elongated mandorla; in the 12th and 13th cc., in cycles of anecdotal painting, she appears in glory, sometimes within a radiant cloud (most often in the 14th and 15th cc.).

Finally, from the 13th c., the saints too can be represented in glory: sometimes in scenes of posthumous appearance (*St Francis at the Chapter of Arles*, upper church of *Assisi), death, survival of the soul, or glorification on a throne (*St Thomas Aquinas*, Florence, Santa Maria Novella, chapter hall, 1366-1368).

A. Grabar, *Les Voies de la création en iconographie chrétienne*, Paris, 1979.

Daniel Russo

**GLOSSARIES, JEWISH.** Several bilingual (Hebrew-vernacular) lexicons of biblical terms were established by *Jews in the Middle Ages, notably in *France and *Italy. Written for both languages in *Hebrew characters, they provide an interesting contribution to Romance philology. The French glossaries (13th c.) may have made use of a vernacular Jewish translation of the *Bible, used in elementary teaching; the best known are those called "of Basel" and "of Leipzig". A 12th-c. Hebrew-Italian philosophical glossary has recently been discovered.

M. Banitt, "L'Étude des glossaires bibliques des juifs de France au Moyen Âge", *PIASH*, 2, 1968, 188-210. – G. Sermoneta, *Un glossario filosofico*, Rome, 1969. – M. Banitt, *Le Glossaire de Bâle*, Jerusalem, 1972.

Gilbert Dahan

**GLOSSARIES, LATIN.** During the Latin Middle Ages, glossaries were an indispensable educational tool, serving both as sources of vocabulary (often of rare and exotic vocabulary, which was used for ornamentation by authors with stylistic pretensions) and as accessories to the study of Latin school texts. Glossaries took various forms: at the simplest level, they consisted of *glossae collectae* drawn from marginal and interlinear glosses to lemmata in particular source-texts, and presented in the same order as they occur in the source-texts. But the lemmata might also be arranged in alphabetical order, according to the first letter of the word (hence called a-order glossaries), the first two letters (ab-order) or, more rarely, the first three (abc-order). Words in a glossary might also be classified in lexical categories: *e.g.* words for plants, animals, houses, etc.; such glossaries are called 'class glossaries'. Finally, glossaries might contain extensive entries (rather than one- or two-word explanations); such glossaries would perhaps better be described as encyclopedias. Although countless glossaries were produced during the Middle Ages, characteristically for the individual use of schoolmasters, only a small number have been adequately described or edited.

The main sources of unusual vocabulary in medieval glossaries were lexical compilations of classical antiquity, such as Festus, *De significatu verborum* (a text that circulated in a redaction made by *Paul the Deacon in the late 8th c.), Nonius Marcellus, *De compendiosa doctrina*, and *Isidore's *Etymologiae*, as well as scholia to antique authors who were studied in schools (Vergil, Terence, Persius, etc.). Another source of numerous medieval glossaries were the so-called *Hermeneumata pseudo-Dositheana*, a collection of Greek-Latin entries arranged as a class glossary, which may have originated in late Antiquity as a bilingual phrasebook for Latin-speaking students of Greek.

Various phases in the development of medieval Latin glossaries can be identified. Two early glossaries, which may have originated in 7th-c. Spain, and which drew on Festus, are known (from their first entries) as "Abolita" and "Abstrusa"; these two glossaries were apparently used in some form at the late 7th-c. *Canterbury school of *Theodore and Hadrian. The teaching of their Canterbury school is represented by various corpora of glosses, of which the most important witness is the so-called "Leiden Glossary", which preserves *glossae collectae* to some 48 texts (pre-eminently biblical and Christian-Latin texts), which illustrate the school-room explanations of the Canterbury masters. However, the glossary that had the greatest influence on later lexicography was the *Liber glossarum,* a massive compilation drawing on "Abolita" and "Abstrusa" as well as Isidore's *Etymologiae,* apparently compiled at *Corbie by one Ansileubus in the late 8th century. During the 9th c., scholars and school-masters such as *John Scotus Eriugena, Martin of Laon and *Remigius of Auxerre commented extensively on school-texts such as Priscian, Martianus Capella and *Boethius, and many of their comments found their way into glossaries.

Later glossaries drew on this earlier tradition. Thus the 11th-c. *Elementarium doctrinae rudimentum* of Papias draws on the *Liber glossarum* and Remigius's commentary on Priscian. In the early 12th c., Osbern of Gloucester in his *Panormia* used Festus in the redaction of Paul the Deacon as well as Isidore. *Huguccio of Pisa († 1210) compiled his massive *Liber derivationum* from Papias and Osbern; although it survives in more than 200 manuscripts, the *Liber derivationum* has never been printed in its entirety. Finally, the *Catholicon* of John Balbus of Genoa († 1298) draws in its turn on Papias and Huguccio. There was thus an uninterrupted tradition of medieval Latin lexicographical scholarship, extending from late Antiquity to the late Middle Ages.

*Corpus Glossarium Latinorun*, G. Goetz (ed.), 7 vols., Leipzig, 1888-1923. – *Glossaria Latina*, W. M. Lindsay (ed.), 5 vols. (London, 1926-1931).

G. Loewe, *Prodromus Corporis Glossariorum Latinorum*, Leipzig, 1876. – M. Lapidge, "The School of Theodore and Hadrian", *Anglo-Saxon England*, 15, 1986, 45-72. – J. D. Pheifer, "Early Anglo-Saxon Glossaries and the School of Canterbury", *Anglo-Saxon England,* 16, 1987, 17-44. – C. Dionisotti, "Greek Grammars and Dictionaries in Carolingian Europe", *The Sacred Nectar of the Greeks*, M. Herren (ed.), London, 1988, 1-56. – W. M. Lindsay, *Studies in Early Medieval Latin Glossaries*, M. Lapidge (ed.), Aldershot, 1996. – P. Lendinara, *Anglo-Saxon Glosses and Glossaries*, Aldershot, 1999.

Michael Lapidge

**GLOSSES, LEGAL.** In the primary sense of the term, a gloss is a short explanation given by the commentator of a text. It is called interlinear when it is put between the lines, marginal when put in the margin, authentic when it cites the terms of the law, magistral when borrowed from the sayings of a professor. The procedure was perfected by the *masters of the school of *Bologna to explain to their pupils the group of texts of *Roman law rediscovered during the 11th c., whence the name "school of glossators" given to the authors who employed this method.

Very rapidly, the explanations given in this form took on breadth and gave rise to various types of glosses which ended by constituting particular literary genres. The earliest were merely etymological or grammatical remarks intended to account for unfamiliar words. Then glosses were applied to giving a true legal interpretation by indicating parallel or contrary passages to be encountered in other legal texts, which gave different solutions to identical or similar situations. These were *allegationes*. As the rules of *university teaching were specified, a clearer specialization appeared. For each text of law, a summary (**summa*) emerged, glossing the official paragraph title; *notabilia* were added which were later detached from the gloss to form a special genre. In the strict sense, they designated a rule of law extracted from the text, but in the broad sense, any important remark made in connection with it. They were so called because they were introduced by the words *nota, notandum est*. The sets constituted by them were later called by the more poetic names of *gemma*, *margarita*, *flos* or, more prosaically, *tabulae* or *repertoria*. The *casus* were also an integral part of the gloss. They consisted of a brief exposition of a real or fictitious difficulty reflecting a phenomenon or a reality of social life that demanded a legal solution. Finally, in time, the *master inserted into the gloss **quaestiones* that came originally from practical exercises in the schools: after the exposition of two opponents on a point of law, the master summed up the arguments *pro* and *contra* and gave the solution.

Glosses became so abundant that certain authors brought together those they had formulated in the course of their teaching into collections or *apparatus*. Under this form has come down the work of the greatest glossators of the 12th and 13th cc. such as Placentino, Azo, Odofredus and many others.

Each master's most characteristic glosses were introduced by copyists into manuscripts of the *Corpus juris civilis*, identifying the author by a sign indicating the glossator's name. In the manuscripts, the legal text commented on was transcribed in relatively prominent characters in the centre of the page; the glosses filled the margins.

In the middle of the 13th c., one of the best known Bolognese professors, Accursius, undertook to bring together the glosses of his predecessors and drew up the *Glossa ordinaria* of the *Corpus*, also called the *Great Gloss*. The *Glossa ordinaria* was accepted and commented on in the schools; it was also used by the *courts. Later manuscripts and editions of the *Corpus juris civilis* reproduced it until the revision undertaken by Denis Godefroy at the end of the 16th century.

The margins of the manuscripts were then covered with a second layer of glosses much more difficult to read. The opinion of many representatives of the French schools of *Orléans, *Montpellier or *Toulouse whose *apparatus* have not been preserved are known to us only through this medium. The early 14th c. was thus the second golden age of glosses (manuscripts called Glossed Digests or Glossed Codes).

But the methods of teaching civil law began to evolve at this time; the professors increasingly abandoned the too analytic procedure of the gloss in favour of much more systematic expositions which they grouped together in treatises bearing on important questions of law or in *summae* more independent of the actual text of the *Corpus*.

In *canon law, we see the same evolution: the canonists glossed the whole of the *Corpus juris canonici*. They began in the 12th c. by explaining Gratian's **Decretum* according to this method. Soon after 1215, *John Teutonicus drew up an *apparatus* of these glosses which, revised in 1236 by Bartholomew of Brescia, from now on formed the *Glossa ordinaria Decreti*. The other parts of the *Corpus* also gave rise to innumerable glosses which were also the object of syntheses. In the middle of the 13th c., the *apparatus* of Bernardo Bottoni (*Bernard of Parma, † 1266) was chosen to form the *Glossa ordinaria* on *Gregory IX's *Decretals, which in the next century received the additions of *Johannes Andreae. The author of the Ordinary Gloss (completed between 1334 and 1338) on the *Liber Sextus*, completed in 1301, was Johannes Andreae. Also by Johannes Andreae is the Ordinary Gloss on the *Clementines. The edition of the *Corpus juris canonici* published at Paris by Jean Chappuis in 1500 contains glosses by Josselin de Cassagne on the Extravagantes of *John XXII and by Guillaume de Montlauzun on the *Extravagantes communes*.

Though the various glosses did not by themselves have the force of law, *jurists were called to take the greatest account of them in their application of the law, since they figured among the official additions to the different *Corpus* and they had the merit of providing precious information both on the sense of the words and on the interpretation of the texts.

S. Kuttner, *Prodromus corpus glossarum*, Vatican, 1937. – C. Lefebvre, "Glose", *Cath.*, 5, 1962, 64-66. – G. Astuti, "La glossa Accursiana", *Atti del convegno internazionale di Studi Accursiani*, Milan, 1968, 287-379. – G. R. Dolezalek, "Les gloses des manuscrits de droit: reflet des méthodes d'enseignement", *Manuels, programmes de cours et techniques d'enseignement dans les universités médiévales*, Louvain-la-Neuve, 1994, 235-255.

Henri Gilles

**GLOSSES ON THE BIBLE, LATIN.** More than a genre, the gloss was a literary form characteristic of the teaching and interpretation of the manuals used in the medieval *schools of the West, in particular for *exegesis of the *Bible.

The natural form of exegesis in the 3rd and 4th cc. was the commentary or "*treatise": this was the personal work of an ecclesiastical authority, who organised the interpretative matter into a continuous discourse punctuated by literary citations following the letter of the *Bible. He expounded a book of the Bible sentence by sentence, without necessarily being obliged to respect the integrality of the text. From the 4th and 5th cc., a new literary form appeared in the Eastern Empire, the **catena* ("chain"), or *florilegium of biblical exegesis, composed of patristic extracts, *sermons as well as commentaries, whose authorship was generally established at the beginning of the citation. At *Constantinople and in the great monastic centres of the West that inherited it, this form at first occupied the full page of the manuscript; it was soon arranged in a column parallel to the biblical text (Western examples are known from the 8th and 9th cc.). Around 750, in the East, a type of marginal arrangement appeared in which the biblical text was written in one column and the catena on the three margins around it, without any interference of glosses in the column of text; this arrangement, strongly resembling that of manuscripts of the *Talmud, was dominant in the *Byzantine Empire in the 10th century.

However, the commentary and the catena soon took on a new appearance in the West. Borrowed from school manuals, notably those of *grammar and *rhetoric which may have experimented with it from late Antiquity, the form of the gloss, distributing morsels of commentary around and between the lines of the text, first appeared applied to the Bible in the late 8th c. in *psalters and works of biblical exegesis of Insular origin (New York, Pierpont Morgan Library, ms. 776; Zurich, Staatsarchiv AG 19, no. XII) and was widely adopted in the 9th c. in East Francia. This innovation of the gloss received a favourable welcome in the cathedral and monastic *schools, attracted by the potentialities of a flexible form which was suited to the exercise of the commented *lecture (vulgarized by *Remigius of Auxerre, † *c.*908) and which easily assimilated personal additions and course notes. However the gloss remained much more commonly used for the study of grammarians and the Latin *classics than for that of the Bible.

Glosses on the Bible borrowed their material from patristic commentaries and "interpretations of names" as well as from the *glossaries of the 8th and 9th cc. (*Abavus*, *Abrogans*, Glosses *Rz*) which gave synonyms and sometimes allegorical interpretations for a choice of biblical words, classified by alphabetical order. Unlike the Byzantine East, Western scholars soon stopped using non-exegetical sources in the biblical commentary or gloss, until the university explosion of the 13th c., which obliged intellectuals to conduct their reasoning otherwise. In the reign of the Capetian *Philip I (1060-1108), at first in the Île-de-France and *Normandy, then around the more active *cathedrals, there spread an intensive use of the "gloss" form for the most studied books of the Bible, the *Psalms, Pauline *epistles, *Song of Songs and *Apocalypse: based on citations of indisputable authorities – *Fathers, but also moderns –, the gloss served the new needs of churchmen favourable to the religious *reform of the 11th century. From the first decades of the 12th c., many copyists adopted it, doubtless at the request of the *masters who gave an increased place to the teaching of the Bible. The very idea of a complete gloss of the Bible probably arose in the circle of Anselm of Laon, around 1100. Under *Louis VI (1108-1137), the main centre of production of glossed books seems to have been the abbey of *Saint-Victor at *Paris, closely connected with the royal *chancery. Precisely at this time, the content of these glosses tended to crystallize, to become uniform from one manuscript to another, while references to earlier authors were removed from the recopied text and masters faded into anonymity: these were the visible signs of a standardization taking place in the second quarter of the 12th c. in the Capetian capital, though there was no real identity of content before the 1220s. The most modern biblical exegesis thus tended to fall into a particular form, though without being confined to it. Around 1115, the manuscripts presenting this form still had no name. We can distinguish them perfectly under their name of "glossed books" (*e.g. Genesis glossata*) in all the *library catalogues of the second half of the 12th c. as well as in the works of Parisian masters like *Peter Comestor and *Peter Cantor in the years 1170-1180.

The biblical gloss of the 12th c. was at once a *codicological and a literary form; it restored the primacy of the text, which was reproduced in its entirety and no longer "lemmatized", in accordance with the best manuscripts (unfortunately we still know little about the sources used by those responsible for the Parisian gloss), and it distilled the information necessary for the sense in a very visible way, between the lines and in the margins of the page. The effect sought was that of a dynamic reading, in which the reader was placed at a crossroads, face to face with the text and yet helped by the assortment of glosses which supplemented each other or revealed divergences of interpretation, up to him to resolve. The traditional form of the commentary rapidly lost its primacy; from the 1140s, *Gilbert of Poitiers, then *Peter Lombard, judged it opportune to present their exegeses of the book of Psalms and the Pauline epistles by following the codicological model of the gloss (text in the centre, commentary in the margin, in smaller writing). Concern for the text and its letter thus appears to have prevailed over the desire to impose a personal thought, for which the most natural vehicle was the continuous commentary. Scholars were animated by fervour for the *littera*, the letter of the text in the strictest philological sense, which was itself the consequence of the device of the gloss; but the 1150s saw a return to an exegesis more respectful of traditional thought. The example of *Andrew of Saint-Victor is illuminating: he was criticized by his colleagues at the abbey, *Richard and then Geoffrey. Exegesis from the late 12th c. reacted against earlier tendencies and showed a return to *allegory.

The success of the gloss was dazzling; it is attested by the rapid multiplication of glossed books in the second third of the 12th century. The Parisian workshop bequeathed its recipes to **scriptoria* capable of confronting the specific difficulties of a complex page layout, and the *scriptoria* redistributed glossed books through all the lands of Latin *Christendom. The gloss did not just affect the schools: princes showed an interest in glossed books and procured examples (Henry, son of *Louis VI, gave a series to *Clairvaux, now preserved in the libraries of *Troyes and *Montpellier; there are some among the *books of Henry the Liberal, count of *Champagne). In the early 13th c., there was hardly an important *cathedral or monastery that did not possess a glossed Bible. The *universities and the great *convents of the *mendicant orders also devoted themselves to putting complete sets at the disposal of their professors and students. From the second quarter of the 13th c., the gloss of the Bible entered the common stock of studies of *theology, in a triad associating it with *Peter Lombard's *Book of *Sentences* and *Peter Comestor's *Scholastic history*.

The status of the exegete himself benefited from such fortune: though standardization limited the field of interpretations, the authorized commentator, holder of a *licence to teach, acquired an authentic power over the text and its interpretation. From now on, the text would no longer be diffused without an authorial "gloss" – to the great scandal of the more religious (*Francis of Assisi forbade his disciples to gloss the text of his Rule). The ideal was to produce clear messages, presenting the least possible ambiguity: in consequence, drifts in interpretation also had to be prevented.

The success of biblical glosses went together with their contribution to the general history of written culture. Indeed they were at the source of several vernacular literatures, since the first translations were devoted to the Bible, of which they were generally free adaptations sprinkled with interpretative glosses. It is known that *Waldes of Lyon, after his *conversion, commissioned a translation not of the New Testament itself, but of its gloss: he thus allied prudence with a sense of modernity.

P. Riché, G. Lobrichon, *Le Moyen Âge et la Bible*, Paris, 1984. – M. Zier, "The Manuscript Tradition of the Glossa Ordinaria for Daniel", *Scr.*, 47, 1993, 3-25.

Guy Lobrichon

**GLOSSES ON THE BIBLE, VERNACULAR.** The teaching of the *Bible in the Middle Ages, in *Latin or in *Hebrew, often resorted to the vernacular to explain certain difficult terms; thus the written commentaries have preserved vernacular glosses; they are numerous in Hebrew texts, more rare in Latin texts.

**Jewish glosses.** Elementary teaching was done in the vernacular, perhaps with the help of an established translation; higher teaching was probably in Hebrew, but resorted, though more periodically, to the secular language, as is shown by the French glosses (in

Gloucester cathedral. Gallery of the cloister, *c.*1370.

Hebrew characters) present in medieval *rabbinic literature; they are called *laazim* (sing. *laaz*). The first texts to preserve them are undoubtedly those attributed to Gershom of Metz (960-1028), but actually of the 11th century. The most important are those in the commentaries of *Rashi (1040-1106); numerous, contemporary with the first works of French literature, they considerably enrich our knowledge of 11th-c. vocabulary, notably that of daily life and the natural *sciences. Moreover, by virtue of being transcriptions (and despite the difficulties connected with Hebrew writing), they can help us reconstruct the old pronunciation of French. The glosses reflect regional variations; those of Rashi are in the dialect of *Champagne. The 12th-c. commentaries from northern France (Joseph Qara, Eliezer of Beaugency, Joseph Bekhor Shor) and those of the 13th c. (Samson of Sens) also contain French glosses; they are more rare in the Midi. Apart from biblical exegesis, all rabbinic literature made use of the vernacular. This immense field has not yet been exploited (*e.g.* the codes of Moses of Coucy).

**Christian glosses.** The presence of vernacular glosses is much more sporadic in Latin commentaries; it may be significant to call attention to those in *Andrew of Saint-Victor: is this the influence of a characteristic of Jewish exegesis? In the 13th c., glosses mainly concern the vocabulary of feudal institutions. They allow us to localize certain texts, but French is used by authors who are not from *France.

A. Darmesteter, L. Brandin, *Les Gloses françaises de Raschi dans la Bible*, Paris, 1909. – A. Darmesteter, D. S. Blondheim, *Les Gloses françaises dans les commentaires talmudiques de Raschi*, Paris, 1929. – R. Levy, *Contribution à la lexicographie française*. . ., Syracuse, 1960. – M. Banitt, "Le renouvellement lexical de la Version Vulgate des juifs de France", *Rom.*, 102, 1981, 433-455. – R. Berndt, *André de Saint-Victor*, Paris-Turnhout, 1991, 196-201.

Gilbert Dahan

**GLOUCESTER.** A former Roman *castrum*, Gloucester was one of the towns that commanded access to the Welsh frontier and it always had an important military role. Though *Henry II dealt severely with its burghers who had tried to create a *commune in 1170, it was a borough that benefited from the urban franchises usual in *England; it was governed by a *merchant oligarchy, which led to social tensions. The town, which dominated the mouth of the Severn, also enjoyed relative economic prosperity; it was in an important area of *animal husbandry and controlled the trade of charcoal and iron produced in the great *forest of Dean. It was the 15th town in England in 1377 with a population of about 3400 inhabitants, and the 17th in 1524 in the number of taxpayers.

But the essence of its prestige came from its ecclesiastical role. Gloucester was the place where Osric, with the help of King Æthelred of Mercia, had founded the monastery of Sts Peter and Paul in *c.*680. Destroyed early in the 11th c., it was restored as a Benedictine monastery in *c.*1022 with the help of King *Cnut. It had about 100 monks at the start of the 12th c. and about 50 in the 14th. In 1534, the *abbot and 35 monks accepted the Act of Supremacy; the *abbey was suppressed, but the abbey church was turned into a *cathedral and a bishopric of Gloucester was founded. Though the abbey was only the 15th Benedictine abbey in wealth (with a revenue of 1430 pounds a year in 1536), it possessed one of the finest abbey churches. In essence it was a *Romanesque church, whose nave was finished in *c.*1160; but the choir was enlarged in the 14th c., then the façade, the central tower and especially a great perpendicular-style *cloister were added in the 15th century. The chronicler Robert of Gloucester, author of a *chronicle relating English history from Brutus to 1270, of which a dozen manuscripts survive, was probably a monk here in the late 13th century. Another chronicle, perhaps by Abbot Walter Frocester, covers local history from 681 to 1412, while *Annales* from Creation to 1469 also exist.

But there was also at Gloucester an Augustinian *priory, St Oswald's, which had a glorious history: it was an important secular church in the *Anglo-Saxon period, since King *Alfred's daughter Æthelflæd had transferred the body and *relics of St *Oswald there; in 1153, Henry Murdac, archbishop of *York, turned this church into a priory of Augustinian *canons. The *mendicant orders made their appearance very early; the *Franciscan *convent was founded before 1230 under the guidance of Agnellus of Pisa himself, that of the *Dominicans before 1241, and that of the *Carmelites before 1268. Between them they had about a hundred friars in 1331-1337. There were also two *hospitals, one of which, St Bartholomew, was very important, since it had 90 patients in 1333, and a *leper-house (St Mary Magdalene).

*Medieval Art and Architecture at Gloucester and Tewkesbury*, T.A. Heslop (ed.), V.A. Sekules (ed.), London, 1985. – R. Holt, "Gloucester in the Century after the Black Death", *Transactions of the Bristol and Gloucestershire Archaeological Society*, 103, 1985, 149-61. – C. Heighway, *Anglo-Saxon Gloucestershire*, Gloucester, 1987. – D. Welander, *The History, Art and Architecture of Gloucester Cathedral*, Stroud, 1991.

Jean-Philippe Genet

**GNIEZNO.** Gniezno (Gnesen), in Great Poland, was the centre of the tribal community of the Polani and the seat of their legendary princes. From the 9th c., a fortified settlement is attested there by *archaeology, composed of a princely residence surrounded by *suburbia* which were extended in the course of the 10th century. After the *baptism of *Mieszko I, a palatine *chapel of St George was built, as well as an urban church dedicated to the Assumption in which, in 997, *Boleslas the Brave deposed the *relics of St *Adalbert, *martyred in Prussia. Under the double patronage of the Virgin and St Adalbert, the building attained the rank of metropolitan *cathedral under *Otto III, who visited it in the year 1000. Richly endowed by the duke of *Poland, it saw his royal *coronation and that of his son and successor Mieszko II, but it was destroyed in 1038 by Bretislav of *Bohemia who took St Adalbert's relics away to *Prague. Soon rebuilt, following the discovery of St Adalbert's head in 1127 it once more prevailed as a high place of the cult of that saint, promoted to patron of Poland, whose life was illustrated there by scenes cast in the bronze of a sumptuous door in the *Mosan style in 1175.

Gniezno remained the metropolitan see of *Poland, while the political capital was established at *Cracow before the middle of the 11th c., and *Poznań was chosen as residence of the dukes of Great Poland after the partition of the country. However, it was at Gniezno that the *coronations of Přemysł II, king of a reunified Poland (1295), and Wenceslas II of Bohemia (1300) took place. The *cathedral was rebuilt in a new style, under the influence of the French cathedrals and the architectural styles known at Prague, *Vienna and in *Swabia; it became an active intellectual centre, notably in the sphere of *historiography. Still visible today, after important restorations following the Second World War, as well as the relics of St Adalbert it houses a rich treasure, the archives of the *archbishopric and numerous *objets d'art*, which make it an important place of the Polish national memory.

As well as the archiepiscopal quarter, the town of Gniezno comprised several centres of population, sites of *markets, seats of five or six *parishes. A new town was created in 1238-1239 to the east of the cathedral: governed by the law of *Magdeburg, it had a great market-place, a town hall, a *convent of *Franciscans and one of *Poor Clares, a parish church, a *hospital and, outside the walls, a community of Canons of the *Holy Sepulchre. The town was burned and pillaged in 1331 by the *Teutonic Knights, who spared the cathedral in exchange for thirty masses promised them by an altarist (a priest who lived by celebrating remunerated masses).

*Dzieje Gniezna* [History of Gniezno], J. Topolski (ed.), Warsaw, 1965. – *Katedra Gnieznieriska* [Gniezno cathedral], A. Swiechowska (ed.), Poznań, 1970 (2 vol.). – M. Aleksandrowicz, "Gniezno", *DHGE*, 21, 1986, 247-262.

Aleksander Gieysztor †

## GOD

**Theology.** In the religious and cultural context of the Jewish, Christian and Muslim civilizations, "God" designates the creator of the universe who governs the world and cares for the destiny of each human being. From the beginnings of philosophical thought in Greece, there developed, in parallel with practice and theological reflection, a philosophical advance that not only put human discourse on God to the test but also tried to found a theology philosophically and hence on rational and universally valid bases. This effort of foundation and legitimation was pursued throughout the Middle Ages, a period of particularly fertile dialogue between *philosophy, for which "God" designated firstly and principally the ultimate reponse to a question, and the data of revealed religion. In the Christian setting, such a rational investigation could find support in Rom 1, 19 f., where St *Paul asserts that the human *intellect is capable of knowing God. Three orientations of this specific questioning can be discerned in medieval thought.

Firstly, starting from observation and analysis of the physical world, a first type of advance arrived, especially through an interpretation of the phenomenon of movement, at the discovery of a first *cause that explained the universe in its totality. From the discovery of *Aristotle's major works in the 13th c., this first cause was called, following *Physics* VIII and *Metaphysics* XII, the "unmoved mover". But the use made of the Aristotelian argument by St *Thomas Aquinas, especially in the *Summa theologiae* (I$^{a}$, q. 2, a. 3), attests that it was not a purely physicistic conception, since St Thomas proposed to interpret the movement perceived by the senses in terms of *act and potency: "To move is to make something pass from potency to act": thus the unmoved mover, "which is not itself moved by any other", can be identified with pure act. We can nevertheless speak of a cosmological conception, since God is discovered in the context of investigation of the structure, functioning and existence of the universe as it appears to *man in his daily experience. There is an undeniable link between this form of philosophical *theology, of which traces are found in most authors from the 13th c. on, and the *astronomical ideas inherited from Antiquity through the intermediary of Arab *science, according to which the supralunary part of the world is more perfect.

Secondly, the philosophical discovery of a first principle was linked to the problem of *being, and more particularly to the question of the radical origin of that which is: we can speak of an onto-theology for which the analysis of "that which is" culminates in a first being which, unlike finite and contingent beings, cannot not exist and is consequently necessary and self-subsistent. Among the major representatives of this form of philosophical theology in which the distinctions between necessary and contingent, and especially between being and essence, play a preponderant role, must be counted *Avicenna and St Thomas Aquinas. By an original *ontological analysis, the latter tried to demonstrate that every being whose existence is not part of its essence requires a first cause: "All that does not enter into the concept of the essence or quiddity comes to it from outside and enters into composition with the essence; for no essence can be conceived without its elements, but any essence or quiddity can be conceived without its being: I can conceive what man or phoenix is without knowing whether it possesses being in the order of the real. Hence it is evident that being differs from essence or quiddity, unless a thing exist whose quiddity is its very being. Such a thing can only be unique and first" (*De ente et essentia*, ch. 5). Since being *qua* existing "is the act of acts and the perfection of perfections" (*De potentia* 7, 2 ad 9) and since every finite thing participates in being, God as the source of all being is subsistent being *per se* (*ipsum esse per se subsistens*), the pure act of existing, the reality "whose essence is to be", the "absolutely perfect cause of all being" (*In Ioh.*, prol.) which possesses in itself all the perfections of being, viz. unity, goodness and truth.

Finally, following Augustine, medieval thought developed another method of philosophical theology that may conveniently be called "noölogical", to the extent that reflection on *knowledge

*The Trinity ("Pity of Our Lord")*, woodcut from Johann Gielemans's *Sanctilogium*, second half of 15th c. Vienna, Österreichische Nationalbibliothek (SN 12812, fol. 8 r°).

and its final conditions was thought to lead to the discovery of a first principle. The second book of St Augustine's *De libero arbitrio* provided an adequate paradigm of this step, which conceived God as the ultimate foundation of knowledge. St *Anselm of Canterbury explored this path especially in the *Monologion*, in which he explained the proportionality of self-knowledge and knowledge of God (ch. 66). The Bonaventurian idea that God is the first thing known attests this same tendency, which entirely dominates the work of *Nicholas of Cusa, who does not hesitate to say that God is what is presupposed in every question (*Idiota de sapientia*, II, beginning). When Meister *Eckhart, in his celebrated Parisian *disputation of 1302, claimed that God is not an existing thing but *intelligere*, this was very evidently a critique of onto-theology in the sense mentioned above: "It now no longer seems to me that God knows because he is, but he is because he knows. Thus God is *intellect and knowledge, and it is this intellective knowledge itself that is the basis of his being."

While integrating elements of the ancient, Jewish and Arab tradition, medieval philosophical theology in Christian lands profoundly innovated not just as to the interpretation of the nature of God, in which trinitarian theology played an important role, but especially as to the relationship between God and the world. The exploration of the idea of *creation, according to which every existing thing depends as such on the first principle, entailed as a consequence new conceptions of relation; and since creation is a free act of both the divine intellect and the divine will, it was indispensable to rethink the *Platonist doctrine of ideas in a new way.

Towards the end of the Middle Ages, we may remark, notably in *Duns Scotus and William of *Ockham, a heavy stress on divine freedom. Divine omnipotence, though it could not be proved by *reason, was the corner-stone of the Ockhamite conception of God. Creation and *grace are free acts that are beyond the need for human justification. God is no-one's debtor, Ockham never ceases to repeat; what God does and what he has done, he does because he wants to, and it is because he has willed it that it is just.

The contribution of medieval thought in the field of the proofs of the existence of God is probably even more important. *Anselm of Canterbury, in an astonishing effort of conciseness, sought and found "an argument that, to be probative, needs nothing but itself" (*Proslogion*, proem). Defining God as "something than which nothing greater can be thought", he wished to show that we cannot even think that He is not, since he who says that God is not, if he understands what he says, must recognise that "that than which nothing greater can be thought" exists both in the intellect and in reality. The validity of this argument, interpreting a necessity of thought as a necessity in reality, was contested by *Thomas Aquinas, for whom God's existence is demonstrable only from its effects, since "from any effect, it can be demonstrated that the cause exists" (*Summa theologiae* Iª, q. 2, a. 2). The five ways (Iª, q. 2, a. 3) by which St Thomas demonstrated that God exists follow this method. Thomas thus tried to prove that there exists a first unmoved mover, a first efficient cause, which is a necessary, perfect and intelligent being. As in other fields, Duns Scotus profoundly transformed the parameters of the problem: he tried to prove that infinite being exists. To do this, he had to proceed in two steps: first, the intellect must demonstrate that there is a first in the order of being, since this first is infinite. Though that Franciscan admitted that it is necessary to go from the effects to the cause, the effects on which he wanted to base his proof were not the contingent beings given in sense experience, but all modes of being *qua* being. That is why he showed firstly that there is a first in the order of efficacy, finality and eminence, and that this triple primacy belongs to a single *nature, before proving that this first is infinite. It was by reason of an ever stricter idea of the nature of demonstration that Ockham criticized the proofs of his predecessors. According to him, it is impossible to prove the unicity of God rigorously, but it is licit to infer from effects the existence of a cause that maintains beings in existence (*causa conservans*).

Nearly every author insisted on the limits of human knowledge of God, both by implementing a theory of knowledge of God and by an appeal to the demands of *apophatic theology, following *Dionysius the Areopagite or *Maimonides. Thomas Aquinas was not the only one to insist on the fact that, for man, what God is in himself remains always hidden, just as he is beyond human representations.

É. Gilson, *Jean Duns Scot. Introduction à ses positions fondamentales*, Paris, 1952. – É. Gilson, *God and philosophers*, New Haven, 1955. – É. Gilson, *L'Etre et l'essence*, Paris, 1962. – É. Gilson, *L'Esprit de la philosophie médiévale*, Paris, 1969. – K. Flasch, *Die Metaphysik des Einen bei Nikolaus von Kues*, Leiden, 1973. – *Maître Eckhart à Paris. Une critique médiévale de l'ontothéologie. Études, textes et introduction*, Paris, 1984. – W. J. Hankey, *God in himself: Aquinas' doctrine of God as expounded in the "Summa theologiae"*, Oxford, 1987. – J. Aertsen, *Nature and Creature. Thomas Aquinas's Way of Thought*, Leiden, 1988. – L. J. Elders, *The philosohical theology of St Thomas Aquinas*, Leiden, 1990. – P. Magnard, *Le Dieu des philosophes*, Paris, 1992. – A. de Libera, *La Philosophie médiévale*, Paris, 1993. – V. Boland, *Ideas in God according to Saint Thomas Aquinas*, Leiden, 1996. – N. Kretzmann, *The metaphysics of theism: Aquinas' natural theology in the "Summa contra gentiles"*, Oxford, 1997.

Ruedi Imbach

**Iconography.** From the Carolingian period to the end of the Romanesque period, the perception of God in the Western religious mentality seems to have been that of a power of life, light and judgment both adored and dreaded. The plastic *image that responded to this perception was that of the *Majestas Domini* on tympana (*Autun, *Conques, *Vézelay, *Saint-Denis, *Chartres). Images of the *Trinity remained rare, as did those of the suffering *Christ.

From the 11th c. and especially from the 12th c., a radical change appeared in the image of God, in the religious mentality as well as in art, with the increasingly frequent appearance of the suffering Crucified, *God the Father as an old man, and various images of the Trinity: the Throne of Grace (the Father presents the Son on the *cross between his knees, the dove flying between them), the Trinity of the Psalter (Father and Son sitting side by side, the dove between them), the Triandric Trinity (the three persons rendered by three men more or less differing in their ages and attributes), the Tricephalous Trinity (God with one body and three heads, or three faces).

These images of the Trinity were to have great popularity in the West from the 12th c. and would become encrusted in the collective memory, notably, in the 15th c., figures of divine Persons endowed with the insignia of political power (*crown, sceptre, *throne, dais) or sacerdotal power (alb and cord, cape and stole, *tiara). During the same period, due to the focusing of *mysticism and devotion on the Saviour's humanity and his redemptive *Passion, the marks of suffering on Christ's body were magnified by art with a realism that often attained the pathetic (**Pietà*).

The religious imagery of the second half of the Western Middle Ages appears marked by a humanization of God. This allowed the faithful a feeling of proximity in mysticism and religious *theatre. The first reservations about these images and the attitudes they reflected were expressed by representatives of the nascent *humanism (*Gerson, *Antoninus of Florence, Erasmus) before being developed by the reformers (Luther, Zwingli and especially Calvin). The modern period coincided with a certain destructuring of this imagery.

W. Braunfels, *Die heilige Dreifaltigkeit*, Düsseldorf, 1954. – F. Boespflug, "Dieu en pape. Une singularité de l'art religieux de la fin du Moyen Âge", *RMab*, new series, 2, 1991, 167-205. – A. M. d'Achille, "Sulla iconografia trinitaria medievale: La Trinità del santuario sul Monte Autore presso Vallepietra", *Arte medievale*, 1, Rome, 1991, 49-73. – F. Boespflug, Y. Zaluska, "Le Dogme trinitaire et l'essor de son iconographie en Occident de l'époque carolingienne au concile de Latran IV (1215)", *CCM*, 3, 1994, 181-240. – B. C. Raw, *Trinity and Incarnation in Anglo-Saxon Art and Thought*, Cambridge, 1997.

François Boespflug

**GOD THE FATHER.** The Church *Fathers, and following them the medieval theologians, taught that God the Father, unlike the incarnate Son, could not be represented, and hence condemned the rare attempts made to depict him (*e.g.* Augustine, *De fide et symbolo*, 7). This doctrine explains why, over the centuries, God the Father had no recognised *image in art: "The visible face of the Father is the Son" (Irenaeus). It was only from the Carolingian period, *e.g.* in the *Utrecht Psalter and then in the Roda Bible, that the Father and the Son started to be depicted alongside each other. Gradually in the West, by invoking his appearances to the *prophets, the first *person of the *Trinity was given the traits of the Ancient of Days (Dan 7) of Byzantine iconography. With the popularity, from the 13th c., of the iconographical types of the Throne of Grace and the Trinity of the Psalter, then, from the second half of the 14th c., that of the *Majesty of the Father, the late Middle Ages saw the rise of the image of the Father as an old man with white hair and beard, which triumphed at the Renaissance (*e.g.* Michelangelo and Raphael) often replacing the figure of *Christ as *God.

I. Correll, *Gottvater. Untersuchungen über seine bildlichen Darstellungen bis zum Tridentinum, zugleich ein Beitrag zur östlichen und westlichen Bildauffassung*, Heidelberg, 1958 (Thesis). – F. Boespflug, "Du Père au Fils nulle différence", *Les Chartreux et l'Art*, A. Girard (ed.), D. Le Blevec (ed.), Paris, 1989, 325-345. – F. Boespflug, "Apophatisme théologique et abstinence figurative. Sur l'irreprésentabilité de Dieu (le Père)", *Revue des sciences religieuses*, 72, 4, 1998, 446-468.

François Boespflug

**GODFREY OF BOUILLON (*c.*1061-1100).** Son of Eustace of Boulogne and Ida of Ardenne, grandson of Duke Godfrey the Bearded and nephew of Godfrey the Hunchback, Godfrey (Godefroi) of Bouillon became duke of Lower *Lorraine in 1087 and exercised his ducal function with authority. He pledged his *castle of Bouillon to the bishop of *Liège in order to raise the necessary money to go on *crusade, where he commanded one of the Western armies. Chosen as ruler of the new kingdom of *Jerusalem, he opted for the simple title "advocate of the *Holy Sepulchre". He used the one year of his reign to consolidate the conquests of the Westerners. He was renowned for his physical strength and his piety (judged excessive), and was respected by his companions and his adversaries. His submission to the Church was in line with princes attached both to the papal and to the imperial power.

P. Aube, *Godefroi de Bouillon*, Paris, 1985. – J. Riley-Smith, *The First Crusade and the Idea of Crusading*, London, 1986.

Michel Parisse

**GODFREY OF FONTAINES (before 1250 - *c.*1306 or 1309).** Coming from the principality of *Liège to *Paris (a pupil of *Siger of Brabant?), regent master in *theology in 1285, Godfrey (Godefroid) of Fontaines left a vast and dispersed body of theological and philosophical work (**Quaestiones*; a university *sermon). He opposed the privileges accorded to the *mendicant orders. A convinced *Aristotelian, he took up *metaphysical positions that were original compared to those of *Thomas Aquinas. His farsighted approval of Margaret Porete's *Mirror of Simple Souls* attests his freedom of spirit. He left his rich *library to the *Sorbonne College.

P. Verdeyen, "Le procès d'inquisition contre Marguerite Porete et Guiart de Cressonessart (1309-1310)", *RHE*, 81, 1986, 47-94. – J. F. Wippel, *The Metaphysical Thought of Godfrey of Fontaines*, Washington (DC), 1989.

Nicole Bériou

**GODFREY OF HUY (died 1173/1174).** Godfrey (Godefroy) of Huy or of Claire, a *goldsmith of the *Mosan school, active *c.*1150, worked there in the service of the *abbot of Stavelot (Belgium); he also worked for Abbot *Suger at *Saint-Denis where he made the giant crucifix (lost) decorated with scenes from both Testaments in concordance (*typological exegesis): from this work dates the birth of *Gothic decoration and the Gothic manner in sculpture. He is known essentially for his works as an enameller: the *Baptism of Christ and the Crucifixion (Metropolitan Museum of Arts, New York), but also a bronze *reliquary of Pope St Alexander (Brussels).

Jean-Pierre Nicol

**GODFREY OF SAINT-VICTOR (died *c.*1194).** Having received an intellectual training before joining the abbey of *Saint-Victor around 1155-1160, Godfrey is known for his philosophical works, the *Microcosmos* and the *Fons philosophiae*. The latter follows *Hugh of Saint-Victor's *Didascalicon* with regard to the systematization of the *sciences, while the *Microcosmos* is a commentary on the Hexaemeron. In the second half of the 12th c., he was the last representative of Victorine humanism. Within the community of *canons of Saint-Victor, he held the office of librarian as well as that of *canonist.

H. Santiago Otero, "Gualterio y Godofredo de San Victor. Su tesis acerca del conocimiento de Cristo hombre", *Div.*, 18, 1974, 168-179. – F. Gasparri, "Godefroy de Saint-Victor: une personnalité peu connue du monde intellectuel et artistique parisien du XIIe siècle", *Scr.*, 41, 1985, 57-69.

Rainer Berndt

**GODPARENTS.** Those who – according to forms that varied over the thousand years of the Middle Ages – assisted the candidate for *baptism and *confirmation. Over the centuries their role, fundamentally religious and liturgical to begin with, took on a social dimension, which sometimes became essential in the late Middle Ages.

In the early Church, the godparent (designated by no particular term) was one who, after having converted an adult pagan, presented him to the Christian community and brought him before it as guarantor of his *conversion. He accompanied him during the long period of instruction as a catechumen. But he does not seem to have played any particular role in the liturgy of baptism proper.

A first evolution came about between the 4th and the 8th c., under the dual effect of the generalization of Christianity and the development of infant baptism, which led to a profound transformation of the catechumenate. If the godparent apparently continued to have no privileged place in the administration of baptism, he henceforth had to exercise his role after the reception of the *sacrament: he was considered responsible for the quality of the Christian life of the newly-baptized. At the same time, he began to be spoken of as a spiritual relative of the latter, which led to a search for prestigious godparents, such as saints or sovereigns.

The Carolingians, anxious to reinforce the religious instruction and direction of the Christian people, put great stress, in their reflection on baptism, on the function of godparenthood, whose theological and institutional foundations they laid for centuries to come. In the first place, the properly liturgical role of the godparents, until then very little known, was clearly laid out. From now on solely to do with infant baptism, throughout the baptismal cycle they replaced the natural parents, who were disqualified by the carnal act of procreation. Thus there were those who, during the baptism proper, carried the *child and took the required commitments on his behalf. There were also those who clothed him in the white garment (later called "chrismal") that he would wear for the next week. Then, after the baptism, godparents were supposed to look after the religious instruction of their godchild. This role supposed a minimum of instruction and of moral qualities: the frequent mention of these requirements in 9th-c. *capitularies and conciliar canons shows very well that the reality must have been quite wide of the mark. It was also in the Carolingian period that the West worked out a real doctrine of spiritual parenthood – created by godparenthood – presented as a model of ideal parenthood, exempt from any carnal stain. It was just at this moment (8th c. at the latest) that a specific terminology of godparenthood, derived from the vocabulary of parenthood, appeared (*patrinus/patrina*; *filiolus/filiola*; *compater/commater*). To this spiritual parenthood were then applied, in an extended form, the rules already laid down by Justinian in the 6th c., which prohibited any matrimonial union between godparents of the same godchild, or between godparent and godchild, or between godchildren and the children of their godparents. This also led to allowing (late 9th c.) only a single pair of spiritual parents per child. This last prescription was very little observed, since spiritual parenthood in fact created bonds of solidarity – essential in that society – which people very soon sought to develop by multiplying the number of godparents and/or by choosing different godparents for the catechumenate, the baptism proper and the confirmation. Thus compaternity often became more important than godparenthood proper, *i.e.* the choice of the godparent could be made more in terms of the surplus of relatives it brought to the parents than by reason solely of the child's spiritual interests. The "political" godparenthoods practised by the *Carolingian and *Ottonian rulers are a good example of this.

The doctrine, if not the rules of practice, hardly evolved subsequently. At the most we discern some clarifications, reminders and retouches. If at first the principles were held to, the *scholastics (notably *Hugh of Saint-Victor) pushed Carolingian thought to its limit by making the godparents the actual authors of the new birth

The Lamb triumphant over the Beast.
From *Commentary on the Apocalypse* by Beatus of Liébana (fol 117 r°). 10th c. Library of the Escorial, Spain

Creation of Adam.
Relief from the casket of the relics of Isidore, dated 1063, from the Treasury of St Isidore, León.

of the one they presented for baptism and by reaffirming their function as guarantors. More concretely, the role of the godparent was reinforced by the custom, attested at any rate from the 10th c. (save in *Italy), that had him give his own name to his godchild, thus creating a veritable spiritual lineage. The importance of the social bonds created by compaternity ceaselessly gained ground and was expressed in the multiplication of godparents, against which the synodal *statutes of the 13th c. found it hard to struggle. The social advantages procured by the spiritual parenthood that resulted from godparenthood took on a particular prominence at the end of the Middle Ages. We observe at first that, nearly everywhere in the West, godparents were chosen from outside the natural relations; godparenthood was in effect supposed to extend *kinship, not limit it to corroborate blood ties. Meanwhile the number of godparents remained sometimes – despite prohibitions – high; as at *Florence, where people sought to have four, five or anything up to twenty godfathers – godmothers were in a minority – for their children, taken from outside the natural *family, in such a way as to reinforce the clientelism inherent in Florentine society. Mendicant *preaching denounced in vain this social drift of the institution of godparenthood. However this inflation was not general, and examples of godparenthood limited to a single couple are not rare outside Italy in the late Middle Ages. As for relations between godparents and godchildren, the picture is equally contrasting. At Florence again, godparents gave presents to the mother of their godchild, but took no further interest in them after the baptism had been celebrated. Elsewhere, the links between godparents and godchildren seem sometimes better preserved. Not that the former ensured, as they were supposed to, the religious instruction of the latter; but at least they remembered them at the time of their own *death, *e.g.* in the Toulousain, where godchildren figure in the *testaments of their godparents, admittedly for a modest sum, but at a place that made them privileged intercessors for the testator. Despite its drifts, godparentage thus remained an essential institution of Christian society at the end of the Middle Ages.

P. Niles, "Baptism and the Naming of Children in Late Medieval England", *Medieval Prosopography*, 3/1, Spring 1982, 95-107. – J. H. Lynch, *Godparents and Kinship in Early Medieval Europe*, Princeton (NJ), 1986. – L. Haas, "Social Connections between Parents and Godparents in Late Medieval Yorkshire", *Medieval Prosopography*, 10/1, Spring 1989, 1-21. – C. Klapisch-Zuber, *La Maison et le Nom. Stratégies et rituels dans l'Italie de la Renaissance*, Paris, 1990. – B. Jussen, *Patenschaft und Adoption im frühen Mittelalter. Künstliche Verwandtschaft als soziale Praxis*, Göttingen, 1991. – B. Jussen, "Le Parrainage à la fin du Moyen Âge. Savoir public, attentes théologiques et usages sociaux", *Annales*, 48, 1992, 467-502. – C. Maurel, "Prénomination et parenté baptismale du Moyen Âge à la Contre-Réforme. Modèles religieux et logiques familiales", *RHR*, 209, 1992, 393-412.

Michel Rubellin

**GOLD.** Fabulous *metal, fetish metal, gold performed two social functions in the Middle Ages: it was an instrument of exchange and also an object conferring prestige and power; hence its symbolic role was of the first importance.

In the same way as silver, but to a higher degree, gold was a medium of exchange: it enabled the acquisition of all goods, was the object of free gifts or the pay for services rendered, and manifested the bounty of a prince. The Western Middle Ages situated its provenance in the East, in a mythical Arabia, in the fabulous Colchis of the ancient Greeks or in regions close to the equator, because, according to the ideas of the time, heat favoured the birth of gold. In fact, the West had access to metal coming by caravan from Sudan to the shores of the Mediterranean, the resources of the mines of *Transylvania, but especially the profits of trade with the Byzantine and Muslim worlds, familiar with gold coin from the start of the Middle Ages, when it disappeared from the West under the *Merovingians. The pillage of *Constantinople by the crusaders in 1204, but especially the fabulous commercial profits obtained by the Italians, enabled the West to escape from the sterile hoarding previously practised and allowed a return to minting gold in the 13th century. The yellow metal now animated large-scale international *commerce, but also regional exchanges, and sometimes even the transactions of everyday life, at the end of the Middle Ages.

Social prestige was naturally linked to the possession of gold and the largesse that it permitted. The Byzantine emperors bought tranquillity from barbarian tribes at the price of gold; they recovered the metal by selling the products of Byzantine industry. They rewarded their officials by annually distributing purses filled with the yellow metal. It was the mark of power; it embellished the table (cups, vases, plate) and *clothing of kings, for whom fabrics woven with gold were a sign of excellence and *wealth; it adorned arms and even horses' harnesses. It enhanced *beauty and glorified valour; it was associated with victory, feasting, *love.

Gold also had an essential symbolic function. In medieval painting, it was synonymous with *spirituality. It expressed the splendour of the divine world, depicted the sky, aureoled the saints: the Byzantine *icon was not just the *image of a saint, but almost the living reality of a divine companionship which it invited humans to join. Gold symbolized a link with perfection, wealth and eternity; it was a veritable substitute for *immortality. It is hardly astonishing that it occupied a preponderant place in the alchemical corpus, since it was associated with political and economic power and also with the desire for immortality. Though *Christendom saw gold as an instrument of *charity, on the other hand it condemned the cupidity and *usury to which the yellow metal gave rise.

M. Bloch, "Le problème de l'or au Moyen Âge", *AHES*, 5, 1933, 1-34. – E. Fournial, *Histoire monétaire de l'Occident médiéval*, Paris, 1970. – *L'or au Moyen Âge (monnaie, métal, objets, symbole), Colloques du CUERMA*, Marseille, 1983. – J. Favier, *De l'or et des épices*, Paris, 1987.

Michel Balard

**GOLDEN HORDE.** A *Mongol khanate. In the inheritance of *Genghis Khān, the sons of his eldest son Juchi received the lands situated between Lake Balkhash and the Urals: the eldest, Orda, and the youngest, Cheïban, were given *ulus* later called the White Horde and the Blue Horde (from *ordu*, "encampment"); the second, Batu, cantonned in the west, between the Aral Sea and the Urals, increased his share of the conquests carried out under his direction (1236-1242): Cumania (Qipchaq), Bulgaria on the Volga (Great Bulgaria), and the tributary Russian principalities. He established his capital Saraï on the Volga and his *ulus* was called the "Golden Horde". But the Mongol manpower at his disposal, too weak to resume the conquest of Europe, was soon submerged in the Turkish element. His son Sartaq (1255-1256) had himself baptized; but his brother Berke (1257-1267), undoubtedly the son of a Muslim woman, embraced *Islam and made war on the khan of Persia in an attempt to take Azerbaijan from him. Christian influence became predominant once more with Toqtaï who, on his death (1312), is

*The Golden Legend* by Jacobus de Voragine, French translation by Jehan de Vignay, *c.*1480-1490. Paris, BNF (Ms fr. 244, fol. 1).

said to have been buried in the *Franciscan church of Saraï. It was with Özbäg (1312-1340) and especially Jani-bäg (1342-1357) that Islam prevailed. The former eliminated the Buddhist priests and forbade the ringing of *bells; the latter tried to take *Caffa (in *Crimea) from the Genoese. His failure permitted the Italian colonies to maintain themselves on the Sea of Azov (Tana) and the Black Sea coast.

The Islamization of the nomads put an end to the progress made by missionaries in *Tartaria aquilonia*, where the papacy had erected several *bishoprics and even, in 1362, an archbishopric of Saraï. An active *commerce had developed, participated in by Frankish or Armenian *merchants who went in search of *silks in *China. But in 1380 the grand duke of *Moscow, who was entrusted with the raising of tribute from the other Russian duchies, victoriously confronted Mamaï at *Kulikovo. He was soon brought back to obedience by Toqtamish, of the White Horde, who supplanted Batu's descendants and burned Moscow in 1382. *Timur invaded and ravaged his territories, including Saraï and Tana; but another descendant of Orda, Timur Qutlug, re-established himself there and in 1399 drove back the Lithuanians, who had tried to profit from the weakening of the khanate. The khanate broke up in the next century: khans made themselves independent in Crimea (*c.*1430), at Kazan (1445) and at Astrakhan (*c.*1466); the grand duke of Moscow *Ivan III freed himself from tribute in 1480. Saraï finally fell into the hands of the khan of Crimea in 1502.

P. Pelliot, *Notes sur l'histoire de la Horde d'Or*, L. Hambis (ed.), Paris, 1950. – B. Spuler, *Die goldene Horde*, Wiesbaden, 1965 (2nd ed.). – J. Richard, "La conversion de Berke et les débuts de l'islamisation de la Horde d'Or", *RESl*, 1967, 167-184. – J. Richard, *La papauté et les Missions d'Orient au Moyen Âge*, Rome, 1977. – C.J. Halperin, *Russia and the Golden Horde*, Bloomington, 1985. – D. DeWeese, *Islamization and Native Religion in the Golden Horde*, University Park (PA), 1994. – L. de Hartog, *Russia and the Mongol Yoke: the history of Russian principalities and the Golden Horde 1221-1502*, London, 1996.

Jean Richard

**GOLDEN LEGEND.** The *Legenda aurea* or *Golden Legend*, a hagiographical compilation completed in *c.*1265 by the Dominican *Jacobus de Voragine, was one of the most important monuments of Christian culture of the Middle Ages. Its circulation was enormous: more than 1000 *Latin manuscripts have survived; *translations into most of the vernacular languages appear in more than 500 manuscripts. This popularity bridged the gap of the *Renaissance (97 Latin incunabula). Instances of the text being used for the production of *images, in *preaching and even in *theology appear innumerable. And yet the text hardly seems new: the sanctoral seldom strays into the contemporary period; many chapters textually recopy a source or closely summarize an old source. This popularity can be explained by two major reasons: the totalizing character of the work and its suitability for various appropriations and transformations. In fact, the *Golden Legend* is presented as a synthetic compendium of the Christian religion presented in order of the *calendar, starting from the beginning of *Advent.

The original text comprises more than 150 Saints' Lives, each preceded by a symbolic *etymology, among which are intercalated some 30 chapters dedicated to the *feasts in celebration of *Christ, the Virgin and the great liturgical commemorations. The narrative, though very susceptible to the (Christian) marvellous, frequently gives way to doctrinal expositions, nourished by patristic citations. A long chapter on Pope Pelagius provides a veritable summary of ecclesiastical history. The *sanctoral manifests no regional preference; that is why the *Legend* could serve as a basis for numerous local *legendaries, thanks to a system of additions or grafts: in *c.*1290, it permitted the construction of the first English legendary, the *South English Legendary*, which kept its own autonomy (twenty per cent of the *legends come from Voragine). A Latin edition of 1470 had 448 chapters, instead of the original 180! Yet the redaction of the *Legend* was not an isolated phenomenon: it was part of a vast movement of lively Christian vulgarization early in the 13th c. in the newly created *mendicant orders. The "new legend" (*legenda nova*) of the *Dominicans, an abridged compilation of hagiographical narratives, allowed the friars to find material for *sermons on the saint of the day or to follow up the refectory *readings in the *convents. The first collection of this kind was drawn up by Jean de Mailly, a *cleric and then a Preacher, in two stages (1225-1230 and *c.*1243); later, the Dominican Bartholomew of Trent composed another abridgment in 1245. But only Voragine was able to attain the universality and the synthesis that were also being aimed at, at the same time, by the *Franciscan Haymo of Faversham, charged with working out a universal *Roman liturgy. The perfect functionality of the *Legend* was able to develop within the efficent Dominican network, characterised by strong centralization and great capillarity.

Jacobus de Voragine, *The Golden Legend: Readings on the Saints*, W. G. Ryan (ed.), Princeton (NJ), 1993 (2 vol.).

*The Lombard king Agilulf on his throne.* Fragment of a golden helmet from Valdinievole, 6th-7th c. Monza, Tesoro del Duomo.

A. Boureau, *La Légende dorée. Le système narratif de Jacques de Voragine (mort en 1298)*, Paris, 1984. – S. L. Reames, *The Legenda aurea*, Madison (WI), 1985. – B. Fleith, *Studien zur Uberlieferungsgeschichte der lateinischen Legenda Aurea*, Brussels, 1991.

Alain Boureau

**GOLDSMITHRY.** Goldsmithry is the art of enhancing the value of so-called precious metals. While in the modern period these metals are exclusively *gold and silver, it was not so in the Middle Ages. Then *liturgical objects and *reliquaries were frequently made of copper, whether gilded, *enamelled or just bare. Moreover, the distinction between goldsmithry and jewelry did not exist in the Middle Ages: the goldsmith habitually provided jewels, tableware and works intended to ornament churches. Texts regulating the profession of goldsmith are preserved for numerous towns. The earliest are those of *Venice (1233) and *Paris (1260). These texts mention a great variety of works provided by goldsmiths: religious and secular objects of all sorts, but also *seals or elements of horses' harness. These same regulations often give specific authorization to use less precious materials for religious works, and also sometimes mention the minimum content of gold and silver used as well as the obligation laid on the goldsmith to affix a hallmark: at first that of the town to which he belonged, then also his own. In France, the first text enjoining goldsmiths to strike their works with the mark of their town is an *ordinance of (1275). Letters patent of 1355 specify that goldsmiths must "*avoir poinçon à contre saing*". But these measures seem to have been only very progressively and partially applied.

The techniques used by medieval goldsmiths were very varied: formation by casting or hammering, decoration embossed in relief, engraved, chiselled or stamped, addition of filigrees or foliated scrolls enriched with various motifs, niello, brown glaze etc. One of the characteristics of medieval goldsmithry is incontestably the taste for enamelled decoration that allowed works to be enhanced with various colours and lent itself particularly well to narration. Numerous objects associate a great number of these techniques. The majority, moreover, were enriched with precious or semi-precious stones, or failing that with coloured *glass, which added to their brilliance.

The sole surviving work to describe the techniques used by goldsmiths in the Middle Ages is the *Schedula diversarum artium* of the monk *Theophilus, written in Lower Saxony in the first half of the 12th century. The writings of Benvenuto Cellini, a 16th-c. Florentine goldsmith, also contain precious information on certain techniques known earlier.

The diversity of forms was as great as that of techniques and types of decoration: royal or princely inventories of the 14th and 15th cc. describe a considerable number of pieces of extreme inventiveness, which the rare surviving works allow us only partially to perceive.

Theophilus, *The Various Arts: De Diversibus Artibus*, C. R. Dodwell (ed.), Oxford, 1986.

L. Lanel, *L'Orfèvrerie*, 1943 ("QSJ"). – J. M. Fritz, *Goldschmiedekunst der Gotik im Mitteleuropa*, Munich, 1982. – É. Taburet-Delahaye, *L'Orfèvrerie gothique – XIII$^{e}$-début XV$^{e}$ siècle – au musée de Cluny. Catalogue*, Paris, 1989.

Élisabeth Taburet-Delahaye

**GOLIARDS.** The very etymology of "Goliard" is disputed; does the word refer to *gula* ("gluttony"), to the giant Goliath, biblical symbol of *evil, or to a mythical poet named Golias? The name "goliards" was given to those *clerics who, abandoning their places because they had squandered their *prebends or been hit by disciplinary measures, wandered from town to town associating with groups of students; in some 13th-c. texts, goliards appear as clerics or students of depraved morals, threatened by the Church with the loss of their clerical status. But the term serves mainly to designate a current of medieval Latin *poetry that flourished especially in the 12th century.

Fictitiously attributed to "Golias" and his disciples, these were rhythmical poems, mainly in *Latin, often of fine literary craftsmanship and great freedom of versification: rhythm and regularity of stress progressively replaced quantity, leading up to the introduction of rhyme. These poems, which had illustrious antecedents in the Merovingian *Joca monachorum* and the *Cambridge Song Book*, developed hedonistic themes, sometimes in open opposition to Christian morality: *wine, play, free *love;

not without some secret bitterness, the Goliard sang of *youth, the joy of living, the gifts of nature, love of his home country.

But the goliardic poems were also satirical works that criticized, often virulently, the excessive *wealth of the Church (the *Evangelium secundum marcas argenti*), the vices of clerics, the arrogance of the powerful, the omnipotence of *money. Parody, *e.g.* of liturgical texts, was one of their favourite procedures.

Goliardic poetry also contained numerous references to ancient authors, notably Ovid. Brought together in collections, the best known being that of ms. Munich 4660 (the *Carmina Burana), some of these poems are anonymous, others have been more or less reliably attributed to known authors such as Hugh Primas (*c.*1093-*c.*1160), a professor of grammar in the *Orléans region, or the "Archpoet", a former medical student at *Salerno whose nickname was derived from his belonging to the entourage of the imperial archchancellor and archbishop of *Cologne, Rainald of Dassel (attested *c.*1130-1170).

Others, like Peter of Blois (*c.*1130-*c.*1200) or Gauthier of Châtillon (*c.*1135-*c.*1200), were scholars and professors who often also had prestigious ecclesiastical careers, and the goliardic poems represent only a small part of their work. Most of these works seem to come from *langue d'oïl* *France, from where they spread into *England and *Germany; *Italy had no goliardic poetry proper, but some late echoes such as Morando da Padova's *Vinum dulce gloriosum* or, in some verses, *Pietro della Vigna's satire *Vehementi nimium*.

The themes of goliardic poetry certainly evoke a climate of innovation widespread in the 12th c., with increased mobility, the development of the schools, the growing role of the monetary economy and the discovery of the feeling for nature; but it is hard to establish a precise sociology of the Goliards and, in many of them, inspiration seems to come as much from literary invention as from lived experience. However, the themes conveyed by this poetry were sufficiently audacious to arouse, in the next century, the Church's mistrust of those who continued to peddle it.

O. Dobiache-Rojdesvensky, *Les Poésies des goliards*, Paris, 1931. – H. Waddell, *The Wandering Scholars*, London, 1949 (7th ed.). – E. Massa, *Carmina Burana e altri canti della Goliarda medievale*, Rome, 1979. – *Love Lyrics from the Carmina Burana*, P.G. Walsh (ed.), Chapel Hill, 1993.

Jacques Verger

**GONZALO OF BERCEO (*c.*1198 - after 1264).** The first poet in the Castilian language whose name is known, Gonzalo, a *secular cleric, native of the village of Berceo in the Rioja, was educated at the abbey of *San Millán de la Cogolla, to which he remained attached all his life.

Berceo is the most perfect representative of the *mester de clerecía*, learned and clerical *poetry as opposed to the *mester de juglaría*, popular and secular poetry. The "métier of clergy" associated the use of the vernacular, necessary for the edification of "unlettered" believers, with the forms of learned prosody. Exclusively religious in content, Berceo's poems adopt the Alexandrian strophe of four (14-syllable) mono-rhymed lines called *cuaderna vía*. In this form, he wrote hagiographical accounts, Marian poems and two exegetical poems. But the poet incorporates in his learned poetry numerous traits of oral poetry and manifests a real talent as a storyteller, describing with equal spontaneity the daily life of the inhabitants of the Rioja and the irruption of the supernatural. A cleric, Berceo was also a "**jongleur* of God" or a "*jongleur* of saints".

*A New Berceo Manuscript*, B. Dutton (ed.), Exeter, 1982.

G. Giménez Resano, *El mester poético de Gonzalo de Berceo*, Logrono, 1976. – J.E. Keller, *Pious Brief Narrative in Medieval Castilian and Galician Verse: from Berceo to Alfonso X*, Lexington, 1978. – J. A. Ruiz Domínguez, *La historia de la salvación en la obra de Gonzalo de Berceo*, Riojanos, 1990.

Michel Zimmermann

**GOOD.** The conception of the good as developed in the Middle Ages was heavily marked by Plato, for whom the Good was the source and principle of everything, and by *Aristotle, for whom the good was what every being desired. This dual interpretation of the good, transcendent and immanent, gave rise to different currents of thought: the school of *Chartres on one hand, Thomism on the other. But *Thomas Aquinas too was marked by *Platonism and, in his reflection on the good, he made, as was his habit, a synthesis of different thoughts and thus envisaged all the meanings of the good: *ontological good, man's supreme Good, *i.e.* *beatitude, and moral good.

Here we will deal only with ontological good, good as a property of *being, which leads us to consider the relationship between good and *God and to reflect on the goodness of creatures. In the late Middle Ages, in 1442, *Eugenius IV's *bull *Cantate Domino*, which reiterated the condemnation of any form of Manicheeism, provided a solution to these problems, emphasizing that there are not two principles, but only one (so identifying God with the Good) and recalling that *creation is fundamentally good. But this was already the teaching of the *Fathers, whose full capacity had been shown by St Augustine, explaining that if God created, it was because he wanted to (*quia voluit*) and because he was good (*quia bonus*).

However, though the good was nearly always identified with being, before onto-theology existed the medievals put God above and beyond being. Thus, in the 9th c., *John Scotus Eriugena wrote in the *De divisione naturae* (I, 459 D): "We call God goodness, but properly speaking God is not goodness: for goodness is opposed to badness, so God will be more than good and more than goodness." Following *Dionysius the Areopagite, John Scotus makes clear that God surpasses every category including the Good, in which everything participates and which itself participates in nothing, being the Good in itself (622 B).

As source of *participation, the Good is identified with being, as the final *cause that has the property of diffusing itself. Thus the good is *diffusivum sui* according to Thomas Aquinas (*Summa theologiae*, I$^a$, q. 5, 19-20). God is even in the first good, He alone is good by essence (*Summa theologiae*, I$^a$, q. 6); in the *Trinity it is the *Holy Spirit that is the expression of goodness. As for creatures, they are good by *nature and by *participation, and it behoves them to choose to fulfil themselves.

For St Thomas, the good has a principle role and reflects the nature of God, while for other authors, like *Durand of Saint-Pourçain, the good is essentially relative: it expresses a relation of suitability, but it is no longer situated alongside being, and we begin to move away from the medieval conception of the good.

J. Pieper, *Die Wirklichkeit und das Gut*, Munich, 1963. – J.-P. Jossua, "L'axiome *bonum diffusiva sui* chez saint Thomas d'Aquin", *RevSR*, 40, 1966, 127-153.

Marie-Anne Vannier

**GOOD SHEPHERD.** From the mid 3rd to the late 4th c., the Shepherd (depiction of a young, beardless shepherd, alone or carrying a *lamb on his shoulders, holding a pail of milk, etc.) was, with the *Orans*, one of the favourite themes of Christian artists: thus it recurs 113 times in the catacomb paintings and often on sarcophagi. This success is explained by the fact that *Christ himself was called the Good Shepherd (Jn 10, 11), but it also stems from the fact that the image was already known to the Ancients, who saw in it the symbol of *philanthropia*. Hence the mere presence of a shepherd on a *tomb is not sufficient to determine the Christian faith of the deceased.

W.-N. Schumacher, *Hirt oder "Guter Hirt"?*, Rome-Fribourg-Vienna, 1977. – *La Bible et les saints: Guide iconographique*, Paris, 1990, 65-66.

Jean Guyon

**GORZE.** Situated 15 kilometres south-west of *Metz, the *abbey of Gorze was founded before 757 by Bishop *Chrodegang and received from the start the Rule of St *Benedict at the same time as it was closely attached to the episcopal see. The abbacy of this richly endowed monastery was monopolized in the 9th c. by the *bishops.

A first *reform was carried out in 863 by Bishop Adventius, a second in 934. This was due to a group of seven *clerics from Metz and Toul, supported by Bishop Adalbero I. With the support of Abbot Einold and its *provost, John of Vandières (whose *Vita* recounts this period), the abbey enjoyed great success and rapidly sent out some of its monks to restore neighbouring monasteries (Saint-Arnoul at Metz, Stavelot, Saint-Hubert in Ardenne). In the following decades, the reform successively affected the monasteries of the *diocese and bishopric of Metz, the whole of *Lotharingia and even some establishments outside the *Empire. Gorze had close relations with the movement of *Fleury-sur-Loire through the intermediary of Saint-Evre de Toul and the abbot of Saint-Clément, Cadroé; it was asked for help by the abbeys of *Ghent. The reform and expansion of Gorze took place simultaneously with those of *Brogne and Saint-Maximin at *Trier.

The revival rested on a strict application of the Rule, a regular *abbot coming from the ranks of the monks, and good relations with the ecclesiastical and lay authorities (king, duke). A network of relationships was created, but did not give rise to an *order. During the 11th c., the abbey, entrusted at one time to *William of Volpiano, abbot of Saint-Bénigne at *Dijon, continued to have influence and to provide abbots for the monasteries of *Lorraine and the Empire (*Siegburg, *Saxony, *Bavaria) but without creating a congregation. Its customs, whose text does not survive, were close to those of Fleury, but we do not know how far they formed an original whole. Having restored its temporality in 934-945, it enriched it and created *priories in the 11th and 12th cc., from *Champagne to the district of *Worms (Varangéville, Amel, Saint-Nicolas-de-Port, Apremont, Vanault-le-Châtel, Pfeddersheim). Its abbots kept aloof from the *Investiture Contest and began an inconspicuous life from the 12th c., after the abbacy of Theoduin, future *cardinal of Santa Rufina. Although it had had a place in the redaction of several hagiographical works in the 10th c., the abbey later ceased to be an intellectual centre, and its *library was already old-fashioned in the late 11th century. The bishop of Metz was able to draw on the resources of Gorze for his personal needs in the late 13th century.

From the 15th c., the abbey fell into *commendation, even belonging to a Borgia, then to members of the ducal house of Lorraine. Having given rise to the creation of a small monastic principality, the Terre-de-Gorze, around the abbey, it was considered pro-French, served as a garrison for troops and was finally destroyed while its dismantled temporality was used to endow the primatial *chapter of Nancy. All that remain are some modern buildings and the parish church, a former *collegiate church of the town.

F. Chaussier, *L'Abbaye de Gorze*, Metz, 1894. – J. Schneider, "Gorze", *DHGE*, 21, 1986. – *L'Abbaye de Gorze au Xe siècle*, Nancy, 1993. – A. Wagner, *L'Abbaye de Gorze au XIe siècle*, Nancy, 1993 (thesis).

Michel Parisse

**GOSCELIN (died *c.*1100).** A monk of Saint-Bertin at *Saint-Omer, Goscelin came to *England in *c.*1058 at the invitation of a compatriot, Bishop Herman of Wiltshire. Shortly after this patron's death (1078), Goscelin left the Wiltshire area and, during an itinerant phase, apparently visited Peterborough, Barking, Ely and *Ramsey, finally settling in *c.*1090 at St Augustine's, *Canterbury, where he died very early in the 12th century. Having probably already composed a *Vita* of St Amelberga at Saint-Bertin, Goscelin undertook many hagiographical commissions on the lives of English saints while in England. He also wrote a *Liber confortatorius* for Eva, an enclosed *anchoress and former *nun of Wilton Abbey.

C.H. Talbot, "The *Liber Confortatorius* of Goscelin of Saint-Bertin", *Analecta Monastica*, 37, 1955, 1-117. – F. Barlow, *The Life of King Edward who rests at Westminster*, Oxford, 1992, 133-149 (2nd ed.).

Rosalind C. Love

**GOSPELS, SYNOPTIC.** For the Middle Ages, the four Gospels formed a homogeneous whole; though commentaries on John tend to be doctrinally richer, it is difficult to study them separately. Due to their place in the liturgy and the importance for Christian thought of the themes expounded in them, the synoptic gospels (Matthew, Mark and Luke; the term is recent) played a major role in *preaching and *exegesis. The parables, repeated and expounded in *sermons aimed at the people, contributed to the formation of a Christian mentality modelled by its biblical inspiration (12th-15th c.). The narratives, also known through iconographical representations or the *theatre, were an important element in medieval culture.

Very early, exegetes were struck by the dissimilarities between the three synoptic gospels and John; "concordances of the gospels" were rapidly put together (Tatian, *Diatessaron*; Augustine, *De consensu evangelistarum*; Pseudo-Ammonius); for the Middle Ages, those of Zachary of Besançon (or Chrysopolitanus, O. Praem., † 1157); *Super unum ex quattuor* (of Pseudo-Ammonius); *Joachim of Fiore (?), *Tractatus super IV Evangelium*; *Peter Cantor, *Super Unum ex quattuor*; Jean *Gerson, *Unus ex quattuor*.

Commentaries generally gave a place to historical considerations and developed theological considerations. The main sources of medieval exegetes were Ambrose (Lk), Jerome (Mt), Augustine (*Quaestiones Evangeliorum*) and Pseudo-Chrysostom (*Opus imperfectum in Matthaeum*). *Gregory the Great's *XL Homilies on the Gospels* and the commentaries of *Bede (Mk, Lk) were often cited. Apart from those who commented on the whole *Bible, some 12th-c. authors gave *glosses (notably Bruno of Segni), but exegesis of the Gospels was of more interest to those of the 13th c.: *Alexander of Hales, *John of La Rochelle, Walter of Château-Thierry, *Albert the Great, Nicholas of Gorran and

*Peter John Olivi commented on the three synoptics. A particular place must be given to *Peter Comestor's *Historia evangelica*, St *Bonaventure's commentary on Luke and St *Thomas Aquinas's *Catena aurea*, which brought together many passages from the Greek *Fathers.

F. Stegmüller, *RBMA*, 2-5, 1950-1955. – B. Smalley, *The Gospels in the Schools, c.1100-c.1280*, London, 1985. – G. Conticello, "San Tommaso ed i Padri. . .", *AHDL*, 57, 1990, 31-92.

Gilbert Dahan

**GOTHIC ART.** To define Gothic art is a complex undertaking, so diverse is the geographical and chronological reality that it covers, from the mid 12th c. to the *Renaissance. It was precisely at the Renaissance that the term appeared, to express the disdain felt in those times for forms considered as barbarous as the Goths to whom their imaginary paternity was attributed.

Gothic art was born in the Île-de-France, a region that had previously been less conspicuous than others for its artistic inventiveness, but which then profited from the establishment of Capetian power and its centralizing tendencies, from peace and returning prosperity, in a place that became the commercial and intellectual crossroads of Europe. With the birth of the *university, a lay education developed, in which the desire for an encyclopedic knowledge replaced the former *meditation on sacred texts, *theology rediscovered Greek *logic and abandoned the monasteries for the debates of the *towns, and literature opened itself up to the vernacular tongue, *courtly love and *nature.

Among the initiators of the new artistic current was the *abbot of *Saint-Denis, *Suger, who found in his reading of Pseudo-*Dionysius the inspiration for an aesthetic marked by a fascination with *light and the hierarchy of forms. Thus in 1140 he rebuilt his *abbey church, breaking down the divisions between the radiating chapels, which threw the light of their windows onto the choir. This conquest of light was underpinned by architectural techniques ceaselessly perfected: intersecting ribs to lighten the vaults and better distribute the thrusts, the pointed arch, whose effectivenes was quickly seen by the rational spirit of the *Cistercians, flying buttresses, which allowed the hollowing out of walls and the opening up of large windows.

The first experiments were carried out in a fever of emulation: at *Sens, from 1140, the sexpartite vault was combined with alternation of strong and weak springing on the pillars, as at Notre-Dame, *Paris (1163); *Noyon (1150-1235) inaugurated a quadruple elevation – arcades, tribunes, blind arcading and high windows; at *Chartres (after 1194) the adoption of a quadripartite vaulting and the disappearance of tribunes marked a decisive step forward: it determined the structures of *Reims (finished in 1275) and *Amiens, which marked the apogee of the *rayonnant* style. But at *Beauvais in 1284 the collapse of the vaults of the choir punished the excesses of an ever more vertiginous search for verticality. After 1260 activity shifted towards the East (*Metz), *Normandy (Saint-Ouen at *Rouen), *Burgundy and the Midi (*Narbonne, *Clermont-Ferrand, *Limoges, *Toulouse). There, churches with a single nave were often preferred. After a period of latency, in the early 14th c. Gothic became *flamboyant*, with exuberant decoration on the outside and a new monumentality on the inside (Saint-Séverin and Saintt-Germain l'Auxerrois at Paris, basilica of Saint-Nicolas-de-Port).

These new architectural forms found varying expressions in Europe: *England, where intersecting ribbed vaults had become general from the late 11th c., at *Durham, then at Peterborough and *Gloucester, preferred compartmentalized plans to the French unification of interior volumes, while retaining at *Canterbury a model based on Sens. Soon its originality showed itself in forms called "decorated", at *Wells (from 1185) or *Lincoln (*c.*1192). The inventiveness of artists was deployed in spectacular systems of vaulting (transept crossing at Ely) which led in the mid 14th c. to the style called "curvilinear", whose effects of curves and counter-curves were later contradicted by the perpendicular style, which allowed the opening up of immense bays (Gloucester).

One of the first buildings of German Gothic was *Magdeburg cathedral (1209). *Opus francigenum* penetrated local traditions, asserted itself in the nave of *Strasbourg (1240) and found new formulations at *Cologne, Halberstadt or *Regensburg. The *Cistercian spirit had been determinative for the building of hall-churches, of which the nave of *Marburg is a fertile example, and which was the manifestation of German originality: there, in an edifice of rectangular plan, without ambulatory or transept, the central body and side-aisles culminate at the same height.

In *Spain, Gothic was at first indebted to France, as at *Toledo, *Burgos or *León. But it asserted its autonomy in the choice of volumes simplified with the help of single naves.

In *Italy, the influence of the *mendicant orders determined the development of Gothic architecture, as in the upper basilica at *Assisi (consecrated in 1253) and the Umbrian area generally, though *Romanesque resistance was still vigorously manifested, as at *Siena cathedral or at Sant'Antonio in *Padua (1236-1270). In Italy, architectural works in the pure Gothic style were rare and later than French models; *Cistercian architecture had better luck, as in the abbeys of *Fossanova, *Casamari and San Galgano.

These new definitions of space had enormous consequences for decoration. The window, which had the complex task of illuminating as well as decorating, supplanted mural *painting. *Stained glass became a major art which, in the 13th c., conditioned the graphic and chromatic choices of the other media. After the success, *e.g.* at Chartres in *c.*1200, of bays divided into a multitude of historiated panels, and then the alternation of tall coloured figures standing out on a grisaille background (Saint-Urbain at *Troyes, *c.*1270), the evolution of architecture led in the 14th c. to the employment of silvered yellow and engraved *glass, which allowed subtle colour harmonies.

One of the most obvious manifestations of the Gothic spirit can be seen in the *ambo of *Klosterneuburg (1181), where *Nicholas of Verdun renewed in *enamel the antique forms of deep, supple draperies, easy movements and clear logical structures, translating an erudite and systematically organised thought. More than other arts, that of *goldsmiths' work served the taste of a society that was becoming courteous and mannerist (**châsse* of St Taurinus at *Évreux, 1240-55), before being renewed by the technique of *cloisonné* enamel on *gold and of translucent enamels (*corporal of Bolsena in *Orvieto cathedral).

*Illumination continued to attract the most prestigious *artists. The *crusades gave them a better knowledge of the Byzantine style which nourished the renaissance of the 1200s, *e.g.* in the *Psalter painted for Queen Ingeborg. The precise and mannered drawing style of the time of *Louis IX contrasts with the harsher forms of German painters, on whom the *Romanesque heritage left a lasting mark. Italian artists preferred painting on wood and in *fresco, rather than illumination. They displayed their autonomy from the time of *Cimabue and especially *Giotto (1266-1337), who freed

Abbey church of Saint-Denis. Vaulting of the ambulatory, 1140-1145.

himself from Byzantine influence to rediscover the values of Latin monumentality: his taste for architectural and natural spaces, conveyed on a simplified palette, and his knowledge of bodies and faces combined with the *Franciscan spirit to announce a new *humanism. This spectacular Italian renaissance fertilized the art of Europe when Jean *Pucelle borrowed its perspective, or when Simone *Martini and Matteo Giovanetti went to *Avignon to work on the decorations of the papal *palace. It was then that the conditions for an international style came together: from Paris to Prague, from Flanders to Spain, an ever more realistic vision of life led to the emergence of Flemish art, in which devotion and the expression of the true was served by the technique of oil painting, where the superimposition of coats of transparent varnish undertook to make the inner world glow. Thus the brothers *van Eyck, Rogier *van der Weyden and Hans *Memling, who, at the dawn of the *Renaissance, preceded Dürer's attempted synthesis of Nordic attention to minute detail and the Italian sense of space.

The evolution of sculpture led from the statue-columns of the first Gothic portals, where Biblical heroes were set in architectural monumentality, to the bourgeois *portraits of the waning Middle Ages. It is the history of a patient emancipation, helped by the observation of antique examples, from architecture and from a mystique of eternity. From the childish grace of the *angels who awaken the Virgin on the portal of *Senlis (1175-85) to the tragic power of the *prophets who surround Klaus *Sluter's "Well of Moses" at *Dijon, it was humanity that awoke in stone. And this stone was now able to express the sweetness of life, and above all the sadness of *death: because it was to the sculptor more than to other artists that funerary art, so important in that age obsessed by suffering and death, was entrusted.

W. Sauerländer, *La Sculpture gothique en France, 1140-1270*, Paris, 1972. –A. Erlande-Brandenburg, *L'Art gothique*, Paris, 1983. – L. Grodecki, A. Prache, R. Recht, *Gothic Architecture*, London, 1986. – A. Erlande-Brandenburg, *La Conquête de l'Europe*, Paris, 1987. – R. Recht, A. Châtelet, *Automne et Renouveau*, Paris, 1988. – W. Sauerländer, *Le Siècle des cathédrales, 1140-1260*, Paris, 1989. – M. Camille, *The Gothic Idol: Ideology and Image-Making in Medieval Art*, Cambridge, 1991.

Colette Deremble

**GOTHIC SCULPTURE.** Northern France had not ignored sculpture in the *Romanesque period: its workshops had produced capitals decorated with foliage or animals, but rarely with the human figure, and the great sculpted tympanum had remained unknown there. It was in this region that Gothic art came into being, and from its beginning sculpted works of very high quality appeared, notably on the façade of *Saint-Denis. What still exists of the masterpieces produced by these northern provinces of France before the end of the 13th c. is considerable, despite important losses caused by revolutionary vandalism. In all this output, sculpture was strictly subordinated to *architecture: after the death of *Louis IX, profound changes took place.

The Gothic sculptors of the 12th c. naturally took up of their own accord the tradition that aimed to expound for Christians, on church façades, the great themes of their faith. The multiplication of portals on western and transept façades allowed them to broaden their perspectives and aim to present a coherent and synthetic doctrinal whole; though it was really only at *Chartres and *Amiens that this aim could be realized, since elsewhere the programmes were disturbed by the fact that it was necessary to re-use elements initially provided for earlier programmes (thus at *Paris or *Reims). Each portal was deeper than it had been before: it included a tympanum that provided the central theme; on its vast surface, the single scene of the Romanesque period was replaced by rows of superimposed scenes in which multitudes of chararacters were lined up: the legibility of the whole lost a great deal. The multiplication of arch mouldings allowed the main theme to be supplemented and enriched by statuettes often sheltered under canopies. For the embrasures, the Gothic masters at first followed the *Romanesque form of ressauts with reflex angles in which were lodged columns associated with statues (Saint-Denis, Chartres. . .); then the backgrounds became smooth, the statues, still associated with columns, more autonomous, their bodies more natural, their feet resting on small consoles while small canopies crowned their heads. Beneath these statues, the bases were ornamented with complementary scenes (*Senlis, *Amiens) or geometrical decorations inspired by Antiquity (Mantes, *Rouen), or even with hangings evoking those with which façades were covered on feast days. Very quickly too, programmes overflowed this traditional framework and occupied the buttresses both on the façade (Amiens) and on the side elevations (Reims). Enthusiasm for the human figure meant that statues were also associated with columns on *cloister supports (Châlons) or at the entrances to *chapter houses (Boscherville, *Cambrai). By contrast, the historiated capital was replaced by more or less realistic foliage. Soon, the gables encasing the portals were also enriched by sculptures (*Laon) and the great iconographical themes were moved onto these when, to improve the internal lighting of the nave, the traditional historiated tympanum of the portal was replaced by a glazed tympanum.

Romanesque tympana had mainly been dedicated to apocalyptic themes. In the Gothic period, *Christ surrounded by the *tetramorph is hardly found except at Chartres and Saint-Loup-de-Naud, while the *Ascension appears only at Chartres and Étampes. Everywhere else, starting with Saint-Denis, the *Last Judgment is retained, but in its Gothic version: Christ has conquered death, and the instruments of the *Passion are the trophies of this victory; the Apostles are no longer the Judge's assessors, they have descended to the embrasures as witnesses and kneel as intercessors alongside Christ, the Virgin and St John; on the trumeau, Christ the redeemer treads on the asp and the basilisk; the wise and foolish virgins and the combat of *virtues and *vices remind men that they have the freedom to accept or refuse the benefits of Christ's sacrifice. The 12th c. was a great Marian century; traditionally, the Virgin offered her son, seated frontally on her knees, for the adoration of the *Magi or the faithful (Chartres and Paris). But rapidly another theme was substituted for this; since the Virgin was not soiled by *sin, she could not suffer the *death that was its consequence. At Byzantium, Christ came himself to gather his mother's *soul. In the West, scenes of the *Dormition were associated with scenes of the *Assumption to *heaven by *angels and the Coronation by Christ himself; this theme, appearing in *c.*1170 at Senlis and Cambrai, was followed by most of the great Gothic façades. Their third portal was often devoted to the saints of the *diocese. However, façades presenting a coherent iconographical programme are rare, with the exception of Amiens and Chartres.

From 1140 to 1270, the style evolved considerably. To begin with, *artists borrowed from other disciplines like *goldsmithry and *illumination; then gradually sculpture acquired real autonomy and became capable of influencing other artistic expressions. From the start it sought to observe *nature, the anatomical reality of bodies and the psychology of the persons represented; this was because *creation proved the existence of *God. The hieratic style of the royal portals of Chartres and Saint-Denis were succeeded by that of Senlis, full of life, and that of the antiquizing workshops of the end of the century at Laon and *Sens. Very soon however, at Paris, another tendency asserted itself: that of immobile characters, impassible and clothed in garments with broad folds falling vertically. After 1240, the court style characterised by smiles, almond eyes and undulating locks and moustaches imposed itself in the workshops of Paris and Reims (the Smiling Angel).

After the death of St *Louis, sculpture became more autonomous and less monumental and, in liaison with the evolution of religious mentalities, iconographical themes were renewed. Though great portals were still executed, they became more narrative and their legibility suffered greatly (Rouen). The isolated statue spread to the interior of buildings; apostolic processions clung to piers as at *Jumièges, devotional statues multiplied; Virgins standing with the weight on one leg (the "Gothic slouch"), graciously holding the Child who played with a rabbit, a bunch of grapes or the clasp of his mother's garment, multiplied to satisy the refined taste of the clientele. But art also had to take part in the glorification of the ruler, symbol of the *State; at Vincennes as at the Louvre, the royal family was everywhere commemorated by statues, the language of the emblem appeared. The funerary statue too took part in this exaltation of the *monarchy. The idealized faces of previous decades were replaced by genuine *portraits of the deceased (*Beauneveu's *Gisant de Charles V*). The misfortunes of the time (war, *epidemics, *famine) meant that death became a subject of anguish. Instead of the idealized dead person lying on his gravestone as he would appear on the day of *resurrection, there was the horror of the degradation of the flesh (*tomb of Cardinal La Grange at *Avignon); the weepers who surround the monument recall the sorrow expressed during the *funeral procession (tombs of the dukes of *Burgundy). In the last centuries of the Middle Ages, this very fear of the misfortunes of the time multiplied devotional statues, including those of the anti-plague saints *Roch and Sebastian; this also explains the vogue of themes linked to Christ's death: Christ in bonds, Crucifixion, Deposition from the Cross, Virgins of pity, Entombments (Chaource, Saint-Mihiel). These subjects were translated into stone and into wood. The taste of the time for miniaturization explains the vogue for great *altarpieces in which all the episodes of the *Passion were minutely recounted. Produced all over the place, these works were sometimes the object of a veritable export industry (*Brabant).

The sculpture of the *cathedrals, intimately linked to architecture, was succeeded at the end of the Middle Ages by a more varied output, with renewed themes, in which realism replaced idealization. The new conditions of production explain why humble rural churches could house great works of art at this time.

W. Sauerlander, *La Sculpture gothique en France, 1140-1270*, Paris, 1972. – *Le Monde gothique*, Paris, 1987-1989 (3 vol.; "Univers des Formes"). – P. Williamson, *Northern Gothic Sculpture, 1200-1400*, London, 1988. – P. G. Lindley, *Gothic to Renaissance: Essays on Sculpture in England*, Stamford, 1995. – W. H. Forsyth, *The Pietà in French Late Gothic Sculpture*, New York, 1995. – P. Williamson, *Gothic Sculpture, 1140-1300*, New Haven, 1995.

Jacques Thiébaut

**GOTLAND.** From the *Viking period, this great Baltic island was a tributary territory of *Sweden, but in the Middle Ages it enjoyed wide autonomy. The local sources, *Gutasaga* (*Saga of the Gotlanders) and *Gutalagen* (Law of the Gotlanders), insist on the free consent of links with Sweden. In 1285, the annual tribute was transformed into an obligatory tax; nevertheless Gotland remained an oligarchical republic of peasant proprietors whose Assembly (*aldra manna samtalan*) dispensed justice. The king of Sweden collected no share of the fines and kept no representatives on the island, where he had no estate. After *conversion in the 11th c., Gotland was attached to the *diocese of *Linköping, but the *bishop's powers there were limited. The great density of *parishes (some 90) indicates that the *Eigenkirche* system was very widespread there.

Gotland's wealth is explained by its important commercial role in the Baltic, up to the 14th century. At *Novgorod, the Gotlanders possessed a counter (*Gotenhof*) and a church (St Óláfr), attested in the 11th century. In 1161, *Henry the Lion renewed the privileges granted to the Gotland *merchants by the Emperor *Lothar III, and a community of German merchants was established in the island, at Visby, which became the embryo of the *Hanse. The influence of Visby lasted just over a century, then *Lübeck and also *Riga eclipsed it. The civil war between Visby and the inhabitants of the island (1288) weakened the position of Gotland, victim in 1361 of the Danish conquest during which Valdemar Atterdag crushed the army of Gotland *peasants. In the late 14th c., the exactions of the Vitalian pirates led to the occupation of Gotland by the *Teutonic Order from 1398 to 1407. The island later came back under Danish rule and the efforts of Sweden to conquer it remained vain until 1645.

A. Andersson, *L'Art scandinave*, 2, Saint-Léger-Vauban, 1968, 127-141 ("La Nuit des temps"). – H. Yrwing, *Gotlands medeltid*, Visby, 1978. – H. Yrwing, *Visby. Hansestad på Gotland*, Stockholm, 1986. – E. Nylen, *Stones, Ships and Symbols: the Picture Stones of Gotland*, Stockholm, 1988. – T. Gannholm, *Gutarnas historia*, Stånga, 1990.

Jean-Marie Maillefer

**GOTTFRIED VON STRASSBURG (13th c.).** In the late 12th c., the theme of fatal *love was reproduced in the various English and French versions of the story of Tristan and Iseult. Gottfried took it up early in the 13th c. (*c.*1210-1220) and adapted it for German court society. He is known only through his work; he offers the originality of sticking to the model for the theme and multiplying inventions to modify certain episodes; he favours the love story to the detriment of warlike actions.

Gottfried von Strassburg, *Tristan*, A. T. Hatto (tr.), Harmondsworth, 1960. – Gotfried von Strassburg, *Tristan und Isold*, F. Ranke (ed.), Dublin, 1967. – Gottfried de Strasbourg, *Tristan et Iseut*, D. Buschinger (tr.), J.-M. Pastré (tr.), Göppingen, 1980 (Fr. tr.).

*Tristan et Iseut, mythe européen et mondial*, Göttingen, 1987. – *Gottfried von Strassburg and the Medieval Tristan Legend*, A. Stevens (ed.), R. Wisbey (ed.), Cambridge, 1990. – M. Chinca, *Gottfried von Strassburg, Tristan*, Cambridge, 1997.

Michel Parisse

**GÖTTWEIG.** A Benedictine *abbey near Krems in Lower Austria, founded in several phases from 1070 by Bishop Altman of Passau (1065-1091). The monastery, richly endowed with possessions in Lower and Upper Austria as well as *Bavaria, was occupied by regular *canons. From before 1094, the Rule of St *Benedict was adopted there and it enjoyed papal protection from 1098. Göttweig's medieval cultural and economic apogee was in the 12th century. The *priors often became *abbots to neighbouring monasteries. The **scriptorium* had a great reputation; historical works were written there, notably the account of the election of *Lothar III in 1125 and the *Vita* of the founder, very interesting in content, and "Traditionum codices". Material and spiritual difficulties appeared in the 13th c., but were overcome after the *exemption from the episcopal authority of *Passau in 1401 and the adoption of the reform of *Melk. The medieval conventual buildings disappeared when the abbey was rebuilt in the baroque style.

G. M. Lechner, *Stift Göttweig und seine Kunstschatze*, Vienna, 1983. – *900 Jahre Stift Göttweig 1083-1983*, Vienna, 1983 (exhibition catalogue). – G. Hödl, "Göttweig im Mittelalter und in der frühen Neuzeit", *SMBO* 94, 1983, 1-231. – W. Telesko, *Göttweiger Buchmalerei des 12. Jhs.*, Augsburg, 1995.

Werner Maleczek

**GOYIM.** Hebrew term meaning "peoples" (singular *goy*), equivalent to "gentiles", then designating non-Jews. It was applied in *rabbinic literature to those among whom the *Jews lived. At the disputation of Paris in 1240, the term led to dispute: the accusers of Talmudic literature thought the term specifically designated Christians, with a pejorative connotation. In fact, in the *Talmud it designates both non-Jews and more specifically pagans (*e.g.* the Romans). This *controversy was pursued until the end of the Middle Ages: in many *Hebrew manuscripts, the word *goy* (or the plural *goyim*) has been crossed out by the censor.

I. Loeb, "La Controverse de 1240 sur le Talmud", *REJ*, 1, 1880, 257-259. – J. Katz, *Exclusiveness and Tolerance*, Oxford, 1961.

Gilbert Dahan

**GRACE.** The term "grace", which designates the gift of the *Holy Spirit necessary for man to obtain *salvation, designates in itself the gratuitous character of this divine action. Already in the New Testament with St *Paul, but still more in St Augustine's controversies with Pelagius, the first Christian centuries were marked by bitter debates on the relationship between this gift of *God and human capacities, between the action of the *Holy Spirit and *man's efforts.

These debates on the difficult division between gratuity and *merit apropos of salvation were continued during the Middle Ages. There we find the heirs of the different protagonists of the early centuries. Some, like William of *Ockham, followed Pelagius in affirming the determinative role of the human *will in the process of salvation. Others, like *Bonaventure, followed Augustine and insisted on God's gift. *Thomas Aquinas sought to make a synthesis by basing his theology of grace on his *Aristotelian approach to *virtue and *habitūs*. Grace, like moral law, is an exterior principle of human acts. Like *habitūs*, it is apt to render man capable of doing good. In this, it perfects and heals a human nature limited and wounded by *sin.

Apart from this debate on the distinction between *nature and grace, we must equally emphasize St Thomas's position in the history of *theology apropos of the place he assigns to grace in the *Summa*. The treatise on grace is integrated into the *prima secundae*, *i.e.* moral theology. The most original point of this integration of grace into moral reflection is the treatise on the new law, in which St Thomas states that, in the new covenant, the new law is "the grace of the Holy Spirit given to Christ's faithful" ($I^{a}$ $II^{ae}$, q. 106, a. 1). Gradually, the theologians of the next generations disconnected grace from the intimate links it had had with the other dimensions of morality, particularly law and the virtues, so as to fit it into treatises on dogmatic theology.

This set of theological debates was resumed with particular keenness at the time of the Reformation. To understand its complexity in the 16th c., it is important to perceive the diversity of Christian approaches to this question in the previous centuries. The distinctions made by the *scholastics were recapitulated in the decree of the 6th session of the council of Trent on *justification.

Thomas Aquinas, *Summa theologiae*, $I^{a}$ $II^{ae}$, q. 106-114.

J. Van Der Meersch, "Grâce", *DThC*, 6, 1924, 1554-1687.

Jean-Marie Gueullette

**GRADUAL.** The chant of the gradual belonged to the category of chants of the proper of the *mass, of which it was the earliest. Its text and melody varied from one feast to another. In the celebration of mass, it was performed just after the first *reading, the epistle, by the soloist. He did not mount to the summit of the *ambo, a place reserved for the proclamation of the Gospel, but to an intermediate step, the *gradus*, whence the chant took its name. Its content consisted of a gradual-response, often a *psalm, and its accompanying *verse. The gradual also had the function of introducing the chant of the *Alleluia* which preceded the reading of the gospel.

R.-J. Hesbert, "Le graduel. Chant responsorial", *EL*, 95, 1981, 316-350. – A. Ekenberg, *Cur cantatur? Die Funktion des liturgischen Gesanges nach den Autoren der Karolingerzeit*, Stockholm, 1987, 61-68.

Éric Palazzo

**GRAIL.** At the centre of the silent procession that, in *Chrétien de Troyes's *Conte du Graal*, passes before the feasters in the castle of the Fisher King, walks a young girl carrying a "graal". Though not frequent, the term is not exceptional in the Middle Ages: it designates a hollow dish, in which meat or fish could be put. So the object is not incongruous in a room where people eat, but several elements combine to surround it with mystery. This dish is not intended for the feasters present; it is solemnly carried: the young girl who holds it is surrounded by young people who provide light with candlesticks; it is preceded by a young man who carries a white lance whose point lets fall a drop of blood, constantly renewed; finally the Grail is made of precious material, *gold enriched with precious stones, and spreads such clarity that it eclipses the light of the candles. This object, for Chrétien, is the occasion for a decisive question (who is served with the dish?), but it is already connected with the Christian *mystery, since it contains a *host, mystical nourishment intended for the Fisher King's father. With *Wolfram von Eschenbach and his *Parzival*, the Grail becomes marvellous: a stone with prodigious virtues, it takes its power from a host laid on it every Good Friday. A first synthesis is made here between Celtic tradition – the talisman of abundance, which heals and gives food and drink at will – and Christian conceptions. But the choice of the magical stone poses a problem, since it proposes a double origin for the Grail's virtue.

Robert de Boron, in the late 12th c., gave a decisive orientation to the representation of the Grail by making it a sacred object, linked to the *Passion and death of *Christ. For Robert, the Grail is a *vessel* in which Christ offered the Holy Thursday sacrifice and in which Joseph of Arimathea later collected the blood flowing from Jesus' *wounds at the time of the descent from the cross. A Christian relic, before which the Fisher King bows respectfully when the procession passes, it is also the emblem of a genealogy both carnal and mystical linking the Grail hero to the witness of the mystery of the Incarnation and *Redemption, Joseph of Arimathea. It is in fact Joseph's descendants – he left Palestine and came to Britain to evangelize the country – who are called to be the guardians of the Grail. In the *Queste del saint Graal*, penultimate part of the prose **Lancelot-Graal* *romance (1220), the mystical evolution of the conception of the Grail is pushed to its limit, without disavowing its Celtic origins: the Grail spreads secular nourishment and delicious perfumes around itself, but it is likened to the *chalice of the *mass and allows the heroes of the quest to see the mystery of *Transubstantiation; Galahad, the purest, is allowed to approach in *ecstasy the *contemplation of the divine.

*The High History of the Holy Grail*, S. Evans (ed.), Cambridge. – La *Queste del Saint Graal*, A. Pauphilet (ed.), Paris, 1967 (*CFMA*, 33). – *The Quest of the Holy Grail*, P. M. Matarasso (tr.), Harmondsworth, 1969. – Wolfram von Eschenbach, *Parzival*, Harmondsworth, 1980. – Chrétien de Troyes, *The Story of the Grail*, New York, 1990.

*Lumière du Graal, Cahiers du Sud*, Paris, 1951. – J. Frappier, *Chrétien de Troyes et le mythe du Graal*, Paris, 1972. – J. Frappier, *La Légende du Graal: origine et évolution*, *GRLMA*, 4, 1979, 197-218. – C. Mela, *La Reine et le Graal*, Paris, 1984. – A. Groos, *Romancing the Grail*, Ithaca (NY), 1995.

François Suard

**GRAMMAR.** Medieval grammar had as its primary aim the oral and written teaching of *Latin, language of the Church. First developed in the British Isles, grammar later established itself on the soil of the former Gaul, around *Charlemagne. At this same time the *classics were rediscovered, which aroused varied reactions among the lettered. The grammarian *Smaragdus tried, in his commentary on Donatus, to replace classical examples with examples taken from the *Bible.

*Grammar.* Sculpture of the royal portal (right bay) of Chartres cathedral, 12th c.

The turn of the 11th-12th cc. was an important moment in that it saw the development of a new type of grammar, more theoretical than pedagogical in orientation. In their commentaries on Priscian's *Institutiones grammaticales*, grammarians, who knew *logic well, introduced new reflections, on the causes of the invention of the parts of speech, on meaning and reference, even on the form that grammatical definitions should take. In these commentaries – of which the most important are the anonymous *Glosulae super Priscianum* (late 11th c.), the *Glosae* of *William of Conches (in two redactions, *c.*1230 and *c.*1240) and Peter Helias's *Summa super*

*Priscianum* (*c.*1240) – were introduced new notions that would persist in the grammatical tradition, such as those of subject (*subjectum*, *suppositum*) and predicate (*praedicatum*, *appositum*), antecedent or government (*regimen*). Interferences between grammar, logic and *theology were a characteristic of the period, as witness the current that developed around *Gilbert of Poitiers.

The second half of the 12th c. saw the appearance of independent treatises, oriented more towards syntax than towards the semantic questions that had occupied the grammarians of the previous period. At the end of the century and in the early 13th were composed two versified grammars, Alexander of Villedieu's *Doctrinale* and Évrard of Béthune's *Grecismus*. Normative in character, setting out rules and paradigms, they would be used in *schools and *universities until the 15th c., giving rise to numerous commentaries.

With the creation of universities, grammar in the 13th c. became one of the materials of the programme of the arts *faculty, alongside *logic and *philosophy. It then moved away from the teaching of the classics, except in certain centres such as *Orléans, and was oriented towards a more theoretical approach, starting from commentaries or sophismatical *disputations (argued discussions taking a difficult example as starting-point). Philosophical questions (on the status of grammar as a *science, on the nature of its method, of its principles, etc.) accompanied properly grammatical formulations, mainly on linguistic categories (with the new notion of "mode of signifying") and on syntax (see *Robert Kilwardby, *Roger Bacon, *Boethius of Dacia, Raoul le Breton).

J. N. Miner, *The Grammar Schools of Medieval England*, Montreal, 1990. – *The Teaching of Grammar in Late Medieval England*, C.R. Bland (ed.), Woodbridge, 1991. – A. de Libera, I. Rosier, "La pensée linguistique médiévale", *Histoire des idées linguistiques*, S. Auroux (ed.), Liège, 1992 ("Histoire des idées linguistiques", 2). . – V. Law, *The Insular Latin Grammarians*, Woodbridge, 1992. – I. Rosier, *La parole comme acte. Sur la grammaire et la sémantique au XIIIe siècle*, Paris, 1994. – V. Law, *Grammar and Grammarians in the Early Middle Ages*, London, 1997.

Irène Rosier

**GRANADA.** The history of Christian Granada (Illiberis or Elvira up to the 11th c., which was an episcopal see) was, more than any other city of al-Andalus (Andalusia), that of the *Mozarabs: the Christians of the city and the Genil valley remained under Muslim rule for 781 years, from 711 to 1492. Their history, often described but little known, can be written in two ways.

The first accompanies the slow movement of Mozarab decline from the persecutions of the 9th c. – especially at *Cordova, but also at Granada – up to the sombre period of the *Almoravid and *Almohad dynasties. After the failure of the siege of the city by Alfonso I of *Aragon early in 1126, the Mozarabs who did not return with him to *Saragossa were exiled to Meknès and Salé in accordance with the **fatwā* of the grand *cadi of Cordova, Abū l-Walīd b. Rushd. Their representative, the *kūmis*, was suppressed, and those who remained formed from now on a community of peasants "who were long habituated to humiliation and contempt". The suppression of the episcopal framework of al-Andalus under the Almohads completed the dislocation of the community. Finally, the Nasrid period (1238-1492) merely accelerated its decline, with the influx of Muslims forced back by the *Reconquista* into the last Muslim enclave in the Peninsula and the unfortunate missionary attempts ending in a number of executions (Pedro Pascual in 1300; J. de Cetina and P. de Dueñas in 1397). At this time, the Christian community was essentially formed of birds of passage such as *merchants, well received, and mercenaries, and slaves whom the charitable orders came to redeem.

The few traces of the Mozarabic history of Elvira-Granada, perhaps less glorious than that of the city's *Jews, impel us, despite the indications given earlier, not to consider their position solely from the angle of a slow decomposition. The Mozarabs of Granada, probably because of their social and economic difficulties, showed a spirit of resistance that brings out their relative importance and their cohesion. They helped Ibn Hafsūn in his revolt of the 9th-10th centuries. Again, it was their representative, Ibn al-Qallās, who appealed to the king of Aragon in 1125-1126 to take possession of the town. In 1162, they formed a militia with the Jews to resist the Almohad troops. The Mozarab group of Granada was also distinguished by its social cohesion in the city, occupying the quarter of the present *parish of San Cecilio and in the Vega where they were grouped around numerous churches. The Christians of Granada seem to have paid dearly for their spirit of initiative from the 12th c., but during the 10th and 11th cc. they formed one of the rare Mozarab communities, with those of Cordova and *Toledo, to have shown signs of vigour.

R. Arié, *L'Espagne musulmane au temps des Nasrides*, Paris, 1973, 314-328. – V. Lagardère, "Communautés mozarabes et pouvoir almoravide", *StIsl*, 67, 1988, 99-119. – P. Guichard, V. Lagardère, "La vie sociale et économique de l'Espagne musulmane aux XIe et XIIe siècles à travers les fatwās du Miyār d'al-Wansharīshī", *Mélanges de la Casa de Velásquez*, Paris, 1990, 197-236.

Christophe Picard

**GRANDMONT.** It was at Grandmont, some leagues north of *Limoges, that clerical and lay disciples of the hermit *Stephen of Muret († 1124) established themselves in full independence. They wrote down the teachings of their master, inspired by the Gospel and *Gregory the Great, a writing that has survived. The next two generations systematized the usages and principles of the founder by attributing to him a rule that was clearly distinct from the canonical and monastic practices of the time. Not only were the brothers forbidden the charges and profits of those churches which it was then being made a duty for the *laity to disseize themselves of, but they had to be content to live on the products of a modest cleared enclosure and occasional *alms, to the exclusion of productive land, livestock that might annoy neighbours, fixed external revenues and even written titles to defend any right in law. In case of want, they begged on the roads or resorted to the *bishop. The Rule of Grandmont was a sort of manual for evangelical groups wishing to settle in the woods, which were the *desert of the Latin West.

The formula enjoyed rapid success in the 12th c. in a good hundred "*cells" or small monasteries of identical model, from *Normandy to *Provence, from *Aquitaine to *Champagne. But clergy and *laity lived there on an equal footing, except in the case of the liturgy, and this situation became less acceptable to the former as the latter came to be called **conversi* as among other religious. A first crisis failed to end a schism between the establishments of the Plantagenet domain and those of the Capetian domain and Champagne. The apostolic see restored order in 1189 by canonizing the founder and textually approving the Rule.

All through the 13th c., this same apostolic see remedied other crises by amending the excesses of the Rule, and endowing the order with institutions tested elsewhere, especially among the *Cistercians; for reasons of discipline and management, authority in the cells passed gradually from the lay steward to a priestly "corrector". In 1317, Pope *John XXII erected Grandmont into an

*St Stephen of Muret and his disciple Hugo Lacerta.* Altar-plaque from Grandmont. Enameled and gilded copper, 12th c. Paris, Musée du Moyen Âge et des Thermes de Cluny.

*abbey of 60 monks and reduced its dependencies to 39 conventual *priories of 16 to 18 members by amalgamating suppressed cells; later these occasionally received administrators to look after their demesnial rights and their ritual or charitable obligations. The *abbot of Grandmont received the papal insignia as did the heads of *orders, in 1353, but *commendation, which had affected a number of priories by way of the beneficial system, reached the abbey in its royal form in 1476. It was to a conscientious commendatory abbot like Cardinal Guillaume Briçonnet that Grandmont owed its last general *chapter of the Middle Ages, in 1497.

J. Becquet, "Grandmont", *DHGE*, 21, Paris, 1986, 1129-1140 (repr. *Etudes grandmontaines*, Ussel, 1999). – C. Hutchison, *The Hermit Monks of Grandmont*, Kalamazoo (MI), 1989. – *L'Ordre de Grandmont: art et histoire*, G. Durand (ed.), J. Nougaret (ed.), Montpellier, 1992.

Jean Becquet

**GRANGE.** Until about the 10th c. the word "grange" designated the building in which grain and crops were stored. By extension it signified the whole of an agricultural *estate (buildings and land), among the Benedictines, *Carthusians and *Premonstratensians, with their own characteristics. Anxious to rehabilitate manual *labour, the *Cistercians made granges a veritable institution for managing their temporality.

An original ruling, later clarified and modified by the general *chapter of the *order, allows us to discern the theoretical facts: status, layout, buildings, personnel (timetable, alimentary regime), management, hospitality.

Until about 1220, the system functioned well. Each male *abbey possessed between half a dozen and two dozen granges, created by a patient assemblage of lands or by acquisition of a major nucleus, often on lands brought into cultivation, sometimes by displacing the existing population. Self-sufficiency necessitated a wise complementarity of resources and soils. Viticulture (Clos Vougeot), cereal production (Vaulerent), *animal husbandry for meat or wool, *forest management rather than *clearance called for variable areas of a few tens to several hundred hectares, even thousands in the Eastern regions. The great rectangular cereal barns with triple aisles and triangular stone gables should not make us forget that the majority of granges were much more modest, adapted to their primary function, and evolved with time. A dozen lay brothers per grange, sometimes many more, handled the work, seconded by paid workers if necessary, using methods remarkable for their efficiency. Certain granges specialized in mining, *metallurgy or *salt production; others were created in *towns.

The diminution of the number of lay brothers obliged a gradual renunciation of direct exploitation: partial commutation to quit-rent, allotment among new *villages and farms, parcelling out into smaller farms, slow transformation into lordships: these were the common lot between 1250 and 1300. The crises of the 14th c. and the internal evolution of the order made the granges the centres of a solid landed and financial power which, even curtailed, often lasted until the suppression of the abbeys. Notable evidence remains in the landscape, detailed surveys and toponomy of Europe.

M. Aubert, *L'Architecture cistercienne en France*, 2, Paris, 1947, 159-171. – A. Dimier, "Grange", *DDC*, 5, 1953, 987-993. – C. Higounet, *La Grange de Vaulerent. . .*, Paris, 1965. – C. Platt, *The Monastic Grange in Medieval England*, London, 1969. – *Archeologia*, 58, Paris, May 1973, 52-62; *ibid.*, 65, Dec 1973, 52-63; *ibid.*, 74, Sept 1974, 46-57. – B. Chauvin, "Granges", *Cîteaux*, 24-38, 1973-1987. – J. Dubois, "Grangia", *DIP*, 4, 1977, 1391-1402. – C. Higounet, "Essai sur les granges cisterciennes", *L'Économie cistercienne*, Auch, 1983, 157-180. – "Les abbayes cisterciennes et leurs granges", *Cahiers de la Ligue urbaine et rurale*, 109, Paris, 1990.

Benoît Chauvin

Grange-infirmary at Voisinlieu, Oise, France. 13th c.

**GREAT BRITAIN.** The mainland island of the British Isles, also sometimes used to include the offshore islands except for *Ireland and the islands adjacent thereto. There has never been a unified Christian *province of Great Britain.

The origins of Christianity in the different parts of the British Isles were disparate, and threw up different structures and authorities. The Roman imperial province of the 4th c. was Christian, with bishops in major towns. Archaeological evidence for Christianity beyond the Roman frontier is slender, but Christianity survived on the fringes of the province when it was destroyed by pagan *Angles and Saxons in the 5th century. British missionaries, like St *Patrick in the 5th c. and St Finnian or Finnbarr in the early 6th, carried Christianity into Ireland, where its structures were adapted to Irish society and returned to mainland Britain during the 6th c., most notably under St *Columba. Thus, before Pope *Gregory the Great sent St *Augustine to convert the Angles and Saxons in 597 (the year of Columba's death), large parts of west and north Britain had long established autonomous Christian churches.

Pope Gregory envisaged a church for Great Britain with metropolitan *archbishops based in the old imperial cities of *London and *York, each with twelve subject diocesan *bishops. This never came about: due to the hostility of the Londoners, Augustine and his successors settled at *Canterbury under the protection of the sympathetic Kentish kings, and the York mission of Paulinus was short-lived. Gregory intended that Augustine should have *authority over "all the *sacerdotes* of Britain"; but Augustine's meeting with seven British (*i.e.* Welsh) bishops in 601 failed to produce agreement on co-operation, and atrocities by Northumbrian kings against British clergy led to further hostility and suspicion. Northumbria was converted by Irish monks from *Iona during the 630s and '40s independently of the papal mission. For a short time the *abbot of Iona may have been the most powerful churchman in the British Isles, appealed to by the Irish on the *Easter question and with authority over the church in Northumbria, whose bishop, according to *Bede, was "held in veneration" by Bishop Honorius of Canterbury and other bishops among the English. At the synod of *Whitby (664) the Northumbrian kings removed their churches from Iona's authority, but this did not lead to the completion of Pope Gregory's scheme. The bishop of York was raised to archiepiscopal dignity in 735, but never had more than three or four diocesans at any one time.

The aftermath of the *Viking invasions saw the emergence of strong dynasties in Wessex and in *Scotland who carved up the Scandinavian kingdom of York between them, and were anxious to promote the pretensions of their own churches; but the archbishopric of York survived, and in the 12th c. its archbishops even renewed claims to authority over the Scottish bishops. These were successfully resisted by the Scottish *Crown and bishops, and in 1192 Scotland became an autonomous province without a *metropolitan. Part of the reason for this success was the fact that the Scots were able to play off the rivalries of York and Canterbury.

The church in *Wales was less fortunate. In the 12th c., following the Norman conquest of Wales, archbishops of Canterbury brought the four Welsh *dioceses under their control, and thereafter many of the higher clergy were English and opposed to the nationalism of Welsh leaders such as *Llywelyn ap Gruffydd († 1282) and *Owain Glyndŵr († 1415), though some *secular clergy supported the latter. Throughout the medieval and Reformation periods the church in Wales always had an alien, anglicized character, and this contributed greatly to the rise of nonconformity among the Welsh in more recent times.

The archbishops of Canterbury succeeded in subjugating the Welsh bishoprics while the archbishops of York failed to do the same in Scotland. Meanwhile, the two archbishops waged a long and fruitless controversy over primacy in the church of *England. This was only settled when Pope *Innocent VI (1352-1362) awarded precedence to Canterbury with the title "*primate of all England", while York was styled "primate of England".

Several factors prevented the development of a unified ecclesiastical province of Great Britain in the Middle Ages: one was the disparate origins of the different local churches in England, Scotland and Wales; another was the success of the Scots in resisting English attempts at conquest; a third was the wasteful rivalry between the English archbishops of Canterbury and York.

Alan Macquarrie

**GREAT CHURCH.** Hagia Sophia in *Constantinople, the Great Church, was the *cathedral church of the bishop of Constantinople, *i.e.* the *patriarch.

A first church was built under Constantius II and inaugurated in 360. At first just called the Great Church, it was later given the name of Divine Wisdom (Christ): Hagia Sophia. With a simple *basilica plan, it was situated near the Great *Palace, in the heart of the City. Burned in 404 during the riots that accompanied the exile of St John Chrysostom, then rebuilt on the same plan by Theodosius II, it was burned again under Justinian during the Nika rebellion. Justinian had the basilica rebuilt by Anthemius of Tralles and Isidore of Miletus. It is this new Hagia Sophia, begun in 532 and inaugurated in 537, that we still see, turned into a *mosque since 1453.

It was a basilica of new and bold conception, whose dome, said the historian Procopius in his *De aedificiis*, seemed "suspended from heaven by a golden chain". At the time of its inauguration, Justinian is said to have cried: "I have beaten you, Solomon". In 558 the dome collapsed after an earthquake and was rebuilt, for reasons of stability, seven metres higher (54 metres from the ground with a diameter of 31 metres) by Isidore the Younger. The dome collapsed several more times in the course of its history: in 869, 989 and 1346.

Preceded by a *narthex, the church consists of a nave dominated by the vast dome which represents the vault of heaven. It is flanked on the west by an atrium surrounded by colonnades, with a fountain at the centre, a *baptistery at the north-east, and a *sacristy (*skevophylakion*) at the south-east. To the south it adjoined the patriarchal palace. At the south-east, a passage to the Great Palace gave the emperor access to the basilica.

In the interior of the church, the pavement of *mosaics and polychrome marbles which originally covered the ground (cf. Procopius's description) has been replaced by marble flagging. The walls, which under Justinian had only a non-figurative decoration, were covered with figured mosaics mainly after the *iconoclast crisis. The dome was ornamented with a Christ *Pantocrator (ruler of the universe). In the apse, the cross was replaced by a seated Virgin and Child, with the archangels *Michael and *Gabriel on the springing of the arches. Processions of *prophets, Church *Fathers, patriarchs and bishops ornamented the tympana. In the vestibules leading to the nave, one of the doors was surmounted by *Christ enthroned in Wisdom, between medallions of *Mary and Gabriel, with the Emperor Leo VI prostrate; above another door, the Emperor *Constantine offered the city and Justinian the basilica to the Mother of God. Other emperors were represented in the church: Constantine IX Monomachus and the Empress Zoe, John II *Comnenus and the empress Irene with their son Alexius. A great mosaic represented the theme of *Deêsis.

Hagia Sophia was used for religious ceremonies and imperial ceremonial. There the *coronation of the emperor or the *baptism of the *porphyrogenete prince was performed by the patriarch. But an imperial liturgy existed for the whole year, centred on the Palace and the Great Church, described by Constantine VII Porphyrogenitus in his *De ceremoniis*. On great *feast days, this liturgy took the form of a *procession in which the emperor went from the Palace to Hagia Sophia, escorted by his dignitaries.

The detail of the religious festivals, of which the most important were celebrated by the patriarch, is given in the **Synaxarion of Hagia Sophia*. The splendour of the festivals at Hagia Sophia was renowned. A legend relates that it was this splendour, intended to reproduce the heavenly liturgy on earth, that dazzled the ambassadors of Grand Prince *Vladimir of Kiev and led him to choose the *Byzantine rite at the time of Russia's *conversion in the 10th century.

If the cathedral or episcopal liturgy was long distinguished from the monastic liturgy, the growing importance of *monasticism resulted, at the end of the Empire, in a direct influence of the latter on the liturgy of the Great Church. In the 14th c., the patriarchs of Constantinople adopted for the *offices of Hagia Sophia the **typikon* (liturgical rule) of *Jerusalem, itself modelled on the monastic liturgy. The cathedral rite was thus enriched by innumerable psalmodies, *hymns and *gestures characteristic of the great monasteries. Such magnificence required a numerous personnel, strictly hierarchized: canonarchs, ecclesiarchs, *deacons, cantors, lectors, archons of the Gospel, officials in charge of *lighting, *incense, etc.

The clergy of the Great Church also had an administrative role, which became heavier and heavier as the patriarch's jurisdiction increased. It was he in particular who handled the secretariat of the permanent *synod. From the 7th c., a distinction was made between the ministers of the church (clerics of Hagia Sophia in charge of the liturgy) and those with administrative functions (*offikia*), the most important of whom were called archons.

The great officials were in charge of the administration of the Great Church. The *great oeconomus* administered the estates of the Great Church and appointed the local administrators of these estates; he gathered the produce and taxes that came from these estates, paid the salaries and procured the necessary equipment for the liturgy (oil for the lamps, wax for candles, *incense. . .). His role decreased after 1204. The **sacellarius* was in charge of the monasteries dependent on the Great Church. The *skevophylax* was responsible for the sacred furniture, *vestments and *liturgical books; he exercised authority over the liturgical personnel and presented candidates for minor *orders or for positions of archon. The *sakelliou* controlled the property deeds and leases of the estates, as well as the churches of Constantinople and their ministers. The *protekdikos* represented the Great Church in the secular courts; he defended the accused, redeemed slaves, administered the right of *asylum and catechized converts. The services of the *chancery* were assigned rather to the duties of the patriarchate and the synod. The *chartophylax*, originally a mere keeper of the patriarchal and synodal archives, gradually became

Interior of Hagia Sophia, Istanbul. 6th c.

the patriarch's secretary. He served as intermediary between the patriarch and the bishops of the synod. His role decreased at the end of the Empire. The *protonotarius* saw to the formulation of deeds and presented them for the patriarch's signature. The *logothete*, whose original role was to make speeches on feast days in the patriarch's name, gradually became the patriarch's official spokesman. The *hypomnematographer* drew up the minutes of synodal sessions. The *hieromnemon* was in charge of *ordinations. Besides the major officials, a whole host of secondary officials contributed to the smooth working of the services of the patriarchate and the synod.

To make these services function, the Great Church possessed estates granted by the emperors over the centuries. In 1204 these estates were confiscated by the crusaders. On the restoration of the Empire in 1261, Michael VIII *Palaeologus undertook to restore these estates, but they did not recover their past importance. Michael VIII's *chrysobull (1271) specified that the revenues (products and taxes) of these estates should provide for the salary of the officials of the patriarchate and the ministers of the church, the expenses of the liturgy (lighting) and the upkeep of the patriarch and his household.

The Great Church suffered as much as the State from the repercussions of the economic crisis. The ruin of the countryside deprived it of a great part of its revenues. In 1307, Patriarch *Athanasius reached the point where he could no longer guarantee the salaries of his clergy. There ensued an insurrection, led by the archons but widely followed by the clerics of the liturgical service, since the patriarch complained to the emperor that he could no longer find clerics to celebrate the liturgy. The settlement of this crisis, which was done to the detriment of the clergy of the Great

Church, marked an important step in the decline of that clergy, gradually confined to its liturgical functions, the patriarchs of the late Empire preferring to govern through the intermediary of confidential agents, most often monks, rather than depend on that caste represented by the personnel of the Great Church.

R. Janin, *La géographie ecclésiastique de l'Empire byzantin, 1, Le Siège de Constantinople et le patriarcat oecuménique*, 3, *Les églises et les monastères*, Paris, 1969. – J. Darrouzès, *Recherches sur les Offikia de l'Église byzantine*, Paris, 1970. – K. Theoharidou, *The Architecture of Hagia Sophia*, Thessaloniki, Oxford, 1988. – *Hagia Sopia from the Age of Justinian to the Present*, Cambridge, 1992.

Marie-Hélène Congourdeau

**GREAT SCHISM OF THE WEST.** The period in the history of the Latin Church called the "Great Schism of the West" lasted from 20 Sept 1378 to 8 Nov 1417; it was marked by the joint presence of several pontiffs, each claiming legitimacy. The *popes of *Rome – Urban VI, Boniface IX, Innocent VII, Gregory XII – were opposed by those of *Avignon – Clement VII and Benedict XIII. To Gregory XII and Benedict XIII was added the pope chosen by the council of *Pisa: Alexander V, then John XXIII. The council of *Constance managed to reduce this triple authority by electing *Martin V. The term "*schism" applied to this crisis of the Church is not theologically adequate. It means "rupture, tearing" and would imply a break with the Holy See. But the authority of the supreme pontiff as head of the Church was not called into question as such. *Christendom was divided on the question of who was *Peter's true successor. Since every Christian recognised one or other of the pontiffs, neither was schismatic in the strict sense of the word.

During the last months of the pontificate of *Gregory XI, *Italy suffered profound troubles due to the war between the papacy and the towns of central Italy; the political situation of Rome was equally confused. At the announcement of the pope's decease, agitation grew and the pressure of the Romans on the *cardinals was manifested in the streets, notably by this exclamation cited by numerous witnesses: "We want a Roman, or at least an Italian". In this climate of excitement, the cardinals present at Rome assembled in *conclave and, on 8 April, chose Bartolomeo Prignano, archbishop of *Bari, who took the name of *Urban VI. Were the cardinals constrained to this choice? On the morrow of the *election, no document questioned its regularity, while its turbulent circumstances were not concealed. Cardinal Pedro de Luna expressed himself thus: "We have elected a true pope. The Romans could tear my limbs off before they would make me go back on today's election".

On the morrow of his *coronation, Urban VI attacked the luxury and ostentation of the cardinals' lives, which gave rise to feelings of hostility. In June, only the Italian cardinals remained with Urban while the others, meeting at *Anagni, proclaimed that Bartolomeo's election was void. Supported by Queen Joanna of Naples and her *chancellor Nicola Spinelli da Giovinazzo, as well as by baron Onorato *Caetani, count of Fondi, and Duke Louis of Anjou, the dissident cardinals were joined on 15 Sept by the Italian fraction of the *Sacred College. On 20 Sept, at Fondi, Cardinal Robert of Geneva was elected pope under the name of *Clement VII. From then on there were two supreme pontiffs at the head of *Christendom.

For all the faithful, the question posed was whether Urban VI or Clement VII was the legitimate pope. The Emperor *Charles IV and *England recognised Urban VI, while *Charles V of France, encouraged by Louis of Anjou, pronounced his support, after the assembly of Vincennes (7 May), for Clement VII. The obediences were gradually organised in accordance with political affinities. *Poland, *Bohemia, *Hungary, Austria, the bishops of *Flanders and *Florence rallied to Urban VI, while *Savoy, *Scotland, *Ireland and the Flemish regions joined Clement VII. The kingdoms of *Aragon, *Navarre, *Castile and *Portugal opted at first for an attitude of neutrality. Certain regions oscillated between the two obediences, like *Milan or *Bologna; in the *Empire, Clement VII obtained support in the Palatinate, *Hesse and *Thuringia, as well as in the bishopric of Basel, while the rest of the country recognised Pope Urban VI.

In order to put an end to this split within the Church, each party sent *legates or preachers instructed to convince the rulers and clergy who had been won over to the rival pope. The granting of promises, *expectative graces and *subsidies in favour of churchmen in the provinces of rival obedience was another means of action, used by both pontiffs.

Recourse to force, called "*via de facto*", was also preached by both popes. In April 1379, Clement VII promised the duke of *Anjou a kingdom that would comprise all the *States of the Church save *Latium and would be a vassal of the Holy See. The duke of Anjou was to help Clement VII recover these territories. But the project aborted. Queen Joanna of Naples, by her new adhesion to Clement VII, relaunched the *via de facto* in Italy by inciting the duke of Anjou to take possession of *Naples which was then in the hands of Charles of Durazzo, a supporter of Urban VI. In 1383, the bishop of *Norwich began a military operation in *Flanders that ended in failure. The "crusade" waged in Castile by the duke of *Lancaster had no more success. But England managed to bring Portugal into the Urbanist party. In *Germany, an Urbanist leage was created, bringing together the king of the Romans, *Wenceslas of Bohemia, the Rhenish electors and the bishops of *Liège, *Utrecht and *Würzburg. Although Urban VI encouraged Wenceslas to go to Italy to be crowned emperor there, he never made the journey. At this time, the Iberian peninsula underwent a change of obedience and rallied to the party of Clement VII: Castile in 1381, Aragon in 1387 and Navarre in 1390. Yet despite these changes of obedience and these different armed actions, neither of the two popes succeeded in resolving the schism.

The death of Urban VI (15 Oct 1389) provided an occasion to put an end to it. On 2 Nov, the Urbanist cardinals chose a new pope in the person of Pietro Tomacelli, cardinal of Naples, who took the name *Boniface IX. The financial difficulties that confronted him led him to extend the levying of *annates to all *benefices provided by the papacy with or without *cure of souls. Likewise, the success of the *jubilee of 1390 and the extension of *indulgences offered new financial returns. The *via de facto* was continued.

At the same time, a new way of resolving the schism opened up, that of negotiation. On 1 March 1391, Boniface IX, while rejecting the idea of a *council, invited France to a reconciliation. The sudden illness of King *Charles VI prevented the pursuit of these contacts, which were not encouraged by the king's uncles. At this same period numerous works appeared expressing the need to restore unity. Eustache Deschamps, in his *Dolente et piteuse complainte de l'Église*, envisaged resolving the schism by "*concile général ou aultrement*". In Jan 1394, the university of *Paris set up a chest in which all its members could put slips containing their proposals to resolve the schism. The majority of slips pronounced in favour of cession, *i.e.* the *resignation of both pontiffs.

Clement VII died on 16 Sept 1394. Although the king of France appealed to the cardinals to suspend the election, on 28 Sept they elected Pedro de Luna, under the name of *Benedict XIII. From that autumn, the king of France, through the intermediary of *Pierre d'Ailly, incited the new pope to enter the way of cession, but he expressed his preference for the way of convention. Negotiations continued and a common request coming from Castile, France and England (June 1397) did nothing to modify Benedict XIII's position.

The king of France now convoked the French clergy (*abbots, *bishops, cathedral *chapters, *Dominicans, *Franciscans, *universities) to an assembly. On 22 May 1398, 300 people took part in this meeting that had to choose between a total or partial *subtraction of obedience from Benedict XIII. *Simon de Cramaud, author of the treatise *De substractione obedientie*, managed to obtain a vote for total subtraction of obedience. On 28 July 1398 this was proclaimed, thus denying Benedict XIII the right to designate titulars to benefices or to levy taxes on the clergy of the kingdom of France. Only five cardinals remained faithful to the pontiff while the others waged a violent war against him. Marie de Blois, countess of *Provence, and Henry of Castile followed France in their subtraction.

The deposition of the king of the Romans, Wenceslas, and his replacement by the Elector Palatine, Robert III of Bavaria (20 Aug 1400), marked a passing reconciliation between the Empire and France. However, following the death of the count of *Milan, Robert resumed contact with Boniface and consequently broke off his contacts with France. The pope demanded that he no longer concern himself about the schism without his agreement. The talks entered into between France and England came to nothing, France proposing only subtraction. Thus this way ended in failure, and a contrary movement began. From August 1402, Anjou restored its obedience to Benedict. Castile followed on 29 April 1403. On 30 May 1403, Pierre d'Ailly announced the return of the kingdom of France to Benedict's obedience, a decision approved by the king and the universities.

In the years following this restitution, each pope experienced growing difficulties. Benedict XIII, who wanted to organise a triumphal march to Italy, sent ambassadors to Boniface. They were finally received, but the sick pope insulted them and rejected the idea of a meeting. The day after this interview, Boniface died. Though Benedict XIII had several times promised to resign in case of his rival's death, he did nothing. As for the cardinals, they swore an *oath to restore unity by any means, cession included. On 7 Oct 1404, Cardinal Cosma Megliorati was elected and took the name of Innocent VII.

From then on Benedict XIII had once more to confront the French university which rebelled against him. Overwhelmed by the pope's fiscal demands, the university of Paris conducted protests and strikes during the winter of 1406, resulting in the convocation of a new assembly of the French clergy in November. For three months, Guillaume Fillâtre, Pierre d'Ailly, Pierre Leroy and Simon de Cramaud faced each other. The *ordinances of 18 Feb 1407 officially gave rise to *Gallicanism: while retaining his spiritual power, Benedict XIII was deprived of any collation of benefices and dignities.

During the meeting of this assembly, 6 Nov 1406, Innocent VII died at Rome. Though the way of cession appeared to the cardinals to be worth encouraging, they entered into conclave. But they promised that the new pope would abdicate as soon as the cession or death of his rival was known, on condition that the adverse cardinals would rally to him. On 30 Nov, Cardinal Angelo Correr was elected and took the name Gregory XII. The new pope hastened to transmit to Benedict XIII his conviction that cession had to be rapidly envisaged. Benedict XIII, prefering to engage in discussion, received the Roman ambassadors on 3 April 1407. An interview between the two popes was envisaged at Savona, in the five months following. However this meeting was not supported by the princes. Arguing financial difficulties, Gregory XII rejected this meeting. Despite numerous attempts to find a new place that would satisfy all parties, no agreement was reached. Gregory, aware that his cardinals opposed his policy, forbade them to leave *Lucca and engage in discussions with the ambassadors of the king of France or of Benedict. Scorning these prohibitions, the cardinal of Liège left the town and, very rapidly, other members of the Sacred College followed him to Pisa. Joined by certain Avignonese cardinals, they announced to rulers, bishops and both popes their decision to call a *council.

Opening on 25 March 1409, the council of *Pisa proclaimed by its decisions its wish to put an end to the schism: first summoning the popes to appear, the council pronounced against them a sentence of condemnation for contumacy (23 May). On 5 June 1409, Angelo Correr and Pedro de Luna were deposed. The conclave opened on 15 June. Directed by Baldassare Cossa, it elected Philargis of Candia, archbishop of Milan, who took the name Alexander V. Following the council of Pisa, Latin Christendom thus found itself divided into three obediences, of which that of Pisa was admittedly the strongest: it included in its ranks France, the dukes of Bavaria and Austria, the archbishops of Mainz, Hamburg, Magdeburg, Prague, Tuscany, the kingdom of England, Venice, Savoy and the Comtat Venaissin. For his part, Benedict XIII was supported by the kingdom of Aragon and by Scotland, while Gregory XII kept some support from Germany (town of Frankfurt, some bishops around Trier and in Bavaria), the lord of Malatesta and Naples.

Alexander V did not engage in *reform and his short pontificate was marked by the struggle between Louis of Anjou and Ladislas, king of Naples, in the Papal States. At the theological level, the pope, in granting the *mendicant orders, by the *bull *Regnans in excelsis* (12 Oct 1409), the right to preach and confess in any place in spite of the ordinaries, provoked a strong movement of disapproval against him. His death, 3 May 1410, quelled a new subject of discord. On 17 May Baldassare Cossa was elected under the name *John XXIII. The new pope convoked a council at Rome for April 1412, but it was not until December that the work began. From 3 March, under pressure from Ladislas, king of Naples, the council was deferred. Following the pillage of Rome organised by Ladislas, John XXIII fled to Florence.

Despite the failure of the council of Rome, the pope wished to pursue the work, and it was through the intermediary of *Sigismund, king of the Romans, that the council was continued at *Constance. On 1 Nov 1414, Francesco *Zabarella read the decree opening it. Very soon, discussions were committed to the *council's superiority over the *pope, proclaimed on 6 April 1415 by the decree *Sacrosancta*. From the beginning of March 1415, John XXIII promised to abdicate but, supported by Frederick of Austria, he managed to flee the town. Taking refuge at Fribourg, he nevertheless had to submit to the orders of the council which brought him back to *Constance and imprisoned him. On 29 May, John XXIII was deposed. As for Gregory XII, he chose to abdicate on 4 July, but before doing so he convoked the council, thus giving it legitimacy. Negotiations carried out at *Perpignan under Sigismund's leadership to bring Benedict XIII to cession led to nothing (Sept-Nov 1415), and it was the council that deposed him, 3 Sept 1417, after which Aragon, Navarre, Castile and the county of Foix abandoned him and joined Constance. Before seeking to nominate a new pope, the different *nations and the fathers fixed his mode of *election: the electoral body would be composed of the *cardinals and thirty delegates, six of each nation. The electors were finally able to go into *conclave on 8 Nov 1417. Oddone *Colonna, the future *Martin V, was elected on 11 Nov, putting an end to the schism of the West. But from 1439 Christendom was once more divided between two papal obediences. By electing *Felix V, the council of *Basel created a new rupture, since the council of *Florence continued to recognise *Eugenius IV and then *Nicholas V. With the abdication of Felix V (7 April 1449), Christendom found itself led once more by a single pontiff.

This division of Christendom naturally had consequences on religious life. Ecclesiastical staff sometimes had a double hierarchy, since a single *benefice could be claimed by the candidates of both obediences. By the use of *expectatives, each pope could introduce his candidate, even in provinces in which he was not recognised. Local conflicts broke out at the level of *dioceses and *parishes. Likewise, the religious *orders suffered the adverse consequences of the schism: the obedience of the mother *abbeys did not always correspond to that of their daughters, which hindered the holding of general *chapters.

At the individual level, the schism doubtless had repercussions on the *conscience of Christians. Alongside the *jubilees and *indulgences linked to it, *processions and other collective *prayers were celebrated in order to accelerate the end of the schism; in this context we can mention the *flagellant movement. Moreover, the religious life of certain regions was profoundly hampered, the Urbanists refusing to attend masses celebrated by Clementines. It was in this context that *Gerson wrote his treatise *De modo se habendi tempore schismatis*, in order to tranquillize consciences.

The secular powers intervened widely in the conduct of ecclesiastical affairs, in particular in the collation of benefices, during periods of *subtraction of obedience. Thus, progressively, a State Church was substituted for the centralizing policy of the papacy. Likewise, assemblies of the clergy, convoked by the king of France, functioned as representative of the Church of the realm. This movement culminated in the development of national Churches, of which *Gallicanism is an example. The role played by the *universities in the resolution of the schism sometimes had grave consequences on their personnel. In the staff of a single institution, several obediences could in fact exist alongside each other and hence numerous departures marked the university of *Paris at the time of its adhesion to the party of Clement VII. By contrast, new creations saw the light of day, like that of the universities of Heidelberg or *Cologne. Sharp quarrels, tainted by *politics and secular influences, from then on opposed universities of different obediences, thus hindering their intellectual development.

Finally, the Great Schism had ecclesiological repercussions, since the Universal Church, distinguishing itself from the Roman Church, was able to justify the idea of the superiority of the *council over the *pope (*Henry of Langenstein, *Conrad of Gelnhausen, *Pierre d'Ailly, Jean *Gerson).

N. Valois, *La France et le Grand Schisme d'Occident*, Paris, 1896 (4 vol.). – J. Favier, *Les Finances pontificales à l'époque du Grand Schisme d'Occident 1378-1409*, Paris, 1966. – R.N. Swanson, *Universities, Academics and the Great Schism*, Cambridge, 1979. – J. Favier, *Genèse et débuts du Grand Schisme d'Occident (1362-1394)*, Avignon, 1980. – H. Kaminsky, *Simon de Cramaud and the Great Schism*, New Brunswick (NJ), 1983. – H. Millet, "Du conseil au Concile (1395-1408). Recherche sur la nature des assemblées du clergé en France pendant le Grand Schisme d'Occident", *JS*, 1985, 137-159. – H. Millet, E. Poulle, *Le Vote de la soustraction d'obédience en 1398*, Paris, 1988. – W. Brandmüller, *Papst und Konzil im grossen Schisma (1378-1431)*, Paderborn, 1990. – H. Millet, "Le Grand Schisme d'Occident vu par les contemporains: crise de l'Église ou crise de la papauté?", *Recherches sur l'économie ecclésiale à la fin du Moyen Âge autour des collégiales de Savoie. Actes de la table ronde internationale d'Annecy, 26-28 avril 1990*, Annecy, 1991, 27-42.

Véronique Pasche

**GREECE.** In the late Roman Empire, Greece, cut up into several provinces, was part of the *diocese of Macedonia and the prefecture of Illyricum; but its influence was important. It was one of the last refuges of paganism when, in 529, Justinian closed the Academy of Athens.

The first Slav *invasions affected it from the mid 6th c.; in the 580s, it was submerged by these peoples, except for some towns which, like *Thessalonica, resisted several sieges, a narrow fringe along the Aegean coast as far as Cape Malea, and some islands. Entire cities emigrated, like Lacedaemonia which moved to Monemvasia. The Byzantine reconquest began from the north; at the end of the 7th c., the creation of the *themes of Macedonia and Hellas indicates that the eastern part of northern and central Greece was once more Byzantine. The reconquest of the Peloponnese was completed in 805 by the return of Patras to its metropolitan status and the submission of the last revolted *Slavs. All over Greece an effective policy of *conversion and Hellenization was practised, helped at need by transfers of population, Slavs being deported to Asia Minor and Hellenophones installed in Greece. But the Arabs occupied *Crete from 827 to 961. The presence on the throne at the end of the 8th c. of an Athenian, the empress *Irene, shows that Greece had regained its place in the Byzantine world, as witness the growing number of saints from this region who attained wide renown (Peter of Argos, Luke the Younger, Nikon the Metanoeite). If we except some *Bulgar raids or the sack of *Thessalonica by Leo of Tripoli in 904, central and northern Greece were sheltered from invasions until the end of the 11th century. The building of churches and monasteries multiplied; *Athos became the centre of Byzantine *monasticism.

At the turn of the 11th/12th cc., then again in 1185, central and northern Greece suffered Norman attacks. The fourth *crusade led to the greater part of Greece falling into the hands of the Latins, Frankish knights or Venetians. Though Byzantine sovereignty was rapidly restored starting from Epirus and totally in northern Greece under Michael VIII from 1261, the region of Athens and especially the Peloponnese, which became the Frankish Morea, suffered Latin occupation for a long time. But, starting from *Mistra, near Sparta, where a despotate was based, the Byzantines progressively reconquered the Peloponnese. Mistra became the seat of a brilliant court, held by one of the branches of the *Palaeologus dynasty, and sent several of its princes to occupy the throne of *Constantinople. Though northern Greece was occupied from the late 14th c. by the *Turks, the Morea resisted several years longer than the capital and fell into their hands only in 1460, four years after Athens. This was the beginning of the Turcocracy.

A. Bon, *Le Péloponnèse byzantin jusqu'en 1204*, Paris, 1951. – A. Avraméa, *Byzantine Thessaly up to 1204*, Athens, 1974 (in Greek). – B. K. Panagopoulos, *Cistercian and Mendicant Monasteries in Medieval Greece*, Chicago, 1979. – D. M. Nicol, *The Despotate of Epiros, 1267-1497*, Cambridge, 1984. – *The Archaeology of Medieval Greece*, P. Lock (ed.), G. D. R. Sanders (ed.), Oxford, 1996.

Michel Kaplan

**GREENLAND.** In 985, a great Icelandic dignitary, Eiríkr the Red, who had been proscribed for crimes, chose to be exiled to an unknown land whose coasts had been glimpsed by navigators blown off course by the wind. Thus he reached a land whose south-west coast he decided to colonize, and baptized it Groenland (Green Land) on the pretext that if he gave this country a pretty name he would find it easier to persuade people to go and live there! So he set out to *Iceland to announce this news and found friends and relations to colonize the new country, partly on the extreme south-west coast (Vestribyggd, around the present Godthåb), partly on the extreme south-east coast ('Eystribyggd, near the present Julianehåb). This was the start of a movement that brought to Greenland a certain number of Icelandic families who had decided to settle there. Its resources were admittedly meagre, but the trade in walrus *ivory seems to have enjoyed particular favour in the Middle Ages, at least for a certain time. A *bishopric was founded at Gardarr, where a church was built: the Vatican preserves the plans of it, and its ruins are still visible. Two monasteries were added, and a dozen churches. The country, whose population was in any case extremely limited in number, passed under the *Crown of *Norway, then of *Denmark at the same time as its mother country, *Iceland.

Then night fell on the destiny of Greenland and it remains one of the great mysteries of the history of the West. For reasons that remain unexplained, this country purely and simply disappeared from the map in the course of the 15th or early 16th century. Was it a systematic eradication due to foreign invasions (but then, by whom?) or collisions with Inuit (but what we know of their naturally peaceful ways goes against this "explanation") or extinction due to the *Black Death? The mystery remains unsolved. . . .

*The Norse Atlantic Saga*, G. Jones (ed.), Oxford, 1986.

K.A. Seaver, *Frozen Echo*, Stanford (CA), 1996. – R. Bergerson, *Vinland Bibliography*, Tromsø, 1997.

Régis Boyer

**GREGORIAN CHANT.** The term "Gregorian chant" designates the monophonic liturgical chant of the Latin *Catholic Church, which came into being from the beginnings of Christianity and throughout the Middle Ages. Its name comes from its legendary attribution to Pope *Gregory I (590-604), who is supposed to have received it from the *Holy Spirit by the agency of a dove.

The origin of this chant was long disputed. We may say summarily that it was a repertory of Roman origin, introduced into Gaul in the 8th c. by the political will of *Pippin the Short, then of *Charlemagne. It was then confronted with the *Gallican liturgical and musical tradition. Interferences were produced, which gave rise in the 9th c. to what was later called Romano-Frankish chant. It is this repertory that, *stricto sensu*, is called Gregorian chant. By extension, this name is also given to the whole of the corpus that gradually came into being throughout the Middle Ages, though from the stylistic point of view the chants of the 15th c. have little in common with the old Gregorian foundation. The more recent layers are mainly in the *sanctoral, progressively enriched with new proper *offices for recently canonized saints, and new musical forms that appeared in the 9th c., mainly *tropes and sequences.

The characteristic of Gregorian chant is to belong to a liturgy. It comments on the texts, with which it hence keeps up a close relationship, and the musical pieces belonging to the same liturgical genre are related in their writing. The majority of these texts, especially in the older parts, are borrowed from the *psalms. The psalmody, inherited from the synagogue chant, is an early musical form of Gregorian chant. Originally, the singing of psalms was reserved for the *cantor, then the assembly was progressively invited to respond by brief refrains. This responsorial psalmody was the origin of the main musical forms, with the exception of *hymns, strophic chants attested from the 4th century. From the 10th c., the connection that united *music closely to text was sometimes altered by *polyphony, writing in which one or more voices were added to the Gregorian melody. The text was thus more or less obscured, and, from the 13th c., its *rhythm was modified to allow the ordered progression of all the voices. The *popes legislated several times against this musical evolution, considered a hindrance to the liturgical vocation of the pieces thus put into polyphony.

Gregorian chant was transmitted orally until the late 9th c., at which time the first signs of notation appeared. But the spread of writing was very gradual, and the oral tradition remained preponderant throughout the Middle Ages.

W. Apel, *Gregorian Chant*, Bloomington, 1958. – R. Steiner, "Gregorian Chant", *The New Grove Dictionary*, 7, London, 1980, 697-698. – P. Jeffrey, *Re-envisioning Past Musical Cultures,* Chicago, 1992.

Claire Maître

**GREGORIAN REFORM.** The expression "Gregorian reform" designates the *reform of the Church, as conceived and applied by *Gregory VII (1073-1085), but it also covers the ecclesastical reform that developed from the mid 11th to the mid 12th century. It affected every area of the Church's life.

At the highest level, Gregory VII wanted to give the papacy great independence from the imperial power. From 1059, the election of the *pope was in the hands of the *cardinals alone: the **Dictatus papae* of 1075 defined the pope's superiority in the spiritual sphere and his *authority over the emperor, which unleashed the quarrel between *priesthood and *Empire. The papacy wanted to have control over both powers, spiritual and *temporal, and at the same time gave itself a right of intervention in the political life of the States.

Reform of the life of the clergy, especially the struggle against *simony and *nicolaitism, began well before the pontificate of Gregory VII and were supported by all the popes of the 11th c.; *Leo IX personally concerned himself with applying the decisions taken. The Gregorian reform concerned only the question of relations with the *laity and that of *investitures. There too the movement was set in motion before 1073 and was largely prolonged after 1100; the first mention of a prohibition of lay investiture of *clerics dates from 1078.

The choice of prelates (*bishops and *abbots) and benefice-holders (*canons, *parish priests) was to be the fruit of an *election in accordance with the canons: election by the clergy and the people for the bishop, by the monks for the abbot, appointment to *prebends according to capacities and without money changing hands or any kind of pressure. Finally, investiture given by the lay authority was in no case to bear on the spiritual aspect of the function exercised. In 1095, it was forbidden for any cleric to pay *homage to a layman.

The complete resumption of Church properties by their holders led to a clear distinction being made between the temporality and the spirituality. Thus, in the *parishes, the church building received a distinct treatment from the *altar, place of exercise of the pastoral office and of levying of special charges. A movement of redistribution of churches to ecclesiastical institutes (*bishoprics, *chapters, monasteries) took place, whether *donations pure and simple or the *restitution of churches received in *benefice by laymen.

The ecclesiastical reform of the 11th and 12th cc. and more particularly the Gregorian reform had the effect of giving the clergy great independence, taking it out of the lay society in which it was deeply roooted, giving religious life a new *spirituality, creating a church in which the hierarchy (pope, bishops) acquired a considerable force in the conduct of men's lives. The success of the new monastic *orders, totally independent of the feudal system in comparison to the old Benedictines who remained immersed in it, was a manifestation of the success of the new spirit that the so-called Gregorian reform brought to them.

The main protagonists of this reform were popes *Leo IX, *Alexander II, *Gregory VII, *Urban II, *Paschal II and *Calixtus II, and the most striking events were the council of *Reims (1049), the *Canossa affair (1077) and the *concordat of *Worms (1122).

A. Fliche, *La Réforme grégorienne*, Louvain, 1924-1937. – G. Tellenbach, *Libertas. Kirche und Weltordnung im Zeitalter des Investiturstreites*, Stuttgart, 1936. – G. Ladner, *The Idea of Reform*, Florence, 1959. – G. Miccoli, *Chiesa gregoriana*, Cambridge (MA), 1966. – H.E.J. Cowdrey, *The Cluniacs and the Gregorian Reform*, Oxford, 1970. – R. Morghen, *Gregorio VII e la riforma della chiesa nel secolo XI*, Palermo, 1974. – G. Tellenbach, "Gregorianische Reform. Kritische Besinnungen", *Reich und Kirche vor dem Investiturstreit*, Sigmaringen, 1985. – W. Hartmann, *Der Investiturstreit*, Munich, 1993.

Michel Parisse

**GREGORY I THE GREAT (*c.*540-604).** An outstanding figure in the Church, of which he has been declared a *Doctor, and a careful and energetic spiritual leader for 14 years (*pope from 3 Sept 590 to 12 Mar 604), Gregory can rightly be numbered among the pillars of the Middle Ages, and has gone down in history as the Great.

The information on his life comes mainly from three biographical works: an Anglo-Saxon life (pre-710), an 8th-c. life by *Paul the Deacon and another by John the Deacon (873-876).

**The years before the pontificate.** Born at *Rome in *c.*540 to the noble family of the Anicii, he was given a sound education, typical of a scion of the *Roman patriciate close to the Church. His adolescence covered one of the most dramatic periods of the 6th c., when the Italian peninsula was ravaged by the Gothic war and Rome itself risked being destroyed by King Totila.

Beginning a career as an official of the Byzantine government of Rome, in 573 Gregory became *Praefectus Urbis*, a civil post of unlimited prestige. He worked conscientiously for the city and gained precious experience in the administrative and bureaucratic field, as well as a profound respect for discipline and law, which he treasured for the years to come. Completely immersed in this kind of *active life, at the same time he felt a strong call to the contemplative life until, around 574-575, without abandoning Rome, he withdrew to his palace on the Coelian, which became the monastery of St Andrew, in order to lead a monastic life. Gregory had happy memories of this period: in the serenity of that secure port where he had escaped shipwreck, he could profitably devote himself to the inner life, substantiating it by ascetic exercises and assiduous reading and *meditation on the texts of Scripture, the Latin exegetes and the *Fathers generally. The spiritual gains of this experience would also shortly bear fruit.

Pope Pelagius II, who had divined his qualities and the extent of the contribution he could make at such a delicate historical moment, first promoted him *deacon and then entrusted him with a task of great responsibility as his *apocrisiary at *Constantinople. This period, from 579 to 586, put Gregory in direct contact with the Byzantine world, in which he met widespread esteem and *friendship, beginning with that of two emperors, Tiberius II and Maurice. He took some monks from St Andrew's to Constantinople with him, and these were the main recipients of the spiritual conferences he held on the reading of the book of *Job, which, touched up later, would become the precious *Expositio in beatum Job*, better known as *Moralia in Job*. These 35 books of commentary on the biblical text, following a historical and moral interpretation that made the theme of suffering the centre of interest, formed a work that had imense popularity in the Middle Ages and beyond. The value of the *Moralia* lay in the incisiveness of the teachings taken from the biblical book, which, thanks to the simple form in which they were expounded, lent themselves to being reduced to extracts and used as epitomes of morality: not by chance did authors like *Isidore of Seville, *Alcuin and *Hincmar of Reims refer to this work.

In 586, Pelagius II recalled Gregory to Rome as counsellor and secretary, at a moment when he faced the thorny question of the Three Chapters and the approaching resumption of the war against the *Lombards. In this period, Gregory seems to have combined the intense work he did alongside Pelagius II with the experience of ascetic life in the monastery of St Andrew. This fact indicates an essential trait of Gregory's personality: that capacity to reconcile the *active and the contemplative life which he recommended to pastors, but which he was able to incarnate in his own person even after his elevation to the papacy, which happened in 590, after Pelagius's death.

**The years of the pontificate (590-604).** The historical moment was extremely delicate, given the difficulties deriving from the devastation due to the Gothic war and the mutinies and robberies of the imperial soldiers, to which were added natural catastrophes (rains, overflowing of rivers, including the Tiber) and various *sicknesses such as the plague. Gregory overcame his initial reservations and faced the material situation with awareness and intelligent determination, without disjoining them from a pastoral and missionary programme of immense scope. The administrative, diplomatic and spiritual experiences matured up to that moment bore fruit in the 14 years of his pontificate and supported a variegated pastoral activity that began in Rome and reached out to *Italy and the Churches of Africa, Illyricum and the kingdoms of the West, to which was added a particular concern for relations with the Eastern Churches.

A precious documentary source for all Gregory's intense activity is the collection of his *letters, known by the title of *Registrum epistolarum*. Of the 14 volumes collected by Gregory himself (as many as the years of his pontificate), there remain today only three extracts (848 letters), a precious reflection of his personality and gifts. What emerges is a personality attentive to the material needs, the reordering of the administration and the development of the *patrimony of the Roman Church through a programme worthy of the best administrative official, but also attentive to the needs of the poorest. A personality solicitous in keeping religious life alive by exercises of piety (the "Stations"), alert to the behaviour of the clergy and careful to control the *election of the *bishops of the whole Italian peninsula.

His overall activity in reference to the Lombard question was mainly one of mediation with the *Byzantine Empire with a view to peaceful coexistence in the peninsula. He saved Rome and the imperial territories from Lombard occupation in 592 and 593 by courageous strategic and political operations undertaken autonomously and through incisive diplomatic activity. He later managed to agree a truce with Agilulf that lasted from 598 to 601 and, after two years of new hostilities, mediated the armistice of 603 with the *exarch Smaragdus. Once peace had been reached, the best conditions were in place for the profitable missionary work among the Lombards at which Gregory aimed.

Gregory gave particular attention to the Western barbarian kingdoms, especially the Visigothic kingdom of *Spain and the Frankish kingdoms: in the former case, the council of *Toledo (589) decreed the *conversion of the *Visigoths to *Catholicism and their abjuration of the *Arian heresy; in the Frankish kingdoms, he acted incisively to educate and regenerate the Church, an activity hinging on the restoration of the vicariate of *Arles.

But one of the most important successes of his vast missionary activity was surely the *evangelization of the *Angles and Saxons in *Great Britain. In 595 he arranged for the acquisition of some young British *slaves in the market of *Marseille with the intention of forming them in the Christian faith and then sending them to Britain to preach the Gospel. Seeing the good reception accorded to the message in that island, in 596 he sent there *Augustine of Canterbury, prior of St Andrew's, with 40 monks. Thus, starting from the kingdom of Kent, and thanks to the good disposition of King *Æthelbert, were laid the bases of the Church of *England, headed by Augustine and organised into two ecclesiastical *provinces, that of *London and that of *York.

Finally, Gregory's diplomatic ability showed itself to be balanced and enormously precious in his relations with the Eastern Churches and the imperial authorities at Constantinople. His relations with the Churches of *Jerusalem, *Alexandria, *Antioch and *Constantinople were always marked by respect and deference, while standing firm in claiming the primacy of the Roman See on all occasions when it was necessary to impress this. Particularly severe, in this sense, was his intervention against patriarch John IV of Constantinople, who had given himself the title of "ecumenical *patriarch" in the acts of the *council of 595; the question was resolved thanks to the mediation of the emperor Maurice. Towards the State authorities of Constantinople too, respect and deference were not disjoined from firm positions in defence of the ecclesiastical sphere, through the express distinction between temporal interests and spiritual interests.

Gregory's reforming activities also extended his influence in the liturgical field: they were manifested in the composition of a *Sacramentary and an *Antiphonary, as well as in the impetus given to the "*Schola Cantorum" by the introduction of singing reforms that led to the chant still known as *Gregorian Chant.

*Gregory the Great.* Miniature from a sacramentary. School of Saint-Denis, 9th c. Paris, BNF (Ms lat. 1141, fol. 3).

**The works.** Overall, by the extent, farsightedness and incisiveness of his activity, Gregory overshadowed the whole of the Middle Ages with his influence, all the more marked in that it was backed up by a literary output whose character was essentially practical, exegetical and moral. Apart from the vast scope of the *Moralia in Job*, the medievals read and deeply meditated on another fundamental work, written during the first years of his pontificate, the *Liber regulae pastoralis*, considered "the code of bishops and priests as the *Rule of St *Benedict was of monks" (B. Mondin). Divided into four parts, the work deals diffusely with what for Gregory was the most difficult art, that of the ruler and guide of souls, concentrated in the figure of the pastor (*ars est artium regimen animarum*).

Around the same period, Gregory wrote the *Dialogues,* four books carrying a rich cargo of saints' lives. The work is interesting for many reasons: the author uses the dialogue form to offer profusely lavish dogmatic, ascetic, moral and exegetical explanations; book II, on St Benedict, helped propagate his Rule throughout the West.

Among his exegetical works are a series of commentaries on several books of the *Bible: the homilies on the Gospels (*Homiliae in Evangelia*), a collection of 40 *homilies given during the first years of his pontificate; that on the text of the prophet *Ezekiel (*Homiliae in Ezechielem prophetam*) in two books; the commentary (*Expositio*) on the first eight verses of the *Song of Songs; and that on the first 16 chapters of the first book of *Kings.

*Opera Omnia* of Gregory the Great in *PL*, 66, 125-203; *PL*, 75-79; *CChrSL*, 140-144; *SC*, 32, 212, 221, 251, 260, 265. – *Morals on the Book of Job*, C. Marriott (ed.), Oxford, 1844-1837 (3 vol.). – *Selected Epistles*, J. Barmby (tr.), Oxford, New York, 1898 (2 vol.). – *Pastoral Care*, H. Davis (tr.), Westminister (MD), 1950. – *Dialogues of Saint Gregory the Great*, O. J. Zimmermann (tr.), New York, 1959. – *Opera Omnia* on CD-ROM, CETEDOC, Louvain-la-Neuve.

R. Gillet, *DSp*, 6, 1967. – V. Recchia, *L'esegesi di Gregorio Magno al Cantico dei Cantici*, Turin, 1967. – C. Dagens, *Saint Grégoire le Grand, culture et expérience chrétiennes*, Paris, 1977. – V. Recchia, *Gregorio Magno e la società agricola*, Rome, 1978. – S. Boesch Gajano, "La proposta agiografica dei "Dialoghi" di Gregorio Magno", *Stud. Med.*, 3, 21, 1978, 623-664. – J. Richards, *Consul of God. Life and Times of Gregory the Great*, London, 1980. – *Colloque Grégoire le Grand*, Paris, 1986. – G. R. Evans, *The Thought of Gregory the Great*, Cambridge, 1986. – R. Gillet, *DHGE*, 21, 1988. – C. Straw, *Gregory the Great: Perfection in Imperfection*, Berkeley (CA), 1988. – W. D. McCready, *Signs of Sanctity: Miracles in the Thought of Gregory the Great*, Toronto, 1989. – R. Godding, *Bibliografia di Gregorio Magno 1890-1989*, Rome, 1990. – Y. Recchia, "Gregory the Great", *EEC*, 1, 1992, 365-368. – *Gregory the Great: a Symposium*, J. C. Cavadini (ed.), Notre Dame (IN), 1995. – V. Monachino, *BSS*, 7, 222-287, 1996. – R. A. Markus, *Gregory the Great and his World*, Cambridge, 1997.

Roberto Buccoliero

**GREGORY VII, POPE (before 1029? - 1085).** Hildebrand was born into a Tuscan family, perhaps from Soana. Entrusted to his maternal uncle, *abbot of Santa Maria on the Aventine, he had as his masters Lawrence, archbishop of *Amalfi, and the future Gregory VI. *Leo IX appointed him *oeconomus*, *cardinal subdeacon of the Roman Church and *rector* of the abbey of San Paolo fuori le Mura (1050). At the death of *Alexander II, Hildebrand's *election (22 April 1073) was approved by the clergy of *Rome, in the presence of the cardinal-bishops.

The *pope held a first reforming *council at the Lateran (9-17 March 1074). Scorning the strong resistance encountered, a second council (Lateran, Lent 1075) renewed the decrees against simoniac and concubinary priests, and condemned a large number of *bishops. All secular authorities were now forbidden to "make a gift" of a bishopric. The *excommunication of *Robert Guiscard was confirmed.

On 24 Jan 1076, an assembly of German *bishops meeting at *Worms declared the pope unworthy of his papal office. The response was immediate. The emperor was deposed and excommunicated at the Lateran *synod of 14 Feb. Writing on 25 Aug 1076 to *Hermann of Metz, Gregory VII clarified his thought on the doctrinal level: the power to bind and loose given to St *Peter also affects *kings; the apostolic see has the power to judge spiritual things; *a fortiori* he can judge secular things.

Having agreed to take part in an assembly of the kingdom, the pope left Rome between November and December 1076. The emperor, fearing an *entente* between Gregory and the princes, went to meet him. Surprised, Gregory withdrew to *Canossa, a castle belonging to Countess *Matilda. The king finally arrived at Canossa on 25 Jan, barefoot, in the habit of a *penitent. After three days of penance, he was admitted to the pope's presence. The latter, after having obtained *Henry IV's written *oath that he would accept his arbitration, raised the emperor, prostrate before him, and restored him to the Church. Canossa had enabled the *pope to set himself up as judge of lay princes and great temporal affairs.

In February 1079, a new Roman synod tried to find a solution to the problem of the kingdom, but the king's evasiveness led the pope to pronounce a second *excommunication of *Henry IV (7 March 1080).

After a long siege, on 21 March 1084 the emperor made himself master of Rome. The pope, a prisoner in Castel Sant'Angelo, was freed by *Robert Guiscard. He left the city and took refuge on *Monte Cassino, then at Salerno where he died on 25 May 1085. On his deathbed he uttered the words that have become famous: "I have loved justice and hated iniquity, therefore I die in exile".

G. Miccoli, "Gregorio VII, papa", *BSS*, 7, 1966, 293-378. – *La riforma gregoriana e l'Europa*, 1, 1989 ("SGSLE", 13). – I. S. Robinson, *The Papacy, 1073-1198*, Cambridge, 1990. – A. Paravicini Bagliani, *HChr*, 5, 1993.

Agostino Paravicini Bagliani

**GREGORY IX, POPE (*c.*1170-1241).** Ugo (or Ugolino) was born *c.*1170 into the family of the Conti de Segni, who held possessions in the region of *Anagni. His degree of kinship with *Innocent III is unclear. Ugolino studied at *Paris. A contemporary source calls him *iuris peritus*, which is confirmed by his activity as a judge under Innocent III, who brought him into his *chapel, appointed him cardinal of Sant'Eustachio (1198) and charged him with difficult missions, political (negotiations with Markward of Anweiler) and legal. Bishop of Ostia from 1206, he was one of the most influential cardinals.

A first legation (1207-1209) took him to *Germany, where he had to persuade the two claimants to the throne (*Otto of Brunswick and *Philip of Swabia) to accept papal arbitration. His most important legation concerned northern *Italy: in 1217, he tried to resolve local political conflicts (*Pisa, *Genoa, *Lucca, Volterra); in 1218, he worked at *Florence, *Bologna and in the Lombard towns to impose the authority of *Frederick II; in 1221, he sought the support of the Lombard towns for the *crusade to the *Holy Land and the struggle against *heresies. At the death of Cardinal John of St Paul, *Francis of Assisi, who may have met Ugolino at *Subiaco in 1222 (which would explain the presence of the cardinal's portrait in the chapel of San Gregorio), chose him as protector of his young community. Ugolino apparently took part in the redaction of the *Regula bullata*. From 1218, he was also occupied with the community of St *Clare, whose Rule he drew up (1219-1227). Without ever becoming their protector, Ugolino kept up excellent relations with the Friars Preachers. He met their founder, St *Dominic, several times (in 1215, perhaps at the fourth *Lateran council; in 1217, in 1219-1220 and in *Lombardy in 1221).

Elected *pope 19 March 1227, he remained faithful to the broad lines of his activity as a cardinal. To support the crusading movement, whose military aspects he tempered, he turned to the *Teutonic Order; opening up new geographical horizons to the Church's expansion, he encouraged the missionary efforts of Franciscans and Dominicans, from *Finland to Romania, and encouraged the *Premonstratensians to settle in *Latvia. At his death (22 Aug 1241), the cardinals were divided. To force them to take a decision, the senator Matteo Rosso *Orsini shut them up in the Roman palace of the Septizonium. This act may be considered history's first *conclave.

*Les Registres de Grégoire IX (1227-1241)*, L. Auvray (ed.), Paris, 1890-1955. – E. Brem, *Papst Gregor IX. bis zum Beginn seines Pontifikats*, Heidelberg, 1911. – W. Maleczek, *Papst und Kardinalskolleg von 1191 bis 1216*, Vienna, 1984, 126-133. – B. Schimmelpfennig, "Papst- und Bischofswahlen seit dem 12. Jahrhundert", *Wahlen und Wählen im Mittelalter*, Sigmaringen, 1990, 173-196. – A. Paravicini Bagliani, *HChr*, 5, 1993, 531-532.

Agostino Paravicini Bagliani

**GREGORY X, POPE (*c.*1210-1276).** Tedaldo Visconti was born at *Piacenza in *c.*1210. *Archdeacon of *Liège, he was elected *pope (1271) by the *conclave of *Viterbo, after three years of vacancy. He was then in the *Holy Land. At the second council of *Lyon (1275), he got the constitution *Ubi periculum* adopted as "constitutional charter" of the conclave, and sought an accord with the Byzantine Emperor Michael VIII to guarantee the safeguard of the Holy Places. He distanced himself from *Charles I of Anjou and supported *Rudolf of Habsburg, whom he met (Lausanne, 1275) to prepare his *coronation. He died at Arezzo, 10 Jan 1276.

*1274. Année charnière. Mutations et continuités*, Paris, 1977. – B. Roberg, *Das Zweite Konzil von Lyon (1274)*, Paderborn, 1990.

Agostino Paravicini Bagliani

**GREGORY XI, POPE (*c.*1330-1378).** Born at Rosiers-d'Égletons in Limousin, Pierre Roger was the nephew of *Clement VI; appointed *cardinal of Santa Maria Novella very young (1348), he studied law for several years at *Perugia. Elected *pope on 29 Dec 1370, he was crowned on 5 Jan 1371. In accordance with the cardinals' vow, he returned to a more traditional policy than that of *Urban V, a number of whose measures he revoked, but he resumed the project of returning the papacy to *Rome.

He gave the *Sacred College due importance and, in two promotions, created 21 cardinals, among them relations and former *familiares*. He kept and even accelerated centralization in the matter of *benefices by the practice of special *reservations, but showed himself more liberal to petitioners, imposing *residence only exceptionally and sometimes authorizing *pluralism.

He resumed the struggle against *heresy in *Dauphiné, Lyonnais, *Provence and *Corsica; he developed the *Inquisition in *Spain with Nicholas Eymerich. He sent *Dominicans to *Armenia and *Franciscans to *Bosnia and founded new episcopal sees in north-eastern Europe.

Through the intermediary of his *legates and nuncios and the arrival of ambassadors at *Avignon, Gregory XI carried on a great diplomatic activity. In Spain, Cardinal Guy of Boulogne tried to restore harmony between the kings of *Aragon, *Castile and *Navarre. The mission of Cardinals Simon of Langham and Jean de Dormans in favour of peace between *France and *England (1371) failed; but the negotiations culminated in a one-year truce signed at *Bruges (1375) where an agreement was also reached between England and the papacy, which moderated its *taxation in England, suspended *expectative graces and reservations and legitimized the *provision of benefices accorded by the king; but the English clergy remained discontent, as witness also the violent attacks of *Wycliffe against the Roman Church.

Gregory XI ratified the agreement concluded between Joanna of Naples and Frederick of Aragon, who was officially recognised as king of Trinacria (island of *Sicily) but had to accept the *suzerainty of queen and pope and pay an annual *rent; the *interdict that had weighed on the island for nearly a century was lifted.

In northern *Italy, Bernabò and Galeazzo Visconti, lords of *Milan, had resumed their intrigues; the pope condemned them in 1372 and 1373 and preached a crusade against them; an *army of mercenaries, led by the pope's brother and nephew as well as by captains John Hawkwood and Enguerran de Coucy, was raised; defeated in Piedmont and *Lombardy, the *Visconti came to terms at *Bologna in 1375.

In the *States of the Church a serious rebellion broke out at the instigation of *Florence, its pretext being the pope's *vicar general's prohibition against importing corn from the *Patrimony of St Peter at a time of severe shortage; the bad government of legates and rectors and the excesses of papal officials had led to general discontent. An *interdict was pronounced against Florence (1376). The mercenaries of the legate Robert of Geneva and captain John Hawkwood, after having been defeated before Bologna, massacred the population of Cesena, while some months later Sylvestre Bude's Bretons did the same at Bolsena. The Florentines ended by accepting the mediation of Bernabò Visconti with a view to peace, which was finally concluded at Sarzana.

Meanwhile, Gregory XI had left *Avignon on 13 Sept 1376, after having long put off the court's departure; on 17 Jan 1377, after a difficult journey, he entered Rome where he was received with great solemnities. He died there on 27 March 1378.

*Gregoire XI, 1370-1378: lettres communes*, A.-M. Hayez (ed.), Rome, 1992 (3 vol.).

E. Dupré-Theseider, *I papi d'Avignone e la questione romana*, Florence, 1939. – *Genèse et débuts du Grande Schisme d'Occident*, Paris, 1980. – P. R. Thibault, *Pope Gregory XI: the Failure of Tradition*, Lanham (MD), 1986. – A. M. Hayez, "D'Urbain V à Grégoire XI: un dangereux retour au passé?", *L'Écrit dans la Societé médiévale. Textes en hommage à Lucie Fossier*, Paris, 1991, 151-164. – M. Hayez, A. M. Hayez, "Les débuts du pontificat de Grégoire XI: un premier bilan administratif d'après les lettres communes", *Les prélats, l'Eglise et la société, XIe-XV[e] siècles. Hommage à Bernard Guillemain*, Bordeaux, 1994, 173-183. – A. M. Hayez, "Un aperçu de la politique bénéficiale de Grégoire XI: première moitié du pontificat (1371-1378)", *Forschungen zur Reichs-, Papst- und Landsgeschichte Peter Herde zum 65. Geburtstag von Freunden, Schülen und Kollegen dargebracht*, 2, Stuttgart, 1998, 685-698.

Anne-Marie Hayez

**GREGORY OF RIMINI (*c.*1300-1358).** Born at Rimini, an Augustinian, Gregory studied and taught *theology in *Italy, *England and *France, receiving the title of bachelor (1341) and *magister* (1345) at the university of *Paris. In 1357, a year before his death, he was appointed *prior general of his order. Often considered a representative of "the right wing of the *nominalist movement", Gregory was in reality the initiator of an autonomous tendency of thought, which had a lasting influence: we find disciples of the *via Gregorii* in many European *universities, and his main work, the commentary on the first two books of the **Sentences*, was republished several times between 1482 and 1522.

Among Gregory's most characteristic philosophical positions were the primacy of intuitive consciousness, the renunciation of **species* as intermediaries in the *knowledge of present objects, the rejection of the distinction between the *soul and its *faculties and the possibility of the infinite in act. In theology he forcefully emphasized the role of *grace, opposing, like *Thomas Bradwardine, any form of neopelagianism. But the most celebrated *doctrine usually attached to Gregory's name concerns the problem of the object of scientific knowledge: as object of knowing, it is for Gregory neither the extra-mental thing nor the proposition, but the total meaning of the proposition (*complexe significabile*), irreducible to the meaning of the terms it involves.

G. Leff, *Gregory of Rimini: Tradition and Innovation in Fourteenth Century Thought*, Manchester, 1961. – M. Dal Pra, "La teoria del 'significato totale' della proposizione nel pensiero di Gregorio da Rimini", *Logica e realtà. Momenti del pensiero medievale*, Rome-Bari, 1974, 121-153. – *Gregor von Rimini: Werk und Wirkung bis zur Reformation*, H. A. Obermann (ed.), Berlin-New York, 1981.

Luca Bianchi

**GREGORY OF TOURS (538-594).** Georgius Florentius Gregorius was born on 30 Nov, probably 538, to a family of the Arvernian senatorial aristocracy. When he was ten, his father died and he was entrusted to his paternal uncle, Bishop Gallus of *Clermont, until the latter's death in 551. Later, he lived at *Lyon with his maternal uncle Bishop Nicetius. These years were devoted to study. His ecclesiastical career began before 551; in 563, when he went on *pilgrimage to *Saint-Martin, he was a *deacon. He remained some time with Bishop Euphronius of Tours, a relative. On the latter's death, he was designated by King Sigebert of *Austrasia to replace him; he was consecrated at *Reims.

During the 21 years of his episcopate (573-594) he acted as pastor, heir to St *Martin. Until 585 he was opposed by the coalition of part of the Touraine clergy, the *count of the city and the enemies of the Austrasian family. The *Merovingian princes were then disputing Touraine. Though he respected established *authority, he was obliged to get involved in political quarrels in order to defend the privileges of Saint-Martin, particularly its right of *asylum, and in 579 he was even compromised in a plot against Fredegund; exculpated by the council of Berny, he regained Chilperic's confidence. His relations were more serene with Chilperic's successors, who were reconciled after 585. He even acted as counsellor to Guntram, then to Childebert II; in 589 he appealed to them to pacify the revolt of the nuns of the Holy Cross at *Poitiers. He died in 594. He innovated little at *Tours; he extended Saint-Martin's influence, but could not maintain his authority over the whole ecclesiastical *province, divided between several kingdoms.

His greatness pertains to his literary work, which is that of a Christian and a witness. All through his episcopate, he wrote to preserve the memory of his times and also to edify his readers. He had a narrative sense, a taste for anecdote. In his *History of the Franks*, which goes from the creation of the world to 591, he introduces the Frankish people into the economy of *Revelation; but the essential part – nine books out of ten – is devoted to the 6th c., especially the period 575-591. The victory of the *Franks is interpreted as the success of *Clovis's alliance with God and Martin's patronage of Gaul. In the majority of his hagiographical writings – the *Book of the Miracles of St Martin*, the *Book of the Miracles of St Julian*, *To the Glory of the Martyrs*, *To the Glory of the Confessors*, the *Lives of the Fathers* – he favours the *virtutes* (miraculous powers) of saints to whom he can bear witness, *i.e.* those of Auvergne and Touraine. He also wrote a *Book of the Miracles of St Andrew*, a *Passion of the Seven Sleepers*, a treatise on the course of the stars and an explanation of the title of the *psalms: of these only fragments remain.

Gregorii Turonensis, *Libri historiarum, miracula et opera omnia*, B. Krusch (ed.), *MGH.SRM*, 1, 1-2, 1937-1969 (2 vol.; re-ed. 1988-1992). – Gregory of Tours, *History of the Franks*, L. Thorpe (tr.), Harmondsworth, 1977. – Gregory of Tours, *Life of the Fathers*, 2nd ed., Liverpool, 1991.

L. Pietri, *La Ville de Tours du IVe au VIe siècle*, Rome, 1983. – W. Goffart, *The Narrators of Barbarian History A.D. 500-900, Jordanes, Gregory of Tours, Bede and Paul the Deacon*, Princeton (NJ), 1988. – J. Verdon, *Grégoire de Tours*, Paris, 1989. – A. H. B. Breukelaar, *Historiography and Episcopal Authority in Sixth-Century Gaul*, Gottingen, 1994. – M. Heinzelmann, *Gregor von Tours*, Darmstadt, 1994.

Brigitte Beaujard

**GROENENDAAL, SCHOOL OF.** There is a manifest link between the great Brabantine mystic Jan van *Ruysbroeck (1293-1381) and several writers belonging to his religious community, but the relationshiop is unclear. The main figures are:

1. Jan van Leeuwen († 1378), called the "good cook of Groenendaal". Before his entry into religious life, he served in the household of John III, duke of *Brabant. At that time he could neither read nor write. Jan van Ruysbroeck was concerned as much with his literary formation as with his spiritual advancement, so the good cook was put to write in his leisure hours. In his many writings, still largely unedited, he vulgarized his master's *doctrine. Ruysbroeck greatly esteeemed the writings of *Hadewijch of Antwerp, but had reservations about the testimony of Meister *Eckhart, as Jan van Leeuwen tells us in "A little book on the doctrine of Meister Eckhart, a doctrine in which he errs".

2. William Jordaens (*c.*1320-1372). Master William was born at *Brussels, the son of Jordaens d'Heerzele, cup-bearer at the *court of duchess Joan of Brabant (1355-1406). Before entering Groenendaal in 1352, he had passed his mastership in *theology, probably at the university of *Paris. He translated three of Ruysbroeck's works into Latin: the **Spiritual Espousals*, the *Seven Degrees* and the *Spiritual Tabernacle*. He also wrote personal works, of which we may mention the *Planctus super obitu fratris Johannis de Speculo* (*AnBoll* 4, 1885, 323-333) and a spiritual treatise in Middle Dutch entitled *De mystieke mondkus*, edited by the Ruysbroeck society in 1967.

3. Godefroid Wevel († 1396). Godefroid was the son of a rich family of Louvain. He entered Groenendaal before 1360, aged about 40. He was the author of the treatise *The Twelve Virtues*, long considered a work of Ruysbroeck and, as such, translated into Latin by the Carthusian Surius. Wevel borrowed widely from Ruysbroeck's *Spiritual Espousals* and Meister Eckhart's first published text, *Reden der Unterscheidung*. The religious of Groenendaal did not all have the same estimation of that great German master.

4. Jan van Schoonhoven (1356-1432). Jan was a native of Schoonhoven near Gouda in Holland. He studied at Paris and there obtained the mastership of arts, before entering Groenendaal in 1376. He is known mainly for his defence of Ruysbroeck against the objections of *Gerson (1363-1429). This apologia is entitled *Commendatio sive defensio libri fratris Johannis Ruusbroec De ornatu spiritualium nuptiarum*. The controversy has been studied in depth by A. Combes (*Essai sur la critique de Ruusbroec par Gerson*). Jan van Schoonhaven left many other spiritual works. In 1413 there fell to him the signal honour of preaching the inaugural sermon at the general chapter of *Windesheim.

5. Henry Pomerius (1382-1469), a native of Brussels. He directed the schools, first at Brussels and then at Louvain, a town of which he had been appointed sworn secretary. Aged 30, he retired to the monastery of Groenendaal. Around 1420 he set to write the history of his monastery's foundation. He completed this history with the biographies of Jan van Ruysbroeck and Jan van Leeuwen. All these texts have been edited in *AnBoll* 4 (1885). Henry was prior at Groenendaal and at Sept-Fontaines. He wrote many spiritual works, of which the most important is his *Pomerium spirituale*.

6. Sayman van Wijc (1374-1438). A native of Zaltbommel, he entered Groenendaal on 12 May 1398 and became the community's archivist. To his pen we owe the Inventory and the *Obituary of the Groenendaal community. He is more a historian than a spiritual writer.

7. Jan Wisse (died after 1416). Jan Wisse came from Leiden in Holland. He was the first *provost of the monastery of Eemsteyn, founded in 1382 with the intention of following the rules and

customs of Groenendaal. In 1414, he was elected as third prior of Groenendaal. In manuscript D of Ruysbroeck's works, he is called "the disciple" (*de nacomelinc*), because he did not know Ruysbroeck personally. He left several accounts typical of the oral tradition concerning Ruysbroeck.

All these authors were contemporaries or immediate successors of Ruysbroeck. In the second half of the 15th c., the level of the community seems to have fallen. We find fewer authors there and their interest is less in *spirituality. Nevertheless we may cite Arnould Gheylhoven († 1492), who had studied at *Padua where he became a doctor in *canon law. He is known mainly for his *Gnotosolitos*, also called *Speculum conscientiae*.

P. Verdeyen, *Ruusbroec and his Mysticism*, Collegeville (MN), 1994, 64-82.

Paul Verdeyen

**GROOTE, GERHARD (1340-1384).** "Father of the *Devotio moderna*", Gerhard (Geert) Groote was born at *Deventer (Yssel). He studied at *Paris and became master of arts in 1358. He continued his studies (law, *medicine, *theology) until 1368 and obtained two *prebends, at *Aachen and *Utrecht. After his *conversion to a more ascetic life (*c.*1374), he renounced his *benefices, made a gift of his house to some "poor women", germ of the *foundation of the Sisters of the Common Life, and withdrew for some years to the Charterhouse of Monnikhuizen near Arnhem. Back in Deventer, he began a great reforming activity among young *clerics whom he gathered round himself, and among the *secular and regular clergy. In his preaching tours, he vehemently called the people to conversion. He also, not without violence, took issue with "*heretics". In 1383, at the synod of Utrecht, he attacked concubinary priests and was penalized by the *bishop who, indirectly, withdrew his right to preach. In his retreat, he devoted himself to the translation of the *Hours* which he glossed for the Sisters and the *laity. He died of the plague in 1384, but not before he had laid the foundations of the *Brethren of the Common Life and the congregation of *canons of *Windesheim.

His work, nourished by scriptural, patristic and juridical references, is entirely dedicated to his apostolate: his *letters allow us to follow his activity as a reformer and spiritual guide. Part of his treatises aim at denouncing ecclesiastical abuses (*simony, lack of *pastoral care, concubinage) and violations of monastic *Rules. He also wrote two treatises on *marriage, one in Dutch, and more spiritual works such as a small treatise on common life among the *beguines (*De Simonia ad baguttas*), a *sermon on *poverty (*De paupertate in die Palmarum*) and a treatise on the subjects of *meditation, more philosophical (*De quatuor generibus meditabilium*). We also owe him a Latin translation of Jan van *Ruysbroeck's **Spiritual Espousals*.

A man full of contrasts, rigorously ascetic, Groote genuinely wished to cure the ills of the Church at the time of the *Great Schism. He advocated a return to the Gospel and the *Fathers and the simplicity of the early Church. He insisted on self-knowledge and the need for a lucid choice in all the circumstances of life and saw the common life, even outside canonical *vows, as the means of realising his ideal of imitation of *Christ. His criticism of the clergy was not anti-ecclesial, but proof of a moral exactingness and of the wish to provide the faithful with an authentic pastoral presence.

*Gerardi Magni Epistolae*, W. Mulder (ed.), Antwerp, 1933. – Geert Grote, *Devotia moderna: Basic Writings*, New York, 1988. – Gérard Grote, *Lettres et traités*, G. Epiney-Burgard (ed., tr.), Turnhout, 1998. J. G. Tiecke, *De werken van Geert Grote*, Utrecht-Nijmegen, 1941. – J. G. Tiecke, "Gérard Grote", *DSp*, 6, 1967, 265-274. – T. Van Zijl, *Gerard Groote, Ascetic and Reformer (1340-1348)*, Washington (DC), 1963. – G. Épiney-Burgard, *Gérard Grote (1340-1384) et les débuts de la Dévotion moderne*, Wiesbaden, 1970. – "Geert Grote & Moderne Devotie", *OGE*, 59, 1985.

Georgette Épiney-Burgard

**GROTTAFERRATA, SANTA MARIA DI.** An *abbey of Greek rite founded in 1004 in the territory of *Tusculum, near *Rome, by St *Nilus of Rossano. The original building, which still exists, resembled a cave and had bars on the windows, whence the name Grottaferrata. The earliest document to mention this name *Crypta ferrata* is a *bull of Benedict IX dated 1037. Abbot Bartholomew, third successor of St Nilus, built the abbey church, consecrated in 1024 by Pope John XIX of the counts of Tusculum. During the 9th c. the abbey gradually enlarged its possessions until 1222 when Pope *Calixtus II established its autonomy, subjecting it to the Church of Rome alone. It was the first monastery in Latium to enjoy *exemption. In 1131, its *abbot was invested by *Roger II of Sicily with a barony in the Salernitano. In the 12th c. the abbey was devastated during the disputes between Tusculum, Albano and Rome, and in 1163 its monks had to go to the monastery of San Speco at *Subiaco, where they remained until 1188. In 1240 Grottaferrata was occupied for over a year by *Frederick II. After a period of decline in the 14th and early 15th cc., the abbey recovered under its first commendatory abbot, the Greek cardinal *Bessarion (1462-1472). *Pius II had given the abbey in *commendation to this cultivated Byzantine humanist, who not only took possession of all its usurped property, but gave a great impetus to the monastery's cultural life. His successor, Cardinal Giuliano della Rovere (the future Pope Julius II), surrounded it with fortified walls, giving it the appearance of a great medieval fortress, and built the abbot's palace (1492). The commendation later passed to cardinals of the *Colonna, Farnese and Barberini families before being finally suppressed under Pope Leo XII. The last commendatory abbot was Ercole Consalvi.

The heart of the abbey is the church, dedicated to the Madonna. After recent restorations, the façade keeps the original *rose window. The 11th/12th-c. Romanesque campanile has five storeys of three-light windows over one of single-light windows, and is ornamented with polychrome disks. On the left of the *narthex is a marble baptismal *font with bas-reliefs depicting fishing scenes, alluding to the sacrament of *baptism, from around the year 1000. In the centre is the early 11th-c. entrance door, the "Porta speciosa", with contemporary wooden panels. Above it is the *mosaic of the *Deêsis (intercession): Jesus blessing with the Virgin and St John the Baptist at each side; on the left, in smaller proportions, the figure of Abbot Bartholomew who built the church. The church has three aisles. The right aisle gives access to the *vetus aedicula* (1004), the abbey's original nucleus. On the triumphal arch, still well preserved, is the 12th/13th-c. mosaic of the *Etimasia* (preparation). It depicts the 12 apostles beside the empty throne in whose lower part is the apocalyptic *lamb. Over the *altar is the venerated 13th-c. *icon of the Mother of God, of Byzantine derivation but with Latin elements in the sweetness of the face and the Child's *gesture of blessing.

Besides the Museum with its exhibits of ancient and medieval history, there is the famous *Library, which holds many precious manuscripts, some illuminated, especially on Byzantine liturgy and music, evidence of intense literary activity. By transcribing *codices, the monks kept alive the Italo-Greek calligraphical and iconographical tradition.

L. Ferrara, "S. Maria di Grottaferrata", *EC*, 11, 1830-1833. – "Nilo da Rossano", *BSS*, 9, 995-1008. – M. Petta, *MonIt*, 1, 1981, 144-145. – P. Giannini, *DHGE*, 22, 1988, 388-396. – M. Petta, *LdM*, 4, 1989, 1733 f.

Marcello Terzano

**GRUNWALD or TANNENBERG.** Grunwald (Tannenberg in German historiography), a place belonging in the 15th c. to the State of the *Teutonic Order, is now in *Poland. It was the site of the battle of 15 July 1410, during the great war of 1409-1411, in which the Polish-*Lithuanian troops led by the king of Poland, *Ladislas Jagiello (Władisław Jagiełło), faced the *army of the Teutonic Knights commanded by the grand master of the order, Ulrich von Jungingen. The Polish-Lithuanian army numbered nearly 29,000 men, to which the Teutonics opposed some 31,000: a total of nearly 60,000 men in arms, 50,000 of them horsemen and 10,000 footsoldiers. After a combat that lasted all day, the Teutonic Knights were beaten and Ulrich von Jungingen met his death on the field of battle along with a good number of high dignitaries of the order.

The Polish-Lithuanian side were unable to profit from the victory, neither militarily – Malbork (*Marienburg), the capital of the Teutonic State, was not conquered – nor politically – the advantages obtained by the peace treaty of Toruń in 1411 were relatively meagre. However, this battle began the decline of the rule of the Teutonic State in that part of Europe.

M. Kuczyński, *Wielka wojna z Zakonem Krzyżackim w latach 1409-1411*, Warsaw, 1980. – S. Ekdahl, *Die Schlacht bei Tannenberg, 1410. Quellenkritische Untersuchungen*, 1, Berlin, 1983.

Zbigniew Piłat

**GUARDIAN.** The name "guardian" was given by St *Francis of Assisi (1182-1226) to the person reponsible for the community containing both laymen and *clerics. A lay brother could become a guardian, but the church hierarchy quite rapidly encouraged the clericalization of the nascent Order. Nevertheless, the definitive rule of 1223 maintained the right of laymen to attain elective office. In 1239, Albert of Pisa was the first cleric to be elected minister general. His successor Haymo of Faversham excluded laymen from the position of guardian. The Constitutions of Narbonne (1260) did not deal with the problem of the eligibility of laymen. The council of Trent, by the decree *De reformatione*, reserved superiority in all clerical religious families for priests. Despite the protests and efforts of the Capuchin reform in the 16th c., the order conformed to the conciliar decree.

*The Writings of St. Francis of Assisi*, H. Backhouse (ed.), London, 1994.

Élisabeth Lopez

**GUELFS AND GHIBELLINES.** The terms "Guelfs" and "Ghibellines" spread shortly before the middle of the 13th c., starting from *Tuscany, to refer to a major cleavage in the political and social life of central and northern *Italy in the 13th-14th cc., between partisans of the papacy (*pars Ecclesie*) and partisans of the emperor (*pars Imperii*), in the trial of strength that opposed these two powers in the peninsula. Their etymology, readily enriched by fantastic explanations ever since the Middle Ages, goes back to the names of two families, taken as rallying-signs and perhaps as war-cries: the Welfs, Bavarian dukes from whom sprung the Emperor *Otto IV, who was crowned by the *pope in 1209 and died in 1218, soon opposed to *Innocent III, but primarily, as posterity remembered, a constant rival of the *Staufen; and the Waiblingen family, otherwise called the *Salians, whose authority the Staufen appealed to. Beginning in the 1170s under *Frederick Barbarossa and the first *Lombard League, the fracture was aggravated during the conflict between the papacy and the Staufen *Frederick II († 1250). It was prolonged with the wars between his heirs and the Guelf forces, revived and unified for a time around *Charles I of Anjou, victorious in 1266-1268. Handicapped, the Ghibellines were on the defensive from now on, not without pugnacity or occasional victories, in particular at the time of the descents into Italy of the kings, then emperors, *Henry VII (1310-1313) and Louis of Bavaria (1327-1330).

The essence and the difficulty lie less here than in comprehending the bipolarization of communal societies, which overflowed the milieu of the elites, conditioned the whole life of the cities and took root in their institutions. The conflict between the pope and the emperor only partially provided its motives and themes. It was grafted onto regional rivalries (Florentine Guelfism against Sienese Ghibellinism), family rivalries within towns (the Montagues and Capulets of *Verona have become their literary prototypes), but also rivalries within *families, conditioning each man's positioning on a complex chessboard: a positioning, moreover, more and more changeable, especially when it interfered with the strategies of power at the dawn of the regional *signorie*, and further complicated by the faults that broke up the political landscape when Guelfism came to power ("black" and "white" Guelfs at *Florence, *pars inferior* and *pars superior* at Reggio Emilia, etc.). In these conditions, it is vain to assign any sort of programme to these groups that had become veritable parties (*partes*), or to attach a reductive social reading to them, though the ranks of the Ghibellines, soon thinned out and more affected by exile (*fuorusciti*), included a considerable number of *signori* rooted, with their clienteles, in the *contado*.

The historiographical fortune of the phenomenon is at the height of its hold and has even led to the birth of "neo-Guelfism" in the contemporary period.

P. Herde, *Guelfen und Neoguelfen: Zur Geschichte einer nationalen Ideologie vom Mittelalter zum Risorgimento*, Stuttgart, 1986 ("SbWGF", 22, 2). – E. Voltmer, "Gibelins" et "Guelfes", *Dictionnaire historique de la papauté*, Paris, 1994, 726-729 and 773-775.

Olivier Guyotjeannin

**GUERRIC OF IGNY (before 1080-1157).** Born at *Tournai, he was educated at St Martin's cathedral *school, of which he became a *canon, then **scholasticus*. When he had retired to solitude and prayer, two friends spoke to him of *Clairvaux, which he decided to enter in 1125. He was sent to Igny to succeed the retiring Abbot Humbert, and died in 1157. His 54 liturgical *sermons reveal an author steeped in philosophical and theological culture. A disciple of St *Bernard, he developed the themes of the intermediary coming of *Christ and the spiritual progress that leads, by stages, from *faith to the *beatific vision. Purified thanks to faith which is light, the believer accomplishes works of light and thus gives birth to Christ as does *Mary, image of the Church.

Guerric, *Sermons*, *SC*, 166 and 202, 1970-1973 (2 vol.). – Guerric of Igny, *Liturgical Sermons*, 1, Shannon, 1971; 2, Spencer (MA), 1971.

*DSp*, 6, 1967, 1113-1121. – J. Morson, *Christ the Way: the Christology of Guerric of Igny*, Kalamazoo (MI), 1978. – *DSp*, 13, 1988, 747.

Jean-Baptiste Auberger

*Christ in Majesty.* Miniature from Guibert of Nogent's *Tropologiae in Osee, Jeremiam et Amos*, 1120-1124. Paris, BNF (Ms lat. 2502, fol. 1).

**GUIBERT OF NOGENT (1053-*c*.1130).** Born 15 April 1053 shortly before the death of his father, a knight of the Beauvaisis, Guibert, vowed to the clerical life, received a careful *education from his mother, completed after 1067 by a sound instruction at the monastery of Saint-Germer-de-Fly (Oise). Abbot of Nogent-sous-Coucy (Aisne) from 1104 to 1125, he was witness and actor in the events of the *commune of *Laon (1111-1112) of which he left a vivid account in his *Autobiography*. A curious character, obsessed with the corruption of the world, he observed his contemporaries with a rare critical sense tinged with irony. His work consists of historical and theological works of quality (*Gesta Dei per Francos*, *De laude Sanctae Mariae*).

*A Monk's Confession: the Memoirs of Guibert of Nogent*, P. J. Archambault (ed.), University Park (PA), 1996. – Guibert of Nogent, *The Deeds of God through the Franks*, R. Levine (ed.), Woodbridge, 1997.

Alain Saint-Denis

**GUIBERT OF TOURNAI (*c*.1200-1284).** A *Franciscan from *Tournai, he succeeded his close friend *Bonaventure when the latter was elected minister general, doubtless in 1257-1260. Guibert is known by his theological works and *sermons. His most important treatise in content and influence is the *Rudimentum doctrinae*, in which he demonstrates that *God is the "first thing remarked by the *intellect and that the rest is known in him" (C. Bérubé). We have 457 of his sermons for *Sundays and saints' days, as well as for the various states of life.

D. L. d'Avray, *The Preaching of the Friars*, Oxford, 1985. – S. Gieben, "Il 'Rudimentum doctrinae' di Gilberto di Tournai con l'edizione del suo 'Registro': Tavola della materia", *Bonaventuriana*, Rome, 1988, 621-680.

Jacques-Guy Bougerol

**GUIDO OF AREZZO (*c*.991-1031).** The most influential theoretician of *music in the Middle Ages. A monk of the abbey of *Pomposa, in *c*.1025 he moved to Arezzo under the protection of Bishop Theodald, and in 1028 he presented the *pope with the results of his researches on notation and teaching.

In his major work, the *Micrologus*, he revised the teaching of his predecessors on the scale of sounds: seven notes, of which he proposed two modes of distribution on the Monochord. His theory of *organum* (descant), which authorized the passage of the accompanying voice above the other, was decisive for the evolution of *polyphony. An excellent pedagogue, he proposed an original method of improvisation and a new principle of writing music: the notes were placed in relation to coloured lines, Fa and Ut, drawn above the semitone and set between letter-clefs (*Aliae Regulae*). His invention of the syllables of *solmization, *Ut re mi fa sol la* (*Epistola de ignoto cantu*); his description of their transpositions laid the basis for the teaching of the "Sol-fa" in the Middle Ages.

Guidonis Aretini, *Micrologus*, J. Smits van Waesbergue (ed.), Rome, 1955 ("Corpus Scriptorum de Musica", 4). – *Hucbald, Guido and John on Music*, C.V. Palsca (ed.), New Haven, 1978. – Gui d'Arezzo. *Micrologus*, M.-N. Colette (Fr. tr., commentary), J.-C. Jolivet (Fr. tr., commentary), Paris, 1993.

C. V. Palisca, "Guido of Arezzo", *The New Grove Dictionary of Music and Musicians*, S. Sadie (ed.), 7, London, 1980 (repr. 1998), 803-807.

Marie-Noël Colette

**GUIGO THE CARTHUSIAN (1083-1136).** Born in the castle of Saint-Romain-du-Val-Mordane (commune of Saint-Barthélemy-le-Plain, Ardèche), he entered the Grande Chartreuse in 1106. Three years later, he became its fifth *prior. His priorate was marked by the *foundation of seven new Charterhouses, for whom the authorities, led by Bishop Hugh of Grenoble, asked him to set down in writing the usages followed at the Grande Chartreuse in order to imitate its observance. Drawn up between 1121 and 1128, the *Customs* gave the nascent *Carthusian Order its stability and its unity, based on a communion of specific vocation. They gave it a definitive character, despite the adaptations made at various times, and remain the foundation of Carthusian life.

Endowed with exceptional intellectual qualities, a talented legislator and efficient administrator, Guigo was also an acknowledged spiritual master, whose influence went beyond Carthusian circles. The friendly exchanges he had notably with *Peter the Venerable and St *Bernard allowed him to explore more deeply, by formulating them clearly, the particularities of the *propositum* of the Chartreuse: the daily problems of the monk's life were subjected to an imperative, that of the vocation to *contemplation in solitude. Hence all the observances were arranged so as to favour the pursuit of an ideal, the meeting of the *soul with *God; they had to permit the solitary in peace in his cell, freed from the material contingencies of existence, to open himself up to the only realities that mattered, those of *heaven.

Guigo died, still in charge, in 1136. He left several writings: *Meditations*, drawn up at the beginning of his priorate, intimate thoughts on the interior perfecting of the contemplative and the role of the *prior as spiritual guide of his community; nine *Letters addressed to various personages, especially memorable among them being the "Letter to an unknown friend on the solitary life", in which the author sums up the essence of his thought on the Carthusian vocation; the *Life of Bishop Hugh* of Grenoble, written at the request of *Innocent II who had just canonized him, in 1135, three years after his death. But the *Customs of Chartreuse* remain the prior's essential work, one of the finest expressions of monastic legislation in the West in its eremitical version, as still attested today by the Statutes of the Order of Carthusians, which see Guigo's prescriptions as "sparks struck from a soul: that of the monk to whom the *Holy Spirit entrusted the mission of drawing up the first laws of our order".

Guigo I, *Lettres des premiers Chartreux*, *SC*, 88, 1962, 97-133. – Guigo I, *Coutumes de Chartreuse*, *SC*, 313, 1984, 13-24. – *The Meditations of Guigo I, prior of the Charterhouse*, Kalamazoo (MI), 1995.

M. Laporte, "Guigues Ier", *DSp*, 6, Paris, 1967, 1169-1175. – [Un chartreux], "La Jeunesse de Guigues le Chartreux", *Revue drômoise*, 83, Valence, 1983, 313-332. – G. Hocquard, "Les idées maîtresses des *Meditationes* du prieur Guigues Ier", *Historia et spiritualitas cartusiensis*, Destelbergen, 1983, 247-256. – G. Mursell, *The Theology of the Carthusian Life in the Writings of St. Bruno and Guigo I*, Salzburg, 1988.

Daniel Le Blévec

**GUILD.** Mutual aid association of a type dominant in the Middle Ages in the countries that bordered the North Sea.

The guilds were long considered societies of *merchants arising in the 11th c., stimulators of the renewal of the *towns and of urban freedoms. But a *capitulary of 779, and an instruction of Archbishop *Hincmar of Reims of 852, show the *gildae* or *geldoniae* as groups based on an *oath, as much given to drinking sessions as to works of piety, and hence suspect to the civil and ecclesiastical authorities; no doubt they were connected with the – notably pecuniary – mutual aid groups, cemented by rites of shared carousal, attested in ancient Germany, but proper to many other stateless societies. At the same epoch the Anglo-Saxon laws show a number of guilds of the same type, but where collective responsibility held an important place.

The guilds we subsequently meet in *Scandinavia or in the 10th c. at Tiel (Gueldre), in the 11th at Valenciennes, *Saint-Omer, *Arras, *Ghent or *Cologne and, later, at *Bruges, *Rouen, *Tournai and *London have a more marked mercantile character by reason of their members' way of life, but they remained essentially religious solidarities. Being also "peace associations" and leagues, it is not astonishing that they were able to play an active role in the emergence of those groupings of a similar nature, the communes.

In the 12th c., the growing self-assertion of the civil powers in their role of preservers of public peace restricted the guilds to their social function, in which they were soon overtaken by other, more specialized organisations, whether in fraternal *charity like the *confraternities, or in large-scale *commerce like the *Hanses with which they are too often confused. Professional solidarity took the lead from the others and they slipped down towards trade communities. From the 13th c., the guilds appear to be obsolete institutions nearly everywhere, except in *England. There, in numerous boroughs, the *gilda mercatoria* was a community of notables led by its aldermen, knit together by the fiscal and commercial privileges that it enjoyed, and an effectual relay of royal power. In the next two centuries, this eminent role was often contested on the economic level by the appearance of other guilds composed of artisans (craft guilds), the appearance of real *confraternities like those of *Corpus Christi, and the setting up of municipal organisations embodying the whole urban community.

S. L. Thrupp, "Medieval Gilds Reconsidered", *JEconHist*, 2, 1942, 164-173. – E. Coornaert, "Les ghildes médiévales (Ve-XIVe siècles. Définition-Évolution", *RH*, 199, 1948, 22-55, 208-243. – S. L. Thrupp, "The Gilds", *Economic Organization and Policies in the Middle Ages*, M. M. Postan (ed.), E. E. Rich (ed.), E. Miller (ed.), Cambridge, 1963, 230-280 ("The Cambridge Economic History of Europe", 3). – S. Epstein, *Wage Labor and Guilds in Medieval Europe*, Chapel Hill, 1991. – V.R. Bainbridge, *Gilds in the Medieval Countryside*, Woodbridge, 1996.

Bernard Chevalier

**GUILLAUME DE MACHAUT (1300-1377).** A major musician and poet of the 14th c., born *c.*1300 in *Champagne and died 1377 at *Reims. In *c.*1323 Machaut entered the service of John of Luxemburg, king of *Bohemia, as secretary; he travelled to *Poland, *Lithuania and *Italy before settling at Reims. When John of Luxemburg died in 1346, Machaut passed into the service of his daughter Bonne of Luxemburg, then that of Charles the Bad, king of *Navarre, and finally of *Charles V, king of *France. He also had as patrons such princes as *John of Berry and Amadeus of Savoy. In the course of his life, he received canonries at Reims, *Verdun and *Arras.

We possess more works by him than by any other 14th-c. composer. His literary inspiration was courtly by nature and erudite in make. In *music, he wrote in all the genres, religious and secular, practised in his time; he introduced or developed new procedures of composition, known under the name *Ars Nova*: binary *rhythms, shorter rhythmic values than in the 13th c., use of motifs all through a single piece, isorhythm or construction of one or more voices on a long sequence several times repeated.

The *Remede de fortune* is a long poem, perhaps didactic. The main secular lyrical forms of the time – *lais*, *ballades*, *rondeaux*, *virelais*, a *chanson royale*, a *complainte* – are represented in it. The *Voir Dit* is an autobiographical or allegorical poem, perhaps his most important literary work. In it the aged Machaut evokes his *love for a young girl, real or fictitious: Péronne d'Armentières. The *Prise d'Alexandrie* is his last work, a long *chronicle devoted to Peter I de *Lusignan, king of *Cyprus and *Jerusalem.

The secular songs follow the *formes fixes*, as was then the custom. Machaut put some of them into *music: 19 *lais*, two of them *polyphonic; 33 *virelais*, of which half are polyphonic, often syllabic and in binary rhythm; 42 *ballades* and 21 *rondeaux*, two very innovative forms in Machaut. All the *ballades* save one and all the *rondeaux* are polyphonic, but the number of voices can vary.

The *Messe De Nostre Dame* is the oldest surviving *mass that deals polyphonically – in four voices – with the six pieces sung at the ordinary of the mass: **Kyrie*, **Gloria*, **Credo*, **Sanctus*, **Agnus Dei* and *Ite missa est*. Historically, the grouping together of these pieces, which do not follow each other in the mass, appears in the *Franciscan *gradual, in the mid 13th century. Their polyphonic treatment was at first done in pairs: *Gloria* and *Credo*, *Sanctus* and *Agnus Dei*. But Machaut seems to have been the first to compose a polyphonic music intended to make a single work out of these six pieces. Lastly, the *Hoquet David* is a work that uses a writing procedure in which the notes are separated by silences and are out of phase from one voice to another.

Finally, we also have 24 *motets by Machaut, usually in three

*Nature, wishing to reveal the honourable benefits that there are in Love, comes to Guillaume, orders him to make new love-songs on this theme and gives him three of her children as advisers: Sense, Rhetoric and Music.* Miniature from Guillaume de Machaut's *Poésies*, *c.*1370. Paris, BNF (Ms fr. 1584, fol. E).

voices, sometimes four. The genre was not necessarily religious in the 14th c., and the majority of these motets associate the use of Latin and French.

*The Works of Guillaume de Machaut*, L. Schrade (ed.), Monaco, 1956 ("Polyphonic Music of the Fourteenth Century", 2-3). – G. Reaney, *Machaut*, London, 1971 ("Oxford Studies of Composers", 9). – G. Becker, S. Lefevre, "Guillaume de Machaut", *DLFMA*, 1992. – D. Leech-Wilkinson, *Machaut's Mass: an Introduction*, Oxford, 1992. – L. Earp, *Guillaume de Machaut: a Guide to Research*, New York, 1995. – Y. Plumley, *The Grammar of 14th Century Melody*, New York, 1996.

Claire Maître

**GUTENBERG, JOHANNES (*c.*1400-1468).** Johannes Gensfleisch called Gutenberg was the first to respond, by dedicating his existence to working out the art of printing, to the expectations he shared with the society of his time. Banished from his home town for having refused to bow to the fiscal demands of a municipality dominated by tradesmen, this son of Mainz patricians devoted himself at the beginning of his *Strasbourg exile (1434-1448), after having cut precious stones for a time, to the mass production of the mirrors that *pilgrims going to *Aachen brought away with them. This activity confronted him with the challenge of reduction, while he had acquired (or proved) in the exercise of his first activity his aptitude for precision work. It matters little whether he printed for the first time after his return to *Mainz (which is generally admitted) or at Strasbourg (A. Kapr). From 1438, in any case, he used his different skills to work out the four operations that were to give rise to typography: the cutting of punches (*patrices*) from a letter, the engraving of type moulds (*matrices*) with the help of a *patrix*, the casting of moveable characters on the basis of a *matrix*, and finally the infinity of textual combinations allowed by moveable characters.

That in 1455 he had to cede his workshop to his creditor and then associate Johannes Fust attests that printing could not have come into existence without the mobilization of a considerable *capital: what was possible in the towns of the Rhine valley was shown, by contrast, to be fragile at *Avignon, where a contemporary initative was short-lived. Gutenberg failed because he had been unable to pay off his investment. For that, it was necessary to develop a book market whose cultural landmarks were in that area rather than elsewhere, *i.e.* not just a considerable demand (which could in any case be partly satisfied by the copying of manuscripts), but especially a uniformization of perception (again defying a clerical cultural monopoly already well breached) and, especially, the concomitant wish to communicate, and not to capitalize on, memory. The 42-line *Bible may well have been a typographical masterpiece, but it corresponded only little to these conditions. It was to commissions better adapted to this growing market and hence to the possibilities of his art (*indulgences or more important productions printed with his original, less elaborate type, as was the 36-line Bible) that Gutenberg owed the success of his first workshop, which he directed no doubt until his death, and the spread of his invention, notably through the sale of characters.

F. Geldner, *Die deutschen Inkunabeldrucker*, 1, Stuttgart, 1968. – *Joh. Gutenbergs 42zeilige Bibel. Kommentarband*, W. Schmidt (dir.), F. A. Schmidt-Künsemüller (dir.), Munich, 1979. – *Gutenberg. 550 Jahre Buchdruck in Europa*, Wolfenbüttel, 1990, 9-52. – A. Kapr, *Johann Guttenberg: the Man and his Invention*, Aldershot, 1996.

Martial Staub

**GUY DE LUSIGNAN (1297/1300-1344).** King of Armenia (*Cilicia). Son of Amalric de *Lusignan, lord of Tyre, and Isabella of Armenia, he entered the service of the Emperor Andronicus II, who made him *strategos* of the West; but on the death of King Leo IV of Armenia, he was called to the throne and crowned under the name of Constantine IV (1342). To improve relations between the Church of Armenia and the papacy, he sent his brother Bohemund and the Franciscan Daniel of Tabriz to *Avignon. But his policy of resistance to the *Mamluks alienated certain barons, who killed him and Bohemund at Adana during *mass (17 Nov 1344). His son Leo V ascended the throne in 1373 and was to be the last king of Armenia.

S. Binon, "Guy d'Arménie et Guy de Chypre. Isabelle d'Arménie à la cour de Mistra", *Mélanges Boisacq*, Brussels, 1937, 125-142.

Jean Richard

**GUY OF SPOLETO (died 894).** Of a family of Alsatian origin established partly in *Brittany, partly in central *Italy, marquis of *Spoleto (like his father and namesake) and married to a Beneventan princess (whence interventions in the Mezziogiorno), Guy got himself elected king of West Francia in 888; but he abandoned the throne to his rival Eudes and turned to Italy, which had chosen Berengar of Friuli as king; he repulsed him, became king in 889 and was recognised by nearly all the kingdom. But, the better to establish his power in central and southern Italy, and inspired by *Louis II, he had himself crowned emperor (though he was not of the *Carolingian family) in 891. He issued *capitularies in the Carolingian tradition; in 891 he associated on the throne his son Lambert, whom Pope *Formosus crowned emperor at *Ravenna in 892. But the *pope, worried by his too active policy in central Italy, appealed to the Carolingian *Arnulf, who took *Pavia early in 894. Guy died suddenly at the end of that year.

G. Fasoli, *I re d'Italia (888-962)*, Florence, 1949.

Jean-Marie Martin

**GYROVAGUE.** Used of the wandering monk who "turned round and round", in the East this term characterised the monk who moved around continually, whereas the rule and ecclesiastical discipline prescribed stability: he went from monastery to monastery, village to village, town to town, and in a town he was always on visits or in public places. Hence the accusation of vagabondage launched against these monks, who were a source of troubles and sometimes scandal. In hagiographical literature, they are called "peripatetic" monks in the *Life of Paul the Younger* (ed. I. Sirmondi, 92) and compared in the *Life of Cyril the Phileote* (ed. E. Sargologos, 136) to transplanted trees that bear no fruit.

É. Malamut, *Sur la route des saints byzantins*, Paris, 1993, 187-192.

Élisabeth Malamut

# H

**HABITUS.** The term *habitus*, of Aristotelian origin, either designates one of the ten categories (that of having: see *Categories* 4) or a quality by which, according to *Aristotle, "a being is well- or ill-disposed with regard either to itself or to something else" (*Metaphysics* V, 20). The notion of *habitus* signifying a given or acquired disposition is fundamental both for epistemological doctrine (*habitus* of principles, intellectual virtues) and for *ethics, notably in St *Thomas Aquinas, since *virtues and their contrary are defined as *habitus*: "human virtue, which is a *habitus* of action, is a naturally good *habitus* and one that does good" (*Summa theologiae* I[a] I[ae], 55, 3).

Thomas Aquinas, *Summa theologiae*, I[a] II[a], 49-54.

Ruedi Imbach

**HABSBURG.** A dynasty originally from the upper Rhine region (upper *Alsace, Breisgau, Klettgau), also established in Austria from the 13th century. From 1438, the Habsburgs *de facto* monopolized the imperial *Crown and acquired a European dimension unequalled in the *Empire.

Its first known members go back to the 10th c. and seem to be related to the Etichonids. The eponymous *castle (*Habichtsburg*, later becoming *Habsburg*, in the Aargau) was built in *c.*1020 and the title "count of Habsburg" appeared in 1108. The Habsburgs built up their establishment in south-west *Germany through war, *money, marriage and the support of the *Staufen. They thus took the place, in whole or in part, of extinct dynasties (Lenzburg, Kiburg, Zähringen, then Staufen itself).

Rudolf IV of Habsburg, elected king of the Romans (Rudolf I) in 1273, managed to concede Austria and Styria to his sons as *fiefs of the *Empire; this gave the dynasty a second point of territorial anchorage, in the south-west of the Empire, and brought it into the group of Princes of the Empire. Yet the crown finally escaped Rudolf's successors: his son Albert I obtained it with difficulty and was assassinated, his grandson *Frederick the Fair never managed to make anything of the chances opened up by a double election.

However, the Habsburgs remained among the dominant dynasties of the Empire, allied by marriage to most of the German rulers. They arrogated to themselves the title of "archdukes" on the basis of a *forgery (*privilegium maius*, 1358-1359) and dedicated themselves wholly to establishing a junction between their western and eastern properties. Their territorial successes (Carinthia, Tyrol, Vorarlberg, upper *Swabia) led to clashes with the Swiss cantons (already victors over the Habsburgs in 1315 at Morgarten), against whom the Habsburgs suffered several defeats (Sempach, Näfels, loss of Habsburg). The ratio of strength with the Swiss could not subsequently be corrected, largely by reason of successoral divisions, which engendered three lines whose geopolitical horizons diverged (Balkans, central Europe, south-east Germany), and in 1474 (*Ewige Richtung*) the Habsburgs had to accept the territorial consequences of their successive defeats.

The return of the Habsburgs to the German throne inaugurated their entry into the concert of first-rank European dynasties. *Frederick III, at one time gravely menaced by conflicts in Austria (against his brother and part of the *nobility), in the Empire (against the *Wittelsbachs) and by the military successes of the king of *Hungary, *Matthias Corvinus, managed to restore the situation to his advantage. Obtaining the expectancy of the Hungarian Crown (1463 and 1491) and the hand of the daughter of the duke of *Burgundy for his son Maximilian (who also harvested the fruits of the patrimonial assemblage), Frederick III thus gave the Habsburgs the means to carry out (at least partly) the programme of his device *AEIOU* (*Austriae est imperare orbi universo* or, in German, *Alles Erdreich ist Österreich unterthan*: "The whole world is subject to Austria").

*NDB*, 7, 1966, 400-402. – A. Wandruszka, *Die Haus Habsburger*, Vienna, 1978. – B. Hamann, *Die Habsburger. Ein biographisches Lexikon*, Munich, 1988. – G. Hödl, *Habsburg und Österreich, 1273-1493*, Vienna, 1988. – *LdM*, 4, 1989, 1815-1816. – W. Baum, *Die Habsburger in den Vorlanden*, 1993. – W. Baum, *Reichs- und Territorialgewalt*, Vienna, 1993. – K. F. Krieger, *Die Habsburger im Mittelalter*, Stuttgart, 1994.

Joseph Morsel

**HADEWIJCH OF ANTWERP (13th c.).** A mystical Dutch poetess, for whose life we are reduced to conjectures, Hadewijch of Antwerp was undoubtedly active, according to clues found in her work, in the first half of the 13th c. (1220-1240). Her literary and theological culture undoubtedly testifies to an *education in an aristocratic milieu. To judge from her *letters, she was the spiritual guide of a small group of *women, probably *beguines.

Preserved in four manuscripts and rediscovered in the 19th c. both by medievalists and by the poet Maeterlinck, her work is important because Hadewijch is one of the creators of Dutch prose, a brilliant poetess, and even more imposing as a "mistress of *spirituality". To her we owe *Visions* (*Visioenen*), *Strophic Poems* (*Strofische Gedichten*) and *Poems* in rhyming couplets collected under the name of *Mengeldichten*.

The strophic poems, 45 in number, are inspired by contemporary courtly *poetry, all of whose formal wealth (images, rhymes and rhythms) she uses with virtuosity. They offer a ceaselessly repeated variation on the theme of *love (*minne*) and of her "adventures", the passionate quest for union with *God beyond tangible experience. The first 16 poems in rhyming couplets are in general more didactic. The next 13 poems are not by Hadewijch, but by one or more unknown authors (Hadewijch II). More recent, they are marked by a more speculative note, with a scholastic vocabulary and a more abstract content which implies an outstripping of forms and images.

The 14 *Visions* draw their images from the *Apocalypse, evoking the dynamism of divine love in its action on the world (vision 13) and describe the *visionary's own spiritual experience: passing from practice of the *virtues to fruitive union in the divine abyss.

Finally, 30 letters of direction or small spiritual *treatises give a summary of her *doctrine: "to become God with God", *i.e.* to participate in God's *being in order to rediscover there the nobility that the creature had in him from all eternity. Union conforms the creature to *Christ's humanity at the same time as his divinity.

The plunge into the divine Essence ravishes it into a state in which it is "without God by excess of God, unstable by excess of constancy, ignorant by excess of knowing" (Letter 28).

Nourished on the *Cistercian doctrine of *William of Saint-Thierry and that of the Victorines, Hadewijch created a Dutch theological vocabulary that would be taken up with more precision by *Ruysbroeck. She also influenced some members of the congregation of *Windesheim.

Hadewijch, *Visioenen*, J. Van Mierlo (ed.), Louvain, 1924-1925 (2nd ed., 2 vol.). – Hadewijch, *Strofische Gedichten*, J. Van Mierlo (ed.), Louvain, 1942 (2nd ed., 2 vol.). – Hadewijch, *Brieven*, J. Van Mierlo (ed.), Louvain, 1947 (2nd ed., 2 vol.). – Hadewijch, *Mengeldichten*, J. Van Mierlo (ed.), Louvain, 1952 (2nd ed.). – Hadewijch, *Poèmes mystiques des béguines*, J. B. Porion (tr.), Paris, 1954. – Hadewijch, *Lettres spirituelles*, J. B. Porion (tr.), Geneva, 1972. – *Hadewijch: the complete works*, London, 1981. – Hadewijch, *Visions*, J. B. Porion (tr.), Paris, 1987. – *Poetry of Hadewijch*, M. Van Baest (ed.), Leuven, 1998.

J. B. Porion, "Hadewijch", *DSp*, 7, 1968, 13-23. – F. Willaert, M. J. Govers, *Bibliographie zur deutschen Frauenmystik des Mittelalters*, Anhang 2, G. J. Lewis (ed.), Berlin 1989, 351-410. – S.M. Murk Jansen, *The Measure of Mystic Thought: a Study of Hadewijch's Mengeldichten*, Goppingen, 1991. – J.G. Milhaven, *Hadewijch and her Sisters*, Albany, 1993. – S.M. Murk Jansen, *Brides in the Desert: the Spirituality of the Beguines*, London, 1998.

Georgette Épiney-Burgard

***HADĪTH.*** The term *hadīth* means "recital", "talk"; with the article (*al-hadīth*), it designates the tradition relating the acts or the words of *Muḥammad. The **sunna*, "normative custom of the Prophet" is handed down in it. In *Islam, the "science of *hadīth*" is the science *par excellence*, in that the *hadīth* relate what the Prophet, or sometimes one of his companions or even a person of the next generation ("follower"), is held to have said or done. Moreover, they occupy a central place in Muslim law and jurisprudence. In a word, they continue the mission of Muḥammad as individual model and the paradigmatic function of the original community. From the 2nd century of the *hejira (8th c. AD), a *hadīth* consisted of two parts: a chain of guarantees (*isnād*) attesting the veracity of the transmission, and a text (*matn*) relating what was said or done.

The first age of putting the *hadīth* into writing was the period of the companions and followers. This writing down was much less developed than was claimed later, when the argument of writing was used to support the idea that all these traditions were authentic. Moreover, some elders were opposed to the writing down of the prophetic traditions, probably so that the Prophet's words should not be confused with the Koranic text, a distinction that was not always clear at that early period, when the intellectual arsenal intended to affirm the divine origin of the *Koran was not yet matured.

The systematic organisation of the collected materials began at the end of the 2nd century of the hejira (8th c. AD) and in the first half of the 3rd century (9th c.). One of the most important "summae" was that of Ibn Hanbal († 855), called *al-Musnad* (a work provided with chains of guarantees going back to the companions; it contains 30,000 traditions); it is classified according to the names of the companions who were its direct transmitters.

At the end of a period of codification, several of these collections acquired a particular flavour, notably the "six books", of which the most prized were the *Sahīh* (collection of "authentic" traditions) of al-Bukhārī († 870) and of Muslim († 875).

Certain transmitters (*muhaddith*) of traditions asked the question of their authenticity, developing a discipline in which it was possible to pronounce on the degree of trustworthiness to be accorded to this or that transmitter, but also on the veracity of the content. The criteria of this critique are not always the same as those of Western scholars, in that the former bring in theological and ideological judgments. It was this concern for approval and disapproval that gave rise to works of onomastic ordered by "classes" (*tabaqāt*, "generations" of transmitters) or alphabetically. The question of the authenticity of the traditions is one of those that has aroused most passion in Islam.

J. Robson, "Ḥadīth", *EI(E)*, 3, 1971, 23-28. – A. von Denffer, *Literature on Hadith in European Languages: a bibliography*, Leicester, 1981. – G. H. A. Juynboll, *Muslim Tradition: studies in chronology provenance and authorship of early "hadith"*, Cambridge, 1983. – L. T. Librande, "Ḥadīth", *EncRel(E)*, 6, 1987, 143-151. – J. Burton, *An Introduction to the Ḥadīth*, Edinburgh, 1994. – G. H. A. Juynboll, *Studies on the Origins and Uses of Islamic Hadith*, Aldershot, 1996.

Claude Gilliot

**HADRIAN OF CANTERBURY (*c.*630-709).** Abbot of Sts Peter and Paul, *Canterbury (670-709). A Greek-speaking African by birth, Hadrian probably left Africa as a refugee from the Arab *invasions of North Africa (642-645) and settled in *Naples, where he became *abbot of a monastery on Nisida (an islet on the outskirts of Naples). Perhaps as a result of his Greek background, he became an adviser to the Byzantine emperor Constans II after the Byzantine invasion of *Italy in 663, and conducted at least two embassies to Gaul on the emperor's behalf. Through the emperor he met Pope Vitalian and, as *Bede informs us (*Historia Ecclesiastica*, IV, 1-2), Hadrian was invited to become archbishop of Canterbury in 667; he declined the invitation and proposed the name of *Theodore (a Greek monk then living in *Rome), whom he was subsequently to join in *England, where he spent the remainder of his life. No writings of Hadrian survive, but he contributed to the teaching reflected in a large corpus of biblical commentaries from Canterbury, and his influence may be seen in the commemorations of Neapolitan saints in early Anglo-Saxon *liturgical books.

B. Bischoff, M. Lapidge, *Biblical Commentaries from the Canterbury School of Theodore and Hadrian*, Cambridge, 1994, 82-132.

Michael Lapidge

**HAGIOGRAPHY**

**The West.** Under the name of hagiography are designated all the texts in which are recounted the life and *miracles of the saints. It is not a literary genre but a "converging bundle of complex narrative modes with the common objective of exalting the memory or power of a saint" (A. Boureau). The most widespread forms are Lives (*vita*, *legenda*, *historia*), collections of miracles, and accounts of translation. These texts may be in prose or in verse, in *Latin or in the *vernacular (from the 12th c. in the West).

In the first centuries of Christianity, hagiography had an essentially devotional character. From the 3rd or 4th c., the main Christian Churches (Carthage, *Rome, *Antioch, etc.) established and updated their *martyrology, a *calendar arranged by months and days containing, opposite certain dates, the name of one or more saints, with an indication of their place of death. Later, these rather dry lists were enriched with information containing a summary of the life of the *martyr or, soon, of the confessor, as well as a description of the circumstances of his death. These are the historical martyrologies, the most famous of which is the "Hieronymian" martyrology – falsely attributed to St Jerome – compiled at Rome in the 6th c. from earlier texts drawn up in *Italy, Africa and Gaul. Other later ones enjoyed wide circulation, like those of the Venerable *Bede, *Florus of Lyon, *Ado and especially that of *Usuard, composed in 875 at Paris. In the Eastern Church, we find the same process in slightly different forms (menologies and *synaxaria, the most famous of which is that of Hagia Sophia, the "*Great Church" of *Constantinople).

At the same time we see a development, more or less rapid according to region, of the role given to the commemoration of saints in the liturgy. Very early in Africa, the custom spread among *clerics of reading at the *office a summary of the life of the servant of God whose *anniversary (*dies natalis*) was being celebrated. In this perspective were composed texts intended for public reading (*legendae*, *legends), which were divided into narrative lessons incorporated into *matins. To compose them, the initial inspiration was taken from the acts of the martyrs, *i.e.* the minutes of their trial and execution established by the civil authorities. On this model were later drawn up numerous accounts given the name of Passions (*Passiones*), epic and romantic amplifications in which the role of imagination and imitation were greater in proportion as the personages whose merits they claimed to celebrate were less known. Their authors spared no details about the cruelty of magistrates and executioners, the harshness of interrogations and punishments and the admirable resistance opposed to the persecutors by the servants of God. The search for edification at any price is attested by a series of *miracles each more extraordinary than the last, which aim to arouse the admiration of auditors or readers. These texts have sometimes been presented as the epic of nascent *Christendom: they are rather its soap-opera. In them the behaviour of the saints is increasingly reduced to stereotyped behaviour and a number of conventional attitudes, veritable commonplaces inspired by the rhetoric of the antique panegyrics that were to characterise hagiography until the end of the Middle Ages and make it a coded language that today's historian must avoid taking literally.

Up to the 8th c., the Roman Church manifested a certain reticence towards the Passions, but, with the rise of the cult of *relics in the Carolingian period, most of the barriers fell and the narrative sources relating to the saints made a massive entry into the liturgy, which makes it difficult, after 900, to establish clear-cut distinctions between texts intended for celebration of the *office and hagiographical "romances". Many *Vitae* of this period are not outstanding for their originality and are inspired, sometimes very closely, by a few prestigious texts such as Sulpicius Severus's *Life of St Martin*, an obligatory reference for any *biography of a saintly prelate, or that of St *Benedict in the *Dialogues* of *Gregory the Great. But just as important for the lasting influence they exercised were texts of Eastern origin, such as the *Lives of the Fathers of the Egyptian Desert* (*Vitae Patrum*) or Palladius's *Lausiac History*. What these works had in common was that they exalted the prestige of asceticism and presented the "man of God" (*vir Dei*) as both prophet, playing the role of a mediator between God and men, and *thaumaturge, performing miracles by virtue of the power he had acquired by *fasting, *mortification and *prayer.

In parallel with the *Vitae* we see a multiplication, after the year 1000, of collections of miracles, often linked to a sanctuary that wanted to vaunt the powers of the saint whose *relics it held in order to attract *pilgrims and offerings. The most famous are the *Book of the Miracles of St Faith*, composed in *c.*1035, and that of St James at *Compostela (early 12th c.). Accounts of inventions and especially of translations of relics also abound, especially with the Norse and *Saracen invasions in the 10th c., which led to frequent movements of relics, and the initiatives taken by certain *bishops anxious to reinforce their influence over the city through the exaltation of the remains of their predecessors.

Apparently immutable, hagiographical texts did in fact undergo an important evolution between the 12th and the 14th c. in the West, in connection with the emergence of a new conception of *sanctity and an evolution at the level of their use and circulation. The saint still remains a hero, *i.e.* an extraordinary man or woman, but more than in the past he becomes a model proposed for the imitation of monks, *clerics and the *laity. Thus, while in nearly all cases the saints of the early Middle Ages were *noble or reputed to be so, in the 12th c. we see the appearance in *Italy of saints of modest origin, sometimes simple artisans like St Homobonus († 1197), a tailor of Cremona who was canonized by *Innocent III in 1199. This change was favoured by the development of penitential spirituality: the saint was no longer necessarily perfect from the beginning; he became so at the price of a *conversion the more remarkable the deeper he was sunk in *sin, like *Mary Magdalene, Thaïs or Pelagia.

Under the influence of the *Cistercians and especially of the *mendicant orders in the 13th c., the pastoral dimension of hagiography was ceaselessly accentuated, the aim being to present to the faithful, through the Lives of the saints, models of behaviour and orthodoxy, at a time when the *Cathar "perfect" or *Waldensian preachers were exercising a considerable seduction over the masses. One of the most important texts in this respect was the Life of the *beguine *Marie of Oignies († 1213), composed in 1215 by the future bishop and cardinal *Jacques de Vitry. Throughout Christendom, especially from the 1230s, papacy and preachers stressed the fact that the perfection of the saints resided in their lives, not in their *miracles, and that the extraordinay powers they had were the culmination of a process of imitation of *Christ, pushed to the point of physical conformity in the case of St *Francis of Assisi, the first stigmatized saint in history, whose life and miracles were written down between 1229 and 1255 by *Thomas of Celano. In this perspective, collections of miracles of a new type, not linked to a specific sanctuary but to a saint such as the Virgin *Mary, to a religious *order (*Dialogus miraculorum* of the *Cistercian *Caesarius of Heisterbach, *Vitae fratrum* of the Dominican Gerard de Frachet) or to a *sacrament such as the *Eucharist, began to be drawn up. Moreover, *Dominicans like Jean de Mailly and Bartholomew of Trent composed abridged *legendaries that aimed to put at the disposal of the parish clergy texts that had previously been difficult of access, since only fortunate *abbeys or *chapters could afford the luxury of possessing the enormous magnificently-illuminated legendaries that covered the whole of the *sanctoral throughout the *liturgical year. But the main instrument of circulation of these compilations of abridged texts (*Flores sanctorum*) was undoubtedly the *Golden Legend* of the Dominican *Jacobus de Voragine, composed *c.*1260-1265 in Italy. This work, of which more than a thousand *Latin manuscripts still exist today, enjoyed an extraordinary success up to the middle of the 16th century. During the 14th c., it was translated into all the vernacular languages of Christendom. For this reason, it affected not just priests for whom it provided *exempla* to illustrate their *sermons, but also the *laity for whom it soon constituted a reading both attractive and edifying; the *Golden Legend* also inspired *artists and profoundly influenced the iconographical representation of saints in the last centuries of the Middle Ages.

During the 13th and early 14th cc., we also see the appearance and rise of mystical *biographies, seeking to reconstitute the inner lives of saints from the more spectacular manifestations of their devotion: *visions, *revelations, prophetic announcements, various paramystical phenomena. The most accomplished examples of this hagiography, whose circulation was quite limited, were the Lives of the beguine saints of the *Netherlands in the 13th c. and those of St *Margaret of Cortona († 1297) and St *Catherine of Siena († 1380) in Italy. At the end of the Middle Ages, hagiographical literature in its various forms was widespread in all circles. It comprised both fabulous accounts of mysterious or fictitious personages and spiritual biographies that constituted what we would call today "the journal of a soul". This vast collection of texts, whose vernacular output is still badly catalogued, is a way of access to the *spirituality and mentality of the Middle Ages.

R. Aigrain, *L'Hagiographie, ses sources, ses méthodes, son histoire*, Paris, 1953. – S. Boesch Gajano, *Agiografia medievale*, Bologna, 1976. – J. Dubois, *Les Martyrologes historiques du Moyen Âge latin*, Louvain, 1978. – M. Heinzelmann, *Translationsberichte und andere Quellen des Reliquienkultes*, Louvain, 1979. – B. Ward, *Miracles and the Medieval Mind*, Philadelphia (PA), 1982. – A. Boureau, *La Légende dorée. Le système narratif de Jacques de Voragine*, Paris, 1984. – G. Philippart, *Les Légendiers et autres manuscrits hagiographiques*, Louvain, 1985 (2nd ed.). – R. Grégoire, *Manuale di agiologia*, Fabriano, 1987. – *Raccolte di Vite di santi dal XIII al XVIII secolo*, S. Boesch Gajano (ed.), Fasano, 1990. – *Saints and their Authors*, J.E. Connolly (ed.), A. Deyermond (ed.), B. Dutton (ed.), Madison, 1990. – T. Head, *Hagiography and the Cult of Saints*, Cambridge, 1990. – J. Dubois, J.-L. Lemaître, *Sources et méthodes de l'hagiographie médiévale*, Paris, 1993 ("Histoire"). – *Hagiographies*, 1, G. Philippart (ed.), Turnhout, 1994-1996 (2 vol.). – *Saints: Studies in Hagiography*, S. Sticca (ed.), Binghamton (NY), 1996. – P. Fouracre, *Late Merovingian France: History and Hagiography 640-720*, Manchester, 1996. – L. L. Coon, *Sacred Fictions: Holy Women and Hagiography in Late Antiquity*, Philadelphia (PA), 1997.

André Vauchez

**Byzantium, 6th-10th centuries.** Byzantine hagiography brings together a considerable number of texts belonging to various literary genres, whose common characteristic is the commemoration and glorification of the saints, often proposed as models to the Christian people.

Hagiography, older than the Christianization of the Empire, enjoyed a spectacular flowering in the protobyzantine period as the cult of saints developed. We can distinguish several literary genres. Eulogies, which follow the rules of ancient eloquence, find their classical models from the 4th century. This rhetorical genre contrasts with several narrative genres: Lives of saints; collections of *miracles; accounts of the invention or translation of *relics. Liturgical poetry also occupies an important place: some of Romanus the Melode's *kontakia* (6th c.) are hagiographical. Another distinction can be made according to the type of *sanctity celebrated by the hagiographical work. To *martyrs are consecrated Acts (*praxeis*) or Passions (*martyrion*), sometimes clothed in particular forms (the *Martyrdom of Polycarp* and that of the Christians of Lyon are *letters); monk saints and bishop saints are celebrated in Lives (*bios, bios kai politeia*). The diversity of the monastic Life in turn aroused several variants. Alongside Athanasius's *Life of Anthony* which, from the 4th c., provided the classic model of the anchoritic Life, we can see works of a more *coenobitic nature: Lives of Pachomius or, in the 6th c., Life of St Dositheus. Certain spectacular forms of *ascesis are well represented: *e.g.* *stylitism (Life of Symeon the Stylite the Elder [5th c.]; of Symeon the Younger [6th c.]). Finally, we must distinguish according to the historical value of the documents. While some Acts of martyrs come with good guarantees of authenticity, others belong to the category of legendary Passions: it was very often these that had the greatest success. Likewise monastic hagiography, alongside more historical accounts, produced works whose sole concern was to demonstrate a type of sanctity, and which spread from one end of *Christendom to the other: *e.g.*, in the 6th c., the Life of St Pelagia, or in the 7th, that of Mary the Egyptian. The best known works are often anonymous or pseudepigraphical. But several hagiographers deserve a mention: *e.g.*, in the 6th c., Cyril of Scythopolis wrote seven Lives of saintly monks of *Palestine; in the 7th c., Leontius of Neapolis was the author of two major works (Life of John the Almsgiver, patriarch of *Alexandria; Life of Symeon Salos). Up to the Arab conquest, output was dense, geographically and linguistically dispersed (Greek, *Coptic, Syriac), and creative. To judge by its language, it sometimes addressed a cultivated public, but often it confined itself to quite a humble level.

The Middle Byzantine period opened with the Arab conquest (7th c.). The Empire lost its oriental provinces, though they continued to produce hagiography: several Palestinian texts, written in Greek, acquaint us with neomartyrs, victims of the Arabs. But output was centred in the Empire. It was henceforth exclusively in Greek. The iconoclast crisis (730-787, 815-843) played an important role: hostile to certain forms of the *cult of the saints, the iconoclasts may have contributed to a decrease in the hagiographical output in the 8th and early 9th centuries. It is disputable whether they produced their own models of lay sanctity, which the Life of Philarete may reflect. Above all, *iconoclasm was the occasion for the iconophiles to write, on the model of the old Passions, the Lives of confessors of *images (Life of St *Stephen the Younger between the two iconoclast crises).

Monastic Lives (or Lives combining confession of *Orthodoxy and monastic career) are abundant and of good quality after 843. They allow us to follow the history of the great monastic centres: in the 9th c., Life of *Theodore the Studite for *Constantinople, and Lives of saintly monks living in Bithynia (*e.g.* St Joannice). In the 10th c., Latros (Life of St Paul) and *Athos saw the appearance of works of high quality, whose masterpiece is perhaps the Life of St Athanasius of Lavra, written shortly after the year 1000. At the same time, Lives of saintly *patriarchs, of very high quality, reveal contacts between hagiography and pamphlet (Life of St *Ignatius by Nicetas David) or between hagiography and *chronicle (Life of St *Euthymius the Patriarch).

This contemporary hagiography was not alone. At Byzantium, in the 9th and 10th cc. the hagiography of previous centuries was brought together. It was then that great collections appeared: hagiographical manuscripts grouping together Lives of saints in order of the *calendar (menologies); *synaxaria. The rebirth of culture made the low linguistic level of certain early works insupportable. They were unhesitatingly rewritten in a more noble style: this was the phenomenon of metaphrasis. The most illustrious representative of this genre was Symeon the Logothete, active in the late 10th c., whose menologion, very widely circulated, supplanted the older menologia.

F. Halkin, *BHG*, 1957 ("SHG", 8; repr. 1986); *ibid.*, *Novum supplementum*, 1984 ("SHG", 65). – H. Delehaye, *Les Passions des martyrs et les genres littéraires*, 1966 (2nd ed.; "SHG", 13 b). – L. Ryden, "New Forms of Hagiography: Heroes and Saints"), *The 17th International Byzantine Congress. Major Papers*, New York, 1986, 532-536. – H. Delehaye, *L'Ancienne hagiographie byzantine: les sources, les premiers modèles, la formation des genres*, 1991 ("SHG", 73).

Bernard Flusin

**Byzantium, 11th-15th centuries.** In the 11th c., the dominant model of sanctity remained the monastic life. Michael *Psellus thus exalted Auxentius, a 5th-c. ascetic and *thaumaturge, founder of the hermitages on the mountain that bore his name, and Nicholas, founder of the monastery of the Beautiful Spring on Mount *Olympus. But these hagiographical works served mainly as pretexts for developments on *demonology (*Life* of St Auxentius, *BHG*, 203) and *philosophy (*Eulogy of Nicholas*, *BHG*, 2313). Other founders are known through their disciples, and this smacks of a more traditional hagiography: such as Bartholomew of Grottaferrata, in southern *Italy, who maintained fraternal links with the Benedictines of *Monte Cassino (*BHG*, 233), or Lazarus the Galesiot (*BHG*, 979), a *pilgrim and then *stylite who founded various monasteries on mount Galesius in Asia Minor, one of them by imperial privilege to escape the pettifogging of the metropolitan of Ephesus. In the same period, with the support of Alexius *Comnenus, Christodoulos built the monastery of St John the Theologian at *Patmos: he is known by his autobiographical **Typikon* (*BHG*, 303). Alongside these saints in the standard mould, well integrated, despite some originalities, into contemporary society (Lazarus and Christodoulos negotiated with emperors), *Symeon the New Theologian, known as much by his writings as by the *Life* by his disciple Nicetas Stethatus (*BHG*, 1692), represents a form of sanctity that dissented from Studite coenobitism (he claimed the freedom to choose his spiritual father) and from the official forms of the *cult of the saints ("uncouth" cult of his spiritual father Symeon the Studite) or of the relationship between mystical life and theology (necessity of experience of the *Holy Spirit).

In the 12th c., alongside more traditional saints – Bishop Lucas of Isola Capro Rizzuto (*BHG*, 2237), Hegumen Cyprian of Calabria (*BHG*, 2089) or his colleague Irene of Chrysovalantôn (*BHG*, 952) – there persisted "originals" like Neophytus the Recluse, a Cypriot hero who gathered an entire monastery around his *recluse's cell and naively organised his own cult, known by his *Typikon* (*BHG*, 1325 m); Meletius the Younger, an itinerant charismatic ascetic (*Life* by Nicholas of Methone, *BHG*, 1247); Leontius of Jerusalem, who began as a holy fool and ended as patriarch of *Jerusalem (*Life* by the monk Theodosius, *BHG*, 985). Particular mention must be made of Cyril the Phileot (*Life* by Nicholas Kataskepenos, *BHG*, 468), a lay hesychast, married and father of a family (one of his sons died in the monastic habit), who became a monk only late in life, worked *miracles and advised the great men of this world.

In the 13th c., the Empire of *Nicaea was made illustrious by the Emperor John Vatatzes the Merciful (*BHG*, 933), model of a saintly prince renowned for his charity, whose popularity nourished hostility to the *Palaeologus dynasty in Asia Minor. Other saintly princes of the same period were Symeon and *Sava of Serbia (*BHG*, 1693), founders of the Serbian monastery of Chilandar on mount *Athos and organisers of the Serbian church.

The end of the century, marked by the Palaeologan restoration and the Union of Lyon, boasted confessors of the *Orthodox faith, a type of sanctity that went back to the beginnings: Nicephorus the Hesychast and Meletius the Galesiot (*BHG*, 1246a) combined monastic virtues with that of resistance to the *Union. Other martyrs, due this time to the Turkish conquest, were Nicetas the Younger at Nyssa in *Cappadocia (*BHG*, 2303) and Arsenius, *metropolitan of Berroea, killed during the capture of his town.

The 14th and the early 15th c. saw the triumph of hesychast hagiography. The Palamite patriarchs contributed to the hagiographical flowering, which glorified especially the heroes of the hesychast quarrel: Philotheus wrote the *Life* of Isidore Bucheiras the Patriarch (*BHG*, 962) and the *Eulogy* of Gregory *Palamas (*BHG*, 718); Patriarch Nilus also wrote a eulogy of Palamas (*BHG*, 719); Callistus wrote the *Life* of his master Gregory the Sinaite (*BHG*, 722). This last, a spiritual master rather than a controversialist, had several disciples who spread *hesychasm beyond the frontiers of the Empire: such as the Bulgars Romylos (*BHG*, 2384) and Theodosius of Tŭrnovo. Other monks lived out a charismatic hesychasm, in which extraordinary manifestations (visions of light, miracles, prophecies) appeared as the habitual fruits of interior *prayer: Maximus the Kausokalybite (*Life* by his disciple Niphon: *BHG*, 1236 z), the monk Niphon (*BHG*, 1371), Germanus Maroulis the Hagiorite (*BHG*, 2164), Sabas the Younger of Vatopedi (*BHG*, 1606). All these monks lived at least a part of their life on Mount Athos. Besides these solitaries, other monks, less marked by hesychasm, continued the tradition of founder monks: Dionysius, founder of the Athonite monastery that bears his name (*BHG*, 559 a), and Athanasius the Meteorite who, forced out of Athos by Turkish incursions, founded hermitages on the rocky pillars of Meteora (*BHG*, 195).

On the margin of hesychast hagiography, but quickly annexed by it, there also developed the cult of Patriarch *Athanasius of Constantinople, who tried to reform the Church at the start of the 14th c., and whose *relics worked cures (*BHG*, 194).

The hagiographical model of this period was mainly but not exclusively Palamite. One of this movement's main adversaries, Nicephorus Gregoras, was also a hagiographer, writing the life of his uncle John of Heraclea, an imperial official who became a monk and then a *bishop, and lived in *poverty and *humility (*BHG*, 2188). The last years of the Empire (mid 15th c.) saw the flowering of more dramatic forms of sanctity. Mark Eugenicus, metropolitan of Ephesus, is numbered among the saints for the devotion he showed to his flock under the *Ottoman yoke, but above all for his determined opposition to the union of Florence (*BHG*, 2551). The Constantinopolitan monk Macarius Makrès exhorted to martyrdom the Christians under *Islam tempted by *apostasy (*BHG* 1001, 1002).

By its insistence on *ascesis, *miracles and interior *prayer, but also on martyrdom, the hagiography of the late *Byzantine Empire perhaps rediscovered, after centuries of greater political and social conformism, the enthusiasm of the early centuries.

*The Byzantine Saint. University of Birmingham Fourteenth Spring Symposium of Byzantine Studies*, S. Hackel (ed.), Birmingham, 1981. – *HChr*, 6, 1990, 549-557 . – *HChr*, 5, 1993. – *Holy Women of Byzantium*, A.M. Talbot (ed.), Washington (DC), 1996.

Marie-Hélène Congourdeau

**HAIMO OF AUXERRE (died *c.*865/866).** Founder and prestigious *master of the Carolingian *school of *Auxerre, Haimo was a monk of the abbey of Saint-Germain in that town, where his literary activity is situated between *c.*840 and *c.*860. His disciple

Heiric presents him as a brilliant master, with a wide knowledge of the pagan *classics, but subordinating them to the authority of the *Fathers. He contributed to fixing the methods of medieval *exegesis, and we can see in his teaching a prefiguration of *scholasticism.

His main works are hence works of exegesis, nourished by the great patristic commentaries and dedicated to St Paul's *epistles, the *Apocalypse, the *Song of Songs and several *prophets. We also have by him an important *homiliary on the gospels.

H. Barré, "Haimon d'Auxerre", *DSp*, 7, 1969, 91-97. – D. Iogna-Prat, C. Jeudy, G. Lobrichon, *L'École carolingienne d'Auxerre, de Muretach à Remi (830-908)*, Paris, 1991.

Michel Sot

**HAIRSHIRT.** A garment of rough material made of goat's hair (from *Cilicia, hence the French name *cilice*), camel's hair or any coarse fibre (tow, horsehair), the hairshirt was worn as penance from biblical times. It was frequently employed as an instrument of penitential *mortification by the Desert Fathers (Anthony, Basil, Hilarion, Theodore) and, following their example, spread in medieval *Christendom. In the Middle Ages, the wearing of the hairshirt was a *topos* of Lives of hermits, ascetics and *penitents and of their iconography. Out of asceticism and *humility, it was generally worn next to the skin under the normal garments, and was discovered only after the master's death by his disciples who saw in it a proof of his *sanctity and an object of devotion.

L. Gougaud, "Cilice", *DSp*, 2, 1953, 899-902.

Cécile Caby

***HAJJ.*** The great pilgrimage to *Mecca (*Hajj*) is one of the five pillars of *Islam, distinct from the *'umra* or little pilgrimage. The *Hajj* is collective and obligatory for all Muslims, men and women, who are able to perform it (*Koran*, III, 91-97). It takes place once a year from the 8th to the 12th of the month of dhū l-hijja. The pilgrim must undergo a rite of sacralization (*ihrām*) in which he is purified, changes his clothes, pronounces the formula of consecration. From then on he must abstain from all sexual relations for the time of the pilgrimage. Arrival at Mecca often comprises an *'umra*, consisting firstly of a circumambulation seven times (*ṭawāf*) round the Ka'ba, a cubical building situated at the heart of the sanctuary (*al-masjid al haram*). These circuits are followed by a prayer, then by a run between Safa and Marwa. The *Hajj* itself begins on the 8th of dhū l-hijja; on the 9th, the pilgrims meet at Arafāt for the station (the *wuqūf*), culminating point of the *Hajj*, followed by another station at Muzdalifa. At Mina, on the 10th, take place rites of stoning of a pillar symbolizing the devil. Then the pilgrim sacrifices a victim, usually a sheep, and shaves his head to bring about desacralization. The pilgrimage ends with another *ṭawāf* around the Ka'ba.

The Muslim *Hajj* follows most of the rites of the important pre-Islamic pilgrimage to Mecca, imposing an Abrahamic reading on them. Access to the interior of the Ka'ba, still open on Mondays and Fridays in the 12th c., and during all the days of *rajab*, was more and more restricted. The custom of a *siqāya* where the pilgrims were given to drink disappeared after the 8th c. and was supplanted by the veneration of the spring of Zemzem, not obligatory. Constructions and enlargements by the different caliphs modified the appearance of the Mecca sanctuary. The Ka'ba notably was rebuilt in 693 by the *Umayyad governor Yūsuf al-Hajjāj.

The *Hajj* still played a political role. The Prophet fixed its rites by taking part in them on his farewell pilgrimage in 632. Then the presence of the *caliph, his representative or his rival, punctuated each *Hajj*. From 969 the *Fatimids controlled the sanctuary. From then on, the *Abbasid caliph's authority over the pilgrimage was constantly breached. After 1260, the *Mamluk sultans of Egypt dominated the ceremonies and the caravan was accompanied by the *mahmal*, a palanquin symbolizing their power.

An assembly of Muslims, the *Hajj* was also the centre of a vast fair and contributed to the mixing of the Muslim elites.

M. Gaudefroy-Demombynes, *Le Pèlerinage à La Mecque, étude d'histoire religieuse*, Paris, 1923; re-ed. Philadelphia (PA), 1977. – J. Jomier, A. Wensinck, "Ḥadjdj", *EI(E)*, 3, 1971, 31-38. – J. Jomier, "Aspects politiques et religieux du pèlerinage de La Mekke", *Livre du Centenaire de l'IFAO*, Cairo, 1980, 391-401. – M. N. Pearson, *Pious Passengers and the Hajj in Earlier Times*, London, 1994.

Catherine Mayeur-Jaouen

**HĀKIM, AL- (985-1021).** Al-Hākim b. Amr Allāh Abū 'Alī al-Mansūr, born at *Cairo, became the sixth *Fātimid *caliph in 996 on the death of his father, al-'Azīz. In his youth, opposed to his Christian sister Sitt al-Mulk, he frequented the popular *Sunni circles of Fustāt Misr; then, in a fit of unitarian madness, he executed the *Shi'ite Berber court dignitaries, persecuted Christians (destruction of the *Holy Sepulchre at *Jerusalem in 1009) and Jews, banned alcohol and forbade women to go out in public. In 1017, some Persians tried to make him a god, but failed, except in *Syria where the *Druze sect was founded. In 1020 he burned down Fustāt. Then al-Hākim abandoned all pomp to a cousin, his designated successor, restored property and religious freedom to the minorities and disappeared in the desert near Cairo.

"al-Ḥākim", *EI(E)*, 3, 1971, 76-82 (new ed.). – T. Bianquis, *Damas et la Syrie sous la domination fâtimide*, Damascus, 1989 (index).

Thierry Bianquis

**ḤALLĀJ, AL- (244 [858] - 309 [922]).** The great martyr-figure of *Sufism, Abū-l-Mughīth al-Ḥusayn son of Manṣūr was surnamed the Carder, al-Ḥallāj, probably because of his father's occupation. Born in Persia, he spent his youth in southern *Iraq where his family had emigrated. He had been trained in mysticism by the Sufi of Susiana, Sahl of Tustar, before receiving at Bassora the "rags", *khirqa*, symbol of initiation. In contrast to the Sufis of that time, al-Ḥallāj seems to have chosen public expression. At first he preached on the spot, before making several pilgrimages and long journeys to *Iran, even to India. His very extrovert Sufism attracted large audiences, but got him accused of charlatanry. Certain paradoxical aphorisms ("I am Truth", *i.e.* God) made him suspect of "incarnationism", *Ḥulūl*. He was imprisoned for nine years. A victim of court intrigues, finally he was publicly executed under atrocious conditions. His followers were persecuted. A number of them went into exile, particularly in Iran. The propositions attributed to him were preserved by his disciples in several collections.

L. Massignon, *The Passion of al-Hallaj*, Princeton (NJ), 1982.

Jacqueline Chabbi

**HAMBURG.** Town and *archbishopric. After the integration of *Saxony into the Frankish *Empire (772-804), probably between 810 and 822, a more important Frankish stronghold – Hammaburg – arose on the site of a former Saxon castle near the right bank of the Elbe, on the Alster-Bille delta.

Hamburg at first depended on the *bishoprics of Werden (archbishopric of *Mainz) and *Bremen (archbishopric of *Cologne). At the expense of these bishoprics, the town became canonically independent between 831 and 864. The monk *Anskar, of the abbey of *Corvey, probably began by founding a "bishopric" of Hamburg in 831-832. After the destruction of Hamburg by Danish *Vikings in 845, Anskar obtained the vacant bishopric of Bremen, which was united to the reconstructed *diocese of Hamburg (848-864), leading to the creation of an archbishopric in 864. For reasons of ecclesiastical politics, this archdiocese kept the name "Hamburg" although, even in Anskar's lifetime († 865), Bremen was preferred as the episcopal residence. To the diocese and then archdiocese of Hamburg belonged the Christianization of, and the claims to dominate, the distant lands of *Scandinavia and the Baltic countries, particularly *Denmark and *Sweden, as well as the land of the *Wends on the south shore of the Baltic and the peoples to the east of the Baltic. Archbishop Adalbert (1043-1072) tried to push this claim even further by attempting to erect Hamburg into the patriarchate of the Nordic lands. Only the creation of independent archbishoprics in these regions (*Lund for *Denmark in 1104; *Uppsala for Sweden in 1164; and *Riga for Livonia) put an end to the Nordic ambitions of the archbishopric of Bremen-Hamburg. In the 13th c., the name "archbishopric of Bremen" prevailed.

From the 9th c., a *market was held at "Hammaburg". The destruction of the town by the Vikings in 845 was only partly prejudicial to this. Alongside the old town of Hamburg, whose lord was the archbishop of Hamburg-Bremen, Count Adolf III of Holstein founded the new town of Hamburg on the Alster (1186-1187). It was more oriented towards the Elbe than was the old town. *Commerce and *navigation towards the lower Elbe and the North Sea intensified. In *c.*1220, the old and new towns fused together under the power of the Holstein. Hamburg obtained wide legal autonomy in 1292; it was probably an Imperial Town from the mid 14th c., but certainly so only from 1618. From the 13th c., it formed contractual commercial links with *Lübeck. Both towns were part of the union of Wendish towns; but within the *Hanse, their interests very often diverged.

*Hamburg. Geschichte der Stadt und ihrer Einwohner*, H. D. Loose (ed.), 1, Hamburg, 1982. – G. Theuerkauf, "Urkundenfälschungen der Stadt und des Domkapitels Hamburg in der Stauferzeit", *SMGH*, 1988, 397-431. – R. Aubert, "Hambourg", *DHGE*, 23, 1990, 208-219.

Gerhard Theuerkauf

**HANSE, HANSEATIC TOWNS.** The Hanse, a very old Germanic term, designated in *c.*1250 the group of North German *merchants residing at *London. In a broader sense, it covered a historical, commercial and political reality that maintained its existence for half a millennium: as the community of all the merchants of northern *Germany, from the late 13th c. the Hanse controlled all the traffic of the Baltic and the North Sea on the *Novgorod-London axis and engaged in defence of its interests 180 to 200 maritime and continental *towns, from the *Netherlands to the gulf of *Finland.

A flexible and durable organisation, the Hanse responded to the structural facts of long-distance *commerce between the Baltic and the Atlantic or even, from the 15th c., the Mediterranean coasts. Exchanges in one direction involved *forest products – weighty e.g. wood, precious e.g. *furs – growing quantities of cereals in the later Middle Ages and the modern period, *metallurgical products like Swedish steel and copper; in the other direction, the sea-*salt of the Atlantic coasts from *Brittany to *Portugal, the *wine of Poitou and Bordeaux, and English, French and Flemish cloth.

The German merchants were masters of the seas thanks to the technical superiority of their ships; at the end of the 15th c. the Hanseatic long-distance fleet represented a thousand boats and sixty thousand tons of freight. Participating in numerous distinct concerns at once, they specialized in certain directions – *e.g.* the *Bergenfahrer* going to seek fish in *Norway – but possessed shares in ships and shared the risks between several societies. They could count on the support of a political force, the Hanse often intervening, in the late Middle Ages and the 16th c., by blockade and military engagement to maintain or increase the commercial privileges acquired from towns or princes.

Made up of *Wendish and *Pomeranian towns (Rostock, Stralsund), Saxon towns (*Bremen, Brunswick, *Magdeburg), Prussian and Livonian towns (*Gdańsk, Königsberg, *Riga), Westphalian and Rhenish towns (*Münster, Dortmund and especially *Cologne), for centuries the Hanse recognised the *de facto* hegemony of *Lübeck, which was the usual seat of the general diets dealing with questions of common interest (negotiations, arbitrations, ratifications of treaties, financial and military measures) and the more frequent regional diets, preparing and carrying out decisions. The essential mainstays of Hanseatic *commerce, subordinate to the diet after the middle of the 14th c., were the four counters, each with elected heads, a *court of law and a treasury, established at Novgorod, *Bergen, London and *Bruges.

The rise of the Hanse, which culminated in the late 14th c., went hand in hand with urban development and manifested the extent of a cultural unity attested by the language of the *chronicles and of maritime law, the brick of the main public monuments, woodwork ranging from naval shipyards to church *altarpieces.

These signs of unity survived the economic and political association which, from the 15th c., struggled against rivals such as the Dutch and the South Germans who breached its monopoly, while the power of the princes prevailed from the Burgundian *Netherlands to *Moscow. The system of the Hanse had had its day: the last Hanseatic diet was held in 1669.

P. Dollinger, *La Hanse (XII^e-XVII^e siècles)*, Paris, 1964.

Philippe Braunstein

**HARALD BLUETOOTH (*c.*910-985).** The Danish king Harald (Haraldr Blátand, "Bluetooth", *i.e.* black tooth, or Haraldr Gormsson) was the son of Gormr who reigned around 940 and of Thyri who seems to have left a vivid memory in legend. Harald must have reigned from *c.*940 to *c.*985, and we know very little about him, except that under his reign *Denmark was officially converted to Christianity. At least this is what emerges from the *runic inscription on the Jelling Stone, in which Harald is celebrated as "he who led all Denmark and *Norway and made the Danes Christians". A contemporary source of events has it that the German priest Poppo, after having submitted victoriously to an *ordeal, baptized Harald. It is probable, however, that the latter adopted the new religion to avoid German intrusions into his kingdom.

L. Demidoff, "The Poppo Legend", *Mediaeval Scandinavia*, 6, 1973, 39-67. – E. Roesdahl, *Viking Age Denmark*, London, 1982. – P. Sawyer, "The Christianisation of Scandinavia", *Beretning fra femte tvaerfaglige Vikingesymposium*, T. Kisbye (ed.), E. Roesdahl (ed.), Arhus, 1986, 23-37.

Régis Boyer

**HARPHIUS (*c.*1400-1477).** At first a Brother of the Common Life at Delft and Gouda, then a Friar Minor of the *Observance from 1450, Harphius (Henry Herp, or of Erp) held several posts in the province of *Cologne. Apart from two collections of *sermons intended for priests (on the *liturgical year, on the *decalogue), he wrote some spiritual treatises circulated from 1538 by the Cologne Charterhouse under the general title of *Theologia mystica*, the most important of which was the *Mirror of Perfection*.

Harphius tried to reconcile scholastic *theology with the mystical theology of *Ruysbroeck. To it he added the practice of "aspirations", formulae of devotion which, tirelessly repeated, lead to detachment and unification of soul. The *Theologia mystica* went through numerous editions in northern and southern Europe and had considerable influence on Spanish and French spirituality in the 16th and 17th centuries.

*Theologia mystica*, M. Novesianus (ed.), Cologne, 1538 (repr. 1966). – Henri Herp, *De processu humani profectus*, G. Epiney-Burgard (ed.), Wiesbaden, 1982.

L. Mees *et al.*, "Herp (Henri de, Harphius). Vie, Oeuvres", *DSp*, 7, 1968, 346-366.

Georgette Épiney-Burgard

**HASTINGS.** The battle of Hastings was fought at Battle, Sussex, on Saturday 14 Oct 1066. On that day *William the Conqueror, duke of *Normandy (1035-1087), killed Harold Godwineson (6 Jan - 14 Oct 1066) and with him most of the male aristocracy of *England. On Christmas Day, William was crowned king of the English. The Normans had disputed Harold's coronation as King *Edward's successor on the grounds that Harold, having previously promised to be faithful to William, was a perjurer. According to canon law, a perjured ruler was a tyrant against whom a *just war could be fought. Pope *Alexander II's backing provided William with crucial moral justification. After his victory, as a token of *penance William built Battle Abbey on the site of the bloodshed.

*The Carmen de Hastingae Proelio of Guy Bishop of Amiens*, F. Barlow (ed., tr.), Oxford, 1999.

R. A. Brown, "The Battle of Hastings", *Anglo-Norman Studies*, 3, 1981, 1-21.

Elisabeth van Houts

**HATFIELD.** The site of a church *council (perhaps Hatfield in Hertfordshire, perhaps that in South Yorkshire) convened by Archbishop *Theodore in 680 in response to a request by Pope *Agatho to ascertain the opinion of the English church on the *monothelete controversy (Agatho was then conducting negotiations with the Emperor Constantine IV with the aim of ending the *schism that the controversy had provoked). As reported by *Bede (*Historia Ecclesiastica*, IV, 17-18), the council of Hatfield under Theodore's presidency endorsed the dyothelete doctrine of the *Acta* of the Lateran council of 649, where papal opposition to the imperial monothelete doctrine had been formally expressed; in particular, the council at Hatfield endorsed the notion of the double procession of the *Holy Spirit.

H. Chadwick, "Theodore, the English Church and the Monothelete Controversy", *Archbishop Theodore*, M. Lapidge (ed.), Cambridge, 1995, 88-95. – C. Cubitt, *Anglo-Saxon Church Councils, c.650-c.850*, Leicester, 1995.

Michael Lapidge

**HEARTS, EXCHANGE OF.** The renewal of heart promised by *God to those who love him (Ps 50, 12; Ezek 11, 19; 18, 31; 36, 26) became, in the language of many women mystics from the 13th c., a literal exchange of hearts. Usually, the biblical metaphor of the "new heart" had been interpreted by commentators as a figure of inner *conversion. For these holy *women, the experience of conversion was expressed by the acute consciousness of a brutal and radical physiological change: their heart, withdrawn from their breast, had been replaced by another heart. St *Gertrude the Great, a *nun at *Helfta, suggests it in her *Revelations*, where she declares that she has felt in her breast the beatings of Jesus' heart. There is clearer evidence of an exchange of hearts in Lutgard of Aywières and Osanna of Mantua. Then *Catherine of Siena and *Dorothea of Montau enjoyed the same privilege.

In the late 14th c., the entourage of these two women saints admitted the prodigy of *extractio cordis* in its physiological reality. In the *canonization trial of Dorothea of Montau, one of the articles even bore on this singular event, which thus became one of the criteria of the *recluse's authentic *sanctity. As for Catherine of Siena, the authorized testimony of her confessor contributed to accrediting the physiological reality of the phenomenon. Indeed *Raymond of Capua complacently reproduced, or even enriched, Catherine's confidences. According to the official text of the *Legenda maior* (*c.*1385-1395), one day, after having solicited this favour in her *prayers, she felt that *Christ took her heart to himself and carried it away. Two days later he returned, holding a shining vermilion heart, and opened her breast declaring: "My daughter, the other day I took your heart; today I give you mine, which will serve you from now on in place of your own." And a scar remained as the visible *sign of this invisible grafting of Jesus' heart into the body of the young *mantellata*.

In the *Legenda maior*, Raymond of Capua sought to show the constructive and unifying force of mystical experience in the life of his *penitent. Mystical marriage, in the course of which Catherine of Siena received from Christ's hands the ring of espousal, here inaugurated a process in which the exchange of hearts was a decisive moment. In that event was clearly manifested the precise reality of mystical union, *i.e.* the annihilation of self and the loving fusion of wills. Image-makers, quite naturally, later made this "new heart" one of the saint's habitual attributes.

A. Cabassut, "Coeurs (changement, échange des)", *DSp*, 2, Paris, 1953, 1046-1051. – A. Vauchez, *Sainthood in the Later Middle Ages*, Cambridge, 1997.

Nicole Bériou

**HEAVEN.** While the doctrine of heaven took on its full importance in the Middle Ages, it was not invented at that time. It goes back to the 2nd c., when the *Fathers chose the emblem of the flight of the dove to signify the *soul's entry into heaven. This symbolic dimension was inevitable, since heaven corresponds to an indescribable eschatological experience that fulfils the human being's desire for transcendence, whence the many pictorial representations from Herrad of Landsberg's **Hortus deliciarum* to Fra *Angelico's *Paradise*, via the evocations of the heavenly *Jerusalem, the *visions of *Hildegard of Bingen, etc. But one constant recurs in all these pictures: the expression of an ideal place, all joy and beauty. This place, which crystallizes all desires, is the country of the blessed and, from now on, according to St *Bernard, that of monks, whence the *ipso facto* promotion of the monastic life as the way of *salvation.

By proposing this definition of heaven, the medievals distanced themselves from *cosmology. Though they took it from a rereading of *Dionysius the Areopagite's *Celestial Hierarchy*, they agreed for the most part (*Thomas Aquinas, *Richard de Mediavilla, *Duns Scotus, *Durand of Saint-Pourçain. . .) that the empyrean heaven was merely a hypothesis. In the *Summa theologiae* ($I^a$ $II^{ae}$, q. 5, a. 8, ad 3), St Thomas set out to clarify this proposition, explaining that "heaven is presented in theological thought primarily as a moral and religious notion, *i.e.* as a state rather than a place". The many treatises on heaven by Pseudo-Alcuin, Eadmer, John of Fécamp, etc., thus take on their full meaning. Moreover, their final reference is the *Bible, rather than classical literature or philosophy, though Plato's intelligible world may have influenced some interpretations.

They referred essentially, in fact, to the themes of the heavenly *Jerusalem, the *contemplation of *God's glory, the *Transfiguration. Thus the monk was understood as an inhabitant of that new Jerusalem which was *Clairvaux. By his life, he was wholly oriented towards the contemplation of God's glory, but this contemplation was not reserved for him alone: it could belong to all, as *Dante emphasized in the *Divine Comedy*. Moreover, the manifestation of God's glory was not confined to the afterlife, it was already present in the liturgy, in particular the Eastern liturgy "which brings heaven down to earth". *Peter the Venerable perceived this, which is why he accorded such a place to the *mystery of the *Transfiguration, whose *feast he introduced at *Cluny and for which he composed an *office and a beautiful *meditation, thus celebrating it in the Latin Church three centuries before its official recognition.

By thus stressing the desire for heaven, the medievals broached, in a dynamic way that spoke for all, the question of intuitive vision and union with God.

N. Wicki, *Die Lehre von der himmlischen Seligkeit in der mittelalterlischen Scholastik von Petrus Lombardus bis Thomas von Aquin*, 1954. – J. Leclercq, *The Love of Learning and the Desire for God*, London, 1978. – E. Gardiner, *Medieval Visions of Heaven and Hell: a Sourcebook*, New York, 1993.

Marie-Anne Vannier

**HEBDOMADARY.** In medieval and post-medieval vocabulary, the term *hebdomadarius* designates the priest who, in a community, was charged with celebrating *mass and presiding over the *divine office for a week in rotation. It was likewise for the *office in communities of *nuns. The practice of hebdomadary tasks, liturgical or other, in monasteries went back to Christian antiquity. In the Middle Ages, the term "hebdomadary" was also used for various usages more extensive than that of officiating priest.

C. Ducange, "Hebdomadarius", *Glossarium mediae et infimae latinitatis*, Paris, 1733-1736. – "Hebdomadier", *Cath.*, 5, 1962, 544.

Pierre-Marie Gy

***HEBRAICA VERITAS.*** In the Middle Ages, the expression nearly always refers to St Jerome's *Latin translation of the *Bible (*Vulgate), made directly from the *Hebrew (for Jerome himself, it designated the Hebrew text). In some 12th- or 13th-c. commentators, however, *hebraica veritas* can also designate the Hebrew text or the Jewish (literal) interpretation of this Hebrew text.

H. de Lubac, *Exégèse médiévale* 2, 1, Paris, 1961, 238-285. – B. Smalley, *The Study of the Bible in the Middle Ages*, Oxford, 1983 (3rd ed.).

Gilbert Dahan

**HEBREW, KNOWLEDGE OF.** One of the three sacred languages, sometimes considered the most holy and often (from the 13th c.) the original or natural language (*e.g.* by *Dante), Hebrew never ceased to arouse the curiosity of the Christian world, to a varying extent. During the early Middle Ages, only the rudiments were known, and those at second hand: we find crudely traced alphabets, some lexicons and lists of **Interpretationes nominum Hebraicorum* (following Jerome); *Theodulf corrected the text of the *Vulgate using the Hebrew, but with the collaboration of a converted Jew. Interest became keener in the 12th c., by way of biblical studies: *Stephen Harding and Nicholas of Maniacoria amended their *Latin manuscripts by referring to the Hebrew, read to them by *Jews. Likewise, *Andrew of Saint-Victor ceaselessly referred to the Hebrew text in his commentaries, but he was not a Hebraist and worked with Jewish colleagues. The same is true of *Ralph Niger († *c.*1200), many of whose works show an interest in Hebrew and who paid tribute to the help provided by a (converted) Jewish friend. Herbert of Bosham was undoubtedly the first true Hebraist: his commentary on the *Psalms shows a real knowledge of the Hebrew language. In the late 12th and early 13th c., notably in *England, we have evidence of a more active study, with a series of Hebrew psalters whose *Latin annotation certainly corresponds to "lecture notes" taken by Christians from the dictation of Jews.

Study became systematic in the 13th c.: it was not just a *desideratum*, as we see it in *Roger Bacon (himself author of a Hebrew grammar), but a reality with *studia*, notably *Dominican ones (those of *Barcelona, where *Raymond Martini, the best Hebraist of the Middle Ages, taught, and Jativa). *Raymond of Peñafort seems to have given the impetus. The objective was not just to enrich biblical studies, but to provide better weapons for the mission to the Jews. Another man played an important role in the development of linguistic studies: the Arabist (but not Hebraist) Raymond *Lull never ceased to implore the authorities (the university of *Paris, the *pope) to set up chairs in languages; the council of *Vienne (1311-12) gave him satisfaction, and the *universities of *Paris, *Oxford, *Bologna, *Salamanca and of the seat of the papal court were ordered not to stint the teaching of Hebrew, Aramaic, Greek and Arabic. We have little information about the effective results, but Hebrew never ceased to be taught, privately or at university, as is proved in the late 15th c. by the example of Jacques Legrand. Among the other Hebraists of the Middle Ages, we may cite especially the Franciscan William of Mara († *c.*1290), *Nicholas of Lyra, Nicholas Trivet (*c.*1258-*c.*1330) and Henry of Hesse († 1397).

S. Berger, *Quam notitiam linguae hebraicae habuerint Christiani*, Nancy, 1893. – R. Loewe, "The Medieval Christian Hebraists of England", *TJHSE*, 17, 1953, 225-249. – M. Thiel, *Grundlagen und Gestalt der Hebräischkenntnisse des frühen Mittelalters*, Spoleto, 1973. – B. Smalley, *The Study of the Bible in the Middle Ages*, Oxford, 1983 (3rd ed.). – G. Dahan, "L'Enseignement de l'hébreu en Occident médiéval", *Histoire de l'éducation*, 57, Paris, 1993, 3-22. – *Hebrew Bible/Old Testament: the History of its Interpretation*, 1, M. Saebo (ed.), Göttingen, 1996.

Gilbert Dahan

**HEBREW MANUSCRIPTS.** Though Hebrew manuscripts produced in the West are known only from the 10th or 11th cc., numerous indications suggest that this output began several centuries earlier. In their formal aspect, these manuscripts are distinguished from their Latin homologues of the same period by their script and by the fact that, since Hebrew writing goes from

*Hedwig, duchess of Silesia.* Ostrov manuscript, 1353. Malibu (CA), Paul Getty Museum.

right to left, the volumes follow the same direction. All other formal criteria – preparation of *parchment, assemblage of quires, procedures and systems of ruling – are common to all manuscripts of a single region, whatever method of writing may be employed.

In Jewish culture, the manuscript enjoyed a particularly important status. It was the sole vehicle for the safeguard and transmission of religious tradition, knowledge and the rules of social and family morality. The manuscript had also permitted the survival of Hebrew, the only language that was cultivated over nearly 2000 years without a State to protect it and without being linked to any definite geographical area. The manuscript also served to ensure the link between communities dispersed throughout the world, living amidst foreign societies and cultures.

Centres of production flourished wherever important communities were settled. The trade of copyist was a family craft, transmitted from father to son: no stable organisation like the Christian **scriptoria* (workshops of copyists) is attested in Jewish civilization. Between the 11th and 15th cc., the most important centres were in the Iberian peninsula – *Toledo, Soria, *Barcelona, Lisbon –, northern *France – *Paris, *Troyes –, *Normandy and the Rhineland. The rise of Italian centres – *Rome, *Florence, *Padua, *Venice, *Bologna – took place mainly from the 14th-15th centuries.

Hebrew manuscripts also served as a means of communication between *Jews and Christians. At the time of the great renewal of biblical studies in the 11th and 12th cc., Christian scholars engaged in correcting the Latin text of the *Bible were quite willing to resort to the Hebrew text as reference. They also got Jews or converted Jews to copy bilingual biblical texts – notably the *psalter –, the Hebrew version appearing opposite the Latin version. The Bibles copied for the use of *Theodulf, bishop of *Orléans (750-821), bore marginal annotations in Hebrew. The Victorine exegetes – *Hugh, *Richard and *Andrew of Saint-Victor – refer more than once in their writings to "rabbi Solomon" (rabbi Solomon ben Isaac, called *Rashi) or to his pupils, and the evidence suggests that this was not just a matter of theoretical exchanges, but of encounters around Hebrew manuscripts.

T. Metzger, *Jewish Life in the Middle Ages: Illuminated Hebrew Manuscripts of the 13th to 16th Centuries*, New York, 1982. – G. Sed-Rajna, *The Hebrew Bible in Medieval Illuminated Manuscripts*, New York, 1987. – G. Dahan, *Les Intellectuels chrétiens et les Juifs au Moyen Âge*, Paris, 1990. – M. Beit Arie, *Hebrew Manuscripts of East and West*, London, 1992.

Gabrielle Sed-Rajna

**HEDWIG OF POLAND (1374-1399).** Hedwig (Jadwiga) was queen of *Poland. Her *tomb is at *Cracow (Wawel cathedral). She was the daughter of Louis the Great of Anjou, king of Poland and *Hungary, and Princess Elizabeth of Bosnia. After her father's death, Hedwig was crowned king (*rex*) of Poland in 1384. In 1386 she married *Ladislas Jagiełło, grand duke of *Lithuania, a marriage that cemented the Polish-Lithuanian alliance and permitted the start of the Christianization of Lithuania. Hedwig played an active role in the restoration of royal power in Ruthenia and in relations with the *Teutonic Order. Her gifts permitted the reopening of the *university of Cracow. The cult of Hedwig, a cultivated woman of profound piety, always considered *beata*, spread after her death. It was confirmed in 1979 by Pope John Paul II and she was canonized in Cracow in 1997.

A. Strzelecka, *O królowej Jadwidze* [Queen Hedwig], 1933. – G. Labuda, "Hedwig", *LdM*, 4, 1989, 1986. – O. Halecki, *Jadwiga of Anjou and the Rise of East Central Europe*, Boulder (CO), 1991.

Teresa Dunin-Wąsowicz

**HEDWIG OF SILESIA (*c.*1178/1180-1243).** Daughter of Berthold IV, count of Andechs, and Agnes of Meissen, Hedwig (Jadwiga) was brought up in the Benedictine monastery of Kitzingen, which she left at the age of 13 to marry the duke of *Silesia, Henry the Bearded. In 1202, she and her husband founded the *Cistercian abbey of Trzebnica, not far from *Wrocław, of which their daughter Gertrude later became *abbess. After 20 years of marriage and seven children, only one of whom survived, she took a *vow of *chastity and retired to Trzebnica where she died in 1243, after the tragedy of losing her son Henry the Pious, defeated and killed by the *Mongols at the battle of Legnica in 1241. At the request of the archbishop of *Gniezno, an inquiry into her life and *miracles was ordered in 1262, and she was canonized in 1267 by Pope *Clement IV. With St *Elizabeth of Thuringia (or of Hungary), she was one of the rare married *women and mothers to attain such an honour in the Middle Ages. Towards the end of the 13th c., an anonymous author compiled an important *biography of Hedwig and added a genealogy to it. In 1353, a manuscript of this Life – that of Ostrov, now in the J. Paul Getty Museum in California – was illuminated with 64 scenes. It is one of the fundamental sources for the religious and cultural history of medieval Silesia.

T. Dunin-Wąsowicz, *Legenda śląska*, Wrocław, 1967 (ed. of the illuminated manuscript of the *Vita*).

J. Gottschalk, *St Hedwig Herzogin von Schlesien*, Cologne-Graz, 1964. – A. Vauchez, *Les Laïcs au Moyen Âge*, Paris, 1987, 203-209. – T. Dunin-Wąsowicz, "Hedwig", *LdM*, 4, 1989, 1985-1986.

Teresa Dunin-Wąsowicz

**HEILIGENKREUZ.** A *Cistercian *abbey near Baden, in Lower Austria, founded in 1133 by the Austrian Margrave Leopold III who settled monks from *Morimond there. It rose rapidly and very soon became the mother house of numerous Cistercian monasteries (Zwettl, Baumgartenberg, Lilienfeld and others). It had numerous possessions in Austria, Carinthia, Styria and *Hungary. The medieval church, consecrated in 1187 and given a *Gothic choir in 1295, and the *cloister (1220-1240), housing the *tombs of some Austrian dukes of the Babenberg dynasty, still exist. A very active **scriptorium* and the production of theological and literary works by the monks of Heiligenkreuz (*e.g.* Gutolf, 1245-*c.*1300, or Nicholas Vischel, early 14th c.) attest the monastery's cultural importance. In the 15th c. a certain decline set in due to the political uncertainties of the time.

H. Watzl, *Das Stift Heiligenkreuz*, Vienna, 1967. – *Handbuch der historischen Stätten, Österreich*, 1, K. Lechner (ed.), Stuttgart, 1970, 313-316. – H. Watzl, *"In loco, qui nunc ad Sanctam Crucem vocatur"*, Heiligenkreuz, 1987.

Werner Maleczek

**HEJIRA.** The *hejira* designates the beginning of the Muslim era and corresponds with the year 622 of the Christian *calendar. The Latinized form *hejira* or *hegira* is derived from the Arabic *hijra* which means "migration", "separation", "breaking of relations" (and not "flight" as is still sometimes said).

The event of reference is the clandestine migration organised by the founder of *Islam, *Muḥammad, from his home town of *Mecca to the more northerly oasis of Yathrib, which later became *Medina. Muḥammad's religious teaching and the social role it conferred on him disturbed the commercial aristocracy of Mecca, which showed its hostility more and more emphatically. By contrast, the different tribes of Medina, Jews among them, in search of a federator and more or less in commercial rivalry with Mecca, contrived to propose a politico-military alliance to Muḥammad and his *hijra* companions. These were called *muhājirūn*, "migrants", a title later coveted, since it offered its beneficiaries advantages linked to a high social rank, that of the first Muslims.

Muḥammad's departure took place by night, on camel-back, with Abū Bakr, future successor to the Prophet and first *caliph of Islam. During this march of about 350 kilometres by unfrequented routes, the legendary episode of the spider occurred. Having taken refuge in a cave, the two companions escaped their pursuers only thanks to a spider which rapidly wove its web in the hollows of the entrance, with led them to believe that the cave was unoccupied. The legend has its origin in a passage of the *Koran, revealed later: "Now Allah certainly brought him [Muḥammad] help . . . when they were both in the cave, when he said to his companion: Do not be distressed, yes, Allah is with us" (IX, 40).

The arrival at Medina took place on 24 Sept 622 of the Christian era. But the Muslim year was lunar, and the new era was made to begin not in September 622 but on the first day of the current lunar year, *i.e.* 16 July 622. This decision was taken in year 16 of the hejira (637 of the Christian era), by the second caliph of Islam, 'Umar. Customarily, texts give the hejiran date followed by an H (for Hejira): *e.g.* 1308 H, or followed by the corresponding date of the Christian era: *e.g.* 114/732. Mathematical formulae allow us to pass from the Hejiran dating system to the Christian or *vice versa*, but in practice we consult tables of concordance or, better still, data-processing.

H. G. Cattenoz, *Tables de concordance des ères chrétienne et hégirienne*, Rabat, 1961 (3rd ed.). – M. Rodinson, *Mahomet*, Paris, 1967 (2nd ed.). – W. M. Watt, "Hidjra", *EI(E)*, 3, 1971, 366-367. – G.S.P. Freeman-Grenville, *The Islamic and Christian Calendars, AD 622-2222 (AH 1-1650)*, Reading, 1995.

Constant Hamès

**HELFTA.** The celebrated monastery *Beatae Mariae Virginis* (of the Blessed Virgin *Mary) at Helfta (active from 1229 to 1545), erected by Count Burchard of Mansfeld near the castle of the Mansfelds, was really established in 1229 with seven *nuns coming from the monastery of St Burcharda of Halberstadt, and provided with rich endowments. From 1234 it was transferred to Rossdorf, then, under the abbacy of Gertrude of Hackeborn, to Helpede (Helfta), east of Eisleben. The inauguration of the monastery took place on 3 June 1258, in the presence of the counts of Mansfeld and Querfurt, the archbishop of *Magdeburg, Volrad, bishop of Halberstadt, and "other lords and prelates", which attests its importance. During the episcopal quarrel of Halberstadt, the monastery, which was rich and had more than 100 nuns, was devastated and transferred, in 1346, immediately outside the town ramparts, to Neuhelfta (New Helfta). This new *foundation was sacked and burned during the Peasants' War, in 1525. The same year, the sisters, who had fled, returned to the place, but settled in the monastery's dependencies, at Althelfta (Old Helfta). After the death of the last *abbess, Walburge Reuber, in 1545, the monastery was suppressed by the local lord.

Under the second abbess, Gertrude of Hackeborn (abbess 1251-1292), the monastery developed until it became the shrine of German women's *mysticism. Perhaps in 1270-1271, the 60-year-old *Mechthild of Magdeburg came to spend the last 12 years of her life there, during which she wrote the seventh and last book of her *Flowing Light of the Godhead*. She influenced the writings in which the sisters *Mechthild of Hackeborn and *Gertrude (the Great) of Helfta related their mystical experiences, though their works were very different. Mechthild of Magdeburg's work, written in popular language, reveals in its language as well as in its spirit the clear influence of the education and culture of the feudal courts, while the *Latin writings of the younger sisters are the products of a serious education in the *liberal arts, heavily influenced by the liturgy. Abbess Gertrude of Hackeborn attached great importance to a sound education for the sisters, since "if zeal for the sciences were to disappear, care for religion would disappear, since they would no longer understand Holy Scripture in all its profundity", as Mechthild of Hackeborn asserts in her *Liber specialis gratiae* (VI, 1). Helfta being a monastery dedicated to the Virgin, Marian devotion took an important place there, alongside marriage-mysticism and the cult of the Sacred Heart, very widely developed in the literature of women mystics over the centuries.

F. Schrader, "Helfta", *Marienlexikon*, 3, Sankt Ottilien, 1991, 136. – M. J. Finnegan, *The Women of Helfta*, Athens (GA), 1991. – S. B. Spitzlei, *Erfahrungen Herz. Zur Mystik des Zisterzienserinnenklosters Helfta im 13. Jahrhundert*, Stuttgart-Bad Cannstatt, 1991. – M. Hubrath, *Schreiben und Erinnern. Zur "memoria" im Liber specialis gratiae Mechthilds von Hackeborn*, Paderborn, 1996. – M. Bangert (ed.), H. Keul (ed.), *"Vor dir steht die leerer Schale meiner Sehnsucht". Die Mystik der Frauen von Helfta*, Leipzig, 1998.

Margot Schmidt

***HELIAND.*** The anonymous biblical *epic poem *Heliand* (Old Saxon for *Heiland*, "saviour") consists of some 6000 alliterative verses, recounting the life of Christ. Inspired by Tatian's *Diatessaron* and *Rabanus Maurus's *Commentary on Matthew's Gospel*, it was written around 830, perhaps at *Fulda or Werden (Ruhr). Heir to the Latin biblical poetry of late Antiquity and part of the monastic evangelistic tradition, the work renews and vulgarizes the genre by the use of a vernacular literary language and a Germanized representation of Christianity, whose universe, though without betraying the theological thought, is confused with that of the ancient indigenous lays.

*The Heliand: the Saxon Gospel*, G.R. Murphy (ed.), Oxford, 1992. – O. Behaghel, *Heliand und Genesis*, 1882 (9th ed. revised by B. Taeger, Tübingen, 1984).

G.R. Murphy, *The Saxon Saviour*, Oxford, 1989. – D. Hofmann, *Die Versstrukturen der altsachsischen stabreimgedichte Heliand und Genesis*, Heidelberg, 1991.

Monique Goullet

## HELL

**Doctrine.** Medieval Christianity inherited from the New Testament (cf. Mt 25, Rev 20) the perspective of eternal punishment in the other world for the non-baptized and for Christians who died in a state of mortal *sin. However, such a notion was not easily imposed and St Augustine needed a whole book of the *City of God* to refute the idea of a final return of all creatures to *God, the sentiment of those whom he calls the merciful, and thus to found, for the whole medieval period, the doctrine of the eternity of punishment.

After Augustine and *Gregory the Great, only the situation of the damned souls before the *Last Judgment raised real theological difficulties. At first, it was admitted with difficulty that *souls could go directly to hell proper. Only in the late 12th c. did Western theologians, unlike the Byzantines, abandon "dilation" – deferred access to hell and *paradise – an abandonment confirmed by the second council of *Lyon in 1274 and the *bull *Benedictus Deus* of 1336. One of the difficulties consisted in conceiving the torturing action of the material fire of Gehenna on the soul, which is spiritual. At first admitted to be inexplicable, this question was elaborately worked out in St *Thomas Aquinas's *Summa theologiae*.

*Hell, punishment of the proud.* Fresco of the *Last Judgment* in the cathedral of Sainte-Cécile, Albi. Late 15th c.

For the rest, the analysis of the destiny of the damned was largely homogeneous, admitting the eternity and materiality of the infernal fire, as well as its locality in the centre of the earth. Two types of punishment were distinguished: the most terrible was the pain of *damnation* – privation of *God – to which were added psychological torments like despair, remorse or the rage of seeing the elect in *heaven (until the Last Judgment, but not after); among the pains of the senses, the main one was fire, but worms, cold and darkness were often added. Clerics sometimes admitted a greater diversity of pains, as in the model of the nine pains of hell worked out by *Honorius Augustodunensis, and still more in the preaching that, by way of **exempla*, incorporated certain descriptions of *visions of the afterlife. Though it was not for theologians to describe the detail of the punishments, they admitted, especially from the 13th c., the principle of a diversity of pains and, still more, of an adaptation of punishments to sins punished, quantitatively as well as qualitatively.

Gradually, particularly during the 13th, 14th and 15th cc.,

reference to the threat of eternal damnation became more present in the writings of *clerics, in *sermons and iconography, at the same time as the structuring of hell became more rigorous. However, we see no major imbalance to the detriment of the promise of *paradise, and hell was far from arousing a panic fear. It was more a part of the attempt at social control waged by the Church and the prospect of *salvation that it held out to the faithful.

"Enfer", *DThC*, 5, 1924, 28-120. – A. E. Bernstein, "The Invocation of Hell in 13th Century Paris", *Supplementum festivum. Studies in Honor of O. Kristeller*, New York, 1987, 13-54. – J. Le Goff, *The Birth of Purgatory*, Aldershot, 1990. – J. Baschet, *Les Justices de l'au-delà. Les représentations de l'enfer en France et en Italie (XIIe-XVe siècle), BEFAR*, 1993.

Jérôme Baschet

**Iconography.** Domain of absolute horror, reputed to be unspeakable and unportrayable, hell seems hardly amenable to representation before the 9th c., and had only a moderate presence before the 11th century. The themes in which it appeared were diversified at that time: to the *Last Judgment were added the fall of the *angels, the parable of Lazarus, the final episodes of the *Apocalypse and, especially in the late Middle Ages, pictures of the places of the afterlife, outside the perspective of the Last Judgment. In the Romanesque period – apart from exceptional works like the tympanum of Sainte-Foy at *Conques – its place was still very restricted. It was the rise of the Last Judgment in the Gothic period that ensured the massive circulation of *images of hell. This period saw the triumph of the motif of the throat of *Leviathan. The devouring monster evoked, metaphorically and synthetically, the formidable power of hell, while the confused clutter of bodies inside its jaws was not allowed to draw real attention to the destiny of the damned. *Italy however, faithful to Byzantium, opted for another model: hell was a zone of fire where the damned burned around the enthroned Satan, sometimes with the addition, as at Torcello, of the depiction of the principal pains admitted by the theologians.

An important transformation took place in the course of the 14th c. (first in the *frescos of the Camposanto at *Pisa, *c.*1330-1340, then in the rest of Italy and, with a more or less perceptible time-lag, in the other parts of the West; similarly in the East, but in a less radical way). At this time we see a development and diversification of punishments; the sight of the body, tortured, beheaded, violated, reaches its climax. Then again, hell was the object of an internal structuring that manifests the constitution of a veritable penal system. It was a matter of designating the whole of the sins that led to damnation: a division inspired by the model of the seven *capital sins was favoured at this time, but it was also possible, notably at Byzantium, to make use of a distinction of the different social categories, in particular the trades. Finally, the image aimed to bring out the correspondence between the nature of the punishment and the fault that it punished (gluttons before a groaning table but forbidden to eat, misers force-fed with gold, the lustful joined in an eternal embrace). Echoing both the descriptions of the afterlife and certain penitential practices, the adaptation of the penalty to the fault conferred on the image an increased effectiveness; it guaranteed the legitimacy of punishment and turned the spectacle of cruelty into a moral lesson.

Hell thus came to the aid of a *pastoral care more and more obsessed with the denunciation of sins. But hell was never an end in itself; it was more an incitement to confess the sins denounced by the image, to make the *confession that would permit one to escape from the pains represented.

J. Le Don, "Structure et signification de l'imagerie médiévale de l'enfer", *CCM*, 22, 1979, 363-372. – *The Iconography of Hell*, C. Davidson (ed.), T.H. Seiler (ed.), Kalamazoo (MI), 1992. – J. Baschet, *Les Justices de l'au-delà. Les représentations de l'enfer en France et en Italie (XIIe-XVe siècle)*, Rome, 1993. – G.D. Schmidt, *The Iconography of the Mouth of Hell*, London, 1995.

Jérôme Baschet

**HELOISE (*c.*1100-1164).** Heloise was born of a noble family. In 1116 her uncle Fulbert, a *canon of Notre-Dame, engaged as her preceptor *Abelard, the most famous *master of the cathedral *school, to teach her the *liberal arts. Such an *education was rare for a young girl, even among the aristocracy. A violent passion soon arose between the master and his young pupil. A son being born, the lovers agreed to a secret marriage, but this did not appease the anger of Fulbert, who had Abelard emasculated. After this drama, Abelard made Heloise enter the monastery of Argenteuil, then himself became a monk at *Saint-Denis (1118). Of Heloise's youth we remember, apart from her enthusiasm for study, the strength of an amorous passion deeply experienced and proudly assumed even in its carnal aspect and its hostility to *marriage; she resigned herself to this, but saw it as a brake on Abelard's vocation of "philosopher" and an obstacle to their own *love. "She preferred the title of mistress to that of wife and thought it more honourable for me", said Abelard; "she wished to be be attached to me by tenderness alone, not by the constraint of the nuptial tie." This reaction, which expressed Heloise's passion and her character in love with *freedom, also shows something of the resistance aroused by the Church's wish to enforce marriage as a social institution and the decisive criterion of distinction between *clerics and laymen.

In 1129, the abbot of Saint-Denis recovered Argenteuil and expelled the *nuns from it. Abelard, who had just been elected abbot of Saint-Gildas, offered Heloise his Champenois hermitage of the Paraclete in which to establish a women's monastery. She became its *abbess; under her direction, the Paraclete received numerous properties and created several *priories. Between 1130 and 1135, Abelard and Heloise resumed regular relations, direct or epistolary. In this correspondence appear three *letters of Heloise. In them she recalls with spirit, though in a refined style, the memory of a still burning passion, mingling regrets, reproaches and amorous protestations; she worries about her *salvation and asks herself what her intentions were; but she ends by giving in to the reasons of Abelard, who presses her to dedicate herself above all to her duties as abbess. After 1136, Heloise and Abelard seem to have finally separated. At Abelard's death (1142), she had him buried at the Paraclete. She died 16 May 1164, not without perhaps having assembled and revised the complete dossier of her correspondence with Abelard.

Heloise was a "heroine" whose unhappy love-affair seems to have touched her contemporaries even before moving posterity, and an exemplary figure of what has been called "12th-c. feminism".

*The Last Love Letters of Abelard and Heloïse* Constant J Mews (ed), London, 2000 – *The Letters of Abelard and Heloïse*, B. Radice (tr.), Harmondsworth, 1974.

E. McLeod, *Héloïse*, Paris, 1941. – É. Gilson, *Heloïse and Abelard*, London, 1953. – P. Dronke, *Abelard and Heloïse in Medieval Testimonies*, Glasgow, 1976. – P. Bourgain, "Héloïse", *Abélard en son temps*, Paris, 1981, 211-237. – P. Dronke, "Héloïse", *Women Writers in the Middle Ages*, Cambridge, 1984, 107-143.

Jacques Verger

**HENRY I OF GERMANY (*c.*875-936).** Henry I, 'the Fowler', was king of *Germany from 919 to 936. Duke of *Saxony on the death of his father Otto (912), Henry was elected king by the magnates in May 919, after having been designated by his predecessor Conrad I. He refused to be crowned and consecrated. With his neighbours, he maintained relations based on "friendship" (agreement of Bonn in 921 with Charles the Simple). He enlarged his kingdom by attaching *Lotharingia to it (925), gaining military successes against the Danes and *Slavs, fortified the eastern frontier and signed a truce with the Hungarians. He left the succession to the eldest son of his second marriage, *Otto I.

G. Althoff, H. Keller, *Heinrich I. und Otto der Grosse*, Göttingen, 1985. – H. Beumann, *Die Ottonen*, Stuttgart, 1987.

Michel Parisse

**HENRY II, EMPEROR (973-1024).** Henry II the Saint, son and successor of Henry the Quarrelsome, duke of *Bavaria. He was elected king of *Germany after the death of *Otto III, 7 July 1002, and crowned. Crowned king of *Italy in 1004, he was consecrated emperor in 1014. He had to fight long against *Poland which he made a vassal, and thrice went to Italy to get his authority respected. He leaned on the imperial Church, which was put at the service of the *Empire, supported monastic *reform, restored the see of Merseburg and created that of *Bamberg. He had no child by his wife *Cunegund of Luxemburg, who like him was canonized.

"Vita Heinrici II. imperatoris", *MGH.SS*, 4, 1841, 679-695 and 792-814 (re-ed. 1982).

T. Schieffer, "Heinrich II. und Konrad II.", *DA*, 1951, 384-437. – R. Klauser, *Der Heinrichs- und Kunigundenkult im mittelalterlichen Bistum Bamberg*, Bamberg, 1957. – R. Schneider, "Die Königserhebung Heinrichs II. im Jahre 1002", *DA*, 28, 1972, 74-104. – H. Zimmermann, "Heinrich II.", *TRE*, 15, 1986, 1-3. – K. Guth, *Die heiligen Heinrich und Kunigunde*, Bamberg, 1986.

Michel Parisse

**HENRY III, EMPEROR (1017-1056).** Son of the Emperor Conrad II, Henry was crowned and consecrated king at the age of ten (1028); he received the duchies of *Bavaria and *Swabia, became king of *Burgundy in 1038 and succeeded his father in June 1039. He received the imperial *crown in *Rome at Christmas 1046, from the *pope whom he had appointed. Greatly attached to a Church at the service of the *Empire, he chose the popes from 1046 to 1054 from among German *bishops, and supported the Cluniac movement. He defended his kingdom against the Hungarians. His marriage to Agnes of Poitou was criticized because of their *kinship (1043). He was the first to take the title of king of the Romans and to add the *ring to the *crozier for the *investiture of bishops.

E. Boshof, *Die Salier*, Stuttgart, 1987. – F. Prinz, "Kaiser Heinrich III.", *HZ*, 1988, 529-548.

Michel Parisse

**HENRY IV, EMPEROR (1050-1106).** Son of *Henry III and Agnes of Poitou, the young Henry, crowned in 1054, was put, on his father's death in 1056, under his mother's tutelage until 1062. Archbishop Anno of Cologne then tried to remove her in order to exercise power, which eventually precipitated the declaration of majority in 1065. The baton of authority then passed to Archbishop Adalbert of Bremen. Well educated, Henry IV was a man of fine stature but contrasting character. He had been marked by the events of his youth and the threats that had weighed on his life. To give

*The Coronation of Henry II.* Miniature from the *Sacramentary of Henry II.* Munich, Bayerische Staatsbibliothek (Ms lat. 4456).

himself a firmer territorial base, he wanted to make himself sole master of *Saxony, and hence found himself involved in a difficult war from which he emerged as victor of the Unstrut (1075).

He then had leisure to turn his efforts against Pope *Gregory VII who denied the emperor any right over the papacy and over the Church itself, while the system of the imperial Church was still functioning. Having had Hildebrand-Gregory condemned by his bishops at *Worms in Jan 1076, Henry IV, threatened with deposition, made his submission at *Canossa (Jan 1077). The German princes elected anti-kings (1077-1088), and the king could not hide much longer his profound hostility to the Gregorian policy. At Brixen, in 1080, he got an *antipope elected in the person of Clement III who crowned him emperor at *Rome in 1084. In order to get to Rome, he had to launch into a long and difficult conquest of northern *Italy, where his cousin *Matilda of Tuscany, an indefectible supporter of the *pope, provided men and money to his opponents. The capture of Rome and the death of Gregory VII in exile (1085) did not improve his situation. *Urban II resumed the struggle and raised up against him Welf of Bavaria, who married Matilda. Illness and setbacks made him renounce his project and he returned north. His son and successor Conrad had himself crowned king of Italy and made an alliance with the pope. After Conrad's premature death, his brother Henry led the opposition, forcing his father to abdicate in 1105. He died, isolated and deprived of his power, at *Liège in 1106. His body was later transported to the *Speyer *cathedral which he and his predecessors had contributed to make a memorial to the *Salian dynasty.

*Vita Heinrici IV. imperatoris*, *MGH.SRG*, 58, 1899 (re-ed. 1990).

*Canossa als Wende*, H. Kämpf (ed.), Darmstadt, 1963. – *Investiturstreit und Reichsverfassung*, J. Fleckenstein (ed.), Sigmaringen, 1973. – E. Boshof, *Heinrich IV. Herrscher an einer Zeitenwende*, Göttingen, 1979. – H. Zimmermann, "Heinrich IV.", *Kaisergestalten des Mittelalters*, Munich, 1984, 116-134. – H. Zimmermann, "Heinrich IV.", *TRE*, 15, 1986, 6-9. – E. Boshof, *Die Salier*, Stuttgart, 1987. – I. S. Robinson, *Henry IV of Germany, 1056-1106*, Cambridge, 1999.

Michel Parisse

**HENRY V, EMPEROR (1081-1125).** Younger son of *Henry IV, Henry, already elected king and crowned (1098-1099), rose up aged 19 against his father, whose place he took in 1105. Married to *Matilda of England (1114), he maintained good relations with that country. His main preoccupation was the regulation of the conflict with the papacy; he first opposed *Paschal II, then came to an understanding with him and forced him to crown him emperor (1111). He claimed to obtain the inheritance of Countess *Matilda. His uncertain policy, which at one time envisaged dismantling the *bishoprics, aroused strong opposition from the lay and ecclesiastical princes. Henry V ended by signing an agreement with Pope *Calixtus II to regulate the problem of Investitures (*concordat of *Worms, 1122).

E. Boshof, *Die Salier*, Stuttgart, 1987.

Michel Parisse

**HENRY VI, EMPEROR (1165-1197).** Son of *Frederick Barbarossa, Henry was crowned king in 1169 (aged four). Dubbed a knight in 1184, he married *Constance, heiress to the kingdom of *Sicily, in 1186 and became emperor in 1191. In his kingdom he had to face opposition from the Welfs of Brunswick. In 1194, he took possession of the kingdom of Sicily and was crowned king at *Palermo. His political ambitions were fruitless. Wishing to play a role in the Mediterranean, he married his brother to a daughter of the emperor of Byzantium; he also dreamed of taking part in a *crusade, but died prematurely of malaria and dysentery, leaving only one son, *Frederick II.

O. Engels, *Die Staufer*, Stuttgart, 1993.

Michel Parisse

**HENRY VII, EMPEROR (*c.*1274-1313).** Count of *Luxemburg, Henry was elected king of the Romans by the *Prince Electors led by the archbishops of *Trier and *Mainz, with anti-French intentions. The king was anxious above all to restore the *Empire and give it back all its prestige in *Christendom. After having obtained positive results in the east of the kingdom and the promise of *Bohemia by the marriage of his son John to the heiress Elizabeth, he set out in 1310 for *Italy, where he hoped to gather the money necessary for his policy. He received the iron *crown of *Lombardy (1311), but had to fight to get into *Rome where he was crowned emperor (29 June 1312). He died of malaria the next year.

F. Schneider, *Kaiser Heinrich VII*, 1924-1928. – W. M. Bowsky, *Henry VII in Italy*, Lincoln (NE), 1960. – *Balduin von Luxemburg*, F. J. Heyen (ed.), Mainz, 1985.

Michel Parisse

**HENRY I OF ENGLAND (1068-1135).** The third son of *William I (the Conqueror), Henry seized the throne on the death of his brother *William II (2 Aug 1100). His was a crucially important reign: *Normandy was reattached to the English *Crown, baronial opposition was crushed, the Church was reconciled (compromise of Bec), and the foundations of a highly efficient fiscal and legal system were laid in the organisation of the Curia Regis and *Exchequer. On his death (1 Dec 1135) the barons repudiated his daughter, the empress *Matilda (widow of the Emperor *Henry V), preferring his nephew *Stephen of Blois.

*NCE*, 6, 1021-1022. – M. Brett, *The English Church under Henry I*, Oxford, 1975. – *DMA*, 6, 1985, 154-156. – J. A. Green, *The Government of England under Henry I*, Cambridge, 1986. – C.A. Newman, *The Anglo-Norman Nobility in the Reign of Henry I*, Philadelphia, 1988.

Anne J. Duggan

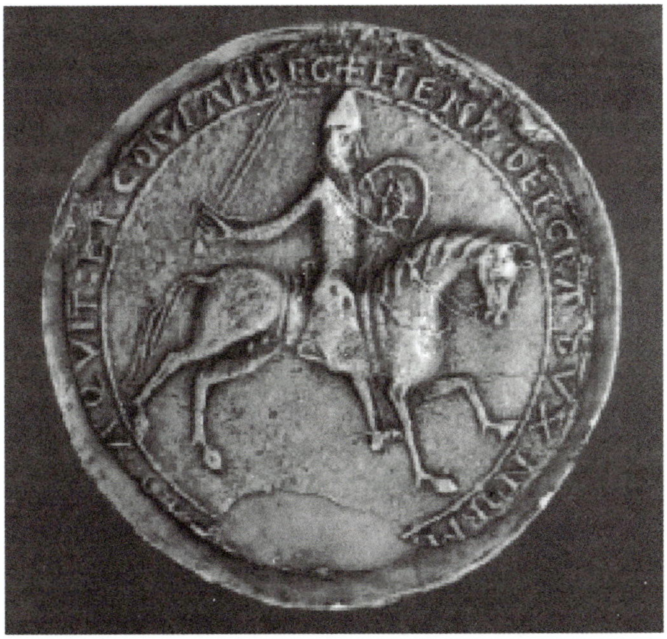

*Seal of Henry II Plantagenet* (1133-1189). Reverse. Paris, Archives Nationales.

**HENRY II OF ENGLAND (1133-1189).** Eldest son of Count Geoffrey of Anjou and *Matilda, widow of the emperor *Henry V and daughter and heiress of *Henry I of England, Henry II became master of what historians call the Angevin Empire by a combination of marriage, inheritance, diplomacy and conquest – duke of *Normandy (1149-1150), count of *Anjou (1151), duke of *Aquitaine (by marriage to *Eleanor of Aquitaine, 1152), king of *England (Oct 1154), thus ruling a territory that extended from the North Sea to the *Pyrenees and embraced the whole western sea-board of France, from *Brittany to *Gascony. He was as much a French prince as an English king, and French was his mother tongue. Succeeding King Stephen was both a challenge and an opportunity. On the one hand, the period of "anarchy" in Stephen's reign had undermined orderly monarchical rule; on the other, there was a longing for peace and order, to which the energetic young king responded with a programme of recuperation of royal rights and major reconstruction of the processes of law and government. This latter formed the context of the Becket controversy, where the king's policies conflicted with the Church's claim to jurisdictional *immunity, then more clearly defined by *canon law, especially in Gratian's *Decretum* (*c.*1140). The murder of *Thomas Becket (29 Dec 1170) forced Henry to make concessions to the Church on *appeals to *Rome and the treatment of criminous clerks, but he survived the crisis.

The governance of the "Angevin Empire", united neither by *custom, language nor mutual interest and at different stages of pacification, demanded constant vigilance; and the competing ambitions of his four legitimate adult sons (Henry, Richard, Geoffrey, John), who conspired with the many discontented elements in the "Empire", with one another and with King *Louis VII of France to advance their ambitions against their father, caused serious difficulties (rebellions in 1173-1174, 1183, 1188-1189). Only ceaseless activity, the judicious use of force and fear, and the loyalty of his administration preserved Henry's dominions intact. To his reign belongs the beginning of English common law – of a royal *justice available to all free men, dependent on royal writs, sworn juries and itinerant justices – and the consolidation of the *Exchequer and *chancery. He declared that he was merely restoring the customs of his grandfather Henry I, but he did much more. He created a framework of government, law and justice that survived the absence of one son (*Richard I) and the great rebellion against another (John), and became the basis of later medieval government in England and Normandy.

J. E. A. Jolliffe, *Angevin Kingship*, London, 1955. – J. Boussard, *Le Gouvernement d'Henri II Plantagenêt*, Paris, 1956. – *NCE*, 6, 1967, 1022-1023. – W. L. Warren, *Henry II*, London, 1973. – J. Gillingham, *The Angevin Empire*, London-New York, 1984. – *DMA*, 6, 1985, 156-158. – J. Gillingham, "Conquering Kings: some Twelfth-Century Reflections on Henry II and Richard I", *Warriors and Churchmen in the Middle Ages*, T. Reuter (ed.), London, 1992. – E. Amt, *The Accession of Henry II in England*, Woodbridge, 1993.

Anne J. Duggan

**HENRY III OF ENGLAND (1207-1272).** Eldest son of King *John and Isabella of Angoulême, Henry III succeeded in 1216 at the age of nine to a troubled inheritance, following *Magna Carta and the loss of most of the "Angevin Empire". Although he failed to recover the lost provinces, by the treaty of Paris (1259) he secured possession of Guienne/*Gascony in return for *homage to the king of *France. His misjudged support for his younger son Edmund's claim to the Sicilian crown precipitated the baronial rebellion of 1258-1265, but he defeated the opposition. A patron of the arts, he is best remembered for the rebuilding of *Westminster Abbey.

*NCE*, 6, 1967, 1023. – *DMA*, 6, 1985, 158-159. – R.C. Stacey, *Politics, Policy and Finance under Henry III, 1216-1245*, Oxford, 1987. – D. A. Carpenter, *The Minority of Henry III*, London, 1990. – D. A. Carpenter, *The Reign of Henry III*, London, 1996.

Anne J. Duggan

**HENRY IV OF ENGLAND (1367-1413).** Son of the richest man in *England, John of Gaunt (himself third son of *Edward III) and of Blanche of *Lancaster, Henry of Bolingbroke, earl of Derby, was soon involved in English *politics. Heir to the Bohun family through his wife Mary, in 1386 he rallied to the "appellants", those lords who "appealed" *Richard II's favourites of treason. That did not prevent him gaining glory and popularity in *tournaments (joust of Saint-Inglevert) and *crusades (*Lithuania, *Holy Land). Though reconciled with Richard, he was, like all the appellants, a victim of his revenge. Exiled in 1397 over the confused affair of a *duel with Thomas Mowbray, duke of Norfolk, on the death of John of Gaunt in 1399 he was refused his inheritance.

Richard II had alienated opinion by the arbitrariness of his measures; but imprudently he set out to lead an expedition to *Ireland, leaving his realm in the keeping of the indecisive duke of *York. When Henry landed with some followers (including the archbishop of *Canterbury, Thomas *Arundel) at Ravenspur, reclaiming his inheritance, he was well received and rallied to: Richard reacted too late and, on his return from Ireland, had to surrender (August 1399). Instead of contenting himself with his inheritance, Henry then decided to take the *crown, though he was not its legitimate heir: that was the great-grandson of Edward III's second son Lionel of Antwerp, the eight-year-old Edmund Mortimer, earl of March, whose sister Anne had married the son of the duke of York.

On 29 September, Richard II renounced the crown before a committee presided over by Arundel; on the 30th, *Parliament, which was no more than a mere assembly, the throne being vacant, acclaimed Henry and, reconvened by him for 6 October as Parliament in its entirety, ratified the change without the question of the Lancastrian "title" to the Crown being ruled on. On the 13th Henry was crowned, and Richard died soon after, probably murdered. All this was nebulous, and the new sovereign's authority was immediately contested. The *nobles who supported Richard II fomented a plot: but on its discovery (Jan 1400), they were massacred. Then *Wales was inflamed by a *revolt led by *Owain Glyndŵr: though the revolt was contained, troops had to be maintained there throughout the reign; Henry's son *Henry V had a harsh military apprenticeship there. Yesterday's allies, the Percies, revolted: defeated in 1403 at Shrewsbury, they did so again in 1405 and again in 1408, with the complicity of the Scots. Henry IV also had to cope with the hostility of *France, allied to Richard II. Finally, his relations with Parliament were bad, since his campaigns and the need to reward his followers obliged him to demand *money ceaselessly.

Moreover, the *Lollard danger obliged the king to grant the archbishop of Canterbury, Thomas Arundel, exceptional means to fight against that *heresy (statute *De heretico comburendo* in 1401). And from 1409 the Council was deeply divided by factional struggle, Arundel and Clarence opposing Prince Henry and Henry Beaufort. Henry IV's reign was difficult, and the illness that struck the king from 1405 obscures the reckoning still further.

*DNB*, 1885-1900. – J. L. Kirby, *Henry IV of England*, London, 1970. – S. Pistono, "Henry IV and Charles VI: the Confirmation of the Twenty-Eight-Year Truce", *JMH*, 3, 1977, 353-65. – P. McNiven, "Legitimacy and Consent: Henry IV and the Lancastrian Title, 1399-1406", *MS*, 44, 1982, 470-88. – P. McNiven, *Heresy and Politics in the Reign of Henry IV*, Woodbridge, 1987.

Jean-Philippe Genet

**HENRY V OF ENGLAND (1386-1422).** Henry was already an experienced soldier in *Wales when his father *Henry IV died (March 1413). The *Lollard revolt of Sir John *Oldcastle (1414) and the plot of Richard of Cambridge (1415) failed, but revealed the fragility of his *crown. A great leader of men, pious and patriotic, Henry knew that, to consolidate his power, he had to conquer abroad. Reclaiming the continental inheritance of the English kings, he took Harfleur and triumphed at Agincourt (25 Oct 1415), thus ensuring the support of *Parliament. Between 1416 and 1419 (capture of *Rouen), he completed the conquest of *Normandy. The murder of John the Fearless (1419) cemented his alliance with Philip the Good, duke of *Burgundy; the government of *Charles VI had to accept the treaty of Troyes (1420). Henry married Catherine, daughter of the king of France, the dauphin *Charles being practically disowned; on the death of Charles VI, Henry and his successors were to inherit the kingdom of *France. But Henry's premature death (31 Aug 1422), of a dysentery contracted at the siege of Melun, left his victory incomplete.

*Gesta Henrici Quinti*, F. Taylor (ed.), J. S. Roskell (ed.), Oxford, 1975 (*OMT*).

G. L. Harriss, *Henry V. The Practice of Kingship*, Oxford, 1985. – T. B. Pugh, *Henry V and the Southampton Plot of 1415*, Southampton, 1988. – E. Powell, *Kingship, Law and Society: Criminal Justice in the Reign of Henry V*, Oxford, 1989. – C. T. Allmand, *Henry V*, Berkeley (CA), 1992 (re-ed. New Haven, 1997).

Jean-Philippe Genet

**HENRY VI OF ENGLAND (1421-1471).** Henry VI was nine months old at the death of his father *Henry V (August 1422). On the death of *Charles VI (Oct 1422) he was also, by his mother Catherine de Valois and by virtue of the treaty of Troyes (1420), king of *France. In France his uncle the duke of Bedford was an energetic regent, but in *England Cardinal Beaufort, bishop of *Winchester, and another uncle, Humphrey of Gloucester, opposed each other. When in 1429 the French regained a new dynamism, English power vacillated. Bedford's death and the Franco-Burgundian reconciliation (congress of Arras, 1435) led to the loss of *Paris (1436). Henry showed himself both indecisive and vindictive. Devout, he founded Eton College as well as King's College, *Cambridge. Suffolk negotiated a rapprochement with France at the truces of Tours (1444) and Henry's marriage to Margaret of Anjou; he eliminated his opponents: Gloucester was assassinated (1447), Richard of *York sent into semi-exile in *Ireland (1449). But the defeats of Formigny (1450) and Castillon (1453) necessitated the evacuation of *Normandy and then *Gascony.

Suffolk paid for his failure with his life (1450). As for Henry VI, struck down by the same illness as Charles VI, he had to be periodically removed from power: York was thus three times protector of England. During the Wars of the Roses, the queen's party supported by the Beauforts faced the party of York supported by the Nevilles; but in October 1460 York claimed the *crown, denouncing the illegitimacy of the Lancastrian claim. York was killed, but his son *Edward IV triumphed (1461). Henry VI took refuge in the North, but was arrested in 1465. Restored by *Warwick in 1470-1471, he was murdered when Edward IV regained power. Henry VII undertook to have the martyr king canonized.

*DNB*, 1885-1900. – R. A. Griffiths, *The Reign of King Henry VI*, London, 1981. – B. Wolffe, *Henry VI*, London, 1981. – D. Styles, C.T. Allmand, "The Coronation of Henry VI", *History Today*, 32, May 1982, 28-33. – J. Watts, *Henry VI and the Politics of Kingship*, Cambridge, 1996.

Jean-Philippe Genet

**HENRY VII OF ENGLAND (1457-1509).** Henry was the son of Margaret Beaufort, sole survivor of the *Lancaster family after 1471, and of Edmund *Tudor, earl of Richmond, himself a son of Catherine de Valois, widow of *Henry V, and the Welshman Owen Tudor. After fleeing to France, then *Brittany, he landed in *England where the excesses of *Richard III had wearied public opinion: victorious at Bosworth (22 Aug 1485) where Richard was killed, Henry took the *crown and, by marrying Elizabeth of *York, daughter of *Edward IV, added a Yorkist legitimacy to his Lancastrian legitimacy. *Revolts were at first numerous: Lovells and Staffords (1486), and the false princes Lambert Simnel (1487) and Perkin Warbeck (1491-1497), but gradually the king imposed strict control on the aristocracy, strengthening his finances while reducing the role of *Parliament. He followed a very prudent foreign policy, avoiding war while conducting a skilful policy of balance between *Spain, *France and the *Empire. He left his son Henry VIII a pacified and stabilized kingdom.

*DNB*, 1885-1900. – S. B. Chrimes, *Henry VII*, London, 1982 (new ed.). – A. Fox, *Politics and Literature in the Reigns of Henry VII and Henry VIII*, Oxford, 1989. – *The Reign of Henry VII*, B. Thompson (ed.), Stamford, 1995.

Jean-Philippe Genet

**HENRY OF BLOIS (*c.*1090/1100-1171).** Fourth son of Stephen of Blois and thus brother of King *Stephen (1135-1154), Henry was professed at *Cluny, abbot of *Glastonbury (1126-1171), bishop of *Winchester (1129-1171) and papal *legate (1136-1143). In addition to playing a full part in the political events of his brother's reign, Henry was very much a princely *bishop, renowned for extravagant building and patronage of art; at the same time, he was an energetic administrator and reformer, and a defender of the rights of the Church.

L. Voss, *Heinrich von Blois, Bischof von Winchester, 1129-1171*, Berlin, 1932. – D. Knowles, *The Monastic Order in England*, Cambridge, 1963, 281-297 (2nd ed.). – *NCE*, 6, 1967, 1034.

Anne J. Duggan

**HENRY OF GHENT (1217-1293).** Henry of Ghent, a secular theologian, is known mainly for his opposition to the thought of St *Thomas Aquinas and *Duns Scotus. The influence of the "solemn *doctor", perceptible up to the end of the Middle Ages, was exercised notably in the distinction he established between the essence and the *being of the creature, their distinction being only intentional. Only *God is Being, and the being of the creature supposes the creator and remains affected by the act of *creation. God is also the first object of *knowledge. Henry of Ghent, both a logician and a commentator on *Aristotle, contributed to the condemnation of the *Averroism taught at the *faculty of arts from 1266 to 1277 by *Siger of Brabant.

"Quodlibet I", R. Macken (ed.), *Henrici de Gandavo Opera omnia*, E. J. Brill (dir.), Leiden, 1979. – S. P. Marrone, *Truth and Scientific Knowledge in the Thought of Henry of Ghent*, Cambridge (MA), 1985.

Edgard Weber

**HENRY OF LANGENSTEIN (1325-1397).** Henry of Langenstein taught at the *universities of *Paris and *Vienna. He was one of the first protagonists of the movement in favour of a conciliar solution to the *Great Schism (1378-1383). To this end he wrote the *Concilium pacis de unione ac reformatione Ecclesiae in concilio universali quaerenda* and the *Epistola concilii pacis*.

Stress has recently been put on his theological works dealing with relations between *Jews and Christians; thus he wrote a treatise *De idiomate ebraico* (1388), in which he declares that he learned *Hebrew in order to convert the Jews, and a *Tractatus de contractibus* (1390-1391), in which he discusses social and economic relations between Jews and Christians.

With Henry of Oyta and *Nicholas of Dinkelsbühl, Henry was, after 1381, one of the most important theologians of the university of Vienna; he was considered an *Ockhamizing *nominalist. But he was also one of those who cast doubt on the universality of Aristotelian *logic, notably calling it powerless to demonstrate the trinitarian paradoxes and consequently to deal with the fundamental problems of *faith. This logic nevertheless remained valuable for the sphere of *creation, if one confined oneself to the level of the arts *faculty.

The work of Henry of Langenstein is important evidence of the questioning of papal power in this period of *schism and the choice of *conciliarism that was its direct consequence, but also of the dissolution of a *theology of Thomist and rationalist type by means of a re-evaluation of Aristotelian logic, confronted by the problems of the data of faith. As such, and as a defector from the university of Paris to that of Vienna, he is a significant representative of the 14th century as it ended.

*Concilium pacis de unione ac reformatione Ecclesiae in concilio universali quaerenda*, H. Von der Hardt (ed.), *MOCC*, 2, 1696-1742, 2-61. – *Advocates of Reform*, "Epistola concili pacis", Spinka (ed.), London, 1953, 135-136. – G. Kreuzer, *Heinrich von Langenstein*, Paderborn, 1987. – M. Shank, *Unless you Believe, you shall not Understand*, Princeton (NJ), 1988.

Jeannine Quillet

**HENRY OF LAUSANNE (12th c.).** Variously called (Henry of Le Mans, of Toulouse, of Lausanne, or, in more pertinent form, the monk Henry), he began his preaching activity in *c.*1116 in the city of *Le Mans. Initially received favourably by the local bishop, *Hildebert of Lavardin, he was held responsible for a citizen uprising against the clergy that we may call "*Patarine" in type. We later find him at *Pisa in 1134 before an ecclesiastical *synod: here he seems to have abjured all "*heresy" and agreed to join the *Cistercian monks of *Clairvaux after a period of suitable *penance. We do not know what actually happened. But in 1145 *Bernard of Clairvaux wrote to the count of *Saint-Gilles to warn him of Henry's impending arrival at *Toulouse with the aim of putting an end to the disastrous effects caused by Henry's preaching: in this letter the prestigious Cistercian briefly outlines the steps of the itinerant life of one whom he ironically calls "*insignis praedicator*", whom he accuses of being an apostate and practising hypocritical and sinful behaviour. Not only this: Henry is held responsible for the disastrous religious and ecclesiastical situation of the Toulouse region (churches deserted by the faithful and without priests, cure of souls neglected, sacramental and liturgical celebrations almost non-existent). After Bernard's letter we lose track of Henry and know no more of him.

Some interesting information on his religious ideas can, however, be foundin a short polemical work written by an equally little-known monk, William. At the centre of Henry's evangelical universe seems to be the taking of full responsibility by every believer in his relationship with God. We also find the demand for "*sanctity" in the priest for the *sacrament to be valid, a choice of *poverty that seems to have an institutional extension (is a poor *priesthood the premise for a poor church?), the claim that loyalty to God takes precedence over any other human obedience, the imperative of *love of neighbour and evangelistic mission. Finally, certain doctrinal positions (denial of efficacity of works for the *dead, superfluity of sacred buildings) seem to be related to the extremism of *Peter of Bruys, with whom he must for some time have had relations, if not indeed a relation of discipleship.

R. Manselli, "Il monaco Enrico e la sua eresia", *BISI*, 65, 1953, 1-63. – A. H. Bredero, "Henri de Lausanne: un réformateur devenu hérétique", *Pascua mediaevalia*, Louvain, 1983, 108-123. – G. G. Merlo, *Eretici ed eresie medievali*, Bologna, 1989, 27-31.

Grado G. Merlo

**HENRY OF NÖRDLINGEN (mid 14th c.).** Our sources for the life and spiritual work of Henry of Nördlingen are his 58 surviving *letters, dated from 1332/1338 to 1350. A *secular priest of the *diocese of *Augsburg, he is described in contemporary sources as *honestus vir, magnae discretionis*. His life is closely linked to that of Margaret *Ebner. When he met her for the first time on 28 Oct 1332 at the monastery of Medingen, he had already exercised for some time a highly esteemed pastoral *ministry in the surrounding monastic communities. For reasons of ecclesiastical *politics (the quarrel between Louis of Bavaria and the *pope), Henry, loyal to the supreme pontiff, had to leave his Swabian homeland in 1338. Passing through *Constance and Königsfelden (Aargau), he went to Basel. There, thanks to *Tauler, he found a new circle of influence as an almoner and preacher for ten years and united around himself a circle of "Friends of God". It was at this time that, on his initiative, *Mechthild of Magdeburg's *Flowing Light of the Godhead* was translated into the High German dialect. From Basel, Henry went to *Alsace and only returned to his homeland in 1350. During his exile, he could only visit Margaret four times. It is to this exile that we owe the first exchange of correspondence in German with Margaret, attesting their spiritual *friendship. After Margaret's death, 20 May 1351, we have little information on Henry other than what we find in the notes of Christine *Ebner, and we know neither the date nor the place of his death.

The exchange of correspondence does not just show us Henry's efforts in *pastoral care and *spiritual direction, they are also a testimony of great historical and cultural value. These letters reflect the characteristic spirit of the "Friends of God" as they appear in Southern *Germany, and allow us to guess at the close relations they had among themselves. Moreover, this epistolary heritage reveals how Henry, from a heeded and venerated *spiritus rector*, gradually evolved to become the figure of a man overwhelmed by *graces and spiritual gifts through contact with Margaret *Ebner, to the point of recognising her as a guide to *God not just for himself, but for the whole Church.

P. Strauch, *Margaretha Ebner und Heinrich von Nördlingen. Ein Beitrag zur Geschichte der deutschen Mystik*, Freiburg im Breisgau, Tübingen, 1882, 169-270 (re-ed. Amsterdam, 1966). – *VerLex*, 3, 845-852 (2nd ed.; bibliog.). – M. R. Schneider, *Die selige Margaretha Ebner*, Sankt Ottilien, 1985. – *Marienlexikon*, 3, Sankt Ottilien, 1991, 130 f. – M. Schmidt, Introduction, *Margaretha Ebner*, L. P. Hindsley (ed., tr.), New York-Mahwah (NJ), 1993.

Margot Schmidt

**HENRY THE LION (died 1195).** Son of Henry the Proud, duke of *Bavaria and *Saxony, Henry, becoming head of a family opposed to the *Staufen, successively received the two paternal duchies (1140 and 1152) and thus became the greatest prince in the *Empire, after the king. His attitude to *Frederick I Barbarossa, his cousin, was long one of loyalty. His policy took him mainly to his lands of Saxony, which led him to neglect somewhat his other possessions, his Bavarian *duchy and his Swabian properties. In the North, he set out to regroup his patrimony, various inheritances from vanished lineages, new acquisitions as well as *fiefs, in order to make them into a territorial whole that he intended to govern as sovereign, which earned him the hostility of a number of vassals, lay and ecclesiastical. He obtained a right of control of the three *bishoprics of Nordalbingia (Oldenburg-Lübeck, Mecklenburg-Schwerin, Ratzeburg) which he endowed. In the economic and

*Reliquary cross of Henry the Lion,* 13th c. Hildesheim, cathedral treasury.

urban sphere, he played a decisive role whose main beneficiary, *Lübeck, became a great Baltic *port. A second brilliant marriage to Matilda of England, a prestigious journey to *Constantinople and *Jerusalem and a dazzling patronage gave him increased importance and he erected in the middle of the renovated town of Brunswick a bronze lion, heraldic symbol of his family.

Having refused to send reinforcing troops at the request of Frederick I, then in difficulties in *Italy, he became the target of numerous attacks and the emperor seized the occasion of a complaint by the bishop of Halberstadt (spoliation of Church properties) to summon Henry before his *court and, after a long procedure, have him condemned to the loss of his duchies and exile (Gelnhausen, 1186). Henry took refuge in *Normandy and then *England, only finally returning to his lands in 1192. He was able to hand down to his children only the *duchy of Brunswick. Resting their case on the illustrations of his *evangeliary, historians have sometimes mooted the idea that the Lion had royal ambitions; this hypothesis has not been confirmed. In any case, the double duke left the memory of a powerful prince, whose power and ambitions could in the long run only be looked at askance by the emperor. His *tomb and that of his wife are in the church of Brunswick, which he built near his *castle of Dankwarderode and the bronze lion of his family.

*Die Urkunden Heinrichs des Löwen, Herzogs von Sachsen und Bayern*, K. Jordan (ed.), *MGH.LF*, 1, 1949 (re-ed. 1995).

K. Jordan, *Die Bistumgründungen Heinrichs des Löwen*, Leipzig, 1939. – *Heinrich der Löwe*, W.-D. Mohrmann (ed.), Göttingen, 1980. – *Der Reichstag von Gelnhausen. Ein Markstein in der deutschen Geschichte, 1180-1980*, H. Patze (ed.), Marburg, Cologne, 1981. – K. Jordan, *Henry the Lion. A Biography*, Oxford, 1986. – O. Engels, "Heinrich der Löwe", *LdM*, 5, 1991, 2076-2078. – J. Ehlers, "Heinrich der Löwe und der sächsische Episcopat", *Friedrich Barbarossa. Handlungsspielräume und Wirkungsweisen des staufischen Kaisers*, A. Haverkamp (ed.), *VKAMAG*, 40, 1992, 435-466.

Michel Parisse

**HERACLIUS, EMPEROR (*c.*575-641).** Son of the exarch of Africa Heraclius the Elder, Heraclius (Hèrakleios) arrived at *Constantinople at the head of a fleet and took power. Crowned emperor by Patriarch *Sergius (5 Oct 610), he took some time to establish himself. The external situation was alarming. To the north, the *Avars, a people of Turkic origin, were penetrating into the Balkans. To the south and east, the danger came from Sasanid Persia. The King of Kings, Chosroes II, taking as pretext the assassination of the Emperor Maurice (602), had begun a war with the Empire. The start of Heraclius's reign was marked by Persian successes: *Syria, *Palestine and Egypt were lost. *Jerusalem was taken and sacked in 614; the *relic of the True *Cross was taken to Persia. The Persians advanced deep into Asia Minor. The danger was at its height in 626; Constantinople, defended by the patrician Bonos and Patriarch Sergius, was besieged from the European side by the Avars, from the Asiatic side by Shahrbaraz's Persians. The deliverance of the city seemed miraculous to the Byzantines, who attributed it to the *Theotokos. After several years of inactivity, Heraclius – who had dreamed of making Carthage his capital – managed to raise an *army and, going by the north, invaded Persia (622-628). In 627 he won an important victory at Nineveh. Early in 628 he took Dastagerd, residence of the King of Kings, and went on to threaten the capital, Seleucia-Ctesiphon. Chosroes, fleeing, was assassinated; his son Kavadh-Siroes succeeded him and signed a peace with Heraclius, who resumed possession of the provinces occupied by the Persians. In spring 630, Heraclius restored the relic of the True Cross to Jerusalem. But this triumph was short-lived. The armies of *Islam, issuing from the Arabian peninsula, invaded the Empire. In 636, the Roman troops were overwhelmed at the battle of Yarmuk. Palestine, Syria and soon Egypt were again lost to the Empire. Heraclius had abandoned Syria in 634. The Holy Cross was transferred to *Constantinople.

Heraclius's domestic achievement is harder to discern. He has been seen as the creator of the system of *themes (new administrative areas, at once military and civil). But this hypothesis is now abandoned. In the religious sphere, Heraclius, inspired by Patriarch Sergius, made a final attempt to reconcile monophysites and Chalcedonians: not without hesitation, he became the promoter of *monothelism. This policy led to a new religious crisis.

Married firstly to Eudocia, secondly – not without scandal – to his own niece Martina, Heraclius had numerous children and founded a dynasty. Martina tried to impose her own children: Heraclius II Heraclonas was sole emperor from 25 May 641 to the end of September. But it was the descendants of Heraclius's first wife who won: Heraclius the New Constantine (Constantine III) reigned from 11 Feb 641 to 24 May 641; his son Constans II from 641 to 668; and Constans's son Constantine IV from 668 to 685. Finally Justinian II, son of Constantine IV, reigned from 685 to 695 and from 705 to 711.

A. N. Stratos, *Byzantium in the 7th Century* 1-5, Amsterdam, 1968-1980. – A. N. Stratos, *Studies in 7th Century Byzantine Political History*, London, 1983.

Bernard Flusin

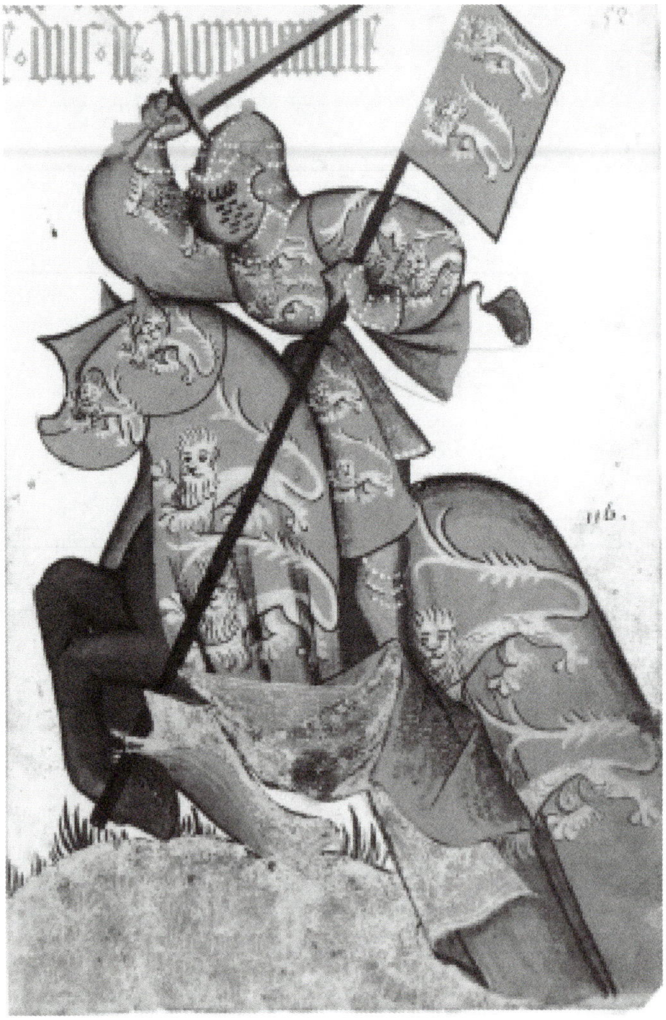

*Armorial bearings of the duke of Normandy.* Miniature from the *Armorial of Europe and of the Golden Fleece*, 15th c. Paris, Bibliothèque de l'Arsenal (Ms 4790, fol. 52).

**HERALDRY.** Heraldry is the historical science whose object is the study of armorial bearings. These may be defined as emblems in colours, proper to an individual, a *family or a collective group and subject in their composition to particular rules which are those of blazonry. It is the existence of these rules, few in number, the main rule concerning the use of colours, that differentiates the European heraldic system from all other systems of emblems.

The appearance of armorial bearings in the West in the first half of the 12th c. was primarily linked to a material cause: the evolution of military equipment. As transformations of the helmet and the hauberk made the knight unrecognisable in battle and tourney, he gradually got into the way of having figures (animals, plants, geometrical) painted onto the great surface of his buckler to aid his recognition in the heart of the mêlée. We can speak of armorial bearings from the moment when a single knight made constant use, over a long period of his life, of the same figures and the same colours. Yet this material cause does not explain everything. The appearance of armorial bearings is more profoundly connected with the new *social order that affected Western society in the seignorial period. Like patronyms or vestimentary attributes, it brought new signs of identity to a society in the process of reorganising itself.

At first individual and reserved for combatants only, armorial bearings progressively became hereditary. Then, in the course of the 13th c., their use was extended to *women, churchmen, townsmen, artisans and even, in certain regions, *peasants (*Normandy, *Flanders, southern *England, *Switzerland); finally, a little later, to moral persons: *towns, trade *corporations, religious communities, various institutions and administrations. The Church, at first mistrustful of this system which had developed entirely outside its own influence – as emphasized by the use, from the start, of the vernacular to describe armorial bearings – became fully part of it from the 14th century.

On the socio-juridical level, it is necessary to correct an error that is widespread but rests on no historical reality: the limitation to the *nobility of the right to armorial bearings. At no time, in no country, were armorial bearings the appanage of a *social class. Each individual, each *family, each group or community was always and everywhere free to adopt the armorial bearings of its choice, the sole condition being not to usurp those of others.

At once marks of possession and decorative ornaments, armorial bearings found a place, from the 12th to the 15th c., on innumerable objects, monuments and documents to which, by doing so, they brought a sort of civil status. Indeed their study is very often the sole means at our disposal today of situating these objects and monuments in space and time so as to rediscover their original or successive possessors, to retrace their history and vicissitudes. It is in matters of dating that the contribution of heraldry appears most precious, since the dates of a person's wearing of an armorial shield generally form a more reduced bracket of dates than those of his life and death. In the case of an object, a work of art or monument ornamented with several shields belonging to several people, it is possible to attain great precision in establishing a date resulting from the dates of birth, *marriage, beginning of "reign", entry into title or position and decease of each of them. Every archaeologist, every art-historian, every conservationist thus has recourse to the study of armorial bearings to try to date, localize or attribute objects, monuments and works of art.

This "archaeological" aspect of heraldic studies belongs to what may be called "traditional" heraldry. This bears primarily on the identity of the persons who made use of armorial bearings. But armorial bearings do not just tell us the identity of those who bore them: they can also reflect their personality. It is to this latter that a "new" heraldry now seeks to devote itself. Profiting from the lowering of the barriers between the different human sciences, over the last twenty years it has renewed the methods and enlarged the fields of investigation of traditional heraldry. It studies, *e.g.*, the motives that presided over the choice of colours or figures composing the armorial bearings of a family or an individual. The relationship between the signifying element and the idea signified can be situated at various levels (linguistic, political, allegorical, symbolic), but its study always provides pertinent information on the aspirations, beliefs, culture or modes of sensibility of those who created or were formed by armorial bearings.

Likewise, the new heraldry seeks to know why and how at such a time, such or such an imaginary personage or one who lived before the appearance of armorial bearings (heroes of *romance, biblical figures, mythological creatures, kings and emperors of Antiquity, saints or *popes of the early Middle Ages, etc.) was provided with armorial bearings and how these were composed, represented, imitated and transformed. Then, going beyond individual cases, it bases itself on quantitative – medieval documents make known to us about a million different armorial bearings –

and statistical methods to draw up indexes of frequency and rarity in the armorial bearings of a time, a region, a class or social category. By interpreting the results obtained, by comparing them with those provided by other disciplines, it brings out phenomena of fashion and taste and merges with the history of cultural systems and the facts of sensibility. Examination of, *e.g.*, the frequency of colours allows us to follow the astonishing promotion of the colour blue which, in armorial bearings as in *clothing, artistic creation and vocabulary, over the centuries takes the place of red as the most valued colour. In the same way, analysis of the frequency of figures allows us to bring out traits of cultural order going far beyond the mere framework of blazonry. We may cite, *e.g.*, the political opposition between the eagle and the lion in the armorial bearings of the 12th and 13th cc., the permanence in the role of king of beasts held by the bear throughout Northern Europe, the pejorative character of certain figures (leopard, cat and diabolical animals, structures in checks and broken lines) and "snobbery" in the choice of other figures (*lily, rose, *unicorn, greyhound) at the end of the Middle Ages.

Finally, in a perspective at once semiological and anthropological, the new heraldry proposes to study blazonry as a system of signs. Resting on a language with its own vocabulary and syntax, and on codes of representation that make the armorial bearing the most theorized of medieval images, the heraldic system offers future research numerous, original and seductive fields of investigation.

G. A. Seyler, *Geschichte der Heraldik*, Nuremberg, 1885-1889 (2 vol.). – R. Mathieu, *Le Système héraldique français*, Paris, 1946. – A. R. Wagner, *Heralds and Heraldry in the Middle Ages*, Oxford, 1956. – G. J. Brault, *Early Blazon. Heraldic Terminology in the XIIth and XIIIth Centuries*, Oxford, 1972. – M. Pastoureau, *Les Armoiries*, 1976 ("TSMÂO", 20). – G. L. Galbreath, L. Jequier, *Manuel du blason*, Lausanne, 1977. – R. Marks, A. Payne, *British Heraldly from its Origins to c. 1800*, London, 1978. – M. Pastoureau, *Traité d'héraldique*, Paris, 1993.

Michel Pastoureau

**HEREFORD.** Situated in the Wye valley, Hereford was the capital of Herefordshire and had a strategic importance in the defence of the frontier against the Welsh, then in the various attempts to conquer *Wales. It was one of *Alfred's "burghs", powerfully fortified, and a Norman *castle was later built there. For this reason the earls of Hereford always played an important political role: William FitzOsbern and Roger FitzWilliam, Miles of Gloucester and the members of the Bohun family up to the end of the 14th century. The region was favourable to sheep-rearing and hence to the rise of the wool industry. Hereford was the 19th town in *England by population in 1377 with 2900 inhabitants, and the 14th for wealth in 1334; it was essentially a *market town, on a regional scale.

But its importance also stemmed form its status as the seat of a *bishopric. The first known bishop of Hereford was Putta, in 676; in 794, King Æthelbert of East Anglia was beheaded by Offa not far from there and buried in the *cathedral, where *miracles took place on his *tomb. Several churches followed each other on the site, but after the Welsh sack of 1056 Robert Losinga began to build a great *Romanesque cathedral in 1079. Work continued until the end of the 15th century. The cathedral houses one of the finest medieval **mappae mundi*, made by Richard of Haldingham. It was served by a college of 32 *canons led by a dean, assisted by a college of 27 *vicars. The bishopric and the college were of middling wealth for England (respectively 831 and 426 pounds at the start of the 16th c.), and the bishops of Hereford were often only transitory: out of 18 bishops between 1317 and 1516, nine were transferred to other sees. No fewer than eight *hospitals (one of which depended on the Order of *Hospitallers), *Franciscan and especially *Dominican *convents and an important Benedictine *priory (St Guthlac) contributed to make the town a great ecclesiastical centre. This concentration doubtless explains why the town was an important cultural centre, notably in the 12th c. when, with Worcester, it was the most active centre for the study of *astrology and *astronomy; *Robert Grosseteste was a member of the household of the bishop of Hereford when the comet of winter 1196-1197 aroused general astonishment.

*Medieval Art, Architecture and Archaeology at Hereford*, D. Whitehead (ed.), Leeds, 1995. – W. J. Dohar, *The Black Death and Pastoral Leadership: the Diocese of Hereford in the Fourteenth Century*, Philadelphia (PA), 1995.

Jean-Philippe Genet

**HERESY, HERETIC.** In a strictly historical perspective, to speak of "heresy" and "heretics" requires us to go beyond a theological viewpoint. The historian does not have to evaluate the consistency, or inconsistency, of the doctrines with the characteristics of the message to which they refer. He takes note that certain doctrines were considered "orthodox" and others "heterodox", and seeks to understand the reasons for this within specific contexts and in a diachronic dimension. He has the further task of establishing periodizations to determine the continuity, changes, breaks and historical incidence of heretical phenomena in that immense period traditionally called the *Middle Ages. This gives rise to difficulties of a general and particular nature. Not the least difficulty is that of being able to arrive at a heretical "history" of the Middle Ages, in which we attempt to leave behind mere description and get to the heart of the phenomena analysed. Moreover, the heresiological medievalist finds himself obliged to use rather unreliable sources and documents, the great majority of which come from orthodox circles and from a culture that tended to reproduce ancient and well-established models and reject "novelties" (since the inheritance of *faith received from Antiquity contained everything necessary to *salvation). Finally, a serious complication arises from the evolution of the concept of heresy and of its wide-ranging applications with the rise of the papal monarchy, in other words the vertical construction of Catholicity culminating in the Roman papacy: heresy then assumed disciplinary, ecclesiological and "political" connotations.

On the level of contents, the first years of the 11th c. undoubtedly represent a turning-point. Heterodox groups were discovered in various parts of *Italy, *France and *Germany. Until recent years, historiography identified the deviant religious ideas of such groups as "popular heresies" to indicate that they stood outside the currents of elite thought and belonged to modest social strata. Today such an interpretation is considered inadequate and partial, since we think we can perceive some links with the thought of the Carolingian period (*e.g.*, with a *John Scotus Eriugena) and with "spiritualistic" tendencies widespread even among the upper classes. Heretical ideas revolved around the key concept, the value of purity obtainable only by a radical detachment from the values of the world, of materiality. From this derived a *dualism, whose origins some see in Eastern culture and others in Western traditions. What is certain is that, with the rise of the *reform movement in the mid 11th c., anti-heretical polemic began to be directed against the clergy: the heresies were *nicolaitism and *simony and were wholly inside the ecclesial organism. Operating here was a demand for rationality, on both an institutional and an ethical level. *Patarine tensions moved on this second level, capable of fully involving the world of the *laity. Purity and rationality met to generate forms of religiosity in whose eyes consistency of behaviour with the Gospel legitimated them and their separation from the hierarchical Church when, in the 12th c., this "closed itself off" as part of the self-consolidation and sacralization of society. This institutional hardening contrasts singularly with the multiplication of religious experiments in every direction and the emergence of an "individual" *conscience: "*sanctity" was no longer intrinsic to the fact of belonging to a *status*; "sanctity" became a personal dimension, a consistent adherence to the Gospel, to *sequela Christi*.

In the 12th c., the reformist and Patarine drives, *i.e.* those directed towards a reform of religious life and the Church in the direction of evangelical poverty, thus exhausted themselves. They made way for religious groups of a different orientation: some were structured according to an antagonistic theology of their own and according to models that imitated the hegemonic Church; others, though condemned by the ecclesiastical authorities, remained inside the *Catholic theological and sacramental tradition. The former, the dualistic "good Christians" – those who as a whole were called "*Cathars" – and the latter (formations called by various names) were confused by the Church hierarchies into an indistinct and flattened heterodox universe, which underwent some attempts at distinction during the papacy of *Innocent III. The *Decretal *Ad abolendam* issued at *Verona by Lucius III in 1184 seems discriminatory: it excommunicates "*catharos et patarinos et eos qui se humiliatos vel pauperes de Lugduno falso nomine mentiuntur, passaginos, iosephinos, arnaldistas*" and all those who exercise the ministry of preaching "either prohibited, or not authorized", independently, we note, of the content of their actual message, and naturally also those who preach differently from the Roman Church about the *sacraments.

The absence of necessary distinctions left a heavy inheritance that obliged especially those who intended to become "new apostles" to make difficult choices about their own situation in relation to the hegemonic Church: how could they return to communion with it without denaturing or even losing their own peculiar characteristics? On the other hand, how could they consent to be definitively classed among the heterodox? To this dilemma, few had time to respond (positively or negatively). With the 13th c., the papacy embittered the anti-heretical struggle on both the theoretical and the practical level: once heresy was defined as a "crime of *lèse-majesté*", it took on a "political" connotation, being a violation of order. And not just this: henceforth any disobedience to the papacy (in other words any injury done to the divine majesty in the person of its earthly representative) became heresy. Finding that space for it to spread in society was closed off, heresy accentuated its eschatological and apocalyptic tensions and, at the same time, became more interior. So the episode of the Dolcinian "resistance" may be taken as the final moment of the heretical parabola that lasted from the early 12th to the early 14th century. With Fra *Dolcino's dream of spiritual rebirth was exhausted a great part of the innovative movement of Christian life, which opened on the wave of the reforming drive that had swept through and modified the ecclesiastical organism in the second half of the 11th century.

Not that *Waldenses, *beguines, *beghards and *fraticelli did not remain here and there in Europe; but their presence no longer made "history". A new heretical wave was inaugurated at the end of the 14th c. in *England and *Bohemia, connected with social and economic crises and coinciding with processes of assertion of national realities. Particularly with the Hussite movement, old themes of polemic against the "carnality" of the hierarchical Church were renewed. A further novelty was the contribution to, and participation in, religious movements by "professional" thinkers; the ideas of a *Wycliffe or a Jan *Hus, as well as the masters of the *Carolinum* who became officially responsible for the theological line of the Bohemian religious movement. Intellectuals succeeded in finding and stimulating interlocutors, protagonists of transformations: heretical ideas, which appeared historically defeated, manifested an unforeseeable vitality, not just on the evangelical level, but actively entering into processes of emancipation and national identity.

W. L. Wakefield, A. P. Evans, *Heresies of the High Middle Ages*, New York, London, 1969 (re-ed. New York, Oxford, 1991). – *The Concept of Heresy in the Middle Ages (11th-13th c.)*, W. Lourdaux (ed.), D. Verhelst (ed.), Louvain-Paris-The Hague, 1976. – *Medioevo ereticale*, O. Capitani (ed.), Bologna, 1977. – *Heresy and Authority in Medieval Europe*, E. Peters (ed.), Philadelphia, 1980. – C. T. Berkhout, J. B. Russell, *Medieval Heresies: a Bibliography, 1960-1979*, Toronto, 1981. – G. Gracco, "Gli eretici nella 'societas christiana' dei secoli XI e XII", *La Cristianità dei secoli XI e XII in Occidente: coscienza e strutture di una società*, Milan, 1983, 339-373. – R. Manselli, *Il secolo XII: religione popolare ed eresia*, Rome, 1983. – R. I. Moore, *The origins of European dissent*, Oxford, 1985. – G. G. Merlo, *Eretici ed eresie medievali*, Bologna, 1989. – M. D. Lambert, *Medieval Heresy*, London, 1992 (2nd ed.). – H. Fichtenau, *Ketzer und Professoren. Häresie und Vernunftglaube im Hochmittelalter*, Munich, 1992. – J.B. Russell, *Dissent and Order in the Middle Ages*, New York, 1992. – *Heresy and Literacy 1000-1530*, P. Biller (ed.), A. Hudson (ed.), Cambridge, 1994. – L. George, *The Encyclopedia of Heresies and Heretics*, London, 1995. – M. Barber, *Crusaders and Heretics, 12th – 14th Centuries*, Aldershot, 1995.

Grado G. Merlo

**HEREWARD (11th c.).** Hereward is renowned as one of the leaders of the English resistance to the Normans after the *Norman Conquest of England in 1066. In *Domesday Book he is listed as a pre-conquest landholder and tenant in Lincolnshire (at Laughton, Rippingdale and Witham) and two of these entries refer to his (undated) outlawry. During his exile he spent some time in *Flanders. In the late 1060s he returned to England where his leadership in Ely and Peterborough in the years 1070-1071 and his subsequent escape from the Normans are mentioned by all main chroniclers. According to his 12th-c. Latin biography, parts of which are of dubious validity, he was eventually pardoned by *William the Conqueror. The year of his death is unknown.

A. Williams, *The English and the Norman Conquest*, Woodbridge, 1995. – E. Van Houts, "Hereward and Flanders", *Anglo-Saxon England*, 28, 1999, 201-203.

Elisabeth van Houts

**HERFORD.** Herford is a town in Westphalia south-east of Osnabrück. Originally it was a monastery of Benedictine *nuns founded *c.*789 in Carolingian *Saxony. Refounded in 823 on the model of Notre-Dame at *Soissons, it later became an institution of *canonesses of the *nobility (at first under the patronage of the Virgin, then of St Pusinne). In 860 occurred the translation of the *relics of St Pusinne from northern France. Herford became a

Carolingian royal *court. In 868 it was accorded *immunity and free *election of the *abbess. At the same period, under the influence of Soissons and *Corvey, Herford became a centre of Christianization of the Saxon *nobility and for the *mission in the Nordic lands (Isleif, bishop of *Iceland) until the 11th century. In 940, it was accorded commercial, customs and monetary rights. In 1011, a female *foundation came into being for the lesser aristocracy, Maria auf dem Berge. In 1427, the *Brethren of the Common Life settled there. From the mid 12th c. appeared the institution of citizenship, while the municipal council was heavily influenced by the abbess of St Pusinne. It reached its apogee in the 14th and 15th cc. with the production of cloth and was attached to the *Hanse.

R. Pape, *Santa Herfordia*, Herford, 1979. – *1200 Jahre Herford*, T. Helmert-Corvey (ed.), Herford, 1989. – "Herford", *Westfälisches Klosterbuch*, K. Hengst (ed.), Münster, 1992, 404-438 (bibliog.).

Franz Neiske

**HERMANN OF METZ (died 1090).** Offspring of the Ardennais *nobility, Hermann, future bishop of *Metz (1073-1090), received his education and began his career at *Liège. He was always connected with the family of Countess *Matilda, who welcomed him on his journeys to *Italy. Bishop of Metz after Adalbero III, he refused to follow King *Henry IV at *Worms (1076) in his condemnation of *Gregory VII, and received a long *letter from Gregory explaining the papal position. He was expelled from his town in 1078 and spent some time in Italy and *Rome and then in the *diocese of Liège. He was deposed by Henry IV in 1085 and had against him Walo, then Bruno as intruded *bishops. He was able to re-enter Metz in 1089 and proceeded before his death to the translation of the *relics of St Clement.

S. Salloch, *Hermann von Metz*, Berlin, 1931. – F. R. Erkens, *Die Trierer Kirchenprovinz im Investiturstreit*, Cologne, 1987, 45-66.

Michel Parisse

**HERMANN CONTRACTUS (*c.*1013-1049).** Hermann was the son of a count of *Swabia. Paralytic from infancy, he was entrusted at the age of seven to the *abbot of *Reichenau, Berno, and remained in the community until his death in 1049. He was the most famous **scholasticus* of his time and was remarked by the Emperor *Henry III and Pope *Leo IX on their visit to the *abbey. His Universal *Chronicle is a model of the genre. The author set out to speak objectively of events, particularly those concerning southern *Germany and neighbouring countries like *Bohemia and *Hungary. Hermann was also a great scholar. He wrote a work on *computus and on division, a commentary on the abacus and a treatise on the measurement of the *astrolabe, using Arabic translations. We also have from him a work on *music. His encyclopedic curiosity astonished his contemporaries.

M. Manitius, *Geschichte der lateinischen Literatur des Mittelalters*, 2, Munich, 1923, 786. – J. C. Didier, "Hermann Contract", *Cath.*, 5, 1957, 663-664.

Pierre Riché

**HERMITS OF SAINT AUGUSTINE, ORDER OF.** *Augustinian influence deeply marked Western *monasticism. It inspired the majority of the great *Rules, like those of *Isidore of Seville or St *Benedict of Nursia. But St Augustine had left no proper normative text, only a series of general recommendations. In the second half of the 11th c., when Benedictine power touched its apogee, these orientations inspired the spiritual search of communities of *canons and then guided the first steps of the *Premonstratensians, before being taken up by congregations of hermits, particularly numerous in central and northern *Italy.

In 1252, *Alexander IV, taking up on his own account a policy of regrouping undertaken by *Innocent IV, presided over the union of the hermits of the Milanese and *Romagna. From 1256, he decided on the creation of a new order, likened to the *mendicant orders, and convoked the *chapter charged with the *election of the first superior general. The most important obstacle encountered on the way to union was the resistance of the Guillemite congregations, perhaps disappointed not to have obtained the office of superior despite their numerical importance; it was smoothed out from 1265, when the Guillemites individually received the right to join the Hermits of St Augustine. In 1257, the *pope exempted the new order from episcopal tutelage. The general chapters of Florence (1287) and Regensburg (1290) put the final touches to constitutions that were to undergo no further notable evolution until the 16th century.

The first mention of Augustinian *nuns dates from 1264. The existence of secular tertiaries is also attested from the 13th century. The female *Third Order was officially recognised by *Boniface IX in 1399. The male branch had to await the decision of Paul II, dated 1470. The Order of Hermits of St Augustine soon attracted many vocations and aroused fervent devotion. In 1329, it numbered 24 provinces, from only four in 1256.

The evolution of the *order gave rise in the 14th c. to desires for *reform. The communities that agreed to submit to it grouped themselves into congregations of regular *observance, directed by a *vicar general. The first appeared in 1387 (congregation of Lecceto). Reforming enthusiasm later reached Germany (1419) and the Iberian peninsula (1431). These measures provoked high tensions within the order. In 1497, the congregation of Lombardy claimed to make itself independent; in 1503, the congregation of Saxony got itself exempted from the jurisdiction of the superior general.

But the Order of Hermits of St Augustine was at the dawn of the most brilliant period of its history. One of its members – Martin Luther – contributed to break the unity of the Church, but its missionaries played a decisive part in the apostolic effort in the Far East as well as in the New World.

M. T. Disdier, *DHGE*, 5, 1931, 499-581. – B. Rano, "Agostiniani", *DIP*, 1, 1974, 278-381.

Daniel Baloup

**HEROLT, JOHANNES (died 1486).** A *Dominican, Johannes Herolt was one of the foremost figures of the new Dominican *spirituality of 15th-c. Germany, combining pastoral aims with mystical spirituality. Though his career was confined to *Nuremberg, his works – in Latin – had great success (many manuscripts, printed editions), like the *Book of Instruction of Christ's Faithful* (1416), the *Sermons of the Time* (1418), or the *Manual of Exemplary Narrations* (*Promptuarium exemplorum*, 1440). This last work, composed (according to the printed edition of Ulm, 1480) of 99 *rubrics classified in alphabetical order, comprises 867 **exempla*. These anecdotes, borrowed from some twenty collections (*Caesarius of Heisterbach, *Stephen of Bourbon, *Thomas of Cantimpré, etc.), belong to various genres, from the strict moral history to the humorous story, secular in character.

A. Brückner, "Herolt, Johannes", *LdM*, 6, 1989, 858-863.

Jacques Berlioz

**HERSFELD.** The Life of Sturm tells how *Boniface sent his disciple in search of a favourable place to build an *abbey. He stopped at the confluence of the Geisa and the Fulda at Hersfeld, but Boniface, fearing the *Saxons, preferred the site of *Fulda. It was Lull, another disciple of Boniface, who later founded a monastery at Hersfeld. To it were transferred in 780 the *relics of Wigbert of Fritzlar, then those of Lull. The abbey benefited from Carolingian favours and enjoyed a brilliant development under Abbot Brunwart († 865). *Henry I the Fowler respected its privileges of *immunity and conceded regalian rights to the *abbot. The walls of Hersfeld were rebuilt and the abbey became a veritable monastic city.

Under Abbot Hagano (935-959), the *Miracles of St Wigbert* were written; from the mid 10th c. date the *Annals of Hersfeld. In the late 11th c., the monk *Lambert († 1077) used the resources of the monastery's *library to write a *History of good quality. We also owe him the Life of Lull and the Book of Institutions of the church of Hersfeld. In the *Investiture Contest, Lambert sided with *Henry IV against *Gregory VII. The abbey's history for the rest of the Middle Ages is less brilliant.

T. Struve, "Hersfeld", *LdM*, 4, 1989, 2182-2183.

Pierre Riché

**HERTFORD.** The site of a church *council convoked in 672 or 673 by Archbishop *Theodore, the first national council of the English Church. As reported by *Bede (*Historia Ecclesiastica*, IV, 5), the council under Theodore's presidency promulgated ten canons drawn from a *liber canonum*; the canons legislate *inter alia* against *bishops interfering in the *dioceses of other bishops, against monks leaving their monasteries without their *abbot's permission, and lay down various regulations pertaining to *divorce. Although some of the stipulations are found in earlier church canons, the identity of Theodore's *liber canonum* has proved elusive, though it evidently bore some resemblance to the second *canonical collection of Dionysius Exiguus.

M. Brett, "Theodore and the Latin Canon Law", *Archbishop Theodore*, M. Lapidge (ed.), Cambridge, 1995, 120-140. – C. Cubitt, *Anglo-Saxon Church Councils, c.650-c.850*, Leicester, 1995.

Michael Lapidge

**HESSE.** The region of the rivers Eder, Lahn and Fulda, later extending to *Mainz and the Rheingau (Rheinhessen). The *pagus Hassorum* was evangelized by St *Boniface from 721. The region was Franconian from the first half of the 6th c. and hence part of the *diocese of Mainz. In 744 Boniface founded the monastery of *Fulda and installed his pupil Sturm as *abbot. Another pupil, Lull, founded the abbey of *Hersfeld in 775. In the Middle Ages, both monasteries remained important religious, cultural and economic centres of Hesse. The extension of Franconian sovereignty, supported by powerful fortifications intended for protection against the *Saxons (Büraburg near *Fritzlar), favoured Hesse's role as a region of deployment of military troops during *Charlemagne's Saxon wars. Its central position with its imperial *palaces (Fritzlar, Cassel) and its Imperial monasteries (Fulda, Hersfeld, Helmarshausen) contributed to make Hesse in the 10th and 11th cc. a region of great importance for the German *monarchy. During the *Investiture Contest, the confrontation between *Henry IV and the Saxons took place there. On the other hand, the transformation of Hesse into a *duchy could not come about, probably because most of the power over these territories belonged to the king and the Imperial monasteries in the region.

*John Cantacuzenus at the council of Constantinople (1351)*, with ecclesiastical dignitaries and civil and military officials, one of whom carries the imperial sword and buckler. Miniature from the *Theological works* of John VI Cantacuzenus, 1370-1375. Paris, BNF (Ms gr. 1242, fol. 5 v°).

Early in the 12th c., the counts of *Thuringia obtained possession by inheritance of *Marburg, Cassel and the banks of the Eder and Fulda, as well as the **bailliage* of several monasteries (Hersfeld, Fritzlar, Hasungen). This constant seignorial appurtenance allowed Marburg to become the residence of St *Elizabeth of Thuringia († 1231) during her widowhood (her *tomb is in the church of St Elizabeth at Marburg). Elizabeth was venerated as patron saint of Hesse; this is why she also became an important political figure of integration. Indeed, beginning with the alliance of the landgraves of Thuringia-Hesse with the *Teutonic Order and *Frederick II, the landgraviate of Hesse developed under the symbolic aegis of Elizabeth in the time of her daughter Sophia and her husband Duke Henry II of *Brabant († 1284). The rich territorial possessions of the *diocese of Mainz went to the landgraves from 1263. In 1526, Landgrave Philip introduced the Reformation into Hesse.

W. Diehl, *Hassia sacra*, Friedberg-Darmstadt, 1921-1951 (12 vol.). – *Schrifttum zur Geschichte und geschichtlichen Landeskunde von Hessen*, E. Demandt (ed.), Wiesbaden, 1965-1968 (3 vol.). – *Althessen im Frankenreich*, H. Schlesinger (ed.), Sigmaringen, 1975. – *Die Geschichte Hessens*, U. Schultz (ed.), Stuttgart, 1983. – *Das Werden Hessens*, W. Heinemayer (ed.), Marburg, 1986.

Franz Neiske

**HESYCHASM.** Hesychasm was a movement going back to the origins of the Christian East. Derived from a Greek word, *hesuchia*, meaning "calm", "peace", "recollection", it designated the state of mind propitious to the *contemplation of *God. "Hesychasm" designated both this spiritual current and the way of life that was most favourable to it: Byzantine sources commonly use "hesychasts" to refer to *anchorites who had abandoned the world to dedicate themselves to contemplation, and *hesychia* to mean life in solitude as opposed to life in community.

Most of the hesychast writings have been collected into the **Philocalia of the Neptic Fathers*. They insist on interior silence and continual *prayer, obtained by the repetition of a short formula centred on the *Name of Jesus; the fruits of this are contemplation of *God in a vision of light, and spiritual joy. Among the best-known followers of this movement are Evagrius Ponticus (4th c.), Diadochus of Photice (5th c.), *John Climacus (6th c.) and *Symeon the New Theologian (10th c.).

Towards the end of the 13th c., after a period of dormancy, hesychasm enjoyed a great revival. Its initiator was Nicephorus the Hesychast, author of a *Treatise on Sobriety and Custody of the Heart* that had great success, mainly on Mount *Athos. In it he described a method of prayer that gave great importance to bodily attitudes: control of the breath, continual invocation of the Name of Jesus, concentration on the interior kingdom. Another Athonite spiritual master made numerous disciples: Gregory the Sinaite. For him, the aim of hesychast prayer was to make the *grace received at *baptism and buried beneath the cares of life, spring up anew. Others (like the future Patriarch Isidore Bucheiras) strove to show that hesychast prayer was not reserved for monks, but open to all the baptized.

The great success of the hesychast movement in a monastic world where the contemplative dimension seemed asleep aroused both imitation and hostility. A derivative can be found in the *Method of Holy Prayer and Attention*, attributed to Symeon the New Theologian, which insists, with a crudity that contrasts with the discretion of other authors, on the monk's concentration on the "interior of the bowels", or even "the navel". This text provoked the virulent attacks of a philosopher, Barlaam the Calabrian, who styled the hesychast monks *omphalopsychics* ("those whose soul is their navel"). This was the beginning of a quarrel that would occupy the greater part of the 14th c.: the hesychast quarrel.

The hesychasts found a defender in Gregory *Palamas, an Athonite monk, then *metropolitan of *Thessalonica, who wrote *Triads for the Defence of the Hesychast Saints*, in which he based hesychast prayer and the contemplation of God which is its fruit on the distinction in God between incommunicable essence and participable *energies. Summoned by the *synod of the *patriarch of *Constantinople in 1341 to account for his *doctrine, he emerged the victor in the controversy. Supported by the Emperor *John VI Cantacuzenus, Palamism, the theological justification of hesychasm, ended by prevailing as the official doctrine of the *Orthodox Church in 1351.

J. Meyendorff, *Introduction à l'étude de Grégoire Palamas*, Paris, 1959. – *La Philocalie, présentée par Olivier Clément. Les écrits fondamentaux des Pères du désert aux pères de l'Eglise (IVe-XIVe siècle)*, Paris, 1995 (2 vol.). – *HChr*, 6, 1990, 557-563. – M. L. Hebert, *Hesychasm, Word-weaving, and Slavic Hagiography*, Munich, 1992.

Marie-Hélène Congourdeau

**HEYNLIN, JEAN (*c.*1430-1496).** Jean Heynlin or de Lapide is situated at the crossroads of the *via antiqua*, which he imposed at Basel and taught at *Paris (1464-1465 and 1472-1474), a **Devotio moderna* strongly implanted in the Rhine valley and of which certain traits appear in the *sermons he gave at Basel from 1474, and that Christian *humanism of Northern Europe with which he was connected at Basel and at Paris, where he contributed to the introduction of printing (1472). His synthesis recalls that of the *Carthusians whom he finally joined (1484) and is expressed more in the 1,410 sermons he left them, together with his *library (now in the university library of Basel), than in his theological and pastoral works, an immediate success of the printing-press.

B. von Scarpatetti, "Heynlin", *VerLex*, 3, 1981, 1213-1219 (2nd ed.).

Martial Staub

## HIERONYMITES (ORDER OF SAINT JEROME)

**In Spain.** The Order of St Jerome arose out of Spanish eremitical congregations very active in the region of *Toledo in the mid 14th century. Two factors allowed their federation: their reinforcement by Italian and Iberian disciples of the blessed Tommasuccio of Siena († at Foligno, 1377) towards the middle of the century, and again after their teacher's death; while the entry into this movement of Fernando Yañez de Figueroa, a *canon of Toledo, and Pedro Fernandez Pecha, son of a royal *chamberlain, led to a more solid settlement of the group near Guadalajara, at Lupiana.

By the *bulls *Sane petitio* (Oct 1373) and *Divini cultus augmentum* (Feb 1374), *Gregory IX confirmed the foundation of the *order, which was given the Rule of St *Augustine, constitutions borrowed from the Florentine monastery of San Sepolcro, and a maroon and white habit.

Between 1374 and 1415, 25 houses were founded or joined them, notably in 1389 the sanctuary of Our Lady of Guadaloupe, near Cáceres, centre of a very active *pilgrimage throughout the Middle Ages. From 1415 the order was united and structured, with a *prior general (the prior of Lupiana) at its head and a general *chapter that met every three years. At the same time a female branch developed, strictly subordinate to the neighbouring male monasteries.

Protected and enriched by the Spanish and Portuguese sovereigns, by the reforming higher clergy and by the aristocracy, the Hieronymites enjoyed a rapid development, which did not exclude certain grave crises: secession of an observant branch in 1418, led by the former general Lope de Olmedo and established around *Seville (San Isidore del Campo); and above all the discovery of crypto-*Judaizers in the order, which led the Hieronymites to adopt one of the first Statutes of Purity of Blood (1486).

The order surmounted these difficulties thanks to the constant support of the monarchy, which it furnished with counsellors and confessors, such as Alonso de Oropesa and above all Fernando de Talavera. Recognising their value, Charles V chose Yuste for his retreat, and his son Philip II installed them in his new palace-monastery, the Escorial.

**In Italy.** In the mid 14th c., some Italian eremitical congregations also adopted the patronage of St Jerome and a rule of St Augustine, notably the *Jesuates of the blessed Giovanni Colombini (founded 1335), the Hermits of St Jerome (Fiesole, 1360) and the *Fratres Heremitae Sancti Hieronymi* of the blessed Pietro Gambacorta (Montebello, 1380). The greater part of them joined together or disappeared in 1668.

A. A. Sicroff, *Les Controverses des statuts de "pureté de sang" en Espagne du XVe au XVIIe siècle*, Paris, 1960. – O. d'Allerit, "Hiéronymites", *DSp*, 7, 1969, 451-462. – *Studia Hieronymiana. Études à l'occasion du sixième centenaire de l'Ordre de Saint-Jérôme*, Madrid, 1973 (2 vol.). – J. M. Revuelta Sotomalo, *Los Jerónimos. Una orden religiosa nacida en Guadalajara 1373-1415*, Guadalajara, 1982.

Sophie Coussemacker

*The man Adam subject to the forces of the universe (water, air, fire).* Miniature from Hildegard of Bingen's *Book of the works of God.* Latin codex, 11th-12th c. Lucca, Civic Library.

**HILARION OF KIEV (11th c.).** First Russian *metropolitan of *Kiev, Hilarion was raised to that dignity by Prince *Iaroslav in 1051, perhaps without the approval of *Constantinople. Hilarion's name is attached to the *Sermon on Law and Grace* (*Slovo o zakone i blagodati*), a *homily composed in *c.*1049 in which the author celebrates Russia's *conversion to Christianity and eulogizes *Vladimir, prince and confessor. By its structure and style, the work testifies to a great mastery of Byzantine *rhetoric. Hilarion's originality lay in the fact that, using Byzantine models, he was able to express the ideas of his milieu and his time. The *Slovo* is the first known Russian text to evoke *Rus' as a geographical and political unit.

S. Franklin, *Sermons and Rhetorics of Kievan Rus'*, Cambridge (MA), 1991, XV-XLIV and 3-29.

Irène Sorlin

**HILDEBERT OF LAVARDIN (1056-1133).** Born at Lavardin en Vendômois, **scholasticus*, *archdeacon (1091), then *bishop (1096) of *Le Mans, finally metropolitan archbishop of *Tours (from 1125 to 1133, date of his death). The progress of the fine ecclesiastical career reserved for a man of rather modest birth reveals the prestige attached to his person and his thought. A zealous propagator of the *Gregorian reform – which earned him some disappointments –, a sagacious director of conscience and a much heeded preacher, he was also esteemed for his remarkable talent as a writer nourished on classical reading: so he traditionally passes, and rightly, for one of the precursors of the "12th-c. renaissance". He appears to posterity as a fine figure of a Christian humanist. His work, whose canon is still ill-established, comprised *poetry, *letters, *sermons, Saints' Lives, liturgical and moral *treatises, sacred and profane writings.

*PL*, 171, 1854, 1-1462 (edition – alas execrable – of all Hildebert's works).

P. von Moos, *Hildebert von Lavardin, 1056-1133. Humanitas an der Schwelle des höfischen Zeitalters*, Stuttgart, 1965. – *DLFMA*, 1992, 681-682.

Jean-Yves Tilliette

**HILDEGARD OF BINGEN (1098-1179).** Hildegard of Bingen was undoubtedly one of the most astonishing *women the Middle Ages produced. Her work and her personality impressed her contemporaries, ensuring her a wide posterity over the centuries, including our own. Daughter of a family of lesser Rhineland *nobility, she was offered to God by her parents at the age of eight. Living at first with a *recluse together with other young girls, she became *abbess in 1136 and in 1150 founded her own monastery, St Rupert's, at Bingen. Her reputation was already well established: had she not since the age of three been affected by astonishing *visions which she began to set down in writing in the *Scivias* from 1146? Her first texts were approved by Pope *Eugenius III and St *Bernard in 1147. Immediately, her fame extended beyond the restricted setting of Bingen. She simultaneously led the life of an abbess, whose rule was praised by all, that of a writer and that of a prophetess engaged in the conflicts of her time. Several times she travelled through *Germany, *preaching in public, visiting the monasteries, everywhere exhorting people to piety and admonishing indolent or corrupt priests. Thus she forcefully opposed the undertakings of the *Cathars at *Cologne and *Mainz.

The abundant correspondence (more than 450 *letters) that she maintained with *popes, with the Emperor *Frederick Barbarossa (whom she condemned with a stupefying violence), with *bishops, monks or simple laypeople, testifies to the force of her message. Always upheld by divine visions, she exercised a role as consoler or director of conscience, even outside the *Empire, as far as *Prague or *Jerusalem. Moreover, she wrote two more visionary books: the *Book of Life of Merits* and the *Book of Divine Works*, devoted to salvation-history, which, like the *Scivias*, ended with a splendid description of the end of the world, since Hildegard was fascinated by the mysteries of *creation, whether concerned with the origins or the *final ends. If these works sometimes appear obscure, this is not so with her book on *medicine or that on the natural *sciences, in which we find popular beliefs, shrewd observations on human psychopathology, even kitchen recipes! Short texts and two Saints' Lives complete this *oeuvre*, which also contains *hymns and a musical drama (the *Game of the Virtues*) with the original notes. She was the first woman in the West to compose *music.

Hildegard was undisputably a visionary and prophetess, engaged in the conflicts and crises of her time, but was no mystic, and it would be an error to make her the origin of the current of the 13th and 14th centuries. Her work remained isolated, taken up and deformed over the centuries by unquiet souls who stressed its apocalyptic aspects. Though she was the object of a popular devotion that has followed her to our own day, she was never canonized, but her designation as "St Hildegard" rapidly prevailed.

Hildegard of Bingen, *The Book of Divine Works*, M. Fox (ed.), Santa Fe (NM), 1987. – Hildegard of Bingen, *Scivias*, (C. Hart (tr.), J. Bishop (tr.), New York, Mahwah, 1990. – Hildegard of Bingen, *The Book of the Rewards of Life*, B. W. Hozeski (tr.), Oxford, New York, 1994. – *The Letters of Hildegard of Bingen*, (J. L. Baird (ed.), R. K. Ehrmann (ed.), 1, Oxford, 1994; 2, 1998 (3 and 4 in preparation). – *The Life of the Holy Hildegard by the Monks Gottfried and Theoderic*, Collegeville (MN), 1995.

M. Schrader, "Hildegarde de Bingen", *DSp*, 7, 1969, 505-521. – A. Führkötter, *Hildegard von Bingen. Eine Biographie*, Salzburg, 1972. – A. Führkötter, C. Meyer *et al.*, *Festschrift zum 800. Todestag der heiligen*, Mainz, 1979 (collection of articles in honour of the 800th anniversary of the saint's death). – S. Flanagan, *Hildegard of Bingen, 1098-1179: a visionary life*, London, 1989. – S. Gougenheim, *La Sibylle du Rhin: Hildegarde de Bingen abbesse et prophétesse rhénane*, Paris, 1996. – *Hildegarde of Bingen: the Context of her Thought and Art*, C. Burnett (ed.), P. Dronke (ed.), London, 1998.

Sylvain Gouguenheim

**HILDESHEIM.** After the conquest of *Saxony, *Charlemagne occupied himself with its *conversion to Christianity and the creation of *dioceses. Among others, the see originally founded at Elze was moved to Hildesheim by *Louis the Pious, who entrusted it to Gunthar of Reims (815). The diocese, small in size, extended between the Leine and the Oker, between the Aller in the north and the diocese of *Mainz in the south. This last border was soon disputed around the year 1000, the *archbishop wishing to keep under his jurisdiction the *chapter of *Gandersheim which in fact belonged to the bishop of Hildesheim. The *cathedral, built beside the east-west road on a height dominating marshy lands and dedicated in 872, had a chapter whose **mensa* became independent in *c.*910. Bishop Altfrid (851-874) had established a *school, but renown came with Bernward (993-1022), preceptor of *Otto III, who established Benedictines at St Michael's, fortified the town and commissioned numerous works of art (bronze doors and column, manuscripts, *goldsmiths' work). After him Godehard, Dithmar, Azelin and Hezilo were also part of the royal *chapel and remained connected with the *Ottonian and *Salian dynasties. The proximity of Goslar and the Harz made the *bishops partisans of the *Staufen against the Welfs. The bishop built up a solid *territorial principality, infeudated numerous **ministeriales*, created *towns (Peine, Dassel) and consolidated his power in the 13th and 14th centuries. From the 12th c. his diocese saw an increase in the number of *parishes (334 in the 15th c.). *Annals and a *chronicle were composed to trace the history of the bishops (10th-15th cc.).

A town slowly arose. The Altstadt, the old town, was attached to the original core. An urban area of Flemish artisans (Dammstadt) was established, but was made subject to a new centre (Neustadt), grouping patricians around the cathedral *provost. These three centres remained distinct until the 16th c. (75 hectares, 10,000 inhabitants). From the 11th c. a *market developed beside the road, for trade in cloth, beer and *salt. Hildesheim later joined the ranks of the *Hanse. It was given a council (1236), a constitution (1249), and pushed back the episcopal authority (more and more limited in its prerogatives) and even the prelate, who built himself two residential castles at Steurwald (1310) and Meirenburg (1350).

J. H. Gebauer, *Geschichte der Stadt Hildesheim*, 1, 1922. – W. Klewitz, *Studien zur territorialen Entwicklung des bistums Hildesheim*, Göttingen, 1932. – H. Goetting, *Die Hildesheimer Bischöfe von 815-1221*, *GermSac*, new series, 20, 1984.

Michel Parisse

Hildesheim (Saxony). Bronze door of the westwork of the cathedral, *c.*1015.

**HILDUIN (died 840/844).** Hilduin, *abbot of *Saint-Denis, was the first translator of the *Corpus dionysiacum*. In 827, at Compiègne, *Louis the Pious received a complete Greek *codex of *Dionysius's works from the Eastern Emperor Michael the Stammerer and asked the abbot of Saint-Denis to translate it. In *c.*832 he gave him an almost unreadable translation. Before 835, Hilduin used his work in the *Areopagitica* (*PL*, 106, 29-37), which give the chapter-titles of Dionysius's works, a long fragment of the eighth and the whole of the tenth letter.

He wrote the *Passio sanctissimi Dionysii* (*PL*, 106, 23-50), in which St Paul's convert on the Areopagus (Acts 17, 34), author of sublime treatises and letters on theology, also became the glorious *martyr of *Paris. It was thus that the legend of the identity of St Paul's convert, the author of the *Corpus dionysiacum* and the bishop of Paris was accredited in the West.

*Dionysiaca* , P. Chevalier (ed.), Solesmes, 1937, 249-262 (2 vol.); repr., Stuttgart, 1989.

G. Théry, "Recherches pour un édition critique historique du Pseudo-Denys", *NSchol*, 3, 1929, 353-442. – G. Théry, *Études dionysiennes*, Paris, 1932-1937 (2 vol.). – A. Siegmund, *Die Überlieferung der griechischen christlichen Literatur in der lateinischen Kirche bis zum zwölften Jahrhundert*, Munich, 1949. – H. F. Dondaine, *Le Corpus dionysien de l'Université de Paris au XIII^e siècle*, Rome, 1953. – M. Lapidge, "The Lost 'Passio Metrica S. Dionysii' by Hilduin of Saint-Denis", *Mittellateinisches Jahrbuch*, 22, 1987, 56-79. – J. Pycke, "Hilduin", *DHGE*, 24, 1993, 515-522.

Ysabel de Andia

**HILTON, JOHN (14th c.).** John Hilton, a *Franciscan known from 1357 to 1376, studied at the Franciscan *convent of *Oxford. A *doctor of *theology, he was famous mainly for his *Determinationes de paupertate fratrum et de statu minorum*, now lost, but of which John Bale claimed to have seen a manuscript at *Norwich; it is further attested that he maintained two *determinationes* in favour of his order against the theologian (and Benedictine monk of *Durham) Uhtred of Boldon, who had attacked the positions of the *mendicant orders, unleashing a violent controversy.

*BRUO*, 2, 1958, 936-937.

Jean-Philippe Genet

**HILTON, WALTER (died 1396).** Walter Hilton was born in the north of the *diocese of *Lincoln: he was thus, like the archbishop of *York, John Thoresby, a native of the same district as *Richard Rolle, one of his models and a northerner. He began by studying *canon law at *Cambridge, and may even have begun to practise law in the household of Thomas *Arundel, then bishop of Ely but soon archbishop of York. It was probably at Cambridge, under the dual influence of the *Franciscans and William Flete, that he began to write: from this time date the *De imagine peccati* for *nuns or *recluses, and the translation of a text by the Aragonese Franciscan Lluis de Font (*Tretes of VIII chaptitres necessarye for men . . .*). He adapted and translated Jacopo da Milano's *Stimulus Amoris*, then made a translation of William Flete's *De remediis contra temptacionem*: but when he left Cambridge in *c.*1384, it was to become a hermit. Yet he ended by becoming an Augustinian *canon at Thurgarton *priory where he remained until his death in 1396, writing a series of works of which the most famous is *The Scale of Perfection* (45 manuscripts; printed in 1494).

Through the intermediary of two *recluses, Margaret Pensax – who received a pension from *Henry IV in 1399, lived in a little cell at *London (Bishop's Gate) until 1415 and bequeathed the manuscript to Syon – and the royal confessor Thomas Fishbourne, who was also the confessor of the *Bridgettines of Syon, the work was known at the Lancastrian *court, as was the *Epistle on Mixed Life (media vita)*; a spiritual guide sought after throughout Yorkshire in his lifetime, Hilton's readers included many great ladies like Blanche of Lancaster, Cecily Neville and Lady Eleanor Roos, but also a Yorkshire gentleman, Sir Thomas Cumbeworth, and a London grocer, John Killum; so his work reached a very wide public.

Among his other works are the *Epistola aurea de origine religionis*, addressed in *c.*1385 to the baron of the *Exchequer Adam de Horsley when he took the *Carthusian habit at Beauvale; the *Expositions* on *Qui habitat* and on *Bonum est*; *De adoratione imaginum*, in defence of the veneration of *images; *De habenda consolatione in tentatione spirituali*; *A Devoute Treatyse of the Song of Aungels*; but he was not the author of *The Cloud of Unknowing*, which has often been attributed to him. Like the other English mystics of the period, Hilton was strongly anti-intellectual, very individualistic and passionately attached to the example of *Christ, to whom he refers ceaselessly; finally, *Latin was a means of communication less important to him than the English vernacular.

*DNB*, 1885-1900. – M. D. Knowles, *The English Mystics*, London, 1927. – *BRUO*, 1, 1957, 305-306. – C. Riehle, *The Middle English Mystics*, London, 1981. – J. Hugues, *Pastors and Visionaries*, Woodbridge, 1988.

Jean-Philippe Genet

**HINCMAR OF REIMS (*c.*806-882).** The most famous *archbishop of the 9th c. was a product of the monastery of *Saint-Denis where he was a disciple of Abbot *Hilduin. Having gained the confidence of King *Charles the Bald, he was part of his *court when, in 845, he was elected and consecrated archbishop of *Reims: the see had been vacant for ten years following the deposition of *Ebbo, who had supported *Lothar's revolt against his father, the Emperor *Louis the Pious.

During the 36 years of his episcopate, Hincmar fought to impose his *authority as *bishop and *metropolitan in his *diocese and in his ecclesiastical *province, against other archbishops and against the papacy. His very abundant output is primarily that of a jurist, keen on order for the Church and society as a whole. His voluminous correspondence is addressed to the *kings and archbishops of the various kingdoms that emerged from the partition of Verdun (843), just as if the recent frontiers had not divided the Carolingian *Empire.

Asserting his authority as bishop, Hincmar degraded the *clerics ordained by his predecessor Ebbo after his deposition. They appealed to *Rome. Consolidating the authority of the metropolitan over his *suffragans, he came into conflict with Bishop Rothad of Soissons and then with his own nephew, Bishop Hincmar of Laon. In both cases, the bishops appealed to the pope against the decisions inspired by the metropolitan. Lastly, Hincmar defended the doctrine of the "primacy" of the archbishop of Reims, especially over the archbishops of *Trier and *Sens. In Hincmar's view, no other archbishop could have authority over that of Reims, who was subject only to the *pope.

His constant relations with the papacy were often very strained, since *Nicholas I and *John VIII were both interlocutors of the same weight as Hincmar and both intended to strengthen Roman centralization and hence limit the authority of the metropolitan.

Anxious to maintain order in society, the archbishop also developed a doctrine of the good prince, strove to limit the exactions of warriors and promoted the Christian model of *marriage, firmly opposing *divorce, that of King *Lothar II in particular. A loyal supporter of King Charles the Bald, though not sparing in his criticism, he formulated for him a ritual of *consecration that was held at *Metz in 869.

In the theological sphere, Hincmar fought against the doctrines on *predestination and the *Trinity developed by the monk Godescalc of Orbais, partly supported by Abbot *Ratramnus of

Corbie, while the great minds of the time (Prudentius of Troyes, *Lupus of Ferrières, *Rabanus Maurus) and the episcopate of Francia in general did not adopt the archbishop's intransigent positions.

Hincmar thus appears a very controversial man, passionate for the authority of the metropolitan, which he saw as the keystone of authority in the whole Church. A man of action, Hincmar was also a historian: he wrote the last part of the **Annals of Saint-Bertin* and composed a *Life of St Remigius*, *c.*878. To complete his many works, Hincmar had to assemble an enormous mass of evidence: he was responsible for establishing the *library of Reims, which still preserves manuscripts annotated in his hand.

G. Mathon, "Hincmar", *Cath.*, 5, 1962. – J. Devisse, *Hincmar, archevêque de Reims*, Geneva, 1976.

Michel Sot

**HIRSAU.** A Benedictine monastery in the Black Forest (on the Nagold, "Kreis" of Calw). After a first *foundation in 830 as a monastery for aristocrats (St Aurelian), it was refounded on the initiative of Pope *Leo IX (1049) by Count Adalbert II of Calw (1059). Abbot Frederick of *Einsiedeln in Switzerland was replaced by Abbot *William of Hirsau (1069-1091), who came from Sankt Emmeran at *Regensburg. His aim was to establish *integra libertas coenobii*: free *election of the *abbot, freedom from the lord, free *advocacy, which was granted in the so-called "formulary of Hirsau" in 1075, under the protection of the *pope. During the *Investiture Contest, Hirsau supported *Gregory VII, whom William met at *Rome in 1075. The monastery was transferred to the left bank of the Nagold and the church of Sts Peter and Paul was consecrated in 1091. This building influenced the *architecture of *Romanesque churches in the reforming monasteries, the "school of Hirsau" seeking to conform to the Cluniac model. Its **scriptorium* was very important.

Through the intermediary of Ulrich of Zell (Sankt Ulrich im Schwarzwald) and the papal *legate Bernard (abbot of *Saint-Victor at *Marseille), William opened up Hirsau to the influence of *Cluny. The Constitutions of Hirsau were drawn up in the years 1083-1088 on the model of the *consuetudines* in use at Cluny in the time of Abbot *Hugh I. They modified Cluny's way of life to adapt it to the conditions of Hirsau: strictly regulated use of daily time, obligatory silence and sign language, description of offices and duties in the monastery, introduction of **conversi*. This attractive way of life was behind a movement of *reform and creations of monasteries that lasted until the end of the 11th c. and extended over more than 120 religious houses, mainly in the south-west of the *Empire, but also in *Thuringia and *Saxony. But, unlike Cluny, it gave rise to no monastic federation since, under pressure from the *bishops, the monasteries of the "Constitution of Hirsau" were not exempt (*investiture of the *abbot by the ordinary bishop) and since the tutelary lords, as **baillis*, had a growing influence.

The crisis the monastery suffered in the 12th c. was followed in the 15th c. by a revival, after decisions of reform issued by the provincial *chapter of Petershausen (1417). The monastery was attached to the reform of *Melk and, from 1458, the union of *Bursfeld. In the late 15th c., Johannes Trithemius wrote very circumstantial *chronicles of Hirsau.

K. Schmid, *Kloster Hirsau und seine Stifter*, Freiburg-im-Breisgau, 1959. – H. Jakobs, *Die Hirsauer. Ihre Ausbreitung und Rechtsstellung im Zeitalter des Investiturstreites*, Cologne, Graz, 1961. – K. Schreiner, "Hirsau", *Germania benedictina V (Baden-Würtemberg)*, Augsburg, 1975, 281-303. – *Hirsau. St. Peter und Paul, 1091-1991, Teil I. Zur Archäologie und Kunstgeschichte, Teil II. Geschichte, Lebens- und Verfassungsformen eines Reformklosters*, Stuttgart, 1991.

Franz Neiske

**HISPANIC LITURGY.** More prudent than the traditional terms "Mozarabic" or "Visigothic", the term "Hispanic" prevails today to designate the former Latin rite of the Church of *Spain. The original stages of its construction are little known, but the rite, which may have undergone oriental and African influences, was already well outlined at the time of *Isidore of Seville, who describes it in his *De ecclesiasticis officiis*. It was doubtless during the 7th c. that most of the work of organising the annual cycle, compiling formularies and unifying the rite was done. After the *conversion of the *Visigoths, the anxiety to superimpose liturgical unity on the kingdom's political unity was confirmed by the fourth council of *Toledo (633) and led to a liturgical undertaking of great breadth, in particular under the episcopate of *Julian of Toledo (680-690). The distance of three or four centuries that separates this "Julian" reform from the first surviving manuscripts explains why the corpus of texts underwent more modifications and additions in the *Mozarabic period.

Solicited in the late 7th c. by *Elipandus of Toledo, certain equivocal christological formulae, probably old, put the texts of the Hispanic liturgy at the centre of the controversy over *adoptianism. At the time of *Gregory VII's *reform, carried out in *Spain by Cluniacs, the old – apparently excessive – suspicion of dogmatic uncertainty that weighed on the Hispanic rite was one of the main arguments – or pretexts – for its replacement in 1080 by the *Roman liturgy.

Preserved at Toledo, the old rite slowly fell into disuse, until its restoration by the Toledan cardinal Jiménez de Cisneros, who had the "Mozarabic" *breviary and *missal edited in 1498 and 1500 and obtained the preservation of the rite in the primatial city, at the cost of serious concessions to Roman tradition. It is this restored rite that is still celebrated today under the name of "Mozarabic", in a chapel of Toledo cathedral.

Unlike the Roman canon, that of the Hispanic *mass is entirely variable. The number and length of the formularies of the *sacramentary and of the *Liber ordinum*, as well as the extreme wealth of their rhetorical and literary elaboration, have sometimes earned the Hispanic rite the modern reproach of verbosity. Today we see it rather as one of the most eminent expressions of the aesthetics and spirituality of Visigothic and Mozarabic Spain.

M. Férotin, *Le Liber ordinum en usage dans l'Église wisigothique et mozarabe*, Paris, 1904. – M. Férotin, *Le Liber mozarabicus sacramentorum et les manuscrits mozarabes*, Paris, 1912. – J. Vives, *Oracional visigótico*, Barcelona, 1946. – J. Pinell, "Liturgia hispánica", *DHEE*, 2, 1972, 1303-1320. – J. Janini, *Liber ordinum sacerdotal*, Silos, 1981. – J. Janini, *Liber missarum de Toledo y libros místicos*, Toledo, 1982-1983 (2 vol.). – J. Janini, *Liber ordinum episcopal*, Silos, 1991.

Jean-Michel Rabotin

**HISPANO-ARABIC LITERATURE.** The Arabic literature of *Spain occupies a considerable place in the enormous output of medieval *Islam. Here it will be discussed only in terms of its relations with the West. The influences this Andalusian literature received from Antiquity and the influence it had on the Christian world have long been subjects of debate.

That *bishops wrote in Arabic – as happened in the 10th c. –

does not imply that they introduced Latin ideas into it. Medieval Islam, in fact, showed as much passionate interest in the sciences of the Ancients as indifference to their literature. The Arabs knew this: they translated the *mathematics, not the poetry. If they wished to enrich their prose, they sought their themes in Persia or India rather than in Greece or Rome. Direct heir of *Baghdad, the Arabic literature of Spain was as resolutely oriental as its precursor and as ignorant of the heritage of the Christians it lived alongside – in its treatises of *theology, it called the Catholics "Melkites", as it did the Orthodox in the East. The only Latin text whose translation is attested, the *Histories* of Orosius, was offered to the *caliph of *Cordova in 948 by the emperor of *Constantinople.

One single slight exception: a hundred or so verses in the Romance language – of which they are the earliest evidence – placed as refrain (*kharja*, "exit") at the end of 10th- and 11th-cc. Arabic or Hebrew poems, denote a probable folkloristic interest in indigenous popular speech.

On the other hand, at first sight Arabic influence on the literatures of the West seems well established. The latter's courtly *Platonism has often been compared with the *udhri* love vaunted by Bedouin poetry. Certain poetic forms (the final rhyme), certain themes (the "aubade" or dawn song, which reappears in *Romeo and Juliet*) indisputably come to us from the Arabs. But some would emphasize the weight, in "courtesy", of social realities (lordship, the warrior caste) and ideological realities (the code of *chivalry) that were alien to Islam and essentially limited the borrowings that the West of the *troubadours might have made from it. And these influences were perhaps more marked in the more urbanized Europe of the 14th and 15th centuries.

Don Manuel in *Castile and *Boccaccio in *Italy "translated" the oriental prose that passed through Spain, like the famous *Celestina* (1498), whose character of the procuress had already appeared in the Andalusian *Ibn Hazm. Miguel Asin has shown everything that the *Divine Comedy* owes to Arabic representations of the afterlife. But, here too, we must be able to distinguish: analogy of themes does not imply similarity of meaning.

There remains the undeniable Maurophilia of the 14th- and 15th-c. Castilian elites, still attested by the *romancero*: Andalusian Islam truly became more amiable the more it was vanquished.

Ibn Hazm, *Tawq al-hamâma (De l'amour et des amants)*, G. Martinez (tr.), Paris, 1992.

M. Asin Palacios, *La Escatologia musulmana en la Divina Comedia*, Madrid, 1919 (re-ed. 1984). – H. Peres, *La poésie andalouse en arabe classique au XI^e siècle*, Paris, 1953.

Gabriel Martinez

## HISTORY, HISTORIOGRAPHY

**The West.** History is the account of things that have happened. This definition given by *Isidore of Seville in the 7th c. was ceaselessly repeated in the Middle Ages, until the *Renaissance. From the early Middle Ages to the 15th c., history was not an autonomous discipline. It was never taught as such in medieval *schools and *universities. It was present there, however, as an auxiliary science of the *liberal arts, law or *theology. When they wished to clarify the literal sense of a text, whether biblical or not, they applied themselves to the study of its historical meaning. This was the first, lowest, level of interpretation. To define it, medieval historians followed the words of the ancient authors, but in a different spirit: while, for the ancients, history was cyclical, civilizations being born, developing and dying one after another, for Christian historians it had become linear and took place in a single *time, from the *creation of the world to its end. They applied themselves mainly to the account of things past, leaving to the prophets the business of divining the future, which did not prevent some of them, like *Otto of Freising or *Vincent of Beauvais, from devoting the last chapter of their work to the end of time.

History, "lamp of truth" in Cicero's much-cited words, should above all be true, simple, exemplary and useful. However, its field of investigation was very limited. For *Hugh of Saint-Victor, in the 12th c., history was a knowledge of the actors, places and times of past events, in short an account without any other form of explanations. Indeed, it could not go very far in its ambitions, since its place in medieval culture did not allow it to. When they departed from the simple recital of facts to attempt the explanation of their causes, historians entered the field of *theology, *philosophy or *ethics. Besides, they were well aware of the modesty and humility of their task: in the 12th c., *Orderic Vitalis declared in his *Ecclesiastical History*: "I cannot clarify the divine will, by which all happens. I do not wish to divulge the hidden causes of things. For . . . I write a mere history in which I recount the facts year after year."

And yet history was actively practised. During the early Middle Ages, this was mainly done by bishops – like *Gregory of Tours in the 6th c. – who had the education, the political position and also the library necessary for this activity. The *Carolingian Renaissance turned bishops into men much occupied with their political and religious functions, but this did not prevent some of them from writing remarkable *chronicles, *e.g.* Thietmar of Merseburg or Otto of Freising. They then encouraged their canons to make the history they no longer had the time to write, but which was indispensable to root their Church in time. In the 9th, 10th and 11th cc., from Cesena to *Cambrai, cathedral *chapters were breeding-grounds of historians. Towards the year 1000, political changes and the development of monastic *reform gradually pushed history towards monastic *cloisters and *libraries, firstly among Benedictines, then, around 1200, *Cistercians. Monastic historiography ran out of breath from the 13th c., but the baton was taken up by some representatives of the new orders: *Dominicans like *Martin of Opava (Troppau) or *Bernard Gui actively cultivated it, and some produced veritable historical *encyclopedias whose finest example is undoubtedly *Vincent of Beauvais's *Speculum historiale*. Some *Franciscans did the same, like Paulinus of Venice who wrote a universal history in the 14th c.; others, like *John of Plano Carpini or John of Marignola, turned more particularly towards new horizons, the East or the Far East.

At the same time, history aroused the interest of an ever wider public, especially of laypeople. In order to be understood by them, historians gradually abandoned *Latin to express themselves in the vernacular. Historians had patrons: the place of history was still admittedly modest, but the historical arguments that fed the political debates of the time conferred a new status on it. Historians were more numerous, their training more varied. From now on history was made not just by religious, but also by cultivated *merchants or knights. Finally the official historian was invented: disengaged in part from the tutelage of the Church, history entered the modern period in the service of the *State.

The enlargement of the public, like that of the circle of historians, went hand in hand with the progress of scholarship and the wish to cite sources better. Throughout the Middle Ages, the prologue to the historical work was the privileged space in which the author expressed his view of his own work. As such, it was also the place where the history of history, historiography, took its first steps. By the 10th and 11th cc., some historians, Richer in his *History of France* or *Rodulfus Glaber in his *Histories*, were citing here or there some names of other historians whom they had used, but this was not yet a systematic exposition of sources. Historiography was born in the 12th century. Around 1130, *Hugh of Saint-Victor was the first to give a list of 33 names of historians, whom he enumerated at the beginning of his brief universal chronicle. This list, both logically and chronologically disordered, cites, pell-mell, historians of classical Antiquity (Suetonius, Livy, Josephus, etc.) and the 5th c. (Orosius) whom he may well have read. But at least a score of names were taken haphazardly from his reading and are cited in the order in which he found them. Many of these names are faulty, because copyists before him had read them badly. Finally the list is incomplete and some authors used are not even cited. Despite all these faults, this list was the first of its kind and led some of Hugh's pupils and readers to pursue the way he had opened up. Half a century later, in 1185, Geoffrey of Viterbo had the idea of classifying chronologically the names of the list of authorities that he gave in the preface to his work, offering his reader a sketch of universal historiography. Finally, in 1190, Ralph Diceto, who may have been a pupil of Hugh of Saint-Victor at Paris, gave a list of 42 historians, each accompanied by a brief note indicating the subject of his work, the date when he wrote and the date up to which he took his *chronicle.

Historiography, which took its first steps thanks to Hugh of Saint-Victor, had reached its maturity. Two reasons enable us to explain its birth in the 12th c.: at this moment, each historian began to claim his place in the hierarchy of his predecessors, which thus needed to be given, but above all he felt the need to cite his sources in order to convince his reader, more cultivated and more demanding than heretofore, of their validity. There are many discrepancies between the sources cited by historians and those they actually used. This is to do with the nature of historical criticism, which, in the 12th c., was based on a hierarchy of authorities, the earlier ones being also the best. Many historians thus judged it indispensable to cite the ancient authors, often omitting their modern sources who did not possess the required prestige. From the 12th c., the first duty of the historian was to cite his sources.

In the 19th and 20th cc., historians often gave little consideration to their medieval predecessors. Mistrusting them, they did not seek to understand their work and used their chronicles as a mere reservoir of facts. The regained interest in medieval history and historiography has grown over the last thirty years. We now know that history as we practice it today was born in the **scriptoria*, round about the 12th century.

G. Arnaldi, *Studi sui cronisti della marca trevigiana nell'età di Ezzelino da Romano*, Rome, 1963. – O. Capitani, "Motivi e momenti di storiografia medioevale italiana: sec. V-XIV", *Nuove questioni di storia medievale*, Milan, 1964, 729-800. – "La storiografia altomedievale, 10-16 aprile 1969", *SSAM*, 1970 (2 vol.). – B. Smalley, *Historians in the Middle Ages*, London, 1974. – J.-P. Bodmer, *Chroniken und Chronisten im Spätmittelalter*, Bern, 1976. – A. Paravicini Bagliani, "La Storiografia pontifica del secolo XIII. Prospettive di ricerca", *RöHM*, 18, 1976, 45-54. – "L'Historiographie en Occident du Ve au XVe siècle", *ABret*, 87, 1980, 163-417. – I. Sterns, *The Greater Medieval Historians*, Washington (DC), 1981. – *L'historiographie médiévale en Europe*, J.-P. Genet (ed.), Paris, 1991. – B. Guenée, *Histoire et culture historique dans l'Occident médiéval*, Paris, 1991 (2nd ed.). – E.M.C. Van Houts, *Local and Regional Chronicles*, Turnhout, 1995.

Isabelle Heullant-Donat

**Byzantium.** History at Byzantium was a brilliant and productive literary genre that accompanied the Empire from its birth to its death. Historians, even when distinguished from *chroniclers, form a chain interrupted only by the dark centuries.

History belonged to learned literature and obeyed its laws. The most constricting of these was imitation (*mimesis*) of the ancients. Its language, Atticizing, a vehicle of dead forms and terms, avoided the terms of contemporary language. Choice of subjects and rhetorical devices was also fixed. But mimesis had its limits. The contemporary world and Christianity also marked the work of Byzantine historians. In imitation of their models, they took for object the recent past of which they had been witnesses or actors. Their works sometimes have the appearance of memoirs.

Authors were recruited from the little world of scholars and from the ruling circles: high officials, rarely churchmen, aristocrats, emperors. From the middle Byzantine period, they were Constantinopolitans and their works were centred on the capital. A notable exception are the three accounts of the capture of *Thessalonica (904, by the corsair Leo of Tripoli; 1185, by the *Normans; 1430, by the *Turks). Of their three authors – John Kaminiates, Eustathius of Thessalonica, John the Anagnostic – only the second came from the capital.

The protobyzantine period saw the coexistence of the last *pagan historians (Zosimus, *c.*500) and the Christians, of whom the most remarkable was Procopius of Caesarea, a jurist who left three works on the reign of Justinian (527-565): a pamphlet, the *Secret History*; a eulogy, the *Buildings*; and a properly historical work, the *Wars*. The *Histories* of the advocate Agathias follow up the *Wars* from the period 552-559. Under *Heraclius, the *Histories* of Theophylact Simokattes recount the reign of Maurice (582-602) in a very tortuous style.

The chain is then interrupted for a century and a half, to resume in the late 8th c. with the *Brief History* of *Nicephorus, future *patriarch of *Constantinople, covering the period 602-769. The next century and a half saw the appearance of *chronicles rather than histories. Not until well into the Macedonian renaissance did history flourish once more around Constantine VII Porphyrogenitus (920-959). This emperor composed several works, on the margins of the historical genre or belonging to it (*Life of Basil I*). He encouraged a group of scholars to write to show the emergence of the *Macedonian dynasty. By so doing, he was responsible for the *Continuation of Theophanes* (the *Life of Basil* is book V) as well as the *Reigns* of Genesius. We also owe Constantine a great encyclopedia that preserves extracts of historians.

The *History* of Leo the Deacon covers the period 959-976 and forms a bridge between the age of Porphyrogenitus and the major historical work of the 11th c.: the *Chronography* of Michael *Psellus. This, written by the most learned man of his time, a perfect stylist and powerful minister, reads like a memoir, but has gaps. These are corrected by Michael Attaliates, who presents a more balanced account of the years 1034-1080.

The age of the *Comneni is marked by two aristocratic works. Caesar Nicephorus Bryennius, son-in-law of the Emperor Alexius I Comnenus, wrote at his mother-in-law's request the *Materials for a History*, to the glory of Alexius. The work was resumed by his wife Anna Comnena, Alexius's daughter, a learned princess who wrote the *Alexiad* to the glory of her father in the monastery of Kecharitomene. The period 1118-1176 was dealt with by John Kinnamos, imperial secretary to Manuel I. Finally *Nicetas Choniates, witness to the sack of Constantinople in 1204 by the crusaders, devoted his work to the period 1118-1206.

The Empire of *Nicaea and the recapture of Constantinople in 1261 are known through George Acropolites, a scholar and high official. His pupil George *Pachymeres, deacon of the *Great Church, related the decline of the Empire up to 1308. The following years are clarified by two authors with opposite points of view. Nicephorus Gregoras, an opponent of Gregory *Palamas, gave *theology an important place in his *Roman History* (1204-1358). The Emperor *John VI Cantacuzenus, a supporter of Palamas, wrote *Histories* (1320-1356) with a markedly *apologetic character during his time as a monk.

Finally, the last hours of Byzantium are known through four authors: Laonikos Chalkokondyles, marked by the intellectual influence of *Mistra; Ducas, in the service of the Gattilusi of Lesbos; George Sphrantzes, who kept a personal journal; and Michael Kritobulos, governor of Imbros under the *Turks, whose *Histories* (1451-1467), dedicated to Mehmet II, belong only literarily to Byzantium.

H. Hunger, *Die hochsprachliche profane Literatur der Byzantiner*, 1978, 243-504 ("HAW", 12, 5, 1).

Bernard Flusin

**HOHENZOLLERN.** German dynasty originally from *Swabia (castle of Zollern in the Schwäbischer Alb). The first Zollern are mentioned in 1061. Connected with the *Staufen, Count Frederick III was made burgrave of *Nuremberg in 1191-1192 by King *Henry VI. His sons shared his possessions in 1204: Konrad I received the burgraviate and founded the Franconian (then also Brandenburg) branch, while Frederick IV obtained the Swabian possessions. The Franconian branch rapidly stopped calling itself Zollern: the designation "Hohenzollern" appeared in the Swabian branch in 1350, but did not designate all the Zollern (notably those of Brandenburg-Prussia) until the 18th century. The rise of the Franconian Hohenzollern combined two principal means: on the one hand the recovery by way of inheritance or obtaining in *fief of the property of extinct dynasties (dukes of Andechs-Meran, counts of Raabs, Abenberg and Orlamünde); on the other hand imperial proximity, which resulted in fiefs of the *Empire and especially in the elevation by the Emperor *Charles IV of the burgraves of Nuremberg (at the time Frederick V) to the rank of Prince of the Empire in 1363, followed in 1415 by the feudal *investiture of Frederick VI with the margraviate of *Brandenburg, which gave him the title of Elector. This imperial proximity was the original foundation on which was built the dynastic propaganda of the 15th-c. Hohenzollern, who could not count, like the other Princes of the Empire, on a claimed immemorial antiquity of their princely rank.

Supplemented by various acquisitions, the Franconian possessions were divided into two groups: the lands "this side the mountains" (*unter dem Gebirge*), governed from Ansbach, and the lands "beyond the mountains" (*ob dem Gebirge*), governed from Kulmbach. These two groups corresponded to two Franconian branches excluded from succession to the Electorate, reserved since the successoral arrangement of 1473 (*Dispositio Achillea*, taken by Margrave Albrecht Achilles) for the eldest male of the Brandenburg branch.

The efforts of the Hohenzollern to acquire a position of political primacy also in Franconia came up in particular against the imperial town of Nuremberg, which they did not succeed in bending to their will ("margravial war" of 1449-1450), and the bishops of *Würzburg who had arrogated to themselves the title of "dukes of Franconia" coveted (in vain) by the Hohenzollern. The Swabian counts of Hohenzollern suffered important successoral, military and financial rebuffs until the beginning of the 15th century. Thanks to the help of the Franconia-Brandenburg Hohenzollern and also to that of the *Habsburgs, they managed to restore their power and, in the late 15th c., recovered a brilliant position in the *Empire.

*Fränkische Bibliographie*, 1, G. Pfeiffer (ed.), Würzburg, 1965, 1161-1526; *ibid.*, 6147-6476, 7615-8363; *ibid.*, 2, 1, 1969, 22035-22088; *ibid.*, 2, 2, 1970, 35101-35175. – *NDB*, 9, 1972, 496-501. – W. Bernhardt, "Bibliographie für Hohenzollerische Geschichte", *Zeitschrift für Hohenzollerische Geschichte*, 10/11, Sigmaringen, 1974-1975. – J. M. Moeglin, "Toi, Burgrave de Nuremberg, misérable gentilhomme à la grandeur si récente", *JS*, 1991, 91-131.

Joseph Morsel

**HOLY BLOOD.** The problem of the Saviour's *relics, though they were the most sought after, was insoluble. One could have recourse to the blood shed by *Christ in his lifetime (*tears of blood, blood of the *flagellation or crowning with thorns, scarce) or at his death (blood shed from his side by the centurion's lance – the *Holy Lance, privileged instrument of mankind's *salvation – , very early believed to have been collected in a mysterious chalice, the *Grail), or to the sacramental blood, since at the *mass (type of St Gregory's mass) the wine became Christ's blood. Save for an astonishing *miracle, this renewable source was for a long time less appreciated than others, all the more since it presupposed a clear definition of *transubstantiation, which took time. The blood could also be that of a mistreated *image (that of Beirut in 787 was the most celebrated).

Christ's blood had multiple functions in the history of *Christendom; it nourished *bodies as well as *souls, it saved and healed; the place where this incomparable treasure was kept was another *Jerusalem. He who kept it was a priest-king. Possession of Christ's blood was a source of legitimacy. But in certain cases the blood could also denounce (bleeding *host).

The main cult centres of the Holy Blood were *Fécamp, *Mantua, *Bruges and Saint-Bavon at *Ghent. The abbey of Fécamp, dedicated to the *Trinity, played the role of religious capital of the duchy of *Normandy. But for a long time it hardly had sufficient relics. The holy blood miraculously appeared there during the *dedication of the new church before Duke Richard II in 990, according to the *Libellus* of 1090. The eucharistic wine was changed into real blood, placed in a *chalice and incorporated in the *altar. Fécamp also possessed a phial of Christ's blood attributed to Nicodemus and rediscovered in 1171 in the presence of *Henry II. The monastery's spring was soon confused with that of *Rollo's founding dream. At Fécamp, a ducal necropolis until 1066, until 1204 the duke-king played the role of priest-king which the possession of these relics authorized him to hold. The events of 1204 were fatal for Fécamp, the *Capetians preferring the blood of the holy *crown.

Less political was the holy blood of Ghent, brought back from the *crusade by the counts of Flanders, entrusted to one of their main towns and illustrated in the 15th c. by *van Eyck's *Mystic Lamb*, or that of *Mantua, venerated throughout Italy, and attributed to the centurion Longinus, himself healed and converted by Christ's blood. The legend dates from the 8th or 9th century. In the 15th c. it was the object of an active *pilgrimage launched by the healing of Pope *Pius II. But the veneration of Christ's blood, a very popular devotion, was also the subject of a lively controversy in the late Middle Ages between *Franciscans and *Dominicans. The former thought that, during the three days between his *death and *Resurrection, Christ was just a *body without a *soul. Thus the blood from the wound in his side made after his death was just human blood to which was owed not *latreia* but simple veneration. Conversely, the Dominican churches multiplied *images to the glory of Christ's blood in their most doleful versions (cult of Christ's *wounds, mystical *winepress or instruments of the *Passion). Around 1500, Christ's blood had lost none of its power of fascination but, theoretically, the existence of this type of relic provoked more and more reservations.

M. Rubin, *Corpus Christi. The Eucharist in Late Medieval Culture*, Cambridge, 1991.

Colette Beaune

**HOLY DAYS OF OBLIGATION.** Among the many *feasts of the *Catholic liturgical cycle, holy days of obligation – also called holy days of precept – are likened to *Sundays and, as such, characterised by the dual obligation of attendance at *mass and abstention from certain activities.

From the apostolic age, Sunday, the "Lord's day", commemorating the *Resurrection and day of the liturgical assembly, was solemnized and made a public holiday. To this holy Sunday period, two imperatives for Christians were added over the centuries: attendance at mass, mentioned by *Caesarius of Arles (*Sermo in parochiis necessarius*, ed. *CChr.SL.*, 103, 66) and prescribed in the acts of several 6th-c. *councils – Agde (506), Orléans (511 and 541), Clermont (535) – and obligatory abstention from certain works. While this forced idleness had undeniable antecedents in the Roman **feriae* and the Jewish sabbath, it took on a new dimension during the 6th c. and seems, by its rigorism, one of the symptoms of the more ritualist redefinition of Christianity that took place in the West at this time (G. Philippart). The ever more numerous prohibitions were applied mainly to commercial, judicial and legal activities and agricultural tasks, *opera ruralia*.

From the 6th c., the proliferation of the number of feasts led the Church to solemnize some of them and accord them a particular status comparable to that of Sunday. The word *sabbatizare*, which designated the observance of Sunday and the duties associated with it, now also concerned holy days of obligation. Throughout the Middle Ages, the list of these days varied from one *diocese to another: originally it often comprised Christmas, Epiphany and Ascension, later the Nativity of the Virgin, the Assumption, *Pentecost and certain feasts of apostles, local *martyrs or patron saints. The frequency of these public holidays was constantly increasing: in *c.*620, Sonnatius of Reims mentions eleven days *in quibus sabbatizandum*, the rule of *Chrodegang in 735 details thirteen (*De solemnitatibus praecipuis colendis*, ch. LXXIV), the council of *Mainz in 813 more than twenty, and Gratian's **Decretum* in *c.*1140 forty-one. Criticisms were raised against this inflation of feast-days, the damaging consequences for agricultural output and the subsistence of small folk, but not before the 13th century. The first concessions relating to the prohibition of work were granted by the councils of Oxford in 1222 and Worcester in 1240, and the issue was developed over the following centuries (council of Reims, 1405). But effective reduction in the number of holy days of precept did not come about until the modern period.

*DACL*, 5, 1, 1922, 1403-1452. – *DThC*, 5, 1924, 2183-2191. – *DDC*, 5, 1953, 833-835. – *EC*, 11, 1954, 1902-1906. – *Cath.*, 4, 1956, 1225-1226. – G. Philippart, "Temps sacré. Temps chômé. Jours chômés en Occident de Caton l'Ancien à Louis le Pieux", *Le Travail au Moyen Âge*, Louvain-la-Neuve, 1990, 23-24.

François de Vriendt

**HOLY FACE.** The Middle Ages were marked by an incessant search for direct proofs of Christ's existence. Among these, besides bodily *relics of the Saviour, a great role was played by representations of him, which provided an important basis for iconography. There were two categories of *images of *Christ, real or supposed: *acheropitae* (**acheiropoieta*) images, not made by human hand but obtained from a direct imprint of Christ's face or entire body, and *chiropitae* images, representations made by artists.

To the former category belonged the Holy Face, the effigy of Christ's face impressed on a cloth, and the Holy *Shroud, the winding-sheet that enclosed Christ's body and preserved entire the imprint of his body. Concerning the Holy Face, there were substantially two types of *legends circulating in the Middle Ages, one relating to what was called the "mandylion of Abgar", king of Edessa, the other to the "veil" of Veronica. The story of Abgar is told in the **Golden Legend* of *Jacobus de Voragine, which greatly influenced medieval imagery: this Syrian king offered Jesus asylum to protect him from persecution, but, Christ not accepting his invitation, he contented himself with sending a painter to Jerusalem to paint his portrait. The painter failed to carry out his task, since Jesus' luminous face dazzled the canvas; Christ then took a piece of his cloak and passed it over his face, which remained imprinted on it. After Christ's death Abgar received the miraculous portrait which, by mere contact, cured him of leprosy.

The legend, attested in the 6th c., gained great popularity from the 12th c., particularly influencing the Byzantine world, where representations of it multiplied. In the West, it was the story of *Veronica's veil – Jesus' face impressed on a linen cloth – that was most often told. The legend had it that during Christ's ascent to Calvary, a woman named Veronica (the name is simply a personification of *vera icona*, the true image of Christ) dried his perspiring face with a linen cloth (*sudarium*). The Saviour's portrait remained miraculously imprinted on the cloth. This tradition appears in 1300 in Roger d'Argenteuil's Bible and enjoyed great popularity in the late Middle Ages, to the point that Veronica's veil became one of the most famous relics preserved in *St Peter's at *Rome, where it remained until 1527 when it disappeared during the sack of the city. Unlike the mandylion of Abgar, the veil showed the face of the Christ of the Passion, crowned with thorns. In the Middle Ages, the so-called Holy Face of *Lucca enjoyed a particular reputation, though its name was equivocal, since it was not a portrait, but a crucifix.

G. Schiller, *Ikonographie der christlichen Kunst*, Gütersloh, 1976. – *Il Volto Santo. Storia e culto*, Lucca, 1982. – E. Kuryluk, *Veronica and her Cloth*, Oxford, 1991. – O. Celier, *Le signe du linceul, la saint suaire de Turin*, Paris, 1992.

Monica Chiellini Nari

**HOLY FAMILY.** The gospels clearly assert the existence of the small society formed of Jesus, *Mary and his foster-father *Joseph. But for a long time it was not made the object of commentaries, nor did it give rise to representation. Apropos of Jesus' hidden life, the author of the *Meditations* on the life of Christ and Rudolf the Carthusian († 1377) developed considerations on the work, the meals taken in common, the conversations that formed the staple of life at Nazareth: but both described them in abstraction from the family setting.

Attention was only drawn to the group formed of Jesus, Mary and Joseph after having fixed on the latter: in speaking of Joseph's exemplary values, the existence he led with his family at Nazareth was described. Jean *Gerson mentioned it in the exposition he gave before the council of *Constance (1416) (*Sermo de nativitate gloriosae Virginis*): without speaking of "family", Gerson used the term "trinity" which, since St Augustine, had been reserved for the three divine Persons. Thus he tried to make explicit "a *mystery so deep and hidden for centuries, this trinity so worthy of astonishment and veneration, Jesus, Joseph and Mary". He also insisted, before *Bernardino of Siena (*Sermo de S. Joseph*, *Sermones de sanctis*), on the *graces that St Joseph received by the fact of his continual presence alongside Jesus and Mary.

In iconography, the representation developed mainly in the 15th c.: the Holy Family was a more restricted group than that formed by the Holy Kindred (which, especially in the 16th c., could comprise 23 figures). In it were the Child Jesus and his close relations: Mary and Anne, or Mary and Joseph (notably in the *Flight into Egypt and the Return from Egypt). The representation of the trinitarian group of Mary, Anne and the Child Jesus followed modes of depiction adopted for the divine *Trinity: superposition (St *Anne carries *Mary who carries the little *Christ) or juxtaposition (the little Christ seated between Anne and Mary). In the former case, two variants appear: St Anne, standing, supports Mary and the Child on each of her arms; or, sitting, she holds on her knees Mary, who in turn presents the Child. In the case of juxtaposition, the proportions of the characters are respected and the two women are seated on a bench, each on one side of the little Christ who both separates them and unites them. This latter type of composition prevailed in the second half of the 15th century. At the end of the century and in the first third of the 16th, the enlarged Holy Family was more often represented: around Mary and the little Christ were grouped St Elizabeth and the little *John the Baptist; behind Anne and Mary, ranged around the bench, were the figures composing Christ's and Mary's relatives (altarpiece of the Master of the Holy Kindred, late 15th c., Cologne; now in the Wallraf-Richartz Museum).

This iconographical type would later serve as basis for the representation of the *portrait of an important person surrounded by his family (Bernhard Strigel, *Portrait of Maximilian and his Family*, 1515; now in the Kunsthistorisches Museum, Vienna).

T. Dehau, *Famille et Sainte Famille*, Paris, 1947. – J. Wirth, *L'Image médiévale. Naissance et développement (Ve-XVe s.)*, Paris, 1989, 302-322 (IVe part, ch. 2). – K. Ashley, P. Sheingorn, *Interpreting Cultural Symbols: Saint Anne in Late Medieval Society*, Georgia, 1991.

Daniel Russo

**HOLY LANCE.** According to Christian tradition, a Roman legionary, who was given the name of Longinus, pierced *Christ's side with his lance on Calvary. This lance later disappeared. Several centuries later, a lance, considered to be that of the *Passion and supposedly rediscovered in the 4th c. at the same time as the holy *cross, was venerated at *Constantinople. According to another tradition, followed by Armenian historians from the 13th c., the holy lance was brought to *Armenia by St Thaddeus and deposited at the monastery of Gueghart, near *Ejmiacin. But in 1098, during the first *crusade, the discovery of another lance, also held to be that of Longinus, restored hope to the crusaders besieged in *Antioch by the army of Karbôgâ and permitted a victorious counter-offensive.

On 10 June 1098 Peter Bartholomew, a simple peasant in the army of Raymond of Saint-Gilles, announced that St Andrew had appeared to him several times to reveal to him the place where the holy lance was buried, at Antioch. Despite the scepticism of the *legate *Adhemar of Le Puy, the main leaders of the crusade believed his story and, on 14 June, excavations undertaken in St Peter's church at Antioch ended in the discovery of the presaged lance, an event which the crusaders saw as a sign from God. Subsequently, the leaders of the crusade who opposed Raymond of Saint-Gilles cast doubt on the authenticity of the Antioch lance and on Peter Bartholomew, who was challenged and submitted to the *ordeal by fire, from which he died. These events are related by several *chroniclers of the crusades, notably Raymond of Aguilers.

Though the idea of a fraud quite quickly prevailed in the West, the Christians of the East, by contrast, guarded the memory of the discovery of an important *relic at Antioch. Some saw it as a *nail of the holy cross, others thought it was the lance which, according to a sermon of St Athanasius, the Jews had used to pierce the image of Christ.

What became of the lance of Antioch? According to Eastern sources, it was given by Raymond of Saint-Gilles to the Emperor Alexius *Comnenus and became part of the imperial treasure. According to the Genoese Caffaro, Raymond of Saint-Gilles recovered it and later lost it on the occasion of his defeat in Anatolia in 1101. If the lance remained at Constantinople, it may have been the one that appears among the relics of the Passion bought in 1241 from the Emperor Baldwin II by St *Louis, since one of the relics is described as a "holy lance". As for the original holy lance of Constantinople, it fell into the hands of the *Turks at the siege of 1453 and was offered by Sultan Bayezid II to Pope Innocent VIII in 1492. It has been in *Rome since that date.

F. Chalandon, *Histoire de la première croisade*, Paris, 1925. – S. Runciman, "The Holy Lance Found at Antioch", *AnBoll*, 68, 1950, 197-209.

Pierre-André Sigal

**HOLY LAND.** In the *Bible, only the Lord is truly holy, and holy is his name (Is 6, 3). It is on *God's *sanctity that the different sanctity of men and things is founded: holy is his heavenly throne, holy the places on earth where he manifested himself (Gen 28, 17; Ex 3, 5 and 19, 10 ff.); holy are the Temple, the altars, the sabbath. Holy is the city of *Jerusalem which he has chosen as favoured seat of his glory on earth.

"Holy", therefore, for the Christians, were the places touched by the divine and human experience of Jesus, and "holy" was the land in which the main episodes of the Bible and the Gospel had taken place. This led to the identification between the *Terra promissionis* of *Exodus and *Terra sancta*. It seems that already in 2nd- and 3rd-c. Jerusalem – despite its destruction by Hadrian, who had built the Roman centre of Aelia Capitolina on its ruins – there was a tradition of some "Holy Places" that pilgrims connected with the death, *Resurrection and Ascension of the Saviour. After the empress Helena's journey to Jerusalem (326) and the building of the *basilica of the Anastasis (Resurrection) on the site traditionally held to be that of Jesus' crucifixion and burial, in the years between the empire of *Constantine and that of Justinian (4th-6th cc.) all the places that Jesus, *Mary and the apostles had lived in or in some way frequented were gradually identified in Judaea, Samaria and Galilee: needless to say, legend took possession of the space thus sacralized and, together with the places of the New Testament, those of the Old were also identified and venerated, partly by taking up Jewish traditions and partly by creating new ones with the help of oral memory handed down *in loco*, or presented as such.

Eusebius, in his *Demonstratio evangelica* and *Historia ecclesiastica*, recalled that the tradition of Christian *pilgrimage to *Jerusalem – evidently based on the Jewish model – was old, dating at least to the second half of the 2nd century. But it was St Jerome, residing in the last years of the 4th c. near the basilica of the *Nativity at Bethlehem, who encouraged pilgrimage and with it veneration for the Holy Places. In the symbolic **mappae mundi*, drawn in great numbers in the Middle Ages, Jerusalem was at the centre of the circle depicting the *oecumenos*, immediately above the horizontal line of waters that represented the Don, the Indian Ocean and the Nile, *i.e.* the borders of Asia, Europe and Africa.

The *Itineraria* described by pilgrims from the 4th to the 15th c. configured around Jerusalem a Holy Land in which pilgrims made "circles", *i.e.* visits to sanctuaries connected with the life of Jesus and with episodes of the New and Old Testaments: a "sacred geography" of the Near East was gradually formed, within which we can situate two meanings of the expression *Terra sancta*: one more literal and restricted, essentially evangelical in sign and in value, which concerned the episodes of Jesus' life and was thus limited to Jerusalem, with the nearby "places" of Bethlehem, *Montana Iudaeae* (Ain Karem) and *Emmaus; Galilee with Tabor and the shores of Lake Tiberias; Samaria with Shechem and "Jacob's well"; and a wider one, which also comprised the places consecrated by biblical memories and thus went from Egypt and *Sinai, through Hebron, city of the patriarchs, north to *Damascus, where St *Paul's memory was venerated, Edessa, sacred to the memory of St Thomas and original site of the **acheiropoieta* image of Christ's face called the "Mandylion", and Ephesus, a city consecrated by the presence of the Virgin. During the 12th and 13th cc., *i.e.* when *Palestine was controlled by the Latin kingdom of Jerusalem (though after 1187 its centre moved to the coast, around the two great cities of *Acre and Tyre), pilgrims usually contented themselves with visiting the "Holy Places" in the hands of the West; but when, in the late 13th c., the whole of *Palestine had fallen under the power of the *Mamluk Sultans of *Cairo, pilgrims could reach Jerusalem by starting from the port cities of the Nile delta, *Alexandria and *Damietta, and visiting Sinai.

Present in exegetical, liturgical and "popular" tradition, the concept of *Terra sancta* – which had also fired crusading propaganda – finally attained a legal systemization thanks to the thought of the great 13th-c. *canonists, especially the *Apparatus* of Pope *Innocent IV, composed between 1245 and 1253. The successive setbacks of the *crusades and the fact that the concept of crusade was extended to objectives outside the Holy Land, as well as the struggle for control of the Holy Places, had obliged the Church to regulate with great precision the doctrine of the crusading *vow: and many voices had been raised to contest the legitimacy of a war that no longer seemed favoured by the divine will. To these doubts, Innocent replied that the crusade was a legitimate war since it aimed, among other things, at enabling *Christendom – considered the legitimate heir of the Roman Empire – to resume

Holy Land. Interior of St Anne's church at Jerusalem.

possession of that *Terra* that was *sancta* not just from a religious, but also from a legal point of view: he argued from the fact that the Holy Land had been conquered, before and after the Incarnation, by the Roman armies of Pompey, Titus and Hadrian and, as an old imperial possession, now belonged by right to Christendom, like any other inheritance of the Empire. Moreover, in the *Institutiones*, Justinian had defined that everything that belonged directly to God was *res sancta*: and the *Terra sancta* was evidently an essential part of these.

The apocalyptic and eschatological spirit that dominated some circles of the Christian world and often prevailed in Christian society between the 11th and the 15th-16th cc., saw the Holy Land as the real geographical theatre of the final phase of history, that of the *Last Judgment, which would be held in the Valley of Jehoshaphat, under the eastern walls of Jerusalem: hence the tension that often led throngs of *pauperes* towards Palestine on *"popular" crusades which – like the children's crusade of 1212 or those of the **pastoureaux* in 1251 and 1320 – regularly failed.

The birth of the *Franciscan Order created a new element in the history of the concept of the Holy Land. On one hand, the fact that *Francis was proposed as an *alter Christus* was translated into the conception of a new *Terra sancta* that was his, in which *Assisi – where he was born and buried – was at once a "new Bethlehem" and a "new Jerusalem", and the mountain of *Alverna, where the Poor Man of Assisi had received the *stigmata, became a new Calvary. On the other hand, for a long time in Europe veritable *Jerusalem translatae* had been formed around *relics from the Holy Land, or sanctuaries that more or less reproduced the form of the *Holy Sepulchre or the basilica of the Resurrection. The Eucharistic cult, which in the 13th c. enjoyed a period of great success all over Europe, ended by opposing to the role of the historical Holy Land a "metahistorical Holy Land": any *altar on which the divine sacrifice was celebrated was in reality an authentic Calvary on which Christ was *truly* immolated: what need was there to travel overseas to visit a bare rock, an empty sepulchre? These voices were joined to an age-old mystical tradition, which had always deprecated pilgrimage as an occasion of *temptation and *sin rather than of sanctification. And, from the 13th c., the *popes had conceded to a number of Western sanctuaries *indulgences similar or equal to those one could gain in the Holy Land. This seemed to prelude a decline in devotion to the Holy Places.

But that was not what happened. Francis had shown a strong affection for the Holy Land, and he was still living when his friars were installed there. In 1333, thanks to the insistence of *Robert the Wise, king of *Naples, the Mamluk Sultan of Egypt, Malik an-Naser Muhammad, had allowed the Franciscans to settle on Mount Zion and take possession of the Cenacle, and gave them the right to officiate in the sanctuaries of the *Holy Sepulchre and the Tomb of the Virgin in Jerusalem and that of the Nativity in Bethlehem. Thus was born the Franciscan custody of the Holy Places, henceforth reponsible for the assistance of Catholic pilgrims, and guarantee of the continued existence of the concept of the Holy Land throughout the Middle Ages and into our own day.

M. Halbwachs, *la topographie légendaire des Evangiles en Terre Sainte*, Paris, 1941. – P. Deschamps, *Terre Sainte romane*, Paris, 1964. – B. Collin, *Les lieux saints*, Paris, 1969. – D. Baldi, *Enchiridion Locorum Sanctorum*, Jerusalem, 1982. – *La Custodia di Terra Santa e l'Europa*, M. Piccirillo (dir.), Rome, 1983. – A. Dupront, *Du Sacré. Croisades et pèlerinages. Images et langages*, Paris, 1987.

Franco Cardini

**HOLY SEPULCHRE.** The complex of Golgotha and the tomb in which Christ's body was laid on the evening of Good Friday form the major sanctuary of *Christendom. The sacred rocks, the hill of Golgotha and the monolithic tomb, hidden in the Roman period, were developed under *Constantine from 326: around the tomb was built the rotunda (or rather a semi-rotunda whose east wall intersected the central circle composed of alternate columns and pillars) of the *Anastasis*, provided with an ambulatory that allowed a processional liturgy and, further to the east, a great five-aisled *basilica, where was set the *omphalos*, symbolic centre of the Earth. The Persian invasion of 614 caused a first phase of destruction, followed by a restoration by Patriarch Modestus. It is this building that is described by the pilgrim Arculf in an extremely schematic plan (670). The whole suffered from the eschatological passion of Caliph al-*Hākim – *Fatimid *imām and nephew of the patriarch of *Jerusalem – who ordered the destruction of the Holy Sepulchre in 1009. While the tomb itself seems to have been badly damaged, the structure of the rotunda still exists though the great *basilica disappeared, to be replaced by a porticoed court that served the holy places. In 1048 the Emperor Constantine Monomachos managed to negotiate the indispensable restorations, establishing a great courtyard between the *Anastasis* and the reduced basilica. This *atrium*, of which a portico called the "arcade of the Virgin" is probably a survival, gave access to Golgotha. The crusaders unified the whole, prolonging the *Anastasis*, untouched in its broad lines, by a choir in the western manner, which was consecrated in 1149 for the fiftieth anniversary of the capture of Jerusalem by the Latins. To this period also belong the decoration of the main façade, on the south side, with a double portal with sculpted lintel, as well as a clock. The Latin clergy also constructed buildings for *canons around a great *cloister, situated to the east. After the fall of the Latin kingdom, the various vicissitudes, in particular the necessary sharing of the area between the different Christian communities, entailed compartmentalizations of space, some destruction and especially the camouflage of the original parts under more recent decorations. In 1808, a fire ravaged the *Anastasis*, and the kiosk that housed the tomb itself was rebuilt. A complex and controversial restoration has been under way for the last 20 years.

The Holy Sepulchre is the seat of the *patriarchate of Jerusalem. At the time of the Arab conquest, the Caliph 'Umar refused to pray there so that the place could remain in future the responsibility of the Christians (638). The Greek patriarch of Jerusalem, who resided to the north of the Holy Sepulchre, was put in charge of the holy places. Under the kingdom of Jerusalem (1099-1187), the Greek clergy were joined by a Latin clergy, in a dominant position. The Latin patriarch was at the head of a *chapter of canons, charged with serving the holy places. But certain parts of the sanctuary remained entrusted to other rites, Greek, *Jacobite, etc. The Holy Sepulchre, direct cause of the *crusade, became the centre of the new State. *Godfrey de Bouillon took the title of Advocate of the Holy Sepulchre. Later, the kings of Jerusalem were consecrated there. The first four kings of Jerusalem were buried in the lower chapel of Calvary. The fall of Jerusalem (1187) led to the departure of the patriarch and the chapter. *Frederick II, who crowned himself at the Holy Sepulchre on 18 March 1229, negotiated the restitution of Jerusalem (1219-1244). The holy places having been bought back by *Robert the Wise (1333), the Sepulchre was served by the *Franciscans, to whom *Clement VI granted custody of the *Holy Land (1342).

Goal of *pilgrimages, the *Anastasis* was the setting for the liturgy of the "holy fire" on *Easter night, when fire from heaven came to light the lamps in the course of a symbolic ceremony, which became falsely miraculous through the medium of a wire smeared with an inflammable product. Attested from the 9th c., the ceremony was forbidden to the Latins in the 13th century. In the Latin usage, the custom was established in the 15th c. of certain pilgrims to the Holy Sepulchre arming knights. Carried on by *confraternities of "palmers" (pilgrims), this custom was the origin of an order of chivalry of the Holy Sepulchre, totally distinct from the Augustinian Canons who formed the cathedral chapter of Jerusalem.

The sanctuaries are well known from the descriptions of pilgrims, from the laconic Egeria of Bordeaux (333) to the *Evagatorium* of Friar Felix Fabri (Schmitt), who in 1483-1484 described the many secondary holy places and the legends current about them, which he criticized severely. For a series of subsidiary places had been grafted onto Golgotha and the tomb. Some were related to the *Passion: the prison where Christ awaited execution, the column of the *flagellation, the place where he was stripped of his clothing, where his clothing was shared out, the *stabat mater*, the stone where his body was anointed after deposition, the places where he appeared to *Mary Magdalene, the Virgin, the holy women. Others insisted on the *typological link between the Old and New *Testaments: Adam's tomb, the place of *Abraham's sacrifice (though normally situated in the Temple). The underground chapel with columns of Byzantine date is reputed to be that of the *inventio* of the *cross and is dedicated to St Helena.

C. Coüasnon, *The Church of the Holy Sepulchre in Jerusalem (The Schweich Lectures of the British Academy, 1972)*, London, 1974. – V. Corbo, *Il Santo Sepolcro di Gerusalemme. Aspetti dalle origini al periodo crociato*, Jerusalem, 1981-1982. – M. Piccirillo, *La Custodia di Terra Santa e l'Europa. I rapporti politici e l'attivita culturale dei Francescani in Medio Oriente*, Rome, 1983. – M. Biddle, *The tomb of Christ*, Stroud, 1999.

Geneviève Bresc-Bautier

**HOLY SEPULCHRE, ORDER OF CANONS OF.** On their arrival at *Jerusalem, the crusaders installed a Latin clergy to serve the *Holy Sepulchre. The *chroniclers give contradictory evidence on the constitution of the cathedral *chapter of Jerusalem, charged with electing the *patriarch, so it is difficult to specify exactly the chronology and circumstances of institution, but it is certain that *Godfrey of Bouillon played a determining role, handing over to the chapter a temporality of twenty-one *casalia* around Jerusalem, probably corresponding to the *prebends since Albert of Aachen cites the figure of twenty *canons, to whom must have been added the *archdeacon. In 1103, the prebends were reorganised and the offices regulated: sub-dean, *cantor, sub-cantor, **primicerius*, treasurer, sacrist.

In April 1112, Patriarch Gibelin on his deathbed recommended that community of board be established. The following years saw the difficult institution of the Rule of St *Augustine within the chapter and the reform of the offices (*prior, sub-prior, *cellarer, **scholasticus*). However the temporality increased rapidly, both in the *Holy Land and in the West, thanks particularly to the reception of confrères, male and female, who handed over their property in exchange for board, lodging and participation in spiritual benefits.

The fall of Jerusalem (1187) dealt a rude blow to the chapter, which was able to settle at *Acre in 1191. But some canons left to serve the Sepulchre at the time of the truce negotiated by *Richard Coeur de Lion and during the brief period of peace obtained by *Frederick II (1231-1244). In 1291 they fell back on the West. From 1313 the prior, who took the title of prior general or archprior, had his seat at *Perugia. There, on 28 March 1489, it was struck by the *bull of suppression of the order, promulgated by Innocent VIII and ordering the properties of the Holy Sepulchre to be handed over to the Order of *Hospitallers.

The canons had in fact constituted an order of canons. From 1156 we observe the setting up of a hierarchy, in a temporality organised in the West into provinces entrusted to provincial priors, and into houses run by priors, sometimes called commanders in Spain in imitation of the *military orders. But the canons had no military role, though they seem sometimes to have had *hospital duties. The most active provinces were Aragon (around Calatayud), Castile (Segovia), Catalonia (Santa Ana de Barcelona), Apulia (Barletta), Sicily (Piazza), Poland (Miechow), Bohemia (Zderas) and Germany (Denkendorf). The French *priory of La Vinadière (Corrèze) was very minor, as were the English houses.

By reason of their vitality, the provinces of Aragon, Germany and Poland were excluded from the bull of suppression and continued to live autonomously after 1489.

Under the direction of Jan van Abroek, a spiritual revival animated the provinces of Germany and the Netherlands in the late 15th c., which not only helped them escape the suppression but led to a movement of foundation of new houses, mainly female, throughout the 16th c. and even in the 17th c. (mostly in Belgium, fewer in France: Charleville, Paris, Vierzon).

*Le Cartulaire du chapitre du Saint-Sépulcre de Jérusalem*, G. Bresc-Bautier (ed.), Paris, 1984 ("Documents relatifs à l'histoire des croisades", 15).

M. Hereswitha, *Orde van het Heilig-Graf. Inleidung tot de Geschiedenis van het Kloosterwezen in de Nederlander*, Bruxelles, 1975. – K. Elm, "Kanoniker und Ritter von Heiligen Grab", *Die Geistlichen Ritterorden Europas*, Sigmaringen, 1980, 141-169 ("Vorträge und Forschungen", 26).

Geneviève Bresc-Bautier

**HOLY SPIRIT.** In comparison with *christology, reflection on the Holy Spirit came late to the *Fathers. Sketched out by Tertullian and *Origen, it reached its full extent in the East with the Cappadocians, St Basil and St Gregory Nazianzen who, by their response to the heresy of the pneumatomachi, prepared the council of Constantinople, and in the West with St Augustine.

In the Middle Ages, perspectives changed and a lively awareness developed of the specific role of the Holy Spirit in the liturgy (in *baptism, *confirmation, the *Eucharist, *ordination) and in Christian life. *Prayers to the Holy Spirit multiplied in the West: the **Veni Creator* in the 9th c., the antiphon of the *Veni Sancte Spiritus* in the 12th c., the *sequence **Veni Sancte Spiritus* in the 13th, and so on; the efflorescence of religious *orders was recognised as a work of the Spirit and, more generally, the seven *gifts of the Holy Spirit were implored and studied, as attested by, *e.g.*, *Rupert of Deutz's *De Trinitate*.

In the East, the Holy Spirit, already very important for *John of Damascus, took a preponderant place with *Symeon the New Theologian. Principle of spiritual life, the Spirit was "the key to the door . . . . By it and in it, first our mind is enlightened and purified and we are illumined by the light of knowledge, then we are baptized from on high, regenerated and made children of God" (*Catechesis* 33, 113). This experience of the Spirit was at the same time a decisive ecclesial experience in the East. It was also in these terms that St Gregory *Palamas evoked it several centuries later, but he went further in his formulation, distinguishing *energies and hypostasis in the Spirit and specifying that the Spirit has the role of manifesting the divine energy and deifying Christians. He also proposed a whole *economy of the Spirit.

However, a question divided East and West, that of whether the Spirit proceeded from the Father alone or from the Father and the Son, whence the painful problem of the **Filioque* that consummated the break between the two groups.

But Western *theology developed in other directions. Heavily marked by St Augustine, it was oriented either towards an analysis of the activities of the Spirit – *knowledge, *love – or towards an understanding of the Spirit as charity, bond of love. Thus St *Anselm, in the *Monologion* (ch. 49), used the Augustinian analogies to deduce the Spirit as memory, understanding and love of itself, while *Richard of Saint-Victor defined the Spirit as love received, and explained that "the Holy Spirit is given to man when the due love (*amor debitus*) that is in the divinity is inspired into the *soul . . . . When we give back to our Creator the love due to him, we are certainly configured to the property of the Spirit" (*De Trinitate* VI, 14). Finally, St *Thomas Aquinas took up his predecessors' positions and reinterpreted them to define the Holy Spirit as the mutual love of the Father and the Son, the well of Love that gives itself graciously.

Y. Congar, *I Believe in the Holy Spirit*, London, 1983.

Marie-Anne Vannier

**HOLY WEEK.** The week before *Easter was the holiest week in the year, and each of its days (Holy Monday, etc.) was called a "holy day", but especially the last three. In ancient Christianity, the *triduum* designated the three days of the death and *Resurrection, from Friday to *Sunday, as indissociable. In the Middle Ages, the *triduum* was considered as formed of Holy Thursday (when the holy *oils were consecrated, public *penitents reconciled, the Last Supper commemorated), the Friday of Christ's crucifixion, the *adoration of the Cross and the great *fast, and the Saturday when Christ was in the tomb.

*CaP*, 4, *The Liturgy and Time*, London, 1986, ch. 1.

Pierre-Marie Gy

**HOMAGE.** Homage (*hominium* or *homagium*) was one of the fundamental moments of the ceremony sanctioning vassalic commitment. It characterised the establishment of a personal bond and usually preceded an *oath of loyalty. Some of the elements constituting this ceremony probably originated in the *recommendation customary in the early Middle Ages, but recommendation by hands may have existed from the start independently of that.

In the 12th c., *gestures of homage were fixed from North-West Europe to *Catalonia, except for other Mediterranean regions in which it seems to have been much less common than the oath of loyalty. Homage began with the dedication of the vassal to his lord, a moment characterised by a gesture of submission: *immixtio* or *datio manuum*, during which the disarmed and kneeling vassal put his joined hands in those of his lord and avowed himself his vassal. Then the lord raised up the vassal and sometimes gave him the *kiss (*osculum*) which marked, now that agreement was concluded between equals, the fact that it was an honourable commitment between members of the same aristocratic social group. The faith (*fides*) that followed the homage proper was the occasion for both contracting parties to swear an oath and signify their mutual commitments. For the lord, this was the duty of protection and assistance. He also had to provide for the upkeep of his vassal, which he increasingly did by conceding him rights over a piece of land. For his part, the vassal owed obedience and devotion, aid and counsel (*auxilium* and *consilium*). Aid was often military service, while counsel evoked the vassal's duty to be present at the lord's council. Homage thus created a bond that was not natural, but many of whose aspects recalled the carnal bonds of sonship, and to which mutual obligations were attached.

As cases of breaking of homage and faith multiplied in the course of the 11th c. due to the fact of one vassal paying homage to different lords, attempts were made to remedy this by reservation of loyalty and by liege homage, *solidantia* in *Catalonia. In these latter cases, a principal lord reserved to himself the essential services of his liege or "solid" man. This method was used with profit by the king of *France or the count of *Barcelona. We also know types of homage exchanged by princes on the margins of a territory and sanctioning a return to peace, in *Normandy, *Burgundy and *Champagne. Finally there was a servile homage paid by a free man in becoming a serf, some aspects of which recall recommendation.

J. F. Lemarignier, *Recherches sur l'hommage en marche et les frontières féodales*, Lille, 1945. – G. Fourquin, *Seigneurie et féodalité au Moyen Âge*, Paris, 1970. – J. Le Goff, "Le rituel symbolique de la vassalité", *Simbolo e simbologia nell'alto medioevo*, *SSAM*, 23, 1976, 679-788. – S. Reynolds, *Fiefs and Vassals*, Oxford, 1994.

Thierry Pécout

**HOMICIDE.** Homicide was the act of killing in the course of a brawl, with or without the intention of causing death. Up to the end of the Middle Ages, it could be confused with murder: both were *occisiones*. Nevertheless, from the 13th c., *customaries tended to dissociate them, allying murder with treason, *i.e.* a premeditation that infringed the normal laws of vengeance and approached the "crime of blood" of assassination (a term unknown in our modern sense). By deduction, homicide followed the laws of a vengeance carried out either in the heat of the fray or to assuage a "mortal" hatred: it was not ashamed to break out in broad daylight and it obeyed the code of *honour that, in the system of challenges that fed ordinary *violence, set equally-armed adversaries against each other. The link that thus existed between homicide and "*beau fait*" – avenging wounded honour – explains why it was late in entering public legislation. In the *barbarian period, the laws punished homicide with *death only in two cases: when the infractions were directed against the *king, who alone had no **wergild*, and when the guilty party could not pay the composition imposed on him. Later, in the *seigneuries hautes justicières*, it is uncertain whether homicide was pursued in a systematic way, and certain communal *charters neglect or punish the guilty party with banishment rather than death. That is to say that the vengeance of which it was the culmination remained respected and that justice, then in its infancy, hesitated whether to classify homicide as a private offence or an infringement of public order.

Linked to the laws of honour, homicides were the most numerous offences among the "heinous" crimes, and for a long time they tended to be resolved by transactions that facilitated the flight of the culprit. In the last two centuries of the Middle Ages, the setting up of a repressive system anxious to be effective necessitated the refining of a hierarchy within this type of crime. Judges took account of premeditation, "lying in wait", legitimate defence. Thus involuntary homicide seems to have been defined right at the end of the 15th c., undoubtedly earlier in *England than in *France. In countries where the authorities could grant letters of remission, a discussion took place as to the conditions in which a homicide must be considered irremissible. In France, letters of remission seem to have been more selective and reserved for involuntary homicides; but the presence of a royal pardon that remained all-powerful incontestably paralyzed the efforts of jurists to proceed to a fine analysis of homicide.

J. M. Given, *Society and Homicide in Thirteenth-Century England*, Stanford, 1977. – C. Gauvard, *"De grace especial". Crime, État et Société en France à la fin du Moyen Âge*, Paris, 1991 (2 vol.). – X. Rousseaux, "Ordre moral, justices et violence: l'homicide dans les sociétés européennes XIII$^{e}$-XVIII$^{e}$ siècle", *Ordre moral et délinquance de l'Antiquité au XX$^{e}$ siècle*, B. Garnot (ed.), Dijon, 1994, 65-82.

Claude Gauvard

## HOMILY, HOMILIARY

**The West.** Homilies are commentaries on biblical texts read in the liturgy, in particular at the *office, alongside Holy Scripture and hagiographical texts. The authors of the homilies were generally the Church *Fathers or the great theologians of Antiquity and the Middle Ages. For the West, the four great Fathers of the Church, whose authority was one of the main foundations of medieval culture, were Ambrose (bishop of Milan, † 397), Jerome († 420), Augustine (bishop of Hippo, † 430) and Pope *Gregory the Great († 604). To these names were added those of medieval theologians like the Venerable *Bede, *Alcuin or *Rabanus

Maurus. Their commentaries on Holy Scripture were the primary source of Christian reflection and knowledge. Every medieval *library possessed numerous manuscripts of patristic commentaries to serve the most diverse reflections (philosophical, moral, historical, astronomical, geographical, etc.) as well as for reading during the liturgy.

Patristic reading at the office is attested in the West from the 6th c. in the Rule of St *Benedict which prescribes commentaries on biblical texts for daily vigils on long nights. It is supposed, however, that the custom of patristic readings in the liturgy was known at *Rome perhaps from the 5th century. *Ordo Romanus* XIV (second half of 7th c.), which represents the usage of the monasteries serving *St Peter's basilica, suggests the existence of texts intended to comment on Holy Scripture. In the 8th c., the annual cycle of biblical *readings was in place, as was the *cursus* of patristic readings, with a fair number of local variants.

The homiliary contained the homilies on the various books of the *Bible read in the liturgy, at *mass or at the office. For the practice of *lectio continua*, one of the two ways of reading the Fathers at the office, no particular book was necessary. It was enough to go to the monastery's library and use a manuscript containing the works of *e.g.* St Augustine or St Jerome, and to add in the margin the divisions into lessons according to the rhythm of the offices. The increasingly rigorous allocation of proper readings, according to *hours and *feasts, necessitated the compilation of appropriate collections. Thus homiliaries came into being, in order to offer the celebrant a choice of patristic commentaries conveniently accessible for the patristic reading at the office.

In the homiliary, the texts of the Fathers, divided into longer or shorter lessons, were transcribed in order of their use during the *liturgical year, often distinguishing the summer part (from *Easter to the end of ordinary time preceding *Advent) from the winter part (from Advent to Easter). Sometimes, identification of authors was made possible thanks to an alphabetical system in which each letter referred to an author. Some collections were simply used for the spiritual *meditation of the monks or as an aid to preparation of *sermons for the preacher. Others were produced with a view to their use at mass. The Roman homiliary of the 6th and 7th cc. has been reconstructed on the basis of medieval manuscript evidence. Comparison with other old Roman books, like lectionaries, enables us to reconstruct the liturgical structure (organisation of the *temporal and *sanctoral) of the homiliary of St Peter's. For each celebration, it offered collections of sermons from which the celebrant could choose. From the old Roman homiliary, four types were established in the 8th century.

Starting from the adaptation of *Roman liturgical usages in Gaul from the 8th c., the *cursus* of patristic readings was gradually specified, in accordance with local usages as well as the nature of the offices, longer or shorter. In the great *reform movement that he animated, *Charlemagne played a determinant role in the establishment of a homiliary type that was to be used for all the churches of his *Empire. The commission was given to *Paul the Deacon who, between 786 and 792, produced an official homiliary whose success was immediate. Compared to earlier collections, Paul the Deacon's homiliary innovated on two essential points: on one hand, he strictly allotted a single patristic text to each day; on the other, he provided for every *Sunday of the year and many other *feasts a homily on the gospel of the day, of which one or two verses recalled the opening.

From the 9th c., particular traditions multiplied and asserted themselves, depending on the choice of monasteries and Churches in matters of patristic reading at the office. From the 10th and 11th cc., texts of recent or contemporary authors came to be added to the lessons taken from the Fathers, with the effect of strengthening the identity of the various traditions. At this time too, homiliaries began to be included in the lectionary of the office in which the biblical, patristic and hagiographical readings were grouped together.

R. Grégoire, *Les Homéliaires du Moyen Âge. Inventaire et analyse des manuscrits*, Rome, 1966. – H. Barré, "Homéliaires", *DSp*, 7, 1, 1969, 597-606. – R. Grégoire, *Homéliaires liturgiques médiévaux*, Spoleto, 1980. – A.-G. Martimort, *Les Lectures liturgiques et leurs livres*, *TSMÂO*, 64, 1991, 77-96.

Éric Palazzo

**Byzantium.** The first duty of the *bishop was to teach his people (cf. canon 19 of the *council *in Trullo* which recommended bishops to preach every day). The *preaching and composition of homilies thus fell to him by right. The great bishops of the patristic period (the Cappadocians, John Chrysostom, Cyril of Alexandria, etc.) composed an immense number of homilies. Output subsequently dried up a bit, but all through the *Byzantine Empire bishops continued to practise this literary genre with more or less success and originality: among the great preachers were *Germanus of Constantinople, *Photius, Theophanes Kerameus, Macarius Chrysokephalos, etc. Homilies were on a variety of subjects: liturgical *feasts, points of *doctrine or morals, eulogy of a saint or a deceased person.

But not every bishop was an orator. The bishop was able to delegate this function to *clerics, *didaskaloi*. The corps of *didaskaloi* of the patriarchal school of *Constantinople was created in 1107 by Alexius *Comnenus (cf. P. Gautier, *REByz*, 31, 1973, 165-201). In the 15th c., Joseph Bryennius held the post of *didaskalos of the didaskaloi* at the patriarchal school, *i.e.* he trained future preachers. Though the canons forbade laymen to preach in churches, as *Symeon of Thessalonica reminded them in the 15th c., we do find some laymen charged with preaching in the emperor's palace: such as *George Scholarius, future *patriarch of Constantinople, who was official palace preacher while not yet a cleric.

For preachers short of inspiration, from the 9th c., collections of homilies of the great patristic authors were formed: homiliaries. In them homilies were grouped together following the cycle of the *liturgical year, so that each bishop could find what he wanted there. Byzantine homiliaries were divided into several categories, the most important being the *Panegyrics* (homilies for the great fixed feasts of the year and the feasts of the saints) and the *Homiliaries* (homilies for the movable feasts of the *Easter cycle). The *Menologia* and **Synaxaria* gave summaries of Saints' Lives that could also be used by the preacher. Under the name of "Catecheses" we also find monastic homilies addressed by the hegumen to his monks; the most celebrated are those of *Theodore the Studite and *Symeon the New Theologian. Finally, the *Patriarchal homiliary* was a manual that compiled, for most *Sundays of the liturgical year, homilies from different periods (going back mainly to the 11th c.) from which the patriarchs of Constantinople drew inspiration for their own *preaching.

A. Ehrhard, *Überlieferung und Bestand der hagiographischen und homiletischen Literatur der griechischen Kirche*, Leipzig, 1936-1939 (3 vol.). – *HChr*, 6, 1990, 399-409. – T. Antonopoulou, *The Homilies of the Emperor Leo VI*, Leiden, 1997. – *Preacher and audience. Studies in Early Christian and Byzantine Homiletics*, M. B. Cunningham (ed.), P. Allen (ed.), *A New History of the Sermon*, 1, Leiden-Boston-Cologne, 1998.

Marie-Hélène Congourdeau

**HOMOSEXUALITY.** The medieval taboo against sexual relations between men (women are almost completely ignored) was enshrined in the Mosaic holiness code found in Leviticus 20, 13: "If anyone lie with a man as with a woman, both have committed an abomination, let them be put to death; their blood be upon them," and Leviticus 18, 22: "Thou shalt not lie with mankind as with womankind: it is an abomination"). St *Paul (Rom 1, 24-27 and 1 Cor 6, 9) also described those who perform "acts against nature" as idolators who may not inherit the Kingdom of *Heaven. The wrath of *God was invoked against such sinners, whose behaviour had allegedly brought about the destruction of Sodom and Gomorrah; and it was feared that *famine, earthquakes and pestilence would result from such *sin.

The perceived rise of homosexuality in the later Middle Ages, particularly in such urban areas as *Paris, *Venice and *Florence, may have encouraged such penitential movements as the *flagellants and the spread of secular legislation against same-sex relations. The ancient Israelites regarded sodomy as a vice of idolators, and its practice was associated in the Middle Ages with *witchcraft and *heresy. It therefore ranked among the charges levelled against such heretical sects as the Albigenses, and was often used against political foes. Pope *Boniface VIII was so accused by the allies of *Philip the Fair; the charge was a major ground for the persecution and dissolution of the *Templars (1312). Christianized *Roman law warned against "acts against nature", which were linked with *blasphemy, and suggested severe, though unclear, punishment of persistent offenders. Early medieval tribal law, however, except for the Visigothic code, is generally silent on the subject. It was therefore not until the 13th c. that secular legislation demanded such punishments as castration and execution for sodomites. Sexual misdemeanours were largely dealt with in the context of the *penitential code, which ranked sodomy among the most infamous of the venial sins, requiring the severest acts of *penance. The clergy and *nobility were regarded as the prime offenders, and the 11th and 12th centuries witnessed a flowering of vernacular and Latin *poetry with homosexual themes, particularly in *Anglo-Norman circles. The council of Nablus (1120) also suggested that contact with the Muslim world (which was regarded as prone to sexual deviance) during the *Crusades had added respectability to homosexuality. The most thorough polemical attack on homosexuality, especially among the clergy, was *Peter Damian's *Liber Gommorrhianus*. The uneven treatment of offenders by both Church and State suggests, however, that demographic and economic factors may have strongly influenced the condition of persons performing homosexual acts, despite the severe prohibition.

Peter Damian, *Book of Gomorrah: an Eleventh-Century Treatise against Clerical Homosexual Practices*, Waterloo (Ont), 1982.

M. Goodich, *The Unmentionable Vice: Homosexuality in the Later Medieval Period*, Santa Barbara (CA), 1979. – J. Boswell, *Christianity, Social Tolerance, and Homosexuality*, Chicago (IL), 1980. – J. Brundage, *Law, Sex, and Christian Society in Medieval Europe*, Chicago (IL), 1987. – J. Boswell, *The Marriage of Likeness*, London, 1996.

Michael Goodich

**HONORIUS III, POPE (died 1227).** Roman by birth, Cencius (Savelli?) directed the *Camera and the *chancery (1194-1198) and composed (1191) the *Liber censuum*, which assembled the property rights of the papacy. Cardinal-deacon of Santa Lucia in Orthea from 1192, in 1200 he was promoted *cardinal-priest of Sts John and Paul. Elected *pope at Perugia, 18 July 1216, he continued the crusading project decided on by *Lateran IV (1215). In 1216, he recognised the Order of Preachers and in 1223 that of the Minors, whose Rule he approved. In 1219, he forbade the study of civil law at *Paris. He died on 18 March 1227.

J. Sayers, *Papal Government and England during the Pontificate of Honorius III (1216-1227)*, Cambridge, 1984. – A. Paravicini Bagliani, *HChr*, 5, 1993.

Agostino Paravicini Bagliani

**HONORIUS AUGUSTODUNENSIS (*c.*1080-*c.*1157).** Recent research now allows us to discern with precision the figure of this person long considered enigmatic, despite the volume of his work (a whole volume of the *Patrologia*) and the popularity it enjoyed in the Middle Ages.

Born in *England where he followed the lessons of *Anselm of Canterbury, he crossed the Channel in 1097 to establish himelf as a *recluse in an Irish monastery on the outskirts of *Regensburg (*Augustodunum*, Regensburg, and not *Autun or *Augsburg as was once thought). There he died in *c.*1157. His numerous and varied work is less that of an original thinker than of a pedagogue and vulgarizer. It comprises notably: the **Elucidarium*, a systematic exposition of the truths of faith in the form of a dialogue between master and pupil, which probably reflects the teaching of St Anselm; the *Clavis physicae*, which repeats and summarizes for a not too erudite public the *Periphyseon* of *John Scotus Eriugena; theological opuscula on questions discussed at the time, free *will (*Inevitabile*), the eucharistic mystery (*Eucharistion*), the degrees of knowledge (*Scala coeli*); three collections of *sermons; several biblical commentaries; liturgical treatises (*Gemma animae*, *Sacramentarium*); polemical booklets favourable to the papacy in conflict with the *Empire; a critical catalogue of ecclesiastical writers (*De luminaribus Ecclesiae*). On the level of secular letters, if we may speak thus of a writer so penetrated with *mysticism, Honorius was the author of an *encyclopedia impregnated with allegorical thought, the *Imago mundi*, and a universal *chronicle. For good measure, we should also add some works of less certain attribution, or even altogether doubtful, like the famous *Visio Tnugdali*.

The mere enunciation of this long list helps us outline the intellectual traits of a man on the hinge of two cultures: by the methodical clarity of his exposition, he already heralds the onset of *scholasticism; but his thought, which sets out to illuminate the symbolic correspondences between the objects of the visible world and spiritual realities, is still that of previous centuries. In this respect, Honorius may be considered a late representative of "*monastic theology". As such, and by reason of his marginal position, his works find few echoes within the scholastic institution; but outside it, quickly translated into the vernaculars, they made a considerable stir and made no small contribution to the revival of *spirituality, especially in the lands of the Empire.

*PL*, 172, 1854 (complete works of Honorius).

J. A. Endres, *Honorius Augustodunensis*, Munich, 1906. – Y. Lefèvre, *L'Elucidarium et les lucidaires*, Paris, 1955. – M.-O. Garrigues, "L'oeuvre d'Honorius Augustodunensis: inventaire critique", *Abhandlungen der braunschweigischen wissenschaftlichen Gesellschaft*, 38, Göttingen, 1986, 7-138; *ibid.*, 39, 1987, 113-228. – V. I. J. Flint, *Ideas in the Medieval West. Texts and their Contexts*, London, 1988 (collection of articles, mostly devoted to Honorius). – *DLFMA*, 1992, 687. – *Elucidarium und Lucidaires*, E. Ruhe (ed.), Wiesbaden, 1993. – V. I. J. Flint, *Honorius Augustodunensis of Regensburg*, Aldershot, 1995.

Jean-Yves Tilliette

**HONOUR.** In the Middle Ages as now, the word "honour" had a double sense. Shortly after the year 1000, Bishop *Fulbert of Chartres, in a still celebrated letter on the obligations of *vassalage, played on the two senses of the term *honor*: "I would prefer to die honoured than to live without honour". So honour was indeed, as now, "a feeling that makes one act so as to preserve one's own esteem and consideration and that of others", a feeling very strong in a society based on ties of loyalty; but honour was also an office, a position, and the privileges that went with it, as at Rome with its "career of honours", *cursus honorum*, the hierarchy of high State offices. In the early Middle Ages, in continuity with the late Empire and the Carolingian period, an *honor* in the second sense was a landed property granted as salary for the exercise of a function, and whose enjoyment lasted only during the time of exercise of that function. It must not be confused with the *benefice, *beneficium*. A Carolingian *count could thus "possess" three sorts of *property: his family or personal properties, received by succession or dowry, or acquired; benefices received for life after a personal, "private" *oath of *recommendation; and *honores*, properties received on a temporary basis for his "public" service as count.

In 844, the emperor took back the *honores* of Bernard of Septimania who had rebelled against his authority; in 878 he did the same to Bernard of Gothia who had recovered them, over and above those that had already been entrusted to him. For the authorities at this time had got into the dangerous habit of grouping together several counties under the authority of a single count, who became a duke or marquis; in the 9th c., this accumulation of offices, concentration of *honores* in the hands of a few, was the origin of *territorial principalities. *Charles the Bald thus divided *Aquitaine and *Septimania among three counts Bernard, clan chieftains rather than princes. By an irreversible movement in the course of the 9th c., *honores* came to be likened to the benefices of vassals, and a lifetime character insensibly attributed to them. In 843, at the assembly of Coulaines, Charles the Bald promised not to despoil the Church of its properties and not to take their offices away from the great. And it became more and more difficult for the king to take his "honours" away from a count, even in cases of manifest rebellion, as was the case of Bernard of Septimania in 844. The *capitulary of Quierzy-sur-Oise of 878 did not confirm the hereditary nature of offices, as has wrongly been claimed, but it did establish that this had become the common norm, while trying to safeguard the royal right of disposal of *honores* and benefices.

But insensibly, heredity was installed and led to the disappearance of the personal bond behind the real bond. The benefice became the real cause of vassalic obligations, and it slid further and further from the hands of the proprietor to those of the holder. Power and its prerogatives followed the same path: after having passed from the *Empire to the *crown, they descended from the *king to the local magnates. Thus, well before the feudal revolution and as one of the major causes of the new system, "honorable dependence" had changed its meaning.

J. Dhondt, M. Rouche, *Le Haut Moyen Âge (VIIIe-XIe siècles)*, Paris, 1976. – J.-P. Poly, É. Bournazel, *The Feudal Transformation: 900-1200*, New York, 1991. – J.-P. Poly (dir.), É. Bournazel (dir.), *Les Feudalités*, Paris, 1998.

Christian Lauranson-Rosaz

**HONOUR, SENSE OF.** The use of the term "honour" in the modern sense appears only very late in the Middle Ages. In medieval Latin, *honor* meant an ecclesiastical dignity or a *fief granted by a lord to his supporter. At most, the derivatives of this noun – *honorabilis, honorifice* – were used with the less material meaning of personal dignity. The Latin *decus* seems to have covered what we call "honour", with the strong moral connotation that led Cicero to write: "*Verum decus in virtute positum est*". In the 14th and 15th cc., the word "honourability" was used in the sense of due reverence and respect, and the polite and respectful man was called "honourable". Jean *Froissart first used the term "honour" in the figurative sense: "*Bien disoient plusieurs vaillans chevaliers, usites d'armes, que point ne faisoyent leur honneur*".

Though the word did not exist before, the value was deeply rooted in the medieval mentality. Honour was not just the individual virtue dear to Cicero; it was above all a social quality, recognised by the community, which accorded its marks of esteem to those who deserved them: it depended directly on group approval. In knightly circles, a man preserved the honour that came to him from his noble ancestors by his courage in combat, his fidelity to his given word and the prodigality of his largesse. If he was valiant, loyal and generous, he gained the affection of his companions in arms: by contrast the coward, the perjurer and the miser were dishonoured and lost the reputation that came to them from their ancestors. Woman's honour was rather more passive: it resolved itself mainly into her *chastity. This conception of honour was deeply rooted in the aristocracy, the category of combatants. Its main pattern – "active honour" of virility and "passive honour" of femininity – recurs, in other forms, in the *merchant class and the *peasantry.

An affront could dishonour the individual and his lineage. A slap in the face, an insult or an attack on his precedence put a man's valour in question; the rape or seduction of a woman threw suspicion on the capacity of the males of her house to protect her or watch over her. The code of honour required that this affront be wiped out either by the man directly concerned – the defied knight or the deceived husband – or by the whole aggrieved *family group. The affair was private: so would be the *violence; no recourse to public justice could be envisaged. The infernal cycle of aggression and response was unleashed: untiring vengeance, the settling of accounts between two family groups from generation to generation, was set in place as we still see it in certain Mediterranean societies.

From the 13th c., the sentiment of honour was affected by the repercussions of the affirmation of the values of *humility, detachment and renunciation in Christian *spirituality.

G. Duby, *Hommes et Structures du Moyen Âge*, Paris, 1973. – C. Gauvard, *"De grace especial". Crime, État et Société en France à la fin du Moyen Âge*, Paris, 1991 (2 vol.).

Martin Aurell

**HOPE.** At the dawn of the 12th c. in the West, commentaries clarified the act of hoping, leaving the *virtue in shadow. Man hoped as he lived.

Starting from the theme of 1 Corinthians 13, 13, the *mystery of hope would advance slowly towards theological definition throughout the Middle Ages. In the 12th c., *William of Champeaux († 1121) gave his thoughts an expression that would be cited by *Bonaventure and *Thomas Aquinas: "Hope of pardon,

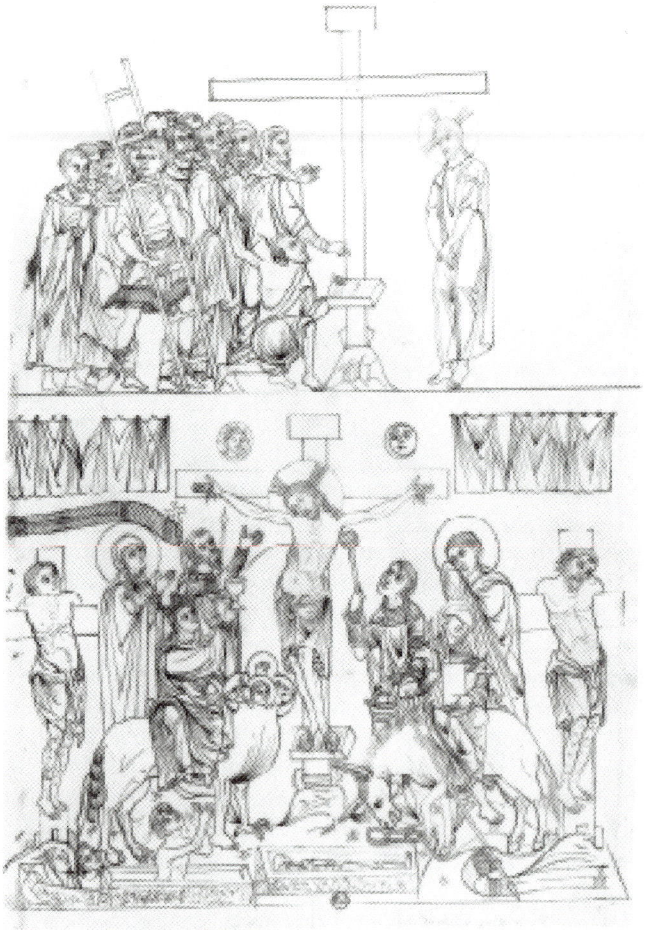

Copies of miniatures from Herrad of Landsberg's *Hortus deliciarum*, fol. 150. Paris, BNF (Dpt des Estampes, Ad 144 a/fol.).

grace and glory". These three hopes punctuated the rhythm of man's spiritual destiny. A slow and difficult progress continued with Peter *Abelard († 1142), for whom hope was the expectation of some profit to be gained in a confidence that rested totally on *God's fidelity. This progress culminated in the definitions of *Peter Lombard († 1160) in his *Book of *Sentences*.

By now the schools of *theology were studying the content of these definitions. As a theology of virtues was established, first by defining them, then by classifying them, hope appeared as one of the three theological virtues (the term **theologalis* first appeared in the early 14th c. with William Wheatley). Alongside the Abelardian school, the Porretan school insisted on the priority between hope and charity and on the certainty of expectation.

The problem posed in the 13th c. was linked to the evolution of ideas, *i.e.* the change from the Platonic view of the irascible power to a positive view of the arduous good that constitutes the eternal and permanent *good.

St *Bonaventure and St *Thomas Aquinas appear simultaneously at the apogee of the Latin Middle Ages. For Bonaventure, the certainty of hope is personal; I hope for myself the *beatitude promised by *God if I persevere to the end, and this hope is personal to me. Its object is the difficult, the "arduous" and the great, it is God himself. St Thomas proceeds differently. First he studies the passion of hope and shows how *man transcends his own nature in magnanimity, the highest form of human hope and self-confidence. With the help of *grace, hope becomes the theological virtue whose object is God himself. Its seat is the irascible appetite inasmuch as this appetite participates in *reason. In this way, the voluntary passion of hope tends towards the status of a virtue: it accedes to the supernatural promotion of the theological virtue. Man is thus ordered towards God.

In the late 13th and early 14th cc., a more positive problematic manifested itself. But theological reflection on hope remained very classical in its development. *Henry of Ghent situated hope in the irascible. *Duns Scotus based his thought on the text of 1 Corinthians 13, 13. He distinguished the virtue from its act. We experience this act in ourselves in desiring infinite good for ourselves, thanks to God's free gift. Hope is thus a personal virtue.

R. A. Gauthier, *Magnanimité. L'idéal de la grandeur dans la philosophie païenne et dans la théologie chrétienne*, Paris, 1951. – O. Lottin, *Psychologie et morale aux XIIe et XIIIe siècles*, Gembloux, 1954-1960 (8 vol.). – J. G. Bougerol, *La Théologie de l'espérance aux XIIe et XIIIe siècles*, 1, *Études*; 2, *Textes*, Paris, 1985 (2 vol.). – B. Studer, "Hope", *EEC*, 1, 1992, 397-399.

Jacques-Guy Bougerol

***HORTUS DELICIARUM.*** The astonishing illustrated *encyclopedia entitled *Hortus deliciarum* was composed by Abbess Herrad of Landsberg († 1195), who exercised her office at Hohenburg, on St *Odile's Mount. Very little is known of her life. She apparently ruled her monastery with great firmness, putting the *nuns under the *spiritual direction of the *Premonstratensians. The *Hortus deliciarum* was written between 1159 and 1175 and is known to us only by a single manuscript miraculously preserved.

The work is voluminous (nearly 600 pages) and is distinguished both by its content and its internal architecture. Constantly, the text is associated with the illustrations: 336 superb designs that give the work an exceptional quality. It is a compilation of extracts from numerous writings. In it are citations from the *Song of Songs, the Gospels and the *Apocalypse, as well as a wide use of the Church *Fathers (from Irenaeus to *Isidore of Seville, going through Ambrose and Augustine). Recent or even contemporary authors are not disdained, and Herrad leans *e.g.* on *Rabanus Maurus and *Ivo of Chartres, *Rupert of Deutz and *Peter Lombard. Chapter after chapter, the *abbess unfurls the story of sacred history, from *Genesis to the *Apocalypse, while establishing in parallel a **summa* of the knowledge of her time. Thus we find expositions on secular *history, but also on *agriculture or the *calendars, etc. In doing this, she offers us a vision of the world that is admittedly her own, but which could doubtless be extended to numerous abbesses and nuns. The stress put on the history of the Church, including that of *heresies, as well as the numerous clarifications of the respective *duties of *clerics and laymen (*nobles as well as *peasants) shows clearly that the author wanted mainly to write a book of morality in order to give a eulogy of the religious *virtues. The poems and *hymns that complete the whole are among the finest lyrical texts of the 12th c. (Christmas hymns, poems on the fall, *prayers addressed to *Christ).

In this work we admire the evocative power of the miniatures and the quality of the information transmitted about daily life; the strength that emerges from the whole book makes the *Garden of delights* one of the texts that can best help us to get into the spirit of medieval Europe.

Herrad of Hohenburg, *Hortus deliciarum*, R. Green (ed.), M. Evans (ed.), C. Bischoff (ed.) and M. Curschmann (ed.), London, 1979 (2 vol.); 1, *Reconstitution*; 2, *Commentary*.

J. Walter, *Herrade de Landsberg (1167-1195). Hortus deliciarum*, Strasbourg, 1952.

Sylvain Gouguenheim

**HOSPITAL, HOSPICE.** The first hospital establishments in the West date from the Frankish period: their existence is attested at that time in numerous towns. They were put under the responsibility of the *bishops, but benefited from a regime of legal autonomy that allowed them freely to receive gifts and *legacies, at that time the essential part of their resources. The political and economic difficulties of the time were favourable neither to their prosperity nor to their multiplication: Carolingian *capitularies mention the lamentable situation in which a number of them lived; the measures advocated to remedy this were not put into effect. Not until the 11th and especially the 12th c. was there a veritable flowering of hospitals, linked to the rise of the *towns.

Linked to the economic revival and the rise of the towns, but also to the "urgency of *charity" in favour of those left behind by growth, a need whose new awareness was not unrelated to the evangelical revival of the time, *foundations of hospitals were numerous, especially from the 12th century. Founders (princes, lords, *bishops, but also rich townsfolk) wished in this way to leave their memory attached to a work witnessing to their charitable sentiments and their piety. In the late Middle Ages, ordinary individuals, notably small urban artisans, would go so far as to bequeath their modest dwelling for the institution of a house of hospitality for the sick poor, a wish that very often could not be realized by reason of the insufficiency of the *donation.

These establishments were considered from the outset as religious places and, as such, subject to Church law, *i.e.* the more or less strict tutelage of the episcopal authorities. Exempted from taxes and *tithes, protected from all patrimonial alienation, they moreover enjoyed various rights (their own *chapel and *cemetery, right of *asylum). Their beneficiaries were all the victims of misfortune, *sickness, old age, joined together in current vocabulary under the term "Christ's poor", as well as *pilgrims. In most regions of the West, there was a distinction betwen hospices, numerous in towns and *villages, where poor passers-by and pilgrims were fed and housed for the night, and hospitals, where the sick, women in labour, orphans and abandoned *children were received and cared for. In the Mediterranean countries, this distinction was much less clear, since hospital establishments, rural or urban, generally accepted all miseries, all sufferings (except that of *lepers, houses being reserved for them close to most built-up areas).

The care dispensed consisted mainly in providing, for whoever turned up, material and moral comfort for the wellbeing of *body and *soul: after having confessed and communicated, the lodger was washed, then taken to a soft bed – which he admittedly sometimes had to share with one or two companions, according to affluence. . . – and from then on benefited from the attentive solicitude of the hospital personnel. Choice and regular *food, warmth of a room provided with a chimney, therapy founded on a traditional plant-based pharmacopeia: the minimal conditions came together to procure a temporary solace to these beings suffering mainly from cold and chronic undernourishment. Hospitals remained powerless in the face of severe illness: admittedly they could appeal to the services of a local surgeon or doctor, but most of the time it was better to trust to divine *mercy and *intercession of the healing saints.

The Hôtel-Dieu at Beaune, founded in 1443 by chancellor Nicolas Rolin. View of the timber-framed gallery and the cloister. Burgundian-Flemish art.

The tutelage of bishops over hospitals was always more or less theoretical. An important number of establishments were free from it: those founded by rulers, in particular the king of France, those set up by communal authorities who exercised a strict control over them, those dependent on the great religious *orders which benefited from the privilege of *exemption. But the tutelary authority, whoever it might be, strove to take care that each house of hospitality was well administered, both on the financial and on the disciplinary level. In a great number of cases, notably in small rural hospices, the management was entrusted to an administrator (rector, master, governor), appointed by the lay or ecclesiastical patron for a fixed length of time. The establishment was often entrusted to a couple, husband and wife: they engaged themselves under *oath to administer the house correctly and look after the poor with compassion, an inventory of the *furniture being taken on entering and leaving the position.

But in many cases, since caring for the sick was an essentially religious function, the charge of a hospital was considered an ecclesiastical *benefice. The titular was then appointed by the bishop or elected by the hospital community of brothers and sisters. He exercised his functions for life, could be dismissed only for a serious offence and benefited from clerical privilege. Abuses were often introduced into such a system: non-*residence of titulars, appropriation of the house's revenues for personal ends, lack of zeal etc. The highest authorities of the Church tried to react

(*Decretal *Quia contingit* of *Clement V in 1311), but in most cases with no real result.

Apart from small establishments entrusted to the management of one or two individuals, hospital personnel usually consisted of brothers and sisters, living in community according to particular statutes inspired by monastic *Rules (noviciate, specific habit, *vows, participation in *offices). The orientation towards a greater regularity of life for caring personnel was particularly affirmed in the communities of canons hospitallers (Aubrac, Roncevaux) and in veritable hospitaller orders (Order of the Holy Spirit, *Antonines and *Trinitarians).

Few traces survive of small hospices – the most numerous – whose appearance resembled that of many private houses. By contrast, some fine examples of town hospitals survive (Tonnerre, Lille, Angers, Beaune), revealing a type of *architecture marked by a religious imprint (importance of the chapel) and by common characteristics: vast hall of the sick, sometimes divided into several aisles by rows of columns, thick massive walls, narrow openings, paved floors.

As to location, the preferred sites were close to town gates and on the banks of rivers, which facilitated the provisioning of *water and the elimination of refuse.

The essential part of the resources of medieval hospitals came from their endowments, instituted by the founders, added to over the years by the donations and charitable legacies of the faithful, for whom the hospitalized sick, suffering image of Christ, were symbolic intercessors with a view to *salvation. Made up of landed property, cultivated directly or granted to tenants, and rentable houses, this *patrimony provided establishments with fixed revenues, to which were added various additional resources of a more contingent nature: the product of *collections, offerings granted by pious visitors, all the more important since *indulgences were sometimes granted by the ecclesiastical authorities, goods in kind (*clothing, sheets) voluntarily given or levied on the effects of sick people who died in the hospital, or confiscated as a fine on the property of the condemned.

The temporalities of hospitals suffered much from the crises and wars that marked the last centuries of the Middle Ages: their revenues diminished, like those of all landed lordships; buildings were damaged or destroyed, precisely at a time when needs were being felt with increased acuteness. Many hospitals disappeared, their property being joined to that of establishments which resisted better. Unable to cope with these disruptions and the abuses that accompanied them, hospital administrators and their ecclesiastical patrons gradually had to admit the intervention of municipal or royal authorities in the management of houses. The laicization of the hospital institution which characterises modern times really began in the 15th c., notably in the Mediterranean lands (*Italy, *Provence, *Languedoc).

J. Imbert, *Les Hôpitaux en droit canonique*, Paris, 1947. – *Histoire des hôpitaux en France*, J. Imbert (dir.), Toulouse, 1982. – *The Hospital in History*, L. Granshaw (ed.), R. Porter (ed.), London, 1989. – E. Prescott, *The English Medieval Hospital, c. 1050-1640*, London, 1992. – C. Rawcliffe, *The Hospitals of Medieval Norwich*, Norwich, 1995.

Daniel Le Blévec

**HOSPITALLERS OF ST JOHN OF JERUSALEM.** The Order of Hospitallers of St John of Jerusalem originated in a modest *foundation intended to shelter *pilgrims, established at *Jerusalem in *c.*1070 by *merchants from *Amalfi, dependent on the Benedictines of Santa Maria Latina. From 1099 the community was endowed by the Latins of Jerusalem in order to provide hospitality there, under the stimulus of its head, Gerard, who appears to have been the founder of the Hospital. It formed the embryo of a new order with St *John the Baptist as its patron. By a privilege of 1113, considered the order's act of foundation, *Paschal II took the brethren under his protection and confirmed all the *donations that had been made to them. From *c.*1120, under the influence of its master, Raymond du Puy, the order's hospital vocation was progressively accompanied by military activity. The Hospital comprised three categories of brethren: knights, sergeants and priests. It adopted a rule inspired by that of St Augustine and confirmed by *Eugenius III before 1153. Up to the end of the 13th c., the Hospitallers took part in the *crusades and in Latin life in the *Holy Land. Benefiting from the enthusiasm aroused by this movement, they received many privileges, rights and lands. All over Latin Europe, they created *commanderies intended to procure men and subsidies for the Holy Land. In 1291, after the fall of *Acre, the Hospitallers fell back on *Cyprus. From 1306 they undertook the conquest of the island of *Rhodes and settled there in *c.*1310. In 1312, after the dissolution of the Temple, *Clement V assigned the Hospital all the properties of the abolished order, except those in the Iberian peninsula. The Hospital's *patrimony in the West was considerably increased.

Each *preceptory* (commandery) comprised a lodging for the brethren, a *chapel, a *cemetery, sometimes a *hospice, often an agricultural estate; indeed the Hospital's pattern of settlement seems to have been more rural than urban. At the head of the commandery was a *preceptor* (commander), responsible for the management of the patrimony and hierarchical superior of the brethren. The commanderies were grouped together into districts called priories, themselves grouped into "langues" corresponding approximately to geographical areas speaking the same idiom: Provence, France, Auvergne, England, Italy, Spain, Germany. The order's government was in the East, successively at Jerusalem, Acre, Cyprus and then Rhodes, the master assisted by the great officials constituting the "convent". These dignitaries were joined at periodical meetings by the priors of the West, to form the general *chapter, supreme *authority of the order.

During the 14th and 15th cc., the Hospital continued to provide hospitality to *pilgrims passing through Rhodes and took part in various military actions against the infidel. In 1522, after a long siege, the Hospitallers had to capitulate before Suleiman's *Turks and abandon Rhodes. In 1530 Charles V gave the Hospital the island of *Malta, and the knights of Rhodes became the knights of Malta.

J. Delaville Le Roux, *Cartulaire général des Hospitaliers de S. Jean de Jérusalem (1100-1310)*, Paris, 1894-1906 (4 vol.). – J. Delaville Le Roux, *Les Hospitaliers en Terre Sainte et à Chypre (1100-1310)*, Paris, 1904. – J. Delaville Le Roux, *Les Hospitaliers à Rhodes (1310-1421)*, Paris, 1913 (re-ed. London, 1974). – J. Riley-Smith, *The Knights of St John in Jerusalem and Cyprus* c.*1050-1310*, London, 1967. – A. Luttrell, *The Hospitallers in Cyprus, Rhodes, Greece and the West: 1291-1440*, London, 1978. – A. Luttrell, *Latin Greece, the Hospitallers and the Crusades: 1291-1440*, London, 1982. – A.-M. Legras, *L'enquête pontificale de 1373 sur l'ordre des Hospitaliers de Saint-Jean de Jérusalem. Vol. I: L'enquête dans le prieuré de France*, Paris, 1987. – A. Luttrell, *The Hospitallers of Rhodes and their Mediterranean World*, Aldershot, 1992. – H. Nicholson, *Templars, Hospitallers, and Teutonic Knights*, Leicester, 1993. – A. Luttrell, *The Hospitaller State on Rhodes and its Western Provinces: 1306-1462*, Aldershot, 1999.

Anne-Marie Legras

**HOST, DESECRATION OF.** Stories about desecration of the *host by doubting Christians or unbelievers circulated in medieval Europe, particularly after the year 1200 as interest in the nature of the *Eucharist grew. From 1215 the doctrine of *transubstantiation was taught throughout *Christendom, expounding the claim that after the *consecration at the *altar the host turned into Christ's real flesh and blood, the historic body that suffered on the cross. Liturgy, *theology and popular *preaching disseminated and explained these claims, often using miracle-tales to illustrate the powers of the consecrated Eucharist. Stories also circulated of accidental abuse or intended desecration perpetrated by *Jews, *Cathars or unbelieving Christians, which always resulted in some miraculous manifestation of the host's power and demonstrated the doctrine.

Within this world of belief, tale and doubt, a particularly powerful narrative developed in the late 13th c., that of profanation of the host at the hand of Jews. From the 1280s we encounter the recurrent accusation of a Jew procuring the host (through *theft, purchase or bribery) and then inflicting harm on it (with boiling water, knives, axes, needles). The claim was that the Jew did this either to ridicule Christ or to re-enact the pains of the *Passion on the Eucharist, Christ's body. An early and famous accusation took place in Paris in 1290, when a Jew was thus accused, arrested and executed, while his wife and children and other Parisian Jews were said to have converted. Similar tales were also developing in German-speaking lands, primarily in the Rhineland, where the *ritual murder accusation had already become entrenched throughout the 13th century.

The accusation of host desecration, and particularly the case at Paris, spread in a variety of medieval media – preaching, collections of religious tales, the iconography of religious art, vernacular drama – and became well-established among the religious narratives of late medieval culture. It was particularly endemic as a form of accusation which led to regional pogroms in Franconia, *Bavaria, Austria, and in the later 14th and 15th cc. moved into *Bohemia and *Silesia. The first and most notorious such regional pogrom is usually known as the Rintfleisch movement which swept Franconia and the Lower Rhineland in 1298-1300, and it was followed by the Armleder movement of *c.* 1338. In such cases most typically an alleged insult perpetrated by Jews to the Eucharist, in public (during eucharistic *processions) or in private, was turned into a violent mass movement that purported to take revenge "for Christ's sake". Lynching and mass executions began in a single town and then spread into villages and towns in the vicinity. In the 15th c. almost as a matter of course, accusations of host desecration were made as a prelude to *expulsion of Jewish communities from imperial towns.

P. Browe, "Die Hostienschändungen der Juden im Mittelalter", *RQ*, 34, 1926, 167-197. – M. Rubin, "Desecration of the Host: the Birth of an Accusation", *SCH*, 29, 1992, 169-185. – M. Rubin, *Gentile tales: the narrative assault on late medieval Jews*, New Haven, London, 1999.

Miri Rubin

**HOST, EUCHARISTIC.** From the Latin *hostia*, which means "victim", the word gradually supplanted, from the 9th c. in *Ordo romanus* V, the term *oblatio*, "offering", used in previous centuries to designate the "altar bread".

The affirmation of Christ's real presence in the host led to the introduction, early in the 13th c., of the gesture of *elevation that marked the moment of *consecration and satisfied the dominant tendency of devotion: "the desire to see the host". At the same time, it gave rise to a number of measures concerning the practice of the liturgy: exposition of the blessed *sacrament, preservation of the sacred *species, rhythms of *communion. However, communion remained infrequent throughout the Middle Ages, annual communion being the minimum made obligatory by the Church at the fourth *Lateran council (1215). In the West the use of unleavened bread was general from the 9th century. The host had to be made with wheat, to the exclusion of all other cereals, as specified by Pope *Eugenius IV at the council of *Florence. Though in the Latin church from the 9th c. we see the practice of preparing great hosts for the celebrant and smaller ones for the congregation, the dimensions of hosts vary at different times, as do the figures, symbols or inscriptions reproduced on them in relief, whose trace is preserved on the baking moulds called "host-irons". However, the preferred iconography was the *Cross or the Crucifixion. The making of hosts was often reserved for religious, who cultivated a field whose harvest was specially set aside for this use: it was called the field of Corpus Domini. From the 15th c., we note a mistrust of hosts prepared by the *laity and especially by *women. But, in general, *nuns escaped this prohibition. Between the moment of preparation and that of consecration, care was taken that the altar bread be put in the best possible conditions for preservation. The Middle Ages went to great expense to lodge the *bread intended to be consecrated, making boxes or *repositoria* of carved wood or bone, *ivory, *enamelled copper and even silver and *gold, a few specimens of which remain.

The fear of corruption of the sacred species, and still more of its profanation, was a veritable obsession. Many varieties of regulations fixed the renewal of consecrated hosts. But the respect accorded by the faithful to the holy reservation also attracted *superstitions. To look at the consecrated bread became the surest way not to be carried off by sudden death or to lose one's sight. And the multiplication of eucharistic *miracles in the late Middle Ages, in which hosts bled between the hands of an incredulous priest or under the blows of a "sacrilegious" Jew attests the deviations that were grafted onto the devotion to the Real Presence.

E. Dumoutet, *Le Désir de voir l'hostie*, Paris, 1926. – P. Browe, *Die Verehrung der Eucharistie im Mittelalter*, Munich, 1933, 137-169. – J. Corblet, *Histoire du sacrement de l'eucharistie*, 1, Paris, 449-513. – E. Dumoutet, *Corpus Domini*, Paris, 1942. – *L'Hostie et le Denier*, Geneva, 1991 (conference). – M. Rubin, *Corpus Christi: the Eucharist in late Medieval Culture*, Cambridge, 1991. – G. J. C. Snoek, *Medieval Piety from Relics to the Eucharist*, Leiden, 1995.

Dominique Rigaux

**HOST, MILITARY.** Derived from the Latin *hostis*, the term "host" evolved, originally designating an armed expedition against an enemy, then the *army itself, and finally, by extension, the obligation to serve in arms.

In the Frankish military organisation, service was due in principle by all free men capable of bearing arms. In the Carolingian period a complex system was perfected in order not to weigh too heavily on the humblest of those liable. In 808, a *capitulary of *Charlemagne indicates that the levy of troops was organised on a landed basis: four "clothed" *manses (worked by *coloni* or slaves) were to provide a completely equipped combatant. Below this threshold, the proprietors of manses were grouped together and owed host service turn and turn about. The refractory were subject to a fine of 60 sous levied by the king by virtue of his right to convoke the army (*heriban*).

The power to levy the host, originally exercised solely by the ruler or in his name, was the object from the late 10th c., at the same time as the other powers of command, of an appropriation by the territorial princes, counts and finally lords of *castles. Having become one of the principal rights of the *seigneur banal*, it was also integrated into the feudal organisation. From the 11th and 12th cc., host service became one of the great vassalic obligations. The vassal owed, by virtue of *homage and for his *fief, military aid to his lord (*auxilium*); gradually, the content of this aid was specified: guard service, *chévauchée* and the host. *Chévauchée* was a military service limited in time and space while the host, much heavier, represented a service whose duration, fixed by *custom, was commonly of thirty or forty days in the year. Later, from the 13th c., the distinction between host and *chévauchée* does not always appear very clearly. The two terms sometimes ended by being confused. The host was due for the fief, basis of the military system, and gave rise in principle to a personal service. In certain cases, notably in *England, the vassal could redeem his obligation to serve in arms by paying a tax called scutage.

The destiny of host service in the later Middle Ages varied according to country: in England it was replaced at the end of the 13th c. by a system resting on contracts of engagement taking the form of indentures, while elsewhere, *e.g.* in *France, the summons of the feudal host remained one of the bases of the constitution of armies until the 15th c., despite the existence of paid service and engagement by contract.

B. D. Lyon, *From Fief to Indenture. The Transition from Feudal to Non-Feudal Contract in Western Europe*, Cambridge (MA), 1957. – J.-F. Verbruggen, "L'armée et la stratégie de Charlemagne", *Karl der Grosse. Lebenswerke und Nachleben, I, Persönlichkeit und Geschichte*, Düsseldorf, 1965-1966, 420-436. – P. Contamine, *War in the Middle Ages*, Oxford, 1984.

Bertrand Schnerb

**HOSTIENSIS or HENRY OF SUSA (died 1270).** Henry of Susa – his surname was Bartolomei, while his date of birth is unknown – followed the career of those 13th-c. *clerics whose rise was due to their *university training and legal competence. Born at Susa, he studied *canon law at *Bologna, then taught at *Paris where he held the post of *archdeacon. He may also have taught at Bologna. He evolved in the same intellectual milieu as prelates such as Ugolino de' Segni, later Pope *Gregory IX, or Sinibaldo *Fieschi, *Innocent IV. He probably benefited from their beneficent protection, and initially he climbed the ecclesiastical hierarchy in his home region. Bishop of Sisteron in 1244, he was archbishop of Embrun from 1250 to 1261. From then on, in the entourage of *Urban IV († 1264) and *Clement IV († 1268), *popes of French origin, he pursued his career in *Rome as *cardinal-bishop of Ostia from 1262 to his death in 1270.

Hostiensis (so surnamed from his cardinalate) was one of the principal 13th-c. *doctors of canon law. He provided the papacy with solid theoretical arguments by which to assert its *authority against the *temporal power, that of the emperor in particular. His *Summa aurea*, probably written *c.*1250, and his commentary on the *Decretals written towards the end of his life (*Lectura in quinque libros decretalium*) nourished reflection on the nature of sovereignty. This could not be divisible, and only the pope possessed *imperium* absolutely. In this, Hostiensis was in line with the doctrine of *plenitudo potestatis* formulated in the 12th c. and pushed to its extreme by Innocent IV. Yet he did not confine himself to the latter's mere enunciation of papal supremacy. For Hostiensis, the *potestas* held by the pope could be exercised not just absolutely, but also in respect of existing temporal laws. However, this did not reveal the coexistence of several sources of sovereignty. This distinction was exercised only in practice, and the unicity of sovereignty that only the pope possessed, in collaboration with the *Sacred College, was in no doubt. Consequently, the pope could legally intervene in temporal matters, the emperor being merely his vicar. Hostiensis's reflection also covered the notion of licit war, of which he risked a definition in his *Summa aurea*. Finally, the great canonist attempted to establish a legal status for the notion of *indulgence: here too, the pope occupied a central place, an argument that illustrates the penetration of legal thought into the clarification of theological notions.

In Hostiensis we see an attempt to synthesize "quoad utrumque ius", *i.e.* all law, canon and civil, which he did by "renovando et prosequendo diversorum Doctorum summas" (*Proem.* to the *Liber Extra*) in order to seek out those "principia et radices" that are the "fundamentum" of "omnis legalis scientia".

A. Rota, "Enrico Bartolomei (Hostiensis)", *EC*, 2, 914-915. – F. Calasso, *Medioevo del diritto*, 1, *Le fonti*, Milan, 1954, 528, 551, 562, 568. – DDC, 5, 1953, 1215. – F. Calasso, *I Glossatori e la teoria della sovranità*, Milan, 1957 (3rd ed.). – J. Gaudemet *et al.*, *L'Age classique*, 1965, 312-316 ("HDIEO", 7). – J. A. Watt, *The Theory of Papal Monarchy in the Thirteenth Century. The Contribution of the Canonists*, London, 1965. – C. Gallagher, *Canon Law and the Christian Community: the Role of Law in the Church according to the Summa aurea of Cardinal Hostiensis*, Rome, 1978. – D. Quaglioni, *"Civilis sapientia". Dottrine giuridiche e dottrine politiche fra medioevo ed età moderna*, Rimini, 1989.

Thierry Pécout

**HOUR.** Up to the 12th c., "hour" designated a moment in the day, more particularly that of a change of activity (work, repose). The perception of the hour as a unit of measurement of *time did not exist. *Rabanus Maurus's division of an hour, in the 9th c., into 22,560 flickers of the eyelid was an experiment without a future. If the ancient system, *i.e.* the division of the day into 12 hours of day and 12 hours of night varying according to the seasons, was used only very little among the *laity, this was not the case in religious communities, where "*hours" in the plural designated the *prayers said at precise and regular times.

From the 12th c., "hour" also began to designate a unit of duration. But not until the 14th c. was this new designation generally accepted. In order to deal with the numerous social conflicts, middle class and workers would seek to determine more precisely the duration of work. From now on it was a question of giving the working day a regular and immutable rhythm. In the *towns we see the invention and then spread of the mechanical clock, the only *bell that gave "the certain hour".

J. Le Goff, *Pour un autre Moyen Âge*, Paris, 1977.

Pierre Bonnerue

**HOURS, PRAYER OF THE.** At the renovation of the Roman liturgy after Vatican II, the name "liturgy of the hours" was happily chosen to designate what had previously been called the "*divine office" or more commonly "*breviary". It is in fact the proper character of this liturgy to organise times of *prayer according to the rhythm of day and night. This practice is rooted in the Jewish Temple tradition, structured by the morning and evening sacrificial offering, to which the synagogue usage would add an afternoon prayer (*mussaf*). These customs were taken up in the Christian communities; already attested by the *Didachè* in the form of a triple recitation of the *Pater*, they were organised from the 3rd c., particularly in monastic circles. Soon this liturgy of the Hours was structured along two lines: ecclesiastical – often called "cathedral" – celebration morning and evening, triple prayer in the course of the day (terce, *sext, *none), and night *office of Vigils, consisting mainly of psalmody, in monastic communities. Quite a wide diversification was manifested when liturgical traditions became fixed according to place. Through the intermediary of urban monasteries, both at *Rome and *Constantinople, monastic usages came to provide the structure of the liturgy of the hours in all the Churches, distributed among a septenary framework in accordance with Psalm 118 (119), 164.

This diversification was accentuated in the course of the Middle Ages and, in monasteries and *collegiate churches, the celebration of the hours was overburdened with new elements, both in the psalmody and by the addition of new prayers or the development of the hymnody, which had long remained very sober in the *Latin liturgies, by contrast with what it had become in the Eastern liturgies, *Byzantine or Syriac. In those Churches, the properly monastic element was maintained primarily in the form of the reading of a section of the *psalter, while there developed a hymnody overflowing with hymnic strophes (*troparia*) originally intercalated between the verses of the *psalms or scriptural canticles of the morning Office (the "odes" of the canon). In the West, the hymnodic element had very early taken a versified form, whose main instigator and model was St Ambrose of Milan. From the Carolingian period, the phrases, biblical or otherwise, chanted at the start of the psalms (*antiphons) or intercalated between the readings as vestiges of responsorial psalmody, were enriched by *neumatic melodies that accentuated their lyrical character. The biblical *readings, reduced to a few verses in the hours of the day, took place primarily in the night office (called "*matins" or "vigils"). In the *Roman liturgy, the habit grew up of combining them with the reading of a *sermon or another work by recognised ecclesiastical writers: the "*Fathers". Detached from the rhythm of the Hours, this *office became, in the renovation of the liturgy, properly an "office of readings".

*CaP*, 4, *The Liturgy and Time*, London, 1986. – R. Taft, *The Liturgy of the Hours in East and West*, Collegeville (MN), 1986.

Irénée-Henri Dalmais

**HOUSE.** The term "house" designates the concrete whole, building(s) and open spaces, in which the family group lives and works. That is why the "house" is also the *family that it represents in society. It is *par excellence* the setting of private life. For a long time, historians paid attention only to the finest dwellings, but the *archaeology of deserted *villages overturned this earlier approach. In return, historians became more attentive to information on settlement, and the study of houses became a subject on its own.

The *peasant houses of the early Middle Ages, often excavated, used earth and wood for the walls and vegetable matter for the roofs; they were built without the help of professional builders. Fruit of long traditions, the long-house of the Nordic lands, sheltering men and beasts, or the elementary house with one or two rooms forming a block reveal this continuity of peasant knowledge. The expansion of the 11th-12th centuries was marked by the organisation of the farm: separate buildings (dwelling, granges, stables) distributed around an often closed courtyard. Construction became more solid, and the carpenter or the *mason took a hand in it. Progress, however, spread slowly: few chimneys replacing the earthen hearth, and few openings (rooms without windows); many houses were dark and smoky. What came first was security.

City houses, at least in the first phase of urbanization, retained the traits of the peasant house. From the 13th c., houses had to be adapted to *towns whose population was growing while the urban territory remained limited: the custom spread of building upwards, and houses were divided into separate lodgings. Built of light materials, houses projected over the street. On the ground floor opened the shop or the workplace, in direct contact with the street and its customers. The hall was the room for living and working. The chambers were the family's private domain. In general, these rooms were of modest dimensions (at *Paris, between 10 and 20 square metres). In the 14th and 15th cc., certain rooms were differentiated (kitchen, garde-robe, bath-house) and the houses of prominent or great men stood out amidst the ordinary houses: larger, provided with *gardens and stables, they sometimes possessed a *chapel or a private *oratory. These mansions accelerated the spread of progress, such as window-panes, chimneys, the use of tiles or brick.

The furnishings of houses were extremely simple: *furniture was of wood, solid and robust; the important elements were the chest – which held clothing, family papers and *money – and the bed, which for the poor was more of a box filled with straw, while for the better-of it consisted of a pallet and feather cushions. Wardrobes were made from niches in the wall, closed by doors; chairs were very rudimentary in structure and not very common, preference going to benches set along the wall; tables were movable: resting on trestles, they were dismantled after meals. Internal illumination was scanty, mostly ensured by candles and torches or the flames of the stove, and only in a few cases by oil lamps or lanterns.

Ceaselessly rebuilt, and adapted to the needs of successive generations, peasant or city houses evolved constantly. Thus accumulated the slow transformations that culminated in the traditional house, of which some examples have survived into our own day.

M. Beresford, J. G. Hurst, *Deserted Medieval Villages*, London, 1971. – S. Roux, *La Maison dans l'histoire*, Paris, 1976. – J. Chapelot, R. Fossier, *The Village and House in the Middle Ages*, London, 1985. – J. Heers, *La Ville au Moyen Âge*, Paris, 1990. – J. Schofield, *Medieval London Houses*, New Haven, 1994.

Simone Roux

**HROSWITHA OF GANDERSHEIM (*c.*935 - after 973).** The first German poetess, Hroswitha wrote at *Gandersheim (Saxony) a Latin work rediscovered in the last years of the 15th c. by the German humanist Celtes. The first two books are a eulogy of *chastity and consist of poems in dactylic metres with interior rhymes, called *Legends*, as well as dramatic dialogues in rhymed prose, or *Dramas*, which the poetess presents as a *retractatio* (reworking) of Terence: the two historical poems, *Gesta Oddonis* and *Primordia Coenobii Gandeshemensis*, subordinate the success of political power to dynastic piety. The whole is a fine monument to learned Ottonian culture.

C. Magnin, *Théâtre de Hroswitha*, Paris, 1845 (bilingual edition). – *Hrotsvithae Opera*, P. von Winterfeld (ed.), Berlin, 1902 (new ed. 1965). – *Hrotsvithae Opera*, K. Strecker (ed.), Leipzig, 1930 (1st ed. 1906). –

*Hrotsvithae Opera*, H. Homeyer (ed.), Munich, 1970. – *The Plays of Hrotsvit of Gandersheim*, New York, 1989. – *Hrotsvita de Gandersheim. Six drames hagiographiques*, M. Goullet (ed. and tr.), Paris, 1997.

K.M. Wilson, *Hrotsvit of Gandersheim*, Leiden, 1988.

Monique Goullet

**HUCBALD OF SAINT-AMAND (*c.*850-930).** This Benedictine monk, was born and died at the abbey of Elnone (Saint-Amand, near Valenciennes). A fellow-pupil of *Remigius and Heiric of Auxerre, he shone as a poet (dedications of the "Second Bible of Charles the Bald" and of the *De sobrietate* of Milo of Saint-Amand, his first teacher; *Ecloga de calvis* or "Eulogy of the Bald", a verbal tour de force in which each word of the 148 hexameters starts with the letter C, initial of *calvus*), computist (*De diebus aegyptiacis*, an astrological and zodiacal *calendar in verse), hagiographer (*Passions* of St Cyrus, St Juliet and St Cassian of Imola; *Lives* of St Rictrude, *abbess of Marchiennes; St Lebwin, apostle of the *Saxons; St Amatus of Douai; and St Jonas), composer (prose or *sequence *Pangat simul* in honour of St Cyrus; two *hymns in honour of St Thierry of Reims, where he taught; troped *Gloria *Quem vere pia laus*, the oldest non-anonymous *trope; versified *offices for St *Peter and St Thierry) and musical theorist (*Musica*, also known by the title *De Harmonica Institutione*, *c.*880); but the anonymous and more celebrated treatises *Alia Musica* and *Musica et Scolica Enchiriadis* are wrongly attributed to him.

Highly esteemed by his contemporaries, his rich and varied work attests various influences, among others those of *John Scotus Eriugena and of Irish teachers active in the region of Saint-Amand.

Hucbaldus, "Notitia historica et bibliographica" *PL*, 132, 1953, 815-825. – *MGH.PL*, 3-4, 1895-1923 (4 vol.; re-ed. 1978). – *Hucbald, Guido and John on Music*, C.V. Palisca (ed.), New Haven, 1978.

Y. Chartier, *L'oeuvre musicale d'Hucbald de Saint-Amand: les compositions et le traité de musique*, Montréal, 1995 ("Cahiers d'études médiévales", 5).

Yves Chartier

**HUGH OF DIE (*c.*1030-1106).** *Prior of the monastery of Saint-Marcel at Chalon-sur-Saône, then *camerarius* of the *chapter of *Lyon, in 1073 Hugh succeeded the bishop of Die deposed for *simony by the papal *legate Gerald of Ostia. Consecrated at Rome by *Gregory VII (March 1074) and designated legate, he was one of the most rigorous and effective "Gregorians" thanks to his roots in the former kingdom of *Burgundy from which he came.

Straightaway multiplying *councils (Anse, Dijon, Autun, Poitiers, Toulouse, Avignon, Lyon) in which a vigorous policy was applied against simony, Hugh played a decisive role in the renewal of the episcopal body from before 1080 – the choice of Gebuin of Lyon (1077), of Hugh of Grenoble and the deposition of Manasses of Reims (1080) – before himself becoming archbishop of Lyon and, as such, holder of the primacy of the Gauls. Designated among his possible successors by Gregory VII (1085), he suffered difficulties at Rome under the pontificate of Victor III, the former Abbot *Desiderius of Monte Cassino (1087), but then obtained a new legation under *Urban II (1093-1094), marked by the *excommunication of King *Philip I. Active in favour of the new *monasticism – the Grande Chartreuse, whose establishment (1084) and maintenance he favoured (1088-1089), and *Cîteaux (evidence of the little Exordium) – he went to Santiago de *Compostela (1095) and the *Holy Land and died at Susa in 1106.

B. Bligny, *L'Église et les Ordres religieux dans le royaume de Bourgogne*, Grenoble, 1960, 57-61. – T. de Morembert, "Bourgogne (Hugues de)", *DBF*, 6, 1964, 1493-1494; *ibid.*, 102, 1989, 1481. – P. R. Gaussin, "Hugues de Die et l'épiscopat franco-bourguignon (1075-1085)", *CH*, 13, 1968, 77-98. – *HChr*, 5, 1993, 105-107.

Pierrette Paravy

**HUGH OF PROVENCE (died 947).** Son of Theobald, duke of *Arles and count of *Provence, and Bertha. His widowed mother married Adalbert II, marquis of *Tuscany, by whom she had three children: Guy, Lambert and Ermengard. Hugh was called to *Italy by the Lombard nobles against Rudolf II, king of Burgundy (himself called to Italy by lords rebelling against Berengar, he had become king of Italy in 924). With the Lombard aristocracy was associated Pope John X, who wished to oppose the party of *Marozia. Hugh landed at *Pisa and in 926 was crowned king of Italy at *Pavia, the former capital of the Lombard kingdom. It was allegedly the charm and intrigues of his stepsister Ermengard, second wife and now widow of Adalbert of Ivrea, that transferred the Lombard crown from Rudolf to Hugh. In 928 he ceded Provence to Rudolf in exchange for a promise not to interfere in Italy.

Marozia then offered her hand to Hugh, lured by the idea of becoming, from *senatrix*, queen and even empress, since the son of her first marriage, Pope John XI, had not denied his step-father the imperial crown. The marriage was canonically illicit since Hugh, as the half-brother of her second husband Guy of Tuscany, was Marozia's brother-in-law. His other half-brother Lambert, who had become marquis of Tuscany on Guy's death, was hence hostile to the marriage. Hugh then removed Lambert and gave the marquisate to his brother Boso (born of the same father). On the death of his wife Alda, Hugh came to *Rome in 932 to marry Marozia. The rite was celebrated in the Castel Sant'Angelo, the most secure fortress in the city. But *Alberic II, another son of Marozia and her first husband Alberic, marquis of Spoleto, incited the Romans to revolt against the "foreigner". Hugh then decided to flee and Alberic became prince of the Romans. Though Hugh had enlarged the kingdom of central Italy, he never managed to impose himself on Rome. His repeated diplomatic and military efforts (he came to Rome with an army in 933, and again in 936 and 941) were always in vain; indeed he had to give his own legitimate daughter Alda as wife to his hated stepson Alberic. From 931 Hugh associated his son Lothar in the kingdom. With the intention of strengthening the tottering throne, in 937 he had married Bertha, widow of the king of *Burgundy, while Lothar married her daughter Adelaide. But the Italian grandees were by now disgusted with his tyrannical behaviour. He therefore left the kingdom to Lothar and returned to Provence, where he died in 947. Lothar died poisoned by Berengar II, marquis of Ivrea, who wore the Lombard crown together with his son Adalbert. Lothar's wife Adelaide avenged him by marrying *Otto I, king of Germany, who descended on Italy and overwhelmed Berengar.

G. Arnaldi, "Alberico di Roma", *DBI*, 1, 1980, 647-653. – *HChr*, 4, 1993.

Marcello Terzano

**HUGH OF SAINT-CHER (died 1263).** *Doctor of law and bachelor of *theology, Hugh of Saint-Cher took the *Dominican habit in 1225 and was twice provincial of France (1227-1230, 1236-1244), *reader of the **Sentences* and master of theology at *Paris (1229-1233). Appointed *cardinal in 1244, *legate at *Liège and in *Germany, he played an important role in the spread of devotion to the Blessed *Sacrament; he died in 1263. He composed a commentary on *Peter Lombard's *Sentences*, theological treatises, but above all he directed the work of producing biblical *concordances and a commentary on all the books of Scripture, very widely circulated.

*SOPMA*, 2, 1975, 269-281, no. 1983-1994. – J.-P. Torrell, *Théorie de la prophétie et philosophie de la connaissance aux environs de 1230. La contribution d'Hugues de Saint-Cher*, *SSL*, 40, 1977.

Louis Jacques Bataillon

**HUGH OF SAINT-VICTOR (late 11th c. - 1141).** Born in *Saxony in the very late 11th or early 12th c., Hugh of Saint-Victor received his first instruction from the regular *canons of St Pancras, Hamersleben, representatives in Saxon territory of the *Gregorian reform, and remained on friendly terms with them. Entering *Saint-Victor at *Paris very young, after 1115, by 1127 he exercised an intensive teaching activity there that made him the founder of the "school of Saint-Victor": *Richard, Achard and *Andrew of Saint-Victor each developed an aspect of his thought.

From this period dates one of his most famous works, the *Didascalicon*. This is an art of "reading", *i.e.* learning or teaching. We may see in it the programme of studies at Saint-Victor and of the *master's lessons. The disciplines of the *trivium* and *quadrivium* surveyed in it were intended to contribute to restoring God's image in man by reordering it to the true and the *good. A scholastic programme, the *Didascalicon* is thus also a spiritual directory. Written around the same time, the *De institutione novitiorum* regulates the discipline of deed and that of word: this manual of cloistered living had a clear influence on later normative literature.

Hugh's work was closely linked to his teaching activities, whether *lectures given impromptu and then copied down, lessons or spiritual talks given orally and then rewritten. It also reflects an organisation of knowledge and sacred science based on the doctrine of the three *senses of Scripture: *history, *allegory and tropology or moral teaching. Anagogy – upper part, so to speak, of allegory and tropology united – is present in several works in which spiritual experience crops up (*De arrha animae*, *Homilies on Ecclesiastes*).

His pedagogical methods made use of figured representations, whether for expounding a geography lesson in front of a *map, or for spiritual conferences that took place at the same time as a drawing was made. The latter was the object of a visual *exegesis, *i.e.* a meditative reading which, going beyond the *sign, was supposed to end in the *contemplation of the reality signified. These spiritual exercises took place in an intellectual ambience inherited from Augustine and *Dionysius and in a resolutely Christian atmosphere. It shared with the *Cistercian movement an emphasis on the role of the person of *Christ, but was distinguished from it by its particular insistence on the sacramental order and by its ecclesiological character: it is by penetrating into the current of *sanctity that is the Church that the Christian is both in and of the Church. This perspective was the basis not just of a sociology of *ordines*, but of various spiritual classifications. Finally, the dimension of salvation-history and its periodizations (*nature, law, *grace) were taken into account, and not just the succession, but the coexistence of these states in *souls as well as in *Christendom was affirmed.

A modest and attractive personality, Hugh had the confidence of many of his contemporaries and kept up an abundant correspondence, notably with St *Bernard. Early on, he put his students on guard against the seduction of *Abelard's positions, against theories of pure *love and against the "doctors of *allegory" and their speculations with no foundation in *history.

Hugh of Saint Victor, *On the Sacraments of the Christian Faith*, R. J. Deferrari (ed.), Cambridge (MA), 1951. – *The Didascalicon of Hugh of St Victor*, J. Taylor (ed.), New York, Chichester, 1961 (repr. 1991; "Records of Western Civilization"). – P. Gautier Dalché, *La "Descriptio mappe mundi" de Hugues de Saint-Victor. Texte inédit avec introduction et commentaire*, Paris, 1988. – *L'Oeuvre de Hugues de Saint-Victor*, 1, Turnhout, 1997 ("Sous la règle de saint Augustin", 3).

J. Châtillon, *Le Mouvement canonial au Moyen Âge. Réforme de l'Église, spiritualité et culture*, Turnhout, 1990, 395-435 ("Bibliotheca victorina", 3). – P. Sicard, *Exégèse visuelle, diagrammes médiévaux et exercices spirituels: le "Libellus de formatione arche" de Hugues de Saint-Victor*, Turnhout, 1993 ("Bibliotheca victorina", 4).

Patrice Sicard

**HUGH OF SEMUR (1024-1109).** Hugh of Semur, also called St Hugh the Great, belonged to the Burgundian higher aristocracy, his father, Dalmatius of Semur, being the half-brother of the count of Chalon. After having frequented the cathedral *school of *Auxerre or Chalons-sur-Saône (1030-1035), Hugh decided, aged 15, to enter *Cluny. In 1047 he became grand *prior of the monastery, and in 1049 he was the first Cluniac *abbot elected by the monks (and not designated by his predecessor in office, as were the previous five abbots). His abbacy represents the period of apogee of Cluniac history. Apparently giving form to an initative of *Odilo, Hugh had the monastery's first *cartularies drawn up. He gave Cluny new customs (drawn up by Bernard and Ulrich of Zell). He built Cluny III, the most important monument of Latin *Christendom before *St Peter's in Rome, at the end of the 11th century. The "Cluniac Church" was vigorously extended under his abbacy, gaining new lands, in particular *England, conquered by William of Normandy, and the pioneering front of Latin Christendom represented by the kingdom of *León-*Castile. He obtained from the papacy a statute of exception for Cluny: reinforcement of *immunity and *exemption, handing over of papal insignia by *Urban II (a former Cluniac). In return, Hugh of Semur was, as *legate, an active supporter of the papacy at a tragic moment in the history of Christendom, the *Investiture Contest. Like all Cluniac abbots of the first generations, he had close relations with the *Empire. He was the godfather of *Henry IV; hence he served as intermediary between his spiritual son and *Gregory VII in 1077, at the time of the *Canossa episode.

His writings are relatively few. We have nine *letters (to, among others, *William the Conqueror, *Philip I of France and *Anselm of Canterbury), some statutes and a *sermon. His feast is 29 April.

*Memorials of Abbot Hugh of Cluny (1049-1109)*, H. E. J. Cowdrey (ed.), *SGSLE*, 11, 1978, 9-175.

N. Hunt, *Cluny under St Hugh 1049-1109*, London, 1967. – *Le Gouvernement d'Hugues de Semur à Cluny. Actes du colloque scientifique international, Cluny, septembre 1988*, Cluny, 1990. – A. Kohnle, *Abt Hugo von Cluny (1049-1109)*, Sigmaringen, 1993 ("Beihefte der Francia", 32).

Dominique Iogna-Prat

**HUGO SPERONI (12th c.).** Little is known of Hugo Speroni. In all probability he was a member of the consular aristocracy of the commune of *Piacenza, with a legal and theological education. At a mature age (*c.*1185), giving up public duties, he devoted himself to a broad reflection on Christian thought, formulating a theological text that he sent to the *jurist Master Vacario, his former fellow-student at *Bologna, now settled in England. It is from the latter's confutation of this text that we know the fundamental elements of Speroni's heretical thought. This stressed the dimension of divine *grace and *predestination: communion with God takes place in interior sanctification on the basis of the inscrutable divine plan; there is no place for ascetic practices and good works, nor for the mediation of the hierarchical Church, nor for the division into *clerics and *laity (which indeed, in a harsh expression, he compares to the ancient distinction between masters and slaves). It may be supposed that he had few followers and that his ideas had no important and lasting consequences.

I. da Milano, *L'Eresia di Ugo Speroni nella confutazione del maestro Vicario. Testo inedito del secolo XII con studio storico e dottrinale*, Vatican, 1945. – G. G. Merlo, *Eretici ed eresie medievali*, Bologna, 1989, 63-67.

Grado G. Merlo

**HUGUCCIO (*c.*1140-1210).** Huguccio (Hugh of Pisa) studied *theology and probably *canon law at *Bologna, before teaching there; among his pupils was the future Pope *Innocent III. He was elected bishop of *Ferrara in 1190 and remained so until his death. Among other works, we owe him the *Liber derivationum*, a dictionary of *etymology, the *Expositio symboli apostolorum*, and above all a very celebrated *Summa on Gratian's *Decretum*, drawn up between 1180 and 1190, which is a synthesis of the ideas of the School (and notably of the thought of Rufinus and Simon of Bisignano), the thought of the French *Decretalists, political practice as it had developed at the time of *Alexander III, and *Roman law. Huguccio's work constitutes a sort of apogee that would influence not just the Anglo-Norman school but also, directly or indirectly, all later canon law (the *bull *Per venerabilem* is a good example of this) and indeed the whole political and religious reality of Europe. An ardent defender of the independence of the Church, he put the *pope at the summit of the Catholic hierarchy, though the Church, in his eyes, consisted in the mass of believers (since the Church was founded mainly on Christ and only secondarily on St Peter); he considered that the Church could have "neither spot nor stain" and that it could not err. The pope could not be judged, save in case of *heresy (determined by the *cardinals) since he then became "less than the last of Christians" (but the heresy must be public); otherwise, the pope's judgment prevailed over that of the *council (likewise, in case of opposition between all the *bishops of a Church and the pope, it was the latter who prevailed). In relations between Church and *Empire, Huguccio comes across as a partisan of the Holy See; thus, against the *communis opinio*, he alleged that *clerics could not be brought before a lay court in feudal matters. Nevertheless he accorded an independence to the emperor (and he put *kings and cities on the same level), since both powers came from God: he thought that the emperor drew his legitimacy from election and that *coronation by the pope simply authorized him to change his title from "king of *Germany" to "emperor". The pope could depose the emperor (*ratione peccati* or *casualiter*), but his subjects could never do so; nevertheless, the emperor did not have the same faculty vis-à-vis the pope (the privilege accorded by Pope *Adrian I to *Charlemagne created no vested right for the emperor) since, although both powers came from God (Christ had acted as king and priest) and although the Empire had existed before the papacy, the spiritual sword remained superior to temporal *authority and it was this superiority that authorized the (measured) intervention of the pope in temporal affairs. Huguccio was also interested in the sources of law, the theory of contracts, and *marriage.

S. Kuttner, *Repertorium der Kanonistik*, Vatican, 1936. – N. Del Re, *I codici vaticani della "summa decretorum" di Uguccione da Pisa*, Rome, 1938. – A. Mariago, *I codici manoscritti delle "Derivationes" di Uguccione Pisano*, Rome, 1938. – M. Maccarrone, *Chiesa e Stato nella dottrina di papa Innocenzo III*, Rome, 1940. – A. Stikler, "Der Schwerterbegriff bei Huguccio", *Ephemerides iur. can.*, 3, 1940, 201-242. – H. D. Austin, "Uguccione Miscellany", *Italica*, 27, 1950, 12-17. – S. Mochi Onory, *Fonti canonistiche dell'idea moderna dello Stato*, Milan, 1951.

Jacques Bouineau

**HUMANISM, HUMANISTS**

**Italy.** From the middle of the 14th c., Francesco Petrarca (*Petrarch) (1304-1374), with his interest in reading the *classics, his epistolary contacts with friends and various contemporary personalities, and finally his own literary output, increasingly centred on the rediscovery and application of what the ancients had called *studia humanitatis*, indicated a way of approaching culture that was outside the traditional schemes in use in the schools before him. So those forms of innovation that a limited group of Paduan intellectuals meeting around Albertino Mussato (1261-1329) had practised by reading the classical texts in the *libraries of *Padua – and the nearby ones of *Verona and *Pomposa – found, with Petrarch, a revival that succeeded in taking them outside strictly municipal and civic limits. Giovanni *Boccaccio (1313-1375) and then Coluccio *Salutati (1331-1406) also developed the germs of the movement that referred itself to *humanae litterae*, understood as fundamental and irreplaceable in the formation of the man and the citizen. By a fortunate series of political and cultural circumstances, *Florence, the city of *Dante, Petrarch, Boccaccio and Salutati – from 1375 chancellor of the Republic – became the driving centre of this intellectual renaissance.

Two essential factors concurred to the definition of the process of renewal under way: the recovery and re-evaluation of the classical culture of Rome and then Greece: and the certainty that man, with his strength and rationality, was capable of choosing his destiny and his place in the world. These convictions were the hinges of the culture that was set up in antithesis and disharmony with that of the medieval schools. Indeed a lively polemic developed towards the entire Middle Ages, since to it – understood as a formless period of ignorance lasting from the 600s to the 1200s – the humanists attributed the loss of the memory and use of the letters of ancient Rome, which had disappeared under the rule of ignorant and indifferent *barbarians.

The rebirth of classical culture – which at its beginnings encountered sometimes violent forms of opposition, caused by the fear that the circulation of the texts of the "pagans" could lead to negative consequences on the moral and religious plane – brought with it a different way of reading the ancient authors, as well as ancient documents. The most famous case was that of the work of Lorenzo *Valla (1407-1457), which demonstrated the falsity of the act on which was based the emperor Constantine's *donation to Pope Silvester I of the territory that formed the beginning of the temporal power of the Church. Texts – including those widespread in the Middle Ages, *e.g.* Virgil or Cicero – were now compared with those transmitted by other manuscripts, while those unknown to the Middle Ages were sought out and works such as Cicero's *Pro Archia*, *Familiares* and *Brutus*, Lucretius's *De rerum natura*, Quintilian's *Institutiones oratoriae*, Valerius Flaccus's *Argonautica* and Tacitus's *Annales* and *Historiae*, to cite just the most significant, were recovered.

A method of reading increasingly took shape that no longer trusted any particular codex, but sought to arrive at the genuineness of the original text. Humanistic philology produced extraordinary examples of methodological ability, as appears from the researches of Valla, who also worked on the sacred texts, Angelo Poliziano (1454-1494) and Ermolao Barbaro (1453/1454-1493), to whom may be added at least Cristoforo Landino (1424-1498), Giorgio Merula (1430/1431-1494), Domizio Calderini (1446-1478) and Filippo Beroaldo (1453-1505). Even in the production of *books, they sought to go back to ancient models of *script, which they considered those of the classics themselves: the distancing from earlier "Gothic" models was due, in particular, to the graphic reform brought about mainly by *Poggio Bracciolini (1380-1459), which then became current in the workshops of all Italy. Outstanding among these was the Florentine workshop of Vespasiano da Bisticci (1421-1498), which furnished its products to emperors, popes and kings all over Europe.

The extension of literary knowledge and the need for an increasingly widespread intellectual and civil education led to the *translation of Greek works into Latin and Latin ones into the vernacular, continuing a habit that had developed from the 13th century. It is not without significance that they chose to translate Greek authors who also had civil values – *i.e.* Plutarch, Demosthenes, Isocrates, as well as Aristotle and Plato –, useful at a time of reconstruction of a society that was no longer communal. Hence the translations of *e.g.* Uberto Decembrio (*c.*1350-1427), Iacopo Angeli (*c.*1360-1410/1411), Leonardi Bruni (1370/1374-1444), Guarino Guarini (1370-1460), Pier Candido Decembrio (1392-1477) and many more, while the *Camaldolese friar Ambrogio *Traversari (1386-1439) made the Greek works of the Church *Fathers accessible in Latin. In the second half of the *Quattrocento, in the Florence of the *Medici, Marsilio *Ficino (1433-1499) translated and spread the writings of Plato and then those of the Hermetics.

The classical works were seen not just as rhetorical and stylistic models, but also as ethical and moral examples on which to base the formation of society in general and the education of the citizen in particular. The city, often with its signorial courts, always with its commercial traffic, with its centres of culture – no longer *schools of grammar but often *universities of ancient fame or new institution –, with its private coteries – sometimes gathered around an interested *patronage, a monastery rich in books, a prelate sensitive to the reading of the classics, even if pagan –, acquired an increasingly decisive role in the diffusion of culture.

It appeared indispensable to choose and organise political life, which differed according to whether the government of the city was in the hands of republican cliques or under the will of a lord. Cities like *Venice and Florence (before the rise to power of the Medici in 1434) represent precious evidence of the constant relationship between political life and cultural interests: in these two environments, especially the Florentine – where, among others, worked Matteo Palmieri (1406-1475), author of a *Vita civile* – humanism took on a clearly civil dimension that characterised it on the ideological as well as on the literary level; recourse to study was seen as an irreplaceable means for the formation of men engaged in the life and conduct of the State. Exemplars of this may be the *Books of the Family* of Leon Battista Alberti (1404-1472), one of the most significant humanist authors, and engaged not just in literary but also in architectural activity, of which he left extraordinary proofs at Florence, *Mantua and Rimini.

Fundamental manifestations of humanistic ideals were works like the *De ingenuis moribus* of Pietro Paolo Vergerio (1370-1444) or the *De studiis et litteris* of Leonardo Bruni, both of whom absorbed and developed the idea that *man, architect of his own history, must tend towards his own good and that of his fellows, and hence to elevation, if not perfection. This was also expounded in treatises on the dignity of man, like those of Giannozzo Manetti (1396-1459), Bartolomeo Facio (*c.*1420-1457) and Giovanni *Pico della Mirandola (1463-1494). Whether they referred to *Platonism or to *Aristotle, their fundamental aim was always to put man at the centre of the universe: around him revolved the whole creation since he was made in the image and likeness of *God, as being endowed with rationality and intelligence, as *e.g.* the whole work of Leonardo da Vinci (1452-1519) demonstrated.

In the second half of the century, the unconditioned supremacy of the use of *Latin, typical of the first half of the Quattrocento, gave way to a growing and progressive recovery of the *Italian language: a language that did not appear, like Latin, crystallized in the patterns formulated by Valla in his *Elegantie lingue latine*, but much closer to the requirements of civil society and hence to its intellectual concerns. Thus humanism – which towards the end could still show writers in Latin like Poliziano, Ficino, Pico, Giovanni Pontano (1426-1503) or Iacopo Sannazzaro (1457-1530) – ended with an author like Niccolò Machiavelli (1469-1527) who, before Pietro Bembo (1470-1547), brought new impetus and new solutions to the Italian language. But humanistic culture, especially the Latin – which within itself had produced two *popes, *Nicholas V (1447-1453) and *Pius II (1458-1463) –, had left a germ that would reach maturity even far beyond the geographical borders of the Italian vernacular.

R. Sabbadini, *Storia del ciceronianismo e di altre questioni letterarie dell'età della Rinascenza*, Turin-Florence-Rome, 1885. – G. Voigt, *Die Wiederbelebung des classischen Alterthums oder das erste Jahrhundert des humanismus*, Berlin, 1893 (3rd ed.; 2 vol.). – R. Sabbadini, *Il metodo degli Umanisti*, Florence, 1920. – R. Burdach, *Riforma, Rinascimento, Umanesimo*, Florence, 1935 (It. tr.). – N. Festa, *Umanesimo*, Milan, 1940 (2nd ed.). – G. Toffanin, *Storia dell'Umanesimo (dal XIII al XVI secolo)*, Rome, 1940 (2nd ed.). – G. Saitta, *Il pensiero italiano nell'Umanesimo e nel Rinascimento*, Florence, 1949-1951. – J. Burckhardt, *The Civilization of the Renaissance in Italy*, L. Goldscheider (ed.), London, 1950 (3rd ed.). – M. P. Gilmore, *The World of Humanism, 1453-1517*, New York, 1952. – E. R. Curtius, *European Literature and the Latin Middle Ages*, London, 1953. – P. O. Kristeller, *Renaissance Thought. The Classic, Scholastic and Humanist Strains*, New York, 1961. – E. Garin, *Italian Humanism. Philosophy and Civic Life in the Renaissance*, Oxford, 1965. – R. Sabbadini, *Le scoperte dei codici latini e greci ne' secoli XIV e XV*, Florence, 1967 (anast. repr.). – H. Baron, *The Crisis of the early Italian Renaissance. Civic Humanism and Republican Liberty in an Age of Classicism and Tyranny*, Princeton (NJ), 1967. – W. K. Ferguson, *Il Rinascimento nella critica storica* (It. tr.), Bologna, 1969. – R. Sabbadini, *Storia e critica dei testi latini*, Padua, 1971 (2nd ed.). – E. Garin, *Medioevo e Rinascimento. Studi e ricerche*, Bari, 1973 (4th ed.). – E. Garin, *La cultura del Rinascimento. Profilo storico*, Bari, 1973 (3rd ed.). – S. Rizzo, *Il lessico filologico degli Umanisti*, Rome, 1973. –L. D. Reynolds, N. G. Wilson, *Scribes and Scholars. A Guide to the Transmission of Greek and Latin Literature*, Oxford, 1991 (3rd ed.). – J. Huizinga, *the Waning of the Middle Ages*, Harmondsworth, 1976. – C. Vasoli, *Umanesimo e Rinascimento*, Palermo, 1976 (2nd ed.). – E. Garin, *La cultura filosofica nel Rinascimento italiano. Ricerche e documenti*, Florence, 1979. – V. Rossi, *Il Quattrocento*, R. Bessi (revised), M. Martelli (intro.), Padua-Milan, 1992. – R. Sabbadini, *Opere Minori*, 1, T. Toffano (ed.), Padua, 1995.

Paolo Viti

**Northern Europe.** The Italian term *umanesimo* means the intellectual movement oriented to the study of the humanities, while *umanismo* means a doctrine, asserting the primacy of the human, and *ipso facto* opposed to the values of Christianity. In English, French, and various other languages, most conspicuously German, the ambiguity exists.

The predominantly French humanism of the century that began in the 1380s and ended with the entry onto the stage of Erasmus began to be truly studied only a few decades ago, and even today it remains very little known outside a restricted circle of specialists; so it would be useful for us to interest ourselves particularly in that. Like Italian humanism, it was a very complex, sometimes even contradictory cultural phenomenon, made up of a multitude of components that never came together in a single person: thus, Nicolas de Clamanges (*c.*1362-1437) gave himself up passionately to philological work, covering the margins of his manuscripts of Cicero with variants; Jean *Gerson (1353-1429) did not devote himself to that activity but, like his friend Clamanges or Laurent de Premierfait (*c.*1360-1418), he wrote Latin poems, even practising imitating all the metres formerly used by *Boethius. Jean de Montreuil (1354-1418) does not seem to have tried verses but, like Gerson – and unlike Clamanges – he readily passed from *Latin to French according to the public he was addressing, using the vernacular with great clarity and vigour. Montreuil and the brothers Gontier (*c.*1350-1418) and Pierre Col proclaimed their admiration for Jean de Meung, while Gerson, like *Christine de Pizan (*c.*1364-*c.*1435), was indignant at the immorality of the *Roman de la Rose*. Moreover, if real subjects of disagreement were lacking, the French humanists invented them, any quarrel being a pretext for brilliant epistolary jousts.

A simple examination of the manuscripts – among which are many autographs – makes clear that several of the characteristic traits of Italian humanism also appeared in northern Europe, and this well before the dates generally assigned to them: philological work did not remain the appanage of the Italians alone until Guillaume Budé (1468-1540) or the Estiennes; humanistic writing did not have to await the return of Guillaume *Fichet (1433-1480) from his stay in *Rome before penetrating among the French, and interest in the Greek language had begun to manifest itself nearly half a century before the arrival of Tipherna at Paris.

The study of texts – some particularly important ones have been identified only recently – confirms the need for a profound revision of the traditional division into periods. For example, the reappearance of the Virgilian eclogue in France had always been put in the reign of François I; we now know two eclogues written at Paris in the late 14th c.: one composed *c.*1382 by the adolescent Gerson, the other written by Clamanges in 1394. It is also very interesting to observe that the French humanists, when they in turn adopted this literary genre already made illustrious decades earlier by Petrarch, used it to oppose some of the latter's key ideas: thus, against Petrarch who proclaimed the primacy of the Eternal City, they took up the old theme of *translatio studii*, maintaining that *Paris was the heir to the glorious traditions of Athens and Rome.

In the Netherlands the *Devotio Moderna and the *Brethren of the Common Life coalesced with Italian and Greek ideas to produce in the person of Desiderius Erasmus (1467-1536) a figure whose influence was to extend across many fields. Through him humanistic ideas spread to England and Germany. In the former, St Paul's School, founded by John Colet, and new colleges at *Oxford and *Cambridge betokened a new interest in education and scholarship directly inspired by humanism. In Germany, too Erasmus's influence was felt through his personal connections, for example Johannes Reuchlin.

Humanist ideas merged in northern Europe with the new technology of printing, with the expansion of Europe across the Atlantic, and in the persons of monarchs such as Francis I of France and Henry VIII of England to produce a character different from that in Italy. The rapid spread of Reformation ideas took place in countries where humanist ideas had made rapid progress.

B. G. Kohl, *Renaissance Humanism, 1300-1500: a Bibliography of Materials in English*, New York, 1985. – D. Cecchetti, *Il Primo Umanesimo francese*, Turin, 1987. – *L'Époque de la Renaissance, L'avènement de l'esprit nouveau (1400-1480)*, T. Klaniczay (dir.), E. Kushner (dir.) and A. Stegmann (dir.), Budapest, 1988 (bibliog.). – *Préludes à la Renaissance, aspects de la vie intellectuelle en France au XV<sup>e</sup> siècle*, C. Bozzolo (ed.), E. Ornato (ed.), Paris, 1992. – G. Ouy, "Les recherches sur l'humanisme français des XIV<sup>e</sup> et XV<sup>e</sup> siècles", *La Filologia medievale e umanistica greca e latina nel secolo XX* (Atti del Congresso Internazionale, Roma . . . 11-15 dicembre 1989), Rome, 1993, 275-327. – G. Ouy, "Humanism and Nationalism in France at the Turn of the Fifteenth Century", *The Birth of Identities*, B. P. McGuire (ed.), Copenhagen, 1996, 107-125.

Gilbert Ouy

**HUMANISTS, BYZANTINE.** The conventional term "Byzantine humanists" designates those scholars who, in the 9th and 10th cc., revived the knowledge of Antiquity at Byzantium.

The late 7th c. and the 8th c. were a dark age at Byzantium. *Islam threatened Asia Minor, while the *Slavs penetrated into the Balkans. The Empire was agitated by the first *iconoclast crisis (730-787). Literary output was at its lowest: few ecclesiastical writers; no trace of secular culture. The intellectual movement of the following age must be judged against this background.

From the restoration of *Orthodoxy (787-814), the situation improved: *Nicephorus, the future *patriarch, wrote his *Brief History*, George Syncellus and Theophanes their *chronicles, *Theodore the Studite was at work. This renewal continued under the second *iconoclasm (815-842). At the same time, a technical innovation revolutionized the production of *books: minuscule writing replaced uncial. Secular culture, meanwhile, slept.

From the first half of the 9th c., Leo the Philosopher (or the Mathematician), who was largely self-taught, taught *mathematics and *philosophy at *Constantinople, at first as a private professor. Metropolitan of *Thessalonica from 840 to 843, he then returned to the capital, where Caesar Bardas, reviving higher education, founded the palace school of the Magnaura. Leo, with three professors under him (mathematics and grammar), reserved philosophy for himself. He died after 869. His culture was mainly scientific (mathematics, *astrology, *astronomy), but he also corrected the text of Plato.

Interest in ancient culture appears in broad daylight with *Photius (*c.*810-after 890), whose wealth allowed him to collect books. His *Bibliotheca* (Library), which brings together 279 reviews: Christian authors, but also 122 secular prose works, shows his knowledge of ancient literature.

In the same period, secular texts were copied from uncial models into the new *script. To this transliteration we owe many texts of Greek Antiquity.

For the following period, Arethas, metropolitan of Caesarea (*c.*850-944?) shows that the movement made famous by Photius continued. His works and his scholia attest his culture and his philological activity. Some of the books he owned still exist: Euclid,

Plato, Lucian, Christian apologists, *Aristotle, *Nicephorus and Photius.

The 10th c. saw the appearance of an encylopedist movement that culminated with Constantine VII Porphyrogenitus (913-959). This emperor was a scholar to whom we owe several works, often compilations (*Book of Ceremonies*, *On the Themes*, *On the Administration of the Empire*). He also brought about the creation of a vast *encyclopedia, moral and practical in aim, which, made up of extracts of historians, comprised 53 sections. Two survive (*On Embassies*; *Virtues and Vices*), as well as parts of three more.

L. Lemerle, *Le Premier Humanisme byzantin*, Paris, 1971. – W. T. Treadgold, *The Nature of the Biblioteca of Photius*, Washington (DC), 1980. – *The Chronicle of Theophanes Confessor*, C. Mango (ed.), R. Scott (ed.), Oxford, 1997.

Bernard Flusin

**HUMBERT OF MOYENMOUTIER (late 10th c.-1061).** Humbert of Moyenmoutier, "a stiff and linear mind, cold . . . but vigorous and logical" (Y. Congar) was, with *Peter Damian, one of the main figures of the first generations of the *Gregorian reform.

Humbert was in 1015 a Benedictine at the abbey of Moyenmoutier, in the *diocese of Toul, an establishment reformed by Bishop Bruno, the future Pope *Leo IX. From the latter's election in 1049, Humbert followed him to *Rome where he became if not his secretary, at least his confidant. He was rapidly promoted archbishop of all *Sicily, then in the hands of the Muslims, and *cardinal-bishop of Silva Candida (or Santa Rufina), the name by which he is sometimes designated.

In *Lorraine, a region of contacts that gave rise to partisans of both the imperial and papal camps, Humbert soon came into contact with a reforming circle for which the renewal of the Church was not to be carried out solely on the moral level. The undertaking, underpinned by sound canonical principles, could not fail to lead onto political terrain, in order to put an end to lay *investiture and the abuses to which this gave rise: did not Humbert go so far as to reject the validity of *orders conferred by simoniacal prelates? In such a perspective, the universal Church was conceived as a single diocese under the responsibility of the papacy, an office in which the *bishops were nothing but participants. These ideas, which he adapted and hardened, are enunciated in his work, the *Libri tres contra simoniacos* as well as in the *canonical collection *Collection in Seventy-Four Titles* (or *Diversorum patrum sententiae*) of which, according to A. Michel, he must have been the author.

It is not astonishing, then, to see Humbert preparing for the *pope a reply to the attacks on Latin usages formulated by *Leo of Ohrid on the initiative of the *patriarch of *Constantinople, *Michael Cerularius. Likewise he was, with Frederick, *chancellor of the Roman Church, and Peter, archbishop of *Amalfi, part of the embassy sent to the banks of the Bosphorus in 1054, to carry out a negotiation which was cut short and at the end of which, despite the pope's death, a *bull of *excommunication against the patriarch and his followers was laid on the *altar by the *legates.

On his return to Rome, appointed in 1057 chancellor and librarian of the Church of Rome – a post he kept until his death – Humbert remained influential, though Hildebrand, (later *Gregory VII), began to occupy centre stage. Some would even see the cardinal's hand in the decree of 1059 that modified the procedure of papal *elections. We should finally note that he also intervened in the eucharistic quarrel unleashed by *Berengar of Tours.

A. Michel, "Die folgenschweren Ideen des Kardinales Humbert und ihr Einfluss auf Gregor VII", *SGSG*, 1, 1947, 65-92. – A. Michel, "Die Anfänge des Kardinales Humbert bei Bischof Bruno von Toul", *SGSG*, 3, 1948, 299-319. – Y. Congar, "Humbert de Silva Candida", *Cath.*, 5, 1962, 1090-1093. – U. Blumenthal, "Humbert von Silva Candida", *TRE*, 15, 1986, 682-685 (bibliography).

Catherine Vincent

**HUMBERT OF ROMANS (*c.*1200-1277).** Born at Romans (*Dauphiné), master of arts at *Paris, Humbert entered the Friars Preachers in 1225. *Reader (1226), then *prior (1237) at the *convent of *Lyon, provincial of the Roman province (1240-1244) and of France (1244-1254), fifth master of the order from 1254, he resigned on 20 May 1263. He retired to Lyon, where he devoted himself to his writings: he died at Valence. A skilful organiser, irenic and tenacious, he governed an order rich in strong personalities, faced with the most varied tasks and the dangerous opposition of the *seculars to the *mendicant orders at *Paris (1254-1258); supported by the *popes, making common front with the Friars Minor, he knew how to hold his own against the enemy as well as moderating his own friars. He completed (1254-1256) and got adopted (1267) the codification of the Dominican liturgy; gave a strong impetus to distant *missions (separated Christians, *Jews, Muslims) and, to prepare his friars, founded the *studia linguarum* (1255-1256); he put an end to the disengagement of the order from its *nuns, for whom in 1259 he procured their Constitutions for the next seven centuries; he ensured that studies flourished in the order without neglecting the contemplative life; finally, he applied his friars everywhere to the proclamation of the Word of God and the perfection of the regular life.

His literary activity was connected with his government and shows the same qualities of judgment, balance and pedagogy. He did not write *a priori*, but communicated what he had experienced in *ministry and government. With the exception of the *De dono timoris*, a collection of **exempla* composed before his provincialate, his writings date from his generalate and especially his retirement. 1) Writings as general, such as the 14 encyclicals to the order and the Prototype of the Dominican liturgy: *Ecclesiasticum officium secundum O. F. P.*, 14 books that regulated the Dominican liturgy until Vatican II. 2) On the regular life: *Epistola de regularis observantia disciplinae* (1254-1260); *Instructiones officialium O. F. P.* (1257-1267), the celebrated *customary of the order's *offices; *Expositio regulae B. Augustini episcopi* (1248-1254); *Expositio super constitutiones Fr. praed.* (before 1267); *Quaestiones quinque circa statuta O. P.* 3) On *preaching: the *Tractatus de dono timoris*, already cited; *De predicatione crucis* (1266-1268); *De eruditione predicatorum* (1266-1277), a very rich **summa* on preaching. 4) A report requested by *Gregory X to prepare the second council of *Lyon: *Opus tripartitum* (the *crusade; the Greeks; *reform). These last works are especially useful to history; they benefit from the information and judgment of the master of the *Dominicans on the order, on regular life, on Western society and its ecclesiastical and political problems, and reflect the attractive personality of the animator and educator of a great order at a privileged time.

T. Kaeppeli, *SOPMA*, 2, 1975, 283-295.

A. Mortier, *Histoire des maîtres généraux de l'ordre des Frères prêcheurs*, 1, Paris, 1903, 415-644. – F. Heintke, *Humbert von Romans, der fünfte Ordenmeister der Dominikaner*, Berlin, 1933 ("HS", 222). – M.-H. Vicaire, *Dsp*, 7, 1969, 1108-1116. – E. T. Brett, *Humbert of Romans*, *STPIMS*, 67, 1984.

Marie-Humbert Vicaire †

**HUMILIATI.** The name Humiliati designates a religious movement that developed in northern *Italy from the late 12th to the 14th c., whose members wore a poor-quality (*umile*) woollen garment. Like several other groups of that time (*penitents, *Poor Catholics, *Waldenses), it appealed to the evangelical ideal of *apostolic life.

Appearing in the towns of *Lombardy, in lay circles, the first Humiliati consisted of married people who remained in the world and mixed communities practising *continence. They lived poorly from the fruits of their labour, abstained from swearing *oaths or bearing arms, were clothed in grey, fasted more frequently than the ordinary faithful, mutually edified each other at Sunday meetings and gave themselves to public preaching. These religious activities exposed them to the suspicion of the *magisterium and they were condemned at the same time as the Waldenses in 1184. They differed from these, however, in the spiritual value they accorded to manual *labour and the esteem in which they held the state of matrimony. The return of most of them to the Church was the work of *Innocent III who, in 1201, organised them into three orders governed by a common general *chapter: the first, of *clerics (*canons and sisters), and the second, of continent laypeople living in double houses, adopted a monastic rule; the third, that of married people, was given a regulation or *Propositum*, the first document for the use of this form of life. From the mid 13th c., the movement was clericalized: the first order gradually absorbed the second; the third dwindled away, victim of the rivalry of the *Franciscan and *Dominican *Third Orders. The male branch was suppressed in 1571, but some female communities still exist in Italy.

During its phase of apogee, the movement enjoyed an influence that was not limited to the urban world but extended to the countryside: the communities of the *Bergamo region were as numerous in the city as in the *contado*. The Humiliati took an active part in economic life, particularly in the sector of the *textile industry, where they produced cloth of various qualities, not just high-quality textiles, as used to be thought. But the landed *patrimony they accumulated and their rural installations also involved them in agricultural work. Enjoying good social integration by reason of a varied recruitment, they were requested to fill various public offices. They enjoyed real favour among the faithful but it is hard to measure their religious influence, except by the preaching against *heresy to which they devoted themselves under episcopal control. In an original way, they testify to the efforts of the lay world to seek a way of perfection proper to itself.

A. Mens, "Humiliés", *DSp*, 7, 1, 1969, 1129-1136. – M. T. Brolis, *Gli Umiliati a Bergamo nei secoli XIII e XIV*, Milan, 1991. – F. Andrews, *The Early Humiliati*, Cambridge, 1999.

Catherine Vincent

**HUMILITY.** The Latin *humilitas* corresponds to the English "humility". To give an account of the exact content of the medieval concept of humility, it is best to expound the thought of three great teachers, St Bernard, St Thomas Aquinas and St Bonaventure.

For St *Bernard, humility is a *virtue acquired at the end of a dual approach. The first starts from true self-knowledge: "*Ego sum via, veritas et vita. Viam dicit humilitatem quae ducit ad veritatem* (I am the way, the truth and the life. [Christ] calls the way that leads to truth, humility)" (*De grad. hum.*, c. 1, n. 1: *PL*, 182, 941). The second starts from the *love that leads to the self-abasement of *Christ. It is his example that draws us: "We must be converted to the child God to learn of him that he is meek and humble of heart. The child has been given to us for that" (*Serm. 2 in quadrag.*: *PL*, 183, 171). The Virgin *Mary gives an admirable example: she esteemed herself lowly and at the same time she was magnanimous to believe in the divine promises (*Dom. infra oct. assumpt.*, *sermon [*PL*, 183, 457]). Thus, St Bernard can exhort us: "*Studete humilitati, quae fundamentum est custosque virtutum* (Cultivate humility which is the foundation and guardian of the virtues)" (*In nativ. dei*, serm. 1 [*PL*, 183, 115]).

In the *secunda secundae*, *Thomas Aquinas develops his *theology of the virtues. He studies humility as a kind of modesty. It is a virtue that tempers the *soul and prevents it from excessive desire of greatness and, in this sense, it is complementary to magnanimity which fortifies the soul and draws it to the pursuit of great things proposed to it by right *reason (q. 161, a. 1). It is evident that knowledge of our weakness is an element of humility and, as it were, a rule for the *will (a. 2). While acknowledging at their right value *God's gifts in oneself and in others, humility does not require us to put ourselves below our neighbour (a. 3). In this sense, humility suppresses self-confidence, and so it is connected with temperance as well as gentleness (a. 4). After the theological virtues, after the intellectual virtues, after *justice, especially legal justice, comes humility, the first of the other virtues (a. 5). It prepares the soul to rise freely towards spiritual goods (a. 6, ad 4).

The point of view adopted by *Bonaventure is altogether different. A faithful disciple of *Francis of Assisi for whom humility was the sister of *poverty, at the beginning of his disputed questions *De perfectione evangelica* he raises the question of the foundation of Christian perfection, humility that consists in external and internal contempt of self for the love of Jesus Christ. Biblical texts abound: Mt 18, 3 and 20, 27; Lk 17, 10 and 22, 26; Jn 13, 13-14; and above all Phil 2, 8-9 with a commentary by St Bernard. In conclusion, Bonaventure asserts that the sum of all Christian perfection consists in humility whose act is external and internal annihilation of self. It is the gate of *wisdom, the foundation of justice, the abode of *grace, since grace makes man acceptable to God; he who is acceptable to God is he who knows the gift that makes him worthy and the divine love that descends to him. To know this makes him conscious of his own unworthiness and confident in the power of God's love.

Thomas Aquinas, *Summa Theologiae*, II[a] II[ae], q. 161. – St Bonaventure, *Quaestiones disputatae de perfectione evangelica*, q. 1 (V, 117-124).

R. A. Gauthier, *Magnanimité. L'idéal de la grandeur dans la philosophie païenne et dans la théologie chrétienne*, Paris, 1951. – P. Adnes, "Humilité", *DSp*, 2, 1, 1969, 1136-1187.

Jacques-Guy Bougerol

**HUNAYN IBN ISHĀQ (808-873).** The greatest *Nestorian translator, from Greek to Syriac and from Syriac to Arabic. Born at al-Hīra (*Iraq), in the Christian tribe of the Ibād, he studied *medicine at *Baghdad, then Greek in Byzantine territory. Returning to Baghdad, he remained the official doctor of some ten *caliphs until his death. He made numerous translations in the spheres of medicine (Hippocrates and Galen) and philosophy (Plato and *Aristotle), *astronomy, *mathematics and oneiromancy. He composed several original works, including the *Book of Questions on Medicine* (translated into *Latin and *Hebrew), the *Book of Questions on the Eye* and a short defence of Christianity.

Hunayn ibn Ishāq, *The Book of the Ten treatises on the Eye*, M. Meyerhof (ed.), Cairo, 1928. – Hunayn ibn Ishāq, "Apologie du christianisme", K. Samir (ed.), P. Nwyia (ed.), *PO*, 40, 687-723.

Gérard Troupeau

**HUNDRED YEARS' WAR.** In 1328, the extinction of the line of "direct" *Capetians does not seem to have been felt in the kingdom of *France as a break in dynastic continuity. The *consecration of *Philip VI of Valois, the nearest heir in the male line, gave rise to no contention. But twelve years later, *Edward III of England, engaged for three years in an armed conflict with the king of France in *Flanders and Guyenne, chose to carry the struggle from the feudal terrain to the dynastic terrain. To destabilize his enemy's political situation, he claimed the French *crown as the nearest heir through the female line. Did this claim really correspond to Edward III's objectives, or was it just a polemical argument?

Against all expectation, the conflict was prolonged because of the weakness of the means employed by both opponents. The kings of France, Philip VI and then his son John II, could not triumph over their competitor. Despite the numerical superiority of their armies, they suffered a series of reverses: Sluys in 1340, Crécy in 1346 and above all Poitiers, a disaster marked by the capture of the king (1356). Despite this success and the political, social and economic crisis into which France was then plunged, Edward III, at the conclusion of the treaty of Brétigny in 1360, made only territorial gains that were admittedly substantial, but which revealed the limits of his French ambitions.

After a period of troubles (1360-1364), the king of France, *Charles V, was able to envisage a restoration of order and a plan of reconquest. After having regulated the Navarrese (1364) and Breton questions (1365), he opened a new phase of the struggle (1369-1380). Seconded by valiant men of war, such as Bertrand du Guesclin, advocating a tactic based on the defence of strongholds and a systematic refusal to confront the enemy in open country, the king let his enemy exhaust himself in vain expeditions. In 1380, on the death of Charles V, the English held nothing in France but Calais, Cherbourg and Bordeaux.

The years 1380-1390 saw a phase of reconciliation between the two kingdoms, *Charles VI in France and *Richard II in England both desiring appeasement. But this détente did not survive changes in both countries. In France, the madness of Charles VI left a free hand to princely rivalries, which turned into civil war between Armagnacs and Burgundians. In *England, the fall of Richard II and the rise to power of the Lancastrians were followed by new English claims on the crown of France.

*Henry V's victory at Agincourt (1415) and the treaty of *Troyes (1420), marking the rallying of the Burgundian party to the English cause, threatened the kingdom with partition. But the duration of the war and the peril in which the French Crown found itself had given rise to a hatred of the English and attachment to the king's cause. Combined, these two elements would take the place of "national feeling" and find an enthusiastic interpreter in *Joan of Arc.

The retreat of the English and the *consecration of *Charles VII (1429) marked a turning-point. The movement that had begun precipitated when, in 1435 (treaty of Arras), the king of France succeeded in detaching the duke of *Burgundy from the English alliance. From then on, after a profound reform of military institutions, profiting from the exhaustion of the enemy, Charles VII was able to expel him from the realm, recapturing *Normandy and the Bordelais between 1449 and 1453.

J. Favier, *La Guerre de Cent Ans*, Paris, 1980. – C. Allmand, *The Hundred Years War*, Cambridge, 1988. – P. Contamine, *War in the Middle Ages*, Oxford, 1984. – *Arms, Armies and Fortifications in the Hundred Years War*, A. Curry (ed.), M. Hughes (ed.), Woodbridge, 1994.

Bertrand Schnerb

**HUNGARY.** The *conversion of the Hungarian people and the establishment of the Christian kingdom of Hungary came about during the second half of the 10th century, in the reign of Duke Géza and that of his son Vajk, baptized *Stephen and crowned king in the year 1000. The Hungarian people already had a long history behind it, with its distant origin, its Finno-Ugric and Turkic components, its long migration from the direction of the Urals to the Caspian region, its affiliation to the State of the *Khazars, its continued migrations across the steppes ending in its occupation of the Carpathian basin at the end of the 9th c. under the leadership of Duke Árpád. The semi-nomadic state of the *Árpáds, established on the basis of seven Hungarian tribes and three "allied" tribes, threatened the whole *Empire with its military incursions at the beginning of the 10th century. Then, following the defeats of Merseburg (933) and Augsburg (955), the Hungarian people underwent a profound transformation, of which Christianization was the main instrument.

Missionaries arrived at that time from East and West. The Greek Church sought to convert the south-east parts (especially *Transylvania) from the middle of the 10th c., and its impact was felt over the centuries through half a dozen Greek monasteries. The conquests of Latin *Christendom were the work of Slav neighbours, but also of Germans and Italians. They were symbolized by three protagonists: the Czech St *Adalbert (Voytech, d. 997), second bishop of *Prague, who baptized St Stephen in 995; Gisela, Stephen's Bavarian wife, sister of the Emperor *Henry II, to whom German traditions ascribe the credit for the conversion of the Hungarians; and finally St Gerard (Gellért), bishop of Csanád († 1046), a product of the Venetian monastery of San Giorgio Maggiore, who was the effective organiser of the young Church of Hungary and also its first *martyr at the time of the *pagan uprising of 1046. Indeed the conversion of the Hungarians was not without violent elements; Stephen prevailed over his dynastic rivals and adversaries at the end of a bloody war of succession and imposed the new monastic and Christian order by often harsh measures. His main acts of foundation were the creation of the Benedictine monastery of *Pannonhalma (supposed birthplace of St *Martin) in the year 1000, the organisation of the first ten *bishoprics, the promulgation of decrees that obliged all the villages (in groups of "tens") to build churches, and the writing of a *Mirror of Princes, the *Libellus de instructione morum*, in which he brought together his personal admonitions on the principles of Christian royal government for the benefit of his son Imre.

These acts earned him *canonization in 1083. With Stephen, were canonised his son Imre, the *martyr bishop Gerard and two hermits, Andrew-Zoerard and Benedict. The canonisations were performed at the initiative of King *Ladislas (1077-1095) to end a long series of *revolts and religious and dynastic troubles after Stephen's death (1038). This consolidation of the gains of Christianity was reinforced by a second collection of laws, and by new ecclesiastical *foundations. The stabilizing work of Ladislas was continued by his nephew and successor Coloman (1095-1116).

The 12th century saw the development of new dynastic rivalries, reinforced by the domineering ambitions of the German Empire and that of Byzantium in the time of the *Comneni. The great king who put an end to these troubles, Béla III (1172-1196), had been raised at the court of Manuel Comnenus (who was moreover the grandson of St Ladislas). But Béla III managed to maintain Hungary's independence while forming links with the West. His second wife was Margaret Capet, daughter of *Louis VII, and his palace of *Esztergom was enlarged according to the plans of French architects. Under his chancery, an embryo of modern administration appeared in this kingdom, and his court gave a welcome to the first wave of chivalrous culture and courtly literature. In 1192 he obtained the canonization of St Ladislas, who at the same time incarnated a chivalrous ideal. His monastic foundations (Egres, Pilis, Szentgotthárd, Pásztó, Zirc) gave real support to the *Cistercian Order, present in Hungary since the middle of the century (Cikádor, 1142). Béla III's sons, Imre (1196-1204) and *Andrew II (1204-1235), brought the spirit of the *crusades to central Europe. This expedition, prepared for decades, was carried out by Andrew, who took part in the fifth crusade in 1217. The reign of Andrew II also saw important movements of the *nobility: he had to ratify, by the Golden Bull of 1222, the constitutional rights of the greater and lesser nobility and the Church – first European parallel to the English *Magna Carta of 1215. The tensions between the king and his *nobility during this time were also illustrated by the court intrigues that culminated in 1213 in the tragedy of the assassination of Queen Gertrude of Meran, mother of St *Elizabeth.

The first half of the 13th c. put Hungary in an important position for the policy of the Holy See. Its kings were entrusted with the task of organising a crusade against the Bosnian "*heretics". They also had to take part in the *conversion of the Cuman nomads coming from the East. All this explains the interest of the new *mendicant orders in Hungary, where they very quickly established themselves. The Dominican Paul of Hungary was the author of one of the first *confessors' manuals and it was an exploratory *mission by four Dominican friars, who set out in 1232 to renew links with the Hungarians who remained "in the former eastern homeland", that towards the end of the 1230s brought the news to the West of the disasters caused by the *Mongol invasion approaching from the East.

In fact, the troops of Batu Khan failed to annihilate the kingdom of Hungary. After the defeat of Muhi (1241), Béla IV had to leave the country and find refuge in *Dalmatia (at Trogir and Split) until the departure of the Mongol troops, who had no desire to conquer Hungary and rapidly left the country with their booty. Béla IV's main work was the reconstruction of the country after this devastation. This new beginning allowed him to undertake structural reforms at the level of power and of society. Thus he encouraged the building of fortresses and fortified towns, as had happened in the West in the 10th c. in reaction to the Hungarian invasions. In doing so, he sought to promote the formation of an aristocracy committed to the defence of the country, as well as the development of *towns, supported by the granting of new privileges. The mendicant orders enjoyed considerable influence in the policy of Béla IV, whose confessors were chosen first from the *Dominicans, then from the *Franciscans. He had himself buried by the latter in the monastery of *Esztergom. His daughter, St Margaret (1240-1270), born in Dalmatia, was vowed to the service of God with the aim of obtaining the country's liberation from the Tatars. She spent her life in a convent of Dominican *nuns, built for her on an island in the Danube near the new fortified town of *Buda, founded by Béla IV in 1243, which became the capital of Hungary from the end of the 14th century.

During the last ten years of his reign, Béla had had to share power with his son Stephen V (1270-1272) who in 1262 had been given the title of *rex iunior* and had taken possession of the eastern half of the country. Father and son opposed each other in a veritable war in 1264-1265, but neither of the two managed to prevail until the death of Béla IV. This situation favoured the dispersal of royal power and the setting up of autonomous territories in the hands of the barons, who relied on the multitude of new fortresses built after the invasion of the Tatars. The last decades of the 13th c., especially the reign of Ladislas IV surnamed the Cuman (1272-1290), were characterised by the growing influence of these territorial powers and a resurgence of orientalizing ethnic traditions. The theory of the kinship between the Hungarians and the *Huns was the central motif of the *chronicle of master Simon of Kéza, written in *c.*1282-1285; there was a fashion for Cuman clothes and hairstyles (adopted even by Ladislas IV's court circles), which recalled the distant nomadic past and gave substance to the idea of the Hungarians' Scythian origin.

The male line of the Árpáds was extinguished in 1301 after an agitated *interregnum*, and the claimant supported by the papacy, Charles Robert of Anjou (1309-1342), managed to install himself on the Hungarian throne, thus extending the dynastic power of the Neapolitan *Angevins in central Europe. After a series of victorious wars against the barons, he was able to follow a policy of economic and political reforms. Profiting from the great demand for *gold and silver in the early 14th c., the new mines opened at this time became the basis of the wealth of the kingdom of Hungary, expressed by the striking of a gold florin (1325). For the promotion of external trade, Charles Robert entered into negotiations with the neighbouring rulers: with *Casimir the Great of *Poland and John of Luxemburg, king of *Bohemia, he organised the famous meeting of Visegrád in 1335. Their political alliance was reinforced by dynastic links, which finally gave Charles Robert's son Louis the Great (1340-1382) the inheritance of the Polish throne in 1378 and allowed John of Luxemburg's grandson *Sigismund (1387-1437) finally to acquire the Hungarian throne. These alliances also indicate that, from the 14th c., these new dynasties sought to construct a conglomeration of *kingdoms in central Europe, united by a personal union around the reigning dynasty, an ambition which was lastingly realized by the *Habsburgs in the modern period.

The second half of the reign of Sigismund of Luxemburg was marked by the coexistence of the royal and imperial frameworks (he also became king of the Romans in 1410, Czech king in 1420 and emperor in 1433). At this time Hungary suffered the repercussions of the wars against the *Hussites, whose ideas had spread to the country. So in 1437 two ex-students of *Prague prepared the first translation of the New Testament and *Psalms into Hungarian. The peasant *revolts of 1437 in *Transylvania, though we find no trace of Hussite doctrines in them, saw the use of their most dreaded strategic weapon: entrenchments formed by wagons.

In the 14th and 15th cc., Hungary experienced a late flowering of chivalrous culture, manifested by the foundation of the Orders of St George (1326) and the Dragon (1408), the multiplication of *tournaments and the appearance of legendary warrior heroes (like Nicholas Toldy, a knight of Louis the Great). The cultural *patronage of Louis and Sigismund made itself felt in several fields. The kings' favourite order was that of the Hermits of St Paul (the one religious order of Hungarian foundation), for which King Louis obtained in 1381, at the time of a peace agreement with *Venice, bodily *relics of its patron saint.

The Hungarian kings were not so effective in promoting their country's university culture as were the Czechs (*Prague, 1347), Austrians (*Vienna, 1365) or Poles (*Cracow, 1367). The foundations of the *university of Pécs (Fünfkirchen) and the *studium* of Óbuda (1389, 1410) were not followed up. On the other hand, the *court of these kings became a centre of influence for the new Italian *humanism: Sigismund received, among others, *Poggio Bracciolini in Hungary.

Hungary's major problem towards the end of the Middle Ages was soon the advance of *Ottoman power over the Balkan peninsula, posing a threat to the Empire. The danger was already felt in 1396, when Sigismund's knights suffered a humiliating defeat at *Nicopolis. The career of 15th-c. Hungary's greatest military figure, John *Hunyadi, a native of *Transylvania born to a family of lesser nobility of Romanian origin, was connected with the effective wars of defence against the Turkish attacks, waged from 1439. With his private mercenary *army, John Hunyadi rapidly rose to the heights of power. In 1443-1444 he commanded campaigns of counter-attack as far as *Bulgaria, but these ended in a political tragedy: at the battle of Varna, the young and ambitious King Ladislas Jagiellon (1440-1444) was killed. In 1446, John Hunyadi was elected governor of the country alongside the young King Ladislas V (1444-1458), son of Albert of Habsburg (1437-1440), first king of that dynasty in Hungary. Continuing his military activity, he won an important victory at Belgrade in 1456, which halted the Turkish advance for several decades, but died shortly afterwards during an *epidemic.

John Hunyadi's prestige allowed him to get his son *Matthias Corvinus elected king, despite the ambitions of the Habsburgs. The reign of Matthias (1458-1490), with his famous court peopled by Italian humanists (Galeotto Marzio, Antonio Bonfini) and the first generation of Hungarian humanists (John Vitéz, Janus Pannonius, Johannes Regiomontanus), with his famous "Corvinian" *library, with his formidable Black Army which advanced as far as Vienna in 1485, with a policy of efficient centralization and with a new increase in urban evolution and especially in the prosperity of his capital *Buda, crowned the evolution of medieval Hungary and marked the opening of a new period, that of the *Renaissance.

*Catalogus fontium historiae Hungariae*, F. Gombos (ed.), 1-4, Budapest, 1937-1940. – *Scriptores rerum Hungaricarum*, E. Szentpétery (ed.), 1-2, Budapest, 1938. – J. M. Bak, L. S. Domonkos, J. S. Sweeney, *Decreta regni mediaevalis Hungariae*, 1-3, Idyllwild (CA), 1992-1997.

S. de Vajay, *Der Eintritt des ungarischen Stämmebundes*, Mainz, 1968. – J. Deér, *Heidnisches und Christliches in der altungarischen Monarchie*, Darmstadt, 1969 (2nd ed.). – G. Moravcsik, *Byzantium and the Magyars*, Amsterdam, 1970. – J. Szűcs, *Theoretical Elements in Master Simon of Kéza's Gesta Hungarorum*, Budapest, 1975. – J. Szűcs, *Nation und Geschichte*, Budapest, 1981. – J. M. Bak, B. Király, *From Hunyadi to Rákóczi: War and Society*, New York, 1982. – J. Szűcs, *Les Trois Europes*, Paris, 1985. – E. Fügedi, *Castle and Society in Medieval Hungary*, Budapest, 1986. – E. Fügedi, *Kings, Bishops, Nobles and Burghers in Medieval Hungary*, London, 1986. – G. Klaniczay, "From Sacral Kingship to Self-Representation", *The Uses of Supernatural Power*, Cambridge, 1990, 79-128. – *L'histoire de la Transylvanie*, B. Köpeczi (ed.), Budapest, 1992. – G. Kristó, P. Engel, F. Makk, *Korai magyar történeti lexikon*, Budapest, 1994. – G. Kristó, *Hungarian History in the Ninth Century*, Szeged, 1996.

Gábor Klaniczay

**HUNS.** Originally from central Asia, the Huns do not appear in Western sources until Ptolemy (AD 160-170), when they were settled between the Volga and the Don. At the end of the 4th c., they moved towards the *Caucasus and subjected the Alans, who helped them destroy the Gothic kingdom in 375; from then on, part of the Goths remained subject to them.

Hunnic civilization is known from Western written sources and from archaeological sites occupied by the Huns and other nomads between the late 4th and early 5th centuries. These sites are concentrated in the regions of the middle and lower Danube, in the steppes to the north of the Black Sea and the Volga. They are mainly isolated tombs, with cremation or inhumation, mostly under tumuli (kurgans), and deposits of offerings of a ritual character. Funerary furnishings were composed of a great number of elements of harness (but neither stirrups nor spurs, which the nomads did not use), double-edged swords, bone arrow-heads and polychrome ornaments of a fashion attested among the aristocracy of the European *barbarian kingdoms up to the 6th century.

From 425, the Huns formed a veritable State in *Pannonia. Attila, coming to power with his brother Bleda in 434, then sole king from 445, regularly launched raids against the Eastern Empire between 441 and 448; he obliged the emperor to pay him ever heavier tributes. Until 450, thanks to his friendship with the *magister militum* Aetius, he maintained good relations with the Western emperor, for whom he even provided soldiers. But, following a call for help by Honoria, sister of Valentinian III, he launched a first raid against the Roman Empire in 451, the aim of which was not to make conquests but to pick up as much booty as possible and to force Valentinian III to grant him Honoria's hand. The Huns crossed the Rhine near *Mainz, ravaged the province of Belgica Prima (*Metz was burned on 7 April) and, from the end of May, beseiged *Orléans. The town was delivered only in mid-June by Aetius's troops, the Visigothic army and Frankish troops. The Huns made an about-turn and confronted the "Romans" near *Troyes, on the Campus Mauriacus. The battle was murderous on both sides (Theodoric, king of the *Visigoths, was killed) and so the Huns, though defeated, were able to re-enter Pannonia without being harried. In spring 452 they entered *Italy and pillaged the whole north of the peninsula; Attila died shortly after their return to Pannonia (453). His empire, disputed among his sons, was then dismembered. The Huns were driven back to the steppes of south Russia where they fused with other nomadic peoples of Turkic origin coming from Asia, with whom they formed a new confederation of nomads, the *Bulgars.

E. Demougeot, *La Formation de l'Europe et les Invasions Barbares*, 3, Paris, 1979, 521-557. – L. Musset, *Les Invasions, les vagues germaniques*, Paris, 1995, 74-78 (3rd ed.). – E.A. Thompson, *The Huns*, Oxford, 1996.

Michèle Gaillard

**HUNTING.** In the Middle Ages, hunting still fulfilled its old functions of protection from an omnipresent animal world (protection of crops and livestock) and complementary source of *food and *clothing. But it was also for many an important distraction, or even the "diversion" *par excellence*, a sport and a passion. Indeed all social groups were attracted to it and practised it as they had opportunity. For *peasants, this meant traps and snares, from simple nooses to vast nets for migrating birds, pits filled with pikes or enclosures containing haunches of meat to attract wild beasts. On occasion the *nobility practised this "knaves'" hunting, but they marked their distinction by their devotion to hunting with hawk and hound. The former, codified in the West by *Frederick II of Hohenstaufen in the 13th c., involved the training of birds of prey and sophisticated techniques. The latter was done on horseback with packs of hounds; it was inseparable from the pleasure of galloping and living with dogs. Hence it demanded luck, endurance and the art of combat, since, *e.g.*, to kill a boar nobly consisted of running it through with a sword without leaving the saddle. Preceded and followed by a common meal, it was also a time of masculine conviviality, though women were sometimes invited to take part in falconing. From the mid 14th c., of animals hunted with hounds, the stag became the prey *par excellence*; it was the royal chase with an obvious social connotation. Consequently, great men sought to enclose the *forests for their exclusive use, like that of Compiègne in the Île-de-France. The phenomenon was not new, but it had not yet taken on the dimensions it did between the 16th and 18th cc., when it tended to exclude the peasant world from hunting and confine it to the shameful practice of poaching.

In these conditions a hunting literature arose in the 14th c., whose great classic, up to the mid 16th c., was the *Livre de chasse* that Gaston Phoebus, lord of Foix-Béarn, began to dictate in 1387. This work begins with an outline of the natural history of the animals to be hunted, then minutely describes the world of dogs and the art of training them and caring for them, before starting on the hunt itself, followed by a section on trapping and snaring. It is also an *apologia* that dwells on all the virtues of the chase. This is not just a propaedeutic for war, but allows men to live joyously, in good health and in communion with *nature. Better still, its virtue extends beyond this. Indeed Phoebus claims that all hunters – rich or poor, great or small – will be lodged "at least in the outskirts of paradise", always providing they do not neglect the offices of religion. Why such a dignity? Laziness is the source of all the sins that lead to *hell; but the hunter is never lazy: he always has his "bad imagination" held in check. Thus protected from *sin, he will go to *paradise. The author concludes with this formula: "Never did I see a man who loved working with dogs who did not have good qualities in himself, for this comes to him of right *noblesse* and *gentillesse* of heart."

*The Art of Falconry by Frederick II of Hohenstaufen*, C. A. Wood (ed.), F. M. Fyfe (ed.), Stanford (CA), 1943 (repr. 1981). – Gaston Phébus, *Livre de Chasse*, G. Tilander (ed.), Karlshamn, 1971 ("Cynegetica", 18).

J.M. Gilbert, *Hunting and Hunting Reserves in Medieval Scotland*, Edinburgh, 1979. – *La Chasse au Moyen Âge*, Paris, 1980. – A. Rooney, *Hunting in Middle English Literature*, Woodbridge, 1993.

Pierre Tucoo-Chala

**HUNYADI.** A family of southern *Transylvania, the Hunyadi ("of Hunyad") saw one of their members become king of *Hungary under the name of *Matthias I.

The glorious political and military career of Matthias's father John Hunyadi marked the social rise of this Romanian family of lesser *nobility. Born *c.*1409, John Hunyadi soon got himself noticed by King *Sigismund of Luxemburg (1387-1437) by his skill in fighting the *Ottoman enemy, which led to his being appointed voivode of Transylvania. Regent of the kingdom during the captivity of the young King Ladislas V (1446), then "supreme captain" on the latter's liberation in 1453, he made himself famous throughout *Christendom by his last victory against the *Turks, at Belgrade (1456) – on this occasion the *pope conferred on him the title of "defender of the faith" – but he died soon after.

Z. Teke, *Hunyadi János és kora* [John Hunyadi and his Time], Budapest, 1980. – *From Hunyadi to Rakoczi*, J. M. Bak (ed.), B. K. Kiraly (ed.), Boulder (CO), 1982. – J. Held, *Hunyadi: Legend and Reality*, Boulder (CO), 1985.

Marie-Madeleine de Cevins

**HUS, JAN (*c.*1370-1415); HUSSITES.** The Hussites were a Czech reforming movement who bore the name of their founder and tribune. Jan Hus (*c.*1370-6 July 1415), a professor at the *university of *Prague and preacher at Bethlehem chapel, continued in some ways the actions of his compatriots *Milíč of Kroměříž († 1374) and Matthew of Janov († 1394), but the source of his ideas was the work of the *Oxford theologian John *Wycliffe. After the reorganisation of the system of self-government at the university of Prague, which favoured the Czech national group and to which he made a decisive contribution in Jan 1409, the ecclesiastical authorities intensified their proceedings against Hus. From 1412, when he opposed King *Wenceslas IV in the matter of the trade in plenary *indulgences, he lived mostly in the countryside.

From this period date his major works, notably the treatise *De ecclesia*, in which Hus, following his Oxford master, demanded a radical *reform of the schismatic Church with the co-operation of the secular powers, invoking the validity for everyone of the strict norms of "divine law". But the ideal that he aimed at was not the establishment of a new *social order, but rather the amelioration of the existing situation through the overall harmonization of the relations between rich and poor or between lords and serfs. Trusting in the victory of his truth, Hus agreed in autumn 1414 to go to the council of *Constance which wished to hear him. But shortly after his arrival, he was arrested and then judged for *heresy.

His death at the stake (6 July 1415) aroused a powerful wave of protest in *Bohemia and favoured the rapid propagation of the reform movement, whose rallying-sign would be the *communion of the *laity in both kinds (*utraquism). Thanks to the resolute support of the *nobility won over to their ideas, the teaching of the university reformers became equally rooted in the countryside. The growing pressure of the university authorities against the movement contributed to hardening it, notably in southern *Bohemia where the very influential community of the *Taborites was founded in spring 1420. The declaration of a crusade launched against them obliged all the Hussite currents to unite in a "holy war" to defend their common programme, contained in the "Four Articles of Prague" (freedom to confess the divine word, *chalice for the laity, secularization of Church property, chastisement of mortal sins). At the end of 14 years of wars, crusades and Hussite expeditions into the neighbouring countries, these four articles, though much watered-down, would serve as basis for the peace accords (called **compactata*) concluded by the delegates of the Hussite federations with Emperor *Sigismund of Luxemburg and the representatives of the council of *Basel.

The Hussite wars formed moreover the centre of gravity of a process of internal upheavals, whose long-term repercussions often had a revolutionary character. In the first place, we must emphasize the great importance of the coexistence, legalized at the cost of numerous sacrifices, of two Christian confessions in the same country, with a degree of religious *toleration unique for the time. The Hussite period hardly improved, but nor did it make worse, the living conditions of the small people of the *towns and *villages. At Prague and in the other Hussite cities, the Czech nation consolidated its positions, while in the main towns of *Moravia the German *Catholics retained all their influence. The secularized goods of the clergy would mainly go to enrich the nobility. Before the revolution, only the higher barons opposed the sovereign in struggles for power, while the post-Hussite *monarchy henceforth had to reckon with the two perfectly constituted estates of the greater and lesser nobility. And little by little, the royal towns were

*Jan Hus condemned to the stake.* Miniature from Ulrich of Richental's *Chronicle*, 15th c. Prague, University National Library.

organised in their turn into an autonomous third estate. The pact of general religious compromise (March 1485) set the seal on the Hussite period and accelerated the transition to the rise of a monarchy based on the system of estates general.

M. Spinka, *John Hus's Concept of the Church*, Princeton (NJ), 1966. – H. Kaminsky, *A History of the Hussite Revolution*, Berkeley-Los Angeles, 1967. – J. Macek, *Jean Hus et les traditions hussites*, Paris, 1973. – P. de Vooght, *L'Hérésie de Jean Huss*, 1-2, Louvain, 1975. – F. Šmahel, *La Révolution hussite, une anomalie historique*, Paris, 1985. – F. Bartoš, *The Hussite Revolution, 1424-1437*, Boulder (CO), 1986. – F. Seibt, *Hussitica. Zur Struktur einer Revolution*, Cologne-Vienna, 1990. – E. Werner, *Jan Hus*, Weimar, 1991. – T. A. Fudge, *The Magnificent Ride. The First Reformation in Hussite Bohemia*, Aldershot-Brookfield-Singapore-Sydney, 1998.

František Šmahel

**HYACINTH (late 12th c. – 13th c.).** St Hyacinth, a *Dominican, was canonized in 1594. His real name was Jacek (changed to Hyacinth in the 14th c.) of Opole (*Silesia). Entering the order at Rome, he was sent to *Poland by St *Dominic in 1221. He founded the *convent of *Cracow (1222) and, with missionary aims, those of *Gdańsk (1227) and *Kiev (1228), where he preached from 1229 to 1233. *Definitor at the *chapter *generalissimus* of 1228, he preached the *crusade at *Gniezno in 1238. His fame as founder, preacher and apostle of the *Slavs and his reputation as a *thaumaturge, known through *Bernard Gui (from 1277) and lists of *miracles (1268-1290), triggered off an aberrant *hagiography in the 16th and 17th centuries.

R. Loenertz, *AFP*, 27, 1957, 5-38. – B. Stasiewski, *LThK*, 5, 1960, 553. – A. Duval, *Cath.*, 5, 1962, 1121-1122.

Marie-Humbert Vicaire †

**HYLOMORPHISM.** The term "hylomorphism", coined in the 19th c., designates the doctrine going back to *Aristotle according to which everything that exists or moves – *i.e.* that is mobile in the broadest sense of the term – is determined by two principles: that of the "mobility" of matter (in Greek *hyle*; in Latin *materia*) and that of *ontological form (in Greek *morphè*; in Latin *forma*). The main object of debate was to ascertain whether hylomorphism was a universal theory, *i.e.* whether everything that existed was constructed on the form-matter principle (as *Bonaventure and *Roger Bacon thought, following *Avicebron) or whether it was valid only for material substances (*Thomas Aquinas).

F. Brunner, *Platonisme et aristotélisme. La critique d'Ibn Gabirol par saint Thomas d'Aquin*, Louvain-Paris, 1965. – F. Van Steenberghen, *La Philosophie au XIII^e^ siècle*, Louvain, 1966.

Rolf Schönberger

## HYMN, HYMNOLOGY

**The West.** From the Latin *hymnus*, a hymn is a lyrical chant, in metrical or rhythmical verses, intended to enrich the *spirituality of the *office. It expresses the mystery of the day in poetic terms, while being a solemn act of profession of faith. It may take place at the beginning of the office or after the *reading, when it favours reflection on the Word. Its essential function is to introduce a lyrical element into the liturgy. The alternation of hymns with *psalms, the practice of relating them to the hour of the day so as to express its meaning better, and the omnipresent trinitarian praise, characterise the profound essence of hymns. Some were written by great figures of Latin Christianity, like Hilary of Poitiers or St Ambrose.

The old monastic *Rules, notably that of St *Benedict, specify the liturgical role of hymns from the 6th c. and suggest the existence of repertoires proper to the different *hours of the liturgy of the office. Before the 11th c., hymns were used exclusively by monks, before also being adopted by communities of *canons and by every *cleric celebrating the office.

The question of the origin of a liturgical hymnal, hence of an appropriate book, is not yet entirely clear. Though we cannot go back to the Benedictine hymnal, up to the mid 8th c. we know fragments of repertoires from which we must exclude the *Ambrosian hymns, which in the Middle Ages were not circulated in the form of a collection. Only in the late 8th and early 9th cc. was the first Frankish monastic hymnal put in place, soon to be supplanted by the "official" hymnal of St *Benedict of Aniane, the great Carolingian reformer. This official hymnal may have been prepared by *Alcuin († 804) at *Tours under Ambrosian influence.

Several creations came into being in the Carolingian period, such as the **Veni Creator Spiritus*, quite likely by *Rabanus Maurus, and enriched the repertoire, increasingly organised according to the hours and days of the *liturgical year. Certain hymns were sometimes the occasion for their author to take up a position on contemporary theological debates. From this time, the repertoire of hymns was ceaselessly enriched by pieces, each new *feast or office entailing a creation of its own.

In the manuscript tradition, the earliest known hymnals (8th c.) are in the form of composite books. Many are psalter-hymnals, or are found twinned with other pieces of the *office (collects, canticles, readings). In non-liturgical *psalters, the hymnal part generally closes the manuscript. In liturgical psalters, the hymns are apportioned within hours and feasts.

The first independent hymnals appeared in the 9th c. References in old *library catalogues confirm the existence of this book as an independent *codicological entity at that time. In the 10th and 11th cc., meet references to the same effect in monastic *customaries.

Most often, these manuscripts transmit the repertoire of this or that tradition, in which the pieces are ordered according to the liturgical year, but without notation. Through the whole of the Western Middle Ages, no original repertoire imposed itself on all the liturgical traditions. This diversity was reinforced by the great variety of melodies that existed for the same hymn.

In the second half of the Middle Ages, the hymnal was, like the other books of the office, integrated into the *breviary.

Hypogeum "of the Dunes", Poitiers. At the bottom of the access stairway, the foot of a monumental cross. 8th c.

J. Szöverffy, *Die Annalen der lateinischen Hymnendichtung. Ein Handbuch, I. Die lateinischen Hymnen bis zum Ende des 11. Jahrhunderts, II. Die lateinischen Hymnen vom Ende des 11. Jahrhunderts bis zum Ausgang des Mittelalters*, Berlin, 1964. – H. Gneuss, *Hymnar und Hymnen im englischen Mittelalter*, Tübingen, 1968. – J. Fontaine, *Naissance de la poésie dans l'Occident chrétien. Esquisse d'une histoire de la poésie latine chrétienne du III^e^ au VI^e^ siècle*, Paris, 1981. – *The Canterbury Hymnal*, G. R. Wieland (ed.), Toronto, 1982. – J. Szoverffy, *A Concise History of Medieval Latin Hymnody*, Leiden, 1985. – J. Szöverffy, *Latin Hymns, TSMÂO*, 55, 1989. – I. B. Milfull, *The Hymns of the Anglo-Saxon Church*, Cambridge, 1996.

Éric Palazzo

**Byzantium.** The Greek word *humnos* (Latin equivalent *hymnus*) signified generically any song of praise. In this sense it was used in the Septuagint, by St *Paul, who recommended the use of "psalms, hymns and inspired canticles", and by patristic writers. The use of the word hymn only of sacred poems, intended to be chanted or sung, that are neither *psalms nor biblical odes. is modern convenience.

The earliest Byzantine hymns were known as *troparia*, sung during *orthros* and *vespers and inserted after each verse of a psalm. Another word commonly in use was *sticheron*, a form of **troparion* written in rhythmic prose and offering a *meditation suitable for the day. One of the most beautiful of the *troparia* is the *phôs hilarón* (joyful light), probably written in *Palestine as early as the 5th c. but only introduced into *Constantinople with the 9th-c. Studite reform of the *office. Perhaps as early as the 5th c., *kontakia* were introduced into the recitation of *orthros*. The *kontakion* was probably of Syrian origin. One of the most prolific composers of *kontakia* at Byzantium was Romanus the Melode (born in Emesa, *Syria, died after 555). These *homilies in verse began with an introduction (*prooimion*), followed by a series of stanzas (*oikoi*), linked to the *prooimion* by a refrain. The *oikoi* were linked by an *acrostic. Although Romanus the Melode was revered and canonized by the *Byzantine Church, *kontakia*, with one exception, were not permanently integrated into Byzantine worship. This exception was the *Akathistos* hymn. It owes its name to the fact that it was sung standing. According to legend it was first sung in thanksgiving for the failure of the *Avar siege of *Constantinople. Specialists, however, attribute an earlier date to it; they do not consider Romanos to have been its author. The *Akathistos*, which includes 24 *oikoi* linked acrostically, is further embellished with a series of salutations to the *Theotokos. The theme of the first 12 *oikoi* is the history of the Incarnation. The second 12 *oikoi* constitute a meditation on its *mystery. When other *kontakia* fell out of use, the *Akathistos* continued to be sung on the feast of the Annunciation and during *Lent. From the 8th c., both biblical odes and *kontakia* disappeared from *orthros*, being replaced by Kanons, which paraphrase the biblical odes.

Original chant was monophonic, unaccompanied and in free *rhythm, intended to be sung by all. From the mid 9th c., specialized *music for professional choirs was introduced.

E. Wellesz, *A History of Byzantine Music and Hymnography*, Oxford, 1961. – K. Mitsakis, *Byzantine Hymnographia*, Thessalonica, 1971. – J. Szoverffy, *A Guide to Byzantine Hymnography*, Brookline (MA), 1978. – D. E. Conomos, *Byzantine Hymnography and Byzantine Chant*, Brookline, 1984. – A.F. Gove, *The Slavic Akathistos Hymn*, Munich, 1988.

Christopher Walter

**HYPAPANTE (PRESENTATION OF JESUS IN THE TEMPLE).** This Greek term means "meeting"; at *Constantinople from the 6th c., it designated a *feast celebrated at *Jerusalem from the second half of the 4th c. to commemorate the meeting of the aged Symeon with the child Jesus on the day of his *Presentation in the Temple, 40 days after his birth, a feast accompanied from 450 by a *procession with candles.

Accepted at *Rome in the 7th c. under its original name, in the Frankish lands it received the name "*Purification of the Virgin", which it kept until the 20th c. when it recovered its original meaning as a feast of the Lord under the title "Presentation in the Temple", which had been given it by the French liturgies of the 17th century.

At Rome, the characteristic procession with candles had by 1970 taken on a penitential character and remained immovably attached to the date of 2 Feb, though the feast itself was transferred to another date. We must doubtless see here the desire to superimpose a Christian feast on the pagan fertility rites traditional at the start of this month. The chants that accompanied it retain traces of their Greek origin.

"Présentation", *DACL*, 14, 2, 1948, 1722-1729. – "Présentation", *Cath.*, 11, 1988, 847-849.

Irénée-Henri Dalmais

**HYPOGEUM.** The Greek word "hypogeum", meaning "underground", was used by the Ancients to designate *e.g.* the chambers and galleries of catacombs. In modern archaeological usage, it designates sunken rooms for funerary use, dug in the ground or built and sometimes provided with superstructures: for the early Middle Ages, the best example in France is the hypogeum of Les Dunes at *Poitiers, which housed the *tomb of Abbot Mellebaude, *relics and an *altar. The *crypts and confessions of medieval churches are like substitutes for the old hypogea.

C. de La Croix, *Monographie de l'hypogée-martyrium de Poitiers*, Paris, 1883. – H. Leclercq, "Hypogée", *DACL*, 6, 2, 1925, 3932-3945.

Jean Guyon

# I

**IAROSLAV THE WISE (*c.*978-1054).** Son of *Vladimir I and Rogneda, Iaroslav occupied the throne of *Kiev in 1019, and in 1036 reigned alone over *Rus'. Under his aegis, Kievan Rus' enjoyed a political and cultural rise made illustrious by the matrimonial alliances that united his children to the reigning families of the West and Byzantium, by the rebuilding of the *cathedral of St Sophia (1037-1046), which became the model for Russian stone architecture, and by an important intellectual activity (translation of various Byzantine works into Slavonic and, perhaps, first redaction of a Russian law).

G. Vernadsky, *Kievian Russia*, New Haven, 1948, 74-83. – A. Poppe, "The Building of the Church of St Sophia in Kiev", *JMH*, 7, 1981, 15-66.

Irène Sorlin

**IBN BĀJJA (late 11th c. – 1139).** Andalusian philosopher, scholar, poet and musician (born at *Saragossa, died at *Fez). Reacting against the criticism of *philosophy made by al-*Ghazālī in the name of religious orthodoxy, he asserted that it was possible for man to attain *beatitude by uniting his *intellect with the divine – not *God himself but the Active Intellect – by a continual process of *abstraction through a hierarchy of "spiritual forms". He influenced *Averroes and through him was received by the West under the name of Avempace. *Albert the Great seems to have known his work directly and refers to him also on the scientific level. *Thomas Aquinas dedicated a chapter of the *Contra gentiles* to refuting his likening of the *knowledge of an essence abstracted from the sensible to that of an intelligible *substance.

J. Lomba, *Avempace*, Saragossa, 1989.

Dominique Urvoy

**IBN HAZM (994-1064).** Andalusian thinker and polygraph (born at *Cordova, died at Huelva). His *Dove's Neck Ring* (*Tawk al-hamama*), which details the psychological topics of *love, may have indirectly influenced the *troubadours. His *Chapters on the Religions* insist on the internal contradictions of biblical texts in order to invalidate them. With him the interpretation of the Koranic concept of *tahrīf* of the biblical Scriptures no longer just as "alteration of sense", but as "textual alteration", became general in *Islam. Though not admitted by all, this acceptation incited Christian missionaries (notably Raymond *Lull) to abandon Scriptural arguments in favour of rational proofs.

Ibn Hazm, *Tawq al-hamâma (De l'amour et des amants)*, G. Martinez (tr.), Paris, 1992.

R. Arnaldez, *Grammaire et théologie chez Ibn Hazm de Cordoue*, Paris, 1956. – C. Adang, *Islam frente a judaismo*, Cordoba, 1994. – C. Adang, *Muslim Writers on Judaism and the Hebrew Bible*, New York, 1996.

Dominique Urvoy

**IBN KHALDŪN (1332-1406).** Abū Zayd Abd ar-Rahmān ibn Khaldūn al-Hadramī, a great 14th-c. Maghrebian historian, author of a theory of society that, since its rediscovery early in the 19th c., has been rightly regarded by the moderns as a major work, forerunner of most of the human sciences. Born at Tunis to a family of high officials of Andalusian origin, he received a sound legal, literary and scientific education. In the first period of his life, spent in the *Maghreb, he held high office in the kingdoms of Tunis, *Fez and Tlemçen, and travelled to *Spain. He had opportunity to gain an intimate knowledge of court life and the functioning of States, and to observe the world of the Arab and Berber tribes. But at the age of 43 he decided to retire from public life and dedicate himself to *science. In the space of five months he wrote the first version of the *Muqaddima*, an "introduction" to his Universal history, the *Kitāb al-Ibar* (the Book of Examples). Some years later he left Tunis to settle permanently at *Cairo, where the *Mamluk sultan az-Zāhir Barqūq put him in charge of education and justice. At the same time he continued, until the end of his life, toiling to finish his historical work. Five years before his death in 1406, he met *Timur Lenk. Of his long negotiations with him, he left a gripping account in his *Autobiography*.

Ibn Khaldūn's work thus has two sides: one theoretical, the other historical. He started from the project of writing a new synthesis of the history of the Maghreb, which finally took on the dimensions of a universal history. But, dissatisfied with the traditional methods of authentification and verification of facts, he worked out a science of society (*ilm al-ijtimā al-insānī*) as a preliminary to all writing of history. After having defined the bases of human civilization in general (*al-umrān*) – necessity of life in society, influence of geography and *climate, relation to the transcendent – he successively presents the laws governing agro-pastoral (*al-badāwa*) and urban (*al-hadāra*) societies, which constitute, according to him, the two great stages of human evolution. He shows how the transition from one to the other is effected, through the formation of central power and States. Most of the concepts that he forged for the needs of his analyses, like those of *asabiya* (team spirit, solidarity), *istinā* (adoption of clients), *mulk* (central power), *jāh* (social prestige), as well as the explanatory models that he proposed for a great number of social phenomena, still retain all their pertinence and continue to inspire the anthropological and sociological labours of Muslim countries.

Ibn Khaldūn's historical work is no less important. By his original organisation, his critical point of view and the mass of information that he provides, especially on the Maghreb countries and Mamluk Egypt in the time of az-Zāhir Barqūq, he remains essential to the historian.

Ibn Khaldūn, *Histoire des Berbères et des dynasties musulmanes de l'Afrique septentrionale*, W. de Slane (tr.), Paris, 1863 (4 vol.). – Ibn Khaldūn, *Les Prolégomènes*, W. de Slane (tr.), Paris, 1863 (3 vol.). – Ibn Khaldun, *The Muqqadinah*, F. Rosenthal (ed., tr.), Princeton (NJ), 1967. – Ibn Khaldūn, *Discours sur l'Histoire universelle*, V. Monteil (tr.), Beirut, 1967-1968 (3 vol., 2nd ed. Paris, 1978). – Ibn Khaldūn, *Le Voyage d'Occident et d'Orient. Autobiographie*, A. Cheddadi (tr.), Paris, 1980.

A. Cheddadi, "Le système de pouvoir en Islam d'après Ibn Khaldûn", *Annales*, May-August 1980, 534-550. – A. Al-Azmeh, *Ibn Khaldûn in Modern Scholarship*, London, 1981. – J. W. Anderson, "Conjuring with Ibn Khaldûn: From an Anthropological Point of View", *Journal of Asian and African Studies*, 18, Leiden, 3-4, 1983. – *Ibn Khaldun and Islamic Theology*, B.B. Lawrence (ed.), Leiden, 1984.

Abdesselam Cheddadi

**IBN PAKŪDA (1040-1110).** The Jewish philosopher Bahya ibn Pakūda lived at *Saragossa, capital of the tolerant Hudid *taifa*, where he held the post of judge of the Jewish community. He was the author of the *Duties of the Heart*, an extremely popular treatise on mysticism, in which he appears as a man of fervent piety and immense trust in God. Going beyond simple religious practices, he emphasizes the rational dimension of religious life and affirms that God has given man the means to attain knowledge of him by the way of *contemplation, without having to renounce the world. Written in Arabic, his work was translated into *Hebrew by Ibn Tibbon in 1161.

Ibn Pakuda, *The Book of Direction to the Duties of the Heart*, M. Mansoor (tr.), London, 1973.

G. Vajda, *La Théologie ascétique de Bahya ibn Paqūda*, Madrid, 1950. – L. Suarez Fernández, *Judios españoles en la edad Media*, Madrid, 1980 (Fr. tr., *Les Juifs espagnols au Moyen Âge*, Paris, 1983). – J. Lomba Fuentes, *Filosofía judía en Zaragoza*, Saragossa, 1988.

Philippe Sénac

**ICELAND.** Iceland was colonized by a mixture of Norwegians (from the south-east of their country) and Celts (recruited in the North Atlantic islands, Orkneys, Hebrides, Shetlands, and in northern *Scotland or northern *Ireland) from 874. Modern *archaeology demonstrates, however, that Celts, probably Irish, had discovered and inhabited the island before the Scandinavians. What is certain is that from 874 (at which date a certain Ingólfr Arnarson settled at the place now called Reykjavík) and until 930, a certain number of families – about forty in all, seemingly – came to settle in Iceland for various reasons, the primary one being certainly bound up with the attraction that any new land exercised on the Scandinavians of the time (but not, to put paid to a legend accredited since the 13th c., to flee the tyranny of the Norwegian king Harald Fairhair). This manner of establishment and the rites that presided over it are described in detail by a book that has no equivalent elsewhere, the *Book of the Colonization of Iceland*. In 930, this little society decided to give itself a legislation. To this end, it sent to *Norway a "specialist" who returned with a code that gave rise to the future Icelandic legislation. In effect there was set up, from 930, a society perfectly original for the Middle Ages, which wanted no king nor any kind of obedience and which entrusted the exercise of power to those of its nationals who, at the time, could prove the antiquity of their family and were possessed of evident wealth: these peasant-fishermen free proprietors, who in any case certainly constituted the backbone of all the old Scandinavian societies, were called *boendr* (singular *bóndi*). They erected a curious state, with no equivalent elsewhere in the Middle Ages, which was not, contrary to a common error, a republic, any more than a democracy, but rather a plutocratic oligarchy. This "State" gave itself a highly original popular assembly, the *althing*, charged with discussing in common, among *boendr*, all questions of an executive (though Iceland never had a military or police force), legislative and judicial nature.

The Icelandic *sagas or related texts allow us to follow how this society came to be set up and then survive, despite being rent by the intestine quarrels which the Icelanders, excellent litigants, succeeded admirably in bringing to a successful conclusion. The essential event of their history was the adoption in 999, by unanimous consent, of Christianity. The Church brought them not just a form of writing that was preferable to *runes, but especially all the treasure of its own texts, biblical and classical. We are struck by the speed and depth with which two *bishoprics were set up, as well as an impressive number of churches and monasteries, the whole crowned by the nomination of two local saints, bishops *Thorlákr Thórhallsson and *Jón Ögmundarson. From then on, Iceland was provided with a national Church, also original (the great lay chiefs becoming also the main dignitaries of the Church), and with *clerics who had the skill not just to set down Christian traditions, but also to draw up in the vernacular the great local *chronicles, firstly in the form of books of "*history" in the sense that this word could have at the time, then in the form of all kinds of *sagas, to which must be added the recording of the *Eddas and the collation or original composition of *scaldic poems, not to speak of a whole learned literature of immense richness. It is perfectly fair to say that the Icelandic literature of the Middle Ages is by far the richest, in quantity at least, of the whole Christian West. So much so that Iceland has been called the "conservatory of Nordic antiquities", and this literary phenomenon, with no equivalent elsewhere, treated as an "Icelandic miracle". It gradually ceased when in 1262-1264 the island, riven by internal rivalries, passed under Norwegian and then Danish rule. Not until the 20th c. did the Icelanders regain the original political and intellectual status that they had acquired in the Middle Ages.

*Le Livre de la colonisation de l'Islande*, R. Boyer (ed. and tr.), Turnhout, 2000. – K. Hastrup, *Culture and History in Medieval Iceland*, Oxford, 1985. – J. L. Byock, *Medieval Iceland*, Berkeley, 1988. – E. P. Durrenberger, *The Dynamics of Medieval Iceland*, Iowa City, 1992.

Régis Boyer

**ICON.** Nowadays the term "icon" suggests a movable, portable image in painting or *mosaic on a wooden panel, representing either a portrait (*Christ, Virgin, saint) or a religious scene. In the Byzantine period, "icon", which in Greek means "image" or "resemblance", designated any religious image, portable or fixed, that was the object of a cult, whatever its technique (painting, mosaic, marble, *ivory, *enamel, *goldsmithry, bronze, cloth, etc.) or scale. A religious *image with religious value, the icon was also a work of art – the Byzantines praised especially the realism of the portrait and the painter's skill in expressing the spiritual qualities of the model – and an object of value, at least for those with precious cladding or those reputed to be miraculous.

Mode of expression *par excellence* of the *Orthodox faith, icons were omnipresent at Byzantium: in churches, monks' cells, private houses, shops, public monuments and in the imperial *palace; they participated in all the manifestations of private and public life. Icons continued the tradition of Greco-Roman portraits, perpetuating their technique – encaustic (coloured pigments mixed with heated wax) or tempera –, their hieratic frontality, their commemorative function, but also their magical and religious value. Doubtless appearing early, despite the hesitations of the early Church, they multiplied especially from the 6th c.; it is moreover from this time that the oldest surviving icons date (in St Catherine's monastery at *Sinai, at *Kiev or at *Rome). Stories of *miracles connected with icons proliferated at this time, showing that a supernatural power and protective and beneficent virtues were ascribed to them. The icon became the equivalent of or substitute for the *relic, the vehicle of supernatural powers. The distinction between the image and the person represented tended to be obliterated and a whole series of ritual and magical practices developed. Mediators between men and God, source of succour against all sorts of evils, icons also defended cities during wars

*Christ and Abbot Menas.* Distemper painting, 7th c. Paris, Louvre

and were present in battles. Also around the middle of the 6th c. apeared legends about miraculous images called **acheiropoieta* (not made by [human] hand), the most famous of which was the Mandylion: an image of Christ on a cloth sent by Christ himself to King Abgar, it saved Edessa from a Persian assault in 544 and was transferred to *Constantinople in the 10th century. More or less contemporary was the legendary tradition concerning images of the Virgin attributed to the evangelist Luke. One of the most renowned icons of Constantinople, venerated as the palladium of the city, that of the Virgin Hodighitria (conductress) – so-called from the name of the monastery (Hodegon: "of the Guides") that housed it – was thus attributed to St Luke; its iconographical type, many times reproduced, shows *Mary carrying the Child on her left arm and pointing with her right hand to him who is "the Way, the Truth and the Life" (Jn 14, 6).

The condemnation of icons and their cult in the *iconoclastic period (726-843) led the defenders of icons (*John of Damascus, the patriarchs of Constantinople *Germanus and *Nicephorus, *Theodore the Studite) to formulate a doctrine of religious images justifying them. In 787, the second council of *Nicaea declared the cult of images to be in accordance with the *tradition of the Church and useful to *salvation, raising the one who contemplated the *image to veneration of the one represented, according to the adage of St Basil: "Honour given to the image goes back to the prototype". The icon of Christ is justified by the visions of the *prophets and, especially, by the Incarnation: God being manifested in the flesh, we can represent this "character", this visible aspect. There is no identity of nature between image and prototype, but the image is linked to its model by resemblance; mediative, it allows man to enter into communion with the divine or sacred personage that it represents and whose presence it ensures; it transmits the divine energy, the spiritual *grace of the prototype.

From this conception of the icon – reflection of the prototype and vehicle of divine grace and energy – flowed certain characteristics of the art of the icons, firstly the loyalty to iconographical types hallowed by *tradition and considered to resemble the prototypes: to be effective, an icon had to be the authentic representation of the personages represented; this was the necessary condition for divine grace to be transmitted. The link between *image and model was confirmed by the inscription, which confirmed this resemblance. This will to realism went hand in hand with the choice of a hieratic, severe style, marked by a tendency to abstraction and the immaterial, proper to express the presence of the sacred and to reveal the divine nature. Frontality, immobility and accentuated spiritualization characterise these portraits. The desire to show an ideal world, a transfigured state of creation, was manifested by recourse to simple, harmoniously balanced compositions: concise images, where immobility or a balance of rhythmic movements reigned, reflecting *order, peace, calm, marks of the divine nature. The laws that ruled the visible world did not apply: depth of field tended to disappear, the *image being constructed on a single plane, standing out on an abstract background, often gilded; elements of landscape or architecture, when they existed, did not imitate reality, and the whole was bathed in an even and diffused light. Undoubtedly, these general characteristics must be nuanced: the style of icons evolved over the centuries in parallel with that of mural *painting or miniatures, the painters often being the same.

At first mainly intended for private devotion, icons were soon multiplied in places of worship. Some, kept in an annexe, were exposed on the proskynetarion (a sort of lectern situated in the nave) on the day of the saint's *feast or the event commemorated. In the late 10th or early 11th c. appeared calendar-icons, permanently exposed, that grouped together, in order of the liturgical *calendar, the images of the saint celebrated each day and sometimes the fixed feasts of the year, in twelve (one per month), four (tetraptych) or two panels (diptych). Fine examples of this type of icons are preserved in St Catherine's monastery on *Sinai, which houses the most important collection of Byzantine icons. But it was on the iconostasis that the icons were mainly concentrated. This barrier that separated the nave, where the congregation stood, from the choir reserved for the clergy, originally without icons (templon), was transformed over the centuries. From the 10th c., if not earlier, epistyle icons, arranged in one, then two registers, appeared on the architrave of the enclosure, above the columns. The *Deêsis (*Christ between the Virgin and St *John the Baptist in prayer), illustrating prayer of *intercession, often decorated the centre, surrounded by scenes from the cycle of the Dodekaorton or twelve great feasts of the *liturgical year, corresponding to the main events of the life of Christ and the Virgin. The epistyle icons could also compose a Marian or hagiographical cycle, or again a Great Deêsis, saints associating their *prayers with those of the Virgin and the Prodrome. No doubt from the 11th c., but more commonly from the time of the *Palaeologi, great icons – often four (representing the three figures of the Deêsis and the titular saint of the church) – were placed beneath the epistyle, between the columns of the templon, which thus tended to become a solid wall concealing the liturgy from the congregation. The royal doors, in the centre, were also decorated (often by the Annunciation). The iconostasis, a partition henceforth usually of wood, gained in height from the late 14th c. and acquired its classic form: crowned by a cross, it was covered with several rows of icons – Great Deêsis, Dodekaorton, and finally, directly offered to the veneration of the congregation, the great icons of proskynesis (veneration), placed between the columns. Two supplementary rows showing the patriarchs and prophets could still be added above the Deêsis, particularly in Russia where the iconostasis took on very important proportions.

K. Weitzmann, *The Icon, Holy Images, Sixth to Fourteenth Century*, London, 1978. – D. Mouriki, "Icons", *Sinai. Treasures of the Monastery of Saint Catherine*, K. A. Manafis (ed.), Athens, 1990, 91-227. – K. Weitzmann, G. Alibegašvili, A. Volskaya *et al.*, *Les Icônes*, Paris, 1982. – C. Schönborn, *L'Icône du Christ. Fondements théologiques*, Paris, 1986. – H. Belting, *Likeness and Presence. A History of the Image before the Era of Art*, Chicago, 1994. – R. Cormack, *Painting the Soul. Icons, Death Masks and Shrouds*, London, 1997.

Catherine Jolivet-Lévy

**ICONOCLASM.** The term "iconoclasm", which etymologically means the breaking (*kla-ô*, I break) of *images (*eikôn*), has been given by modern historians to a period of the *Byzantine Empire during which the emperors ordered the destruction of *icons (images representing *Christ, the Virgin, the saints or angels, to which worship was given). So the word designates two different things, a historical period and the ideology that marked that period.

**History.** Iconoclasm was the religious doctrine of the Byzantine Empire at two periods, between 730 and 787 (first iconoclasm, under the *Isaurian dynasty) and between 815 and 843 (second iconoclasm under the Amorian dynasty). The precursory signs of Byzantine iconoclasm were the prohibition of icons by two *bishops of Asia Minor (Thomas of Synnada and Constantine of Nacolea), who were called to order by Patriarch Germanus, and a series of speeches given by the Emperor Leo III from 726; perhaps we should add, at that date, the destruction of an image of Christ that had been over the gate of the imperial *palace, called the Chalke.

Its official beginning dates from 17 Jan 730, when Leo III ordered the high officials of the Empire to sign a declaration hostile to icons and pursued those who refused; Patriarch *Germanus of Constantinople, who was among them, was deposed and replaced. The *popes (Gregory II and Gregory III) rejected Leo III's new policy all the more vigorously in that its condemnation provided them with a dogmatic pretext to distance themselves from the Empire and justified their temporal ambitions. Leo III's son, *Constantine V, made iconoclasm the religious law of the Empire by calling a *council, called that of Hiereia (754), which forbade the making and veneration of icons. The council's decisions seem to have been accepted without difficulty in the Empire, but in 765 the participation of an influential monk, *Stephen the Younger, in a plot against the emperor unleashed the imperial anger. An iconoclast oath was then required from all the subjects of the Empire and persecution descended on the refractory, monks and laymen. It took the form of exiles, corporal punishments, confiscations, ceremonies of derision of monks in the hippodrome, and monks being publicly deprived of their attributes, beard and habit.

The council of *Nicaea II (787), convoked by the empress *Irene, annulled the decisions of the council of Hiereia: icons were justified and their cult imposed. The Empire remained iconodule, *i.e.* favourable to icons (*doulos*, "servant", "slave"), until 815. At that date, the Emperor *Leo V returned to iconoclasm. He repeated Leo III's gesture – or, if that never happened, innovated – by having soldiers destroy the image of Christ over the Chalke gate of the palace, and then called a local council at Constantinople that rehabilitated the council of Hiereia and annulled the decisions of *Nicaea II. The reaction was much stronger than in 754. Patriarch *Nicephorus, several bishops (Euthymius of Sardis, Michael of Synnada, Joseph of Thessalonica, brother of Theodore the Studite) and a number of hegumens including *Theodore the Studite rejected the council's decisions: Nicephorus was deposed and the others exiled. They were recalled from exile on the accession of Michael II, but did not regain their posts.

Michael II (820-829) was a moderate iconoclast, in contrast to his son Theophilus (829-842), who chose John the Grammarian as *patriarch (837-843) and resumed persecution of his opponents (the future Patriarch *Methodius, Michael Syncellus, the brothers Graptoi). On Theophilus's death (842), his wife Theodora, though favourable to the restoration of icons, did not accept it until she had obtained *absolution for her husband. The restoration was carried out without a *council by the newly-promoted Patriarch Methodius in a simple liturgical ceremony, a *procession and a *mass at Hagia Sophia, on 11 March 843, the first Sunday of *Lent, which later became the feast of *Orthodoxy or "Orthodoxy Sunday".

**Ideology.** We know little about this, because the iconoclast writings have disappeared and because the iconodules, having won, presented iconoclasm in a diabolical light as they rewrote the history of the period. However, at the council of Nicaea II, the acts of Hiereia were cited in order to be refuted, which ensured their preservation, while Patriarch Nicephorus, in his treatises against the iconoclasts, cited some phrases of Constantine V (known under the name of *Peuseis*) and the decisions of the council of Constantinople.

The *theology of Constantine V was strong and clearly expounded. The main accusation brought against the worship of icons was that of idolatry: "the devil urged Christians to prostrate themselves before the creature, to honour it and to think that the work called by the name of Christ was God" (*Mansi*, 13, 221). The council also placed itself in line with the christological debates and demonstrated that to represent Christ was to fall into the *Nestorian heresy, since only the man could be represented; besides, by separating what in Christ was inseparable, his divinity from his humanity, those who made icons of Christ were creating a particular hypostasis of him and inventing a fourth person of the *Trinity; finally, since Christ's divinity was present in his body, to represent his body was to give a limit to the divinity, which was impossible and heretical. For Constantine V and the council of Hiereia, a true image of Christ existed: the *Eucharist, *i.e.* the body and blood of Christ. "Christ said, after having blessed the bread and shared it out: 'Take and eat, this is my body . . .' and likewise for the wine, 'this is my blood, do this in memory of me', so that no other kind can be the image of his incarnation nor was chosen by him on this earth, nor any other model [*typos*]" (*Mansi*, 13, 264). Well-argued in connection with Christ's image, the theology of Hiereia is weaker when it attacks the images of the saints and the Virgin: it is not fitting that the Mother of God and the saints, who live always in God, should be represented by a dead and pagan art. The council of Constantinople, abandoning the accusation of idolatry and the christological dilemma, was more occupied with defining the nature of the true image. In its view, the true image was *man, whom God had made in his image, which allowed man to work to resemble God; this was to push to its limit the thought of Constantine V, "the image is consubstantial with what is represented" (*PG*, 100, 225), and to justify the ban on representing the saints and the Virgin as well as Christ. Iconoclast theology was thus not the caricature that is presented by iconodule sources.

Opinions differ as to the reasons that suddenly led Leo III to adopt an iconoclast religious policy. Though we all now agree that *Islam and *Judaism had no direct influence on the beginnings of iconoclasm and we are less inclined to think that iconoclasm arose in Asia Minor on the rather disputable grounds that the peoples of Asia Minor would have been aniconic because they were oriental, we do not really understand what motivated Leo III's choice. However, there are numerous traces of hostility to the excesses of the *cult of the saints in the 7th and early 8th centuries. Then again, the cult of icons was a centrifugal cult, which required no recourse to any clergy and which diluted devotion into so many personal practices; the cult of the saints, whose guardians were the monks, had the same characteristics. It is probable that Leo III's decision, which restored the imperial authority misused before 717, was motivated by the desire to unify the religious practice of the inhabitants of the Empire under the banner of the secular clergy, who were easily controlled. All in all, Byzantine iconoclasm must doubtless be considered not as an inexplicable crisis, but as a reform, comparable to the Protestant Reformation, with which it has many points in common.

A. Grabar, *L'Iconoclasme byzantin, Dossier archéologique*, Paris, 1957 (1st ed.). – P. Brown, "A Dark Age Crisis: Aspects of the Iconoclastic Controversy", *EHR*, 88, 1973, 1-34. – S. Gero, *Byzantine Iconoclasm during the reign of Leo III with particular attention to oriental sources, CSCO*, 346, Subs. 41, Louvain, 1973. – S. Gero, *Byzantine Iconoclasm during the reign of Constantine V, CSCO*, 384, Subs. 52, Louvain, 1977. – P. J. Alexander, *Religious and Political History and Thought in the Byzantine Empire*, London, 1978. – P. J. Alexander, *The patriarch Nicephorus of Constantinople, Ecclesiastical policy and Image worship in the Byzantine Empire*. – J. Moorhead, "Iconoclasm, the Cross and the Imperial Image", *Byz.*, 55, 1985, 165-79. – M.-F. Auzépy, "La destruction de l'icône du Christ de la Chalcé par Léon III: propagande ou réalité?", *Byz.*, 60, 1990, 445-492. – G. Dagron, *HChr*, 4, 1993, 93-165.

Marie-France Auzépy

**IDIORRHYTHM.** In the 10th c., *coenobitic *monasticism prevailed on Mount *Athos. Meanwhile small colonies of hermits lived in the shadow of the great monasteries, rejoining the community for the great feasts. In the 14th c., under the pressure of growing insecurity, these colonies of hermits regrouped within the monasteries. They lived at their own pace (*idiorrhythm*), administering their own property and being free from the authority of the hegumen. This practice, which gradually ruined community life, was opposed by the *patriarchs and the emperors, but the fall of the Empire contributed to its development.

P. de Meester, *De Monachico statu. . .*, Vatican, 1942, 68 f. – V. Kravari, *Actes du Pantocrator*, 22, 1991 ("ArAt", 17; 2 vol.).

Marie-Hélène Congourdeau

**IDRĪSIDS.** The dynasty of the Idrīsids reigned over the far *Maghreb (*Morocco) from 789 to the end of the 10th century. Its founder, Idrīs I, was a descendant of *'Alī who, fleeing the *Abbasid persecutions, got himself acknowledged as **imām* by the Berbers of the region of Volubilis. Yet the Idrīsids did not develop *Shi'ism and were content to venerate the Prophet's family. They founded the town of *Fez, peopled it with *Kairouanis and Andalusians and made it a great centre of Arabic and religious culture in Berber territory. But from the 9th c. the far Maghreb was weakened by dynastic quarrels, and from the 10th c. to the death of the last Idrīsid in 985 it was the stake of rivalries between the *Fatimids of Ifrīkiya and the Umayyads of *Spain.

"Idrīsids", *EI(E)*, 3, 1971, 1035-1037.

Philippe Gourdin

**IGNATIUS OF CONSTANTINOPLE (*c.*797-877).** Son of the Emperor Michael I, at the time of his father's deposition the young Nicetas was castrated and became a monk under the name of Ignatius. He was appointed *patriarch of *Constantinople by the empress Theodora (24 July 847), but Caesar Bardas forced him to retire and appointed *Photius in his place (23 Oct 858). The supporters of the two patriarchs confronted each other. In 867, the emperor Basil deposed Photius and recalled Ignatius (23 Nov). He followed an active policy: the Church of *Bulgaria once more became a zone of Byzantine influence. An agreement was reached with Photius, who succeeded Ignatius (23 Oct 877) and contributed to the recognition of his *sanctity. His feast day is 23 October.

R. Janin, "Ignace (saint)", *DThC*, 7, 2, 1930, 713-722.

Bernard Flusin

**ILDEFONSUS OF TOLEDO (died 667).** Born to an aristocratic family, Ildefonsus entered the monastery of Agali, near *Toledo, very young. He became its *abbot before becoming *archbishop of the Visigothic capital in 657. His theological, liturgical, epistolary and literary work was extremely abundant. They include particularly a treatise in defence of *Mary's *virginity (*De virginitate Sanctae Mariae*), first landmark of Iberian mariology, and a text of liturgical and pastoral nature on *baptism (*Annotationum de cognitione baptismi liber*). Ildefonsus was the object of a fervent cult, relaunched in the 13th c. by the rediscovery of his *relics in a church at Zamora.

*DHEE*, 2, 1972, 1188-1189. – J.F. Rivera Recio, *San Ildefonso de Toledo*, Madrid, 1985. – R. Aubert, "Hildefonse de Tolède", *DHGE*, 25, 1995, 806-807.

Daniel Baloup

**ILLUMINATION.** "Illumination", "miniature" or "manuscript painting" are so many terms designating the same thing: decoration drawn or painted by hand on manuscripts. The preferred term is the one that appeared in the 11th c., "illumination" – from *illuminatio, illuminare, illuminator* – which means: "to make luminous, light up"; it is especially preferable to "miniature", derived from "minium" – *miniare*, "to write in red" – which, though it applies wonderfully well to rubrication in the etymological sense, is a bit restrictive.

Taken in the broad sense, the decoration of a manuscript includes historiated scenes as well as decorative elements such as ornamented letters, frames, borders, etc.; in short, it includes all that concurs to facilitate reading through the medium of colour and design.

Illumination was a medieval phenomenon, which affected every country in Western Europe. It began to come into prominence only in late Antiquity, and ended when printing supplanted the manuscript and the incunabulum.

*Saint John the Evangelist.* Miniature from the *Gospels of Ebbo*, archbishop of Reims. *C.*820-830. Épernay, Municipal Library.

With the use of *parchment, illuminators had at their disposal a medium that favoured technical refinements and the exploitation of colour; it was with the generalization of the **codex* that they would find a surface that allowed them to use all the possibilities offered by division into pages.

In later antiquity, manuscript illumination was still rudimentary. But technical works dealing with medicine or architecture required illustration, which has come down to us through copies made in the Middle Ages. Early Christian biblical images also survive in the decoration of Spanish, Carolingian and *Anglo-Saxon manuscripts. This period bequeathed two types of decoration whose use persisted: Eusebius of Caesarea's tables of concordance set in a painted frame, and portraits of the *evangelists.

Illumination was a natural response to the wish to beautify the manuscript, and the aesthetic concerns of its author can be evident, as in the "carpet-pages" that served as frontispieces to the Irish and Northumbrian gospel-books of the 7th and 8th cc., but it would be reductive to confine ourselves to that: little by little, illumination came to illustrate and explain the text; sometimes it went even further and illustrated the concept or the symbol as well as the text. The title-page too quite quickly became the object of particular care, and the *incipit* was sometimes written in capital letters made up of a maze of spirals and interlacings (in *Ireland and *England), interlaced bands, birds and fish (*Merovingian area). Ornamented *initials were still rare and usually confined to a large capital painted in one or two colours at the head of the chapter. Decorative though it may have been, the initial also brought out the division into chapters and made the handling and reading of the work more convenient.

It was only really from the Carolingian period that illumination appeared as an element in the reading of the text: this was doubtless for pedagogical reasons, to transmit the content by the image. This concern would grow until, in the *Bibles moralisées*, it reached proportions worthy of the comic strip.

The *scholastic period introduced *glosses and commentaries by *masters and students; the transcription of these manuscripts (*Bibles, *Decreta, *Decretals) was accomplished by playing about with page-divisions and character sizes. But it would have remained obscure without the use of different-coloured initials (blue and red) and the introduction of colour signs (paragraph marks), to mark its subdivisions. Finally, the 14th c. closed up the space by adding line endings.

L. Reau, *La miniature*, Melun, 1946. – M. Smeyers, *La miniature*, 1974 ("TSMÂO", 8). – F. Unterkirchner, *Die Buchmalerei, Entwicklung, Technik, Eigenart*, Vienna, 1974. – *The Place of Book Illumination in Byzantine Art*, K. Weitzmann (ed.), Princeton (NJ), 1975. – J. de Mahuet, "Miniature", *Cath.*, 9, 1982. – H. Mayr-Harting, *Ottonian Book Illumination*, London, 1991. – J.J.G. Alexander, *Medieval Illuminators and their Methods of Work*, New Haven, 1992. – T. Ohlgren, *Anglo-Saxon Textual Illustration*, Kalamazoo, 1993. – J. Backhouse, *The Illuminated Page*, London, 1997.

Guy Lanoë

## IMAGE, RELIGIOUS

**Status.** The term "image" (*imago*), which covers many meanings in which medieval *philosophy was greatly interested (*forma, figura, similitudo, *species, exemplar, effigies, phantasma, ratio*, etc.), was marked throughout the Middle Ages by a double ambiguity. The first hesitated between image in the plastic sense and image in the theological sense, the latter being descended from the *Neoplatonist concept of the sensible world as a "reflection" of the intelligible world, *man created "in the image of *God", *Christ as "*icon" of the father, the Church as "figure" of the coming Kingdom, and finally the image insofar as it referred to a prototype (past and/or to come); even the expression "visual image" was not sufficiently specific, since it referred equally to the sense (the percepts) of sight, and to the first two of the three categories of vision distinguished by St Augustine (*De Genesi ad litteram*, 1, XII). The other ambiguity was that between image in the sense of work of art, a sense that appealed to an aesthetic quality, and image in the general (and undifferentiated) sense of figured document. The first of these ambiguities reveals one of the characteristics of the medieval image: even if this was secular, it was part of a world of images that supposed a symbolic system, and it was capable of an interpretation that referred to medieval techniques of *exegesis (*typology, doctrine of the four *senses of Scripture, etc.); one of its main aspects lay in its relational character and hence its relation to the prototype, in whose essence it participated in some way; to believe numerous hagiographical accounts, this relationship could even become so close that the image sometimes came, like the *relic, to possess the properties of its model, that is to say it listened, spoke, wept, moved, threatened and punished, protected and performed *miracles (thus the painted crucifix of *San Damiano, which spoke to *Francis of Assisi). And the second ambiguity was in turn the reflection of the will of the medieval *artist no longer to appear to depend solely on the mechanical arts, but to tend towards the prestigious status of the *liberal arts.

Images occupied a great place in the medieval West, which was a resolutely iconophile civilization, a declared friend of images, as materially shown by the extent of the medieval artistic heritage surviving today, which attests an incessant creation of images and a constant renewal of styles, in the most varied contexts and for the most varied ends, covering an immense work of exploration of artistic genres and forms. The Middle Ages saw the inventive resumption of many ancient techniques, in particular monumental sculpture (tympanum of *Vézelay), statuary (the *Majesty of Sainte-Foy de *Conques) and *illumination (gospels of Saint-Médard at Soissons) which too enjoyed a prodigious development thanks to the *codex. But we also see the creation of new media (*stained glass: Head of Christ, Strasbourg) and then the invention of the multiple image (engraving). Nor should we forget intellectual, aesthetic and financial efforts, attested by *patronage and great collections (libraries of *Charles V of France or Duke *John of Berry).

From a theoretical point of view, the importance of images was fully recognised and accepted. A unanimous conviction of medieval theologians was that the Incarnation of God's *Word in Jesus Christ had abolished the prohibition on images in the Old Testament. From *Gregory the Great (*Letter to Serenus of Marseille*) to the *scholastic theologians (*Thomas Aquinas, *Summa theologiae*, III[a], 25, 3; Guillaume *Durand, *Rationale divinorum officiorum*, I, 3), there developed a triple justification of the role of images (didactic, mnemonic, affective) which, beyond differences of presentation and emphasis, was widely shared. The decisions of the council of *Nicaea II (787) were "received" by *Rome: and the pontiffs of the 8th and 9th cc. in turn restated, not without solemnity, their full agreement with the famous *horos* on the veneration of *icons, thereby giving it the force of law. The theologians of the court of *Aachen, however, on the strength of a defective translation, harboured resentment against this *council – very wrongly – for having encouraged the worship of images; worship, they thought they should point out, belonged only to *God, who could not be painted. Thus the **Libri Carolini* and the council of *Frankfurt (794) took a pedagogical approach to the image, save in what concerned the *cross. And many later theologians, in *controversies or dialogues with *Jews, Muslims and *heretics, forcefully emphasized the difference between worship of the image, which risked transforming it into an idol, and its veneration, which alone was to be recommended.

In any case, the West was not led to make a dogma of the veneration of religious images: there was, properly speaking, no quarrel over images and no *theology of the image. Neither idol nor icon, it never took on an essential role in the course of the liturgy. In law, everyone was free to have them or not: it was a matter of indifference (*adiaphoron*). In fact, the image was prized by most. Its questioning, before that brought about by the Reformation, was always the work of isolated individuals or limited groups (*Claudius of Turin, *Hussites, *Lollards, *Savonarola) or else was limited to certain contexts (*Bernard of Clairvaux, for the decoration of monasteries; *Eckhart in the context of *mysticism), certain iconographical types (*Antoninus of Florence objecting to the type of the tricephalous *Trinity), or certain objects (*Gerson taking issue with statuettes of the Virgin that opened up). The late Middle Ages were marked on the contrary by the triumph of the religious image in devotion, its omnipresence in churches and the central place of the image-principle in *philosophy (*e.g.* in *Nicholas of Cusa).

***Realia.*** Any attempt to understand the status of the medieval image must, however, without prejudice to the fundamental unity of the iconocosm of that period, avoid considering it in a uniform way and take into account its variations according to:

– the nature of the image, linked among other things to its technique, size, position, which determined its accessibility and visibility. One of the clearest signs of the importance of images in the Middle Ages is seen, from the 13th to the 15th c., in public devotion, with the phenomenon of the *altarpiece, in which an image of growing size and complexity from now on dominated the *altar. Consequently, we should not compare the public image and the private image (*e.g.* in *Books of Hours for devout layfolk); the image conceived for everyone and that intended for a particular social category or religious *order; the image with a fixed content and the image that changed according to the liturgical *calendar (altarpiece with side-panels, like that of the *van Eyck brothers at *Ghent); the fixed image (monumental relief, mural *painting, *mosaic) and the moveable image (*tapestry, portable altar); the single image and the multiple image (*seal, lead token, *Flugblatt*, illustrations of printed *books); the finished image and the temporary image (preparatory drawing, project).

– the type of representation, whether we think of the most common case, the narrative image, or, at one extreme, an ornamental or decorative image, or, at the other, the transformation of an element extracted from the narrative into an image of devotion (*Andachtsbild*) or its expression in a theological or moral diagram, or even its reduction to a symbol or a *sign.

– the use of the image: decoration-image or illustration; representation-image (*portrait); didactic image; model for an *artist; secular image (object, playing card. . .); image carried in *procession; image of protection or *intercession, before which one prayed; image prayed to; image carried on the person (*pilgrim's badge, sign of belonging to a religious *order, a *confraternity. . .); a place apart belongs to images that express deviant beliefs or *superstitious practices.

– the place in a chronological evolution, to take account of the incessant and often cumulative enrichment of medieval iconography in the West, but also the very marked stylistic evolutions. The evolution towards naturalism, the expression of visible appearances and the search for a realistic or even illusionistic effect in the late Middle Ages are not synonymous with lack of interest in any symbolic content: the very elaborate iconography of the Flemish *Primitives proves the contrary.

Finally we must take into account the freedom of the medieval image. It would be too much to describe it as autonomy, at least until the late Middle Ages: its content was usually dependent on theological texts and concepts, and images were readily organised into groups, cycles and series that respected great patterns, like the typological principle which juxtaposed Old *Testament and New Testament images. But the application of such principles was done with great freedom. The medieval image was at the heart of a system of creation in which the individual occupied a central place. The grip of *theology on medieval art and the control of theologians over *artists have undoubtedly been exaggerated. The freedom of the latter must be reclaimed. One and the same biblical text (*e.g.* the hospitality of *Abraham in Gen 18), read according to the same interpretative principle (*typology), could be treated by artists as a prefiguration of the *Annunciation, the *baptism of Christ, his *Transfiguration, the *washing of feet at the Last Supper, the *Eucharist, the *Trinity, etc.

The way in which we now look at medieval images seeks to combine all these aspects. It can no longer be limited to the narrative, didactic or symbolic content, but takes into account the function of images and the social and anthropological aspects of their manufacture and uses. And it no longer takes as its sole object the "great" works of art, but also takes an interest in productions of poor artistic quality. Equally, it must be kept free from any restrictive reading. To privilege the functional, socio-anthropological or even documentary dimension of medieval images would be to risk erasing their fundamental meaning and ignoring their place in a history of ideas. In reality, the different frames of reading that have been formulated since the 19th c. supplement without supplanting each other. Though it often possesses great historical and documentary interest, the medieval image is not a document but a work of art, which participates, in its singularity, in an effort of ceaselessly renewed creation.

Molanus, *Traité des saintes images*, F. Boespflug (ed.), O. Christin (ed.), B. Tassel (ed.), Paris, 1996.

A. C. Esmeijer, *"Divina quaternitas". A Preliminary Study in the Method and Application of Visual Exegesis*, Amsterdam, 1978. – É. Mâle, *Religious Art in France: the Twelfth Century*, Princeton (NJ), 1978. – H. Belting, *Das Bild und sein Publikum im Mittelalter*, Berlin, 1981. – S. Sinding-Larsen, *Iconography and Ritual. A Study of Analytical Perspectives*, Oslo, 1981. – F. O. Büttner, *Imitatio Pietatis. Motive der christlichen Ikonographie als Modelle zur Verähnlichung*, Berlin, 1983. – É. Mâle, *Religious Art in France: the Thirteenth Century*, Princeton (NJ), 1984. – S. Ringbom, *Icon to Narrative: The Rise of the Dramatic Close-Up in Fifteenth-Century Devotional Painting*, Doorspijk, 1984 (2nd ed.); tr. 1997. – É. Mâle, *Religious Art in France: the late Middle Ages*, Princeton (NJ), 1986 . – M. Camille, *The Gothic Idol. Ideology and Image-Making in Medieval Art*, Cambridge, 1989. – J. Wirth, *L'Image médiévale. Naissance et développements (VIe-XV[e] siècles)*, Paris, 1989. –L. Grodecki, *Le Moyen Âge retrouvé*, Paris, 1990 and 1991 (2 vol.). – D. Menozzi, *Les Images. L'Église et les arts visuels*, Paris, 1991. – A. Chastel, *La Pala, ou le Retable italien des origines à 1500*, Paris, 1993. – H. Belting, *Likeness and Presence: a History of the Image before the Era of Art*, Chicago, 1994. – *Moyen Âge. Chrétienté et Islam*, C. Heck (dir.), Paris, 1996. – J. Wirth, *L'Image à l'époque romane*, forthcoming.

François Boespflug and Christian Heck

***IMĀM.*** In Arabic, *imām* designates a leader, a guide, an example to follow; in Muslim Arabic vocabulary, its uses can be summed up in four main meanings.

Firstly it is the leader, the guide of a group or a community. Thus for the *Koran (2, 214), *Abraham is "a guide for men". Among *Sunnis, the *caliph is the supreme head (*imām*) of the community.

Next, among the twelver Shi'ites (imamites), the conception of the imamate is based on mankind's permanent need for an infallible leader, guided by God, and an undisputed teacher in the religious sciences. They consequently reject the caliphates, apart from the imamate of *'Alī. This imamate is merited only by the twelve imāms descended from the Prophet's family. Having said that, each Shi'ite group in the broad sense of the term (Zaydites, septiman Isma'ilites, etc.) has its own conception of the imamate; the same goes for the *Khārijites.

Moreover, the founders of the schools of law, some of the jurists and the most respected theologians had this title ascribed to them out of reverence, both in Sunnism and in *Shi'ism. Thus one can speak of Imām Ahmad, *i.e.* Ibn Hanbal, or Imām al-*Ghazālī. The same goes for heads of *confraternities or other religious movements. But this designation is sometimes extended to other disciplines (grammar, prosody, *belles-lettres*, etc.) to affirm the outstanding excellence of a scholar.

Finally, the leader of the community's canonical prayer in a *mosque or with a group of believers is also called an *imām*. The caliph presided over prayer; as *imām*, he led in war, headed the administration and led the common prayer. Likewise, provincial governors were leaders of prayer, especially the Friday prayers at which, like the caliph, they preached the sermon. The ministers of mosques also bore this title; it was they who usually presided over prayer.

The question of the supreme direction (imamate) of the community is one of those that have most divided Muslims. While the Sunnis were mainly concerned to guarantee supreme power to the current caliph in order to ensure the unity of the community, the Shi'ites insisted mainly on the legitimacy of the imām, who had to come from the Prophet's family. But the majority of the Shi'ite imāms, apart from the Zaydites, never exercised supreme power over the Muslims. It was probably partly due to this situation that the Shi'ites had a tendency to attribute great religious authority to them and to place the imamate at the centre of the religion. The twelver imamites, whose twelfth imām disappeared (*ghayba*, occultation) in 874, have since then lived in expectation of his return, but he still ensures their spiritual guidance. His legal rights and duties are partly assumed by the religious scholars (*'*ulamā'*, imāms).

T. P. Hughes, *Dictionary of Islam*, London, 1896, 203-204 (2nd ed.). – W. Madelung, "Imāma", *EI(E)*, 3, 1971, 1163-1169. – J. Pedersen, "Masdjid", *EI(E)*, 6, 1991, 674-675.

Claude Gilliot

***IMITATION OF CHRIST.*** The *Imitation of Christ* is the most influential writing of the **Devotio moderna*, composed by *Thomas a Kempis. Originally, it consisted of four independent treatises, each with its specific spiritual character: *Admonitiones ad spiritualem vitam utiles* (25 chapters), *Admonitiones ad interna trahentes* (12), *Devota exhortatio ad sacram communionem* (59) and *Liber internae consolationis* (18). The autograph manuscript contains the particulars that Thomas introduced into the original text between 1420 and 1441. Only in 1441, according to the autograph colophon, did he consider the book finished. Given that the treatises were copied several times from the autograph before 1441, there exist many manuscripts earlier than the final autograph and whose text differs from it.

The *Imitation* seems to be the most mature fruit of the **Devotio moderna*. More than 700 manuscripts and about 4000 printed editions are known. It has been translated into many languages and is part of world literature; up to 1960 or so it was, after the *Bible, the most read book of the Christian tradition. It contains no systematic teaching, but deals with different spiritual themes, like the vanity of the world, false happiness, selfishness, disordered passions, *temptations, alongside peace of heart, inner freedom, purification of the senses and mind, trust in God, patience, *obedience, frequent *communion. *Humility, *contrition and simplicity make a man fit to enter the Kingdom of *Heaven. The Christian model of "imitation" is centred on *Christ who, by the incarnation of God, has made possible our union with God, in and after this life.

As far as the work's authorship is concerned, there have been a multitude of opinions since the 15th century. Among the 40 or so names that have been advanced as the author, that of Thomas a Kempis has the best title. Johannes *Busch (1400-1480), who in 1464 finished the second redaction of his *Chronicon Windes-*

*heimense*, called him the author of the *Imitation*: his testimony was never contradicted in *Windesheim circles, but always confirmed. As the *Imitation* was often copied or printed (especially at Venice, in 1483 and subsequently) with the works of a famous author, it has often been taken for the work of that author. Thus the *Imitation* was attributed, wrongly, to Jean *Gerson (1363-1429), *chancellor of the *university of *Paris. Even now, ink is still spilt over the question of the author. It is generally recognised that, by its content, the *Imitation* reflects the inheritance of the first generation of "devout moderns" (including *Groote); over 20 years, Thomas completed and reworked this material, which doubtless came from a number of *rapiaria*, up to the moment when, in 1441, he reckoned its redaction complete.

L. M. J. Delaisse, *Le Manuscrit autographe de Thomas a Kempis et "l'Imitation de Jésus-Christ". Examen archéologique et édition diplomatique du bruxellensis 5855-61*, *PSc*, 2, 1956. – *The Imitation of Christ*, W.C. Creasy (ed.), Macon (GA), 1989.

A. Ampe, B. Spaapen, "Imitatio Christi", *DSp*, 7, 1971, 2338-2368. – S. G. Axters, *De imitatione Christi. Een handschrifteninventaris bij et vijfhondertste verjaren van Thomas Hemerken van Kempen († 1471)*, Kempen, 1971. – J. Sudbrack, "Das geistliche Gesicht der vier Bücher der Nachfolge Christi", *Thomas van Kempen. Beiträge zum 500. Todesjahr 1471-1971*, Kempen, 1971, 14-36.

Rudolf T. M. Van Dijk

**IMMANENCE.** The term "immanence" (that which remains in) is not current in classical Latin. It is a technical term which seems to appear in the medieval commentaries on the Pauline *epistles or on I John and which designates, by contrast with the transcendent, that which is proper to the world, tangible and of the created order. Transcendence being defined as that which is higher, separate or distinct, immanence cannot but evoke the human limitation of *knowledge and the finitude of all that is created. *Scholasticism defines human life as *actio immanens* as opposed to *actio transiens*, which is not linked to an organism. Immanence is the state of the human mind that can apprehend transcendent verities, but can never know them in plenitude. St *Thomas Aquinas evokes the distinction between the divine intellect and the human *intellect, which does not have the same relation to things. The human intellect is marked by immanence, *i.e.* it is "measured by things" (*Summa theologiae*, $I^a II^{ae}$, q. 93, a. 1).

E. Coreth, "Immanenz", *LThK*, 5, 1960, 629-631 (2nd ed.). – A. Billecoq, "Immanence", *Les notions philosophiques. Dictionnaire*, S. Auroux (dir.), Paris, 1990, 1239-1240 ("Encyclopédie philosophique universelle", 2).

Michel Deneken

**IMMORTALITY.** Although the Middle Ages were marked by the encounter with Aristotelian *philosophy, the (*Neo-)platonism that was the basis of the notion of immortality (in fact always understood "of the soul") was not questioned. For medieval thinkers, immortality had to do with the divine, which, in *man, corresponded to the *soul.

In the 13th c., the theme of the migration of the soul appeared in funerary art, *death being understood as a separation of the soul from the *body, whereas previously it was not rare to see *tombs representing the deceased taken body and soul to *heaven (St Saturninus near Limoux or Randulph at Saint-Nazaire at Carcassonne in the 12th c.). So the evolution of Western thought led to the favouring of the immortality of the soul. At a time of troubles, great wars and great plagues, the contempt for the body preached by certain spiritual currents, a popular Stoicism, made immortality an evident fact for all, even a hope. As certain sins could lead to damnation, whose effect was eternal death, people were obsessed by *salvation. The theme of judgment developed in iconography from the 11th century. In the late Middle Ages, it culminated in a particular *judgment at the moment of death: the soul is weighed, then led to the immortal condition of the blessed, sent to *purgatory or damned by eternal death.

Among theologians and philosophers, the debates on Plato and *Aristotle as well as on Arabic philosophy show that the idea of immortality was sometimes questioned. Thus *Averroism, opposed by *Thomas Aquinas, did not acknowledge immortality (of the soul). By contrast *Avicenna (980-1037), whose thought was very compatible with that of many *Platonists, insisted on the immortality of the soul. Immortality was also a quest, and the *Eucharist was the food of immortality. The nascent *scholasticism understood the soul as a *pars hominis* which was not man as such (*person) but which was man's immortal principle. Man truly died, but his soul was immortal. *Bonaventure, opposing the Aristotelian and Averroist conceptions of the soul and the divine essence, strongly affirmed the immortality of the soul in connection with the immortality of *God. St Thomas explained the traditional doctrine of the immortality of the soul on the basis of the positive property of the *intellect. For him the soul held man's different components together. He distinguished between the immortality conferred on man in the state of paradisal innocence and the immortality of glory, promised for the future life (resurrection) (*Summa theologiae*, $I^a$, q. 97, a. 1). Thomas sought solutions to a dichotomy not previously overcome: that between the Platonic principle of immortality of the soul and the Christian principle of *resurrection of the dead. In the *Summa contra gentiles*, he showed that resurrection was not an addition, but a new *informatio* of the body by the soul (IV, 81). The council of *Vienne (*Fidei Catholica* of 1312) affirmed that "the immortal soul is the form of the body" (*DzS* 904). For *mysticism, the man who lives totally in God is told by Him with what *love He loves the creature and that He thereby gives him immortality (*Eckhart, *Reden der Unterweisung*, 15).

*Il dolore e la morte nella spiritualità dei secoli XII e XIII*, *CCSSM*, 5, 1967. – A. Solignac, "Immortalité", *DSp*, 7, 1971, 1601-1614.

Michel Deneken

**IMMUNITY.** In its historical and etymological meaning, the term immunity – from the Latin *immunis*, *immunitas* – meant an exemption from *munera*, *i.e.* fiscal burdens. And as such burdens were managed by the authority that set them and periodically demanded them, by extension the term immunity took on the meaning of exemption from the jurisdiction necessarily connected with them. The first application of immunity appeared in the Late Empire and concerned the imperial properties declared immune and entrusted to a *procurator*, to whom were delegated administration and the exercise of justice.

Later, it formed the third element of the *fief together with the *beneficium* and *vassaticum*, a legal-historical confluence of very different institutions. Immunity was thus exemption from *munera*, which were distinguished into *personalia* and *patrimonialia* according to whether the immunity concerned persons or things, patrimonial goods. Concretely, immunity meant that the imposition of taxes and the exercise of *justice fell outside the royal or imperial authority – and hence the *State – and were concentrated in the hands of the feudal lord or the ecclesiastical body, while *introitus*, *exactio* and *districtio* were prohibited, *i.e.* the central authority was forbidden to cross the boundaries of the *benefice, collect taxes (*functiones*) or execute legal sentences in it. Obviously the application of immunity would not be peaceful, and an example of this is the *Edictum de beneficiis* that Conrad II the *Salian promulgated in 1037 in an attempt to discipline the heated matter. Immunity underwent a separate historical development in France, especially under the *Carolingians; a fact that beset the *king's relationship with the aristocracy and especially with the Church.

Here, immunity was a privilege by which the king removed, at least in part, an ecclesiastical establishment and its estates from the ordinary jurisdiction of the *count, who in turn was exempt. The privilege, "fiscal" in origin, alienated with the public estates to which it was attached, would become primarily legal. Immunity already existed in the *Merovingian period. The Carolingians made it a useful instrument of decentralization, as well as a way of controlling churches. For this reason they extended it to a great number of establishments, even when not former royal fiscs, and to every region of their *Empire. Thus *Corbie and its 10 or 12 estates situated between Amiens and *Arras, or *Saint-Germain-des-Prés and its estates south of the Seine, would constitute a sort of island endowed with franchises: the *abbot or his representative examined legal cases, judged minor cases and referred major ones to the judgment of the count; he levied public taxes in the king's name and for him, and summoned and led the free men in the royal *host.

From the time of *Charlemagne, immunity became general, diplomas of concession and confirmation multiplied and the privilege came to be considered exclusively ecclesiastical. *Immunitas* was understood at that time as a privilege by which a named estate, or more often all the estates belonging to a church, sometimes even its present and future properties (so that further increases in the temporality, by *donation or purchase, would automatically enjoy *exemption) were removed from the interference of the king's ordinary agents. The establishment was exempt (*immunis*) from the intervention of officials and, at least in theory, was directly attached to the central authority: its proprietor was personally responsible to the sovereign for performing administrative and legal services in place of the count, whose powers hence passed to the immunist. By thus massively removing Church lands from comital authority, the ruler thought to lose nothing. By opposing counts and immunists, he thought to weaken the always great autonomy of these great men. In fact, the authorities' hold on the immunist estates crumbled rapidly: the excessive generosity of rulers and the seizure of immunist territories by the *laity through the intermediary of *advocates or **vidames* – obligatory representatives of churchmen by virtue of *canon law – ended by increasing the grip of the aristocracy over Church properties; the advocates, rather than devoted agents of the establishments concerned, became more and more invasive, and the control that the immunist lords could exercise over their subordinates was hardly more effective than that which the ruler had over his counts. The phenomenon was less felt in the Midi, where the absence of advocacy in the Carolingian sense of the term and the exercise by the count of the powers devolved in the North to the advocate corresponded to the persistence of a different ecclesiastical tradition. This does not alter the fact that it was generally through immunity that the Church succeeded in integrating itself into vassalic society shortly after the year 1000.

In the Lombard principalities of Capua, Salerno and *Benevento, and in southern *Italy generally, immunity was applied later than in Italy subject to the *Franks. Moreover the struggles of the *Communes against ecclesiastical privileges, especially fiscal ones, remain memorable. Yet in the late Middle Ages these privileges ended in a decisive affirmation and even found legal formulation, especially with *Urban V's *bull *In coena Domini*, and were later confirmed by Urban VIII (*Pastoralis romanorum pontificum vigilantia*, 1627). It is superfluous to add that such principles would be repudiated by modern legislation, with the sole safeguard of the immunity kept by religious buildings and regulated by *concordat.

R. Schröder, *Lehrbuch der deutschen Rechtsgeschichte*, Berlin, 1932 (7th ed.). – M. Conte Coronata, *Introductio in ius ecclesiasticum*, Turin, 1948 (3rd ed.). – F. Calasso, *Medioevo del diritto*, 1, *Le fonti*, Milan, 1954, 188-197. – F. L. Ganshof, *L'Immunité dans la monarchie franque*, *RSJB*, 1, 1958, 171. – G. Tabacco, *Egemonie sociali e strutture del potere nel Medioevo italiano*, Turin, 1979. – L. Gatto, *Il Feudalismo*, Rome, 1997, 47-59.

Christian Lauranson-Rosaz and Attilio Stendardi

**IMPROPERIA.** "Improperia" is the name given to a text sung on Good Friday, during the *adoration of the *cross. These are the reproaches (*improperare* means "to reproach") addressed by *Christ to his people for their ingratitude. Their source of inspiration is biblical (Mic 6, 3-4; 8, 2. 3. 7). There are two series of chants: the first, which uses some Greek *acclamations, dates from the 8th c. and is manifestly inspired by the *Byzantine liturgy; the second series, finer from a literary point of view, takes up and develops the substance of the first. There is no manuscript evidence of the second series before the 11th c. and its first attestation is that of the liturgy of *Benevento. It has been ignored by numerous diocesan or religious liturgies (*Dominicans, *Premonstratensians).

G. Jaquemet, "Impropères", *Cath.*, 5, 1963, 1374-1377.

Guy-Marie Oury

***INCASTELLAMENTO.*** In the strict sense, the Italian word *incastellamento* designates the act of fortifying a building or a larger settlement. Italian historiography has progressively enriched the notion, applying the word as a term of contrast to that of *inurbamento* and using it to express the appearance of *castles and fortified *villages (*castrum*, *castellum*) and the consecutive birth of territories subject to feudal lordship, conceived primarily as abstract legal entities. Pierre Toubert's research on *Latium has shown how the phenomenon was at the centre of the transformations of population, settlement, and rural society between the 10th and 12th centuries. *Castra*, grouped together in small areas often on hilltops, defended by walls, commanded areas organised in accordance with the requirements of concentration and integration of the feudal lordship into the socio-legal system. The beginnings of the phenomenon can be ascribed to the 920s and, although the essential part of its manifestations, with the creation of the major *castra*, was complete by the mid 11th c., it continued until the end of the 12th century. A response to defensive needs, but primarily a rational solution to the tensions provoked in land occupation and the management of resources at a time of demographic growth and favourable economic circumstances, *incastellamento* was the material expression of the nascent territorial lordships that were taking over from the great

Carolingian *estates. The phenomenon was linked to a profound transformation of the landscape: the peasants gradually abandoned their houses scattered in the countryside and came to live next to the lord's fortress. For this reason, *incastellamento* was connected to the gradual disappearance of the latifundiary system; lands were differently organised to comply with land use and the demands of cultivation: the orchard, which needed continuous care, was placed immediately next to the wall or even inside the wall; the *vines were further off; while the land furthest from the settlement was left to cereal cultivation. The break with the previous organisation was all the clearer since it was accompanied by the systematic adoption of stone in rural construction.

Since the publication of Pierre Toubert's work (1973), the notion of *incastellamento* has been generally accepted as a descriptive and explanatory model for the evolution of social life in the Christian West Mediterranean basin; but in recent years it has been subjected to continuous verification in the light of certain observations and considerations. In some regions, for example, the building of the *castrum* seems to have been merely an element imposed on pre-existing structures and forms of settlement (*e.g.* in Friuli and, in some respects, *Tuscany); other regions knew only a "hybrid" *incastellamento*. The modifications of the concept mainly concern the intensity and chronology of the concentration of settlements: it seems to have been a movement of long duration, beginning at the end of Antiquity and failing to eliminate every form of dispersal. The impact on the old manorial forms, on the traditional network of *parishes, on the change in building materials, was neither so immediate nor so heavy as had been thought. Some have even denied the exclusive responsibility of the signorial class for the promotion of the phenomenon of *castra*, instead ascribing to *peasant communities an unsuspected capacity for initiative. In the present state of research, it is more advisable to restore the term to its original meaning, so as to avoid projecting onto the 10th c. a conceptual pattern fully applicable only in the 12th and 13th centuries. This does not alter the fact that the *castrum* was the visible manifestation of a complex series of evolutions; by bringing them together into a single concept, scholars have been able to recognise the common dynamic that was at the basis of the phenomenon.

P. Toubert, *Les structures du Latium médiéval. Le Latium méridional et la Sabine du IXᵉ siècle à la fin du XIIᵉ siècle*, Rome, 1973, 2 vol. – *Castrum*, 1-7, Lyon-Rome-Madrid, 1983-2000. – A. A. Settia, *Castelli e villaggi nell'Italia padana. Popolamento, potere e sicurezza fra IX e XIII secolo*, Naples, 1984. – P. Toubert, "Incastellamento", *LdM*, 5, 1991. – *"L'incastellamento". Actes des rencontres de Gérone (26-27 nov. 1992) et de Rome (5-7 mai 1994)*, Rome, 1998.

François Bougard

**INCENSE.** The use of incense was introduced into the Christian liturgies from at least the 4th c., with various meanings. At first it was in the Syrian and Egyptian churches, in reference to the Mosaic tradition of offering incense morning and evening (Ex 30, 7 ff.). This tradition was perpetuated and amply developed in the *Coptic liturgy which knew an "offering of incense evening and morning" each time the eucharistic liturgy was to be celebrated. It was the same in the Antiochene Syrian liturgies with a more clearly penitential accent (*hussayé*) and in the setting of a *prayer both doxological and didactic (*sedro*). It was in the same perspective that censing took place at various moments of the eucharistic liturgy.

In the *Roman liturgical tradition, a trace of this tradition was maintained during the singing of the gospel canticles of *lauds and *vespers. But the most usual meaning, inherited from pre-Christian Roman usages, made it a rite of honour during the *mass or various ceremonies.

C. Atcheley, *A History of the Use of Incense in Divine Worship*, London, 1909. – E. Fehrenbach, "Encens", *DACL*, 5, 1, 1922, 2-21.

Irénée-Henri Dalmais

**INCENSE BOAT.** The name "boat" was given to the recipient containing incense, carried by the *thurifer. This recipient often took the form of a small ship, or boat, whence its name *navicula*; incense was taken from it with the help of a spoon.

*Les Trésors des églises de France. Musée des Arts décoratifs, 1965*, Paris, 1965.

Guy-Marie Oury

**INCEST.** In the strict sense, incest designates sexual relations between a man and a woman linked by bonds of *kinship, a situation variously estimated according to times and places. The notion of incest held an important place in *canon law and in medieval society, firstly because it was applied to a wide circle of kinship, but also because the incestuous character of a union was often alleged in order to have a *marriage pronounced null, since the path of *divorce was rejected by the Church, sole judge of matrimonial cases in the Middle Ages.

In the name of morality and "natural law", *Roman law had suppressed incest, in the penal code as a *crimen publicum* punished by relegation to an island, and in the civil code by obligation to cease such a union, which could not constitute a legitimate marriage. Jewish law enumerated at length the degrees of kinship that forbade sexual relations (Lev 18, 6-18). Disapproval of incest was expressed in the multitude of provisions issued by *councils in the early Middle Ages, sometimes supported by the civil law. Union was forbidden between relatives in direct line *ad infinitum*, in collateral line to the sixth degree, according to the Roman computation of kinship. The violation of these prohibitions exposed a person to *excommunication and confiscation of property. "Classical" canon law, from the 11th to the 13th c., returned repeatedly to the question. With hesitations as to the extent of the prohibition: infinite in direct line, in collateral line it oscillated between the seventh degree (canonical computation) and the fourth degree (*Lateran IV, 1215, canon 50). The weapon of prohibition was moreover two-edged: extending the prohibition penalized any shocking relationship, but it allowed people, by invoking its discovery, to end a union and set aside the principle of indissolubility. Examples of this practice abound (*Philip Augustus and Ingeborg). To get a wide prohibition of kinship respected was difficult at a time when marriage could be contracted without publicity (bans became obligatory for all *Christendom only at the fourth Lateran council, and their absence did not entail the nullity of a marriage). Moreover, there was no register of civil status proving kinship. The conditions of life (narrowness of rural communities, absence of social mobility) and the prejudices of the *nobility (marriage among noble or princely families) limited choices and led to endogamy. Nevertheless, the kinship taken into account was widely extended: "blood" kinship, but also adoptive kinship from the 1180s. The extent of this latter remains disputed. Prohibition was certain for marriage between adoptants and adoptive children as well as between brothers and sisters by adoption. Beyond that, there is no unanimity. Finally, a spiritual kinship resulted from *baptism or *confirmation: so marriage was forbidden between godfather and godmother, and between godfather or godmother and their godchildren. All in all, the Middle Ages knew a certain disapproval of incest, through a legislation that was abundant but hardly coherent; the effectiveness of these measures is difficult to estimate, but they left room for many tolerances and facilitated the break-up of marriages.

J. Gaudemet, *Le Mariage en Occident*, Paris, 1987.

Jean Gaudemet

**INDIA.** For the Greeks, India was at the eastern extremity of the earth. According to Herodotus, Asia was inhabited only as far as India, beyond which were unknown deserts; in reaching the Indus, Alexander arrived at one of the ends of the world. This doubtless explains why, ever since Ctesias's *Indica* (5th c. BC), India has been the land of all marvels, with fabulous plants and animals and monstrous men like the famous Cynocephali.

These old traditions, brought together in the works of Pliny and Solinus, were known from the early Middle Ages. Basic texts like those of Orosius (*Historia adversum paganos*, 5th c.) and *Isidore of Seville (*Etymologiarum libri XIII*, 7th c.) established the geographical nomenclature of India, with its two rivers, Indus and Ganges (assimilated to Phison, one of the four rivers of the earthly *Paradise), and the list of its riches and marvels, *ivory, precious stones, elephants, *dragons and griffons.

The 13th c. saw all this marvellous stuff enriched still further by the literature on Alexander, notably the famous *Roman d'Alexandre* which presents a fantastic fauna and the oracle-trees of the sun and the moon, as well as the Brahmin sages endowed with all virtues. From this century also dates the *Letter of *Prester John*, whose empire was situated in India, with its fairy trees, its rivers of precious stones, its sumptuous palace.

India was also a land evangelized by the apostle Thomas, according to a legend going back to the 7th c. with Pseudo-Abdias's *Acts of St Thomas*. This same text distinguished three Indias, one opposite *Ethiopia, one opposite the land of the Medes, the third at the end of the world. This distinction, followed in *Orderic Vitalis's *Historia ecclesiastica*, would engender all sorts of errors. Post-Ptolemaean geographers were already failing to distinguish properly between Ethiopia and India. Despite a better knowledge of the continent of Asia due to the voyages of Westerners from the mid 13th c., there were still many hesitations, attested by cartography and missionaries' letters or travellers' tales, and this until the middle of the 14th century.

India still kept its mythical character. *Pierre d'Ailly devoted a long chapter of his *Imago mundi* (1410) to its marvels. And it was in the Indies that Christopher *Columbus thought to disembark after crossing the Ocean.

Cosmas Indicopleustes, *Topographie chrétienne*, W. Wolska-Conus (ed.), 1968-1973 (3 vol.; "SC", 141, 159 and 197). – Oderic de Pordenone, *Les voyages en Asie du bienheureux frère Oderic de Pordenone, religieux de saint François*, H. Cordier (ed.), Paris, 1891.

J. Richard, "L'extrême-Orient légendaire au Moyen Âge, roi David et Prêtre Jean", *AEt*, 2, 1957, 225-244. – J. K. Wright, *The Geographical Lore of the Time of the Crusades*, New York, 1965. – M. Mollat, M. de La Roncière, *Les Portulans. Cartes marines du XIII^e au XVII^e siècle*, Paris, 1984. – L.N. Gumilev, *Searches for an Imaginary Kingdom: the Legend of the Kingdom of Prester John*, Cambridge, 1987.

Christiane Deluz

**INDIA, CHRISTIANS IN.** The tradition relative to the preaching and martyrdom of St Thomas in India is uncertain; but the presence of Christians at Taprobane is attested by Cosmas Indicopleustes, and the catholicos of *Baghdad Timothy I takes notice of journeys by monks to *China and India (between 780 and 829); it is probable that Christianity followed the same route as Christian merchants who went to seek *spices and pearls in Southern India. These frequented the port of Quilon, where a king of Travancore gave them land to build a church (825), doubtless the one, built by Sabr'iso, that received a *charter (on a copper plaque) exempting its ministers from taxes and giving the Christians control of the market, which they still possessed in the 14th c.; at that time they had a leader called *dominus Nascarinorum*. Other communities, with their churches, were strung out along the route from the Persian Gulf, notably in Gujerat. In the 9th c., a metropolis and *bishops were designated for India; their flocks were especially numerous in Cochin and Travancore.

Meanwhile, St Thomas's tomb at Meliapur was famous for the *miracles that *Gregory of Tours learned about from an eyewitness, and it attracted *pilgrims even from the West, like Bernard the Penitent and Henry of Morungen (12th-13th cc.). Latin *merchants followed the same route as their predecessors from the 13th century. Quilon was an obligatory stage on the maritime route to China. So missionaries going to China touched at Quilon, like *John of Montecorvino (1290-1291), *Odoric of Pordenone (1322) and John of Marignolla (1346-1347). The latter found a church of St John of the Latins there and decorated it with paintings. Four *Franciscans and a *Dominican, also on their way to China, put into Thana (Salsette) and were the first to be martyred there in 1321. The fifth, Jordan Cathala of Severac, devoted himself first to the small, religiously unsupported *Nestorian communities of Gujerat and Konkan, where preaching was made difficult by the progress of the rule of the Sultans of Delhi; then he went to the lands beyond their rule, where his success led to him being made bishop of Quilon in 1329.

The presence of this Latin-rite Christendom doubtless did not survive the interruption of commercial relations between the West and the Far East in the late 14th c., though episodic contacts seem to have taken place early in the next century.

J. Dauvillier, "Les provinces chaldéennes 'de l'extérieur' au Moyen Âge", *Mélanges Cavallera*, Toulouse, 1948, 312-314. – B. Colless, "The Traders of the Pearl", *Abr-n.*, 9, 1969-1970, 17-38. – J. Richard, "Les missionnaires latins dans l'Inde au XIV^e siècle", *StVen*, 12, 1970, 231-242. – J. Richard, *La Papauté et les Missions d'Orient au Moyen Âge*, Rome, 1977. – L. Brown, *The Indian Christians of St Thomas*, Cambridge, 1982 (2nd ed.).

Jean Richard

**INDICTION.** Starting from the year AD 312, the indiction indicated, by a figure from 1 to 15, the place of a year in a 15-year cycle whose rank, unlike the Greek Olympiads, was not indicated: from 1 Sept 312 to 31 Aug 313, the indiction was 1 (as it was again from 1 Sept 327, 342, etc.). At first linked to the periodic revision of taxation quotas, the indiction was soon used as a subsidiary system of dating, then it was made obligatory in private documents by Justinian in 537. It was subsequently kept up by tradition: in the West, quite common up to the 11th and 12th cc., not without frequent errors in calculation, it remained in use among those who, directly or indirectly, had been influenced by Justinian's legislation (public *notaries, pontifical *chancery) or Greek culture (southern *Italy, where it long remained the only way of designating years, *e.g.* in the Angevin Registers). The starting-point of the computation (style) also evolved: the original style, called Greek (1 Sept), could be replaced by the so-called Western, imperial or *Bede's style (24 Sept) or the so-called Roman or pontifical style (25 Dec), adopted by the papal chancery in 1088.

M. Del Piazzo, *Manuale di cronologia*, Rome, 1981.

Olivier Guyotjeannin

**INDULGENCES.** In the Theodosian Code, *indulgentia* designated an amnesty granted by the Christian emperors. From 1215, the meaning of the term "indulgence" corresponded to its present use, which may be defined as "an extra-sacramental remission, granted by the Church, of the temporal penalty due to sins already pardoned" (P. Galtier). In the pardon of *sin, the guilt, *i.e.* the moral fault, the offense to *God, is wiped out by *confession, by *absolution, while the temporal penalty persists and has to be paid in this world or in *purgatory. Indulgence thus allows this burden to be diminished. The principle of indulgence rests on the idea of the "*treasure of the Church", laid up by the favours of *Christ, the Virgin and the saints. Each Christian's membership of the body of the Church implies a communion among persons and a communion of spiritual goods. Thus, each one's sin harms the whole body. The treasure of the Church allows an exchange of spiritual goods, the *merits of some helping the remission of the sins of others. The granting of indulgences is in the hands of the *pope, trustee of the Church's treasure. The pope can also delegate this power to *cardinals or *bishops. Though the indulgence is granted by the Church, the sinner remits his fault before God.

Indulgence is closely linked to the practice of penitence. The *penance known to the first Christians was performed by expiatory works (*fasts, long *prayers, *mortifications), more or less tiring according to the gravity of the fault. Very early on, the Church envisaged the remission of this penalty. The council of Carthage (251) decided that *lapsi* could be reconciled through long penance, after precise examination of their *contrition by the bishop. The councils of Ancyra (314) and Nicaea (325) confirmed this acceleration of reconciliation through the intercession of the bishop. From the 5th c., penance underwent profound modifications. Tariffed penance, practised in Celtic lands, spread: from now on the penalty corresponded to the gravity of the fault committed. It could go from fasts, *flagellations, almsgiving or prayers to exile for life or for a limited period. But the system was lightened by the principle of redemption confirmed by the council of Tribur in 895. From now on it could be replaced by the penalty of good works such as pilgrimage to Rome or maintenance of churches, *abbeys or *hospitals.

In the 11th and 12th cc., general remissions developed, no longer linked to individual penalties. They were granted, whatever the sin committed, on the occasion of the *consecration of a church, the construction of an abbey, an *anniversary, the translation of *relics. These indulgences were considered partial: they remitted a part of the penalty required. Plenary indulgence, on the other hand, pardoned the fault and remitted the penalty; it was granted by the pope on the occasion of *e.g.* a *crusade: such was the case of that granted by *Urban II in 1095 at the council of *Clermont.

The 13th c. saw a spread of the plenary indulgence: at the fourth *Lateran council (1215), *Innocent IV granted such an indulgence to the crusaders and to those who offered *subsidies. Visitors to the church of Santa Maria degli Angeli at *Assisi benefited from the indulgence of the *Portiuncula.

Partial indulgences also multiplied through the activity of preachers of indulgences who collected *alms at the same time. The papacy tried to control their actions by requiring them to be furnished with papal or episcopal letters (decision of Lateran IV, of the council of Béziers) or by seeking to limit the scope of the indulgences. Lateran IV limited these to 40 days for bishops.

In the 12th c., theologians took hardly any interest in indulgence: *Peter Lombard and Gratian's **Decretum* gave it little importance. In the 13th c., however, a more systematic reflection was put in place: *Thomas Aquinas developed a theoretical reflection on the concept, the beneficiary and the dispenser of indulgence. *Henry of Ghent put forward a complete definition: "Indulgence is the remission or mitigation of the temporal penalties incurred by actual sins, which still remain to be paid after sacramental *absolution: remission or mitigation made in compensation for reasonable considerations by a legitimate ecclesiastical authority and drawn from the treasure of the Church in the superabundance of the *satisfactions of the just."

In the 14th c., the number of indulgences grew considerably. Requests addressed to the pope by monasteries, churches, *confraternities, prelates and princes multiplied: the grant of indulgences could accompany the desire to develop the cult devoted to a particular saint, the celebration of certain *feasts or the organisation of *pilgrimages. The celebration of the *jubilee was also intimately linked to the obtaining of a plenary indulgence, acquired by visiting the churches of *Rome. On the occasion of that of 1300, celebrated by *Boniface VIII, numerous faithful flocked to Rome and were thus admitted to the benefit of this favour. The frequency of jubilees increased in the course of the 14th c., thus multiplying the possibility of obtaining plenary indulgences: initially fixed by Boniface VIII every hundred years, the jubilee was prescribed by *Clement VI every fifty years and by *Urban VI every thirty.

The 14th c. also saw the development of indulgences linked to *confessionalia* which authorized their beneficiaries to choose a confessor outside those whom the Church recognised, viz. the bishop, the *parish priest or the rural dean. From the middle of the century, such confessors obtained the power to remit, with the sins, the whole of the penalties linked to them.

Yet the papacy sought to stay the multiplication of indulgences. The *Decretal *Abusionibus* of the council of *Vienne of 1312 severely condemned the abuses committed by the collectors. But this increase in indulgences continued throughout the 15th c., through the actions of bishops and *legates who regularly organised tours of *collection accompanied by the granting of indulgences. Papal concessions saw the same evolution on the occasion of the jubilees, whose frequency increased once more: Paul II decided that they should take place every 25 years. At this time, plenary indulgences could also be granted on the occasion of the building of churches. Furthermore, in 1480 appeared the first attestation of a plenary indulgence on the occasion of a pilgrimage to *Jerusalem.

The *dead also became beneficiaries of indulgences. In a letter to Henry IV of Castile, *Calixtus III granted a plenary indulgence in favour of the souls in *purgatory, in order to encourage the crusade. *Sixtus IV repeated a similar indulgence on the occasion of the rebuilding of *St Peter's basilica.

The concession of indulgences granted conjointly with almsgiving saw an evolution that sometimes favoured the lucrative dimension of the operation: as when from 1515 to 1518 the Emperor Charles V organised a preaching of indulgences for the upkeep of the maritime dikes. The distribution of indulgences was the occasion of numerous abuses, like the use of the money collected for other purposes or the suppression of the value of certain indulgences. These practices were reproved many times by theologians like *Berthold of Regensburg or by movements which the Church condemned. John *Wycliffe rejected the role of the pope in granting indulgences, stating that only *God could choose the beneficiaries of his *grace. Jan *Hus also rebelled against the practice of indulgences. Finally, the excesses occasioned by their collection were present in Luther's revolt. This was set off by the collection for indulgences organised by the archbishop of *Magdeburg and intended half for *St Peter's in Rome, half to reimburse a loan he had contracted with the *banking house of Fugger.

N. Paulus, *Geschichte des Ablasses im Mittelalter vom Ursprung bis zur Mitte des 14. Jahrhunderts*, Paderborn, 1922-1923. – E. Jombart, "Indulgences", *DDC*, 5, 1953, 1331-1352. – P. Adnès, "Indulgences", *DSp*, 7, 2, 1971, 1713-1728. – G. A. Benrath, "Ablass", *TRE*, 1, 1977, 347-364. – N. Orme, "Indulgences in the Diocese of Exeter, 1100-1536", *Transactions of the Devonshire Association*, 120, 1988, 15-32. – B. Matray, "Les indulgences au XIVe siècle: Étude des lettres de Jean XXII (1316-1334) et d'Urbain V (1363-1370)", *CH*, 33, 1988, 135-151.

Véronique Pasche

**INDULT.** Among the numerous categories of papal *letters called *communes* that the *chancery established in the course of the 14th c. with a view to their registration, that of "indults, privileges and *dispensations" was part of the limitless field of graces. With the exception of *indulgences *in articulo mortis* or linked to pious visits to sanctuaries, it was the faculty to derogate from common law, as in matrimonial dispensations, dispensations accorded to *clerics otherwise barred by age or illegitimate birth or *pluralism of *benefices, time allowed for episcopal *consecration and abbatial benediction, the validation of collations of benefices by the ordinaries, the fiscal relief of religious establishments, the reconciliation of profaned churches and *cemeteries, and the lifting of *interdicts that put towns and countries under the ban of the Church.

Michel Hayez

**INFALLIBILITY, PAPAL.** The idea of papal infallibility – not the dogma, which dates from the late 19th c. – took shape in the 12th c. with the doctrines of *Gregory VII. According to that great *pope, the Holy See judges spiritual as well as temporal affairs. The pope possesses primacy in the Church, since he is the vicar of Christ. The Roman pontiff represents on earth the *authority instituted immediately by *God. Finally he is, in the name of the Church, the sole interpreter of God's will; his person is inviolable; he can be judged by no-one, not even by the Church which might nevertheless be empowered to do so, though Gregory rejects this (**Dictatus papae*: Registrum, II, 55a, ed. Caspar, Berlin, 1930).

Was this a personal infallibility? Gregory's texts do not allow us to state this with certainty. The *Decretists, *c.*1200, admitted that papal primacy had been established firstly by *Christ himself and secondly by the *councils, though the pope could not contest the truth of Scripture: he was the supreme guide within the framework of divine *Revelation, especially in matters of jurisdiction. Such was the traditional doctrine, which was distinct from the idea of papal infallibility. For the *canonists, indeed, the pope was not of himself the guarantee of the stability of the faith; Christ did not promise *Peter that he would never err in his **magisterium* at the head of the Church, but only that he would have the *grace to persevere in the faith. It was the universal Church that possessed not infallibility but, *stricto sensu*, indefectibility.

The idea of papal infallibility emerged from the discussions concerning the relations between the pope and the general council. On this question, the Decretists and *canonists did not teach that the pope was infallible. That was not believed in the 12th c.; only the Church and the first four general councils were so. In matters of *faith, the general council was superior to the pope. Then, under the influence of St *Bonaventure's thought, the idea of papal infallibility became preponderant, thanks to his doctrine of papal monarchy. If the universal Church could not err, he who was its head, the pope, could not logically do so either. For Bonaventure, the pope's supreme authority was obviously jurisdictional; it was also doctrinal. Bonaventure does not use the word: "infallible" pope, but he affirms the idea, viz. "the inerrancy of the pope".

Among the *Franciscan masters, it was *Peter John Olivi who clearly formulated the question of papal infallibility, in a text entitled *De infallibilitate romani pontificis*. The essence of his argument consists in establishing that the pope cannot err and that he thus possesses the *clavis scientiae* as long as he is the true pope and the head of the Church. In the 14th c., this position would be taken up by supporters of the plenitude of papal power, like *Augustine of Ancona.

For *Marsilius of Padua, on the contrary, in his *Defensor pacis*, the pope was not at all infallible, since his power was, in a way, of human origin; only the general council was infallible in matters of faith. William of *Ockham contested the pope's power of revoking the decisions and decrees of his predecessors in matters of faith. In his eyes, only Holy Scripture and the doctrine of the universal Church, which cannot err, constituted the rule in matters of faith (*Tractatus contra Ioannem*, in: William of Ockham, *Opera politica*, ed. G. Sikes *et al.*, t. III, p. 72).

M. Maccarrone, "Una questione inedita dell'Olivi sull'infallibilità del Papa", *RSCI*, 3, 1949, 309-343. – M. Pacaut, *La théocratie. L'Eglise et le pouvoir au Moyen-Age*, Paris, 1957. – Y. Congar, *L'Église, de saint Augustin à l'époque moderne*, Paris, 1968, 221-223. – B. Tierney, *The Origins of Papal Infallibility (1150-1350)*, Leiden, 1972.

Jeannine Quillet

**INITIALS.** Initials could be painted, ornamented, historiated or filigreed. This element of decoration – the initial was its first element – must be seen in relation to the evolution of the practice of reading.

The first ornamented initials – dated to the 6th c. – were placed at the head of the work to decorate it; they gradually appeared at the head of large sections of the text, of chapters and then of paragraphs, and from then on their function was to emphasize the divisions of the text and guide the reading of it. They served as points of reference.

Historiated initials made their appearance in the 8th c. and enjoyed great success in the *Romanesque period. Note that they were not necessarily intended to illustrate the text. Their format and decoration often had a hierarchical value in relation to the text: a 15th-c. *Ordo scribendi secundum artem* contains indications prescribing the dimensions and decor of the initials with a view to a hierarchy of ornamentation of the *book.

C. Nordenfalk, *Die spätantike Zierbuchstaben*, Stockholm, 1970. – J. J. G. Alexander, *The Decorated Letter*, London, 1978.

Guy Lanoë

**INNOCENT II, POPE (died 1143).** At the death of Honorius II in 1130, Gregorio Papareschi could legitimately hope to ascend the throne of St *Peter. A *cardinal since 1116, his capacity as a negotiator had been shown by his participation in the preparation of the *concordat of *Worms (1122) and an important legation to the king of *France. At *Rome, he enjoyed the favours of the Frangipani family, represented in the *Sacred College by the enterprising *chancellor Haimeric. But the hostility of the *Pierleoni clan led to a double *election. Conscious of the approaching difficulties, Haimeric tried to force the hand of the Sacred College by precipitately organising the election of Cardinal Papareschi, who took the name of Innocent II. His main rival, Cardinal Pietro Pierleoni, reacted without delay: the same day, 14 Feb 1130, he assembled those members of the College who had not taken part in the choice of Gregorio Papareschi and had himself proclaimed *pope under the name of *Anacletus II.

Constrained by force to abandon Rome, Innocent went to *Pisa and embarked for France. Both parties then worked to find support among the regular powers. To try and see more clearly into the matter, *Louis VI decided to call a *council at Étampes. From a legal point of view, the situation appeared inextricable: in the name of different interpretations of the decree of *Nicholas II (1059) which at that time regulated papal election, Anacletus's supporters, like those of Innocent, claimed to have right on their side. It was by defending the moral qualities of his favourite that *Bernard of Clairvaux carried the decision of the assembly. Supported by one who could pass for the most important religious personality of his time, Innocent had won the day. The king of *France recognised him as the new supreme pontiff. *Lothar, king of the Romans, did the same in October 1130. The kings of *England, *Castile and *Aragon were not slow to rally. Lothar headed a military expedition to allow Innocent to return to Rome. But hardly had he left the city than Innocent was obliged to flee once more: Anacletus resisted, and the dénouement of the crisis had to wait until his death, 25 Jan 1138.

Innocent II's pontificate continued the reforming policy initiated by *Gregory VII. He held the second *Lateran council in 1139, and settled one of the most famous theological quarrels of his century by condemning *Abelard (1140). The rigour of character shown by Innocent II earned him a war against *Roger of Sicily, at the end of which the pontiff was obliged to confirm the royal title accorded to his opponent by Anacletus to ensure his support. He fiercely opposed *Louis VII over episcopal *investitures, and managed only to nourish the discontent of the Romans. He died 13 Sept 1143.

E. Amann, *DThC*, 7, 2, 1927, 1950-1961. – A. Fliche, *HE*, 9, 1, 1948, 50-88. – M. Pacaut, "Innocent II", *DHP*, 1994, 875-876.

Daniel Baloup

**INNOCENT III, POPE (1160/1161-1216).** Lotario de Comitibus (Conti), born at Gavignano near Segni, was elected *pope 8 Jan 1198, consecrated 22 Feb of that year and died 16 July 1216 at *Perugia. After studying *theology at *Paris and *canon law at *Bologna, he was made *cardinal-deacon of SS. Sergio e Baccho. He was the author of theological writings, of little importance in content but very widely circulated (*De miseria humane conditionis*; *De missarum mysteriis*; *De quadripartita specie nuptiarum*). His major preoccupation was the *crusade decided in 1198, whose organisation he arranged, committing himself much more than his predecessors, but he quickly lost control of the enterprise, which

*Innocent III*. 13th-c. mosaic at Rome.

in the long term was a bitter failure. At first he enthusiastically hailed the capture of *Constantinople in 1204, thinking of a *union with the Greek Church, as well as the new ecclesiastical and political organisation of the Latin Empire, but he very soon expressed great reservations. Not until 1213 could he call a new crusade. In the struggle against *heresies, on one hand he strengthened measures of repression, but on the other he gained the return to the Church of radical reformist groups (like the *Humiliati). Recognising their promise for the future, he favoured new religious movements (St *Francis of Assisi, St *Dominic). The murder of the papal legate *Peter of Castelnau was the occasion for him to call the crusade against the Albigenses in 1209, which stained Innocent III's image by reason of the abuses committed by the crusaders under the protection of papal privileges.

The pope's activities, mingling political and religious questions, affected practically every country in *Christendom. Thus, in central *Italy, after the collapse of the power of the *Staufen, Innocent became the *de facto* founder of the *Patrimonium Petri*. The regency that lasted until 1208 in the kingdom of *Sicily, which was handed down by testament to the pope by Queen *Constance in 1198, swallowed up much money and energy. In *Germany, which from 1198 lived under the regime of double kingship, Innocent, fearing lest the policy of the Staufen be pursued in Italy, quickly sided with *Otto IV, but tried only moderately to influence the division of powers. The accession of the *Guelfs to the kingship, then to the *Empire (*coronation in Oct 1209) after the murder of *Philip of Swabia in 1208, soon aroused the opposition of the pope who, after Otto's *excommunication, favoured the election of *Frederick II in Dec 1212. In *England, the battle for the see of the archbishop of *Canterbury led Innocent to launch an *interdict that lasted from 1207 to 1213 and only the threat of a French invasion ended by forcing King *John to hand over his kingdom to the pope, to have it restored to him in *fief. In *France, Innocent tried several times to undertake peace mediations in the war between France and England. But his relations with *Philip Augustus were envenomed until 1213 by the affair of his repudiated wife, Ingeborg. Innocent's pontificate reached its apogee with the fourth *Lateran council (1215), very well attended, whose canons were essentially to do with pastoral questions.

With Innocent III, the medieval papacy reached the summit of its power, but setbacks in the temporal domain already showed up the limits of its influence. In the properly religious domain, the concentration of papal power would in the long run lead to ultra-conservatism.

*PL*, 1855, 214-217 (*Gesta Innocentii III papae*; works; registers). – *Regestum Innocentii III papae super negotio Romani imperii*, F. Kempf (ed.), Rome, 1947. – *Die Register Innocenz'III*, O. Hageneder (ed.) *et al.*, Vienna, 1964, 1979, 1993, 1995, 1997 (1st, 2nd, 5th-7th years of pontificate). – *The Letters of Pope Innocent III concerning England and Wales*, C. R. Cheney (ed.), M. G. Cheney (ed.), London, 1967. – Lotario dei Segni (Pope Innocent III), *De Miseria Condicionis Humanae*, R.E. Lewis (ed.), Athens (GA), 1978. – *Innocent III: Selected Documents on the Pontificate 1198-1216*, B. Bolton (ed.), Manchester, 1999.

A. Fliche, C. Thouzellier, Y. Azais, *La Chrétienté romaine (1198-1274)*, *HE*, 10, Paris, 1950. – H. Tillmann, *Pope Innocent III*, Amsterdam, 1980. –H. Roscher, *Papst Innocenz III und die Kreuzzüge*, Göttingen, 1969. – M. Maccarrone, *Studi su Innocenzo III*, Padua, 1972. – M. Maccarrone, *Nuovi studi su Innoocenzo III*, Rome, 1995. – H. Wolter, *HKG(J)*, 3, 2, Freiburg, 1973, 168-213. – C. R. Cheney, *Innocent III and England*, Stuttgart, 1976. – W. Imkamp, *Das Kirchenbild Innocenz'III*, Stuttgart, 1983. – W. Maleczek, *Papst und Kardinalskolleg von 1191 bis 1216*, Vienna, 1984. – T. Holzapfel, *Papst Innozenz III. Philipp II. August, König von Frankreich und die englischwelfische Verbindung, 1198-1216*, Frankfurt am Main, 1991. – R. Foreville, *Le Pape Innocent III et la France*, Stuttgart, 1993. – *Innocent III: Vicar of Christ or Lord of the World?*, J. M. Powell (ed.), Washington (DC), 1994. – J. Sayers, *Innocent III. Leader of Europe*, London, 1994. – B. Bolton, *Innocent III*, Aldershot, 1995.

Werner Maleczek

**INNOCENT IV, POPE (*c.*1190-1254).** Sinibaldo *Fieschi came from a noble Ligurian family. Born in *c.* 1190, he studied at *Parma and then followed a career comparable to that of numerous 13th-c. prelates. It was as a *canonist, a training acquired at the *university of *Bologna, that he climbed the hierarchy of the Church's administrative machine. After 1226 he was *jurist to the Roman *Curia, before directing the pontifical *chancery.

Elevated to the dignity of *cardinal in 1227, he was close to *Gregory IX, with whom he shared a similar training and a great mistrust of the projects of *Frederick II: the heredity of the imperial office, which would mean a weakening of the *authority of the pontiff. He was rector of the *march of Ancona from 1234 to 1239. On the death of Celestine IV in 1241, a fragile and laborious compromise came into being in the *Sacred College.

After his *election as supreme pontiff in June 1243 under the name of Innocent IV, Sinibaldo Fieschi left the Peninsula for *Lyon where he held a *council from June to July 1245. There, with the encyclical *Cum simus super*, he formulated the project of reunifying the Roman and Eastern Churches, but he also inaugurated a policy of absolute opposition to Frederick II by deposing him, getting an anti-king, William of Holland, elected in his place in 1248 and supporting all the opponents of the *Staufen in *Italy. Striving to make the papacy the main political power in Italy, he thwarted the attempts of Frederick's successors to establish their power in *Germany against the rivalry of the great aristocratic families or in the kingdom of *Sicily.

Innocent IV tried to enrich the doctrinal and legal apparatus of papal power. As well as an abundant collection of *Decretals, he left commentaries on those of Gregory IX (*Apparatus super quinque libros decretalium*). In them he developed the doctrine of the *plenitudo potestatis* of the *pope, who holds without restriction the power of *Christ whose vicar he is. He gave this conception an absolute dimension. He thus broke in his favour the balance of the *temporal and spiritual powers, since his *authority participated in another order. As such, he had the capacity to depose monarchs and release their vassals from all *oaths, and even to intervene among the infidel.

Innocent died at *Naples in December 1254, while the presence of the Staufen in southern Italy dwindled and the papal monarchy asserted itself, not just as sole head of *Christendom, but also as the chief actor in the power politics of the Italian peninsula.

M. Pacaut, "L'autorité pontificale selon Innocent IV", *MA*, 66, 1960, 185-219. – C. Lefebvre, "Sinibalde dei Fieschi", *DDC*, 7, 1965, 1029-1062. – G. Le Bras, "Innocent IV romaniste. Examen de l'*Apparatus*", *StGra*, 11, 1967, 305-326. – A. Melloni, *Innocenzo IV. La concezione e l'esperienza della cristianità come* regimen unius personae, Genoa, 1990.

Thierry Pécout

**INNOCENT VI, POPE (1285/95-1362).** Of Limousin origin, Étienne Aubert, *juge-mage* in the **sénéchaussée* of *Toulouse in 1328, became bishop of *Noyon in 1338, then of *Clermont-Ferrand in 1340, was created *cardinal in 1342 and appointed grand *penitentiary. He was finally elected *pope on 18 Dec 1352.

The greatest success of his pontificate was the restoration of order in the *States of the Church in *Italy, carried out by Cardinal Gil *Albornoz whom he had appointed *legate. By contrast, Innocent failed in his attempts to restore peace between the kings of *France and *England. After the battle of Poitiers (1356), he had *Avignon, threatened by armed bands, surrounded by walls. All these expenses exhausted the resources of the papal treasury, and the plague *epidemic of 1361 deprived the pope of his closest collaborators. He died on 12 Sept 1362 and was buried in the Chartreuse of Villeneuve-lès-Avignon, which he had founded.

Innocent VI, *Lettres secrètes*, P. Gasnault (ed.), Paris, 1959-1976.

B. Guillemain, *La Cour pontificale d'Avignon*, Paris, 1966. – D. Williman, "Memoranda and sermons of Etienne Aubert (Innocent VI) as bishop (1338-1341)", *MS*, 37, 1975, 7-41. – P. Gasnault, "Innocenzo VI, papa", *Enciclopedia dei papi*, forthcoming.

Pierre Gasnault

**INNOCENTS, FEAST OF THE HOLY.** The episode of the massacre of the Innocents, ordered by Herod to ensure the destruction of the Infant King of the Jews, was frequently evoked by the Church *Fathers, notably in homiletic, where it was the object of reflections on suffering and innocence. It enjoyed a certain popularity in the last centuries of the Middle Ages. Fixed on 28 Dec, the liturgical *feast of the Holy Innocents followed imme-

*Ecumenical council held at Lyon by Pope Innocent IV against the emperor Frederick II.* Miniature from *Passages d'Outre-Mer* by Sébastien Mamerot of Soissons, 15th c. Paris, BNF

diately after that of Christmas. Referring to the themes, current in common piety, of *Christ's infancy and the sufferings for which he was destined, the massacre of the Innocents inspired an abundant iconography (from *frescos to the miniatures in *Books of Hours) and gave rise to dramatic representations.

From the 12th c., each year between the feast of the Holy Innocents and that of the *Circumcision (1 Jan), sometimes until Epiphany (6 Jan), the *canons, *deacons, scholars and choirboys of cathedral *schools, subject all year round to the authority of the *bishop or of their elders, gave themselves up to ritual pleasantries, parodying the episcopal offices and electing a false bishop. These collective rejoicings, going under a variety of names: "feast of the Innocents", "feast of Fools", "of Children", "of Deacons", or even "feast of the *ass", were repeatedly condemned by the ecclesiastical authorities (in 1198 by Bishop Eudes of Paris, in 1444 by the *faculty of theology at *Paris. . .). However in the 12th c., in his *Summa of ecclesiastical offices*, the *liturgist *John Beleth mentions these parodies as a regular custom. And various documents attest that up to the end of the Middle Ages, feasts of the Innocents or of Fools were regularly celebrated.

It is probable that a parallel was made between the Holy Innocents, victims of King Herod, and the "infants" who, around 28 Dec, took a symbolic ritual revenge on their superiors.

J. Heers, *Fêtes des fous et Carnavals*, Paris, 1983. – J. C. Schmitt, "Les Superstitions", *Histoire de la France religieuse*, J. Le Goff (dir.), R. Rémond (dir.), 1, Paris, 1988, 543-544. – *Bambini santi: rappresentazioni dell'infanzia e modelli agiografici*, A. Benvenuti Papi (ed.), E. Giannarelli (ed.), Turin, 1991. – P. A. Hayward, "Suffering and Innocence in Latin Sermons for the Feast of the Holy Innocents, c. 400-800", *The Church and Childhood*, D. Wood (ed.), Oxford, 1994, 67-80. – M. R. Dudley, "Natalis Innocentum: the Holy Innocents in Liturgy and Drama", *ibid.*, 233-242.

Michel Lauwers

**INQUISITION.** The defence of orthodoxy was among the tasks of the ecclesiastical hierarchy. With the affirmation of the papal monarchy, this task was gradually assumed by the papacy. Church historians generally tend to distinguish two types of inquisition: an episcopal inquisition and a papal inquisition. The episcopal

*Pope Gregory IX receives the list of those accused by the inquisitor.* Miniature from the *Decreta* of Gregory IX. 14th-c. Latin manuscript. Venice, Biblioteca Marciana.

inquisition lasted until the institution, under *Gregory IX, of inquisitors specifically delegated by the apostolic see for the repression of *heretics.

The problem of formulating norms that would regulate forced return to orthodoxy was posed in the last quarter of the 12th c., when the heterodox peril was perceived as urgent. With the *Decretal *Ad abolendam* issued at Verona by Lucius III in 1184 in agreement with the Swabian Emperor *Frederick I, *archbishops and *bishops were obliged to provide for the pursuit of heretics present in their respective ecclesiastical districts, and holders of public *authority, when requested by the Church authorities, to collaborate with them. The traditional collaboration between *sacerdotium* and *regnum* was here given an anti-heretical orientation, while *Innocent III's subsequent *Decretal *Vergentis in senium* in 1199 demonstrates the will of the papacy to place itself above the civil power. By equating heresy with the "crime of *lèse-majesté*" and doing so in his capacity as both pontiff and temporal lord, the pope as a "prince" imposed the model on other "princes": repression of heresy became one of the tasks that constituted and connoted political power, which, consequently and conversely, was delegitimized when it did not provide for the repression of heretics. But beware: judgment as to orthodoxy or heterodoxy was the responsibility of the ecclesiastical hierarchy, or rather of its head, the *pope.

So we can understand how Innocent III, faced with the resistance he met from the lords of the French Midi, personally took the initiative in the struggle against the dualist "good Christians" of that area, proclaiming in 1208 the notorious crusade against the Albigenses. We can understand how in 1213 *Frederick II promised the pope to give his active support to the eradication of the error of *heretica pravitas* and why he issued the *Constitutio in basilica Sancti Petri* on the day of his *coronation in Rome in Nov 1220, taking up and incorporating into imperial legislation earlier ecclesiastical provisions that had become part of *canon law. In neither case was this mere opportunism: the emperor was fully convinced that the repression of heresy and heretics was part of the prerogatives and functions of his high office. In doing so, however, he put himself, on the legal level, in a subordinate position to the papacy, while in fact expressing a spirit of competitiveness with the head of Roman Catholicity. Some have even thought that the decisions of *Gregory IX that led to the birth of the papal inquisition were taken in order to oppose imperial rivalry more effectively.

In the years between 1227 and 1231 emerges the figure of the inquisitor delegated by the apostolic see: the Dominicans *Conrad of Marburg and *Robert le Bougre were the first to operate under this title in the respective kingdoms of *Germany and *France. They were followed by innumerable friars, no longer just *Dominicans but also *Franciscans, who would hold the office of inquisitors of *heretica pravitas*. In support of repressive activity, the papacy issued increasingly precise norms for the regulation of this office. At the same time earlier legislation was assimilated, among which stand out the provisions taken by the ecclesiastical *synods that met in the French Midi. So inquisitorial activity conformed to canonistic principles; and an increasingly precise and articulate legal literature flourished. From this set of norms derived the so-called inquisitorial "manuals", *i.e.* works containing the formal elements to which the friars who held the repressive office had to conform.

Despite efforts at normalization, it is not easy to offer a complete picture of inquisitorial activity. But we can say that the inquisitor worked within large administrative areas gradually fixed and assigned by the papacy, and worked where someone or something called him. As a rule, when he appeared in a place, he held a "general *sermon" at which, among other things, he proclaimed the *tempus gratiae*, or the time during which anyone who had had anything to do with heretics and heresies had to appear to "confess" what he knew, declare his "external" repentance and thus avoid any condemnation. On the basis of information gathered on the spot, which completed what the inquisitor already knew (through having been orally informed of it, perhaps by spies paid for the purpose, or by the acts of his predecessors), he summoned the "suspects" (heretics or sympathizers): in reality, by the fact of not having appeared spontaneously before the inquisitor, these were *already* guilty. Nothing remained for them but to take note of the inquisitorial logic, either accepting or rejecting it. In the former case, the inquisitor would demand concrete information (not so much on religious ideas as on individuals) that would attest recognition of past "faults" and hence the desire to return to communion with the Roman Catholic Church: this involved the acceptance of certain penances (*prayers, *fasts, *pilgrimages, etc., up to the assumption of yellow crosses sewn visibly onto the clothing, or "voluntary" incarceration). In the latter case, the heretic "chose" the extreme penalty, the stake. Having completed his activity in one place, the inquisitor, after another "general sermon", publicly pronounced the sentences, beginning with the minor punishments and moving on to the capital ones, according to a ceremonial of great theatrical effect and emotional intensity: this would culminate in the "*auto-da-fé*". Admittedly, the inquisitors' procedures were not always and everywhere borrowed from the "model" we have summarily expounded. Often, especially in the central decades of the 13th c., procedures were more rapid and casual.

We should not forget that the accusation of heresy had a very broad application and was often used to assail opponents, political or otherwise (inside and outside the Church organisation), of the papacy and the ecclesiatical hierarchy. On the other hand, the inquisitors usually operated not in a perspective of attack, but more of preservation, to maintain *Catholic hegemony where it had already managed to impose itself. They also worked to bring religious conditions back to normality and to reinforce the hegemony of the Roman Catholic apparatus. A particularly unscrupulous use of inquisitorial instruments can be seen in the quarrels that afflicted the Order of Friars Minor at the turn of the 13th-14th cc. and in the processes of social and political reorganisation of the late medieval period. It was in this last period that the culture of *clerics and inquisitors gave shape to the *witch scare with its associated "witch-hunts".

A. Dondaine, "Le Manuel de l'inquisiteur (1230-1330)", *AFP*, 17, 1947, 85-194. – H. Maisonneuve, *Études sur les origines de l'Inquisition*, Paris, 1960 (2nd ed.). – A. Patschovsky, *Die Anfänge einer ständigen Inquisition in Böhmen*, Berlin-New York, 1975. – G. G. Merlo, *Eretici e inquisitori nella società piemontese del Trecento*, Turin, 1977. – *Bernard Gui et son monde*, Toulouse, 1981. – A. Patschovsky, "Zur Ketzerverfolgung Konrads von Marburg", *DA*, 37, 1981, 641-693. – L. Kölmer, *Ad capiendas vulpes. Die Ketzerbekämpfung in Südfrankreich in der ersten Hälfte des 13. Jahrhunderts und die Ausbildung des Inquisitionsverfahrens*, Bonn, 1982. – M. d'Alatri, *Eretici e inquisitori in Italia*, 1-2, Rome, 1986-1987. – G. G. Merlo, *Contro gli eretici*, Bologna, 1996. – J. B. Given, *Inquisition and Medieval Society*, Ithaca (NY), 1997.

Grado G. Merlo

**INTELLECT.** "Intellect", *intellectus*, means firstly the content of the operation of *knowledge and then the supreme *faculty or power of knowledge in *man. The meaning of faculty and that of object of intellection are often indissociable, as for St Augustine: "*Intellectus* is that which is made up of the intelligent subject and its object of intellection" (*Soliloquia*, VI, 13; *BAug*, 5, 52). The alliteration *intellectus-intus legere*, "to read inwardly", characterises the intellect in its capacity to link up with the thing known in its inmost essence (see Thomas Aquinas, *De veritate*, q. 15, a. 12, Resp., t. 22, 35, 24 and ff.). In *Albert the Great and *Thomas Aquinas, the *Augustinian heritage was enriched by Greek or Arab contributions, hence debates and disagreements. The supreme intellective instance – which, being apt to know all things, is in itself nothing of the reality known, which it becomes intentionally by its integral self-reflectiveness (which attests its superiority to the human organism) – is the sole basis of the *immortality of the human *soul, according to Thomas.

For Thomas, the human intellect is in the lowest rank of the hierarchy of intelligent living beings – the supreme one being *God, intellect by essence (which entails loving will) –, since the intelligibles accessible to man are received only in humble corporeal realities. Hence there is a necessary negativity in formulating critical notions about God and transcendant realities, which gives our *language about God an inadequacy expressed by the negative meaning of *analogical notions. Further disagreement then arises with the traditionalists who, in their poverty-stricken noetic of univocal representation, and in order to explain *freedom (considered threatened by the *Averroist theory of the intellect), opt for the thesis of the priority of *will over intellect. From this issue stems disagreement on eschatological *beatitude between the Thomist school who situate it in the intellective knowledge of God aroused by the light of glory, and the voluntarist traditionalists who postulate the thesis (contrary to Augustine) of an intuitive vision of God through *love.

J. Péghaire, *Intellectus et ratio selon saint Thomas d'Aquin*, Paris, Ottawa, 1936. – A. J. Backes, "Der Geist als höherer Teil der Seele nach Albert dem Grossen", *Studia Albertina*, H. Ostlender (ed.), Münster, 1952, 52-67 ("BGPhMA", suppl. 4). – J. E. Naus, *The Nature of the Practical Intellect according to Saint Thomas Aquinas*, Rome, 1959. – Z. Kuksewicz, *De Siger de Brabant à Jacques de Plaisance. La théorie de l'intellect chez les averroïstes latins des XIIIe et XIVe siècles*, Ossolineum, 1968. – E. H. Wéber, *L'Homme en discussion à l'université de Paris en 1270*, Paris, 1970. – R. Imbach, *Deus est intelligere. Das Verhältnis von Sein und Denken und seine Bedeutung für das Gottesverständnis bei Thomas von Aquin und in der Pariser Quaestionen Meister Eckharts*, Fribourg, 1976. – A. de Libera, *Introduction à la mystique rhénane d'Albert le Grand à Maître Eckhart*, Paris, 1984.

Édouard-Henri Wéber

**INTELLIGENCES.** According to *Aristotelian *cosmology, the intelligences or separate substances were the movers of the celestial spheres (*Metaphysics*, XII, 8; *De caelo*, I, 9). Arabic *philosophy (al-*Fārābī) made a synthesis between this cosmology and Plotinian *metaphysics in order to harmonize Greek philosophy with the religious doctrine of *creation: from the first principle, there proceeded by way of emanation ten intelligences, mediators between it and the sublunary world they governed. This synthesis reached the medieval West through the intermediary of *Avicenna. The majority of Latin thinkers admitted the existence of separate *substances having the same cosmological function, and some of them identified these with the *angels of biblical tradition, modifying the conception in accordance with Christian *theology. This adaptation worked out by recourse to Pseudo-*Dionysius led to a very elaborate angelology.

P. Merlan, "Aristotle's Unmoved Movers", *Traditio*, 4, 1946, 1-30. – R. Roques, *L'Univers dionysien. Structure hiérarchique du monde selon le Pseudo-Denys*, Paris, 1954. – H. A. Wolfson, "The Plurality of Immovable Movers in Aristotle and Averroes", *Harvard Studies in Classical Philology*, 63, 1958, 233-253. – J. A. Weisheipl, "The Celestial Movers in Medieval Physics", *Thom.*, 24, 1961, 286-326. – T. Litt, *Les Corps célestes dans l'univers de saint Thomas d'Aquin*, Louvain, 1963. – O. Blanchette, *The Perfection of the Universe according to Aquinas*, University Park (PA), 1992. – J. Jolivet, *Philosophie médiévale arabe et latine*, Paris, 1995.

Tiziana Suarez-Nani

**INTERCALARY FRUITS.** Between the late 13th and early 15th cc., the papal administration monopolized the revenues of *benefices on the occasion of a change of holder. The intercalary fruits (*fructus medii temporis*, *fructus intercalares*. . .) that it claimed represented the revenue during the vacancy; they came between the *spoils (what the deceased benefice-holder left of his revenue) and the *annates (what the new benefice-holder owed of the revenues of his first year of enjoyment).

J. Favier, *Les Finances pontificales à l'époque du Grand Schisme*. . ., Paris, 1966, 291-340.

Jean-Daniel Morerod

**INTERCESSION OF SAINTS.** According to a belief going back to Christian origins and the first developments of the cult of the *martyrs, the saints, in return for the sufferings they endured and the witness of *faith they gave to *Christ, were gratified by *God with a power of supernatural origin (called *virtus* by medieval authors) that remained present in their *relics and continued to act after their death. Thus God's servants, promoted to the role of celestial protectors of communities and individuals who were attached to them by a bond of particular devotion, mysteriously continued to live and intervene in events.

In the 12th and 13th cc., these traditional conceptions were influenced by the dominant feudal and monarchical socio-cultural models. As St *Louis declared to his entourage (*Vie de Saint Louis* by Guillaume de Saint-Pathus, ch. 7) – but his opinions on this point were shared by the least of his subjects – "It is with the saints in *Paradise as it is with the counsellors of kings. Whoever has to do with a king in this world makes inquiries to find out who is well regarded by him and, having his ear, is able to approach him usefully. He then goes to find that favoured person and prays him to transmit his request. It is the same with the saints in Paradise who, being intimate with our Lord and his familiars, can invoke him in all assurance since he cannot fail to hear them". The theme of the celestial court, so important in the religious iconography of the late Middle Ages, is not a mere figure of style, but well expresses the idea commonly held of the afterlife: God, in *heaven, was never alone. The world above, like that below, was conceived as a society connected with the earth by the *angels and saints. The latter, before being models, were considered as more or less powerful intercessors who, with the Virgin *Mary, were capable of bending God's will by reason of the *merits they had acquired in his eyes and the familiarity they had with him. From the 14th c., however, in certain milieux animated by a more spiritual piety, like that of the *beguines, appeared the idea that man could only benefit from the intercession of the saints if he repented of his faults and was converted to a better life. In this perspective, the role of God's servants was limited to favouring by their *prayers the action of *grace in man's heart.

P. Brown, *The Cult of the Saints: its Rise and Function in Latin Christianity*, London, 1981. – *Le Peuple des saints. Croyance et dévotions en Provence et Comtat, Mémoires de l'Académie de Vaucluse*, 6, Avignon, 1985. – B. F. Abou-El-Haj, *The Medieval Cult of Saints*, Cambridge, 1994. – A. Vauchez, *Sainthood in the Later Middle Ages*, Cambridge, 1997.

André Vauchez

**INTERDICT.** Interdict was, with *excommunication and suspension, one of the three ecclesiastical *censures. Personal interdict, which we meet already in St Ambrose, was akin to excommunication. More specific was general interdict, which suspended religious services in a particular place (*parish, *town, *diocese, *kingdom) until such time as the guilty did *penance. This punishment was rare until about 1100: in a letter to *Paschal II, *Ivo of Chartres speaks of this "unaccustomed remedy".

In the 12th and 13th cc., the interdict became a chosen weapon of the papacy in its struggle against intractable lay powers. In 1129, the bishop of *Paris could thus put his *diocese under an interdict because the king did not allow certain abuses to be reformed there. In 1142, *Innocent II did the same with any places (towns, *villages, *castles) where *Louis VII stayed. It was undoubtedly *Innocent III (1198-1216) who most systematically used this procedure against his adversaries. In the first year of his pontificate, he used it against the town of Cremona and against *Philip Augustus, Alfonso IX of *León and Sancho VI, king of *Navarre.

One of the most celebrated interdicts was that which struck Philip Augustus in 1198; aimed at the whole kingdom of *France, its aim was to force the sovereign to repudiate Agnes of Meran and recall his legitimate wife, Ingeborg of Denmark. Philip resisted for two years before submitting (1200). The text of the sentence, pronounced by the *legate Peter of Capua, shows that the interdict always allowed some exceptions since it affected thousands of innocents. Thus, a weekly *mass could be celebrated on Fridays, but without attendance; *Sunday was reserved for *preaching in front of the church; only *communion of the dying was authorized; though *confessions could not take place in the church, they were legitimate in the porch or on the threshold. These arrangements, though attenuated, were still terrible: the sick were deprived of *extreme unction and the *dead of *burial in consecrated ground.

At the end of the Middle Ages, the harshness of these measures was relaxed a little thanks to the mitigations consented to by *Boniface VIII (1294-1303), *Martin V (1429) and *Eugenius IV (1433). Interdict was then a weapon less and less used, and in the 15th c. it served mainly as a threat to unify *Christendom against the *Turks. However we find episodic examples until the beginning of the 20th century.

Innocentii III, *PL*, 214, 1855, 97, n. 60 (interdict against the kingdom of France, 1198).

E. Martène, V. Durand, *Thesaurus novus anecdotorum*, 4, Paris, 1717, 147. – "Interdit", *DThC*, 7, 2, 1927, 2280-2290. – "Interdit", *DDC*, 5, 1953, 1464-1475.

Patrick Henriet

***INTERPRETATIONES NOMINUM HEBRAICORUM.*** "Interpretations" (translations) of the proper names of the *Bible. Consulted all through the Middle Ages, these lexicons often accompanied the biblical text. Their model was St Jerome's *Liber interpretationum hebraicorum nominum*, which gave the words in order of the biblical books (summary alphabetical classification within each book). From the 12th c., these lexicons were organised in strict alphabetical order: the matter was enriched, in some cases from a knowledge of *Hebrew. These collections are designated by their first entry; the most widespread, "Aaz apprehendens", has been wrongly attributed to *Bede and to *Remigius of Auxerre, then to *Stephen Langton, but must date rather from the early 12th century. Among the other collections are "Aaron mons fortitudinis" and "Adam homo sive terrenus". The author of "Abba interpretatur pater" presents himself as a *Carthusian; a certain Jehannot Rossignol compiled another lexicon at the end of the 13th century. *Ralph Niger's *Philippicus* shows a certain knowledge of Hebrew.

*Interpretatio* was a frequent exegetical method in the 12th and 13th cc., especially in monastic *exegesis: reflection on the meaning of the name justified the exegesis of a given passage or served as starting-point for a tropological commentary. It was a procedure parallel with (but not identical to) *etymologia* (of common names), which sought the essence of the reality considered from the starting-point of an explanation that was not truly linguistic (*etymologia* does not correspond to our term "etymology").

M. Thiel, *Grundlagen und Gestalt der Hebräischkenntnisse des frühen Mittelalters*, Spoleto, 1973. – A. d'Esneval, "Le perfectionnement d'un instrument de travail. . . : les trois glossaires bibliques d'Étienne Langton", *Culture et travail intellectuel dans l'Occident médiéval*, G. Hasenohr (ed.), J. Longère (ed.), Paris, 1981, 163-175. – G. Dahan, *Les intellectuels chrétiens et les juifs au Moyen Âge*, Paris, 1990, 244-248.

Gilbert Dahan

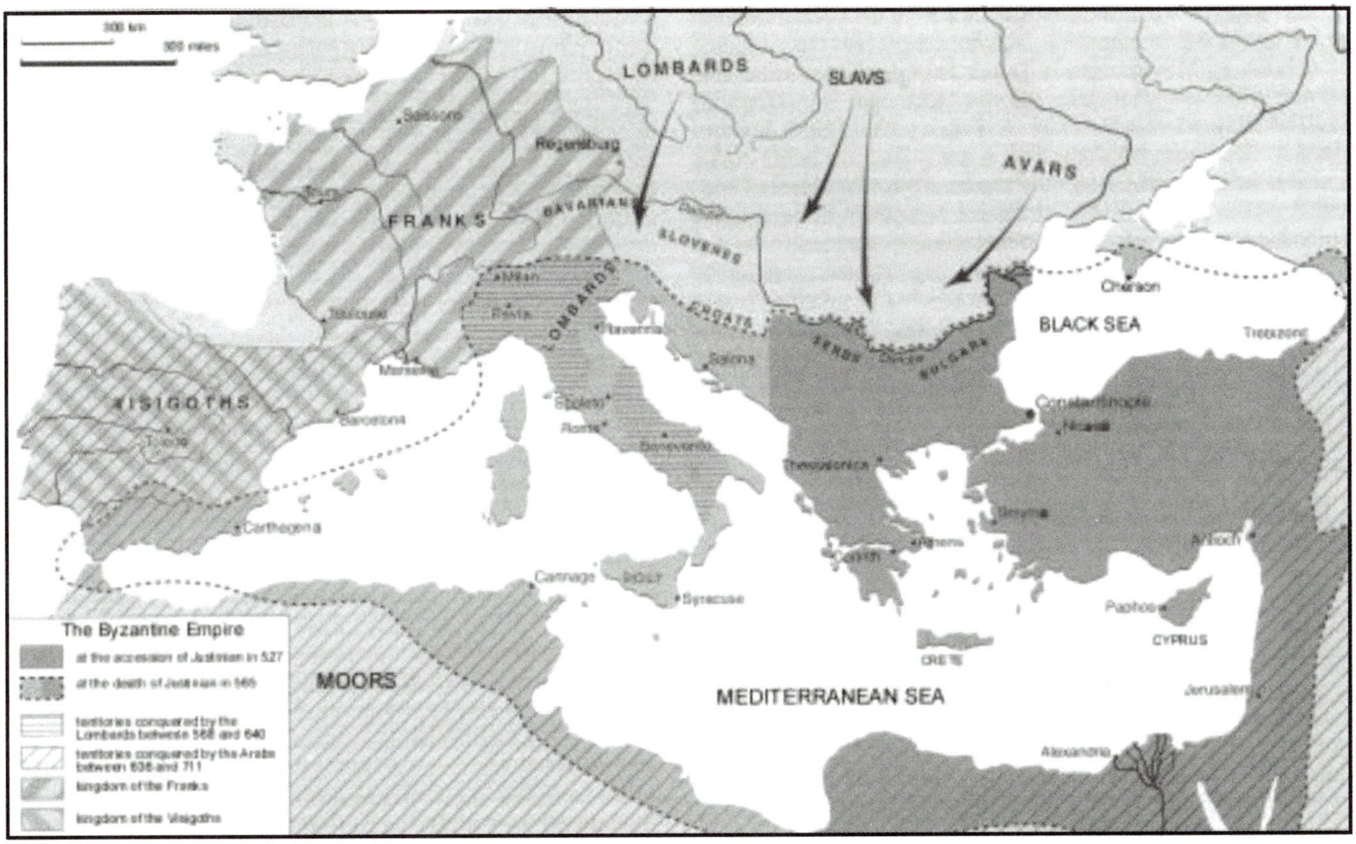


The Roman world and the barbarian invasions, 4th-8th cc.

**INTINCTION.** The term "intinction", which designates the steeping of an object in a liquid, received the technical sense of steeping a consecrated *host in consecrated wine to permit communion in both kinds without risk of spilling the precious blood. Medieval documents seem to consider such a way of doing things as a limited case rather than a normal practice. In rigour of terms, intinction must be distinguished from commixtion, by which, at any *mass, before communicating, the priest drops a fragment of consecrated bread in the *chalice. Intinction must also be distinguished from immixtion, a widespread practice in the early Middle Ages, consisting of adding some not yet consecrated wine to that already consecrated in order to consecrate the former.

M. Andrieu, *Immixtion et consecratio*, Paris, 1924. – J. Gaillard, "Intinction", *Cath.*, 6, 1966, 6-8.

Pierre-Marie Gy

**INTROIT.** The first chant of the *mass, the introit belongs to the proper, *i.e.* it is particular to each mass. Nowadays it is composed of an *antiphon and a *verse of a *psalm, but originally it accompanied the *procession of the clergy that, at the beginning of mass, went from the *sacristy to the foot of the *altar, and the number of verses varied according to its duration. Then, in the course of the Middle Ages, it was gradually brought down to a single verse, at the same time as it became general to have it recited by the celebrant, even in masses with no entrance procession.

For this chant reserved for the *schola*, the psalmody is a bit more ornate than that of the night *office. The texts of the antiphons come mostly from the psalms that they accompany. The liturgical function of this chant, marks the entrance of the celebrant and announces the proper character of the *feast of the day.

J. A. Jungmann, *The Mass of the Roman Rite*, Westminster (MD), 1986. – A. Hughes, *Medieval Manuscripts for Mass and Office*, Toronto, 1995.

Claire Maître

**INVASIONS.** During the first millennium, Europe was the theatre of a vast movement of migrations of peoples, ordered in two phases between the 4th and the 11th century.

The settlement of the *Huns in *Pannonia in the 4th c. unleashed the migration of Germanic peoples traditionally called the Great Invasions. These began on 31 Dec 406 with the crossing of the Rhine by hordes of Vandals, Alans and *Suevi, followed by *Alamanni and *Burgundians, and the sack of Rome by the *Visigoths, 24 Aug 410, while the *Anglo-Saxons began to settle in Britain. With the consent of the Emperor Honorius, the Visigoths created a federated kingdom in *Aquitaine, then extended their rule over *Spain, whence they expelled the Vandals. The latter conquered the Roman provinces of Africa between 431 and 439. Throughout the 5th c., *Italy was ceaselessly devastated: by the Huns in 452, by the Vandals who pillaged Rome in 455, by the revolt of the Germanic mercenaries ruled by the Scyrran Odoacer who in 476 dethroned the last Roman emperor of the West, Romulus, before himself being ousted by the *Ostrogoths between 489 and 493. From the reign of *Clovis (481-511), the Salian *Franks, previously cantonned in the region of *Tournai, threw themselves into the conquest of Gaul at the expense of the Alamanni, Burgundians and Visigoths. At this time the Byzantine reconquest began in Africa (532-534), then in Italy (535-562). But the *Lombards established themselves in northern Italy (568-572); with them ends the period of the great Germanic migrations.

The second phase, from the 8th to the 11th c., did not overturn

Europe in depth; with the exception of the *Slavs, the peoples who took part in it did not have the essential aim of occupying new territories. The Iberian peninsula once conquered (711) and their progress stopped by the Franks (Poitiers, 732), the Arabs and Berbers, then called *Saracens, were mainly occupied in making pillaging raids from their Provençal and Italian bases, from which they were not dislodged until the end of the 9th century. The Scandinavian invasions began at the end of the 8th century. The *Vikings made fruitful raids on the coasts and in the great river valleys and imposed tributes, *danegeld*, on the terrorized populations and weakened governments. Of all the States founded by the Danes, only the duchy of *Normandy survived beyond the 11th century. The Scandinavian raids were not yet ended when there appeared, in Germany in 862 and Italy in 898, Hungarian horsemen whose almost annual incursions ceased only with the victory of *Otto I on the Lechfeld in 955. The 11th c. was no longer troubled except by some Saracen raids on *Provence and Scandinavian naval expeditions against *England; but the horsemen of the steppes long remained a threat: Western Europe would suffer the *Mongol onslaught once more in the time of St *Louis and, in eastern Europe, arrivals of Asiatic nomads would last until the 18th century.

L. Musset, *Les Invasions, le second assaut contre l'Europe chrétienne (VII^e-XI^e siècles)*, Paris, 1971 (2nd ed.). – H. Wolfram, *History of the Goths*, Berkeley, 1988. – F.M. Clover, *The Late Roman West and the Vandals*, Aldershot, 1993. – N. Christie, *The Lombards*, Oxford, 1995. – L. Musset, *Les Invasions, les vagues germaniques*, Paris, 1995 (3rd ed.).

Michèle Gaillard

**INVESTITURE.** Investiture (*vestitio*) is the act by which a man or a woman entering religious life is clothed in the distinctive habit of this state. Originally, entry into religious life was not yet, or not necessarily, distinguished from commitment by religious *vows at the end of a period of probation. From the 13th c. (*Innocent III, 1198), vows could no longer be contracted except at the end of a year. Meanwhile the blessing of the religious garment gradually became general.

E. Martène, *De antiquis monachorum ritibus*, L. V, ch. 2, (Venice, 1783, 218-222).

*CaP*, 3, *The Sacraments*, London, 1988.

Pierre-Marie Gy

**INVESTITURE.** A public and symbolic act by which a person conferred a *property, office or right on another person by means of a material symbol. The object of investiture was eminently variable: indeed anything could be the object of this act by which a benefice-holder was "invested". The property could be a piece of land, from a *manse to a principality, a means of production (*mill, oven), a right to levy revenues (*advocacy, *tithe), an office to be exercised (comital, episcopal, abbatial, presbyterial). The persons involved were not legally fixed, unless by the fact that there was one actor who gave the investiture and one who received it. The symbolic gift, more convenient than taking real possession, was a material object such as a sceptre, a lance, a *staff, a *crozier, a straw, a branch, a knife, a lump of earth, a cord, according to the quality of the benefice-holder, the *fief conceded and the position entrusted. The act of putting in possession (*traditio*, *vestitura*) had its contrary; in case of resumption, conflict or confiscation, there was divestiture, by breaking or restoration of the material symbol: a glove thrown back, a straw broken. Investiture existed at all levels of medieval society and in all countries; it was a fundamental act on which the management of lordships and States rested; it was a node in a network of relations.

The most important investitures concerned the handing over of positions of power, whether exercised by laymen or churchmen. At the higher level, they were usually complementary to the act of vassalic *homage. It was these that had an impact on the government of States and principalities. Investiture, as an oral and visual manifestation, had its full weight in the early and central Middle Ages. Later, writing replaced the symbolic ceremony; a *charter sealed by the ruler determined the fief and its beneficiary.

The king conferred on his representatives powers analogous to his own, which allowed their holders to be all-powerful in the territory designated to them. Conferring a lance on a *count in the 10th c. was equivalent to investiture with the comital office, in no case to investiture with a precise territory, even if that territory was subsequently designated. It was the same with the *crozier (*baculum*) given to a *bishop or an *abbot, which represented his dignity (*episcopatus*, *abbatia*) and supposed the right of use of the *honor*; the *oath of fidelity came later to complement it.

In the early Middle Ages, the king exercised the same control over counts as over bishops, the former having a vocation to exercise strictly lay powers, the latter a sacramental office, both receiving their dignity from the ruler. For a long time no-one really contested the right of rulers to exercise strict control over the choice of holders of these positions, even religious ones, since these were accompanied by the exercise of *authority over men, which could not leave the king indifferent. From the 11th c., however, the Church did not remain unreactive to the acceleration of royal control over primarily sacramental offices, which were essentially a matter for the ecclesiastical authorities alone. The conferring of the crozier, when that of the *ring was added to it by the Emperor *Henry III, unveiled the usurpatory character of the investiture and provoked the vigorous reaction of the defenders of the Church's "*freedom". The so-called Investiture Contest thus turned on the conferring by laymen of the sacramental office symbolized by the crozier (and the ring): behind the rejection of the ceremony of investiture was really the refusal to see rulers or proprietors of churches themselves choosing the titulars or closely controlling that choice. The biting criticism made by the theoretician *Humbert of Moyenmoutier, who took up and reinforced an old theme, was that the current system favoured the illegal acquisition of the spiritual office by way of *money, *family and political pressure, the consequence of this being the *election of bad candidates, at all levels of the ecclesiastical hierarchy. This conflict appeared insoluble since rulers could not totally abandon their right of supervision over men who held a great part of their territory directly in their hands. In the 11th c., the phenomenon was all the more visible since, with the development of lordships and the exercise of the privilege of *immunity, the *temporal power of the holders of religious offices was reinforced and as it were institutionalized. Bishops in the *Empire, abbots all over Europe held an important, though variable, proportion of the land and its revenues.

It fell notably to the jurist *Ivo, bishop of Chartres, to formulate a solution that provided for the splitting of the religious office (episcopal, abbatial, presbyterial) into a spiritual part and a temporal part, each one being the object of a distinct investiture, the former by an ecclesiastical superior, the latter by a lay holder. The question then posed was: who would act first, the hierarchical superior in the Church or the superior in the world? To safeguard

Isle of Iona (Scotland). Romanesque chapel and abbey (background).

the "*freedom" of the Church, it was necessary that the layman should act second. The *concordat of *Worms (1122), which regulated the problem of episcopal elections in the Empire, put an end to what was rightly described as a conflict between *sacerdotium* and *regnum*, religious power and lay power. The crozier and the ring could no longer be conferred except by a prelate, the lay prince being confined to investiture of the *patrimony by a sceptre, a standard or even a crozier (the crozier was the pastoral *staff). In certain *abbeys, the lay prince laid the "abbatial staff" on the *altar of the patron saint, whence the abbot elect went to take it, thus seeming to receive his office from the saint himself.

For laymen, the principle of heredity pushed the necessity of investiture into the background. For a long time indeed, no office could be exercised as long as the benefice-holder had not received investiture. The *custom of letting the son succeed his father in the office allowed him to hold power without having been invested with it beforehand, regularization taking place after the event with a variable delay and according to circumstances. It was the same with homage, whose performance was supposed always to take place shortly after a new accession, whether that of the lord or that of the vassal, but which was deferred or sometimes no longer took place at all, as was the case at the end of the Middle Ages.

A. Fliche, *La Querelle des Investitures*, Paris, 1945. – A. Dumas, "Investiture", *DDC*, 6, 1957, 17-42. – *The Investiture Controversy*, K.F. Morrison (ed.), Huntingdon (NY), 1978. – "Investitur", *LdM*, 3, 1986. – U. R. Blumenthal, *The Investiture Controversy: Church and Monarchy from the Ninth to the Twelfth Century*, Philadelphia (PA), 1988. – H. Keller, "Die Investitur. Ein Beitrag zum Problem der 'Staatssymbolik'", *FMSt*, 27, 1993, 51-86.

Michel Parisse

**INVITATORY.** At the *office, the invitatory designates psalm 94 (95), *Venite*, a mutual invitation to *prayer that begins *matins; the custom is attested since the Rule of St *Benedict (530-555), ch. 9. In the other liturgical fuctions, the invitatory is an admonition addressed to the assembly to invite them to prayer, and to specify its object or its beneficiaries. It is normally followed by a time of silent prayer, before this is "collected" (a Gallican term) by the priest. We find invitatories in the "solemn intercessions" of Good Friday, before the prayers of *ordination, before the *Pater* of the *mass. They have great importance in the *Gallican and *Hispanic liturgies.

J. Pascher, "Das Invitatorium", *LJ*, 10, 1960, 149-158. – P. Rouillard, "Invitatoire", *Cath.*, 6, 1967, 49-50.

Paul De Clerck

Courtyard of the Royal Mosque at Ispahan (Iran).

**IONA.** A small island lying adjacent to the Scottish Isle of Mull (Inner Hebrides), it was known in the Middle Ages as Hy, and was a centre of great importance in the history of the Irish and English churches. Iona was granted to St *Columba by the king of Dalriada (a kingdom embracing north-eastern *Ireland and the Western Isles of Scotland), and the monastery which Columba established there came in time to be regarded as the principal monastery of the *paruchia* or federation of Columban monasteries (also including Kells and Derry in Ireland). Iona's influence extended far beyond Dalriada: several Northumbrian kings were nurtured there, and it was from Iona that the monk Aidan came to *Lindisfarne in 635. We are moderately well informed about the early history of Iona from the *Vita S. Columbae* of *Adomnán, its ninth *abbot; and recent excavations have revealed something of the monastery's conventual buildings. In the 8th and 9th cc., Iona was a centre of *pilgrimage, until *Viking depredations forced the monks to remove the *relics of the founder to Ireland. It was arguably at Iona that the "Book of Kells", the most lavish manuscript of the Irish Middle Ages, was written.

"Iona", *DACL*, 7, 2, 1927, 1426-1461. – M. Herbert, *Iona, Kells and Derry*, Oxford, 1988. – T.O. Clanchy, G. Markus, *Iona. The Earliest Poetry of a Celtic Monastery*, Edinburgh, 1995. – R. Sharpe, *Adomnan of Iona: Life of St Columba*, Harmondsworth, 1995. – A. Ritchie, *Iona*, London, 1997.

Michael Lapidge

**IRAN.** The word Iran, forged in the Sasanian period (3rd-7th c.), while properly meaning "Aryans", is synonymous with Persia, though etymologically the latter term designates only a province in the south-west of modern Iran, Fârs.

With the progressive advance of the Arab armies eastward, pushing towards Merv the last of the Sasanian kings, Yezdegerd III, who was finally murdered by one of his subjects in 651, Iran became a divided empire, subject to provincial governors and a more or less rapid Islamization. It was an Iranian, Abū Muslim, who, setting out from Khorasan, put an end to the rule of the *Umayyads, replaced in 750 by the *Abbasids. Resistance to *Islam was stronger in the Caspian regions and Central Asia. But it was in Khorasan that Iranian culture flourished once more from the 10th c., with the blossoming of Persian court poetry and of a classical language that borrowed its script from the conquerors and was enriched by the considerable contribution of Arabic vocabulary. During these first centuries of the *hejira, revolts like that of Māzyār, governor of Tabaristān, or Bābak, in the 9th c., might have led to the birth of hope in a saviour who would restore Zoroastrianism. They are in any case a proof of resistance to Islamization.

The *Shi'ite movement developed in Iran more than elsewhere, among those who were recognised as descendants of *'Alī and avengers of the murder of his son Husayn. Thus was born the messianic idea of the Mahdī, the saviour to come, of considerable importance in Iranian Islam, and the role of the twelve *Imāms, spiritual leaders and symbols of the perfect man, which constitute the basic belief of twelver Shi'ism. Equally we should not underestimate the place of *Sufi mysticism, so present in all classical literature and in Muslim hagiography. H. Corbin has particularly brought out the gnostic and esoteric character of this current of medieval thought.

But religious particularisms had not disappeared: in the 9th and 10th cc., the Zoroastrians, still numerous, drew up the main surviving *Pahlavī works; then, victims of persecution, many emigrated to *India. Subject to the same difficulties, the *Nestorian Christians, constituted into an autocephalous Oriental Church since their separation from *Constantinople in the 5th c., also left a very rich literature.

With the *Seljuk Turks, who became masters of the country in the 12th c., there was a considerable displacement of culture towards the west, prolonged during the *Mongol period (13th-15th cc.) during which the devastations ruined agriculture and led to a process of nomadization.

A. Bausani, *Persia religiosa*, Milan, 1959. – H. Corbin, *En Islam iranien: aspects spirituels et philosophiques*, Paris, 1971-1972 (4 vol.). – C.E. Bosworth, *The Medieval History of Iran, Afghanistan and Central Asia*, London, 1977. – V. Minorsky, *Medieval Iran and its Neighbours*, London, 1982. – A.K.S. Lambton, *Continuity and Change in Medieval Persia*, London, 1988. – D. Morgan, *Medieval Persia, 1040-1797*, London, 1988.

Philippe Gignoux

**IRAQ.** Iraq is a modern Arab State in the Near East, extending over both parts of ancient Mesopotamia: the northern part, Jazīra (former Assyria), and the southern part, Iraq proper or Sawād (former Babylonia), whose name also applies to Mesopotamia as a whole. The frontier between the two regions is at the latitude of Takrīt, limit of palm cultivation. From the geographical point of view, Iraq consists, on one hand, of the alluvial plains of the Tigris and Euphrates, whose waters lose themselves in the marshes of the Shatt al-Arab; on the other hand, of the mountainous massifs of the north-east whence descend the three affluents of the Tigris: great Zāb, little Zāb and Diyāla. From Antiquity, Iraq has been an extremely fertile region, thanks to the floods carried down by the two rivers, which allow irrigated cultivation.

From the political point of view, Iraq in the Middle Ages had a chequered history and saw numerous dynasties succeed each other on its soil. Mesopotamia had been conquered by the Arabs at the victory of al-Qādisiyya, won in 637 by Sa'd ibn Abī Waqqās over the Sasanid armies. In 638 the new masters founded the town of al-Basra on the Shatt al-Arab, then in 639, near al-Hīra, that of al-Kūfa, which became the capital of the province in place of Seleucia-Ctesiphon. Subsequently, Iraq was the scene of bloody encounters between the fourth *caliph, *'Alī, and his opponents: it was at al-Kūfa that he was assassinated, and it was at Karbalā that his son al-Husayn was killed in 680.

Under the *Umayyads (661-750), the governors, the most famous of whom was al-Hajjāj, had to put down several rebellions, like those of Ibn al-Zubayr, al-Mukhtār, the *Khārijites and Ibn al-Muhallab. With the accession of the *Abbasids (750-1258), Iraq became the central province of the Muslim Empire whose capital was installed in the new town of *Baghdad. Founded by al-Mansūr in 762, Baghdad was eclipsed as capital of the Empire only by Samarra, founded by al-Mu'tasim, between 836 and 872. Under the Abbasid dynasty, Iraq enjoyed a remarkable economic and intellectual development, but this did not prevent it also being the scene of many troubles, like the rising of the 'Alids, the revolts of the Zanj and the periodic raids of the Qarmates. This political instability culminated in the establishment of the regime of the Buyid *emirs, Shi'ite by confession, who governed in place of the Abbasid caliphs from 947 to 1055. Then, favoured by a Sunni reaction, the *Seljuk sultans took power and set to work to restore Sunnism, thanks in particular to the Nizāmiyya **madrasa* which they founded in 1067. The Seljuks governed Iraq until Caliph al-Nāsir (1180-1225) resumed power, but the *Mongols invaded Iraq and took *Baghdad in 1258, putting an end to the Abbasid caliphate.

From the religious point of view, the majority of the inhabitants of Iraq were *Sunni, but the Shi'ite element was extremely important, especially in the south, where the two greatest sanctuaries of *Shi'ism were situated: al-Najaf and Karbalā. The Aramean Christian population belonged to two Churches: the majority to the *Nestorian Church of the East, whose *catholicos* resided first at Seleucia-Ctesiphon, then at Baghdad, and governed six metropolises comprising some 40 *dioceses; and a minority to the *Jacobite Church of Antioch, whose primate (*maphrian*) resided at Takrīt and governed some ten dioceses.

G. Le Strange, *The Lands of the Eastern Caliphate*, Cambridge, 1905, 24-83. – A. Miquel, D. Sourdel, "'Irāḳ", *EI(E)*, 3, 1971, 1250-1257 (repr. New York, 1976). – M.M. Ahsan, *Social Life under the Abbasids, 170-289 AH, 786-902 AD*, London, 1979. – G.R. Hawting, *The First Dynasty of Islam: the Umayyad Caliphate AD 661-750*, London, 1986.

Gérard Troupeau

**IRELAND.** Ireland emerges from prehistory in the 5th c., with the formal establishment of Christianity in 431 by Palladius, sent by Pope Celestine I as first *bishop "to the Irish believing in *Christ" (*ad Scottos in Christum credentes*). A second 5th-c. missionary, *Patrick, has left the only indisputably contemporary written sources (*Confessio* and *Epistola ad Coroticum*), as almost no trace of Palladius's activity has survived. The earliest native documentary sources (*annals, genealogies, legal texts) preserve archaic elements perhaps as old as the 6th c., but for the most part reflect Irish society between *c.*600 and *c.*800. These historical texts and the earliest quasi-historical literary *saga material (*Táin Bó Cuailnge*) indicate that the prehistoric political framework was dominated by the "Pentarchy" of five large provincial kingdoms (*cóiceda*), Ulster, Leinster, Connacht, Munster and Mide, with their "capitals" at Emain Macha, Tara, Cruachu, Emly and Uisnech. On the eve of the historical period, however, this older structure gave way to a new pattern in which the country was divided up amongst some 150 petty kingdoms (*tuatha*), each a separate and autonomous political entity with its own king. Parallel with this development was a shift from an earlier, tribal polity to one in which political loyalties were based on the activities of dynasties and families. Indicative of this change is the disappearance of the word *moccu* (denoting tribal affiliation) in family *names; whereas up to that time the *moccu*-formula was universal (*e.g.* in the ogam inscriptions, the oldest written memorials of the *Irish language), it disappears entirely from the annals after 690. A new political vocabulary comes into use in which terms like *Uí* (Latin *nepotes*) indicates descent from known historical personages, rather than the tribal gods of prehistory.

The radical changes that took place in the 5th and 6th cc. were probably precipitated by outbreaks of severe plague, which devastated many population-groups and forced many others into

Portal of the Romanesque cathedral of Clonfert (Ireland).

exile. The annals and genealogies preserve the names of many peoples of which no historical record survives; they cannot even be located on the landscape. Amongst these were possibly the Mairtine, at one time the dominant political group in Munster, who fade from the picture by *c.*600. The effects of plague doubtless differed in different regions of the country; it is noteworthy, however, that in Connacht (for which the sources are most meagre), the older tribal conglomeration of Connachta (which gave its name to the province) produced an offshoot in the Uí Néill, which came to dominate Irish politics in the period *c.*600-*c.*800.

The expansion of the Uí Néill, and their conquest of large parts of the northern half of the country, can be followed – at least in outline – in a series of annual notices of 5th- and 6th-c. battles, mainly against Ulster and Leinster. The rise of the Uí Néill is invariably linked in tradition with the collapse of the old northern province of Ulster and the destruction of its capital, Emain Macha. In fact, Emain Macha had been abandoned long before, but the Uí Néill incorporated the overthrow of the Ulster kings into their origin-legends, and fashioned a history for themselves in later centuries which was almost entirely fictional. In their two branches, northern and southern, the Uí Néill expanded across Ireland in a band stretching from Ailech in the far north-west to the eastern seaboard at Brega (County Meath). In fact, however, Ulster kings were still powerful down to the end of the 6th c. and relinquished their ambition to reconquer their former lands only after defeat at the hands of the Uí Néill in the battle of Moyra (637).

In the southern half of the country, the upheavals of the 5th and 6th cc. saw the emergence and rapid disappearance of several Leinster population-groups in succession, as the Uí Néill ground them down one by one. The relentless expansion of the Uí Néill was only halted in the 7th c., when the Uí Dúnlainge in the north of the province and the Uí Cennselaig in the south emerged as the dominant political and military forces, and halted the Uí Néill incursions. These two gradually ousted the older population-groups (*e.g.* Uí Enechglaiss, Uí Failge, Uí Bairrche) from their strategic lands and established control over their territories and their principal churches. The Uí Dúnlainge and Uí Cennselaig retained control in Leinster until the arrival of the Anglo-Normans in the 12th century.

In Munster the political scene in the 6th and 7th cc. is dominated by the rise of the Eóganachta. These replaced older population-groups such as the Mairtine and the Déisi, which in previous centuries had stretched in a band of kingdoms from County Clare in the west to County Waterford in the south-east. The earlier upheavals, followed by the expansion of the Eóganachta, probably precipitated the movements of some Irish population-groups, such as the Uí Liatháin, across the Irish Sea to *Wales and Cornwall. The survival of many bilingual Latin-Irish ogam stones in these areas bears witness to these emigrations. The Eóganachta kingdoms extended from the Aran islands (off the coast of County Galway, in the west) to Cashel (County Tipperary) and farther east. But although Munster was probably the most extensive and richest of the new lordships, the Eóganachta never exerted the same dominance in the south as the Uí Néill did in the north and, with the rise of the Dál Cais in the late 10th c., their power went into decline.

From the mid 7th c., the concept of high-kingship began to take hold and was propagated in a series of Uí Néill-inspired texts; the following centuries were characterised by the attempts of successive provincial rulers to carve out a place for themselves as kings of Ireland. The earlier claims of Uí Néill kings were met with competition from Munster in the 8th c., and the arrival of the *Vikings in 795 further complicated matters. By 1000 a new Munster dynasty, the Dál Cais, had emerged as a dominant power, and its principal leader, *Brian Bóruma, during a visit to *Armagh in 1008, had his name and title (*imperator Scottorum*) inscribed in the famous Book of Armagh. The two centuries that followed, before the arrival of the Anglo-Normans, were marked by the constant clashes of rival claimants to the high-kingship. All that came to an end, however, in 1172, with the arrival of *Henry II, king of *England.

*Táin Bó Cúalnge from the Book of Leinster*, C. O'Rahilly (ed.), Dublin, 1967.

D. Ó Corráin, *Ireland before the Normans*, Dublin, 1972. – G. MacNiocaill, *Ireland before the Vikings*, Dublin, 1972. – F. J. Byrne, *Irish Kings and High-Kings*, London, 1973. – *A New History of Ireland, 2: Medieval Ireland, 1169-1534*, A. Cosgrove (ed.), Oxford, 1993. – *Colony and Frontier in Medieval Ireland*, T.B. Barry (ed.), R. Frame (ed.), K. Sims (ed.), London, 1995. – D. Ó Cróinín, *Early Medieval Ireland 400-1200*, London, 1995. – B. Smith, *Colonisation and Conquest in Medieval Ireland*, Cambridge, 1999.

Dáibhí Ó Cróinín

**IRENE, EMPRESS (752-803).** Irene (reigned 797-802), called the Athenian because born at Athens, was the first woman emperor at Byzantium and the only one before Zoe and Theodora in the 11th century. A saint (feast: 7 Aug), she attained the imperial dignity because she had married *Constantine V's son, Leo IV (775-780), and at her husband's death her son Constantine VI, aged ten, was too young to reign. She exercised power conjointly with her son from 780 to 790, then from 792 to 797: on 15 August 797 she had him blinded in a way that led to his death. She was then "emperor" until October 802 when she was dethroned by *Nicephorus I (802-811) and exiled to Lesbos where she died, 9 Aug 803. The reign of Constantine VI and Irene, then that of Irene alone, was disastrous for the Empire: the gains of Constantine V's reign, both in the defence of the Empire against the Arabs and *Bulgars and in the reorganisation of the *army and the balance of finances, were lost (reductions in *taxation, free gifts to the monasteries). In domestic policy, the struggle for power, first between mother and son and then between the two eunuchs whom Irene put in charge of the government, entailed an incessant intestine war. In foreign policy, Irene paid tribute to Hārūn al-Rashīd (782 and 798) and broke off her son's betrothal to *Charlemagne's daughter (788); she was hesitating to refuse the hand of Charlemagne, who had sent an embassy on this subject, when she was dethroned. Her sole success was the recovery of *Greece, disorganised by the invasion of *Slav tribes (784).

However, Byzantine sources are very favourable to her because she called the council of *Nicaea II which restored the cult of *icons (787), forbidden since the council of Hiereia (754). To impose the cult of icons after 50 years of *iconoclasm was no easy task. First Irene appointed Tarasius *patriarch (784): this appointment was contrary to the canons since Tarasius, a high palace official, was a layman; he accepted the post only on condition that an ecumenical *council restore the icons. Irene subsequently showed her determination in favour of icons by employing a ruse to send home the soldiers of the elite regiments who had risen up and interrupted the council as it met for its first session in the church of the Holy Apostles at *Constantinople, 7 Aug 786. Though the measure was detrimental to the defence of the Empire, it enabled the council to be held the next year at Nicaea. Irene insisted that the council's definition (*horos*) be officially presented to the people of Constantinople, and called Tarasius and the bishops into the capital to do so as soon as the council ended. The *horos* was read to the high civil officials, military officers and representatives of the people, who acclaimed it before "the emperors Constantine and Irene" in the Magnaura palace, 23 Oct 787. A bad emperor and a bad mother, Irene was yet a remarkable person who gave the Eastern church its definitive configuration and its originality by imposing the cult of icons.

C. Diehl, *Impératrices de Byzance*, Paris, 1959, 59-86. – P. Speck, *Kaiser Konstantin VI. Die Legitimation einer Fremden und der Versuch einer eigenen Herrschaft*, Munich, 1978. – W. Treadgold, *The Byzantine Revival (780-842)*, Stanford, 1988.

Marie-France Auzépy

*The empress Irene.* Mosaic in the tribune of Hagia Sophia, Istanbul. 11th c.

**IRISH LANGUAGE.** Irish belongs to the Celtic branch of the Indo-European family of languages. On areal criteria, Celtic can be subdivided into Continental Celtic (Lepontic, 700-400 BC; Celtiberian, 300-100 BC; Gaulish, 300 BC - *c.*200 AD) and Insular Celtic, with the latter's two branches, Brythonic (*Welsh, Breton, Cornish) and Goidelic, phonologically differentiated by their treatment of $^{*}k^{w}$ ($^{*}k^{w}$etwor > Welsh *pedwar*, Irish *cethair*, "four"). The Goidelic group began to split into a Western branch (Irish) and an Eastern branch (Scottish Gaelic, Manx) in the time between the 10th and the 13th centuries. The periods of Irish are: Ogam Irish (the language of the ogam inscriptions of the 5th-7th cc.), Archaic Irish (to *c.*700), Old Irish (to mid 10th c.), Middle Irish (to late 12th c.), Classical Modern Irish (to *c.*1600) and Modern Irish. Old Irish is attested in glosses and short texts in contemporary manuscripts; most texts which can linguistically be dated to the Archaic, Old and Middle Irish periods are transmitted in manuscripts written after 1100. The oldest surviving manuscript entirely in Irish is *Lebor na hUidre* (*c.*1100); the earliest known manuscript of vernacular texts, the lost *Cín Dromma Snechta*, is conventionally dated to the first half of the 8th century. The writing of Irish texts appears to have begun before 600. The orthography of Old Irish is based on *Latin and its local pronunciation. Among the characteristics of Irish which it shares with Brythonic languages are initial mutations (systematic, syntactically conditioned changes of initial consonants of stressed words or syllables, *e.g. cenn*, "head" [*c* = /k/], *a chenn*, "his head" [*ch* = /χ/]), lexicalized prepositions with suffixed pronouns (*do*, "to", *dom*, "to me"), and basic verb-initial constituent order. Old Irish is a fully inflected language of the ancient Indo-European type. Nouns still have five cases (including a vocative), and a singular, a plural, as well as a residual dual. Its outstanding morphological feature is a complex verbal paradigm, with a syntactically conditioned system of double inflection for each slot and pronouns and most syntactic markers behaving as clitics (*e.g. berid*, "he carries", *ni-beir*, "he does not carry" [*b* = /b/], *beirthi*, "he carries it", *ni-beir*, "he does not carry it" [*b* = /ß/], *connach-beir*, "so that he does not carry it" [*b* = /ß/]). The remarkable grammatical consistency of Old Irish has been interpreted as reflecting a conservative and learned standard which lagged behind developments in popular speech. Middle Irish is characterised by a variety of processes of morphological simplification, analogical levelling, and literary hypercorrection.

Classical Modern Irish represents a new literary standard based on the innovative patterns of popular speech. Evidence for the spoken dialects of Modern Irish first appears in the late 16th century. The grammatical system of Modern Irish shows a significant reduction of morphological categories; nouns have, at the most, two different forms in the singular and plural respectively, and the verbal system is radically simplified and regularized after the erosion of the double system of verbal inflexion and the emergence of independent subject and object pronouns.

R. Thurneysen, *A Grammar of Old Irish*, Dublin, 1946. – K. H. Jackson, "Common Gaelic. The Evolution of the Goidelic Languages", *PBA*, 37, 1951, 71-97. – K. McCone, *The Early Irish Verb*, Maynooth, 1987. – G. MacEoin, "Irish", *The Celtic Languages*, M. J. Ball (ed.), London-New York, 1993, 101-144.

Erich Poppe

**ISAAC.** A biblical patriarch (Gen 21-28), Isaac was the miraculous son of *Abraham and Sarah in their old age. He was exposed to death by his father whose faith Yahweh wished to test (episode of the sacrifice of Isaac). He was the husband of Rebecca and the father of Esau and *Jacob.

The character of Isaac plays a great role in Christian symbolism and iconography by reason of his sacrifice which, representing absolute trust in God, was interpreted as a prefiguration of *Christ's sacrifice on the Cross.

The episode of the sacrifice was depicted by two great Italian artists of the early 15th c., Ghiberti and Brunelleschi, as part of the competition to decorate the portal of the Florence baptistery: both sculpted a relief representing the sacrifice of Isaac, using a nude of classical inspiration for the character of Isaac.

E.G. Tasker, "Abraham and Isaac", *Encyclopedia of Medieval Church Art*, J. Beaumont (ed.), London, 1993, 9-12.

Frédérique Trouslard

**ISAAC ISRAELI (*c.*855-*c.*955).** Ishaq ben Sulayman or Isaac Iudaeus, Jewish philosopher and doctor, was born in Egypt and died in Tunis, where he was the court doctor. His works, written in Arabic, translated into Latin, had considerable influence on *medicine and *philosophy. His medical works were translated by *Constantine the African in the 11th c., then retranslated in the 12th and 13th cc.: *Book of Fevers*, *Book of Urines* (very widely circulated), *Universal Diets* and *Particular Diets*, *Viatica*. . . His philosophical works include the *Book of Definitions (Liber de definitionibus)*, Latin *translation by *Gerard of Cremona, abridged by Dominic Gundisalvi (?), which served as a philosophical lexicon to the Latin world in the 13th and 14th cc. (cited by *Robert Grosseteste, *Albert the Great, *Thomas Aquinas, etc.). His other works are less common (*Book of Elements*, translated into Latin).

A. Altmann, S. M. Stern, *Isaac Israeli. A Neoplatonic Philosopher*. . ., Oxford, 1958. – G. Dahan, *Les Intellectuels chrétiens et les juifs au Moyen Âge*, Paris, 1990, 311-313 and 333-335.

Gilbert Dahan

**ISAAC OF NINEVEH (7th c.).** The most celebrated of the Syro-oriental monks. A native of Beth Qatraya (now Qatar, Persian gulf), he was a monk there before becoming bishop of Nineveh. He remained only five months on the episcopal throne before finally retiring as an *anchorite to Beth Huzzaye (south-west *Iran) and finally to the monastery of Rabban Shabbur. He wrote spiritual works of which we have translations, some of them into Arabic and then Ethiopic, some from Syriac into Greek. Like that of all the mystics, the goal of his doctrine is to lead the monk to *contemplation of God. His thought is rich and subtle, hence the difficulties we find in trying to reconcile sometimes divergent statements.

P. Bedjan, *Mar Isaacus Ninivita, De Perfectione religiosa*, Paris, 1909 (Syriac text). – A. J. Wensinck, *Mystic Treatises by Isaac of Nineveh*, Amsterdam, 1923 (Eng. tr.; repr. Wiesbaden, 1969). – *On Ascetical Life*, Crestwood (NY), 1989. – S. Brock, *Isaac of Niniveh (Isaac the Syrian). "The Second Part", chapters IV-XII, CSCO*, 554 (Syriac text) and 555 (Eng. tr.), Louvain, 1995.

E. Kalifé-Hachem, *DSp*, 7, 1971, 2041-2054.

Micheline Albert

**ISAAC OF STELLA (*c.*1105/1120-*c.*1178).** Born in England, he went to France in *c.*1130 to follow the teaching of the great *masters of *Chartres and *Paris: *Abelard, *William of Conches, *Gilbert of Poitiers; whence his taste for *disputation and freedom of thought. Entering *Pontigny in *c.*1143, he was sent to L'Étoile (Stella) in 1146 and then, to find more solitude and *poverty, founded Les Châteliers (île de Ré) where he died at an unknown date. Though drawing on the best sources of the *Fathers and ancient philosophy, his works had a limited influence in the Middle Ages, except for his letter on the *canon of the mass. He has now been rediscovered as "one of the profoundest metaphysicians of his century" (H. de Lubac).

Isaac de L'Étoile, *Sermons*, *SC*, 130, 1967; 207, 1974; 339, 1987.

*DSp*, 7, 1969-1971, 2011-2038.

Jean-Baptiste Auberger

**ISAIAH.** Isaiah is considered the first of the major *prophets. He was active in Jerusalem between 766 and 701 BC.

Isaiah's popularity in Christian art in the Middle Ages was due to three passages in his prophecies, interpreted as predictions of the Annunciation to the Virgin and the birth of *Christ: "a young woman shall conceive and bear a son" (Is 7, 14), "unto us a child is born, unto us a son is given" (Is 9, 6) and "there shall come forth a rod out of the stem of Jesse" (Is 11, 1). Isaiah was also the prophet of the *Last Judgment: "The lord standeth to judge the people" (Is 3, 13; also Is 63, 1-6). It was also one of his visions that served as point of departure for the iconography of *God in *Majesty: "Thus says the Lord, The heaven is my throne, and the earth is my footstool" (Is 66, 1).

The iconographical type of Isaiah is the same as that of the prophets: he is represented as an old man with a long beard. However, there may be distinguishing elements like the phylactery bearing one of his prophecies or the stem of the *Tree of Jesse. A 12th-c. statue on the portal of Cremona cathedral shows the prophet with a phylactery bearing the inscription: *Ecce Virgo concipiet et pariet filium*. Isaiah holding a branch of the Tree of Jesse was placed in the 13th c. at the north crossing of the transept of *Chartres cathedral. Representations of Isaiah are often integrated with those of other prophets among which he occupies first place, as in Klaus *Sluter's *Well of Moses*.

Isaiah was also associated with the Marian programme by reason of his prophecies, as various statues attest, the first dating from *c.*1130, in the church of Souillac, and another on the left side-pillar of the south portal of the church of Notre-Dame-du-Port at *Clermont-Ferrand, also of the 12th century.

Different visions of his book could be illustrated, among them the vision of the Lord among the seraphim (Is 6, 1-4), represented *e.g.* in the 7th c. in a miniature of Cosmas Indicopleustes in the Vatican Library. A window of the *Sainte-Chapelle in Paris illustrates the episode of the purification of the prophet's lips (Is 6, 5-7). As for Isaiah's execution, sawn alive in the crook of a cedar, which could be interpreted as a prefiguration of Christ's death on the Cross, a detailed and realistic version of it is given in miniature in a *Book of Hours in Cherbourg library.

M. Simonetti, "Uno sguardo d'insieme sull'esegesi patristica di Isaia fra IV e V secolo", *Annali di storia esegetica*, 1, 1984, 9-44.

Frédérique Trouslard

**ISAURIANS.** The Isaurian dynasty was a dynasty of Byzantine emperors whose founder was Leo III (717-741): he was succeeded by his son *Constantine V (741-775), his grandson Leo IV (775-780), called the Khazar, and his great-grandson Constantine VI, who shared power with his mother *Irene before she blinded him, causing his death (797).

The Isaurian emperors Leo III and Constantine V have been subjected to a *damnatio memoriae* by the sources, all monastic or ecclesiastical by origin, because their work of renewing the Empire was accompanied by an innovative religious policy, *iconoclasm (council of Hiereia, 754), finally rejected in 843. The defeat of iconoclasm had two consequences: the Isaurian sources have all disappeared, with the exception of a legislative code, the *Ecloga*, and part of the acts of the council of Hiereia, refuted at the council of *Nicaea II (787); later sources, written by partisans of the cult of *icons, have rewritten the history of the period by blackening the Isaurians to the utmost and misrepresenting their work. They have reduced the history of the dynasty to the history of iconoclasm, whereas this was really just one aspect among others.

The Isaurians were primarily great warrior emperors. Leo III inaugurated his reign in 717-718 by lifting the siege laid to *Constantinople by the troops of the *Umayyad caliphate. This victory, which had considerable repercussions, marked the end of the caliphs' hopes of conquering the *Byzantine Empire. It was consolidated by the defeat of the Arab-Muslim troops before Nicaea (727), and allowed the Isaurians to pass from defence to attack (victory of Akroïnon, 740; Constantine V in *Syria, 745).

Constantine V fought against the Arabs in Asia Minor and, in the West, against a new danger, the *Bulgars (victory of Anchialos, 763), whom he tried to ward off by repopulating Thrace with Armenians and Syrians. In *Italy, however, *Ravenna fell into the hands of the *Lombards (751). The warlike valour of Constantine V, which gave rise to the legend of the *dragon-slaying emperor, explains the attachment of the soldiers to his religious policy, which they defended in 786 when Irene wanted to impose the cult of icons.

The Isaurians did not just fight, they reorganised the Empire by centralizing it under the effective authority of the emperor in the administrative (division of *themes), military (transformation of the *scholarii* into elite regiments), legislative (creation of a simplified code applied by salaried judges) and economic spheres (abolition of *silk farms); their religious policy, iconoclasm, was one aspect of this vast work of reform.

*Prayer of Isaiah, between Night and Dawn* (in the form of a little child). Miniature from the Psalter with commentaries known as the *Paris Psalter*, early 10th c.

The attachment of Illyricum, which depended on the *patriarchate of Rome, to the patriarchate of Constantinople proceeded from the same intention; it gained the Isaurians the lasting hostility of the papacy and hastened, even more than did imperial heterodoxy, the rallying of the papacy to the *Carolingians. Behind the caricature put forward by the sources, we can see that Leo III and Constantine V did a work comparable to what the Carolingians were doing in the West at the same time. The Byzantines were not deceived: when the Bulgars threatened Constantinople in 812, they ran to the tomb of Constantine V and begged him to save the city and the Empire.

*Ecloga. Das Gesetzbuch Leons III und Konstantinos' V*, L. Burgmann (ed.), 1983 ("FBRG", 10).

J. Haldon, *Byzantine Praetorians*, *Poikila Byzantina*, 3, Bonn, 1984.

Marie-France Auzépy

**ĪSHŌ'DĀD OF MERV (died after 852).** A Syro-oriental bishop, born at Merv in Persia (now in north Khorasan), then installed in the see of Hedatta near Mosul (*Iraq), he wrote *Commentaries on the Old and New Testament* in Syriac: these, which form his main work, constitute a good summary of oriental exegesis.

C. Van Den Eynde, *Commentaire d'Ishodad de Merw sur l'Ancien Testament*, I, *Genèse*, *CSCO*, 126 (Syriac text) and 156 (Fr. tr.), Louvain, 1950 and 1955; II, *Exode, Deutéronome*, *CSCO*, 176 (Syriac text) and 179 (Fr. tr.), Louvain, 1958; III, *Livre des Sessions*, *CSCO*, 229 (Syriac text) and 230 (Fr. tr.), Louvain, 1962-1963; IV, *Isaïe et les Douze*, *CSCO*, 303 (Syriac text) and 304 (Fr. tr.), Louvain, 1969; V, *Jérémie, Ézéchiel, Daniel*, *CSCO*, 328 (Syriac text) and 329 (Fr. tr.), Louvain, 1972; VI, *Psaumes*, *CSCO*, 433 (Syriac text) and 434 (Fr. tr.), Louvain, 1981. – *The Commentary on the Books of the Holy Prophets*, C. Molenberg (ed.), Louvain, 1987.

Micheline Albert

*Isidore on horseback setting out to fight the Visigoths.* Banner of San Isidoro. 10th c. embroidered fabric. León, treasury of San Isidoro.

**ISIDORE OF KIEV (died 1462).** Metropolitan of *Kiev and all *Rus' (1436-1439), prelate and Byzantine *humanist, Isidore was appointed head of the ecclesiastical *province of Rus' on the eve of the unionist council of Ferrara-*Florence. Having gone there at the head of the Russian delegation, he was an ardent advocate of *Union with Rome. Made *cardinal and *legate by Pope *Eugenius IV, he was coolly received in Poland and Lithuania; at *Moscow, as soon as the union was proclaimed, Isidore was deposed and imprisoned by Grand Prince Basil II. He managed to escape and ended his days, like other Greek humanists, in Italy, without seeking to return to Eastern Europe.

G. Alef, *Slavic Review*, 20, 1961, 389-401. – J. Gill, *Personalities of the Council of Florence*, Oxford, 1964.

Vladimir Vodoff

**ISIDORE OF SEVILLE (570-636).** Born into an illustrious Roman family of Carthagena, Isidore was brought up by his elder brother *Leander at *Seville, where the family had fled after the loss of their father. He received an austere education. In 600 he succeeded Leander in the see of the Baetican metropolis. As *bishop, he pursued three aims: to preserve ancient knowledge; to complete the recent triumph of Catholicism (council of Toledo of 589); and to favour a profound Romano-Gothic fusion. In 619 he took part in the synod held at Seville under the aegis of King Sisebut, and in 633 he presided over the important 4th council of Toledo, in the presence of King Sisenand.

In 600, the Church of Spain had recently suffered the rivalry of an *Arian clergy supported by the Gothic aristocracy; cure of souls remained patchy, by reason of the mediocrity of the pastoral framework. Profiting from the emergence of a Catholic Hispanic *monarchy, Isidore decided to provide the Church with the intellectual tools indispensible for its renewal. Faithful to the methods of the ancient scholars, based on wide reading, he collected referenced extracts and summaries, before putting them together in a continuous text, drawing on an exceptional *library and served by a considerable staff of copyists.

On ordinary knowledge, Isidore wrote a brief treatise on Christian *numerology (*Liber numerorum*). At the request of the lettered King Sisebut, he wrote *De natura rerum*, an exposition of physical geography. He composed a two-book synthesis *De differentiis*, in which he applied himself methodically to sorting out words whose usage had become confused. He devoted himself to an exercise of *copia dicendi* in two books of *Synonyma*, a long lamentation (inspired by the *Psalms) of the sinful soul.

As for religious knowledge, the bishop composed a summary *De haeresibus*, took issue with the Jewish religion in *De fide catholica*, gave a list *De ortu et obitu patrum*, and fixed a *Major Chronicle* faithful to the *Augustinian division of the six ages of the world. Following Jerome and Gennadius, he listed the annals *De viris illustribus*, Christian authors of the West. Braulio of Saragossa, his friend and pupil, admired his talents as a preacher. Two treatises of scriptural *exegesis have come down under his name.

In the matter of national teaching, in his *De origine Gothorum* Isidore maintained that the Goths (not the Byzantines) were the spiritual heirs of the Roman Empire; ethnic opposition was blotted out in Hispanic unity, Latin and *Catholic. Taking an active part in *synods and *councils, he influenced the drawing up of various canons of the fourth council of *Toledo (633).

In Christian discipline, Isidore, as a legislator, established a short *Regula monachorum*, set out (following Ambrose and *Gregory I) in two books *De ecclesiasticis officiis* the ends and means of pastoral ministry in *Spain, and traced the programme of a Christian life for all the baptized in his three books of *Sententiae*.

Finally, in the form of a synthesis, in the last part of his life Isidore built up an *encyclopedia – the *Etymologiae* – an extraordinary work for 7th-c. Europe and exceptional in the history of medieval Latin culture. His method was faithful to ancient tradition: he started from words, their meaning and history, to establish an immense dictionary of knowledge, structured by a dual aim: to transmit the contents of a secular scholarship ranging over the seven *liberal arts and to perfect this tradition through an appropriate Christian training.

*PL*, 81-84, 1862. – "Chronica, Historia Gothorum", *MGH.AA*, 11, 2, 1894, 241 f. – *Etymologiarum libri XX*, W. Lindsay (ed.), Oxford, 1911 (2 vol.; new ed. in progress in the "Alma" collection, Paris). – *De natura rerum*, J. Fontaine (ed.), Bordeaux, 1960. – *De viris illustribus*, C. Codoñer (ed.), Salamanca, 1964. – *De ecclesiasticis officiis*, *CChr*, 113, 1989.

J. Fontaine, *Isidore de Séville et la culture classique dans l'Espagne wisigothique*, Paris, 1983 (3 vol.; 1st ed. 1959). – M. C. Diaz y Diaz, *Introducción general, San Isidoro de Sevilla. Etymologias*, J. Oroz Reta (ed.), A. Marcos Casquero (ed.), Madrid, 1983-1984, 1-257. – F. Brunhölzl, *Histoire de la littérature latine du Moyen Âge*, 1, Turnhout, 1991, 78-93 and 257-260.

Michel Banniard

**ISLAM.** The Arabic root *slm* means "to be at peace", "to be safe". The verb *aslama*, which is derived from it, acquired in Muslim Arabic vocabulary the sense of "to submit to God's law and thus be safe". In this theological context, Islam is thus submission to God and to his Prophet. M. Bravmann has shown that, in its pre-Koranic, but also partly Koranic, origins, this term is connected with the ideas of combat, war effort (**jihād*), notably in oaths of allegiance to *Muḥammad: "to defy death", "to sacrifice one's life for".

*Muslim*, which gave the Persian *musulmān*, is the present participle of the verb *aslama* and means: "one who submits, who puts himself in the hands of God". At the time of Muḥammad, this term kept a certain ambivalence, since he who became a *muslim* often did no more than recognise Muḥammad as a sort of supratribal chieftain more powerful than the others. This word also conveys one of the fundamental Muslim conceptions of mankind's religious history, according to which the prophets before Muḥammad and their followers were "submitted to God". As such, Adam, Moses, Jesus, etc., were "Muslims". The *Koran (22, 78) even claims that the name *muslim* was given by Abraham.

The word "Islam" (and Muslim) as we will use it here refers to Islam as a religion, rather than to Islam as a society and a culture.

In the Koran, some verses emphasize the interiority of Islam (6, 125); others, often cited, bring out the connection between *islam* and *dīn* ("religion", "worship and law", 5, 3). Islam supposes a "return to God" (*tawba*, 9, 74). In the traditions ascribed to the Prophet, in defining Islam the stress is put on the submission to God expressed by works, mainly the prescribed acts of worship, but also all good works. Thus, in one of these traditions, after having defined faith (*īmān*) as "to believe in God, his angels, the future life, the prophets, the resurrection", to the question: "What is Islam?" Muḥammad replies: "Islam is to worship God without associating anything with him, to observe the canonical prayer, to give the legal alms, to fast during the month of Ramadan." This leads to the consequence that "Islam is external, while faith is of the heart". This distinction gave rise to debates within the schools of dialectical theology (*kalām*) and law (**fiqh*). Was it or was it not necessary to distinguish between Islam and faith, and what was the relation between the two? Was faith just verbal confession or did it also include adherence of the heart and works?

Despite the diversity of Islam, which appears not just in the different religious groups that make it up (*Sunnism, *Shi'isms, *Khārijism), but also within each of these groups (theological and legal currents, *Sufism, geopolitical and inter-racial division), there is an institutional common denominator, the five pillars (*arkān*): confession of faith (**shahāda*), canonical prayer (**salāt*), legal almsgiving (**zakāt*), the *Ramadan fast (*sawm/siyām*) and pilgrimage (**Hajj*). These are the five individual obligations to which all Muslims whose age permits them are subject. To these we must add the communal obligation that is **jihād*, the "effort" to defend or even propagate this religion, holy war.

As for the Muslim religion as such, it is often summed up in six constituents: 1. Faith in the divine unicity and the divine attributes. 2. Faith in the "prophets" and "messengers" who have all delivered the same message, but of whom Muḥammad represents the seal and the fulfilment. 3. Faith in angels. 4. Faith in the "holy books", particularly those that were revealed to the Jews and Christians before they "falsified" them (since that is the Muslim view). 5. Faith in the *Last Judgment or day of *resurrection. 6. Faith in *predestination (*qadar*). These articles of faith, notably the question of the divine attributes, with their corollary, the debate over whether the *Koran is created (the *Mu'tazilites) or uncreated, and the debate over predestination (the Mu'tazilites professing free will), have given rise to often passionate theological debates.

As for theological thought itself, its birth and development took place in a polemical and apologetic ambience in the face of rival confessions (*Judaism, Christianity and Zoroastrianism), but also among disputes within the Muslim community. This gave it a largely dialectical aspect, whence the name *kalām* (word, dispute) borne by speculative *theology in Islam. Moreover, one current of thought, often dominant in Sunnism, rejects the application of rational argument to revealed doctrine. The opponents of this speculative theology are called the "people of tradition and of the community". It has also been said, not without reason, that, while theology occupies a central place in Christianity, in Islam this role belongs to law (Fazlur Rahman, following certain Orientalists). Does not Islam consider itself both a religion and a socio-political institution (*dīn wa dawla*)? This appeared from the earliest centuries, when confrontations within the community were a matter for politico-religious opposition groups (*firaq*, a term improperly translated "sects" or "schisms").

M. M. Bravmann, *The Spiritual Background of Early Islam*, Leiden, 1972, 1-38. – L. Gardet, J. Jomier, "Islām", *EI(E)*, 4, 1978, 171-177. – J. Jomier, *How to Understand Islam*, London, 1989. – T. Izutsu, *The Concept of Belief in Islamic Theology*, New York, 1980 (Tokyo, 1965). – W. M. Watt, *Early Islam*, Edinburgh, 1990. – J. Van Ess, *Theologie und Gesellschaft im 2. und 3. Jahrhundert Hidschra*, 1-6, Berlin-New York, 1991-1997. – S. von Sicard, "Muslimūn" [Muslims], *EI(E)*, 7, 1993, 695-704. – *Medieval Christian Perceptions of Islam*, New York, 1996.

Claude Gilliot

**ISLAMIC ART.** Islamic art, as the emanation of a religion still in full expansion today, cannot be defined as the art of a period of revolution, limited in time. Moreover, if the art of the first centuries of Islam shows an apparent unity, it was soon splintered by the numerous regional evolutions.

Islamic art developed rapidly in all the territories conquered and converted to Islam. The first great monument was the Dome of the Rock, completed on the Temple esplanade at *Jerusalem in 692. Octagonal in plan with a double ambulatory, it employed an architectural vocabulary that came directly from the recently conquered Byzantine world. As a religious monument associated with the rock of *Abraham's Sacrifice and the Jewish Temple, the dome was not a *mosque, but rather a commemorative building signaling the victorious presence of Islam in a Jewish and Christian town. However, it was mosques that marked the Islamized world in the most visible way. Over the medieval period, several types of plan were employed, varying according to geographical areas.

The establishment of three types of plan for mosques took place under the reign of the *Umayyad caliph al-Walid (705-715), who was responsible for building the three mosques that provided the essentials of models to come. The house of the Prophet at *Medina doubtless provided the first type, called "Bedouin". This consisted of a central court (*sahn*) around which were arranged porticos (*riwaq*) on three sides and on the fourth side the prayer hall, oriented towards *Mecca. This orientation (*qibla*) was later materialized by a niche enshrined in the wall, the *mihrāb*. On the very site of the Prophet's house, Caliph al-Walid built a mosque that was in fact an enlargement of its original plan.

The second model was that called "Mediterranean"; it comprised a prayer hall of *basilica plan, with aisles perpendicular to the *qibla* wall. The prayer hall was preceded by a court. The earliest example of this is given by the al-Aksa mosque, built on the Temple esplanade at Jerusalem, facing the Dome of the Rock. This Mediterranean plan recurs, among other places, in the mosques of *Kairouan (836) and *Cordova (785-961).

The last prototype, which may be called "Syrian", is shown by the mosque of *Damascus; this has a prayer hall formed of three aisles parallel to the *qibla* wall, cut by a transverse aisle starting in front of the *mihrāb*. A court bordered by porticos faces the prayer hall.

Few variations break in on the plans of mosques until the 12th c., at which time a new plan known as "Iranian" developed in *Iran. This followed the Bedouin plan, but added, on the four sides of the court, great arches preceding rooms closed on three sides and open onto the court: the *eyvān*(s). The type and example of this is provided by the Friday mosque of Isfahan.

Minarets, recognisable signs of Muslim presence, hardly take on a monumental aspect before the 9th c., when that of the great mosque of Kairouan was built. The immense minaret with spiral ramp at Samarra (*Iraq) was built some years later (848). In Western Islam, the minarets of *Seville (the Giralda) and Marrakesh (the Kutubiyya) have a square base and graceful proportions, as well as a decoration of panels covered with tracery, sometimes set off by squares of colours. In the oriental world, several great minarets with circular or star-shaped plan are remarkable for their monumental appearance, outstanding among them the Kalān minaret of Bukhara (1127), that of Jam in Afghanistan (*c.*1180) or the Qutub minar at Delhi, begun in 1199.

Palace architecture also enjoyed an important role in the development of a properly Islamic style. The first Umayyad palaces hesitated, in their plan as well as their decoration, between the Roman *castrum* and the Sasanid palace. In the *Abbasid period, the immense palaces of Samarra (9th c.) evolved towards forms that became characteristic: structures with axial symmetry for the plan; development of hanging decorations of "arabesque" type. In western Islam, the palaces of Medina az-Zahra (10th c., Cordova), the Aljaferia of *Saragossa (11th c.) and the Alhambra of *Granada (13th-14th c.) are conspicuous examples of this palace art.

In the field of the so-called minor arts, Islamic ceramics occupy a special place. Muslim potters introduced certain techniques to the Western world, notably faience and ceramics with metallic lustre. During the 9th c., the Abbasid period saw the appearance of the first Islamic faience pieces. They show a great variety of decorations, comprising "blues and whites" as well as motifs in metallic lustre. This procedure enjoyed considerable development in Iran as well as in *Syria, Egypt and *Spain. These different techniques were used not just for pieces in the round but also for architectural decorations (squares painted or cut out, then assembled into a *mosaic).

From Antiquity, oriental *objets d'art* were highly prized in the West. So it is hardly astonishing to find in the church treasuries of France textiles, rock crystals or enamelled glass brought back especially from the *crusades. Thus, the fragment of *silk samite known as the "sudarion of St Josse" (Louvre museum) was undoubtedly offered by Stephen of Blois. On this tissue appear two elephants framed by an inscription in the name of a governor of Khorasan (Eastern Iran) who died in 961. "St Mexme's cope", a piece of silk depicting cheetahs preserved in the church of Saint-Étienne at Chion, was woven in Egypt in the 11th century. "King Robert's cope", preserved at Saint-Sernin in *Toulouse, is a tissue ornamented with facing peacocks made in Spain in the 12th century.

Syrian goblets in enamelled glass like the so-called "glass of Charlemagne" (late 12th c., Chartres museum) or the goblet "of eight priests" (Douai museum) are evidence of the mastery of the glass-makers of Raqqa (Syria), also brought back from crusades. Among cut crystals, the ewer of the treasury of *Saint-Denis, from Fatimid Egypt, is one of the most famous examples. Finally, the Mamluk basin in engraved bronze encrusted with silver called the "baptistery of St Louis" (early 14th c.; Louvre museum) is a remarkable specimen of Islamic bronze.

*Arabic Calligraphy was undoubtedly the art most prized by the Muslims. This fact is explained in the first place by Koranic Revelation and by the role the *Koran played in the formation of Arabic writing. Calligraphy is also one of the sole traits that characterise all Islamic art. In fact, whether discreetly, in the form of an invocation on a ceramic, or monumentally, to emphasize an architectural setting, this art is omnipresent. The first Korans were transcribed on *parchment under Caliph 'Uthman (644-656). At

Kufa, in Lower Mesopotamia, a style developed from the 8th c. that was at once sober and elegant, Kufic. It was characterised by its angular appearance, its tendency to horizontal elongation of letters and the absence of diacritical points. Until the 12th c., it was used for copying the Koran. Kufic was later replaced by other styles, more cursive and more easily readable, like *naskhī*.

We know few illustrated Islamic manuscripts before the 12th century. However, several historical sources mention their existence. For, contrary to received ideas, the prohibition of images in Islam – at least in secular spheres – was extremely relative. Iconographical traditions were deeply rooted in many countries affected by the Muslim conquest, which, most of the time, retained their habits. The Umayyad and then Abbasid *caliphs did not hesitate to decorate their palaces with mural paintings or stucco reliefs, some fragments of which still exist. This fact is verified also for the *Fatimid caliphs of Egypt (909-1171). Closer to home, the ceilings of the Sala de los Reyes, in the Alhambra of Granada (14th c.), show a strange synthesis of *Gothic and Islamic elements.

*Arts de l'Islam des origines à 1700 dans les collections publiques françaises*, Paris, 1971. – R. Ettinghausen, *Arab Painting*, London, 1977. – D. and J. Sourdel, *La Civilisation de l'islam classique*, Paris, 1983. – R. Ettinghausen, O. Grabar, *The Art and Architecture of Islam, 650-1250*, London, 1987. – O. Grabar, *The Formation of Islamic Art*, New Haven, 1987. – J. D. Hoag, *Islamic Architecture*, London, 1987. – M. Bernus-Taylor, *L'Art en terre d'Islam. 1. Les premiers siècles*, Paris, 1988. – S. Blair, *The Art and Architecture of Islam, 1250-1800*, New Haven, 1994.

Yves Porter

**ISRAEL.** The term "Israel" was used by medieval authors essentially apropos of two themes (the word did not generally designate contemporary *Jews).

1) The question of the *Verus Israel* was one of the major themes of *controversy between Jews and Christians: which was the true Israel, depositary of divine truth, the Jews, faithful to the Old Testament whose prescriptions they scrupulously observed, or the Christians, who recognised the new Law and believed in the Son of God? At the centre of polemical works, this theme received a particular illustration with the allegorical *exegesis of the story of *Jacob (whose other name was Israel), considered by Jews and Christians as a figure of themselves, notably in his opposition to Esau (Edom: for the Jews, pagan and Christian Rome; for the Christians, the Jews).

2) The future conversion of the "remnants of Israel" (cf. Rom 9, 27 and 11, 26) was at the heart of Christian doctrine on *Judaism: the hope of this conversion at the end of *time justified the maintenance of the Jewish people as such and the rites of Judaism, to allow the *prophecy to be fulfilled. Certain authors (including Peter *Abelard and *Duns Scotus), while leaning on Rom 9, 27 (*reliquiae Israel*), restricted its scope and saw in the "remnants" of Israel a limited number of representatives of Judaism, preserved so as not to make the Apostle a liar (Duns Scotus wished that the other Jews had been baptized, by persuasion or force). Other Christian thinkers spoke of the survival of the Jewish people in its entirety (thus *Peter Lombard, *Peter Cantor, *Joachim of Fiore, *Thomas Aquinas).

F. J. Caubet Iturbe, "*Et sic omnis Israel salvus fieret*, Rom 11, 26. Su interpretación . . . s. III-XII", *EstB*, 21, 1963, 127-150. – G. Dahan, *Les Intellectuels chrétiens et les juifs au Moyen Âge*, Paris, 1990.

Gilbert Dahan

**ISTRIA.** A peninsula of the former Yugoslavia, at the northern end of the Adriatic, at present divided between Slovenia (the north) and Croatia (the south), it was invaded by the Istri at the end of the 2nd millennium BC. After encounters with the Romans, probably between 18 and 12 BC, part of its territory was incorporated in Roman Italy (with the border at the river Arsa), until in 6 BC (?) Augustus included it with Venetia in "regio X". With the colonies of Pola, Trieste and Parenzo, *romanitas* was present with public works and new possibilities of work, including the Via Flavia (AD 78/79) that joined Trieste and Pola. At the same time the way was open to Christianity, which spread very quickly probably from Aquileia: the earliest known bishop of Parenzo, Maurus, was martyred under Diocletian (293); other *martyrs included Justus of Trieste. Their inclusion in the ecclesiastical *province of Aquileia shows the importance of the Istrian *bishoprics, particularly those of Parenzo, Pola, Cisa, Pedena, Sipar and, later, Emona and Capodistria.

The 5th c. saw an attempted invasion by *Visigoths and occupation by *Ostrogoths from 493 to the arrival of the Byzantines before the middle of the 6th century. The precise centralized government of the Byzantines united the military command with the civil and financial administration. This period saw the penetration of *Avars and *Slavs, who broke into Istria between the late 6th c. and the first decade of the 7th. Around 770 there was a brief *Lombard occupation, before the Frankish conquest (787) which radically transformed it socially and politically, though the region was soon united with the March of Friuli (803). Subsequently subject to the duchies of *Bavaria and Carinthia, in 1040 Istria was an autonomous *march, enfeoffed to other dynasties, without excluding the influence of the patriarchate of Aquileia and of lay lordships.

The coastal cities could not fail to have relations with *Venice, because of their common Byzantine past and their identical maritime interests, a connection which, in the 12th c., ended in subordination. In 1208, Istria was enfeoffed by the emperor to the patriarch of Aquileia: in reality, the internal zone remained under the count of Gorizia, while the coast was under Venetian control from the late 13th c., before becoming totally so in 1451 (except for the county of Pisino, which went to the house of Austria with Carnia and Gorizia).

*Codice diplomatico istriano*, P. Klander (ed.), Trieste, 1986 (5 vol.; phot. repr.).

*Atti e memorie della Società di archeologia e Storia patria*, 1884 f. – Contributions in *Antichità Altoadriatiche*, 2, Udine, 1972; 26, 1985; 28, 1986. – P. Zavotto, P. A. Passolunghi, *Bibliografia storico-religiosa su Trieste e l'Istria, 1864-1974*, Rome, 1978.

Giorgio Fedalto

**ITALIAN LANGUAGE, ORIGINS OF.** The formation of the Italian language was part of the more general process of evolution that led from *Latin to the multiplicity of the Romance languages. In this process, the consolidation of national languages, understood as languages of reference for literary and institutional communication, did not come first: in every region we see a longer or shorter primary phase of great dialectal differentiation, followed only later by the crystallization of a regional variety as a unitary language. In *Italy this process was set in motion, on the literary level, from the 14th c., with the great age of Tuscan literary culture, which through its peaks – *Dante, *Petrarch and *Boccaccio – imposed a model that would not be superseded. But before this phase, to speak of the origins of the Italian language involves making a distinction at least between the great dialectal areas of the peninsula: the north (Gallo-Italic and Venetian dialects), *Tuscany and the centre-south (median, southern and Sicilian dialects), not to mention the Sard unit: a distinction that, in the spoken language, has lasted into the present.

The common matrix of this dialectal variety was the so-called "vulgar" Latin, the spoken Latin of late Roman Antiquity and the early Middle Ages, profoundly changed from the classical language both due to the variety of peoples who had become part of the Empire and through ever closer contact with the Germanic languages of the invaders, in Italy mainly Goths, *Lombards and *Franks. The evolution was slow but profound: towards the end of the first millennium, starting from the *Carolingian reform of writing and orthography, which aimed to restore the "correctness" of classical Latin (8th-9th c.), there was an increasing awareness of the coherence of a "rustic Roman language" by now autonomous from and contrasted with Latin.

Already in the written evidence of the previous centuries we can make out numerous elements that would be typical of the *vernacular languages (in Italy, Lombard charters abound in them), but only from the 9th c. is there evidence of a situation of effective bilingualism, as appears from the emergence of the first texts explicitly written in the vernacular. For the Italian area, it is doubtful whether the Veronese *Indovinella* (8th-9th c.), which still shows strong Latin elements, can be considered such. More decidedly vernacular is the brief graffito found in the catacomb of Domitilla at Rome: *Non dicere ille secrita a bboce* (first half of 9th c.), a sort of liturgical admonition to the celebrant, which inaugurates the strand of vernacular writing in Italy. Certainly vernacular, and hence traditionally considered the first documents in Italian, are the testimonial formulae contained in some Campanian **Placita* relating to disputes over territories belonging to the abbey of *Monte Cassino (the first is that of Capua, March 960): *Sao ke kelle terre, per kelle fini que ki contene, trenta anni le possette parte Sancti Benedicti*. As in many other documents of the Romance origins, the vernacular – inserted into a rigorously Latin legal context – emerges here because of the need to reproduce a testimony faithfully; though the language here is formularistic, and certainly does not mirror the spoken language (indeed the existence of a supra-regional vernacular for the median area has been hypothesized even in the *Placita*). Much more extensive, and less rigid even in the analogous repetitiveness of its content, is the later Umbrian *Formula* of confession (mid 11th c.) that inaugurates another of the major strands of the first vernacular documentation, connected with the needs of religious *pastoral care (from the 10th c. at Monte Cassino it was recommended that *confession take place *rusticis verbis*). The typology of these first texts finally comprises documents of a practical nature, beginning with the Pisan naval account (11th-12th c.), listing the payments relative to the armament of one or more ships, detailing the items of expense in a vernacular that seems free from any formularistic rigidity, as one would expect from the mercantile ambience to which the document belongs.

From the same Pisan area of influence (Volterra?) comes the first vernacular literary text, the so-called *Ritmo laurenziano* (late 12th c.), whose **jongleur* character and metrical structure echo French tradition. In Tuscany it is an isolated case, and we cannot yet talk of a formed literary language, but other texts from the southern – more specifically Cassinese – area are more or less contemporary, such as the so-called Cassinese *Ritmo* (a moralizing dialogue between an Eastern sage and a Westerner) and the *Pianto di Maria* (lament beneath the cross), followed by the more important *Ritmo* on St *Alexius (a legendary *hagiography of the ascetic saint). Here we have homogeneous texts, even linguistically, all belonging to the area of influence of Benedictine *monasticism headed by the abbey of Monte Cassino, an area that extended throughout median Italy as far as the *Marches. So this first vernacular literary tradition evidently emerged for reasons of *pastoral care, and the first great Italian text, *Francis of Assisi's *Laudes creaturarum* ("Canticle of the creatures", composed in 1244) would not have been alien to it, since the sources assert that the saint wanted his friars to sing it among the people.

Alongside these first surviving evidences of a literary language, practical documents in the vernacular become more frequent in these decades straddling the two centuries, with a particular density in central Italy, between Tuscany and the median area; proof of a total diffusion of the language, even in its written sedimentation.

But, more or less at the same time as Francis's death, the first true organic experience of the literary use of an Italian vernacular arose in *Sicily, with the poetic *corpus* of the Sicilian School at the court of *Frederick II. It is still debated whether the language of this first poetic season reflected more or less rigorously the Sicilian of the time, or whether it was not already a supra-regional *koinè*, in conformity with the cosmopolitan character of the imperial *Magna Curia*. The fact is that this *poetry has come down to us almost exclusively in the transcriptions made at the end of the century in Tuscany, hence clothed in a heavy linguistic patina. This became the model for the first secular poetic season in Tuscany (Guittone d'Arezzo, Bonagiunta da Lucca) and in Emilia (Guido Guinizzelli), still partly linked linguistically to the influence of various dialectal areas; until the next generation, that of Guido Cavalcanti and Dante with their "Stil Nuovo", by now specialized in a Florentine direction.

With Dante, at the end of the 13th c., we see the first methodological reflection on the use of the vernacular (in particular in the treatise *De vulgari eloquentia* where, together with a list of the various Italian dialects, he sets out the value of a supra-regional "volgare illustre" that could aspire to expressive and communicative functions parallel to those of Latin itself). Though Dante's vernacular work would in fact only partially correspond to this ideal programme, it was the language of his *Rime* and of the *Commedia* that, partly through the mediation and new impetus provided by Petrarch and Boccaccio, would become the basis of the Italian language.

*Poeti del Duecento*, G. Contini (ed.), Milan-Naples, 1960. – A. Castellani, *I più antichi testi italiani. Edizione e commento*, Bologna, 1973 (2nd ed. 1976). – A. Castellani, *La prosa italiana delle origini*, 1, *Testi toscani di caracttere pratico*, Bologna, 1982 (2 vol.). – I. Baldelli, "La letteratura dell'Italia mediana dalle origini al XIII secolo", *Letteratura italiana*, 1, *Storia e geografia*, Turin, 1987, 27-63. – I. Baldelli, "La letteratura volgare in Toscana dalle origini ai primi decenni del secolo XIII", *ibid.*, 65-77. – L. Petrucci, "Il problema delle Origini e I più antichi testi italiani", *Storia della lingua italiana*, 3, *Le altre lingue*, Turin, 1994, 5-72. – "Profilo linguistico dei volgari medievali", *ibid.*, 75-489. – A. Fassò, "I primi documenti della letteratura italiana", *Storia della letteratura italiana*, 1, Rome, 1995, 233-264. – F. Sabatini, *Italia linguistica delle origini. Saggi editi dal 1956 al 1996*, Lecce, 1996. – M. L. Meneghetti, *Le origini delle letterature medievali romanze*, Bari, 1997.

Lino Leonardi

**ITALY.** After the deposition of Romulus Augustulus by Odoacer in 476 and the latter's recognition of Eastern authority, Italy lost its position as heart of the Western Empire. The *Ostrogothic invasion (489-493) hardly changed the regime set up at that time: *Theodoric, based at *Ravenna, always used the services of the Roman aristocracy to run his kingdom, while entrusting military responsibilities to Goths alone; he managed until his death (526) to ensure great political stability. Justinian's reconquest (535-553) ruined this equilibrium and left a country sucked dry, easy prey for the *Lombards. Their invasion (569) established a lasting partition between the "Germanized" lands and those that remained in Byzantine hands (centred on Ravenna, seat of an exarch with both civil and military functions, they also comprised the Ligurian coast, which fell in the 7th c.; the *Pentapolis; *Rome and its *duchy, linked to Ravenna by the Perugian corridor; the young *Venice and *Istria; *Naples, *Apulia and *Calabria), which left traces in spheres as varied as the occupation and management of the land, styles of building, the notarial and legal systems. The Lombard regime radically subjugated the Roman populations, who were systematically refused civil responsibilities, while the Church hierarchy was ignored by an *Arian power whose administrative divisions (*duchies and gastaldates) deliberately broke up the former episcopal geography. This situation gradually evolved, helped by the political unification of the kingdom under the aegis of rulers won over to Roman Catholicism and by a temporary improvement in relations with Byzantium (680). A limited process of fusion of populations took place, attested by modifications regularly made to legislation (from the edict of Rothari in 643 to the last additions of *Aistulf in 750).

But hopes of detaching the whole peninsula from Greek influence with the help of the tensions of the *iconoclast crisis were in vain: the papacy, at one time attracted by Liutprand's support against the decrees of Leo the *Isaurian, very soon preferred the Frankish alliance, which alone, in its eyes, was capable of preserving the future of a nascent "Papal State". Absorption into the Carolingian political sphere, which was rapid (774), sealed for several centuries the dependence of a large part of Italy on a German Empire that was physically distant but always very concerned to maintain quite strong links with the capital of *Christendom, which became the obligatory site of nearly all *coronations after 800. In the 9th c., transalpine elites replaced the Lombard aristocracy of the *regnum Italiae*, bringing with them the essentials of Frankish institutions (comital system, *vassalage, *capitularies, etc.) – bipartite organisation of the great *estates became general in the countryside – while remaining largely open to earlier local influences. As in the rest of the *Empire, *social order and interior peace were guaranteed by a close collaboration between *counts and *bishops, though this quite quickly turned to the advantage of the latter. These profited widely from the troubled period that, from the late 880s to the middle of the 10th c., saw the territorial fragmentation of the Empire, a recrudescence of external dangers (Hungarian invasion, Arab raids), and an ever more rapid succession of rival claimants to the leadership of the kingdom. Though all linked by family ties to the *Carolingians, they usually owed their political position to nothing more than a fairly massive transfer of the prerogatives and revenues of the State in fiscal and legal matters to the hands of the most influential prelates, who, to the *immunity enjoyed by their rural estates, added ever more extensive jurisdiction over the chief towns of their *dioceses.

Italy in the 11th century

When the *Ottonian dynasty managed to impose itself (951-1024), it was no longer in any state to reverse the tendency, any more than were the *Salian emperors: at the most it attempted to lay the bases of a new institutional equilibrium, ratifying the advancement of episcopal powers by a series of solemn *charters, while giving active support to some newly promoted comital families. But, for the most part weakened, the former civil officials were mainly concerned with maintaining and developing their financial grip on the countryside, within the nascent *signorie*; only the most powerful among them came out of it well, controlling whole regions under the title of duke or marquis (in *Tuscany) or, like the *Canossa and Obertenghi families, changing aggregates of districts.

In the 11th c., these old oppositions rapidly gave way to other social gulfs, against the background of a continually maintained demographic and economic growth. The progress of urbanization; the role played by *notaries, judges, *merchants and vassal clienteles who increasingly claimed the right to participate in decisions that concerned them; the spread of watchwords linked on the one hand to the Peace movement coming from the north, on the other to ideas of ecclesiastical *reform (episode of the **pataria* at *Milan), led to the creation of communal organisations, whose idea, present from the 1050s, attained its first institutional expression from the last two decades of the 11th c. and real maturity in the years 1120-1140 (collective *oath, elections of consuls, emergence of a communal *historiography and a new civic culture, etc.). Beyond an often common vocabulary, each town also worked out its own solution in the new political and social equilibrium that was set up: the Milanese model, characterised by a relative loss of power by the *archbishop and the wish to restore a deeply compromised civil peace, may be contrasted with the non-conflictual cases of *Pisa and *Genoa, where the convergent interests of a whole population led to a better development of commercial activity, and those of small towns in the interior where the role of the military clienteles had always been secondary.

Recognition of communal autonomy did not take place without resistance on the part of the Empire. Already losing to the papacy in the affair of religous *investitures (*concordat of *Worms, 1122), it saw with an ill grace the expulsion of all higher public authority in the towns of the realm and the growing submission that these towns imposed on the rural aristocracy of the *contado*. But the efforts of *Frederick Barbarossa, both legislative and military (diet of Roncaglia, 1158, destruction of Milan, 1162), were powerless to subdue the *communes united in a league, whose customs ended by being recognised in 1183 in exchange for a very formal loyalty (peace of *Constance). Victorious against the Empire, the towns nevertheless went through a difficult period in the late 12th c., when they had to make room for the middle and lower social classes (the *popolo*), until then little concerned with the running of local affairs. To resolve their internal conflicts, many of them, renouncing consular regimes, entrusted their rule at that time to a **podestà* not involved in the interests of the various parties. This solution was powerless to counteract the ever more pronounced narrowness of urban power, monopolized from the 1250s by "bourgeois" patrician oligarchies or by individual representatives of the greater families who, in the 14th c., even managed to impose their "signoria" on veritable principalities (*Visconti, *Sforza, *Medici, etc.), profiting from the political void caused by the Empire's lack of interest in Italy at that time.

Yet, on the threshold of the 13th c., it had still seemed possible to unify the two parts of the peninsula, despite the obstacle of the papal territories. No more than their Lombard predecessors had the German rulers been able to impose themselves in a lasting way on southern Italy. The efforts of *Charlemagne, *Louis II and then the *Ottonians to impose their authority on the lands of Capua, *Benevento and Salerno had led only to an episodic and formal recognition, which did not mask the independence of these principalities with their very troubled internal political life. The Byzantines, whose presence had been reduced from the mid 7th c. to the *terra d'Otranto* and the southern half of *Calabria, had reconquered Lucania, *Apulia and northern Calabria at the end of the 9th c. on the pretext of liberating their populations from the Arab danger (*Sicily was under the Muslim yoke from 827, and several emirates were installed in the peninsula) and had given these provinces a sound administrative structure, based on a division into *themes (Calabria, Longobardia and perhaps Lucania), dependent from 975 on a catapan residing at *Bari.

This organisation had not resisted Norman expansion: pilgrims who soon became mercenaries, in 1029 the *Normans were officially put at the head of the Campanian county of Aversa, which served them as a base for the conquest of the whole Italian South, under the aegis of the Hauteville family. *Robert Guiscard became master of southern Italy in the last decade of the 11th c., while his brother *Roger, called the Great Count, took possession of Sicily. Both were united into a single kingdom by *Roger II (1130-1154) who, despite his active support of the schism of *Anacletus, was clever enough to return to *Innocent II's good graces, maintaining the link of vassalic dependence on the Holy See created by Robert Guiscard (synod of Melfi, 1059). He was able to keep the essentials of Byzantine and Arab experience in matters of government, ruling a *court in which all the cultural influences mingled in the service of a single power. In 1186, however, *Constance of Hauteville's marriage to the Emperor *Henry VI gave the latter rights over the Norman succession, which he effectively received in 1194 before dying four years later, leaving his son *Frederick II with the problem of holding together the three *Crowns of *Germany, *Pavia and *Palermo. Greatly attached to southern Italy, the land of his birth, Frederick II was nevertheless unable to save this tricephalous empire. Contested in the north by the second *Lombard League (1226) and in the south by the intrigues of the *pope aiming to loosen the pincers that threatened him, he was unable to profit from his military successes against both (San Germano 1230, Cortenuova 1237). In 1263, the papacy used its *suzerainty over Sicily to disinherit his heir *Manfred in favour of the house of Anjou, which transferred the capital to *Naples, but itself quickly lost control of the situation and in the end had to leave Sicily to the crown of *Aragon (war of the *Sicilian Vespers from 1282, peace of Caltabellotta 1302), followed by Naples itself (1442). The attempts at recovery made at the end of the 15th c. did not result in any lasting success.

*Il Medioevo, Storia d'Italia*, N. Valeri (dir.), Turin, 1967 (2nd ed.). – *Dalla caduta dell'impero romano al secolo XVIII, Storia d'Italia*, 2, Turin, 1974. – D. Herlihy, *Cities and Society in Medieval Italy*, London, 1980. – *Storia d'Italia*, G. Galasso (dir.), 1-10, Turin, 1980-1987. – C. Wickham, *Early Medieval Italy. Central Power and Local Society, 400-1000*, London, 1981. – O. Capitani, *Storia dell'Italia medievale*, Bari, 1988 (2nd ed.). – "Italien", *LdM*, Munich-Zurich, 1991, 706-762. – E.M. Jamison, *Studies on the History of Medieval Sicily and Southern Italy*, D. Clementi (ed.), T. Kolzer (ed.), Aalen, 1992. – P. Amory, *People and Identity in Ostrogothic Italy, 489-554*, Cambridge, 1997.

François Bougard

**ITINERARIES, BYZANTINE.** The itineraries used by the military, by soldiers and *pilgrims, followed the *road network inherited from the Roman world. Nevertheless, the centre of the East Roman world now being *Constantinople, travellers set out from the capital westward by the Via Egnatia or by Adrianople across the Balkans, eastward by the great road going through Chalcedon and Nicomedia. The *chronicles testify to the modification of military itineraries over the centuries. To go to war against the Persians, soldiers took the Ancyra route through Juliopolis, then went towards Caesarea; later, faced with the Arabs and *Turks, they took the road to Amorion and Ikonion. From 1350, Asia Minor being entirely *Ottoman, itineraries now concerned only the European part, of which Adrianople and Philippopolis, situated on the royal road, were the strategic nodes.

Itineraries also followed the sea-routes, which made up a large part of the traffic from Constantinople, hinge betwen the Black Sea and the Propontis. The route that, after Abydos, crossed the Aegean from north to south, rejoined the old itineraries to *Rome, *Alexandria and *Palestine. These, going via *Cyprus, *Rhodes (sometimes the Cyclades), *Crete and Syracuse, continued to be widely used in the medieval period and enjoyed a new vigour with the arrival of the Venetians. Descriptions of trajectories are given in the *Stadiodromikon of Constantine VII* in the mid 10th c., the *Geography of Edrisi* and the *Russian Itineraries* in the early 12th c., the *Narrative of Saewulf* in 1102-1103 and the *Itinerary of Benjamin of Tudela* in the second half of the 12th century. Chroniclers mention the itineraries of Bohemund in 1126, William of Tyre in 1180, *Philip Augustus and *Richard Coeur de Lion in 1191.

Religious itineraries followed these great routes, but impressed the specific characters of their vocation. Saints' Lives and Miracles relate journeys of monks and pilgrims. Until the 7th c., they led to Egypt and Palestine. From the 8th c., at a time when Palestine was no longer accessible, they now led to famous sanctuaries and holy mountains in Asia Minor (Ephesus, Chônai, Euchaïte, Myra, Patara, *Olympus, Galesios, Latros), *Greece (*Athos, St Luke of Phocis) and the islands (*Patmos). From the 11th c., a time of regained security in the East Mediteranean, and at the time of the settlement of the Franks in the *Holy Land, pilgrims embarked once more with *merchants and the military for *Antioch and the *ports of Palestine.

N. Schur, *Jerusalem in Pilgrims' and Travellers' Accounts*, Jerusalem, 1980. – P. Maraval, *Lieux saints et pèlerinages d'Orient*, Paris, 1985. – É. Malamut, *Les Îles de l'empire byzantin*, Paris, 1989. – É. Malamut, *Sur la route des saints byzantins*, Paris, 1993.

Élisabeth Malamut

**IVAN III (1440-1505).** Grand prince of *Moscow (1462-1505). Inheriting the necessary means from his father, Basil II, Ivan imposed an autocratic power, with the help of a new class of servants (the *dvorjane*), and transformed the grand principality of Moscow into a "centralized Russian State", according to today's historical terminology, notably by annexing the vast republic of *Novgorod (1478) and the old rival, the grand principality of Tver' (1485). The *Mongol yoke having collapsed (1480), Ivan took from *Lithuania the *Belarusian and *Ukrainian territories that he considered "Russian". This led him to establish contacts and alliances in southern and central Europe.

J. Fennell, *Ivan the Great of Moscow*, London, 1961. – G. Alef, *The Origins of Muscovite Autocracy: The Age of Ivan III*, 1986 ("FOEG", 39).

Vladimir Vodoff

**IVO OF CHARTRES (*c.*1040-1115).** Ivo was born in *c.*1040, probably at *Chartres. He studied at the monastery of *Bec under *Lanfranc, and later at *Paris. He obtained a *benefice in the church of Nesle in *Picardy, and in *c.*1078 became *prior of the *collegiate church of Saint-Quentin in *Beauvais. Elected bishop of Chartres in 1090, he was refused *consecration by the *metropolitan of *Sens and it was *Urban II who consecrated him, at Capua, late in 1090. Taking possession of his Beauce see was not easy. In conflict with local lords, he was supported by *Philip I. But the king's *divorce and his new union were denounced by the bishop of Chartres: so, from 1092, good relations between the king and the bishop ceased. However, Ivo contributed to sorting out the king's matrimonial difficulties in 1104 thanks to his knowledge of the interpretation of *canon law. Having died on 23 Dec 1115, Ivo was soon venerated at Chartres as a saint.

We have 23 of his *sermons, which deal mainly with dogmatic and liturgical questions and were not without influence on the scholastic literature of the school of *Laon. We also have a correspondence of some 300 *letters, mostly dating from the time of his episcopate. Their credit is attested by the numerous manuscripts of them, not just in France but also in Germany and England. These letters, which deal with *theology and canon law, show us the position of a pastor in the presence of the difficulties of daily life, and their attitude is not always that revealed by his works as a *Doctor.

But the reputation of Ivo of Chartres comes mainly from his three *canonical collections, only two of which are edited. The *Decretum* (probably *c.*1094) is a large compilation of 3760 chapters, divided into 17 parts, in an order that leaves much to be desired. Ivo reproduces a number of texts from the first two parts of his *Tripartita* and from *Burchard of Worms's *Decretum*. He makes wide use of *Roman law. Though we have few manuscripts of it, the *Decretum* was widely circulated in France, England, the Rhineland and even the Scandinavian countries.

A "warehouse of texts", the *Decretum* was used by Ivo for his *Panormia*, a more modest collection (some 1200 chapters, divided into eight books and systematically ordered). Slightly later than the *Decretum* (*c.*1095), the *Panormia* is greatly superior to it in its methodical classification of texts. It had a great success: we know more than a hundred manuscripts of it.

The *Tripartita* owes its (modern) name to the fact that it is composed of three parts. The first contains *Decretals, authentic and false, from Clement I to *Urban II, and some conciliar texts. The second gives conciliar canons. The third is an extract from the *Decretum*. It was composed between 1093 and 1095.

"Yves de Chartres", *DDC*, 7, 1966, 1641-1666. – B. Basdevant-Gaudemet, "Le Mariage d'après la correspondance d'Yves de Chartres", *RHD*, 61, 1983, 195-215. – M. Grandjean, *Laïcs dans l'Église: regards de Pierre Damien, Anselme de Cantorbéry, Yves de Chartres*, Paris, 1994. – J. Werckmeister, "Le premier 'canoniste' Yves de Chartres", *RDC*, 47, en hommage à J. Bernhard, 1997, 53-70. – J. Werckmeister (ed.), Le "Prologue", coll. "Sources canoniques", 1, 1997.

Jean Gaudemet

**IVORIES.** Ivory sculpture was one of the major fields of medieval artistic creation. In this sphere as in many others, medieval *artists borrowed from the ancient world a material, a technique, even types of objects and stylistic models, but they also profoundly adapted them to their own genius.

Thus, the material used was primarily the elephant's tusk, coming from *India in the early Middle Ages and more from *Africa from the 13th century. But because of the frequent scarcity of this rare and costly material, artists did not hesitate to find substitutes for it, in particular walrus tusks or deers' antlers, an infallible mark of Nordic output in the *Romanesque period. In the late 14th c., the Embriachi family in north Italy developed a technique based on the juxtaposition of sheets of bone in a framework of marquetry.

The use of these materials involved complex constraints, connected with the curve of the tusks and more generally with their thinness. As well as the translucent whiteness of the material, gilding and polychromy enriched the works with a supplementary brilliance. The sculptors, whose names are rarely known, were nonetheless artists in their own right and their links with monumental sculpture, particularly in the *Gothic period, are evident.

The Eastern Empire of Byzantium retained from the antique inheritance primarily a serene classicism, which flourished fully under the *Macedonian dynasty. The 10th-11th cc. thus saw an extensive output of small plaques and triptychs for religious use, or caskets with secular decoration, whose manufacture could be divided among several workshops. In the West, where output had suffered a net regression at the time of the *barbarian kingdoms, the Carolingian and then Ottonian Empires would revive the old tradition in this sphere too. Essentially intended to ornament the

Ivory comb. Burgundian school, 14th c. Florence, Bargello Museum.

bindings of sumptuous *liturgical books, ivories at this time revived the classical aesthetic in all its diversity.

In the *Romanesque period, when artists produced mainly crosses and *reliquaries but also, in the secular sphere, chessmen or backgammon counters, the variety of plastic expressions is striking; it corresponds to the plurality of production sites. In the 13th and 14th cc. on the contrary, alongside secondary centres (Rhineland, England, Italy), *Paris occupied a primary place. At the height of their means, artists created independent statuettes as well as sculpted groups; bas-relief diptychs and triptychs; or mirror backs, writing tablets and caskets ornamented with secular subjects. This output, which suffered a sort of exhaustion from the 1400s, was not really replaced by 15th-c. Italian work, which at first created impressive *altarpieces but later specialized in increasingly stereotyped secular objects.

A. Goldschmidt, *Die Elfenbeinskulpturen aus der Zeit karolingischen und sächsischen Kaiser*, Berlin, 1914-1926 (4 vol.). – R. Koechlin, *Les Ivoires gothiques français*, Paris, 1924 (3 vol.). – A. Goldschmidt, K. Weitzmann, *Byzantinische Elfenbeinskulpturen*, Berlin, 1930-1934 (2 vol.). – W. F. Volbach, *Elfenbeinarbeiten der Spätantike und des frühen Mittelalters*, Mainz, 1976 (3rd ed.). – D. Gaborit-Chopin, *Ivoires du Moyen Âge*, Fribourg, 1978.

Pierre-Yves Le Pogam

# J

**JACOB.** Son of *Isaac and grandson of *Abraham, Jacob was the third of the great patriarchs. He bought the birthright from his brother Esau, and was the husband of Leah and Rachel. His struggle with the angel (Gen 32) preceded his reconciliation with Esau. The end of his life is associated with that of his son *Joseph.

The usurpation of Isaac's blessing, interpreted as the substitution of the New Covenant for the Old, is rare in the Middle Ages. But it can be seen on a capital at *Vézelay (12th c.) and an arch moulding of the portal of the gilded Virgin at *Amiens (13th c.). Symbolic art attached itself especially to Jacob's dream (*Jacob's ladder) and his struggle with the angel. The latter episode could be perceived in different ways, so its iconography varies: on a 12th-c. bas-relief of *Modena cathedral, the *angel is shown as a *demon.

E.G. Tasker, "Jacob and Esau", *Encyclopedia of Medieval Church Art*, J. Beaumont (ed.), London, 1993.

Frédérique Trouslard

*The hospitality of Abraham, the sacrifice of Isaac, Jacob's ladder.* Miniature from the *Lambeth Bible.* London, Lambeth Palace Library (Ms 3, fol. 6).

**JACOB ANATOLI (13th c.).** Jacob ben Abba Mari Anatoli, Jewish translator and exegete, was allied to the family of Ibn Tibbon, celebrated translators (dates unknown). In 1231 he was doctor to *Frederick II at the court of *Naples; there he formed a lasting *friendship with Michael Scot. We owe him translations (from Arabic to *Hebrew) of works of *Averroes (middle commentary on *Isagoge*, *De interpretione*, *Analytica* I and II) and of the abridgment of Ptolemy's *Almagest*. His *Malmad ha-Talmidim* (Goad of the Disciples) proposes a philosophical exegesis of biblical pericopes; it cites interpretations of Michael Scot and Frederick II.

E. Renan, A. Neubauer, "Les rabbins français du commencement du XIVe siècle", *HLF*, 27, 1877, 580-589. – C. Sirat, "Les Traducteurs juifs à la cour des rois de Sicile et de Naples", *Traductions et traducteurs au Moyen Âge*, Paris, 1989, 169-191.

Gilbert Dahan

**JACOB BEN REUBEN (late 12th c.).** The Jew Jacob ben Reuben seems to have lived in the late 12th c. in northern *Spain or southern France. His polemical work *Sefer Milhamoth Adonay* (Book of the Wars of the Lord) is one of the first to show the influence of the philosophical method of *apologetic. The preface states that the work was written to counter the arguments of a learned priest whom the author held in high esteem. The twelve chapters contain an imaginary debate between a "monotheist" and a "dissimulator" or "destroyer" (of the divine unity). The Christian arguments, marshalled in order of the biblical books, are refuted; one section examines those drawn from the gospels.

G. Dahan, *Les Intellectuels chrétiens et les juifs au Moyen Âge*, Paris, 1990, 345-346, 416, 488-489.

Sonia Fellous

**JACOB OF EDESSA (*c.*633-708).** One of the chief Syriac writers of the 7th century, Jacob (or James) became a monk at the monastery of Qinnasrīn where he studied the Scriptures and Greek. Appointed bishop of Edessa in *c.*684, he wished to reform monastic life in his *diocese; having failed, he abandoned his see and retired to the monastery of Kaysūm where he expounded the Scriptures. He later moved to the monastery of Teleda where he continued his work on the Old Testament and, after having resumed possession of his see, died on 5 June 708. A polygraph, Jacob of Edessa composed numerous works: revision of the Simple version of the Old Testament (Pešitta), Hexaemeron on creation, Enchiridion of philosophical terms, *Chronicle up to 692, translation of 125 *homilies of Severus of Antioch, Grammar of the Syriac language.

C. Kayser (ed., tr.), *Die Canones Jacobs von Edessa*, Leipzig, 1886.

Gérard Troupeau

**JACOB'S LADDER.** The two main elements of the account of Gen 28, 10-22 are the divine promise during Jacob's dream at Bethel, and the sacred foundation and vow that follow it. But the vision of the ladder set on earth, whose summit touched heaven, which the angels ascended and descended, while God stood above it, had an immense diffusion in the Middle Ages, particularly in *exegesis and art. It symbolized the foundation of places of worship. It was also the basis of the theme of the *spiritual ladder, allegory of the way of return to *heaven proposed to men, whose best-known examples were, in the West, ch. 7 of the Rule of St *Benedict, or the *illumination of the *Ladder of virtues* in the **Hortus deliciarum*; in the East, the *Holy Ladder* of *John Climacus.

E. Bertaud, A. Rayez, "Échelle spirituelle", *DSp*, 4, 1958, 62-86. – C. M. Kauffmann, "Jakob", *LCI*, 2, 1970, 373-375. – C. Heck, *L'échelle céleste dans l'art du Moyen Âge. Une image de la quête du ciel*, Paris, 1997.

Christian Heck

**JACOBELLUS OF STŘÍBRO (?-1429).** Jakoubek ze Stříbra, front-rank *Hussite theologian, the greatest thinker among the Prague *Utraquists, and professor at the university of *Prague (master of *liberal arts). His works form a solidly argued justification of a whole series of Hussite articles of faith and rites, but he was primarily the initiator of the return to early Christian sources with communion in both kinds (*chalice for the laity). He occupied an eminent position in the organisation of the structures of the Utraquist clergy at Prague, and also took a prominent part in the political events that agitated his country at that time.

P. de Vooght, *Jacobellus de Stříbro, premier théologien du hussitisme*, Louvain, 1972.

Jaroslav Boubín

**JACOBITES.** These adherents of the Church founded by Jacob Bar-Addai or Baradaeus († 578) were derisively called "Jacobites" by their opponents: their own name for themselves is "orthodox".

The Syrian Church had had a brilliant start, especially in Osrhoene: from the 2nd c. it had blossomed in an original way through the philosophical or poetical works of various authors, especially Ephrem († 373), whose theology had shown itself to be of an astonishing doctrinal sureness.

In the 5th c., however, the christological debates to clarify the nature of the union of the two natures in the person of Christ, following the *Arian crisis, had made it necessary to call the council of Ephesus (431) which deposed Nestorius, patriarch of Constantinople; these debates led to the discovery by the Oriental world of Greek thought and its requirements, obliging each to define their dogmatic positions: for the Incarnation, Cyril had sought to impose his central intuition of an indissociable unity between *God and *man, and the brutal energy he had deployed to this end had, at first, got the better of his adversary. But, for all that, feelings were not pacified: if the radical heresy of Eutyches, which suppressed one of the two natures in Christ in favour of the divine, was at the origin of "monophysitism" proper, this last was condemned from 448 and definitively condemned at the council of Chalcedon in 451. Then followed a long confrontation between the Chalcedonian party, upheld by the authorities, and the monophysites, taken in the broad sense of anti-Chalcedonians.

In the East, the monophysites found here in addition a justification for opposing the central government; they also had the advantage of counting among their ranks the strong personalities of Peter the Fuller, the passionate Philoxenus, bishop of Mabbug († 523), and the much more moderate Severus, patriarch of *Antioch († 538). After attempts at reconciliation, made by the emperors over some 70 years, Justin's terrible repression in 518-519 failed to win the day: many bishops and archimandrites of monasteries were deposed and exiled, as Michael the Syrian relates: the party seemed threatened with extinction, when it was saved by the energy of Jacob Bar-Addaï (the surname means "beggar" or "old rags" and was given him on account of his garments).

This Jacob, son of a priest, was originally a monk in the monastery of Phesilta (the "cut [stone]") near Tella. With the protection of the Eastern empress Theodora and at the request of the king of the Ghassanid Arabs, he got himself consecrated *bishop. With no fixed residence, he travelled through *Syria, Asia Minor and even Egypt, ordaining priests everywhere and consecrating bishops, among them the historian John of Ephesus from whom we have an account of these events; in Persia, he even managed to set up a separate Church with its own network of bishops and monasteries, mainly in northern Mesopotamia, unified from 559 under the authority of the see of Tagrit, whose titular would receive in the 7th c. the title of *maphrien* (the fertilizer). Subsequently, missions extended still further east as far as Afghanistan and even Chinese Turkestan. By his death in 578, Jacob had set up a Church powerful enough to impose on the patriarchal see a parallel hierarchy uninterrupted to this day: it rightly bears the name "Jacobite" in honour of its founder. In 1783, part of its membership rallied behind Rome, becoming the "Syro-Catholics", while the others remained the "Syro-Orthodox".

This Church also enjoyed great renown; after the christological struggles of the 5th-6th cc. and the arrival of *Islam in the 7th, it enjoyed periods of fertile intellectual work: it had revisers of the Scriptures, such as Philoxenus of Mabbug who made the so-called Philoxenian version of the New Testament around 500-505; commentators, like Philoxenus himself and above all *Dionysius bar Salibi († 1171); grammarians, who fixed the Syriac language, which from now on was rivalled by Arabic: *Jacob of Edessa († 708) and *Bar Hebraeus († 1286); and great historians like John of Ephesus († 586), Patriarch *Michael the Syrian († 1199) and again Bar Hebraeus, the celebrated encyclopedist who summed up in his work all the thought and the literary and scientific attainments of the Syrians.

J. B. Chabot, *Chronique de Michel le Syrien*, Paris, 1899-1910 (re-ed. Brussels, 1963, 4 vol.).

C. Sélis, *Les Syriens orthodoxes et catholiques*, Turnhout, 1988.

Micheline Albert

**JACOBUS DE VORAGINE (*c.*1228/1229-1298).** Born doubtless at Varazze near *Genoa, Jacobus entered the Order of Preachers in 1244. Without having been through the *universities, he climbed all the rungs of the order: perhaps sub-prior of the *convent of Genoa in 1258 and *prior of that of Asti in 1266, he directed the *Dominican province of Lombardy in 1267-1277, then in 1281-1286. Meanwhile he had taken part in the council of *Lyon in 1274. Then, on the death of John of Vercelli, he was interim master general of the Order of Preachers between 1283 and 1285. In 1292 he was elected archbishop of Genoa, where he tried to promote Church *reform and peace between the *Guelf and Ghibelline factions until his death. His firm support for the master general Muño de Zamora between 1285 and 1293, at a critical moment for the order, places him in a fideist and rigorist current, hostile to the Thomist "university" tendency. For him, the essential thing was the pastoral mission of the Friars Preachers.

Voragine's name remains rightly attached to his work of Christian vulgarization and particularly to his **Golden Legend*, compiled in the mid 1260s, an immensely successful hagiographical collection that was part of a Dominican effort to circulate and unify the Christian *legendary. The compiler shows himself more concerned with an overall grasp of tradition than with hagiographical innovation. Voragine continued his work with three collections of *sermons (between 1275 and 1285): the 306 sermons on 81 saints (*Sermones de sanctis et festis*), treated according to the order of the *calendar, repeat some of the material of the *Golden Legend*, mixing it with numerous scriptural and patristic texts. The coherence of the undertaking shows very well that the primary function of the legendary was to prepare for *preaching, the order's essential task. It was doubtless the success of this collection that encouraged Jacobus to continue, with the 159 sermons on the Dominical gospels (*Sermones de tempore per annum*) and finally the 98 lenten sermons (*Sermones quadragesimales*). These are model sermons, firmly structured, entirely written out, but without developments (the **exempla* are only sketched out). This preaching well illustrates the "scholastic-thematic" tendency used in the 13th c. by the *mendicant orders, based on a series of lexical and conceptual distinctions, ramified from the starting-point of the initial verse (the theme). These three collections had great success in the Middle Ages (from 100 to 200 manuscripts each). A fourth collection, in a different style, the *Mariale*, written during the period of his archiepiscopate, groups together 161 considerations on the words ascribed to the Virgin *Mary, in alphabetical order; this text is related to the collections of "*distinctions" used for preaching. Voragine's last six works are connected with his archiepiscopate: these are five opuscula consecrated to the *sanctoral and the liturgy of Genoa (on St Cyrus, bishop of Genoa, on St John *Cassian, on the *relics of St *John the Baptist, Florentius and various other saints), but especially a *Chronicle of the City of Genoa* (finished in 1297) which takes up the annalistic civic tradition and Christianizes it.

*The Golden Legend*, W. G. Ryan (tr.), Princeton (NJ), 1993 (2 vol.). – Jacopo da Varazze, *Legenda Aurea*, G. P. Maggioni (ed.), Florence, 1998.

G. Monleone, *Jacopo di Varagine e la sua Cronaca de Genova*, Rome, 1941.

Alain Boureau

**JACOPONE DA TODI (*c.*1230-1306).** Jacobus de Benedictis, better known as Jacopone da Todi, was born in *Umbria, probably in the early 1230s. We have little sure information about his life. His religious *conversion in 1269 – he was a *jurist by profession – seems to have resulted from his discovery of a *hairshirt on the body of his dying wife after the ground gave way in a castle where a banquet was being held.

For a decade he led a life of *poverty as a mendicant. In 1278 he was accepted into the Order of Friars Minor, where he quickly adhered to the positions of the "zealots" of the Rule, otherwise called the *Spirituals: he shared their hopes and disappointments at the time of the pontificate of *Celestine V. With the pontificate of *Boniface VIII, Jacopone personally committed himself – by signing the manifesto of Lunghezza, 10 May 1297 – to the party of those who contested not just the *pope's religious choices, but the very legitimacy of his *election. The pope's victory over his opponents, led by the *Colonna cardinals, meant, for Jacopone, condemnation in 1298-1299 to perpetual imprisonment, served in the underground cells of a Franciscan *convent, probably at San Fortunato in his own town. Despite a number of *appeals addressed by him to Boniface VIII, the sentence of *excommunication against him was not lifted until the accession of *Benedict XII late in 1303. Jacopone died a few years later, Dec 1306, in the convent of the *Poor Clares at Collazzone, not far from Todi.

*Adoration of the magi*. Miniature by Jacquemart of Hesdin from the *Petites Heures de Jean de Berry*, *c.*1390. Paris, BNF (Ms lat. 18014, fol. 42 v°).

Jacopone da Todi is known mainly for his collection of vernacular lauds, whose manuscripts enjoyed wide circulation in the 14th and 15th cc. among the *Franciscans: the first printed edition by Francesco Bonaccorsi dates from 1490 at Florence. The *Laudes* of Jacopone da Todi belong to the history of literature as well as of *spirituality and religious feeling. Tension towards the divine is expressed through a "Franciscanism" not without traits of pessimism and anguish, interpreted and experienced in a troubled and rigorous way, marked by ecclesiological elements.

Iacopone da Todi, *Laude*, F. Mancini (ed.), Rome-Bari, 1977.

*Iacopone e il suo tempo*, Todi, 1959. – E. Menesto, *Le Prose latine attribuite a Iacopone da Todi*, Bologna, 1979. – *Atti del Convegno storico iacoponico in occasione del 750e anniversario della nascita di Iacopone da Todi*, Florence, 1981 (re-ed. Spoleto, 1992).

Grado G. Merlo

**JACQUEMART OF HESDIN (14th-15th cc.).** A painter from Artois, Jacquemart of Hesdin was active between 1384 and 1414 at Bourges, at the *court of Duke *John of Berry, where his whole career developed. With the *Boucicaut Master and the de *Limbourg brothers, he set his mark on the illustration of illuminated *books for *Charles V's brother. He manifests a certain mastery in the representation of space, thus showing that he had suitably assimilated the lesson of *Siena; he also attests the new northern naturalist tendencies, in contrast to the idealized art of Jean *Pucelle. He was one of the best authors of the *Très belles heures de Jean de Berry* (Brussels, Bibliothèque royale, ms. 11060-11061), the *Grandes heures* for which he painted the *Carrying of the cross* in the Louvre museum, the *Petites heures* and the *Psalter* (Paris, BNF, lat. 18014 and fr. 13091).

J. Porcher, *L'Enluminure française*, Paris, 1959. – M. Meiss, *French Painting in the Time of Jean de Berry*, New York, 1967.

Anne Granboulan

**JACQUERIES.** The term "Jacquerie" evoked "Jacques Bonhomme", an insulting surname given to rustics, or the "*jaque*", the short jacket of the *peasants. Primarily, it designated the *revolt of the peasants of the *Paris region in May and June 1358. But this rising caused such a stir that the word became synonymous with peasant revolt.

Unleashed by an affray between looters and peasants on 29 May 1358 at Saint-Leu-d'Esserent, the Jacquerie was propagated in a few days in the villages around Paris and its influence was felt as far as *Champagne and *Normandy. Immediately characterised by great *violence against the *nobles, it attacked *castles, tried to capture the *market of Meaux and was finally defeated on 10 June at Mello, near Creil, by an army of nobles led by the king of *Navarre, Charles the Bad. An aristocratic counter-Jacquerie then developed whose ferocity betrayed the hatred and fear felt by the nobles for the "non-nobles", or even the awareness of a questioning of society by the rebels.

A revolt of misery for some, the Jacquerie is interpreted by others as the reaction of a once-prosperous rural world to the "misfortunes of the times", to an economic and political crisis (defeat of Poitiers in 1356, captivity of King John the Good, failure of the elites). Its leaders were largely village notables, rural artisans or country priests who, willingly or unwillingly, followed their parishioners in the revolt. However, the Jacques only very fleetingly obtained an alliance with the revolted Parisians, led by Étienne Marcel who preferred Charles the Bad to them. This social isolation, the Jacques' lack of organisation, their improvised armament and their inexperience against the warrior solidarity of the nobles explain their rapid failure.

Before and after this episode there were many other peasant risings. During the early Middle Ages, "jacqueries" developed especially at a time when the policy of the *Peace of God – whose ambition was actually to protect non-combatants – was in fact amplifying antagonisms between lords and peasants. In the 12th and 13th cc., peasant communities opposed the seignorial will to the point of revolt. In particular, the late Middle Ages were scoured by a succession of popular movements many of which had aspects of jacquerie: from the revolt of the Karls of maritime *Flanders in the early 14th c. to the revolts of the 1380s – Tuchins of the Massif Central and *Languedoc, workers of *England in 1381 – and those of the 15th c., *Hussite revolts in *Bohemia or "*Bundschuh* period" in the *Empire. All had varied and complex motivations: the revolt of the workers of England was that of people liable to the capitation ("poll-tax") and of unfree peasants against an archaic status; it also revealed egalitarian aspirations and the wish for a return to an authentic Christian society, in conformity with the evangelical model ("When Adam delved and Eve span, who was then the gentleman?"). Indeed, from the late 14th c., *millenarian demands frequently slid into revolutionary discourse.

M. Dommanget, *La Jacquerie*, Paris, 1971. – R. Fossier, "Les mouvements populaires en Occident au XIe siècle", *CRAI*, April-June 1971, 257-269. – M. Mollat, P. Wolff, *The Popular Revolutions of the Late Middle Ages*, London, 1973. – R. Hilton, *Bond Men Made Free*, London, 1977. – M. T. de Medeiros, *Jacques et chroniqueurs*, Paris, 1980. – D.M. Bessen, "The Jacquerie: Class War or Co-opted Rebellion?", *JMH*, 11, 1985, 43-59.

Jean Tricard

**JACQUES DE VITRY (*c.*1160/70 - 1240).** Born between 1160 and 1170, in a locality hard to identify, Jacques de Vitry obtained the cure of Argenteuil (*diocese of *Paris) without yet being a priest. Attracted by the reputation of *Marie of Oignies († 1213), in *c.*1208 he settled at Oignies, in the Sambre valley some 10 kilometres east of Charleroi, at that time in the diocese of *Liège. Ordained priest at Paris, he returned to Oignies and entered Saint-Nicolas, an *abbey of regular *canons, in *c.*1211.

He preached in France against the Albigensian *heretics, then took an active part in the preparations for the fifth *crusade. Appointed bishop of St John of *Acre in 1216, he was active in *Palestine. He was in the West in 1222-1223, then in *c.*1226. In 1228, *Gregory IX accepted his *resignation from the bishopric of Acre. He was in the diocese of Liège, created *cardinal of Tusculum in 1229, and was associated with the activities of the Roman *Curia until his death, 1 May 1240. He was buried at Oignies.

His works consist of the following:

*Life of Marie of Oignies*. Written before Jacques de Vitry left for the East in 1216. This is among the earliest medieval *biographies of a woman. In *c.*1231, the Dominican *Thomas of Cantimpré added a third book relating the *miracles worked by Marie.

Seven *letters, written in the East between 1216 and 1221; four letters (2, 4, 6, 7) had several recipients. Their reputation has remained slight. In his *Historia orientalis*, Jacques de Vitry partly re-used the documentation on the *Holy Land assembled in *Ep.* 2.

*Historia hierosolimitana abbreuiata*. An ambiguous title that in fact designates two books. The *Historia orientalis* is a brief account of the first three crusades and the main events up to 1212. The work is also a guide to the Holy Land: peoples, fauna, flora. It had an excellent circulation and was translated into French in the 13th century. The *Historia occidentalis*, much less circulated, vigorously denounces the "fauna" of the West and of the Church. It then deals with several people (Fulk of Neuilly, *Peter Cantor), contemporary religious *orders, sacramental theology.

Some 400 *sermons, listed in J.-B. Schneyer (*RLS*, 3, 1971, 179-221) and divided into four series of unequal length: 194 sermons called *dominical*, three for each *Sunday and feast-day: gospel, epistle and – something rare – *introit (old edition by Damien Du Bois, Antwerp, 1575, 932 pp.); 115 sermons *de sanctis* dealing with the *sanctoral of the *liturgical year (from one to three sermons according to the *feast) and the common (apostles, confessors), known in six almost complete manuscripts (sermons unedited, except the three for 2 Nov, ed. by J. Longère for the conferences on *death in the Middle Ages, Orléans, 1982, and Lille, 1992); 74 sermons *ad status* or *uulgares*: this collection, Jacques de Vitry's most widely circulated and most famous (more than fifteen manuscripts survive), contains instructions appropriate to the various states and conditions of life, prelates and priests, monks, *nuns, *canons, students, *pilgrims, crusaders, *merchants and labourers, *widows and married *women (J. Longère has published several sermons and is preparing the critical edition of the whole collection); and 27 *common* sermons: little circulated, they comment on the first chapters of *Genesis, and are unedited.

A celebrated preacher before his departure to the Holy Land, Jacques de Vitry surely used his past experience to write his sermons, which by common consent are generally placed in the last part of his life; they are certainly the work of the author himself, given the homogeneity of the textual tradition of all the series.

*Lettre de Jacques de Vitry (1160/1170-1240), évêque de Saint-Jean-d'Acre*, R. B. C. Huygens (crit. ed.), Leiden, 1960 [*Ep.* 2]. – J. F. Hinnebusch, *The Historia occidentalis of Jacques de Vitry. A Critical Edition*, Fribourg, 1972. – Jacques de Vitry, *Vie de Marie d'Oignies*, Thomas de Cantimpré, *Supplément*, A. Wankenne (Fr. tr., preface), Namur, 1989. – Jacques de Vitry, *The Life of Marie d'Oignies*, M. H. King (ed.), M. Marsolais (ed.), Toronto, 1993. – Jacques de Vitry, *Histoire occidentale*, G. Duchet-Suchaux (Fr. tr.), J. Longère (intro., notes), Paris, 1997.

M. Coens, "Jacques de Vitry", *BNBelg*, 31, suppl. 3, 1962, 465-473. – H. Platelle, "Jacques de Vitry", *DSp*, 8, 1974, 60-62. – J. Longère, *Oeuvres oratoires de maîtres parisiens au XII^e siècle. Étude historique et doctrinale*, 1, Paris, 1975, 31-33, 168-176, 346-351; *ibid.*, 2, 32-34, 129-136, 256-261.

Jean Longère

**JAGIELLONIANS.** The dynasty of kings of *Poland and grand dukes of *Lithuania going back to *Ladislas Jagiello, king from 1386 to 1434. In the 15th and 16th cc. they were also kings of *Hungary and *Bohemia (until 1526). They were a branch of the Gedyminids, descendants of Gedymin (born *c.*1275), grand duke of Lithuania from 1316 to 1341, the real creator of this great State. Putting up a resistance to the *Teutonic Knights, he extended his power over the Ruthenian lands (*Belarus, *Ukraine) particularly through the marriages of his children, 12 sons and daughters. One of Gedymin's sons, Olgierd, strengthened the State as grand duke (1345-1377) by sharing supreme power with his younger brother Kejstut. Olgierd had 21 sons and daughters, one of whom, Jogaïla – who received the name Ladislas (Władysław) on the occasion of his *baptism at *Cracow in 1386 – took the title and power of grand duke in 1377. Until 1392 Ladislas united the throne of Poland and the sovereignty of Lithuania as grand duke – he called himself *princeps supremus* of Lithuania. In this way, Lithuania found itself united to Poland by a personal union, which, having regard to the very powerful position of the reigning dynasty of Lithuania, could not have been more advantageous to the Jagiellonians. Witold (Vytautas), an exceptional ruler, extremely enterprising, ruling over Eastern Europe, maintained good relations with Jagiello until the end of his life, thus making lasting the *de facto* close link that united the two States. Differences, and even intestine wars, broke out after Witold's death in 1430, but finally the Jagiellonians, in the person of Jagiello's son Casimir, established themselves firmly from 1440 over the grand duchy of Lithuania. Casimir's elder brother Ladislas became king of Poland (1434-1444) after his father's death, and was also king of Hungary from 1440. The young king's heroic death at the head of the Polish-Hungarian army at the battle of Varna against the *Turks in 1444 put an end to a new attempt at Polish-Hungarian union, at the same time strengthening Turkish rule over the Balkans.

At the request of the Poles, Grand Duke Casimir then took possession of the throne of Cracow, fully keeping a distinct power over Lithuania. He had a long reign (1446-1492). Married in 1454 to Elizabeth of Habsburg, by her he had six sons and seven daughters. Dynastic policy – which consisted in securing thrones and making good marriages – occupied an important place in his way of life. His eldest son Ladislas became king of Bohemia in 1471 despite the *pope's protests over the preponderance there of the *Hussite *Utraquists, considered *heretics. In 1490, Ladislas also mounted the throne of Hungary; Jagiellonians held both kingdoms until the death of Ladislas's son and successor Louis at the battle of *Mohács against the Turks (1526). In Poland, after the death of King Casimir, the new ruler was his son John Albert (Jan Olbracht, 1492-1501), while in Lithuania his brother Alexander (1492-1506, also king of Poland from 1501) became grand duke. From 1490 to 1526, the Jagiellonians reigned over three great countries of East-Central Europe, getting the best in the rivalry that existed between them and the *Habsburgs over Bohemia and Hungary. This was facilitated by the traditional *toleration of the dynasty's representatives and their taking account of regional aspirations, especially those of the *nobility, whose power was strengthened everywhere in their countries. Casimir Jagiello's son, St *Casimir, still enjoys a cult which is very much alive as patron of both Lithuania and Poland.

*Polski Słownik Biograficzny*, Cracow, 1935 f. – W. Dworzaczek, *Genealogia*, Warsaw, 1959. – F. Dvornik, *Les Slaves*, Paris, 1970. – N. Davies, *God's Playground. A History of Poland*, 1, Oxford, 1981. – J. Kłoczowski, *Młodsza Europa*, Warsaw, 1998.

Jerzy Kłoczowski

**JAKUB OF PARADYŻ (died 1464).** Formerly wrongly called Jakub of Jüterborg. Cistercian, Carthusian, professor at the university of *Cracow and author of some 80 important treatises on *reform, which were widely known throughout central Europe. He came from a family of German peasants who had settled in Great Poland, and it was there that he entered the *Cistercians of Paradyż. He lived at Cracow in the years 1420-1441; from 1432, as professor of the university, he joined in the conciliar movement that was then very powerful there. Among other things he collaborated in drawing up the pro-conciliar and reforming collective treatise sent by the university of Cracow to the council of *Basel in 1440. He also wrote in favour of the reform of the religious *orders, going so far as to project the suppression of their property. After 1441, he left Cracow and then the Cistercian Order, and ended in *c.*1447 by settling with the *Carthusians of *Erfurt, where he wrote abundantly. He was one of the most eminent representatives of the reforming intellectual current that strongly marked this generation, both at Cracow and in the other university clerical milieux of central Europe. There is still no fully satisfactory study of Jakub's work and of this whole movement.

*Polski słownik biograficzny*, 10, Cracow, 1962-1964, 363-364.

*Dzieje teologii katolickiej w Polsce*, 1, M. Rechowicza (ed.), Lublin, 1974.

Jerzy Kłoczowski

**JAMES OF LAUSANNE (died 1321).** A native of Vaudens (Switzerland), he entered the *Dominicans at Lausanne. At *Paris from 1303, he taught at the *convent of Saint-Jacques (1311-1316). Provincial of France in 1318, he died, according to the *obituary of the Lausanne Dominicans, on 17 Nov 1321. He was the author of commentaries on the **Sentences* and the Scriptures, as well as *sermons of rare verve.

*Opus moralitatum*, Limoges, 1528. – *Sermons dominicaux et festifs*, Paris, 1530.

G. T. Bedouelle, *DSp*, 8, 1974, 45-46. – T. Kaeppeli, *SOPMA*, 2, 1975, 323-329.

Ansgar Wildermann

**JAMES OF THE MARCHES (1394-1476).** Born in the Italian Marches, of a poor family. Having studied seriously, James became a Franciscan in 1416. An admirer and imitator of St *Bernardino, a popular preacher, with a very lively and sound doctrine, inquisitor in the *Marches, he was thrice sent on *missions to *Hungary and the Slav lands, first as companion to *John of Capestrano, then alone. He propagated devotion to the *Name of Jesus, preached the *crusade against the *Turks and favoured the creation of *Monti di Pietà*. He was beatified in 1624 and canonized in 1726.

Iacobus de Marchia, *Sermones dominicales*, R. Lioi (ed.), Falconara, 1978.

R. Lioi, P. Cannato, "Giacomo della Marchia", *BSS*, 6, 1965, 388-401. – R. Lioi, "Jacques de la Marche", *DSp*, 8, 1974, 41-45.

Louis Jacques Bataillon

**JAMES OF VITERBO (*c.*1260-1307/1308).** An Augustinian friar, James of Viterbo (Jacopo Capucci) studied at *Paris from 1281 and taught at the *faculty of *theology. His principal work, *De regimine christiano*, was dedicated to Pope *Boniface VIII, then at odds with the king of France, *Philip the Fair. James was archbishop of *Benevento, then of *Naples.

His treatise forms part of the writings to the glory of the papal monarchy and of *theocracy. It is centred on the concept of the Church, which has two powers, priestly (power of order) and royal (power of jurisdiction). The unity of the Church is symbolized by its head, *Christ, whose vicar is the *pope; it is he whose job it is to assume responsibility for both powers.

James of Viterbo analyses *temporal power which, according to him, is of natural origin, like the *State that exercises it; however, only the Church possesses power in the full sense of the term, since it is a perfect *regnum*. Its activity extends to the present and the future life. Although temporal power is of divine origin, to be exercised fully, it needs *grace, spiritual by definition. This subordinates the temporal power to the spiritual. Temporal princes are within the Church, which James of Viterbo sees as a kingdom whose prince is the pope. The spiritual power commands, judges and informs the temporal. The exaltation of the plenitude of papal power is at the centre of a *doctrine for which the *respublica christiana* is the Church; the Christian people is directed by its spiritual head, the *pope, to whom temporal princes owe both respect and submission.

*Le Plus Ancient Traité de l'Église, le "De regimine christiano" (1301-1302)*, H. X. Arguillière (ed.), Paris, 1926. – James of Viterbo, *On Christian Government*, R.W. Dyson (ed.), Woodbridge, 1995.

Y. Congar, *L'Église, de saint Augustin à l'époque moderne*, Paris, 1970.

Jeannine Quillet

**JEAN DESCHAMPS (13th c.).** The name of the *architect Jean Deschamps is connected with religious buildings south of the Loire, in the so-called southern Gothic style. Though he may be considered the conceiver of *Clermont-Ferrand cathedral, *c.*1248, which also drew on the repertoire of northern *Gothic to make an original synthesis, the other buildings with which the name Deschamps is connected must be attributed to a whole family of *architects: Jean Deschamps at *Narbonne (attested in 1286, perhaps the same as the former), Jean and Bertrand at Bordeaux (before 1309 and in 1320), Guillaume at Rodez (1355), Pierre at Clermont again (1357). Doubtless they also worked on other *cathedrals including those of *Toulouse and *Limoges.

R. Ray, *L'Art gothique du Midi de la France*, Paris, 1934. – C. Freigang, "Jean Deschamps et le Midi", *BM*, 149-III, 1991, 265-298.

Thierry Soulard

**JEAN LEMOINE (*c.*1250-1313).** Politician and "intermediary", Jean Lemoine studied *philosophy and *theology and was received as *doctor *in utroque*. His ecclesiastical career began at Amiens (canon) before taking him to *Rome (auditor of the *Rota), then back to France, to *Bayeux (dean of the church); but he is known mainly as a *cardinal. With the dual title of cardinal and *legate, the papacy dispatched him to *Philip the Fair to make him accept the *bull *Unam sanctam*. Cardinal Lemoine founded a *college. He left the first apparatus on the Sext, a commentary on the "Extravagantes" of *Boniface VIII and sixteen *glosses. In his eyes, the Roman Church consisted of an association between *pope (head) and cardinals (members).

Jacques Bouineau

**JEAN PETIT (*c.*1360-1411).** Born near Caux, master of theology in 1402, endowed with a powerful eloquence, Jean Petit, a professor of the university of *Paris, was involved in the affairs of the *Great Schism and the French civil war. Pensioned by John the Fearless, in 1406 he was the University's spokesman against *Benedict XIII. On 8 March 1408, he pronounced before the king's council at Paris the justification of the duke of Burgundy over the murder of the duke of Orléans. His speech, based on the idea that one guilty of *lèse-majesté* was a traitor and a *tyrant, was widely circulated. The duke's master of requests, he died on 15 July 1411.

A. Coville, *Jean Petit. La question du tyrannicide au commencement du XV^e^ siècle*, Paris, 1932. – B. Guenée, *Un meutre, une société. L'assassinat du duc d'Orléans, 23 novembre 1407*, Paris, 1992.

Claude Gauvard

**JEAN QUIDORT (died 1306).** Jean Quidort, or John of Paris, played an important role in the controversies of the 13th and 14th cc. on the relations between the spiritual and *temporal powers, notably at the time of the "difference" between Pope *Boniface VIII and King *Philip the Fair in the early 14th century. He is generally considered a sort of mediator between opposed positions, viz. *theocracy on one hand and its adversaries on the other, partisans of autonomy and the independence of the civil power.

His work written in 1302, *De potestate regia et papali* (ed. J. Leclercq, Paris, 1942), is the illustration of the dualism of powers that he affirmed: that of the prince and that of the *pope. Just as *man pursues two ends in this world, that of his happiness on earth and that of his *salvation in view of *eternal life, so he lives in society in accordance with his nature, but he also needs a spiritual authority for his salvation: this authority is that of the Christian *priesthood, heir to *Christ. The unity of the Church requires the unity of the spiritual power incarnated by the pope; on the other hand, political society is diverse and the *regna* are diverse. There is no subordination, but coordination between the two powers, it being understood that the spiritual power has a superior dignity. But the royal power too comes directly from *God. The two powers are hence distinct, as Pope Gelasius said in the 5th c.; they are complementary and mutually related. The doctrine of John of Paris would inspire the nascent *Gallicanism and open the way to the dualism of *Dante's *De monarchia*. However, this dualism was not without ambiguity, since John of Paris acknowledged to the papal power a dignity superior to that of the civil authority.

J. Rivière, *Le Problème de l'Église et de l'État au temps de Philippe le Bel*, Louvain, Paris, 1926. – J. Quillet, *La Philosophie politique du Songe du vergier, Sources doctrinales*, Paris, 1977.

Jeannine Quillet

**JEREMIAH.** The book of Jeremiah was commented on at length in the Middle Ages, after St Jerome, in particular by *Rabanus Maurus, *Walafrid Strabo, *Paschasius Radbertus, *Peter Damian, *Guibert of Nogent, *Rupert of Deutz and *Hugh of Saint-Victor, who extoll the prophet of the *Passion, or even, following Tertullian and *Isidore of Seville, relate his legendary stoning.

In art, when no inscription identifies him, Jeremiah, who has no distinctive physiognomy, can be recognised by the cross he brandishes, the manticore – a fabulous animal from the depths of the earth – under his feet, or the early almond branch of his vocation (Jer 1, 11). Extolled on the *Moissac trumeau, he appears among the series of prophetic characters in the splays of the great Gothic portals. Three important cycles were dedicated to him, in the Roda Bible (Paris, BNF, lat. 6, vol. I, XI f.), the *Bible moralisée* (Toledo cathedral treasury, *c.*1230, and BNF ms. lat. 11560) and, in *stained glass, the east window of the *Sainte-Chapelle in Paris, influenced by the choices of the annotated *Bible. Among isolated motifs, the most represented is that of his lamentations over the destroyed Jerusalem, accompanied by the blinding of Zedekiah on the orders of Nebuchadnezzar. Moreover, he is clearly used for his *typological value.

L. Réau, *Iconographie de l'art chrétien*, 2, 1, Paris, 1956, 370-372. – A. Heimann, *LCI*, 2, 1970, 387-392.

Colette Deremble

**JEROME (*c.*347-419/420; iconography).** Born at Strido in *Dalmatia, died at Bethlehem. St Jerome is a well-known character in the iconographical tradition of Christian art: author, monk, valued adviser of the *Roman patriciate. Four Lives form the basis of his representation: the *Chronicle of Marcellinus* (6th c.), the *Vita Hieronymi nostri* (6th-7th c.); the *Vita plerosque nimirum* (second half of 6th c.), Niccolo Maniacoria's *Beati Hieronymi vita* (12th c.). They follow a common thread, the dominant themes being those of the defender of the Church and the learned monk.

Up to the 12th c., Jerome remained the sacred author represented according to the old tradition of the portrait of a scholar. From then on, his iconography was attached to the earlier iconography of the *evangelist: both exalted the authority of the written word. In the 13th c., other contributions enriched the established type: the *Legenda aurea* of the Dominican *Jacobus de Voragine; the *De sancto Hieronymo* of another Dominican, Fra Pietro Calo da Chioggia (1340), on whom depends the account written by Petrus de Natalibus in his *Catalogus sanctorum et gestorum eorum* (VIII, 132); finally, written shortly before 1348, the *Hieronymianus* of the Bolognese *jurist *Johannes Andreae. This created a complete synthesis of the previous Lives and set itself the task of fixing the saint's representation in the visual art of the time: as *Doctor of the Church and cardinal-priest, draped in purple, wearing the *cardinal's hat and flanked by a lion (borrowed from Gerasimus). Furthermore, Johannes Andreae drew on a mass of hagiographical material composed between the late 12th and late 13th cc.: namely the apocryphal *Letters* of Eusebius of Cremona, St Augustine and Cyril of Jerusalem, to which was added the *Translatio Romam* describing the transfer of Jerome's remains to the church of *Santa Maria Maggiore in Rome. Within the *Dominican Order, St Jerome sanctioned an ancient attitude – spiritual work, study and biblical translation – then being revalued: as such, he often appears on the order's great *altarpieces, in the province of Lombardy, in the guise of a Preacher. Long an afterthought in overall programmes, only in the 15th c. did he reach the centre of the altarpiece, alongside the Virgin and Child or in a Holy Conversation.

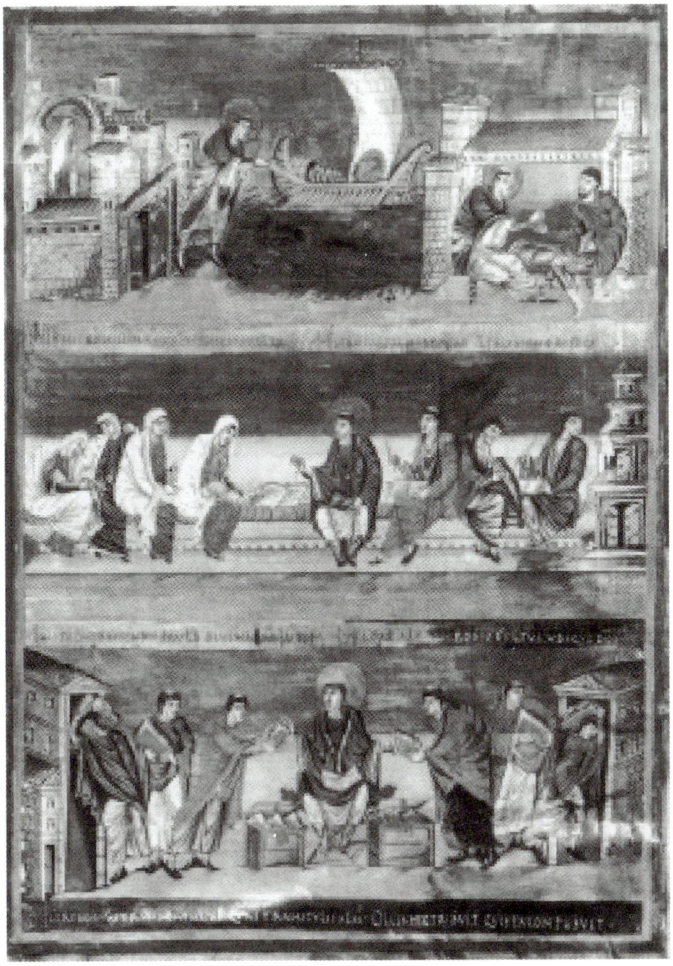

*Story of St Jerome*: St Jerome leaves Rome, embarking for Jerusalem. He learns Hebrew from a converted Jew. He teaches his disciples and gives exemplars of his translation of the Bible. Miniature from the *Bible of Charles the Bald*, early 9th c. Paris, BNF (Ms lat. 1, fol. 3 v°).

At the very moment when he was being represented in Florence enthroned in *majesty (in Giovanni del Biondo's Strozzi chapel at Santa Maria Novella, *c.*1380-1390), St Jerome as a figure of authority was gradually transformed under the influence of new forms of devotion inspired by the *Observance: the hitherto neglected aspect of the penitent in the *desert of Chalchis came into the foreground. The type of the ascetic beating his breast in the arid solitudes, standing or kneeling, at the entrance to a cave, took on its full meaning and became general all through the 15th c., and even beyond. In connection with this type of religious *reform and under the impetus of new orders appealing to his patronage (*Jesuates, Friars Hermits of St Jerome, all later brought together under the generic name of *Hieronymites), painted hagiographical cycles developed. For a brief instant, the saint in the desert abandoned the wide-open solitudes to enclose himself within the walls of an elegant, refined study: from the late 1430s in Flanders, *c.*1480-1500 at Florence and Venice, St Jerome became the exemplary image of good patrician government, and took his traits from men already illustrious. In these late Middle Ages, the representation of St Jerome returned to the initial portrait of an author.

F. Cavallera, *Saint Jérôme, sa vie et son oeuvre*, 1, Louvain-Paris, 1922 (2 vol.). – G.J. Campbell, "St. Jerome's Attitude towards Marriage and Women", *American Ecclesiastical Review*, 143, 1960, 31-20, 184-394. – D. Russo, *Saint Jérôme en Italie. Étude d'iconographie et de spiritualité, XIII^e-XV^e siècle*, Paris-Rome, 1987. – *Jerome entre l'Occident et l'Orient*, Y.-M. Duval (ed.), Paris, 1988.

Daniel Russo

**JEROME OF PRAGUE (died 1416).** Czech reformer and one of the leaders of the *reform movement at the university of *Prague, burned at the stake at *Constance as a *heretic, 31 May 1416. During his stay at *Oxford, he familiarized himself with the *doctrine of John *Wycliffe; he later developed Wycliffe's *realist concept of *universals and defended it before the *universities of *Paris, Heidelberg, *Cologne and Prague. In Jan 1409, he worked successfully, with his friend Jan *Hus, for the administrative reorganisation of Prague university in favour of the Czech national group, whose mission and social outlines he defined. Subsequently, Jerome of Prague would be remarked for the radicalism of his statements, in *Bohemia and in the neighbouring countries.

F. Šmahel, *Leben und Werk des Magisters Hieronymus von Prag, Hist(P)*, 13, 1966, 81-111. – R. R. Betts, "Jerome of Prague", *Essays in Czech History*, London, 1969, 195-235. – Z. Kaluza, *Le Chancelier Gerson et Jérôme de Prague, AHDL*, 51, 1984, 81-126.

František Šmahel

## JERUSALEM

**History.** During the Byzantine rule, Jerusalem (whose official name was Aelia Capitolina from 135) was one of the cities of the province of *Palestine, whose metropolis was and would remain Caesarea, even when in 451, through the urging of its bishop Juvenal, Jerusalem became the seat of a *patriarchate whose territory consisted of the three Palestines. The development of the Christian holy places, which began from the time of *Constantine, would make it the most important Holy City and *pilgrimage centre in *Christendom.

After the discovery of the *relic of the *cross and of Christ's tomb near Golgotha in 324 during a journey by the *augusta* Helena, mother of the emperor, imperial generosity built the *basilica of the Martyrium (where the cross was deposited) and the round church of the Anastasis (above the tomb) as well as the basilica of the Eleona on the Mount of Olives (above the grotto where Christ spoke to his disciples), not to mention that of the Nativity in the nearby town of Bethlehem.

During the 4th c., at the initiative of the *bishops of Jerusalem or of rich benefactors, basilicas also arose at Zion (on the site of Christ's appearances after the Resurrection and the descent of the Spirit, later also held to be that of the Last Supper), at Gethsemane (on the site of the agony) and on the summit of the Mount of Olives (on the site of the Ascension). In the 5th c., the palace of Caiaphas (St Peter's), Pilate's praetorium (St Sophia), the Virgin's tomb, the pool of Siloam, the probatic pool, the tomb of *Lazarus at Bethany and other sites of lesser importance received churches; another was built by the *augusta* Eudocia to receive the relics of St Stephen discovered in 415.

In the 6th c., Justinian built New St Mary's, where relics of the Virgin were deposited. With these churches were also built hospices and hostelries intended to receive pilgrims. The town also saw the multiplication of monastic establishments, particularly on the Mount of Olives. In 450, Eudocia restored the town's ramparts, following its most extended outline, including Mount Zion. The town was then mostly Christian: Jews were forbidden access to it, save for the anniversary of the destruction of the Temple and during the brief reign of Julian (361-363), when the attempt to rebuild the Temple ended in failure. Pilgrims from all over the Christian world were numerous there. Through them, the Jerusalem liturgy would influence many churches. The *feast of the Dedication of the Martyrium, celebrated every year on 13 Sept, was the occasion for a veritable international fair.

In 614, the town was taken by the Persians after a long siege; many inhabitants were massacred, most of the sanctuaries were pillaged and burned. The Persian occupation ended in 629; the next year, *Heraclius triumphantly brought back the relic of the Cross that they had taken to Seleucia-Ctesiphon. Patriarch Modestus then partly restored a number of sanctuaries. But soon after, in 638, the Arab conquerors besieged the town: after seven months, the town capitulated into the hands of Caliph 'Umar, on fairly lenient conditions: civil and religious freedom was granted in exchange for an annual tribute; a double tax – personal tax and capitation – affected non-Muslims.

The Muslims laid claim to the esplanade of Solomon's temple, held (perhaps not yet at this period) to be the place of *Muḥammad's ascent, and immediately built a modest *mosque there; it was only under Caliph Abd-al-Malik ibn Marwan (685-705) that the Dome of the Rock would be built (Qubbet es-Sakhra, wrongly called the mosque of Omar), and under his son al-Walid (705-715) the el-Aqsa mosque. Jerusalem thus became one of the three Holy Cities of *Islam, with *Mecca and *Medina. The Jews were authorized to live there again; they established their quarter near the Wailing Wall and built a synagogue on Mount Zion. Relations between the Muslim occupants and the Christians remained relatively good under the *Umayyads, then under the *Abbasids, despite frequent annoyances and occasional violence. In 803, *Charlemagne obtained from Hārūn al-Rashīd the, at least symbolic, possession of the church of the *Holy Sepulchre, of which the patriarch of Jerusalem sent him the keys (with those of the city and the Mount of Olives), and a right of protection over the Latin establishments of Palestine; a *capitulary of 810 provided for the periodic levying of *alms that would be sent to Jerusalem. Several establishments were founded there at this time – an abbey on the Mount of Olives, a hospice at Akeldama, a church and a hospice (Sancta Maria Latina) near the Holy Sepulchre. This latter, which had been damaged by an earthquake in the 8th c., was restored. A document of this time, the *Commemoratorium*, shows the state of the Christian establishments of Jerusalem. Some sanctuaries had disappeared – St Peter's, St Sophia, the church of the Agony at Gethsemane, that of Siloam – but a great number of them still remained.

The Frankish "protectorate" (which must be understood in the broad sense) was kept up in the 9th c.; traces of it still existed in the 10th. However a mosque was built early in the 10th c. in the quarter of the Holy Sepulchre, in violation of the agreements concluded. The consequence of the Byzantine conquests of Nicephorus Phocas (which led to a repairing of the ramparts at Christian expense in 968) and the campaign of John Tzimisces (who retook Caesarea in 975, but did not dare push on to Jerusalem) was a more repressive policy towards the Christians. In 1009, the *Fatimid caliph al-*Hākim confiscated the property of the churches and forbade the *Palm Sunday *processions; the Martyrium (St Constantine) and the Anastasis were burned and partly demolished;

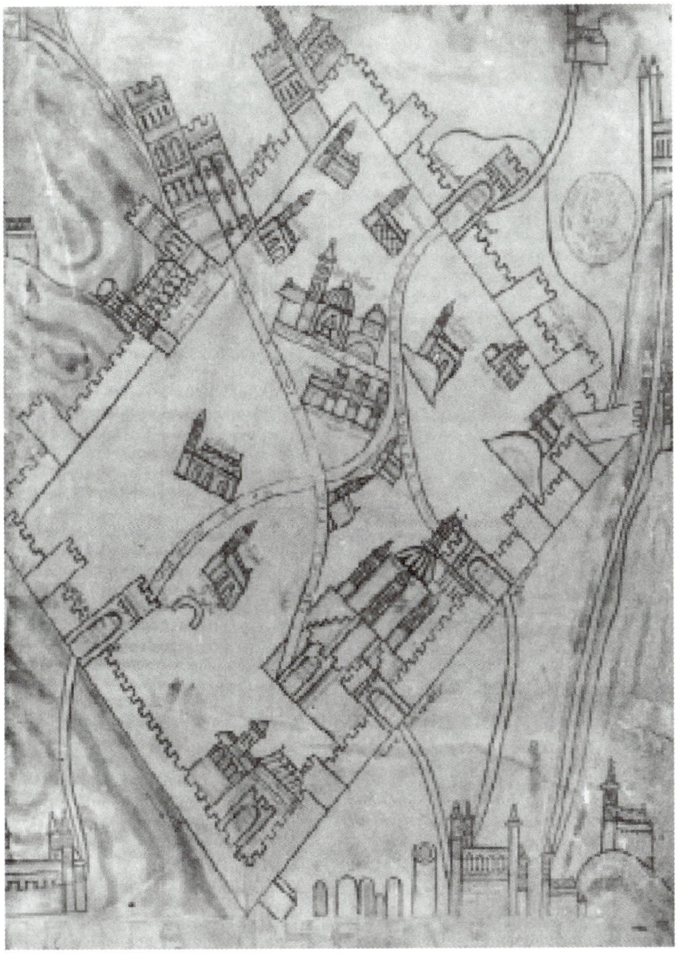

*Plan of Jerusalem*. 13th-c. manuscript. Cambrai, Municipal Library (Ms B 466, fol. 1 v°).

in this building, nothing was left of the chapel that contained Christ's tomb but the lower part of the walls and the sepulchral bed. The Anastasis (but not the Martyrium) was rebuilt in 1049 thanks to the gifts of Constantine IX Monomachos, the emperors of Byzantium having resumed the role of protectors of the Holy Places previously held by the *Franks. Gifts from King *Stephen of *Hungary also permitted the restoration of several Latin establishments. But new destructions took place at the time of the capture of Jerusalem by the *Seljuks in 1071; the town was again occupied by the *Fatimids in 1098.

On 15 July 1099, after a siege of a month, the army of the first *crusade took Jerusalem. The capture of the town was accompanied by three days of massacres of Muslims and Jews (perhaps 20,000 victims) and the pillage of the Muslim sanctuaries. The crusaders made Jerusalem, from which they expelled Jews, Muslims and non-Christians, the capital of a Latin kingdom; *Godfrey of Bouillon, who took the title of "advocate of the Holy Sepulchre", in fact exercised royal power. They also installed a Latin patriarch (the Greek patriarch had just died; his successor would reside at Constantinople until 1187) and substituted a Latin clergy for the Greek clergy. A good many sanctuaries were restored and repaired. The church of the Holy Sepulchre was rebuilt in 1149 and took the form it still has today; St Anne's replaced the Byzantine basilica of the Probatica. The Dome of the Rock became a church (the "Lord's Temple"). The Syrians, Armenians and Georgians built churches (St Mark of the Syrians, St James, St James Intercisus). The town's fortifications were restored and strengthened; a citadel was built (the "Tower of David").

The crusaders made practically no changes to the urban structure, save for the utilisation as churches of the two mosques on the Temple esplanade, and the reduction of other Muslim buildings to Christian worship. The town was now divided into quarters, Christian, Jewish and Muslim. But the crusaders expelled the Jews and Muslims, and the latter in turn, after the reconquest by *Saladin in 1187, readmitted the Jews and left the Eastern Christians in peace, but expelled the Latins. In 1229, following the treaty between the Emperor *Frederick II and the sultan of Egypt, al-Malik al-Kāmil, and after the urban defences had been dismantled, Jerusalem became once more a possession of the Latins, except for the Temple esplanade (called by the Arabs al-Haram as-Sharif, "the Noble Enclosure").

The fragile equilibrium established by the treaty of 1229 could not last. Deprived of defences, the town was assaulted in 1239 by the sultan's troops, and in 1244 it was finally occupied by nomad mercenaries from Khwarezm; from then on it remained under the control of the sultans of *Cairo, who in 1342 – following a treaty with King *Robert of Naples – allowed some Latin religious, *Franciscans, to come and settle on Mount Zion and take possession of the Cenacle. Thus was born the Custody of the *Holy Land, whose friars were soon granted the right to officiate at the altars and in the chapels of the church of the Holy Sepulchre assigned to the Latin Church, and to assist Western pilgrims. Save at rare moments of tension, the flood of pilgrims never slowed down: the Muslims contented themselves with imposing a "right of entry" to the Holy Places, which they levied at the *port of Jaffa and at the gates of Jerusalem. The journals of pilgrims, of which we have dozens and dozens of examples – some still unedited – going uninterruptedly from the 4th to the 15th c. (and indeed to this day), is precious evidence for anyone wishing to study the architectural and planning evolution of Jerusalem.

G. Le Strange, *Palestine under the Moslems*, Boston, 1890. – H. Vincent, F.-M. Abel, *Jérusalem nouvelle*, 2, Paris, 1926. – J. Wilkinson, *Jerusalem Pilgrims before the Crusades*, Warminster, 1977. – J. Prawer, *The Latin Kingdom of Jerusalem*, Amsterdam, 1979 (tr. from Hebrew). – B. Hamilton, *The Latin Church in the Crusader States*, London, 1980. – "Al Kuds", *EI(E)*, 5, 1986, 322-344. – "Jérusalem", *LdM*, 5, 1991. – H.E. Mayer, *Kings and Lords in the Latin Kingdom of Jerusalem*, Aldershot, 1994. – *The History of Jerusalem: the early Muslim Period, 638-1099*, J. Prawer (ed.), H. Ben-Shammai (ed.), New York, 1996.

Pierre Maraval and Franco Cardini

**Place in the medieval imagination.** The Christian liturgy and biblical *exegesis of the Middle Ages (Is 52, 1; 60, 1-6; Ps 122, 3-6) never cease to raise their solemn and joyful song to Jerusalem. Jerusalem is the city of victory and peace, it is to Jerusalem that the King comes, there the just will be crowned. The whole *Easter liturgical service is a hymn to the Holy City. And, though the exegetical doctrine may be clear and the *Fathers never cease to put the faithful on guard, the earthly Jerusalem holds in its distant mirage all the reflections of the heavenly City, the Jerusalem of the *Apocalypse, the divine city of gold and crystal eternally founded on precious stones, which comes down to earth and in which the faithful are glorified.

The reality was different. From the pages of Josephus it was already easy to draw an image of a Jerusalem different from the biblical one, though not wholly unlike it; and hardly – by the 3rd c., and certainly from the 4th – had Christian *pilgrims begun to flock to Jerusalem, taking up and renewing the tradition of Jewish pilgrimage, than they became aware that the Holy City was quite another thing from that dreamed through the prophets and the Apocalypse. And yet, even in it – and perhaps especially in it – they recognised the signs of the Saviour: this was the *Hierusalem miserabilis* over which Jesus had wept, there was the Temple whose final destruction he had foretold. The Jerusalem that had killed the prophets and stoned God's envoys, and that for this had been destroyed and its people dispersed.

But with the victory of Christianity in the Empire, a new Chosen People was born, a new *Israel – the Church – had arisen: to it belonged a new Jerusalem, waiting for the blessed hope to be fulfilled and the authentic and desired Jerusalem, gloriously built on precious stones, to descend from heaven.

The Holy city subsequently remained at the centre of the medieval imagination. It was the "*Jerusalem miserabilis, quae est in Syria*", the *Jerusalem inferior* often prey to *sin. But for all that it did not cease to be the image and pledge of the *Jerusalem superior*, the kingdom of *heaven announced in the Apocalypse. The pilgrims of the first *crusade, and subsequently many other crusading pilgrims, in particular those belonging to the lower classes, did not always succeed in properly distinguishing the two holy cities, the heavenly and the earthly, and they confused them in a single eschatological expectation. This was why the possession of the town, between 1099 and 1187, signified for Western *Christendom a sure pledge of election and *salvation; this was also why, in the 12th and 13th cc., several crusades were organised. Even after the crusaders had been expelled from the Syro-Palestinian coast in 1291, there were further crusading projects and attempts: in the Middle Ages, the last organised project for an armed expedition was that of Pope *Pius II, halted by his death in 1464; but crusading programmes continued to be drawn up until the end of the 17th century.

Western pilgrims in the early Middle Ages – but this remained true later – usually reached Jerusalem from Egypt, taking a route that passed through *Sinai and St Catherine's monastery at the foot of the "Mountain of Moses"; but during the crusading period this route was impracticable, and then the Holy City was reached by sea via the port of Jaffa (today the old part of Tel Aviv) and the road that went up to Jerusalem from Lydda, seat of the famous sanctuary dedicated to St George. The town had many *hospices for the Latins, the most famous of which – legendarily founded by *Charlemagne when he had received Jerusalem as a gift from the Caliph Hārūn al-Rashīd, but in fact going back at least to the 11th c. – was that of Santa Maria Latina, very close to the *Holy Sepulchre, held since the start of the 12th c. by the *Hospitallers of St John of Jerusalem (later "of *Rhodes", and then "of *Malta"). The most visited Holy Places in Jerusalem were naturally the Holy Sepulchre and Calvary in the basilica of the Resurrection, and the church of St Anne, traditionally built over the house in which the Virgin *Mary was born; immediately outside the city wall, the church of St Stephen and that of the Tomb of the Virgin in the Valley of Jehoshaphat, the church of the *Dormitio Mariae* and the Cenaculum on Mount Zion, the "pool of Siloam" at the foot of that hill; and, near the city, the basilica of the Nativity at Bethlehem and the church of the Visitation (built over the house of St Elizabeth, mother of *John the Baptist) in the place called *Montana Judaeae* (Ain Karem).

But those who went on pilgrimage to Jerusalem wished to preserve a tangible record of it and to relive what had been for them a splendid adventure of the spirit. So they took from the Holy City *relics which they then gave to churches back home; and for the edification of those who were unable to make the pilgrimage they built votive sanctuaries some of which were more or less faithful "copies" (often purely symbolic) of the basilica of the Resurrection or the chapel of the Holy Sepulchre that was at its centre. This devotion, accompanied by special forms of liturgy that were performed around those monuments during *Holy Week and by "*indulgences" that the *popes began to distribute from the 13th c. at least, gave rise to substitutive pilgrimages; in the late 15th c., the *Franciscans thought to perfect these *Jerusalem translatae* by reproducing, in sanctuaries founded for the purpose, all the "Holy Places" of Jerusalem, which were visited in a circuit called a "circle". Thus were born the *Sacri Monti*, of which the first example was that of Varallo Sesia in Lombardy.

But *Jerusalem translata* was not the only type of Hierosolymitan devotion to reach the West. It became a common thing for cities to proclaim themselves, in their own *statutes, *Nova Jerusalem* or *Jerusalem minor*, naturally with reference to the heavenly Jerusalem, signifying by this their will to appear as a kingdom of peace and justice: but their "Hierosolymitan" vocation then led them to multiply, within their city walls, references to the earthly Jerusalem to the point of reproducing within themselves, at least symbolically, the sites of the Holy Places. Late Medieval Europe lived in this climate of translation of Hierosolymitan sacrality to the West, which explains a quantity of monuments, *dedications and folklore traditions otherwise incomprehensible and yet endowed with a rigorous value on the symbolic level.

L.-H. Vincent, F. M. Abel, *Jérusalem. Recherches de topographie, d'archéologie et d'histoire*, 2, Paris, 1914-1922. – A. R. Bredero, "Jérusalem dans l'Occident médiéval", *Mélanges offerts à René Crozet*, 1, Poitiers, 1966. – D. Neri, *Il Santo Sepolcro riprodotto in Occidente*, Jerusalem, 1971. – G. Bresc-Bautier, "Les imitations du Saint-Sépulcre de Jérusalem (IXe-XIVe siècle)", *RHSp*, 50, 1974, 319-341. – J. Prawer, "Jerusalem in the Christian and Jewish Perspectives of the Early Middle Ages", *Gli ebrei nell'Alto Medioevo*, 2, Spoleto, 1980, 739-795. – A. I. Galletti, "Gerusalemme o la città desiderata", *Images et mythes de la ville médiévale*, Rome, 1984, 459-487. – A. I. Galletti, "Modelli urbani dell'età comunale: Gerusalemme", *Modelli nella storia del pensiero politico*, V. I. Comparato (dir.), Florence, 1987, 89-101. – A. Dupront, *Du Sacré. Croisades et pèlerinages. Images et langages*, Paris 1987. – L. Zanzi, *Sacri Monti e dintorni*, Milan, 1990. – S. Schein, J. Riley-Smith, *Jerusalem*, *LdM*, 5, 2, 1991, 351-359. – M. Biddle, *The tomb of Christ*, Stroud, 1999.

Franco Cardini

**JESUATES.** The name "Jesuates" was given to the "Brigade of the Poor of Jesus Christ" established at *Siena by Giovanni Colombini († 1367). An influential public figure, married with two children, he underwent a profound spiritual crisis on the morrow of the great political changes that convulsed Sienese civil life from 1355; with other notables who adhered to his movement, he wanted to demonstrate the penitential signs of *conversion by assuming degrading attitudes in places where he had occupied prestigious public offices; voluntary humiliations which he also imposed on the neophytes of the group, like the parodistic inversion of knightly *dubbing that constituted initiation to the Brigade of the Poor. Freed from family duties after the death of his only son, separated from his wife and with his daughter in a monastery, Giovanni submitted to the exile to which the Sienese republic briefly condemned him and his followers in the climate of suspicion that followed the change of political regime. With his departure from his natal city, Columbini, now aged 60, and the Brigade, on whose margins many *women were now active – including his cousin Caterina, later foundress of the female branch of the movement – expanded the apostolate of *poverty and ardent invocation of the *Name of Jesus beyond the Sienese borders.

But the movement's heavy concentration on poverty created suspicions and mistrust that quickly became a problem: ever more urgently seeking a religious legitimacy that would put him and his followers beyond suspicion of connivance with the **fraticelli*, the old knight of Christ sought the support of the nearest prelates (the bishops of Siena, Arezzo, Città di Castello) who advised him to submit his group to the approval of *Urban VI, then on the point of returning to *Italy. His meeting with the *Curia, prejudiced against pauperism, was so harsh that many abandoned the Brigade. The inquiry opened into the movement was resolved positively and the *pope took the Poor Sienese under his protection, allowing them as distinctive sign a habit, but not a rule. On the way back to Siena, Giovanni died (1367), leaving his spiritual sons to inherit ill-defined institutions. This did not prevent the movement spreading, beyond Siena and *Tuscany, to *Romagna and *Veneto, where Jesuate *foundations, both male and female, multiplied.

Characterised by a lay status and a specialization in craftsmanship (they were famous as glaziers, clockmakers and distillers), the Jesuates did not survive the regularizing winds of the *Quattrocento. Assimilated to the Augustinians, they became Hermits of St Jerome (*Hieronymites), losing with their name the particularity that linked them to the extraordinary spiritual experience of their founder.

G. Dufner, *Geschichte der Jesuaten*, Rome, 1975.

Anna Benvenuti Papi

**JEWISH QUARTER.** A topographical space (one or several streets) in the medieval town that housed a Jewish population, provided with communal facilities indispensable for religious practice (*synagogue, school, *mikvé* or ritual bath, butchery, oven, extra-mural cemetery) and social life (*hospital, almshouse, especially for important communities).

Jewish quarters had a Latin (*Judearia*, *Judaica*) or a vernacular designation (for France, in langue d'oïl, *Juerie*; in langue d'*oc, *Juatarle*, *Juzatarie* and their variants), the imprint of the surrounding milieu being taken from specific terms of Latin origin. The most frequent term, *rue des Juifs*, thus appears in the Midi in its Latin form *carreria judeorum* or Provençalized as *carreyre dels jusieus*. The Provençal term *carreyre* ended by designating the Jewish quarter of the *Comtat Venaissin, just as the Catalan term *call* would describe the Jewish quarter of *Perpignan.

Early in the Middle Ages, Jewish occupation developed as much in *villages as in *towns; in very modest places, their small number (four, six or even ten *houses) would not always justify grouping them together in a particular street or establishing religious facilities. It was occasional vicissitudes (like the prohibition of Jews in 1276 from living in small places in the kingdom of France, or the *Black Death with its train of riots) that would affect this rural occupation, at the same time, of course, as the revival of urban life would already have pushed the *Jews irresistibly towards the towns.

In towns, Jewish occupation was originally mixed and not confined to a particular imposed perimeter. However, it is admitted that this community with a distinct confession grouped itself together spontaneously; this behaviour characteristic of any minority, reinforced by the desire to satisfy communal needs, entailed a voluntarily chosen concentration based on the topography of the city, in no way excluding the neighbourhood of Christians. The site of Jewish occupation in towns was multiple and varied; it knew no rules (peripheral as well as central, close to the *market, the *cathedral or monastery, the *castle, etc.). Its history, closely linked to local conditions, is inseparable from the history of the towns that housed the Jews.

Then came obligatory compartmentalization: the relegation of the Jews to a defined and then compartmentalized area came about progressively in the second half of the 12th c., a century of segregation. Christian authorities aimed to confine their Jewish minorities within well-defined limits. A restrictive apparatus put in place at the time of the *Lateran council of 1215 preached distinction in living space and clothing, and denounced all promiscuity. But there too, legislation fluctuated according to place.

South of the Loire, in a more amenable climate, such regulation would be late and would know compromises. Besides, the hardening came from the North: the origin of compartmentalization was German (*Speyer, 1084). In French *Languedoc, though it is true that from 1294 (at Beaucaire) a royal order formally prescribed obligatory concentration, it was mainly in the 14th c., at the time of the permitted returns of the Jews, that a certain rigidity was accentuated, heralding the measures of *expulsion that would follow in 1394.

In southern Europe with its still tolerated Jewish presence, the late 15th c. saw here and there the enforcing of spatial segregation by a *Christendom avid for unity, which would end by rejecting elements foreign to it. As for the maintained Jewish settlements, those of *Avignon and the Comtat Venaissin, they would become closely surveyed spaces, limited and closed off on all sides. It was in this ultimate papal asylum, reduced to four authorized towns, that the Jews of the Midi would experience in the 16th c. a real ghetto like their Italian coreligionists of *Venice (1516) or *Rome (1555). The "ghetto" – a rigorously closed quarter – was not a medieval word; of Venetian origin, it came into use later (16th c.).

Though Jewry and *rue des Juifs* remain numerous in modern towns, genuine vestiges of religious buildings (synagogues, ritual baths, cemeteries) are rarer: *Rouen (11th-c. synagogue), *Speyer, Bésalu or *Montpellier (12th- and 13th-c. *mikvaoth*) are places with Jewish memories among the oldest in medieval Europe.

B. Blumenkranz, "Quartiers juifs en France (XIIe, XIIIe et XIVe siècles)", *MPhLJ*, 3-5, 1958-1962, 77-86. – D. Iancu-Agou, "Topographie des quartiers juifs en Provence médiévale", *REJ*, 1-2, 1974, 11-56. – G. Nahon, "Archéologie juive de la France médiévale", *ArMed*, 5, 1975, 139-159. – G. Dahan, "Quartiers juifs et Rues des Juifs", in *Art et Archéologie des Juifs en France médiévale*, B. Blumenkranz (dir.), Toulouse, 1980, 15-32. – "Le mikvé et l'évolution du quartier juif médiéval à Montpellier", *Les Juifs à Montpellier et dans le Languedoc*, C. Iancu (ed.), Montpellier, 1988, 72-92.

Danièle Iancu-Agou

## JEWS IN THE MIDDLE AGES

**The West.** The history of the Jews in medieval Europe is of a minority at first integrated into that vast, nebulous whole which was the Christian West, but which ended by being rejected, because it presented a world in search of its identity the image of an otherness, at the very moment when it thought it had found its unity.

The origin of the Jewish part of the population of the Christian West is not clearly established; it seems probable that all through

*Two rabbis celebrate Passover according to the Seder rite.* Miniature from a 15th-c. Hebrew manuscript, *Agada Pascalis.* Parma, Palatine Library.

Antiquity and the early centuries Jewish families had come to settle in Italy, southern France and the Iberian peninsula, a movement that may have developed with the end of a Jewish state in the East (1st-2nd cc.). But the majority of Western Jews in the early Middle Ages were the product of *conversions: hence an absence of distinctive physical or cultural traits, observed by medieval authors. The difference was religious: this explains both the integration of Jews into the medieval landscape (their activities were those of other Westerners, though they tended to specialize in *commerce) and the crises they had to suffer, like the wave of forced baptisms in Gaul (late 6th and early 7th c.); the worst crisis of the early Middle Ages was the attempted suppression of Judaism in Spain after the conversion of the *Visigoths to Catholicism: royal laws and councils tried to reduce the role that the Jewish minority could play. These crises were not passively submitted to, as is shown by the setback encountered by *Agobard, *archbishop of *Lyon, and his successor Amolo, ill-content with the privileges showered on the Jews by the imperial court. Indeed the reign of the *Carolingians (*Charlemagne, *Louis the Pious) corresponds to a happy period for the Jews of the West, whose communities grew and multiplied, notably in the Rhine valley.

It was precisely these Rhineland communities that suffered most from the first wave of persecutions, when the situation began to be called in question: the date 1096 marks a turning-point in the history of the Western Jews. On the route of the first *crusade, bands on the fringe of the official troops turned on the Jews and annihilated the communities of *Worms, *Mainz and Neuss. Elsewhere (*Speyer, *Cologne), more out of common interest than for theological reasons, churchmen or townsmen successfully protected the Jews. Despite this alert, the 12th c. still remained a period of integration, but signs of deterioration multiplied: the first accusations of *ritual murder, the onset of persecution at the time of the second crusade (the vigorous intervention of St *Bernard stopped all the outbursts), more virulent *antijudaism, bordering on antisemitism (*e.g.* in *Peter the Venerable or *Gautier de Coincy). On the economic level, evolution did not work in their favour; whereas they had had an energizing role in the mutation of the Western economy by permitting a circulation of coin that *canon law made otherwise impossible, other solutions in the 13th c. meant that their contribution was marginalized; Christian *bankers succeeded them. In the same period, the organisation of trade associations into religious *confraternities forbade them access to the ranks of the craftsmen. For its part, the Church tried to isolate the Jews: the fourth *Lateran council decreed several measures to this end; they were not immediately put into effect, but the date 1215 is still a turning-point: Western Christianity, triumphant, wanted to be homogeneous and sought to marginalize heterogeneous elements: the Jews were marked out in their singularity (wearing of a distinctive sign) and isolated (cohabitation and meals in common forbidden). The royal powers contributed to this deterioration: the Jews were surtaxed in England and finally expelled in 1290; in France, *Louis IX dreamed of integrating them into his Christian universe; *Philip the Fair, after having subjected them to a multitude of financial exactions, expelled them in 1306. The late Middle Ages were a difficult period for Western *Judaism: in a world in crisis (economic, social, religious) they played the role of scapegoats, as witness the accusations of collusion with *lepers in poisoning wells (1321) and, above all, the persecutions at the time of the *Black Death (1348-49), which they were accused of propagating. Assaults against Jewish communities multiplied, religiously motivated (*pastoureaux*, *flagellants) or otherwise. The worst crisis was the persecution of 1391 in the Iberian peninsula, which marked the decline of Spanish Judaism. Alternately called back and chased out all through the 14th c., the final *expulsion of the Jews from France came in 1394. In Germany and Italy (and in the Papal States of southern France), communities existed and even developed, but not without crises. After a century of tension, the Jews were expelled from *Spain in 1492; this date marks the end of the history of the Jews in the medieval West.

The legal status of the Jews conveys this degradation. As far as personal rights went, their ancient status of "Roman citizens [thus free men] of Jewish religion [enjoying privileges and suffering restrictions]" had never been abolished; the Carolingian *capitularies echoed this and the *jurists who rediscovered *Roman law reaffirmed it. But the reality was otherwise, and it was a quite different status that took shape (without being rigorously defined) in the 13th century. Two expressions sum it up: one Latin, *Iudei nostri*, clearly marks how the Jews belonged to the lords; the other German, *Kammerknechtschaft* (the Jews were "serfs of the imperial Chamber") describes a state of dependence; although, in Germany, Italy and southern France, certain cities considered them "citizens", these were contradicted by the royal or imperial power. Curiously enough, it was at the very moment when feudal structures were becoming exhausted that the new status of the Jews was formulated, constituting a survival of *feudalism, since the Jews were in a certain way likened to *serfs. To this personal condition was added a communal status: the Jewish community was considered a *universitas* (*corporation), the sole legal relay between individuals and the authorities; it was represented by a syndic, charged with assessing and collecting taxes and serving as interlocutor with the authorities. Within itself, it was organised according to its own customs, its members being subject to rabbinic law.

This minority lived in a Christian setting; before the discriminatory measures of the 13th c., nothing distinguished Jews from Christians (same language, same clothes, same preoccupations, same mental structures) except, of course, their religion. Their separation had a primarily religious motivation: the economic and social conditions of the 13th and 14th cc. would allow this discrimination to take effect. However, to the restrictive side of the Church's doctrine on the Jews there corresponded a positive side: *canon law, taking its cue from *Gregory the Great, affirmed the legitimacy of Jewish worship (the *Inquisition condemned only reversions and *conversions to *Judaism) and laid the basis for the protection of the persons and *property of Jews (*bull *Sicut Iudeis*); likewise, it forbade forced conversions, notably of Jewish children (*Thomas Aquinas); these principles were put into practice, notably by the papal authorities: *Innocent IV rejected accusations of *ritual murder; *Clement VI protected the communities in his domains during the *Black Death; we have already seen the role of St Bernard during the second crusade.

The whole period was marked by encounters between Christians and Jews: collaboration between scientists (astronomers, astrologers, doctors) and philosophers, notably in Italy, Spain and southern France (the Jews contributed to the introduction of *Averroes' commentaries to the Latin world, and *Maimonides' *Guide to the Perplexed* helped Christian thought to resolve the problems posed by *Aristotelianism); continual discussions between ordinary men or scholars on the fundamental problems of the two religions and especially encounters around the *Bible (the Jews were consulted with a view to the improvement of the Latin text; there were reciprocal influences in *exegesis: challenged by the recourse to *ratio* at the time of St *Anselm and *Abelard, the Jews developed a literal approach to biblical texts, and this was taken up in turn by Christian exegetes, who abundantly cited Jewish interpretations).

Clashes were not lacking, however. To the physical clashes we have mentioned was added ideological confrontation in the **disputatio* or debate. Moreover, Christian literature developed a certain number of anti-Jewish themes; these seem to have had a lasting effect on the Western mentality and contributed to the hardening and deepening of the theological *antijudaism of the *clerics; the literature of Miracles and the dramatic *Passions multiplied anti-Jewish connotations. Gradually a fantastic image of the Jew was built up in the Christian West: his otherness became total (e.g. a *quodlibetal question of the early 14th c. asked whether Jews had a menstrual cycle); the process continued: from being different, the Jew became adversarial and then diabolical. The modern mentality preserves this diabolized image of the Jew, but it does not correspond to the way in which Jews were perceived during the greater part of the Middle Ages: companions in misfortune exposed to the infinite evils due to nature or man, fellow guests at the feast of rediscovered knowledge, the Jews shared the joys and miseries of their neighbours. The turning in of the Christian world on itself, the crises it had to face, modified the data and gave the Jew a role to play that he did not have during the whole of the first part of the Middle Ages.

J. Parkes, *The Conflict of the Church and the Synagogue*, London, 1934. – J. Parkes, *The Jew in the Medieval Community*, Baltimore (MD), 1938. – S. W. Baron, *A Social and Religious History of the Jews*, 4-12, New York, 1959-1968. – B. Blumenkranz, *Juifs et chrétiens dans le monde occidental, 430-1096*, Paris-The Hague, 1960. – G. Dahan, *Les intellectuels chrétiens et les juifs au Moyen Âge*, Paris, 1990. – E. Taitz, *The Jews of Medieval France*, Westport (CT), 1994. – Y.T. Assis, *Jewish Economy in the Medieval Crown of Aragon, 1213-1327*, Leiden, 1997. – R.R. Mundill, *England's Jewish Solution*, Cambridge, 1998. – N. Golb, *The Jews in Medieval Normandy*, Cambridge, 1998.

Gilbert Dahan

**Byzantium.** The Jewish communities at Byzantium remained numerous and relatively flourishing, thanks to the official attitude that maintained the essentials of the Roman status of *religio licita* accorded to *Judaism – while in the West the Jews lost their status as citizens with the fall of the Empire. This *toleration was nonetheless different from that formerly accorded by the pagan

Empire: the Jews and their worship had to be protected because they were living evidence of the victory of Christianity, and because their community was called to be converted at the end of *time, after the *conversion of the pagans, according to St *Paul (Rom 11, 25-26). But, especially from the reign of Justinian, various measures (prohibition on building new *synagogues, *de facto* prohibition of proselytism, exclusion from public employment) marked their subordination to *Orthodox Christians and encouraged conversion; the Jews were second-class citizens, though they escaped the proscription that overtook pagans and heretical Christians. The special tax on the Jews, which some have seen at various times in the Middle Ages as a mark of discrimination, existed for certain only in the early centuries of Byzantium, in the form of a devolution to the State of the contribution previously paid to the Jewish patriarchate of Palestine, whose last titular died in 429 – actually in order to prevent this money going to the exilarch of Babylon, thus profiting the Persian rival.

So the Jews were not excluded from society or affected by legal incapacities comparable to those existing in the West; their concentration in autonomous communities in certain quarters of *Constantinople (Chalcoprateia, then Pera) was certainly imposed by the State, but not as a ghetto. The Jews played a normal part in everyday life, in the circus games; we often encounter warnings by the Church against Jewish magicians and doctors, or even against the frequenting of *synagogues by Christians; we know of Jewish sailors and artisans; many were *merchants, and the 7th-c. *Doctrina Jacobi* shows us a Jew named Jacob, trusted agent of a rich Christian who sent him to sell costly fabrics in *Africa. Lending at interest was not forbidden to Christians, but the Jews did not specialize in it, in contrast to the West; on the other hand, it is doubtless no accident that they seem to be the only people in 9th-c. *Constantinople to practise the "ignoble" activity of tanning; nevertheless, Benjamin of Tudela on his journey to Constantinople in the 12th c. also remarked, alongside the tanners, specialists in *silk working.

If this almost peaceful coexistence between Jews and Christians sometimes disappeared, the causes doubtless had more to do with the evolution of the Christians than that of the Jews. Only the revolts of the Samaritans in 529 and 555 under Justinian replicated those of the Jews in the first centuries of the Christian era, aiming to expel the occupying power from the Promised Land. Admittedly, the Jews remained hostile to the Byzantine State. The Jewish apocalypses of the time liken Rome to Edom (the Byzantines considered themselves "Romans") and the final *Antichrist to "Hermolaus", a corruption of Romulus: the essential mission of the Messiah would be to annihilate him. The Christian texts of anti-Jewish polemic that multiplied from the 6th c. reflected a certain aggression among Jewish critics, in particular against the Christian cult of *relics, crosses and *icons, then in the ascendant. Further Christian initiatives reflected not antisemitism in the modern sense, but a desire to bring an end to the scandal of Jewish rejection of Christianity at a time when the historic, even eschatological, moment of *conversion was thought to have come. The first great enterprise of forced *baptism, by *Heraclius in 630-632, closely followed the great victories over the Persians (who, it was thought, might be converted to Christianity) and accompanied the *monothelite attempt to restore unity among Christians: it took place at that fleeting moment when it was possible to believe that a finally reunified Christianity would dominate the inhabited world – the eschatological moment foretold for the conversion of *Israel. Furthermore, the help – ill paid in return – given by the Jews to the Persians during the war had shown that their religion made them a foreign body in the Empire. Barely applied, the measure aroused the opposition of a contemporary, *Maximus Confessor, who saw in it both a risk of soiling the Christian *sacraments by giving them forcibly to opponents, thus sowing impiety in the Church, and a risk of bringing about the end of the world, *i.e.* not so much the expected conversion of *Israel as the coming of *Antichrist who would be supported by the Jews.

On the whole the *Byzantine Church would follow the prudence of Maximus, and the other known attempts at forced *baptism were the fruit of imperial initiatives, linked to an effort at reorganisation that went far beyond the mere problem of the existence of Jews in a Christian Empire. Convergent but undetailed sources tell us that Leo III, the initiator of *iconoclasm, resumed *Heraclius's project around 721-722, to the point of creating an exodus to the Islamic lands; canon 8 of the 2nd council of *Nicaea in 787, obliging these converts either to leave the Church or to truly renounce all Jewish identity and practice, repeated Maximus's fears. We understand all the better how, when in *c.*873-874 Basil I, founder of the *Macedonian dynasty, anxious to ensure his legitimacy, threw himself into an analogous enterprise, he operated with more prudence, exercising all sorts of indirect pressures – promises of gifts of *money, social promotion, public debates – instead of the physical *violence of previous attempts (except perhaps in *Italy). This was not enough to spare him the criticism of at least Gregory of Nicaea, whose treatise against this *baptism is our principal source, together with a Jewish *chronicle from Italy: *conversions could not be achieved, and such converts would be not a gain but a detriment to the Church. The even less well known enterprise of Romanus Lecapenus around 940 must have had no more success (the absence of Greek sources suggests that it may only have involved frontier zones).

From then on, the Byzantine Jewish communities enjoyed almost complete tranquillity and even became, from the late 10th c., a centre of attraction for Jews from Islamic countries in search of better living conditions; an apocalypse of this time, the *Vision of Daniel*, gives a positive version of recent Byzantine *history, visibly borrowed from the official *historiography of the *Macedonians, and imagines that the Messiah will take his seat at *Constantinople after the destruction of Old *Rome, which takes on the role of the power of *evil. The "schism" introduced at that time among the Jews by the appearance of the Karaïtes does not seem to have hindered the growth of their communities. The latent hostility of the Christian population had few consequences, and Byzantium would not experience the equivalent of the volte-face that took place in the West at the time of the *crusades, the identification of the Jews as enemies within who had to be exterminated like the infidels in *Palestine. On the contrary, the accession of the dynasty of the *Palaeologi would confirm their status as a minority specially protected by the emperor. The gradual passing under the domination of *Islam, officially tolerant of *Judaism, would confirm this situation, which was enviable compared to that of the Jews of the West.

M. Avi-Yonah, *The Jews under Roman and Byzantine Rule*, Jerusalem-New York, 1984. – S. B. Bowman, *The Jews of Byzantium, 1204-1453*, Tuscaloosa (AL), 1985. – G. Dagron, V. Déroche, "Juifs et Chrétiens dans l'Orient du VIIe siècle", *TMCB*, 11, 1991, 17-273. – G. Dagron, "Le traité de Gregoire de Nicée sur le baptême des Juifs", *ibid.*, 313-357.

Vincent Déroche

***JIHĀD.*** The common translation "holy war" does no justice to the meaning and scope of this concept in *Islam. Taken from an Arabic root that refers primarily to the idea of effort and struggle, *jihād* is man's mobilization of all his strength in view of an ideal. Thus the expression "*jihād* of souls" designates the effort to overcome self in the way of perfection. More commonly, *jihād* is extended to any struggle to defend and exytend Islam, generally but not exclusively through arms. Over the centuries, *jihād* was thus able to take on forms of very variable intensity.

When *Muḥammad appealed for *jihād*, it expressly designated armed struggle against the inhabitants of *Mecca: "Fight for the sake of Allah those who fight you . . . Kill them wherever you meet them and drive them from the places whence they drove you . . . But do not fight them near the sacred *mosque, unless they attack you there. In that case kill them" (Sura II, 190-191). This passage mentions the Ka'ba ("the sacred mosque") and the **hejira* ("whence they drove you"). But the Muslims soon extended the application of these Koranic appeals to all infidel territories, and the armies of conquering Arabs, who in the decades following Muḥammad's death created a vast empire from the Atlantic to the Indus, were largely mobilized by this appeal to "fight for the sake of Allah". Offensive war thus found its justification: to extend the territory of Islam (*dār al-islām*) at the expense of the territory of infidelity or territory of war (*dār al-harb*). The faithful who died in battle were witnesses, martyrs, to whom paradise was promised.

The great waves of the first conquests once over, *Sunni jurists distinguished offensive war, a collective obligation, which was incumbent on the whole community, but which only a few had to fulfil in the name of all, from defensive war which was a personal obligation, weighing on every male adult Muslim. In the reality of things, *jihād* was then limited to an annual incursion into infidel territory, carried out by *ghāzīs*, voluntary combatants who made war on the *Turks on the eastern borders or the *Byzantine Empire on the Taurus frontier. Thus, in the 10th c., the collective consciousness of *jihād* seems much weakened.

It was attacks by the Christian powers – *Reconquest in *Spain, *crusades in the East – that restored *jihād* propaganda to its proper place. Rulers appealed to the Muslim conscience to push back the infidels, stating that in case of defensive war combat was imposed on everyone, thus returning the *jihād* to its full mobilizing force. The *Almoravids and *Almohads, those great dynasties of Berber origin, used the theme of *jihād* to justify their invasion of Spain. Likewise the rulers of *Syria, Zengī, Nūr al-Dīn and especially *Saladin, appealed to the *jihād* against the Franks: moral rearmament, application of strict religious orthodoxy, unity of Muslims (Syria and Egypt) against the crusaders were constantly put forward by these rulers to justify and support their policy.

But, from the 13th c., in the West with the reflux of Muslims after the Christian victory of Las *Navas de Tolosa in 1212, in the East with the policy of coexistence followed by the *Ayyubids, mobilization in favour of *jihād* once more suffered a certain retreat, though it was brought back to the fore by the *Mamluks in their struggle against the *Mongols.

E. Tyan, "*Dj̲ihād*", *EI(E)*, 2, 1965, 538-540 (2nd ed.). – B. Lewis, *The Political Language of Islam*, Chicago, 1988 (bibl.). – *The Jihad and its Times*, H. Dajani-Shakeel (ed.), R.A. Messier (ed.), Ann Arbor (MI), 1991. – A. Morabia, *Le Ǧihād dans l'Islam médiéval. Le "combat sacré" des origines au XIIe siècle*, Paris, 1993. – M. Bonner, *Aristocratic Violence and Holy War: Studies in the Jihad and the Arab-Byzantine Frontier*, New Haven, 1996.

Françoise Micheau

**JOACHIM OF FIORE (*c.*1132-1202)**

**Biography.** Joachim of Fiore was born at Celico near Cosenza (*Calabria) in *c.*1132. Son of a *notary, perhaps with some Jewish ancestry, he seems to have followed his father's profession at Cosenza and at *Palermo, in the *chancery of *William II. Between 1156 and 1157, he made a *pilgrimage to the East which was the central episode of his life, and of which we find clear evidence in the *Tractatus super quatuor evangelia*. During the journey his *conversion to *monasticism took place in extraordinary circumstances, and he went through some experiences crucial to his formation. He had contacts with the Greek world at *Constantinople; he decided to adopt extreme *poverty and for a time he lived with a *Saracen community; he arrived in *Palestine where he wished to become a hermit, and had his first *visions in a cave on Mount Tabor. Back in *Calabria, he entered the *Cistercian monastery of *Sambucina in 1159; he was a lay brother there for a year, with the job of doorkeeper. Soon afterwards, though not yet a priest, he began *preaching. Recalled to ecclesiastical discipline, he prepared for the *priesthood at Corazzo (1168) where, ten years later, he became *abbot. In 1182-1183 he was at *Casamari, mother *abbey of Sambucina, where he composed the *Liber concordiae Novi et Veteris Testamenti* and the *Expositio in Apocalypsim*.

His conflict with the Cistercian Order emerged in those years. The era of *Bernard was over: the concrete demands that presided over the organisation of the institution, now very strong, became dominant. After new eremitical experiences, he decided to found a congregation of his own, still under the Rule of St *Benedict; his first centre was at San Giovanni in Fiore, in the Sila, and the Florenses saw their statutes recognised in 1196 by *Celestine III and later confirmed by *Innocent III and *Honorius III.

In the last years of his life, Joachim gained some *authority among the powerful, who consulted him to interpret portents, in particular on crusading expeditions (on whose advisability he gave ambiguous judgment, disapproving of their *violence). Contemporary chroniclers record his meeting with *Richard Coeur de Lion near Messina in winter 1190-1191, with *Henry VI, and with the emperor's wife *Constance who came to him as a *penitent. With the *popes he long had positive relations: he explained a *prophecy to Lucius III at Veroli in 1184 and met Urban III at *Verona in 1186, seeking approval for his writings: this approval would come with Clement III, who exhorted him to continue his exegetical work.

*Celestine III supported him more than anyone, and it was only at Celestine's death and *Innocent III's accession in 1198 that his position at the Roman *Curia deteriorated, so much so as to induce him in 1200 to prepare a famous testamentary letter in which he protested his absolute loyalty and submission to the Church. It was precisely at this moment that the premises were being created for the condemnation of some of his trinitarian views, a condemnation that would come later, in 1215 during the fourth *Lateran council, and would throw a shadow of heterodoxy over him. It was the final proof of the incommunicability between *scholastic theology, now dominant, and *monastic theology, which seemingly could not survive the decline of the institutions that had permitted it, or respond to the cultural requirements of the new century. Joachim died on 30 March 1202, while composing the *Tractatus super quatuor evangelia* and working to spread his message and strengthen the congregation of Fiore, with the help of a group of monks and friends, among them his faithful biographer Luca da Cosenza.

**Historiography.** Two tendencies have characterised historiography on Joachim's thought in our century: Ernesto Buonaiuti on one hand and Herbert Grundmann on the other have outlined the two possible readings from which, despite the clear progress of philological work, there has been no movement. For Buonaiuti, Joachim represented one of the highest experiences of Catholicism: he denounced his violent conflict with the institutional Church, but this conflict was merely the consequence of an extreme assertion of the necessarily universal and mystical nature of Christian experience. Catholicism, for Buonaiuti, was the authentic form of Christian life, because in it there was no conception of even the possibility of a separate community of the elect, but a tendency to recognise the *de facto* reality of the total belonging of human life to the life of *Christ. Hence the historiographical comparison of Joachim's *doctrine with the lay and minorite experience of *Francis of Assisi, united both in the theme of the religious meaning of human history (from which would come so many themes dear to the Friars Minor) and in that of conflictual fidelity to the *pope (a sign of universality, but also an institutional stumbling-block). According to Buonaiuti, Joachim understood that *history was not only directed towards the future, but was an intertwining of multiple meanings. It had no end outside itself, but was an actual end in itself. In history, the divine manifested itself, and this statement should not necessarily be considered a precocious form of historicism, but rather a recognition of the eternal in *time, drawing symbols of universality from history.

For H. Grundmann, on the other hand, Joachim was the theoretician of ecclesiastical secession and temporal succession. If his challenge was fragile in practical terms, in theoretical terms he laid down the premises for every other challenge. The surpassing of previous levels of religious awareness, and the recognition of the necessity of a successive series of breaks, defined his Christianity as a walk towards the end and his *theology as a theology of time.

Other historiographical tendencies have more recently performed a parallel labour, even judging the problems confronted by Buonaiuti and Grundmann to be insoluble or irrelevant to historiographical truth. The labours of Marjorie Reeves and Bernard McGinn have a completely different cultural bckground. In general, the reconstruction of the sources of Joachim's thought, the description of the character of his mental procedures, the mechanics of his symbols and the techniques of transmission have become the dominant problems of historiography. It has thus been possible to re-evaluate the absolute character of the Joachite innovation, by tracing some of his demands for a positive exposition of history in one or other of his contemporaries and predecessors. Much work has been done on the heavy formal demands of his mind, showing how he attests a form of rationalism within the monastic world.

Joachim's theological discoveries were undoubtedly based on his ecstatic experience, but they also bear the imprint of a rationalistic mind. His rationalism is different from that exemplified by *Abelard, *Gilbert of Poitiers or *Peter Lombard some decades earlier, and recalls rather the modes of thought of *William of Saint-Thierry's *Aenigma fidei*. At first sight his discourse is essentially the proclamation of the era of the Spirit, which must apparently mark the time of a new Gospel, which will bring that of Christ to completion. But this declaration is subsequent to another, that of the primacy of the *Trinity in history; the divine Trinity in fact appears to be the sole reality of time, even human time, and therefore it involves history in itself, marking three stages in it. In this, the very figure of *God is modified, manifesting itself as Father in the Old Testament, Son in the New Testament and Spirit at the end of time.

The discovery of Joachim, who with lucid optimism overturned the *Augustinian image of the meaning of human history, had a hermeneutical side. The era of the Spirit would not give a new Gospel, but a new collective understanding of the Scriptures: "collective" because experienced by a group of monks who would inaugurate the new era; "understanding" because through a spiritual *intellect would be created the figures and figurative mechanisms in which was manifested the perfect internal *order of the Christian message, its perfect congruity with history, in a system of references that created the perfect design.

Francesco Santi

**Joachism.** Joachim's ideas were not destined for rapid oblivion: after his death, a "pseudo-Joachite" literature quickly spread. Its most important examples were the two apocryphal works *Super Hieremiam* and *super Isaiam*. Preaching the imminent coming of *Christ as Judge, they celebrated the saving function of the *Franciscan and *Dominican Orders, and criticized the hierarchical Church. Joachim's innovative *exegesis especially favoured the placing of the book of the *Apocalypse in a historical dimension; through this, the appeal he made to men with a view to the age of the Spirit had profound repercussions throughout the 13th century.

Joachim's appeal was appropriated in no uncertain way by the Franciscan movement: the stigmatized *Francis, the *Alter Christus*, could be none other than the one deputed to inaugurate the age of the Spirit, which was to mark the renewal of the Church. *Gerard of Borgo San Donnino, in his *Introductorius ad Evangelium aeternum*, identified Joachim's work with the eternal Gospel mentioned in the Apocalypse (14, 5) and assigned the mission of regenerating the Church to the Franciscan Order; his ideas were condemned by a papal commission and he died in prison. A similar line was taken by *John of Parma, minister general of the order, who aligned himself mainly with the apocryphal Joachim and confirmed the providential conception of the Franciscan Order; his friend Hugh of Digne, a provincial, contributed to spreading Joachism in France, particularly in *Provence. Through Hugh of Digne and Gerard of Borgo San Donnino, the Franciscan *Salimbene of Parma, known mainly as the author of an interesting *Chronicle, also approached Joachite positions. But the most interesting personalities to gravitate towards Joachism were *Arnold of Villanova and *Peter John Olivi. Arnold was certainly formed on Joachim's books and, while his long commentary on the Apocalypse, written around 1290, was centred on the figure of the *angelic pope, that holy and humble pope who would accompany men to the kingdom of God, it also echoed themes and aspects of Joachism. Olivi took from Joachim mainly the idea of history as a development of divine rationality, whose culmination was no longer the age of the Spirit, but Christ, the central figure to whom and from whom history flowed. Olivi's was not a scholastic Joachism, but an occasion to meditate on the Church of his own time; his apocalyptic interpretation inspired *Ubertino da Casale and *Angelo Clareno. Joachim's apocalyptic awareness also cut into the historical dimension and the spiritual consciousness of the Franciscans at deeper levels: thus *Bonaventure, while his orthodoxy was opposed to Joachism, recovered its line of historical develpment and its apocalyptic vision, giving form to them through his *Legenda maior*.

*Joan of Arc before the Dauphin.* From the *Vigils of Charles VII* by Martial of Paris, called Dauvergne. Rouen, Municipal Library.

*Liber concordiae Novi ac Veteris Testamenti*, Venice, 1519 (repr. Frankfurt, 1964). – *Expositio super Apocalypsim*, Venice, 1527 (repr. Frankfurt, 1964). – *Psalterium decem chordarum*, Venice, 1527 (repr. Frankfurt, 1965). – *Tractatus super quatuor evangelia*, E. Buonaiuti (ed.), Rome, 1930, XXXI-363. – E. R. Daniel, *Abbot Joachim of Fiore: Liber de concordia Novi ac Veteris Testamenti*, Philadelphia (PA), 1983.

H. Grundmann, *Studien über Joachim von Floris*, Leipzig-Berlin, 1927. – E. Buonaiuti, *Gioacchino da Fiore. I tempi, la vita, il messaggio*, Rome, 1931 (re-ed. Cosenza, 1980). – H. Grundmann, *Neue Forschungen über Joachim von Fiore*, Marburg, 1950. – B. Töpfer, *Das kommende Reich des Friedens. Zur Entwicklung chiliastischer Zukunftshoffnungen im Hochmittelalter*, Berlin, 1964. – M. Reeves, *The Influence of Prophecy in the Later Middle Ages. A Study in Joachimism*, Oxford, 1969. – M. Reeves, B. Hirsch-Reich, *The Figurae of Joachim of Fiore*, Oxford, 1972. – H. Mottu, *La Manifestation de l'Esprit selon Joachim de Flore. Herméneutique et théologie de l'histoire d'après le "Traité sur les quatre évangiles"*, Neuchâtel-Paris, 1977. – B. McGinn, *The Calabrian Abbot Joachim of Fiore in Western Thought*, London, 1985. – E. Pispisa, *Gioacchino da Fiore e i cronisti medievali*, Messina, 1988. – S. E. Wessley, *Joachim of Fiore and Monastic Reform*, New York, 1990.

Lucia Velardi

**JOAN OF ARC (1412?-1431).** If we consider the two trial documents, that of condemnation (1431) and that of rehabilitation (1451-1455), together with all the surviving contemporary sources, the life of Jeanne la Pucelle, called Joan of Arc, is undoubtedly the best documented French life of the 15th century. Yet we have no authentic portrait of her, and the year of her birth – 1412 – is more probable than certain. Having said that, neither her origin (born at Domrémy, on the border of the duchies of Bar and *Lorraine, the daughter of Isabelle Romeé and Jacques d'Arc) nor her death (publicly burnt in the Old Market Square at *Rouen, 30 May 1431) are in any doubt.

The activities of Joan of Arc are explicable in a context of profound uncertainty on the part of the political world and tragic disarray on that of the people. *Charles VII, the "king of Bourges" (1422-1461), found himself radically threatened by the alliance of John, duke of Bedford, regent of the kingdom of *France for *Henry VI, king of France and *England, and Philip the Good, duke of *Burgundy. Not only did the war and its miseries go on for ever, but many people were persuaded that it was the end of the "holy realm of France". Meeting Charles VII at Chinon in March 1429, Joan of Arc presented herself with strength and simplicity as God's envoy sent to lift the siege of *Orléans, to take the king to *Reims to be consecrated and crowned, and to "boot" the English out of his kingdom. At *Poitiers, she was accepted after a thorough examination by churchmen. Orléans was indeed liberated (8 May 1429) and Charles VII consecrated (17 July). Hope was at its height. But the enthusiasm she had aroused was insufficiently exploited.

A part of Charles VII's entourage judged it imprudent and impolitic to further affront the duke of Burgundy. The assault on *Paris failed (8 Sept 1429).

The spell seemed broken. Still overflowing with energy, Joan went to the rescue of Compiègne, besieged by the Anglo-Burgundians. A victim of her impressive courage, she was taken prisoner (24 May 1430). Bedford, skilfully advised by Pierre *Cauchon, bishop of Beauvais, and by the *university of Paris, had her judged by a tribunal of *inquisition, solely on religious grounds. Sitting at Rouen, this court formulated many sorts of grievances against her, the most serious being her apparent refusal to submit to the Church. At first she denied her voices (24 May 1431), then rallied and re-affirmed the inspired character of her mission. She was then condemned to the stake as a backslider. In a posthumous report intended for the widest circulation, Cauchon claimed that before dying she had again abjured and asked pardon from the English and Burgundians for the harm she had done them.

During the period of her captivity, Charles VII's passivity on her behalf was total. However, after 1450, the king, having become aware of the contents of the minute of condemnation, asked the *pope for new proceedings to be instituted. Memoirs were drawn up, tens of witnesses interrogated. The verdict of Rouen was annulled and Joan cleared of any charge. Undoubtedly a current of opinion wanted her to be raised to the altar there and then.

Over the centuries the memory of Joan of Arc was perpetuated. She was long celebrated mainly as a heroine. From 1869, on the initiative of Mgr Dupanloup, bishop of Orléans, a movement developed among French Catholics which culminated in her beatification in 1909 and canonization in 1920. That year the French Republic, in its enthusiasm for the victory of 1918, made the feast of Joan of Arc a national holiday.

*Procés de condemnation de Jeanne d'Arc*, P. Tisset (ed.), Y. Lanhers (ed.), Paris, 1960-1971 (3 vol.). – *Procés en nullité de la condemnation de Jeanne d'Arc*, P. Dupart (ed.), Paris, 1977-1988 (5 vol.).

F. Grayeff, *Joan of Arc*, London, 1978. – M. Warner, *Joan of Arc: the Image of Female Heroism*, New York, 1981. – R. Pernoud, M.-V. Clin, *Jeanne d'Arc*, Paris, 1986. – P. Marot, "De la réhabilitation à la glorification de Jeanne d'Arc. Essai sur l'historiographie et le culte de l'héroïne en France pendant cinq siècles", in *Hommage à Pierre Marot...*, Paris, 1988, 33-150. – S. Tanz, *Jeanne d'Arc*, Weimar, 1991. – P. Contamine, "Jeanne d'Arc dans la mémoire des droites", in *Cultures, Histoire des droites en France*, J.-F. Sirinelli (dir.), 2, Paris, 1992, 399-435 and 721-722. – M. Winock, "Jeanne d'Arc", in *Les France, 3, Les Lieux de mémoire*, 3, Paris, 1992, 674-733. – G. Krumeich, *Jeanne d'Arc in der Geschichte. Historiographie – Politik – Kultur*, Sigmaringen, 1989. – P. Contamine, *De Jeanne d'Arc aux guerres d'Italie*, Orléans, Caen, 1994. – *Joan of Arc: Reality and Myth*, J. van Herwaarden (ed.), Hilversum, 1994.

Philippe Contamine

**JOAN OF FRANCE (1464-1505).** A Capetian princess and saint, Joan of France illumines by her Marian *mysticism the medieval *spirituality of the "flamboyant" period. Infirm from birth, she was obliged by her father, *Louis XI, to marry her cousin, Louis of Orléans. The king wished, by a union considered sterile, to extinguish this rival collateral dynasty. In 1498, Louis XII obtained from the pope a declaration of the nullity of his marriage in order to unite *Brittany with the kingdom of France. Becoming apanagist duchess of Berry and venerated in her own lifetime, Joan founded the Order of the Annunciad or Order of the Virgin Mary in 1502 and contributed actively to the church reform movement. She died on 4 Feb 1505 and was canonized in 1950. St Joan's spirituality invites the Christian to "imitate *Mary in order to please God".

J.-F. Drèze, *Raison d'État, raison de Dieu. Politique et mystique chez Jeanne de France*, Paris, 1991.

Jean-François Drèze

**JOAN, POPE.** A woman is supposed to have occupied the papal see in male disguise in the 9th century. This fiction, whose first traces occur around 1255, was taken for reality through the later Middle Ages. The gradual refutation of the legend began in the 16th century. This episode, whose memory remains alive in our own day, had immense popularity; apart from its romantic aspect, it put the spotlight on a fundamental taboo of Catholic culture: the rejection of women priests. It also posed the troubling question of imposture: what happened when a supreme and divinely sanctioned power was allowed to be usurped? So we can understand that the legend played a powerful role in the controversies that came to a head from the 13th c. around the status of the Roman Church and its *magisterium. At the time of the *Great Schism, the anecdote, treated as a legal case, was used to justify the necessity to declare a papal *election null. Later, the *Hussite movement and then the Reformation found in Joan a striking image of the corruption of the Roman Church. The account was rapidly fixed in a stable form.

So here is the version that could be read from the late 13th c.: around 850, a woman from Mainz, but of English origin, dressed herself as a man in order to follow her lover who was devoted to studies and so to an exclusively male world; she herself was so successful in them that, after a period of study at Athens, she met with a warm and admiring welcome at Rome which allowed her to enter the hierarchy of the Curia and finally to be elected pope. Her pontificate lasted more than two years and was interrupted by a scandal: Joan, who had not renounced the pleasures of the flesh, found herself pregnant and died during a procession from *St Peter's to *St John Lateran, after having publicly given birth to a child. Various versions of the story produced traces, proofs, a memory of the female pope: such as that, from that time, the sex of the popes was supposed to have been manually verified during their coronation. Or that papal processions were supposed to have left the direct route from the Vatican to the Lateran, on a level with the church of San Clemente, to avoid the place of the *accouchement*. Or that a statue or an inscription in that place immortalized the memory of this deplorable incident.

It is very difficult to establish the origins of this story, which appeared for the first time in a chronicle of the convent of *Metz written around 1255 by the Dominican Jean de Mailly. The rapidity and geographical breadth of the legend's circulation suggest that the rumour of the female pope had circulated for some time, notably at *Rome, before being fixed in writing. However this may be, the legend was widely circulated in *Dominican (*Stephen of Bourbon, Arnold of Liège and especially *Martin of Opava [Troppau], author of a much-read universal *chronicle) and *Franciscan circles. The papacy itself cherished the legend: the commemorative detour was maintained in the *coronation ritual and, in 1474, the history of Joan came into the official *Lives of the Popes* written by the humanist *Platina.

A. Boureau, *La Papesse Jeanne*, Paris, 1988.

Alain Boureau

## JOB

**Exegesis.** The figure of Job fascinated medieval man thanks especially to *Gregory the Great's (*c.*540-604) *Moralia in Job*, one of the texts most used by medieval commentators.

Job is an allegorical prefiguration of *Christ, among other just figures of the Old Testament, as well as of the Church and the Christian (*Moralia*, *Praefatio*, VI, 13-14). The story of his unjust suffering and the trials to which he was subjected was the occasion, in the theological project of the *Moralia*, for a pedagogy of charity and faith for the pastors of the Church, the community of Christians and the individual believer.

Job was also the man of *mercy who helped the poor, *widows and orphans (Job 31, 16; *Moralia*, *Epist. missoria ad Leandrum*, 4), living without the Law but, thanks to his *virtue, according to the Law. His example was offered "to confound our impudence" as men subject to the Law but "disdainful of obeying that law" (*Praefatio*, 4-5). Up to the 12th and 13th cc., commentators interpreting the book of Job favoured the allegorical method, often forgetting the moralizing intention of Gregory the Great's work. *Thomas Aquinas's (1225-1274) commentary, *Expositio super Iob ad litteram*, was the first literal interpretation of the book of Job. The history of the just sufferer was no longer considered an exhortation to patience in trials, but became a theme for discussion on the metaphysical problem of *providence.

The person of Job – figure of Christ, the Christian and the Church in times of trial, symbol of fidelity in adversity, image of patience in misfortune – gave rise to a particularly rich iconography in the monumental art of the Middle Ages: e.g. cloister capitals of Pamplona cathedral (*c.*1140), of the church of the Daurade at *Toulouse (*c.*1180), bas-relief of the central portal of Notre-Dame cathedral in *Paris (early 13th c.).

Gregory the Great, *Moralia in Job*, *PL*, 75-76, 509-782; Peter of Blois († 1204), *Compendium in Job*, *PL*, 207, 795-826; Thomas Aquinas, *Expositio super Job ad litteram*, 26, Rome, 1965. – S.E. Schreiner, *Where Shall Wisdom be Found?: Calvin's Exegesis of Job from Medieval and Modern Perspectives*, Chicago, 1994.

R. Wasselynck, *L'Influence des Moralia in Job de saint Grégoire le Grand sur la théologie morale entre le VII<sup>e</sup> et le XII<sup>e</sup> siècle*, Lille, 1956. – "Les Compilations des Moralia in Job. . .", *RThAM*, 29, 1962, 5-32. – L. L. Besserman, *The Legend of Job in the Middle Ages*, Cambridge (MA), 1979.

Giambattista Livi

**Iconography.** The story of Job and his trials occupies a whole book of the *Bible, the book of Job, which recounts the challenge launched by Satan at God, who puts his servant to the test (Job 1, 6-12). The calamities that struck Job were many and varied: he lost his property, his children and was struck down by boils. In Byzantine and Western art, Job was represented as an old man with a beard and long hair.

Different episodes of the book of Job were illustrated, like the banquet with his children preceding the calamities, of which we can see a representation on a 12th-c. capital at Pamplona (Museum of Navarre). Representations of Job's sufferings were more frequent, since they were interpreted as a prefiguration of Christ's *Passion. Job on his dungheap was the iconographical type that predominated from 1500. Jean *Fouquet represented him, *c.*1450, in the Hours of Étienne Chevalier (Musée Condé at Chantilly).

S. L. Terrain, *The Iconography of Job throught the Centuries*, University Park (PA), 1996.

Frédérique Trouslard

*Job, his wife and friends and the devil.* Miniature from Gregory the Great's *Moralia in Job*, early 12th c. Douai, Municipal Library (Ms 301, fol. 107 v°).

**JOHANN NIDER (1380-1438).** An Observant Friar Preacher, born in *Swabia in 1380, died at *Nuremberg in 1438, Johann Nider entered the *Dominican Order at the *convent of *Colmar which *Raymond of Capua, inaugurating the *Observance in German territory, had reformed in 1389. He studied at *Cologne and then *Vienna (1422), where he became master of theology in 1425, before directing the theology *faculty as *dean in 1436. Before that, succeeding Francis of Retz, his master at Vienna († 1427), as *vicar of the reformed convents of the province of Teutonia, he was *prior of Nuremberg (1428) and then Basel (1429) and worked for the progress of the Observance among friars (convent of Vienna) and sisters (convents of Nuremberg and Colmar).

A contemporary of major crises in the Church and of the flowering of the Observance, his whole life was lived in the geographical area of the Imperial lands sensitized by the *councils: that of *Constance where he may have met *John Dominici, propagator of the Lombard reform in 1414, then that of *Basel (1429) of which he was nuncio in 1431 for *Bohemia ravaged by the *Hussite wars. So his activity, both practical and speculative, took place at the heart of lively, bracing milieux, propitious to debate and open to the problems of the time. His priority was *reform and, at the request of Bartholomew Textier who became master of the Dominican Order in 1426, he produced the *De* *reformatione status coenobitici*, destined to remain a reference-point of observant practice until the late 16th century. A spiritual master, he defined its ideals in the numerous works that make him less an original author than the fertile representative of a broad and deep current, as witness the difficulties of attribution from which he has sometimes suffered. Thus, with the *Twenty-four Golden Harps* written in German (*Die XXIV goldenen Harfen*), a paraphrase of John *Cassian's *Conferences*, appears the *Alphabeticum divini amoris*, sometimes attributed to *Gerson, as the *Liber de modo bene vivendi* has been to St *Bernard.

By vocation and training a specialist in moral theology, in fact he spoke to wider circles than those of the *convents, and his reflections and treatises *Manuale confessorum* (*confessors' manual), *Consolatorium timorate conscientiae* and *Preceptorium divinae legis* (exposition of the *Decalogue) belong to a work on society as a whole, as does his most famous work: the *Formicarius*. An ordered reflection on the practice and conditions of the good moral life, whose first book intends to give examples, it is constructed on a rigorous balance of contraries whose content must be explored if we are to have any chance of defining its path. Thus good *revelations (book II) are opposed to false and illusory *visions (book III), companions of the world of *heresy; the works of the good (book IV) are opposed to those of the tools of the devil (book V). The work's celebrity comes from this fifth book, *De maleficiis et errores deceptionibus*, considered a major step in the structuring of witch-hunts, to the extent that it is a fundamental reference of the **Malleus maleficarum*, with which it was sometimes published. In fact, unlike exactly contemporary treatises, the anonymous *Errores Gazariorum* and the Dauphinois judge Claude Tholosan's *Ut magorum et maleficiorum errores*, strictly ordered with a view to the identification and pursuit of sorcerers, the *Formicarius*, born out of Johann Nider's interests and encounters, appears more as a sonorous echo of the preoccupations of the time in this matter. Well placed to receive testimonies, Johann Nider propagated them, and this is what gives him his major importance in the analysis of a deep current which he both revealed and multiplied by the publicity which the very audience of its author ensured the work.

T. Kaeppeli, "Johannes Nider", *SOPMA*, 2, 1975, 500-515. – G. T. Bedouelle, "Nider (Jean)", *DSp*, 11, 1981, 322-325. – A. Duval, "Nider (Jean)", *Cath.*, 1982, 1262-1263.

Pierrette Paravy

**JOHANNES ANDREAE (*c.*1270-1348).** Born at Rifredo near *Florence, Johannes Andreae (Giovanni di Andrea) died of plague at *Bologna. He studied *theology, *canon law (he was received as *doctor "despite himself" between 1296 and 1300) and civil law. Professor of *Decretals and of *Decretum, he exercised his art alternately at Bologna and *Padua; he was the second married professor of canon law known to history. He said himself that he consulted his wife Melancia on legal questions. Father of three sons and four daughters, he used the talents of his younger daughter Novella (born 1312) to read his *lectures in his place when he was ill, though the lecturess had to conceal herself behind a curtain to avoid distracting the audience's attention by her beauty (*Christine de Pizan relates this anecdote). "*Fons et turba juris*" for some of his contemporaries, he was without general culture in *Petrarch's eyes, and has since been considered a "useful and heavy compiler". His work is immense; he is known mainly for his *Glosa in Sextum* (completed later) and the novella on the decree of *Gregory IX dating from the years 1321-1338, but we may also cite the *Quaestiones mercuriales*, various treatises on canon law, an important work on legal *procedure and a biography of St Jerome (the *Summa de ordine et processu judicii spiritualis* has been attributed to him in error). An ardent defender of papal supremacy (he speaks of the *pope in these terms: "*Papa stupor mundi . . . . Nec Deus est nec homo, quasi neuter est inter utrumque* [the pope, wonder of the world . . . neither God nor man, he is as it were half-way between the two]"). He thought that all should obey the Holy See, including the Infidels, and that canon law was of universal application; the deposition of the emperor by the pope seemed to him evident since the Holy Father acted in the name of God. In fact his thought does not shine by its originality (he recopied, so to speak, John of Paris [*Jean Quidort] in certain passages of his *Novella in Sextum*), but the breadth of his work would spread a number of agreed arguments to future generations; thus, copying *Hostiensis, he stated that the pope, successor of *Christ and St *Peter, could not err – *Zabarella would reproduce this confident truth, while introducing a slight difference: if the Church could not err, the pope could. The pope was in his eyes the veritable master of the world: "*Apostolicus totius orbis est dominus* (The apostolic [*vicar] is the master of the whole world)"; any order of the supreme pontiff, coming from God, was thus of immediate application; he was not subject to the laws of *councils as mere mortals were, since he gave *authority to councils while the reverse was not true (though a heretical or criminal pope could be subjected to the jurisdiction of a council), and could change conciliar laws by his mere will; he was the judge of all and could be judged by none; the Church never dying, the authority of a papal *legate did not cease with the death of the pope who had invested him with it.

L. Sorrenti, *Testimonianze di Giovanni d'Andrea sulle Quaestiones civilistiche*, Catania, 1980.

Jacques Bouineau

**JOHN THE BAPTIST.** In the tradition of interpretation, from the Church *Fathers to *Honorius Augustodunensis and *Dante, the Precursor (in Greek, *Prodromos*) occupies a pre-eminent place in the iconography of Christian art. In a miniature (6th c., 7th c.?) of manuscript Greek 699 of the Vatican Library, St John the Baptist is at the centre of the composition, with *Christ the Saviour on his right, *Mary on his left. Commonly he figures among the *prophets in the great decorative programmes (thus at the Palatine Chapel in *Palermo, *mosaic, 12th c.). He is also among the messengers who announce the coming of Christ and the New Law; at *Clermont-Ferrand, on the south portal of Notre-Dame-du-Port, he is opposite *Isaiah, on the engaged piers; at *Chartres, in the splays of the north portal, he is the last of the Prophets, followed immediately by the apostle *Peter, the vicar of Christ, who from now on testifies to the fulfilment of the prophecies. By virtue of the same conception, in the 15th c., he is associated with Calvary, as the prophet who assists at the *revelation of what he has announced (at *Colmar, in the former convent of the Dominican nuns of *Unterlinden, the *Crucifixion* of Matthias Grünewald).

But St John the Baptist is also the equal of the evangelists: he is considered the first of them. On the throne of Bishop Maximilian in the chapel of the archiepiscopal palace of *Ravenna, he appears with the four *evangelists; later, on the bronze doors of the new *sacristy of Florence cathedral, he dominates by his stature the double college of evangelists and *Doctors of the Latin Church:

*Beheading of John the Baptist.* Miniature from a 9th-c. gospel. School of Chartres. Paris, BNF (Ms lat. 9386, fol. 146 v°).

Luca Della *Robbia represents him in the act of *preaching, while below him the evangelists prepare to transcribe his words. By reason of his pre-eminence, he sits opposite Mary, in the first rank of the saints, on *altarpieces (*Adoration of the Mystic Lamb* by Hubert and Jan *van Eyck in *Ghent cathedral; *Last Judgment* by Rogier *van der Weyden at the hôtel-Dieu of Beaune, 1443).

In the pose and attitude of the desert preacher, John the Baptist resumes the role he held in the scene of the *Deêsis*, opposite Mary, on the other side of *Christ, with whom he too intercedes. In 15th-c. Italian altarpices, he always occupies the place of honour, facing the observer, pointing his index finger towards the central scene or the main character. It is he again who recommends a devotee or a kneeling saint to Mary (most often) or to Christ (Wilson diptych, late 14th c.: London, National Gallery: he presents the young King *Richard II of England to Mary). Between the 13th and 14th cc., in painting and sculpture, he became the one who baptized Christ. Finally, he was the subject of numerous hagiographical cycles: at *Florence, which chose him for its patron saint, there are no fewer than eight cycles dedicated to him (in the *baptistery; at Santa Croce, in the Peruzzi and Castellani chapels; at Santa Maria Novella, in the choir of the church; on liturgical embroideries, in the Opera del Duomo; and in the *cloister of the Scalzo). Especially in the 15th c., it is the little St John who converses with the Infant Christ.

P. M. Paciaudi, *De cultu S. Johannis Baptistae*, Rome, 1755. – A. Masseron, *Saint Jean Baptiste dans l'art*, Paris, 1957. – M. Aronberg-Lavin, "San Giovannino Battista: a Study in Renaissance Religious Symbolism", *ArtB*, 43, 1961, 319-326. – J.S. Cwi, *St. John, Mustair and St. Benedict, Malles*, Ann Arbor (MI), 1981.

Daniel Russo

## JOHN THE EVANGELIST

**History and cult.** John, whom the New Testament makes known to us as one of the twelve apostles, son of Zebedee, brother of James the Great, with him nicknamed by Jesus "sons of thunder", witness of the *Transfiguration (Mk 9, 1), the agony (Mk 14, 33) and the appearances of the Risen Christ (Jn 21, 2), one of the "pillars of the Church" after Pentecost (Gal 2, 9), associated with *Peter (Acts 3 and 4), is also traditionally venerated as the disciple whom Jesus loved, leaning on his bosom at the Last Supper (Jn 13, 23 and 21, 20), to whom his Master on the cross entrusted the Virgin *Mary (Jn 19, 27), discoverer of the empty tomb on Easter morning (Jn 20, 4), author of the fourth gospel, the three canonical epistles and the *Apocalypse, who penetrated like no other into the *mystery of Christ's divinity, represented by the figure of the eagle for the depth and strength of his contemplative gaze.

From the patristic period, accounts of him were added to these biblical data: in the 2nd c., Irenaeus of Lyon attests his sojourn and apostolate at Ephesus. Tertullian (*c.*220) describes his torture under Domitian: taken to Rome and plunged into a cauldron of boiling oil, he emerged unscathed and was then exiled to an island. In the 4th c., Eusebius of Caesarea relates other anecdotes taken from Clement of Alexandria (John in old age going in search of a young Christian who had become a leader of brigands) or Irenaeus (meeting the heretic Cerinthus in the public baths, John left precipitately crying: "Let us get out, for fear the baths will collapse, since Cerinthus, enemy of the Truth, is within").

*Jacobus de Voragine's **Golden Legend* (composed shortly before 1264), relying on Miletus of Laodicea and on *Isidore of Seville's († 636) treatise on the birth and death of the Fathers, brings together the legendary data that inspired painters and glaziers (raising of the widow Drusiana; disputes with the philosopher Crato and with Aristodemus, priest of Diana: to confound the latter, he agrees to drink a poisoned cup without suffering any ill-effects; account of his death: John has a grave dug and goes down into it himself). In the *Divine Comedy*, *Dante contested the belief in a bodily assumption of the apostle (*Paradiso*, 25, 122-129).

From the 4th c. in the East and at least the 6th c. in the West (attestation in the Leonian *sacramentary), John was liturgically feasted on 27 December. In the 8th c. we see a second *feast appear in the West, 8 May, commemorating his *martyrdom at Rome. Several *guilds (copyists, printers, gunsmiths, candlemakers etc.) placed themselves under his patronage.

L. Reau, *Iconographie de l'art chrétien. Iconographie des saints*, 2, Paris, 1958, 708-720. – F.-M. Braun, *Jean le théologien et son évangile dans l'église ancienne*, Paris, 1959. – G. Marsot, "Jean (saint) l'Apôtre ou l'Évangéliste", *Cath.*, 6, 1966, 377-381.

Gilles Berceville

**Iconography.** Apostle and evangelist, John, son of the fisherman Zebedee and brother of St James the Great, appears in various scenes from the New Testament.

After having followed the preaching of *John the Baptist, he was called by Christ to become one of the twelve apostles and became his favourite disciple. Present at the episode of the miraculous draught of fishes, he took part in the wedding-feast of Cana and the *Transfiguration, and was near Jesus at the Last Supper, the Mount of Olives and at the foot of the Cross. He later went to Ephesus before being summoned to Rome, scene of the episode in which he was thrown into boiling oil. He was subsequently exiled to the isle of Patmos (Sporades) where he wrote

*The Evangelist John.* Miniature from a Moldavian manuscript (*Tetraevangelia*) from the monastery of Putna, written by the monk Spiridon, 1502.

the *Apocalypse. On his return to Ephesus, he composed his gospel. Ephesus was also the scene of the test of the poisoned cup which the high priest of Diana wanted him to drink and from which he emerged victorious. His death and elevation are to be compared to those of the Virgin, according to a tradition popularized by the **Golden Legend*, doubtless the product of an erroneous interpretation of a passage in his gospel.

In the 11th c., St Christodoulos founded a monastery dedicated to him on *Patmos. His cult developed, in the West, notably at the Porta Latina in *Rome, place of the torture of the boiling oil, where an *oratory was built, San Giovanni in Oleo; but the chief church dedicated to him was that of *St John Lateran which claimed to possess, among other *relics, the cup of poison.

In the West he was represented young and beardless, while in the Byzantine East he appeared with the characteristics of a bald old man with a white beard. The symbols associated with him were the eagle which characterised him as *evangelist, the cup of poison as apostle; but the caldron of boiling oil and the palm of *paradise were frequent.

In France, the cathedral of *Besançon was put under his patronage. The St John window in *Chartres cathedral was given by the armourers, whose protector he was, notably against burns, frequent in that profession. As writer of a gospel and of the Apocalypse that bears his name, St John was also the patron of theologians and writers.

St John could be depicted alone, as *e.g.* in the 11th c. on a *mosaic of the archbishop's chapel at *Ravenna. In the 14th c., a miniature of the Hours of the Marshal de Boucicaut (Musée Jacquemart-André, Paris) shows him in front of a background decorated with gold eagles in lozenges. Donatello shows him, *c.*1415, with the characteristics of a wild man, with a long beard, sitting with his hand resting on his gospel (Opera del Duomo, Florence).

More often, St John is part of a group, with the Virgin at the foot of the *Cross (window of the Crucifixion in the cathedral of Châlons-sur-Marne), or with John the Baptist (grisailles of the polyptych of the *Mystic Lamb* by the *van Eyck brothers, 1432: Saint-Bavon cathedral, *Ghent), or even in cycles linked to the life of *Christ, as *e.g.* in the 13th c. at Chartres cathedral, at *Bourges or at the *Sainte-Chapelle in Paris.

M. Meis, *Painting in Florence and Siena*, Princeton, 1951, 7-9; 19-45. – C. Cecchelli, *La pittura dei cemeteri cristiani dal V al VII secolo*, 2, Ravenna, 1958, 45-46. – H. Hausshert, "Christus-Johannes-Gruppen der 'Bible moralisée'", *ZfKG*, 27, 1964, 133-152.

Frédérique Trouslard

**JOHN VIII, POPE (late 8th c. - 882).** Roman, *pope from 14 Dec 872 to 15 Dec 882. In the decomposition of the Carolingian politico-institutional edifice after the death of *Louis II (875) and in the climate of continual war that characterised southern *Italy in those years (Arab attacks, internal struggles among the *Lombard states), John sought to keep alive a high-profile policy.

He worked to avoid interrupting the Carolingian succession at the head of the *Empire (election of *Charles the Bald) and intervened repeatedly, but with few effective results, in the Mezzogiorno to organise anti-Islamic resistance on the basis of a sort of "holy war". He kept up an active political and religious dialogue with the Eastern Empire on the themes of papal primacy and the *evangelization of the *Bulgars, which had the secondary effect of stimulating theological thought within the Church of *Rome.

P. Balan, *Il pontificato di Giovanni VIII*, Rome, 1880. – *DEP*, 114-117. – G. Arnaldi, *Natale 875: politica, ecclesiologia, cultura del papato altomedievale*, Rome, 1990.

Federico Marazzi

**JOHN XXII, POPE (*c.*1245-1334).** Jacques Duèse, son of a middle-class family of Cahors, bishop of Fréjus (1300), of *Avignon (1310), then cardinal of San Vitale (1312), was elected at the *conclave of Lyon, 7 Aug 1316, through the support of the future *Philip V of France; he fixed the residence of the papal court at Avignon, though without abandoning the prospect of a return to Italy: a project to establish himself at Bologna failed in 1330.

A judicious administrator, he reorganised the services of the *Curia after the long vacancy that had followed the death of *Clement V, redressed the financial situation, the apostolic treasury having been put in a bad way by his predecessor's excessive liberality; he created a fiscal system fed by taxes levied on ecclesiastical *benefices. He inaugurated a great centralization in the Church which allowed him, by playing with *reservations, to assign numerous appointments to himself: from now on, progress in careers passed through Avignon. John XXII condemned *pluralism of benefices by the *bull *Execrabilis* (1317), though with exceptions for those close to him, *cardinals and their families, apostolic officials or protégés of rulers.

There was no lack of difficulties: firstly, a plot hatched by Hugh Géraud, bishop of Cahors, guilty of embezzlement, soon unmasked but which may have cost the life of the pope's nephew Jacques de Via (1317).

*Franciscan partisans of complete *poverty sometimes to the point of extravagance (the *Spirituals) were called to order (1317-1318); shortly afterwards the order's minister general, *Michael of Cesena, condemned and imprisoned at *Avignon, fled to the court of Louis of Bavaria.

John XXII maintained good relations with *France and more than once proposed his mediation in the conflict with the count of *Flanders and the king of *England.

In *Italy, the situation was difficult both inside and outside the Papal States: it was necessary to support the *Guelfs against the Ghibellines and moderate the ambition of the tyrants (the *Visconti at *Milan, Can Grande della Scala at *Verona), more than once excommunicated; this was the work of the *legate *Bertrand du Poujet, who had varying success; he managed to recapture *Modena, *Parma, Reggio and above all *Bologna (1326-1327), whence he exercised an authoritarian and beneficial administration, but had to flee at the time of the uprising of 1334.

The Emperor Louis of Bavaria, though excommunicated by the pope, had himself crowned at *Rome by schismatic bishops (1328), opened a trial that pronounced the deposition of John XXII for *heresy and replaced him with the Franciscan Pietro da Corbara; the latter, under the name of *Nicholas V, set up a court and a *Sacred College, but could not maintain himself after Louis's departure and came to ask John's pardon at Avignon, where he died three years later.

John XXII created several *bishoprics in south-western France and erected *Toulouse into a metropolis. He reformed the Orders of the *Hospital of St John of Jerusalem and *Grandmont and created *military orders in Spain. He made several *canonizations, including that of St *Thomas Aquinas (1323).

In 1331, the pope developed on his own account a theory that the *souls of the just would enjoy the "*beatific vision" only after the *Last Judgment, a doctrine fiercely opposed by the majority of theologians; John XXII retracted on his deathbed and expired on 4 Dec 1334, aged 90.

An energetic and skilful politician, John XXII was a pontiff whose activities were often beneficial. His *nepotism – six nephews out of some thirty cardinals created, Quercynois in nearly all the positions of the Curia – did not detract from the quality of his choices. Throughout *Christendom he set up a strong, competent administration, very attached to the person of the pope and the papal court, with the dangers that could result from that.

B. Guillemain, *La Cour pontificale d'Avignon*, Paris, 1962. – G. Mollat, *Les Papes d'Avignon*, Paris, 1964 (10th ed.). – M. Dykmans, *Les Sermons de Jean XXII sur la vision béatifique*, Rome, 1973. – L. Caillet, *La Papauté d'Avignon et l'Église de France*, Paris, 1975. – J. Heft, *John XXII and Papal Teaching Authority*, Lewiston (NY), 1986. – T. Turley, "John XXII and the Franciscans", *Popes, Teachers, and Canon Law in the Middle Ages. Essays in Honour of B. Tierney*, Ithaca (NY), 1989, 74-88. – U. Holst, *Evangelische Armut und papstliches Lehramt*, Stuttgart, 1996.

Anne-Marie Hayez

**JOHN (XXIII), POPE (*c.*1360-1419).** Baldassare Cossa was born to a noble Neapolitan family. *Canon and then *archdeacon of *Bologna, he was created *cardinal in 1402 and sent on legation to Bologna. To put an end to the *Great Schism that divided the Church between the Roman and Avignonese *popes, out of his own pocket he supported the holding of the council of *Pisa (1409). He succeeded Alexander V as pope of the Pisan obedience (1410). Pressed by *Sigismund, king of *Germany, he agreed to hold a new council at *Constance. Hostile to the idea of resigning, he took flight and was taken prisoner. The *council, which had proclaimed itself superior to the pope, deposed him in 1415. Freed by *Martin V in 1419, he died the same year as a submissive son of the Church.

E. J. Kitts, *Pope John the Twenty-third and Master John Hus of Bohemia*, London, 1910.

Hélène Millet

**JOHN VIII XIPHILINUS (11th c.).** Patriarch of *Constantinople (1064-1075). Born at *Trebizond, he studied law and *philosophy at Constantinople in the school of John Mauropus, where Michael *Psellus was a fellow-student. In 1045 the Emperor Constantine Monomachos appointed him *nomophylax* (guardian of the laws) and director of the new School of Law. In 1054, following controversies, he retired to a monastery on Mt *Olympus. He became *patriarch of Constantinople in 1064 and replied to Psellus's congratulations by reproaching him for not having sacrificed philosophy to Christ. We owe him some treatises on law and some *homilies.

P. Lemerle, *Cinq études sur le XIe siècle byzantin*, Paris, 1977, 203-212.

Marie-Hélène Congourdeau

**JOHN XI BECCUS (1235-1297).** Born at *Nicaea, John Beccus (Bekkos) belonged to the clergy of the *Great Church, in the service of the patriarchal chancery. As *chartophylax* and *skevophylax* of Patriarch *Joseph I, he carried out several diplomatic missions, in *Serbia and to the king of *France. On one of these missions, he was present at the death of St *Louis at Tunis in 1270. Hostile to the unionist policy of the Emperor Michael VIII, whom he felt was selling off the *Orthodox faith for political reasons, he was put in prison. There he had brought to him various manuscripts of the Church *Fathers on the questions disputed between Latins and Greeks, in particular the **Filioque*. Finding no irreconcilable dogmatic difference between the two Churches, he convinced himself of the merits of union. When Patriarch Joseph resigned in order to avoid signing the *union of the Churches, he recommended Beccus to the emperor as his successor.

Becoming *patriarch (1275), Beccus collaborated fully in the emperor's unionist policy, striving to convince his compatriots. His position was conciliatory: he recognised the primacy of the *pope and the orthodoxy of the *Filioque*, while refusing to abandon the *traditions of the East and in particular to include the *Filioque* in the liturgy. Hoping to reconcile everybody, he attracted the hostility of both the *Byzantine Church, which accused him of ambition and treachery, and the Roman Church, which blamed him for not applying the union strictly.

Positions hardened: depositions and *excommunications of anti-unionist bishops by the patriarch merely reinforced resistance; the emperor provided martyrs and confessors by multiplying arrests.

The emperor's support, Beccus's only trump card, soon failed him: the patriarch's interventions in favour of the poor and condemned and protests against imperial encroachments on ecclesiastical affairs antagonized Michael VIII. In 1279 Beccus resigned retiring to a monastery. But Michael VIII, who could not do without his unionist patriarch, obtained his recall after several months.

Michael's death in 1282 led to a reversal of policy. His son Andronicus II denounced the union of the Churches and dismissed John Beccus, who was exiled and imprisoned in Bithynia. The altar of Hagia Sophia was publicly "purified" from the defilements of the "heretical" patriarch. The Union of Lyon was denounced, the bishops ordained by Beccus deposed. From his exile, Beccus wrote pamphlets refuting the texts that condemned him. He was condemned again by a *synod held at Blachernae in 1285. He died in exile in 1297.

V. Laurent, J. Darrouzès, *Dossier grec de l'Union de Lyon*, Paris, 1976, 59 f. – *HChr*, 6, 1990, 176.

Marie-Hélène Congourdeau

**JOHN XIV CALECAS (1282-1347).** Of modest origin, he belonged to the married clergy attached to the imperial palace of *Constantinople. The protection of John Cantacuzenus (the future Emperor *John VI) was instrumental in his appointment as *patriarch by Andronicus III in 1334 despite the opposition of the *synod. He showed great concern for the Churches situated in Turkish territory, but his patriarchate was marked mainly by the *hesychast quarrel and the civil war between John VI and the young John V. The patriarch supported John V and the anti-Palamites against John VI and the partisans of Gregory *Palamas. He got Palamas condemned by the synod, but the political victory of John VI entailed his deposition, while Palamas was rehabilitated.

*HChr*, 6, 1990, 182-183.

Marie-Hélène Congourdeau

**JOHN III OF ALEXANDRIA (died 689).** *Coptic *patriarch of *Alexandria from 681 to 689. A native of Samannūd in the Delta, he had been a monk in the monastery of St Macarius. Under his patriarchate, the *Umayyad *caliph Marwān I (684-685) appointed his son Abd al-Azīz governor of Egypt. Coming to Alexandria to levy the land tax, the new governor taxed John III 100,000 dinars; but thanks to the intervention of the Coptic secretaries, the patriarch only paid 10,000 dinars. John rebuilt and embellished the church of St Mark at Alexandria, and acquired properties in the town and in the country; this allowed him to give alms twice a week during a rise in the price of foodstuffs that lasted three years. Coming to Fustāt to greet the governor Abd al-Azīz, he fell ill; taken back to Alexandria, he died there and was buried in the church of St Mark which he had restored.

Gérard Troupeau

**JOHN VI CANTACUZENUS (*c.*1295-1383).** John was a Byzantine general and statesman under Andronicus III *Palaeologus, after whose death he fought, from 1341 to 1347, a devastating civil war against the young successor to the throne, John V (for whom he claimed the regency) and his followers. He was recognised by him as principal emperor in 1347. In 1351, a *synod was held under his direction at *Constantinople which raised Gregory *Palamas's doctrine of *energies to the rank of a dogma. In 1354, John V forced him to abdicate and he became a monk. He wrote memoirs defening his political and religious positions, as well as polemical writings against anti-Palamites, *Jews and *Islam.

A.-M. Talbot, "John VI Kantakouzenos", *Oxford Dictionary of Byzantium*, 2, New York, Oxford, 1991, 1050-1051. – K.-P. Todt, *Kaiser Johannes VI. Kantakuzenos und der Islam*, Wurzburg, 1991. – F. Tinnefeld, "Idealizing Self-centered Power Politics in the Memoirs of Emperor John VI Kantakouzenos", *To Ellenikon, Studies in Honor of Speros Vryonis, Jr.*, 1, New Rochelle (NY), 1993, 387-415. – D. M. Nicol, *The Reluctant Emperor*, Cambridge, 1996.

Franz Tinnefeld

**JOHN, KING OF ENGLAND (1167-1216).** The youngest son of *Henry II and *Eleanor of Aquitaine, John inherited all the Angevin dominions in 1199, but was obliged to acknowledge that he held them of the king of *France (Treaty of Le Goulet, May 1200). *Philip Augustus used this to justify his invasion of *Normandy (1204) and of nearly all the rest of the continental dominions in 1214. In 1203 John disposed of his only rival, Arthur, duke of *Brittany, but in circumstances which left him widely suspected of a brutal murder. John's relations with the Church were also troubled: in 1209 he was *excommunicated by Pope *Innocent III over the archbishopric of *Canterbury. The misfortunes of his reign provoked baronial rebellion from 1212, forcing John to agree to the provisions of *Magna Carta in June 1215. England was still in a state of civil war when John died on 18 Oct 1216.

J. C. Holt, *Magna Carta*, 2nd ed., Cambridge, 1992. – W. L. Warren, *King John*, New Haven, London, 1997. – S. D. Church (ed.), *King John: New Interpretations*, Woodbridge, 1999.

Judith Everard

**JOHN BELETH (12th c.).** A disciple of the theologian *Gilbert of Poitiers and master of *Stephen Langton, John Beleth composed a treatise on liturgy linked to the nascent *scholasticism, the *Summa de ecclesiasticis officiis* (*Rationale divinorum officiorum*), whose third state is put between 1160 and 1164. This treatise was the most popular on the subject up to the end of the 13th century.

Joannes Beleth, "Rationale divinorum officiorum", *PL*, 202, 1855, 13-166 (defective text). – J.-F. Maurel, "Jean Beleth et la *Summa de eccl. officiis*", *Position des thèses de l'École des Chartes*, Paris, 1953, 77-80. – *CChr.CM*, 41-41A, 1976. – N. Häring, "Chartres and Paris Revisited", *Essays in Honour of A. C. Pegis*, J. R. O'Donnell (ed.), Toronto, 1974, 306. – *Johannis Beleth Summa de ecclesiasticis officiis*, H. Douteil (ed.), Turnhout, 1976.

Pierre-Marie Gy

**JOHN BONUS (1168-1249).** Born at *Mantua in 1168, orphaned of his father at the age of 15, Giovanni Bono took up the nomadic life of the **jongleurs*; converted in 1208, he decided to withdraw to a hermitage near Cesena where, over ten years, his reputation drew numerous proselytes and led him to an apostolate of peacemaking, as in 1225 between the towns of *Ravenna and Cervia. With the adoption of the Rule of St *Augustine, his community took a regular form and the "Giamboniti" began to expand in *Romagna and *Tuscany. In 1249 he abandoned Cesena to return to Mantua, where he died in the hermitage of Santa Maria in Porto, 23 Oct 1249. He was the object of a *canonization trial, but his *sanctity was not confirmed by the papacy.

A. Vauchez, *Sainthood in the Later Middle Ages*, Cambridge, 1997.

Anna Benvenuti Papi

**JOHN BURIDAN (*c.*1300 - after 1358).** John Buridan taught all his life at the arts *faculty of *Paris. His philosophy of *language rested on an intransigent *nominalism and a logical analysis based on the reference of terms. He put the analysis of language at the centre of philosophical thought. In natural *philosophy, he proposed a new theory of movement of projectiles (theory of *impetus*) and formulated the hypothesis of an initial impulse given by God to all the heavenly spheres, which subsequently continued to move without resistance; he favoured efficient causes over any final *cause. He commented on the *Ethics*, where he defended the human being's *freedom of choice against all determinism. His influence was very great, not just at the university of Paris, but also in the new *universities of central Europe.

Johannes Buridanus, *Sophismata*, T. K. Scott (ed.), Stuttgart, 1967. – Johannes Buridanus, *Tractatus de consequentiis*, H. Hubien (ed.), Louvain-Paris, 1976. – Johannes Buridanus, *Questiones longe super Perihermeneias*, R. van der Lecq (ed.), Nijmegen, 1983. – Johannes Buridanus, *Questiones in Predicamenta*, J. Schneider (ed.), Munich, 1983. – John Buridan's *Tractatus de infinito*, J. M. M. H. Thijssen (ed.), Nijmegen, 1991. – B. Patar, *Le Traité de l'âme de Jean Buridan*, Louvain-la-Neuve-Longeuil, 1991. – *John Buridan, A Master of arts*, Nijmegen, 1993. – Johannes Buridanus, *Questiones Elenchorum*, R. van der Lecq (ed.), H. A. G. Braakhuis (ed.), Nijmegen, 1994. – Johannes Buridanus, *Summulae in Praedicamenta*, E. P. Bos (ed.), Nijmegen, 1994. – Johannes Buridanus, *Summulae de Praedicabilibus*, L. M. De Rijk (ed.), Nijmegen, 1995. – Iohannis Buridani *Expositio et Quaestiones in Aristotelis De caelo*, B. Patar (ed.), Louvain-la-Neuve-Louvain-Paris.

Joël Biard

**JOHN CLIMACUS (7th c.).** A monk at *Sinai, then hegumen of the monks of the Holy Mountain in the mid 7th c., John seems to have resigned his office and passed the last years of his life in reclusion. We owe him the most widely circulated spiritual work in the Byzantine world: the *Ladder of Divine Ascent* (*Klimax théias anodou*), or *Ladder of Paradise*, to which he owes the surname Climacus. This treatise, which concentrates the spiritual teaching of ancient *monasticism, is divided into thirty steps, the number being that of the years of *Christ's life before his *baptism. The first step is devoted to the renunciation of the world, the thirtieth to divine *love; the Ladder takes the monk from the beginning of the spiritual life to its end. The first steps are more especially addressed to *coenobites, the later ones to *hesychasts. At the end of the *Ladder*, we find another treatise by John, the *Letter to the Pastor*, on the role of the hegumen. The work of St *John Climacus exercised a considerable influence on Byzantine and Slav *spirituality, particularly at the time of the hesychast revival of the 14th century.

Jean Climaque, *L'Échelle sainte*, P. Deseille (tr.), *SpOr*, 24, 1978. – *The Ladder of Divine Ascent*, London, 1982.

W. Völker, *Scala Paradisi*, Wiesbaden, 1968. – G. Couilleau, "Jean Climaque", *DSp*, 8, 1974, 369-389.

Bernard Flusin

**JOHN DOMINICI (*c.*1355/1356-1419).** Son of a *merchant and a noble Venetian lady, born at *Florence, Giovanni Dominici or Banchini entered the *Dominican convent of Santa Maria Novella as a *novice in 1373. At Florence and Pisa, he saw and heard *Catherine of Siena. This meeting was decisive for him. In his writings he explains that, being a stammerer, he received the *grace of speech at that time through Catherine's intercession. Ordained priest in 1380, he was *prior of Santa Maria Novella between 1385 and 1387.

In 1388 Dominici left Florence for *Venice. He then undertook the *reform of his order and of Venetian society. With the support of *Raymond of Capua, he managed to restore the former discipline in three convents on the lagoon. In 1393 he was nominated vicar general of the reformed convents in Italy. His tireless *preaching in the churches of Venice, bearing notably on the themes of *marriage and *wisdom in the Old and New Testaments, borrowing examples from the Lives of the saints and St Catherine's *Legenda maior*, was much appreciated by the Venetian aristocracy. Between 1397 and 1398, in his *Libro d'amor di caritá*, he made a synthesis of his ideas and drew up a balance-sheet of his Venetian mission. The severity of the principles of reform that he preached, going so far as to forbid the brothers the use of *books, were considered excessive by some and provoked a split in the group of the reformed.

In late 1399, a procession of *penitents, the Whites, made its entry into Venice. Suspect in the eyes of the authorities, the Whites were condemned. But on 18 November of the same year, Dominici headed another – unauthorized – procession, which brought together 150 persons, "women and men, religious and *seculars", clothed in white and crying "Misericordia!". Dominici was arrested, with the other organisers of the procession, and condemned to exile for five years. Daniel Bornstein has recently tried to show that the procession led by Dominici can only partially be associated with that of the Whites. The piety of the former, for example, was christocentric, while that of the Whites was Marian.

The same year, Pope *Boniface IX firstly confirmed John Dominici in his office of vicar-general, then revoked it by reason of the opposition of the Preachers of Italy. Dominici's ecclesiological vision then became more and more sombre, taking on apocalyptic accents. He settled at *Florence and, with the future archbishop of that city, *Antonino Pierozzi (St *Antoninus), boosted the *observance of his order and founded a *convent at Fiesole (1406). Elected *vicar of Santa Maria Novella, he recommenced his preaching.

Dominici also played a role in the events of the *Great Schism. After the death of Innocent VII (1406), he was sent to *Rome by

Above: *St Paul preaching to the Romans.* Below: *David and St Andrew.* Miniature from the *Petites Heures de Jean de Berry, c.*1390. Paris, BNF (Ms lat. 18014, fol. 1 v°).

the Florentines, with the aim of bringing together the two *popes, Gregory XII and *Benedict XIII, at Florence. The failure of this mission, as well as his favourable position towards Gregory XII, who had made him a *cardinal, earned him the enmity of the Florentines. Ordered by Pope *Martin V to combat the *Hussites in *Bohemia, he died at *Buda on 10 June 1419.

His best-known works are the *Libro d'amor di carità*, the *Regola del governo di cura familiare* (written between 1401 and 1403 for Bartolomea degli Obizzi), widely circulated in the late Middle Ages, and the *Lucula noctis* (1405), in which he warned against the dangers of the *pagan culture that he believed was being revived by *humanism.

P. Stella, "Saggio bio-bibliografico", *MDom*, new series, 1, 1970. – R. L. Oelchslin, "Jean Dominici", *DSp*, 8, 1974, 473-480. – D. Bornstein, "Giovanni Dominici, the Bianchi, and Venice", *JMRS*, 23, 1993, 143-171.

Rosa Maria Dessì

**JOHN IBN SABBĀ' (14th c.).** *Copto-Arab author of the 14th c., whose life is virtually unknown. We know only that he wrote a short encyclopedia of the religious sciences, entitled the *Precious Pearl Treating of the Ecclesiastical Sciences*. Divided into 115 short chapters, this manual deals with the following subjects: the *Trinity, sacred history (from the creation of Adam to the coming of Christ), commentary on the *Lord's Prayer and the *Apostles' Creed, Christian morality and discipline, ecclesiastical law, administration of the *sacraments and liturgical ceremonies. Published twice at Cairo, the work is of real interest for knowledge of the Coptic rite and its historical evolution. Chapters 1-56 have been edited and translated by J. Périer (*PO*, 16, 591-760).

J. Périer, *La perle précieuse traitant des sciences ecclésiastiques, chapitres I-LVI, par Jean, fils d'Abou Zakariyâ, surnommé Ibn Sabâ'* (Arabic text, Fr. tr.), *PO*, 16, 591-760.

Gérard Troupeau

**JOHN OF BERRY (1340-1416).** John, duke of Berry, was the third son of John II the Good, king of *France, and Bonne of Luxemburg. During his father's reign he was count of Poitou (present at the battle of Poitiers in 1356), knight of the ephemeral Order of the Star in 1356, lieutenant of his elder brother Charles, duke of *Normandy and dauphin of Viennois, "this side the Loire and throughout the *langue d'*oc*". He received the peerage-duchies of Berry and Auvergne in 1360. The same year he married Jeanne d'Armagnac. Following the treaty of Brétigny, he was sent as a hostage to *England until 1369. On his return to France, his brother *Charles V established him as lieutenant general for Berry, Auvergne, Bourbonnais, Forez, Sologne, Touraine, *Anjou, Maine and Normandy, etc. He commanded the royal *army against the English. On the king's death in 1380, he was part of the council of regency. The same year he was appointed governor and lieutenant general in *Languedoc. He remained so despite *revolts (the Tuchins) until 1388. This position was taken from him when the "Marmousets", *Charles VI's mainstay, gained power. Widowed of Jeanne d'Armagnac, in 1389 he married Jeanne de Boulogne. It was a failure. When the king became mad, John shared authority with his brother Philip of Burgundy and his nephew Louis of Orléans, the king's brother. He attempted to reconcile the two houses, condemned the murder of the duke of Orléans by John the Fearless in 1407 and favoured the Armagnacs in 1410. The league of Gien constituted the Armagnac party of which, despite himself, he became head. During the revolt of the Cabochiens at *Paris, his goods at the castle of Bicêtre and the hôtel de Nesles were pillaged in 1411. He died in 1416.

John of Berry left a reputation as a sumptuous and enlightened patron, a lover of *belles-lettres* and *illuminations. His contemporaries mainly remembered his grasping nature. His *castles, *palaces, hôtels and *houses were connected with his estates: palaces at *Poitiers, Bourges and Riom, castles at Concressault, Mehun-sur-Yèvre, Lusignan, Nonette, Bicêtre, near Paris, residences at Dourdan, Étampes, Genouilly and Hôtel de Nesles at Paris. The luxury of these monuments and the quality of the *artists were famous in his lifetime. Philip the Bold sent Klaus *Sluter to Mehun-sur-Yèvre to "see and admire" the creations of André *Beauneveu.

John of Berry employed the greatest artists of the time: the sculptors André Beauneveu and Jean de Cambrai, the *goldsmiths Jean de Morselles, Hermann Riu and Jean Chenu, the painters Beauneveu, *Jacquemart of Hesdin, the *Boucicaut Master and the de *Limbourg brothers. Of his sumptuous collection, of which detailed inventories were drawn up in the first years of the 15th c., little remains. Some manuscripts are preserved in the French National Library (*Grandes Heures*, *Très Belles Heures*, Psalter), at Chantilly (*Très Riches Heures*), in the Royal Library of Brussels (*Book of Hours) and the New York Cloisters (*Belles Heures*).

Like his brothers Louis of Anjou and Philip the Bold and his nephew Louis of Orléans, he tried to found a house, but had no male successor. Only his emblems, the bear, the wounded swan, the *monogram "E. V." and the device *le temps verra*, sometimes associated with his arms (the *semé* of France broken by a border engrailed with gules), his crest as a son of France (the double *lily) and the prestigious arms of his mother, Bonne of Luxemburg, perpetuate his memory by their imprint on the manuscripts, monuments, paving-stones, his *tomb which ornaments the *Sainte-Chapelle of Bourges, and other works of art.

F. Lehoux, *Jean de France, duc de Berry, sa vie, son action politique (1340-1416)*, Paris, 1966-1968 (4 vol.). – M. Meiss, *French Painting in the Time of Jean de Berry, the Late Fourteenth Century and the Patronage of the Duke*, London, New York, 1967 (2 vol.). – M. Meiss, *French Painting in the Time of Jean de Berry*, 2nd ed., 2 vol., London, 1969. – J. Longnon, R. Cazelles, *The Très Riches Heures of Jean, Duke of Berry*, New York, 1969. – C. Sterling, *La Peinture médiévale à Paris, 1300-1500*, 1, Paris, 1987.

Christian de Mérindol

**JOHN OF BRIDLINGTON (*c.*1320-1379).** John Thweng was born in *c.*1320 at Thweng-on-the-Wolds (Yorkshire). He seems to have belonged to a family of gentry, the Thwengs of Kilton. He appears to have known the celebrated hermit *Richard Rolle, who had a strong influence on him before his death in 1349. In 1340 he entered the Augustinian *priory of Bridlington in Yorkshire, where he remained until his death in 1379, becoming firstly novice-master, *cellarer, then *prior from 1361 until his death, so he was neither a *recluse nor a hermit like Rolle.

His *spirituality seems to be influenced both by the mystical tradition of northern England, well represented by authors like Richard Rolle and Walter *Hilton, and by the traditions of his order as they developed on the continent, notably in the Netherlands by Jan van *Ruysbroeck and Gerhard *Groote; but none of the works attributed to him seems to have survived. After his death, anecdotes of his life were systematically copied and circulated at Bridlington, while from 1377 he was credited with authorship of the prophecies of Robert of Bridlington on which John Erghome, an Augustinian, had written a political commentary (for Humphrey Bohun, earl of *Hereford). Canon Hugh collected the saint's *miracles in a *biography from 1380 and his cult took off: it was promoted first by the lords Neville of Raby (whose confessor was an Austin canon of Bridlington, William Sleightholme), then by the archbishop of *York, Alexander Neville; *Richard II also took an interest in it. Bridlington rapidly became one of the most popular English *pilgrimages and remained so throughout the 15th century. In 1401, Thweng was officially canonized; a second life of the saint was later drawn up by John Capgrave and inserted in his *Nova Legenda Angliae*.

Certain aspects of this cult sometimes took on an anti-Lancastrian tone, as did another cult, that of "Saint" Richard Scrope, the archbishop of York executed by order of *Henry IV. But that did not prevent the Lancastrians, particularly *Henry VI, from having a special devotion to him; Thomas Beaufort, duke of Exeter, and *Henry V made the pilgrimage to Bridlington. Lives of the saint insist on his kindness, his humanity and good sense: Thweng was primarily a cellarer generous to beggars and to his *peasants, and a model prior, sharply dressing down those who came to congratulate him on his "miracles".

*Vita S. Joannis de Bridlingtona, ActaSS Oct., Collecta Digesta*, 5, Brussels, 1786. – J. Capgrave, *Nova Legenda Angliae*, C. Horstman (ed.), Oxford, 1901. *DNB*, 1885-1900. – J. S. Purvis, "Saint John of Bridlington", *Journal of Bridlington and Augustinian Society*, 2, 1924. – J. Hughes, *Pastors and Visionaries*, Woodbridge, 1988. – A.G. Rigg, "John of Bridlington's Prophecy: a New Look", *Spec.*, 63, 1988, 596-613.

Jean-Philippe Genet

**JOHN OF BRIENNE (*c.*1144-1237).** John of Brienne was king of *Jerusalem from 1212 to 1225 by his marriage to Mary, heiress to the *crown. During his reign, the monarchical power weakened in comparison with the strength of the *military orders (*Templars and *Hospitallers) and the Italian communes. During the fifth *crusade (1217-1221), he tried in vain to prevent the stranglehold of the legate Pelagius on the Frankish *army. He had no more luck in his expedition against *Armenia (1220), which he claimed in the name of his second wife Stephanie, daughter of Leo II of Armenia. In 1225, the marriage of his daughter Isabelle-Yolande to *Frederick II rebounded on him, since he was obliged to abdicate in their favour. He died in 1237 after having got himself crowned co-emperor of the Latin Empire of Constantinople in 1231.

J. M. Buckley, "The Problematical Octogenarianism of John of Brienne", *Spec.*, 1957, 315-322. – J. Prawer, *Histoire du royaume latin de Jérusalem*, 2, Paris, 1975, 124-197 (2 vol.).

Anne-Marie Eddé

**JOHN OF CAPESTRANO (1386-1456).** Born at Capestrano (L'Aquila), John studied law at *Perugia and became a judge there in 1413-1414. In 1415, he took the habit of the Friars Minor and became part of the movement of the *Observance, of which he became an eminent representative. In 1426 he intervened successfully to defend *Bernardino of Siena against the accusation of *heresy. After having tried in vain to favour the unity of the order by drawing up the Martinian Constitutions of 1430, in 1443 he became *vicar general of the Italian observants (to whom he addressed a circular letter) and in 1446 he facilitated the order's *de facto* separation into *conventuals and observants. He acted as inquisitor against dissident *Franciscan elements, against the **fraticelli* (in 1426-1427 and in 1449) and against the adherents of the sect of the *Free Spirit (1437); from 1436 he favoured the regular reform of the tertiaries, for whom he wrote in 1440 the *Defensorium tertii ordinis beati Francisci*.

Also very active in promoting the observant reform within the Order of *Poor Clares, in 1445 he wrote a commentary on the Rule of the Franciscan *nuns: at *Besançon he met *Colette of Corbie, during a political mission to *Burgundy and *Flanders (1442-1443) which gave him a way to promote the spread of the Minorite Observance in those regions. He did the same in 1451-1453 in Austria, *Germany and *Poland, where he had been sent by Pope *Pius II to slow down the spread of *Hussite *doctrine. Appointed preacher of the crusade against the *Turks after the fall of *Constantinople (1453), he took part in the victorious siege of Belgrade in 1456, but died soon after at Ilok (*Slovenia), 23 October.

As itinerant preacher in various regions of *Italy, he was intensely active in pacification in his own home country (at Lanciano, Sulmona, L'Aquila) and particularly outstanding for his ethical and social *preaching, against luxury: of his numerous writings, only the *Tractatus de cupiditate*, which reflects the content of his preaching at *Verona during *Lent 1438, was edited in the 15th c. (Cologne, 1480). The *Speculum clericorum* derives from a synodal preaching held at *Trent in 1439, while the *Tractatus de* *conscientia serenanda* was written in preparation for Lenten preaching at *Milan in 1441. A defender of papal primacy, between 1438 and 1444 he wrote a treatise *De auctoritate pape et concilii*. He was canonized only in 1690, by Pope Alexander VIII.

A. Chiappini, *La produzione letteraria di S. Giovanni da Capestrano. Trattati, lettere, sermoni*, Gubbio, 1927. – L. Luszcki, *De sermonibus S. Ioannis a Capistrano. Studium historico-criticum*, Rome, 1961. – J. Hofer, *Johannes Kapistran. Ein Leben im Kampf um die Reform der Kirche*, Rome, 1964-1965 (2nd ed.). – *S. Giovanni da Capestrano nella Chiesa e nella società del suo tempo*, E. and L. Pásztor (ed.), L'Aquila, 1989. – *S. Giovanni da Capestrano: un bilancio storiografico*, E. Pásztor (ed.), 1999.

Roberto Rusconi

**JOHN OF CHELLES (died *c.*1258).** We know practically nothing of the life and work of the *architect John of Chelles. The sole information concerning him is the inscription on the base of the south portal of the transept of Notre-Dame at *Paris, probably engraved by *Pierre de Montreuil in homage to his predecessor. It suggests that John of Chelles, put in charge of building the new transept in *c.*1250, finished the north arm but died *c.*1258 before having finished the south arm, completed on a different plan by his successor Pierre de Montreuil. John of Chelles is also thought to be the author of the nave *chapels adjoining the north transept. Certain archaeologists, basing themselves on the analysis of the tracery of the bays, attribute to him the upper parts of the choir of *Le Mans cathedral, the chapel of Saint-Germain-en-Laye and, at the abbey church of *Saint-Denis, the south arm of the transept except for the *rose window, and the rose of the north transept. A text dated 9 Sept 1416 cites an architect named Pierre de Chelles, also master of works of Paris cathedral. He may be a descendant.

A. Prache, "Un architecte du XIIIe siècle et son oeuvre: Pierre de Montreuil", *Dossiers de l'archéologie*, 47, Paris, 1980, 29. – M. Bouttier, "La reconstruction de l'abbatiale de Saint-Denis au XIIIe siècle", *BM*, 145, 1987, 357-386. – A. Erlande-Brandenburg, *Notre-Dame de Paris*, Paris, 1991, 155-163.

Philippe Plagnieux

**JOHN OF DALYATHA or JOHN SABAS (second half of 8th c.).** Syro-oriental monk of El Qardou (south-east Turkey) and then in the nearby mountain of Dalyatha, *i.e.* "the vine shoots". He left 25 *sermons and 51 *letters; the latter, recently edited, reveal a very great mystical author. Little inclined to general views and systematic expositions, he is more a careful master of the advancement of souls along the steps of a way leading to the "mystical life, conceived by the author as the anticipated *resurrection, fruit of *baptism and the *Eucharist" (*DSp*, 8, 1974, 451).

R. Beulay, *La Collection des lettres de Jean de Dalyatha*, *PO*, 39, fasc. 3, no. 180, Turnhout, 1978 (Syriac text and Fr. tr.).

R. Beulay, *DSp*, 8, 1974, 449-452. – R. Beulay, *L'Enseignement spirituel de Jean de Dalyatha, mystique syro-oriental du VIIIe siècle*, Paris, 1990.

Micheline Albert

**JOHN OF DAMASCUS (second half of 7th c. - before 753?).** Born to a family of Christian Arabs who played an important role under the *Umayyad *caliphs, John, son of Mansur, received a sound education in Greek. Active at the court of *Damascus, he later retired to the laura of St Sabas, east of *Jerusalem, where he composed works that make him one of the most important Orthodox theologians.

His fundamental work, the *Fount of Knowledge*, has three parts: a philosophical introduction, the *Dialectic*; a treatise *On the Heresies*; and an *Exposition of the Faith*. This work, which recapitulates the heritage of Chalcedonian orthodoxy, had considerable influence in the East and was also known in the West (*Thomas Aquinas). It also reflected the contemporary world: chapter 101 of the treatise *On the Heresies* is given over to *Islam. Damascene also composed a vast *florilegium, the *Sacra parallela* (*Hiera*), in three books: the first two – *On God*, *On Man* – were organised alphabetically, while the third opposed *vices and virtues in parallel chapters. This florilegium, lost in its original form, is known only by derived collections. Among the numerous treatises and *homilies surviving under John's name, we must also mention the *Discourses on Images*, dating from the 730s – the earliest surviving extended apologia for holy *images. These respond – from Palestine, land of Islam – to the *iconoclast heresy that had just made its appearance in the Empire under Leo III. These discourses earned John a condemnation – doubtless posthumous – at the iconoclast council of Hiera in 753. However, his memory was acclaimed at the 2nd council of *Nicaea (787).

Since then, John, common *doctor of the Orthodox and Roman churches, has been in the first rank among the Fathers of *Orthodoxy. His poetic work, which contains important liturgical pieces, is still ill-defined. The memory of St John of Damascus (or John Damascene) is celebrated on 4 December.

J. Nasrallah, *Saint Jean de Damas. Son époque, sa vie, son oeuvre*, Harissa, 1950. – B. Studer, "Jean Damascène", *DSp*, 8, 1974, 452-466. – A. Siclari, *Giovanni di Damasco*, Perugia, 1978. – A. Louth, *A Christian Theologian at the Court of the Caliph*, London, 1995.

Bernard Flusin

**JOHN OF FREIBURG (died 1314).** Born near *Freiburg im Breisgau, Johann Rumsik, a *Dominican, studied at *Strasbourg where he had *Ulrich as professor. Around 1280, he was assigned to the convent of Freiburg, where he held the offices of *prior and *reader; he died on 10 March 1314. His contemporaries ranged him among the most illustrious theologians of the time; today he is considered a particularly eminent representative of medieval penitential literature. All his work tends to help confessors in the exercise of their *ministry. He began by updating *Raymond of Peñafort's *Summa de casibus poenitentia*; to it he added an index to facilitate consultation.

Around 1290, he wrote his own work: *Summa confessorum*, from which he made an abridgement, *Manuale confessorum* (*confessors' manual). For the benefit of priests "with no training and little experience", he wrote a *Confessionale*.

Finally, after 1298, he supplemented the *Summa confessorum* with *Statuta* inspired by *Boniface VIII's *Sext*, *i.e.* the complements added to the *Corpus* of *canon law. Only the *Summa confessorum* and the *Statuta* have been published (*Augsburg, 1476).

In his works, John of Freiburg appeals to the authority of the canonists (especially Henry of Susa, called *Hostiensis, † 1271), but also to the masters of the theology faculty: *Albert the Great, *Peter of Tarentaise, *Ulrich of Strasbourg and *Thomas Aquinas (his preferred author).

P. Michaud-Quantin, *Sommes de casuistique et manuels de confession au Moyen Âge (XIIe-XVIe siècles)*, Louvain-Lille-Montreal, 1962, 43-50. – P. Michaud-Quantin, "Jean de Fribourg", *DSp*, 8, 1974, 529-531. – T. Kaeppeli, *SOPMA*, 2, 1975, 428-436; *ibid.*, 4, 1993, 151-152.

Jean Longère

**JOHN OF GARLAND (*c.*1195-*c.*1272).** Teacher of *grammar and *rhetoric at the university of *Paris, John of Garland, born in England in *c.*1195, lived in Paris from 1220. Author of treatises on grammar, a treatise on poetics, *Dictionarii*, a treatise on the allegorical interpretation of Ovid's *Metamorphoses*, an *epic poem (*De triumphis Ecclesiae*), poems dedicated to the Virgin, etc., he celebrated the transfer of the knowledge of the Ancients to France – "Paris, like a living spring, irrigates the whole West" – but deplored the decline of literary studies.

*De triumphis Ecclesiae*, T. Wright (ed.), London, 1856. – T. Lawler, *The "Parisiana Poetria" of John of Garland*, New Haven-London, 1974. – *Epithalamium beate virginis Marie*, A. Saiani (ed.), Florence, 1995.

A.G. Rigg, "John of Garland", *A History of Anglo-Latin Literature 1066-1422*, Cambridge, 1992, 163-76.

Michel Stanesco

**JOHN OF GENOA (late 13th c.).** John of Genoa (Johannes de Janua or Giovanni Balbi) was one of the representatives of the late 13th-c. Italian Thomist school. This *Dominican who died in the odour of *sanctity became famous thanks mainly to his *Catholicon*, a grammatical and lexical treatise, completed in 1286. The work pursues a purely practical aim such as was required by the study of law. He was also the author of a dialogue between *soul and spirit (*Dialogus de quaestionibus anime ad spiritum*, 1272). The soul asks questions of the spirit, which represents the rational part of *man. Divided into nine parts and drawing widely on the patristic and Arabic sources then known, the dialogue embraces the essential questions of Thomist *theology.

M. Grabmann, *Mittelalterliches Geistesleben. Abhandlungen zur Geschichte der Scholastik und Mystik*, Munich, 1926, 369-373. – T. Kaeppeli, *SOPMA*, 2, 1975, 379-383.

Coloman Viola

**JOHN OF GORZE (*c.*900-974).** John was born at Vandières, *c.*900, to a family of rich *peasants, dependent on St Peter's abbey at *Metz. He received an *education among the Benedictine monks of Saint-Mihiel (Meuse) and completed it at Metz. After having had to return to run the paternal farm and look after his mother and brothers, he came into contact with Bishop Dado and Count Ricuin of *Verdun, entered the clerical state, received a church at Fontenoy, then began to search for a religious life that accorded with his aspirations. He frequented the *canons of Toul cathedral, a hermit of the Argonne, the *nuns of St Peter's, Metz, where he was hebdomadary, proposed with his friends to retire to a monastery, went to southern Italy to look for a refuge, and finally entered *Gorze in spring 934 with six companions at the instigation of Bishop Adalbero I of Metz. Assisting Abbot Einold, he put all his efforts into re-establishing and managing the temporality of the *abbey, to which he gave the necessary material *foundation to carry through the enterprise of restoring Benedictine life. After having held other positions in the monastery, he became *abbot at the end of his life and succeeded Einold.

His life is told by Abbot John of Saint-Arnoul. The work shows the tribulations of the initial search, John's embassy to the *emir of *Cordova in 953-956, and portraits of the reformed monks. That of John appears to conform to the model of the Benedictine abbot as seen in St *Benedict. He combined the practical efficiency of a peasant with the *ascesis of a monk very demanding on himself, entirely at the service of others, firm in his rule and charitable at the same time, avid of reading and *prayers. Tradition wrongly attributes to him the *Miracles of St Gorgo*, where he is often portrayed running the abbey and which repeat part of his Life. John was the object of a local cult.

*Vita Johannis abbatis gorziensis*, *MGH.SS*, 4, 1841, 335-377.

J. Leclercq, "Jean de Gorze et la vie religieuse au X^e^ siècle", *Saint Chrodegang*, Metz, 1967, 133-152. – W. Goez, *Gestalten des Hochmittelalters*, Darmstadt, 1983, 54-69. – *L'Abbaye de Gorze au X^e^ siècle*, Nancy, 1993. – Jean de Saint-Amand, *La Vie de Jean abbé de Gorze*, M. Parisse (ed.), Paris, 1999.

Michel Parisse

**JOHN OF JANDUN (died 1328).** John of Jandun was one of the most representative figures of what has been called "Latin *Averroism" or "heterodox Aristotelianism" (E. Van Steenberghen), at the arts *faculty of the university of *Paris at the dawn of the 14th century. Friend of the doctor and astrologer Pietro d'Abano and of *Marsilius of Padua, one of the leaders of the anti-curialist opposition, he was long thought to be the co-author of the *Defensor pacis*, since he was excommunicated by *John XXII at the same time as his friend Marsilius. This opinion is now contested, but the close connection between Jandun, a master of arts at the university of Paris, and Marsilius of Padua is well attested: both fled to the court of the Emperor Louis of Bavaria and John XXII's three *bulls of *excommunication against the *Defensor pacis* condemn them together. John of Jandun's known work consists mainly of commentaries on the works of *Aristotle, notably the *Metaphysics* and the *De anima* in which he adopts the Averroist doctrine of the one *Intellect for all men, eternal and separate. On the political level, his preference was for a city governed by sages, in which the most perfect felicity would reign. Demonstration of *creation *ex nihilo* is impossible. Happiness in this world consists in *wisdom.

A. Gewirth, "John of Jandun and the Defensor Pacis", *Spec.*, 23, 1948, 267-272. – J. McClintock, *Perversity and Error, Studies in the "Averroist" John of Jandun*, Bloomington, 1956. – L. Schmugge, *Johannes von Jandun, 1285/1289-1328*, Stuttgart, 1966.

Jeannine Quillet

**JOHN OF LA ROCHELLE (*c.*1190/1200-1245).** The age and career of the *Franciscan John of La Rochelle (de Rupella) remain mysterious. He was already a Franciscan and a master of theology under *William of Auxerre in 1238 (*Chartularium univ. Paris*, I, Paris, 1889, 158, n. 108). *Alexander of Hales made him share his chair as regent master of the *Paris *studium*. He died in Lyon on 3 Feb 1245 while preparing the first council of *Lyon.

John of La Rochelle composed *Postillae in Danielem*, *in Matthaeum*, *in Marcum*, *in Lucam*, and the *Summa super epistolas beati Pauli*. He was able, with remarkable clarity, to condense the knowledge of his time into *tractatus* or **summae*: the *Summa de anima*, the *Tractatus de divisione multiplici potentiarum animae*, the *Summa de vitiis*, the *Summa de sacramentis*, *Quaestiones disputatae* and *Sermones de tempore*, *de sanctis* and *de communi*. It is almost certain that manuscript Vat. lat. 691 represents the fair copy of his commentary on the *Sentences.

Situated at the very heart of the break-up of the traditional framework in which the 12th c. had cast the study of the *soul within the Christian project of *salvation, he was the last witness to that tradition, in the *Tractatus* written after 1233, the *Summa de vitiis* written before 1236 and the *Summa de anima* after 1236. He favoured the change from the *Platonist view of the irascible power of flight to a positive and "aggressive" view of the irascible power, a power of daring according to *William of Auxerre, a power of the "arduous" according to John of La Rochelle. Thus the theological *virtue of *hope finds its specific object there.

He created the treatise on eternal law, synthesizing the texts of Augustine, a synthesis that *Thomas Aquinas perfected. Finally he witnessed to the exploration of the theology of *grace, the virtues and the gifts in his *Quaestiones disputatae de gratia*.

But his greatest merit comes from his role as producer and redactor-in-chief of the *Summa theologiae*, under the direction of Alexander of Hales and with the materials accumulated by him, a summa called for that reason the *Summa fratris Alexandri*.

*Summa fratris Alexandri. Tomus IV. Liber Tertius. Prolegomena*, V. Doucet (ed.), Quaracchi, 1948. – Jean de La Rochelle, *Tractatus de divisione multiplici potentiarum animae*, P. Michaud-Quantin (ed.), Paris, 1964. – Jean de La Rochelle, *Summa de anima*, J.-G. Bougerol (ed.), Paris, 1995.

P. Minges, "De quibusdam scriptis fr. Ioannis de Rupella", *AFH*, 6, 1913, 597-622. – L. Hödl, *Die neuen Quästionen der Gnadentheologie des Iohannes von Rupella OM († 1245) in cod. lat. Paris 14726*, Munich, 1964. – I. Brady, "Jean de La Rochelle", *DSp*, 8, 1974, 599-602. – J.-G. Bougerol, "La Glose sur les Sentences du manuscrit Vat. lat. 691", *Anton.*, 55, 1980, 108-173. – J.-G. Bougerol, "Inventaire du fonds Jean de La Rochelle aux archives de l'Évêché de La Rochelle", *AFH*, 76, 1993.

Jacques-Guy Bougerol

**JOHN OF MATHA (*c.*1160-1213/1214).** St John of Matha, a Provençal, died at *Rome in 1213-1214. At *Paris he was trained in the milieu of the Victorines, held the post of master of theology and was ordained priest in 1193-1194. During his first *mass, he conceived the project of freeing Christians fallen into Muslim hands. This was the time of the unsuccessful third *crusade, the victories of *Saladin and the Muslim capture of *Jerusalem. With the aim of setting up his organisation – a sort of International Red Cross – he spent four or five years at Cerfroid (Aisne) looking for followers and benefactors, and wrote a Rule of Life with the help of Absalon of St Victor, Eudes of Sully and *Innocent III. The organisation was known as the Order of the Holy Trinity for the Redemption of Captives (*Trinitarians), and is considered a singular phenomenon as coming into being totally unarmed and with humanitarian aims in a context of Holy War: crusade and **jihād*.

J. W. Baldwin, "Masters at Paris from 1179 to 1215: a Social Perspective", *Renaissance and Renewal in the Twelfth Century*, Oxford, 1985, 138-172. – J. Pujana, "Trinitaires", *DSp*, 15, 1991, 1261-1269. – G. Cipollone, *Cristianità-Islam, cattività e liberazione in nome di Dio. Il tempo di Innocenzo III dopo 'il 1187'*, *MHP*, 60, 1992 (repr., Rome, 1996), 393 f. – G. Cipollone, "Jean de Matha", *DHGE*, fasc. 156-157, 1998, 263-276.

Giulio Cipollone

**JOHN OF MONTECORVINO (1247-1328).** A missionary. Born near Salerno, before entering religion John had been a knight, a judge and a doctor; so he had had a *university education. Becoming a Friar Minor, he held the position of *reader in theology; he seems to have belonged to the spiritual current.

He doubtless came into contact with the East before 1288. That year, the *pope sent him to carry an exposition of the faith to Argun, khan of Persia; he may have travelled with Bishop Barsauma who set out for the East. John visited Catholicos Yahballaha III and other prelates, as well as King Hethum of Armenia, and brought their letters to Rieti where *Nicholas IV was living. Nicholas entrusted him with his replies and letters of recommendation, in July 1289. From *Venice, John passed through Cilician *Armenia and Tabriz and reached *India in company with the Dominican Nicholas of Pistoia and the *merchant Pietro da Lucalongo. Staying three months at Quilon, he visited the tomb of St Thomas and baptized a hundred pagans. Nicholas died; John embarked for *China and brought a letter from the pope to the Qaghan *Qubilai (Kublai); in his capital, Khanbaliq, he built a church and a *convent which he peopled with some 40 children ransomed from slavery, translating and copying *liturgical books for them thanks to his knowledge of Turkish. At the same time, he built another church at Olon-süme, capital of the *Öngüt, whither he had been called by King George who embraced Catholicism; but the king's death put an end to that enterprise.

John suffered difficulties from the *Nestorians and from a Lombard surgeon; he had nevertheless baptized 6000 persons when he sent a first letter to the West (1305) and another 400 before the second (1306). This news decided *Clement V to erect Khanbaliq into an *archbishopric and to provide for it, by giving him six *suffragan bishops (of which only three were able to join him); he assigned one of them to the see of Zayton.

John had meanwhile built a second convent and been invited to *Ethiopia. The arrival of his co-workers (1309-1310) allowed him to discharge the Latin-rite community onto them and devote himself first to the Armenians, numerous in the *Mongol Empire, and then to the Alans of Greek rite, who had come from the *Caucasus and formed the imperial guard. These regarded him as their religious leader. John held an eminent rank at Khanbaliq, as *Odoric of Pordenone, who lived there in 1322-1326, tells us; the qaghan surrounded him with consideration and supplied his needs. He also benefited from the help of Lucalongo, who had built one of the convents at his own expense, and doubtless from the liberality of other passing merchants, "Franks" or Armenians.

He died in 1328, regarded as a saint by the Alans who, soon after, asked the pope for a new archbishop. The Latin Church has beatified him.

A. Van den Wyngaert, *Jean de Montecorvin, o.m., premier archevêque de Khanbaliq (Pékin). 1247-1328*, Lille, 1924 (taken from *FrFr*, 6, 1923). – J. Richard, *La Papauté et les Missions d'Orient au Moyen Âge*, Rome, 1977.

Jean Richard

**JOHN OF MONTREUIL (1354-1418).** John of Montreuil (Jean Charlin, in Latin Johannes de Monasterio Sicco, de Monsterolio), French *humanist, was born at Monthureux-le-Sec (Vosges) in 1354 and died at *Paris in 1418. Beneficiary of a scholarship at the *Collège de Navarre* in Paris, one of his fellow-students was *Pierre d'Ailly. A master of arts, he did not study theology, but, being a priest, he received various *benefices, including that of *provost of the *chapter of Saint-Pierre at Lille.

Entering the royal *chancery, he soon specialized in diplomacy. His first mission (1384) took him to *Tuscany, where he came into contact with the chancellor of Florence, Coluccio *Salutati, the most illustrious *humanist of the time. This meeting left a profound mark on one who is sometimes called "the first true humanist in France". All his life he was in contact with Italian scholars, including the Milanese Ambrogio Migli, secretary of

Louis of Orléans, with whom he was not slow to get embroiled. Even with his best friends, like Nicolas de Clamanges, he sometimes quarrelled, but these were primarily literary jousts. One quarrel remains famous: the "debate over the *Roman de la Rose*" (1401-1403) which set him and the Col brothers, Gontier and Pierre, against *Christine de Pizan and chancellor *Gerson. Some see this as proof of a deep-seated antagonism between "humanists" and "theologians"; in reality, being closely connected with Pierre d'Ailly, a master of theology, John did not hide his admiration for Gerson, a friend and former student of d'Ailly's, whose political opinions were indeed quite close to his own. On the professional level, Montreuil took part in numerous embassies and one of his main fields of activity was that of relations between Church and kingdom and hence the problems of the *Great Schism. This had just ended when, in June 1418, he perished in the massacres that followed the capture of *Paris by the Burgundians; his *library – probably one of the richest of the time – disappeared with him.

Among his *books were certainly precious manuscripts of works by Cicero and other authors of Antiquity, which he sought as avidly as his friend Clamanges; like the latter, he had undertaken to introduce the custom of humanistic writing into France.

By chance, autographs of his main works have survived, probably because he did not keep them with him, but in his office at the chancery. In particular there are two collections of his Latin epistles, a first-rate source for knowledge of the political and intellectual life of the time, as well as polemical treatises against the claims of the king of *England to the throne of *France, sometimes written in a clear and vigorous French, greatly superior to his *Latin which does not attain the elegance of Clamanges's.

Jean de Montreuil, *Opera*, 1: *Epistolario*, E. Ornato (ed.), Turin, 1966; 2: *L'Oeuvre historique et polémique*, N. Grevy (ed.), E. Ornato (ed.), G. Ouy (ed.), Turin, 1975; 3: *Textes divers, appendices et tables*, N. Grevy-Pons (ed.), E. Ornato (ed.), G. Ouy (ed.), Paris, 1981; 4: *Monsteroliana*, E. Ornato (ed.), G. Ouy (ed.), N. Pons (ed.), Paris, 1986 (bibl.).

Gilbert Ouy

**JOHN OF NAPLES (14th c.).** An Italian *Dominican, an indirect disciple of St *Thomas Aquinas, he taught at *Paris between 1315 and 1317, then at *Naples, and concerned himself with the *canonization of his master. Author of a commentary – now lost – on the *Sentences*, composed between 1311 and 1337. We also owe him *Quaestiones disputatae* and *Quaestiones de quodlibet*. In connection with *theology, he explored questions of *metaphysics: the problem of continual becoming and permanence of *being; the real distinction between the existence and the essence of creatures. He also took part in discussions on the supremacy of the *pope's power over the *temporal power of the emperor and princes.

*Ioannis de Neapoli Quaestiones Variae*, Ridgewood (NJ), 1966.

M. Grabmann, *Mittelalterliches Geistesleben. Abhandlungen zur Geschichte der Scholastik und Mystik*, Munich, 1926, 374-384. – T. Kaeppeli, *SOPMA*, 2, 1975, 495-498.

Coloman Viola

**JOHN OF NEPOMUK (*c.*1340-1393).** Born at Pomuk (now Nepomuk), a large village in *Bohemia where his father was mayor, he worked for several years in the archiepiscopal chancery before being appointed curate of a *parish of the Old Town of *Prague. In 1383, he left to study *canon law at the university of *Padua, where in 1387 he obtained the title of *doctor decretorum*. On his return to Bohemia, he held important ecclesiastical posts and in 1389 became *vicar general of John of Jenstein, archbishop of Prague. Arrested on 20 March 1393 by order of King *Wenceslas IV, he was tortured to death and his body thrown into the river Vltava. The reasons for the royal anger have not been entirely elucidated: according to the pious version, John Nepomuk was punished for his refusal to divulge the secrets of the confessional; but a more realistic explanation presents him as expiatory victim of the political struggles between the archbishop of Prague and the king of Bohemia. Oral tradition has even deformed the date of his death, and the *chronicle of Hajek (1541) speaks of two people struck down by the king's vengeance: John Nepomucenus († 1383) and *Doctor Johanek of Pomuk († 1393). This erroneous information also appears in the *canonization trial of John Nepomucenus (canonized 19 March 1729).

P. de Vooght, *Jean de Pomuk*, *RHE*, 48, 1953, 777-795. – H.L. Zollner, *Johannes von Nepomuk zu Ehren*, Karlsruhe, 1992. – *Johannes von Nepomuk 1393-1993*, R. Baumstark (ed.), J. Von Herzogenberg (ed.), P. Volk (ed.), Munich, 1993. – V. Vlnas, *Jan Nepomucký, česká legenda* [John of Nepomuk, a Czech legend], Prague, 1993.

Jana Zachová

**JOHN OF NEUMARKT (before 1320-1380).** John of Neumarkt or of Středa, *chancellor of *Charles IV from 1353 to 1374 (save 1364-1365), contributed to establishing the imperial power by bringing representatives of the new forces of society into the *chancery and introducing a formulary destined for great success. His translations (including *prayers) found interest with the emperor (whose links with the **Devotio moderna* remain to be elucidated) more than they belonged to the *friendship between Neumarkt and the first *humanists (*Petrarch). His services to the court gained him the *bishoprics of Leitomischl and Olmütz.

W. Höver, "Johann von Neumarkt", *VerLex*, 3, 1983, 686-695 (2nd ed.). – P. Moraw, "Grundzüge der Kanzleigeschichte Kaisers Karl IV.", *Zeitschrift für historische Forschung*, 12, Berlin, 1985, 11-42.

Martial Staub

**JOHN OF NIKIU (7th c.).** A *Coptic *bishop (second half of 7th c.) whose see was in Upper *Egypt. He was appointed administrator of the monasteries of Egypt in the late 7th c.; but, accused of excessive severity, he was deposed and must have died early in the 8th century. John was the author of a *Byzantine Chronicle*, written in Greek and Coptic, now lost; we possess only an Ethiopic translation made in 1602 from an Arabic version, itself lost. Divided into 122 chapters, this work is a universal history whose last 12 chapters contain authentic information on the situation of Egypt in the 7th c., as well as an account of some episodes in the conquest of Egypt by the Arabs, of which John was an eyewitness.

*The Chronicle of John, Bishop of Nikiu, translated from Zotenberg's Ethiopic text by R. H. Charles*, London, 1916.

Gérard Troupeau

**JOHN OF PARMA (died 1288).** Friar Minor and minister general of the *Franciscan Order. After having taught in the *studia* of *Bologna, *Naples and *Paris, he was elected minister general in 1247. To inspire more rigorous observance in the order, he undertook visits of inspection, interrupted when *Innocent IV sent him to *Constantinople with a mission to reconcile the Greek and Latin Churches. He was popular among the friars, but *Alexander

IV obliged him to resign in Feb 1257, because of his Joachite opinions. *Bonaventure, who was designated as his successor, put him on trial in 1262-1263, after which he retired to a hermitage at Greccio. As he was setting out again for Constantinople in 1288, he died en route, at Cammarino.

Renée de Nantes, "Le bienheureux Jean de Parme", *EtFr*, 15, 1906, 148-167, 277-300.

Michael Cusato

**JOHN OF PLANO CARPINI (*c.*1180-1252).** Traveller, born at Piano di Carpine, near *Perugia (Italy). St *Francis sent him to *Saxony as *guardian of the *Franciscan Order (1221); he was provincial of Germany (1228), Spain (1230) and finally Saxony (1233) and played an important role in the spread of the order to Scandinavia, Bohemia, Poland and Hungary. Despite his age (and corpulence), his experience and his knowledge of Holy Scripture led *Innocent IV to choose him to bear letters to the Russian princes inviting them to the *union of Churches, and others to the *Mongols to propose a non-aggression pact and expound the Christian faith to them. Leaving *Lyon, at *Wrocław he took a companion, Benedict of Poland, and passed through *Prague, *Cracow, Halych and *Kiev, which he left on 3 Feb 1246. The Mongol Khan Batu sent him to his nephew, the Qaghan Güyük; on 22 July, Plano Carpini arrived at Sira-Ordo, where he was present at Güyük's coronation and met numerous rulers. He had talks with Güyük's advisers, several of whom were Christians, and received from them an invitation addressed to the *pope and the kings, to accept Mongol sovereignty. He set out on 13 Nov, crossed Asia in mid-winter (Güyük's mother had fortunately provided him with a fur coat), reached Kiev on 9 June 1247 and Lyon in November. Innocent IV sent him to St *Louis, then made him archbishop of Antivari (1248). He died on 1 Aug 1252.

During his *journey and his sojourn, he had gathered, either by himself or by interrogating Russians, *Cumans and Hungarians, a great deal of information, in particular on the armaments, tactics and customs of the Mongols, a new attack by whom on Europe was then feared. During his return, he had to satisfy the curiosity of those who received him. A monk, C. of Brzeg, set down in writing a first version of his *Account of the Tatars*; John wrote another for the king of *Hungary, and finally at Lyon he drew up his *Hystoria Mongalorum*, supplemented by a succinct account of his journey in which he gave the names of witnesses who could attest his veracity. This text, of which two versions exist, was used by *Vincent of Beauvais concurrently with the *Historia Tartarorum* of Simon of Saint-Quentin, a *Dominican who had accompanied Ascelin of Cremona, who had performed a similar mission, but without going beyond the lands of the *Caucasus. A courageous traveller, Plano Carpini shows himself an attentive and well-informed observer to whom the medieval West owed its first precise knowledge of the Mongols and Central Asia.

C. Dawson (ed.), *The Mongol Mission*, London, 1955 (re-ed. as *Mission to Asia*, Toronto, 1980). – Jean de Plan Carpin, *Histoire des Mongols*, J. Becquet (tr.), L. Hambis (tr.), Paris, 1965. – *Historia Tartarorum C. de Bridia monachi*, A. Önnefors (ed.), Berlin, 1967. – Giovanni di Pian del Carpine, *Storia dei Mongoli*, E. Menesto (ed.), M. C. Lungarotti (tr.), L. Petech (intro.), Spoleto, 1989.

P. Pelliot, "Les Mongols et la papauté", *ROC*, 23, 1922-1923, 3-30. – A. Van den Wyngaert, *Sinica franciscana*, 3, Quaracchi, 1929, 190. – D. Sinor, "John of Plano Carpini's Return from the Mongols", *JRAS*, 1957, 193-206.

Jean Richard

**JOHN OF POUILLY (late 13th - early 14th c.).** A secular priest, professor of theology at *Paris from 1301, he was the author of **Quodlibeta* and **Quaestiones* still unedited. His *doctrine, though generally close to Thomism, was tinged with *nominalism. Mixed up in the trial of the *Templars in 1308 and later in the quarrels between *seculars and mendicants, he opposed the *Dominican Pierre de la Palu. In 1321, several of his ideas about the administration of the sacrament of *penance – "exclusive divine right of *parish priests" to hear the *confession of their congregation, restriction of the *pope's universal jurisdiction – were condemned by Pope *John XXII in the *bull *Vas electionis*, but he continued his teaching after having solemnly retracted his errors.

A. Thouvenin, "Jean de Pouilly", *DThC*, 8, 1924, 797-799.

Coloman Viola

**JOHN OF RIPA (14th c.).** An Italian *Franciscan, an important figure in 14th-c. *theology, John of Ripa (or of Marchia) taught at *Paris in 1357-1358. Of the works attributed to him, we have only a Commentary on the **Sentences* and *Determinationes* (or **Quodlibeta*, 1354). The latter represent the essential theses of his original *doctrine concerning the *metaphysics of the universe, the foundation of *faith, divine simplicity and *God's knowledge of future contingents, which surpass in subtlety the doctrine of his master *Duns Scotus and some of which – according to *Gerson – were condemned in 1362. In his theology, he used mathematical concepts borrowed from the masters of arts of the time.

A. Combes, "Présentation de Jean de Ripa", *AHDL*, 23, 1956, 145-242. – F. Ruello, *La Theologie Naturelle de Jean de Ripa*, Paris, 1992.

Coloman Viola

**JOHN OF ROQUETAILLADE (died after 1365).** Born near Aurillac, at Marcolès, in the first years of the 14th c., John of Roquetaillade (de Rupescissa) entered the *Franciscan Order in 1332 and there continued the philosophical studies begun five years before at the university of *Toulouse. He was at the *convent of Aurillac in 1340 and doubtless remained there until 1344. On 2 Dec 1344 he was "snatched from his native land" (*Liber ostensor*, fol. 83 v°) and imprisoned in the convent of Figeac. Later incarcerated in half a dozen conventual prisons and pursued by the ceaseless hostility of the provincial of Aquitaine, Guillaume Farinier, the friar minor escaped from the justice of his order only in 1349 when he was taken to *Avignon to defend himself before the *pope in public *consistory. He presented himself there on 2 Oct 1349. The same day, he was incarcerated in the papal *prison of Soudan where he remained until at least the end of 1356 and perhaps Dec 1365, at which date we lose trace of him.

The chequered career of John of Roquetaillade is explained as much by his belonging to the dissident branches of the Franciscan Order as by his vocation as visionary and prophet. The friar was doubtless accused of associating with the order's dissident movements who demanded a strict observance of the Rule of St Francis and preached radical evangelical *poverty in the manner of the Italian Franciscans or the *beguines of *Provence. His public predictions, furnished with numerous *visions and *revelations of all sorts, unquestionably added to his discredit. They also contributed to furthering the ambiguity of his position at the Avignon *Curia. Despite his incarceration, the friar held in effect the role of a court prophet, officiously interrogated by the most prestigious *cardinals such as Elias of Talleyrand-Périgord († 1364) on questions of immediate policy like the *election of the future pope or the peace missions between *France and *England.

Drawing on the prophetic works and *millenarian predictions of his predecessors, in particular *Joachim of Fiore († 1202) and *Peter John Olivi († 1298), John of Roquetaillade left a diverse oeuvre composed essentially of *alchemical books (*De quinta essentia*, *Liber lucis* . . .) and prophetic books (*Commentary on the Oracle of the Blessed Cyril*, written between 1345 and 1349, *Liber secretorum eventuum* completed in 1349, *Liber ostensor* finished in September 1356, *Vade mecum in tribulatione* completed late in 1356 . . .). The whole of his work fits into the climate of eschatological expectation characteristic of the years preceding the start of the *Great Schism (1378).

J. Bignami-Odier, *Études sur Jean de Roquetaillade*, Paris, 1952. – J. Bignami-Odier, "Jean de Roquetaillade théologien, polémiste, alchimiste", *HLF*, 41, 1981, 75-240 (repeat of the preceding study). – R. Halleux, "Les Ouvrages alchimiques de Jean de Rupescissa", *HLF*, 41, 1981, 241-284. – L. Boisset, "Roquetaillade", *DSp*, XIII, Paris, 1988, 933-938. – R. E. Lerner, "Popular Justice: Rupescissa in Hussite Bohemia", *Eschatologie und Hussitismus*, A. Patchovsky (ed.), F. Šmahel (ed.), Prague, 1996, 39-51.

Sylvie Barnay

**JOHN OF SALISBURY (*c.*1115-1180).** Born near *Salisbury, England, to a non-noble family, John studied at *Paris and then at *Chartres under *William of Conches where he acquired a great mastery of the literary disciplines, particularly *rhetoric. He returned to Paris, where he received a sound theological training. In 1148, he was recruited as a cleric by Pope *Eugenius III, who was then in France, and consequently took part in the council of *Reims. In 1153, he entered the service of the archbishop of *Canterbury, *Theobald, who put him in charge of relations with the Roman *Curia where he went several times. Distanced from ruling circles by King *Henry II Plantagenet whom he had supported since his accession, in 1159 he wrote a treatise on political morality, the *Policraticus*, and a plea for the *liberal arts entitled *Metalogicon*. Having sided with Archbishop *Thomas Becket, he had to leave England in 1163 returning only in 1170, just before Becket's assassination, which he witnessed. From then on he dedicated himself to the defence of the latter's memory and wrote his Life. Thanks to the support of the king of France, *Louis VII, he became bishop of Chartres in 1176 and took part in the third *Lateran council (1179), on his return from which he died.

Defender of a Christian humanism on a literary basis, John of Salisbury was also one of the first minds of his time to formulate a concept close to the notion of the *State, by distinguishing the physical person of the king from the power he incarnated and transmitted to his successors.

John of Salisbury, *Policraticus*, C. C. J. Webb (ed.), Oxford, 1909. – *The Metalogicon of John of Salisbury*, D. D. McGarry (ed.), Berkeley (CA), Los Angeles, 1955. – *The Letters of John of Salisbury*, 1, W. J. Millar (ed.), S. J. Butler (ed.), H. E. Butler (ed.), 2nd ed., Oxford, 1986; 2, W. J. Millar (ed.), C. N. L. Brooke (ed.), Oxford, 1979 (*OMT*). – *The Historia Pontificalis of John of Salisbury*, M. Chibnall (ed.), Oxford, 1986 (*OMT*). – *John of Salisbury's Entheticus Maior and Minor*, J. van Laarhoven (ed.), Leiden, 1987 (3 vol.). – John of Salisbury, *Policraticus*, C. J. Nederman (ed., tr.), Cambridge, 1990.

"Jean de Salisbury", *DSp*, 8, 1974, 716-721. – W. Ullmann, *John of Salisbury's Policraticus in the Later Middle Ages*, Cologne, 1978. – M. Wilks, *The World of John of Salisbury*, 1984 ("SCH(L).S", 3).

André Vauchez

**JOHN OF TRANI (11th c.).** John, bishop of Trani in Byzantine *Apulia, is known for his role in the *schism of 1054. In 1053 he received a letter from the *metropolitan of *Bulgaria, *Leo of Ohrid, probably inspired by *Michael Cerularius and intended for the *pope, violently criticizing certain Latin customs. John was considered by the Greek Church its main defender in Italian territory against Roman ambitions, which earned him the title of imperial *syncellus* (official of the *patriarchate). In reality, John mainly supported the catapan of Italy, Argyros, who preached an alliance between Rome and Constantinople against the Norman conquest. He may have been deposed for *simony at the council of Melfi (1058).

J. Gay, *L'Italie méridionale et l'Empire byzantin*, Paris, 1904.

Anne-Françoise Loué

**JOHN PECKHAM (*c.*1240-1292).** Born *c.*1240, John Peckham became a *Franciscan and studied under the direction of St *Bonaventure at *Paris, where he held the position of a theologian from 1270, as well as at *Oxford and at the *Curia, before being appointed archbishop of *Canterbury in succession to *Robert Kilwardby. As such, in 1283 he renewed the "condemnations" of Thomist theses pronounced by his predecessor.

Peckham's output was multiform. Alongside works of *theology, he dealt with problems of natural *science, several times defended the Francisan ideal of *poverty and composed *hymns. He was a relentless enemy of any attempt to recognise the autonomy of *philosophy and fought for a return to *Augustinianism (neo-Augustinianism) against what he saw as the dangerous drift of *Aristotelianism. One of the examples of this return to Augustine is given by the doctrine of illumination. The human mind, being finite, cannot by itself know necessary and, as such, eternal truths. But since there exists an activity of human *reason that permits it to understand, we must admit a special influence of what Augustine calls the "inner master", *i.e.* the reasonable understanding of the divinity. Though each man enjoys this potential, which Aristotle calls the "agent *intellect" (*De anima*, III, 5), we must add to it, according to Peckham – following *Roger Bacon and *Albert the Great –, a more eminent agent intellect: *God.

Peckham was not concerned with *light merely as a metaphor in the doctrine of *knowledge, but also as a phenomenon of *nature, in line with the Oxford tradition (*Robert Grosseteste, Roger Bacon), just as he was interested in the spheres or planets. But at the centre of his thought is the doctrine of *form. This does not relate to matter as Aristotle envisaged, as the sole reality for the possible: several forms can subsist perfectly in the same being at the same time. In this sense, matter also has a certain reality, so that in all logic it would not be impossible for it to have been created and to exist separately from form. Finally, his theory of self-knowledge is remarkable. Like Bonaventure, Peckham admits the existence of an immediate presence-to-self; so knowledge of self is not mediated by the forms of concrete objects. His **Quodlibeta* contain numerous citations from the patristic tradition.

Ioannis Pecham, *Quodlibeta quatuor*, G. J. Etzkorn (ed.), F. Delorme (ed.), Grottaferrata, 1989. – John Peckham, *Questions concerning the Eternity of the World*, V.G. Potter (ed.), New York, 1993.

A. Callebaut, "Jean Peckham et l'augustinisme", *AFH*, 18, 1925, 441-472. – D. Douie, *Archbishop Peckham*, Oxford, 1952. – D. E. Sharp, *Franciscan Philosophy at Oxford in the Thirteenth Century*, New York, 1964. – A. G. Rigg, "John Pecham", *A History of Anglo-Latin Literature 1066-1422*, Cambridge, 1992, 222-6.

Rolf Schönberger

**JOHN SCOTUS ERIUGENA (9th century).** What we know of the life of John Scotus, surnamed Eriugena, does not amount to much. When we have said that he was Irish, that he lived at the court of *Charles the Bald in the third quarter of the 9th c., taught the *liberal arts there and took part in the controversy over *predestination raised by Godescalc (Gottschalk) of Orbais, we have said nearly all that can be said for certain about his life. In the 12th c., *William of Malmesbury tried to fill the gaps in this biography by some anecdotes of his own invention. One of the most famous takes place at a dinner during which Charles the Bald and Eriugena, sitting opposite each other at the same table, chat familiarly. The king puts him the following question: "What separates a 'Scot' (Irishman) from a 'sot'?" The Irishman replies: "Nothing but a table". William of Malmesbury especially exercised his ingenuity to make Eriugena die in the *abbey whose librarian he himself was. It was there that the master of the Palatine school was supposed to have ended his days, teaching the rudiments to the children of the monastic *school and receiving for his pains the treatment that had been reserved for St Cassian of Imola: to die stabbed by the pens of his pupils. These anecdotes, arising from William of Malmesbury's imagination, lack any foundation.

Eriugena's thought is worked out from the reading of a dual book: that of *Nature and that of Scripture, both written by the same divine Author. Preference is given to the book of Scripture, which is the starting-point of all philosophical or theological speculation. Adherence by *faith to revealed truths is an indispensable condition of the search: "If you do not believe, you will not understand" (Is 7, 9, according to the Septuagint). But we cannot remain there. The Christian thinker is condemned to go beyond this first stage, his task is to seek to understand what he believes. This quest for understanding is the work of human *reason, helped by divine *grace and guided by the experience of those who have interpreted Scripture before us, the *Fathers of the Church, both Latin and Greek. Among the Latins, the one whom Eriugena cites most often is incontestably Augustine. In the end, however, he prefers Ambrose, whose allegorical *exegesis, in line with Philo and *Origen, corresponds better to his tastes. He also prefers the Greeks to the Latins and avows that he would have gone to sleep over the latter, had not his protector, King Charles, encouraged him to draw "on the very pure and very abundant sources" of the Greek Fathers. As such he is profoundly original, since in him, and for the first time in the West, two distinct *Neoplatonist currents converge: the first, coming from Porphyry, reached him through Augustine, the second, coming from Proclus, was handed down to him by *Dionysius. Despite the reverence that Eriugena accords to the Church Fathers, their authority is not in his eyes the supreme rule: "Authority derives from true reason, but reason does not derive from authority. . . . The real authority, in my opinion, is none other than a truth that has been found by the power of reason and that the holy Fathers have handed down in writing to posterity."

In one sense, we could say that all Eriugena's work is a commentary on Scripture. But the interpretation of Scripture is an infinite task: "Since what we seek is infinite, we must seek it indefinitely" (*Commentary on the "Celestial Hierarchy"*, VI, 38-39). Each verse of the *Bible is capable of multiple interpretations which, far from contradicting each other, supplement each other. Scripture is like the peacock's feather, iridescent with infinite nuances in a single point (749C). It is a labyrinth whose thousand turnings aim, not to lead us astray, but to stimulate our ardour to search for the truth. The seeker's reward is to understand the sacred text. For Eriugena, the joy of knowing surpasses all others: "Nothing is sweeter to listen to than true reason, nothing is more delectable to explore for him who seeks, nothing is more beautiful to contemplate for him who finds" (512B).

If preference is given to the book of Scripture, that does not mean that the book of *nature is disdained. In the created universe, as in the inspired Book, God is manifest in a multiplicity of ways. Each of these manifestations is what Eriugena calls a "*theophany". And just as in reading Scripture our understanding discovers an infinity of hidden senses, so in reading the book of Nature it contemplates an infinity of theophanies. Each of these theophanies gives rise to a different perspective – Eriugena says a "theory". None of these perspectives gives us the totality of the knowable. Whatever the profundity or elevation of a "theory", it can and must be overtaken by a more profound or more elevated "theory". Expressed in Dionysian terms, the movement of *contemplation is a circular movement, while the movement that makes us go from one given "theory" to a more elevated "theory" is a rectilinear movement. The combination of the two engenders what geometers call a "helix". So Eriugenian thought follows a helicoid curve. The temptation, for one who considers it from outside, is to fix its movement. We can stop, *e.g.* (point A), on this proposition: "Master: Will you deny that Creator and creature are one? Disciple: It is difficult to deny it" (528B). If we hold on to this declaration, we will be inclined to conclude that Eriugena was a pantheist. But if we go a bit further on the helicoid curve (point B), we will find an unequivocal affirmation of *God's absolute transcendence: "He surpasses all that is and all that is not" (572D).

Those who have accused Eriugena of *pantheism have succumbed to the temptation of stopping at point A. Thus from 1271, nearly all the *chroniclers assert that the pantheism of *Amalric of Bene (condemned in 1210) has its source in the writings of Eriugena. Paolo Lucentini has shown that nothing justifies this interpretation. But it was to receive a favourable reception, all the more since Eriugena was suspect on two counts: because of *De corpore et sanguine Domini*, falsely attributed to him but whose true author was *Ratramnus of Corbie, and because of a work whose author he incontestably was, viz. the *Periphyseon*. Condemned in 1225 by Pope *Honorius III to be burned, the *Periphyseon* long remained suspect to the Roman *magisterium.

H. J. Floss, *PL*, 122, 1853, 441-1022. – Dionysius the Areopagite, *PL*, 122, 1853, 1029-1194. – *Carmina*, L. Traube (ed.), *MGH.PL*, 3, 1896, 518-556. – *Annotationes in Marcianum*, E. Lutz (ed.), Cambridge (MA), 1939 (unabridged ed. according to the Paris manuscript, BNF, ms. lat. 12960). – *Vox spiritualis*, É. Jeauneau (ed.), *SC*, 151, 1961. – Gregory of Nyssa, *De imagine*, M. Cappuyn (ed.), *RThAM*, 32, 1965, 205-262. – *Periphyseon* (improperly called *De diuisione naturae*), I. P. Sheldon-Williams (ed.), *SLH*, 7, 9, 11, 13, 1968, 1972, 1981, 1995. – Jean Scot, *Commentaire sur l'évangile de Jean*, É. Jeauneau (ed.), *SC*, 180, 1970. – Jean Scot, *Commentaire sur la "Hiérarchie céleste"*, J. Barbet (ed.), *CChrCM*, 31, 1975. – Jean Scot, *De praedestinatione*, G. Madec (ed.), *CChrCM*, 50, 1978. – *Quatre thèmes érigéniens*, É. Jeauneau (ed.), Montreal-Paris, 1978, 91-166 (partial ed. from the Oxford manuscript, Bodleian Library Auct. T. 2.19). – Maximus Confessor, *Quaestiones ad Thalassium*, C. Laga (ed.), C. Steel (ed.), *CChrSG*, 7-22, 1980-1990 (2 vol.). – Maximus Confessor, *Ambigua ad Iohannem*, É. Jeauneau (ed.), *CChrSG*, 18, 1988. – G. H. Allard, *Periphyseon. Indices generales*, Montreal-Paris, 1983 (table). – *Carmina*, M. Herren (ed.), *SLH*, 12, 1993. – *Homily on the Prologue of St John's Gospel* (Latin text and Russian tr. by V. Petroff), Moscow, 1995. – *Periphyseon*, É. Jeauneau (ed.), *CChr.CM*, 161-163, 1996, 1997, 1999. – *Glossae diuinae historiae*, J. Contreni (ed.),

P. O'Neill (ed.) Florence, 1997. – John Scotus, *Commentary on Priscian*, A. Luhtala (ed.), P Dutton (ed.), (in preparation).

G. Schrimpf, *Das Werk des Johannes Scottus Eriugena im Rahmen des Wissenschaftsverständnisses seiner Zeit*, Münster, 1982. – *Eriugena Rediuiuus*, W. Beierwaltes, Heidelberg, 1987 ("AHAW.PH", 1). – É. Jeauneau, *Études érigéniennes*, Paris, 1987. – J. J. O'Meara, *Eriugena*, Oxford, 1988. – G. Madec, *Jean Scot et ses auteurs*, Paris, 1988. – *Giovanni Scoto nel suo tempo*, C. Leonardi (ed.), Spoleto, 1989. – M. Brennan, *Guide des études érigéniennes. Bibliographie commentée des publications 1930-1987*, Fribourg-Paris, 1989 (bibliography). – D. Moran, *The Philosophy of John Scottus Eriugena. A Study of Idealism in the Middle Ages*, Cambridge, 1989. – *Begriff und Metapher*, W. Beierwaltes (ed.), Heidelberg, 1990. – W. Otten, *The Anthropology of Johannes Scottus Eriugena*, Leiden, 1991. – *From Athens to Chartres. Neoplatonism and Medieval Thought*, H. Westra (ed.), Leiden, 1992. – P. E. Dutton, A. Luhtala, "Eriugena in Priscianum", *MS*, 56, 1994, 153-163. – W. Beierwaltes, *Eriugena: Grundzüge seines Denkens*, Frankfurt am Main, 1994. – A. Kijewska, *Neoplatonizm Jana Szkota Eriugeny*, Lublin, 1994. – É. Jeauneau, P. E. Dutton, *The Autograph of Eriugena*, Turnhout, 1996. – *Iohannes Scottus Eriugena. The Bible and Hermeneutics*, G. Van Riel (ed.), C. Steel (ed.), J. McEvoy (ed.), Louvain, 1996.

Édouard Jeauneau

**JOHN STOJKOVIĆ OF RAGUSA (*c.*1393-1443).** John Stojković (Stoici) of Ragusa entered the *Dominicans of *Dubrovnik, his home town, which – on the frontiers of Eastern and Western *Christendom – had served as a link between the Eastern and Western Churches. There he acquired the first elements of learning at the school of the Friars Preachers, then – at the expense of the Republic of Ragusa – continued his studies at the university of *Padua (1414-1417) and the theology *faculty of *Paris (1417-1420).

*Doctor and professor of the university of Paris, a persuasive orator, renowned theologian and one of the main protagonists of the council of *Basel (1431-1439), a man of great erudition and an experienced diplomat, John of Ragusa managed to convince the Easterners to open a serious dialogue on the *union of the Churches.

John Stojković was one of the defenders of *conciliarism in the wake of *Gerson. Convinced of the utility and benefit of *councils in the history of the Church, he asserted that it was through them that *heresies were condemned, reforms instituted and order ensured, while negligence in holding councils had led to many disorders. He justified the participation in councils, with right to vote, of minor *clerics having jurisdiction and especially of *doctors who had not just this title, but also the capacity of true theologians.

In 1433, at the council of Basel, John of Ragusa held long discussions with the *Hussites, from which his best works emerged.

On 10 June 1434, on the announcement of the arrival of representatives of the Bosnian Church, he declared before the conciliar assembly that an "excellent occasion [offered itself] for the *conversion of the whole kingdom of *Bosnia, which for three hundred years and more [had been] infested by the heresy of the Manichees and that of Arius".

John of Ragusa was well aware that union with the Greeks could come about only in and by a truly ecumenical council. On 10 March 1436, he warned the assembly of Basel that "if they ceased to negotiate with the *Byzantine Church and if they failed to take an interest in the union of the Churches, *Constantinople would fall; and that the kingdom of *Hungary and all central Europe would soon be devastated by the enemy of Christianity".

The *humanist activity of John of Ragusa, to which the Latin West was so indebted, has been acknowledged by numerous scholars, beginning with Beatus Rhenanus and Erasmus. His centres of interest covered a vast field, from the principles of biblical hermeneutics to the knowledge of *Islam. From his distant embassies, John of Ragusa brought back the *Meditations* of Marcus Aurelius (Zurich, 1558, *editio princeps*), Athenagoras's *Apologia*, the *Epistle to Diognetus*, the *Koran (Latin version of Robert of Ketton and Herman the Dalmatian), and precious biblical *codices that would be studied by Erasmus.

Johannis Stojković de Ragusio, "Tractatus de Ecclesia", F. Šanjek (ed.), A. Krchnák (ed.), M. Biškup (ed.), Zagreb, 1983 ("*editio princeps*").

A. Krchnák, *De vita et operibus Ioannis de Ragusio*, Rome, 1960. – Y. Congar, *L'Église, de saint Augustin à l'époque moderne*, Paris, 1970, 328-330. – W. Krämer, "Konsens und Rezeption. Verfassungsprinzipien der Kirche im Basler Konziliarismus", *BGPhMA*, 19, Münster, 1980. – "Croatie-France. Relations historiques et culturelles", *The Bridge*, 12, The Hague, 1995, 156-159 and 179-187. – J. Santiago Madrigal Terrazas, *La eclesiología de Juan de Ragusa OP (1390/95-1443)*, Madrid, 1995. – F. Šanjek, "Jean Stojković de Raguse et l'idée de l'integration européenne au XVe siècle", *Mémoire dominicaine*, 9/1996, 31-40.

Franjo Šanjek

**JOHN TEUTONICUS (1180-1245).** John Zemeke (Semeca in Latin), alias John of Strasbourg, studied civil and canon law at *Bologna (under the guidance of Azzo in civil law) and spoke German, Italian, French and Latin. His works comprise the *gloss on Gratian's **Decretum* and that on the constitutions of the fourth *Lateran council. Successively *canon, *provost of the *chapter of Halberstadt, provincial of the *Dominicans for Hungary, then for Lombardy (while the province was leagued against *Frederick II), and general of the Dominicans, he was a close friend of the emperor of *Germany. He was obliged to part from him, which explains his political contradictions: no *Empire outside the Church, but an imperial power coming from *God.

John Teutonicus, *Apparatus glossarum in compilationem tertiam*, K. Pennington (ed.), Vatican, 1981.

Jacques Bouineau

**JON ÖGMUNDARSON (died 1121).** The Icelandic bishop Jon Ögmundarson was the first titular (1106-1121) of the see of Hólar in the north-west of the island, *Iceland's second *bishopric. Extremely popular, he earned two *sagas (in the category of *Sagas of Bishops*, one in *Latin by the monk Gunnlaugr Leifsson) and a book of *miracula* and was canonized shortly after his death. He was celebrated for having founded, at Hólar, a *school that attracted numerous pupils, where the *trivium* and *quadrivium* were taught and for which he brought, among other learned men, a Frenchman, Rikini, charged with teaching *Gregorian chant and Latin versification. He took equal care to maintain purity of morals by forbidding secular *dances or *dansar*.

R. Boyer, *La Vie religieuse en Islande (1116-1264) d'après la Sturlunga Saga et les Sagas des Évêques*, Paris, 1979.

Régis Boyer

**JONAS OF BOBBIO (*c.*600 - after 659).** Jonas entered the monastery of *Bobbio in 618, became secretary of Abbot Attalus and then of Abbot Bertulf who commissioned from him a Life of St *Columbanus. To write it, he visited *Luxeuil under Abbot Eustasius († 629) and the Rhineland regions. He later joined St

*Amandus at Elnone (now Saint-Amand-les-Eaux) before 639 and finished the *Vita* of Columbanus in 642, adding to it information on Attalus, Bertulf, Eustasius and the *nuns of Columbanian obedience at Faremoutiers in Brie. We also owe him a *Life* of St Vaast (Vedastus) of Arras. Crossing *Burgundy, he stopped at Réôme (Moûtiers-Saint-Jean) where he wrote a *Life* of St John of Réôme (659). We do not know where he died.

*Ionae vitae sanctorum Colombani, Vedasti, Iohannis*, B. Krusch (ed.), *MGH.SRG*, 37, 1905. – *The Life of St. Columban*, D.C. Munro (ed.), Felinfach, 1993.

J. Marilier, *Cath.*, 23, 1967.

Bruno Judic

**JONAS OF ORLÉANS (before 780 - 841/843).** Jonas of Orléans, one of the great names of the "*Carolingian Renaissance", is one of the undisputed masters of the literature of Mirrors, treatises of edification and moral and *spiritual direction essentially intended for princes or laymen, popular in the 9th century. Born in *Aquitaine, doubtless some years before 780, in his youth he was probably part of the court of *Louis the Pious, son of *Charlemagne and king of Aquitaine from 781, who for a time made him the preceptor of his young son Pippin. He owed it to the favour of Louis, now emperor, that he succeeded another strong personality, *Theodulf, in the important episcopal see of *Orléans, doubtless in 818. From then on he divided his time between the administration of his *diocese, the service of the Emperor Louis – to whom he seems to have remained loyal, though tested by the tribulations of the reign and his participation in the great religious events of the time, in particular the councils of Paris (829) and Aachen (836) – and the production of a literary output on which he worked until his death, which must be put in 841 or 843.

His purely religious works are admittedly not his best known: a Life of St Hubert (bishop of Tongres, died 725) written in 825 on the occasion of the transfer of the saint's *relics, a treatise in defence of Church *property (*De rebus ecclesiasticis non invadendis*) and another on the cult of *images. He owes his place in Carolingian literature to his didactic work, which rests on two essential texts. *De institutione laicali* ("On the edification of the laity") – of which A. Dubreucq proposes to distinguish two versions, one written doubtless soon after Jonas's arrival at Orléans and dedicated to the *count of that town, Matfrid, and a second, more developed, to be dated from the first half of 829 – is a veritable *treatise on matrimonial and conjugal ethics in a society in which the *laity were essentially classed as *conjugati* (married people) by a Church that strove to propose to them a Christian way of life modelled on those defined for *clerics; it assuredly offers one of the most perfect expressions of what E. Delaruelle has called "Carolingian moralism". *De institutione regia*, sent by Jonas to King Pippin I of Aquitaine in autumn 831, *i.e.* in the aftermath of the troubles that affected the *Empire in 829-830, is a *Mirror of Princes that draws widely on the full range of scriptural and patristic texts, and in which the bishop of Orléans, formulating a veritable theory of the royal office in a Christian Empire, gives one of the most complete expositions of the politico-religious ideas of the clerics of the Carolingian Renaissance, sometimes known, perhaps incorrectly, as "political *Augustinianism".

*A Ninth-Century Political Tract: the "De institutione regia" of Jonas of Orléans*, Smithtown, 1983. – Jonas d'Orleans, *Le Métier de roi ("De institutione regia")*, A. Dubreucq (ed.), Paris, 1995.

J. Reviron, *Les Idées politico-religieuses d'un évêque du IX^e siècle. Jonas d'Orléans et son "De institutione regia". Étude et texte critique*, Paris, 1930. – J. Chélini, *L'Aube du Moyen Âge. La vie religieuse des laïcs dans l'Europe carolingienne*, Paris, 1991. – M. Banniard, "Jonas d'Orléans", *DLFMA*, 1992, 869-870.

Charles Vulliez

***JONGLEUR.*** The word *jongleur* (from Latin *joculator*) designated any professional entertainer, generally itinerant, the reciter of a work, the mime, the showman, the jester, the animal trainer, the charlatan. The *jongleur* was the descendant of the ancient *histriones*, the Celtic and Germanic bards, the wandering clerics. He was condemned by the Church and distrusted by the clergy. Not until the 12th c. would the *scientia ludorum* gain respectability in the field of knowledge, and not until the 14th c. would the *jongleur* no longer be considered a diabolical being.

*Jongleurs* were not excluded from society, however: they played before lords, churchmen, the crowd at the *fair. Their reputation depended on their repertoire: the texts distinguish between *nobles jongleurs*, the ignorant, the indecent. They were recruited from all *social classes: we know of *nobles, *clerics and townsmen who became *jongleurs*. Not all were needy, as they often liked to represent themselves: some were richly rewarded, others held a permanent place at *court, where they took the more respectable name of minstrels.

The role of the *jongleur* in poetic activity is still disputed. The distinction between composition and representation is not always very clear: was the *jongleur* content to reproduce the work he had memorized or did he improvise during representation? According to Edmond Faral, he "found and executed" at the same time. Further research into the poetic tradition in traditional societies tends to confirm this hypothesis. This explains the existence of a "customary rhetoric", the flexibility of formulae, the multiplicity of variants.

The *jongleur* was also a frequent literary character. This or that epic hero was accompanied by his *jongleur*. In the first Arthurian *romance, *Chrétien de Troyes's *Érec et Énide*, musician *jongleurs* arrive at King *Arthur's court from all over the country for the marriage of the protagonists. An Occitan **chanson de geste*, *Daurel et Beton* (late 12th c.), presents a *jongleur* as a faithful servant and the guardian of tradition. In the romance of William of Dole (early 13th c.), a *jongleur* is the confidant of the emperor of Germany. In the Occitan romance of *Flamenca*, *jongleurs* play *music, sing love poems, recite stories of *Brittany, "ancient romances" and *chansons de geste*.

It goes without saying that, with the progress of writing and the growing prestige of written culture, the "oral" *jongleur* became an unnecessary figure. In the late Middle Ages, people deplored the decline of minstrels and their art.

E. Faral, *Les Jongleurs en France au Moyen Âge*, Paris, 1910. – P. Zumthor, *La Lettre et la Voix. De la "littérature" médiévale*, Paris, 1987.

Michel Stanesco

**JORDAN OF SAXONY (*c.*1185-1237).** German, a student, master of arts and bachelor of theology at *Paris, Jordan became a Friar Preacher in 1220, provincial of Lombardy in 1221 and succeeded St *Dominic in 1222 at the head of the order, which he governed by visiting alternately the provinces, the *chapters, the *universities and the *Curia; he was drowned while returning from the *Holy Land. Supported by *Rome, he developed the order in the spirit of St Dominic. He is remarkable for constitutional work (1220 and

1228), the promotion and organisation of studies, apostolic contact and missionary spirit. His *Letters to Diana*, foundress of the Sisters of Bologna, and his *Little Book on the Origins of the Order of Preachers* reveal his mind and are the basis of the order's history.

*Libellus de principiis Ordinis Fratrum Praedicatorum*, H. C. Scheeben (ed.), *MOFPH*, 16, 1935. – *Epistulae*, A. Walz (ed.), Rome, 1951.

M. Aron, *Un animateur de la jeunesse au XIIIe siècle*, Paris, 1930. – H. C. Scheeben, *Beiträge zur Geschichte Jordan von Sachsen*, Vechta, 1938 ("Quellen und Forschungen zur Geschichte des Dominickaner-ordens in Deutschland", 35). – J. Kaeppeli, *SOPMA*, 3, 1980, 55-58. – I. W. Frank, "Jordanus v. Sachsen", *LThK*, 5, 1996, 994-995 (3rd ed.).

Marie-Humbert Vicaire †

**JOSEPH.** Joseph, called the Patriarch to avoid confusing him with *Joseph of Nazareth, was the son of *Jacob and Rachel. The numerous episodes of his life (Gen 37-50) were interpreted as prefiguring the life of the Messiah. Isolated representations of Joseph were rare, though he sometimes had a place on *cathedral portals alongside the *prophets. The cycle of Joseph's story was popularized from the 5th c. and could provide matter for numerous episodes, like the 22 bas-reliefs on the foundation of the façade of *Auxerre cathedral. But scenes from the story could be represented on their own; they were connected with his childhood, trials and triumph. Joseph thrown by his brothers into a cistern, an important episode of his childhood, appears on the 10th-c. ivory **châsse* in the treasury of *Sens cathedral, as does that of Joseph and Potiphar's wife, a well-known scene of his trials. The windows of *Bourges show various episodes of Joseph's triumph in Egypt.

G. Vikan, "Joseph Iconography on Coptic Textiles", *Gesta*, 18, 1979, 99-108.

Frédérique Trouslard

## JOSEPH OF NAZARETH

**Theology.** Joseph occupies an inconspicuous place in the Infancy gospels (Mt and Lk). It is the *apocrypha that flesh out his identity. They make him an aged widower who already had children (Jesus' "brothers"), miraculously designated to be *Mary's chaste husband. Joseph thus entered popular devotion and iconography with the characteristics of an old man. 14th- and 15th-c. preachers such as Jean *Gerson, anxious to ascribe a more spiritual dimension to Joseph, describe him rather as a young man, object of a particular sanctification allowing him to exercise the responsibility of father and husband to Jesus and his mother. Both old and new representations were grounded in the growing cult of the *Holy Family.

R. Gauthier *et al.*, "Joseph", *DSp*, 8, 1974, 1289-1316.

Marielle Lamy

**Iconography.** The iconography of Joseph was of little inspiration to medieval *artists, who depicted him essentially in cycles of the Life of the Virgin or the Infancy of Christ: his First Dream, which announced the Incarnation, sometimes put in parallel with the *Annunciation to Mary, the Betrothal, Test of the bitter water, Journey to Bethlehem, *Nativity, *Presentation in the Temple, Adoration of the *Magi, Second Dream, and *Flight into Egypt.

P. Testini, "Alle origini dell'iconografia di Giuseppe di Nazareth", *RivAC*, 48, 1972, 271-347. – C. Klapasch-Zuber, *Women, family and ritual in Renaissance Italy*, Chicago, 1985.

Colette Deremble

*Nativity and bathing of Jesus in Joseph's presence.* 13th-c. marble bas-relief in the church called Pieve di Santa Maria, Arezzo.

**JOSEPH I OF CONSTANTINOPLE (13th c.).** A member of the clergy of Irene, wife of the Emperor John III Vatatzes, Joseph became a monk on Mount Galesios after the death of his wife. Confessor and counsellor of Michael VIII, he became *patriarch of *Constantinople in 1266 and, on 2 Feb 1267, lifted the *excommunication that Arsenius had declared against the emperor, but he had to renounce the patriarchal throne in Jan 1275, after the conclusion of the Union of *Lyon. Already moribund, he regained his office for some months after the death of Michael VIII (1282-1283) and presided over the rejection of unionism at the beginning of the reign of Andronicus II.

V. Laurent, *Les Regestes de 1208 à 1309*, Paris, 1971, no. 1383-1423 and 1453-1459 ("RAPC", 4). – *PLP*, 4, 1980, 205-206, no. 9072.

Albert Failler

**JOSEPH ALBO (died *c.*1444).** A Jewish philosopher and preacher originally from Daroca (province of *Saragossa), Joseph Albo played a preponderant role at the disputation of Tortosa and San Mateo (1412-1413) against the convert Jerome of Santa Fé (previously Joshua ha-Lorqi). After this confrontation, he wrote the *Sefer ha-Ikkarim* (Book of Precepts), a treatise on the problem of the principles of the Jewish faith on which Jewish scholars found no commmon opinion. In his writings and sermons, he denounced the spread of *Averroism. He professed that the reward of the future

Crypt of the former abbey of Jouarre, 7th c. On the right, the tomb of Theodehild; at the back, that of bishop Agilbert.

world would be reserved for those whose accomplishments were religious rather than philosophical.

J. Albo, *Sefer ha-'Iqqarim: Book of Roots*, I. Husik (ed., tr.), Philadelphia (PA), 1946 (5 vol.).

C. Sirat, *A History of Jewish Philosophy in the Middle Ages*, Cambridge, 1985.

Sonia Fellous

**JOSEPH BEN NATHAN THE OFFICIAL (13th c.).** French Jewish apologist called the *Official or agent of the archbishop of *Sens. A disciple of *Yehiel ben Joseph of Paris, he composed an account of the Jewish-Christian disputation of 1240 and, in *c.*1260, the *Sefer Yosef ha-Meqaneh* or Book of Joseph the Zealot, a biblical commentary refuting the christological interpretations and the Gospels. This book cites dialogues with various interlocutors like the duke of Vitry and the bishops of Vannes, Le Mans and Saint-Malo. It reflects the ecclesiastical policy of *conversion, Jewish reactions and an atmosphere of relative *toleration. It reveals a Jewish knowledge of *Latin, the *Vulgate and the Christian liturgy. It draws on the *Talmud as well as on Saadya Gaon, Nissim, Solomon ibn Gabirol, *Rashi, Joseph Qara, *Samuel ben Meir and Joseph Bekhor Shor of Orléans. It influenced later polemical literature including the *Sefer ha-Nisaḥon* of Yom Tov Lipmann Mülhausen († 1459).

Z. Kahn, "Étude sur le livre de Joseph le Zélateur, recueil de controverses religieuses du Moyen Âge", *REJ*, 1, 1880, 222-246; 3, 1881, 1-38. – *R. Joseph ben R. Nathan l'Official, Sepher Joseph hamekane*, J. Rosenthal (ed.), Jerusalem, 1970 (in Hebrew).

Gérard Nahon

**JOSEPH HAZZAYA (THE SEER) (died before 786).** Syro-oriental mystic of Persian and Mazdean origin. A converted slave, he became a monk at Beth Nuhadra (northern *Iraq) and superior of the monastery of Mar Bassima in El Qardu (south-east Turkey). In his spiritual *doctrine, he seems to have been the first to make the synthesis between the tripartite divisions of John of Apamea, a 5th-c. Syrian monk, still free from Hellenic influences, and those of the three *contemplations of Evagrius Ponticus († 399). He was condemned by Patriarch Timothy in 786-787 for having maintained *Origenist or Messalian opinions. His main works are a treatise on the *Divine Essence*, *Chapters of Knowledge* (science), the *Book of Questions and Answers* and a *Letter on the Three Stages of the Monastic Life*.

*Joseph Hazzaya ? Lettre sur les trois étapes de la vie monastique*, P. Harb (ed.), F. Graffin (ed.), M. Albert (collab.), *PO*, 45, fasc. 2, no. 202, Turnhout, 1992 (Syriac text and Fr. tr.).

R. Beulay, *DSp*, 8, 1974, 1341-1349.

Micheline Albert

**JOSHUA.** Joshua, son of Nun, was given his name by Moses (Num 13, 16) whom he succeeded as head of the Israelites. He brought the children of Israel across the Jordan and led them to the Promised Land. Christian *theology hence considers him a second Moses, but also a prefiguration of the Messiah, the crossing of the Jordan being interpreted as a symbol of Christ's *baptism. The iconographical type of the character of Joshua is not well defined in comparison to that of Moses. Both are observed on the miniature painted by the Master of Rolin on folio 156 of the *Clock of Wisdom* (Brussels, Bibliothèque royale, ms. IV.111). The four most popular episodes of the account of Joshua's life are the crossing of the Jordan, the fall of the walls of Jericho, the capture of Ai and the stopping of the sun during the battle against the Amoreans. The Joshua Scroll in the Vatican Library at Rome is the most complete illustration of his *legend.

K. Weitzmann, *The Joshua Roll*, Princeton (NJ), 1970.

Frédérique Trouslard

**JOUARRE.** Forced to leave his abbey of *Luxeuil by his conflict with Brunhild, St *Columbanus halted shortly after 610 at Vulviacum (Ussy-sur-Marne), with the great landowner Autharius. The latter's three sons Dado (the future St *Audoin), Rado and Ado were influenced by him: Ado founded Jouarre in *c.*630. It was a *double monastery, directed by an *abbess and regulated by the rule of Luxeuil. As was customary, the establishment had three buildings. Of the Merovingian period, only the *crypt of St Paul's church survives. The sanctuary is a rectangle of 8.2 by 6.2 metres. It is divided into three aisles by two rows of three columns, surmounted by elegant marble capitals of Aquitanian style.

Its construction was decided on and financed by Agilbert, who had occupied the episcopal see of Dorchester before being made bishop of *Paris in 665. In *c.*670, he retired near his sister, Theodechilde, first abbess of Jouarre. The crypt served as a family necropolis, housing the remains of Agilbert, Theodechilde and the abbesses who succeeded her.

Of the seven surviving *tombs, two are exceptional works. The sarcophagus of Agilbert (*c.*680) has been placed since the 8th c. in the north recess. Cut in local stone, it is sculpted on two faces: a Christ in *Majesty surrounded by the *tetramorph occupies a short side, while on a long side is the earliest representation of the *Last Judgment north of the Alps. The risen, enveloped in short tunics, have their arms raised in the position of *orantes*. Nothing distinguishes the damned from the elect, distributed around the enthroned *Christ. Independent of the sarcophagus, the "stele of Agilbert" represents an archangel leading a man (Agilbert?) to *paradise. These bas-reliefs show strong Coptic influence, due no doubt to a transitory workshop.

In the east bay, a funerary dais built in *c.*750-760 holds the bodies of the first abbesses, whose sarcophagi are surmounted by cenotaphs. That of Theodechilde (mid 8th c.) is decorated on its two faces by two rows of shells, contained by three bands bearing an inscription to the saint's glory: ". . . Virgin without stain, of noble race, sparkling with *merits, zealous in her morals, she burned for the lifegiving dogma. . . . Dead, she finally exults in the triumph of Paradise." The quality of the lettering heralds the Carolingian majuscules.

The crypt was profoundly altered in the 8th c. (funerary dais, access gallery the length of the church's nave, rebuilding of the north wall) and in the first third of the 12th, with the replacement of the ceiling by groined vaults, as well as the adjustment of the 10th-c. crypt of St Ebrégésile (7th-c. bishop of Meaux) towards the south wall.

A. de Maillé, *Les Cryptes de Jouarre*, Paris, 1971. – C. Heitz, *La France pré-romane. Archéologie et architecture religieuse du Haut Moyen Âge. IVe siècle-an mille*, Paris, 1987, 96-103.

Pierre Kerbrat

**JOURNEYS.** Apart from *pilgrimages, which began to *Jerusalem from the 4th c., the period of great medieval journeys was between the 13th and 15th centuries.

The continental route to Asia was opened from 1204 when the conquest of *Constantinople gave the West access to the Black Sea, starting-point for the steppes of Central Asia. Moreover, the *Mongol conquest, making peace reign in those previously insecure regions, made possible the crossing of Asia at the same time as the anxieties aroused by the Mongol raids in Western Europe incited the sending of embassies to them.

The first journeys were those of two Friars Minor, *John of Plano Carpini (1246-1247) and William of Rubruck (1253-1255). They stayed several months at the residence of the Great Khan, Karakorum in Mongolia. Their accounts of their journeys, with their observations on the Tatars (Mongols), the one dedicated to Pope *Innocent IV, the other to St *Louis, made the immensity of the Asian continent known for the first time in the West, and allowed some errors of the ancient authorities to be corrected (the Caspian Sea was finally defined as a closed sea).

Alongside them must be cited many others whose journeys are known only by fragmentary texts or summed up in other works. We also possess *letters sent by missionaries when, in the late 13th c., the Avignon papacy created Latin *dioceses in *China (*e.g.* *John of Montecorvino, archbishop of Cambaluc, now Peking).

The exploration of Asia was also the work of *merchants, among them the celebrated *Marco Polo (*Devisement du monde*) and Francesco Balduccio Pegolotti (*Pratica della mercatura*). Missionaries and merchants also took the Indian Ocean route and contributed their knowledge of *India and the Indonesian world, not without mingling it with innumerable marvels.

Voyages to *Africa also began in the 13th c. with the failure of the Atlantic attempt of the Vivaldi brothers who set out from Genoa in 1291. That of Jaime Ferrer on the coast of Mauretania in 1346 had no more success. Africa was not truly breached until the 15th century. The interior of the continent remained almost unknown, except for the journey of Antonio Malfante, a Genoese, to Sigilmassa and Touat. Journeys to *Ethiopia were undertaken by missionaries or merchants, whose accounts have survived only indirectly: the only really important text is that of Pero da Covilham who reached India by the Red Sea route (1487).

But the essential discoveries were made via the Atlantic. The French expedition of Jean de Béthencourt and Gadifer de la Salle (1402-1406) landed in the Canaries. The main impetus came from Prince Henry the Navigator, who launched the Portuguese on the assault of Cape Bojador, crossed in 1434 by Gil Eanes. From then on, mariners mastered the techniques that permitted the return journey by using or running before the trade winds. The accounts of the official historian Eanes de Zurara and of Italian navigators in the service of *Portugal, the Venetian Alvise Cadamosto and the Genoese Antonietto Usodimare, are our main sources of knowledge for these explorations: in 1444, the mouth of the Senegal and Cape Verde; in 1460, Sierra Leone, then the Cape Verde Isles and the coast of Guinea, finally the crossing of the equator in 1471-1472. Exploration continued in the southern hemisphere, marking out the coast with landmarks, the *padroes*. In 1487-1488, Bartholomeu Dias passed the Cape of Storms, rebaptized the Cape of Good Hope after Vasco da Gama had managed to reach India on his great voyage of 1497-1499.

*Asia.* Miniature from the *Catalan Atlas* attributed to Crescas, 1375. Paris, BNF.

Alvise Cadamosto, *The Voyages of Cadamosto*, G. H. Crone (ed.), London, 1937. – Eanes de Zurara, *Chronique de Guinée*, L. Bourdon (ed.), R. Richard (ed.), Dakar, 1960. – Jean du Plan Carpin, *Histoire des Mongols*, J. Becquet (ed.), L. Hambis (ed.), Paris, 1965. – *The Mission of Friar William of Rubruck*, P. Jackson (ed.), London, 1990.

P. Chaunu, *European Expansion in the Later Middle Ages*, Amsterdam, 1979. – M. Mollat, *Les Explorateurs du XIIIe au XVe siècle. Premiers regards sur des mondes nouveaux*, Paris, 1984. – M. Mollat, *Sea Charts of the Early Explorers*, New York, 1984. – H. Watanabe, *Marco Polo Bibliography, 1477-1983*, Tokyo, 1986. – N. Ohler, *The Medieval Traveller*, Woodbridge, 1989.

Christiane Deluz

**JUBILEE.** In Jewish tradition, the jubilee year came every 50 years and marked a moment of general pacification, remission of debts and liberation of slaves; it was announced by the priests to the sound of the *jobhêl*, a ram's horn. In Christian tradition, from the year 1300, a jubilee meant the plenary remission of all pains in the afterlife for the Christian who, after having duly confessed and obtained *absolution of his sins, went to pray at *Rome. The process that led to the proclamation of the first jubilee are still not wholly clear; according to the sole surviving contemporary evidence, that of Cardinal Stefaneschi in his *de Centesimo seu Jubileo anno liber*, from Christmas 1299 a crowd of *pilgrims went to Rome, drawn by the news of an extraordinary remission of penalties, which was said to have happened in the years 1100 and 1200. Researches made in the archives of the Holy See were fruitless, but *Boniface VIII decided that he too would grant the "great pardon", in order to discipline this spontaneous religious movement and give it a solemn form. By the papal *bull *Antiquorum habet fidem* of 22 Feb 1300, it was established that during that year and every hundred years, beginning from Christmas night, whoever wanted to gain the *indulgence was bound to visit the basilicas of *St Peter's and *St Paul's, thirty times for Romans and fifteen times for pilgrims coming from a distance. Contemporary sources describe the grandiose success of this first jubilee celebration, which brought in a million pilgrims and considerably enriched the Romans, who were transformed into hotel-keepers and room-letters. Under *Clement VI, the interval of time for the celebration of the so-called *Holy Year* was reduced to 50 years; in 1389 *Urban VI reduced the interval to 33 years, in reference to the life of Jesus; and in 1470 Paul II reduced it to 25, to allow each generation a chance to gain the extraordinary indulgence. Meanwhile the faithful were required to visit, not just the apostolic basilicas, but also the cathedral of *St John Lateran and, later, the basilica of *Santa Maria Maggiore.

The jubilee was often also the occasion for a progressive modification of Rome's town plan, with the rebuilding of the city's gates and *bridges and the construction of new roads. It also favoured the birth of *confraternities that gave free assistance to pilgrims (Companies of the Gonfalon and of the Holy Saviour), charitable institutions created by individual national groups (*scholae* and *xenodochiae*) and *hospices (*e.g.* the English hospice of St Thomas of Canterbury or the Aragonese hospice of Santa Maria in Monterone). While, in Boniface VIII's mind, the jubilee was to make the necessary mediation between *man and *God exercised by *Peter's successor evident to all and hence confirm his *plenitudo potestatis*, according to many specialists the new indulgence marked the end of the medieval dream of a collective *salvation of mankind and opened the era of the search for individual salvation. The first jubilee of 1300 thus responded to a great expectation of *renovatio*, salvation and pardon widespread in the disoriented collective consciousness and confirmed the action of the Church in the world, repositary of the gifts necessary for salvation. It is in any case very significant that *Dante situated his "journey of salvation" to the other world in the year of the first jubilee and that the pilgrimage to Rome left a deep impression on its participants, *e.g.* the chronicler Giovanni *Villani, who drew from his visit to the city the inspiration to compose his *chronicle. After a crisis at the time of the *Great Schism, which in this too created rivalry between the *pope of Rome and that of *Avignon, the jubilee of 1450 marked the revived power of the Renaissance papacy.

A. Frugoni, *Il Giubileo di Bonifacio VIII*, *BISI*, 62, 1950, 1-121. – R. Morghen, *Medioevo cristiano*, Bari, 1968, 265-282 (5th ed.). – P. Brezzi, *Storia degli Anni Santi*, Milan, 1975 (2nd ed.). – M. Maccarrone, *Il pellegrinaggio a S. Pietro e il Giubileo del 1300*, *RSCI*, 34, 1980, 363-429. – A. Menholdt, H. Smolinsky, "Jubeljhar", *TRE*, 17, 1988, 280-285.

Giulia Barone

**JUDAH HA-LEVI (*c.*1075-1140).** The Jewish poet and philosopher Judah ha-Levi was born at Tudela (?), lived in Muslim and Christian *Spain and died in the *Holy Land soon after his arrival there. His poetical work (in *Hebrew) comprises secular and religious works, notably liturgical poems and a series of superb poetry on his journey to Zion. His philosophical work (written in Arabic, translated into Hebrew in the second half of the 12th c.), the *Kuzari* or *Book of Proof in Favour of the Despised Religion*, is a classic of Jewish thought. In dialogue form, it describes the religious quest of the king of the *Khazars, who successively questions a philosopher, a Christian, a Muslim and a Jew; he lets himself be persuaded by the latter and is converted to *Judaism with his people. The *Kuzari* has been compared to *Abelard's *Dialogue* and Raymond *Lull's *Book of the Gentile and the Three Sages*, but the resemblance is only thematic: there is no possibility of any influence on these Christian works.

Judah ben Samuel, ha-Levi, *Kitab al Khazari*, H.Hirschfeld (ed., tr.), London, 1931. – Juda Hallevi, *Kuzari. Apologie de la religion méprisée*, C. Touati (Fr. tr.), Paris, 1994.

A. Graboïs, "Un chapitre de tolérance intellectuelle...", *Pierre Abélard, Pierre le Vénérable*, Paris, 1975, 641-654. – C. Sirat, *La philosophie juive médiévale en terre d'Islam*, Paris, 1988, 127-151.

Gilbert Dahan

**JUDAISM.** By Judaism we understand the whole of the doctrines (religious, moral, philosophical) and rules of life (in Hebrew, *halakhah*) generally recognised by the *Jews. After the biblical and Hellenistic periods, Judaism progressively took shape: in the West, it took its definitive form (at least such as we know it today) around the 13th century. Various factors created it. Firstly, the biblical heritage provided both a monotheistic thought (God creator of the universe) and a ritual practice (Sabbath, feasts, alimentary code, ceremonial laws, etc.). The *Talmud (the Mishnah, codification of moral, social and religious laws, whose redaction was completed early in the 3rd c.; then the Gemara, a discussion of the propositions of the Mishnah, completed early in the 6th c.) attempted to elucidate these practices in a situation different from that described in the *Bible (no more Temple, a dispersed people) and initiated a doctrinal reflection, while providing various options. The still new situation of the Jews in the West (Christian context) obviously led to another elucidation of rites and *doctrines. The ceremonial laws, adapted to the new context, were fixed in Codes (*Maimonides's *Mishneh Torah*, *c.*1180; Moses of Coucy's *sefer mizvoth gadol*, first half of 13th c.; the definitive code, Joseph Karo's *Shulhan 'arukh*, was drawn up in the 16th c.). The doctrines were re-examined in the light of Arab and Greek philosophy; attempts were made to fix dogma (notably Maimonides's 13 "articles of faith"), but none became canonical. On the level of biblical exegesis, under the influence of Christian hermeneutics the traditional modes tended to be abandoned for a more literal exegesis that permitted dialogue with the Christian world.

Despite constant physical proximity, the Christian world of the medieval West had only a mediocre knowledge of Judaism. It realized very slowly (without ever admitting it) that between the Hebrew religion of the Bible and contemporary Judaism there was a wide margin. Though certain authors (*Peter the Venerable) cited it earlier, Talmudic literature was not known in the Christian West until the 13th century. Jewish *philosophy was relatively better known (the *Guide to the Perplexed* was translated into Latin between 1225 and 1230); it procured solutions to the opposition between *Aristotelianism and monotheistic thought. Jewish exegesis stimulated the revival of Christian *exegesis in the 12th c. (notably *Hugh and *Andrew of Saint-Victor), but contacts were mainly oral before the 13th c.; early in the 14th c., *Nicholas of Lyra incorporated part of the results of *Rashi's exegesis in his **Postilla*. Jewish rites remained little known and were most often perceived through the Bible.

S. W. Baron, *A Social and Religious History of the Jews*, 4-15, New York, 1957-1973. – C. Touati, *Prophètes, talmudistes, philosophes*, Paris, 1990.

Gilbert Dahan

**JUDAIZERS.** In the world of Christian authors, the term *iudaizantes* covered several different realities.

1) In *exegesis of the *Bible, commentators who, occasionally or systematically, gave the greater share to *littera* or *historia* (literal sense): *e.g.* *Andrew of Saint-Victor, whose exegesis of the Prophets was judged too close to the Jewish commentaries (his interpretation of Is 7, 14 provoked a controversy); Guerric of Saint-Quentin says that "Andrew expounds this verse [Is 9, 6] no differently from the Jews, indeed he expounds the explanation of the Jews and talks like them".

2) Those who extolled practices that could be inspired by *Judaism or have connections with it; thus, in the controversies over the Saturday *fast, each party taunted the other with Judaizing; and the Greeks accused the Latins of consuming *azyme or unleavened bread at the *Eucharist. The term *iudaizantes* was also used polemically to designate those who manifested some sympathy for Jewish practices (cf. *Guibert of Nogent, apropos of Count John of Soissons).

3) Finally, this term covered certain currents, considered heretical, that literally appealed to the authority of Old Testament practices. The most important was undoubtedly that of the Passagians, known mainly through the *Summa contra haereticos* attributed to *Praepositinus of Cremona (*c.*1200), which devotes 15 chapters to them; the opening of ch. 5 sums up their doctrine: "They say that Christ is a mere creature, the first to be created, that the Old Testament must be observed with regard to solemnities, circumcision, alimentary laws and nearly all the other points, except the sacrifices". So the Passagians rejected the divinity of Christ and the *Trinity and observed to the letter the Sabbath and the prescriptions of the Mosaic law; moreover they rejected ecclesiastical institutions. They seem to have been active in *Lombardy at the end of the 12th century. On the other hand we have no information about the Circumcizers, named in several lists of heretical movements in the 13th century.

L. I. Newman, *Jewish influence on Christian Reform Movements*, New York, 1925. – J. N. Garvin, J. A. Corbett, *The* Summa contra haereticos *ascribed to Praepositinus of Cremona*, Notre Dame, 1958. – B. Blumenkranz, *Juifs et chrétiens dans le monde occidental, 430-1096*, Paris-The Hague, 1960. – H. de Lubac, *Exégèse médiévale. Les quatre sens de l'Écriture*, 2, 1, Paris, 1961, 128-153. – R. Manselli, "I passagini", *BISI*, 75, 1963, 189-210.

Gilbert Dahan

*The kiss of Judas*. 12th-c. Romanesque fresco in the church of St Martin, Vic.

**JUDAS.** One of Jesus' twelve apostles, "who betrayed him" for a sum of money: 30 pieces of silver, specifies Matthew (Mt 26, 15). His sin was made more odious by the fact that it was associated with cupidity. He even became the symbol of it. From the 4th c., the idea prevailed that Judas was the emblematic figure of the Jewish people, whom the Christians never ceased to accuse of having killed the Messiah. The phonic identity between the name "Judas" and the word "Jew" (Latin *Judaeus*) encouraged this assimilation. All the Church *Fathers developed the theme of the traitor, personification of "the audacious Jew, blind and avid". In medieval society, in which *merchants took an increasing place, the representation of the *traditor* tended to be confused with that of the *mercator pessimus*. Under this description Judas appears, richly dressed, purse at his waist and pieces of money in his hands, in a miniature of the **Hortus deliciarum* (12th c.). This was in vogue in the Christian West. Urged on by a growing *antijudaism, in the final centuries of the Middle Ages the image of Judas, whose *suicide illustrated the ultimate sin – that of despair –, became a veritable caricature.

W. D. Hand, *A Dictionary of Words and Idioms Associated with Judas Iscarioth*, Berkeley (CA)-Los Angeles (CA), 1942. – B. Blumenkranz, *Le Juif médiéval au miroir de l'art chrétien*, Paris, 1966. – D. Rigaux, "De l'apôtre félon au *mercator pessimus*. L'image de Judas Iscarioth dans les Cènes italiennes de la fin du Moyen Âge", *Cahiers d'études juives*, 2, Paris, 1990, 109-126.

Dominique Rigaux

**JUDGES, BOOK OF.** One of the historical books of the Old Testament, sometimes grouped with the *Pentateuch and *Joshua (Heptateuch). It is little used in the liturgy, but several episodes were well known in the Middle Ages: Song of Deborah (ch. 4; figure of the Church), story of Gideon (ch. 6-8; the dry fleece of 6, 36-40, image of the virgin birth or of *grace), stories of Jephthah and Samson (Samson a figure of *Christ, Delilah a figure of the *Jews; the foxes of ch. 15 a figure of the *heretics); the fable of the trees who want a king (9, 8-15) was often cited as an example of metaphorical style. The commentators were inspired by *Origen's homilies (translated by Rufinus) and Augustine's *Quaestiones*. For the early Middle Ages, we note the commentaries of *Isidore of Seville and *Rabanus Maurus. In the 12th c., the book of Judges was commented on several times (*Rupert of Deutz, Rainald of Saint-Éloi, *Hugh and *Andrew of Saint-Victor, Osbern of Gloucester, *Peter Cantor, *Stephen Langton). The text of the *Glossa ordinaria* seems to have been due to Gilbert the Universal; it would be supplanted by *Hugh of Saint-Cher's **Postilla* and then by that of *Nicholas of Lyra. Commentaries were more rare in the 13th and 14th cc. (William of Alton, Thomas Waleys, Dominic Grima). Several *sermons (*e.g.* of *Caesarius of Arles) were dedicated to passages from the book of Judges, notably those relating to Samson.

A. M. Dubarle, "Les renards de Samson", *RMAL*, 7, 1951, 174-176; *ibid.*, 8, 1952, 138. – G. Dahan, "Guillaume de Flay et son commentaire du Livre des Juges", *RechAug*, 13, 1978, 37-104 (52-55, list of commentaries). – G. Dahan, "Les Figures des Juifs et de la Synagogue. L'exemple de Dalila", *RechAug*, 23, 1988, 125-150.

Gilbert Dahan

**JUDGMENT, PARTICULAR.** By contrast with the *Last Judgment which, at the end of *time, must involve the whole human race, the expression "particular judgment" or "individual judgment" designates the evaluation to which each man is subject just after his *death, in order to determine his destiny in the afterlife. It would be more correct to speak of "judgment of the soul", since this judgment is sometimes collective; its most distinctive characteristic is the fact that it is applied to separated *souls, not to *bodies raised and reunited with their souls, like the Last Judgment.

In the first Christian centuries, the eschatological perspective announced in St Matthew's gospel (ch. 25) and the *Apocalypse (ch. 19) predominated. A great uncertainty enveloped the fate of the souls of the *dead awaiting the end of time. Yet the *Fathers, like St Augustine and *Gregory the Great, had to admit that souls received rewards or punishments from the time of death, and the contrary thesis, that souls were in a state of sleep until the *Last Judgment, was considered heterodox. So an implicit form of evaluation was admitted very early. But not until the 12th c. did theologians like *Abelard or *Robert of Melun formalize the conception of a legal trial and apply the term *iudicium* to it.

The judgment of the soul was described, earlier, by accounts of *visions, or shown in image. It could take the form of a combat between *angels and *demons, who assembled round the dying man to dispute his soul. Next could come a comparative measuring of sins and virtues: by comparison of two books, as in an account by the Venerable *Bede, or more often, from the 7th c., by the use of the balance. An iconography corresponding to these procedures appeared in the 10th c. and was developed particularly from the 12th century. Finally, complex legal scenarios were formulated, very early in the East (Greek versions of the *Apocalypse of Paul* in the 3rd c.), from the 12th c. in the West (*Guibert of Nogent). Gradually, ever more eminent figures came to intervene in the judgment of the soul (important saints, the Virgin, *Christ, even *God the Father) and it gave rise to procedural refinements (evidence, pleading, appeal), as in Guillaume de Digulleville's *Pèlerinage de l'âme* (1355) or the mural *painting of Zseliz (*Slovakia, 1388). In the course of the Middle Ages, the judgment of the soul acquired a growing importance, though this rise was not accompanied by an eclipse of the Last Judgment. We must rather think, in *theology as in image, of a *iudicium duplex*, *i.e.* the necessary association of two judgments, which did not have exactly the same importance, or altogether the same object.

C. Viola, "Jugements de Dieu et Jugement dernier. Saint Augustin et la scolastique naissante", *The Use and Abuse of Eschatology in the Middle Ages*, W. Verbeke (ed.), D. Verhelst (ed.), A. Welkenhuysen (ed.), Louvain, 1988, 241-298. – J. Le Goff, *The Birth of Purgatory*, Aldershot, 1990. – J. Baschet, "Jugement de l'âme, Jugement dernier: contradiction, complémentarité, chevauchement?", *RMab*, 6, 1995, 159-203.

Jérôme Baschet

**JUDICATE.** The name of each of the kingdoms (Torres, Gallura, Cagliari, Arborèa) into which *Sardinia was divided during the 11th to 14th centuries. The term is derived from *Judex*, the island's most important civil and military post during the Byzantine period (from 534). The origin of the judicates (*giudicati*)goes back to an unspecified time somewhere between the 9th and 10th cc. when, following the Arab expansion, relations between *Constantinople and the island grew slack, favouring the development of four kingdoms whose rulers took the name of Judges. The first three kingdoms disappeared during the second half of the 13th c. following the progressive increase in the political and economic control of the island by *Pisa and *Genoa. The judicate of Arborèa was extinguished in 1420 when the island was under Aragonese rule.

M. Guidetti (ed.), *Storia dei Sardi e della Sardegna*, 2, *Il Medioevo*, Milan, 1988.

Mauro Sanna

**JULIAN OF NORWICH (1342-1416?).** English *recluse, mystic and visionary. From her youth, she desired to live Christ's *Passion, to suffer the pains that presage death and to receive a triple wound: *contrition, compassion, thirst for God. Aged 30, her prayer was heard. During a grave illness, she had 16 *visions of the crucified *Christ. She transmitted her experience in two versions: one short, close to the initial event (London, BL, Add. 37790: Amherst manuscript); the other long (Paris, BNF, fonds anglais ms 40; BM, Sloane ms 2499; Sloane ms 3705), filled out with the seer's later *meditations.

The *Revelations* present an original *theology and pedagogy of looking. For Julian, sinful man is blind and must learn to see *God in all things, by awakening the look of loving *faith. In a multiplicity of ways, she tries to uncover for her reader the infinite presences of the Triune God: in the trinitarian *circulus*, in *creation and creatures, and in the history of *salvation. "God is the centre point of everything, he does everything" (ch. 11). Anguished by *sin, by the problems of suffering and *hell, she received from God the assurance of final universal transfiguration: every man is inserted into the Christ of glory; there exists at *man's deepest level a fundamental presence – God himself, united to his creature – that is always working to lead him back to his divine sources; "the power of Satan is locked up in the hand of God" (ch. 13); the Church's just judgment is inscribed within the continually recreative *love of God. Mother Jesus will finally give birth to a beautiful child. Divine love will turn all things to *good. "All shall be well".

Julian of Norwich is a mystic of divine joy. The exercise of looking in loving faith makes her exult, because she sees God present everywhere. "He creates. He loves. He guards". "He is for us what is good and comforting. He is our garment of love. He encompasses us. He encloses us. He surrounds us with a tender love. He never leaves us" (ch. 5). Living at a time of great tribulations (*Hundred Years' War, *Great Schism, *Black Death,

English defeats on the continent, *Peasants' Revolt, heresy of *Wycliffe), she centres all her soul on union with the All-Present God, who gives light, force, peace, the *grace of the Spirit, allowing each one to go fruitfully through hard times.

E. Colledge, J. Walsh, *A Book of Showings to the Anchoress Julian of Norwich*, Toronto, 1978. – Julian of Norwich, *A Revelation of Divine Love*, M. Glascoe (ed.), Exeter, 1993.

G. Jantzen, *Julian of Norwich, Mystic and Theologian*, London, 1987. – R. Maisonneuve, *L'Univers visionnaire de Julian of Norwich*, Paris, 1987. – F. Beer, *Women and Mystical Experience in the Middle Ages*, Woodbridge, 1992. – M.D.F. Krantz, *The Life and Text of Julian of Norwich*, New York, 1997.

Roland Maisonneuve

**JULIAN OF TOLEDO (642-690).** Trained at the episcopal school of *Toledo under the tutelage of Eugenius, Julian became *archbishop in 680. A brilliant intellectual, he dedicated himself to *theology (*Prognosticon futuri saeculi*) and secular *history (*Historia Wambae*). Author and compiler of a collection of masses and a book of *prayers, he is considered by some as the father of the *Mozarabic liturgy. Like other prelates of the Visigothic church, he governed on good terms with kings Wamba and Euric, but clashed with the papacy. A misunderstanding over the decrees of the third council of *Constantinople gave rise to a conflict finally settled in 688.

J. Madoz, "S. Julien de Toledo", *EE*, 26, 1952, 39-69. – *HChr*, 4, 1993.

Daniel Baloup

**JULIANA FALCONIERI (1270-1341).** Considered the foundress of the women's branch of the *Servites, she has left little trace in the historical record. Even her kinship with the Falconieri and in particular with one of the seven founders of the Servites, St Alexius, is unproven. Born in the second half of the 13th c., according to her 15th-c. *legend, she was converted by hearing the apocalyptic *preaching of her relative, and joined the group of pious women who met at the Servites' little church outside the walls of *Florence (later the Annunziata) and whom the Florentine lexicon called *Mantellate* on account of the mantle they used to wear. Rejecting *marriage and adopting a rigid style of penitential life, she was the protagonist of a eucharistic *miracle at the point of death (19 June 1341). St Juliana's feast day is 19 June.

D. M. Brown, "St Juliana Falconieri: Selected Bibliography (1613-1694)", *Contributi di storiografia servitana*, Vicenza, 1964.

Anna Benvenuti Papi

**JULIANA OF MONT-CORNILLON (1192-1258).** Born in 1192 at Rétine near *Liège, aged five Juliana was offered (with her sister) to the *double monastery of Mont-Cornillon outside Liège. In this Augustinian house she was educated, received as a sister in 1207 and elected prioress of the female community in 1222. Sometime in the 1220s she became the recipient of recurrent *visions, which she finally divulged to her confessor. These were interpreted as *Christ's requests for a eucharistic *feast in the Christian *calendar. The visions stirred an interest that culminated in the foundation of the feast of *Corpus Christi, first in the *diocese of Liège (from 1246) and then throughout *Christendom (from 1264). Juliana had a fervent following of male and female religious, but she faced opposition at Mont-Cornillon. She was expelled in 1246 and then again (after restoration under a friendly bishop) in 1248. During

Interior of the abbey church of Notre-Dame de Jumièges, 11th c.

her last years she moved between *Cistercian nunneries in the diocese of Liège which offered her protection, such as Salzinnes and Fosses. At her death in 1258 she was buried at the nunnery of *Villers.

*The Life of Juliana of Mont-Cornillon*, Toronto, 1988.

E. Denis, *La Vraie Histoire de sainte Julienne de Liège et de l'institution de la Fête-Dieu*, Paris-Tournai, 1935. – M. Rubin, *Corpus Christi: the Eucharist in Late Medieval Culture*, Cambridge, 1991, 169-179.

Miri Rubin

**JUMIÈGES.** Founded in 654 by St Philibert at the request of St *Audoin, archbishop of *Rouen, the *abbey of Jumièges prospered from the 7th to the 9th century. At that time it had three churches, Saint-Pierre, Notre-Dame and Saint-Germain, to which was added in the 9th c. a *chapel of Saint-Sauveur (doubtless the western block of the abbey of Notre-Dame), and its buildings housed 900 monks. Pillaged by the *Vikings in 841, abandoned by its occupants who fled to Haspres, it was revived by monks from *Fleury, on the initiative of William Longsword (928). In *c.*990 the church of Saint-Pierre was rebuilt.

At the start of the 11th c., Jumièges enjoyed a new grandeur under the impetus of reforming *abbots, *William of Volpiano and his disciple Thierry, and an important *chronicle was written there. The abbey church of Notre-Dame, rebuilt from 1040 at the latest by Abbot Robert Champart, was completed and dedicated in 1067. The abbey's prosperity in the 13th c. allowed the rebuilding of the choir of this church and, in the 14th c., of its transept. Though the monastery suffered from the *Hundred Years' War, its abbot, Simon du Bosc (1390-1418), played an essential role in the events of the *Great Schism and was a deputy at the council of *Constance. In the 15th c., Jumièges benefited from the liberality of *Charles VII who lived there with Agnès Sorel in 1450.

Sold as national property at the Revolution, used as a stone quarry after 1802, then saved from total destruction by the Lepel-Cointet family, Jumièges offers grandiose ruins: the abbey church of Saint-Pierre presents a massive two-towered porch, a tribune at the back of the façade, a triforium passage looking towards a nave with rectangular piers (*c.*990), a choir and the south wall of the nave rebuilt in the 14th century. The abbey church of Notre-Dame (1040-1067) offers a chevet with ambulatory (disappeared), a western block with tribune, façade towers and a projecting porch evoking the Carolingian and Ottonian tradition, a nave with tribunes and high windows with alternating supports, whose composite piers announce the maturity of Norman *Romanesque architecture; its transept shows one of the first upper passages cut into the thickness of the wall. The sculpted decoration attests the links with the *Anglo-Saxon world forged through the intermediary of Robert Champart, who became bishop of *London in 1045 and then archbishop of *Canterbury. The *Gothic choir, almost entirely vanished, had an ambulatory and radiating chapels, with a two-storey elevation. We can still see a Romanesque *chapter house, a 12th-c. cellar and vestiges of all the other buildings.

*Jumièges, congrès scientifique du XIII*[e] *centenaire*, Rouen, 1954. – L. Jouen, G. Lanfry, J. Lafond, *Jumièges, à travers l'histoire, à travers les ruines*, Rouen, 1955. – J. Vallery-Radot, "Le deuxième colloque international", *BM*, 1969, 125-147. – J. Taralon, *L'Abbaye de Jumièges*, Paris, 1979. – M. Baylé, *Sculpture romane en Normandie*, Caen, 1992.

Maylis Baylé

**JURISDICTION, CONFLICTS OF.** Conflicts could arise between secular jurisdictions of a different order or competence. They were also encountered in ecclesiastical society by reason of the parties in dispute or the nature of the litigation between different instances (conflict of jurisdiction between *archdeacons and *bishops, bishops and *metropolitans, bishops and *abbots, etc.). Both had to find their solution within secular or ecclesiastical society. More serious and with more political resonance in the Middle Ages were conflicts which, apropos of judicial litigation, opposed the two societies to each other.

Such conflicts supposed the existence on both sides of judicial instances already clearly structured and anxious to safeguard – sometimes to extend – their competence; behind them, secular authorities (emperors, *kings, princes, *towns, etc.) and religious authorities (papacy, episcopate) who measured the importance of the stake (the sovereignty of the *State, the independence of the Church) and backed them; litigations that concerned both societies at once. Such conditions were hardly achieved before the 13th century. This means that conflicts of jurisdiction attained no great extent until the 12th c., when they provoked very serious crises. The conflict between *Thomas Becket and *Henry II of England (1164-1170) and the Bernard Saisset affair in France were among the most dramatic. By the start of the 13th c., *Philip Augustus was laying down the basis of an agreement between *clerics and barons to put an end to the attacks of clerics on the secular *justices, and canon 42 of the *Lateran council of 1215 "forbids all clerics in future from extending their jurisdiction, on the pretext of ecclesiastical freedom, at the expense of the secular justices". Particularly numerous, sometimes very serious, were the conflicts of jurisdiction aroused by *privilegium fori*, which put *clerics out of reach of the secular justices. But who was a "cleric", and who had the competence to judge him one? Hence the ceaseless *trials about the status of cleric, the frauds, the scandals, the *violence to which they gave rise. Against *privilegium fori*, proof of the "*freedom of the Church", were ranged the needs of public order and the suppression of crimes, which pertained to the secular authorities, guardians of social peace. These could not renounce the right to pursue criminous clerks (case of Bernard *Saisset, bishop of Pamiers, accused of "*lèse-majesté*, treason, *simony, *heresy and *blasphemy" in October 1301).

*Canonists did admit some derogations from *privilegium fori*, allowing the secular judge to take cognizance of cases in which a cleric was implicated (*e.g.*, in civil cases, in case of the bishop's refusal to judge; in criminal cases, if the cleric had been degraded beforehand).

Other disputed cases were: those relating to right of *patronage, of which the Church claimed to take cognizance since they involved a *ius spirituali annexum* and which the secular courts wished to judge since they concerned "real cases" (questions of real estate); inventories after decease when there were pious *legacies; in penal cases, infractions committed in "holy places" (churches, *cemeteries, monasteries), *theft, scandal, commerce or manual occupation, spectacles and dances, etc.; application of the right of *asylum. These conflicts of jurisdiction occurred in France, England, the Empire, Italy, Sweden, etc. They nourished political controversies and doctrinal debates (*e.g.* the **Songe du vergier*).

R. Genestal, *Le Procès sur l'état de clerc au Moyen Âge*, *BEHE*, 1909. – R. Wright, *The Church and the English Crown, 1305-1335*, 177-185. – G. Inger, *Kirchliche Visitationsinstitut im . . . Schweden*, 1961, 164 f. ("BTP"). – J.A. Guy, "The Development of Equitable Jurisdiction 1450-1550", *Law, Litigants and the Legal Profession*, E.W. Ives (ed.), A.H. Manchester (ed.), London, 1983, 80-6.

Jean Gaudemet

**JURISTS, ITALIAN.** In the juridical experience of the Middle Ages the jurists (civilists, canonists and feudists) of the Italian school occupy a central place, so much so that the dominant jurisprudential movement in classical common law is usually called the "Italian tradition". If we leave out the doctrinal currents north of the Alps, important as they were, especially in 13th-c. civil law, the Italian schools of law provided the dominant interpretative models, until the crisis of common law in the complex intellectual movement of juridical Humanism and its subsequent rationalistic systematization.

But the "Italian tradition" cannot be exhausted, is is often maintained for convenience, in the historical vicissitudes of the "school of *Bologna" and its fortunes. Modern legal historiography has now established the existence of a very broad range of schools and doctrinal movements, in which we can distinguish (not just on the basis of the geographical distribution of *universities) "regional" areas characterised by particular experiences". Think of the importance of the Lombard area in the feudistic tradition, or that of the South for some aspects of the study of *ius proprium*, or the importance of *Perugia as a centre of that intellectual movement still known as "Bartolism", from the name of its founder,

Bartolo da Sassoferrato (1314-1357).

There is room here to list only the most eminent of the Italian jurists belonging to these scholastic traditions. A brief mention of the greatest and most characteristic figures must begin with the protagonists of the pre-Accursian science of civil law, from the almost legendary Pepo ad Irnerio († *c.*1125) with his school (the "four doctors", Martin, Bulgarus, Iacobus and Hugo), from Piacentino († 1192) to Pillio da Medicina († *c.*1207), the first jurist to develop a strong interest in feudal law, from Giovanni Bassiano († *c.*1193) to Azzo († *c.*1220). Special reference must obviously be made to Accursius († 1263), the compiler of the great consolidation of the exegetical tradition on Justinian's *Corpus Iuris* known as the *Magna Glossa*, material on which later schools would draw for centuries. Another outstanding figure is Odofredo († 1265), author of a *Summa feudorum* and an apparatus to the book of the Peace of Constance (25 June 1183) as well as his two glosses on the Digests, sources (not always reliable) of rare information on the origin of the Bolognese Studio and the activities of the first masters of civil and canon law.

Equally rich and broad is the range of the Italian schools of *canon law, beginning with the exegetical tradition on Gratian's **Decretum* (*c.*1140), begun by his pupils Paucapalea and Rolando, and on the subsequent collections of papal *Decretals. Among the most important personalities were *Bernard of Pavia and the Beneventan Pietro Collevaccino, respectively redactors of the *Compilatio I* (*c.*1191) and the *Compilatio III*, the first official collection of papal Decretals ordered by *Innocent III (1209), and above all the great *Huguccio of Pisa, author of the monumental *Summa Decretorum* (1188-1190) and perhaps the teacher of Innocent III himself. To Bartolomeo da Brescia, a scholar of Tancredi, we owe, around 1245, the updating of the apparatus to the *Decretum* prepared some thirty years earlier by *John Teutonicus. The author of the ordinary *Gloss on *Gregory IX's *Liber Extra* was *Bernard of Parma († *c.*1266). Great 13th-c. interpreters of canon law were Goffredo da Trani († 1245), Sinibaldo *Fieschi (later Pope *Innocent IV) and Henry of Susa called *Hostiensis († 1271), author of the famous *Summa* known as *aurea*. Between the late 13th and early 14th cc. flourished Guido da Baisio, called the Archdeacon (*c.*1250-1313), author of the fundamental *Rosarium* on the *Decretum Gratiani* and teacher of the great canonist *Johannes Andreae († *c.*1348), in whose school were formed Paolo de' Liazari and Giovanni Calderini, with their disciple Giovanni da Legnano († 1383).

In the field of civil law, separate mention should be made of the authors of **quaestiones*, the literary genre that bridged school and practice and would provide food for the genre of the *treatise as well as for the first collections of doctrine on the fundamental theme of the relationship between particular law (*ius proprium*) and common law. Among these jurists was the author of the first great summary of penal law, Alberto da Gandino († 1310). Among the great interpreters of particular law, we should not forget Alberico da Rosciate of *Bergamo (1290-1360).

But the full flowering of the Italian tradition belongs to the period of the civilist Commentators. Among these must be mentioned first of all Cino da Pistoia (1270-1336), linked to transalpine doctrinal circles and responsible for the introduction of the techniques of the commentary to Italy. His disciple was Bartolo da Sassoferrato, to whose school belonged the Perugian Baldo degli Ubaldi (1327-1400), a professor in the Studio Viscontea at *Pavia, author of commentaries of a strong philosophical stamp on the *Corpus Iuris Civilis* and part of the *Liber Extra* and a great feudist. Other outstanding personalities were Iacopo Bottrigari, Luca da Penne, commentator on the *Tres Libri Codicis*, Raniero Arsendi, Bartolo's adversary in the doctrine of statutes, and the feudist Andrea d'Isernia.

The 14th c. saw the consolidation of the Italian school, characterised by a strongly dialectical tendency in the exposition of the legal books and by the nexus between science and practice, which gave rise to a vast production of *consilia* (not just in the sphere of civil law, but also that of canon law, as in the case of Oldrado da Ponte from Lodi).

The figure of Bartolo looms over the rest. Under his name remains a monumental *corpus*, manuscript and printed (the 10-volume editions of the 16th c. contain his *lecturae* on the Digests, on the *Code, on the Instutitions and on the Authentics, as well as a rich series of *quaestiones*, *consilia* and *tractatus*). The authenticity of many works is disputed, because of the phenomenon of historical concentration, which has led to texts of varying nature and provenance being put under his name. The *lecturae* on the Digests and the Code and the *quaestiones* are certainly his, as are most of the *consilia* and the treatises.

His political treatises, devoted to the constitutional order of cities (*De regimine civitatis*), political parties (*De Guelphis et Gebellinis*), *tyrannicide (*De tyranno*) and reprisals (*De represaliis*) are of great importance for the thought of the late Middle Ages, since some theoretical positions formulated by Bartolo in the field of public common law provided nourishment for the politico-juridical doctrines of the 14th, 14th and 16th centuries. Also noteworthy are the glosses on the Pisan constitutions of *Henry VII, which form a sort of monographic treatment of the law of resistance and *crimen maiestatis* (*Tractatus super Constitutione Ad reprimendum* and *qui sint rebelles*). Bartolo's thought is characterised by a translation into juristic language of positions already widespread in Aristotelian-Thomistic circles. His doctrine is connected with the crisis of the Avignonese period and is one of the most important and influential examples of the juridical thought of the late Middle Ages. There also remains a rich series of his *consilia*, very important for the development of private law until at least the end of the 16th century.

The 15th c., despite the presence of some doctors of great stature, both in civil law, such as Raffaele Fulgioso (1367-1427), Paolo di Castro († 1441), Angelo Gambiglioni († 1461), Bartolomeo Cepolla (1420-1475), Alessandro Tartagni († 1477) and Andrea Barbazza (*c.*1400-1479), and in canon law, such as *Antonio da Butrio († 1408), Pietro d'Ancarano (*c.*1330-1416), Francesco *Zabarella (1360-1417), Giovanni da Imola († 1436) and Niccolò de' Tudeschi known as *Panormitanus (1386-1445), tended towards a preponderance of practical interests and the exhaustion of the genuinely creative motifs of the tradition. With Felino Sandei (1444-1503) in canon law and especially with Giason del Maino and Andrea Alciato in the study of civil law, we leave the world of the commentators and the Italian tradition comes to an end, opening that cultural phenonenon known as juridical Humanism, the watershed between medieval and modern law.

Thomae Diplovatatii, *Liber de claris iuris consultis*. Pars posterior curantibus F. Schulz, H. Kantorowicz, G. Rabotti, Bononiae, 1968 (for biographies of Italian jurists).

F. C. von Savigny, *Geschichte des römischen Rechts im Mittelalter*, Heidelberg, 1834-1851 (2nd ed.). – F. Calasso, *Medioevo del diritto*, 1, *Le fonti*, Milan, 1954. – F. Calasso, *I Glossatori e la teoria della sovranità*,

Milan, 1957 (3rd ed.). – *Bartolo da Sassoferrato. Studi e documenti per il VI centenario*, Milan, 1962. – M. Sbriccoli, *L'interpretazione dello statuto. Contributo allo studio della funzione dei giuristi nell'età comunale*, Milan, 1969. – F. Calasso, *Introduzione al diritto comune*, Milan, 1970 (repr.). – D. Maffei, *Gli inizi dell'Umanesimo giuridico*, Milan, 1972 (repr.). – D. Quaglioni, *Politica e diritto nel Trecento italiano*, Florence, 1983. – D. Quaglioni, *"Civilis sapientia". Dottrine giuridiche e dottrine politiche fra medioevo ed eta modernà*, Rimini, 1989. – E. Cortese, *Il rinascimento giuridico medievale*, Rome, 1992. – E. Cortese, *Il diritto nella storia medievale*, Rome, 1995.

Diego Quaglioni

**JUST WAR.** A number of texts suggests that the Church of the early centuries, which did not have the responsibility of power – the Church of the martyrs and catacombs – was more than reserved towards war and the profession of arms, whatever the conditions of its exercise. The great change must have come about with the Christianization of power in the 4th c. and, on the intellectual level, with St Augustine, for whom the prince's soldiers, charged with fighting the "visible *barbarians", could legitimately exist and act alongside the soldiers of Christ charged with fighting the "invisible enemies". For him a war could be just if it was waged in self-defence or to restore peace and justice, and with no desire either for cruelty or cupidity. St Ambrose echoed him when he praised "the courage that protects its native land in war against the barbarians, which defends the weak within the country or the allies against the brigands".

Starting from this *Augustinian reflection and parallel with the notion of "holy war", which was to find its full bloom in the *crusades, the notion of "just war" underwent a certain development in the course of the medieval centuries. Gratian's **Decretum* (*c.*1140) expressed the four conditions of the just war: authorized by the prince, *clerics taking no part, for the defence of one's native land under attack or the recovery of despoiled property, to the exclusion of all useless *violence. From the early 13th c., these four conditions became five, summed up in the following terms: "person", "thing", "cause", "spirit", "authority". In the 14th c., the Italian Baldus de Ubaldis, a *doctor in *canon law and civil law, commented thus on these five terms: "The person, viz. whether he is secular and not a churchman; the object, such that the war be made to recover property or to defend one's native land; the cause, such that one fights out of necessity. . . ; the spirit, such that it be waged neither in hatred nor out of insatiable cupidity; the authority, because without the prince's authority war cannot be declared".

A double practical problem must then have been posed: did such a real conflict correspond to a just war (necessarily on one side only), or was it unjust on both sides? what *authority could settle the question? It will be remarked that anyhow it was a question of absolving or condemning persons and not, on the whole, situations. The fact is, in any case, that the papacy, which might have been considered a sort of international tribunal in this sphere, refused to play this role; perhaps it felt that no war within *Christendom could be considered just and that only the "Roman" war conducted in its name, in the name of the Church, in the name of God, could be so. So during the *Hundred Years' War, the papacy, while proposing its own arbitration, refused, despite pressure, to choose, in the name of the notion of a just war, between the English and the French. In the later Middle Ages, rather than "just war", people spoke of a "just quarrel", which implied that only the cause and the thing were just, independent of the spirit.

An interesting, but exceptional, case is that of *Joan of Arc: in the memoirs drawn up on the occasion of the trial that rehabilitated her, theologians and *canonists examined Joan's warlike behaviour according to the five classical criteria and concluded that the Maid had waged, wholly, a just war.

Though this was the orthodox doctrine, it nevertheless remains that heterodox currents – *Waldenses, *Cathars, *Lollards, *Hussites – considered all war a *sin.

F. H. Russell, *The Just War in the Middle Ages*, Cambridge, 1975. – P. Bellini, *Il gladio bellico. Il tema della guerra nella riflessione canonistica dell'età classica*, Turin, 1989. – P. Contamine, *War in the Middle Ages*, Oxford, 1984.

Philippe Contamine

**JUSTICE.** In medieval thought, the problem of justice was approached in a properly theological context (as an attribute of *God or in connection with the *justification of the sinner) and in moral *philosophy, as a *virtue. With Prudence, Fortitude and Temperance, Justice formed the group of cardinal virtues whose conceptualization went back to Plato but whose doctrine was known to the medievals, before the translation and circulation of *Aristotle's *Nicomachean Ethics*, through Roman and patristic sources. The famous definition of justice given by Ulpian († 228) and taken up by *Roman law (*Digest* I, 1, 10; *Institutes* I, pr.) enjoyed immense success: "Justice is the constant and perpetual will to assign to each his right [*suum ius cuique tribuendi*]".

While St *Anselm of Canterbury organised his conception of justice around the idea of rectitude, notably asserting that only the *will that seeks rectitude for its own sake can be called just (*De veritate*, ch. 12), the interpretation of St *Thomas Aquinas was heavily dependent on the Aristotelian theory of justice (*Nicomachean Ethics*, book V). In agreement with the Stagyrite, St Thomas distinguished legal justice from particular justice. Granted that justice as such concerns everyone who is in relationship with another, and hence requires a diversity of subjects, "general justice" or "legal justice" is understood as that which orders man to the common good: "by it, man concurs with the law that orders the acts of all the virtues to the common good" (*Summa theologiae* $II^{a}$ $II^{ae}$, q. 58, a. 5). Particular justice, in contrast, regulates the subject's relations with persons other than himself. But this relationship can again be considered in two ways, either as a relation of one individual to another, or as a relationship of what is common to individuals. Distributive justice shares out proportionately the common good of society, and the equality of this form of justice "consists in according the various parts to different persons in proportion to their *merits" (*Summa theologiae* $II^{a}$ $II^{ae}$, q. 63, a. 1); it thus excludes consideration of persons. Commutative justice, whose object is mutual exchanges, voluntary and involuntary, between two persons, regulates the equity of those exchanges. Faults committed against all justice are: *homicide, but also other forms of *violence against others, verbal injuries and injustices in *court and outside, as well as *theft, rapine and *usury. In the Thomist perspective, *religion, whose role is to render to God the honour that is due to him, is a virtue attached to justice. In this way, St Thomas actually integrates an ancient perspective expressed by Cicero when he stated that "piety is justice towards the gods" (*De natura deorum* I, 41). So it is not surprising that St Thomas can claim with Aristotle that justice surpasses in value all the moral virtues: the other virtues, in fact, excel by reason of the perfection they bring to the subject, while justice "is also praised for the *good that the virtuous man achieves in his relations with others" and, thus, it is in some way "the good of others" (*Summa theologiae* $II^{a}$ $II^{ae}$, q. 58, a. 12).

With Meister *Eckhart, we meet a very original interpretation of justice since, in his exegesis of John's Prologue, he conceives the relationship between the just man and justice as a paradigm for our understanding of the relationship between the Father and the Divine *Word, as well as that between God and man.

Maître Eckhart, *Le Commentaire de l'évangile selon Jean*, A. de Libera (ed.), E.-H. Wéber (ed.), E. Zum Brunn (ed.), Paris, 1989.

É. Gilson, *Saint Thomas moraliste*, Paris, 1974. – *Ancient and Medieval Economic Ideas and Concepts of Social Justice*, S.T. Lowry (ed.), B. Gordon (ed.), Leiden, 1998.

Ruedi Imbach

**JUSTICES.** Medieval justice was plural. This had to do with the nature of justiciary power and the parcelling out of its exercise. Civil was opposed to criminal, high to low justice, lay justices to ecclesiastical justices. These distinctions, however, were far from clear.

The frontier between the civil and the criminal remained confused until the end of the Middle Ages, even in the best-organised *monarchies. In the *Parlement of Paris, where in the early 14th c. there was a criminal chamber – the *Tournelle* – whose registers were entrusted to specific clerks, it still happened that *trials that would normally be adjudged criminal were adjudged civil, by reason of the personality of the culprit or of political circumstances.

The distinction between high and low justice prevailed from the time of the development of the **seigneurie* in the 11th century. High justice dealt in principle with the more important civil cases, crimes of blood and offences engendering a disorder that struck at the sacred, like deliberate arson, *abduction, rape or treason. It could decide on the death of the culprits or levy fines equal to or over 60 pence, whereas low justice could only impose lesser fines. In reality, this distinction was not always respected. To know what types of offences pertained to one or other of these justices, it would have been necessary to have a strict hierarchy of crimes to which a hierarchy of penalties was applied, and this was not the case throughout the Middle Ages. The same crime, *e.g.* *theft, could be judged indifferently by the lords who were custodians of low or of high justice, and its author could, by either of them, be punished by *death. Land justice, whose definition appeared in the early 13th c. and which concerned offences relating to *property, was also very ill distinguished from low justice. As for middle justice, it hardly appeared before the late Middle Ages. It was a convenient means thought up by practitioners to liberate low justice, choked by offences, from fines of between 6 and 60 pence. From a concrete point of view, high justice brought in less than low justice, which was based on fines. But to hold it was an element of prestige, symbolically marked by the construction of a gallows. Indeed, the difference between high and low justice contributed to the establishment of the seignorial hierarchy.

The only distinction for which theory coincided with reality was that between the justice of the lay courts and that of the ecclesiastical courts or *officialities. The *Gregorian reform, by giving *clerics their social autonomy, and *canon law, by providing them with a technical arsenal, permitted the expansion of officialities. Not until the late Middle Ages do we see their competence denied by the lay power, which considered them too

Justice according to Aristotle. Miniature from the *Libro secreto dei secreti*, from which eight citations on the theme of justice surround and teach Alexander the Great. Tuscany, late 13th c. Paris, BNF (Ms it. 917, fol. 26 v°).

laxist. The *death penalty was forbidden them.

The exercise of justiciary power increased this plurality still further. The Carolingian organisation had been based on the exercise of a public justice intended for free men and dispensed within the *mallus publicus*. Privileges of *immunity, by forbidding the entry of public officials and giving all power to the *advocate on immunist territory, had done little to breach this. This system, which corresponded to the administrative division into counties, *vigueries* or hundreds, was succeeded by that of private justices exercised within *seigneuries* whose most perfect judicial form was the castellan lordship. Justice emanated in principle from him who held the *ban (to command, to punish, to constrain); the latter had been the object of rivalries by reason of the power it supposed and the very lucrative profits that its exercise could entail. Under the effect of these violent competitions and of infeudations, the ban was pulverized and private justices multiplied. Thus was created a tangle of *jurisdictions that seemed to lend itself to confusion. But the parcelling out of justice was only apparent, in particular when we look at the local level, that of the *village. It was rare, even in the late Middle Ages, for justices in one and the same village to be shared out in a clear-cut and harmonious way. The tangle of subinfeudations and rivalries was translated into relations of forces that imposed a hierarchy on the *seigneurs justiciers*. Above all, reality gave the preponderance to what the texts call *justicia loci*, local justice. It could be in the hands of the mayor and the representatives of the inhabitants, in which case it served as a natural guarantee against the arbitrary will of the lords while serving their interests since it controlled the transmission of tenures and levied fines. It was also a springboard for the exercise of high justice, which was in many cases dispensed on the spot by the same judgers, to whom might be added the *milites* (knights) of the *seigneur haut justicier* when the latter moved around. To increase the effectiveness of his justice, the *seigneur haut justicier* had an interest in this unification and he was often content to have the thief taken before his court, once he had been judged by the local justice. The fragmentation of powers led in fact to a multiplication of fines, which were brought together and levied locally at the expense of the *peasants.

These forces of disintegration finally encountered limits imposed by communities of inhabitants and by legal thinking about public order. From the late 11th c., urban communities obtained *charters of franchise that guaranteed legal privileges to the townspeople. New justices in the hands of **échevins* or consuls thus arose and came to be added to the seignorial justices. The need to maintain public order also made itself felt and contributed to defining blood justice and the cognizance of cases concerning *roads or *fairs. This activity was nourished by the public principles which it had been possible to safeguard, in particular the "*Peace of God" movement, or whose revival was permitted by legal thought from the 12th century. Finally it was disciplined by political theory, especially in the great monarchies. From the 13th c., the idea tended to prevail that all justice emanated from the prince. In France, the hand of justice was the first of the royal insignia (the **regalia*) that the king received after the anointing of *consecration. It followed from this that the royal power was in essence a justiciary power and that the judges were merely delegates of the prince. Delegated justice was hence distinguished from retained justice.

Delegated justice was exercised by men whose competence was recognised by the prince, whether they acted directly in his name because they had been appointed by him, like the **baillis* and **sénéchaux* from the 13th c. in France, or whether they exercised justice for lords or towns that recognised the king's *authority. Delegated judges thus acted in the name of whoever fundamentally held the right of justice in a given area. But the prince could also judge any case whatever, whether by himself or by transferring it to other judges. The right of pardon exercised by numerous kings or princes, in *France, *England, *Castile or *Portugal, pertained to retained justice. The ruler could in fact decide to pardon the petitioner who avowed his crime, no matter what *court might have condemned him or risked doing so, no matter who the individual, cleric or layman, and no matter what type of crime. In the late 15th c., pardon seems to have been reserved for involuntary *homicides, the least serious of the "crimes of blood". This evolution had less to do with the weakening of retained justice than with the desire to come down hard on serious criminality.

The evolution of justices thus went in the direction of a clarification and a centralization, but we must not forget that, throughout the Middle Ages, their activity was only a slender aspect of the legal field. A very great number of resolutions escaped them since they were regulated by private transactions.

R. Boutruche, *Seigneurie et féodalité*, Paris, 1959 and 1970 (2 vol.). – B. Guenée, *Tribunaux et gens de justice dans le bailliage de Senlis à la fin du Moyen Âge (vers 1380 – vers 1550)*, Paris, 1963. – H. Platelle, *La Justice seigneuriale de l'abbaye de Saint-Amand*, Louvain, 1965. – P. Toubert, *Les Structures du Latium médiéval. Le Latin méridional et la Sabine du IXᵉ siècle à la fin du XIIᵉ siècle*, Rome-Paris, 1973 (2 vol.). – D. Barthelemy, *Les Deux Ages de la seigneurie banale, Coucy (XIᵉ-XIIIᵉ siècle)*, Paris, 1984. – J. Chiffoleau, *Les Justices du Pape. Délinquance et criminalité dans la région d'Avignon au XIVᵉ siècle*, Paris, 1984. – J.-M. Carbasse, *Introduction historique au droit pénal*, Paris, 1990. – C. Gauvard, *"De grace especial". Crime, État et Société en France à la fin du Moyen Âge*, Paris, 1991 (2 vol.). – E. Cohen, *The Crossroads of Justice*, Leiden, 1993. – N. Gonthier, *Délinquance. Justice et Société dans le Lyonnais médiéval*, Paris, 1993. – R. Jacob, *Images de la Justice. Essai sur l'iconographie judiciaire du Moyen Âge à l'âge classique*, Paris, 1994. – *Le pénal dans tous les Etats. Justice, Etats et sociétés en Europe (XIIᵉ-XXᵉ siècles)*, X. Rousseaux (dir.), R. Lévy (dir.), Brussels, 1997.

Claude Gauvard

**JUSTIFICATION.** Before the Reformation, the debate on justification was far from having the breadth that it later acquired. The theologians of the Middle Ages received as a basic datum the *Augustinian doctrine of *grace, born of the anti-Pelagian struggle, insisting on *God's freedom in the justification of the sinner by sanctifying grace. The Middle Ages treated this question usually in the context of original sin. For *Anselm, the justification of the sinner was the work of *redemption by *Christ who satisfies for sinful man. St *Thomas Aquinas (*Summa theologiae* Iª IIªᵉ, q. 68, a. 1) considered that justification involves, on God's part, the remission of sins and the insufflation of the Spirit and, on man's part, *faith and *contrition. *Bonaventure, and following him the *Franciscans, insisted on the wholly free will of God and on the liberation from *sin that justification entailed. Medieval preaching on *merits maintained that we must acquire them by the conduct of our lives, but must leave them out of consideration so as to make no demands on God.

J. Rivière, "Justification", *DThC*, 8, 2, 1925, 2042-2228. – J. Auer, "Rechtfertigung", *LThK*, 8, 1963, 1037-1042 (2nd ed.).

Michel Deneken

**JUSTINA OF PADUA (3rd-early 4th c.).** Member of an important Paduan family and daughter of a certain Vitalian "king" of Padua, Justina was arrested towards the end of the reign of Maximian and martyred on 7 Oct 304 (the first redaction of the *Passio* says 5 Oct, but the date of 7 Oct is common to later redactions and to tradition). The *martyr's body was later interred in the *pomerium*, east of the town, near the Roman theatre. Certain hypotheses have recently corrected this biography: *Vitalis* or *Vitalianus* will have been *consularis* and hence governor of *Padua, but he may also be identified with the bishop of Padua present at the synod of Rome in 370. In consequence, Justina will have been a consecrated virgin rather than a martyr, and she will not have been martyred but simply driven out and exiled. The account of the cruel martyrdom will have been introduced later, though rapidly and doubtless before the 5th century.

The earliest evidence of her cult dates from the first half of the 6th c.: this is the dating suggested by the existing inscription in the *basilica of Santa Giustina at Padua, concerning the foundation by the praetorian prefect Opilius of a small sanctuary dedicated to the saint. Opilius, at first *iudex* (he was to be one of *Boethius's accusers), then consul in 524, became patrician and praetorian prefect after 529. The sanctuary (probably set up over Justina's grave) and the inscription would thus date from between 529 and 533, when *Cassiodorus returned to court and was made praetorian prefect of Italy. The lettering of the inscription also inclines us to this dating.

The second evidence of Justina's cult, the introduction of the saint's name into the Milanese canon, was long attributed to Bishop Lawrence and hence to the years between 489 and 510-511. This date too is now rejected, and specialists prefer to date the introduction of her cult into the *Ambrosian liturgy to the time of the schism of the Three Chapters (547-551), when the saint henceforth appeared as the patron of Venetian Christianity. Later, her name also entered the *calendar of *Ravenna.

From these same years date the first *images of the saint: on the intrados of the apse of the Euphrasian basilica of Parenzo (539-543), and in the procession of virgins in Sant'Apollinare Nuovo at Ravenna (556-569).

Also from the 6th c. seems to date the original core of the *Passio beatae Iustinae virginis et martyris*, which uses many passages of *Sedulius's *Epistola ad Macedonium*, preface to the *Paschale Carmen* (*CSEL* 10). The author of the *Passio* was Florianus, a disciple of the deacon Ennodius. But the other hagiographical text, viz. the *Vita sancti Prosdocimi*, dates from the 11th century. Later *hagiography conforms substantially to this tradition, especially in the works of Pietro Calo, Bartholomew of Trent, *Jacobus de Voragine and Filippo Ferrari.

The saint's cult took on new life in the 15th and 16th cc.: with the *reform introduced in 1419 by the Venetian Lodovico Barbo and the creation of the congregation of Santa Giustina, of which she became the co-patron with St *Benedict; and with the Venetian victory of Lepanto on 7 Oct 1571. 7 Oct became an important festival throughout the Venetian State, and a silver coin dedicated to the saint was struck until the end of the Republic. From the 15th c., finally, date the first attestations of the current iconography in which Justina is depicted with a sword planted in her breast.

*AnBoll*, 10, *Passio Sanctae Iustinae virginis et martyris*, 1981, 467-470. – H. Delehaye, "Vita s. Prosdocimi", *Acta SS. Novembris*, III, 1910, 350-359. – H. Delehaye, "Martyrologium Romanum", *Acta SS. Decembris*, 1940, 440. – "Giustina, santa martire di Padova", *BSS*, 1965, 1345-1349. – G. Prevedello, *S. Giustina vergine e martire di Padova. Note di iconografia e di iconologia*, Padua, 1972. – G. Prevedello, *S. Giustina martire di Padova. Note biografiche*, Padua, 1972. – A. Barzon, "Santa Giustina vergine e martire di Padova", *Santi padovani*, Padua, 1975 ("Scrittori padovani", 1). – A. Barzon, *Padova cristiana dalle origini all'anno 800*, Cittadella, 1979, 211-219 ("Scrittori padovani", 1-2). – M. P. Billanovich, *San Prosdocimo "metropolitanus multarum civitatum". Acquisizioni e problemi delle ricerche storiche*, 1989, 133-147 ("Archivio veneto", 120). – M. P. Billanovich, "Il formulario dell'epigrafe di Opilione (CIL, V 3100). Rassegna critica di recenti pubblicazioni sulle origini di Padova cristiana", *Fonti e ricerche di storia ecclesiastica padovana*, 23, 1991, 63-104. – A. Tilatti, *Istituzioni e culto dei santi a Padova fra VI e XII secolo*, Rome, 1997 (Italia Sacra, 56), 58-80.

Laura Gaffuri

# K

**KABBALA.** The term "kabbala" (from Hebrew *Qabbalah*, "received tradition") designates all the manifestations of Jewish mysticism. Jewish mysticism in the Middle Ages had two great orientations: one of a devotional nature, which led the mystic to *ecstasy and, in some cases, mystical union; the second orientation was that of the theosophical kabbala, centred on knowledge of the divine insofar as it allowed itself to be apprehended by man. This second way proceeded by a symbolic reading of the text of the Scriptures and of the whole content of tradition. This theosophical interpretation was made concrete by a theurgical activity of the kaballist.

Geographically, this mysticism arose in three places: Egypt, the Rhineland and Provence. Medieval Jewish thought as a whole was heavily marked by Islamic *Arab culture. As far as mysticism was concerned, it was evidently the influence of *Sufism that counted most. Its asceticism led man to detach himself from the world and progressively approach God. Bahya *ibn Pakūda (Spain, 11th c.), author of the *Introduction to the Duties of the Heart*, summed up the stations of the Sufi's journey, which culminated for him in the love of God. But it was in Egypt that veritable mystical confraternities were formed, with personalities like Abraham Maimonides († 1217) and his son Obadiah.

Another pietist movement came into being between 1150 and 1250 in the Rhine valley. The core of the movement was a family of scholars, the Kalonymids, with two legendary figures: Rabbi Judah the Pious (1146-1217) and his disciple Rabbi Eleazar of Worms. Their *theology distinguished between the hidden aspect of the divine designated as Creator, *Bore*, and its manifest aspect: glory, *Kabôd*. It was marked by a particularly lively sense of the *immanence of *God and was expressed on the level of practice by a very elaborate theory of prayer and a penitential practice close to the *penitential tariffs used in Irish monasticism.

But the dominant current of medieval Jewish mysticism was that of the theosophical kabbala that came into being in Provence and later flourished in Spain before spreading all over the Jewish world. The *Sefer ha-Bahir* (Book of Light) and the writings of Isaac the Blind (1165-1235) and his pupils are the earliest evidences of it. Great kabbalistic centres flourished firstly at Gerona in Catalonia, then in Castile. It was in this latter region that the best-known book of the medieval kabbala appeared, around 1293: the *Sefer ha-Zohar* (Book of splendour). The theosophical kabbala distinguished between *Eyn Sof* (Infinite), the hidden and unspeakable aspect of God, and the ten fundamental manifestations that emanate from him, the ten *sefirôth*. *Man is made in the image of the sefirothic world, and the Torah is the interface that allows man to act upon the divine and thus to achieve the end in view of which the world came about.

G. Scholem, *Les Grands Courants de la mystique juive*, Paris, 1950. – S.A. Spector, *Jewish Mysticism: an Annotated Bibliography on the Kabbalah in English*, New York, 1984. – G. Scholem, *La Mystique juive. Les thèmes fondamentaux*, Paris, 1985. – G. Scholem, *Origins of the Kabbalah*, Princeton (NJ), 1987. – C. Mopsik, *La Cabale*, Paris, 1988. – R. Goetschel, *La Kabbale*, Paris, 1992 ("QSJ", 1105).

Roland Goetschel

Porticos of the hall of prayer of the great mosque of Kairouan (Tunisia), 9th c.

**KAIROUAN.** A town in the centre of Ifrīkiya, Kairouan was founded in 670 by Ubka ben Nafi during the conquest of the *Maghreb (Kayrawān means "military camp"). It was the capital of the Maghrebian province of the Muslim empires, then capital of the *Aghlabid state in the 9th c., when the town was at its apogee. The great *mosque was enlarged; immense reservoirs were built to provide it with water; the jurist Sahnūn developed Malikism there and made it one of the greatest religious centres of the Muslim world. In the 10th c., the *Fatimids forsook Kairouan, considered too *Sunni, in favour of the twin city of Sabra-Mansūriyya and especially Mahdiyya. It was a town in serious decline that the Hilalians devastated in 1057. Kairouan was henceforth just a modest provincial centre.

"Al-Ḳayrawān", *EI(E)*, 4, 1978, 824-832.

Philippe Gourdin

**KALOCSA.** A small town in central *Hungary (modern county of Bács-Kiskun), Kalocsa housed the seat of Hungary's second ecclesiastical *province. It was in *c.*1008 that King *Stephen I founded a *bishopric there; its first titular, the missionary *abbot of German origin, Astric, made it from 1009 the seat of a probably autocephalous *archbishopric. In the late 11th c., King *Ladislas I attached the bishopric of Bács (of Byzantine rite) to the archbishopric of Kalocsa. From then on, the archbishoprics resided more at Bács than at Kalocsa. They traditionally occupied the curial position of grand *chancellor to the king. In the 14th and 15th cc., the province of Kalocsa, extending over 155,000 square kilometres, comprised some 1600 *parishes, half as many as the province of *Esztergom.

G. Györffy, *Az Arpád-kori Magyarország történeti földrajza* [Historical geography of Hungary in the Árpád period], 2, Budapest, 1987, 427-432.

Marie-Madeleine de Cevins

**KARAITES.** Karaism was a current of medieval *Judaism whose origins remain debated, but which crystallized in 8th-c. Babylon. The Karaites (in Hebrew *qara'im* or *ba'alei ha-miqra*, "people of Scripture") rejected *a priori* the authority of the Jewish oral tradition, mainly incarnate in the Mishnah and then the *Talmud. Heavily influenced by *Islam at the outset, Karaism, still alive today, developed in a great variety of geographical and cultural contexts: the Arab-Muslim East, the Holy Land, North Africa, Spain, Byzantium, Eastern Europe. It produced an abundant philosophical, exegetical, legal and poetic literature, notably in Aramaean, Arabic and *Hebrew.

L. Nemoy, *Karaite Anthology. Excerpts from the Early Literature*, New Haven-London, 1952. – E. Trevisan-Semi, *Les Caraïtes. Un autre judaïsme*, Paris, 1992. – N. Schur, *The Karaite Encyclopedia*, Frankfurt am Main, 1995. – J. Olszowy-Schlanger, *Karaite Marriage Documents from the Cairo Geniza*, Leiden, 1998.

Jean-Christophe Attias

**KEMPE, JOHN (*c.*1380-1454).** A prototype careerist political prelate, Kempe was educated at *Oxford (fellow of Merton College, 1395) and was *doctor of laws by 1414, when he was in the service of the archbishop of Canterbury and administering ecclesiastical courts. On diplomatic missions by 1415, he later served *Henry V as *chancellor of conquered *Normandy (1417-1422). Thereafter he served the *Crown in politics and diplomacy, being continuously on the Council and twice chancellor (1426-1432 and 1450-1454). He passed rapidly through the sees of Rochester, Chichester and *London (1419-1425) to the archbishoprics of *York (1426-1452) and *Canterbury (1452-1454), and was made *cardinal in 1439. Usually associated with Cardinal Henry Beaufort and the party of negotiation and peace in the politics of the *Hundred Years' War, he outlived his mentor to represent stability and experience in a turbulent period of English government right up to his death.

*DNB*, 30, 384-388. – G. L. Harriss, *Cardinal Beaufort: a Study of Lancastrian Ascendancy and Decline*, Oxford, 1988. – M. A. Hicks, *Who's Who in Late Medieval England (1271-1485)*, London, 1991, 261-262.

Benjamin Thompson

**KENTIGERN (died *c.*612).** Founder and patron saint of the church of *Glasgow. The *obit* of a Conthigirnus, probably the same person, is entered *c.*612 in the Welsh *Annals. 12th-c. *hagiography by Jocelin of Furness and others contains much mythological material, but probably factual material as well. He appears to have been a British *bishop active in Strathclyde in the late 6th c., but possibly not the first Christian missionary there. His shrine in Glasgow cathedral became a popular *pilgrimage centre.

K. H. Jackson, "The Sources for the Life of St Kentigern", N. K. Chadwick *et al.*, *Studies in the Early British Church*, Cambridge, 1958. – A. Macquarrie, *The Saints of Scotland*, Edinburgh, 1997, ch. 5.

Alan Macquarrie

**KERAITS.** A Turkik people, the Keraits (Kereyit) lived as nomads in central Mongolia. Their king, miraculously saved in a snowstorm and instructed by *merchants, was converted to Christianity and in 1009 asked the *metropolitan of Merv to relax the rules of *fasting for his people. The kings bore Christian names (Mark, Cyriac). The last king, Toghrul, having defeated the Tatars, received the title of Wang from the Kin emperor of China (1199); but he got embroiled with his ally *Genghis Khān, was defeated and perished in 1203. The Kerait people was dispersed, but gave the *Mongols princesses and a governmental personnel that long remained Christian.

P. Pelliot, "Chrétiens d'Asie centrale et d'Extrême-Orient", *TP*, 15, 1914, 623-644. – I. Togan, *Flexibility and Limitation in Steppe Formations: the Kerait Khanate and Chinggis Khan*, Leiden, 1998.

Jean Richard

**KHĀRIJITES.** The Khārijites were followers of a heterodox Muslim sect whose origin went back, like that of *Shi'ism, to the earliest times of *Islam. After the murder of 'Uthmān in 656, the partisans of *'Alī and those of Mu'āwiya faced each other at the battle of Siffīn, then decided to submit to arbitration; one group, which had so far supported 'Alī, rejected this procedure; some of its members secretly left the town of Kūfa in February-March 658, whence their name of Khārijites ("those who went out").

The conflict turned on the nomination and role of the *caliph; against the partisans of 'Alī (the Shi'ites), for whom the caliph could only be a descendant of the Prophet, and those of Mu'āwiya who preached the legitimacy of the new *Umayyad dynasty, the Khārijites claimed that the caliph should be chosen on purely religious and moral criteria; so he must be the best of the Muslims. Hence any irreproachable believer could be designated, even if he were not of the family of the Prophet and even if he were not an Arab; this doctrine seduced the converted peoples (*mawālī*), especially the Iranians and Berbers. Moreover, the Khārijites asserted their originality on another point; for them, every Muslim was responsible for his acts (doctrine of justification by faith and by works); the caliph who had committed faults must be killed; it was religious murder. The Khārijites were thus idealists living according to a rigorous morality, according man a certain freedom and practising holy war against bad Muslims. Far from forming a single movement, they divided into a great number of sects who fought against the established States.

In the East, the Khārijites never stopped struggling against the Umayyads and then against the *Abbasids; the more extremist ones, the Azrakites, held Fars for a time. Under the last Umayyads, their revolts favoured the change of dynasty. In the 9th c., the Abbasids managed to reduce them to the status of minority sects in the whole of the Empire, except for the region of Omān and a part of Yemen.

The Khārijites received their best welcome in the freshly Islamized lands of the *Maghreb; the Berbers were seduced by their egalitarian doctrine and adopted it as a sign of independence. Extremist Khārijites, the Sufrites, took possession of *Kairouan. But it was Ibadism (moderate Khārijism) that triumphed; in 777, Ibn Rustām, an Iranian chief who had lived at Kairouan, founded a principality at Tahert; other Ibadite principalities arose at Sijilmassa and Tlemcen; the whole Saharan border of the Maghreb was in the hands of Khārijites who spread Islam in black Africa. In the 10th c., these States did not resist *Fatimid expansion; the last political manifestation of the Khārijites was the revolt of the Man on the Ass that threatened Ifrīkiya in the middle of the 10th century. Opposed by the new empires, the Khārijites were reduced to the status of residual communities existing in Berber-speaking regions like M'zab, Jerba, Kabylia and Aurès.

H. Laoust, *Les Schismes dans l'Islam*, Paris, 1965. – "Kharidjites", *EI(E)*, 4, 1978, 1074-1077.

Philippe Gourdin

**KHAYYĀM, 'UMAR (died 1123 or 1132).** Persian poet and mathematician born at Nishāpūr in Khurāsān, 'Umar Khayyām became the official astronomer of the *Seljuk sultan Malik-Shāh. He is known mainly for his *Rubāīyāt* (a poetical collection composed of quatrains in which the first, second and fourth lines have the same rhyme). Khayyām died probably in 1123. The first manuscript containing his poems dates only from the 14th c. and contains 13 quatrains, while later traditions attribute to him up to 800. In his quatrains, the poet generally adopts a free attitude towards religion. Dāya's mystic work, *Mirsād al-Ibād* (1223), says of Khayyām that, while much appreciated "for his talent and wisdom, he is close to the errors of the philosophers and materialists".

*Les Quatrains d'Omar Khayyam*, M. Fouladvand (tr.), Paris, 1959. – *The Rubáiyat of Omar Khayyam*, P. Avery (tr.), J. Heath-Stubbs (tr.), London, 1979.

A. Dashti, *In Search of Omar Khayyam*, London, 1971. – R. Levy, *Introduction à la littérature persane*, Paris, 1973.

Michel Balivet

**KHAZARS.** A Turkik people, the Khazars appeared at the time of the dismemberment of the Empire of the Western *Turks (early 7th c.), associating Turkish, Oghuz and Sabir elements under the leadership of a royal clan from which was chosen the qaghan, a sacred figure who was put to death if fortune failed him. Their leader Zichel helped *Heraclius against the Persians (625); but their capital Balandja, south of the *Caucasus, was taken in 642 by the Arabs; from then on their rule extended from the Caucasus to the middle Volga and Khwarezm, with Itil on the Volga as capital. In 737 the Caliph Marwan had obliged their qaghan, a prisoner, to embrace *Islam, but he abjured it, and the Khazars tolerated the raids made by the Russians across their territory against the neighbouring Muslims of the Caspian, except in 922 when one of their clans, which had embraced Islam, massacred the pillagers. Their relations with the Byzantines were in general cordial; two emperors married Khazar princesses and it was a Byzantine, Petronas, who built for the qaghan the fortress of Sarkel on the Don, to contain the Hungarians and *Pechenegs who had taken the eastern part of their territory from them. They also had to suffer from the Russians, who managed to establish themselves in *Kiev. In 965, Sviatoslav destroyed Itil and Sarkel; and in 1015 the Russians helped Basil II conquer *Crimea from the Khazars who were established there and who left it their name (Khazaria). The Khazar power thus disappeared in the first half of the 11th c.; but Khazar chiefs maintained themselves, *e.g.* at Tmutorakan.

This empire was at the confluence of commercial routes, and the Khazars acquired a reputation as merchants; they were open to various religious influences. Islam had won over some clans and Masūdī states that the "vizirs" were traditionally Muslim. The *Jews managed to convert the ruler and, for quite a long period from the early 9th c., the qaghan was habitually Jewish. Recently-discovered letters have confirmed the existence of a considerable Jewish element, and the reputation of the Khazar kings spread far in the Jewish world. Christianity also progressed among them from their close neighbours, Alans, Abkhazians, etc. From Byzantium, Constantine the Philosopher (St *Cyril) came in *c.*861 to evangelize them, without success; but in 1015 the khan of Taman was a Christian, and the Byzantines had founded a *bishopric at Matrakha from which Christian preaching spread out among the Khazars. So *Judaism had not become the religion of the State among them.

D. M. Dunlop, *The History of the Jewish Khazars*, New York, 1967. – O. Pritsak, "The Khazar Conversion to Judaism", *Harvard Ukrainian Studies*, 2, Cambridge (MA), 1971, 261-281. – P. B. Golden, *Khazar Studies*, Budapest, 1980 (2 vol.). – P. B. Golden, "The Khazars", *Cambridge History of Early Inner Asia*, Cambridge, 1990, 263-270.

Jean Richard

**KIEV.** The beginnings of Kiev as the capital of Kievan *Rus', originally the base of the *Varangians and a transit commercial counter, date from the late 9th century. Situated high above the right bank of the Dniepr, downstream from its main tributaries, Kiev controlled the river routes joining the Baltic to the Black Sea. In the 10th c., it became an important commercial and political centre. At the time of *Vladimir the Great, it was already an important urban centre with a multi-ethnic population of 15-20,000 inhabitants, with eight markets serving local *commerce and merchandise from far away. The core of Kiev was a *burg* or borough of 10 hectares. *Iaroslav the Wise enlarged Kiev's fortified area by 70 supplementary hectares, so that with its suburbs the town's total territory exceeded 300 hectares and the population reached nearly 35,000 inhabitants, 45,000 in the 12th century. The social configuration of the town consisted of the prince's court with guard and domestics; a numerous *nobility of great landowners who also took part in operations of commerce and credit; the domestics and clientele surrounding this social class; *merchants and artisans, a few thousand people connected with Church institutions, the population drawn to the town, and finally travellers passing through.

There was a Christian community at Kiev from the first half of the 10th century. Thirty years after the *baptism of Vladimir the Great (988), the view of Kiev was dominated by the *crosses of more than 400 churches, according to a Saxon knight. Apart from one stone church, that of the *palace (Our Lady of the Tithe), and about fifteen wooden public churches, these were mainly private *chapels erected next to important houses. Six hundred of these were consumed by the fire of 1124. The number of monumental stone churches, beginning with the magnificent *cathedral of Divine Wisdom (St Sophia, 1037-1046), grew to more than ten in the second half of the 11th c.; by the early 13th c., there were nearly forty. In the suburbs were some fifteen important monasteries and *convents, including the monastery of the *Caves.

In secular architecture too, Kiev remained a wooden town. The town that grew up in the 11th c. under the patronage of the Mother of God, called *Blachernitissa* ("She who intercedes"), venerated as the "Indestructible Wall", aimed to conform to the model of *Constantinople, a fact remarked in Western Europe: *Adam of Bremen called Kiev "an ornament of the Greek Christian world" and described the town as an imitation (*aemula*) of the capital of the Empire. The ambitions of Kiev, surnamed the "second Constantinople" or "second Jerusalem" in the 12th c., engendered the attribution to the town of an apostolic "act of baptism": according to the tradition handed down in the *Narrative of Bygone Years*, the apostle Andrew came up the Dniepr from Cherson, planted a cross at a certain place and blessed the hills, prophecying the appearance of a great town and numerous churches in that place.

The modification of commercial routes in the 12th c. following the *crusades, and the division of Rus' into principalities, reduced Kiev's political and economic supremacy in the second half of the 12th c., but it remained the nominal capital of Rus' until the *Mongol invasion. Despite the considerable destruction suffered by the town, taken by the invaders on 6 Dec 1240, Kiev and its archiepiscopal see remained the residence of the *metropolitans and the centre of religious life until 1299. In the mid 15th c., Kiev regained this religious role for the *Orthodox population of the Polish-Lithuanian State following the division of the Russian Church and the separation of the metropolitanate of *Moscow. From *c.*1362, under the supremacy of the rulers of *Lithuania, the town emerged from its decline, saw its importance increase in commerce with the East and in 1494 was granted the urban law of *Magdeburg.

V. Lazarev, "Regards sur l'art russe ancien", *CCM*, 13, 1970, 195-203; *ibid.*, 14, 1971, 221-238. – H. Ivakin, *Kiev XIII-XV vv.*, Kiev, 1982. – W. Philipps, "Die religiöse Begründung der altrussischen Haupstadt", *FOEG*, 33, 1983, 227-238. – P. Točko, *Drevnij Kiev*, Kiev, 1983. – J. Fennell, *The Crisis of Medieval Russia 1200-1304*, London, 1983. – V. Mezentzev, "The Development of Medieval Kiev", *The Russian Review*, 48, London, 1989, 145-170. – V. Mezentzev, *Harvard Ukrainian Studies*, 14, Cambridge (MA), 1990, 176-179. – S. Franklin, J. Shepard, *The Emergence of Rus, 750-1200*, London, New York, 1996 (index).

Andrzej Poppe

**KILIAN (died *c.*639).** Kilian, an Irish missionary *bishop, carried out his *mission in liaison with the ducal family of the *Thuringians, which was already baptized but whose morals were still hardly Christian. He is said to have been murdered for having insisted that Duke Gozbert separate from his wife who had previously been his brother's wife. But the details of his *Vita* written in *c.*840, which make him a *martyr, are often hardly credible. However, his *relics were elevated from 752 by Burchard, first bishop of *Würzburg. The cult of Kilian, supported by the *Carolingians, spread particularly to *Paderborn and *Bamberg.

A. Wendehorst, "Die Iren und die Christianisierung Mainfrankens", *Die Iren und Europa im früheren Mittelalter*, H. Löwe (ed.), Stuttgart, 1982, 319-349.

Geneviève Bührer-Thierry

**ḲIMḤI, DAVID (*c.*1160-1235).** Important Jewish grammarian and exegete. Son of the well-known scholar Josef Kimhi (or Qimhi), in his youth he composed the *Miklol* ("Summa"), a grammatical work destined to have great success, also among Christians. He then devoted himself to biblical exegesis, commenting on the *Torah*, Chronicles, the Psalms, the former and latter Prophets. In particular, his commentaries on the Psalms and Prophets are masterpieces of medieval Jewish exegesis.

His exegetical works were presented as a paraphrase of the biblical text, aimed at favouring their exact understanding. The author's first intention was to expound the "literal sense", which he defined with rigorous method, using his excellent knowledge of Hebrew. Constant attention was reserved for the authoritative Rabbinic heritage, so much so that midrashic interpretations form an important component of all the commentaries. Also amply developed was the eschatological reading, since Kimhi – a direct witness of the terrible sufferings of Israel in exile – was able to give voice to the hopes of his people, who awaited with indestructible faith the coming of the messianic redemption.

David Kimchi, *Commento ai Salmi. I. Sal 1-50*, L. Cattani (ed.), Rome, 1991; *II. Sal 51-100*, L. Cattani (ed.), Rome, 1995.

F. Talmage, *David Kimhi: the Man and the Commentaries*, Cambridge (MA), London, 1975.

Luigi Cattani

**KINDĪ, AL- (*c.*801-*c.*866).** An Arab philosopher and scholar who lived at *Baghdad as a familiar of the *caliphs, at a time of great theological controversies and intense activity of translating Greek works into Arabic. He is considered the initiator of *falsafa*, *i.e.* *philosophy expressed in Arabic and appealing to the authority of the Greek heritage. He left numerous opuscula on philosophy and on all the sciences, and even on certain techniques. Only a small part of this circulated in the West, notably his *De intellectu*, of which two Latin *translations are known. Under the influence of Alexander of Aphrodisias, he distinguished a single Agent *Intellect for all men and the potential intellect possessed by everyone, which passes into act under the action of the former.

A. L. Ivry (ed., tr.), *Al-Kindi's Metaphysics: a Translation of Ya'qub ibn Ishaq al-Kindi's Treatise "On First Philosophy"*, Albany (NY), 1974.

A. Cortabarria, "Al-Kindi vu par Albert le Grand", *MIDEO*, 13, 1977, 117-146.

Dominique Urvoy

**KING, KINGDOM.** In the early Middle Ages, the Frankish or Anglo-Saxon king belonged to an elect family of divine origin. Kingship was sacred, though without any Christian reference. The king was the mediator between his people of free warriors and the gods who gave victory and prosperity. In each generation, the great men made a choice, and whichever brother prevailed was considered to have succeeded by divine will. So kingship was discontinuous and each generation saw the sharing out of lands conquered by the father often at the price of civil wars. Power was conquered more than it was inherited. So the kingdom had no strength, and its borders were ceaselessly revised, though there were holy places that focused loyalties (*Paris and *Saint-Denis).

The appearance of *consecration led to great changes. The *Visigothic bishops were the first to anoint the elect of the magnates in imitation of the kings of Israel in order to fortify particularly weak princes. At the same time, the new practice increased the power of the *clerics who held the power to anoint or not (and so if necessary to depose), and allowed them to make good their ministerial conception of kingship in which the Christian king, guarantor of peace and *justice, led his people to *salvation by following the advice of the clerics. The *Carolingians had themselves consecrated in 751 and 754 to mark the change of elect family that ratified an established fact. The practice was generalized slowly but imperfectly. The kings of *Castile were sometimes consecrated, the kings of *Portugal never. Indeed, a simple handing over of royal insignia might be found preferable. In a way, consecration aligned the type of designation of kings on that of *bishops. It consequently formalized the election (in the medieval sense of the word, which meant any choice inspired by *God, that of the *maior et sanior pars* or even that of a single person) by the magnates. Royal anointing was not originally linked to any particular chrism and it was renewable, to reaffirm the alliance between the king and God and to reinforce tottering powers. The holy **ampulla* appeared in the late 9th c. in West Francia in the works of *Hincmar. The period 888-987 saw the alternation of two families, the Robertians, victors on the battlefield, and the Carolingians, handicapped by numerous minorities, who were successively consecrated and recognised by all. That is to say that in 987, while it was admitted that kingship was always hereditary, provided the great men elected the sons of the deceased king, it was also necessary to be victorious and possess regal qualities. So Hugh Capet was logically chosen to the detriment of Charles of

Lower Lorraine, distant and unconsidered.

The election of 987 was for the moment a non-event. But in the long term it would change the conception both of the kingdom and of the king. *Francia occidentalis* was permanently separated from the *Empire, and the first *Capetians were far too weak to be able to continue to look east. The frontier of 843 thus became assured (Scheldt, Meuse, Saône, Rhône) and the *regnum* gained in stability of basis, even if the custom of appanages for cadets multiplied the risks of division. The Capetians put all their energy into creating a continuous dynasty. They could hardly get rid of election, but they got round it by organising the consecration of their successor and his association on the throne in their own lifetime, up to the reign of *Philip Augustus. By chance, and by multiplying marriages, for ten generations they nearly always had grown-up sons. Masculinity was unproblematically imperative for a position where the role of war leader and judge was capital. Primogeniture was hardly contested any longer after the 11th century. The exclusion of *women became an established fact between 1316 and 1328. Thus a dynastic right took shape quite quickly in *France while other kingships remained elective. Moreover, French consecration never ended by putting the king under the tutelage of the *pope (distant) or the archbishop of *Reims (losing ground from the 12th c.). The consecration oath in France was more of a declaration of intention, and election was finally replaced by a rather formal *acclamation. In the late Middle Ages, it was even envisaged that consecration, a costly ceremony, should be done away with. Blood now made the king, consecration was of little further use to a hereditary kingship. Thus, sooner in France than elsewhere (but the evolution was the same for all princes), kingship possessed chronological continuity and territorial stability.

The kingship of the feudal period was no longer that of the early Middle Ages. The king now ruled a society clearly divided into three orders: *oratores, bellatores, laboratores*. The king made a synthesis of the three functions. He was sacred, pious, if possible saintly. He persecuted *Jews, went on *crusade, showered attention on the pope (the emperor could hardly do this), dispensed *justice to the poor. He was slightly more than a layman, all the more so since he worked *miracles in France and England. He was also a fighter and a warrior who led his vassals to war in person and multiplied exploits and conquests. To lose a battle was always to face the judgment of God. And war was merely the ultimate way to maintain justice. The king also had to guarantee prosperity to all, feed all the hungry and care for the sick. St *Louis gave an example of this. But feudal kingship quite soon acknowledged that the prince had a position apart in this hierarchy. The king was at the summit of the pyramid of *fiefs. All the land in the kingdom depended on him, directly or indirectly. As head of this hierarchy, the king was outside it. He swore *homage to no-one, even if a fief *escheated to him and he did not reassign it. He was the lord of all the inhabitants of the kingdom. From the 13th c., the majority of princes were considered not just *suzerains but sovereigns. Independence from the two universal powers was gradually acknowledged to all kings by the *jurists. Likewise, royal power was inspired by imperial power. All *justice derived from the king, possessor of grace, all law flowed from him. It followed that royal power became everywhere theoretically imperial and absolute. But in general the king did not have the means for his declarations, his Christian *conscience limiting his excesses. It was also possible to appeal to his *authority by urging respect for his consecration *oath or the privileges of individuals or communities. The effectiveness of these counterweights to the growth of royal power was extremely variable. The rights of the community were only liable to threaten royal power where a social group (the *nobility or the inhabitants of the *towns) took charge of them and where there was a regular representation of that community (parliaments, general or regional estates). England was more favoured than France in this matter.

The 14th and 15th cc. were marked by a fitful dialogue between the king and his kingdom. The institutional innovations plunged into by a kingship more and more organised into *monarchy aroused strong reservations. Against these, all kingships, especially if they were also threatened from outside, issued massive propaganda to make their function visible and legitimate. The use of monarchical symbols became massive (leopards, *lilies, towers of *Castile, royal colours); everywhere in the 13th c. a national history was written in the vernacular, justifying the king and the kingdom. If war threatened, pamphlets, communiqués of victory and *Te Deums* were distributed. The royal spectacle gained in pomp and organisation. Consecration changed little in substance but became more ostentatious, royal *funerals were turned upside down. The king no longer died like an ordinary Christian. The royal death became a necessary spectacle followed by a long exposition, then a funeral cortège that took the body, and later the royal mannequin (in England from 1327, in France after 1422), from the *palace to the *cathedral, then to the royal necropolis. Mannequin and *gens de Parlement* in red affirmed on this occasion that the king never died, even if his person was mortal. In France, royal entries, easy to stage, became the most popular ceremony, all the more since they permitted a dialogue between the kingdom and its king which, in France, had hardly any institutional channels. The people went to seek the king outside the walls to bring him in *procession through the decorated streets. Public *games and discourses expressed the grievances of some and the certainties of others. All this was to allow the whole of the kingdom to be persuaded of both the excellence of the king and the permanence of the *crown. The bond between the king and his kingdom remained very strong in the late Middle Ages, and a whole policy tended to celebrate it and reactivate it if need be.

W. A. Chaney, *The Cult of Kingship in Anglo-Saxon England*, Manchester, 1970. – S. Reynolds, *Kingdoms and Communities in Western Europe, 900-1300*, Oxford, 1984. – B. Yorke, *Kings and Kingdoms in Early Anglo-Saxon England*, London, 1990. – D. P. Kirby, *The Earliest English Kings*, London, 1991. – J. Barbey, *Être roi. Le roi et son gouvernement en France de Clovis à Louis XVI*, Paris, 1992. – B. Guenée, *L'Occident aux XIV^e^ et XV^e^ siècles. Les états*, Paris, 1993 (re-ed.). – J. Krynen, *L'Empire du roi. Idées et croyances politiques en France, XIII^e^-XV^e^ siècle*, Paris, 1993.

Colette Beaune

**KINGS, BOOKS OF.** Part of the "Former Prophets" (in the Hebrew Bible) or of the "historic books", in some Latin Bibles (following the Septuagint) Kings also include the two books of Samuel; but the distinction was made in the 12th c. (*Hugh of Saint-Victor [*Didascalicon* IV, 2] separated the books of Samuel from the books of Kings, which he called by their Hebrew name, *Malachim*). Mainly narrative (apart from some lyrical pieces like the prayer of Hannah), throughout the Middle Ages they aroused the interest of the Christian West, providing some emblematic models of rulers, such as *David, *Solomon, Josiah, etc., whose ambiguous values were sometimes noted. The history of the kings of Judah gave the *chroniclers of the great monarchies the opportunity for parallels. So the *exegesis of these biblical books had a dual orientation: on the one hand, it was interested in historic details (facts, successions and genealogies of rulers. . .), on the other, it explored the analysis of the characters of the protagonists (Saul, Solomon, *Elijah).

Medieval exegesis made considerable use of the commentaries of *Claudius of Turin and *Gregory the Great's *Homilies on Kings*. The **Quaestiones* on 1 and 2 Samuel and 1 Kings by a converted Jew of the early 9th c., which introduced a great number of Jewish interpretations and considerations on the Hebrew, also exercised a certain influence, due to the fact of their attribution to Jerome. The main commentaries were: for the early Middle Ages, those of the Venerable *Bede, *Isidore of Seville (*Quaestiones*) and *Rabanus Maurus (the most voluminous); for the 12th c., the *Glossa ordinaria*, *Rupert of Deutz, *Stephen Langton; for the 13th c., *Hugh of Saint-Cher, William of Alton; for the 14th c., *Nicholas of Lyra, Dominic Grima.

M. L. W. Laistner, "Some early Comments on the Old Testament", *HThR*, 46, 1953, 27-46. – M. Bloch, *Mélanges historiques*, 2, Paris, 1963, 920-938. – A. Saltman, *Pseudo-Jerome Quaestiones. . .*, Leiden, 1975. – P. Riché, "La Bible et la vie politique dans le haut Moyen Âge", *Le Moyen Âge et la Bible*, Paris, 1984, 385-400. – J. Le Goff, "Saint Louis et Josias", *Mélanges B. Blumenkranz*, Paris, 1985, 157-167.

Gilbert Dahan

**KINSHIP, DEGREES OF.** All systems of kinship are faced with the necessity of employing criteria that allow kin to be distinguished from non-kin and, where necessary, to evaluate the "distance" between two kinsfolk.

The Middle Ages had recourse to a method already in force at Rome, that of counting the number of generations separating either two individuals one of whom descended from the other or, in the collateral line, two individuals having a common ancestor. Yet the principles of this computation evolved during the medieval period. For collateral kinship, the Roman system used the notion of *gradus* (degree) on a "dual scale": starting from an individual, called *Ego*, they counted the number of generations going back to the common ancestor, then going down to the kinsperson being identified; two first cousins were thus separated by four degrees (two degrees from *Ego* to his grandfather, two from the grandfather to the cousin). This method of calculation was kept up during the first centuries of the Middle Ages; but in the 8th c. the ecclesiastical texts seem to have adopted what would become the canonical method of computation: the generations were then counted on a single line; first cousins were then kin to the second degree; when the distance from the common ancestor was of unequal length, classical *canon law held to the higher figure.

This counting by generation on a "simple scale" – the degree being designated indifferently by the terms *geniculum*, *generatio*, *gradus* and *linea* – is considered a Germanic practice and it is attested in various "Germanic laws". The conditions under which the Church adopted this computation are not clear; we are entitled to challenge the idea, formerly accepted, of a "popular" influence and we can only state that this modification was in keeping with the continual movement of broadening of kinship in ecclesiastical regulations between the 5th and 12th centuries.

In the medieval system, the counting of degrees was in fact used to designate kinsfolk whom a person could not marry, but also an individual's potential heirs. The former point was a major preoccupation of the Church, which progressively extended the circle of prohibited marriage partners; even when the change to computation on the "simple scale" automatically halved the distance between two kinsfolk, it was the same values that were preserved: in the 11th and 12th cc., *marriage was forbidden to the seventh canonical degree, in direct line as well as in collateral line – equivalent to the 14th degree on the Roman computation. Moreover, the notion of "one flesh" between spouses allowed the same prohibitions to be projected onto allied families: if my wife is one with me, her blood relations become mine and *vice versa*.

In 1215, at the fourth *Lateran council, the limit of prohibitions was brought down to the fourth canonical degree; the reason for this apparent retreat by the Church is often attributed to the impossibility of applying the rules; it seems more likely that the Church succeeded henceforward in imposing the idea that a too close marriage was negative, and that the new canonical rules were adjusted to marriage practices which, in the aristocracy at least, avoided alliances between kinsfolk closer than the fourth degree.

A. Esmein, *Le Mariage en droit canonique*, Paris, 1929-1935 (2nd ed.). – H. Schadt, *Die Darstellungen des Arbores Consanguinitatis und des Arbores Affinitatis*, Tübingen, 1982.

Anita Guerreau-Jalabert

**KINSHIP STRUCTURES.** While they share a common biological factor, human societies have defined kinship very differently; the conceptions and rules that regulate it are thus largely social in nature. They are organised into sets whose elements are structurally linked; which obliges us to examine, for each society, the facts of kinship in their diversity and coherence, remembering that our own categories correspond only to one system among many and that projection onto what we observe in medieval times is anachronistic.

According to the definition given by anthropology, "the study of kinship is that of the relations that unite men to each other by links based on consanguinity and alliance" (F. Héritier). By consanguinity, we mean the relationship between two individuals one of whom descends from the other or who have (or acknowledge) a common ancestor; this relationship is defined in a very variable way according to society. Alliance is the whole of the links forged between kinship groups by means of and around the matrimonial union of two of their members. But careful examination of the field of kinship in medieval Europe obliges us to take into account a third type of relationship that cannot be reduced to one of the former two, spiritual kinship, fraternity or paternity based on union of souls alone. The generalization and importance of these relationships in Christian society, to which we will return, seems an essential and original aspect of the kinship structures put in place in the West from the 5th century.

The rules that define consanguinity determine membership of a group of relatives and a sort of automatic access to the *property, privileges, status and name that characterise this group. In the medieval system, as in our own, these elements were transmitted equally by men and by *women (whereas some societies only recognise – or strongly favour – one of the ways of circulation of kinship and what accompanies it). Thus, a *child born of a legitimate *marriage was equally the grandson of its father's parents and of its mother's parents and was equally able to inherit from either of them. The evolution of vocabulary at the time when the Romance languages were formed shows the elimination of the distinction between paternal and maternal relatives that existed in a part of the Roman terminology. The limits of each person's *parentela* (set of socially recognised kin) were fixed, in the medieval case, by the counting of a certain number of degrees on the line of consanguinity, a number that went on increasing up to the seventh canonical degree, before being fixed at the fourth degree by the *Lateran council of 1215.

But this character of filiation in the Middle Ages, called cognatic or undifferentiated, seems to have been hidden from view by the preferential transmission to the sons of the most important elements of material or symbolic property – and this probably at all levels of society. This phenomenon flowed from social domination by men and not from any sort of principle regulating filiation and favouring transmission by men. Daughters took up a portion of the inheritance with their dowries, and inherited and transmitted fully in the absence of sons. Also, at certain periods, patrimonial strategies likewise reduced, sometimes drastically, the inheritance of younger sons. From the 11th c. at least, the settlement of the aristocracy on lands whose name they ended by taking led to the formation of what we may call "lineages of heirs" or "topolineages" made up of those who successively (but not necessarily from father to son) occupied a land and the duties attaching to it. The line thus defined became, for each generation, a part of the vast networks woven by consanguinity and alliance: "lineages". Phenomena linked to transmission are easier to observe in the dominant groups, where there was more to transmit. But the whole of medieval society was caught up in this system in which an undifferentiated filiation coexisted with a domination by men.

Part of the questions to do with alliance having been treated under "Marriage", they will not be repeated here. Alliance was hemmed in more and more tightly in the course of the Middle Ages by the regulations and prohibitions voiced by the Church. Though little studied as yet, its practical functioning, which here as elsewhere organised the circulation of women between kinship groups, was an essential element of the social fabric; the more so since in the medieval system there was an added equivalence, which was probably not just one of principle, between blood-relatives and allies in the definition of a *parentela*. Forming the context of biological reproduction, alliance was also an instrument of social reproduction, for which reason it served to support patrimonial strategies and was a means of social ascent.

Conveyed by *sexuality or associated with it, consanguinity and alliance were united in the Middle Ages in the category of "carnal kinship". But the language of kinship was widely used to represent and bring into play a vast set of social relationships that belonged to a different level, since they were based on the circulation of spiritual love and the union of souls. These representations and practices were not marginal phenomena. On the contrary, they were generalized and occupied a central place and a founding role in a Christian society. On them rested the notions of *Christendom and Church, as well as the functioning of baptismal kinship: all Christians, spiritually engendered in *baptism by *God and the Church, were mutual brothers; likewise *clerics, excluded from sexual reproduction, had the capacity to engender spiritually, in the rites of baptism and the *Eucharist, the whole community and each of its members. In the last centuries of the Middle Ages, we see several manifestations of the weight of the spiritual principle, the importance of this specific form of kinship in the organisation and functioning of social relationships: the formation of village communities fulfilling themselves in the context of the *parish, around the church and its *parish priest; the remarkable success of *confraternities and links of godparenthood and sponsorship.

Spiritual kinship rested on the conception of *caritas* as paradigm of every social relationship. The bond of spiritual *love that united the divine persons to each other, but also *God to men, men to God and men to each other through the intermediary of God, was by definition independent of kinship by the flesh, *i.e.* of consanguinity and alliance. So here we see a system that no longer used these two as the principal matrix of creation and reproduction of social bonds, which was still the case at Rome. Admittedly, kinship in the flesh was one of the possible conveyors of *caritas*, but insofar as it included a union of souls. But the latter, which had its origin in God and the *Holy Spirit, could be realized outside any carnal form of kinship, and it was there that it was at its purest; thus, the spiritual engendering of the Christian in *baptism produced a spiritual union between *godparents and godchildren, between godparents and carnal parents of godchildren, a union so strong that, like carnal kinship, it entailed prohibitions on *marriage. It must be remembered that baptism was also the rite that confirmed the *child's entry into society; the creation by the Church of baptismal kinship in the 6th c. was one of the marks of the inauguration of the domination of spiritual principles in the representations and practices of social reproduction.

These conceptions, which went hand in hand with a marked devaluation of the flesh and carnal kinship, very probably played an essential role in an evolution of the social structures of Europe that gradually limited the structuring role of relationships based exclusively on consanguinity and alliance.

H.R. Loyn, "Kinship in Anglo-Saxon England", *Anglo-Saxon England*, 3, 1974, 197-209. – F. Héritier, *L'Exercice de la parenté*, Paris, 1981. – J. Goody, *The Development of the Family and Marriage in Europe*, Cambridge, 1983. – A.C. Murray, *Germanic Kinship Structure*, Toronto, 1983. – J.M. Lynch, *Godparents and Kinship in Early Medieval Europe*, Princeton (NJ), 1986. – F. Héritier, *Le Mouvement confraternel au Moyen Âge: France, Italie, Suisse*, Rome, 1987. – S.D. White, *Custom, Kinship and Gifts to Saints*, Chapel Hill (NC), 1988. – A. Guerreau-Jalabert, "La Parenté dans l'Europe médiévale et moderne: à propos d'une synthèse récente", *L'Homme*, 2, 1989, 69-92. – *Cofradias, gremios, solidaridades en la Europa Medieval (XIX Semana de Estudios Medievales. Estella 1992)*, Pamplona, 1993. – A. Guerreau-Jalabert, "*Spiritus et caritas.* Le baptême dans la société médiévale", *La parenté spirituelle*, F. Héritier-Augé (ed.), E. Copet (ed.), Paris, 1995, 133-203. – "L'Arbre de Jessé et l'ordre chrétien de la parenté", *Marie. Le culte de la Vierge dans la société médiévale*, D. Iogna-Prat (ed.), É. Palazzo (ed.), D. Russo (ed.), Paris, 1996.

Anita Guerreau-Jalabert

**KISS.** The kiss (*osculum*) was one of the fundamental *gestures marking the conclusion of certain rites of association and alliance with the divinity or between persons or social groups. The kiss had several functions corresponding perhaps to distinct origins, but which overlapped and were mutually enriched, and which we will distinguish for the needs of our analysis.

In the first place, the presence of the kiss of peace in the liturgy of the *mass, where it accompanied the *communion, seems early. An act of devotion, it was also given by the believer to the *relics he venerated, or to the *altar. Here the kiss suggests a certain idea of submission or at least of unequal exchange with the divine, a nuance that may allow us to compare this gesture with the kissing of feet at the *investiture of prelates. It probably also provided a model for the kiss of peace attested from the 11th and 12th cc. to conclude and regulate conflicts. In this case it belonged to the private ritual practiced between families, which comprised

Enameled altar of Nicholas of Verdun, 1181, Klosterneuburg (near Vienna). Chapter of the Canons Regular of St Augustine.

elements borrowed from another type of kiss.

Indeed, there was also a kiss that sealed an alliance between individuals and which was frequent at rites accompanying betrothals. This practice seems attested before Christianization. It was perhaps the origin of the kiss present during the ritual of *homage, which confirmed entry into *vassalage. In fact, the kiss was one of the principal moments of homage that linked the vassal to his lord, and it thus belonged to the set of gestures proper to the aristocracy. It was a gesture of reciprocity that accompanied or followed the homage proper and the ritual of hands, *immixtio manuum*, which itself was a gesture of subordination and dedication. Also, by the *osculum*, vassalic submission was itself sealed between two equals, members of the same social group; it was honourable. As with betrothals, it was a matter of manifesting by this gesture the conclusion of a union that was outside natural filiation. The custom of kissing was gradually abandoned as the practice of homage faded out and that of the *oath prevailed, from the 14th c. and especially in the 15th.

D. Cabrol, "Baiser", *DACL*, 2, 1, 1910, 117-130. – L. Gougaud, "Baiser", *DSp*, 1, 1937, 1203-1204. – J. Le Goff, "Le rituel symbolique de la vassalité", *Simbolo e Simbologia nell'Alto Medioevo*, *SSAM*, 23, 1976, 679-788. – J. C. Schmitt, *La Raison des gestes dans l'Occident médiéval*, Paris, 1990. – Y. Carre, *Le Baiser sur la bouche au Moyen Âge. Rites, symboles, mentalités, XI^e-XV^e siècle*, Paris, 1992.

Thierry Pécout

**KLOSTERNEUBURG.** A *convent of regular *canons near *Vienna. Founded in 1114 by margrave Leopold III of Austria, in liaison with his *castle, as a secular *collegiate church, in 1133 it was transformed into a convent of regular canons. Siding with the *Gregorian reform, but at the same time always supported by the dukes, Klosterneuburg was among the most important spiritual centres in Austria, with an intense scientific activity and a very productive **scriptorium*, not to mention major works of art like the enamel altar of *Nicholas of Verdun (late 12th c.) or the Babenberg family tree. The monastery's apogee extended throughout the Middle Ages and its founder was canonized in 1485. The convent of *canonesses founded at the same time survived from 1133 to 1568. The medieval buildings were integrated into those rebuilt in the baroque period.

F. Röhrig, *Klosterneuburg*, Vienna, 1975. – F. Röhrig, *Stift Klosterneuburg und seine Kunstschätze*, Vienna, 1994. – *Der heilige Leopold. Landesfürst und Staatssymbol: Stift Klosterneuburg*, 1985 (exhibition catalogue).

Werner Maleczek

**KNIGHTS OF THE SWORD.** The *military-religious order of the *Fratres milicie Christi de Livonia* was founded in 1202 to protect the *missions and converted populations of Livonia and *Latvia. The knights' emblem was a red sword and red cross *patée* on a white cloak (hence their name). Following the rule and organisation of the Temple, it recruited among the crusaders of northern *Germany. It subjected and converted the *pagans of *Estonia and tried to erect its conquests into a State (first adumbration of an *Ordenstaat*) while it was dependent on the bishop of *Riga. Its defeat by the *Lithuanians in 1236 and the weakness of its roots in Germany led to its fusion with the Order of *Teutonic Knights in 1237.

F. Benninghoven, *Der Orden der Schwertbrüder*, Cologne-Graz, 1965. – C.-E. Perrin, "Une histoire de l'ordre des chevaliers Porte-Glaive", *MA*, 74, 1968, 73-85. – F. Benninghoven, "Milizia di Cristo", *DIP*, 5, 1978, 1323-1327. – E. Christiansen, *The Northern Crusades, 1100-1525*, London, 1980.

Alain Demurger

**KNOWLEDGE.** In 1324, when John Lutterell, *chancellor of *Oxford university, drew up an act of accusation against the *doctrine of William of *Ockham, he understood the danger posed by the new *philosophy to the traditional view of the world and of *God. From the outset, he fixed the debate in the sphere of the doctrine of knowledge.

An expression of the insecurity of the world it was born into (*famine, economic crisis), the thought of William of Ockham († 1349/1350) effected a radical critique of the scope of human *language. Though Ockham never cast doubt on the relation between the words of our language and the world, to the extent that the term logically exercises a function of substitute for (*supponere pro*) things, he did deny that there was between the two an intrinsic relation of meaning that assigned to each term a universal in reality; this is why we say of this philosophy that it is a "non-*realism": Ockham would track down the universal everywhere in reality in order to dislodge it. The thesis that each thing is singular in itself was backed up by a *logic that forbade itself to multiply explanatory principles needlessly (*pluralitas non est ponenda sine necessitate*): in this way we avoid taking abstractions for realities, *i.e.* projecting a human conceptual construct on God or the world. So knowledge, which necessarily starts from sense-experience, has to start by establishing itself with confidence in an immediate apprehension of things: an intuition. (The primary intellectual intuition is that of the internal experience of "I think", which could never open up the possibility of an intuitive knowledge of a non-existent). The *metaphysical point of this debate is what would continue to be called the "question of *universals": for Ockham, knowledge is not a reproduction of the world, and the universal exists nowhere in the world.

Where in all this do we find a trace of that scepticism of which Ockham has so readily been accused, making him a 14th-c. precursor of the critical philosophy?

Though the Ockhamist critique of knowledge was aimed primarily at *Henry of Ghent († 1293) and John *Duns Scotus († 1308), John Lutterell, who could not bring himself to deny that language expressed the order of the world, remarked that with the same blow it overthrew the doctrine of *Thomas Aquinas († 1274).

Thomas received from *Aristotle a *doctrine of concept* according to which the agent intellect produces the universality in act of objects of knowledge by following a process of *abstraction: receiving its food through the senses, the human *intellect frees the universal nature from the matrix of materiality that encloses it in things; knowledge is the object itself with which the understanding is united vitally in act according to the mode of the knower (*secundum modum recipientis*).

But he received from Augustine a *doctrine of truth*, which he modified in consequence. Formally defined as "adequation between the intellect and the thing", truth is properly human only when it is known in an act of reflection, at the very centre of self-knowledge.

However, knowledge is measured by things themselves which, as works of God, are essentially pervaded by intelligibility: "Natural things are constituted between two intellects (that of God and that of *man)"; hence it is because *being is an imitation of God that the human intellect is capable of knowing it in a second-degree imitation, and of restoring in himself the *order willed by God; since "everything has been made to imitate the divine *beauty", man's highest perfection, in the natural order accessible to philosophy, is to know as well as possible that order of things perceived as an imitation of God: "So the ultimate perfection to which the soul can attain, according to the philosophers, is that the whole order of the universe is inscribed within this soul (*ut in ea describatur totus ordo universi*)".

It can readily be imagined that John Lutterell was alarmed to see that Ockham's thought contained in germ a criticism of this view: if all the distinctions made by Thomas Aquinas (or, differently, by Duns Scotus) were merely projections of an order that was the order of *reason but not the order of the world, the ruin of the theory of knowledge would entail with it the collapse of a "harmonicist" conception of the world and cognition, of philosophy and *theology, of reason and *faith.

Given this, it is not surprising that the 14th c. should have turned again towards the Augustinian doctrine of knowledge.

Beyond *Bonaventure (†1274) and his disciples such as *Matthew of Aquasparta (†1302), who integrated the Aristotelian novelties rediscovered in the 13th c. while following the Bonaventurian doctrine of the idea, men looked to Augustine (†430) to safeguard knowledge beyond the contingency of the world. Indeed the *Contra academicos* contained a refutation of scepticism that Augustine considered definitive: sense-knowledge is infallibly credible if we ask it to give what it is in a position to provide, viz. appearance; only when we make sense-knowledge the criterion of all knowledge does lead us into error: I am mistaken when I affirm that things are as they appear to me. Beyond this point, the certainty of knowledge is immediately based in the certainty of the existence of thought, which is given as the primary certainty. Given this, scepticism is no longer possible: whatever happens, "if I am mistaken, I am".

This critique of the scepticism of the Academy (which gained renewed interest in 1328 when, in a world suffering the painful experience of contingency, the book by the Arab philosopher al-*Ghazālī [† 1111] entitled *The Incoherence of the Philosophers* was translated into Latin) nevertheless remained incapable of founding a stable cognition: indeed, in the same way as that of sensible things, knowledge of self is a contingent and inevitably changing *donnée*. It is impossible that a temporal soul should produce eternal truths within itself. Hence we must explain how the human soul finds within itself something greater than itself.

If communication permits agreement between individuals (*e.g.* in teaching – this is the theme of the *De magistro*, much prized in the Middle Ages), it is because the substratum on which they agree is distinct from the concept they produce. The "inner teacher", who assures us of the truth and guarantees that men can understand each other, can be none other than absolute and immutable truth, the eternal *wisdom of God: from the outset, human knowledge ends in affirmation of the existence of God.

Throughout the early Middle Ages, this unconditioned necessity of all knowledge appealed to the doctrine of *illumination*: knowledge supposes in us a source that is given to us, more "interior than our own interiority and above what is highest in us". Here we have a reason for the primacy of self-knowledge in all the variants of medieval *Augustinianism, up to *Theodoric of Freiberg († *c.*1319).

This illumination natural to all intellect is immediate and ascribes to human cognition a dependence on divine Ideas, archetypes of every created thing; this is what gives human knowledge the irreducible characteristics of immutability, necessity and universality that belong to it: by divine illumination, the understanding can read the truth in things.

Augustinianism lacked a doctrine of the concept, something that became imperative to the philosophers of the 13th c.; having failed to find in Augustine's work a doctrine of generalization of ideas, medieval thinkers attributed to Augustine a doctrine of the concept that was to modify its original ideas profoundly. Indeed Augustine's epistemology, so impregnated with the doctrine of Plotinus, brought with it a major difficulty: how can the divine and immutable truth be that of a mutable creature infinitely distant from God? According to Étienne Gilson, the only way to escape from this was by resolutely abandoning Plotinus for Aristotle.

Wilhelm von Ockham, *Texte zur Theorie der Erkenntnis und der Wissenschaft*, R. Imbach (ed.), Stuttgart, 1984.

É. Gilson, *L'Esprit de la philosophie médiévale*, Paris, 1969 (2nd ed.). – G. Leff, *William of Ockham*, Manchester, 1975. – M. M. Adams, *William Ockham*, Notre Dame (IN), 1987. – P. Alféri, *Guillaume d'Ockham, le singulier*, Paris, 1989. – F.-X. Putallaz, *La Connaissance de soi au XIII*e *siècle. De Matthieu d'Aquasparta à Thierry de Freiberg*, Paris, 1991. – K. Flasch, *Introduction à la philosophie médiévale*, Fribourg, Paris, 1992. – H. Klocker, *William of Ockham and the Divine Freedom*, Milwaukee (WI), 1992. – R. Pasnau, *Theories of Cognition in the Later Middle Ages*, Cambridge, 1997.

François-Xavier Putallaz

**KORAN.** In Arabic, *Qur'ân*. The sacred book of the Muslims, it is considered the "uncreated" word of God, even in its objective materiality, by the greater part of Muslim opinion. This dogma was imposed not without resistance in the 9th century. The whole of the revelation to *Muḥammad during the prophetic period of his life constitutes the Koran. As a common noun the term refers to the "faithful oral utterance" of a "Writing", *Kitāb*. In this, the term is contrasted to the poetic word, which was given no fixed reference. In the original strict Koranic context, the Writing that imparts the revelation is to be likened to the expression of the destiny of the tribes. This would later be broadened to the destiny of the world through the vision of Muslim societies. The dating of the revelation is unverifiable. We can only accept what sacred tradition tells us: *Mecca period from 610 to the *hejira in 622; *Medina period from the year 1 (622) to the death of Muḥammad in 11 (632). The revelation to Muḥammad was collected in one volume by order of 'Uthmān, third *caliph of Medina, less than a quarter of a century after the death of the prophet. But no evidential document survives from *Islam's Arabian and peninsular period. However, despite some passages that might appear suspect, the Koran, by its content and language, seems to be the product of the western Arabia with which Muslim tradition connects it.

The Koranic text of the Vulgate is divided into 114 *surās*, very unequal in length. They are arranged – after the first *surā*, called "opening" – from the longest (286 verses) to the shortest (less than five verses) and from the most recent to the earliest. Some very short *surās* belong nevertheless to the Medina rather than the Mecca period. The word *surā* is a borrowing from the Aramean and designates "putting in order". Each *surā* is considered to go back to a revelatory moment which is reproduced just as it is. Numerous Koranic passages nevertheless appear to have been the object of rearrangements or displacements, probably when the Vulgate was being put in order. Each *surā* constitutes a text in itself and supposes no sequel. This procedure of composition has produced a text of dispersed subject-matter. Its incessant repetitions and internal contradictions make it difficult to read. But they give a hold to the analysis of modern historical criticism.

The Koranic representations, if considered in themselves, without interference from the texts of a later time (exegesis, historiography, even the tradition called "prophetic"), appear rooted in a tribal milieu. The Koran's biblical borrowings are numerous (eschatology, prophetic and royal legends). But they lose their original identity to be integrated into a peculiarly Koranic functionality and imagery. During the Mecca period, the biblical subject-matter illustrates Muḥammad's mission in the face of his tribe's persistent unbelief. During the Medina period, the biblical subject-matter fits into the polemic against the Medina Jews who refused to recognise Muḥammad as the continuer of their prophets and patriarchs. Moreover, to the extent that the Prophet now played a role as tribal chief and war leader of Medina, the Koranic discourse becomes much more political. It deals equally with the internal problems of the intertribal confederation which is gradually constituted under the name of **umma*, "the rightly-guided group".

*Le Coran*, R. Blachère (tr.), Paris, 1947-1951 (3 vol.). – *The Koran*, N. J. Dawood (tr.), Harmondsworth, 1956. – *Der Koran*, R. Paret (ed.), Stuttgart, 1971.

R. Bell, *Bell's Introduction to the Qur'an*, Edinburgh, 1977. – R. Blachère, *Introduction au Coran*, Paris, 1977. – R. Paret, *Mohammed und der Koran: Geschichte und Verkündigung den arabischen Propheten*, Stuttgart, 1985.

Jacqueline Chabbi

**KOSOVO POLJE ("BLACKBIRDS' FIELD").** A great plain in the valley of the rivers Sitnica and Lab in southern *Serbia, where a bloody battle took place on 23 June 1389, in which Prince Lazar, ruler of the Serbs, and Sultan Murad I were killed and both armies suffered enormous losses. Its immediate consequence was the establishment of the *Turks in the Balkans, which facilitated their expansion towards central Europe.

Serbia thus became a vassal State of the Turkish Empire, Lazar's successors having acknowledged the power of Bayezid. This battle was sung by *epic poetry that glorified the exploits of Lazar and the Serb gentry, transforming the defeat into a moral victory.

In 1448, at Kosovo Polje, Murad II defeated John *Hunyadi.

N. Radojčić, "Die griechischen Quellen zur Schlacht am Kosovo polje", *Byz.*, 6, 1931, 241-246. – T. A. Emmert, *Serbian Golgotha: the Battle of Kosovo*, New York, 1990. – *Kosovo: Legacy of a Medieval Battle*, W. S. Vucinich (ed.), T. A. Emmert (ed.), Minneapolis, 1991.

Gordana Babić †

**KREMLIN.** The term "kremlin" (Russian *kreml'*) is attested in Russian texts only after 1331 to designate the fortified core of the towns of old Russia, *i.e.* the fortress, citadel or *burg*. Before this period, the word *detinec* was used. The etymology of both terms is still disputed, but for *kreml'* the most probable is that formerly advanced by the historian Karamzin: *kremen'*, stone, flint, though other hypotheses have been advanced. As for *detinec*, among the etymologies advanced have been *dne*, "interior space", or *det'*, "to place", "to hide".

Though Westerners know only the Moscow Kremlin, most old Russian towns had a detinec or kremlin, in some cases from the 10th c., or even the 9th. Originally simple earth banks, they were later reinforced and surmounted by palisades of stakes, only later by stone or brick walls.

The best-known kremlin is obviously that of *Moscow, whose history is long and complex. Situated on an abrupt eminence overlooking the Moskova, it has known several stages, starting with the earth banks surmounted by stakes that characterised it from the 12th to the early 14th c., covering an area of 3 to 4 hectares. It was surrounded by stone walls from the late 14th c., then with brick walls with swallow-tail crenellations, in the Italian style, in the late 15th. These were restored early in the 17th c., when they were flanked by towers. Its vast territory housed the residence of the grand princes of Moscow and their entourage, then the first *tsars, as well as churches, monasteries, an armoury, workshops, guards and reserves. In the 17th c., the length of the walls surpassed 2 kilometres, and the Kremlin covered nearly 30 hectares. Italians worked there at that time (Ruffo, Solari, Fioravanti, etc.). When Peter the Great transferred the capital to St Petersburg, the Kremlin remained the place where the tsars were crowned and their imperial residence when they were in Moscow. It became the seat of Soviet government after 1918 and is still the seat of the Russian government, only the part with the museums being open to the public since the Khruschev period.

Among Russian towns that have retained a monumental kremlin, nearly always rebuilt several times over the centuries, we must mention *Novgorod. Its first stone walls seem to have been raised in 1044, housing the beautiful cathedral of St Sophia (1045-1050) and the faceted palace. The kremlin was later surrounded by brick walls, restored several times between the 15th and 18th centuries. The Novgorod kremlin became the residence of the *bishop and doubtless of certain boyars rather than of the prince.

Apart from some traces of earth banks, little remains of the original kremlin of Suzdal'. Though it has not kept the name of kremlin, the fortress of Prince *Vladimir Monomakh at *Vladimir, abruptly dominating the river Kljaz'ma, core of the princely residence, had all the functions of a kremlin and still houses two of the town's most monumental churches.

Kazan', Nijni-Novgorod and Astrakhan' on the Volga have preserved monumental kremlins going back, in their present state, to the 16th, 17th and 18th centuries. Old Rostov (Jaroslavskij) had a medieval kremlin encircled by earth banks, but what is today wrongly called the kremlin is in fact the metropolis, a vast group of palaces and churches surrounded by walls, built to the north of Lake Nero in the second half of the 17th c. by Metropolitan Iona.

*Istorija Moskvy*, 1, Moscow, 1952. – V. Ivanov, *Moskovskij kreml'*, Moscow, 1971. – M. Karger, *Novgorod the Great*, Moscow, 1973.

Jean Blankoff

**KREMSMÜNSTER.** A Benedictine *abbey in Upper Austria, founded in 777 by Duke Tassilo III of *Bavaria as a centre of colonization and *mission, richly endowed with surrounding territories and erected into an imperial monastery in the Carolingian period (788). Works of art from the time of foundation are still preserved (*chalice and luminary of Tassilo, Codex Millenarius). The monastery's decline came about in the 10th c. with the Hungarian *invasions and its transformation into the private monastery of the bishops of *Passau.

It enjoyed a new flowering with the *reform movement of *Gorze in the 11th c. and at the time of its attachment to the Cluniac customs from 1160. Until the end of the Middle Ages, Kremsmünster remained a spiritually and economically flourishing monastery (**scriptorium*, *library, *chronicles – Bernardus Noricus [*c.*1270-1326] – and collections of works of art). The *Romanesque church (built from 1232) still exists, but most of today's conventual buildings are baroque .

*Kremsmünster, 1200 Jahre Benediktinerstift*, Linz, 1976. – *Cremifanum 777-1977 (Festschrift zur 1200-Jahr-Feier des Stiftes Kremsmünster*, Mainz, 1977. – *Die Anfänge des Klosters Kremsmünster*, Linz, 1978 ("Mitteilungen d. Oberösterreichischen Landesarchivs", suppl. 2).

Werner Maleczek

**KULIKOVO.** *Kulikovo pole*, "Field of the snipe": this place, on the right bank of the upper Don, saw the victory of the grand prince of *Moscow, Dmitrii Donskoi (of the Don), over a *Mongol troop commanded by a usurper, Mamay. This episode, despite having no decisive consequences, inspired an abundant literature: the *Zadonshchina*, a prose poem on the battle "beyond the Don" (*c.*1406) – comparison of this poem with Igor's "Dit on the Ost", dated to the 12th c., calls in question the latter's authenticity – and the *Tale of the Battle with Mamay* (*Skazanie o Mamaevom poboishche*), a late work, rich in apocryphal details to the glory of Moscow.

A. Vaillant, *La Zadonščina, épopée russe du XV^e siècle*, Paris, 1967. – A. Vaillant, *RESl*, 39, 1961, 59-89.

Vladimir Vodoff

**KYRIE ELEISON.** The *Kyrie eleison* (Lord, have mercy) was introduced to the West most probably as an independent chant (Rule of St *Benedict for the little *hours; canon 3 of the council of Vaison, 529). Subsequently, the piece could be joined to a *litany (Rule of St Benedict, matins). Finally the *Kyrie eleison* became the response of litanies, but not of the *Deprecatio Gelasii* as Capelle claimed on the basis of a defective edition.

*Gregory the Great attests the alternation of *Kyries* and *Christes* (*Ep.* 9, 26). *Amalarius (9th c.) gives it a trinitarian sense in his *Liber officialis*. Later, the *Kyrie* would be "stuffed" with *tropes.

E. Bishop, "Kyrie eleison", *Liturgica historica*, Oxford, 1918, 116-136. – B. Capelle, "Le Kyrie de la messe et le pape Gélase", *RB*, 46, 1934, 126-144, reprinted in *Travaux liturgiques*, 2, Louvain, 1962, 116-134. – P. De Clerck, *La "prière universelle" dans les liturgies latines anciennes. . .*, Münster, 1977, 282-295.

Paul De Clerck

Germany
Main locations listed in the encyclopedia
•Towns •Monasteries
Denmark
Lubeck
Hamburg
Pomerania
Brandenburg
Frisia
Bremen
Saxony
Amsterdam
Utrecht
Brandenburg
Gniezno
Poznan
Poland
Herford
Hildesheim
Munster
Gandersheim
Corvey
Paderborn
Magdeburg
Quedlinburg
Silesia
Essen
Fritzlar
Leipzig
Wroclaw
Maastricht
Cologne
Liege
Aachen
Siegburg
Hersfeld
Erfurt
Marburg
Fulda
Thuringia
Bohemia
Prum
Frankfurt
Prague
Echternach
Mainz
Trier
Windesheim
Wurzburg
Bamberg
Worms
Franconia
Luxemburg
Nuremburg
Moravia
Metz
Verdun
Ellwangen
Regensburg
Hirsau
Passau
Swabia
Bavaria
Augsburg
Gottweig
Vienna
Melk
Murbach
Freiburg
Munich
Kremsmunster
Heiligenkreuz
Reichenau
Luxeuil
Staufen
Tegernsee
Salzburg
Austria
Constance
Besancon
St Gallen
Admont
Einsiedeln
0 25 50 75 100 miles
0 50 100 150 kms